RIDGEWATER COLLEGE LIBRARY
HUTCHINSON CAMPUS

Encyclopedia
of Legal
Information Sources

Encyclopedia of Legal Information Sources

A Bibliographic Guide to Approximately 29,000 Citations for Publications, Organizations, and Other Sources of Information on 480 Law-Related Subjects

Includes: Statutes, Codes, Standards, and Uniform Laws; Restatements; Looseleaf Services and Reporters; Handbooks, Manuals, and Formbooks; Textbooks and General Works; Encyclopedias and Dictionaries; Digests, Indexes, Abstracts, and Citators; Annuals and Surveys; Law Reviews and Periodicals; Newsletters and Newspapers; Bibliographies; Directories; Biographical Sources; Associations and Professional Societies; Research Centers, Institutes, and Clearinghouses; Online Databases; Statistics Sources; Audiovisuals; Computer-Assisted Legal Software; and Other Sources of Information on Each Topic

SECOND EDITION

Edited by

Brian L. Baker and **Patrick J. Petit**

Robert J. White Law Library
Catholic University of America

Editors:	Brian L. Baker and Patrick J. Petit
Consulting Editor:	Paul Wasserman
Editorial Assistant:	Marilyn L. Baker

Gale Research Inc. Staff

Senior Editor:	Donna Wood
Coordinating Editor:	Jennifer Mossman
Associate Editor:	Allison K. McNeill
Assistant Editors:	Jacqueline L. Gural, Matt Merta, Lou Ann Shelton, Kelle S. Sisung, Rita H. Skirpan, Phyllis Spinelli, Alice M. Walsh, Grace E. Wright
Production Manager:	Mary Beth Trimper
Production Assistant:	Shanna Heilveil
Art Director:	Arthur Chartow
Keyliners:	C.J. Jonik, Yolanda Y. Latham

While every effort has been made to ensure the reliability of the information presented in this publication, Gale Research Inc. does not guarantee the accuracy of the data contained herein. Gale accepts no payment for listing; and inclusion in the publication of any organization, service, or individual does not imply endorsement of the editors or publisher.

Errors brought to the attention of the publisher and verified to the satisfaction of the publisher will be corrected in future editions.

This publication is a creative work copyrighted by Gale Research Inc. and fully protected by all applicable copyright laws, as well as by misappropriation, trade secret, unfair competition, and other applicable laws. The authors and editors of this work have added value to the underlying factual material herein through one or more of the following: unique and original selection, coordination, expression, arrangement, and classification of the information.

Gale Research Inc. will vigorously defend all of its rights in this publication.

Copyright © 1993 by Gale Research Inc.
835 Penobscot Building
Detroit, MI 48226

All rights reserved including the right of reproduction in whole or in part in any form.

∞™ This book is printed on acid-free paper that meets the minimum requirements of American National Standard for Information Sciences—Permanence Paper for Printed Library Materials, ANSI Z39.48-1984.

♻ This book is printed on recycled paper that meets Environmental Protection Agency standards.

Library of Congress Cataloging-in-Publication Data

Encyclopedia of legal information sources: a bibliographic guide to approximately 29,000 citations for publications, organizations, and other sources of information on 480 law-related subjects. . . / edited by Brian L. Baker and Patrick J. Petit. — 2nd ed.
    p. cm.
ISBN 0-8103-7439-0 : $165.00
1. Law—United States—Bibliography.   2. Law—United States—Information services.   I. Baker, Brian L.   II. Petit, Patrick J.
KF1.E53
016.34973—dc20
[016.3473]
                                            92-18907
                                                CIP

Printed in the United States of America

Published simultaneously in the United Kingdom
by Gale Research International Limited
(An affiliated company of Gale Research Inc.)

Contents

Highlights vii

Introduction ix

User's Guide xi

Outline of Contents xiii

Legal Information Sources 1

Highlights

> 29,000 Citations
> 480 Topics

As the information needs of lawyers, librarians, and researchers continue to increase, timely access is crucial. Publication of this edition of *Encyclopedia of Legal Information Sources (ELIS)* allows you to keep pace with the rapidly-changing legal profession. Highlights include:

- New law-related topics - 20 added since the previous edition

- New material for a wide range of established topics - all first edition topics have been expanded

- Extensive updating - thousands of changes have been made to ensure that addresses, publication dates, and other vital details will be as accurate as possible.

- Computer-assisted legal software listed for many topics

- Phone numbers added for associations and research centers

New Topics

Topics were selected for inclusion based upon their timeliness and importance in the field of law. Those appearing for the first time are:

Asbestos	European Economic Community
Black Lung	Funerals and Burial
Canon Law	Homelessness
Church and State	Law Examinations
Colleges and Universities	Law in Art
Courthouses	Mentally Handicapped
Drug Testing	Money Laundering
Electronic Funds Transfer	Notaries Public
Engineers and Engineering Law	Sexual Harassment
Entrapment	Veterinarians

Introduction

Lawyers and law-related professionals need an easy-to-use tool that leads to the books, periodicals, databases, and organizations that can answer their questions. Those outside the legal profession may also require a tool that directs them to the more basic law books and to the organizations of, and related to, the legal profession.

The *Encyclopedia of Legal Information Sources (ELIS)* is able to meet the needs of both professionals and laypersons. For example, under the topic "Partnership," *ELIS* citations range from *Partnership Basis and Basis Adjustments*, a highly technical tax management portfolio published by the Bureau of National Affairs, to *The Partnership Book: How to Write Your Own Small Business Partnership Agreement*, published by Nolo Press, which specializes in self-help law books.

Method of Compilation

Extensive research was required in order to gather the sources of information on the hundreds of topics included in this publication. A wide range of sources was consulted, including online databases, bibliographies, indexes of the legal literature, and publishers' promotional brochures. In each instance, the details have been carefully verified and corroborated.

Because of the crucial importance of timeliness in the legal field, only the most recent and up-to-date sources have been cited. Material published prior to 1980 has been excluded, unless considered a landmark or classic contribution in the field.

Headings Narrowly Defined

To assure that information can be located easily, headings have been kept as specific as possible. This edition of *ELIS* includes citations under 480 different topics and is supplemented by numerous cross-references.

Topics were selected for inclusion based upon their timeliness and importance in the field of law. To make *ELIS* as useful as possible, the entire range of legal concerns has been incorporated, including specific crimes (Fraud, Libel and Slander); legal specialties (Antitrust Law, Environmental Law, Family Law); trial procedures (Appellate Procedure, Cross-Examination, Sentencing); and current legal issues (Capital Punishment, Euthanasia, Legal Ethics and Malpractice).

Topics Provide Special Assistance

While most of the topics contained in *ELIS* are fairly self-explanatory, a few require special mention:

–The user who is unfamiliar with legal materials is advised to consult the topic "Legal Research." Under this heading are listed "how to" books as well as statutes, reporters, digests, encyclopedias, and dictionaries basic to a legal collection. Entries are briefly annotated.

–While subject-specific formbooks, restatements, and uniform laws are listed under each topic, they are also gathered under the topics "Legal Forms," "Restatements," and "Uniform and Model Acts."

–Basic legal materials of each state can be found under the topic "States."

–Under "State Law Compilations" are listed sources that compile state laws by subject or sources that cite compilations.

–The topic "Treaties and Conventions" includes a special subheading "Collections" under which are listed general and subject-specific collection of treaties.

Bibliography Covers 20 Kinds of Sources

Under each heading, citations are found for a wide variety of sources, both print and nonprint, on a particular topic. A complete list of the kinds of sources cited is outlined below, in the sequence in which they appear (although not all types of sources are listed for each topic).

Statutes, Codes, Standards, Uniform Laws	Bibliographies
Restatements	Directories
Looseleaf Services and Reporters	Biographical Sources
Handbooks, Manuals, Formbooks	Associations and Professional Societies
Textbooks and General Works	Research Centers, Institutes, Clearinghouses
Encyclopedias and Dictionaries	Online Databases
Digests, Indexes, Abstracts, Citators	Statistics Sources
Annuals and Surveys	Audiovisuals
Law Reviews and Periodicals	Computer-Assisted Legal Software
Newsletters and Newspapers	Other Sources

Type of source categories are arranged in order of importance to the user. Legal researchers would begin an information search by consulting the primary sources—statutes, restatements and reporters. Additional data could be gathered from secondary bibliographic sources—proceeding from handbooks to textbooks to encyclopedias, etc. Beyond the printed information sources, researchers may find it helpful to contact individual organizations, either by consulting directories and biographical sources or scanning the lists of associations and research centers found in *ELIS*. Online databases can be extremely helpful for legal research. However, because of the cost involved, such an information-gathering device is often impractical. Statistical data is perhaps the least important source, while audiovisuals and computer-assisted legal software are primarily teaching tools.

Acknowledgments

The editors are extremely grateful to many people for their assistance. We would especially like to thank all the fine people at Gale Research, Incorporated, but especially Jennifer Mossman and Ann Evory, whose encouragement and gentle nudging really made this book a possibility.

Most importantly, however, the editors would like to dedicate this work to our wonderful wives, Marilyn Baker and Elizabeth Petit. They were forced to deal with this upheaval in their lives and came away, we believe, with mostly smiles. Without their support, encouragement and forgiveness, this book would never have gotten finished.

Suggestions are Welcome

In spite of the considerable care that has been taken to keep errors and inconsistencies to a minimum, some may have occurred. It would be appreciated if users would send to the editors any information, suggestions, comments, or corrections that might improve future editions. Please address remarks to:

Editors
Encyclopedia of Legal Information Sources
Gale Research Inc.
835 Penobscot Bldg.
Detroit, MI 48226-4094

User's Guide

Entries are arranged alphabetically by [1] topic, and further subdivided by [2] type of source, and [3] publication title or organization name. Complete citations are provided for each information source. Citations for publications include title, author or editor, publisher's name and address, and publication date or frequency. For databases, citations include database name, producer, and producer's address. Citations for organizations include name and address. For example:

---

[1] ABORTION

[2] TEXTBOOKS AND GENERAL WORKS

[3] *Abortion Decisions of the Supreme Court, 1973 Through 1989: A Comprehensive Review With Historical Commentary.* Dan Drucker. McFarland and Company, P.O. Box 611, Jefferson, North Carolina 28640. 1990.

Abortion: The Clash of Absolutes. Lawrence H. Tribe. W.W. Norton and Company, 500 Fifth Avenue, New York, New York 10110. 1990.

DIRECTORIES

National Abortion Federation — Directory. National Abortion Federation, 1436 U Street, Northwest, Washington, D.C. 20003. Annual.

ASSOCIATIONS AND PROFESSIONAL SOCIETIES

National Right to Life Committee. 419 Seventh Street, Northwest, Suite 500, Washington, D.C. 20004. (202) 626-8800.

Physicians for Choice. c/o Planned Parenthood Federation of America, 810 Seventh Avenue, 7th Floor, New York, New York 10019. (212) 541-7800.

"Outline of Contents" Speeds Access to Topics

For the most efficient use of this publication, do not go directly to the text to look up the topic on which information is sought. Instead, consult the extensive and detailed Outline of Contents, where it is possible to determine the exact form that has been used and to be guided by cross-references to related topics.

Outline of Contents

Abbreviations— *See* Legal Research
Abduction— *See* Kidnapping; Terrorism
Abortion 1
Accidents 5
Accountants and Accounting 6
Acquisitions, Corporate— *See* Consolidation and Merger; Corporations
Actions and Defenses 11
Administration of Justice 12
Administrative Conference of the United States 14
Administrative Law 15
Administrative Office of the United States Courts 18
Administrative Procedure 19
Admiralty 20
Admissibility of Evidence— *See* Evidence
Admission to the Bar 22
Admissions— *See* Evidence
Adoption 24
Advertising 26
Aeronautics— *See* Aviation
Affirmative Action— *See* Discrimination, Employment; Discrimination, Race; Discrimination, Sex; Equal Employment Opportunity
Age Discrimination 30
Aged and Aging 31
Aged and Crime 35
Aged and Employment 35
Aged and Health Care 36
Aged and Retirement 36
Agency 37
Agriculture 38
Agriculture Department 42
AIDS 43
Air Force— *See* Aviation; Military Law and Service
Air Law— *See* Aviation; Aviation Accidents
Airliner Hijacking— *See* Terrorism
Alcohol Control and Drinking Behavior 45
Alcohol, Tobacco and Firearms Bureau 49
Aliens— *See* Citizens and Citizenship; Emigration and Immigration
Alimony— *See* Family Law
Alternative Dispute Resolution— *See* Dispute Resolution

American Bar Association 49
Amusements— *See* Entertainment Law
Anarchism— *See* Political Crimes and Offenses; Terrorism
Animals 56
Annuities— *See* Insurance, Life
Annulment— *See* Family Law
Antenuptial Contracts— *See* Family Law
Anti-Dumping Duties— *See* Export and Import
Antitrust and Economics 57
Antitrust Law 58
Appellate Procedure 63
Arbitration and Award 65
Arbitration, Industrial— *See* Labor Arbitration
Arbitration, International— *See* International Arbitration
Architects 69
Armed Forces— *See* Military Law and Service; Veterans
Arms— *See* Firearms and Ballistics
Arms Control— *See* Intenational Law and Relations; Treaties and Conventions
Army— *See* Military Law and Service
Arrest 70
Arson 71
Art 72
Artificial Insemination— *See* Family Law
Asbestos 74
Assassination— *See* Murder; Political Crimes and Offenses
Assembly— *See* Freedom of Assembly and Association
Assignment for Benefit of Creditors — *See* Bankruptcy
Association— *See* Freedom of Assembly and Association
Associations and Non-Profit Corporations 76
Asylum— *See* Emigration and Immigration
Atomic Energy— *See* Nuclear Energy
Attachment and Garnishment 77
Attorney-General 78

Attorneys— *See* Admission to the Bar; American Bar Association; Law Office Management; Law Practice; Lawyer and Client; Lawyers' Fees; Legal Aid; Legal Ethics and Malpractice; Legal Profession in Fiction; Prepaid Legal Services; Public Prosecutors
Auditing— *See* Accountants and Accounting
Authors and Publishers 78
Automobiles— *See* Insurance, Motor Vehicles and Aviation; Motor Vehicles
Aviation 79
Aviation Accidents 81
Award— *See* Arbitration and Award
Bail 83
Ballistics— *See* Firearms and Ballistics
Bankruptcy 85
Bankruptcy Court— *See* Bankruptcy; District Courts
Banks and Banking 90
Bar Associations— *See* American Bar Association; States
Bar Examiners and Examinations— *See* Admission to the Bar
Bars and Taverns— *See* Alcohol Control and Drinking Behavior
Battered Children— *See* Child Abuse and Neglect; Family Violence
Battered Women— *See* Family Violence
Bill Drafting— *See* Statutory Construction and Drafting
Bills of Lading— *See* Negotiable Instruments
Bioethics 99
Birth Control 102
Black Lung 103
Blood Tests— *See* Evidence; Health Care; Medical Jurisprudence and Malpractice
Blue Sky Laws— *See* Securities
Boats and Boating— *See* Admiralty
Bonds— *See* Securities
Boycotts— *See* Export and Import; Labor and Labor Relations
Bribery— *See* Corruption, Political
Briefs— *See* Legal Writing
Broadcasting— *See* Television and Radio
Brokers— *See* Real Property; Securities
Budgets— *See* Public Finance
Building and Loan Associations— *See* Banks and Banking
Building Laws— *See* Construction Industry
Burden of Proof— *See* Civil Procedure; Criminal Procedure
Bureau of Alcohol, Tobacco and Firearms— *See* Alcohol, Tobacco and Firearms Bureau
Business Crime 104
Business Law— *See* Commercial Law; Corporations; Joint Ventures; Partnership; Small Business

Business Secrets— *See* Trade Secrets
Cable Television— *See* Television and Radio
Campaign Funds— *See* Election Law
Canon·Law 107
Capital Punishment 108
Carriers— *See* Interstate Commerce Commission; Railroads; Transportation; Transportation Department
Cars— *See* Insurance, Motor Vehicle and Aviation; Motor Vehicles
Cartels— *See* Antitrust Law
Censorship 111
Central Intelligence Agency 113
Character Licensing— *See* Licensing, Industrial and Intellectual
Charitable Trusts— *See* Charities; Wills, Trusts and Inheritance
Charities 113
Checks— *See* Banks and Banking; Commercial Law; Negotiable Instruments
Chemical Industries 115
Child Abuse and Neglect 116
Child Custody 119
Child Labor— *See* Children; Labor and Labor Relations
Child Support— *See* Family Law
Children 121
Church and State 125
Circuit Courts of Appeal 127
Citizens and Citizenship 129
City Government— *See* Local Government
City Planning— *See* Historic Preservation; Zoning and Planning
Civil Law 130
Civil Procedure 131
Civil Rights and Liberties 133
Civil Service 139
Claims Against the Government— *See* Government Immunity and Liability
Class Actions 143
Clergy— *See* Religion
Coal— *See* Mines and Minerals
Cohabitation 144
Collaboration— *See* Treason
Collection Laws 145
Collective Bargaining— *See* Labor and Labor Relations
Colleges and Universities 146
Commerce— *See* Commerce Department; Commercial Law
Commerce Department 147
Commercial Arbitration— *See* Arbitration and Award
Commercial Crimes— *See* Business Crime; Fraud
Commercial Law 147

Encyclopedia of Legal Information Sources • 2nd Ed.   **OUTLINE OF CONTENTS**

Commodity Futures Trading Commission	150
Commodity Trading	151
Common Law	153
Communications Law— *See* Federal Communications Commission; Telecommunications; Television and Radio	
Community Property	153
Comparable Worth— *See* Equal Employment Opportunity	
Comparative Law	154
Comparative Negligence— *See* Torts	
Compensation of Crime Victims— *See* Crime Victims	
Competition and Unfair Competition — *See* Antitrust Law; Trade Secrets	
Complex Litigation	156
Compromise and Settlement	156
Comptroller General	158
Computer Contracts	159
Computer Crimes	159
Computer Software Protection and Licensing	161
Computers	162
Computers and Legal Research	164
Conciliation— *See* Arbitration and Award; Compromise and Settlement; International Arbitration; Labor Arbitration	
Condemnation of Land— *See* Eminent Domain	
Condominiums and Cooperative Buildings	166
Confessions	167
Confidential Communications	167
Confiscation— *See* Eminent Domain; Government Ownership	
Conflict of Interest	169
Conflict of Laws	170
Congress— *See* Legislative History and Process	
Conscientious Objectors	171
Conservation— *See* Energy; Natural Resources	
Conservatorship— *See* Guardian and Ward	
Consolidation and Merger of Corporations— *See* Antitrust Law; Corporations, Consolidation and Merger	
Conspiracy	172
Constitutional History	172
Constitutional Law	175
Constitutions	179
Construction Industry	180
Consumer Credit	184
Consumer Protection	187
Continental Shelf— *See* Law of the Sea	
Contraception— *See* Birth Control; Family Law	
Contracts	190
Contributory Negligence— *See* Torts	
Controlled Substances— *See* Drug Laws	
Conventions, International— *See* Treaties and Conventions	

Cooperatives— *See* Condominiums and Cooperative Buildings	
Copyright	194
Copyright Office	200
Coroners and Medical Examiners	200
Corporations	201
Corporations, Consolidation and Mergers	206
Corporations, Foreign and Multinational	209
Corporations, Formation	210
Corporations, Officers and Directors	211
Corporations, Taxation	213
Corrections— *See* Prisons and Prisoners	
Corruption, Political	218
Cosmetics— *See* Drug Laws	
Counsel, Right to— *See* Due Process of Law	
Counterclaim— *See* Damages	
Counterfeiting	220
Countervailing Duties— *See* Export and Import	
County Government— *See* Local Government	
Court Clerks— *See* Circuit Courts of Appeal; District Courts; States; Supreme Court	
Court-Martial— *See* Military Law and Service	
Court Opinions— *See* Circuit Courts of Appeal; District Courts; States; Supreme Court	
Court Rules— *See* Administrative Office of the United States Courts; Circuit Courts of Appeal; District Courts; States; Supreme Court	
Courthouses	221
Courts	221
Covenants— *See* Contracts; Real Property	
Credit	228
Crime Victims	232
Criminal Investigation	234
Criminal Justice, Administration of	236
Criminal Law	244
Criminal Procedure	247
Critical Legal Studies	253
Crops— *See* Agriculture	
Cross-Examination	254
Cruel and Unusual Punishment— *See* Punishment	
Currency— *See* Money and Monetary Control	
Custody— *See* Child Custody; Guardian and Ward; Habeas Corpus; Prisons and Prisoners	
Customs— *See* Customs Service; Export and Import	
Customs Service	255
Damages	257
Databases— *See* Bioethics; Computer Software; Computers; Legal Research	
Death	258
Death Penalty— *See* Capital Punishment	
Debtor and Creditor— *See* Attachment and Garnishment; Bankruptcy; Collection Laws; Credit	
Decendents' Estates— *See* Wills, Trusts, and Inheritance	

Deceit— *See* Fraud
Declaratory Judgments— *See* Judgments
Deeds— *See* Real Property
Deeds of Trust— *See* Mortgages; Real Property
Defamation— *See* Libel and Slander
Defense Department 260
Defenses— *See* Actions and Defenses
Demonstrations— *See* Freedom of Assembly and Association
Demonstrative and Visual Evidence 261
Dental Jurisprudence 262
Department of Agriculture— *See* Agriculture Department
Department of Commerce— *See* Commerce Department
Department of Defense— *See* Defense Department
Department of Education— *See* Education Department
Department of Energy— *See* Energy Department
Department of Health and Human Services— *See* Health and Human Services Department
Department of the Interior— *See* Interior Department
Department of Justice— *See* Justice Department
Department of Labor— *See* Labor Department
Department of State— *See* State Department
Department of Transportation— *See* Transportation Department
Department of Treasury— *See* Treasury Department
Deportation— *See* Emigration and Immigration
Depositions— *See* Discovery; Witnesses
Descent and Distribution— *See* Wills, Trusts, and Inheritance
Desertion— *See* Family Law
Dictionaries— *See* Legal Research; Heading "Encyclopedias and Dictionaries" under specific topics
Diplomatic Privileges and Immunities 264
Directories— *See* Legal Directories
Disability Insurance— *See* Insurance, Health, and Unemployment
Disabled— *See* Mental Health and Disability; Physically Handicapped
Disbarment of Attorneys— *See* Legal Ethics and Malpractice
Discovery 265
Discrimination, Education 266
Discrimination, Employment 268
Discrimination, Housing 272
Discrimination, Race 273
Discrimination, Sex 274
Dispute Resolution 278
Distressed Property— *See* Landlord and Tenant; Real Property
District Attorneys— *See* Public Prosecutors
District Courts 281

Dividends— *See* Securities
Divorce, Separation, and Marriage 283
Doctors— *See* Discrimination, Sex; Medical Jurisprudence and Malpractice
Documents— *See* Evidence; Freedom of Information
Domestic Relations— *See* Family Law
Domestic Violence— *See* Child Abuse and Neglect; Family Violence
Domicile— *See* Jurisdiction
Double Jeopardy 287
Dower and Curtesy 288
Draft, Military— *See* Conscientious Objectors; Military Law and Service
Drinking and Drunkenness— *See* Alcohol Control and Drinking Behavior
Drug Laws 288
Drug Testing 291
Drunkenness— *See* Alcohol Control and Drinking Behavior
Due Process of Law 292
Dumping— *See* Export and Import
Easements— *See* Real Property
Eavesdropping 295
Ecclesiastical Law— *See* Canon Law; Religion
Economics— *See* Antitrust and Economics; Money and Monetary Control; Torts
Education 295
Education Department 300
Education Finance— *See* Education; Federal Aid to Education
Election Finance— *See* Election Law
Election Law 300
Electricity— *See* Energy; Public Utilities
Electronic Funds Transfer 302
Embezzlement 303
Emigration and Immigration 303
Eminent Domain 308
Employee Fringe Benefits 309
Employees' Compensation Appeals Board 313
Employer and Employee— *See* Agency; Employment Law; Labor and Labor Relations; Workers' Compensation
Employer's Liability— *See* Workers' Compensation
Employment Discrimination— *See* Discrimination, Employment
Employment Law 313
Endangered Species— *See* Animals; Wildlife
Energy 317
Energy Department 319
Enforcement of Judgments— *See* Judgments
Engineers and Engineering Law 320
Entertainment Law 321
Entrapment 322
Environmental Law 322
Environmental Protection Agency 329

Equal Employment Opportunity 329
Equal Employment Opportunity Commission 332
Equal Pay— *See* Equal Employment Opportunity; Discrimination, Sex
Equal Protection— *See* Discrimination, Employment; Discrimination, Housing; Discrimination, Race; Discrimination, Sex; Due Process of Law
Equipment Leasing— *See* Leases
Equity Pleading and Procedure— *See* Civil Procedure; Restitution
Escheat— *See* Wills, Trusts and Inheritance
Estate, Inheritance and Transfer Taxes 333
Estates— *See* Estate, Inheritance and Transfer Taxes; Real Property; Wills, Trusts and Inheritance
Estoppel— *See* Actions and Defenses; Judgments
Ethics— *See* Legal Ethics and Malpractice; Professional Ethics and Liability
European Economic Community (EEC) 336
Euthanasia 341
Eviction— *See* Landlord and Tenant
Evidence 343
Excise Taxes 349
Execution— *See* Capital Punishment; Judgments
Executive Power 350
Executors and Administrators— *See* Wills, Trusts, and Inheritance
Expatriation and Deportation— *See* Citizens and Citizenship; Emigration and Immigration
Expert Witnesses— *See* Trial Practice; Witnesses
Explosives— *See* Fires and Fire Prevention; Hazardous Substances
Export and Import 352
Expropriation— *See* Eminent Domain; Government Ownership
Extradition and Asylum— *See* Emigration and Immigration
Extraterritoriality— *See* International Law and Relations
Fair Employment Practices 357
Fair Trial, Right to 359
Family Law 359
Family Violence 362
Farms and Farming— *See* Agriculture
Federal Aid 365
Federal Aid to Education 366
Federal Aviation Administration 368
Federal Bureau of Investigation 368
Federal Communications Commission 369
Federal Contracts— *See* Government Contracts
Federal Courts 369
Federal Energy Regulatory Commission 371
Federal Judicial Center 371
Federal Jurisdiction— *See* Jurisdiction
Federal Labor Relations Authority 373
Federal Maritime Commission 374

Federal Mine Safety and Health Review Commission . 374
Federal Reserve Board 374
Federal Trade Commission 375
Federalism 376
Fees— *See* Lawyers' Fees
Fiction— *See* Legal Profession in Fiction
Fiduciary Relationship— *See* Guardian and Ward; Wills, Trusts, and Inheritance
Finance— *See* Credit; Loans; Mortgages; Public Finance
Financial Responsibility Laws— *See* Insurance, Motor Vehicle and Aviation
Firearms and Ballistics 378
Fires and Fire Prevention 380
Fish and Fishing 382
Fixtures— *See* Landlord and Tenant; Real Property
Flammable Substances— *See* Fires and Fire Prevention; Hazardous Substances
Food and Drug Administration 384
Food Laws 385
Foreclosures 387
Foreign Affairs— *See* International Law and Relations
Foreign Corporations— *See* Corporations, Foreign and Multinational; International Trade
Foreign Investments— *See* International Trade
Foreign Law 388
Foreign Relations— *See* International Law and Relations
Foreign Trade— *See* Export and Import
Forensic Medicine— *See* Coroners and Medical Examiners; Medical Jurisprudence and Malpractice
Forests and Forestry 410
Forgery 412
Forms— *See* Legal Forms
Foster Care 413
Foundations— *See* Associations and Nonprofit Corporations; Charities
Franchising 413
Fraud 414
Freedom of Assembly and Association 415
Freedom of Association— *See* Freedom of Assembly and Association
Freedom of Information 416
Freedom of Press 419
Freedom of Religion— *See* Church and State; Religion
Freedom of Speech 420
Freight— *See* Trade Regulation; Transportation
Funerals and Burial 422
Future Interests— *See* Real Property; Wills, Trusts and Inheritance
Futures— *See* Commodity Trading
Gambling 425

Game— *See* Wildlife
Garnishment— *See* Attachment and Garnishment
Gas— *See* Oil and Gas
Gays— *See* Sexual Orientation
General Accounting Office 426
Genetic Engineering— *See* Medical Jurisprudence and Malpractice
Genocide 426
Gerontology— *See* Aged and Aging
Gifts— *See* Wills, Trusts and Inheritance
Government— *See* Administrative Law; Government Contracts; Government Corporations; Government Immunity and Liability; Government Ownership; Local Government; States
Government Contracts 427
Government Corporations 432
Government Employees— *See* Public Officials and Employees
Government Immunity and Liability 433
Government Information— *See* Freedom of Information
Government Liability— *See* Government Immunity and Liability
Government Ownership 434
Grand Jury 434
Grants-In-Aid 435
Guaranty— *See* Suretyship and Guaranty
Guardian and Ward 437
Gun Control— *See* Firearms and Ballistics
Habeas Corpus 439
Handicapped— *See* Mental Health and Disability; Physically Handicapped
Handwriting— *See* Evidence
Hazardous Substances 440
Health and Human Services Department 444
Health Care 445
Hearsay— *See* Evidence
Heirs— *See* Wills, Trusts and Inheritance
High Technology 449
Hijacking of Airlines— *See* Terrorism
Historic Preservation 450
History— *See* Historic Preservation; Legal History
Homelessness 451
Homestead Law— *See* Real Property
Homicide— *See* Murder; Suicide
Homosexuality— *See* Sexual Orientation
Hospitals 453
Hostages— *See* Kidnapping; Terrorism
Hotels, Restaurants, etc. 456
Housing 457
Housing Discrimination— *See* Discrimination, Housing
Human Rights 460
Humor— *See* Legal Humor

Husband and Wife— *See* Community Property; Divorce, Separation and Marriage; Family Law; Family Violence
Identification— *See* Evidence; Firearms and Ballistics
Illegitimacy— *See* Family Law
Immigration— *See* Emigration and Immigration
Immigration and Naturalization Service 467
Immunity— *See* Diplomatic Privileges and Immunity; Government Immunity and Liability
Impeachment of Public Officials— *See* See President (United States); Public Officials and Employees
Implied Trusts— *See* Wills, Trusts and Inheritance
Imports— *See* Exports and Imports
Incapacity— *See* Children; Mental Health and Disability; Physically Handicapped
Income Tax, Federal 468
Incompetents— *See* Guardian and Ward
Incorporation— *See* Corporations, Formation
Independent Contractors— *See* Agency
Indians of North America 479
Indigence 482
Industrial Arbitration— *See* Labor Arbitration
Industrial Diseases— *See* Occupational Safety and Health
Industrial Property— *See* Patents; Trademarks and Trade Names
Industrial Relations— *See* Labor and Labor Relations
Industrial Safety— *See* Occupational Safety and Health
Infants— *See* Children
Information, Freedom— *See* Freedom of Information
Information Storage and Retrieval Systems— *See* Computers; Legal Research
Inheritance— *See* Wills, Trusts and Inheritance
Inheritance and Transfer Taxes 484
Initiative and Referendum— *See* Election Law; Legislative History and Process
Injunctions— *See* Civil Procedure; Remedies
Injuries— *See* Personal Injuries; Torts
Inns— *See* Hotels, Restaurants, etc.
Insanity— *See* Mental Health and Disability
Insemination, Artificial— *See* Family Law
Insolvency— *See* Bankruptcy
Instructions to Juries— *See* Jury; States
Insurance 485
Insurance, Disability— *See* Insurance, Health and Unemployment
Insurance, Health and Unemployment 492
Insurance, Liability 493
Insurance, Life 495
Insurance, Motor Vehicle and Aviation 496
Insurance, Property 496
Insurance, Unemployment— *See* Insurance, Health and Unemployment
Integration— *See* Segregation and Integration

Intellectual Property— *See* Copyright; Licensing, Industrial and Intellectual; Patents; Trademarks and Trade Names
Interest and Usury— *See* Banks and Banking; Consumer Credit; Loans
Interior Department 498
Internal Revenue Service 498
International Agencies and Organizations 500
International Agreements— *See* Treaties and Conventions
International Arbitration 503
International Claims— *See* Government Immunity and Liability
International Commerce— *See* Export and Import
International Conventions— *See* Treaties and Conventions
International Courts and Tribunals 505
International Crime 506
International Criminal Law— *See* International Crime
International Jurisprudence— *See* International Law and Relations
International Law and Relations 507
International Organizations— *See* International Agencies and Organizations
International Trade 516
International Trade Administration 524
International Trade Commission 525
Interpretation of Statutes— *See* Statutory Construction and Drafting
Interrogatories— *See* Discovery, Civil; Discovery, Criminal
Interstate Agreements— *See* State Government
Interstate Commerce— *See* Interstate Commerce Commission; Trade Regulation; Transportation
Interstate Commerce Commission 526
Intoxicating Liquors— *See* Alcohol Control and Drinking Behavior
Inventions— *See* Patents
Investments 526
Investments, Foreign— *See* Corporations, Foreign and Multinational; International Trade
Irrigation— *See* Water Law
Job Discrimination— *See* Discrimination, Employment
Job Safety— *See* Occupational Safety and Health
Joint Ventures 533
Judge-Made Law— *See* Common Law
Judges and Judicial Process 535
Judgments 542
Judicial Opinions— *See* Judgments
Judicial Process— *See* Administration of Justice; Courts; Judges and Judicial Process
Judicial Review— *See* Common Law; Judges and Judicial Process; Separation of Powers

Jurisdiction 543
Jurisdiction, International Law— *See* International Arbitration; International Courts and Tribunals; Jurisdiction
Jurisprudence 544
Jury 549
Justice Department 553
Justices of the Peace— *See* Courts; Judges
Juvenile Courts— *See* Children; Courts; Juveniles
Juvenile Delinquency— *See* Children; Criminal Law
Juveniles 554
Kidnapping 561
Labor and Labor Relations 563
Labor Arbitration 571
Labor Department 574
Labor Relations— *See* Labor and Labor Relations
Land Use— *See* Agriculture; Public Land; Zoning and Planning
Landlord and Tenant 575
Law Enforcement 576
Law Examinations 579
Law in Art 579
Law Libraries 579
Law of the Sea 583
Law Office Management 586
Law Practice 590
Law Schools— *See* Legal Education
Law Societies 595
Lawyer and Client 603
Lawyers— *See* Admission to the Bar; American Bar Association; Law Office Management; Law Practice; Lawyer and Client; Lawyers' Fees; Legal Aid; Legal Ethics and Malpractice; Legal Profession in Fiction; Prepaid Legal Services; Public Prosecutors
Lawyers' Fees 605
Learning Disabled— *See* Mental Health and Disability
Leases 606
Legal Abbreviations— *See* Legal Research
Legal Aid 608
Legal Assistants 610
Legal Dictionaries— *See* Legal Research
Legal Directories 611
Legal Drafting— *See* Legal Writing; Statutory Construction and Drafting
Legal Education 614
Legal Ethics and Malpractice 618
Legal Forms 622
Legal History 625
Legal Humor 628
Legal Malpractice— *See* Legal Ethics and Malpractice; Professional Ethics and Liability

Legal Profession— *See* American Bar Association; Law Practice; Lawyer and Client; Legal Assistants; Legal Directories; Legal Ethics and Malpractice; Legal Profession in Fiction; Legal Secretaries
Legal Profession in Fiction 629
Legal Quotations 629
Legal Research 630
Legal Secretaries 636
Legal Services Corporation— *See* Federal Aid; Legal Aid
Legal Terminology— *See* Legal Research; Statutory Construction and Drafting
Legal Writing 637
Legislative History and Process 639
Legislative Process— *See* Legislative History and Process
Lesbians— *See* Sexual Orientation
Letters of Credit 643
Liability— *See* Criminal Law; Damages; Government Immunity and Liability; Products Liability and Safety; Torts
Liability Insurance— *See* Insurance, Liability; Insurance, Motor Vehicle and Aviation
Libel and Slander 644
Libraries 645
Licensing, Industrial and Intellectual 648
Licensing, Occupational— *See* Professional Ethics and Liability
Lie Detectors and Detection 650
Liens— *See* Admiralty; Construction Industry; Mortgages; Secured Transactions
Life Estates— *See* Real Property; Wills, Trusts and Inheritance
Life Insurance— *See* Insurance, Life
Limitations of Actions— *See* Civil Procedure
Liquidation 651
Liquor Laws— *See* Alcohol Control and Drinking Behavior
Literary Property— *See* Authors and Publishers; Copyright
Litigation— *See* Complex Litigation; Trial Practice
Loans 652
Lobbying 654
Local Government 656
Local Transit 658
Lockouts— *See* Labor and Labor Relations
Lost Property— *See* Personal Property
Lotteries— *See* Gambling
Loyalty Oaths— *See* Constitutional Law; Political Crimes and Offenses
Lumber— *See* Forests and Forestry
Magistrates— *See* Federal Judicial Center
Malicious Prosecution— *See* Torts

Malpractice— *See* Legal Ethics and Malpractice; Medical Jurisprudence and Malpractice
Management-Labor Relations— *See* Labor and Labor Relations
Manslaughter— *See* Murder
Maritime Law— *See* Admiralty; Law of the Sea
Marriage and Divorce— *See* Child Custody; Cohabitation; Community Property; Divorce, Separation and Marriage; Family Law
Master and Servant— *See* Agency; Labor and Labor Relations
Materialmen's Liens— *See* Construction Industry
Mechanic's Liens— *See* Construction Industry
Mediation— *See* Arbitration and Award; Labor Arbitration
Medical Examiners— *See* Coroners and Medical Examiners
Medical Jurisprudence and Malpractice 661
Medical Malpractice— *See* Medical Jurisprudence and Malpractice
Medicare and Medicaid— *See* Aged and Health Care; Health Care; Hospitals; Insurance, Health and Unemployment; Social Security
Mental Health and Disability 669
Mental Illness— *See* Mental Health and Disability
Mentally Handicapped 672
Merchandise Licensing— *See* Licensing, Industrial and Intellectual
Merchant Marine— *See* Admiralty
Merger— *See* Antitrust Law; Corporations, Consolidation and Merger
Merit Systems Protection Board 675
Migrant Labor— *See* Agriculture; Agriculture Department; Labor and Labor Relations
Military Law and Service 675
Mining Law 677
Minorities— *See* Civil Rights and Liberties; Discrimination, Education; Discrimination, Employment; Discrimination, Housing; Discrimination, Race; School Integration; Segregation and Integration
Minors— *See* Children
Model Codes— *See* Uniform and Model Acts
Money and Monetary Control 680
Money Laundering 683
Monopolies— *See* Antitrust Law
Monuments— *See* Historic Preservation; Public Land
Mortgages 684
Motels— *See* Hotels, Restaurants, etc.
Motion Pictures— *See* Copyright; Entertainment Law
Motions— *See* Civil Procedure
Motor Vehicle Accidents— *See* Accidents; Motor Vehicles
Motor Vehicle Insurance— *See* Insurance, Motor Vehicle and Aviation

Motor Vehicles	687
Motor Vehicles and Drinking— *See* Alcohol Control and Drinking Behavior; Motor Vehicles	
Multinational Corporations— *See* Corporations, Foreign and Multinational	
Multinational Litigation— *See* Complex Litigation	
Multistate Litigation— *See* Complex Litigation	
Municipal Corporations— *See* Local Government	
Municipal Courts— *See* Courts; Local Government	
Murder	690
Museums— *See* Art	
Mutual Funds— *See* Investments and Investment Companies	
Narcotics— *See* Drug Laws	
National Defense— *See* International Law and Relations; Military Law and Service; Political Crimes and Offenses; President (United States); Terrorism	
National Labor Relations Board	693
National Parks— *See* Parks and Monuments	
National Security— *See* Central Intelligence Agency; International Law and Relations; Military Law and Service; Political Crimes and Offenses; President (United States); Terrorism	
National Telecommunications and Information Administration	694
National Transportation Safety Board	694
Nationality— *See* Citizens and Citizenship	
Nationalization of Industry— *See* Eminent Domain; Government Ownership	
Native Races— *See* Indians of North America	
Natural Gas— *See* Oil and Gas	
Natural Law	695
Natural Resources	696
Naturalization— *See* Citizens and Citizenship	
Navy— *See* Admiralty; Military Law and Service	
Negligence— *See* Accidents; Admiralty; Aviation; Motor Vehicles; Personal Injuries; Products Liability and Safety; Torts; Wrongful Death	
Negotiable Instruments	699
Negotiation— *See* Arbitration and Award; Compromise and Settlement; Dispute Resolution; International Arbitration; Labor Arbitration	
Newspapers	700
Noise— *See* Environmental Law	
Nonprofit Corporations— *See* Associations and Nonprofit Corporations	
Notaries Public	703
Nuclear Energy	704
Nuclear Regulatory Commission	706
Nuisance— *See* Torts	
Nurses and Nursing	707
Nursing Homes	708
Obscenity	711

Occupational Diseases— *See* Occupational Safety and Health	
Occupational Safety and Health	712
Occupational Safety and Health Administration	714
Occupational Safety and Health Review Commission	715
Occupations— *See* Occupational Safety and Health; Professional Ethics and Liability	
Office of Personnel Management	715
Officers— *See* Corporations, Officers and Directors; Public Officials and Employees	
Oil and Gas	716
Open Meetings— *See* Freedom of Information	
Opinions, Judicial— *See* Judgments	
Organized Crime	720
Paralegals— *See* Legal Assistants	
Pardon— *See* Criminal Law; President (United States); Probation and Parole; Rehabilitation of Offenders	
Parent and Child— *See* Adoption; Child Abuse and Neglect; Child Custody; Children; Family Law; Guardian and Ward	
Parks and Monuments— *See* Historic Preservation; Public Land	
Parole— *See* Criminal Law; Probation and Parole; Rehabilitation of Offenders	
Partition— *See* Real Property	
Partnership	723
Patent and Trademark Office	726
Patents	726
Paternity— *See* Family Law	
Peace Officers— *See* Law Enforcement; Police	
Penology— *See* Prisons and Prisoners	
Pensions— *See* Employee Fringe Benefits; Insurance, Life; Social Security	
Performing Arts— *See* Entertainment Law	
Perjury— *See* Criminal Law	
Personal Injuries	731
Personal Property	735
Pharmacists and Pharmacy	736
Philosophy of Law— *See* Jurisprudence; Natural Law	
Photographs and Photography	737
Physically Handicapped	737
Physicians— *See* Medical Jurisprudence and Malpractice	
Picketing— *See* Freedom of Assembly and Association; Freedom of Speech; Labor and Labor Relations	
Pipelines— *See* Oil and Gas	
Planned Parenthood— *See* Birth Control	
Planning— *See* Zoning and Planning	
Pleading— *See* Civil Procedure; Legal Forms	
Poisons— *See* Hazardous Substances	
Police	739
Police Magistrates— *See* Police	
Police Power— *See* Constitutional Law; Police	

Political Crimes and Offenses 743
Political Offenses— *See* Political Crimes and Offenses
Politics— *See* Election Law; Lobbying
Pollution— *See* Environmental Law
Poor People— *See* Indigence; Legal Aid
Pornography— *See* Obscenity
Post-Conviction Remedies 744
Poverty Law— *See* Indigence
Practice of Law— *See* Admission to the Bar; Law Office Management; Law Practice; Lawyer and Client; Lawyers' Fees; Legal Ethics and Malpractice; Legal Forms; Legal Profession in Fiction; Prepaid Legal Services
Precedent, Judicial— *See* Judgments
Prepaid Legal Services 744
Pre-Marital Agreements— *See* Family Law
Pretrial Procedure— *See* Civil Procedure; Criminal Procedure; Trial Practice
President (United States) 744
Price Regulation— *See* Consumer Protection
Principal and Agent— *See* Agency
Prisons and Prisoners 750
Privacy, Right of 753
Private International Law and Relations— *See* Conflict of Laws
Privileged Communications— *See* Confidential Communications
Privileges and Immunities— *See* Diplomatic Privileges and Immunities; Government Immunity and Liability
Probate Law and Practice— *See* Wills, Trusts and Inheritance
Probation and Parole 755
Process Service— *See* Civil Procedure
Products Liability and Safety 757
Professional Corporations 761
Professional Ethics and Liability 761
Profit-Sharing— *See* Employee Fringe Benefits
Property— *See* Personal Property; Public Land; Real Property; Time-Share Property
Prosecuting Attorneys— *See* Public Prosecutors
Prostitution 765
Proximate Cause— *See* Torts
Psychiatry 765
Psychology 767
Public Administration 769
Public Assistance— *See* Federal Aid; Indigence
Public Contracts— *See* Government Contracts
Public Corporations— *See* Government Corporations; Local Government
Public Debts— *See* Public Finance
Public Defenders— *See* Legal Aid
Public Employees— *See* Public Officials and Employees
Public Finance 772

Public Health— *See* Health Care
Public Housing— *See* Housing
Public Land 774
Public Legal Services— *See* Legal Aid
Public Meetings— *See* Freedom of Assembly and Association; Freedom of Information
Public Officials and Employees 775
Public Property— *See* Public Land
Public Prosecutors 776
Public Records— *See* Freedom of Information
Public Utilities 777
Public Welfare— *See* Federal Aid; Indigence
Publishers and Authors— *See* Authors and Publishers; Copyright
Punishment 779
Quasi-Contract— *See* Restitution
Quotations— *See* Legal Quotations
Race Discrimination— *See* Discrimination, Race
Racketeering— *See* Organized Crime
Radio— *See* Television and Radio
Railroads 783
Rape 785
Real Estate Business— *See* Real Property
Real Property 786
Real Property Taxation 793
Recidivism— *See* Rehabilitation of Offenders
Records— *See* Evidence; Freedom of Information
Referendum— *See* Election Law; Legislative History and Process
Refugees— *See* Emigration and Immigration
Regional Planning— *See* Zoning and Planning
Rehabilitation of Offenders 796
Religion 798
Remainders— *See* Real Property; Wills, Trusts and Inheritance
Remedies 800
Removal of Causes— *See* Civil Procedure
Rent and Rent Control— *See* Landlord and Tenant
Renvoi— *See* Conflict of Laws
Reorganization, Corporate— *See* Bankruptcy
Res Judicata— *See* Civil Procedure; Judgments
Residence— *See* Jurisdiction
Restatements 801
Restaurants— *See* Hotels, Restaurants, etc.
Restitution 801
Restraint of Trade— *See* Antitrust Law
Restraints on Alienation— *See* Real Property
Restrictive Convenants— *See* Contracts; Real Property
Resulting Trusts— *See* Wills, Trusts and Inheritance
Retardation— *See* Mental Health and Disability
Retirement Communities— *See* Aged and Aging; Aged and Retirement
Retirement Income— *See* Social Security
Revenue Sharing— *See* Federal Aid

Reversions— *See* Real Property
Right of Assembly— *See* Freedom of Assembly and Association
Right of Privacy— *See* Privacy, Right of
Right to Counsel— *See* Due Process of Law
Right to Die— *See* Death; Euthanasia; Medical Jurisprudence and Malpractice
Right to Fair Trial— *See* Due Process of Law
Right to Life— *See* Abortion; Euthanasia
Right to Trial by Jury— *See* Due Process of Law; Jury
Right to Work— *See* Labor and Labor Relations
Riots— *See* Criminal Law
Riparian Rights— *See* Water Law
Roman Law 803
Safety Laws— *See* Consumer Protection; Drug Laws; Fires and Fire Prevention; Food Laws; Hazardous Substances; Occupational Safety and Health; Products Liability and Safety
Sales— *See* Commercial Law; Secured Transactions
Sales and Use Taxes 805
Salvage— *See* Admiralty
Savings and Loan Associations— *See* Banks and Banking
School Integration 805
School Violence and Discipline 807
Schools— *See* Education; Mental Health and Disability; School Integration; School Violence and Discipline
Science 808
Seamen— *See* Admiralty
Search and Seizure 810
Seas— *See* Admiralty; Law of the Sea
Section 1983— *See* Civil Rights and Liberties; Civil Rights Commission
Secured Transactions 811
Securities 813
Securities and Exchange Commission 819
Segregation and Integration 820
Selective Service— *See* Military Law and Service
Self-Incrimination— *See* Criminal Procedure
Senior Citizens— *See* Aged and Aging
Sentencing 821
Separation, Marital— *See* Family Law
Separation of Powers 823
Service of Process— *See* Civil Procedure
Servitudes— *See* Real Property
Settlement— *See* Arbitration and Award; Compromise and Settlement
Set-Off and Counterclaims— *See* Damages
Sex Crimes 824
Sex Discrimination— *See* Discrimination, Sex
Sexual Harassment 825
Sexual Orientation 827
Sexual Preference— *See* Sexual Orientation
Shareholders— *See* Corporations; Securities

Shipping— *See* Transportation
Ships and Boats— *See* Admiralty
Slander— *See* Libel and Slander
Slavery 828
Small Business 829
Small Claims Courts 833
Smog— *See* Environmental Law
Social Science 833
Social Security 835
Social Security Administration 837
Social Welfare— *See* Indigence
Societies— *See* Associations and Nonprofit Corporations; Law Societies
Solar Energy 837
Soldiers— *See* Military Law and Service; Veterans
Solicitors— *See* Admission to the Bar; Law Office Management; Law Practice; Lawyer and Client; Lawyers' Fees; Legal Ethics and Malpractice; Legal Profession in Fiction; Prepaid Legal Services
Sovereignty— *See* Government Immunity and Liability; International Law and Relations
Space Law 838
Special Education— *See* Mental Health and Disability; Physically Handicapped
Specific Performance— *See* Contracts
Speedy Trial, Right to— *See* Due Process of Law
Sports Law 839
Standing to Sue— *See* Civil Procedure
Stare Decisis— *See* Judgment and Judicial Opinions
State Courts 841
State Department 847
State Government 848
State Law Compilations 851
Stateless Persons— *See* Citizens and Citizenship; Emigration and Immigration
States - Alabama 852
States - Alaska 854
States - Arizona 856
States - Arkansas 857
States - California 859
States - Colorado 865
States - Connecticut 867
States - Delaware 869
States - District of Columbia 870
States - Florida 873
States - Georgia 877
States - Hawaii 880
States - Idaho 881
States - Illinois 882
States - Indiana 885
States - Iowa 888
States - Kansas 890
States - Kentucky 891
States - Louisiana 893

States - Maine	895
States - Maryland	897
States - Massachusetts	900
States - Michigan	903
States - Minnesota	906
States - Mississippi	909
States - Missouri	910
States - Montana	913
States - Nebraska	914
States - Nevada	915
States - New Hampshire	916
States - New Jersey	918
States - New Mexico	920
States - New York	922
States - North Carolina	927
States - North Dakota	929
States - Ohio	930
States - Oklahoma	934
States - Oregon	936
States - Pennsylvania	938
States - Rhode Island	941
States - South Carolina	942
States - South Dakota	943
States - Tennessee	944
States - Texas	947
States - Utah	951
States - Vermont	952
States - Virginia	953
States - Washington	956
States - West Virginia	959
States - Wisconsin	961
States - Wyoming	963

States' Rights— See State Government
Statutes— See Legislative History and Process; State Law Compilations; States; Statutory Construction and Drafting
Statutes of Limitation— See Civil Procedure

Statutory Construction and Drafting	965
Sterilization	965

Stocks— See Securities
Strict Liability— See Products Liability and Safety; Torts
Strikes— See Labor and Labor Relations
Study of Law— See Legal Education
Subversive Activities— See Political Crimes and Offenses; Terrorism
Succession— See Wills, Trusts and Inheritance

Suicide	966

Summary Proceedings— See Civil Procedure
Sunset Legislation— See Administrative Law
Support of Dependants— See Family Law

Supreme Court (United States)	967
Surety and Guaranty	972

Surgeons— See Medical Jurisprudence and Malpractice
Surrogate Motherhood— See Family Law
Survival of Actions— See Wrongful Death
Taverns— See Alcohol Control and Drinking Behavior; Hotels, Restaurants, etc.
Tax— See Corporations, Taxation; Estate, Inheritance and Transfer Taxes; Excise Taxes; Income Tax, Federal; Internal Revenue Service; Real Property Taxation; Sales and Use Taxes; Tax and Estate Planning; Tax Court; Tax Exempt Organizations; Tax Legislation and Policy; Tax Practice and Enforcement; Tax Returns; Tax Shelters; Taxation, International; Taxation, State and Local

Tax and Estate Planning	973
Tax Court	981
Tax Exempt Organizations	982
Tax Legislation and Policy	983
Tax Practice and Enforcement	986
Tax Returns	990
Tax Shelters	993

Taxation— See Corporations, Taxation; Estate, Inheritance and Transfer Taxes; Excise Taxes; Income Tax, Federal; Internal Revenue Service; Real Property Taxation; Sales and Use Taxes; Tax and Estate Planning; Tax Court; Tax Exempt Organizations; Tax Legislation and Policy; Tax Practice and Enforcement; Tax Returns; Tax Shelters; Taxation, International; Taxation, State and Local

Taxation, International	995
Taxation, State and Local	998

Teachers— See Education; School Integration; School Violence and Discipline

Telecommunications	999

Telephones— See Telecommunications

Television and Radio	1003

Tenancy— See Landlord and Tenant
Tender Offers— See Corporations, Consolidation and Merger
Terminology— See Legal Research; Statutory Construction and Drafting
Territorial Waters— See Law of the Sea

Terrorism	1007

Theaters— See Entertainment Law

Time-Share Property	1009

Title to Land— See Real Property
Tort Claim Act— See Government Immunity and Liability

Torts	1010

Town Government— See Local Government
Toxic Substances— See Hazardous Substances
Trade— See Commercial Law; Trade Regulation
Trade and Professional Associations — See Associations and Nonprofit Corporations

Trade Regulation	1014

Trade Secrets	1016
Trade Unions— *See* Labor and Labor Relations	
Trademarks and Trade Names	1017
Traffic— *See* Motor Vehicles	
Transnational Litigation— *See* Conflict of Laws	
Transportation	1020
Transportation Department	1022
Travel and Travel Agency	1022
Treason	1023
Treasury Department	1024
Treaties and Conventions	1024
Trees— *See* Forests and Forestry	
Trial by Jury, Right to— *See* Due Process of Law	
Trial Practice	1027
Trials, Noteworthy	1034
Trusts and Trustees— *See* Wills, Trusts and Inheritance	
Trusts, Industrial— *See* Antitrust Law	
Unemployment— *See* Labor and Labor Relations	
Unfair Competition— *See* Antitrust Law	
Unfair Labor Practices— *See* Labor and Labor Relations	
Uniform and Model Acts	1037
Unions— *See* Labor and Labor Relations	
United Nations	1048
United States Government— *See* Attorney-General (United States); Circuit Courts of Appeal (United States); District Courts (United States); Federal Courts; President (United States); Supreme Court (United States)	
Universities— *See* Education; School Integration; School Violence and Discipline	
Unjust Enrichment— *See* Restitution	
Unmarried Couples— *See* Cohabitation	
Urban Renewal— *See* Historic Preservation; Local Government; Zoning and Planning	
Usury— *See* Banks and Banking	
Vehicles— *See* Motor Vehicles	
Venue— *See* Civil Procedure; Trial Practice	
Verdicts— *See* Jury	
Veterans	1055
Veterinarians	1056
Vicarious Liability— *See* Agency	
Victims of Crime— *See* Crime Victims	
Videogames— *See* Entertainment Law	
Videotape— *See* Television and Radio	
Voting— *See* Election Law	
Wages— *See* Labor and Labor Relations	
War and War Crimes— *See* International Law and Relations; Military Law and Service	
Ward— *See* Guardian and Ward	
Water Law	1059
Weapons— *See* Criminal Law; Firearms	
Welfare— *See* Indigence	
White Collar Crime— *See* Business Crime	
Wife Abuse— *See* Family Violence	
Wildlife	1061
Will, Trusts and Inheritance	1063
Wiretapping— *See* Eavesdropping	
Witnesses	1069
Women	1071
Workers' Compensation	1078
World Trade— *See* Export and Import	
Writs— *See* Civil Procedure	
Wrongful Death	1080
Zoning and Planning	1081

Encyclopedia of Legal Information Sources

A

ABBREVIATIONS
See: LEGAL RESEARCH

ABDUCTION
See: KIDNAPPING; TERRORISM

ABORTION
See also: BIRTH CONTROL

LOOSELEAF SERVICES AND REPORTERS

REPORTER ON HUMAN REPRODUCTION AND THE LAW. Legal-Medical Studies Incorporated, P.O. Box 8219, JFK Station, Boston, Massachusetts 02114. 1971- . (Bimonthly Supplements).

HANDBOOKS, MANUALS, FORMBOOKS

ABORTION GUIDE: A HANDBOOK FOR WOMEN AND MEN. Carole Cornblaser and Uta Landry. Berkley Publishing Group, 200 Madison Avenue, New York, New York 10016. 1982.

TEXTBOOKS AND GENERAL WORKS

ABORTED WOMEN: SILENT NO MORE. David C. Reardon. Loyola University Press, 3441 North Ashland Avenue, Chicago, Illinois 60657. 1987.

ABORTING AMERICA. Bernard N. Nathanson and Richard N. Ostling. Doubleday and Company, 666 Fifth Avenue, New York, New York 10103. 1979.

ABORTION. Janet Podell, Editor. H.W. Wilson and Company, 950 University Avenue, Bronx, New York 10452. 1990.

ABORTION: A CASE STUDY IN LAW AND MORALS. Fred Frohock. Greenwood Publishing Group, Incorporated, 88 Post Road West, P.O. Box 5007, Westport, Connecticut 06881. 1983.

ABORTION AND DIVORCE IN WESTERN LAW. Mary Ann Glendon. Harvard University Press, 79 Garden Street, Cambridge, Massachusetts 02138. 1987.

ABORTION AND MORAL THEORY. L.W. Sumner. Princeton University Press, 41 William Street, Princeton, New Jersey 08540. 1981.

ABORTION AND PROTECTION OF THE FETUS: LEGAL PROBLEMS IN A CROSS-CULTURAL PERSPECTIVE. Paul Sachev. Kluwer Academic Publishers, 101 Philip Drive, Assinippi Park, Norwell, Massachusetts 02061. 1987.

ABORTION AND THE CONSCIENCE OF THE NATION. Ronald Reagan. Thomas Nelson, Incorporated, Nelson Place at Elm Hill Pike, Nashville, Tennessee 37214. 1984.

ABORTION AND THE CONSTITUTION: REVERSING ROE V. WADE THROUGH THE COURTS. Dennis J. Horan and others. Georgetown University Press, Intercultural Center, Room 111, Washington, D.C. 20057. 1987.

ABORTION AND THE POLITICS OF MOTHERHOOD. Kristin Luker. University of California Press, 2120 Berkeley Way, Berkeley, California 94720. 1984.

ABORTION AND THE PRIVATE PRACTICE OF MEDICINE. Jonathan B. Imber. Yale University Press, 302 Temple Street, New Haven, Connecticut 06520. 1986.

ABORTION AND THE STATUS OF THE FETUS. William B. Bondesor and H. Tristan Engelhardt. Kluwer Academic Publishers, 101 Philip Drive, Assinippi Park, Norwell, Massachusetts 02061. 1983.

ABORTION AND WOMEN'S CHOICE: THE STATE, SEXUALITY AND REPRODUCTIVE FREEDOM. Rosalind P. Petchesky. Northeastern University Press, 272 Huntington Plaza, 360 Huntington Avenue, Boston, Massachusetts 02115. 1990.

ABORTION DECISIONS OF THE SUPREME COURT, 1973 THROUGH 1989: A COMPREHENSIVE REVIEW WITH HISTORICAL COMMENTARY. Dan Drucker. McFarland and Company, P.O. Box 611, Jefferson, North Carolina 28640. 1990.

THE ABORTION DISPUTE AND THE AMERICAN SYSTEM. Gilbert Steiner, Editor. Brookings Institution, 1775 Massachusetts Avenue, Northwest, Washington, D.C. 20036. 1983.

ABORTION: FACING THE ISSUES. Susan Neiburg Terkel. Franklin Watts, Incorporated, 387 Park Avenue, South, New York, New York 10016. 1988.

ABORTION IN NINETEENTH CENTURY AMERICA. Arno Publishers, c/o Ayer Company, P.O. Box 958, Salem, New Hampshire 03079. 1974.

ABORTION: MORAL AND LEGAL PERSPECTIVES. Jay L. Garfield and Patricia Hennessey, Editors. University of Massachusetts Press, P.O. Box 429, Amherst, Massachusetts 01004. 1985.

ABORTION, POLITICS, AND THE COURTS: ROE V. WADE AND ITS AFTERMATH. Eva R. Rubin. Greenwood Publishing Group, Incorporated, 88 Post Road West, P.O. Box 5007, Westport, Connecticut 06881. 1987.

ABORTION: POLITICS, MORALITY, AND THE CONSTITUTION. Stephen M. Krason. University Press of America, 4720 Boston Way, Lanham, Maryland 20706. 1984.

ABORTION POLITICS: PRIVATE MORALITY AND PUBLIC POLICY. Frederick S. Jaffe and Barbara L. Lindheim. McGraw-Hill Publishing Company, 1221 Avenue of the Americas, New York, New York 10020. 1981.

ABORTION PRACTICE. Warren M. Hern. J.B. Lippincott Company, East Washington Square, Philadelphia, Pennsylvania 19105. 1990.

THE ABORTION PRIVACY DOCTRINE: A COMPARISON AND CRITIQUE OF FEDERAL COURT ABORTION CASES. Lynn D. Wardle. William S. Hein and Company, Hein Building, 1285 Main Street, Buffalo, New York 14209. 1980.

THE ABORTION QUESTION. Hyman Rodman, Betty Sarvis and Joy Walker Bonar. Columbia University Press, 562 West One Hundred Thirteenth Street, New York, New York 10025. 1990.

ABORTION: THE CLASH OF ABSOLUTES. Lawrence H. Tribe. W.W. Norton and Company, 500 Fifth Avenue, New York, New York 10110. 1991.

ABORTION: THE SILENT HOLOCAUST. John Powell. Tabor Publishing, P.O. Box 5000, Allen, Texas 75002. 1981.

ABORTION: UNDERSTANDING DIFFERENCES. Sid Callahan and Daniel Callahan, Editors. Plenum Publishing Corporation, 233 Spring Street, New York, New York 10013. 1984.

ABORTION WITHOUT APOLOGY: RADICAL HISTORY FOR THE 1990s. Ninea Baehr. South End Press, 116 Saint Botolph Street, Boston, Massachusetts 02115. 1990.

ADOLESCENT ABORTION: PSYCHOLOGICAL AND LEGAL ISSUES. Gary B. Melton, Editor. University of Nebraska Press, 901 North Seventeenth Street, Lincoln, Nebraska 68588. 1986.

BACK ROOMS: VOICES FROM THE ILLEGAL ABORTION ERA. Ellen Messer. St. Martin's Press, 175 Fifth Avenue, New York, New York 10010. 1989.

CONCEPTS OF SELF AND MORALITY: WOMEN'S REASONING ABOUT ABORTION. Judith G. Smetana. Praeger Publishers, One Madison Avenue, New York, New York 10010. 1982.

CONTESTED LIVES: THE ABORTION DEBATE IN AN AMERICAN COMMUNITY. Faye D. Ginsburg. University of California Press, 2120 Berkeley Way, Berkeley, California 94720. 1989.

THE COURT VS. CONGRESS: PRAYER, BUSING, AND ABORTION. Edward Keynes. Duke University Press, Box 6697, College Station, Durham, North Carolina 27708. 1989.

DECODING ABORTION RHETORIC: COMMUNICATING SOCIAL CHANGE. Celeste Michelle Condit. University of Illinois Press, 54 East Gregory Drive, Champaign, Illinois 61820. 1990.

ENEMIES OF CHOICE: THE RIGHT-TO-LIFE MOVEMENT AND ITS THREAT TO ABORTION. Andrew Merton. Beacon Press, 25 Beacon Street, Boston, Massachusetts 02108. 1981.

THE ETHICS OF ABORTION: PRO-LIFE! VS. PRO-CHOICE! Robert M. Baird and Stuart E. Rosenbaum. Prometheus Books, 700 East Amherst Street, Buffalo, New York 14215. 1989.

AN EVALUATION OF THE CONSEQUENCES FOR MATERNAL AND INFANT HEALTH. Jerome S. Legge, Jr. State University of New York Press, State University Plaza, Albany, New York 12246. 1985.

FROM ABORTION TO REPRODUCTIVE FREEDOM: TRANSFORMING A MOVEMENT. South End Press, 116 Saint Botolph Street, Boston, Massachusetts 02115. 1990.

FROM CRIME TO CHOICE: THE TRANSFORMATION OF ABORTION IN AMERICA. Nanette J. Davis. Greenwood Publishing Group, Incorporated, 88 Post Road West, P.O. Box 5007, Westport, Connecticut 06881. 1985.

THE GLOBAL POLITICS OF ABORTION. Jodi L. Jacobsen. Worldwatch Institute, 1776 Massachusetts Avenue, Northwest, Washington, D.C 20036. 1990.

HUMAN ABORTION: GUIDE FOR MEDICINE, SCIENCE AND RESEARCH. Brenda Reynolds. ABBE Publishers Association, 4111 Gallows Road, Annandale, Virginia 22003. 1984.

IDEOLOGY AND ABORTION POLICY POLITICS. Marilyn Falik. Praeger Publishers, One Madison Avenue, New York, New York 10010. 1983.

INTERNATIONAL HANDBOOK ON ABORTION. Paul Sachev. Greenwood Publishing Group, Incorporated, 88 Post Road West, P.O. Box 5007, Westport, Connecticut 06881. 1988.

THE LAW GIVETH: LEGAL ASPECTS OF THE ABORTION CONTROVERSY. Barbara Milbauer and Bert N. Obrentz. Atheneum Publishers, 866 Third Avenue, New York, New York 10022. 1983.

A LAWYER LOOKS AT ABORTION. Lynn D. Wardle and Mary A. Wood. Brigham Young University Press, 205 University Press Building, Provo, Utah 84602. 1982.

THE MORAL QUESTION OF ABORTION. Stephen D. Schwarz. Loyola University Press, 3441 North Ashland Avenue, Chicago, Illinois 60657. 1990.

MOTHER-LOVE AND ABORTION. Robert D. Goldstein. University of California Press, 2120 Berkeley Way, Berkeley, California 94720. 1988.

NEW PERSPECTIVES ON HUMAN ABORTION.
Thomas W. Hilgers, Dennis J. Horan and D. Mall, Editors.
University Press of America, Incorporated, 4720 Boston Way,
Lanham, Maryland 20706. 1981.

NOBODY'S BUSINESS: PARADOXES OF PRIVACY.
Alida Brill. Addison-Wesley Publishing Company,
Incorporated, Route 128, Reading, Massachusetts 01867.
1990.

OUR RIGHT TO CHOOSE! TOWARD A NEW ETHIC
OF ABORTION. Beverly W. Harrison. Beacon Press, 25
Beacon Street, Boston, Massachusetts 02108. 1991.

A PRIVATE CHOICE, ABORTION IN AMERICA IN
THE SEVENTIES. John Thomas Noonan. Free Press, 866
Third Avenue, Ilew York, New York 10022. 1979.

THE PROBLEM OF ABORTION. Joel Feinberg, Editor.
Wadsworth Publishing Company, 10 Davis Drive, Belmont,
California 94002. 1984.

ROE V. WADE: THE UNTOLD STORY OF THE
LANDMARK SUPREME COURT DECISION THAT
MADE ABORTION LEGAL. Marian Faux. MacMillan
Publishing Company, Incorporated, 866 Third Avenue, New
York, New York 10022. 1988.

WOMEN, SOCIETY, THE STATE, AND ABORTION.
Patrick J. Sheehan. Praeger Publishers, One Madison Avenue,
New York, New York 10010. 1987.

DIGESTS, INDEXES, ABSTRACTS, CITATORS

ABRIDGED INDEX MEDICUS. National Library of
Medicine, 8600 Rockville Pike, Bethesda, Maryland 20894.
Monthly.

BIHEP: BIBLIOGRAPHIC INDEX OF HEALTH
EDUCATION PERIODICALS. William J. Bailey, Editor.
Department of Health and Safety Education, Indiana
University, HPER Building, Room 116, Bloomington,
Indiana 47405. Quarterly.

BIORESEARCH TODAY: POPULATION, FERTILITY
AND BIRTH CONTROL. BioSciences Information Service
(BIOSIS), 2100 Arch Street, Philadelphia, Pennsylvania
19103. Monthly.

CURRENT LITERATURE ON FAMILY PLANNING.
Gloria A. Roberts. Katharine Dexter McCormick Library,
810 Seventh Avenue, New York, New York 10019. Monthly.

EXERPTA MEDICA. FORENSIC SCIENCE
ABSTRACTS SECTION 49. Exerpta Medica, Users Aids
Department, 52 Vanderbilt Avenue, New York, New York
10017. Monthly.

EXERPTA MEDICA. OBSTETRICS AND
GYNECOLOGY SECTION 10. Exerpta Medica, Users Aids
Department, 52 Vanderbilt Avenue, New York, New York
10017. Monthly.

GENERAL SCIENCE INDEX. Joyce Howard, Editor.
H.W. Wilson Company, 950 University Avenue, Bronx, New
York 10452. Monthly.

HEALTH MEDIA REVIEW INDEX: A GUIDE TO
REVIEWS AND DESCRIPTIONS OF COMMERCIALLY
AVAILABLE NON-PRINT MATERIAL FOR THE
MEDICAL, MENTAL, ALLIED HEALTH, HUMAN
SERVICES AND RELATED COUNSELLING
PROFESSIONS. Jill E. Proven and Joy W. Hunter, Editors.
Scarecrow Press, Incorporated, 52 Liberty Street, Box 4167,
Metuchen, New Jersey 08840. 1985.

INDEX MEDICUS. National Library of Medicine, 8600
Rockville Pike, Bethesda, Maryland 20894. Monthly.

SCIENCE CITATION INDEX. Institute for Scientific
Information, 3501 Market Street, Philadelphia, Pennsylvania
19104. Bimonthly.

WOMEN'S STUDIES ABSTRACTS. Rush Publishing
Company, Incorporated, P.O. Box 1, Rush, New York 14543.
Quarterly.

LAW REVIEWS AND PERIODICALS

AMERICAN JOURNAL OF LAW AND MEDICINE.
American Society of Law and Medicine, Incorporated and the
Boston University School of Law, 765 Commonwealth
Avenue, Boston, Massachusetts 02215. Quarterly.

HASTINGS CENTER REPORT. 255 Elm Road, Briarcliff,
New York 10706. Bimonthly.

JOURNAL OF CONTEMPORARY HEALTH LAW AND
POLICY. The Catholic University of America, Columbus
School of Law, 620 Michigan Avenue, Northeast,
Washington, D.C. 20064. Annual.

JOURNAL OF FAMILY LAW. University of Louisville,
2301 South Third Street, Louisville, Kentucky 40292.
Quarterly.

LEX VITAE. Americans United for Life, Legal Defense
Fund, 230 North Michigan Avenue, Chicago, Illinois 60601.
Quarterly.

PRO-LIFE REPORTER. United States Coalition for Life,
Box 315, Export, Pennsylvania 15632. Quarterly.

WOMEN'S RIGHTS LAW REPORTER. Womens Rights
Law Reporter, Incorporated, 15 Washington Street, Newark,
New Jersey 07109. Quarterly.

WOMEN'S STUDIES QUARTERLY. Women's Studies
Quarterly, Box 334, Old Westbury, New York 11568.
Quarterly.

BIBLIOGRAPHIES

ABORTION, AN ANNOTATED INDEXED
BIBLIOGRAPHY. Third Edition. Maureen Muldoon. Edwin
Mellen Press, P.O. Box 450, Lewiston, New York 14092.
1980.

ABORTION BIBLIOGRAPHY FOR 1984. Polly T. Goode.
Whitson Publishing Company, P.O. Box 958, Troy, New
York 12181. 1986.

BIBLIOGRAPHY OF BIOETHICS. LeRoy Walters, Editor.
Kennedy Institute of Ethics, Georgetown University,
Washington, D.C. 20057. Annual.

ABORTION

HASTINGS CENTER'S BIBLIOGRAPHY OF ETHICS, BIOMEDICINE AND PROFESSIONAL RESPONSIBILITY. Hastings Center, 255 Elm Road, Briarcliff Manor, New York 10510. 1984.

PSYCHOLOGICAL AND MEDICAL ASPECTS OF INDUCED ABORTION: A SELECTIVE, ANNOTATED BIBLIOGRAPHY, 1970-1986. Eugenia B. Winter. Greenwood Publishing Group, Incorporated, 88 Post Road West, P.O. Box 5007, Westport, Connecticut 06881. 1988.

DIRECTORIES

NATIONAL ABORTION FEDERATION DIRECTORY. National Abortion Federation, 1436 U Street, Northwest, Washington, D.C. 20009. Annual.

ASSOCIATIONS AND PROFESSIONAL SOCIETIES

ALTERNATIVES TO ABORTION INTERNATIONAL. 4680 Lake Underhill, Orlando, Florida 32807. (407) 277-1942.

AMERICAN LIFE LOBBY. P.O. Box 490, Stafford, Virginia 22554. (703) 659-4171.

BIRTHRIGHT, U.S.A. 686 North Broad Street, Woodbury, New Jersey 08096. (609) 848-1819.

CATHOLICS FOR A FREE CHOICE. 1436 U Street, Northwest, Suite 301, Washington, D.C. 20009. (202) 638-1706.

EAGLE FORUM. P.O. Box 618, Alton, Illinois 62002. (618) 462-5415.

NATIONAL ABORTION FEDERATION. 1436 U Street, Northwest, Washington, D.C. 20009. (202) 667-5881.

NATIONAL ABORTION RIGHTS ACTION LEAGUE. 1101 Fourteenth Street, 5th Floor, Northwest, Washington, D.C. 20005. (202) 371-0779.

NATIONAL ORGANIZATION FOR WOMEN. 1000 Sixteenth Street, Northwest, Washington, D.C. 20036. (202) 331-0066.

NATIONAL RIGHT TO LIFE COMMITTEE. 419 Seventh Street, Northwest, Suite 500, Washington, D.C. 20004. (202) 626-8800.

PHYSICIANS FOR CHOICE. c/o Planned Parenthood Federation of America, 810 Seventh Avenue, 7th Floor, New York, New York 10019. (212) 541-7800.

PRO-LIFE ACTION LEAGUE. 6160 N. Cicero, Chicago, Illinois 60646. (312) 777-2900.

RELIGIOUS COALITION FOR ABORTION RIGHTS. 100 Maryland Avenue, Suite 307, Northeast, Washington, D.C. 20002. (202) 543-7032.

RESEARCH CENTERS, INSTITUTES, CLEARINGHOUSES

ALAN GUTTMACHER INSTITUTE. 111 Fifth Avenue, New York, New York 10003. (212) 254-5656

AMERICAN CITIZENS CONCERNED FOR LIFE EDUCATION FUND/ACCL COMMUNICATIONS CENTER. P.O. Box 179, Excelsior, Minnesota 55331. (612) 474-0885.

HUMAN LIFE CENTER. University of Steubenville, Steubenville, Ohio 43952. (614) 282-9953.

HUMAN LIFE INTERNATIONAL. 7845 E. Airpark Road, Gaithersburg, Maryland 20879. (301) 670-7884.

ONLINE DATABASES

BIOETHICSLINE. Kennedy Institute of Ethics, Georgetown University, Washington, D.C. 20057.

EMBASE. Elsevier Science Publishers, P.O. Box 1527, 1000 BM Amsterdam, The Netherlands.

HUMAN SEXUALITY. Clinical Communications, Incorporated, P.O. Box 88, 132 Hutchin Hill, Shady, New York 12409.

MEDIS. Mead Data Central, P.O. Box 933, Dayton, Ohio 45401.

MEDLINE. National Library of Medicine, 8600 Rockville Pike, Bethesda, Maryland 20894.

POPLINE (POPULATION INFORMATION ONLINE). National Library of Medicine, 8600 Rockville Pike, Bethesda, Maryland 20894.

POPULATION BIBLIOGRAPHY. Carolina Population Center, University Square West 300A, Chapel Hill, North Carolina 27514.

SCISEARCH. Institute for Scientific Information, 3501 Market Street, Philadelphia, Pennsylvania 19104.

STATISTICS SOURCES

ABORTION SERVICES IN THE UNITED STATES: EACH STATE AND METROPOLITAN AREA, 1984-1985. Stanley K. Henshaw and Jennifer van Vort. Guttmacher Institute, 111 Fifth Avenue, New York, New York 10003. 1988.

ABORTION SURVEILLANCE REPORT -- LEGAL ABORTIONS. Centers for Disease Control, 1600 Clifton Road, Northeast, Atlanta, Georgia 30333. 1982. (Annual).

FAMILY PLANNING PERSPECTIVES. Alan Guttmacher Institute, 111 Fifth Avenue, South, New York, New York 10003. 1982.

HOSPITAL STATISTICS. American Hospital Association, 840 North Lake Shore Drive, Chicago, Illinois 60611. Annual.

INDUCED ABORTIONS, A WORLD REVIEW, 1986. Sixth Edition. Christopher Tietze. Guttmacher Institute, 111 Fifth Avenue, New York, New York 10003. 1986.

INDUCED TERMINATIONS OF PREGNANCY: REPORTING STATES, 1981. Kate Prager. National Center for Health Statistics. Superintendent of Documents, United States Government Printing Office, Washington, D.C. 20402. Monthly.

POPULATION REPORTS, SERIES F: PREGNANCY TERMINATION. Population Information Program. Johns Hopkins University, Hampton House, 624 North Broadway, Baltimore, Maryland 21205. 1973- . (Irregular Supplements).

VITAL STATISTICS OF THE UNITED STATES. National Center for Health Statistics. Superintendent of Documents, United States Government Printing Office, Washington, D.C. 20402. Annual.

OTHER SOURCES

1988 LEGAL DOCKET. Diana Traub, Editor. American Civil Liberties Union Foundation, 132 West Forty-third Street, New York, New York 10036. 1988.

ACCIDENTS
See also: AVIATION ACCIDENTS; OCCUPATIONAL SAFETY AND HEALTH ADMINISTRATION; OCCUPATIONAL SAFETY AND HEALTH REVIEW COMMITTEE; PERSONAL INJURIES; TORTS

LOOSELEAF SERVICES AND REPORTERS

EMPLOYMENT SAFETY AND HEALTH GUIDE. Commerce Clearing House, Incorporated, 4025 West Peterson Avenue, Chicago, Illinois 60646. 1971- . (Weekly).

TRIAL OF ACCIDENT CASES. Third Edition. Louis E. Schwartz. Matthew Bender and Company, Incorporated, 11 Penn Plaza, New York, New York 10001. 1958- . (Annual Supplements).

TEXTBOOKS AND GENERAL WORKS

THE COST OF ACCIDENTS: A LEGAL AND ECONOMIC ANALYSIS. Guido Calabresi. Yale University Press, 302 Temple Street, New Haven, Connecticut 06520. 1970.

MOTOR VEHICLE ACCIDENT RECONSTRUCTION AND CAUSE ANALYSIS. Third Edition. Rudolf Limpert. Michie Company, P.O. Box 7587, Charlottesville, Virginia 22906. 1989.

DIGESTS, INDEXES, ABSTRACTS, CITATORS

HEALTH AND SAFETY SCIENCE ABSTRACTS JOURNAL. Cambridge Scientific Abstracts, 7200 Wisconsin Avenue, Bethesda, Maryland 20814. 1987- . (Five issues per year).

LAW REVIEWS AND PERIODICALS

ACCIDENT ANALYSIS AND PREVENTION. Pergamon Press, Incorporated, Maxwell House, Fairview Park, Elmsford, New York 10523. Quarterly.

ACCIDENT PREVENTION. Flight Safety Foundation, 2200 Wilson Boulevard, Arlington, Virginia 22201. Monthly.

ELECTRONIC AND ELECTRICAL EQUIPMENT. National Safety Council Research and Statistical Services. 444 North Michigan Avenue, Chicago, Illinois 60611. Quarterly.

EMPLOYMENT SAFETY AND HEALTH GUIDE SUMMARY. Commerce Clearing House, 4025 West Peterson Avenue, Chicago, Illinois 60646. Weekly.

FAMILY SAFETY AND HEALTH. National Safety Council Research and Statistical Services. 444 North Michigan Avenue, Chicago, Illinois 60611. Quarterly.

HUMAN FACTORS AND AVIATION MEDICINE. Flight Safety Foundation, Incorporated, 2200 Wilson Boulevard, Arlington, Virginia 22201. Bimonthly.

JOB SAFETY AND HEALTH. Bureau of National Affairs, Incorporated, 1231 Twenty-fifth Street, Northwest, Washington, D.C. 20037. Biweekly.

JOURNAL OF SAFETY RESEARCH. National Safety Council Research and Statistical Services. 444 North Michigan Avenue, Chicago, Illinois 60611. Quarterly.

OCCUPATIONAL HAZARDS. Penton Publishing, Incorporated, 1100 Superior Avenue West, Cleveland, Ohio 44114. Monthly.

SAFETY AND HEALTH. National Safety Council, 444 North Michigan Avenue, Chicago, Illinois 60611. Monthly.

SAFETY AND HEALTH VOICE. National Safe Workplace Institute, 122 South Michigan Avenue, Chicago, Illinois 60603. Bimonthly.

TRAFFIC SAFETY. National Safety Council, 444 North Michigan Avenue, Chicago, Illinois 60611. Monthly.

ASSOCIATIONS AND PROFESSIONAL SOCIETIES

HEALTH INSURANCE ASSOCIATION OF AMERICA. 1250 Connecticut Avenue, Northwest, Suite 1200, Washington, D.C. 20036. (202) 223-7780.

INTERNATIONAL ASSOCIATION OF DEFENSE COUNSEL. 20 North Wacker Drive, Suite 3100, Chicago, Illinois 60606. (312) 368-1494.

INTERNATIONAL ASSOCIATION OF INDUSTRIAL ACCIDENT BOARDS AND COMMISSIONS. P.O. Box 13449 Jackson, Mississippi 39236. (601) 366-4582.

NATIONAL ASSOCIATION OF HEALTH UNDERWRITERS. 1000 Connecticut Avenue, Northwest, Suite 1111, Washington, D.C. 20036. (202) 223-5533.

NATIONAL FIRE PROTECTION ASSOCIATION. One Batterymarch Park, P.O. Box 9101, Quincy, Massachusetts 02269. (617) 770-3000.

NATIONAL SAFETY COUNCIL. 444 North Michigan Avenue, Chicago, Illinois 60611. (312) 527-4800.

NATIONAL SAFETY MANAGEMENT SOCIETY. 3871 Piedmont Avenue, Oakland, California 94611. (415) 653-4148.

NATIONAL TRANSPORTATION SAFETY BOARD. 800 Independence Avenue, Southwest, Washington, D.C. 20594. (202) 382-6600.

ACCIDENTS

RESEARCH CENTERS, INSTITUTES, CLEARINGHOUSES

AMERICAN AUTOMOBILE ASSOCIATION FOUNDATION FOR TRAFFIC SAFETY. 1730 M Street, Northwest, Washington, D.C. 20036. (202) 775-1456.

AVIATION SAFETY INSTITUTE. 6797 North High Street, P.O. Box 304, Worthington, Ohio 43085. (614) 885-4242.

CENTER FOR AUTO SAFETY. 2001 S Street, Northwest, Suite 410, Washington, D.C. 20009. (202) 328-7700.

INSURANCE INSTITUTE FOR HIGHWAY SAFETY. 1005 North Glebe Road, Arlington, Virginia 22201. (703) 247-1500.

NATIONAL SAFE WORKPLACE INSTITUTE. 122 South Michigan Avenue, Suite 1450, Chicago, Illinois 60603. (312) 527-4800.

NATIONAL SAFETY COUNCIL RESEARCH AND STATISTICAL SERVICES. 444 North Michigan Avenue, Chicago, Illinois 60611. (312) 527-4800.

ONLINE DATABASES

ASI. (American Statistics Index). Congressional Information Service, Incorporated, 4520 East-West Highway, Suite 800, Bethesda, Maryland 20814.

AVIATION SAFETY INSTITUTE. Aviation Safety Institute, 6797 North High Street, P.O. Box 304, Worthington, Ohio 43085.

HEALTH AND SAFETY SCIENCE ABSTRACTS. Cambridge Scientific Abstracts, 7200 Wisconsin Avenue, Bethesda, Maryland 20814.

LABORDOC. International Labour Office, Central Library and Document Branch, 4 Route des Marillons, 1211 Geneva 22, Switzerland.

RIMSNET. Risk and Insurance Management Society, 205 East Forty-second Street, New York, New York 10017.

STATISTICS SOURCES

ACCIDENT BULLETIN. United States Interstate Commerce Commission, Twelfth Street and Constitution Avenue, Northwest, Washington, D.C. 20423. Annual.

ACCIDENT FACTS. National Safety Council, 444 North Michigan Avenue, Chicago, Illinois 60611. Annual.

ACCIDENT/INCIDENT BULLETIN: SUMMARY STATISTICS AND ANALYSIS OF ACCIDENTS ON RAILROADS IN THE UNITED STATES. Federal Railroad Administration, United States Department of Transportation, 400 Seventh Street, Southwest, Washington, D.C. 20590. Annual.

DRIVERS LICENSES. Federal Highway Administration, 400 Seventh Street, Southwest, Washington, D.C. 20590. Annual.

FATAL ACCIDENT REPORTING SYSTEM ANNUAL REPORT. United States Department of Transportation, National Highway Traffic Safety Administration, 400 Seventh Street, Southwest, Washington, D.C. 20590. Annual.

HEALTH CARE FINANCING REVIEW. United States Department of Health and Human Services, Health Care Financing Administration, Superintendent of Documents, United States Government Printing Office, Washington, D.C. 20402. 1979- . (Quarterly).

MINERAL YEARBOOK. United States Department of the Interior, Bureau of Mines, 12201 Sunrise Valley Drive, Reston, Virginia 22092. 1933- . (Annual).

OCCUPATIONAL INJURIES AND ILLNESSES BY INDUSTRY. Bureau of Labor Statistics, United States Department of Labor. Superintendent of Documents, United States Government Printing Office, Washington, D.C. 20402. Annual.

RAIL-HIGHWAY CROSSING ACCIDENT/INCIDENTAL AND INVENTORY BULLETIN. United States Department of Transportation, Federal Railroad Administration, 400 Seventh Street, Southwest, Washington, D.C. 20590. Annual.

SOCIAL SECURITY BULLETIN. United States Department of Health and Human Services, Social Security Administration, 6401 Security Boulevard, Baltimore, Maryland 21235. 1938- . (Monthly).

SOURCE BOOK OF HEALTH INSURANCE DATA. Health Insurance Association of America, 1025 Connecticut Avenue, Northwest, Washington, D.C. 20036. Biennial.

STATISTICAL BULLETIN. Metropolitan Life Insurance Company, One Madison Avenue, New York, New York 10010. April-June 1982 (and unpublished data).

TRANSPORT STATISTICS IN THE UNITED STATES. United States Interstate Commerce Commission, Twelfth Street and Constitution Avenue, Northwest, Washington, D.C. 20423. Annual.

TRAVELERS BOOK OF STREET AND HIGHWAY ACCIDENT DATA. Travelers Insurance Companies, One Tower Square, Hartford, Connecticut 06115. Annual.

VITAL STATISTICS OF THE UNITED STATES. Public Health Service, United States Department of Health and Human Services. Superintendent of Documents, Government Printing Office, Washington, D.C. 20402. Annual.

OTHER SOURCES

FUNDAMENTALS OF HANDLING A PERSONAL INJURY CASE: PROGRAM MATERIALS. Georgetown University Law Center, Continuing Legal Education, 600 New Jersey Avenue, Northwest, Washington, D.C. 20001. 1982.

ACCOUNTANTS AND ACCOUNTING

STATUTES, CODES, STANDARDS, UNIFORM LAWS

ACCOUNTING STANDARDS - ORIGINAL PRONOUNCEMENTS. Financial Accounting Standards Board, 401 Merritt, Norwalk, Connecticut 06856. 1984- .

AICPA PROFESSIONAL STANDARDS. American Institute of Certified Public Accountants. Commerce Clearing House, Incorporated, 4025 West Peterson Avenue, Chicago, Illinois 60646. 1974- . (Periodic Supplements).

CODE OF PROFESSIONAL ETHICS. American Institute of Certified Public Accountants, 1211 Avenue of the Americas, New York, New York 10036. 1967.

FASB ACCOUNTING STANDARDS. Financial Accounting Standards Board, 401 Merritt, Norwalk, Connecticut 06856. 1982- . (Periodic Supplements).

LOOSELEAF SERVICES AND REPORTERS

ACCOUNTANCY LAW REPORTS. Commerce Clearing House, Incorporated, 4025 West Peterson Avenue, Chicago, Illinois 60646. 1938- . (Monthly Supplements).

ACCOUNTANTS BUSINESS MANUAL. William H. Behrenfeld and Andrew R. Biebl. American Institute of Certified Public Accountants, 1211 Avenue of the Americas, New York, New York 10036-8775. 1988- . (Semiannual Supplements).

ACCOUNTANT'S SEC PRACTICE MANUAL. Morton Poloway and Dane Charles. Commerce Clearing House, Incorporated, 4025 West Peterson Avenue, Chicago, Illinois 60646. 1976- . (Monthly Supplements).

ACCOUNTANT'S WORKBOOK SERIES. J. Loebbecke and E. Luria. Matthew Bender and Company, Incorporated, 11 Penn Plaza, New York, New York 10001. 1986- . (Periodic Supplements).

ACCOUNTING FOR BANKS. James M. Koltveit. Matthew Bender and Company, Incorporated, 11 Penn Plaza, New York, New York 10001. 1982- . (Periodic Supplements).

ACCOUNTING FOR GOVERNMENT CONTRACTS - COST ACCOUNTING STANDARDS. Lane K. Anderson. Matthew Bender and Company, Incorporated, 11 Penn Plaza, New York, New York 10001. 1981- . (Periodic Supplements).

ACCOUNTING FOR GOVERNMENT CONTRACTS - FEDERAL ACQUISITION REGULATION. Matthew Bender and Company, Incorporated, 11 Penn Plaza, New York, New York 10001. 1985- . (Periodic Supplements).

ACCOUNTING FOR PUBLIC UTILITIES. Robert Hahne and others. Matthew Bender and Company, Incorporated, 11 Penn Plaza, New York, New York 10001. 1983- . (Periodic Supplements).

APPLYING GAAP AND GAAS. Paul Munter and Thomas Ratcliffe. Matthew Bender and Company, Incorporated, 11 Penn Plaza, New York, New York 10001. 1985- . (Annual Supplements).

S & L ACCOUNTING AND AUDITING SERVICE. Sheshunoff Information Services, Incorporated. Capitol Station, P.O. Box 13203, Austin, Texas. 78711. 1989- . (Monthly Supplements).

SEC ACCOUNTING RULES. Commerce Clearing House, Incorporated, 4025 West Peterson Avenue, Chicago, Illinois 60646. 1968- . (Periodic Supplements).

WORLD ACCOUNTING SERIES. L.L. Orfini and others. Matthew Bender and Company, Incorporated, 11 Penn Plaza, New York, New York 10001. 1986- . (Periodic Supplements).

HANDBOOKS, MANUALS, FORMBOOKS

ACCOUNTANTS' COST HANDBOOK: A GUIDE FOR MANAGEMENT ACCOUNTING. Third Edition. James Bullock, Donald E. Keller and Louis Vlasho, Editors. John Wiley and Sons, Incorporated, 605 Third Avenue, New York, New York 10158. 1983.

ACCOUNTANT'S DESK HANDBOOK. Third Edition. Albert P. Ameiss and Nichlas A. Kargas. Prentice-Hall, Incorporated, 113 Sylvan Avenue, Englewood Cliffs, New Jersey 07632. 1988.

ACCOUNTANTS' HANDBOOK. Seventh Edition. Lee J. Seidler and D.R. Carmichael, Editors. John Wiley and Sons, Incorporated, 605 Third Avenue, New York, New York 10158. 1991.

ACCOUNTANT'S LAW, TAX, ACCOUNTING AND BUSINESS MANAGEMENT MANUAL WITH FORMS. David Minars and others. Garland Publishing, Incorporated, 136 Madison Avenue, New York, New York 10016. 1987- .

ACCOUNTANTS' TAX PRACTICE HANDBOOK. William H. Westphal. Prentice-Hall, Incorporated, 113 Sylvan Avenue, Englewood Cliffs, New Jersey 07632. 1978.

ACCOUNTING AND AUDITING DISCLOSURE MANUAL. Allan B. Afterman. Warren, Gorham, and Lamont, Incorporated, One Penn Plaza, New York, New York 10119. Annual.

ACCOUNTING DESK BOOK: THE ACCOUNTANT'S EVERY-DAY INSTANT ANSWER BOOK. Ninth Edition. Revised by Douglas L. Blensly and Tom M. Plank. Institute for Business Planning, Prentice-Hall, Incorporated, 113 Sylvan Avenue, Englewood Cliffs, New Jersey 07632. 1989.

ACCOUNTING HANDBOOK FOR NONACCOUNTANTS. Third Edition. Clarence B. Nickerson. Van Nostrand Reinhold Company, Incorporated, 115 Fifth Avenue, New York, New York 10003. 1986.

AICPA AUDIT AND ACCOUNTING MANUAL. American Institute of Certified Public Accountants. Commerce Clearing House, Incorporated, 4025 West Peterson Avenue, Chicago, Illinois 60646. 1979- . (Periodic Supplements).

AICPA TECHNICAL PRACTICE AIDS. American Institute of Certified Public Accountants. Commerce Clearing House, Incorporated, 4025 West Peterson Avenue, Chicago, Illinois 60646. 1975- . (Periodic Supplements).

ATTORNEY'S HANDBOOK OF ACCOUNTING. Third Edition. Henry Sellin. Matthew Bender and Company, Incorporated, 11 Penn Plaza, New York, New York 10001. 1979- . (Periodic Supplements).

GAAP PRACTICE MANUAL. Allan B. Afterman. Warren, Gorham and Lamont, Incorporated, One Penn Plaza, New York, New York 10119. 1985- . (Quarterly Supplements).

ACCOUNTANTS AND ACCOUNTING

HANDBOOKS, MANUALS, FORMBOOKS

GOVERNMENT CONTRACT ACCOUNTING. Second Edition. James Bedingfield and Louis Rosen. Federal Publications, 1120 Twentieth Street, Northwest, Washington, D.C. 20036. 1985- .

HANDBOOK FOR INTERNAL AUDITORS. William E. Perry. Matthew Bender and Company, Incorporated, Matthew Bender and Company, Incorporated, 11 Penn Plaza, New York, New York 10001. 1985- .

HANDBOOK OF MODERN ACCOUNTING. Third Edition. Sidney Davidson and Roman L. Weil, Editors. McGraw-Hill Publishing Company, 1221 Avenue of the Americas, New York, New York 10020. 1983.

HANDBOOK OF SAMPLING FOR AUDITING AND ACCOUNTING. Third Edition. Herbert Arkin. McGraw-Hill Publishing, Company, 1221 Avenue of the Americas, New York, New York 10020. 1984.

INTRODUCTION TO FINANCIAL ACCOUNTING FOR LAWYERS. Samuel P. Gunther, Chairman. Practising Law Institute, 810 Seventh Avenue, New York, New York 10019. 1985.

MILLER'S COMPREHENSIVE GAAS GUIDE: A COMPREHENSIVE RESTATEMENT OF GENERALLY ACCEPTED AUDITING STANDARDS. Martin A. Miller and Larry P. Bailey. Harcourt Brace Jovanovich, Incorporated, 6277 Sea Harbor Drive, Orlando, Florida 32821. Annual.

MODERN ACCOUNTING AND AUDITING CHECKLISTS. Revised Edition. Margaret A. Loscalzo and Paul J. Wendell. Warren, Gorham and Lamont, Incorporated, One Penn Plaza, New York, New York 10119. 1981- . (Semiannual Supplements).

QUALITY REVIEW PROGRAM MANUAL. Commerce Clearing House, 4025 West Peterson Avenue, Chicago, Illinois 60646. 1989- . (Semiannual Supplements).

SEC ACCOUNTING AND REPORTING MANUAL. William J. Badecker and R.F. Harnek. Warren, Gorham and Lamont, Incorporated, One Penn Plaza, New York, New York 10119. 1983. (Three supplements per year).

TAX ACCOUNTING. Durwood L. Alkire. Matthew Bender and Company, Incorporated, 11 Penn Plaza, New York, New York 10001. 1982- . (Annual Supplements).

TEXTBOOKS AND GENERAL WORKS

ACCOUNTANTS AND THE LAW OF NEGLIGENCE. R.W.V. Dickerson. Garland Publishing, Incorporated, 136 Madison Avenue, New York, New York 10016. 1982.

AN ACCOUNTANT'S GUIDE TO MALPRACTICE LIABILITY. Duke Nordlinger Stern. Michie Company, P.O. Box 7587, Charlottesville, Virginia 22906. 1979.

ACCOUNTANTS MALPRACTICE: COURSE MANUAL. Michael J. Silverberg, Ira B. Rose and George P. Birnbaum. Federal Publications, 1120 Twentieth Street, Northwest, Washington, D.C. 20036. 1978.

ACCOUNTING AND THE LAW IN A NUTSHELL. E. McGruder Faris. West Publishing Company, 50 West Kellogg Boulevard, Saint Paul, Minnesota 55164. 1984.

ACCOUNTING FOR LAWYERS. Fourth Edition. E. McGruder Faris. Michie Company, P.O. Box 7587, Charlottesville, Virginia 22906. 1982.

ACCOUNTING: THE BASIS FOR BUSINESS DECISIONS. Eighth Edition. Walter B. Meigs and Robert F. Meigs. McGraw-Hill Publishing Company, 1221 Avenue of the Americas, New York, New York 10020. 1990.

BASIC ACCOUNTING FOR LAWYERS. Fourth Edition. Anthony Philips and others. American Law Institute/American Bar Association, 4025 Chestnut Street, Philadelphia, Pennsylvania 19104. 1988.

DUTIES AND LIABILITIES OF PUBLIC ACCOUNTANTS. Fourth Edition. Denzil Y. Causey. Accountants Press, P.O. Box 753, Mississippi State, Mississippi 39762-0753. 1991.

EXECUTIVE'S ACCOUNTING PRIMER. Second Edition. Robert L. Dixon. McGraw-Hill Publishing Company, 1221 Avenue of the Americas, New York, New York 10020. 1982.

FINANCIAL ACCOUNTING: AN INTRODUCTION TO CONCEPTS, METHODS, AND USES. Sidney Davidson and others. Dryden Press, 465 South Lincoln Drive, Troy, Missouri 63379. 1988.

FINANCIAL REPORTING: AN ACCOUNTING REVOLUTION. Second Edition. William H. Beaver. Prentice-Hall, Incorporated, Englewood Cliffs, New Jersey 07632. 1989.

FUNDAMENTAL ACCOUNTING PRINCIPLES. Twelfth Edition. William W. Pyle and Kermit D. Larson. Dow-Jones-Irwin, 1818 Ridge Road, Homewood, Illinois 60430. 1990.

FUNDAMENTALS OF FINANCIAL ACCOUNTING. Sixth Edition. Glenn A. Welsch and others. Dow-Jones-Irwin, 1818 Ridge Road, Homewood, Illinois 60430. 1989.

PRINCIPLES OF ACCOUNTING. J. Cerapac and D. Taylor. Prentice-Hall, Incorporated, 113 Sylvan Avenue, Englewood Cliffs, New Jersey 07632. 1987.

SIMPLIFIED ACCOUNTING FOR NON-ACCOUNTANTS. Rick Stephan Hayes and C. Richard Baker. Jove Publications, Incorporated, 200 Madison Avenue, New York, New York 10016. 1986.

A STUDENT'S GUIDE TO ACCOUNTING FOR LAWYERS. David A. Lipton and Daniel Lipsky. Matthew Bender and Company, Incorporated, 11 Penn Plaza, New York, New York 10001. 1985.

ENCYCLOPEDIAS AND DICTIONARIES

ACCOUNTANT'S ENCYCLOPEDIA. Revised by Jerome K. Pescow. Prentice-Hall, Incorporated, 113 Sylvan Avenue, Englewood Cliffs, New Jersey 07632. 1981.

COMPLETE EXECUTIVE'S ENCYCLOPEDIA OF ACCOUNTING, FINANCE, INVESTING, BANKING AND ECONOMICS. Albert N. Link and Charles J. Woelfel. Probus Publishing Company, Incorporated, 118 North Clinton, Chicago, Illinois 60606. 1989.

DESKTOP ENCYCLOPEDIA OF CORPORATE FINANCE AND ACCOUNTING. Charles J. Woelfel. Probus Publishing Company, 118 North Clinton, Chicago, Illinois 60606. 1987.

DICTIONARY FOR ACCOUNTANTS. Sixth Edition. Eric Kohler. Prentice-Hall, Incorporated, 113 Sylvan Avenue, Englewood Cliffs, New Jersey 07632. 1983.

DICTIONARY OF ACCOUNTING. Second Edition. Ralph Estes. MIT Press, 55 Hayward Street, Cambridge, Massachusetts 02142. 1985.

DICTIONARY OF ACCOUNTING TERMS. Joel G. Siegel and Jae K. Shim. Barron's Educational Series, Incorporated, P.O. Box 8040, 250 Wireless Boulevard, Hauppauge, New York 11788. 1987.

ENCYCLOPEDIA OF ACCOUNTING SYSTEMS. Jerome K. Pescow, Editor. Prentice-Hall, Incorporated, 113 Sylvan Avenue, Englewood Cliffs, New Jersey 07632. 1976.

ENCYCLOPEDIC DICTIONARY OF ACCOUNTING AND FINANCE. Jae K. Shim and Joel G. Siegel. Prentice-Hall, Incorporated, 113 Sylvan Avenue, Englewood Cliffs, New Jersey 07632. 1989.

MACMILLAN DICTIONARY OF ACCOUNTING. R.H. Parker. MacMillan Publishing Company, Incorporated, 866 Third Avenue, New York, New York 10022. 1984.

DIGESTS, INDEXES, ABSTRACTS, CITATORS

ACCOUNTANTS DIGEST. Germain Publishing Company, Incorporated, Box 6549, Syracuse, New York 13217. Quarterly.

ACCOUNTANTS' INDEX. American Institute of Certified Public Accountants, 1211 Avenue of the Americas, New York, New York 10036. 1975- . (Annual Supplements).

ACCOUNTING ARTICLES. Commerce Clearing House, Incorporated, 4025 West Peterson Avenue, Chicago, Illinois 60646. 1965- . (Monthly Supplements).

BUSINESS PERIODICALS INDEX. H.W. Wilson Company, 950 University Avenue, Bronx, New York 10452. Monthly Supplements.

LAW REVIEWS AND PERIODICALS

ACCOUNTING REVIEW. American Accounting Association, 5719 Bessie Drive, Sarasota, Florida 33583. Quarterly.

GOVERNMENT ACCOUNTANTS JOURNAL. Association of Government Accountants, 727 South Twenty-third Street, Suite 120, Arlington, Virginia 22202. Quarterly.

JOURNAL OF ACCOUNTANCY. American Institute of Certified Public Accountants, 1211 Avenue of the Americas, New York, New York 10036-8775. Monthly.

JOURNAL OF ACCOUNTING AND PUBLIC POLICY. Elsevier Science Publishing Company, Incorporated, 52 Vanderbilt Avenue, New York, New York 10017. Quarterly.

JOURNAL OF ACCOUNTING RESEARCH. Institute of Professional Accounting, University of Chicago, Graduate School of Business, 1101 East Fifty-eighth Street, Chicago, Illinois 60637. Semiannual.

MANAGEMENT ACCOUNTING. National Association of Accountants, 919 Third Avenue, New York, New York 10022. Monthly.

NATIONAL PUBLIC ACCOUNTANT. National Society of Public Accountants, 1717 Pennsylvania Avenue, Northwest, Suite 1200, Washington, D.C. 20006. Monthly.

NSPA WASHINGTON REPORTER. National Society of Public Accountants, 1717 Pennsylvania Avenue, Northwest, Suite 1200, Washington, D.C. 20006. Eleven Supplements Per Year.

TAXATION FOR ACCOUNTANTS. Tax Research Group, Limited. Warren, Gorham and Lamont, 210 South Street, Boston, Massachusetts 02111. Monthly.

NEWSLETTERS AND NEWSPAPERS

ACCOUNTANTS' LIABILITY REVIEW. Timeline Publishing Company, Incorporated., P.O. Box 1435, Bellevue, Washington. 98009. Monthly.

ACCOUNTANT'S WEEKLY REPORT. Prentice-Hall Professional Newsletters, Englewood Cliffs, New Jersey 07632. Weekly.

ACCOUNTING AND AUDITING UPDATE SERVICE. Warren, Gorham and Lamont, Incorporated, 210 South Street, Boston, Massachusetts 02111. Quarterly.

ACCOUNTING FOR LAW FIRMS. Leader Publications, 111 Eighth Avenue, New York, New York 10011. Monthly.

ACTION REPORT. Governmental Accounting Standards Board. 401 Merritt Seven, Norwalk, Connecticut 06856. Bimonthly.

ATTORNEY-CPA. American Association of Attorneys-CPAs, 24196 Alicia Parkway, Mission Viejo, California 92691. Bimonthly.

BUSINESS ACCOUNTING FOR LAWYER'S NEWSLETTER. Practising Law Institute, 810 Seventh Avenue, New York, New York 10019. Eight issues per year.

FORENSIC ACCOUNTING REVIEW. Computer Protection Systems, Incorporated, 150 North Main Street, Plymouth, Michigan 48170. Monthly.

PRACTICAL ACCOUNTANT ALERT. Warren, Gorham and Lamont, Incorporated, 210 South Street, Boston, Massachusetts 02111. Biweekly.

SEC ACCOUNTING AND REPORTING UPDATE SERVICE. Warren, Gorham and Lamont, Incorporated, 210 South Street, Boston, Massachusetts 02111. Monthly.

SEC ACCOUNTING REPORT. Warren, Gorham and Lamont, Incorporated, 210 South Street, Boston, Massachusetts 02111. Monthly.

ACCOUNTANTS AND ACCOUNTING

BIBLIOGRAPHIES

ACCOUNTING ARTICLES. Commerce Clearing House, Incorporated, 4025 West Peterson Avenue, Chicago, Illinois 60646. 1965- . (Monthly Supplements).

ACCOUNTING RESEARCH DIRECTORY: THE DATABASE OF ACCOUNTING LITERATURE. Second Enlarged Edition. Lawrence D. Brown and others. Markus Wiener Publishing, Incorporated, 114 Jefferson Road, Princeton, New Jersey 08540. 1989.

FINANCIAL JOURNALS AND SERIALS: AN ANALYTICAL GUIDE TO ACCOUNTING, BANKING, FINANCE, INSURANCE AND INVESTMENT PERIODICALS. William Fisher, Compiler. Greenwood Publishing Group, Incorporated, 88 Post Road, P.O. Box 5007, Westport, Connecticut 06881. 1986.

MANAGEMENT ACCOUNTING RESEARCH, 1926-1983. Charles F. Klemstine and Michael W. Maher. American Accounting Association, 5717 Bessie Drive, Sarasota, Florida 34233-2399. 1984.

DIRECTORIES

ACCOUNTING FIRMS AND PRACTITIONERS. American Institute of Certified Public Accountants, 1211 Avenue of the Americas, New York, New York 10036-8775. Biennial.

EMERSON'S DIRECTORY OF LEADING U.S. ACCOUNTING FIRMS. James C. Emerson. Emerson's Professional Services Review, 12356 Northrup Way, Bellevue, Washington 98009. 1990.

MEMBERSHIP LIST. American Institute of Certified Public Accountants, 1211 Avenue of the Americas, New York, New York 10036-8775. Annual.

NATIONAL SOCIETY OF PUBLIC ACCOUNTANTS MEMBERSHIP DIRECTORY. National Society of Public Accountants, 1010 North Fairfax Street, Alexandria, Virginia 22314. Annual.

WHO AUDITS AMERICA. Data Financial Press, Box 668, Menlo Park, California 94025. Annual.

ASSOCIATIONS AND PROFESSIONAL SOCIETIES

AMERICAN ACCOUNTING ASSOCIATION. 5717 Bessie Drive, Sarasota, Florida 34233. (813) 921-7747.

AMERICAN ASSOCIATION OF ATTORNEY-CERTIFIED PUBLIC ACCOUNTANTS. 24196 Alicia Parkway, Mission Viejo, California 92691. (714) 768-0336.

AMERICAN INSTITUTE OF CERTIFIED PUBLIC ACCOUNTANTS. 1211 Avenue of the Americas, New York, New York 10036. (212) 575-6200.

ASSOCIATION OF GOVERNMENT ACCOUNTANTS. 601 Wythe Street, Suite 204, Alexandria, Virginia 22314. (703) 684-6931.

FINANCIAL EXECUTIVES INSTITUTE. Ten Madison Avenue, P.O. Box 1938, Morristown, New Jersey 07960. (201) 898-4600.

GOVERNMENT ACCOUNTING STANDARDS BOARD. 401 Merritt Seven, P.O. Box 5116, Norwalk, Connecticut 06856. (203) 847-0700.

INSTITUTE OF INTERNAL AUDITORS. 249 Maitland Avenue, Altamonte Springs, Florida 32701. (407) 830-7600.

NATIONAL ASSOCIATION OF ACCOUNTANTS. Ten Paragon Drive, Montvale, New Jersey 07645. (201) 573-9000.

NATIONAL SOCIETY OF PUBLIC ACCOUNTANTS. 1010 North Fairfax Street, Alexandria, Virginia 22314. (703) 549-6400.

RESEARCH CENTERS, INSTITUTES, CLEARINGHOUSES

ACCOUNTING INFORMATION SYSTEMS RESEARCH PROGRAM. Graduate School of Management, University of California, Los Angeles, California 90024. (213) 206-8187.

ACCOUNTING RESEARCH CENTER. College of Business Administration, University of Florida, Gainesville, Florida 32611. (904) 392-0229.

CENTER FOR INTERNATIONAL EDUCATION AND RESEARCH IN ACCOUNTING. University of Illinois, 320 Commerce West, Champaign, Illinois 61820. (217) 333-4545.

FINANCIAL ACCOUNTING FOUNDATION. 401 Merritt Seven, P.O. Box 5116, Norwalk, Connecticut 06856. (203) 847-0700.

FINANCIAL EXECUTIVES RESEARCH FOUNDATION. P.O. Box 1938, Ten Madison Avenue, Morristown, New Jersey 07962. (201) 898-4608.

FOUNDATION FOR ACCOUNTING EDUCATION. Pan-Am Building, 200 Park Avenue, New York, New York 10166. (212) 973-8300.

INSTITUTE OF PROFESSIONAL ACCOUNTING. University of Chicago, 1101 East Fifty-eighth Street, Chicago, Illinois 60637. (312) 702-0458.

ONLINE DATABASES

ACCOUNTANTS. American Institute of Certified Public Accountants, Library, 1211 Avenue of the Americas, New York, New York 10036-8775. 1974- .

MANAGEMENT CONTENTS. Information Access Corporation, 362 Lakeside Drive, Foster City, California 94404. 1974- .

NAARS. American Institute of Certified Public Accountants, National Automated Accounting Research System, 1211 Avenue of the Americas, New York, New York 10036-8775. 1978.

USCOM. Comshare, P.O. Box 1588, 3001 South State Street, Ann Arbor, Michigan 48106. 1947- .

STATISTICS SOURCES

ACCOUNTING TRENDS AND TECHNIQUES: ACCOUNTING SURVEY OF 525 CORPORATE REPORTS. American Institute of Certified Public Accountants, 1211 Avenue of the Americas, New York, New York 10036-8775. 1948- . (Annual).

AUDIOVISUALS

ACCOUNTING FOR LAWYERS. William D. Kilboun, Jr. National Practice Institute, 330 Second Avenue South, Minneapolis, Minnesota 55401. Audiotape.

COMPUTER-ASSISTED LEGAL INSTRUCTION

ACCOUNTING INTRODUCTION. Donald T. Trautman. Center for Computer-Assisted Instruction, 229 Ninteenth Avenue South, University of Minnesota, Minneapolis, Minnesota 55455. Machine-readable computer file.

TELEPHONE POLES EXPENSE: SOME PROBLEMS OF DEFERRAL. Donald T. Trautman. Center for Computer-Assisted Instruction, 229 Ninteenth Avenue South, University of Minnesota, Minneapolis, Minnesota 55455. Machine-readable computer file.

OTHER SOURCES

ACCOUNTING RESEARCH STUDIES. American Institute of Certified Public Accountants, 1211 Avenue of the Americas, New York, New York 10036-8775. Irregular.

LAWYERS AND CERTIFIED PUBLIC ACCOUNTANTS: A STUDY OF INTERPROFESSIONAL RELATIONS. National Conference of Lawyers and CPAs. Distributed by the American Bar Association and American Institute of Certified Public Accountants, 1211 Avenue of the Americas, New York, New York 10036-8775. 1981- .

MANAGEMENT ADVISORY SERVICES GUIDELINE SERIES. American Institute of Certified Public Accountants, 1211 Avenue of the Americas, New York, New York 10036-8775. Irregular.

ACQUISITIONS, CORPORATE
See: CORPORATIONS; CONSOLIDATION AND MERGER

ACTIONS AND DEFENSES
See also: LEGAL FORMS; REMEDIES; TRIAL PRACTICE

LOOSELEAF SERVICES AND REPORTERS

ACTIONS AND REMEDIES. Charles E. Friend. Callaghan and Company, 155 Pfingsten Road, Deerfield, Illinois 60015. 1985- . (Periodic Supplements).

CIVIL RIGHTS ACTIONS. Joseph G. Cook and John L. Sobieski. Matthew Bender and Company, Incorporated, 11 Penn Plaza, New York, New York 10001. 1983- . (Periodic Supplements).

COMMERCIAL DAMAGES: A GUIDE TO REMEDIES IN BUSINESS LITIGATION. Charles L. Knapp, Editor. Matthew Bender and Company, Incorporated, 11 Penn Plaza, New York, New York 10001. 1986- . (Periodic Supplements).

DEFENSE AGAINST A PRIMA FACIE CASE. Callaghan and Company, 155 Pfingsten Road, Deerfield, Illinois 60015. 1982- . (Annual Supplements).

FEDERAL LITIGATION GUIDE. Matthew Bender and Company, 11 Penn Plaza, New York, New York 10001. 1985- . (Periodic Supplements).

IMMIGRATION LAW AND DEFENSE. Third Edition. National Lawyers Guild. Clark Boardman Company, Limited, 375 Hudson Street, New York, New York 10014. 1988. (Annual Supplements).

LIBEL AND PRIVACY: THE PREVENTION AND DEFENSE OF LITIGATION. Bruce W. Sanford. Prentice-Hall Law and Business, Incorporated. 910 Sylvan Avenue, Englewood Cliffs, New Jersey 07632. 1985- . (Periodic Supplements).

LITIGATION AND TRIAL OF AIR CRASH CASES. John J. Kennelly. Callaghan and Company, 155 Pfingsten Road, Deerfield, Illinois 60015. 1968- . (Periodic Supplements).

LITIGATION OF INTERNATIONAL DISPUTES IN U.S. COURTS. Ved P. Nanda and David K. Pansius. Clark Boardman Company, Limited, 375 Hudson Street, New York, New York 10014. 1986- . (Annual Supplements).

NECESSARY ELEMENTS. Louis A. Kass. Gould Publications, 199 State Street, Binghamton, New York 13901-2782. 1979- . (Periodic Supplements).

PERSONAL INJURY--ACTIONS, DEFENSES, DAMAGES. Louis R. Frumer and others. Matthew Bender and Company, Incorporated, 11 Penn Plaza, New York, New York 10001. 1957- . (Three supplements per year).

PROSECUTION AND DEFENSE OF A LENDER LIABILITY LAWSUIT. American Law Institute-American Bar Association, 4025 Chestnut Street, Philadelphia, Pennsylvania 19104. 1989.

HANDBOOKS, MANUALS, FORMBOOKS

PARALEGAL LITIGATION FORMS. Marcy Davis Fawcett. James Publishing, Incorporated, 3520 Costa Mesa, California 92626. Annual Supplements.

WILMER, CUTLER AND PICKERING MANUAL ON LITIGATION SUPPORT. Second Edition. Deanne Siemer and Douglas Land. John Wiley and Sons, Incorporated, 605 Third Avenue, New York, New York 10158. 1989.

TEXTBOOKS AND GENERAL WORKS

ALIMONY: NEW STRATEGIES FOR PURSUIT AND DEFENSE. Practising Law Institute, 810 Seventh Avenue, New York, New York 10019. 1988.

AVIATION LITIGATION. Windle Turley. Shepard's/McGraw-Hill, 420 North Cascade Avenue, Colorado Springs, Colorado 80901. 1986.

CIVIL ACTIONS AGAINST THE UNITED STATES, ITS AGENCIES, OFFICES, AND EMPLOYEES. Shepard's/McGraw-Hill, 420 North Cascade Avenue, Colorado Springs, Colorado 80901. 1982- . (Periodic Supplements).

ACTIONS AND DEFENSES

CIVIL PRACTICE AND EFFECTIVE LITIGATION TECHNIQUES IN FEDERAL AND STATE COURTS: ALI-ABA COURSE OF STUDY MATERIALS. American Law Institute-American Bar Association, 4025 Chestnut Street, Philadelphia, Pennsylvania 19104. 1985.

COMPARATIVE NEGLIGENCE DEFENSE TACTICS. James G. McConnell. John Wiley and Sons, Incorporated, 605 Third Avenue, New York, New York 10158. 1985- . (Annual Supplements).

CONDUCTING COMPLEX FACT INVESTIGATIONS: TECHNIQUES AND ISSUES FOR LAWYERS. Practising Law Institute, 810 Seventh Avenue, New York, New York 10019. 1987.

CRASH CASES: A GUIDE TO VEHICLE COLLISION LITIGATION. American Bar Association, 750 North Lake Shore Drive, Chicago, Illinois 60611. 1989.

DEFENDING A PERSONAL INJURY CASE, 1990. Practising Law Institute, 810 Seventh Avenue, New York, New York 10019. 1990.

EMPLOYEE BENEFITS CLAIMS: LAW AND PRACTICE. Henry H. Perritt. John Wiley and Sons, Incorporated, 605 Third Avenue, New York, New York 10158. 1990.

EMPLOYEE BENEFITS LITIGATION. American Law Institute-American Bar Association, 4025 Chestnut Street, Philadelphia, Pennsylvania 19104. 1990.

EMPLOYMENT DISCRIMINATION LITIGATION. Andrew J. Ruzicho, Louis A. Jacobs and Louis M. Thrasher. Anderson Publishing Company, P.O. Box 1576, Cincinnati, Ohio 45201. 1989.

GENERAL AVIATION ACCIDENT LITIGATION. Practising Law Institute, 810 Seventh Avenue, New York, New York 10019. 1986.

GUIDE TO MULTISTATE LITIGATION. Victor E. Schwartz, Patrick W. Lee and Kathryn Kelly. Shepard's/McGraw-Hill, 420 North Cascade Avenue, Colorado Springs, Colorado 80901. 1985- . ((Periodic Supplements).

INSURANCE CLAIMS AND DISPUTES. Allen D. Windt. Shepard's/McGraw-Hill, 420 North Cascade Avenue, Colorado Springs, Colorado 80901. 1988.

LAWSUIT. Stuart M. Speiser. Horizon Press, 7272 East Broadway Boulevard, Suite 400, Tucson, Arizona 85710. 1980.

LITIGATING PRIVATE ANTITRUST ACTIONS. Philip C. Jones. Shepard's/McGraw-Hill, 420 North Cascade Avenue, Colorado Springs, Colorado 80901. 1984- . (Periodic Supplements).

NEGLIGENCE LITIGATION HANDBOOK: FEDERAL AND STATE. Mark A. Dombroff, Patricia K. Gilmore and Juanita M. Madole. John Wiley and Sons, Incorporated, 605 Third Avenue, New York, New York 10158. 1986.

NEWBERG ON CLASS ACTIONS: A MANUAL FOR GROUP LITIGATION AT FEDERAL AND STATE LEVELS. Herbert B. Newberg. Shepard's/McGraw-Hill, 420 North Cascade Avenue, Colorado Springs, Colorado 80901. 1977- .

RECOVERY OF DAMAGES FOR WRONGFUL DISCHARGE. Second Edition. John C. McCarthy. Lawpress, P.O. Box 596, Kentfield, California 94914. 1990.

SHEPARD'S CAUSES OF ACTION. Shepard's Editorial Staff. Shepard's/McGraw-Hill, 420 North Cascade Avenue, Colorado Springs, Colorado 80901. 1983- .

STATISTICS IN LITIGATION: PRACTICAL APPLICATIONS FOR LAWYERS. Richard A. Wehmhoefer. Shepard's/McGraw-Hill, 420 North Cascade Avenue, Colorado Springs, Colorado 80901. 1985.

STOCKHOLDERS SUITS AND CLASS ACTIONS. Stuart D. Wechsler, Chairman. Practising Law Institute, 810 Seventh Avenue, New York, New York 10019. 1986.

TRANSNATIONAL COMMERCIAL AND TRADE LITIGATION. American Law Institute-American Bar Association, 4025 Chestnut Street, Philadelphia, Pennsylvania 19104. 1986.

WINNING THE SLIP AND FALL CASE. Practising Law Institute, 810 Seventh Avenue, New York, New York 10019. 1989.

WOMEN'S ORGANIZATIONAL USE OF THE COURTS. Karen O'Connor. Lexington Books, 125 Spring Street, Lexington, Massachusetts 02173. 1980.

ANNUALS AND SURVEYS

ANNUAL INSTITUTE ON EQUAL EMPLOYMENT OPPORTUNITY COMPLIANCE. Practising Law Institute, 810 Seventh Avenue, New York, New York 10019. Annual.

CIVIL RICO. Practising Law Institute, 810 Seventh Avenue, New York, New York 10019. 1984- .

LIBEL LITIGATION. Richard N. Winfield, Chairman. Practising Law Institute, 810 Seventh Avenue, New York, New York 10019. Annual.

NEWSLETTERS AND NEWSPAPERS

LITIGATION NEWS. American Bar Association, 750 North Lake Shore Drive, Chicago, Illinois 60611. Quarterly.

ADMINISTRATION OF JUSTICE
See also: COURTS; CRIMINAL LAW; JUDGES AND JUDICIAL PROCESS

STATUTES, CODES, STANDARDS, UNIFORM LAWS

STANDARDS RELATING TO COURT DELAY REDUCTION. National Conference of State Trial Judges. American Bar Association, 750 North Lake Shore Drive, Chicago, Illinois 60611. 1985.

STANDARDS RELATING TO COURT ORGANIZATION. Judicial Administration Division, American Bar Association, 750 North Lake Shore Drive, Chicago, Illinois 60611. 1974.

UNIFORM JUVENILE COURT ACT. National Conference of Commissioners on Uniform State Laws, Uniform Laws Annotated, West Publishing Company, P.O. Box 64526, 50 West Kellogg Boulevard, St. Paul, Minnesota 55164-0526. 1976- . (Annual Supplements).

HANDBOOKS, MANUALS, FORMBOOKS

THE IMPROVEMENT OF THE ADMINISTRATION OF JUSTICE: JUDICIAL ADMINISTRATION DIVISION HANDBOOK. Lawyers Conference, Judicial Administration Division, American Bar Association, 750 North Lake Shore Drive, Chicago, Illinois 60611. 1981.

UNITED STATES ATTORNEYS MANUAL. United States Department of Justice. Superintendent of Documents, United States Government Printing Office, Washington, D.C. 20402. 1976- .

TEXTBOOKS AND GENERAL WORKS

THE AMERICAN JUDICIAL TRADITION: PROFILES OF LEADING AMERICAN JUDGES. Expanded Edition. G. Edward White. Oxford University Press, 200 Madison Avenue, New York, New York 10016. 1988.

THE AMERICAN LEGAL SYSTEM. Second Edition. Blair J. Kolasa and Bernadine Meyer. Prentice-Hall, Incorporated, 113 Sylvan Avenue, Englewood Cliffs, New Jersey 07632. 1987.

ATTACKING LITIGATION COSTS AND DELAYS. Lawyers Conference, Judicial Administration Division, American Bar Association, 750 North Lake Shore Drive, Chicago, Illinois 60611. 1984.

BEFORE THE LAW: AN INTRODUCTION TO THE LEGAL PROCESS. Fourth Edition. John J. Bonsignore and others. Houghton Mifflin Company, 1 Beacon Street, Boston, Massachusetts 02108. 1989.

CAUSATION, PREDICTION AND LEGAL ANALYSIS. Stuart S. Nagel. Quorum Books, Greenwood Publishing Group, Incorporated, 88 Post Road West, P.O. Box 5007, Westport, Connecticut 06881. 1986.

COURTS ON TRIAL: MYTH AND REALITY IN AMERICAN JUSTICE. Jerome Frank. Princeton University Press, 41 William Street, Princeton, New Jersey 08540. 1949.

DEFEATING DELAY: DEVELOPING AND IMPLEMENTING A COURT DELAY REDUCTION PROGRAM. American Bar Association, 750 North Lake Shore Drive, Chicago, Illinois 60611. 1986.

DISPUTES AND SETTLEMENTS: LAW AND HUMAN RELATIONS IN THE WEST. John Bossy, Editor. Cambridge University Press, 40 West Twentieth Street, New York, New York 10011. 1984.

THE ECONOMICS OF JUSTICE. Richard A. Posner. Harvard University Press, 79 Garden Street, Cambridge, Massachusetts 02138. 1981.

EQUAL JUSTICE UNDER LAW. Harold M. Hyman and William M. Wiecek. HarperCollins Publishers, Incorporated, 10 East Fifty-third Street, New York, New York 10022. 1986.

THE HIGH COST AND EFFECT OF LITIGATION. Kenneth R. Feinberg, Jack M. Kress and Gary L. McDowell. National Legal Center for the Public Interest, 1000 Sixteenth Street, Northwest, Suite 301, Washington, D.C. 20036. 1986.

THE IMPACT OF SOCIAL PSYCHOLOGY ON PROCEDURAL JUSTICE. Martin F. Kaplan, Editor. Charles C. Thomas, Publishers, 2600 South First Street, Springfield, Illinois 62794-9265. 1986.

JUDICIAL POLICIES: IMPLEMENTATION AND IMPACT. Charles A. Johnson and Bradley C. Canon. Congressional Quarterly Books, Incorporated, 1414 Twenty-second Street, Northwest, Washington, D.C. 20037. 1984.

JUSTICE AND THE MODERN LAW. Everett B. Abbot. Fred B. Rothman and Company, 10368 West Centennial Road, Littleton, Colorado 80127. 1987, c1913.

JUSTICE DENIED: THE CASE FOR REFORM OF THE COURTS. Leonard Downie, Jr. Praeger Publications, One Madison Avenue. New York, New York 10010. 1971.

JUSTICE IN AMERICA: COURTS, LAWYERS AND THE JUDICIAL PROCESS. Fourth Edition. Herbert Jacob. Little, Brown and Company, 34 Beacon Street, Boston, Massachusetts 02108. 1984.

JUSTICE WITHOUT LAW. Jerald S. Auerbach. Oxford University Press, 200 Madison Avenue, New York, New York 10016. 1983.

LAW, COURTS AND POLICY. Mitchell S. Klein. Prentice-Hall, Incorporated, 113 Sylvan Avenue, Englewood Cliffs, New Jersey 07632. 1984.

LAW, POLICY AND OPTIMIZING ANALYSIS. Stuart S. Nagel. Quorum Books, Greenwood Publishing Group, Incorporated, 88 Post Road West, P.O. Box 5007, Westport, Connecticut 06881. 1986.

MONEY AND JUSTICE: WHO OWNS THE COURTS? Lois G. Forer. W.W. Norton and Company, Incorporated, 500 Fifth Avenue, New York, New York 10110. 1986.

PROCEDURES IN THE JUSTICE SYSTEM. Third Edition. Gilbert B. Stuckley. C.E. Merrill Publishing Company, 1300 Alum Creek Drive, Columbus, Ohio 43216. 1986.

REDEFINING THE SUPREME COURT'S ROLE: MANAGING THE FEDERAL JUDICIAL PROCESS. Samuel Estreicher and John Sexton. Yale University Press, 302 Temple Street, New Haven, Connecticut 06520. 1988. Reprint of 1986 edition.

TOTAL JUSTICE. Laurence M. Friedman. Russell Sage Foundation, 112 East Sixty-fourth Street, New York, New York 10021. 1985.

UNEQUAL JUSTICE. Jerold S. Auerbach. Oxford University Press, 200 Madison Avenue, New York, New York 10016. 1976.

LAW REVIEWS AND PERIODICALS

JUSTICE QUARTERLY: JQ. Academy of Criminal Justice Sciences, Omaha, Nebraska 68108. Quarterly.

ADMINISTRATION OF JUSTICE

NEWSLETTERS AND NEWSPAPERS

CITIZEN'S FORUM ON THE COURT: A NEWSLETTER OF THE AMERICAN JUDICATURE SOCIETY. American Judicature Society, 25 East Washington, Suite 1600, Chicago, Illinois 60602. Quarterly.

FROM THE STATE CAPITALS: JUSTICE POLICIES. Wakeman Walworth, Incorporated, P.O. Box 1939, New Haven, Connecticut 06509. Weekly.

BIBLIOGRAPHIES

THE ADMINISTRATION OF JUSTICE IN THE COURTS: A SELECTED ANNOTATED BIBLIOGRAPHY. Oceana Publications, Incorporated, 75 Main Street, Dobbs Ferry, New York 10522. 1976.

ASSOCIATIONS AND PROFESSIONAL SOCIETIES

ALLIANCE FOR JUSTICE. 25 E Street, Northwest, Washington, D.C. 20001. (202) 662-9548.

AMERICAN BAR FOUNDATION. 750 North Lake Shore Drive, Chicago, Illinois 60611. (312) 988-6500.

AMERICAN JUDICATURE SOCIETY. 25 East Washington Street, Suite 1600, Chicago, Illinois 60602. (312) 588-6900.

AMERICAN TORT REFORM ASSOCIATION. 1015 Fifteenth Street, Northwest, Washington, D.C. 20005. (202) 682-1163.

CENTER FOR STUDY OF RESPONSIVE LAW. P.O. Box 19367, Washington, D.C. 20036. (202) 387-8030.

FEDERAL BAR ASSOCIATION. 1815 H Street, Northwest, Washington, D.C. 20006. (202) 638-0252.

JUDICIAL ADMINISTRATION DIVISION. American Bar Association, 750 North Lake Shore Drive, Chicago, Illinois 60611. (312) 988-5000.

NATIONAL LEGAL CENTER FOR THE PUBLIC INTEREST. 1000 Sixteenth Street, Northwest, Washington, D.C. 20036. (202) 296-1683.

WASHINGTON LEGAL FOUNDATION. 1705 N Street, Northwest, Washington, D.C. 20036. (202) 857-0240.

RESEARCH CENTERS, INSTITUTES, CLEARINGHOUSES

DELINQUENCY CONTROL INSTITUTE. University of Southern California, Center for the Administration of Justice, Tyler Building, 3601 South Flower Street, Los Angeles, California 90007. (213) 743-2497.

STATISTICS SOURCES

FEDERAL COURT MANAGEMENT STATISTICS. Director of the Administrative Office of the United States Courts. Superintendent of Documents, United States Government Printing Office, Washington, D.C. 20402. 1983- . (Annual).

SOURCEBOOK OF CRIMINAL JUSTICE STATISTICS. United States Department of Justice, Bureau of Statistics. Superintendent of Documents, United States Government Printing Office, Washington, D.C. 20402. 1973- . (Annual).

ADMINISTRATIVE CONFERENCE OF THE UNITED STATES

STATUTES, CODES, STANDARDS, UNIFORM LAWS

CODE OF FEDERAL REGULATIONS, TITLE 1. Office of the Federal Register, National Archives and Records Administration. Superintendent of Documents, United States Government Printing Office, Washington, D.C. 20402. Annual. (Updated by use of monthly *List of Sections Affected* and daily *Federal Register*).

HANDBOOKS, MANUALS, FORMBOOKS

GUIDE TO FEDERAL AGENCY RULEMAKING. Administrative Conference of the United States, Office of the Chairman. Superintendent of Documents, United States Government Printing Office, Washington, D.C. 20402. 1983.

AN INTERPRETATIVE GUIDE TO THE GOVERNMENT IN THE SUNSHINE ACT. Richard K. Berg. Administrative Conference of the United States, Office of the Chairman. Superintendent of Documents, United States Government Printing Office, Washington, D.C. 20402. 1978.

MANUAL FOR ADMINISTRATIVE LAW JUDGES. Merritt Ruhlen. Administrative Conference of the United States. Superintendent of Documents, United States Government Printing Office, Washington, D.C. 20402. 1982.

TEXTBOOKS AND GENERAL WORKS

AGENCY ARBITRATION: CONSTITUTIONAL AND STATUTORY ISSUES. Administrative Conference of the United States, Office of the Chairman. Superintendent of Documents, United States Government Printing Office, Washington, D.C. 20402. 1988.

FEDERAL ADMINISTRATIVE PROCEDURE SOURCEBOOK: STATUTES AND RELATED MATERIALS. Administrative Conference of the United States, Office of the Chairman. Superintendent of Documents, United States Government Printing Office, Washington, D.C. 20402. 1985.

REPORT TO THE ADMINISTRATIVE CONFERENCE OF THE UNITED STATES: REFORMING ASYLUM ADJUDICATION. David A. Martin. Administrative Conference of the United States, Superintendent of Documents, United States Government Printing Office, Washington, D.C. 20402. 1989.

ANNUALS AND SURVEYS

ANNUAL REPORT - ADMINISTRATIVE CONFERENCE OF THE UNITED STATES. Administrative Conference of the United States, Office of the Chairman. Superintendent of Documents, United States Government Printing Office, Washington, D.C. 20402. 1983- . (Annual).

RECOMMENDATIONS AND REPORTS - ADMINISTRATIVE CONFERENCE OF THE UNITED STATES. Administrative Conference of the United States, Office of the Chairman. Superintendent of Documents, United States Government Printing Office, Washington, D.C. 20402. 1978- . (Annual).

NEWSLETTERS AND NEWSPAPERS

ADMINISTRATIVE CONFERENCE NEWS. Administrative Conference of the United States, 2120 L Street, Northwest, Washington, D.C. 20037. Quarterly.

RESEARCH CENTERS, INSTITUTES, CLEARINGHOUSES

ADMINISTRATIVE CONFERENCE OF THE UNITED STATES, LIBRARY. 2120 L Street, Northwest, Suite 500, Washington, D.C. 20037. (202) 254-7020.

ADMINISTRATIVE LAW
See also: ADMINISTRATIVE CONFERENCE OF THE UNITED STATES; ADMINISTRATIVE PROCEDURE

STATUTES, CODES, STANDARDS, UNIFORM LAWS

ADMINISTRATIVE CODES AND REGISTERS. State/Federal Survey. National Association of Secretaries of State, Administrative Codes and Registers Committee, c/o Council of State Governments, P.O. Box 11910, Iron Works Pike, Lexington, Kentucky 40578. Annual.

CODE OF FEDERAL REGULATIONS (CFR). Office of the Federal Register. National Archives and Records Administration, Superintendent of Documents, United States Government Printing Office, Division of Public Documents, Washington, D.C. 20402. Annual. (Updated by use of monthly *List of Sections Affected* and daily *Federal Register*).

FEDERAL REGISTER. Office of the Federal Register, National Archives and Records Administration. Superintendent of Documents, United States Government Printing Office, Washington, D.C. 20402. Daily (except Saturday and Sunday).

LOOSELEAF SERVICES AND REPORTERS

ADMINISTRATIVE LAW. Basil Mezines and others. Matthew Bender and Company, Incorporated, 11 Penn Plaza, New York, New York 10001. 1977- . (Annual Supplements).

BNA ADMINISTRATIVE PRACTICE MANUAL. Bertram R. Cottine. Bureau of National Affairs, Incorporated, 1231 Twenty-fifth Street, North West, Washington, D.C. 20037. 1988- . (Periodic Supplements).

FEDERAL REGULATORY PROCESS: AGENCY PRACTICES AND PROCEDURES. Gary J. Edles and Jerome Nelson. Prentice Hall Law and Business, Incorporated, 910 Sylvan Avenue, Englewood Cliffs, New Jersey 07632. 1989- . (Periodic Supplements).

PIKE AND FISHER ADMINISTRATIVE LAW, THIRD SERIES. John W. Willis and others. Pike and Fischer, Incorporated, 4550 Montgomery Avenue, Suite 433N, Bethesda, Maryland 20814. 1989- . (Biweekly Supplements).

HANDBOOKS, MANUALS, FORMBOOKS

FEDERAL ADMINISTRATIVE PROCEDURE SOURCEBOOK: STATUTES AND RELATED MATERIALS. Richard K. Berg and others. Administrative Conference of the United States, Office of the Chairman. United States Government Printing Office, Division of Public Documents, Washington, D.C. 20402. 1985.

GOVERNMENT REGULATION OF BUSINESS: AN INFORMATION SOURCEBOOK. Robert Goehlert and Nels Gunderson. Oryx Press, 2214 North Central Avenue, Phoenix, Arizona 85004. 1987.

A GUIDE TO FEDERAL AGENCY RULEMAKING. Administrative Conference of the United States, Office of the Chairman. United States Government Printing Office, Division of Public Documents, Washington, D.C. 20402. 1983.

MANUAL FOR ADMINISTRATIVE LAW JUDGES. Revised Edition. Merritt Ruhlen. Administrative Conference of the United States. United States Government Printing Office, Division of Public Documents, Washington, D.C. 20402. 1982.

SOURCEBOOK: FEDERAL AGENCY USE OF ALTERNATIVE MEANS OF DISPUTE RESOLUTION. Prepared for the Office of the Chairman, Administrative Conference of the United States. Superintendent of Documents, United States Government Printing Office, Washington, D.C. 20402. 1987.

WORKING ON THE SYSTEM: A COMPREHENSIVE MANUAL FOR CITIZEN ACCESS TO FEDERAL AGENCIES. James R. Michael and Ruth C. Fort, Editors. Ralph Nader's Center for the Study of Responsive Law. Basic Books, 10 East Fifty-third Street, New York, New York 10022. 1974.

TEXTBOOKS AND GENERAL WORKS

ADMINISTRATIVE AGENCIES AND THE COURTS. Frank E. Cooper. University of Michigan Law School, 1020 Green Street, Ann Arbor, Michigan 48109. 1982. Reprint of 1951.

ADMINISTRATIVE DISCRETION AND PUBLIC POLICY IMPLEMENTATION. Douglas H. Shumavon and H. Kenneth Hibbeln, Editors. Greenwood Publishing Group, Incorporated, 88 Post Road West, P.O. Box 5007, Westport, Connecticut 06881. 1985.

ADMINISTRATIVE LAW: A CASEBOOK. Third Edition. Bernard Schwartz. Little, Brown and Company, 34 Beacon Street, Boston, Massachusetts 02108. 1988.

ADMINISTRATIVE LAW AND GOVERNMENT. Second Edition. Kenneth Culp Davis. West Publishing Company, 50 West Kellogg Boulevard, St. Paul, Minnesota 55164. 1975.

ADMINISTRATIVE LAW AND PRACTICE. Charles H. Koch, Jr. West Publishing Company, P.O. Box 43526, 50 West Kellogg Boulevard, St. Paul, Minnesota 55164. 1985- . (Annual Supplements).

ADMINISTRATIVE LAW AND PROCESS. Richard J. Pierce, Jr., Sydney A. Shapiro and Paul R. Verkuil. Foundation Press, 615 Merrick Avenue, Westbury, New York 11590. 1985.

ADMINISTRATIVE LAW AND PROCESS IN A NUTSHELL. Ernest Gellhorn and Barry B. Boyer. Third Edition. West Publishing Company, 50 West Kellogg Boulevard, St. Paul, Minnesota 55164. 1990.

ADMINISTRATIVE LAW IN THE AMERICAN POLITICAL SYSTEM. Kenneth F. Warren. Second Edition. West Publishing Company, 50 West Kellogg Boulevard, St. Paul, Minnesota 55164. 1988.

ADMINISTRATIVE LAW, ITS GROWTH, PROCEDURE, AND SIGNIFICANCE. Roscoe Pound. Fred B. Rothman and Company, 10368 West Centennial Road, Littleton, Colorado 80127. 1981.

ADMINISTRATIVE LAW: PRACTICE AND PROCEDURE. Lee Modjeska. Lawyers Cooperative Publishing Company, Aqueduct Building, Rochester, New York 14694. 1982.

ADMINISTRATIVE LAW: RETHINKING JUDICIAL CONTROL OF BUREAUCRACY. Christopher F. Edley. Yale University Press, 302 Temple Street, New Haven, Connecticut 06520. 1990.

ADMINISTRATIVE LAW TEXT. Third Edition. Kenneth Culp Davis. West Publishing Company, 50 West Kellogg Boulevard, St. Paul, Minnesota 55164. 1972.

ADMINISTRATIVE LAW: THE INFORMAL PROCESS. Peter Woll. University of California Press, 2120 Berkeley Way, Berkeley, California 94720. 1974.

ADMINISTRATIVE LAW TREATISE. Second Edition. Kenneth Culp Davis. K.C. Davis Publishing Company, University of San Diego, Alcala Park, San Diego, California 92110. 1978- .

THE ADMINISTRATIVE REGULATORY PROCESS. Florence Heffron with Neil McFeeley. Longman Publishing Group, Incorporated, 95 Church Street, White Plains, New York 10601. 1983.

ADVICE TO THE PUBLIC FROM FEDERAL ADMINISTRATIVE AGENCIES. Michael Asimov. Matthew Bender and Company, Incorporated, 11 Penn Plaza, New York, New York 10001. 1973.

AFTER THE RIGHTS REVOLUTION: RECONCEIVING THE REGULATORY STATE. Cass R. Sunstein. Harvard University Press, 79 Garden Street, Cambridge, Massachusetts 01238. 1990.

THE AMERICAN LAW SCHOOL AND THE RISE OF ADMINISTRATIVE GOVERNMENT. William C. Chase. University of Wisconsin Press, 114 North Murray Street, Madison, Wisconsin 53706. 1982.

BUREAUCRATIC AND GOVERNMENT REFORM. Donald J. Calista. JAI Press, Incorporated, 55 Old Post Road, Number 2, P.O. Box 1678, Greenwich, Connecticut 06830. 1986.

BUREAUCRATIC DISCRETION: LAW AND POLICY IN FEDERAL REGULATORY AGENCIES. Gary C. Bryner. Pergamon Press, Incorporated, Maxwell House, Fairview Park, Elmsford, New York 10523. 1987.

BUREAUCRATIC JUSTICE: MANAGING SOCIAL SECURITY DISABILITY CLAIMS. Jerry L. Mashaw. Yale University Press, 302 Temple Street, New Haven, Connecticut 06520. 1983.

BUREAUCRATIC RESPONSIBILITY. John P. Burke. Johns Hopkins University Press, 701 West Fortieth Street, Suite 275, Baltimore, Maryland 21211-2190. 1988.

COURTS AND ADMINISTRATORS: A STUDY IN JURISPRUDENCE. Michael J. Detmold. Weidenfeld and Nicholson, Distributed by Fred B. Rothman and Company, 10368 West Centennial Road, Littleton, Colorado 80127. 1989.

CONTROLLING THE FEDERAL BUREAUCRACY. Dennis D. Riley. Temple University Press, 1601 North Broad Street, University Services Building, Philadelphia, Pennsylvania 19122. 1990.

DEMOCRATIC PROCESS AND ADMINISTRATIVE LAW. Robert Stuart Lorch. Wayne State University Press, Leonard N. Simons Building, 5959 Woodward Avenue, Detroit, Michigan 48202. 1980.

DUE PROCESS IN THE ADMINISTRATIVE STATE. Jerry L. Mashaw. Yale University Press, 302 Temple Street, New Haven, Connecticut 06520. 1985.

ENFORCING REGULATION. Keith Hawkins and John M. Thomas. Martinus Nijhoff, Kluwer Academic Publishers, 101 Philip Drive, Assinippi Park, Norwell, Massachusetts 02061. 1983.

FEDERAL STANDARDS OF REVIEW: CIVIL, CRIMINAL AND ADMINISTRATIVE. S.A. Childress, M.S. Davis. John Wiley and Sons, Incorporated, 605 Third Avenue, New York, New York 10158. 1986.

GOING BY THE BOOK: THE PROBLEM OF REGULATORY UNREASONABLENESS. Eugene Bardach and Robert A. Kagan. Temple University Press, 1601 North Broad Street, Philadelphia, Pennsylvania 19122. 1982.

AN INTRODUCTION TO ADMINISTRATIVE JUSTICE IN THE UNITED STATES. Peter L. Strauss. Carolina Academic Press, P.O. Box 51879, Durham, North Carolina 27717. 1989.

LAW AND DYNAMIC ADMINISTRATION. Marshall Edward Dimock. Praeger Publishers, Greenwood Publishing Group, Incorporated, 88 Post Road West, P.O. Box 5007, Westport, Connecticut 06881. 1980.

LEGAL FOUNDATIONS OF PUBLIC ADMINISTRATION. Second Edition. Donald D. Barry. West Publishing Company, 50 West Kellogg Boulevard, St. Paul, Minnesota 55164. 1987.

LEGAL IDENTITY: THE COMING OF AGE OF PUBLIC LAW. Joseph Vining. Yale University Press, 302 Temple Street, New Haven, Connecticut 06520. 1978.

PERSPECTIVES ON THE ADMINISTRATIVE PROCESS. Robert L. Rabin, Editor. Little, Brown and Company, 34 Beacon Street, Boston, Massachusetts 02108. 1979.

POLITICS AND BUREAUCRACY: POLICY MAKING IN THE 4TH BRANCH OF GOVERNMENT. Second Edition. Brooks/Cole Publishing Company, 511 Forest Lodge Road, Pacific Grove, California 93950. 1986.

PUBLIC ADMINISTRATION AND LAW: BENCH V. BUREAU IN THE UNITED STATES. David H. Rosenbloom. Marcel Dekker, 270 Madison Avenue, New York, New York 10016. 1983.

PUBLIC LAW AND PUBLIC ADMINISTRATION. Second Edition. Phillip J. Cooper. Mayfield Publishing Company, 1240 Villa Street, Mountain View, California 94041. 1988.

REGULATION AND ITS REFORM. Stephen Breyer. Harvard University Press, 79 Garden Street, Cambridge, Massachusetts 02138. 1982.

REGULATION AND THE COURTS: THE CASE OF THE CLEAN AIR ACT. R. Shep Melnick. Brookings Institution, 1775 Massachusetts Avenue, Northwest, Washington, D.C. 20036. 1983.

THE REGULATORS: WATCHDOG AGENCIES AND THE PUBLIC INTEREST. Louis M. Kohlmeier. HarperCollins Publishers, Incorporated, 10 East Fifty-third Street, New York, New York 10022. 1969.

RESEARCH ESSENTIALS OF ADMINISTRATIVE LAW. H.B. Jacobini. Palisades Publishers, P.O. Box 744, Pacific Palisades, California 90272. 1983.

STATE ADMINISTRATIVE RULE MAKING. Arthur Earle Bonfield. Little, Brown and Company, 34 Beacon Street, Boston, Massachusetts 02108. 1986.

TRIAL OF AN ADMINISTRATIVE CASE. Law and Business, Incorporated, Harcourt Brace Jovanovich, 6277 Sea Harbor Drive, Orlando, Florida 32821. 1985.

UNDERSTANDING ADMINISTRATIVE LAW. William F. Fox. Matthew Bender and Company, Incorporated, 11 Penn Plaza, New York, New York 10001. 1986.

DIGESTS, INDEXES, ABSTRACTS, CITATORS

CIS FEDERAL REGISTER INDEX. Congressional Information Service, 4520 East-West Highway, Suite 800, Bethesda, Maryland 20814. 1984- .

PAIS (PUBLIC AFFAIRS INFORMATION SERVICE, INCORPORATED). 521 West Forty-third Street, New York, New York 10036-4396. Semimonthly.

PIKE AND FISHER ADMINISTRATIVE LAW, THIRD SERIES, CURRENT DIGEST. Pike and Fischer, Incorporated, 4550 Montgomery Avenue, Suite 433N, Bethesda, Maryland 20014. 1989- .

SHEPARD'S CODE OF FEDERAL REGULATIONS CITATIONS. Shepard's/McGraw-Hill, 425 North Cascade Avenue, Colorado Springs, Colorado 80901. Bimonthly Supplements.

SHEPARD'S UNITED STATES ADMINISTRATIVE CITATIONS. Shepard's/McGraw-Hill, 425 North Cascade Avenue, Colorado Springs, Colorado 80901. Bimonthly Supplements.

ANNUALS AND SURVEYS

SUNSET: A SCHEDULE OF STATE SUNSET REVIEWS. The Council of State Governments, Iron Works Pike, P.O. Box 11910, Lexington, Kentucky 40578. 1983.

LAW REVIEWS AND PERIODICALS

ADMINISTRATIVE COURT DIGEST. Juridical Digest Institute, 1860 Broadway, Suite 1401, New York, New York 10023. Monthly.

ADMINISTRATIVE LAW REVIEW. Administrative Law Section, American Bar Association, 1800 M Street, Northwest, Washington, D.C. 20036. Quarterly.

REGULATION. American Enterprise Institute, 1150 Seventeenth Street, Northwest, Washington, D.C. 20016. Bimonthly.

NEWSLETTERS AND NEWSPAPERS

THE ADMINISTRATIVE JUDICIARY NEWS AND JOURNAL. National Conference of Administrative Law Judges, Judicial Administration Division. American Bar Association, 750 North Lake Shore Drive, Chicago, Illinois 60611. Quarterly.

ADMINISTRATIVE LAW NEWS. Administrative Law Section, American Bar Association, 750 N. Lake Shore Drive, Chicago, Illinois 60611. Quarterly.

FEDERAL REGISTER ABSTRACTS. National Standards Association, 1200 Quince Orchard Road, Gaithersburg, Maryland 20878. Daily.

FEDERAL REGISTER HIGHLIGHTS NEWSLETTER. National Clearinghouse for Legal Services, Incorporated, 407 South Dearborn Street, Chicago, Illinois 60605. Semimonthly.

FEDERAL REGISTER INTERNATIONAL DIGEST. International Business Reports, Incorporated, P.O. Box 1009, Falls Church, Virginia 22041. Weekly.

BIBLIOGRAPHIES

ADMINISTRATIVE AGENCIES AND INDEPENDENT REGULATORY COMMISSIONS: A BIBLIOGRAPHY. Vance Bibliographies, P.O. Box 229, 112 North Charter Street, Monticello, Illinois 61856. 1981.

ADMINISTRATIVE LAW: MONOGRAPHS PUBLISHED IN THE ENGLISH LANGUAGE, 1980-1987. Mary Vance. Vance Bibliographies, P.O. Box 229, 112 North Charter Street, Monticello, Illinois 61856. 1988.

THE CODE OF FEDERAL REGULATIONS: BIBLIOGRAPHY AND GUIDE. Second Edition. Erwin C. Surrency. Oceana Publications, Incorporated, 75 Main Street, Dobbs Ferry, New York 10522. 1986.

COURT SUPERVISION AND OVERSIGHT OF GOVERNMENT AGENCIES: A SELECTED BIBLIOGRAPHY. Anthony G. White. Vance Bibliographies, P.O. Box 229, 112 North Charter Street, Monticello, Illinois 61856. 1982.

ADMINISTRATIVE LAW

Encyclopedia of Legal Information Sources • 2nd Ed.

UNION LIST OF STATE ADMINISTRATIVE CODES AND REGISTERS. New England Law Library Consortium. Compiled by Donald Dunn. Western New England College, Springfield, Massachusetts 01119. 1983.

DIRECTORIES

FEDERAL EXECUTIVE DIRECTORY. Nancy Cahill, Editor. Carroll Publishing Company, 1058 Thomas Jefferson Street, Northwest, Washington, D.C. 20007. Bimonthly.

FEDERAL FAST FINDER: A KEY WORD TELEPHONE DIRECTORY OF THE FEDERAL GOVERNMENT. Washington Researchers Publishing, 2612 P Street, Northwest, Washington, D.C. 20007. Annual.

NATIONAL DIRECTORY OF STATE AGENCIES. Nancy D. Wright and Gene P. Allen. Information Resources Press, 1110 North Glebe Road, Suite 550, Arlington, Virginia 22201. Biennial.

RESEARCHER'S GUIDE TO WASHINGTON EXPERTS. Washington Researchers Publishing, Division of Washington Researchers, Limited, 2612 P Street, Northwest, Washington, D.C. 20007. 1981- . Annual.

STATE ADMINISTRATIVE OFFICIALS CLASSIFIED BY FUNCTION. The Council of State Governments, Iron Works Pike, P.O. Box 11910, Lexington, Kentucky 40578. Biennial.

STATE EXECUTIVE DIRECTORY. Pauline Green, Editor. Carroll Publishing Company, 1058 Thomas Jefferson Street, Northwest, Washington, D.C. 20007. Bimonthly.

UNITED STATES GOVERNMENT MANUAL. Office of the Federal Register. United States Government Printing Office, Division of Public Documents, Washington, D.C. 20402. Annual.

WASHINGTON INFORMATION DIRECTORY. Congressional Quarterly Books, Incorporated, 1414 Twenty-second Street, Northwest, Washington, D.C. 20037. Annual.

ASSOCIATIONS AND PROFESSIONAL SOCIETIES

CENTER FOR STUDY OF RESPONSIVE LAW. P.O. Box 19367, Washington, D.C. 20036. (202) 387-8030.

FEDERAL ADMINISTRATIVE LAW JUDGES CONFERENCE. 424 National Lawyers Club, 1815 H Street, Northwest, Washington, D.C. 20006. (202) 357-9251.

RESEARCH CENTERS, INSTITUTES, CLEARINGHOUSES

ANNE BLAINE HARRISON INSTITUTE FOR PUBLIC LAW. Georgetown University, 25 E Street, Northwest, Washington, D.C. 20001. (202) 662-9070.

INSTITUTE FOR ADMINISTRATIVE JUSTICE. University of the Pacific, McGeorge School of Law, 3287 Fifth Avenue, Sacramento, California 95817. (916) 739-7049.

ONLINE DATABASES

WESTLAW ADMINISTRATIVE LAW DATABASE. West Publishing Company, 50 West Kellogg Boulevard, P.O. Box 64526, St. Paul, Minnesota 55164.

OTHER SOURCES

ADMINISTRATIVE CONFERENCE OF THE UNITED STATES: RECOMMENDATIONS AND REPORTS. Administrative Conference of the United States. United States Government Printing Office, Division of Public Documents, Washington, D.C. 20402. Annual.

ADMINISTRATIVE LAW ANNUAL REPORT OF COMMITTEES. American Bar Association, 1800 M Street, Northwest, Washington, D.C. 20036. Annual.

PARALLEL GRAND JURY AND ADMINISTRATIVE AGENCY INVESTIGATIONS. American Bar Association, Section of Criminal Justice, 1800 M Street, Northwest, Washington, D.C. 20036. 1981.

RULES IN THE MAKING: A STATISTICAL ANALYSIS OF REGULATORY AGENCY BEHAVIOR. Wesley A. Magat, Alan J. Krupnik and Winston Harrington. Resources for the Future, Incorporated, 1616 P Street, Northwest, Washington, D.C. 20036. 1986.

ADMINISTRATIVE OFFICE OF THE UNITED STATES COURTS

See also: ADMINISTRATION OF JUSTICE

LOOSELEAF SERVICES AND REPORTERS

FEDERAL CRIMINAL PRACTICE MANUAL. Administrative Office of the United States Courts. Superintendent of Documents, United States Government Printing Office, Washington, D.C. 20402. 1977- .

HANDBOOKS, MANUALS, FORMBOOKS

UNITED STATES TITLE AND CODE CRIMINAL OFFENSE CITATIONS: FOR USE OF U.S. MAGISTRATES, CLERKS OF COURT, FEDERAL PROBATION OFFICES, PRETRIAL SERVICE AGENCIES, FEDERAL PUBLIC DEFENDERS, COMMUNITY DEFENDERS. Fourth Edition. Administrative Office of the United States Courts. Superintendent of Documents, United States Government Printing Office, Washington, D.C. 20402. 1982.

TEXTBOOKS AND GENERAL WORKS

PRESENTENCE INVESTIGATION REPORT. Administrative Office of the United States Courts, Probation Division. Superintendent of Documents, United States Government Printing Office, Washington, D.C. 20402. 1984.

THE UNITED STATES COURTS: THEIR JURISDICTION AND WORK. Administrative Office of the United States Courts. Superintendent of Documents, United States Government Printing Office, Washington, D.C. 20402. 1989.

ANNUALS AND SURVEYS

FEDERAL OFFENDERS IN THE UNITED STATES DISTRICT COURTS. Administrative Office of the United States Courts. Superintendent of Documents, United States Government Printing Office, Washington, D.C. 20402. 1962- . (Annual).

REPORT OF THE PROCEEDINGS OF THE JUDICIAL CONFERENCE OF THE UNITED STATES. Administrative Office of the United States Courts. Superintendent of Documents, United States Government Printing Office, Washington, D.C. 20402. Annual.

SEMI-ANNUAL REPORT OF THE DIRECTOR - ADMINISTRATIVE OFFICE OF THE UNITED STATES COURTS. Superintendent of Documents, United States Government Printing Office, Washington, D.C. 20402. 1940- .

UNITED STATES DISTRICT COURTS SENTENCES IMPOSED CHART. Administrative Office of the United States Courts. Superintendent of Documents, United States Government Printing Office, Washington, D.C. 20402. 1976- . (Annual).

LAW REVIEWS AND PERIODICALS

FEDERAL PROBATION: A JOURNAL OF CORRECTIONAL PHILOSOPHY AND PRACTICE. Administrative Office of the United States Courts. Superintendent of Documents, United States Government Printing Office, Washington, D.C. 20402. Quarterly.

NEWSLETTERS AND NEWSPAPERS

THE THIRD BRANCH: A BULLETIN OF THE FEDERAL COURTS. Administrative Office of the United States Courts and the Federal Judicial Center. Superintendent of Documents, United States Government Printing Office, Washington, D.C. 20402. Quarterly.

DIRECTORIES

UNITED STATES COURT DIRECTORY. Administrative Office of the United States Court, Administrative Services Division. Superintendent of Documents, United States Government Printing Office, Washington, D.C. 20402. Biannual.

RESEARCH CENTERS, INSTITUTES, CLEARINGHOUSES

ADMINISTRATIVE OFFICES OF THE UNITED STATES COURTS LIBRARY. 811 Vermont Avenue, Northwest, Washington, D.C. 20544. (202) 633-6314.

ADMINISTRATIVE PROCEDURE
See also: ADMINISTRATIVE CONFERENCE OF THE UNITED STATES; ADMINISTRATIVE LAW

STATUTES, CODES, STANDARDS, UNIFORM LAWS

MODEL STATE ADMINISTRATIVE PROCEDURE ACT. National Conference of Commissioners on Uniform State Laws. Uniform Laws Annotated. West Publishing Company, 50 West Kellogg Boulevard, St. Paul, Minnesota 55164-0526. 1976- . (Annual Supplements).

LOOSELEAF SERVICES AND REPORTERS

BNA ADMINISTRATIVE PRACTICE MANUAL. Bertram R. Cottine. Bureau of National Affairs, Incorporated, 1231 Twenty-fifth Street, Northwest, Washington, D.C. 20037. 1988- . (Periodic Supplements).

FEDERAL REGULATORY PROCESS: AGENCY PRACTICES AND PROCEDURES. Gary J. Edles and Jerome Nelson. Prentice-Hall Law and Business, Incorporated, 910 Sylvan Avenue, Englewood Cliffs, New Jersey 07632. 1989- . (Periodic Supplements).

HANDBOOKS, MANUALS, FORMBOOKS

ADMINISTRATIVE PRACTICE MANUAL. Second Edition. David H. Baker, Editor. Bar Association of the District of Columbia. Young Lawyers Section, 1819 H Street, Northwest, Washington, D.C. 20006. 1989.

A GUIDE TO FEDERAL AGENCY RULEMAKING. Administrative Conference of the United States, Office of the Chairman. Superintendent of Documents, United States Government Printing Office, Division of Public Documents, Washington, D.C. 20402. 1983.

RESEARCH ESSENTIALS OF ADMINISTRATIVE LAW. H.B. Jacobini, Albert P. Melone and Carl Kalvelage. Palisades Publishers, P.O. Box 744, Pacific Palisades, California 90272. 1983.

STATE AND FEDERAL ADMINISTRATIVE AGENCY PRACTICE. Indiana Continuing Legal Education Forum, 230 East Ohio Street, Indianapolis, Indiana 46204. 1989.

TEXTBOOKS AND GENERAL WORKS

ADMINISTRATIVE LAW AND PRACTICE. Charles H. Koch. West Publishing Company, 50 West Kellogg Boulevard, St. Paul, Minnesota 55164-0526. 1985- . (Annual Supplements).

ADMINISTRATIVE LAW: PRACTICE AND PROCEDURE. Lee Modjeska. Lawyers Cooperative Publishing Company, Aqueduct Building, Rochester, New York 14694. 1982.

ADMINISTRATIVE PROCESS. Second Edition. Stephen P. Robbins. Prentice-Hall, Incorporated, 113 Sylvan Avenue, Englewood Cliffs, New Jersey 07632. 1980.

THE ADMINISTRATIVE REGULATORY PROCESS. Florence A. Heffron and Neel McFeeley. Longman Publishing Group, Incorporated, 95 Church Street, White Plains, New York 10601. 1983.

ADMINISTRATIVE RULEMAKING: POLITICS AND PROCESSES. William F. West. Greenwood Publishing Group, Incorporated, 88 Post Road West, P.O. Box 5007, Westport, Connecticut 06881. 1985.

ADMINISTRATIVE RULEMAKING: STRUCTURING, OPPOSING AND DEFENDING FEDERAL AGENCY REGULATIONS. James T. O'Reilly. Shepard's/McGraw-Hill, Incorporated, 420 North Cascade Avenue, Colorado Springs, Colorado 80901. 1983- .

BUREAUCRATIC DISCRETION: LAW AND POLICY IN FEDERAL REGULATORY AGENCIES. Garry C. Bryner. Pergamon Press, Incorporated, Maxwell House, Fairview Park, Elmsford, New York 10523. 1987.

CONTROLLING REGULATORY SPRAWL: PRESIDENTIAL STRATEGIES FROM NIXON TO REAGAN. Howard Ball. Greenwood Publishing Group, Incorporated, 88 Post Road West, P.O. Box 5007, Westport, Connecticut 06881. 1984.

CRISIS AND LEGITIMACY: THE ADMINISTRATIVE PROCESS AND AMERICAN GOVERNMENT. James O. Freedman. Cambridge University Press, 40 West Twentieth Street, New York, New York 10011. 1978.

DISMANTLING AMERICA: THE RUSH TO DEREGULATE. Susan Tolchin and Martin Tolchin. Oxford University Press, 200 Madison Avenue, New York, New York 10016. 1985.

DUE PROCESS IN THE ADMINISTRATIVE STATE. Jerry L. Mashaw. Yale University Press, 302 Temple Street, New Haven, Connecticut 06520. 1985.

ENFORCING REGULATION. Keith Hawkins and John M. Thomas, Editors. Martinus Nijhoff, Kluwer Academic Publishers, 101 Philip Drive, Assinippi Park, Norwell, Massachusetts 02061. 1983.

FEDERAL PROCEDURE: A PROBLEM-SOLVING TEXTUAL ANALYSIS OF FEDERAL JUDICIAL AND ADMINISTRATIVE PROCEDURE. Lawyers Cooperative Publishing Company, Aqueduct Building, Rochester, New York 14694. 1981- . (Periodic Supplements).

MAKING BUREAUCRACIES THINK: THE ENVIRONMENTAL IMPACT STATEMENT STRATEGY OF ADMINISTRATIVE REFORM. Stanford University Press, Stanford, California 94305-2235. 1984.

PERSPECTIVES ON THE ADMINISTRATIVE PROCESS. Robert L. Rabin. Little, Brown and Company, 34 Beacon Street, Boston, Massachusetts 02108. 1979.

REFORMING FEDERAL REGULATION. Robert E. Litan and William D. Nordhaus. Yale University Press, 302 Temple Street, New Haven, Connecticut 06520. 1983.

REGULATORY REFORM: NEW VISION OR OLD CURSE. Margaret N. Maxey and Robert L. Kuhn. Praeger Publishers, Greenwood Publishing Group, Incorporated, 88 Post Road West, P.O. Box 5007, Westport, Connecticut 06881. 1985.

ASSOCIATIONS AND PROFESSIONAL SOCIETIES

ASSOCIATION OF ADMINISTRATIVE LAW JUDGES. Department of Health and Human Services, 1715 Sixty-second Court, Spokane, Washington 99223. (509) 448-1597.

FEDERAL ADMINISTRATIVE LAW JUDGES CONFERENCE. 424 National Lawyers Club, 1815 H Street, Northwest, Washington, D.C. 20006. (202) 357-9251.

OTHER SOURCES

LEGISLATIVE HISTORY MANUAL FOR THE ADMINISTRATIVE PROCEDURE ACT. United States National Labor Relations Board, 1717 Pennsylvania Avenue, Northwest, Washington, D.C. 20570. 1947.

SYMPOSIUM--THE LEGACY OF THE NEW DEAL: PROBLEMS AND POSSIBILITIES IN THE ADMINISTRATIVE STATE. Yale Law Journal Company, 92A Yale Station, New Haven, Connecticut 06520. June, 1983.

ADMIRALTY
See also: COMMERCIAL LAW; FEDERAL MARITIME COMMISSION; LAW OF THE SEA; NATIONAL TRANSPORTATION SAFETY BOARD; OCCUPATIONAL SAFETY AND HEALTH ADMINISTRATION; TRANSPORTATION DEPARTMENT

STATUTES, CODES, STANDARDS, UNIFORM LAWS

LAWS RELATING TO SHIPPING AND MERCHANT MARINE. Gerard P. Walsh, Junior. United States Government Printing Office, Division of Public Documents, Washington, D.C. 20402. 1981.

WORLD SHIPPING LAWS. David C. Jackson, Editor. Oceana Publications, Incorporated, 75 Main Street, Dobbs Ferry, New York 10522. 1979- .

LOOSELEAF SERVICES AND REPORTERS

BENEDICT ON ADMIRALTY. Revised Seventh Edition. Michael Marks Cohen, Martin J. Norris, Steven F. Friedell, John R. Geraghy and the Publisher's Editorial Staff. Matthew Bender and Company, Incorporated, 11 Penn Plaza, New York, New York 10001. 1974- .

FEDERAL MARITIME COMMISSION SERVICE. Hawkins Publishing Company, 310 Tahiti Way, Number 108, Marina Del Rey, California 90291.

MARINE OPERATIONS REPORTER. Sherry Stossel. Marine Advisory Services, Incorporated, 10 Signal Road, Stamford Connecticut 06902. 1980- .

MARITIME TAX REPORTER. Commerce Clearing House, Incorporated, 4025 West Peterson Avenue, Chicago, Illinois 60646. 1950- .

SHIPPING REGULATION. Pike and Fischer, Incorporated, 4550 Montgomery Avenue, Suite 433N, Bethesda, Maryland 20814. 1961- .

HANDBOOKS, MANUALS, FORMBOOKS

HANDBOOK OF ADMIRALTY LAW. Second Edition. Robert Morton Hughes. West Publishing Company, P.O. Box 43526, 50 West Kellogg Boulevard, St. Paul, Minnesota 55164-0526. 1970.

HANDBOOK OF ADMIRALTY LAW IN THE UNITED STATES. Gustavus H. Robinson. West Publishing Company, P.O. Box 43526, 50 West Kellogg Boulevard, St. Paul, Minnesota 55164-0526. 1939.

TEXTBOOKS AND GENERAL WORKS

ADMIRALTY AND FEDERALISM: HISTORY AND ANALYSIS OF PROBLEMS OF FEDERAL-STATE RELATIONS IN THE MARITIME LAW OF THE UNITED STATES. David W. Robertson. Foundation Press, 615 Merrick Avenue, Westbury, New York 11590. 1970.

ADMIRALTY AND MARITIME LAW. Thomas J. Schoenbaum. West Publishing Company, 50 W. Kellogg, St. Paul, Minnesota 55164-0526. 1987.

ADMIRALTY IN A NUTSHELL. Second Edition. Frank L. Maraist. West Publishing Company, P.O. Box 43526, 50 West Kellogg Boulevard, St. Paul, Minnesota 55164-0526. 1987.

ADMIRALTY LAW OF THE SUPREME COURT. Third Edition. Herbert R. Baer. The Michie Company, P.O. Box 7587, Charlottesville, Virginia 22906-7582.

THE CARRIAGE OF DANGEROUS GOODS BY SEA: THE ROLE OF INTERNATIONAL MARITIME ORGANIZATION IN INTERNATIONAL LEGISLATION. St. Martin's Press, Incorporated, 175 Fifth Avenue, New York, New York 10010. 1985.

CONSENSUS AND CONFRONTATION: THE UNITED STATES AND THE LAW OF THE SEA CONVENTION. Jon M. Van Dyke, Editor. The Law of the Sea Institute, University of Hawaii Press, 2840 Kolowalu Street, Honolulu, Hawaii 96822. 1985.

THE DEVELOPMENT OF ADMIRALTY JURISDICTION AND PRACTICE SINCE 1800: AN ENGLISH STUDY WITH AMERICAN COMPARISONS. F.L. Wiswall. Cambridge University Press, 40 West Twentieth Street, New York, New York 10011. 1970.

THE LAW OF ADMIRALTY. Second Edition. Grant Gilmore and Charles L. Black. Foundation Press 615 Merrick Avenue, Westbury, New York 11590. 1975.

THE LAW OF SEAMEN. Fourth Edition. Martin J. Norris. Bancroft Press, 27 McNear Drive, San Rafael, California 94901. 1985.

LAW OF THE SEA IN A NUTSHELL. Louis B. Sohn and Kristen Gustafson. West Publishing Company, P.O. Box 43526, 50 West Kellogg Boulevard, St. Paul, Minnesota 55164-0526. 1984.

MARITIME LAW. Third Edition. Christopher Hill. Lloyds of London Maritime and Business Publishing Incorporated, 611 Broadway, New York, New York 10012.

MARITIME LAW: THE NEED FOR A COMPREHENSIVE MARITIME CODE. Gerald A. Malia. Associated Faculty Press, 90 South Bayles Avenue, Port Washington, New York 11050. 1983.

MERCHANTMAN? OR SHIP OF WAR: A SYNOPSIS OF LAWS, U.S. STATE DEPARTMENT POSITIONS AND PRACTICES WHICH ALTER THE PEACEFUL CHARACTER OF U.S. MERCHANT VESSELS IN TIME OF WAR. Charles Dana Gibson. Ensign Press, P.O. Box 638, Camden, Maine 04843. 1986.

NEGOTIATING THE LAW OF THE SEA. James K. Sebenius. Harvard University Press, 79 Garden Street, Cambridge, Massachusetts 02138. 1984.

REGULATION AND POLICIES OF AMERICAN SHIPPING. Ernst G. Frankel. Auburn House Publishing Company, Greenwood Publishing Group, Incorporated, 88 Post Road West, P.O. Box 5007, Westport, Connecticut 06881. 1982.

SUPERPOWER AT SEA: UNITED STATES OCEAN POLICY. Finn Laursen. Greenwood Publishing Group, Incorporated, 88 Post Road West, P.O. Box 5007, Westport, Connecticut 06881. 1983.

U.S. FOREIGN POLICY AND THE LAW OF THE SEA. Ann L. Hollick. Princeton University Press, 41 William Street, Princeton, New Jersey 08540. 1981.

ENCYCLOPEDIAS AND DICTIONARIES

CHARTERING AND SHIPPING TERMS. Seventh Edition. J. Bes. William S. Hein and Company, Incorporated, 1285 Main Street, Buffalo, New York, 14209. 1970.

DIGESTS, INDEXES, ABSTRACTS, CITATORS

DIGEST: LLOYD'S LAW REPORTS. Lloyd's of London Press, 611 Broadway, New York, New York 10012. 1947.

FIVE-YEAR INDEX -- DIGEST OF AMERICAN MARITIME CASES. Maritime Law Association of the United States. 1 Battery Park Plaza, 25th Floor, New York, New York 10004. 1923- .

INDEX TO MARITIME TREATIES. John King Gamble. University of Washington Press, P.O. Box C50096, Seattle, Washington 98145. 1972.

ANNUALS AND SURVEYS

YEARBOOK MARITIME LAW. Kluwer Academic Publishers, 101 Philip Drive, Assinippi Park, Massachusetts 02061. 1986- .

LAW REVIEWS AND PERIODICALS

JOURNAL OF MARITIME LAW AND COMMERCE. Jefferson Law Book Company, Colorado Building, 1341 G Street, Northwest, Suite 408, Washington, D.C. 20005. Quarterly.

TULANE MARITIME LAW JOURNAL. Tulane University, School of Law, New Orleans, Lousiana 70118. Quarterly.

NEWSLETTERS AND NEWSPAPERS

ADMIRALTY LAW NEWSLETTER. American Bar Association, Young Lawyers Division, 750 North Lake Shore Drive, Chicago, Illinois 60611. Semiannual.

ADMIRALTY

CIB NEWSLETTER. Congressional Information Bureau, Incorporated, 1325 G Street, Northwest, Suite 1005 Washington, D.C. 20005. Daily.

LLOYDS' MARITIME LAW, NORTH AMERICAN EDITION. Lloyd's of London Press, Incorporated, 611 Broadway, Suite 523, New York, New York 10012. Biweekly.

LLOYDS' SHIP ARREST INTERNATIONAL. Lloyds' of London Press, Incorporated, 611 Broadway, Suite 523, New York, New York 10012. Monthly.

LONGSHORE NEWSLETTER AND CHRONICLE OF MARITIME INJURY LAW. Longshore Newsletter, 15 Fowler Court, #100, San Rafael, California 94903. Monthly.

MARINE OPERATIONS REPORTER. Marine Advisory Services, Incorporated, 2 Greenwich Plaza, Greenwich, Connecticut 06830. Monthly.

MARITIME ADVISOR ARBITRATION AWARD DIGEST. Marine Advisory Services, Incorporated, 2 Greenwich Plaza, Greenwich, Connecticut 06830. Monthly.

MARITIME ADVISOR COURT CASE DIGEST. Marine Advisory Services, Incorporated, 2 Greenwich Plaza, Greenwich, Connecticut 06830. Monthly.

MARITIME LAW REPORTER. Butterworth Legal Publishers, 90 Stiles Road, Salem, New Hampshire 03079. Bimonthly.

MARITIME PERSONAL INJURY REPORT. Marine Advisory Services, Incorporated, 2 Greenwich Plaza, Greenwich, Connecticut 06830. Monthly.

MIB UPDATE. Marine Index Bureau, Incorporated, 44 East Thirty-second Street, New York, New York 10016. Bimonthly.

MLA REPORT. Maritime Law Association of the United States, 1 Battery Park Plaza, New York, New York 10004. Semiannual.

PROCTOR-IN-ADMIRALTY NEWSLETTER. Florida Bar Admiralty Law Committee, 650 Apalachee Parkway, Tallahassee, Florida 32399. Semiannual.

SOUNDINGS. Admiralty and Maritime Law Section, Illinois State Bar Association, Illinois Bar Center, Springfield, Illinois 62701. (Five issues per year).

ASSOCIATIONS AND PROFESSIONAL SOCIETIES

MARITIME LAW ASSOCIATION OF THE UNITED STATES. 956 Public Ledger Building, 600 Chestnut Street, Philadelphia, Pennsylvania 96822. (215) 625-9900.

RESEARCH CENTERS, INSTITUTES, CLEARINGHOUSES

CENTER FOR SEAFARERS' RIGHTS. 50 Broadway, New York, New York 10004. (212) 269-2710.

UNIVERSITY OF HAWAII AT MANOA LAW OF THE SEA INSTITUTE. Richardson School of Law, 2515 Dole Street, Honolulu, Hawaii 96822. (808) 948-6750.

UNIVERSITY OF OREGON OCEAN AND COASTAL LAW CENTER. University of Oregon Law School, Eugene, Oregon 97403. (503) 686-3845.

UNIVERSITY OF SOUTHERN MAINE MARINE LAW INSTITUTE. 246 Deering Avenue, Portland, Maine 04102. (207) 780-4474.

ONLINE DATABASES

LEXIS ADMIRALTY LIBRARY. Mead Data Central, P.O. Box 933, Dayton, Ohio 45401.

WESTLAW ADMIRALTY LIBRARY. West Publishing Company, P.O. Box 64526, 50 West Kellogg Boulevard, St. Paul, Minnesota 55164-0526.

OTHER SOURCES

MARITIME LAW ASSOCIATION OF THE UNITED STATES PROCEEDINGS. Maritime Law Association of the United States, One Battery Park Plaza, Twenty-fifth Floor, New York, New York 10004. Semiannual.

THE UNCTAD LINER CODE: UNITED STATES MARITIME POLICY AT THE CROSSROADS. Lawrence Juda. Westview Press, 5500 Central Avenue, Boulder, Colorado 80301. 1983.

WHAT LAW NOW FOR THE SEAS? Program Proceedings (1982 Annual Meeting, San Francisco, California). Carlyle E. Maw, Editor. American Bar Association, Section of International Law and Practice, 1800 M Street, Northwest, Washington, D.C. 20036. 1984.

ADMISSIBILITY OF EVIDENCE
See: EVIDENCE

ADMISSION TO THE BAR
See also: AMERICAN BAR ASSOCIATION

STATUTES, CODES, STANDARDS, UNIFORM LAWS

RULES FOR ADMISSION TO THE BAR IN THE UNITED STATES. West Publishing Company, P.O. Box 64526, 50 West Kellogg Boulevard, St. Paul, Minnesota 55164-0526. 1982.

HANDBOOKS, MANUALS, FORMBOOKS

COMPREHENSIVE GUIDE TO BAR ADMISSION REQUIREMENTS, 1990. American Bar Association, Section on Legal Education and Admissions to the Bar, 750 North Lake Shore Drive, Chicago, Illinois 60611. 1990.

MULTISTATE BAR EXAMINATION QUESTIONS VIII. Lucas Brothers, 909 Lowry Street, Columbia, Missouri 65201. 1985.

ANNUALS AND SURVEYS

ANNUAL COMPILATION OF BAR EXAMINATION QUESTIONS AND ANSWERS. The Institute for Bar Review Study, 86 Norwood Road, West Hartford, Connecticut 06117. Annual.

LAW REVIEWS AND PERIODICALS

THE BAR EXAMINER. National Conference on Bar Examiners, 333 North Michigan Avenue, Chicago, Illinois 60601. Quarterly.

ASSOCIATIONS AND PROFESSIONAL SOCIETIES

ALABAMA STATE BAR. Admissions Office, P.O. Box 671, Montgomery, Alabama 36101. (205) 269-1515.

ALASKA BAR ASSOCIATION. P.O. Box 100279, Anchorage, Alaska 99510. (907) 272-7469.

AMERICAN BAR ASSOCIATION. Section on Legal Education and Admissions to the Bar. 750 North Lake Shore Drive, Chicago, Illinois 60611. (312) 988-5000.

ARKANSAS BAR ASSOCIATION. State Board of Law Examiners, P.O. Box 5581, Little Rock, Arkansas 72215-5581. (501) 225-1070.

BOARD OF EXAMINERS OF THE STATE OF DELAWARE. P.O. Box 8965, Wilmington, Delaware 19899. (302) 888-6989.

BOARD OF LAW EXAMINERS OF THE STATE OF TENNESSEE. Tenth Floor, L & C Tower, 401 Church Street, Nashville, Tennessee 37219. (615) 741-3234.

CONNECTICUT BAR EXAMINING COMMITTEE. P.O. Box 6430, Hartford, Connecticut 06106. (203) 566-3770.

DISTRICT OF COLUMBIA COURT OF APPEALS. Committee on Admissions, 500 Indiana Avenue, Northwest, Room 6000, Washington, D.C. 20001. (202) 879-2710.

FLORIDA BOARD OF BAR EXAMINERS. 1300 East Park Avenue, Tallahassee, Florida 32399-1750. (904) 487-1292.

IDAHO STATE BAR. P.O. Box 895, Boise, Idaho 83701. (208) 342-8958.

ILLINOIS STATE BAR ASSOCIATION. State Board of Bar Examiners, 340 INB Center, Springfield, Illinois 62701. (217) 522-5917.

INDIANA STATE BAR ASSOCIATION. State Board of Law Examiners, 150 West Ohio Street, Suite 450, Indianapolis, Indiana 46204. (317) 232-2552.

IOWA SUPREME COURT CLERK. State Capital, Des Moines, Iowa 50319. (515) 281-5911.

KANSAS SUPREME COURT CLERK. Kansas Judicial Center, 301 West Tenth, Topeka, Kansas 66612. (913) 296-3229.

KENTUCKY STATE BOARD OF BAR EXAMINERS. 801 Lexington Building, 201-215 West Short Street, Lexington, Kentucky 40507. (606) 253-2733.

LOUISIANA STATE BAR ASSOCIATION. Committee on Bar Admissions, 601 St. Charles Avenue, New Orleans, Louisiana 70130. (504) 566-1600.

MAINE STATE BAR ASSOCIATION. Board of Bar Examiners, P.O. Box 30, Augusta, Maine 04332-0030. (207) 623-2464.

MARYLAND STATE BOARD OF LAW EXAMINERS. The District Court Building, Suite 403, 580 Taylor Avenue, Annapolis, Maryland 21401. (301) 975-2140.

MASSACHUSETTS BAR ASSOCIATION. Board of Bar Examiners, 77 Franklin Street, Boston, Massachusetts 02110. (607) 482-4467.

MINNESOTA STATE BAR ASSOCIATION. State Board of Law Examiners, One West Water Street, Suite 250, Saint Paul, Minnesota 55107. (612) 297-1800.

MISSISSIPPI STATE BAR. Board of Bar Admissions, P.O. Box 1449, Jackson, Mississippi 39215-1449. (601) 359-1268.

MISSOURI SUPREME COURT. Office of the Clerk, P.O. Box 150, Jefferson City, Missouri 65102. (314) 751-4144.

NATIONAL CONFERENCE OF BAR EXAMINERS. 333 North Michigan, Suite 1025, Chicago, Illinois 60601. (312) 641-0963.

NEBRASKA STATE BAR COMMISSION. 635 South Fourteenth Street, P.O. Box 81809, Lincoln, Nebraska 68501. (402) 475-7091.

NEW JERSEY STATE BAR ASSOCIATION. Board of Bar Examiners, CN 973, Trenton, New Jersey 08625. (609) 984-7783.

NEW YORK STATE BAR ASSOCIATION. State Board of Law Examiners, 7 Executive Center Drive, Albany, New York 12203. (518) 452-8700.

NORTH CAROLINA STATE BAR. Board of Law Examiners, 208 Fayetteville Street Mall, P.O. Box 2946, Raleigh, North Carolina 27602. (919) 828-4886.

OKLAHOMA BAR ASSOCIATION. Board of Bar Examiners, 1901 North Lincoln Boulevard, P.O. Box 53036, Oklahoma City, Oklahoma 73152. (405) 524-2365.

OREGON STATE BOARD OF BAR EXAMINERS. 5200 Southwest Meadows Road, P.O. Box 1689, Lake Oswego, Oregon 97035-0889. (503) 620-0222.

PENNSYLVANIA BOARD OF BAR EXAMINERS. Public Ledger Building, Sixth and Chestnut Streets, Philadelphia, Pennsylvania 19106. (215) 627-3246.

PUERTO RICO BAR ASSOCIATION. Executive Director, Board of Bar Examiners of Puerto Rico, P.O. Box 2392, San Juan, Puerto Rico 00903. (809) 723-1630.

RHODE ISLAND SUPREME COURT CLERK. Providence County Courthouse, 250 Benefit Street, Providence, Rhode Island 02903. (401) 277-3272.

STATE BAR ASSOCIATION OF NORTH DAKOTA. State Board of Bar Examiners, First Floor, Judicial Wing, 600 East Boulevard Avenue, Bismarck, North Dakota 58505-0530. (701) 224-4201.

STATE BAR OF ARIZONA. Committee on Character and Fitness, 363 North First Avenue, Phoenix, Arizona 85003. (602) 252-4804.

THE STATE BAR OF CALIFORNIA. Committee of Bar Examiners, 555 Franklin Street, P.O. Box 7908, San Francisco, California 94120. (415) 561-8303.

THE STATE BAR OF CALIFORNIA. Committee of Bar Examiners, 333 South Beaudry, Los Angeles, California 90017. (213) 975-1200.

STATE BAR OF GEORGIA. Office of Bar Admissions, P.O. Box 38466, Atlanta, Georgia 30334. (404) 656-3490.

STATE BAR OF MICHIGAN. Board of Law Examiners, P.O. Box 30104, Lansing, Michigan 48909. (517) 334-6992.

STATE BAR OF MONTANA. P.O. Box 577, Helena, Montana 59624. (406) 442-7660.

STATE BAR OF NEVADA. 295 Holcomb Avenue, Suite 2, Reno, Nevada 89502. (702) 329-4100.

STATE BAR OF SOUTH DAKOTA. Board of Bar Examiners, 400 East Capitol, Pierre, South Dakota 57501. (605) 773-4898.

STATE BAR OF TEXAS. Board of Law Examiners, Eligibility and Examination, P.O. Box 13486, Austin, Texas 78711. (512) 463-1621.

STATE BAR OF WISCONSIN. Board of Attorneys Professional Competence, 119 Martin Luther King, Jr. Boulevard, Room 405, Madison, Wisconsin 53703. (608) 266-9760.

STATE OF COLORADO SUPREME COURT. Board of Law Examiners, 600 Seventeenth Street, Suite 520-S, Denver, Colorado 80202. (303) 893-8096.

SUPREME COURT OF HAWAII. Office of the Clerk, P.O. Box 2560, Honolulu, Hawaii 96804. (808) 548-7430.

SUPREME COURT OF NEW HAMPSHIRE. Office of the Clerk, Concord, New Hampshire 03301. (603) 271-2646.

SUPREME COURT OF NEW MEXICO. Clerk, P.O. Box 848, Santa Fe, New Mexico 87504-0848. (505) 827-4860.

SUPREME COURT OF OHIO. Admissions Office, 30 East Broad Street, Columbus, Ohio 43215. (614) 466-1541.

THE SUPREME COURT OF SOUTH CAROLINA. Office of the Clerk, P.O. Box 11330, Columbia, South Carolina 29211. (803) 734-1080.

UTAH STATE BAR. 645 South 200 East, Salt Lake City, Utah 84111. (801) 531-9077.

VERMONT BAR ASSOCIATION. Board of Bar Examiners, 111 State Street, Montpelier, Vermont 05602. (802) 828-3281.

VIRGINIA BOARD OF BAR EXAMINERS. Suite 303, Mutual Building, Ninth and Main Streets, Richmond, Virginia 23219. (804) 786-7490.

WASHINGTON STATE BAR ASSOCIATION. 500 Westin Building, 201 Sixth Avenue, Seattle, Washington 98121-2599. (206) 448-0563.

WEST VIRGINIA STATE BAR. Board of Law Examiners, E400 Capitol Building, Charleston, West Virginia 25305. (304) 348-7815.

WYOMING STATE BAR. State Board of Law Examiners, P.O. Box 109, Cheyenne, Wyoming 82003-0109. (307) 632-9061.

ADMISSIONS
See: EVIDENCE

ADOPTION
See also: FAMILY LAW

STATUTES, CODES, STANDARDS, UNIFORM LAWS

UNIFORM ADOPTION ACT. National Conference of Commissioners on Uniform State Laws. Uniform Laws Annotated. West Publishing Company, P.O. Box 64526, 50 West Kellogg Boulevard, St. Paul, Minnesota 55164-0526. 1976- . (Annual Supplements).

LOOSELEAF SERVICES AND REPORTERS

ADOPTION LAW AND PRACTICE. Joan H. Hollinger, Editor. Matthew Bender and Company, Incorporated, 11 Penn Plaza, New York, New York 10001. 1988.

HANDBOOKS, MANUALS, FORMBOOKS

ADOPTION FACTBOOK 1989: UNITED STATES DATA, ISSUES, REGULATIONS AND RESOURCES. National Committee for Adoption, P.O. Box 33366, Washington, D.C. 20033. 1989.

THE ADOPTION RESOURCE BOOK. Lois Gilman. HarperCollins Publishers, 10 East Fifty-third Street, New York, New York 10022. 1987.

ADOPTION WITHOUT AGENCIES: A STUDY OF INDEPENDENT ADOPTIONS. William Meegan, Sanford Katz and Eva M. Russo. Child Welfare League of America, 440 First Street, Northwest, Suite 310, Washington, D.C. 20001. 1978.

ADOPTIONS: AN ATTORNEY'S GUIDE TO HELPING ADOPTIVE PARENTS. Joseph H. Gitlin. Callaghan and Company, 155 Pfingsten Road, Deerfield, Illinois 60015. 1987.

IDEAL ADOPTION: A COMPREHENSIVE GUIDE TO FORMING AN ADOPTIVE FAMILY. Shirley Samuels. Plenum Publishing Corporation, 233 Spring Street, New York, New York 10013. 1990.

A PARENT'S GUIDE TO ADOPTION. Robert S. Lasnik. Sterling Publishing Company, 387 Park Avenue South, New York, New York 10016-8810. 1979.

THE PENGUIN ADOPTION HANDBOOK: A GUIDE TO CREATING YOUR NEW FAMILY. Edmund Blair Bolles. Viking-Penguin, Incorporated, 375 Hudson Street, New York, New York 10014. 1984.

THE PRIVATE ADOPTION HANDBOOK: A STEP-BY-STEP GUIDE TO THE LEGAL, EMOTIONAL, AND PRACTICAL DEMANDS OF ADOPTING A BABY. Stanley B. Michelman and Meg Schneider. Villard Books, Random House, Incorporated, 201 East Fiftieth Street, New York, New York 10022. 1988.

SEARCH: A HANDBOOK FOR ADOPTEES AND BIRTHPARENTS. Second Edition. Jayne Askin and Bob Oskam. Oryx Press, 2214 North Central Avenue, Phoenix, Arizona 85004. 1992.

TEXTBOOKS AND GENERAL WORKS

THE ADOPTED ONE. Sara B. Stein. Walker and Company, 720 Fifth Avenue, New York, New York 10019. 1979.

AN ADOPTER'S ADVOCATE. Patricia Irwin Johnston. Perspectives Press, P.O. Box 90318, Indianapolis, Indiana 46290-0318. 1984.

ADOPTING CHILDREN WITH SPECIAL NEEDS. Patricia Kravik, Editor. North American Council on Adoptable Children, 1821 University Avenue, Suite N-498, St. Paul, Minnesota 55104. 1976.

ADOPTING OLDER CHILDREN. Alfred Kadushin. Columbia University Press, 562 West One Hundred Thirteenth Street, New York, New York 10025. 1970.

THE ADOPTION ADVISER. Joan McNamara. Hawthorn Books, 2 Park Avenue, New York, New York 10016. 1975.

ADOPTION ASSISTANCE: JOINING THE FAMILY OF EMPLOYEE BENEFITS. Bureau of National Affairs, Incorporated, 1231 Twenty-fifth Street, Northwest, Washington, D.C. 20037. 1988.

ADOPTION: ESSAYS IN SOCIAL POLICY, LAW AND SOCIOLOGY. Philip Bean, Editor. Tavistock Books Limited, Routledge, Chapman and Hall, Incorporated, 29 West Thirty-Fifth Street, New York, New York 10001. 1984.

ADOPTION IN AMERICA COMING OF AGE. Hal Aigner. Paradigm Press, 127 Greenbrae Boardwalk, Greenbrae, California 94904. 1986.

ADOPTION IN WORLDWIDE PERSPECTIVE: A REVIEW OF PROGRAMS, POLICIES, AND LEGISLATION IN FOURTEEN COUNTRIES. R.A.C. Hoksberger, Editor. Swets North America, Box 517, Berywn, Pennsylvania 19132. 1986.

ADOPTION LAW. Hamline University School of Law, Advanced Legal Education, 1536 Hewitt Avenue, St. Paul, Minnesota 55104. 1982.

ADOPTION OF CHILDREN WITH SPECIAL NEEDS: ISSUES IN LAW AND POLICY. National Legal Resource Center for Child Advocacy, American Bar Association, 750 North Lake Shore Drive, Chicago, Illinois 60611. 1985.

THE ADOPTION TRIANGLE. Arthur D. Sorosky, Annette Baran and Reuben Pannor. Doubleday and Company, Incorporated 666 Fifth Avenue, New York, New York 10103. 1984.

THE ART OF ADOPTION: Linda Cannon Burgess. W.W. Norton and Company, Incorporated, 500 Fifth Avenue, New York, New York 10110. 1981.

THE BABY BROKERS: THE MARKETING OF WHITE BABIES IN AMERICA. Lynne McTaggart. Dial Press, Doubleday and Company, Incorporated, 666 Fifth Avenue, New York, New York 10103. 1980.

BABYSELLING: THE SCANDAL OF BLACK-MARKET ADOPTION. Nancy C. Baker. Vanguard Press, Incorporated, c/o M. Greenspan, 201 East Fiftieth Street, Second Floor, New York, New York 10022. 1978.

BEATING THE ADOPTION GAME. Cynthia Martin. Harcourt Brace Jovanovich, Incorporated, 6277 Sea Harbor Drive, Orlando, Florida 32821. 1988.

BEYOND THE BEST INTEREST OF THE CHILD. Joseph Goldstein, Anna Freud and Albert J. Solnit. Free Press, MacMillan Publishing Company, Incorporated, 866 Third Avenue, New York, New York 10022. 1984.

CHOSEN CHILDREN: NEW PATTERNS OF ADOPTIVE RELATIONSHIPS. William Feigelman and Arnold R. Silverman. Praeger Publishers, Greenwood Publishing Group, Incorporated, 88 Post Road West, P.O. Box 5007, Westport, Connecticut 06881. 1983.

THE FIFTEEN MOST ASKED QUESTIONS ABOUT ADOPTION. Laura L. Valenti. Herald Press, 616 Walnut Avenue, Scottdale, Pennsylvania 15683. 1985.

THE FOSTER CHILD, FROM ABANDONMENT TO ADOPTION. Joseph R. Carrieri. Practising Law Institute, 810 Seventh Avenue, New York, New York 10019. 1977.

INTERCOUNTY ADOPTIONS: WHERE DO THEY GO FROM HERE? Gerald B. Adcock. North American Council on Adoptable Children, 1821 University Avenue, Suite N-498, St. Paul, Minnesota 55104. 1979.

LAW OF ADOPTION. Fourth Edition. Morton L. Leavy and Roy David Weinberg. Oceana Publications, 75 Main Street, Dobbs Ferry, New York 10522. 1979.

THE LAW OF ADOPTION AND SURROGATE PARENTING. Irving J. Sloan. Oceana Publications, 75 Main Street, Dobbs Ferry, New York 10522. 1988.

LOST AND FOUND: THE ADOPTION EXPERIENCE. Betty Jean Lifton. Perennial Library, HarperCollins Publishers, 10 East Fifty-Third Street, New York, New York 10022. 1988.

NEW DEVELOPMENTS IN FOSTER CARE AND ADOPTION. John Triseliotis, Editor. Routledge, Chapman and Hall, Incorporated, 29 West Thirty-fifth Street, New York, New York 10001. 1980.

ON THE FRONTIERS OF ADOPTION: A STUDY OF SPECIAL NEEDS ADOPTIVE FAMILIES. Katherine A. Nelson. Child Welfare League of America Research Center, 475 Riverside Drive, New York, New York 10115. 1985.

THE POLITICS OF ADOPTION. Mary Kathleen Benet. The Free Press, MacMillan Publishing Company, Incorporated, 866 Third Avenue, New York, New York 10022. 1976.

THE RIGHTS OF FOSTER PARENTS. Center on Children and the Law, American Bar Association, 750 Lake Shore Drive, Chicago, Illinois 60611. 1989.

WORKING WITH ADOPTIVE FAMILIES BEYOND PLACEMENT. Ann Hartman. Child Welfare League, 475 Riverside Drive, New York, New York 10115. 1984.

ADOPTION

BIBLIOGRAPHIES

ADOPTION: AN ANNOTATED BIBLIOGRAPHY AND GUIDE. Lois Ruskai Melina. Garland Publishing, Incorporated, 136 Madison Avenue, New York, New York 10016. 1987.

ADOPTION BIBLIOGRAPHY AND MULTI-ETHNIC SOURCEBOOK. Open Door Society of Connecticut, Incorporated, Box 478, Hartford, Connecticut 06101. 1977.

SPECIAL NEEDS: AN ANNOTATED BIBLIOGRAPHY ON TRANSRACIAL, TRANSCULTURAL, AND NONCONVENTIONAL ADOPTION AND MINORITY CHILDREN. Peter S. Kim. National Institute of Mental Health, 5600 Fishers Lane, Rockville, Maryland 20857. 1981.

DIRECTORIES

THE ADOPTION DIRECTORY: THE MOST COMPREHENSIVE GUIDE TO FAMILY-BUILDING OPTIONS. Second Edition. Ellen Paul, Editor. Gale Research, Incorporated, 835 Penobscot Building, Detroit, Michigan 48226. 1993.

CWLA'S GUIDE TO ADOPTION AGENCIES: A NATIONAL DIRECTORY OF ADOPTION AGENCIES AND ADOPTION RESOURCES. Julia L. Posner. Child Welfare League of America, 440 First Street, Northwest, Washington, D.C. 20001. 1993.

ASSOCIATIONS AND PROFESSIONAL SOCIETIES

ADVOCATING LEGISLATION FOR ADOPTION REFORM MOVEMENT. 1161A Southeast Forty-seventh Terrace, Cape Coral, Florida 33904. (813) 542-1342.

AMERICAN ADOPTION CONGRESS, P.O. Box 20137, Cherokee Station, New York, New York 10028. (212) 988-0110.

CHILD WELFARE LEAGUE OF AMERICA. 440 First Street, Northwest, Suite 310, Washington, D.C. 20001. (202) 638-2952.

COMMITTEE FOR SINGLE ADOPTIVE PARENTS. P.O. Box 15084, Chevy Chase, Maryland 20815. (202) 966-6367.

CONCERNED PERSONS FOR ADOPTION. P.O. Box 179, Whippany, New Jersey 07981. (914) 651-7075.

CONCERNED UNITED BIRTHPARENTS. 2000 Walker Street, Des Moines, Iowa 50317. (515) 263-9558.

INTERNATIONAL CONCERNS COMMITTEE FOR CHILDREN. 911 Cypress Drive, Boulder, Colorado 80303. (303) 494-8333.

LATIN AMERICAN PARENTS ASSOCIATION. P.O. Box 72, Seaford, New York 11783. (718) 236-8689.

NATIONAL ADOPTION CENTER, 1218 Chestnut Street, Second Floor, Philadelphia, Pennsylvania 19107. (215) 925-0200.

NATIONAL COMMITTEE FOR ADOPTION. 1930 Seventeenth Street, Northwest, Washington, D.C. 20007-6207. (202) 328-1200.

NORTH AMERICAN COUNCIL ON ADOPTABLE CHILDREN. 1821 University Avenue, Suite N-498, St. Paul, Minnesota 55104. (612) 644-3036.

STARS OF DAVID INTERNATIONAL. 9 Hampton Street, Cranford, New Jersey 07016. (201) 272-3156.

RESEARCH CENTERS, INSTITUTES, CLEARINGHOUSES

CHILD WELFARE LEAGUE OF AMERICA - RESEARCH CENTER. 440 First Street, Northwest, Suite 310, Washington, D.C. 20001. (202) 638-2952.

NATIONAL ADOPTION INFORMATION CLEARINGHOUSE. 1400 I Street, Northwest, Suite 600, Washington, D.C. 20005. (202) 842-1919.

ONLINE DATABASES

THE NATIONAL ADOPTION NETWORK. The National Adoption Exchange, 1218 Chestnut Street, Philadelphia, Pennsylvania 19107.

ADVERTISING

LOOSELEAF SERVICES AND REPORTERS

THE LAW OF ADVERTISING. George Eric Rosden and Peter E. Rosden. Matthew Bender and Company, Incorporated, 11 Penn Plaza, New York, New York 10001. 1973- .

LEGAL PROBLEMS IN ADVERTISING. Felix W. Kent and Douglas J. Wood. Matthew Bender and Company, Incorporated, 11 Penn Plaza, New York, New York 10001. 1984- .

PROVISIONS OF STATE CODES OF PROFESSIONAL RESPONSIBILITY GOVERNING LAWYER ADVERTISING AND SOLICITATION. Second Edition. American Bar Association, Commission on Advertising, 750 North Lake Shore Drive, Chicago, Illinois 60611. 1987.

HANDBOOKS, MANUALS, FORMBOOKS

ADVERTISING COMPLIANCE HANDBOOK. Kenneth A. Plevan. Practising Law Institute, 810 Seventh Avenue, New York, New York 10019. 1988.

ADVERTISING COMPLIANCE LAW: HANDBOOK FOR MARKETING PROFESSIONALS AND THEIR COUNSEL. John Lichtenberger. Quorum Books, Greenwood Publishing Group, Incorporated, 88 Post Road, Westport, Connecticut 06881. 1986.

ADVERTISING COST CONTROL HANDBOOK. Ovid Riso. Van Nostrand Reinhold Company, Incorporated, 115 West Fiftieth Street, New York, New York 10003. 1973.

ADVERTISING MANAGER'S HANDBOOK. Richard H. Stansfield. Dartnell Corporation, 4660 Ravenswood Avenue, Chicago, Illinois 60640. 1982.

BAR ASSOCIATION ADVERTISING: A HOW-TO MANUAL. American Bar Association, Commission on Advertising, 750 North Lake Shore Drive, Chicago, Illinois 60611. 1979.

BUT THE PEOPLE IN LEGAL SAID--: A GUIDE TO CURRENT LEGAL ISSUES IN ADVERTISING. Dean Keith Fueroghne. Richard D. Irwin, Incorporated, 1818 Ridge Road, Homewood, Illinois 60430. 1988.

HANDBOOK OF ADVERTISING AND MARKETING SERVICES. Executive Communications, Incorporated, 411 Lafayete Street, New York, New York 10003. 1987.

HANDBOOK OF INDEPENDENT ADVERTISING AND MARKETING SERVICES. Executive Communications Incorporated, 411 Lafayette Street, New York, New York 10003. Annual.

INDIVIDUAL LAWYER ADVERTISING: A HOW-TO MANUAL. American Bar Association, Commission on Advertising, 750 North Lake Shore Drive, Chicago, Illinois 60611. 1979.

INTERNATIONAL ADVERTISING HANDBOOK: A USER'S GUIDE TO RULES AND REGULATIONS. Barbara Sundberg Baudot. Lexington Books, 125 Spring Street, Lexington, Massachusetts 02173. 1989.

MARKETING YOUR LAW PRACTICE: A PRACTICAL GUIDE TO CLIENT DEVELOPMENT. Austin G. Anderson. American Bar Association, Section of Economics of Law Practice, 750 North Lake Shore Drive, Chicago, Illinois 60611. 1986.

MATURE ADVERTISING: A HANDBOOK OF EFFECTIVE ADVERTISING COPY. Robert B. Parker. Addison-Wesley Publishing Company, Incorporated, Route 128, Jacob Way, Reading, Massachusetts 01867. 1981.

REGULATION OF ADVERTISING BY LAWYERS: COMPARISONS OF THE ABA CODE OF PROFESSIONAL RESPONSIBILITY, ABA PROPOSAL B, AND STATE CODES. American Bar Association, Commission on Advertising, 750 North Lake Shore Drive, Chicago, Illinois 60611. 1978.

TEXTBOOKS AND GENERAL WORKS

ADVERTISING. Second Edition. William H. Bolen. John Wiley and Sons, Incorporated, 605 Third Avenue, New York, New York 10158. 1984.

ADVERTISING. Fifth Edition. John S. Wright and Sherilyn K. Zeigler. McGraw-Hill Publishing Company, 1221 Avenue of the Americas, New York, New York 10020. 1982.

ADVERTISING AND THE FIRST AMENDMENT. Michael Gartner. Priority Press Publications, 41 East Seventieth Street, New York, New York 10021. 1989.

ADVERTISING AND THE PUBLIC INTEREST. John C. Daly. American Enterprise Institute for Public Policy Research, 1150 Seventeenth Street, Northwest, Washington, D.C. 20036. 1976.

ADVERTISING CAMPAIGNS: FORMULATION AND TACTICS. Second Edition. Leon Quera. Grid, Incorporated, 4666 Indianola Avenue, Columbus, Ohio 43214. 1977.

ADVERTISING MANAGEMENT. Third Edition. David A. Aaker and John G. Myers. Prentice-Hall, Incorporated, 113 Sylvan Avenue, Englewood Cliffs, New Jersey 07632. 1987.

ADVERTISING PRINCIPLES AND PROBLEMS. Sixth Edition. Charles J. Dirksen and Arthur Kroeger. Richard D. Irwin Incorporated, 1818 Ridge Road, Homewood, Illinois 60430. 1983.

ADVERTISING, PURE AND SIMPLE: THE NEW EDITION. Hank Seiden. American Management Association, 135 West Fiftieth Street, New York, New York 10020. 1990.

COMPARISON ADVERTISING: A WORLDWIDE STUDY. J.J. Boddewyn and Katherine Morton. Hastings House Publishers, Incorporated, 141 Halstead Avenue, Mamaroneck, New York 10543. 1978.

CONTEMPORARY ADVERTISING. Third Edition. Courtland L. Bovee and William F. Arens. Richard D. Irwin, 1818 Ridge Road, Homewood, Illinois 60430. 1988.

CORPORATE AND COMMERCIAL FREE SPEECH: FIRST AMENDMENT PROTECTION OF EXPRESSION IN BUSINESS. Edwin P. Roome and William H. Roberts. Quorum Books, 88 Post Road, Westport, Connecticut 06881. 1985.

CORPORATE FIRST AMENDMENT RIGHTS AND THE S.E.C. Nicholas Wolfson. Quorum Books, 88 Post Road, Westport, Connecticut 06881. 1990.

CREATIVE STRATEGY AND TACTICS IN ADVERTISING. Sherilyn K. Zeigler and Douglas J. Johnson. Grid, Incorporated, 4666 Indianola Avenue, Columbus, Ohio 43214. 1981.

CREATIVE STRATEGY IN ADVERTISING: WHAT THE COPYWRITER SHOULD KNOW ABOUT THE CREATIVE SIDE OF THE BUSINESS. Third Edition. A. Jerome Jewler. Wadsworth Publishing Company, 10 Davis Drive, Belmont, California 94002. 1989.

DECEPTIVE ADVERTISING: A BEHAVIORAL STUDY OF A LEGAL CONCEPT. Jef I. Richard. L. Erlbaum Associates, 365 Broadway, Hillsdale, New Jersey 07642. 1990.

FUNDAMENTALS OF ADVERTISING RESEARCH. Fourth Edition. Alan D. Fletcher and Thomas A. Bowers. Wadsworth Publishing Company, 10 Davis Drive, Belmont, California 94002. 1991.

HONESTY AND COMPETITION: FALSE ADVERTISING LAW AND POLICY UNDER FTC ADMINISTRATION. George J. Alexander. Books on Demand, 300 North Zeeb Road, Ann Arbor, Michigan 48106-1346. 1967.

INTERNATIONAL TRADE IN BUSINESS SERVICES: ACCOUNTING, ADVERTISING, LAW, AND MANAGEMENT CONSULTING. Thierry J. Noyelle. Ballinger Division, HarperCollins Publishers, 10 East Fifty-third Street, New York, New York 10022. 1988.

ISSUES IN ADVERTISING: ECONOMICS OF PERSUASION. David G. Tuerck, American Enterprise Institute for Public Policy Research, 1150 Seventeenth Street, Northwest, Washington, D.C. 20036. 1978.

LEGAL AND BUSINESS ASPECTS OF THE ADVERTISING INDUSTRY. Felix H. Kent and Elhanan C. Stone. Practising Law Institute, 810 Seventh Avenue, New York, New York 10019. 1986.

MARKETING AND LEGAL ETHICS: THE RULES AND RISKS. Revised Edition. Harry J. Haynsworth. American Bar Association, 750 North Lake Shore Drive, Chicago, Illinois 60611. 1990.

MASS MEDIA AND ELECTIONS. Richard Joslyn. The Wesley Foundation, 211 North School Street, Normal, Illinois 61761. 1984.

MASS MEDIA, FREEDOM OF SPEECH, AND ADVERTISING: A STUDY IN COMMUNICATION LAW. Daniel M. Rohrer. Kendall-Hunt Publishing Company, 2460 Kerper Road, Dubuque, Iowa 52001. 1979.

MASS MEDIA LAW. Don R. Pember. Brown Book Company, P.O. Box 69-3883, Miami, Florida 33269 1987.

THE MIRROR MAKERS: A HISTORY OF AMERICAN ADVERTISING AND ITS CREATORS. Stephen Fox. William Morrow and Company, Incorporated, 105 Madison Avenue, New York, New York 10016. 1984.

PACKAGING THE PRESIDENCY: A HISTORY AND CRITICISM OF PRESIDENTIAL CAMPAIGN ADVERTISING. Kathlenn H. Jameison. Oxford University Press, Incorporated, 200 Madison Avenue, New York, New York 10016. 1988.

REPORT ON THE SURVEY OF LEGAL CLINICS AND ADVERTISING LAW FIRMS. American Bar Association, Special Committee on the Delivery of Legal Services, 750 North Lake Shore Drive, Chicago, Illinois 60611. 1990.

REPORT ON THE SURVEY ON THE IMAGE OF LAWYERS IN ADVERTISING. American Bar Association, Commission on Advertising, 750 North Lake Shore Drive, Chicago, Illinois 60611. 1990.

THE SPOT: THE RISE OF POLITICAL ADVERTISING ON TELEVISION. Revised Edition. Edwin Diamond and Stephen Bates. MIT Press, 55 Hayward Street, Cambridge, Massachusetts 02142. 1988.

STUDY ON INSTITUTIONAL ADVERTISING. American Bar Association, Committee on Advertising, 750 North Lake Shore Drive, Chicago, Illinois 60611. 1980.

TELEVISED MEDICINE ADVERTISING AND CHILDREN. Thomas S. Robertson and John R. Rossiter. Praeger Publishers, Greenwood Publishing Group, Incorporated, 88 Post Road West, P.O. Box 5007, Westport, Connecticut 06881. 1979.

DIGESTS, INDEXES, ABSTRACTS, CITATORS

BUSINESS PERIODICALS INDEX. H.W. Wilson Company, 950 University Avenue, Bronx, New York 10452. Monthly.

TOPICATOR: CLASSIFIED ARTICLE GUIDE TO THE ADVERTISING / COMMUNICATIONS / MARKETING PERIODICAL PRESS. Thompson Bureau, Box 127, Golden, Colorado 80401. Monthly.

ANNUALS AND SURVEYS

ADVERTISER'S ANNUAL. International Publications Service, 1900 Frost Road, Suite 101, Bristol, Pennsylvania 19007. Annual.

ADVERTISING LAW ANTHOLOGY. National Law Anthology Series. International Library, Incorporated, 2425 Wilson Boulevard, Arlington, Virginia 22201. Annual.

EXPENDITURES OF NATIONAL ADVERTISING IN NEWSPAPERS. Media Records, Incorporated, 370 Seventh Avenue, New York, New York 10001. Annual.

HANDBOOK OF SMALL BUSINESS ADVERTISING. Michael Anthony. Addison-Wesley Publishing Company, Incorporated, Route 128, Reading, Massachusetts 01867. 1981.

WORLD ADVERTISING EXPENDITURES. Starch INRA Hooper, 420 Lexington Avenue, New York, New York 10017. Biennial.

LAW REVIEWS AND PERIODICALS

AAF EXCHANGE. American Advertising Federation, 1225 Connecticut Avenue, Northwest, Washington, D.C. 20036. Monthly.

ADVERTISING AGE. Crain Communications, 740 Rush Street, Chicago, Illinois 60611. Weekly.

IAA AIRLETTER. International Advertising Association, Incorporated, 475 Fifth Avenue, New York, New York 10017. Bimonthly.

JOURNAL OF ADVERTISING. University of Kansas, School of Journalism, Lawrence, Kansas 66045. Quarterly.

JOURNAL OF ADVERTISING RESEARCH. Advertising Research Foundation, Three East Fifty-fourth Street, New York, New York 10022. Bimonthly.

PUBLISHING, ENTERTAINMENT, ADVERTISING AND ALLIED FIELDS LAW QUARTERLY. PEAL, Box 4134, Pittsburgh, Pennsylvania 15202. Quarterly.

SAM (SERVING ADVERTISING IN THE MIDWEST). 435 North Michigan Avenue, Suite 1333, Chicago, Illinois 60611. Weekly.

NEWSLETTERS AND NEWSPAPERS

AAF WASHINGTON REPORT. American Advertising Federation, 1400 K Street, Northwest, Suite 1000, Washington, D.C. 20005. Monthly.

BIBLIOGRAPHIES

ATTORNEY ADVERTISING IN THE UNITED STATES: A COMPREHENSIVE BIBLIOGRAPHY OF ARTICLES, BOOKS, AND OTHER PUBLICATIONS. Nathan Aaron Rosen. Vance Bibliographies, P.O. Box 229, 112 North Charter Street, Monticello, Illinois 61856. 1987.

MEASURING PAYOUT: AN ANNOTATED BIBLIOGRAPHY ON THE DOLLAR EFFECTIVENESS OF ADVERTISING. Advertising Research Foundation, Three East Fifty-fourth Street, New York, New York 10022. 1973.

100 BOOKS ON ADVERTISING. Compiled and Annotated by Robert W. Haverfield. University of Missouri, School of Journalism, 108 Journalism Building, Columbia, Missouri 65201. 1976. (Biennial).

Encyclopedia of Legal Information Sources • 2nd Ed. **ADVERTISING**

WHAT'S NEW IN ADVERTISING AND MARKETING. c/o Special Libraries Association, 1700 Eighteenth Street, Northwest, Washington, D.C. 20009. Ten issues per year.

DIRECTORIES

BUSINESS/PROFESSIONAL ADVERTISING ASSOCIATIONS DIRECTORY OF MEMBERS. 100 Metroplex Drive, Edison, New Jersey 08817. Biennial.

FINANCIAL PUBLICISTS DIRECTORY. Investment Dealers' Digest, Incorporated, 150 Broadway, New York, New York 10038. Annual.

INTERNATIONAL ADVERTISING ASSOCIATION MEMBERSHIP DIRECTORY. 342 Madison Avenue, New York, New York 10017. Annual.

MADISON AVENUE EUROPE. Peter Glenn Publications, 17 East Forty-eighth Street, New York, New York 10017. Annual.

MADISON AVENUE HANDBOOK. Peter Glenn Publications, 17 East Forty-eighth Street, New York, New York 10017. Annual.

MADISON AVENUE WEST. Peter Glenn Publications, 17 East Forty-eighth Street, New York, New York 10017. Annual.

STANDARD DIRECTORY OF ADVERTISERS AND SUPPLEMENTS. Geographical Edition and Classified Edition. National Register Publishing Company, 3004 Glenview Road, Wilmette, Illinois 60091. Monthly Supplements and Annual Cumulation.

TOP 100 NATIONAL ADVERTISERS. Advertising Age, Crain Communications, 740 Rush Street, Chicago, Illinois 60611. Annual.

BIOGRAPHICAL SOURCES

WHO'S WHO IN ADVERTISING. Redfield Publishing Company, Incorporated, Box 325, Monroe, New York 10950. Biennial.

ASSOCIATIONS AND PROFESSIONAL SOCIETIES

ADVERTISING COUNCIL. 825 Third Avenue, New York, New York 10022. (212) 758-0400.

ADVERTISING RESEARCH FOUNDATION. Three East Fifty-fourth Street, New York, New York 10022. (212) 751-5656.

AMERICAN ADVERTISING FEDERATION. 1400 K Street, Northwest, Washington, D.C. 20005. (202) 898-0089.

ASSOCIATION OF NATIONAL ADVERTISERS. 155 East Forty-fourth Street, New York, New York 10017. (212) 697-5950.

DIRECT MARKETING ASSOCIATION. 11 West Forty-second Street, New York, New York 10036-8096. (212) 768-7277.

INTERNATIONAL ADVERTISING ASSOCIATION. 342 Madison Avenue, Suite 2000, New York, New York 10017. (212) 557-1133.

NATIONAL ADVERTISING REVIEW BOARD. 845 Third Avenue, New York 10022. (212) 832-1320.

RESEARCH CENTERS, INSTITUTES, CLEARINGHOUSES

ADVERTISING RESEARCH CENTER. P.O. Box 4710, Lubbock, Texas 79409. (806) 742-2315.

MARKETING SCIENCE INSTITUTE. 1000 Massachusetts Avenue, Cambridge, Massachusetts 02138. (617) 491-2060.

ONLINE DATABASES

ABC ONLINE SERVICE. Audit Bureau of Circulations, 900 North Meacham Road, Schaumburg, Illinois 60173-4968.

ADTRACK. DIALOG Information Services, 4360 Hillview Avenue, Palo Alto, California 94394.

ADVERTISING AND MARKETING INTELLIGENCE SERVICES. New York Times Company, 229 West Forty-third Street, New York, New York 10036.

ADWEEK. Available on NEXIS. Mead Data Central, Incorporated, P.O. Box 933, Dayton, Ohio 45401.

AMI. 1719A Mount Pleasant Office Park, Route 10, Parsippany, New Jersey 07054.

MANAGEMENT CONTENTS. Management Contents, Incorporated, Box 1054, Skokie, Illinois 60076.

MRI. Mediamark Research, 341 Madison Avenue, New York, New York 10017.

PTS MARKETING AND ADVERTISING REFERENCE SERVICE. Predicasts, 11001 Cedar Avenue, Cleveland, Ohio 44106.

PUBLIC RELATIONS JOURNAL. Available on NEXIS, Mead Data Central, P.O. Box 933, Dayton, Ohio 45401.

TARGET GROUP INDEX, MAJOR MARKET INDEX, TARGET TEEN INDEX. Simmons Market Research Bureau, 219 East Forty-second Street, New York, New York 10017.

STATISTICS SOURCES

LNA MULTI-MEDIA REPORT SERVICE. Leading National Advertisers, Incorporated, 347 Madison Avenue, New York, New York 10017. Quarterly.

WORLD ADVERTISING EXPENDITURES. International Advertising Association, 342 Madison Avenue, New York, New York 10017. Biennial.

AUDIOVISUALS

INDIVIDUAL LAWYER AND BAR ASSOCIATION ADVERTISING. American Bar Association, Commission on Advertising, 750 Lake Shore Drive, Chicago, Illinois 60611. 1981. Videocassette.

LAWYER ADVERTISING: HOW FAR CAN REGULATION GO? American Bar Association, 750 North Lake Shore Drive, Chicago, Illinois 60611. Videotape.

LEGAL ADVERTISING: OF THE PEOPLE, BY THE PEOPLE, FOR THE PEOPLE. American Bar Association, 750 North Lake Shore Drive, Chicago, Illinois 60611. 1985. Videotape.

OTHER SOURCES

THE BOOZE MERCHANTS: THE INEBRIATING OF AMERICA. Michael Jacobson, Robert Atkins and George Hacker. (A Report from the Center for Science in the Public Interest). CSPI Books, 1501 Sixteenth Street, Northwest, Washington, D.C. 20036. 1983.

AERONAUTICS
See: AVIATION

AFFIRMATIVE ACTION
See: DISCRIMINATION, EMPLOYMENT; DISCRIMINATION, RACE; DISCRIMINATION, SEX; EQUAL EMPLOYMENT OPPORTUNITY

AGE DISCRIMINATION
See also: AGED AND AGING; AGED AND EMPLOYMENT; DISCRIMINATION, EMPLOYMENT; FAIR EMPLOYMENT PRACTICES

LOOSELEAF SERVICES AND REPORTERS

AGE DISCRIMINATION. Howard C. Eglit. Shepard's/McGraw-Hill, 420 North Cascade Avenue, Colorado Springs, Colorado 80901. 1981- . (Periodic Supplements).

EMPLOYMENT DISCRIMINATION. Arthur Larson. Matthew Bender and Company, Incorporated, 11 Penn Plaza, New York, New York 10001. 1975- .

LITIGATING AGE DISCRIMINATION CASES. Andrew J. Ruzicho. Callaghan and Company, 155 Pfingsten Road, Deerfield, Illinois 60015. 1986- .

HANDBOOKS, MANUALS, FORMBOOKS

AGE AND SEX DISCRIMINATION: COURSE MANUAL. Gerald Hartman and Richard Schnadig. Federal Publications, Incorporated, 1120 Twentieth Street, Northwest, Washington, D.C. 20036. 1986.

AGE DISCRIMINATION IN EMPLOYMENT ACT, ADEA: A SYMPOSIUM HANDBOOK FOR LAWYERS AND PERSONNEL PRACTITIONERS. American Bar Association Commission on Legal Problems of the Elderly and National Council on Aging, 750 North Lake Shore Drive, Chicago, Illinois 60611. 1983.

AGE DISCRIMINATION LITIGATION: COURSE MANUAL. Ellen Epstein and others. Federal Publications, Incorporated, 1120 Twentieth Street, Northwest, Washington, D.C. 20036. 1983.

AGE DISCRIMINATION WORKSHOP 1985: STATE AND FEDERAL LITIGATION: A COURSE HANDBOOK. Practising Law Institute, 810 Seventh Avenue, New York, New York 10019. 1985.

EMPLOYMENT DISCRIMINATION: A CLAIMS MANUAL FOR EMPLOYEES AND MANAGERS. Andrew J. Maikovich and Michele D. Brown. McFarland and Company, Incorporated, Box 611, Jefferson, North Carolina 28640. 1989.

THE LAW OF AGE DISCRIMINATION: A REFERENCE MANUAL. Burton D. Fretz and Neal S. Dudovitz. National Clearinghouse for Legal Services, 407 South Dearborn, Chicago, Illinois 60605. 1987.

SOCIAL SECURITY, MEDICARE AND PENSIONS. Fifth Edition. Joseph L. Matthews. Nolo Press, 950 Parker Street, Berkeley, California 94710. 1990.

TEXTBOOKS AND GENERAL WORKS

ADVANCED STRATEGIES IN LITIGATING, SETTLING AND AVOIDING UNJUST DISMISSAL AND AGE DISCRIMINATION CLAIMS. Jerome B. Kauff and Maureen E. McClain, Chairpersons. Practising Law Institute, 810 Seventh Avenue, New York, New York 10019. 1987.

AGE DISCRIMINATION AND THE MANDATORY RETIREMENT CONTROVERSY. Martin Lyon Levine. Johns Hopkins University Press, 701 West Fortieth Street, Baltimore, Maryland 21211. 1989.

AGE DISCRIMINATION IN EMPLOYMENT LAW. Joseph E. Kalet. Bureau of National Affairs, Incorporated, 1231 Twenty-fifth Street, Northwest, Washington, D.C. 20037. 1990.

DISCRIMINATION IN PUBLIC EMPLOYMENT: THE EVOLVING LAW. Martha M. McCarthy. National Organization on Legal Problems of Education, Southwest Plaza Building, 3601 West Thirty-ninth Street, Topeka, Kansas 66601. 1983.

FEDERAL AGE DISCRIMINATION IN EMPLOYMENT LAW. Charles D. Edelman and Ilene C. Siegler. Michie Company, P.O. Box 7587, Charlottesville, Virginia 22906-7582. 1980.

FORCED OUT: WHEN VETERAN EMPLOYEES ARE DRIVEN FROM THEIR CAREERS. Juliet P. Brudney and Hilda Scott. Simon and Schuster, Incorporated, 1230 Avenue of the Americas, New York, New York 10020. 1987.

LITIGATING AGE AND SEX DISCRIMINATION CASES. Gerald Hartman and Richard Schnadig. Federal Publications, Incorporated, 1120 Twentieth Street, Northwest, Washington, D.C. 20036. 1985.

OLD AGE, HANDICAPPED, AND VIETNAM-ERA ANTIDISCRIMINATION LEGISLATION. James P. Northrup. Books on Demand, 300 North Zeeb Road, Ann Arbor, Michigan 48106-1346. 1980.

OLD AND OBSOLETE: AGE DISCRIMINATION AND THE AMERICAN WORKER: 1860-1920. Judith C. Hushbeck. Garland Publishing, Incorporated, 136 Madison Avenue, New York, New York 10016. 1990.

OLDER AMERICANS IN THE WORKFORCE: CHALLENGES AND SOLUTIONS. Bureau of National Affairs, Incorporated, 1231 Twenty-fifth Street, Northwest, Washington, D.C. 20037. 1987.

YOUR TIME WILL COME: THE LAW OF AGE DISCRIMINATION AND MANDATORY RETIREMENT. Russell Sage Foundation, 112 East Sixty-fourth Street, New York, New York 10021. 1985.

BIBLIOGRAPHIES

AGE DISCRIMINATION AND THE AGE DISCRIMINATION IN EMPLOYMENT ACT AMENDMENTS OF 1978. Karen Fair Harrell. Vance Bibliographies, P.O. Box 229, 112 North Charter Street, Monticello, Illinois 61856. 1983.

ASSOCIATIONS AND PROFESSIONAL SOCIETIES

AMERICAN ASSOCIATION OF RETIRED PEOPLE. 1909 K Street, Northwest, Washington, D.C. 20005. (202) 872-4700.

AMERICAN BAR ASSOCIATION. Commission on Legal Problems of the Elderly. 1800 M Street, Northwest, Washington D.C. 20036. (202) 331-2258.

GRAY PANTHERS. 311 South Juniper Street, Suite 601, Philadelphia, Pennsylvania 19107. (215) 545-6555.

HEALTH AND HUMAN SERVICES DEPARTMENT. Administration on Aging. 330 Independence Avenue, Southwest, Washington D.C. 20201. (202) 619-0641.

HEALTH AND HUMAN SERVICES DEPARTMENT. Federal Council on the Aging. 330 Independence Avenue, Southwest, Washington, D.C. 20201. (202) 619-2451.

LEGAL COUNCIL FOR THE ELDERLY. 1909 K Street, Northwest, Washington, D.C. 20049. (202) 662-4933.

NATIONAL ASSOCIATION OF STATE UNITS ON AGING. 2033 K Street, Northwest, Suite 304, Washington, D.C. 20006. (202) 785-0707.

NATIONAL CAUCUS AND CENTER ON BLACK AGED. 1424 K Street, Northwest, Suite 500, Washington, D.C. 20005. (202) 637 8400.

NATIONAL COUNCIL ON THE AGING. 600 Maryland Avenue, Southwest, West Wing, Suite 100, Washington, D.C. 20024. (202) 479-1200.

NATIONAL COUNCIL ON SENIOR CITIZENS. 925 Fifteenth Street, Northwest, Washington, D.C. 20005. (202) 347-8800.

NATIONAL SENIOR CITIZENS LAW CENTER. 1052 West Sixth Street, Suite 700, Los Angeles, California 90017. (213) 482-3550.

RESEARCH CENTERS, INSTITUTES, CLEARINGHOUSES

LEADERSHIP COUNCIL OF AGING ORGANIZATIONS. c/o National Council on Senior Citizens, 925 Fifteenth Street, Northwest, Washington, D.C. 20005. (202) 347-8800.

NATIONAL INSTITUTE ON AGING. National Institutes of Health, Federal Building, Room 6C12, 9000 Rockville Pike, Bethesda, Maryland 20892. (301) 496-1752.

ONLINE DATABASES

AGELINE. American Association of Retired People, 1909 K Street, Northwest, Washington, D.C. 20049.

AUDIOVISUALS

AGING AND THE LAW: IS AGE DISCRIMINATION REALLY DISCRIMINATION? Robert N. Brown, Chair/Speaker. Recorded Resources Corporation, Crofton, Maryland 21114. 1986. (2 Audiocassettes).

OTHER SOURCES

EQUAL EMPLOYMENT OPPORTUNITY COMMISSION ENFORCEMENT OF THE AGE DISCRIMINATION IN EMPLOYMENT ACT 1979 TO 1982. An Information Paper, Prepared by the Staff of the Special Committee on Aging, United States Senate. United States Government Printing Office, Division of Public Documents, Washington, D.C. 20402. 1982.

FINAL REPORT TO CONGRESS ON AGE DISCRIMINATION IN EMPLOYMENT ACT STUDIES. Report to the Congress required by Section Five of Age Discrimination in Employment Act, submitted to Congress in 1982. United States Department of Labor Employment Standards Administration. United States Government Printing Office, Washington, D.C. 20402. 1982.

AGED AND AGING

See also: AGED AND CRIME; AGED AND EMPLOYMENT; AGED AND HEALTH CARE; AGED AND RETIREMENT

LOOSELEAF SERVICES AND REPORTERS

THE LAW AND AGING RESOURCE GUIDE. American Bar Association, 750 North Lake Shore Drive, Chicago, Illinois 60611. 1981- .

LEGAL ISSUES, GOVERNMENT PROGRAMS AND THE ELDERLY: A MANUAL FOR ADVOCATES. Revised Edition. The Center for Government Responsibility. Holland Law Center, University of Florida, D and S Publications, Incorporated, 6334 St. Andrews Circle, Fort Myers, Florida 33907. 1987- .

SOCIAL SECURITY PRACTICE GUIDE. National Organization of Social Security Claimants' Representatives. Matthew Bender and Company, Incorporated, 11 Penn Plaza, New York, New York 10001. 1983- .

TAX, ESTATE AND FINANCIAL PLANNING FOR THE ELDERLY. John J. Regan. Matthew Bender and Company, Incorporated, 11 Penn Plaza, New York, New York 10001. 1985- .

AGED AND AGING

HANDBOOKS, MANUALS, FORMBOOKS

ESTATE AND FINANCIAL PLANNING FOR THE AGING OR INCAPACITATED CLIENT 1990: A COURSE HANDBOOK. Practising Law Institute, 810 Seventh Avenue, New York, New York 10019. 1990.

A HANDBOOK FOR SENIOR CITIZENS: RIGHTS, RESOURCES, AND RESPONSIBILITIES. Ramona Walhof. American Brotherhood for the Blind, 1800 Johnson Street, Baltimore, Maryland 21230. 1981.

LAW AND AGING RESOURCE GUIDE. American Bar Association, Commission of Legal Problems of the Elderly, 750 North Lake Shore Drive, Chicago, Illinois 60611. 1985.

LCE ELDERLY LAW MANUAL. Legal Counsel for the Elderly, 1909 K Street, Northwest, Washington, D.C. 20049. 1982- . (Periodic Supplements).

THE RIGHTS OF OLDER PERSONS. Robert N. Brown and the Legal Counsel for the Elderly. Revised Edition. Southern Illinois University Press, P.O. Box 3697, Carbondale, Illinois 62902-3697. 1988.

SOCIAL SECURITY LAW AND PRACTICE. Lawyers Cooperative Publishing Company, Aqueduct Building, 50 East Broad Street, Rochester, New York 14694. 1987- .

SOCIAL SECURITY, MEDICARE AND PENSIONS. Fifth Edition. Joseph L. Matthews. Nolo Press, 950 Parker Street, Berkeley, California 94710. 1990.

YOUR RIGHTS IN LATER LIFE. John J. Regan and Legal Counsel for the Elderly. American Association of Retired Persons, 1909 K Street, Northwest, Washington, D.C. 20049. 1989.

TEXTBOOKS AND GENERAL WORKS

ABUSE AND MALTREATMENT OF THE ELDERLY: CAUSES AND INTERVENTIONS. Jordan I. Kosberg, Editor. PSG Publishing Company, Incorporated, P.O. Box 6, Littleton, Massachusetts 01460. 1983.

THE AGED CLIENT AND THE LAW. John J. Regan. Columbia University Press, 562 West One Hundred Thirteenth Street, New York, New York 10025. 1990.

AGING AND THE LAW. Peter J. Strauss, Robert Wolf and Dana Shilling. Commerce Clearing House, Incorporated, 4025 West Peterson Avenue, Chicago, Illinois 60646. 1990.

AGING AND PUBLIC POLICY: SOCIAL CONTROL OR SOCIAL JUSTICE. John B. Williamson, Judith A. Shindul and Linda Evans. Charles C. Thomas Publishers, 2600 South First Street, Springfield, Illinois 62794. 1985.

AGING, THE INDIVDUAL, AND SOCIETY. Georgia Barrow and Patricia Smith. West Publishing Company, P.O. Box 43526, 50 West Kellogg Boulevard, St. Paul, Minnesota 55164-0526. 1983.

BEYOND SIXTY-FIVE: THE DILEMMA OF OLD AGE IN AMERICA'S PAST. Carole Haber. Cambridge University Press, 40 West Twentieth Street, New York, New York 10011. 1985.

COMMON-SENSE SUICIDE: THE FINAL RIGHT. Doris Portwood. Grove Weidenfeld, 841 Broadway, Fourth Floor, New York, New York 10003-4793. 1983.

ELDER ABUSE: CONFLICT IN THE FAMILY. Karl A. Pillemer and Rosalie S. Wolf, Editors. Auburn House Publishing Company, Incorporated, 14 Dedham, Dover, Massachusetts 02030. 1986.

THE EXTREME AGED IN AMERICA: A PORTRAIT OF AN EXPANDING POPULATION. Ira Rosenwaike. Greenwood Publishing Group, Incorporated, 88 Post Road West, P.O. Box 5007, Westport, Connecticut 06881. 1985.

INCOME TAX BENEFITS FOR OLDER TAXPAYERS. Commerce Clearing House, Incorporated, 4025 West Peterson Avenue, Chicago, Illinois 60646. 1983.

JUSTICE AND OLDER AMERICANS. Marlene A. Young-Rifai. Lexington Books, 125 Spring Street, Lexington, Massachusetts 02173. 1977.

LAW AND THE ELDERLY. Richard Grimes. Croom Helm, Paul H. Brookes Publishing Company, P.O. Box 10624, Baltimore, Maryland 21285. 1985.

LEGAL SERVICES FOR THE ELDERLY: WHERE THE NATION STANDS. Fourth Edition. American Bar Association, Commission on Legal Problems of the Elderly, 1800 M Street, Northwest, Washington, D.C. 20036. 1988.

ORGANIZATION AND ADMINISTRATION OF SERVICE PROGRAMS FOR THE OLDER AMERICAN. Richard Hardy and John G. Cull. Charles C. Thomas Publishers, 2600 South First Street, Springfield, Illinois 62794. 1975.

THE POLITICAL ECONOMY OF AGING: THE STATE, PRIVATE POWER AND SOCIAL WELFARE. Laura K. Olson. Columbia University Press, 562 West One Hundred Thirteenth Street, New York, New York 10025. 1982.

PUBLIC GUARDIANSHIP AND THE ELDERLY. Winsor C. Schmidt and others. Ballinger Division, HarperCollins Publishers, 10 East Fifty-third Street, New York, New York 10022. 1981.

PUBLIC POLICIES FOR AN AGING POPULATION. Elizabeth W. Markson and Gretchen R. Barta, Editors. Lexington Books, 125 Spring Street, Lexington, Massachusetts 02173. 1980.

SETTING LIMITS: MEDICAL GOALS IN AN AGING SOCIETY. Daniel Callahan. Simon and Schuster Publishing Company, 1230 Avenue of the Americas, New York, New York 10020. 1988.

SHADES OF GRAY: OLD AGE, AMERICAN VALUES, AND FEDERAL POLICIES SINCE 1920. W. Andrew Achenbaum. Little, Brown and Company, 34 Beacon Street, Boston, Massachusetts 02108. 1983.

WOMEN AND AGING: AN ANTHOLOGY. Jo Alexander, Editor. Calyx Books, P.O. Box B, Corvallis, Oregon 97339. 1986.

LAW REVIEWS AND PERIODICALS

JOURNAL OF CONTEMPORARY HEALTH LAW AND POLICY. The Catholic University of America, Columbus School of Law, 620 Michigan Avenue, Northeast, Washington, D.C. 20064. Annual.

QUARTERLY JOURNAL OF THE WESTERN GERONTOLOGICAL SOCIETY. 833 Market Street, Suite 516, San Francisco, California 94103. Quarterly.

NEWSLETTERS AND NEWSPAPERS

AGING ACTION ALERT. CD Publications, 8555 Sixteenth Street, Suite 100, Silver Spring, Maryland 20910. Monthly.

AGING SERVICES NEWS. Business Publishers, Incorporated, 951 Pershing Drive, Silver Spring, Maryland 20910. Weekly.

BIFOCAL. American Bar Association, Committee on Legal Problems of the Elderly, 1800 M Street Northwest, Washington D.C. 20036. Quarterly.

ESTATE ADMINISTRATION AND TAX PLANNING FOR THE ELDERLY AND DISABLED. Garland Law Publishing, 136 Madison Avenue, New York, New York 10011. Quarterly.

NSCLC WASHINGTON WEEKLY. National Senior Citizens Law Center, 2025 M Street, Suite 400, Northwest, Washington, D.C. 20036. Weekly.

OLDER AMERICANS REPORTS. Business Publishers, Incorporated, 951 Pershing Drive, Silver Spring, Maryland 20910. Weekly.

RETIREMENT HOUSING REPORT. Federal Research Press, 210 Lincoln Street, Boston, Massachusetts 02111. Monthly.

SENIOR LAW REPORT. CD Publications, 8555 Sixteenth Street, #100, Silver Spring, Maryland 20910. Biweekly.

WEST'S SOCIAL SECURITY NEWS. West Publishing Company, 50 West Kellogg Boulevard, St. Paul, Minnesota 55164. Biweekly.

BIBLIOGRAPHIES

ELDER NEGLECT AND ABUSE: AN ANNOTATED BIBLIOGRAPHY. Tanya F. Johnson, James G. O'Brien and Margaret F. Hudson. Greenwood Publishing Group, Incorporated, 88 Post Road West, P.O. Box 5007, Westport, Connecticut 06881. 1985.

HOUSING FOR THE ELDERLY: A SELECTED BIBLIOGRAPHY. David A. Spaeth. Vance Bibliographies, P.O. Box 229, 112 North Charter Street, Monticello, Illinois 61856. 1980.

LIBRARY ON LAW AND AGING: CATALOGUE OF MATERIALS IN THE LAW AND AGING LIBRARY OF THE CHICAGO-KENT COLLEGE OF LAW. Howard Eglit and Georgia Strohm. Illinois Institute of Technology, 10 West Thirty-second Street, Chicago, Illinois 60616. 1983.

PUBLICATIONS LIST. Prepared by the Staff of the Special Committee on Aging, United States Senate, Eighty-seventh to Ninety-eighth Congresses, February, 1961 to December 1984. United States Government Printing Office, Division of Public Documents, Washington, D.C. 20402. Annual.

WORDS ON AGING: A BIBLIOGRAPHY OF SELECTED ANNOTATED REFERENCES. Dorothy Mounce Jones and United States Administration on Aging. Greenwood Publishing Group, Incorporated, 88 Post Road West, P.O. Box 5007, Westport, Connecticut 06881. 1981.

DIRECTORIES

AGING: A GUIDE TO RESOURCES. John B. Balkema, Editor. Gaylord Professional Publications in association with Neal-Schuman Publishers, Incorporated, 100 Varick Street, New York, New York 10013. 1983.

DIRECTORY OF LAW AND AGING COURSES IN U.S. LAW SCHOOLS. American Bar Association, Commission on Legal Problems of the Elderly, Public Services Division, 750 North Lake Shore Drive, Chicago, Illinois 60611. 1989.

A DIRECTORY OF STATE AND AREA AGENCIES ON AGING. United States House of Representatives Committee on Aging. United States Congress House Select Committee on Aging. Superintendent of Documents, United States Government Printing Office, Washington, D.C. 20402. Annual.

LAW AND AGING RESOURCE GUIDE. Young Lawyers Division, American Bar Association, 750 North Lake Shore Drive, Chicago, Illinois 60611. 1981.

ASSOCIATIONS AND PROFESSIONAL SOCIETIES

ADMINISTRATION ON AGING. United States Health and Human Services Department, 330 Independence Avenue, Southwest, Washington, D.C. 20024. (202) 619-0641.

AMERICAN ASSOCIATION OF RETIRED PERSONS. 1909 K Street, Northwest, Washington, D.C. 20049. (202) 872-4700.

BAR ASSOCIATIONS IN FOCUS ON AGING AND THE LAW (BIFOCAL). Commission on Legal Problems of the Elderly, American Bar Association, 1800 M Street, Northwest, Washington, D.C. 20036. (202) 331-2258.

CENTER ON SOCIAL WELFARE POLICY AND LAW. 821 Fifteenth Street, Northwest, Suite 638, Washington, D.C. 20005. (202) 347-5615.

FEDERAL COUNCIL ON AGING. United States Health and Human Services Department, 330 Independence Avenue, Southwest, Washington, D.C. 20024. (202) 619-2451.

GRAY PANTHERS. 3635 Chestnut Street, Philadelphia, Pennsylvania 19104. (215) 545-6555.

LEGAL COUNSEL FOR THE ELDERLY. 1909 K Street, Northwest, Washington, D.C. 20049. (202) 662-4933.

LEGAL SERVICES FOR THE ELDERLY. 132 West Forty-third Street, Third floor, New York, New York 10036. (212) 595-1340.

AGED AND AGING

NATIONAL CAUCUS AND CENTER ON BLACK AGED. 1424 K Street, Northwest, Washington, D.C. 20036. (202) 637-8400.

NATIONAL COUNCIL OF SENIOR CITIZENS. 925 Fifteenth Street, Northwest, Washington, D.C. 20005. (202) 347-8800.

NATIONAL COUNCIL ON THE AGING. 600 Maryland Avenue, Southwest, West Wing, Washington, D.C. 20024. (202) 479-1200.

NATIONAL SENIOR CITIZENS LAW CENTER. 1052 West Sixth Street, Suite 700, Los Angeles, California 90017. (213) 482-3550.

SENIOR ACTION IN A GAY ENVIRONMENT (SAGE). 208 West Thirteenth Street, New York, New York 10011. (212) 741-2247.

RESEARCH CENTERS, INSTITUTES, CLEARINGHOUSES

NATIONAL INSTITUTE ON AGING. National Institutes of Health, Federal Building, Room 6C12, 9000 Rockville Pike, Bethesda, Maryland 20892. (301) 496-1752.

ONLINE DATABASES

AGELINE. American Association of Retired Persons, National Gerontology Resource Center, 1909 K Street, Northwest, Washington, D.C. 20049.

STATISTICS SOURCES

AGING AMERICA: TRENDS AND PROJECTIONS. United States Senate Special Committee on Aging in Conjunction with AARP. United States Government Printing Office, Division of Public Documents, Washington, D.C. 20402. 1983.

STATISTICAL HANDBOOK ON AGING AMERICANS. Frank L. Schick, Editor. Oryx Press, 2214 North Central Avenue, Phoenix, Arizona 85004-1483. 1986.

U.S. CENSUS OF POPULATION: 1980. CURRENT POPULATION REPORTS. UNPUBLISHED DATA. United States Department of Commerce, Bureau of the Census, Suitland, Maryland 20233.

AUDIOVISUALS

PERSONAL AND ESTATE PLANNING FOR THE ELDERLY. American Bar Association, 750 North Lake Shore Drive, Chicago, Illinois 60611. 1989. Videotape.

YOU'RE IN CONTROL: OLDER AMERICANS AND THE LAW. American Bar Association, 750 North Lake Shore Drive, Chicago, Illinois 60611. 1986.

OTHER SOURCES

AMERICA IN TRANSITION: AN AGING SOCIETY. An Information Paper Prepared by the Staff of the Special Committee on Aging, United States Senate. United States Government Printing Office, Washington, D.C. 20402. Annual.

DEVELOPMENTS IN AGING: A REPORT OF THE SPECIAL COMMITTEE ON AGING. United States Senate. United States Government Printing Office, Division of Public Documents, Washington, D.C. 20402. Annual.

ELDER ABUSE: THE HIDDEN PROBLEM. House Select Committee on Aging. Superintendent of Documents, United States Government Printing Office, Washington, D.C. 20402. 1979.

HOUSE RICH, BUT CASH POOR: HOME EQUITY CONVERSION OPTIONS FOR OLDER HOMEOWNERS: A SALE LEASEBACK FACT FINDING SESSION. Federal Council on the Aging, Department of Health and Human Services. United States Government Printing Office, Division of Public Documents, Washington, D.C. 20402. 1984.

IMPACT OF FEDERAL ESTATE TAX POLICIES ON RURAL WOMEN. United States Senate Special Committee on Aging. United States Government Printing Office, Division of Public Documents, Washington, D.C. 20402. 1981.

PROBLEMS OF AGING WOMEN. Hearing before the Select Committee on Aging, House of Representatives, 97th Congress, Second Session, July 26, 1982. United States Government Printing Office, Washington, D.C. 20402. 1982.

REAUTHORIZATION ISSUES FOR THE OLDER AMERICANS ACT. Joint Hearing before the Select Committee on Aging, House of Representatives, 98th Congress, Second Session, February 21, 1984. United States Government Printing Office, Washington, D.C. 20402. 1984.

REAUTHORIZATION OF OLDER AMERICANS ACT: A RURAL PERSPECTIVE. Hearing before the Subcommittee on Retirement Income and Employment of the Select Committee on Aging, House of Representatives, 98th Congress, First Session, December 2, 1983. United States Government Printing Office, Washington, D.C. 20402. 1984.

SHELTERING AMERICA'S AGED: OPTIONS FOR HOUSING AND SERVICES. Hearing before the Special Committee on Aging, United States Senate, 98th Congress, Second Session, Boston, Massachusetts, April 23, 1984. United States Government Printing Office, Washington, D.C. 20402. 1984.

SOCIAL SERVICE NEEDS OF ELDER MINORITIES. Hearing before the Subcommittee on Housing and Consumer Interests of the Select Committee on Aging, House of Representatives, 96th Congress, Second Session, September 13, 1980. United States Government Printing Office, Washington, D.C. 20402. 1981.

TAX COUNSELING FOR THE ELDERLY: APPLICATION PACKAGE. Department of Treasury, Internal Revenue Service. Superintendent of Documents, United States Government Printing Office, Washington, D.C. 20402. 1983. (Periodic Supplements).

A TENTH ANNIVERSARY REVIEW OF THE SUPPLEMENTARY SECURITY INCOME PROGRAM. Hearing before the Special Committee on Aging, United States Senate, Ninety-Eighth Congress, Second Session, May 17, 1984. United States Government Printing Office, Washington, D.C. 20402. 1984.

AGED AND CRIME
See also: CRIME VICTIMS

TEXTBOOKS AND GENERAL WORKS

CRIME AND GERONTOLOGY. Alan A. Malinchak. Prentice-Hall, Incorporated, 113 Sylvan Avenue, Englewood Cliffs, New Jersey 07632. 1980.

ELDERLY CRIMINALS. Evelyn S. Newman, Donald J. Newman, Mindy Gewirtz and Associates. Oelgeschlager, Gunn, and Hain Publishers, 245 Mirriam Street, Weston, Massachusetts 02193. 1984.

ELDERLY CRIMINALS. William Wilbanks and Paul K.H. Kim, Editors. University of America Press, 4720 Boston Way, Lanham, Maryland 20706. 1984.

THE ELDERLY VICTIM OF CRIME. David Lester, Editor. Charles C. Thomas, 2600 South First Street, Springfield, Illinois 62794. 1981.

JUVENILE CRIMES AGAINST THE ELDERLY. Frank P. Morello. Charles C. Thomas, 2600 South First Street, Springfield, Illinois 62794. 1982.

BIBLIOGRAPHIES

THE ELDERLY AND CRIME--A DISHEARTENING DILEMMA: A SELECTED BIBLIOGRAPHY. Carol Ann Martin. Vance Bibliographies, P.O. Box 229, 112 North Charter Street, Monticello, Illinois 61856. 1980.

VIOLENT CRIME AND THE ELDERLY: A BIBLIOGRAPHY. Patricia L. Ormiston. Vance Bibliographies, P.O. Box 229, 112 North Charter Street, Monticello, Illinois 61856. 1981.

STATISTICS SOURCES

CRIME AGAINST THE ELDERLY IN TWENTY-SIX CITIES. Ellen Hochstedler. Department of Justice, Bureau of Justice Statistics. Superintendent of Documents, United States Government Printing Office, Washington, D.C. 20402. 1981.

OTHER SOURCES

CRIME AGAINST THE ELDERLY. Hearing before the Subcommittee on Federal, State, and Community Services of the Select Committee on Aging, House of Representatives, 94th Congress, Second Session, December 13, 1976. Superintendent of Documents, United States Government Printing Office, Washington, D.C. 20402. 1976.

CRIME AND THE ELDERLY: WHAT YOUR COMMUNITY CAN DO. Hearing before the Special Committee on Aging, Senate, 96th Congress, Second Session, June 23, 1980. Superintendent of Documents, United States Government Printing Office, Washington, D.C. 20402. 1981.

ELDERLY CRIME VICTIMIZATION (CRIME PREVENTION PROGRAMS). Hearing before the Subcommittee on Housing and Consumer Interests of the Select Committee on Aging, House of Representatives, 94th Congress, Second Session, March 29, 1976. Superintendent of Documents, United States Government Printing Office, Washington, D.C. 20402. 1976.

ELDERLY CRIME VICTIMIZATION: FEDERAL LAW ENFORCEMENT AGENCIES, LEAA AND FBI. Hearings before the Subcommittee on Housing and Consumer Interests of the Select Committee on Aging, House of Representatives, 94th Congress, Second Session, April 12-13, 1976. Superintendent of Documents, United States Government Printing Office, Washington, D.C. 20402. 1976.

ELDERLY CRIME VICTIMIZATION: LOCAL POLICE DEPARTMENT CRIME PREVENTION PROGRAMS. Hearing before the Subcommittee on Housing and Consumer Interests of the Select Committee on Aging, House of Representatives, 94th Congress, Second Session, April 28, 1976. Superintendent of Documents, United States Government Printing Office, Washington, D.C. 20402. 1976.

ELDERLY CRIME VICTIMIZATION, RESIDENTIAL SECURITY. Hearing before the Subcommittee on Housing and Consumer Interests of the Select Committee on Aging, House of Representatives, 94th Congress, Second Session, March 15, 1976. Superintendent of Documents, United States Government Printing Office, Washington, D.C. 20402. 1976.

FRAUDS AGAINST THE ELDERLY: NEW YORK. Hearing before the Subcommittee on Retirement Income and Employment of the Select Committee on Aging, House of Representatives, 96th Congress, Second Session, October 23, 1980. Superintendent of Documents, United States Government Printing Office, Washington, D.C. 20402. 1981.

VIOLENT CRIME AGAINST THE ELDERLY. Briefing by the Select Committee on Aging, House of Representatives, 95th Congress, Second Session. Superintendent of Documents, United States Government Printing Office, Washington, D.C. 20402. 1978.

AGED AND EMPLOYMENT
See also: AGE DISCRIMINATION; EQUAL EMPLOYMENT OPPORTUNITY; FAIR EMPLOYMENT PRACTICES

TEXTBOOKS AND GENERAL WORKS

POLICY ISSUES IN WORK AND RETIREMENT. Herbert S. Parnes, Editor. W.E. Upjohn Institute for Employment Research, 300 South Westnedge Avenue, Kalamazoo, Michigan 49007. 1983.

WORK, HEALTH AND INCOME AMONG THE ELDERLY. Gary Burtless, Editor. Brookings Institution, 1775 Massachusetts Avenue, Northwest, Washington D.C. 20036. 1987.

BIBLIOGRAPHIES

AGE AND EMPLOYMENT: A BIBLIOGRAPHY. Marian Dworaczek. Vance Bibliographies, P.O. Box 229, 112 North Charter Street, Monticello, Illinois 61856. 1983.

OTHER SOURCES

THE UNEMPLOYMENT CRISIS FACING OLDER AMERICANS. Hearing before the Select Committee on Aging, House of Representatives, Ninety-Seventh Congress, Second Session, October 8, 1982. United States Government Printing Office, Division of Public Documents, Washington, D.C. 20402. 1982.

AGED AND HEALTH CARE
See also: HEALTH CARE; NURSING HOMES

STATUTES, CODES, STANDARDS, UNIFORM LAWS

A MODEL ACT REGULATING BOARD AND CARE HOMES: GUIDELINES FOR STATES. Jane Beyer, Josephine Bukley and Paula Hopkins. American Bar Association, 1800 M Street, Northwest, Washington, D.C. 20036. 1984.

TEXTBOOKS AND GENERAL WORKS

GERIATRICS AND THE LAW: PATIENT RIGHTS AND PROFESSIONAL RESPONSIBILITIES. Marshall B. Kapp and Arthur Bigot. Springer Publishing Company, Incorporated, 536 Broadway, New York, New York 10012. 1985.

HEALTH INSURANCE FOR THE AGED: THE 1965 PROGRAM FOR MEDICARE, ITS HISTORY AND A SUMMARY OF OTHER PROVISIONS OF PUBLIC LAW 89-97. Margaret Greenfield and University of California. Institute of Governmental Studies, 109 Moses Hall, Berkeley, California 94720. 1966.

HEALTH ISSUES AFFECTING THE ELDERLY. Intergovernmental Health Policy Project, George Washington University for the American Association of Retired Persons, 1909 K Street, Northwest, Washington, D.C. 20049.

LEGAL AND ETHICAL ASPECTS OF HEALTH CARE FOR THE ELDERLY. Marshall B. Kapp and others. Health Administration Press, Department KW, 1021 East Huron Street, University of Michigan, Ann Arbor, Michigan 48104. 1986.

MEDICARE AND THE AMERICAN RHETORIC OF RECONCILIATION. Max J. Skidmore, University of Alabama Press, P.O. Box 870380, Tuscaloosa, Alabama 35487. 1970.

MENTAL CAPACITY: MEDICAL AND LEGAL ASPECTS OF THE AGING. J. Brooke Aker, Arthur C. Walsh and James R. Beam. Shepard's/McGraw-Hill, 420 North Cascade Avenue, Colorado Springs, Colorado 80901. 1977- . (Periodic Supplements).

SETTING LIMITS: MEDICAL GOALS IN AN AGING SOCIETY. Daniel Callahan. Simon and Schuster Publishing Company, Incorporated, 1230 Avenue of the Americas, New York, New York 10020. 1988.

LAW REVIEWS AND PERIODICALS

JOURNAL OF CONTEMPORARY HEALTH LAW AND POLICY. The Catholic University of America, Columbus School of Law, 620 Michigan Avenue, Northeast, Washington, D.C. 20064. Annual.

BIBLIOGRAPHIES

LEGAL ASPECTS OF HEALTH CARE FOR THE ELDERLY: AN ANNOTATED BIBLIOGRAPHY. Marshall B. Kapp. Greenwood Publishing Group, Incorporated, 88 Post Road West, P.O. Box 5007, Westport, Connecticut 06881. 1988.

ASSOCIATIONS AND PROFESSIONAL SOCIETIES

NATIONAL HEALTH LAW PROGRAM. 2639 South La Cienega Boulevard, Los Angeles, California 90034. (213) 204-6010.

STATISTICS SOURCES

SELECTED CHARACTERISTICS OF THE LIVING ARRANGEMENTS AND INSTITUTIONALIZATION OF THE ELDERLY IN THE STATES, HEW REGIONS, AND THE UNITED STATES: 1970 CENSUS DATA. Office of Policy, Planning and Research, Health Care Financing Administration. Superintendent of Documents, United States Government Printing Office, Washington, D.C. 20402. 1978.

OTHER SOURCES

THE CRISIS IN MEDICARE: EXPLORING THE CHOICES. Hearing before the Special Committee on Aging, United States Senate, Ninety-Eighth Congress, Second Session, Rock Island, Illinois, August 20, 1984. Superintendent of Documents, United States Government Printing Office, Washington, D.C. 20402. 1985.

HEALTH AND EXTENDED WORKLIFE. An information paper prepared for use by the Special Committee on Aging, United States Senate. February, 1985. Superintendent of Documents, United States Government Printing Office, Washington, D.C. 20402. 1985.

HEALTHY ELDERLY AMERICANS: A FEDERAL, STATE, AND PERSONAL PARTNERSHIP. Hearing before the Special Committee on Aging, United States Senate, Ninety-Eighth Congress, Second Session, Albuquerque, New Mexico, October 12, 1984. Superintendent of Documents, United States Government Printing Office, Washington, D.C. 20402. 1985.

PROTECTING MEDICARE AND MEDICAID PATIENTS FROM SANCTIONED HEALTH PRACTITIONERS. Hearing before the Special Committee on Aging, United States Senate, Ninety-Eighth Congress, Second Session, May 1, 1984. Superintendent of Documents, United States Government Printing Office, Washington, D.C. 20402. 1984.

AGED AND RETIREMENT
See also: EMPLOYEE FRINGE BENEFITS; SOCIAL SECURITY

HANDBOOKS, MANUALS, FORMBOOKS

THE RETIREMENT HANDBOOK: A COMPLETE PLANNING GUIDE TO YOUR FUTURE. Joseph C. Buckley. HarperCollins Publishers, Incorporated, 10 East Fifty-third Street, New York, New York 10022. 1977.

TEXTBOOKS AND GENERAL WORKS

AGE DISCRIMINATION AND THE MANDATORY RETIREMENT CONTROVERSY. Martin Lyon Levine. Johns Hopkins University Press, 701 West Fortieth Street, Suite 275, Baltimore, Maryland 21211-2190. 1989.

AGE DISCRIMINATION WORKSHOP 1985: STATE AND FEDERAL LITIGATION. Samuel Estreicher, Chairman. Practising Law Institute, 810 Seventh Avenue, New York, New York 10019. 1985.

THE CHANGING PROFILE OF PENSIONS IN AMERICA. Emily S. Andrews. Employee Benefit Research Institute, 2121 K Street, Northwest, Washington, D.C. 20037-2121. 1985.

THE END OF MANDATORY RETIREMENT: IMPLICATIONS FOR MANAGEMENT. James W. Walker and Harriet L. Lazer. Books on Demand, 1300 North Zeeb Road, Ann Arbor, Michigan 48106-1346. 1978.

THE GRAYING OF AMERICA: RETIREMENT AND WHY YOU CAN'T AFFORD IT. James J. Jorgenson. Dial Press, Doubleday and Company, Incorporated, 666 Fifth Avenue, New York, New York 10103. 1980.

LAW OF RETIREMENT. Second Edition. Libby F. Jessup. Oceana Publications, 75 Main Street, Dobbs Ferry, New York 10522. 1979.

A LAWYER'S ADVICE TO RETIREES. Thomas Tinsley. Doubleday and Company, Incorporated, 666 Fifth Avenue, New York, New York 10103. 1981.

POLICY ISSUES IN WORK AND RETIREMENT. Herbert S. Parnes, Editor. W.E. Upjohn Institute for Employment Research, 300 South Westridge Avenue, Kalamazoo, Michigan 49007. 1983.

RETIREMENT AND ECONOMIC BEHAVIOR. Henry J. Aaron and Gary Burtless, Editors. Brookings Institution, 1775 Massachusetts Avenue, Washington, D.C. 20036. 1984.

RETIREMENT, PENSIONS AND SOCIAL SECURITY. Gary S. Field and Olivia S. Mitchell. MIT Press, 55 Hayward Street, Cambridge, Massachusetts 02142. 1985.

SOCIAL SECURITY AND RETIREMENT: PRIVATE GOALS, PUBLIC POLICY. Congressional Quarterly Books, Incorporated, 1414 Twenty-second Street, Northwest, Washington, D.C. 20037. 1983.

YOUR TIME WILL COME: THE LAW OF AGE DISCRIMINATION AND MANDATORY RETIREMENT. Russell Sage Foundation, 112 East Sixty-fourth Street, New York, New York 10021. 1985.

ASSOCIATIONS AND PROFESSIONAL SOCIETIES

AMERICAN ASSOCIATION OF RETIRED PERSONS. 1909 K Street, Northwest, Washington, D.C. 20049. (202) 872-4700.

INSTITUTE FOR RETIRED PROFESSIONALS. New School for Social Research, 66 West Twelfth Street, New York, New York 10011. (212) 741-5682.

NATIONAL ASSOCIATION OF RETIRED FEDERAL EMPLOYEES. 1424 K Street, Northwest, Washington, D.C. 20036. (202) 234-0832.

PENSION RIGHTS CENTER. 1346 Connecticut Avenue, Room 1019, Washington, D.C. 20036. (202) 296-3776.

OTHER SOURCES

PROHIBITION OF MANDATORY RETIREMENT AND EMPLOYMENT RIGHTS ACT OF 1982. Hearing before the Subcommittee on Labor of the Committee on Labor and Human Resources, Senate, 97th Congress. Superintendent of Documents, United States Government Printing Office, Washington, D.C. 20402. 1982.

AGENCY
See also: AUTHORS AND PUBLISHERS; ENTERTAINMENT LAW; JOINT VENTURES; PARTNERSHIP; REAL ESTATE PROPERTY; SPORTS LAW

RESTATEMENTS

RESTATEMENT OF THE LAW: AGENCY SECOND. Adopted and Promulgated by the American Law Institute. American Law Institute, 4025 Chestnut Street, Philadelphia, Pennsylvania 19104. 1958- . (Annual Supplements).

LOOSELEAF SERVICES AND REPORTERS

AGENCY, PARTNERSHIP AND EMPLOYMENT: A TRANSACTIONAL APPROACH. John J. Slain, Charles A. Thompson and Freda F. Bein. Matthew Bender and Company, Incorporated, 11 Penn Plaza, New York, New York 10001. 1980- .

TEXTBOOKS AND GENERAL WORKS

AGENCY. William E. Sell. Foundation Press, 615 Merrick Avenue, Westbury, New York 11590. 1975.

AGENCY AND PARTNERSHIP. Richard J. Conviser. Gilbert Law Summaries. Harcourt Brace Jovanovich, Incorporated, 6277 Sea Harbor Drive, Orlando, Florida 32821. 1982.

AGENCY. Barry Josephson. Josephson-Kluwer Legal Education Centers, Incorporated, Center for Creative Educational Services, Culver City, California 90232. 1987.

AGENCY, PARTNERSHIP, AND OTHER UNINCORPORATED BUSINESS ENTERPRISES. Harry G. Henn. West Publishing Company, P.O. Box 43526, 50 West Kellogg Boulevard, St. Paul, Minnesota 55164-0526. 1972.

AGENCY-PARTNERSHIP IN A NUTSHELL. Roscoe T. Steffen. West Publishing Company, P.O. Box 43526, 50 West Kellogg Boulevard, St. Paul, Minnesota 55164-0526. 1977.

HANDBOOK OF THE LAW OF AGENCY. Warren A. Seavey. West Publishing Company, P.O. Box 43526, 50 West Kellogg Boulevard, St. Paul, Minnesota 55164-0526. 1964.

HANDBOOK ON THE LAW OF AGENCY AND PARTNERSHIP. Harold G. Reuschlein and William A. Gregory. West Publishing Company, P.O. Box 43526, 50 West Kellogg Boulevard, St. Paul, Minnesota 55164-0526. 1979- . (Periodic Supplements).

AN INTRODUCTION TO AGENCY AND PARTNERSHIP. Melvin Aron Eisenberg. Foundation Press, 615 Merrick Avenue, Westbury, New York 11590. 1987.

THE LAW OF AGENCY. Leonard Lakin and Martin Schiff. Kendall/Hunt Publishing Company, 2460 Kerper Boulevard, Dubuque, Iowa 52001. 1990.

THE LAW OF AGENCY AND PARTNERSHIP. Second Edition. Harold G. Reuschlein and William A. Gregory. West Publishing Company, P.O. Box 43526, 50 West Kellogg Boulevard, St. Paul, Minnesota 55164-0526. 1990.

THE LAW OF AGENCY, INCLUDING THE LAW OF PRINCIPAL AND AGENT AND THE LAW OF MASTER AND SERVANT. Second Edition. Ernest Wilson Huffent. Little, Brown and Company, 34 Beacon Street, Boston, Massachusetts 02108. 1901.

PRINCIPALS AND AGENTS: THE STRUCTURE OF BUSINESS. Harvard Business School Press, Harvard Business School, Gallatin Hall, E117, Boston, Massachusetts 02163. 1991.

STUDIES IN AGENCY. Warren A. Seavey. West Publishing Company, P.O. Box 43526, 50 West Kellogg Boulevard, St. Paul, Minnesota 55164-0526. 1949.

A TREATISE ON THE LAW OF PRINCIPAL AND AGENT, CHIEFLY WITH REFERENCE TO MERCANTILE TRANSACTIONS. William Paley. Fred B. Rothman and Company, 10368 West Centennial Road, Littleton, Colorado 80127. 1982.

DIRECTORIES

PARKER DIRECTORY OF ATTORNEYS. Parker and Sons Publications, P.O. Box 60001, Los Angeles, California 90060. 1978- . (Annual).

AGRICULTURE
See also: AGRICULTURE DEPARTMENT

STATUTES, CODES, STANDARDS, UNIFORM LAWS

COMPILATION OF STATUTES RELATING TO THE AGRICULTURAL MARKETING SERVICE AND CLOSELY RELATED ACTIVITIES. Agricultural Marketing Service. Superintendent of Documents, United States Government Printing Office, Washington, D.C. 20402. 1986.

FEDERAL FARM LOAN ACT WITH AMENDMENTS AND FARM MORTGAGE AND FARM CREDIT ACTS. Compiled by Gerard P. Walsh, Jr. Superintendent of Documents, United States Government Printing Office, Washington, D.C. 20402. 1981.

LOOSELEAF SERVICES AND REPORTERS

AGRIBUSINESS PLANNING FOR FARMERS AND RANCHERS. Institute for Business Planning, IBP Plaza, Englewood Cliffs, New Jersey 07632. 1979- .

AGRICULTURAL ESTATE, TAX AND BUSINESS PLANNING. Neil E. Harl. Matthew Bender and Company, Incorporated, 11 Penn Plaza, New York, New York 10001. 1982- .

AGRICULTURAL LAW. Neil E. Harl. Matthew Bender and Company, Incorporated, 11 Penn Plaza, New York, New York 10001. 1980- . (Fifteen Volumes).

AGRICULTURAL LAW MANUAL. Neil E. Harl. Matthew Bender and Company, Incorporated, 11 Penn Plaza, New York, New York 10001. 1985- .

AGRICULTURE DECISIONS. Decisions of the Secretary of Agriculture Under Regulatory Laws Administered in the United States Department of Agriculture. Superintendent of Documents, United States Government Printing Office, Washington, D.C. 20402. 1942- .

CATTLEMAN'S TAX MANUAL. Tad David. National Cattleman's Association, 5420 South Quebec Street, Englewood, Colorado 80155. 1984- .

HANDBOOKS, MANUALS, FORMBOOKS

AGRICULTURAL LAW: A LAWYER'S GUIDE TO REPRESENTING FARM CLIENTS. J.W. Looney and others. American Bar Association, Section of General Practice, 750 North Lake Shore Drive, Chicago, Illinois 60611. 1989.

FARM INCOME TAX MANUAL. Charles Davenport. Michie Company, P.O. Box 7587, Charlottesville, Virginia 22906-7582. 1990.

FEDERAL TAXATION OF AGRICULTURE. Third Edition. Harry M. Halstead and others. American Law Institute-American Bar Association, 4025 Chestnut Street, Philadelphia, Pennsylvania 19104. 1979.

FEDERAL TAXATION OF FARMERS AND RANCHERS: A PRACTICAL GUIDE FOR THE PREPARATION OF AN INCOME TAX RETURN. John L. Kramer and Ted D. Englebrecht. Lawyers and Judges Publishing Company, P.O. Box 2744, Del Mar, California 92014-5744. 1980.

TAX GUIDE FOR FARMERS. Revised Edition. John C. O'Byrne and Charles Davenport. Doane Western, 8900 Manchester Road, St. Louis, Missouri 63144. 1981.

TEXTBOOKS AND GENERAL WORKS

AGRICULTURAL DEVELOPMENT: AN INTERNATIONAL PERSPECTIVE. Revised Edition. Yujiro Hayami and Vernon W. Rultan. Johns Hopkins University Press, 701 West Fortieth Street, Suite 275, Baltimore, Maryland 21211-2190. 1985.

AGRICULTURAL LAW. John H. Davidson. McGraw-Hill Book Company, 1221 Avenue of the Americas, New York, New York 10020. 1981. (Two Volumes).

AGRICULTURAL LAW. Julian Juergensmeyer and James Wadley. Little, Brown and Company, 34 Beacon Street, Boston, Massachusetts 02108. 1982.

AGRICULTURAL RESEARCH POLICY. Vernon W. Ruttan. University of Minnesota Press, 2037 University Avenue, Southeast, St. Paul, Minnesota 55414. 1982.

AGRICULTURAL WORKOUTS AND BANKRUPTCIES. Practising Law Institute, 810 Seventh Avenue, New York, New York 10019. 1986.

AGRICULTURE AND THE GAAT: REWRITING THE RULES. Dale E. Hathaway. Institute for International Economics, 11 Dupont Circle, Washington, D.C. 20036. 1987.

ALTERED HARVEST: AGRICULTURAL GENETICS AND THE FATE OF THE WORLD'S FOOD SUPPLY. Jack Doyle. Viking Penguin, Incorporated, 375 Hudson Street, New York, New York 10014. 1985.

THE DECLINE IN BLACK FARMING IN AMERICA: A REPORT. United States Commission on Civil Rights. Superintendent of Documents, United States Government Printing Office, Washington, D.C. 20402. 1982.

DISHARMONIES IN EC AND U.S. AGRICULTURAL POLICY MEASURES. European Community Information Service, 2100 M Street, Northwest, Suite 707, Washington, D.C. 20037. 1988.

FARM AND RANCH REAL ESTATE LAW. John M. Cartwright. Lawyers Cooperative Publishing Company, Aqueduct Building, One Graves Street, Rochester, New York 14694. 1972.

FARM REORGANIZATION AFTER CHAPTER TWELVE. Minnesota Institute of Legal Education, 29 South Fifth Street, Minneapolis, Minnesota 55402. 1987.

THE GOVERNING OF AGRICULTURE. Bruce L. Gardner. University Press of Kansas, 329 Carruth, Lawrence, Kansas 66045. 1981.

THE LAW AND PRESERVATION OF AGRICULTURAL LAND. E.F. Roberts. Northeast Center for Rural Development, Ithaca, New York 14850. 1982.

THE LAW OF THE LAND: TWO HUNDRED YEARS OF AMERICAN FARM POLICY. John Opie. University of Nebraska Press, 901 North Seventeenth Street, Lincoln, Nebraska 68588. 1987.

LEGAL ASPECTS OF AGRICULTURE IN THE EUROPEAN COMMUNITY. J.A. Usher. Oxford University Press, 200 Madison Avenue, New York, New York 10016. 1988.

MODERN AGRICULTURE MANAGEMENT: A SYSTEMS APPROACH TO FARMING. Revised Edition. Donald E. Osburn and Kenneth C. Schneeberger. Reston Publishing Company, Division of Prentice-Hall, 15 Columbus Circle, New York, New York 10023. 1983.

THE POPULIST REVOLT: A HISTORY OF THE FARMERS' ALLIANCE AND THE PEOPLE'S PARTY. John D. Hicks. Greenwood Publishing Group, Incorporated, 88 Post Road West, P.O. Box 5007, Westport, Connecticut 06881. 1981.

RESOURCE AND ENVIRONMENTAL EFFECTS OF U.S. AGRICULTURE. Pierre R. Crosson, Sterling Brubaker. Resources for the Future, Johns Hopkins University Press, 701 West Fortieth Street, Suite 275, Baltimore, Maryland 21211. 1982.

TAXING THE RURAL LANDSCAPE: IMPROVING STATE AND FEDERAL POLICIES FOR PRIME FARMLAND. Justin R. Ward. National Resources Defense Council, 40 West Twentieth Street, New York, New York 10011. 1988.

THIRD ANNUAL FARM, RANCH AND AGRI-BUSINESS BANKRUPTCY INSTITUTE. Texas Tech University School of Law, Lubbock, Texas 79409-1037. 1987.

VANISHING FARMLAND: A LEGAL SOLUTION FOR THE STATES. Sarah E. Redfield. Lexington Books, 125 Spring Street, Lexington, Massachusetts 02173. 1984.

ENCYCLOPEDIAS AND DICTIONARIES

DICTIONARY OF AGRICULTURE: GERMAN / ENGLISH / FRENCH / SPANISH / RUSSIAN. Fifth Edition. Gunther Haensch and Gisela Haberkamp de Anton. Elsevier Science Publishing Company, P.O. Box 882, Madison Square Station, New York, New York 10159. 1986.

McGRAW-HILL ENCYCLOPEDIA OF FOOD, AGRICULTURE AND NUTRITION. Daniel N. Lapedes, Editor in chief. McGraw-Hill Book Company, 1221 Avenue of the Americas, New York, New York 10020. 1977.

DIGESTS, INDEXES, ABSTRACTS, CITATORS

AGRINDEX. Unipub, Incorporated, Division of Kraus Organization Limited, 4611-F Assembly Drive, Lanham, Maryland 20706-4391. Monthly.

BIOLOGICAL AND AGRICULTURAL INDEX. H.W. Wilson Company, 950 University Avenue, Bronx, New York 10452. Monthly.

WEEKLY GOVERNMENT ABSTRACTS: AGRICULTURE AND FOOD. National Technical Information Service, 5285 Port Royal Road, Springfield, Virginia 22151. Weekly.

ANNUALS AND SURVEYS

ALMANAC OF BUSINESS AND INDUSTRIAL FINANCIAL RATIOS. Leo Troy. Prentice-Hall, Incorporated, 113 Sylvan Avenue, Englewood Cliffs, New Jersey 07632. Annual.

FACT BOOK OF U.S. AGRICULTURE. United States Department of Agriculture. Superintendent of Documents, United States Government Printing Office, Washington, D.C. 20402. Annual.

REVIEW OF AGRICULTURAL POLICIES: GENERAL SURVEY. Organization for Economic Cooperation and Development, 2000 L Street, Northwest, Washington, D.C. 20036. Annual.

AGRICULTURE

YEARBOOK OF AGRICULTURE. United States Department of Agriculture. Superintendent of Documents, United States Government Printing Office, Washington, D.C. 20402. 1895- . Annual.

LAW REVIEWS AND PERIODICALS

ACA UPDATE. Agriculture Council of America, 1625 I Street, Northwest, Suite 708, Washington, D.C. 20006. Monthly.

AGRICULTURAL LAW JOURNAL. Callaghan and Company, 155 Pfingsten Road, Deerfield, Illinois 60015. 1979 to 1983. (Volumes 1 to 4).

AGRICULTURAL RESEARCH. Science and Education Administration, United States Department of Agriculture. United States Government Printing Office, Division of Public Documents, Washington, D.C. 20402. Monthly.

AGRONOMY JOURNAL. American Society of Agronomy, 677 South Segoe Road, Madison, Wisconsin 53711. Bimonthly.

BUSINESS FARMING. Business Farming, Incorporated, P.O. Box 229, Raleigh, North Carolina 27601. Seven issues per year.

JOURNAL OF AGRICULTURAL TAXATION AND LAW. Research Institute of America, Incorporated, 210 South Street, Boston, Massachusetts 02111. Quarterly.

NEWSLETTERS AND NEWSPAPERS

ADC NEWSLETTER. Agricultural Development Council, Incorporated, 1290 Avenue of the Americas, New York, New York 10019. Quarterly.

AGRICULTURAL LAW UPDATE. Maynard Printing Company, 299 New York Avenue, Des Moines, Iowa 50313. Monthly.

FARMERS FEDERAL TAX ALERT. Research Institute of America, 90 Fifth Avenue, New York, New York 10011. Monthly.

THE FOOD AND FIBER LETTER. Webster Communications Corporation, P.O. Box 9153, Arlington, Virginia 22209. Biweekly.

WASHINGTON AGRICULTURAL RECORD. Washington Agricultural Record, P.O. Box 25001, Georgetown Station, Washington, D.C. 20007. Biweekly.

BIBLIOGRAPHIES

AGRICULTURAL ECONOMIC BIBLIOGRAPHY. United States Department of Agriculture, Bureau of Agriculture Economics Editors. Arno Publishers, c/o Ayer Company, 99 Main Street, Salem, New York 03079. 1975. (Fourteen Volumes).

AGRICULTURAL JOURNAL TITLES AND ABBREVIATIONS. Second Edition. Oryx Press, 2214 North Central Avenue, Phoenix, Arizona 85004. 1983.

AGRICULTURAL POLICY: A BIBLIOGRAPHIC OVERVIEW. Coppa and Avery Consultants. Vance Bibliographies, P.O. Box 229, 112 North Charter Street, Monticello, Illinois 61856. 1980.

AGRICULTURE: A BIBLIOGRAPHY. E.A. Bush. Beekman Publishers, Incorporated, Box 888, Woodstock, New York 12498. 1975. (Two Volumes).

AGRICULTURE: A BIBLIOGRAPHY OF BIBLIOGRAPHIES. Theodore Besterman. Rowman and Littlefield, Incorporated, 8705 Bollman Place, Savage, Maryland 20763. 1971.

BIBLIOGRAPHY OF AGRICULTURAL AND FOOD LAW, 1960-1978. Winston W. Grant and Dale C. Dahl. Minnesota Agricultural Experiment Station, St. Paul, Minnesota 55101. 1978.

BIBLIOGRAPHY OF AGRICULTURE. United States Science and Education Administration, Technical Information Systems. Oryx Press, 2214 North Central Avenue, Phoenix, Arizona 85004. Monthly.

FOOD BIBLIOGRAPHY: REFERENCES TO REPORTS AND OTHER DOCUMENTS. Issued by the United States General Accounting Office, 441 G Street, Northwest, Washington, D.C. 20548. Annual.

FORMULATION OF FEDERAL FARM POLICY SINCE THE GREAT DEPRESSION: A Bibliography. Tim J. Watts. Vance Bibliographies, P.O. Box 229, 112 North Charter Street, Monticello, Illinois 61856. 1986.

GUIDE TO SOURCES FOR AGRICULTURAL AND BIOLOGICAL RESEARCH. J. Richard Blanchard and Lois Farrell, Editors. University of California Press, 2120 Berkeley Way, Berkeley, California 94720. 1981.

STRUCTURE OF U.S. AGRICULTURE BIBLIOGRAPHY. Compiled by Ronald C. Wimberly and Charles N. Bebee. United States Department of Agriculture, Science and Education Administration, Fourteenth Street and Independence Avenue, Southwest, Washington, D.C. 20250. 1981.

DIRECTORIES

CDE STOCK OWNERSHIP DIRECTORY: AGRIBUSINESS. Corporate Data Exchange, Incorporated, 198 Broadway, Seventh Floor, New York, New York 10038. 1976- .

DIRECTORY OF MAJOR U.S. CORPORATIONS INVOLVED IN AGRIBUSINESS. A.V. Krebs. Agribusiness Accountability Publications, 3410 Nineteenth Street, San Francisco, California 94110. 1976- . (Annual).

FOOD AND AGRICULTURAL EXPORT DIRECTORY. Export Programs Division, Foreign Agricultural Service, Agriculture Department, Fourteenth Street and Independence Avenue, Southwest, Washington, D.C. 20250. 1972- .

FOOD PRODUCTION AND AGRICULTURE: A LISTING OF U.S. NON-PROFIT ORGANIZATIONS IN FOOD PRODUCTION AND AGRICULTURAL ASSISTANCE ABROAD. Technical Assistance Information, American Council of Voluntary Agencies for Foreign Service, 200 Park Avenue, New York, New York 10003. 1981.

NATIONAL DIRECTORY OF FARMLAND PROTECTION ORGANIZATIONS. Nancy Boshwick. Farmland Project, National Association of State Departments of Agricultural Research Foundation, 1616 H Street, Northwest, Washington, D.C. 20006. 1983.

USDA DATA BASE DIRECTORY. Office of Automated Data Systems, United States Department of Agriculture, Fourteenth Street and Independence Avenue, Southwest, Washington, D.C. 20250. Irregular.

ASSOCIATIONS AND PROFESSIONAL SOCIETIES

AGRICULTURE COUNCIL OF AMERICA. 1250 I Street, Northwest, Suite 601, Washington, D.C. 20005. (202) 296-4563.

AMERICAN AGRICULTURAL LAW ASSOCIATION. Leflar Law Center, University of Arkansas, Fayetteville, Arkansas 72701. (501) 575-7389.

NATIONAL ASSOCIATION OF STATE DEPARTMENTS OF AGRICULTURE. 1616 H Street, Northwest, Washington, D.C. 20006. (202) 628-1566.

NATIONAL FARMERS UNION. 10065 East Harvard Avenue, Denver, Colorado 80231. (303) 337-5500.

NATIONAL INSTITUTE FOR SCIENCE, LAW, AND PUBLIC POLICY. 1424 Sixteenth Street, Northwest, Suite 105, Washington, D.C. 20036. (202) 462-8800.

RESEARCH CENTERS, INSTITUTES, CLEARINGHOUSES

AGRICULTURAL EXPERIMENT STATION. Cornell University, 292 Roberts Hall, Ithaca, New York 14853. (607) 255-5420.

AGRICULTURAL LAW AND POLICY INSTITUTE. 1920 N Street, Northwest, Washington, D.C. 20036. (202) 857-0211.

CALIFORNIA AGRICULTURAL EXPERIMENT STATION. University of California, 300 Lakeside Drive, Oakland, California 94612-3560. (415) 987-0026.

CENTER FOR AGRICULTURE LAW. University of Florida, Holland Law Center, Gainesville, Florida 32611. (904) 392-0082.

FLORIDA AGRICULTURAL EXPERIMENT STATION. University of Florida, 1022 McCarty Hall, Gainesville, Florida 32611. (904) 392-1784.

MICHIGAN AGRICULTURAL EXPERIMENT STATION. Michigan State University, 109 Agriculture Hall, East Lansing, Michigan 48224-1039. (517) 355-0123.

NATIONAL AGRICULTURE LIBRARY. National Agriculture Library Building, Beltsville, Maryland 20705. (301) 344-3755.

OHIO AGRICULTURAL RESEARCH AND DEVELOPMENT CENTER. Wooster, Ohio 44691. (216) 263-3700.

TENNESSEE AGRICULTURAL EXPERIMENT STATION. University of Tennessee at Knoxville, 103 Morgan Hall, P.O. Box 1071, Knoxville, Tennessee 37901. (615) 974-7121.

WISCONSIN AGRICULTURAL EXPERIMENT STATION. University of Wisconsin, 140 Agricultural Hall, Madison, Wisconsin 53706. (608) 262-2349.

ONLINE DATABASES

AGRICOLA. National Agricultural Library, Beltsville, Maryland 20705.

AGRIDATA NETWORK. Agridata Resources, Incorporated, 330 East Kilbourn Avenue, Milwaukee, Wisconsin 53202.

AGRIS. Food and Agriculture Organization of the United Nations, AGRIS Coordinating Centre, Via delle Terme di Caracalla, 00100 Rome, Italy.

CRIS (CURRENT RESEARCH INFORMATION SYSTEM). (Agricultural research projects database). United States Department of Agriculture, Cooperative State Research Service, Room 6818 S Building, Twelfth and Independence Avenue, Washington, D.C. 20250.

USDA ONLINE. United States Department of Agriculture. Fourteenth Street and Independence Avenue, Southwest, Washington, D.C. 20250.

STATISTICS SOURCES

AGRICULTURAL OUTLOOK. Economics, Statistics, and Cooperatives Services, United States Department of Agriculture. Available from United States Government Printing Office, Division of Public Documents, Washington, D.C. 20402. Monthly.

AGRICULTURAL PRICES. Economics, Statistics and Cooperatives Service, United States Department of Agriculture, Fourteenth Street and Independence Avenue, Southwest, Washington, D.C. 20250. Monthly. (With Annual Summary).

AGRICULTURAL STATISTICS. United States Department of Agriculture. United States Government Printing Office, Division of Public Documents, Washington, D.C. 20402. Annual.

CROP PRODUCTION. Crop Reporting Board. United States Department of Agriculture, Fourteenth Street and Independence Avenue, Southwest, Washington, D.C. 20250. Monthly. (With Annual Summary).

ECONOMIC INDICATORS OF THE FARM SECTOR: INCOME AND BALANCE SHEET STATISTICS. United States Department of Agriculture, Economic Research Service, Fourteenth Street and Independence Avenue, Southwest, Washington, D.C. 20250. Annual.

FARM LABOR. United States Department of Agriculture, Statistical Reporting Service. Fourteenth Street and Independence Avenue, Southwest, Washington, D.C. 20250. Quarterly.

MONTHLY LABOR REVIEW. Bureau of Labor Statistics, United States Department of Labor. United States Government Printing Office, Division of Public Documents, Washington, D.C. 20402. Monthly.

NATIONAL FOOD REVIEW. Economics, Statistics and Cooperatives Service, United States Department of Agriculture. United States Government Printing Office, Division of Public Documents, Washington, D.C. 20402. Quarterly.

PERIODIC REPORTS OF AGRICULTURAL ECONOMICS AND STATISTICS. United States Department of Agriculture, Office of Management Services, Fourteenth Street and Independence Avenue, Southwest, Washington, D.C. 20250. 1973- .

SPECIAL ANALYSES, BUDGET OF THE UNITED STATES GOVERNMENT. Executive Office of the President, Office of Management and Budget, Executive Office Building, Washington, D.C. 20503. Annual.

UNITED STATES CENSUS OF AGRICULTURE. Bureau of the Census, United States Department of Commerce. Available from Subscriber Services Section, Bureau of the Census, Fourteenth Street between Constitution Avenue and East Street, Northwest, Washington, D.C. 20233. Every five years.

U.S. FOREIGN AGRICULTURAL TRADE STATISTICAL REPORT. Economics, Statistics and Cooperatives Service, United States Department of Agriculture, Fourteenth Street and Independence Avenue, Southwest, Washington, D.C. 20250. Annual.

AUDIOVISUALS

AGRIBUSINESS: DEBTOR/CREDITOR RELATIONS. Neil E. Harl. National Practice Institute, 330 Second Avenue South, Minneapolis, Minnesota 55401. Audiotape.

FARM BANKRUPTCIES UNDER CHAPTER 12: RECENT DEVELOPMENTS. American Bar Association, 750 North Lake Shore Drive, Chicago, Illinois 60611. 1987. Videotape.

OTHER SOURCES

ADVANCES IN AGRONOMY. Academic Press, Incorporated, 1250 Sixth Avenue, San Diego, California 92101. Irregular.

DEVELOPING STRATEGIES FOR RANGELAND MANAGEMENT: A REPORT. Committee on Developing Strategies for Rangeland Management, National Research Council/National Academy of Sciences, Westview Press, Incorporated, 5500 Central Avenue, Boulder, Colorado 80301. 1985.

STATE INCORPORATION STATUTES FOR FARMER COOPERATIVES. James R. Baarda. United States Department of Agriculture, Agricultural Cooperative Service, Fourteenth Street and Independence, Southwest, Washington, D.C. 20250. 1982.

TAX PLANNING FOR AGRICULTURE. ALI-ABA Course of Study Materials. American Law Institute-American Bar Association, 4025 Chestnut Street, Philadelphia, Pennsylvania 19104. 1983.

WASHINGTON AGRICULTURAL PROCEEDINGS. Agro-Info, 8215 Donset Drive, Springfield, Virginia 22152. Weekly. (When Congress is in session).

AGRICULTURE DEPARTMENT
See also: FOOD LAWS

STATUTES, CODES, STANDARDS, UNIFORM LAWS

CODE OF FEDERAL REGULATIONS, TITLE 7. Office of the Federal Register, National Archives and Records Administration. Superintendent of Documents, United States Government Printing Office, Washington, D.C. 20402. Annual. (Updated by use of monthly List of Sections Affected and daily Federal Register).

COMPILATION OF STATUTES RELATING TO THE AGRICULTURAL MARKETING SERVICE AND CLOSELY RELATED ACTIVITIES. Agriculture Department, Agricultural Marketing Service. Superintendent of Documents, United States Government Printing Office, Washington, D.C. 20402. 1986.

COMPILATION OF STATUTES RELATING TO THE AGRICULTURAL STABILIZATION AND CONSERVATION SERVICE. Agriculture Department, Agricultural Stabilization and Conservation Service, Office of the General Counsel. Superintendent of Documents, United States Government Printing Office, Washington, D.C. 20402. 1983- .

PRINCIPAL LAWS RELATING TO FOREST SERVICE ACTIVITIES. Agriculture Department, Forest Service, Legislative Affairs Staff. Superintendent of Documents, United States Government Printing Office, Washington, D.C. 20402. 1983.

LOOSELEAF SERVICES AND REPORTERS

AGRICULTURAL DECISIONS. Superintendent of Documents, United States Government Printing Office, Washington, D.C. 20402. 1942- .

TEXTBOOKS AND GENERAL WORKS

IMMIGRATION REFORM AND AGRICULTURAL LABOR. Robert Coltrane. Agriculture Department, Economic Research Service, Economic Development Division. Superintendent of Documents, United States Government Printing Office, Washington, D.C. 20402. 1984.

PROVISIONS OF THE FOOD SECURITY ACT OF 1985. Lawrence K. Glaser. Agriculture Department, Economic Research Service, National Economics Division. Superintendent of Documents, United States Government Printing Office, Washington, D.C. 20402. 1986.

STATE MINERAL TAXES, 1982. Thomas F. Stinson. Agricultural Department, Economic Research Service. Superintendent of Documents, United States Government Printing Office, Washington, D.C. 20402. 1983.

DIGESTS, INDEXES, ABSTRACTS, CITATORS

DIGEST OF STATE FOREST FIRE LAWS. Agriculture Department, Forest Service, Northeastern Area, State and Private Forestry. Superintendent of Documents, United States Government Printing Office, Washington, D.C. 20402. 1979.

RESEARCH CENTERS, INSTITUTES, CLEARINGHOUSES

NATIONAL AGRICULTURE LIBRARY. National Agriculture Library Building, Beltsville, Maryland 20705. (301) 344-3755.

UNITED STATES DEPARTMENT OF AGRICULTURE, OFFICE OF GENERAL COUNSEL LIBRARY. Room 2043, South Agriculture Building, Washington, D.C. 20250. (202) 447-7219.

AIDS (Acquired Immune Deficiency Syndrome)
See also: HEALTH CARE

STATUTES, CODES, STANDARDS, UNIFORM LAWS

LAWS GOVERNING CONFIDENTIALITY OF HIV-RELATED INFORMATION: 1983-1988. Mona J. Rowe and Bethany Bridgham. AIDS Policy Center, Intergovernmental Health Policy Project, George Washington University, 2011 I Street, Northwest, Washington, D.C. 20006. 1989.

LEGISLATIVE RESPONSES TO AIDS. World Health Organization. Kluwer Academic Publishers, 101 Philip Drive, Asinippi Park, Norwell, Massachusetts 02061. 1989.

STATE AIDS LEGISLATION RELATED TO WORK NOTIFICATION AND EXPOSURE: 1983-1988. Mona J. Rowe and Rita M. Keintz. Intergovernmental Health Policy Project, George Washington University, 2011 I Street, Northwest, Suite 200, Washington, D.C. 20006. 1989.

LOOSELEAF SERVICES AND REPORTERS

AIDS IN THE WORKPLACE: RESOURCE MATERIAL. Third Edition. Bureau of National Affairs, Incorporated, 1231 Twenty-fifth Street, Northwest, Washington, D.C. 20037. 1989- .

AIDS LAW AND LITIGATION REPORTER. Christopher J. Collins. University Publications of America, 4520 East West Highway, Suite 600, Bethesd, Maryland 20814. 1986- .

HOSPITAL LAW MANUAL, ATTORNEY'S VOLUMES. Aspen Systems Corporation, 1600 Research Boulevard, Rockville, Maryland 20850. 1959- . (Quarterly Supplements).

SEXUAL ORIENTATION AND THE LAW. Clark Boardman Company, Limited, 435 Hudson Street, New York, New York 10014. 1985- . (Periodic Supplements).

HANDBOOKS, MANUALS, FORMBOOKS

AIDS: A COMPREHENSIVE LEGAL MANUAL. Second Edition. Jeff G. Peters and Deborah H. Wagner. Florida AIDS Legal Defense and Education Fund, 1353 East Lafayette, Tallahassee, Florida 32306. 1989.

AIDS AND THE LAW. William H. L. Dornette, Editor. John Wiley and Sons, Incorporated, 605 Third Avenue, New York, New York 10158. 1987.

AIDS AND THE LAW: A GUIDE FOR THE PUBLIC. Harlon L. Dalton, Scott Burris and the Yale AIDS Law Project. Yale University Press, 302 Temple Street, New Haven, Connecticut 06520. 1987.

THE AIDS BENEFITS HANDBOOK: EVERYTHING YOU NEED TO KNOW TO GET SOCIAL SECURITY, WELFARE, MEDICAID, MEDICARE, FOOD STAMPS, HOUSING, DRUGS, AND OTHER BENEFITS. Thomas P. McCormack. Yale University Press, 302 Temple Street, New Haven, Connecticut 06520. 1990.

AIDS INFORMATION SOURCEBOOK. Second Edition. H. Robert Malinowsky and Gerald J. Perry. Oryx Press, 2214 North Central Avenue, Phoenix, Arizona 85004. 1989.

AIDS LAW IN A NUTSHELL. Robert M. Jarvis and others. West Publishing Company, 50 West Kellogg Boulevard, St. Paul, Minnesota 55164-0526. 1990.

AIDS LEGAL GUIDE: A PROFESSIONAL RESOURCE ON AIDS-RELATED ISSUES AND DISCRIMINATION. Second Edition. Lambda Legal Defense and Education Fund, Incorporated. 666 Broadway, New York, New York 10012. 1987.

AIDS NETWORK MANUAL. Bay Area Anti-sexism Committee of the National Lawyers Guild. 211 Gough Street, Third Floor, San Francisco, California 94102. 1985. Defunct.

AIDS PRACTICE MANUAL: A LEGAL AND EDUCATIONAL GUIDE. Second Edition. Paul Albert, Leonard Graff, Benjamin Schatz. National Lawyers Guild, 55 Sixth Avenue, New York, New York 10013. 1988.

AIDS REFERENCE AND RESEARCH COLLECTION. Robert F. Hummel, Editor. University Publishing Group, 107 East Church Street, Frederick, Maryland 21701. 1986- .

AIDS REFERENCE GUIDE. Atlantic Information Services, Incorporated, 1050 Seventeenth Street, Northwest, Washington, D.C. 20036. 1988- .

TEXTBOOKS AND GENERAL WORKS

AIDS AND HOSPITALS: THE EMERGENCY LEGAL ISSUES. E.J. Holland, Jr. and David L. Wing. Health Law Center, Aspen Publishers, Incorporated, 1600 Research Boulevard, Rockville, Maryland 20850. 1986.

AIDS AND THE COURTS. Clark C. Abt and Kathleen M. Hardy. ABT Books, University Press of America, 4720 Boston Way, Lanham, Maryland 20706. 1990.

AIDS AND THE HEALTH CARE SYSTEM. Lawrence O. Gostin, Editor. Yale University Press, 302 Temple Street, New Haven, Connecticut 06520. 1990.

AIDS AND THE LAW. William H.L. Dornette, Editor. John Wiley and Sons, Incorporated, 605 Third Avenue, New York, New York 10158. 1987.

AIDS: EMPLOYER RIGHTS AND RESPONSIBILITIES. Commerce Clearing House, Incorporated, 4025 West Peterson Avenue, Chicago, Illinois 60646. 1985.

THE AIDS EPIDEMIC: PRIVATE RIGHTS AND THE PUBLIC INTEREST. Padraig O'Malley. Beacon Press, 25 Beacon Street, Boston, Massachusetts 02108. 1989.

AIDS IN THE MIND OF AMERICA. Dennis Altman. Anchor Press/Doubleday, 666 Fifth Avenue, New York, New York 10103. 1987.

AIDS IN THE WORKPLACE: LEGAL QUESTIONS AND PRACTICAL ANSWERS. William F. Banta. Free Press, 866 Third Avenue, New York, New York 10022. 1987.

AIDS: LEGAL POLICIES. Legal-Medical Studies, Incorporated. Box 8219, Boston, Massachusetts 02114. 1984.

AIDS: TESTING AND PRIVACY. Mayo Gunderson and Rhame Gunderson. University of Utah Press, 101 U.U.P., Salt Lake City, Utah 84112. 1989.

AIDS, THE LEGAL ISSUES. American Bar Association, AIDS Coordinating Committee, 750 North Lake Shore Drive, Chicago, Illinois 60611. 1988.

AND THE BAND PLAYED ON: POLITICS, PEOPLE AND THE AIDS EPIDEMIC. Randy S. Shilts. St. Martin's Press, Incorporated, 175 Fifth Avenue, New York, New York 10010. 1987.

COMMUNICABLE DISEASES IN THE WORKPLACE: LEGAL, MEDICAL, ECONOMIC, AND HUMAN RESOURCE ISSUES. Richard J. Cureale and Samuel Estreicher, Co-Chairmen. Practising Law Institute, 810 Seventh Avenue, New York, New York 10019. 1986.

CONFRONTING AIDS: DIRECTIONS FOR PUBLIC HEALTH, HEALTH CARE, AND RESEARCH. National Academy Press, 2101 Constitution Avenue, Northwest, Washington, D.C. 20418. 1986.

EMPLOYMENT PROBLEMS IN THE WORKPLACE. Jerome B. Kauff, Chairman. Practising Law Institute, 810 Seventh Avenue, New York, New York 10019. 1986.

GAYS/JUSTICE: A STUDY OF ETHICS, SOCIETY, AND LAW. Richard D. Mohr. Columbia University Press, 562 West One Hundred Thirteenth Street, New York, New York 10025. 1988.

LEGAL, MEDICAL AND GOVERNMENTAL PERSPECTIVES ON AIDS AS A DISABILITY. David Rappaport and John Parry, Editors. American Bar Association, Commission on the Mentally Disabled, 750 North Lake Shore Drive, Chicago, Illinois 60611. 1987.

MOBILIZING AGAINST AIDS: THE UNFINISHED STORY OF A VIRUS. Eve K. Nichols. Institute of Medicine, National Academy of Sciences, Harvard University Press, 79 Garden Street, Cambridge, Massachusetts 02138. 1989.

THE QUESTION OF AIDS. Richard Liebmann-Smith. Academy of Sciences, Publications Department, 2 East Sixty-third Street, New York, New York 10021. 1985.

SEX AND GERMS: THE POLITICS OF AIDS. Cindy Patton. South End Press, 116 St. Boloph Street, Boston, Massachusetts 02115. 1985.

THE SEXUALLY TRANSMITTED DISEASES. Charles E. Rinear. McFarland and Company, Incorporated, P.O. Box 611, Jefferson, North Carolina 28640. 1986.

A SYNOPSIS OF STATE AIDS RELATED LEGISLATION. George Washington University, Intergovernmental Health Policy Project, 2011 I Street, Northwest, Washington, D.C. 20036. 1987.

TOWARD A NATIONAL POLICY ON DRUG AND AIDS TESTING. Mathea Falco and Warren I. Cikins. Brookings Institution, 1775 Massachusetts Avenue, Washington, D.C. 20036. 1989.

UNDERSTANDING AIDS: A COMPREHENSIVE GUIDE. Victor Gong, Editor. Rutgers University Press, 109 Church Street, New Brunswick, New Jersey. 08901. 1985.

DIGESTS, INDEXES, ABSTRACTS, CITATORS

INDEX MEDICUS. United States Department of Health and Human Services, National Library of Medicine. Superintendent of Documents, United States Government Printing Office, Washington, D.C. 20402. 1960- . Monthly.

LAW REVIEWS AND PERIODICALS

AIDS AND PUBLIC POLICY JOURNAL. University Publishing Group, 107 East Church Street, Frederick, Maryland 21701. Quarterly.

HASTINGS CENTER REPORT. The Hastings Center, 255 Elm Road, Briarcliff Manor, New York 10510. Bimonthly.

JAMA: THE JOURNAL OF THE AMERICAN MEDICAL ASSOCIATION. American Medical Association, 535 North Dearborn Street, Chicago, Illinois 60610. Monthly.

JOURNAL OF CONTEMPORARY HEALTH LAW AND POLICY. The Catholic University of America, Columbus School of Law, 620 Michigan Avenue, Northeast, Washington, D.C. 20064. Annual.

LAW, MEDICINE AND HEALTH CARE. American Society of Law and Medicine, 765 Commonwealth Avenue, Boston, Massachusetts 02215. Quarterly.

NEWSLETTERS AND NEWSPAPERS

AIDS EMPLOYMENT ALERT. University Publishing Group, 107 East Church Street, Frederick, Maryland 21701. Quarterly.

THE AIDS LAW REPORTER. National Legal Research Group, Incorporated, 2421 Ivy Road, Charlottesville, Virginia 22906. Monthly.

AIDS LITIGATION REPORTER. Andrews Publications, Incorporated, P.O. Box 200, Edgemont, Pennsylvania 19028. Biweekly.

AIDS POLICY AND LAW. Buraff Publications, Incorporated, 1350 Connecticut Avenue Northwest, Washington D.C. 20036. Biweekly.

AIDS UPDATE. Lambda Legal Defense and Education Fund, Incorporated, 666 Broadway, New York, New York 10012. Bimonthly.

LESBIAN/GAY LAW NOTES. Bar Association for Human Rights, P.O. Box 1899, Grand Central Station, New York, New York 10163. Monthly.

DIRECTORIES

AIDS RESOURCES. DJM Publishers, Incorporated, 1111 Third Avenue, Suite 700, Seattle, Washington 98101. 1985- .

ASSOCIATIONS AND PROFESSIONAL SOCIETIES

ACT UP. 496A Hudson Street, Suite G4, New York, New York 10014. (212) 989-1114.

AIDS ACTION COUNSEL. 2033 M Street, Northwest, Suite 801, Washington, D.C. 20036. (202) 293-2886.

NATIONAL ASSOCIATION OF PEOPLE WITH AIDS. 2025 I Street, Northwest, Suite 1118, Washington, D.C. 20006. (202) 429-2856.

NATIONAL GAY AND LESBIAN TASK FORCE. 1517 U Street, Northwest, Washington, D.C. 20009. (202) 332-6483.

NATIONAL HEALTH LAWYERS ASSOCIATION. 1620 I Street, Northwest, Suite 900, Washington, D.C. 20036. (202) 833-1100.

NATIONAL MINORITY AIDS COUNCIL. 300 I Street, Northeast, Suite 400, Washington, D.C. 20002. (202) 544-1076.

NATIONAL RESOURCE CENTER ON WOMEN AND AIDS. 2000 P Street, Northwest, Suite 508, Washington, D.C. 20036. (202) 872-1770.

WORLD HEALTH ORGANIZATION COLLABORATING CENTRE ON AIDS. Centers for Disease Control, 1600 Clifton Road, Northeast, Atlanta, Georgia 30333. (404) 639-3311.

RESEARCH CENTERS, INSTITUTES, CLEARING HOUSES

ACQUIRED IMMUNE DEFICIENCY SYNDROME (AIDS) INFORMATION. United States Department of Health and Human Services, P.O. Box 1133, Washington, D.C. 20013. (202) 245-0471.

CENTERS FOR DISEASE CONTROL. 1600 Clifton Road, Northeast, Atlanta, Georgia 30033. (404) 639-0965.

GEORGE WASHINGTON UNIVERSITY INTERGOVERNMENTAL HEALTH POLICY PROJECT. 2011 I Street, Northwest, Suite 200, Washington, D.C. 20006. (202) 872-1445.

INSTITUTE FOR HEALTH POLICY STUDIES. University of California-San Francisco, 1326 Third Avenue, San Francisco, California 94143. (415) 476-4921.

LAMBDA LEGAL DEFENSE AND EDUCATION FUND. 666 Broadway, New York, New York 10012. (212) 995-8585.

NATIONAL GAY RIGHTS ADVOCATES. 640 Castro Street, San Francisco, California 94114. (415) 863-3624.

ODPHP NATIONAL HEALTH INFORMATION CENTER. P.O. Box 1133, Washington, D.C. 20013-1133. (301) 565-4167.

UCLA AIDS CLINICAL RESEARCH CENTER/AIDS CLINICAL TRIALS GROUP. 18033 Le Conte Avenue, Room 60-051 CHS, Los Angeles, California 90024-1793. (213) 206-6414.

ONLINE DATABASES

AIDS. Bureau of Hygiene and Tropical Diseases (BHTD), Keppel Street, London, WC1E 7HT, England.

AIDS POLICY AND LAW. Buraff Publications, Incorporated, 1350 Connecticut Avenue Northwest, Washington D.C. 20036.

AIDS UPDATE. Bureau of Hygiene and Tropical Diseases (BHTD), Keppel Street, London, WC1E 7HT, England

CENTERS FOR DISEASE CONTROL INFORMATION SERVICE. American Medical Association (AMA) and United States Department of Health and Human Services, Public Health Service Centers for Disease Control, 535 North Dearborn Street, Chicago, Illinois 60610.

OTHER SOURCES

AMERICAN BAR ASSOCIATION POLICY ON AIDS AND THE CRIMINAL JUSTICE SYSTEM. American Bar Association, 750 North Lake Shore Drive, Chicago, Illinois 60611. 1989.

1988 UPDATE: AIDS IN CORRECTIONAL FACILITIES. Theodore M. Hammett. Office of Justice Programs, National Institute of Justice, United States Department of Justice. Superintendent of Documents, United States Government Printing Office, Washington, D.C. 20402. 1989.

AIR FORCE
See: AVIATION; MILITARY LAW AND SERVICE

AIR LAW
See: AVIATION; AVIATION ACCIDENTS

AIRLINER HIJACKING
See: TERRORISM

ALCOHOL CONTROL AND DRINKING BEHAVIOR
See also: ALCOHOL, TOBACCO AND FIREARMS BUREAU

STATUTES, CODES, STANDARDS, UNIFORM LAWS

QUARTERLY BULLETIN: U.S. BUREAU OF ALCOHOL, TOBACCO, AND FIREARMS. Department of the Treasury. Superintendent of Documents, United States Government Printing Office, Washington, D.C. 20402. Quarterly.

UNIFORM ALCOHOLISM AND INTOXICATION TREATMENT ACT. National Conference of Commissioners on Uniform State Laws. Uniform Laws Annotated. West Publishing Company, P.O. Box 64526, 50 West Kellogg Boulevard, St. Paul, Minnesota 55164-0526. 1976- . (Annual Supplements).

ALCOHOL CONTROL AND DRINKING BEHAVIOR

LOOSELEAF SERVICES AND REPORTERS

DEFENDING DRINKING DRIVERS. Second Edition. John Tarantino. James Publishing, Incorporated, 3520 Cadillac Avenue, Suite A, Costa Mesa, California 92626. 1986- .

DEFENSE OF DRUNK DRIVING CASES: CRIMINAL-CIVIL. Third Edition. Richard E. Erwin and Marilyn K. Minzer. Matthew Bender and Company, Incorporated, 11 Penn Plaza, New York, New York 10001. 1971- .

DRINKING/DRIVING LITIGATION: CRIMINAL AND CIVIL. Donald H. Nichols. Callaghan and Company, 155 Pfingsten Road, Deerfield, Illinois 60015. 1985- .

DRINKING/DRIVING LITIGATION NOTEBOOK. Donald H. Nichols. Callaghan and Company, 155 Pfingsten Road, Deerfield, Illinois 60015. 1987- .

DRUGS AND ALCOHOL IN THE WORKPLACE: TESTING AND PRIVACY. Craig M. Cornish. Callaghan and Company, 155 Pfingsten Road, Deerfield, Illinois 60015. 1988.

LIQUOR CONTROL LAW REPORTS. Commerce Clearing House, Incorporated, 4025 West Peterson Avenue, Chicago, Illinois 60646. 1934- .

LIQUOR LIABILITY LAW. James F. Mosher. Matthew Bender and Company, Incorporated, 11 Penn Plaza, New York, New York 10001. 1987- .

HANDBOOKS, MANUALS, FORMBOOKS

AN INTRODUCTORY HANDBOOK FOR STATE TASK FORCES TO COMBAT DRUNK DRIVING. C.W. Lynn and Rosemarie L. Hauter. Virginia Highway and Transportation Research Council, 1221 East Broad Street, Richmond, Virginia 23219. 1983.

LEGAL ISSUES IN ADDICT DIVERSION: A LAYMAN'S GUIDE. Harvey S. Perlman. Lexington Books, 125 Spring Street, Lexington, Massachusetts 02173. 1976.

A PRACTITIONER'S GUIDE TO ALCOHOLISM AND THE LAW. David G. Evans. Hazelden Foundation, 15245 Pleasant Valley Road, P.O. Box 11, Center City, Minnesota 55012. 1983.

PRACTITIONER'S GUIDE TO LIQUOR LIABILITY LITIGATION. American Law Institute-American Bar Association, 4025 Chestnut Street, Philadelphia, Pennsylvania 19104. 1987.

RIGHTS OF ALCOHOLICS AND THEIR FAMILIES: A HANDBOOK FOR SOCIAL WORKERS. New York City Affiliate, National Council on Alcoholism, 730 Fifth Avenue, New York, New York 10019. 1982.

TEXTBOOKS AND GENERAL WORKS

ALCOHOL AND DRUGS: ISSUES IN THE WORKPLACE. Tia Denenberg and Richard Denenberg. Bureau of National Affairs, Incorporated, 1231 Twenty-fifth Street, Northwest, Washington, D.C. 20037. 1983.

ALCOHOL AND PUBLIC POLICY: BEYOND PROHIBITION. National Research Council Assembly of Behavioral Social Sciences. National Academy Press, 2101 Constitution Avenue, Northwest, Washington, D.C. 20418. 1981.

ALCOHOL, REFORM AND SOCIETY: THE LIQUOR ISSUE IN SOCIAL CONTEXT. Jack S. Blocker. Contributions in American History Series, No. 83. Greenwood Publishing Group, Incorporated, 88 Post Road West, P.O. Box 5007, Westport, Connecticut 06881. 1979.

ALCOHOL STILLS, MOONSHINING MADE LEGAL. Jean Cram. Washburn Press, 2753 Upland Court, Plymouth, Minnesota 55447. 1981.

ALCOHOL: THE CRUTCH THAT CRIPPLES. Brent Q. Hafen. West Publishing Company, P.O. Box 43526, 50 West Kellogg Boulevard, St. Paul, Minnesota 55164-0526. 1977.

ALCOHOL, THE PREVENTION DEBATE. Marcus Grant and Bruce Ritson, Editors. St. Martin's Press, Incorporated, 175 Fifth Avenue, New York, New York 10010. 1983.

ALCOHOL USE AND CRIMINAL BEHAVIOR: AN EXECUTIVE SUMMARY. James J. Collins. United States Department of Justice, National Institute of Justice. Superintendent of Documents, United States Government Printing Office, Washington, D.C. 20402. 1981.

ALCOHOLISM AND EMPLOYEE RELATIONS. Bureau of National Affairs, Incorporated, 1231 Twenty-fifth Street, Northwest, Washington, D.C. 20037. 1978.

ALCOHOLISM AND THE LAW. Frank P. Grad, Audrey L. Goldberg and Barbara A. Shapiro. Oceana Publications, 75 Main Street, Dobbs Ferry, New York 10522. 1971.

BEYOND ALCOHOLISM: ALCOHOL AND PUBLIC HEALTH POLICY. Dan E. Beauchamp. Temple University Press, 1601 North Broad Street, University Services Building, Philadelphia, Pennsylvania 19122. 1982.

THE CULTURE OF PUBLIC PROBLEMS: DRINKING, DRIVING AND THE SYMBOLIC ORDER. Joseph R. Gusfield. University of Chicago Press, 5801 Ellis Avenue, Chicago, Illinois 60637. 1984.

DETERRING THE DRINKING DRIVER: LEGAL POLICY AND SOCIAL CONTROL. Revised Edition. H. Lawrence Ross. Free Press, 866 Third Avenue, New York, New York 10022. 1984.

DRINKING AND CRIME: PERSPECTIVES ON THE RELATIONSHIPS BETWEEN ALCOHOL CONSUMPTION AND CRIMINAL BEHAVIOR. James J. Collins, Editor. Guilford Publications, Incorporated, 72 Spring Street, New York, New York 10012. 1981.

DRIVING THE DRUNK OFF THE ROAD: A HANDBOOK FOR ACTION. Sandy Golden. Quince Mill Books, 21 Quince Mill Court, Gaithersburg, Maryland 20878. 1983.

DRUGS AND ALCOHOL IN THE WORKPLACE: LEGAL DEVELOPMENTS AND MANAGEMENT STRATEGIES. Victor Schachter, Thomas E. Geidt and Susan Grody Ruben. Executive Enterprises Publishing Company, Incorporated, 22 West Twenty-first Street, New York, New York 10010-6904. 1986.

DRUNK DRIVING DEFENSE. Second Edition. Lawrence E. Taylor. Little, Brown and Company, 34 Beacon Street, Boston, Massachusetts 02108. 1986- . (Periodic Supplements).

DRUNK DRIVING LAWS AND ENFORCEMENT: AN ASSESSMENT OF EFFECTIVENESS. Criminal Justice Section, American Bar Association, 750 North Lake Shore Drive, Chicago, Illinois 60611. 1986.

IN SEARCH OF NIRVANA, A NEW PERSPECTIVE ON ALCOHOL AND DRUG DEPENDENCY. A. Ghairian. George Ronald Publisher, Limited, P.O. Box 447, St. Louis, Missouri 63166. 1989.

LAW, ALCOHOL, AND ORDER: PERSPECTIVES ON NATIONAL PROHIBITION. David E. Kyvig. Greenwood Publishing Group, Incorporated, 88 Post Road West, P.O. Box 5007, Westport, Connecticut 06881. 1985.

LEGAL ASPECTS OF CHEMICAL TESTING FOR INTOXICATION. Second Edition. James C. Drennan. University of North Carolina Institute on Government, Knapp Building, 059A, Chapel Hill, North Carolina 27514. 1983.

MINIMUM-DRINKING-AGE LAWS: AN EDUCATION. Henry Wechsler, Editor. Lexington Books, 125 Spring Street, Lexington, Massachusetts 02173. 1980.

PUBLIC POLICY AND POLICE DISCRETION. David E. Aaronson. Clark Boardman Company, Limited, 435 Hudson Street, New York, New York 10014. 1984.

TREATING THE CRIMINAL OFFENDER. Third Edition. Alexander B. Smith and Louis Berlin. Plenum Publishing Corporation, 233 Spring Street, New York New York 10013. 1988.

ANNUALS AND SURVEYS

STATE LAWS ON EARLY LICENSE REVOCATION FOR DRIVING WHILE UNDER THE INFLUENCE: MODEL REVOCATION ON ADMINISTRATIVE DETERMINATION LAW. Revised Edition. United States Department of Transportation, National Highway Traffic Safety Administration, 400 Seventh Street, Southwest, Washington, D.C. 20590. 1984.

LAW REVIEWS AND PERIODICALS

CONTEMPORARY DRUG PROBLEMS. Xerox/University Microfilms, Incorporated, 300 North Zeeb Road, Ann Arbor, Michigan 48106. Annual.

DRUG ABUSE AND ALCOHOLISM REVIEW. The Hayworth Press, Incorporated, 12 West Thirty-second Street, New York, New York 10001. Quarterly.

DRUG ABUSE LAW REVIEW. Clark Boardman Company, Limited, 435 Hudson Street, New York, New York 10014. Annual.

DRUG ENFORCEMENT. Drug Enforcement Administration, United States Department of Justice. Superintendent of Documents, United States Government Printing Office, Washington, D.C. 20402. Quarterly.

JOURNAL OF DRUG ISSUES. P.O. Box 4021, Tallahassee, Florida 32315. Quarterly.

JOURNAL OF STUDIES ON ALCOHOL. Journal of Studies on Alcohol, Incorporated, New Brunswick, New Jersey 08901. Quarterly.

NEWSLETTERS AND NEWSPAPERS

ALCOHOL AND DRUG ABUSE REPORT. National Association of State Alcohol and Drug Abuse Directors, 444 North Capitol Street, Northwest, Suite 520, Washington, D.C. 20001. Monthly.

ALCOHOL BEVERAGE LEGAL BRIEFS. National Alcohol Beverage Control Association, 4216 King Street West, Alexandria, Virginia 22302. Bimonthly.

ALCOHOL WEEK. Inside Washington Publishers, P.O. Box 7167, Ben Franklin Station, Washington, D.C. 20004. Weekly.

ALCOHOLISM AND DRUG ABUSE WEEK. Manisses Communications Group, Incorporated, P.O. Box 3357, Wayland Square, Providence, Rhode Island 02906. Four issues per month.

ALCOHOLISM REPORT. Manisses Communications Group, Incorporated, P.O. Box 3357, Wayland Square, Providence, Rhode Island 02906. Seventeen issues per year.

DRAM SHOP AND ALCOHOL REPORTER. Seak, Incorporated, P.O. Box 590, Falmouth, Massachusetts 02541. Monthly.

FROM THE STATE CAPITALS - ALCOHOLIC BEVERAGE CONTROL. Wakeman Walworth, Incorporated, 300 North Washington Street, Suite 204, Alexandria, Virginia 22314. Weekly.

THE NATIONAL REPORT ON SUBSTANCE ABUSE. Buraff Publications, Incorporated, 1350 Connecticut Avenue, Northwest, Suite 1000, Washington, D.C. 20036. Semimonthly.

NATIONAL ASSOCIATION OF STATE ALCOHOL AND DRUG ABUSE DIRECTORS. Monthly Report. National Association of State Alcohol and Drug Abuse Directors, 918 F Street, Northwest, Suite 400, Washington, D.C. 20004. Monthly.

SUBSTANCE ABUSE REPORT. Business Research Publications, 817 Broadway, New York, New York 10003. Semimonthly.

WASHINGTON BEVERAGE INSIGHT. George Wells and Associates, Incorporated, 1120 Connecticut Avenue Northwest, Suite 270, Washington, D.C. 20036. Thirty-six issues per year.

BIBLIOGRAPHIES

A BIBLIOGRAPHY OF DRUG ABUSE, INCLUDING ALCOHOL AND TOBACCO. Theodora Andrews. Libraries Unlimited, Incorporated. P.O. Box 3988, Englewood, Colorado 80155-3988. 1977.

LIQUOR LAW VIOLATORS. In Handling Misdemeanor Cases . F. Lee Bailey and Henry R. Rothblatt. Lawyers Cooperative Publishing Company, Aqueduct Building, Rochester, New York 14694. 1978.

NOBODY'S CLIENTS: FEMALES, ALCOHOL AND SKID ROW. Harvey A. Moore and Bonnie Yegidis. Journal of Drug Issues, Volume 12, Number 3, Summer 1982, Tallahassee, Florida 32306. Quarterly.

YOUTH AND THE FORBIDDEN FRUIT: EXPERIENCES WITH CHANGES IN LEGAL DRINKING AGE IN NORTH AMERICA. Evelyn R. Vingilis and Katherine DeGenova. Journal of Criminal Justice, Volume 12, Number 2, 1984, Pergamon Press, Maxwell House, Farfield Park, Elmsford, New York 10523. Quarterly.

ASSOCIATIONS AND PROFESSIONAL SOCIETIES

ALCOHOL AND DRUG PROBLEMS ASSOCIATION OF NORTH AMERICA. 444 North Capitol Street, Northwest, Suite 706, Washington, D.C. 20001. (202) 737-4340.

ALCOHOL POLICY COUNCIL. P.O. Box 148, Waterford, Virginia 22190. (703) 882-3933.

JOINT COMMITTEE OF THE STATES TO STUDY ALCOHOLIC BEVERAGE LAWS. c/o National Alcoholic Beverage Control Association, 4216 King Street, West Alexandria, Virginia 22302. (703) 578-4200.

NATIONAL ASSOCIATION OF STATE ALCOHOL AND DRUG ABUSE DIRECTORS. 444 North Capitol Street, Northwest, Suite 520, Washington, D.C. 20001. (202) 783-6868.

NATIONAL BLACK ALCOHOLISM COUNCIL. 53 West Jackson, Suite 828, Chicago, Illinois 60604. (312) 663-5780.

NATIONAL CATHOLIC COUNCIL ON ALCOHOLISM AND RELATED DRUG PROBLEMS. 1200 Varnum Road, Northeast, Washington, D.C. 20017. (202) 832-3811.

RESEARCH CENTERS, INSTITUTES, CLEARINGHOUSES

AL-ANON FAMILY GROUP HEADQUARTERS. P.O. Box 862, Midtown Station, New York, New York 10018. (212) 302-7240.

ALCOHOLICS ANONYMOUS WORLD SERVICES. P.O. Box 459, Grand Central Station, New York, New York 10163. (212) 686-1100.

ALCOHOL RESEARCH INFORMATION SERVICE. 1106 East Oakland, Lansing, Michigan 48906. (517) 485-9900.

AMERICAN COUNCIL ON ALCOHOLISM. White Marsh Business Center, 5024 Campbell Boulevard, Baltimore, Maryland 21236. (301) 931-9393.

BEER INSTITUTE. 1225 I Street, Northwest, Washington, D.C. 20005. (202) 737-2337.

CENTER OF ALCOHOL STUDIES. Rutgers University, Smithers Hall, Busch Campus, Piscataway, New Jersey 08854. (201) 932-2190.

DISTILLED SPIRITS COUNCIL OF THE UNITED STATES. 1250 I Street, Northwest, Washington, D.C. 20005. (202) 628-3544.

DRUG LAW UNIT/UNIT IN LAW AND DENTISTRY/UNIT IN LAW AND PHARMACY. Temple Law School, 1719 North Broad Street, Philadelphia, Pennsylvania 19122. (215) 787-1278.

DRUGINFO: ALCOHOL USE/ABUSE. University of Minnesota, College of Pharmacy, Drug Information Services, 3-160 Health Services Center, Unit F, 308 Harvard Street, Southeast, Minneapolis, Minnesota 55455. (612) 624-6492.

LICENSED BEVERAGE INFORMATION COUNCIL. 1250 I Street, Northwest, Washington, D.C. 20005. (202) 682-8826.

NATIONAL CLEARINGHOUSE ON ALCOHOL AND DRUG INFORMATION. 6000 Executive Boulevard, Rockville, Maryland 20857. (301) 468-2600.

NATIONAL COUNCIL ON ALCOHOLISM. 12 West Twenty-first Street, New York, New York 10010. (212) 206-6770.

NATIONAL INSTITUTE ON ALCOHOL ABUSE AND ALCOHOLISM. Parklawn Building, 5600 Fishers Lane, Rockville, Maryland 20857. (301) 443-3885.

OFFENDER REHABILITATION. Division of the Public Defender Service, 451 Indiana Avenue, Northwest, Washington, D.C. 20001. (202) 628-1200.

STATISTICS SOURCES

ADVANCE DATA FROM VITAL HEALTH AND STATISTICS. United States Department of Health and Human Services, Public Health Service, 200 Independence Avenue, Southwest, Washington, D.C. 20201.

ALCOHOL AND DRUGS IN THE WORKPLACE: COSTS, CONTROLS AND CONTROVERSIES. Bureau of National Affairs, Incorporated, 1231 Twenty-fifth Street, Northwest, Washington, D.C. 20037.

DRUG USE AMONG AMERICAN HIGH SCHOOL STUDENTS. Lloyd D. Johnston, Jerald G. Bachman and Patrick M. O'Malley. National Institute on Drug Abuse, Division of Research, 5600 Fishers Lane, Rockville, Maryland 20857. 1977.

NATIONAL REPORT ON SUBSTANCE ABUSE. Buraff Publications, 2445 M Street, Northwest, Suite 275, Washington, D.C. 20037.

NATIONAL SURVEY ON DRUG ABUSE: MAIN FINDINGS 1979. United States Department of Health and Human Services, Alcohol, Drug Abuse, and Mental Health Administration, 200 Independence Avenue, Southwest, Washington, D.C. 20201.

OTHER SOURCES

ALCOHOL AND DRUG ABUSE PROGRAMS FOR LAWYERS AND JUDGES. Standing Committee on Bar Activities and Services, Division of Bar Services. American Bar Association, 750 North Lake Shore Drive, Chicago, Illinois 60611. 1982.

FIFTH SPECIAL REPORT TO THE U.S. CONGRESS ON ALCOHOL AND HEALTH. United States Department of Health and Human Services, Public Health Service, Alcohol, Drug Abuse, and Mental Health Administration, National Institute on Alcohol Abuse and Alcoholism. United States Government Printing Office, Superintendent of Documents, Washington, D.C. 20402. 1984.

LEGAL OPINIONS ON THE CONFIDENTIALITY OF ALCOHOL AND DRUG ABUSE PATIENT RECORDS 1975-1978. National Institute of Drug Abuse, 5600 Fishers Lane, Rockville, Maryland 29857. 1980.

THE NEW HOPE OF SOLUTION. Presidential Committee on Drunk Driving. Final Report available from the Superintendent of Documents, United States Government Printing Office, Washington, D.C. 20402. 1983.

TASK FORCE REPORT: DRUNKENNESS, ANNOTATIONS, CONSULTANTS' PAPERS AND RELATED MATERIALS. United States Task Force on Drunkenness. Superintendent of Documents, United States Government Printing Office, Washington, D.C. 20402. 1967.

YOUTH, ALCOHOL, AND SOCIAL POLICY. Howard T. Blane and Morris E. Chafetz, Editors. Plenum Publishing Corporation, 233 Spring Street, New York, New York 10013. 1979.

ALCOHOL, TOBACCO AND FIREARMS BUREAU
See also: LICENSING, INDUSTRIAL AND INTELLECTUAL

STATUTES, CODES, STANDARDS, UNIFORM LAWS

ALCOHOL, TOBACCO AND FIREARMS: EXPLOSIVES LAW AND REGULATIONS, 1982. Treasury Department, Bureau of Alcohol, Tobacco and Firearms. Superintendent of Documents, United States Government Printing Office, Washington, D.C. 20402. 1982.

STATE LAWS AND PUBLISHED ORDINANCES: FIREARMS, 1989. Treasury Department, Bureau of Alcohol, Tobacco and Firearms. Superintendent of Documents, United States Printing Office, Washington, D.C. 20402. 1990.

HANDBOOKS, MANUALS, FORMBOOKS

ALCOHOL, TOBACCO AND FIREARMS ARSON INVESTIGATIVE GUIDE. Treasury Department, Bureau of Alcohol, Tobacco and Firearms. Superintendent of Documents, United States Government Printing Office, Washington, D.C. 20402. 1986.

IDENTIFICATION OF FIREARMS WITHIN THE PURVIEW OF THE NATIONAL FIREARMS ACT. Treasury Department, Bureau of Alcohol, Tobacco and Firearms. Superintendent of Documents, United States Government Printing Office, Washington, D.C. 20402. 1984.

YOUR GUIDE TO FEDERAL FIREARMS REGULATION, 1984-85. Treasury Department, Bureau of Alcohol, Tobacco and Firearms. Superintendent of Documents, United States Government Printing Office, Washington, D.C. 20402. 1984.

NEWSLETTERS AND NEWSPAPERS

BUREAU OF ALCOHOL, TOBACCO AND FIREARMS QUARTERLY BULLETIN. Treasury Department, Bureau of Alcohol, Tobacco and Firearms. Superintendent of Documents, United States Government Printing Office, Washington, D.C. 20402. Quarterly.

ALIENS
See: CITIZENS AND CITIZENSHIP; EMIGRATION AND IMMIGRATION

ALIMONY
See: FAMILY LAW

ALTERNATIVE DISPUTE RESOLUTION
See: DISPUTE RESOLUTION

AMERICAN BAR ASSOCIATION

STATUTES, CODES, STANDARDS, UNIFORM LAWS

AMERICAN BAR ASSOCIATION CONSTITUTION AND BYLAWS, RULES OF PROCEDURE OF THE HOUSE OF DELEGATES. Policy Administration Office, American Bar Association, 750 North Lake Shore Drive, Chicago, Illinois 60611. Annual.

CODE OF PROFESSIONAL RESPONSIBILITY BY STATE. Center for Professional Responsibility, American Bar Association, 750 North Lake Shore Drive, Chicago, Illinois 60611. 1981.

STANDARDS FOR APPROVAL OF LAW SCHOOLS WITH INTERPRETATIONS REVISIONS. Legal Education and Admissions to the Bar Section, American Bar Association, 750 North Lake Shore Drive, Chicago, Illinois 60611. 1989.

STANDARDS FOR CRIMINAL JUSTICE. Second Edition. Criminal Justice Section, American Bar Association, 750 North Lake Shore Drive, Chicago, Illinois 60611. 1986.

STANDARDS FOR IMPOSING LAWYER SANCTIONS. Center for Professional Responsibility, American Bar Association, 750 North Lake Shore Drive, Chicago, Illinois 60611. 1986.

STANDARDS FOR JUDICIAL EDUCATION. Judicial Administration Division, American Bar Association, 750 North Lake Shore Drive, Chicago, Illinois 60611. 1984.

AMERICAN BAR ASSOCIATION

STANDARDS FOR PROVIDERS OF CIVIL LEGAL SERVICES TO THE POOR. Standing Committee on Lawyer Referral and Information Service, American Bar Association, 750 North Lake Shore Drive, Chicago, Illinois 60611. 1986.

LOOSELEAF SERVICES AND REPORTERS

ABA/BNA LAWYERS' MANUAL ON PROFESSIONAL CONDUCT. Bureau of National Affairs, 1231 Twenty-fifth Street, Northwest, Washington, D.C. 20037. 1984- .

FORMAL AND INFORMAL ETHICS OPINIONS. American Bar Association, Committee on Ethics and Professional Responsibility, 750 North Lake Shore Drive, Chicago, Illinois 60611. 1985.

INFORMAL ETHICS OPINIONS. American Bar Association, Committee on Ethics and Professional Responsibility, 750 North Lake Shore Drive, Chicago, Illinois 60611. 1975. (Volumes one and two).

INITIATIVE: A RESOURCE GUIDE TO DEVELOPING SUCCESSFUL MINORITY PROGRAMS. Commission on Opportunities for Minorities in the Profession, American Bar Association, 750 North Lake Shore Drive, Chicago, Illinois 60611. 1989.

MAP PACKAGE: ALTERNATIVE DISPUTE RESOLUTION. Bar Services Division and Special Committee on Dispute Resolution, American Bar Association, 750 North Lake Shore Drive, Chicago, Illinois 60611. 1983.

MAP PACKAGE: NON-DUES SOURCES OF INCOME. American Bar Association, Bar Services Division, 750 North Lake Shore Drive, Chicago, Illinois 60611. 1983.

OPINIONS ON PROFESSIONAL ETHICS. American Bar Association, Committee on Ethics and Professional Responsibilities, 750 North Lake Shore Drive, Chicago, Illinois 60611. 1967.

PRIVATE BAR INVOLVEMENT IN THE DELIVERY OF LEGAL SERVICES: ABA MAP PROGRAM MODELS AND PACKAGES. American Bar Association, Division of Bar Services, 750 North Lake Shore Drive, Chicago, Illinois 60611. 1982.

HANDBOOKS, MANUALS, FORMBOOKS

THE BAR FOUNDATION HANDBOOK. Bar Services Division, American Bar Association, 750 North Lake Shore Drive, Chicago, Illinois 60611. 1986.

RESOURCE: A PRO BONO MANUAL. Special Committee on Lawyers' Public Service Responsibility, American Bar Association, 750 North Lake Shore Drive, Chicago, Illinois 60611. 1983.

LAW REVIEWS AND PERIODICALS

ABA JOURNAL. American Bar Association, 750 North Lake Shore Drive, Chicago, Illinois 60611. Monthly.

ADMINISTRATIVE LAW REVIEW. Administrative Law Section, American Bar Association, 750 North Lake Shore Drive, Chicago, Illinois 60611. Quarterly.

ANIMAL LAW REPORT. Young Lawyers Division, American Bar Association, 750 North Lake Shore Drive, Chicago, Illinois 60611. Quarterly.

ANTITRUST LAW JOURNAL. Section of Antitrust Law, American Bar Association, 750 North Lake Shore Drive, Chicago, Illinois 60611. Quarterly.

BAR LEADER. Bar Services Division, American Bar Association, 750 North Lake Shore Drive, Chicago, Illinois 60611. Bimonthly.

BARRISTER. Young Lawyers Division, American Bar Association, 750 North Lake Shore Drive, Chicago, Illinois 60611. Quarterly.

BRIEF. Section of Tort and Insurance Practice, American Bar Association, 750 North Lake Shore Drive, Chicago, Illinois 60611. Quarterly.

BUSINESS LAWYER. Section on Business Law, American Bar Association, 750 North Lake Shore Drive, Chicago, Illinois 60611. Quarterly.

CHINA LAW REPORTER. International Law and Practice Section, American Bar Association, 750 North Lake Shore Drive, Chicago, Illinois 60611. Quarterly.

COMPLEAT LAWYER. General Practice Section, American Bar Association, 750 North Lake Shore Drive, Chicago, Illinois 60611. Quarterly.

CRIMINAL JUSTICE. Section on Criminal Law, American Bar Association, 750 North Lake Shore Drive, Chicago, Illinois 60611. Quarterly.

DISPUTE RESOLUTION. Standing Committee on Dispute Resolution, American Bar Association, 750 North Lake Shore Drive, Chicago, Illinois 60611. Quarterly.

FAMILY ADVOCATE. Section of Family Law, American Bar Association, 750 North Lake Shore Drive, Chicago, Illinois 60611. Quarterly.

FAMILY LAW QUARTERLY. Section of Family Law, American Bar Association, 750 North Lake Shore Drive, Chicago, Illinois 60611. Quarterly.

FIDELITY AND SURETY NEWS. Tort and Insurance Practice Section, American Bar Association, 750 North Lake Shore Drive, Chicago, Illinois 60611. Quarterly.

FRANCHISE LAW JOURNAL. Forum on Franchising, American Bar Association, 750 North Lake Shore Drive, Chicago, Illinois 60611. Quarterly.

HUMAN RIGHTS. Individual Rights and Responsibilities Section, American Bar Association, 750 North Lake Shore Drive, Chicago, Illinois 60611. Three issues per year.

INTER-AMERICAN LEGAL MATERIALS. International Law and Practice Section, American Bar Association, 750 North Lake Shore Drive, Chicago, Illinois 60611. Quarterly.

INTERNATIONAL LAWYER. Section of International Law and Practice, American Bar Association, 750 North Lake Shore Drive, Chicago, Illinois 60611. Quarterly.

THE JUDGES JOURNAL. Judicial Administrative Division, American Bar Association, 750 North Lake Shore Drive, Chicago, Illinois 60611. Quarterly.

JURIMETRICS: JOURNAL OF LAW, SCIENCE AND TECHNOLOGY. Science and Technology Section, American Bar Association, 750 North Lake Shore Drive, Chicago, Illinois 60611. Quarterly.

JUVENILE AND CHILD WELFARE LAW REPORTER. National Legal Resource Center for Child Advocacy and Protection, American Bar Association, 750 North Lake Shore Drive, Chicago, Illinois 60611. Monthly.

THE LABOR LAWYER. Labor and Employment Law Section, American Bar Association, 750 North Lake Shore Drive, Chicago, Illinois 60611. Quarterly.

LAW AND SOCIAL INQUIRY. Journal of the American Bar Foundation, American Bar Association, 750 North Lake Shore Drive, Chicago, Illinois 60611. Quarterly.

LAW PRACTICE MANAGEMENT. Law Practice Management Section, American Bar Association, 750 North Lake Shore Drive, Chicago, Illinois 60611. Eight times a year.

LITIGATION. Section of Litigation, American Bar Association, 750 North Lake Shore Drive, Chicago, Illinois 60611. Quarterly.

MEMBERNET. Young Lawyers Division, American Bar Association, 750 North Lake Shore Drive, Chicago, Illinois 60611. Quarterly.

MENTAL AND PHYSICAL DISABILITY LAW REPORTER. Commission on the Mentally Disabled, American Bar Association, 750 North Lake Shore Drive, Chicago, Illinois 60611. Bimonthly.

NATURAL RESOURCES AND ENVIRONMENT. Section of Natural Resources Law, American Bar Association, 750 North Lake Shore Drive, Chicago, Illinois 60611. Quarterly.

PREVIEW OF UNITED STATES SUPREME COURT CASES. Public Education Division, American Bar Association, 750 North Lake Shore Drive, Chicago, Illinois 60611. 12-14 issues from September to June.

PROBATE AND PROPERTY. Real Property, Probate and Trust Law Section, American Bar Association, 750 North Lake Shore Drive, Chicago, Illinois 60611. Bimonthly.

PROFESSIONAL LAWYER. Center for Professional Responsibility, American Bar Association, 750 North Lake Shore Drive, Chicago, Illinois 60611. Quarterly.

PUBLIC CONTRACT LAW JOURNAL. Section of Public Contract Law, American Bar Association, 750 North Lake Shore Drive, Chicago, Illinois 60611. Semiannual.

REAL PROPERTY, PROBATE AND TRUST JOURNAL. Section of Real Property, Probate and Trust Law, American Bar Association, 750 North Lake Shore Drive, Chicago, Illinois 60611. Quarterly.

RECENT ETHICS OPINIONS. American Bar Association, Committee on Ethics and Professional Responsibility, 750 North Lake Shore Drive, Chicago, Illinois 60611. 1985- .

STUDENT LAWYER. Law Student Division, American Bar Association, 750 North Lake Shore Drive, Chicago, Illinois 60611. Monthly.

TAX LAWYER. Section of Taxation, American Bar Association, 750 North Lake Shore Drive, Chicago, Illinois 60611. Quarterly.

THE URBAN LAWYER. Urban, State and Local Government Law Section, American Bar Association, 750 North Lake Shore Drive, Chicago, Illinois 60611. Quarterly.

NEWSLETTERS AND NEWSPAPERS

ADMINISTRATIVE LAW NEWS. American Bar Association, Administrative Law Section, 750 North Lake Shore Drive, Chicago, Illinois 60611. Quarterly.

ADMIRALTY LAW NEWSLETTER. Young Lawyers Division, American Bar Association, 750 North Lake Shore Drive, Chicago, Illinois 60611. Semiannually.

THE AFFILIATE. Young Lawyers Division, American Bar Association, 750 North Lake Shore Drive, Chicago, Illinois 60611. Bimonthly.

AIR AND SPACE LAWYER. Forum on Air and Space, American Bar Association, 750 North Lake Shore Drive, Chicago, Illinois 60611. Quarterly.

ALTERNATIVES NEWSLETTER. Young Lawyers Division, American Bar Association, 750 North Lake Shore Drive, Chicago, Illinois 60611. Three times a year.

ANTITRUST. Antitrust Law Section, American Bar Association, 750 North Lake Shore Drive, Chicago, Illinois 60611. Quarterly.

ARSON REPORTER. Young Lawyers Division, Arson Project Committee, American Bar Association, 750 North Lake Shore Drive, Chicago, Illinois 60611. Monthly.

BIFOCAL. Young Lawyers Division, American Bar Association, 750 North Lake Shore Drive, Chicago, Illinois 60611. Quarterly.

BULLETIN OF LAW, SCIENCE AND SCIENCE TECHNOLOGY. Science and Technology Section, American Bar Association, 750 North Lake Shore Drive, Chicago, Illinois 60611. Bimonthly.

BUSINESS LAWYER UPDATE. Business Law Section, American Bar Association, 750 North Lake Shore Drive, Chicago, Illinois 60611. Bimonthly.

CHILD ADVOCACY AND PROTECTION NEWSLETTER. Young Lawyers Division, American Bar Association, 750 North Lake Shore Drive, Chicago, Illinois 60611. Semiannually.

CHILD SUPPORT PROSECUTORS' BULLETIN. Center for Children and the Law, American Bar Association, 750 North Lake Shore Drive, Chicago, Illinois 60611. Bimonthly.

CLIENT COUNSELING UPDATE. Client Counseling Competition Committee, American Bar Association, 750 North Lake Shore Drive, Chicago, Illinois 60611. Irregular.

COMMUNICATIONS LAWYER. Forum Committee on Communications Law of the American Bar Association, 750 North Lake Shore Drive, Chicago, Illinois 60611. Quarterly.

COMMUNITY LAW WEEK NEWSLETTER. Young Lawyers Division, American Bar Association, 750 North Lake Shore Drive, Chicago, Illinois 60611. Semiannually.

THE CONSTRUCTION LAWYER. Forum on the Construction Industry, American Bar Association, 750 North Lake Shore Drive, Chicago, Illinois 60611. Quarterly.

COURT OF APPEALS FOR THE FEDERAL CIRCUIT NEWSLETTER. Litigation Section, American Bar Association, 750 North Lake Shore Drive, Chicago, Illinois 60611. Bimonthly.

DIS/ABILITY LAW BRIEFS. Commission on the Mentally Disabled, American Bar Association, 750 North Lake Shore Drive, Chicago, Illinois 60611. Quarterly.

ENTERTAINMENT AND SPORTS LAWYER, Forum Committee on Entertainment and Sports Industries, American Bar Association, 750 North Lake Shore Drive, Chicago, Illinois 60611. Three times per year.

ENVIRONMENTAL LAW. Standing Committee on Environmental Law, American Bar Association, 750 North Lake Shore Drive, Chicago, Illinois 60611. Quarterly.

FEDERAL TRIAL NEWS. National Conference of Federal Trial Judges, American Bar Association, 750 North Lake Shore Drive, Chicago, Illinois 60611. Irregular.

HEALTH LAWYER. Forum on Health Law, American Bar Association, 750 North Lake Shore Drive, Chicago, Illinois 60611. Three to four times per year.

INTELLIGENCE REPORT. Standing Committee on Law and National Security, American Bar Association, 750 North Lake Shore Drive, Chicago, Illinois 60611. Monthly.

INTERNATIONAL LAW NEWS. Section of International Law and Practice, American Bar Association, 750 North Lake Shore Drive, Chicago, Illinois 60611. Quarterly.

LABOR AND EMPLOYMENT LAW. Labor and Employment Law Section, American Bar Association, 750 North Lake Shore Drive, Chicago, Illinois 60611. Quarterly.

LAMPLIGHTER. Standing Committee on Legal Assistance for Military Personnel, American Bar Association, 750 North Lake Shore Drive, Chicago, Illinois 60611. Quarterly.

LAWYERS FOR THE ARTS NEWSLETTER. Young Lawyers Division, American Bar Association, 750 North Lake Shore Drive, Chicago, Illinois 60611. Semiannually.

LAWYERS' PROFESSIONAL LIABILITY UPDATE. Standing Committee on Lawyers' Professional Liability, American Bar Association, 750 North Lake Shore Drive, Chicago, Illinois 60611. Annual.

LAWYERS TITLE GUARANTY FUNDS NEWSLETTER. Standing Committee on Lawyers' Title Guaranty Funds, American Bar Association, 750 North Lake Shore Drive, Chicago, Illinois 60611. Irregular.

LITIGATION COMMITTEE NEWSLETTER. Young Lawyers Division, American Bar Association, 750 North Lake Shore Drive, Chicago, Illinois 60611. Quarterly.

LITIGATION NEWS. Litigation Section, American Bar Association, 750 North Lake Shore Drive, Chicago, Illinois 60611. Quarterly.

LRE PROJECT EXCHANGE. Special Committee on Youth Education for Citizenship, American Bar Association, 750 North Lake Shore Drive, Chicago, Illinois 60611. Three times per year.

LRE REPORT. Special Committee on Youth Education for Citizenship, American Bar Association, 750 North Lake Shore Drive, Chicago, Illinois 60611. Three times per year.

NATURAL RESOURCES LAW NEWSLETTER. Natural Resources Law Section, American Bar Association, 750 North Lake Shore Drive, Chicago, Illinois 60611. Five times per year.

PARASCOPE. Committee of Appellate Staff Attorneys, American Bar Association, 750 North Lake Shore Drive, Chicago, Illinois 60611. Quarterly.

PASSPORT TO LEGAL UNDERSTANDING: THE NEWSLETTER ON PUBLIC EDUCATION PROGRAMS AND MATERIALS. Commission on Public Understanding About the Law, American Bar Association, 750 North Lake Shore Drive, Chicago, Illinois 60611. Semiannually.

PREVIEW OF UNITED STATES SUPREME COURT CASES. Public Education Division, American Bar Association, 750 North Lake Shore Drive, Chicago, Illinois 60611. Sixteen issues from September to June.

PTC NEWSLETTER. Section of Patent, Trademark and Copyright Law, American Bar Association, 750 North Lake Shore Drive, Chicago, Illinois 60611. Quarterly.

PUBLIC CONTRACT NEWSLETTER. Public Contract Law Section, American Bar Association, 750 North Lake Shore Drive, Chicago, Illinois 60611. Quarterly.

SECTION OF TAXATION NEWSLETTER. Taxation Section, American Bar Association, 750 North Lake Shore Drive, Chicago, Illinois 60611. Quarterly.

SENIOR LAWYER. Senior Lawyers Division, American Bar Association, 750 North Lake Shore Drive, Chicago, Illinois 60611. Quarterly.

SPECIAL COURT NEWS. National Conference of Special Court Judges, American Bar Association, 750 North Lake Shore Drive, Chicago, Illinois 60611. Quarterly.

UTILITY SECTION NEWSLETTER. Public Utility Law Section, American Bar Association, 750 North Lake Shore Drive, Chicago, Illinois 60611. Quarterly.

WASHINGTON LETTER. Governmental Affairs Office, American Bar Association, 750 North Lake Shore Drive, Chicago, Illinois 60611. Monthly.

BIBLIOGRAPHIES

AMERICAN BAR ASSOCIATION CATALOG: BOOKS, PERIODICALS, PAMPHLETS AND AUDIOVISUAL MATERIALS. American Bar Association, 750 North Lake Shore Drive, Chicago, Illinois 60611. Annual.

DIRECTORIES

AMERICAN BAR ASSOCIATION DIRECTORY. American Bar Association, 750 North Lake Shore Drive, Chicago, Illinois 60611. Annual.

DIRECTORY OF ASSOCIATIONS OF WOMEN LAWYERS. Division for Bar Services, American Bar Association, 750 North Lake Shore Drive, Chicago, Illinois 60611. 1987.

DIRECTORY OF BAR ACTIVITIES. Division of Bar Services, American Bar Association, 750 North Lake Shore Drive, Chicago, Illinois 60611. 1983.

DIRECTORY OF BAR ASSOCIATIONS. Division of Bar Services, American Bar Association, 750 North Lake Shore Drive, Chicago, Illinois 60611. Annual.

ASSOCIATIONS AND PROFESSIONAL SOCIETIES

AMERICAN BAR ASSOCIATION, COMMISSION ON ADVERTISING. 750 North Lake Shore Drive, Chicago, Illinois 60611. (312) 988-5000.

AMERICAN BAR ASSOCIATION, COMMISSION ON DISPUTE RESOLUTION. 750 North Lake Shore Drive, Chicago, Illinois 60611. (312) 988-5000.

AMERICAN BAR ASSOCIATION, COMMISSION ON FEDERAL JUDICIAL COMPENSATION. 750 North Lake Shore Drive, Chicago, Illinois 60611. (312) 988-5000.

AMERICAN BAR ASSOCIATION, COMMISSION ON THE MENTALLY DISABLED. 750 North Lake Shore Drive, Chicago, Illinois 60611. (312) 988-5000.

AMERICAN BAR ASSOCIATION, COMMISSION ON PUBLIC UNDERSTANDING ABOUT THE LAW. 750 North Lake Shore Drive, Chicago, Illinois 60611. (312) 988-5000.

AMERICAN BAR ASSOCIATION, COMMITTEE ON CONTINUING EDUCATION OF THE BAR. 750 North Lake Shore Drive, Chicago, Illinois 60611. (312) 988-5000.

AMERICAN BAR ASSOCIATION, COMMITTEE ON CUSTOMS LAW. 750 North Lake Shore Drive, Chicago, Illinois 60611. (312) 988-5000.

AMERICAN BAR ASSOCIATION, COMMITTEE ON ENVIRONMENTAL LAW. 750 North Lake Shore Drive, Chicago, Illinois 60611. (312) 988-5000.

AMERICAN BAR ASSOCIATION, COMMITTEE ON ETHICS AND PROFESSIONAL RESPONSIBILITY. 750 North Lake Shore Drive, Chicago, Illinois 60611. (312) 988-5000.

AMERICAN BAR ASSOCIATION, COMMITTEE ON FEDERAL JUDICIAL IMPROVEMENTS. 750 North Lake Shore Drive, Chicago, Illinois 60611. (312) 988-5000.

AMERICAN BAR ASSOCIATION, COMMITTEE ON FEDERAL JUDICIARY. 750 North Lake Shore Drive, Chicago, Illinois 60611. (312) 988-5000.

AMERICAN BAR ASSOCIATION, COMMITTEE ON INTERNATIONAL LAW. 750 North Lake Shore Drive, Chicago, Illinois 60611. (312) 988-5000.

AMERICAN BAR ASSOCIATION, COMMITTEE ON JUDICIAL SELECTION, TENURE AND COMPENSATION. 750 North Lake Shore Drive, Chicago, Illinois 60611. (312) 988-5000.

AMERICAN BAR ASSOCIATION, COMMITTEE ON LAW AND NATIONAL SECURITY. 750 North Lake Shore Drive, Chicago, Illinois 60611. (312) 988-5000.

AMERICAN BAR ASSOCIATION, COMMITTEE ON LAWYER REFERRAL AND INFORMATION SERVICES. 750 North Lake Shore Drive, Chicago, Illinois 60611. (312) 988-5000.

AMERICAN BAR ASSOCIATION, COMMITTEE ON LAWYER'S IN THE ARMED FORCES. 750 North Lake Shore Drive, Chicago, Illinois 60611. (312) 988-5000.

AMERICAN BAR ASSOCIATION, COMMITTEE ON LAWYER'S PROFESSIONAL LIABILITY. 750 North Lake Shore Drive, Chicago, Illinois 60611. (312) 988-5000.

AMERICAN BAR ASSOCIATION, COMMITTEE ON LAWYER'S PUBLIC SERVICE RESPONSIBILITY. 750 North Lake Shore Drive, Chicago, Illinois 60611. (312) 988-5000.

AMERICAN BAR ASSOCIATION, COMMITTEE ON LAWYER'S RESPONSIBILITY FOR CLIENT PROTECTION. 750 North Lake Shore Drive, Chicago, Illinois 60611. (312) 988-5000.

AMERICAN BAR ASSOCIATION, COMMITTEE ON LAWYER'S TITLE GUARANTY FUNDS. 750 North Lake Shore Drive, Chicago, Illinois 60611. (312) 988-5000.

AMERICAN BAR ASSOCIATION, COMMITTEE ON LEGAL AID AND INDIGENT DEFENDANTS. 750 North Lake Shore Drive, Chicago, Illinois 60611. (312) 988-5000.

AMERICAN BAR ASSOCIATION, COMMITTEE ON LEGAL ASSISTANTS. 750 North Lake Shore Drive, Chicago, Illinois 60611. (312) 988-5000.

AMERICAN BAR ASSOCIATION, COMMITTEE ON MILITARY LAW. 750 North Lake Shore Drive, Chicago, Illinois 60611. (312) 988-5000.

AMERICAN BAR ASSOCIATION, COMMITTEE ON PATENT, COPYRIGHT AND TRADEMARK LAW. 750 North Lake Shore Drive, Chicago, Illinois 60611. (312) 988-5000.

AMERICAN BAR ASSOCIATION, COMMITTEE ON PROFESSIONAL DISCIPLINE. 750 North Lake Shore Drive, Chicago, Illinois 60611. (312) 988-5000.

AMERICAN BAR ASSOCIATION, COMMITTEE ON PROFESSIONAL UTILIZATION AND CAREER DEVELOPMENT. 750 North Lake Shore Drive, Chicago, Illinois 60611. (312) 988-5000.

AMERICAN BAR ASSOCIATION, COMMITTEE ON PUBLIC EDUCATION. 750 North Lake Shore Drive, Chicago, Illinois 60611. (312) 988-5000.

AMERICAN BAR ASSOCIATION, COMMITTEE ON RETIREMENT OF LAWYERS. 750 North Lake Shore Drive, Chicago, Illinois 60611. (312) 988-5000.

AMERICAN BAR ASSOCIATION, COMMITTEE ON SPECIALIZATION, 750 North Lake Shore Drive, Chicago, Illinois 60611. (312) 988-5000.

AMERICAN BAR ASSOCIATION, COMMITTEE ON WORLD ORDER UNDER THE LAW. 750 North Lake Shore Drive, Chicago, Illinois 60611. (312) 988-5000.

AMERICAN BAR ASSOCIATION, CONSORTIUM ON LEGAL SERVICES AND THE PUBLIC. 750 North Lake Shore Drive, Chicago, Illinois 60611. (312) 988-5000.

AMERICAN BAR ASSOCIATION, CONSORTIUM ON PROFESSIONAL COMPETENCE. 750 North Lake Shore Drive, Chicago, Illinois 60611. (312) 988-5000.

AMERICAN BAR ASSOCIATION, COORDINATING COMMITTEE ON IMMIGRATION LAW. 750 North Lake Shore Drive, Chicago, Illinois 60611. (312) 988-5000.

AMERICAN BAR ASSOCIATION, COORDINATING COMMITTEE ON RICO. 750 North Lake Shore Drive, Chicago, Illinois 60611. (312) 988-5000.

AMERICAN BAR ASSOCIATION, COORDINATING GROUP ON ENERGY LAW. 750 North Lake Shore Drive, Chicago, Illinois 60611. (312) 988-5000.

AMERICAN BAR ASSOCIATION, FORUM COMMITTEE ON AIR AND SPACE LAW. 750 North Lake Shore Drive, Chicago, Illinois 60611. (312) 988-5000.

AMERICAN BAR ASSOCIATION, FORUM COMMITTEE ON COMMUNICATIONS LAW. 750 North Lake Shore Drive, Chicago, Illinois 60611. (312) 988-5000.

AMERICAN BAR ASSOCIATION, FORUM COMMITTEE ON CONSTRUCTION INDUSTRY. 750 North Lake Shore Drive, Chicago, Illinois 60611. (312) 988-5000.

AMERICAN BAR ASSOCIATION, FORUM COMMITTEE ON FRANCHISING. 750 North Lake Shore Drive, Chicago, Illinois 60611. (312) 988-5000.

AMERICAN BAR ASSOCIATION, FORUM COMMITTEE ON HEALTH LAW. 750 North Lake Shore Drive, Chicago, Illinois 60611. (312) 988-5000.

AMERICAN BAR ASSOCIATION, FORUM COMMITTEE ON THE ENTERTAINMENT AND SPORTS INDUSTRIES. 750 North Lake Shore Drive, Chicago, Illinois 60611. (312) 988-5000.

AMERICAN BAR ASSOCIATION, JUDICIAL ADMINISTRATION DIVISION. 750 North Lake Shore Drive, Chicago, Illinois 60611. (312) 988-5000.

AMERICAN BAR ASSOCIATION, JUDICIAL ADMINISTRATION DIVISION, COMMITTEE ON THE TRAFFIC COURT PROGRAM. 750 North Lake Shore Drive, Chicago, Illinois 60611. (312) 988-5000.

AMERICAN BAR ASSOCIATION, JUDICIAL ADMINISTRATION DIVISION, LAWYERS CONFERENCE. 750 North Lake Shore Drive, Chicago, Illinois 60611. (312) 988-5000.

AMERICAN BAR ASSOCIATION, JUDICIAL ADMINISTRATION DIVISION, NATIONAL CONFERENCE OF FEDERAL TRIAL JUDGES. 750 North Lake Shore Drive, Chicago, Illinois 60611. (312) 988-5000.

AMERICAN BAR ASSOCIATION, JUDICIAL ADMINISTRATION DIVISION, NATIONAL CONFERENCE OF SPECIAL COURT JUDGES. 750 North Lake Shore Drive, Chicago, Illinois 60611. (312) 988-5000.

AMERICAN BAR ASSOCIATION, JUDICIAL ADMINISTRATION DIVISION, NATIONAL CONFERENCE OF STATE TRIAL JUDGES. 750 North Lake Shore Drive, Chicago, Illinois 60611. (312) 988-5000.

AMERICAN BAR ASSOCIATION, LAW STUDENT DIVISION. 750 North Lake Shore Drive, Chicago, Illinois 60611. (312) 988-5000.

AMERICAN BAR ASSOCIATION, NATIONAL CONFERENCE GROUP OF LAWYERS AND COLLECTION AGENCIES. 750 North Lake Shore Drive, Chicago, Illinois 60611. (312) 988-5000.

AMERICAN BAR ASSOCIATION, NATIONAL CONFERENCE GROUP OF LAWYERS AND CORPORATE FIDUCIARIES. 750 North Lake Shore Drive, Chicago, Illinois 60611. (312) 988-5000.

AMERICAN BAR ASSOCIATION, NATIONAL CONFERENCE GROUP OF LAWYERS AND ENVIRONMENTAL DESIGN PROFESSIONS. 750 North Lake Shore Drive, Chicago, Illinois 60611. (312) 988-5000.

AMERICAN BAR ASSOCIATION, NATIONAL CONFERENCE GROUP OF LAWYERS AND LIFE INSURANCE COMPANIES. 750 North Lake Shore Drive, Chicago, Illinois 60611. (312) 988-5000.

AMERICAN BAR ASSOCIATION, NATIONAL CONFERENCE GROUP OF LAWYERS AND REALTORS. 750 North Lake Shore Drive, Chicago, Illinois 60611. (312) 988-5000.

AMERICAN BAR ASSOCIATION, NATIONAL CONFERENCE GROUP OF LAWYERS AND REPRESENTATIVES OF THE MEDIA. 750 North Lake Shore Drive, Chicago, Illinois 60611. (312) 988-5000.

AMERICAN BAR ASSOCIATION, NATIONAL CONFERENCE GROUP OF LAWYERS, INSURANCE COMPANIES AND ADJUSTERS. 750 North Lake Shore Drive, Chicago, Illinois 60611. (312) 988-5000.

AMERICAN BAR ASSOCIATION, SECTION OF ADMIRALTY AND MARITIME LAW. 750 North Lake Shore Drive, Chicago, Illinois 60611. (312) 988-5000.

AMERICAN BAR ASSOCIATION, SECTION OF ANTITRUST LAW. 750 North Lake Shore Drive, Chicago, Illinois 60611. (312) 988-5000.

AMERICAN BAR ASSOCIATION, SECTION OF BUSINESS LAW. 750 North Lake Shore Drive, Chicago, Illinois 60611. (312) 988-5000.

AMERICAN BAR ASSOCIATION, SECTION OF FAMILY LAW. 750 North Lake Shore Drive, Chicago, Illinois 60611. (312) 988-5000.

AMERICAN BAR ASSOCIATION, SECTION OF GENERAL PRACTICE. 750 North Lake Shore Drive, Chicago, Illinois 60611. (312) 988-5000.

AMERICAN BAR ASSOCIATION, SECTION OF INDIVIDUAL RIGHTS AND RESPONSIBILITIES. 750 North Lake Shore Drive, Chicago, Illinois 60611. (312) 988-5000.

AMERICAN BAR ASSOCIATION, SECTION OF LABOR AND EMPLOYMENT LAW. 750 North Lake Shore Drive, Chicago, Illinois 60611. (312) 988-5000.

AMERICAN BAR ASSOCIATION, SECTION OF LEGAL EDUCATION AND ADMISSION TO THE BAR. 750 North Lake Shore Drive, Chicago, Illinois 60611. (312) 988-5000.

AMERICAN BAR ASSOCIATION, SECTION OF LITIGATION. 750 North Lake Shore Drive, Chicago, Illinois 60611. (312) 988-5000.

AMERICAN BAR ASSOCIATION, SECTION OF NATURAL RESOURCES, ENERGY AND ENVIRONMENTAL LAW. 750 North Lake Shore Drive, Chicago, Illinois 60611. (312) 988-5000.

AMERICAN BAR ASSOCIATION, SECTION OF PATENT, TRADEMARK, AND COPYRIGHT LAW. 750 North Lake Shore Drive, Chicago, Illinois 60611. (312) 988-5000.

AMERICAN BAR ASSOCIATION, SECTION OF PUBLIC UTILITY LAW. 750 North Lake Shore Drive, Chicago, Illinois 60611. (312) 988-5000.

AMERICAN BAR ASSOCIATION, SECTION OF REAL PROPERTY, PROBATE AND TRUST LAW. 750 North Lake Shore Drive, Chicago, Illinois 60611. (312) 988-5000.

AMERICAN BAR ASSOCIATION, SECTION OF SCIENCE AND TECHNOLOGY. 750 North Lake Shore Drive, Chicago, Illinois 60611. (312) 988-5000.

AMERICAN BAR ASSOCIATION, SECTION OF TAXATION. 750 North Lake Shore Drive, Chicago, Illinois 60611. (312) 988-5000.

AMERICAN BAR ASSOCIATION, SECTION OF TORTS AND INSURANCE PRACTICE. 750 North Lake Shore Drive, Chicago, Illinois 60611. (312) 988-5000.

AMERICAN BAR ASSOCIATION, SECTION OF URBAN, STATE AND LOCAL GOVERNMENT. 750 North Lake Shore Drive, Chicago, Illinois 60611. (312) 988-5000.

AMERICAN BAR ASSOCIATION, SPECIAL COMMITTEE ON COOPERATION WITH THE NEWSPAPER PUBLISHERS ASSOCIATION. 750 North Lake Shore Drive, Chicago, Illinois 60611. (312) 988-5000.

AMERICAN BAR ASSOCIATION, SPECIAL COMMITTEE ON DELIVERY OF LEGAL SERVICES. 750 North Lake Shore Drive, Chicago, Illinois 60611. (312) 988-5000.

AMERICAN BAR ASSOCIATION, SPECIAL COMMITTEE ON EVALUATION OF DISCIPLINARY ENFORCEMENT. 750 North Lake Shore Drive, Chicago, Illinois 60611. (312) 988-5000.

AMERICAN BAR ASSOCIATION, SPECIAL COMMITTEE ON HOUSING AND URBAN DEVELOPMENT LAW. 750 North Lake Shore Drive, Chicago, Illinois 60611. (312) 988-5000.

AMERICAN BAR ASSOCIATION, SPECIAL COMMITTEE ON LAWYERS IN GOVERNMENT. 750 North Lake Shore Drive, Chicago, Illinois 60611. (312) 988-5000.

AMERICAN BAR ASSOCIATION, SPECIAL COMMITTEE ON PREPAID LEGAL SERVICE. 750 North Lake Shore Drive, Chicago, Illinois 60611. (312) 988-5000.

AMERICAN BAR ASSOCIATION, YOUNG LAWYERS DIVISION. 750 North Lake Shore Drive, Chicago, Illinois 60611. (312) 988-5000.

ONLINE DATABASES

ABA/NET. American Bar Association, ABA/Net, 14800 Conference Center Drive, Chantilly, Virginia 22021-3805.

AMBAR. Information Services, American Bar Association, 750 North Lake Shore Drive, Chicago, Illinois 60611.

AMERICAN BAR ASSOCIATION DATABASE. Available on WestLaw, West Publishing Company, P.O. Box 64526, 50 West Kellogg Boulevard, St. Paul, Minnesota 55164-0526.

AMERICAN BAR ASSOCIATION LIBRARY. Available on Lexis, Mead Data Central, P.O. Box 933, Dayton, Ohio 45401.

AUDIOVISUALS

LAWYERING TO HOUSE THE HOMELESS: CREATIVE TOOLS. Consortium for Professional Education, American Bar Association, 750 North Lake Shore Drive, Chicago, Illinois 60611. 1990. (2 Videocassettes).

PEOPLE'S COURT. Consortium for Professional Education, American Bar Association, 750 North Lake Shore Drive, Chicago, Illinois 60611. 1977. (1 Videocassette).

PERCEPTIONS - MINORITY LAWYERS: WHERE ARE WE NOW? Young Lawyers Division, American Bar Association, 750 North Lake Shore Drive, Chicago, Illinois 60611. 1983. (1 Videocassette).

REDUCING COSTS AND DELAYS IN TRIAL COURTS. Consortium for Professional Education, American Bar Association, 750 North Lake Shore Drive, Chicago, Illinois 60611. 1988. (2 Videocassettes).

SUPREME COURT. Young Lawyers Division, American Bar Association, 750 North Lake Shore Drive, Chicago, Illinois 60611. 1979. (1 Videocassette).

OTHER SOURCES

ATTACKING LITIGATION COSTS AND DELAY: FINAL REPORT OF THE ACTION COMMISSION TO REDUCE COURT COSTS AND DELAY. American Bar Association, Commission to Reduce Court Costs and Delays, 750 North Lake Shore Drive, Chicago, Illinois 60611. 1984.

ATTACKING LITIGATION COSTS AND DELAY: PROJECT REPORTS AND RESEARCH FINDINGS SUPPORTING THE FINAL REPORT OF THE ACTION COMMITTEE TO REDUCE COURT COSTS AND DELAY. American Bar Association, Commission to Reduce Court Costs and Delays, 750 North Lake Shore Drive, Chicago, Illinois 60611. 1984.

REPORT OF THE ABA TASK FORCE ON THE GENERAL PRACTITIONER AND THE ORGANIZED BAR. General Practice Section, American Bar Association, 750 North Lake Shore Drive, Chicago, Illinois 60611. 1984.

REPORT OF THE AMERICAN BAR ASSOCIATION'S TASK FORCE AND ADVISORY BOARD ON INTEREST ON LAWYER TRUST ACCOUNTS. Interest on Lawyer Trust Accounts Task Force and Advisory Board, American Bar Association, 750 North Lake Shore Drive, Chicago, Illinois 60611. 1982.

AMUSEMENTS
See: ENTERTAINMENT LAW

ANARCHISM
See: POLITICAL CRIMES AND OFFENSES; TERRORISM

ANIMALS
See also: WILDLIFE

TEXTBOOKS AND GENERAL WORKS

ANIMAL LAW. David S. Favre and Murray Loring. Quorum Books, Greenwood Publishing Group, Incorporated, 88 Post Road West, Westport, Connecticut 06881. 1983.

ANIMAL RIGHTS AND HUMAN OBLIGATION. Tom Regan and Peter Singer. Prentice-Hall, Incorporated, 113 Sylvan Avenue, Englewood Cliffs, New Jersey 07632. 1976.

ANIMAL RIGHTS AND THE LAW. Daniel S. Moretti. Oceana Publications, 75 Main Street, Dobbs Ferry, New York 10522. 1984.

ANIMALS' RIGHTS: CONSIDERED IN RELATION TO SOCIAL PROGRESS. Revised Edition. Henry S. Salt. Society for Animal Rights, 421 South State Street, Clarks Summit, Pennsylvania 18411. 1980.

THE CASE FOR ANIMAL RIGHTS. Tom Regan. University of California Press. 2120 Berkeley Way, Berkeley, California 94720. 1983.

ETHICS AND ANIMALS. Harlan B. Miller and William H. Williams. The Humana Press, P.O. Box 2148, Clifton, New Jersey 07015. 1983.

THE EXTENDED CIRCLE: A COMMONPLACE BOOK OF ANIMAL RIGHTS. Jon Wynne-Tyson, Editor. Paragon House Publications, 90 Fifth Avenue, New York, New York 10011. 1988.

IN DEFENSE OF ANIMALS. Peter Singer, Editor. Perennial Library, HarperCollins Publishers, Incorporated, 10 East Fifty-third Street, New York, New York 10022. 1986.

INTERESTS AND RIGHTS: THE CASE AGAINST ANIMALS. R.G. Frey. Oxford University Press, 200 Madison Avenue, New York, New York 10016. 1980.

OF MICE, MODELS, AND MEN: A CRITICAL EVALUATION OF ANIMAL RESEARCH. Andrew N. Rowman. State University of New York Press, State University Plaza, Albany, New York 12246. 1984.

ON THE FIFTH DAY: ANIMAL RIGHTS AND HUMAN ETHICS. Centaur Books, Incorporated, 799 Broadway, New York, New York 10003. 1983.

RETURNING TO EDEN: ANIMAL RIGHTS AND HUMAN RESPONSIBILITY. Michael W. Fox. Robert E. Kreiger Publishing Company, Incorporated, P.O. Box 9542, Malabar, Florida 32902-9542. 1986.

LAW REVIEWS AND PERIODICALS

ANIMAL LAW REPORT. American Bar Association, Young Lawyers Division, 750 North Lake Shore Drive, Chicago, Illinois 60611. Quarterly.

INTERNATIONAL SOCIETY FOR ANIMAL RIGHTS REPORT. International Society for Animal Rights, Incorporated, 421 South State Street, Clarks Summit, Pennsylvania 18411. Annual.

NEWSLETTERS AND NEWSPAPERS

ACTIONLINE. Friends of Animals, Incorporated, P.O. Box 1244, Norwalk, Connecticut 06856. Five issues per year.

ANIMAL LEGAL DEFENSE FUND NEWSLETTER. Animal Legal Defense Fund, 1363 Lincoln Avenue, San Rafael, California 94901. Quarterly.

HUMAN RESEARCH REPORT. The Deem Corporation, P.O. Box 44069, Omaha, Nebraska 68144. Monthly.

BIBLIOGRAPHIES

ANIMAL WELFARE LEGISLATION: BILLS AND PUBLIC LAWS 1980-1988. Animal Welfare Information Center, National Agricultural Library, Beltsville, Maryland 20705. 1988.

A BIBLIOGRAPHY ON ANIMAL RIGHTS AND RELATED MATTERS. Charles R. Magel. University Press of America, 4720 Boston Way, Lanham, Maryland 20706. 1981.

LAW, LEGISLATION, AND PROBLEMS OF ANIMAL BEHAVIOR AND ANIMAL CONTROL: A BIBLIOGRAPHY. Lorna Peterson. Vance Bibliographies, P.O. Box 229, 112 North Charter Street, Monticello, Illinois 61856. 1989.

DIRECTORIES

ANIMAL ORGANIZATIONS AND SERVICE DIRECTORY. Animal Stories, 3004 Maple, Manhattan Beach, California 90266. Annual.

DIRECTORY OF ANIMAL CARE AND CONTROL AGENCIES. American Humane Association, Animal Protection Division, 63 Inverness Drive, East, Englewood, Colorado 80112. 1985.

ASSOCIATIONS AND PROFESSIONAL SOCIETIES

ACTIVISTS FOR PROTECTIVE ANIMAL LEGISLATION. P.O. Box 11743, Costa Mesa, California 92627. (714) 540-0583.

AMERICAN ANTI-VIVISECTION SOCIETY. Noble Plaza, Suite 204, 801 Old York Road, Jenkintown, Pennsylvania 19046. (215) 887-0816.

AMERICAN HUMANE ASSOCIATION. 9725 East Hampden, Denver, Colorado 80231. (303) 695-0811.

AMERICAN SOCIETY FOR THE PREVENTION OF CRUELTY TO ANIMALS. 441 East Ninety-second Street, New York, New York 10128. (212) 876-7700.

ANIMAL LEGAL DEFENSE FUND. 1363 Lincoln Avenue, Suite 7, San Rafael, California 94901. (415) 459-0885.

ANIMAL PROTECTION INSTITUTE OF AMERICA. P.O. Box 22505, Sacramento, California 95822. (916) 731-5521.

COMMITTEE FOR HUMANE LEGISLATION. 1506 Nineteenth Street, Northwest, Washington, D.C. 20009. (202) 483-8998.

FUND FOR ANIMALS. 200 West Fifty-seventh Street, New York, New York 10019. (212) 246-2096.

INTERNATIONAL SOCIETY FOR ANIMAL RIGHTS. 421 South State Street, Clark Summit, Pennsylvania 18411. (717) 586-2200.

NATIONAL ANTI-VIVISECTION SOCIETY. 53 West Jackson, Suite 1550, Chicago, Illinois 60604. (312) 427-6065.

PEOPLE FOR THE ETHICAL TREATMENT OF ANIMALS. P.O. Box 42516, Washington, D.C. 20015. (301) 770-7444.

RETIRED GREYHOUNDS AS PETS. P.O. Box 111, Camby, Indiana 46113. (317) 996-2154.

AUDIOVISUALS

EQUINE LAW. National Practice Institute, 330 Second Avenue South, Minneapolis, Minnesota 55401. Audiotape.

ANNUITIES
See: INSURANCE, LIFE

ANNULMENT
See: FAMILY LAW

ANTENUPTIAL CONTRACTS
See: FAMILY LAW

ANTI-DUMPING DUTIES
See: EXPORT AND IMPORT

ANTITRUST AND ECONOMICS
See also: ANTITRUST LAW

TEXTBOOKS AND GENERAL WORKS

ANTITRUST ECONOMICS AND LEGAL ANALYSIS. Eugene M. Singer. Grid, Incorporated, 4666 Indianola Avenue, Columbus, Ohio 43214. 1981.

ANTITRUST LAW, AN ECONOMIC PERSPECTIVE. Richard A. Posner. University of Chicago Press, 5801 Ellis Avenue, Third Floor, Chicago, Illinois 60637. 1978.

ANTITRUST LAW AND ECONOMICS IN A NUTSHELL. Third Edition. Ernest Gellhorn. West Publishing Company, P.O. Box 43526, 50 West Kellogg Boulevard, St. Paul, Minnesota 55164-0526. 1986.

ANTITRUST LAWS OF THE U.S.A. Third Edition. Alan D. Neale and D.G. Goyder. Cambridge University Press, 40 West Twentieth Street, New York, New York 10011. 1981.

THE ANTITRUST PENALTIES: A STUDY IN LAW AND ECONOMICS. Kenneth G. Elzinga and William Breit. Books on Demand, 300 North Zeeb Road, Ann Arbor, Michigan 48106-1346. 1989.

ANTITRUST PENALTY REFORM: AN ECONOMIC ANALYSIS. William Breit and Kenneth G. Elzinga. American Enterprise Institute for Public Policy Research, 1150 Seventeenth Street, Northwest, Washington, D.C. 20036. 1986.

ANTITRUST POLICIES AND ISSUES. Roger Sherman. Addison-Wesley Publishing Company, Incorporated, Route 128, Reading, Massachusetts 01867. 1978.

ANTITRUST POLICY: AN ECONOMIC AND LEGAL ANALYSIS. Carl Kaysent and Donald F. Turner. Harvard University Press, 79 Garden Street, Cambridge, Massachusetts 02138. 1965.

ANTITRUST POLICY IN TRANSITION: THE CONVERGENCE OF LAW AND ECONOMICS. Eleanor M. Fox and James T. Halverson, Editors. American Bar Association, 750 North Lake Shore Drive, Chicago, Illinois 60611. 1984.

ECONOMIC ANALYSIS OF ANTITRUST LAW. Second Edition. Terry Calvani and John J. Siegfried. Little, Brown and Company, 34 Beacon Street, Boston, Massachusetts 02108. 1988.

ECONOMIC THEORY AND THE ANTITRUST DILEMMA. Peter Asch. Robert E. Krieger Publishing Company, Incorporated, P.O. Box 9542, Malabar, Florida 32902-9542. 1984.

ECONOMICS AND FEDERAL ANTITRUST LAW. Herbert Hovenkamp. West Publishing Company, P.O. Box 43526, 50 West Kellogg Boulevard, St. Paul, Minnesota 55164-0526. 1985- . (Periodic Supplements).

FAIR COMPETITION: THE LAW AND ECONOMICS OF ANTITRUST POLICY. Joel B. Dirlam and Alfred Edward Kahn. Greenwood Publishing Group, Incorporated, 88 Post Road West, P.O. Box 5007, Westport, Connecticut 06881. 1970.

LAW AND ECONOMIC POLICY IN AMERICA: THE EVOLUTION OF THE SHERMAN ANTITRUST ACT. William Letwin. Greenwood Publishing Group, Incorporated, 88 Post Road West, P.O. Box 5007, Westport, Connecticut 06881. 1980.

PATENT AND ANTITRUST LAW: A LEGAL AND ECONOMIC APPRAISAL. Ward S. Bowman, Jr. University of Chicago Press, 5801 Ellis Avenue, Chicago, Illinois 60637. 1973.

LOOSELEAF SERVICES AND REPORTERS

ANTITRUST, AN ECONOMIC APPROACH. Richard Givens. Law Journal Seminars-Press, 111 Eighth Avenue, Suite 900, New York, New York 10011. 1983.

LAW REVIEWS AND PERIODICALS

ANTITRUST AND MACROECONOMICS REVIEW. Antitrust Law and Economics Review, Incorporated, P.O. Box 6134, Washington, D.C. 20044. Biannually.

ANTITRUST BULLETIN. Federal Legal Publications, 157 Chambers Street, New York, New York 10007. Quarterly.

ANTITRUST LAW AND ECONOMICS REVIEW. Beach Press, P.O. Box 3532, Vero Beach, Florida 52964. Quarterly.

ANTITRUST LAW JOURNAL. Antitrust Law Section, American Bar Association, 750 North Lake Shore Drive, Chicago, Illinois 60611. Quarterly.

JOURNAL OF LAW AND ECONOMICS. University of Chicago, 1111 East Sixtieth Street, Chicago, Illinois 60637. Semiannually.

THE JOURNAL OF REPRINTS FOR ANTITRUST LAW AND ECONOMICS. Federal Legal Publications, 157 Chambers Street, New York, New York 10007. Quarterly.

RESEARCH IN LAW AND ECONOMICS: A RESEARCH ANNUAL. Richard O. Zerbe, Jr. JAI Press, Incorporated, P.O. Box 1678, Greenwich, Connecticut 06836. Annual.

ASSOCIATIONS AND PROFESSIONAL SOCIETIES

ANTITRUST LAW SECTION. American Bar Association, 750 North Lake Shore Drive, Chicago, Illinois 60611. (312) 988-5000.

COMMITTEE TO SUPPORT THE ANTITRUST LAWS. 1300 I Street, Northwest, Suite 480, Washington, D.C. 20005. (202) 962-3862.

RESEARCH CENTERS, INSTITUTES, CLEARINGHOUSES

CENTER FOR LAW AND ECONOMIC STUDIES. Columbia University, 435 West One Hundred Sixteenth Street, Box E-2, School of Law, New York, New York 10027. (212) 854-3739.

COMPETITIVE ENTERPRISE INSTITUTE. 233 Pennsylvania Avenue, Southwest, Suite 200, Washington, D.C. 20003. (202) 547-1010.

INSTITUTE FOR LAW AND ECONOMICS. University of Pennsylvania, 3400 Chestnut Street, Philadelphia, Pennsylvania 19104-6204. (215) 898-7852.

LAW AND ECONOMICS CENTER. George Mason University, School of Law, 3401 North Fairfax Drive, Arlington, Virginia 22201-4498. (703) 841-7171.

RESEARCH PROGRAM IN COMPETITION AND BUSINESS POLICY. University of California, Los Angeles, John F. Anderson Graduate School of Management, Los Angeles, California 90024-1481. (213) 825-2200.

AUDIOVISUALS

ANTITRUST AND ECONOMICS. American Bar Association, 750 North Lake Shore Drive, Chicago, Illinois 60611. 1984. Videotape.

OTHER SOURCES

ANTITRUST POLICY IN TRANSITION: THE CONVERGENCE OF LAW AND ECONOMICS. American Bar Association, 750 North Lake Shore Drive, Chicago, Illinois 60611. 1984.

THE USE OF ECONOMISTS IN ANTITRUST LITIGATION. Jay Greenfield, Editor. American Bar Association, 750 North Lake Shore Drive, Chicago, Illinois 60611. 1984.

ANTITRUST LAW
See also: ANTITRUST AND ECONOMICS; COMMERCE DEPARTMENT; CORPORATIONS, CONSOLIDATION AND MERGER; FEDERAL TRADE COMMISSION; INTERSTATE COMMERCE COMMISSION; JUSTICE DEPARTMENT; TRADE REGULATION

STATUTES, CODES, STANDARDS, UNIFORM LAWS

UNIFORM STATE ANTITRUST ACT. National Conference of Commissioners on Uniform State Laws. Uniform Laws Annotated. West Publishing Company, P.O. Box 64526, 50 West Kellogg Boulevard, St. Paul, Minnesota 55164-0526. 1976- . (Annual Supplements).

LOOSELEAF SERVICES AND REPORTERS

ACQUISITIONS UNDER THE HART-SCOTT-RODINO ANTITRUST IMPROVEMENTS ACT. Revised Edition. Stephan M. Axinn. Law Journal Seminars-Press, Incorporated, 111 Eighth Avenue, Suite 900, New York, New York 10011. 1988- .

ANTITRUST: AN ECONOMIC APPROACH. Richard Givens. Law Journal Seminars-Press, Incorporated, 111 Eighth Avenue, Suite 900, New York, New York 10011. 1983- .

ANTITRUST AND RESTRICTIVE BUSINESS PRACTICES: INTERNATIONAL, REGIONAL AND NATIONAL REGULATION. Compiled and Edited by Julius J. Marke and Najeeb Samie. Oceana Publications, 75 Main Street, Dobbs Ferry, New York 10522. 1982- .

ANTITRUST AND TRADE REGULATION. Julian O. von Kalinowski. Matthew Bender and Company, Incorporated, 11 Penn Plaza, New York, New York 10001. 1969- .

ANTITRUST AND TRADE REGULATION REPORT. Bureau of National Affairs, Incorporated, 1231 Twenty-fifth Street, Northwest, Washington, D.C. 20037. 1961- .

ANTITRUST ASPECTS OF MERGERS AND ACQUISITIONS. Phillip A. Proger and John J. Miles. Bureau of National Affairs, Incorporated, 1231 Twenty-fifth Street, Northwest, Washington, D.C. 20037. 1990- .

ANTITRUST BASICS. Thomas V. Vakerics. Law Journal Seminars-Press, Incorporated, 111 Eighth Avenue, Suite 900, New York, New York 10011. 1985- .

ANTITRUST COUNSELING AND LITIGATION TECHNIQUES. Julian O. von Kalinowski, Editor. Matthew Bender and Company, Incorporated, 11 Penn Plaza, New York, New York 10001. 1984- .

ANTITRUST DISCOVERY HANDBOOK. Section on Antitrust Law, American Bar Association, 750 North Lake Shore Drive, Chicago, Illinois 60611. 1981- .

ANTITRUST DIVISION MANUAL. Revised Edition. United States Department of Justice, Antitrust Division. Superintendent of Documents, United States Government Printing Office, Washington, D.C. 20402. 1987- .

ANTITRUST LAWS AND TRADE REGULATION: DESK EDITION. Julian O. von Kalinowski. Matthew Bender and Company, Incorporated, 11 Penn Plaza, New York, New York 10001. 1981- .

COMPETITION LAW IN WESTERN EUROPE AND THE UNITED STATES OF AMERICA. Douwe Gijlstra and F. Murphy, Editors. West Publishing Company, P.O. Box 43526, 50 West Kellogg Boulevard, St. Paul, Minnesota 55164-0526. 1976- .

COMPLYING WITH INTERNATIONAL ANTITRUST REGULATIONS. J. Vogelsohn and others. Matthew Bender and Company, Incorporated, 11 Penn Plaza, New York, New York 10001. 1988- .

INTELLECTUAL PROPERTY AND ANTITRUST LAW. William C. Holmes. Clark Boardman Company, Limited, 435 Hudson Street, New York, New York 10014. 1983- .

MATERIALS ON ANTITRUST COMPLIANCE PROGRAMS. W.A. Hancock, Editor. Business Laws, Incorporated, P.O. Box 185, Chesterland, Ohio 44026. 1986- .

STATE ANTITRUST LAW. William T. Lifland. Law Journal Seminars-Press, Incorporated, 111 Eighth Street, Suite 900, New York, New York 10011. 1984- .

TRADE REGULATION REPORTS. Commerce Clearing House, Incorporated, 4025 West Peterson Avenue, Chicago, Illinois 60646. 1914- .

U.S. COMMON MARKET AND INTERNATIONAL ANTITRUST: A COMPARATIVE GUIDE. Second Edition. Barry E. Hawk. Harcourt Brace Jovanovich, Incorporated, 6277 Sea Harbor Drive, Orlando, Florida 32821. 1985.

HANDBOOKS, MANUALS, FORMBOOKS

ANTITRUST COMPLIANCE: A LEGAL AND BUSINESS GUIDE. James J. Garrett. Practising Law Institute, 810 Seventh Avenue, New York, New York 10019. 1978.

ANTITRUST COMPLIANCE MANUAL: A GUIDE FOR COUNSEL, MANAGEMENT, AND PUBLIC OFFICIALS. Walker B. Comegys. Practising Law Institute, 810 Seventh Avenue, New York, New York 10019. 1986.

ANTITRUST COMPLIANCE MANUAL (CORPORATE PRACTICE SERIES). John C. Scott. Bureau of National Affairs, Incorporated, 1231 Twenty-fifth Street, Northwest, Washington, D.C. 20037. 1978- .

ANTITRUST CONSENT DECREE MANUAL. Committee on Civil Practice and Procedure. American Bar Association, 750 North Lake Shore Drive, Chicago, Illinois 60611. 1979.

ANTITRUST DISCOVERY HANDBOOK. American Bar Association, 750 North Lake Shore Drive, Chicago, Illinois 60611. 1981- .

ANTITRUST EXEMPTIONS, SPECIFIC INDUSTRIES AND ACTIVITIES. Earl W. Kintner and Joseph P. Bauer. Anderson Publishing Company, 2035 Reading Road, Cincinnati, Ohio 45202. 1989.

THE ANTITRUST GOVERNMENT CONTRACTS HANDBOOK. William E. Kovacic. American Bar Association, Section of Antitrust Law, 750 North Lake Shore Drive, Chicago, Illinois 60611. 1990.

ANTITRUST GUIDE FOR HEALTH CARE COALITIONS. H. Robert Halper and John J. Miles. National Health Policy Forum, 2011 I Street, Northwest, Suite 200, Washington, D.C. 20006. 1983.

ANTITRUST GUIDE FOR INTERNATIONAL MARKETING AND DISTRIBUTION. Joel Davidow, Earl M. Prater, Jr. and Donald E. Schwartz. Bureau of National Affairs, Incorporated, 1231 Twenty-fifth Street, Northwest, Washington, D.C. 20037. 1983.

ANTITRUST LAW AND PRACTICE. Philip Marcus. West Publishing Company, P.O. Box 43526, 50 West Kellogg Boulevard, St. Paul, Minnesota 55164-0526. 1980- .

ANTITRUST LAW DEVELOPMENTS. Second Edition. American Bar Association, 750 North Lake Shore Drive, Chicago, Illinois 60611. 1984- . (Periodic Supplements).

ANTITRUST LAW DEVELOPMENTS: 1983-1988 SUPPLEMENT. Second Edition. American Bar Association, 750 North Lake Shore Drive, Chicago, Illinois 60611. 1988.

ANTITRUST LAW HANDBOOK. William C. Holmes. Clark Boardman Company, Limited, 435 Hudson Street, New York, New York 10014. 1983- .

ANTITRUST POLICY AND INTEREST-GROUP POLITICS. William F. Shughart II. Quorum Books, Greenwood Publishing Group, Incorporated, 88 Post Road West, P.O. Box 5007, Westport, Connecticut 06881. 1990.

COMPLIANCE MANUALS FOR THE NEW ANTITRUST ERA. American Bar Association, Section of Antitrust Law, 750 North Lake Shore Drive, Chicago, Illinois 60611. 1990.

CRIMINAL ANTITRUST LITIGATION MANUAL. Antitrust Section's Criminal Practice and Procedure Committee. American Bar Association, 750 North Lake Shore Drive, Chicago, Illinois 60611. 1983.

HANDBOOK ON ANTITRUST GRAND JURY INVESTIGATIONS. Second Edition. American Bar Association, 750 North Lake Shore Drive, Chicago, Illinois 60611. 1988.

MERGER STANDARDS UNDER U.S. ANTITRUST LAWS. Merger Standards Task Force, Section of Antitrust Law. American Bar Association, 750 North Lake Shore Drive, Chicago, Illinois 60611. 1981.

STATE ANTITRUST LAW AND PRACTICE. Ralph H. Folsom. Prentice-Hall, Incorporated, 113 Sylvan Avenue, Englewood Cliffs, New Jersey 07632. 1988.

TEXTBOOKS AND GENERAL WORKS

ANTITRUST. Eighth Edition. Thomas M. Jorde and Robert H. Mnookin. Gilberts Law Summaries, distributed by Law Distributors, 14415 South Main Street, Gordena, California 90248. 1983-1984.

ANTITRUST ACTION AND MARKET STRUCTURE. Don E. Waldeman. Lexington Books, 125 Spring Street, Lexington, Massachusetts 02173. 1978.

ANTITRUST ADVISER. Third Edition. Carla A. Hills, Editor. McGraw-Hill Publishing Company, 1221 Avenue of the Americas, New York, New York 10020. 1985- . (Periodic Supplements).

ANTITRUST AND MONOPOLY: ANATOMY OF POLICY FAILURE. Second Edition. Dominick T. Armentano. John Wiley and Sons, Incorporated, 605 Third Avenue, New York, New York 10158. 1990.

ANTITRUST AND REGULATED INDUSTRIES. D.C. Hjelmfelt. John Wiley and Sons, Incorporated, 605 Third Avenue, New York, New York 10158. 1985.

ANTITRUST AND THE U.S. SUPREME COURT 1829-1980. Second Edition. Michael A. Duggan. Federal Legal Publications, Incorporated, 157 Chambers Street, New York, New York 10007. 1981.

ANTITRUST COUNSELING FOR THE 1980s. Edwin S. Rockefeller. Bureau of National Affairs, Incorporated, 1231 Twenty-fifth Street, Northwest, Washington, D.C. 20037. 1983.

ANTITRUST FEDERALISM. Antitrust Law Section, American Bar Association, 750 North Lake Shore Drive, Chicago, Illinois 60611. 1988.

ANTITRUST LAW: AN ANALYSIS OF ANTITRUST PRINCIPLES AND THEIR APPLICATION. Phillip Areeda and Donald F. Turner. Little, Brown and Company, 34 Beacon Street, Boston, Massachusetts 02108. 1980- .

ANTITRUST LAW AND LOCAL GOVERNMENT. Mark R. Lee. Greenwood Publishing Group, Incorporated, 88 Post Road West, P.O. Box 5007, Westport, Connecticut 06881. 1985.

ANTITRUST LAW DEVELOPMENTS (SECOND). American Bar Association, 750 North Lake Shore Drive, Chicago, Illinois 60611. 1984- . (Periodic Supplements).

THE ANTITRUST PARADOX: A POLICY AT WAR WITH ITSELF. Robert H. Bork. Basic Books, Incorporated, 10 East Fifty-third Street, New York, New York 10022. 1980.

CRITICAL ISSUES IN INTERNATIONAL ANTITRUST AND UNFAIR COMPETITION LAW. American Bar Association, 750 North Lake Shore Drive, Chicago, Illinois 60611. 1981.

ECONOMIC ANALYSIS AND ANTITRUST LAW. Second Edition. Terry Calvani and John Siegfried. Little Brown and Company, 34 Beacon Street, Boston, Massachusetts 02108. 1988.

ECONOMICS AND ANTITRUST POLICY. Robert J. Larner and James W. Meehan, Jr. Quorum Books, Greenwood Publishing Group, Incorporated, 88 Post Road West, P.O. Box 5007, Westport, Connecticut 06881. 1989.

ECONOMIC LAW AND ECONOMIC GROWTH: ANTITRUST, REGULATION, AND THE AMERICAN GROWTH SYSTEM. George E. Garvey and Gerald J. Garvey. Greenwood Publishing Group, Incorporated, 88 Post Road West, P.O. Box 5007, Westport, Connecticut 06881. 1990.

ENTERPRISE LAW OF THE 80s: EUROPEAN AND AMERICAN PERSPECTIVES ON COMPETITION AND INDUSTRIAL ORGANIZATION. Frederick M. Rowe. American Bar Association, 750 North Lake Shore Drive, Chicago, Illinois 60611. 1980.

THE EVOLUTION OF THE SHERMAN ANTITRUST ACT. William Letwin. Greenwood Publishing Group, Incorporated, 88 Post Road West, P.O. Box 5007, Westport, Connecticut 06881. 1980.

EXTRATERRITORIAL ANTITRUST: THE SHERMAN ANTITRUST ACT AND U.S. BUSINESS ABROAD. James B. Townsend. Westview Press, 5500 Central Avenue, Boulder, Colorado 80301. 1980.

FEDERAL ANTITRUST LAW: A TREATISE ON THE ANTITRUST LAWS OF THE UNITED STATES. Earl W. Kintner. Anderson Publishing Company, 2035 Reading Road, Cincinnati, Ohio 45202. 1980.

FEDERAL CONTROL OF BUSINESS ANTITRUST LAWS. Austin T. Sticketts. Lawyers Cooperative Publishing Company, Aqueduct Building, One Graves Street, Rochester, New York 14694. 1972- .

THE FEDERAL TRADE COMMISSION: UNFAIR METHODS OF COMPETITION AND OTHER PRACTICES. Earl W. Kintner. Anderson Publishing Company, 2035 Reading Road, Cincinnati, Ohio 45202. 1988.

FOREIGN COMMERCE AND ANTITRUST LAWS. Fourth Edition. Wilbur Fugate. Little, Brown and Company, 34 Beacon Street, Boston, Massachusetts 02108. 1991.

HANDBOOK OF THE LAW OF ANTITRUST. Lawrence Anthony Sullivan. West Publishing Company, P.O. Box 43526, 50 West Kellogg Boulevard, St. Paul, Minnesota 55164-0526. 1977.

ISSUES AFTER A CENTURY OF FEDERAL COMPETITION POLICY. Robert L. Wills, Julie A. Caswell and John D. Culbertson, Editors. Free Press, 866 Third Avenue, New York, New York 10022. 1987.

THE LAW OF INTERNATIONAL CARTELS. Heinrich Kronstein. Cornell University Press, 124 Roberts Place, Ithaca, New York 14850. 1973.

LEGAL ASPECTS OF GOVERNMENT REGULATION OF BUSINESS. Third Edition. Thomas W. Dunfee and Frank Gibson. John Wiley and Sons, Incorporated, 605 Third Avenue, New York, New York 10158. 1984.

LEGAL ASPECTS OF MARKETING STRATEGY: ANTITRUST AND CONSUMER PROTECTION ISSUES. Louis W. Stern and Thomas L. Eavaldi. Prentice-Hall, Incorporated, 113 Sylvan Avenue, Englewood Cliffs, New Jersey 07632. 1984.

MARKET POWER, COMPETITION, AND ANTITRUST POLICY. William M. Baldwin. Richard D. Irwin, Incorporated, 1818 Ridge Road, Homewood, Illinois 60430. 1987.

MERGER STANDARDS UNDER U.S. ANTITRUST LAWS. American Bar Association, 750 North Lake Shore Drive, Chicago, Illinois 60611. 1981.

NEW TECHNOLOGIES IN ACQUISITIONS AND TAKEOVERS. Kenneth J. Bialkin, Arthur Fleischer, Jr. and Edward F. Greene. Law and Business/Harcourt, Brace, Jovanovich, Incorporated, 6277 Sea Harbor Drive, Orlando, Florida 32821. 1984.

NEWSPAPERS AND THE ANTITRUST LAWS. S. Chesterfield Oppenheim and Carrington Shields. Michie/Bobbs-Merrill Law Publishing, P.O. Box 7587, Charlottesville, Virginia 22906-7582. 1982.

NON-HORIZONTAL MERGERS: LAW AND POLICY. Wayne D. Collins and James R. Loftis. American Bar Association, Section of Antitrust Law, 750 North Lake Shore Drive, Chicago, Illinois 60611. 1988.

PATTERN DISCOVERY: ANTITRUST. Douglas Danner. Lawyers Cooperative Publishing Company, Aqueduct Building, One Graves Street, Rochester, New York 14694. 1981- . (Periodic Supplements).

PERSPECTIVES ON THE EXTRATERRITORIAL APPLICATION OF U.S. ANTITRUST AND OTHER LAWS. Joseph P. Griffin. American Bar Association, 750 North Lake Shore Drive, Chicago, Illinois 60611. 1979.

A PRIMER TO ANTITRUST LAW AND REGULATORY POLICY. Kenneth M. Parzych. University Press of America, 4720 Boston Way, Lanham, Maryland 20706. 1987.

PRIVATE ANTITRUST LITIGATION: NEW EVIDENCE, NEW LEARNING. Lawrence J. White, Editor. MIT Press, 55 Hayward Street, Cambridge, Massachusetts 02142. 1988.

PRIVATE LITIGATION UNDER SECTION 7 OF THE CLAYTON ACT: LAW AND POLICY. American Bar Association, Section of Antitrust Law, 750 North Lake Shore Drive, Chicago, Illinois 60611. 1989.

PROFESSIONAL SPORTS AND ANTITRUST. Warren Freedman. Quorum Books, Greenwood Publishing Group, Incorporated, 88 Post Road West, P.O. Box 5007, Westport, Connecticut 06881. 1987.

REFUSALS TO DEAL AND EXCLUSIVE DISTRIBUTORSHIPS. American Bar Association, 750 North Lake Shore Drive, Chicago, Illinois 60611. 1983.

THE ROBINSON-PATMAN ACT: POLICY AND LAW. American Bar Association, 750 North Lake Shore Drive, Chicago, Illinois 60611. 1980.

A ROBINSON-PATMAN PRIMER: A GUIDE TO THE LAW AGAINST PRICE DISCRIMINATION. Earl W. Kintner. Second Edition. Macmillan Publishing, Company, Incorporated, 866 Third Avenue, New York, New York 10022. 1979.

STATE ANTITRUST LAW. William T. Lifland. Law Journal Seminars-Press, Incorporated, 111 Eighth Avenue, Suite 900, New York, New York 10011. 1984.

STATE ANTITRUST LAWS. William J. Haynes, Jr. Bureau of National Affairs, Incorporated, 1231 Twenty-fifth Street, Northwest, Washington, D.C. 20037. 1988.

A TREATISE ON STATE ANTITRUST LAW AND ENFORCEMENT. Robert C. Fellmeth and Thomas A. Papageorge. Bureau of National Affairs, Incorporated, 1231 Twenty-fifth Street, Northwest, Washington, D.C. 20037. 1978.

THE TRIAL OF AN ANTITRUST PRICE-FIXING CASE. American Bar Association, 750 North Lake Shore Drive, Chicago, Illinois 60611. 1981.

TWENTY-FIVE YEARS OF ANTITRUST. Milton Handler. Matthew Bender and Company, Incorporated, 11 Penn Plaza, New York, New York 10001. 1973.

U.S. ANTITRUST LAW IN INTERNATIONAL PATENT AND KNOW-HOW LICENSING. American Bar Association, 750 North Lake Shore Drive, Chicago, Illinois 60611. 1981.

VERTICAL RESTRICTIONS UPON BUYERS LIMITING PURCHASES OF GOODS FROM OTHERS. American Bar Association, 750 North Lake Shore Drive, Chicago, Illinois 60611. 1982.

DIGESTS, INDEXES, ABSTRACTS

MERGER CASE DIGEST 1982. Brian E. Moran and Bruce J. Prager. American Bar Association, 750 North Lake Shore Drive, Chicago, Illinois 60611. 1984- .

ANNUALS AND SURVEYS

ANTITRUST LAW INSTITUTE (CORPORATE LAW AND PRACTICE COURSE HANDBOOK SERIES). Practising Law Institute, 810 Seventh Avenue, New York, New York 10019. Annual.

LAW REVIEWS AND PERIODICALS

ANTITRUST AND MACROECONOMICS REVIEW. Antitrust Law and Economics Review, Incorporated, P.O. Box 6134, Washington, D.C. 20044. Biannually.

ANTITRUST BULLETIN. Federal Legal Publications, Incorporated, 157 Chambers Street, New York, New York 10007. Quarterly.

ANTITRUST LAW AND ECONOMICS REVIEW. Antitrust Law and Economics, Incorporated, Box 3532, Vero Beach, Florida 32964. Quarterly.

ANTITRUST LAW JOURNAL. Antitrust Law Section, American Bar Association, 750 North Lake Shore Drive, Chicago, Illinois 60611. Quarterly.

JOURNAL OF REPRINTS FOR ANTITRUST LAW AND ECONOMICS. Federal Legal Publications, Incorporated, 157 Chambers Street, New York, New York 10007. Quarterly.

NEWSLETTERS AND NEWSPAPERS

ANTITRUST. American Bar Association, 750 North Lake Shore Drive, Chicago, Illinois 60611. Four to five issues per year.

ANTITRUST AND COMMERCE REPORT. National Association of Attorneys General, 444 North Capitol Street, Suite 403, Washington, D.C. 20001. Monthly.

ANTITRUST FOIA LOG. Washington Regulatory Reporting Associates, P.O. Box 2220, Springfield, Virginia 22152. Weekly.

BIBLIOGRAPHIES

ANTITRUST POLICY: A BIBLIOGRAPHICAL OVERVIEW. Coppa and Avery Consultants. Vance Bibliographies, P.O. Box 229, 112 North Charter Street, Monticello, Illinois 61856. 1980.

CORPORATE COUNSEL'S ANNUAL. Matthew Bender and Company, Incorporated, 11 Penn Plaza, New York, New York 10001. Annual.

FRANCHISE LAW BIBLIOGRAPHY. Section of Antitrust Law, American Bar Association, 750 North Lake Shore Drive, Chicago, Illinois 60611. 1984.

MERGER LAW BIBLIOGRAPHY: 1950 - 1980. Section of Antitrust Law, American Bar Association, 750 North Lake Shore Drive, Chicago, Illinois 60611. 1982.

ASSOCIATIONS AND PROFESSIONAL SOCIETIES

ANTITRUST LAW SECTION. American Bar Association, 750 North Lake Shore Drive, Chicago, Illinois 60611. (312) 988-5000.

COMMITTEE TO SUPPORT THE ANTITRUST LAWS. 1300 I Street, Northwest, Suite 480, Washington, D.C. 20005. (202) 737-1534.

RESEARCH CENTERS, INSTITUTES, CLEARINGHOUSES

CENTER FOR LAW AND ECONOMIC STUDIES. Columbia University, 435 West One Hundred Sixteenth Street, Box E-2, School of Law, New York, New York 10027. (212) 854-3739.

COMPETITIVE ENTERPRISE INSTITUTE. 233 Pennsylvania Avenue, Southwest, Suite 200, Washington, D.C. 20003. (202) 547-1010.

INSTITUTE FOR LAW AND ECONOMICS. University of Pennsylvania, 3400 Chestnut Street, Philadelphia, Pennsylvania 19104-6204. (215) 898-7852.

LAW AND ECONOMICS CENTER. George Mason University, School of Law, 3401 North Fairfax Drive, Arlington, Virginia 22201-4498. (703) 841-7171.

RESEARCH PROGRAM IN COMPETITION AND BUSINESS POLICY. University of California, Los Angeles, John F. Anderson Graduate School of Management, Los Angeles, California 90024-1481. (213) 825-2200.

ONLINE DATABASES

ANTITRUST AND BUSINESS REGULATIONS LIBRARY. Available on WestLaw. West Publishing Company, P.O. Box 43526, 50 West Kellogg Boulevard, St. Paul, Minnesota 55164.

ANTITRUST AND TRADE REGULATION REPORT. Bureau of National Affairs. Available on Lexis. Mead Data Central, P.O. Box 933, Dayton, Ohio 45401.

ANTITRUST AND TRADE REGULATION REPORT. Bureau of National Affairs. Available on WestLaw. West Publishing Company, 50 West Kellogg Boulevard, P.O. Box 64526, St. Paul, Minnesota 55164-0526.

ANTITRUST FOIA LOG. Washington Regulatory Reporting Associates, P.O. Box 2220, Springfield, Virginia 22152.

TRADE REGULATION LIBRARY. Lexis. Mead Data Central, 9443 Springboro Pike, P.O. Box 933, Dayton, Ohio 45401.

AUDIOVISUALS

ANTITRUST AND ECONOMICS. Videolaw Seminars, American Bar Association, 750 North Lake Shore Drive, Chicago, Illinois 60611. 1983. (4 Videocassettes).

ANTITRUST COUNSELING AND THE MARKETING PROCESS. American Bar Association, 750 North Lake Shore Drive, Chicago, Illinois 60611. 1981. Videotape.

ANTITRUST MINEFIELD. American Bar Association, 750 North Lake Shore Drive, Chicago, Illinois 60611. 1987. Videotape.

LEGAL IMPLICATIONS OF MARKETING PLANS: PRICING, PROMOTION, AND DISTRIBUTION. American Bar Association, 750 North Lake Shore Drive, Chicago, Illinois 60611. 1981.

LITIGATING RULE OF REASON CASES. American Bar Association, 750 North Lake Shore Drive, Chicago, Illinois 60611. 1987. Videotape.

PREVENTIVE ANTITRUST: CONDENSED PROGRAM. American Bar Association, 750 North Lake Shore Drive, Chicago, Illinois 60611. 1979.

PREVENTIVE ANTITRUST -- CORPORATE COMPLIANCE PROGRAMS. American Bar Association, 750 North Lake Shore Drive, Chicago, Illinois 60611. 1979.

TRIAL OF AN ANTITRUST BID-RIGGING CASE. Videolaw Seminars, American Bar Association, 750 North Lake Shore Drive, Chicago, Illinois 60611. 1985. (2 Videocassettes).

TRIAL OF AN ANTITRUST CASE. American Bar Association, 750 North Lake Shore Drive, Chicago, Illinois 60611. 1977.

OTHER SOURCES

ADVANCED ANTITRUST SEMINAR. Practising Law Institute, 810 Seventh Avenue, New York, New York 10019. Annual.

ANTITRUST CIVIL JURY INSTRUCTIONS (1980). American Bar Association, 750 North Lake Shore Drive, Chicago, Illinois 60611. 1980- . (Periodic Supplements).

THE EFFICIENCY OF PRIVATE ANTITRUST ENFORCEMENT: THE ILLINOIS BRICK DECISION. Valerie Sarris. Garland Publishing, Incorporated, 136 Madison Avenue, New York, New York 10016. 1984.

INTERLOCKING DIRECTORATES UNDER SECTION 8 OF THE CLAYTON ACT. American Bar Association, 750 North Lake Shore Drive, Chicago, Illinois 60611. 1984.

JURY INSTRUCTIONS IN CRIMINAL ANTITRUST CASES 1964-1976. American Bar Association, 750 North Lake Shore Drive, Chicago, Illinois 60611. 1978- . (Periodic Supplements).

MANUAL OF CLASS ACTION NOTICE FORMS: A PROJECT OF THE CIVIL PRACTICE COMMITTEE, ANTITRUST SECTION, AMERICAN BAR ASSOCIATION. American Bar Association, 750 North Lake Shore Drive, Chicago, Illinois 60611. 1979.

SAMPLE JURY INSTRUCTIONS IN CRIMINAL ANTITRUST CASES. American Bar Association, 750 North Lake Shore Drive, Chicago, Illinois 60611. 1984.

APPELLATE PROCEDURE
See also: CIVIL PROCEDURE; POST CONVICTION REMEDIES; TRIAL PRACTICE

STATUTES, CODES, STANDARDS, UNIFORM LAWS

FEDERAL RULES OF APPELLATE PROCEDURE, WITH FORMS. United States Supreme Court. United States Government Printing Office, Division of Public Documents, Washington, D.C. 20402. 1990.

STANDARDS RELATING TO APPELLATE COURTS. American Bar Association, 750 North Lake Shore Drive, Chicago, Illinois 60611. 1977.

LOOSELEAF SERVICES AND REPORTERS

APPEALS. (ART OF ADVOCACY SERIES). Matthew Bender and Company, Incorporated, 11 Penn Plaza, New York, New York 10001. 1981- .

APPEALS IN ALL COURTS: THE ARTS AND PITFALLS OF APPELLATE PROCEDURE. Hamline University School of Law, Advanced Legal Education, 1536 Hewitt Avenue, St. Paul, Minnesota 55104. 1985.

APPEALS TO THE ELEVENTH CIRCUIT MANUAL. Larry M. Ruth and George K. Rohdert. Butterworth Legal Publishers, 90 Stiles Road, Salem, New Hampshire 03079. 1984- .

APPEALS TO THE FIFTH CIRCUIT MANUAL. Larry M. Ruth and George K. Rohdert. Butterworth Legal Publishers, 90 Stiles Road, Salem, New Hampshire 03079. 1977- .

APPEALS TO THE THIRD CIRCUIT MANUAL. Ellen Wertheimer. Butterworth Legal Publishers, 90 Stiles Road, Salem, New Hampshire 03079. 1986- .

CALLAGHAN'S APPELLATE ADVOCACY MANUAL: A DESIGN APPROACH. John W. Cooley. Callaghan and Company, 155 Pfingsten Road, Deerfield, Illinois 60015. 1989.

HANDBOOKS AND MANUALS

APPELLATE ADVOCACY. Peter J. Carre, Azike A. Ntephe and Helen C. Trainor, Editors. American Bar Association, 750 North Lake Shore Drive, Chicago, Illinois 60611. 1981.

APPELLATE ADVOCACY IN A NUTSHELL. Alan D. Hornstein. West Publishing Company, 50 West Kellogg Boulevard, St. Paul, Minnesota 55164-0526. 1984.

APPELLATE COURTS AND LAWYERS: INFORMATION GATHERING IN THE ADVERSARY SYSTEM. Thomas B. Marvell. Greenwood Publishing Group, Incorporated, 88 Post Road West, P.O. Box 5007, Westport, Connecticut 06881. 1978.

APPELLATE LITIGATION. Richardson R. Lynn. John Wiley and Sons, Incorporated, 605 Third Avenue, New York, New York 10158. 1984.

APPELLATE PRACTICE IN THE UNITED STATES. Second Edition. Robert L. Stern. Bureau of National Affairs, Incorporated, 1231 Twenty-fifth Street, Northwest, Washington, D.C. 20037. 1989.

ATTITUDES OF UNITED STATES JUDGES TOWARD LIMITATION OF ORAL ARGUMENT AND OPINION WRITING IN THE UNITED STATES COURTS OF APPEALS. Jerry Goldman. United States Federal Judicial Center, 1520 H Street, Northwest, Washington, D.C. 20005. 1975.

BRIEFING AND ARGUING FEDERAL APPEALS. Frederick Bernays Wiener. Bureau of National Affairs, Incorporated, 1231 Twenty-fifth Street, Northwest, Washington, D.C. 20037. 1967.

CALLAGHAN'S APPELLATE ADVOCACY MANUAL: A DESIGN APPROACH. John W. Cooley. Callaghan and Company, 155 Pfingsten Road, Deerfield, Illinois 60015. 1989.

THE COMMON LAW TRADITION: DECIDING APPEALS. Karl Nickerson Llewellyn. Little, Brown and Company, 34 Beacon Street, Boston, Massachusetts 02108. 1960.

COMPARATIVE REPORT ON INTERNAL OPERATING PROCEDURES OF UNITED STATES COURTS OF APPEAL. James E. Langer and Steven Planders. United States Federal Judicial Center, 1520 H Street, Northwest, Washington, D.C. 20005. 1973.

COURTS OF APPEALS IN THE FEDERAL JUDICIAL SYSTEM. J. Woodford Howard. Princeton University Press, 41 William Street, Princeton, New Jersey 08540. 1981.

AN EVALUATION OF THE CIVIL APPEALS MANAGEMENT PLAN: AN EXPERIMENT IN JUDICIAL ADMINISTRATION. Jerry Goldman. United States Federal Judicial Center, 1520 H Street, Northwest, Washington, D.C. 20005. 1982.

FEDERAL APPELLATE PRACTICE. James D. Crawford. Practising Law Institute, 810 Seventh Avenue, New York, New York 10019. 1984- . (Annual).

FEDERAL COURTS OF APPEALS MANUAL. Second Edition. David G. Knibb. West Publishing Company, 50 West Kellogg Boulevard, St. Paul, Minnesota 55164-0526. 1990.

FUNDAMENTALS OF MODERN APPELLATE ADVOCACY. Richard J. Martineau. Lawyers Cooperative Publishing Company, Aqueduct Building, Rochester, New York 14694. 1985.

HANDBOOK OF APPELLATE ADVOCACY. UCLA Moot Court Honors Program. West Publishing Company, 50 West Kellogg Boulevard, St. Paul, Minnesota 55164-0526. 1986.

HOW TO HANDLE AN APPEAL. Third Edition. Herbert Monte Levy. Practising Law Institute, 810 Seventh Avenue, New York, New York 10019. 1990.

INEFFECTIVE JUSTICE: EVALUATING THE PRE-APPEAL CONFERENCE. Sage Publications, Incorporated, 2455 Teller Road, Newbury Park, California 91320. 1980.

INTERNAL OPERATING PROCEDURES OF APPELLATE COURTS. Robert Allen Leflar. American Bar Foundation, 750 North Lake Shore Drive, Chicago, Illinois 60611. 1976.

POST CONVICTION REMEDIES: A SELF-HELP MANUAL. Daniel E. Manville and George N. Brezna. Oceana Publications, Incorporated, 75 Main Street, Dobbs Ferry, New York 10522. 1988.

THE PRACTICAL LAWYER'S MANUAL OF TRIAL AND APPELLATE PRACTICE. American Law Institute-American Bar Association, 4025 Chestnut Street, Philadelphia, Pennsylvania 19104. 1986.

STANDARDS RELATING TO APPEALS AND COLLATERAL REVIEW. Michael C. Moran. Ballinger Division, HarperCollins Publishers, 10 East Fifty-third Street, New York, New York 10022. 1977.

SUPREME COURT PRACTICE. Sixth Edition. Robert Stern. Bureau of National Affairs, Incorporated, 1231 Twenty-fifth Street, Northwest, Washington, D.C. 20037. 1986.

WINNING AN APPEAL: A STEP-BY-STEP EXPLANATION OF HOW TO PREPARE AND PRESENT YOUR CASE EFFICIENTLY AND WITH MAXIMUM EFFECTIVENESS, WITH A SAMPLE BRIEF. Myron Moskovitz. Michie Company, P.O. Box 7587, Charlottesville, Virginia 22906-7582. 1985.

TEXTBOOKS AND GENERAL WORKS

A CASE ON APPEAL: A JUDGE'S VIEW. Herbert Funk Goodwich and Ralph M. Carson. American Law Institute--American Bar Association Committee on Continuing Professional Education. American Law Institute, 4025 Chestnut Street, Philadelphia, Pennsylvania 19104. 1967.

EFFICIENCY AND JUSTICE IN APPEALS: METHODS AND SELECTED MATERIALS. American Bar Association, Task Force on Appellate Advocacy, 750 North Lake Shore Drive, Chicago, Illinois 60611. 1978.

FEDERAL APPELLATE PRACTICE. Minnesota Institute of Legal Education, 29 South Fifth Street, Minneapolis, Minnesota 55402. 1989.

MANAGING APPEALS IN FEDERAL COURTS. Federal Judicial Center, 1520 H Street, Northwest, Washington, D.C. 20005. 1988.

MODERN APPELLATE PRACTICE: FEDERAL AND STATE CIVIL APPEALS. Robert J. Martineau. Lawyers Cooperative Publishing Company, Aqueduct Building, Rochester, New York 14694. 1983- .

PROBLEMS AND MATERIALS ON MOTION AND APPELLATE ADVOCACY. Paul J. Zwier. National Institute for Trial Advocacy, Notre Dame Law School, Notre Dame, Indiana 46556. 1990.

LAW REVIEWS AND PERIODICALS

APPELLATE COURT ADMINISTRATION REVIEW. National Conference of Appellate Court Clerks, c/o National Center for State Courts, 300 Newport Avenue, Williamsburg, Virginia 23187. Annual.

Encyclopedia of Legal Information Sources • 2nd Ed. — ARBITRATION AND AWARD

NEWSLETTER AND NEWSPAPERS

COURT OF APPEALS FOR THE FEDERAL CIRCUIT NEWSLETTER. Litigation Section, American Bar Association, 750 North Lake Shore Drive, Chicago, Illinois 60611. Semiannually.

THE THIRD BRANCH: NEWSLETTER OF THE FEDERAL COURTS. Administrative Office of the United States Courts, Office of Legislative and Public Affairs, 811 Vermont Avenue, Northwest, Room 655, Washington, D.C. 20544.

BIBLIOGRAPHIES

ANNOTATED BIBLIOGRAPHY FOR USE OF COMMISSION ON REVISION OF THE FEDERAL COURT APPELLATE SYSTEM. United States Federal Judicial Center, 1520 H Street, Northwest, Washington, D.C. 20005. 1973.

APPELLATE PROCEDURE: A BIBLIOGRAPHY OF APPELLATE ADVOCACY. Randall T. Bell, Peter J. Carre, Azike A. Ntephe and Helen C. Trainor. American Bar Association, 750 North Lake Shore Drive, Chicago, Illinois 60611. 1981.

BIBLIOGRAPHY: STATE APPELLATE COURT WORKLOAD AND DELAY. National Center for State Courts, 300 Newport Avenue, Williamsburg, Virginia 23185. 1983.

ASSOCIATIONS AND PROFESSIONAL SOCIETIES

COMMITTEE OF APPELLATE STAFF ATTORNEYS. American Bar Association, 750 North Lake Shore Drive, Chicago, Illinois 60611. (312) 988-5000.

NATIONAL CONFERENCE OF APPELLATE COURT CLERKS. National Center for State Courts, 300 Newport Avenue, Williamsburg, Virginia 23185. (804) 253-2000.

RESEARCH CENTERS, INSTITUTES, CLEARINGHOUSES

AMERICAN JUDICATURE SOCIETY. 25 East Washington, Chicago, Illinois 60602. (312) 558-6900.

AUDIOVISUALS

APPELLATE ADVOCACY. National Institute for Trial Advocacy, Notre Dame Law School, Notre Dame, Indiana 46556. 1980. Videotape.

EFFECTIVE APPELLATE ADVOCACY. Myron H. Bright. National Practice Institute, 330 Second Avenue South, Minneapolis, Minnesota 55401. Videotape.

EFFECTIVE ARGUMENT TO THE COURT. American Bar Association, 750 North Lake Shore Drive, Chicago, Illinois 60611. 1989. Videotape.

NEW PERSPECTIVES IN ADVOCACY: TRIAL AND APPELLATE. Myron Bright. National Practice Institute, 330 Second Avenue South, Minneapolis, Minnesota 55401. Videotape.

OTHER SOURCES

APPELLATE JUSTICE IMPROVEMENT PROJECT: COLLECTED PAPERS. National Center for State Courts, 300 Newport Avenue, Williamsburg, Virginia 23187. 1981.

THE APPELLATE PROCESS: ALI-ABA COURSE OF STUDY. American Law Institute-American Bar Association, 4025 Chestnut Street, Philadelphia, Pennsylvania 19104. 1990.

CERTIFYING QUESTIONS OF STATE LAW: EXPERIENCE OF FEDERAL JUDGES. Carroll Seron. United States Federal Judicial Center, 1520 H Street, Northwest, Washington, D.C. 20005. 1983.

FEDERAL APPELLATE PRACTICE: ALI-ABA COURSE OF STUDY MATERIALS. American Law Institute-American Bar Association Course of Study. American Law Institute, 4025 Chestnut Street, Philadelphia, Pennsylvania 19104. 1983.

ARBITRATION AND AWARD
See also: DISPUTE RESOLUTION; LABOR ARBITRATION

LOOSELEAF SERVICES AND REPORTERS

ARBITRATION AND THE LICENSING PROCESS. Robert Goldscheider and Michel de Haas, Editors. Clark Boardman Company, Limited, 435 Hudson Street, New York, New York 10014. 1984- . (Periodic Supplements).

ARBITRATOR'S QUALIFICATIONS REPORT. R.C. Simpson Company, 25 North Maple Avenue, Ridgewood, New Jersey 07451. 1956- .

BNA'S ALTERNATIVE DISPUTE RESOLUTION REPORT. Bureau of National Affairs, Incorporated, 1231 Twenty-fifth Street, Northwest, Washington, D.C. 20037. 1987- . (Biweekly).

DOMKE ON COMMERCIAL ARBITRATION (THE LAW AND PRACTICE OF COMMERCIAL ARBITRATION). Martin Domke. Callaghan and Company, 155 Pfingsten Road, Deerfield, Illinois 60015. 1984- .

INDUSTRIAL RELATIONS GUIDE. Prentice-Hall, Incorporated, 113 Sylvan Avenue, Englewood Cliffs, New Jersey 07632. 1969- . (Biweekly Supplements).

INTER-AMERICAN COMMERCIAL ARBITRATION. Charles R. Norberg. Oceana Publications, 75 Main Street, Dobbs Ferry, New York 10522. 1988.

INTERNATIONAL CHAMBER OF COMMERCE ARBITRATION. W. Lawrence Craig and others. Oceana Publications, 75 Main Street, Dobbs Ferry, New York 10522. 1984- .

INTERNATIONAL COMMERCIAL ARBITRATION. Clive Schnitthoff, Editor. Oceana Publications, 75 Main Street, Dobbs Ferry, New York 10522. 1974- .

INTERNATIONAL COMMERCIAL ARBITRATION: CASES UNDER THE NEW YORK CONVENTION. Giorgio Gaja. Oceana Publications, 75 Main Street, Dobbs Ferry, New York 10522. 1978- .

INTERNATIONAL COMMERCIAL ARBITRATION: COMMERCIAL ARBITRATION LAW IN ASIA AND THE PACIFIC. Kenneth R. Simmonds and Brian H.W. Hill. Oceana Publications, 75 Main Street, Dobbs Ferry, New York 10522. 1987- .

INTERNATIONAL COMMERCIAL ARBITRATION REFERENCE AND FINDING TOOLS. Brian H.W. Hill, Editor. Oceana Publications, 75 Main Street, Dobbs Ferry, New York 10522. 1988.

LABOR ARBITRATION AWARDS. Commerce Clearing House, Incorporated, 4025 West Peterson Avenue, Chicago, Illinois 60646. 1961- .

LABOR ARBITRATION INFORMATION SYSTEM. Labor Relations Press, P.O. Box 579, Fort Washington, Pennsylvania 19034. 1970- .

LABOR ARBITRATION REPORTS. Bureau of National Affairs, Incorporated, 1231 Twenty-fifth Street, Northwest, Washington, D.C. 20037. 1946- .

RESPONDING TO UNION ORGANIZING CAMPAIGNS. Robert Lewis, Roger S. Kaplan and Philip Rosen. Matthew Bender and Company, Incorporated, 11 Penn Plaza, New York, New York 10001. 1984- .

UNCITRAL MODEL LAW OF INTERNATIONAL COMMERCIAL ARBITRATION: A DOCUMENTARY HISTORY. Igor I. Kavass and Arno Liivak. William S. Hein and Company, 1285 Main Street, Buffalo, New York 14209. 1985- .

USING ARBITRATION IN COMMERCIAL DISPUTES. Norman Solovay, David R. Foley and Amy R. Ignatin. Matthew Bender and Company, Incorporated, 11 Penn Plaza, New York, New York 10001. 1984- .

WORLD ARBITRATION REPORTER. Hans Smit and Vratislav Pechota. Butterworth Legal Publishers, 90 Stiles Road, Salem, New Hampshire 03079. 1988- .

HANDBOOKS, MANUALS, FORMBOOKS

COLLECTIVE BARGAINING: HOW IT WORKS AND WHY: A MANUAL OF THEORY AND PRACTICE. Thomas R. Colosi and Arthur E. Berkeley. American Arbitration Association, 140 West Fifty-first Street, New York, New York 10020. 1986.

CONSTRUCTION ARBITRATION HANDBOOK. James Acret. Shepard's/McGraw-Hill, P.O. Box 1235, Colorado Springs, Colorado 80901. 1985- . (Periodic Supplements).

INTERNATIONAL ARBITRATION. Thomas Oehnmke. Lawyers Cooperative Publishing Company, Aqueduct Building, Rochester, New York 14694. 1990.

INTERNATIONAL COMMERCIAL AGREEMENTS: A FUNCTIONAL PRIMER ON DRAFTING, NEGOTIATING, AND RESOLVING DISPUTES. William F. Fox, Jr. Kluwer Academic Publishers, 101 Philip Drive, Assinippi Park, Norwell, Massachusetts 02061. 1988.

A LAWYER'S GUIDE TO COMMERCIAL ARBITRATION. Second Edition. American Law Institute-American Bar Association, 4025 Chestnut Street, Philadelphia, Pennsylvania 19104. 1983.

MEDIATION OF ENVIRONMENTAL DISPUTE: A SOURCEBOOK. Scott Mernitz. Praeger Publishers, One Madison Avenue, New York, New York 10010. 1980.

POWER NEGOTIATING TACTICS AND TECHNIQUES. David V. Lewis. Prentice-Hall, Incorporated, 113 Sylvan Avenue, Englewood Cliffs, New Jersey 07632. 1984.

TEXTBOOKS AND GENERAL WORKS

ALTERNATIVE DISPUTE RESOLUTION AND RISK MANAGEMENT: CONTROLLING CONFLICT AND ITS COSTS. Practising Law Institute, 810 Seventh Avenue, New York, New York 10019. 1987.

ALTERNATIVE DISPUTE RESOLUTION: MELTING THE LANCES AND DISMOUNTING THE STEEDS. Thomas E. Carbonneau. University of Illinois Press, 54 East Gregory Drive, Champaign, Illinois 61820. 1989.

ARBITRATION AND THE LICENSING PROCESS. Robert Goldscheider and Michel De Hass, Editors. Clark Boardman Company, Limited, 435 Hudson Street, New York, New York 10014. 1981.

ARBITRATION IN PRACTICE. Arnold M. Zack, Editor. ILR Press, New York State School of Industrial and Labor Relations, Cornell University, Ithaca, New York 14850. 1984.

ARBITRATION STRATEGY AND TECHNIQUE. Craig A. Peterson and Claire McCarthy. Michie/Bobbs-Merrill Law Publishing Company, P.O. Box 7587, Charlottesville, Virginia 22906-7582. 1986.

BUSINESS ARBITRATION: WHAT YOU NEED TO KNOW. Third Edition. Robert Coulson. American Arbitration Association, 140 West Fifty-first Street, New York, New York 10020. 1986.

COMMERCIAL ARBITRATION OF FORMS. Robert M. Rodman. West Publishing Company, P.O. Box 64526, 50 West Kellogg Boulevard, St. Paul, Minnesota 55164-0526. 1984- . (Periodic Supplements).

DISPUTE RESOLUTION. Stephen B. Goldberg, Eric D. Green and Frank A.E. Sander. Little, Brown and Company, 34 Beacon Street, Boston, Massachusetts 02108. 1985.

EMPLOYER'S GUIDE TO STRIKE PLANNING AND PREVENTION. Mark A. Hutcheson. Practising Law Institute, 810 Seventh Avenue, New York, New York 10019. 1985.

EVIDENCE IN ARBITRATION. Second Edition. Marvin Hill and Anthony V. Sinicropi. Bureau of National Affairs, Incorporated, 1231 Twenty-fifth Street, Northwest, Washington, D.C. 20037. 1987.

HOW ARBITRATION WORKS. Fourth Edition. Frank Elkouri and Edna A. Elkouri. Bureau of National Affairs, Incorporated, 1231 Twenty-fifth Street, Northwest, Washington, D.C. 20037. 1985- . (Periodic Supplements).

INTERNATIONAL ARBITRATION REPORT. Fred B. Rothman and Company, 10368 West Centennial Road, Littleton, Colorado 80127. 1986.

INTERNATIONAL COMMERCIAL ARBITRATION. Practising Law Institute, 810 Seventh Avenue, New York, New York 10019. 1988.

THE PRACTICAL NEGOTIATOR. William I. Zartman and Maurceu Burman. Yale University Press, 302 Temple Street, New Haven, Connecticut 06520. 1982.

THE PRACTICE AND LAW OF LABOR ARBITRATION. Fourth Edition. John Kagel and Douglas H. Barton. Stanford University School of Law, Stanford, California 94305. 1985.

REMEDIES IN ARBITRATION. Second Edition. Marvin Hill and Anthony V. Sinicropi. Bureau of National Affairs, Incorporated, 1231 Twenty-fifth Street, Northwest, Washington, D.C. 20037. 1990.

RESOLVING DISPUTES WITHOUT LITIGATION: A BNA SPECIAL REPORT. Bureau of National Affairs, Incorporated, 1231 Twenty-fifth Street, Northwest, Washington, D.C. 20037. 1988.

SECURITIES ARBITRATION. Practising Law Institute, 810 Seventh Avenue, New York, New York 10019. 1988.

SUCCESSFUL ARBITRATION: EXPERIENCE IN THE PREPARATION AND PRESENTATION OF ARBITRATION CASES. Randy D. Elkin and Thomas Hewitt. Reston Publishing Company, Incorporated, distributed by Prentice-Hall, Incorporated, 113 Sylvan Avenue, Englewood Cliffs, New Jersey 07632. 1980.

TECHNIQUES OF MEDIATION IN LABOR DISPUTES. W. Maggiolo. Oceana Publications, 75 Main Street, Dobbs Ferry, New York 10522. 1985.

DIGESTS, INDEXES, ABSTRACTS, CITATORS

ARBITRATION AWARD INDEX. The Newspaper Guild, 8611 Second Avenue, Silver Spring, Maryland 20910. 1983- .

STEEL ARBITRATION DIGEST. John W. Willis. Pike and Fisher, Incorporated, 4550 Montgomery Avenue, Suite 433N, Bethesda, Maryland 20814. 1960- .

A SUMMARY OF COURT DECISIONS AND INTERNATIONAL COMMERCIAL ARBITRATION. American Arbitration Association, 140 West Fifty-first Street, New York, New York 10020. 1984- .

LAW REVIEWS AND PERIODICALS

THE ARBITRATION JOURNAL. American Arbitration Association, 140 West Fifty-first Street, New York, New York 10020. Quarterly.

DISPUTE RESOLUTION. Standing Committee on Dispute Resolution, American Bar Association, 750 North Lake Shore Drive, Chicago, Illinois 60611. Quarterly.

MISSOURI JOURNAL OF DISPUTE RESOLUTION. University of Missouri School of Law, Columbia, Missouri 65211. Annual.

OHIO STATE JOURNAL ON DISPUTE RESOLUTION. Ohio State University, College of Law, 1659 North High Street, Columbus, Ohio 43210-1391. Semiannual.

NEWSLETTERS AND NEWSPAPERS

ARBITRATION IN THE SCHOOLS. American Arbitration Association, 140 West Fifty-first Street, New York, New York 10020. Monthly.

INTERNATIONAL ARBITRATION REPORT. Mealey Publications, Incorporated, P.O. Box 446, Wayne, Pennsylvania 19087. Monthly.

LABOR ARBITRATION IN GOVERNMENT. American Arbitration Association, 140 West Fifty-first Street, New York, New York 10020. Monthly.

LAWYERS ARBITRATION LETTER. American Arbitration Association, 140 West Fifty-first Street, New York, New York 10020. Quarterly.

SUMMARY OF LABOR ARBITRATION AWARDS. American Arbitration Association, 140 West Fifty-first Street, New York, New York 10020. Monthly.

BIBLIOGRAPHIES

ARBITRATION, MEDIATION, AND OTHER FORMS OF ALTERNATIVE DISPUTE RESOLUTION: A SELECTIVE BIBLIOGRAPHY. Vance Bibliographies, P.O. Box 229, 112 North Charter Street, Monticello, Illinois 61856. 1987.

A SELECTED BIBLIOGRAPHY ON GRIEVANCES AND INTEREST ARBITRATION IN EDUCATION. Jeannine R. Esswein. American Arbitration Association, 140 West Fifty-first Street, New York, New York 10020. 1979.

DIRECTORIES

COMMERCIAL ARBITRATION INSTITUTIONS: AN INTERNATIONAL DIRECTORY AND GUIDE. Ludwik Kos-Rabcevicz-Zubkowski. Oceana Publications, 75 Main Street, Dobbs Ferry, New York 10522. 1986.

DIRECTORY OF U.S. LABOR ARBITRATORS. Courtney D. Gifford and William P. Hobgood. Bureau of National Affairs, Incorporated, 1231 Twenty-fifth Street, Northwest, Washington, D.C. 20037. 1985.

ASSOCIATIONS AND PROFESSIONAL SOCIETIES

ACADEMY OF FAMILY MEDIATORS. P.O. Box 10501, Eugene, Oregon 97440. (503) 345-1205.

ALTERNATIVE DISPUTE RESOLUTION COMMITTEE. Family Law Section, American Bar Association, 750 North Lake Shore Drive, Chicago, Illinois 60611. (312) 988-5000.

AMERICAN ARBITRATION ASSOCIATION. 140 West Fifty-first Street, New York, New York 10020. (212) 484-4000.

CENTER FOR DISPUTE SETTLEMENT. 1666 Connecticut Avenue, Northwest, Suite 501, Washington, D.C. 20009. (202) 265-9572.

ARBITRATION AND AWARD

COMMUNITY DISPUTE SERVICES. 140 West Fifty-first Street, New York, New York 10020. (212) 484-4000.

CONFLICT RESOLUTION CENTER INTERNATIONAL. 7514 Kensington Street, Pittsburgh, Pennsylvania 15221. (412) 371-1000.

ENVIRONMENTAL MEDIATION INTERNATIONAL. 1775 Pennsylvania Avenue, Northwest, Suite 1000, Washington, D.C. 20006. (202) 457-0457.

INTER-AMERICAN COMMERCIAL ARBITRATION COMMISSION. 1889 F Street, Northwest, Room LL-3, Washington, D.C. 20006. (202) 293-1455.

INTERNATIONAL CENTRE FOR SETTLEMENT OF INVESTMENT DISPUTES. 1818 H Street, Northwest, Washington, D.C. 20433. (202) 477-1234.

NATIONAL ACADEMY OF ARBITRATORS. Office of the Secretary, Graduate School of Business Administration, University of Michigan, Ann Arbor, Michigan 48109. (313) 763-9714.

NATIONAL ACADEMY OF CONCILIATORS. 7315 Wisconsin Avenue, Suite 1255N, Bethesda, Maryland 20814. (301) 907-7000.

NATIONAL CENTER FOR MEDIATION EDUCATION. 2083 West Street, Suite 3C, Annapolis, Maryland 21401. (301) 261-8445.

NATIONAL INSTITUTE FOR DISPUTE RESOLUTION. 1901 L Street, Northwest, Suite 600, Washington, D.C. 20036. (202) 466-4764.

SOCIETY OF MARITIME ARBITRATORS. 26 Broadway, New York, New York 10004. (212) 483-0616.

SOCIETY OF PROFESSIONALS IN DISPUTE RESOLUTION. 1730 Rhode Island Avenue, Northwest, Suite 909, Washington, D.C. 20036. (202) 833-2188.

STANDING COMMITTEE ON DISPUTE RESOLUTION. American Bar Association, 750 North Lake Shore Drive, Chicago, Illinois 60611. (312) 988-5000.

RESEARCH CENTERS, INSTITUTES, CLEARINGHOUSES

CENTER FOR COMMUNITY JUSTICE. 1666 Connecticut Avenue, Northwest, Suite 501, Washington, D.C. 20009. (202) 265-9572.

CENTER FOR NEGOTIATION AND CONFLICT RESOLUTION. Rutgers University, S.I. Newhouse Center for Law and Justice, Newark, New Jersey 07102. (201) 648-5048.

CONFLICT RESOLUTION CENTER INTERNATIONAL. 7514 Kensington Street, Pittsburgh, Pennsylvania 15221. (412) 371-1000.

DISPUTE RESOLUTION RESEARCH CENTER. Northwestern University, J.L. Kellogg Graduate School of Management, Leverone Hall, 3-191, Evanston, Illinois 60208. (708) 491-8068.

HARVARD NEGOTIATION PROJECT. Harvard University, Harvard Law School, Pound Hall 500, Cambridge, Massachusetts 02138. (617) 495-1684.

INSTITUTE FOR MEDIATION AND CONFLICT RESOLUTION. 99 Hudson Street, Eleventh Floor, New York, New York 10013. (212) 966-3660.

INSTITUTE OF INDUSTRIAL RELATIONS. Loyola University of Chicago, 820 North Michigan Avenue, Chicago, Illinois 60611. (312) 670-3134.

NATIONAL INSTITUTE FOR DISPUTE RESOLUTION. 1901 L Street, Northwest, Suite 600, Washington, D.C. 20036. (202) 466-4764.

ONLINE DATABASES

COMPUTERIZED LABOR ARBITRATION INFORMATION MANAGEMENT. Axon Group, LRP Publications, 1035 Camphill Road, Fort Washington, Pennsylvania 19034.

LABOR RELATIONS WEEK. Bureau of National Affairs. Available on Lexis. Mead Data Central, P.O. Box 933, Dayton, Ohio 45401.

AUDIOVISUALS

LABOR ARBITRATION OF A DRUG TESTING CASE. National Practice Institute, 330 Second Avenue South, Minneapolis, Minnesota 55401. Videotape.

LABOR ARBITRATION OF A SEXUAL HARASSMENT CASE. National Practice Institute, 330 Second Avenue South, Minneapolis, Minnesota 55401. Videotape.

LABOR ARBITRATION: THE 1987 CONFERENCE. National Practice Institute, 330 Second Avenue South, Minneapolis, Minnesota 55401. Audiotape.

LABOR ARBITRATION: THE 1988 CONFERENCE. National Practice Institute, 330 Second Avenue South, Minneapolis, Minnesota 55401. Audiotape.

LABOR ARBITRATION: THE 1989 CONFERENCE. National Practice Institute, 330 Second Avenue South, Minneapolis, Minnesota 55401. Audiotape.

LABOR ARBITRATION: THE 1989 MIDWEST CONFERENCE. National Practice Institute, 330 Second Avenue South, Minneapolis, Minnesota 55401. Audiotape.

LABOR ARBITRATION: THE 1989 SAN FRANCISCO CONFERENCE. National Practice Institute, 330 Second Avenue South, Minneapolis, Minnesota 55401. Audiotape.

LABOR ARBITRATION: THE 1990 CONFERENCE. National Practice Institute, 330 Second Avenue South, Minneapolis, Minnesota 55401. Audiotape.

MODEL NEGOTIATIONS. Consortium for Professional Education, American Bar Association, 750 North Lake Shore Drive, Chicago, Illinois 60611. (2 videocassettes).

NEGOTIATION - CAN YOU TRUST YOUR INSTINCTS. Consortium for Professional Education, American Bar Association, 750 North Lake Shore Drive, Chicago, Illinois 60611. (4 videocassettes).

COMPUTER-ASSISTED LEGAL INSTRUCTION

ARBITRATION EXERCISES. Thomas G. Field, Jr. Center for Computer- Assisted Instruction, 229 19th Avenue South, University of Minnesota, Minneapolis, Minnesota 55455. Machine-readable computer file.

OTHER SOURCES

BASIC DOCUMENTS ON COMMERCIAL ARBITRATION. Diane T. Olsson. American Arbitration Association, 140 West Fifty-first Street, New York, New York 10020. 1984.

COMMERCIAL ARBITRATION RULES OF THE AMERICAN ARBITRATION ASSOCIATION ANNOTATED. American Arbitration Association, 140 West Fifty-first Street, New York, New York 10020. 1984.

INTERNATIONAL CENTRE FOR SETTLEMENT OF INVESTMENT DISPUTES -- ANNUAL REPORT. 1818 H Street, Northwest, Washington, D.C. 20433. Annual.

MANAGING AND RESOLVING DOMESTIC AND INTERNATIONAL BUSINESS DISPUTES: ALI-ABA COURSE OF STUDY MATERIALS. American Law Institute-American Bar Association, 4025 Chestnut Street, Philadelphia, Pennsylvania 19104. 1988.

REMOVING THE BARRIERS TO THE USE OF ALTERNATIVE METHODS OF DISPUTE RESOLUTIONS: CONFERENCE PROCEEDINGS. Vermont Law School, Dispute Resolution Project, South Royalton, Vermont 05068. 1986.

ARBITRATION, INDUSTRIAL
See: LABOR ARBITRATION

ARBITRATION, INTERNATIONAL
See: INTERNATIONAL ARBITRATION

ARCHITECTS

STATUTES, CODES, STANDARDS, UNIFORM LAWS

CODES AND STANDARDS. Kelly P. Reynolds and Associates, Incorporated, 1105 West Chicago Avenue, Chicago, Illinois 60622. 1980- . Monthly.

LOOSELEAF SERVICES AND REPORTERS

ARCHITECT'S HANDBOOK OF PROFESSIONAL PRACTICE. 11th edition. David Haviland. American Institute of Architects, 1735 New York Avenue, N.W., Washington, D.C. 20006. 1988- .

FORMS AND AGREEMENTS FOR ARCHITECTS, ENGINEERS AND CONTRACTORS. Albert Dib. Clark Boardman Callaghan, 1155 Pfingsten Road, Deerfield, Illinois 60015. 1976- .

MODERN CONSTRUCTION AND DEVELOPMENT FORMS. Second edition. James Douglas and others. Research Institute of America, Incorporated, 210 South Street, Boston, Massachusetts 02111. 1982- .

ARCHITECT'S GUIDE TO LAW AND PRACTICE. Bob Greenstreet and Karen Greenstreet. Van Nostrand Reinhold Company, Incorporated, 115 5th Avenue, New York, New York 10003. 1984.

HANDBOOKS, MANUALS, FORMBOOKS

ARCHITECT'S LEGAL HANDBOOK: THE LAW FOR ARCHITECTS. Fifth edition. Anthony Speaight and Gregory Stone, editors. Butterworth Legal Publishers, 90 Stiles Road, Salem, New Hampshire 03079. 1990.

LEGAL HANDBOOK FOR ARCHITECTS, ENGINEERS AND CONTRACTORS. Clark Boardman Callaghan, 1155 Pfingsten Road, Deerfield, Illinois 60015. 1986- .

PRACTICAL ARCHITECT-ENGINEER LAW: COURSE MANUAL. John D. Sours and W. Hensell Harris. Federal Publications, Incorporated, 1120 20th Street, N.W., Washington, D.C. 20036. 1983.

TEXTBOOKS AND GENERAL WORKS

ARCHITECTS/ENGINEER'S ROLE UNDER SUPERFUND, AND SELECTING A PROFESSIONAL LIABILITY INSURANCE POLICY. James A. Thompson and Frank J. Baltz. Public Contract Law Section, American Bar Association, 750 North Lake Shore Drive, Chicago, Illinois 60611. 1984.

ARCHITECTURAL PRACTICE. John J. Scott. Butterworth Legal Publishers, 90 Stiles Road, Salem, New Hampshire 03079. 1985.

DESIGN AND CONSTRUCTION CONTRACTS: NEW FORMS, NEW REALITIES. Real Property, Probate and Trust Law Section, American Bar Association, 750 North Lake Shore Drive, Chicago, Illinois 60611. 1988.

ENGINEERING EVIDENCE. Second edition. Max Schwartz and Neil F. Schwartz. Shepard's/McGraw-Hill, P.O. Box 35300, Colorado Springs, Colorado 80935. 1987.

LEGAL AND CONTRACTUAL PROCEDURES FOR ARCHITECTS. Third edition. Bob Greenstreet and Karen Greenstreet. Butterworth Legal Publishers, 90 Stiles Road, Salem, New Hampshire 03079. 1989.

DIGESTS, INDEXES, ABSTRACTS, CITATORS

AIA BUILDING CONSTRUCTION LEGAL CITATOR. American Institute of Architects, 1735 New York Avenue, N.W., Washington, D.C. 20006.

LIEN LAWS FOR DESIGN PROFESSIONALS. Second edition. Daniel S. Roth. American Institute of Architects, 1735 New York Avenue, N.W., Washington, D.C. 20006. 1984.

NEWSLETTERS AND NEWSPAPERS

A/E LEGAL NEWLETTER. Victor O. Schinnerer & Company, Incorporated, 2 Wisconsin Circle, Chevy Chase, Maryland 20815. 1981- . Monthly.

CONSTRUCTION INDUSTRY LITIGATION REPORTER. Andrews Publications, 1646 West Chester Pike, Westtown, Pennsylvania 19395.

LAST WORD. American Consulting Engineers Council, 1015 15th Street, N.W., Washington, D.C. 20005. 1971- . Weekly.

LEGAL BRIEFS FOR THE CONSTRUCTION INDUSTRY. McGraw-Hill, Incorporated, 11 West 19th Street, New York, New York 10011. 1975- . Bimonthly.

BIBLIOGRAPHIES

ARCHITECTS AND ENGINEERS: ARTICLES FROM LAW JOURNALS. Mary A. Vance. Vance Bibliographies, P.O. Box 229, 112 North Charter Street, Monticello, Illinois 61856. 1986.

ARCHITECTS--LEGAL STATUS, LAWS, ETC. Mary A. Vance. Vance Bibliographies, P.O. Box 229, 112 North Charter Street, Monticello, Illinois 61856. 1985.

ARCHITECTURAL DESIGN REVIEW COMMITTEES: A SELECTED BIBLIOGRAPHY. Anthony G. White. Vance Bibliographies, P.O. Box 229, 112 North Charter Street, Monticello, Illinois 61856. 1987.

COPYRIGHT, DESIGN PROTECTION, AND THE ARCHITECT: PERIODICAL LITERATURE, 1976-1986. Carole Cable. Vance Bibliographies, P.O. Box 229, 112 North Charter Street, Monticello, Illinois 61856. 1987.

ASSOCIATIONS AND PROFESSIONAL SOCIETIES

AMERICAN INSTITUTE OF ARCHITECTS. 1735 New York Avenue, N.W., Washington, D.C. (202) 626-7300.

SOCIETY OF AMERICAN REGISTERED ARCHITECTS. 1245 South Highland Avenue, Lombard, Illinois 60148. (708) 932-4622.

ONLINE DATABASES

ARCHITECTURAL PERIODICALS INDEX. Royal Institute of British Architects, 66 Portland Place, London W1N 4AD, England.

MASTERSPEC. American Institute of Architects, Professional Systems Division, 1735 New York Avenue, N.W., Washington, D.C.

ARMED FORCES
See: MILITARY LAW AND SERVICE; VETERANS

ARMS
See: FIREARMS AND BALLISTICS

ARMS CONTROL
See: INTERNATIONAL LAW AND RELATIONS; TREATIES AND CONVENTIONS

ARMY
See: MILITARY LAW AND SERVICE

ARREST
See also: ADMINISTRATION OF JUSTICE; DUE PROCESS OF LAW

LOOSELEAF SERVICES AND REPORTERS

SEARCHES AND SEIZURES, ARRESTS AND CONFESSIONS. Second Edition. William E. Ringel. Clark Boardman Company, Limited, 435 Hudson Street, New York, New York 10014. 1979- .

TEXTBOOKS AND GENERAL BOOKS

ARREST IN DOMESTIC VIOLENCE CASES: A STATE-BY-STATE SUMMARY. National Center on Women and Family Law, 799 Broadway, Room 402, New York, New York 10003. 1987.

ARREST, SEARCH AND SEIZURE. Calvin W. Berry. Michie Company, P.O. Box 7587, Charlottesville, Virginia 22906-7582. 1973.

ARREST: THE DECISION TO TAKE A SUSPECT INTO CUSTODY. Wayne R. LaFave, Frank J. Remington, Editor. Little, Brown and Company, 34 Beacon Street, Boston, Massachusetts 02108. 1974.

ARRESTS WITHOUT CONVICTION: HOW OFTEN THEY OCCUR AND WHY. Floyd Feeney, Forest Dill and Adrianne Weir. United States Department of Justice, National Institute of Justice. Superintendent of Documents, United States Government Printing Office, Washington, D.C. 20402. 1983.

CITIZEN'S ARREST: THE LAW OF ARREST, SEARCH, AND SEIZURE FOR PRIVATE CITIZENS AND PRIVATE POLICE. M. Cherif Bassiouni. Charles C. Thomas, Publishers, 2600 South First Street, Springfield, Illinois 62794. 1977.

HOUSE ARREST AND CORRECTIONAL POLICY: DOING TIME AT HOME. Richard A. Ball, C. Ronald Huff and J. Robert Lilly. Sage Publications, Incorporated, 2455 Teller Road, Newbury Park, California 91320. 1988.

THE LAW OF ARREST, SEARCH, AND SEIZURE. Third Edition. J. Shane Creamer. Holt, Rinehart and Winston, Incorporated, 6277 Sea Harbor Drive, Orlando, Florida 32821. 1980.

POLICE GUIDE TO SEARCH AND SEIZURE, INTERROGATION AND CONFESSION. First Edition. Arlen Specter and Marvin Katz. Chilton Book Company, 201 King of Prusia Road, Radnor, Pennsylvania 19089-0230. 1967.

SEARCHES, SEIZURES AND IMMUNITIES. Second Edition. Joseph A. Varon. Bobbs-Merrill Company, Incorporated, 4300 West Sixty-second Street, Indianapolis, Indiana 46206. Defunct. 1974.

TWO CLASSES OF ACCUSED: A STUDY OF BAIL AND DETENTION IN AMERICAN JUSTICE. John S. Goldkamp. Harvard University Press, 79 Garden Street, Cambridge, Massachusetts 02138. 1979.

NEWSLETTERS AND NEWSPAPERS

ARREST LAW BULLETIN. Quinlan Publishing Company, Incorporated, 23 Drydock Avenue, Boston, Massachusetts 02110. Monthly.

BIBLIOGRAPHIES

ELECTRONIC DETENTION, HOUSE ARREST AS A CORRECTIONAL ALTERNATIVE: A SELECTED BIBLIOGRAPHY. Verna Casey. Vance Bibliographies, P.O. Box 229, 112 North Charter Street, Monticello, Illinois 61856. 1988.

DIRECTORIES

CLEAN SLATE: A STATE-BY-STATE GUIDE TO EXPUNGING AN ARREST RECORD. Tom Ballinger. Harmony Books, Crown Publishers, Incorporated, 225 Park Avenue, South, New York, New York 10003. 1979.

AUDIOVISUALS

HOUSE ARREST. Police Foundation, National Institute of Justice, 1001 Twenty-second Street, Northwest, Suite 200, Washington, D.C. 20037. 1986. (Videocassette).

ARSON

See also: CRIMINAL LAW; INSURANCE, PROPERTY; ALCOHOL, TOBACCO AND FIREARMS BUREAU

LOOSELEAF SERVICES AND REPORTERS

ARSON LEGISLATION REFERENCE MANUAL. Young Lawyer's Division, American Bar Association, 750 North Lake Shore Drive, Chicago, Illinois 60611. 1985- .

FIRE LITIGATION SOURCEBOOK: TECHNICAL, MEDICAL AND LEGAL ASPECTS. Alexander J. Patton. Garland Publishing, Incorporated, 136 Madison Avenue, New York, New York 10016. 1986- .

HANDBOOKS, MANUALS, FORMBOOKS

ENFORCEMENT MANUAL: APPROACHES FOR COMBATTING ARSON-FOR-PROFIT SCHEMES. Clifton L. Karchmer and James Greenfield. United States Department of Justice, Law Enforcement Assistance Administration. Superintendent of Documents, United States Government Printing Office, Washington, D.C. 20402. 1980.

PRACTICAL FIRE AND ARSON INVESTIGATION. John J. O'Conner. Elsevier Science Publishing Company, P.O. Box 882, Madison Square Station, New York, New York 10159. 1986.

TEXTBOOKS AND GENERAL WORKS

THE ANATOMY OF ARSON. Harvey M. French. Arco Publishing, Incorporated, Division of Prentice-Hall, Incorporated, 15 Columbus Circle, New York, New York 10023. 1979.

ARSON: DETECTION AND INVESTIGATION. Brendan P. Battle and Paul B. Weston. Arco Publishing, Incorporated, Division of Prentice-Hall, Incorporated, 15 Columbus Circle, New York, New York 10023. 1978.

ARSON VICTIMS: SUGGESTIONS FOR A SYSTEM RESPONSE. Victim Witness Assistance Project of the American Bar Association Section of Criminal Justice. American Bar Association, 750 North Lake Shore Drive, Chicago, Illinois 60611. 1983.

BOMBERS AND FIRESETTERS. John M. MacDonald. Charles C. Thomas, Publishers, 2600 South First Street, Springfield, Illinois 62794-9265. 1977.

CHILDREN AND ARSON: AMERICA'S MIDDLE CLASS NIGHTMARE. Wayne S. Wooden and Martha L. Berkey. Plenum Publishing Corporation, 233 Spring Street, New York, New York 10013. 1984.

FIRE, ARSON AND EXPLOSION INVESTIGATION. John Kennedy. Investigations Institution, 53 West Jackson Boulevard, Chicago, Illinois 60604. 1977.

FIRE LITIGATION SOURCEBOOK: TECHNICAL, MEDICAL, AND LEGAL ASPECTS. Alexander J. Patton and John C. Russell. John Wiley and Sons, Incorporated, 605 Third Avenue, New York New York 10158. 1986.

FIRES AND EXPLOSIONS: DETERMINING CAUSE AND ORIGIN. John Kennedy and Patrick Kennedy. Investigations Institution, 53 West Jackson Boulevard, Chicago, Illinois 60611. 1985.

INVESTIGATING ARSON. Wayne Bennett and Karen M. Hess. Charles C. Thomas, Publishers, 2600 South First Street, Springfield, Illinois 62794-9265. 1984.

LAW REVIEWS AND PERIODICALS

ARSON REPORTER: ARSON LEGISLATION. Young Lawyers Division. American Bar Association, 750 North Lake Shore Drive, Chicago, Illinois 60611. Monthly.

BIBLIOGRAPHIES

ARSON AND ARSON INVESTIGATION: A BIBLIOGRAPHY. Mary Vance. Vance Bibliographies, P.O. Box 229, 112 North Charter Street, Monticello, Illinois 61856. 1987.

ARSON, FOR INSURANCE AND PROTEST: A BIBLIOGRAPHY, 1965-1977. Joseph Lee Cook and Earleen Cook. Council of Planning Librarians, 1313 East Sixtieth Street, Chicago, Illinois 60637. 1978.

ARSON, THE CRIME FOR PROFIT. Carol A. Martin. Vance Bibliographies, P.O. Box 229, 112 North Charter Street, Monticello, Illinois 61856. 1981.

ARSON

DIRECTORIES

ARSON CONTROL: DIRECTORY. Insurance Committee for Arson Control, 85 John Street, New York, New York 10038. 1977.

ARSON LEGAL RESOURCES DIRECTORY. Young Lawyers Division, American Bar Association, 750 North Lake Shore Drive, Chicago, Illinois 60611. 1985.

ARSON RESOURCE DIRECTORY. Second Edition. Arson Resource Center, United States Fire Administration, 16825 South Seton, Emmittsburg, Maryland 21727. 1982.

ASSOCIATIONS AND PROFESSIONAL SOCIETIES

INTERNATIONAL ASSOCIATION OF ARSON INVESTIGATORS. 5428 Del Maria Way, Suite 201, P.O. Box 91119, Louisville, Kentucky 40291. (502) 491-7482.

INTERNATIONAL FIRE PHOTOGRAPHERS ASSOCIATION. P.O. Box 8337, Rolling Meadows, Illinois 60008. (708) 394-835.

NATIONAL ARSON PREVENTION AND ACTION COALITION. Urban Educational Systems, P.O. Box 1146, Jamaica Plain, Massachusetts 02130. (617) 522-7118.

STATISTICS SOURCES

EXPLOSIVE INCIDENTS: ANNUAL REPORT BY THE BUREAU OF ALCOHOL, TOBACCO AND FIREARMS. Department of the Treasury, 1500 Pennsylvania Avenue, Northwest, Washington, D.C. 20220. Annual.

AUDIOVISUALS

ARSON FOR PROFIT: THE INSURER'S DEFENSE. Tort and Insurance Practice Section. American Bar Association, 750 North Lake Shore Drive, Chicago, Illinois 60611. 1981. (1 Videocassette).

ART

HANDBOOKS, MANUALS, FORMBOOKS

ART LAW: THE GUIDE FOR COLLECTORS, INVESTORS, DEALERS, AND ARTISTS. Practising Law Institute, 810 Seventh Avenue, New York, New York 10019. 1989.

COLLECTORS AND ARTISTS: PLANNING AND PROBATING THE ESTATE. Ralph E. Lerner. Practising Law Institute, 810 Seventh Avenue, New York, New York 10019. 1978.

THE LAW OF ART AND ANTIQUES: A PRIMER FOR ARTISTS AND COLLECTORS. Scott Hodes. Oceana Publications, 75 Main Street, Dobbs Ferry, New York 10522. 1966.

REPRESENTING ARTISTS, COLLECTORS, AND DEALERS. Practising Law Institute, 810 Seventh Avenue, New York, New York 10019. 1981.

THE RIGHTS OF AUTHORS AND ARTISTS. Southern Illinois University Press, P.O. Box 3697, Carbondale, Illinois 62902-3697. 1984.

TEXTBOOKS AND GENERAL WORKS

ART LAW, DOMESTIC AND INTERNATIONAL. Leonard D. Duboff, Editor. Fred B. Rothman and Company, 10368 West Centennial Road, Littleton, Colorado 80127. 1975.

ART LAW IN A NUTSHELL. Leonard D. DuBoff. West Publishing Company, P.O. Box 43526, 50 West Kellogg Boulevard, St. Paul, Minnesota 55164-0526. 1984.

ART LAW: REPRESENTING ARTISTS, DEALERS AND COLLECTORS. Practising Law Institute, 810 Seventh Avenue, New York, New York 10019. 1977.

ART LAW: RIGHTS AND LIABILITIES OF CREATORS AND COLLECTORS. Franklin Feldman and Stephen E. Weil. Little, Brown and Company, 34 Beacon Street, Boston, Massachusetts 02108. 1986. (Two Volumes).

ART ON TRIAL: FROM WHISTLER TO ROTHKO. Laurie Adams. Walker and Company, 720 Fifth Avenue, New York, New York 10019. 1976.

ART WORKS: LAW, POLICY, PRACTICE. Franklin Feldman and Stephen E. Weil. Practising Law Institute, 810 Seventh Avenue, New York, New York 10019. 1974.

THE ARTIST-GALLERY PARTNERSHIP: A PRACTICAL GUIDE TO CONSIGNMENT. Tad Crawford and Susan Mellon. American Council for the Arts, 1285 Avenue of the Americas, Third Floor, Area M, New York, New York 10019. 1981.

BEAUTY AND THE BEASTS: ON MUSEUMS, ART, THE LAW AND THE MARKET. Stephen E. Weil. Smithsonian Institution Press, 470 L'Enfant Plaza, Southwest, Suite 7100, Washington, D.C. 20560. 1983.

COMMISSIONING A WORK OF PUBLIC ART: AN ANNOTATED MODEL AGREEMENT. The Committee on Art Law of the Association of the Bar of the City of New York. American Council for the Arts, 1285 Avenue of the Americas, Third Floor, Area M, New York, New York 10019. 1985.

THE DESKBOOK OF ART LAW. Leonard D. DuBoff. Federal Publications, 1120 Twentieth Street, Northwest, Washington, D.C. 20036. 1977- . (Periodic Supplements).

FEAR OF ART: CENSORSHIP AND FREEDOM OF EXPRESSION IN ART. Moshe Carmilly-Weinberger. R.R. Bowker and Company, 121 Chanlon Road, New Providence, New Jersey 07974. 1986.

THE INTERNATIONAL TRADE IN ART. Paul M. Bator. University of Chicago Press, 5801 Ellis Avenue, Chicago, Illinois 60637. 1988.

THE LAW AND BUSINESS OF ART. Practising Law Institute, 810 Seventh Avenue, New York, New York 10019. 1990.

LAW AND THE ARTS -- ART AND THE LAW. Tem Horwitz, Editor. Lawyers for the Creative Arts: Distributed by Chicago Review Press, 814 North Franklin Street, Chicago, Illinois 60610. 1979.

LEGAL GUIDE FOR THE VISUAL ARTIST: THE PROFESSIONAL'S HANDBOOK. Tad Crawford. Allworth Press, 10 East Twenty-third Street, New York, New York 10010. 1989.

A LEGAL PRIMER ON MANAGING MUSEUM COLLECTIONS. Marie D. Malaro. Smithsonian Institute Press, 470 L'Enfant Plaza, Southwest, Suite 7100, Washington, D.C. 20560. 1985.

LEGAL RIGHTS IN THE ART COLLECTORS' WORLD. Second Edition. Scott Bodes. Oceana Publications, Incorporated, 75 Main Street, Dobbs Ferry, New York 10522. 1986.

LINDEY ON ENTERTAINMENT, PUBLISHING, AND THE ARTS: ARGUMENTS AND THE LAW. Second Edition. Alexander Lindey. Clark Boardman Company, Limited, 435 Hudson Street, New York, New York 10014. 1980- .

LOCAL GOVERNMENT AND THE ARTS. Luisa Kriesberg. American Council for the Arts, 1285 Avenue of the Americas, Third Floor, Area M, New York, New York 10019. 1979.

PICTURES AND PUNISHMENT: ART AND CRIMINAL PROSECUTION DURING THE FLORENTINE RENAISSANCE. Samuel Y. Edgerton, Jr. Cornell University Press, 124 Roberts Place, P.O. Box 250, Ithaca, New York 14851. 1984.

THE VISUAL ARTIST AND THE LAW. Revised Edition. Associated Councils of the Arts, The Association of the Bar of the City of New York and Volunteer Lawyers for the Arts, 1285 Avenue of the Americas, Suite 300, New York, New York 10019. 1974.

WHAT EVERY ARTIST AND COLLECTOR SHOULD KNOW ABOUT THE LAW. Scott Hodes. NAL/Dutton, 375 Hudson Street, New York, New York 10014-3657. 1974.

LAW REVIEWS AND PERIODICALS

ART RESEARCH NEWS. International Foundation for Art Research, 46 East Seventieth Street, New York, New York 10021. Monthly.

CARDOZO ARTS AND ENTERTAINMENT LAW JOURNAL. Benjamin N. Cardozo School of Law, Yeshiva University, New York, New York 10003. Biannual.

COLUMBIA-VLA JOURNAL OF LAW AND THE ARTS. Columbia University School of Law and Volunteer Lawyers for the Arts, 435 West One Hundred Sixteenth Street, New York, New York 10027. Quarterly.

THE JOURNAL OF ARTS MANAGEMENT AND LAW. Helen D. Reid Educational Foundation, 4000 Albemarle Street, Northwest, Washington, D.C. 20016. Quarterly.

LAWYERS FOR THE ARTS. Young Lawyers Division, American Bar Association, 750 North Lake Shore Drive, Chicago, Illinois 60611. Quarterly.

NEWSLETTERS AND NEWSPAPERS

ACA UPDATE. American Council for the Arts, 1285 Avenue of the Americas, New York, New York 10019. Monthly.

ART LAW AND ACCOUNTING REPORTER. Texas Accountants and Lawyers for the Arts, 1540 Sul Ross, Houston, Texas 77006. Quarterly.

ARTS AND CULTURE FUNDING REPORT. Education Funding Research Council, 1611 North Kent Street, Arlington, Virginia 22209. Monthly.

THE E.A.S.L. Entertainment, Arts and Sports Law Section, Florida Bar Association, 650 Apalachee Parkway, Tallahassee, Florida 32399. Quarterly.

ENTERTAINMENT LAW REPORTER. Entertainment Law Reporter Publishing Company, 2210 Wilshire Boulevard, Suite 311, Santa Monica, California 90403. Quarterly.

LAWYERS FOR THE ARTS NEWSLETTER. American Bar Association, Young Lawyers Division, 750 Lake Shore Drive, Chicago, Illinois 60611. Semiannual.

BIBLIOGRAPHIES

LAW AND FINE ART: A SELECTED BIBLIOGRAPHY. Wendy Waldron Brandow. John Marshall Publishing Company, 4888 Loop Central Drive, Suite 800, Houston, Texas 77081. 1984.

REFERENCE SOURCES FOR ART LAW. Jane Chittendon Minor. Legal Reference Services Quarterly, Volume 3, Number 3, p.53 (Fall 1983). Hayworth Press, 75 Griswold Street, Binghamton, New York 13904.

DIRECTORIES

INTERNATIONAL DIRECTORY OF ARTS. R.R. Bowker Company, 121 Chanlon Road, New Providence, New Jersey 07974. Biennial.

NATIONAL ARTS GUIDE. National Arts Guide, Incorporated, 200 East Ontario Street, Suite 607, Chicago, Illinois 60611. Bimonthly.

ASSOCIATIONS AND PROFESSIONAL SOCIETIES

AMERICAN ARTS ALLIANCE. 1319 F Street, Northwest, Washington, D.C. 20004. (202) 737-1727.

AMERICAN COUNCIL FOR THE ARTS. 1285 Avenue of the Americas, New York, New York 10019. (212) 245-4510.

AMERICAN FEDERATION OF ARTS. 41 East Sixty-fifth Street, New York, New York 10021. (212) 988-7700.

ARTISTS UNITED AGAINST APARTHEID. The African Fund, 198 Broadway, New York, New York 10038. (212) 962-1210.

ARTS FOR AMERICA, NATIONAL ASSEMBLY OF LOCAL ARTS AGENCIES. 1420 K Street, Northwest, Washington, D.C. 20005. (202) 371-2830.

ART

INTERNATIONAL FOUNDATION FOR ART RESEARCH. 46 East Seventieth Street, New York, New York 10021. (212) 879-1780.

NATIONAL ASSEMBLY OF STATE ARTS AGENCIES. 1010 Vermont Avenue, Northwest, Washington, D.C. 20005. (202) 347-6352.

VOLUNTEER LAWYERS FOR THE ARTS. 1285 Avenue of the Americas, New York, New York 10019. (212) 977-9270.

ONLINE DATABASE

ART INDEX: WILSONLINE. H.W. Wilson Company, 950 University Avenue, Bronx, New York 10452.

ART LITERATURE INTERNATIONAL. J. Paul Getty Trust, RILA, Clark Art Institute, Williamstown, Massachusetts 01267.

ARTBIBLIOGRAPHIES MODERN. ABC-CLIO Information Sources. 2040 Alameda Padre Serra, P.O. Box 4397, Santa Barbara, California 93140.

ARTQUEST. Pergamon Financial Data Services. Pergamon ORBIT InfoLine Limited, Achilles House, Western Avenue, London, England W3 0UA.

ARTIFICIAL INSEMINATION
See: FAMILY LAW

ASBESTOS
See also: HAZARDOUS SUBSTANCES; OCCUPATIONAL SAFETY AND HEALTH ADMINISTRATION

LOOSELEAF SERVICES AND REPORTERS

ASBESTOS ABATEMENT REGULATORY SERVICE. National Insulation and Abatement Contractors Association, 99 Canal Center Plaza, Suite 222, Alexandria, Virginia 22314. 1988- . (Bimonthly Supplements).

CHEMICAL REGULATION REPORTER. Bureau of National Affairs, Incorporated, 1231 Twenty-fifth Street, Northwest, Washington, D.C. 20037. 1977- . (Weekly Supplements).

CHEMICAL SUBSTANCE CONTROL. Bureau of National Affairs, Incorporated, 1231 Twenty-fifth Street, Northwest, Washington, D.C. 20037. 1980- .

HANDBOOKS, MANUALS, FORMBOOKS

ASBESTOS ABATEMENT RESOURCE GUIDE. Second Edition. Bureau of National Affairs, Incorporated, 1231 Twenty-fifth Street, Northwest, Washington, D.C. 20037. 1989.

ASBESTOS ABATEMENT: RISKS AND RESPONSIBILITIES. Bureau of National Affairs, Incorporated, 1231 Twenty-fifth Street, Northwest, Washington, D.C. 20037. 1987.

Encyclopedia of Legal Information Sources • 2nd Ed.

ASBESTOS CASE MANAGEMENT: PRETRIAL AND TRIAL PROCEDURES. Thomas E. Willging. Federal Judicial Center, 1520 H Street, Northwest, Washington, D.C. 20005. 1985.

ASBESTOS HANDBOOK FOR REMODELING: HOW TO PROTECT YOUR BUSINESS AND YOUR HEALTH. National Association of Home Builders, Fifteenth and M Streets, Northwest, Washington, D.C. 20034. 1989.

ASBESTOS IN THE SCHOOLS: A GUIDE FOR SCHOOL ADMINISTRATORS, TEACHERS, AND PARENTS. Carolyn Harvey and Mark Rollinson. Praeger Publishers, Greenwood Publishing Group, Incorporated, 88 Post Road West, P.O. Box 5007, Westport, Connecticut 06881. 1987.

ASBESTOS REGULATION, REMOVAL, AND PROHIBITION. Practising Law Institute, 810 Seventh Street, New York, New York 10019. 1987.

ASBESTOS REVIEW AND UPDATE. George A. Peters and Barbara J. Peters. Garland Law Publishing, 136 Madison Avenue, New York, New York 10016. 1987.

ASBESTOS SAMPLING AND ANALYSIS. Gyan S. Rajhans and John L. Sullivan. Ann Arbor Science Publishers, Ann Arbor, Michigan 48104. 1981.

INDUSTRYWIDE LITIGATION: DEFENSE OF ASBESTOS LAWSUITS: ADVANCED TRIAL TECHNIQUES AND MEDICAL ASPECTS. Defense Research Institute, 750 North Lake Shore Drive, Suite 500, Chicago, Illinois 60611. 1981.

SOURCEBOOK ON ASBESTOS DISEASES: MEDICAL, LEGAL AND ENGINEERING ASPECTS. George A. Peters and Barbara J. Peters. Garland Legal Publishers, 136 Madison Avenue, New York, New York 10016. 1986.

TEXTBOOKS AND GENERAL WORKS

ASBESTOS: GROWTH OF FEDERAL CLAIMS, COURT CASES, AND LITIGATION COSTS. United States General Accounting Office, United States Government Printing Office, Washington, D.C. 20402. 1988.

ASBESTOS IN THE COURTS: THE CHALLENGE OF MASS TOXIC TORTS. Deborah R. Hensler and others. Rand Corporation, Institute for Civil Justice, 1700 Main Street, P.O. Box 2138, Santa Monica, California 90406. 1985.

ASBESTOS IN THE NATURAL ENVIRONMENT. H. Schreider. Elsevier Science Publishing Company, P.O. Box 882, Madison Square Station, New York, New York 10159. 1989.

ASBESTOS LITIGATION: INSURANCE ISSUES, LIABILITY, DAMAGES. Law & Business, Prentice-Hall, Incorporated, 113 Sylvan Avenue, Englewood Cliffs, New Jersey 07632. 1986.

ASBESTOS: MEDICAL AND LEGAL ASPECTS. Second Edition. Barry I. Castleman. Law and Business, Prentice-Hall, Incorporated, 113 Sylvan Avenue, Englewood Cliffs, New Jersey 07632. 1986.

ASBESTOS PROPERTY DAMAGE LITIGATION: THIRD ANNUAL TOXIC TORTS ADVOCACY INSTITUTE. Harcourt, Brace, Jovanovich, Incorporated, 6277 Sea Harbor Drive, Orlando, Florida 32821. 1985.

ASBESTOS-RELATED INJURY CLAIMS ... FACTORS THAT EXPLAIN HOW THE CASES CAME OUT: A SUMMARY OF RESEARCH RESULTS. James S. Kakalik. Rand Corporation, Institute for Civil Justice, 1700 Main Street, P.O. Box 2138, Santa Monica, California 90406. 1984.

ASBESTOS: THE HAZARDOUS FIBER. Melvin A. Benardes, Editor. CRC Press, Incorporated, 2000 Corporate Boulevard, Northwest, Boca Raton, Florida 33431. 1989.

CONTROLLING ASBESTOS IN BUILDINGS: AN ECONOMIC INVESTIGATION. Donald N. Dewees. Resources for the Future, Incorporated, 1616 P Street, Northwest, Washington, D.C. 20036. 1986.

COSTS OF ASBESTOS LITIGATION. James S. Kakalik and others. Rand Corporation, Institute for Civil Justice, 1700 Main Street, P.O. Box 2138, Santa Monica, California 90406. 1983.

CURRENT ISSUES IN ASBESTOS REMOVAL. American Society of Civil Engineers, 345 East Forty-seventh Street, New York, New York 10017. 1988.

DEFUSING THE ASBESTOS LITIGATION CRISIS: THE RESPONSIBILITY OF THE U.S. GOVERNMENT. Joseph A. Artabane and Catherine R. Baumer. Washington Legal Foundation, 1705 N Street, Northwest, Washington, D.C. 20036. 1986.

FOURTH ANNUAL TOXIC TORT ADVOCACY INSTITUTE: TOBACCO PRODUCT LIABILITY: AFFIRMATIVE AND DEFENSIVE TOOLS, ASBESTOS PROPERTY DAMAGE LITIGATION. Prentice-Hall, Incorporated, 113 Sylvan Avenue, Englewood Cliffs, New Jersey 07632. 1986.

HEALTH HAZARDS OF ASBESTOS EXPOSURE. Irving J. Selikoff and E. Cuyler Hammond, Editors. Volume 330 of the Annals of the New York Academy of Sciences. New York Academy of Sciences, Publications Department, 2 East Sixty-third Street, New York, New York 10021. 1979.

THE IMPACT OF ASBESTOS ON REAL ESTATE. Practising Law Institute, New York, 810 Seventh Avenue, New York, New York 10019. 1989.

INTERNATIONAL REINSURANCE: ASBESTOS CLAIMS. Kluwer Academic Publishers, 101 Philip Drive, Assinippi Park, Norwell, Massachusetts 02061. 1988.

JUDICIAL ADMINISTRATION WORKING GROUP ON ASBESTOS LITIGATION: FINAL REPORT WITH RECOMMENDATIONS. National Center for State Courts, 300 Newport Avenue, Williamsburg, Virginia 23187-8798. 1984.

LEGAL ASPECTS OF ASBESTOS ABATEMENT: RESPONSES TO THE THREAT OF ASBESTOS-CONTAINING MATERIALS IN SCHOOL BUILDINGS. Kristin Olson. National Organization on Legal Problems of Education, Southwest Plaza Building, 3601 West Twenty-ninth Street, Suite 223, Topeka, Kansas 66614. 1986.

OUTRAGEOUS MISCONDUCT: THE ASBESTOS INDUSTRY ON TRIAL. Paul Brodeur. Pantheon Books, 201 East Fiftieth Street, New York, New York 10022. 1985.

SPECIAL PROBLEMS IN TOXIC SUBSTANCES LITIGATION AFTER MANVILLE. Practising Law Institute, 810 Seventh Avenue, New York, New York 10019. 1983.

TRENDS IN ASBESTOS LITIGATION. Thomas E. Willging. Federal Judicial Center, 1520 H Street, Northwest, Washington, D.C. 20005. 1987.

VARIATIONS IN ASBESTOS LITIGATION COMPENSATION AND EXPENSES. James S. Kakalik and others. Rand Corporation, Institute for Civil Justice, 1700 Main Street, P.O Box 2138, Santa Monica, California 90406. 1984.

NEWSLETTERS AND NEWSPAPERS

ASBESTOS ABATEMENT REPORT. Buraff Publications, Incorporated, 1350 Connecticut Avenue, Northwest, Washington, D.C. 20036. Biweekly.

ASBESTOS CONTROL REPORT. Business Publishers, Incorporated, 951 Pershing Drive, Silver Spring, Maryland 20910. Biweekly.

ASBESTOS LITIGATION REPORTER. Andrews Publications, Incorporated, P.O. Box 200, Edgemont, Pennsylvania 19028. Biweekly.

ASBESTOS PROPERTY LITIGATION REPORTER. Andrews Publications, Incorporated, P.O. Box 200, Edgemont, Pennsylvania 19028. Biweekly.

INDOOR POLLUTION LAW REPORT. Leader Publications, 111 Eighth Avenue, New York, New York 10011. Monthly.

INDOOR POLLUTION NEWS. Buraff Publications, Incorporated, 1350 Connecticut Avenue, Northwest, Washington, D.C. 20036. Biweekly.

MEALEY'S LITIGATION REPORT: ASBESTOS. Mealey Publications, Incorporated, P.O. Box 446, Wayne, Pennsylvania 19087. Biweekly.

MEALEY'S LITIGATION REPORT: ASBESTOS PROPERTY ACTIONS. Mealey Publications, Incorporated, P.O. Box 446, Wayne, Pennsylvania 19087. Biweekly.

NATIONAL JOURNAL OF ASBESTOS IN BUILDINGS LITIGATION. McGuire Publications Incorporated, P.O. Box 315, Springfield, Pennsylvania 19064. Biweekly.

BIBLIOGRAPHIES

ASBESTOS: A SELECTED BIBLIOGRAPHY. Marian Dworaczek. Vance Bibliographies, P.O. Box 229, 112 North Charter Street, Monticello, Illinois 61856. 1984.

ASBESTOS: A SELECTED BIBLIOGRAPHY OF JOURNAL ARTICLES. David R. Baca. Vance Bibliographies, P.O. Box 229, 112 North Charter Street, Monticello, Illinois 61856. 1989.

ASBESTOS: JOURNAL ARTICLES. Robert W. Lockerby. Vance Bibliographies, P.O. Box 229, 112 North Charter Street, Monticello, Illinois 61856. 1986.

ASBESTOS

DIRECTORIES

ASBESTOS, DIRECTORY OF RESEARCH AND DOCUMENTATION CENTRES. Sandro Amaducci, Editor. Kluwer Academic Publishers, 101 Philip Drive, Assinippi Park, Norwell, Massachusetts 02061. 1982.

ASSOCIATIONS AND PROFESSIONAL SOCIETIES

ASBESTOS LITIGATION GROUP. Ness, Motley, Loadholt, Richardson, and Poole, P.O. Box 1137, Charleston, South Carolina 29402. (803) 577-6747.

ASBESTOS VICTIMS OF AMERICA. P.O. Box 559, Capitola, California 95010. (408) 476-3646.

WHITE LUNG ASSOCIATION. 1114 Cathedral, Baltimore, Maryland 21201. (301) 727-6059.

RESEARCH CENTERS, INSTITUTES, CLEARINGHOUSES

ASBESTOS INFORMATION ASSOCIATION/NORTH AMERICA. 1745 Jefferson Davis Highway, Arlington, Virginia 22202. (703) 979-1150.

ASBESTOS INSTITUTE. 1130 Sherbrooke Street West, Suite 410, Montreal, PQ, Canada H3A 2M8. (514) 844-3956.

AUDIOVISUALS

ASBESTOS: A LETHAL LEGACY. Ambrose Video, 381 Park Avenue South, Suite 1601, New York, New York 10016. 1983. (1 Videocassette).

ASSASSINATION
See: MURDER; POLITICAL CRIMES AND OFFENSES

ASSEMBLY
See: FREEDOM OF ASSEMBLY AND ASSOCIATION

ASSIGNMENT FOR BENEFIT OF CREDITORS
See: BANKRUPTCY

ASSOCIATION
See: FREEDOM OF ASSEMBLY AND ASSOCIATION

ASSOCIATIONS AND NON-PROFIT CORPORATIONS
See also: CHARITIES; CORPORATIONS, TAXATION; LAW SOCIETIES; TAX EXEMPT ORGANIZATIONS

STATUTES, CODES, STANDARDS, UNIFORM LAWS

1986 REVISED MODEL NONPROFIT CORPORATION ACT. The Committee on Nonprofit Corporations, Section of Corporation, Banking and Business Law, American Bar Association, 750 North Lake Shore Drive, Chicago, Illinois 60611. 1986.

LOOSELEAF SERVICES AND REPORTERS

THE LAW OF ASSOCIATIONS. Second Edition. George D. Webster. Matthew Bender and Company, Incorporated, 11 Penn Plaza, New York, New York 10001. 1975- .

NONPROFIT ENTERPRISES: LAW AND TAXATION. Marilyn E. Phelan. Callaghan and Company, 155 Pfingsten Road, Deerfield, Illinois 60015. 1985- .

PLANNING TAX-EXEMPT ORGANIZATIONS. Robert J. Desiderio and Scott A. Taylor. Shepard's/McGraw-Hill, 420 North Cascade Avenue, Colorado Springs, Colorado 80901. 1983- .

HANDBOOKS, MANUALS, FORMBOOKS

ASSOCIATION LAW HANDBOOK. Second Edition. Jerald A. Jacobs. Bureau of National Affairs, Incorporated, 1231 Twenty-fifth Street, Northwest, Washington, D.C. 20037. 1986.

LEGAL HANDBOOK FOR NON-PROFIT ORGANIZATIONS. Marc J. Lane. Amacom, 135 West Fiftieth Street, New York 10020. 1980.

THE NONPROFIT SECTOR: A RESEARCH HANDBOOK. Walter W. Powell, Editor. Yale University Press, 302 Temple Street, New Haven, Connecticut 06520. 1989.

TEXTBOOKS AND GENERAL WORKS

CHARITABLE GIVING AND TAX-EXEMPT ORGANIZATIONS: THE IMPACT OF THE 1981 TAX ACT. Bruce R. Hopkins. John Wiley and Sons, Incorporated, 605 Third Avenue, New York, New York 10158. 1981.

THE ECONOMICS OF NONPROFIT INSTITUTIONS: STUDIES IN STRUCTURES AND POLICY. Susan Rose-Ackerman. Oxford University Press, 200 Madison Avenue, New York, New York 10016. 1986.

EFFECTIVE FINANCIAL MANAGEMENT IN PUBLIC AND NON-PROFIT AGENCIES: A PRACTICAL AND INTEGRATIVE APPROACH. Jerome B. McKinney. Quorum Books, Greenwood Publishing Group, Incorporated, Incorporated, 88 Post Road West, P.O. Box 5007, Westport, Connecticut 06881. 1986.

GROUP DYNAMIC LAW: EXPOSITION AND PRACTICE. Law Arts Publishers, 159 West Fifty-third Street, New York, New York 10019. 1988.

IF NOT FOR PROFIT, FOR WHAT?: A BEHAVIORAL THEORY OF THE NONPROFIT SECTOR BASED ON ENTREPRENEURSHIP. Dennis R. Young. Lexington Books, 125 Spring Street, Lexington, Massachusetts 02173. 1983.

THE LAW OF TAX-EXEMPT ORGANIZATIONS. Fifth Edition. Bruce R. Hopkins. John Wiley and Sons, Incorporated, 605 Third Avenue, New York, New York 10158. 1987.

NONPROFIT BOARDS OF DIRECTORS: ANALYSES AND APPLICATIONS. Robert D. Herman and Jon Van Til, Editors. Transaction Books, Rutgers University, New Brunswick, New Jersey 08903. 1988.

NONPROFIT CORPORATIONS ORGANIZATIONS, AND ASSOCIATIONS. Fifth Edition. Howard L. Oleck. Prentice-Hall, Incorporated, 113 Sylvan Avenue, Englewood Cliffs, New Jersey 07632. 1988.

NON-PROFIT ORGANIZATIONS: CURRENT ISSUES AND DEVELOPMENTS. Jonathan A. Small, Chairman. Prentice-Hall, Incorporated, 113 Sylvan Avenue, Englewood Cliffs, New Jersey 07632. 1986.

RIGHTS, PERSONS, AND ORGANIZATIONS: A LEGAL THEORY FOR BUREAUCRATIC SOCIETY. Meir Dan-Cohen. University of California Press, 2120 Berkeley Way, Berkeley, California 94720. 1986.

TAX-EXEMPT CHARITABLE ORGANIZATIONS. Third Edition. Paul E. Treusch and Norman A. Sugarman. American Law Institute-American Bar Association, 4025 Chestnut Street, Philadelphia, Pennsylvania 19104. 1988.

TAX EXEMPT ORGANIZATIONS. E.C. Lashbrooke, Jr. Quorum Books, Greenwood Publishing Group, Incorporated, Incorporated, 88 Post Road West, Westport, Connecticut 06881. 1985.

A WORKING GUIDE FOR DIRECTORS OF NOT-FOR-PROFIT ORGANIZATIONS. Charles N. Waldo. Quorum Books, Greenwood Publishing Group, Incorporated, Incorporated, 88 Post Road West, Westport, Connecticut 06881. 1986.

ENCYCLOPEDIAS AND DICTIONARIES

ENCYCLOPEDIA OF ASSOCIATIONS. Twenty-sixth Edition. Gale Research Incorporated, 835 Penobscot Building, Detroit, Michigan 48226. 1991- . (Periodic Supplements).

NEWSLETTERS AND NEWSPAPERS

ASSOCIATION LAW AND POLICY. American Society of Association Executives, 1575 I Street, Northwest, Washington, D.C. 20005. Biweekly.

EXEMPT TAX ORGANIZATION REVIEW. Tax Analysts, 6830 North Fairfax Drive, Arlington, Virginia 22213. Monthly.

NON-PROFIT ORGANIZATION TAX LETTER. Organization Management, Incorporated, 13234 Pleasantview Lane, Fairfax, Virginia 22033. Eighteen issues per year.

THE NONPROFIT COUNSEL. John Wiley and Sons, Incorporated, 605 Third Avenue, New York, New York 10158. Monthly.

TAX-EXEMPT NEWS. Whitaker Newsletters, 313 South Avenue, Fanwood, New Jersey 07023. Biweekly.

BIBLIOGRAPHIES

NON-PROFIT CORPORATIONS: SELECTED BIBLIOGRAPHY. Howard Oleck. Stetson Law Library, 1401 Sixty-first Street South, St. Petersburg, Florida 33707. 1986.

OTHER SOURCES

REPRESENTING AND MANAGING TAX-EXEMPT ORGANIZATIONS: PROGRAM MATERIALS, APRIL 17-18, 1983. Third Annual Program. Georgetown University Law Center, Continuing Legal Education, 25 East Street, Northwest, First Floor, Washington, D.C. 20001. 1986.

ASYLUM
See: EMIGRATION AND IMMIGRATION

ATOMIC ENERGY
See: NUCLEAR ENERGY

ATTACHMENT AND GARNISHMENT

TEXTBOOKS AND GENERAL WORKS

DEBTOR-CREDITOR LAW IN A NUTSHELL. Third Edition. David G. Epstein. West Publishing Company, 50 West Kellogg Boulevard, St. Paul, Minnesota 55164-0526. 1985.

DEBTOR-CREDITOR RELATIONS: MANUAL AND FORMS. Leo O. Myers. Shepard's/McGraw-Hill Publishing Company, 420 North Cascade Avenue, Colorado Springs, Colorado 80901. 1986.

ENFORCING STATE AND FEDERAL MONEY JUDGMENTS AND COMMERCIAL CLAIMS. Practising Law Institute, 810 Seventh Avenue, New York, New York 10019. 1988.

FAIR DEBT COLLECTION. Robert J. Hobbs. National Consumer Law Center, 11 Beacon Street, Boston, Massachusetts 02108. 1987.

FEDERAL REGULATION OF CONSUMER-CREDITOR RELATIONS. Kenneth R. Reddan and James McClellan. Michie Company, P.O. Box 7587, Charlottesville, Virginia 22906-7582. 1982.

A TREATISE ON AMERICAN LAW OF ATTACHMENT AND GARNISHMENT: A COMPLETE STATEMENT OF THE GENERAL PRINCIPLES APPLIED BY COURTS OF REVIEW AND OF THE COMMON RULES GOVERNING THE PRACTICE UNDER ALL STATUTES. Bobbs-Merrill Company, Incorporated, 4300 West Sixty-second Street, Indianapolis, Indiana 46206. Defunct.

ATTACHMENT AND GARNISHMENT

A TREATISE ON THE LAW OF ATTACHMENT AND GARNISHMENT, AN APPENDIX CONTAINING A COMPILATION OF THE STATUTES OF THE DIFFERENT STATES AND TERRITORIES NOW IN FORCE GOVERNING SUITS BY ATTACHMENT. Bancroft-Whitney, P.O. Box 7005, San Francisco, California 94120. 1886.

A TREATISE ON THE LAW OF SUITS BY ATTACHMENT IN THE UNITED STATES. Seventh Edition. Charles David Drake. Little, Brown and Company, 34 Beacon Street, Boston, Massachusetts 02108. 1891.

COMPUTER-ASSISTED LEGAL INSTRUCTION

DEBTOR CREDITOR GAME. Lynn M. LoPucki. Center for Computer- Assisted Instruction, 229 19th Avenue South, University of Minnesota, Minneapolis, Minnesota 55455. Machine-readable computer file.

ATTORNEY-GENERAL (UNITED STATES)
See also: JUSTICE DEPARTMENT

LOOSELEAF SERVICES AND REPORTERS

OPINIONS OF THE ATTORNEY GENERAL OF THE UNITED STATES. Justice Department. Superintendent of Documents, United States Government Printing Office, Washington, D.C. 20402. Irregular.

TEXTBOOKS AND GENERAL WORKS

ATTORNEY GENERAL'S COMMISSION ON PORNOGRAPHY, FINAL REPORT, VOLUMES 1 AND 2. Justice Department. Superintendent of Documents, United States Government Printing Office, Washington, D.C. 20402. 1986.

REPORT OF THE TORT POLICY WORKING GROUP ON THE CAUSES, EXTENT AND POLICY IMPLICATIONS OF THE CURRENT CRISIS IN INSURANCE AVAILABILITY AND AFFORDABILITY. Tort Policy Working Group. Superintendent of Documents, United States Government Printing Office, Washington, D.C. 20402. 1986.

ANNUALS AND SURVEYS

ATTORNEY GENERAL OF THE UNITED STATES ANNUAL REPORT. Justice Department, Office of the Attorney General. Superintendent of Documents, United States Government Printing Office, Washington, D.C. 20402. Annual.

ONLINE DATABASES

LEXIS, GENERAL FEDERAL LIBRARY, U.S. ATTORNEY GENERAL FILE. Mead Data Central, P.O. Box 933, Dayton, Ohio 45401.

WESTLAW, GENERAL FEDERAL LIBRARY, U.S. ATTORNEY GENERAL OPINIONS FILE. West Publishing Company, P.O. Box 64526, 50 West Kellogg Boulevard, St. Paul, Minnesota 55164-0526.

ATTORNEYS
See: ADMISSION TO THE BAR; AMERICAN BAR ASSOCIATION; LAW OFFICE MANAGEMENT; LAW PRACTICE; LAWYER AND CLIENT; LAWYERS' FEES; LEGAL AID; LEGAL ETHICS AND MALPRACTICE; LEGAL PROFESSION IN FICTION; PREPAID LEGAL SERVICES; PUBLIC PROSECUTORS

AUDITING
See: ACCOUNTANTS AND ACCOUNTING

AUTHORS AND PUBLISHERS
See also: COPYRIGHT; COPYRIGHT OFFICE

LOOSELEAF SERVICES AND REPORTERS

AUTHORS AND PUBLISHERS: AGREEMENTS AND LEGAL ASPECTS OF PUBLISHING. Lazar Sarnar. Butterworth Legal Publishers, 90 Stiles Road, Salem, New Hampshire 03079. 1980.

LINDEY ON ENTERTAINMENT, PUBLISHING AND THE ARTS. Second Edition. Alexander Lindey. Clark Boardman Company, Limited, 435 Hudson Street, New York, New York 10014. 1980- .

THE PUBLISHER'S LEGAL HANDBOOK. John Taylor Williams and E. Gabriel Perle. Prentice Hall Law and Business, Incorporated, 1873 Western Avenue, Albany, New York 12203. 1987- .

RECORD AND MUSIC PUBLISHING FORMS OF AGREEMENT IN CURRENT USE. Irwin O. Spiegel and Jay L. Cooper. Law-Arts Publishers, 159 West Fifty-third Street, No. 14F, New York, New York 10019. 1971- .

RIGHTS AND LIABILITIES OF PUBLISHERS, BROADCASTERS AND REPORTERS. Slade R. Metcalf. Shepard's/McGraw-Hill, P.O. Box 1235, Colorado Springs, Colorado 80901. 1982- .

HANDBOOKS, MANUALS, FORMBOOKS

BOOKS PUBLISHERS' LEGAL GUIDE. Leonard D. Duboff. Butterworth Legal Publishers, 90 Stiles Road, Salem, New Hampshire 03079. 1980.

ENTERTAINMENT, PUBLISHING AND THE ARTS HANDBOOK. Michael Myer and John D. Viera. Clark Boardman Company, Limited, 435 Hudson Street, New York, New York 10014. 1989.

TEXTBOOKS AND GENERAL WORKS

BOOK PUBLISHING. Practising Law Institute, 810 Seventh Avenue, New York, New York 10019. Annual.

LAW AND THE WRITER. Updated Edition. Kirk Polking and Leonard S. Meranus. Writer's Digest Books, 1507 Dana Avenue, Cincinnati, Ohio 45207. 1981.

MAKING IT LEGAL: A LAW PRIMER FOR AUTHORS, ARTISTS AND CRAFTS PEOPLE. Marion Davidson and Martha Blue. Northland Press, P.O. Box 1187, Springfield, Virginia 22151-0187. 1988.

PRESSING BUSINESS: AN ORGANIZATIONAL MANUAL FOR INDEPENDENT PUBLISHERS. Barbara S. Taylor. Volunteer Lawyers for the Arts, 1285 Avenue of the Americas, Third Floor, New York, New York 10019. 1984.

DIRECTORIES

AMERICAN SOCIETY OF JOURNALISTS AND AUTHORS DIRECTORY. 1501 Broadway, Suite 1907, New York, New York 10036. Annual.

DIRECTORY FOR SUCCESSFUL PUBLISHING IN LEGAL PERIODICALS. Al Joyner. Qucoda Publishing Company, R.R. 5, #16, P.O. Box 146, Charleston, Illinois 61920.

PUBLISHERS, DISTRIBUTORS AND WHOLESALERS OF THE UNITED STATES 1991-92. R.R. Bowker Company, 121 Chanlon Road, New Providence, New Jersey 07974. 1991.

WRITER'S DIRECTORY. St. Martin's Press, 175 Fifth Avenue, New York, New York 10010. Biennial.

ASSOCIATIONS AND PROFESSIONAL SOCIETIES

AMERICAN BOOKSELLERS ASSOCIATION, 137 West Twenty-fifth Street, New York, New York 10001. (212) 463-8450.

AMERICAN CIVIL LIBERTIES UNION FOUNDATION, 132 West Forty-third Street, New York, New York 10036. (212) 944-9800.

AMERICAN LIBRARY ASSOCIATION, 50 East Huron Street, Chicago, Illinois 60611. (312) 944-6780.

AMERICAN SOCIETY OF JOURNALISTS AND AUTHORS, 1501 Broadway, Suite 1907, New York, New York 10036. (212) 997-0947.

ASSOCIATION OF AMERICAN PUBLISHERS, 220 East Twenty-third Street, New York, New York 10010. (212) 689-8920.

BLACK WOMEN IN PUBLISHING, P.O. Box 6275, F.D.R. Station, New York, New York 10150. (212) 772-5951.

MAGAZINE PUBLISHERS OF AMERICA, 575 Lexington Avenue, New York, New York 10022. (212) 752-0055.

SOCIETY OF AUTHORS' REPRESENTATIVES, 10 Astor Place, New York, New York 10003. (212) 924-6023.

RESEARCH CENTERS, INSTITUTES, CLEARINGHOUSES

BOOK INDUSTRY STUDY GROUP, 160 Fifth Avenue, New York, New York 10010. (212) 929-1393.

CENTER FOR ELECTRONIC PUBLISHING RESEARCH. Box 381, Cambridge, Massachusetts 02142.

AUTOMOBILES
See: INSURANCE, MOTOR VEHICLES AND AVIATION; MOTOR VEHICLES

AVIATION
See also: AVIATION ACCIDENTS; FEDERAL AVIATION ADMINISTRATION; INSURANCE, MOTOR VEHICLE AND AVIATION; NATIONAL TRANSPORTATION SAFETY BOARD; SPACE LAW; TERRORISM; TRANSPORTATION DEPARTMENT

STATUTES, CODES, STANDARDS, UNIFORM LAWS

AIR AND AVIATION TREATIES OF THE WORLD. S. Houston Lay. Oceana Publications, 75 Main Street, Dobbs Ferry, New York 10522. 1986- .

FEDERAL AVIATION ADMINISTRATION - CODIFIED REGULATIONS. Rules Service Company, 7658 Standish Place, Suite 106, Rockville, Maryland 20855. 1962- .

FEDERAL AVIATION REGULATIONS. United States Federal Aviation Administration. United States Government Printing Office, Washington, D.C. 20402. 1978- . (Annual).

LOOSELEAF SERVICES AND REPORTERS

AVIATION CASES IN THE COURTS. Hawkins Publishing Company, Incorporated, 1207B 310 Tahiti Way, Number 108, Marina Del Rey, California 90291. 1980. (Periodic Supplements).

AVIATION LAW REPORTS. Commerce Clearing House, Incorporated, 4025 West Peterson Avenue, Chicago, Illinois 60646.

AVIATION REGULATORY DIGEST SERVICE. Carl R. Eyler. Hawkins Publishing Company, Incorporated, 310 Tahiti Way, Number 108, Marina Del Rey, California 90291.

REGULATION OF INTERNATIONAL COMMERCIAL AVIATION: THE INTERNATIONAL REGULATORY STRUCTURE. Stanley Rosenfield. Oceana Publications, Incorporated, 75 Main Street, Dobbs Ferry, New York 10522. 1984. (Periodic Supplements).

HANDBOOKS, MANUALS, FORMBOOKS

THE AIRLINE DEREGULATION HANDBOOK: WITH THE COMPLETE TEXT OF THE AIRLINE DEREGULATION ACT OF 1978. Jeffrey R. Miller. Merton House Publishing Company, 937 West Liberty Drive, Wheaton, Illinois 60187. 1981.

AVIATION LAWYER'S MANUAL: REPRESENTING THE PILOT IN FAA PROCEEDINGS. John S. Yodice. Maryland Historical Press, 9205 Tuckerman Street, Lanham, Maryland 20706. 1986.

PILOTS AND AIRCRAFT OWNERS LEGAL GUIDE. Fourth Edition. Jay C. White. Aviation Book Company, 25133 Anza Drive, Unit E, Santa Clarita, California 91355. 1984.

PILOT'S DIGEST OF FAA REGULATIONS. Second Edition. John L. Nelson. TAB Books, Incorporated, P.O. Box 40, Blue Ridge Summit, Pennsylvania 17294-0850. 1981.

TEXTBOOKS AND GENERAL WORKS

AERIAL HIJACKING AS AN INTERNATIONAL CRIME. Nancy Douglas Joyner. Oceana Publications, 75 Main Street, Dobbs Ferry, New York 10522. 1974.

AIRLINE DEREGULATION. Melvin A. Brenner, James O. Feet and Elibu Schott. ENO Foundation for Transportation, P.O. Box 2055, Westport, Connecticut 06880. 1985.

AIRLINE DEREGULATION: THE EARLY EXPERIENCE. John R. Meyer, Clinton V. Oster, Jr. and others. Auburn House Publishing Company, Incorporated, Greenwood Publishing Group, Incorporated, 88 Post Road West, P.O. Box 5007, Westport, Connecticut 06881. 1981.

AIRLINES IN TRANSITION. Nawal K. Taneja. Lexington Books, 125 Spring Street, Lexington, Massachusetts 02173. 1981.

AVIATION AND THE LAW. Laurence E. Gesell. Coast Aire Publications, 2823 North Yucca Street, Chandler, Arizona 85224-1867. 1989.

AVIATION ANTITRUST: THE EXTRATERRITORIAL APPLICATION OF THE UNITED STATES ANTITRUST LAWS AND INTERNATIONAL AIR TRANSPORTATION. Patricia M. Barlow. Kluwer Law Book Publishers, 36 West Forty-fourth Street, New York, New York 10036. 1988.

AVIATION INDUSTRY BANKRUPTCY ISSUES. Practising Law Institute, 810 Seventh Avenue, New York, New York 10019. 1986.

AVIATION INDUSTRY: CURRENT PERSPECTIVES AND PROBLEMS. Ruth J. Weinstein. Practising Law Institute, 810 Seventh Avenue, New York, New York 10019. 1978.

AVIATION INDUSTRY REGULATION. Harry P. Wolfe and Daved A. Newmyer. Southern Illinois University Press, P.O. Box 3697, Carbondale, Illinois 62902-3697. 1985.

AVIATION TORT LAW. Stuart M. Speiser, Charles F. Krause and Alfred W. Gans. Lawyers Co-Operative Publishing Company, Aqueduct Building, One Graves Street, Rochester, New York 14694. 1978- . (Periodic Supplements).

BLIND TRUST: THE HUMAN CRISIS IN AIRLINE SAFETY. John J. Nance. William Morrow and Company, Incorporated, 105 Madison Avenue, New York, New York 10016. 1987.

CLEARED FOR TAKEOFF: AIRLINE LABOR RELATIONS SINCE DEREGULATION. Jean T. McKelvey, Editor. ILR Press, New York State School of Industrial and Labor Relations, Cornell University, Ithaca, New York 14850. 1988.

DEREGULATING THE AIRLINES. Elizabeth E. Bailey, David R. Graham and Daniel P. Kaplan. MIT Press, 55 Hayward Street, Cambridge, Massachusetts 02142. 1985.

DEREGULATION AND THE NEW AIRLINE ENTREPRENEURS. John R. Meyer and Clinton V. Oster, Jr. MIT Press, 55 Hayward Street, Cambridge, Massachusetts 02142. 1984.

DISCRIMINATORY REFUSAL OF CARRIAGE IN NORTH AMERICA. Barbara Reukema. Kluwer Law Book Publishers, 36 West Forty-fourth Street, New York, New York 10036. 1982.

THE ECONOMIC EFFECTS OF AIRLINE DEREGULATIONS. Steven A. Morrison and Clifford Winston. The Brookings Institution, 1775 Massachusetts Avenue, Northwest, Washington, D.C. 20036. 1986.

INTERNATIONAL AIR TRANSPORT IN A CHANGING WORLD. Jacques Naveau. Martinus Nijhoff, Kluwer Academic Publishers, 101 Philip Drive, Assinipi Park, Norwell, Massachusetts 02061. 1989.

INTRODUCTION TO AIR LAW. Fourth Revised Edition. I.H. Philepina Diederiks-Verschoor. Kluwer Law Book Publishers, 36 West Forty-fourth Street, New York, New York 10036. 1991.

LAW AND FOREIGN POLICY IN INTERNATIONAL AVIATION. Paul Stephen Dempsey. Transnational Publishers, P.O. Box 7281, Ardsley-on-Hudson, New York 10503. 1987.

THE POLITICS OF AIRLINE DEREGULATION. Anthony E. Brown. University of Tennessee Press, 293 Communications Building, Knoxville, Tennessee 37996-0325. 1987.

THE POLITICS OF INTERNATIONAL AIR TRANSPORTATION. Betsy Gidwitz. Lexington Books, 125 Spring Street, Lexington, Massachusetts 02173. 1980.

TRAVEL INDUSTRY PROBLEMS: TRAVEL LITIGATION, TERRORISM, DEREGULATION, AND THE PUBLIC INTEREST. Practising Law Institute, 810 Seventh Avenue, New York, New York 10019. 1987.

TREATISE ON AIR-AERONAUTICAL LAW. Nicholas Mateesco Matte. Carswell Company, Limited, 145 Adelaide Street West, Toronto, Ontario MSH 3114, Canada. 1981.

U.S. INTERNATIONAL AVIATION POLICY. Nawal K. Taneja. Lexington Books, 125 Spring Street, Lexington, Massachusetts 02173. 1980.

LAW REVIEWS AND PERIODICALS

AIR AND SPACE LAWYER. Forum Committee on Air and Space Law, American Bar Association, 750 North Lake Shore Drive, Chicago, Illinois 60611. Quarterly.

AIR LAW. Kluwer Law and Taxation Publishers, 190 Derby Street, Hingham, Massachusetts 02043. Bimonthly.

ANNALS OF AIR AND SPACE LAW. Institute of Air and Space Law, Toronto. Carswell Company, Limited, 145 Adelaide Street West, Toronto, Ontario MSH 3H4, Canada. Annual.

NORTHROP UNIVERSITY LAW JOURNAL OF AEROSPACE, ENERGY AND THE ENVIRONMENT. School of Law, Northrop University, Arbor Vitae Boulevard, Inglewood, California 90306. Annual.

NEWSLETTERS AND NEWSPAPERS

AEROSPACE DAILY. McGraw-Hill, Incorporated, 1156 Fifteenth Street, Northwest, Washington, D.C. 20005. Daily (weekdays).

AIR SAFETY LAW AND TECHNOLOGY. Bureau of National Affairs, 1231 Twenty-sixth Street, Northwest, Washington, D.C. 20036. Bimonthly.

AVIATION DAILY. McGraw-Hill Incorporated, 1156 Fifteenth Street, Northwest, Washington, D.C. 20005. Daily (weekdays).

AVIATION LITIGATION REPORTER. Andrews Publications, 1646 West Chester Pike, Westtown, Pennsylvania 19395. Weekly.

GENERAL AVIATION ACCIDENT REPORT. Andrews Publications, 1646 West Chester Pike, Westtown, Pennsylvania 19395. Monthly.

LLOYD'S AVIATION LAW. Lloyd's of London Press, 611 Broadway, New York, New York 10012. Semimonthly.

NASAO STATE AVIATION NEWSLETTER. National Association of State Aviation Officials, 8401 Colesville Road, Silver Spring, Maryland 20910. Monthly.

BIBLIOGRAPHIES

AEROSPACE BIBLIOGRAPHY. Seventh Edition. Jean F. Blashfield, Editor. National Aeronautics and Space Administration. Superintendent of Documents, United States Government Printing Office, Washington, D.C. 20402. 1982.

AIR TRANSPORTATION--AIRCRAFT AND EQUIPMENT, SERVICES, SAFETY MEASURES, AIR FREIGHT: A BIBLIOGRAPHY. E. Willard Miller and Ruby W. Miller. Vance Bibliographies, P.O. Box 229, 112 North Charter Street, Monticello, Illinois 61856. 1987.

AIR TRANSPORTATION--REGULATIONS, COMPUTER SYSTEMS, AIR TRAFFIC CONTROL, LABOR: A BIBLIOGRAPHY. E. Willard Miller and Ruby W. Miller. Vance Bibliographies, P.O. Box 229, 112 North Charter Street, Monticello, Illinois 61856. 1987.

INTERNATIONAL BIBLIOGRAPHY OF AIR LAW 1900-1971. Wybo P. Heere. Oceana Publications, 75 Main Street, Dobbs Ferry, New York 10522. 1972.

INTERNATIONAL BIBLIOGRAPHY OF AIR LAW: SUPPLEMENT 1977-1980. Wybo P. Heere. Kluwer Academic Publishers, 101 Philip Drive, Assinippi Park, Norwell, Massachusetts 02061. 1980.

ASSOCIATIONS AND PROFESSIONAL SOCIETIES

AIRCRAFT OWNERS AND PILOTS ASSOCIATION. 421 Aviation Way, Frederick, Maryland 21701. (301) 695-2000.

AMERICAN BAR ASSOCIATION. Forum Committee on Air and Space Law, 750 North Lake Shore Drive, Chicago, Illinois 60611. (312) 988-5000.

LAWYER-PILOTS BAR ASSOCIATION. 500 E Street, Southwest, Suite 930, Washington, D.C. 20024. (202) 863-1000.

NATIONAL ASSOCIATION OF STATE AVIATION OFFICIALS. 8401 Colesville Road, Suite 505, Silver Spring, Maryland 20910. (301) 588-0587.

RESEARCH CENTERS, INSTITUTES, CLEARINGHOUSES

BATTELLE MEMORIAL INSTITUTE. 505 King Avenue, Columbus, Ohio 43201. (614) 424-6424.

NASAO CENTER FOR AVIATION RESEARCH AND EDUCATION, INCORPORATED. Metro Plaza One, 8401 Colesville Road, Silver Spring, Maryland 20910. (301) 495-2848.

OFFICE OF AVIATION SAFETY ANALYSIS. Federal Aviation Administration, 800 Independence Avenue, Southwest, Washington, D.C. 20591. (202) 267-7770.

ONLINE DATABASES

AVIATION SAFETY INSTITUTE. P.O. Box 304, Worthington, Ohio 43085.

FAA RULES AND REGULATIONS. Jay C. White, P.O. Box 1148, Redwood City, California 94064.

AVIATION ACCIDENTS
See also: FEDERAL AVIATION ADMINISTRATION; NATIONAL TRANSPORTATION SAFETY BOARD

LOOSELEAF SERVICES AND REPORTERS

AVIATION ACCIDENT LAW. Lee S. Krindler. Matthew Bender and Company, Incorporated, 11 Penn Plaza, New York, New York 10001. 1963- .

AVIATION CASES IN THE COURTS. Hawkins Publishing Company, Incorporated, 310 Tahiti Way, Number 108, Marina Del Rey, California 90291. 1980. (Periodic Supplements).

AVIATION LAW REPORTS. Commerce Clearing House, Incorporated, 4025 West Peterson Avenue, Chicago, Illinois 60646. 1931- .

LITIGATION AND TRIAL OF AIR CRASH CASES. John J. Kennelly. Callaghan and Company, 155 Pfingsten Road, Deerfield, Illinois 60015. 1968- .

TEXTBOOKS AND GENERAL WORKS

AIRCRASH LITIGATION TECHNIQUES. Daniel C. Cathcart. Michie Company, P.O. Box 7587, Charlottesville, Virginia 22906-7582. 1985- .

AVIATION LITIGATION. Windle Turley. Shepard's/McGraw-Hill, P.O. Box 1235, Colorado Springs, Colorado 80901. 1986- . (Annual Supplements).

AVIATION TORT LAW. Stuart M. Spieser and Charles F. Krause. Lawyers Cooperative Publishing Company, Aqueduct Building, One Graves Street, Rochester, New York 14694. 1978- . (Annual Supplements).

AVIATION ACCIDENTS

GENERAL AVIATION ACCIDENT LITIGATION. Practising Law Institute, 810 Seventh Avenue, New York, New York 10019. 1986.

KAL FLIGHT 007: THE HIDDEN STORY. Oliver Clubb. The Permanent Press, RD2 Noyac Road, Sag Harbor, New York 11963. 1985.

LITIGATING THE AVIATION CASE: FROM PRETRIAL TO CLOSING ARGUMENT. Juanita M. Madole, Editor. American Bar Association, Tort and Insurance Practice Section, 750 North Lake Shore Drive, Chicago, Illinois 60611. 1987.

THE UNFRIENDLY SKIES: AN AVIATION WATERGATE. Second Revised Edition. Rodney Stitch, Editor. Diablo Western Press, P.O. Box 5, Alamo, California 94507. 1980.

WILLFUL MISCONDUCT: AN UNTOLD STORY. William Norris. W.W. Norton and Company, Incorporated, 500 Fifth Avenue, New York, New York 10110. 1984.

ANNUALS AND SURVEYS

AIRCRAFT CRASH LITIGATION. Practising Law Institute, 810 Seventh Avenue, New York, New York 10019. Annual.

LAW REVIEWS AND PERIODICALS

AIR LAW. Kluwer Law and Taxation Publishers, 190 Derby Street, Hingham, Massachusetts 02043. Bimonthly.

NEWSLETTERS AND NEWSPAPERS

AVIATION LITIGATION REPORTER. Andrews Publications, Incorporated, P.O. Box 200, Edgemont, Pennsylvania 19028. Semimonthly.

GENERAL AVIATION ACCIDENT REPORT. Andrews Publications, Incorporated, P.O. Box 200, Edgemont, Pennsylvania 19028. Weekly.

BIBLIOGRAPHIES

THE AIRLINE BIBLIOGRAPHY: THE SALEM COLLEGE GUIDE TO SOURCES ON COMMERCIAL AVIATION. VOLUME 1: THE UNITED STATES. Myron J. Smith. Locust Hill Press, P.O. Box 260, West Cornwall, Connecticut 06796. 1988.

RESEARCH CENTERS, INSTITUTES, CLEARINGHOUSES

OFFICE OF AVIATION SAFETY ANALYSIS. Federal Aviation Administration, 800 Independence Avenue, Southwest, Washington, D.C. 20591. (202) 267-7770.

ONLINE DATABASES

AVIATION SAFETY INSTITUTE. P.O. Box 304, Worthington, Ohio 43085.

FAA RULES AND REGULATIONS. Jay C. White, P.O. Box 1148, Redwood City, California 94604.

AWARD
See: ARBITRATION AND AWARD

B

BAIL

STATUTES, CODES, STANDARDS, UNIFORM LAWS

A MODEL CODE OF PRE-ARRAIGNMENT PROCEDURE. James Vorenberg, Chief Reporter. American Law Institute, 4025 Chestnut Street, Philadelphia, Pennsylvania 19104. 1975.

STANDARDS RELATING TO PRETRIAL RELEASE. Kenneth J. Hodson, Chairman, Project on Standards for Criminal Justice. Task Force on Pretrial Release, American Bar Association, 1800 M Street, Northwest, Washington, D.C. 20036. 1979.

LOOSELEAF SERVICES AND REPORTE RS

FEDERAL BAIL AND DETENTION HANDBOOK. John L. Weinberg. Practising Law Institute, 810 Seventh Avenue, New York, New York 10019. 1988.

HANDBOOKS, MANUALS, FORMBOOKS

BOND PRACTICE MANUAL. National Lawyers Guild, National Immigration Project, 55 Sixth Avenue, New York, New York 10013. 1986.

CONSTITUTIONAL RIGHTS OF THE ACCUSED: PRETRIAL RIGHTS. Joseph G. Cook. Second Edition. Lawyers Cooperative Publishing Company, Aqueduct Building, Rochester, New York 14694. 1985.

A FEDERAL PROSECUTOR'S GUIDE TO BOND AND SENTENCING ISSUES: PRETRIAL DETENTION, SENTENCE ENHANCEMENT, PAROLE ELIGIBILITY, AND PENAL DESIGNATION IN FEDERAL PROSECUTIONS. Gregory Bruce English. United States Department of Justice, Criminal Division. Superintendent of Documents, United States Government Printing Office, Washington, D.C. 20402. 1984.

HOW TO IMPLEMENT CRIMINAL JUSTICE STANDARDS FOR PRETRIAL RELEASE. Bruce Beaudin. American Bar Association, Section on Criminal Justice, 1800 M Street, Northwest, Washington, D.C. 20036. 1976.

TEXTBOOKS AND GENERAL WORKS

AMERICA'S COURTS AND THE CRIMINAL JUSTICE SYSTEM. Second Edition. David W. Neubauer. Brooks/Cole Publishing Company, 511 Forest Lodge Road, Pacific Grove, California 93924. 1988.

ARREST BY POLICE COMPUTER: THE CONTROVERSY OVER BAIL AND EXTRADITION. John J. Murphy. Lexington Books, 125 Spring Street, Lexington, Massachusetts 02173. 1975.

BAIL AND ITS REFORM: A NATIONAL SURVEY. Paul B. Wice. National Institute of Law Enforcement and Criminal Justice. Superintendent of Documents, United States Government Printing Office, Washington, D.C. 20402. 1973.

BAIL AND PREVENTIVE DETENTION IN NEW YORK. Edward J. Shaughnessy. University Press of America, 4720 Boston Way, Lanham, Maryland 20706. 1982.

BAIL DECISION-MAKING: THE STUDY OF POLICY GUIDELINES. John S. Goldkamp, Michael R. Gottfredson and Susan Mitchell-Herzfeld. Criminal Justice Research Center, State University of New York at Albany, 135 Western Avenue, Albany, New York 12222. 1981.

BAIL REFORM ACT OF 1984. Deirdre Golash. Federal Judicial Center. Superintendent of Documents, Government Printing Office, Washington, D.C. 20402. 1987.

BAIL REFORM IN AMERICA. Wayne H. Thomas. University of California Press, 2120 Berkeley Way, Berkeley, California 94720. 1977.

THE CONSTITUTIONALITY OF PREVENTIVE DETENTION. Philip E. Secret. University Press of America, 4720 Boston Way, Lanham, Maryland 20706. 1977.

DECISION THEORY AND THE LEGAL PROCESS. Stuart S. Nagel. Lexington Books, 125 Spring Street, Lexington, Massachusetts 02173. 1979.

DEVELOPMENT AND IMPLEMENTATION OF BAIL GUIDELINES: HIGHLIGHTS AND ISSUES. John S. Goldkamp. United States Department of Justice, National Institute of Justice. Superintendent of Documents, United States Government Printing Office, Washington, D.C. 20402. 1984.

THE EFFECTIVENESS OF BAIL SYSTEMS: AN ANALYSIS OF FAILURE TO APPEAR IN COURT AND RE-ARREST WHILE ON BAIL. Stevens H. Clarke, Jean L. Freeman and Gary G. Koch. United States Department of Justice, National Institute of Law Enforcement and Criminal Justice. Superintendent of Documents, United States Government Printing Office, Washington, D.C. 20402. 1976.

FREEDOM FOR SALE. Paul B. Wice. Lexington Books, 125 Spring Street, Lexington, Massachusetts 02173. 1974.

INSTEAD OF JAIL: PRE- AND POST-TRIAL ALTERNATIVES TO JAIL INCARCERATION. John J. Galvin, Walter H. Busher, William Greene and others. United States Department of Justice, National Institute of Law Enforcement and Criminal Justice. Superintendent of Documents, United States Government Printing Office, Washington, D.C. 20402. 1977.

JUDICIAL GUIDELINES FOR BAIL: THE PHILADELPHIA EXPERIMENT. John S. Goldkamp and Michael Gottfredson. United States Department of Justice, National Institute of Law Enforcement and Criminal Justice. Superintendent of Documents, Government Printing Office, Washington, D.C. 20402. 1984.

POLICY GUIDELINES FOR BAIL: AN EXPERIMENT IN COURT REFORM. John S. Goldkamp and Michael R. Gottfredson. Temple University Press, 1601 North Broad Street, University Services Building, Room 305, Philadelphia, Pennsylvania 19122. 1985.

PRETRIAL RELEASE: A NATIONAL EVALUATION OF PRACTICES AND OUTCOMES. Mary A. Toborg. United States Department of Justice, National Institute of Law Enforcement and Criminal Justice. Superintendent of Documents, United States Government Printing Office, Washington, D.C. 20402. 1981.

PRETRIAL RELEASE AND DETENTION: THE BAIL REFORM ACT OF 1984. United States Department of Justice, Bureau of Justice Statistics. Superintendent of Documents, United States Government Printing Office, Washington, D.C. 20402. 1988.

PRETRIAL RELEASE PROGRAM OPTIONS. Andy Hall, Elizabeth Gayner, D. Alan Henry and Walter F. Smith. Superintendent of Documents, United States Government Printing Office, Washington, D.C. 20402. 1984.

PRETRIAL RELEASE PROGRAMS. Wayne H. Thomas, Victoria Cashman and others. United States Department of Justice, National Institute of Law Enforcement and Criminal Justice, Law Enforcement Assistance Administration. Superintendent of Documents, United States Government Printing Office, Washington, D.C. 20402. 1977.

PRETRIAL RELEASE PROGRAMS: ISSUES AND TRENDS. Chris W. Eskridge. Clark Boardman Company, Limited, 435 Hudson Street, New York, New York 10014. 1983.

PUBLIC DANGER AS A FACTOR IN PRETRIAL RELEASE: A COMPARATIVE ANALYSIS OF STATE LAWS. Barbara Gottlieb. United States Department of Justice, National Institute of Law Enforcement and Criminal Justice. Superintendent of Documents, United States Government Printing Office, Washington, D.C. 20402. 1985.

PUNISHMENT BEFORE TRIAL: AN ORGANIZATIONAL PERSPECTIVE OF FELONY BAIL PROCESSES. Longman Publishing Group, 95 Church Street, White Plains, New York 10601. 1982.

RANSON: A CRITIQUE OF THE AMERICAN BAIL SYSTEM. Ronald Goldfarb. HarperCollins Publishers, 10 East Fifty-third Street, New York, New York 10022. 1965.

SELECTED READINGS IN PROSECUTION, DEFENSE AND BAIL. Allan Ashman and Tina Asperk, Editors. American Judicature Society, 25 East Washington Street, Suite 1600, Chicago, Illinois 60602. 1971.

TWO CLASSES OF ACCUSED: A STUDY OF BAIL AND DETENTION IN AMERICAN JUSTICE. John S. Goldkamp. Ballinger Division, HarperCollins Publishers, 10 East Fifty-third Street, New York, New York 10022. 1979.

NEWSLETTERS AND NEWSPAPERS

BONDSMAN. American Bail Bondsman Association, Lock Box 28185, Las Vegas, Nevada 89126. Annual.

BIBLIOGRAPHIES

BAIL: A SELECTED BIBLIOGRAPHY OF LAW REVIEW ARTICLES. Dittakavi Nagasankara Rao. Vance Bibliographies, P.O. Box 229, 112 North Charter Street, Monticello, Illinois 61856. 1987.

PRE-TRIAL SERVICES: AN EVALUATION OF POLICY RELATED RESEARCH. Joan Mullen and others. Abt Books, Incorporated, 146 Mt. Auburn Street, Cambridge, Massachusetts 02138. 1974.

DIRECTORIES

ABBA DIRECTORY. American Bail Bondsman Association, Lock Box 28185, Las Vegas, Nevada 89126. Annual.

STATISTICS SOURCES

STATISTICAL RESULTS OF THE BAIL PROCESS IN EIGHT FEDERAL DISTRICT COURTS: A STUDY. United States General Accounting Office, 441 G Street, Northwest, Washington, D.C. 20548. 1978.

AUDIOVISUALS

OUT ON BAIL. National Institute of Justice. Washington, D.C. 20530. Videocassette.

OTHER SOURCES

BAIL REFORM ACT: HEARINGS BEFORE THE SUBCOMMITTEE ON COURTS, CIVIL LIBERTIES, AND THE ADMINISTRATION OF JUSTICE OF THE COMMITTEE ON THE JUDICIARY, HOUSE OF REPRESENTATIVES, NINETY-EIGHTH CONGRESS, FIRST AND SECOND SESSIONS, ON H.R. 1098, H.R. 3005, AND H.R. 3491 ... JUNE 16, JULY 27, 1983; AND MAY 24, 1984. Superintendent of Documents, United States Government Printing Office, Washington, D.C. 20402. 1985.

CONSTITUTIONAL RIGHTS AND FEDERAL BAIL PROCEDURES: SUMMARY REPORT OF HEARINGS AND INVESTIGATIONS BY THE SUBCOMMITTEE ON CONSTITUTIONAL RIGHTS AND THE SUBCOMMITTEE ON IMPROVEMENTS IN JUDICIAL MACHINERY OF THE COMMITTEE ON THE JUDICIARY, EIGHTY-EIGHTH CONGRESS, SECOND SESSION, PURSUANT TO S. RES. 265. Superintendent of Documents, United States Government Printing Office, Washington, D.C. 20402. 1965.

FEDERAL BAIL PROCEDURES: HEARINGS BEFORE THE SUBCOMMITTEE ON CONSTITUTIONAL RIGHTS AND THE SUBCOMMITTEE ON IMPROVEMENTS IN JUDICIAL MACHINERY OF THE COMMITTEE ON THE JUDICIARY, UNITED STATES SENATE, EIGHTY-NINTH CONGRESS, FIRST SESSION. Superintendent of Documents, United States Government Printing Office, Washington, D.C. 20402. 1965.

FEDERAL BAIL PROCESS FOSTERS INEQUITIES: REPORT TO THE CONGRESS. Comptroller General of the United States. United States General Accounting Office, 441 G Street, Northwest, Washington, D.C. 20548. 1978.

BALLISTICS
See: FIREARMS AND BALLISTICS

BANKRUPTCY
See also: ATTACHMENT AND GARNISHMENT; COLLECTION LAWS

STATUTES, CODES, STANDARDS, UNIFORM LAWS

BANKRUPTCY CODE AND RULES. West Publishing Company, P.O. Box 43526, 50 West Kellogg Boulevard, St. Paul, Minnesota 55164-0562. Annual.

BANKRUPTCY CODE. Collier Pamphlet Edition. Matthew Bender and Company, Incorporated, 11 Penn Plaza, New York, New York 10001. Annual.

BANKRUPTCY CODE, RULES AND FORMS: INCLUDING FEDERAL RULES OF CIVIL PROCEDURE AND FEDERAL RULES OF EVIDENCE. West Publishing Company, P.O. Box 43526, 50 West Kellogg Boulevard, St. Paul, Minnesota 55164-0562. 1991.

BANKRUPTCY CODE, RULES AND OFFICIAL FORMS. West Publishing Company, P.O. Box 43526, 50 West Kellogg Boulevard, St. Paul, Minnesota 55164-0562. 1991.

BANKRUPTCY REFORM ACT OF 1978: A LEGISLATIVE HISTORY. Alan N. Resnick and Eugene M. Wypyski. William S. Hein and Company, 1285 Main Street, Buffalo, New York 14209. 1979. (Microfiche).

BANKRUPTCY RULES: INCLUDING RULES OF BANKRUPTCY PROCEDURE AND FORMS. Collier Pamphlet Edition. Matthew Bender and Company, Incorporated, 11 Penn Plaza, New York, New York 10001. Annual.

LOOSELEAF SERVICES AND REPORTERS

BANKRUPTCY. Joe Lee. Lawyers Co-Operative Publishing Company, Aqueduct Building, Rochester, New York 14694. 1981- . (Annual Supplements).

BANKRUPTCY. Second Edition. Robert E. Ginsberg. Prentice-Hall, Incorporated, 113 Sylvan Avenue, Englewood Cliffs, New Jersey 07632. 1988- . (Annual Supplements).

BANKRUPTCY: ANNOTATED FORMS. Robert E. Ginsberg. Prentice-Hall, Incorporated, 113 Sylvan Avenue, Englewood Cliffs, New Jersey 07632. 1989- . (Periodic Supplements).

BANKRUPTCY COURT DECISIONS. Frances P. Hays, Editor. CRR Publishing Company/LRP Publications, 747 Dresher Road, Horsham, Pennsylvania 19044. 1974- . (Biweekly Supplements).

BANKRUPTCY LAW AND PROCEDURE: A FUNDAMENTAL GUIDE FOR LAW OFFICE PROFESSIONALS. Thomas Salerno and others. Professional Education Systems, Incorporated, 200 Spring Street, Eau Claire, Wisconsin 54702. 1989- . (Annual Supplements).

BANKRUPTCY LAW FUNDAMENTALS. Richard I. Aaron. Clark Boardman Company, Limited, 435 Hudson Street, New York, New York 10014. 1984- . (Annual Supplements).

BANKRUPTCY LAW REPORTS. Commerce Clearing House, Incorporated, 4025 West Peterson Avenue, Chicago, Illinois 60646. 1929- . (Semimonthly Supplements).

BANKRUPTCY LITIGATION AND PRACTICE: A PRACTITIONER'S GUIDE. Thomas J. Salerno. Professional Education Systems, Incorporated, 200 Spring Street, Eau Claire, Wisconsin 54702. 1987- . (Annual Supplements).

BANKRUPTCY LITIGATION MANUAL. Michael L. Cook. Prentice-Hall, Incorporated, 113 Sylvan Avenue, Englewood Cliffs, New Jersey 07632. 1990. (Periodic Supplements).

BANKRUPTCY PRACTICE FOR THE GENERAL PRACTITIONER. W. Homer Drake, Jr. and A.L. Mullins, Jr. Shepard's/McGraw-Hill, P.O. Box 1235, Colorado Springs, Colorado 80901. 1980- .

BANKRUPTCY PRACTICE HANDBOOK. Rosemary E. Williams. Callaghan and Company, 155 Pfingsten Road, Deerfield, Illinois 60015. 1983- . (Annual Supplements).

BANKRUPTCY PRACTICE MANUAL. Richard H.W. Maloy. Butterworth Legal Publishers, 90 Stiles Road, Salem, New Hampshire 03079. 1982- . (Semiannual Supplements).

BANKRUPTCY SERVICE, LAWYERS EDITION. Lawyers Co-Operative Publishing Company, Aqueduct Building, Rochester, New York 14694. 1979- . (Quarterly Supplements).

BANKRUPTCY STAY MANUAL. Richard Ralston. Book Publishing Company, 201 Westlake Avenue North, Seattle, Washington 98109. 1989- . (Annual Supplements).

BANKRUPTCY STRATEGIES FOR LENDERS. Michael J. Sutherland and John R. Blinn. Professional Education Systems, Incorporated, 200 Spring Street, Eau Claire, Wisconsin 54702. 1988- . (Annual Supplements).

CHAPTER 11 REORGANIZATIONS. John C. Anderson. Shepard's/McGraw- Hill, P.O. Box 1235, Colorado Springs, Colorado 80901. 1983- . (Annual Supplements).

CHAPTER 12: FARM REORGANIZATIONS. John C. Anderson and Jeffrey W. Morris. Shepard's/McGraw-Hill, P.O. Box 1235, Colorado Springs, Colorado 80901. 1987- . (Annual Supplements).

CHAPTER 13 PRACTICE AND PROCEDURE. Homer W. Drake and Jeffrey W. Morris. Shepard's/McGraw-Hill, P.O. Box 1235, Colorado Springs, Colorado 80901. 1983- . (Annual Supplements).

COLLIER BANKRUPTCY CASES, SECOND SERIES. Matthew Bender and Company, Incorporated, 11 Penn Plaza, New York, New York 10001. 1979- . (Bimonthly Supplements).

COLLIER BANKRUPTCY COMPENSATION GUIDE. Stanley B. Bernstein. Matthew Bender and Company, Incorporated, 11 Penn Plaza, New York, New York 10001. 1988- . (Annual Supplements).

COLLIER BANKRUPTCY EXEMPTION GUIDE. Lawrence P. King, Editor. Matthew Bender and Company, Incorporated, 11 Penn Plaza, New York, New York 10001. 1982- . (Annual Supplements).

COLLIER BANKRUPTCY FORMS MANUAL. Third Edition. Lawrence P. King and A.L. Mollar. Matthew Bender and Company, Incorporated, 11 Penn Plaza, New York, New York 10001. 1979- . (Annual Supplements).

COLLIER BANKRUPTCY PRACTICE GUIDE. Asa S. Herzog and Lawrence P. King. Matthew Bender and Company, Incorporated, 11 Penn Plaza, New York, New York 10001. 1981- . (Periodic Supplements).

COLLIER FARM BANKRUPTCY GUIDE. R. Rogers. Matthew Bender and Company, Incorporated, 11 Penn Plaza, New York, New York 10001. 1989- . (Annual Supplements).

COLLIER HANDBOOK FOR CREDITOR'S COMMITTEES. Lawrence P. King, Editor. Matthew Bender and Company, Incorporated, 11 Penn Plaza, New York, New York 10001. 1988- . (Annual Supplements).

COLLIER LABOR LAW AND THE BANKRUPTCY CODE. Mark S. Pulliam and Richard A. Conn, Jr. Matthew Bender and Company, Incorporated, 11 Penn Plaza, New York, New York 10001. 1989- . (Annual Supplements).

COLLIER ON BANKRUPTCY. Fifteenth Edition. Lawrence P. King, Editor. Matthew Bender and Company, Incorporated, 11 Penn Plaza, New York, New York 10001. 1979- . (Periodic Supplements).

COLLIER REAL ESTATE TRANSACTION AND BANKRUPTCY CODE. Laurence D. Cherkis and others. Matthew Bender and Company, Incorporated, 11 Penn Plaza, New York, New York 10001. 1984- . (Periodic Supplements).

COLLIER'S LENDING INSTITUTIONS AND THE BANKRUPTCY CODE. Robert J. Rosenberg and Lawrence P. King. Matthew Bender and Company, Incorporated, 11 Penn Plaza, New York, New York 10001. 1985- . (Periodic Supplements).

CREDITORS' RIGHTS IN BANKRUPTCY. Second Edition. Patrick A. Murphy. Shepard's/McGraw-Hill, 420 North Cascade Avenue, Colorado Springs, Colorado 80901. 1988- . (Annual Supplements).

DRAFTING BANKRUPTCY REORGANIZATION PLANS. John K. Pearson and others. Professional Education Systems, Incorporated, 200 Spring Street, Eau Claire, Wisconsin 54702. 1988- . (Annual Supplements).

FEDERAL RULES OF BANKRUPTCY. Third Edition. Joseph Patchan. Clark Boardman Company, Limited, 435 Hudson Street, New York, New York 10014. 1988- . (Annual Supplements).

FEDERAL TAX ASPECTS OF BANKRUPTCY. C. Richard McQueen and Jack Crestol. Shepard's/McGraw-Hill, 420 North Cascade Avenue, Colorado Springs, Colorado 80901. 1984- . (Annual Supplements).

GUIDE TO EFFECTIVE BANKRUPTCY LITIGATION. David W. Pollard and Joseph J. Burton. Shepard's/McGraw-Hill, 420 North Cascade Avenue, Colorado Springs, Colorado 80901. 1988- . (Annual Supplements).

GUIDELINES FOR FULFILLING THE REQUIREMENTS OF THE UNITED STATES TRUSTEE. United States Department of Justice, Office of the United States Trustees, Constitution Avenue and Tenth Street, Northwest, Washington, D.C. 20530. 1989- .

HERZOG'S BANKRUPTCY FORMS AND PRACTICE. Eighth Edition. Asa S. Herzog and others. Clark Boardman Company, Limited, 435 Hudson Street, New York, New York 10014. 1987- . (Annual Supplements).

NORTON BANKRUPTCY LAW AND PRACTICE. William L. Norton, Jr. Callaghan and Company, 155 Pfingsten Road, Deerfield, Illinois 60015. 1981- . (Periodic Supplements).

A PRACTICAL GUIDE TO THE BANKRUPTCY REFORM ACT. Harvey Miller and Michael Cook. Prentice-Hall, Incorporated, 113 Sylvan Avenue, Englewood Cliffs, New Jersey 07632. 1979- . (Periodic Supplements).

REORGANIZATIONS UNDER CHAPTER 11 OF THE BANKRUPTCY CODE. Richard F. Broude. Law Journal Seminars-Press, Incorporated, 111 Eighth Avenue, Suite 900, New York, New York 10011. 1986- . (Periodic Supplements).

WEST'S BANKRUPTCY REPORTER. West Publishing Company, P.O. Box 64526, 50 West Kellogg Boulevard, St. Paul, Minnesota 55164-0526. 1980- . (Monthly Supplements).

HANDBOOKS, MANUALS, FORMBOOKS

ADVANCED BANKRUPTCY WORKSHOP. Practising Law Institute, 810 Seventh Avenue, New York, New York 10019. 1991.

AGRICULTURAL WORKOUTS AND BANKRUPTCIES 1987. Practising Law Institute, 810 Seventh Avenue, New York, New York 10019. 1987.

THE ATTORNEY'S HANDBOOK ON CONSUMER BANKRUPTCY AND CHAPTER 13. Twelfth Edition. John H. Williamson. Argyle Publishing Company, 1955 Hoyt Street, Lakewood, Colorado 80215. 1988.

THE ATTORNEY'S HANDBOOK ON SMALL BUSINESS REORGANIZATION UNDER CHAPTER 11. John H. Williamson. Argyle Publishing Company, 1955 Hoyt Street, Lakewood, Colorado 80215. 1987.

AVIATION INDUSTRY BANKRUPTCY ISSUES. Practising Law Institute, 810 Seventh Avenue, New York, New York 10019. 1986.

BANKRUPTCY, A CONCISE GUIDE FOR CREDITORS AND DEBTORS. Richard B. Herzog, Jr. Arco Publishing, Incorporated, Division of Prentice-Hall, Incorporated, 15 Columbus Circle, New York, New York 10023. 1983.

BANKRUPTCY AND INSOLVENCY ACCOUNTING: PRACTICE AND PROCEDURE. Fourth Edition. John Wiley and Sons, Incorporated, 605 Third Avenue, New York, New York 10158. 1989.

BANKRUPTCY AND REORGANIZATION, 1986: THE SUBSTANTIVE AND PROCEDURAL BASICS. Practising Law Institute, 810 Seventh Avenue, New York, New York 10019. 1986.

BANKRUPTCY CODE AND REAL ESTATE LENDERS: TROUBLED REAL ESTATE LOANS AND DOCUMENTATION. Practising Law Institute, 810 Seventh Avenue, New York, New York 10019. 1983.

BANKRUPTCY CODE REEXAMINED AND UPDATED: ALI-ABA COURSE OF STUDY MATERIALS. American Law Institute-American Bar Association, 4025 Chestnut Street, Philadelphia, Pennsylvania 19104. 1985.

BANKRUPTCY DESKBOOK. Second Edition. Harvey M. Lebowitz. Practising Law Institute, 810 Seventh Avenue, New York, New York 10019. 1990.

BANKRUPTCY DEVELOPMENTS FOR WORKOUT OFFICERS AND LENDERS COUNSEL. Practising Law Institute, 810 Seventh Avenue, New York, New York 10019. 1989.

BANKRUPTCY: DO IT YOURSELF. Third Edition. Janice Kosel. Nolo Press, 950 Parker Street, Berkeley, California 94710. 1984.

BANKRUPTCY EVIDENCE MANUAL. 1990 Edition. Barry Russell. West Publishing Company, 50 West Kellogg Boulevard, St. Paul, Minnesota 55164-0526. 1990.

BANKRUPTCY LAW FUNDAMENTALS. Richard I. Aaron. Clark Boardman Company, Limited, 435 Hudson Street, New York, New York 10014. 1984.

BANKRUPTCY LAW MANUAL. Revised Edition. Benjamin Weintraub and Alan N. Resnick. Research Institute of America, Incorporated, One Penn Plaza, New York, New York 10119. 1986- . (Periodic Supplements).

BANKRUPTCY: PRACTICE AND PROCEDURE, 1984. Lewis Kruger and Arnold M. Quittner. Practising Law Institute, 810 Seventh Avenue, New York, New York 10019. 1984.

BANKRUPTCY PRACTICE FOR BANK COUNSEL. Michael S. Lurey and Robert J. Rosenberg. Practising Law Institute, 810 Seventh Avenue, New York, New York 10019. Annual.

BANKRUPTCY PRACTICE FOR THE GENERAL PRACTITIONER. Homer W. Drake. Shepard's/McGraw-Hill, P.O. Box 1235, Colorado Springs, Colorado 80901. 1980.

BANKRUPTCY PRACTICE HANDBOOK. Rosemary E. Williams. Callaghan and Company, 155 Pfingsten Road, Deerfield, Illinois 60015. 1990.

BANKRUPTCY PROCEDURE AND FORMS. Harold Lavien. West Publishing Company, 50 West Kellogg Boulevard, St. Paul, Minnesota 55164-0526. 1985.

CHAPTER 11 BUSINESS REORGANIZATIONS. Harold S. Novikoff. Practising Law Institute, 810 Seventh Avenue, New York, New York 10019. 1983.

CHAPTER 13 PRACTICE AND PROCEDURE. Homer W. Drake. Shepard's/McGraw-Hill, P.O. Box 1235, Colorado Springs, Colorado 80901. 1983.

COLLIER FORMS MANUAL. Third Edition. Laurence P. King and Arthur L. Moller, Editors. Matthew Bender and Company, Incorporated, 11 Penn Plaza, New York, New York 10001. 1973- . (Periodic Supplements).

COMPLEX LITIGATION IN THE CONTEXT OF THE BANKRUPTCY LAWS. Michael F. Perlis. Practising Law Institute, 810 Seventh Avenue, New York, New York 10019. 1984.

CONSUMER BANKRUPTCY MANUAL. Arnold B. Cohen and Mitchell W. Miller. Research Institute of America, Incorporated, One Penn Plaza, New York, New York 10119. 1985- . (Annual Supplements).

CREDITOR-DEBTOR LAW MANUAL. Thomas D. Crandall and others. Research Institute of America, Incorporated, One Penn Plaza, New York, New York 10119. 1985.

FUNDAMENTALS OF BANKRUPTCY LAW. Second Edition. George M. Treister. American Law Institute and American Bar Association, Committee on Continuing Professional Education, 4025 Chestnut Street, Philadelphia, Pennsylvania 19104. 1988.

GARLAND'S ANNOTATED BANKRUPTCY HANDBOOK. Robert J. D'Agostino and others. Garland Publishing, Incorporated, 136 Madison Avenue, New York, New York 10016. 1988.

HERZOG'S BANKRUPTCY FORMS AND PRACTICE. Eighth Edition. Asa S. Herzog and others. Clark Boardman Company, Limited, 435 Hudson Street, New York, New York 10014. 1987- . (Annual Supplements).

REAL ESTATE AND THE BANKRUPTCY CODE. Practising Law Institute, 810 Seventh Avenue, New York, New York 10019. 1985.

RESOLUTION TRUST CORPORATION: BANKRUPTCIES, LIQUIDATIONS, AND SALE OF ASSETS. Practising Law Institute, 810 Seventh Avenue, New York, New York 10019. 1990.

SECURED CREDITORS AND LESSORS UNDER THE BANKRUPTCY REFORM ACT OF 1990. Patrick A. Murphy. Practising Law Institute, 810 Seventh Avenue, New York, New York 10019. 1990.

WEST'S FEDERAL FORMS. BANKRUPTCY PROCEDURE FORMS. West Publishing Company, P.O. Box 64526, 50 West Kellogg Boulevard, St. Paul, Minnesota 55164-0526. 1985- . (Annual Supplements).

BANKRUPTCY

TEXTBOOKS AND GENERAL WORKS

AS WE FORGIVE OUR DEBTORS: BANKRUPTCY AND CONSUMER CREDIT IN AMERICA. Teresa A. Sullivan. Oxford University Press, 200 Madison Avenue, New York, New York 10016. 1989.

BANKRUPTCY PRACTICE AND STRATEGY. Alan N. Resnick, Editor. Research Institute of America, Incorporated, One Penn Plaza, New York, New York 10119. 1987- . (Periodic Supplements).

BANKRUPTCY, SECURED TRANSACTIONS AND OTHER DEBTOR-CREDITOR MATTERS. Arnold B. Cohen. Michie Company, P.O. Box 7587, Charlottesville, Virginia 22906-7582. 1981- . (Annual Supplements).

BUSINESS OPPORTUNITIES FROM CORPORATE BANKRUPTCIES. Rees W. Morrison. John Wiley and Sons, Incorporated, 605 Third Avenue, New York, New York 10158. 1986.

COLLIER REAL ESTATE TRANSACTIONS AND THE BANKRUPTCY CODE. Laurence D. Cherkis. Matthew Bender and Company, Incorporated, 11 Penn Plaza, New York, New York 10001. 1984.

CONSUMER BANKRUPTCY LAW AND PRACTICE. Second Edition. Henry J. Sommer. National Consumer Law Center, 11 Beacon Street, Boston, Massachusetts 02108. 1985- . (Annual Supplements).

COWANS BANKRUPTCY LAW AND PRACTICE. Daniel R. Cowans. West Publishing Company, P.O. Box 64526, 50 West Kellogg Boulevard, St. Paul, Minnesota 55164-0526. 1989- . (Periodic Supplements).

DEBTOR-CREDITOR LAW IN A NUTSHELL. Third Edition. David G. Epstein. West Publishing Company, P.O. Box 64526, 50 West Kellogg Boulevard, St. Paul, Minnesota 55164-0526. 1985.

FUNDAMENTALS OF BANKRUPTCY LAW: ALI-ABA COURSE OF STUDY MATERIALS. American Law Institute-American Bar Association, Committee on Continuing Professional Education, 4025 Chestnut Street, Philadelphia, Pennsylvania 19104. 1986.

HANDBOOK OF THE LAW OF BANKRUPTCY. (Hornbook Series). James A. MacLachlan. West Publishing Company, P.O. Box 64526, 50 West Kellogg Boulevard, St. Paul, Minnesota 55164-0526. 1956.

THE LAW OF CORPORATE GROUPS: BANKRUPTCY LAW. Phillip I. Blumberg. Little, Brown and Company, 34 Beacon Street, Boston, Massachusetts 02108. 1985.

LAW OF DISTRESSED REAL ESTATE: FORECLOSURES, WORKOUTS, PROCEDURES. Baxter Dunaway. Clark Boardman Company, Limited, 435 Hudson Street, New York, New York 10014. 1985- .

LIQUIDATING BANKRUPTCY: CORPORATE AND BUSINESS APPLICATIONS. (Corporate Practice Series). Richard F. Broude. Bureau of National Affairs, Incorporated, 1231 Twenty-fifth Street, Northwest, Washington, D.C. 20037. 1984- . (Periodic Supplements).

THE LOGIC AND LIMITS OF BANKRUPTCY LAW. Thomas H. Jackson. Harvard University Press, 79 Garden Street, Cambridge, Massachusetts 02138. 1986.

PURCHASE AND SALE OF ASSETS IN BANKRUPTCY CASES. Richard N. Tilton. John Wiley and Sons, Incorporated, 605 Third Avenue, New York, New York 10158. 1990.

REAL ESTATE BANKRUPTCIES AND WORKOUTS: A PRACTICAL PERSPECTIVE. Anthony B. Kuklin and Paul E. Roberts. American Bar Association, Section on Real Property, Probate and Trust Law, 450 North Lake Shore Drive, Chicago, Illinois 60611. 1983.

STRATEGIES FOR CREDITORS IN BANKRUPTCY PROCEEDINGS. Lynn M. LoPucki. Little, Brown and Company, 34 Beacon Street, Boston, Massachusetts 02108. 1985.

DIGESTS, INDEXES, ABSTRACTS, CITATORS

SHEPARD'S BANKRUPTCY CITATIONS. Shepard's/McGraw-Hill, P.O. Box 1235, Colorado Springs, Colorado 80901. 1980- . (Quarterly Supplements).

WEST'S BANKRUPTCY DIGEST. West Publishing Company, P.O. Box 43526, 50 West Kellogg Boulevard, St. Paul, Minnesota 55164-0526. 1980- . (Monthly Supplements).

ANNUALS AND SURVEYS

ANNUAL SURVEY OF BANKRUPTCY LAW. William L. Norton, Jr. Callaghan and Company, 155 Pfingsten Road, Deerfield, Illinois 60015. Annual.

CURRENT DEVELOPMENTS IN BANKRUPTCY AND REORGANIZATION: A COURSE HANDBOOK. Practising Law Institute, 810 Seventh Avenue, New York, New York 10019. Annual.

LENDING TRANSACTIONS AND THE BANKRUPTCY ACT: A COURSE HANDBOOK. Practising Law Institute, 810 Seventh Avenue, New York, New York 10019. Annual.

LAW REVIEWS AND PERIODICALS

AMERICAN BANKRUPTCY LAW JOURNAL. National Conference of Bankruptcy Judges, c/o Judge George C. Paine, Customs House, Room 218, 701 Broadway, Nashville, Tennessee 37203. Quarterly.

BANKRUPTCY DEVELOPMENTS JOURNAL. Emory University School of Law, Atlanta, Georgia 30322. Semiannual.

COMMERCIAL LAW JOURNAL. Commercial Law League of America, 222 West Adams Street, Chicago, Illinois 60606-5278. Quarterly.

NEWSLETTERS AND NEWSPAPERS

ABI NEWSLETTER. American Bankruptcy Institute, 510 C Street, Northeast, Washington, D.C. 20002. Bimonthly.

BANKRUPTCY COUNSELLOR. Counsellor Publications, Incorporated, P.O. Box 19070, Alexandria, Virginia 22320. Bimonthly.

BANKRUPTCY INSOLVENCY - CREDITORS RIGHTS. State Bar of Wisconsin, Bankruptcy, Insolvency and Creditors Rights Section, 402 West Wilson Street, Madison, Wisconsin 53703. Monthly.

BANKRUPTCY LAW LETTER. Research Institute of America, Incorporated, 210 South Street, Boston, Massachusetts 02111. Monthly.

BANKRUPTCY SERVICE, LAWYERS EDITION - CURRENT AWARENESS ALERT. Clark Boardman Co. Ltd. 435 Hudson St. New York, NY 10014. Monthly.

THE BANKRUPTCY STRATEGIST. Leader Publications, 111 Eighth Avenue, New York, New York 10011. Monthly.

BNA'S BANKRUPTCY LAW REPORTER. Bureau of National Affairs, 1231 Twenty-fifth Street, Northwest, Washington, D.C. 20037. Weekly.

BROKEN BENCH REVIEW. Whitman Publishing Company, 10 Water Street, Box 573, Lebanon, New Hampshire 03766. Quarterly.

COMMERCIAL BANKING AND BANKRUPTCY LAW. Illinois State Bar Association, Section on Commercial Banking and Bankruptcy Law, Illinois Bar Center, Springfield, Illinois 62701. Bimonthly.

COMMERCIAL LAW ADVISER. Business Laws Incorporated, 11630 Chillicothe Road, Chesterland, Ohio 44026. Monthly.

FAILED BANK AND THRIFT LITIGATION. Andrews Publications, 1646 West Chester Pike, Westtown, Pennsylvania 19395. Bimonthly.

FAILED LBO LITIGATION REPORTER. Andrews Publications, 1646 West Chester Pike, Westtown, Pennsylvania 19395. Monthly.

GARLAND'S BANKRUPTCY BULLETIN. Garland Law Publishing, 136 Madison Avenue, New York, New York 10016. Bimonthly.

LENDER LIABILITY LITIGATION REPORTER. Andrews Publications, 1646 West Chester Pike, Westtown, Pennsylvania 19395. Bimonthly.

MEALEY'S LITIGATION REPORT: INSURANCE INSOLVENCY. Mealey Publications, Incorporated, P.O. Box 446, Wayne, Pennsylvania 19087. Bimonthly.

NORTON BANKRUPTCY LAW ADVISOR. Callaghan and Company, 155 Pfingsten Road, Deerfield, Illinois 60015. Monthly.

TURNAROUNDS AND WORKOUTS. Beard Group, P.O. Box 9867, Washington, D.C. 20016. Semimonthly.

BIBLIOGRAPHIES

BANKRUPTCY REFORM ACT OF 1978: ANALYSIS, LEGISLATIVE HISTORY, AND SELECTED BIBLIOGRAPHY. Mickie A. Voges and Kathy E. Shimpock. Tarleton Law Library, University of Texas School of Law, 727 East Twenty-sixth Street, Austin, Texas 78705-5799. 1981.

ORGANIZATIONAL CLOSINGS: A BIBLIOGRAPHY. Robert I. Sutton. Vance Bibliographies, P.O. Box 229, 112 North Charter Street, Monticello, Illinois 61856. 1982.

SELECTED BIBLIOGRAPHY ON THE BANKRUPTCY REFORM ACT OF 1978. Herbert L. Ho. John Marshall Law School Library, 315 South Plymouth Court, Chicago, Illinois. 60604. 1983.

ASSOCIATIONS AND PROFESSIONAL SOCIETIES

AMERICAN BANKRUPTCY INSTITUTE, 107 Second Street, Northeast, Washington, D.C. 20002. (202) 543-1234.

COMMERCIAL LAW LEAGUE OF AMERICA. 175 West Jackson Boulevard, Suite 1545, Chicago, Illinois 60604-2703. (312) 431-1305.

NATIONAL ASSOCIATION OF BANKRUPTCY TRUSTEES. 3008 Millwood Avenue, Columbia, South Carolina 29205. (803) 252-5646.

NATIONAL CONFERENCE OF BANKRUPTCY JUDGES. c/o Judge George C. Paine, Customs House, Room 218, 701 Broadway, Nashville, Tennessee 37203. (615) 736-5587.

RESEARCH CENTERS, INSTITUTES, CLEARINGHOUSES

CENTER FOR RISK MANAGEMENT AND INSURANCE EDUCATION AND RESEARCH. University of Wisconsin - Madison, School of Business, Madison, Wisconsin 53706. (608) 263-5717.

ONLINE DATABASES

FEDERAL BANKRUPTCY LIBRARY. LEXIS. Mead Data Central, 9393 Springboro Pike, P.O. Box 933, Dayton, Ohio 04540.

WESTLAW BANKRUPTCY LIBRARY. West Publishing Company, P.O. Box 64526, 50 West Kellogg Boulevard, St. Paul, Minnesota 55164-0526.

STATISTICS SOURCES

BANKRUPTCIES FILED AND PENDING. Administrative Office of the United States Courts, United States Supreme Court Building, One First Street, Northeast, Washington, D.C. 20543. Annual.

AUDIOVISUALS

BANKRUPTCY AND CREDITOR'S RIGHTS. Douglas Bashkoff. Josephson Center for Creative Educational Centers, Incorporated, Culver City, California 90232. 1986. (Four Audiocassettes).

BANKRUPTCY IN THE 90'S. David G. Epstein. National Practice Institute, 330 Second Avenue South, Minneapolis, Minnesota 55401. Audiotape.

FARM BANKRUPTICIES UNDER CHAPTER 12: RECENT DEVELOPMENTS. American Bar Association, 750 North Lake Shore Drive, Chicago, Illinois 60611. 1987. Videotape.

REAL ESTATE BANKRUPTCY CASSETTE PROGRAM. Real Estate Bankruptcies and Workouts. American Bar Association, 750 North Lake Shore Drive, Chicago, Illinois 60611. (Eight Audiocassettes).

REPRESENTING REAL ESTATE INTERESTS IN BANKRUPTCY REORGANIZATIONS. American Bar Association, 750 North Lake Shore Drive, Chicago, Illinois 60611. 1990. Videotape.

COMPUTER-ASSISTED LEGAL INSTRUCTION

DEBTOR CREDITOR GAME. Lynn M. LoPucki. Center for Computer- Assisted Instruction, 229 19th Avenue South, University of Minnesota, Minneapolis, Minnesota 55455. Machine-readable computer file.

OTHER SOURCES

BANKRUPTCY CODE REEXAMINED AND UPDATED: ALI-ABA COURSE OF STUDY MATERIALS. American Law Institute, 4025 Chestnut Street, Philadelphia, Pennsylvania 19104. 1984.

BUSINESS REORGANIZATIONS UNDER THE BANKRUPTCY CODE: ALI-ABA COURSE OF STUDY MATERIALS. American Law Institute, 4025 Chestnut Street, Philadelphia, Pennsylvania 19104. 1985.

DEBTOR AND CREDITOR RELATIONS: BANKRUPTCY. George F. Bason, Jr. West Publishing Company, P.O. Box 43526, 50 West Kellogg Boulevard, St. Paul, Minnesota 55164-0526. 1984.

THE SELECTION AND APPOINTMENT OF UNITED STATES BANKRUPTCY JUDGES. Administrative Office of the United States Courts, Bankruptcy Division, Washington, D.C. 20544. 1988.

BANKRUPTCY COURT
See: BANKRUPTCY; DISTRICT COURTS

BANKS AND BANKING
See also: CONSUMER CREDIT; FEDERAL RESERVE BOARD; LOANS; MONEY AND MONETARY CONTROL; NEGOTIABLE INSTRUMENTS; TREASURY DEPARTMENT

LOOSELEAF SERVICES AND REPORTERS

AMERICAN BANKERS ASSOCIATION'S COMPLIANCE SOURCEBOOK. American Bankers Association, 1120 Connecticut Avenue, Northwest, Washington, D.C. 20036. 1984- .

ACCOUNTING FOR BANKS. James M. Koltveit. Matthew Bender and Company, Incorporated, 11 Penn Plaza, New York, New York 10001. 1982- . (Periodic Supplements).

BANK ACCOUNTING AND AUDITING SERVICE. Charles D. Mecimore. Sheshunoff Information Services, Incorporated, Capitol Station, P.O. Box 13203, Austin, Texas 78711. 1989- . (Monthly Supplements).

BANK CAPITAL SERVICE. Sheshunoff Information Services, Incorporated, Capitol Station, P.O. Box 13203, Austin, Texas 78711. 1989- . (Periodic Supplements).

BANK HOLDING COMPANY COMPLIANCE MANUAL. J.G. Beckford. Matthew Bender and Company, Incorporated, 11 Penn Plaza, New York, New York 10001. 1986- . (Periodic Supplements).

BANK LOAN AGREEMENTS. Sidney S. Goldstein. Matthew Bender and Company, Incorporated, 11 Penn Plaza, New York, New York 10001. 1990.

BANKING CRIMES. John K. Villa. Clark Boardman Company, Limited, 435 Hudson Street, New York, New York 10014. 1987- . (Annual Supplements).

BANKING LAW. Fredric Solomon. Matthew Bender and Company, Incorporated, 11 Penn Plaza, New York, New York 10001. 1981- . (Periodic Supplements).

BANKING LAW MANUAL. Matthew Bender and Company, Incorporated, 11 Penn Plaza, New York, New York 10001. 1983- . (Periodic Supplements).

BNA'S BANKING REPORT. Bureau of National Affairs, Incorporated, 1231 Twenty-fifth Street, Northwest, Washington, D.C. 20037. 1987- . Weekly.

CHECKS, DRAFTS, NOTES. Matthew Bender and Company, Incorporated, 11 Penn Plaza, New York, New York 10001. 1984- . (Annual Supplements).

COMMERCIAL ASSET-BASED FINANCING. Raymond Nimmer. Callaghan and Company, 155 Pfingsten Road, Deerfield, Illinois 60015. 1988- . (Annual Supplements).

COMMUNITY REINVESTMENT ACT MANUAL. Roland E. Brandel and David E. Teitelbaum. Prentice-Hall, Incorporated, 113 Sylvan Avenue, Englewood Cliffs, New Jersey 07632. 1989- . (Periodic Supplements).

COMPLIANCE EXAMINATIONS UPDATE FOR FINANCIAL INSTITUTIONS. Drew V. Tidwell and John H. Mancuso. Research Institue of America, Incorporated, One Penn Plaza, New York, New York 10119. 1988- . (Semimonthly Supplements).

COMPTROLLER'S HANDBOOK FOR NATIONAL BANK EXAMINERS. United States Comptroller of the Currency, Administrator of the National Banks, Washington, D.C. 20062. 1977- . (Periodic Supplements).

COMPTROLLER'S HANDBOOK FOR NATIONAL TRUST EXAMINERS. United States Comptroller of the Currency, Administrator of the National Banks, Washington, D.C. 20062. 1976- . (Periodic Supplements).

COMPTROLLER'S MANUAL FOR NATIONAL BANKS. United States Comptroller of the Currency, Administrator of the National Banks, Washington, D.C. 20062. 1979- . (Periodic Supplements).

CONTROL OF BANKING. Prentice-Hall, Incorporated, 113 Sylvan Avenue, Englewood Cliffs, New Jersey 07632. 1962- . (Biweekly Supplements).

EFT REGULATION E COMPREHENSIVE COMPLIANCE MANUAL. American Bankers Association, 1120 Connecticut Avenue, Northwest, Washington, D.C. 20036. 1982- . (Periodic Supplements).

THE EVOLVING FINANCIAL SERVICES INDUSTRY. Harvey L. Pitt. Prentice-Hall, Incorporated, 113 Sylvan Avenue, Englewood Cliffs, New Jersey 07632. 1987- .

EXPEDITED FUNDS AVAILABILITY REGULATION CC COMPLIANCE MANUAL. Sheshunoff Information Services, Incorporated, Capitol Station, P.O. Box 13203, Austin, Texas 78711. 1989- . (Semiannual Supplements).

FDIC ENFORCEMENT DECISIONS. Prentice-Hall, Incorporated, 113 Sylvan Avenue, Englewood Cliffs, New Jersey 07632. 1988- . (Periodic Supplements).

FEDERAL BANK HOLDING COMPANY LAW. Pauline B. Heller. Law Journal Seminars-Press, Incorporated, 111 Eighth Avenue, Suite 900, New York, New York 10011. 1986- . (Periodic Supplements).

FEDERAL BANKING LAW REPORTS. Commerce Clearing House, Incorporated, 4025 West Peterson Avenue, Chicago, Illinois 60646. 1914- . (Weekly Supplements).

FEDERAL BANKING LAW SERVICE. A.S. Pratt and Sons, Incorporated, 1117 North Nineteenth Street, Arlington, Virginia 22209. 1878- . (Biweekly Supplements).

FEDERAL GUIDE. Robert Wiorski. United States League of Savings Institutions, 1709 New York Avenue, Northwest, Suite 801, Washington D.C. 20006. 1953- . (Monthly Supplements).

FEDERAL INCOME TAXATION OF BANKS AND FINANCIAL INSTITUTIONS. Sixth Edition. Lance W. Rook. Research Institute of America, Incorporated, One Penn Plaza, New York, New York 10119. 1990.

FEDERAL REGULATION OF BANKING--BANK HOLDING COMPANIES. Paul Allen Schott. , Research Institute of America, Incorporated, One Penn Plaza, New York, New York 10119. 1988- . (Annual Supplements).

FEDERAL REGULATION OF BANKING--THE DEPOSITORY INSTITUTIONS ACT. , Research Institute of America, Incorporated, One Penn Plaza, New York, New York 10119. 1982- . (Annual Supplements).

FEDERAL REGULATION OF DEPOSITORY INSTITUTIONS: ENFORCEMENT POWERS AND PROCEDURES. Miles A. Cobb. , Research Institute of America, Incorporated, One Penn Plaza, New York, New York 10119. 1983- . (Periodic Supplements).

FEDERAL RESERVE REGULATORY SERVICE. Federal Publications, 1120 Twentieth Street, Northwest, Washington, D.C. 20036. 1981- . (Monthly Supplements).

FEDERAL RESERVE SYSTEM COMPLIANCE HANDBOOK. Federal Publications, 1120 Twentieth Street, Northwest, Washington, D.C. 20036. 1990- . (Periodic Supplements).

GUIDE TO THE FEDERAL LAW OF BANKING AND INSURANCE. James E. Scott and Richard M. Whiting. Prentice-Hall, Incorporated, 113 Sylvan Avenue, Englewood Cliffs, New Jersey 07632. 1989.

HOME EQUITY LENDING SERVICE. , Research Institute of America, Incorporated, One Penn Plaza, New York, New York 10119. 1988- . (Quarterly Supplements).

THE LAW OF FINANCIAL SERVICES. Harvey L. Pitt and others. Prentice-Hall, Incorporated, 113 Sylvan Avenue, Englewood Cliffs, New Jersey 07632. 1989- . (Annual Supplements).

LAWS, REGULATIONS, RELATED ACTS. Federal Deposit Insurance Corporation, 550 Fifteenth Street, Northwest, Washington, D.C. 20429. 1983- . (Semiannual Supplements).

LENDER LIABILITY. A. Barry Cappello and Frances E. Komoroske. Parker and Sons Publications, Incorporated, P.O. Box 60001, Los Angeles, California 90060. 1987- . (Periodic Supplements).

LENDER LIABILITY AND BANK LITIGATION. Edward Mannino. Law Journal Seminars-Press, Incorporated, 111 Eighth Avenue, Suite 900, New York, New York 10011. 1989- . (Periodic Supplements).

LENDER LIABILITY LAW AND LITIGATION. J. Norton. Matthew Bender and Company, Incorporated, 11 Penn Plaza, New York, New York 10001. 1989- . (Annual Supplements).

LENDER LIABILITY: THEORY AND PRACTICE. Thomas Bucknell and others. Professional Education Systems, Incorporated, 200 Spring Street, Eau Claire, Wisconsin 54702. 1988- . (Annual Supplements).

LETTERS OF CREDIT. Barton B. McCullough. Matthew Bender and Company, Incorporated, 11 Penn Plaza, New York, New York 10001. 1987- . (Periodic Supplements).

MODERN BANKING CHECKLISTS. Third Edition. Jack Kusnet. , Research Institute of America, Incorporated, One Penn Plaza, New York, New York 10119. 1981- . (Semiannual Supplements).

MONETARY POLICY AND RESERVE REQUIREMENTS HANDBOOK. Federal Publications, 1120 Twentieth Street, Northwest, Washington, D.C. 20036. 1981- . (Monthly Supplements).

S & L ACCOUNTING AND AUDITING SERVICE. Sheshunoff Information Services, Incorporated, Capitol Station, P.O. Box 13203, Austin, Texas 78711. 1989- . (Monthly Supplements).

S & L CAPITAL SERVICE. Sheshunoff Information Services, Incorporated, Capitol Station, P.O. Box 13203, Austin, Texas 78711. 1989- . (Periodic Supplements).

SAVINGS INSTITUTIONS: MERGERS, ACQUISITIONS AND CONVERSIONS. Julie L. Williams. Law Journal Seminars-Press, Incorporated, 111 Eighth Avenue, Suite 900, New York, New York 10011. 1988- . (Periodic Supplements).

STATE TAXATION OF BANKS AND THRIFT INSTITUTIONS. Second Edition. American Bar Association, Section on Taxation, 750 North Lake Shore Drive, Chicago, Illinois 60611. 1983- .

TAXATION OF FINANCIAL INSTITUTIONS. Henry W. Schmidt. Matthew Bender and Company, Incorporated, 11 Penn Plaza, New York, New York 10001. 1983- . (Periodic Supplements).

TRUST DEPARTMENT ADMINISTRATION AND OPERATIONS. Matthew Bender and Company, Incorporated, 11 Penn Plaza, New York, New York 10001. 1981- . (Periodic Supplements).

TRUTH IN LENDING: A COMPREHENSIVE GUIDE. Prentice-Hall, Incorporated, 113 Sylvan Avenue, Englewood Cliffs, New Jersey 07632. 1984- . (Periodic Supplements).

UNDERSTANDING FIRREA: A PRACTICAL GUIDE TO PLANNING AND COMPLIANCE. Prentice-Hall, Incorporated, 113 Sylvan Avenue, Englewood Cliffs, New Jersey 07632. 1989- . (Periodic Supplements).

HANDBOOKS, MANUALS, FORMBOOKS

THE BANK DIRECTOR'S HANDBOOK. Second Edition. Auburn House, Greenwood Publishing Group, Incorporated, 88 Post Road West, P.O. Box 5007, Connecticut 06881. 1986.

BANKER'S HANDBOOK. Third Edition. William H. Baughn and Charles E. Walker. Business One Irwin, Incorporated, 1818 Ridge Road, Homewood, Illinois 60430. 1988.

FEDERAL BANKING LAWS. Fourth Edition. James A. Douglas and Sylvia Parker. , Research Institute of America, Incorporated, One Penn Plaza, New York, New York 10119. 1990.

THE FINANCIAL DESK BOOK. Consolidated Communications Group, Incorporated, 2000 Powell Street, Emeryville, California 94608. 1985.

HANDBOOK FOR BANKING STRATEGY. Richard C. Aspinwall and Robert A. Eisenbeis, Editors. John Wiley and Sons, Incorporated, 605 Third Avenue, New York, New York 10158. 1985.

HANDBOOK OF MODERN FINANCE. Dennis E. Logue, Editor. , Research Institute of America, Incorporated, One Penn Plaza, New York, New York 10119. 1984- . (Periodic Supplements).

THE LENDER'S HANDBOOK. Richard T. Nassberg. American Law Institute, American Bar Association, 750 North Lake Shore Drive, Chicago, Illinois 60611. 1986.

MODERN BANKING FORMS. Third Edition. Jack Kusnet. , Research Institute of America, Incorporated, One Penn Plaza, New York, New York 10119. 1981- .

MOODY'S BANK AND FINANCE MANUAL. Moody's Investors Service, 99 Church Street, New York, New York 10007. Annual.

TERM LOAN HANDBOOK. John J. McCann, Editor. Prentice Hall, Incorporated, 113 Sylvan Avenue, Englewood Cliffs, New Jersey 07632. 1983.

TEXTBOOKS AND GENERAL WORKS

THE AUTOMATED TELLER MACHINE (ATM) AS A NATIONAL BANK "BRANCH" UNDER THE FEDERAL LAW. Kirk Peterson. William S. Hein and Company, 1285 Main Street, Buffalo, New York 14209. 1988.

BANK DEREGULATION AND THE NEW COMPETITION IN FINANCIAL SERVICES. S. Kerry Cooper. Ballinger Division, HarperCollins Publishers, 10 East Fifty-third Street, New York, New York 10022. 1984.

THE BANKERS. Martin Mayer. Ballantine Books, Incorporated, 201 East Fiftieth Street, New York, New York 10022. 1984.

BANKING AND COMMERCIAL LENDING LAW. Richard T. Nassberg, Editor. American Law Institute, American Bar Association, Committee on Continuing Professional Education, 4025 Chestnut Street, Philadelphia, Pennsylvania 19104. 1984.

BANKING AND FINANCIAL INSTITUTIONS LAW IN A NUTSHELL. Second Edition. William A. Lovett. West Publishing Company, P.O. Box 64526, 50 West Kellogg Boulevard, St. Paul, Minnesota 55164-0526. 1988.

BANKING LAW IN THE UNITED STATES. Alfred M. Pollard. Butterworth Legal Publishers, 90 Stiles Road, Salem, New Hampshire 03079. 1988.

BANKING POLICY AND STRUCTURE: A COMPARATIVE ANALYSIS. J.S.G. Wilson. New York University Press, 70 Washington Square South, New York, New York 10012. 1986.

BLUEPRINT FOR REFORM: THE REPORT OF THE TASK GROUP ON REGULATION OF FINANCIAL SERVICES. Superintendent of Documents, United States Government Printing Office, Washington, D.C. 20402. 1984.

BRADY ON BANK CHECKS. Fifth Edition. Henry J. Bailey. , Research Institute of America, Incorporated, One Penn Plaza, New York, New York 10119. 1979- . (Annual Supplements).

COMMENTARIES ON BANKING REGULATION. John D. Hawke, Jr. Harcourt, Brace, Jovanovich, Incorporated, 6277 Sea Harbor Drive, Orlando, Florida 32821. 1985.

COMMERCIAL BANKING. Fourth Edition. Edward W. Reed. Prentice-Hall, Incorporated, 113 Sylvan Avenue, Englewood Cliffs, New Jersey 07632. 1989.

CONSUMER FINANCIAL SERVICES IN THE 1990'S. Section on Business Law, Division of Professional Education, American Bar Association, 750 North Lake Shore Drive, Chicago, Illinois 60611. 1990.

THE CORPORATE LAW OF BANKS: REGULATION OF CORPORATE AND SECURITIES ACTIVITIES OF DEPOSITORY INSTITUTIONS. Michael P. Malloy. Little, Brown and Company, 34 Beacon Street, Boston, Massachusetts 02108. 1987.

DEALING WITH THE RESOLUTION TRUST CORPORATION AND FDIC. Prentice-Hall, Incorporated, 113 Sylvan Avenue, Englewood Cliffs, New Jersey 07632. 1990.

DOMESTIC AND MULTINATIONAL BANKING: THE EFFECTS OF MONETARY POLICY. Rae Weston. Columbia University Press, 562 West One Hundred Thirteenth Street, New York, New York 10025. 1980.

THE ECONOMICS OF MONEY AND BANKING. Eighth Edition. Stephen M. Goldfeld and Lester V. Chandler. HarperCollins Publishers, Incorporated, 10 East Fifty-third Street, New York, New York 10022. 1981.

FEDERAL BANKING LAWS. Revised Edition. Duncan A. MacDonald and Robert L. Geltzer. , Research Institute of America, Incorporated, One Penn Plaza, New York, New York 10119. 1979- . (Annual Supplements).

THE GATHERING CRISIS IN FEDERAL DEPOSIT INSURANCE. Edward J. Kane. MIT Press, 55 Hayward Street, Cambridge, Massachusetts 02142. 1985.

THE GREAT AMERICAN BANKING SNAFU. Mary L. King. Free Press, 866 Third Avenue, New York, New York 10022. 1985.

IN BANKS WE TRUST. Penny Lernoux. Doubleday and Company, Incorporated, 666 Fifth Avenue, New York, New York 10103. 1984.

LAW OF BANK DEPOSITS, COLLECTIONS AND CREDIT CARDS. Third Edition. Barkley Clark. , Research Institute of America, Incorporated, One Penn Plaza, New York, New York 10119. 1990.

LITIGATING FOR OR AGAINST THE FDIC AND THE RTC. Practising Law Institute, 810 Seventh Avenue, New York, New York 10019. 1990.

MICHIE ON BANKS ON BANKING. Michie/Bobbs-Merrill Law Publishing Company, P.O. Box 7587, Charlottesville, Virginia 22906-7582. 1956- . (Annual Supplements).

MONEY AND BANKING. Third Edition. Dudley G. Luckett. McGraw-Hill Book Company, 1221 Avenue of the Americas, New York, New York 10020. 1984.

MONEY, BANKING, AND THE UNITED STATES ECONOMY. Sixth Edition. Harry D. Hutchinson. Prentice-Hall, Incorporated, 113 Sylvan Avenue, Englewood Cliffs, New Jersey 07632. 1988.

THE MONEY BAZAARS: UNDERSTANDING THE BANKING REVOLUTION AROUND US. Martin Mayer. E.P. Dutton, 2 Park Avenue, New York, New York 10016. 1984.

PERSPECTIVES ON SAFE AND SOUND BANKING: PAST, PRESENT, AND FUTURE. George J. Benston. MIT Press, 55 Hayward Street, Cambridge, Massachusetts 02142. 1986.

PRINCIPLES OF MONEY, BANKING AND FINANCIAL MARKETS. Second Revised Edition. Lawrence S. Ritter and William L. Silber. Basic Books, Incorporated, 10 East Fifty-third Street, New York, New York 10022. 1983.

RESOLUTION TRUST CORPORATION: BANKRUPTCIES, LIQUIDATIONS AND SALES OF ASSETS. Practising Law Institute, 810 Seventh Avenue, New York, New York 10019. 1990.

RETAIL FINANCIAL SERVICES. Practising Law Institute, 810 Seventh Avenue, New York, New York 10019. 1987- .

THE RETENTION OF BANK RECORDS. Revised Edition. American Bankers Association, 1120 Connecticut Avenue, Northwest, Washington, D.C. 20036. 1984.

TECHNOLOGICAL INNOVATION, REGULATION, AND THE MONETARY ECONOMY. Colin Lawrence and Robert P. Shay, Editors. HarperCollins Publishers, Incorporated, 10 East Fifty-third Street, New York, New York 10022. 1986.

TECHNOLOGY AND THE REGULATION OF FINANCIAL MARKETS: SECURITIES, FUTURES, AND BANKING. Anthony Saunders and Lawrence J. White, Editors. Free Press, 866 Third Avenue, New York, New York 10022. 1985.

THE THRIFT INDUSTRY RESTRUCTURED: THE NEW REGULATORS AND OPPORTUNITIES FOR THE FUTURE. Practising Law Institute, 810 Seventh Avenue, New York, New York 10019. 1989.

WHAT SHOULD BANKS DO? Robert E. Litan. The Brookings Institution, 1775 Massachusetts Avenue, Northwest, Washington, D.C. 20036. 1987.

ENCYCLOPEDIAS AND DICTIONARIES

BANKING LANGUAGE: A RUNNING PRESS GLOSSARY. Laila Batz. Running Press, 125 South Twenty-second Street, Philadelphia, Pennsylvania 19103. 1977.

BANKING TERMINOLOGY. Third Revised Edition. American Bankers Association, 1120 Connecticut Avenue, Northwest, Washington, D.C. 20036. 1989.

DICTIONARY OF BANKING AND FINANCE. Lewis Davids. Rowman and Littlefield, Incorporated, 8705 Bollman Place, Savage, Maryland 20763. 1980.

DICTIONARY OF BANKING AND FINANCE. Terry M. Rosenberg. John Wiley and Sons, Incorporated, 605 Third Avenue, New York, New York 10158. 1982.

DICTIONARY OF BANKING AND FINANCIAL SERVICES. Second Edition. Jerry M. Rosenberg. John Wiley and Sons, Incorporated, 605 Third Avenue, New York, New York 10158. 1985.

ELSEVIER'S BANKING DICTIONARY IN SIX LANGUAGES. ENGLISH/AMERICAN, FRENCH, ITALIAN, SPANISH, DUTCH, AND GERMAN. Second Edition. Elsevier Scientific Publishing Company, P.O. Box 882, Madison Square Station, New York, New York 10159. 1980.

ENCYCLOPEDIA OF BANKING AND FINANCE. Eighth Revised Edition. Glenn G. Munn and Ferdinand L. Garcia. Bankers Publishing Company, 210 South Street, Boston, Massachusetts 02111. 1983.

GLOSSARY OF FIDUCIARY TERMS. Second Edition. American Bankers Association, 1120 Connecticut Avenue, Northwest, Washington, D.C. 20036. 1984.

THE MONEY ENCYCLOPEDIA. Harvey Rachlin. HarperCollins Publishers, Incorporated, 10 East Fifty-third Street, New York, New York 10022. 1984.

THOMSON'S DICTIONARY OF BANKING. Twelfth Edition. F.R. Ryder and D.B. Jenkins. Pitman Publishing Corporation, 6 Davis Drive, Belmont, California 94002. 1974.

THE THORNDIKE ENCYCLOPEDIA OF BANKING AND FINANCIAL TABLES. Revised Edition. David Thorndike. , Research Institute of America, Incorporated, One Penn Plaza, New York, New York 10119. Annual.

DIGESTS, INDEXES, ABSTRACTS, CITATORS

AMERICAN BANKER INDEX. American Banker Incorporated, 1 State Street Plaza, New York, New York 10004. Monthly.

BANK EXECUTIVES REPORT. , Research Institute of America, Incorporated, One Penn Plaza, New York, New York 10119. Semimonthly.

BANKING LAW JOURNAL DIGEST. , Research Institute of America, Incorporated, One Penn Plaza, New York, New York 10119. 1984- .

BANKING LITERATURE INDEX. American Bankers Association, 1120 Connecticut Avenue, Northwest, Washington, D.C. 20036. 1982- . Monthly.

BUSINESS PERIODICALS INDEX. H.W. Wilson Company, 950 University Avenue, Bronx, New York 10452. Monthly.

ANNUALS AND SURVEYS

BANK COMPLIANCE. Practising Law Institute, 810 Seventh Avenue, New York, New York 10019. 1989- . Annual.

BANKERS ALMANAC. Richard B. Miller. Bankers Publishing Company, 210 South Street, Boston, Massachusetts 02111. 1985- . Annual.

BANKERS' ALMANAC AND YEARBOOK. International Publications Service, 1900 Frost Road, Suite 101, Bristol, Pennsylvania 19007. Annual.

BANKING LAW AND REGULATION. Practising Law Institute, 810 Seventh Avenue, New York, New York 10019. 1988- . Annual.

FINANCIAL SERVICES INSTITUTE. Practising Law Institute, 810 Seventh Avenue, New York, New York 10019. Annual.

INSTITUTE ON BANKING LAW AND REGULATION. Practising Law Institute, 810 Seventh Avenue, New York, New York 10019. 1989- . Annual.

VALUE LINE INVESTMENT SURVEY. Arnold Bernhard and Company, 711 Third Avenue, New York, New York 10017. Weekly.

WORLD CURRENCY YEARBOOK. Phillip P. Cowitt, Editor. International Currency Analysis, Incorporated, 7239 Avenue North, Brooklyn, New York 11234. 1984- . Annual.

LAW REVIEWS AND PERIODICALS

ABA BANKERS WEEKLY. American Bankers Association, 1120 Connecticut Avenue, Northwest, Washington, D.C. 20036. Weekly.

ABA BANKING JOURNAL. American Bankers Association. 1120 Connecticut Avenue, Northwest, Washington, D.C. 20036. Monthly.

BANK FRAUD. Bank Administration Institute, 60 Gould Center, Rolling Meadows, Illinois 60008. Monthly.

THE BANKER. F.T. Business Information, LTD. Greystoke Place, Fetter Lane, London, EC4A IND, England. Monthly.

BANKERS LAW JOURNAL. , Research Institute of America, Incorporated, 210 South Street, Boston, Massachusetts 02111. Ten issues per year.

THE BANKERS MAGAZINE. , Research Institute of America, Incorporated, 210 South Street, Boston, Massachusetts 02111. Bimonthly.

BANKERS MONTHLY. Bankers Monthly, Incorporated, 601 Skokie Boulevard, Northbrook, Illinois 60062. Monthly.

BANKING AND FINANCE LAW REVIEW. The Carswell Company, Limited, 2330 Midland Avenue, Agincourt, Ontario, Canada M1S 1P7. Three issues per year.

BANKING LAW JOURNAL. , Research Institute of America, Incorporated, 210 South Street, Boston, Massachusetts 02111. Quarterly.

EXECUTIVE FINANCIAL WOMEN. National Association for Bank Women, 500 North Michigan Avenue, Suite 1400, Chicago, Illinois 60611. Bimonthly.

FEDERAL RESERVE BULLETIN. Federal Reserve Board. Superintendent of Documents, United States Government Printing Office, Washington, D.C. 20402. Monthly.

THE INDEPENDENT BANKER: THE NATIONAL VOICE OF AMERICA'S INDEPENDENT BANKERS. Independent Bankers Association, One Thomas Circle, Northwest, Suite 950, Washington, D.C. 20005. Monthly.

ISSUES IN BANK REGULATION. Bank Administration Institute, 60 Gould Center, Rolling Meadows, Illinois 60008. Quarterly.

JOURNAL FOR BANK COST AND MANAGEMENT ACCOUNTING. National Association for Bank Cost and Management Accounting, P.O. Box 458, Northbrook, Illinois 60065. Monthly.

JOURNAL OF BANK RESEARCH. Bank Administration Institute, 60 Gould Center, Rolling Meadows, Illinois 60008. Quarterly.

JOURNAL OF COMMERCIAL BANKING LENDING. Robert Morris Associates, Philadelphia National Bank Building, Philadelphia, Pennsylvania 19107. Monthly.

JOURNAL OF MONEY, CREDIT, AND BANKING. Ohio State University Press, 1050 Carmack Road, Columbus, Ohio 43210. Quarterly.

JOURNAL OF RETAIL BANKING. 3945 Holcomb Bridge Road, Suite 301, Norcross, Georgia 30092. Quarterly.

LEGAL BULLETIN. United States League of Savings Institutions, 1709 New York Avenue, Northwest, Suite 801, Washington, D.C. 20006. Bimonthly.

MAGAZINE OF BANK ADMINISTRATION. Bank Administration Institute, 60 Gould Center, Rolling Meadows, Illinois 60008. Monthly.

REGULATORY REPORT. United States League of Savings Institutions, 1709 New York Avenue, Northwest, Suite 801, Washington, D.C. 20006. Monthly.

THE REVIEW OF FINANCIAL SERVICES REGULATION: AN ANALYSIS OF CURRENT LAWS AND REGULATIONS AFFECTING BANKING AND RELATED INDUSTRIES. Standard and Poor's Corporation, 25 Broadway, New York, New York 10004. 1985- . Semimonthly.

SAVINGS BANK JOURNAL. National Association of Mutual Savings Banks, 200 Park Avenue, New York, New York 10017. Monthly.

THE WORLD OF BANKING. Bank Administration Institute, 60 Gould Center, Rolling Meadow, Illinois 60008. Bimonthly.

NEWSLETTERS AND NEWSPAPERS

ABA'S FINANCIAL MANAGER. American Bankers Association, 1120 Connecticut Avenue, Northwest, Washington, D.C. 20036. Monthly.

ADVISOR NEWSLETTER. American Bankers Association, 1120 Connecticut Avenue, Northwest, Washington, D.C. 20036. Monthly.

AMERICAN BANKER. American Banker Incorporated, 1 State Street Plaza, New York, New York 10004. Daily.

THE BANK ATTORNEY. American Banker-Bond Buyer Newsletter Division, P.O. Box 30240, Bethesda, Maryland 20814. Weekly.

BANK BAILOUT LITIGATION NEWS. Buraff Publications, 1350 Connecticut Avenue, Northwest, Suite 1000, Washington, D.C. 20036. Bimonthly.

THE BANK DIGEST. Washington Service Bureau, 655 Fifteenth Street, Northwest, Washington, D.C. 20005. Daily.

BANK INSURANCE AND PROTECTION BULLETIN. American Bankers Association, 1120 Connecticut Avenue, Northwest, Washington, D.C. 20036. Monthly.

BANK LETTER. Institutional Investor, Incorporated, 488 Madison, Avenue, New York, New York 10022. Weekly.

BANK OPERATIONS BULLETIN. American Bankers Association, 1120 Connecticut Avenue, Northwest, Washington, D.C. 20036. Monthly.

BANK PERSONNEL NEWS. American Bankers Association, 1120 Connecticut Avenue, Northwest, Washington, D.C. 20036. Monthly.

BANK TAX REPORT. , Research Institute of America, Incorporated, 210 South Street, Boston, Massachusetts 02111. Monthly.

BANK/THRIFT LITIGATION AND ENFORCEMENT NEWS. Atlantic Information Services, Incorporated, 1050 Seventeenth Street, Northwest, Suite 480, Washington, D.C. 20036. Weekly.

THE BANKERS LETTER OF THE LAW. , Research Institute of America, Incorporated, 210 South Street, Boston, Massachusetts 02111. Monthly.

BANKERS NEWS WEEKLY. American Bankers Association, 1120 Connecticut Avenue, Northwest, Washington, D.C. 20036. Weekly.

BANKERS RESEARCH. Bankers Research, Incorporated, 12 Avery Place, Westport, Connecticut 06880. Semimonthly.

BANKING EXPANSION REPORTER. Prentice Hall Law and Business, 270 Sylvan Avenue, Englewood Cliffs, New Jersey 07632. Bimonthly.

BANKING LAW BRIEFS. Elsah Associates, P.O. Box 426, Lenox Station, New York, New York 10021. Semimonthly.

BANKING LAW REPORT. Executive Enterprises, Incorporated, 22 West Twenty-first Street, New York, New York 10010. Monthly.

BANKING LAW SECTION NEWSLETTER. New Jersey State Bar Association, One Constitution Square, New Brunswick, New Jersey 08901-1500. Irregular.

BANKING REGULATOR. Reports Publications, 700 Orange Street, Wilmington, Delaware 19801. Weekly.

BANKS IN INSURANCE REPORT. Executive Enterprises Publications Company, Incorporated, 22 West Twenty-first Street, New York, New York 10010. Weekly.

BNA'S BANKING REPORT. Bureau of National Affairs, 1231 Twenty-fifth Street, Northwest, Washington, D.C. 20037. Weekly.

CAPITAL UPDATE. Mortgage Insurance Companies of America, 805 Fifteenth Street, Northwest, Suite 1110, Washington, D.C. 20005. Semimonthly.

CASE LAW UPDATE. United States League of Savings Institutions, 111 East Wacker Drive, Chicago, Illinois 60601. Monthly.

COMMERCIAL, BANKING AND BANKRUPTCY LAW. Illinois State Bar Association, Section on Commercial, Banking and Bankruptcy Law, Illinois Bar Center, Springfield, Illinois 62701. Semimonthly.

COMPLIANCE ALERT. Bank Administration Institute, 60 Gould Center, Rolling Meadow, Illinois 60008. Biweekly.

CONSUMER LENDING REPORT. , Research Institute of America, Incorporated, 210 South Street, Boston, Massachusetts 02111. Monthly.

CSBS NEWS. Conference of State Bank Supervisors, 1015 Eighteenth Street, Northwest, Suite 1100, Washington, D.C. 20036. Quarterly.

EFT REPORT. Phillips Publishing, Incorporated, 7811 Montrose Road, Potomac, Maryland 20854. Biweekly.

EXECUTIVE REPORT. Electronic Funds Transfer Association, 1726 M Street, Northwest, Washington, D.C. 20036. Monthly.

FAILED BANK AND THRIFT LITIGATION REPORTER. Andrews Publications, Incorporated, P.O. Box 200, Edgemont, Pennsylvania 19063. Semimonthly.

THE FDIC WATCH. American Banker-Bond Buyer Newsletter Division, P.O. Box 30240, Bethesda, Maryland 20814. Weekly.

FINANCIAL SERVICES WEEK. Phillips Publishing Incorporated, 7811 Montrose Road, Potomac, Maryland 20854. Weekly.

INTERNATIONAL BANK ACCOUNTANT. American Banker-Bond Buyer Newsletter Division, P.O. Box 30240, Bethesda, Maryland 20814. Weekly.

LENDER LIABILITY LAW REPORT. , Research Institute of America, Incorporated, 210 South Street, Boston, Massachusetts 02111. Monthly.

LOAN OFFICER'S LEGAL ALERT. Executive Enterprises Publications Company, Incorporated, 22 West Twenty-first Street, New York, New York 10010. Weekly.

MONEY LAUNDERING LAW REPORT. Leader Publications, 111 Eighth Avenue, New York, New York 10011. Monthly.

NATIONAL FINANCING LAW DIGEST. National Property Law Digests, Incorporated, 7200 Wisconsin Avenue, Suite 314, Bethesda, Maryland 20814. Monthly.

ONE-HUNDRED HIGHEST YIELDS AMONG FEDERALLY-INSURED BANKS AND SAVINGS INSTITUTIONS. Advertising News Service, Incorporated, P.O. Box 088888, North Palm Beach, Florida 33408. Weekly.

PRATTS LETTER. A.S. Pratt and Sons, Incorporated, 1117 North Nineteenth Street, P.O. Box 9655, Arlington, Virginia 22209. Weekly.

RESOLUTION TRUST REPORTER. The Dorset Group, Incorporated, 225 West Thirty-fourth Street, Room 918, New York, New York 10001. Bimonthly.

THE REVIEW OF BANKING AND FINANCIAL SERVICES REGULATION. Standard and Poor's, 25 Broad Street, New York, New York 10004. Semimonthly.

THE THRIFT ATTORNEY. American Banker-Bond Buyer Newsletter Division, P.O. Box 30240, Bethesda, Maryland 20814. Weekly.

THE THRIFT REGULATOR. American Banker-Bond Buyer Newsletter Division, P.O. Box 30240, Bethesda, Maryland 20814. Weekly.

TRENDS. American Bankers Association, 1120 Connecticut Avenue, Northwest, Washington, D.C. 20036. Weekly.

WASHINGTON BOND AND MONEY MARKET LETTER. Newsletter Services, Incorporated, 1545 New York Avenue, Northeast, Washington, D.C. 20002. Biweekly.

WASHINGTON MEMO. National Council of Savings Institutions, 1101 Fifteenth Street, Northwest, Suite 400, Washington, D.C. 20005. Weekly.

WASHINGTON NOTES. United States League of Savings Institutions, 111 East Wacker Drive, Chicago, Illinois 60601. Monthly.

WASHINGTON REGULATORY REPORT. Clark Boardman Company, Limited, 375 Hudson Street, New York, New York 10014. Monthly.

WASHINGTON WEEKLY REPORT. Independent Bankers Association of America, One Thomas Circle, Northwest, Suite 950, Washington, D.C. 20005. Weekly.

BIBLIOGRAPHIES

BANKING DEREGULATION, 1979-1984: A SELECT BIBLIOGRAPHY. Nels L. Gunderson. Vance Bibliographies, P.O. Box 229, 112 North Charter Street, Monticello, Illinois 61856. 1984.

THE FED IN PRINT. Public Information Department, Federal Reserve Bank of Philadelphia, Pennsylvania 19106. Semiannual.

FINANCIAL JOURNALS AND SERIALS: AN ANALYTICAL GUIDE TO ACCOUNTING, BANKING, FINANCE, INSURANCE, AND INVESTMENT PERIODICALS. William Fisher, Compiler. Greenwood Publishing Group, Incorporated, 88 Post Road West, P.O. Box 5007, Westport, Connecticut 06881. 1986.

MONEY, BANKING, AND MACROECONOMICS: A GUIDE TO INFORMATION SOURCES. James M. Rock. Gale Research, Incorporated, 835 Penobscot Building, Detroit, Michigan 48226. 1977.

NONBANK BANKS: REGULATING CREDIT UNIONS, SAVINGS AND LOANS AND OTHER THRIFT INSTITUTIONS. Tim J. Watts. Vance Bibliographies, P.O. Box 229, 112 North Charter Street, Monticello, Illinois 61856. 1988.

SELECTIVE BIBLIOGRAPHY ON INTERNATIONAL BANKING. American Bankers Association, 1120 Connecticut Avenue, Northwest, Washington, D.C. 20036. 1987.

SOURCES OF WORLD FINANCIAL AND BANKING INFORMATION. G.R. Dicks. Greenwood Publishing Group, Incorporated, 88 Post Road West, P.O. Box 5007, Westport, Connecticut 06881. 1981.

DIRECTORIES

AMERICAN BANK DIRECTORY. McFadden Business Publications, 6195 Crooked Creek Road, Norcross, Georgia 30092. Semiannual.

AMERICAN BANKERS ASSOCIATION KEY TO ROUTING NUMBERS. Rand McNally and Company, P.O. Box 7600, Chicago, Illinois 60680. Annual.

BANKERS SCHOOLS DIRECTORY. Professional Services Division, American Bankers Association, 1120 Connecticut Avenue, Northwest, Washington, D.C. 20036. 1982.

COMMITTEE DIRECTORY OF THE SECTION ON BUSINESS LAW OF THE AMERICAN BAR ASSOCIATION. Section on Business Law, American Bar Association, 750 North Lake Shore Drive, Chicago, Illinois 60611. 1988- . (Annual).

DIRECTORY OF AMERICAN SAVINGS AND LOANS ASSOCIATIONS. T.K. Sanderson Organization, 200 East Twenty-fifth Street, Baltimore, Maryland 21218. 1982.

SOURCES OF WORLD FINANCIAL AND BANKING INFORMATION. G.R. Dicks, Editor. Greenwood Publishing Group, Incorporated, 88 Post Road West, P.O. Box 5007, Westport, Connecticut 06881. 1981.

BIOGRAPHICAL SOURCES

WHO'S WHO IN BANKING: DIRECTORY OF THE BANKING PROFESSION. Third Edition. Business Press, 200 Park Avenue, South, New York, New York 10003. 1966- . (Irregular).

ASSOCIATIONS AND PROFESSIONAL SOCIETIES

AMERICAN BANKERS ASSOCIATION. 1120 Connecticut Avenue, Northwest, Washington, D.C. 20036. (202) 663-5000.

AMERICAN COUNCIL OF STATE SAVINGS SUPERVISORS. 1400 L Street, Northwest, Suite 600, Washington, D.C. 20005-4905. (202) 371-0666.

AMERICAN INSTITUTE OF BANKING. 1120 Connecticut Avenue, Northwest, Washington, D.C. 20036. (202) 362-5510.

AMERICAN LEAGUE OF FINANCIAL INSTITUTIONS. 1709 New York Avenue, Northwest, Suite 201, Washington, D.C. 20006. (202) 628-5624.

ASSOCIATION OF BANK HOLDING COMPANIES. 730 Fifteenth Street, Northwest, Washington, D.C. 20005. (202) 393-1158.

ASSOCIATION OF MILITARY BANKS OF AMERICA. 10205 Eisenhower Lane, Great Falls, Virginia 22066. (703) 759-4037.

ASSOCIATION OF RESERVE CITY BANKERS. 1710 Rhode Island Avenue, Northwest, Suite 500, Washington, D.C. 20036. (202) 296-5709.

BANK ADMINISTRATION INSTITUTE. 60 Gould Center, Rolling Meadows, Illinois 60008. (708) 228-6200.

BANKERS ASSOCIATION FOR FOREIGN TRADE. 1600 M Street, Northwest, Seventh Floor, Washington, D.C. 20036. (202) 452-0952.

CONFERENCE OF STATE BANK SUPERVISORS. 1015 Eighteenth Street, Northwest, Suite 1100, Washington, D.C. 20036-5275. (202) 296-2840.

CONSUMER BANKERS ASSOCIATION. 1000 Wilson Boulevard, 30th Floor, Arlington, Virginia 22209. (703) 276-1750.

COUNCIL OF MUTUAL SAVINGS INSTITUTIONS. 521 Fifth Avenue, Suite 1714, New York, New York 10017. (212) 867-2776.

FARM CREDIT COUNCIL. 50 F Street, Northwest, Suite 900, Washington, D.C. 20001. (202) 626-8710.

INDEPENDENT BANKERS ASSOCIATION OF AMERICA. One Thomas Circle, Northwest, Suite 950, Washington, D.C. 20005. (202) 659-8111.

MORTGAGE BANKERS ASSOCIATION OF AMERICA. 1125 Fifteenth Street, Northwest, Washington, D.C. 20005. (202) 861-6500.

NATIONAL ASSOCIATION FOR BANK COST AND MANAGEMENT ACCOUNTING. P.O. Box 458, Northbrook, Illinois 60065. (708) 272-4233.

NATIONAL ASSOCIATION OF BANK WOMEN. 500 North Michigan Avenue, Suite 1400, Chicago, Illinois 60611. (312) 661-1700.

NATIONAL ASSOCIATION OF URBAN BANKERS. 122 C Street, Northwest, Suite 580, Washington, D.C. 20001. (202) 783-4743.

NATIONAL BANKERS ASSOCIATION. 122 C Street, Northwest, Suite 580, Washington, D.C. 20001. (202) 783-3200.

NATIONAL COUNCIL OF SAVINGS INSTITUTIONS. 1101 Fifteenth Street, Northwest, Suite 600, Washington, D.C. 20005. (202) 857-3100.

UNITED STATES LEAGUE OF SAVINGS INSTITUTIONS. 1709 New York Avenue, Northwest, Suite 800, Washington, D.C. 20006. (202) 637-8900.

RESEARCH CENTERS, INSTITUTES, CLEARINGHOUSES

AMERICAN INSTITUTE FOR ECONOMIC RESEARCH. Division Street, Great Barrington, Massachusetts 01230. (413) 528-1216.

MID AMERICA INSTITUTE FOR PUBLIC POLICY RESEARCH, INCORPORATED. 175 West Jackson Boulevard, Suite 1801, Chicago, Illinois 60604. (312) 786-9575.

MORIN CENTER FOR BANKING LAW STUDIES. Boston University, School of Law, 765 Commonwealth Avenue, Boston, Massachusetts 02215. (617) 353-3023.

NATIONAL BUREAU OF ECONOMIC RESEARCH. 1050 Massachusetts Avenue, Cambridge, Massachusetts 02138. (617) 868-3900.

NORC: A SOCIAL SCIENCE RESEARCH CENTER. 1155 East Sixtieth Street, Chicago, Illinois 60637. (312) 702-1200.

ONLINE DATABASES

ABA BANKING JOURNAL. Simmons Boardman Publishing Company, 345 Hudson Street, New York, New York 10014.

AMERICAN BANKER: FULL TEXT. American Banker-Bond Buyer Database Services, One State Street Plaza, New York, New York 10004. (Available on NEXIS).

AMERICAN BANKER NEWS SERVICE. American Banker-Bond Buyer Database Services, One State Street Plaza, New York, New York 10004.

BANK VALUATION. Bank Valuation, 2130 Jackson Street, San Francisco, California 94115.

BANKING EXPLOSION REPORTER. Law and Business, Incorporated, 855 Valley Road, Clifton, New Jersey 07013.

BANKING REGULATOR. CoVest Reports, Incorporated, 1001 Connecticut Avenue, Northwest, Suite 1238, Washington, D.C. 20036.

BANKROLL II. Federal Reserve Board, Flow of Funds Section, Stop 95, Twentieth and Constitution Avenues, Northwest, Washington, D.C. 20551.

BNA BANKING DAILY. Bureau of National Affairs, 1231 Twenty-fifth Street, Northwest, Washington, D.C. 20037.

BNA'S BANKING REPORT. Bureau of National Affairs, 1231 Twenty-fifth Street, Northwest, Washington, D.C. 20037.

FEDERAL BANKING LIBRARY. Available on LEXIS. Mead Data Central, 9443 Springboro Pike, P.O. Box 933, Dayton, Ohio 45401.

THE FINANCIAL SERVICES INDUSTRY COMPETITIVE INTELLIGENCE DATABASE. Strategic Intelligence Systems, Incorporated, 404 Park Avenue South, Suite 1301, New York, New York 10016.

FINANCIAL SERVICES LIBRARY. Available on WestLaw, West Publishing Company, P.O. Box 64526, 50 West Kellogg Boulevard, St. Paul, Minnesota 55164-0526.

ISSUES IN BANK REGULATION. Bank Administration Institute, 60 Gould Center, Rolling Meadows, Illinois 60008.

STATE CAPITALS: BANKING POLICIES. Wakeman/Walworth, Incorporated, P.O. Box 1939, New Haven, Connecticut 06509.

UNITED STATES BANKER. Kalo Communications, Incorporated, 10 Valley Drive, Greenwich, Connecticut 06831.

STATISTICS SOURCES

BANK OPERATING STATISTICS. Federal Deposit Insurance Corporation, 550 Seventeenth Street, Northwest, Washington, D.C. 20429. Annual.

CONCORDANCE OF STATISTICS AVAILABLE IN SELECTED FEDERAL RESERVE PUBLICATIONS. Board of Governors of the Federal Reserve System, Twentieth Street and Constitution Avenue, Washington, D.C. 20551. 1982.

ECONOMIC INDICATORS. Council of Economic Advisors, Executive Office of the President. Superintendent of Documents, United States Government Printing Office, Washington, D.C. 20402. Monthly.

FEDERAL RESERVE BULLETIN. Board of Governors of the Federal Reserve System, Publications Services, Twentieth Street and Constitution Avenue, Washington, D.C. 20551. Monthly.

MORTGAGE BANKING: FINANCIAL STATEMENTS AND OPERATING RATIOS. Mortgage Bankers Association of America, 1125 Fifteenth Street, Northwest, Washington, D.C. 20005. Annual.

STATISTICAL INFORMATION ON THE FINANCIAL SERVICES INDUSTRY. Second Edition. American Bankers Association, 1120 Connecticut Avenue, Northwest, Washington, D.C. 20036. 1983.

TREASURY BULLETIN. Office of the Secretary, United States Department of the Treasury. Superintendent of Documents, United States Government Printing Office, Washington, D.C. 20402. Monthly.

OTHER SOURCES

BANK POWERS: ISSUES RELATED TO REPEAL OF THE GLASS STEAGALL ACT. United States General Accounting Office, 441 G Street, Northwest, Washington, D.C. 20548. 1988.

BANK RATES ON SHORT TERM BUSINESS LOANS. United States Board of Governors of the Federal Reserve System, Twentieth Street and Constitution Avenue, Washington, D.C. 20551. Quarterly.

THE BANK RATINGS OF ALL U.S. BANKS. Sheshunoff Rating Services, Incorporated, Capitol Station, P.O. Box 13203, Austin, Texas 78711. Annual.

BANK WATCH. Keefe, Bruyette, and Woods, Incorporated, Two World Trade Center, Suite 8566, New York, New York 10048.

BANKS OF YOUR STATE. Sheshunoff Rating Services, Incorporated, Capitol Station, P.O. Box 13203, Austin, Texas 78711. Annual.

DOCUMENTARY HISTORY OF BANKING AND CURRENCY IN THE UNITED STATES. Herman E. Kroos, Chelsea House Publishers, 1974 Sproul Road, Suite 400, Broomall, Pennsylvania 19008. 1969.

MODERNIZING THE FINANCIAL SYSTEM: U.S. TREASURY DEPARTMENT RECOMMENDATIONS FOR SAFER, MORE COMPETITIVE BANKS. Commerce Clearing House, Incorporated, 4025 West Peterson Avenue, Chicago, Illinois 60646. 1991.

WOMEN AND MINORITIES IN BANKING. Council on Economic Priorities and Tina Simcich. Praeger Publishers, 88 Post Road, West, Box 5007, West Port, Connecticut 06881. 1977.

BAR ASSOCIATIONS
See: AMERICAN BAR ASSOCIATION; STATES

BAR EXAMINERS AND EXAMINATIONS
See: ADMISSION TO THE BAR

BARS AND TAVERNS
See: ALCOHOL CONTROL AND DRINKING BEHAVIOR

BATTERED CHILDREN
See: CHILD ABUSE AND NEGLECT; FAMILY VIOLENCE

BATTERED WOMEN
See: FAMILY VIOLENCE

BILL DRAFTING
See: STATUTORY CONSTRUCTION AND DRAFTING

BILLS OF LADING
See: NEGOTIABLE INSTRUMENTS

BIOETHICS
See also: MEDICAL JURISPRUDENCE AND MALPRACTICE; PROFESSIONAL ETHICS AND LIABILITY

STATUTES, CODES, STANDARDS, UNIFORM LAWS

UNIFORM PARENTAGE ACT. National Conference of Commissioners on Uniform State Laws. Uniform Laws Annotated. West Publishing Company, P.O. Box 64526, 50 West Kellogg Boulevard, St. Paul, Minnesota 55164-0526. 1976- . (Annual Supplements).

LOOSELEAF SERVICES AND REPORTERS

BIOETHICS REPORTER: ETHICAL AND LEGAL ISSUES IN MEDICINE, HEALTH CARE ADMINISTRATION, AND HUMAN EXPERIMENTATION. University Publications of America, 4520 East West Highway, Suite 600, Bethesda, Maryland 20814. 1983- .

BIOLAW: A LEGAL AND ETHICAL REPORTER ON MEDICINE, HEALTH CARE, AND BIOENGINEERING. James F. Childress, Patricia King, Karen Rothenberg, and Walter Wadlington, Editors. University Publications of America, 4520 East West Highway, Suite 600, Bethesda, Maryland 20814. 1986- .

BIOTECHNOLOGY AND THE LAW. Clark Boardman Company, Limited, 435 Hudson Street, New York, New York 10014. 1982- . (Annual Supplements).

BIOTECHNOLOGY: PRINCIPLES, PATENTS AND PROMISES. Hamline University School of Law, Advanced Legal Education, 1536 Hewitt Avenue, St. Paul, Minnesota 55104. 1987- .

HANDBOOKS, MANUALS, FORMBOOKS

HANDBOOK FOR HOSPITAL ETHICS COMMITTEES. Judith Wilson Ross, American Hospital Publishing, Incorporated, 211 East Chicago, Illinois 60611. 1986.

HEALTH AND HUMAN VALUES: A GUIDE TO MAKING YOUR OWN DECISIONS. Frank Harron, John Burnside and Tom Beauchamp. Yale University Press, 302 Temple Street, New Haven, Connecticut 06520. 1983.

TEXTBOOKS AND GENERAL WORKS

AGRICULTURAL BIOETHICS: IMPLICATIONS OF AGRICULTURAL BIOTECHNOLOGY. Steven M. Gendel and others. Iowa State University Press, 2121 South State Avenue, Ames, Iowa 50010. 1990.

BIOMEDICAL ETHICS: AN ANGLO-AMERICAN DIALOGUE. Daniel Callahan and G.R. Dunstan. New York Academy of Sciences, 2 East Sixty-third Street, New York, New York 10021. 1988.

BIOMEDICAL TECHNOLOGY AND PUBLIC POLICY. Robert H. Blank and Miriam K. Mills. Greenwood Publishing Group, Incorporated, 88 Post Road West, P.O. Box 5007, Westport, Connecticut 06881. 1989.

BRAVE NEW PEOPLE: ETHICAL ISSUES AT THE COMMENCEMENT OF LIFE. Revised Edition. D. Gareth Jones. William B. Eerdmans Publishing Company, 255 Jefferson Avenue, Southeast, Grand Rapids, Michigan 49503. 1985.

CASES IN BIOETHICS: SELECTIONS FROM THE HASTINGS CENTER. Revised Edition. Carol Levine and Robert M. Veatch, Editors. St. Martin's Press, Incorporated, 175 Fifth Avenue, New York, New York 10010. 1984.

CHOOSING LIFE OR DEATH: A GUIDE FOR PATIENTS, FAMILIES, AND PROFESSIONALS. William J. Winslade and Judith Wilson Roth. Free Press, 866 Third Avenue, New York, New York 10022. 1986.

CONTEMPORARY ISSUES IN BIOETHICS. Third Edition. Tom L. Beauchamp and LeRoy Walters. Wadsworth Publishing Company, 10 Davis Drive, Belmont, California 94002. 1989.

DEATH, BRAIN DEATH, AND ETHICS. David Lamb. State University of New York Press, State University Plaza, Albany, New York 12246. 1985.

DECIDING FOR OTHERS: THE ETHICS OF SURROGATE DECISIONMAKING. Allen E. Buchanan and Dan W. Brock. Cambridge University Press, 40 West Twentieth Street, New York, New York 10011. 1990.

DECIDING TO FOREGO LIFE-SUSTAINING TREATMENT: A REPORT ON ETHICAL, MEDICAL AND LEGAL ISSUES IN TREATMENT DECISIONS. President's Commission for the Study of Ethical Problems in Medicine and Biomedical and Behavioral Research. Superintendent of Documents, United States Government Printing Office, Washington, D.C. 20402. 1983.

DEFINING HUMAN LIFE: MEDICAL, LEGAL, AND ETHICAL IMPLICATIONS. Margery W. Shaw and A. Edward Doudera. Health Administration Press, Department KW, 1021 East Huron Street, The University of Michigan, Ann Arbor, Michigan 48104. 1983.

ETHICAL, LEGAL AND SOCIAL CHALLENGES TO A BRAVE NEW WORLD. George P. Smith, II, Editor. Associated Faculty Press, 19 West Thirty-sixth Street, New York, New York 10018. 1982.

ETHICS AND REGULATION OF CLINICAL RESEARCH. Robert J. Levine. Yale University Press, 302 Temple Street, New Haven, Connecticut 06520. 1988.

EUTHANASIA AND THE RIGHT TO DEATH: THE CASE FOR VOLUNTARY EUTHANASIA. A.B. Downing, Editor. Peter Owen, Limited, 12 Kendrick Mews, Kendrick Place, London, England SW7. 1977.

THE FOUNDATION OF BIOETHICS. H. Tristram Engelhardt, Jr. Oxford University Press, 200 Madison Avenue, New York, New York 10016. 1986.

THE FOUNDATIONS OF JUSTICE: WHY THE RETARDED AND THE REST OF US HAVE CLAIMS TO EQUALITY. Robert M. Veatch. Oxford University Press, 200 Madison Avenue, New York, New York 10016. 1986.

GENETICS, ETHICS AND THE LAW. George P. Smith, II. Associated Faculty Press, Incorporated, 19 West Thirty-sixth Street, New York, New York 10018. 1981.

HEALTH CARE ETHICS: AN INTRODUCTION. Donald Van DeVeer and Tom Regan. Temple University Press, 1601 North Broad Street, Philadelphia, Pennsylvania 19122. 1987.

HOW BRAVE A NEW WORLD?: DILEMMAS IN BIOETHICS. Richard A. McCormick. Georgetown University Press, Intercultural Center, Room 111, Washington, D.C. 20007. 1985.

HUMAN LIFE: CONTROVERSIES AND CONCERNS. Bruce Bohle, Editor. H.W. Wilson Press, 950 University Avenue, Bronx, New York 10452. 1979.

LAW AND BIOETHICS: TEXTS WITH COMMENTARY ON MAJOR U.S. COURT DECISIONS. Thomas A. Shannon and Jo Ann Manfra. Paulist Press, 997 MacArthur Boulevard, Mahwah, New Jersey 07430. 1982.

LAW AND ETHICS IN THE MEDICAL OFFICE: INCLUDING BIOETHICAL ISSUES. Marcia A. Lewis and Carol D. Warden. F.A. Davis Company, 1915 Arch Street, Philadelphia, Pennsylvania 19103. 1988.

LEGAL AND ETHICAL ASPECTS OF TREATING CRITICALLY AND TERMINALLY ILL PATIENTS. Edward Doudera and J. Douglas Peters, Editors. Health Administration Press, Department KW, 1021 East Huron Street, The University of Michigan, Ann Arbor, Michigan 48104. 1982.

MAKING HEALTH CASE DECISIONS. President's Commission for the Study of Ethical Problems in Medicine and Biomedical and Behavioral Research. Superintendent of Documents, United States Government Printing Office, Washington, D.C. 20402. 1982.

MEDICAL ETHICS AND THE LAW: IMPLICATIONS FOR PUBLIC POLICY. Marc D. Hiller. Ballinger Division, HarperCollins Publishers, 10 East Fifty-third Street, New York, New York 10022. 1981.

MORAL THEORY AND MORAL JUDGMENTS IN MEDICAL ETHICS. Baruch A. Brody, Editor. Kluwer Academic Publishers, 101 Philip Drive, Assinippi Park, Norwell, Massachusetts 02061. 1988.

MORTAL CHOICES: BIOETHICS IN TODAY'S WORLD. Ruth Macklin. Pantheon Books, 201 East Fiftieth Street, New York, New York 10022. 1987.

PRINCIPLES OF BIOMEDICAL ETHICS. Third Edition. Tom L. Beauchamp and James F. Childress, Oxford University Press, 200 Madison Avenue, New York, New York 10016. 1989.

REFUSING TREATMENT IN MENTAL HEALTH INSTITUTIONS--VALUES IN CONFLICT. Edward Doudera and Judith P. Swazey. Health Administration Press, Department KW, 1021 East Huron Street, The University of Michigan, Ann Arbor, Michigan 48104. 1982.

SCIENCE AND MORALITY: NEW DIRECTIONS IN BIOETHICS. Doris Teichler-Zallen and Colleen D. Clements. Free Press, 866 Third Avenue, New York, New York 10022. 1982.

SELECTIVE NON-TREATMENT OF HANDICAPPED NEWBORNS: MORAL DILEMMAS IN NEONATAL MEDICINE. Robert F. Weir. Oxford University Press, 200 Madison Avenue, New York, New York 10016. 1984.

SPLICING LIFE: A REPORT ON THE SOCIAL AND ETHICAL ISSUES OF GENETIC ENGINEERING WITH HUMAN BEINGS. President's Commission for the Study of Ethical Problems in Medicine and Biomedical and Behavioral Research. Superintendent of Documents, United States Government Printing Office, Washington, D.C. 20402. 1982.

SUMMING UP: FINAL REPORT ON STUDIES OF THE ETHICAL AND LEGAL PROBLEMS IN MEDICINE AND BIOETHICAL AND BEHAVIORAL RESEARCH. President's Commission for the Study of Ethical Problems in Medicine and Biomedical and Behavioral Research. Superintendent of Documents, United States Government Printing Office, Washington, D.C. 20402. 1983.

TAKING SIDES: CLASHING VIEWS ON CONTROVERSIAL BIOETHICAL ISSUES. Fourth Edition. Carol Levine, Editor. Dushkin Publishing Group, Incorporated, Sluice Dock, Guilford, Connecticut 06437. 1991.

TO TREAT OR NOT TO TREAT: BIOETHICS AND THE HANDICAPPED NEWBORN. Richard C. Sparks. Paulist Press, 997 MacArthur Boulevard, Mahwah, New Jersey 07430. 1988.

TOWARD AN AMERICAN CATHOLIC MORAL THEOLOGY. Charles E. Curran. University of Notre Dame Press, Notre Dame, Indiana 46556. 1987.

TOWARD A MORE NATURAL SCIENCE: BIOLOGY AND HUMAN AFFAIRS. Leon R. Kass. Free Press, 866 Third Avenue, New York, New York 10022. 1985.

THE VALUE OF LIFE. John Harris. Routledge and Kegan Paul, Limited, 39 Store Street, London WC1E, England. 1985.

ENCYCLOPEDIAS AND DICTIONARIES

A DICTIONARY OF MEDICAL ETHICS AND PRACTICE. William A.R. Thomson. John Wright and Sons, Limited, 42-44 Triangle West, Bristol B58, England. 1977.

ENCYCLOPEDIA OF BIOETHICS. T. Reich, Editor. Macmillan Publishing Company, Incorporated, 866 Third Avenue, New York, New York 10022. 1982. (2 Volumes).

LAW REVIEWS AND PERIODICALS

BIOETHICS. Basil Blackwell Limited, P.O. Box 1320, Murray Hill Station, New York 10156. Quarterly.

BIOETHICS QUARTERLY. Human Sciences Press, Incorporated, 72 Fifth Avenue, New York, New York 10011. Quarterly.

HASTINGS CENTER REPORT. 255 Elm Road, Briarcliff Manor, New York 10510. Bimonthly.

ISSUES IN LAW AND MEDICINE. National Legal Center for the Medically Dependent and Disabled, Incorporated, P.O. Box 1586, Terra Haute, Indiana 47808-1586. Bimonthly.

ISSUES IN SCIENCE AND TECHNOLOGY. National Academy of Sciences, 2101 Constitution Avenue, Northwest, Washington, D.C. 20418. Quarterly.

JOURNAL OF LEGAL MEDICINE. Pharmaceutical Communications, Incorporated, 42-15 Crescent Street, Long Island City, New York 11101. Quarterly.

JOURNAL OF MEDICAL HUMANITIES AND BIOETHICS. Human Sciences Press, 72 Fifth Avenue, New York, New York 10011. Biannual.

NEWSLETTERS AND NEWSPAPERS

BIOTECHNOLOGY LAW REPORT. Mary Ann Liebert, Incorporated, 157 East Eighty-sixth Street, New York, New York 10028. Monthly.

BIOTECHNOLOGY NEWSWATCH. McGraw-Hill Publishing Company, 1221 Avenue of the Americas, New York, New York 10020. Semimonthly.

GENETIC ENGINEERING LETTER. Environs, Incorporated, 1331 Pennsylvania Avenue, Northwest, Suite 509, Washington, D.C. 20004. Semimonthly.

KENNEDY INSTITUTE NEWSLETTER. Kennedy Institute of Ethics, Georgetown University, Washington, D.C. 20057. Bimonthly.

MEDICAL ETHICS ADVISOR. American Health Consultants, Incorporated, 67 Peachtree Park Drive, Northeast, Atlanta, Georgia 30309. Monthly.

THE MEDICO-LEGAL ADVISOR. Health Law Research Group, Incorporated, 140 East Division Road, Health Law Plaza, Suite C-3, Oak Ridge, Tennessee 37830. Monthly.

NEWSLETTER OF BIOETHICAL SAFETY AND STANDARDS. Quest Publishing Company, 1351 Titan Way, Brea, California 92621. Semimonthly.

BIBLIOGRAPHIES

BIBLIOGRAPHY OF BIOETHICS, VOLUME 16. LeRoy Walters and Tamar Joy Kahn, Editors. Kennedy Institute of Ethics, Georgetown University, Washington, D.C. 20057. 1990.

BIOETHICS: A GUIDE TO INFORMATION SOURCES. Doris Mueller Goldstein. Gale Research, Incorporated, 835 Penobscot Building, Detroit, Michigan 48226. 1982.

BIOETHICS LITERATURE REVIEW. University Publications of America, 4520 East West Highway, Suite 600, Bethesda, Maryland 20814. 1986- . (Monthly).

THE HASTINGS CENTER'S BIBLIOGRAPHY OF ETHICS, BIOMEDICINE, AND PROFESSIONAL RESPONSIBILITY. Staff of the Hastings Center. Greenwood Publishing Group, Incorporated, 88 Post Road West, P.O. Box 5007, Westport, Connecticut 06881. 1984.

NEW TITLES IN BIOETHICS. Kennedy Institute of Ethics, Georgetown University, Washington, D.C. 20057. Monthly.

A SELECTED AND PARTIALLY ANNOTATED BIBLIOGRAPHY OF SOCIETY, ETHICS AND THE LIFE SCIENCES, 1979-80. Sharmon Sollitto, Robert M. Veatch and Ira D. Singer. Hastings Center, 255 Elm Road, Briarcliff Manor, New York 10510. 1980.

DIRECTORIES

DIRECTORY OF EXPERTS AND CONSULTANTS IN SCIENCE AND ENGINEERING. Second Edition. Research Publications, 12 Lunar Drive, Drawer AB, Woodbridge, Connecticut 06525.

RESEARCH CENTERS, INSTITUTES, CLEARINGHOUSES

BIOTECHNOLOGY COUNCIL. Iowa State University, Office of Biotechnology, 1010 Agronomy Building, Ames, Iowa 50011. (515) 294-9818.

CENTER FOR BIOETHICS. Kennedy Institute of Ethics, Georgetown University, 1437 Thirty-seventh Street, Northwest, Washington, D.C. 20057. (202) 687-3885.

CENTER FOR BIOMEDICAL ETHICS. Case Western Reserve University, 1101 Cedar Avenue, Cleveland, Ohio 44106. (216) 844-3936.

CENTER FOR THE STUDY OF SOCIETY AND MEDICINE. Columbia University, College of Physicians and Surgeons, 630 West One Hundred Sixty-eighth Street, New York, New York 10032. (212) 305-4184.

CENTER FOR VALUES AND SOCIAL POLICY. University of Colorado - Boulder, CB 232, Boulder, Colorado 80309-0232. (303) 492-6364.

COMMISSION ON THE MENTALLY DISABLED. American Bar Association, 1800 M Street, Northwest, Suite 200, Washington, D.C. 20036. (202) 331-2200.

COUNCIL FOR THE STUDY OF ETHICS AND PUBLIC POLICY. Queens College of City University of New York, Powdermaker Hall, Room 360, Flushing, New York 11367. (718) 520-7402.

DIVISION OF HUMAN GENETICS. University of California, Irvine, UCI Medical Center, 101 The City Drive, Orange, California 92668. (714) 634-5791.

THE HASTINGS CENTER. 255 Elm Road, Briarcliff Manor, New York 10510. (914) 762-8500.

HUMAN GENETICS AND BIOETHICS EDUCATION LABORATORY. Ball State University, 2000 University Avenue, Muncie, Indiana 47306. (317) 285-8840.

POPE JOHN XXIII MEDICAL - MORAL RESEARCH AND EDUCATION CENTER. 186 Forbes Road, Braintree, Massachusetts 02184. (617) 848-6965.

PROGRAM FOR BIOSOCIAL RESEARCH. Northern Illinois University, Dekalb, Illinois 60115. (815) 753-1907.

PROGRAM ON SCIENCE, TECHNOLOGY AND SOCIAL POLICY. Cornell University, 632 Clark Hall, Ithaca, New York 14853. (607) 255-3810.

SCIENTISTS CENTER FOR ANIMAL WELFARE. 4805 St. Elmo Avenue, Bethesda, Maryland 20814. (301) 654-6390.

ONLINE DATABASES

BIOETHICSLINE. Kennedy Institute of Ethics, Georgetown University, Washington, D.C. 20057.

BIRTH CONTROL
See also: ABORTION; STERILIZATION

LOOSELEAF SERVICES AND REPORTERS

FAMILY LAW REPORTER. Bureau of National Affairs, Incorporated, 1231 Twenty-fifth Street, Northwest, Washington, D.C. 20037. 1974- .

FAMILY PLANNING/POPULATION REPORTER. Center For Family Planning Program Development, Planned Parenthood - World Population, 1660 L Street, Northwest, Washington, D.C. 20036. 1972-1981.

REPORTER ON HUMAN REPRODUCTION AND THE LAW. Legal-Medical Studies, Incorporated, P.O. Box 8219, JFK Station, Boston, Massachusetts 02114. 1971- . (Bimonthly Supplements).

TEXTBOOKS AND GENERAL WORKS

ABORTION, FERTILITY, AND CHANGING LEGISLATION: AN INTERNATIONAL REVIEW. Jean Van der Tak. Lexington Books, 125 Spring Street, Lexington, Massachusetts 02173. 1974.

CONTRACEPTION: A HISTORY OF ITS TREATMENT BY THE CATHOLIC THEOLOGIANS AND CANONISTS. John T. Noonan, Jr. Belknap Press, Harvard University Press, 79 Garden Street, Cambridge, Massachusetts 02138. 1986.

FAMILY PLANNING, CONTRACEPTION, AND VOLUNTARY STERILIZATION: AN ANALYSIS OF LAWS AND POLICIES IN THE UNITED STATES. National Center for Family Planning Services, Public Health Service, Superintendent of Documents, United States Government Printing Office, Washington, D.C. 20402. 1974.

FROM PRIVATE VICE TO PUBLIC VIRTUE: THE BIRTH CONTROL MOVEMENT AND AMERICAN SOCIETY SINCE 1830. James Reed. Basic Books, Incorporated, 10 East Fifty-third Street, New York, New York 10022. 1978.

LAW GOVERNING ABORTION, CONTRACEPTION AND STERILIZATION. Irving J. Sloan. Oceana Publications, 75 Main Street, Dobbs Ferry, New York 10522. 1988.

LAW, POLITICS, AND BIRTH CONTROL. C. Thomas Dienes. University of Illinois Press, 54 East Gregory Drive, Champaign, Illinois 61820. 1972.

POPULATION LAW AND POLICY: SOURCE MATERIALS AND ISSUES. Stephen L. Isaacs. Human Sciences Press, Incorporated, 233 Spring Street, New York, New York 10013. 1981.

SEXUAL RIGHTS OF ADOLESCENTS: COMPETENCE, VULNERABILITY, AND PARENTAL CONTROL. Hyman Rodman, Susan H. Lewis and Saralyn B. Griffith. Columbia University Press, 562 West One Hundred Thirteenth Street, New York, New York 10025. 1988.

TEENAGE PREGNANCY: A RESEARCH GUIDE TO PROGRAMS AND SERVICES. Patrice A. Gillotti. William S. Hein and Company, 1285 Main Street, Buffalo, New York 14209. 1987.

WOMAN'S BODY, WOMAN'S RIGHT: BIRTH CONTROL IN AMERICA. Linda Gordon. Viking Penguin, Incorporated, 375 Hudson Street, New York, New York 10014. 1977.

ANNUALS AND SURVEYS

ANNUAL REVIEW OF POPULATION LAW. United Nations Fund for Population Activities, United Nations Sales Section, Publishing Division, Room DC2-853, New York, New York 10017. 1974- . (Annual).

FAMILY PLANNING PERSPECTIVES. Alan Guttmacher Institute, 111 Fifth Avenue, New York, New York 10003-1089. 1969- . (Bimonthly).

NEWSLETTERS AND NEWSPAPERS

PLANNED PARENTHOOD--WORLD POPULATION WASHINGTON MEMO. The Alan Guttmacher Institute, 2010 Massachusetts Avenue, Northwest, Washington, D.C. 20036. 1967- .

BIBLIOGRAPHIES

WRONGFUL LIFE: A BIBLIOGRAPHY OF LAW REVIEW ARTICLES. Dittakavi Nagasankara Rao. Vance Bibliographies, P.O. Box 229, 112 North Charter Street, Monticello, Illinois 61856. 1988.

ASSOCIATIONS AND PROFESSIONAL SOCIETIES

ALAN GUTTMACHER INSTITUTE. 111 Fifth Avenue, New York, New York 10003. (212) 254-5656.

ASSOCIATION FOR VOLUNTARY SURGICAL CONTRACEPTION. 122 East Forty-second Street, New York, New York 10168. (212) 351-2500.

ASSOCIATION OF REPRODUCTIVE HEALTH PROFESSIONALS. 409 Twelfth Street, Southwest, Washington, D.C. 20024. (202) 863-2475.

CATHOLICS FOR A FREE CHOICE. 1436 U Street, Northwest, Suite 301, Washington, D.C. 20009. (202) 638-1706.

NATIONAL ABORTION FEDERATION. 1436 U Street, Northwest, Washington, D.C. 20009. (202) 667-5881.

NATIONAL ABORTION RIGHTS ACTION LEAGUE. 1101 Fourteenth Street, Northwest, 5th Floor, Washington, D.C. 20005. (202) 371-0779.

NATIONAL FAMILY PLANNING AND REPRODUCTIVE HEALTH ASSOCIATION. 122 C Street, Northwest, Suite 380, Washington, D.C. 20001. (202) 628-3535.

ORAL CONTRACEPTIVE COUNCIL. 4775 Peachtree-Dunwoody Road, Suite 500-D, Atlanta, Georgia 30392. (404) 252-3663.

PLANNED PARENTHOOD FEDERATION OF AMERICA. 810 Seventh Avenue, New York, New York 10019. (212) 541-7800.

PHYSICIANS FOR CHOICE. c/o Planned Parenthood Federation of America, 810 Seventh Avenue, 7th Floor, New York, New York 10019. (212) 541-7800.

PRO-CHOICE DEFENSE LEAGUE. 131 Fulton Avenue, Hempstead, New York 11550. (516) 538-2626.

PROGRAM FOR APPROPRIATE TECHNOLOGY IN HEALTH. 4 Nickerson Street, Seattle, Washington 98109. (206) 285-3500.

RELIGIOUS COALITION FOR ABORTION RIGHTS. 100 Maryland Avenue, Northeast, Suite 307, Washington, D.C. 20002. (202) 543-7032.

BLACK LUNG

STATUTES, CODES, STANDARDS, UNIFORMS LAWS

UNITED STATES LONGSHORE AND HARBOR WORKERS' COMPENSATION LAW OF THE DISTRICT OF COLUMBIA AND BLACK LUNG BENEFITS ACT INCLUDING DIGESTS AND SUPPLEMENTARY LAWS. American Insurance Association, 1130 Connecticut Avenue, N.W., Washington, D.C. 20636. 1990.

LOOSELEAF SERVICES AND REPORTERS

BLACK LUNG REPORTER. Alexander Sann. Matthew Bender and Company, Incorporated, 11 Penn Plaza, New York, New York 10001. 1980.

RULINGS. United States Social Security Administration. Superintendent of Documents, United States Government Printing Office, Washington, D.C. 20402. 1960- .

HANDBOOKS, MANUALS, FORMBOOKS

SOCIAL SECURITY HANDBOOK: RETIREMENT INSURANCE, SURVIVORS INSURANCE, DISABILITY INSURANCE, HEALTH INSURANCE, BLACK LUNG BENEFITS AND SUPPLEMENTAL SECURITY INCOME. Tenth Edition. United States Social Security Administration. Superintendent of Documents, United States Government Printing Office, Washington, D.C. 20402. 1988.

TEXTBOOKS AND GENERAL WORKS

DIGGING OUR OWN GRAVES: COAL MINERS AND THE STRUGGLE OVER BLACK LUNG DISEASE. Barbara E. Smith. Temple University Press, Broad and Oxford Streets, University Services Building, Room 305, Philadelphia, Pennsylvania 19122. 1987.

DUST AND PNEUMOCONIOSIS: MEDICAL SUBJECT ANALYSIS AND RESEARCH GUIDEBOOK WITH BIBLIOGRAPHY. Paul O. Parker. ABBE Publishers Association of Washington, D.C., 1215 31st Street, N.W., Washington, D.C. 20007. 1987.

FEDERAL BLACK LUNG: TEN YEARS OF LEGISLATION AND LITIGATION. Section of Tort and Insurance Practice, American Bar Association, 750 North Lake Shore Drive, Chicago, Illinois 60611. 1980.

FEDERAL DISABILITY LAW AND PRACTICE. Frank S. Bloch. Wiley Law Publications, P.O. Box 1777, Colorado Springs, Colorado 80901. 1984.

INHALED DUST AND DISEASE. Paul F. Holt. John Wiley & Sons, Incorporated, One Wiley Drive, Somerset, New Jersey 08873. 1987.

OCCUPATIONAL LUNG DISEASES. Second edition. W. Keith C. Morgan and Anthony Seaton. W. B. Saunders Company, Curtis Center, Independence Square West, Philadelphia, Pennsylvania 19106. 1984.

OCCUPATIONAL LUNG DISORDERS. Second edition. W. Raymond Parkes. Butterworth Legal Publishers, 90 Stiles Road, Salem, New Hampshire 03079. 1982.

RECENT DEVELOPMENTS IN BLACK LUNG CASE LAW. Kilcullen, Wilson, and Kilcullen, 1800 M Street, N.W., Washington, D.C. 20036. 1984.

THE TRAGEDY OF BLACK LUNG: FEDERAL COMPENSATION FOR OCCUPATIONAL DISEASE. Peter S. Barth. W.E. Upjohn Institute for Employment Research, 300 South Westnedge Avenue, Kalamazoo, Michigan 49007. 1987.

WE OFFER OURSELVES AS EVIDENCE: TOWARD WORKERS' CONTROL OF OCCUPATIONAL HEALTH. Bennett M. Judkins. Greenwood Publishing Group, Incorporated, 88 Post Road West, P.O. Box 5007, Westport, Connecticut 06881. 1986.

ANNUALS AND SURVEYS

BLACK LUNG BENEFITS ACT: ANNUAL REPORT ON ADMINISTRATION OF THE ACT. United States Department of Labor. Superintendent of Documents, United States Government Printing Office, Washington, D.C. 20402. 1977- .

LAW REVIEWS AND PERIODICALS

FEDERAL BLACK LUNG JOURNAL. Black Lung Association, 907 West Neville Street, Beckley, West Virginia 25801. Bimonthly.

NEWSLETTERS AND NEWSPAPERS

BLA NEWSLETTER. Black Lung Association, 907 West Neville Street, Beckley, West Virginia 25801. Monthly.

BLACK BULLETIN. Black Lung Association, 907 West Neville Street, Beckley, West Virginia 25801. Biweekly.

BIBLIOGRAPHIES

HEALTH AND SAFETY ASPECT OF MINING: A BIBLIOGRAPHY. Elizabeth Hendryson. University of New Mexico, Medical Center Library, Albuquerque, New Mexico. 1980.

ASSOCIATIONS AND PROFESSIONAL SOCIETIES

BLACK LUNG ASSOCIATION. c/o Bill Bailey, P.O. Box 872, Craborchard, West Virginia 25827. (304) 252-9654.

NATIONAL COALITION OF BLACK LUNG AND RESPIRATORY DISEASE CLINICS. P.O. Box 209, Jacksboro, Tennessee 37757. (615) 562-1156.

STATISTICS SOURCES

BLACK LUNG BENEFITS ACT: ANNUAL REPORT ON ADMINISTRATION OF THE ACT. Employment Standards Administration, Washington, D.C. Annual.

SAMPLE SURVEY OF ALL SOURCES OF BOTH MONETARY AND NON-MONETARY INCOME OF BLACK LUNG BENEFICIARIES. Employment Standards Administration, U.S. Department of Labor, Washington, D.C. 1983.

BLOOD TESTS
See: EVIDENCE; HEALTH CARE; MEDICAL JURISPRUDENCE AND MALPRACTICE

BLUE SKY LAWS
See: SECURITIES

BOATS AND BOATING
See: ADMIRALTY

BONDS
See: SECURITIES

BOYCOTTS
See: EXPORT AND IMPORT; LABOR AND LABOR RELATIONS

BRIBERY
See: CORRUPTION, POLITICAL

BRIEFS
See: LEGAL WRITING

BROADCASTING
See: TELEVISION AND RADIO

BROKERS
See: REAL PROPERTY; SECURITIES

BUDGETS
See: PUBLIC FINANCE

BUILDING AND LOAN ASSOCIATIONS
See: BANKS AND BANKING

BUILDING LAWS
See: CONSTRUCTION INDUSTRY

BURDEN OF PROOF
See: CIVIL PROCEDURE; CRIMINAL PROCEDURE

BUREAU OF ALCOHOL, TOBACCO AND FIREARMS
See: ALCOHOL, TOBACCO AND FIREARMS BUREAU

BUSINESS CRIME
See also: COMPUTER CRIMES; EMBEZZLEMENT; FRAUD

LOOSELEAF SERVICES AND REPORTERS

CORPORATE CRIME REPORTER. American Communications and Publishing Company, P.O. Box 18384, Washington, D.C. 20036. 1987- . (Weekly).

WHITE COLLAR CRIME REPORTER. Meckler Corporation, White Collar Crime Reporter, 11 Ferry Lane, West, West Port, Connecticut 06880. 1987- . (Monthly).

TEXTBOOKS AND GENERAL WORKS

ADVANCED WHITE COLLAR CRIMINAL PRACTICE. Frederick P. Hafetz, Chairman. Practising Law Institute, 810 Seventh Avenue, New York, New York 10019. 1983.

BUSINESS CRIMES: A GUIDE FOR CORPORATE AND DEFENSE COUNSEL. Jeffrey Glekel. Practising Law Institute, 810 Seventh Avenue, New York, New York 10019. 1982.

CONTROLLING UNLAWFUL ORGANIZATIONAL BEHAVIOR: SOCIAL STRUCTURE AND CORPORATE MISCONDUCT. Diane Vaughan, University of Chicago Press, 5801 Ellis Avenue, Chicago, Illinois 60637. 1985.

CORPORATE AND GOVERNMENTAL DEVIANCE: PROBLEMS OF ORGANIZATIONAL BEHAVIOR. Third Edition. M. David Ermann and Richard J. Lundman. Oxford University Press, Incorporated, 200 Madison Avenue, New York, New York 10016. 1987.

CORPORATE CRIME AND VIOLENCE: BIG BUSINESS POWER AND THE ABUSE OF THE PUBLIC TRUST. Russell Mokhiber. Sierra Club Books, 730 Polk Street, San Francisco, California 94109. 1989.

CORPORATE ETHICS AND CRIME: THE ROLE OF MIDDLE MANAGEMENT. Marshall B. Clinard. Sage Publications, 2455 Teller Road, Newbury Park, California 91320. 1983.

CORRIGIBLE CORPORATIONS AND UNRULY LAW. Brent Fisse and Peter A. French. Trinity University Press, 715 Stadium Drive, San Antonio, Texas 78284. 1985.

THE CRIMINAL ELITE: THE SOCIOLOGY OF WHITE COLLAR CRIME. James William Coleman. St. Martin's Press, 175 Fifth Avenue, New York, New York 10010. 1988.

DEFENDING BUSINESS AND WHITE COLLAR CRIMES: FEDERAL AND STATE. Second Edition. F. Lee Bailey and Henry B. Rothblatt. Lawyers Cooperative Publishing Company, Aqueduct Building, Rochester, New York 14694. 1984.

DEFENDING WHITE-COLLAR CRIME: A PORTRAIT OF ATTORNEYS AT WORK. Kenneth Mann. Yale University Press, 302 Temple Street, New Haven Connecticut 06520. 1988.

DEFENDING WHITE COLLAR CRIMINAL PROSECUTIONS: FROM INVESTIGATION TO TRIAL: ALI-ABA COURSE OF STUDY MATERIAL. American Law Institute, American Bar Association Committee on Continuing Legal Education, 4025 Chestnut Street, Philadelphia, Pennsylvania 19104. 1984.

ELITE DEVIANCE. Third Edition. David R. Simon and D. Stanley Eitzen. Allyn and Bacon, 160 Gould Street, Needham Heights, Massachusetts 02194. 1990.

FRAUD AUDITING AND FORENSIC ACCOUNTING: NEW TOOLS AND TECHNIQUES. G. Jack Bologna and Robert J. Lindquist. John Wiley and Sons, Incorporated, 605 Third Avenue, New York, New York 10158. 1987.

A GUIDE TO INTERNAL LOSS PREVENTION. Roy L. Wesley. Butterworth Legal Publishers, 90 Stiles Road, Salem, New Hampshire 03079. 1986.

GUIDE TO WHITE COLLAR CRIME: A PRACTICAL GUIDE FOR THE CORPORATE COUNSELOR. Marvin G. Pickholz, Stephen Horn and Justin D. Simon. Bureau of National Affairs, Incorporated, 1231 Twenty-fifth Street, Northwest, Washington, D.C. 20037. 1986.

"ILLEGAL BUT NOT CRIMINAL": BUSINESS CRIME IN AMERICA. John E. Conklin. Prentice-Hall, Incorporated, 113 Sylvan Avenue, Englewood Cliffs, New Jersey 07632. 1977.

MODERN SECURITY AND LOSS PREVENTION MANAGEMENT. Philip P. Purpura. Butterworth Legal Publishers, 90 Stiles Road, Salem, New Hampshire 03079. 1989.

NEW DEVELOPMENTS AND PERSPECTIVES ON CORPORATE CRIME LAW ENFORCEMENT IN AMERICA. Leonard Orland and Harold R. Tyler, Co-chairmen. Practising Law Institute, 810 Seventh Avenue, New York, New York 10019. 1987.

OCCUPATIONAL CRIME. Gary S. Green. Nelson-Hall, 111 North Canal Street, Chicago, Illinois 60606. 1990.

THE POLITICS AND ECONOMICS OF ORGANIZED CRIME. Herbert E. Alexander and Gerald E. Caiden. Lexington Books, 125 Spring Street, Lexington, Massachusetts 02173. 1985.

POST-CONVICTION LAWYERING IN WHITE COLLAR CASES. Michael F. Armstrong. Practising Law Institute, 810 Seventh Avenue, New York, New York 10019. 1981.

PREVENTATIVE COUNSELING ON BUSINESS CRIMES: PROGRAM MATERIAL, FEBRUARY 1982. Michael Brooks Carroll. California Continuing Education of the Bar, 2300 Shattuck Avenue, Berkeley, California 94704. 1982.

REGULATING FRAUD: WHITE-COLLAR CRIME AND THE CRIMINAL PROCESS. Tavistock Publications, Limited, Routledge, Chapman and Hall, Incorporated, 29 West Thirty-fifth Street, New York, New York 10001. 1990.

SITTING IN JUDGMENT: THE SENTENCING OF WHITE-COLLAR OFFENDERS. Stanton Wheeler. Yale University Press, 302 Temple Street, New Haven, Connecticut 06520. 1988.

VESCO: FROM WALL STREET TO CASTRO'S CUBA: THE RISE, THE FALL, AND EXILE OF THE KING OF WHITE COLLAR CRIME. Arthur Herzog. Doubleday and Company, 666 Fifth Avenue, New York, New York 10103. 1987.

WAYWARD CAPITALISTS: TARGET OF THE SECURITIES AND EXCHANGE COMMISSION. Susan P. Shapiro. Yale University Press, 302 Temple Street, New Haven, Connecticut 06520. 1987.

WHITE-COLLAR AND ECONOMIC CRIME: MULTI DISCIPLINARY AND CROSS-NATIONAL PERSPECTIVES. Peter Wickman and Timothy Dailey. Lexington Books, 125 Spring Street, Lexington, Massachusetts 02173. 1982.

WHITE COLLAR CRIME: BUSINESS AND REGULATORY OFFENSES. Otto G. Obermaier and Robert G. Morvillo. Richard D. Irwin, Incorporated, 1818 Ridge Road, Homewood, Illinois 60430. 1990.

WHITE COLLAR CRIME: THE UNCUT VERSION. Edwin Sutherland. Yale University Press, 302 Temple Street, New Haven, Connecticut 06520. 1985.

WHITE COLLAR CRIME: THEORY AND RESEARCH. Gilbert Geis and Ezra Stotland, Editors. Sage Publications, 2455 Teller Road, Newbury Park, California 91320. 1980.

WHITE COLLAR CRIMINAL PRACTICE, 1985. Frederick P. Hafetz, Chairman. Practising Law Institute, 810 Seventh Avenue, New York, New York 10019. 1985.

NEWSLETTERS AND NEWSPAPERS

CORPORATE CRIME REPORTER. American Communications and Publishing Company, incorporated, P.O. Box 18384, Washington, D.C. 20036. Weekly.

CORPORATE CRIMINAL LIABILITY REPORTER. Federal Litigators Group, 8530 Wilshhire Boulevard, Suite 404, Beverly Hills, California 90211. Quarterly.

WHITE COLLAR CRIME REPORTER. Meckler Publishing, 11 Ferry Lane West, Westport, Connecticut 06880. Monthly.

ASSOCIATIONS AND PROFESSIONAL SOCIETIES

NATIONAL ASSOCIATION OF CERTIFIED FRAUD EXAMINERS. 716 West Avenue, Austin, Texas 78701. (512) 478-9070.

RESEARCH CENTERS, INSTITUTES AND CLEARINGHOUSES

INTERNATIONAL CENTRE FOR COMPARATIVE CRIMINOLOGY. University of Montreal, P.O. Box 6128, Montreal, PQ, Canada H3C 3J7. (514) 343-7065.

OTHER SOURCES

THE HUTTON REPORT: A SPECIAL INVESTIGATION INTO THE CONDUCT OF E.F. HUTTON AND COMPANY, INCORPORATED THAT GAVE RISE TO THE PLEA OF GUILTY ENTERED ON MAY 2, 1985. Griffin B. Bell. King and Spaulding, 2500 Trust Company Tower, Atlanta, Georgia 30303. 1985.

BUSINESS LAW
See: COMMERCIAL LAW; CORPORATIONS; JOINT VENTURES; PARTNERSHIP; SMALL BUSINESS

BUSINESS SECRETS
See: TRADE SECRETS

C

CABLE TELEVISION
See: TELEVISION AND RADIO

CAMPAIGN FUNDS
See: ELECTION LAW

CANON LAW
See also: CHURCH AND STATE; RELIGION

STATUTES, CODES, STANDARDS, UNIFORM LAWS

THE CODE OF CANON LAW: A TEXT AND COMMENTARY. James A. Coriden, Thomas J. Green, and Donald E. Heintschel, Editors. Paulist Press, The Plough Publishing House, 300 Rosenthal Lane, Ulster Park, New York 12487. 1985.

THE CODE OF CANON LAW, IN ENGLISH TRANSLATION. William B. Eerdmans Publishing Company, 255 Jefferson Street, Southeast, Grand Rapids, Michigan 49503. 1983.

THE CODE OF CANON LAW: LATIN-ENGLISH EDITION. Canon Law Society of America, The Catholic University of America, 620 Michigan Avenue, Northeast, Washington, D.C. 20064. 1983.

TEXTBOOKS AND GENERAL WORKS

CANON LAW FOR RELIGIOUS: AN EXPLANATION. Joseph F. Gallen. Alba House, 2187 Victory Boulevard, Staten Island, New York 10314. 1983.

CATHOLIC INSTITUTIONS IN THE UNITED STATES; CANONICAL AND CIVIL LAW STATUS. John J. McGrath. The Catholic University of America Press, 620 Michigan Avenue, Northeast, Washington, D.C. 20064. 1968.

CONFIDENTIALITY IN THE UNITED STATES: A LEGAL AND CANONICAL STUDY. Donna Krier Ioppolo and others. Canon Law Society of America, The Catholic University of America, 620 Michigan Avenue, Northeast, Washington, D.C. 20064. 1988.

AN INTRODUCTION TO ENGLISH CANON LAW. E. Garth Moore. Oxford University Press, 200 Madison Avenue, New York, New York 10016. 1967.

MARRIAGE IN CANON LAW. Ladislas M. Orsy. Michael Glazier, Incorporated, 1925 West Fourth Street, Wilmington, Delaware 19805. 1986.

POPES, TEACHERS, AND CANON LAW IN THE MIDDLE AGES. James R. Sweeney and Stanley Choldorow, Editors. Cornell University Press, 124 Roberts Place, Ithaca, New York 14850. 1989.

THE PRINCIPLES OF CANON LAW. Hubert S. Box. Greenwood Publishing Group, Incorporated, 88 Post Road West, P.O. Box 5007, Westport, Connecticut 06881. 1986. (Reprint of 1949 edition).

ROMAN CANON LAW IN REFORMATION ENGLAND. R.H. Helmholz. Cambridge University Press, 40 West Twentieth Street, New York, New York 10011. 1990.

THE STATUS OF THE CHURCH IN AMERICAN CIVIL LAW AND CANON LAW. Thomas F. Donovan. The Catholic University of America Press, 620 Michigan Avenue, Northeast, Washington, D.C. 20064. 1966.

LAW REVIEWS AND PERIODICALS

BULLETIN OF MEDIEVAL CANON LAW. Institute of Research and Study in Medieval Canon Law, University of California, Berkeley, Boalt Hall, Berkeley, California 94720. 1971- . (Annual).

THE JURIST. Department of Canon Law, The Catholic University of America, 620 Michigan Avenue, Northeast, Washington, D.C. 20064. 1941- . (Annual).

STUDIA CANONICA. Faculte de Droit Canonique, University Saint-Paul, Ottawa, Canada. 1967- . (2 issues per year).

BIBLIOGRAPHIES

AN ANNOTATED BIBLIOGRAPHY OF THE WORK OF THE CANON LAW SOCIETY OF AMERICA, 1965-1980. Richard G. Cunningham. Canon Law Society of America, The Catholic University of America, 620 Michigan Avenue, Northeast, Washington, D.C. 20064. 1982.

BIBLIOGRAPHY ON CANON LAW, 1965-1971. Leslie W. Sheridan. University of Texas, Tarlton Law Library, 727 East Twenty-sixth Street, Austin, Texas 78705. 1971.

THE CANON LAW COLLECTION OF THE LIBRARY OF CONGRESS: A GENERAL BIBLIOGRAPHY WITH SELECTIVE ANNOTATIONS. Dario C. Ferreira-Ibarra. Library of Congress. Superintendent of Documents, United States Government Printing Office, Washington, D.C. 20402. 1981.

ASSOCIATIONS AND PROFESSIONAL SOCIETIES

CANON LAW SOCIETY OF AMERICA. The Catholic University of America, Room 431, Caldwell Hall, 620 Michigan Avenue, Northeast, Washington, D.C. 20064. (202) 269-3491.

RESEARCH CENTERS, INSTITUTES, CLEARINGHOUSES

INSTITUTE OF MEDIEVAL CANON LAW, University of California, Berkeley, Boalt Hall, Berkeley, California 94720. (415) 642-5094.

CAPITAL PUNISHMENT
See also: CRIMINAL LAW

STATUTES, CODES, STANDARDS, UNIFORM LAWS

AMERICAN BAR ASSOCIATION GUIDELINES FOR THE APPOINTMENT AND PERFORMANCE OF COUNSEL IN DEATH PENALTY CASES. American Bar Association, 750 North Lake Shore Drive, Chicago, Illinois 60611. 1989.

HANDBOOKS, MANUALS, FORMBOOKS

CAPITAL CASE SENTENCING: HOW TO PROTECT YOUR CLIENT. Ursula Bentele. Section on Criminal Justice, American Bar Association, 750 North Lake Shore Drive, Chicago, Illinois 60611. 1988.

TEXTBOOKS AND GENERAL WORKS

ABOLITION AND CAPITAL PUNISHMENT: THE UNITED STATES' JUDICIAL, POLITICAL AND MORAL BAROMETER. Roger E. Schwed. AMS Press, 56 East Thirteenth Street, New York, New York 10003. 1983.

ARBITRARINESS OF THE DEATH PENALTY. Barry Nakell and Kenneth A. Hardy. Temple University Press, 1601 North Broad Street, University Services Building, Philadelphia, Pennsylvania 19122. 1987.

CAPITAL PUNISHMENT. Charles Lund Black. W. W. Norton and Company, Incorporated, 500 Fifth Avenue, New York, New York 10110. 1981.

CAPITAL PUNISHMENT. Thomas Draper, Editor. H. W. Wilson and Company, 950 University Avenue, Bronx, New York 10452. 1985.

CAPITAL PUNISHMENT AND THE AMERICAN AGENDA. Franklin E. Zimring and Gordon Hawkins. Cambridge University Press, 40 West Twentieth Street, New York, New York 10011. 1989.

CAPITAL PUNISHMENT: CRIMINAL LAW AND SOCIAL EVOLUTION. Jan Gorecki. Columbia University Press, 562 West One-hundred and thirteenth Street, New York, New York 10025. 1983.

CAPITAL PUNISHMENT: THE INEVITABILITY OF CAPRICE AND MISTAKE. Revised Edition. Charles L. Black. W. W. Norton and Company, Incorporated, 500 Fifth Avenue, New York, New York 10110. 1982.

THE CASE AGAINST THE DEATH PENALTY. Hugh Adam Bedau. American Civil Liberties Union, 132 West Forty-third Street, New York, New York 10036. 1984.

CAUSING DEATH AND SAVING LIVES. Jonathan Glover. Viking Penguin, Incorporated, 375 Hudson Street, New York, New York 10014. 1977.

CONDEMNED TO DIE: LIFE UNDER SENTENCE OF DEATH. Robert Johnson. Waveland Press, Incorporated, P.O. Box 400, Prospect Heights, Illinois 60070. 1989.

THE COURTS, THE CONSTITUTION, AND CAPITAL PUNISHMENT. Hugo Adam Bedau. Lexington Books, 125 Spring Street, Lexington, Massachusetts 02173. 1977.

CRIME AND CAPITAL PUNISHMENT. Robert H. Loeb. Franklin Watts, Incorporated, 387 Park Avenue, New York, New York 10016. 1986.

CRUEL AND UNUSUAL: THE SUPREME COURT AND CAPITAL PUNISHMENT. Michael Meitsner. Random House, Incorporated, 201 East Fiftieth Street, New York, New York 10022. 1973.

DEATH AND DISCRIMINATION: RACIAL DISPARITIES IN CAPITAL SENTENCING. Sam R. Gross and Robert Mauro. Northeastern University Press, 360 Huntington Avenue, Huntington Plaza, Suite 272, Boston, Massachusetts 02115. 1989.

DEATH IS DIFFERENT. Hugo Adam Bedau, Editor. Northeastern University Press, 272 Huntington Plaza, 360 Huntington Avenue, Boston, Massachusetts 02115. 1987.

DEATH PENALTIES: THE SUPREME COURT'S OBSTACLE COURSE. Raoul Berger. Harvard University Press, 79 Garden Street, Cambridge, Massachusetts 02138. 1982.

THE DEATH PENALTY. Irwin Isenberg, Editor. H. W. Wilson Company, 950 University Avenue, Bronx, New York 10452. 1977.

THE DEATH PENALTY: A DEBATE. Ernest Van den Haag and John P. Conrad. Plenum Publishing Corporation, 233 Spring Street, New York, New York 10013. 1983.

DEATH PENALTY AND CRIME: EMPIRICAL STUDIES. Kilman Shin. George Mason University, Center for Economic Analysis, 4400 University Drive, Fairfax, Virginia 22201. 1978.

DEATH PENALTY FOR JUVENILES. Victor L. Streib. Indiana University Press, Tenth and Morton Streets, Bloomington, Indiana 47405. 1987.

THE DEATH PENALTY IN AMERICA. Third Edition. Hugo Adam Bedau. Oxford University Press, 200 Madison Avenue, New York, New York 10016. 1982.

THE DEATH PENALTY IN THE EIGHTIES: AN EXAMINATION OF THE MODERN SYSTEM OF CAPITAL PUNISHMENT. Welsh S. White. University of Michigan Press, P.O. Box 1104, Ann Arbor, Michigan 48106. 1987.

THE DEATH PENALTY: OPPOSING VIEWPOINTS. Bonnie Szumski, Lynn Hall and Susan Bursell, Editors. Greenhaven Press, Incorporated, P.O. Box 289, San Diego, California 92128-9009. 1986.

DEATH PENALTY: THE CASE OF LIFE VERSUS DEATH IN THE UNITED STATES. Leonard A. Stevens. Coward, McCann, and Geoghegan, 200 Madison Avenue, New York, New York 10016. 1978.

DETERRENCE AND INCAPACITATION: ELIMINATING THE EFFECTS OF CRIMINAL SANCTIONS ON CRIME RATES. Alfred Blumstein, Jacqueline Cohen, and Daniel Nagin, Editors. National Academy of Sciences, 2101 Constitution Avenue, Northwest, Washington, D.C 20418. 1978.

EQUAL JUSTICE AND THE DEATH PENALTY: A LEGAL AND EMPIRICAL ANALYSIS. David C. Baldus, George Woodwoth, Charles A. Pulaski, Jr. Northeastern University Press, 360 Huntington Avenue, Huntington Plaza, Suite 272, Boston, Massachusetts 02115. 1990.

THE ETHICS OF LAW ENFORCEMENT AND CRIMINAL PUNISHMENT. Edward A. Malloy. University Press of America, 4720 Boston Way, Lanham, Maryland 20706. 1983.

EXECUTIONS IN AMERICA. William J. Bowers. Northeastern University Press, 272 Huntington Plaza, 360 Huntington Avenue, Boston, Massachusetts 02115. 1981.

AN EYE FOR AN EYE: THE MORALITY OF PUNISHING BY DEATH. Stephen Nathanson. Rowman and Littlefield, 4720 Boston Way, Lanham, Maryland 20706. 1987.

FOR CAPITAL PUNISHMENT: CRIME AND THE MORALITY OF THE DEATH PENALTY. Walter F. Berns. University Press of America, 4720 Boston Way, Lanham, Maryland 20706. 1991.

THE HISTORY OF CAPITAL PUNISHMENT. John Laurence. Carroll Publishing Company, 1058 Thomas Jefferson Street, Northwest, Washington, D.C. 20007. 1983.

HUMANE RECIPROCITY: THE MORAL NECESSITY OF THE CAPITAL PENALTY. Barney R. Josephson. Ann Arbor Books, P.O. Box 8064, Ann Arbor, Michigan 48107. 1979.

LAST RIGHTS: 13 FATAL ENCOUNTERS WITH THE STATE'S JUSTICE. Joseph B. Ingle. Abingdon Press, P.O. Box 801, 201 Eighth Avenue, Nashville, Tennessee 37202. 1990.

LEGAL HOMICIDE: DEATH AS PUNISHMENT IN AMERICA, 1964-1982. William J. Bowers. Northeastern University Press, 272 Huntington Plaza, 360 Huntington Avenue, Northeastern University, Boston, Massachusetts 02115. 1984.

LIFE IN THE BALANCE: PROCEDURAL SAFEGUARDS IN CAPITAL CASES. Welsh S. White. University of Michigan Press, P.O. Box 1104, Ann Arbor, Michigan 48106. 1984.

NEITHER CRUEL NOR UNUSUAL: THE CASE FOR CAPITAL PUNISHMENT. Frank G. Carrington. Crown Publications, Incorporated, 225 Park Avenue, South, New York, New York 10003. 1978.

A PUNISHMENT IN SEARCH OF A CRIME: AMERICANS SPEAK OUT AGAINST THE DEATH PENALTY. Ian Gray and Moira Stanley for Amnesty International. Avon Books, 105 Madison Avenue, New York, New York 10016. 1989.

THE PENALTY OF DEATH. Johan Thorsten Sellin. Books on Demand, 300 North Zeeb Road, Ann Arbor, Michigan 48106-1346. 1980.

THE QUESTION OF CAPITAL PUNISHMENT. Sandra Nicolai. Contact, Incorporated, P.O. Box 81826, Lincoln, Nebraska 68501. 1981.

THE RIGHT TO LIFE. Norman St. John-Stevas. Holt, Rinehart, Winston, 6277 Sea Harbor Drive, Orlando, Florida 32821. 1964.

RITES OF EXECUTION: CAPITAL PUNISHMENT AND THE TRANSFORMATION OF AMERICAN CULTURE, 1776-1865. Louis P. Masur. Oxford University Press, 200 Madison Avenue, New York, New York 10016. 1989.

STATE COURTS AND THE DEATH PENALTY AFTER FURMAN V. GEORGIA. National Center for State Courts Staff. National Center for State Courts, 300 Newport Avenue, Williamsburg, Virginia 23187-8798. 1973.

TOWARD A MORE JUST AND EFFECTIVE SYSTEM OF REVIEW IN STATE DEATH PENALTY CASES. American Bar Association, 750 North Lake Shore Drive, Chicago, Illinois 60611. 1990.

ULTIMATE PENALTIES: CAPITAL PUNISHMENT, LIFE IMPRISONMENT, PHYSICAL TORTURE. Leon Shaskolsky Sheleff. Ohio State University Press, 1070 Carmack Road, Room 180 Pressey Hall, Columbus, Ohio 43210. 1987.

UNITED STATES OF AMERICA: THE DEATH PENALTY. Amnesty International of the USA, Incorporated, 322 Eighth Avenue, New York, New York 10001. 1987.

THE URGE TO PUNISH: NEW APPROACHES TO THE PROBLEM OF MENTAL IRRESPONSIBILITY FOR CRIME. Henry Weihofen. Greenwood Publishing Group, Incorporated, 88 Post Road West, P.O. Box 5007, Westport, Connecticut 06881. 1979.

VOICES AGAINST DEATH: AMERICAN OPPOSITION TO CAPITAL PUNISHMENT 1787-1975. Burt Franklin Publications, 235 East Forty-fourth Street, New York, New York 10017. 1976.

WHEN MEN PLAY GOD: THE FALLACY OF CAPITAL PUNISHMENT. Eugene B. Block. Cragmont Publications, 4124 Lincoln Avenue, Oakland, California 94602-2525. 1984.

CAPITAL PUNISHMENT

WHEN THE STATE KILLS--: THE DEATH PENALTY, A HUMAN RIGHTS ISSUE. Amnesty International of the USA, Incorporated, 322 Eighth Avenue, New York, New York 10001. 1989.

NEWSLETTERS AND NEWSPAPERS

THE DEATH PENALTY EXCHANGE. National Coalition to Abolish the Death Penalty. 1419 V Street, Northwest, Washington, D.C. 20009. Irregular.

EXECUTION ALERT. National Coalition to Abolish the Death Penalty. 1419 V Street, Northwest, Washington, D.C. 20009. Irregular.

LIFELINES. National Coalition to Abolish the Death Penalty. 1419 V Street, Northwest, Washington, D.C. 20009. Bimonthly.

PENNY RESISTANCE. Penny Resistance, 8319 Fulham Court, Richmond, Virginia 23227. Irregular.

BIBLIOGRAPHIES

CAPITAL PUNISHMENT AS A DETERRENT: A SELECTED BIBLIOGRAPHY. Allan V. Miller. Vance Bibliographies, P.O. Box 229, 112 North Charter Street, Monticello, Illinois 61856. 1980.

CAPITAL PUNISHMENT IN AMERICA: AN ANNOTATED BIBLIOGRAPHY. Michael L. Radelet and Margaret Vandiver. Garland Publishing, Inc., 136 Madison Avenue, New York, New York 10016. 1988.

DEATH PENALTY (CAPITAL PUNISHMENT) AND THE LAW: A SELECTED BIBLIOGRAPHY OF ARTICLES. Dittakavi Nagasankara Rao. Vance Bibliographies, P.O. Box 229, 112 North Charter Street, Monticello, Illinois 61856. 1986.

DIRECTORIES

THE ABOLITIONISTS DIRECTORY. National Coalition to Abolish the Death Penalty, 1419 V Street, Northwest, Washington, D.C. 20009. Annual.

BIOGRAPHICAL SOURCES

DEATHMAN PASS ME BY: TWO YEARS ON DEATH ROW. Philip Brasfield and Jeffrey M. Elliot. Borgo Press, P.O. Box 2845, San Bernadino, California 92406-2845. 1983.

FATAL ERROR: THE MISCARRIAGE OF JUSTICE THAT SEALED THE ROSENBERG'S FATE. Joseph H. Sharlitt. Charles Scribner Sons, MacMillan Publishing Company, Incorporated, 866 Third Avenue, New York, New York 10022. 1989.

ASSOCIATIONS AND PROFESSIONAL SOCIETIES

NATIONAL COALITION TO ABOLISH THE DEATH PENALTY. 1419 V Street, Northwest, Washington, D.C. 20009. (202) 797-7090.

NATIONAL EXECUTION ALERT NETWORK. c/o National Coalition to Abolish the Death Penalty, 1419 V Street, Northwest, Washington, D.C. 20009. (202) 797-7090.

PENNY RESISTANCE. 8319 Fulham Court, Richmond, Virginia 23227. (804) 266-7400.

RESEARCH CENTERS, INSTITUTES, CLEARINGHOUSES

AMERICAN CIVIL LIBERTIES UNION. 132 West Forty-third Street, New York, New York 10036. (212) 944-9800.

CAPITAL PUNISHMENT PROJECT. 132 West Forty-third Street, New York, New York 10036. (212) 944-9800.

LOYOLA DEATH PENALTY RESEARCH CENTER. 348 Baronne Street, Suite 421, New Orleans, Louisiana 70112. (504) 522-0578.

NAACP LEGAL DEFENSE FUND, INCORPORATED. 99 Hudson Street, Sixteenth Floor, New York, New York 10013. (212) 219-1900.

CENTER FOR APPLIED SOCIAL RESEARCH. Northeastern University, 301 Cushing Hall, Boston, Massachusetts 02115. (617) 437-3310.

SOUTHERN CENTER FOR HUMAN RIGHTS. 83 Poplar, Northwest, Atlanta, Georgia 30303. (404) 688-1202.

TEAM DEFENSE PROJECT, INCORPORATED. P.O. Box 1978, Atlanta, Georgia 30301. (404) 688-8116.

STATISTICS SOURCES

CAPITAL PUNISHMENT. United States Justice Department, Bureau of Justice Statistics. Superintendent of Documents, United States Government Printing Office, Division of Public Documents, Washington, D.C. 20402. Annual.

DEATH ROW, U.S.A. NAACP Legal Defense and Education Fund, Incorporated, 99 Hudson Street, 16th Floor, New York, New York 10013. 1980- .

NATIONAL CRIMINAL JUSTICE INFORMATION AND STATISTICS SERVICE. Superintendent of Documents, United States Government Printing Office, Washington, D.C. 20402. 1975- . Annual.

OTHER SOURCES

CAPITAL TRIALS: JUROR ATTITUDES AND SELECTION STRATEGIES COMPILED. Emily DeFalla, Lois Heaney, and Terri Walker. National Jury Project, 1540 San Pablo Avenue, Ninth Floor, Oakland, California 94612. 1984.

CARRIERS
See: INTERSTATE COMMERCE COMMISSION; RAILROADS; TRANSPORTATION; TRANSPORTATION DEPARTMENT

CARS
See: INSURANCE, MOTOR VEHICLE AND AVIATION; MOTOR VEHICLES

CARTELS
See: ANTITRUST LAW

CENSORSHIP
See also: FREEDOM OF INFORMATION; FREEDOM OF PRESS; FREEDOM OF SPEECH

HANDBOOKS, MANUALS, FORMBOOKS

INTELLECTUAL FREEDOM MANUAL. Third Edition. Office for Intellectual Freedom, American Library Association, 50 East Huron Street, Chicago, Illinois 60611. 1989.

PROTECTING THE FREEDOM TO LEARN: A CITIZEN'S GUIDE. Barbara Parker and Stefanie Weiss. People for the American Way, 2000 M Street, Northwest, Suite 400, Washington, D.C. 20036. 1983.

TEXTBOOKS AND GENERAL WORKS

BANNED BOOKS, 387 B.C. TO 1978 A.D. Fourth Edition. Anne L. Haight. R.R. Bowker Company, 121 Chanlon Road, New Providence, New Jersey 07974. 1978.

BATTLE OF THE BOOKS: LITERARY CENSORSHIP IN THE PUBLIC SCHOOLS, 1950-1985. Lee Burress. Scarecrow Press, Incorporated, 52 Liberty Street, Box 4167, Metuchen, New Jersey 08840. 1989.

BOOKBANNING IN AMERICA: WHO BANS BOOKS?--AND WHY? William Noble. Paul S. Eriksson Publishers, 208 Battell Building, Middlebury, Vermont 05753. 1990.

CENSORSHIP AND OBSCENITY. Rajeev Dhavan and Christie Davies. Rowman and Littlefield, Publishers, Incorporated, 8705 Bollman Place, Savage, Maryland 20763. 1978.

CENSORSHIP AND PUBLIC MORALITY. Peter Macmillan. Gower Publishing Company, Old Post Road, Brookfield, Vermont 05036. 1983.

CENSORSHIP, LIBRARIES, AND THE LAW. Haig A. Bosmajian. Neal-Schuman Publications, Incorporated, 23 Leonard Street, New York, New York 10013. 1983.

THE DAME IN THE KIMONO: HOLLYWOOD, CENSORSHIP, AND THE PRODUCTION CODE FROM THE 1920s TO THE 1960s. Weidenfeld and Nicolson, c/o Fred B. Rothman and Company, 10368 West Centennial Road, Littleton, Colorado 80127. 1990.

DEFENDING INTELLECTUAL FREEDOM: THE LIBRARY AND THE CENSOR. Eli M. Oboler. Greenwood Publishing Group, Incorporated, 88 Post Road West, P.O. Box 5007, Westport, Connecticut 06881. 1980.

EROTIC COMMUNICATIONS: STUDIES IN SEX, SIN, CENSORSHIP. George N. Gordon. Hastings Books, 116 North Wayne Avenue, Wayne, Pennsylvania 19087. 1980.

THE FEAR OF THE WORD: CENSORSHIP AND SEX. Eli M. Oboler. Scarecrow Press, Incorporated, 52 Liberty Street, P.O. Box 4167, Metuchen, New Jersey 08840. 1974.

THE FIRST FREEDOM: LIBERTY AND JUSTICE IN THE WORLD OF BOOKS AND READING. Robert B. Downs. American Library Association, 50 East Huron Street, Chicago, Illinois 60611. 1960.

THE FIRST FREEDOM TODAY: CRITICAL ISSUES RELATING TO CENSORSHIP AND TO INTELLECTUAL FREEDOM. Robert B. Downs and Ralph E. McCoy, Editors. American Library Association, 50 East Huron Street, Chicago, Illinois 60611. 1984.

THE FLIGHT FROM REASON: ESSAYS ON INTELLECTUAL FREEDOM IN THE ACADEMY, THE PRESS, AND THE LIBRARY. David K. Berninghausen. American Library Association, 50 East Huron Street, Chicago, Illinois 60611. 1975.

FREE EXPRESSION AND CENSORSHIP: PUBLIC POLICY AND THE LAW. Ralph D. Mawdsley. National Organization on Legal Problems in Education, 3601 Southwest Twenty-ninth Street, Topeka, Kansas 66614. 1988.

FREEDOM AT RISK: SECRECY, CENSORSHIP, AND REPRESSION IN THE 1980S. Temple University Press, Broad and Oxford Streets, University Services Building, Room 305, Philadelphia, Pennsylvania 19122. 1988.

FREEDOM OF THE HIGH SCHOOL PRESS. Nicholas D. Kristof. University Press of America, 4720 Boston Way, Lanham, Maryland 20706. 1983.

AN INTELLECTUAL FREEDOM PRIMER. Charles H. Busha. Libraries Unlimited, Incorporated, P.O. Box 3988, Englewood, Colorado 80155-3988. 1977.

THE LEGAL ASPECTS OF CENSORSHIP OF PUBLIC SCHOOL LIBRARY AND INSTRUCTIONAL MATERIALS. Joseph E. Bryson and Elizabeth W. Detty. Michie/Bobbs-Merrill Law Publishing, P.O. Box 7587, Charlottesville, Virginia 22906-7582. 1982.

LIBERTY DENIED: THE CURRENT RISE OF CENSORSHIP IN AMERICA. Donna A. Demac. PEN American Center, 568 Broadway, New York, New York 10012. 1988.

OBSCENITY AND PUBLIC MORALITY: CENSORSHIP IN A LIBERAL SOCIETY. Harry M. Clor. Midway Reprint Edition. University of Chicago Press, 5801 Ellis Avenue, Third Floor, Chicago, Illinois 60637. 1985, c1969.

PORNOGRAPHY AND CENSORSHIP. David Copp and Susan Wendell. Prometheus Books, 700 East Amherst Street, Buffalo, New York 14215. 1982.

A QUESTION OF SEDITION: THE FEDERAL GOVERNMENT'S INVESTIGATION OF THE BLACK PRESS DURING WORLD WAR II. Patrick S. Washburn. Oxford University Press, Incorporated, 200 Madison Avenue, New York, New York 10016. 1986

SEVEN DIRTY WORDS AND SIX OTHER STORIES: CONTROLLING CONTENT OF PRINT AND BROADCAST. Matthew L. Spitzer. Yale University Press, 302 Temple Street, New Haven, Connecticut 06520. 1986.

STORM IN THE MOUNTAINS: A CASE STUDY OF CENSORSHIP, CONFLICT, AND CONSCIOUSNESS. James Moffett. Southern Illinois University Press, P.O. Box 33697, Carbondale, Illinois 62902. 1988.

THE WICKED STAGE: A HISTORY OF THEATER CENSORSHIP AND HARASSMENT IN THE UNITED STATES. Abe Laufe. Ungar Publishing Company, 370 Lexington Avenue, New York, New York 10017. 1978.

ENCYCLOPEDIAS AND DICTIONARIES

ENCYCLOPEDIA OF CENSORSHIP. Jonathan Green. Facts on File, Incorporated, 460 Park Avenue, South, New York, New York 10016. 1990.

HISTORICAL DICTIONARY OF CENSORSHIP IN THE UNITED STATES. Leon Hurwitz. Greenwood Publishing Group, Incorporated, 88 Post Road West, P.O. Box 5007, Westport, Connecticut 06881. 1985.

LAW REVIEWS AND PERIODICALS

BOOKS ON TRIAL: A SURVEY OF RECENT CASES. National Coalition Against Censorship, 2 West Sixty-fourth Street, New York, New York 10023. Quarterly.

NEWSLETTERS AND NEWSPAPERS

ADULT VIDEO ASSOCIATION NEWSLETTER. 270 North Canon Drive, Suite 1370, Beverly Hills, California 90210. Monthly.

CENSORSHIP NEWS. National Coalition Against Censorship, 2 West Sixty-fourth Street, New York, New York 10023. Quarterly.

FREE SPIRIT. First Amendment Consumer and Trade Association, 1000 Connecticut Avenue, Northwest, Suite 9, Washington, D.C. 20036. Monthly.

FREEDOM TO READ FOUNDATION NEWS. Freedom to Read Foundation, 50 East Huron Street, Chicago, Illinois 60611. Quarterly.

NEWSLETTER ON INTELLECTUAL FREEDOM. American Library Association, 50 East Huron Street, Chicago, Illinois 60611. Bimonthly.

BIBLIOGRAPHIES

CABLE TELEVISION AND CENSORSHIP; A BIBLIOGRAPHY. Patrick Henry Kellough. Vance Bibliographies, P.O. Box 229, 112 North Charter Street, Monticello, Illinois 61856. 1985.

CONTROL OF INFORMATION IN THE UNITED STATES: AN ANNOTATED BIBLIOGRAPHY. James R. Bennett. Meckler Corporation, 11 Ferry Lane West, Westport, Connecticut 06880. 1987.

FEMINISTS, PORNOGRAPHY, AND THE LAW: AN ANNOTATED BIBLIOGRAPHY OF CONFLICT, 1970-1986. Betty-Carol Sellen. Library Professional Publications, Shoe String Press, P.O. Box 4327, Hamden, Connecticut 06514.

FREE SPEECH BIBLIOGRAPHY; INCLUDING EVERY DISCOVERED ATTITUDE TOWARD THE PROBLEM COVERING EVERY METHOD OF TRANSMITTING IDEAS AND OF ABRIDGING THEIR PROMULGATION UPON EVERY SUBJECT MATTER. Theodore A. Schroeder. Burt Franklin Publishers, 235 East Forty-fourth Street, New York, New York 10017. 1969.

INTELLECTUAL FREEDOM AND CENSORSHIP: AN ANNOTATED BIBLIOGRAPHY. Frank W. Hoffman. Scarecrow Press, Incorporated, 52 Liberty Street, P.O. Box 4167, Metuchen, New Jersey 08840. 1989.

A SELECTED BIBLIOGRAPHY OF BOOKS AND ARTICLES ON CENSORSHIP (1950-1983). Denise Rogers. Washington University, Freund Law Library, St. Louis, Missouri 63130. 1983.

ASSOCIATIONS AND PROFESSIONAL SOCIETIES

ADULT VIDEO ASSOCIATION. 270 North Canon Drive, Suite 1370, Beverly Hills, California 90210. (213) 631-1600.

AMERICAN CIVIL LIBERTIES UNION. 132 West Forty-third Street, New York, New York 10036. (212) 944-9800.

COMMITTEE ON INTERNATIONAL FREEDOM TO PUBLISH. Association of American Publishers, 220 East Twenty-third Street, New York, New York 10010. (212) 689-8920.

FIRST AMENDMENT CONSUMER AND TRADE SOCIETY. 1000 Connecticut Avenue, Northwest, Suite 9, Washington, D.C. 20036. (202) 780-6860.

FREEDOM TO READ FOUNDATION. 50 East Huron Street, Chicago, Illinois 60611. (312) 944-6780.

INTELLECTUAL FREEDOM COMMITTEE. American Library Association, 50 East Huron Street, Chicago, Illinois 60611. (312) 280-4223.

MEDIA COALITION. 900 Third Avenue, Suite 1600, New York, New York 10022. (212) 891-2070.

NATIONAL COALITION AGAINST CENSORSHIP. 2 West Sixty-fourth Street, New York, New York 10023. (212) 724-1500.

PROJECT CENSORED, Department of Communications Studies, Sonoma State University, Rohnert Park, California 94928. (707) 664-2500.

RESEARCH CENTERS, INSTITUTES, CLEARINGHOUSES

INSTITUTE OF BILL OF RIGHTS. College of William and Mary, Marshall-Wythe School of Law, Williamsburg, Virginia 23185. (804) 221-3810.

NATIONAL CENTER FOR FREEDOM OF INFORMATION STUDIES. Loyola University of Chicago, 820 North Michigan Avenue, Chicago, Illinois 60611. (312) 670-3116.

WOMENS' INSTITUTE FOR FREEDOM OF THE PRESS. 3306 Ross Place, Northwest, Washington, D.C. 20008. (202) 966-7783.

ONLINE DATABASES

INTELLECTUAL FREEDOM ALERT. American Library Association, 50 East Huron Street, Chicago, Illinois 60611.

OTHER SOURCES

THE FINAL REPORT OF THE ATTORNEY GENERAL'S COMMISSION ON PORNOGRAPHY. Rutledge Hill Press, 513 Third Avenue, South, Nashville, Tennessee 37210. 1986.

POLLUTING THE CENSORSHIP DEBATE: A SUMMARY AND CRITIQUE OF THE FINAL REPORT OF THE ATTORNEY GENERAL'S COMMISSION ON PORNOGRAPHY. Barry W. Lynn. American Civil Liberties Union, 132 West Forty-third Street, New York, New York 10036. 1986.

CENTRAL INTELLIGENCE AGENCY

STATUTES, CODES, STANDARDS, UNIFORM LAWS

CODE OF FEDERAL REGULATIONS, TITLE 32. Office of the Federal Register, National Archives and Records Administration. Superintendent of Documents, United States Government Printing Office, Washington, D.C. 20402. Annual. (Updated by use of monthly List of Sections Affected and daily Federal Register.)

TEXTBOOKS AND GENERAL WORKS

THE CENTRAL INTELLIGENCE AGENCY: A PHOTOGRAPHIC HISTORY. John P. Quirk and others. Foreign Intelligence Press, P.O. Box 306, Guilford, Connecticut 06437. 1986.

THE CENTRAL INTELLIGENCE AGENCY, AN INSTRUMENT OF GOVERNMENT, TO 1950. Arthur B. Darling. Pennsylvania State University Press, 820 North University Drive, Barbara Building, University Park, Pennsylvania 16802. 1990.

THE CENTRAL INTELLIGENCE AGENCY, HISTORY AND DOCUMENTS. William M. Leary, Editor. University of Alabama Press, P.O. Box 870380, Tuscaloosa, Alabama 35487. 1984.

DECEPTION: THE INVISIBLE WAR BETWEEN THE KGB AND THE CIA. Edward Jay Epstein. Simon and Schuster, Incorporated, 1230 Avenue of the Americas, New York, New York 10020. 1989.

DONOVAN AND THE CIA: A HISTORY OF THE ESTABLISHMENT OF THE CENTRAL INTELLIGENCE AGENCY. Thomas F. Troy. Aletheia Books, P.O. Box 1178, Northampton, Massachusetts 01060. 1981.

VEIL: THE SECRET WARS OF THE CIA, 1981-1987. Bob Woodward. Simon and Schuster, Incorporated, 1230 Avenue of the Americas, New York, New York 10020. 1987.

RESEARCH CENTERS, INSTITUTES, CLEARINGHOUSES

UNITED STATES CENTRAL INTELLIGENCE AGENCY, OFFICE OF GENERAL COUNSEL LIBRARY. Washington, D.C. 20505. (703) 874-3200.

CHARACTER LICENSING
See: LICENSING, INDUSTRIAL AND INTELLECTUAL

CHARITABLE TRUSTS
See: CHARITIES; WILLS, TRUSTS AND INHERITANCE

CHARITIES
See also: ASSOCIATIONS AND NONPROFIT CORPORATIONS

STATUTES, CODES, STANDARDS, UNIFORM LAWS

AMERICAN LAW OF CHARITIES. Carl F.G. Zollman. Bruce Publishing Company, 17337 Ventura Boulevard, Encino, California 91316. 1924.

STATE REGULATION OF CHARITABLE TRUSTS AND SOLICITATIONS. Committee on the Office of Attorney General. National Association of Attorneys General, 444 North Capitol Street, Northwest, Washington, D.C. 20001. 1977.

SURVEY OF STATE LAWS REGULATING CHARITABLE SOLICITATION. Philanthropy Monthly, P.O. Box 989, New Milford, Connecticut 06776. 1976- .

LOOSELEAF SERVICES AND REPORTERS

CHARITABLE GIFTS. James Colliton. Garland Publishing, Incorporated, 136 Madison Avenue, New York, New York 10016. 1990- . (Periodic Supplements).

CHARITABLE GIVING AND SOLICITATION. Sue S. Stern. Research Institute of America, Incorporated, 910 Sylvan Avenue, Englewood Cliffs, New Jersey 07632. 1981- . (Monthly Supplements).

CHARITABLE LEAD TRUSTS - EXPLANATION, SPECIMEN AGREEMENTS, FORMS. Conrad Teitell. Taxwise Giving, 13 Arcadia Road, Old Greenwich, Connecticut 06870. 1983- . (Annual Supplements).

DEFERRED GIVING - EXPLANATION, SPECIMEN AGREEMENTS, FORMS. Conrad Teitell. Taxwise Giving, 13 Arcadia Road, Old Greenwich, Connecticut 06870. 1971- . (Annual Supplements).

EXEMPT ORGANIZATIONS REPORTS. Commerce Clearing House, Incorporated, 4025 West Peterson Avenue, Chicago, Illinois 60646. 1971- . (Semimonthly Supplements).

OUTRIGHT CHARITABLE GIFTS - EXPLANATION, SUBSTANTIATING, FORMS. Conrad Teitell. Taxwise Giving, 13 Arcadia Road, Old Greenwich, Connecticut 06870. 1986- . (Annual Supplements).

PLANNED GIVING - STARTING, MARKETING, ADMINISTERING. Conrad Teitell. Taxwise Giving, 13 Arcadia Road, Old Greenwich, Connecticut 06870. 1986- . (Periodic Supplements).

PRIVATE FOUNDATIONS, TERMINATION. Christopher L. Hartwell and Fred M. Hartwick. (Tax Management Portfolio, #272-3rd) Bureau of National Affairs, Incorporated, 1231 Twenty-fifth Street, Northwest, Washington, D.C. 20037. 1986- . (Periodic Supplements).

HANDBOOKS, MANUALS, FORMBOOKS

THE HANDBOOK ON PRIVATE FOUNDATIONS. David F. Freeman. Published for the Council on Foundations by Seven Locks Press, P.O. Box 27, Cabin John, Maryland 20818. 1981.

HANDBOOK ON TAX-EXEMPT ORGANIZATIONS. Howard Godfrey. Prentice-Hall, Incorporated, 113 Sylvan Avenue, Englewood Cliffs, New Jersey 07632. 1983.

THE NONPROFIT ORGANIZATION HANDBOOK. Tracy Daniel Connors, Editor. McGraw-Hill Publishing Company, 1221 Avenue of the Americas, New York, New York 10020. 1980.

TEXTBOOKS AND GENERAL WORKS

THE ART OF WINNING FOUNDATION GRANTS. Howard Hillman and Karin Abarbanel. Vanguard Press, Incorporated, 201 East Fiftieth Street, New York, New York 10022. 1975.

BEFORE YOU GIVE ANOTHER DIME. Robert Sharpe. Thomas Nelson, Publishers, P.O. Box 141000, Nelson Place at Elm Hill Pike, Nashville, Tennessee 37214-1000. 1980.

CHARITIES AND CHARITABLE FOUNDATIONS. Edith L. Fisch and Doris Jonas. Lond Publications, Pomona, New York 10970. 1974.

COUNSELING TAX-EXEMPT CHARITABLE ORGANIZATIONS: PROGRAM MATERIAL, OCTOBER/NOVEMBER 1985. Boyd J. Black, et al. California Continuing Education of the Bar, 2300 Shattuck Avenue, Berkeley, California 94704. 1985.

FEDERAL TAX POLICY AND CHARITABLE GIVING. Charles T. Clotfelter. University of Chicago Press, 5801 Ellis Avenue, Fourth Floor, Chicago, Illinois 60637. 1985.

FOUNDATIONS. Harold M. Keele and Joseph C. Kiger. Greenwood Publishing Group, Incorporated, 88 Post Road, P.O. Box 5007, West Westport, Connecticut 06881. 1984.

FOUNDATIONS AND GOVERNMENT: STATE AND FEDERAL LAW AND SUPERVISION. Marion R. Fremont-Smith. Russell Sage Foundation, 112 East Sixty-fourth Street, New York, New York 10021. 1965.

FOUNDATIONS, PRIVATE GIVING, AND PUBLIC POLICY: REPORT AND RECOMMENDATIONS. Commission on Foundations and Private Philanthropy. University of Chicago Press, 5801 Ellis Avenue, Fourth Floor, Chicago, Illinois 60637. 1971.

GIVE! WHO GETS YOUR CHARITY DOLLARS? Harvey Katz. Anchor Press, 666 Fifth Avenue, New York, New York 10103. 1974.

HOW TO SOLICIT BIG GIFTS. Daniel L. Conrad. Public Management Associates, 2014 Siegle Drive, Lemon Grove, California 92045. 1978.

THE LAW OF TAX-EXEMPT ORGANIZATIONS. Fifth Edition. Bruce R. Hopkins. John Wiley and Sons, Incorporated, 605 Third Avenue, New York, New York 10158. 1987.

THE PLANNED GIVING IDEA BOOK. Robert Sharpe. Thomas Nelson Publishers, P.O. Box 141000, Nelson Place, at Elm Hill Pike, Nashville, Tennessee 37214-1000. 1978.

PRIVATE FOUNDATIONS: BEFORE AND AFTER THE TAX REFORM. William H. Smith and Carolyn P. Chiechi. American Enterprise Institute for Public Policy Research, 1150 Seventeenth Street, Northwest, Washington, D.C. 20036. 1969.

TAX-EXEMPT CHARITABLE ORGANIZATIONS. Third Edition. Paul E. Treusch. American Law Institute-American Bar Association, 4025 Chestnut Street, Philadelphia, Pennsylvania 19104. 1988.

TRUSTEESHIP AND THE MANAGEMENT OF FOUNDATIONS. Donald Ramsey Young and Wilbert Ellis Moore. Russell Sage Foundation, 112 East Sixty-fourth Street, New York, New York 10021. 1969.

WITH CHARITY FOR ALL: WELFARE AND SOCIETY FROM ANCIENT TIMES TO THE PRESENT. Merritt Ierley. Praeger Publishers, One Madison Avenue, New York, New York 10010-3603. 1984.

ENCYCLOPEDIAS AND DICTIONARIES

FOUNDATIONS. Harold M. Keele and Joseph C. Kiger. Greenwood Publishing Group, Incorporated, 88 Post Road West, P.O. Box 5007, Westport, Connecticut 06881. 1984.

ANNUALS AND SURVEYS

NEW YORK UNIVERSITY BIENNIAL CONFERENCE ON TAX PLANNING FOR THE CHARITABLE SECTOR. Matthew Bender and Company, Incorporated, 11 Penn Plaza, New York, New York 10001. 1956- . (Biennial).

LAW REVIEWS AND PERIODICALS

LEGISLATIVE MONITOR. American Association of Fund-Raising Counsel, 25 West Forty-third Street, Suite 1519, New York, New York 10036. Irregular.

NEWSLETTERS AND NEWSPAPERS

CONSUMER PROTECTION REPORT. National Association of Attorneys General, 444 North Capitol Street, Northwest, Suite 403, Washington, D.C. 20001. Monthly.

TAXWISE GIVING. Taxwise Giving, 13 Arcadia Road, Old Greenwich, Connecticut 06870. Monthly.

BIBLIOGRAPHIES

FOUNDATIONS, GRANTS AND FUND-RAISING: A SELECTED BIBLIOGRAPHY. Charlotte Georgi. Vance Bibliographies, P.O. Box 229, 112 North Charter Street, Monticello, Illinois 61856. 1981.

SOCIAL WELFARE IN AMERICA: AN ANNOTATED BIBLIOGRAPHY. Walter I. Trattner and W. Andrew Achenbaum. Greenwood Publishing Group, Incorporated, 88 Post Road West, P.O. Box 5007, Westport, Connecticut 06881. 1983.

ASSOCIATIONS AND PROFESSIONAL SOCIETIES

AMERICAN ASSOCIATION OF FUND-RAISING COUNSEL. Twenty-five West Forty-third Street, Suite 1519, New York, New York 10036. (212) 354-5799.

NATIONAL ASSOCIATION OF STATE CHARITY OFFICIALS. c/o Sheila Fishman, Assistant Attorney General, 340 Bremer Tower, Seventh Place and Minnesota Street, St. Paul, Minnesota 55101. (612) 297-4608.

NATIONAL CENTER FOR CHARITABLE STATISTICS, 1828 L Street, Northwest, Washington, D.C. 20036. (202) 223-8100.

RESEARCH CENTERS, INSTITUTES, CLEARINGHOUSES

THE AMERICAN NATIONAL RED CROSS. Seventeenth Street and D Street, Northwest, Washington, D.C. 20006. (202) 737-8300.

THE FOUNDATION CENTER. 79 Fifth Avenue, New York, New York 10003. (212) 620-4230.

INDEPENDENT SECTOR. 1828 L Street, Northwest, Washington, D.C. 20036. (202) 223-8100.

NATIONAL CHARITIES INFORMATION BUREAU. 19 Union Square, West, Sixth Floor, New York, New York 10003. (212) 929-6300.

STATISTICS SOURCES

AMERICAN ASSOCIATION OF FUND-RAISING COUNSEL. 25 West Forty-third Street, Suite 1519, New York, New York 10036. (212) 354-5799.

CHARITABLE DONATIONS. The American National Red Cross, Seventeenth Street and D Street, Northwest, Washington, D.C. 20006.

CHARITABLE DONATIONS. The Foundation Center, 79 Fifth Avenue, New York, New York 10003.

CHARITABLE DONATIONS. United Way of America, Incorporated, 701 North Fairfax Street, Alexandria, Virginia 22314.

DIMENSIONS OF THE INDEPENDENT SECTOR: A STATISTICAL PROFILE. Virginia Ann Hodgkinson and Murray S. Weitzman, Independent Sector, 1828 L Street, Northwest, Washington, D.C. 20036. 1984.

OTHER SOURCES

GIVING IN AMERICA: TOWARD A STRONGER VOLUNTARY SECTOR: REPORT OF THE ADVISORY COMMITTEE ON PRIVATE PHILANTHROPY AND PUBLIC NEEDS. Superintendent of Documents, United States Government Printing Office, Washington, D.C. 20402. 1977.

TAX-EXEMPT CHARITABLE ORGANIZATIONS: ALI-ABA COURSE OF STUDY MATERIALS. Third Edition. American Law Institute, 4025 Chestnut Street, Philadelphia, Pennsylvania 19104. 1988.

CHECKS
See: BANKS AND BANKING; COMMERCIAL LAW; NEGOTIABLE INSTRUMENTS

CHEMICAL INDUSTRIES
See also: ENVIRONMENTAL LAW; ENVIRONMENTAL PROTECTION AGENCY; HAZARDOUS SUBSTANCES

STATUTES, CODES, STANDARDS, UNIFORM LAWS

THE BUSINESS GUIDE TO TOSCA EFFECTS AND ACTIONS. George S. Dominguez. Books on Demand, 300 North Zeeb Road, Ann Arbor, Michigan 48106-1346. 1979.

LOOSELEAF SERVICES AND REPORTERS

CHEMICAL REGULATION REPORTER. Bureau of National Affairs, Incorporated, 1231 Twenty-fifth Street, Northwest, Washington, D.C. 20037. 1977- . (Weekly Supplements).

FEDERAL REGULATION OF THE CHEMICAL INDUSTRY. James T. O'Reilly. McGraw-Hill Book Company, 1221 Avenue of the Americas, New York, New York 10020. 1980- . (Annual Supplements).

TOXIC CHEMICALS LITIGATION REPORTER. Andrews Publications, 1646 West Chester Pike, Westtown, Pennsylvania 19395. 1983- .

TEXTBOOKS AND GENERAL WORKS

CONTROLLING CHEMICALS: THE POLITICS OF REGULATION IN EUROPE AND THE UNITED STATES. Ronald Brickman, Sheila Sanoff, and Thomas Ilgen. Cornell University Press, 124 Roberts Place, P.O. Box 250, Ithaca, New York 14851. 1985.

GOVERNMENT AND THE CHEMICAL INDUSTRY: A COMPARATIVE STUDY OF BRITAIN AND WEST GERMANY. Wyn Grant and others. Oxford University Press, 200 Madison Avenue, New York, New York 10016. 1988.

HAZARDOUS WASTE SITES IN THE UNITED STATES. H. Pishdadazav and A. Alan Moghissi. Pergamon Press, Maxwell House, Fairview Park, Elmsford, New York 10523. 1981.

PERIL ON THE JOB: A STUDY OF HAZARDS IN THE CHEMICAL INDUSTRIES. Ray Davidson. Public Affairs Press, 419 New Jersey Avenue, Washington, D.C. 20003. 1970.

SAFETY REGULATION OF CHEMICALS IN THE UNITED STATES. F. Homberger and Judith K. Marquis, Editors. S. Karger, 26 West Avon Road, Box 529, Farmington, Connecticut 06085. 1985.

TRENDS IN BIOTECHNOLOGY AND CHEMICAL PATENT LAW: A COURSE HANDBOOK. Practising Law Institute, 810 Seventh Avenue, New York, New York 10019. 1985.

ASSOCIATIONS AND PROFESSIONAL SOCIETIES

CHEMICAL INDUSTRY FOR MINORITIES IN ENGINEERING. P.O. Box 1310, Wilmington, Delaware 19899. (412) 777-2484.

SOCIETY OF CHEMICAL INDUSTRY, AMERICAN SECTION. 425 Park Avenue, Thirty-first floor, New York, New York 10022. (212) 685-9410.

RESEARCH CENTERS, INSTITUTES, CLEARINGHOUSES

CHEMICAL INDUSTRY INSTITUTE OF TOXICOLOGY. P.O. Box 12137, Research Triangle Park, North Carolina 27709. (919) 541-2070.

ONLINE DATABASES

CEH ONLINE. SRI International, Process Industries Division, Chemical Economics Handbook Program, 333 Ravenswood Avenue, AE208, Menlo Park, California 94025.

CHEMICAL ENGINEERING. McGraw-Hill Book Company, 1221 Avenue of the Americas, New York, New York 10020.

CHEMICAL INDUSTRY NOTES. Chemical Abstracts Service, 2540 Olentangy River Road, P.O. Box 3012, Columbus, Ohio 43210.

CHEMICAL REGULATION REPORTER. Bureau of National Affairs, Incorporated, Data Base Publishing Unit, 1231 Twenty-fifth Street, Northwest, Washington, D.C. 20037.

CHEMICAL REGULATIONS AND GUIDELINES SYSTEM. CRC Systems, Incorporated, 2550 M Street, Northwest, Suite 699, Washington, D.C. 20037.

CHEMICAL WEEK. Chemical Week Associates, 810 Seventh Avenue, New York, New York 10018.

CHEMICALS INDUSTRY COMPETITIVE INTELLIGENCE TRACKING SERVICE. Strategic Intelligence Systems, Incorporated, 404 Park Avenue South, Suite 301, New York, New York 10016.

CSCHEM. Directories Publishing Company, Incorporated, P.O. Box 1824, Clemson, South Carolina 29633.

CSCORP. Directories Publishing Company, Incorporated, P.O. Box 1824, Clemson, South Carolina 29633.

FINE CHEMICALS DIRECTORY. Pergamon Infoline, Incorporated, 1340 Old Chain Bridge Road, McLean, Virginia 22101.

HAZARDLINE, OCCUPATIONAL HEALTH SERVICES, INCORPORATED (HAZARD). Occupational Health Services, Incorporated, 400 Plaza Drive, P.O. Box 1505, Secaucus, New Jersey 07094.

LEXIS. BNA Energy File. Mead Data Central, 9393 Springboro Pike, P.O. Box 933, Dayton, Ohio 45401. (Contains BNA's Chemical Regulation Reporter and Environment Reporter)

WESTLAW. BNA Environmental Law Library. West Publishing Company, P.O. Box 64526, 50 West Kellogg Boulevard, St. Paul, Minnesota 55164-0526.

CHILD ABUSE AND NEGLECT
See also: CHILDREN; FAMILY VIOLENCE

LOOSELEAF SERVICES AND REPORTERS

CHILD CUSTODY AND VISITATION LAW AND PRACTICE. Matthew Bender and Company, Incorporated, 11 Penn Plaza, New York, New York 10001. 1983- . (Periodic Supplements).

DOMESTIC VIOLENCE TRAINING MANUAL. House of Ruth Domestic Violence Clinic. MICPEL, 520 West Fayette Street, Baltimore, Maryland 21201. 1988- . (Periodic Supplements).

FAMILY LAW AND PRACTICE. Matthew Bender and Company, Incorporated, 11 Penn Plaza, New York, New York 10001. 1985- . (Periodic Supplements).

FAMILY LAW PRACTICE MANUAL. Charles P. Kindregan. Legal-Medical Studies, Incorporated, P.O. Box 8219, JFK Station, Boston, Massachusetts 02114. 1988- . (Annual Supplements).

THE FAMILY LAW REPORTER. Bureau of National Affairs, Incorporated, 1231 Twenty-fifth Street, Northwest, Washington, D.C. 20037. 1974- . (Weekly Supplements).

TEXTBOOKS AND GENERAL WORKS

THE BATTERED CHILD. Fourth Edition. Ray E. Helfer, M.D. and Ruth S. Kempe, M.D., University of Chicago Press, 5801 Ellis Avenue, Chicago, Illinois 60637. 1988.

CHILD ABUSE. A. Carmi and H. Zimrin. Springer and Verlag, Inc., 175 Fifth Avenue, New York, New York 10010. 1984.

CHILD ABUSE. Ruth S. Kempe and C. Henry Kempe. Harvard University Press, 79 Garden Street, Cambridge, Massachusetts 02138. 1978.

CHILD ABUSE: A POLICE GUIDE. Doulgas J. Besharov, American Bar Association, National Legal Resource Center for Child Advocacy and Protection, 1800 M Street, Northwest, Washington, D.C. 20036. 1987.

CHILD ABUSE: AN AGENDA FOR ACTION. George Gerbner, Catherine J. Ross, and Edward Zigler. Oxford University Press, 200 Madison Avenue, New York, New York 10016. 1980.

CHILD ABUSE AND NEGLECT. Practising Law Institute, 810 Seventh Avenue, New York, New York 10019. 1988.

CHILD ABUSE AND NEGLECT REPORTING AND INVESTIGATION: POLICY GUIDELINES FOR DECISION MAKING. Douglas J. Besharov. American Bar Association, 750 North Lake Shore Drive, Chicago, Illinois 60611. 1988.

CHILD ABUSE AND NEGLECT: SHARING RESPONSIBILITY. Pamela D. Mayhall, Katherine Eastlack Norgard. Macmillan Publishing Company, Incorporated, 866 Third Avenue, New York, New York 10022. 1983.

CHILD ABUSE, NEGLECT, AND THE FOSTER CARE SYSTEM. Practising Law Institute, 810 Seventh Avenue, New York, New York 10019. 1990.

DAMAGED PARENTS, AN ANATOMY OF CHILD NEGLECT. Norman A. Polansky. University of Chicago Press, 5801 Ellis Avenue, Fourth Floor, South, Chicago, Illinois 60637. 1983.

EXPLORING THE RELATIONSHIP BETWEEN CHILD ABUSE AND DELINQUENCY. Robert J. Hunner and Yvonne Elder Walker. Rowman and Littlefield, Publishers, Incorporated, 8705 Bollman Place, Savage, Maryland 20763. 1981.

FOUNDATIONS OF ADVOCACY: LEGAL REPRESENTATION OF THE MALTREATED CHILD. Donald C. Bross and Laura F. Michaels. Bookmakers Guild, Incorporated, 9655 West Coilfax Avenue, Lakewood, Colorado 80215. 1987.

INSTITUTIONAL ABUSE OF CHILDREN AND YOUTH. Ranae Hanson, Editor. Haworth Press, Incorporated, 10 Alice Street, Binghamton, New York 13904. 1982.

MAKING AN ISSUE OF CHILD ABUSE: POLITICAL AGENDA SETTING FOR SOCIAL PROBLEMS. Barbara J. Nelson. University of Chicago Press, 5801 Ellis Avenue, Fourth Floor, South, Chicago, Illinois 60637. 1986.

ON TRIAL: AMERICA'S COURTS AND THEIR TREATMENT OF SEXUALLY ABUSED CHILDREN. Billie W. Dziech and Charles B. Schudson. Beacon Press, 25 Beacon Street, Boston, Massachusetts 02108. 1989.

THE POLITICS OF CHILD ABUSE. Nigel Parton. St. Martin's Press, 175 Fifth Avenue, New York, New York 10010. 1985.

PROTECT YOUR CHILD: A PARENT'S SAFEGUARD AGAINST CHILD ABDUCTION AND SEXUAL ABUSE. Laura M. Huchton. Prentice-Hall, Incorporated, 113 Sylvan, Englewood Cliffs, New Jersey 07632. 1985.

REPRESENTATION FOR THE ABUSED AND NEGLECTED CHILD: THE GUARDIAN AD LITEM AND LEGAL COUNSEL. Marlene H. Alderman. National Center on Child Abuse and Neglect, Children's Bureau, National Center on Child Abuse. Superintendent of Documents, United States Government Printing Office, Washington, D.C. 20402. 1980.

REPRESENTING PARENTS IN CHILD PROTECTION CASES: A BASIC INTRODUCTION FOR ATTORNEYS. Lisa A. Granik. American Bar Association, 750 North Lake Shore Drive, Chicago, Illinois 60611. 1988.

SEXUAL ASSAULT OF CHILDREN AND ADOLESCENTS. Ann Wolbert Burgess and A. Nichols Groth. C. Henry Kempe National Center for the Prevention and Treatment of Child Abuse and Neglect, University of Colorado Health Science Center, Department of Pediatrics, 1205 Oneida Street, Denver, Colorado 80220. 1978.

SEXUAL VICTIMIZATION OF ADOLESCENTS. Ann Wolbert Burgess and United States Department of Health and Human Services. Alcohol, Drug Abuse and Mental Health Administration, National Institute of Mental Health, Superintendent of Documents, United States Government Printing Office, Division of Public Documents, Washington, D.C. 20402. 1985.

SEXUALLY VICTIMIZED CHILDREN. David Finkelhor. Free Press, 866 Third Avenue, New York, New York 10022. 1981.

TRAUMATIC ABUSE AND NEGLECT OF CHILDREN. Abridged Edition. Gertrude J. Williams and John Money. Johns Hopkins University Press, 701 West Fortieth Street, Baltimore, Maryland 21211. 1980.

THE VIOLENT HOME. Richard J. Gelles. Sage Publications, 2455 Teller Road, Newbury Park, California 91320. 1985.

ENCYCLOPEDIAS AND DICTIONARIES

CHILD ABUSE AND NEGLECT THESAURUS. U.S. Department of Health and Human Services, Administration for Children, Youth and Families, Children's Bureau, National Center on Child Abuse. Superintendent of Documents, United States Government Printing Office, North Capitol and H Streets, Northwest, Washington, D.C. 20401. 1986.

INTERDISCIPLINARY GLOSSARY ON CHILD ABUSE AND NEGLECT: LEGAL, MEDICAL, SOCIAL WORK TERMS. United States Department of Health and Human Services. Superintendent of Documents, United States Government Printing Office, Division of Public Documents, Washington, D.C. 20402. 1980.

LAW REVIEWS AND PERIODICALS

ABA JUVENILE AND CHILD WELFARE LAW REPORTER. American Bar Association, Center on Children and the Law, 1800 M Street, Northwest, Washington, D.C. 20036. Monthly.

CHILD ABUSE AND NEGLECT: THE INTERNATIONAL JOURNAL. International Society for the Prevention of Child Abuse and Neglect, 1205 Oneida Street, Denver, Colorado 80220. Quarterly.

CHILD PROTECTION EXCHANGE. American Association for Protecting Children, c/o American Humane Association, 9725 East Hampden Avenue, Denver, Colorado 80231. Quarterly.

CHILDREN'S LEGAL RIGHTS JOURNAL. American Bar Association, Center on Children and the Law, 1800 M Street, Northwest, Washington, D.C. 20036. Quarterly.

FAMILY LAW QUARTERLY. American Bar Association, 750 North Lake Shore Drive, Chicago, Illinois 60611. 1964- . Quarterly.

FAMILY LAW QUARTERLY. University of Denver, College of Law, Denver, Colorado 80220. Quarterly.

JUVENILE AND FAMILY COURT JOURNAL. National Council of Juvenile Family Court Judges, Judicial College Building, University of Nevada, Reno, Nevada 89507. Quarterly.

PROTECTING CHILDREN. American Association for Protecting Children, c/o American Humane Association, 9725 East Hampden Avenue, Denver, Colorado 80231. Quarterly.

STATE STATUTES RELATED TO CHILD ABUSE AND NEGLECT. Clearinghouse on Child Abuse and Neglect Information, P.O. Box 1182, Washington, D.C. 20013. Annual.

YOUTH LAW NEWS. National Center for Youth Law, 1663 Mission Street, Fifth floor, San Francisco, California 94103. Bimonthly.

NEWSLETTERS AND NEWSPAPERS

CALMWORD. Child Abuse Listening and Mediation, P.O. Box 90754, Santa Barbara, California 93190. Quarterly.

CHILD ABUSE INSTITUTE UPDATE. Child Abuse Institute of Research, P.O. Box 1217, Cincinnati, Ohio 45201. Quarterly.

CHRONICLE. Child Abuse Listening and Mediation, P.O. Box 90754, Santa Barbara, California 93190. Monthly.

THE PUN. Parents United, P.O. Box 952, San Jose, California 95108. Quarterly.

BIBLIOGRAPHIES

ANNOTATED BIBLIOGRAPHY OF LEGAL ARTICLES ON CHILD ABUSE. Richard Cozzola. National Committee for the Prevention of Child Abuse, 332 South Michigan Avenue, Suite 1600, Chicago, Illinois 60604-4357. 1979.

ANNOTATED BIBLIOGRAPHY OF LEGAL ARTICLES ON CHILD ABUSE: AN UPDATE. Sandra L. Kopels and Gary L. Shaffer. National Committee for Prevention of Child Abuse, 332 South Michigan Avenue, Suite 1600, Chicago, Illinois 60604-4357. 1983.

ANNUAL REVIEW OF CHILD ABUSE AND NEGLECT RESEARCH. Children's Bureau. Superintendent of Documents, United States Government Printing Office, Washington, D.C. 20402. 1978.

CHILD ABUSE: A SELECTED BIBLIOGRAPHY OF AN ALARMING SOCIAL PROBLEM. Phyllis Cohen. Vance Bibliographies, P.O. Box 229, 112 North Charter Street, Monticello, Illinois 61856. 1981.

CHILD ABUSE: AN ANNOTATED BIBLIOGRAPHY. Dorothy Pearl Wells. Scarecrow Press, Incorporated, 52 Liberty Street, Box 4167, Metuchen, New Jersey 08840. 1980.

CHILD ABUSE AND NEGLECT: A LITERATURE REVIEW AND SELECTED BIBLIOGRAPHY. Marian Eskin and Marjorie Kravitz. National Criminal Justice Reference Service. Superintendent of Documents, United States Government Printing Office, Washington, D.C. 20402. 1980.

CHILD ABUSE AND NEGLECT: AN ANNOTATED BIBLIOGRAPHY. Beatrice Kalisch, Greenwood Publishing Group, Incorporated, 88 Post Road West, P.O. Box 5007, Westport, Connecticut 06881. 1978.

CHILD ABUSE AND NEGLECT. (SUBJECT BIBLIOGRAPHY SB309). Superintendent of Documents, United States Government Printing Office, Division of Public Documents, Washington, D.C. 20402. 1987.

DIRECTORIES

THE CHILD ABUSE HELP BOOK. James Haskins. Addison-Wesley Publishing Company, Route 128, Reading, Massachusetts 01867. 1981.

ENCYCLOPEDIA OF MEDICAL ORGANIZATIONS AND AGENCIES. Fourth Edition. Gale Research, Incorporated, 835 Penobscot Building, Detroit, Michigan 48226. 1991.

HOW AND WHERE TO RESEARCH AND FIND INFORMATION ABOUT CHILD ABUSE. Robert D. Reed. R & E Publishers, P.O. Box 2008, Saratoga, California 95070-2008. 1983.

NATIONAL DIRECTORY OF CHILDREN AND YOUTH SERVICES. CPR Directory Services Company, 1301 Twentieth Street, Northwest, Washington, D.C. 20036. Biennial.

NATIONAL DIRECTORY OF PROGRAMS PROVIDING COURT REPRESENTATION TO ABUSED AND NEGLECTED CHILDREN. National Legal Resource Center for Child Advocacy and Protection, American Bar Association, 1800 M Street, Northwest, Washington, D.C. 20036. 1983.

ASSOCIATIONS AND PROFESSIONAL SOCIETIES

AMERICAN ASSOCIATION FOR PROTECTING CHILDREN. c/o American Humane Association, 9725 East Hampden Avenue, Denver, Colorado 80231. (303) 695-0811.

CHILD ABUSE LISTENING AND MEDIATION. P.O. Box 90754, Santa Barbara, California 93190. (805) 965-2376.

INTERNATIONAL SOCIETY FOR PREVENTION OF CHILD ABUSE AND NEGLECT. 1205 Oneida Street, Denver, Colorado 80220. (303) 321-3963.

NATIONAL COMMITTEE FOR PREVENTION OF CHILD ABUSE. 332 South Michigan Avenue, Suite 1250, Chicago, Illinois 60604. (312) 663-3520.

PARENTS UNITED. P.O. Box 952, San Jose, California 95108. (408) 280-5055.

RESEARCH CENTERS, INSTITUTES, CLEARINGHOUSES

ADAM WALSH CHILD RESOURCE CENTER. 5111 South Dixie Highway, Suite 244, West Palm Beach, Florida 33405. (407) 833-9080.

AMERICAN BAR ASSOCIATION, CENTER ON CHILDREN AND THE LAW. 1800 M Street, Northwest, Washington, D.C. 20036. (202) 331-2250.

CENTER FOR LAW AND HEALTH SCIENCES. Boston University, 765 Commonwealth Avenue, Boston, Massachusetts 02215. (617) 353-2904.

CHILD ABUSE INSTITUTE OF RESEARCH. P.O. Box 1217, Cincinnati, Ohio 45201. (606) 441-7409.

CLEARINGHOUSE ON CHILD ABUSE AND NEGLECT INFORMATION. P.O. Box 1182, Washington, D.C. 20013. (703) 821-2086.

INSTITUTE FOR URBAN AFFAIRS AND RESEARCH. Howard University, 2900 Van Ness Street, Northwest, Washington, D.C. 20008. (202) 686-6770.

INSTITUTE FOR FAMILY AND CHILD STUDY. Michigan State University, Pablucci Building 2, East Lansing, Michigan 48824. (517) 353-6617.

NATIONAL CENTER ON CHILD ABUSE AND NEGLECT. United States Department of Health and Human Services, Children's Bureau, P.O. Box 1182, Washington, D.C. 20013. (202) 245-0856.

NATIONAL CENTER FOR YOUTH LAW. 1663 Mission Street, Fifth floor, San Francisco, California 94103. (415) 543-3307.

ONLINE DATABASES

CHILD ABUSE AND NEGLECT. United States National Center on Child Abuse and Neglect, Information Clearinghouse, P.O. Box 1182, Washington, D.C. 20013.

AUDIOVISUALS

REPRESENTING THE STATE IN CHILD ABUSE AND NEGLECT PROCEEDINGS. American Bar Association, 750 North Lake Shore Drive, Chicago, Illinois 60611. 1981. Videotape.

OTHER SOURCES

CHILD ABUSE AND NEGLECT: STATE REPORTING LAWS. United States Department of Health and Human Services. Superintendent of Documents, United States Government Printing Office, Washington, D.C. 20402. 1979.

CHILD CUSTODY
See also: CHILDREN; FAMILY LAW

STATUTES, CODES, STANDARDS, UNIFORM LAWS

UNIFORM CHILD CUSTODY JURISDICTION ACT. National Conference of Commissioners on Uniform State Laws. Uniform Laws Annotated. West Publishing Company, 50 West Kellogg Boulevard, St. Paul, Minnesota 55164-0526. 1976- . (Annual Supplements).

LOOSELEAF SERVICES AND REPORTERS

CHILD CUSTODY AND VISITATION LAW AND PRACTICE. John P. McCahey, Martin Kaufman, Celeste Kraut, David Gaffner, Maris Silverman, Robert Schwartz, James Zett. Matthew Bender and Company, Incorporated, 11 Penn Plaza, New York, New York 10001. 1983- . (Periodic Supplements).

CONTEMPORARY FAMILY LAW. Lynn Wardle and others. Callaghan and Company, 155 Pfingsten Road, Deerfield, Illinois 60015. 1988- . (Annual Supplements).

DETERMINING CHILD AND SPOUSAL SUPPORT. Jeanne W. Smith and Elizabeth S. Beninger. Callaghan and Company, 155 Pfingsten Road, Deerfield, Illinois 60015. 1986- . (Annual Supplements).

DISPUTED PATERNITY PROCEEDINGS. Sidney Schatkin. Fourth Edition. Matthew Bender and Company, Incorporated, 11 Penn Plaza, New York, New York 10001. 1975- . (Annual Supplements).

FAMILY LAW AND PRACTICE. Matthew Bender and Company, Incorporated, 11 Penn Plaza, New York, New York 10001. 1985- . (Periodic Supplements).

FAMILY LAW PRACTICE MANUAL. Charles P. Kindregan. Legal-Medical Studies, Incorporated, P.O. Box 8219, JFK Station, Boston, Massachusetts 02114. 1988- . (Annual Supplements).

THE FAMILY LAW REPORTER. Bureau of National Affairs, Incorporated, 1231 Twenty-fifth Street, Northwest, Washington, D.C. 20037. 1974- . (Weekly Supplements).

IMPROVING CHILD SUPPORT PRACTICE. National Legal Resource Center for Child Advocacy and Protection, 1800 M Street, Northwest, Washington, D.C. 20036. 1986.

HANDBOOKS, MANUALS, FORMBOOKS

BEST OF FAMILY ADVOCATE: A PRACTICE MANUAL FOR MATRIMONIAL AND FAMILY LAWYERS. Arnold H. Rutkin, Editor. Section of Family Law, American Bar Association, 750 North Lake Shore Drive, Chicago, Illinois 60611. 1989.

CHILD CUSTODY EVALUATIONS: A PRACTICAL MANUAL. Dianne Skafte. Sage Publications, 2455 Teller Road, Newbury Park, California 91320. 1985.

CUSTODY CASES AND EXPERT WITNESSES: A MANUAL FOR ATTORNEYS: Melvin G. Goldzband. Prentice-Hall Law and Business, Route 9W, Englewood Cliffs, New Jersey 07632. 1988.

INTERNATIONAL CHILD ABDUCTIONS: A GUIDE TO APPLYING THE 1988 HAGUE CONVENTION, WITH FORMS. Gloria F. DeHart, Editor. Section of Family Law, American Bar Association, 750 North Lake Shore Drive, Chicago, Illinois 60611. 1989.

LESBIAN MOTHER LITIGATION MANUAL. Second Edition. National Center for Lesbian Rights, 1370 Mission Street, 4th floor, San Francisco, California 94103. 1990.

REASONABLE EFFORTS: A MANUAL FOR JUDGES. Debra Ratterman. American Bar Association, 750 North Lake Shore Drive, Chicago, Illinois 60611. 1987.

CHILD CUSTODY

TEXTBOOKS AND GENERAL WORKS

BEFORE THE BEST INTERESTS OF THE CHILD. Joseph Goldstein, Anna Frend, and Albert J. Solnit. Free Press, 866 Third Avenue, New York, New York 10022. 1980.

CHILD CUSTODY. James C. Black and Donald J. Cantor. Columbia University Press, 562 West One Hundred Thirteenth Street, New York, New York 10025. 1989.

CHILD CUSTODY DISPUTES. Gary E. Stollak and Michael G. Lieberman, Editors. Irvington Publishers, 195 McGregor Street, Manchester, New Hampshire 03103. 1985.

CHILD CUSTODY DISPUTES: SEARCHING FOR SOLOMON. Section of Family Law, American Bar Association, 750 North Lake Shore Drive, Chicago, Illinois 60611. 1989.

CHILD CUSTODY MEDIATION: TECHNIQUES FOR COUNSELORS, ATTORNEYS, AND PARENTS. Florence Bienenfeld. Science and Behavior Books, P.O. Box 60519, Palo Alto, California 94306. 1983.

CHILD SNATCHING: THE LEGAL RESPONSE TO THE ABDUCTION OF CHILDREN. Sanford N. Katz. American Bar Association, Section of Family Law, 750 North Lake Shore Drive, Chicago, Illinois 60611. 1981.

CUSTODY LITIGATION: NEW DIRECTIONS. Henry H. Foster, Jr. and Gary N. Skoloff. Prentice-Hall Law and Business, Route 9W, Englewood Cliffs, New Jersey 07632. 1981.

DILEMMAS IN CHILD CUSTODY: FAMILY CONFLICTS AND THEIR RESOLUTION. Andrew P. Musetto. Nelson-Hall, 111 North Canal Street, Chicago, Illinois 60606. 1982.

FAMILY EVALUATION IN CHILD CUSTODY MEDIATION, ARBITRATION, AND LITIGATION. Richard A. Gardner. Creative Therapeutics, 155 County Road, Cresskill, New Jersey. 1989.

HANDLING CHILD CUSTODY CASES. Ann M. Haralambie. McGraw-Hill Publishing Company, 1221 Avenue of the Americas, New York, New York 10020. 1983.

IMPROVING CHILD SUPPORT PRACTICE. Diane Dodson, Compiler, American Bar Association, 1800 M Street, Northwest, Washington, D.C. 20036. (2 volumes--includes forms). 1986.

INTERSTATE AND INTERNATIONAL CHILD CUSTODY DISPUTES: A COLLECTION OF MATERIALS: A MONOGRAPH. Fourth Edition. Child Custody Clearinghouse and Information Exchange. American Bar Association, National Legal Resource Center for Child Advocacy and Protection, 1800 M Street, Northwest, Washington, D.C. 20036. 1984.

INTERSTATE CHILD CUSTODY DISPUTES AND PARENTAL KIDNAPPING: POLICY, PRACTICE AND LAW. National Clearinghouse for Legal Services, Incorporated, 407 South Dearborn, Chicago, Illinois 60605. 1982.

INTERSTATE CUSTODY LITIGATION: A GUIDE TO USE AND COURT INTERPRETATION OF THE UNIFORM CHILD CUSTODY JURISDICTION ACT. Richard E. Crouch. Bureau of National Affairs, Incorporated, 1231 Twenty-fifth Street, Northwest, Washington, D.C. 20037. 1981.

ISSUES IN FORENSIC PSYCHIATRY: INSANITY DEFENSE, HOSPITALIZATION OF ADULTS, MODEL CIVIL COMMITMENT LAW, SENTENCING PROCESS, CHILD CUSTODY CONSULTATION. Books on Demand, 300 North Zeeb Road, Ann Arbor, Michigan 48106-1346. 1984.

THE LAW OF CHILD CUSTODY: DEVELOPMENT OF THE SUBSTANTIVE LAW. Shirley Wohl Kram and Neil A. Frank. Lexington Books, 125 Spring Street, Lexington, Massachusetts 02173. 1982.

LEGAL RIGHTS OF CHILDREN. Robert M. Horowitz and Howard A. Davidson. Shepard's/McGraw Hill, P.O. Box 1235, Colorado Springs, Colorado 80901. 1983- . (Annual Supplements).

MEDIATING CHILD CUSTODY DISPUTES. Donald T. Saposnek. Jossey-Bass, Incorporated, Publishers, 350 Sansome Street, San Francisco, California 94104. 1983.

MOTHERS ON TRIAL: THE BATTLE FOR CHILDREN AND CUSTODY. Phyllis Chesler. Harcourt Brace Jovanovich, Incorporated, 6277 Sea Harbor Drive, Orlando, Florida 32821. 1991.

PSYCHOLOGY AND CHILD CUSTODY DETERMINATIONS: KNOWLEDGE, ROLES, AND EXPERTISE. Lois A. Weithorn, Editor. University of Nebraska Press, 901 North Seventeenth Street, Lincoln, Nebraska 68588. 1987.

THE SACRED BOND: THE LEGACY OF BABY M. Phyllis Chesler. Times Books, Random House, Incorporated, 201 East Fiftieth Street, New York, New York 10022. 1988.

SEXUAL ABUSE ALLEGATIONS IN CUSTODY AND VISITATION CASES: A RESOURCE BOOKS FOR JUDGES AND COURT PERSONNEL. E. Bruce Nicholson, Editor. National Legal Resource Center for Child Advocacy and Protection, American Bar Association, 1800 M Street, Northwest, Washington, D.C. 20036. 1988.

ANNUALS AND SURVEYS

IN THE BEST INTEREST OF THE CHILD: A GUIDE TO STATE CHILD SUPPORT AND PATERNITY LAWS. Carolyn Royce Kastner and Lawrence R. Young. Child Support Enforcement Beneficial Laws Project, National Conference of State Legislatures, 1125 Seventeenth Street, Suite 2100, Denver, Colorado 80265-2101. 1981.

NEWSLETTERS AND NEWSPAPERS

NEWSLETTER -- ASSOCIATION OF FAMILY AND CONCILIATION COURTS. Association of Family and Conciliation Courts, 329 West Wilson Street, Madison, Wisconsin 53703. Quarterly.

SPEAK OUT FOR CHILDREN. National Council for Children's Rights, 721 Second Street, Northeast, Washington, D.C. 20002. Quarterly.

THE WOMEN'S ADVOCATE. National Center on Women and Family Law, 799 Broadway, New York, New York 10003. Bimonthly.

BIBLIOGRAPHIES

BIBLIOGRAPHY OF ARTICLES ON THE UNIFORM CHILD CUSTODY JURISDICTION ACT. Richard E. Crouch. Bureau of National Affairs, Incorporated, 1231 Twenty-fifth Street, Northwest, Washington, D.C. 20037. 1981.

LESBIAN MOTHER AND GAY FATHER CUSTODY ISSUES: BIBLIOGRAPHY. Advanced Legal Education, Hamline University School of Law, 1536 Hewitt Avenue, St. Paul, Minnesota 55104. 1983.

ASSOCIATIONS AND PROFESSIONAL SOCIETIES

AMERICAN BAR ASSOCIATION, CENTER ON CHILDREN AND THE LAW, 1800 M Street, Northwest, Washington, D.C. 20036. (202) 331-2250.

COMMITTEE FOR MOTHER AND CHILD RIGHTS. Route 1, Box 256A, Clear Brook, Virginia 22624. (703) 722-3652.

FATHERS FOR EQUAL RIGHTS. P.O. Box 010847, Flagler Station, Miami, Florida 33101. (305) 895-6351.

JOINT CUSTODY ASSOCIATION. 10606 Wilkins Avenue, Los Angeles, California 90024. (213) 475-5352.

NATIONAL CHILD SUPPORT ENFORCEMENT ASSOCIATION. Hall of States, 444 North Capitol Street, Northwest, Suite 613, Washington, D.C. 20001. (202) 624-8180.

NATIONAL COUNCIL FOR CHILDREN'S RIGHTS. 721 Second Street, Northeast, Washington, D.C. 20002. (202) 547-6227.

NATIONAL INSTITUTE FOR CHILD SUPPORT ENFORCEMENT. 7200 Wisconsin Avenue, Suite 500, Bethesda, Maryland 20814. (301) 654-8338.

ORGANIZATION FOR THE ENFORCEMENT OF CHILD SUPPORT. 119 Nicodemus Road, Reisterstown, Maryland 21136. (301) 833-2458.

PARENTS AND CHILDREN'S EQUALITY. 1816 Florida Avenue, Palm Harbor, Florida 34683. (813) 787-3875.

RESEARCH CENTERS, INSTITUTES, CLEARINGHOUSES

CANADIAN RESEARCH INSTITUTE FOR LAW AND THE FAMILY. University of Calgary, Room 596, Bio Sciences Building, 2500 University Drive, Northwest, Calgary, AB, Canada T2N 1N4. (403) 220-6653.

CENTER FOR FAMILY LEARNING. 16 Ryeridge Plaza, Ryebrook, New York 10573. (914) 253-9190.

INSTITUTE FOR THE STUDY OF MATRIMONIAL LAWS. 11 Park Place, Suite 1116, New York, New York 10007. (212) 766-4030.

NATIONAL CENTER FOR LESBIAN RIGHTS. 1370 Mission Street, 4th Floor, San Francisco, California 94103. (415) 621-0674.

NATIONAL CENTER ON WOMEN AND FAMILY LAW. 799 Broadway, New York, New York 10003. (212) 674-8200.

UNIVERSITY CENTER FOR THE CHILD AND FAMILY. University of Michigan, 1007 East Huron Street, Ann Arbor, Michigan 48104. (313) 764-9466.

STATISTICS SOURCES

CHILD SUPPORT PAYMENTS AND ALIMONY. Current Population Reports. United States Department of Commerce, Bureau of the Census. Superintendent of Documents, United States Government Printing Office, Washington, D.C. 20402. (Irregular).

AUDIOVISUALS

PREPARING AND TRYING A CHILD CUSTODY CASE. American Bar Association, 750 North Lake Shore Drive, Chicago, Illinois 60611. 1981. Videotape.

CHILD LABOR
See: CHILDREN; LABOR AND LABOR RELATIONS

CHILD SUPPORT
See: FAMILY LAW

CHILDREN
See also: CHILD ABUSE AND NEGLECT; CHILD CUSTODY; FAMILY LAW; FAMILY VIOLENCE

STATUTES, CODES, STANDARDS, UNIFORM LAWS

STANDARDS RELATING TO RIGHTS OF MINORS, RECOMMENDED BY THE IJA-ABA JOINT COMMISSION ON JUVENILE JUSTICE STANDARDS. Ballinger Division, HarperCollins Publishers, 10 East Fifty-third Street, New York, New York 10022. 1980.

HANDBOOKS, MANUALS, FORMBOOKS

ADVOCATING FOR THE CHILD IN PROTECTION PROCEEDINGS: A HANDBOOK FOR LAWYERS AND COURT APPOINTED SPECIAL ADVOCATES. Donald N. Duquette and others. Lexington Books, 125 Spring Street, Lexington, Massachusetts 02173. 1990.

CHILD WITNESS LAW AND PRACTICE. John E.B. Myers. John Wiley and Sons, Incorporated, 605 Third Avenue, New York, New York 10158. 1987.

EVALUATING AND IMPROVING CHILD WELFARE AGENCY LEGAL REPRESENTATION: SELF-ASSESSMENT INSTRUMENT AND COMMENTARY. National Legal Resource Center for Child Advocacy and Protection, American Bar Association, 750 North Lake Shore Drive, Chicago, Illinois 60611. 1988.

LEGAL DIRECTORY OF CHILDREN'S RIGHTS. Thomas A. Jacobs, Editor. Greenwood Publishing Group, Incorporated, 88 Post Road West, P.O. Box 5007, Westport, Connecticut 06881. 1989.

LEGAL RIGHTS OF CHILDREN. Robert M. Horowitz, Howard A. Davidson, Editors. Shepard's/McGraw-Hill, P.O. Box 1235, Colorado Springs, Colorado 80901. 1983- . (Annual Supplements).

REPRESENTING THE CHILD CLIENT. Matthew Bender and Company, Incorporated, 11 Penn Plaza, New York, New York 10001. 1987- .

THE RIGHTS OF YOUNG PEOPLE. Martin Guggenheim and Alan Sussman. (ACLU Handbook). Southern Illinois University Press, P.O. Box 3697, Carbondale, Illinois 62902-3697. 1985.

TEXTBOOKS AND GENERAL WORKS

BEFORE THE BEST INTERESTS OF THE CHILD. Joseph Goldstein, Anna Freud, and Albert J. Solnit. Free Press, 866 Third Avenue, New York, New York 10022. 1980.

BEYOND THE BEST INTERESTS OF THE CHILD. Joseph Goldstein, Anna Freud, and Albert J. Solnit. Free Press, 866 Third Avenue, New York, New York 10022. 1984.

CHILD ADVOCACY. Gary B. Melton. Plenum Publishing Corporation, 233 Spring Street, New York, New York 10013. 1983.

THE CHILD AND THE LAW. Roberta Gottesman. West Publishing Company, 50 West Kellogg Boulevard, St. Paul, Minnesota 55164-0526. 1981.

CHILD CARE: EMERGING LEGAL ISSUES. Mary Frank. Haworth Press, Incorporated, 10 Alice Street, Binghamton, New York 13904. 1983.

CHILD PORNOGRAPHY AND PROSTITUTION: BACKGROUND AND ANALYSIS. Howard A. Davidson and Gregory A. Loken. National Center for Missing and Exploited Children, National Obscenity Enforcement Unit, U.S. Department of Justice. Superintendent of Documents, United States Government Printing Office, Washington, D.C. 20402. 1987.

CHILD SNATCHING: THE LEGAL RESPONSE TO THE ABDUCTION OF CHILDREN. Sanford N. Katz, American Bar Association, 750 North Lake Shore Drive, Chicago, Illinois 60611. 1981.

CHILDREN BEFORE THE COURT: REFLECTIONS ON ISSUES AFFECTING MINORS. Paul R. Kfoury. Butterworth Legal Publishers, 90 Stiles Road, Salem, New Hampshire 03079. 1987.

CHILDREN, EDUCATION AND THE FIRST AMENDMENT. David Moshman. University of Nebraska Press, 901 North Seventeenth Street, Lincoln, Nebraska 68588. 1989.

CHILDREN, FAMILIES, AND GOVERNMENT: PERSPECTIVES ON AMERICAN SOCIAL POLICY. Edward F. Zigler, Sharon Lynn Kagan, and Edgar Klugman. Cambridge University Press, 40 West Twentieth Street, New York, New York 10011. 1983.

CHILDREN, MENTAL HEALTH, AND THE LAW. N. Dickon Reppucci. Books on Demand, 300 North Zeeb Road, Ann Arbor, Michigan 48106-1346. 1984.

CHILDREN'S EYEWITNESS MEMORY. Stephen J. Ceci and others, Editors. Springer-Verlag New York, Incorporated, 175 Fifth Avenue, New York, New York 10010. 1987.

CHILDREN'S RIGHTS: A PHILOSOPHICAL STUDY. C.A. Wringe. Routledge, Chapman & Hall, 29 West Thirty-fifth Street, New York, New York 10001. 1981.

CHILDREN'S RIGHTS AND THE LAW. Samuel M. Davis and Mortimer D. Schwartz. Free Press, 866 Third Street, New York, New York 10022. 1987.

CHILDREN'S RIGHTS IN AMERICA: U.N. CONVENTION ON THE RIGHTS OF THE CHILD COMPARED WITH UNITED STATES LAW. Cynthia P. Price and Howard A. Davidson, Editors. American Bar Association, Center on Children and the Law, 750 North Lake Shore Drive, Chicago, Illinois 60611. 1990.

DIVORCE AND YOUR CHILD: PRACTICAL SUGGESTIONS FOR PARENTS. Sonja Goldstein and Albert J. Solnit. Yale University Press, 302 Temple Street, New Haven, Connecticut 06520. 1984.

DRUG EXPOSED INFANTS AND THEIR FAMILIES: COORDINATING RESPONSES OF THE LEGAL, MEDICAL, AND CHILD PROTECTION SYSTEM. American Bar Association, 750 North Lake Shore Drive, Chicago, Illinois 60611. 1990.

EDUCATORS, CHILDREN AND THE LAW. Lynn Sametz and Caver McLaughlin, Editors. Charles C. Thomas Publishers, 2600 South First Street, Springfield, Illinois 62794. 1985.

EMERGING ISSUES IN CHILD PSYCHIATRY AND THE LAW. Elissa P. Benedek and Diane Schetky. Brunner/Mazel Publishers, 19 Union Square, West, New York, New York 10003. 1985.

EQUAL RIGHTS FOR CHILDREN. Howard Cohen. Rowman and Littlefield Publishers, Incorporated, 8705 Bollman Place, Savage, Maryland 20763. 1980.

GROWING UP DIVORCED. Linda Bird Francke. Fawcett Book Group, 201 East Fiftieth Street, New York, New York 10022. 1984.

GUARDIANS AD LITEM IN CRIMINAL COURTS. Debra Whitcomb. National Institute of Justice, U.S. Department of Justice. Superintendent of Documents, United States Government Printing Office, Washington, D.C. 20402. 1988.

HOW OLD IS ENOUGH?: THE AGES OF RIGHTS AND RESPONSIBILITIES. Committee on Child Psychiatry, Group for the Advancement of Psychiatry. Brunner/Mazel Publications, 19 Union Square, West, New York, New York 10003. 1989.

IN DEFENSE OF CHILDREN: UNDERSTANDING THE RIGHTS, NEEDS, AND INTERESTS OF THE CHILD: A RESOURCE FOR PARENTS AND PROFESSIONALS. Thomas A. Nazario and others. Charles Scribner Sons, MacMillan Publishing Company, Incorporated, 866 Third Avenue, New York, New York 10022. 1988.

IN THE BEST INTEREST OF THE CHILD: A GUIDE TO STATE SUPPORT AND PATERNITY LAWS. Carolyn R. Kastner and Lawrence R. Young, Editors. National Conference of State Legislatures, 1050 Seventeenth Street, Suite 2100, Denver, Colorado 80265. 1981.

IN THE INTEREST OF CHILDREN: ADVOCACY LAW, REFORM, AND PUBLIC POLICY. Robert H. Mnookin. W.H. Freeman & Company, 41 Madison Avenue, East Twenty-sixth, Thirty-fifth Floor, New York, New York 10010. 1985.

IN WHOSE BEST INTEREST? CHILD WELFARE REFORM IN THE PROGRESSIVE ERA. Susan Tiffin. Greenwood Publishing Group, Incorporated, 88 Post Road West, P.O. Box 5007, Westport, Connecticut 06881. 1982.

INVESTING IN CHILDREN: NEW ESTIMATES OF PARENTAL EXPENDITURES. Thomas J. Espenshade. Urban Institute Press, 2100 M Street, Northwest, Washington, D.C. 20037. 1984.

THE KID BUSINESS AND HOW IT EXPLOITS THE CHILDREN IT SHOULD HELP. Ronald B. Taylor. Houghton Mifflin Company, One Beacon Street, Boston, Massachusetts 02108. 1981.

LAWYERS FOR CHILDREN. ABA Center on Children and the Law, American Bar Association, 750 North Lake Shore Drive, Chicago, Illinois 60611. 1990.

LEGAL ADVOCACY FOR CHILDREN AND YOUTH: REFORMS, TRENDS AND CONTEMPORARY ISSUES. Robert M. Horowitz and Howard A. Davidson, Editors. American Bar Association, National Legal Resource Center for Child Welfare Programs, 1800 M Street, Northwest, Washington, D.C. 20036. 1986.

THE LIMITS OF LAW AND PSYCHOLOGY IN DECISIONS CONCERNING THE WELFARE OF CHILDREN. Michael King. Macmillan Publishing Company, Incorporated, 866 Third Avenue, New York, New York 10022. 1981.

PERSPECTIVE ON CHILDREN'S TESTIMONY. S.J. Ceci and others, Editors. Springer-Verlag New York, Incorporated, 175 Fifth Avenue, New York, New York 10010. 1989.

REASONABLE EFFORTS TO PREVENT FOSTER PLACEMENT: A GUIDE TO IMPLEMENTATION. Second Edition. Debra Ratterman and others. National Legal Resource for Child Advocacy and Protection, American Bar Association, 750 North Lake Shore Drive, Chicago, Illinois 60611. 1987.

REFORMING THE LAW: IMPACT OF CHILD DEVELOPMENT RESEARCH. Gary B. Melton, Editor. Guilford Press, 72 Spring Street, New York, New York 10012. 1987.

REPRESENTATION OF PARENTS IN CHILD PROTECTION CASES: A BASIC INTRODUCTION FOR ATTORNEYS. Lisa A. Granik. American Bar Association, 750 North Lake Shore Drive, Chicago, Illinois 60611. 1988.

THE RIGHTS OF CHILDREN: LEGAL AND PSYCHOLOGICAL PERSPECTIVES. James S. Henning. Charles C. Thomas, 2600 South First Street, Springfield, Illinois 62794-9265. 1982.

UNACCOMPANIED CHILDREN: CARE AND PROTECTION IN WARS, NATURAL DISASTERS AND REFUGEE MOVEMENTS. Everett M. Ressler, Neil Boothby and Daniel J. Steinbock. Oxford University Press, 200 Madison Avenue, New York, New York 10016. 1987.

UNEQUAL PROTECTION: WOMEN, CHILDREN, AND THE ELDERLY IN COURT. Lois G. Forer. W.W. Norton and Company, Incorporated, 500 Fifth Avenue, New York, New York 10110. 1991.

UP AGAINST THE LAW: YOUR LEGAL RIGHTS AS A MINOR. Ross R. Olney and Patricia J. Olney. E.P. Dutton, 375 Hudson Street, New York, New York 10014. 1985.

WHOSE CHILD? CHILDREN'S RIGHTS, PARENTAL AUTHORITY, AND STATE POWER. William Aiken and Hugh LaFollette. Rowman and Littlefield Publishers, Incorporated, 8705 Bollman Place, Savage, Maryland 20763. 1980.

DIGESTS, INDEXES, ABSTRACTS, CITATORS

KINDEX: AN INDEX TO LEGAL PERIODICAL LITERATURE CONCERNING CHILDREN, 1965/1975. National Center for Juvenile Justice, 1309 Cathedral of Learning, Pittsburgh, Pennsylvania 15260.

ANNUALS AND SURVEYS

ADVANCES IN LAW AND CHILD DEVELOPMENT: A RESEARCH ANNUAL. JAI Press, Incorporated, 55 Old Post Road, Number 2, P.O. Box 1678, Greenwich, Connecticut 06830. Annual.

THE OUT-OF-STATE PLACEMENT OF CHILDREN: A NATIONAL SURVEY. John C. Hall. Academy for Contemporary Problems, 1501 Neal Avenue, Columbus, Ohio 43201 1982.

LAW REVIEWS AND PERIODICALS

CHILDREN'S LEGAL RIGHTS JOURNAL. Children's Legal Rights Information and Training Program, 2008 Hillyer Place, Northwest, Washington, D.C. 20009. Bimonthly.

FAMILY LAW QUARTERLY. American Bar Association, Section of Family Law, 750 North Lake Shore Drive, Chicago, Illinois 60611. Quarterly.

JUVENILE AND FAMILY COURT JOURNAL. National Council of Juvenile and Family Court Judges. University of Nevada, P.O. Box 8978, Reno, Nevada 89507. Quarterly.

CHILDREN

BIBLIOGRAPHIES

THE CHILD WITNESS. Earleen H. Cook. Vance Bibliographies, P.O. Box 229, 112 North Charter Street, Monticello, Illinois 61856. 1987.

CHILDREN AND DIVORCE: AN ANNOTATED BIBLIOGRAPHY AND GUIDE. Evelyn B. Hausstein. Garland Publishing, Incorporated, 136 Madison Avenue, New York, New York 10016. 1983.

CHILDREN AND THE LAW: A SELECTED BIBLIOGRAPHY. Edward Stanek. Vance Bibliographies, P.O. Box 229, 112 North Charter Street, Monticello, Illinois 61856. 1986

DIRECTORIES

AMERICAN ASSOCIATION OF CHILDREN'S RESIDENTIAL CENTERS -- DIRECTORY OF ORGANIZATIONAL MEMBERS. American Association of Children's Residential Centers, 440 First Street, Northwest, Suite 310, Washington, D.C. 20001. Annual.

CHILD WELFARE LEAGUE OF AMERICA -- DIRECTORY OF MEMBER AGENCIES AND ASSOCIATES. Child Welfare League of America, 440 First Street, Northwest, Suite 310, Washington, D.C. 20001. Annual.

CHILDHOOD INFORMATION RESOURCES. Marda Woodbury. Information Resources Press, 1110 North Glebe Road, Suite 550, Arlington, Virginia 22201. 1985.

DIRECTORY OF RESIDENTIAL TREATMENT FACILITIES FOR EMOTIONALLY DISTURBED CHILDREN. Barbara Smiley Sherman. Oryx Press, 2214 North Central Avenue, Phoenix, Arizona 85004. 1985.

DIRECTORY OF SERVICES FOR HANDICAPPED CHILDREN AND ADULTS. Coordinating Council for Handicapped Children, 220 South State Street, Room 412, Chicago, Illinois 60604. Irregular.

DIRECTORY: SUPPORT SERVICES AND RESOURCES FOR MISSING AND EXPLOITED CHILDREN. National Center for Missing and Exploited Children, 2101 Wilson Boulevard, Suite 550, Arlington, Virginia 22201. 1985.

INTERNATIONAL HALFWAY HOUSE ASSOCIATION -- DIRECTORY OF RESIDENTIAL TREATMENT CENTERS. International Halfway House Association, P.O. Box 2337, Reston, Virginia 22090. Annual.

NATIONAL DIRECTORY OF CHILDREN AND YOUTH SERVICES. CPR Directory Services Company, 1301 Twentieth Street, Northwest, Washington, D.C. 20036. Biennial.

NATIONAL DIRECTORY OF RUNAWAY PROGRAMS. National Youth Work Alliance, 1346 Connecticut Avenue, Northwest, Suite 502, Washington, D.C. 20036. 1983- . (Irregular).

SOCIAL SERVICE ORGANIZATIONS AND AGENCIES DIRECTORY. Gale Research, Incorporated, 835 Penobscot Building, Detroit, Michigan 48226. 1982.

ASSOCIATIONS AND PROFESSIONAL SOCIETIES

AMERICAN CIVIL LIBERTIES UNION CHILDREN'S RIGHTS PROJECT. 132 West Forty-third Street, New York, New York 10036. (212) 944-0801.

BIG BROTHERS/BIG SISTERS OF AMERICA. 230 North Thirteenth Street, Philadelphia, Pennsylvania 19107. (215) 567-7000.

CHILD TRENDS. 2100 M Street, Northwest, Washington, D.C. 20037. (202) 223-6288.

CHILD WELFARE LEAGUE OF AMERICA. 440 First Street, Northwest, Suite 310, Washington, D.C. 20001. (202) 638-2952.

CHILDREN OF THE AMERICAS. c/o W.O. Mills, III, P.O. Box 140165, Dallas, Texas 75214. (214) 823-3922.

CHILDREN'S DEFENSE FUND. 122 C Street, Northwest, Washington, D.C. 20001. (202) 628-8787.

CHILDREN'S RIGHTS GROUP. 543 Howard Street, San Francisco, California 94105. (415) 495-7283.

MAKE-A-WISH FOUNDATION OF AMERICA. 2600 North Central Avenue, Suite 936, Phoenix, Arizona 85004. (602) 240-6600.

NATIONAL ASSOCIATION OF COUNSEL FOR CHILDREN. 1205 Oneida Street, Denver, Colorado 80220. (303) 321-3963.

SAVE THE CHILDREN FEDERATION. 54 Wilton Road, Westport, Connecticut 06880. (203) 221-4000.

UNITED NATIONS CHILDREN FUND. 3 United Nations Plaza, New York, New York 10017. (212) 326-7000.

RESEARCH CENTERS, INSTITUTES, CLEARINGHOUSES

AMERICAN BAR ASSOCIATION, CENTER ON CHILDREN AND THE LAW. 1800 M Street, Northwest, Washington, D.C. 20036. (202) 331-2250.

CANADIAN COUNCIL ON CHILDREN AND YOUTH. 2211 Riverside Drive, Suite 14, Ottawa, ON, Canada K1H 7X5. (613) 738-0200.

CHILD STUDY CENTER. Yale University, P.O. Box 3333, New Haven, Connecticut 06510. (203) 785-5759.

JOHN F. KENNEDY CHILD DEVELOPMENT CENTER. University of Colorado, 4200 East Ninth Avenue, Campus Box C234, Denver, Colorado 80262. (303) 270-7224.

NATIONAL CENTER ON CHILD ABUSE AND NEGLECT INFORMATION CLEARINGHOUSE. P.O. Box 1182, Washington, D.C. 20013. (202) 245-0856.

NATIONAL COUNCIL FOR CHILDREN'S RIGHTS. 721 Second Street, Northeast, Washington, D.C. 20002. (202) 547-6227.

ONLINE DATABASES

CHILD ABUSE AND NEGLECT. United States National Center on Child Abuse and Neglect, Information Clearinghouse, P.O. Box 1182, Washington, D.C. 20013. (202) 245-0856.

HRAF DATA ARCHIVE. Human Relations Area Files, Incorporated, 755 Prospect Street, P.O. Box 2054, Yale Station, New Haven, Connecticut 06520. (203) 777-2334.

THE NATIONAL REPORT ON WORK AND FAMILY. The Bureau of National Affairs, Incorporated, BNA ONLINE, 1231 Twenty-fifth Street, Northwest, Washington, D.C. 20037. (202) 452-4132.

STATISTICS SOURCES

CURRENT POPULATION REPORTS. United States Department of Commerce, Bureau of Census. Superintendent of Documents, United States Government Printing Office, Washington, D.C. 20402.

EMPLOYMENT AND EARNINGS. United States Department of Labor, Bureau of Labor Statistics, 200 Constitution Avenue, Northwest, Washington, D.C. 20212. Monthly.

UNITED STATES DEPARTMENT OF HEALTH AND HUMAN SERVICES. Social Security Administration, 6401 Security Boulevard, Baltimore, Maryland 21235.

VITAL STATISTICS OF THE UNITED STATES, MONTHLY VITAL STATISTICS REPORTS. United States Department of Health and Human Services, Public Health Service, 200 Independence Avenue, Southwest, Washington, D.C. 20201. Annual.

OTHER SOURCES

A CHILDREN'S DEFENSE BUDGET: AN ANALYSIS OF THE PRESIDENT'S FISCAL YEAR BUDGET AND CHILDREN. Second Edition. Children's Defense Fund, 122 C Street, Northwest, Washington, D.C. 20001. Annual.

FEDERAL PROGRAMS AFFECTING CHILDREN. Thomas J. Bliley, Junior. Superintendent of Documents, United States Government Printing Office, Division of Public Documents, Washington, D.C. 20402. 1984.

REDUCING POVERTY AMONG CHILDREN. United States Congressional Budget Office. Superintendent of Documents, United States Government Printing Office, Washington, D.C. 20402. 1985.

CHURCH AND STATE
See also: CANON LAW; CONSTITUTIONAL LAW; RELIGION

LOOSELEAF SERVICES AND REPORTERS

RELIGIOUS FREEDOM REPORTER. Center for Law and Religious Freedom, P.O. Box 2069, Oak Park, Illinois 60603. 1981- .

TEXTBOOKS AND GENERAL WORKS

AMERICAN PLURALISM AND THE CATHOLIC CONSCIENCE. Richard J. Regan. MacMillan Publishing Company, Incorporated, 866 Third Avenue, New York, New York 10022. 1963.

AMERICA'S UNWRITTEN CONSTITUTION: SCIENCE, RELIGION, AND POLITICAL RESPONSIBILITY. Don K. Price. Louisiana State University Press, Highland Road, Baton Rouge, Louisiana 70893. 1983.

ARTICLES OF FAITH, ARTICLES OF PEACE: THE RELIGIOUS LIBERTY CLAUSES AND THE AMERICAN PUBLIC PHILOSOPHY. Brookings Institution, 1775 Massachusetts Avenue, Northwest, Washington, D.C. 20037. 1990.

THE BELIEVER AND THE POWERS THAT ARE: CASES, HISTORY, AND OTHER DATA BEARING ON THE RELATION OF RELIGION AND GOVERNMENT. John T. Noonan. MacMillan Publishing Company, Incorporated, 866 Third Avenue, New York, New York 10022. 1987.

BETWEEN GOD AND CAESAR: PRIESTS, SISTERS, AND POLITICAL OFFICE IN THE UNITED STATES. Paulist Press, 997 MacArthur Boulevard, Mahwah, New Jersey 07430. 1985.

CAESAR'S COIN: RELIGION AND POLITICS IN AMERICA. Richard P. McBrien. MacMillan Publishing Company, Incorporated, 866 Third Avenue, New York, New York 10022. 1987.

CHURCH AND STATE IN THE UNITED STATES. Revised Edition. Anson P. Stokes. Harper and Row, 10 East Fifty-third Street, New York, New York 10022. 1964.

CHURCH, STATE, AND AMERICAN CULTURE. University of North Carolina, Chapel Hill, North Carolina 27599. 1985.

CHURCH, STATE, AND EDUCATION. University of North Carolina, Chapel Hill, North Carolina 27599. 1985.

CHURCH, STATE, AND FREEDOM. Revised Edition. Leo Pfeffer. Beacon Press, 25 Beacon Street, Boston, Massachusetts 02108. 1967.

CHURCH, STATE, AND PUBLIC POLICY: THE NEW SHAPE OF THE CHURCH-STATE DEBATE. Jay Mechling. American Enterprise Institute for Public Policy Research, 1150 Seventeenth Street, Northwest, Washington, D.C. 20036. 1978.

CHURCH-STATE RELATIONSHIPS IN AMERICA. Gerald V. Bradley. Greenwood Publishing Group, Incorporated, 88 Post Road West, P.O. Box 5007, Westport, Connecticut 06881. 1987.

CONSTITUTIONAL ISSUES IN THE CASE OF REV. MOON: AMICUS BRIEFS PRESENTED TO THE UNITED STATES SUPREME COURT. Edwin Mellen Press, P.O. Box 450, Lewiston, New York 14029. 1984.

ECUMENICAL PERSPECTIVES ON CHURCH AND STATE: PROTESTANT, CATHOLIC, AND JEWISH. Jay Mechling, Editor. J.M. Dawson Institute of Church-State Studies, Baylor University, Waco, Texas 76798. 1988.

EQUAL SEPARATION: UNDERSTANDING THE RELIGION CLAUSES OF THE FIRST AMENDMENT. Paul J. Weber. Greenwood Publishing Group, Incorporated, 88 Post Road West, P.O. Box 5007, Westport, Connecticut 06881. 1990.

FREEDOM AND FAITH: THE IMPACT OF LAW ON RELIGIOUS LIBERTY. Christian Legal Society. Crossway Books, Good News Publications, 9825 West Roosevelt Road, Westchester, Illinois 60154. 1982.

PASTOR, CHURCH AND LAW. Richard R. Hammar. Gospel Publishing House, 1445 Boonville Avenue, Springfield, Missouri 65802. 1983.

PRIVATE CHURCHES AND PUBLIC MONEY: CHURCH-GOVERNMENT FISCAL RELATIONS. Paul J. Weber. Greenwood Publishing Group, Incorporated, 88 Post Road West, P.O. Box 5007, Westport, Connecticut 06881. 1981.

PUBLIC VIRTUE: LAW AND THE SOCIAL CHARACTER OF RELIGION. Christopher F. Mooney. University of Notre Dame Press, Notre Dame, Indiana 46556. 1986.

RELIGION AND POLITICS: THE INTENTIONS OF THE AUTHORS OF THE FIRST AMENDMENT. Michael J. Malbin. American Enterprise Institute for Public Policy Research, 1150 Seventeenth Street, Northwest, Washington, D.C. 20036. 1978.

RELIGION AND THE CONSTITUTION. Paul G. Kauper. Louisiana State University Press, Highland Road, Baton Rouge, Louisiana 70893. 1964.

RELIGION AND THE STATE: ESSAYS IN HONOR OF LEO PFEFFER. Baylor University Press, P.O. Box 7363, Waco, Texas 76798. 1985.

RELIGION, MORALITY, AND THE LAW. New York University Press, 70 Washington Square, South, New York, New York 10012. 1988.

RELIGION, THE COURTS, AND PUBLIC POLICY. Robert F. Drinan. McGraw-Hill Publishing Company, 1221 Avenue of the Americas, New York, New York 10020. 1963.

RELIGION, THE STATE, AND EDUCATION. James E. Wood, Editor. Baylor University, Institute on Church-State Studies, Waco, Texas 76798.

RELIGIOUS FREEDOM IN AMERICA. Charles C. Haynes. American United Research Foundation in Celebration of the Bicentennial Observances of the United States Constitution and Bill of Rights, 8120 Fenton Street, Silver Spring, Maryland 20910. 1986.

RELIGIOUS LIBERTY UNDER THE FREE EXERCISE CLAUSE. Office of Legal Policy, U.S. Department of Justice. Superintendent of Documents, United States Government Printing Office, Washington, D.C. 20402. 1988.

SEPARATION OF CHURCH AND STATE: GUARANTOR OF RELIGIOUS FREEDOM. Robert L. Maddox. Crossroad Publishing Company, 370 Lexington Avenue, New York, New York 10017. 1987.

THE UNEASY ALLIANCE: RELIGION, REFUGEE WORK, AND U.S. FOREIGN POLICY. J. Bruce Nichols. Oxford University Press, 200 Madison Avenue, New York, New York 10016. 1988.

THE WALL BETWEEN CHURCH AND STATE. Dallin H. Oaks, Editor. University of Chicago Press, 5801 Ellis Avenue, Chicago, Illinois 60637. 1963.

THE WALL OF SEPARATION: THE CONSTITUTIONAL POLITICS OF CHURCH AND STATE. Frank J. Sorauf. Princeton University Press, P.O. Box 190, Princeton, New Jersey 08544. 1976.

WE HOLD THESE TRUTHS: CATHOLIC REFLECTIONS ON THE AMERICAN PROPOSITION. John Courtney Murray. Sheed and Ward, Eastview Editions, P.O. Box 783, Westfield, New Jersey 07091. 1960.

LAW REVIEWS AND PERIODICALS

CHRISTIAN LEGAL SOCIETY QUARTERLY. P.O. Box 1492, Merrifield, Virginia 22116.

JOURNAL FOR THE SCIENTIFIC STUDY OF RELIGION. Society for the Scientific Study of Religion, The Catholic University of America, Marist Hall, Room 108, Washington, D.C. 20064. Quarterly.

JOURNAL OF CHURCH AND STATE. Baylor University, Box 380, Waco, Texas 76798. Triannually.

NEWSLETTERS AND NEWSPAPERS

ADL LAW REPORT. Anti-Defamation League of B'nai Brith, 823 United Nations Plaza, New York, New York 10017. Irregular.

THE RELIGION AND SOCIETY REPORT. Rockford Institute Center on Religion and Society, 934 North Main Street, Rockford, Illinois 61103. Monthly.

RELIGIOUS FREEDOM REPORTER. Center for Law and Religious Freedom, P.O. Box 505, Buies Creek, North Carolina 27506. Monthly.

BIBLIOGRAPHIES

CHURCH AND STATE IN AMERICA: A BIBLIOGRAPHICAL GUIDE. John F. Wilson, Editor. Greenwood Publishing Group, Incorporated, 88 Post Road West, P.O. Box 5007, Westport, Connecticut 06881. 1987.

ASSOCIATIONS AND PROFESSIONAL SOCIETIES

AMERICANS UNITED FOR SEPARATION OF CHURCH AND STATE. 8120 Fenton Street, Silver Spring, Maryland 20910. (301) 589-3707.

CHRISTIAN LAW ASSOCIATION. P.O. Box 30, Conneaut, Ohio 44030. (216) 599-8900.

CHRISTIAN LEGAL SOCIETY. P.O. Box 1492, Merrifield, Virginia 22116. (703) 642-1070.

COALITION FOR RELIGIOUS FREEDOM. 515 Wythe Street, Alexandria, Virginia 22314. (703) 684-9010.

FREEDOM FROM RELIGION FOUNDATION. P.O. Box 750, Madison, Wisconsin 53701. (608) 256-8900.

NATIONAL LEAGUE FOR SEPARATION OF CHURCH AND STATE. P.O. Box 2832, San Diego, California 92112. (619) 239-9043.

RESEARCH CENTERS, INSTITUTES, CLEARINGHOUSES

CENTER FOR LAW AND RELIGIOUS FREEDOM. 4208 Evergreen Lane, Annandale, Virginia 22003. (703) 642-1070.

CENTER FOR RELIGION, ETHICS AND SOCIAL POLICY. Anabel Taylor Hall, Cornell University, Ithaca, New York 14853. (607) 255-6486.

INSTITUTE ON RELIGION AND PUBLIC LIFE. 156 Fifth Avenue, Suite 400, New York, New York 10010. (212) 627-2288.

J.M. DAWSON INSTITUTE OF CHURCH-STATE STUDIES. Baylor University, B.U. Box 7308, Waco, Texas 76798. (817) 755-1510.

ROCKFORD INSTITUTE CENTER ON RELIGION AND SOCIETY. 934 North Main Street, Rockford, Illinois 61103. (815) 964-5811.

RUTHERFORD INSTITUTE. P.O. Box 7482, Charlottesville, Virginia 22906. (804) 978-3888.

THOMAS JEFFERSON INSTITUTE FOR THE STUDY OF RELIGIOUS FREEDOM. P.O. Box 1777, Fredricksburg, Virginia 22402. (703) 373-2370.

OTHER SOURCES

CHURCH, STATE, AND POLITICS: FINAL REPORT OF THE 1981 CHIEF JUSTICE EARL WARREN CONFERENCE ON ADVOCACY IN THE UNITED STATES. John Wesley Baker, A.E. Dick Howard, and Thomas S. Derr. Roscoe Pound-American Trial Lawyers Foundation, 1050 Thirty-first Street, Northwest, Washington, D.C. 20007. 1981.

CIRCUIT COURTS OF APPEAL (UNITED STATES)

See also: ADMINISTRATIVE OFFICE OF THE UNITED STATES COURTS; COURTS; FEDERAL COURTS

STATUTES, CODES, STANDARDS, UNIFORM LAWS

FEDERAL CIVIL PROCEDURE AND RULES. West Publishing Company, P.O. Box 64526, 50 West Kellogg Boulevard, St. Paul, Minnesota 55164-0526. Annual.

FEDERAL LOCAL COURT RULES FOR CIVIL AND ADMIRALTY PROCEEDINGS. Pike and Fischer, Incorporated, Callaghan and Company, 155 Pfingsten Road, Deerfield, Illinois 60015. 1972- .

FEDERAL PROCEDURE RULES SERVICE. Lawyers Cooperative Publishing Company, Aqueduct Building, Rochester, New York 14694. Annual.

JUDICIARY AND JUDICIAL PROCEDURE, FEDERAL RULES OF CIVIL PROCEDURE, FEDERAL RULES OF APPELLATE PROCEDURE AND FEDERAL COURT RULES. United States Code, Title 28 and Title 28 Appendices. Superintendent of Documents, United States Government Printing Office, Washington, D.C. 20402. Annual Supplements.

JUDICIARY AND JUDICIAL PROCEDURE, FEDERAL RULES OF CIVIL PROCEDURE, FEDERAL RULES OF APPELLATE PROCEDURE AND FEDERAL COURT RULES. United States Code Annotated, Title 28 and Title 28 Appendices. West Publishing Company, 50 West Kellogg Boulevard, St. Paul, Minnesota 55164. Annual Supplements.

JUDICIARY AND JUDICIAL PROCEDURE, FEDERAL RULES OF CIVIL PROCEDURE, FEDERAL RULES OF APPELLATE PROCEDURE AND FEDERAL COURT RULES. United States Code Service, Title 28 and Court Rules Volumes. Lawyers Cooperative Publishing Company, Aqueduct Building, Rochester, New York 14694. Annual Supplements.

MOORE'S FEDERAL PRACTICE: RULES PAMPHLET. Matthew Bender and Company, Incorporated, 11 Penn Plaza, New York, New York 10001. Annual.

LOOSELEAF SERVICES AND REPORTERS

FEDERAL REPORTER: CASES ARGUED AND DETERMINED IN THE UNITED STATES COURTS OF APPEALS. West Publishing Company, 50 West Kellogg Boulevard, St. Paul, Minnesota 55164. 1891- .

HANDBOOKS, MANUALS, FORMBOOKS

APPEALS TO THE ELEVENTH CIRCUIT MANUAL. Larry M. Roth and George K. Rahdert. Butterworth Legal Publishers, 90 Stiles Road, Salem, New Hampshire 03079. 1984- . (Periodic Supplements).

APPEALS TO THE FIFTH CIRCUIT MANUAL. George K. Rahdert and Larry M. Roth. Butterworth Legal Publishers, 90 Stiles Road, Salem, New Hampshire 03079. 1977- . (Periodic Supplements).

APPEALS TO THE THIRD CIRCUIT. Ellen Wertheimer. Butterworth Legal Publishers, 90 Stiles Road, Salem, New Hampshire 03079. 1986- . (Periodic Supplements).

D.C. FEDERAL COURTS HANDBOOK. Prentice-Hall Law and Business, Route 9W, Englewood Cliffs, New Jersey 07632. 1988.

GUIDE TO THE FEDERAL COURTS: AN INTRODUCTION TO THE FEDERAL COURTS AND THEIR OPERATION (INCLUDES EXPLANATION OF HOW A CASE IS LITIGATED). Want Publishing Company, 1511 K Street, Northwest, Washington, D.C. 20005. 1982.

PRACTICING BEFORE THE COURT OF APPEALS FOR THE FEDERAL CIRCUIT. Donald R. Dunner, Chairman. Practising Law Institute, 810 Seventh Avenue, New York, New York 10019. 1985.

CIRCUIT COURTS OF APPEAL (UNITED STATES)

TEXTBOOKS AND GENERAL WORKS

A COURT DIVIDED: THE FIFTH CIRCUIT COURT OF APPEALS AND THE POLITICS OF JUDICIAL REFORM. Deborah J. Barrow. Yale University Press, 302 Temple Street, New Haven, Connecticut 06520. 1988.

THE FIRST DECADE OF THE CIRCUIT COURT EXECUTIVE: AN EVALUATION. John W. Macy. Federal Judicial Center, Superintendent of Documents, United States Government Printing Office, Washington, D.C. 20402.

ANNUALS AND SURVEYS

ADMINISTERING THE FEDERAL JUDICIAL CIRCUITS: A SURVEY OF CHIEF JUDGES' APPROACHES AND PROCEDURES. Russell R. Wheeler and Charles W. Nihan. Federal Judicial Center, Dolley Madison House, 1520 H Street, Northwest, Washington, D.C. 20005. 1982.

REPORT OF THE PROCEEDINGS OF THE JUDICIAL CONFERENCE OF THE UNITED STATES. Administrative Office of the United States Courts. Superintendent of Documents, United States Government Printing Office, Washington, D.C. 20402. Annual.

NEWSLETTERS AND NEWSPAPERS

D.C. COURT REVIEW. Barclay's Law Publishers, 400 Oyster Point Boulevard, Suite 500, South San Francisco, California 94080. Biweekly.

EIGHTH CIRCUIT REVIEW. Barclay's Law Publishers, 400 Oyster Point Boulevard, Suite 500, South San Francisco, California 94080. Biweekly.

FIFTH CIRCUIT REPORTER. West Publishing Company, 50 West Kellogg Boulevard, St. Paul, Minnesota 55164. Monthly.

FOURTH CIRCUIT REPORT. Barclay's Law Publishers, 400 Oyster Point Boulevard, Suite 500, South San Francisco, California 94080. Biweekly.

NINTH CIRCUIT REVIEW. Barclay's Law Publishers, 400 Oyster Point Boulevard, Suite 500, South San Francisco, California 94080. Biweekly.

NINTH CIRCUIT UPDATE. Judicial Update, 559 Douglas Street, San Francisco, California 94114. Weekly.

SECOND CIRCUIT DIGEST. Federal Bar Council, 145 East Forty-ninth Street, New York, New York 10017. Monthly.

SECOND CIRCUIT REVIEW. Barclay's Law Publishers, 400 Oyster Point Boulevard, Suite 500, South San Francisco, California 94080. Biweekly.

SEVENTH CIRCUIT REVIEW. Barclay's Law Publishers, 400 Oyster Point Boulevard, Suite 500, South San Francisco, California 94080. Biweekly.

SIXTH CIRCUIT REVIEW. Barclay's Law Publishers, 400 Oyster Point Boulevard, Suite 500, South San Francisco, California 94080. Biweekly.

STARE DECISIS FOR THE SECOND CIRCUIT. Stare Decisis, P.O. Box 368, Cassville, New York 13318. Weekly.

TENTH CIRCUIT REVIEW. Barclay's Law Publishers, 400 Oyster Point Boulevard, Suite 500, South San Francisco, California 94080. Biweekly.

DIRECTORIES

THE AMERICAN BENCH: JUDGES OF THE NATION. Reginald Bishop Forster and Associates, 3287 Ramos Circle, Sacramento, California 95827. Biennial.

FEDERAL JUDICIARY ALMANAC. Stuart Dornette and Robert R. Cross. John Wiley and Sons, Incorporated, 605 Third Avenue, New York, New York 10158. 1986.

UNITED STATES COURT DIRECTORY. Administrative Office of the United States Courts. Superintendent of Documents, United States Government Printing Office, Washington, D.C. 20402. Semiannual.

WANT'S FEDERAL-STATE COURT DIRECTORY. Want Publishing Company, 1511 K Street, Northwest, Washington, D.C. 20005. Annual.

BIOGRAPHICAL SOURCES

ALMANAC OF THE FEDERAL JUDICIARY: PROFILES OF ALL ACTIVE UNITED STATES DISTRICT JUDGES. Lawletters, Incorporated, 332 South Michigan Avenue, Suite 1460, Chicago, Illinois 60604. Semiannual.

BIOGRAPHICAL DICTIONARY OF THE FEDERAL JUDICIARY. Harold Chase, Samuel Krislov, Keith O. Boyum and Jerry N. Clark. Gale Research, Incorporated, 835 Penobscot Building, Detroit, Michigan 48226. 1976. (Retrospective).

ASSOCIATIONS AND PROFESSIONAL SOCIETIES

FEDERAL COURT CLERKS ASSOCIATION. c/o Candice Clark Quinn, 120 Oriole Lane, La Plata, Maryland 20646.

RESEARCH CENTERS, INSTITUTES, CLEARINGHOUSES

ADMINISTRATIVE OFFICE OF THE UNITED STATES COURTS LIBRARY. 811 Vermont Avenue, Northwest, Washington, D.C. 20544. (202) 633-6314.

AMERICAN JUDICATIVE SOCIETY. 25 East Washington, Chicago, Illinois 60602. (312) 558-6900.

FEDERAL JUDICIAL CENTER LIBRARY. Dolley Madison House, 1520 H Street, Northwest, Washington, D.C. 20005. (202) 633-6011.

ONLINE DATABASES

LEXIS, GENERAL FEDERAL LIBRARY. Mead Data Central, 9393 Springboro Pike, P.O. Box 933, Dayton, Ohio 45401.

WESTLAW, FEDERAL DATABASES. West Publishing Company, P.O. Box 64526, 50 West Kellogg Boulevard, St. Paul, Minnesota 55164-0526.

CITIZENS AND CITIZENSHIP
See also: EMIGRATION AND IMMIGRATION; IMMIGRATION AND NATURALIZATION SERVICE

STATUTES, CODES, STANDARDS, UNIFORM LAWS

1986 IMMIGRATION AND NATIONALITY ACTS. National Immigration Project of the National Lawyers Guild. Clark Boardman Company, Limited, 435 Hudson Street, New York 10014. 1987.

LOOSELEAF SERVICES AND REPORTERS

PATEL'S DIGEST OF ADMINISTRATIVE DECISIONS UNDER IMMIGRATION AND NATIONALITY LAWS. Second Edition. P. J. Patel. Clark Boardman Company, Limited, 435 Hudson Street, New York, New York 10014. 1982- .

HANDBOOKS, MANUALS, FORMBOOKS

BASIC GUIDE TO NATURALIZATION AND CITIZENSHIP. Immigration and Naturalization Service. Superintendent of Documents, United States Government Printing Office, Washington, D.C. 20402. 1990.

CITIZEN COMMITTEES: A GUIDE TO THEIR USE IN LOCAL GOVERNMENT. Joseph Lee Rodgers. Ballinger Division, HarperCollins Publishers, 10 East Fifty-third Street, New York, New York 10022. 1977.

HOW TO BECOME A UNITED STATES CITIZEN: A STEP BY STEP GUIDEBOOK FOR SELF-INSTRUCTION. Second Edition. Sally A. Abel. Nolo Press, 950 Park Street, Berkeley, California 94710. 1986.

PRACTICE FOR UNITED STATES CITIZENSHIP: EVERYTHING YOU NEED TO KNOW ABOUT THE TEST. Second Edition. Carlos F. Paz. Arco Publishing, Incorporated, Division of Prentice-Hall, Incorporated, 15 Columbus Circle, New York, New York 10023. 1981.

REFERENCE MANUAL FOR CITIZENSHIP INSTRUCTORS. Immigration and Naturalization Service. Superintendent of Documents, United States Government Printing Office, Washington, D.C. 20402. 1987.

TEXTBOOKS AND GENERAL WORKS

THE ALIEN AND THE ASIATIC IN AMERICAN LAW. Milton Rodvas Konvitz. Johnson Reprint Corporation, 111 Fifth Avenue, New York, New York 10003. 1946.

AND JUSTICE FOR ALL: AN ORAL HISTORY OF THE JAPANESE AMERICAN DETENTION CAMPS. John Tateishi. Random House, Incorporated, 201 East Fiftieth Street, New York, New York 10022. 1984.

BELONGING TO AMERICA: EQUAL CITIZENSHIP AND THE CONSTITUTION. Kenneth L. Karst. Yale University Press, 302 Temple Street, New Haven, Connecticut 06520. 1989.

CITIZENSHIP AND THE AMERICAN EMPIRE: NOTES ON THE LEGISLATIVE HISTORY OF THE UNITED STATES CITIZENSHIP OF PUERTO RICANS. Jose A. Cabranes. Yale University Press, 302 Temple Street, New Haven, Connecticut 06520. 1979.

CITIZENSHIP OF THE UNITED STATES. Frederick Van Dyne. Fred B. Rothman and Company, 10368 West Centennial Road, Littleton, Colorado 80127. 1980.

FOR THE PEOPLE: U.S. CITIZENSHIP EDUCATION AND NATURALIZATION INFORMATION. Immigration and Naturalization Service. Superintendent of Documents, United States Government Printing Office, Washington, D.C. 20402. 1988.

FREEDOM AND THE PUBLIC: PUBLIC AND PRIVATE MORALITY IN AMERICA. Donald Meiklejohn. Books on Demand, 300 North Zeeb Road, Ann Arbor, Michigan 48106-1346. 1965.

IMMIGRATION AND THE POLITICS OF CITIZENSHIP IN EUROPE AND NORTH AMERICA. University Press of America, 4720 Boston Way, Lanham, Maryland 20706. 1989.

NATIVE AMERICAN ALIENS: RENUNCIATION OF CITIZENSHIP BY JAPANESE AMERICANS DURING WORLD WAR II. Donald D. Collins. Greenwood Publishing Group, Incorporated, 88 Post Road West, P.O. Box 5007, Westport, Connecticut 06881. 1985.

OBLIGATIONS: ESSAYS ON DISOBEDIENCE, WAR AND CITIZENSHIP. Michael Walzer. Harvard University Press, 79 Garden Street, Cambridge, Massachusetts 02138. 1982.

OPEN BORDERS? CLOSED SOCIETIES?: THE ETHICAL AND POLITICAL ISSUES. Mark Gibney, Editor. Greenwood Publishing Group, Incorporated, 88 Post Road West, P.O. Box 5007, Westport, Connecticut 06881. 1988.

STRONG DEMOCRACY: PARTICIPATORY POLITICS FOR A NEW AGE. Benjamin R. Barber. University of California Press, 2120 Berkeley Way, Berkeley, California 94720. 1984.

A TREATISE ON THE LAW OF CITIZENSHIP IN THE UNITED STATES. Prentise Webster. Fred B. Rothman and Company, 10368 West Centennial Road, Littleton, Colorado 80127. 1980.

NEWSLETTERS AND NEWSPAPERS

AMERICAN CITIZENSHIP. American Citizenship Center, Box 11000, Oklahoma City, Oklahoma 73136. Monthly.

CITIZENSHIP EDUCATION NEWS. Council for the Advancement of Citizenship, 1724 Massachusetts Avenue, Northwest, Suite 300, Washington, D.C. 20036. Quarterly.

CLOSE UP CHRONICLE. Close Up Foundation, Director of Development, 1235 Jefferson Davis Highway, Arlington, Virginia 22202. Quarterly.

BIBLIOGRAPHIES

IMMIGRATION, NATURALIZATION AND CITIZENSHIP. (SUBJECT BIBLIOGRAPHY SB-069). Superintendent of Documents, United States Government Printing Office, Division of Public Documents, Washington, D.C. 20402. 1981.

CITIZENS AND CITIZENSHIP

ASSOCIATIONS AND PROFESSIONAL SOCIETIES

ASSOCIATION FOR PUBLIC JUSTICE. 806 Fifteenth Street, Northwest, Suite 440, Washington, D.C. 20005. (202) 737-2110.

CLOSE UP FOUNDATION. Director of Development, 1235 Jefferson Davis Highway, Arlington, Virginia 22202. (703) 892-5400.

NATIONAL CONFERENCE ON CITIZENSHIP. Bank of Florida, Suite 5048, 3550 Biscayne Boulevard, Miami, Florida 33137. (305) 576-4310.

NATIONAL INSTITUTE FOR CITIZEN EDUCATION IN THE LAW. 25 E Street, Northwest, Suite 400, Washington, D.C. 20001. (202) 662-9620.

RESEARCH CENTERS, INSTITUTES, CLEARINGHOUSES

AMERICAN CITIZENSHIP CENTER. P.O. Box 11100, Oklahoma City, Oklahoma 73136. (405) 425-5040.

CENTER FOR THE STUDY OF CITIZENSHIP. Syracuse University, 216 Maxwell Hall, Syracuse, New York 13244. (315) 443-2126.

COUNCIL FOR THE ADVANCEMENT OF CITIZENSHIP. 1724 Massachusetts Avenue, Northwest, Suite 300, Washington, D.C. 20036. (202) 857-0580.

STATISTICS SOURCES

UNITED STATES DEPARTMENT OF COMMERCE. Bureau of the Census, Fourteenth Street between Constitution Avenue and East Street, Northwest, Washington, D.C. 20230. 1980.

UNITED STATES DEPARTMENT OF JUSTICE. Immigration and Naturalization Service, 425 I Street, Northwest, Washington, D.C. 20536.

CITY GOVERNMENT
See: LOCAL GOVERNMENT

CITY PLANNING
See: HISTORIC PRESERVATION; ZONING AND PLANNING

CIVIL LAW
See also: ROMAN LAW

TEXTBOOKS AND GENERAL WORKS

THE CIVIL LAW IN ITS NATURAL ORDER. Jean Domat. Fred B. Rothman and Company, 10368 West Centennial Road, Littleton, Colorado 80127. 1981. (Reprint).

THE CIVIL LAW: INCLUDING THE TWELVE TABLES, THE INSTITUTES OF GAIUS, THE RULES OF ULPIAN, THE OPINIONS OF PAULUS, THE ENACTMENTS OF JUSTINIAN, AND THE CONSTITUTIONS OF LEO. Samuel P. Scott, Editor. AMS Press, Incorporated, 56 East Thirteenth Street, New York, New York 10003. Reprint of 1932 Edition.

THE CIVIL LAW SYSTEM: AN INTRODUCTION TO THE COMPARATIVE STUDY OF LAW. Second Edition. Arthur T. von Mehren and James R. Gordley. Little, Brown and Company, 34 Beacon Street, Boston, Massachusetts 02108. 1977.

THE CIVIL LAW TRADITION: AN INTRODUCTION TO THE LEGAL SYSTEMS OF WESTERN EUROPE AND LATIN AMERICA. Second Edition. John H. Merryman. Stanford University Press, Stanford, California 94305-2235. 1985.

CONSCIENCE, OBLIGATION, AND THE LAW: THE MORAL BINDING POWER OF THE CIVIL LAW. David C. Bayne. Loyola University Press, 3441 North Ashland Avenue, Chicago, Illinois 60657. 1966.

A HISTORY OF THE LOUISIANA CIVIL CODE: THE FORMATIVE YEARS, 1803-1839. Richard H. Kilbourne. Louisiana State University Law School, Publications Institute, Baton Rouge, Louisiana 70803. 1987.

AN INTRODUCTION TO THE LOUISIANA CIVIL LAW SYSTEM. Fourth Edition. Symeon Symeonides. Louisiana State University Law School, Publications Institute, Baton Rouge, Louisiana 70803. 1988.

THE MAKING OF THE CIVIL LAW. Alan Watson. Harvard University Press, 79 Garden Street, Cambridge, Massachusetts 02138. 1981.

MAXIMS OF THE CIVIL LAW: ESSAYS IN THE EVOLUTION OF LAW. Walter S. Johnson. W. W. Gaunt and Sons, Inc., 3011 Gulf Drive, Holmes Beach, Florida 34217-2199. 1970. (Reprint 1973).

POLITICS AND THE LAW IN LATE NINETEENTH-CENTURY GERMANY: THE ORIGINS OF THE CIVIL CODE. Michael John. Oxford University Press, 200 Madison Avenue, New York, New York 10016. 1989.

SOVIET CIVIL LAW. O.S. Ioffe. Kluwer Academic Publishers, 101 Philip Drive, Assinippi Park, Norwell, Massachusetts 02061. 1988.

STUDIES IN THE CIVIL LAW AND ITS RELATIONS TO THE LAW OF ENGLAND AND AMERICA. William W. Howe. Fred B. Rothman and Company, 10368 West Centennial Road, Littleton, Colorado 80127. 1980.

RESEARCH CENTERS, INSTITUTES, CLEARINGHOUSES

CENTER OF CIVIL LAW STUDIES. Louisiana State University, Paul M. Hebert Law Center, Room 382, Baton Rouge, Louisiana 70803. (504) 388-1126.

INSTITUTE OF COMPARATIVE LAW. McGill University, 3674 Peel Street, Montreal, PQ, Canada H3A 1X1. (514) 398-6646.

INTERNATIONAL COMMISSION ON CIVIL STATUS. Faculte de Droit, Place d'Athenes, F-67084 Strasbourg Cedex, France. 88 414200.

LOUISIANA STATE LAW INSTITUTE. Louisiana State University, Paul M. Hebert Law Center, Room 382, Baton Rouge, Louisiana 70803. (504) 342-6360.

QUEBEC RESEARCH CENTRE FOR PRIVATE AND COMPARATIVE LAW. McGill University, 3647 Peel Street, Montreal, PQ, Canada H3A 1X1. (514) 398-3546.

CIVIL PROCEDURE

See also: ACTIONS AND DEFENSES; APPELLATE PROCEDURE; CLASS ACTIONS; JUDGMENTS; JURISDICTION; LEGAL FORMS; REMEDIES; TRIAL PRACTICE

STATUTES, CODES, STANDARDS, UNIFORM LAWS

FEDERAL CIVIL PROCEDURE AND RULES. West Publishing Company, P.O. Box 64526, 50 West Kellogg Boulevard, St. Paul, Minnesota 55164-0526. Annual.

FEDERAL PROCEDURE RULES SERVICE. Lawyers Cooperative Publishing Company, Aqueduct Building, Rochester, New York 14694. Annual.

JUDICIARY AND JUDICIAL PROCEDURE, FEDERAL RULES OF CIVIL PROCEDURE, FEDERAL RULES OF APPELLATE PROCEDURE AND FEDERAL COURT RULES. United States Code, Title 28 and Title 28 Appendices. Superintendent of Documents, United States Government Printing Office, Washington, D.C. 20402. Annual Supplements.

JUDICIARY AND JUDICIAL PROCEDURE, FEDERAL RULES OF CIVIL PROCEDURE, FEDERAL RULES OF APPELLATE PROCEDURE AND FEDERAL COURT RULES. United States Code Annotated, Title 28 and Title 28 Appendices. West Publishing Company, P.O. Box 64526, 50 West Kellogg Boulevard, St. Paul, Minnesota 55164-0526. Annual Supplements.

JUDICIARY AND JUDICIAL PROCEDURE, FEDERAL RULES OF CIVIL PROCEDURE, FEDERAL RULES OF APPELLATE PROCEDURE AND FEDERAL COURT RULES. United States Code Service, Title 28 and Court Rules Volumes. Lawyers Cooperative Publishing Company, Aqueduct Building, Rochester, New York 14694. Annual Supplements.

LOOSELEAF SERVICES AND REPORTERS

BNA CIVIL TRIAL MANUAL. Bureau of National Affairs, 1231 Twenty-fifth Street, Northwest, Washington, D.C. 20037. 1985- . (Bi-weekly Supplements).

FEDERAL LITIGATION GUIDE. Matthew Bender and Company, Incorporated, 11 Penn Plaza, New York, New York 10001. 1985- . (Periodic Supplements).

FEDERAL RULES DECISIONS. West Publishing Company, P.O. Box 64526, 50 West Kellogg Boulevard, St. Paul, Minnesota 55164-0526. 1938- .

FEDERAL RULES OF CIVIL PROCEDURE. Thomas A. Coyle. Clark Boardman Company, Limited, 435 Hudson Street, New York, New York 10014. 1982- . (Annual Supplements).

FEDERAL RULES SERVICE, THIRD SERIES. Callaghan and Company, 155 Pfingsten Road, Deerfield, Illinois 60015. 1985- .

JURISDICTION AND FORUM SELECTION. Robert Casad. Callaghan and Company, 155 Pfingsten Road, Deerfield, Illinois 60015. 1988- . (Annual Supplements).

MANUAL FOR COMPLEX LITIGATION. Federal Judicial Center. Clark Boardman Company, Limited, 435 Hudson Street, New York, New York 10014. 1982- . (Periodic Supplements).

MOORE'S FEDERAL PRACTICE. Second Edition. James William Moore and others. Matthew Bender and Company, Incorporated, 11 Penn Plaza, New York, New York 10001. 1948- . (Quarterly Supplements).

MOORE'S MANUAL - FEDERAL PRACTICE AND PROCEDURE. James William Moore and others. Matthew Bender and Company, Incorporated, 11 Penn Plaza, New York, New York 10001. 1962- . (Annual Supplements).

MOORE'S MANUAL - FORMS. James William Moore and others. Matthew Bender and Company, Incorporated, 11 Penn Plaza, New York, New York 10001. 1964- . (Periodic Supplements).

PRACTICE BEFORE FEDERAL MAGISTRATES. Kent Sinclair, Jr. Matthew Bender and Company, Incorporated, 11 Penn Plaza, New York, New York 10001. 1984- . (Periodic Supplements).

HANDBOOKS, MANUALS, FORMBOOKS

BENDER'S FEDERAL PRACTICE FORMS: ANNOTATIONS AND CROSS REFERENCES TO MOORE'S FEDERAL PRACTICE. Second Edition. Louis R. Frumer and Marvin Waxner. Matthew Bender and Company, Incorporated, 11 Penn Plaza, New York, New York 10001. 1951- . (Semiannual Supplements).

BENDER'S FEDERAL PRACTICE MANUAL. Second Edition. Irwin Hall and Marvin Waxner. Matthew Bender and Company, Incorporated, 11 Penn Plaza, New York, New York 10001. 1953- . (Annual Supplements).

BENDER'S FORMS FOR THE CIVIL PRACTICE. Louis L. Frumer and others. Matthew Bender and Company, Incorporated, 11 Penn Plaza, New York, New York 10001. 1963- . (Semiannual Supplements).

CIVIL TRIAL MANUAL II. Ralph C. McCullough II and James L. Underwood. American Law Institute-American Bar Association, Committee on Continuing Professional Education, 4025 Chestnut Street, Philadelphia, Pennsylvania 19104. 1980- . (Periodic Supplements).

FEDERAL CIVIL PROCEDURE. Edward I. Niles. Parker and Sons Publications, Incorporated, P.O. Box 60001, Los Angeles, California 90060. 1985- . (Annual Supplements).

FEDERAL LAWYER'S MANUAL. Roger A. Needham. Callaghan and Company, 155 Pfingsten Road, Deerfield, Illinois 60015. 1980- . (Annual Supplements).

FEDERAL PRACTICE MANUAL FOR LEGAL SERVICES ATTORNEYS. Michael R. Masinter, Arthur B. LaFrance, and Florence Wagman Roisman. National Clearinghouse for Legal Services, 407 South Dearborn, Chicago, Illinois 60605. 1989.

FEDERAL PROCEDURAL FORMS, LAWYER'S EDITION. Lawyers Cooperative Publishing Company, Aqueduct Building, Rochester, New York 14694. 1975- . (Periodic Supplements).

FEDERAL TRIAL HANDBOOK. Second Edition. Robert S. Hunter. Lawyers Cooperative Publishing Company, Aqueduct Building, Rochester, New York 14694. 1984.

NICHOLS CYCLOPEDIA OF FEDERAL PROCEDURE FORMS. Clark Asahel Nichols. Callaghan and Company, 155 Pfingsten Road, Deerfield, Illinois 60015. 1936- . (Annual Supplements).

UNDERSTANDING CIVIL PROCEDURE. Gene R. Shreve and Peter Raven-Hansen. Matthew Bender and Company, Incorporated, 11 Penn Plaza, New York, New York 10001. 1989.

WEST'S FEDERAL FORMS. Third Edition. West Publishing Company, P.O. Box 64526, 50 West Kellogg Boulevard, St. Paul, Minnesota 55164-0526. 1982-1983- . (Annual Supplements).

WEST'S FEDERAL PRACTICE MANUAL. Second Edition. Marlin M. Volz. West Publishing Company, P.O. Box 64526, 50 West Kellogg Boulevard, St. Paul, Minnesota 55164-0526. 1970- . (Annual Supplements).

TEXTBOOKS AND GENERAL WORKS

BASIC CIVIL PROCEDURE. Second Edition. Milton D. Green. Foundation Press, Incorporated, 615 Merrick Avenue, Westbury, New York 11590. 1979.

CIVIL PRACTICE AND LITIGATION IN FEDERAL AND STATE COURTS: RESOURCE MATERIALS. Sol Schreiber, Editor. American Law Institute-American Bar Association, Committee on Continuing Professional Education, 4025 Chestnut Street, Philadelphia, Pennsylvania 19104. 1987.

CIVIL PROCEDURE. Second Edition. Kevin M. Clermont. West Publishing Company, P.O. Box 64526, 50 West Kellogg Boulevard, St. Paul, Minnesota 55164-0526. 1987.

CIVIL PROCEDURE. (Hornbook Series). Fourth Edition. Jack H. Friedenthal, Mary Jay Kane and Arthur R. Miller. Herbert Legal Series, 2060 Huntington Drive, Number 4, San Marino, California 91108. 1988.

CIVIL PROCEDURE. Third Edition. Fleming James, Jr. and Geoffrey C. Hazard, Jr. Little, Brown, and Company, 34 Beacon Street, Boston, Massachusetts 02108. 1985.

CIVIL PROCEDURE: A MODERN APPROACH. Richard L. Marcus, Martin H. Redish and Edward F. Sherman. West Publishing Company, P.O. Box 64526, 50 West Kellogg Boulevard, St. Paul, Minnesota 55164-0526. 1989.

CIVIL PROCEDURE IN A NUTSHELL. Second Edition. West Publishing Company, P.O. Box 64526, 50 West Kellogg Boulevard, St. Paul, Minnesota 55164-0526. 1991.

COMPUTER-AIDED EXERCISES ON CIVIL PROCEDURE. Second Edition. Roger Park. West Publishing Company, P.O. Box 64526, 50 West Kellogg Boulevard, St. Paul, Minnesota 55164-0526. 1983.

CURRENT PROBLEMS IN FEDERAL CIVIL PRACTICE. Barry H. Garfinkel, Chairman. Practising Law Institute, 810 Seventh Avenue, New York, New York 10019. 1988.

CYCLOPEDIA OF FEDERAL PROCEDURE. Third Edition. Callaghan and Company, 155 Pfingsten Road, Deerfield, Illinois 60015. 1951- . (Annual Supplements).

FEDERAL CIVIL PRACTICE. Second Edition. Kent Sinclair. Practising Law Institute, 810 Seventh Avenue, New York, New York 10019. 1986.

FEDERAL PRACTICE AND PROCEDURE. Second Edition. Charles Alan Wright. West Publishing Company, P.O. Box 64526, 50 West Kellogg Boulevard, St. Paul, Minnesota 55164-0526. 1982- . (Annual Supplements).

FEDERAL PROCEDURE: A PROBLEM-SOLVING TEXTUAL ANALYSIS OF FEDERAL JUDICIAL AND ADMINISTRATIVE PROCEDURE. Lawyers Cooperative Publishing Company, Aqueduct Building, Rochester, New York 14694. 1981- . (Annual Supplements).

INTRODUCTION TO CIVIL LITIGATION. Second Edition. Mark I. Weinstein. West Publishing Company, P.O. Box 64526, 50 West Kellogg Boulevard, St. Paul, Minnesota 55164-0526. 1986.

JURISDICTION IN CIVIL ACTIONS: TERRITORIAL BASIS AND PROCESS LIMITATIONS ON JURISDICTION OF STATE AND FEDERAL COURTS. Second Edition. Robert C. Casad. Butterworth Legal Publishers, 90 Stiles Road, Salem, New Hampshire 03079. 1991.

JUSTICE FOR ALL: REDUCING COSTS AND DELAY IN CIVIL LITIGATION. Brookings Task Force on Civil Justice Reform. Brookings Institution, 1775 Massachusetts Avenue, Washington, D.C. 20036. 1989.

THE LAW OF FEDERAL COURTS HANDBOOK. Fourth Edition. Charles A. Wright. West Publishing Company, P.O. Box 64526, 50 West Kellogg Boulevard, St. Paul, Minnesota 55164-0526. 1983.

MOTIONS IN FEDERAL COURT, CIVIL PRACTICE. Shepard's/McGraw-Hill, P.O. Box 1235, Colorado Springs, Colorado 80901. 1982.

THE NEW AND PROPOSED FEDERAL RULES OF CIVIL PROCEDURE. Alvin K. Hellerstein, Melvin R. Goldman, Abraham D. Sofaer. Practising Law Institute, 810 Seventh Avenue, New York, New York 10019. 1984.

PREPARATION AND PURSUANCE OF CIVIL LITIGATION. Leon Rock. National Center for Paralegal Training, 1271 Avenue of the Americas, New York, New York 10020. 1983.

DIGESTS, INDEXES, ABSTRACTS, CITATORS

FEDERAL RULES DIGEST. Third Edition. Callaghan and Company, 155 Pfingsten Road, Deerfield, Illinois 60015. 1954- . (Supplemented).

COMPUTER-ASSISTED LEGAL INSTRUCTION

ANALYSIS OF A DIVERSITY CASE. Roger C. Park. Center for Computer-Assisted Instruction, 229 Nineteenth Avenue South, University of Minnesota, Minneapolis, Minnesota 55455. Computer program.

ANALYSIS OF A DIVERSITY JURISDICTION CASE. Roger C. Park and Douglas D. McFarland. Center for Computer-Assisted Instruction, 229 19th Avenue South, University of Minnesota, Minneapolis, Minnesota 55455. Machine-readable computer file.

BUFFALO CREEK: A GAME OF DISCOVERY. Owen M. Fiss, Thomas Glocer and Ronald F. Wright. Center for Computer-Assisted Instruction, 229 19th Avenue South, University of Minnesota, Minneapolis, Minnesota 55455. Machine-readable computer file.

CONEY ISLAND: A GAME OF DISCOVERY. Owen M. Fiss, Thomas Glocer, and Ronald F. Wright, Jr. Center for Computer-Assisted Instruction, 229 Nineteenth Avenue South, University of Minnesota, Minneapolis, Minnesota 55455. Computer program.

DEMURRERS AND JUDGMENTS ON THE PLEADINGS. Roger C. Park and Douglas D. McFarland. Center for Computer-Assisted Instruction, 229 19th Avenue South, University of Minnesota, Minneapolis, Minnesota 55455. Machine-readable computer file.

DIRECTED VERDICTS. Roger C. Park and Douglas D. McFarland. Center for Computer-Assisted Instruction, 229 Nineteenth Avenue South, University of Minnesota, Minneapolis, Minnesota 55455. Machine-readable computer file.

DRAFTING A COMPLAINT. Roger C. Park and Douglas D. McFarland. Center for Computer-Assisted Instruction, 229 Nineteenth Avenue South, University of Minnesota, Minneapolis, Minnesota 55455. Machine-readable computer file.

AN EXERCISE IN CIVIL PROCEDURE. William P. Kratzke. Center for Computer-Assisted Instruction, 229 Nineteenth Avenue South, University of Minnesota, Minneapolis, Minnesota 55455. Machine-readable computer file.

JURISDICTION AND VENUE. Roger C. Park and Douglas D. McFarland. Center for Computer-Assisted Instruction, 229 Nineteenth Avenue South, University of Minnesota, Minneapolis, Minnesota 55455. Machine-readable computer file.

MOTION SKILLS ILLUSTRATED. CLE Group, 274 Willow Road, Menlo Park, California 94025. Interactive videodisc.

MOTIONS TO DISMISS ON THE PLEADINGS. Roger C. Park. Center for Computer-Assisted Instruction, 229 Nineteenth Avenue South, University of Minnesota, Minneapolis, Minnesota 55455. Computer program.

A REVIEW OF JOINDER CONCEPTS. David S. Welkowitz. Center for Computer-Assisted Instruction, 229 Nineteenth Avenue South, University of Minnesota, Minneapolis, Minnesota 55455. Machine-readable computer file.

SUMMARY JUDGMENT. Roger C. Park and Douglas D. McFarland. Center for Computer-Assisted Instruction, 229 19th Avenue South, University of Minnesota, Minneapolis, Minnesota 55455. Machine-readable computer file.

SURVEY OF EVIDENCE -- CIVIL PROCEDURE VERSION. Roger C. Park and Douglas D. McFarland. Center for Computer-Assisted Instruction, 229 Nineteenth Avenue South, University of Minnesota, Minneapolis, Minnesota 55455. Machine-readable computer file.

WAIVER UNDER RULE 12. Roger C. Park and Douglas D. McFarland. Center for Computer-Assisted Instruction, 229 Nineteenth Avenue South, University of Minnesota, Minneapolis, Minnesota 55455. Machine-readable computer file.

CIVIL RIGHTS AND LIBERTIES
See also: CONSTITUTIONAL LAW; DISCRIMINATION, EDUCATION; DISCRIMINATION, EMPLOYMENT; DISCRIMINATION, HOUSING; DISCRIMINATION, RACE; DISCRIMINATION, SEX; DOUBLE JEOPARDY; HUMAN RIGHTS; JUSTICE DEPARTMENT; SEGREGATION AND INTEGRATION; SLAVERY

STATUTES, CODES, STANDARDS, UNIFORM LAWS

CIVIL RIGHTS ACT OF 1957, 1968 (AS AMENDED THROUGH THE END OF THE 96TH CONGRESS); VOTING RIGHTS ACT OF 1965 (AS AMENDED THROUGH THE END OF THE 96TH CONGRESS). Committee on the Judiciary, House of Representatives. Superintendent of Documents, United States Government Printing Office, Division of Public Documents, Washington, D.C. 20402. 1981.

INTERNATIONAL HUMAN RIGHTS INSTRUMENTS: A COMPILATION OF TREATIES, AGREEMENTS AND DECLARATIONS OF ESPECIAL INTEREST TO THE UNITED STATES. Second Edition. Hein and Company, 1285 Main Street, Buffalo, New York 14209. 1990.

LOOSELEAF SERVICES AND REPORTERS

CIVIL RIGHTS ACTIONS. Joseph G. Cook and John L. Sobieski. Matthew Bender and Company, Incorporated, 11 Penn Plaza, New York, New York 10001. 1983- . (Periodic Supplements).

GOVERNMENT DISCRIMINATION. James A. Kushner. Clark Boardman Company, Limited, 435 Hudson Street, New York, New York 10014. 1988- . (Annual Supplements).

POLICY GUIDE OF THE AMERICAN CIVIL LIBERTIES UNION. American Civil Liberties Union, 132 West Forty-third Street, New York, New York 10036. 1986- . (Periodic Supplements).

SECTION 1983 LITIGATION IN STATE COURTS. Steven H. Steinglass. Clark Boardman Company, Limited, 435 Hudson Street, New York, New York 10014. 1987- . (Annual Supplements).

STATE AND LOCAL GOVERNMENT CIVIL RIGHTS LIABILITY. Ivan E. Bodensteiner and Rosalie B. Levinson. Callaghan and Company, 155 Pfingsten Road, Deerfield, Illinois 60015. 1987- . (Annual Supplements).

HANDBOOKS, MANUALS, FORMBOOKS

CIVIL RIGHTS AND CIVIL LIBERTIES LITIGATION: THE LAW OF SECTION 1983. Second Edition. Sheldon Nahmod. McGraw-Hill Book Company, 1221 Avenue of the Americas, New York, New York 10020. 1986- . (Annual Supplements).

CIVIL RIGHTS LITIGATION: AN INVESTIGATION, PREPARATION AND TRIAL MANUAL. Andrew J. Ruzicho and Louis A. Jacobs. Anderson Publishing Company, 2035 Reading Road, Cincinnati, Ohio 45202. 1976.

CIVIL RIGHTS LITIGATION AND ATTORNEY FEES ANNUAL HANDBOOK. Frederic A. Strom. Clark Boardman Company, Limited, 435 Hudson Street, New York, New York 10014. 1985- . (Annual).

FEDERAL CIVIL RIGHTS LAWS: A SOURCEBOOK. Subcommittee on the Constitution of the Committee on the Judiciary. Superintendent of Documents, United States Government Printing Office, Division of Public Documents, Washington, D.C. 20402. 1984.

SECTION 1983 CIVIL RIGHTS LITIGATION 1985: DEVELOPMENTS, TRENDS, AND PROBLEMS: A COURSE HANDBOOK. Practising Law Institute, 810 Seventh Avenue, New York, New York 10019. 1985.

TEXTBOOKS AND GENERAL WORKS

THE AGE OF RIGHTS. Louis Henkin. Columbia University Press, 562 West One Hundred Thirteenth Street, New York, New York 10025. 1990.

THE ANTAGONISTS: HUGO BLACK, FELIX FRANKFURTER AND CIVIL LIBERTIES IN MODERN AMERICA. James F. Simon. Simon and Schuster, Incorporated, 1230 Avenue of the Americas, New York, New York 10020. 1989.

BEFORE THE CIVIL RIGHTS REVOLUTION: THE OLD COURT AND INDIVIDUAL RIGHTS. John Braeman. Greenwood Publishing Group, Incorporated, 88 Post Road West, P.O. Box 5007, Westport, Connecticut 06881. 1988.

BELONGING TO AMERICA: EQUAL CITIZENSHIP AND THE CONSTITUTION. Kenneth L. Karst. Yale University Press, 302 Temple Street, New Haven, Connecticut 06520. 1989.

BLACKS AND SOCIAL JUSTICE. Bernard R. Boxill. Rowman and Littlefield, 4720 Boston Way, Lanham, Maryland 20706. 1984.

A CENTURY OF CIVIL RIGHTS. Milton R. Konvitz. Greenwood Publishing Group, Incorporated, 88 Post Road West, P.O. Box 5007, Westport, Connecticut 06881. 1983.

CIVIL LIBERTIES AND AMERICAN DEMOCRACY. John Brigham. Congressional Quarterly Books, Incorporated, 1414 Twenty-second Street, Northwest, Washington, D.C. 20037. 1984.

CIVIL LIBERTIES UNDER THE CONSTITUTION. Fifth Edition. Glenn Abernathy. University of South Carolina Press, Columbia, South Carolina 29208. 1989.

THE CIVIL RIGHTS ERA: ORIGINS AND DEVELOPMENT OF NATIONAL POLICY, 1960-1972. Hugh Davis Graham. Oxford University Press, 200 Madison Avenue, New York, New York 10016. 1990.

THE CIVIL RIGHTS SOCIETY: THE SOCIAL CONSTRUCTION OF VICTIMS. Kristin Bumiller. Johns Hopkins University Press, 701 West Fortieth Street, Baltimore, Maryland 21211. 1988.

CIVIL RIGHTS, THE CONSTITUTION, AND CONGRESS. Earl M. Maltz. University of Press of Kansas, 329 Carruth, Lawrence, Kansas 66045.

CONFRONTING THE COLOR LINE: THE BROKEN PROMISE OF THE CIVIL RIGHTS MOVEMENT IN CHICAGO. Alan B. Anderson and George W. Pickering. University of Georgia Press, Terrell Hall, Athens, Georgia 30602. 1986.

THE CONSTITUTION AND AMERICAN LIFE. David P. Thelen. Cornell University Press, 124 Roberts Place, P.O. Box 350, Ithaca, New York 14850. 1988.

THE CONSTITUTIONAL BASES OF POLITICAL AND SOCIAL CHANGE IN THE UNITED STATES. Shlomo Slonim, Editor. Praeger Publishers, Greenwood Publishing Group, Incorporated, 88 Post Road West, P.O. Box 5007, Westport, Connecticut 06881. 1990.

CONSTITUTIONAL CIVIL LIBERTIES. C. Herman Pritchett. Prentice- Hall, Incorporated, 113 Sylvan Avenue, Englewood Cliffs, New Jersey 07632. 1984.

CONSTITUTIONAL CIVIL RIGHTS IN A NUTSHELL. Second Edition. Norman Vieira. West Publishing Company, P.O. Box 43526, 50 West Kellogg Boulevard, St. Paul, Minnesota 55164-0526. 1990.

CONTEMPORARY DEBATES ON CIVIL LIBERTIES: ENDURING CONSTITUTIONAL QUESTIONS. Glenn A. Phelps and Robert A. Pirier. Free Press, 866 Third Avenue, New York, New York 10022. 1985.

CONTEXTS OF THE BILL OF RIGHTS. Stephen L. Schechter and Richard B. Bernstein. New York State Commission on the Bicentennial of the United States Constitution, Madison House, P.O. Box 3100, Madison, Wisconsin 53704. 1990.

THE CRUCIBLE OF RACE: BLACK/WHITE RELATIONS IN THE AMERICAN SOUTH SINCE EMANCIPATION. Joel Williamson. Oxford University Press, 200 Madison Avenue, New York, New York 10016. 1984.

DISABLING AMERICA: THE RIGHTS INDUSTRY IN OUR TIME. Richard E. Morgan. Basic Books, 10 East Fifty-third Street, New York, New York 10022. 1986.

THE FOURTEENTH AMENDMENT AND THE BILL OF RIGHTS. Raoul Berger. University of Oklahoma Press, 1005 Asp Avenue, Norman, Oklahoma 73019. 1989.

THE FOURTEENTH AMENDMENT: FROM POLITICAL PRINCIPLE TO JUDICIAL DOCTRINE. William E. Nelson. Harvard University Press, 79 Garden Street, Cambridge, Massachusetts 02138. 1988.

FREEDOM AND THE COURT: CIVIL RIGHTS AND LIBERTIES IN THE UNITED STATES. Fifth Edition. Henry J. Abraham. Oxford University Press, 200 Madison Avenue, New York, New York 10016. 1988.

FREEDOM UNDER FIRE: U.S. CIVIL LIBERTIES IN TIMES OF WAR. Michael Linfield. South End Press, 116 St. Botolph Street, Boston, Massachusetts 02115. 1990.

HUMAN RIGHTS IN THE STATES: NEW DIRECTIONS IN CONSTITUTIONAL POLICYMAKING. Greenwood Publishing Group, Incorporated, 88 Post Road West, P.O. Box 5007, Westport, Connecticut 06881. 1988.

IMPLEMENTATION OF CIVIL RIGHTS POLICY. Charles S. Bullock III and Charles M. Lamb, Editors. Brooks/Cole Publishing Company, 511 Forest Lodge Road, Pacific Grove, California 93924. 1984.

IN OUR DEFENSE: THE BILL OF RIGHTS IN ACTION. Ellen Alderman. William Morrow and Company, 105 Madison Avenue, New York, New York 10016. 1991.

INALIENABLE RIGHTS: A DEFENSE. Diana T. Meyers. Columbia University Press, 562 West One Hundred Thirteenth Street, New York, New York 10025. 1985.

INTERNATIONAL COOPERATION FOR SOCIAL JUSTICE: GLOBAL AND REGIONAL PROTECTION OF ECONOMIC/SOCIAL RIGHTS. Glenn A. Mower. Greenwood Publishing Group, Incorporated, 88 Post Road West, P.O. Box 5007, Westport, Connecticut 06881. 1985.

THE LAW AND POLITICS OF CIVIL RIGHTS AND LIBERTIES. Richard E. Morgan. Alfred A. Knopf, 201 East Fiftieth Street, New York, New York 10022. 1985- . (Annual Supplements).

MINORITY VOTE DILUTION. Chandler Davidson, Editor. Howard University Press, 2900 Van Ness Street, Northwest, Washington, D.C. 20008. 1989.

MORAL RIGHTS IN THE WORKPLACE. Gertrude Ezorsky, Editor. State University of New York Press, University Plaza, Albany, New York 12246. 1986.

THE NATIONALIZATION OF THE BILL OF RIGHTS: FOURTEENTH AMENDMENT DUE PROCESS AND PROCEDURAL RIGHTS. Roald Y. Mykkeltvedt. Associated Faculty Press, 824 President Street, Brooklyn, New York 11215. 1983.

NO PLACE TO HIDE: THE SOUTH AND HUMAN RIGHTS. Cal Logue, Editor. Mercer University Press, Macon, Georgia 31207. 1984.

ONE NATION, INDIVISIBLE: THE CIVIL RIGHTS CHALLENGE FOR THE 1990s. Reginald C. Govan and William L. Taylor. Citizen's Commission on Civil Rights, 2000 M Street, Northwest, Washington, D.C. 20036. 1989.

THE ORIGINS OF THE CIVIL RIGHTS MOVEMENT: BLACK COMMUNITIES ORGANIZING FOR CHANGE. Aldon D. Morris. Free Press, 866 Third Avenue, New York, New York 10022. 1984.

OUR ENDANGERED RIGHTS: THE ACLU REPORT ON CIVIL LIBERTIES TODAY. Norman Dorsen, Editor. Pantheon Books, 201 East Fiftieth Street, New York, New York 10022. 1984.

PERSONS, RIGHTS, AND THE MORAL COMMUNITY. Loren E. Lomaskey. Oxford University Press, 200 Madison Avenue, New York, New York 10016. 1990.

THE POLITICS OF JUDICIAL INTERPRETATION: THE FEDERAL COURTS, DEPARTMENT OF JUSTICE AND CIVIL RIGHTS. Robert J. Kaczorowski. Oceana Publications, 75 Main Street, Dobbs Ferry, New York 10522. 1985.

PROMISES TO KEEP: AFRICAN-AMERICANS AND THE CONSTITUTIONAL ORDER, 1776 TO THE PRESENT. Donald G. Nieman. Oxford University Press, 200 Madison Avenue, New York, New York 10016. 1991.

PROTECTING CONSTITUTIONAL FREEDOMS: A ROLE FOR FEDERAL COURTS. Daan Braveman. Greenwood Publishing Group, Incorporated, 88 Post Road West, P.O. Box 5007, Westport, Connecticut 06881. 1989.

PROTESTERS ON TRIAL: CRIMINAL JUSTICE IN THE SOUTHERN CIVIL RIGHTS AND VIETNAM ANTIWAR MOVEMENTS. Steven E. Barkan. Rutgers University Press, 109 Church Street, New Brunswick, New Jersey 08901. 1985.

RACE, REFORM, AND REBELLION: THE SECOND RECONSTRUCTION IN BLACK AMERICA. Manning Marable. University Press of Mississippi, 3825 Ridgewood Road, Jackson, Mississippi 39211. 1984.

RECENT DEVELOPMENTS IN SECTION 1983 CIVIL RIGHTS LITIGATION. George C. Pratt, Alvin B. Rubin, Sol Schreiber, and Martin A. Schwartz. Practising Law Institute, 810 Seventh Avenue, New York, New York 10019. 1984.

REMEDIAL LAW: WHEN COURTS BECOME ADMINISTRATORS. Robert C. Wood, Editor. University of Massachusetts Press, P.O. Box 429, Amherst, Massachusetts 01004. 1990.

THE RIGHTS OF FREE MEN: AN ESSENTIAL GUIDE TO CIVIL LIBERTIES. Alan Barth. Knopf Publishers, 201 East Fiftieth Street, New York, New York 10022. 1984.

THE STEALING OF AMERICA. John W. Whitehead. Crossway Books, Good News Publishers, 1300 Crescent Street, Wheaton, Illinois 60187. 1983.

THE SUPREME COURT AND INDIVIDUAL RIGHTS. Second Edition. Elder Witt. Congressional Quarterly, Incorporated, 1414 Twenty-second Street, Northwest, Washington D.C. 20036. 1988.

SUPPRESSING THE KU KLUX KLAN: THE ENFORCEMENT OF THE RECONSTRUCTION AMENDMENTS, 1870-1877. Everette Swinney. Garland Publishing Company, 136 Madison Avenue, New York, New York 10016. 1987.

TAKING LIBERTIES: A DECADE OF HARD CASES, BAD LAWS, AND BUM RAPS. Alan M. Dershowitz. Contemporary Books, 180 North Michigan Avenue, Chicago, Illinois 60601. 1988.

CIVIL RIGHTS AND LIBERTIES

THEORIES OF RIGHTS. Jeremy Waldron, Editor. Oxford University Press, 200 Madison Avenue, New York, New York 10016. 1984.

A THEORY OF RIGHTS: PERSONS UNDER LAWS, INSTITUTIONS, AND MORALS. Carl Wellman. Rowman and Littlefield, 4720 Boston Way, Lanham, Maryland 20706. 1985.

UNFINISHED BUSINESS: A CIVIL RIGHTS STRATEGY FOR AMERICA'S THIRD CENTURY. Clint Bolick. Pacific Research Institute for Public Policy, 177 Post Street, San Francisco, California 94108. 1990.

THE VOTING RIGHTS ACT: CONSEQUENCES AND IMPLICATIONS. Lorn S. Foster, Editor. Praeger Publishers, One Madison Avenue, New York, New York 10010. 1985.

WHEN THE MARCHING STOPPED: THE POLITICS OF CIVIL REGULATORY AGENCIES. Hanes Walton. State University of New York Press, State University Plaza, Albany, New York 12246.

ENCYCLOPEDIAS AND DICTIONARIES

THE CONSTITUTIONAL LAW DICTIONARY, VOLUME ONE: INDIVIDUAL RIGHTS. Ralph C. Chandler, Richard A. Enslen, and Peter G. Renstrom. ABC-CLIO Information Services, Riviera Campus, P.O. Box 1911, Santa Barbara, California 93116-1911. 1985- . (Periodic Supplements).

ENCYCLOPEDIA OF THE AMERICAN CONSTITUTION. Leonard W. Levy, Editor. MacMillan Publishing Company, Incorporated, 866 Third Avenue, New York, New York 10022. 1986.

LAW REVIEWS AND PERIODICALS

BILL OF RIGHTS JOURNAL. National Civil Liberties Union, 175 Fifth Avenue, New York, New York 10010. 1968- . Annual.

THE BLACKLETTER JOURNAL. Harvard Law School. Harvard University Press, 79 Garden Street, Cambridge, Massachusetts 02138. 1985- . Annual.

CHICANO LAW REVIEW. Chicano Law Student Association, School of Law, University of California at Los Angeles, 405 Highland Avenue, Los Angeles, California 90024. Annual.

HARVARD CIVIL RIGHTS -- CIVIL LIBERTIES LAW REVIEW. Harvard Law School. Harvard University Press, 79 Garden Street, Cambridge, Massachusetts 02138. Biannual.

HUMAN RIGHTS MAGAZINE. American Bar Association, Section on Individual Rights and Responsibilities, 1800 M Street, Northwest, Suite 200, Washington, D.C. 20036. Three times per year.

LAW REPORT. Southern Poverty Law Center, P.O. Box 2087, Montgomery, Alabama 36102. Bimonthly.

NEW PERSPECTIVES. United States Commission on Civil Rights. Superintendent of Documents, United States Government Printing Office, Division of Public Documents, Washington, D.C. 20402. Quarterly.

VANGUARD. Trade Union Leadership Council, 8670 Grand River Avenue, Detroit, Michigan 48204. Quarterly.

WORKERS' DEFENSE LEAGUE NEWS. Workers' Defense League, 100 East Seventeenth Street, New York, New York 10003. Quarterly.

NEWSLETTERS AND NEWSPAPERS

AFFIRMATIVE ACTION/EEO NOTES. NYPER Publications, P.O. Box 662, Latham, New York 12110. Monthly.

ARROW. International Committee Against Racism, P.O. Box 904, Brooklyn, New York 11202. Bimonthly.

THE BILL OF RIGHTS IN ACTION. Constitutional Rights Foundation, 601 South Kingsley Avenue, Los Angeles, California 90005. Quarterly.

CAPITAL NOTES. Commission for Social Justice, 219 E Street, Northeast, Washington, D.C. 20002. Bimonthly.

CIVIL LIBERTIES. American Civil Liberties Union, 132 West Forty-third Street, New York, New York 10036. Quarterly.

CIVIL LIBERTIES ALERT. American Civil Liberties Union, 122 Maryland Avenue, Northeast, Washington, D.C. 20002. Monthly.

THE CIVIL RIGHTS. United Church of Christ Commission for Racial Justice, 105 Madison Avenue, New York, New York 10016. Weekly.

CIVIL RIGHTS JOURNAL. Commission for Racial Justice, 105 Madison Avenue, New York, New York 10016. Quarterly.

CIVIL RIGHTS MONITOR. Leadership Conference on Civil Rights, 2027 Massachusetts Avenue, Northwest, Washington, D.C. 20036. Bimonthly.

COMMITTEE REPORT. Lawyers' Committee for Civil Rights Under Law, 1400 I Street, Northwest, Suite 400, Washington, D.C. 20005. Quarterly.

EQUAL JUSTICE. National Association for the Advancement of Colored People, Legal Defense and Education Fund, Incorporated, 99 Hudson Street, New York, New York 10013. Quarterly.

FIRST PRINCIPLES. Center for National Security Studies, 122 Maryland Avenue, Northeast, Washington, D.C. 20002. Bimonthly.

KLANWATCH INTELLIGENCE REPORT. Klanwatch, P.O. Box 548, Montgomery, Alabama 36195. Monthly.

LAW STUDENTS CIVIL RIGHTS RESEARCH COUNCIL NEWSLETTER. Law Students Civil Rights Research Council, 132 West Forty-third Street, New York, New York 10036. Quarterly.

LAWYERS COMMITTEE FOR INTERNATIONAL HUMAN RIGHTS BULLETIN. Lawyers' Committee for International Human Rights, 36 West Forty-Fourth Street, New York, New York 10036. Quarterly.

LEX VITAE. Americans United for Life Legal Defense Fund, 343 South Dearborn Street, Suite 1804, Chicago, Illinois 60604. Quarterly.

MALDEF NEWSLETTER. Mexican-American Legal Defense and Educational Fund, 634 South Spring Street, Eleventh floor, Los Angeles, California 90014. Three times per year.

POLICE MISCONDUCT AND CIVIL RIGHTS LAW REPORT. National Lawyers' Guild Civil Liberties Committee. Clark Boardman Company, Limited, 435 Hudson Street, New York, New York 10014. Bimonthly.

RELIGIOUS FREEDOM REPORTER. Center for Law and Religious Freedom, P.O. Box 505, Buies Creek, North Carolina 27506. Monthly.

SOUTHERN CHRISTIAN LEADERSHIP COUNCIL NEWSLETTER. Southern Christian Leadership Council, 334 Auburn Avenue, Northwest, Atlanta, Georgia 30312. Monthly.

VOICE OF REASON NEWSLETTER. Americans for Religious Liberty, P.O. Box 6656, Silver Spring, Maryland 20906. Quarterly.

BIBLIOGRAPHIES

THE CONSTITUTION OF THE UNITED STATES: A GUIDE AND BIBLIOGRAPHY TO CURRENT SCHOLARLY RESEARCH. Bernard D. Reams and Stuart D. Yoak. Oceana Publications, 75 Main Street, Dobbs Ferry, New York 10522. 1987.

DIRECTORIES

CIVIL RIGHTS DIRECTORY. United States Commission on Civil Rights, 1121 Vermont Avenue, Northwest, Washington, D.C. 20425. 1981- .

HUMAN RIGHTS ORGANIZATIONS AND PERIODICALS DIRECTORY, 1979-1980. Meiklejohn Civil Liberties Institute, P.O. Box 673, Berkeley, California 94701. 1981.

THE NEW ENGLAND HUMAN RIGHTS DIRECTORY. New England Human Rights Network Directory Collective. 2161 Massachusetts Avenue, Cambridge, Massachusetts 02140. Annual.

NORTH AMERICAN HUMAN RIGHTS DIRECTORY. Third Edition. Laurie S. Wiseberg and Hazel Sirett. Human Rights Internet, Harvard Law School, Pound Hall, Room 401, Cambridge, Massachusetts 02138. 1984.

BIOGRAPHICAL SOURCES

BEARING THE CROSS: MARTIN LUTHER KING, JR. AND THE SOUTHERN CHRISTIAN LEADERSHIP CONFERENCE. David J. Garrow. William Morrow and Company, Incorporated, 105 Madison Avenue, New York, New York 10016. 1986.

FATHER DIVINE AND THE STRUGGLE FOR RACIAL EQUALITY. Robert Weisbrot. University of Illinois Press, 54 East Gregory Drive, Champaign, Illinois 61820. 1983.

LAY BARE THE HEART: AN AUTOBIOGRAPHY OF THE CIVIL RIGHTS MOVEMENT. James Farmer. NAL/Dutton, 375 Hudson Street, New York, New York 10014-3657. 1986.

THE WAY OUT MUST LEAD IN: LIFE HISTORIES IN THE CIVIL RIGHTS MOVEMENT. William R. Beardslee. Lawrence Hill Books, 230 Park Place, Suite 6A, Brooklyn, New York 11238. 1983.

ASSOCIATIONS AND PROFESSIONAL SOCIETIES

AMERICAN-ARAB ANTI-DISCRIMINATION COMMITTEE. 4201 Connecticut Avenue, Northwest, Suite 500, Washington, D.C. 20008. (202) 244-2990.

AMERICAN-ARAB RELATIONS COMMITTEE. P.O. Box 416, New York, New York 10017. (212) 972-0460.

AMERICAN CIVIL LIBERTIES UNION. 132 West Forty-third Street, New York, New York 10036. (212) 944-9800.

AMERICANS FOR CONSTITUTIONAL FREEDOM. 500 Fifth Avenue, Suite 1406, New York, New York 10110. (212) 302-0067.

AMERICANS FOR RELIGIOUS LIBERTY. P.O. Box 6656, Silver Spring, Maryland 20906. (301) 598-2447.

ANTI-DEFAMATION LEAGUE OF B'NAI B'RITH. 823 United Nations Plaza, New York, New York 10017. (212) 490-2525.

ANTI-REPRESSION RESOURCE TEAM. P.O. Box 122, Jackson, Mississippi 39205. (601) 969-2269.

ASIAN AMERICAN LEGAL DEFENSE AND EDUCATION FUND. 99 Hudson Street, New York, New York 10013. (212) 966-5932.

ASSOCIATION OF AMERICAN LAW SCHOOLS, Section on Minority Groups, One Dupont Circle, Northwest, Suite 370, Washington, D.C. 20036. (202) 296-8851.

ASSOCIATION EXECUTIVES HUMAN RIGHTS CAUCUS. P.O. Box 31, Evanston, Illinois 60204. (708) 869-0299.

CATHOLIC INTERRACIAL COUNCIL OF NEW YORK. 899 Tenth Avenue, New York, New York 10019. (212) 237-8255.

INTERNATIONAL COMMITTEE AGAINST RACISM. P.O. Box 904, Brooklyn, New York 11202. (212) 629-0003.

LAWYERS COMMITTEE FOR CIVIL RIGHTS UNDER LAW. 1400 I Street, Northwest, Suite 400, Washington, D.C. 20005. (202) 371-1212.

MEXICAN-AMERICAN LEGAL DEFENSE AND EDUCATIONAL FUND (MALDEF). 635 South Spring Street, Twelfth floor, Los Angeles California 90014. (213) 629-2512.

NAACP LEGAL DEFENSE AND EDUCATIONAL FUND. 99 Hudson Street, Sixteenth floor, New York, New York 10013. (212) 219-1900.

CIVIL RIGHTS AND LIBERTIES

NATIONAL LAWYERS' GUILD CIVIL LIBERTIES COMMITTEE. c/o David Rudovsky, 636 Westview Street, Philadelphia, Pennsylvania 19119. (215) 972-0909.

NATIONAL RIGHT TO WORK LEGAL DEFENSE AND EDUCATIONAL FOUNDATION. 8001 Braddock Road, Suite 600, Springfield, Virginia 22160. (703) 321-8510.

PEOPLE FOR THE AMERICAN WAY. 2000 M Street, Northwest, Suite 400, Washington, D.C. 20036. (202) 467-4999.

SECTION OF INDIVIDUAL RIGHTS AND RESPONSIBILITIES, American Bar Association, 1800 M Street, Northwest, Suite 200, Washington, D.C. 20036. (202) 331-2279.

SOUTHERN POVERTY LAW CENTER. P.O. Box 2087, Montgomery, Alabama 36102. (205) 264-0286.

TRADE UNION LEADERSHIP COUNCIL. 8670 Grand River Avenue, Detroit, Michigan 48204. (313) 894-0303.

UNITED CHURCH OF CHRIST COMMISSION FOR RACIAL JUSTICE. 105 Madison Avenue, New York, New York 10016. (212) 683-5656.

RESEARCH CENTERS, INSTITUTES, CLEARINGHOUSES

A. PHILIP RANDOLPH EDUCATIONAL FUND. 260 Park Avenue, South, Sixth floor, New York, New York 10010. (212) 533-8000.

ALLIANCE TO END REPRESSION. 220 State Street, Suite 1430, Chicago, Illinois 60604. (312) 427-4064.

AMERICAN CIVIL LIBERTIES UNION FOUNDATION. 132 West Forty-Third Street, New York, New York 10036. (212) 944-9800.

AMERICAN CONSTITUTIONAL AND CIVIL RIGHTS UNION. 18055 Southwest Jay Street, Aloha, Oregon 97006. (503) 649-9310.

AMERICAN-ISRAELI CIVIL LIBERTIES COALITION. 275 Seventh Avenue, Suite 1776, New York, New York 10001. (212) 696-9603.

CENTER FOR CONSTITUTIONAL RIGHTS. 666 Broadway, Seventh floor, New York, New York 10012. (212) 614-6464.

CENTER FOR LAW AND RELIGIOUS FREEDOM. P.O. Box 505, Buies Creek, North Carolina 27506. (919) 893-4111.

CITIZENS COMMISSION ON CIVIL RIGHTS. 2000 M Street, Northwest, Washington, D.C. 20036. (202) 659-5565.

COMMISSION FOR SOCIAL JUSTICE. 219 E Street, Northeast, Washington, D.C. 20002. (202) 547-2900.

DEPARTMENT OF CIVIL RIGHTS, AFL-CIO. 815 Sixteenth Street, Northwest, Washington, D.C. 20006. (202) 637-5270.

FIRST AMENDMENT RESEARCH INSTITUTE. 821 Massachusetts Avenue, Northeast, Washington, D.C. 20002. (202) 547-4090.

INSTITUTE FOR POLICY STUDIES. 1901 Q Street, Northwest, Washington, D.C. 20009. (202) 234-9382.

INSTITUTE OF BILL OF RIGHTS LAW. College of William and Mary, Marshall-Wythe School of Law, Williamsburg, Virginia 23185. (804) 221-3810.

KLANWATCH. P.O. Box 548, Montgomery, Alabama 36195. (205) 264-0286.

LAW STUDENTS CIVIL RIGHTS RESEARCH COUNCIL. 132 West Forty-Third Street, New York, New York 10036. (212) 736-9270.

LEADERSHIP CONFERENCE ON CIVIL RIGHTS (LCCR). 2027 Massachusetts Avenue, Northwest, Washington, D.C. 20036. (202) 667-1780.

MEIKLEJOHN CIVIL LIBERTIES INSTITUTE. P.O. Box 673, Berkeley, California 94701. (415) 848-0599.

NATIONAL ASSOCIATION FOR THE ADVANCEMENT OF COLORED PEOPLE (NAACP). 4805 Mt. Hope Drive, Baltimore, Maryland 21215. (212) 481-4100.

NATIONAL COUNCIL OF LA RAZA. Office of Research Advocacy and Legislation, 20 F Street, Northwest, Washington, D.C. 20001. (202) 289-1380.

NATIONAL URBAN LEAGUE. 500 East Sixty-Second Street, New York, New York 10021. (212) 310-9000.

SOUTHERN CHRISTIAN LEADERSHIP CONFERENCE. 334 Auburn Avenue, Northeast, Atlanta, Georgia 30312. (404) 522-1420.

SOUTHERN REGIONAL COUNCIL. 60 Walton Street, Northwest, Atlanta, Georgia 30303. (404) 522-8764.

WORKERS' DEFENSE LEAGUE. 100 East Seventeenth Street, New York, New York 10003. (212) 533-7870.

OTHER SOURCES

CIVIL LIBERTIES IN REAGAN'S AMERICA: A SPECIAL TWO-YEAR REPORT ON THE ACLU'S DEFENSE OF THE BILL OF RIGHTS AGAINST THE ATTACKS OF THE ADMINISTRATION AND ITS ALLIES. American Civil Liberties Union, 132 West Forty-third Street, New York, New York 10036. 1982.

THE EISENHOWER ADMINISTRATION AND BLACK CIVIL RIGHTS. Robert Fredrick Burk. University of Tennessee Press, 239 Communications Building, Knoxville, Tennessee 37996-0325. 1984.

FEDERAL CIVIL RIGHTS ENFORCEMENT EFFORTS IN MID-AMERICA: A REPORT. United States Commission on Civil Rights, 1121 Vermont Avenue, Northwest, Washington, D.C. 20425. 1983.

IN CONTEMPT OF CONGRESS AND THE COURTS: CIVIL RIGHTS RECORD. Muriel Morisey Spence. American Civil Liberties Union, 132 West Forty-third Street, New York, New York 10036. 1984.

LOBBYING FOR FREEDOM IN THE 1980's: A GRASS-ROOTS GUIDE TO PROTECTING YOUR RIGHTS. Kenneth P. Norwick, Editor. Putnam Publishing Group, 200 Madison Avenue, New York, New York 10016. 1983.

THE MARCUS GARVEY AND UNIVERSAL NEGRO IMPROVEMENT ASSOCIATION PAPERS. Robert A. Hill, Editor. University of California Press, 2120 Berkeley Way, Berkeley, California 94720. 1986.

MEDICAL SCREENING OF WORKERS. Mark A. Rothstein. Bureau of National Affairs, Incorporated, 1231 Twenty-fifth Street, Northwest, Washington, D.C. 20037. 1984.

PERSONAL JUSTICE DENIED: REPORT OF THE COMMISSION ON WARTIME RELOCATION AND INTERMENT OF CIVILIANS. The Commission. Superintendent of Documents, United States Government Printing Office, Division of Public Documents, Washington, D.C. 20402. 1983.

REPORT OF THE UNITED STATES COMMISSION ON CIVIL RIGHTS ON THE CIVIL RIGHTS ACT OF 1990. United States Commission on Civil Rights, 1121 Vermont Avenue, Northwest, Washington, D.C. 20425. 1990.

STATE OF CIVIL RIGHTS, 1957-1983: THE FINAL REPORT OF THE UNITED STATES COMMISSION ON CIVIL RIGHTS. United States Commission on Civil Rights. Superintendent of Documents, United States Government Printing Office, Washington, D.C. 20402. 1983.

UNITED STATES COMMISSION ON CIVIL RIGHTS. United States Commission on Civil Rights. Superintendent of Documents, United States Government Printing Office, Washington, D.C. 20402. 1983.

THE UNITED STATES DEPARTMENT OF JUSTICE AND INDIVIDUAL RIGHTS, 1937-1962. John T. Elliff. Garland Publishing Company, 136 Madison Avenue, New York, New York 10016. 1987.

CIVIL SERVICE
See also: INDIVIDUAL AGENCIES AND STATES; MERIT SYSTEMS PROTECTION BOARD; NATIONAL LABOR RELATIONS BOARD; U.S. OFFICE OF PERSONNEL MANAGEMENT

STATUTES, CODES, STANDARDS, UNIFORM LAWS

CODE OF FEDERAL REGULATIONS, TITLE 5. Office of the Federal Register, National Archives and Records Administration. Superintendent of Documents, United States Government Printing Office, Washington, D.C. 20402. Annual. (Updated by monthly List of Sections Affected and daily Federal Register).

POSITION CLASSIFICATION STANDARDS FOR POSITIONS AND GENERAL SCHEDULE CLASSIFICATION SYSTEM. Office of Personnel Management. Superintendent of Documents, United States Government Printing Office, Washington, D.C. 20402. Looseleaf.

LOOSELEAF SERVICES AND REPORTERS

DECISIONS OF THE FEDERAL LABOR RELATIONS AUTHORITY. Federal Labor Relations Authority. United States Government Printing Office, Division of Public Documents, Washington, D.C. 20402. 1979- .

DECISIONS OF THE UNITED STATES MERIT SYSTEMS PROTECTION BOARD. Merit Systems Protection Board. Superintendent of Documents, United States Government Printing Office, Washington, D.C. 20402. 1979- .

ETHICS IN GOVERNMENT REPORTER. Washington Service Bureau, 655 Fifteenth Street, Northwest, Washington, D.C. 20005. 1980- . (Monthly Supplements).

FEDERAL PAY AND BENEFITS REPORTER. LRP Publications, 747 Dresher Road, Horsham, Pennsylvania 19044. 1974- . (Monthly Supplements).

FEDERAL SERVICE IMPASSES PANEL RELEASES. Superintendent of Documents, United States Government Printing Office, Washington, D.C. 20402. 1970- .

GOVERNMENT EMPLOYEE RELATIONS REPORT. Bureau of National Affairs, Incorporated, 1231 Twenty-fifth Street, Northwest, Washington, D.C. 20037. 1963- . (Weekly Supplements).

MERIT SYSTEMS PROTECTION BOARD SERVICE. Hawkins Publishing Company, Incorporated, 310 Tahiti Way, Number 108, Marina Del Rey, California 90291. 1984- . (Monthly Supplements).

NATIONAL PUBLIC EMPLOYMENT REPORTER. LRP Publications, 747 Dresher Road, Horsham, Pennsylvania 19044. 1979- . (Quarterly Supplements).

PUBLIC EMPLOYEE BARGAINING. Commerce Clearing House, Incorporated, 4025 West Peterson Avenue, Chicago, Illinois 60646. 1977- . (Semi-Monthly Supplements).

PUBLIC PERSONNEL ADMINISTRATION - POLICIES AND PRACTICES FOR PERSONNEL. Prentice-Hall, Incorporated, 113 Sylvan Avenue, Englewood Cliffs, New Jersey 07632. 1973- .

UNITED STATES CIVIL SERVICE COMMISSION. United States Government Printing Office, Division of Public Documents, Washington, D.C. 20402. 1978- .

UNITED STATES MERIT SYSTEMS PROTECTION BOARD REPORTER. West Publishing Company, P.O. Box 64526, 50 West Kellogg Boulevard, St. Paul, Minnesota 55164-0526. 1979- .

HANDBOOKS, MANUALS, FORMBOOKS

CIVILIAN PERSONNEL LAW MANUAL. Second Edition. Office of General Counsel, United States General Accounting Office. United States Government Printing Office, Division of Public Documents, Washington, D.C. 20402. 1983.

FEDERAL CIVIL SERVICE LAW AND PROCEDURES: A BASIC GUIDE. Second Edition. Ellen M. Bussey and others. Bureau of National Affairs, Incorporated, 1231 Twenty-fifth Street, Northwest, Washington, D.C. 20037. 1990.

FEDERAL ETHICS HANDBOOK. The Michie Company, P.O. Box 7587, Charlottesville, Virginia 22906-7582. 1981.

FEDERAL GRATUITIES POLICIES: A CONTRACTOR GUIDE. Robert J. Kenney and Douglas R. Duberstein. Federal Publications, 1120 Twentieth Street, Northwest, Washington, D.C. 20036. 1990.

FEDERAL PERSONNEL MANUAL. Office of Personnel Management. Superintendent of Documents, United States Government Printing Office, Washington, D.C. 20402. Looseleaf.

GUIDE TO THE FEDERAL SERVICE LABOR MANAGEMENT RELATIONS STATUTE. Federal Labor Relations Authority. Superintendent of Documents, United States Government Printing Office, Washington, D.C. 20402. 1990.

A GUIDE TO THE MERIT SYSTEMS PROTECTION BOARD: LAW AND PRACTICE, 1979-1986. Third Edition. Peter B. Broida. Dewey Publications, Incorporated, 353 North Edison Street, Arlington, Virginia 22203. 1986.

HANDBOOK OF REASONABLE ACCOMMODATION. Office of Personnel Management, Office of Affirmative Action Programs, Office of Selective Placement Programs. Superintendent of Documents, United States Government Printing Office, Washington, D.C. 20402. 1984.

HANDBOOK ON PUBLIC PERSONNEL ADMINISTRATION AND LABOR RELATIONS. Jack Rabin, Editor. Marcel Dekker, Incorporated, 270 Madison Avenue, New York, New York 10016. 1983.

POLICY AND SUPPORTING POSITIONS: UNITED STATES GOVERNMENT. Superintendent of Documents, United States Government Printing Office, Washington, D.C. 20402. 1988.

REPRESENTING THE AGENCY BEFORE THE UNITED STATES MERIT SYSTEMS PROTECTION BOARD, A HANDBOOK ON MSPB PRACTICE AND PROCEDURE. Harold J. Ashner and William C. Jackson. Office of Personnel Management, Office of Employee, Labor, and Agency Relations, Appellate Policies Division. Superintendent of Documents, United States Government Printing Office, Washington, D.C. 20402. 1984.

TEXTBOOKS AND GENERAL WORKS

BLOWING THE WHISTLE IN THE FEDERAL GOVERNMENT: A COMPARATIVE ANALYSIS OF 1980 AND 1983 SURVEY FINDINGS. Merit Systems Protection Board, Office of Merit Systems Review and Studies. Superintendent of Documents, United States Government Printing Office, Washington, D.C. 20402. 1984.

DEMOCRACY AND THE PUBLIC SERVICE. Second Edition. Frederick C. Mosher. Oxford University Press, 200 Madison Avenue, New York, New York 10016. 1982.

ETHICS FOR BUREAUCRATS: AN ESSAY ON LAW AND VALUES. Second Edition. Marcel Dekker, 720 Madison Avenue, New York, New York 10016. 1989.

EXECUTIVES FOR GOVERNMENT: CENTRAL ISSUES OF FEDERAL PERSONNEL ADMINISTRATION. Paul T. David and Ross Pollock. Greenwood Publishing Group, Incorporated, 88 Post Road West, P.O. Box 5007, Westport, Connecticut 06881. 1977.

THE FAST TRACK PROMOTION PLAN FOR GOVERNMENT EMPLOYEES: FEDERAL, LOCAL, STATE, EDUCATORS. Robert G. Smith. Helix Press, P.O. Box 5144, Springfield, Virginia 22150. 1986.

FEDERAL EQUAL EMPLOYMENT OPPORTUNITY POLICY AND NUMERICAL GOALS AND TIMETABLES: AN IMPACT ASSESSMENT. J. Edward Kellough. Praeger Publishers, Greenwood Publishing Group, Incorporated, 88 Post Road West, P.O. Box 5007, Westport, Connecticut 06881. 1989.

THE HATCH ACT AND THE AMERICAN BUREAUCRACY. James R. Eccles. Vantage Press, Incorporated, 516 West Thirty-fourth Street, New York, New York 10001. 1981.

LABOR/MANAGEMENT RELATIONS AMONG GOVERNMENT EMPLOYEES. Harry Kershen, Editor. Baywood Publishing Company, Incorporated, 26 Austin Avenue, P.O. Box 337, Amityville, New York 11701. 1983.

LEGISLATING BUREAUCRATIC CHANGE: THE CIVIL SERVICE REFORM ACT OF 1978. Patricia W. Ingraham and Carolyn Ban, Editors. State University of New York Press, State University Plaza, Albany, New York 12246. 1985.

MANAGING HUMAN RESOURCES: AN INTRODUCTION TO PUBLIC PERSONNEL ADMINISTRATION. N. Joseph Cayer. St. Martin's Press, Incorporated, 175 Fifth Avenue, New York, New York 10010. 1980.

MERIT SYSTEMS PROTECTION BOARD: RIGHTS AND REMEDIES. Robert C. Vaughn. Law Journal Seminars-Press, Incorporated, 111 Eighth Avenue, Suite 900, New York, New York 10011. 1984- . (Periodic Supplements).

THE NEW PUBLIC PERSONNEL ADMINISTRATION. Third Edition. Felix A. Nigro. F.E. Peacock Publishers, Incorporated, 115 North Prospect Avenue, Itasca, Illinois 60143-0397. 1986.

THE PARTICIPATORY BUREAUCRACY: WOMEN AND MINORITIES IN A MORE REPRESENTATIVE PUBLIC SERVICE. Harry Kranz. Lexington Books, 125 Spring Street, Lexington, Massachusetts 02173. 1976.

PERSONAL LIABILITY OF PUBLIC OFFICIALS UNDER FEDERAL LAW. Fourth Edition. Paul T. Hardy and J. Devereux Weeks. Carl Vinson School of Government, University of Georgia, Terrell Hall, Athens, Georgia 30602. 1988.

PERSONNEL MANAGEMENT IN GOVERNMENT: POLITICS AND PROCESS. Jay M. Shafritz, Albert C. Hyde, and David H. Rosenbloom. Marcel Dekker, Incorporated, 270 Madison Avenue, New York, New York 10016. 1985.

POLITICAL ACTIVITY AND THE FEDERAL EMPLOYEE. Merit Systems Protection Board, Office of the Special Counsel. Superintendent of Documents, United States Government Printing Office, Washington, D.C. 20402. 1984.

POLITICAL ACTIVITY AND THE STATE AND LOCAL EMPLOYEE. Merit Systems Protection Board, Office of the Special Counsel. Superintendent of Documents, United States Government Printing Office, Washington, D.C. 20402. 1984.

THE PROFESSIONS IN GOVERNMENT. Frederick C. Mosher. Richard J. Stillman, Transaction Books, Rutgers University, 109 Church Street, New Brunswick, New Jersey 08901. 1982.

PUBLIC ADMINISTRATION: UNDERSTANDING MANAGEMENT, POLITICS AND LAW IN THE PUBLIC SECTOR. Second Edition. David H. Rosenbloom and Deborah D. Goldman. Random House, Incorporated, 201 East Fiftieth Street, New York, New York 10022. 1989.

PUBLIC EMPLOYMENT IN WESTERN NATIONS. Richard Rose and Edward Page. Cambridge University Press, 40 West Twentieth Street, New York, New York 10011. 1985.

PUBLIC PERSONNEL ADMINISTRATION: A VALUES PERSPECTIVE. Robert H. Elliot. Reston Publishing Company, Prentice-Hall, Incorporated, 113 Sylvan Avenue, Englewood Cliffs, New Jersey 07632. 1985.

PUBLIC PERSONNEL POLICY: THE POLITICS OF CIVIL SERVICE. David H. Rosenbloom, Editor. Associated Faculty Press, 19 West Thirty-sixth Street, New York, New York 10018. 1985.

RIGHTS OF THE PUBLIC EMPLOYEE. Robert P. Dworskin. American Library Association, 50 East Huron Street, Chicago, Illinois 60611. 1978.

SEX AND PAY IN THE FEDERAL GOVERNMENT: USING JOB EVALUATION SYSTEMS TO IMPLEMENT COMPARATIVE WORTH. Doris M. Werwie. Greenwood Publishing Group, Incorporated, 88 Post Road West, P.O. Box 5007, Westport, Connecticut 06881. 1987.

SEXUAL HARASSMENT IN THE FEDERAL GOVERNMENT: AN UPDATE. Merit Systems Protection Board, Office of Merit Systems Review and Studies. Superintendent of Documents, United States Government Printing Office, Washington, D.C. 20402. 1988.

SEXUAL HARASSMENT IN THE FEDERAL WORKPLACE: IS IT A PROBLEM? Merit Systems Protection Board, Office of Merit Systems Review and Studies. Superintendent of Documents, United States Government Printing Office, Washington, D.C. 20402. 1981.

THE UNFINISHED AGENDA FOR CIVIL SERVICE REFORM: IMPLICATIONS OF THE GRACE COMMISSION REPORT. Charles H. Levine, Editor. Brookings Institution, 1775 Massachusetts Avenue, Northwest, Washington, D.C. 20036-2188. 1985.

THE UNFINISHED BUSINESS OF CIVIL SERVICE REFORM. William Seal Carpenter. Greenwood Publishing Group, Incorporated, 88 Post Road West, P.O. Box 5007, Westport, Connecticut 06881. 1980.

WASHINGTON STORY: BEHIND THE SCENES IN THE FEDERAL GOVERNMENT: AN OFFICIAL UNDER CIVIL SERVICE DESCRIBES HIS EXPERIENCES. A.C. Roseander. National Directions, 500 Twenty-sixth Street, Greeley, Colorado 80631. 1985.

WOMEN, MINORITIES, AND UNIONS IN THE PUBLIC SECTOR. Norma Riccucci. Greenwood Publishing Group, Incorporated, 88 Post Road West, P.O. Box 5007, Westport, Connecticut 06881. 1990.

WORKING FOR THE SOVEREIGN: EMPLOYEE RELATIONS IN THE FEDERAL GOVERNMENT. Sar A. Levitan and Alexandra B. Noden. Johns Hopkins University Press, 701 West Fortieth Street, Suite 275, Baltimore, Maryland 21211-2190. 1983.

DIGESTS, INDEXES, ABSTRACTS, CITATORS

DIGEST. Merit Systems Protection Board, Office of the Board, Information Services Division. Superintendent of Documents, United States Government Printing Office, Washington, D.C. 20402. Monthly.

DIGEST AND TABLES OF CASES FOR DECISIONS OF THE FEDERAL LABOR RELATIONS AUTHORITY. Federal Labor Relations Authority. United States Government Printing Office, Division of Public Documents, Washington, D.C. 20402. 1983- .

DIGEST OF SIGNIFICANT CLASSIFICATION DECISIONS AND OPINIONS. Office of Personnel Management. Superintendent of Documents, United States Government Printing Office, Washington, D.C. 20402. Three issues per year.

QUARTERLY DIGESTS OF UNPUBLISHED DECISIONS OF THE COMPTROLLER GENERAL OF THE UNITED STATES. PERSONNEL LAW, CIVILIAN PERSONNEL AND MILITARY PERSONNEL. United States General Accounting Office. Superintendent of Documents, United States Government Printing Office, Washington, D.C. 20402. Quarterly.

SHEPARD'S FEDERAL LABOR LAW CITATIONS. Shepard's/McGraw-Hill, P.O. Box 1235, Colorado Springs, Colorado 80901. Monthly.

UNITED STATES MERIT SYSTEMS PROTECTION BOARD DIGEST. West Publishing Company, P.O. Box 64526, 50 West Kellogg Boulevard, St. Paul, Minnesota 55164-0526. 1979- .

ANNUALS AND SURVEYS

REPORT ON CASE HANDLING DEVELOPMENTS OF THE OFFICE OF THE GENERAL COUNSEL. Federal Labor Relations Authority, Office of the General Counsel. Superintendent of Documents, United States Government Printing Office, Washington, D.C. 20402. Annual.

A SURVEY OF SIGNIFICANT COURT DECISIONS OF THE RIGHTS OF FEDERAL EMPLOYEES SINCE THE CIVIL REFORM ACT OF 1978. Arthur L. Burnett. Federal Bar Association, 1815 H Street, Northwest, Washington, D.C. 20006. 1981.

LAW REVIEWS AND PERIODICALS

GOVERNMENT UNION REVIEW. 8330 Old Courthouse Road, Suite 600, Vienna, Virginia 22180. Quarterly.

PUBLIC ADMINISTRATION REVIEW. American Society for Public Administration, 1120 G Street, Northwest, Suite 500, Washington, D.C. 20005. Bimonthly.

WEEKLY FEDERAL EMPLOYEES' NEWS DIGEST. Federal Employees' News Digest, Incorporated, 510 North Washington Street, Suite 200, Falls Church, Virginia 22046. Weekly.

NEWSLETTERS AND NEWSPAPERS

CIVIL SERVICE PERSONNEL NOTES. NYPER Publications, P.O. Box 662, Latham, New York 12110. Monthly.

DISCIPLINE AND GRIEVANCES (GOVERNMENT EDITION). The Bureau of Business Practices, Incorporated, 24 Rope Ferry Road, Waterford, Connecticut 06386. Monthly.

FEDERAL EMPLOYEE/RETIREE NEWSLETTER. Federal Employee/Retiree News Service, 53 Rollingwood Court, Gulfport, Mississippi 39503. Weekly.

FEDERAL LABOR AND EMPLOYEE RELATIONS UPDATE. FPMI Communications, Incorporated, 3322 South Memorial Parkway, Suite 40, Huntsville, Alabama 35802. Monthly.

THE GOVERNMENT MANAGER. The Bureau of National Affairs, Incorporated, 1231 Twenty-fifth Street, Northwest, Washington, D.C. 20037. Biweekly.

MUNICIPAL WORKERS LAW BULLETIN. Quinlan Publishing Company, Incorporated, 23 Drydock Avenue, Boston, Massachusetts 02110. Monthly.

THE PUBLIC ADMINISTRATOR AND THE COURTS. Research Publications, Incorporated, P.O. Box 9267, Asheville, North Carolina 28815. Quarterly.

PUBLIC EMPLOYMENT LAW NOTES. NYPER Publications, P.O. Box 662, Latham, New York 12110. Monthly.

PUBLIC EMPLOYMENT LAW REPORT. Data Research, Incorporated, P.O. Box 490, Rosemount, Minnesota 55068. Monthly.

WEEKLY FEDERAL EMPLOYEES' NEWS DIGEST. Federal Employees' News Digest, Incorporated, 510 North Washington Street, Suite 200, Falls Church, Virginia 22046. Weekly.

BIBLIOGRAPHIES

LABOR MANAGEMENT RELATIONS IN THE PUBLIC SECTOR: AN ANNOTATED BIBLIOGRAPHY. N. Joseph Cayer and Sherry S. Dickerson. Garland Publishing, Incorporated, 136 Madison Avenue, New York, New York 10016. 1984.

LAWYERS AS PUBLIC ADMINISTRATORS: A SELECTED BIBLIOGRAPHY. Anthony G. White. Vance Bibliographies, P.O. Box 229, 112 North Charter Street, Monticello, Illinois 61856. 1982.

DIRECTORIES

ASPA WOMEN IN PUBLIC MANAGEMENT DIRECTORY. Committee on Women, American Society for Public Administration. 1120 G Street, Northwest, #500, Washington, D.C. 20005. 1980.

DIRECTORY OF UNIONS AND ASSOCIATIONS WITH EXCLUSIVE RECOGNITION IN THE FEDERAL SERVICE. Office of Labor Management Relations. Office of Personnel Management, 1900 E Street, Northwest, Washington, D.C. 20415-0001. Irregular.

FEDERAL CAREER OPPORTUNITIES. Federal Research Service, Incorporated, P.O. Box 1059, Vienna, Virginia 22180. Biweekly.

FEDERAL EMPLOYEES ALMANAC. Federal Employees' News Digest, Incorporated, P.O. Box 7528, Falls Church, Virginia 22046. Annual.

FEDERAL EXECUTIVES DIRECTORY. Carroll Publishing Company, 1058 Thomas Jefferson Street, Northwest, Washington, D.C. 20007. Biweekly.

FEDERAL FAST FINDER: A KEY WORD TELEPHONE DIRECTORY TO THE WASHINGTON RESEARCHERS LIMITED. 918 Sixteenth Street, Northwest, Washington, D.C. 20006.

FEDERAL JOB INFORMATION CENTERS DIRECTORY. Office of Personnel Management, 1900 East Street, Northwest, Washington, D.C. 20415-0001. 1981.

FEDERAL JOBS. Federal Jobs, Incorporated, P.O. Box 1438, Leesburg, Virginia 22075. Biweekly.

FEDERAL ORGANIZATION SERVICE. Carroll Publishing Company, 1058 Thomas Jefferson Street, Northwest, Washington, D.C. 20007. 1979- . (Updated every six months).

FEDERAL YELLOW BOOK. Washington Monitor, Incorporated. National Press Building, Number 499, Washington, D.C. 20045.

UNITED STATES GOVERNMENT DIRECTORY. Want Publishing Company, 1511 K Street, Northwest, Washington, D.C. 20005. Annual.

BIOGRAPHICAL SOURCES

RUNNING AND FIGHTING: WORKING IN WASHINGTON. Brett Duval Fromson. Simon and Schuster, Incorporated, 1230 Avenue of the Americas, New York, New York 10020. 1981.

ASSOCIATIONS AND PROFESSIONAL SOCIETIES

AMERICAN FEDERATION OF STATE, COUNTY AND MUNICIPAL EMPLOYEES (AFSCME). 1625 L Street, Northwest, Washington, D.C. 20036. (202) 452-4800.

BLACKS IN GOVERNMENT. 1424 K Street, Northwest, Suite 604, Washington, D.C. 20005. (202) 638-7767.

CIVIL SERVICE EMPLOYEES ASSOCIATION. P.O. Box 125, Capitol Station, 143 Washington Avenue, Albany, New York 12210. (518) 434-0191.

INTERNATIONAL PERSONNEL MANAGEMENT ASSOCIATION. 1617 Duke Street, Alexandria, Virginia 22314. (703) 549-7100.

NATIONAL ASSOCIATION OF CIVIL SERVICE EMPLOYEES. 7185 Navajo Road, Suite C, San Diego, California 92119. (619) 464-1014.

NATIONAL ASSOCIATION OF GOVERNMENT EMPLOYEES. 1313 L Street, Northwest, Washington, D.C. 20005. (202) 371-6644.

NATIONAL ORGANIZATION OF LEGAL SERVICES WORKERS. 13 Astor Place, Room 910, New York, New York 10003. (212) 475-8931.

PUBLIC EMPLOYEE DEPARTMENT OF THE AFL-CIO. 815 Sixteenth Street, Northwest, Room 308, Washington, D.C. 20006. (202) 393-2820.

PUBLIC EMPLOYEES ROUNDTABLE. P.O. Box 6184, Ben Franklin Station, Washington, D.C. 20044. (202) 535-4324.

RESEARCH CENTERS, INSTITUTES, CLEARINGHOUSES

PUBLIC SERVICE RESEARCH FOUNDATION. 8330 Old Courthouse Road, Suite 600, Vienna, Virginia 22180. (703) 790-0700.

UNITED STATES FEDERAL LABOR RELATIONS AUTHORITY LIBRARY, 500 C Street, Southwest, Room 234, Washington, D.C. 20434. (202) 382-0748.

ONLINE DATABASES

LEXIS, FEDERAL LABOR LIBRARY. Mead Data Central, P.O. Box 933, Dayton, Ohio 45401.

WESTLAW, LABOR LIBRARY. West Publishing Company, P.O. Box 64526, 50 West Kellogg Boulevard, St. Paul, Minnesota 55164-0526.

STATISTICS SOURCES

UNION RECOGNITION IN THE FEDERAL GOVERNMENT: STATISTICAL SUMMARY, SUMMARY REPORTS WITHIN AGENCIES, LISTINGS WITHIN AGENCIES OF EXCLUSIVE RECOGNITIONS AND AGREEMENTS AS OF JANUARY, 1985. Office of Personnel Management, Office of Policy and Communications, Office of Employee, Labor and Agency Relations. Superintendent of Documents, United States Government Printing Office, Washington, D.C. 20402. 1985.

UNITED STATES DEPARTMENT OF COMMERCE. Bureau of the Census, Suitland, Maryland 20233. 1980.

UNITED STATES DEPARTMENT OF LABOR. Bureau of Labor Statistics, Department of Labor, Room 2822, 441 G Street, Northwest, Washington, D.C. 20212. Monthly.

UNITED STATES OFFICE OF PERSONNEL MANAGEMENT. 1900 E Street, Northwest, Washington, D.C. 20415-0001. Monthly.

OTHER SOURCES

FEDERAL EMPLOYEES IN WAR AND PEACE: SELECTION, PLACEMENT AND REMOVAL. Frances Cahn. Greenwood Publishing Group, Incorporated, 88 Post Road West, P.O. Box 5007, Westport, Connecticut 06881. 1978.

HOW TO GET A JOB IN THE FEDERAL GOVERNMENT. Inter-Agency Minority and Female Recruiters Association. United States Government Printing Office, Division of Public Documents, Washington, D.C. 20402. 1981.

TO SERVE WITH HONOR: A REPORT AND RECOMMENDATIONS TO THE PRESIDENT. President's Commission on Federal Reform. United States Government Printing Office, Washington, D.C. 20402. 1989.

U.S. OFFICE OF PERSONNEL MANAGEMENT AND THE MERIT SYSTEM: A RETROSPECTIVE ASSESSMENT: A REPORT TO THE PRESIDENT AND THE CONGRESS OF THE UNITED STATES. Merit Systems Protection Board, Office of Merit Systems Review and Studies. Superintendent of Documents, United States Government Printing Office, Washington, D.C. 20402. 1989.

CLAIMS AGAINST THE GOVERNMENT
See: GOVERNMENT IMMUNITY AND LIABILITY

CLASS ACTIONS
See also: CIVIL PROCEDURE

STATUTES, CODES, STANDARDS, UNIFORM LAWS

UNIFORM CLASS ACTIONS ACT. National Conference of Commissioners on Uniform State Laws. Uniform Laws Annotated. West Publishing Company, P.O. Box 64526, 50 West Kellogg Boulevard, St. Paul, Minnesota 55164-0526. 1976- . (Annual Supplements).

LOOSELEAF SERVICES AND REPORTERS

CIVIL RIGHTS ACTIONS. Joseph Cook and John L. Sobieski. Matthew Bender and Company, Incorporated, 11 Penn Plaza, New York, New York 10001. 1983- . (Periodic Supplements).

CLASS ACTIONS: LAW AND PRACTICE WITH FORMS. Carl R. Aron and others. Callaghan and Company, 155 Pfingsten Road, Deerfield, Illinois 60015. 1987- . (Annual Supplements).

CLASS ACTIONS: THE LAW OF THE 50 STATES. Thomas A. Dickerson. Law Journal Seminars-Press, Incorporated, 111 Eighth Avenue, Suite 900, New York, New York 10011. 1988- . (Periodic Supplements).

MANUAL FOR COMPLEX LITIGATION. Judicial Panel on Multidistrict Litigation. Second Edition. Matthew Bender and Company, Incorporated, 11 Penn Plaza, New York, New York 10001. 1948- . (Periodic Supplements).

HANDBOOKS, MANUALS, FORMBOOKS

CONSUMER CLASS ACTIONS: A PRACTICAL LITIGATION GUIDE. Joel Stein. National Consumer Law Center, 11 Beacon Street, Boston, Massachusetts 02108. 1987.

MANUAL FOR COMPLEX LITIGATION. Commerce Clearing House, Incorporated, 4025 West Peterson Avenue, Chicago, Illinois 60646. 1985.

CLASS ACTIONS

MANUAL OF CLASS ACTIONS NOTICE FORMS: A PROJECT OF THE CIVIL PRACTICE AND PROCEDURES COMMITTEE, ANTITRUST SECTION, AMERICAN BAR ASSOCIATION, COMMITTEE FOR CLASS ACTION NOTICE MANUAL. Robert B. Gosline. American Bar Association, 750 North Lake Shore Drive, Chicago, Illinois 60611. 1979- .

TEXTBOOKS AND GENERAL WORKS

CLASS ACTION AS A MECHANISM FOR ENFORCING THE FEDERAL SECURITIES LAWS: AN EMPIRICAL STUDY OF THE BURDENS IMPOSED. Barbara Ann Arnoff and Benjamin S. Duval, Junior. American Bar Association, 750 North Lake Shore Drive, Chicago, Illinois 60611. 1985.

A CLASS-ACTION SUIT THAT WORKED: THE CONSUMER REFUND IN THE ANTIBIOTIC ANTITRUST LITIGATION. Thomas C. Bartsh. Lexington Books, 125 Spring Street, Lexington, Massachusetts 02173. 1978.

FROM MEDIEVAL GROUP LITIGATION TO THE MODERN CLASS ACTION. Stephen C. Yeazell. Yale University Press, 302 Temple Street, New Haven, Connecticut 06520. 1987.

MANAGEMENT OF MASS TORT LITIGATION. Lawrence H. Curtis and Edward D. Tanenhaus. Practising Law Institute, 810 Seventh Avenue, New York, New York 10019. 1983.

NEWBERG ON CLASS ACTIONS. Second Edition. Herbert B. Newberg. Shepard's/McGraw-Hill Book Company, P.O. Box 1235, Colorado Springs, Colorado 80901. 1985- . (Periodic Supplements).

PROSECUTING THE CLASS ACTION. Washington State Bar Association, 505 Madison Street, Seattle, Washington 98104. 1981.

REPRESENTING GOVERNMENT OFFICIALS IN LITIGATION. Dennis R. Yeager. Practising Law Institute, 810 Seventh Avenue, New York, New York 10019. 1981.

SOCIAL SCIENCE IN THE COURTROOM: STATISTICAL TECHNIQUES AND RESEARCH METHODS FOR WINNING CLASS ACTION SUITS. James W. Loewen. Lexington Books, 125 Spring Street, Lexington, Massachusetts 02173. 1982.

NEWSLETTERS AND NEWSPAPERS

CLASS ACTION REPORTS. Class Action Reports, Incorporated, 4900 Massachusetts Avenue, Northwest, Suite 205, Washington, D.C. 20016. Bimonthly.

NEW YORK CLASS ACTION DIGEST. New York Bar Association, Insurance, Negligence and Compensation Law Section, One Elk Street, Albany, New York 12207. Semiannual.

SECURITIES CLASS ACTION ALERT. Investors Research Bureau, 100 Union Avenue, Cresskill, New Jersey 07626. Monthly.

DIRECTORIES

GETTING ORGANIZED: A DIRECTORY OF ACTION ALLIANCES, PUBLICATIONS AND INFORMATION SERVICES. Ruth M. Edone. Neal-Schuman Publications, Incorporated, 23 Leonard Street, New York, New York 10013. 1982.

RESEARCH CENTERS, INSTITUTES, CLEARINGHOUSES

PUBLIC CITIZEN LITIGATION GROUP. 2000 P Street, Northwest, Suite 700, Washington, D.C. 20036. (202) 785-3704.

OTHER SOURCES

ATTORNEYS FEES IN CLASS ACTIONS: A REPORT TO THE FEDERAL JUDICIAL CENTER. Arthur R. Miller. United States Federal Judicial Center, Dolly Madison House, 1520 H Street, Northwest, Washington, D.C. 20005. 1980.

CIVIL LITIGATION IN MASS DISASTERS: THE HYATT SKYWALKS COLLAPSE. U.M.K.C. Law Review, Volume 52, #2. University of Missouri-Kansas City, Kansas City, Missouri 64110. 1984.

CLERGY
See: RELIGION

COAL
See: MINES AND MINERALS

COHABITATION

LOOSELEAF SERVICES AND REPORTERS

FAMILY LAW REPORTER. Bureau of National Affairs, Incorporated, 1231 Twenty-fifth Street, Northwest, Washington, D.C. 20037. 1974- .

HANDBOOKS, MANUALS, FORMBOOKS

COHABITATION CONTRACTS. Christopher Barton. Gower Publishing Company, Old Post Road, Brookfield, Vermont 05036. 1984.

COMMUNITY PROPERTY LAW IN THE UNITED STATES. W.S. McClanahan. Lawyers Co-Operative Publishing Company, Aqueduct Building, Rochester, New York 14694. 1982- . (Periodic Supplements).

HOW TO DRAW UP YOUR OWN LEGAL SEPARATION, PROPERTY, SETTLEMENT, OR COHABITATION AGREEMENT WITHOUT A LAWYER. Benji O. Anosike. Do-It-Yourself Legal Publications, 298 Fifth Avenue, New York, New York 10001. 1981.

LIVING TOGETHER. Marvin Mitchelson. Simon and Schuster, Incorporated, 1230 Avenue of the Americas, New York, New York 10020. 1981.

TEXTBOOKS AND GENERAL WORKS

AMERICAN FAMILY LAW IN TRANSITION. Walter O. Weyruch and Sanford N. Katz. Bureau of National Affairs, Incorporated, 1231 Twenty-fifth Street, Northwest, Washington, D.C. 20037. 1983.

COHABITEES. Stephen Parker. Kluwer Academic Publishers, 101 Philip Drive, Assinippi Park, Norwell, Massachusetts 02061. 1987.

FAMILY LAW IN A NUTSHELL. Second Edition. Harry D. Krause. West Publishing Company, P.O. Box 64526, 50 West Kellogg Boulevard, St. Paul, Minnesota 55164-0526. 1986.

FATHERS, HUSBANDS, AND LAWYERS. LEGAL RIGHTS AND RESPONSIBILITIES, Family Law Section, American Bar Association, 750 North Lake Shore Drive, Chicago, Illinois 60611. 1979.

INFORMAL MARRIAGE, COHABITATION, AND THE LAW. Stephen Parker. MacMillan Press, VCH Publications, 220 East Twenty-third Street, New York, New York 10010. 1990.

THE LEGALITY OF LOVE. Jerry Sonenblick and Martha Sowerwine. Jove Publications, 200 Madison Avenue, New York, New York 10016. 1981.

MARRIAGE AND COHABITATION IN CONTEMPORARY SOCIETIES: AREAS OF LEGAL, SOCIAL, AND ETHICAL CHANGE. John M. Ekelaar and Sanford N. Katz, Editors. Butterworth Legal Publishers, 90 Stiles Road, Salem, New Hampshire 03079. 1980.

BIBLIOGRAPHIES

COMMON LAW MARRIAGE AND THE LEGAL REGULATION OF COHABITATION: SPECIAL BIBLIOGRAPHY. Ronald L. Brown. Women's Rights Law Reporter, Rutgers University, 15 Washington Street, Newark, New Jersey 07102. Spring 1978.

COLLABORATION
See: TREASON

COLLECTION LAWS

LOOSELEAF SERVICES AND REPORTERS

THE COMPLETE CREDIT AND COLLECTION SYSTEM. Arnold Goldstein. Enterprise Publishing Company, 725 North Market Street, Wilmington, Delaware 19801. 1984- .

DEBTOR-CREDITOR LAW. Matthew Bender and Company, Incorporated, 11 Penn Plaza, New York, New York 10001. 1982- . (Periodic Supplements).

HANDBOOKS, MANUALS, FORMBOOKS

THE COMPLETE GUIDE FOR CREDIT AND COLLECTION LETTERS. Sol Barzman. National Association of Credit Management, Publications Division, 8815 Centre Park Drive, Columbia, Maryland 21045. 1983.

CONSUMER CREDIT GRANTOR'S GUIDE TO CREDIT GRANTING, BILLING, AND COLLECTING. John W. Johnson. Prentice-Hall, Incorporated, P.O. Box 500, Englewood Cliffs, New Jersey 07632. 1984.

DEBT COLLECTION PRACTICE IN CALIFORNIA. California Continuing Education for the Bar, 2300 Shattuck Avenue, Berkeley, California 94704. 1987.

DUN AND BRADSTREET HANDBOOK OF CREDITS AND COLLECTIONS. Harold T Redding and G. H. Knight, III. Thomas Y. Crowell Company, Incorporated, 10 East Fifty-third Street, New York, New York 10022. 1974.

EXECUTIVE'S CREDIT AND COLLECTION GUIDE. Executive Reports Corporation, 190 Sylvan Avenue, Englewood Cliffs, New Jersey 07632. 1980.

THE MANUAL OF MODERN CREDIT AND COLLECTION PRACTICES: A PRACTICAL GUIDE TO HELP YOU IMPROVE AND ACCELERATE CASH FLOW, BASED ON EXTENSIVE INTERVIEWS WITH CREDIT EXPERTS. Alexander Hamilton Institute, 197 West Spring Valley Avenue, Maywood, New Jersey 07607-1700. 1976.

TEXTBOOKS AND GENERAL WORKS

CREDIT AND COLLECTIONS: POLICY AND PROCEDURES. United States Small Business Administration, 1441 L Street, Northwest, Washington, D.C. 20416. 1983.

DEBT-COLLECTION HARASSMENT. Robert J. Hobbs. National Consumer Law Center, 11 Beacon Street, Boston, Massachusetts 02108. 1982- . (Annual Supplements).

DEBT COLLECTION LAW AND PRACTICE: ALI-ABA COURSE OF STUDY MATERIALS. American Law Institute-American Bar Association, 4025 Chestnut Street, Philadelphia, Pennsylvania 19104. 1983.

DEBTOR-CREDITOR LAW IN A NUTSHELL. Fourth Edition. David G. Eptstein. West Publishing Company, 50 West Kellogg Boulevard, St. Paul, Minnesota 55164-0526. 1990.

HANDLING CONSUMER CREDIT CASES. Third Edition. John R. Fonesca. Lawyers Co-Operative Publishing Company, Aqueduct Building, Rochester, New York 14694. 1986- . (Periodic Supplements).

HARASSMENT AND OTHER COLLECTION TABOOS. Lipman G. Feld. National Association of Credit Management, 8815 Centre Park Drive, Columbia, Maryland 21045. 1976.

HOW TO COLLECT WHAT OTHERS OWE YOU. Phillip Fry and Susan Fry. Tax Information Center, Route One, New Concord, Ohio 43762. 1976.

PROFITABLE CONSUMER LENDING: A GUIDE TO LENDING, COLLECTION AND COMPLIANCE. Robert D. Hall, Jr. and F. Blake Cloonen. Bankers Publishing Company, 210 South Street, Boston, Massachusetts 02111. 1984.

YOUR CHECK IS IN THE MAIL: HOW TO STAY LEGALLY AND PROFITABLY IN DEBT. Revised Edition. Bruce Goldman and Kenneth Pepper. Warner Books, Incorporated, 666 Fifth Street, New York, New York 10103. 1984.

ANNUALS AND SURVEYS

CONSUMER ACTIONS. Shepard's Lawyers Reference Manual. Shepard's/McGraw-Hill, P.O. Box 1235, Colorado Springs, Colorado 80901. 1983- . (Annual Supplements).

LAW REVIEWS AND PERIODICALS

COLLECTOR. American Collectors Association, 4040 West Seventieth Street, Minneapolis, Minnesota 55435. Monthly.

CREDIT AND COLLECTION LESSON SHEET. Credit Research Institute, Drawer 758, Federal National Bank Building, Shawnee, Oklahoma 74801. Semimonthly.

ASSOCIATIONS AND PROFESSIONAL SOCIETIES

AMERICAN COLLECTORS ASSOCIATION. 4040 West Seventieth Street, Minneapolis, Minnesota 55435. (612) 926-6547.

AMERICAN COMMERCIAL COLLECTORS ASSOCIATION. 4040 West Seventieth Street, Minneapolis, Minnesota 55435. (612) 925-0760.

NATIONAL ASSOCIATION OF CREDIT MANAGEMENT. 8815 Centre Park Drive, Columbia, Maryland 21045. (301) 740-5560.

COMPUTER-ASSISTED LEGAL INSTRUCTION

THE DEBTOR CREDITOR GAME. Lynn M. LoPucki. Center for Computer-Assisted Instruction, 229 Nineteenth Avenue South, University of Minnesota, Minneapolis, Minnesota 55455. Machine-readable computer file.

COLLECTIVE BARGAINING
See: LABOR AND LABOR RELATIONS

COLLEGES AND UNIVERSITIES

HANDBOOKS, MANUALS, FORMBOOKS

STUDENT SERVICES AND THE LAW: A HANDBOOK FOR PRACTITIONERS. Margaret J. Barr. Jossey-Bass, 350 Sansome Street, San Francisco, California 94104. 1988.

TEXTBOOKS AND GENERAL WORKS

LAW OF HIGHER EDUCATION 1980. William A. Kaplin. Jossey-Bass, 350 Sansome Street, San Francisco, California 94104. 1980.

LAW OF HIGHER EDUCATION: A COMPREHENSIVE GUIDE TO LEGAL IMPLICATIONS OF ADMINISTRATIVE DECISION MAKING. Second edition. William A. Kaplin. Jossey-Bass, 350 Sansome Street, San Francisco, California 94104. 1985.

LECHEROUS PROFESSOR: SEXUAL HARASSMENT ON CAMPUS. Second edition. Billie W. Dziech and Linda Weiner. University of Illinois Press, 54 East Gregory Drive, Champaign, Illinois 61820. 1990.

PENSION AND RETIREMENT POLICIES IN COLLEGES AND UNIVERSITIES: AN ANALYSIS AND RECOMMENDATION. Oscar Ruebhausen. Jossey-Bass, 350 Sansome Street, San Francisco, California 94104. 1990.

RESOLVING CONFLICT IN HIGHER EDUCATION. Jane E. McCarthy. Jossey- Bass, 350 Sansome Street, San Francisco, California 94104. 1980.

STUDENT AFFAIRS AND THE LAW. Margaret J. Barr, editor. Jossey- Bass, 350 Sansome Street, San Francisco, California 94104. 1983.

UNDERSTANDING ACADEMIC LAW. Walter C. Hobbs, editor. Jossey-Bass, 350 Sansome Street, San Francisco, California 94104. 1982.

NEWSLETTERS AND NEWSPAPERS

AGB NOTES. Association of Governing Boards of Universities and Colleges, 1 Dupont Circle, N.W., Washington, D.C. 20036. 1975- . Bimonthly.

CAMPUS CRIME. Business Publishers, Incorporated, 951 Pershing Drive, Silver Spring, Maryland 20910. 1991- . Monthly.

CAPITAL COMMENTS. Association of Independent Colleges & Schools, 1 Dupont Circle, N.W. Washington, D.C. 20036. 1984- . Bimonthly.

COLLEGE ADMINISTRATOR AND THE COURTS. College Administration Publications, Incorporated, P.O. Box 8492, Asheville, North Carolina 28814. 1978- . Quarterly.

COLLEGE LAW DIGEST. National Association of College & University Attorneys, 1 Dupont Circle, N.W., Washington, D.C. 20036. 1971- . Monthly.

COLLEGE STUDENT AND THE COURTS: CASES AND COMMENTARY. College Administration Publications, Incorporated, P.O. Box 8492, Asheville, North Carolina 28814. 1973- . Quarterly.

LEX COLLEGII. College Legal Information, Incorporated, P.O. Box 150541, Nashville, Tennessee 37202. 1978- . Quarterly.

NCSCBHEP NEWSLETTER. NCSCBHEP, Baruch College, CUNY, 17 Lexington Avenue, Box 322, New York, New York 10010. 1973- . Quarterly.

Encyclopedia of Legal Information Sources • 2nd Ed.   **COMMERCIAL LAW**

PERSPECTIVE: THE CAMPUS LEGAL MONTHLY. Magna Publications, Incorporated, 2718 Dryden Drive, Madison, Wisconsin 53704. 1986- . Monthly.

SCHOOL LAW NEWSLETTER. School Law Newsletter, Box 199, Ranger, Texas 76470. 1970- . Three times per year.

STUDENT AID NEWS. Capitol Publications, Incorporated, 1101 King Street, Alexandria, Virginia 22314. 1974- . Bimonthly.

SYNTHESIS: LAW AND POLICY IN HIGHER EDUCATION. College Administration Publications, Incorporated, P.O. Box 8492, Asheville, North Carolina 28814. 1989- . Quarterly.

BIBLIOGRAPHIES

ON THE LEGAL, FINANCIAL, AND PUBLIC POLICY ASPECTS OF HIGHER EDUCATION: A BIBLIOGRAPHY OF M. M. CHAMBERS. Richard H. Quay. Vance Bibliographies, P.O. Box 229, 112 North Charter Street, Monticello, Illinois 61856. 1983.

COMMERCE
See: COMMERCE DEPARTMENT; COMMERCIAL LAW

COMMERCE DEPARTMENT
See also: FEDERAL TRADE COMMISSION; INTERNATIONAL TRADE ADMINISTRATION; NATIONAL TELECOMMUNICATION AND INFORMATION ADMINISTRATION; PATENT AND TRADEMARK OFFICE

STATUTES, CODES, STANDARDS, UNIFORM LAWS

CODE OF FEDERAL REGULATIONS, TITLE 15. Office of the Federal Register, National Archives and Records Administration. Superintendent of Documents, United States Government Printing Office, Washington, D.C. 20402. Annual. (Updated by use of monthly List of Sections Affected and daily Federal Register.)

UNIFORM LAWS AND REGULATIONS AS ADOPTED BY THE NATIONAL CONFERENCE ON WEIGHTS AND MEASURES. Commerce Department, National Bureau of Standards. Superintendent of Documents, United States Government Printing Office, Washington, D.C. 20402. Annual.

TEXTBOOKS AND GENERAL WORKS

FROM LIGHTHOUSES TO LASERBEAMS: A HISTORY OF THE U.S. DEPARTMENT OF COMMERCE, 1913-1988. Helen Bowers, Editor. United States Department of Commerce. Superintendent of Documents, United States Government Printing Office, Washington, D.C. 20402. 1988.

DIRECTORIES

DIRECTORY OF LAW ENFORCEMENT AND CRIMINAL JUSTICE ASSOCIATIONS AND RESEARCH CENTERS. Sharon Lyles, Editor. Commerce Department, National Bureau of Standards, National Engineering Laboratory, Law Enforcement Standards Laboratory. Superintendent of Documents, United States Government Printing Office, Washington, D.C. 20402. 1986.

RESEARCH CENTERS, INSTITUTES, CLEARINGHOUSES

UNITED STATES DEPARTMENT OF COMMERCE LAW LIBRARY. Fifteenth Street and Pennsylvania Avenue, Northwest, Room 1894, Washington, D.C. 20230. (202) 377-1916.

COMMERCIAL ARBITRATION
See: ARBITRATION AND AWARD

COMMERCIAL CRIMES
See: BUSINESS CRIME; FRAUD

COMMERCIAL LAW
See also: ADMIRALTY; BANKS AND BANKING; COMMERCE DEPARTMENT; COMMODITY TRADING COMMISSION; FEDERAL TRADE COMMISSION; FRANCHISES; INTERSTATE COMMERCE COMMISSION; LAW OF THE SEA; NEGOTIABLE INSTRUMENTS; SALES AND USE TAXES; SECURITIES AND EXCHANGE COMMISSION; TRADE REGULATION

STATUTES, CODES, STANDARDS, UNIFORM LAWS

COMMERCIAL AND DEBTOR-CREDITOR LAW: SELECTED STATUTES. Foundation Press, 615 Merrick Avenue, Westbury, New York 11590. 1989.

SELECTED COMMERCIAL STATUTES. West Publishing Company, P.O. Box 64526, 50 West Kellogg Boulevard, St. Paul, Minnesota 55164-0526. Annual.

UNIFORM COMMERCIAL CODE. American Law Institute. National Conference of Commissioners on Uniform State Laws. Fred B. Rothman and Company, 10368 West Centennial Road, Littleton, Colorado 80127. 1976.

LOOSELEAF SERVICES AND REPORTERS

ANDERSON ON THE UNIFORM COMMERCIAL CODE. Ronald A. Anderson. Third Edition. Lawyers Cooperative Publishing Company, Aqueduct Building, Rochester, New York 14694. 1981- .

BUSINESS LAW MONOGRAPHS. Matthew Bender and Company, Incorporated, 11 Penn Plaza, New York, New York 10001. 1984- . (Periodic Supplements).

BUSINESS STRATEGIES. Sidney Kess, Bertil Westlin. Commerce Clearing House, Incorporated, 4025 West Peterson Avenue, Chicago, Illinois 60646. 1983- .

COMMERCIAL, BUSINESS AND TRADE LAWS OF THE UNITED STATES OF AMERICA. Oceana Publications, Incorporated, 75 Main Street, Dobbs Ferry, New York 10522. 1983- .

COMMERCIAL FINANCE GUIDE. Laurel Shifin. Matthew Bender and Company, Incorporated, 11 Penn Plaza, New York, New York 10001. 1990- . (Annual Supplements).

COMMERCIAL LOAN DOCUMENTATION GUIDE. J. Norton. Matthew Bender and Company, Incorporated, 11 Penn Plaza, New York, New York 10001. 1988- . (Annual Supplements).

COMMERCIAL PAPER AND PAYMENT SYSTEMS. William E. Lawrence. Butterworth Legal Publishers, 90 Stiles Road, Salem, New Hampshire 03079. 1990- . (Annual Supplements).

COMMERCIAL PAPER UNDER THE UNIFORM COMMERCIAL CODE. F.M. Hart and W.F. Willier. Matthew Bender and Company, Incorporated, 11 Penn Plaza, New York, New York 10001. 1972- . (Annual Supplements).

COMPENDIUM OF COMMERCIAL FINANCE LAW. National Commercial Finance Association, 225 West Thirty-fourth Street, New York, New York 10001. (Periodic Supplements).

CONSUMER AND COMMERCIAL CREDIT - INSTALLMENT SALES. Research Institute of America, Incorporated, 910 Sylvan Avenue, Englewood Cliffs, New Jersey 07632. 1932- . (Biweekly Supplements).

CONSUMER CREDIT GUIDE. Commerce Clearing House, Incorporated, 4025 West Peterson Avenue, Chicago, Illinois 60646. 1969- . (Biweekly Supplements).

DOING BUSINESS IN THE UNITED STATES. Jeremiah J. Spires and others. Matthew Bender and Company, Incorporated, 11 Penn Plaza, New York, New York 10001. 1978- . (Annual Supplements).

DRAFTING EFFECTIVE CONTRACTS. R.A. Feldman. Prentice-Hall Law and Business, Route 9W, Englewood Cliffs, New Jersey 07632. 1989- . (Periodic Supplements).

FEDERAL BUSINESS LAWS. W.A. Hancock. Business Laws, Incorporated, 11630 Chillicothe Road, Chesterland, Ohio 44026. 1970- . (Monthly Supplements).

THE LAW OF PURCHASING. Second Edition. W.A. Hancock. Business Laws, Incorporated, 11630 Chillicothe Road, Chesterland, Ohio 44026. 1986. (Annual Supplements).

LEGAL COMPLIANCE CHECKUPS: BUSINESS CLIENTS. Robert B. Hughes. Callaghan and Company, 155 Pfingsten Road, Deerfield, Illinois 60015. 1985- . (Periodic Supplements).

PURCHASER'S FORMBOOK OF CONTRACTS AND AGREEMENTS. W.A. Hancock. Business Laws, Incorporated, 11630 Chillicothe Road, Chesterland, Ohio 44026. 1985- . (Annual Supplements).

SALES AND BULK TRANSFERS UNDER THE UNIFORM COMMERCIAL CODE. Matthew Bender and Company, Incorporated, 11 Penn Plaza, New York, New York 10001. 1980- . (Annual Supplements).

SECURED TRANSACTIONS GUIDE. Commerce Clearing House, Incorporated, 4025 West Peterson Avenue, Chicago, Illinois 60646. 1969- . (Semimonthly Supplements).

SECURED TRANSACTIONS UNDER THE UNIFORM COMMERCIAL CODE. Peter F. Coogan and others. Matthew Bender and Company, Incorporated, 11 Penn Plaza, New York, New York 10001. 1963- . (Semiannual Supplements).

STRUCTURING COMMERCIAL LOAN AGREEMENTS. Sandra Stern. Research Institute of America, Incorporated, One Penn Plaza, New York, New York 10119. 1990- . (Annual Supplements).

UNIFORM COMMERCIAL CODE REPORTING SERVICE. Callaghan and Company, 155 Pfingsten Road, Deerfield, Illinois 60015. 1964- . (Monthly Supplements).

UNIFORM COMMERCIAL CODE SERIES. William D. Hawkland and others. Callaghan and Company, 155 Pfingsten Road, Deerfield, Illinois 60015. 1982- . (Annual Supplements).

HANDBOOKS, MANUALS, FORMBOOKS

CORPORATE AND COMMERCIAL FINANCE AGREEMENTS. Starr L. Tomezak, Editor. Shepard's/McGraw Hill, P.O. Box 1235, Colorado Springs, Colorado 80901. 1984- .

CREDIT MANUAL OF COMMERCIAL LAWS. National Association of Credit Management, 8815 Centre Park Drive, Columbia, Maryland 21045. Annual.

FORMS AND PROCEDURES UNDER THE UNIFORM COMMERCIAL CODE. Matthew Bender and Company, Incorporated, 11 Penn Plaza, New York, New York 10001. 1963- . (Periodic Supplements).

FORMS OF COMMERCIAL AGREEMENTS. Herbert Schlagman. Garland Publishing, Incorporated, Law Division, 136 Madison Avenue, New York, New York 10016. 1986- . (Periodic Supplements).

FORMS OF COMMERCIAL AGREEMENTS OF THE WORLD. National Association of Credit Management. Oceana Publications, Incorporated, 75 Main Street, Dobbs Ferry, New York 10522. 1984- . (Periodic Supplements).

A GUIDE TO MODERN BUSINESS AND COMMERCIAL LAW: A COMPREHENSIVE AND PRACTICAL HANDBOOK. Bernard M. Kaplan. Commerce Clearing House, Incorporated, 4025 West Peterson Avenue, Chicago, Illinois 60646. 1985.

MODERN UCC LITIGATION FORMS. Matthew Bender and Company, Incorporated, 11 Penn Plaza, New York, New York 10001. 1969- . (Annual Supplements).

QUINN'S UCC FORMS AND PRACTICE. Thomas M. Quinn. Research Institute of America, Incorporated, One Penn Plaza, New York, New York 10119. 1986- . (Annual Supplements).

WARREN'S FORMS OF AGREEMENTS, BUSINESS FORMS. Matthew Bender and Company, Incorporated, 11 Penn Plaza, New York, New York 10001. 1976- .

WEST'S LEGAL FORMS. West Publishing Company, 50 West Kellogg Boulevard, St. Paul, Minnesota 55164. 1976- . (Annual Supplements).

TEXTBOOKS AND GENERAL WORKS

THE BUSINESSPERSON'S LEGAL ADVISOR. Cliff Roberson. Liberty House Press, Blue Ridge Summit, Pennsylvania 17294. 1990.

COMMERCIAL ARBITRATION. Thomas Oehmke, Lawyer's Cooperative Publishing Company, Aqueduct Building, Rochester, New York 14694. 1987- . (Periodic Supplements).

COMMERCIAL LAW. Douglas Whitman and Clyde Stoltenberg. John Wiley and Sons, Incorporated, 605 Third Avenue, New York, New York 10158. 1985.

COMMERCIAL PAPER IN A NUTSHELL. Third Edition. Charles M. Weber and Richard E. Speidel. West Publishing Company, 50 West Kellogg Boulevard, St. Paul, Minnesota 55164. 1982.

COMMERCIAL TRANSACTIONS UNDER THE UNIFORM COMMERCIAL CODE. Fourth Edition. Donald B. King. Matthew Bender and Company, Incorporated, 11 Penn Plaza, New York, New York 10001. 1987.

COMMON LAW AND EQUITY UNDER THE UNIFORM COMMERCIAL CODE. Robert A. Hillman, Julian B. McDonnell and Steve H. Nickles. Research Institute of America, Incorporated, One Penn Plaza, New York, New York 10119. 1985.

A DOCUMENTARY GUIDE TO COMMERCIAL LEASING. American Law Institute, American Bar Association Continuing Professional Education, 4025 Chestnut Street, Philadelphia, Pennsylvania 19104. 1985. (1989 and 1990 Supplements)

DOING BUSINESS IN THE UNITED STATES. Frank G. Opton and Herbert Feiler. Kluwer Law and Taxation, 36 West Forty-fourth Street, New York, New York 10036. 1984.

FUNDAMENTALS OF BUSINESS LAW. Fourth Edition. Robert N. Corley, Peter J. Shedd and Eric M. Holmes. Prentice Hall, Incorporated, 113 Sylvan Avenue, Englewood Cliffs, New Jersey 07632. 1986.

GUIDE TO INTERNATIONAL COMMERCE LAW. Paul H. Vishny. Shepard's/McGraw-Hill, P.O. Box 1235, Colorado Springs, Colorado 80901. 1981- .

HANDBOOK OF THE LAW UNDER THE UNIFORM COMMERCIAL CODE (Hornbook Series). Third Edition. James J. White and Robert S. Summers. West Publishing Company, 50 West Kellogg Boulevard, St. Paul, Minnesota 55164. 1988.

INTERNATIONAL BUSINESS TRANSACTIONS IN A NUTSHELL. Third Edition. Ralph H. Folsom. West Publishing Company, 50 West Kellogg Boulevard, St.Paul, Minnesota 55164. 1988.

LAW AND BUSINESS. Lawrence S. Clark and Peter D. Kinder. McGraw-Hill Book Company, 1221 Avenue of the Americas, New York, New York 10020. 1988.

THE LAW OF SALES. Ray D. Henson. American Law Institute-American Bar Association Committee on Continuing Professional Education, 4025 Chestnut Street, Philadelphia, Pennsylvania 19104. 1985.

LEGAL ASPECTS OF INTRODUCING PRODUCTS TO THE UNITED STATES MARKET. John Richards and Robert Alpert. Kluwer Academic Publishers, 101 Philip Drive, Assinippi Park, Norwell, Massachusetts 02061. 1988.

THE LEGAL ENVIRONMENT OF BUSINESS. Second Edition. Rate A. Howell. Dryden Press, 465 South Lincoln Drive, Troy, Missouri 63379. 1987.

LETTERMAN'S LAW OF PRIVATE INTERNATIONAL BUSINESS. G. Gregory Letterman. Lawyers Cooperative Publishing Company, Aqueduct Building, Rochester, New York 14694. 1990.

LITIGATING COMMERCIAL CASES UP TO TRIAL. Allan M. Pepper and Mark C. Zauderer, Chairmen. Practising Law Institute, 810 Seventh Avenue, New York, New York 10019. 1986.

PURCHASER'S GUIDE TO THE UNIFORM COMMERCIAL CODE. W.A. Hancock. Business Laws, Incorporated, 11630 Chillicothe Road, Chesterland, Ohio 44026. 1985.

SALES AND SALES FINANCING (Black Letter Series). Richard E. Speidel. West Publishing Company, 50 West Kellogg Boulevard, St. Paul, Minnesota 55164-0526. 1984.

SALES OF GOODS AND SERVICES. Second Edition. Yvonne W. Rosmarin. National Consumer Law Center, 11 Beacon Street, Boston, Massachusetts 02108. 1989.

SIGNIFICANT BUSINESS DECISIONS OF THE SUPREME COURT, 1986-87 TERM. Henry N. Butler. Washington Legal Foundation, 1705 N Street, Northwest, Washington, D.C 20036. 1988.

A TRANSACTIONAL GUIDE TO THE UNIFORM COMMERCIAL CODE. Second Edition. Richard M. Alderman. American Law Institute-American Bar Association Committee on Continuing Professional Education, 4025 Chestnut Street, Philadelphia, Pennsylvania 19104. 1983- .

UCC SKILLS: ARTICLES 3, 4, 5, AND 9: A COURSE HANDBOOK. Practising Law Institute, 810 Seventh Avenue, New York, New York 10019. 1985.

UNIFORM COMMERCIAL CODE IN A NUTSHELL. Third Edition. Bradford Stone. West Publishing Company, 50 West Kellogg Boulevard, St. Paul, Minnesota 55164-0526. 1989.

ENCYCLOPEDIAS AND DICTIONARIES

A FRENCH-ENGLISH DICTIONARY OF LEGAL AND COMMERCIAL TERMS. Graham Oliver. Fred B. Rothman and Company, 10368 West Centennial Road, Littleton, Colorado 80127. 1988.

DIGESTS, INDEXES, ABSTRACTS, CITATORS

BUSINESS LAW ARTICLES. Commerce Clearing House, Incorporated, 4025 West Peterson Avenue, Chicago, Illinois 60646. 1966- .

COMMERCIAL LAW

DIGEST OF COMMERCIAL LAWS OF THE WORLD: STATE VARIATIONS OF COMMERCIAL LAW. Oceana Publications, Incorporated, 75 Main Street, Dobbs Ferry, New York 10522. 1985- .

UNIFORM COMMERCIAL CODE CASE DIGEST. Callaghan and Company, 155 Pfingsten Road, Deerfield, Illinois 60015.

UNIFORM COMMERCIAL CODE COMMENTARY AND LAW DIGEST. Thomas Quinn and Louis F. Del Duca. Research Institute of America, Incorporated, One Penn Plaza, New York, New York 10119. 1978- . (Periodic Supplements).

UNIFORM COMMERCIAL CODE REPORTER -- DIGEST. Matthew Bender and Company, Incorporated, 11 Penn Plaza, New York, New York 10001. 1965- .

LAW REVIEWS AND PERIODICALS

COMMERCIAL LAW BULLETIN. Commercial Law League of America, 222 West Adams Street, Chicago, Illinois 60606. Bimonthly.

COMMERCIAL LAW JOURNAL. Commercial Law League of America, 222 West Adams Street, Chicago, Illinois 60606. Quarterly.

COMMERCIAL LAW REPORT. Matthew Bender and Company, Incorporated, 11 Penn Plaza, New York, New York 10001. Monthly.

NORTH CAROLINA JOURNAL OF INTERNATIONAL LAW AND COMMERCIAL REGULATION. University of North Carolina, School of Law, Chapel Hill, North Carolina 27514. Three times per year.

UNIFORM COMMERCIAL CODE LAW JOURNAL. Research Institute of America, Incorporated, 1633 Broadway, New York, New York 10002. Quarterly.

NEWSLETTERS AND NEWSPAPERS

DAILY COMMERCIAL RECORD. 706 Main Street, Dallas, Texas 75202. Daily.

JOURNAL OF COMMERCE AND COMMERCIAL. 445 Marshall Street, Phillipsburg, New Jersey 08865-2695. Daily.

ASSOCIATIONS AND PROFESSIONAL SOCIETIES

COMMERCIAL LAW LEAGUE OF AMERICA. 175 Jackson Boulevard, Suite 1541, Chicago, Illinois 60604. (312) 431-1305.

NATIONAL ASSOCIATION OF SECURITIES AND COMMERCIAL LAW ATTORNEYS. 1300 I Street, Northwest, East Tower, Suite 480, Washington, D.C. 20005. (202) 962-3863.

RESEARCH CENTERS, INSTITUTES, CLEARINGHOUSES

AMERICAN LAW INSTITUTE. 4025 Chestnut Street, Philadelphia, Pennsylvania 19104. (800) 253-6397.

INSTITUTE FOR LAW AND ECONOMICS. University of Pennsylvania, 3400 Chestnut Street, Philadelphia, Pennsylvania 19104. (215) 898-7852.

LOUISIANA STATE LAW INSTITUTE. Louisiana State University, Paul M. Hebert Law Center, Room 382, Baton Rouge, Louisiana 70803. (504) 342-6360.

AUDIOVISUALS

BASICS OF CONSUMER LAW: EFFECTIVE REPRESENTATION FOR BUYERS AND SELLERS. American Bar Association, 750 North Lake Shore Drive, Chicago, Illinois 60611. 1986. Videotape.

BUSINESS LITIGATION. National Institute for Trial Advocacy, Notre Dame Law School, Notre Dame, Indiana 46556. 1987. Videotape.

PURCHASE AND SALE OF COMMERCIAL REAL ESTATE. American Bar Association, 750 North Lake Shore Drive, Chicago, Illinois 60611. 1988. Videotape.

USING FINANCIAL EXPERTS IN BUSINESS LITIGATION. National Institute for Trial Advocacy, Notre Dame Law School, Notre Dame, Indiana 46556. 1988. Videotape.

COMMODITY FUTURES TRADING COMMISSION
See also: SECURITIES AND EXCHANGE COMMISSION

STATUTES, CODES, STANDARDS, UNIFORM LAWS

CODE OF FEDERAL REGULATIONS, TITLE 17. Office of the Federal Register, National Archives and Records Administration. Superintendent of Documents, United States Government Printing Office, Washington, D.C. 20402. Annual. (Updated by use of monthly List of Sections Affected and daily Federal Register .)

TEXTBOOKS AND GENERAL WORKS

THE COMMODITY FUTURES TRADING COMMISSION: CURRENT ISSUES. Practising Law Institute, 810 Seventh Avenue, New York, New York 10019. 1985.

RESEARCH CENTERS, INSTITUTES, CLEARINGHOUSES

UNITED STATES COMMODITY FUTURES TRADING COMMISSION LIBRARY. 2033 K Street, Northwest, Room 540, Washington, D.C. 20581. (202) 254-8630.

ONLINE DATABASES

LEXIS, FEDERAL SECURITIES. Mead Data Central, P.O. Box 933, Dayton, Ohio 45401.

WESTLAW, SECURITIES LIBRARY. West Publishing Company, P.O. Box 64526, 50 West Kellogg Boulevard, St. Paul, Minnesota 55164-0526.

COMMODITY TRADING
See also: COMMODITY FUTURES TRADING COMMISSION; SECURITIES AND EXCHANGE COMMISSION

STATUTES, CODES, STANDARDS, UNIFORM LAWS

CODE OF FEDERAL REGULATIONS, TITLE 17. Office of the Federal Register, National Archives and Records Administration. Superintendent of Documents, United States Government Printing Office, Washington, D.C. 20402. (Updated by use of monthly List of Sections Affected and daily Federal Register). Annual.

LOOSELEAF SERVICES AND REPORTERS

CFTC ADMINISTRATIVE REPORTER. Washington Service Bureau, Incorporated, 655 Fifteenth Street, Northwest, Washington, D.C. 20005. 1983- . (Monthly Supplements).

COMMODITIES REGULATION: FRAUD, MANIPULATION AND OTHER CLAIMS. Jerry W. Markham. Clark Boardman Company, Limited, 435 Hudson Street, New York, New York 10014. 1987- . (Annual Supplements).

COMMODITY FUTURES LAW REPORTS. Commerce Clearing House, 4025 West Peterson Avenue, Chicago, Illinois 60646. 1974- . (Semimonthly Supplements).

LAW AND POLICY OF INTER-GOVERNMENTAL PRIMARY COMMODITY AGREEMENTS. Charles R. Johnston. Oceana Publications, Incorporated, 75 Main Street, Dobbs Ferry, New York 10522. 1976- .

MID AMERICA COMMODITY EXCHANGE RULES AND REGULATIONS. Mid America Commodity Exchange, 141 West Jackson Boulevard, Chicago, Illinois 60606. 1976- . (Periodic Supplements).

NATIONAL FUTURES ASSOCIATION MANUAL. Prentice-Hall Law and Business, Route 9W, Englewood Cliffs, New Jersey 07632. 1983- .

NEW YORK MERCANTILE EXCHANGE GUIDE. Commerce Clearing House, Incorporated, 4025 West Peterson Avenue, Chicago, Illinois 60646. 1986- . (Monthly Supplements).

REGULATION OF THE COMMODITIES FUTURES AND OPTION MARKETS. Thomas A. Russo. Shepard's/McGraw-Hill, P.O. Box 1235, Colorado Springs, Colorado 80901. 1983- . (Annual Supplement).

RULES AND REGULATIONS OF THE CHICAGO BOARD OF TRADE. Chicago Board of Trade, 141 West Jackson Boulevard, Chicago, Illinois 60604. (Monthly Supplements).

RULES AND REGULATIONS OF THE CHICAGO MERCANTILE EXCHANGE. 30 South Wacker Drive, Chicago, Illinois 60606. (Periodic Supplements).

RULES AND REGULATIONS OF THE MINNEAPOLIS GRAIN EXCHANGE. Minneapolis Grain Exchange, 150 Grain Exchange Building, 400 South Fourth Street, Minneapolis, Minnesota 55415. 1981- .

SECURITIES AND COMMODITIES DEALERS. Mark Rachleff. Commerce Clearing House, Incorporated, 4025 West Peterson Avenue, Chicago, Illinois 60646. 1987- .

SECURITIES FRAUD AND COMMODITIES FRAUD. Alan R. Bromberg and Lewis D. Lowenfels. Shepard's/McGraw Hill, P.O. Box 1235, Colorado Springs, Colorado 80901. 1967- . (Annual Supplements).

HANDBOOKS, MANUALS, FORMBOOKS

THE DOW JONES-IRWIN GUIDE TO COMMODITIES TRADING. (Revised Edition). Bruce G. Gould. Dow Jones-Irwin, Incorporated, 1818 Ridge Road, Homewood, Illinois 60430. 1981.

WORLD'S MAJOR STOCK EXCHANGES: LISTING REQUIREMENTS. Price Waterhouse Center for Transnational Taxation, New York, New York. 10984. 1984- .

TEXTBOOKS AND GENERAL WORKS

COMMODITIES REGULATION. Second Edition. Philip F. Johnson. Little, Brown and Company, 34 Beacon Street, Boston, Massachusetts 02108. 1982.

THE COMMODITY FUTURES TRADING COMMISSION: CURRENT ISSUES. Susan M. Phillips, Chairman, Practising Law Institute, 810 Seventh Avenue, New York, New York 10019. 1985.

COMMODITY PRICES AND THE NEW INFLATION. Barry P. Bosworth and Robert Z. Lawrence. The Brookings Institution, 1775 Massachusetts Avenue, Northwest, Washington, D.C. 20036-2188. 1982.

COMMODITY TEXTURES: AN EXPANDING REGULATORY WORLD. Practising Law Institute, 810 Seventh Avenue, New York, New York 10019. 1984.

FUTURES MARKETS: REGULATORY ISSUES. Anne E. Peck, Editor. American Enterprise Institute for Public Policy Research, 1150 Seventeenth Street, Northwest, Washington, D.C. 20036. 1985.

HEDGING WITH FINANCIAL FUTURES FOR INSTITUTIONAL INVESTORS: THEORY AND PRACTICE. Stephen Figlewski. HarperCollins Publishers, 10 East Fifty-third Street, New York, New York 10022. 1985.

THE HISTORY OF COMMODITY FUTURES TRADING AND ITS REGULATION. Jerry W. Markham. Praeger Publishers, Greenwood Publishing Group, Incorporated, 88 Post Road West, P.O. Box 5007, Westport, Connecticut 06881. 1987.

INTERNATIONAL COMMODITY AGREEMENTS: A LEGAL STUDY. B.S. Chimni. Croom Helm, Paul H. Brookes Publishing Company, P.O. Box 10624, Baltimore, Maryland 21285. 1987.

INTERNATIONAL COMMODITY AGREEMENTS: THE SYSTEM OF CONTROLLING THE INTERNATIONAL COMMODITY MARKET. Ervin Ernst. Kluwer Academic Publishers, 101 Philip Drive, Assinippi Park, Norwell, Massachusetts 02061. 1982.

INTERNATIONAL COMMODITY CONTROL: A CONTEMPORARY HISTORY AND APPRAISAL. Fiona Gordon-Ashworth. St. Martin's Press, Incorporated, 175 Fifth Avenue, New York, New York 10010. 1984.

INTRODUCTION TO TAXATION OF FINANCIAL INSTRUMENTS: FEDERAL INCOME TAXATION OF CAPITAL TRANSACTIONS IN SECURITIES, STRADDLES, OPTIONS, AND FUTURES. Henry D. Shereff. American Law Institute-American Bar Association, 4025 Chestnut Street, Philadelphia, Pennsylvania 19104. 1990.

AN INVESTOR'S GUIDE TO COMMODITIES FUTURES MARKET. David Courtney and Eric Bettelheim. Butterworth Legal Publishers, 90 Stiles Road, Salem, New Hampshire 03079. 1986.

MANAGING INTERNATIONAL MARKETS: DEVELOPING COUNTRIES AND COMMODITY TRADE REGIME. Jock A. Finlayson. Columbia University Press, 562 West One Hundred Thirteenth Street, New York, New York 10025. 1988.

NEW DEVELOPMENTS IN COMMODITY FUTURES REGULATION AND ENFORCEMENT. Practising Law Institute, 810 Seventh Avenue, New York, New York 10019. 1989- .

REGULATION OF COMMODITIES FUTURES AND OPTIONS MARKETS. Thomas A. Russo, Shepard's/McGraw Hill, P.O. Box 1235, Colorado Springs, Colorado 80901. 1983- .

SECURITIES AND COMMODITIES ENFORCEMENT: CRIMINAL PROSECUTIONS AND CIVIL INJUNCTIONS. Howard M. Friedman. Lexington Books, 125 Spring Street, Lexington, Massachusetts 02173. 1981.

TAX ASPECTS OF COMMODITY AND FINANCIAL FUTURES TRANSACTIONS. Geoffrey Pink. Butterworth Legal Publishers, 90 Stiles Road, Salem, New Hampshire 03079. 1985.

TAXATION OF SECURITIES, COMMODITIES, AND OPTIONS. Andrea Kramer. John Wiley and Sons, Incorporated, 605 Third Avenue, New York, New York 10158. 1986.

TECHNOLOGY AND THE REGULATION OF FINANCIAL MARKETS: SECURITIES, FUTURES AND BANKING. Anthony Saunders and Lawrence J. White, Editors. Free Press, 866 Third Avenue, New York, New York 10022. 1985.

LAW REVIEWS AND PERIODICALS

FIA REVIEW. Futures Industry Association, 1825 I Street, Northwest, Suite 1040, Washington, D.C. 20006. Bimonthly.

THE JOURNAL OF FUTURES MARKETS. Center for the Study of Futures Markets, Columbia University. John Wiley and Sons, Incorporated, 605 Third Avenue, New York, New York 10158. Quarterly.

MFTA JOURNAL. Managed Futures Trade Association, One Glendinning Place, Westport, Connecticut 06880. Semiannual.

NEWSLETTERS AND NEWSPAPERS

COMMODITIES LAW LETTER. Commodities Law Press Associates, 900 Third Avenue, New York, New York 10022. Monthly.

COMMODITIES LITIGATION REPORTER. Andrews Publications, 1646 West Chester Pike, Westtown, Pennsylvania 19395. Semimonthly.

MFTA NEWSLETTER. Managed Futures Trade Association, One Glendinning Place, Westport, Connecticut 06880. Monthly.

NAFTA NEWSLETTER. National Association of Futures Trading Advisors, 1919 Pennsylvania Avenue, Northwest, Suite 300, Washington, D.C. 20006. Monthly.

NFA - NEWS, FACTS, ACTIONS. National Futures Association, 200 West Madison Street, Suite 1600, Chicago, Illinois 60606. Bimonthly.

REVIEW OF SECURITIES AND COMMODITIES REGULATION. Standard and Poor's, 25 Broadway, New York, New York 10004. Semimonthly.

SAC AWARD REPORTER. Securities Arbitration Commentator, P.O. Box 112, Maplewood, New Jersey 07040. Monthly.

SECURITIES REGULATION AND LAW REPORT. Bureau of National Affairs, Incorporated, 1231 Twenty-fifth Street, Northwest, Washington, D.C. 20037. Weekly.

WEEKLY BULLETIN. Futures Industry Association, 1825 I Street, Northwest, Suite 1040, Washington, D.C. 20006. Weekly.

ASSOCIATIONS AND PROFESSIONAL SOCIETIES

FUTURES INDUSTRY ASSOCIATION. 1825 I Street, Northwest, Suite 1040, Washington, D.C. 20006. (202) 466-5460.

MANAGED FUTURES TRADE ASSOCIATION. One Glendinning Place, Westport, Connecticut 06880. (203) 221-1260.

NATIONAL ASSOCIATION OF FUTURES TRADING ADVISORS. 1919 Pennsylvania Avenue, Northwest, Suite 300, Washington, D.C. 20006. (202) 872-9186.

NATIONAL FUTURES ASSOCIATION. 200 West Madison Street, Suite 1600, Chicago, Illinois 60606. (312) 781-1300.

RESEARCH CENTERS, INSTITUTES, CLEARINGHOUSES

CENTER FOR RESEARCH IN FUTURES MARKETS. University of Chicago, 1101 East Fifty-Eighth Street, Chicago, Illinois 60637. (312) 702-7275.

CENTER FOR THE STUDY OF FINANCIAL INSTITUTIONS AND MARKETS. Southern Methodist University, Cox School of Business, Dallas, Texas 72575. (214) 692-2627.

CENTER FOR THE STUDY OF FUTURES MARKETS. Columbia University, Columbia Business School, 802 Uris Hall, New York, New York 10027. (212) 854-4202.

GLUCKSMAN INSTITUTE FOR RESEARCH IN SECURITIES MARKETS. New York University, Saloman Brothers Center, 90 Trinity Place, New York, New York 10006. (212) 285-6100.

COMMON LAW
See also: JUDGMENTS

TEXTBOOKS AND GENERAL WORKS

BENTHAM AND THE COMMON LAW TRADITION. Gerald J. Postema. Clarendon Press, Oxford University Press, 200 Madison Avenue, New York, New York 10016. 1989.

CODIFIED AND JUDGE MADE LAW: THE ROLE OF COURTS AND LEGISLATORS IN CIVIL AND COMMON LAW SYSTEMS. J.G. Sauveplanne. Elsevier Science Publishing Company, Incorporated, P.O. Box 882, Madison Square Station, New York, New York 10159. 1982.

COMMON LAW AND EQUITY UNDER THE UNIFORM COMMERCIAL CODE. Robert A. Hillman, Julian McDonald and Steve Nickles. Research Institute of America, Incorporated, 210 South Street, Boston, Massachusetts 02111. 1985. (Annual Supplements).

A COMMON LAW FOR THE AGE OF STATUTES. Guido Calabresi. Harvard University Press, 79 Garden Street, Cambridge, Massachusetts 02138. 1982.

HANDBOOK OF COMMON LAW PLEADING. Joseph A. Koffler and Alison Reppy. West Publishing Company, 50 West Kellogg Boulevard, St. Paul, Minnesota 55164. 1969.

HISTORICAL INTRODUCTION TO ANGLO-AMERICAN LAW IN A NUTSHELL. Second Edition. Frederick G. Kempin, Jr. West Publishing Company, 50 West Kellogg Boulevard, St. Paul, Minnesota 55164. 1990.

HOLMES AND THE COMMON LAW: A CENTURY LATER: THREE LECTURES. Benjamin Kaplan, Patrick Atiyah and Jan Vetter. Harvard Law School, Harvard University Press, 79 Garden Street, Cambridge, Massachusetts 02138. 1983.

AN INTRODUCTION TO THE ANGLO-AMERICAN LEGAL SYSTEM: READINGS AND CASES. Second Edition. West Publishing Company, 50 West Kellogg Boulevard, St. Paul, Minnesota 55164. 1988.

JUDGES, LEGISLATORS, AND PROFESSORS: CHAPTERS IN EUROPEAN LEGAL HISTORY. R.C. van Caenegem. Cambridge University Press, 40 West Twentieth Street, New York, New York 10011. 1987.

LAW'S EMPIRE. Ronald Dworkin. Belknap Press, 79 Garden Street, Cambridge, Massachusetts 02138. 1986.

THE LEGAL PROFESSION AND THE COMMON LAW: HISTORICAL ESSAYS. John Hamilton Baker. Hambledon Press, P.O. Box 162, Rio Grande, Ohio 45674-0162. 1986.

LEGAL THEORY AND COMMON LAW. Michael Twining, Editor. Basil Blackwell, Incorporated, 3 Cambridge Center, Cambridge, Massachusetts 02142. 1986.

LEGAL THEORY AND LEGAL HISTORY: ESSAYS ON THE COMMON LAW. A.W.B. Simpson. Hambledon Press, 309 Greenbriar Avenue, Ronceverte, West Virginia 24970. 1987.

THE NATURE OF THE COMMON LAW. Melvin A. Eisenberg. Harvard University Press, 79 Garden Street, Cambridge, Massachusetts 02138. 1988.

OUR LADY THE COMMON LAW: AN ANGLO-AMERICAN LEGAL COMMUNITY, 1870-1930. Richard A. Cosgrove. New York University Press, distributed by Columbia University Press, 70 Washington Square, South, New York, New York 10012. 1986.

STUDIES IN THE HISTORY OF COMMON LAW. S.E.C. Milsom. Hambledon Press, P.O. Box 162, Rio Grande, Ohio 45674-0162. 1985.

COMMUNICATIONS LAW
See: FEDERAL COMMUNICATIONS COMMISSION; TELECOMMUNICATIONS; TELEVISION AND RADIO

COMMUNITY PROPERTY

STATUTES, CODES, STANDARDS, UNIFORM LAWS

UNIFORM MARITAL PROPERTY ACT. National Conference of Commissioners on Uniform State Laws. Uniform Laws Annotated. West Publishing Company, P.O. Box 64526, 50 West Kellogg Boulevard, St. Paul, Minnesota 55164-0526. 1976- . (Annual Supplements).

LOOSELEAF SERVICES AND REPORTERS

CALIFORNIA COMMUNITY PROPERTY WITH TAX ANALYSIS. Joseph J. Stein and Jack Zuckerman. Matthew Bender and Company, Incorporated, 11 Penn Plaza, New York, New York 10001. 1985- . (Periodic Supplements).

VALUATION AND DISTRIBUTION OF MARITAL PROPERTY. John P. McCahey, Editor. Matthew Bender and Company, Incorporated, 11 Penn Plaza, New York, New York 10001. 1984- . (Periodic Supplements).

TEXTBOOKS AND GENERAL WORKS

THE CHANGING RIGHTS OF MARRIED WOMEN, 1800-1861. Elizabeth B. Warbasse. Garland Publishing, Incorporated, 136 Madison Avenue, New York, New York 10016. 1987.

COMMUNITY PROPERTY. Twelfth Edition. William A. Reppy, Jr., Gilberts Law Summaries, distributed by Law Distributors, 14415 South Main Street, Gardena, California 90248. 1982.

COMMUNITY PROPERTY IN A NUTSHELL. Second Edition. Robert L. Mennell. P.O. Box 64526, West Publishing Company, 50 West Kellogg Boulevard, St. Paul, Minnesota 55164-0526. 1988.

COMMUNITY PROPERTY

COMMUNITY PROPERTY IN THE UNITED STATES. Second Edition. William A. Reppy, Jr. and Cynthia A. Samuel. Michie/Bobbs-Merrill Law Publishing, P.O. Box 7587, Charlottesville, Virginia 22906-7582. 1982.

COMMUNITY PROPERTY LAW IN THE UNITED STATES. W.S. McClanahan. Lawyers Co-Operative Publishing Company, Aqueduct Building, Rochester, New York 14694. 1982- . (Periodic Supplements).

COMPARATIVE STUDIES IN COMMUNITY PROPERTY LAW. Jan P. Charmatz and Harriet Daggett. Greenwood Publishing Group, Incorporated, 88 Post Road West, P.O. Box 5007, Westport, Connecticut 06881. 1977.

THE MARITAL DEDUCTION. James B. Lewis. Practising Law Institute, 810 Seventh Avenue, New York, New York 10019. 1984.

MARITAL PROPERTY IN NEW ENGLAND. Sanford Katz and Samuel V. Schoonmaker. Butterworth Legal Publishers, 90 Stiles Road, Salem, New Hampshire 03079. 1984.

MARRIED WOMEN'S SEPARATE PROPERTY IN ENGLAND, 1660-1833. Susan Staves. Harvard University Press, 79 Garden Street, Cambridge, Massachusetts 02138. 1990.

PRINCIPLES OF COMMUNITY PROPERTY. Second Edition. William Q. De Funiak and Michael J. Vaughn. Books on Demand, 300 North Zeeb Road, Ann Arbor, Michigan 48106-1346. 1971.

TEXAS MATRIMONIAL PROPERTY LAW. Joseph W. McKnight. Michie/Bobbs- Merrill Law Publishing, P.O. Box 7587, Charlottesville, Virginia 22906-7582. 1983.

A TREATISE ON THE PROPERTY RIGHTS OF HUSBAND AND WIFE, UNDER THE COMMUNITY OF GANANCIAL SYSTEM: ADAPTED TO THE STATUTES AND DECISIONS OF LOUISIANA, TEXAS, CALIFORNIA, NEVADA, WASHINGTON, IDAHO, ARIZONA, AND NEW MEXICO. Richard Achilles Ballinger. Fred B. Rothman and Company, 10368 West Centennial Road, Littleton, Colorado 80127. 1981.

VALUATION AND DISTRIBUTION OF MARITAL PROPERTY. Matthew Bender and Company, Incorporated, 11 Penn Plaza, New York, New York 10001. 1985- .

WOMEN AND THE LAW OF PROPERTY IN EARLY AMERICA. Marylynn Salmon. University of North Carolina Press, P.O. Box 2288, Chapel Hill, North Carolina 27515. 1986.

LAW REVIEWS AND PERIODICALS

COMMUNITY PROPERTY JOURNAL. Aspen Publishers, Incorporated, 16792 Oakmont Avenue, Gaithersburg, Maryland 20877. 1974- . Quarterly.

BIBLIOGRAPHIES

GONZAGA LAW REVIEW: COMMUNITY PROPERTY BIBLIOGRAPHY. Lorraine E. Rodich. Gonzaga University School of Law, Spokane, Washington 99202. 1983-1984.

COMPARABLE WORTH
See: EQUAL EMPLOYMENT OPPORTUNITY

COMPARATIVE LAW
See also: CONFLICT OF LAWS

LOOSELEAF SERVICES AND REPORTERS

FOREIGN LAW: CURRENT SOURCES OF CODES AND BASIC LEGISLATION IN JURISDICTIONS OF THE WORLD. Thomas H. Reynolds. Fred B. Rothman and Company, 10368 West Centennial Road, Littleton, Colorado 80127. 1989- .

HANDBOOKS, MANUALS, FORMBOOKS

GUIDE TO INTERNATIONAL LEGAL RESEARCH. Butterworth Legal Publishers, 90 Stiles Road, Salem, New Hampshire 03079. 1990.

LEGAL TRADITIONS AND SYSTEMS: AN INTERNATIONAL HANDBOOK. Alan N. Katz. Greenwood Publishing Group, Incorporated, 88 Post Road West, P.O. Box 5007, Westport, Connecticut 06881. 1986.

TEXTBOOKS AND GENERAL WORKS

COMPARATIVE LAW AND LEGAL SYSTEMS: HISTORICAL AND SOCIO-LEGAL PERSPECTIVES. W.E. Butler and V.N. Kudriavtsev, Editors. Oceana Publications, Incorporated, 75 Main Street, Dobbs Ferry, New York 10522. 1985.

COMPARATIVE LEGAL TRADITIONS IN A NUTSHELL. Mary Ann Glendon, Wallace Gordon and Christopher Osakwe. West Publishing Company, P.O. Box 64526, 50 West Kellogg Boulevard, St. Paul, Minnesota 55164-0526. 1982.

COUNTRIES AND CONCEPTS: AN INTRODUCTION TO COMPARATIVE POLITICS. Third Edition. Prentice-Hall, Incorporated, 113 Sylvan Avenue, Englewood Cliffs, New Jersey 07632. 1989.

CRIMINAL LAW IN ACTION: AN OVERVIEW OF CURRENT ISSUES IN WESTERN SOCIETIES. Jan van Dijk, Editor. Kluwer Academic Publishers, 101 Philip Drive, Assinippi Park, Norwell, Massachusetts 02061. 1986.

DEMOCRACY: A WORLDWIDE SURVEY. Robert Wesson, Editor. Praeger Publishers, One Madison Avenue, New York, New York 10010. 1987.

EASTERN IMPORTATION OF WESTERN CRIMINAL LAW: THAILAND AS A CASE STUDY. Apirat Petchsiri. Fred B. Rothman and Company, 10368 West Centennial Road, Littleton, Colorado 80127. 1987.

ESSAYS ON INTERNATIONAL AND COMPARATIVE LAW IN HONOUR OF JUDGE ERADES. Kluwer Academic Publishers, 101 Philip Drive, Assinippi Park, Norwell, Massachusetts 02061. 1983.

FORMATION OF CONTRACT: A COMPARATIVE STUDY OF ISLAMIC, IRANIAN, ENGLISH AND FRENCH LAW. P. Owsia. Kluwer Academic Publishers, 101 Philip Drive, Norwell, Massachusetts 02061. 1988.

AN INTRODUCTION TO COMPARATIVE LAW. Second Edition. Konrad Zweigert. Oxford University Press, 200 Madison Avenue, New York, New York 10016. 1987.

LAW IN RADICALLY DIFFERENT CULTURES. John H. Barton. West Publishing Company, P.O. Box 64526, 50 West Kellogg Boulevard, St. Paul, Minnesota 55164-0526. 1983.

THE SOVIET WAY OF CRIME: BEATING THE SYSTEM IN THE SOVIET UNION AND THE U.S.A. Lydia S. Rosner. Greenwood Publishing Group, Incorporated, 88 Post Road, West, P.O. Box 5007, Westport, Connecticut 06881. 1986.

THE STRENGTH AND WEAKNESS OF COMPARATIVE LAW. Bernhard Grossfeld. Oxford University Press, 200 Madison Avenue, New York, New York 10016. 1990.

ENCYCLOPEDIAS AND DICTIONARIES

INTERNATIONAL ENCYCLOPEDIA OF COMPARATIVE LAW. Kluwer Academic Publishers, 101 Philip Drive, Assinippi Park, Norwell, Massachusetts 02061. 1971- .

ANNUALS AND SURVEYS

COMPARATIVE LAW YEARBOOK. Center for International Legal Studies. Kluwer Academic Publishers, 101 Philip Drive, Assinippi Park, Norwell, Massachusetts 02061. Annual.

THE FINE IN COMPARATIVE LAW: A SURVEY OF 21 COUNTRIES. Gerhardt Grebing. Cambridge University Press, 40 West Twentieth Street, New York, New York 10011. 1982.

LOYOLA OF LOS ANGELES INTERNATIONAL AND COMPARATIVE LAW ANNUAL. Loyola of Los Angeles School of Law, 1441 Olympic Boulevard, Los Angeles, California 90015. Annual.

LAW REVIEWS AND PERIODICALS

AMERICAN JOURNAL OF COMPARATIVE LAW. American Foreign Law Association, c/o Richard E. Lutringer, Whitman and Ransom, 200 Park Avenue, New York, New York 10166. Quarterly.

THE AMERICAN JOURNAL OF COMPARATIVE LAW. American Association for the Comparative Study of Law, c/o Honorable Edward D. Re, United States Court of International Trade, One Federal Plaza, New York, New York 10017. Quarterly.

ARIZONA JOURNAL OF INTERNATIONAL AND COMPARATIVE LAW. University of Arizona College of Law, Tucson, Arizona 85721. Semiannual.

BOSTON COLLEGE INTERNATIONAL AND COMPARATIVE LAW REVIEW. Boston College School of Law, 885 Centre Street, Newton Centre, Massachusetts 02159. Semiannual.

COLUMBIA JOURNAL OF TRANSNATIONAL LAW. Box D-25, Columbia University, School of Law, 435 West One Hundred Sixteenth Street, New York, New York 10027. Three issues per year.

GEORGIA JOURNAL OF INTERNATIONAL AND COMPARATIVE LAW. University of Georgia School of Law, Athens, Georgia 30602. Three issues per year.

HASTINGS INTERNATIONAL AND COMPARATIVE LAW REVIEW. Hastings College of Law, 200 McAllister Street, San Francisco, California 94102. Three issues per year.

LOYOLA OF LOS ANGELES INTERNATIONAL AND COMPARATIVE LAW JOURNAL. Loyola of Los Angeles School of Law, 1441 Olympic Boulevard, Los Angeles, California 90015. Three issues per year.

NEW YORK LAW SCHOOL JOURNAL OF INTERNATIONAL AND COMPARATIVE LAW. New York Law School, 57 Worth Street, New York, New York 10013. Three issues per year.

SUFFOLK UNIVERSITY TRANSNATIONAL LAW JOURNAL. Suffolk University, School of Law, 41 Temple Street, Boston, Massachusetts 02114. Three issues per year.

BIBLIOGRAPHIES

A BIBLIOGRAPHY ON FOREIGN AND COMPARATIVE LAW: BOOKS AND ARTICLES IN ENGLISH, 1790-1953; 1953-1959; 1960-1965; 1966-1971; 1972-1978; 1979-83. Charles Szladits, Compiler. Oceana Publications, Incorporated, 75 Main Street, Dobbs Ferry, New York 10522. 1955-1981. (Annual Supplements).

SZLADITS' BIBLIOGRAPHY ON FOREIGN AND COMPARATIVE LAW: BOOKS AND ARTICLES IN ENGLISH, 1984-86. Vratislav Pechota, Compiler. Oceana Publications, Incorporated, 75 Main Street, Dobbs Ferry, New York 10522. 1990- .

ASSOCIATIONS AND PROFESSIONAL SOCIETIES

AMERICAN ASSOCIATION FOR THE COMPARATIVE STUDY OF LAW. c/o Honorable Edward D. Re, United States Court of International Trade, One Federal Plaza, New York, New York 10017. (212) 264-2800.

AMERICAN FOREIGN LAW ASSOCIATION. c/o Richard E. Lutringer, Whitman and Ransom, 200 Park Avenue, New York, New York 10166. (212) 351-3277.

INTERNATIONAL THIRD WORLD LEGAL STUDIES ASSOCIATION. c/o International Center for Law in Development, 777 United Nations Plaza, New York, New York 10017. (212) 687-0036.

JAPANESE AMERICAN SOCIETY FOR LEGAL STUDIES. c/o Professor Daniel H. Foote, University of Washington School of Law, Seattle, Washington 98105. (206) 545-1897.

SECTION OF COMPARATIVE LAW, ASSOCIATION OF AMERICAN LAW SCHOOLS. One Dupont Circle, Northwest, Washington, D.C. 20036. (202) 296-8851.

SECTION OF INTERNATIONAL LAW AND PRACTICE. American Bar Association, 1800 M Street, Northwest, Suite 200, Washington, D.C. 20036. (202) 331-2239.

SOUTHWESTERN LEGAL FOUNDATION, INTERNATIONAL AND COMPARATIVE LAW CENTER. c/o Cindie J. Burkel, P.O. Box 830707, Richardson, Texas 75083. (214) 690-2370.

RESEARCH CENTERS, INSTITUTES, CLEARINGHOUSES

CENTER OF CIVIL LAW STUDIES. Louisiana State University, Paul M. Hebert Law Center, Baton Rouge, Louisiana 70803. (504) 388-1126.

DEAN RUSK CENTER FOR INTERNATIONAL AND COMPARATIVE LAW. University of Georgia, Athens, Georgia 30602. (404) 542-7875.

INSTITUTE OF COMPARATIVE LAW. McGill University, 3674 Peel Street, Montreal, PQ, Canada H3A 1X1. (514) 398-6646.

INTERNATIONAL AND COMPARATIVE LEGAL STUDIES PROGRAMS. Harvard University, 1557 Massachusetts Avenue, Cambridge, Massachusetts 02138. (617) 495-3117.

INTERNATIONAL LAW INSTITUTE. 1615 New Hampshire Avenue, Northwest, Washington, D.C. 20009. (202) 483-7979.

INTERNATIONAL LEGAL STUDIES PROGRAM. Cornell University, Myrom Taylor Hall, Ithaca, New York 14853. (607) 255-3469.

COMPARATIVE NEGLIGENCE
See: TORTS

COMPENSATION OF CRIME VICTIMS
See: CRIME VICTIMS

COMPETITION AND UNFAIR COMPETITION
See: ANTITRUST LAW; TRADE SECRETS

COMPLEX LITIGATION
See also: CLASS ACTIONS

LOOSELEAF SERVICES AND REPORTERS

MANUAL FOR COMPLEX LITIGATION. Second Edition. Commerce Clearing House, Incorporated, 4025 West Peterson Avenue, Chicago, Illinois 60646. 1985- .

MANUAL FOR COMPLEX LITIGATION. Second Edition. Clark Boardman Company, Limited, 435 Hudson Street, New York, New York 10014. 1986. (Periodic Supplements).

HANDBOOKS, MANUALS, FORMBOOKS

COMPLEX LITIGATION RESEARCH MANUAL. Terrence F. Kiely. John Wiley and Sons, Incorporated, 605 Third Avenue, New York, New York 10158. 1987.

GUIDE TO MULTISTATE LITIGATION. Victor E. Schwartz, Patrick W. Lee and Kathryn Kelly. Shepard's/McGraw-Hill, P.O. Box 1235, Colorado Springs, Colorado 80901. 1985- . (Periodic Supplements).

USING LITIGATION DATABASES. Terrence F. Kiely. John Wiley and Sons, Incorporated, 605 Third Avenue, New York, New York 10158. 1987.

TEXTBOOKS AND GENERAL WORKS

ASBESTOS IN THE COURTS: THE CHALLENGE OF MASS TOXIC TORTS. Deborah R. Hemsler. Rand Corporation, 1700 Main Street, P.O. Box 2138, Santa Monica, California 90406-2138. 1985.

CIVIL PRACTICE AND LITIGATION IN FEDERAL AND STATE COURTS: RESOURCE MATERIALS. Third Edition. American Law Institute - American Bar Association, 4025 Chestnut Street, Philadelphia, Pennsylvania 19104. 1985.

COMPLEX LITIGATION CONFRONTS THE JURY SYSTEM: A CASE STUDY. Arthur D. Austin. Greenwood Publishing Group, Incorporated, 88 Post Road, West, P.O. Box 5007, Westport, Connecticut 06881. 1984.

LITIGATION FOR THE NON-LITIGATOR: THE ROLE OF THE CORPORATE LAWYER IN THE LITIGATION PROCESS. Practising Law Institute, 810 Seventh Avenue, New York, New York 10019. 1987.

MANAGEMENT OF COMPLEX MASS TORT LITIGATION: PREPARING FOR TRIAL. Practising Law Institute, 810 Seventh Avenue, New York, New York 10019. 1986.

MULTIDISTRICT LITIGATION: HANDLING CASES BEFORE THE JUDICIAL PANEL ON MULTIDISTRICT LITIGATION. David F. Herr. Little, Brown and Company, 34 Beacon Street, Boston, Massachusetts 02108. 1986- . (Periodic Supplements).

OTHER SOURCES

COMPLEX LITIGATION PROJECT: REPORTERS' PRELIMINARY MEMORANDUM ON CHAPTER SIX. American Law Institute, 4025 Chestnut Street, Philadelphia, Pennsylvania 19104. 1990.

PRELIMINARY STUDY OF COMPLEX LITIGATION. American Law Institute, 4025 Chestnut Street, Philadelphia, Pennsylvania 19104. 1987.

COMPROMISE AND SETTLEMENT
See also: DISPUTE RESOLUTION

LOOSELEAF SERVICES AND REPORTERS

ART OF ADVOCACY. SETTLEMENT. Henry G. Miller. Matthew Bender and Company, Incorporated, 11 Penn Plaza, New York, New York 10001. 1983- . (Periodic Supplements).

STRUCTURED SETTLEMENTS AND PERIODIC PAYMENTS JUDGMENTS. Daniel W. Hindert. Law Journal Seminars-Press, Incorporated, 111 Eighth Avenue, Suite 900, New York, New York 10011. 1986- . (Periodic Supplements).

STRUCTURED SETTLEMENTS: DESIGN AND EVALUATION. Steven Cooper and others. Structured Benefit Consultants, P.O. Box 1976, Topeka, Kansas 66601. 1983- . (Annual Supplements).

HANDBOOKS, MANUALS, FORMBOOKS

ADR AND THE COURTS: A MANUAL FOR JUDGES AND LAWYERS. Erika S. Fine, Editor. Butterworth Legal Publishers, 90 Stiles Road, Salem, New Hampshire 03079. 1987.

EFFECTIVE APPROACHES TO SETTLEMENT: A HANDBOOK FOR LAWYERS AND JUDGES. Wayne D. Brazil. Prentice-Hall Law and Business, Route 9W, Englewood Cliffs, New Jersey 07632. 1988.

TEXTBOOKS AND GENERAL WORKS

COMPROMISE IN ETHICS, LAW AND POLITICS: NOMOS XXI. J. Roland Pennock and John W. Chapman. New York University Press, 70 Washington Square, South, New York, New York 10012. 1979.

CORPORATE DISPUTE MANAGEMENT, 1982: A MANUAL OF INNOVATIVE CORPORATE STRATEGIES FOR THE AVOIDANCE AND RESOLUTION OF LEGAL DISPUTES. Center for Public Resources, Matthew Bender and Company, Incorporated, 11 Penn Plaza, New York, New York 10001. 1982.

EDUCATION AND MEDIATION: EXPLORING THE ALTERNATIVES. Standing Committee on Dispute Resolution, American Bar Association, 1800 M Street, Northwest, Washington, D.C. 20037. 1988.

EFFECTIVE LEGAL NEGOTIATION AND SETTLEMENT. Charles B. Craver. The Michie Company, P.O. Box 7587, Charlottesville, Virginia 22906-7582. 1986.

EVALUATING AND NEGOTIATING SETTLEMENTS IN PERSONAL INJURY CASES. Practising Law Institute, 810 Seventh Avenue, New York, New York 10019. 1981- . (Annual).

HOW TO KEEP YOUR COMPANY OUT OF COURT: THE PRACTICAL LEGAL GUIDE FOR GROWING BUSINESSES. Paul A. Allen. Prentice-Hall, Incorporated, 113 Sylvan Avenue, Englewood Cliffs, New Jersey 07632. 1984.

LEGISLATION ON DISPUTE RESOLUTIONS. Lawrence Freedman. Special Committee on Alternative Means of Dispute Resolution, American Bar Association, 1800 M Street, Northwest, Washington, D.C. 20036. 1984.

THE MANAGER'S GUIDE TO RESOLVING LEGAL DISPUTES: BETTER RESULTS WITHOUT LITIGATION. James F. Henry and Jethro K. Lieberman. HarperCollins Publishers, 10 East Fifty-third Street, New York, New York 10022. 1985.

NEGOTIATING TO SETTLEMENT IN DIVORCE. Sanford N. Katz, Editor. Prentice Hall Law and Business, Incorporated, 113 Sylvan Avenue, Englewood Cliffs, New Jersey 07632. 1987.

NEGOTIATION PRACTICE. Roger S. Haydock. John Wiley and Sons, Incorporated, 605 Third Avenue, New York, New York 10158. 1984.

PROJECT EARLY SETTLEMENT: AN ALTERNATIVE TO THE COURTS. Special Committee on Dispute Resolution, American Bar Association, 1800 M Street, Northwest, Washington, D.C. 20036. 1984.

THE RESOLUTION OF CONFLICT: CONSTRUCTIVE AND DESTRUCTIVE PROCESSES. Morton Deutsch. Yale University Press, 302 Temple Street, New Haven, Connecticut 06520. 1973.

RESOLVING DISPUTES WITHOUT LITIGATION. Bureau of National Affairs, Incorporated, 1231 Twenty-fifth Street, Northwest, Washington, D.C. 20037. 1985.

THE ROLE OF THE JUDGE IN THE SETTLEMENT PROCESS. Federal Judicial Center, 1520 H Street, Northwest, Washington, D.C. 20005. 1977.

SETTLEMENT STRATEGIES FOR FEDERAL DISTRICT JUDGES. D. Marie Provine. Federal Judicial Center, 1520 H Street, Northwest, Washington, D.C. 20005. 1986.

SETTLEMENTS INCLUDING DEFERRED PAYMENTS. Practising Law Institute, 810 Seventh Avenue, New York, New York 10019. 1984.

SETTLING CIVIL SUITS: LITIGATORS' VIEWS ABOUT APPROPRIATE ROLES AND EFFECTIVE TECHNIQUES FOR FEDERAL JUDGES. Wayne D. Brazil. American Bar Association, 750 North Lake Shore Drive, Chicago, Illinois 60611. 1984.

STATE LEGISLATION ON DISPUTE RESOLUTION. Lawrence Freidman, with Larry Ray. Special Committee on Alternative Means of Dispute Resolution, American Bar Association, 1800 M Street, Northwest, Washington, D.C. 20036. 1982.

STRUCTURED SETTLEMENTS. Paul J. Lesti, Brent B. Danninger and Robert W. Johnson. Lawyers Cooperative Publishing Company, Aqueduct Building, Rochester, New York 14694. 1986- . (Periodic Supplements).

STRUCTURING SETTLEMENTS. Howard L. Nations. American Trial Lawyers Association Press, 1050 Thirty-first Street, Northwest, Washington, D.C. 20007. 1987

ANNUALS AND SURVEYS

OUTSIDE THE COURTS: A SURVEY OF DIVERSION ALTERNATIVES IN CIVIL CASES. National Center for State Courts, 300 Newport Avenue, Williamsburg, Virginia 23187-8798. 1977.

YEARBOOK: COMMERCIAL ARBITRATION. American Arbitration Association, 140 West Fifty-first Street, New York, New York 10020. Annual.

LAW REVIEWS AND PERIODICALS

ARBITRATION JOURNAL. American Arbitration Association, 140 West Fifty-first Street, New York, New York 10020. Quarterly.

DISPUTE RESOLUTION. Standing Committee on Dispute Resolution. American Bar Association, 1800 M Street, Northwest, Washington, D.C. 20036. Quarterly.

MEDIATION QUARTERLY. Academy of Family Mediators, P.O. Box 10501, Eugene, Oregon 97440. Quarterly.

NEWSLETTERS AND NEWSPAPERS

ARBITRATION IN SCHOOLS. American Arbitration Association, 140 West Fifty-first Street, New York, New York 10020. Monthly.

CONFLICT RESOLUTION NOTES. Conflict Resolution Center International, 7514 Kensington Street, Pittsburgh, Pennsylvania 15221. Quarterly.

MEDIATION NEWS. Academy of Family Mediators, P.O. Box 10501, Eugene, Oregon 97440. Quarterly.

NAC NEWSLETTERS. 7315 Wisconsin Avenue, Suite 1255N, Bethesda, Maryland 20814. Quarterly.

NATIONAL ACADEMY OF ARBITRATORS NEWSLETTER. Graduate School of Business Administration, University of Michigan, Ann Arbor, Michigan 48109. Quarterly.

NEWS FROM ICSID. International Centre for Settlement of Disputes. 1818 H Street, Northwest, Washington, D.C. 20433. Semiannual.

VERDICTS AND SETTLEMENTS. Litigation Research Group, 822 D Street, San Rafael, California 94901. Monthly.

BIBLIOGRAPHIES

ALTERNATIVE METHODS OF DISPUTE SETTLEMENT: A SELECTED BIBLIOGRAPHY. Frank E.A. Sander and Frederick E. Snyder. Division of Public Services Activities, American Bar Association, 1800 M Street, Northwest, Washington, D.C. 20036. 1982.

MEDIATION: A SELECT ANNOTATED BIBLIOGRAPHY. Frank E.A. Sander. Special Committee on Dispute Resolution, American Bar Association, 1800 M Street, Northwest, Washington, D.C. 20036. 1984.

ASSOCIATIONS AND PROFESSIONAL SOCIETIES

ACADEMY OF FAMILY MEDIATORS. P.O. Box 10501, Eugene, Oregon 97440. (503) 345-1205.

AMERICAN ARBITRATION ASSOCIATION. 140 West Fifty-first Street, New York, New York 10020. (212) 484-4000.

CONFLICT RESOLUTION CENTER INTERNATIONAL. 7514 Kensington Street, Pittsburgh, Pennsylvania 15221. (412) 371-1000.

INSTITUTE FOR MEDIATION AND CONFLICT RESOLUTION. 99 Hudson Street, Eleventh floor, New York, New York 10013. (212) 966-3660.

NATIONAL ACADEMY OF ARBITRATORS. Graduate School of Business Administration, University of Michigan, Ann Arbor, Michigan 48109. (313) 763-9714.

NATIONAL ACADEMY OF CONCILIATORS. 7315 Wisconsin Avenue, Suite 1255N, Bethesda, Maryland 20814. (301) 907-7000.

RESEARCH CENTERS, INSTITUTES, CLEARINGHOUSES

CENTER FOR NEGOTIATION AND CONFLICT RESOLUTION. Rutgers University, S.I. Newhouse Center for Law and Justice, Newark, New Jersey 07102. (201) 648-5048.

HARVARD NEGOTIATION PROJECT. Harvard University, Harvard Law School, Pound Hall 500, Cambridge, Massachusetts 02138. (617) 495-1684.

COMPUTER-ASSISTED LEGAL INSTRUCTION

HAWKINS I & II. Center for Computer-Assisted Instruction, 229 19th Avenue South, University of Minnesota, Minneapolis, Minnesota 55455. Interactive videodisc.

NEGOTIATOR PRO. Beacon Expert System, Incorporated, 35 Gardner Road, Brookline, Massachusetts 02146. Machine-readable computer file.

OTHER SOURCES

DISPUTE RESOLUTION DEVICES IN A DEMOCRATIC SOCIETY: FINAL REPORT OF THE 1985 CHIEF JUSTICE EARL WARREN CONFERENCE ON ADVOCACY IN THE UNITED STATES. Roscoe Pound-American Trial Lawyers Foundation, 1050 Thirty-first Street, Northwest, Washington, D.C. 20007.

COMPTROLLER GENERAL (UNITED STATES)

LOOSELEAF SERVICES AND REPORTERS

DECISIONS OF THE COMPTROLLER GENERAL OF THE UNITED STATES. General Accounting Office. Superintendent of Documents, United States Government Printing Office, Washington, D.C. 20402. 1921- .

TEXTBOOKS AND GENERAL WORKS

WATCHDOG ON THE POTOMAC: A STUDY OF COMPTROLLER GENERALS OF THE UNITED STATES. Joseph Pois. University Press of America, 4720 Boston Way, Lanham, Maryland 20706. 1979.

ONLINE DATABASES

LEXIS, GENERAL FEDERAL LIBRARY, COMPTROLLER DECISIONS FILE. Mead Data Central, P.O. Box 933, Dayton, Ohio 45401.

WESTLAW, ADMINISTRATIVE MATERIALS LIBRARY. West Publishing Company, P.O. Box 64526, 50 West Kellogg Boulevard, St. Paul, Minnesota 55164-0526.

COMPUTER CONTRACTS
See also: GOVERNMENT CONTRACTS

LOOSELEAF SERVICES AND REPORTERS

COMPUTER LAW - DRAFTING AND NEGOTIATING FORMS AND AGREEMENTS. Peter Brown and Richard Raysman. Law Journal Seminars-Press, Incorporated, 111 Eighth Avenue, Suite 900, New York, New York 10011. 1984- . (Periodic Supplements).

COMPUTER SOFTWARE AGREEMENTS: FORMS AND COMMENTARY. John Matuszeski and others. Research Institute of America, Incorporated, 210 South Street, Boston, Massachusetts 02111. 1987- . (Annual Supplements).

COMPUTER SOFTWARE: PROTECTION, LIABILITY, LAW. L.J. Kutten. Clark Boardman Company, Limited, 435 Hudson Street, New York, New York 10014. 1987- . (Annual Supplements).

DATA PROCESSING AGREEMENTS. W.A. Hancock, Editor. Business Laws, Incorporated, 11630 Chillicothe Road, Chesterland, Ohio 44026. 1983- . (Quarterly Supplements).

THE SOFTWARE LEGAL BOOK. Paul S. Hoffman. Shafer Books, 139 Grand Street, P.O. Box 40, Croton-on-Hudson, New York 10520. 1991.

A USER'S GUIDE TO COMPUTER CONTRACTING: FORMS, TECHNIQUES, AND STRATEGIES. Lanny J. Davis, Don A. Allen, Terry Bowman, and Joseph Armstrong. Prentice-Hall Law and Business, Route 9W, Englewood Cliffs, New Jersey 07632. 1984- . (Annual Supplements).

USER'S GUIDE TO SOFTWARE LICENSES. W.A. Hancock. Business Laws, Incorporated, 11630 Chillicothe Road, Chesterland, Ohio 44026. 1985- . (Annual Supplements).

HANDBOOKS, MANUALS, FORMBOOKS

LAW AND THE SOFTWARE MARKETER. Fredrick L. Cooper. Prentice-Hall, Incorporated, Route 9W, Englewood Cliffs, New Jersey 07632. 1988.

RESOLVING COMPUTER DISPUTES: A GUIDE TO ARBITRATION. Computer Disputes Committee, American Arbitration Association, 140 West Fifty-first Street, New York, New York 10020. 1988.

SOFTWARE CONTRACT FORMS 1987 COLLECTION. Software Licensing Practices Committee, Computer Law Division, Section of Science and Technology, American Bar Association, 750 North Lake Shore Drive, Chicago, Illinois 60611. 1987.

TEXTBOOKS AND GENERAL WORKS

COMPUTER CONTRACT NEGOTIATIONS. Joseph Auer and Charles E. Harris. Van Nostrand Reinhold Company, Incorporated, 115 Fifth Avenue, New York, New York 10003. 1981.

COMPUTER LAW: PURCHASING, LEASING, AND LICENSING SOFTWARE AND SERVICES. Practising Law Institute, 810 Seventh Avenue, New York, New York 10019. 1980.

COMPUTER USER'S LEGAL GUIDE. R. Lee Hagelshaul. Chilton Book Company, 201 King of Prussia Road, Radnor, Pennsylvania 19089-0230. 1985.

NEGOTIATING COMPUTER CONTRACTS. Lanny J. Davis and Charles B. Ortner. Prentice-Hall Law and Business, Route 9W, Englewood Cliffs, New Jersey 07632. 1984.

PROGRAM LICENSING AGREEMENT WITH END USER: A FORM CONTRACT WITH ALTERNATIVE CLAUSES. Esther R. Schachter. Association of Data Processing Service Organizations, 1300 North Seventeenth Street, Arlington, Virginia 22209. 1979- .

PROTECT YOURSELF: THE GUIDE TO UNDERSTANDING AND NEGOTIATING CONTRACTS FOR BUSINESS COMPUTERS. Dennis S. Deutsch. John Wiley and Sons, Incorporated, 605 Third Avenue, New York, New York 10158. 1984.

COMPUTER CRIMES
See also: BUSINESS CRIMES; COMPUTER SOFTWARE PROTECTION AND LICENSING

LOOSELEAF SERVICES AND REPORTERS

COMPUTER CRIME LAW REPORTER. Buck BloomBecker, Editor. National Center for Computer Crime Data, 1222-B Seventeenth Avenue, Santa Cruz, California 95062. 1989- . (Annual Supplements).

COMPUTER LAW: EVIDENCE AND PROCEDURE. David Bender. Matthew Bender and Company, Incorporated, 11 Penn Plaza, New York, New York 10001. 1977- . (Annual Supplements).

LAWYER'S GUIDE TO COMPUTER SECURITY: A SOURCEBOOK. Mark W. Greenia. Lexikon Services Publications, 8042 Singleterry Way, Sacramento, California 95842. 1991- . (Annual Supplements).

PREVENTION AND PROSECUTION OF COMPUTER AND HIGH TECHNOLOGY CRIME. Stanley Arkin and others. Matthew Bender and Company, Incorporated, 11 Penn Plaza, New York, New York 10001. 1988- . (Annual Supplements).

HANDBOOKS, MANUALS, FORMBOOKS

COMPUTER CRIME-EXPERT WITNESS MANUAL. Bureau of Justice Statistics, Department of Justice. Superintendent of Documents, United States Government Printing Office, Washington, D.C. 20402. 1981.

COMPUTER CRIME-LEGISLATIVE RESOURCE MANUAL. Bureau of Justice Statistics, Department of Justice. Superintendent of Documents, United States Government Printing Office, Washington, D.C. 20402. 1981.

GUIDE TO THE PROSECUTION OF TELECOMMUNICATIONS FRAUD BY THE USE OF COMPUTER CRIME STATUTES. Section of Technology, American Bar Association, 750 North Lake Shore Drive, Chicago, Illinois 60611. 1989.

TEXTBOOKS AND GENERAL WORKS

COMMITMENT TO SECURITY. National Center for Computer Crime Data, 1222-B Seventeenth Avenue, Santa Cruz, California 95062. 1989.

THE COMPUTER AND THE LAW. Irving J. Sloan, Editor. Oceana Publications, Incorporated, 75 Main Street, Dobbs Ferry, New York 10522. 1984.

COMPUTER CRIME. August Bequai. Lexington Books, 125 Spring Street, Lexington, Massachusetts 02173. 1978.

COMPUTER CRIME: COMPUTER SECURITY TECHNIQUES. Superintendent of Documents, United States Government Printing Office, Division of Public Documents, Washington, D.C. 20402. 1982.

COMPUTER CRIME: PREVENTION, DETECTION, PROSECUTION. Daniel T. Brooks and Susan H. Nycum. Prentice-Hall Law and Business, Route 9W, Englewood Cliffs, New Jersey 07632. 1983.

COMPUTER CRIMES: ELECTRONIC FUND TRANSFER SYSTEMS AND CRIME. Kent W. Colton. Superintendent of Documents, United States Government Printing Office, Division of Public Documents, Washington, D.C. 20402. 1982.

COMPUTER INSECURITY. Adrian R.D. Norman. Routledge, Chapman and Hall, 29 West Thirty-fifth Street, New York, New York 10001-2291. 1985.

DATATHEFT: COMPUTER FRAUD, INDUSTRIAL ESPIONAGE AND INFORMATION CRIME. Hugo Cornwall. Heinmann Educational Books, Incorporated, 361 Hanover Street, Portsmouth, New Hampshire 03801. 1987.

THE INVESTIGATION OF COMPUTER CRIME. Jay J. Becker. Law Enforcement Assistance Agency. Superintendent of Documents, United States Government Printing Office, Division of Public Documents, Washington, D.C. 20402. 1980.

THE MARKET FOR INFORMATION SECURITY SYSTEMS IN THE UNITED STATES. Frost and Sullivan, 106 Fulton Street, New York, New York 10038. 1985.

ORGANIZING FOR COMPUTER CRIME INVESTIGATION AND PROSECUTION. Catherine H. Conly. United States Department of Justice, National Institute of Justice. Superintendent of Documents, United States Government Printing Office, Washington, D.C. 20402. 1989.

PROTECTION OF COMPUTER SYSTEMS AND SOFTWARE. Frank HuBand and R. D. Shelton. Law and Business, Incorporated, 113 Sylvan Avenue, Englewood Cliffs, New Jersey 07632. 1986.

WHITE COLLAR CRIME: THEORY AND RESEARCH. Gilbert Geis and Ezra Statland, Editors. Sage Publications, P.O. Box 6944, San Mateo, California 94403. 1980.

LAW REVIEWS AND PERIODICALS

COMPUTER CRIME DIGEST. Washington Crime News Services, 7620 Little River Turnpike, Annandale, Virginia 22003. 1982- . (Monthly Supplements).

COMPUTER SECURITY JOURNAL. Computer Security Institute, 360 Church Street, Northboro, Massachusetts 01532. Semiannual.

NEWSLETTERS AND NEWSPAPERS

COMPUCRIME VIEWS. International Association of Computer Crime Investigators, c/o Jack Bologna, 150 North Main Street, Plymouth, Michigan 48170. Quarterly.

COMPUTER INDUSTRY LITIGATION REPORTER. Andrews Publications, 1646 West Chester Pike, Westtown, Pennsylvania 19395. Semimonthly.

COMPUTER LAW REPORTER. Law Reporters, 1519 Connecticut Avenue, Northwest, Suite 200, Washington, D.C. 20036. Monthly.

COMPUTER LAW STRATEGIST. Leader Publications, 111 Eighth Avenue, New York, New York 10011. Monthly.

COMPUTER SECURITY DIGEST. Computer Protection Systems, Incorporated, 150 North Main Street, Plymouth, Michigan 48170. Monthly.

COMPUTER SECURITY NEWSLETTER. Computer Security Institute, 360 Church Street, Northboro, Massachusetts 01532. Bimonthly.

BIBLIOGRAPHIES

COMPUTER CRIME: A BIBLIOGRAPHY. Revised Edition. Mary Vance. Vance Bibliographies, P.O. Box 229, 112 North Charter Street, Monticello, Illinois 61856. 1988.

COMPUTER CRIME, ABUSE, LIABILITY, AND SECURITY: A COMPREHENSIVE BIBLIOGRAPHY, 1970-1985. Reba A. Best and D. Cheryn Picquet. McFarland and Company, Incorporated, P.O. Box 611, Jefferson, North Carolina 28640. 1985.

ASSOCIATIONS AND PROFESSIONAL SOCIETIES

COMPUTER SECURITY INSTITUTE. 360 Church Street, Northboro, Massachusetts 01532. (508) 393-2600.

INTERNATIONAL ASSOCIATION OF COMPUTER CRIME INVESTIGATORS. c/o Jack Bologna, 150 North Main Street, Plymouth, Michigan 48170. (313) 459-8787.

NATIONAL CENTER FOR COMPUTER CRIME DATA. 1222 Seventeenth Avenue, Suite B, Santa Cruz, California 95062. (408) 874-8233.

RESEARCH CENTERS, INSTITUTES, CLEARINGHOUSES

CENTER FOR COMPUTER SECURITY AND FAULT TOLERANCE. Florida Atlantic University, Department of Computer Engineering, Boca Raton, Florida 33431. (407) 367-3466.

NATIONAL CENTER FOR COMPUTER CRIME DATA. 4053 J.F.K. Library, California State University, 5151 State University Drive, Los Angeles, California 90032. (213) 874-8233.

OTHER SOURCES

COMPUTER CAPERS: TALES OF ELECTRONIC THIEVERY, EMBEZZLEMENT, AND FRAUD. Thomas Whiteside. Thomas Y. Crowell Company, 10 East Fifty-third Street, New York, New York 10022. 1978.

COMPUTER VIRUS LEGISLATION: HEARING BEFORE THE SUBCOMMITTEE ON CRIMINAL JUSTICE OF THE COMMITTEE OF THE JUDICIARY, HOUSE OF REPRESENTATIVES, 101ST CONGRESS, FIRST SESSION. Superintendent of Documents, United States Government Printing Office, Washington, D.C. 20402. 1989.

REPORT ON COMPUTER CRIME. American Bar Association Task Force on Computer Crime, Criminal Justice Section, 750 North Lake Shore Drive, Chicago, Illinois 60611. 1984.

COMPUTER SOFTWARE PROTECTION AND LICENSING
See also: COMPUTER CRIMES

LOOSELEAF SERVICES AND REPORTERS

COMPUTER SOFTWARE AGREEMENTS: FORMS AND COMMENTARY. John Matuszeski and others. Research Institute of America, Incorporated, 210 South Street, Boston, Massachusetts 02111. 1987- . (Annual Supplements).

COMPUTER SOFTWARE PROTECTION LAW. Cary H. Sherman and others. Bureau of National Affairs, Incorporated, 1231 Twenty-fifth Street, Northwest, Washington, D.C. 20037. 1989- . (Periodic Supplements).

COMPUTER SOFTWARE: PROTECTION, LIABILITY, LAW. L.J. Kutten. Clark Boardman Company, Limited, 435 Hudson Street, New York, New York 10014. 1987- . (Annual Supplements).

SEMICONDUCTOR CHIP PROTECTION. Richard H. Stern. Prentice-Hall Law and Business, Route 9W, Englewood Cliffs, New Jersey 07632. 1986- . (Periodic Supplements).

HANDBOOKS, MANUALS, FORMBOOKS

AMERICAN STANDARD HANDBOOK OF SOFTWARE LAW. John C. Lautsch. Reston Publishing Company, Incorporated, c/o Prentice-Hall, Incorporated, P.O. Box 500, Englewood Cliffs, New Jersey 07632. 1985.

COMPUTER LAW HANDBOOK: SOFTWARE PROTECTION, LITIGATION, FORMS. David F. Simon. American Law Institute-American Bar Association, 4025 Chestnut Street, Philadelphia, Pennsylvania 19104. 1990.

THE SEMICONDUCTOR CHIP PROTECTION ACT OF 1984. Jon A. Baumgarten. Harcourt, Brace, and Jovanovich, 1250 Sixth Avenue, San Diego, California 92101. 1984.

SOFTWARE CONTRACT FORMS 1987 COLLECTION. Software Licensing Practices Committee, Computer Law Division, Section of Science and Technology, American Bar Association, 750 North Lake Shore Drive, Chicago, Illinois 60611. 1987.

SOFTWARE OWNERSHIP/CONFIDENTIALITY FORMS. American Bar Association, 750 North Lake Shore Drive, Chicago, Illinois 60611. 1984.

TEXTBOOKS AND GENERAL WORKS

COMPUTER LAW INSTITUTE 1990: A COURSE HANDBOOK. Eleventh Edition. Practising Law Institute, 810 Seventh Avenue, New York, New York 10019. 1990.

COMPUTER SOFTWARE AND CHIPS 1990: A COURSE HANDBOOK. Practising Law Institute, 810 Seventh Avenue, New York, New York 10019. 1990.

COMPUTER SOFTWARE 1984: PROTECTION AND MARKETING. Practising Law Institute, 810 Seventh Avenue, New York, New York 10019. 1984.

COMPUTER SOFTWARE PROTECTION AND SEMICONDUCTOR CHIPS. Dirk Schroeder. Butterworth Legal Publishers, 90 Stiles Road, Salem, New Hampshire 03079. 1990.

COPYRIGHT, CONGRESS AND TECHNOLOGY: THE PUBLIC RECORD. Nicholas Henry, Editor. Oryx Press, 2214 North Central Avenue, Phoenix, Arizona 85004-1483. 1979.

INTELLECTUAL PROPERTY PROTECTION OF COMPUTER TECHNOLOGY. Michigan Yearbook of International Legal Studies, University of Michigan Law School, Ann Arbor, Michigan. 48109. 1988.

INTRODUCTION TO COMPUTER LAW: A COURSE HANDBOOK. Practising Law Institute, 810 Seventh Avenue, New York, New York 10019. 1985.

LEGAL ASPECTS -- ACQUIRING AND PROTECTING SOFTWARE. Bruce K. Brickman. Carnegie Press, Incorporated, 100 Kings Road, Madison, New Jersey 07940. 1984- . (Annual Supplements).

MODERN COPYRIGHT FUNDAMENTALS: KEY WRITINGS ON TECHNOLOGICAL AND OTHER ISSUES. Ben H. Weil and Barbara Friedman Polansky, Editors. Learned Publications, Incorporated, 83-53 Manton Street, Jamaica, New York 11435. 1989.

THE PATENTABILITY OF COMPUTER SOFTWARE: AN INTERNATIONAL GUIDE TO THE PROTECTION OF COMPUTER RELATED INVENTIONS. Henri W.A.M. Hanneman. Kluwer Law and Taxation, 6 Bigelow Street, Cambridge, Massachusetts 02139. 1985.

PROTECTION OF COMPUTER SOFTWARE: ITS TECHNOLOGY AND APPLICATIONS. Derrick Grover, Editor. Cambridge University Press, 40 West Twentieth Street, New York, New York 10011. 1989.

PROTECTION OF COMPUTER SYSTEMS AND SOFTWARE. Frank Huband and R.D. Shelton. Prentice-Hall Law and Business, Route 9W, Englewood Cliffs, New Jersey 07632. 1985.

SCUTTLE THE COMPUTER PIRATES: SOFTWARE PROTECTION SCHEMES. Richard H. Baker. Tab Books, Monterey Lane, Blue Ridge Summit, Pennsylvania 17214-0850. 1984.

SOFTWARE, COPYRIGHT, AND COMPETITION: THE LOOK AND FEEL OF THE LAW. Anthony L. Clapes. Quorum Books, Greenwood Publishing Group, Incorporated, 88 Post Road West, P.O. Box 5007, Westport, Connecticut 06881. 1989.

A SOFTWARE LAW PRIMER. Frederick William Neitzke. Van Nostrand Reinhold, 135 West Fiftieth Street, New York, New York 10020. 1984.

THE SOFTWARE LEGAL BOOK. Paul S. Hoffman. Shafer Books, Incorporated, 139 Grand Street, P.O. Box 40, Croton-on-Hudson, New York 10520. 1986.

SOFTWARE PROTECTION: PRACTICAL AND LEGAL STEPS TO PROTECT AND MARKET COMPUTER PROGRAMS. Gervaise G. Davis. Van Nostrand Reinhold, 115 Fifth Avenue, New York, New York 10003. 1991.

THIRD PARTY PROTECTION OF SOFTWARE AND FIRMWARE: DIRECT PROTECTION OF ZEROS AND ONES. J.J. Borking. Elsevier Science Publishing Company, P.O. Box 882, Madison Square Station, New York, New York 10159. 1985.

UNDERSTANDING SOFTWARE LAW. Jonathan D. Wallace. Alfred Publishing Company, Incorporated, 16380 Roscoe Boulevard, Suite 200, P.O. Box 10003, Van Nuys, California 91406-1215. 1984.

ANNUALS AND SURVEYS

COMPUTER LAW INSTITUTE. Practising Law Institute, 810 Seventh Avenue, New York, New York 10019. 1983- . (Annual).

NEWSLETTERS AND NEWSPAPERS

COMPUTER INDUSTRY LITIGATION REPORTER. Andrews Publications, 1646 West Chester Pike, Westtown, Pennsylvania 19395. Semimonthly.

SOFTWARE PROTECTION. Law and Technology Press, Incorporated, P.O. Box 3280, Manhattan Beach, California 90266.

ASSOCIATIONS AND PROFESSIONAL SOCIETIES

PATENT, TRADEMARK, AND COPYRIGHT LAW SECTION. American Bar Association, 750 North Lake Shore Drive, Chicago, Illinois 60611.

OTHER SOURCES

COMPUTER SOFTWARE AND INTELLECTUAL PROPERTY. Office of Technology Assessment. Superintendent of Documents, United States Government Printing Office, Washington, D.C. 20402. 1990.

COMPUTERS (GENERAL)
See also: COMPUTER CONTRACTS; COMPUTER CRIMES; COMPUTER SOFTWARE PROTECTION AND LICENSING; COMPUTERS AND LEGAL RESEARCH; HIGH TECHNOLOGY INDUSTRIES

LOOSELEAF SERVICES AND REPORTERS

BERNACCHI ON COMPUTER LAW - A GUIDE TO THE LEGAL AND MANAGEMENT ASPECTS OF COMPUTER TECHNOLOGY. Richard L. Bernacchi and others. Little Brown and Company, 34 Beacon Street, Boston, Massachusetts 02108. 1986- . (Periodic Supplements).

COMPUTER LAW. David Bender. Matthew Bender and Company, Incorporated, 11 Penn Plaza, New York, New York 10001. 1978- . (Annual Supplements).

COMPUTER LAW. Michael D. Scott. John Wiley and Sons, Incorporated, 605 Third Avenue, New York, New York 10158. 1984- . (Annual Supplements).

GUIDE TO COMPUTER LAW. Commerce Clearing House, Incorporated, 4025 West Peterson Avenue, Chicago, Illinois 60646. 1989- . (Semi-monthly Supplements).

INTERNATIONAL COMPUTER LAW. Jozef A. Keustermans and others. Matthew Bender and Company, Incorporated, 11 Penn Plaza, New York, New York 10001. 1988- . (Annual Supplements).

HANDBOOKS, MANUALS, FORMBOOKS

THE AUTOMATED LAW FIRM: A COMPLETE GUIDE TO SOFTWARE AND SYSTEMS. Richard L. Robbins. Prentice-Hall Law and Business, Route 9W, Englewood Cliffs, New Jersey 07632. 1989- . (Periodic Supplements).

COMPUTER BUYER'S PROTECTION GUIDE: HOW TO PROTECT YOUR RIGHTS IN THE COMPUTER MARKETPLACE. L.J. Kutten. Prentice-Hall, Incorporated, 113 Sylvan Avenue, Englewood Cliffs, New Jersey 07632. 1983.

THE COMPUTER DATABASE THESAURUS AND DICTIONARY: THE COMPLETE ONLINE USERS GUIDE TO THE DATABASE FOR COMPUTERS, TELECOMMUNICATIONS AND ELECTRONICS. Management Contents, Northbrook, Illinois. 1983- . (Periodic Supplements).

COMPUTER FUNDAMENTALS FOR LEGAL PROFESSIONALS. Second Edition. John A. Gurdak. Pearson Publications Company, 5910 North Central Expressway, Dallas, Texas 75206. 1989- . (Semiannual Supplements).

THE COMPUTER USER'S LEGAL GUIDE. Lee R. Hagelshaw. Chilton Books Company, 201 King of Prussia Road, Radnor, Pennsylvania 19089-0230. 1985.

COMPUTERS AND THE LAW: AN INTRODUCTORY HANDBOOK. Robert P. Bigelow, Editor. Commerce Clearing House, Incorporated, Section of Science and Technology, 4025 West Peterson Avenue, Chicago, Illinois 60646. 1981.

LAW OF COMPUTER TECHNOLOGY. Raymond T. Nimmer. Research Institute of America, Incorporated, One Penn Plaza, New York, New York 10119. 1985. (1991 Supplement).

LAW OFFICE GUIDE TO COMPUTER ABBREVIATIONS AND ACRONYMS. Mark W. Greenia. Lexikon Services Publications, 8042 Singleterry Way, Sacramento, California 95842. 1991- . (Semiannual Supplements).

LEGAL CARE FOR YOUR SOFTWARE: A STEP-BY-STEP GUIDE FOR COMPUTER SOFTWARE WRITERS. Nolo Press, 950 Parker Street, Berkeley, California 94710. 1987.

A LEGAL GUIDE TO EDP MANAGEMENT. Michael C. Gemignani. Quorum Books, Greenwood Publishing Group, Incorporated, 88 Post Road West, P.O. Box 5007, Westport, Connecticut 06881. 1989- .

TEXTBOOKS AND GENERAL WORKS

ACCOUNTING AND TAX ASPECTS FOR COMPUTER SOFTWARE MANUFACTURERS. Robert W. McGee. Praeger Publishers, Greenwood Publishing Group, Incorporated, 88 Post Road West, P.O. Box 5007, Westport, Connecticut 06881.

ADVANCED TOPICS OF LAW AND INFORMATION TECHNOLOGY. Kluwer Academic Publishers, 101 Philip Drive, Assinippi Park, Norwell, Massachusetts 02061. 1988.

COMPUTER LAW. Michael C. Genignami. Lawyers Co-Operative Publishing Company, Aqueduct Building, Rochester, New York 14694. 1985- . (Annual Supplements).

COMPUTER LAW. Chris Reed. Blackstone Publishing Company, 1507 Cochise Drive, Arlington, Texas 76012. 1989.

COMPUTER LAW. Fourth Edition. Colin Tapper. Longman, Incorporated, 95 Church Street, White Plains, New York 10601. 1989.

COMPUTER LAW 1981: ACQUIRING COMPUTER GOODS AND SERVICES. Daniel T. Brooks. Practising Law Institute, 810 Seventh Avenue, New York, New York 10019. 1981.

COMPUTER LAW: PURCHASING, LEASING, AND LICENSING HARDWARE, SOFTWARE, AND SERVICES. Daniel T. Brooks. Practising Law Institute, 810 Seventh Avenue, New York, New York 10019. 1980.

COMPUTER TECHNOLOGY AND THE LAW. John T. Soma. Shepard's/McGraw-Hill, P.O. Box 1235, Colorado Springs, Colorado 80901. 1983.

COMPUTERS AND THE LAW. Richard B. Mawrey. Bancroft-Sage Publishing, Incorporated, 533 Eighth Street, South, Naples, Florida 33939. 1988.

COMPUTERS, DATA PROCESSING, AND THE LAW. Steven L. Mandell. West Publishing Company, P.O. Box 43526, 50 West Kellogg Boulevard, St. Paul, Minnesota 55164-0526. 1984.

LEGAL ASPECTS -- ACQUIRING AND PROTECTING SOFTWARE. Bruce K. Brickman. Carnegie Press, 100 Kings Road, Madison, New Jersey 08940. 1984- . (Annual Supplements).

PRIVATE RIGHTS, PUBLIC WRONGS: THE COMPUTER AND PERSONAL PRIVACY. Michael R. Rubin. Ablex Publications Corporation, 355 Chestnut Street, Norwood, New Jersey 07648. 1988.

THE RIGHT OF PRIVACY IN THE COMPUTER AGE. Warren Freedman. Quorum Books, Greenwood Publishing Group, Incorporated, 88 Post Road West, P.O. Box 5007, Westport, Connecticut 06881. 1987.

TARGETING THE COMPUTER: GOVERNMENT SUPPORT AND INTERNATIONAL COMPETITION. Kenneth Flamm. Brookings Institution, 1775 Massachusetts Avenue, Washington, D.C. 20037. 1987- .

DIGESTS, INDEXES, ABSTRACTS, CITATORS

AMERICAN COMPUTER LAW DIGEST. American Computer Law Digest, Incorporated, P.O. Box 39235, Friendship Station, Washington, D.C. 20016-0035. Quarterly.

COMPUTER INDUSTRY LITIGATION REPORTER. Andrews Publications, Incorporated, 1646 West Chester Pike, Westtown, Pennsylvania 19395. Bimonthly.

ANNUALS AND SURVEYS

THE COMPUTER LAW ANNUAL 1985: AN ANTHOLOGY OF CURRENT THINKING ON THE MAJOR ISSUES. Miles R. Gilburne, Ronald L. Johnson, and Allen R. Grogan, Editors. Harcourt, Brace, and Jovanovich, Incorporated, 6277 Sea Harbor Drive, Orlando, Florida 32821. 1985.

COMPUTER LAW: CURRENT TRENDS AND DEVELOPMENTS. Practising Law Institute, 810 Seventh Avenue, New York, New York 10019. 1989- . (Annual).

COMPUTER LAW INSTITUTE. Practising Law Institute, 810 Seventh Avenue, New York, New York 10019. 1983- . (Annual).

LAW REVIEWS AND PERIODICALS

COMPUTER LAW AND TAX REPORT. Research Institute of America, Incorporated, 210 South Street, Boston, Massachusetts 02111. Monthly.

COMPUTER/LAW JOURNAL. Center for Computer Law, 1112 Ocean Drive, Suite 101, Manhattan Beach, California 90266. Quarterly.

THE COMPUTER LAW MONITOR. Research Publications, Incorporated, P.O. Box 9267, Asheville, North Carolina 28815. Quarterly.

COMPUTER LAW STRATEGIST. Leader Publications, 111 Eighth Avenue, New York, New York 10011. Monthly.

COMPUTERS (GENERAL)

THE COMPUTER LAWYER. Law and Business, Incorporated, 855 Valley Road, Clifton, New Jersey 07013. Monthly.

HIGH TECHNOLOGY LAW JOURNAL. University of California School of Law, Boalt Hall, Room 225, Berkeley, California 94720. Biannual.

JOURNAL OF LAW AND TECHNOLOGY. Georgetown University Law Center, Computer Law Group, 600 New Jersey Avenue, Northwest, Washington, D.C. 20001. Quarterly.

JURIMETICS JOURNAL. American Bar Association, Section of Science and Technology and the Arizona State College of Law, 750 North Lake Shore Drive, Chicago, Illinois 60611. Quarterly.

RUTGERS COMPUTER AND TECHNOLOGY LAW JOURNAL. Rutgers Law School, 15 Washington Street, Newark, New Jersey 07102. Biannual.

BIBLIOGRAPHIES

COMPUTER LAW READING LIST. Second Edition. Michael D. Scott. Law and Technology Press, P.O. Box 3280, Manhattan Beach, California 90266. 1981.

DIRECTORIES

COMPUTER PUBLISHERS AND PUBLICATIONS 1985-1986: AN INTERNATIONAL DIRECTORY AND YEARBOOK. Communication Trends, Incorporated, Two East Avenue, New Rochelle, New York 10538. Annual.

ASSOCIATIONS AND PROFESSIONAL SOCIETIES

CENTER FOR COMPUTER-ASSISTED LEGAL INSTRUCTION. 229 Nineteenth Avenue, South, Minneapolis, Minnesota 55455. (612) 625-2552.

COMPUTER LAW ASSOCIATION. 103 Rowell Court, Falls Church, Virginia 22046. (703) 560-7747.

SECTION OF SCIENCE AND TECHNOLOGY. American Bar Association, 750 North Lake Shore Drive, Chicago, Illinois 60611. (312) 988-5000.

ONLINE DATABASES

COMPUT. Information Access Company, 11 Davis Drive, Belmont, California 94002.

THE COMPUTER DATABASE MANAGEMENT CONTENTS. P.O. Box 3014, 2265 Carlson Drive, North Brook, Illinois 60062.

OTHER SOURCES

ADVANCED COMPUTER LAW STRATEGIES. Journal of Law and Technology and Georgetown University Law Center, Washington, D.C. 20001. Quarterly.

COMPUTER LAW: ALI-ABA COURSE OF STUDY MATERIALS. American Law Institute-American Bar Association, 4025 Chestnut Street, Philadelphia, Pennsylvania 19104. 1984.

DEFENDING SECRETS, SHARING DATA: NEW LOCKS AND KEYS FOR ELECTRONIC INFORMATION. Office of Technology Assessment. Superintendent of Documents, United States Government Printing Office, Washington, D.C. 20402. 1987- .

COMPUTERS AND LEGAL RESEARCH
See also: COMPUTER SOFTWARE PROTECTION AND LICENSING; LEGAL RESEARCH

LOOSELEAF SERVICES AND REPORTERS

THE AUTOMATED LAW FIRM: A COMPLETE GUIDE TO SOFTWARE AND SYSTEMS. Richard L. Robbins. Prentice-Hall Law and Business, Route 9W, Englewood Cliffs, New Jersey 07632. 1989- . (Periodic Supplements).

COMPUTER FUNDAMENTALS FOR LEGAL PROFESSIONALS. Second Edition. John A. Gurdak. Pearson Publications Company, 5910 North Central Expressway, Dallas, Texas 75206. 1989- . (Semiannual Supplements).

COMPUTER LAW. David Bender. Matthew Bender and Company, Incorporated, 11 Penn Plaza, New York, New York 10001. 1984- . (Periodic Supplements).

COMPUTERS FOR LAW OFFICES. Peter and Rainer Luedtke. Harcourt, Brace, and Jovanovich, 6277 Sea Harbor Drive, Orlando, Florida 32821. 1984.

LAW OFFICE GUIDE TO COMPUTER ABBREVIATIONS AND ACRONYMS. Mark W. Greenia. Lexikon Services Publications, 8042 Singleterry Way, Sacramento, California 95842. 1991- . (Semiannual Supplements).

MODERN VISUAL EVIDENCE. Gregory P. Joseph. Law Journal-Seminars Press, 111 Eighth Avenue, Suite 900, New York, New York 10011. 1984- . (Periodic Supplements).

HANDBOOKS, MANUALS, FORMBOOKS

AUTOMATED LAW OFFICE SYSTEMS: A SURVEY OF TODAY'S TOOLS AND TECHNIQUES. Sidney W. Frost and James C. Dunlap. West Publishing Company, P.O. Box 43526, 50 West Kellogg Boulevard, St. Paul, Minnesota 55164-0526. 1983.

COMMUNICATING WITH LEGAL DATABASES: TERMS AND ABBREVIATIONS FOR THE LEGAL RESEARCHER. Anne L. McDonald and others. Neal-Schuman Publications, Incorporated, 23 Leonard Street, New York, New York 10013. 1987.

HANDBOOK OF LEGAL INFORMATION RETRIEVAL. Jon Bing, Editor. Elsevier Science Publishing Company, P.O. Box 882, Madison Square Station, New York, New York 10159. 1984.

LEARNING LEXIS: A HANDBOOK FOR MODERN LEGAL RESEARCH. Mead Data Central, P.O. Box 933, Dayton, Ohio 45401. 1990.

LEXIS: A RESEARCH MANUAL. Kathleen M. Carrick. Mead Data Central, P.O. Box 933, Dayton, Ohio 45401. 1989.

REFERENCE MANUAL: FOR LEXIS/NEXIS. Mead Data Central, P.O. Box 933, Dayton, Ohio 45401. 1988- .

WESTLAW FOR LAW STUDENTS. Fourth Edition. West Publishing Company, 50 West Kellogg Boulevard, St. Paul, Minnesota 55164. 1990.

WESTLAW REFERENCE MANUAL. Fourth Edition. West Publishing Company, 50 West Kellogg Boulevard, St. Paul, Minnesota 55164. 1990.

WHAT A LAWYER NEEDS TO KNOW TO BUY AND USE A COMPUTER. Robert P. Wilkins. R.P.W. Publishing Corporation, P.O. Box 1108, Lexington, South Carolina 29072. 1984.

WILMER, CUTLER & PICKERING MANUAL ON LITIGATION SUPPORT DATABASES. Second Edition. Deanne C. Siemer. John Wiley and Sons, Incorporated, 605 Third Avenue, New York, New York 10158. 1989- .

TEXTBOOKS AND GENERAL WORKS

AUTOMATED LITIGATION SUPPORT: A PRACTICAL INTRODUCTION. Fred M. Greguras. Bureau of National Affairs, Incorporated, 1231 Twenty-fifth Street, Northwest, Washington, D.C. 20037. 1984.

CHOOSING AND USING COMPUTERS TO IMPROVE YOUR LAW PRACTICE. Kline D. Strong, American Bar Association, 750 North Lake Shore Drive, Chicago, Illinois 60611. 1983.

COMPUTER LITIGATION 1984: RESOLVING COMPUTER RELATED DISPUTES AND PROTECTING PROPRIETARY RIGHTS. William A. Fenwick. Practising Law Institute, 810 Seventh Avenue, New York, New York 10019. 1984.

COMPUTERIZED LEGAL RESEARCH: GETTING YOUR MONEY'S WORTH OUT OF THE WESTLAW AND LEXIS DATABASES. Terry Thomas and Marlene G. Weinstein. Holt, Rinehart and Winston, Incorporated, 6277 Sea Harbor Drive, Orlando, Florida 32821. 1985.

FROM YELLOW PADS TO COMPUTERS: TRANSFORMING YOUR LAW PRACTICE WITH A COMPUTER. Kathryn M. Braiman and Fran Shellenberger, Editors. Section of Economics of Law Practice, American Bar Association, 750 North Lake Shore Drive, Chicago, Illinois 60611. 1987.

LAW OFFICE GUIDE TO SMALL COMPUTERS. Forrest D. Rhoads and John Edwards. Shepard's/McGraw-Hill, P.O. Box 1235, Colorado Springs, Colorado 80901. 1984.

LEGAL DATABASES ONLINE: LEXIS AND WESTLAW. John E. Kinsock. Little, Brown and Company, 34 Beacon Street, Boston, Massachusetts 02108. 1985.

LITIGATION SUPPORT SYSTEMS: AN ATTORNEY'S GUIDE. E. Hugh Kinney. Callaghan and Company, 155 Pfingsten Road, Deerfield, Illinois 60015. 1990.

MINICOMPUTERS: HARDWARE, SOFTWARE, AND SELECTION. Udo W. Pooch and Rahul Chattergy. West Publishing Company, P.O. Box 43526, 50 West Kellogg Boulevard, St. Paul, Minnesota 55164-0526. 1984, c1980.

PLANNING FOR COMPUTERS: EVALUATING DATA PROCESSING NEEDS FOR MEDIUM AND LARGE LAW FIRMS. American Bar Association, Economics of Law Practice Section, 750 North Lake Shore Drive, Chicago, Illinois 60611. 1981.

THE USE OF COMPUTERS IN LITIGATION. John H. Young, Michael E. Kris, and Helen C. Trainor. American Bar Association, Young Lawyers Division, Section on Science and Technology, 750 North Lake Shore Drive, Chicago, Illinois 60611. 1979.

USING COMPUTERS IN THE LAW: AN INTRODUCTION AND PRACTICAL GUIDE. Second Edition. Mary Ann Mason. West Publishing Company, P.O. Box 43526, 50 West Kellogg Boulevard, St. Paul, Minnesota 55164. 1988.

NEWSLETTERS AND NEWSPAPERS

THE LAWYER'S P.C. Shepard's/McGraw-Hill, P.O. Box 1235, Colorado Springs, Colorado 80901. Semimonthly.

BIBLIOGRAPHIES

COMPUTER ASSISTED LEGAL RESEARCH: A SELECTED BIBLIOGRAPHY. Vance Bibliographies, P.O. Box 229, 112 North Charter Street, Monticello, Illinois 61856. 1984.

SELECTED BIBLIOGRAPHICAL MATERIAL ON COMPUTER-ASSISTED LEGAL ANALYSIS. Guy M. Bennett and Signa Treat. In Jurimetrics Journal, Volume 24, Number 3. (Spring 1984). American Bar Association, Section of Science and Technology, 750 North Lake Shore Drive, Chicago, Illinois 60611. Quarterly.

DIRECTORIES

DATABASE LIST. (WESTLAW). West Publishing Company, 50 West Kellogg Boulevard, St. Paul, Minnesota 55164. 1990- . (Updated Regularly).

DIRECTORY OF PERIODICALS ONLINE. Federal Document Retrieval, Incorporated, 810 First Street, Northeast, Washington, D.C. 20002. 1985- . (Annual).

THE FEDERAL DATA BASE FINDER. Information U.S.A., Incorporated, Computer Data Service, P.O. Box E, Kensington, Maryland 20895. Annual.

LAW DATABASES, 1988. Diana Raper. Aslib, Gale Research, Incorporated, 835 Penobscot Building, Detroit, Michigan 48226. 1988.

LEXIS/NEXIS LIBRARY CONTENTS AND ALPHABETICAL LIST. Mead Data Central, P.O. Box 933, Dayton, Ohio 45401. 1991- . (Regularly Updated).

LOCATE: A DIRECTORY OF LAW OFFICE COMPUTER SOFTWARE. American Bar Association, Economics of Law Practice Section, 750 North Lake Shore Drive, Chicago, Illinois 60611. 1985.

RESEARCH CENTERS, INSTITUTES, CLEARINGHOUSES

IIT CENTER FOR LAW AND COMPUTERS. Illinois Institute of Technology, 77 South Wacker Drive, Chicago, Illinois 60606.

AUDIOVISUALS

COMPUTER-ASSISTED LEGAL RESEARCH TECHNIQUES. American Bar Association, 750 North Lake Shore Drive, Chicago, Illinois 60611. 1983.

COMPUTERIZING YOUR LAW PRACTICE. American Bar Association, Economics of Law Practice Section, 750 North Lake Shore Drive, Chicago, Illinois 60611. 1984.

INTRODUCING COMPUTER-ASSISTED LEGAL RESEARCH. American Bar Association, 750 North Lake Shore Drive, Chicago, Illinois 60611. 1978.

USE OF COMPUTERS IN COMPLEX LITIGATION. American Bar Association, 750 North Lake Shore Drive, Chicago, Illinois 60611. 1980.

USE OF COMPUTERS IN COMPLEX LITIGATION: CONDENSED SEMINAR. American Bar Association, 750 North Lake Shore Drive, Chicago, Illinois 60611. 1980.

COMPUTER-ASSISTED LEGAL INSTRUCTION

LEARNING LEXIS: COMPUTER-BASED TRAINING FOR LAW STUDENTS. Version 2.0. Mead Data Central, P.O. Box 933, Dayton, Ohio 45401. 1989- . (Computer program).

PC WESTRAIN II. West Publishing Company, 50 West Kellogg Boulevard, St.Paul, Minnesota 55164. 1990- . (Computer program).

CONCILIATION
See: ARBITRATION AND AWARD; COMPROMISE AND SETTLEMENT; INTERNATIONAL ARBITRATION; LABOR ARBITRATION

CONDEMNATION OF LAND
See: EMINENT DOMAIN

CONDOMINIUMS AND COOPERATIVE BUILDINGS

STATUTES, CODES, STANDARDS, UNIFORM LAWS

UNIFORM CONDOMINIUM ACT. National Conference of Commissioners on Uniform State Laws, Uniform Laws Annotated. West Publishing Company, P.O. Box 64526, 50 West Kellogg Boulevard, St. Paul, Minnesota 55164-0526. 1976- . (Annual Supplements).

UNIFORM LAND TRANSACTIONS ACT. National Conference of Commissioners on Uniform State Laws, Uniform Laws Annotated. West Publishing Company, P.O. Box 64526, 50 West Kellogg Boulevard, St. Paul, Minnesota 55164-0526. 1985- . (Annual Supplements).

LOOSELEAF SERVICES AND REPORTERS

CONDOMINIUM DEVELOPMENT GUIDE: PROCEDURES, ANALYSIS, FORMS. Keith B. Romney and Brad Romney. Research Institute of America, Incorporated, One Penn Plaza, New York, New York 10119. 1983- . (Periodic Supplements).

CONDOMINIUM LAW AND PRACTICE: FORMS. Patrick J. Reskin, Jr. and Patrick J. Rohan. Matthew Bender and Company, Incorporated, 11 Penn Plaza, New York, New York 10001. 1965- . (Biannual Supplements).

CONDOMINIUMS, COOPERATIVES AND CLUSTER DEVELOPMENTS. Ralph Boyer and William Sklar. Butterworth Legal Publishers, 90 Stiles Road, Salem, New Hampshire 03079. 1986- . (Semiannual Supplements).

COOPERATIVE HOUSING LAW AND PRACTICE: FORMS. Melvin A. Reskin and Patrick J. Rohan. Matthew Bender and Company, Incorporated, 11 Penn Plaza, New York, New York 10001. 1967- . (Periodic Supplements).

LAW OF CONDOMINIUM OPERATIONS. Gary A. Poliakoff. Callaghan and Company, 155 Pfingsten Road, Deerfield, Illinois 60015. 1988- . (Annual Supplements).

TAX ANGLES FOR CONDOMINIUMS, COOPERATIVES, AND VACATION HOMES. Commerce Clearing House, Incorporated, 4025 West Peterson Avenue, Chicago, Illinois 60646. 1981- . (Periodic Supplements).

HANDBOOKS, MANUALS, FORMBOOKS

ATTORNEYS' AND LENDERS' GUIDE TO COMMON INTEREST OWNERSHIP ACTS: CONDOMINIUMS, COOPERATIVES, AND PLANNED COMMUNITIES. Dennis P. Anderson and Gurdon H. Buck. Real Estate, Real Property, Probate and Trust Section, American Bar Association, 750 North Lake Shore Drive, Chicago, Illinois 60611. 1989.

COMMERCIAL AND MIXED USE CONDOMINIUMS. F. Scott Jackson. Practising Law Institute, 810 Seventh Avenue, New York, New York 10019. 1982.

CONDOMINIUM AND HOMEOWNER ASSOCIATION PRACTICE: COMMUNITY ASSOCIATION LAW. Second Edition. Wayne S. Hyatt. American Law Institute-American Bar Association, 4025 Chestnut Street, Philadelphia, Pennsylvania 19104. 1988.

CONDOMINIUM AND HOMEOWNERS ASSOCIATION LITIGATION: COMMUNITY ASSOCIATION LAW. Wayne S. Hyatt. John Wiley and Sons, Incorporated, 605 Third Avenue, New York, New York 10158. 1987.

CONDOMINIUMS AND HOME OWNER ASSOCIATIONS: A GUIDE TO THE DEVELOPMENT PROCESS. Wayne S. Hyatt. Shepard's/McGraw-Hill, P.O. Box 1235, Colorado Springs, Colorado 80901. 1985- . (Annual Supplements).

CONDOS AND CO-OPS/MULTI-USE STRUCTURES: TECHNIQUES. Lewis R. Kastel and William Jay Lippman. Practising Law Institute, 810 Seventh Avenue, New York, New York 10019. 1983.

COOPERATIVES AND CONDOMINIUMS. Oceana Publications, 75 Main Street, Dobbs Ferry, New York 10522. 1974- . (Periodic Supplements).

RESIDENTIAL CONDOMINIUM AND COOPERATIVE DEVELOPMENT. Practising Law Institute, 810 Seventh Avenue, New York, New York 10019. 1982.

TEXTBOOKS AND GENERAL WORKS

ALI-ABA COURSE OF STUDY: REAL ESTATE CONDOMINIUMS AND PLANNED UNIT DEVELOPMENTS. American Law Institute, 4025 Chestnut Street, Philadelphia, Pennsylvania 19104. 1982.

CONDOMINIUMS AND COOPERATIVES. Second Edition. John Wiley and Sons, Incorporated, 605 Third Avenue, New York, New York 10158. 1984.

OTHER SOURCES

RESOURCE MATERIALS: CONDOMINIUM, PLANNED UNIT DEVELOPMENT AND CONVERSION DOCUMENTS. Third Edition. American Law Institute, 4025 Chestnut Street, Philadelphia, Pennsylvania 19104. 1985.

CONFESSIONS

TEXTBOOKS AND GENERAL WORKS

CONFESSION STANDARDS. Nathan R. Sobel. Gould Publications, 199/300 State Street, Binghamton, New York 13901. 1966.

CRIMINAL INTERROGATIONS AND CONFESSIONS. Third Edition. Fred E. Inbau and John E. Reid. Williams and Wilkins Company, 428 East Preston Street, Baltimore, Maryland 21202. 1986.

INTERROGATIONS AND CONFESSIONS, WHITE'S PA. Welsh S. White. Harrison Company, 3110 Crossing Park, Norcross, Georgia 30091. 1985.

LAW OF CONFESSIONS. David M. Nissman, Ed Hagen and Pierce R. Brooks. Lawyers Cooperative Publishing Company, Aqueduct Building, Rochester, New York 14694. 1985- . (Periodic Supplements).

PRE-TRIAL CRIMINAL PROCEDURE: A SURVEY ON CONSTITUTIONAL RIGHTS. Marc W. Tobias and David R. Petersen. Charles C. Thomas, Publishers, 2600 South First Street, Springfield, Illinois 62794-9265.

A SCOTTSBORO CASE IN MISSISSIPPI: THE SUPREME COURT AND BROWN v. MISSISSIPPI. Richard C. Cortner. University of Mississippi, University, Mississippi 38677. 1986.

THE SUPREME COURT AND CONFESSIONS OF GUILT. Otis H. Stevens, Jr. University of Tennessee Press, 293 Communications Building, Knoxville, Tennessee 37996-0325. 1973.

WHY MEN CONFESS. O. John Rogge. Da Capo Press, Incorporated, 233 Spring Street, New York, New York 10013. 1975, c1959.

OTHER SOURCES

REPORT TO THE ATTORNEY GENERAL ON THE LAW OF PRE-TRIAL INTERROGATION: TRUTH IN CRIMINAL JUSTICE. United States Department of Justice, Office of Legal Policy. Superintendent of Documents, United States Government Printing Office, Washington, D.C. 20402. 1986.

CONFIDENTIAL COMMUNICATIONS
See also: EVIDENCE

STATUTES, CODES, STANDARDS, UNIFORM LAWS

LAWS GOVERNING CONFIDENTIALITY OF HIV-RELATED INFORMATION: 1983 TO 1988. Mona Rowe and Bethany Bridgham. AIDS Policy Center, Intergovernmental Health Policy Project, George Washington University, Washington, D.C. 20052.

RESTATEMENTS

RESTATEMENT OF THE LAW (THIRD), THE LAW GOVERNING LAWYERS: TENTATIVE DRAFT. American Law Institute, 4025 Chestnut Street, Philadelphia, Pennsylvania 19104. 1988- .

LOOSELEAF SERVICES AND REPORTERS

BANKING CRIMES: FRAUD, MONEY LAUNDERING, AND EMBEZZLEMENT. John K. Villa. Clark Boardman Company, Limited, 435 Hudson Street, New York, New York 10014. 1987- . (Annual Supplements).

FEDERAL TESTIMONIAL PRIVILEGES. Murl A. Larkin. Clark Boardman and Company, Limited, 435 Hudson Street, New York, New York 10014. 1982- . (Annual Supplements).

HANDBOOKS, MANUALS, FORMBOOKS

CONFIDENTIALITY IN MEDIATION: A PRACTITIONER'S GUIDE. Lawrence Freedman, Christopher Hacle and Howard Bookstaff. American Bar Association, Alternative Dispute Resolution Committee, Young Lawyers Division, Special Committee on Dispute Resolution, Public Services Division, 1800 M Street, Northwest, Washington, D.C. 20036. 1985.

EMPLOYEE PRIVACY: LAWS, PROCEDURE, AND POLICIES. John Wiley and Sons, Incorporated, 605 Third Avenue, New York, New York 10158. 1989.

PRACTICAL GUIDE TO ACCESS, DISCLOSURE, AND LEGAL REQUIREMENTS RELATING TO HOSPITAL PATIENT, MEDICAL STAFF, AND EMPLOYEE RECORDS. Forum Committee on Health Law, American Bar Association, 750 North Lake Shore Drive, Chicago, Illinois 60611. 1987.

PROTECTING WORKPLACE SECRETS: MANAGER'S GUIDE TO CONFIDENTIALITY AND THE RIGHT TO KNOW. James T. O'Reilly. Executive Enterprises, 5811 La Jolla Corona Drive, La Jolla, California 92037. 1985.

TEXTBOOKS AND GENERAL WORKS

THE ATTORNEY-CLIENT PRIVILEGE AND THE WORK-PRODUCT DOCTRINE: A PROJECT OF THE TRIAL EVIDENCE COMMITTEE. Second Edition. Edna S. Epstein. Section on Litigation, American Bar Association, 750 North Lake Shore Drive, Chicago, Illinois 60611. 1989.

THE ATTORNEY-CLIENT PRIVILEGE UNDER SIEGE: PRESERVING AND PROTECTING IT IN CIVIL CASES. Tort and Insurance Practice Section, American Bar Association, 750 North Lake Shore Drive, Chicago, Illinois 60611. 1989.

THE ATTORNEY-CORPORATE CLIENT PRIVILEGE. Second Edition. John W. Gergacz. Garland Publishing, Incorporated, 136 Madison Avenue, New York, New York 10016. 1990.

BANK ACCOUNTS: A WORLD GUIDE TO CONFIDENTIALITY. Edouard Chambost. Wiley Interscience, 605 Third Avenue, New York, New York 10158. 1983.

BANK CONFIDENTIALITY. F.W. Neate and Roger McCormick. International Bar Association, Butterworth Legal Publishers, 90 Stiles Road, Salem, New Hampshire 03079. 1990.

BREACH OF CONFIDENCE. Francis Gurry. Oxford University Press, 200 Madison Avenue, New York, New York 10016. 1984.

CONFIDENTIAL AND OTHER PRIVILEGED COMMUNICATIONS. Roy D. Weinberg. Oceana Publications, Incorporated, 75 Main Street, Dobbs Ferry, New York, New York 10522. 1967- .

CONFIDENTIALITY AND THE LAW. Brian C. Reid. Pergamon Press, Incorporated, Maxwell House, Fairview Park, Elmsford, New York 10523. 1986.

CONFIDENTIALITY IN SOCIAL WORK. Joseph T. Alves. Greenwood Publishing Group, Incorporated, Incorporated, 88 Post Road, Westport, Connecticut 06881. 1984, c1959.

CONFIDENTIALITY VERSUS THE DUTY TO PROTECT: FORESEEABLE HARM IN THE PRACTICE OF PSYCHIATRY. James C. Beck. American Psychiatric Press, 1400 K Street, Northwest, Washington, D.C. 20005. 1990.

CORPORATE DISCLOSURE AND ATTORNEY CLIENT PRIVILEGE. Dennis J. Block and Jerold S. Solovy, Chairmen. Practising Law Institute, 810 Seventh Avenue, New York, New York 10019. 1984.

CORPORATE INFORMATION MANAGEMENT. Ivan T. Jackson. Prentice-Hall, 113 Sylvan Avenue, Englewood Cliffs, New Jersey 07632. 1986.

EMPLOYEE PRIVACY LAW AND PRACTICE. Kurt H. Decker. John Wiley and Sons, Incorporated, 605 Third Avenue, New York, New York 10158. 1987.

THE POTENTIALLY VIOLENT PATIENT AND THE TARASOFF DECISION IN PSYCHIATRIC PRACTICE. James Beck, Editor. Books on Demand, 300 North Zeeb Road, Ann Arbor, Michigan 48106-1346. 1985.

PRIVACY AND CONFIDENTIALITY OF HEALTH CARE INFORMATION. Second Edition. Jo Anne C. Bruce. American Hospital Publishing Incorporated, 211 East Chicago Avenue, Chicago, Illinois 60611. 1988.

PRIVILEGED COMMUNICATION AND THE PRESS: THE CITIZEN'S RIGHT TO KNOW VS. THE LAW'S RIGHT TO CONFIDENTIAL NEWS SOURCE EVIDENCE. Maurice Van Gerpen. Greenwood Publishing Group, Incorporated, 88 Post Road West, P.O. Box 5007, Westport, Connecticut 06881. 1979.

PRIVILEGED COMMUNICATIONS AS A BRANCH OF LEGAL EVIDENCE. John T. Hageman. Fred B. Rothman and Company, 10368 West Centennial Road, Littleton, Colorado 80127. 1983, c1889.

PRIVILEGED COMMUNICATIONS IN THE MENTAL HEALTH PROFESSIONS. Samuel Knapp and Leon Vande Creek. Van Nostrand Reinhold Company, Incorporated, 115 Fifth Avenue, New York, New York 10003. 1987.

PROTECTING THE CONFIDENTIALITY OF BUSINESS INFORMATION SUBMITTED TO THE FEDERAL GOVERNMENT. Kevin R. McCarthy and John W. Kornmeier. Matthew Bender and Company, Incorporated, 11 Penn Plaza, New York, New York 10001. 1984- . (Periodic Supplements).

THE PSYCHOTHERAPIST-PATIENT PRIVILEGE: A CRITICAL EXAMINATION. Daniel W. Shuman. Charles C. Thomas, Publishers, 2600 South First Street, Springfield, Illinois 62794. 1987.

THE RIGHT TO SILENCE: PRIVILEGED CLERGY COMMUNICATION AND THE LAW. Third Edition. John C. Bush. Abingdon Press, 201 Eighth Avenue South, Nashville, Tennessee 37202. 1989.

SCIENCE AS INTELLECTUAL PROPERTY: WHO CONTROLS RESEARCH? Dorothy Nelkin. MacMillan Publishing Company, Incorporated, 866 Third Avenue, New York, New York 10022. 1983.

THE SECRET MONEY MARKET: INSIDE THE DARK WORLD OF TAX EVASION, FINANCIAL FRAUD, INSIDER TRADING, MONEY LAUNDERING, AND CAPITAL FLIGHT. Ingo Walter. Ballinger Division, HarperCollins, 10 East Fifty-third Street, New York, New York 10022. 1990.

TESTIMONIAL PRIVILEGES. Scott N. Stone and Ronald S. Liebman. Shepard's/McGraw-Hill, P.O. Box 1235, Colorado Springs, Colorado 80901. 1983- . (Periodic Supplements).

WORKPLACE PRIVACY: EMPLOYEE TESTING, SURVEILLANCE, WRONGFUL DISCHARGE AND OTHER AREAS OF VULNERABILITY. Ira M. Shepard and Robert L. Duston. Bureau of National Affairs, Incorporated, 1231 Twenty-fifth Street, Northwest, Washington, D.C. 20037. 1987.

BIBLIOGRAPHIES

CONFIDENTIALITY - PRIVACY I: THE PRIVACY ACT OF 1974: A SELECTED BIBLIOGRAPHY. Vance Bibliographies, P.O. Box 229, 112 North Charter Street, Monticello, Illinois 61856. 1982.

EMPLOYEE PRIVACY: A BIBLIOGRAPHY. Marian Dworaczek. Vance Bibliographies, P.O. Box 229, 112 North Charter Street, Monticello, Illinois 61856. 1989.

PRIVACY - CONFIDENTIALITY IV: MEDICAL RECORDS AND INFORMATION: A SELECTED BIBLIOGRAPHY. Vance Bibliographies, P.O. Box 229, 112 North Charter Street, Monticello, Illinois 61856. 1983.

CONFISCATION
See: EMINENT DOMAIN; GOVERNMENT OWNERSHIP

CONFLICT OF INTEREST
See also: LEGAL ETHICS AND MALPRACTICE; PROFESSIONAL ETHICS AND LIABILITY

LOOSELEAF SERVICES AND REPORTERS

ETHICS IN GOVERNMENT REPORTER. Washington Service Bureau, 655 Fifteenth Street, Northwest, Washington, D.C. 20005. 1980- . (Monthly Supplements.)

OPINIONS OF THE OFFICE OF LEGAL COUNSEL OF THE UNITED STATES DEPARTMENT OF JUSTICE. Office of the Legal Counsel of the United States Department of Justice. Superintendent of Documents, United States Government Printing Office, Washington, D.C. 20402. 1977- .

HANDBOOKS, MANUALS, FORMBOOKS

FEDERAL ETHICS HANDBOOK. Michie/Bobbs-Merrill Law Publishing, P.O. Box 7587, Charlottesville, Virginia 22906-7582. 1981- . (Periodic Supplements).

TEXTBOOKS AND GENERAL WORKS

ABUSE ON WALL STREET: CONFLICTS OF INTEREST IN THE SECURITIES MARKETS: REPORT TO THE TWENTIETH CENTURY FUND STEERING COMMITTEE ON CONFLICTS OF INTEREST IN THE SECURITIES MARKETS. Quorum Books, Greenwood Publishing Group, Incorporated, 88 Post Road West, P.O. Box 5007, Westport, Connecticut 06881. 1980.

CONFLICT OF INTEREST AND THE FEDERAL SERVICE ASSOCIATION OF THE BAR OF THE CITY OF NEW YORK. Special Committee on the Federal Conflict of Interest Laws. Harvard University Press, 79 Garden Street, Cambridge, Massachusetts 02138. 1960.

CONFLICT OF INTEREST REGULATION IN THE FEDERAL EXECUTIVE BRANCH. Robert G. Vaughn. Lexington Books, 125 Spring Street, Lexington, Massachusetts 02173. 1979.

CONFLICTS OF INTEREST: MULTIPLE REPRESENTATIONS. Robin Alexander-Smith. American Bar Association, 750 North Lake Shore Drive, Chicago, Illinois 60611. 1983.

CONFLICTS OF INTEREST: TRIAL LAWYER'S DILEMMA. American Bar Association, Section of Litigation, 750 North Lake Shore Drive, Chicago, Illinois 60611. 1981.

CONGRESS AND THE PUBLIC TRUST: REPORT. Association of the Bar of the City of New York, Special Committee on Congressional Ethics. Atheneum Publishers, 115 Fifth Avenue, New York, New York 10003. 1970.

CONGRESSIONAL ETHICS: THE CONFLICT OF INTEREST ISSUE. Robert S. Getz. Van Nostrand Reinhold Company, Incorporated, 115 Fifth Avenue, New York, New York 10003. 1966.

FEDERAL CONFLICT OF INTEREST LAW. Bayless Manning. Harvard University Press, 79 Garden Street, Cambridge, Massachusetts 02138. 1964.

GUIDANCE ON ETHICS AND CONFLICTS OF INTEREST. Environmental Protection Agency, Office of General Counsel. Superintendent of Documents, United States Government Printing Office, Washington, D.C. 20402. 1984.

A MODEL LAW FOR CAMPAIGN FINANCE, ETHICS, AND LOBBYING REGULATION. Council on Governmental Ethics Laws. Council of State Governments, Iron Works Pike, P.O. Box 11910, Lexington, Kentucky 40578. 1990.

1990 UPDATE ON ETHICS LITIGATION. Council on Governmental Ethics Laws. Council of State Governments, Iron Works Pike, P.O. Box 11910, Lexington, Kentucky 40578. 1990.

PERSONAL CONFLICTS OF INTEREST IN GOVERNMENT CONTRACTING. L. James D'Agostino and Roger G. Darley. Conflicts of Interest and Ethics Committee, American Bar Association, 750 North Lake Shore Drive, Chicago, Illinois 60611. 1988.

POLITICS AND MONEY: THE NEW ROAD TO CORRUPTION. Elizabeth Drew. Macmillan Publishing Company, Incorporated, 866 Third Avenue, New York, New York 10022. 1983.

WHITE HOUSE ETHICS: THE HISTORY OF THE POLITICS OF CONFLICT OF INTEREST REGULATION. Robert N. Roberts. Greenwood Publishing Group, Incorporated, 88 Post Road West, P.O. Box 5007, Westport, Connecticut 06881. 1988.

DIGESTS, INDEXES, ABSTRACTS, CITATORS

INDEX OF ADVISORY OPINIONS ON CONFLICT OF INTEREST LAWS AND FINANCIAL DISCLOSURE LAWS. Third Edition. Page Elizabeth Bigelow. National Civic League, 1601 Grant Street, Suite 250, Denver, Colorado 80203. 1978.

BIBLIOGRAPHIES

CONFLICT OF INTEREST (PUBLIC OFFICE): A BIBLIOGRAPHY. Mary Vance. Vance Bibliographies, P.O. Box 229, 112 North Charter Street, Monticello, Illinois 61856. 1982.

CONFLICTS OF INTEREST: A TRIAL LAWYER'S GUIDE. Edna Selan Epstein. National Law Publishing Corporation, 428 Preston Street, Baltimore, Maryland 21201. 1984.

OTHER SOURCES

REPORT OF THE BIPARTISAN TASK FORCE ON ETHICS ON H.R. 3660: TO AMEND THE RULES OF THE HOUSE OF REPRESENTATIVES AND ETHICS IN GOVERNMENT ACT OF 1978 TO PROVIDE FOR GOVERNMENT-WIDE ETHICS REFORM, AND FOR OTHER PURPOSES. Bipartisan Task Force on Ethics, United States Congress, House of Representatives. Superintendent of Documents, United States Government Printing Office, Washington, D.C. 20402. 1989.

CONFLICT OF LAWS
See also: COMPARATIVE LAW; JURISDICTION

RESTATEMENTS

RESTATEMENT OF THE LAW (SECOND), CONFLICT OF LAWS: AS ADOPTED AND PROMULGATED BY THE AMERICAN LAW INSTITUTE AT WASHINGTON, D.C., MAY 23, 1969. American Law Institute-American Bar Association, 4025 Chestnut Street, Philadelphia, Pennsylvania 19104. 1986- . (Annual Supplements).

LOOSELEAF SERVICES AND REPORTERS

PUBLIC POLICY IN TRANSNATIONAL RELATIONS. Mauro Rubino-Sammartano. Kluwer Academic Publishers, 101 Philip Drive, Assinippi Park, Norwell, Massachusetts 02061. 1990. (Periodic Supplements).

TRANSNATIONAL CONTRACTS: APPLICABLE LAW OF SETTLEMENT IN DISPUTES. Georges R. Delaume. Oceana Publications, Incorporated, 75 Main Street, Dobbs Ferry, New York 10522. 1979- . (Annual Supplements).

TEXTBOOKS AND GENERAL WORKS

ACROSS STATE LINES: APPLYING THE CONFLICT OF LAWS TO YOUR PRACTICE. Robert A. Sedler. Section of General Practice, American Bar Association, 750 North Lake Shore Drive, Chicago, Illinois 60611. 1989.

AVIATION ANTITRUST: THE EXTRATERRITORIAL APPLICATION OF THE UNITED STATES ANTITRUST LAWS AND INTERNATIONAL AIR TRANSPORTATION. Patricia M. Barlow. Kluwer Academic Publishers, 101 Philip Drive, Assinippi Park, Norwell, Massachusetts 02061. 1987.

BEYOND LEX LOCI DELICTI: CONFLICTS METHODOLOGY AND MULTISTATE TORTS IN AMERICAN CASE LAW. T.M. de Boer. Kluwer Academic Publishers, 101 Philip Drive, Assinippi Park, Norwell, Massachusetts 02061. 1987.

THE CHOICE OF LAW: SELECTED ESSAYS, 1933-1983. David F. Cavers. Duke University Press, P.O. Box 6697, College Station, Durham, North Carolina 27708. 1985.

COMMENTARY ON THE CONFLICT OF LAWS. Third Edition. Russell J. Weintraub. Foundation Press, Incorporated, 615 Merrick Avenue, Westbury, New York 11590. 1986.

CONFLICT OF LAWS. Eugene F. Scoles and Peter Hay. West Publishing Company, P.O. Box 64526, 50 West Kellogg Boulevard, St. Paul, Minnesota 55164-0526. 1982- . (Annual Supplements).

CONFLICT OF LAWS: THEORY AND PRACTICE. Second Edition. David H. Vernon. Matthew Bender and Company, Incorporated, 11 Penn Plaza, New York, New York 10001. 1982- . (Periodic Supplements).

FOREIGN PLAINTIFFS IN PRODUCTS LIABILITY ACTIONS: THE DEFENSE OF FORUM NON CONVENIENS. Warren Freedman. Quorum Books, Greenwood Publishing Group, Incorporated, 88 Post Road West, P.O. Box 5007, Westport, Connecticut 06881. 1988.

HANDBOOK OF THE CONFLICT OF LAWS. Herbert F. Goodrich. West Publishing Company, P.O. Box 64526, 50 West Kellogg Boulevard, St. Paul, Minnesota 55164-0526. 1927.

INTERNATIONAL CIVIL LITIGATION IN UNITED STATES COURTS: COMMENTARY AND MATERIALS. Gary Born and David Westin. Kluwer Academic Publishers, 101 Philip Drive, Assinippi Park, Norwell, Massachusetts 02061. 1989.

INTRODUCTION TO THE CONFLICT OF LAWS. A.J.E. Jaffey. Butterworth Legal Publishers, 90 Stiles Road, Salem, New Hampshire 03079. 1988.

LAW OF CONFLICT OF LAWS. Robert A. Leflar. Bobbs-Merrill Company, 866 Third Avenue, New York, New York 10022. 1968.

LAW OF CONFLICTS IN A NUTSHELL. David D. Seigel. West Publishing Company, P.O. Box 64526, 50 West Kellogg Boulevard, St. Paul, Minnesota 55164-0526. 1982.

PERSPECTIVES ON CONFLICT OF LAWS: CHOICE OF LAW. James A. Martin, Little Brown and Company, 34 Beacon Street, Boston, Massachusetts 02108. 1980.

PRINCIPLES OF THE CONFLICT OF LAWS: NATIONAL AND INTERNATIONAL. K. Lipstein. Martinus Nijhoff, 101 Philip Drive, Assinippi Park, Norwell, Massachusetts 02061. 1981.

PRODUCTS LIABILITY ACTIONS BY FOREIGN PLAINTIFFS IN THE UNITED STATES. Warren Freedman. Kluwer Academic Publishers, 101 Philip Drive, Assinippi Park, Norwell, Massachusetts 02061. 1988.

SUING FOREIGN GOVERNMENTS AND THEIR CORPORATIONS. Joseph W. Dellapenna. Bureau of National Affairs, Incorporated, 1231 Twenty-fifth Street, Northwest, Washington, D.C. 20037. 1988.

SUM AND SUBSTANCE OF CONFLICT OF LAWS. Third Edition. Robert A. Sedler. Herbert Legal Series, 1231 Third Street Promenade, Santa Monica, California 90401. 1987.

A TREATISE ON THE CONFLICT OF LAWS. Albert A. Ehrenzweig. West Publishing Company, P.O. Box 64526, 50 West Kellogg Boulevard, St. Paul, Minnesota 55164-0526. 1962.

UNDERSTANDING CONFLICT OF LAWS. William M. Richman and William L. Reynolds. Matthew Bender and Company, Incorporated, 11 Penn Plaza, New York, New York 10001. 1984- . (Periodic Supplements).

CONGRESS
See: LEGISLATIVE HISTORY AND PROCESS

CONSCIENTIOUS OBJECTORS

HANDBOOKS, MANUALS, FORMBOOKS

DRAFT COUNSELOR'S MANUAL. Robert A. Seeley, Editor. Central Committee for Conscientious Objectors, 2208 South Street, Philadelphia, Pennsylvania 19146. 1982.

DRAFT, REGISTRATION AND THE LAW: A GUIDEBOOK. Charles R. Johnson. Nolo Press, 950 Parker Street, Berkeley, California 94710. 1991.

HANDBOOK FOR CONSCIENTIOUS OBJECTORS. Thirteenth Edition. Robert A. Seeley. Central Committee for Conscientious Objectors, 2208 South Street, Philadelphia, Pennsylvania 19146. 1981.

NISBCO DRAFT COUNSELOR'S MANUAL. Fifth Edition. Charles A. Maresca, Jr. National Interreligious Service Board for Conscientious Objectors, 1601 Connecticut Avenue, Northwest, Washington, D.C. 20009. 1989- . (Periodic Supplements).

TEXTBOOKS AND GENERAL WORKS

ADVICE FOR CONSCIENTIOUS OBJECTORS IN THE ARMED FORCES. Fifth Edition. Robert Seeley, Editor. Central Committee for Conscientious Objectors, 2208 South Street, Philadelphia, Pennsylvania 19146. 1984.

ANOTHER PART OF THE WAR: THE CAMP SIMON STORY. Gordon C. Zahn. University of Massachusetts Press, P.O. Box 429, Amherst, Massachusetts 01004. 1979.

CHOICE OF CONSCIENCE: VIETNAM ERA MILITARY AND DRAFT RESISTERS IN CANADA. David Surrey. Praeger Publishers, One Madison Avenue, New York, New York 10010. 1982.

CONSCIENTIOUS OBJECTION TO MILITARY SERVICE. Amnesty International, 322 Eighth Avenue, New York, New York 10001. 1988.

CONSCIENTIOUS OBJECTOR. Walter G. Kellogg. Jerome S. Ozer Publishers, Incorporated, Tenafly Road, Englewood, New Jersey 07631. 1972.

FIGHTING FOR PEACE: THE WAR RESISTANCE MOVEMENT. William J. Chamberlain. Garland Publishing, Incorporated, 136 Madison Avenue, New York, New York 10016. 1971.

JAILED FOR PEACE: THE HISTORY OF AMERICAN DRAFT LAW VIOLATORS 1658-1985. Stephen M. Kohn. Greenwood Publishing Group, Incorporated, 88 Post Road West, P.O. Box 5007, Westport, Connecticut 06881. 1986.

A JUST WAR NO LONGER EXISTS: THE TEACHING AND TRIAL OF DON LORENZO MILIANI. James T. Burtchaell. University of Notre Dame Press, P.O. Box L, Notre Dame, Indiana 46556. 1988.

MY COUNTRY RIGHT OR WRONG?: SELECTIVE CONSCIENTIOUS OBJECTION IN THE NUCLEAR AGE. Eileen P. Flynn. Loyola University Press, 3441 North Ashland Avenue, Chicago, Illinois 60657. 1985.

NOT SHOOTING AND NOT CRYING: PSYCHOLOGICAL INQUIRY INTO MORAL DISOBEDIENCE. Ruth Linn. Greenwood Publishing Group, Incorporated, 88 Post Road West, P.O. Box 5007, Westport, Connecticut 06881. 1989.

PROPHETS WITHOUT HONOR: PUBLIC POLICY AND SELECTIVE CONSCIENTIOUS OBJECTORS. John A. Rohr. Abingdon Press, P.O. Box 801, 201 Eighth Avenue South, Nashville, Tennessee 37202. 1971.

THE RESISTANCE. Michael Ferber and Staughton Lynd. Beacon Press, 25 Beacon Street, Boston, Massachusetts 02108. 1971.

SELECTIVE CONSCIENTIOUS OBJECTION: ACCOMMODATING CONSCIENCE AND SECURITY. Michael F. Noone, Jr., Editor. Westview Press, 5500 Central Avenue, Boulder, Colorado 80301. 1989.

TROUBLESOME PEOPLE: THE WARRIORS OF PACIFISM. Caroline Moorehead. Adler and Adler Publication, Incorporated, 4550 Montgomery Avenue, Bethesda, Maryland 20814. 1987.

UNSUNG HERO OF THE GREAT WAR: THE LIFE AND WITNESS OF BEN SALMON. Torin R.T. Finney. Paulist Press, 997 MacArthur Boulevard, Mahwah, New Jersey 07430. 1989.

WE WOULD NOT KILL. Hobart Mitchell. Friends United Press, 101 Quaker Hill Drive, Richmond, Indiana 47374. 1983.

LAW REVIEWS AND PERIODICALS

CONSCIENTIOUS OBJECTOR, VOLUMES 1-8, 1939-46. The War Resisters League. Greenwood Publishing Group, Incorporated, 88 Post Road West, P.O. Box 5007, Westport, Connecticut 06881. 1968.

REPORTER FOR CONSCIENCE SAKE. National Interreligious Service Board for Conscientious Objectors, 1601 Connecticut Avenue, Northwest, Suite 750, Washington, D.C. 20009. Monthly.

NEWSLETTERS AND NEWSPAPERS

CONSCIENCE. Conscience and Military Tax Campaign, 4534 1/2 University Way, Northeast, Suite 204, Seattle, Washington 98105. Quarterly.

NEWS NOTES. CCCO/An Agency for Military and Draft Counseling, 2208 South Street, Philadelphia, Pennsylvania 19146. Quarterly.

THE OBJECTOR: JOURNAL OF DRAFT AND MILITARY COUNSELING. CCCO/An Agency for Military and Draft Counseling, 2208 South Street, Philadelphia, Pennsylvania 19146. Bimonthly.

DIRECTORIES

MILITARY COUNSELOR'S DIRECTORY. CCCO/An Agency for Military and Draft Counseling (formerly Central Committee for Conscientious Objectors), 2208 South Street, Philadelphia, Pennsylvania 19146. Annual.

ASSOCIATIONS AND PROFESSIONAL SOCIETIES

CCCO/AN AGENCY FOR MILITARY AND DRAFT COUNSELING. 2208 South Street, Philadelphia, Pennsylvania 19146. (215) 545-4626.

CONSCIENCE AND MILITARY TAX CAMPAIGN. 4534 1/2 University Way, Suite 204, Seattle, Washington 98105. (206) 547-0952.

NATIONAL INTERRELIGIOUS SERVICE BOARD FOR CONSCIENTIOUS OBJECTORS. 1601 Connecticut Avenue, Northwest, Suite 750, Washington, D.C. 20009. (202) 483-4510.

CONSERVATION
See: ENERGY; NATURAL RESOURCES

CONSERVATORSHIP
See: GUARDIAN AND WARD

CONSOLIDATION AND MERGER OF CORPORATIONS
See: ANTITRUST LAW; CORPORATIONS, CONSOLIDATION AND MERGER

CONSPIRACY

LOOSELEAF SERVICES AND REPORTERS

PROSECUTION AND DEFENSE OF CRIMINAL CONSPIRACY CASES. Paul Marcus. Matthew Bender and Company, Incorporated, 11 Penn Plaza, New York, New York 10001. 1979- . (Annual Supplements).

TEXTBOOKS AND GENERAL WORKS

ARCHITECTS OF FEAR: CONSPIRACY THEORIES AND PARANOIA IN AMERICAN POLITICS. George Johnson. J.P. Tarcher, Incorporated, 5858 Wilshire Boulevard, Suite 200, Los Angeles, California 90036. 1984.

CONSPIRACY: HISTORICAL PERSPECTIVES. Phyllis Flug and Michael J. Miller. Ayer Company Publishers, Incorporated, 382 Main Street, P.O. Box 958, Salem, New Hampshire 03079. 1987.

HISTORY OF AMERICAN CONSPIRACIES. Orville J. Victor. Charles E. Tuttle Company, Incorporated, P.O. Box 410, 28 South Main Street, Rutland, Vermont 05701-0410. 1973.

THE LAW OF CRIMINAL CONSPIRACIES AND AGREEMENTS. Robert S. Wright. Fred B. Rothman and Company, 10368 West Centennial Road, Littleton, Colorado 80127. 1986. (Reprint of 1873 Edition).

CONSTITUTIONAL HISTORY
See also: CONSTITUTIONAL LAW; CONSTITUTIONS

HANDBOOKS, MANUALS, FORMBOOKS

DOCUMENTS OF AMERICAN CONSTITUTIONAL AND LEGAL HISTORY. Temple University Press, Broad and Oxford Streets, University Services Building, Room 305, Philadelphia, Pennsylvania 19122. 1989.

THE FOUNDERS' CONSTITUTION. University of Chicago Press, 5801 Ellis Avenue, Chicago, Illinois 60637. 1987.

THE FRAMING OF THE CONSTITUTION OF THE UNITED STATES. Max Farrand. Yale University Press, 302 Temple Street, New Haven, Connecticut 06520. 1925.

A REFERENCE GUIDE TO THE UNITED STATES SUPREME COURT. Stephen P. Elliot, Editor. Facts on File, Incorporated, 460 Park Avenue, South, New York, New York 10016. 1986.

THE UNITED STATES CONSTITUTION FOR EVERYONE. Mort Gerberg. Putnam Publishing Group, 200 Madison Avenue, New York, New York 10016. 1991.

WE HOLD THESE TRUTHS: UNDERSTANDING THE IDEAS AND IDEALS OF THE CONSTITUTION. Mortimer J. Adler. Macmillan Publishing Company, Incorporated, 866 Third Avenue, New York, New York 10022. 1987.

TEXTBOOKS AND GENERAL WORKS

THE AMERICAN CONSTITUTION AND THE ADMINISTRATIVE STATE: CONSTITUTIONAL LAW IN THE LATE 20TH CENTURY. University Press of America, 4720 Boston Way, Lanham, Maryland 20706. 1989.

THE AMERICAN CONSTITUTION: FOR AND AGAINST: THE FEDERALIST AND ANTI-FEDERALIST PAPERS. J.R. Pole. Hill and Wang, Incorporated, 19 Union Square West, New York, New York 10003. 1987.

THE AMERICAN CONSTITUTION: ITS ORIGINS AND DEVELOPMENT. Sixth Edition. Alfred A. Kelly, Winfred A. Harbison and Herman Belz. W.W. Norton and Company, Incorporated, 500 Fifth Avenue, New York, New York 10110. 1982.

AMERICAN CONSTITUTIONAL HISTORY: ESSAYS. Essays by Edward S. Corwin. Alpheus T. Mason and Gerald Garvey, Editors. Peter Smith Publishing Company, 6 Lexington Avenue, Magnolia, Massachusetts 01930. 1970.

AMERICAN CONSTITUTIONALISM ABROAD: SELECTED ESSAYS IN COMPARATIVE CONSTITUTIONAL HISTORY. George A. Billias. Greenwood Publishing Group, Incorporated, 88 Post Road West, P.O. Box 5007, Westport, Connecticut 06881. 1990.

THE AMERICAN FOUNDING: ESSAYS ON THE FORMATION OF THE CONSTITUTION. J. Jackson Barlow, Editor. Greenwood Publishing Group, Incorporated, 88 Post Road West, P.O. Box 5007, Westport, Connecticut 06881. 1988.

AMERICAN LAW AND CONSTITUTIONAL ORDER: HISTORICAL PERSPECTIVES. Enlarged Edition. Lawrence M. Friedman and Harry N. Scheiber, Editors. Harvard University Press, 79 Garden Street, Cambridge, Massachusetts 02138. 1988.

THE AMERICAN SOLUTION: ORIGINS OF THE UNITED STATES CONSTITUTION. Library of Congress. Superintendent of Documents, United States Government Printing Office, Washington, D.C. 20402. 1987.

THE ANTI-FEDERALIST: AN ABRIDGEMENT. Murray Dry. University of Chicago University Press, 5801 Ellis Avenue, Chicago, Illinois 60637. 1985.

THE ANTIFEDERALISTS. Cecelia M. Kenyon, Editor. Northeastern University Press, 360 Huntington Avenue, Huntington Plaza, Suite 272, Boston, Massachusetts 02115. 1985.

ARE WE TO BE A NATION? THE MAKING OF THE CONSTITUTION. Richard B. Bernstein. Harvard University Press, 79 Garden Street, Cambridge, Massachusetts 02138. 1987.

BEYOND CONFEDERATION: ORIGINS OF THE CONSTITUTION AND AMERICAN NATIONAL IDENTITY. Richard Beeman, Stephen Botein, and Edward C. Carter, Editors. University of North Carolina Press, P.O. Box 2288, Chapel Hill, North Carolina 27515-2288. 1987.

BEYOND THE CONSTITUTION. Hadley Arkes. Princeton University Press, 41 William Street, Princeton, New Jersey 08540. 1990.

THE BLESSINGS OF LIBERTY: AN ENDURING CONSTITUTION IN A CHANGING WORLD. Random House, Incorporated, 201 East Fiftieth Street, New York, New York 10022. 1989.

THE BLESSINGS OF LIBERTY: THE CONSTITUTION AND THE PRACTICE OF LAW. American Law Institute-American Bar Association, 4025 Chestnut Street, Philadelphia, Pennsylvania 19104. 1988.

THE CONCEPT OF LIBERTY IN THE AGE OF THE AMERICAN REVOLUTION. John P. Reid. University of Chicago Press, 5801 Ellis Avenue, Chicago, Illinois 60637. 1988.

CONCEPTUAL CHANGE AND THE CONSTITUTION. University Press of Kansas, 329 Carruth, Lawrence, Kansas 66045. 1988.

THE CONSTITUTION AND THE STATES: THE ROLE OF THE ORIGINAL THIRTEEN IN THE FRAMING AND ADOPTION OF THE FEDERAL CONSTITUTION. Patrick T. Conley. Madison House, P.O. Box 3100, Madison, Wisconsin 53604. 1988.

THE CONSTITUTION IN THE SUPREME COURT: THE SECOND CENTURY, 1888-1986. David P. Currie. University of Chicago Press, 5801 Ellis Avenue, Chicago, Illinois 60637. 1990.

CONSTITUTION MAKING: CONFLICT AND CONSENSUS IN THE FEDERAL CONVENTION OF 1787. Calvin C. Jillson. Agathon Press, 111 Eighth Avenue, New York, New York 10011. 1988.

CONSTITUTIONAL BRINKSMANSHIP: AMENDING THE CONSTITUTION BY NATIONAL CONVENTION. Russell L. Caplan. Oxford University Press, 200 Madison Avenue, New York, New York 10016. 1988.

CONSTITUTIONAL HISTORY OF THE AMERICAN REVOLUTION: THE AUTHORITY TO TAX. John P. Reid. University of Wisconsin Press, 114 North Murray Avenue, Madison, Wisconsin 53715. 1987.

A CONSTITUTIONAL HISTORY OF THE UNITED STATES. Forrest McDonald. Robert E. Krieger Publishing Company, P.O. Box 9542, Malabar, Florida 32902-9542. 1986.

CONSTITUTIONAL MAKERS ON CONSTITUTION MAKING: THE EXPERIENCE OF EIGHT NATIONS. American Enterprise Institute for Public Policy Research, University Press of America, 4720 Boston Way, Lanham, Maryland 20706. 1988.

CONSTITUTIONAL OPINIONS: ASPECTS OF THE BILL OF RIGHTS. Leonard W. Levy. Oxford University Press, 200 Madison Avenue, New York, New York 10016. 1985.

CONSTITUTIONALISM: FOUNDING AND FUTURE. Kenneth W. Thompson, Editor. University Press of America, 4720 Boston Way, Lanham, Maryland 20706. 1989.

THE CONVENTION AND THE CONSTITUTION: THE POLITICAL IDEAS OF THE FOUNDING FATHERS. David G. Smith. University Press of America, 4720 Boston Way, Lanham, Maryland 20706. 1987.

DECISION IN PHILADELPHIA: THE CONSTITUTIONAL CONVENTION OF 1787. First Edition. Christopher Collier and James Lincoln Collier. Random House Publicity, 201 East Fiftieth Street, New York, New York 10022. 1986.

THE ENDURING CONSTITUTION: A BICENTENNIAL PERSPECTIVE. Jethro K. Lieberman. West Publishing Company, 50 West Kellogg Boulevard, St. Paul, Minnesota 55164. 1987.

THE ENDURING CONSTITUTION: AN EXPLORATION OF THE FIRST TWO HUNDRED YEARS. Jethro K. Lieberman. Harper and Row, 10 East Fifty-third Street, New York, New York 10022. 1987.

ESSAYS ON THE MAKING OF THE CONSTITUTION. Leonard W. Levy, Editor. Oxford University Press, 200 Madison Avenue, New York, New York 10016. 1987.

THE ESSENTIAL ANTIFEDERALIST. W.B. Allen and Gordon Lloyd, Editors. University Press of America, 4720 Boston Way, Lanham, Maryland 20706. 1985.

FEDERALISTS AND ANTIFEDERALISTS: THE DEBATE OVER THE RATIFICATION OF THE CONSTITUTION. Madison House, P.O. Box 3100, Madison, Wisconsin 53604. 1989.

FIFTY-FIVE MEN: THE STORY OF THE CONSTITUTION: BASED ON THE DAY-BY-DAY NOTES OF JAMES MADISON. Fred Rodell. Stackpole Books, Incorporated, P.O. Box 1831, Cameron and Kelker Streets, Harrisburg, Pennsylvania 17105. 1986.

THE FORGING OF THE UNION, 1781-1789. Richard B. Morris. HarperCollins, Publishers, 10 East Fifty-third Street, New York, New York 10022. 1988.

THE FORMATION AND RATIFICATION OF THE CONSTITUTION: MAJOR HISTORICAL INTERPRETATIONS. Kermit L. Hall. Garland Publishing Company, 136 Madison Avenue, New York, New York 10016. 1987.

THE FOUNDING: A DRAMATIC ACCOUNT OF THE WRITING OF THE CONSTITUTION. Fred Barbash. Simon and Schuster, Incorporated, 1230 Avenue of the Americas, New York, New York 10020. 1987.

THE FRAMING AND RATIFICATION OF THE CONSTITUTION. Leonard W. Levy and Dennis J. Mahoney. MacMillan Publishing Company, Incorporated, 866 Third Avenue, New York, New York 10022. 1987.

FREE GOVERNMENT IN THE MAKING: READINGS IN AMERICAN POLITICAL THOUGHT. Fourth Edition. Alpheus Thomas Mason and Gordon E. Baker, Editors. Oxford University Press, 200 Madison Avenue, New York, New York 10016. 1985.

THE GENIUS OF THE PEOPLE. Charles L. Mee, Jr. HarperCollins, Publishers, 10 East Fifty-third Street, New York, New York 10022. 1987.

THE GREAT REHEARSAL: THE STORY OF THE MAKING AND RATIFYING OF THE CONSTITUTION OF THE UNITED STATES. Carl Van Doren. Penguin Books, Incorporated, 375 Hudson Street, New York, New York 10014. 1986.

HOW BLACKSTONE LOST THE COLONIES: ENGLISH LAW, COLONIAL LAWYERS, AND THE AMERICAN REVOLUTION. Beverly Zweiben. Garland Publishing, Incorporated, 136 Madison Avenue, New York, New York 10016. 1990.

JAMES MADISON: CREATING THE AMERICAN CONSTITUTION. Neal Riemer. Congressional Quarterly, Books, 1414 Twenty-second Street, Northwest, Washington, D.C. 20037. 1986.

JAMES MADISON ON THE CONSTITUTION AND BILL OF RIGHTS. Robert J. Morgan. Greenwood Publishing Group, Incorporated, 88 Post Road West, P.O. Box 5007, Westport, Connecticut 06881. 1988.

LIBERTY AND COMMUNITY: CONSTITUTION AND RIGHTS IN THE EARLY AMERICAN REPUBLIC. William E. Nelson. Oceana Publications, 75 Main Street, Dobbs Ferry, New York 10522. 1987.

A MACHINE THAT WOULD GO OF ITSELF: THE CONSTITUTION IN AMERICAN CULTURE. First Edition. Michael Kammen. Alfred A. Knopf, Incorporated, 201 East Fiftieth Street, New York, New York 10022. 1986.

THE MAKING OF AMERICA: THE SUBSTANCE AND MEANING OF THE CONSTITUTION. W. Cleon Skousen. National Center for Constitutional Studies, 5288 South, 320 West, Number B-158, Salt Lake City, Utah 84107. 1985.

A MARCH OF LIBERTY: A CONSTITUTIONAL HISTORY OF THE UNITED STATES. Melvin I. Urofsky. Alfred A. Knopf, Incorporated, 201 East Fiftieth Street, New York, New York 10022. 1988.

MIRACLE AT PHILADELPHIA: THE STORY OF THE CONSTITUTIONAL CONVENTION, MAY TO SEPTEMBER, 1787. Catherine Drinker Bowen. Little, Brown and Company, 34 Beacon Street, Boston, Massachusetts 02108. 1986.

ORIGINAL INTENT AND THE FRAMERS' CONSTITUTION. Leonard W. Levy. MacMillan Publishing Company, Incorporated, 866 Third Avenue, New York, New York 10022. 1988.

THE ORIGINS OF AMERICAN CONSTITUTIONALISM. Donald S. Lutz. Louisiana State University Press, Highland Road, Baton Rouge, Louisiana 70893.

ORIGINS OF THE CONSTITUTION AND AMERICAN NATIONAL IDENTITY. Richard Beeman, Stephen Botein and Edward C. Carter, II, Editors. University of North Carolina Press, P.O. Box 2288, Chapel Hill, North Carolina 27515-2288. 1987.

RATIFYING THE CONSTITUTION. University Press of Kansas, 329 Carruth, Lawrence, Kansas 66045. 1989.

RENEWING THE DREAM: NATIONAL ARCHIVES BICENTENNIAL '87 LECTURES ON CONTEMPORARY CONSTITUTIONAL ISSUES. Ralph S. Pollock. University Press of America, 4720 Boston Way, Lanham, Maryland 20706. 1987.

THE SUPREME COURT AND THE CONSTITUTION: READINGS IN AMERICAN HISTORY. Third Edition. Stanley I. Kutler. W.W. Norton and Company, Incorporated, 500 Fifth Avenue, New York, New York 10110. 1984.

THIS CONSTITUTION: FROM RATIFICATION TO THE BILL OF RIGHTS. Congressional Quarterly, Incorporated, 1414 Twenty-second Street, Northwest, Washington, D.C. 20037. 1988.

AN UNCERTAIN TRADITION: CONSTITUTIONALISM AND THE HISTORY OF THE SOUTH. University of Georgia Press, Terrell Hall, Athens, Georgia 30602. 1989.

UNFOUNDED FEARS: MYTHS AND REALITIES OF THE CONSTITUTIONAL CONVENTION. Paul J. Weber. Greenwood Publishing Group, Incorporated, 88 Post Road West, P.O. Box 5007, Westport, Connecticut 06881. 1989.

WITNESSES AT THE CREATION: HAMILTON, MADISON, JAY AND THE CONSTITUTION. Holt, Rinehart, and Winston, Incorporated, 301 Commerce Street, Suite 3700, Fort Worth, Texas 76102. 1985.

LAW REVIEWS AND PERIODICALS

AMERICAN HISTORICAL REVIEW. American Historical Association, 400 A Street, Southeast, Washington, D.C. 20003. Bimonthly.

BEHIND THE SCENES IN WASHINGTON. National Center for Constitutional Studies, P.O. Box 37110, Washington, D.C. 20013. Monthly.

CONSTITUTION. Foundation for the U.S. Constitution, 1271 Avenue of the Americas, New York, New York 10020. Monthly.

THE CONSTITUTION. National Center for Constitutional Studies, P.O. Box 37110, Washington, D.C. 20013. Monthly.

SUPREME COURT HISTORICAL SOCIETY YEARBOOK. Supreme Court Historical Society, 111 Second Street, Northeast, Washington, D.C. 20002. Annual.

BIBLIOGRAPHIES

BIBLIOGRAPHY OF ORIGINAL MEANING OF THE UNITED STATES CONSTITUTION. Office of Legal Policy, U.S. Department of Justice. Superintendent of Documents, United States Government Printing Office, Washington, D.C. 20402. 1988.

A COMPREHENSIVE BIBLIOGRAPHY OF AMERICAN CONSTITUTIONAL AND LEGAL HISTORY, 1896-1979. Kermit L. Hall. Kraus International Publications, Route 100, Millwood, New York 10546. 1984.

ASSOCIATIONS AND PROFESSIONAL SOCIETIES

AMERICAN HISTORICAL ASSOCIATION. 400 A Street, Southeast, Washington, D.C. 20003. (202) 544-2422.

RESEARCH CENTERS, INSTITUTES, CLEARINGHOUSES

COMMISSION ON THE BICENTENNIAL OF THE UNITED STATES CONSTITUTION. 808 Seventeenth Street, Northwest, Washington, D.C. 20036. (202) 872-1787.

FOUNDATION FOR THE U.S. CONSTITUTION. 1271 Avenue of the Americas, New York, New York 10020. (212) 522-5522.

NATIONAL CENTER FOR CONSTITUTIONAL STUDIES. P.O. Box 37110, Washington, D.C. 20013. (800) 365-1776.

AUDIOVISUALS

EQUAL JUSTICE UNDER LAW. WQED, Public Broadcasting Service, Pittsburgh, Pennsylvania. 1988. 6 Videocassettes.

CONSTITUTIONAL LAW

See also: CHURCH AND STATE; CIVIL RIGHTS AND LIBERTIES; CONSTITUTIONAL HISTORY; CONSTITUTIONS; DISCRIMINATION, RACE; DISCRIMINATION, SEX; DUE PROCESS OF LAW; EXECUTIVE POWER; FEDERALISM; FREEDOM OF ASSEMBLY AND ASSOCIATION; FREEDOM OF INFORMATION; FREEDOM OF PRESS; FREEDOM OF RELIGION; FREEDOM OF SPEECH; JURY; SEPARATION OF POWERS; SUPREME COURT

STATUTES, CODES, STANDARDS, UNIFORM LAWS

THE CONSTITUTION OF THE UNITED STATES OF AMERICA: ANALYSIS AND INTERPRETATIVE ANNOTATIONS OF CASES DECIDED BY THE SUPREME COURT OF THE UNITED STATES. Legislative Reference Service, Library of Congress. Superintendent of Documents, United States Government Printing Office, Washington, D.C. 20402. 1988- . (Periodic Supplements).

UNITED STATES CODE ANNOTATED: CONSTITUTION OF THE UNITED STATES ANNOTATED: ANNOTATIONS FROM FEDERAL AND STATE COURTS. West Publishing Company, P.O. Box 64526, 50 West Kellogg Boulevard, St. Paul, Minnesota 55164-0526. 1987- . (Annual Supplements).

LOOSELEAF SERVICES AND REPORTERS

CRIMINAL CONSTITUTIONAL LAW. Helen Jenkins. Matthew Bender and Company, Incorporated, 11 Penn Plaza, New York, New York 10001. 1990- . (Annual Supplements).

UNITED STATES LAW WEEK. Bureau of National Affairs, Incorporated, 1231 Twenty-fifth Street, Northwest, Washington, D.C. 20037. 1932- .

HANDBOOKS, MANUALS, FORMBOOKS

CONSTITUTIONAL CHOICES. Laurence H. Tribe. Harvard University Press, 79 Garden Street, Cambridge, Massachusetts 02138. 1985.

DOCUMENTS OF AMERICAN CONSTITUTIONAL AND LEGAL HISTORY. Temple University Press, Broad and Oxford Streets, University Services Building, Room 305, Philadelphia, Pennsylvania 19122. 1989.

GUIDELINES ON CONSTITUTIONAL LITIGATION. Office of Legal Policy, United States Department of Justice. Superintendent of Documents, United States Government Printing Office, Washington, D.C. 20402. 1988.

ORIGINAL MEANING JURISPRUDENCE: A SOURCEBOOK. Office of Legal Policy, United States Department of Justice. Superintendent of Documents, United States Government Printing Office, Washington, D.C. 20402. 1988.

TREATISE ON CONSTITUTIONAL LAW: SUBSTANCE AND PROCEDURE. Ronald D. Rotunda, John E. Nowak, and J. Nelson Young. West Publishing Company, P.O. Box 64526, 50 West Kellogg Boulevard, St. Paul, Minnesota 55164-0526. 1986- . (Periodic Supplements).

THE UNITED STATES CONSTITUTION FOR EVERYONE: A GUIDE TO THE MOST IMPORTANT DOCUMENT WRITTEN BY AND FOR THE PEOPLE OF THE UNITED STATES. Mort Gerberg. Putnam Publishing Group, 200 Madison Avenue, New York, New York 10016. 1991.

TEXTBOOKS AND GENERAL WORKS

ADJUDICATING CONSTITUTIONAL ISSUES. Chester J. Antieau. Oceana Publications, 75 Main Street, Dobbs Ferry, New York 10522. 1985.

THE AMERICAN CONSTITUTION: ITS ORIGINS AND DEVELOPMENT. Seventh Edition. Alfred A. Kelly, Winifred A. Harbison and Herman Belz. W.W. Norton Company, Incorporated, 500 Fifth Avenue, New York, New York 10110. 1991.

AMERICAN CONSTITUTIONAL INTERPRETATION. Walter F. Murphy, James E. Fleming and William F. Harris, III. Foundation Press, 615 Merrick Avenue, Westbury, New York 11590. 1986.

AMERICAN CONSTITUTIONAL LAW. Second Edition. Laurence H. Tribe. Foundation Press, 615 Merrick Avenue, Westbury, New York 11590. 1987.

AMERICAN CONSTITUTIONAL LAW: INTRODUCTORY ESSAYS AND SELECTED CASES. Ninth Edition. Alpheus Thomas Mason. Prentice-Hall, Incorporated, 113 Sylvan Avenue, Englewood Cliffs, New Jersey 07632. 1990.

AMERICAN CONSTITUTIONALISM ABROAD: SELECTED ESSAYS IN COMPARATIVE CONSTITUTIONAL HISTORY. George A. Billias. Greenwood Publishing Group, Incorporated, 88 Post Road West, P.O. Box 5007, Westport, Connecticut 06881. 1990.

A COMMENTARY ON THE CONSTITUTION OF THE UNITED STATES. PART I: THE POWERS OF GOVERNMENT. Bernard Schwartz. Macmillan Publishing Company, Incorporated, 866 Third Avenue, New York, New York 10022. 1963.

A COMMENTARY ON THE CONSTITUTION OF THE UNITED STATES. PART II: THE RIGHTS OF PROPERTY. Bernard Schwartz. Macmillan Publishing Company, Incorporated, 866 Third Avenue, New York, New York 10022. 1965.

A COMMENTARY ON THE CONSTITUTION OF THE UNITED STATES. PART III: RIGHTS OF THE PERSON. Bernard Schwartz. Macmillan Publishing Company, Incorporated, 866 Third Avenue, New York, New York 10022. 1968.

THE CONSERVATIVE CONSTITUTION. Russell Kirk. Regnery Gateway, Incorporated, 1130 Seventeenth Street, Northwest, Washington, D.C. 20036. 1990.

THE CONSTITUTION AND THE REGULATION OF SOCIETY. Gary C. Bryner and Dennis L. Thompson. Brigham Young University Press, 205 UPB, Provo, Utah 84602. 1988.

THE CONSTITUTION IN THE YEAR 2000: CHOICES AHEAD IN CONSTITUTIONAL INTERPRETATION. Office of Legal Policy, United States Department of Justice. Superintendent of Documents, United States Government Printing Office, Washington, D.C. 20402. 1988.

THE CONSTITUTION OF THE UNITED STATES: A PRIMER FOR THE PEOPLE. David P. Currie. University of Chicago Press, 5801 Ellis Avenue, Chicago, Illinois 60637. 1988.

THE CONSTITUTION: THAT DELICATE BALANCE. First Edition. Fred W. Friendly and Martha J.H. Elliott. McGraw-Hill Publishing Company, 1221 Avenue of the Americas, New York, New York 10020. 1984.

CONSTITUTIONAL ANALYSIS IN A NUTSHELL. Jerre S. Williams. West Publishing Company, P.O. Box 64526, 50 West Kellogg Boulevard, St. Paul, Minnesota 55164-0526. 1979.

THE CONSTITUTIONAL BASES OF POLITICAL AND SOCIAL CHANGE IN THE UNITED STATES. Praeger Publishers, Greenwood Publishing Group, Incorporated, 88 Post Road West, P.O. Box 5007, Westport, Connecticut 06881. 1990.

CONSTITUTIONAL CONFLICTS BETWEEN CONGRESS AND THE PRESIDENT. Third Revised Edition. Louis Fisher. Princeton University Press, 41 William Street, Princeton, New Jersey 08540. 1991.

CONSTITUTIONAL CULTURES: THE MENTALITY AND CONSEQUENCES OF JUDICIAL REVIEW. Robert F. Nagel. University of California Press, 2120 Berkeley Way, Berkeley, California 94720. 1989.

CONSTITUTIONAL FAITH. Sanford Levinson. Princeton University Press, 41 William Street, Princeton, New Jersey 08540. 1988.

CONSTITUTIONAL FEDERALISM IN A NUTSHELL. Second Edition. David E. Engdahl. West Publishing Company, P.O. Box 64526, 50 West Kellogg Boulevard, St. Paul, Minnesota 55164-0526. 1987.

CONSTITUTIONAL LAW. Third Edition. John E. Nowak, Ronald D. Rotunda and J. Nelson Young. West Publishing Company, P.O. Box 64526, 50 West Kellogg Boulevard, St. Paul, Minnesota 55164-0526. 1987.

CONSTITUTIONAL LAW IN A NUTSHELL. Second Edition. Jerome A. Barron and C. Thomas Dienes. West Publishing Company, P.O. Box 64526, 50 West Kellogg Boulevard, St. Paul, Minnesota 55164-0526. 1991.

CONSTITUTIONAL LITIGATION. Kenneth F. Ripple. Michie Company, P.O. Box 7587, Charlottesville, Virginia 22906-7582. 1984.

CONSTITUTIONAL OPINIONS: ASPECTS OF THE BILL OF RIGHTS. Leonard W. Levy. Oxford University Press, 200 Madison Avenue, New York, New York 10016. 1989.

CONSTITUTIONALISM AND RIGHTS: THE INFLUENCE OF THE UNITED STATES CONSTITUTION ABROAD. Albert J. Rosenthal and Louis Henkin. Columbia University Press, 562 West One Hundred Thirteenth Street, New York, New York 10025. 1990.

CONSTITUTIONALISM, DEMOCRACY, AND FOREIGN AFFAIRS. Louis Henkin. Columbia University Press, 562 West One Hundred Thirteenth Street, New York, New York 10025. 1990.

CONSTITUTIONALISM: THE PHILOSOPHICAL DIMENSION. Alan S. Rosenbaum. Greenwood Publishing Group, Incorporated, 88 Post Road West, P.O. Box 5007, Westport, Connecticut 06881. 1988.

CONSTITUTIONS IN CRISIS: POLITICAL VIOLENCE AND RULE OF LAW. John E. Finn. Oxford University Press, 200 Madison Avenue, New York, New York 10016. 1991.

CORWIN AND PELTASON'S UNDERSTANDING THE CONSTITUTION. Twelfth Edition. J.W. Peltason. Harcourt, Brace, Jovanovich, Incorporated, 6277 Sea Harbor Drive, Orlando, Florida 32821. 1991.

THE COURT AND THE CONSTITUTION. Archibald Cox. Houghton Mifflin Company, 1 Beacon Street, Boston, Massachusetts 02108. 1988.

CREATING THE BILL OF RIGHTS: THE DOCUMENTARY RECORD FROM THE FIRST FEDERAL CONGRESS. Helen E. Veit and Kenneth R. Bowling. Johns Hopkins University Press, 701 West Fortieth Street, Baltimore, Maryland 21211. 1991.

DEMOCRATIC THEORIES AND THE CONSTITUTION. Martin Edelman. State University of New York Press, State University Plaza, Albany, New York 12246. 1985.

THE ENDURING CONSTITUTION: A BICENTENNIAL PERSPECTIVE. Jethro K. Lieberman. West Publishing Company, P.O. Box 64526, 50 West Kellogg Boulevard, St. Paul, Minnesota 55164-0526. 1987.

THE FOURTEENTH AMENDMENT AND THE BILL OF RIGHTS. Raoul Berger. University of Oklahoma Press, 105 Asp Avenue, Norman, Oklahoma 73019. 1989.

THE FOURTEENTH AMENDMENT: FROM POLITICAL PRINCIPLE TO JUDICIAL DOCTRINE. William E. Nelson. Harvard University Press, 79 Garden Street, Cambridge, Massachusetts 02138. 1988.

THE GENIUS OF THE PEOPLE. Charles L. Mae. HarperCollins Publishers, 10 East Fifty-third Street, New York, New York 10022. 1987.

GOD SAVE THIS HONORABLE COURT: HOW THE CHOICE OF SUPREME COURT JUSTICES CAN SHAPE OUR HISTORY. Random House Publicity, 201 East Fiftieth Street, New York, New York 10022. 1985.

INTERPRETING THE CONSTITUTION: THE SUPREME COURT IN THE PROCESS OF ADJUDICATION. Harry H. Wellington. Yale University Press, 302 Temple Street, New Haven, Connecticut 06520. 1991.

JAMES MADISON ON THE CONSTITUTION AND THE BILL OF RIGHTS. Robert J. Morgan. Greenwood Publishing Group, Incorporated, 88 Post Road West, P.O. Box 5007, Westport, Connecticut 06881. 1988.

JUSTICE REHNQUIST AND THE CONSTITUTION. Sue Davis. Princeton University Press, 41 William Street, Princeton, New Jersey 08540. 1989.

LIBERALISM AND AMERICAN CONSTITUTIONAL LAW. Rogers M. Smith. Harvard University Press, 79 Garden Street, Cambridge, Massachusetts 02138. 1985.

THE LIVING UNITED STATES CONSTITUTION. Second Revised Edition. Jacob W. Landynski. The New American Library, 1633 Broadway, New York, New York 10019. 1983.

THE LOGIC OF AMERICAN GOVERNMENT: APPLYING THE CONSTITUTION TO THE CONTEMPORARY WORLD. Daniel L. Feldman. William Morrow and Company, 105 Madison Avenue, New York, New York 10016. 1990.

MODERN CONSTITUTIONAL LAW: THE INDIVIDUAL AND THE GOVERNMENT. Chester J. Antieau. Lawyers Co-Operative Publishing Company, Aqueduct Building, Rochester, New York 14694. 1969.

ON WHAT THE CONSTITUTION MEANS. Sotirios A. Barber. Johns Hopkins University Press, 701 West Fortieth Street, Baltimore, Maryland 21211-2190. 1984.

THE ORDEAL OF THE CONSTITUTION. Robert Allan Rutland. University of Oklahoma Press, 105 Asp Avenue, Norman, Oklahoma 73019. 1966.

ORIGINAL INTENT AND THE FRAMERS' CONSTITUTION. Leonard W. Levy. MacMillan Publishing Company, Incorporated, 866 Third Avenue, New York, New York 10022. 1988.

PHILOSOPHIC DIMENSIONS OF THE CONSTITUTION. Diana T. Meyers and Kenneth Kipnis. Westview Press, 5500 Central Avenue, Boulder, Colorado 80301. 1988.

PHILOSOPHY, THE FEDERALIST, AND THE CONSTITUTION. Norton White. Oxford University Press, 200 Madison Avenue, New York, New York 10016. 1989.

QUARRELS THAT HAVE SHAPED THE CONSTITUTION. Revised Edition. HarperCollins Publishers, 10 East Fifty-third Street, New York, New York 10022. 1987.

STATE CONSTITUTIONAL LAW IN A NUTSHELL. Thomas C. Marks. West Publishing Company, 50 West Kellogg Boulevard, St. Paul, Minnesota 55164. 1988.

STATE CONSTITUTIONS IN THE FEDERAL SYSTEM. Advisory Commission on Intergovernmental Relations. Superintendent of Documents, United States Government Printing Office, Washington, D.C. 20402. 1989.

SUPREME COURT POLICYMAKING AND CONSTITUTIONAL LAW. Sidney S. Ulmer. Shepard's/McGraw-Hill, P.O. Box 1235, Colorado Springs, Colorado 80901. 1985.

SUPREME COURT STATECRAFT: THE RULE OF LAW AND MEN. First Edition. Wallace Mendelson. Iowa State University Press, 2121 South State Avenue, Ames, Iowa 50010. 1985.

THE SUPREME COURT'S CONSTITUTION. Bernard H. Siegan. Transaction Books, Rutgers University, New Brunswick, New Jersey 08903. 1987.

TAKING THE CONSTITUTION SERIOUSLY: ESSAYS ON THE CONSTITUTION AND CONSTITUTIONAL LAW. Gary L. McDowell. Kendall/Hunt Publishing Company, 2460 Kerper Boulevard, Dubuque, Iowa 52001. 1981.

THE TEMPTING OF AMERICA: THE POLITICAL SEDUCTION OF THE LAW. Robert H. Bork. Free Press, 866 Third Avenue, New York, New York 10022. 1990.

TOLERATION AND THE CONSTITUTION. David A.J. Richards. Oxford University Press, 200 Madison Avenue, New York, New York 10016. 1989.

ENCYCLOPEDIAS AND DICTIONARIES

THE CONSTITUTIONAL LAW DICTIONARY. Ralph C. Chandler. ABC-Clio, Incorporated, P.O. Box 1911, Santa Barbara, California 93116-1911. 1987.

ENCYCLOPEDIA OF THE AMERICAN CONSTITUTION. Leonard W. Levy, Editor. Macmillan Publishing Company, Incorporated, 866 Third Avenue, New York, New York 10022. 1990.

THE FOUNDER'S CONSTITUTION. Philip Kurland and Ralph Lerner, Editors. University of Chicago Press, 5801 Ellis Avenue, Chicago, Illinois 60637. 1987.

ANNUALS AND SURVEYS

CONSTITUTIONAL COMMENTARIES. Center for Judicial Studies, P.O. Box 17248, Richmond, Virginia 23226. 1984- . Annual.

LAW REVIEWS AND PERIODICALS

CONSTITUTIONAL COMMENTARY. University of Minnesota Law School, 229 Nineteenth Avenue, South, Minneapolis, Minnesota 55455. Biannual.

CRISIS. National Association for the Advancement of Colored People, 4805 Mt. Hope Drive, Baltimore, Maryland 21215. Monthly.

HASTINGS CONSTITUTIONAL LAW QUARTERLY. University of California, Hastings College of Law, 200 McAllister Street, San Francisco, California 94102. Quarterly.

JOURNAL OF CHURCH AND STATE. Baylor University, Box 380, Waco, Texas 76798. Three times per year.

SUPREME COURT HISTORICAL SOCIETY YEARBOOK. Supreme Court Historical Society, 111 Second Street, Northeast, Washington, D.C. 20002. Annual.

THE SUPREME COURT REVIEW. University of Chicago Law School, 1111 East Sixtieth Street, Chicago, Illinois 60637. Annual.

NEWSLETTERS AND NEWSPAPERS

CIVIL LIBERTIES. American Civil Liberties Union, 132 West Forty-third Street, New York, New York 10036. Quarterly.

CIVIL LIBERTIES ALERT. American Civil Liberties Union, 132 West Forty-third Street, New York, New York 10036. Monthly.

THE CORPORATE CRIMINAL AND CONSTITUTIONAL LAW REPORTER. Lexline Publishing Company, 233 Broadway, Suite 944, New York, New York 10279. Semimonthly.

EQUAL JUSTICE. National Association for the Advancement of Colored People, Legal Defense and Education Fund, 99 Hudson Street, 16th Floor, New York, New York 10013. Quarterly.

FREEDOM OF EXPRESSION FOUNDATION -- NEWSLETTER. c/o Dr. Craig R. Smith, 5220 South Marina Pacifica, Long Beach, California 90803. Quarterly.

STATE CONSTITUTIONAL LAW BULLETIN. National Association of Attorneys General, 444 North Capitol Street, Northwest, Suite 403, Washington, D.C. 20001. Monthly.

BIBLIOGRAPHIES

BIBLIOGRAPHY OF ORIGINAL MEANING OF THE UNITED STATES CONSTITUTION. Office of Legal Policy, United States Department of Justice. Superintendent of Documents, United States Government Printing Office, Washington, D.C. 20402. 1988.

EDWARD S. CORWIN AND THE AMERICAN CONSTITUTION: A BIBLIOGRAPHICAL ANALYSIS. Kenneth D. Crews. Greenwood Publishing Group, Incorporated, 88 Post Road West, P.O. Box 5007, Westport, Connecticut 06881. 1985.

ASSOCIATIONS AND PROFESSIONAL SOCIETIES

AMERICAN CIVIL LIBERTIES UNION. 132 West Forty-third Street, New York, New York 10036. (212) 944-9800.

AMERICAN CIVIL LIBERTIES UNION FOUNDATION. 132 West Forty-third Street, New York, New York 10036. (212) 944-9800.

NAACP LEGAL DEFENSE AND EDUCATIONAL FUND. 99 Hudson Street, Sixteenth Floor, New York, New York 10013. (212) 219-1900.

NATIONAL ASSOCIATION FOR THE ADVANCEMENT OF COLORED PEOPLE. 4805 Mt. Hope Drive, Baltimore, Maryland 21215. (301) 358-8900.

RESEARCH CENTERS, INSTITUTES, CLEARINGHOUSES

CATO INSTITUTE. 224 Second Street, Southeast, Washington, D.C. 20003. (202) 546-0200.

CENTER FOR CONSTITUTIONAL RIGHTS. 666 Broadway, 7th Floor, New York, New York 10012. (212) 614-6464.

CENTER FOR JUDICIAL STUDIES. P.O. Box 15449, Washington, D.C. 20003. (202) 544-1776.

CENTER ON CONSTITUTIONAL STUDIES. Mercer University, 1400 Coleman Avenue, Macon, Georgia 31207. (912) 752-2774.

FREEDOM OF EXPRESSION FOUNDATION. c/o Dr. Craig R. Smith, 5220 South Marina Pacifica, Long Beach, California 90803. (213) 985-4301.

GOVERNMENT LAW CENTER. University of Louisville, Louisville, Kentucky 40292. (502) 588-6482.

INSTITUTE OF BILL OF RIGHTS LAW. College of William and Mary, Marshall-Wythe School of Law, Williamsburg, Virginia 23185. (804) 221-3810.

LAW AND ECONOMICS CENTER. George Mason University, School of Law, 3401 North Fairfax Drive, Arlington, Virginia 22201. (703) 841-7171.

MEIKLEJOHN CIVIL LIBERTIES INSTITUTE. P.O. Box 673, Berkeley, California 94701. (415) 848-0599.

NATIONAL ALLIANCE AGAINST RACIST AND POLITICAL REPRESSION. 126 West One Hundred Nineteenth Street, Suite 101, New York, New York 10026. (212) 866-8600.

NATIONAL CENTER FOR CONSTITUTIONAL STUDIES. 5288 South 320 West, Suite B-158, Salt Lake City, Utah 84107. (800) 261-1776.

ONLINE DATABASES

WESTLAW: JURISPRUDENCE AND CONSTITUTIONAL LAW. (Texts and Periodicals). West Publishing Company, P.O. Box 64526, 50 West Kellogg Boulevard, St. Paul, Minnesota 55164-0526.

AUDIOVISUALS

THE CONSTITUTION, THAT DELICATE BALANCE. Fred W. Friendly and Martha J.H. Elliot. Media and Society Seminars, New York, New York 10013. 1984. (1 Videotape).

CONSTITUTIONAL LITIGATION IN FEDERAL AND STATE COURTS. Paul M. Bator. National Practice Institute, 330 Second Avenue South, Minneapolis, Minnesota 55401. Audiotape.

PRACTICAL ASPECTS OF CONSTITUTIONAL LITIGATION. Rex E. Lee. National Practice Institute, 330 Second Avenue South, Minneapolis, Minnesota 55401. Audiotape.

THIS HONORABLE COURT. Greater Washington Educational Telecommunications Association, Washington, D.C. 20036. 1988. (2 Videotapes).

COMPUTER-ASSISTED LEGAL INSTRUCTION

SEARCH AND SEIZURE. Center for Computer-Assisted Instruction, 229 19th Avenue South, University of Minnesota, Minneapolis, Minnesota 55455. Interactive videodisc.

OTHER SOURCES

BLESSINGS OF LIBERTY: THE CONSTITUTION AND THE PRACTICE OF LAW. American Law Institute-American Bar Association, 4025 Chestnut Street, Philadelphia, Pennsylvania 19104. 1988.

CONSTITUTIONS
See also: CONSTITUTIONAL HISTORY; CONSTITUTIONAL LAW

LOOSELEAF SERVICES AND REPORTERS

CONSTITUTIONS OF AMERICAN DENOMINATIONS. Robert L. Schenck. William S. Hein and Company, Incorporated, 1285 Main Street, Buffalo, New York 14209. 1984- . (Periodic Supplements).

CONSTITUTIONS OF CANADA. Oceana Publications, Incorporated, 75 Main Street, Dobbs Ferry, New York 10522. 1979- . (Periodic Supplements).

CONSTITUTIONS OF DEPENDENCIES AND SPECIAL SOVEREIGNTIES. Albert P. Blaustein and Eric B. Blaustein. Oceana Publications, Incorporated, 75 Main Street, Dobbs Ferry, New York 10522. 1975- . (Periodic Supplements).

CONSTITUTIONS OF THE COUNTRIES OF THE WORLD. Albert P. Blaustein and Gisbert H. Flanz. Oceana Publications, Incorporated, 75 Main Street, Dobbs Ferry, New York 10522. 1971- . (Quarterly Supplements).

CONSTITUTIONS OF THE UNITED STATES, NATIONAL AND STATE. Second Edition. Columbia University Legislative Drafting Research Fund. Oceana Publications, Incorporated, 75 Main Street, Dobbs Ferry, New York 10522. 1974- . (Periodic Supplements).

FRENCH LAW - CONSTITUTION AND SELECTIVE LEGISLATION. Parker School of Comparative Law. Matthew Bender and Company, Incorporated, 11 Penn Plaza, New York, New York 10001. 1981- .

TEXTBOOKS AND GENERAL WORKS

CONSTITUTIONS AND CONSTITUTIONAL TRENDS SINCE WORLD WAR II: AN EXAMINATION OF SIGNIFICANT ASPECTS OF POSTWAR PUBLIC LAW WITH PARTICULAR REFERENCE TO THE NEW CONSTITUTIONS OF WESTERN EUROPE. Arnold J. Zurcher. Greenwood Publishing Group, Incorporated, 88 Post Road, West, P.O. Box 5007, Westport, Connecticut 06881. 1975, c1955.

CONSTITUTIONS THAT MADE HISTORY. Albert P. Blaustein and Jay A. Sigler. Paragon House Publishers, 90 Fifth Avenue, New York, New York 10011. 1988.

GOVERNMENTAL INSTITUTIONS AND PROCESSES. Fred I. Greenstein and Nelson W. Polsby. Addison-Wesley, Publishing Company, Incorporated, Route 128, Reading, Massachusetts 01867. 1975.

MODERN CONSTITUTIONS. Second Edition. K. C. Wheare. Oxford University Press, Incorporated, 200 Madison Avenue, New York, New York 10019. 1966.

STATE CONSTITUTIONAL CONVENTIONS: THE POLITICS OF THE REVISION PROCESS IN SEVEN STATES. Elmer E. Cornwell, Jr., Jay S. Goodman and Wayne R. Swanson. Praeger Publishers, One Madison Avenue, New York, New York 10010. 1975.

CONSTITUTIONS   *Encyclopedia of Legal Information Sources • 2nd Ed.*

STATE CONSTITUTIONS IN A FEDERAL SYSTEM. John Kincaid, Editor. Sage Publications, P.O. Box 6944, San Mateo, California 94403. 1988.

BIBLIOGRAPHIES

THE CONSTITUTIONS OF THE STATES: A STATE BY STATE GUIDE AND BIBLIOGRAPHY TO CURRENT SCHOLARLY RESEARCH. Bernard D. Reams, Jr. and Stuart D. Yoak, Editors. Oceana Publications, Incorporated, 75 Main Street, Dobbs Ferry, New York 10522. 1988.

SOURCES AND DOCUMENTS OF UNITED STATES CONSTITUTIONS. Second Series. William F. Swindler, Editor and Annotator. Oceana Publications, Incorporated, 75 Main Street, Dobbs Ferry, New York 10522. 1982- .

STATE CONSTITUTIONAL CONVENTION FROM INDEPENDENCE TO THE COMPLETION OF THE PRESENT UNION, 1776-1959: A BIBLIOGRAPHY. Cynthia E. Browne. Greenwood Publishing Group, Incorporated, 88 Post Road, West, P.O. Box 5007, Westport, Connecticut 06881. 1973.

STATE CONSTITUTIONAL CONVENTIONS, 1979-1988: AN ANNOTATED BIBLIOGRAPHY. Congressional Information System, 4520 East-West Highway, Bethesda, Maryland 20814. 1988.

STATE CONSTITUTIONAL CONVENTIONS, 1959-1975: A BIBLIOGRAPHY. Susan Rice Yarger. Greenwood Publishing Group, Incorporated, 88 Post Road, West, P.O. Box 5007, Westport, Connecticut 06881. 1976.

STATE CONSTITUTIONAL CONVENTIONS, REVISIONS AND AMENDMENTS, 1959-1976: A BIBLIOGRAPHY. Bonnie Canning. Greenwood Publishing Group, Incorporated, 88 Post Road, West, P.O. Box 5007, Westport, Connecticut 06881. 1977.

NEWSLETTERS AND NEWSPAPERS

ACROSS FRONTIERS. World Constitution and Parliament Association, 1480 Hoyt Street, Suite 31, Lakewood, Colorado 80215. Bimonthly.

ASSOCIATIONS AND PROFESSIONAL SOCIETIES

WORLD CONSTITUTION AND PARLIAMENT ASSOCIATION. 1480 Hoyt Street, Suite 31, Lakewood, Colorado 80215. (303) 233-3548.

OTHER SOURCES

STATE CONSTITUTIONS IN THE FEDERAL SYSTEM: SELECTED ISSUES AND OPPORTUNITIES FOR STATE INITIATIVES. Advisory Commission on Intergovernmental Relations. Superintendent of Documents, United States Government Printing Office, Washington, D.C. 20402. 1989.

CONSTRUCTION INDUSTRY
See also: LABOR DEPARTMENT; OCCUPATIONAL SAFETY AND HEALTH

STATUTES, CODES, STANDARDS, UNIFORM LAWS

CONSTRUCTION SAFETY STANDARDS. Interior Department, Bureau of Reclamation, Division of Safety, Engineering and Research Center. Superintendent of Documents, United States Government Printing Office, Division of Public Documents, Washington, D.C. 20402. 1982.

DIRECTORY OF STATE BUILDING CODES AND REGULATIONS. National Conference of States on Building Codes and Standards, 481 Carlisle Drive, Herndon, Virginia 22070. 1987.

UNIFORM BUILDING CODES. International Conference of Building Officials, 5360 South Workman Mill Road, Whittier, California 90601. 1988- .

LOOSELEAF SERVICES AND REPORTERS

AIA BUILDING CONSTRUCTION LEGAL CITATOR. Spencer, Whalen and Graham. American Institute of Architects, 1735 New York Avenue, Northwest, Washington, D.C. 10108. 1982- . (Biennial Supplements).

ATTORNEY'S GUIDE TO ENGINEERING. Ira Kuperstein and Neil Salters. Matthew Bender and Company, Incorporated, 11 Penn Plaza, New York, New York 10001. 1986- . (Periodic Supplements).

CONSTRUCTION AND DESIGN LAW. National Institute of Construction Law, Incorporated. Michie/Bobbs-Merrill Law Publishing, P.O. Box 7587, Charlottesville, Virginia 22906-7582. 1984- . (Periodic Supplements).

CONSTRUCTION DELAY CLAIMS. Barry B. Bramble and Michael T. Callahan. John Wiley and Sons, Incorporated, 605 Third Avenue, New York, New York 10158. 1987.

CONSTRUCTION INDUSTRY STANDARDS AND INTERPRETATIONS. United States Department of Labor, Occupational Safety and Health Administration. Superintendent of Documents, United States Government Printing Office, Division of Public Documents, Washington, D.C. 20402. 1980- . (Periodic Supplements).

CONSTRUCTION LABOR REPORT. Bureau of National Affairs, Incorporated, 1231 Twenty-fifth Street, Northwest, Washington, D.C. 20037. 1955- . (Weekly Supplements).

CONSTRUCTION LAW. Steven G.M. Stein, Editor. Matthew Bender and Company, Incorporated, 11 Penn Plaza, New York, New York 10001. 1986- . (Periodic Supplements).

CONSTRUCTION RISK MANAGEMENT. Jeffrey Woodward and others. International Risk Management Institute, 12222 Merit Drive, Dallas, Texas 75251. 1984- . (Quarterly Supplements).

FINANCING TRANSNATIONAL PROJECTS. Ronald F. Sullivan. Matthew Bender and Company, Incorporated, 11 Penn Plaza, New York, New York 10001. 1988- . (Periodic Supplements).

HANDBOOKS, MANUALS, FORMBOOKS

AVOIDING AND RESOLVING CONSTRUCTION CLAIMS. Barry B. Bramble, Michael F. D'Onofrio, and John B. Stetson. R.S. Means Company, Incorporated, 100 Construction Plaza, Kingston, Massachusetts 02364. 1990.

CONSTRUCTION ACCIDENT: PLEADING AND PRACTICE. Turner W. Branch, Editor. John Wiley and Sons, Incorporated, 605 Third Avenue, New York, New York 10158. 1988.

CONSTRUCTION AND DEVELOPMENT FINANCING: LAW PRACTICE FORMS. Richard Harris. Research Institute of America, Incorporated, One Penn Plaza, New York, New York 10119. 1982.

CONSTRUCTION ARBITRATION HANDBOOK. James Acret. Shepard's/McGraw-Hill, P.O. Box 1235, Colorado Springs, Colorado 80901. 1985- . (Periodic Supplements).

CONSTRUCTION DEFAULTS: RIGHTS, DUTIES, AND LIABILITIES. Robert F. Cushman and Charles A. Meeker, Editors. John Wiley and Sons, Incorporated, 605 Third Avenue, New York, New York 10158. 1989.

CONSTRUCTION INDUSTRY CONTRACTS: LEGAL CITATOR AND CASE DIGEST. John Wiley and Sons, Incorporated, 605 Third Avenue, New York, New York 10158. 1988.

CONSTRUCTION INDUSTRY FORMBOOK: A PRACTICAL GUIDE TO REVIEWING AND DRAFTING FORMS FOR THE CONSTRUCTION INDUSTRY. Second Edition. James Acret. Shepard's/McGraw-Hill, P.O. Box 1235, Colorado Springs, Colorado 80901. 1990- . (Periodic Supplements).

CONSTRUCTION INDUSTRY FORMS. Robert F. Cushman and George L. Blick, Editors. John Wiley and Sons, Incorporated, 605 Third Avenue, New York, New York 10158. 1988.

CONSTRUCTION LAW: PRINCIPLES AND PRACTICE. Bruce M. Jervis and Paul Levin. McGraw-Hill Publishing Company, 1221 Avenue of the Americas, New York, New York 10020. 1988.

CONSTRUCTION LITIGATION HANDBOOK. James Acret. Shepard's/McGraw-Hill, P.O. Box 1235, Colorado Springs, Colorado 80901. 1986- . (Annual Supplements).

CONSTRUCTION LITIGATION: TRIAL STRATEGIES AND TECHNIQUES. Barry B. Bramble and Albert E. Phillips, Editors. John Wiley and Sons, Incorporated, 605 Third Avenue, New York, New York 10158. 1989.

CONTRACTOR'S PROJECT GUIDE TO PUBLIC AGENCY CONTRACTS. Edward R. Fisk and James R. Negele. John Wiley and Sons, Incorporated, 605 Third Avenue, New York, New York 10158. 1988.

DESKBOOK OF CONSTRUCTION CONTRACT LAW WITH FORMS. Murray H. Hohns. Prentice-Hall, Incorporated, 113 Sylvan Avenue, Englewood Cliffs, New Jersey 07632. 1981.

FORMS AND AGREEMENTS FOR ARCHITECTS, ENGINEERS AND CONTRACTORS. Albert Dib. Clark Boardman Company, Limited, 435 Hudson Street, New York, New York 10014. 1983- . (Annual Supplements).

HANDBOOK OF CONSTRUCTION LAW. Irv Richter and Roy Mitchell. Reston Publishing Company, Incorporated, 113 Sylvan Avenue, Englewood Cliffs, New Jersey 07632. 1982.

HANDBOOK OF CONSTRUCTION LAW, SECOND: WITH FORMS. Stuart J. Faber. Lega Books, 3255 Wilshire Boulevard, Suite 1514, Los Angeles, California 90010. 1984.

HANDBOOK OF MODERN CONSTRUCTION LAW. Jeremiah D. Lambert and Lawrence White. Prentice-Hall, Incorporated, P.O. Box 500, Englewood Cliffs, New Jersey 07632. 1982.

HAZARDOUS MATERIAL AND HAZARDOUS WASTE: A CONSTRUCTION REFERENCE MANUAL. Francis J. Hopcroft, David L. Vitale and Donald L. Anglehart. R.S. Means Company, Incorporated, 100 Construction Plaza, Kingston, Massachusetts 02364. 1989.

LEGAL HANDBOOK FOR ARCHITECTS, ENGINEERS AND CONTRACTORS. Albert Dib and James K. Grant, Editors. Clark Boardman Company, Limited, 435 Hudson Street, New York, New York 10014. 1986.

THE McGRAW-HILL CONSTRUCTION BUSINESS HANDBOOK: A PRACTICAL GUIDE TO ACCOUNTING, CREDIT, FINANCE, INSURANCE, AND LAW FOR THE CONSTRUCTION INDUSTRY. Second Edition. Robert F. Cushman and John P. Bigada. Shepard's/McGraw-Hill, P.O. Box 1235, Colorado Springs, Colorado 80901. 1985.

UNCITRAL: LEGAL GUIDE ON DRAWING UP INTERNATIONAL CONTRACTS FOR THE CONSTRUCTION OF INDUSTRIAL WORKS. United Nations Commission on International Trade Law. United Nations, 2 United Nations Plaza, New York, New York 10017. 1988.

TEXTBOOKS AND GENERAL WORKS

THE ARCHITECT/ENGINEER'S CHANGING ROLE IN THE CONSTRUCTION INDUSTRY: THE 1980'S AND BEYOND. American Bar Association, 750 North Lake Shore Drive, Chicago, Illinois 60611. 1984.

ARCHITECTS AND ENGINEERS. Second Edition. James Acret, Shepard's/McGraw-Hill, P.O. Box 1235, Colorado Springs, Colorado 80901. 1984- . (Periodic Supplements).

CONSTRUCTION BID RIGGING: COURSE MANUAL. Federal Publications, Incorporated and Judah Lifschitz. Federal Publications, Incorporated, 1120 Twentieth Street, Northwest, Washington, D.C. 20036. 1984.

CONSTRUCTION CLAIMS: A QUANTITATIVE APPROACH. James J. Adrian. Prentice-Hall, Incorporated, Route 9W, Englewood Cliffs, New Jersey 07632. 1988.

CONSTRUCTION CLAIMS WORKSHOP. Practising Law Institute Staff and Luther P. Cochrane. Practising Law Institute, 810 Seventh Avenue, New York, New York 10019. 1983.

CONSTRUCTION CONTRACT LITIGATION: COURSE MANUAL. Luther House and George A. Smith. Federal Publications, Incorporated, 1120 Twentieth Street, Northwest, Washington, D.C. 20036. Annual.

CONSTRUCTION CONTRACTS AND CLAIMS. Michael S. Simon. Shepard's/McGraw-Hill, P.O. Box 1235, Colorado Springs, Colorado 80901. 1979.

CONSTRUCTION INDUSTRY. James Acret. Shepard's/McGraw-Hill, P.O. Box 1235, Colorado Springs, Colorado 80901. 1985.

CONSTRUCTION LABOR RELATIONS. Arthur B. Smith. Commerce Clearing House, Incorporated, 4025 West Peterson Avenue, Chicago, Illinois 60646. 1984.

CONSTRUCTION LITIGATION: REPRESENTING THE OWNER. Robert F. Cushman and Kenneth M. Cushman, Editors. John Wiley and Sons, Incorporated, 605 Third Avenue, New York, New York 10158. 1984.

CONSTRUCTION SCHEDULES: ANALYSIS, EVALUATION, AND INTERPRETATION OF SCHEDULES IN LITIGATION. Michael T. Callaghan. Michie/Bobbs-Merrill Law Publishing, P.O. Box 7587, Charlottesville, Virginia 22906-7582. 1983.

DISCOVERY IN CONSTRUCTION LITIGATION. Second Edition. Michael T. Callahan, Barry B. Bramble and Frank M. Rapoport. Michie/Bobbs-Merrill Law Publishing, P.O. Box 7587, Charlottesville, Virginia 22906-7582. 1987- . (Periodic Supplements).

ENGINEERING EVIDENCE. Max Schwartz and Neil Forrest Schwartz. Shepard's/McGraw-Hill, P.O. Box 1235, Colorado Springs, Colorado 80901. 1987- . (Annual Supplements).

INTRODUCTION TO CONSTRUCTION LAW. Steven M. Siegfried. American Law Institute-American Bar Association, 4025 Chestnut Street, Philadelphia, Pennsylvania 19104. 1987.

INTRODUCTION TO CONSTRUCTION LAW: SUPPLEMENT. Steven M. Siegfried. American Law Institute-American Bar Association, 4025 Chestnut Street, Philadelphia, Pennsylvania 19104. 1989.

MAXIMIZING TAX BENEFITS IN BUSINESS CONSTRUCTION. Donald E. Swanton. John Wiley and Sons, Incorporated, 605 Third Avenue, New York, New York 10158. 1986.

NEW CONCEPTS IN CONSTRUCTION LAW FOR THE 80'S. American Bar Association, 750 North Lake Shore Drive, Chicago, Illinois 60611. 1981.

PROSECUTING CONSTRUCTION CLAIMS AGAINST PUBLIC OWNERS. American Bar Association, 750 North Lake Shore Drive, Chicago, Illinois 60611. 1982.

STATE AND MUNICIPAL CONSTRUCTION LAW. American Bar Association, 750 North Lake Shore Drive, Chicago, Illinois 60611. 1976.

TRANSNATIONAL CORPORATIONS IN THE CONSTRUCTION AND DESIGN ENGINEERING INDUSTRY. United Nations, 2 United Nations Plaza, New York, New York 10017. 1989.

UNDERSTANDING CONSTRUCTION LAW. Alonzo Wass. Reston Publishing Company, Incorporated, 113 Sylvan Avenue, Englewood Cliffs, New Jersey 07632. 1982.

DIGESTS, INDEXES, ABSTRACTS, CITATORS

AMERICAN INSTITUTE OF ARCHITECTS BUILDING CONSTRUCTION LEGAL CITATOR. American Institute of Architects, 1735 New York Avenue, Northwest, Washington, D.C. 20006. 1982- . (Biennial Supplements).

CONSTRUCTION AND DESIGN LAW DIGEST. National Institute of Construction Law, Incorporated. Michie/Bobbs-Merrill Law Publishing, P.O. Box 7587, Charlottesville, Virginia 22906-7582. (Eleven issues per year).

THE CONSTRUCTION CLAIMS CITATOR. Construction Industry Press, 1105-F Spring Street, Silver Spring, Maryland 20910. 1982- . (Six issues per year).

CONSTRUCTION INDUSTRY OSHA SAFETY AND HEALTH STANDARDS DIGEST. United States Government Printing Office, Division of Public Documents, Washington, D.C. 20402. 1983.

CONSTRUCTION LAW DIGESTS. James Acret. Shepard's/McGraw-Hill, P.O. Box 1235, Colorado Springs, Colorado 80901. 1990- . (Quarterly Supplements).

ANNUALS AND SURVEYS

CONSTRUCTION CONTRACTS. Practising Law Institute, 810 Seventh Avenue, New York, New York 10019. 1984- . Annual.

ENGINEERING NEWS-RECORD -- TOP 400 CONSTRUCTION CONTRACTORS ISSUE. Shepard's/McGraw-Hill, P.O. Box 1235, Colorado Springs, Colorado 80901. Annual.

NEWSLETTERS AND NEWSPAPERS

BOCA BULLETIN. Building Officials and Code Administrators International, 4051 West Flossmoor Road, Country Club Hills, Illinois 60478. Bimonthly.

CAPITAL COMMENTS. National Lumber and Building Materials Dealers Association, 40 IVy Street, Southeast, Washington, D.C. 20003. Monthly.

CONSTRUCTION AND DESIGN LAW DIGEST. The Michie Company, P.O. Box 7587, Charlottesville, Virginia 22906. Monthly.

CONSTRUCTION BRIEFINGS. Federal Publications, Incorporated, 1120 Twentieth Street, Northwest, Washington, D.C. 20036. Monthly.

CONSTRUCTION CLAIMS CITATOR. Construction Industry Press, P.O. Box 9838, San Rafael, California 94912. Monthly.

CONSTRUCTION CLAIMS MONTHLY. Business Publishers, Incorporated, 951 Pershing Drive, Silver Spring, Maryland 20910. Monthly.

THE CONSTRUCTION CONTRACTOR. Federal Publications, Incorporated, 1120 Twentieth Street, Northwest, Washington, D.C. 20036. Biweekly.

CONSTRUCTION INDUSTRY LIABILITY MONTHLY. Business Publishers Incorporated, 951 Pershing Drive, Silver Spring, Maryland 20910. Monthly.

CONSTRUCTION LABOR REPORT. The Bureau of National Affairs, 1231 Twenty-fifth Street, Northwest, Washington, D.C. 20037. Weekly.

CONSTRUCTION LAW ADVISOR. Callaghan and Company, 155 Pfingsten Road, Deerfield, Illinois 60015. Monthly.

THE CONSTRUCTION LAWYER. American Bar Association, Forum Committee on the Construction Industry, 750 North Lake Shore Drive, Chicago, Illinois 60611. Quarterly.

CONSTRUCTION LITIGATION LAW BULLETIN. Quinlan Publishing Company, Incorporated, 23 Drydock Avenue, Boston, Massachusetts 02110. Monthly.

CONSTRUCTION LITIGATION REPORTER. Shepard's/McGraw-Hill, Incorporated, 420 North Cascade Avenue, Colorado Springs, Colorado 80903. Monthly.

LEGAL BRIEFS FOR THE CONSTRUCTION INDUSTRY. McGraw-Hill, Incorporated, 11 West Nineteenth Street, New York, New York 10016. Semimonthly.

NATION'S BUILDING NEWS. NAHB, P.O. Box 1627, Rockville, Maryland 20850. Semimonthly.

NCSBCS NEWS. National Conference of States on Building Codes and Standards, Incorporated, 505 Huntmar Park Drive, Herndon, Virginia 22070. Bimonthly.

THE PUNCH LIST. American Arbitration Association, 140 West Fifty-first Street, New York, New York 10020. Quarterly.

SUBCONTRACTOR NEWSPAPER. American Subcontractors Association, 1004 Duke Street, Alexandria, Virginia 22314. Monthly.

DIRECTORIES

ASSOCIATED BUILDERS AND CONTRACTORS -- MEMBERSHIP DIRECTORY AND ASSOCIATION GUIDE. Associated Builders and Contractors, 729 Fifteenth Street, Northwest, Washington, D.C. 20005. Annual.

ASSOCIATED GENERAL CONTRACTORS OF AMERICA -- NATIONAL DIRECTORY. Associated General Contractors of America, 1957 E Street, Northwest, Washington, D.C. 20006. Annual.

BUILDING AND CONSTRUCTION TRADES DEPARTMENT, AMERICAN FEDERATION OF LABOR-CONGRESS OF INDUSTRIAL ORGANIZATIONS -- OFFICIAL DIRECTORY. American Federation of Labor-Congress of Industrial Organizations, 815 Sixteenth Street, Northwest, Washington, D.C. 20006. Semiannual.

DIRECTORY OF CONSTRUCTION ASSOCIATIONS. Metadata, Incorporated, 310 East Forty-fourth Street, New York, New York 10017. Biennial.

DIRECTORY OF CONSTRUCTION INDUSTRY CONSULTANTS. Robert F. Cushman and George L. Blick, Editors. John Wiley and Sons, Incorporated, 605 Third Avenue, New York, New York 10158. 1989.

DIRECTORY OF EXPERTS AND CONSULTANTS IN SCIENCE AND ENGINEERING. Research Publications, 12 Lunar Drive, Drawer AB, Wood Bridge, Connecticut 06525. 1987- .

INTERNATIONAL CONFERENCE OF BUILDING OFFICIALS -- MEMBERSHIP ROSTER. International Conference of Building Officials, 5360 South Workman Mill Road, Whittier, California 90601. 1981- . Annual.

ASSOCIATIONS AND PROFESSIONAL SOCIETIES

AMERICAN SUBCONTRACTORS ASSOCIATION. 1004 Duke Street, Alexandria, Virginia 22314. (703) 684-3450.

ASSOCIATED BUILDERS AND CONTRACTORS. 729 Fifteenth Street, Northwest, Washington, D.C. 20005. (202) 637-8800.

ASSOCIATED GENERAL CONTRACTORS OF AMERICA. 1957 E Street, Northwest, Washington, D.C. 20006. (202) 393-2040.

CONSTRUCTION MANAGEMENT ASSOCIATION OF AMERICA. 12355 Sunrise Valley Drive, Suite 640, Reston, Virginia 22091. (703) 391-1200.

FEDERAL CONSTRUCTION COUNCIL. c/o National Academy of Sciences, 2101 Constitution Avenue, Northwest, Washington, D.C. 20418. (202) 334-3378.

FORUM COMMITTEE ON THE CONSTRUCTION INDUSTRY. American Bar Association, 750 North Lake Shore Drive, Chicago, Illinois 60611. (312) 988-5158.

NATIONAL ASSOCIATION OF HOME BUILDERS OF THE UNITED STATES. Fifteenth and M Streets, Northwest, Washington, D.C. 20005. (202) 822-0200.

NATIONAL ASSOCIATION OF MINORITY CONTRACTORS. 806 Fifteenth Street, Northwest, Suite 340, Washington, D.C. 20005. (202) 347-8259.

PROFESSIONAL WOMEN IN CONSTRUCTION. 342 Madison Avenue, Suite 453, New York, New York 10173. (212) 687-0610.

RESEARCH CENTERS, INSTITUTES, CLEARINGHOUSES

CONSTRUCTION INDUSTRY INSTITUTE. 3208 Red River Road, Suite 300, University of Texas at Austin, Austin, Texas 78705. (512) 471-4319.

CONSTRUCTION INSTITUTE. University of Hartford, 312 Bloomfield Avenue, West Hartford, Connecticut 06117. (203) 243-4445.

CONSTRUCTION RESEARCH CENTER. Georgia Institute of Technology, College of Architecture, Atlanta, Georgia 30332. (404) 894-2070.

ENGINEERING RESEARCH CENTER. University of Colorado -- Boulder, Campus Box 423, Boulder, Colorado 80309. (303) 492-7427.

FLORIDA ARCHITECTURE AND BUILDING RESEARCH COUNCIL. University of Florida, 360 Architecture Building, Gainesville, Florida 32611. (904) 392-0221.

CONSTRUCTION INDUSTRY

JOINT CENTER FOR HOUSING STUDIES OF HARVARD UNIVERSITY. 53 Church Street, Cambridge, Massachusetts 02138. (617) 495-7908.

MIT-REMERGENCE LABORATORY. Massachusetts Institute of Technology, Department of Civil Engineering, E15-109, 20 Ames Street, Cambridge, Massachusetts 02139. (617) 253-3598.

NAHB NATIONAL RESEARCH CENTER. 400 Prince George's Boulevard, Upper Marlboro, Maryland 20772. (301) 249-4000.

NATIONAL INSTITUTE OF BUILDING SCIENCES (NIBS). 1201 L Street, Northwest, Suite 400, Washington, D.C. 20005. (202) 289-7800.

RESEARCH AND DEVELOPMENT LABORATORY. National Concrete Masonry Association, 2302 Horse Pen Road, P.O. Box 781, Herndon, Virginia 22070. (703) 435-4900.

ONLINE DATABASES

CONSTRUCTION COST INDEXES. The Robnor Group, Limited, P.O. Box 112, Coudersport, Pennsylvania 16915.

CONSTRUCTION CRITERIA BASE. National Institute of Building Sciences, 1201 L Street, Northwest, Room 400, Washington, D.C. 20005.

CONSTRUCTION LABOR REPORT. The Bureau of National Affairs, Incorporated, BNA ONLINE, 1231 Twenty-fifth Street, Northwest, Washington, D.C. 20037.

CONTRACTOR PROFIT NEWS. Construction Industry Press, P.O. Box 9838, San Rafael, California 94912.

COUNTY BUILDING PERMITS. The WEFA Group, 150 Monument Road, Bala Cynwyd, Pennsylvania 19004.

DODGE CONSTRUCTION ANALYSIS SYSTEM. McGraw-Hill, Incorporated, Construction Information Services Group, F.W. Dodge Division, 1221 Avenue of the Americas, New York, New York 10020.

DODGE DATALINE. McGraw-Hill, Incorporated, Construction Information Services Group, F.W. Dodge Division, 1221 Avenue of the Americas, New York, New York 10020.

DODGE/DRI DATALINE. McGraw-Hill, Incorporated, Construction Information Services Group, F.W. Dodge Division, 1221 Avenue of the Americas, New York, New York 10020.

MSA AND STATE HOUSING AND CONSTRUCTION. The WEFA Group, 150 Monument Road, Bala Cynwyd, Pennsylvania 19004.

MSA BUILDING PERMITS. The WEFA Group, 150 Monument Road, Bala Cynwyd, Pennsylvania 19004.

PUBLICATIONS OF THE INSTITUTE FOR RESEARCH IN CONSTRUCTION. National Research Council of Canada, Institute for Research in Construction, Building M-20, Ottawa, ON, Canada K1A 0R6.

TRADE AND INDUSTRY INDEX. Information Access Company, 362 Lakeside Drive, Foster City, California 94404.

STATISTICS SOURCES

CENSUS OF CONSTRUCTION. Superintendent of Documents, United States Government Printing Office, Division of Public Documents, Washington, D.C. 20402. 1985. (Every 18 months).

CONSTRUCTION REPORTS. United States Department of Commerce, Subscriber Services Section, Bureau of the Census, Washington, D.C. 20233. 1970. (Monthly).

NATIONAL CENTER FOR CONSTRUCTION STATISTICS. Indiana University, Indiana Business Research Center, Room 426, School of Business, Bloomington, Indiana 47405. (812) 855-5507.

OCCUPATIONAL INJURIES AND ILLNESSES IN THE UNITED STATES BY INDUSTRY. United States Department of Labor, Bureau of Labor Statistics, Washington, D.C. 20212. Annual.

UNION WAGES AND BENEFITS. United States Department of Labor, Bureau of Labor Statistics, Superintendent of Documents, United States Government Printing Office, Washington, D.C. 20402. Annual.

UNITED STATES CENSUS OF CONSTRUCTION INDUSTRIES: (Year). United States Department of Commerce, Bureau of the Census, Washington, D.C. 20233. Annual.

YEARBOOK OF CONSTRUCTION STATISTICS. United Nations, Sales Section, Publishing Division, Room DC2-853, New York, New York 10017. Annual.

OTHER SOURCES

BANKRUPTCY -- CRISIS IN THE CONSTRUCTION INDUSTRY. Forum Committee on the Construction Industry. American Bar Association, 750 North Lake Shore Drive, Chicago, Illinois 60611. 1983.

EMERGING TRENDS IN CONSTRUCTION LAW. American Bar Association Forum Committee on the Construction Industry. American Bar Association, 750 North Lake Shore Drive, Chicago, Illinois 60611. 1984.

ISSUES IN CONSTRUCTION LAW: NEW PERSPECTIVES ON LIABILITY AND CONTRACTS. Real Property, Probate and Trust Law Section, American Bar Association, 750 North Lake Shore Drive, Chicago, Illinois 60611. 1988.

OPEN SHOP CONSTRUCTION REVISITED. Herbert R. Northrup. Industrial Research Unit, Wharton School, University of Pennsylvania, 418 Service Drive, Blockly Hall, 13th Floor, Philadelphia, Pennsylvania 19104-6097. 1984.

AN OUTLINE OF THE LAW AND PRACTICE OF ARBITRATION UNDER THE CONSTRUCTION INDUSTRY ARBITRATION RULES OF THE AMERICAN ARBITRATION ASSOCIATION. American Arbitration Association, 140 West Fifty-first Street, New York, New York 10020. 1982.

CONSUMER CREDIT
See also: LOANS

STATUTES, CODES, STANDARDS, UNIFORM LAWS

COMPENDIUM OF COMMERCIAL FINANCE LAW. National Commercial Finance Association, 225 West 34th Street, New York, New York 10001.

EQUAL CREDIT OPPORTUNITY ACT. Second Edition. Gerry Azzata. National Consumer Law Center, 11 Beacon Street, Boston, Massachusetts 02108. 1988.

FAIR CREDIT REPORTING ACT. National Consumer Law Center, Incorporated, 11 Beacon Street, Boston, Massachusetts 02108. 1988.

FEDERAL CONSUMER CREDIT LAWS AND REGULATIONS. NILS Publishing Company, 21625 Prairie Street, Chatsworth, California 91311. 1987- . Annual supplements.

LOOSELEAF SERVICES AND REPORTERS

ADMINISTRATIVE INTERPRETATIONS OF THE UNIFORM CONSUMER CREDIT CODE. Frederick H. Miller, compiler. Butterworth Legal Publishers, 90 Stiles Road, Salem, New Hampshire 03079. 1989- .

COMPLIANCE EXAMINATION UPDATE FOR FINANCIAL INSTITUTIONS. Drew V. Tidwell and John H. Mancuso. Research Institute of America, One Penn Plaza, New York, New York 10119. 1988- . Semimonthly supplements.

CONSUMER AND BORROWER PROTECTION: AM JUR PRACTICE GUIDE. Lawyers Cooperative Publishing Company, Aqueduct Building, Rochester, New York 14694. 1991.

CONSUMER AND COMMERCIAL CREDIT -- INSTALLMENT SALES. Research Institute of America, Incorporated, 910 Sylvan Avenue, Englewood Cliffs, New Jersey 07632. 1932- . Biweekly Supplements.

CONSUMER CREDIT. Kenneth M. Lapine. Matthew Bender and Company, Incorporated, 11 Penn Plaza, New York, New York 10001. 1984- . Annual Supplements.

CONSUMER CREDIT AND THE LAW. Dee Pridgen. Clark Boardman Company, Limited, 435 Hudson Street, New York, New York 10014 1990- . Annual Supplements.

CONSUMER CREDIT GUIDE. Commerce Clearing House, Incorporated, 4025 West Peterson Avenue, Chicago, Illinois 60646. 1969- . Biweekly Supplements.

CONSUMER CREDIT REGULATIONS. Second edition. Dan Nicewander and others. PESI Legal Publishing, 200 Spring Street, Eau Claire, Wisconsin 54702. 1989- . Annual supplements.

COST OF PERSONAL BORROWING IN THE UNITED STATES. Financial Publishing Company, 82 Brookline Avenue, Boston Massachusetts 02215. 1971- . Monthly supplements.

FAIR HOUSING--FAIR LENDING. Prentice-Hall Law and Business, Route 9W, Englewood Cliffs, New Jersey 07632. 1985- . Monthly supplements.

REGULATION Z: TRUTH IN LENDING COMPREHENSIVE COMPLIANCE MANUAL. Robert P. Chamness. American Banker's Association, 1120 Connecticut Avenue, Northwest, Washington, D.C. 20036. 1989. Periodic supplements.

TRUTH IN LENDING: A COMPREHENSIVE MANUAL. Second edition. Roland E. Brandel and others. Prentice-Hall Law and Business, Route 9W, Englewood Cliffs, New Jersey 07632. 1991- . Periodic Supplements.

TRUTH IN LENDING FOR THE COMMUNITY BANK: A PRACTICAL APPROACH TO REGULATION Z. T. Herbert Stevenson. Bank Administration Institute, 60 Gould Center, Rolling Meadows, Illinois 60008. 1989- . Periodic supplements.

HANDBOOKS, MANUALS, FORMBOOKS

BILLPAYERS' RIGHTS. Eighth Edition. Ralph Warner and Stephen Elias. Nolo Press, 950 Parker Street, Berkeley, California 94710. 1988.

COMPLIANCE HANDBOOK FOR CONSUMER CREDIT. Ninth edition. Milton W. Schober, editor. Business Publishers, Incorporated, 951 Pershing Drive, Silver Spring, Maryland 20910. 1984.

COMPLYING WITH THE CREDIT PRACTICES RULE. Federal Trade Commission, Superintendent of Documents, U.S. Government Printing Office, Washington, D.C.20402. 1987.

CONSUMER CREDIT COMPLIANCE MANUAL. Second edition. John R. Fonseca. Lawyers Cooperative Publishing Company, Aqueduct Building, Rochester, New York 14694. 1984.

CONSUMER CREDIT 1985. Richard Fischer. Practising Law Institute, 810 Seventh Avenue, New York, New York 10019. 1985.

EQUAL CREDIT OPPORTUNITY MANUAL: SPECIAL REPORT: FEDERAL REGULATIONS OF DEBT COLLECTION PRACTICES. Fourth Edition. Ralph C. Clontz. Research Institute of America, Incorporated, One Penn Plaza, New York, New York 10119. 1988.

FAIR CREDIT REPORTING ACT. Second edition. Willard Ogburn. National Consumer Law Center, 11 Beacon Street, Boston, Massachusetts 02108. 1988.

FEDERAL REGULATION OF CONSUMER CREDIT. Frank M. Salinger and Robert W. Green. Executive Enterprises Publications Company, 22 West Twenty-first Street, New York, New York 10010-6904. 1989.

A GUIDE TO STATE CONSUMER REGULATIONS. Frank M. Salinger and Robert W. Green. Executive Enterprises Publications Company, 22 West Twenty-first Street, New York, New York 10010-6904. 1989.

THE GUIDE TO SUCCESSFUL CONSUMER BANKING STRATEGY. Robert G. Stemper. John Wiley and Sons, Incorporated, 605 Third Avenue, New York, New York 10158. 1990.

A GUIDE TO THE CONSUMER BANKRUPTCY CODE. Frank M. Salinger, Alvin O. Wiese, Jr. and Robert E. McKew. Executive Enterprises Publications Company, 22 West Twenty-first Street, New York, New York 10010-6904. 1989.

HANDBOOK OF CONSUMER BANKING LAW. Michael G. Hales. Prentice-Hall, Incorporated, 113 Sylvan Avenue, Englewood Cliffs, New Jersey 07632. 1989.

HANDLING CONSUMER CREDIT CASES. John R. Fonseca. Third edition. Lawyers Cooperative Publishing Company, Aqueduct Building, Rochester, New York 14694. 1987.

HOW TO BORROW MONEY AND USE CREDIT. Martin Weiss. Houghton Mifflin Company, 1 Beacon Street, Boston, Massachusetts 02108. 1990.

A PRACTICAL GUIDE TO THE FEDERAL TRUTH-IN-LENDING ACT. Joseph W. Gelb, Sheldon Feldman and Peter N. Cubita. Executive Enterprises Publications Company, 22 West Twenty-first Street, New York, New York 10010-6904. 1990.

PROTECTING CONSUMER RIGHTS. Tang Thanh Trai Le. Shepard's/McGraw-Hill, P.O. Box 1235, Colorado Springs, Colorado 80901. 1987.

SIMPLIFIED CONSUMER CREDIT FORMS. Carl Felsenfeld and Alan Siegel. Research Institute of America, Incorporated, One Penn Plaza, New York, New York 10119. 1978- . Semiannual Supplements.

TRUTH IN LENDING CASE SUMMARIES. Third edition. National Consumer Law Center, 11 Beacon Street, Boston, Massachusetts 02108. 1983.

TRUTH IN-LENDING MANUAL. Sixth Edition. Ralph C. Clontz, Jr. and James A. Douglas. Research Institute of America, Incorporated, One Penn Plaza, New York, New York 10119. 1991.

USURY AND CONSUMER CREDIT REGULATION. Kevin W. Brown. National Consumer Law Center, 11 Beacon Street, Boston, Massachusetts 02108. 1987.

YOUR LEGAL GUIDE TO CONSUMER CREDIT: WITH A SPECIAL SECTION ON BANKRUPTCY. Robert Willard Johnson. American Bar Association, Public Education Division, 750 North Lake Shore Drive, Chicago, Illinois 60611. 1988.

TEXTBOOKS AND GENERAL WORKS

AS WE FORGIVE OUR DEBTORS: BANKRUPTCY AND CONSUMER CREDIT IN AMERICA. Teresa A. Sullivan, Elizabeth Warren and Jay L. Westbrook. Oxford University Press, 200 Madison Avenue, New York, New York 10016. 1989.

BUY NOW, PAY LATER: ADVERTISING, CREDIT, AND CONSUMER DURABLES IN THE 1920S. Martha L. Olney. University of North Carolina Press, P.O. Box 2288, 116 South Boundary Street, Chapel Hill, North Carolina 27515-2288. 1991.

CONSUMER AND COMMERCIAL CREDIT MANAGEMENT. Ninth Edition. Robert H. Cole. Richard D. Irwin, Incorporated, 1818 Ridge Road, Homewood, Illinois 60430. 1992.

THE CONSUMER AND THE CREDIT TRANSACTIONS. Lee D. Chavis, editor. Legal Researcher, 1377 K Street, Northwest, Washington, D.C. 20005. 1983.

CONSUMER LAW: CASES AND MATERIALS. John A. Spanogle, Ralph Rohner and others. Second edition. West Publishing Company, 50 West Kellogg Boulevard, St.Paul, Minnesota 55164. 1991.

THE CREDIT CARD INDUSTRY: A HISTORY. Lewis Mandell. Twayne Publishers, 70 Lincoln Street, Boston, Massachusetts 02111. 1990.

THE DECLINE OF THRIFT IN AMERICA: OUR CULTURAL SHIFT FROM SAVING TO SPENDING. David M. Tucker. Praeger Publishers, One Madison Avenue, New York, New York 10010-3603. 1991.

FAIR DEBT COLLECTION. Robert J. Hobbs. National Consumer Law Center, 11 Beacon Street, Boston, Massachusetts 02108. 1987.

GIVE YOURSELF CREDIT: GUIDE TO CONSUMER CREDIT LAWS. Subcommittee on Consumer Affairs and Coinage of the Committee on Banking, Finance, and Urban Affairs, House of Representatives, Ninety-eighth Congress, First Session. Superintendent of Documents, U.S. Government Printing Office, Washington, D.C. 20402. 1983.

THE INDEBTED SOCIETY: CREDIT AND DEFAULT IN THE 1980S. Janet Ford. Routledge, Chapman and Hall, 29 West Thirty-fifth Street, New York, New York 10001. 1988.

THE LAW OF TRUTH IN LENDING. Ralph J. Rohner, editor. Research Institute of America, Incorporated, One Penn Plaza, New York, New York 10119. 1984.

THE LEGAL SIDE OF CREDIT AND COLLECTION. Bureau of Business Practices, Incorporated, 24 Rope Ferry Road, Waterford, Connecticut 06386. 1989.

MATERIALS FOR UNDERSTANDING CREDIT AND PAYMENT SYSTEMS. Steve H. Nickles. West Publishing Company, 50 West Kellogg Boulevard, St.Paul, Minnesota 55164. 1987.

RETAIL FINANCIAL SERVICES: CURRENT DEVELOPMENTS. Practising Law Institute, 810 Seventh Avenue, New York, New York 10019. 1987.

TRUTH-IN-LENDING AND REGULATION Z: A PRACTICAL GUIDE TO CLOSED-END CREDIT. Dennis Replansky. American Law Institute-American Bar Association, 4025 Chestnut Street, Philadelphia, Pennsylvania 19104. 1984.

UNDERSTANDING THE CONSUMER CREDIT ENVIRONMENT. A. Charlene Sullivan. Executive Enterprises Publications Company, 22 West Twenty-first Street, New York, New York 10010-6904. 1989.

Encyclopedia of Legal Information Sources • 2nd Ed.   **CONSUMER PROTECTION**

LAW REVIEWS AND PERIODICALS

CONSUMER FINANCE LAW QUARTERLY REPORT. Conference on Consumer Finance Law, Peapack, New Jersey. 1984- . Quarterly.

CONSUMER TRENDS. International Credit Union, 243 North Lindbergh Boulevard, St. Louis, Missouri 63141. Monthly.

NATIONAL FOUNDATION FOR CONSUMER CREDIT - MEMBERS BULLETIN. National Foundation for Consumer Credit, 8701 Georgia Avenue, Suite 507, Silver Spring, Maryland 20910. Quarterly.

NEWSLETTERS AND NEWSPAPERS

CONSUMER CREDIT AND TRUTH-IN-LENDING COMPLIANCE REPORT. Research Institute of America, Incorporated, One Penn Plaza, New York, New York 10119. Monthly.

CONSUMER FINANCE LAW BULLETIN. American Financial Services Association, 1101 Fourteenth Street, Northwest, Washington, D.C. 20005. Monthly.

CONSUMER FINANCE NEWSLETTER. Financial Publishing Company, 82 Brookline Avenue, New York, New York 02215. Monthly.

CONSUMER LENDING REPORT. Research Institute of America, Incorporated, One Penn Plaza, New York, New York 10119.

CREDIT WORLD. International Credit Association, 243 North Lindbergh Boulevard, St. Louis, Missouri 63141. Bimonthly.

NCLC REPORTS. National Consumer Law Center, Incorporated, 11 Beacon Street, Boston, Massachusetts 02108. Bimonthly.

ASSOCIATIONS AND PROFESSIONAL SOCIETIES

CONFERENCE ON CONSUMER FINANCE LAW. c/o Lawrence X. Pusateri, Peterson, Ross, Schoerb, and Seidel, 200 East Randolph Drive, Suite 7300, Chicago, Illinois 60601. (312) 861-1400.

CONSUMER CREDIT INSURANCE ASSOCIATION. 542 South Dearborn, Suite 400, Chicago, Illinois 60605. (312) 939-2242.

INTERNATIONAL CREDIT ASSOCIATION. 243 North Lindbergh Boulevard, St. Louis, Missouri 63141. (314) 991-3030.

NATIONAL ASSOCIATION OF CONSUMER CREDIT ADMINISTRATORS. P.O. Box 4068, Santa Fe, New Mexico 87502. (505) 438-0219.

NATIONAL FOUNDATION FOR CONSUMER CREDIT. 8701 Georgia Avenue, Suite 507, Silver Spring, Maryland 20910. (301) 589-5600.

SOCIETY OF CERTIFIED CREDIT EXECUTIVES. P.O. Box 27357, St. Louis, Missouri 63141-1757. (314) 991-3030.

RESEARCH CENTERS, INSTITUTES, CLEARINGHOUSES

CONSUMER CREDIT COUNSELING SERVICE. National Foundation for Consumer Credit, 8701 Georgia Avenue, Suite 507, Silver Spring, Maryland 20910. (301) 589-5600.

CREDIT RESEARCH CENTER. Purdue University, Kernnert Graduate School of Management, West Lafayette, Indiana 47907. (317) 494-4380.

CREDIT RESEARCH FOUNDATION, INCORPORATED. 8815 Centre Park Drive, Suite 206, Columbia, Maryland 21045-2117. (301) 740-5499.

STATISTICS SOURCES

CONSUMER CREDIT. Board of Governors of Federal Reserve System, Twentieth Street and Constitution Avenue, Northwest, Washington, D.C. 20551. Monthly.

CONSUMER LOANS. Board of Governors of Federal Reserve System, Twentieth Street and Constitution Avenue, Northwest, Washington, D.C. 20551. Monthly.

CONSUMER PROTECTION
See also: ADVERTISING; CREDIT; MOTOR VEHICLES; PRODUCTS LIABILITY AND SAFETY

LOOSELEAF SERVICES AND REPORTERS

CONSUMER AND BORROWER PROTECTION: AM JUR PRACTICE GUIDE. Lawyers Cooperative Publishing Company, Aqueduct Building, Rochester, New York 14694. 1991- .

CONSUMER AND COMMUNITY AFFAIRS HANDBOOK. Federal Publications, 1120 20th Street, Northwest, Washington, D.C. 20036. 1981- . Monthly supplements.

CONSUMER PROTECTION AND THE LAW. Dee Pridgen. Clark Boardman Company, Limited, 435 Hudson Street, New York, New York 10014. 1986- . Annual supplements.

FEDERAL CONSUMER PROTECTION: LAWS, RULES, AND REGULATIONS. Bernard D. Reams, Jr. and J.R. Ferguson. Oceana Publications, 75 Main Street, Dobbs Ferry, New York 10522. 1978- . Periodic supplements.

THE LEMON FILE: AN AUTO WARRANTY LITIGATION CASE REFERENCE SERVICE. Center for Auto Safety, 2001 S Street, Northwest, Suite 410, Washington, D.C. 20009. 1982- . Quarterly supplements.

HANDBOOKS, MANUALS, FORMBOOKS

BARBARA KAUFMAN'S CONSUMER ACTION GUIDE. Barbara Kaufman. Nolo Press, 950 Parker Street, Berkeley, California 94710. 1991.

A BUSINESSPERSON'S GUIDE TO FEDERAL WARRANTY LAW. Federal Trade Commission, Superintendent of Documents, U.S. Government Printing Office, Washington, D.C. 20402. 1987.

CONSUMER CLASS ACTIONS: A PRACTICAL LITIGATION GUIDE. Second Edition. Yvonne W. Rosmarin and Daniel A. Edelman. National Consumer Law Center, 11 Beacon Street, Boston, Massachusetts 02108. 1990.

THE CONSUMER PROTECTION HANDBOOK: A LEGAL GUIDE. Charles F. Hemphill. Prentice-Hall, Incorporated, 113 Sylvan Avenue, Englewood Cliffs, New Jersey 07632. 1981.

THE CONSUMER PROTECTION MANUAL. Andrew Eiler. Facts on File, 460 Park Avenue, New York, New York 10016. 1983.

THE CONSUMER SOURCEBOOK. Fifth edition. Kay Gill and Robert Wilson. Gale Research, Incorporated, 835 Penobscot Building, Detroit, Michigan 48226. 1989.

FIGHTING BACK: A CONSUMER'S GUIDE FOR GETTING SATISFACTION, INCLUDING PLAINTEXT FORM LETTERS TO RIP OUT WHEN YOU'RE RIPPED OFF. Dana Shilling. Quill, 105 Madison Avenue, New York, New York 10016. 1982.

LET THE SELLER BEWARE!: THE COMPLETE CONSUMER GUIDE TO GETTING YOUR MONEY'S WORTH. J. Elias Portnoy. Macmillan Publishing Company, Incorporated, 866 Third Avenue, New York, New York 10022. 1990.

MUGGED BY MR. BADWRENCH: AN INSIDER'S GUIDE TO SURVIVING THE SHARK-INFESTED WATERS OF BUYING, MAINTAINING, AND REPAIRING YOUR CAR. Sal Fariello. St. Martin's Press, 175 Fifth Avenue, New York, New York 10010. 1991.

PROTECTING CONSUMER RIGHTS. Tang Thanh Trai Le. Shepard's/McGraw-Hill, P.O.Box 1235, Colorado Springs, Colorado 80901. 1987.

TEXTBOOKS AND GENERAL WORKS

CIVIL WAR ON CONSUMER RIGHTS. Laurence E. Drivon. Conari Press, Berkeley, California. 1990.

CONSUMER DISPUTE RESOLUTION: EXPLORING THE ALTERNATIVES. Larry Ray and Deborah Smolover, editors. American Bar Association, 750 North Lake Shore Drive, Chicago, Illinois 60611. 1983.

CONSUMER ECONOMIC ISSUES IN AMERICA. E. Thomas Garman. Houghton Mifflin Company, 1 Beacon Street, Boston, Massachusetts 02108. 1991.

THE CONSUMER INTEREST: DIMENSIONS AND POLICY IMPLICATIONS. J.D. Forbes. Croom Helm, Paul H. Brookes Publishing Company, P.O. Box 10624, Baltimore, Maryland 21285. 1987.

CONSUMER LAW. Iain Ramsay. New York University Press, 70 Washington Square South, New York, New York 10012. Reprint of 1970 edition.

CONSUMER LAW. Second Edition. Daniel Jay Baum and Robert Force. South-Western Publishing Company, 5101 Madison Road, Cincinnati, Ohio 45227. 1988.

CONSUMER LAW: CASES AND MATERIALS. Second Edition. John A. Spanogle. West Publishing Company, 50 West Kellogg Boulevard, St. Paul, Minnesota 55164. 1991.

CONSUMER LAW, COMMON MARKETS, AND FEDERALISM IN EUROPE AND THE UNITED STATES. Thierry Bourgoignie and David Trubek. Walter de Gruyter, Incorporated, 200 Saw Mill Road, Hawthorne, New York 10532. 1987.

CONSUMER LAW IN A NUTSHELL. Second edition. David G. Epstin and Steve H. Nickles. West Publishing Company, P.O. Box 64526, 50 West Kellogg Boulevard, St. Paul, Minnesota 55164-0526. 1981.

CONSUMER MOVEMENT: GUARDIANS OF THE MARKETPLACE. Robert N. Mayer. Twayne Publishers, 70 Lincoln Street, Boston, Massachusetts, 02111. 1989.

CONSUMER PRODUCT WARRANTIES UNDER FEDERAL AND STATE LAWS. Second edition. Curtis R. Reitz. American Law Institute-American Bar Association, 4025 Chestnut Street, Philadelphia, Pennsylvania 19104. 1987.

CONSUMER PRODUCTS: GOVERNMENT REGULATION AND PRODUCT LIABILITY. Practising Law Institute, 810 Seventh Avenue, New York, New York 10019. 1984.

CONSUMER PROTECTION LEGISLATION AND THE UNITED STATES FOOD INDUSTRY. Melvin J. Hinich and Richard Staelin. Pergamon Press, Maxwell House, Fairview Park, Elmsford, New York, New York 10523. 1980.

CONSUMER SAFETY REGULATION: PUTTING A PRICE ON LIFE AND LIMB. Peter Asch. Oxford University Press, 200 Madison Avenue, New York, New York 10016. 1988.

CONSUMER TRANSACTIONS. Second Edition. Michael M. Greenfield. Foundation Press, 615 Merrick Avenue, Westbury, New York 11590. 1991.

CONSUMERS, COMMISSIONS, AND CONGRESS: LAW, THEORY, AND THE FEDERAL TRADE COMMISSION, 1968-1985. Bernice R Hasin. Transaction Books, Rutgers University, New Brunswick, New Jersey 08903. 1986.

DESIGN OF WARNING LABELS AND INSTRUCTIONS. Joseph P. Ryan. Van Nostrand Reinhold Company, Incorporated, 115 Fifth Avenue, New York, New York 10003. 1991.

DISMANTLING AMERICA: THE RUSH TO DEREGULATE. Susan J. Tolchin and Martin Tolchin. Oxford University Press, 200 Madison Avenue, New York, New York 10016. 1985.

FAIR PLAY IN THE MARKET PLACE: THE FIRST BATTLE FOR PURE FOOD AND DRUG. Mitchell Okun. Northern Illinois University Press, Williston, 320A, DeKalb, Illinois 60115. 1986.

FEDERAL REGULATION OF REAL ESTATE. Revised edition. Paul Barron. Research Institute of America, Incorporated, One Penn Plaza, New York, New York 10119. 1983.

LEARNING ABOUT RISK: CONSUMER AND WORKER RESPONSES TO HAZARD INFORMATION. W. Kip Viscusi. Harvard University Press, 79 Garden Street, Cambridge, Massachusetts 02138. 1987.

LEGAL PROTECTION FOR TODAY'S CONSUMER. Second Edition. Si Horvitz. Kendall/Hunt Publishing Company, 2460 Kerper Boulevard, Dubuque, Iowa 52001. 1989.

PROBLEMS AND MATERIALS ON CONSUMER LAW. Douglas J. Whaley. Little, Brown and Company, 34 Beacon Street, Boston, Massachusetts 02108. 1991.

REGULATING CONSUMER PRODUCT SAFETY. W. Kip Viscusi. American Enterprise Institute for Public Policy Research, 1150 17th Street, Northwest, Washington, D.C. 20036. 1984.

SATISFACTION GUARANTEED: THE ULTIMATE GUIDE TO CONSUMER SELF-DEFENSE. Ralph Charell. Simon and Schuster, Incorporated, 1230 Avenue of the Americas, New York, New York 10020. 1985.

TRUTH-IN-LENDING AND REGULATION Z: A PRACTICAL GUIDE TO CLOSE-END CREDIT. Dennis Replansky. American Law Institute, 4025 Chestnut Street, Philadelphia, Pennsylvania 19104. 1984.

UNFAIR AND DECEPTIVE ACTS AND PRACTICES. Second Edition. Jonathon Sheldon. National Consumer Law Center, Incorporated, 11 Beacon Street, Boston, Massachusetts 02108. 1988.

UNFAIR TRADE PRACTICES AND CONSUMER PROTECTION: CASES AND COMMENTS. Fifth Edition. Glen E. Weston, Peter B. Maggs and Roger E. Schechter. West Publishing Company, 50 West Kellogg Boulevard, St. Paul, Minnesota 55164. 1992.

DIGESTS, INDEXES, ABSTRACTS, CITATORS

ANALYSIS AND DIGEST OF CONSUMER PROTECTION CASE LAW. National Association of Attorneys General, Committee on the Office of Attorney General and Reginald Watkins. National Association of Attorneys Generals, 444 North Capitol Street, Northwest, Washington, D.C. 20001. 1976.

ANNUALS AND SURVEYS

CONSUMERS REPORT BUYING GUIDE. Consumer's Union. Doubleday and Company, Incorporated, 666 Fifth Avenue, New York, New York 10103. Annual.

LAW REVIEWS AND PERIODICALS

CONSUMER PROTECTION: GAINS AND SETBACKS. Congressional Quarterly Staff, editors. Congressional Quarterly, Incorporated, 1414 22nd Street, Northwest, Washington, D.C. 20037. 1978- .

CONSUMER REPORTS. Consumer's Union of United States, Incorporated, 250 Washington Street, Mt. Vernon, New York 10553. Monthly.

JOURNAL OF CONSUMER POLICY. Dordrecht, Holland, New York, New York. 1983- . Quarterly.

NATIONAL CONSUMER LAW CENTER REPORTS. National Consumer Law Center, 11 Beacon Street, Boston, Massachusetts 02108. 36 issues per year.

NEWSLETTERS AND NEWSPAPERS

ACCI NEWSLETTER. American Council on Consumer Interests, 240 Stanley Hall, University of Missouri, Columbia, Missouri 65211. Nine times a year.

COMMERCIAL PROTECTION REPORTING SERVICE. Consumer H-E-L-P, Incorporated, National Law Center, 1424 Sixteenth Street, Northwest, Suite 105, Washington, D.C. 20036. Monthly.

CONSUMER PRODUCT LITIGATION REPORTER. Andrews Publications, 1646 West Chester Pike, Westtown, Pennsylvania 19395. Monthly.

CONSUMER PROTECTION REPORT. National Association of Attorneys General, 444 North Capitol Street, Suite 403, Washington, D.C. 20001. Monthly.

FROM THE STATE CAPITALS: CONSUMER PROTECTION AND MERCHANDISING. Wakeman/Walworth, Incorporated, P.O. Box 1939, New Haven, Connecticut 06509. Weekly.

LEMON TIMES. Center for Auto Safety, 2001 S Street, Northwest, Suite 410, Washington, D.C. 20009. Quarterly.

LOYOLA CONSUMER LAW REPORTER. Loyola University School of Law, 1 East Delaware Street, Chicago, Illinois 60611. Quarterly.

NCLC REPORTS. National Consumer Law Center, Incorporated, 11 Beacon Streets, Boston, Massachusetts 02108. Bimonthly.

TEXAS CONSUMER LAW REPORTER. Texas Law Letter, P.O. Box 12841, Capitol Station, Austin, Texas 78711. Monthly.

BIBLIOGRAPHIES

THE MODERN CONSUMER MOVEMENT: REFERENCES AND RESOURCES. Stephen Brobeck. G.K. Hall and Company, Incorporated, 70 Lincoln Street, New York, New York 10119. 1990.

POLICY STUDIES ON CONSUMERISM: A SELECTED BIBLIOGRAPHY. Robert Goehlert. Vance Bibliographies, 112 North Charter Street, Monticello, Illinois 61856. 1983.

DIRECTORIES

AMERICAN COUNCIL ON CONSUMER INTERESTS--MEMBERSHIP LIST. Stanley Hall, Room 240, University of Missouri, Columbia, Missouri 65211.

CONSUMER PROTECTION DIRECTORY. Second edition. Marquis Academic Media, 200 East Ohio Street, Chicago, Illinois 60611. 1975- .

DIRECTORY OF BETTER BUSINESS BUREAUS. Council of Better Business Bureaus, 4200 Wilson Boulevard, Suite 800, Arlington, Virginia 22203. Irregular.

DIRECTORY OF STATE AND LOCAL CONSUMER ORGANIZATIONS. Consumer Federation of America, 1424 Sixteenth Street, Northwest, Suite 604, Washington, D.C. 20036. Irregular.

EVERYBODY'S MONEY COMPLAINT DIRECTORY FOR CONSUMERS. Credit Union National Association, P.O. Box 431, Madison, Wisconsin 53701. Annual.

WEBSTER'S 21ST CENTURY CONSUMER'S RESOURCE GUIDE. Thomas Nelson, Incorporated, Nelson Place at Elm Hill Pike, P.O. Box 141000, Nashville, Tennessee 37214. 1992.

ASSOCIATIONS AND PROFESSIONAL SOCIETIES

CONFERENCE ON CONSUMER FINANCE LAW. c/o Lawrence X. Pusateri, Peterson, Ross, Schloerb, and Seidel, 200 East Randolph Drive, Suite 7300, Chicago, Illinois 60601. (312) 861-1400

CONSUMER CREDIT. c/o Lawrence X. Pusateri, Peterson, Ross, Schloerb, and Seidel, 200 East Randolph Drive, Suite 7300, Chicago, Illinois 60601. (312) 861-1400.

COUNCIL OF BETTER BUSINESS BUREAUS. 1515 Wilson Boulevard, Arlington, Virginia 22209.

NATIONAL ASSOCIATION OF CONSUMER AGENCY ADMINISTRATORS. 1511 K Street, Northwest, Washington, D.C. 20005.

NATIONAL CONSUMER LAW CENTER. 11 Beacon Street, Boston, Massachusetts 02108.

RESEARCH CENTERS, INSTITUTES, CLEARINGHOUSES

AMERICAN COUNCIL ON CONSUMER AWARENESS, INCORPORATED. 1251 Kent Street North, P.O. Box 17291, St. Paul, Minnesota 55117. (612) 489-2835.

CENTER FOR RESPONSIVE LAW. P.O. Box 19367, Washington, D.C. 20036.

CONSUMERS HEALTH AND MEDICAL INFORMATION CENTER. P.O. Box 2138, Clearwater, Florida 34617. (813) 441-8952.

FAMILY AND CONSUMER SCIENCES RESEARCH INSTITUTE. Iowa State University, 126 MacKay, Ames, Iowa 50011. (515) 294-5982.

NATIONAL CONSUMER LAW CENTER. 236 Massachusetts Avenue, Northeast, Washington, D.C. 20002. (202) 543-6060.

NATIONAL RESOURCE CENTER FOR CONSUMER STUDIES. 3254 Jones Court, Washington, D.C. 20007.

UNITED STATES CONSUMER PRODUCT SAFETY COMMISSION. 5401 Westbard Avenue, Room 625, Bethesda, Maryland 20816. (800) 638-2772.

AUDIOVISUALS

BASICS OF CONSUMER LAW: EFFECTIVE REPRESENTATION FOR BUYERS AND SELLERS. American Bar Association, 750 North Lake Shore Drive, Chicago, Illinois 60611. 1986. Videotape.

CONTINENTAL SHELF
See: LAW OF THE SEA

CONTRACEPTION
See: BIRTH CONTROL; FAMILY LAW

CONTRACTS
See also: AUTHORS AND PUBLISHERS; COMPUTER CONTRACTS; CONSTRUCTION INDUSTRY; GOVERNMENT CONTRACTS; RESTITUTION; UNIFORM COMMERCIAL CODE

STATUTES, CODES, STANDARDS, UNIFORM LAWS

UNIFORM COMMERCIAL CODE (Master edition). Ninth Edition. National Conference of Commissioners on Uniform State Laws, Uniform Laws Annotated, West Publishing Company, Post Office Box 64526, 50 West Kellogg Boulevard, St. Paul, Minnesota 55164-0526. 1976- . (Annual Supplements).

UNIFORM COMMERCIAL CODE. 1978 Official text with comments. National Conference of Commissioners on Uniform State Laws, West Publishing Company, Post Office Box 64526, 50 West Kellogg Boulevard, St. Paul, Minnesota 55164-0526. 1978.

RESTATEMENTS

RESTATEMENT OF THE LAW (SECOND): CONTRACTS. American Law Institute, 4025 Chestnut Street, Philadelphia, Pennsylvania 19104. 1981- .

LOOSELEAF SERVICES AND REPORTERS

BASIC LEGAL TRANSACTIONS. Vincent DiLorenzo. Research Institute of America, Incorporated, One Penn Plaza, New York, New York 10119. 1985- . (Annual supplements).

COMPUTER SOFTWARE AGREEMENTS: FORMS AND COMMENTARY. John Matuszeski and others. Research Institute of America, Incorporated, One Penn Plaza, New York, New York 10119. 1987- . (Annual supplements).

CONTRACT CHECKLISTS. Albert Kritzer. Kluwer Academic Publishers, 101 Philip Drive, Assinippi Park, Norwell, Massachusetts 02061. 1990- . (Periodic supplements).

CORPORATE COUNSEL'S GUIDE TO EMPLOYMENT CONTRACTS. W.A.Hancock. Business Laws, Incorporated, 11630 Chillicothe Road, Chesterland, Ohio 44026. 1990- . (Annual supplements).

DRAFTING EFFECTIVE CONTRACTS. R.A. Feldman. Prentice-Hall Law and Business, Route 9W, Englewood Cliffs, New Jersey 07632. 1989- . (Periodic supplements).

DRAFTING THE UNION CONTRACT. Peter Laureau. Matthew Bender and Company, Incorporated, 11 Penn Plaza, New York, New York 10001. 1988- . (Annual supplements).

ENTERTAINMENT INDUSTRY CONTRACTS: NEGOTIATIONS AND DRAFTING GUIDE. D.C. Farber. Matthew Bender and Company, Incorporated, 11 Penn Plaza, New York, New York 10001. 1986- . (Periodic supplements).

EXECUTIVE AND PROFESSIONAL EMPLOYMENT CONTRACTS. L.J. Kutten and Bernard D. Reams, Jr. Butterworth Legal Publishers, 90 Stiles Road, Salem, New Hampshire 03079. 1988- . (Periodic supplements).

GUIDE TO GOVERNMENT CONTRACTING. Commerce Clearing House, Incorporated, 4025 West Peterson Avenue, Chicago, Illinois 60646. 1991- .

GUIDE TO PRACTICAL APPLICATIONS OF THE UN CONVENTION ON CONTRACTS FOR THE INTERNATIONAL SALE OF GOODS. Albert Kritzer. Kluwer Academic Publishers, 101 Philip Drive, Assinippi Park, Norwell, Massachusetts 02061. 1990- . (Periodic supplements).

HOSPITAL CONTRACTS MANUAL. Baker and Hostetler. Aspen Publishers Incorporated, 200 Orchard Ridge Drive, Gaithersburg, Maryland 20878. 1982- . (Semiannual supplements).

INTERNATIONAL HANDBOOK ON CONTRACTS OF EMPLOYMENT. John S. Bradley. Box 358, Accord Station, Hingham, Massachusetts 02018. 1988- . (Periodic supplements).

MODERN LAW OF EMPLOYMENT RELATIONSHIPS. Second edition. Charles D. Bakaly, Jr. and Joel M. Grossman. Prentice-Hall Law and Business, Route 9W, Englewood Cliffs, New Jersey 07632. 1989- . (Periodic supplements).

NATURAL GAS CONTRACTS. Stephen Munro. Thompson Publishing Group, 1725 K Street, N.W., Washington, D.C. 20006. 1984- . (Quarterly supplement).

WARREN'S FORMS OF AGREEMENT. Oscar Leroy Warren, and others. Matthew Bender and Company, Incorporated, 11 Penn Plaza, New York, New York 10001. 1954- . (Annual Supplements).

HANDBOOKS, MANUALS, FORMBOOKS

ALLEN AND DAVIS ON COMPUTER CONTRACTING: A USER'S GUIDE WITH FORMS AND STRATEGIES. Second Edition. Don A. Allen and Lanny J. Davis. Prentice-Hall, Incorporated, 113 Sylvan Avenue, Englewood Cliffs, New Jersey 07632. 1992- .

THE ANTITRUST GOVERNMENT CONTRACTS HANDBOOK: A PROJECT OF THE SHERMAN ACT SECTION 1 COMMITTEE. William E. Kovacic. American Bar Association, Section of Antitrust Law, 750 North Lake Shore Drive, Chicago, Illinois 60611. 1990.

BUSINESS CONTRACT FORMS. Robert J. English. John Wiley and Sons, Incorporated, 605 Third Avenue, New York, New York 10158. 1984- . (Periodic Supplements).

THE COMPACT GUIDE TO CONTRACT LAW: A CIVILIZED APPROACH TO THE LAW. Jefferson Hane Weaver. West Publishing Company, 50 West Kellogg Boulevard, St. Paul, Minnesota 55164. 1990.

CONSTRUCTION INDUSTRY FORMBOOK. Second Edition. James Acret. Shepard's/McGraw-Hill, P.O. Box 1235, Colorado Springs, Colorado 80901. 1990.

CONSTRUCTION OWNER'S HANDBOOK OF PROPERTY DEVELOPMENT. Robert F. Cushman and Peter J. King. John Wiley and Sons, Incorporated, 605 Third Avenue, New York, New York 10158. 1992.

DRAFTING CONSTRUCTION CONTRACTS: STRATEGY AND FORMS FOR CONTRACTORS. Samuel Frank Schoninger. John Wiley and Sons, Incorporated, 605 Third Avenue, New York, New York 10158. 1990.

DRAFTING CONTRACTS: A GUIDE TO THE PRACTICAL APPLICATION OF THE PRINCIPLES OF CONTRACT LAW. Scott J. Burnham. Michie Company, P.O. Box 7587, Charlottesville, Virginia 22906. 1987.

EVERYDAY CONTRACTS: PROTECTING YOUR RIGHTS: A STEP-BY-STEP GUIDE. Revised Edition. George Milko, Kay Ostberg and Theresa Rudy. Random House, Incorporated, 201 East Fiftieth Street, New York, New York 10022. 1991.

THE GOVERNMENT CONTRACT COMPLIANCE HANDBOOK. Federal Publications, 1120 Twentieth Street, Northwest, Washington, D.C. 20036. 1990.

GUIDE TO PRACTICAL APPLICATIONS OF THE UN CONVENTION ON CONTRACTS FOR THE INTERNATIONAL SALE OF GOODS. Albert H. Kritzer. Kluwer Law Book Publishers, Incorporated, 36 West Forty-fourth Street, New York, New York 10036. 1988.

HANDBOOK FOR CONTRACT LITIGATION. Valera Grapp. Prentice-Hall, Incorporated, 113 Sylvan Avenue, Englewood Cliffs, New Jersey 07632. 1988.

THE INSIDER'S GUIDE TO CONTRACTING WITH THE FEDERAL GOVERNMENT. Richard L. Porterfield. John Wiley and Sons, Incorporated, 605 Third Avenue, New York, New York 10158. 1992.

INTERNATIONAL CONTRACT MANUAL: CONTRACT CHECKLIST. Albert H. Kritzer, Editor. Kluwer Law Book Publishers, Incorporated, 36 West Forty-fourth Street, New York, New York 10036. 1990.

PORTFOLIO OF BUSINESS FORMS, AGREEMENTS, AND CONTRACTS. Valera Grapp. Prentice-Hall, 113 Sylvan Avenue, Englewood Cliffs, New Jersey 07632. 1985- . (Periodic Supplements).

SIMPLE CONTRACTS FOR PERSONAL USE. Stephen Elias and Marcia Stewart. Nolo Press, 950 Parker Street, Berkeley, California 94710. 1991.

WEST'S LEGAL FORMS. West Publishing Company, P.O. Box 64526, 50 West Kellogg Boulevard, St. Paul, Minnesota 55164-0526. 1971- . (Annual Supplements).

TEXTBOOKS AND GENERAL WORKS

BASIC CONTRACT LAW. Fifth Edition. Lon L. Fuller and Melvin Aron Eisenberg. West Publishing Company, 50 West Kellogg Boulevard, St. Paul, Minnesota 55164. 1990.

CASES AND MATERIALS ON CONTRACTS. Second Edition. Robert W. Hamilton, Alan Scott Rau and Russell J. Weintraub. West Publishing Company, 50 West Kellogg Boulevard, St. Paul, Minnesota 55164. 1992.

CONTRACTS

COMMERCIAL GUIDE TO GC-WORKS-CONDITIONS OF CONTRACT. Brian Meopham. Pergamon Press, Incorporated, Maxwell House, Fairview Park, Elmsford, New York 10523. 1985.

CONCEPTS AND CASE ANALYSIS IN THE LAW OF CONTRACTS. Marvin A. Chirelstein. Foundation Press, 615 Merrick Avenue, Westbury, New York 11590. 1990.

CONSTRUCTION CONTRACTS. Jimmie Hinze. McGraw-Hill Publishing Company, 1221 Avenue of the Americas, New York, New York 10020. 1992.

CONSTRUCTION CONTRACTS AND LITIGATION IN THE ECONOMICALLY TROUBLED 90'S. Kenneth M. Cushman. Practising Law Institute, 810 Seventh Avenue, New York, New York 10019. 1991.

CONTRACT AND RELATED OBLIGATION: THEORY, DOCTRINE, AND PRACTICE. Second Edition. Robert S. Summers and Robert A. Hillman. West Publishing Company, 50 West Kellogg Boulevard, St. Paul, Minnesota 55164. 1992.

CONTRACT AS PROMISE: A THEORY OF CONTRACTUAL OBLIGATION. Charles Fried. Harvard University Press, 79 Garden Street, Cambridge, Massachusetts 02138. 1981.

CONTRACT LAW AND THEORY. Robert E. Scott and Douglas L. Leslie. Michie Company, P.O. Box 7587, Charlottesville, Virginia 22906. 1988.

CONTRACT REMEDIES IN A NUTSHELL. Jane M. Friedman. West Publishing Company, Post Office Box 64526, 50 West Kellogg Boulevard, St. Paul, Minnesota 55164-0526. 1981.

CONTRACTING WITH THE FEDERAL GOVERNMENT. Third Edition. Frank M. Alston, Margaret M. Worthington and Louis P. Goldsman. John Wiley and Sons, Incorporated, 605 Third Avenue, New York, New York 10158. 1992.

CONTRACTS. Second Edition. John D. Calamari and Joseph M. Perillo. West Publishing Company, 50 West Kellogg Boulevard, St. Paul, Minnesota 55164. 1990.

CONTRACTS. Second Edition. Steven Emanuel and Steven Knowles. Emanuel Law Outlines, 1865 Palmer Avenue, Larchmont, New York 10538.

CONTRACTS. Second Edition. E. Allan Farnsworth. Little, Brown and Company, 34 Beacon Street, Boston, Massachusetts 02108. 1990.

CONTRACTS AND SPECIFICATIONS FOR PUBLIC WORKS PROJECTS. Edward R. Fisk and Julius C. Calhoun. John Wiley and Sons, Incorporated, 605 Third Avenue, New York, New York 10158. 1991.

A CONTRACTS ANTHOLOGY. Peter Linzer, Editor. Anderson Publishing Company, 2035 Reading Road, Cincinnati, Ohio 45202. 1989.

CONTRACTS: CASES AND MATERIALS. Fourth Edition. John Edward Murray, Jr. Michie Company, P.O. Box 7587, Charlottesville, Virginia 22906. 1991.

CONTRACTS IN A NUTSHELL. Third Edition. Gordon D. Schaber and Claude D. Rohwer. West Publishing Company, 50 West Kellogg Boulevard, St. Paul, Minnesota 55164. 1990.

CORBIN ON CONTRACTS (Hornbook Edition). Arthur L. Corbin. West Publishing Company, Post Office Box 64526, 50 West Kellogg Boulevard, St. Paul, Minnesota 55164-0526. 1952.

DEATH OF CONTRACT. Grant Gilmore. Ohio State University Press, 1070 Carmack Road, Columbus, Ohio 43120-1002. 1976.

THE ECONOMICS OF CONTRACT CHOICE: AN AGRARIAN PERSPECTIVE. Yujiro Hayami and Keijiro Otsuka. Oxford University Press, 200 Madison Avenue, New York, New York 10016. 1991.

ECONOMICS OF CONTRACT LAW. Anthony T. Kronman and Richard A. Posner, compilers. Little, Brown and Company, 34 Beacon Street, Boston, Massachusetts 02108. 1979.

ELECTRONIC CONTRACTING LAW: EDI AND BUSINESS TRANSACTIONS. L.J. Kutten, Bernard D. Reams and Allen E. Strehler. Clark Boardman Company, Limited, 435 Hudson Street, New York, New York 10014. 1991.

ESSAYS ON CONTRACT. P.S. Atiyah. Oxford University Press, 200 Madison Avenue, New York, New York 10016. 1986.

FEDERAL CONSTRUCTION CONTRACTING. James F. Nagle. John Wiley and Sons, Incorporated, 605 Third Avenue, New York, New York 10158. 1992.

THE FRENCH LAW OF CONTRACT. Second Edition. Barry Nicholas. Oxford University Press, 200 Madison Avenue, New York, New York 10016. 1992.

FUNDAMENTALS OF FEDERAL CONTRACT LAW. Eugene W. Massengale. Quorum Books, Greenwood Publishing Group, Incorporated, 88 Post Road West, P.O. Box 5007, Westport, Connecticut 06881. 1991.

GOVERNMENT CONTRACTS IN A NUTSHELL. Second Edition. W. Noel Keyes. West Publishing Company, 50 West Kellogg Boulevard, St. Paul, Minnesota 55164. 1990.

HANDBOOK FOR THE TRIAL OF CONTRACT LAWSUITS: STRATEGIES AND TECHNIQUES. Edward J. Imwinkelried. Prentice-Hall, Incorporated, 113 Sylvan Avenue, Englewood Cliffs, New Jersey 07632. 1981.

HANDBOOK OF THE LAW OF CONTRACTS. Second Edition. (Hornbook Series). Laurence P. Simpson. West Publishing Company, Post Office Box 64526, 50 West Kellogg Boulevard, St. Paul, Minnesota 55164-0526. 1965.

A HISTORY OF THE ANGLO-AMERICAN COMMON LAW OF CONTRACT. Kevin M. Teeven. Greenwood Publishing Group, Incorporated, 88 Post Road West, P.O. Box 5007, Westport, Connecticut 06881. 1990.

HOW TO HANDLE YOUR OWN CONTRACTS: A LAYMAN'S GUIDE TO CONTRACTS, LEASES, WILLS AND OTHER LEGAL AGREEMENTS. Revised Edition. Christopher Neubert and Jack Withiam, Jr. Greenwich House. Distributed by Sterling Publishing Company, Incorporated, 387 Park Avenue, New York, New York, 10016-8810. 1991.

INTERNATIONAL COMMERCIAL AGREEMENTS: A FUNCTIONAL PRIMER ON DRAFTING, NEGOTIATING, AND RESOLVING DISPUTES. William F. Fox, Jr. Kluwer Law Book Publishers, Incorporated, 36 West Forty-fourth Street, New York, New York 10036. 1988.

INTERNATIONAL STANDARD CONTRACTS: THE PRICE OF FAIRNESS. Antonio Boggiano. Graham and Trotman Limited. Distributed by Kluwer Academic Publishers, 101 Philip Drive, Assinippi Park, Norwell, Massachusetts 02061. 1991.

THE INTERPRETATION OF CONTRACTS. Kim Lewison. Sweet and Maxwell Limited, South Quay Plaza, 183 Marsh Wall, London E14 9FT, England. 1989.

INTRODUCTION TO CONTRACTS. Second Edition. Thomas W. Dunfee, Frank F. Givson. John Wiley and Sons, Incorporated, 605 Third Avenue, New York, New York 10158. 1984.

INTRODUCTION TO CONTRACTS AND RESTITUTION FOR PARALEGALS. Martin A Frey and Terry H. Bitting. West Publishing Company, 50 West Kellogg Boulevard, St. Paul, Minnesota 55164. 1988.

AN INTRODUCTION TO THE LAW OF CONTRACT. Fourth Edition. P.S. Atiyah. Oxford University Press, 200 Madison Avenue, New York, New York 10016. 1989.

LAW, ECONOMY, AND THE POWER OF CONTRACT: MAJOR HISTORICAL INTERPRETATIONS. Kermit L. Hall. Fred B. Rothman and Company, 10368 West Centennial Road, Littleton, Colorado 80127.

THE LAW OF CONTRACTS. Third Edition. John D. Calamari and Joseph M. Perillo. West Publishing Company, Post Office Box 64526, 50 West Kellogg Boulevard, St. Paul, Minnesota 55102-1611. 1987.

THE LEGAL ENVIRONMENT OF BUSINESS: REGULATORY LAW AND CONTRACTS. Douglas Whitman, John William Gergacz and Murray Levin. McGraw-Hill Publishing Company, 1221 Avenue of the Americas, New York, New York 10020. 1992.

LETTERS OF INTENT AND OTHER PRECONTRACTUAL DOCUMENTS: COMPARATIVE ANALYSIS AND FORMS. Ralph B. Lake and Ugo Draetta. Butterworth Legal Publishers, 90 Stiles Road, Salem, New Hampshire 03079. 1989.

MATERIALS IN THE LAW OF BUSINESS CONTRACTS. Second Edition. Leonard Lakin and Leona Beane. Kendall/Hunt Publishing Company, 2460 Kerper Boulevard, Dubuque, Iowa 52001. 1989.

MODERN LAW OF CONTRACTS. Howard O. Hunter. Research Institute of America, Incorporated, One Penn Plaza, New York, New York 10119. 1987.

MORAL DEALING: CONTRACT, ETHICS, AND REASON. David Gauthier. Cornell University Press, 124 Roberts Place, Ithaca, New York 14850. 1990.

MURRAY ON CONTRACTS, Third Edition of Grismore on Contracts. John E. Murray. Michie Company, Post Office Box 7587, Charlottesville, Virginia 22906-7582. 1990.

THE NEW SOCIAL CONTRACT: AN INQUIRY INTO MODERN CONTRACTUAL RELATIONS. Ian R. Macneil. Yale University Press, 302 Temple Street, New Haven, Connecticut 06520. 1980.

THE PHILOSOPHICAL ORIGINS OF MODERN CONTRACT DOCTRINE. James Gordley. Oxford University Press, 200 Madison Avenue, New York, New York 10016. 1991.

SIGN HERE? EVERYTHING YOU NEED TO KNOW ABOUT CONTRACTS. Mari W. Privette. Doubleday and Company, Incorporated, 666 Fifth Avenue, New York, New York 10103. 1985.

SIMPLE CONTRACTS FOR PERSONAL USE. Stephen Elias. Nolo Press, 950 Parker Street, Berkeley, California 94710. 1991.

STUDIES IN CONTRACT LAW. Fourth Edition. Edward J. Murphy and Richard E. Speidel. Foundation Press, 615 Merrick Avenue, Westbury, New York 11590. 1991.

A TREATISE ON THE LAW OF CONTRACTS. Fourth Edition. Samuel Williston. Lawyers Cooperative Publishing Company, Aqueduct Building, Rochester, New York 14694. 1990- .

UNEQUAL BARGAINING: A STUDY OF VITIATING FACTORS IN THE FORMATION OF CONTRACTS. John Cartwright. Oxford University Press, 200 Madison Avenue, New York, New York 10016. 1991.

UNIFORM COMMERCIAL CODE IN A NUTSHELL. Third Edition. Bradford Stone. West Publishing Company, Post Office Box 64526, 50 West Kellogg Boulevard, St. Paul, Minnesota 55164-0526. 1989.

UNITED STATES CONTRACT LAW. E. Allan Farnsworth. Transnational Publishers, P.O. Box 7282, Ardsley-on-Hudson, New York 10503. 1991.

ENCYCLOPEDIAS AND DICTIONARIES

ENCYCLOPEDIC DICTIONARY OF CONTRACT AND PROCUREMENT LAW. Fourth edition. W. Noel Keyes. Oceana Publications, 75 Main Street, Dobbs Ferry, New York 10522. 1987.

AUDIOVISUALS

MEDIATION: SIMULATION OF A CONSTRUCTION DISPUTE. National Practice Institute, 330 Second Avenue South, Minneapolis, Minnesota 55401. Videotape.

COMPUTER-ASSISTED LEGAL INSTRUCTION

CONTRACT FORMATION I AND II. Matthew C. McKinnon. Center for Computer-Assisted Instruction, 229 19th Avenue South, University of Minnesota, Minneapolis, Minnesota 55455. Machine-readable data file.

DAVIS V. JACOBY. Center for Computer-Assisted Instruction, 229 19th Avenue South, University of Minnesota, Minneapolis, Minnesota 55455. Interactive videodisc.

DRAFTING A CONTRACT: THE SALE OF GOODS. Scott J. Burnham. Center for Computer-Assisted Instruction, 229 19th Avenue South, University of Minnesota, Minneapolis, Minnesota 55455. Machine- readable computer file.

EASERLY V. LETWIN. Center for Computer-Assisted Instruction, 229 19th Avenue South, University of Minnesota, Minneapolis, Minnesota 55455. Interactive videodisc.

HAWKINS I & II. Center for Computer-Assisted Instruction, 229 19th Avenue South, University of Minnesota, Minneapolis, Minnesota 55455. Interactive videodisc.

NEGOTIATOR PRO. Beacon Expert System, Incorporated, 35 Gardner Road, Brookline, Massachusetts 02146. Machine-readable computer file.

PRE-EXISTING DUTY RULE, CONTRACT MODIFICATION, AND ACCORD AND SATISFACTION. John A. Humbach. Center for Computer-Assisted Instruction, 229 19th Avenue South, University of Minnesota, Minneapolis, Minnesota 55455. Machine-readable computer file.

THIRD PARTY BENEFICIARIES. Matthew C. McKinnon. Center for Computer-Assisted Instruction, 229 19th Avenue South, University of Minnesota, Minneapolis, Minnesota 55455. Machine-readable data file.

TRIAL EVIDENCE AND DIRECT EXAMINATION SKILLS. CLE Group, 274 Willow Road, Menlo Park, California 94025. Interactive videodisc.

YOU BE THE JUDGE. CLE Group, 274 Willow Road, Menlo Park, California 94025. Interactive videodisc.

CONTRIBUTORY NEGLIGENCE
See: TORTS

CONTROLLED SUBSTANCES
See: DRUG LAWS

CONVENTIONS, INTERNATIONAL
See: TREATIES AND CONVENTIONS

COOPERATIVES
See: CONDOMINIUMS AND COOPERATIVE BUILDINGS

COPYRIGHT
See also: COPYRIGHT OFFICE

STATUTES, CODES, STANDARDS, UNIFORM LAWS

CODE OF FEDERAL REGULATIONS. TITLE 37. Office of the Federal Register, Superintendent of Documents, U.S. Government Printing Office, Washington, D.C. 20402. Annual.

COPYRIGHT REVISION ACT OF 1976: P. L. 94-553, AS SIGNED BY THE PRESIDENT, OCTOBER 19, 1976: LAW, EXPLANATION, COMMITTEE REPORTS. Commerce Clearing House, Incorporated, 4025 West Peterson Avenue, Chicago, Illinois 60646. 1976.

THE FIRST FEDERAL COPYRIGHT LAW: A FACSIMILE. Library of Congress, Copyright Office, 101 Independence Avenue, Southeast, Washington, D.C. 20540. Reprint of 1790 edition.

THE KAMINSTEIN LEGISLATIVE HISTORY PROJECT: A COMPENDIUM AND ANALYTICAL INDEX OF MATERIALS LEADING TO THE COPYRIGHT ACT OF NINETEEN SEVENTY-SIX. Alan Latman and James F. Lightstone, editors. Fred B. Rothman and Company, 10368 West Centennial Road, Littleton, Colorado 80127. 1981-1985.

LEGISLATIVE HISTORY OF THE 1909 COPYRIGHT ACT. E. Fulton Brylawski and Abe Goldman. Fred B. Rothman and Company, 10368 West Centennial Road, Littleton, Colorado 80127. 1976.

OMNIBUS COPYRIGHT REVISION: LEGISLATIVE HISTORY 1960-1976. George S. Grossman, editor. W. S. Hein and Company, Incorporated, Hein Building, 1285 Main Street, Buffalo, New York 14209. 1976.

PATENT, TRADEMARK, AND COPYRIGHT LAWS. Jeffrey M. Samuels, editor. Bureau of National Affairs, Incorporated, 1231 Twenty-fifth Street, Northwest, Washington, D.C. 20037. 1989.

LOOSELEAF SERVICES AND REPORTERS

COMPUTER SOFTWARE PROTECTION LAW. Cary H. Sherman, Hamish R. Sandison and Marc D. Guren. Bureau of National Affairs, Incorporated, 1231 Twenty-fifth Street, Northwest, Washington, D.C. 20037. 1989-

COMPUTER SOFTWARE: PROTECTION, LIABILITY, LAW, FORMS. L.J. Kutten. Clark Boardman Company, Limited, 435 Hudson Street, New York, New York 10014. 1987- . (Periodic supplements).

THE COPYRIGHT LAW JOURNAL: AN ANALYSIS OF CURRENT CASES AND DEVELOPMENTS AFFECTING INTEL-LECTUAL PROPERTY RIGHTS. Copyright Law Journal, P.O. Box 3897, San Fransisco, California 94119. 1984- . (Ten issues per year).

COPYRIGHT LAW REPORTS. Commerce Clearing House, Incorporated, 4025 West Peterson Avenue, Chicago, Illinois 60646. 1978- . (Monthly supplements).

COPYRIGHT LAWS AND TREATIES OF THE WORLD. Bureau of National Affairs, Incorporated, 1231 Twenty-fifth Street, Northwest, Washington, D.C. 20037. 1957- . (Periodic supplements).

COPYRIGHT PROTECTION IN THE AMERICAS. Organization of American States, General Legal Division. Oceana Publications, Incorporated, 75 Main Street, Dobbs Ferry, New York 10522. 1979- . (Periodic supplements).

COPYRIGHT REGISTRATION PRACTICE. James E. Hawes. Clark Boardman Company, Limited, 435 Hudson Street, New York, New York 10014. 1990- . (Annual supplements).

DECISIONS OF THE UNITED STATES COURTS INVOLVING COPYRIGHT. Copyright Office. Library of Congress, Superintendent of Documents, United States Government Printing Office, Washington, D.C. 20402. 1909- .

INTERNATIONAL COPYRIGHT LAW AND PRACTICE. Meville Nimmer and P. Geller. Matthew Bender and Company, Incorporated, 11 Penn Plaza, New York, New York 10001. 1988- . (Annual supplements).

THE LAW AND BUSINESS OF COMPUTER SOFTWARE. D.C. Toedt, III, Editor. Clark Boardman Company, Limited, 435 Hudson Street, New York, New York 10014. 1990.

THE LAW OF COPYRIGHT. Howard B. Abrams. Clark Boardman Company, Limited, 435 Hudson Street, New York, New York 10014. 1991- .

LINDEY ON ENTERTAINMENT, PUBLISHING AND THE ARTS: AGREEMENTS AND THE LAW. Alexander Lindey. Second edition. Clark Boardman Company, Limited, 435 Hudson Street, New York, New York 10014. 1983- . (Biannual supplements).

MODERN INTELLECTUAL PROPERTY. Michael A. Epstein. Prentice-Hall Law and Business, Route 9W, Englewood Cliffs, New Jersey 07632. 1984.

NIMMER ON COPYRIGHT: A TREATISE ON THE LAW OF LITERARY, MUSICAL AND ARTISTIC PROPERTY AND THE PROTECTION OF IDEAS. Melville B. Nimmer. Matthew Bender and Company, Incorporated, 11 Penn Plaza, New York, New York 10001. 1963- . (Annual supplements).

PATENT, TRADEMARK AND COPYRIGHT JOURNAL. Bureau of National Affairs, Incorporated, 1231 Twenty-fifth Street, Northwest, Washington, D.C. 20037. 1970- . (Weekly supplements).

PATENT, TRADEMARK, AND COPYRIGHT REGULATIONS. James D. Crowne, Editor. Bureau of National Affairs, Incorporated, 1231 Twenty-fifth Street, Northwest, Washington, D.C. 20037. 1991- .

PERFORMING ARTS MANAGEMENT AND THE LAW. Joseph Taubman. Law-Arts Publishers, Incorporated, 159 West Fifty-third Street, New York, New York 10019. 1971- . (Periodic supplements).

SCOTT ON COMPUTER LAW. Second Edition. Michael D. Scott. Prentice-Hall, Incorporated, 113 Sylvan Avenue, Englewood Cliffs, New Jersey 07632. 1991.

SEMICONDUCTOR CHIP PROTECTION. Richard H. Stern. Prentice-Hall Law and Business, Route 9W, Englewood Cliffs, New Jersey 07632. 1986- . (Periodic supplements).

TAXATION OF PATENTS, TRADEMARKS, COPYRIGHTS AND KNOW-HOW. Jon E. Bischel. Research Institute of America, Incorporated, One Penn Plaza, New York, New York 10119. 1974- .

HANDBOOKS, MANUALS, FORMBOOKS

AN ARTIST'S HANDBOOK ON COPYRIGHT. Robert C. Lower and Jeffrey E. Young. Georgia Volunteer Lawyers for the Arts, 501 William-Oliver Building, 32 Peachtree Street, Northwest, Atlanta, Georgia 30303. 1981.

AN AUTHORS GUIDE TO THE COPYRIGHT LAW. Warren L. Patton. Lexington Books, 125 Spring Street, Lexington, Massachusetts 02173. 1980.

THE BEGINNING CREATOR'S COPYRIGHT MANUAL: A PRACTICAL GUIDE FOR AUTHORS, POETS, COMPOSERS, PROGRAMMERS, PLAYWRIGHTS, ARTISTS, AND PHOTOGRAPHERS, IN ORDINARY LANGUAGE. H.P. Killough. Harlo Press, 50 Victor Avenue, Detroit, Michigan 48203. 1988.

COMPUTER LAW HANDBOOK: SOFTWARE PROTECTION, CONTRACTS, LITIGATION, FORMS. David F. Simon. American Law Institute-American Bar Association, Committee on Continuing Professional Education, 4025 Chestnut Street, Philadelphia, Pennsylvania 19104. 1990.

COPYRIGHT AND INSTRUCTIONAL TECHNOLOGIES: A GUIDE TO FAIR USE AND PERMISSIONS PROCEDURES. Second Edition. R.S. Talab. Association for Educational Communications and Technology, 1025 Vermont Avenue, Suite 820, Washington, D.C. 20005. 1989.

THE COPYRIGHT BOOK: A PRACTICAL GUIDE. Third Edition. William S. Strong. MIT Press, 55 Hayward Street, Cambridge, Massachusetts 02142. 1990.

COPYRIGHT HANDBOOK. Second Edition. Donald F. Johnston. R. R. Bowker and Company, 121 Chanlon Road, New Providence, New Jersey 07974. 1982.

THE COPYRIGHT HANDBOOK: HOW TO PROTECT AND USE WRITTEN WORKS. Stephen Fishman. Nolo Press, 950 Parker Street, Berkeley, California 94710. 1991.

COPYRIGHT LAW: A PRACTITIONER'S GUIDE. Second Edition. Harry G. Henn. Practising Law Institute, 810 Seventh Avenue, New York, New York 10019. 1988.

THE COPYRIGHT PRIMER FOR LIBRARIANS AND EDUCATORS. Mary Hutchings Reed. American Library Association, 50 East Huron Street, Chicago, Illinois 60611. 1987.

EVERY WRITER'S GUIDE TO COPYRIGHT AND PUBLISHING LAW. Ellen M. Kozak. Henry Holt and Company, 115 West Eighteenth Street, New York, New York 10011. 1990.

HOW TO REGISTER A COPYRIGHT AND PROTECT YOUR CREATIVE WORK: A BASIC GUIDE TO THE NEW COPYRIGHT LAW AND HOW IT AFFECTS ANYONE WHO WANTS TO PROTECT CREATIVE WORK. Robert B. Chickering and Susan Hartman. Macmillan Publishing Company, Incorporated, 866 Third Avenue, New York, New York 10022. 1987.

HOW TO PROTECT YOUR CREATIVE WORK: ALL YOU NEED TO KNOW ABOUT COPYRIGHT. David A. Weinstein. John Wiley and Sons, Incorporated, 605 Third Avenue, New York, New York 10158. 1987.

LEGAL CARE FOR YOUR SOFTWARE: A STEP-BY-STEP GUIDE FOR COMPUTER SOFTWARE WRITERS AND PUBLISHERS. Third Edition. Daniel Remer and Stephen Elias. Nolo Press, 950 Parker Street, Berkeley, California 94710. 1987.

MAKE IT LEGAL. Lee Wilson. Allworth Press, 10 East Twenty-third Street, New York, New York 10010. 1990.

MUSICIAN'S GUIDE TO COPYRIGHT. Second edition. J. Gunnar Erickson, Edward R. Hearn and Mark E. Halloran. Charles Scribner's Sons, 866 Third Avenue, New York, New York 10022. 1983.

A PRACTICAL GUIDE TO COPYRIGHTS AND TRADEMARKS. Frank H. Andorka. World Almanac. Distributed by St. Martin's Press, 175 Fifth Avenue, New York, New York 10010. 1989.

RESEARCHING COPYRIGHT RENEWAL: A GUIDE TO INFORMATION AND PROCEDURE. Iris J. Wildman and Rhonda Carlson. Fred B. Rothman and Company, 10368 West Centennial Road, Littleton, Colorado 80127. 1989.

UNITED STATES COPYRIGHT DOCUMENTS: AN ANNOTATED COLLECTION FOR USE BY EDUCATORS AND LIBRARIANS. Jerome K. Miller. Libraries Unlimited, Incorporated, P.O. Box 3988, Englewood, Colorado 80155-3988. 1981.

A WRITER'S GUIDE TO COPYRIGHT. Second Edition. Elizabeth Preston, compiler. Writer, Incorporated, 120 Boylston Street, Boston, Massachusetts 02116. 1990.

THE WRITER'S LAWYER: ESSENTIAL LEGAL ADVICE FOR WRITERS AND EDITORS IN ALL MEDIA. Ronald L. Goldfarb and Gail E. Ross. Times Books/Random House, Incorporated, 201 East Fiftieth Street, New York, New York 10022. 1989.

TEXTBOOKS AND GENERAL WORKS

ADVANCED WORKSHOP ON COPYRIGHT LAW. Richard Dannay. Practising Law Institute, 810 Seventh Avenue, New York, New York 10019. 1990.

CASES AND MATERIALS ON COPYRIGHT. Sheldon W. Halpern, David E. Shipley and Howard B. Abrams. West Publishing Company, 50 West Kellogg Boulevard, St. Paul, Minnesota 55164. 1992.

CASES AND MATERIALS ON COPYRIGHT AND OTHER ASPECTS OF ENTERTAINMENT LITIGATION INCLUDING UNFAIR COMPETITION, DEFAMATION, PRIVACY, ILLUSTRATED. Fourth Edition. Melville B. Nimmer. West Publishing Company, 50 West Kellogg Boulevard, St. Paul, Minnesota 55164. 1991.

CASES ON COPYRIGHT, UNFAIR COMPETITION, AND OTHER TOPICS BEARING ON THE PROTECTION OF LITERARY, MUSICAL, AND ARTISTIC WORKS. Fifth Edition. Ralph S. Brown and Robert C. Denicola. Foundation Press, 615 Merrick Avenue, Westbury, New York 11590. 1990.

CD-ROM LICENSING AND COPYRIGHT ISSUES FOR LIBRARIES. Meta Nissley and Nancy Melin Nelson, Editors. Meckler Corporation, 11 Ferry Lane West, Westport, Connecticut 06880. 1990.

COMPENSATING CREATORS OF INTELLECTUAL PROPERTY: COLLECTIVES THAT COLLECT. Stanley M. Besen and Sheila Nataraj Kirby. Rand Corporation, Institute for Civil Justice, 1700 Main Street, P.O. Box 2138, Santa Monica, California 90406. 1989.

COMPUTER AND HIGH TECHNOLOGY LAW. Pennsylvania Bar Institute, 104 South Street, P.O. Box 1027, Harrisburg, Pennsylvania 17108-1027. 1990.

COMPUTER SOFTWARE 1984: PROTECTION AND MARKETING. Morton David Goldberg. Practising Law Institute, 810 Seventh Avenue, New York, New York 10019. 1984.

CONTEMPORARY COPYRIGHT ISSUES: FOCUS ON 'WORK-FOR-HIRE' DOCTRINE AFTER CCNV V. REID. Jon A. Baumgarten and E. Gabriel Perle. Prentice-Hall, Incorporated, 113 Sylvan Avenue, Englewood Cliffs, New Jersey 07632. 1989.

COPYRIGHT AND DESIGNS LAW: A QUESTION OF BALANCE: THE COPYRIGHT, DESIGNS AND PATENTS ACT 1988. Peter Groves. Graham and Trotman Limited, Sterling House, 66 Wilton Road, London SW1V 1DE, England. 1991.

COPYRIGHT FOR THE NINETIES: CASES AND MATERIALS. Third Edition. Alan Latman, Robert A. Gorman and Jane C. Ginsburg. Michie Company, P.O. Box 7587, Charlottesville, Virginia 22906. 1989.

COPYRIGHT LAW. Neil Boorstyn. Lawyers Co-Operative Publishing Company, Aqueduct Building, Rochester, New York 14694. 1981- . (Annual Supplements).

COPYRIGHT LAW. Robert A. Gorman. Federal Judicial Center. Superintendent of Documents, United States Government Printing Office, Washington, D.C. 20402. 1991.

THE COPYRIGHT LAW: HOWELL'S COPYRIGHT LAW REVISED AND THE 1976 ACT. Fifth edition. Alan Latman. Bureau of National Affairs, 1231 25th Street, Northwest, Washington, D.C. 20037. 1979.

COPYRIGHT LAW IN THE UNITED KINGDOM AND THE EUROPEAN COMMUNITY. Peter Stone. Athlone Press, Atlantic Highlands, New Jersey. 1990.

COPYRIGHT LITIGATION. Richard Dannay. Practising Law Institute, 810 Seventh Avenue, New York, New York 10019. 1983.

COPYRIGHT, PATENTS, AND TRADEMARKS: THE PROTECTION OF INTELLECTUAL AND INDUSTRIAL PROPERTY. Richard Wincor and Irving Mandell. Oceana Publications, 75 Main Street, Dobbs Ferry, New York 10522. 1980.

COPYRIGHT PRIMER. Harry C. Henn. Practising Law Institute, 810 Seventh Avenue, New York, New York 10019. 1979.

COPYRIGHT: PRINCIPLES, LAW, AND PRACTICE. Paul Goldstein. Little, Brown and Company, 34 Beacon Street, Boston, Massachusetts 02108. 1989.

COPYRIGHT PROBLEMS OF SATELLITE AND CABLE TELEVISION IN EUROPE. Marie Helen Pichler. Martinus Nijhoff, Kluwer Academic Publishers, 101 Philip Drive, Assinippi Park, Norwell, Massachusetts 02061. 1987.

COPYRIGHTS IN THE WORLD MARKETPLACE: SUCCESSFUL APPROACHES TO INTERNATIONAL MEDIA RIGHTS. Richard Wincor. Prentice-Hall, Incorporated, 113 Sylvan Avenue, Englewood Cliffs, New Jersey 07632. 1990.

THE ECONOMICS OF INTELLECTUAL PROPERTY IN A WORLD WITHOUT FRONTIERS: A STUDY OF COMPUTER SOFTWARE. Meheroo Jussawalla. Greenwood Publishing Group, Incorporated, 88 Post Road West, P.O. Box 5007, Westport, Connecticut 06881. 1992.

ELECTRONIC AND COMPUTER PATENT LAW. Robert Greene Sterne. Practising Law Institute, 810 Seventh Avenue, New York, New York 10019. 1990.

EXAMINING THE IMPLICATIONS OF THE FEIST AND KINKO'S DECISIONS. I. Fred Koenigsberg. Practising Law Institute, 810 Seventh Avenue, New York, New York 10019. 1991.

FAIR USE AND FREE INQUIRY: COPYRIGHT LAW AND THE NEW MEDIA. Second Edition. John Shelton Lawrence and Bernard Timberg. Ablex Publishing Corporation, 355 Chestnut Street, Norwood, New Jersey 07648. 1989.

THE FAIR USE PRIVILEGE IN COPYRIGHT LAW. William F. Patry. Bureau of National Affairs, Incorporated, 1231 Twenty-fifth Street, Northwest, Washington, D.C. 20037. 1985.

GLOBAL INTELLECTUAL PROPERTY SERIES: PRACTICAL STRATEGIES-TRADEMARK AND COPYRIGHT. Practising Law Institute, 810 Seventh Avenue, New York, New York 10019. 1991.

HOW TO COPYRIGHT LITERARY WORKS: FOR WRITERS AND PUBLISHERS. Second edition. Lee Ward. Lee Ward Institute, Route 2, Box 62, Piggott, Arizona 72454. 1980.

HOW TO COPYRIGHT SOFTWARE. Third Revised Edition. M. J. Salone. Nolo Press, 950 Parker Street, Berkeley, California 94710. 1989.

HOW TO HANDLE BASIC COPYRIGHT AND TRADEMARK PROBLEMS. Richard Dannay. Practising Law Institute, 810 Seventh Avenue, New York, New York 10019. 1989.

INFORMATION LAW AND PRACTICE. Paul Marett. Gower Publishing Company, Old Post Road, Brookfield, Vermont 05036. 1991.

INFRINGEMENT OF COPYRIGHTS. David Goldberg. Practising Law Institute, 810 Seventh Avenue, New York, New York 10019. 1981.

INTELLECTUAL PROPERTIES AND THE PROTECTION OF FICTIONAL CHARACTERS: COPYRIGHT, TRADEMARK, OR UNFAIR COMPETITION? Dorothy J. Howell. Quorum Books, Greenwood Publishing Group, Incorporated, 88 Post Road West, P.O. Box 5007, Westport, Connecticut 06881. 1990.

AN INTELLECTUAL PROPERTY LAW PRIMER. Second edition. Earl W. Kintner and Jack Lahr. Clark Boardman Company, Limited, 435 Hudson Street, New York, New York 10014. 1982.

INTELLECTUAL PROPERTY: PATENTS, TRADEMARKS, AND COPYRIGHTS IN A NUTSHELL. Second Edition. Arthur R. Miller and Michael H. Davis. West Publishing Company, P.O. Box 43526, 50 West Kellogg Boulevard, St. Paul, Minnesota 55164-0526. 1990.

INTRODUCTION TO COPYRIGHT AND TRADEMARK LAW. Richard Dannay. Practising Law Institute, 810 Seventh Avenue, New York, New York 10019. 1987.

LAW AND HIGH-TECHNOLOGY INNOVATION. Aryeh S. Friedman. Butterworth Legal Publishers, 90 Stiles Road, Salem, New Hampshire 03079. 1989.

LAW AND THE SOFTWARE MARKETER. Frederick L. Cooper III. Prentice-Hall, Incorporated, 113 Sylvan Avenue, Englewood Cliffs, New Jersey 07632. 1988.

LAW AND THE WRITER. Kirk Polking and Leonard S. Meranus. Writer's Digest, 9933 Alliance Road, Cincinatti, Ohio 45242. 1985.

THE LAW OF COPYRIGHT. Don R. Pember. William C. Brown Publishers, 2460 Kerper Boulevard, Dubuque, Iowa 52001. 1982.

THE LAW OF GRAY AND COUNTERFEIT GOODS. David Bender and David Gerber. Practising Law Institute, 810 Seventh Avenue, New York, New York 10019. 1987.

LAWYERING FOR THE ARTS. Richard C. Allen. Massachusetts Continuing Legal Education, 20 West Street, Boston, Massachusetts 10119. 1991.

LEGAL AND BUSINESS ASPECTS OF THE MAGAZINE INDUSTRY, 1984. Peter C. Gould and Stephen H. Gross. Practising Law Institute, 810 Seventh Avenue, New York, New York 10019. 1984.

LEGAL AND BUSINESS ASPECTS OF THE MUSIC INDUSTRY: MUSIC, VIDEOCASSETTES, AND RECORDS. Practising Law Institute, 810 Seventh Avenue, New York, New York 10019. 1980.

LITERARY AUTHORSHIP AND THE COMPARATIVE LAW OF COPYRIGHT: A DESCRIPTIVE CULTURAL HISTORY AND AN ARGUMENT FOR SETTING LIMITS TO THEORY. David Saunders. Routledge, Chapman and Hall, 29 West Thirty-fifth Street, New York, New York 10001. 1992.

LITIGATING COPYRIGHT, TRADEMARKS, AND UNFAIR COMPETITION CASES: A COURSE HANDBOOK. Practising Law Institute, 810 Seventh Avenue, New York, New York 10019. 1990.

MODERN COPYRIGHT FUNDAMENTALS: KEY WRITINGS ON TECHNOLOGICAL AND OTHER ISSUES. Ben H. Weil and Barbara Friedman Polansky. Learned Information, Incorporated, 143 Old Marlton Pike, Medford, New Jersey 08055. 1989.

THE NATURE OF COPYRIGHT: A LAW OF USERS' RIGHTS. L. Ray Patterson and Stanley W. Lindberg. University of Georgia Press, Athens, Georgia 30602. 1991.

NEW AND EXTRAORDINARY RELIEF IN INTELLECTUAL PROPERTY CASES. Practising Law Institute, 810 Seventh Avenue, New York, New York 10019. 1985.

OFF-AIR VIDEOTAPING IN EDUCATION: COPYRIGHT ISSUES, DECISIONS, IMPLICATIONS. Esther R. Sinofsky. Copyright Information Services, P.O. Box 1460, Friday Harbor, Washington 98250-1460. 1984.

PATENT PROTECTION FOR COMPUTER SOFTWARE: THE NEW SAFEGUARD. Michael S. Keplinger and Ronald S. Laurie. Prentice-Hall, Incorporated, 113 Sylvan Avenue, Englewood Cliffs, New Jersey 07632. 1989.

PROTECTION FOR DATABASES, COMPUTER PROGRAMS AND RELATED WORKS. Morton David Goldberg. Practising Law Institute, 810 Seventh Avenue, New York, New York 10019. 1984.

THE PROTECTION OF COMPUTER SOFTWARE: ITS TECHNOLOGY AND APPLICATIONS. Second Edition. Derrick Grover, Editor. Cambridge University Press, 40 West Twentieth Street, New York, New York 10011. 1991.

REPRESENTING ARTISTS, COLLECTORS AND DEALERS 1985. Ralph E. Lerner. Practising Law Institute, 810 Seventh Avenue, New York, New York 10019. 1985.

SOFTWARE, COPYRIGHT, AND COMPETITION: THE "LOOK AND FEEL" OF THE LAW. Anthony Lawrence Clapes. Quorum Books, Greenwood Publishing Group, Incorporated, 88 Post Road West, P.O. Box 5007, Westport, Connecticut 06881. 1989.

SOFTWARE PROTECTION: PRACTICAL AND LEGAL STEPS TO PROTECT AND MARKET COMPUTER PROGRAMS. G. Gervaise Davis. Van Nostrand Reinhold Company, Incorporated, 115 Fifth Avenue, New York, New York 10003. 1985.

AN UNHURRIED VIEW OF COPYRIGHT. Benjamin Kaplan. Columbia University Press, 562 West 113th Street, New York, New York 10025.

WHAT EVERY BUSINESS LAWYER NEEDS TO KNOW ABOUT TRADEMARKS, COPYRIGHTS, TRADE SECRETS AND OTHER INTELLECTUAL PROPERTY. Pennsylvania Bar Institute, 104 South Street, P.O. Box 1027, Harrisburg, Pennsylvania 17108-1027. 1990.

YOUR INTRODUCTION TO MUSIC-RECORD COPYRIGHT: CONTRACTS AND OTHER BUSINESS LAW. Walter E. Hurst and William S. Hale. Borden Publishing Company, 2623 San Fernando Road, Los Angeles, California 90065. 1974.

ENCYCLOPEDIAS AND DICTIONARIES

NOLO'S INTELLECTUAL PROPERTY LAW DICTIONARY. Stephen R. Elias. Nolo Press, 950 Parker Street, Berkeley, California 94710. 1985.

DIGESTS, INDEXES, ABSTRACTS, CITATORS

SHEPARD'S UNITED STATES PATENTS AND TRADEMARKS CITATIONS. Second Edition. Shepard's/McGraw-Hill, P.O. Box 1235, Colorado Springs, Colorado 80901. 1988.

ANNUALS AND SURVEYS

COPYRIGHT LAW SYMPOSIUM. Copyright Law Symposium of Composers, Authors, and Publishers. Columbia University Press, 562 West 113th Street, New York, New York 10025. 1939- . Annual.

CURRENT DEVELOPMENTS IN COPYRIGHT LAW. Practising Law Institute, 810 Seventh Avenue, New York, New York 10019. 1982- . Annual.

THIRD ANNUAL U.S. COPYRIGHT OFFICE SPEAKS: CONTEMPORARY COPYRIGHT AND INTELLECTUAL PROPERTY ISSUES. Prentice-Hall, Incorporated, 113 Sylvan Avenue, Englewood Cliffs, New Jersey 07632. 1991.

LAW REVIEWS AND PERIODICALS

AIPLA BULLETIN. American Intellectual Property Law Association, 2001 Jefferson Davis Highway, Suite 203, Arlington, Virginia 22202. Bimonthly. (703) 521-1680.

AIPLA QUARTERLY. American Intellectual Property Law Association, 2001 Jefferson Davis Highway, Suite 203, Arlington, Virginia 22202. Quarterly. (703) 521-1680.

COPYRIGHT. World Intellectual Property Organization, 34 Chemin des Colombettes (Places des Nations), CH-1211 Geneva 20 (Switzerland). Monthly.

COPYRIGHT BULLETIN. United Nations Educational, Scientific, and Cultural Organization, 7 Place de Fontenoy, 75700 Paris. Quarterly.

IIC: INTERNATIONAL REVIEW OF INDUSTRIAL PROPERTY AND COPYRIGHT LAW. Verlag Chemie International, Incorporated, Plaza Center Suite E, 1020 Northwest Sixth Street, Deerfield Beach, Florida 33441.

JOURNAL OF THE COPYRIGHT SOCIETY OF THE U.S.A., New York University Law Center, 40 Washington Square South, New York, New York 10012. Quarterly.

TRADEMARK REPORTER. United States Trademark Association, 6 East Forty-fifth Street, New York, New York 10017. Bimonthly.

NEWSLETTERS AND NEWSPAPERS

CCC REPORT. Copyright Clearance Center, 27 Congress Street, Salem, Massachusetts 01970. Quarterly. (508) 744-3350.

PATENT, TRADEMARK, AND COPYRIGHT NEWSLETTER. Patent, Trademark, and Copyright Law Section of the American Bar Association. American Bar Association, 750 North Lake Shore Drive, Chicago, Illinois 60611. Quarterly.

PIRACY, COUNTERFEITING AND INFRINGEMENT REPORT. Bruce A. Lehman and James L. Bikoff, editors. Law and Business, Incorporated, Harcourt, Brace, and Jovanovich, 855 Valley Road, Clifton, New Jersey 07013. Monthly.

REMARKS: TRADEMARK NEWS FOR BUSINESS. United States Trademark Association, 6 East Forty-fifth Street, New York, New York 10017. Quarterly.

SPA NEWS. Software Publishers Association, 1101 Connecticut Avenue, Northwest, Suite 901, Washington, D.C. 20036. Monthly. (202) 452-1600.

BIBLIOGRAPHIES

COPYRIGHT, DESIGN PROTECTION, AND THE ARCHITECT: PERIODICAL LITERATURE, 1976-1986. Carole Cable. Vance Bibliographies, P.O. Box 229, 112 North Charter Street, Monticello, Illinois 61856. 1987.

PUBLICATIONS ON COPYRIGHT. Copyright Office, Library of Congress, 101 Independence Avenue, Southeast, Washington, D.C. 20540. 1987.

SELECTED BIBLIOGRAPHY OF COPYRIGHT MATERIALS WITH ANNOTATIONS. Paul Lomio and Susan Kuklin. Kuklin and Lomio, Stanford, California. 1984.

DIRECTORIES

THE COPYRIGHT DIRECTORY. Jerome K. Miller. Copyright Information Service, 440 Tucker Avenue, Friday Harbor, Washington 98250-1460. 1990.

ASSOCIATIONS AND PROFESSIONAL SOCIETIES

AMERICAN COPYRIGHT SOCIETY. 345 West Fifty-eighth Street, New York, New York 10019. (212) 582-5705.

AMERICAN INTELLECTUAL PROPERTY LAW ASSOCIATION. 2001 Jefferson Davis Highway, Suite 203, Arlington, Virginia 22202. (703) 521-1680.

AMERICAN SOCIETY OF COMPOSERS, AUTHORS, AND PUBLISHERS. One Lincoln Place, New York, New York 10023. (212) 595-3050.

COPYRIGHT CLEARANCE CENTER. 27 Congress Street, Salem, Massachusetts 01970. (508) 744-3350.

COPYRIGHT ROYALTY TRIBUNAL. Suite 450, 1111 Twentieth Street, Northwest, Washington, D.C. 20036. (202) 635-5175.

COPYRIGHT SOCIETY OF THE UNITED STATES OF AMERICA (INTELLECTUAL PROPERTY). New York University School of Law, 40 Washington Square South, Room 343, New York, New York 10012. (212) 998-6194.

PATENT, TRADEMARK, AND COPYRIGHT SECTION OF THE AMERICAN BAR ASSOCIATION. American Bar Asso-ciation, 750 North Lake Shore Drive, Chicago, Illinois 60611.

SOFTWARE PUBLISHERS ASSOCIATION. 1101 Connecticut Avenue, Northwest, Suite 901, Washington, D.C. 20036. (202) 452-1600.

UNITED STATES TRADEMARK ASSOCIATION. 6 East Forty-fifth Street, New York, New York 10017. (212) 986-5880.

RESEARCH CENTERS, INSTITUTES, CLEARINGHOUSES

COPYRIGHT CLEARANCE CENTER (INTELLECTUAL PROPERTY). 27 Congress Street, Salem, Massachusetts 01970.

INTER-AMERICAN COPYRIGHT INSTITUTE. 1141 Milan Avenue, Coral Gables, Florida 33134.

INTERNATIONAL COPYRIGHT INFORMATION CENTER. Association of American Publishers, 2005 Massachusetts Avenue, Northwest, Washington, D.C. 20036. (202) 232-3335.

INVENTORS WORKSHOP INTERNATIONAL EDUCATION FOUNDATION. HQ, Inventor Center, USA, 3201 Corte Malpaso, Camarillo, California 93010. (805) 484-9786.

LIBRARY OF CONGRESS. Copyright Office, 101 Independence Avenue, Southeast, Washingoton, D.C. 20559. (202) 429-0700.

PTC RESEARCH FOUNDATION. Franklin Pierce Law Center, 2 White Street, Concord, New Hampshire 03301. (603)228-1541.

ONLINE DATABASES

CASSIS. United States Patent and Trademark Office, Office of Patent Depository Library Programs, Crystal Mall, Building 2 - Room 306, Washington, D.C. 20231.

COMPUTERPAT. Pergamon ORBIT Info Line Incorporated, 8000 Westpark Drive, Suite 400, McLean, Virginia 22102.

LEXIS. PATENT TRADEMARK AND COPYRIGHT LIBRARY DATABASE. Mead Data Central, P.O. Box 933, Dayton, Ohio 45401.

LITALERT. Orbit Service, 8000 Westpark Drive, Suite 400, McLean, Virginia 22102.

PATDATA. BRS Information Technologies, 1200 Route 7, Latham, New York 12110.

PHARM PAT. Chemical Abstract Service, 2540 Olentarsy River Road, P.O. Box 3012, Columbus, Ohio 43210.

U.S. PATENTS. Derwent Incorporated, 6845 Elm Street, Suite 500, McLean, Virginia 22101.

USCLASS. Derwent Incorporated, 6845 Elm Street, Suite 500, McLean, Virginia 22101.

WESTLAW, COPYRIGHT AND PATENTS DATABASE. West Publishing Company, P.O. Box 43526, 50 West Kellogg Boulevard, St. Paul, Minnesota 55164.

WPI. Derwent Publications Limited, Rochdale House, 128 Theobalds Road, London, WC 1X 8RP, England.

AUDIOVISUALS

CURRENT DEVELOPMENTS IN COPYRIGHT LAW. Fred Koenigsburg. Practising Law Institute, 810 Seventh Avenue, New York, New York 10019. 1986.

LITIGATING COPYRIGHT, TRADEMARK, AND UNFAIR COMPETITION CASES. Robert G. Sugarman. Practising Law Institute, 810 Seventh Avenue, New York, New York 10019. 1984

COPYRIGHT

COMPUTER-ASSISTED LEGAL INSTRUCTION

COMPUGRAPH V. CHANG. Interactive Video Library, Harvard Law School, Educational Technology Department, 18 Everett Street, Cambridge, Massachusetts 02138. Interactive videodisc.

OTHER SOURCES

CABLE TELEVISION: MEDIA AND COPYRIGHT LAW ASPECTS: REPORTS TO AN ALAI SYMPOSIUM. Herman C. Jehoram. Kluwer Law and Taxation Publishers, 36 West Forty-fourth Street, New York, New York 10036. 1982.

COMPUTER SOFTWARE AND INTELLECTUAL PROPERTY. Congress of the United States, Office of Technology Assessment. Superintendent of Documents, United States Government Printing Office, Washington, D.C. 20402. 1990.

COPYRIGHT LIABILITY OF STATES AND THE ELEVENTH AMENDMENT, JUNE 1988: A REPORT OF THE REGISTER OF COPYRIGHTS. United States Copyright Office, Library of Congress. Superintendent of Documents, United States Government Printing Office, Washington, D.C. 20402. 1988.

TRADEMARK AND COPYRIGHT RESTRICTIONS ON IMPORTATIONS BY CUSTOMS. George Gottlieb. Practising Law Institute, 810 Seventh Avenue, New York, New York 10019. 1978.

UNFAIR COMPETITION, TRADEMARKS, AND COPYRIGHTS: ALI-ABA COURSE OF STUDY MATERIAL. American Law Institute, 4025 Chestnut Street, Philadelphia, Pennsylvania 19104. 1984.

COPYRIGHT OFFICE

STATUTES, CODES, STANDARDS, UNIFORM LAWS

CODE OF FEDERAL REGULATIONS, TITLE 27. Office of the Federal Register, National Archives and Records Administration. Superintendent of Documents, United States Government Printing Office, Washington, D.C. 20402. Annual. (Updated by use of monthly List of Sections Affected and daily Federal Register.)

LOOSELEAF SERVICES AND REPORTERS

COPYRIGHT DECISIONS. Superintendent of Documents, United States Government Printing Office, Washington, D.C. 20402. 1909- .

HANDBOOKS, MANUALS, FORMBOOKS

COMPENDIUM II, COMPENDIUM OF COPYRIGHT OFFICE PRACTICES. Library of Congress, Copyright Office. Superintendent of Documents, United States Government Printing Office, Washington, D.C. 20402. 1984.

RESEARCHING COPYRIGHT RENEWAL: A GUIDE TO INFORMATION AND PROCEDURE. Iris J. Wildman and Rhonda Carlson. Fred B. Rothman and Company, 10368 West Centennial Road, Littleton, Colorado 80127. 1989.

Encyclopedia of Legal Information Sources • 2nd Ed.

DIGESTS, INDEXES, ABSTRACTS, CITATORS

SHEPARD'S UNITED STATES PATENTS AND TRADEMARKS CITATIONS. Shepard's/McGraw-Hill, P.O. Box 1235, Colorado Springs, Colorado 80901. (Bimonthly Supplements).

ANNUALS AND SURVEYS

ANNUAL REPORT OF THE REGISTER OF COPYRIGHTS. Library of Congress. Superintendent of Documents, United States Government Printing Office, Washington, D.C. 20402. Annual.

THIRD ANNUAL U.S. COPYRIGHT OFFICE SPEAKS: CONTEMPORARY COPYRIGHT AND INTELLECTUAL PROPERTY ISSUES. Jon A. Baumgarten, E. Gabriel Perle and Dorothy Schrader. Prentice-Hall, Incorporated, 113 Sylvan Avenue, Englewood Cliffs, New Jersey 07632. 1991.

ONLINE DATABASES

LEXIS, FEDERAL PATENT TRADEMARK AND COPYRIGHT LIBRARY. Mead Data Central, P.O. Box 933, Dayton, Ohio 45401.

WESTLAW, COPYRIGHT AND PATENT DATABASE. West Publishing Company, P.O. Box 64526, 50 West Kellogg Boulevard, St. Paul, Minnesota 55164-0526.

CORONERS AND MEDICAL EXAMINERS
See also: DEATH; MEDICAL JURISPRUDENCE AND MALPRACTICE; PROFESSIONAL ETHICS AND LIABILITY

STATUTES, CODES, STANDARDS, UNIFORM LAWS

UNITED STATES MEDICOLEGAL AUTOPSY LAWS. Third Edition. Cyril H. Wecht. Information Resources Press, Arlington, Virginia. 1989.

LOOSELEAF SERVICES AND REPORTERS

BIOETHICS REPORTER. University Publications of America, Incorporated, 4520 East West Highway, Suite 600, Bethesda 20814. 1984- .

HANDBOOKS, MANUALS, FORMBOOKS

CORONER'S INQUIRIES: A GUIDE TO LAW AND PRACTICE. J.D.K. Burton and D. R. Chambers. Kluwer Law Book Publishers, Incorporated, 36 West Forty-fourth Street, New York, New York 10036. 1985.

DEATH LOG. James Romensko. Police Beat Press, 5526 West Wells Street, Milwaukee, Wisconsin 53208. 1982.

EXAMINER'S RECORDING FORM. Elena Boder and Sylvia Jarrico. Grune and Stratton, c/o Academic Press, Incorporated, 1250 Sixth Avenue, San Diego, California 92101. 1982.

TEXTBOOKS AND GENERAL WORKS

CORONER AT LARGE. Thomas T. Noguchi and Joseph DiMona. Simon and Schuster, Incorporated, 1230 Avenue of the Americas, New York, New York 10020. 1985.

CORONERS: A STATE-BY-STATE SYMPOSIUM OF LEGAL BASES AND ACTUAL PRACTICES. Citizens Forum on Self Government, National Municipal League, 55 West Forty-fourth Street, New York, New York 10036. 1975.

DEATH INVESTIGATION: AN ANALYSIS OF LAWS AND POLICIES OF THE UNITED STATES, EACH STATE AND JURISDICTION. Department of Health, Education, and Welfare, Public Health Services Administration, Bureau of Community Health Services, Rockville, Maryland. 1978.

DEFINING DEATH: A REPORT ON THE MEDICAL, LEGAL, AND ETHICAL ISSUES IN THE DETERMINATION OF DEATH. President's Commission for the Study of Ethical Problems in Medicine and Biomedical Behavioral Research. Superintendent of Documents, U.S. Government Printing Office, Washington, D.C. 20402. 1981.

THE POWERS AND DUTIES OF POLICE OFFICERS AND CORONERS. Robert H. Vickers. Foundation of Criminal Justice Series. AMS Press, Incorporated, 56 East 13th Street, New York, New York 10003. 1975.

A TREATISE ON THE LAW OF SHERIFFS, CORONERS, AND CONSTABLES WITH FORMS. Walter H. Anderson. Fred O. Dennis and Company, Incorporated, Buffalo, New York. 1941.

ENCYCLOPEDIAS AND DICTIONARIES

ENCYLCOPEDIA OF BIOETHICS. Warren T. Reich, editor. Free Press, 866 Third Avenue, New York, New York 10022. 1978- .

LAW REVIEWS AND PERIODICALS

AMERICAN JOURNAL OF FORENSIC MEDICINE AND PATHOLOGY. National Association of Medical Examiners, 1402 South Grand Boulevard, St. Louis, Missouri 63104. (314) 577-8298. Quarterly.

NEWSLETTERS AND NEWSPAPERS

IACME NEWSLETTER. International Association of Coroners and Medical Examiners, County Courthouse, Room 24, Peoria, Illinois 61602. Quarterly.

NATIONAL BOARD EXAMINER. National Board of Medical Examiners, 3930 Chestnut Street, Philadelphia, Pennsylvania 19104. Quarterly. (215) 349-6400.

ASSOCIATIONS AND PROFESSIONAL SOCIETIES

INTERNATIONAL ASSOCIATION OF CORONERS AND MEDICAL EXAMINERS. 6913 West Plank Road, Peoria, Illinois 61604. (309) 697-8100.

NATIONAL ASSOCIATION OF CORONERS AND MEDICAL EXAMINERS. 1402 South Grand Boulevard, St. Louis, Missouri 63104.

NATIONAL ASSOCIATION OF MEDICAL EXAMINERS. 1402 South Grand Boulevard, St. Louis, Missouri 63104. (314) 577-8298.

NATIONAL BOARD OF MEDICAL EXAMINERS. 3930 Chestnut Street, Philadelphia, Pennsylvania 19104. (215) 349-6400.

CORPORATIONS

See also: ASSOCIATIONS AND NON-PROFIT CORPORATIONS; BANKRUPTCY; BUSINESS LAW; CORPORATIONS: CONSOLIDATION AND MERGER; CORPORATIONS: FORMATION; CORPORATIONS: FOREIGN AND MULTINATIONAL; CORPORATIONS: OFFICERS AND DIRECTORS; CORPORATIONS: PRIVATE AND CLOSELY-HELD; CORPORATIONS: TAXATION; FRANCHISING; GOVERNMENT CORPORATIONS; JOINT VENTURES; LIQUIDATION; LOCAL GOVERNMENT; PARTNERSHIPS; PROFESSIONAL CORPORATIONS

STATUTES, CODES, STANDARDS, UNIFORM LAWS

MODEL BUSINESS CORPORATION ACT ANNOTATED. Third edition. Committee on Corporate Law, American Bar Association. Prentice-Hall, Law and Business, 113 Sylvan Avenue, Englewood Cliffs, New Jersey 07632. 1985- .

PRINCIPLES OF CORPORATE GOVERNANCE: ANALYSIS AND RECOMMENDATION: TENTATIVE DRAFT NUMBER TEN. American Law Institute, 4025 Chestnut Street, Philadelphia, Pennsylvania 19104. 1990.

SELECTED CORPORATIONS AND PARTNERSHIP STATUTES, REGULATIONS AND FORMS. West Publishing Company, P.O. Box 43526, 50 West Kellogg Boulevard, St. Paul, Minnesota 55164-0526. Annual.

LOOSELEAF SERVICES AND REPORTERS

THE BUSINESS JUDGMENT RULE. Third edition. Dennis J. Block and others. Prentice-Hall Law and Business, Route 9W, Englewood Cliffs, New Jersey 07632. 1989- . (Periodic supplements).

BUSINESS ORGANIZATIONS WITH TAX PLANNING. Zolman Cavitch. Matthew Bender and Company, Incorporated, 11 Penn Plaza, New York, New York 10001. 1984- . (Quarterly supplements).

CORPORATE CAPITAL RESTRUCTURING: LIQUIDATIONS, REDEMPTIONS AND RECAPITALIZATION. Stanley Hafgendorf. Garland Publishing, Incorporated, 136 Madison Avenue, New York, New York 10016. 1985- . (Periodic supplements).

CORPORATE CAPITAL TRANSACTIONS COORDINATOR. Research Institute of America, 90 Fifth Avenue, New York, New York 10011. 1981- . (Biweekly Supplements).

CORPORATE COUNSEL'S MANAGERIAL GUIDE. W.A. Hancock. Business Laws, Incorporated, 11630 Chillicothe Road, Chesterland, Ohio 44026. 1988- . (Annual supplements).

CORPORATE COUNSELLOR'S DESKBOOK. Third edition. Dennis J. Block and Michael A. Epstein. Prentice-Hall Law and Business, Route 9W, Englewood Cliffs, New Jersey 07632. 1990- . (Periodic supplements).

CORPORATE CRIMINAL LIABILITY. Kathleen I. Brickey. Callaghan and Company, 155 Pfingsten Road, Deerfield, Illinois 60015. 1984- . (Annual supplements).

CORPORATE PRACTICE SERIES. Bureau of National Affairs, Incorporated, 1231 Twenty-fifth Street, Northwest, Washington, D.C. 20037. 1978- . (Periodic supplements).

CORPORATE SECRETARY'S GUIDE. American Society of Corporate Secretaries. Commerce Clearing House, Incorporated, 4025 West Peterson Avenue, Chicago, Illinois 60646. 1988- . (Monthly supplements).

CORPORATE TAXATION. Robert Wood. Research Institute of America, Incorporated, 910 Sylvan Avenue, Englewood Cliffs, New Jersey 07632. 1989- . (Annual supplements).

CORPORATION. Pentice-Hall, Incorporated, Route 9W, Englewood Cliffs, New Jersey 07632. 1986- . (Biweekly Supplements).

CORPORATION FORMS. Research Institute of America, Incorporated, 910 Sylvan Avenue, Englewood Cliffs, New Jersey 07632. 1961- . (Monthly supplements).

CORPORATION LAW GUIDE. Commerce Clearing House, Incorporated, 4025 West Peterson Avenue, Chicago, Illinois 60646. 1959- . (Semi-monthly Supplements).

DELAWARE LAW OF CORPORATIONS AND BUSINESS ORGANIZATIONS: TEXT, FORMS, LAW. R. Franklin Balotti and Jesse A. Finkelstein. Prentice-Hall Law and Business, Route 9W, Englewood Cliffs, New Jersey 07632. 1985- .

DIRECTOR AND OFFICER LIABILITY: INSURANCE AND INDEMNIFICATION. W.A. Hancock. Business Laws, Incorporated, 11630 Chillicothe Road, Chesterland, Ohio 44026. 1988- . (Annual supplements).

FLETCHER CORPORATE PRACTICE DESKBOOK. Harry Golter. Callaghan and Company, 155 Pfingsten Road, Deerfield, Illinois 60015. 1988- . (Annual supplements).

GOING PUBLIC AND THE PUBLIC CORPORATION. Harold S. Bloomenthal. Clark Boardman Company, Limited, 435 Hudson Street, New York, New York 10014. 1986- . (Annual supplements).

LAW OF CORPORATE OFFICERS AND DIRECTORS: INDEMNIFICATION AND INSURANCE. Joseph W. Bishop, Jr. Callaghan and Company, 155 Pfingsten Road, Deerfield, Illinois 60015. 1981- . (Annual supplements.

LAW OF CORPORATE OFFICERS AND DIRECTORS: RIGHTS, DUTIES, AND LIABILITIES. Edward Brodsky and M. Patricia Adamski. Callaghan and Company, 155 Pfingsten Road, Deerfield, Illinois 60015. 1984- . (Periodic supplements).

LAWYER'S BASIC CORPORATE MANUAL. Third edition. Richard E. Deer. American Law Institute-American Bar Association, 4025 Chestnut Street, Philadelphia, Pennsylvania 19104. 1984- . (Periodic supplements).

LEGAL AUDIT: CORPORATE INTERNAL INVESTIGATION. Louis M. Brown and Anne O. Kandel. Callaghan and Company, 155 Pfingsten Road, Deerfield, Illinois 60015. 1990- . (Annual supplements).

LEGAL COMPLIANCE CHECKUPS: BUSINESS CLIENTS. Robert B. Hughes. Callaghan and Company, 155 Pfingsten Road, Deerfield, Illinois 60015. 1985- . (Annual supplements).

MODERN CORPORATION CHECKLISTS. Revised Edition. William Sardell. Research Institute of America, Incorporated, One Penn Plaza, New York, New York 10119. 1982- . (Annual Supplements).

NATIONAL CORPORATION LAW SERIES. Prentice-Hall Law and Business, Route 9W, Englewood Cliffs, New Jersey 07632. 1989- . (Periodic supplements).

O'NEAL'S CLOSE CORPORATIONS, LAW AND PRACTICE. Second edition. F. Hodge O'Neal and Robert B. Thompson. Callaghan and Company, 155 Pfingsten Road, Deerfield, Illinois 60015. 1985- . (Annual supplements).

O'NEAL'S OPPRESSION OF MINORITY SHAREHOLDERS: PROTECTING MINORITY RIGHTS IN SQUEEZE-OUTS AND OTHER INTRACORPORATE CONFLICTS. F. Hodge O'Neal and Robert B. Thompson. Callaghan and Company, 155 Pfingsten Road, Deerfield, Illinois 60015. 1985- . (Annual supplements).

ORGANIZING CORPORATE AND OTHER BUSINESS ENTERPRISES. Revised fifth edition. Chester A. Rohrlich. Matthew Bender and Company, Incorporated, 11 Penn Plaza, New York, New York 10001. 1975- . (Annual supplements).

ORGANIZING THE CORPORATE VENTURE. Jeffrey T. Sheffield and Christian E. Kimball. Commerce Clearing House, Incorporated, 4025 West Peterson Avenue, Chicago, Illinois 60646. 1987- .

PIERCING THE CORPORATE VEIL. Stephen B. Presser. Clark Boardman Company, Limited, 435 Hudson Street, New York, New York 10014. 1991- .

REGULATION OF CORPORATE DISCLOSURE. J. Robert Brown, Jr. Prentice-Hall Law and Business, Route 9W, Englewood Cliffs, New Jersey 07632. 1989- . (Periodic supplements).

S CORPORATION GUIDE. Commerce Clearing House, Incorporated, 4025 West Peterson Avenue, Chicago, Illinois 60646. 1983- .

SECURITIES AND FEDERAL CORPORATE LAW REPORTS. Harold S. Bloomenthal. Clark Boardman Company, Limited, 435 Hudson Street, New York, New York 10014. 1979- . (Monthly Supplements).

SHAREHOLDER DERIVATIVE ACTIONS. Deborah A. DeMott. Callaghan and Company, 155 Pfingsten Road, Deerfield, Illinois 60015. 1987- . (Annual supplements).

SHAREHOLDER LITIGATION. Roger J. Magnuson. Callaghan and Company, 155 Pfingsten Road, Deerfield, Illinois 60015. 1987- . (Annual supplements).

TAX PLANNING FOR DISPOSITIONS OF BUSINESS INTERESTS. Theodore Ness and William F. Indoe. Research Institute of America, Incorporated, One Penn Plaza, New York, New York 10119. 1985- . (Periodic Supplements).

HANDBOOKS, MANUALS, FORMBOOKS

BUSINESS FORMS FROM ALI-ABA COURSE MATERIALS. American Law Institute, American Bar Association Committee on Continuing Professional Education, 4025 Chestnut Street, Philadelphia, Pennsylvania 19104. 1983.

BUSINESS ORGANIZATIONS, WITH TAX ANALYSIS: BUSINESS PLANNING, SOLE PROPRIETORSHIPS, PARTNERSHIPS. Paul Lieberman. (West's Legal Forms, volume one), West Publishing Company, P.O. Box 43526, 50 West Kellogg Boulevard, St. Paul, Minnesota 55164-0526. 1981- . (Annual Supplements).

BUSINESS TRANSFERS: AN ACCOUNTANT'S AND ATTORNEY'S GUIDE. A. S. Goldstein. Ronald Press, distributed by John Wiley and Sons, Incorporated, 605 Third Avenue, New York, New York 10158. 1985- .

THE COMPLETE BOOK OF CORPORATE FORMS. Ted Nicholas. Enterprise Publishing, Incorporated, 725 Market Street, Wilmington, Delaware 19801. 1985- .

CORPORATE AND COMMERCIAL FINANCE AGREEMENTS. Second edition. Dennis J. Block, Alfred H. Hoddinott, Jr. and Michael A. Epstein, editors. Law and Business, Incorporated, 855 Valley Road, Clifton, New Jersey 07013. 1985.

CORPORATE COMMUNICATIONS HANDBOOK: A GUIDE FOR MANAGING UNSTRUCTURED DISCLOSURE IN TODAY'S CORPORATE ENVIRONMENT. Wesley S. Walton and Charles P. Brissman. Clark Boardman Company, Limited, 435 Hudson Street, New York, New York 10014. 1991.

THE CORPORATE COUNSELOR'S DESKBOOK. Dennis J. Block, Alfred H. Hoddinott, Jr. and Michael A. Epstein. Second edition. Law and Business, Incorporated, 855 Valley Road, Clifton, New Jersey 07013. 1982- . (Periodic Supplements).

CORPORATE LAW AND ECONOMIC ANALYSIS. Lucian Arye Bebchuk, Editor. Cambridge University Press, 40 West Twentieth Street, New York, New York 10011. 1990.

CORPORATE SECRETARY'S COMPLETE FORMS HANDBOOK. Miklos S. Nicolson. Prentice-Hall, Incorporated, P.O. Box 500, Englewood Cliffs, New Jersey 07632. 1980.

CORPORATION: FORMS. Prentice-Hall, Incorporated, P.O. Box 500, Englewood Cliffs, New Jersey 07632. 1986- . (Biweekly Supplements).

DEFENDING THE CORPORATION IN CRIMINAL PROSECUTIONS: A LEGAL AND PRACTICAL GUIDE TO THE RESPONSIBLE CORPORATE OFFICER AND COLLECTIVE KNOWLEDGE DOCTRINES. Alan Zarky. Bureau of National Affairs, Incorporated, 1231 Twenty-fifth Street, Northwest, Washington, D.C. 20037. 1990.

FLETCHER CORPORATION FORMS, ANNOTATED. Twelfth Edition. William Fletcher and Cynthia S. Van Swearingen. Callaghan and Company, 155 Pfingsten Road, Deerfield, Illinois 60015. 1980-1990.

FORMS OF BUSINESS AGREEMENTS AND RESOLUTIONS, ANNOTATED, TAX TESTED. Institute for Business Planning, B & P Market, 113 Sylvan, Englewood Cliffs, New Jersey 07632. 1979- .

KEYS TO INCORPORATING. Steven A. Fox. Barron's Educational Series, Incorporated, 250 Wireless Boulevard, Hauppauge, New York 11788. 1989.

THE LAWYER'S BASIC CORPORATE PRACTICE MANUAL. Third edition. Richard E. Deer. American Law Institute, American Bar Association Committee on Continuing Education, 4025 Chestnut Street, Philadelphia, Pennsylvania 19104. 1988.

SHARE VALUATION MANUAL. Roland Gurney. Gower Publishing Company, Old Post Road, Brookfield, Vermont 05036. 1987.

TEXTBOOKS AND GENERAL WORKS

CORPORATE FINANCE AND THE SECURITIES LAWS. Charles J. Johnson, Jr. Prentice-Hall, Incorporated, 113 Sylvan Avenue, Englewood Cliffs, New Jersey 07632. 1990.

CORPORATE RESTRUCTURINGS, REORGANIZATIONS, AND BUYOUTS. Joseph W. Bartlett. John Wiley and Sons, Incorporated, 605 Third Avenue, New York, New York 10158. 1991.

CORPORATIONS. James D. Cox. Sum and Substance Center for Creative Educational Services. Josephson-Kluwer Legal Education Centers, 10101 West Jefferson Boulevard, Culver City, California 90232. 1975.

THE DELAWARE GENERAL CORPORATION LAW: A COMMENTARY AND ANALYSIS. Second edition. Ernest L. Folk, III, Rodman Ward, Jr. and Edward T. Welsch. Little, Brown and Company, 34 Beacon Street, Boston, Massachusetts 02108. 1987.

DELAWARE LAW FOR CORPORATE LAWYERS: RECENT DEVELOPMENTS. A. Gilchrist Sparks, III. Practising Law Institute, 810 Seventh Avenue, New York, New York 10019. 1985.

ECONOMICS OF CORPORATION LAW AND SECURITIES REGULATION. Richard A. Posner and Kenneth E. Scott. Little, Brown and Company, 34 Beacon Street, Boston, Massachusetts 02108. 1981.

FINANCING LEVERAGED BUYOUTS AND ACQUISITIONS. James J. Cunningham and Carl D. Lobell. Practising Law Institute, 810 Seventh Avenue, New York, New York 10019. 1989.

HANDBOOK ON THE LAW OF CORPORATIONS AND OTHER BUSINESS ENTERPRISES. Third edition. Harry G. Henn and John R. Alexander. West Publishing Company, P.O. Box 43526, 50 West Kellogg Boulevard, St. Paul, Minnesota 55164-0526. 1983- . (Periodic Supplements).

HIGH-YIELD BONDS, LEVERAGED BUYOUTS, AND TROUBLED DEBT FINANCING. James E. Spiotto. Practising Law Institute, 810 Seventh Avenue, New York, New York 10019. 1989.

ISRAELS ON CORPORATE PRACTICE. Alan M. Hoffman. Fourth edition. Practising Law Institute, 810 Seventh Avenue, New York, New York 10019. 1983.

THE LAW OF CORPORATE GROUPS: PROCEDURAL PROBLEMS IN THE LAW OF PARENT AND SUBSIDIARY CORPORATIONS. Phillip I. Blumberg. Little, Brown and Company, 34 Beacon Street, Boston, Massachusetts 02108. 1984.

LEGAL CAPITAL: BEING A CONCISE PRACTICAL EXPOSITION WITH ILLUSTRATIVE EXAMPLES ... Third Edition. Bayless Manning and James J. Hanks, Jr. Foundation Press, 615 Merrick Avenue, Westbury, New York 11590. 1990.

THE MODERN CORPORATION AND PRIVATE PROPERTY. Adolf A. Berle and Gardiner C. Means. Transaction Books, Rutgers University, New Brunswick, New Jersey 08903. Reprint of 1932 edition.

PROBLEMS OF PARENT AND SUBSIDIARY CORPORATIONS UNDER STATUTORY LAW OF GENERAL APPLICATION. Phillip I. Blumberg. Little, Brown and Company, 34 Beacon Street, Boston, Massachusetts 02108. 1989.

PROTECTING THE CORPORATE PARENT: AVOIDING LIABILITY FOR ACTS OF THE SUBSIDIARY. Thomas J. Heiden. Practising Law Institute, 810 Seventh Avenue, New York, New York 10019. 1991.

THE PROXY MACHINERY: SOLICITATIONS AND CONTESTS INVOLVING CORPORATE CONTROL ISSUES. Klaus Eppler, and Thomas Gilroy. Practising Law Institute, 810 Seventh Avenue, New York, New York 10019. 1988.

RESPONSIBILITIES OF CORPORATE OFFICERS AND DIRECTORS UNDER FEDERAL SECURITIES LAWS. Fourth Edition. Commerce Clearing House, Incorporated, 4025 West Peterson Avenue, Chicago, Illinois 60646. 1991.

START-UP COMPANIES. Richard D. Harroch, editor. Law Journal Seminars-Press, 111 Eighth Street, New York, New York 10011. 1986- . (Periodic Supplements).

THE STRUCTURE OF POWER IN AMERICA: THE CORPORATE ELITE AS A RULING CLASS. Michael Schwartz, editor. Holmes & Meier Publications, Incorporated, 30 Irving Place, IUB Building, New York, New York 10003. 1987.

TAKEOVER DEFENSES: THE EMERGENCE OF ESOPS, STOCK SWAPS, AND OTHER DEFENSES. Dennis J. Block, William N. Kravitz and Arthur H. Kroll. Prentice-Hall, Incorporated, 113 Sylvan Avenue, Englewood Cliffs, New Jersey 07632. 1989.

TAMING THE GIANT CORPORATION. Ralph Nader and Mark J. Green. W. W. Norton and Company, Incorporated, 500 Fifth Avenue, New York, New York 10110. 1976.

THE TRANSFORMATION OF CORPORATE CONTROL. Neil Fligstein. Harvard University Press, 79 Garden Street, Cambridge, Massachusetts 02138. 1990.

TROUBLED LEVERAGED BUYOUTS. Peter H. Weil. Practising Law Institute, 810 Seventh Avenue, New York, New York 10019. 1989.

ENCYCLOPEDIAS AND DICTIONARIES

ENCYCLOPEDIA OF CORPORATE MEETINGS, MINUTES, AND RESOLUTIONS. Revised edition. William Sardell. Prentice-Hall, Incorporated, P.O. Box 500, Englewood Cliffs, New Jersey 07632. 1986.

FLETCHER CYCLOPEDIA OF THE LAW OF COPRORATIONS. Cynthia Van Swearingen. Callaghan and Company, 155 Pfingsten, Deerfield, Illinois 60015. 1983- . (Annual Supplements).

DIGESTS, INDEXES, ABSTRACTS, CITATORS

SHEPARD'S CORPORATION LAW CITATIONS. Shepard's/McGraw-Hill, P.O. Box 1235, Colorado Springs, Colorado 80901. (Quarterly Supplements).

ANNUALS AND SURVEYS

CORPORATE FILING REQUIREMENTS [A-12] SHEPARD'S LAWYER'S REFERENCE MANUAL. Shepard's/McGraw-Hill, P.O. Box 1235, Colorado Springs, Colorado 80901. 1981- . (Annual Supplements).

INSTITUTE FOR CORPORATE COUNSEL: CORPORATE FINANCIAL TRANSACTIONS: A COURSE HANDBOOK. William E. Huth. Practising Law Institute, 810 Seventh Avenue, New York, New York 10019. Annual.

LAW REVIEWS AND PERIODICALS

ACCA DOCKET. American Corporate Counsel Association, 1225 Connecticut Avenue, Northwest, Suite 302, Washington, D.C. 20036. Quarterly.

CORPORATE PRACTICE COMMENTATOR. F. Hodge O'Neal, editor. Callaghan and Company, 3201 Old Glenview Road, Wilmette, Illinois 60091. Quarterly.

THE CORPORATION JOURNAL. C.T. Corporation System, 1633 Broadway, New York, New York 10019. Monthly.

CORPORATION LAW REVIEW. Research Institute of America, Incorporated, One Penn Plaza, New York, New York 10119. Quarterly.

DELAWARE JOURNAL OF CORPORATE LAW. Delaware Law School of Widener University, P.O. Box 7286, Wilmington, Delaware 19803. (Triannually).

DIRECTORS AND BOARDS. M.L.R. Enterprises, Incorporated, 229 South Eighteenth Street, Philadelphia, Pennsylvania 19103. Quarterly.

JOURNAL OF COMPARATIVE BUSINESS AND CAPITAL MARKET LAW. University of Pennsylvania, 3400 Chestnut Street, Philadelphia, Pennsylvania 19104. Quarterly.

JOURNAL OF CORPORATE TAXATION. Research Institute of America, Incorporated, One Penn Plaza, New York, New York 10119. Quarterly.

JOURNAL OF CORPORATION LAW. University of Iowa College of Law, Iowa City, Iowa 52242. Quarterly.

REVIEW OF LITIGATION. The University of Texas, School of Law, 727 East Twenty-sixth Street, Austin, Texas 78705. Quarterly.

SECURITIES REGULATION LAW JOURNAL. Research Institute of America, Incorporated, One Penn Plaza, New York, New York 10119. Quarterly.

NEWSLETTERS AND NEWSPAPERS

ACCA ALERT. American Corporate Counsel Association, 1225 Connecticut Avenue, Northwest, Suite 302, Washington, D.C. 20036. Eight times per year.

BNA'S CORPORATE COUNSEL WEEKLY. The Bureau of National Affairs, Incorporated, 1231 Twenty-fifth Street, Northwest, Washington, D.C. 20037. Weekly.

BOWNE DIGEST FOR CORPORATE AND SECURITIES LAWYERS. Brumberg Publications, 124 Harvard Street, Brookline, Massachusetts 02146. Monthly.

CORPORATE CONTROL ALERT. American Lawyer Media, L.P., 600 Third Avenue, New York, New York 10016. Monthly.

THE CORPORATE COUNSEL. E.P. Executive Press, Incorporated, P.O. Box 3895, San Francisco, California 94119. Bimonthly.

THE DELAWARE CORPORATE LAW REPORTER. Legal Communications Limited, 1617 John F. Kennedy Boulevard, Suite 1245, Philadelphia, Pennsylvania 19103. Monthly.

FLETCHER CORPORATION LAW ADVISER. Callaghan and Company, 155 Pfingsten Road, Deerfield, Illinois 60015. Monthly.

INTERNATIONAL LAWYER'S NEWSLETTER. c/o Kluwer Publishing, Incorporated, 190 Old Denby Street, Hingham, Massachusetts. Bimonthly.

SECURITIES AND FEDERAL CORPORATE LAW REPORT. Clark Boardman Company, Limited, 375 Hudson Street, New York, New York 10014. Monthly.

BIBLIOGRAPHIES

THE LAW OF GROUPS OF COMPANIES: AN INTERNATIONAL BIBLIOGRAPHY. E. Wymeersch and M. Kruithof, Editors. Martinus Nijhoff, Kluwer Academic Publishers, 101 Philip Drive, Assinippi Park, Norwell, Massachusetts 02061. 1991.

ASSOCIATIONS AND PROFESSIONAL SOCIETIES

AMERICAN ASSOCIATION OF LAW SCHOOLS. Section on Business Associates, One Dupont Circle, Washington, D.C. 20036. (202) 296-8851.

AMERICAN CORPORATE COUNSEL ASSOCIATION. 1225 Connecticut Avenue, Northwest, Suite 302, Washington, D.C. 20036. (202) 296-4522.

COMMITTEE ON CORPORATE LAW, Section on Coporation, Banking and Business Law, American Bar Association, 750 North Lake Shore Drive, Chicago, Illinois 60611.

INTERNATIONAL LAW INSTITUTE. 1615 New Hampshire Avenue, Northwest, Washington, D.C. 20009. (202) 483-7979.

LAW AND ECONOMICS CENTER. George Mason University, School of Law, 3401 North Fairfax Drive, Arlington, Virginia 22201-4498. (703) 841-7171.

RESEARCH CENTERS, INSTITUTES, CLEARINGHOUSES

AMERICAN CORPORATE COUNSEL INSTITUTE. ACCA, 1225 Connecticut Avenue, Northwest, Suite 302, Washington, D.C. 20036. (202) 296-4522.

AMERICAN LAW INSTITUTE. 4025 Chestnut Street, Philadelphia, Pennsylvania 19104. (800) 253-6397.

CANADA - UNITED STATES LAW INSTITUTE. University of Western Ontario, Faculty of Law, London, Ontario, Canada N6A 3K7. (519) 679-2111.

CENTER FOR LAW AND ECONOMIC STUDIES. Columbia University, 435 West One Hundred Sixteenth Street, Box E-2, School of Law, New York, New York 10027. (212) 854-3739.

ONLINE DATABASES

DISCLOSURE ONLINE. Disclosure Information Group, 5161 River Road, Bethesda, Maryland 20816.

LEXIS. DELAWARE CORPORATION LAW LIBRARY FILES. Mead Data Central, 9393 Springboro Pike, Post Office Box 933, Dayton, Ohio 45401.

MOODY'S CORPORATE NEWS -- UNITED STATES. Moody's Investors Service, Incorporated, a subsidiary of the Dun and Bradstreet Corporation, 99 Church Street, New York, New York 10007.

MOODY'S CORPORATE PROFILES. Moody's Investors Service, Incorporated, a subsidiary of the Dun and Bradstreet Corporation, 99 Church Street, New York, New York 10007.

THE REFERENCE SERVICE. Mead Data Central, Incorporated, P.O. Box 933, Dayton, Ohio 45401.

STANDARD AND POOR'S CORPORATE DESCRIPTIONS ONLINE. Standard and Poor's Corporation, 25 Broadway, New York, New York 10004.

STANDARD AND POOR'S REGISTER -- CORPORATE. McGraw-Hill Financial and Economic Information Company (FEICO), 25 Broadway, New York, New York 10004.

VALUE LINE DATABASE II. Value Line, Incorporated, 711 Third Avenue, New York, New York 10017.

COMPUTER-ASSISTED LEGAL RESEARCH

CLOSELY HELD CORPORATIONS. Lewis D. Solomon. Center for Computer- Assisted Instruction, 229 19th Avenue South, University of Minnesota, Minneapolis, Minnesota 55455. Machine-readable data file.

CORPORATE ACQUISITIONS. Thomas L. Hazen. Center for Computer- Assisted Instruction, 229 19th Avenue South, University of Minnesota, Minneapolis, Minnesota 55455. Machine-readable data file.

FUNDAMENTAL CORPORATE TRANSACTIONS AND DISSENTER'S RIGHTS. Lewis D. Solomon and Alan R. Palmiter. Center for Computer-Assisted Instruction, 229 19th Avenue South, University of Minnesota, Minneapolis, Minnesota 55455. Machine-readable data file.

INTRODUCTION TO FIDUCIARY DUTIES. Lewis D. Solomon. Center for Computer-Assisted Instruction, 229 19th Avenue South, University of Minnesota, Minneapolis, Minnesota 55455. Machine-readable data file.

LEGAL CAPITAL. Lewis D. Solomon. Center for Computer-Assisted Instruction, 229 19th Avenue South, University of Minnesota, Minneapolis, Minnesota 55455. Machine-readable data file.

LEGAL SOURCES FOR CORPORATE DISTRIBUTIONS. Lewis D. Solomon. Center for Computer-Assisted Instruction, 229 19th Avenue South, University of Minnesota, Minneapolis, Minnesota 55455. Machine readable data file.

PREVENTING AND HANDLING TROUBLE IN CLOSELY HELD CORPORATIONS. Robert C. Clark. National Practice Institute, 330 Second Avenue South, Minneapolis, Minnesota 55401. Audiotape.

OTHER SOURCES

BASIC CORPORATE PRACTICE. Second Edition. American Bar Association Committee on Continuing Professional Education Second edition. American Law Institute, 4025 Chestnut Street, Philadelphia, Pennsylvania 19104. 1977.

COMMENTARIES ON CORPORATE STRUCTURE AND GOVERNANCE. Donald E. Schwartz, editor. American Law Institute -- American Bar Association, 4025 Chestnut Street, Philadelphia, Pennsylvania 19104. 1979.

CORPORATIONS, CONSOLIDATION AND MERGERS
See also: ANTITRUST LAW

LOOSELEAF SERVICES AND REPORTERS

ACQUISITIONS AND DIVESTITURES. Business Laws, Incorporated, 11630 Chillicothe Road, Chesterland, Ohio 44026. 1990- .

ACQUISITIONS AND MERGERS: NEGOTIATED AND CONTESTED TRANSACTIONS. Simon M. Lorne. Clark Boardman Company, Limited, 435 Hudson Street, New York, New York 10014. 1985- . (Annual supplements).

ACQUISITIONS UNDER THE HART-SCOTT-RODINO ANTITRUST IMPROVEMENTS ACT. Stephen M. Axinn and others. Law Journal Seminars-Press, Incorporated, 111 Eighth Avenue, Suite 900, New York, New York 10011. 1988- . (Periodic supplements).

CORPORATE ACQUISITIONS AND MERGERS. Byron E. Fox and Eleanor M. Fox. Matthew Bender and Company, 11 Penn Plaza, New York, New York 10001. 1986- . (Semiannual supplements).

CORPORATE ACQUISITIONS, MERGERS, AND DIVESTITURES. Lewis D. Solomon. Prentice-Hall, Incorporated, 113 Sylvan Avenue, Englewood Cliffs, New Jersey 07632. 1983- . (Monthly supplements).

SHARK REPELLENTS AND GOLDEN PARACHUTES: A HANDBOOK FOR THE PRACTITIONER. Prentice-Hall, Incorporated, 113 Sylvan Avenue, Englewood Cliffs, New Jersey 07632. 1983- . (Periodic supplements).

TAKEOVER DEFENSE. Fourth Edition. Arthur Fleischer, Jr., Alexander R. Sussman and Henry Lesser. Prentice-Hall, Incorporated, 113 Sylvan Avenue, Englewood Cliffs, New Jersey 07632. 1990- .

TAKEOVERS AND FREEZEOUTS. Martin Lipton and Erica H. Steinberger. Law Journal Seminars- Press, Incorporated, 111 Eighth Avenue, Suite 900, New York, New York 10011. 1978- .

TAX ASPECTS OF BUYING AND SELLING CORPORATE BUSINESSES. Clifton J. Fleming, Jr. Shepard's/McGraw-Hill, P.O.Box 1235, Colorado Springs, Colorado 80901. 1984- . (Annual supplements).

TAX SERVICE FOR CORPORATE ACQUISITONS AND DISPOSITIONS OF BUSINESSES. LaVaughn T. Davis. Mark A. Stepehens, Limited, 10018 Colesville Road, Silver Spring, Maryland 20901. 1974- . (Monthly supplements).

HANDBOOKS, MANUALS, FORMBOOKS

ACQUISITIONS, MERGERS, SALES, BUYOUTS, AND TAKEOVERS: A HANDBOOK WITH FORMS. Fourth Edition. Charles A. Scharf, Edward E. Shea and George C. Beck. Prentice-Hall, Incorporated, 113 Sylvan Avenue, Englewood Cliffs, New Jersey 07632. 1991.

THE ART OF M & A: A MERGER ACQUISITION BUYOUT GUIDE. Stanley Foster Reed. Dow Jones-Irwin, 1818 Ridge Road, Homewood, Illinois 60430. 1989.

BUSINESS ACQUISITIONS DESKBOOK WITH CHECKLISTS AND FORMS. Second Edition. F. T. Davis, Jr. Institute for Business Planning, Incorporated, 113 Sylvan Avenue, Englewood Cliffs, New Jersey 07632. 1981.

THE CORPORATE ACQUISITION PLANNER. Guy D. Kolb, Editor. Executive Enterprises Publications Company, 22 West Twenty-first Street, New York, New York 10010-6904. 1989.

THE HANDBOOK OF INTERNATIONAL MERGERS AND ACQUISITIONS. David J. BenDaniel and Arthur H. Rosenbloom. Prentice-Hall, Incorporated, 113 Sylvan Avenue, Englewood Cliffs, New Jersey 07632. 1990.

HANDBOOK OF MERGERS, ACQUISITIONS AND BUYOUTS. Steven J. Lee and Robert D. Colman. Prentice-Hall, Incorporated, 113 Sylvan Avenue, Englewood Cliffs, New Jersey 07632. 1981.

THE LAWYERS' GUIDE TO TRANSNATIONAL CORPORATE ACQUISITIONS. Dennis Campbell, Editor. Kluwer Law Book Publishers, Incorporated, 36 West Forty-fourth Street, New York, New York 10036. 1991.

MANAGING THE MERGER: MAKING IT WORK. Philip H. Mirvis and Mitchell Lee Marks. Prentice-Hall, Incorporated, 113 Sylvan Avenue, Englewood Cliffs, New Jersey 07632. 1992.

MERGERS AND ACQUISITIONS: A PRACTICAL GUIDE TO TAXATION, CORPORATION, AND SECURITIES LAW. Robert F. Klueger. Executive Enterprises Publications Company, 22 West Twenty-first Street, New York, New York 10010-6904. 1989.

MERGERS AND ACQUISITIONS MANUAL. Simon Partner. Prentice-Hall, Incorporated, 113 Sylvan Avenue, Englewood Cliffs, New Jersey 07632. 1991.

RESEARCH GUIDE TO CORPORATE ACQUISITIONS, MERGERS, AND OTHER RESTRUCTURING. Michael Halperin and Steven J. Bell. Greenwood Publishing Group, Incorporated, 88 Post Road West, P.O. Box 5007, Westport, Connecticut 06881. 1992.

SUCCESSFUL CORPORATE ACQUISITIONS: A COMPLETE GUIDE FOR ACQUIRING COMPANIES FOR GROWTH AND PROFIT. Jerold Freier. Prentice-Hall, Incorporated, 113 Sylvan Avenue, Englewood Cliffs, New Jersey 07632. 1990.

TEXTBOOKS AND GENERAL WORKS

THE ACQUISITION MATING DANCE AND OTHER ESSAYS ON NEGOTIATING. James C. Freund. Prentice-Hall, Incorporated, 113 Sylvan Avenue, Englewood Cliffs, New Jersey 07632. 1987.

ACQUISITIONS AND MERGERS IN A CHANGING ENVIRONMENT. Melvin Katz and Ronald M. Loeb. Practising Law Institute, 810 Seventh Avenue, New York, New York 10019. 1990.

ACQUISITIONS AND MERGERS 1986: TACTICS, TECHNIQUES, AND RECENT DEVELOPMENTS. Melvin Katz and Ronald Loeb, Co-Chairmen. Practising Law Institute, 810 Seventh Avenue, New York, New York 10019. 1986.

ACQUISITIONS AND MERGERS OF HIGH TECHNOLOGY COMPANIES. Gordon K. Davidson, Chairman. Practising Law Institute, 810 Seventh Avenue, New York, New York 10019. 1986.

ACQUISITIONS OF U.S. COMPANIES: A PRACTICAL PRIMER ON THE U.S. FINANCIAL AND LEGAL SYSTEMS AND THEIR TERMINOLOGY. Harvey L. Pitt and Charles M. Nathan. Practising Law Institute, 810 Seventh Avenue, New York, New York 10019. 1987.

ANTITRUST ECONOMICS ON TRIAL: A DIALOGUE ON THE NEW LAISSEZ-FAIRE. Walter Adams and James W. Brock. Princeton University Press, 41 William Street, Princeton, New Jersey 08540. 1991.

APPRAISAL RIGHTS AND FAIRNESS OF PRICE IN MERGERS AND CONSOLIDATIONS. E. Norman Veasey and Jesse A. Enkelstein. Bureau of National Affairs, Incorporated, 1231 Twenty-fifth Street, Northwest, Washington, D.C. 20037. 1984.

BIDDERS AND TARGETS: MERGERS AND ACQUISITIONS IN THE U.S. Leo Herzel and Richard W. Shepro. Basil Blackwell, Incorporated, 3 Cambridge Center, Cambridge, Massachusetts 02142. 1990.

BUYING, SELLING, AND MERGING BUSINESSES. Second Edition. Jere D. McGaffey. American Law Institute-American Bar Association, 4025 Chestnut Street, Philadelphia, Pennsylvania 19104. 1989.

CORPORATE ANTI-TAKEOVER DEFENSES: THE POISON PILL DEVICE. Paul W. Richter. Clark Boardman Company, Limited, 435 Hudson Street, New York, New York 10014. 1987.

CORPORATE MAKEOVER: HOW AMERICAN BUSINESS IS RESHAPING FOR THE FUTURE. Harvey H. Segal. Penguin Books, 375 Hudson Street, New York, New York 10014. 1991.

CORPORATE RESTRUCTURINGS, REORGANIZATIONS, AND BUYOUTS. Joseph W. Bartlett. John Wiley and Sons, Incorporated, 605 Third Avenue, New York, New York 10158. 1991.

CORPORATE TAKEOVERS AND PRODUCTIVITY. Frank R. Lichtenberg. MIT Press, 55 Hayward Street, Cambridge, Massachusetts 02142. 1992.

CORPORATE TAKEOVERS: CAUSES AND CONSEQUENCES. Alan J. Auerbach, Editor. University of Chicago Press, 5801 Ellis Avenue, Chicago, Illinois 60637. 1988.

CORPORATE TAX PLANNING: TAKEOVERS, LEVERAGED BUYOUTS, AND RESTRUCTURINGS. Daniel Q. Posin. Little, Brown and Company, 34 Beacon Street, Boston, Massachusetts 02108. 1990.

DANGEROUS PURSUITS: MERGERS AND ACQUISITIONS IN THE AGE OF WALL STREET. Walter Adams and James W. Brock. Pantheon Books, 201 East Fiftieth Street, New York, New York 10022. 1989.

DEBT, TAXES, AND CORPORATE RESTRUCTURING. John B. Shoven and Joel Waldfogel, Editors. Brookings Institution, 1775 Massachusetts Avenue, Washington, D.C. 20036. 1990.

DETERMINANTS AND EFFECTS OF MERGERS: AN INTERNATIONAL COMPARISON. Dennis C. Mueller. Oelgeschlager, Gunn and Hain, Incorporated, 245 Mirriam Street, Weston, Massachusetts 02193. 1980.

EFFECTIVE TAX STRATEGIES FOR INTERNATIONAL CORPORATE ACQUISITIONS. Philip J. Cooke, Editor. Kluwer Law Book Publishers, Incorporated, 36 West Forty-fourth Street, New York, New York 10036. 1989.

FINANCING LEVERAGED BUYOUTS AND ACQUISITIONS. James J. Cunningham and Carl D. Lobell. Practising Law Institute, 810 Seventh Avenue, New York, New York 10019. 1989.

FRIENDLY MERGERS AND ACQUISITIONS. Edward F. Greene, Harvey L. Pitt. Law and Business/Harcourt Brace. Jovanovich, 1250 Sixth Avenue, San Diego, California 92101. 1986.

THE GREAT MERGER MOVEMENT IN AMERICAN BUSINESS, 1895-1904. Naomi R. Lamoreaux. Cambridge University Press, 40 West Twentieth Street, New York, New York 10011. 1988.

HOSTILE TAKEOVERS: ISSUES IN PUBLIC AND CORPORATE POLICY. David L. McKee, Editor. Praeger Publishers, One Madison Avenue, New York, New York 10010-3603. 1989.

HOW TO DO A LEVERAGED BUYOUT OR ACQUISITION FOR YOURSELF, YOUR CORPORATION, OR YOUR CLIENT. Third Edition. Nicholas Wallner, J. Terrence Greve. Buyout Publications, San Diego, California. 1987.

THE HUMAN SIDE OF MERGERS AND ACQUISITIONS: MANAGING COLLISIONS BETWEEN PEOPLE, CULTURES, AND ORGANIZATIONS. Anthony F. Buono and James L. Bowditch. Jossey-Bass, Incorporated, 350 Sansome Street, San Francisco, California 94104. 1989.

INTEGRATING ACQUISITIONS: MAKING CORPORATE MARRIAGES WORK. James A. Yunker. Praeger Publications, One Madison Avenue, New York, New York 10010-3603. 1983.

INTERNATIONAL LAW OF TAKE-OVERS AND MERGERS: SOUTHERN EUROPE, AFRICA, AND THE MIDDLE EAST. H. Leigh Ffrench. Quorum Books, Greenwood Publishing Group, Incorporated, 88 Post Road West, P.O. Box 5007, Westport, Connecticut 06881. 1987.

INTERNATIONAL MERGERS AND ACQUISITIONS. Terence E. Cooke. Basil Blackwell, Incorporated, 3 Cambridge Center, Cambridge, Massachusetts 02142. 1988.

JOINING FORCES: CREATING AND MANAGING SUCCESSFUL MERGERS AND ACQUISITIONS. Joseph E. McCann and Roderick Gilkey. Prentice-Hall, Incorporated, 113 Sylvan Avenue, Englewood Cliffs, New Jersey 07632. 1988.

THE LAW OF MERGERS, ACQUISITIONS, AND REORGANIZATIONS. Dale A. Oesterle. West Publishing Company, 50 West Kellogg Boulevard, St. Paul, Minnesota 55164. 1991.

LEVERAGED ACQUISITIONS AND BUYOUTS, 1990. Harvey E. Benjamin and Michael B. Goldberg, Co-Chairmen. Practising Law Institute, 810 Seventh Avenue, New York, New York 10019. 1990.

THE LIQUIDATION/MERGER ALTERNATIVE. Michael J. Peel. Avebury, Brookfield, Vermont. 1990.

MEGA-MERGERS: CORPORATE AMERICA'S BILLION-DOLLAR TAKEOVERS. Kenneth M. Davidson. Ballinger Division, HarperCollins Publishers, 10 East Fifty-third Street, New York, New York 10022. 1985.

MERGER. Peter F. Hartz. William Morrow and Company, Incorporated, 105 Madison Avenue, New York, New York 10016. 1985.

MERGER AND COMPETITION POLICY IN THE EUROPEAN COMMUNITY. Alexis Jacquemin. Basil Blackwell, Incorporated, 3 Cambridge Center, Cambridge, Massachusetts 02142. 1991.

MERGER AND JOINT VENTURE ACTIVITIES IN THE EEC: A GUIDE TO DOING BUSINESS UNDER THE NEW REGULATIONS. Mario Siragusa. Practising Law Institute, 810 Seventh Avenue, New York, New York 10019. 1990.

MERGERS, ACQUISITIONS AND DIVESTITURES: A GUIDE TO THEIR IMPACT FOR INVESTORS AND DIRECTORS. Thomas H. Hopkins. Dow Jones-Irwin, Incorporated, 1818 Ridge Road, Homewood, Illinois 60430. 1982.

MERGERS, ACQUISITIONS, AND LEVERAGED BUYOUTS. Robert Lawrence Kuhn, Editor-in-chief. Dow Jones-Irwin, 1818 Ridge Road, Homewood, Illinois 60430. 1990.

MERGERS AND ACQUISITIONS. Alan J. Auerbach, Editor. University of Chicago Press, 5801 Ellis Avenue, Chicago, Illinois 60637. 1988.

MERGERS AND ACQUISITIONS. Gregory P. Marchildon, Editor. E. Elgar Publishers, Brookfield, Vermont. 1991.

MERGERS AND ACQUISITIONS. Patrick A. Gaughan. HarperCollins Publishers, 10 East Fifty-third Street, New York, New York 10022. 1991.

MERGERS AND ACQUISITIONS. Terrence E. Cooke. Basil Blackwell, Incorporated, 3 Cambridge Center, Cambridge, Massachusetts 02142. 1986.

MERGERS AND ACQUISITIONS: GEOGRAPHICAL AND SPATIAL PERSPECTIVES. Milford B. Green. Routledge, Chapman and Hall, 29 West Thirty-fifth Street, New York, New York 10001. 1990.

MERGERS AND ACQUISITIONS IN THE 1980S: ATTACK AND SURVIVAL. Ralph C. Ferrara. Practising Law Institute, 810 Seventh Avenue, New York, New York 10019. 1987.

MERGERS AND ACQUISITIONS: MEETING THE CHALLENGES IN EUROPE AND NORTH AMERICA AFTER 1992. Dennis Campbell and David A. Garbus, Editors. Kluwer Law Book Publishers, Incorporated, 36 West Forty-fourth Street, New York, New York 10036. 1991.

MERGERS AND JOINT VENTURES IN EUROPE: THE LAW AND POLICY OF THE EEC. Frank L. Fine. Graham and Trotman Limited, Sterling House, 66 Wilton Road, London SW1V 1DE, England. 1989.

MERGERS AND MERGER POLICY. James Fairburn and John Kay. Oxford University Press, 200 Madison Avenue, New York, New York 10016. 1989.

MERGERS, RESTRUCTURING, AND CORPORATE CONTROL. J. Fred Weston, Kwang S. Chung and Susan E. Hoag. Prentice-Hall, Incorporated, 113 Sylvan Avenue, Englewood Cliffs, New Jersey 07632. 1990.

MERGERS, SELL-OFFS, AND ECONOMIC EFFICIENCY. David J. Ravenscraft and F.M. Scherer. Brookings Institution, 1775 Massachusetts Avenue, Washington, D.C. 20036. 1987.

NEW DIRECTIONS IN STATE TAKEOVER REGULATIONS: THE SECOND GENERATION STATUTES: ALI-ABA COURSE OF STUDY MATERIAL. American Law Institute, American Bar Association Committee on Professional Education, 4025 Chestnut Street, Philadelphia, Pennsylvania 19104. 1986.

NON-HORIZONTAL MERGERS: LAW AND POLICY. Wayne D. Collins and James R. Loftis, III. American Bar Association, Section of Antitrust Law, 750 North Lake Shore Drive, Chicago, Illinois 60611. 1988.

PERSPECTIVES ON CORPORATE TAKEOVERS. Thomas J. Kopp, Editor. University Press of America, 4720 Boston Way, Lanham, Maryland 20706. 1990.

PRACTICAL MERGER TECHNIQUES FOR BUYING AND SELLING A BUSINESS: SUCCESSFUL TAX AND FINANCIAL STRATEGIES. Albert B. Ellentuck. Commerce Clearing House, Incorporated, 4025 West Peterson Avenue, Chicago, Illinois 60646. 1974.

PRIMER ON THE LAW OF MERGERS: A GUIDE FOR BUSINESSMEN. Earl W. Kintner. Macmillan Publishing Company, Incorporated, 866 Third Avenue, New York, New York 10022. 1973- .

PUBLIC POLICY TOWARD CORPORATE TAKEOVERS. Murray L. Weidenbaum and Kenneth W. Chilton, Editors. Transaction Books, Rutgers University, New Brunswick, New Jersey 08903. 1988.

SUCCESSFUL ACQUISITION OF UNQUOTED COMPANIES: A PRACTICAL GUIDE. Third Edition. Barrie Pearson. Gower Publishing Company, Old Post Road, Brookfield, Vermont 05036. 1989.

TAKEOVER DEFENSES: THE EMERGENCE OF ESOPs, STOCK SWAPS, AND OTHER DEFENSES. Dennis J. Block, William N. Kravitz and Arthur H. Kroll. Prentice-Hall, Incorporated, 113 Sylvan Avenue, Englewood Cliffs, New Jersey 07632. 1989.

TAKEOVER MADNESS: CORPORATE AMERICA FIGHTS BACK. Allan Michel and Israel Shaked. John Wiley and Sons, Incorporated, 605 Third Avenue, New York, New York 10158. 1986.

TAKEOVER MADNESS: THE NEW WALL STREET WARRIORS: THE MEN, THE MONEY, THE IMPACT. Moira Johnston. Arbor House Publishing Company, 1350 Avenue of the Americas, New York, New York 10019. 1986.

TENDER OFFERS: THE SNEAK ATTACK IN CORPORATE TAKEOVERS. Dorman L. Commons. University of California Press, 2120 Berkeley Way, Berkeley, California 94720. 1985.

THE YEAR THEY SOLD WALL STREET. Jim Carrington. Viking Penguin, Incorporated, 375 Hudson Street, New York, New York 10014. 1987.

ANNUALS AND SURVEYS

LEVERAGED ACQUISITIONS. New York Practising Law Institute, 810 Seventh Avenue, New York, New York 10019. 1984.

NEWSLETTERS AND NEWSPAPERS

CORPORATE CONTROL ALERT. Anno-Law Publishing Corporation, 600 Third Avenue, New York, New York 10016. (Monthly).

SECURITIES AND FEDERAL CORPORATE LAW REPORT. Clark Boardman Company, Limited, 435 Hudson Street, New York, New York 10014. (Monthly).

DIRECTORIES

THE MIDDLE-MARKET BUSINESS ACQUISITION DIRECTORY AND SOURCE BOOK. A. David Silver. HarperCollins Publishers, 10 East Fifty-third Street, New York, New York 10022. 1990.

RESEARCH CENTERS, INSTITUTES, CLEARINGHOUSES

INVESTOR RESPONSIBILITY RESEARCH CENTER. 1775 Massachusetts Avenue, Northwest, Suite 600, Washington, D.C. 20036.

ONLINE DATABASES

THE M & A DATA BASE. MLR Publishing Company, Mengers and Acquisitions, 229 South Eighteenth Street, Philadelphia, Pennsylvania 19103.

M & A FILINGS. Charles E. Simon and Company, 1333 H Street, Northwest, Washington, D.C. 20005.

MERGERS AND ACQUISITIONS. Securities Data Company, Incorporated, 62 William Street, Sixth Floor, New York, New York 10005.

COMPUTER-ASSISTED LEGAL INSTRUCTION

CORPORATE ACQUISITIONS. Thomas L. Hazen. Center for Computer- Assisted Instruction, 229 19th Avenue South, University of Minnesota, Minneapolis, Minnesota 55455. Machine-readable data file.

CORPORATIONS, FOREIGN AND MULTINATIONAL
See also: TAXATION, INTERNATIONAL

STATUTES, CODES, STANDARDS, UNIFORM LAWS

MODEL CODE OF CONDUCT FOR TRANSNATIONAL CORPORATIONS. World Peace Through Law Center, 1000 Connecticut Avenue, Northwest, Suite 800, Washington, D.C. 20036. 1977.

LOOSELEAF SERVICES AND REPORTERS

CAPITAL FORMATION AND INVESTMENT INCENTIVES AROUND THE WORLD. Walter H. Diamond and Dorothy B. Diamond. Matthew Bender and Company, Incorporated, 11 Penn Plaza, New York, New York 10001. 1981- . (Periodic supplements).

MULTINATIONAL CORPORATION LAW. Kenneth R. Simmonds. Oceana Publications, Incorporated, 75 Main Street, Dobbs Ferry, New York 10522. 1979- . (Periodic supplements).

MULTINATIONAL CORPORATION LAW: MEXICO AND CENTRAL AMERICA. Michael A. Gordon. Oceana Publications, 75 Main Street, Dobbs Ferry, New York 10522. 1980- . (Annual supplements).

U.S. TAXATION OF INTERNATIONAL OPERATIONS. Prentice-Hall, Incorporated, 113 Sylvan Avenue, Englewood Cliffs, New Jersey 07632. 1973- . (Semimonthly supplements).

TEXTBOOKS AND GENERAL WORKS

EFFECTIVE TAX STRATEGIES FOR INTERNATIONAL CORPORATE ACQUISITIONS. Philip J. Cooke, Editor. Kluwer Law Book Publishers, Incorporated, 36 West Forty-fourth Street, New York, New York 10036. 1989.

EUROPE AND 1992: THE CHALLENGE FOR AMERICAN ENTERPRISE. Dennis Campbell, Editor. Kluwer Law Book Publishers, Incorporated, 36 West Forty-fourth Street, New York, New York 10036. 1989.

THE FINANCE, INVESTMENT AND TAXATION DECISIONS OF MULTINATIONALS. Julian S. Alworth. Basil Blackwell, Incorporated, 3 Cambridge Center, Cambridge, Massachusetts 02142. 1988.

FOREIGN INVESTMENT IN THE UNITED STATES: LAW, TAXATION, FINANCE. Marc M. Levey, Editor. John Wiley and Sons, Incorporated, 605 Third Avenue, New York, New York 10158. 1989.

FUNDAMENTALS OF INTERNATIONAL TAXATION: UNITED STATES TAXATION OF FOREIGN INCOME AND FOREIGN TAXPAYERS. Boris I. Bittker and Lawrence Lokken. Research Institute of America, Incorporated, One Penn Plaza, New York, New York 10119. 1991.

GLOBAL CORPORATE ALLIANCES AND THE COMPETITIVE EDGE: STRATEGIES AND TACTICS FOR MANAGEMENT. Martin K. Starr. Quorum Books, Greenwood Publishing Group, Incorporated, 88 Post Road West, P.O. Box 5007, Westport, Connecticut 06881. 1991.

INTERNATIONAL TAXATION: U.S. TAXATION OF FOREIGN TAXPAYERS AND FOREIGN INCOME. Joseph Isenbergh. Little, Brown and Company, 34 Beacon Street, Boston, Massachusetts 02108. 1990.

INVESTMENT STRATEGIES AND THE PLANT-LOCATION DECISION: FOREIGN COMPANIES IN THE UNITED STATES. Robert W. Haigh. Praeger Publishers, One Madison Avenue, New York, New York 10010-3603. 1989.

THE JAPANESE COMPANY. Rodney Clark. Yale University Press, 302 Temple Street, New Haven, Connecticut 06520. 1979.

JAPAN'S MULTINATIONAL ENTERPRISES. M.Y. Yoshino. Harvard University Press, 79 Garden Street, Cambridge, Massachusetts 02138. 1976.

MULTINATIONAL CORPORATION CHECKLIST FOR SUBSIDIARIES. Leonard J. Theberge. Section of International Law, American Bar Association, 750 North Lake Shore Drive, Chicago, Illinois 60611. 1975.

SUING FOREIGN GOVERNMENTS AND THEIR CORPORATIONS. Joseph W. Dellapenna. Bureau of National Affairs, Incorporated, 1231 Twenty-fifth Street, Northwest, Washington, D.C. 20037. 1988.

TAX RESPONSIBILITIES FOR U.S. CORPORATIONS WITH FOREIGN OWNERSHIP: REPORTING AND RECORDKEEPING. Robert Feinschreiber. John Wiley and Sons, Incorporated, 605 Third Avenue, New York, New York 10158. 1992.

TAXATION OF DOMESTIC SHAREHOLDERS ON UNDISTRIBUTED INCOME OF FOREIGN CORPORATE AFFILIATES: OBJECTIVES, TECHNIQUES, AND CONSEQUENCES: PROCEEDINGS OF A SEMINAR HELD IN NEW YORK IN 1986 DURING THE 40TH CONGRESS OF THE INTERNATIONAL FISCAL ASSOCIATION. Brian J. Arnold, Editor. Kluwer Law Book Publishers, Incorporated, 36 West Forty-fourth Street, New York, New York 10036. 1987.

TRANSFER OF TECHNOLOGY: U.S. MULTINATIONALS AND EASTERN EUROPE. Marilyn L. Liebrenz. Praeger Publications, One Madison Avenue, New York, New York 10010-3603. 1982.

U.S. REGULATION OF THE INTERNATIONAL SECURITIES MARKET: A GUIDE FOR DOMESTIC AND FOREIGN ISSUERS AND INTERMEDIARIES. Edward F. Greene. Prentice-Hall, Incorporated, 113 Sylvan Avenue, Englewood Cliffs, New Jersey 07632. 1991.

BIBLIOGRAPHIES

THE MULTINATIONAL CORPORATION: A GUIDE TO INFORMATION SOURCES. Helga Hernes. Gale Research, Incorporated, 835 Penobscot Building, Detroit, Michigan 48226. 1977.

MULTINATIONAL CORPORATIONS LAW. Oceana Publications, Incorporated, 75 Main Street, Dobbs Ferry, New York 10522. 1979- .

DIRECTORIES

DIRECTORY OF FOREIGN MANUFACTURERS IN THE UNITED STATES. Third edition. Jeffrey S. Arpan and David A. Ricks. Georgia State University Business Publishing, University Plaza, Atlanta, Georgia 30303-3093. 1985.

WASHINGTON'S BEST KEPT SECRETS: A U.S. GOVERNMENT GUIDE TO INTERNATIONAL BUSINESS. Edited by Wiliam A. Delphos. John Wiley and Sons, Incorporated, 605 Third Avenue, New York, New York 10158. 1983.

CORPORATIONS, FORMATION

Encyclopedia of Legal Information Sources • 2nd Ed.   **CORPORATIONS, OFFICERS AND DIRECTORS**

STATUTES, CODES, STANDARDS, UNIFORM LAWS

MODEL BUSINESS CORPORATION ACT ANNOTATED. Third Edition. Prentice-Hall, Law and Business, Incorporated, 113 Sylvan Avenue, Englewood Cliffs, New Jersey 07632. 1985- . (Periodic Supplements).

LOOSELEAF SERVICES AND REPORTERS

CORPORATION LAW GUIDE. Commerce Clearing House, Incorporated, 4025 West Peterson Avenue, Chicago, Illinois 60646. 1959- . (Semimonthly supplements).

THE DELAWARE LAW OF CORPORATIONS AND BUSINESS ORGANIZATIONS. Second edition. R. Franklin Balotti and Jesse A. Finkelstein. Prentice-Hall Law and Business, 113 Sylvan Avenue, Englewood Cliffs, New Jersey 07632. 1990- . (Periodic supplements).

MODERN CORPORATION CHECKLISTS. Second Edition. William Sardell. Research Institute of America, One Penn Plaza, New York, New York 10119. 1982- .

ORGANIZING CORPORATE AND OTHER BUSINESS ENTERPRISES. Fifth Edition. Chester A. Rohrlich. Matthew Bender and Company, Incorporated, 11 Penn Plaza, New York, New York 10001. 1975- . (Annual Supplements).

START-UP COMPANIES: PLANNING, FINANCING, AND OPERATING THE SUCCESSFUL BUSINESS. Richard Harroch. Law Journal Seminars-Press, Incorporated, 111 Eighth Avenue, Suite 900, New York, New York 10011. 1985- . (Periodic Supplements).

HANDBOOKS, MANUALS, FORMBOOKS

CORPORATION FORMS. Prentice-Hall, Incorporated, 113 Sylvan Avenue, Englewood Cliffs, New Jersey 07632. 1961- . (Monthly Supplements).

CORPORATION FORMS, ANNOTATED. Fourth edition. William Meade Fletcher. Callaghan and Company, 155 Pfingsten Road, Deerfield, Illinois 60015.

DESK BOOK FOR SETTING UP A CLOSELY-HELD CORPORATION. Second Edition. Robert Hess. Institute for Business Planning, Incorporated, 113 Sylvan Avenue, Englewood Cliffs, New Jersey 07632. 1986.

EXECUTIVE COMPENSATION STRATEGIES: FOR SMALL AND MEDIUM SIZE BUSINESSES. Paul C. Stein and Lewis Schier. Panel Publishers, 36 Forty-fourth Street, New York, New York 10036. 1985- . (Quarterly Supplements).

HANDBOOK OF BUSINESS STRATEGY. William D. Guth, Editor. Research Institute of America, One Penn Plaza, New York, New York 10019. 1990. (Supplement 1991).

HOW TO FORM YOUR OWN CORPORATION WITHOUT A LAWYER FOR UNDER $75.00. Twentieth Edition. Ted Nicholas. Enterprise Dearborn, Chicago, Illinois. 1992.

HOW TO INCORPORATE: A HANDBOOK FOR ENTREPRENEURS AND PROFESSIONALS. Michael R. Diamond and Julie L. Williams. John Wiley and Sons, Incorporated, 605 Third Avenue, New York, New York 10158. 1987.

HOW TO INCORPORATE AND COUNSEL A BUSINESS. Peter M. Rosenblum. Massachusetts Continuing Legal Education, 20 West Street, Boston, Massachusetts 02111. 1990.

HOW TO INCORPORATE YOUR BUSINESS IN ANY STATE. Hoyt L. Barber. Liberty House, Princeton, New Jersey. 1989.

THE LAWYER'S BASIC CORPORATE PRACTICE MANUAL. Third Edition. American Law Institute - American Bar Association Committee for Continuing Professional Education, 4025 Chestnut Street, Philadelphia, Pennsylvania 19104. 1984.

TEXTBOOKS AND GENERAL WORKS

CHOOSING YOUR CLIENT'S STATE OF INCORPORATION. Pennsylvania Bar Institute, 104 South Street, P.O. Box 1027, Harrisburg, Pennsylvania 17108-1027. 1989.

FORMING CORPORATIONS AND PARTNERSHIPS. John C. Howell. Liberty Publishing Company, Incorporated, 440 South Federal Highway, Suite 202, Deerfield Beach, Florida 33441. 1986.

INCORPORATING YOUR BUSINESS. John Kirk. Contemporary Books, Incorporated, 180 North Michigan Avenue, Chicago, Illinois 60601. 1986.

KEYS TO INCORPORATING. Steven A. Fox. Barron's Educational Series, Incorporated, 250 Wireless Boulevard, Hauppauge, New York 11788. 1989.

LAW OF CORPORATIONS AND OTHER BUSINESS ENTERPRISES. Third Edition. Harry G. Henn and John R. Alexander. West Publishing Company, 50 West Kellogg Boulevard, Post Office Box 64526, St. Paul, Minnesota 55164-0526. 1983- . (Periodic Supplement).

LAW OF CORPORATIONS IN A NUTSHELL. Third Edition. Robert W. Hamilton. West Publishing Company, 50 West Kellogg Boulevard, Post Office Box 64526, St. Paul, Minnesota 55164-0526. 1991.

ORGANIZATIONAL DOCUMENTS: A GUIDE FOR PARTNERSHIPS AND PROFESSIONAL CORPORATIONS. Mark F. Murray. American Institute of Certified Public Accountants, 1211 Avenue of the Americas, New York, New York 10036-8775. 1990.

CORPORATIONS, OFFICERS AND DIRECTORS

LOOSELEAF SERVICES AND REPORTERS

THE BUSINESS JUDGMENT RULE: FIDUCIARY DUTIES OF CORPORATE DIRECTORS. Third edition. Dennis J. Block, Nancy E. Barton, and Stephen A. Radin. Prentice-Hall, Incorporated, 113 Sylvan Avenue, Englewood Cliffs, New Jersey 07632. 1989- .

COUNSELING THE BOARD OF DIRECTORS ON ITS STRUCTURE, FUNCTIONS AND COMPENSATION. Elliott Goldstein. Matthew Bender and Company, Incorporated, 11 Penn Plaza, New York, New York 10001. 1985- .

DIRECTOR AND OFFICER LIABILITY: INDEMNIFICATION AND INSURANCE. John F. Olson and Josiah E. Hatch, III. Clark Boardman Company, Limited, 435 Hudson Street, New York, New York 10014. 1990- .

DIRECTOR AND OFFICER LIABILITY: INSURANCE AND INDEMNIFICATION. W.A. Hacock. Business Laws, Incorporated, 11630 Chillicothe Road, Chesterland, Ohio 44026. 1988- . (Annual supplements).

THE LAW OF CORPORATE OFFICERS AND DIRECTORS: INDEMNIFICATION AND INSURANCE. Joseph W. Bishop, Jr. Callaghan and Company, 155 Pfingsten Road, Deerfield, Illinois 60015. 1982- .

LAW OF CORPORATE OFFICERS AND DIRECTORS: RIGHTS, DUTIES AND LIABILITIES. Edward Brodsky and M. Patricia Adamski. Callaghan and Company, 155 Pfingsten Road, Deerfield, Illinois 60015. 1984- .

PIERCING THE CORPORATE VEIL. Stephen B. Presser. Clark Boardman Company, Limited, 435 Hudson Street, New York, New York 10014. 1991- .

PROTECTING CORPORATE DIRECTORS AND OFFICERS FROM LIABILITY. Jesse A. Finkelstein. Matthew Bender and Company, Incorporated, 11 Penn Plaza, New York, New York 10001. 1989- .

HANDBOOKS, MANUALS, FORMBOOKS

BOARDS OF DIRECTORS AND THE PRIVATELY OWNED FIRM: A GUIDE FOR OWNERS, OFFICERS, AND DIRECTORS. Roger H. Ford. Quorum Books, Greenwood Publishing Group, Incorporated, 88 Post Road West, P.O. Box 5007, Westport, Connecticut 06881. 1992.

THE COMPLETE LEGAL GUIDE FOR CORPORATE OFFICERS AND KEY PERSONNEL. Citizens Law Library, 6 West Loudoun Street, Post Office Box 1745, Leesburg, Virginia 22075. 1980.

D AND O LIABILITY HANDBOOK: LAW, SAMPLE DOCUMENTS, FORMS. Mark A. Sargent. Clark Boardman Company, Limited, 435 Hudson Street, New York, New York 10014. 1990.

DEFENDING THE CORPORATION IN CRIMINAL PROSECUTIONS: A LEGAL AND PRACTICAL GUIDE TO THE RESPONSIBLE CORPORATE OFFICER AND COLLECTIVE KNOWLEDGE DOCTRINES. Alan Zarky. Bureau of National Affairs, Incorporated, 1231 Twenty-fifth Street, Northwest, Washington, D.C. 20037. 1990.

THE DIRECTOR'S AND OFFICER'S GUIDE TO ADVISORY BOARDS. Robert K. Mueller. Quorum Books, Greenwood Publishing Group, Incorporated, 88 Post Road West, P.O. Box 5007, Westport, Connecticut 06881. 1990.

ENCYCLOPEDIA OF CORPORATE MEETINGS, MINUTES, AND RESOLUTIONS. Third Edition. William Sardell, revisor. Prentice-Hall, Incorporated, 113 Sylvan Avenue, Englewood Cliffs, New Jersey 07632. 1986.

THE ESSENTIAL GUIDE TO EFFECTIVE CORPORATE BOARD COMMITTEES. Louis Braiotta, Jr. and A. A. Sommer, Jr. Prentice-Hall, Incorporated, 113 Sylvan Avenue, Englewood Cliffs, New Jersey 07632. 1987.

HOW TO FIND INFORMATION ABOUT COMPANIES: THE CORPORATE INTELLIGENCE SOURCE BOOK. Seventh Edition. Washington Researchers Publishing, 2612 P Street, Northwest, Washington, D.C. 20005. 1988.

THE PARTNERSHIP HANDBOOK. Ellen Lieberman, Editor. New York State Bar Association, One Elk Street, Albany, New York 12207. 1986- .

TEXTBOOKS AND GENERAL WORKS

CONFLICTING INTERESTS: CORPORATE-GOVERNANCE CONTROVERSIES. Fred D. Baldwin. Pennon Press, P.O. Box 206, Carlisle, Pennsylvania 17013-0206. 1984.

THE CORPORATE BOARD: AN EXECUTIVE GUIDE TO MULTINATIONAL LEADERSHIP. R. Duane Hall. Random House, Incorporated, 201 East Fiftieth Street, New York, New York 10022. 1987.

THE CORPORATE BOARD: CONFRONTING THE PARADOXES. Ada Demb and F. Friedrich Neubauer. Oxford University Press, 200 Madison Avenue, New York, New York 10016. 1991.

CORPORATE BOARDS AND NOMINEE DIRECTORS. L.C. Gupta. Oxford University Press, 200 Madison Avenue, New York, New York 10016. 1989.

CORPORATE DIRECTORS AND OFFICERS LIABILITY, INSURANCE, AND RISK MANAGEMENT. Paul Cottrell and Joseph P. Monteleone. Executive Enterprises Publications Company, 22 West Twenty-first Street, New York, New York 10010-6904. 1989.

CORPORATE FINANCE LAW: A GUIDE FOR THE EXECUTIVE. Bruce Wasserstein. McGraw Hill Book Company, 1221 Avenue of the Americas, New York, New York 10020. 1979.

CORPORATE GOVERNANCE AND DIRECTORS' LIABILITIES: LEGAL, ECONOMIC, AND SOCIOLOGICAL ANALYSES ON CORPORATE SOCIAL RESPONSIBILITY. Klaus J. Hopt, Editor. Wallace DeGruyter, Incorporated, 200 Saw Mill River Road, Hawthorne, New York 10532. 1985.

CORPORATE INTERNAL AFFAIRS: A CORPORATE AND SECURITIES LAW PERSPECTIVE. Marc I. Steinberg. Quorum Books, 88 Post Road West, Box 5007, Westport, Connecticut 06881. 1983.

CREATING EFFECTIVE BOARDS FOR PRIVATE ENTERPRISES: MEETING THE CHALLENGES OF CONTINUITY AND COMPETITION. John L. Ward. Jossey-Bass, Incorporated, 350 Sansome Street, San Francisco, California 94104. 1991.

GOVERNING BOARDS: THEIR NATURE AND NURTURE. Cyril O. Houle. Jossey-Bass, Incorporated, 350 Sansome Street, San Francisco, California 94104. 1989.

GUIDELINES FOR DIRECTORS: PLANNING FOR AND RESPONDING TO UNSOLICITED TENDER OFFERS. Committee on Corporate Law, Section of Corporation, Banking and Business Law, American Bar Association, 750 North Lake Shore Drive, Chicago, Illinois 60611. 1986.

INTERCORPORATE RELATIONS: THE STRUCTURAL ANALYSIS OF BUSINESS. Mark S. Mizruchi and Michael Schwartz. Cambridge University Press, 40 West Twentieth Street, New York, New York 10011. 1987.

INTERNAL CORPORATE INVESTIGATIONS. Stephen F. Black, Robert M. Pozin. Matthew Bender and Company, Incorporated, 11 Penn Plaza, New York, New York 10001. 1986- .

LIABILITY OF CORPORATE OFFICERS AND DIRECTORS. Fourth edition. William E. Knepper and Dan A. Bailey. Michie Company, P.O. Box 7587, Charlottesville, Virginia 22906. 1988.

NONPROFIT BOARDS OF DIRECTORS: ANALYSES AND APPLICATIONS. Robert D. Herman and Jon Van Til. Transaction Books, Rutgers University, New Brunswick, New Jersey 08903. 1989.

NONPROFIT ORGANIZATIONS: RIGHTS AND LIABILITIES FOR MEMBERS, DIRECTORS, AND OFFICERS. Elaine M. Hadden and Blaire A. French. Clark Boardman Company, Limited, 435 Hudson Street, New York, New York 10014. 1987.

PAWNS OR POTENTATES: THE REALITY OF AMERICA'S CORPORATE BOARDS. Jay W. Lorsch and Elizabeth MacIver. Harvard Business School Press, Boston, Massachusetts. 1989.

REPRESENTING CORPORATE OFFICERS AND DIRECTORS. Marc J. Lane. John Wiley and Sons, Incorporated, 605 Third Avenue, New York, New York 10158. 1987.

RESPONSIBILITIES OF CORPORATE OFFICERS AND DIRECTORS UNDER FEDERAL SECURITIES LAWS. Fourth edition. Commerce Clearing House, Incorporated, 4025 West Peterson Avenue, Chicago, Illinois 60646. 1991.

THE RULES OF THE GAME: INSIDE THE CORPORATE BOARD ROOM. Thomas L. Whisler. Dow Jones-Irwin, Incorporated, 1818 Ridge Road, Homewood, Illinois 60430. 1984.

STANDARDS FOR REGULATING CORPORATE INTERNAL AFFAIRS. Daniel R. Fischel, editor. Northwestern University School of Law, 37 East Chicago Avenue, Chicago, Illinois 60611. 1981.

THE STRUCTURE OF POWER IN AMERICA: THE CORPORATE ELITE AS A RULING CLASS. Michael Schwartz. Holmes and Meier Publishers, IUB Building, 30 Irving Place, New York, New York 10003. 1987.

DIGESTS, INDEXES, ABSTRACTS, CITATORS

F & S INDEX OF CORPORATIONS AND INDUSTRIES. Predicasts, Incorporated, 11001 Cedar Avenue, Cleveland, Ohio 44106. Weekly.

WALL STREET JOURNAL INDEX. Dow Jones Books, 1818 Ridge Road, Homewood, Illinois 60430. Monthly.

LAW REVIEWS AND PERIODICALS

THE CORPORATE DIRECTOR: THE JOURNAL OF CORPORATE GOVERNANCE. Vanguard Publications, 419 Lentz Court, Lansing, Michigan 48917. (Bimonthly).

NEWSLETTERS AND NEWSPAPERS

THE CORPORATE BOARD. Vanguard Publications, 419 Lentz Court, Lansing, Michigan 48917. 1983- . (Bimonthly).

CORPORATE OFFICERS AND DIRECTORS LIABILITY LITIGATION REPORTER. Andreus Publications, Incorporated, Post Office Box 200, Edgemont, Pennsylvania 19028. 1985- . (Monthly).

DAILY REPORT FOR EXECUTIVES. Bureau of National Affairs, 1231 25th Street, Northwest, Washington, D.C. 20037. (Daily).

DIRECTORIES

STANDARD AND POOR'S REGISTER OF CORPORATIONS, DIRECTORS AND EXECUTIVES. Standard and Poor's Corporation, 25 Broadway, New York, New York 10004. Annual.

ASSOCIATIONS AND PROFESSIONAL SOCIETIES

NATIONAL CONFERENCE GROUP OF LAWYERS AND CORPORATE FIDUCIARIES. American Bar Association, 750 North Lake Shore Drive, Chicago, Illinois 60611.

CORPORATIONS, TAXATION
See also: TAX EXEMPT ORGANIZATIONS; TAX PRACTICE AND ENFORCEMENT; TAX SHELTERS

STATUTES, CODES, STANDARDS, UNIFORM LAWS

INTERNAL REVENUE BULLETIN: CUMULATIVE BULLETIN. United States Department of Treasury, Internal Revenue Code. Superintendent of Documents, United States Government Printing Office, Washington, D.C. 20402. Weekly.

INTERNAL REVENUE CODE. West Publishing Company, P.O. Box 64526, 50 West Kellogg Boulevard, St. Paul, Minnesota 55164-0526. Annual.

FEDERAL INCOME TAX CODE AND REGULATIONS. Commerce Clearing House, Incorporated, 4025 West Peterson Avenue, Chicago, Illinois 60646. Annual.

FEDERAL TAX REGULATIONS. West Publishing Company, P.O. Box 64526, 50 West Kellogg Boulevard, St. Paul, Minnesota 55164-0526. Annual.

LOOSELEAF SERVICES AND REPORTERS

BUSINESS ORGANIZATIONS WITH TAX PLANNING. Zolman Cavitch. Matthew Bender and Company, Incorporated, 11 Penn Plaza, New York, New York 10001. 1983- . (Quarterly supplements).

CONSOLIDATED TAX RETURN. Fourth edition. Jack Crestol and others. Research Institute of America, Incorporated, One Penn Plaza, New York, New York 10119. 1988- . (Annual supplements).

CONSOLIDATED TAX RETURNS: A TREATISE ON THE LAW OF CONSOLIDATED FEDERAL INCOME TAX RETURNS. Third edition. Fred W. Peel, Jr. and others. Callaghan and Company, 155 Pfingsten Road, Deerfield, Illinois 60015. 1984- . (Quarterly supplements).

CORPORATE ACQUISITIONS AND MERGERS. Byron E. Fox and Eleanor M. Fox. Matthew Bender and Company, Incorporated, 11 Penn Plaza, New York, New York 10001. 1968- . (Semiannual supplements).

CORPORATE CAPITAL TRANSACTIONS COORDINATOR: TAXATION, REGULATION, PLANNING. Research Institute of America, 90 Fifth Avenue, New York, New York 10011. 1981- . (Biweekly supplements).

CORPORATE TAX PRACTICE MANUAL. Stephen J. Anderson. Panel Publishers, Incorporated, 36 West Forty-fourth Street, New York, New York 10036. 1989- .

CORPORATE TAXATION. Robert Wood. Research Institute of America, Incorporated, 910 Sylvan Avenue, Englewood Cliffs, New Jersey 07632. 1989- . (Annual supplements).

CORPORATIONS GUIDE. Commerce Clearing House, Incorporated, 4025 West Peterson Avenue, Chicago, Illinois 60646. 1986- .

FEDERAL INCOME TAXATION OF CORPORATE LIQUIDATIONS. Neil M. Goff. Shepard's/McGraw-Hill, P.O.Box 1235, Colorado Springs, Colorado 80901. 1984- . (Annual supplements).

FEDERAL INCOME TAXATION OF CORPORATIONS AND SHAREHOLDERS: FORMS. Third edition. Boris I. Bittker, Meade Emory and William P. Streng. Research Institute of America, Incorporated, One Penn Plaza, New York, New York 10119. 1989- . (Semiannual supplements).

FEDERAL INCOME TAXATION OF CORPORATIONS FILING CONSOLIDATED RETURNS. Herbert J. Lerner. Matthew Bender and Company, Incorporated, 11 Penn Plaza, New York, New York 10001. 1975- . (Annual supplements).

FEDERAL INCOME TAXATION OF LIFE INSURANCE COMPANIES. Second edition. Richard S. Antes. Matthew Bender and Company, Incorporated, 11 Penn Plaza, New York, New York 10001. 1986- . (Annual supplements).

FEDERAL INCOME TAXATION OF S CORPORATIONS. Revised Edition. James S. Eustice and Joel D. Kuntz. Research Institute of America, Incorporated, One Penn Plaza, New York, New York 10119. 1985- .

FEDERAL TAX ASPECTS OF CORPORATE REORGANIZATIONS. Daniel M. Schneider and Paul Hoelschen, Jr. Shepard's/McGraw-Hill, P.O.Box 1235, Colorado Springs, Colorado 80901. 1988- . (Annual supplements).

FEDERAL TAXATION OF CLOSE CORPORATIONS. Edwin T. Hood and John J. Mylan. Callaghan and Company, 155 Pfingsten Road, Deerfield, Illinois 60015. 1990- .

FEDERAL TAXATION OF INSURANCE COMPANIES. Keith A. Tucker and Dennis P. Van Meighem. Prentice-Hall, Incorporated, 113 Sylvan Avenue, Englewood Cliffs, New Jersey 07632. 1983- .

FEDERAL TAXATION OF S CORPORATIONS. Deborah H. Schenk. New York Law Publishers, 111 Eighth Avenue, New York, New York 10011. 1986- . (Periodic supplements).

FEDERAL TAXATION OF S CORPORATIONS AND SHAREHOLDERS. Second Edition. Lorence L. Bravenec. Practising Law Institute, 810 Seventh Avenue, New York, New York 10019. 1988- .

FEDERAL TAXES. Prentice-Hall, Corporation, 113 Sylvan Avenue, Englewood Cliffs, New Jersey 07632. 1919- . (Weekly supplements).

FORMS OF COMMERCIAL AGREEMENTS: ANNOTATED WITH TAX ANALYSIS. Garland Publishing, Incorporated, 136 Madison Avenue, New York, New York 10016. 1986- . (Periodic supplements).

MULTISTATE CORPORATE INCOME TAX GUIDE. Commerce Clearing House, Incorporated, 4025 West Peterson Avenue, Chicago, Illinois 60646. 1986- . (Monthly supplements).

ORGANIZING CORPORATE AND OTHER BUSINESS ENTERPRISES. Fifth Edition. Chester Rohrlich. Matthew Bender and Company, Incorporated, 11 Penn Plaza, New York, New York 10001. 1975- . (Annual supplements).

THE S CORPORATION: PLANNING AND OPERATION. Irving Schreiber and Sydney S. Traum. Panel Publishers, Incorporated, 36 West Forty-fourth Street, New York, New York 10036. 1983- .

S CORPORATION TAX PRACTICE MANUAL. Ira Fox. Panel Publishers, Incorporated, 36 West Forty-fourth Street, New York, New York 10036. 1989- .

S CORPORATIONS GUIDE. Edward C. Foth and Ted D. Englebrecht. Commerce Clearing House, Incorporated, 4025 West Peterson Avenue, Chicago, Illinois 60646. 1983- .

S CORPORATIONS: STATE LAW AND TAXATION. James Edward Maule. Callaghan and Company, 155 Pfingsten Road, Deerfield, Illinois 60015. 1989- .

S CORPORATIONS: TAX CHOICES FOR BUSINESS PLANNING: EXPLANATION, LAW AND REGULATIONS, LEGISLATIVE HISTORY, CASES AND RULINGS. Prentice-Hall, Incorporated, 113 Sylvan Avenue, Englewood Cliffs, New Jersey 07632. 1983- .

STANDARD FEDERAL TAX REPORTS. Commerce Clearing House, Incorporated, 4025 West Peterson Avenue, Chicago, Illinois 60646. 1975- . (Weekly supplements).

STATE CORPORATE INCOME TAX FORMS. Commerce Clearing House, Incorporated, 4025 West Peterson Avenue, Chicago, Illinois 60646. 1975- .

STATE TAX FORMS: CORPORATE. Tax Form Library, 518 West Main Treet, Louisville, Kentucky 40202. 1985- .

SUBCHAPTER S TAXATION. Third Edition. Irving M. Grant and William R. Christian. Shepard's/McGraw-Hill, P.O. Box 1235, Colorado Springs, Colorado 80901. 1990- .

TAX ASPECTS OF BUYING AND SELLING CORPORATE BUSINESSES. J. Clifton Fleming, Jr. Shepard's/McGraw-Hill, P.O.Box 1235, Colorado Springs, Colorado 80901. 1984- .

TAX SERVICE FOR AFFILIATED GROUPS. La Vaughn T. Davis. Stephens, Limited, 10018 Colesville Road, Silver Spring, Maryland 20901. 1988- . (Monthly supplements).

TAX SERVICE FOR CORPORATE ACQUISITIONS AND DISPOSITIONS OF BUSINESSES. La Vaughn T. Davis. Mark A. Stephens, Limited, 10018 Colesville Road, Silver Spring, Maryland 20901. 1978- . (Monthly supplements).

TAX SERVICE FOR S CORPORATIONS AND THEIR SHAREHOLDERS. La Vaughn T. Davis. Mark A. Stephens, Limited. 10018 Colesville Road, Silver Spring, Maryland 20901. 1983- .

TAXATION OF CORPORATE LIQUIDATIONS. Robert W. Wood. Research Institute of America, Incorporated, 910 Sylvan Avenue, Englewood Cliffs, New Jersey 07632. 1987- . (Semiannual supplements).

TAXATION OF FINANCIAL INSTITUTIONS: COMMERCIAL BANKS, THRIFT INSTITUTIONS. Henry W. Schmidt. Matthew Bender and Company, Incorporated, 11 Penn Plaza, New York, New York 10001. 1983- .

TAXATION OF THE CLOSELY HELD CORPORATION. Fourth Edition. Theodore Ness and Eugene L. Vogel. Research Institute of America, Incorporated, One Penn Plaza, New York, New York 10119. 1986- .

UNITED STATES TAXATION OF INTERNATIONAL OPERATIONS. Prentice-Hall, Incorporated, 113 Sylvan Avenue, Englewood Cliffs, New Jersey 07632. 1975- .

HANDBOOKS, MANUALS, FORMBOOKS

THE CLOSELY HELD CORPORATION DESK BOOK: 1987 TAX PLANNING UPDATE. Panel Publishers, Incorporated, 36 West Forty-fourth Street, New York, New York 10036. 1987.

THE CLOSELY HELD CORPORATION TAX WORKBOOK. Stephen J. Anderson. Panel Publishers, Incorporated, 36 West Forty-fourth Street, New York, New York 10036. 1989.

CORPORATION, PARTNERSHIP, FIDUCIARY FILLED-IN TAX RETURN FORMS. Commerce Clearing House, Incorporated, 4025 West Peterson Avenue, Chicago, Illinois 60646. 1989.

CURRENT LEGAL FORMS WITH TAX ANALYSIS. Jacob Rabkin and Mark H. Johnson. Matthew Bender and Company, Incorporated, 11 Penn Plaza, New York, New York 10001. 1985- .

FEDERAL TAX HANDBOOK. Prentice-Hall, Incorporated, 113 Sylvan Avenue, Englewood Cliffs, New Jersey 07632. 1988.

FORMS OF COMMERCIAL AGREEMENTS: ANNOTATED WITH TAX ANALYSIS. Garland Publishing, Incorporated, 136 Madison Avenue, New York, New York 10016. 1986.

HANDBOOK OF UNITARY BUSINESS TAXATION MATERIALS, 1985. Multistate Tax Commission, 1790 Thirtieth Street, Suite 130, Boulder, Colorado 80301. 1985.

KAHN'S HANDBOOK ON CORPORATE TAXATION. Third Edition. Douglas A. Kahn. West Publishing Company, P.O. Box 64526, 50 West Kellogg Boulevard, St. Paul, Minnesota 55164-0526. 1981. (1983 Supplement).

PROFESSIONAL CORPORATIONS AND SMALL BUSINESSES AFTER THE TAX REFORM ACT OF 1984: AN ADVANCED TAX AND BUSINESS PLANNING PROGRAM. Stephen H. Paley, et al. Practising Law Institute, 810 Seventh Avenue, New York, New York 10019. 1984.

THE S CORPORATION WORKBOOK. Panel Publishers, Incorporated, 36 West Forty-fourth Street, New York, New York 10036. 1986.

TAX MANUAL FOR CORPORATE LIQUIDATIONS, REDEMPTIONS, AND ESTATE PLANNING RECAPITALIZATIONS. Stanley Hagendorf. Garland Publishing, Incorporated, 136 Madison Avenue, New York, New York 10016. 1984.

TAX STRATEGIES FOR LEVERAGED BUYOUTS AND OTHER CORPORATE ACQUISITIONS. Louis F. Freeman, et al. Practising Law Institute, 810 Seventh Avenue, New York, New York 10019. 1990.

TEXTBOOKS AND GENERAL WORKS

ACQUISITIONS, DIVESTITURES, AND CORPORATE JOINT VENTURES: AN ACCOUNTING, TAX AND SYSTEMS GUIDE FOR THE FINANCIAL PROFESSIONAL. Joseph M. Morris. John Wiley and Sons, Incorporated, 605 Third Avenue, New York, New York 10158. 1984.

BASIC CORPORATE TAXATION. Third Edition. Douglas A. Kahn. West Publishing Company, P.O. Box 64526, 50 West Kellogg Boulevard, St. Paul, Minnesota 55164-0526. 1981.

CASES AND MATERIALS ON FUNDAMENTALS OF CORPORATE TAXATION. Third Edition. Stephen A. Lind. Foundation Press, 615 Merrick Avenue, Westbury, New York 11590. 1991.

CORPORATE AND PARTNERSHIP TAXATION. Stephen Schwarz and Daniel J. Lathrope. West Publishing Company, 50 West Kellogg Boulevard, St. Paul, Minnesota 55164. 1991.

CORPORATE AND TAX ASPECTS OF CLOSELY HELD CORPORATIONS. William H. Painter. Little, Brown, and Company, 34 Beacon Street, Boston, Massachusetts 02108. 1981.

CORPORATE FINANCIAL POLICY AND TAXATION. Mariateresa Fiocca. Dartmouth, Brookfield, Vermont. 1990.

CORPORATE TAX PLANNING: TAKEOVERS, LEVERAGED BUYOUTS, AND RESTRUCTURINGS. Daniel Q. Posin. Little, Brown and Company, 34 Beacon Street, Boston, Massachusetts 02108. 1990.

CORPORATE TAXATION. James T. O'Hara. Shepard's/McGraw-Hill, P.O. Box 1235, Colorado Springs, Colorado 80901. 1992.

CORPORATE TAXATION. Third Edition. Douglas A. Kahn and Pamela B. Gann. West Publishing Company, 50 West Kellogg Boulevard, St. Paul, Minnesota 55164. 1989.

DEVELOPMENTS IN CORPORATE TAX ACCOUNTING. James P. Fuller, Chairman. Practising Law Institute, 810 Seventh Avenue, New York, New York 10019. 1985.

DIFFERENCES IN TAX TREATMENT OF FOREIGN INVESTORS: DOMESTIC SUBSIDIARIES AND DOMESTIC BRANCHES. John I. Forry, Editor. Kluwer Law Book Publishers, Incorporated, 36 West Forty-fourth Street, New York, New York 10036. 1984.

EFFECTIVE TAX STRATEGIES FOR INTERNATIONAL CORPORATE ACQUISITIONS. Philip J. Cooke, Editor. Kluwer Law Book Publishers, Incorporated, 36 West Forty-fourth Street, New York, New York 10036. 1989.

FEDERAL CORPORATE TAXATION. Second Edition. Howard E. Abrams and Richard L. Doernberg. Foundation Press, 615 Merrick Avenue, Westbury, New York 11590. 1990.

FEDERAL INCOME TAXATION OF BUSINESS ORGANIZATIONS. Paul R. McDaniel. Foundation Press, 615 Merrick Avenue, Westbury, New York 11590.

FEDERAL INCOME TAXATION OF CORPORATE ENTERPRISE. Third Edition. Bernard Wolfman. Little, Brown and Company, 34 Beacon Street, Boston, Massachusetts 02108. 1990.

FEDERAL INCOME TAXATION OF CORPORATIONS. Sixth Edition. Herrick K. Lidstone, Jr., William N. Krems and Richard B. Robinson. American Law Institute-American Bar Association, 4025 Chestnut Street, Philadelphia, Pennsylvania 19104. 1989.

FEDERAL INCOME TAXATION OF CORPORATIONS AND SHAREHOLDERS. Fifth Edition. Boris I. Bittker and James S. Eustice. Research Institute of America, Incorporated, One Penn Plaza, New York, New York 10119. 1987.

FEDERAL INCOME TAXATION OF CORPORATIONS AND STOCKHOLDERS IN A NUTSHELL. Third Edition. Peter P. Weidenbruch, Jr. and Karen C. Burke. West Publishing Company, 50 West Kellogg Boulevard, St. Paul, Minnesota 55164. 1989.

FEDERAL TAXATION OF CORPORATIONS. Second Edition. John L. Kramer, Susan L. Nordhauser. Prentice-Hall, Incorporated, 113 Sylvan Avenue, Englewood Cliffs, New Jersey 07632. 1989.

FEDERAL TAXATION OF CORPORATIONS, PARTNERSHIPS, AND THEIR OWNERS. William C. Holmes. Commerce Clearing House, Incorporated, 4025 West Peterson Avenue, Chicago, Illinois 60646. 1989.

FOREIGN INVESTMENT IN THE UNITED STATES: LAW, TAXATION, FINANCE. Marc M. Levey, Editor. John Wiley and Sons, Incorporated, 605 Third Avenue, New York, New York 10158. 1989.

FOREIGN SALES CORPORATIONS UNDER THE TAX REFORM ACT OF 1984. Commerce Clearing House, Incorporated, 4025 West Peterson Avenue, Chicago, Illinois 60646. 1985.

FUNDAMENTALS OF CORPORATE TAXATION: AVOIDING TRAPS FOR THE UNWARY. Massachusetts Continuing Legal Education, 20 West Street, Boston, Massachusetts 02111. 1988.

FUNDAMENTALS OF INTERNATIONAL TAXATION: U.S. TAXATION OF FOREIGN INCOME AND FOREIGN TAXPAYERS. Boris I. Bittker and Lawrence Lokken. Research Institute of America, Incorporated, One Penn Plaza, New York, New York 10119. 1991.

INTERNATIONAL CORPORATE TAXATION. Phillip F. Postelwaite. Shepard's/McGraw-Hill, P.O. Box 1235, Colorado Springs, Colorado 80901. 1980.

INTERNATIONAL TAXATION IN A NUTSHELL. Richard L. Doernberg. West Publishing Company, 50 West Kellogg Boulevard, St. Paul, Minnesota 55164. 1989.

INTERNATIONAL TAXATION: U.S. TAXATION OF FOREIGN TAXPAYERS AND FOREIGN INCOME. Joseph Isenbergh. Little, Brown and Company, 34 Beacon Street, Boston, Massachusetts 02108. 1990.

MANAGER'S GUIDE TO CORPORATE TAX. William Ruland. John Wiley and Sons, Incorporated, 605 Third Avenue, New York, New York 10158. 1984.

PARTNERSHIP AND S CORPORATION: TAX PLANNING GUIDE. Bruce K. Benesh and M. Kevin Bryant. Panel Publishers, Incorporated, 36 West Forty-fourth Street, New York, New York 10036. 1990.

PRENTICE-HALL'S TAX PRACTICE PROBLEMS FOR CORPORATIONS AND PARTNERSHIPS. Debra Garvin. Prentice-Hall, Incorporated, 113 Sylvan Avenue, Englewood Cliffs, New Jersey 07632. 1990.

PROFESSIONAL CORPORATIONS AND SMALL BUSINESSES AFTER THE TAX REFORM ACT OF 1984. Stephen H. Paley, Chairman. Practising Law Institute, 810 Seventh Avenue, New York, New York 10019. 1984.

SHIFTING THE BURDEN: THE STRUGGLE OVER GROWTH AND CORPORATE TAXATION. Cathie J. Martin. University of Chicago Press, 5801 Ellis Avenue, Chicago, Illinois 60637. 1991.

START-UP COMPANIES: PLANNING, FINANCING AND OPERATING THE SUCCESSFUL BUSINESS. Richard D. Harroch. Law Journal - Seminars Press, Incorporated, 111 Eighth Avenue, New York, New York 10011. 1985- .

STATE CORPORATE INCOME TAX: ISSUES IN WORLDWIDE UNITARY COMBINATION. Charles E. Mclure, Jr., Editor. Hoover Institution Press, Stanford University, Stanford, California 94305-6010. 1984.

STATE TAXATION: CORPORATE INCOME AND FRANCHISE TAXES. Jerome R. Hellerstein. Research Institute of America, Incorporated, One Penn Plaza, New York, New York 10119. 1983.

SUBCHAPTER S CORPORATIONS. Mark S. Rothman. Maryland Institute for Continuing Professional Education of Lawyers, Incorporated, 500 West Baltimore Street, Baltimore, Maryland 21201. 1983.

TAKING CASH OUT OF THE CLOSELY HELD CORPORATION: TAX OPPORTUNITIES, STRATEGIES, AND TECHNIQUES. Fourth Edition. Lawrence C. Silton. Prentice-Hall, Incorporated, 113 Sylvan Avenue, Englewood Cliffs, New Jersey 07632. 1988.

TAX ASPECTS OF FORMING AND OPERATING CLOSELY HELD CORPORATIONS. J. Clifton Fleming, Jr. and Janet R. Spragens. Shepard's/McGraw-Hill, P.O. Box 1235, Colorado Springs, Colorado 80901. 1992.

TAX ASPECTS OF LIQUIDATING THE PRIVATELY HELD CORPORATION. Robert A. Rombro and Stephen L. Owen. Maryland Institute for Continuing Professional Education of Lawyers, Incorporated, 500 West Baltimore Street, Baltimore, Maryland 21201. 1983.

THE TAX ON ACCUMULATED EARNINGS. Commerce Clearing House, Incorporated, 4025 West Peterson Avenue, Chicago, Illinois 60646. 1986.

TAX PLANNING TECHNIQUES FOR THE CLOSELY HELD CORPORATION. Third Edition. Edward A. Stoeber. National Underwriter Company, 420 East Fourth Street, Cincinnati, Ohio 45202. 1987.

TAX, SEC, AND ACCOUNTING ASPECTS OF CORPORATE ACQUISITIONS, 1984. Jack S. Levin, Chairman. Practising Law Institute, 810 Seventh Avenue, New York, New York 10019. 1984.

TAX STRATEGIES FOR CLOSELY HELD BUSINESSES. Steven G. Siegel. John Wiley and Sons, Incorporated, 605 Third Avenue, New York, New York 10158. 1991.

TAX STRATEGIES FOR CORPORATE FINANCINGS AND REFINANCINGS: THE NEW FINANCIAL PRODUCTS. Louis S. Freeman. Practising Law Institute, 810 Seventh Avenue, New York, New York 10019. 1987.

TAX STRATEGIES FOR LEVERAGED BUYOUTS AND OTHER CORPORATE ACQUISITIONS. Practising Law Institute, 810 Seventh Avenue, New York, New York 10019. 1990.

TAXATION OF CORPORATE CAPITAL TRANSACTIONS: A GUIDE FOR CORPORATE, INVESTMENT BANKING, AND TAX ADVISORS. Robert Willens. John Wiley and Sons, Incorporated, 605 Third Avenue, New York, New York 10158. 1985.

TAXATION OF CORPORATIONS AND SHAREHOLDERS. Martin Norr. Kluwer Law Book Publishers, Incorporated, 36 West Forty-fourth Street, New York, New York 10036. 1982.

THE TAXATION OF CORPORATIONS AND THEIR SHAREHOLDERS. David J. Shakow. Foundation Press, 615 Merrick Avenue, Westbury, New York 11590. 1991.

DIGESTS, INDEXES, ABSTRACTS, CITATORS

CORPORATE TAX DIGEST. James A. Douglas and James Stanislaw. Research Institute of America, Incorporated, One Penn Plaza, New York, New York 10119. 1987.

FEDERAL TAX ARTICLES: INCOME, STATE, GIFT, EXCISE, EMPLOYMENT TAXES. Commerce Clearing House, Incorporated, 4025 West Peterson Avenue, Chicago, Illinois 60646. 1969- .

FEDERAL TAXES CITATOR. Prentice-Hall, Incorporated, 113 Sylvan Avenue, Englewood Cliffs, New Jersey 07632. 1943- .

INDEX TO FEDERAL TAX ARTICLES. Prentice-Hall, Incorporated, 113 Sylvan Avenue, Englewood Cliffs, New Jersey 07632. 1975- .

SHEPARD'S FEDERAL TAX CITATIONS. Shepard's/McGraw-Hill, P.O. Box 1235, Colorado Springs, Colorado 80901. 1981- .

SHEPARD'S FEDERAL TAX LOCATOR: COMPLETE INDEX TO ALL THE CURRENT SOURCES OF LAW RELATING TO FEDERAL TAXATIONS. Shepard's/McGraw-Hill, P.O. Box 1235, Colorado Springs, Colorado 80901. 1974- .

ANNUALS AND SURVEYS

CORPORATE COUNSEL'S ANNUAL. Matthew Bender and Company, Incorporated, 11 Penn Plaza, New York, New York 10001. 1966- . Annual.

MULTISTATE CORPORATE TAX ALMANAC. 1989 Edition. Panel Publishers, Incorporated, 36 West Forty-fourth Street, New York, New York 10036. (Supplements).

LAW REVIEWS AND PERIODICALS

AKRON TAX JOURNAL. University of Akron School of Law, Akron, Ohio 44325. Annual.

INTERNATIONAL TAX JOURNAL. Panel Publishers, 14 Plaza Road, Greenvale, New York 11548. Quarterly.

JOURNAL OF AGRICULTURAL TAXATION AND LAW. Research Institute of America, Incorporated, One Penn Plaza, New York, New York 10119. Quarterly.

JOURNAL OF CORPORATE TAXATION. Research Institute of America, Incorporated, One Penn Plaza, New York, New York 10119. Quarterly.

JOURNAL OF REAL ESTATE TAXATION. Research Institute of America, Incorporated, One Penn Plaza, New York, New York 10119. Quarterly.

JOURNAL OF STATE TAXATION. Research Institute of America, Incorporated, One Penn Plaza, New York, New York 10119. Quarterly.

JOURNAL OF TAXATION. Research Institute of America, Incorporated, One Penn Plaza, New York, New York 10119. Monthly.

TAX LAW REVIEW. Research Institute of America, Incorporated, One Penn Plaza, New York, New York 10119. Quarterly.

THE TAX LAWYER. American Bar Association, 750 North Lake Shore Drive, Chicago, Illinois 60611. Quarterly.

CORPORATIONS, TAXATION

TAXATION FOR LAWYERS. Research Institute of America, Incorporated, One Penn Plaza, New York, New York 10119. Bimonthly.

TAXES: THE TAX MAGAZINE. Commerce Clearing House, Incorporated, 4025 West Peterson Avenue, Chicago, Illinois 60646. Bimonthly.

VIRGINIA TAX REVIEW. Virginia Tax Review Association, University of Virginia, School of Law, Charlottesville, Virginia 22901. Semiannual.

NEWSLETTERS AND NEWSPAPERS

THE CORPORATE FINANCING STRATEGIST. Faulkner and Gray, 106 Fulton Street, New York, New York 10038. Monthly.

CORPORATION LAW AND TAX REPORT. Research Institute of America, Incorporated, One Penn Plaza, New York, New York 10119. 1967- . Bimonthly.

DAILY REPORT FOR EXECUTIVES. Bureau of National Affairs, Incorporated, 1231 Twenty-fifth Street, Northwest, Washington, D.C. 20037. Daily.

KIPLINGER TAX LETTER. Kiplinger Washington Editors, Incorporated, 1729 H Street, Northwest, Washington, D.C. 20006. Biweekly.

TAX, FINANCIAL AND ESTATE PLANNING FOR THE OWNER OF A CLOSELY HELD CORPORATION. Panel Publishers, Incorporated, 14 Plaza Road, Greenvale, New York 11548. Monthly.

WEEKLY ALERT. Research Institute of America, 90 Fifth Avenue, New York, New York 10011. Weekly.

ASSOCIATIONS AND PROFESSIONAL SOCIETIES

SECTION ON TAXATION, AMERICAN BAR ASSOCIATION. 750 North Lake Shore Drive, Chicago, Illinois 60611. (319) 988-5000.

SECTION ON TAXATION, ASSOCIATION OF AMERICAN LAW SCHOOLS. One Dupont Circle, Northwest, Suite 370, Washington, D.C. 20036. (202) 296-8851.

RESEARCH CENTERS, INSTITUTES, CLEARINGHOUSES

AMERICAN BAR FOUNDATION. 750 North Lake Shore Drive, Chicago, Illinois 60611. (312) 988-6500.

AMERICAN LAW INSTITUTE. 4025 Chestnut Street, Philadelphia, Pennsylvania 19104. (800) 253-6397.

INSTITUTE FOR CONTINUING EDUCATION IN LAW AND TAXATION. New York University, 11 West Forty-second Street, New York, New York 10036.

INSTITUTE FOR LAW AND ECONOMICS. University of Pennsylvania, 3400 Chestnut Street, Philadelphia, Pennsylvania 19104-6204. (215) 898-7852.

INTERNATIONAL TAX PROGRAM. Harvard University, 400 Pound Hall, Cambridge, Massachusetts 02138. (617) 495-4406.

Encyclopedia of Legal Information Sources • 2nd Ed.

TAX INSTITUTE. University of Southern California, Law Center, University Park, Los Angeles, California 90089-0071.

ONLINE DATABASES

BUSINESS TAX REPORT. The Bureau of National Affairs, Incorporated, 1231 Twenty-fifth Street, Northwest, Washington, D.C. 20037.

LEXIS, TAX LIBRARY. Mead Data Central, P.O. Box 933, Dayton, Ohio 45401.

THE SMALL BUSINESS TAX REVIEW. Hooksett Publishing, Incorporated, P.O. Box 895, Melville, New York 11747.

THE TAX DIRECTORY. Tax Analysts, 6830 North Fairfax Drive, Arlington, Virginia 22213.

WESTLAW, TAX LIBRARY. West Publishing Company, P.O. Box 64526, 50 West Kellogg Boulevard, St. Paul, Minnesota 55164-0526.

AUDIOVISUALS

PROFESSIONAL CORPORATIONS AND SMALL BUSINESSES AFTER THE TAX REFORM ACT OF 1984: AN ADVANCED TAX AND BUSINESS PLANNING PROGRAM. Stephen H. Paley, et al. Practising Law Institute, 810 Seventh Avenue, New York, New York 10019. 1984.

TAX STRATEGIES FOR LEVERAGED BUYOUTS AND OTHER CORPORATE ACQUISITIONS. Louis F. Freeman, et al. Practising Law Institute, 810 Seventh Avenue, New York, New York 10019. 1985.

CORRECTIONS
See: PRISONS AND PRISONERS

CORRUPTION, POLITICAL

LOOSELEAF SERVICES AND REPORTERS

ETHICS IN GOVERNMENT REPORTER. Washington Service Bureau, Incorporated, 655 15th Street, Northwest, Washington, D.C. 20005. 1980- . (Monthly supplements)

FOREIGN CORRUPT PRACTICES ACT REPORTER. W.A. Hancock. Business Laws, Incorporated, 11630 Chillicothe Road, Chesterland, Ohio 44026. 1978- . (Quarterly supplements).

HANDBOOKS, MANUALS, FORMBOOKS

POLITICAL CORRUPTION: A HANDBOOK. Arnold J. Heidenheimer, Michael Johnston and Victor T. LeVine, Editors. Transaction Books, Rutgers University, New Brunswick, New Jersey 08903. 1989.

TEXTBOOKS AND GENERAL WORKS

ALICE IN BLUNDERLAND. Jack Anderson and John Kidner. Illustration by Tom Ramey. Acropolis Books, 11741 Bowman Green Drive, Reston, Virginia 22090. 1983.

THE AMERICAN HOUSE OF SAUD: THE SECRET PETRODOLLAR CONNECTION. Steven Emerson. Franklin Watts, Incorporated, 387 Park Avenue, South, Fourth Floor, New York, New York 10016. 1985.

CAPITAL CORRUPTION: THE NEW ATTACK ON AMERICAN DEMOCRACY. Amitai Efzioni. Transaction Publishers, Rutgers University, New Brunswick, New Jersey 08903. 1988.

THE CASE AGAINST CONGRESS: A COMPELLING INDICTMENT OF CORRUPTION ON CAPITOL HILL. Drew Pearson and Jack Anderson. Simon and Schuster, Incorporated, 1230 Avenue of the Americas, New York, New York 10020. 1968.

COCAINE POLITICS: DRUGS, ARMIES, AND THE CIA IN CENTRAL AMERICA. Peter Dale Scott and Jonathan Marshall. University of California Press, 2120 Berkeley Way, Berkeley, California 94720. 1991.

CONGRESSIONAL ETHICS: HISTORY, FACTS, AND CONTROVERSY. Congressional Quarterly Books, 1414 Twenty-second Street, Northwest, Washington D.C. 20037. 1992.

CONTROLLING CORRUPTION. Robert Klitgaard. University of California Press, 2120 Berkeley Way, Berkeley, California 94720. 1987.

CORRUPTION AND POLITICS IN CONTEMPORARY MEXICO. Stephen D. Morris. University of Alabama Press, P.O. Box 870380, Tuscaloosa, Alabama 35487. 1991.

CORRUPTION--CAUSES, CONSEQUENCES, AND CONTROL. Michael Clarke, editor. St. Martin's Press, Incorporated, 175 Fifth Avenue, New York, New York 10010. 1984.

CORRUPTION, DEVELOPMENT, AND UNDERDEVELOPMENT. Robin Theobald. Duke University Press, Box 6697 College Station, Durham, North Carolina 27708. 1990.

CORRUPTION: ITS NATURE, CAUSES, AND FUNCTIONS. Syed Hussein Alatas. Gower Publishing Company, Old Post Road, Brookfield, Vermont 05036. 1990.

DECISIONS FOR SALE: CORRUPTION IN LOCAL LAND-USE AND BUILDING REGULATION. John A. Gardiner and Theodore R. Lyman. Praeger Publications, One Madison Avenue, New York, New York 10010-3603. 1978.

ETHICS IN GOVERNMENT. Paul Howard Douglas. Greenwood Publishing Group, Incorporated, 88 Post Road West, P.O. Box 5007, Westport, Connecticut 06881. 1972, c1952.

ETHICS-IN-GOVERNMENT LAWS: ARE THEY TOO ETHICAL? Alfred S. Neely. American Enterprise Institute, For Public Policy Research, 1150 17th Street, Northwest, Washington, D.C. 20036. 1984.

FALL FROM GRACE: SEX, SCANDAL, AND CORRUPTION IN AMERICAN POLITICS FROM 1702 TO THE PRESENT. Shelley Ross. Ballantine/Del Rey/Fawcett/Ivy Books, 201 East Fiftieth Street, New York, New York 10022. 1988.

FRAUD, WASTE, AND ABUSE IN GOVERNMENT: CAUSES, CONSEQUENCES, AND CURES. Jerome B. McKinney and Michael Johnston. Institute for the Study of Human Issues, 322 South Sixteenth Street, Philadelphia, Pennsylvania 19102. 1986.

GOVERNMENT, ETHICS, AND MANAGERS: A GUIDE TO SOLVING ETHICAL DILEMMAS IN THE PUBLIC SECTOR. Sheldon S. Steinberg and David T. Austern. Quorum Books, Greenwood Publishing Group, Incorporated, 88 Post Road West, P.O. Box 5007, Westport, Connecticut 06881. 1990.

HIGH CRIMES AND MISDEMEANORS: THE TERM AND TRIALS OF FORMER GOVERNOR EVAN MECHAM. Ronald J. Watkins. William Morrow and Company, 105 Madison Avenue, New York, New York 10016. 1990.

HOW TO GET ELECTED: AN ANECDOTAL HISTORY OF MUD-SLINGING, RED-BAITING, VOTE-STEALING, AND DIRTY TRICKS IN AMERICAN POLITICS. Jack Mitchell. St. Martin's Press, 175 Fifth Avenue, New York, New York 10010. 1992.

HUD SCANDALS: HOWLING HEADLINES AND SILENT FIASCOES. Irving H. Welfeld. Transaction Books, Rutgers University, New Brunswick, New Jersey 08903. 1992.

ISSUES IN AMERICAN POLITICAL LIFE: MONEY, VIOLENCE, AND BIOLOGY. Robert G. Thobaben, Donna M. Schlagheck and Charles Funderburk. Prentice-Hall, Incorporated, 113 Sylvan Avenue, Englewood Cliffs, New Jersey 07632. 1991.

ON THE TAKE: FROM PETTY CROOKS TO PRESIDENTS. Second Edition. William J. Chambliss. Indiana University Press, Tenth and Morton Streets, Bloomington, Indiana 47405. 1988.

OUR MAN IN PANAMA: HOW GENERAL NORIEGA USED THE UNITED STATES AND MADE MILLIONS IN DRUGS AND ARMS. John Dinges. Random House, Incorporated, 201 East Fiftieth Street, New York, New York 10022. 1990.

THE PLUNDERING GENERATION: CORRUPTION AND THE CRISIS OF THE UNION, 1849-1861. Mark W. Summers. Oxford University Press, 200 Madison Avenue, New York, New York 10016. 1987.

POLITICAL MISCHIEF: SMEAR, SABOTAGE, AND REFORM IN U.S. ELECTIONS. Bruce L. Felknor. Praeger Publishers, One Madison Avenue, New York, New York 10010-3603. 1992.

POLITICAL TRIALS: GORDIAN KNOTS IN THE LAW. Ronald S. Christenson. Transaction Books, Rutgers University, New Brunswick, New Jersey 08903. 1989.

POLITICS AND MONEY: THE NEW ROAD TO CORRUPTION. Elizabeth Drew. MacMillan Publishing Company, Incorporated, 866 Third Avenue, New York, New York 10022. 1983.

CORRUPTION, POLITICAL

THE POLITICS OF SCANDAL: POWER AND PROCESS IN LIBERAL DEMOCRACIES. Andrei S. Markovits and Mark Silverstein, Editors. Holmes and Meier Publishers, IUB Building, 30 Irving Place, New York, New York 10003. 1988.

PUBLIC DUTIES: THE MORAL OBLIGATIONS OF GOVERNMENT OFFICIALS. Joel L. Heishman, Lance Liebman and Mark H. Moore. Harvard University Press, 79 Garden Street, Cambridge, Massachusetts 02138. 1981.

SCANDAL: THE CRISIS OF MISTRUST IN AMERICAN POLITICS. Suzanne Garment. Times Books/Random House, Incorporated, 201 East Fiftieth Street, New York, New York 10022. 1991.

STEALING FROM AMERICA: A HISTORY OF CORRUPTION FROM JAMESTOWN TO REAGAN. Nathan Miller. Paragon House Publishers, 90 Fifth Avenue, New York, New York 10011. 1992.

THE STRING MAN: INSIDE ABSCAM. Robert W. Greene. E. P. Dutton, Two Park Avenue, New York, New York 10016. 1981.

THIMBLERIGGERS: THE LAW VS. MARVIN MANDEL. Bradford Jacobs. Johns Hopkins University Press, 701 West 40th Street, Suite 275, Baltimore, Maryland 21211-2190. 1984.

THE TWEED RING. Alexander B. Callow. Greenwood Publishing Group, Incorporated, 88 Post Road West, Box 5007, Westport, Connecticut 06881. 1981 reprint of 1966 edition.

THE WHISTLEBLOWERS: EXPOSING CORRUPTION IN GOVERNMENT AND INDUSTRY. Myron Peretz Glazer and Penina Migdal Glazer. Basic Books, Incorporated, 10 East Fifty-third Street, New York, New York 10022. 1989.

THE WHITE LABYRINTH: COCAINE AND POLITICAL POWER. Rensselaer W. Lee, III. Transaction Books, Rutgers University, New Brunswick, New Jersey 08903. 1989.

BIBLIOGRAPHIES

CORRUPTION IN POLITICS IN THE UNITED STATES: A BIBLIOGRAPHY. Mary Vance. Vance Bibliographies, Post Office Box 229, 112 North Charter Street, Monticello, Illinois 61856. 1982.

POLITICAL CORRUPTION: A SELECTED BIBLIOGRAPHY. Robert Goehlert. Vance Bibliographies, Post Office Box 229, 112 North Charter Street, Monticello, Illinois 61856. 1985.

POLITICAL CORRUPTION: SCOPE AND RESOURCES: AN ANNOTATED BIBLIOGRAPHY. Elaine R. Johansen. Garland Publishing, Incorporated, 136 Madison Avenue, New York, New York 10016. 1990.

POLITICAL SCANDALS AND CAUSES CELEBRES SINCE 1945: AN INTERNATIONAL REFERENCE COMPENDIUM. Louis Allen. St. James Press, 233 East Ontario, Chicago, Illinois 60611. 1990.

OTHER SOURCES

PROSECUTION OF PUBLIC CORRUPTION CASES. United States Department of Justice, Washington, D.C. 1988.

COSMETICS
See: DRUG LAWS

COUNSEL, RIGHT TO
See: DUE PROCESS OF LAW

COUNTERCLAIM
See: DAMAGES

COUNTERFEITING
See also: FORGERY; FRAUD

HANDBOOKS, MANUALS, FORMBOOKS

ABAGNALE'S DOCUMENT VERIFICATION AND CURRENCY TRANSACTIONS MANUAL. Frank W. Abagnale. Abagnale and Associates, Washington, D.C. 1991.

THE STANDARD CATALOG OF UNITED STATES ALTERED AND COUNTERFEIT COINS. Virgil Hancock, Larry Spanbauer. Sanford J. Durst, 29-28 41st Avenue, Long Island City, New York 11101. 1979.

TEXTBOOKS AND GENERAL WORKS

BECKER THE COUNTERFEITER. G. F. Hill. Obol International, 4747 North Spaulding, Chicago, Illinois 60625. 1979.

COUNTERFEITER: THE STORY OF A MASTER FORGER. Charles Black and Michael Horsnell. St. Martin's Press, 175 Fifth Avenue, New York, New York 10010. 1989.

COUNTERFEITING AND FORGERY: A PRACTICAL GUIDE TO THE LAW. Roland Rowell. Butterworth Legal Publications, 90 Stiles Road, Salem, New Hampshire 03079. 1986.

INDUSTRIAL COUNTERFEITING. Colin Haynes. Scott, Foresman and Company, 1900 East Lake Avenue, Glenview, Illinois 60025. 1991.

THE LAW OF GRAY AND COUNTERFEIT GOODS. David Bender and David Gerber. Practising Law Institute, 810 Seventh Avenue, New York, New York 10019. 1987.

MAKING MONEY: THE ROGUES AND RASCALS OF COUNTERFEITING. Edward C. Rochette. Jende Hagan, Incorporated, Post Office Box 177A, Frederick, Colorado 80530. 1986.

PRODUCT COUNTERFEITING: REMEDIES. Practising Law Institute, 810 Seventh Avenue, New York, New York 10019. 1984.

COUNTERVAILING DUTIES
See: EXPORT AND IMPORT

COUNTY GOVERNMENT
See: LOCAL GOVERNMENT

COURT CLERKS
See: CIRCUIT COURTS OF APPEAL (UNITED STATES); DISTRICT COURTS (UNITED STATES); STATES; SUPREME COURT (UNITED STATES)

COURT-MARTIAL
See: MILITARY LAW AND SERVICE

COURT OPINIONS
See: CIRCUIT COURTS OF APPEAL (UNITED STATES); DISTRICT COURTS (UNITED STATES); STATES; SUPREME COURT

COURT RULES
See: ADMINISTRATIVE OFFICE OF THE UNITED STATES COURTS; CIRCUIT COURTS OF APPEAL (UNITED STATES); DISTRICT COURTS (UNITED STATES); STATES; SUPREME COURT (UNITED STATES)

COURTHOUSES

HANDBOOKS, MANUALS, FORMBOOKS

COURTHOUSE CONSERVATION HANDBOOK. National Trust for Historic Preservation in the United States and the National Clearinghouse for Criminal Justice Planning and Architecture.

COURTHOUSE: A PLANNING AND DESIGN GUIDE FOR COURT FACILITIES. Don Hardenbergh, Robert Tobin, Sr., and Chang-Ming Yeh. National Center for State Courts, 300 Newport Avenue, Williamsburg, Virginia 23187. 1991.

SPACE MANAGEMENT AND THE COURTS: DESIGN HANDBOOK. F. Michael Wong. Courthouse Reorganization and Renovation Program. National Institute of Law Enforcement and Criminal Justice, U.S. Government Printing Office, Washington, D.C. 20402. 1973.

TEXTBOOKS AND GENERAL WORKS

COURTHOUSES AND COURTROOMS: SELECTED READINGS. James J. Alfini and Glenn R. Winters, editors. American Judicature Society, 25 East Washington Street, Chicago, Illinois 60602. 1972.

BIBLIOGRAPHIES

COURTHOUSES-CONSERVATION AND RESTORATION: A BIBLIOGRAPHY. Ina J. Weis. Vance Bibliographies, P.O. Box 229, 112 North Charter Street, Monticello, Illinois 61856. 1983.

DIRECTORIES

DIRECTORY OF STATE COURT CLERKS AND COUNTY COURTHOUSES. Want Publishing Company, 1511 K Street, N.W., Washington, D.C. 20005. Annual.

AUDIOVISUALS

REDUCING COSTS AND DELAY IN TRIAL COURTS. American Bar Association, 750 North Lake Shore Drive, Chicago, Illinois 60611. 1988. Videotape.

COURTS
See also: ADMINISTRATION OF JUSTICE; CIRCUIT COURTS OF APPEAL (UNITED STATES); DISTRICT COURTS (UNITED STATES); FEDERAL COURTS; JUDGES AND JUDICIAL PROCESS; JUDGMENTS; SMALL CLAIMS COURTS; STATE COURTS; STATES; SUPREME COURT (UNITED STATES); TAX COURT

STATUTES, CODES, STANDARDS, UNIFORM LAWS

CONGRESS AND THE COURTS: A LEGISLATIVE HISTORY, 1787-1978: DOCUMENTS AND MATERIALS REGARDING THE CREATION, STRUCTURE AND ORGANIZATION OF FEDERAL COURTS AND THE FEDERAL JUDICIARY. Bernard D. Reams, Compiler. William S. Hein and Company, Incorporated, Hein Building, 1285 Main Street, Buffalo, New York 14209. 1978.

CONGRESS AND THE COURTS: A LEGISLATIVE HISTORY, 1978-1984: DOCUMENTS AND MATERIALS REGARDING THE CREATION, STRUCTURE AND ORGANIZATION OF FEDERAL COURTS AND THE FEDERAL JUDICIARY. Bernard D. Reams, Jr., Compiler. William S. Hein and Company, Incorporated, Hein Building, 1285 Main Street, Buffalo, New York 14209. 1985.

MODEL RULES OF PROFESSIONAL CONDUCT AND CODE OF JUDICIAL CONDUCT: AS AMENDED AUGUST 1984. American Bar Association, Center for Professional Responsibility, 750 North Lake Shore Drive, Chicago, Illinois 60611. 1989.

STANDARDS RELATING TO APPELLATE COURTS. American Bar Association Committee on Standards of Judicial Administration. American Bar Association, 750 North Lake Shore Drive, Chicago, Illinois 60611. 1977.

STANDARDS RELATING TO APPELLATE DELAY REDUCTION. Appellate Judges Conference, Lawyers Conference Task Force on the Reduction of Litigation Cost and Delay. American Bar Association, 750 North Lake Shore Drive, Chicago, Illinois 60611. 1988.

STANDARDS RELATING TO COURT ORGANIZATION. American Bar Association, Judicial Administration Division, 750 North Lake Shore Drive, Chicago, Illinois 60611. 1990.

STANDARDS RELATING TO TRIAL COURTS AS AMENDED. American Bar Association, Committee on Standards of Judicial Administration, 750 North Lake Shore Drive, Chicago, Illinois 60611. 1987.

TRIAL COURT PERFORMANCE STANDARDS WITH COMMENTARY. National Center for State Courts, 300 Newport Avenue, Williamsburg, Virginia 23187-8798. 1990.

LOOSELEAF SERVICES AND REPORTERS

BARCLAYS UNITED STATES D.C. CIRCUIT SERVICE. Frank Gomex. Barclays Law Publishers, 400 Oyster Point Boulevard, Suite 500, South San Francisco, California 94080. 1990- . (Biweekly supplements).

BARCLAYS UNITED STATES EIGHTH CIRCUIT SERVICE. Frank Gomex. Barclays Law Publishers, 400 Oyster Point Boulevard, Suite 500, South San Francisco, California 94080. 1987- . (Biweekly supplements).

BARCLAYS UNITED STATES ELEVENTH CIRCUIT SERVICE. Frank Gomez. Barclays Law Publishers, 400 Oyster Point Boulevard, Suite 500, South San Francisco, California 94080. 1990- . (Biweekly supplements).

BARCLAYS UNITED STATES FIFTH CIRCUIT SERVICE. Frank Gomex. Barclays Law Publishers, 400 Oyster Point Boulevard, Suite 500, South San Francisco, California 94080. 1990- . (Biweekly supplements).

BARCLAYS UNITED STATES FIRST CIRCUIT SERVICE. Frank Gomez. Barclays Law Publishers, 400 Oyster Point Boulevard, Suite 500, South San Francisco, California 94080. 1991- . (Biweekly supplements).

BARCLAYS UNITED STATES FOURTH CIRCUIT SERVICE. Frank Gomez. Barclays Law Publishers, 400 Oyster Point Boulevard, Suite 500, South San Francisco, California 94080. 1990- . (Biweekly supplements).

BARCLAYS UNITED STATES NINTH CIRCUIT SERVICE. Frank Gomez. Barclays Law Publishers, 400 Oyster Point Boulevard, Suite 500, South San Francisco, California 94080. 1985- . (Biweekly supplements).

BARCLAYS UNITED STATES SECOND CIRCUIT SERVICE. Frank Gomez. Barclays Law Publishers, 400 Oyster Point Boulevard, Suite 500, South San Francisco, California 94080. 1988- . (Biweekly supplements).

BARCLAYS UNITED STATES SEVENTH CIRCUIT SERVICE. Frank Gomez. Barclays Law Publishers, 400 Oyster Point Boulevard, Suite 500, South San Francisco, California 94080. 1988- . (Biweekly supplements).

BARCLAYS UNITED STATES SIXTH CIRCUIT SERVICE. Frank Gomez. Barclays Law Publishers, 400 Oyster Point Boulevard, Suite 500, South San Francisco, California 94080. 1987- . (Biweekly supplements).

BARCLAYS UNITED STATES TENTH CIRCUIT SERVICE. Frank Gomez. Barclays Law Publishers, 400 Oyster Point Boulevard, Suite 500, South San Francisco, California 94080. 1987- . (Biweekly supplements).

BARCLAYS UNITED STATES THIRD CIRCUIT SERVICE. Frank Gomez. Barclays Law Publishers, 400 Oyster Point Boulevard, Suite 500, South San Francisco, California 94080. 1990- . (Biweekly supplements).

D.C. FEDERAL COURTS HANDBOOK. Prentice-Hall, Incorporated, 113 Sylvan Avenue, Englewood Cliffs, New Jersey 07632. 1988- .

JURISDICTION AND FORUM SELECTION. Robert Casad. Callaghan and Company, 155 Pfingsten Road, Deerfield, Illinois 60015. 1988- . (Annual supplements).

HANDBOOKS, MANUALS, FORMBOOKS

COURT-MARTIAL PROCEDURE. Francis A. Gilligan and Fredric I. Lederer. Michie Company, P.O. Box 7587, Charlottesville, Virginia 22906. 1991.

EVERYBODY'S GUIDE TO SMALL CLAIMS COURT. Fourth Edition. Ralph Warner. Nolo Press, 950 Parker Street, Berkeley, California 94710. 1990.

FEDERAL AND STATE COURT SYSTEMS: A GUIDE. Fannie J. Klein. Ballinger Division, HarperCollins, 10 East Fifty-third Street, New York, New York 10022. 1977.

FEDERAL COURT OF APPEALS MANUAL: A MANUAL ON PRACTICE IN THE UNITED STATES COURT OF APPEALS. Second Edition. David G. Knibb. West Publishing Company, 50 West Kellogg Boulevard, St. Paul, Minnesota 55164. 1990.

TEXTBOOKS AND GENERAL WORKS

ALTERNATIVE FUTURES FOR THE STATE COURTS OF 2020. James A. Dator and Sharon J. Rogers. American Judicature Society, 25 East Washington Street, Suite 1600, Chicago, Illinois 60602. 1991.

AMERICAN COURT MANAGEMENT: THEORIES AND PRACTICES. David J. Saari. Greenwood Publishing Group, Incorporated, 88 Post Road West, Post Office Box 5007, Westport, Connecticut 06881. 1982.

AMERICAN COURT SYSTEMS: READINGS IN JUDICIAL PROCESS AND BEHAVIOR. Second Edition. Sheldon Goldman and Austin Sarat, Editors. Longman Publishing Group, 95 Church Street, White Plains, New York 10601. 1989.

THE AMERICAN COURTS: A CRITICAL ASSESSMENT. John B. Gates and Charles A. Johnson. Congressional Quarterly Books, 1414 Twenty-second Street, Northwest, Washington D.C. 20037. 1991.

AMERICAN COURTS: PROCESS AND POLICY. Second Edition. Lawrence Baum. Houghton-Mifflin Company, One Beacon Street, Boston, Massachusetts 02108. 1990.

AMERICAN JUDICIAL POLITICS. Harry P. Stumpf. Harcourt, Brace, Jovanovich, Incorporated, 6277 Sea Harbor Drive, Orlando, Florida 32821. 1988.

THE AMERICAN JUDICIARY. Simeon E. Baldwin. Fred B. Rothman and Company, 10368 West Centennial Road, Littleton, Colorado 80127. Reprint of 1905 edition.

THE AMERICAN JUDICIARY: CRITICAL ISSUES. A. Leo Levin and Russel R. Wheeler, Editors. Sage Publications, Incorporated, 2455 Teller Road, Newbury, California 91320. 1982.

AMERICA'S COURTS AND THE CRIMINAL JUSTICE SYSTEM. Fourth Edition. David W. Neubauer. Brooks/Cole Publishing Company, 511 Forest Lodge Road, Pacific Grove, California 93950. 1992.

ATTACKING LITIGATION COSTS AND DELAY: PROJECT REPORTS AND RESEARCH FINDINGS SUPPORTING THE FINAL REPORT OF THE ACTION COMMISSION TO REDUCE COURT COSTS AND DELAY. American Bar Association, Action Commission to Reduce Court Costs and Delays, 750 North Lake Shore Drive, Chicago, Illinois 60611. 1984.

THE BILINGUAL COURTROOM: COURT INTERPRETERS IN THE JUDICIAL PROCESS. Susan Berk-Seligson. University of Chicago Press, 5801 Ellis Avenue, Chicago, Illinois 60637. 1990.

COMPARATIVE JUDICIAL SYSTEMS: CHALLENGING FRONTIERS IN CONCEPTUAL AND EMPIRICAL ANALYSIS. John R. Schmidhauser, Editor. Butterworth Legal Publishers, 90 Stiles Road, Salem, New Hampshire 03079. 1987.

CONFLICT, COURTS, AND TRIALS. Third Edition. Linda Riekes. West Publishing Company, 50 West Kellogg Boulevard, St. Paul, Minnesota 55164. 1991.

THE CONSTITUTION, THE COURTS, AND THE QUEST FOR JUSTICE. Robert A. Goldwin and William A. Schambra, Editors. American Enterprise Institute for Public Policy Research, 1150 Seventeenth Street, Northwest, Washington, D.C. 20036. 1989.

THE CONTOURS OF JUSTICE: COMMUNITIES AND THEIR COURTS. James Eisenstein, Roy B. Flemming, and Peter F. Nardulli. Little, Brown and Company, 34 Beacon Street, Boston, Massachusetts 02108. 1988.

THE COURT OF JUSTICE OF THE EUROPEAN COMMUNITIES. Third Edition. L. Neville Brown and Francis G. Jacobs. Sweet and Maxwell Limited, South Quay Plaza, 183 Marsh Wall, London E14 9FT, England. 1989.

COURT OFFICER, SENIOR COURT OFFICER, COURT CLERK. William Goffen, Editor. Arco Publishing, Incorporated, 15 Columbus Circle, New York, New York 10023. 1983.

COURT REFORM ON TRIAL: WHY SIMPLE SOLUTIONS FAIL. Malcolm M. Feeley. Basic Books, Incorporated, 10 East Fifty-third Street, New York, New York 10022. 1984.

COURT SELECTION: STUDENT LITIGATION IN STATE AND FEDERAL COURTS. National Center for State Courts, 300 Newport Avenue, Williamsburg, Virginia 23187-8798. 1982.

THE COURTS. Second Edition. Ted H. Rubin. Random House, Incorporated, Random House Publicity, (11-6) 201 East Fiftieth Street, New York, New York 10022. 1984.

COURTS: A COMPARATIVE AND POLITICAL ANALYSIS. Martin Shapiro. University of Chicago Press, 5801 Ellis Avenue, Third Floor, South, Chicago, Illinois 60637. 1986.

THE COURTS: A FULCRUM OF THE JUSTICE SYSTEM. Second Edition. Random House, Incorporated, Random House Publicity, (11-6) 201 East Fiftieth Street, New York, New York 10022. 1986.

COURTS AND JUDGES. James A. Cramer. Sage Publications, Incorporated, 2455 Teller Road, Newbury Park, California 91320. 1981.

COURTS AND JUDGES: HOW THEY WORK. Katherine J. Lee. HALT, Incorporated, 1319 F Street, Northwest, Suite 300, Washington, D.C. 20004. 1987.

COURTS AND POLITICS: THE FEDERAL JUDICIAL SYSTEM. Second Edition. Howard Ball. Prentice-Hall, Incorporated, P.O. Box 500, Englewood Cliffs, New Jersey 07632. 1987.

COURTS AND THE POOR. Christopher E. Smith. Nelson-Hall Publishers, 111 North Canal Street, Chicago, Illinois 60606. 1991.

THE COURTS IN AMERICAN LIFE: MAJOR HISTORICAL INTERPRETATIONS. Kermit L. Hall, Editor. Garland Publishing, Incorporated, 136 Madison Avenue, New York, New York 10016. 1987.

COURTS IN AMERICAN POLITICS: READINGS AND INTRODUCTORY ESSAYS. Henry R. Glick, Editor. McGraw-Hill Publishing Company, 1221 Avenue of the Americas, New York, New York 10020. 1990.

COURTS, JUDGES AND POLITICS: AN INTRODUCTION TO THE JUDICIAL PROCESS. Fourth Edition. Walter Murphy and C. Herman Pritchet, editors. McGraw-Hill Publishing Company, 1221 Avenue of the Americas, New York, New York 10020. 1986.

COURTS, POLITICS, AND JUSTICE. Second edition. Henry R. Glick. McGraw-Hill Publishing Company, 1221 Avenue of the Americas, New York, New York 10020. 1988.

CREATING THE FEDERAL JUDICIAL SYSTEM. Russell R. Wheeler and Cynthia Harrison. Federal Judicial Center, 1520 H Street, Northwest, Washington, D.C. 20005. 1989.

THE CRIMINAL COURTS: STRUCTURES, PERSONNEL, AND PROCESSES. N. Gary Holten and Lawson L. Lamar. McGraw-Hill Publishing Company, 1221 Avenue of the Americas, New York, New York 10020. 1991.

CURBING THE COURTS: THE CONSTITUTION AND THE LIMITS OF JUDICIAL POWER. Gary L. McDowell. Louisiana State University Press, Highland Road, Baton Rouge, Louisiana 70893. 1988.

DECIDING CASES WITHOUT ARGUMENT: AN EXAMINATION OF FOUR COURTS OF APPEALS. Joe S. Cecil and Donna Stienstra. Federal Judicial Center, 1520 H Street, Northwest, Washington, D.C. 20005. 1987.

DISORDER IN THE COURT: GREAT FRACTURED MOMENTS IN COURTROOM HISTORY. Charles M. Sevilla. W.W Norton and Company, Incorporated, 500 Fifth Avenue, New York, New York 10110. 1992.

DOCUMENTS ON INTERNATIONAL ADMINISTRATIVE TRIBUNALS. C.F. Amerasinghe. Clarendon Press, New York, New York. 1989.

EMPIRICAL THEORIES ABOUT COURTS. Keith O. Boyum and Lynn Mather. Longman, Incorporated, 95 Church Street, White Plains, New York, New York 10601-1566. 1983.

EXPLAINING THE COURTS: MATERIALS AND SOURCES. American Bar Association, 750 North Lake Shore Drive, Chicago, Illinois 60611. 1983.

FACT-FINDING BEFORE INTERNATIONAL TRIBUNALS. Richard B. Lillich, Editor. Transnational Publishers, P.O. Box 7282, Ardsley-on-Hudson, New York 10503. 1992.

THE FEDERAL COURTS. Second Edition. Robert A. Carp and Ronald Stidham. Congressional Quarterly Books, 1414 Twenty-second Street, Northwest, Washington D.C. 20037. 1990.

FEDERAL COURTS AND THE LAW OF FEDERAL-STATE RELATIONS. Second Edition. Peter W. Low and John Calvin Jeffries, Jr. Foundation Press, 615 Merrick Avenue, Westbury, New York 11590. 1989.

THE FEDERAL COURTS IN THE POLITICAL ORDER: JUDICIAL JURISDICTION AND AMERICAN POLITICAL THEORY. Martin H. Redish. Carolina Academic Press, P.O. Box 51879, Durham, North Carolina 27717. 1991.

FEDERAL JURISDICTION. Erwin Chemerinsky. Little, Brown and Company, 34 Beacon Street, Boston, Massachusetts 02108. 1989.

FEDERAL JURISDICTION: POLICY AND PRACTICE: CASE AND MATERIALS. Second Edition. Howard P. Fink and Mark V. Tushnet. Michie Company, P.O. Box 7587, Charlottesville, Virginia 22906. 1987.

HARD JUDICIAL CHOICES: FEDERAL DISTRICT COURT JUDGES AND STATE AND LOCAL OFFICIALS. Phillip J. Cooper. Oxford University Press, 200 Madison Avenue, New York, New York 10016. 1988.

HART AND WECHSLER'S THE FEDERAL COURTS AND THE FEDERAL SYSTEM. Third Edition. Henry Melvin Hart and Herbert Wechsler. Foundation Press, 615 Merrick Avenue, Westbury, New York 11590. 1988.

HISTORY OF THE FEDERAL COURTS. Erwin C. Surrency. Oceana Publications, 75 Main Street, Dobbs Ferry, New York 10522. 1987.

THE HOLLOW HOPE: CAN COURTS BRING ABOUT SOCIAL CHANGE? Gerald N. Rosenberg. University of Chicago Press, 5801 Ellis Avenue, Chicago, Illinois 60637. 1991.

HOW COURTS GOVERN AMERICA. Richard Neely. Yale University Press, 302 Temple Street, New Haven, Connecticut 06520. 1981.

INHERENT POWERS OF THE COURTS. National Judicial College. American Bar Association, 750 North Lake Shore Drive, Chicago, Illinois 60611. 1980.

INTERMEDIATE APPELLATE COURTS: IMPROVING CASE PROCESSING: FINAL REPORT. Joy A. Chapper and Roger A. Hanson. National Center for State Courts, 300 Newport Avenue, Williamsburg, Virginia 23187. 1990.

AN INTRODUCTION TO COURT INTERPRETING: THEORY AND PRACTICE. Elena M. de Jongh. University Press of America, 4720 Boston Way, Lanham, Maryland 20706. 1992.

THE JUDICIAL PROCESS: AN INTRODUCTORY ANALYSIS OF THE COURTS OF THE UNITED STATES, ENGLAND, AND FRANCE. Fifth Edition. Henry J. Abraham. Oxford University Press, Incorporated, 200 Madison Avenue, New York, New York 10016. 1986.

JUDICIAL PROCESS IN AMERICA. Robert A. Carp and Ronald Stidham. Congressional Quarterly Books, 1414 Twenty-second Street, Northwest, Washington D.C. 20037. 1989.

THE JUDICIAL PROCESS IN COMPARATIVE PERSPECTIVE. Mauro Cappelletti. Clarendon Press, New York, New York. 1989.

JUDICIAL REVIEW IN COMPARATIVE LAW. Allan R. Brewer-Carias. Cambridge University Press, 40 West Twentieth Street, New York, New York 10011. 1989.

JUSTICE DELAYED: THE PACE OF LITIGATION IN URBAN TRIAL COURTS. National Center of State Courts, 300 Newport Avenue, Williamsburg, Virginia 23187-8798. 1978

JUSTICE IN AMERICA: COURTS, LAWYERS AND THE JUDICIAL PROCESS. Fourth Edition. Herbert Jacob. Little, Brown, and Company, 34 Beacon Street, Boston, Massachusetts 02108. 1984.

THE JUVENILE JUSTICE SYSTEM: DELINQUENCY, PROCESSING, AND THE LAW. Dean J. Champion. Macmillan Publishing Company, Incorporated, 866 Third Avenue, New York, New York 10022. 1992.

LITIGATION AND INEQUALITY: FEDERAL DIVERSITY JURISDICTION IN INDUSTRIAL AMERICA, 1870-1958. Edward A. Purcell, Jr. Oxford University Press, 200 Madison Avenue, New York, New York 10016. 1992.

MANAGERIAL JUDGES. Judith Resnick. The Rand Corporation, P.O. Box 2138, Santa Monica, California 90406. 1982.

MANAGING APPEALS IN FEDERAL COURTS. Federal Judicial Center, 1520 H Street, Northwest, Washington, D.C. 20005. 1988.

MODELS OF COURT MANAGEMENT. Donald Dahlin. Associated Faculty Press, 19 West Thirty-sixth Street, New York, New York 10018. 1985.

MONEY AND JUSTICE: WHO OWNS THE COURTS? Lois G. Forer. W. W. Norton and Company, Incorporated, 500 Fifth Avenue, New York, New York 10110. 1986.

ON TRIAL: AMERICA'S COURTS AND THEIR TREATMENT OF SEXUALLY ABUSED CHILDREN. Second Edition. Billie Wright Dziech and Charles B. Schudson. Beacon Press, 25 Beacon Street, Boston, Massachusetts 02108. 1991.

ORIGINS OF THE FEDERAL JUDICIARY: ESSAYS ON THE JUDICIARY ACT OF 1789. Maeva Marcus, Editor. Oxford University Press, 200 Madison Avenue, New York, New York 10016. 1992.

PACKING THE COURTS: THE CONSERVATIVE CAMPAIGN TO REWRITE THE CONSTITUTION. Herman Schwartz. Scribner Educational Publishers, 866 Third Avenue, New York, New York 10022. 1988.

THE POLITICAL ROLE OF LAW COURTS IN MODERN DEMOCRACIES. Jerold L. Waltman and Kenneth M. Holland, Editors. St. Martin's Press, 175 Fifth Avenue, New York, New York 10010. 1988.

POLITICS AND THE COURTS: TOWARD A GENERAL THEORY OF PUBLIC LAW. Barbara M. Yarnold. Praeger Publishers, One Madison Avenue, New York, New York 10010-3603. 1992.

THE POLITICS OF JUDICIAL REFORM. Philip L. Dubois, Editor. Lexington Books, 125 Spring Street, Lexington, Massachusetts 02173. 1982.

THE POLITICS OF STATE COURTS. Harry P. Stumpf and John H. Culver. Longman Publishing Group, 95 Church Street, White Plains, New York 10601. 1991.

PRESS AND MEDIA ACCESS TO THE CRIMINAL COURTROOM. Warren Freedman. Quorum Books, Greenwood Publishing Group, Incorporated, 88 Post Road West, P.O. Box 5007, Westport, Connecticut 06881. 1988.

A PRIMER ON THE JURISDICTION OF THE UNITED STATES COURTS OF APPEALS. Thomas E. Baker. Federal Judicial Center, 1520 H Street, Northwest, Washington, D.C. 20005. 1989.

RATIONALIZING JUSTICE: THE POLITICAL ECONOMY OF FEDERAL DISTRICT COURTS. Wolf Heydebrand and Carroll Seron. State University of New York Press, Albany, New York. 1990.

RELATIONS BETWEEN FEDERAL AND STATE COURTS. Mitchell Wendell. AMS Press Incorporated, 56 East Thirteenth Street, New York, New York 10003. Reprint of 1949 Edition.

RESTRUCTURING JUSTICE: THE INNOVATIONS OF THE NINTH CIRCUIT AND THE FUTURE OF THE FEDERAL COURTS. Arthur D. Hellman, Editor. Cornell University Press, 124 Roberts Place, Ithaca, New York 14850. 1990.

REWRITING THE HISTORY OF THE JUDICIARY ACT OF 1789: EXPOSING MYTHS, CHALLENGING PREMISES, AND USING NEW EVIDENCE. Wilfred J. Ritz. University of Oklahoma Press, 105 Asp Avenue, Norman, Oklahoma 73019. 1990.

THE ROLE OF COURTS IN SOCIETY. Shimon Shetreet. Martinus Nijhoff, Kluwer Academic Publishers, 101 Philip Drive, Assinippi Park, Norwell, Massachusetts 02061. 1988.

THE ROLE OF STATE SUPREME COURTS IN THE NEW JUDICIAL FEDERALISM. Susan P. Fino. Greenwood Publishing Group, Incorporated, 88 Post Road West, P.O. Box 5007, Westport, Connecticut 06881. 1987.

THE ROLE OF THE JUVENILE COURT. Francis X. Hartmann, Editor. Springer-Verlag New York, Incorporated, 175 Fifth Avenue, New York, New York 10010. 1987.

SHADOW JUSTICE: THE IDEOLOGY AND INSTI-TUTIONALIZATION OF ALTERNATIVES TO COURT. Christine B. Harrington. Greenwood Publishing Group, Incorporated, 88 Post Road West, Post Office Box 5007, Westport, Connecticut 06881. 1985. (Annual).

SMALL CLAIMS COURTS: A COMPARATIVE STUDY. Christopher J. Whelan, Editor. Oxford University Press, 200 Madison Avenue, New York, New York 10016. 1990.

SPECIALIZED JUSTICE: COURTS, ADMINISTRATIVE TRIBUNALS, AND A CROSS-NATIONAL THEORY OF SPECIALIZATION. Stephen H. Legomsky. Oxford University Press, 200 Madison Avenue, New York, New York 10016. 1990.

SPEEDY DISPOSITION: MONETARY INCENTIVES AND POLICY REFORM IN CRIMINAL COURTS. Thomas W. Church and Milton Heumann. State University of New York Press, State University Plaza, Albany, New York 12246. 1992.

STATE CONSTITUTIONS AND CRIMINAL JUSTICE. Barry Latzer. Greenwood Publishing Group, Incorporated, 88 Post Road West, P.O. Box 5007, Westport, Connecticut 06881. 1991.

STATE SUPREME COURTS IN STATE AND NATION. G. Alan Tarr and Mary Cornelia Aldis Porter. Yale University Press, 302 Temple Street, New Haven, Connecticut 06520. 1988.

SUMMARY ADJUDICATION: DISPOSITIVE MOTIONS AND SUMMARY TRIALS. William Daniel Quarles, Joseph C. Howard and Roger Tehan Scully. John Wiley and Sons, Incorporated, 605 Third Avenue, New York, New York 10158. 1990.

SUPRANATIONAL AND CONSTITUTIONAL COURTS IN EUROPE. Igor I. Kavass. William S. Hein and Company, 1285 Main Street, Buffalo, New York 14209. 1992.

THE SUPREME COURT IN THE FEDERAL JUDICIAL SYSTEM. Third Edition. Stephen L. Wasby. Nelson-Hall Publishers, 111 North Canal Street, Chicago, Illinois 60606. 1988.

THE TRIAL: A PROCEDURAL DESCRIPTION AND CASE STUDY. Howard Myers and Jan Pudlow. West Publishing Company, 50 West Kellogg Boulevard, St. Paul, Minnesota 55164. 1991.

TRIAL AND COURT PROCEDURES WORLDWIDE. Charles Platto, Editor. International Bar Association. Graham and Trotman Limited, Sterling House, 66 Wilton Road, London SW1V 1DE, England. 1991.

THE UNITED STATES COURTS: THEIR JURISDICTION AND WORK. Administrative Office of the United States Courts, Washington, D.C. 20544. 1989.

UNITED STATES DISTRICT COURTS SENTENCES IMPOSED CHART, TWELVE MONTH PERIOD ENDING JUNE 30, 1983. Administrative Office of the United States Courts. Superintendent of Documents, United States Government Printing Office, Washington, D.C. 20402. 1985.

WHY COURTS DON'T WORK. Richard Neely. McGraw-Hill Book Company, 1221 Avenue of the Americas, New York, New York 10020. 1983.

ENCYCLOPEDIAS AND DICTIONARIES

STATE COURT MODEL STATISTICAL DICTIONARY. Conference of State Court Administrators. National Center for State Courts, 300 Newport Avenue, Williamsburg, Virginia 23187-8798. 1989.

LAW REVIEWS AND PERIODICALS

COURT REVIEW. American Judges Association, 300 Newport Avenue, Williamsburg, Virginia 23185. Quarterly.

THE JUDGES JOURNAL. American Bar Association, Judicial Administration Division, 750 North Lake Shore Drive, Chicago, Illinois 60611. Quarterly.

JUDICATURE. American Judicature Society, 25 East Washington Street, Chicago, Illinois 60602. Bimonthly.

STATE COURT JOURNAL. National Center for State Courts, 300 Newport Avenue, Williamsburg, Virginia 23187-8798. Quarterly.

NEWSLETTERS AND NEWSPAPERS

AJA BENCHMARK. American Judges Association, 300 Newport Avenue, Williamsburg, Virginia 23185. Quarterly.

AMERICAN INDIAN COURTLINE. American Indian Court Clerks Association, 1000 Connecticut Avenue, Northwest, Washington, D.C. 20036. (202) 296-0685. Irregular.

CHANGE EXCHANGE. American Bar Association, Judicial Administration Division, 750 North Lake Shore Drive, Chicago, Illinois 60611. Quarterly.

CITATIONS. Court Interpreters and Translators Association, P.O. Box 406, Peck Slip Station, New York, New York 10272. Quarterly.

CITIZENS' FORUM ON THE COURTS. American Judicature Society, 25 East Washington Street, Sixteenth Floor, Chicago, Illinois 60602. Quarterly.

COURT EXCELLENCE. Council for Court Excellence, 1025 Vermont Avenue, Northwest, Suite 510, Washington, D.C. 20005. Three times per year.

COURT IMPROVEMENT BULLETIN. American Judicature Society, 12 East Washington Street, Suite 1600, Chicago, Illinois 60602. Semiannual.

THE COURT MANAGER. National Association for Court Management, 300 Newport Avenue, Williamsburg, Virginia 23187. Quarterly.

COURT OF APPEALS FOR THE FEDERAL CIRCUIT NEWSLETTER. American Bar Association, Litigation Section, 750 North Lake Shore Drive, Chicago, Illinois 60611. Bimonthly.

COURT REVIEW. American Judges Association, 42 Little Horn Road, Westcliffe, Colorado 81252. Quarterly.

IJA REPORT. Institute of Judicial Administration. One Washington Square Village, New York, New York 10012. Quarterly.

LAWYERS LETTER. American Bar Association, Judicial Administration Division, Lawyers Conference, 750 North Lake Shore Drive, Chicago, Illinois 60611. Three times per year.

MODERN COURTS. Fund for Modern Courts, Incorporated, 36 West Forty-fourth Street, New York, New York 10036. Quarterly.

THE NATIONAL SHORTHAND NEWSLETTER. National Shorthand Reporters Association, 118 Park Street, Southeast, Vienna, Virginia 22180. Monthly.

NEWSLETTERS: ASSOCIATION OF FAMILY AND CORCILIATION COURTS. Association of Family and Corciliation Courts, 329 West Wilson Street, Madison, Wisconsin 53703. Quarterly.

NJC NEWSLETTER. National Judicial College, Judicial College Building, University of Nevada, Reno, Nevada 89557. Quarterly.

PARASCOPE. American Bar Association, National Committee of Appellate Court Staff Counsel, 750 North Lake Shore Drive, Chicago, Illinois 60611. Quarterly.

SANCTIONS: A GUIDE TO RULE 11 AND OTHER SANCTIONS IN FEDERAL LITIGATIONS. Judicial Update, 559 Douglas Street, San Francisco, California 94114. Monthly.

SPECIAL COURT NEWS. American Bar Association, National Conference of Special Court Judges, 750 North Lake Shore Drive, Chicago, Illinois 60611. Quarterly.

THE THIRD BRANCH: NEWSLETTER OF THE FEDERAL COURTS. Administrative Office of the United States Courts, Office of Legislative and Public Affairs, 811 Vermont Avenue, Northwest, Room 655, Washington, D.C. 20544. Monthly.

BIBLIOGRAPHIES

COURT ADMINISTRATION MONOGRAPHS. Mary Vance. Vance Bibliographies, P.O. Box 229, 112 North Charter Street, Monticello, Illinois 61856. 1983.

FAMILY COURTS: A BIBLIOGRAPHY. Mary Vance. Vance Bibliographies, P.O. Box 229, 112 North Charter Street, Monticello, Illinois 61856. 1988.

JUVENILE COURTS: A BIBLIOGRAPHY. Mary Vance. Vance Bibliographies, P.O. Box 229, 112 North Charter Street, Monticello, Illinois 61856. 1988.

THE UNITED STATES SUPREME COURT: A BIBLIOGRAPHY. Fenton S. Martin and Robert U. Goehlert. Congressional Quarterly Books, 1414 Twenty-second Street, Northwest, Washington D.C. 20037. 1990.

DIRECTORIES

ALMANAC OF THE FEDERAL JUDICIARY. Law Letters, Incorporated, Suite 1460, 332 South Michigan Avenue, Chicago, Illinois 60604. 1984- . (Periodic Supplements).

THE AMERICAN BENCH. Third edition. Sarah Livermore, editor. Reginald Bishop Forster and Associates, Incorporated, 3287 Ramos Circle, Sacramento, California 95827. Biennial.

BNA'S DIRECTORY OF STATE COURTS, JUDGES, AND CLERKS: A STATE-BY-STATE LISTING. Third Edition. Kamla J. King and Judith Springberg. Bureau of National Affairs, Incorporated, 1231 Twenty-fifth Street, Northwest, Washington, D.C. 20037. 1990.

FEDERAL COURT DIRECTORY. Want Publishing Company, 1511 K Street, Northwest, Washington, D.C. 20005. Annual.

FEDERAL JUDICIARY ALMANAC. Third edition. Stuart Dornette and Robert R. Cross. John Wiley and Sons, 605 Third Avenue, New York, New York 10158. 1987.

LAW AND LEGAL INFORMATION DIRECTORY. Fourth Edition. Steven Wasserman and Jacqueline Wasserman O'Brien. Gale Research, Incorporated, 835 Penobscot Building, Detroit, Michigan 48226. 1991.

NATIONAL DIRECTORY OF COURT MANAGEMENT PERSONNEL. School of Justice, American University Press, 4400 Massachusetts Avenue, Northwest, Andersons Lowel Level, Washington, D.C. 20016. Irregular.

UNITED STATES COURT DIRECTORY. Administrative Office of the United States Courts. Superintendent of Documents, U.S. Government Printing Office, Washington, D.C. 20402. Annual.

WANT'S FEDERAL-STATE COURT DIRECTORY. Want Publishing Company, 1511 K Street, Northwest, Washington, D.C. 20005. Annual.

BIOGRAPHICAL SOURCES

WHO'S WHO IN AMERICAN LAW. Marquis Who's Who, Incorporated, 3002 Glenview Road, Wilmette, Illinois 60091. Biennial.

ASSOCIATIONS AND PROFESSIONAL SOCIETIES

AMERICAN JUDGES ASSOCIATION. 300 Newport Avenue, Williamsburg, Virginia 23185. (804) 253-2000.

AMERICAN JUDICATURE SOCIETY. 25 East Washington Street, Suite 1600, Chicago, Illinois 60602. (312) 558-6900.

CONFERENCE OF STATE COURT ADMINISTRATORS. National Center for State Courts, 300 Newport Avenue, Williamsburg, Virginia 23185. (804) 253-2000.

COUNCIL FOR COURT EXCELLENCE. 1025 Vermont Avenue, Northwest, Suite 510, Washington, D.C. 20005. (202) 783-7736.

FUND FOR MODERN COURTS. 36 West Forty-fourth Street, Room 310, New York, New York 10036. (212) 575-1577.

INSTITUTE OF JUDICIAL ADMINISTRATION. One Washington Square Village, New York, New York 10012. (212) 998-6280.

JUDICIAL ADMINISTRATION DIVISION, AMERICAN BAR ASSOCIATION. 750 North Lake Shore Drive, Chicago, Illinois 60611.

NATIONAL AMERICAN INDIAN COURT CLERKS ASSOCIATION. 1000 Connecticut Avenue, Northwest, Suite 401, Washington, D.C. 20036. (202) 296-0685.

NATIONAL ASSOCIATION FOR COURT MANAGEMENT. National Center for State Courts, 300 Newport Avenue, Williamsburg, Virginia 23187. (804) 253-2000.

NATIONAL ASSOCIATION OF JUDICIARY INTERPRETERS AND TRANSLATORS. 815 East Fourteenth Street, Suite 6B, Brooklyn, New York 11230. (718) 434-0636.

NATIONAL ASSOCIATION OF WOMEN JUDGES. National Center for State Courts, 300 Newport Avenue, Williamsburg, Virginia 23187.

NATIONAL CENTER FOR STATE COURTS. 300 Newport Avenue, Williamsburg, Virginia 23187. (804) 253-2000.

NATIONAL CONFERENCE OF APPELLATE COURT CLERKS. National Center for State Courts, 300 Newport Avenue, Williamsburg, Virginia 23187. (804) 253-2000.

NATIONAL CONFERENCE OF BANKRUPTCY JUDGES. Customs House, Room 218, 701 Broadway, Nashville, Tennessee 37203. (615) 736-5587.

NATIONAL CONFERENCE OF FEDERAL TRIAL JUDGES. American Bar Association, 750 North Lake Shore Drive, Chicago, Illinois 60611. (312) 988-5688.

NATIONAL CONFERENCE OF SPECIAL COURT JUDGES. American Bar Association, 750 North Lake Shore Drive, Chicago, Illinois 60611. (312) 988-5697.

NATIONAL COUNCIL OF JUVENILE AND FAMILY COURT JUDGES. P.O. Box 8970, University of Nevada, Reno, Nevada 89507. (702) 784-6012.

NATIONAL JUDGES ASSOCIATION. 42 Little Horn Road, Westcliffe, Colorado 81252. (719) 783-2274.

NATIONAL JUDICIAL COLLEGE. Judicial College Building, University of Nevada, Reno, Nevada 89557. (702) 784-6747.

NATIONAL SHORTHAND REPORTERS ASSOCIATION. 118 Park Street, Southeast, Vienna, Virginia 22180. (703) 281-4677.

ONLINE DATABASES

PROJECT HERMES. United States Supreme Court, Supreme Court Building, 1 First Street, Northeast, Washington, D.C. 20503.

STATISTICS SOURCES

ANNUAL REPORT OF THE DIRECTOR OF THE ADMINISTRATIVE OFFICE OF THE UNITED STATES COURTS. Administrative Office of the United States Courts. Superintendent of Documents, U.S. Government Printing Office, Washington, D.C. 20402. 1940- . Annual.

AUDIOVISUALS

REDUCING COSTS AND DELAY IN TRIAL COURTS. American Bar Association, 750 North Lake Shore Drive, Chicago, Illinois 60611. 1988. Videotape.

OTHER SOURCES

PROCEEDINGS OF THE NATIONAL CONFERENCE ON GENDER BIAS IN THE COURTS. Dixie K. Knoebel and Marilyn McCoy Roberts, Editors. National Center for State Courts, 300 Newport Avenue, Williamsburg, Virginia 23187. 1990.

COVENANTS
See: CONTRACTS; REAL PROPERTY

CREDIT
See also: BANKRUPTCY; LOANS

STATUTES, CODES, STANDARDS, UNIFORM LAWS

CODE OF FEDERAL REGULATIONS. TITLE 13. BUSINESS CREDIT AND ASSISTANCE. Office of the Federal Register, National Archives and Records Administration, Superintendent of Documents, United States Government Printing Office, Washington, D.C. 20402. Annual. (Updated by use of Monthly List of Sections Affected and daily Federal Register).

FEDERAL CONSUMER CREDIT LAWS AND REGULATIONS. NILS Publishing Company, 21625 Prairie Street, Chatsworth, California 91311. 1987- . (Annual supplement).

LOOSELEAF SERVICES AND REPORTERS

ADMINISTRATIVE INTERPRETATIONS OF THE UNIFORM CONSUMER CREDIT CODE. Frederick H. Miller. Butterworth Legal Publishers, 90 Stiles Road, Salem, New Hampshire 03079. 1989- .

COMPENDIUM OF COMMERCIAL FINANCE LAW. National Commercial Finance Association, 225 West 34th Street, New York, New York 10001. 1967- . (Periodic supplements).

COMPLIANCE EXAMINATIONS UPDATE FOR FINANCIAL INSTITUTIONS. Drew V. Tidwell and John H. Mancuso. Research Institute of America, One Penn Plaza, New York, New York 10119. (Semimonthly supplements).

COMPLYING WITH CONSUMER CREDIT REGULATIONS. Professional Education Systems, Incorporated, 200 Spring Street, Eau Claire, Wisconsin 54702. 1986- .

CONSUMER AND BORROWER PROTECTION: AM JUR PRACTICE GUIDE. Lawyers Cooperative Publishing Company, Aqueduct Building, Rochester, New York 14694. 1991- .

CONSUMER AND COMMERCIAL CREDIT -- INSTALLMENT SALES SERVICE. Research Institute of America, Incorporated, 910 Sylvan Avenue, Englewood Cliffs, New Jersey 07632. 1932- . (Biweekly supplements).

CONSUMER CREDIT AND THE LAW. Dee Pridgen. Clark Boardman Company, Limited, 435 Hudson Street, New York, New York 10014. 1990- .

CONSUMER CREDIT GUIDE. Commerce Clearing House, Incorporated, 4025 West Peterson Avenue, Chicago, Illinois 60646. 1969- . (Weekly supplements).

CONSUMER CREDIT: LAW, TRANSACTIONS, AND FORMS. Kenneth M. Lapine. Matthew Bender and Company, Incorporated, 11 Penn Plaza, New York, New York 10001. 1984- . (Annual supplements).

CONSUMER CREDIT REGULATIONS. Second Edition. D. C. Johnson and Dan L. Nicewander. Professional Education Systems, Incorporated, 200 Spring Street, Eau Claire, Wisconsin 54702. 1989- .

CREDIT UNION LAW SERVICE. Matthew Bender and Company, Incorporated, 11 Penn Plaza, New York, New York 10001. 1984- . (Quarterly supplements).

CREDITORS' RIGHTS IN BANKRUPTCY. Second edition. Patrick A. Murphy. Shepard's/McGraw-Hill, P.O. Box 1235, Colorado Springs, Colorado 80901. 1988- . (Annual supplements).

DEBTOR-CREDITOR LAW. Matthew Bender and Company, Incorporated, 11 Penn Plaza, New York, New York 10001. 1982- . (Periodic supplements).

DEBTOR-CREDITOR LAW MANUAL. Thomas D. Crandall, Richard B. Hagedorn and Frank W. Smith. Research Institute of America, One Penn Plaza, New York, New York 10119. 1985- .

LETTERS OF CREDIT. Gerald T. McLaughlin. Prentice-Hall Law and Business, Route 9W, Englewood Cliffs, New Jersey 07632. 1985- .

REGULATION Z: TRUTH-IN-LENDING COMPREHENSIVE COMPLIANCE MANUAL. Robert P. Chamness. American Bankers Association, 1120 Connecticut Avenue, Northwest, Washington, D.C. 20036. 1987- . (Periodic supplements).

TRUTH IN LENDING: A COMPREHENSIVE GUIDE. Second Edition. Roland E. Brandel, Joseph E. Terraciano and Barry A. Abbott. Prentice-Hall, Incorporated, 113 Sylvan Avenue, Englewood Cliffs, New Jersey 07632. 1991- .

TRUTH-IN-LENDING COMPREHENSIVE COMPLIANCE MANUAL. American Bankers Association, 1120 Connecticut Avenue, Northwest, Washington, D.C. 20036. 1985- .

HANDBOOKS, MANUALS, FORMBOOKS

BANK OFFICER'S HANDBOOK OF GOVERNMENT REGULATION. Second Edition. Stephen K. Huber. Research Institute of America, Incorporated, One Penn Plaza, New York, New York 10119. 1989.

BILLPAYERS' RIGHTS. Eighth Edition. Ralph Warner and Stephen Elias. Nolo Press, 950 Parker Street, Berkeley, California 94710. 1988.

BUSINESS LOANS: A GUIDE TO MONEY SOURCES AND HOW TO APPROACH THEM SUCCESSFULLY. Rick Stephen Hayes. Van Nostrand Reinhold Company, 115 Fifth Avenue, New York, New York 10003. Second edition. 1980.

THE COMPLETE GUIDE FOR CREDIT AND COLLECTION LETTERS. Sol Barzman. National Association of Credit Management, Publications Division, 8815 Central Park Drive, Suite 200, Columbia, Maryland 21045. 1983.

CONSUMER CREDIT COMPLIANCE MANUAL. Second Edition. John R. Fonescca. Lawyers Co-operative Publishing Company, Aqueduct Building, Rochester, New York 14694. 1984- . (Periodic Supplements).

CONSUMER CREDIT 1985: A COURSE HANDBOOK. Practising Law Institute, 810 Seventh Avenue, New York, New York 10019. 1985.

COST OF PERSONAL BORROWING IN THE UNITED STATES. Financial Publishing Company, 82 Brookline Avenue, Boston, Massachusetts 02215. Annual.

CREDIT MANUAL OF COMMERCIAL LAWS. National Association of Credit Management, 8815 Central Park Drive, Suite 200, Columbia, Maryland 21045. Annual.

CREDITORS' RIGHTS HANDBOOK: A CREDITOR-DEBTOR RELATIONSHIP. Don Campbell and D. M. Lynn and Steve A. Youngman. Clark Boardman Company, Limited, 435 Hudson Street, New York, New York 10014. 1987. Annual.

EQUAL CREDIT OPPORTUNITY ACT. Second Edition. Gerry Azzata. National Consumer Law Center, 11 Beacon Street, Boston, Massachusetts 02108. 1988.

EQUAL CREDIT OPPORTUNITY MANUAL: SPECIAL REPORT: FEDERAL REGULATIONS OF DEBT COLLECTION PRACTICES. Fourth Edition. Ralph C. Clontz. Research Institute of America, Incorporated, One Penn Plaza, New York, New York 10119. 1988.

FAIR CREDIT REPORTING MANUAL: TEXT, FORMS AND PROCEDURES FOR COMPLIANCE WITH THE FAIR CREDIT REPORTING ACT. Research Institute of America, One Penn Plaza, New York, New York 10119. 1977- . (Periodic Supplements).

FAIR DEBT COLLECTION. Robert J. Hobbs. National Consumer Law Center, 11 Beacon Street, Boston, Massachusetts 02108. 1987.

A GUIDE TO STATE CONSUMER REGULATIONS. Frank M. Salinger and Robert W. Green. Executive Enterprises Publications Company, 22 West Twenty-first Street, New York, New York 10010-6904. 1989.

A GUIDE TO THE CONSUMER BANKRUPTCY CODE. Frank M. Salinger, Alvin O. Wiese, Jr. and Robert E. McKew. Executive Enterprises Publications Company, 22 West Twenty-first Street, New York, New York 10010-6904. 1989.

HANDBOOK OF CONSUMER BANKING LAW. Michael G. Hales. Prentice-Hall, Incorporated, 113 Sylvan Avenue, Englewood Cliffs, New Jersey 07632. 1989.

HANDBOOK OF CREDIT AND COLLECTION MANAGEMENT FORMS AND PROCEDURES. Jack Horn. Prentice-Hall, Incorporated, 113 Sylvan Avenue, Englewood Cliffs, New Jersey 07632. 1980.

THE LAW OF BANK DEPOSITS, COLLECTIONS, AND CREDIT CARDS. Third Edition. Barkley Clark. Research Institute of America, Incorporated, One Penn Plaza, New York, New York 10119. 1990.

MONEY TROUBLES: LEGAL STRATEGIES TO COPE WITH YOUR DEBTS. Robin Leonard. Nolo Press, 950 Parker Street, Berkeley, California 94710. 1991.

A PRACTICAL GUIDE TO THE FEDERAL TRUTH-IN-LENDING ACT. Joseph W. Gelb, Sheldon Feldman and Peter N. Cubita. Executive Enterprises Publications Company, 22 West Twenty-first Street, New York, New York 10010-6904. 1990.

REGULATION B - EQUAL CREDIT OPPORTUNITY ACT COMPREHENSIVE COMPLIANCE MANUAL. American Bankers Association, 1120 Connecticut Avenue, Northwest, Washington, D.C. 20036. 1980.

SALES AND CREDIT TRANSACTIONS HANDBOOK. T. Le and Edward J. Murphy. Shepard's/McGraw-Hill, Post Office Box 1235, Colorado Springs, Colorado 80901. 1985- . (Periodic Supplements).

SIMPLIFIED CONSUMER CREDIT FORMS. Carl Felsenfeld and Alan Siegel. Research Institute of America, One Penn Plaza, New York, New York 10119. 1978- .

TERM LOAN HANDBOOK. John J. McCann. Law and Business, Incorporated/PH Press, P.O. Box 195, Cambridge, Massachusetts 02139. 1983.

TRUTH IN-LENDING MANUAL. Sixth Edition. Ralph C. Clontz, Jr. and James A. Douglas. Research Institute of America, Incorporated, One Penn Plaza, New York, New York 10119. 1991.

USURY AND CONSUMER CREDIT REGULATION. Kevin W. Brown and Kathleen E. Keest. National Consumer Law Center, 11 Beacon Street, Boston, Massachusetts 02108. 1987.

YOUR LEGAL GUIDE TO CONSUMER CREDIT: WITH A SPECIAL SECTION ON BANKRUPTCY. Robert Willard Johnson. American Bar Association, Public Education Division, 750 North Lake Shore Drive, Chicago, Illinois 60611. 1988.

TEXTBOOKS AND GENERAL WORKS

THE CREDIT GAME: HOW WOMEN CAN WIN IT. (Revised edition). Women's Legal Defense Fund, Washington, D.C. 20036. 1984.

CREDIT: HOW TO GET IT, USE IT, STRETCH IT, SAVE IT. Bert Johnson. Harbor Publishing, 80 North Moore Street, Suite 4J, New York, New York 10013. 1980.

DEBTOR AND CREDITOR RELATIONS: NON-BANKRUPTCY RIGHTS AND REMEDIES. George F. Bason, Jr. West Publishing Company, Post Office Box 64526, 50 West Kellogg Boulevard, St. Paul, Minnesota 55164-0526. 1984.

DEBTORS' AND CREDITORS' RIGHTS. Arnold B. Cohen and Barry L. Zaretsky. The Michie Company, Post Office Box 7587, Charlottesville, Virginia 22906-7582. 1984.

EMERGING THEORIES OF LENDER LIABILITY. Helen D. Chaitman, Editor. American Bar Association, Section of Corporation Banking of Business Law and the Section of Litigation, 750 North Lake Shore Drive, Chicago, Illinois 60611. 1985.

FEDERAL REGULATION OF CONSUMER CREDIT. Frank M. Salinger and Robert W. Green. Executive Enterprises Publications Company, 22 West Twenty-first Street, New York, New York 10010-6904. 1989.

FEDERAL REGULATION OF CONSUMER-CREDITOR RELATIONS. Kenneth R. Redden and James McClellan. The Michie Company, Post Office Box 7587, Charlottesville, Virginia 22906-7582. 1982. (Periodic Supplements).

HANDLING CONSUMER CREDIT CASES. Third Edition. John R. Fonseca. Lawyers Cooperative Publishing Company, Aqueduct Building, Rochester, New York 14694. 1987.

HOW TO GET YOUR CREDITORS OFF YOUR BACK WITHOUT LOSING YOUR SHIRT. Melvin J. Kaplan and Phillip T. Drotning. Contemporary Books, Incorporated, 180 North Michigan Avenue, Chicago, Illinois 60601. 1979.

INTRODUCTION TO SECURED TRANSACTIONS AND LETTERS OF CREDIT, 1991. William C. Hillman. Practising Law Institute, 810 Seventh Avenue, New York, New York 10019. 1991.

THE LAW AND LEGISLATION OF CREDIT CARDS: USE AND MISUSE. Irving J. Sloan. Oceana Publications, Incorporated, 75 Main Street, Dobbs Ferry, New York 10522. 1987.

THE LEGAL SIDE OF CREDIT AND COLLECTION. Bureau of Business Practices, Incorporated, 24 Rope Ferry Road, Waterford, Connecticut 06386. 1989.

MATERIALS FOR UNDERSTANDING CREDIT AND PAYMENT SYSTEMS. Steve H. Nickles, John H. Matheson and John F. Dolan. West Publishing Company, 50 West Kellogg Boulevard, St. Paul, Minnesota 55164. 1987.

MODERN LENDING PRACTICES. John J. McCann, Chairman. Law and Business, Incorporated/Harcourt Brace Jovanovich, 1250 Sixth Avenue, San Diego, California 92101. 1983.

MOST COMMON VIOLATION III: THE MOST COMMON VIOLATIONS FOUND IN CONSUMER COMPLIANCE EXAMINATIONS: WHAT THEY ARE, HOW TO CORRECT THEM. Third Edition. Ralph J. Rohner and Drew V. Tidwell. Consumer Bankers Association, 1000 Wilson Boulevard, Thirtieth Floor, Arlington, Virginia 22209-3908. 1984.

PLAYER'S MANUAL FOR THE DEBTOR CREDITOR GAME. Lynn M. Lopucki. West Publishing Company, Post Office Box 64526, 50 West Kellogg Boulevard, St. Paul, Minnesota 55164-0526. 1985.

PROFITABLE CONSUMER LENDING: A GUIDE TO LENDING, COLLECTION AND COMPLIANCE. Robert D. Hall, Jr. and F. Blake Cloonen. Bankers Publishing Company, 210 South Street, Boston, Massachusetts 02111. 1984.

RETAIL FINANCIAL SERVICES CURRENT DEVELOPMENTS. L. Richard Fischer. Practising Law Institute, 810 Seventh Avenue, New York, New York 10019. 1987.

STAYING SOLVENT: A COMPREHENSIVE GUIDE TO EQUAL CREDITS FOR WOMEN. Emily Card. Holt, Rinehart, and Winston, 6277 Sea Harbor Drive, Orlando, Florida 32821. 1985.

STRUCTURING COMMERCIAL LOAN AGREEMENTS. Rodger Tighe. Research Institute of America, One Penn Plaza, New York, New York 10119. (Looseleaf). 1984- .

ANNUALS AND SURVEYS

FINANCE FACTS YEARBOOK. National Consumer Finance Association, 1101 14th Street, Northwest, Washington, D.C. 20005. Annual.

LAW REVIEWS AND PERIODICALS

CONSUMER CREDIT AND TRUTH-IN-LENDING COMPLIANCE REPORT. Research Institute of America, One Penn Plaza, New York, New York 10119. Monthly.

CONSUMER FINANCE LAW BULLETIN. National Consumer Finance Association, 1101 14th Street, Northwest, Washington, D.C. 20005. Quarterly.

CONSUMER TRENDS. Box 27357, St. Louis, Missouri 63130. Semimonthly.

CREDIT. National Consumer Finance Association, 1101 14th Street, Northwest, Washington, D.C. 20005. Bimonthly.

CREDIT AND FINANCIAL MANAGEMENT. National Associa- tion of Credit Management, 520 Eighth Avenue, New York, New York 10018. Monthly.

CREDIT WORLD. International Consumer Credit Association, Box 27357, St. Louis, Missouri 63141-1757. Bimonthly.

INSTALLMENT CREDIT GUIDE. Commerce Clearing House, Incorporated, 4025 West Peterson Avenue, Chicago, Illinois 60646. Biweekly.

NEWSLETTERS AND NEWSPAPERS

CONSUMER CREDIT AND TRUTH-IN-LENDING COMPLIANCE REPORT. Research Institute of America, Incorporated, One Penn Plaza, New York, New York 10119. Monthly.

CONSUMER FINANCE LAW BULLETIN. American Financial Services Association, 1101 Fourteenth Street, Northwest, Washington, D.C. 20005. Monthly.

CONSUMER FINANCE NEWSLETTER. Financial Publishing Company, 82 Brookline Avenue, Boston, Massachusetts 02215. Monthly.

CONSUMER LENDING REPORT. Research Institute of America, Incorporated, One Penn Plaza, New York, New York 10119. Monthly.

CREDITOR - DEBTOR LAW SECTION NEWSLETTER. Washington State Bar Association, 500 Westin Building, 2001 Sixth Avenue, Seattle, Washington 98121. Quarterly.

LETTER OF CREDIT UPDATE. Government Information Services, 1611 North Kent Street, Arlington, Virginia 22209. Monthly.

LETTERS OF CREDIT REPORT. Executive Enterprises Publications Company, Incorporated, 22 West Twenty-first Street, New York, New York 10010. Bimonthly.

BIBLIOGRAPHIES

CREDIT. National Consumer Finance Association, 1101 14th Street, Northwest, Washington, D.C. 20005.

CREDIT CONTROLS: A SELECTED BIBLIOGRAPHY. Felix Chin. Vance Bibliographies, Post Office Box 229, 112 North Charter Street, Monticello, Illinois 61856. 1981.

CREDITALK. National Retail Merchants Association, 100 West Thirty-first Street, New York, New York 10001. Bimonthly.

NONBANK BANKS: REGULATING CREDIT UNIONS, SAVINGS AND LOANS, AND OTHER THRIFT INSTITUTIONS. Tim J. Watts. Vance Bibliographies, P.O. Box 229, 112 North Charter Street, Monticello, Illinois 61856. 1988.

SELECTED AND ANNOTATED BIBLIOGRAPHY OF REFERENCE MATERIALS IN CONSUMER FINANCE. National Consumer Finance Association, 1101 Fourteenth Street, Northwest, Washington, D.C. 20005. Irregular.

DIRECTORIES

NATIONAL CONSUMER FINANCE ASSOCIATION DIRECTORY. National Consumer Finance Association, 1101 Fourteenth Street, Northwest, Washington, D.C. 20005.

ASSOCIATIONS AND PROFESSIONAL SOCIETIES

AMERICAN FINANCIAL SERVICES ASSOCIATION. 1101 Fourteenth Street, Northwest, Washington, D.C. 20005. (202) 289-0400.

ASSOCIATED CREDIT BUREAUS. 16211 Park Ten Place, P.O. Box 218300, Houston, Texas 77218. (713) 492-8155.

CONSUMER CREDIT INSURANCE ASSOCIATION. 542 South Dearborn, Suite 400, Chicago, Illinois 60605. (312) 939-2242.

CREDIT CARD USERS OF AMERICA. P.O. Box 7100, Beverly Hills, California 90212. (818) 343-4434.

CREDIT RESEARCH FOUNDATION. 8815 Center Park Drive, Columbia, Maryland 21045. (301) 740-5499.

CWI: CREDIT PROFESSIONALS. 6500 Chippewa, Suite 225, St. Louis, Missouri 63109. (314) 752-9535.

FARM CREDIT COUNCIL. 50 F Street, Northwest, Suite 900, Washington, D.C. 20001. (202) 626-8710.

INTERNATIONAL ASSOCIATIONS OF CREDIT CARD INVESTIGATORS. 1620 Grant Avenue, Novato, California 94945. (415) 897-8800.

INTERNATIONAL CREDIT ASSOCIATION, 243 North Lindbergh Boulevard, St. Louis, Missouri 63141. (314) 991-3030.

NATIONAL ASSOCIATION OF CONSUMER CREDIT ADMINISTRATORS. Lew Wallace Boulevard, Santa Fe, New Mexico 87503. (505) 438-0219.

NATIONAL ASSOCIATION OF CREDIT MANAGEMENT. 8815 Center Park Drive, Columbia, Maryland 21045. (301) 740-5560.

NATIONAL CONSUMER CREDIT CONSULTANTS. 2840 West Arthur Drive, Chicago, Illinois 60645. (312) 465-0090.

NATIONAL FOUNDATION FOR CONSUMER CREDIT. 8701 Georgia Avenue, No. 601, Silver Spring, Maryland 20910. (301) 589-5600.

NATIONAL INSTITUTE OF CREDIT. 8815 Centre Park Drive, Columbia, Maryland 21045. (301) 740-5560.

ONLINE DATABASES

CREDIT DATA. TRW Information Services Division, 505 City Parkway, West Orange, California 92668. Contains credit profiles of consumers, updated weekly. Inquire as to online cost and availability.

DUN'S CREDIT GUIDE. Dun and Bradstreet Business Credit Services, One Diamond Hill Road, Murray Hill, New Jersey 07974.

MOODY'S MUNICIPAL NETWORK. Moody's Investors Service, Incorporated, Public Finance Department, 99 Church Street, New York, New York 10007.

THE PAYMENT ANALYSIS REPORT. Dun and Bradstreet Business Credit Services, One Diamond Hill Road, Murray Hill, New Jersey 07974.

TRW BUSINESS PROFILES. TRW Business Credit Division, 500 City Parkway West, Second Floor, Orange, California 92668.

TRW UPDATED CREDIT PROFILE. TRW Business Credit Division, 500 City Parkway West, Second Floor, Orange, California 92668.

STATISTICS SOURCES

CONSUMER CREDIT STATISTICS. National Foundation of Consumer Credit, 1819 H Street, Northwest, Suite 510, Washington, D.C. 20006.

DELINQUENCY RATES ON BANK INSTALLMENT LOANS. American Bankers Association, 1120 Connecticut Avenue, Washington, D.C. 20036.

FEDERAL RESERVE BULLETIN. Board of Governors of the Federal Reserve System, Publications Service, Washington, D.C. 20551. Monthly.

SURVEY OF CONSUMERS. University of Michigan, Institute for Social Research, Post Office Box 1248, Ann Arbor, Michigan 48106-1248. Annual.

CRIME VICTIMS
See also: AGED AND CRIME; JUSTICE DEPARTMENT

STATUTES, CODES, STANDARDS, UNIFORM LAWS

ABA GUIDELINES FOR FAIR TREATMENT OF VICTIMS AND WITNESSES IN THE CRIMINAL JUSTICE SYSTEM. The Victims Committee, Criminal Justice Section, American Bar Association, 750 North Lake Shore Drive, Chicago, Illinois 60611. 1983.

LOOSELEAF SERVICES AND REPORTERS

VICTIM'S RIGHTS: LAW AND LITIGATION. James A. Rapp and Frank Carrington. Matthew Bender and Company, Incorporated, 11 Penn Plaza, New York, New York 10001. 1989- . (annual supplements).

HANDBOOKS, MANUALS, FORMBOOKS

THE CRIME VICTIM'S BOOK. Second edition. Morton Bard and Dawn Sangrey. Brunner/Mazel, Incorporated, 19 Union Square West, New York, New York 10003. 1986.

THE CRIME VICTIM'S HANDBOOK: YOUR RIGHTS AND ROLE IN THE CRIMINAL JUSTICE SYSTEM. David T. Austern. Viking, Penguin, Incorporated, 375 Hudson Street, New York, New York 10014. 1987.

THE RIGHTS OF CRIME VICTIMS. James H. Stark and Howard W. Goldstein. Southern Illinois, University Press, P.O. Box 3697, Carbondale, Illinois 62902-3697. 1985.

VICTIMIZATION AND SURVIVOR SERVICES: A GUIDE TO VICTIM ASSISTANCE. Arlene Bowers Andrews. Springer Publishing Company, 536 Broadway, New York, New York 10012. 1992.

THE VICTIMOLOGY HANDBOOK: RESEARCH FINDINGS, TREATMENT, AND PUBLIC POLICY. Emilio C. Viano, Editor. Garland Publishing, Incorporated, 136 Madison Avenue, New York, New York 10016. 1990.

TEXTBOOKS AND GENERAL WORKS

ADJUSTING THE BALANCE: FEDERAL POLICY AND VICTIM SERVICES. Steven R. Smith and Susan Freinkel. Greenwood Publishing Group, Incorporated, 88 Post Road West, P.O.Box 5007, Westport, Connecticut 06881. 1988.

ARMED ROBBERY: COPS, ROBBERS AND VICTIMS. Thomas Gabor and Andre Normadeau. Charles C. Thomas Publishers, 2600 South First Street, Springfield, Illinois 62794. 1987.

THE BEATEN VICTIM. Howard A. Kurtz. R and E Publications, P.O. Box 2008, Saratoga, California 95070-2008. 1983.

CHILD VICTIMS: CRIME, IMPACT, AND CRIMINAL JUSTICE. Jane Morgan and Lucia Zedner. Oxford University Press, 200 Madison Avenue, New York, New York 10016. 1992.

COUNSELING VICTIMS OF VIOLENCE. Sandra L. Brown. American Association for Counseling and Development, 5999 Stevenson Avenue, Alexandria, Virginia 22304. 1991.

CRIME AND THE FAMILY. Alan Jay Lincoln and Murray A. Staus. Charles C. Thomas Publishers, 2600 South First Street, Springfield, Illinois 62794-9265. 1985.

CRIME VICTIMS: AN INTRODUCTION TO VICTIMOLOGY. Second Edition. Andrew Karmen. Brooks/Cole Publishing Company, 511 Forest Lodge Road, Pacific Grove, California 93950-5098. 1990.

CRISIS INTERVENTION IN CRIMINAL JUSTICE/SOCIAL SERVICE. James E. Hendricks, Editor. Charles C. Thomas, Publishers, 2600 South First Street, Springfield, Illinois 62794. 1991.

CRITICAL ISSUES IN VICTIMOLOGY: INTERNATIONAL PERSPECTIVES. Emilio C. Viano, Editor. Springer Publishing Company, 536 Broadway, New York, New York 10012. 1992.

THE EFFECTS OF CRIME AND THE WORK OF VICTIMS SUPPORT SCHEMES. Mike Maguire and Claire Corbett. Gower Publishing Company, Old Post Road, Brookfield, Vermont 05036. 1987.

EXPERIENCES OF CRIME ACROSS THE WORLD: KEY FINDINGS FROM THE 1989 INTERNATIONAL CRIME SURVEY. J.J.M. van Dijk. Kluwer Academic Publishers, 101 Philip Drive, Assinippi Park, Norwell, Massachusetts 02061. 1990.

FROM CRIME POLICY TO VICTIM POLICY: REORIENTING THE JUSTICE SYSTEM. Ezzas A. Fattah, editor. St. Martin's Press, Incorporated, 175 Fifth Avenue, New York, New York 10010. 1986.

HELPING CRIME VICTIMS: RESEARCH, POLICY, AND PRACTICE. Albert R. Roberts. Sage Publications, 2455 Teller Road, Newbury Park, California 91320. 1990.

INTIMATE INTRUSIONS: WOMEN'S EXPERIENCE OF MALE VIOLENCE. Elizabeth A. Starko. Routledge, Chapman & Hall, 29 West 35th Street, New York, New York 10001. 1985.

INTIMATE VIOLENCE: A STUDY OF INJUSTICE. Julie Blackman. Columbia University Press, 562 West 113th Street, New York, New York 10025. 1989.

INVISIBLE WOUNDS CRIME VICTIMS SPEAK. Shelley Neiderbach. The Haworth Press, Incorporated, 10 Alice Street, Binghamton, New York 13904. 1986.

JOHN BARLEYCORN MUST PAY: COMPENSATING THE VICTIMS OF DRINKING DRIVERS. Paul A. LeBel. University of Illinois Press, 54 East Gregory Drive, Champaign, Illinois 61820. 1992.

MAKING AMENDS: MEDIATION AND REPARATION IN CRIMINAL JUSTICE. Gwynn Davis. Routledge, Chapman & Hall, 29 West Thirty-fifth Street, New York, New York 10001. 1992.

MURDER AMONG THE RICH AND FAMOUS. Jay R. Nash. Arlington House, Crown Publications, Incorporated, 201 East 50th Street, New York, New York 10022. 1987.

THE PLIGHT OF CRIME VICTIMS IN MODERN SOCIETY. Ezzat A. Fattah, Editor. St. Martin's Press, 175 Fifth Avenue, New York, New York 10010. 1989.

THE POLITICS OF VICTIMIZATION: VICTIMS, VICTIMOLOGY AND HUMAN RIGHTS. Robert Elias. Oxford University Press, 200 Madison Avenue, New York, New York 10016. 1986.

RESTORATIVE JUSTICE ON TRIAL: PITFALLS AND POTENTIALS OF VICTIM-OFFENDER MEDIATION: INTERNATIONAL RESEARCH PERSPECTIVES. Heinz Messmer and Hans-Uwe Otto, Editors. Kluwer Academic Publishers, 101 Philip Drive, Assinippi Park, Norwell, Massachusetts 02061. 1992.

TO BE A VICTIM: ENCOUNTERS WITH CRIME AND INJUSTICE. Diane Sank and David I. Caplan, Editors. Plenum Publishing Corporation, 233 Spring Street, New York, New York 10013. 1991.

TOWARDS A CRITICAL VICTIMOLOGY. Ezzat A. Fattah, Editor. St. Martin's Press, 175 Fifth Avenue, New York, New York 10010. 1992.

VICTIMS OF CRIME AND PUNISHMENT: INTERVIEWS WITH VICTIMS, CONVICTS, THEIR FAMILIES, AND SUPPORT GROUPS. Shirley Dicks. McFarland and Company, Incorporated, Box 611, Jefferson, North Carolina 28640. 1991.

VICTIMS OF CRIME: PROBLEMS, POLICIES, AND PROGRAMS. Arthur J. Lurigio, Wesley G. Skogan and Robert C. Davis, Editors. Sage Publications, 2455 Teller Road, Newbury Park, California 91320. 1990.

VICTIMS OF THE SYSTEMS: CRIME VICTIMS AND COMPENSATION IN AMERICAN POLITICS AND CRIMINAL JUSTICE. Robert Elias. Transaction Books, Rutgers University, 109 Church Street, New Brunswick, New Jersey 08901. 1983.

LAW REVIEWS AND PERIODICALS

VICTIMOLOGY: AN INTERNATIONAL LAW JOURNAL. Victimology, Incorporated, 2333 North Vernon Street, Arlington, Virginia 22207. Quarterly.

NEWSLETTERS AND NEWSPAPERS

CRIME VICTIMS DIGEST. Washington Criminal Justice Reports Incorporated, 3918 Prosperity Avenue, Suite 318, Fairfax, Virginia 22031. Monthly.

VICTIMS ADVOCATE. American Bar Association, Young Lawyer's Division, 750 North Lake Shore Drive, Chicago, Illinois 60611. Semiannually.

DIRECTORIES

CRIME VICTIM'S AID. Bloom Books, Incorporated, 1020 Broad Street, Newark, New Jersey 07102. Irregular.

ASSOCIATIONS AND PROFESSIONAL SOCIETIES

AMERICAN BAR ASSOCIATION SECTION OF CRIMINAL JUSTICE, VICTIMS COMMITTEE. American Bar Association, 750 North Lake Shore Drive, Chicago, Illinois 60611.

NATIONAL ASSOCIATION FOR CRIME VICTIMS RIGHTS. P.O. Box 16161, Portland, Oregon 97216. (503) 252-9012.

NATIONAL ASSOCIATION OF CRIME VICTIM COMPENSATION BOARDS. 1900 L Street, Northwest, Suite 500, Washington, D.C. 20036. (202) 293-5420.

NATIONAL INSTITUTE OF VICTIMOLOGY. 2333 North Vernon Street, Arlington, Virginia 22207. (703) 536-1750.

NATIONAL ORGANIZATION FOR VICTIM ASSISTANCE, 717 D Street, Northwest, Washington, D.C. 20004. (202) 393-6682.

NATIONAL VICTIM CENTER. 307 West Seventh Street, Suite 1001, Fort Worth, Texas 76102. (817) 877-3355.

VICTIMS OF CRIME AND LENIENCY. Box 4449, Montgomery, Alabama 36103. (205) 262-7197.

ONLINE DATABASES

FROM THE STATE CAPITALS: JUSTICE POLICIES. Wakeman/Walworth, Incorporated, 300 North Washington Street, Suite 204, Alexandria, Virginia 22314.

STATISTICS SOURCES

APPLICATION OF THE NATIONAL CRIME SURVEY VICTIMIZATION AND ATTITUDE DATA. Analytic Report. United Stated Department of Justice, Bureau of Justice Statistics. Superintendent of Documents, United States Government Printing Office, Washington, D.C. 20402. 1981- .

BLACK VICTIMS. Catherine J. Whitaker. United States Department of Justice, Bureau of Justice Statistics. Superintendent of Documents, United States Government Printing Office, Washington, D.C. 20402. 1990.

CRIMINAL VICTIMIZATION IN THE UNITED STATES: TRENDS. Adolfo L. Paez and Richard W. Dodge. United States Department of Justice, Bureau of Justice Statistics. Superintendent of Documents, United States Government Printing Office, Washington, D.C. 20402. 1982- .

ESTIMATION OF VICTIMIZATION PREVALENCE USING DATA FROM THE NATIONAL CRIME SURVEY. Diane Griffin Saphire. Springer-Verlag New York, Incorporated, 175 Fifth Avenue, New York, New York 10010. 1984.

VICTIMIZATION AND FEAR OF CRIME: WORLD PERSPECTIVES. Richard Block, editor. United States Department of Justice, Bureau of Justice Statistics. Superintendent of Documents, United States Government Printing Office, Washington, D.C. 20402. 1984.

VIOLENT CRIME IN THE UNITED STATES. United States Department of Justice, Office of Justice Programs, Bureau of Justice Statistics, Washington, D.C. 1991.

OTHER SOURCES

INDEXED LEGISLATIVE HISTORY OF THE VICTIMS OF CRIME ACT OF 1984. United States Department of Justice, Office of Justice Programs, Office of the General Counsel, Superintendent of Documents, U.S. Government Printing Office, Washington, D.C. 20402. 1985.

SERVING CRIME VICTIMS AND WITNESSESS. Peter Finn. United States Department of Justice, National Institute of Justice, Superintendent of Documents, U.S.Government Printing Office, Washington, D.C. 20402. 1987.

CRIMINAL INVESTIGATION

LOOSELEAF SERVICES AND REPORTERS

FORENSIC SCIENCES: LAW/SCIENCE, CIVIL/CRIMINAL. Cyril H. Wecht, editor. Matthew Bender and Company, Incorporated, 11 Penn Plaza, New York, New York 10001. 1981- . (Periodic Supplements).

POLICE INVESTIGATION HANDBOOK. Barton L. Ingraham and Thomas P. Mauriello. Matthew Bender and Company, Incorporated, 11 Penn Plaza, New York, New York 10001. 1990- .

HANDBOOKS, MANUALS, FORMBOOKS

CRIME SCENE SEARCH AND PHYSICAL EVIDENCE HANDBOOK. Richard H. Fox and Carl L. Cunningham. Paladin Press, P.O. Box 1307, Boulder, Colorado 80306. 1987.

PRIVATE INVESTIGATOR'S BASIC MANUAL. Richard H. Akin. Charles C. Thomas Publishers, 2600 South First Street, Springfield, Illinois 62794-9265. 1979.

TEXTBOOKS AND GENERAL WORKS

THE ACOUSTICS OF CRIME: THE NEW SCIENCE OF FORENSIC PHONETICS. Harry Hollien. Plenum Publishing Corporation, 233 Spring Street, New York, New York 10013. 1990.

BEYOND THE CRIME LAB: THE NEW SCIENCE OF INVESTIGATION. Jon Zonderman. John Wiley and Sons, Incorporated, 605 Third Avenue, New York, New York 10158. 1990.

CRIMINAL AND CIVIL INVESTIGATION HANDBOOK. Joseph J. Grau and Ben Jacobson. Shepard's/McGraw-Hill, P.O. Box 1235, Colorado Springs, Colorado 80901. 1982.

CRIMINAL INVESTIGATION. Third Edition. Wayne Bennett and Karen M. Hess. West Publishing Company, P.O. Box 43526, 50 West Kellogg Boulevard, St. Paul, Minnesota 55164-0526. 1991.

CRIMINAL INVESTIGATION. Fifth Edition. Charles R. Swanson, Neil C. Chamelin and Leonard Territo. McGraw-Hill Publishing Company, 1221 Avenue of the Americas, New York, New York 10020. 1992.

CRIMINAL INVESTIGATION, A GUIDE TO TECHNIQUES AND SOLUTIONS. James V. Vandiver. Scarecrow Press, Incorporated, 52 Liberty Street, Box 4167, Metuchen, New Jersey 08840. 1983.

CRIMINAL INVESTIGATION: BASIC PERSPECTIVES. Fifth Edition. Paul B. Weston and Kenneth Wells. Prentice-Hall, Incorporated, 113 Sylvan Avenue, P.O. Box 500, Englewood Cliffs, New Jersey 07632. 1990.

CRIMINAL INVESTIGATION: ESSAYS AND CASES. James N. Gilbert. Merrill Publishing Company, P.O. Box 508, Columbus, Ohio 43216. 1990.

CRIMINALISTICS: AN INTRODUCTION TO FORENSIC SCIENCE. Fourth Edition. Richard Saferstein. Prentice-Hall, Incorporated, 113 Sylvan Avenue, Englewood Cliffs, New Jersey 07632. 1990.

DETECTION OF CRIME: STOPPING AND QUESTIONING, SEARCH AND SEIZURE, ENCOURAGEMENT AND ENTRAPMENT. Lawrence P. Tiffany and Donald M. McIntyre. Little, Brown and Company, 34 Beacon Street, Boston, Massachusetts 02108. 1974.

THE DETECTION OF HUMAN REMAINS. Edward W. Killam. Charles C. Thomas, Publishers, 2600 South First Street, Springfield, Illinois 62794. 1990.

FORENSIC EVIDENCE AND THE POLICE: THE EFFECTS OF SCIENTIFIC EVIDENCE ON CRIMINAL INVESTIGATIONS. Joseph L. Peterson, Steven Mihajlovic, and Michael Gilliland. United States Department of Justice, National Institute of Justice, for sale by Superintendent of Documents, U.S. Government Printing Office, Washington, D.C. 20402. 1984.

FUNDAMENTALS OF CRIMINAL INVESTIGATION. Fifth Edition. Charles E. O'Hara and Gregory L. O'Hara. Charles C. Thomas Publishers, 2600 South First Street, Springfield, Illinois 62794-9265. 1988.

HANDBOOK OF CRIME SCENE INVESTIGATION. Alexander Joseph and Harrison C. Allison. Allyn and Bacon, Incorporated, 160 Gould Street, Needham Heights, Massachusetts 02194. 1980.

HENRY C. LEE ON CRIME SCENE INVESTIGATION AND RECONSTRUCTION. Henry C. Lee. Massachusetts Continuing Legal Education, 20 West Street, Boston, Massachusetts 02111. 1988.

HUMAN EVIDENCE IN CRIMINAL JUSTICE. Second edition. Larry Miller, William Bass, and Ramona Miller. Pilgrimage, Incorporated, Route 11, Box 553, Jonesboro, Tennessee 37659. 1985.

INVESTIGATION FOR DETERMINATION OF FACT: A PRIMER ON PROOF. Richard A. Myren and Carol Henderson Garcia. Brooks/Cole Publishing Company, 511 Forest Lodge Road, Pacific Grove, California 93950. 1988.

THE LAW OF CRIMINAL INVESTIGATION: A BOOK FOR LAW ENFORCEMENT PERSONNEL. Lloyd L. Weinreb. Ballinger Division, HarperCollins Publishers, 10 East Fifty-third Street, New York, New York 10022. 1982.

THE POLICE FUNCTION AND THE INVESTIGATION OF CRIME. J. Brian Morgan. Gower Publishing Company, Old Post Road, Brookfield, Vermont 05036. 1990.

PRACTICAL CRIMINAL INVESTIGATION. Manuel S. Pena. Custom Publishing Company, 1590 Lotus Road, Placerville, California 95667. 1982.

PROFILING VIOLENT CRIMES: AN INVESTIGATIVE TOOL. Ronald M. Holmes. Sage Publications, 2455 Teller Road, Newbury Park, California 91320. 1989.

SCIENTIFIC CRIME INVESTIGATION. Jenny Tesar. Franklin Watts, Incorporated, 387 Park Avenue South, New York, New York 10016. 1991.

TECHNIQUES OF CRIME SCENE INVESTIGATION. Fifth Edition. Barry A.J. Fisher. Elsevier Science Publishing Company, P.O.Box 882, Madison Square Station, New York, New York 10159. 1991.

TRUE DETECTIVES: THE REAL WORLD OF TODAY'S P.I. William Parkhurst. Crown Publishers, Incorporated, 225 Park Avenue South, New York, New York 10003. 1989.

UNDERCOVER: POLICE SURVEILLANCE IN AMERICA. Gary T. Marx. University of California Press, 2120 Berkeley Way, Berkeley, California 94720. 1988.

WHO KILLED PRECIOUS?: HOW FBI SPECIAL AGENTS COMBINE HIGH TECHNOLOGY AND PSYCHOLOGY TO IDENTIFY VIOLENT CRIMINALS. H. Paul Jeffers. Pharos Books, 200 Park Avenue, New York, New York 10166. 1991.

LAW REVIEWS AND PERIODICALS

JOURNAL OF CRIMINAL LAW AND CRIMINOLOGY. Northwestern University, School of Law, 357 East Chicago Avenue, Chicago, Illinois 60611. Quarterly.

JOURNAL OF FORENSIC SCIENCE. 1916 Race Street, Philadelphia, Pennsylvania 19103. Bimonthly.

NEWSLETTERS AND NEWSPAPERS

ACADEMY NEWS. American Academy of Forensic Sciences, P.O. Box 669, Colorado Springs, Colorado 80901. Bimonthly.

DRUG ENFORCEMENT REPORT. Pace Publications, 443 Park Avenue South, New York, New York 10016. Biweekly.

SCIENTIFIC SLEUTHING REVIEW. George Washington University National Law Center, c/o Professor J.E. Starrs, Washington, D.C. 20052. Quarterly.

SEARCH AND SEIZURE BULLETIN. Quinlan Publishing Company, Incorporated, 23 Drydock Avenue, Boston, Massachusetts 02110. Monthly.

SEARCH AND SEIZURE LAW REPORT. Clark Boardman Company, Limited, 375 Hudson Street, New York, New York 10014. Monthly.

WADE EXCHANGE. World Association of Document Examiners, 111 North Caral Street, Chicago, Illinois 60606. Monthly.

BIBLIOGRAPHIES

BASICS OF CRIMINAL INVESTIGATION. Carol Ann Martin. Vance Bibliographies, P.O. Box 229, 112 North Charter Street, Monticello, Illinois 61856. 1980.

CRIMINAL INTELLIGENCE AND SECURITY INTELLIGENCE: A SELECTIVE BIBLIOGRAPHY. A. Stuart Farson and Catherine J. Matthews. Centre of Criminology, University of Toronto, Toronto, Ontario, Canada. 1990.

CRIMINAL INVESTIGATION: A SELECTED BIBLIOGRAPHY. Robert Goehlert. Vance Bibliographies, P.O. Box 229, 112 North Charter Street, Monticello, Illinois 61856. 1987.

BIOGRAPHICAL SOURCES

G-MEN, HOOVER'S FBI IN AMERICAN POPULAR CULTURE. Richard Gid Powers. Southern Illinois University Press, Post Office Box 3697, Carbondale, Illinois 62902-3697. 1983.

ASSOCIATIONS AND PROFESSIONAL SOCIETIES

ASSOCIATION OF FEDERAL INVESTIGATORS. 1612 K Street, Northwest, Suite 506, Washington, D.C. 20006. (202) 466-7288.

COUNCIL OF INTERNATIONAL INVESTIGATORS. P.O. Box 75600, Washington, D.C. 20013. (202) 583-4400.

FEDERAL CRIMINAL INVESTIGATORS ASSOCIATION. P.O. Box 1256, Detroit, Michigan 48231. (313) 229-5601.

INTERNATIONAL ASSOCIATION OF ARSON INVESTIGATORS. 5428 Del Maria Way, Suite 201, P.O. Box 91119, Louisville, Kentucky 40291. (502) 491-7482.

INTERNATIONAL ASSOCIATION OF AUTO THEFT INVESTIGATORS. 255 South Vernon, Dearborn, Michigan 48124. (313) 561-8583.

INTERNATIONAL ASSOCIATION OF BOMB TECHNICIANS AND INVESTIGATORS. P.O. Box 6609, Colorado Springs, Colorado 80934. (303) 636-2596.

INTERNATIONAL ASSOCIATION OF COMPUTER CRIME INVESTIGATORS. 150 North Main Street, Plymouth, Michigan 48170. (313) 459-8787.

INTERNATIONAL SECURITY AND DETECTIVE ALLIANCE. P.O. Box 6303, Corpus Christi, Texas 78466. (512) 888-6164.

NATIONAL ASSOCIATION OF INVESTIGATIVE SPECIALISTS. P.O. Box 33244, Austin, Texas 78764. (512) 832-0355.

NATIONAL ASSOCIATION OF LEGAL INVESTIGATORS. P.O. Box 12308, Pensacola, Florida 32581. (904) 435-7060.

SOCIETY OF PROFESSIONAL INVESTIGATORS. P.O. Box 3032, Church Street Station, New York, New York 10008. (212) 889-1656.

ONLINE DATABASES

THE EXPERT AND THE LAW. National Forensic Center, 17 Temple Terrace, Lawrenceville, New Jersey 08648.

FORENSIC SERVICES DIRECTORY. National Forensic Center, 17 Temple Terrace, Lawrenceville, New Jersey 08648.

OTHER SOURCES

THE EVIDENCE NEVER LIES: THE CASEBOOK OF A MODERN SHERLOCK HOLMES. Alfred Allan Lewis and Herbert Leon MacDonell. Dell Publishing Company, Incorporated, 666 Fifth Avenue, New York, New York 10103. 1989.

THE NATIONAL CRIME INFORMATION CENTER: THE INVESTIGATIVE TOOL. United States Department of Justice, Federal Bureau of Investigation, Superintendent of Documents, United States Government Printing Office, Washington, D.C. 20402. 1984.

WHAT DO PROSECUTORS PROSECUTE? AN INITIAL STATISTICAL PROFILE OF FEDERAL PROSECUTORIAL BEHAVIOR AT THE INVESTIGATIVE AND CHARGING STAGES. John C. Coffee, Jr., Richard Gruner, and John J. Hansen. Center for Law and Economic Studies, Columbia University School of Law, 435 West 116th Street, New York, New York 10027. 1984.

CRIMINAL JUSTICE, ADMINISTRATION OF
See also: ADMINISTRATION OF JUSTICE; COMMERCE DEPARTMENT

STATUTES, CODES, STANDARDS, UNIFORM LAWS

ABA STANDARDS FOR CRIMINAL JUSTICE. Second edition. Little, Brown and Company, 34 Beacon Street, Boston, Massachusetts 02108. 1980- . (Periodic Supplements).

THE CRIME CONTROL AND FINE ENFORCEMENT ACTS OF 1984: A SYNOPSIS. Anthony Partridge. Federal Judicial Center, 1500 H Street, Northwest, Washington, D.C. 20005. 1985.

HANDBOOKS, MANUALS, FORMBOOKS

CRIME AND JUSTICE. Second edition. Sir Leon Radzinowicz and Marvin E. Wolfgang. Basic Books, Incorporated, 10 East Fifty-third Street, New York, New York 10022. 1977.

A PRACTICAL GUIDE TO THE COMPREHENSIVE CRIME CONTROL ACT OF 1984. B. James George, Jr. Prentice-Hall Law and Business, Route 9W, Englewood Cliffs, New Jersey 07632. 1985.

TEXTBOOKS AND GENERAL WORKS

ABNORMAL BEHAVIOR AND THE CRIMINAL JUSTICE SYSTEM. Robert G. Meyer. D.C. Heath and Company, 125 Spring Street, Lexington, Massachusetts 02173. 1991.

AIDS: THE IMPACT ON THE CRIMINAL JUSTICE SYSTEM. Mark Blumberg. Merrill Publishing Company, P.O. Box 508, Columbus, Ohio 43216. 1990.

AMERICAN JUSTICE: RESEARCH OF THE NATIONAL INSTITUTE OF JUSTICE. Larry J. Siegel, Editor. West Publishing Company, 50 West Kellogg Boulevard, St. Paul, Minnesota 55164. 1990.

THE AMERICAN SYSTEM OF CRIMINAL JUSTICE. Sixth Edition. George F. Cole. Brooks/Cole Publishing Company, 511 Forest Lodge Road, Pacific Grove, California 93950. 1992.

ARRESTS WITHOUT CONVICTION: HOW OFTEN THEY OCCUR AND WHY. Floyd Feeney, Forrest Dill and Adrianne Weir. United States Department of Justice National Institute of Justice, Superintendent of Documents, U.S. Government Printing Office, Washington, D.C. 20402. 1983.

CAREER PLANNING IN CRIMINAL JUSTICE. Robert C. DeLucia and Thomas J. Doyle. Anderson Publishing Company, 2035 Reading Road, Cincinnati, Ohio 45202. 1990.

CASES AND MATERIALS ON CRIMINAL JUSTICE ADMINISTRATION. Fourth Edition. Frank W. Miller. Foundation Press, 615 Merrick Avenue, Westbury, New York 11590. 1991.

CAUSATION, PREDICTION, AND LEGAL ANALYSIS. Stuart S. Nagel. Quorum Books, Greenwood Publishing Group, Incorporated, 88 Post Road West, P.O. Box 5007, Westport, Connecticut 06881. 1986.

CHAOS IN THE COURTHOUSE: THE INNER WORKINGS OF THE URBAN CRIMINAL COURTS. Paul B. Wice. Praeger Publishers, One Madison Avenue, New York, New York 10010-3603. 1985.

COMPUTERS IN CRIMINAL JUSTICE ADMINISTRATION AND MANAGEMENT: INTRODUCTION TO EMERGING ISSUES AND APPLICATIONS. Second Edition. William G. Archambeault and Betty J. Archambeault. Anderson Publishing Company, 2035 Reading Road, Cincinnati, Ohio 45202. 1989.

COURTS AND CRIMINAL PROCEDURE. Eric H. Monkkonen, Editor. Meckler Corporation, 11 Ferry Lane West, Westport, Connecticut 06880. 1991.

CRIME AND CRIMINAL JUSTICE SINCE 1945. Terence Morris. Basil Blackwell, Incorporated, 3 Cambridge Center, Cambridge, Massachusetts 02142. 1989.

CRIME AND CRIMINOLOGY. Sixth Edition. Sue Titus Reid. Holt, Rinehart, and Winston, Incorporated, 6277 Sea Harbor Drive, Orlando, Florida 32821. 1991.

CRIME AND CRIMINOLOGY: A CRITICAL INTRODUCTION. Nigel Walker. Oxford University Press, 200 Madison Avenue, New York, New York 10016. 1987.

CRIME AND HUMAN NATURE. James A. Wilson and Richard J. Herrnstein. Simon and Schuster, Incorporated, 1230 Avenue of the Americas, New York, New York 10020. 1986.

CRIME AND JUSTICE: AN INTRODUCTION. Second Edition. Howard Abadinsky and L. Thomas Winfree. Nelson-Hall Publishers, 111 North Canal Street, Chicago, Illinois 60606. 1992.

CRIME AND JUSTICE IN AMERICA: A HUMAN PERSPECTIVE. Third Edition. Leonard Territo, James Halsted and Max Bromley. West Publishing Company, 50 West Kellogg Boulevard, St. Paul, Minnesota 55164. 1992.

CRIME IN THE STREETS AND CRIME IN THE SUITES: PERSPECTIVES ON CRIME AND CRIMINAL JUSTICE. Doug A. Timmer and D. Stanley Eitzen. Allyn and Bacon, 160 Gould Street, Needham Heights, Massachusetts 02194. 1989.

THE CRIMES WOMEN COMMIT, THE PUNISHMENTS THEY RECEIVE. Rita J. Simon and Jean Landis. Lexington Books, 125 Spring Street, Lexington, Massachusetts 02173. 1991.

CRIMINAL BEHAVIOR AND THE JUSTICE SYSTEM: PSYCHOLOGICAL PERSPECTIVES. Hermann Wegener, Friedrich Losel and Jochen Haisch, Editors. Springer-Verlag New York, Incorporated, 175 Fifth Avenue, New York, New York 10010. 1989.

CRIMINAL JUSTICE. Second Edition. Joel Samaha. West Publishing Company, 50 West Kellogg Boulevard, St. Paul, Minnesota 55164. 1991.

CRIMINAL JUSTICE. Third Edition. Sue Titus Reid. Macmillan Publishing Company, Incorporated, 866 Third Avenue, New York, New York 10022. 1992.

CRIMINAL JUSTICE. Third Edition. James A. Inciardi. Harcourt, Brace, Jovanovich, Incorporated, 6277 Sea Harbor Drive, Orlando, Florida 32821. 1990.

CRIMINAL JUSTICE. Roland Pennock and John W. Chapman. New York University Press, 70 Washington Square South, New York, New York 10012. 1985.

CRIMINAL JUSTICE AND DRUGS: THE UNRESOLVED CONNECTION. James C. Weissman and Robert L. Dupont, editors. Kennikat Press, 90 South Bayles Avenue, Port Washington, New York 11050. 1982.

CRIMINAL JUSTICE: EMERGING ISSUES. Susette M. Talarico. Sage Publications, Incorporated. 2455 Teller Road, Newbury Park, California 91320. 1985.

CRIMINAL JUSTICE IN AMERICA. Roscoe Pound. Da Capo Press, Incorporated, 233 Spring Street, New York, New York 10013. 1972.

CRIMINAL JUSTICE IN NEW YORK CITY. James R. Davis. McFarland and Company, Incorporated, P.O. Box 611, Jefferson, North Carolina 28640. 1990.

CRIMINAL JUSTICE IN THE UNITED STATES. Dean J. Champion. Merrill Publishing Company, P.O. Box 508, Columbus, Ohio 43216. 1990.

CRIMINAL JUSTICE: INTRODUCTORY CASES AND MATERIALS. Fifth Edition. John Kaplan, Jerome H. Skolnick and Malcolm M. Feeley. Foundation Press, 615 Merrick Avenue, Westbury, New York 11590. 1991.

CRIMINAL JUSTICE ORGANIZATIONS: ADMINISTRATION AND MANAGEMENT. John Klofas, Stan Stojkovic and David Kalinich. Brooks/Cole Publishing Company, 511 Forest Lodge Road, Pacific Grove, California 93950. 1990.

THE CRIMINAL JUSTICE SYSTEM: AN INTRODUCTION. Fourth Edition. Ronald J. Waldron. HarperCollins Publishers, 10 East Fifty-third Street, New York, New York 10022. 1989.

THE CRIMINAL JUSTICE SYSTEM AND BLACKS. Daniel Georges-Abeyie, editor. Clark Boardman Company, Limited, 435 Hudson Street, New York, New York 10014. 1984.

CRIMINAL JUSTICE TODAY: AN INTRODUCTORY TEXT FOR THE TWENTY-FIRST CENTURY. Frank Schmalleger. Prentice-Hall, Incorporated, 113 Sylvan Avenue, Englewood Cliffs, New Jersey 07632. 1991.

CRIMINAL LAW, CRIMINOLOGY, AND CRIMINAL JUSTICE: A CASEBOOK. William J. Chambliss and Thomas F. Courtless. Brooks/Cole Publishing Company, 511 Forest Lodge Road, Pacific Grove, California 93950. 1992.

CRIMINAL VIOLENCE, CRIMINAL JUSTICE. Charles E. Silberman. Random House Publicity, 201 East Fiftieth Street, New York, New York 10022. 1980.

CRIMINOLOGY AND PUBLIC POLICY: AN INTRODUCTION. James F. Gilsinan. Prentice-Hall, Incorporated, 113 Sylvan Avenue, Englewood Cliffs, New Jersey 07632. 1990.

DANGEROUS OFFENDERS: THE ELUSIVE TARGET OF JUSTICE. Mark H. Moore. Harvard University Press, 79 Garden Street, Cambridge, Massachusetts 02138. 1985.

DECISION MAKING IN CRIMINAL JUSTICE: TOWARD THE RATIONAL EXERCISE OF DISCRETION. Second Edition. Michael R. Gottfredson and Don M. Gottfredson. Plenum Publishing Corporation, 233 Spring Street, New York, New York 10013. 1988.

DISCRETIONARY JUSTICE: AN INTRODUCTION TO DISCRETION IN CRIMINAL JUSTICE. Howard Abadinsky. Charles C. Thomas Publishers, 2600 First Street, Springfield, Illinois 62794-9265. 1984.

DOMESTIC VIOLENCE: THE CRIMINAL JUSTICE RESPONSE. Eve S. Buzawa and Carl G. Buzawa. Sage Publications, 2455 Teller Road, Newbury Park, California 91320. 1990.

ESCAPE OF THE GUILTY. Ralph Adam Fine. Dodd, Mead, and Company, 71 Fifth Avenue, New York, New York 10003. 1986.

ETHICS IN CRIME AND JUSTICE: DILEMMAS AND DECISIONS. Joycelyn M. Pollock-Byrne. Brooks/Cole Publishing Company, 511 Forest Lodge Road, Pacific Grove, California 93950. 1989.

ETHNIC MINORITIES AND THE CRIMINAL JUSTICE SYSTEM. Robert Waters. Gower Publishing Company, Old Post Road, Brookfield, Vermont 05036. 1990.

GOD SAVE THIS HONORABLE COURT: HOW THE CHOICE OF JUSTICES AFFECTS OUR LIVES. Laurence H. Tribe. Random House Publicity, 201 East Fiftieth Street, New York, New York 10022. 1985.

THE GREAT AMERICAN CRIME MYTH. Kevin N. Wright. Praeger Publishers, One Madison Avenue, New York, New York 10010-3603. 1987.

HARM TO OTHERS. Joel Feinberg. Oxford University Press, 200 Madison Avenue, New York, New York 10016. 1987.

INTRODUCTION TO CRIMINAL JUSTICE. Lawrence F. Travis, III. Anderson Publishing Company, 2035 Reading Road, Cincinnati, Ohio 45202. 1990.

AN INTRODUCTION TO CRIMINAL JUSTICE RESEARCH. Max Futrell and Cliff Roberson. Charles C. Thomas, Publishers, 2600 South First Street, Springfield, Illinois 62794. 1988.

INTRODUCTION TO CRIMINAL JUSTICE RESEARCH METHODS. Gennaro F. Vito, Edward J. Latessa and Deborah G. Wilson. Charles C. Thomas, Publishers, 2600 South First Street, Springfield, Illinois 62794. 1988.

INTRODUCTION TO THE CRIMINAL JUSTICE SYSTEM. Fourth Edition. Gerald D. Robin and Richard H. Anson. HarperCollins Publishers, 10 East Fifty-third Street, New York, New York 10022. 1990.

JUSTICE, CRIME, AND ETHICS. Michael C. Braswell, Belinda R. McCarthy and Bernard J. McCarthy, Editors. Anderson Publishing Company, 2035 Reading Road, Cincinnati, Ohio 45202. 1991.

JUSTICE WITHOUT TRIAL: LAW ENFORCEMENT IN DEMOCRATIC SOCIETY. Second edition. Jerome H. Skolnick. Macmillan Publishing Company, Incorporated 866 Third Avenue, New York, New York 10022. 1975.

LAW AND DISORDER: CRIMINAL JUSTICE IN AMERICA. Bruce Jackson. University of Illinois Press, 54 East Gregory Drive, Champaign, Illinois 61820. 1984.

LAW, IDEOLOGY, AND PUNISHMENT: RETRIEVAL AND CRITIQUE OF THE LIBERAL IDEAL OF CRIMINAL JUSTICE. Alan W. Norrie. Kluwer Academic Publishers, 101 Philip Drive, Assinippi Park, Norwell, Massachusetts 02061. 1991.

LEGAL ISSUES IN CRIMINAL JUSTICE: THE COURTS. Sloan T. Letman, Dan W. Edwards and Daniel J. Bell, editors. Pilgramage, Incorporated, Route 11, Box 553, Jonesboro, Tennessee 37659. 1984.

LEGAL RIGHTS, DUTIES AND LIABILITIES OF CRIMINAL JUSTICE PERSONNEL: HISTORY AND ANALYSIS. Charles C. Thomas Publishers, 2600 First Street, Springfield, Illinois 62794-9265. 1984.

LETTER TO THE PRESIDENT ON CRIME CONTROL. Norval Morris and Gordon Hawkins. University of Chicago Press, 5801 Ellis Avenue, Chicago, Illinois 60637. 1977.

MAJOR CRIMINAL JUSTICE SYSTEMS: A COMPARATIVE SURVEY. Second Edition. George F. Cole, Stanislaw J. Frankowski and Marc G. Gertz. Sage Publications, 2455 Teller Road, Newbury Park, California 91320. 1987.

MAKING AMENDS: MEDIATION AND REPARATION IN CRIMINAL JUSTICE. Gwynn Davis. Routledge, Chapman & Hall, 29 West Thirty-fifth Street, New York, New York 10001. 1992.

THE MEDIA AND CRIMINAL JUSTICE POLICY: RECENT RESEARCH AND SOCIAL EFFECTS. Ray Surette, Editor. Charles C. Thomas, Publishers, 2600 South First Street, Springfield, Illinois 62794. 1990.

MEDIATION AND CRIMINAL JUSTICE: VICTIMS, OFFENDERS, AND COMMUNITY. Martin Wright and Burt Galaway, Editors. Sage Publications, 2455 Teller Road, Newbury Park, California 91320. 1989.

THE MYTH OF A RACIST CRIMINAL JUSTICE SYSTEM. William Wilbanks. Brooks/Cole Publishing Company, 511 Forest Lodge Road, Pacific Grove, California 93950. 1987.

OFFENDING WOMEN: FEMALE LAWBREAKERS AND THE CRIMINAL JUSTICE SYSTEM. Anne Worrall. Routledge, Chapman and Hall, 29 West Thirty-fifth Street, New York, New York 10001. 1990.

OFFENSE TO OTHERS. Joel Feinberg. Oxford University Press, 200 Madison Avenue, New York, New York 10016. 1988.

PATHS OF NEIGHBORHOOD CHANGE: RACE AND CRIME IN URBAN AMERICA. Richard P. Taub and D. Garth Taylor. University of Chicago Press, 5801 Ellis Avenue, Chicago, Illinois 60637. 1987.

THE POLICE FUNCTION. Fifth Edition. Frank W. Miller. Foundation Press, 615 Merrick Avenue, Westbury, New York 11590. 1991.

THE POLITICS OF CRIME AND CRIMINAL JUSTICE. Erika S. Fairchild and Vincent J. Webb, editors. Sage Publications, Incorporated, 2455 Teller Road, Newbury Park, California 91320. 1985.

POPULAR JUSTICE: A HISTORY OF AMERICAN CRIMINAL JUSTICE. Samuel E. Walker. Oxford University Press, 200 Madison Avenue, New York, New York 10016. 1980.

PREDICTION AND CLASSIFICATION: CRIMINAL JUSTICE DECISION MAKING. Don M. Gottfredson and Michael Tonry, Editors. University of Chicago Press, 5801 Ellis Avenue, Chicago, Illinois 60637. 1987.

PREDICTION IN CRIMINOLOGY. David P. Farrington and Roger Tarling. State University of New York Press, State University Plaza, Albany, New York 12246. 1985.

PRIVATIZING CRIMINAL JUSTICE. Roger Matthews. Sage Publications, 2455 Teller Road, Newbury Park, California 91320. 1989.

PRIVATIZING THE UNITED STATES JUSTICE SYSTEM: POLICE, ADJUDICATION, AND CORRECTIONS SERVICES FROM THE PRIVATE SECTOR. Gary W. Bowman, Simon Hakim and Paul Seidenstat, Editors. McFarland and Company, Incorporated, Box 611, Jefferson, North Carolina 28640. 1992.

PROBATION AND JUSTICE: RECONSIDERATION OF MISSION. Patrick D. McAnany, Doug Thomson and David Fogel. Oelgeschlager, Gunn and Hain, Incorporated, 245 Mirriam Street, Weston, Massachusetts 02193. 1984.

PROCEDURES IN THE JUSTICE SYSTEM. Fourth Edition. Gilbert B. Stuckey. Macmillan Publishing Company, Incorporated, 866 Third Avenue, New York, New York 10022. 1991.

THE PROSECUTORS: INSIDE THE OFFICES OF THE GOVERNMENT'S MOST POWERFUL LAWYERS. James B. Stewart. Simon and Schuster, Incorporated, 1230 Avenue of the Americas, New York, New York 10020. 1987.

PSYCHOLOGY AND THE LEGAL SYSTEM. Second Edition. Lawrence S. Wrightsman. Brooks/Cole Publishing Company, 511 Forest Lodge Road, Pacific Grove, California 93950. 1991.

THE PUBLIC DEFENDER: THE PRACTICE OF LAW IN THE SHADOWS OF REPUTE. Lisa J. McIntyre. University of Chicago Press, 5801 Ellis Avenue, Chicago, Illinois 60637. 1987.

PUBLIC ORDER AND PRIVATE LIVES: THE POLITICS OF LAW AND ORDER. Michael Brake and Chris Hale. Routledge, Chapman & Hall, 29 West Thirty-fifth Street, New York, New York 10001. 1992.

RACE AND CRIMINAL JUSTICE. Michael J. Lynch and E. Britt Patterson. Harrow and Heston, P.O. Box 3934 Stuyvesant Plaza, Albany, New York 12203. 1991.

RACE AND CRIMINAL JUSTICE. Paul Finkelman, Editor. Garland Publishing, Incorporated, 136 Madison Avenue, New York, New York 10016. 1992.

RESEARCH METHODS IN CRIMINAL JUSTICE AND CRIMINOLOGY. Third Edition. Frank E. Hagan. Macmillan Publishing Company, Incorporated, 866 Third Avenue, New York, New York 10022. 1992.

RETHINKING LEGAL NEED: THE CASE OF CRIMINAL JUSTICE. Paul Robertshaw. Dartmouth, Brookfield, Vermont. 1991.

THE RICH GET RICHER AND THE POOR GET PRISON: IDEOLOGY, CLASS, AND CRIMINAL JUSTICE. Jeffery H. Reiman. Second edition. Macmillan Publishing Company, Incorporated, 866 Third Avenue, New York, New York 10022. 1984.

ROUGH JUSTICE: DAYS AND NIGHTS OF A YOUNG D.A. David Heilbroner. Pantheon Books, 201 East Fiftieth Street, New York, New York 10022. 1990.

STATE CONSTITUTIONS AND CRIMINAL JUSTICE. Barry Latzer. Greenwood Publishing Group, Incorporated, 88 Post Road West, P.O. Box 5007, Westport, Connecticut 06881. 1991.

THE STATE POLITICS OF JUDICIAL AND CONGRESSIONAL REFORM: LEGITIMIZING CRIMINAL JUSTICE POLICIES. Thomas Carlyle Dalton. Greenwood Publishing Group, Incorporated, 88 Post Road West, P.O. Box 5007, Westport, Connecticut 06881. 1985.

THE TENOR OF JUSTICE: CRIMINAL COURTS AND THE GUILTY PLEA PROCESS. Peter F. Nardulli, James Eisenstein and Roy B. Flemming. University of Illinois Press, 54 East Gregory Drive, Champaign, Illinois 61820. 1988.

THEORY AND METHODS IN CRIMINAL JUSTICE HISTORY. Eric H. Monkkonen, Editor. K.G. Saur, 245 West Seventeenth Street, New York, New York 10011. 1992.

THINK ABOUT PRISONS AND THE CRIMINAL JUSTICE SYSTEM. Lois Smith Owens and Vivian Verdell Gordon. Walker and Company, 720 Fifth Avenue, New York, New York 10019. 1992.

THINKING ABOUT CRIME. James Q. Wilson. Revised Edition. Random House, Incorporated, 201 East Fiftieth Street, New York, New York 10022. 1985.

TO BE A VICTIM: ENCOUNTERS WITH CRIME AND INJUSTICE. Diane Sank and David I. Caplan. Plenum Publishing Corporation, 233 Spring Street, New York, New York 10013. 1991.

UNEQUAL JUSTICE?: WHAT CAN HAPPEN WHEN PERSONS WITH RETARDATION OR OTHER DEVELOPMENTAL DISABILITIES ENCOUNTER THE CRIMINAL JUSTICE SYSTEM. Robert Perske. Abingdon Press, P.O. Box 801, 201 Eighth Avenue South, Nashville, Tennessee 37202. 1991.

VIGILANTE: THE BACKLASH AGAINST CRIME IN AMERICA. William Tucker. Scarborough House, P.O. Box 459, Chelsea, Michigan 48118. 1987.

WOMEN AND CRIMINALITY: THE WOMAN AS VICTIM, OFFENDER, AND PRACTITIONER. Ronald Barri Flowers. Greenwood Publishing Group, Incorporated, 88 Post Road West, P.O. Box 5007, Westport, Connecticut 06881. 1987.

WOMEN, CRIME, AND CRIMINAL JUSTICE. Ralph Weisheit and Sue Mahan. Anderson Publishing Company, 2035 Reading Road, Cincinnati, Ohio 45202. 1988.

WOMEN, CRIME AND CRIMINAL JUSTICE. Allison Morris. Basil Blackwell, Incorporated, 3 Cambridge Center, Cambridge, Massachusetts 02142. 1987.

WOMEN IN THE CRIMINAL JUSTICE SYSTEM. Second edition. Clarice Feinman. Praeger Publishers, One Madison Avenue, New York, New York 10010-3603. 1985.

ENCYCLOPEDIAS AND DICTIONARIES

CRIMINAL JUSTICE DICTIONARY. Erik Beckman. Second edition. Pierian Press, P.O. Box 1808, Ann Arbor, Michigan 48106. 1983.

DICTIONARY OF AMERICAN PENOLOGY: AN INTRODUCTORY GUIDE. Vergil L. Williams. Greenwood Publishing Group, Incorporated, 88 Post Road West, P.O. Box 5007, Westport, Connecticut 06881. 1979.

DICTIONARY OF CRIME: CRIMINAL JUSTICE, CRIMINOLOGY AND LAW ENFORCEMENT. Jay Robert Nash, Editor. Paragon House Publishers, 90 Fifth Avenue, New York, New York 10011. 1992.

DICTIONARY OF CRIMINAL JUSTICE DATA TERMINOLOGY: THE TERMS AND DEFINITIONS PROPOSED FOR INTERSTATE AND NATIONAL DATA COLLECTION AND EXCHANGE: REPORT OF WORK PERFORMED BY SEARCH GROUPS, INCORPORATED. Second Edition. United States Department of Justice, Bureau of Justice Statistics, Superintendent of Documents, U.S. Government Printing Office, Washington, D.C. 20402. 1981.

DICTIONARY OF CRIMINAL JUSTICE TERMS. Gould Publications, 199/300 State Street, Binghamton, New York 13901-2782. 1984- . (Periodic Supplements).

ENCYCLOPEDIA OF CRIME AND JUSTICE. Sanford H. Kadish. Macmillan Publishing Company, Incorporated, 866 Third Avenue, New York, New York 10022. 1983.

FERDICO'S CRIMINAL LAW AND JUSTICE DICTIONARY. John N. Ferdico. West Publishing Company, 50 West Kellogg Boulevard, St. Paul, Minnesota 55164. 1992.

DIGESTS, INDEXES, ABSTRACTS, CITATORS

CRIMINAL JUSTICE ABSTRACTS. National Council on Crime and Deliquency, 685 Market Street, Number 620, San Francisco, California 94105. Quarterly.

CRIMINAL JUSTICE CITATIONS. Shepard's Editorial Staff. Shepard's/McGraw-Hill, P.O. Box 1235, Colorado Springs, Colorado 80901.

CRIMINAL JUSTICE DIGEST. Washington Crime News Service, 7620 Little River Turnpike, Room 400, Annandale, Virginia 22003. 1985.

CRIMINAL JUSTICE PERIODICAL INDEX. Indexing Services. University Microfilms, 300 North Zeeb Road, Ann Arbor, Michigan 48106-1346. Annual.

ANNUALS AND SURVEYS

CRIME AND JUSTICE: AN ANNUAL REVIEW OF RESEARCH. Michael Tonry and Norval Morris, editors. University of Chicago Press, 5801 Ellis Avenue, Chicago, Illinois 60637. Annual.

CRIMINAL JUSTICE HISTORY: AN INTERNATIONAL ANNUAL. Meckler Corporation, 11 Ferry Lane West, Westport, Connecticut 06880. 1980- . (Annual).

LEADING CONSTITUTIONAL CASES ON CRIMINAL JUSTICE. Foundation Press, 615 Merrick Avenue, Westbury, New York 11590. 1973- . Annual.

LAW REVIEWS AND PERIODICALS

AMERICAN CRIMINAL LAW REVIEW. Georgetown University Law Center, 600 New Jersey Avenue, Northwest, Washington, D.C. 20001. Quarterly.

CRIMINAL JUSTICE. American Bar Association, 750 North Lake Shore Drive, Chicago, Illinois 60611. 1973- . Quarterly.

CRIMINAL JUSTICE AND BEHAVIOR. American Association of Correctional Psychologists. 6712 Evening Street, Worthington, Ohio 43085. Quarterly.

CRIMINAL JUSTICE ETHICS. John Jay College of Criminal Justice, Institute for Criminal Justice Ethics, 444 West Fifty-sixth Street, New York, New York 10019. 1982- . Semiannual.

CRIMIMAL JUSTICE POLICY REVIEW. Indiana University of Pennsylvania, Indiana, Pennsylvania. 1986- . Quarterly.

CRIMINAL JUSTICE QUARTERLY. New Jersey Division of Criminal Justice, Appellate Section, East Orange, New Jersey. Quarterly.

JOURNAL OF THE AMERICAN CRIMINAL JUSTICE ASSOCIATION. P.O. Box 61047, Sacramento, California 95860. Semiannual.

JOURNAL OF CRIMINAL JUSTICE. Pergamnom Press, Incorporated, Maxwell House, Fairview Park, Elmsford, New York 10523. Quarterly.

JOURNAL OF CRIMINAL JUSTICE AND BEHAVIOR. American Association of Correctional Psychologists. Federal Prison System, SCRO, 1607 Main Street, Suite 700, Dallas, Texas. Quarterly.

JOURNAL OF QUANTITATIVE CRIMINOLOGY. Plenum Press, 233 Spring Street, New York, New York 10013. Quarterly.

JUSTICE QUARTERLY: JQ. Academy of Criminal Justice Sciences, 402 Nunn Hall, Northern Kentucky University, Highland Heights, Kentucky 41076. Quarterly.

THE JUSTICE REPORTER. Clark Boardman Company, Limited, 435 Hudson Street, New York, New York 10014. 1980- . Bimonthly.

NATIONAL CRIMINAL JUSTICE ASSOCIATION - LEGISLATIVE REPORT. National Criminal Justice Association, 444 North Capital Street, Northwest, Washington, D.C. 20001. Annual.

NEWSLETTERS AND NEWSPAPERS

ACJS TODAY. Academy of Criminal Justice Sciences, Northern Kentucky University, 402 Nunn Hall, Highland Heights, Kentucky 41076. Quarterly.

CASE COMMENTARIES AND BRIEFS. National District Attorneys Association, 1033 North Fairfax Street, Suite 200, Alexandria, Virginia 22314. Monthly.

C.J. THE AMERICAS. Office of International Criminal Justice, 1333 South Wabash Avenue, Box 53, Chicago, Illinois 60605. Bimonthly.

CJSH FORUM. Criminal Justice Statistics Association, 444 North Capital Street, Northwest, Washington, D.C. 20001. Quarterly.

COMMUNITY CRIME PREVENTION DIGEST. Washington Criminal Justice Reports, Incorporated, 3918 Prosperity Avenue, Suite 318, Fairfax, Virginia 22031. Monthly.

CORRECTIONS COMPENDIUM. Contact Center, Incorporated, P.O. Box 81826, Lincoln, Nebraska 68501. Monthly.

CORRECTIONS DIGEST. Washington Crime News Service, 3918 Prosperity Avenue, Suite 318, Fairfax, Virginia 22031. Biweekly.

CRIMINAL JUSTICE. American Bar Association, Criminal Justice Section, 750 North Lake Shore Drive, Chicago, Illinois 60611. Quarterly.

CRIMINAL JUSTICE DIGEST. Washington Crime News Service, 3918 Prosperity Avenue, Suite 318, Fairfax, Virginia 22031. Monthly.

CRIMINAL JUSTICE JOURNAL. New York State Bar Association, One Elk Street, Albany, New York 12207. Triannual.

CRIMINAL JUSTICE NEWSLETTER. Pace Publications, 443 Park Avenue South, New York, New York 10016. Semimonthly.

CRIMINAL JUSTICE REPORT. National Association of Attorneys-General, 444 North Capitol Street, Suite 403, Washington, D.C. 20001. Monthly.

FORTUNE NEWS. Fortune Society, 39 West Nineteenth, New York, New York 10011. Quarterly.

JUSTICE BULLETIN. National Criminal Justice Association, 444 North Capital Street, Northwest, Washington, D.C. 20001. Monthly.

JUSTICE RESEARCH. National Criminal Justice Association, 444 North Capital Street, Northwest, Washington, D.C. 20001. Bimonthly.

JUVENILE JUSTICE DIGEST. Washington Crime News Service, 3918 Prosperity Avenue, Suite 318, Fairfax, Virginia 22031. Semimonthly.

LAW ENFORCEMENT LEGAL REVIEW. James P. Manaky, 421 Ridgewood Avenue, Gaithersburg, Maryland 20760. Bimonthly.

LOCAL CRIMINAL JUSTICE ISSUES NEWSLETTER. National Association of Blacks in Criminal Justice, P.O. Box 66271, Washington, D.C. 20035. Bimonthly.

NATIONAL ASSOCIATION OF ATTORNEYS GENERAL CRIMINAL JUSTICE NEWSLETTER. Box 11910, Iron Works Pike, Lexington, Kentucky 40578. Monthly.

ORGANIZED CRIME DIGEST. Washington Crime News Service, 3918 Prosperity Avenue, Suite 318, Fairfax, Virginia 22031. Semimonthly.

SEARCH AND SEIZURE BULLETIN. Quinlan Publications Company, Incorporated, 23 Drydock Avenue, Boston, Massachusetts 02110. Monthly.

SEARCH AND SEIZURE LAW REPORT. Clark Boardman Company, Limited, 375 Hudson Street, New York, New York 10014. Monthly.

WEST'S CRIMINAL LAW NEWS. West Publishing Company, 50 West Kellogg Boulevard, St. Paul, Minnesota 55164. Biweekly.

BIBLIOGRAPHIES

ADMINISTRATION OF CRIMINAL JUSTICE: A SELECTED BIBLIOGRAPHY. Robert Goehlert. Vance Bibliographies, P.O. Box 229, 112 North Charter Street, Monticello, Illinois 61856. 1987.

CRIME AND PUNISHMENT IN AMERICA: A HISTORICAL BIBLIOGRAPHY. ABC-Clio Information Services, P.O. Box 1911, Santa Barbara, California 93116-1911. 1983.

CRIMINAL JUSTICE ADMINISTRATION: A BIBLIOGRAPHY. Anna Gnadt. Vance Bibliographies, P.O. Box 229, 112 North Charter Street, Monticello, Illinois 61856. 1991.

CRIMINAL JUSTICE DOCUMENTS: A SELECTIVE, ANNOTATED BIBLIOGRAPHY OF U.S. GOVERNMENT PUBLICATIONS SINCE 1975. John F. Berens. Greenwood Publishing Group, Incorporated, 88 Post Road West, P.O. Box 5007, Westport, Connecticut 06881. 1987.

CRIMINAL JUSTICE ETHICS: ANNOTATED BIBLIOGRAPHY AND GUIDE TO SOURCES. Frank Schmalleger and Robert McKenrick. Greenwood Publishing Group, Incorporated, 88 Post Road West, P.O. Box 5007, Westport, Connecticut 06881. 1991.

CRIMINAL JUSTICE IN AMERICA, 1959-1984: AN ANNOTATED BIBLIOGRAPHY. John D. Hewitt, Eric Poole, and Robert M. Regoli. Garland Publishing, Incorporated, 136 Madison Avenue, New York, New York 10016. 1985.

CRIMINAL JUSTICE REFORM--DETERMINATE SENTENCING: A BIBLIOGRAPHY. Mary E. Huls. Vance Bibliographies, P.O. Box 229, 112 North Charter Street, Monticello, Illinois 61856. 1985.

CRIMINOLOGY AND CRIMINAL JUSTICE IN AMERICA: A GUIDE TO THE LITERATURE. Revised Edition. Social Science and Sociological Resources, P.O. Box 241, Aurora, Illinois 60507. 1978.

EXPANDING KNOWLEDGE IN CRIMINAL JUSTICE: PUBLICATIONS OF THE NATIONAL INSTITUTE OF JUSTICE, CUMMULATIVE SUPPLEMENT 1978-1982. United States Department of Justice, National Institute of Justice. Superintendent of Documents, U.S. Government Printing Office, Washington, D.C. 20402. 1984.

INTERAGENCY AND INTERSTATE COOPERATION IN CRIMINAL JUSTICE: A SELECTED BIBLIOGRAPHY. Mary Ellen Huls. Vance Bibliographies, P.O. Box 229, 112 North Charter Street, Monticello, Illinois 61856. 1985.

PUTTING RESEARCH TO WORK: TOOLS FOR THE CRIMINAL JUSTICE PROFESSIONAL. United States Department of Justice, National Institute of Justice. Superintendent of Documents, U.S. Government Printing Office, Washington, D.C. 20402. 1984.

DIRECTORIES

ANDERSON'S DIRECTORY OF CRIMINAL JUSTICE EDUCATION. Anderson Publishing Company, 2035 Reading Road, Cincinatti, Ohio 45202. 1986- . Biennial.

DIRECTORY OF AUTOMATED CRIMINAL JUSTICE INFORMATION SYSTEMS. United States Department of Justice, Bureau of Justice Statistics. Superintendent of Documents, U.S. Government Printing Office, Washington, D.C. 20402. Annual.

DIRECTORY OF CRIMINAL JUSTICE INFORMATION SERVICES. United States Department of Justice, National Institute of Justice, National Criminal Justice Reference Service. Superintendent of Documents, U.S. Government Printing Office, Washington, D.C. 20402. 1986.

DIRECTORY OF CRIMINAL JUSTICE ISSUES IN THE STATES. Criminal Justice Statistics Association, 444 North Capital Street, Northwest, Suite 606, Washington, D.C. 20001. Annual.

NABCJ MINORITY CRIMINAL JUSTICE PERSONNEL DIRECTORY. National Association of Blacks in Criminal Justice, P.O. Box 66271, Washington, D.C. 20035. Annual.

A NETWORK OF KNOWLEDGE: DIRECTORY OF CRIMINAL JUSTICE INFORMATION SOURCES. Fifth edition. Paula Goldberg, Ronnie Mills, and United States Department of Justice, National Institute of Justice. Superintendent of Documents, U.S. Government Printing Office, Washington, D.C. 20402. 1984.

SNI: SELECTIVE NOTIFICATION OF INFORMATION. United States Department of Justice, Law Enforcement Assistance Administration, National Institute of Law Enforcement and Criminal Justice, National Criminal Justice Reference Service, P.O. Box 6000, Rockville, Maryland 20850. NIJ Reports. Bimonthly.

ASSOCIATIONS AND PROFESSIONAL SOCIETIES

ACADEMY OF CRIMINAL JUSTICE SCIENCES. Northern Kentucky University, 402 Nunn Hall, Highland Heights, Kentucky 41076. (606) 572-5634.

AMERICAN ASSOCIATION FOR CORRECTIONAL PSYCHOLOGY. 6712 Evening Street, Worthington, Ohio 43085. (614) 431-2797.

AMERICAN BAR ASSOCIATION STANDING COMMITTEE ON ASSOCIATION STANDARDS FOR CRIMINAL JUSTICE. American Bar Association, 750 North Lake Shore Drive, Chicago, Illinois 60611. (312) 988-5158.

AMERICAN CRIMINAL JUSTICE ASSOCIATION. P.O. Box 61047, Sacramento, Ohio 95860. (916) 484-6553.

AMERICAN SOCIETY OF CRIMINOLOGY. 1314 Kinnear Road, Suite 212, Columbus, Ohio 43212. (614) 292-9207.

CENTER FOR STUDIES IN CRIMINAL JUSTICE. University of Chicago Law School, 1111 East Sixtieth Street, Chicago, Illinois 60637. (312) 702-9493.

CRIMINAL JUSTICE STATISTICS ASSOCIATION. 444 North Capitol Street, Northwest, Washington, D.C. 20001. (202) 624-8560.

NATIONAL ASSOCIATION OF CRIMINAL JUSTICE PLANNERS. 1511 K Street, Northwest, Suite 445, Washington, D.C. 20005. (202) 347-0501.

NATIONAL CRIMINAL JUSTICE ASSOCIATION. 444 North Capitol Street, Northwest, Washington, D.C. 20001. (202) 347-4900.

NATIONAL LAW ENFORCEMENT COUNCIL. 1140 Connecticut Avenue, Northwest, Washington, D.C. 20036. (202) 223-6850.

WOMEN'S PRISON ASSOCIATION. 110 Second Avenue, New York, New York 10003. (212) 674-1163.

RESEARCH CENTERS, INSTITUTES, CLEARINGHOUSES

ADMINISTRATION OF JUSTICE BUREAU. San Jose State University, MacQuarrie Hall 524, San Jose, California 95192. (408) 924-3330.

BUREAU OF JUSTICE STATISTICS UNITED STATES DEPARTMENT OF JUSTICE. 633 Indiana Avenue, Northwest, Washington, D.C. 20530. (202) 307-0759.

CENTER FOR ADMINISTRATION OF CRIMINAL JUSTICE. University of California - Davis, Davis, California 95616. (916) 752-2893.

CENTER FOR CRIMINAL JUSTICE POLICY AND MANAGEMENT. University of San Diego, Alcala Park, San Diego, California 92110. (619) 260-4600.

CENTER FOR CRIMINAL JUSTICE RESEARCH AND TRAINING. California State University, Long Beach, School of Applied Arts and Science, 1250 Bellflower Boulevard, Long Beach, California 90840. (213) 985-4940.

CENTER FOR LAW AND JUSTICE. University of Washington, 1107 Northeast Forty-fifth Street, Suite 505, Seattle, Washington 98105. (206) 543-1485.

CENTER FOR RESEARCH IN LAW AND JUSTICE. University of Illinois at Chicago, Box 4348, Chicago, Illinois 60680. (312) 996-4632

CENTER FOR STUDIES IN CRIMINAL JUSTICE. University of Chicago, 1111 East Sixtieth Street, Chicago, Illinois 60637. (312) 702-9493.

COLORADO DIVISION OF CRIMINAL JUSTICE, RESEARCH UNIT. 700 Kipling, Suite 3000, Denver, Colorado 80215. (303) 239-4442.

CRIMINAL JUSTICE CENTER. 899 Tenth Avenue, Room 636, New York, New York 10019. (212) 247-1600.

CRIMINAL JUSTICE CENTER. Sam Houston State University, College of Criminal Justice, Huntsville, Texas 77341. (409) 294-1647.

CRIMINAL JUSTICE RESEARCH CENTER. Ohio State University, 1775 College Road, Columbus, Ohio 43210. (614) 292-7468.

HINDELANG CRIMINAL JUSTICE RESEARCH CENTER. State University of New York at Albany, 135 Western Avenue, Albany, New York 12222. (518) 442-5600.

INSTITUTE FOR CRIMINAL JUSTICE ETHICS, John Jay College of Criminal Justice, 899 Tenth Avenue, New York, New York 10019. (212) 237-8415.

INSTITUTE FOR THE STUDY OF LAW AND CRIMINOLOGY. University of Florida, 509 Hume Library, Gainesville, Florida 32611. (904) 392-1025.

INSTITUTE OF CRIMINAL JUSTICE AND CRIMINOLOGY. University of Maryland, 2220 Lefrak Hall, College Park, Maryland 20742. (301) 494-4538.

INSTITUTE OF CRIMINAL LAW AND PROCEDURE. Georgetown University, 600 New Jersey Avenue, Northwest, Washington, D.C. 20001. (202) 662-9070.

NATIONAL CENTER FOR JUVENILE JUSTICE. 701 Forbes Avenue, Pittsburgh, Pennsylvania 15219. (412) 227-6950.

NATIONAL CLEARINGHOUSE FOR CRIMINAL JUSTICE INFORMATION SYSTEMS. 7311 Greenhaven Drive, Suite 145, Sacramento, California 95831. (916) 392-2550.

NATIONAL CRIMINAL JUSTICE REFERENCE CENTER. National Institute of Justice, 633 Indiana Avenue, Northwest, Washington, D.C, 20531. (202) 307-2966.

SCHOOL OF JUSTICE STUDIES. Arizona State University, Tempe, Arizona 85287. (602) 965-7682.

SEARCH GROUP INCORPORATED. 925 Secret River Drive, Sacramento, California 05831.

SELLIN CENTER FOR STUDIES IN CRIMINOLOGY AND CRIMINAL LAW. University of Pennsylvania, 3733 Spruce Street, Room 437, Philadelphia, Pennsylvania 19104. (215) 898-7411.

VERA INSTITUTE OF JUSTICE, INCORPORATED, RESEARCH DEPARTMENT. 377 Broadway, New York, New York 10013. (212) 334-1300.

STATISTICS SOURCES

PREDICTION IN CRIMINOLOGY. David P. Farrington and Roger Tarling. State University of New York Press, State University Plaza, Albany, New York 12246. 1985.

THE PROSECUTION OF FELONY ARRESTS...1979- . United States Department of Justice, Bureau of Justice Statistics. Superintendent of Documents, U.S. Government Printing Office, Washington, D.C. 20402. 1983- .

SOURCEBOOK OF CRIMINAL JUSTICE STATISTICS. National Criminal Justice Information and Statistics Service. Superintendent of Documents, U.S. Government Printing Office, Washington, D.C. 20402. 1973- . Annual.

TRENDS IN EXPENDITURE AND EMPLOYMENT DATA FOR THE CRIMINAL JUSTICE SYSTEM, 1971-1977. United States Department of Justice, Law Enforcement Assistance Adminstration. Superintendent of Documents, U.S. Government Printing Office, Washington, D.C. 20402. 1980- .

ONLINE DATABASES

AUTOMATED INDEX OF CRIMINAL JUSTICE INFORMATION SYSTEMS. National Clearinghouse for Criminal Justice Information Systems, 7311 Greenhaven Drive, Suite 145, Sacramento, California 95831.

CRIMINAL JUSTICE DATA DIRECTORY. University of Michigan, Inter University Consortium for Political and Social Research, P.O. Box 1248, Ann Arbor, Michigan 48106.

CRIMINAL JUSTICE PERIODICAL INDEX. University Microfilms International, 300 North Zeeb Road, Ann Arbor, Michigan 48106.

FROM THE STATE CAPITALS: JUSTICE POLICIES. Wakeman/Walworth, Incorporated, 300 North Washington Street, Suite 204, Alexandria, Virginia 22314.

LAW ENFORCEMENT AND CRIMINAL JUSTICE INFORMATION DATABASE. International Research and Evaluation, 21098 IRE Control Center, Eagan, Minnesota 55121.

NATIONAL CRIMINAL JUSTICE REFERENCE SERVICE. National Institute of Justice, P.O. Box 6000, Rockville, Maryland 20850.

WESTLAW CRIMINAL JUSTICE LIBRARY. West Publishing Company, 50 West Kellog Boulevard, P.O. Box 64526, St. Paul, Minnesota 55164.

OTHER SOURCES

DATA RESOURCES OF THE NATIONAL INSTITUTE OF JUSTICE. Second Edition. Colin Loftin. United States Department of Justice, National Insitute of Justice, Washington, D.C. 1987.

THE INFLUENCE OF CRIMINAL JUSTICE RESEARCH. Joan Petersilia. Rand Corporation, Institute for Civil Justice, 1700 Main Street, P.O. Box 2138, Santa Monica, California 90406. 1987.

RESEARCH METHODS IN CRIMINAL JUSTICE AND CRIMINOLOGY. Frank E. Hagan. Macmillan Publishers Company, Incorporated, 866 Third Avenue, New York, New York 10022. 1989.

USE OF MICROCOMPUTERS IN CRIMINAL JUSTICE AGENCIES. J. Thomas McEwen. United States Department of Justice, National Institute of Justice, Office of Communication and Research Utilization, Washington, D.C. 1990.

WHAT PRICE JUSTICE?: A HANDBOOK FOR THE ANALYSIS OF CRIMINAL JUSTICE COSTS. Billy L. Wayson and Gail S. Funke. United States Department of Justice, Office of Justice Programs, National Institute of Justice, Washington, D.C. 1989.

WORLD CRIMINAL JUSTICE SYSTEMS: AN INTRODUCTION. Richard J. Terrill. Anderson Publishing Company, 2035 Reading Road, Cincinnati, Ohio 45202. 1984.

CRIMINAL LAW

See also: ADMINISTRATION OF JUSTICE; ARSON; CAPITAL PUNISHMENT; CONSPIRACY; COUNTERFEITING; CRIMINAL PROCEDURE; DOUBLE JEOPARDY; EMBEZZLEMENT; FRAUD; JUDGES AND JUDICIAL PROCESS; JUDGMENTS; KIDNAPPING; LIBEL AND SLANDER; MURDER; PROBATION AND PAROLE; PROSTITUTION; SEX CRIMES; SUICIDE; TREASON

STATUTES, CODES, STANDARDS, UNIFORM LAWS

MODEL PENAL CODE: OFFICIAL DRAFT AND EXPLANATORY NOTES: COMPLETE TEXT OF MODEL PENAL CODE AS ADOPTED AT THE 1962 ANNUAL MEETING OF THE AMERICAN LAW INSTITUTE AT WASHINGTON, D.C., MAY 24, 1962. American Law Institute, 4025 Chestnut Street, Philadelphia, Pennsylvania 19104. 1985.

LOOSELEAF SERVICES AND REPORTERS

CONTEMPORARY FEDERAL CRIMINAL PRACTICE: A PRACTICAL GUIDE TO THE COMPREHENSIVE CRIME CONTROL ACT OF 1984. George B. James, Jr. Prentice-Hall Law and Business, Route 9W, Englewood Cliffs, New Jersey 07632. 1986- . (Periodic supplements).

CRIMINAL DEFENSE TECHNIQUES. Michael Eisenstein, editor. Matthew Bender and Company, Incorporated, 11 Penn Plaza, New York, New York 10001. 1984- . (Annual supplements).

CRIMINAL LAW ADVOCACY. Mark J. Kadish. Matthew Bender and Company, Incorporated, 11 Penn Plaza, New York, New York 10001. 1982- . (Periodic Supplements).

CRIMINAL LAW ADVOCACY REPORTER. Matthew Bender and Company, Incorporated, 11 Penn Plaza, New York, New York 10001. 1982- . (Monthly supplements).

CRIMINAL LAW DESKBOOK. Patrick L. McCloskey and Ronald L. Shoenberg. Matthew Bender and Company, Incorporated, 11 Penn Plaza, New York, New York 10001. 1984- . (Periodic supplements).

CRIMINAL LAW REPORTER. Bureau of National Affairs, Incorporated, 1231 25th Street, Northwest, Washington, D.C. 20037. 1967- . (Weekly supplements).

FEDERAL CRIMINAL LAW AND PROCEDURE: ALR ANNOTATIONS. Lawyers Cooperative Publishing Company, Aqueduct Building, Rochester, New York 14694. 1991- .

LAW OF ELECTRONIC SURVEILLANCE. James G. Carr. Clark Boardman Company, Limited, 435 Hudson Street, New York, New York 10014. 1986- . (Annual supplements).

PROSECUTION AND DEFENSE OF CRIMINAL CONSPIRACY CASES. Paul Marcus. Matthew Bender and Company, Incorporated, 11 Penn Plaza, New York, New York 10001. 1978- . (Annual supplements).

TRIAL MANUAL 4 FOR THE DEFENSE OF CRIMINAL CASES. Second edition. Anthony G. Amsterdam, Reporter. American Law Institute-American Bar Association, 4025 Chestnut Street, Philadelphia, Pennsylvania 19104. 1984- . (Periodic Supplements).

UNITED STATES SUPREME COURT CASES AND COMMENTS: CRIMINAL LAW AND PROCEDURE. William H. Erickson, William D. Neighbors and B. J. George. Matthew Bender and Company, Incorporated, 11 Penn Plaza, New York, New York 10001. 1985- .

WHITE COLLAR CRIME: BUSINESS AND REGULATORY OFFENSES. Otto G. Obermaier and Robert G. Morvillo, Editors. Law Journal Seminars-Press, Incoprorated, 111 Eighth Avenue, Suite 900, New York, New York 10011. 1989- . (Periodic supplements).

HANDBOOKS, MANUALS, FORMBOOKS

BNA CRIMINAL PRACTICE MANUAL. Bureau of National Affairs, Incorporated, 1231 25th Street, Northwest, Washington, D.C. 20037. 1987- . (Biweekly Supplements).

HANDBOOK ON THE COMPREHENSIVE CRIME CONTROL ACT OF 1984 AND OTHER CRIMINAL STATUTES ENACTED BY THE 98TH CONGRESS. United States Justice Department, Superintendent of Documents, United States Government Printing Office, Washington, D.C. 20402. 1984.

A PRACTICAL GUIDE TO THE COMPREHENSIVE CRIME CONTROL ACT OF 1984. B. James George. Law and Business, Incorporated, Harcourt Brace Jovanovich, 6277 Sea Harbor Drive, Orlando, Florida 32821. 1985.

THE PRACTICAL LAWYER'S MANUAL ON CRIMINAL LAW AND PROCEDURE. ALI-ABA Committee on Continuing Professional Education, American Bar Association, 4025 Chestnut Street, Philadelphia, Pennsylvania 19104. 1984.

TEXTBOOKS AND GENERAL WORKS

CASES AND COMMENTS ON CRIMINAL LAW. Fifth Edition. Andre A. Moenssens, Fred E. Inbau and Ronald J. Bacigal. Foundation Press, 615 Merrick Avenue, Westbury, New York 11590. 1992.

CASES AND MATERIALS ON CRIMINAL LAW AND APPROACHES TO THE STUDY OF LAW. Second Edition. John M. Brumbaugh. Foundation Press, 615 Merrick Avenue, Westbury, New York 11590. 1991.

CASES AND PROBLEMS IN CRIMINAL LAW. Second Edition. Myron Moskovitz. Anderson Publishing Company, 2035 Reading Road, Cincinnati, Ohio 45202. 1991.

CONSTITUTIONAL RIGHTS OF THE ACCUSED. Second edition. Joseph G. Cook. Lawyers Cooperative Publishing Company, Aqueduct Building, Rochester, New York 14694. 1985- . (Periodic Supplements).

CRIME AND CRIMINAL LAW: MAJOR HISTORICAL INTERPRETATIONS. Kermit L. Hall, Editor. Garland Publishing, Incorporated, 136 Madison Avenue, New York, New York 10016. 1987.

CRIME IN AMERICAN SOCIETY. Second Edition. Charles H. McCaghy and Stephen A. Cernkovich. Macmillan Publishing Company, Incorporated, 866 Third Avenue, New York, New York 10022. 1987.

CRIMES AND PUNISHMENT: CASES, MATERIALS, AND READINGS IN CRIMINAL LAW. Richard G. Singer and Martin R. Gardner. Matthew Bender and Company, Incorporated, 11 Penn Plaza, New York, New York 10001. 1989.

THE CRIMES AND PUNISHMENT PRIMER. Third Edition. B.R. White and Irvin J. Sloan, editors. Oceana Publications, Incorporated, 75 Main Street, Dobbs Ferry, New York 10522. 1986.

CRIMINAL JUSTICE. J. Roland Pennock and John W. Chapman. New York University Press, 70 Washington Square, New York, New York 10012. 1985.

CRIMINAL LAW. Thomas Morawetz, Editor. New York University Press, 70 Washington Square South, New York, New York 10012. 1991.

CRIMINAL LAW. Second Edition. Joseph G. Cook and Paul Marcus. Matthew Bender and Company, Incorporated, 11 Penn Plaza, New York, New York 10001. 1988.

CRIMINAL LAW. Second Edition. Robert Force and Daniel Jay Baum. South-Western Publishing Company, 5101 Madison Road, Cincinnati, Ohio 45227. 1988.

CRIMINAL LAW. Second Edition. Sue Titus Reid. Macmillan Publishing Company, Incorporated, 866 Third Avenue, New York, New York 10022. 1992.

CRIMINAL LAW. Second Edition. Stephen Emanuel. Emanuel Law Outlines, 1865 Palmer Avenue, Larchmont, New York 10538. 1987-88.

CRIMINAL LAW. Third Edition. Joel Samaha. West Publishing Company, 50 West Kellogg Boulevard, St. Paul, Minnesota 55164. 1990.

CRIMINAL LAW. Third Edition. John C. Klotter. Anderson Publishing Company, 2035 Reading Road, Cincinnati, Ohio 45202. 1990.

CRIMINAL LAW. Third Edition. Rollin M. Perkins and Ronald N. Boyce. Foundation Press, Incorporated, 615 Merrick Avenue, Westbury, New York 11590. 1989.

CRIMINAL LAW. Thirteenth Edition. George E. Dix. Gilbert Law Summaries, Distributed by Law Distributors, 14415 South Main Street, Gardena, California 90248. 1984.

CRIMINAL LAW AND ITS ADMINISTRATION. Fifth Edition. Fred E. Inbau. Foundation Press, 615 Merrick Avenue, Westbury, New York 11590. 1990.

CRIMINAL LAW AND ITS PROCESSES: CASES AND MATERIALS. Fifth Edition. Sanford H. Kadish and Stephen J. Schulhofer. Little, Brown and Company, 34 Beacon Street, Boston, Massachusetts 02108. 1989.

CRIMINAL LAW AND PROCEDURE FOR PARALEGALS. Daniel Hall. Lawyers Cooperative Publishing Company, Aqueduct Building, Rochester, New York 14694. 1992.

CRIMINAL LAW: CASES AND MATERIALS. Arnold H. Loewy. Anderson Publishing Company, 2035 Reading Road, Cincinnati, Ohio 45202. 1991.

CRIMINAL LAW: CASES, MATERIALS, AND TEXT. Fourth Edition. Phillip E. Johnson. West Publishing Company, 50 West Kellogg Boulevard, St. Paul, Minnesota 55164. 1990.

CRIMINAL LAW, CRIMINOLOGY, AND CRIMINAL JUSTICE: A CASEBOOK. William J. Chambliss and Thomas F. Courtless. Brooks/Cole Publishing Company, 511 Forest Lodge Road, Pacific Grove, California 93950. 1992.

CRIMINAL LAW FOR POLICE OFFICERS. Fifth Edition. Neil C. Chamelin and Kenneth R. Evans. Prentice-Hall, Incorporated, 113 Sylvan Avenue, Englewood Cliffs, New Jersey 07632. 1991.

CRIMINAL LAW IN A NUTSHELL. Second edition. Arnold H. Loewy. West Publishing Company, Post Office Box 64526, 50 West Kellogg Boulevard, St. Paul, Minnesota 55164-0526. 1987.

CRIMINAL LAW IN ACTION. Second edition. William J. Chambliss. John Wiley and Sons, Incorporated, 605 Third Avenue, New York, New York 10158. 1983.

CRIMINAL LAW: PRINCIPLES AND CASES. Fifth Edition. Thomas J. Gardner and Terry M. Anderson. West Publishing Company, 50 West Kellogg Boulevard, St. Paul, Minnesota 55164. 1992.

CRIMINAL LAW: UNDERSTANDING BASIC PRINCIPLES. Charles W. Thomas and Donna M. Bishop. Sage Publications, Incorporated, 2455 Teller Road, Newbury, California 91320. 1987.

CROSS-EXAMINATION IN CRIMINAL TRIALS. F. Lee Bailey and Henry B. Rothblatt. Lawyer's Co-operative Publishing Company, Aqueduct Building, Rochester, New York 14694. 1978- . (Periodic Supplements).

THE ENTRAPMENT DEFENSE. Paul Marcus. Michie Company, P.O. Box 7587, Charlottesville, Virginia 22906. 1989.

FUNDAMENTALS OF CRIMINAL ADVOCACY. F. Lee Bailey and Henry B. Rothblatt, Lawyer's Co-operative Publishing Company, Aqueduct Building, Rochester, New York 14694. 1973- . (Periodic Supplements).

FUNDAMENTALS OF CRIMINAL LAW. Paul H. Robinson. Little, Brown and Company, 34 Beacon Street, Boston, Massachusetts 02108. 1988.

HANDLING MISDEMEANOR CASES. F. Lee Bailey and Henry B. Rothblatt, Lawyer's Co-operative Publishing Company, Aqueduct Building, Rochester, New York 14694. 1976- . (Periodic Supplements).

LAW OF CONFESSIONS. David M. Nissman, Ed Hagan and Pierce R. Brooks. Lawyer's Co-operative Publishing Company, Aqueduct Building, Rochester, New York 14694. 1985- . (Periodic Supplements).

CRIMINAL LAW

MADNESS AND THE CRIMINAL LAW. Norval Morris. University of Chicago Press, 5801 Ellis Avenue, Chicago, Illinois 60637. 1984.

MEDICO - LEGAL ASPECTS OF CRIMINAL LAW. Evan Stone and Hugh Johnson, editors. Pergamon Press, Incorporated, Maxwell House, Fairview Park, Elmsford, New York 10523. 1987.

THE MORAL LIMITS OF THE CRIMINAL LAW. Joel Feinberg. Oxford University Press, 200 Madison Avenue, New York, New York 10016. 1984.

OFFENSES TO OTHERS. Joel Feinberg. Oxford University Press, Incorporated, 200 Madison Avenue, New York, New York 10016. 1985.

PHILOSOPHY OF CRIMINAL LAW. Douglas N. Husak. Rowman and Littlefield Publishers, Incorporated, 8705 Bollman Place, Savage, Maryland 20763. 1987.

RETHINKING CRIMINAL LAW. George P. Fletcher. Little Brown and Company, 34 Beacon Street, Boston, Massachusetts 02108. 1978.

SEARCH AND SEIZURE. John Wesley Hall, Jr. Lawyer's Co-operative Publishing Company, Aqueduct Building, Rochester, New York 14694. 1982- . (Periodic Supplements).

SEARCH AND SEIZURE: A TREATISE ON THE FOURTH AMENDMENT. Wayne R. LaFave. West Publishing Company, Post Office Box 64526, 50 West Kellogg Boulevard, St. Paul, Minnesota 55164-0526. 1978- . (Periodic Supplements).

SMITH'S REVIEW OF CRIMINAL LAW. Fourth edition. West Publishing Company, Post Office Box 64526, 50 West Kellogg Boulevard, St. Paul, Minnesota 55164-0526. 1986.

SUBSTANTIVE CRIMINAL LAW. Leslie W. Abramson. West Publishing Company, 50 West Kellogg Boulevard, St. Paul, Minnesota 55164. 1990.

SUBSTANTIVE CRIMINAL LAW. M. Cherif Bassiouni. Charles C. Thomas Publishing, 2600 South First Street, Springfield, Illinois 62794-9265. 1978.

UNDERSTANDING CRIMINAL LAW. Joshua Dressler. Matthew Bender and Company, Incorporated, 11 Penn Plaza, New York, New York 10001. 1987.

WHARTON'S CRIMINAL LAW. Fourteenth edition. Charles E. Torcia, editor. Lawyer's Co-operative Publishing Company, Aqueduct Building, Rochester, New York 14694. 1979- . (Annual Supplements).

ENCYCLOPEDIAS AND DICTIONARIES

FERDICO'S CRIMINAL LAW AND JUSTICE DICTIONARY. John N. Ferdico. West Publishing Company, 50 West Kellogg Boulevard, St. Paul, Minnesota 55164. 1992.

WORLD ENCYCLOPEDIA OF POLICE FORCES AND PENAL SYSTEMS. George Thomas Kurian. Facts on File, Incorporated, 460 Park Avenue South, New York, New York 10016. 1988.

DIGESTS, INDEXES, ABSTRACTS, CITATORS

CRIMINAL LAW DIGEST: STATE FEDERAL, CONSTITUTIONAL LAW AND PROCEDURES, A TOPICALLY CLASSIFIED DIGEST OF SIGNIFICANT DECISIONS ON CRIMINAL LAW AND PROCEDURE, INCLUDING THOSE PUBLISHED IN THE CRIMINAL LAW BULLETIN, VOLUMES 1-18. Third edition. Research Institute of America, Incorporated, One Penn Plaza, New York, New York 10119. 1983- .

SCIENTIFIC SLEUTHING NEWSLETTER. James E. Starrs and Charles R. Midkiff, editors. Mid-Atlantic Association of Forensic Scientists, Oakton, Virginia. 1983- . (Quarterly).

ANNUALS AND SURVEYS

AMERICAN CRIMINAL LAW REVIEW. WHITE COLLAR CRIME SURVEY. Georgetown University Law Center, 25 East Street, Northwest, Washington, D.C. 20001. Annual.

CRIMINAL LAW REVIEW (YEAR). James G. Carr, editor. Clark Boardman Company, Limited, 435 Hudson Street, New York, New York 10014. Annual.

LAW REVIEWS AND PERIODICALS

AMERICAN CRIMINAL LAW QUARTERLY. Published Jointly by the University of Southern California Law School and the Section of Criminal Law of the American Bar Association, 750 North Lake Shore Drive, Chicago, Illinois 60611. Quarterly.

AMERICAN CRIMINAL LAW REVIEW. Georgetown University Law Center, 600 New Jersey Avenue, Northwest, Washington, D.C. 20007. Quarterly.

JOURNAL OF CRIMINAL LAW AND CRIMINOLOGY. Northwestern University School of Law, Chicago, Illinois. Quarterly.

NEWSLETTERS AND NEWSPAPERS

CRIMINAL LAW NEWSLETTER. Criminal Law Newsletter, 1561 Peregrino Way, San Jose, California 95125. (20 issues per year).

ORGANIZED CRIME DIGEST. Washington Crime News Services, 7043 Wimsatt Road, Springfield, Virginia 22151. (24 issues per year).

WEST'S CRIMINAL LAW NEWS. West Publishing Company, Post Office Box 64526, 50 West Kellogg Boulevard, St. Paul, Minnesota 55164-0526. (Weekly).

BIBLIOGRAPHIES

CRIMINAL LAW: A SELECTED BIBLIOGRAPHY. Robert Goehlert. Vance Bibliographies, P.O. Box 229, 112 North Charter Street, Monticello, Illinois 61856. 1987.

INSANITY DEFENSE: A BIBLIOGRAPHIC RESEARCH GUIDE. D. Cheryn Picouet and Reba A. Best. The Harrison Company, 3110 Crossing Park, Norcross, Georgia 30071. 1985.

Encyclopedia of Legal Information Sources • 2nd Ed. CRIMINAL PROCEDURE

WHITE COLLAR CRIME: A BIBLIOGRAPHY. Mary A. Vance. Vance Bibliographies, Post Office Box 229, 112 North Charter Street, Monticello, Illinois 61856. 1983.

STATISTICS SOURCES

SOURCEBOOK OF CRIMINAL JUSTICE STATISTICS. United States Department of Justice, Bureau of Justice Statistics. Superintendent of Documents, United States Government Printing Office, Washington, D.C. 20402. Annual.

UNIFORM CRIME REPORTING HANDBOOK. U.S. Department of Justice, Federal Bureau of Investigation. Superintendent of Documents, United States Government Printing Office, Washington, D.C. 20402. 1984.

ASSOCIATIONS AND PROFESSIONAL SOCIETIES

ASSOCIATION OF TRIAL LAWYERS OF AMERICA. 1050 31st Street, Northwest, Washington, D.C. 20007.

NATIONAL ASSOCIATION OF CRIMINAL DEFENSE LAWYERS. 1815 H Street, Northwest, Washington, D.C. 20003.

SECTION OF CRIMINAL LAW OF THE AMERICAN BAR ASSOCIATION. 750 North Lake Shore Drive, Chicago, Illinois 60611.

RESEARCH CENTERS, INSTITUTES, CLEARINGHOUSES

CENTER FOR STUDIES IN CRIMINOLOGY AND CRIMINAL LAW. University of Pennsylvania, 3733 Spruce Street, Room 437, Philadelphia, Pennsylvania 19104.

CENTER FOR THE STUDY OF CRIME, DELINQUENCY AND CORRECTIONS. Southern Illinois University at Carbondale, Carbondale, Illinois 62901.

CORNELL UNIVERSITY CENTER FOR THE STUDY OF RACE, CRIME AND SOCIAL POLICY. Suite 401, 1419 Broadway, Oakland, California 94612.

INSTITUTE OF CRIMINAL LAW AND PROCEDURE. Georgetown University, 600 New Jersey Avenue, Northwest, Washington, D.C. 20001.

MONTANA CRIMINAL LAW INFORMATION RESEARCH CENTER. University of Montana, School of Law, Missoula, Montana 59812.

NATIONAL COUNCIL ON CRIME AND DELINQUENCY RESEARCH AND INFORMATION DIVISION. 760 Market Street, San Francisco, California 94102.

UNITED STATES DEPARTMENT OF JUSTICE BUREAU OF JUSTICE STATISTICS. 633 Indiana Avenue, Northwest, Washington, D.C. 20531.

AUDIOVISUALS

CRIMINAL LAW: CLIENT COUNSELING COMPETITION VIDEOTAPE. American Bar Association, 750 North Lake Shore Drive, Chicago, Illinois 60611. 1986. Videotape.

CRIMINAL LAW AND PROCEDURE: THE COUNTER REVOLUTION. Charles H. Whitebread. National Practice Institute, 330 Second Avenue South, Minneapolis, Minnesota 55401. Audiotape.

COMPUTER-ASSISTED LEGAL INSTRUCTION

DEFENSE FUNCTION-CODE OF PROFESSIONAL RESPONSIBILITY VERSION. Kenneth K. Kirwin and Roger C. Park. Center for Computer-Assisted Instruction, 229 19th Avenue South, University of Minnesota, Minneapolis, Minnesota 55455. Machine-readable computer file.

DEFENSE FUNCTION-RULES OF PROFESSIONAL CONDUCT VERSION. Kenneth K. Kirwin and Roger C. Park. Center for Computer-Assisted Instruction, 229 19th Avenue South, University of Minnesota, Minneapolis, Minnesota 55455. Machine-readable computer file.

PRE-INDICTMENT AND CHARGE; PLEA AND DISCOVERY. Frank M. Tuerkheimer. Center for Computer-Assisted Instruction, 229 19th Avenue South, University of Minnesota, Minneapolis, Minnesota 55455. Machine-readable data file.

SEARCH AND SEIZURE. Center for Computer-Assisted Instruction, 229 19th Avenue South, University of Minnesota, Minneapolis, Minnesota 55455. Interactive videodisc.

STATE V. GILBERT. Center for Computer-Assisted Instruction, 229 19th Avenue South, University of Minnesota, Minneapolis, Minnesota 55455. Interactive videodisc.

STATE V. RODGERS. Center for Computer-Assisted Instruction, 229 19th Avenue South, University of Minnesota, Minneapolis, Minnesota 55455. Interactive videodisc.

STATE V. WILLIAMS I & II. Center for Computer-Assisted Instruction, 229 19th Avenue South, University of Minnesota, Minneapolis, Minnesota 55455. Interactive videodisc.

SUPENDATUR! Daniel G. Moriarty. Center for Computer-Assisted Instruction, 229 19th Avenue South, University of Minnesota, Minneapolis, Minnesota 55455. Machine-readable data file.

OTHER SOURCES

CONGRESS, COURTS, AND CRIMINALS: THE DEVELOPMENT OF FEDERAL CRIMINAL LAW 1801-1829. Dwight F. Henderson. Greenwood Publishing Group, Incorporated, 88 Post Road, Westport, Connecticut 06881. 1985.

SAMPLE JURY INSTRUCTIONS IN CRIMINAL ANTITRUST CASES. American Bar Association, 750 North Lake Shore Drive, Chicago, Illinois 60611.

CRIMINAL PROCEDURE
See also: BAIL; DOUBLE JEOPARDY; SEARCH AND SEIZURE; TRIAL PRACTICE

CRIMINAL PROCEDURE

STATUTES, CODES, STANDARDS, UNIFORM LAWS

ABA STANDARDS FOR CRIMINAL JUSTICE. Second edition. American Bar Association, Standing Committee on Association Standards for Criminal Justice, 1800 M Street, Northwest, Washington, D.C. 20036.

DRAFTING HISTORY OF THE FEDERAL RULES OF CRIMINAL PROCEDURE INCLUDING COMMENTS, RECOMMENDATIONS, AND SUGGESTIONS ON PUBLISHED DRAFTS OF THE RULES ... Madeleine J. Wilken and Nicholas Triffin, Editors. William S. Hein and Company, 1285 Main Street, Buffalo, New York 14209. 1991.

MODEL PENAL CODE. National Conference of Commissioners on Uniform State Laws. Uniform Laws Annotated. West Publishing Company, 50 West Kellogg Boulevard, St. Paul, Minnesota 55164-0526. 1976- . (Annual Supplements).

MODEL SENTENCING AND CORRECTIONS ACT. National Conference of Commissioners on Uniform State Laws. Uniform Laws Annotated. West Publishing Company, 50 West Kellogg Boulevard, St. Paul, Minnesota 55164-0526. 1976- . (Annual Supplements).

RULES OF CRIMINAL PROCEDURE. Robert M. Cipes, editor. Matthew Bender and Company, Incorporated, 11 Penn Plaza, New York, New York 10001. 1965- . (Seminannual supplements).

UNIFORM ACT TO SECURE THE ATTENDANCE OF WITNESSES FROM WITHOUT A STATE IN CRIMINAL PROCEEDINGS. National Conference of Commissioners on Uniform State Laws. Uniform Laws Annotated, West Publishing Company, 50 West Kellogg Boulevard, St. Paul, Minnesota 55164-0526. 1976- . (Annual Supplements).

UNIFORM CRIMINAL STATISTICS ACT. National Conference of Commissioners on Uniform State Laws. Uniform Laws Annotated, West Publishing Company, 50 West Kellogg Boulevard, St. Paul, Minnesota 55164-0526. 1976- . (Annual Supplements).

UNIFORM RENDITION OF PRISONERS AS WITNESSES IN CRIMINAL PROCEEDINGS ACT. Uniform Laws Annotated, West Publishing Company, 50 West Kellogg Boulevard, St. Paul, Minnesota 55164-0526. 1976- . (Annual Supplements).

UNIFORM RULES OF CRIMINAL PROCEDURE. National Conference of Commissioners on Uniform State Laws. Uniform Laws Annotated, West Publishing Company, 50 West Kellogg Boulevard, St. Paul, Minnesota 55164-0526. 1976- . (Annual Supplements).

LOOSELEAF SERVICES AND REPORTERS

BNA CRIMINAL PRACTICE MANUAL. Bureau of National Affairs, 1231 25th Street, Northwest, Washington, D.C. 20037. 1987- . (Biweekly supplements).

CRIMINAL CONSTITUTIONAL LAW. Helen Jenkins. Matthew Bender and Company, Incorporated, 11 Penn Plaza, New York, New York 10001. 1990- . (Annual supplements).

CRIMINAL DEFENSE ETHICS: LAW AND LIABILITY. John M. Burkoff. Clark Boardman Company, Limited, 435 Hudson Street, New York, New York 10014. 1991- . Revised Edition.

CRIMINAL DEFENSE TECHNIQUES. Michael Eisenstein, editor. Matthew Bender and Company, Incorporated, 11 Penn Plaza, New York, New York 10001. 1969- . (Biannual supplements).

CRIMINAL LAW ADVOCACY. Mark J. Kadish and others. Matthew Bender and Company, Incorporated, 11 Penn Plaza, New York, New York 10001. 1982- . (Periodic supplements).

THE CRIMINAL LAW DESKBOOK. Patrick L. McCloskey and Ronald L. Schoenberg. Matthew Bender and Company, Incorporated, 11 Penn Plaza, New York, New York 10001. 1984- . (Annual supplements).

THE CRIMINAL LAW REPORTER. Bureau of National Affairs, Incorporated, 1231 25th Street, Northwest, Washington, D.C. 20037. 1967- . (Weekly supplements).

CRIMINAL PROCEDURE. Second edition. Matthew Bender and Company, Incorporated, 11 Penn Plaza, New York, New York 10001. 1986- .

EYE-WITNESS IDENTIFICATION. Second edition. Nathan R. Sobel. Clark Boardman Company, Limited, 435 Hudson Street, New York, New York 10014. 1981- . (Annual supplements).

FEDERAL CRIMINAL APPEALS. Lissa Griffin. Callaghan and Company, 155 Pfingsten Road, Deerfield, Illinois 60015. 1991.

FEDERAL CRIMINAL LAW AND PROCEDURE: ALR ANNOTATIONS. Lawyers Cooperative Publishing Company, Aqueduct Building, Rochester, New York 14694. 1991.

FEDERAL SENTENCING MANUAL. Gerald McFadden and others. Matthew Bender and Company, Incorporated, 11 Penn Plaza, New York, New York 10001. 1989- . (Annual supplements).

OAKES' CRIMINAL PRACTICE GUIDE. Richard T. Oakes. Professional Education Systems, Incorporated, 200 Spring Street, Eau Claire, Wisconsin 54702. 1987- . (Periodic supplements).

PLEA BARGAINING AND GUILTY PLEAS. Second edition. Clark Boardman Company, Limited, 435 Hudson Street, New York, New York 10014. 1982- .

PRACTICE UNDER THE NEW FEDERAL SENTENCING GUIDELINES. Second edition. Phylis Skloot Bamberger, editor. Prentice-Hall Law and Business, Route 9W, Englewood Cliffs, New Jersey 07632. 1990- . (Periodic supplements).

PREVENTION AND PROSECUTION OF COMPUTER AND HIGH TECHNOLOGY CRIME. Stanley Arkin and others. Matthew Bender and Company, Incorporated, 11 Penn Plaza, New York, New York 10001. 1988- . (Annual supplements).

PROSECUTORIAL MISCONDUCT. Bennett L. Gershman. Clark Boardman and Company, Limited, 435 Hudson Street, New York, New York 10014. 1985- . (Annual supplements).

REPRESENTATION OF WITNESSES BEFORE FEDERAL GRAND JURIES. National Lawyers Guild, Clark Boardman and Company, 435 Hudson Street, New York 10014. 1984- .

SEARCHES AND SEIZURES, ARRESTS AND CONFESSIONS. Second edition. William E. Ringel. Clark Boardman and Company, 435 Hudson Street, New York, New York 10014. 1979- . (Annual Supplements).

SENTENCING DEFENSE MANUAL - ADVOCACY/PRACTICE/PROCEDURE. Marcia G. Shein. Clark Boardman Company, Limited, 435 Hudson Street, New York, New York 10014. 1988- . (Annual supplements).

TRIAL MANUAL FOR THE DEFENSE OF CRIMINAL CASES. Second edition. Anthony G. Amsterdam, et al. American Law Institute, American Bar Association Continuing Professional Education, 4025 Chestnut Street, Philadelphia, Pennsylvania 19104. 1984- . (Periodic Supplements).

VICTIM'S RIGHTS: LAW AND LITIGATION. J. Rapp and F. Carrington. Matthew Bender and Company, Incorporated, 11 Penn Plaza, New York, New York 10001. 1989- . (Annual supplements).

HANDBOOKS, MANUALS, FORMBOOKS

ALTERNATIVE SENTENCING: A PRACTITIONER'S GUIDE. Andrew R. Klein. Anderson Publishing Company, 2035 Reading Road, Cincinnati, Ohio 45202. 1988.

CAPITAL CASE SENTENCING: HOW TO PROTECT YOUR CLIENT. Ursula Bentele. American Bar Association, Section of Criminal Justice, 1800 M Street, Northwest, Washington, D.C. 20036. 1988.

COMPLETE MANUAL OF CRIMINAL FORMS. Second edition. F. Lee Bailey and Henry B. Rothblatt, Lawyer's Co-op, Aqueduct Building, Rochester, New York 14694. 1974- . (Periodic Supplements).

CRIMINAL PROCEDURE: FORMS AND COMMENTARY. David Rudovsky and Leonard Sosnov. West Publishing Company, 50 West Kellogg Boulevard, St. Paul, Minnesota 55164. 1991.

CRIMINAL PROCEDURE HANDBOOK. James G. Carr. Clark Boardman and Company, Limited, 435 Hudson Street, New York, New York 10014. 1987.

CYCLOPEDIA OF FEDERAL PROCEDURE, THIRD. Callaghan and Company, 155 Pfingsten, Deerfield, Illinois 60015. 1951- . (Annual Supplements).

FEDERAL GRAND JURY PRACTICE MANUAL. Veta M. Carney. Justice Department Criminal Division, Narcotics and Dangerous Drugs Section. Superintendent of Documents, United States Government Printing Office, Washington, D.C. 20402. 1983.

FEDERAL SENTENCING GUIDELINES HANDBOOK: TEXT, ANALYSIS, CASE DIGESTS. Shepard's/McGraw-Hill, P.O. Box 1235, Colorado Springs, Colorado 80901. 1990.

HANDBOOK OF CRIMINAL PROCEDURE. Fourth revised edition. Stuart J. Faber. Lega Books, 3255 Wilshire Boulevard, Suite 1514, Los Angeles, California 90010. 1985.

LEGAL GUIDE FOR POLICE: CONSTITUTIONAL ISSUES. Second Edition. John C. Klotter. Anderson Publishing Company, 2035 Reading Road, Cincinnati, Ohio 45202. 1989.

OAKES' CRIMINAL PRACTICE GUIDE. Richard T. Oakes. John Wiley and Sons, Incorporated, 605 Third Avenue, New York, New York 10158. 1991.

WEST'S FEDERAL FORMS. West Publishing Company, 50 West Kellogg Boulevard, St. Paul, Minnesota 55164-0526. 1981- .

TEXTBOOKS AND GENERAL WORKS

AMERICAN CRIMINAL PROCEDURE: CASES AND COMMENTARY. Third Edition. Stephen A. Saltzburg. West Publishing Company, 50 West Kellogg Boulevard, St. Paul, Minnesota 55164. 1988.

AMERICA'S COURTS AND THE CRIMINAL JUSTICE SYSTEM. Fourth Edition. David W. Neubauer. Brooks/Cole Publishing Company, 511 Forest Lodge Road, Pacific Grove, California 93950. 1992.

BETWEEN PRISON AND PROBATION: INTERMEDIATE PUNISHMENTS IN A RATIONAL SENTENCING SYSTEM. Norval Morris and Michael Tonry. Oxford University Press, 200 Madison Avenue, New York, New York 10016. 1990.

CASES AND COMMENTS ON CRIMINAL PROCEDURE. Fourth Edition. James B. Haddad. Foundation Press, 615 Merrick Avenue, Westbury, New York 11590. 1992.

CONSTITUTIONAL CRIMINAL PROCEDURE: AN EXAMINATION OF THE FOURTH, FIFTH, AND SIXTH AMENDMENTS, AND RELATED AREAS. Second Edition. Ronald J. Allen and Richard B. Kuhns. Little, Brown and Company, 34 Beacon Street, Boston, Massachusetts 02108. 1991.

CONSTITUTIONAL CRIMINAL PROCEDURE HANDBOOK. Shelvin Singer, Marshall J. Hartman. John Wiley and Sons, Incorporated, 605 Third Avenue, New York, New York 10158. 1986- . (Periodic Supplement).

CONSTITUTIONAL LIMITATIONS ON CRIMINAL PROCEDURE. Richard B. McNamara. Shepard's/McGraw-Hill, P.O. Box 1235, Colorado Springs, Colorado 80901. 1982- . (Annual Supplement).

CONSTITUTIONAL RIGHTS OF THE ACCUSED. Second edition. Joseph G. Cook. Lawyer's Co-op, Aqueduct Building, Rochester, New York 14694. 1985-1986- . (Annual Supplements).

COURTS AND CRIMINAL PROCEDURE. Eric H. Monkkonen, Editor. Meckler Corporation, 11 Ferry Lane West, Westport, Connecticut 06880. 1991.

THE CRIMINAL COURTS: STRUCTURES, PERSONNEL, AND PROCESSES. N. Gary Holten and Lawson L. Lamar. McGraw-Hill Publishing Company, 1221 Avenue of the Americas, New York, New York 10020. 1991.

CRIMINAL DEFENSE MOTIONS. R. Marc Kantrowitz and Roger Witkin. West Publishing Company, 50 West Kellogg Boulevard, St. Paul, Minnesota 55164. 1991.

CRIMINAL JUSTICE. J. Roland Pennock and John W. Chapman. New York University Press, 70 Washington Square, South, New York, New York 10012. 1985.

CRIMINAL JUSTICE AND THE SUPREME COURT: SELECTIONS FROM THE AMERICAN CONSTITUTION. Leonard W. Levy, Kenneth L. Karst and Dennis J. Mahoney, Editors. Macmillan Publishing Company, Incorporated, 866 Third Avenue, New York, New York 10022. 1990.

CRIMINAL JUSTICE PROCEDURE. Third edition. Ronald L. Carlson. Anderson Publishing Company, 2035 Reading Road, Cincinnati, Ohio 45202. 1985.

CRIMINAL LAW AND ITS ADMINISTRATION. Fifth Edition. Fred E. Inbau and others. Foundation Press, 615 Merrick Avenue, Westbury, New York 11590. 1990.

CRIMINAL LAW AND PROCEDURE FOR PARALEGALS. Daniel Hall. Lawyers Cooperative Publishing Company, Aqueduct Building, Rochester, New York 14694. 1992.

CRIMINAL LAW DEFENSES. Paul H. Robinson. West Publishing Company, 50 West Kellogg Boulevard, St. Paul, Minnesota 55164-0526. 1984- . (Periodic Supplements).

CRIMINAL PRACTICE AND PROCEDURE. Second Edition. Leslie W. Abramson and Terrence R. Fitzgerald. West Publishing Company, 50 West Kellogg Boulevard, St. Paul, Minnesota 55164. 1987.

CRIMINAL PRACTICE AND PROCEDURE. Second Edition. Richard B. McNamara. Equity Publishing Company, Main Street, Orford, New Hampshire 03777. 1991.

CRIMINAL PROCEDURE. Fifth Edition. Steven Emanuel and Steven Knowles. Emanuel Law Outlines, 1865 Palmer Avenue, Larchmont, New York 10538. 1985.

CRIMINAL PROCEDURE. Second Edition. Wayne R. LaFave and Jerold H. Israel. West Publishing Company, 50 West Kellogg Boulevard, St. Paul, Minnesota 55164. 1992.

CRIMINAL PROCEDURE: AN ANALYSIS OF CASES AND COMMENTS. Second edition. Charles H. Whitebread. Foundation Press, Incorporated, 615 Merrick Avenue, Westbury, New York 11590. 1989. (With 1988 Supplement).

CRIMINAL PROCEDURE AND THE CONSTITUTION:: LEADING SUPREME COURT CASES AND INTRODUCTORY TEXT. Jerold H. Israel, Yale Kamisar and Wayne R. LaFave. West Publishing Company, 50 West Kellogg Boulevard, St. Paul, Minnesota 55164. 1991.

CRIMINAL PROCEDURE CHECKLISTS. 1991, Edition. Michele G. Hermann and Barbara Bergman. Clark Boardman Company, Limited, 435 Hudson Street, New York, New York 10014. 1991.

CRIMINAL PROCEDURE: CONSTITUTION AND SOCIETY. Marvin Zalman and Larry J. Siegel. West Publishing Company, 50 West Kellogg Boulevard, St. Paul, Minnesota 55164. 1991.

CRIMINAL PROCEDURE: CONSTITUTIONAL CONSTRAINTS ON INVESTIGATION AND PROOF. Welsh S. White and James J. Tomkovicz. Matthew Bender and Company, Incorporated, 11 Penn Plaza, New York, New York 10001. 1990.

CRIMINAL PROCEDURE FOR LAW ENFORCEMENT PERSONNEL. Rolando V. del Carmen. Brooks/Cole Publishing Company, 511 Forest Lodge Road, Pacific Grove, California 93950. 1987.

CRIMINAL PROCEDURE FOR THE CRIMINAL JUSTICE PROFESSIONAL. Fourth Edition. John N. Ferdico. West Publishing Company, 50 West Kellogg Boulevard, St. Paul, Minnesota 55164-0526. 1989.

CRIMINAL PROCEDURE IN A NUTSHELL: CONSTITUTIONAL LIMITATIONS. Fourth Edition. Jerold H. Israel and Wayne R. LaFave. West Publishing Company, 50 West Kellogg Boulevard, St. Paul, Minnesota 55164-0526. 1988.

CRIMINAL PROCEDURE: LAW AND PRACTICE. Second Edition. Rolando V. del Carmen. Brooks/Cole Publishing Company, 511 Forest Lodge Road, Pacific Grove, California 93950. 1991.

CRIMINAL PROCEDURE, PRETRIAL. William Andrew Kerr. West Publishing Company, 50 West Kellogg Boulevard, St. Paul, Minnesota 55164. 1991.

CRIMINAL TRIAL ADVOCACY. Second edition. T. Eric Smithburn and James H. Seckinger. National Institute for Trial Advocacy, 1602 North Ironwood, South Bend, Indiana 46635. 1985- .

DECISION MAKING IN CRIMINAL JUSTICE: TOWARD THE RATIONAL EXERCISE OF DISCRETION. Second Edition. Plenum Publishing Corporation, 233 Spring Street, New York, New York 10013. 1988.

DISCRETION AND THE CRIMINAL JUSTICE PROCESS. T. Kenneth Moran and John L. Cooper. Associated Faculty Press, 19 West 36th Street, New York, New York 10018. 1983.

EXCULPATORY EVIDENCE: THE ACCUSED'S CONSTITUTIONAL RIGHT TO INTRODUCE FAVORABLE EVIDENCE. Edward J. Imwinkelried. Michie Company, P.O. Box 7587, Charlottesville, Virginia 22906. 1990.

FAIR TRIAL: RIGHTS OF THE ACCUSED IN AMERICAN HISTORY. David J. Bodenhamer. Oxford University Press, 200 Madison Avenue, New York, New York 10016. 1992.

FEDERAL CRIMINAL TRIALS. Second Edition. James C. Cissell. Michie Company, P.O. Box 7587, Charlottesville, Virginia 22906. 1987.

FEDERAL PRACTICE AND PROCEDURE: CRIMINAL 2d. (4 volumes). Charles Alan Wright. West Publishing Company, 50 West Kellogg Boulevard, St. Paul, Minnesota 55164-0526. 1982- . (Annual Supplements).

FEDERAL SENTENCING GUIDELINES. Kenneth R. Feinberg. Practising Law Institute, 810 Seventh Avenue, New York, New York 10019. 1987.

FEDERAL SENTENCING LAW AND PRACTICE. Thomas W. Hutchison and David Yellen. West Publishing Company, 50 West Kellogg Boulevard, St. Paul, Minnesota 55164. 1989.

HANDLING CRIMINAL APPEALS. Jonathan M. Purver and Lawrence E. Taylor. Lawyer's Co-op, Aqueduct Building, Rochester, New York 14694. 1980- . (Periodic Supplements).

HARM TO OTHERS. Joel Feinberg. Oxford University Press, 200 Madison Avenue, New York, New York 10016. 1987.

HARM TO SELF. Joel Feinberg. Oxford University Press, 200 Madison Avenue, New York, New York 10016. 1989.

INSIDE THE CRIMINAL PROCESS. Gary S. Katzmann. W.W Norton and Company, Incorporated, 500 Fifth Avenue, New York, New York 10110. 1991.

INTRODUCTION TO CRIMINAL JUSTICE. Fourth Edition. Donald J. Newman and Patrick Anderson. Random House, Incorporated, 201 East Fiftieth Street, New York, New York 10022. 1988.

INTRODUCTION TO THE CRIMINAL JUSTICE SYSTEM. Fourth Edition. Gerald D. Robin and Richard H. Anson. HarperCollins Publishers, 10 East Fifty-third Street, New York, New York 10022. 1990.

INVESTIGATION AND PREPARATION OF CRIMINAL CASES. F. Lee Bailey and Henry B. Rothblatt. Lawyer's Co-operative Publishing Company, Aqueduct Building, Rochester, New York 14694. 1970- . (Periodic Supplements).

JOSEPHSON'S ESSENTIAL PRINCIPLES OF CRIMINAL PROCEDURE. Michael Josephson. Center for Creative Educational Services, Herbert Legal Series, 2060 Huntington Drive, Number 4, San Marino, California 91108. 1983.

JUDICIAL DISCRETION AND CRIMINAL LITIGATION. Second Edition. Rosemary Pattenden. Oxford University Press, 200 Madison Avenue, New York, New York 10016. 1990.

OFFENSE TO OTHERS. Joel Feinberg. Oxford University Press, 200 Madison Avenue, New York, New York 10016. 1988.

ORFIELD'S CRIMINAL PROCEDURE UNDER THE FEDERAL RULES. Second edition. Mark S. Rhodes. Lawyer's Co-operative Publishing Company, Aqueduct Building, Rochester, New York 14694. 1985- . (Periodic Supplements).

POST CONVICTION REMEDIES IN A NUTSHELL. Robert Popper. West Publishing Company, 50 West Kellogg Boulevard, St. Paul, Minnesota 55164-0526. 1978.

PRACTICAL LAWYER'S MANUAL ON CRIMINAL LAW AND PROCEDURE. American Law Institute-American Bar Association Committee on Continuing Professional Education, 4025 Chestnut Avenue, Philadelphia, Pennsylvania 19104. 1984.

PROCEDURES IN THE JUSTICE SYSTEM. Fourth Edition. Gilbert B. Stuckey. Macmillan Publishing Company, Incorporated, 866 Third Avenue, New York, New York 10022. 1991.

PROFESSIONAL RESPONSIBILITY OF THE CRIMINAL LAWYER. John Wesley Hall, Jr. Lawyers Cooperative Publishing Company, Aqueduct Building, Rochester, New York 14694. 1987.

THE PURSUIT OF CRIMINAL JUSTICE: ESSAYS FROM THE CHICAGO CENTER. Gordon Hawkins and Franklin E. Zimring. University of Chicago Press, 5801 Ellis Avenue, Fourth Floor, Chicago, Illinois 60637. 1986.

SITTING IN JUDGMENT: THE SENTENCING OF WHITE-COLLAR CRIMINALS. Stanton Wheeler, Kenneth Mann and Austin Sarat. Yale University Press, 302 Temple Street, New Haven, Connecticut 06520. 1988.

THE SIXTH AMENDMENT IN MODERN AMERICAN JURISPRUDENCE: A CRITICAL PERSPECTIVE. Alfredo Garcia. Greenwood Publishing Group, Incorporated, 88 Post Road West, P.O. Box 5007, Westport, Connecticut 06881. 1992.

SMITH'S REVIEW OF CRIMINAL PROCEDURE. Fourth Edition. Myron G. Hill, et al. West Publishing Company, 50 West Kellogg Boulevard, St. Paul, Minnesota 55164-0526. 1986.

STATE CONSTITUTIONS AND CRIMINAL JUSTICE. Barry Latzer. Greenwood Publishing Group, Incorporated, 88 Post Road West, P.O. Box 5007, Westport, Connecticut 06881. 1991.

THE STRUCTURE OF CRIMINAL PROCEDURE: LAWS AND PRACTICE OF FRANCE, THE SOVIET UNION, CHINA, AND THE UNITED STATES. Barton L. Ingraham. Greenwood Publishing Group, Incorporated, 88 Post Road West, P.O. Box 5007, Westport, Connecticut 06881. 1987.

SUCCESSFUL TECHNIQUES FOR CRIMINAL TRIALS. Second edition. F. Lee Bailey and Henry B. Rothblatt, Lawyer's Co-operative Publishing Company, Aqueduct Building, Rochester, New York 14694. 1985- . (Periodic Supplements).

A SWORD FOR THE CONVICTED: REPRESENTING INDIGENT DEFENDANTS ON APPEAL. David T. Wasserman. Greenwood Publishing Group, Incorporated, 88 Post Road West, P.O. Box 5007, Westport, Connecticut 06881. 1990.

TEMPERED ZEAL: A COLUMBIA LAW PROFESSOR'S YEAR ON THE STREETS WITH THE NEW YORK CITY POLICE. H. Richard Uviller. Contemporary Books, Incorporated, 180 North Michigan Avenue, Chicago, Illinois 60601. 1988.

THE TENOR OF JUSTICE: CRIMINAL COURTS AND THE GUILTY PLEA PROCESS. Peter F. Nardulli, James Eisenstein and Roy B. Flemming. University of Illinois Press, 54 East Gregory Drive, Champaign, Illinois 61820. 1988.

THE TRIAL: A PROCEDURAL DESCRIPTION AND CASE STUDY. Howard Myers and Jan Pudlow. West Publishing Company, 50 West Kellogg Boulevard, St. Paul, Minnesota 55164. 1991.

TRIAL MANUAL FIVE FOR THE DEFENSE OF CRIMINAL CASES. Fifth Edition. Anthony G. Amsterdam. American Law Institute-American Bar Association, 4025 Chestnut Street, Philadelphia, Pennsylvania 19104. 1988.

TRIAL PREPARATION FOR PROSECUTORS. Michael D. Marcus. John Wiley and Sons, Incorporated, 605 Third Avenue, New York, New York 10158. 1989.

UNDERSTANDING CRIMINAL PROCEDURE. Joshua Dressler. Matthew Bender and Company, Incorporated, 11 Penn Plaza, New York, New York 10001. 1991.

THE UNITED STATES SENTENCING GUIDELINES: IMPLICATIONS FOR CRIMINAL JUSTICE. Dean J. Champion, Editor. Praeger Publishers, One Madison Avenue, New York, New York 10010-3603. 1989.

WHARTON'S CRIMINAL PROCEDURE. Thirteenth Edition. Charles E. Torcia. Lawyer's Co-operative Publishing Company, Aqueduct Building, Rochester, New York 14694. 1989.

WHITE COLLAR CRIME: BUSINESS AND REGULATORY OFFENSES. Otto G. Obermaier and Robert G. Morvillo, Editors. Law Journal Seminars-Press, Incorporated, 111 Eighth Avenue, Suite 900, New York, New York 10011. 1990.

ENCYCLOPEDIAS AND DICTIONARIES

THE CRIMINAL JUSTICE DICTIONARY. Second Edition. Pierian Press, Box 1808, Ann Arbor, Michigan 48106. 1983.

DICTIONARY OF CRIMINAL JUSTICE DATA TERMINOLOGY. Second edition. Search Group, Incorporated. Superintendent of Documents, United States Government Printing Office, Washington, D.C. 20402. 1981.

DIGESTS, INDEXES, ABSTRACTS, CITATORS

CRIMINAL JUSTICE PERIODICAL INDEX. Indexing Services, University Microfilms, P.O. Box 1307, Ann Arbor, Michigan 48106. Annual.

CRIMINAL PROCEDURE: WESTLAW REFERENCES AND TABLES OF CASES. Wayne R. LaFave and Jerold H. Israel West. West Publishing Company, 50 West Kellogg Boulevard, St. Paul, Minnesota 55164-0526. 1985.

MANUAL ON RECURRING PROBLEMS IN CRIMINAL TRIALS. Honorable Donald S. Voorhees. Federal Judicial Center, 1520 H Street, Northwest, Washington, D.C. 20005. 1985- .

SHEPARD'S CRIMINAL JUSTICE CITATIONS. Shepard's/ McGraw-Hill, Post Office Box 1235, Colorado Springs, Colorado 80901. 1975- .

ANNUALS AND SURVEYS

CRIMINAL PROCEDURE HANDBOOK. Clark Boardman and Company, 435 Hudson Street, New York, New York 10014. 1984- . (Annual).

LAW REVIEWS AND PERIODICALS

AMERICAN CRIMINAL LAW REVIEW. Georgetown University Law Center, 600 New Jersey Avenue, Northwest, Washington, D.C. 20001. Quarterly.

AMERICAN JOURNAL OF CRIMINAL LAW. University of Texas School of Law, Austin, Texas. 1972- . (3 issues per year).

NEWSLETTERS AND NEWSPAPERS

CRIME CONTROL DIGEST. Washington Crime News Service. 7043 Winn Salt Road, Springfield, Virginia 22151. Weekly.

CRIMINAL JUSTICE REPORT. National Association of Attorneys General, 444 North Capitol Street, Northwest, Suite 403, Washington, D.C. 20001. Monthly.

SCIENTIFIC SLEUTHING NEWSLETTER. Mid-Atlantic Association of Forensic Scientists, Post Office Box 196, McLean, Virginia 22101. Quarterly.

SEARCH AND SEIZURE BULLETIN. Quinlan Publishing Company, Incorporated, 131 Beverly Street, Boston, Massachusetts 02114. Monthly.

SEARCH AND SEIZURE LAW REPORT. Clark Boardman and Company, Liimited, 435 Hudson Street, New York, New York 10014. 1974- . (11 issues per year).

WEST'S CRIMINAL LAW NEWS. West Publishing Company, Post Office Box 64526, 50 West Kellogg Boulevard, St. Paul, Minnesota 55164-0562. 1984- .

DIRECTORIES

DIRECTORY OF CRIMINAL JUSTICE INFORMATION SOURCES. National Criminal Justice Reference Service, National Institute of Justice, Department of Justice, Box 6000, Rockville, Maryland 20850. 1985- .

NATIONAL DIRECTORY OF LAW ENFORCEMENT ADMINISTRATORS AND CORRECTIONAL INSTITUTIONS. National Police Chiefs and Sheriffs Information Bureau, 152 West Wisconsin Avenue, Suite 727, Milwaukee, Wisconsin 53203. Annual.

NATIONAL TRIAL AND DEPOSITION DIRECTORY. 421 West Franklin, Boise, Idaho 83707. 1986.

BIBLIOGRAPHIES

WHO'S WHO IN AMERICAN LAW ENFORCEMENT. National Association of Chiefs of Police, 1000 Connecticut Avenue, Northwest, Suite 9, Washington, D.C. 20036. Triennial.

STATISTICS SOURCES

DIRECTORY OF CRIMINAL JUSTICE ISSUES IN THE STATES. Criminal Justice Statistics Association. Superintendent of Documents, United States Government Printing Office, Washington, D.C. 20402. 1986.

SOURCEBOOK OF CRIMINAL JUSTICE STATISTICS. United States Department of Justice, Bureau of Justice Statistics. Superintendent of Documents, United States Government Printing Office, Washington, D.C. 20402. 1973- . (Annual).

UNIFORM CRIME REPORTING HANDBOOK. United States Department of Justice, Federal Bureau Investigation. Superintendent of Documents, United States Government Printing Office, Washington, D.C. 20402. 1984.

AUDIOVISUALS

CRIMINAL LAW AND PROCEDURE: THE COUNTER REVOLUTION. Charles H. Whitebread. National Practice Institute, 330 Second Avenue South, Minneapolis, Minnesota 55401. Audiotape.

CRIMINAL LAW FOR THE TRIAL ADVOCATE. Charles E. Moylan, Jr. The National Institute for Trial Advocacy, 1507 Emery Park Drive, St. Paul, Minnesota 55108. (6 video cassettes). 1982.

DEFENSE FUNCTION-CODE OF PROFESSIONAL RESPONSIBILITY VERSION. Kenneth K. Kirwin and Roger C. Park. Center for Computer-Assisted Instruction, 229 19th Avenue South, University of Minnesota, Minneapolis, Minnesota 55455. Machine-readable computer file.

DEFENSE FUNCTION-RULES OF PROFESSIONAL CONDUCT VERSION. Kenneth K. Kirwin and Roger C. Park. Center for Computer-Assisted Instruction, 229 19th Avenue South, University of Minnesota, Minneapolis, Minnesota 55455. Machine-readable computer file.

PRE-INDICTMENT AND CHARGE; PLEA AND DISCOVERY. Frank M. Tuerkheimer. Center for Computer-Assisted Instruction, 229 19th Avenue South, University of Minnesota, Minneapolis, Minnesota 55455. Machine-readable data file.

SEARCH AND SEIZURE. Center for Computer-Assisted Instruction, 229 19th Avenue South, University of Minnesota, Minneapolis, Minnesota 55455. Interactive videodisc.

STATE V. GILBERT. Center for Computer-Assisted Instruction, 229 19th Avenue South, University of Minnesota, Minneapolis, Minnesota 55455. Interactive videodisc.

STATE V. WILLIAMS I & II. Center for Computer-Assisted Instruction, 229 19th Avenue South, University of Minnesota, Minneapolis, Minnesota 55455. Interactive videodisc.

SUPENDATUR! Daniel G. Moriarty. Center for Computer-Assisted Instruction, 229 19th Avenue South, University of Minnesota, Minneapolis, Minnesota 55455. Machine-readable data file.

OTHER SOURCES

FEDERAL CRIMINAL JURY INSTRUCTIONS. Stephen A. Saltzburg and Harvey S. Perlman. The Michie Company, P.O. Box 7587, Charlottesville, Virginia 22906-7582. 1985- . (3 volumes).

FEDERAL RULES, CRIMINAL PROCEDURE, EVIDENCE, APPELLATE PROCEDURE, TITLE 18 U.S. CODE, CRIMES AND CRIMINAL PROCEDURE, TITLE 21 U.S. CODE, CHAPTER 13, DRUG ABUSE PREVENTION AND CONTROL, WITH CONSOLIDATED INDEX. West Publishing Company, 50 West Kellogg Boulevard, St. Paul, Minnesota 55164-0562. 1986- . (Every 2 years).

REPORT TO THE ATTORNEY GENERAL ON DOUBLE JEOPARDY AND GOVERNMENT APPEALS OF ACQUITTALS. United States Department of Justice, Office of Legal Policy. Superintendent of Documents, United States Government Printing Office, Washington, D.C. 20402. 1987.

RULES OF CRIMINAL PROCEDURE. Robert M. Cipes, editor. Matthew Bender and Company, Incorporated, 11 Penn Plaza, New York, New York 10001. 1965- . (Semi-annual Supplements).

UNDERSTANDING REVERSIBLE ERROR IN CRIMINAL APPEALS: FINAL REPORT. SUBMITTED TO THE STATE JUSTICE INSTITUTE BY NATIONAL CENTER FOR STATE COURTS. Joy A. Chapper and Roger A. Hanson. National Center for State Courts, State Justice Institute, 300 Newport Avenue, Williamsburg, Virginia 23187. 1989.

CRITICAL LEGAL STUDIES

TEXTBOOKS AND GENERAL WORKS

THE ALCHEMY OF RACE AND RIGHTS. Patricia J. Williams. Harvard University Press, 79 Garden Street, Cambridge, Massachusetts 02138. 1991.

CIVIL LIBERTIES AND AMERICAN DEMOCRACY. John Brigham. Congressional Quarterly, Incorporated, 1414 22nd Street, Northwest, Washington, D.C. 20037. 1984.

CRITICAL LEGAL STUDIES. Allan C. Hutchinson. Rowman and Littlefield Publishers, Incorporated, 8705 Bollman Place, Savage, Maryland 20763. 1989.

CRITICAL LEGAL STUDIES. James Boyle. New York University Press, 70 Washington Square South, New York, New York 10012. 1992.

CRITICAL LEGAL STUDIES. Peter Fitzpatrick and Alan Hunt. Basil Blackwell, Incorporated, 3 Cambridge Center, Cambridge, Massachusetts 02142. 1988.

CRITICAL LEGAL STUDIES: A LIBERAL CRITIQUE. Andrew Altman. Princeton University Press, 41 William Street, Princeton, New Jersey 08540. 1990.

CRITICAL LEGAL STUDIES: ARTICLES, NOTES AND BOOK REVIEWS SELECTED FROM THE PAGES OF THE HARVARD LAW REVIEW. The Harvard Law Review Association, 79 Garden Street, Cambridge, Massachusetts 02138. 1986.

THE CRITICAL LEGAL STUDIES MOVEMENT. Roberto Mangabeira Unger. Harvard University Press, 79 Garden Street, Cambridge, Massachusetts 02138. 1986.

CRITICAL STUDIES IN PRIVATE LAW: A TREATISE ON NEED-RATIONAL PRINCIPLES IN MODERN LAW. Thomas Wilhelmsson. Kluwer Academic Publishers, 101 Philip Drive, Assinippi Park, Norwell, Massachusetts 02061. 1992.

ESSAYS ON CRITICAL LEGAL STUDIES. Harvard Law Review, 79 Garden Street, Cambridge, Massachusetts 02138. 1986.

CRITICAL LEGAL STUDIES

A GUIDE TO CRITICAL LEGAL STUDIES. Mark Kelman. Harvard University Press, 79 Garden Street, Cambridge, Massachusetts 02138. 1987.

LAW'S EMPIRE. Ronald Dworkin. Harvard University Press, 79 Garden Street, Cambridge, Massachusettes 02138. 1986.

LEGAL EDUCATION AND THE REPRODUCTION OF HIERARCHY: A POLEMIC AGAINST THE SYTEM. Duncan Kennedy. AFAR, Cambridge, Massachusetts 02138. 1983.

MARXISM AND LAW. Piers Beirne and Richard Quinney. John Wiley and Sons, Incorporated, 605 Third Avenue, New York, New York 10158. 1982.

A MATTER OF PRINCIPLE. Ronald Dworkin. Harvard University Press, 79 Garden Street, Cambridge, Massachusetts 02138. 1985.

THE POLITICS OF INFORMAL JUSTICE. Richard Abel. Academic Press, 1250 Sixth Avenue, San Diego, California 92101. 1981. (Two Volumes)

THE POLITICS OF LAW: A PROGRESSIVE CRITIQUE. David Kairys, editor. Pantheon, Division of Random House, Incorporated, 201 East 50th Street, New York, New York 10022. 1982.

READING DWORKIN CRITICALLY. Alan Hunt, Editor. Available From: St. Martin's Press, 175 Fifth Avenue, New York, New York 10010. 1991.

TAKING RIGHTS SERIOUSLY. Ronald Dworkin. Harvard University Press, 79 Garden Street, Cambridge, Massachusetts 02138. 1977.

THE TRANSFORMATION OF AMERICAN LAW 1780-1860. Morton Horwitz. Harvard University Press, 79 Garden Street, Cambridge, Massachusetts 02138. 1977.

NEWSLETTERS AND NEWSPAPERS

CONFERENCE ON CRITICAL LEGAL STUDIES NEWSLETTER. Conference on Critical Legal Studies, c/o Alan Freeman, School of Law, John O'Brian Hall, State University of New York - Buffalo, Amherst Campus, Buffalo, New York 14260. Irregular. (716) 636-3035.

BIBLIOGRAPHIES

BIBLIOGRAPHY OF CRITICAL LEGAL STUDIES. Yale Law Journal, 302 Temple Street, New Haven, Connecticut 06520. (Vol 94, #2, December 1984).

ASSOCIATIONS AND PROFESSIONAL SOCIETIES

CONFERENCE ON CRITICAL LEGAL STUDIES. c/o Alan Freeman, School of Law, John O'Brian Hall, State University of New York - Buffalo, Amherst Campus, Buffalo, New York 14260. (716) 636-3035.

OTHER SOURCES

CRITICAL LEGAL STUDIES SYMPOSIUM. Stanford Law Review. Stanford Law School, Crown Quadrangle, Stanford, California 94305. (Volume 36, #'s 1 & 2, January 1984).

SYMPOSIUM ON CRITICAL LEGAL STUDIES. Cardozo Law Review, Benjamin N. Cardozo School of Law, Yeshiva University, 55 Fifth Avenue, New York, New York 10003. (Volume 6, #4, Summer 1985).

CROPS
See: AGRICULTURE

CROSS-EXAMINATION

LOOSELEAF SERVICES AND REPORTERS

ART OF ADVOCACY. CROSS EXAMINATION OF LAY WITNESSES. John E. Durst, Jr. and Fred Queller. Matthew Bender and Company, Incorporated, 11 Penn Plaza, New York, New York 10001. 1988- .

ART OF ADVOCACY. CROSS-EXAMINATION OF MEDICAL EXPERTS. Marshall Houts. Matthew Bender and Company, Incorporated, 11 Penn Plaza, New York, New York 10001. 1982- . (Periodic supplements).

ART OF ADVOCACY: CROSS EXAMINATION OF NON-MEDICAL EXPERTS. Robert L. Habush. Matthew Bender and Company, Incorporated, 11 Penn Plaza, New York, New York 10001. 1981- . (Periodic supplments.

ART OF ADVOCACY: DIRECT EXAMINATION. Scott Baldwin. Matthew Bender and Company, Incorporated, 11 Penn Plaza, New York, New York 10001. 1981- . (Annual supplements).

LANE'S GOLDSTEIN TRIAL TECHNIQUE. Fred Lane. Matthew Bender and Company, Incorporated, 11 Penn Plaza, New York, New York 10001. 1969- . (Annual supplements).

TEXTBOOKS AND GENERAL WORKS

THE ART OF QUESTIONING: THIRTY MAXIMS OF CROSS-EXAMINATIONS. Peter Megaree Brown. Collier MacMillan, 866 Third Avenue, New York, New York 10022. 1987.

CROSS EXAMINATION IN CRIMINAL TRIALS. F. Lee Bailey and Henry B. Rothblatt. Lawyer's Co-operative Publishing Company, Aqueduct Building, Rochester, New York 14694. 1978- . (Periodic Supplements).

CROSS-EXAMINATION ON TRIAL. Arnold J. Wolf. Butterworth Legal Publishers, 90 Stiles Road, Salem, New Hampshire 03079. 1988.

CROSS EXAMINATION, THE MOSAIC ART. John Nicholas Iannuzzi. Prentice-Hall, Incorporated, 113 Sylvan Avenue, Englewood Cliffs, New Jersey 07632. 1981.

DIRECT AND CROSS-EXAMINATION OF ORTHOPEDIC SURGEONS. Thomas J. Murray, Jr. and Jeffrey D. Robertson. Professional Education Systems, Incorporated, 200 Spring Street, Eau Claire, Wisconsin 54702. 1987.

Encyclopedia of Legal Information Sources • 2nd Ed.   CUSTOMS SERVICE

DOMBROFF ON DIRECT AND CROSS-EXAMINATION. Mark A. Dombroff. John Wiley and Sons, Incorporated, 605 Third Avenue, New York, New York 10158. 1985- . (Periodic Supplements).

EXPERT WITNESSES: DIRECT AND CROSS-EXAMINATION. William G. Mulligan. John Wiley and Sons, Incorporated, 605 Third Avenue, New York, New York 10158. 1987.

AUDIOVISUALS

ART OF CROSS-EXAMINATION. Henry B. Rothblatt. National Practice Institute, 330 Second Avenue South, Minneapolis, Minnesota 55401. Audiotape.

CROSS EXAMINATION. National Institute for Trial Advocacy in Cooperation with the American Bar Association, Consortium for Professional Education, Notre Dame Law School, Notre Dame, Indiana. 1983.

DIRECT AND CROSS EXAMINATION. National Institute for Trial Advocacy, Notre Dame Law School, Notre Dame, Indiana 46556. 1975-1979. 8 videocassettes.

MASTERING THE ART OF CROSS EXAMINATION. Irving Younger. National Institute for Trial Advocacy, Notre Dame Law School, Notre Dame, Indiana 46556. 1987. Videotape.

PRINCIPLES OF EXAMINATION. John A. Burgess. Consortium for Professional Education, American Bar Association, 750 North Lake Shore Drive, Chicago, Illinois 60611. 1978- . 2 videocassettes.

THE TEN COMMANDMENTS OF CROSS EXAMINATION. Irving Younger. Consortium for Professional Education, American Bar Association, 750 North Lake Shore Drive, Chicago, Illinois 60611. 1985. 1 videocassette.

COMPUTER-ASSISTED LEGAL INSTRUCTION

BREW V. HARRIS I, II AND III. Interactive Video Library, Harvard Law School, Educational Technology Department, 18 Everett Street, Cambridge, Massachusetts 02138. Interactive videodisc.

EASERLY V. LETWIN. Center for Computer-Assisted Instruction, 229 19th Avenue South, University of Minnesota, Minneapolis, Minnesota 55455. Interactive videodisc.

TRIAL EVIDENCE AND CROSS-EXAMINATION SKILLS. CLE Group, 274 Willow Road, Menlo Park, California 94025. Interactive videodisc.

TRIAL SKILLS ILLUSTRATED I AND II. CLE Group, 274 Willow Road, Menlo Park, California 94025. Interactive videodisc.

CRUEL AND UNUSUAL PUNISHMENT
See: PUNISHMENT

CURRENCY
See: MONEY AND MONETARY CONTROL

CUSTODY
See: CHILD CUSTODY; GUARDIAN AND WARD; HABEAS CORPUS; PRISONS AND PRISONERS

CUSTOMS
See: CUSTOMS SERVICE; EXPORT AND IMPORT

CUSTOMS SERVICE
See also: COURT OF CUSTOMS AND PATENT APPEALS

STATUTES, CODES, STANDARDS, UNIFORM LAWS

CUSTOMS REGULATIONS OF THE UNITED STATES. Treasury Department, Customs Service. Superintendent of Documents, United States Government Printing Office, Washington, D.C. 20402. 1985.

LOOSELEAF SERVICES AND REPORTERS

CUSTOMS BULLETIN AND DECISIONS. Superintendent of Documents, United States Government Printing Office, Washington, D.C. 20402. 1980- .

TEXTBOOKS AND GENERAL WORKS

IMPORT AND CUSTOMS LAW HANDBOOK. Michael J. Horton. Quorum Books, Greenwood Publishing Group, Incorporated, 88 Post Road West, P.O. Box 5007, Westport, Connecticut 06881. 1992.

NARCOTIC IDENTIFICATION MANUAL. Department of the Treasury, United States Customs Service. Superintendent of Documents, United States Government Printing Office, Washington, D.C. 20402. 1988. Revised.

NEUTRALITY CONFIDENTIAL: THE UNITED STATES CUSTOMS SERVICE, OUR 199TH YEAR. Department of the Treasury, United States Customs Service, Washington, D.C. 1988.

THE UNITED STATES CUSTOMS SERVICE: A BICENTENNIAL HISTORY. Carl E. Prince and Mollie Keller. Department of the Treasury, United States Customs Service, Washington, D.C. 1989.

DIGESTS, INDEXES, ABSTRACTS, CITATORS

SHEPARD'S UNITED STATES ADMINISTRATIVE CITATIONS. Shepard's/McGraw-Hill, P.O. Box 1235, Colorado Springs, Colorado 80901. Bimonthly.

NEWSLETTERS AND NEWSPAPERS

CITBA NEWSLETTER. Customs and International Bar Association, c/o Joseph F. Kaplan, Jr., 26 Broadway, New York, New York 10004. Bimonthly.

ASSOCIATIONS AND PROFESSIONAL SOCIETIES

CUSTOMS AND INTERNATIONAL TRADE BAR ASSOCIATION. c/o Joseph F. Donahue, Jr., 26 Broadway, New York, New York 10004. (212) 269-2330.

ONLINE DATABASES

LEXIS, INTERNATIONAL TRADE LIBRARY. Mead Data Central, P.O. Box 933, Dayton, Ohio 45401.

D

DAMAGES
See also: REMEDIES; RESTITUTION

LOOSELEAF SERVICES AND REPORTERS

BAD FAITH ACTIONS LIABILITY AND DAMAGES. Stephen S. Ashley. Callaghan and Company, 155 Pfingsten Road, Deerfield, Illinois 60015. 1985- .

COMMERCIAL DAMAGES: A GUIDE TO REMEDIES IN BUSINESS LITIGATION. Charles J. Knapp. Matthew Bender and Company, Incorporated, 11 Penn Plaza, New York, New York 10001. 1986- .

COMMERCIAL DAMAGES REPORTER. Matthew Bender and Company, Incorporated, 11 Penn Plaza, New York, New York 10001. 1986- . (Monthly).

DAMAGES IN TORT ACTIONS. Marilyn K. Minzen and others. Matthew Bender and Company, Incorporated, 11 Penn Plaza, New York, New York 10001. 1982- .

DAMAGES UNDER THE UNIFORM COMMERCIAL CODE. Roy R. Anderson. Callaghan and Company, 155 Pfingsten Road, Deerfield, Illinois 60015. 1988- .

HOW TO RECOVER FOR LOSS OR DAMAGE TO GOODS IN TRANSIT. Saul Sorkin. Matthew Bender and Company, Incorporated, 11 Penn Plaza, New York, New York 10001. 1976- .

PERSONAL INJURY -- ACTIONS, DEFENSES, DAMAGES. Louis R. Frumer and others. Matthew Bender and Company, Incorporated, 11 Penn Plaza, New York, New York 10001. 1957- .

PUNITIVE DAMAGES, LAW AND PRACTICE. James J. Ghiardi and John J. Kirchner. Matthew Bender and Company, Incorporated, 11 Penn Plaza, New York, New York 10001. 1981- .

SECURITIES LITIGATION: DAMAGES. Michael J. Kaufman. Callaghan and Company, 155 Pfingsten Road, Deerfield, Illinois 60015. 1989- .

TAX ASPECTS OF LITIGATION AND SETTLEMENTS. Sandy Kasten. Callaghan and Company, 155 Pfingsten Road, Deerfield, Illinois 60015. 1989- .

HANDBOOKS, MANUALS, FORMBOOKS

DETERMINING ECONOMIC LOSS IN INJURY AND DEATH. William Gary Baker. Shepard's/McGraw-Hill, P.O. Box 1235, Colorado Springs, Colorado 80901. 1987.

ECONOMIC DAMAGES: THE HANDBOOK FOR PLAINTIFF AND DEFENSE ATTORNEYS. Michael L. Brookshire. Anderson Publishing Company, 2035 Reading Road, Cincinnati, Ohio 45202. 1987.

ECONOMIC/HEDONIC DAMAGES: THE PRACTICE BOOK FOR PLAINTIFF AND DEFENSE ATTORNEYS. Michael L. Brookshire. Anderson Publishing Company, 2035 Reading Road, Cincinnati, Ohio 45202. 1990.

PERSONAL INJURY DAMAGES: LAW AND PRACTICE. Edward C. Martin. Wiley Law Publications, 605 Third Avenue, New York, New York 10158. 1990.

RECOVERY FOR WRONGFUL DEATH AND INJURY: ECONOMIC HANDBOOK. Third Edition. Stuart M. Speiser. Lawyers Cooperative Publishing Company, Aqueduct Building, Rochester, New York 14694. 1988.

RECOVERY OF DAMAGES FOR FRAUD. Robert L. Dunn. Lawpress Corporation, P.O. Box 596, Kentfield, California 94914. 1988.

REMEDIES: DAMAGES, EQUITY, AND RESTITUTION. Second Edition. Robert S. Thompson. Matthew Bender and Company, Incorporated, 11 Penn Plaza, New York, New York 10001. 1989.

TEXTBOOKS AND GENERAL WORKS

AMA TORT REFORM COMPENDIUM. Nancy K. Bannon. American Medical Association, Public Affairs Group, Division of Legislative Activities, Department of State Legislation, 515 North State Street, Chicago, Illinois 60610. 1989.

ANTITRUST PENALTY REFORM: AN ECONOMIC ANALYSIS. William Breit. American Enterprise Institute for Public Policy Research, 1150 Seventeenth Street, Northwest, Washington, D.C. 20036. 1986.

ASBESTOS IN THE COURTS: THE CHALLENGE OF MASS TOXIC TORTS. Deborah R. Hensler. The Rand Corporation, P.O. Box 2138, Santa Monica, California 90406-2138. 1985.

DAMAGES AND RECOVERY: PERSONAL INJURY AND DEATH ACTIONS. Jacob A. Stein. Lawyers Cooperative Company, One Graves Street, Rochester, New York 14694. 1972. (Periodic Supplements).

DEALING WITH DAMAGES. Norman J. Itzkoff. Practising Law Institute, 810 Seventh Avenue, New York, New York 10019. 1983.

DETERMINING AND PROVING DAMAGES IN BUSINESS LITIGATION. Richard J. Phelan and Donald P. Hilliker. Law Journal Seminars-Press, Incorporated. 111 Eighth Avenue, Suite 900, New York, New York 10011. 1981.

EXTRA-CONTRACTUAL DAMAGES. John R. Groves, Editor. Tort and Insurance Practice Section, American Bar Association, 750 North Lake Shore Drive, Chicago, Illinois 60611. 1983.

FEDERAL TAX ASPECTS OF INJURY, DAMAGE, AND LOSS. Lawrence A. Frolik. Bureau of National Affairs, Incorporated, 1231 Twenty-fifth Street, Northwest, Washington, D.C. 20037. 1987.

HANDBOOK ON THE LAW OF DAMAGES (Hornbook Series). Charles T. McCormick. West Publishing Company, P.O. Box 64526, 50 West Kellogg Boulevard, St. Paul, Minnesota 55164-0526. 1935.

THE LAW OF MARITIME PERSONAL INJURIES. Fourth Edition. Martin J. Norris. Lawyers Cooperative Publishing Company, Aqueduct Building, Rochester, New York 14694. 1990- .

THE LITIGIOUS SOCIETY. Jethro K. Lieberman. Basic Books, Incorporated, 10 East Fifty-third Street, New York, New York 10022. 1981.

MODERN DAMAGES. Melvin M. Belli. Bobbs-Merrill Company, 4300 West Sixty-second Street, Indianapolis, Indiana 46206. Defunct. 1960.

MODERN TRIALS. Second Edition. Melvin M. Belli. West Publishing Company, P.O. Box 64526, 50 West Kellogg Boulevard, St. Paul, Minnesota 55164-0526. 1982- . (Periodic Supplements).

NEW AND EXTRAORDINARY RELIEF IN INTELLECTUAL PROPERTY CASES. J. Joseph Bainton, Chairman. Practising Law Institute, 810 Seventh Avenue, New York, New York 10019. 1985.

PERSONAL INJURY VALUATION HANDBOOKS. Jury Verdict Research, Incorporated, 30700-H Bainbridge Road, Solon, Ohio 44139-2291. 1964- .

THE PRODUCT LIABILITY MESS: HOW BUSINESS CAN BE RESCUED FROM THE POLITICS OF STATE COURTS. Richard Neely. Free Press, 866 Third Avenue, New York, New York 10022. 1988.

PROVING AND DEFENDING AGAINST DAMAGES IN CATASTROPHIC INJURY CASES. David B. Baum and Robert L. Conason, Co-Chairmen. Practising Law Institute, 810 Seventh Avenue, New York, New York 10019. 1983.

RECOVERY OF DAMAGES FOR LOST PROFITS. Third Edition. Robert L. Dunn. Lawpress, P.O. Box 596, Kentfield, California 94914. 1978- . (Periodic Supplements).

TAX ASPECTS OF SETTLEMENTS, JUDGEMENTS, ANTITRUST PAYMENTS AND RECOVERIES (Tax Management Portfolio 121-5th). Robert W. Wood and Simon Noel. Tax Management Incorporated, 1231 Twenty-fifth Street, Northwest, Washington, D.C. 20037. 1986- . (Periodic Supplements).

TRENDS IN LIABILITY AWARDS: HAVE JURIES RUN WILD? Mark N. Cooper. Consumer Federation of America, 1424 Sixteenth Street, Northwest, Washington, D.C. 20036. 1986.

TRENDS IN TORT LITIGATION: THE STORY BEHIND THE STATISTICS. Rand Corporation, 1700 Main Street, P.O. Box 2138, Santa Monica, California 90406. 1987.

VARIATION IN ASBESTOS LITIGATION COMPENSATION AND EXPENSES. James S. Kakalik. The Rand Corporation, P.O. Box 2138, Santa Monica, California 90406-2138. 1984.

WHAT'S IT WORTH? A GUIDE TO CURRENT PERSONAL INJURY AWARDS AND SETTLEMENTS. Robert Harley, Maryann Magee and Fredrick Smith. Kluwer Law Book Publishers, Incorporated, 36 West Forty-fourth Street, New York, New York 10036. 1985- . (Periodic Supplements).

OTHER SOURCES

JURY INSTRUCTIONS ON DAMAGES IN TORT ACTIONS. Second Edition. Graham Douthwaite. Michie Company, P.O. Box 7587, Charlottesville, Virginia 22906. 1988.

DATABASES
See: BIOETHICS; COMPUTER SOFTWARE; COMPUTERS; LEGAL RESEARCH

DEATH
See also: EUTHANASIA; MEDICAL JURISPRUDENCE AND MALPRACTICE; WRONGFUL DEATH

STATUTES, CODES, STANDARDS, UNIFORM LAWS

MODEL SURVIVAL AND DEATH ACT. National Conference of Commissioners on Uniform State Laws. Uniform Laws Annotated. West Publishing Company, P.O. Box 64526, 50 West Kellogg Boulevard, St. Paul, Minnesota 55102-1611. 1976- . (Annual Supplements).

UNIFORM BRAIN DEATH ACT. National Conference of Commissioners on Uniform State Laws. Uniform Laws Annotated. West Publishing Company, P.O. Box 64526, 50 West Kellogg Boulevard, St. Paul, Minnesota 55102-1611. 1976- . (Annual Supplements).

UNIFORM DETERMINATION OF DEATH ACT. National Conference of Commissioners on Uniform State Laws. Uniform Laws Annotated. West Publishing Company, P.O. Box 64526, 50 West Kellogg Boulevard, St. Paul, Minnesota 55102-1611. 1976- . (Annual Supplements).

UNIFORM INTERSTATE ARBITRATION OF DEATH TAXES ACT. National Conference of Commissioners on Uniform State Laws. Uniform Laws Annotated. West Publishing Company, P.O. Box 64526, 50 West Kellogg Boulevard, St. Paul, Minnesota 55102-1611. 1976- . (Annual Supplements).

UNIFORM INTERSTATE COMPROMISE OF DEATH TAXES ACT. National Conference of Commissioners on Uniform State Laws. Uniform Laws Annotated. West Publishing Company, P.O. Box 64526, 50 West Kellogg Boulevard, St. Paul, Minnesota 55102-1611. 1976- . (Annual Supplements).

UNIFORM SIMULTANEOUS DEATH ACT. National Conference of Commissioners on Uniform State Laws. Uniform Laws Annotated. West Publishing Company, P.O. Box 64526, 50 West Kellogg Boulevard, St. Paul, Minnesota 55102-1611. 1976- . (Annual Supplements).

LOOSELEAF SERVICES AND REPORTERS

MANUAL FOR LAWYERS AND LEGAL ASSISTANTS: WRONGFUL DEATH. Ray L. Bishop and Donald E. Shelton. University of Michigan Law School, Institute of Continuing Legal Education, Hutchins Hall, Ann Arbor, Michigan 48109-1215. 1977.

TEXTBOOKS AND GENERAL WORKS

BRAIN DEATH: ETHICAL CONSIDERATIONS. Douglas N. Walton. Purdue University Press, South Campus Courts, Building D, West Lafayette, Indiana 47907. 1980.

DAMAGES AND RECOVERY: PERSONAL INJURY AND DEATH ACTIONS. Jacob A. Stein. Lawyers Cooperative Company, One Graves Street, Rochester, New York 14694. 1984.

DEADLY FORCE: WHAT WE KNOW. William A. Geller. American Bar Foundation, 750 North Lake Shore Drive, Chicago, Illinois 60611. 1982.

DEATH: BEYOND WHOLE-BRAIN CRITERIA. Reidel Publishing Company, 101 Philip Drive, Norwell, Massachusetts 02061. 1988.

DEATH, DYING AND EUTHANASIA. Dennis J. Horan and David Mall, Editors. University Publications of America, Incorporated, 4520 East West Highway, Bethesda, Maryland 20814. 1977.

DEATH, TAXES AND THE LIVING. William H. Pedrick. Commerce Clearing House, Incorporated, 4025 West Peterson Avenue, Chicago, Illinois 60646. 1980.

DEFINING DEATH: A REPORT ON THE MEDICAL, LEGAL AND ETHICAL ISSUES IN DETERMINATION OF DEATH. President's Commission for the Study of Ethical Problems in Medicine and Biomedical and Behavioral Research. Superintendent of Documents, United States Government Printing Office, Washington, D.C. 20402. 1981.

FACING THE DEATH PENALTY: ESSAYS ON A CRUEL AND UNUSUAL PUNISHMENT. Michael L. Radelet. Temple University Press, 1601 North Broad Street, University Services Building, Philadelphia, Pennsylvania 19122. 1989.

LAW OF DEATH AND DISPOSAL OF THE DEAD. Second Edition. H.Y. Bernard. Oceana Publications, 75 Main Street, Dobbs Ferry, New York 10522. 1979.

A LEGAL DEFINITION OF DEATH. Robert A. Carter. New York State Library, Gift and Exchange, Sixth Floor, CEC, Albany, New York 12230. 1982.

THE LEGAL ENFORCEMENT OF MORALITY. Thomas C. Grey, Compiler. Random House, 201 East Fiftieth Street, New York, New York 10022. 1983.

LEGAL FRONTIERS OF DEATH AND DYING. Norman L. Cantor. Indiana University Press, Tenth and Morton Streets, Bloomington, Indiana 47405. 1987.

MEDICO-LEGAL IMPLICATIONS OF DEATH AND DYING: A DETAILED DISCUSSION OF THE MEDICAL AND LEGAL IMPLICATIONS INVOLVED IN DEATH AND/OR CARE OF THE DYING AND TERMINAL PATIENT. David W. Meyers. Lawyers Co-Operative Publishing Company, One Graves Street, Rochester, New York 14694. 1981. (Periodic Supplements).

PUBLIC JUSTICE, PRIVATE MERCY: A GOVERNOR'S EDUCATION ON DEATH ROW. Edmund G. Brown. Weidenfeld and Nicholson, 10 East Fifty-third Street, New York, New York 10022. 1989.

RIGHT TO DIE OR RIGHT TO LIVE: LEGAL ASPECTS OF DYING AND DEATH. Peter J. Riga. Associated Faculty Press, Incorporated, 19 West Thirty-sixth Street, New York, New York 10018. 1983.

SEAMAN'S DAMAGES FOR DEATH AND INJURY. Jack B. Hood and Benjamin A. Hardy. Harrison Company, 3110 Crossing Park, Norcross, Georgia 30071.

WHO DIES? AN INVESTIGATION OF CONSCIOUS LIVING AND CONSCIOUS DYING. Stephen Levine. Doubleday and Company, Incorporated, 666 Fifth Avenue, New York, New York 10103. 1982.

ANNUALS AND SURVEYS

DEATH TAXES [A-13]. Shepard's Lawyer's Reference Manual . Shepard's/McGraw-Hill, P.O. Box 1235, Colorado Springs, Colorado 80901. 1983- . (Annual Supplements).

LAW REVIEWS AND PERIODICALS

ADVANCES IN THANATOLOGY. Foundation of Thanatology, 630 West One Hundred Sixty-eighth Street, New York, New York 10032. Quarterly.

ARCHIVES OF THE FOUNDATION OF THANATOLOGY. Foundation of Thanatology, 630 West One Hundred Sixty-eighth Street, New York, New York 10032. Quarterly.

THANATOLOGY ABSTRACTS. Foundation of Thanatology, 630 West One Hundred Sixty-eighth Street, New York, New York 10032. Annual.

NEWSLETTERS AND NEWSPAPERS

CENTERING. St. Francis Center, 5417 Sherier Place, Northwest, Washington, D.C. 20016. Quarterly.

FORUM NEWSLETTER. Association for Death Education and Counseling, 638 Prospect Avenue, Hartford, Connecticut 06105. Bimonthly.

LIVING/DYING PROJECT NEWSLETTER. P.O. Box 357, Fairfax, California 94930. Bimonthly.

RESEARCH CENTERS, INSTITUTES, CLEARINGHOUSES

ASSOCIATION FOR DEATH EDUCATION AND COUNSELING. 638 Prospect Avenue, Hartford, Connecticut 06105. (203) 232-4825.

CENTER FOR DEATH EDUCATION AND RESEARCH. University of Minnesota, 1167 Social Science Building, 267 Nineteenth Avenue, South, Minneapolis, Minnesota 55455. (612) 624-1895.

FOUNDATION OF THANATOLOGY. 630 West One Hundred Sixty-eighth Street, New York, New York 10032. (212) 928-2066.

INSTITUTE FOR THE INTERDISCIPLINARY STUDY OF DEATH. P.O. Box 8565, Pembroke Pines, Florida 33084. (305) 435-2730.

INTERNATIONAL INSTITUTE FOR THE STUDY OF DEATH. P.O. Box 8565, Pembroke Pines, Florida 33084. (305) 435-2730.

NATIONAL RESEARCH AND INFORMATION CENTER. National Foundation of Funeral Service, 1614 Central Street, Evanston, Illinois 60201. (708) 328-6545.

ST. FRANCIS CENTER. 5417 Sherier Place, Northwest, Washington, D.C. 20016. (202) 363-8500.

STATISTICS SOURCES

VITAL STATISTICS OF THE UNITED STATES. (Death and Death Rates). United States Department of Health and Human Services, Public Health Service. Superintendent of Documents, United States Government Printing Office, Washington, D.C. 20402. Annual.

DEATH PENALTY
See: CAPITAL PUNISHMENT

DEBTOR AND CREDITOR
See: ATTACHMENT AND GARNISHMENT; BANKRUPTCY; COLLECTION LAWS; CREDIT

DECEDENTS' ESTATES
See: WILLS, TRUSTS AND INHERITANCE

DECEIT
See: FRAUD

DECLARATORY JUDGMENTS
See: JUDGMENTS

DEEDS
See: REAL PROPERTY

DEEDS OF TRUST
See: MORTGAGES; REAL PROPERTY

DEFAMATION
See: LIBEL AND SLANDER

DEFENSE DEPARTMENT

STATUTES, CODES, STANDARDS, UNIFORM LAWS

CODE OF FEDERAL REGULATIONS, TITLE 32. Office of the Federal Register, National Archives and Records Administration. Superintendent of Documents, United States Government Printing Office, Washington, D.C. 20402. Annual. (Updated by use of monthly List of Sections Affected and daily Federal Register.)

FEDERAL ACQUISITION REGULATIONS. General Services Administration, Defense Department, National Aeronautics and Space Administration. Superintendent of Documents, United States Government Printing Office, Washington, D.C. 20402. 1987- .

INDUSTRIAL SECURITY REGULATION. Defense Department, Defense Investigative Service. Superintendent of Documents, United States Government Printing Office, Washington, D.C. 20402. 1985.

HANDBOOKS, MANUALS, FORMBOOKS

ARMED SERVICES PRICING MANUAL. Defense Department, Assistant Secretary of Defense (Acquisition and Logistics). Superintendent of Documents, United States Government Printing Office, Washington, D.C. 20402. 1986- .

GUIDE TO DEFENSE CONTRACTING REGULATIONS FOR SMALL BUSINESS, SMALL DISADVANTAGED BUSINESS, WOMEN-OWNED SMALL BUSINESS. Defense Department, Office of the Secretary of Defense, Directorate of Small and Disadvantaged Business Utilization. Superintendent of Documents, United States Government Printing Office, Washington, D.C. 20402. 1985.

GUIDE TO MARKING CLASSIFIED DOCUMENTS. Defense Department Office of the Deputy Under Secretary of Defense for Policy Review, Directorate of Information Security. Superintendent of Documents, United States Government Printing Office, Washington, D.C. 20402. 1982.

MANUAL FOR COURTS-MARTIAL, UNITED STATES, 1984. Defense Department. Superintendent of Documents, United States Government Printing Office, Washington, D.C. 20402. 1984- .

MANUAL FOR COURTS-MARTIAL, UNITED STATES, 1984, CHAPTER TWO. Defense Department. Superintendent of Documents, United States Government Printing Office, Washington, D.C. 20402. 1986- .

TEXTBOOKS AND GENERAL WORKS

BLANK CHECK: THE PENTAGON'S BLACK BUDGET. Tim Weiner. Warner Books, Incorporated, 666 Fifth Avenue, New York, New York 10103. 1990.

CONDUCT AND ACCOUNTABILITY: A REPORT TO THE PRESIDENT. President's Blue Ribbon Commission on Defense Management. The Commission, Washington, D.C. 1986.

KEEPING THE NATION'S SECRETS: A REPORT TO THE SECRETARY OF DEFENSE BY THE COMMISSION TO REVIEW DOD SECURITY POLICIES AND PRACTICES. Defense Department, Security Review Commission. Superintendent of Documents, United States Government Printing Office, Washington, D.C. 20402. 1985.

THE LEGAL STRUCTURE OF DEFENSE ORGANIZATION MEMORANDUM. John Norton Moore. President's Blue Ribbon Commission on Defense Management. Superintendent of Documents, United States Government Printing Office, Washington, D.C. 20402. 1986.

NATIONAL SECURITY PLANNING AND BUDGETING: A REPORT TO THE PRESIDENT. President's Blue Ribbon Commission on Defense Management. The Commission, Washington, D.C. 1986.

THE 1990 DEFENSE BUDGET. William W. Kaufmann. Brookings Institution, 1775 Massachusetts Avenue, Washington, D.C. 20036. 1989.

A QUEST FOR EXCELLENCE: FINAL REPORT TO THE PRESIDENT. President's Blue Ribbon Commission on Defense Management. The Commission, Washington, D.C. 1986.

U.S. DEFENCE CONTRACTS. David B. Dempsey. Longman, Incorporated, 95 Church Street, White Plains, New York 10601. 1987.

DIGESTS, INDEXES, ABSTRACTS, CITATORS

FEDERAL ACQUISITION REGULATIONS, DIGEST AND CROSS INDEXES. Defense Department. Superintendent of Documents, United States Government Printing Office, Washington, D.C. 20402. 1983- .

LAW REVIEWS AND PERIODICALS

DEFENSE LAW JOURNAL. The Michie Company, P.O. Box 7587, Charlottesville, Virginia 22906. Quarterly.

MILITARY LAW REVIEW. The Judge Advocate General's School, Army, Charlottesville, Virginia 22903. Quarterly.

NEWSLETTERS AND NEWSPAPERS

DEFENSE CONTRACT LITIGATION REPORTER. Shepard's/McGraw-Hill, 420 North Cascade Avenue, Colorado Springs, Colorado 80903. Biweekly.

INSIDE THE NAVY. Inside Washington Publishers, P.O. Box 7167, Ben Franklin Station, Washington, D.C. 20044. Weekly.

INSIDE THE PENTAGON. Inside Washington Publishers, P.O. Box 7167, Ben Franklin Station, Washington, D.C. 20044. Weekly.

LEGAL ASSISTANCE NEWSLETTER. Standing Committee on Legal Assistance for Military Personnel, American Bar Association, 750 North Lake Shore Drive, Chicago, Illinois 60611. Irregular.

THE OBJECTOR. CCCO, P.O. Box 42249, San Francisco, California 94142. Bimonthly.

REPORT ON DEFENSE PLANT WASTES. Business Publishers Incorporated, 951 Pershing Drive, Silver Spring, Maryland 20910. Biweekly.

RESEARCH CENTERS, INSTITUTES, CLEARINGHOUSES

PUBLIC LAW EDUCATION INSTITUTE. 1601 Connecticut Avenue, Northwest, Washington, D.C. 20009. (202) 232-1400.

UNITED STATES DEPARTMENT OF THE AIR FORCE, OFFICE OF THE JUDGE ADVOCATE GENERAL LIBRARY. Room 102, Building 5683, Bolling Air Force Base, Washington, D.C. 20332-6128. (703) 614-5732.

UNITED STATES DEPARTMENT OF THE ARMY, THE PENTAGON LIBRARY, LAW SECTION. The Pentagon, Room 1A518, Washington, D.C. 20324. (703) 325-9128.

UNITED STATES DEPARTMENT OF THE NAVY, OFFICE OF THE GENERAL COUNSEL LAW LIBRARY. CP #5, Room 450, Washington, D.C. 20360. (703) 614-1994.

UNITED STATES DEPARTMENT OF THE NAVY, OFFICE OF THE JUDGE ADVOCATE GENERAL LIBRARY. 200 Stoval Street, Alexandria, Virginia 22332. (703) 325-9820.

DEFENSES
See: ACTIONS AND DEFENSES

DEMONSTRATIONS
See: FREEDOM OF ASSEMBLY AND ASSOCIATION

DEMONSTRATIVE AND VISUAL EVIDENCE

LOOSELEAF SERVICES AND REPORTERS

ART OF ADVOCACY: DEMONSTRATIVE EVIDENCE. Ashley S. Lipson. Matthew Bender & Company, Incorporated, 11 Penn Plaza, New York, New York 10001. 1988.

MODERN VISUAL EVIDENCE. Gregory P. Joseph. Law Journal Seminars-Press, Incorporated, 111 Eighth Avenue, Suite 900, New York, New York 10011. 1984- .

TANGIBLE EVIDENCE: HOW TO USE EXHIBITS AT TRIAL. Second Edition. Deanne C. Siemer. Prentice Hall Law and Business, Incorporated, 270 Sylvan Avenue, Englewood Cliffs, New Jersey 07632. 1989.

HANDBOOKS, MANUALS, FORMBOOKS

DOMBROFF ON DEMONSTRATIVE EVIDENCE. Mark A. Dombroff. John Wiley and Sons, Incorporated, 605 Third Avenue, New York, New York 10158. 1983.

ENGINEERING EVIDENCE. Second Edition. Max Schwartz. Shepard's/McGraw-Hill, P.O. Box 1235, Colorado Springs, Colorado 80901. 1987- .

USING DEMONSTRATIVE EVIDENCE IN CIVIL TRIALS. Practicing Law Institute, 810 Seventh Avenue, New York, New York 10019. 1982.

TEXTBOOKS AND GENERAL WORKS

DEMONSTRATIVE EVIDENCE. Richard A. Givens. Shepard's/McGraw-Hill, P.O. Box 35300, Colorado Springs, Colorado 80935. 1989.

DEPOSITIONS, EXPERT WITNESSES, AND DEMONSTRATIVE EVIDENCE IN PERSONAL INJURY CASES. David G. Miller, chairman. Practising Law Institute, 810 Seventh Avenue, New York, New York 10019. 1985.

DOMBROFF ON DEMONSTRATIVE EVIDENCE. Mark A. Dombroff. Wiley Law Publications, P.O. Box 1777, Colorado Springs, Colorado 80901. 1983.

EFFECTIVE USE OF DEMONSTRATIVE EVIDENCE IN COURT: A SHOWCASE OF IDEAS. Massachusetts Continuing Legal Education-New England Law Institute, Incorporated, 20 West Street, Boston, Massachusetts 02111. 1987.

ENGINEERING EVIDENCE. Second edition. Max Schwartz and Neil F. Schwartz. Shepard's/McGraw-Hill, P.O. Box 35300, Colorado Springs, Colorado 80935. 1987.

USING DEMONSTRATIVE EVIDENCE IN CIVIL TRIALS. Mark Dombroff, chairman. Practising Law Institute, 810 Seventh Avenue, New York, New York 10019. 1982.

AUDIOVISUALS

DEMONSTRATIVE EVIDENCE. ABA Division of Professional Education. American Bar Association, 750 North Lake Shore Drive, Chicago, Illinois 60611. 1979. Videocassette.

DEMONSTRATIVE EVIDENCE. Mark A. Dombroff. National Practice Institute, 330 Second Avenue South, Minneapolis, Minnesota 55401. Videotape.

EVIDENTIARY FOUNDATIONS ILLUSTRATED. CLE Group, 274 Willow Road, Menlo Park, California 94025. Interactive videodisc.

INTRODUCTION AND USE OF DEMONSTRATIVE EVIDENCE. ABA Division of Professional Education. American Bar Association, 750 North Lake Shore Drive, Chicago, Illinois 60611. Videocassette.

LASER DISC TECHNOLOGY IN THE COURTROOM. National Institute for Trial Advocacy, Notre Dame Law School, Notre Dame, Indiana 46556. 1990. Videotape.

PRESENTING DOCUMENTARY AND DEMONSTRATIVE EVIDENCE EFFECTIVELY. California Continuing Education of the Bar. Distributed by Division of Professional Education, American Bar Association, 750 North Lake Shore Drive, Chicago, Illinois 60611. Videocassette.

SETTLING CASES FASTER WITH VIDEO EVIDENCE. National Practice Institute, 330 Second Avenue South, Minneapolis, Minnesota 55401. Videotape.

TRIAL EVIDENCE AND DIRECT EXAMINATION SKILLS. CLE Group, 274 Willow Road, Menlo Park, California 94025. Interactive videodisc.

DENTAL JURISPRUDENCE
See also: MEDICAL JURISPRUDENCE

HANDBOOKS, MANUALS, FORMBOOKS

DENTAL JURISPRUDENCE: A HANDBOOK OF PRACTICAL LAW. Oliver C. Schroeder, Jr., Editor. PSG Publishing Company, Incorporated, P.O. Box 6, Littleton, Maine 01460. Defunct. 1980.

MEDICAL MALPRACTICE: HANDLING DENTAL CASES. Norman L. Schafler. Shepard's/McGraw-Hill, P.O. Box 1235, Colorado Springs, Colorado 80901. 1985.

TEXTBOOKS AND GENERAL WORKS

CANADIAN DENTAL LAW. Lorne Elkin Rozovsky. Butterworths, 75 Clegg Road, Markham, Ontario, Canada L3R 9Y6. 1987.

DENTAL LITIGATION. Second Edition. William O. Morris. Michie Company, P.O. Box 7587, Charlottesville, Virginia 22906. 1977.

DENTAL PRACTICE FOR TRIAL LAWYERS. Robert L. Pedarsky. Harrison Company, 3110 Crossing Park, Norcross, Georgia 30071. 1984- .

THE DENTIST AND THE LAW. Third Edition. William W. Howard and Alex Leon Parks. C.V. Mosby Company, 11830 Westline Industrial Drive, St. Louis, Missouri 63146. 1973.

ETHICS, JURISPRUDENCE AND HISTORY FOR THE DENTAL HYGIENIST. Third Edition. Wilma E. Motley. Lea & Febiger, 200 Chester Field Parkway, Malvern, Pennsylvania 19355. 1983.

FORENSIC DENTISTRY. Irvin M. Sopher. Charles C. Thomas, Publishers, 2600 South First Street, Springfield, Illinois 62794-9265. 1976.

INTRODUCTION TO FORENSIC SCIENCES. William G. Eckert. C.V. Mosby Company, 11830 Westline Industrial Drive, St. Louis, Missouri 63141. 1980.

LAW AND ETHICS IN DENTISTRY. Third Edition. John Seear. PSG Publishing Company, Incorporated, P.O. Box 6, Littleton, Maine 01460. Defunct. 1991.

LEGAL CONSIDERATIONS IN DENTISTRY. Sidney H. Willig. Williams & Wilkins, Baltimore, Maryland. 1971.

MEDICAL MALPRACTICE: HANDLING DENTAL CASES. Norman L. Schafler. Shepard's/McGraw-Hill, P.O. Box 1235, Colorado Springs, Colorado 80901. 1985.

MEDICAL PARTNERSHIPS AND PRACTICE DISPOSITION. Martin L. Schulman and Steven Schulman. Praeger Publishers, One Madison Avenue, New York, New York 10010-3603. 1983.

PERSONALIZED GUIDE TO LEGAL ISSUES. Randall K. Berning and Thomas L. Snyder. C.V. Mosby Company, 11830 Westline Industrial Drive, St. Louis, Missouri 63141. 1984.

STATE REGULATORY POLICIES: DENTISTRY AND THE HEALTH PROFESSIONS. Council of State Governments, Iron Works Pike, P.O. Box 11910, Lexington, Kentucky 40578. 1979.

SYMPOSIUM ON LEGAL CONSIDERATIONS IN DENTISTRY. W.B. Saunders Company, West Washington Square, Philadelphia, Pennsylvania 19105. 1982.

ANNUALS AND SURVEYS

MEDICAL, DENTAL AND PHARMACEUTICAL AUXILIARIES: A SURVEY OF LEGISLATION. World Health Organization, Avenue Appia, Ch 1211, Geneva 27, Switzerland. 1968- .

LAW REVIEWS AND PERIODICALS

AMERICAN JOURNAL OF ORTHODONTICS AND DENTO-FACIAL ORTHOPEDICS. American Association of Orthodontists, 460 North Lindbergh Boulevard, St. Louis, Missouri 63141. Monthly.

JOURNAL OF DENTAL RESEARCH. American Association for Dental Research, 1111 Fourteenth Street, Northwest, Suite 1000, Washington, D.C. 20005. Sixteen issues per year.

JOURNAL OF THE AMERICAN ASSOCIATION OF ENDODONTISTS. American Association of Endodontists, 211 East Chicago Avenue, Suite 1501, Chicago, Illinois 60611. Quarterly.

LEGAL ASPECTS OF DENTAL PRACTICE. Unit in Law and Dentistry, Temple University, 1719 North Broad Street, Philadelphia, Pennsylvania 19122. Quarterly.

PEDIATRIC DENTISTRY. American Academy of Pediatric Dentistry, 211 East Chicago Avenue, Suite 1036, Chicago, Illinois 60611. Quarterly.

NEWSLETTERS AND NEWSPAPERS

AAO BULLETIN. American Association of Orthodontists, 460 North Lindbergh Boulevard, St. Louis, Missouri 63141. Bimonthly.

AMERICAN ACADEMY OF PEDIATRIC DENTISTRY -- NEWSLETTER. American Academy of Pediatric Dentistry, 211 East Chicago Avenue, Suite 1036, Chicago, Illinois 60611. Quarterly.

AMERICAN ASSOCIATION OF WOMEN DENTISTS CHRONICLE. American Association of Women Dentists, 111 East Wacker Drive, Suite 600, Chicago, Illinois 60601. Bimonthly.

COMMUNIQUE. American Association of Endodontists, 211 East Chicago Avenue, Suite 1501, Chicago, Illinois 60611. Monthly.

DENTAL RESEARCH NEWSLETTER. American Association for Dental Research, 1111 Fourteenth Street, Northwest, Suite 1000, Washington, D.C. 20005. Biweekly.

ASSOCIATIONS AND PROFESSIONAL SOCIETIES

AMERICAN ACADEMY OF PEDIATRIC DENTISTRY. 211 East Chicago Avenue, Suite 1036, Chicago, Illinois 60611. (312) 337-2169.

AMERICAN ASSOCIATION FOR DENTAL RESEARCH. 1111 Fourteenth Street, Northwest, Suite 1000, Washington, D.C. 20005. (202) 898-1050.

AMERICAN ASSOCIATION OF ENDODONTISTS. 211 East Chicago Avenue, Suite 1501, Chicago, Illinois 60611. (312) 266-7255.

AMERICAN ASSOCIATION OF ORTHODONTISTS. 460 North Lindbergh Boulevard, St. Louis, Missouri 63141. (314) 993-1700.

AMERICAN ASSOCIATION OF WOMEN DENTISTS. 111 East Wacker Drive, Suite 600, Chicago, Illinois 60601. (312) 644-6610.

AMERICAN BOARD OF PERIODONTOLOGY. Baltimore College of Dental Surgery, 666 West Baltimore Street, University of Maryland, Baltimore, Maryland 21201. (301) 328-2432.

AMERICAN COLLEGE OF DENTISTS. 7315 Wisconsin Avenue, Suite 352N, Bethesda, Maryland 20814. (301) 986-0555.

AMERICAN DENTAL ASSOCIATION. 211 East Chicago Avenue, Chicago, Illinois 60611. (312) 440-2500.

RESEARCH CENTERS, INSTITUTES, CLEARINGHOUSES

UNIT IN LAW AND DENTISTRY. Temple University, Temple Law School, 1719 North Broad Street, Philadelphia, Pennsylvania 19122. (215) 787-1278.

DEPARTMENT OF AGRICULTURE
See: AGRICULTURE DEPARTMENT

DEPARTMENT OF COMMERCE
See: COMMERCE DEPARTMENT

DEPARTMENT OF DEFENSE
See: DEFENSE DEPARTMENT

DEPARTMENT OF EDUCATION
See: EDUCATION DEPARTMENT

DEPARTMENT OF ENERGY
See: ENERGY DEPARTMENT

DEPARTMENT OF HEALTH AND HUMAN SERVICES
See: HEALTH AND HUMAN SERVICES DEPARTMENT

DEPARTMENT OF THE INTERIOR
See: INTERIOR DEPARTMENT

DEPARTMENT OF JUSTICE
See: JUSTICE DEPARTMENT

DEPARTMENT OF LABOR
See: LABOR DEPARTMENT

DEPARTMENT OF STATE
See: STATE DEPARTMENT

DEPARTMENT OF TRANSPORTATION
See: TRANSPORTATION DEPARTMENT

DEPARTMENT OF TREASURY
See: TREASURY DEPARTMENT

DEPORTATION
See: EMIGRATION AND IMMIGRATION

DEPOSITIONS
See: DISCOVERY; WITNESSES

DESCENT AND DISTRIBUTION
See: WILLS, TRUSTS AND INHERITANCE

DESERTION
See: FAMILY LAW

DICTIONARIES
See: LEGAL RESEARCH; HEADING "ENCYCLOPEDIAS AND DICTIONARIES" UNDER SPECIFIC TOPICS

DIPLOMATIC PRIVILEGES AND IMMUNITIES
See also: STATE DEPARTMENT

TEXTBOOKS AND GENERAL WORKS

CONCURRING OPINION: THE PRIVILEGES OR IMMUNITIES CLAUSE OF THE 14TH AMENDMENT. Second Edition. Arnold J. Lien. Greenwood Publishing Group, Incorporated, 88 Post Road West, P.O. Box 5007, Westport, Connecticut 06881. 1976 reprint of 1957 edition.

CONSULAR PRIVILEGES AND IMMUNITIES. Irvin Stewart. AMS Press, Incorporated, 56 East Thirteenth Street, New York, New York 10003. 1968 reprint of 1926 edition.

DIPLOMATIC IMMUNITY: PRINCIPLES, PRACTICES, PROBLEMS. Grant V. McClanahan. St. Martin's Press, 175 Fifth Avenue, New York, New York 10010. 1989.

DIPLOMATIC LAW: COMMENTARY ON THE VIENNA CONVENTION ON DIPLOMATIC RELATIONS. Eileen Denza. Oceana Publications, Incorporated, 75 Main Street, Dobbs Ferry, New York 10522. 1976- .

A DIPLOMAT'S HANDBOOK OF INTERNATIONAL LAW AND PRACTICE. Third Edition. B.A. Sen. Kluwer Academic Publishers, 101 Philip Drive, Assinippi Park, Norwell, Massachusetts 02061. 1988.

LAWS AND REGULATIONS REGARDING DIPLOMATIC AND CONSULAR PRIVILEGES AND IMMUNITIES. United Nations, Sales Section, Publishing Division, Room DC2-0853, New York, New York 10017. 1958.

RESEARCH IN INTERNATIONAL LAW. Harvard University Press, 79 Garden Street, Cambridge, Massachusetts 02138. 1932.

STATE AND DIPLOMATIC IMMUNITY. Third Edition. Charles Lewis. Lloyd's of London Press, 611 Broadway, Suite 523, New York, New York 10012. 1990.

STATE IMMUNITY. Gamal M. Badr. Kluwer Academic Publishers, 101 Philip Drive, Assinippi Park, Norwell, Massachusetts 02061. 1984.

AUDIOVISUALS

INTERNATIONAL COURT OF JUSTICE CASE CONCERNING THE IMMUNITY OF A DIPLOMATIC AGENT, AND THE FREEZING OF ASSETS OF AN INTERNATIONAL ORGANIZATION. Philip C. Jessup International Law Moot Court Competition. International Law Students Association, 2223 Massachusetts Avenue, Northwest, Washington, D.C. 20008. 1989.

DIRECTORIES
See: LEGAL DIRECTORIES

DISABILITY INSURANCE
See: INSURANCE, HEALTH AND UNEMPLOYMENT

DISABLED
See: MENTAL HEALTH AND DISABILITY; PHYSICALLY HANDICAPPED

DISBARMENT OF ATTORNEYS
See: LEGAL ETHICS AND MALPRACTICE

DISCOVERY

LOOSELEAF SERVICES AND REPORTERS

ANTITRUST DISCOVERY HANDBOOK. American Bar Association, 750 North Lake Shore Drive, Chicago, Illinois 60611. 1981- .

BENDER'S FORMS OF DISCOVERY (22 VOLUMES). Matthew Bender and Company, Incorporated, 11 Penn Plaza, New York, New York 10001. 1984- .

CIVIL DISCOVERY: A GUIDE TO EFFICIENT PRACTICE. William W. Schwarzer. Prentice-Hall, Incorporated, Route 9W, Englewood Cliffs, New Jersey 07632. 1988.

DEPOSITION STRATEGY, LAW AND FORMS (10 VOLUMES). Alexander Sann and Steven Bellman. Matthew Bender and Company, Incorporated, 11 Penn Plaza, New York, New York 10001. 1981- .

DISCOVERY (Art of Advocacy Series). Arthur Ian Miltz. Matthew Bender and Company, Incorporated, 11 Penn Plaza, New York, New York 10001. 1982- .

PRETRIAL DISCOVERY: STRATEGY AND TACTICS. Edward J. Imwinkelried and Theodore Y. Blumhoff. Callaghan and Company, 155 Pfingsten Road, Deerfield, Illinois 60015. 1986- .

HANDBOOKS, MANUALS, FORMBOOKS

CIVIL DISCOVERY PRACTICE IN CALIFORNIA. California Continuing Education of the Bar, Berkeley, California. 1988.

DISCOVERY PRACTICE. Second Edition. Roger S. Haydock. Little, Brown and Company, 34 Beacon Street, Boston, Massachusetts 02108. 1988.

FEDERAL INFORMATION DISCLOSURE: PROCEDURES, FORMS AND THE LAW (2 VOLUMES). James T. O'Reilly. Shepard's/McGraw-Hill, P.O. Box 1235, Colorado Springs, Colorado 80901. 1977- .

A GUIDE TO FEDERAL DISCOVERY RULES. Second Edition. James L. Underwood. American Law Institute, 4025 Chestnut Street, Philadelphia, Pennsylvania 19104. 1985- . (Periodic Supplements).

PERSONAL INJURY FORMS: DISCOVERY AND SETTLEMENT. John A. Tarantino and David J. Oliveira. James Publishing, Incorporated, P.O. Box 27310, Santa Ana, California 92799. 1985- .

TEXTBOOKS AND GENERAL WORKS

CONFIDENTIALITY ORDERS. Francis Hare. Wiley Law Publications, 605 Third Avenue, New York, New York 10158. 1988.

DISCOVERY. Mark A. Dombroff. Kluwer Law Book Publishers, Incorporated, 36 West Forty-fourth Street, New York, New York 10036. 1986- . (Annual Supplements).

DISCOVERY: A COMPARISON BETWEEN ENGLISH AND AMERICAN CIVIL DISCOVERY LAW WITH REFORM PROPOSALS. Julius B. Levine. Oxford University Press, 200 Madison Avenue, New York, New York 10016. 1982.

DISCOVERY IN CONSTRUCTION LITIGATION. Second Edition. Michael T. Callahan and Barry B. Bramble. Michie Company, P.O. Box 7587, Charlottesville, Virginia 22906. 1987. (Periodic Supplements).

DISCOVERY IN MEDICAL MALPRACTICE, PRODUCTS LIABILITY AND PERSONAL INJURY CASES. Marc J. Bern and Steven E. North, Co-chairmen. Practising Law Institute, 810 Seventh Avenue, New York, New York 10019. 1985.

DISCOVERY PRACTICE. Second Edition. Roger S. Haydock and David F. Herr. Little, Brown and Company, 34 Beacon Street, Boston, Massachusetts 02108. 1988. (Periodic Supplements).

DISCOVERY PROCEEDINGS IN FEDERAL PRACTICE. Shepard's Editorial Staff. Shepard's/McGraw-Hill, P.O. Box 1235, Colorado Springs, Colorado 80901. 1984- . (Annual Supplements).

DISCOVERY TECHNIQUES: OBTAINING AND ANALYZING BUSINESS FINANCIAL DATA. Martin Mellman, Steven B. Lilien and James M. Docherty. Research Institute of America, Incorporated, One Penn Plaza, New York, New York 10119. 1987- .

DISCOVERY

FEDERAL DISCOVERY IN COMPLEX CIVIL CASES: ANTITRUST, SECURITIES, ENERGY. Marvin Pickholtz and Douglas M. Schwab. Law Journal Seminars-Press, 111 Eighth Avenue, New York, New York 10011. 1980.

MAKING DISCOVERY WORK: A HANDBOOK FOR LAWYERS AND JUDGES. William Schwarzer and Lynn Pasanow. Harcourt, Brace, Jovanovich, Incorporated, 6277 Sea Harbor Drive, Orlando, Florida 32821. 1985.

PATTERN DEPOSITION CHECKLISTS. Second Edition. Douglas Danner. Lawyers Cooperative Company, One Graves Street, Rochester, New York 14694. 1984- . (Periodic Supplements).

PATTERN DISCOVERY: ANTITRUST. Douglas Danner. Lawyers Cooperative Company, One Graves Street, Rochester, New York 14694. 1981- . (Periodic Supplements).

PATTERN DISCOVERY: AUTOMOBILES. Second Edition. Douglas Danner. Lawyers Cooperative Company, One Graves Street, Rochester, New York 14694. 1985- .

PATTERN DISCOVERY: MEDICAL MALPRACTICE. Second Edition. Douglas Danner. Lawyers Cooperative Company, One Graves Street, Rochester, New York 14694. 1985- . (Periodic Supplements).

PATTERN DISCOVERY: PREMISES LIABILITY. Second Edition. Douglas Danner. Lawyers Cooperative Company, One Graves Street, Rochester, New York 14694. 1986- . (Periodic Supplements).

PATTERN DISCOVERY: PRODUCTS LIABILITY. Second Edition. Douglas Danner. Lawyers Cooperative Company, One Graves Street, Rochester, New York 14694. 1986- . (Periodic Supplements).

PATTERN DISCOVERY: SECURITIES. Douglas Danner. Lawyers Cooperative Company, One Graves Street, Rochester, New York 14694. 1982- . (Periodic Supplements).

SUCCESSFUL TECHNIQUES FOR CIVIL TRIALS. Ronald L. Carlson. Lawyers Cooperative Company, One Graves Street, Rochester, New York 14694. 1983- . (Periodic Supplements).

THE TORT OF DISCOVERY ABUSE. Warren Freedman. Quorum Books, Greenwood Publishing Group, Incorporated, 88 Post Road West, P.O. Box 5007. Westport, Connecticut 06881. 1989.

TRIAL MECHANICS AND DISCOVERY IN MEDICAL MALPRACTICE, PRODUCTS LIABILITY AND PERSONAL INJURY CASES. Steven E. North and Marc J. Bern, Co-Chairmen. Practising Law Institute, 810 Seventh Avenue, New York, New York 10019. 1986.

AUDIOVISUALS

DISCOVERY. Irving Younger. Practising Law Institute, 810 Seventh Avenue, New York, New York 10019. 1979. (4 videocassettes).

INTRODUCTION TO WRITTEN DISCOVERY. An ABA/NITA VideoLaw Seminar. National Institute For Trial Advocacy, Notre Dame Law School, Notre Dame, Indiana 46556. 1985. (1 videocassette).

THE JUDGE'S ROLE IN DISCOVERY. An ABA/NITA VideoLaw Seminar. National Institute for Trial Advocacy, Notre Dame Law School, Notre Dame, Indiana 46556. 1985. (1 videocassette).

PLANNING INFORMAL INVESTIGATION AND FORMAL DISCOVERY. An ABA/NITA VideoLaw Seminar. National Institute for Trial Advocacy, Notre Dame Law School, Notre Dame, Indiana 46556. 1985. (1 videocassette).

COMPUTER-ASSISTED LEGAL INSTRUCTION

BUFFALO CREEK: A GAME OF DISCOVERY. Owen M. Fiss, Thomas Glocer and Ronald F. Wright. Center for Computer-Assisted Instruction, 229 19th Avenue South, University of Minnesota, Minneapolis, Minnesota 55455. Machine-readable computer file.

COMPUGRAPH V. CHANG. Interactive Video Library, Harvard Law School, Educational Technology Department, 18 Everett Street, Cambridge, Massachusetts 02138. Interactive videodisc.

CONEY ISLAND: A GAME OF DISCOVERY Thomas Glocer, Ronald F. Wright, and Owen M. Fiss. Center for Computer-Assisted Legal Instruction, 229 Nineteenth Avenue South, University of Minnesota, Minneapolis, Minnesota 55455. 1990. Machine-readable computer file.

DISCRIMINATION, EDUCATION
See also: CIVIL RIGHTS AND LIBERTIES; DISCRIMINATION, RACE; EDUCATION DEPARTMENT; FEDERAL AID TO EDUCATION; SCHOOL INTEGRATION; SEGREGATION AND INTEGRATION

HANDBOOKS, MANUALS, FORMBOOKS

DESEGREGATING PUBLIC SCHOOLS: A HANDBOOK FOR LOCAL OFFICIALS. David R. Morgan. Bureau of Government Research, University of Oklahoma, 455 West Lindsey, Norman, Oklahoma 73019. Defunct. 1982.

TEXTBOOKS AND GENERAL WORKS

BEYOND BUSING: INSIDE THE CHALLENGE TO URBAN SEGREGATION. Paul R. Dimond. University of Michigan Press. P.O. Box 1104, Ann Arbor, Michigan 48106. 1985.

THE BURDEN OF BROWN: THIRTY YEARS OF SCHOOL DESEGREGATION. Raymond Wolters. University of Tennessee Press, 293 Communications Building, Knoxville, Tennessee 37996-0325. 1984.

DEAD END: THE DEVELOPMENT OF NINETEENTH CENTURY LITIGATION ON RACIAL DISCRIMINATION IN SCHOOLS: AN INAUGURAL LECTURE DELIVERED BEFORE THE UNIVERSITY OF OXFORD ON 28 FEBRUARY 1985. J. Morgan Kousser. Oxford University Press, 200 Madison Avenue, New York, New York 10016. 1986.

EDUCATION: ASSUMPTIONS VERSUS HISTORY: COLLECTED PAPERS. Thomas Sowell. Hoover Institution Press, Stanford University, Stanford, California 94305-6010. 1986.

EQUAL EDUCATION UNDER LAW: LEGAL RIGHTS AND FEDERAL POLICY IN THE POST-BROWN ERA. Rosemary C. Salamone. St. Martin's Press, Incorporated, 175 Fifth Avenue, New York, New York 10010. 1986.

FROM BROWN TO BAKKE: THE SUPREME COURT AND SCHOOL INTEGRATION, 1954-1978. J. Harvie Wilkinson III. Oxford University Press, 200 Madison Avenue, New York, New York 10016. 1979.

I RESPECTFULLY DISAGREE WITH THE JUDGE'S ORDER: THE BOSTON SCHOOL DESEGREGATION CONTROVERSY. J. Michael Ross and William M. Berg. University Press of America, 4720 Boston Way, Lanham, Maryland 20706. 1981.

JOINING THE CLUB: A HISTORY OF JEWS AND YALE. Dan A. Oren. Yale University Press, 92A Yale Station, New Haven, Connecticut 06520. 1986.

JUSTICE AND SCHOOL SYSTEMS: THE ROLE OF THE COURTS IN EDUCATION LITIGATION. Barbara Flicker. Temple University Press, 1601 North Broad Street, University Services Building, Philadelphia, Pennsylvania 19122. 1990.

LITIGATING INTELLIGENCE: IQ TESTS, SPECIAL EDUCATION, AND SOCIAL SCIENCE IN THE COURTROOM. Rogers Elliott. Auburn House Publishing Company, Greenwood Publishing Group, Incorporated, 88 Post Road West, P.O. Box 5007, Westport, Connecticut 06881. 1987.

THE LITTLE ROCK CRISIS: A CONSTITUTIONAL INTERPRETATION. Tony A. Freyer. Greenwood Publishing Group, Incorporated, 88 Post Road West, P.O. Box 5007, Westport, Connecticut 06881. 1984.

THE MYTH OF BLACK PROGRESS. Alphonso Pinkney. Cambridge University Press, 40 West Twentieth Street, New York, New York 10011. 1986.

THE NAACP'S LEGAL STRATEGY AGAINST SEGREGATED EDUCATION, 1925-1950. Mark V. Tushnet. University of North Carolina Press, P.O. Box 2288, Chapel Hill, North Carolina 27515-2288. 1987.

OUT OF ORDER: AFFIRMATIVE ACTION AND THE CRISIS OF DOCTRINAIRE LIBERALISM. Nicholas Capaldi. Prometheus Books, 700 East Amherst Street, Buffalo, New York 14125. 1985.

RACE, CIVIL RIGHTS, AND THE UNITED STATES COURT OF APPEALS FOR THE FIFTH JUDICIAL CIRCUIT. John Michael Spivack. Garland Publishing, Incorporated, 136 Madison Avenue, New York, New York 10016. 1990.

SCHOOL DESEGREGATION PLANS THAT WORK. Charles Vert Willie. Greenwood Publishing Group, Incorporated, 88 Post Road West, P.O. Box 5007, Westport, Connecticut 06881. 1984.

SWANN'S WAY: THE SCHOOL BUSING CASE AND THE SUPREME COURT. Bernard Schwartz. Oxford University Press, 200 Madison Avenue, New York, New York 10016. 1986.

THE USE OF DATA IN DISCRIMINATION ISSUE CASES. William Rosenthal and Bernard Yancey, Editors. Jossey-Bass, Incorporated, Publishers, 350 Sansome Street, San Francisco, California 94104. 1985.

ANNUALS AND SURVEYS

DESEGREGATING BIG CITY SCHOOLS: STRATEGIES, OUTCOMES, AND IMPACTS. Robert E. England and David R. Morgan. Associated Faculty Press, Incorporated, 19 West Thirty-sixth Street, New York, New York 10018. 1986.

LAW REVIEWS AND PERIODICALS

EDUCATION LAW BULLETIN. Center for Law and Education, Gutman Library, Appian Way, Cambridge, Massachusetts 02138. Semiannually.

HARVARD CIVIL RIGHTS -- CIVIL LIBERTIES LAW REVIEW. Harvard Law School. Harvard University Press, 79 Garden Street, Cambridge, Massachusetts 02138. Biannual.

JOURNAL OF COLLEGE AND UNIVERSITY LAW. Notre Dame Law School, Notre Dame, Indiana 46556. Quarterly.

JOURNAL OF LAW AND EDUCATION. University of South Carolina, Law School, Columbia, South Carolina 29208. Quarterly.

NEWSLETTERS AND NEWSPAPERS

EDUCATION OF THE HANDICAPPED. Capitol Publications, Incorporated, 1101 King Street, Suite 444, Alexandria, Virginia 22314. Biweekly.

EQUAL OPPORTUNITY IN HIGHER EDUCATION. Capitol Publications, Incorporated, 1101 King Street, Suite 444, Alexandria, Virginia 22314. Semimonthly.

REPORT ON EDUCATION AND THE DISADVANTAGED. Business Publishers, Incorporated, 951 Pershing Drive, Silver Spring, Maryland 20910. Biweekly.

SPECIAL EDUCATION AND THE HANDICAPPED. Data Research, Incorporated, P.O. Box 490, Rosemount, Minnesota 55068. Monthly.

THE SPECIAL EDUCATOR. LRP Publications, 747 Dresher Road, Horsham, Pennsylvania 19044. Bimonthly.

DIRECTORIES

AFFIRMATIVE ACTION IN HIGHER EDUCATION: A SOURCEBOOK. Lois Vander Waerdt. Garland Publishing, Incorporated, 136 Madison Avenue, New York, New York 10016. 1989.

DISCRIMINATION, EDUCATION

ASSOCIATIONS AND PROFESSIONAL SOCIETIES

CENTER FOR LAW AND EDUCATION. 955 Massachusetts Avenue, Cambridge, Massachusetts 02139. (617) 876-6611.

DISABILITY RIGHTS CENTER. 2500 Q Street, Northwest, Suite 121, Washington, D.C. 20007. (202) 337-4119.

LAWYERS COMMITTEE FOR CIVIL RIGHTS UNDER LAW. 1400 I Street, Northwest, Suite 400, Washington, D.C. 20005. (202) 371-1212.

NATIONAL ASSOCIATION FOR THE ADVANCEMENT OF COLORED PEOPLE. 4805 Mt. Hope Drive, Baltimore, Maryland 21215. (212) 481-4100.

NATIONAL ASSOCIATION OF PROTECTION AND ADVOCACY SYSTEMS. 900 Second Street, Northeast, Suite 211, Washington, D.C. 20002. (202) 408-9514.

NATIONAL BLACK LAW STUDENTS ASSOCIATION. 1225 Eleventh Street, Northwest, Washington, D.C. 20001. (202) 583-1281.

NATIONAL ORGANIZATION FOR WOMEN. 1000 Sixteenth Street, Northwest, Suite 700, Washington, D.C. 20036. (202) 328-5160.

UNITED STATES COMMISSION ON CIVIL RIGHTS. 1121 Vermont Avenue, Northwest, Washington, D.C. 20425. (202) 376-8582.

STATISTICS SOURCES

STATISTICAL METHODS IN DISCRIMINATION LITIGATION. D.H. Kaye and Mikel Aickin. Marcel Dekker, Incorporated, 720 Madison Avenue, New York, New York 10016. 1986.

DISCRIMINATION, EMPLOYMENT
See also: AGE DISCRIMINATION; CIVIL RIGHTS AND LIBERTIES; DISCRIMINATION, RACE; DISCRIMINATION, SEX; EQUAL EMPLOYMENT OPPORTUNITY; EQUAL EMPLOYMENT OPPORTUNITY COMMISSION

LOOSELEAF SERVICES AND REPORTERS

AGE DISCRIMINATION. Howard Eglit. Shepard's/McGraw-Hill, P.O. Box 1235, Colorado Springs, Colorado 80901. 1981- .

EEOC COMPLIANCE MANUAL. United States Equal Employment Opportunity Commission. Bureau of National Affairs, Incorporated, 1231 Twenty-fifth Street, Northwest, Washington, D.C. 20037. 1975- .

EEOC COMPLIANCE MANUAL: INCLUDING THE EEOC'S GENERAL COUNSEL MANUAL. Commerce Clearing House, Incorporated, 4025 West Peterson Avenue, Chicago, Illinois 60646. 1975- .

EEOC DECISIONS. Commerce Clearing House, Incorporated, 4025 West Peterson Avenue, Chicago, Illinois 60646. 1983.

EMPLOYMENT DISCRIMINATION. Arthur Larson and Lex K. Larson. Matthew Bender and Company, Incorporated, 11 Penn Plaza, New York, New York 10001. 1983- .

EMPLOYMENT DISCRIMINATION. Paul N. Cox. Garland Publishing, Incorporated, 136 Madison Avenue, New York, New York 10016. 1987.

EMPLOYMENT DISRIMINATION: LAW AND LITIGATION. Merrick T. Rossein. Clark Boardman Company, Limited, 435 Hudson Street, New York, New York 10014. 1990- .

EQUAL EMPLOYMENT OPPORTUNITY COMPLIANCE MANUAL. Prentice-Hall, Incorporated, Route 9W, Englewood Cliffs, New Jersey 07632. 1979- .

FEDERAL EQUAL OPPORTUNITY REPORTER. LRP Publications, 747 Dresher Road, Horsham, Pennsylvania 19044. 1987- . 3 vols.

GUIDEBOOK TO FAIR EMPLOYMENT PRACTICES. Commerce Clearing House, Incorporated, 4025 West Peterson Avenue, Chicago, Illinois 60646. 1973- .

INDIVIDUAL EMPLOYMENT RIGHTS CASES. Bureau of National Affairs, Incorporated, 951 Pershing Drive, Silver Spring, Maryland 20910. 1987- .

LABOR LAW REPORTS. Commerce Clearing House, Incorporated, 4025 West Peterson Avenue, Chicago, Illinois 60646. 1960- .

LABOR RELATIONS REPORTER. Bureau of National Affairs, Incorporated, 1231 Twenty-fifth Street, Northwest, Washington, D.C. 20037. 1937- .

MANUAL ON EMPLOYMENT DISCRIMINATION AND CIVIL RIGHTS ACTIONS IN THE FEDERAL COURTS. Attorney's Edition. Charles R. Richey. Kluwer Law Book Publishers, Incorporated, 36 West Forty-fourth Street, New York, New York 10036. 1985- .

A PRACTICAL GUIDE TO EQUAL EMPLOYMENT OPPORTUNITY. Walter B. Connolly, Jr. New York Law Journal Press, Incorporated, 111 Eighth Avenue, Suite 900, New York, New York 10011. 1979- .

RESPONDING TO EMPLOYMENT DISCRIMINATION CHARGES. Bruce S. Harrison and Eric Hemmendinger. Matthew Bender and Company, Incorporated, 11 Penn Plaza, New York, New York 10001. 1985- .

UNJUST DISMISSAL. Lex K. Larson. Matthew Bender and Company, Incorporated, 11 Penn Plaza, New York, New York 10001. 1985- .

HANDBOOKS, MANUALS, FORMBOOKS

AMERICANS WITH DISABILITIES ACT HANDBOOK. Henry H. Perritt. Wiley Law Publications, 605 Third Avenue, New York, New York 10158. 1990.

EEOC AND THE LAWS IT ENFORCES: A REFERENCE MANUAL. Equal Employment Opportunity Commission. Superintendent of Documents, United States Government Printing Office, Washington, D.C. 20402.

EMPLOYMENT DISCRIMINATION: A CLAIMS MANUAL FOR EMPLOYEES AND MANAGERS. Andrew J. Maikovich. McFarland and Company, Incorporated, Box 611, Jefferson, North Carolina 28640. 1989.

EMPLOYMENT DISCRIMINATION LITIGATION. Andrew J. Ruzicho. Anderson Publishing Company, 2035 Reading Road, Cincinnati, Ohio 45202. 1989.

THE EQUAL EMPLOYMENT COMPLIANCE MANUAL. Andrew J. Ruzicho and Louis A. Jacobs. Callaghan and Company, 155 Pfingsten Road, Deerfield, Illinois 60015. 1990.

GOVERNMENT REGULATION OF EMPLOYMENT DISCRIMINATION: A SOURCEBOOK FOR MANAGERS. Richard Trotter and Susan Rawson Zacur. University Press of America, 4720 Boston Way, Lanham, Maryland 20706. 1986.

GUIDEBOOK TO FAIR EMPLOYMENT PRACTICES. Commerce Clearing House, Incorporated, 4025 West Peterson Avenue, Chicago, Illinois 60646. 1980- .

IN DEFENSE OF THE PUBLIC EMPLOYER: CASE LAW AND LITIGATION STRATEGIES FOR DISCRIMINATION CLAIMS. Patricia A. Brandin. American Bar Association, Section of Urban, State, and Local Government Law, 750 North Lake Shore Drive, Chicago, Illinois 60611. 1988.

THE LABOR LAWYER'S GUIDE TO THE RIGHTS AND RESPONSIBILITIES OF EMPLOYEE WHISTLEBLOWERS. Stephen M. Kohn. Quorum Books, Greenwood Publishing Group, Incorporated, 88 Post Road West, P.O. Box 5007, Westport, Connecticut 06881. 1988.

MANUAL ON EMPLOYMENT DISCRIMINATION LAW AND CIVIL RIGHTS ACTIONS IN THE FEDERAL COURTS. Charles R. Richey. Federal Judicial Center. Superintendent of Documents, United States Government Printing Office, Washington, D.C. 20402. 1987.

MANUAL ON THE ADMINISTRATIVE PROCESSING OF FEDERAL SECTOR EEO COMPLAINTS (1988): A GUIDE. Bob Fabia. Federal Bar Association, Washington, D.C. 1988.

PRIMER OF EQUAL EMPLOYMENT OPPORTUNITY. Fourth Edition. Michael D. Levin-Epstein. Bureau of National Affairs, Incorporated, 1231 Twenty-fifth Street, Northwest, Washington, D.C. 20037. 1987.

TEXTBOOKS AND GENERAL WORKS

ACADEMICS IN COURT: THE CONSEQUENCES OF FACULTY DISCRIMINATION LITIGATION. George R. LaNoue. University of Michigan Press, P.O. Box 1104. 839 Greene Street, Ann Arbor, Michigan 48106. 1987.

AFFIRMATIVE ACTION AND PRINCIPLES OF JUSTICE. Kathanne W. Greene. Greenwood Publishing Group, Incorporated, 88 Post Road West, P.O. Box 5007, Westport, Connecticut 06881. 1989.

AVOIDING EMPLOYMENT DISCRIMINATION CHARGES. Stephen D. Shawe and Bruce S. Harrison. Matthew Bender and Company, Incorporated, 11 Penn Plaza, New York, New York 10001. 1984.

COLLECTIVE BARGAINING AND LABOR ARBITRATION. Third Edition. Donald P. Rothschild. Michie Company, P.O. Box 7587, Charlottesville, Virginia 22906. 1988.

CONDUCTING THE LAWFUL EMPLOYMENT INTERVIEW: HOW TO AVOID CHARGES OF DISCRIMINATION WHEN INTERVIEWING JOB CANDIDATES. Alan M. Koral, Editor. Executive Enterprises Publications Company, 22 West Twenty-first Street, New York, New York 10010-6904. 1986.

A CONFLICT OF RIGHTS: THE SUPREME COURT AND AFFIRMATIVE ACTION. Melvin I. Urofsky. Charles Scribner Sons, MacMillan Publishing Company, Incorporated, 866 Third Avenue, New York, New York 10022. 1991.

DEFENSE OF EQUAL EMPLOYMENT CLAIMS. William L. Diedrich and William Gaus. Shepard's/McGraw-Hill, P.O. Box 1235, Colorado Springs, Colorado 80901. 1982- . (Annual Supplements).

DISCRIMINATION IN EMPLOYMENT. Fifth Edition. William P. Murphy, James E. Jones, Jr., and Julius G. Getman. Bureau of National Affairs, Incorporated, 1231 Twenty-fifth Street, Northwest, Washington, D.C. 20037. 1986.

DISCRIMINATION IN PUBLIC EMPLOYMENT: THE EVOLVING LAW. Martha M. McCarthy. National Organization on Legal Problems of Education, 3601 West Twenty-ninth Street, Topeka, Kansas 66614. 1983.

DISCRIMINATION, JOBS, AND POLITICS: THE STRUGGLE FOR EQUAL EMPLOYMENT OPPORTUNITY IN THE UNITED STATES SINCE THE NEW DEAL. Paul Burstein. University of Chicago Press, 5801 Ellis Avenue, Chicago, Illinois 60637. 1985.

EEO POLICIES AND PROGRAMS. Personnel Policies Forum. Bureau of National Affairs, Incorporated, 1231 Twenty-fifth Street, Northwest, Washington, D.C. 20037. 1986.

THE EMPLOYER'S GUIDE TO AVOIDING JOB-BIAS LITIGATION, 1986: HOW TO PINPOINT AND REMEDY DISCRIMINATION BEFORE YOU'RE SUED. Peter C. Reid. Random House, Incorporated, 201 East Fiftieth Street, New York, New York 10022. 1986.

EMPLOYMENT DISCRIMINATION LAW. Second Edition. Lee Modjeska. Lawyers Cooperative Publishing Company, Aqueduct Building, Rochester, New York 14694. 1988.

EMPLOYMENT DISCRIMINATION LAW. Student Edition. Mack A. Player. West Publishing Company, 50 West Kellogg Boulevard, St. Paul, Minnesota 55164. 1988.

EMPLOYMENT DISCRIMINATION LAW. Third Edition. Barbara L. Schlei and Paul Grossman. Bureau of National Affairs, Incorporated, 1231 Twenty-fifth Street, Northwest, Washington, D.C. 20037. 1983- . (Irregular Supplements).

EMPLOYMENT DISCRIMINATION LITIGATION. Andrew J. Ruzicho. Anderson Publishing Company, 2035 Reading Road, Cincinnati, Ohio 45202. 1989.

EMPLOYMENT LITIGATION, 1990: A DEFENSE AND PLAINTIFF'S PERSPECTIVE. Peter M. Pranken and Paul I. Weiner, Co-chairmen. Practising Law Institute, 810 Seventh Avenue, New York, New York 10019. 1990.

EQUALITY TRANSFORMED: A QUARTER-CENTURY OF AFFIRMATIVE ACTION. Herman Belz. Transaction Publishers, Rutgers University, New Brunswick, New Jersey 08903. 1991.

FEDERAL LAW OF EMPLOYMENT DISCRIMINATION IN A NUTSHELL. Second Edition. Mack A. Player. West Publishing Company, P.O. Box 64526, 50 West Kellogg Boulevard, St. Paul, Minnesota 55164-0526. 1981.

FIVE-YEAR CUMULATIVE SUPPLEMENT TO SCHLEI AND GROSSMAN'S EMPLOYMENT DISCRIMINATION LAW. Second Edition. American Bar Association, Section of Labor and Employment Law, 750 North Lake Shore Drive, Chicago, Illinois 60611. 1989.

HANDLING EMPLOYMENT DISCRIMINATION CASES. Lee Modjeska. Lawyers Cooperative Company, One Graves Street, Rochester, New York 14694. 1980.

THE LAW OF EQUAL EMPLOYMENT OPPORTUNITY. Stephen N. Shulman. Research Institute of America, Incorporated, 210 South Street, Boston, Massachusetts 02111. 1990.

MAJOR ISSUES IN THE FEDERAL LAW OF EMPLOYMENT DISCRIMINATION. Second Edition. George Rutherglen. Federal Judicial Center, Washington, D.C. 1987.

MAKING A RIGHT A REALITY: AN ORAL HISTORY OF THE EARLY YEARS OF THE EEOC, 1965-1972. Equal Employment Opportunity Commission. Superintendent of Documents, United States Government Printing Office, Washington, D.C. 20402. 1990.

PATHWAYS IN THE WORKPLACE: THE EFFECTS OF GENDER AND RACE ON ACCESS TO ORGANIZATIONAL RESOURCES. Jon Miller. Cambridge University Press, 40 West Twentieth Street, New York, New York 10011. 1986.

PATTERN DISCOVERY: EMPLOYMENT DISCRIMINATION. Douglas Danner. Lawyers Cooperative Company, One Graves Street, Rochester, New York 14694. 1981- . (Periodic Supplements).

PRIMER OF EQUAL EMPLOYMENT OPPORTUNITY. Third Edition. Michael D. Levin-Epstein. Bureau of National Affairs, Incorporated, 1231 Twenty-fifth Street, Northwest, Washington, D.C. 20037. 1984.

PROTECTING THE GROWING NUMBER OF OLDER WORKERS: DISCRIMINATION IN EMPLOYMENT ACT. Daniel P. O'Meara. Industrial Research Unit, the Wharton School, University of Pennsylvania, 3733 Spruce Street, Philadelphia, Pennsylvania 19104. 1989.

THE QUESTION OF DISCRIMINATION: RACIAL INEQUALITY IN THE U.S. LABOR MARKET. Wesleyan University Press, 110 Mount Vernon Street, Middletown, Connecticut 06457. 1989.

WHISTLEBLOWING: THE LAW OF RETALIATORY DISCHARGE. Daniel P. Westman. Bureau of National Affairs, Incorporated, 1231 Twenty-fifth Street, Northwest, Washington, D.C. 20037. 1991.

WOMEN, MINORITIES, AND UNIONS IN THE PUBLIC SECTOR. Norma Riccucci. Greenwood Publishing Group, Incorporated, 88 Post Road West, P.O. Box 5007, Westport, Connecticut 06881. 1990.

WOMEN, WORK AND PROTEST: A CENTURY OF U.S. WOMEN'S LABOR HISTORY. Ruth Milkman, Editor. Routledge, Chapman and Hall, 29 West Thirty-fifth Street, New York, New York 10001. 1985.

WOMEN'S WORK: DEVELOPMENT AND THE DIVISION OF LABOR BY SEX. Eleanor Leacock and Helen I. Safa. Bergin and Garvey Publishers, Incorporated, 670 Amherst Road, Granby, Massachusetts 01033. 1988.

DIGESTS, INDEXES, ABSTRACTS, CITATORS

MANUAL ON EMPLOYMENT DISCRIMINATION AND CIVIL RIGHTS ACTIONS IN THE FEDERAL COURTS. Charles R. Richey. Kluwer Law Book Publishers, Incorporated, 36 West Forty-fourth Street, New York, New York 10036. 1988.

ANNUALS AND SURVEYS

ANNUAL INSTITUTE ON EMPLOYMENT LAW. Practising Law Institute, 810 Seventh Avenue, New York, New York 10019. 1983- . (Annual).

EMPLOYMENT LAW, COURT INTERPRETATIONS, AND EMPLOYER OBLIGATIONS: A REVIEW OF THE LATEST COURT DECISIONS IN THE AREA OF EMPLOYMENT-AT-WILL DOCTRINE, SEX DISCRIMINATION IN EMPLOYMENT, AGE DISCRIMINATION IN EMPLOYMENT. Donn R. Marston. Machinery and Allied Products Institute, 1200 Eighteenth Street, Northwest, Washington, D.C. 20036. 1984.

LAW REVIEWS AND PERIODICALS

HARVARD CIVIL RIGHTS -- CIVIL LIBERTIES LAW REVIEW. Harvard Law School, Harvard University Press, 79 Garden Street, Cambridge, Massachusetts 02138. Biannual.

SEXUAL HARASSMENT AND DISCRIMINATION IN THE WORKPLACE. Nu-Tec Publishing, Incorporated, 4715 Strack Road, Suite 211, Houston, Texas 77069. Monthly.

NEWSLETTERS AND NEWSPAPERS

AFFIRMATIVE ACTION/EEO NOTES. NYPER Publications, P.O. Box 662, Latham, New York 12110. Monthly.

DISCIPLINE AND GRIEVANCES (GOVERNMENT EDITION). The Bureau of Business Practice, Incorporated, 24 Rope Ferry Road, Waterford, Connecticut 06386. Monthly.

EEO REVIEW. Executive Enterprises Publications Company, Incorporated, 22 West Twenty-first Street, New York, New York 10010. Monthly.

EQUAL EMPLOYMENT COMPLIANCE UPDATE. Callaghan and Company, 155 Pfingsten Road, Deerfield, Illinois 60015. Monthly.

FAIR EMPLOYMENT COMPLIANCE. Management Resources, Incorporated, 379 West Broadway, Fourth floor, New York, New York 10014. Semimonthly.

FAIR EMPLOYMENT PRACTICES GUIDELINES. The Bureau of Business Practice, Incorporated, 24 Rope Ferry Road, Waterford, Connecticut 06386. Monthly.

FAIR EMPLOYMENT PRACTICES: SUMMARY OF LATEST DEVELOPMENTS. The Bureau of National Affairs, Incorporated, 1231 Twenty-fifth Street, Northwest, Washington, D.C. 20037. Biweekly.

FAIR EMPLOYMENT ALERT. Business Publishers, Incorporated, 951 Pershing Drive, Silver Spring, Maryland 20910. Biweekly.

NEW DEVELOPMENTS IN EMPLOYMENT DISCRIMINATION. Garland Law Publishing, 136 Madison Avenue, New York, New York 10016. Quarterly.

SPOTLIGHT ON AFFIRMATIVE EMPLOYMENT PROGRAMS. United States Office of Personnel Management. Superintendent of Documents, United States Government Printing Office, Washington, D.C. 20402. Quarterly.

BIBLIOGRAPHIES

EQUAL OPPORTUNITY IN THE WORKPLACE: A CHECK-LIST, 1980-1983. Dale E. Casper. Vance Bibliographies, P.O. Box 229, 112 North Charter Street, Monticello, Illinois 61856. 1985.

ASSOCIATIONS AND PROFESSIONAL SOCIETIES

DISABILITY RIGHTS CENTER. 2500 Q Street, Northwest, Suite 121, Washington, D.C. 20007. (202) 337-4119.

LAWYERS COMMITTEE FOR CIVIL RIGHTS UNDER LAW. 1400 I Street, Northwest, Suite 400, Washington, D.C. 20005. (202) 371-1212.

NATIONAL ASSOCIATION FOR THE ADVANCEMENT OF COLORED PEOPLE. 4805 Mt. Hope Drive, Baltimore, Maryland 21215. (212) 481-4100.

NATIONAL ASSOCIATION OF PROTECTION AND ADVOCACY SYSTEMS. 900 Second Street, Northeast, Suite 211, Washington, D.C. 20002. (202) 408-9514.

NATIONAL EMPLOYMENT LAW PROJECT. 475 Riverside Drive, Suite 240, New York, New York 10115. (212) 870-2121.

NATIONAL ORGANIZATION FOR WOMEN. 1000 Sixteenth Street, Northwest, Suite 700, Washington, D.C. 20036. (202) 328-5160.

NATIONAL URBAN LEAGUE. 500 East Sixty-second Street, New York, New York 10021. (212) 310-9000.

UNITED STATES COMMISSION ON CIVIL RIGHTS. 1121 Vermont Avenue, Northwest, Washington, D.C. 20425. (202) 376-8582.

RESEARCH CENTERS, INSTITUTES, CLEARINGHOUSES

AMERICAN BAR FOUNDATION. 750 North Lake Shore Drive, Chicago, Illinois 60611. (312) 988-6500.

CENTER FOR EMPLOYMENT RELATIONS AND THE LAW. Florida State University, College of Law, Tallahassee, Florida 32306. (904) 644-4287.

STATISTICS SOURCES

STATISTICAL METHODS IN DISCRIMINATION LITIGATION. D.H. Kaye and Mikel Aickin. Marcel Dekker, Incorporated, 270 Madison Avenue, New York, New York 10016. 1986.

USE OF STATISTICS IN EQUAL EMPLOYMENT OPPORTUNITY LITIGATION. Walter B. Connolly, Jr. and David W. Peterson. Law Journal Seminars-Press, 111 Eighth Avenue, New York, New York 10011. 1980- .

AUDIOVISUALS

THE REMEDIES PHASE OF AN EEO CASE. Co-sponsored by the American Bar Association Litigation and Labor and Employment Law Sections. American Bar Association, 750 North Lake Shore Drive, Chicago, Illinois 60611. 1984. (Nine videocassettes).

COMPUTER-ASSISTED LEGAL INSTRUCTION

AFFIRMATIVE ACTION. Peter N. Swan. Center for Computer-Assisted Instruction, 229 19th Avenue South, University of Minnesota, Minneapolis, Minnesota 55455. Machine-readable data file.

BOTTOM LINE DEFENSE. Peter N. Swan. Center for Computer-Assisted Instruction, 229 19th Avenue South, University of Minnesota, Minneapolis, Minnesota 55455. Machine-readable data file.

EQUAL PAY ACT. Peter N. Swan. Center for Computer-Assisted Instruction, 229 19th Avenue South, University of Minnesota, Minneapolis, Minnesota 55455. Machine-readable data file.

TITLE VII: CLAIMS PATHWAY. Peter N. Swan. Center for Computer- Assisted Instruction, 229 19th Avenue South, University of Minnesota, Minneapolis, Minnesota 55455. Machine-readable data file.

OTHER SOURCES

DISCRIMINATION IN EMPLOYMENT -- LAW AND LEGISLATION -- UNITED STATES CONGRESS. American Bar Association, National Institute on Equal Opportunity Law and Section of Labor Relations, 750 North Lake Shore Drive, Chicago, Illinois 60611. 1982.

LAWS ENFORCED BY THE U.S. EQUAL EMPLOYMENT OPPORTUNITY COMMISSION. Superintendent of Documents, United States Government Printing Office, Washington, D.C. 20402. 1987.

REPORT OF THE UNITED STATES COMMISSION ON CIVIL RIGHTS ON THE CIVIL RIGHTS ACT OF 1990. United States Commission on Civil Rights, Washington, D.C. 1990.

REPORT TO THE ATTORNEY GENERAL: REDEFINING DISCRIMINATION: "DISPARATE IMPACT" AND THE INSTITUTIONALIZATION OF AFFIRMATIVE ACTION. U.S. Department of Justice, Office of Legal Policy. Superintendent of Documents, United States Government Printing Office, Washington, D.C. 20402. 1988.

DISCRIMINATION, HOUSING
See also: CIVIL RIGHTS AND LIBERTIES; DISCRIMINATION, RACE; SEGREGATION AND INTEGRATION

LOOSELEAF SERVICES AND REPORTERS

FAIR HOUSING - FAIR LENDING CASES. Prentice-Hall, Incorporated, Route 9W, Englewood Cliffs, New Jersey 07632. 1989- .

HOUSING DISCRIMINATION: LAW AND LITIGATION. Robert G. Schwemm. Clark Boardman Company, Limited, 435 Hudson Street, New York, New York 10014. 1990- .

TEXTBOOKS AND GENERAL WORKS

A DECENT HOME: A REPORT ON THE CONTINUING FAILURE OF THE FEDERAL GOVERNMENT TO PROVIDE EQUAL HOUSING OPPORTUNITY. Citizens Commission on Civil Rights, 2000 M Street, Northwest, Washington, D.C. 20036. 1983.

DIVIDED NEIGHBOORHOODS: CHANGING PATTERNS OF RACIAL SEGREGATION. Gary A. Tobin. Sage Publications, 2455 Teller Road, Newbury Park, California 91320. 1987.

THE FAIR HOUSING ACT AFTER TWENTY YEARS: A CONFERENCE AT YALE LAW SCHOOL. Robert G. Schwemm. Yale Law School, New Haven, Connecticut. 1989.

FAIR HOUSING AND COMMUNITY DEVELOPMENT DISCRIMINATION LAW AND PRACTICE. Shepard's Citations, Incorporated. Shepard's/McGraw-Hill, P.O. Box 1235, Colorado Springs, Colorado 80901. 1983.

FAIR HOUSING COMES OF AGE. George R. Metcalf. Greenwood Publishing Group, Incorporated, 88 Post Road West, P.O. Box 5007, Westport, Connecticut 06881. 1988.

FAIR HOUSING: DISCRIMINATION IN REAL ESTATE, COMMUNITY DEVELOPMENT, AND REVITALIZATION. James A. Kushner. Shepard's/McGraw-Hill, P.O. Box 1235, Colorado Springs, Colorado 80901. 1983- . (Annual Supplements).

THE HIGH COST OF HOUSING DISCRIMINATION: A REPORT ON DISCRIMINATION CASES IN NEW YORK METROPOLITAN AREA 1981-1985. Open Housing Center of New York, 150 Fifth Avenue, New York, New York 10011. 1986.

HOUSING DISCRIMINATION LAW AND LITIGATION. Robert G. Schwemm. Bureau of National Affairs, Incorporated, 1231 Twenty-fifth Street, Northwest, Washington, D.C. 20037. 1990.

THE LEGACY OF JUDICIAL POLICY-MAKING: GAUTREAUX V. CHICAGO HOUSING AUTHORITY: THE DECISION AND ITS IMPACTS. Elizabeth Warren. University Press of America, 4720 Boston Way, Lanham, Maryland 20706. 1988.

RESIDENTIAL SEGREGATION, THE STATE AND CONSTITUTIONAL CONFLICT IN AMERICAN URBAN AREAS. R.J. Johnston. Academic Press, Incorporated, 1250 Sixth Avenue, San Diego, California 92101. 1984.

SHELTERED CRISIS: THE STATE OF FAIR HOUSING IN THE EIGHTIES. United States Commission on Civil Rights. Superintendent of Documents, United States Government Printing Office, Washington, D.C. 20402. 1984.

LAW REVIEWS AND PERIODICALS

HARVARD CIVIL RIGHTS -- CIVIL LIBERTIES LAW REVIEW. Harvard Law School, Harvard University Press, 79 Garden Street, Cambridge, Massachusetts 02138. Biannual.

LAW BULLETIN. National Housing Law Project, 1950 Addison Street, Berkeley, California 94704. Bimonthly.

BIBLIOGRAPHIES

AN ANNOTATED BIBLIOGRAPHY OF HOUSING AND SCHOOL SEGREGATION ARTICLES AND DOCUMENTS, WITH ADDITIONAL MATERIAL FOR RESEARCH. Housing Advocates, Incorporated and Edward G. Kramer. Vance Bibliographies, P.O. Box 229, 112 North Charter Street, Monticello, Illinois 61856. 1980.

FAIR HOUSING AND FAMILIES: DISCRIMINATION AGAINST CHILDREN. Jim Buchanan. Vance Bibliographies, P.O. Box 229, 112 North Charter Street, Monticello, Illinois 61856. 1985.

RESIDENTIAL SEGREGATION BY RACE AND CONSTITUTIONAL CONFLICT IN THE UNITED STATES: A BIBLIOGRAPHY. Lorna Peterson. Vance Bibliographies, P.O. Box 229, 112 North Charter Street, Monticello, Illinois 61856. 1986.

DIRECTORIES

DIRECTORY OF STATE AND LOCAL FAIR HOUSING AGENCIES. United States Commission on Civil Rights. Superintendent of Documents, United States Government Printing Office, Washington, D.C. 20402. 1985.

ASSOCIATIONS AND PROFESSIONAL SOCIETIES

LAWYERS COMMITTEE FOR CIVIL RIGHTS UNDER LAW. 1400 I Street, Northwest, Suite 400, Washington, D.C. 20005. (202) 371-1212.

NATIONAL ASSOCIATION FOR THE ADVANCEMENT OF COLORED PEOPLE. 4805 Mt. Hope Drive, Baltimore, Maryland 21215. (212) 481-4100.

NATIONAL HOUSING LAW PROJECT. 1950 Addison Street, Berkeley, California 94704. (415) 548-9400.

OPEN HOUSING CENTER. 594 Broadway, Suite 608, New York, New York 10012. (212) 941-6101.

UNITED STATES COMMISSION ON CIVIL RIGHTS. 1121 Vermont Avenue, Northwest, Washington, D.C. 20425. (202) 376-8582.

RESEARCH CENTERS, INSTITUTES, CLEARINGHOUSES

ANNE BLAINE HARRISON INSTITUTE FOR PUBLIC LAW. Georgetown University, 25 E Street, Northwest, Washington, D.C. 20001. (202) 662-9600.

THE FRASER INSTITUTE. 626 Bute Street, Vancouver, BC, Canada V6E 3M1. (604) 688-0221.

STATISTICS SOURCES

STATISTICAL METHODS IN DISCRIMINATION LITIGATION. D.H. Kaye and Mikel Aickin. Marcel Dekker, Incorporated, 270 Madison Avenue, New York, New York 10016. 1986.

DISCRIMINATION, RACE
See also: CIVIL RIGHTS AND LIBERTIES; DISCRIMINATION, EDUCATION; DISCRIMINATION, EMPLOYMENT; DISCRIMINATION, HOUSING; EQUAL EMPLOYMENT OPPORTUNITY; EQUAL EMPLOYMENT OPPORTUNITY COMMISSION; FAIR EMPLOYMENT PRACTICES; SEGREGATION AND INTEGRATION; SLAVERY

TEXTBOOKS AND GENERAL WORKS

BEYOND BUSING: INSIDE THE CHALLENGE TO URBAN SEGREGATION. University of Michigan Press, P.O. Box 1104, Ann Arbor, Michigan 48106. 1985.

BLACK VOTER REGISTRATION EFFORTS IN THE SOUTH. John Lewis and Archie E. Allen. Voter Education Project, 604 Beckwith Street, Southwest, Atlanta, Georgia 30314-4113. 1987.

COMPROMISED COMPLIANCE: IMPLEMENTATION OF THE 1965 VOTING RIGHTS ACT. Howard Ball, Dale Krane and Thomas P. Lauth. Greenwood Publishing Group, Incorporated, 88 Post Road West, P.O. Box 5007, Westport, Connecticut 06881. 1982.

THE CRIMINAL JUSTICE SYSTEM AND BLACKS. Daniel E. Georges-Abeyie. Clark Boardman Company, Limited, 435 Hudson Street, New York, New York 10014. 1984.

EQUALITY AND DISCRIMINATION UNDER INTERNATIONAL LAW. Warwick A. McKean. Oxford University Press, 200 Madison Avenue, New York, New York 10016. 1985.

HUMAN RIGHTS, ETHNICITY AND DISCRIMINATION. Vernon Van Dyke. Greenwood Publishing Group, Incorporated, 88 Post Road West, P.O. Box 5007, Westport, Connecticut 06881. 1985.

PREFERENTIAL POLICIES: AN INTERNATIONAL PERSPECTIVE. Thomas Sowell. William Morrow and Company, 105 Madison Avenue, New York, New York 10016. 1990.

RACE AND CULTURAL MINORITIES: AN ANALYSIS OF PREJUDICE AND DISCRIMINATION. Fifth Edition. George E. Simpson and J. Milton Yinger. Plenum Press, 233 Spring Street, New York, New York 10013-1578. 1985.

RACE RELATIONS AND THE LAW IN AMERICAN HISTORY: MAJOR HISTORICAL INTERPRETATIONS. Kermit L. Hall, Editor. Garland Publishing, Incorporated, 136 Madison Avenue, New York, New York 10016. 1987.

SEXISM, RACISM AND OPPRESSION. Arthur Brittan and Mary Maynard. Blackwell North America, 1001 Fries Mill Road, Blackwood, New Jersey 08012. 1984.

STATE CIVIL RIGHTS AGENCIES: THE UNFULFILLED PROMISE: A CRITICAL APPRAISAL OF STATE CIVIL RIGHTS AGENCIES AND RECOMMENDATIONS FOR CHANGE. Ronald A. Krauss. American Jewish Committee, 165 East Fifty-sixth Street, New York, New York 10022. 1986.

STUDY OF THE PROBLEM OF DISCRIMINATION AGAINST INDIGENOUS POPULATIONS. Jose R. Martinez Cobo. United Nations Publishing Service, Room DC2-0853, New York, New York 10017. 1987.

THE VOTING RIGHTS ACT: CONSEQUENCES AND IMPLICATIONS. Lorn S. Foster. Praeger Publishers, One Madison Avenue, New York, New York 10010-3603. 1985.

DIGESTS, INDEXES, ABSTRACTS, CITATORS

PAY EQUITY SOURCEBOOK: RACE-BASED AND SEX-BASED DISCRIMINATION LAW. Diana L. Stone. Equal Rights Advocates, San Francisco, California. 1987.

LAW REVIEWS AND PERIODICALS

HARVARD CIVIL RIGHTS -- CIVIL LIBERTIES LAW REVIEW. Harvard Law School, Harvard University Press, 79 Garden Street, Cambridge, Massachusetts 02138. Biannual.

LAW REPORT. Southern Poverty Law Center, P.O. Box 2087, Montgomery, Alabama 36102. Bimonthly.

NATIONAL BLACK LAW JOURNAL. University of California at Los Angeles School of Law, Los Angeles, California. Three issues yearly. (Formerly: Black Law Journal).

SOUTHERN WOMEN: THE INTERSECTION OF RACE, CLASS AND GENDER. Center for Research on Women, Memphis State University, Clement Hall-339, Memphis, Tennessee 38152. Semiannual.

NEWSLETTERS AND NEWSPAPERS

ADL LAW REPORT. Anti-Defamation League of B'nai B'rith, 823 United Nations Plaza, New York, New York 10017. Irregular.

AFFIRMATIVE ACTION/EEO NOTES. NYPER Publications, P.O. Box 662, Latham, New York 12110. Monthly.

KLANWATCH INTELLIGENCE REPORT. Southern Poverty Law Center, P.O. Box 2087, Montgomery, Alabama 36102. Monthly.

NEW DEVELOPMENTS IN EMPLOYMENT DISCRIMINATION. Garland Law Publishing, 136 Madison Avenue, New York, New York 10016. Quarterly.

THE ORGANIZER. National Alliance Against Racist and Political Repression, 126 West One Hundred Nineteenth Street, Suite 101, New York, New York 10026. Quarterly.

SOUTHERN CHRISTIAN LEADERSHIP CONFERENCE NEWSLETTER. 334 Auburn Avenue, Northeast, Atlanta, Georgia 30312. Monthly.

SPOTLIGHT ON AFFIRMATIVE EMPLOYMENT PROGRAMS. United States Office of Personnel Management. Superintendent of Documents, United States Government Printing Office, Washington, D.C. 20402. Quarterly.

ASSOCIATIONS AND PROFESSIONAL SOCIETIES

COUNCIL ON INTERRACIAL BOOKS FOR CHILDREN. 1841 Broadway, Room 608, New York, New York 10023. (212) 757-5339.

LAWYERS COMMITTEE FOR CIVIL RIGHTS UNDER LAW. 1400 I Street, Northwest, Suite 400, Washington, D.C. 20005. (202) 371-1212.

NAACP LEGAL DEFENSE FUND. 99 Hudson Street, Sixteenth Floor, New York, New York 10013. (212) 481-4100.

NATIONAL ALLIANCE AGAINST RACIST AND POLITICAL REPRESSION. 126 West One Hundred Nineteenth Street, Suite 101, New York, New York 10026. (212) 866-8600.

NATIONAL ASSOCIATION FOR THE ADVANCEMENT OF COLORED PEOPLE (NAACP). 4805 Mt. Hope Drive, Baltimore, Maryland 21215. (212) 481-4100.

NATIONAL URBAN LEAGUE. 500 East Sixty-second Street, New York, New York 10021. (212) 310-9000.

SOUTHERN CHRISTIAN LEADERSHIP CONFERENCE. 334 Auburn Avenue, Northeast, Atlanta, Georgia 30312. (404) 522-1420.

SOUTHERN POVERTY LAW CENTER. P.O. Box 2087, Montgomery, Alabama 36102. (205) 264-0286.

UNITED STATES COMMISSION ON CIVIL RIGHTS. 1121 Vermont Avenue, Northwest, Washington, D.C. 20425. (202) 376-8582.

WOMEN FOR RACIAL AND ECONOMIC EQUALITY. 198 Broadway, Room 606, New York, New York 10038. (212) 385-1103.

RESEARCH CENTERS, INSTITUTES, CLEARINGHOUSES

AMISTAD RESEARCH CENTER. Tulane University, 6923 St. Charles Avenue, New Orleans, Louisiana 70118. (504) 865-5535.

CENTER FOR AFRO-AMERICAN STUDIES. Ohio University, 300 Lindley Hall, Athens, Ohio 45701. (614) 593-4546.

CENTER FOR RACE AND ETHNICITY. Brown University, 82 Waterman, Box 1886, Providence, Rhode Island 02912. (401) 863-3080.

CENTER FOR URBAN AFFAIRS. Michigan State University, East Lansing, Michigan 48224. (517) 353-9035.

INSTITUTE OF HUMAN RELATIONS. American Jewish Committee, 165 East Fifty-sixth Street, New York, New York 10022. (212) 751-4000.

NATIONAL INSTITUTE AGAINST PREJUDICE AND VIOLENCE. 525 West Redwood Street, Baltimore, Maryland 21201. (301) 328-5170.

NATIONAL INSTITUTE FOR WOMEN OF COLOR. 1400 Twentieth Street, Northwest, Suite 104, Washington, D.C. 20036. (202) 296-2661.

SOUTHWEST CENTER FOR HUMAN RELATIONS STUDIES. University of Oklahoma, 555 Constitution, Building 4, Room 141, Norman, Oklahoma 73037. (405) 325-3936.

STATISTICS SOURCES

STATISTICAL METHODS IN DISCRIMINATION LITIGATION. D.H. Kaye and Mikel Aickin. Marcel Dekker, Incorporated, 270 Madison Avenue, New York, New York 10016. 1986.

OTHER SOURCES

THE LONGEST DEBATE: A LEGISLATIVE HISTORY OF THE 1964 CIVIL RIGHTS ACT. Barbara Whalen and Charles Whalen. Seven Locks Press, P.O. Box 27, Cabin John, Maryland 20818. 1985.

DISCRIMINATION, SEX
See also: CIVIL RIGHTS AND LIBERTIES; DISCRIMINATION, EMPLOYMENT; EQUAL EMPLOYMENT OPPORTUNITY; EQUAL EMPLOYMENT OPPORTUNITY COMMISSION; FAIR EMPLOYMENT PRACTICES; WOMEN

STATUTES, CODES, STANDARDS, UNIFORM LAWS

COMPENDIUM OF INTERNATIONAL CONVENTIONS CONCERNING THE STATUS OF WOMEN. United Nations Publishing Service, Room DC2-0853, New York, New York 10017. 1988.

LOOSELEAF SERVICES AND REPORTERS

SEX-BASED DISCRIMINATION: INTERNATIONAL LAW AND ORGANIZATION. H.J. Taubenfeld and R.F. Taubenfeld. Oceana Publications, 75 Main Street, Dobbs Ferry, New York 10522. 1978.

SEXUAL ORIENTATION AND THE LAW. National Lawyers Guild. Clark Boardman Company, Limited, 435 Hudson Street, New York, New York 10014. 1985- .

UNJUST DISCRIMINATION. Lex K. Larson. Matthew Bender and Company, Incorporated, 11 Penn Plaza, New York, New York 10001. 1985.

WOMEN AND THE LAW. Carol H. Lefourt. Clark Boardman Company, Limited, 435 Hudson Street, New York, New York 10014. 1984- .

HANDBOOKS, MANUALS, FORMBOOKS

LIBRARIAN'S AFFIRMATIVE ACTION HANDBOOK. John H. Harvey and Elizabeth M. Dickinson. Scarecrow Press, Incorporated, 52 Liberty Street, Box 4167, Metuchen, New Jersey 08840. 1983.

TEXTBOOKS AND GENERAL WORKS

ACADEMIC WOMEN: WORKING TOWARDS EQUALITY. Angela Simeone. Bergin and Garvey Publishers, Incorporated, 670 Amherst Road, Granby, Massachusetts 01033. 1987.

BEYOND OPPRESSION: FEMINIST THEORY AND POLITICAL STRATEGY. M.E. Hawkesworth. Continuum Publishing Corporation, 370 Lexington Avenue, New York, New York 10017. 1990.

THE CAMPUS TROUBLEMAKERS: ACADEMIC WOMEN IN PROTEST. Athena Theodore. Cap and Gown Press, Incorporated, P.O. Box 58825, Houston, Texas 77258. 1986.

CAREER PROFILES AND SEX DISCRIMINATION IN THE LIBRARY PROFESSION. Kathleen M. Heim. American Library Association, 50 East Huron Street, Chicago, Illinois 60611. 1983.

THE CHAINS OF PROTECTION: THE JUDICIAL RESPONSE TO WOMEN'S LABOR LEGISLATION. Judith A. Baer. Greenwood Publishing Group, Incorporated, 88 Post Road West, P.O. Box 5007, Westport, Connecticut 06881. 1978.

THE CHRISTIAN CHURCH AND THE EQUAL RIGHTS AMENDMENT. Edward M. Robbins. Winston-Derek Publications, Incorporated, 1717 West End Avenue, Nashville, Tennessee 37203. 1986.

THE CONSTITUTIONAL RIGHTS OF WOMEN: CASES IN LAW AND SOCIAL CHANGE. Second Edition. Leslie Friedman Goldstein. University of Wisconsin Press, 114 North Murray, Madison, Wisconsin 53706. 1988.

THE CRIMES WOMEN COMMIT, THE PUNISHMENTS THEY RECEIVE. Rita James Simon and Jean Landis. Lexington Books, 125 Spring Street, Lexington, Massachusetts 02173. 1991.

CUTTING THE MUSTARD: AFFIRMATIVE ACTION AND THE NATURE OF EXCELLENCE. Marjorie Heins. Faber and Faber Incorporated, 50 Cross Street, Winchester, Massachusetts 01890. 1987.

DISCRIMINATION AGAINST WOMEN: A GLOBAL SURVEY OF THE ECONOMIC, EDUCATIONAL, SOCIAL, AND POLITICAL STATUS OF WOMEN. Eschel M. Rhoodie. McFarland and Company, Incorporated, Box 611, Jefferson, North Carolina 28640. 1989.

DISCRIMINATION AMERICAN STYLE: INSTITUTIONAL RACISM AND SEXISM. Second Edition. Joe R. Feagin and Clairece B. Feagin. Robert E. Krieger Publishing Company, Incorporated, P.O. Box 9542, Melbourne, Florida 32902-9542. 1986.

DIVORCE, A GUIDE FOR MEN. Leonard Kerpelman. Icarus Press, P.O. Box 1225, South Bend, Indiana 46624-1225. 1983.

DOCTORS WANTED - NO WOMEN NEED APPLY: SEXUAL BARRIERS IN THE MEDICAL PROFESSION, 1835-1975. Mary R. Walsh. Yale University Press, 302 Temple Street, New Haven, Connecticut 06520. 1977.

DOING COMPARABLE WORTH: GENDER, CLASS, AND PAY EQUITY. Joan Acker. Temple University Press, 1601 North Broad Street, University Services Building, Philadelphia, Pennsylvania 19122. 1989.

A FEARFUL FREEDOM: WOMEN'S FLIGHT FROM EQUALITY. Wendy Kaminer. Addison-Wesley Publishing Company, Incorporated, Route 128, Reading, Massachusetts 01867. 1990.

THE FEMALE BODY AND THE LAW. Zillah R. Eisenstein. University of California Press, 2120 Berkeley Way, Berkeley, California 94720. 1988.

FEMINISM AND SEXUAL EQUALITY: CRISES IN LIBERAL AMERICA. Zillah R. Eisenstein. Monthly Review Press, 122 West Twenty-seventh Street, New York, New York 10001. 1984.

FOR ALMA MATER: THEORY AND PRACTICE IN FEMINIST SCHOLARSHIP. Paula A. Treichler, Cheris Kramarae and Beth Stafford, Editors. University of Illinois Press, 54 East Gregory Drive, Champaign, Illinois 61820. 1985.

THE FUTURE OF WOMEN. Marlene Dixon. Synthesis Publications, P.O. Box 40099, San Francisco, California 94140. 1983.

GENDER IN THE WORKPLACE. Clair Brown and Joseph A. Pechman. Brookings Institution, 1775 Massachusetts Avenue, Washington, D.C. 20036. 1987.

GENDER INEQUALITY: A COMPARATIVE STUDY OF DISCRIMINATION AND PARTICIPATION. Mino Vianello. Sage Publications, 2455 Teller Raod, Newbury Park, California 91320. 1990.

GENDER JUSTICE. David L. Kirp and Mark G. Yudof. University of Chicago Press, 5801 Ellis Avenue, Chicago, Illinois 60637. 1987.

HANDBOOK FOR ACHIEVING SEX EQUITY THROUGH EDUCATION. Susan S. Klien, Editor. Johns Hopkins University Press, 701 West Fortieth Street, Suite 275, Baltimore, Maryland 21211. 1989.

JUSTICE AND GENDER: SEX DISCRIMINATION AND THE LAW. Deborah L. Rhode. Harvard University Press, 79 Garden Street, Cambridge, Massachusetts 02138. 1989.

LAW, GENDER, AND INJUSTICE: A LEGAL HISTORY OF U.S. WOMEN. Joan Hoff-Wilson. New York University Press, 70 Washington Square South, New York, New York 10012. 1990.

LITIGATING AGE AND SEX DISCRIMINATION CASES. Gerald Hartman and Richard Schnadig. Federal Publications, Incorporated, 1120 Twentieth Street, Northwest, Washington, D.C. 20036. 1985.

LITIGATION, COURTS, AND WOMEN WORKERS. Karen J. Maschke. Praeger Publishers, One Madison Avenue, New York, New York 10010-3603. 1989.

MY TROUBLES ARE GOING TO HAVE TROUBLE WITH ME: EVERYDAY TRIALS AND TRIUMPHS OF WOMEN WORKERS. Karen Sacks and Dorothy Remy. Rutgers University Press, 109 Church Street, New Brunswick, New Jersey 08910. 1984.

ON ACCOUNT OF SEX: THE POLITICS OF WOMEN'S ISSUES, 1945-1968. Cynthia Ellen Harrison. University of California Press, 2120 Berkeley Way, Berkeley, California 94720. 1988.

PATHWAYS IN THE WORKPLACE: THE EFFECTS OF GENDER AND RACE ON ACCESS TO ORGANIZATIONAL RESOURCES. Jon Miller. Cambridge University Press, 40 West Twentieth Street, New York, New York 10011. 1986.

SEX DISCRIMINATION AND EQUAL OPPORTUNITY: THE LABOR MARKET AND EMPLOYMENT POLICY. Gunther Schmid and Renate Weitzel. St. Martin's Press, Incorporated, 175 Fifth Avenue, New York, New York 10010. 1984.

SEX DISCRIMINATION AND THE LAW: CAUSES AND REMEDIES. Barbara Allen Babcock, Ann E. Freedman, Eleanor Holmes Norton, and Susan C. Ross. Little, Brown and Company, 34 Beacon Street, Boston, Massachusetts 02108. 1978.

SEX DISCRIMINATION IN A NUTSHELL. Claire S. Thomas. West Publishing Company, P.O. Box 64526, 50 West Kellogg Boulevard, St. Paul, Minnesota 55164-0526. 1982.

SEX LITIGATION AND THE PUBLIC SCHOOLS. Edward C. Bolmeier. Michie/Bobbs-Merrill Law Publishing Company, P.O. Box 7587, Charlottesville, Virginia 22906. 1975.

SEX SEGREGATION IN LIBRARIANSHIP: DEMOGRAPHIC AND CAREER PATTERNS OF ACADEMIC LIBRARY ADMINISTRATORS. Betty J. Irvine. Greenwood Publishing Group, Incorporated, 88 Post Road West, P.O. Box 5007, Westport, Connecticut 06881. 1985.

SEX SEGREGATION IN THE WORKPLACE: TRENDS, EXPLANATIONS, REMEDIES. Barbara F. Raskin. National Academy Press, 2101 Constitution Avenue, Northwest, Washington, D.C. 20418. 1984.

THE SEXUAL BARRIER: LEGAL, MEDICAL, ECONOMIC AND SOCIAL ASPECTS OF SEX DISCRIMINATION. Marija M. Hughes. Hughes Press, 500 Twenty-third Street, Northwest, Washington, D.C. 20037. 1977.

SEXUAL DISTINCTIONS IN THE LAW: EARLY MAXIMUM HOUR DECISIONS OF THE UNITED STATES SUPREME COURT, 1905-1917. Candice Dalrymple. Garland Publishing, Incorporated, 136 Madison Avenue, New York, New York 10016. 1987.

SEXUAL HARASSMENT IN EMPLOYMENT. Susan M. Omilian. Garland Publishing, Incorporated, 136 Madison Avenue, New York, New York 10016. 1987.

STAYING SOLVENT: A COMPREHENSIVE GUIDE TO EQUAL CREDIT FOR WOMEN. Emily Card. Holt, Rinehart and Winston, Incorporated, 6277 Sea Harbor Drive, Orlando, Florida 32821. 1985.

UNEQUAL COLLEAGUES: THE ENTRANCE OF WOMEN INTO THE PROFESSIONS, 1890-1940. Penina Migdal Glazer and Miriam Slater. Rutgers University Press, 109 Church Street, New Brunswick, New Jersey 08901. 1987.

UNIVERSITY AND WOMEN FACULTY: WHY SOME ORGANIZATIONS DISCRIMINATE MORE THAN OTHERS. Robert F. Szafran. Praeger Publishers, One Madison Avenue, New York, New York 10010-3603. 1984.

WOMEN IN THE CRIMINAL JUSTICE SYSTEM. Second Edition. Clarice Feinman. Praeger Publishers, One Madison Avenue, New York, New York 10010-3603. 1985.

WOMEN IN THE WORLD, 1975-1985: THE WOMEN'S DECADE. Second Edition. Lynne B. Iglitizin and Ruth Ross, Editors. ABC-Clio, Incorporated, 2040 Alameda Padre Serra, P.O. Box 1911, Santa Barbara, California 93116-1911. 1986.

WOMEN OF ACADEME: OUTSIDERS IN THE SACRED GROVE. Nadya Aisenberg. University of Massachusetts Press, P.O. Box 429, Amherst, Massachusetts 01004. 1988.

WOMEN, POLICING, AND MALE VIOLENCE: INTERNATIONAL PERSPECTIVES. Jalna Hanmer. Routledge, Chapman and Hall, 29 West Thirty-fifth Street, New York, New York 10001. 1989.

WOMEN, SEX AND THE LAW. Rosemarie Tong. Rowman and Allenheld, 81 Adams Drive, Totowa, New Jersey 07512. 1984.

WOMEN, THE COURTS, AND EQUALITY. Sage Publications, 2455 Teller Road, Newbury Park, California 91320. 1987.

WOMEN, WORK AND PROTEST: A CENTURY OF U.S. WOMEN'S LABOR HISTORY. Ruth Milkman, Editor. Routledge, Chapman and Hall, 29 West Thirty-fifth Street, New York, New York 10001. 1985.

WOMEN, WORK, AND WAGES: EQUAL PAY FOR JOBS OF EQUAL VALUE. Donald J. Treiman and Heidi I. Hartmann, Editors. National Academy Press, 2101 Constitution Avenue, Northwest, Washington, D.C. 20418. 1981.

WOMEN'S RIGHTS AT WORK: CAMPAIGNS AND POLICY IN BRITAIN AND THE UNITED STATES. St. Martin's Press, 175 Fifth Avenue, New York, New York 10010. 1985.

WOMEN'S WORK: DEVELOPMENT AND THE DIVISION OF LABOR BY GENDER. Eleanor Leacock and Helen L. Safa. Bergin and Garvey Publishers, Incorporated, 670 Amherst Road, Granby, Massachusetts 01033. 1988.

WOMEN'S WORK, MEN'S PROPERTY: THE ORIGINS OF GENDER AND CLASS. Stephanie Coontz and Peta Henderson, Editors. Verso, 29 West Thirty-fifth Street, New York, New York 10001. 1986.

WORKING WOMEN: PAST, PRESENT, FUTURE. Bureau of National Affairs, Incorporated, 1231 Twenty-fifth Street, Northwest, Washington, D.C. 20037. 1987.

YES YOU CAN: THE WORKING WOMAN'S GUIDE TO HER LEGAL RIGHTS, FAIR EMPLOYMENT, AND EQUAL PAY. Emily B. Kirby. Prentice-Hall, Incorporated, Route 9W, Englewood Cliffs, New Jersey 07632. 1984.

DIGESTS, INDEXES, ABSTRACTS, CITATORS

WOMEN'S STUDIES ABSTRACTS. Rush Publishing Company, Incorporated, P.O. Box 1, Rush, New York 14543. Quarterly.

LAW REVIEWS AND PERIODICALS

BERKELEY WOMEN'S LAW REPORTER. Boalt Hall School of Law, University of California-Berkeley, Berkeley, California 94720. Annual.

HARVARD CIVIL RIGHTS -- CIVIL LIBERTIES LAW REVIEW. Harvard Law School, Harvard University Press, 79 Garden Street, Cambridge, Massachusetts 02138. Biannual.

HARVARD WOMEN'S LAW JOURNAL. Harvard Law School, Hastings Hall, Cambridge, Massachusetts 02138. Annual.

SIGNS: JOURNAL OF WOMEN IN CULTURE AND SOCIETY. University of Chicago Press, Journals Division, P.O. Box 37005, Chicago, Illinois 60637. Quarterly.

WISCONSIN WOMEN'S LAW JOURNAL. University of Wisconsin Law School, 975 Bascon Mall, Madison, Wisconsin 53706. Annual.

WOMEN'S RIGHTS LAW REPORTER. 15 Washington Street, Newark, New Jersey 07102. Quarterly.

NEWSLETTERS AND NEWSPAPERS

ACTION ALERT. American Association of University Women, 1111 Sixteenth Street, Northwest, Washington, D.C. 20036. Monthly.

THE EQUAL RIGHTS ADVOCATE. Equal Rights Advocates, 1370 Mission Street, San Francisco, California 94103. Quarterly.

SEXUAL HARASSMENT AND DISCRIMINATION IN THE WORKPLACE. Nu-Tec Publishing, Incorporated, 4715 Strack Road, Suite 211, Houston, Texas 77069. Monthly.

WBA NEWSLETTER. Women's Bar Association of the District of Columbia, 1819 H Street, Northwest, Washington, D.C. 20006. Bimonthly.

BIBLIOGRAPHIES

ACADEMIC WOMEN AND EMPLOYMENT DISCRIMINATION: A CRITICAL ANNOTATED BIBLIOGRAPHY. Jennie Farley. New York State School of Industrial and Labor Relations, Cornell Extension, 15 East Twenty-sixth Street, New York, New York 10010. 1982.

SEX DISCRIMINATION AND LAW: A SELECTED BIBLIOGRAPHY. Dittakavi Nagasankara Rao. Vance Bibliographies, P.O. Box 229, 112 North Charter Street, Monticello, Illinois 61856. 1985.

ASSOCIATIONS AND PROFESSIONAL SOCIETIES

COAL EMPLOYMENT PROJECT. 17 Emory Place, Knoxville, Tennessee 37917. (615) 637-7905.

NATIONAL INSTITUTE FOR WOMEN OF COLOR. 1301 Twentieth Street, Northwest, Suite 702, Washington, D.C. 20036. (202) 296-2661.

NATIONAL ORGANIZATION FOR WOMEN. 1000 Sixteenth Street, Northwest, Suite 700, Washington, D.C. 20036. (202) 331-0066.

NATIONAL WOMEN'S LAW CENTER. 1616 P Street, Northwest, Washington, D.C. 20036. (202) 328-5160.

NOW LEGAL DEFENSE AND EDUCATION FUND. 99 Hudson Street, Twelfth floor, New York, New York 10013. (212) 925-6635.

UNITED STATES COMMISSION ON CIVIL RIGHTS. 1121 Vermont Avenue, Northwest, Washington, D.C. 20425. (202) 376-8582.

WOMEN FOR RACIAL AND ECONOMIC EQUALITY. 198 Broadway, Room 606, New York, New York 10038. (212) 385-1103.

WOMEN'S LAW PROJECT. 125 South Ninth Street, Suite 401, Philadelphia, Pennsylvania 19107. (215) 928-9801.

WOMEN'S LEGAL DEFENSE FUND. 2000 P Street, Northwest, Suite 400, Washington, D.C. 20036. (202) 887-0364.

WOMEN'S RIGHTS PROJECT. c/o American Civil Liberties Union, 132 West Forty-third Street, New York, New York 10036. (212) 944-9800.

RESEARCH CENTERS, INSTITUTES, CLEARINGHOUSES

CENTER FOR RESEARCH ON WOMEN. Memphis State University, Clement Hall-339, Memphis, Tennessee 38152. (901) 678-2770.

CENTER FOR THE STUDY OF WOMEN. University of California - Los Angeles, 236A Kinsey Hall, 405 Hilgard Avenue, Los Angeles, California 90024. (213) 825-0590.

CENTER FOR WOMEN POLICY STUDIES. 2000 P Street, Northwest, Suite 508, Washington, D.C. 20036. (202) 872-1770.

CENTER FOR WOMEN'S EDUCATION. Russell Sage College, Cowee Hall, Room 212, Troy, New York 12180. (518) 270-2306.

WOMEN EMPLOYED INSTITUTE. 22 West Monroe, Suite 1400, Chicago, Illinois 60603. (312) 782-3902.

WOMEN'S CENTER. University of Connecticut, 417 Whitney Road, Box U-118, Storrs, Connecticut 06268. (203) 486-4738.

DISCRIMINATION, SEX

WOMEN'S RESOURCES AND RESEARCH CENTER. University of California - Davis, 10 Lower Freeborn, Davis, California 95616. (916) 752-3372.

STATISTICS SOURCES

STATISTICAL METHODS IN DISCRIMINATION LITIGATION. D.H. Kaye and Mikel Aickin. Marcel Dekker, Incorporated, 270 Madison Avenue, New York, New York 10016. 1986.

DISPUTE RESOLUTION
See also: ARBITRATION AND AWARD; COMPROMISE AND SETTLEMENT

STATUTES, CODES, STANDARDS, UNIFORM LAWS

CODE OF ETHICS FOR ARBITRATORS IN COMMERCIAL DISPUTES. American Arbitration Association and American Bar Association. American Arbitration Association, 140 West Fifty-first Street, New York, New York, New York 10020. 1977.

CODE OF PROFESSIONAL CONDUCT FOR LABOR MEDIATORS. Federal Mediation and Conciliation Service and Association of Labor Mediation Agencies. Superintendent of Documents, United States Government Printing Office, Washington, D.C. 20402. 1971.

LEGISLATION ON DISPUTE RESOLUTION: COMPILED 1990. John R. Price and Kendall Woods. American Bar Association, Standing Committee on Dispute Resolution, 1800 M Street, Northwest, Washington, D.C. 20036. 1990.

LOOSELEAF SERVICES AND REPORTERS

ALTERNATIVES TO THE HIGH COST OF LITIGATION. Law and Business, Incorporated, 855 Valley Road, Clifton, New Jersey 07013. 1983- . (Monthly).

BNA'S ALTERNATIVE DISPUTE RESOLUTION REPORT. The Bureau of National Affairs, Incorporated, 1231 Twenty-fifth Street, Northwest, Washington, D.C. 20037. 1987- .

LAWSUITS AND SETTLEMENTS. Kenneth W. Gideon. Commerce Clearing House, Incorporated, 4025 West Peterson Avenue, Chicago, Illinois 60646. 1989- .

WORLD ARBITRATION AND MEDIATION REPORT. BNA International, Incorporated, London, England. 1990- .

HANDBOOKS, MANUALS, FORMBOOKS

ADR AND THE COURTS: A MANUAL FOR JUDGES AND LAWYERS. Erika S. Fine, editor. Butterworth Legal Publishers, 90 Stiles Road, Salem, New Hampshire 03079. 1987.

ALTERNATIVE DISPUTE RESOLUTION: AN ADR PRIMER. Third Edition. Frank E.A. Sander and Larry Ray. American Bar Association, Standing Committee on Dispute Resolution, 1800 M Street, Northwest, Washington, D.C. 20036. 1989.

THE ARBITRATION GUIDE: A CASE-HANDLING MANUAL OF PROCEDURES AND PRACTICES IN DISPUTE RESOLUTIONS. Raymond L. Britton. Prentice-Hall, Incorporated, Route 9W, Englewood Cliffs, New Jersey 07632. 1982.

DISPUTE RESOLUTION HANDBOOK FOR STATE AND LOCAL BAR ASSOCIATIONS: A DIRECTORY OF PROGRAMS, ACTIVITIES, COMMITTEES AND BAR LEADERS IN DISPUTE RESOLUTION. Michael Hernon and others. American Bar Association, Standing Committee on Dispute Resolution, 1800 M Street, Northwest, Washington, D.C. 20036. 1986.

DONOVAN, LEISURE, NEWTON AND IRVINE ADR PRACTICE BOOK. John Wiley and Sons, Incorporated, 605 Third Avenue, New York, New York 10158. 1990.

EMPLOYMENT LITIGATION AND ITS ALTERNATIVES. Mark S. Dichter and Paul I. Weiner. Practising Law Institute, 810 Seventh Avenue, New York, New York 10019. 1984.

THE MANAGER'S GUIDE TO RESOLVING LEGAL DISPUTES: BETTER RESULTS WITHOUT LITIGATION. James F. Henry and Jethro K. Lieberman. HarperCollins Publishers, Incorporated, 10 East Fifty-third Street, New York, New York 10022. 1985.

MEDIATION: A COMPREHENSIVE GUIDE TO RESOLVING CONFLICTS WITHOUT LITIGATION. Jay Folberg and Alison Taylor. Jossey-Bass, Incorporated, 350 Sansome Street, San Francisco, California 94104. 1984.

SETTLEMENT STRATEGIES FOR FEDERAL DISTRICT JUDGES. D. Marie Provine. Federal Judicial Center, 1520 H Street, Northwest, Washington, D.C. 20005. 1986.

SOURCEBOOK: FEDERAL AGENCY USE OF ALTERNATIVE MEANS OF DISPUTE RESOLUTION. Marguerite S. Millhauser and Charles Pou. Administrative Conference of the United States, Office of the Chairman. Superintendent of Documents, United States Government Printing Office, Washington, D.C. 20402. 1987.

TEXTBOOKS AND GENERAL WORKS

AGENCY ARBITRATION: CONSTITUTIONAL AND STATUTORY ISSUES. Administrative Conference of States. Superintendent of Documents, United States Government Printing Office, Washington, D.C. 20402. 1988.

ALTERNATIVE DISPUTE RESOLUTION: MELTING THE LANCES AND DISMOUNTING THE STEEDS. Thomas E. Carbonneau. University of Illinois Press, 54 East Gregory Drive, Champaign, Illinois 61820. 1989.

ALTERNATIVE MEANS OF FAMILY DISPUTE RESOLUTION. National Legal Resource Center for Child Advocacy and Protection, American Bar Association, Young Lawyers Division, 750 North Lake Shore Drive, Chicago, Illinois 60611. 1982.

ATTORNEYS GENERAL AND NEW METHODS OF DISPUTE RESOLUTION. American Bar Association, Standing Committee on Dispute Resolution, 1800 M Street, Northwest, Washington, D.C. 20036. 1990.

BEYOND THE COURTROOM. Benedict S. Alper and Lawrence T. Nichols. Lexington Books, 125 Spring Street, Lexington, Massachusetts 02173. 1981.

BUSINESS MEDIATION--WHAT YOU NEED TO KNOW. Robert Coulson. American Arbitration Association, 140 West Fifty-first Street, New York, New York 10020. 1987.

CONFLICT RESOLUTION AND PUBLIC POLICY. Miriam K. Mills. Greenwood Publishing Group, Incorporated, 88 Post Road West, P.O. Box 5007, Westport, Connecticut 06881. 1990.

CONSUMER DISPUTE RESOLUTION: EXPLORING THE ALTERNATIVES. Larry Ray. American Bar Association, Special Committee on Alternative Dispute Resolution, Public Services Group, 1800 M Street, Northwest, Suite 200, Washington, D.C. 20036-5886. 1983.

CONTAINING LEGAL COSTS: ADR STRATEGIES FOR CORPORATIONS, LAW FIRMS, AND GOVERNMENT: INNOVATIVE STRATEGIES FOR CASE MANAGEMENT, EARLY SETTLEMENT, AND DISPUTE RESOLUTION. Erika S. Fine and Elizabeth S. Plapinger. Butterworth Legal Publishers, 90 Stiles Road, Salem, New Hampshire 03079. 1988.

THE CORPORATE LITIGATOR. American Bar Association, 750 North Lake Shore Drive, Chicago, Illinois 60611. 1989.

DISPUTE RESOLUTION AND LAWYERS. Abridged Edition. Leonard L. Riskin and James E. Westbrook. West Publishing Company, 50 West Kellogg Boulevard, St.Paul, Minnesota 55164. 1988.

DISPUTE RESOLUTION IN AMERICA: PROCESSES IN EVOLUTION. Jonathan B. Marks, Earl Johnson, Jr. and Peter L. Szanton. National Institute for Dispute Resolution, 1901 L Street, Northwest, Washington, D.C. 20036. 1984.

EDUCATION AND MEDIATION: EXPLORING THE ALTERNATIVES. American Bar Association, Standing Committee on Dispute Resolution, Public Services Division, Governmental Affairs Group, 1800 M Street, Northwest, Washington, D.C. 20036. 1988.

EFFECTIVE DISPUTE RESOLUTION FOR THE INTERNATIONAL COMMERCIAL LAWYER. Peter Summerfield and Dennis Campbell. Kluwer Academic Publishers, 101 Philip Drive, Assinippi Park, Norwell, Massachusetts 02061. 1989.

EMPLOYEE SELECTION: LEGAL AND PRACTICAL ALTERNATIVES TO COMPLIANCE AND LITIGATION. Second Edition. Edward E. Potter, Editor. Equal Employment Advisory Council, 1015 Fifteenth Street, Northwest, Washington, D.C. 20005. 1986.

ENDING IT: DISPUTE RESOLUTION IN AMERICA. Susan M. Leeson and Bryan M. Johnston. Anderson Publishing Company, 2035 Reading Road, Cincinnati, Ohio 45202. 1988.

EXPANDING HORIZONS: THEORY AND RESEARCH IN DISPUTE RESOLUTION. Thomas F. Christian et al. American Bar Association, Standing Committee on Dispute Resolution, Fund for Justice and Education, Public Services Division, Governmental Affairs Group, 1800 M Street, Northwest, Washington, D.C. 20036. 1989.

FEDERAL LEGISLATION ON DISPUTE RESOLUTION: CONGRESSIONAL INITIATIVES ON ALTERNATIVES TO TRADITIONAL ADVERSARIAL PROCESSES. American Bar Association, Standing Committee on Dispute Resolution, 1800 M Street, Northwest, Washington, D.C. 20036. 1988.

FIGHTING FAIR: FAMILY MEDIATION WILL WORK FOR YOU. Robert Coulson. Free Press, 866 Third Avenue, New York, New York 10022. 1983.

JUSTICE WITHOUT LAW? J.S. Auerbach. Oxford University Press, 200 Madison Avenue, New York, New York 10016. 1983.

LEGAL ISSUES AFFECTING THE PRACTICE OF MEDIATION. Stephen K. Erickson. Jossey-Bass, Incorporated, 350 Sansome Street, San Francisco, California 94104. 1989.

LET'S MAKE A DEAL: UNDERSTANDING THE NEGOTIATION PROCESS IN ORDINARY LITIGATION. Herbert M. Kritzer. University of Wisconsin Press, 114 North Murray, Madison, Wisconsin 53715. 1991

MAP PROGRAM PACKAGE: ALTERNATIVE DISPUTE RESOLUTION. Bar Services Division and Special Commission on Dispute Resolution. American Bar Association, 750 North Lake Shore Drive, Chicago, Illinois 60611. 1983.

MEDIATING CHILD CUSTODY DISPUTES. Donald T. Saposnek. Jossey-Bass, Incorporated, Publishers, 350 Sansome Street, San Francisco, California 94104. 1983.

THE MEDIATION PROCESS. Christopher W. Moore. Jossey-Bass, Incorporated, Publishers, 350 Sansome Street, San Francisco, California 94104. 1986.

MEDIATION: THE COMING OF AGE: A MEDIATOR'S GUIDE IN SERVING THE ELDERLY. Second Edition. Erica Wood. American Bar Association, 750 North Lake Shore Drive, Chicago, Illinois 60611. 1990.

MULTI-CRITERIA METHODS FOR ALTERNATIVE DISPUTE RESOLUTION, WITH MICROCOMPUTER SOFTWARE APPLICATIONS. Stuart S. Nagel. Quorum Books, Greenwood Publishing Group, Incorporated, 88 Post Road West, P.O.Box 5007, Westport, Connecticut 06881. 1990.

NEIGHBORHOOD JUSTICE IN CAPITALIST SOCIETY: THE EXPANSION OF THE INFORMAL STATE. Richard Hofrichter. Greenwood Publishing Group, Incorporated, 88 Post Road West, P.O. Box 5007, Westport, Connecticut 06881. 1987.

NO ACCESS TO LAW -- ALTERNATIVES TO THE AMERICAN JUDICIAL SYSTEM. Laura Nader, Editor. Academic Press, 1250 Sixth Avenue, San Diego, California 92101. 1980.

OPTIONS FOR ALL AGES: FAMILY DISPUTE RESOLUTION. American Bar Association, Standing Committee on Dispute Resolution, 1800 M Street, Northwest, Washington, D.C. 20036. 1990.

THE POLITICS OF INFORMAL JUSTICE. Richard L. Abel, Editor. Academic Press, Incorporated, 1250 Sixth Avenue, San Diego, California 92101. 1981.

PROCESSES OF DISPUTE RESOLUTION: THE ROLE OF LAWYERS. John S. Murray and Alan Scott Rau. Foundation Press, 615 Merrick Avenue, Westbury, New York 11590. 1989.

THE RESOLUTION OF CONFLICT: CONSTRUCTIVE AND DESTRUCTIVE PROCESSES. Morton Deutsch. Yale University Press, 92A Yale Station, New Haven, Connecticut 06520. 1973.

RESOLVING COMPUTER DISPUTES: A GUIDE TO ARBITRATION. American Arbitration Association, Computer Disputes Advisory Committee. 140 West Fifty-first Street, New York, New York 10020.

RESOLVING EMPLOYMENT DISPUTES WITHOUT LITIGATION. Alan F. Westin and Alfred G. Feliv. Bureau of National Affairs, Incorporated, 1231 Twenty-fifth Street, Northwest, Washington, D.C. 20037. 1988.

RESOLVING ENVIRONMENTAL DISPUTES: A DECADE OF EXPERIENCE. Gail Bingham. Conservation Foundation, 1250 Twenty-fourth Street, Northwest, Washington, D.C. 20037. 1986.

SETTLING DISPUTES: CONFLICT RESOLUTION IN BUSINESS, FAMILIES, AND THE LEGAL SYSTEM. Linda R. Singer. Westview Press, Incorporated, 5500 Central Avenue, Boulder, Colorado 80301. 1990.

LAW REVIEWS AND PERIODICALS

DISPUTE RESOLUTION FORUM. National Institute for Dispute Resolution, 1901 L Street, Northwest, Washington, D.C. 20036. Quarterly.

EMORY INTERNATIONAL LAW REVIEW. Emory University School of Law, Atlanta, Georgia. 1990- . Semiannual. (Formerly: Emory Journal of International Dispute Resolution).

JOURNAL OF DISPUTE RESOLUTION. University of Missouri-Columbia, School of Law, Columbia, Missouri. 1988- . Annual. (Formerly: Missouri Journal of Dispute Resolution).

MEDIATION QUARTERLY: JOURNAL OF THE ACADEMY OF FAMILY MEDIATORS. Academy of Family Mediators. Jossey-Bass, Incorporated, Publishers, 350 Sansome Street, San Francisco, California 94104. Quarterly.

NEWSLETTERS AND NEWSPAPERS

ALTERNATIVES NEWSLETTER. American Bar Association, Young Lawyers Division, 1800 M Street, Northwest, Washington, D.C. 20036. Quarterly.

ALTERNATIVES TO THE HIGH COST OF LITIGATION. Center for Public Resources, 366 Madison Avenue, New York, New York 10017. Monthly.

ARBITRATION IN THE SCHOOLS. American Arbitration Association, 140 West Fifty-first Street, New York, New York 10020. Monthly.

ARBITRATION TIMES. American Arbitration Association, 140 West Fifty-first Street, New York, New York 10020. Quarterly.

BNA'S ALTERNATIVE DISPUTE RESOLUTION REPORT. The Bureau of National Affairs, Incorporated, 1231 Twenty-fifth Street, Northwest, Washington, D.C. 20037. Biweekly.

THE CLAIMS FORUM. American Arbitration Association, 140 West Fifty-first Street, New York, New York 10020. Quarterly.

DISPUTE RESOLUTION. American Bar Association, 1800 M Street, Northwest, Suite 200, Washington, D.C. 20036. Quarterly.

LAWYER'S ARBITRATION LETTER. American Arbitration Association, 140 West Fifty-first Street, New York, New York 10020. Quarterly.

NEWS FROM THE CENTER. Center for Dispute Resolution, Willamette University, College of Law, 250 Winter Street, Southeast, Salem, Oregon 97301. Semiannually.

THE PUNCH LIST. American Arbitration Association, 140 West Fifty-first Street, New York, New York 10020. Quarterly.

BIBLIOGRAPHIES

ALTERNATIVE METHODS OF DISPUTE RESOLUTION -- A SELECTED BIBLIOGRAPHY. Frank E.A. Sander and Frederick E. Snyder. American Bar Association Committee on Resolution of Minor Disputes, Division of Public Service Activities, 1800 M Street, Washington, D.C. 20036. 1979.

KEEP IT OUT OF COURT: CURRENT SOURCES OF INFORMATION ON ALTERNATE DISPUTE RESOLUTION. Leslie Prather-Forbis. Notes from the Tarlton Law Library, volume 19, number three. (May/June, 1984). University of Texas, School of Law, 727 East Twenty-sixth Street, Austin, Texas 78705.

MEDIATION: A SELECTED BIBLIOGRAPHY. Frank E.A. Sander. American Bar Association, Committee on Dispute Resolution, 1800 M Street, Northwest, Suite 200, Washington, D.C. 20036-5886. 1984.

SELECTED MATERIALS ON DISPUTE RESOLUTION MEDIATION-ARBITRATION. The Record of the Association of the Bar of the City of New York, volume 37, number two. (March 1982). Association of the Bar of the City of New York, 42 West Forty-fourth Street, New York, New York 10036.

SELECTED MEDIATION BIBLIOGRAPHY. Family Law Quarterly, Volume 17, number four. (Winter, 1984). University of Denver, College of Law, 1900 Olive Street, Denver, Colorado 80220.

DIRECTORIES

DIRECTORY OF LAW SCHOOL DISPUTE RESOLUTION COURSES AND PROGRAMS: A DIRECTORY OF COURSES, CLINICS, PROFESSORS, KEY CONTACTS, SAMPLE COURSE DESCRIPTIONS AND TEACHING METHODS IN DISPUTE RESOLUTION. Ellen Conlin, Karen Emlaw and Brian Kumamoto. American Bar Association, Standing Committee on Dispute Resolution, 1800 M Street, Northwest, Washington, D.C. 20036-5886. Annual.

DISPUTE RESOLUTION PROGRAM DIRECTORY. Compiled by the American Bar Association, Special Committee on Alternative Dispute Resolution, 1800 M Street, Northwest, Washington, D.C. 20036-5886. Annual.

DISPUTE RESOLUTION RESOURCE DIRECTORY. National Institute for Dispute Resolution, 1901 L Street, Northwest, Washington, D.C. 20036. Annual.

ASSOCIATIONS AND PROFESSIONAL SOCIETIES

AMERICAN ARBITRATION ASSOCIATION. 140 West Fifty-first Street, New York, New York 10020. (212) 484-4000.

CENTER FOR DISPUTE SETTLEMENT. 1666 Connecticut Avenue, Northwest, Suite 501, Washington, D.C. 20009. (202) 265-9572.

COMMUNITY DISPUTE SERVICES. 140 West Fifty-first Street, New York, New York 10020. (212) 484-4000.

NATIONAL INSTITUTE FOR DISPUTE RESOLUTION. 1901 L Street, Northwest, Suite 600, Washington, D.C. 20036. (202) 466-4764.

SOCIETY OF PROFESSIONALS IN DISPUTE RESOLUTION. 1730 Rhode Island Avenue, Northwest, Suite 909, Washington, D.C. 20036. (202) 833-2188.

STANDING COMMITTEE ON DISPUTE RESOLUTION. American Bar Association, 1800 M Street, Northwest, Suite 200, Washington, D.C. 20036. (202) 331-2258.

RESEARCH CENTERS, INSTITUTES, CLEARINGHOUSES

CENTER FOR DISPUTE RESOLUTION. Willamette University, College of Law, 250 Winter Street, Southeast, Salem, Oregon 97301. (503) 370-6046.

INSTITUTE FOR MEDIATION AND CONFLICT RESOLUTION. 99 Hudson Street, Eleventh Floor, New York, New York 10013. (212) 966-3660.

NATIONAL CENTER FOR MEDIATION EDUCATION. 2083 West Street, Suite 3C, Annapolis, Maryland 21401. (301) 261-8445.

AUDIOVISUALS

MEDIATION: SIMULATION OF A CONSTRUCTION DISPUTE. National Practice Institute, 330 Second Avenue South, Minneapolis, Minnesota 55401. Videotape.

MEDIATION: SIMULATION OF A PERSONAL INJURY CASE. National Practice Institute, 330 Second Avenue South, Minneapolis, Minnesota 55401. Videotape.

THE NEIGHBORHOOD SPAT. Nancy Rogers and Richard A. Salem. Ohio State University College of Law, 1659 North High Street, Columbus, Ohio 43210. 1987. (Videotape).

OUT OF COURT: THE MINI-TRIAL. Center for Public Resources, Butterworth Legal Publishers, U.S. Group Headquarters, 90 Stiles Road, Salem, New Hampshire 03079. 1986. (Videotape).

SCENES FROM A MEDIATION. Gary Friedman. Center for Law and Mediation, 34 Forrest Street, Mill Valley, California 94941. 1986. (Videotape).

COMPUTER-ASSISTED LEGAL RESEARCH

NEGOTIATOR PRO. Beacon Expert System, Incorporated, 35 Gardner Road, Brookline, Massachusetts 02146. Machine-readable computer file.

OTHER SOURCES

ALTERNATIVE DISPUTE RESOLUTION: MEDIATION AND THE LAW: WILL REASON PREVAIL? Larry Ray, Editor. American Bar Association, Special Committee on Dispute Resolution of the Public Services Division, 1800 M Street, Northwest, Suite 200, Washington, D.C. 20036-5886. 1983.

ALTERNATIVE METHODS OF DISPUTE RESOLUTION IN MAJOR DISPUTES: THE STATE OF THE ART: A NATIONAL INSTITUTE. Tort and Insurance Practice Section, Committee on Arbitration. American Bar Association, Division of Professional Education, 750 North Lake Shore Drive, Chicago, Illinois 60611. 1983.

MEDIATION IN THE JUSTICE SYSTEM: CONFERENCE PROCEEDINGS, MAY 20-21, 1983. Maria R. Volpe, Thomas F. Christian and Joyce E. Kowalewski. American Bar Association, Special Committee on Dispute Resolution of the Public Services Division, 1800 M Street, Northwest, Suite 200, Washington, D.C. 20036-5886. 1983.

PATHS TO JUSTICE: MAJOR PUBLIC POLICY ISSUES OF DISPUTE RESOLUTION, REPORT OF THE AD HOC PANEL ON DISPUTE RESOLUTION AND PUBLIC POLICY. National Institute For Dispute Resolution, 1901 L Street, Washington, D.C. 20036. 1983.

DISTRESSED PROPERTY
See: LANDLORD AND TENANT; REAL PROPERTY

DISTRICT ATTORNEYS
See: PUBLIC PROSECUTORS

DISTRICT COURTS (UNITED STATES)
See also: ADMINISTRATIVE OFFICE OF THE UNITED STATES COURTS; COURTS; FEDERAL COURTS

STATUTES, CODES, STANDARDS, UNIFORM LAWS

FEDERAL CIVIL PROCEDURE AND RULES. West Publishing Company, P.O. Box 64526, 50 West Kellogg Boulevard, St. Paul, Minnesota 55164-0526. Annual.

FEDERAL LOCAL COURT RULES FOR CIVIL AND ADMIRALTY PROCEEDINGS. Henry G. Fischer and John W. Willis. Callaghan and Company, 155 Pfingsten Road, Deerfield, Illinois 60015. 1972- .

FEDERAL PROCEDURE RULES SERVICE. Lawyers Cooperative Publishing Company, One Graves Street, Rochester, New York 14694. 1985- . Annual Supplements.

JUDICIARY AND JUDICIAL PROCEDURE, FEDERAL RULES OF CIVIL PROCEDURE, FEDERAL RULES OF APPELLATE PROCEDURE AND FEDERAL COURT RULES. United States Code, Title 28 and Title 28 Appendices. Superintendent of Documents, United States Government Printing Office, Washington, D.C. 20402. Annual Supplements.

JUDICIARY AND JUDICIAL PROCEDURE, FEDERAL RULES OF CIVIL PROCEDURE, FEDERAL RULES OF APPELLATE PROCEDURE AND FEDERAL COURT RULES. United States Code Annotated, Title 28 and Title 28 Appendices. West Publishing Company, P.O. Box 64526, 50 West Kellogg Boulevard, St. Paul, Minnesota 55164-0526. Annual Supplements.

JUDICIARY AND JUDICIAL PROCEDURE, FEDERAL RULES OF CIVIL PROCEDURE, FEDERAL RULES OF APPELLATE PROCEDURE AND FEDERAL COURT RULES. United States Code Service, Title 28 and Court Rules Volumes. Lawyers Cooperative Publishing Company, One Graves Street, Rochester, New York 14694. 1987- . Annual Supplements.

MOORE'S FEDERAL PRACTICE: RULES PAMPHLET. James William Moore, Kathleen D. Harper and Linda J. Folkman. Matthew Bender and Company, Incorporated, 11 Penn Plaza, New York, New York 10001. 1984- . Annual.

RULES OF CIVIL PROCEDURE FOR THE UNITED STATES DISTRICT COURTS: PRACTICE COMMENTS. Thomas A. Coyne. Clark Boardman Company, Limited, 435 Hudson Street, New York, New York 10014. 1983. Annual Supplements.

LOOSELEAF SERVICES AND REPORTERS

DESKBOOK FOR CHIEF JUDGES OF UNITED STATES DISTRICT COURTS. Russell R. Wheeler. Federal Judicial Center, Dolley Madison House, 1520 H Street, Northwest, Washington, D.C. 20005. 1984- .

FEDERAL SUPPLEMENT: CASES ARGUED AND DETERMINED IN THE UNITED STATES DISTRICT COURTS. West Publishing Company, P.O. Box 64526, 50 West Kellogg Boulevard, St. Paul, Minnesota 55164-0526. 1932- .

HANDBOOKS, MANUALS, FORMBOOKS

GUIDE TO THE FEDERAL COURTS: AN INTRODUCTION TO THE FEDERAL COURTS AND THEIR OPERATION: INCLUDES EXPLANATION OF HOW A CASE IS LITIGATED. Want Publishing Company, 1511 K Street, Northwest, Washington, D.C. 20005. 1984.

TEXTBOOKS AND GENERAL WORKS

COURT-ANNEXED ARBITRATION IN TEN DISTRICT COURTS. Barbara Stone Meierhoefer. Federal Judicial Center. Superintendent of Documents, United States Government Printing Office, Washington, D.C. 20402. 1990.

THE DISTRICT COURT EXECUTIVE PILOT PROGRAM: A REPORT ON THE PRELIMINARY EXPERIENCE IN FIVE FEDERAL COURTS. William B. Eldridge. Federal Judicial Center, Dolley Madison House, 1520 H Street, Northwest, Washington, D.C. 20005. 1984.

HARD JUDICIAL CHOICES: FEDERAL DISTRICT COURT JUDGES AND STATE AND LOCAL OFFICIALS. Phillip J. Cooper. Oxford University Press, 200 Madison Avenue, New York, New York 10016. 1988.

IN-COURT ORIENTATION PROGRAMS IN THE FEDERAL DISTRICT COURTS. Barbara S. Meierhoefer. Federal Judicial Center, Dolley Madison House, 1520 H Street, Northwest, Washington, D.C. 20005. 1984.

POLICYMAKING AND POLITICS IN THE FEDERAL DISTRICT COURTS. Robert A. Carp and C.K. Rowland. University of Tennessee Press, 293 Communications Building, Knoxville, Tennessee 37996-0325. 1983.

RATIONALIZING JUSTICE: THE POLITICAL ECONOMY OF FEDERAL DISTRICT COURTS. Wolf V. Heydebrand. State University of New York Press, State University Plaza, Albany, New York 12246. 1990.

THE ROLE OF MAGISTRATES IN FEDERAL DISTRICT COURTS. Carroll Seron. Federal Judicial Center. Superintendent of Documents, United States Government Printing Office, Washington, D.C. 20402. 1983.

SUMMARY JUDGMENT PRACTICE IN THREE DISTRICT COURTS. Joe S. Cecil. Federal Judicial Center. Superintendent of Documents, United States Government Printing Office, Washington, D.C. 20402. 1987.

UNITED STATES DISTRICT COURTS SENTENCES IMPOSED CHART, TWELVE MONTH PERIOD ENDING JUNE 30, 1983. Administrative Office of the United States Courts. Superintendent of Documents, United States Government Printing Office, Washington, D.C. 20402. 1985. (Irregular).

USE OF RULE 12(B) (6) IN TWO FEDERAL DISTRICT COURTS. Federal Judicial Center. Superintendent of Documents, United States Government Printing Office, Washington, D.C. 20402. 1989.

VISITING JUDGES IN FEDERAL DISTRICT COURTS. Donna Stienstra. Federal Judicial Center. Superintendent of Documents, United States Government Printing Office, Washington, D.C. 20402. 1985.

ANNUALS AND SURVEYS

REPORT OF THE PROCEEDINGS OF THE JUDICIAL CONFERENCE OF THE UNITED STATES. Administrative Office of the United States Courts. Superintendent of Documents, United States Government Printing Office, Washington, D.C. 20402. Annual.

NEWSLETTERS AND NEWSPAPERS

FEDERAL TRIAL NEWS. American Bar Association, 750 North Lake Shore Drive, Chicago, Illinois 60611. Irregular.

MODERN COURTS. Fund for Modern Courts, Incorporated, 36 West Forty-fourth Street, New York, New York 10036. Quarterly.

THE THIRD BRANCH: NEWSLETTER OF THE FEDERAL COURTS. Administrative Office of the United States Courts, 811 Vermont Avenue, Northwest, Washington, D.C. 20544. Monthly.

DIRECTORIES

THE AMERICAN BENCH: JUDGES OF THE NATION. Forster Long, Incorporated, 3280 Ramos Circle, Sacramento, California 95827. Biennial.

FEDERAL JUDICIARY ALMANAC. W. Stuart Dornette and Robert R. Cross. John Wiley and Sons, Incorporated, 605 Third Avenue, New York, New York 10158. 1986.

UNITED STATES COURT DIRECTORY. Administrative Office of the United States Courts. Superintendent of Documents, United States Government Printing Office, Washington, D.C. 20402. Semiannual.

WANT'S FEDERAL-STATE COURT DIRECTORY. Want Publishing Company, 1511 K Street, Northwest, Washington, D.C. 20005. Annual.

BIOGRAPHICAL SOURCES

ALMANAC OF THE FEDERAL JUDICIARY: PROFILES OF ALL ACTIVE UNITED STATES DISTRICT JUDGES. Lawletters, Incorporated, 332 South Michigan Avenue, No. 1460, Chicago, Illinois 60604. Semiannual.

BIOGRAPHICAL DICTIONARY OF THE FEDERAL JUDICIARY. Harold Chase, Samuel Krislov, Keith O. Boyum and Jerry N. Clark. Gale Research, Incorporated, 825 Penobscot Building, Detroit, Michigan 48226. 1976. (Retrospective).

RESEARCH CENTERS, INSTITUTES, CLEARINGHOUSES

ADMINISTRATIVE OFFICE OF THE UNITED STATES COURTS. 811 Vermont Avenue, Northwest, Washington, D.C. 21544. (202) 633-6040.

AMERICAN JUDICATURE SOCIETY. 25 East Washington, Chicago, Illinois 60602. (312) 558-6900.

FEDERAL JUDICIAL CENTER. Dolley Madison House, 1520 H Street, Northwest, Washington, D.C. 20005. (202) 633-6011.

ONLINE DATABASES

LEXIS, GENERAL FEDERAL LIBRARY. Mead Data Central, 9393 Springboro Pike, P.O. Box 933, Dayton, Ohio 45401.

WESTLAW, FEDERAL DATABASES. West Publishing Company, P.O. Box 64526, 50 West Kellogg Boulevard, St. Paul, Minnesota 55164-0526.

DIVIDENDS
See: SECURITIES

DIVORCE, SEPARATION AND MARRIAGE
See also: FAMILY LAW

STATUTES, CODES, STANDARDS, UNIFORM LAWS

RETIREMENT EQUITY ACT: DIVORCE AND PENSIONS: A COMPREHENSIVE MANUAL CONTAINING DIVORCE PROVISIONS OF THE RETIREMENT EQUITY ACT OF 1984, FEDERAL RETIREMENT PLANS, CLAUSES AND FORMS, LAW AND REGULATION. Divorce Taxation Education, 1710 Rhode Island Avenue, Northwest, Washington, D.C. 20036. 1985.

UNIFORM DIVORCE REGULATION ACT. National Conference of Commissioners on Uniform State Laws. Uniform Laws Annotated. West Publishing Company, P.O. Box 64526, 50 West Kellogg Boulevard, St. Paul, Minnesota 55102-1611. 1976- . (Annual Supplements).

UNIFORM MARRIAGE AND DIVORCE ACT. National Conference of Commissioners on Uniform State Laws. Uniform Laws Annotated. West Publishing Company, P.O. Box 64526, 50 West Kellogg Boulevard, St. Paul, Minnesota 55102-1611. 1979- . (Annual Supplements).

UNIFORM PREMARITAL AGREEMENT ACT. National Conference of Commissioners on Uniform State Laws. Uniform Laws Annotated. West Publishing Company, P.O. Box 64526, 50 West Kellogg Boulevard, St. Paul, Minnesota 55102-1611. 1983- . (Annual Supplements).

LOOSELEAF SERVICES AND REPORTERS

DIVORCE TAX PLANNING STRATEGIES. William J. Brown. Shepard's/McGraw-Hill, P.O. Box 1235, Colorado Springs, Colorado 80901. 1990- .

DIVORCE TAXATION. Marjorie A. O'Connell. Prentice-Hall, Incorporated, P.O. Box 500, Englewood Cliffs, New Jersey 07632. 1982- .

THE FAMILY LAW REPORTER. Bureau of National Affairs, Incorporated, 1231 Twenty-fifth Street, Northwest, Washington, D.C. 20037. 1974- .

TAX ASPECTS OF DIVORCE AND SEPARATION. Robert S. Taft. Law Journal Seminars-Press, 111 Eighth Avenue, Suite 900, New York, New York 10011. 1984- .

TAX ASPECTS OF MARITAL DISSOLUTION. Harold G. Wren. Callaghan and Company, 155 Pfingsten Road, Deerfield, Illinois 60015. 1987- .

TAX STRATEGIES FOR SEPARATION AND DIVORCE. William J. Brown. Shepard's/McGraw-Hill, P.O. Box 1235, Colorado Springs, Colorado 80901. 1984- .

VALUATION AND DISTRIBUTION OF MARITAL PROPERTY. Matthew Bender and Company, Incorporated, 11 Penn Plaza, New York, New York 10001. 1984- .

DIVORCE, SEPARATION AND MARRIAGE

HANDBOOKS, MANUALS, FORMBOOKS

BEST OF FAMILY ADVOCATE: A PRACTICAL MANUAL FOR MATRIMONIAL AND FAMILY LAWYERS. American Bar Association, Section of Family Law, 750 North Lake Shore Drive, Chicago, Illinois 60611. 1989.

DIVORCE, ALIMONY AND CHILD CUSTODY: WITH FORMS. Second Revised Edition. Walton Garrett. Harrison Company, 3110 Crossing Park, Norcross, Georgia 30071. 1984- . (Annual Supplements).

THE DIVORCE HANDBOOK: YOUR BASIC GUIDE TO DIVORCE. James T. Friedman. Random House, Incorporated, 201 East Fiftieth Street, New York, New York 10022. 1984.

DIVORCE MEDIATION: THEORY AND PRACTICE. Jay Folberg and Ann Milne. Guilford Publications, Incorporated, 72 Spring Street, New York, New York 10012. 1988.

DIVORCE, SEPARATION, AND THE DISTRIBUTION OF PROPERTY. Thomas J. Oldham. Law Journal Seminars-Press, Incorporated, 111 Eighth Avenue, Suite 900, New York, New York 10011. 1987- .

EVERY WOMAN'S LEGAL GUIDE: PROTECTING YOUR RIGHTS AT HOME, IN THE WORKPLACE, AND IN THE MARKETPLACE. Barbara A. Burnett, Editor. Doubleday and Company, Incorporated, 666 Fifth Avenue, New York, New York 10103. 1983.

THE HANDBOOK OF DIVORCE MEDIATION. Lenard Marlow. Plenum Publishing Corporation, 233 Spring Street, New York, New York 10013. 1990.

HANDBOOK OF FAMILY LAW. Lester Wallman and Lawrence J. Schwarz. Prentice-Hall, Incorporated, Route 9W, Englewood Cliffs, New Jersey 07632. 1989.

HOW TO DRAW UP YOUR OWN LEGAL SEPARATION, PROPERTY SETTLEMENT, OR COHABITATION AGREEMENT WITHOUT A LAWYER. Benji O. Anosike. Do-It-Yourself Legal Publishers, 150 Fifth Avenue, New York, New York 10011. 1982.

HOW TO HANDLE YOUR DIVORCE STEP BY STEP: A MARITAL MEDIATION PRIMER. Harold Mitnick. Lone Oak Books, 10101 Old Georgetown Road, Bethesda, Maryland 20814-1857. 1981.

MARRIAGE AND FAMILY LAW AGREEMENTS. Samuel Green and John V. Long. Shepard's/McGraw-Hill, P.O. Box 1235, Colorado Springs, Colorado 80901. 1984- . (Annual Supplements).

NO-FAULT DIVORCE: THE CITIZEN'S LEGAL GUIDE. John Cotton Howell. Prentice-Hall, Incorporated, P.O. Box 500, Englewood Cliffs, New Jersey 07632. 1981.

PARTING SENSE: A COUPLE'S GUIDE TO DIVORCE MEDIATION. Revised Edition. Jack J. Shapiro and Marla S. Caplan. Liberty Publishing Company, Incorporated, P.O. Box 298, Cockeysville, Maryland 21030. 1986.

THE PRACTICAL LAWYER'S MANUAL ON DIVORCE AND SEPARATION. American Law Institute-American Bar Association Committee on Continuing Professional Education, 4025 Chestnut Street, Philadelphia, Pennsylvania 19104. 1985.

SEPARATION AGREEMENTS AND ANTENUPTIAL CONTRACTS. Alexander Lindey. Matthew Bender and Company, Incorporated, 11 Penn Plaza, New York, New York 10001. 1964- .

SUPPORT PRACTICE HANDBOOK: PREPARATION, NEGOTIATION, TRIAL. Neil Hurowitz. Kluwer Law Book Publishers, Incorporated, 36 West Forty-fourth Street, New York, New York 10036. 1985.

WOMAN'S COUNSEL: A LEGAL GUIDE FOR WOMEN. Gayle L. Niles and Douglas H. Snider. Arden Press, Incorporated, 1127 Pennsylvania Street, Denver, Colorado 80203. 1984.

A WOMAN'S LEGAL GUIDE TO SEPARATION AND DIVORCE IN ALL FIFTY STATES. Norma Harwood. Scribner Educational Publishers, 866 Third Avenue, York, New York 10022. 1985.

TEXTBOOKS AND GENERAL WORKS

ABORTION AND DIVORCE IN WESTERN LAW. Mary Ann Glendon. Harvard University Press, 79 Garden Street, Cambridge, Massachusetts 02138. 1987.

CAUGHT IN THE MIDDLE: CHILDREN OF DIVORCE. Velma T. Carter and Lynn J. Leavenworth. Judson Press, P.O. Box 851, Valley Forge, Pennsylvania 19482-0851. 1985.

CHILD CUSTODY. James C. Black. Columbia University Press, 562 West One Hundred Thirteenth Street, New York, New York 10025. 1989.

CHILD CUSTODY AND THE POLITICS OF GENDER. Routledge, Chapman & Hall, 29 West Thirty-fifth Street, New York, New York 10001. 1989.

CLARK'S HORNBOOK ON DOMESTIC RELATIONS. Second Edition. Homer H. Clark. West Publishing Company, P.O. Box 64526, 50 West Kellogg Boulevard, St. Paul, Minnesota 55102-1611. 1988.

CONSULTATION WITH A DIVORCE LAWYER: EVERYTHING YOU MUST KNOW TO PROTECT YOUR RIGHTS. Bernard E. Clair and Anthony R. Daniels. Simon and Schuster, Incorporated, 1230 Avenue of the Americas, New York, New York 10020. 1982.

CONTEMPORARY MATRIMONIAL LAW ISSUES: A GUIDE TO DIVORCE ECONOMICS AND PRACTICE. Henry H. Foster, Jr. and Ronald L. Brown. Law and Business, Incorporated, 855 Valley Road, Clifton, New Jersey 07013. 1985.

DESK GUIDE TO THE UNIFORM MARRIAGE AND DIVORCE ACT. Revised Edition. Bureau of National Affairs, Incorporated, 1231 Twenty-fifth Street, Northwest, Washington, D.C. 20037. 1982.

DIVORCE: A GUIDE FOR MEN. Leonard Kerpelman. Icarus Press, Incorporated, 120 West La Salle Street, Suite 906, South Bend, Indiana 46601. 1983.

DIVORCE--AN AMERICAN TRADITION. Glenda Riley. Oxford University Press, 200 Madison Avenue, New York, New York 10016. 1991.

DIVORCE AND DISSOLUTION OF MARRIAGE LAWS OF THE UNITED STATES. Dan Sitarz. Nova Publishing Company, 1103 West College Street, Carbondale, Illinois 62901. 1990.

DIVORCE AND FAMILY MEDIATION. James C. Hansen, Editor. Aspen Publications, Incorporated, 1600 Research Boulevard, Rockville, Maryland 20850. 1985.

DIVORCE AND YOUR CHILD: PRACTICAL SUGGESTIONS FOR PARTNERS. Sonja Goldstein and Albert J. Solnit. Yale University Press, 92A Yale Station, New Haven, Connecticut 06520. 1984.

THE DIVORCE BOOK. Matthew McKay. New Harbinger Publications, 5674 Shattuck Avenue, Oakland, California 94609. 1984.

THE DIVORCE DECISION: THE LEGAL AND HUMAN CONSEQUENCES OF ENDING A MARRIAGE. Richard Neely. Shepard's/McGraw-Hill, P.O. Box 1235, Colorado Springs, Colorado 80901. 1984.

DIVORCE IN THE PROGRESSIVE ERA. William N. O'Neill. Yale University Press, 92A Yale Station, New Haven, Connecticut 06520. 1967.

DIVORCE MEDIATION: A RATIONAL ALTERNATIVE TO THE ADVERSARY SYSTEM. Howard H. Irving. Universe Publishing, Incorporated, 381 Park Avenue South, New York, New York 10016. 1981.

DIVORCE MEDIATION AND THE LEGAL PROCESS. Oxford University Press, 200 Madison Avenue, New York, New York 10016. 1988.

DIVORCE MEDIATION: PERSPECTIVES ON THE FIELD. Craig A. Everett, Editor. Haworth Press, Incorporated, 10 Alice Street, Binghamton, New York 13904. 1985.

DIVORCE MEDIATION: THE CONSTRUCTIVE NEW WAY TO END A MARRIAGE WITHOUT BIG LEGAL BILLS. Karen L. Schneider and Myles J. Schneider. Acropolis Books, 2400 Seventeenth Street, Northwest, Washington, D.C. 20009. 1984.

DIVORCE REFORM AT THE CROSSROADS. Stephen D. Sugarman and Herma Hill Kay. Yale University Press, 302 Temple Street, New Haven, Connecticut 06520. 1990.

THE DIVORCE REVOLUTION: THE UNEXPECTED SOCIAL AND ECONOMIC CONSEQUENCES FOR WOMEN AND CHILDREN IN AMERICA. Lenore J. Weitzman. Free Press, 866 Third Avenue, New York, New York 10022. 1985.

EQUITABLE DISTRIBUTION OF PROPERTY. Lawrence J. Golden. Shepard's/McGraw-Hill, P.O. Box 1235, Colorado Springs, Colorado 80901. 1983- . (Annual Supplements).

FAMILY LAW IN A NUTSHELL. Second Edition. Harry D. Krause. West Publishing Company, P.O. Box 64526, 50 West Kellogg Boulevard, St. Paul, Minnesota 55164-0526. 1986.

FAMILY MEDIATION: COOPERATIVE DIVORCE SETTLEMENT. Joan Blades. Prentice-Hall, Incorporated, Route 9W, Englewood Cliffs, New Jersey 07632. 1985.

FAMILY MEDIATION PRACTICE. John Lemmon. Free Press, 866 Third Avenue, New York, New York 10022. 1985.

HIS, HERS OR THEIRS? FEDERAL INCOME TAXATION OF DIVORCE PROPERTY SETTLEMENTS: EXISTING LAW, ANALYSIS AND CRITIQUE, PLANNING AND DRAFTING, RESEARCH AIDS. Commerce Clearing House, Incorporated, 4025 West Peterson Avenue, Chicago, Illinois 60646. 1983.

AN HISTORICAL GEOGRAPHY OF THE CHANGING DIVORCE LAW IN THE UNITED STATES. Mary Somerville Jones. Garland Publishing, Incorporated, 136 Madison Avenue, New York, New York 10016. 1987.

THE LAW OF SEPARATION AND DIVORCE. Fourth Edition. Parnell Callahan. Oceana Publications, 75 Main Street, Dobbs Ferry, New York 10522. 1978.

MEDIATE YOUR DIVORCE: A GUIDE TO COOPERATIVE CUSTODY, PROPERTY AND SUPPORT AGREEMENTS. Joan Blades. Prentice-Hall, Incorporated, Route 9W, Englewood Cliffs, New Jersey 07632. 1985.

MOTHERS AND DIVORCE: LEGAL, ECONOMIC AND SOCIAL DILEMMAS. Terry Arendell. University of California Press, 2120 Berkeley Way, Berkeley, California 94720. 1986.

NEGOTIATING TO SETTLEMENT IN DIVORCE. Harcourt, Brace, Jovanovich, Incorporated, 6277 Sea Harbor Drive, Orlando, Florida 32821. 1985.

ON DIVORCE AND ANNULMENT: WITH SELECTED FORMS. Second Edition. William Thomas Nelson. Callaghan and Company, 155 Pfingsten Road, Deerfield, Illinois 60015. 1961.

THE PROCESS OF DIVORCE: HOW PROFESSIONALS AND COUPLES NEGOTIATE SETTLEMENTS. Kenneth Kressel. Basic Books, 10 East Fifty-third Street, New York, New York 10022. 1985.

PSYCHOLOGY AND CHILD CUSTODY DETERMINATIONS: KNOWLEDGE, ROLES, AND EXPERTISE. University of Nebraska Press, 901 North Seventeenth Street, Lincoln, Nebraska 68588. 1987.

PUTTING ASUNDER: A HISTORY OF DIVORCE IN WESTERN SOCIETY. Roderick Phillips. Cambridge University Press, 40 West Twentieth Street, New York, New York 10011. 1988.

RETIREMENT BENEFITS AND DIVORCE. Commerce Clearing House, Incorporated, 4025 West Peterson Avenue, Chicago, Illinois 60646. 1984.

THE ROLE OF MEDIATION IN DIVORCE PROCEEDINGS: A COMPARATIVE PROSPECTIVE (United States, Canada and Great Britain). Vermont Law School Dispute Resolution Project, South Royalton, Vermont 05068. 1987.

DIVORCE, SEPARATION AND MARRIAGE

SILENT REVOLUTION: THE TRANSFORMATION OF DIVORCE LAW IN THE UNITED STATES. Herbert Jacob. University of Chicago Press, 5801 Ellis Avenue, Chicago, Illinois 60637. 1988.

SOLOMON'S CHILDREN: EXPLODING THE MYTH OF DIVORCE. Glynnis Walker. Arbor House, 105 Madison Avenue, New York, New York 10016. 1980.

SURVIVING THE BREAKUP: HOW CHILDREN AND PARENTS COPE WITH DIVORCE. Judith S. Wallerstein and Joan B. Kelly. Basic Books, 10 East Fifty-third Street, New York, New York 10022. 1990.

VALUATION OF DIVORCE ASSETS. Barth H. Goldberg. West Publishing Company, P.O. Box 64526, 50 West Kellogg Boulevard, St. Paul, Minnesota 55164-0526. 1984- . (Irregular Supplements).

ANNUALS AND SURVEYS

DIVORCE [A-15] TO [A15-1]. Shepard's Lawyer's Reference Manual. Shepard's/McGraw-Hill, P.O. Box 1235, Colorado Springs, Colorado 80901. 1983- . (Annual Supplements).

SUBJECT COMPILATIONS OF STATE LAWS: RESEARCH GUIDE AND ANNOTATED BIBLIOGRAPHY. Cheryl Nyberg and Carol Boast. Greenwood Publishing Group, Incorporated, 88 Post Road West, P.O. Box 5007, Westport, Connecticut 06881. 1981. (Periodic Supplements).

LAW REVIEWS AND PERIODICALS

AMERICAN JOURNAL OF FAMILY LAW. Professional Education Systems, Incorporated, 200 Spring Street, Eau Claire, Wisconsin 54702. 1987- . Quarterly.

DIVORCE LITIGATION: CUSTODY, PROPERTY, SUPPORT. Aspen Publishers, Incorporated, 1600 Research Boulevard, Rockville, Maryland 20850. 1989- .

EQUITABLE DISTRIBUTION JOURNAL. National Legal Research Group, Incorporated, P.O. Box 7187, 2421 Ivy Road, Charlottesville, Virginia 22906. Monthly.

FAMILY ADVOCATE. American Bar Association, 750 North Lake Shore Drive, Chicago, Illinois 60611. Quarterly.

FAMILY AND CONCILIATION COURTS REVIEW. Association of Family and Conciliation Courts, 329 West Wilson, Madison, Wisconsin 53703. Semiannually.

FAMILY LAW COMMENTATOR. Federal Legal Publications, Incorporated, 157 Chambers Street, New York, New York 10007. Bimonthly.

FAMILY LAW QUARTERLY. American Bar Association, Section of Family Law, 750 North Lake Shore Drive, Chicago, Illinois 60611. Quarterly.

FAMILY LAW REPORTER. The Bureau of National Affairs, Incorporated, 1231 Twenty-fifth Street, Northwest, Washington, D.C. 20037. Weekly.

THE FAMILY MEDIATOR. Family Mediation Association, 5530 Wisconsin Avenue, Suite 1250, Chevy Chase, Maryland 20815. Quarterly.

JOURNAL OF DIVORCE. Hawthorne Press, Incorporated, 28 East Twenty-second Street, New York, New York 10010-6194. Quarterly.

JOURNAL OF FAMILY LAW. University of Louisville, School of Law, 2301 South Third Street, Louisville, Kentucky 40292. Quarterly.

JOURNAL OF THE AMERICAN ACADEMY OF MATRIMONIAL LAWYERS. The American Academy of Matrimonial Lawyers, 53 West Jackson Boulevard, Suite 1301, Chicago, Illinois 60602. Annual.

NEWSLETTERS AND NEWSPAPERS

AFCC NEWSLETTER. Association of Family and Conciliation Courts, 329 West Wilson, Madison, Wisconsin 53703. Quarterly.

DIVORCE LITIGATION. Aspen Publishers, Incorporated, 200 Orchard Ridge Drive, Gaithersburg, Maryland 20878. Monthly.

DTEXPERT. Divorce Taxation Education, Incorporated, 1710 Rhode Island Avenue, Northwest, Suite 600, Washington, D.C. 20036. Bimonthly.

FAIRSHARE: THE MATRIMONIAL LAW MONTHLY. Prentice-Hall Law and Business, 270 Sylvan Avenue, Englewood Cliffs, New Jersey 07632. Monthly.

THE LIBERATOR. Men's Rights Association, Route 6, Forest Lake, Minnesota 55025. Monthly.

THE MATRIMONIAL STRATEGIST. Leader Publications, 111 Eighth Street, New York, New York 10011. Monthly.

MEDIATION NEWS. Academy of Family Mediators, P.O. Box 10501, Eugene, Oregon 97440. Quarterly.

NATIONAL CHILD SUPPORT ENFORCEMENT ASSOCIATION NEWSLETTER. Hall of States, 444 North Capitol Street, Northwest, Washington, D.C. 20001. Bimonthly.

NATIONAL WOMEN'S LAW CENTER UPDATE. 1616 P Street, Northwest, Washington, D.C. 20036. Quarterly.

THE WOMEN'S ADVOCATE. National Center for Women and Family Law, 799 Broadway, Room 402, New York, New York 10003. Bimonthly.

BIBLIOGRAPHIES

DIVORCE MEDIATION: A SELECTED BIBLIOGRAPHY ON DIVORCE MEDIATION AND RELATED TOPICS. Laura Ferris Brown. American Arbitration Association, 140 West Fifty-first Street, New York, New York 10020. 1982.

DIRECTORIES

DIRECTORY OF MEDIATION SERVICES. Divorce Mediation Research Project, 1720 Emerson, Denver, Colorado 80218. 1982.

LIST OF CERTIFIED FELLOWS OF THE AMERICAN ACADEMY OF MATRIMONIAL LAWYERS. American Academy of Matrimonial Lawyers, 20 North Michigan Avenue, Suite 540, Chicago, Illinois 60604. Annual.

WHERE TO WRITE FOR VITAL RECORDS: BIRTHS, DEATHS, MARRIAGES, AND DIVORCES. National Center for Health Statistics, Public Health Service, Health and Human Services, Washington, D.C. 20201. Biennial.

ASSOCIATIONS AND PROFESSIONAL SOCIETIES

ACADEMY OF FAMILY MEDIATORS. P.O. Box 10501, Eugene, Oregon 97440. (503) 345-1205.

AMERICAN ACADEMY OF MATRIMONIAL LAWYERS. 20 North Michigan Avenue, Suite 540, Chicago, Illinois 60602. (312) 263-6477.

AMERICAN BAR ASSOCIATION, SECTION OF FAMILY LAW. American Bar Association, 750 North Lake Shore Drive, Chicago, Illinois 60611. (312) 988-5584.

ASSOCIATION OF FAMILY AND CONCILIATION COURTS. 329 West Wilson, Madison, Wisconsin 53703. (608) 251-4001.

JOINT CUSTODY ASSOCIATION. 10606 Wilkins Avenue, Los Angeles, California 90024. (213) 475-5352.

MEDIATION QUARTERLY. Academy of Family Mediators, P.O. Box 10501, Eugene, Oregon 97440.

NATIONAL CHILD SUPPORT ENFORCEMENT ASSOCIATION. Hall of States, 444 North Capitol Street, Northwest, Suite 613, Washington, D.C. 20001. (202) 624-8180.

RESEARCH CENTERS, INSTITUTES, CLEARINGHOUSES

CENTER FOR FAMILY IN TRANSITION. Building B, Suite 300, 4725 Paradise Drive, Corte Madera, California 94925. (415) 924-5750.

ERIC CLEARINGHOUSE ON COUNSELING AND PERSONNEL SERVICES. University of Michigan, 2108 School of Education Building, Ann Arbor, Michigan 48109. (313) 764-9492.

INSTITUTE FOR THE STUDY OF MATRIMONIAL LAWS. 11 Park Place, Suite 1116, New York, New York 10007. (212) 766-4030.

NATIONAL CENTER ON WOMEN AND FAMILY LAW. 799 Broadway, Room 402, New York, New York 10003. (212) 674-8200.

NATIONAL COUNCIL ON FAMILY RELATIONS. 3989 Central Avenue, Northeast, Suite 550, Minneapolis, Minnesota 55421. (612) 781-9331.

NATIONAL WOMEN'S CENTER. 1616 P Street, Northwest, Washington, D.C. 20036. (202) 328-5160.

ONLINE DATABASES

FAMILY RESOURCES DATABASE. National Council on Family Relations, 3989 Central Avenue, Northeast, Suite 550, Minneapolis, Minnesota 55421.

MARRIAGE AND DIVORCE TODAY. Atcom, Incorporated. 2315 Broadway, New York, New York 10024. 1974.

STATISTICS SOURCES

BIRTH, MARRIAGE, DIVORCE, DEATH -- ON RECORD. Reymont Associates, 6556 Sweet Maple Lane, Boca Raton, Florida 33433. 1987.

CURRENT POPULATION REPORTS. United States Department of Commerce, Bureau of the Census. Superintendent of Documents, United States Government Printing Office, Washington, D.C. 20402. Annual.

DURATION OF MARRIAGE TO DIVORCE UNITED STATES. Alexander A. Plateria and Audrey Shipp. National Center for Health Statistics, Superintendent of Documents, United States Government Printing Office, Washington, D.C. 20402. 1981.

VITAL STATISTICS OF THE UNITED STATES. United States Department of Health and Human Services, Public Health Service. Superintendent of Documents, United States Government Printing Office, Washington, D.C. 20402. Annual.

OTHER SOURCES

DIVORCE INTERROGATORIES. Matthew Bender and Company, Incorporated, 11 Penn Plaza, New York, New York 10001. 1985- .

DOCTORS
See: DISCRIMINATION, SEX; MEDICAL JURISPRUDENCE AND MALPRACTICE

DOCUMENTS
See: EVIDENCE; FREEDOM OF INFORMATION

DOMESTIC RELATIONS
See: FAMILY LAW

DOMESTIC VIOLENCE
See: CHILD ABUSE AND NEGLECT; FAMILY VIOLENCE

DOMICILE
See: JURISDICTION

DOUBLE JEOPARDY

DOUBLE JEOPARDY

TEXTBOOKS AND GENERAL WORKS

DOUBLE JEOPARDY AND THE FEDERAL SYSTEM. Leonard S. Miller. University of Chicago Press, 5801 Ellis Avenue, Chicago, Illinois 60637. 1968.

DOUBLE JEOPARDY: THE DEVELOPMENT OF A LEGAL AND SOCIAL POLICY. Jay A. Sigler. Cornell University Press, 124 Roberts Place, P.O. Box 250, Ithaca, New York 14851. 1969.

REPORT TO THE ATTORNEY GENERAL ON DOUBLE JEOPARDY AND GOVERNMENT APPEALS OF ACQUITTALS. Department of Justice, Office of Legal Policy. Superintendent of Documents, United States Government Printing Office, Washington, D.C. 20402. 1988.

DOWER AND CURTESY
See also: REAL PROPERTY; WOMEN

TEXTBOOKS AND GENERAL WORKS

A DIGEST OF THE LAW OF EXECUTORS AND ADMINISTRATORS, GUARDIAN AND WARD, AND DOWER. Franklin G. Comstock. H.F. Sumner and Company, Hartford, Connecticut. 1832.

INTRODUCTION TO THE LAW OF REAL PROPERTY: AN HISTORICAL BACKGROUND OF THE CANNON LAW OF REAL PROPERTY AND ITS MODERN APPLICATION. Cornelius J. Moynihan. West Publishing Company, P.O. Box 64526, 50 West Kellogg Boulevard, St. Paul, Minnesota 55164-0526. 1962.

THE LAW OF REAL PROPERTY AND OTHER INTERESTS IN LAND. Third Edition. Herbert Thorndike Tiffany. Callaghan and Company, 155 Pfingsten Road, Deerfield, Illinois 60015. 1962.

PRINCIPLES OF THE LAW OF PROPERTY. Second Edition. John E. Cribbett. Foundation Press, Incorporated, 615 Merrick Avenue, Westbury, New York 11590. 1975.

A TREATISE ON THE LAW OF DOWER. Second Edition. Charles H. Scribner. Scribner Educational Publishers, 866 Third Avenue, New York, New York 10022. 1883.

A TREATISE ON THE SEPARATE PROPERTY OF MARRIED WOMEN UNDER THE RECENT ENABLING STATUTE. J.C. Wells. Robert Clarke and Company, Cincinnati, Ohio. 1878.

WOMEN AND THE LAW OF PROPERTY IN EARLY AMERICA. Marylynn Salmon. University of North Carolina Press, P.O. Box 2288, Chapel Hill, North Carolina 27515-2288. 1986.

DIGESTS, INDEXES, ABSTRACTS, CITATORS

A TREATISE ON DOWER: COMPRISING A DIGEST OF THE AMERICAN DECISIONS, AND THE PROVISIONS OF THE REVISED STATUTES OF THE STATE OF NEW YORK. Eli Lambert. Gould, Banks and Company. Research Publications, Incorporated, 12 Lunar Drive, Woodbridge, Connecticut 06525. Reprint of 1834 edition.

DRAFT, MILITARY
See: CONSCIENTIOUS OBJECTORS; MILITARY LAW AND SERVICE

DRINKING AND DRUNKENNESS
See: ALCOHOL CONTROL AND DRINKING BEHAVIOR

DRUG LAWS
See also: FOOD AND DRUG ADMINISTRATION; FOOD LAWS; HAZARDOUS SUBSTANCES; HEALTH AND HUMAN SERVICES DEPARTMENT; PHARMACISTS AND PHARMACY; PRODUCTS LIABILITY AND SAFETY

STATUTES, CODES, STANDARDS, UNIFORM LAWS

UNIFORM ALCOHOLISM AND INTOXICATION TREATMENT ACT. National Conference of Commissioners on Uniform State Laws. Uniform Laws Annotated. West Publishing Company, P.O. Box 64526, 50 West Kellogg Boulevard, St. Paul, Minnesota 55102-1611. 1976- . (Annual Supplements).

UNIFORM CONTROLLED SUBSTANCES ACT. National Conference of Commissioners on Uniform State Laws. Uniform Laws Annotated. West Publishing Company, P.O. Box 64526, 50 West Kellogg Boulevard, St. Paul, Minnesota 55102-1611. 1976- . (Annual Supplements).

UNIFORM DRUG DEPENDENCE TREATMENT AND REHABILITATION ACT--1973 ACT. National Conference of Commissioners on Uniform State Laws. Uniform Laws Annotated. West Publishing Company, P.O. Box 64526, 50 West Kellogg Boulevard, St. Paul, Minnesota 55102-1611. 1976- . (Annual Supplements).

UNIFORM NARCOTIC DRUG ACT. National Conference of Commissioners on Uniform State Laws. Uniform Laws Annotated. West Publishing Company, P.O. Box 64526, 50 West Kellogg Boulevard, St. Paul, Minnesota 55102-1611. 1976- . (Annual Supplements).

LOOSELEAF SERVICES AND REPORTERS

DEFENSE OF NARCOTICS CASES. David Bernheim. Matthew Bender and Company, Incorporated, 11 Penn Plaza, New York, New York 10001. 1972- . (Annual Supplements).

DRUG PRODUCT LIABILITY. Matthew Bender and Company, Incorporated, 11 Penn Plaza, New York, New York 10001. 1974- . (Annual Supplements).

FOOD, DRUG, COSMETIC LAW REPORTS. Commerce Clearing House, Incorporated, 4025 West Peterson Avenue, Chicago, Illinois 60646. 1938- .

PHARMACY LAW DIGEST. J.L. Fink. Harvard University Press, 79 Garden Street, Cambridge, Massachusetts 02138. 1971- . (Annual Supplements).

PROSECUTION AND DEFENSES OF FORFEITURE CASES. David B. Smith. Matthew Bender and Company, Incorporated, 11 Penn Plaza, New York, New York 10001. 1985- .

HANDBOOKS, MANUALS, FORMBOOKS

THE ALCOHOL, DRUG ABUSE, AND MENTAL HEALTH NATIONAL DATA BOOK: A REFERENCE BOOK ON THE INCIDENCE AND PREVALENCE, FACILITIES, SERVICES, UTILIZATION, PRACTITIONERS, COSTS, AND FINANCING. Thomas R. Vischi. United States Alcohol, Drug Abuse and Mental Health Administration. Superintendent of Documents, United States Government Printing Office, Washington, D.C. 20402. 1980- .

FIGHTING DRUGS IN THE SCHOOLS: A LEGAL MANUAL. National School Boards Association Council of School Attorneys. 1680 Duke Street, Alexandria, Virginia 22314. 1988.

FOOD AND DRUG ADMINISTRATION REGULATORY MANUAL. James O'Reilly. Shepard's/McGraw-Hill, P.O. Box 1235, Colorado Springs, Colorado 80901. 1984- . (Annual Supplements).

HANDBOOK OF FEDERAL DRUG LAW. James R. Nielson. Lea & Febiger, 200 Chester Field Parkway, Malvern, Pennsylvania 19355. 1986.

PHYSICIAN'S DESK REFERENCE. Forty-fifth Edition. Edward R. Barnhart. Physicians Desk Reference, P.O. Box 10689, Des Moines, Iowa 50336. 1991.

A PRACTITIONER'S GUIDE TO THE ANTI-DRUG ABUSE ACT OF 1988. Bernard S. Bailor. American Bar Association, Section of Criminal Justice, 1800 M Street, Northwest, Washington, D.C. 20036. 1989.

REGISTRY OF TOXIC EFFECTS OF CHEMICAL SUBSTANCES. Richard L. Lewis and Doris V. Sweet. United States Health and Human Services Department, Public Health Service, Centers for Disease Control, National Institute for Occupational Safety and Health. Superintendent of Documents, United States Government Printing Office, Washington, D.C. 20402. 1985.

TEXTBOOKS AND GENERAL WORKS

ALCOHOL AND DRUG ABUSE AND THE LAW. Irving J. Sloan. Oceana Publications, 75 Main Street, Dobbs Ferry, New York 10522. 1980.

ALCOHOL AND DRUGS IN THE WORKPLACE. COSTS, CONTROLS, AND CONTROVERSIES (BNA Special Report). Bureau of National Affairs, Incorporated, 1231 Twenty-fifth Street, Northwest, Washington, D.C. 20037. 1986.

ALCOHOL, DRUGS AND ARBITRATION: AN ANALYSIS OF FIFTY-NINE ARBITRATION CASES. Robert Coulson. American Arbitration Association, 140 West Fifty-first Street, New York, New York 10020. 1987.

THE CASE FOR LEGALIZING DRUGS. Richard Lawrence Miller. Praeger Publishers, One Madison Avenue, New York, New York 10010-3603. 1991.

CORPUS JURIS SECUNDUM: DRUGS AND NARCOTICS. West Publishing Company, P.O. Box 64526, 50 West Kellogg Boulevard, St. Paul, Minnesota 55164-0526. Supplement to Volume 28. 1974- . (Annual Supplements).

DORMITORY DRUG DENS AND DUE PROCESS: THE LAW OF SEARCH IN THE FEDERAL SYSTEM. Second Edition. Walfred M. Peterson. Wyndham Hall Press, P.O. Box 877, 52857 C.R. 21, Bristol, Indiana 46507. 1988.

DRUG ABUSE AND ITS CONTROL: GLOSSARY OF SELECTED TERMS. Superintendent of Documents, United States Government Printing Office, Washington, D.C. 20402. 1990.

DRUG CONTROL IN A FREE SOCIETY. James B. Bakalar and Lester Grinspoon. Cambridge University Press, 40 West Twentieth Street, New York, New York 10011. 1988.

DRUG CONTROL IN THE AMERICAS. William O. Walker. University of New Mexico Press, Journalism Building, Room 220, Albuquerque, New Mexico 87131. 1982.

DRUG LITIGATION. Paul D. Rheingold. Practising Law Institute, 810 Seventh Avenue, New York, New York 10019. 1981.

DRUG TRAFFICKING: A REPORT TO THE PRESIDENT OF THE UNITED STATES. Department of Justice, Office of the Attorney General. Superintendent of Documents, United States Government Printing Office, Washington, D.C. 20402. 1989.

DRUGS AND ALCOHOL. A. Carmi and S. Schneider, Editors. Springer-Verlag, Incorporated, 175 Fifth Avenue, New York, New York 10010. 1985.

DRUGS AND AMERICAN SOCIETY. Robert E. Long, Editor. H.W. Wilson, 950 University Avenue, Bronx, New York 10452. 1986.

DRUGS IN LITIGATION: DAMAGE AWARDS INVOLVING PRESCRIPTION AND NON-PRESCRIPTION DRUGS. Richard M. Patterson, Editor. Michie Company, P.O. Box 7587, Charlottesville, Virginia 22906. 1991.

EMPLOYEE DRUG SCREENING: DETECTION OF DRUG USE BY URINALYSIS. Michael J. Walsh. United States Health and Human Services Department, Drug Abuse and Mental Health Administration, National Institute on Drug Abuse. Superintendent of Documents, United States Government Printing Office, Washington, D.C. 20402. 1986.

THE EVOLUTION OF FEDERAL DRUG CONTROL LEGISLATION. Thomas M. Quinn and Gerald T. McLaughlin. Catholic University of America Press, 620 Michigan Avenue, Northeast, Washington, D.C. 20064. 1973.

KIDS, DRUGS AND THE LAW. David G. Evans. Fred B. Rothman and Company, 10368 West Centennial Road, Littleton, Colorado 80127. 1985.

NEW DRUG APPROVAL PROCESS: CLINICAL AND REGULATORY MANAGEMENT. Richard A. Guarino. Marcel Dekker, 720 Madison Avenue, New York, New York 10016. 1987.

PHARMACY AND THE LAW. Second Edition. Carl DeMarco. Aspen Publications, Incorporated, 1600 Research Boulevard, Rockville, Maryland 20850. 1984.

PURE FOOD: SECURING THE FEDERAL FOOD AND DRUGS ACT OF 1906. James Harvey Young. Princeton University Press, 41 William Street, Princeton, New Jersey 08540. 1989.

SEX, DRUGS, DEATH AND THE LAW. David A.J. Richards. Rowman and Littlefield, Publishers, 8705 Bollman Place, Savage, Maryland 20763. 1982.

STATE AND LOCAL EXPERIENCE WITH DRUG PARAPHERNALIA LAWS. Kerry Murphy Healey. Department of Justice, National Institute of Justice. Superintendent of Documents, United States Government Printing Office, Washington, D.C. 20402. 1988.

TAKING YOUR MEDICINE: DRUG REGULATION IN THE UNITED STATES. Peter Temin. Harvard University Press, 79 Garden Street, Cambridge, Massachusetts 02138. 1980.

TRAFFICKING IN DRUG USERS: PROFESSIONAL EXCHANGE NETWORKS IN CONTROL OF DEVIANCE. James R. Beniger. Cambridge University Press, 40 West Twentieth Street, New York, New York 10011. 1984.

URINE TESTING FOR DRUGS OF ABUSE. Richard L. Hawks and Nora C. Chiang. United States Health and Human Services Department, Alcohol, Drug Abuse and Mental Health Administration, National Institute on Drug Abuse, Division of Preclinical Research. Superintendent of Documents, United States Government Printing Office, Washington D.C. 20402. 1991.

ANNUALS AND SURVEYS

NARCOTICS AND DANGEROUS DRUGS. SHEPARD'S LAWYER'S REFERENCE MANUAL. Shepard's McGraw-Hill, P.O. Box 1235, Colorado Springs, Colorado 80901. 1983- . (Annual Supplement).

SUBJECT COMPILATION OF STATE LAWS 1979-1983. RESEARCH GUIDE AND ANNOTATED BIBLIOGRAPHY. Cheryl Nyberg and Carol Boast. Greenwood Publishing Group, Incorporated, 88 Post Road West, P.O. Box 5007, Westport, Connecticut 06881. 1981. (Periodic Supplements).

LAW REVIEWS AND PERIODICALS

CONTEMPORARY DRUG PROBLEMS. Federal Legal Publications, Incorporated, 157 Chambers Street, New York, New York 10007. Quarterly.

FDA DRUG BULLETIN. United States Food and Drug Administration. Superintendent of Documents, United States Government Printing Office, Washington, D.C. 20402. (Irregular).

NEWSLETTERS AND NEWSPAPERS

ALCOHOL AND DRUG ABUSE REPORT. National Association of State Alcohol and Drug Abuse Directors, 444 North Capitol Street, Northwest, Suite 520, Washington, D.C. 20001. Monthly.

ALCOHOLISM AND DRUG ABUSE WEEK. Manisses Communications Group, Incorporated, P.O. Box 3357, Wayland Square, Providence, Rhode Island 02906. Weekly.

DRUG ENFORCEMENT REPORT. Pace Publications, 443 Park Avenue South, New York, New York 10016. Semimonthly.

DRUG LAW REPORT. Clark Boardman and Company, Limited, 375 Hudson Street, New York, New York 10014. Bimonthly.

DRUGS IN THE WORKPLACE. Business Research Publications, Incorporated, 817 Broadway, New York, New York 10003. Monthly.

FORENSIC DRUG ABUSE ADVISOR. Forensic Drug Advisors, P.O. Box 5139, Berkeley, California 94705. Monthly.

INTERNATIONAL DRUG REPORT. International Narcotic Enforcement Officers Association, 112 State Street, Suite 1200, Albany, New York 12207. Monthly.

THE LEAFLET. National Organization for the Reform of Marijuana Laws, 1636 R Street, Northwest, Washington, D.C. 20009. Quarterly.

THE MAINLINE. National District Attorneys Association, National Drug Prosecution Center, 1033 North Fairfax Street, Suite 200, Alexandria, Virginia 22314. Monthly.

NARC OFFICERS. Shamrock Publishing, 112 State Street, Albany, New York, 12207. Monthly.

NARCOTICS CONTROL DIGEST. Washington Crime News Services, 3918 Prosperity Avenue, Suite 318, Fairfax, Virginia 22031. Biweekly.

NARCOTICS DEMAND REDUCTION DIGEST. Washington Crime News Services, 3918 Prosperity Avenue, Suite 318, Fairfax, Virginia 22031. Monthly.

NARCOTICS LAW BULLETIN. Quinlan Publishing Company, 23 Drydock Avenue, Boston, Massachusetts 02110. Monthly.

THE NATIONAL REPORT ON SUBSTANCE ABUSE. Buralf Publications, 1350 Connecticut Avenue, Northwest, Suite 1000, Washington, D.C. 20036. Semimonthly.

SUBSTANCE ABUSE REPORT. Business Research Publications, Incorporated, 817 Broadway, New York, New York 10003. Semimonthly.

DIRECTORIES

NATIONAL DRUG CODE DIRECTORY, 1985. United States Health and Human Services Department, Food and Drug Administration, National Center for Drugs and Biologics, Drug Listing Branch. Superintendent of Documents, United States Government Printing Office, Washington, D.C. 20402. 1985.

ASSOCIATIONS AND PROFESSIONAL SOCIETIES

NATIONAL ASSOCIATION OF STATE ALCOHOL AND DRUG ABUSE DIRECTORS. 444 North Capitol Street, Northwest, Suite 520, Washington, D.C. 20001. (202) 783-6868.

RESEARCH CENTERS, INSTITUTES, CLEARINGHOUSES

ALCOHOL DRUG ABUSE AND MENTAL HEALTH ADMINISTRATION. Department of Health and Human Services, 5600 Fishers Lane, Rockville, Maryland 20857. (301) 443-1910.

CENTER ON DRUGS AND PUBLIC POLICY. University of Maryland, School of Pharmacy, 20 North Pine Street, Baltimore, Maryland 21201. (301) 455-1218.

DRUG LAW UNIT. Temple University, Temple School of Law, 1719 North Broad Street, Philadelphia, Pennsylvania 19122. (215) 787-1278.

DRUG POLICY FOUNDATION. 4801 Massachusetts Avenue, Northwest, Washington, D.C. 20016. (202) 895-1634.

FAMILIES IN ACTION NATIONAL DRUG INFORMATION CENTER. 2296 Henderson Mill Road, Suite 204, Atlanta, Georgia 30345. (404) 934-6364.

NATIONAL CLEARINGHOUSE FOR ALCOHOL AND DRUG INFORMATION. 6000 Executive Boulevard, Suite 402, Rockville, Maryland 20852. (301) 468-2600.

NATIONAL DRUG PROSECUTION CENTER. 1033 North Fairfax Street, Suite 200, Alexandria, Virginia 22314. (703) 549-6790.

ONLINE DATABASES

ALCOHOL AND DRUGS IN THE WORKPLACE: COSTS, CONTROLS, AND CONTROVERSIES. The Bureau of National Affairs, Incorporated, BNA ONLINE, 1231 Twenty-fifth Street, Northwest, Washington, D.C. 20037.

ALCOHOL USE/ABUSE. University of Minnesota, Drug Information Services, 3-160 Health Sciences Center, Unit F, 308 Harvard Street, Southeast, Minneapolis, Minnesota 55455.

THE AMERICAN PSYCHO/INFO EXCHANGE. P.O. Box 20533, New York, New York 10025.

DRUG INFO. University of Minnesota, Drug Information Services, 3-160 Health Sciences Center, Unit F, 308 Harvard Street, Southeast, Minneapolis, Minnesota 55455.

DRUG TOPICS. LEXIS. Mead Data Central, 9393 Springboro Pike, P.O. Box 933, Dayton, Ohio 45401.

HEALTH INDEX. Information Access Company, 362 Lakeside Drive, Foster City, California 94404.

THE NATIONAL REPORT ON SUBSTANCE ABUSE. The Bureau of National Affairs, Incorporated, BNA ONLINE, 1231 Twenty-fifth Street, Northwest, Washington, D.C. 20037.

STATISTICS SOURCES

CRIME IN THE UNITED STATES: DRUG VIOLATIONS. United States Department of Justice, Federal Bureau of Investigation, Ninth Street and Pennsylvania Avenue, Northwest, Washington, D.C. 20535. Annual.

DRUGS VIOLATIONS. Administrative Office of the United States Courts, United States Supreme Court Building, One First Street, Northeast, Washington, D.C. 20544. (Annual Report of the Director).

DRUG VIOLATIONS. United States Department of Justice, Bureau of Justice Statistics, 633 Indiana Avenue, Northwest, Washington, D.C. 20531. (Capital Punishment). Annual.

DRUG VIOLATIONS. United States Department of Justice, Bureau of Prisons, 320 First Street, Northwest, Washington, D.C. 20534. (Statistical Report). Annual.

DRUG VIOLATIONS. United States Department of Justice, Federal Bureau of Investigation, Ninth Street and Pennsylvania Avenue, Northwest, Washington, D.C. 20535. (Crime in the United States). Annual.

DRUG VIOLATIONS -- VALUE OF SEIZURES BY IMMIGRATION BORDER PATROLS. United States Department of Justice, Immigration and Naturalization Service, 525 I Street, Northwest, Washington, D.C. 20531. (Annual Report).

AUDIOVISUALS

DRUG TESTING IN THE WORKPLACE. American Bar Association, 750 North Lake Shore Drive, Chicago, Illinois 60611. 1987. Videotape.

LABOR ARBITRATION OF A DRUG TESTING CASE. National Practice Institute, 330 Second Avenue South, Minneapolis, Minnesota 55401. Videotape.

SUBSTANCE ABUSE: WHAT IS IT? HOW TO DETECT IT? AND ALCOHOL AND OTHER DRUG PROBLEMS IN THE LEGAL PROFESSION. American Bar Association, 750 North Lake Shore Drive, Chicago, Illinois 60611. 1989. Videotape.

TRIAL OF A FEDERAL NARCOTICS CASE. American Bar Association Consortium for Professional Education, 750 North Lake Shore Drive, Chicago, Illinois 60611. 1976-80. (Five videocassettes).

OTHER SOURCES

THE LEGISLATIVE HISTORY OF THE DRUG PRICE COMPETITION AND PATENT TERM RESTORATION ACT OF 1984. Food and Drug Law Institute, 1000 Vermont Avenue, Washington, D.C. 20005. 1987.

NATIONAL STRATEGY FOR PREVENTION OF DRUG ABUSE AND DRUG TRAFFICKING. D.C. Drug Abuse Policy Office, Office of Policy Development. Superintendent of Documents, United States Government Printing Office, Washington, D.C. 20402. 1986.

WHEELER-LEA ACT: A STATEMENT OF ITS LEGISLATIVE RECORD. Charles Wesley Dunn. Food and Drug Law Institute, 1000 Vermont Avenue, Washington, D.C. 20005. 1987.

DRUG TESTING

DRUG TESTING

STATUTES, CODES, STANDARDS, UNIFORM LAWS

DRUG TESTING PROGRAMS BY PUBLIC EMPLOYERS: SUGGESTED GUIDELINES. American Bar Association, Section of Urban, State, and Local Government Law. 750 North Lake Shore Drive, Chicago, Illinois 60611. 1988.

LOOSELEAF SERVICES AND REPORTERS

DRUG TESTING LEGAL MANUAL: GUIDELINES AND ALTERNATIVES. Clark Boardman Company, Limited, 435 Hudson Street, New York, New York 10014. 1988- .

EMPLOYEE TESTING: THE COMPLETE RESOURCE GUIDE. Bureau of National Affairs, 1231 Twenty-fifth Street, Northwest, Washington, D.C. 20037. 1990.

HANDBOOKS, MANUALS, FORMBOOKS

DRUG TESTING AT WORK: A GUIDE FOR EMPLOYERS AND EMPLOYEES. Beverly A. Potter. Ronin Publishing, Incorporated, P.O. Box 1035, Berkeley, California 94701. 1990.

WHAT YOU NEED TO KNOW ABOUT WORKPLACE DRUG TESTING. Gary Tulacz. Prentice-Hall, Incorporated, Route 9W, Englewood Cliffs, New Jersey 07632. 1989.

TEXTBOOKS AND GENERAL WORKS

DRUG TESTING IN THE WORKPLACE. Robert P. De Cresce. American Society of Clinical Pathologists. Bureau of National Affairs, Incorporated, 1231 Twenty-fifth Street, Northwest, Washington, D.C. 20037. 1989.

DRUG TESTING: ISSUES AND OPTIONS. Robert H. Coombs and Louis Jolyon West. Oxford University Press, 200 Madison Avenue, New York, New York 10016. 1991.

STEAL THIS URINE TEST: FIGHTING DRUG HYSTERIA IN AMERICA. Abbie Hoffman and Jonathan Silvers. Penguin Books, 375 Hudson Street, New York, New York 10014. 1987.

TOWARD A NATIONAL POLICY ON DRUG AND AIDS TESTING. Brookings Institution, 1775 Massachusetts Avenue, Washington, D.C. 20036. 1989.

DRUNKENNESS
See: ALCOHOL CONTROL AND DRINKING BEHAVIOR

DUE PROCESS OF LAW
See also: CIVIL RIGHTS AND LIBERTIES; EMINENT DOMAIN

TEXTBOOKS AND GENERAL WORKS

THE CONDITIONS OF DISCRETION: AUTONOMY, COMMUNITY, BUREAUCRACY. Joel F. Handler. Russell Sage Publications, Incorporated, 2455 Teller Road, Newbury Park, California 91320. 1986.

THE CONSTITUTIONAL RIGHT TO A SPEEDY AND FAIR CRIMINAL TRIAL. Warren Freedman. Quorum Books, Greenwood Publishing Group, Incorporated, 88 Post Road West, P.O.Box 5007, Westport, Connecticut 06881. 1989.

CRIMINAL JUSTICE AND THE AMERICAN CONSTITUTION. H. Frank Way. Duxbury Press, 20 Park Plaza, Boston, Massachusetts 02116. 1980.

DUE PROCESS IN THE ADMINISTRATIVE STATE. Jerry L. Mashaw. Yale University Press, 92A Yale Station, New Haven, Connecticut 06520. 1985.

DUE PROCESS: NOMOS XVIII. J. Roland Pennock. New York University Press, 70 Washington Square, South, New York, New York 10012. 1977.

DUE PROCESS OF LAW: A HISTORICAL AND ANALYTICAL TREATISE OF THE PRINCIPLES AND METHODS FOLLOWED BY COURTS IN THE APPLICATION OF THE CONCEPT OF THE "LAW OF THE LAND." Rodney Loomer Mott. Bobbs-Merrill Company, 4300 West Sixty-second Street, Indianapolis, Indiana 46206. Defunct. 1926.

THE 5TH AMENDMENT TODAY: THREE SPEECHES. Harvard University Press, 79 Garden Street, Cambridge, Massachusetts 02138. 1955.

FRANKFURTER AND DUE PROCESS. Richard G. Stevens. University Press of America, 4720 Boston Way, Lanham, Maryland 20706. 1987.

THE HISTORY AND MEANING OF THE FOURTEENTH AMENDMENT: JUDICIAL EROSION OF THE CONSTITUTION THROUGH THE MISUSE OF THE FOURTEENTH AMENDMENT. Hermine Herta Meyer. Vantage Press, Incorporated, 516 West Thirty-fourth Street, New York, New York 10001. 1977.

JUSTICE WITHOUT LAW. Jerold S. Auerbach. Oxford University Press, 200 Madison Avenue, New York, New York 10016. 1983.

THE NATIONALIZATION OF CIVIL RIGHTS: CONSTITUTIONAL THEORY AND PRACTICE IN A RACIST SOCIETY, 1866-1883. Robert J. Kaczorowski. Garland Publishing Company Incorporated, 136 Madison Avenue, New York, New York 10016. 1986.

THE NATIONALIZATION OF THE BILL OF RIGHTS: FOURTEENTH AMENDMENT, DUE PROCESS AND PROCEDURAL RIGHTS. Roald Y. Mykkelt, Editor. Associated Faculty Press, Incorporated, 19 West Thirty-sixth Street, New York, New York 10018. 1983.

THE RATIFICATION OF THE FOURTEENTH AMENDMENT. Joseph B. James. Mercer University Press, 1400 Coleman Avenue, Macon, Georgia 31207. 1984.

RECENT DEVELOPMENTS IN STATE CONSTITUTIONAL LAW. Phyllis Skloot Bamberger. Practising Law Institute, 810 Seventh Avenue, New York, New York 10019. 1985.

THE RIGHTS OF THE ACCUSED IN LAW AND ACTION. Stuart S. Nagel, Editor. Sage Publications, Incorporated, 2455 Teller Road, Newbury Park, California 91320. 1972.

SUBSTANTIVE DUE PROCESS OF LAW: A DICHOTOMY OF SENSE AND NONSENSE. Frank R. Strong. Carolina Academic Press, P.O. Box 51879, Durham, North Carolina 27717-1879. 1987.

THE SUPREME COURT AND THE SECOND BILL OF RIGHTS: THE 14TH AMENDMENT AND THE NATIONALIZATION OF CIVIL LIBERTIES. Richard C. Cortner. University of Wisconsin Press, 114 North Murray Street, Madison, Wisconsin 53715. 1981.

WRONG TURNS ON THE ROAD TO JUDICIAL ACTIVISM: THE AMENDMENT AND THE PRIVILEGES OR IMMUNITIES CLAUSE. Department of Justice, Office of Legal Policy. Superintendent of Documents, United States Government Printing Office, Washington, D.C. 20402. 1988.

DUMPING
See: EXPORT AND IMPORT

E

EASEMENTS
See: REAL PROPERTY

EAVESDROPPING
See also: CRIMINAL INVESTIGATION

STATUTES, CODES, STANDARDS, UNIFORM LAWS

STANDARDS RELATING TO ELECTRONIC SURVEILLANCE. Final Proposed Draft. Recommended by the Advisory Committee on the Police Function. Institute of Judicial Administration, 1 Washington Square Village, New York, New York 10012. 1971.

LOOSELEAF SERVICES AND REPORTERS

THE LAW OF ELECTRONIC SURVEILLANCE. Second Edition. James G. Carr. Clark Boardman Company, Limited, 435 Hudson Street, New York, New York 10014. 1986- .

TEXTBOOKS AND GENERAL WORKS

FEDERAL GOVERNMENT INFORMATION TECHNOLOGY: ELECTRONIC SURVEILLANCE AND CIVIL LIBERTIES. John Bibbons. Superintendent of Documents, United States Government Printing Office, Washington, D.C. 20402. 1985.

HOW TO AVOID EAVESDROPPING AND PRIVACY INVASION. John Gibbons. Gordon Press, P.O. Box 459, Bowling Green Station, New York, New York 10004. 1986.

THE PROBLEMS OF ELECTRONIC EAVESDROPPING. Conrad G. Paulsen. American Law Institute, American Bar Association, 4025 Chestnut Street, Philadelphia, Pennsylvania 19104. 1977.

RAISING AND LITIGATING ELECTRONIC SURVEILLANCE IN CRIMINAL CASES. National Lawyers Guild, Electronic Surveillance Project. Lake Law Books, 915 Linden Street, San Francisco, California 94102. 1977.

WIRE TAPS AND SURVEILLANCE. Michael P. Jones. Crumb Elbow Publishers, P.O. Box 294, Rhododendron, Oregon 92045. 1984.

WIRETAP: LISTENING IN ON AMERICA'S MAFIA. Simon and Schuster, Incorporated, 1230 Avenue of the Americas, New York, New York 10020. 1988.

WIRETAPPING AND EAVESDROPPING. Clifford S. Fishman. Lawyer's Co-operative Publishers, One Graves Street, Rochester, New York 14694. 1978- . (Periodic Supplements).

BIBLIOGRAPHIES

ELECTRONIC EAVESDROPPING. Earleen H. Cook. Vance Bibliographies, P.O. Box 229, 112 North Charter Street, Monticello, Illinois 61856. 1983.

ECCLESIASTICAL LAW
See: CANON LAW; RELIGION

ECONOMICS
See: ANTITRUST AND ECONOMICS; MONEY AND MONETARY CONTROL; TORTS

EDUCATION
See also: DISCRIMINATION, EDUCTION; EDUCATION DEPARTMENT; FEDERAL AID TO EDUCATION; LEGAL EDUCATION; MENTAL HEALTH AND DISABILITY; SCHOOL INTEGRATION; SCHOOL VIOLENCE AND DISCIPLINE

STATUTES, CODES, STANDARDS, UNIFORM LAWS

STANDARDS RELATING TO SCHOOLS AND EDUCATION. William B. Bussand and Stephen R. Goldstein. IJA-ABA Juvenile Justice Standards Project. Ballinger Division, HarperCollins Publishers, 10 East Fifty-third Street, New York, New York 10022. 1982.

LOOSELEAF SERVICES AND REPORTERS

EDUCATION FOR THE HANDICAPPED LAW REPORT. CRR Publishing Company/LRP Publications, 747 Dresher Road, Horsham, Pennsylvania 19044. 1979- .

EDUCATION LAW. James A. Rapp, Editor. Matthew Bender and Company, Incorporated, 11 Penn Plaza, New York, New York 10001. 1984- .

GUIDE TO FEDERAL FUNDING FOR EDUCATION. Education Funding Research Council, 1611 North Kent Street, Suite 508, Arlington, Virginia 22209. 1975- .

WEST'S EDUCATION LAW REPORTER. National Association of College and University Attorneys. West Publishing Company, P.O. Box 64526, 50 West Kellogg Boulevard, St. Paul, Minnesota 55164-9853. 1982- . Biweekly.

HANDBOOKS, MANUALS, FORMBOOKS

LEGAL DESKBOOK FOR ADMINISTRATORS OF INDEPENDENT COLLEGES AND UNIVERSITIES. Center For Constitutional Studies, Mercer University, Macon, Georgia 31207. 1986- .

REPRESENTING LEARNING DISABLED CHILDREN: A MANUAL FOR ATTORNEYS. Matthew B. Bogin and Beth Goodman. National Legal Resource Center for Child Advocacy and Protection, American Bar Association, 1800 M Street, Northwest, Washington, D.C. 20036. 1985.

TEXTBOOKS AND GENERAL WORKS

ABILITY GROUPING OF PUBLIC SCHOOL STUDENTS: LEGAL ASPECTS OF CLASSIFICATION AND TRACKING METHODS. Joseph E. Bryson and Charles P. Bentley. Michie Company, P.O. Box 7587, Charlottesville, Virginia 22906. 1980.

AMERICAN PUBLIC SCHOOL LAW. Second Edition. Kern Alexander and M. David Alexander. West Publishing Company, P.O. Box 64526, 50 West Kellogg Boulevard, St. Paul, Minnesota 55164-0526. 1985.

ASSESSMENT IN SPECIAL AND REMEDIAL EDUCATION. Fourth Edition. John Salvia. Houghton Mifflin Company, 1 Beacon Street, Boston, Massachusetts 02108. 1988.

BOUNDARIES DIMLY PERCEIVED: LAW, RELIGION, EDUCATION, AND THE COMMON GOOD. Christopher F. Mooney. University of Notre Dame Press, Notre Dame, Indiana 46556. 1990.

CHILDREN, EDUCATION, AND THE FIRST AMENDMENT: A PSYCHOLEGAL ANALYSIS. David Moshman. University of Nebraska Press, 901 North Seventeenth Street, Lincoln, Nebraska 68588. 1989.

CLASS, RACE, AND GENDER IN AMERICAN EDUCATION. State University of New York Press, State University Plaza, Albany, New York 12246. 1988.

CLASSROOMS IN THE CROSSFIRE: THE RIGHTS AND INTERESTS OF STUDENTS, PARENTS, TEACHERS, ADMINISTRATORS, LIBRARIANS AND THE COMMUNITY. Robert M. O'Neil. Indiana University Press, Tenth and Morton Streets, Bloomington, Indiana 47405. 1981.

THE CLOSING OF THE AMERICAN MIND. Allan Bloom. Simon and Schuster, Incorporated, 1230 Avenue of the Americas, New York, New York 10020. 1987.

COLLEGE AND UNIVERSITY LAW. Kern Alexander and Erwin S. Solomon. Michie Company, P.O. Box 7587, Charlottesville, Virginia 22906. 1972- . (Irregular Supplements).

COMPARATIVE SCHOOL LAW. Ian Keith Falconer Birch and Ingo Richter. Pergamon Press, Incorporated, Maxwell House, Fairview Park, Elmsford, New York 10523. 1990.

COMPELLING BELIEF: THE CULTURE OF AMERICAN SCHOOLING. Stephen Arons. Shepard's/McGraw-Hill, P.O. Box 1235, Colorado Springs, Colorado 80901. 1983.

THE CONSTITUTION AND AMERICAN PUBLIC EDUCATION. Arval A. Morris. Carolina Academic Press, P.O. Box 51879, Durham, North Carolina 27717. 1989.

A DELICATE BALANCE: CHURCH STATE AND THE SCHOOLS. Martha M. McCarthy. Phi Delta Kappa Educational Foundation, Eighth and Union, Box 789, Bloomington, Indiana 47402. 1983.

DESEGREGATING AMERICA'S COLLEGES AND UNIVERSITIES: TITLE VI REGULATION OF HIGHER EDUCATION. Teachers College Press, New York, New York. 1988.

DESIGNING A COMPREHENSIVE EARLY INTERVENTION SYSTEM: THE CHALLENGE OF PUBLIC LAW 99-457. Gray S. Garwood. PRO-ED, Incorporated, 8700 Shoal Creek, Austin, Texas 78758. 1989.

EDUCATION AND MEDIATION: EXPLORING THE ALTERNATIVES. American Bar Association, Standing Committee on Dispute Resolution, 1800 M Street, Northwest, Washington, D.C. 20036. 1988.

EDUCATION LAW: PUBLIC AND PRIVATE. William D. Valente. West Publishing Company, P.O. Box 64526, 50 West Kellogg Boulevard, St. Paul, Minnesota 55164-0526. 1985.

EDUCATIONAL MALPRACTICE: LIABILITY OF EDUCATORS, SCHOOL ADMINISTRATORS, AND SCHOOL OFFICIALS. John Collis. Michie Company, P.O. Box 7587, Charlottesville, Virginia 22906. 1990.

EDUCATORS, CHILDREN AND THE LAW. Lynn Sametz and Caren S. Mclaughlin, Editors. Charles C. Thomas Publishers, 2600 South First Street, Springfield, Illinois 62794-9265. 1985.

THE GREAT SCHOOL DEBATE: WHICH WAY FOR AMERICAN EDUCATION? Beatrice Gross and Ronald Gross. Simon and Schuster, Incorporated, 1230 Avenue of the Americas, New York, New York 10020. 1985.

ILLIBERAL EDUCATION: THE POLITICS OF RACE AND SEX ON CAMPUS. Dinesh D'Souza. Free Press, 866 Third Avenue, New York, New York 10022. 1991.

JUST SCHOOLS: THE IDEA OF RACIAL EQUALITY IN AMERICAN EDUCATION. David L. Kirp. University of California Press, 2120 Berkeley Way, Berkeley, California 94720. 1982.

JUSTICE, MORALITY AND EDUCATION: A NEW FOCUS IN ETHICS IN EDUCATION. Les Brown. St. Martin's Press, Incorporated, 175 Fifth Avenue, New York, New York 10010. 1985.

LAW AND EDUCATION: CONTEMPORARY ISSUES AND COURT DECISIONS. Third Edition. H.C. Hudgins, Jr. and Richard S. Vacca. Michie Company P.O. Box 7587, Charlottesville, Virginia 22906. 1991.

LAW AND THE SHAPING OF PUBLIC EDUCATION. David B. Tyack, Thomas James and Aaron Benavot. University of Wisconsin Press, 114 North Murray Street, Madison, Wisconsin 53715. 1987.

LAW IN THE SCHOOLS. Second Edition. William D. Valente. Merrill Publishing Company, P.O. Box 508, Columbus, Ohio 43216. 1987.

THE LAW OF HIGHER EDUCATION: A COMPREHENSIVE GUIDE TO LEGAL IMPLICATIONS OF ADMINISTRATIVE DECISION MAKING. Second Edition. William A. Kaplin. Jossey-Bass, Incorporated, Publications, 350 Sansome Street, San Francisco, California 94104. 1985.

THE LAW OF PUBLIC EDUCATION. Third Edition. E. Edmund Reutter, Jr. Foundation Press, Incorporated, 615 Merrick Avenue, Westbury, New York 11590. 1985.

THE LAW OF SCHOOLS, STUDENTS AND TEACHERS IN A NUTSHELL. Kern Alexander and M. David Alexander. West Publishing Company, P.O. Box 64526, 50 West Kellogg Boulevard, St. Paul, Minnesota 55164-0526. 1984.

LEGAL AND EDUCATIONAL ISSUES AFFECTING AUTISTIC CHILDREN. John E.B. Myers, William R. Jenson and William M. McMahon. Charles C. Thomas Publishers, 2600 South First Street, Springfield, Illinois 62794-9265. 1986.

LEGAL FOUNDATIONS OF COMPULSORY SCHOOL ATTENDANCE. Lawrence Kotin and William Aikman. Kennikat Press, 90 South Bayles Avenue, Port Washington, New York 11050. 1980.

THE LEGAL STRUCTURE OF COLLECTIVE BARGAINING IN EDUCATION. Kenneth H. Ostrander. Greenwood Publishing Group, Incorporated, 88 Post Road West, P.O. Box 5007, Westport, Connecticut 06881. 1987.

LIABILITY OF SCHOOL OFFICIALS AND ADMINISTRATORS FOR CIVIL RIGHTS TORTS. Richard S. Vacca and H.C. Hudgins, Jr. Michie Company, P.O. Box 7587, Charlottesville, Virginia 22906. 1982.

MINORITIES ON CAMPUS: A HANDBOOK FOR ENHANCING DIVERSITY. Madeleine F. Green. American Council on Education, One Dupont Circle, Washington, D.C. 20036. 1989.

THE POLITICS OF SCHOOL REFORM: 1870-1940. Paul E. Peterson. University of Chicago Press, 5801 Ellis Avenue, Chicago, Illinois 60637. 1985.

PRIVATIZATION AND ITS ALTERNATIVES. William T. Gormley. University of Wisconsin Press, 114 North Murray, Madison, Wisconsin 53706. 1991.

THE RACIAL CRISIS IN AMERICAN HIGHER EDUCATION. Philip G. Altbach. State University of New York Press, State University Plaza, Albany, New York 12246. 1991.

SCHOOL DAYS, RULE DAYS: THE LEGALIZATION AND REGULATION OF EDUCATION. David L. Kirp and Donald Jensen, Editors. Falmer Press, 242 Cherry Street, Philadelphia, Pennsylvania 19106-1906. 1986.

SCHOOL LAW FOR THE PRACTITIONER. Robert C. O'Reilly and Edward T. Green. Greenwood Publishing Group, Incorporated, 88 Post Road West, P.O. Box 5007, Westport, Connecticut 06881. 1983.

THE SUPREME COURT'S IMPACT ON PUBLIC EDUCATION. Edmund E. Reutter, Jr. National Organization on Legal Problems of Education, 3601 West Twenty-ninth Street, Topeka, Kansas 66614. 1982.

WOMEN IN ACADEME: PROGRESS AND PROSPECTS. Mariam Chamberlain. Russell Sage Foundation, 112 East Sixty-fourth Street, New York, New York 10021. 1988.

ENCYCLOPEDIAS AND DICTIONARIES

DICTIONARY OF EDUCATIONAL ACRONYMS, ABBREVIATIONS, AND INITIALISMS. Second Edition. James C. Palmer and Anita Y. Cooley, Editors. Oryx Press, 2214 North Central Avenue, Phoenix, Arizona 85004-1483. 1985.

THE EDUCATOR'S ENCYCLOPEDIA OF SCHOOL LAW. Daniel Jon Gatti and Richard Dey Gatti. Prentice-Hall, Incorporated, Route 9W, Englewood Cliffs, New Jersey 07632. 1990.

NEW ENCYCLOPEDIC DICTIONARY OF SCHOOL LAW. Richard M. Gatti and Daniel J. Gatti. Prentice-Hall, Incorporated, Route 9W, Englewood Cliffs, New Jersey 07632. 1983.

DIGESTS, INDEXES, ABSTRACTS, CITATORS

RESOURCES IN EDUCATION. Educational Resources Information Center. Department of Health and Human Services, Superintendent of Documents, United States Government Printing Office, Washington, D.C. 20402. 1975- .

SPECIALTY LAW DIGEST-EDUCATION. Bureau of National Affairs, Incorporated, 1231 Twenty-fifth Street, Northwest, Washington, D.C. 20037. 1981- . Monthly.

ANNUALS AND SURVEYS

EDUCATIONAL POLICY: AN INTERNATIONAL SURVEY. J.R. Hough. St. Martin's Press, Incorporated, 175 Fifth Avenue, New York, New York 10010. 1984.

YEARBOOK OF EDUCATION LAW. National Organization on Legal Problems of Education, Southwest Plaza Building, 3601 West Twenty-ninth Street, Topeka, Kansas 66614. 1988- .

LAW REVIEWS AND PERIODICALS

BULLETIN OF THE NATIONAL ASSOCIATION OF AMERICAN SCHOOL EMPLOYEES AND RETIREES LEGAL DEFENSE COUNCIL. 13902 Robson Street, Detroit, Michigan 48227. Quarterly.

COLLEGE LAW DIGEST. National Association of College and University Attorneys, One Dupont Circle, Northwest, Suite 620, Washington, D.C. 20036. Monthly.

COLUMBIA JOURNAL OF LAW AND SOCIAL PROBLEMS. Columbia University, School of Law, 435 West One Hundred Sixteenth Street, Box D 27, New York, New York 10027. Quarterly.

EDUCATION LAW BULLETIN. Center For Law and Education, 955 Massachusetts Avenue, Cambridge, Massachusetts 02139. Irregular.

HARVARD EDUCATIONAL REVIEW. Harvard University Press, 79 Garden Street, Cambridge, Massachusetts 02138. Quarterly.

JOURNAL OF COLLEGE AND UNIVERSITY LAW. Notre Dame Law School, Notre Dame, Indiana 46556. Quarterly.

JOURNAL OF LAW AND EDUCATION. University of South Carolina, Law School, Columbia, South Carolina 29208. Quarterly.

SCHOOL LAW REPORTER. National Organization on Legal Problems of Education. 3601 West Twenty-ninth Street, Suite 223, Topeka, Kansas 66614. Monthly.

SYLLABUS. American Bar Association, 750 North Lake Shore Drive, Chicago, Illinois 60611. Quarterly.

NEWSLETTERS AND NEWSPAPERS

BALDWIN'S OHIO SCHOOL SERVICE. Banks-Baldwin Law Publishing Company, University Center, P.O. Box 1974, Cleveland, Ohio 44106. Bimonthly.

BLACK ISSUES IN HIGHER EDUCATION. Cox, Matthews and Associated, Incorporated, 4002 University Drive, Reston, Virginia. Monthly.

CAPITAL COMMENTS. Association of Independent Colleges and Schools, 1 Dupont Circle, Northwest, Suite 350, Washington, D.C. 20036. Biweekly.

CENTER FOR LAW AND EDUCATION NEWSNOTES. Center for Law and Education, 955 Massachusetts Avenue, Cambridge, Massachusetts 02139. Irregular.

THE CHRONICLE OF HIGHER EDUCATION. The Chronicle, 1255 Twenty-third Street, Washington, D.C. 20037. Weekly.

THE COLLEGE ADMINISTRATOR AND THE COURTS. College Administration Publications, Incorporated, P.O. Box 8492, Asheville, North Carolina 28814. Quarterly.

COLLEGE STUDENTS AND THE COURTS: CASES AND COMMENTARY. College Administration Publications, Incorporated, P.O. Box 8492, Asheville, North Carolina 28814. Quarterly.

EDUCATION DAILY. Capitol Publications, 1101 King Street, Suite 444, Alexandria, Virginia 22314. Daily (weekdays).

EDUCATION FUNDING NEWS. Education Funding Research Council, 1611 North Kent Street, Suite 508, Arlington, Virginia 22209. Weekly.

EDUCATION OF THE HANDICAPPED. Capitol Publications, Incorporated, 1101 King Street, Suite 444, Alexandria, Virginia 22314. Biweekly.

FEDERAL REPORT. American Occupational Therapy Association, Incorporated, 1383 Piccard Drive, Rockville, Maryland 20850.

FOOTNOTES. Education Commission of the States Law and Education Center, 1860 Lincoln Street, Denver, Colorado 80295. 1979- . Quarterly.

HIGHER EDUCATION DAILY. Capitol Publications, Incorporated, 1101 King Street, Suite 444, Alexandria, Virginia 22314. Daily.

LEGAL MEMORANDUM. National Association of Secondary School Principals, 1904 Association Drive, Reston, Virginia 22091. Quarterly.

LEGAL NOTES FOR EDUCATION. Data Research Incorporated, P.O. Box 490, Rosemount, Minnesota 55068. Monthly.

NOLPE NOTES. National Organization on Legal Problems of Education, 3601 West Twenty-ninth Street, Suite 223, Topeka, Kansas 66614. Monthly.

NOLPE SCHOOL LAW REPORTER. National Organization on Legal Problems of Education, 3601 West Twenty-ninth Street, Suite 223, Topeka, Kansas 66614. Monthly.

PRIVATE EDUCATION LAW REPORT. Data Research, Incorporated, P.O. Box 490, Rosemount, Minnesota 55068. Monthly.

REPORT ON EDUCATION OF THE DISADVANTAGED. Business Publishers, Incorporated, 651 Pershing Drive, Silver Spring, Maryland 20910. Biweekly.

SCHOOL LAW BULLETIN. Institute of Government, University of North Carolina, Knapp Building, CB #3330, Chapel Hill, North Carolina 27599. Quarterly.

SCHOOL LAW NEWS. Capitol Publications, Incorporated, 1101 King Street, Suite 444, Alexandria, Virginia 22314. Biweekly.

SCHOOL LAW NEWSLETTER. Box 199, Ranger, Texas 76470. Quarterly.

THE SCHOOLS AND THE COURTS. College Administration Publications, Incorporated, P.O. Box 8492, Asheville, North Carolina 28814. Quarterly.

THE SPECIAL EDUCATOR. LRP Publications, 747 Dresher Road, Horsham, Pennsylvania 19044. Semimonthly.

SYNTHESIS: LAW AND POLICY IN HIGHER EDUCATION. College Administration Publications, Incorporated, P.O. Box 8492, Asheville, North Carolina 28814. Quarterly.

WEST'S LEGAL ALERT FOR EDUCATORS. West Publishing Company, P.O. Box 64526, 50 West Kellogg Boulevard, St. Paul, Minnesota 55164-0526. Biweekly.

BIBLIOGRAPHIES

ERIC CLEARINGHOUSE PUBLICATIONS. Educational Resources Information Center, United States Department of Education, National Institute of Education, 4833 Rugby Avenue, Bethesda, Maryland 20814. Annual

POLICY STUDIES ON EDUCATION: A SELECTED BIBLIOGRAPHY. Robert Goehlert. Vance Bibliographies, P.O. Box 229, 112 North Charter Street, Monticello, Illinois 61856. 1983.

DIRECTORIES

DIRECTORY OF EDUCATIONAL RESEARCH INSTITUTIONS. United Nations Educational, Scientific and Cultural Organization, Case Postale, 199 CH-1211 Geneva 20, Switzerland. 1987.

DIRECTORY OF POSTSECONDARY INSTITUTIONS. United States Department of Education, Office of Educational Research and Improvement, Superintendent of Documents, United States Government Printing Office, Washington, D.C. 20402. 1987- .

GOURMAN REPORT: A RATING OF GRADUATE AND PROFESSIONAL PROGRAMS IN AMERICAN AND INTERNATIONAL UNIVERSITIES. Seventh Edition. Jack Gourman. National Education Standards, One Wilshire Building, Suite 1210, 624 South Grand Avenue, Los Angeles, California 90017. 1989.

HEP: HIGHER EDUCATION DIRECTORY. Higher Education Publications, 6400 Arlington Boulevard, Suite 648, Falls Church, Virginia 22042. Annual.

NATIONAL FACULTY DIRECTORY. Gale Research, Incorporated, 835 Penobscot Building, Detroit, Michigan 48226. Annual.

ASSOCIATIONS AND PROFESSIONAL SOCIETIES

AMERICAN ASSOCIATION FOR HIGHER EDUCATION. One Dupont Circle, Northwest, Washington, D.C. 20009. (202) 293-6440.

NATIONAL ASSOCIATION OF AMERICAN SCHOOL EMPLOYEES AND RETIREES LEGAL DEFENSE COUNCIL. c/o William Bent Johnson, 13902 Robson Street, Detroit, Michigan 48227. (313) 837-0627.

NATIONAL ASSOCIATION OF COLLEGE AND UNIVERSITY ATTORNEYS. One Dupont Circle, Northwest, Suite 620, Washington, D.C. 20009. (202) 833-8390.

NATIONAL EDUCATION ASSOCIATION. 1201 Sixteenth Street, Northwest, Washington, D.C. 20036. (202) 833-4000.

NATIONAL ORGANIZATION ON LEGAL PROBLEMS OF EDUCATION. 3601 West Twenty-ninth Street, Suite 223, Topeka, Kansas 66614. (913) 273-3550.

RESEARCH CENTERS, INSTITUTES, CLEARINGHOUSES

CENTER FOR CONSTITUTIONAL STUDIES. Mercer University, 1400 Coleman Avenue, Macon, Georgia 31207. (912) 752-2774.

CENTER FOR EDUCATIONAL RESEARCH AND SERVICES. 112 Strauss Hall, Monroe, Louisiana 71209. (318) 342-3143.

CENTER FOR LAW AND EDUCATION. 955 Massachusetts Avenue, Cambridge, Massachusetts 02138. (617) 876-6611.

CENTER FOR POLICY AND LAW IN EDUCATION. University of Miami, Box 248065, Coral Gables, Florida 33124. (305) 284-2891.

EDUCATIONAL FREEDOM FOUNDATION. 20 Parkland, Glendale, St. Louis, Missouri 63122. (314) 966-3485.

EDUCATIONAL RESOURCES INFORMATION CENTER. United States Department of Education, 400 Maryland Avenue, Southwest, Washington, D.C. 20202. (202) 219-2289.

NATIONAL EDUCATION ASSOCIATION, RESEARCH DEPARTMENT. 1201 Sixteenth Street, Northwest, Washington, D.C. 20036. (202) 822-7400.

PUBLIC LAW INSTITUTE. University of Tennessee at Knoxville, College of Law, 1505 West Cumberland Avenue, Knoxville, Tennessee 37996. (615) 974-6691.

ONLINE DATABASES

ERIC (EDUCATIONAL RESOURCES INFORMATION CENTER). Eric Processing and Reference Facility, Office of Educational Research and Improvement, Department of Education. 4833 Rugby Avenue, Suite 301, Bethesda, Maryland 20814.

STATISTICS SOURCES

DIGEST OF EDUCATION STATISTICS. United States Department of Education, Office of Educational Research and Improvement. Superintendent of Documents, United States Government Printing Office, Washington, D.C. 20402. Annual.

ESTIMATES OF SCHOOL STATISTICS. National Education Association. 1201 Sixteenth Street, Northwest, Washington, D.C. 20036. Annual.

PROJECTIONS OF EDUCATION STATISTICS. United States Department of Education, 400 Maryland Avenue, Southwest, Washington, D.C. 20202. Biennial.

STATISTICS OF STATE SCHOOL SYSTEMS. United States Department of Education, 400 Maryland Avenue, Southwest, Washington, D.C. 20202. Biennial.

OTHER SOURCES

THE EDUCATION OF STUDENTS WITH DISABILITIES: WHERE DO WE STAND? United States National Council on Disability, Washington, D.C. 1989.

THE EDUCATOR'S QUOTEBOOK. Compiled by Edgar Dale. Phi Delta Kappa Education Foundation, Eighth and Union, Box 789, Bloomington, Indiana 47402. 1984.

EDUCATION

ESSAYS ON EQUALITY, LAW, AND EDUCATION: JOHN STUART MILL. John M. Robson, Editor. University of Toronto Press, 10 St. Mary Street, Toronto, Ontario, Canada M4Y 2WB. 1984.

GRANTS FOR HIGHER EDUCATION. Ruth Kovacs. Foundation Center, 79 Fifth Avenue, New York, New York 10003. 1990.

THE STRUCTURE OF STATE AID TO ELEMENTARY AND SECONDARY EDUCATION. Advisory Commission on Intergovernmental Relations, Washington, D.C. 1990.

TOWARD EQUALITY: EDUCATION OF THE DEAF. United States Commission on Education of the Deaf. Superintendent of Documents, United States Government Printing Office, Washington, D.C. 20402. 1988.

EDUCATION DEPARTMENT
See also: DISCRIMINATION, EDUCATION

STATUTES, CODES, STANDARDS, UNIFORM LAWS

CODE OF FEDERAL REGULATIONS, TITLE 34. Office of the Federal Register, National Archives and Records Administration. Superintendent of Documents, United States Government Printing Office, Washington, D.C. 20402. Annual. (Updated by use of monthly *List of Sections Affected* and daily *Federal Register*.)

TEXTBOOKS AND GENERAL WORKS

EDUCATION GOVERNANCE IN THE STATES: A STATUS REPORT ON STATE BOARDS OF EDUCATION, CHIEF STATE SCHOOL OFFICERS, AND STATE EDUCATION AGENCIES. Education Department, Deputy Under Secretary-Designate for Intergovernmental and Interagency Affairs. Superintendent of Documents, United States Government Printing Office, Washington, D.C. 20402. 1983.

ANNUALS AND SURVEYS

OSFA PROGRAM BOOK. United States Department of Education, Office of Student Financial Assistance, Washington, D.C. Annual.

EDUCATION FINANCE
See: EDUCATION; FEDERAL AID TO EDUCATION

ELECTION FINANCE
See: ELECTION LAW

ELECTION LAW

STATUTES, CODES, STANDARDS, UNIFORM LAWS

FEDERAL ELECTION CAMPAIGN LAWS. Federal Election Commission, Compiler. Superintendent of Documents, United States Government Printing Office, Washington, D.C. 20402. 1985.

UNIFORM VOTING BY NEW RESIDENTS IN PRESIDENTIAL ELECTIONS ACT. Uniform Laws Annotated. West Publishing Company, P.O. Box 64526, 50 West Kellogg Boulevard, St. Paul, Minnesota 55164-0526. 1980- . (Annual Supplements).

THE VOTING RIGHTS ACT: CONSEQUENCES AND IMPLICATIONS. Lorn S. Foster, Editor. Praeger Publishers, One Madison Avenue, New York, New York 10010-3603. 1985.

LOOSELEAF SERVICES AND REPORTERS

CAMPAIGN PRACTICES REPORT. Congressional Quarterly, Incorporated, 1414 Twenty-second Street, Northwest, Washington, D.C. 20037. 1980- .

CORPORATE POLITICAL ACTION COMMITTEE GUIDELINES. United States Chamber of Commerce, 1615 H Street, Northwest, Washington, D.C. 20062. 1979- .

CORPORATE POLITICAL ACTIVITY. Thomas Hale Boggs, Jr. and Katharine R. Boyce. Matthew Bender and Company, Incorporated, 11 Penn Plaza, New York, New York 10001. 1984- .

FEDERAL ELECTION CAMPAIGN GUIDE. Commerce Clearing House, Incorporated, 4025 West Peterson Avenue, Chicago, Illinois 60646. 1976- .

FEDERAL REGULATION OF CAMPAIGN FINANCE AND POLITICAL ACTIVITY. Thomas J. Schwarz and Alan G. Straus. Matthew Bender and Company, Incorporated, 11 Penn Plaza, New York, New York 10001. 1980- .

MATERIALS ON CORPORATE POLITICAL ACTIVITY. W.A. Hancock. Business Laws, Incorporated, 11630 Chillicothe Road, Chesterland, Ohio 44026. 1980- .

UNITED STATES FEDERAL ELECTION LAW. Robert F. Bauer and Doris M. Kafka. Oceana Publications, 75 Main Street, Dobbs Ferry, New York 10522. 1982- .

HANDBOOKS, MANUALS, FORMBOOKS

COGEL BLUE BOOK. Council on Governmental Ethics Laws. Council of State Governments, Iron Work Pike, P.O. Box 11910, Lexington, Kentucky 40578. Annual.

CONGRESSIONAL QUARTERLY'S GUIDE TO UNITED STATES ELECTIONS. Congressional Quarterly, Incorporated, 1414 Twenty-second Street, Northwest, Washington, D.C. 20037. 1985.

ELECTIONS SINCE 1945: A WORLDWIDE REFERENCE COMPENDIUM. Ian Gorvin. St. James Press, 233 East Ontario, Chicago, Illinois 60611. 1989.

THE INTERNATIONAL ALMANAC OF ELECTORAL HISTORY. Third Edition. Thomas T. Mackie and Richard Rose. Congressional Quarterly, Incorporated, 1414 Twenty-second Street, Northwest, Washington D.C. 20037. 1991.

TEXTBOOKS AND GENERAL WORKS

CAMPAIGN GUIDE FOR CORPORATIONS AND LABOR ORGANIZATIONS. Federal Election Commission. Superintendent of Documents, United States Government Printing Office, Washington, D.C. 20402. 1984.

CAMPAIGN GUIDE FOR POLITICAL PARTY COMMITTEES. Federal Election Commission. Superintendent of Documents, United States Government Printing Office, Washington, D.C. 20402. 1984.

COMPETITIVE ELECTIONS IN DEVELOPING COUNTRIES. Myron Weiner and Ergun Ozbudun. Duke University Press, Box 6697 College Station, Durham, North Carolina 27708. 1987.

COMPLIANCE WITH FEDERAL ELECTION CAMPAIGN REQUIREMENTS: A GUIDE FOR CANDIDATES. Fifth Edition. Federal Election Campaign Guide Task Force, Compiler. Federal Election Campaign Task Force, 1221 Avenue of the Americas, New York, New York 10036-8775. 1990.

COMPROMISED COMPLIANCE: IMPLEMENTATION OF THE 1965 VOTING RIGHTS ACT. Howard Ball, Dale Krane and Thomas P. Lauth. Greenwood Publishing Group, Incorporated, 88 Post Road West, P.O. Box 5007, Westport, Connecticut 06881. 1982.

CONGRESSIONAL DISTRICTING: THE ISSUE OF EQUAL REPRESENTATION. Andrew Hacker. Greenwood Publishing Group, Incorporated, 88 Post Road West, P.O. Box 5007, Westport, Connecticut 06881. 1986.

CORPORATE PAC'S AND FEDERAL CAMPAIGN FINANCING LAWS: USE OR ABUSE OF POWER? Ann B. Matasar. Greenwood Publishing Group, Incorporated, 88 Post Road West, P.O. Box 5007, Westport, Connecticut 06881. 1986.

ELECTION COMMUNICATIONS AND THE CAMPAIGN OF 1992. Special Committee on Election Law and Voter Participation. American Bar Association, 750 North Lake Shore Drive, Chicago, Illinois 60611. 1984.

ELECTIONS AMERICAN STYLE. James Reichley. Brookings Institution, 1775 Massachusetts Avenue, Washington, D.C. 20036. 1987.

EXIT POLLS AND EARLY ELECTION PROJECTIONS. Special Committee on Election Law and Voter Participation. American Bar Association, 750 North Lake Shore Drive, Chicago, Illinois 60611. 1984.

FAIR REPRESENTATION: MEETING THE IDEAL OF ONE MAN, ONE VOTE. H. Peyton Young and M.L. Balinski. Yale University Press, 92A Yale Station, New Haven, Connecticut 06520. 1982.

THE FEDERAL ELECTION CAMPAIGN ACT: AFTER A DECADE OF POLITICAL REFORM. Herbert E. Alexander. ABC-CLIO, P.O. Box 1911, Santa Barbara, California 93116-1911. 1981.

FEDERAL PROSECUTIONS OF ELECTION OFFENSES. Fourth Edition. Craig C. Donsanto. United States Department of Justice, Criminal Division, Public Integrating Section. Superintendent of Documents, United States Government Printing Office, Washington, D.C. 20402. 1984.

FINANCING THE 1984 ELECTION. Herbert E. Alexander and Brian A. Haggerty. Lexington Books, 125 Spring Street, Lexington, Massachusetts 02173. 1987.

GUBERNATORIAL TRANSITIONS: THE 1983 AND 1984 ELECTIONS. Thad L. Beyle, Editor. Duke University Press, Box 6697, College Station, Durham, North Carolina 27708. 1988.

MONEY AND POLITICS: THE PRICE OF ADMISSION: AN ILLUSTRATED ATLAS OF CAMPAIGN SPENDING IN THE 1988 CONGRESSIONAL ELECTIONS. Larry Makinson and Ellen S. Miller. Center for Responsive Politics, 1320 Nineteenth Street, Northwest, Washington, D.C. 20036. 1989.

THE MONEY CHASE: CONGRESSIONAL CAMPAIGN FINANCE REFORM. David B. Magleby and Candice J. Nelson. Brookings Institution, 1775 Massachusetts Avenue, Washington, D.C. 20036. 1990.

THE NEW FAT CATS: MEMBERS OF CONGRESS AS POLITICAL BENEFACTORS. Ross K. Baker. Priority Press Publications, 41 East Seventieth Street, New York, New York 10021. 1989.

PRESIDENTIAL SELECTION. Special Committee on Election Law and Voter Participation. American Bar Association, 750 North Lake Shore Drive, Chicago, Illinois 60611. 1982.

REGULATING CAMPAIGN FINANCE. Lloyd N. Cutler, Editor. Sage Publications, Incorporated, 2455 Teller Road, Newbury Park, California 91320. 1986.

REGULATION OF CORPORATE POLITICAL ACTIVITY. Third Edition. Gregory K. Merryman. Bureau of National Affairs, Incorporated, 1231 Twenty-fifth Street, Northwest, Washington, D.C. 20037. 1988.

THUNDER IN AMERICA: THE IMPROBABLE PRESIDENTIAL CAMPAIGN OF JESSE JACKSON. Bob Faw and Nancy Kelton. Texas Monthly Press, P.O. Box 1569, Austin, Texas 78767. 1986.

VOTER MOBILIZATION AND THE POLITICS OF RACE: THE SOUTH AND UNIVERSAL SUFFRAGE, 1952-1984. Harold W. Stanley. Praeger Publishers, One Madison Avenue, New York, New York 10010-3603. 1987.

NEWSLETTERS AND NEWSPAPERS

CAMPAIGN PRACTICES REPORTS. Congressional Quarterly, Incorporated, 1414 Twenty-second Street, Northwest, Washington, D.C. 20037. Semimonthly.

BIBLIOGRAPHIES

VOTING PATTERNS IN THE UNITED STATES: PERIODICAL ARTICLES, 1982-1987. Dale E. Casper. Vance Bibliographies, P.O. Box 229, 112 North Charter Street, Monticello, Illinois 61856. 1988.

ELECTION LAW

ASSOCIATIONS AND PROFESSIONAL SOCIETIES

HONEST BALLOT ASSOCIATION. North Shore Towers, Building Three Arcade, 272-30 Grand Central Parkway, Floral Park, New York 11005. (516) 466-4100.

RESEARCH CENTERS, INSTITUTES, CLEARINGHOUSES

COMMITTEE FOR THE STUDY OF THE AMERICAN ELECTORATE. 421 New Jersey Avenue, Southeast, Washington, D.C. 20003. (202) 546-3221.

ELECTION CENTER. Academy for State and Local Government, 444 North Capitol Street, Northwest, Suite 349, Washington, D.C. 20001. (202) 638-1445.

ELECTIONS RESEARCH CENTER. 5508 Greystone Street, Chevy Chase, Maryland 20815. (301) 654-3540.

FEDERAL ELECTION COMMISSION. 999 E Street, Northwest, Washington, D.C. 20463. (202) 376-5134.

NATIONAL CLEARINGHOUSE ON ELECTION ADMINISTRATION. Federal Election Commission, 999 E Street, Northwest, Washington, D.C. 20463. (202) 376-5670.

OTHER SOURCES

DIRECT LEGISLATION: VOTING ON BALLOT PROPOSITIONS IN THE UNITED STATES. David B. Magle. Johns Hopkins University Press, 701 West Fortieth Street, Suite 275, Baltimore, Maryland 21211. 1984.

ELECTIONS IN THE BALTIC STATES AND SOVIET REPUBLICS: A COMPENDIUM OF REPORTS ON PARLIAMENTARY ELECTIONS HELD IN 1990. Superintendent of Documents, United States Government Printing Office, Washington, D.C. 20402. 1990.

LEGISLATIVE HISTORY OF THE FEDERAL ELECTION CAMPAIGN ACT. Federal Election Commission. Superintendent of Documents, United States Government Printing Office, Washington, D.C. 20402. 1979.

ELECTRICITY
See: ENERGY; PUBLIC UTILITIES

ELECTRONIC FUNDS TRANSFER

STATUTES, CODES, STANDARDS, UNIFORM LAWS

UNIFORM COMMERCIAL CODE: ARTICLE 4A -- FUNDS TRANSFERS: PROPOSED FINAL DRAFT. National Conference of Commissioners on Uniform State Laws and American Law Institute, 4025 Chestnut Street, Philadelphia, Pennsylvania 19104. 1989.

HANDBOOKS, MANUALS, FORMBOOKS

AUTOMATED CLEARING HOUSE OPERATIONS HANDBOOK. New revised edition. National Automated Clearing House Association, 1901 L Street, N.W., Washington, D.C. 20036. 1987.

ELECTRONIC FUND TRANSFER ACT AND FEDERAL RESERVE REGULATION E: A COMPLIANCE GUIDE FOR FINANCIAL INSTITUTIONS. Martin B. Ellis and Fred M. Greguras. Prentice Hall, Incorporated, 270 Sylvan Avenue, Englewood Cliffs, New Jersey 07632. 1983.

FUNDS TRANSFER RISK MANAGEMENT: A GUIDE TO COMPLIANCE WITH FEDERAL RESERVE BOARD POLICY. American Bankers Association, 1120 Connecticut Avenue, N.W., Washington, D.C. 20036. 1985.

LEGAL ASPECTS OF ELECTRONIC FUNDS TRANSFERS. Carl Felsenfeld. Butterworth Legal Publishers, 90 Stiles Road, Salem, New Hampshire 03079. 1988.

REGULATION E: COMPREHENSIVE COMPLIANCE MANUAL. William J. O'Conner, Jr and Allen R. Bivens. American Bankers Association, 1120 Connecticut Avenue, N.W., Washington, D.C. 20036. 1982.

TEXTBOOKS AND GENERAL WORKS

CASHLESS SOCIETY: EFTS AT THE CROSSROADS. August Bequai. John Wiley & Sons, Incorporated, One Wiley Drive, Somerset, New Jersey 08873. 1981.

COMPUTER CRIME: ELECTRONIC FUND TRANSFER SYSTEMS AND CRIME. Kent W. Colton and others. U.S. Department of Justice, Bureau of Justice Statistics, U.S. Government Printing Office, Washington, D.C. 20402. 1982.

COMPUTERS AND BANKING: ELECTRONIC FUNDS TRANSFER SYSTEMS AND PUBLIC POLICY. Kent W. Colton and Kenneth L. Kraemer. Plenum Press. 1980.

DEPOSIT OPERATIONS. Third edition. David H. Friedman. American Bankers Association, 1120 Connecticut Avenue, N.W., Washington, D.C. 20036. 1992.

EFT IN EUROPE. Frost and Sullivan, 106 Fulton Street, New York, New York 10038. 1981.

ELECTRONIC BANKING. Allen H. Lipis, Thomas R. Marschall, and Jan H. Linker. John Wiley & Sons, Incorporated, One Wiley Drive, Somerset, New Jersey 08873. 1985.

ELECTRONIC FUND TRANSFER SYSTEMS FRAUD: COMPUTER CRIME. James M. Tien, Thomas F. Rich, and Michael F. Cahn. U.S. Department of Justice, Bureau of Justice Statistics, U.S. Government Printing Office, Washington, D.C. 20402. 1986.

ELECTRONIC FUNDS TRANSFER AND PAYMENTS: THE PUBLIC POLICY ISSUES. Elinor H. Solomon. Kluwer Academic Publishers, 101 Philip Drive, Assinippi Park, Norwell, Massachusetts 02061. 1987.

ELECTRONIC FUNDS TRANSFER: CURRENT LEGAL DEVELOPMENTS, 1981. Alan R. Feldman. Practising Law Institute, 810 Seventh Avenue, New York, New York 10019. 1981.

ELECTRONIC FUNDS TRANSFER: REGULATION E COMPLIANCE, 1980. Alan R. Feldman. Practising Law Institute, 810 Seventh Avenue, New York, New York 10019. 1980.

ELECTRONIC MONEY FLOWS: THE MOLDING OF A NEW FINANCIAL ORDER. Elinor H. Solomon. Kluwer Academic Publishers, 101 Philip Drive, Assinippi Park, Norwell, Massachusetts 02061. 1991.

FUNDAMENTALS OF COMPUTER-HIGH TECHNOLOGY LAW. James V. Vergari and Virginia V. Shue. ALI-ABA Committee on Continuing Professional Education, 4025 Chestnut Street, Philadelphia, Pennsylvania 19104. 1990.

LAW OF ELECTRONIC FUND TRANSFER SYSTEMS. Second edition. Donald I. Baker and Roland E. Brandel. Research Institute of America, Incorporated, One Pen Plaza, New York, New York 10119. 1988.

PAPER AND ELECTRONIC PAYMENTS LITIGATION: ALI-ABA COURSE OF STUDY MATERIALS, 1983. ALI-ABA Committee on Continuing Professional Education, 4025 Chestnut Street, Philadelphia, Pennsylvania 19104. 1983.

PAPER AND ELECTRONIC PAYMENTS LITIGATION: ALI-ABA COURSE OF STUDY MATERIALS, 1984. ALI-ABA Committee on Continuing Professional Education, 4025 Chestnut Street, Philadelphia, Pennsylvania 19104. 1984.

PAYMENTS SYSTEM DEVELOPMENTS: FUNDS AVAILABILITY AND TRANSFERS. Ernest T. Patrikis and Gilbert T. Schwartz. Practising Law Institute, 810 Seventh Avenue, New York, New York 10019. 1986.

NEWSLETTERS AND NEWSPAPERS

EFT REPORT. Phillips Publishing, Incorporated, 7811 Montrose Road, Potomac, Maryland 20854. 1978- . Bi-weekly.

BIBLIOGRAPHIES

ELECTRONIC BANKING: AN ANNOTATED BIBLIOGRAPHY, 1978-1983. Sybil A. Boudreaux and Marilyn L. Hankel. CPL Bibliographies, Chicago, Illinois. 1985.

ELECTRONIC FUNDS TRANSFER SYSTEMS: A BIBLIOGRAPHY. Lorna Peterson. Vance Bibliographies, P.O. Box 229, 112 North Charter Street, Monticello, Illinois 61856. 1988.

ELECTRONIC FUNDS TRANSFERS: A SELECTED BIBLIOGRAPHY, 1978-1980. Felix Chin. Vance Bibliographies, P.O. Box 229, 112 North Charter Street, Monticello, Illinois 61856. 1981.

ASSOCIATIONS AND PROFESSIONAL SOCIETIES

ELECTRONIC BANKING ECONOMICS SOCIETY. 1317 Third Avenue, New York, New York 10021. (203) 295-9788.

ELECTRONIC FUNDS TRANSFER ASSOCIATION. 1421 Prince Street, Alexandria, Virginia 22314. (703) 549-9800.

OTHER SOURCES

SELECTED ELECTRONIC FUNDS TRANSFER ISSUES: PRIVACY, SECURITY, AND EQUITY. U.S. Congress, Office of Technology Assessment, United States Government Printing Office, Washington, D.C. 20402. 1982.

EMBEZZLEMENT

TEXTBOOKS AND GENERAL WORKS

OTHER PEOPLE'S MONEY: A STUDY IN THE SOCIAL PSYCHOLOGY OF EMBEZZLEMENT. Donald R. Cressey. Patterson Smith Publishing Corporation, 23 Prospect Terrace, Montclair, New Jersey 07042. 1973. Reprint of 1953 Edition.

STICKY FINGERS: A CLOSE LOOK AT AMERICA'S FASTEST-GROWING CRIME. William W. McCollough. Amacom, A Division of American Management Association, 135 West Fiftieth Street, New York, New York 10020. 1981.

THEFT, LAW AND SOCIETY. Second Edition. Jerome Hall. Bobbs-Merrill Company, 4300 West Sixty-second Street, Indianapolis, Indiana 46206. 1952. Defunct.

BIBLIOGRAPHIES

EMBEZZLEMENT: A BIBLIOGRAPHY. Mary Vance. Vance Bibliographies, P.O. Box 229, 112 North Charter Street, Monticello, Illinois 61856. 1983.

EMIGRATION AND IMMIGRATION
See also: CITIZENS AND CITIZENSHIP; IMMIGRATION AND NATURALIZATION SERVICE

STATUTES, CODES, STANDARDS, UNIFORM LAWS

CODE OF FEDERAL REGULATIONS: TITLE 8, ALIENS AND NATIONALITY. Office of the Federal Register, National Archives. Superintendent of Documents, United States Government Printing Office, Washington, D.C. 20402. Annual. (Updated by use of monthly List of Sections Affected and daily Federal Register).

FEDERAL IMMIGRATION LAWS, REGULATIONS, AND FORMS: AS AMENDED TO AUGUST 1, 1987. West Publishing Company, 50 West Kellogg Boulevard, St. Paul, Minnesota 55164. 1988.

IMMIGRATION AND NATIONALITY ACT (AS AMENDED THROUGH JANUARY 1, 1989) WITH NOTES AND RELATED LAWS. Eighth Edition. Superintendent of Documents, United States Government Printing Office, Washington, D.C. 20402. 1989.

THE IMMIGRATION REFORM LAW OF 1986: ANALYSIS, TEXT, AND LEGISLATIVE HISTORY. Nancy Humel Montwieler. Bureau of National Affairs, Incorporated, 1231 Twenty-fifth Street, Northwest, Washington, D.C. 20037. 1987.

LOOSELEAF SERVICES AND REPORTERS

ADMINISTRATIVE DECISIONS UNDER IMMIGRATION AND NATIONALITY LAWS OF THE UNITED STATES. (INS Decisions). United States Department of Justice, Immigration and Naturalization Service, Board of Immigration Appeals. Superintendent of Documents, United States Government Printing Office, Washington, D.C. 20402. 1984.

EMPLOYERS' IMMIGRATION COMPLIANCE GUIDE: NEWSLETTER, COMPLIANCE REQUIREMENTS, PRIMARY SOURCE MATERIALS, FINDING AIDS, FORMS. Ronald H. Klasko. Matthew Bender and Company, Incorporated, 11 Penn Plaza, New York, New York 10001. 1987- .

FEDERAL IMMIGRATION LAW REPORTER. Washington Service Bureau, Incorporated, 655 Fifteenth Street, Northwest, Washington, D.C. 20005. 1983- .

HEIN'S INTERIM DECISION SERVICE TO ADMINISTRATIVE DECISIONS UNDER IMMIGRATION AND NATIONALITY LAWS. William S. Hein and Company, Incorporated, Hein Building, 1285 Main Street, Buffalo, New York 14209. 1983- .

IMMIGRATION AND NATIONALITY LAW. Charles Gordon and Ellen G. Gordon. Matthew Bender and Company, Incorporated, 11 Penn Plaza, New York, New York 10001. 1980- . (Periodic Supplements).

IMMIGRATION LABOR CERTIFICATION REPORTER. Matthew Bender Editorial Staff. Matthew Bender and Company, Incorporated, 11 Penn Plaza, New York, New York 10001. 1983- .

IMMIGRATION LAW AND BUSINESS. Austin T. Fragomen. Clark Boardman Company, Limited, 435 Hudson Street, New York, New York 10014. 1983- . (Annual Supplements).

IMMIGRATION LAW AND CRIMES. National Immigration Project of the National Lawyers Guild. Clark Boardman Company, Limited, 435 Hudson Street, New York, New York 10014. 1984- . (Annual Supplements).

IMMIGRATION LAW AND DEFENSE. Third Edition. Clark Boardman Company, Limited, 435 Hudson Street, New York, New York 10014. 1987- .

IMMIGRATION LAW AND PROCEDURE. Charles Gordon. Matthew Bender and Company, Incorporated, 11 Penn Plaza, New York, New York 10001. 1988- .

IMMIGRATION LAW AND PROCEDURE REPORTER. Allen E. Kaye and Roy J. Watson, Editors. Matthew Bender and Company, Incorporated, 11 Penn Plaza, New York, New York 10001. 1985- . (Monthly Supplements).

IMMIGRATION LAW SERVICE. Lawyers Cooperative Publishing Company. Aqueduct Building, Rochester, New York 14694. 1985- . (Monthly Supplements).

INTERPRETER RELEASES. American Council for Nationalities Service. Federal Publications, Incorporated, 1120 Twentieth Street, Northwest, Washington, D.C. 20036. 1959- . Weekly.

OPERATIONS, INSTRUCTIONS, REGULATIONS, AND INTERPRETATIONS. United States Department of Justice, Immigration and Naturalization Service. Superintendent of Documents, United States Government Printing Office, Washington, D.C. 20402. 1979- . (Periodic Supplements).

HANDBOOKS, MANUALS, FORMBOOKS

GETTING INTO AMERICA: THE UNITED STATES VISA AND IMMIGRATION HANDBOOK. Howard David Deutsch. Random House Incorporated, 201 East Fiftieth Street, New York, New York 10022. 1984.

THE GREENCARD BOOK: A GUIDE TO PERMANENT RESIDENCE THROUGH EMPLOYMENT IN THE USA. Richard Madison. Visa Publishing Corporation, 50 East Forty-second Street, New York, New York 10017. 1981.

GUIDE TO IMMIGRATION BENEFITS. United States Department of Justice, Immigration and Naturalization Service, Outreach Program. Superintendent of Documents, United States Government Printing Office, Washington, D.C. 20402. 1982.

A HANDBOOK FOR CITIZENS LIVING ABROAD. Doubleday and Company, 666 Fifth Avenue, New York, New York 10103. 1990.

HANDBOOK ON INTERNATIONAL MIGRATION. William J. Serow. Greenwood Publishing Group, Incorporated, 88 Post Road West, P.O. Box 5007, Westport, Connecticut 06881. 1990.

HANDLING IMMIGRATION CASES: THE PRACTITIONER'S GUIDE TO IMMIGRATION LAW. Bill Ong Hing. John Wiley and Sons, Incorporated, 605 Third Avenue, New York, New York 10158. 1985- . (Annual Supplements).

HANDBOOK OF IMMIGRATION LAW. Third Edition. Mark A. Ivener. Lega-Books, 658 South Bonnie Brae Street, Los Angeles, California 90057. 1986.

IMMIGRATION COMPLIANCE IN EMPLOYMENT AND BUSINESS. Paul L. Zulkie. Callaghan and Company, 155 Pfingsten Road, Deerfield, Illinois 60015. 1987.

IMMIGRATION LAW AND PROCEDURE. Desk Edition. Charles Gordon and Ellen G. Gordon. Matthew Bender and Company, Incorporated, 11 Penn Plaza, New York, New York 10001. 1980- . (Periodic Supplements).

IMMIGRATION LAWS OF THE UNITED STATES: A TEXTBOOK INTEGRATING STATUTES, REGULATIONS, ADMINISTRATIVE PRACTICES, AND LEADING COURT AND ADMINISTRATIVE DECISIONS WITH A COMPREHENSIVE INDEX AND BIBLIOGRAPHY. Third Edition. Elizabeth J. Harper. Bobbs-Merrill Company, 4300 West Sixty-second Street, Indianapolis, Indiana 46206. Defunct. 1975- . (Periodic Supplements).

IMMIGRATION PROCEDURES HANDBOOK: A HOW TO GUIDE FOR LEGAL AND BUSINESS PROFESSIONALS. Austin T. Fragomen, Alfred J. Del Rey, and Steven C. Bell. Clark Boardman Company, Limited, 435 Hudson Street, New York, New York 10014. 1985- .

THE LAW OF ASYLUM IN THE UNITED STATES: A MANUAL FOR PRACTITIONERS AND ADJUDICATORS. Deborah E. Anker. American Immigration Lawyers Association, 1000 Sixteenth Street, Northwest, Washington, D.C. 20036. 1989.

UNDERSTANDING THE IMMIGRATION ACT OF 1990. Stephen Yale-Loehr. Federal Publications, Washington, D.C. 1991.

UNDERSTANDING THE 1986 IMMIGRATION LAW. Maurice A. Roberts. Federal Publications, Washington, D.C. 1987.

TEXTBOOKS AND GENERAL WORKS

ADMINISTRATION OF IMMIGRATION POLICY. Milton D. Morris. Brookings Institution, 1775 Massachusetts Avenue, Northwest, Washington, D.C. 20036-2188. 1984.

THE CAUTIOUS WELCOME: THE LEGALIZATION PROGRAMS OF THE IMMIGRATION REFORM AND CONTROL ACT. Susan Gonzalez Baker. Rand Corporation, Institute for Civil Justice, 1700 Main Street, P.O. Box 2138, Santa Monica, California 90406. 1990.

CITIZENSHIP WITHOUT CONSENT: ILLEGAL ALIENS IN THE AMERICAN POLITY. Peter H. Schuck and Rogers M. Smith. Fred B. Rothman and Company, 10368 West Centennial Road, Littleton, Colorado 80127. 1985.

CLAMOR AT THE GATES: THE NEW AMERICAN IMMIGRATION. Nathan Glazer, Editor. ICS Press, 243 Kearney Street, San Francisco, California 94108. 1985.

CLOSED BORDERS: THE CONTEMPORARY ASSAULT ON FREEDOM OF MOVEMENT. Alan Dowty. Yale University Press, 302 Temple Street, New Haven, Connecticut 06520. 1987.

ENFORCING EMPLOYER SANCTIONS: CHALLENGES AND STRATEGIES. Michael Fix. Rand Corporation, Institute for Civil Justice, 1700 Main Street, P.O. Box 2138, Santa Monica, California 90406. 1990.

FROM OPEN DOOR TO DUTCH DOOR: AN ANALYSIS OF U.S. IMMIGRATION POLICY SINCE 1820. Michael C. LeMay. Praeger Publishers, One Madison Avenue, New York, New York 10010-3603. 1987.

THE GATEKEEPERS: COMPARATIVE IMMIGRATION POLICY. Michael C. LeMay. Praeger Publishers, One Madison Avenue, New York, New York 10010-3603. 1989.

GETTING IN: A GUIDE TO OVERCOMING THE POLITICAL DENIAL OF NONIMMIGRANT VISAS. National Lawyers Guild, 55 Avenue of the Americas, New York, New York 10013. 1985.

IMMIGRATION AND NATIONALITY LAW. Charles Gordon and Ellen Gittel Gordon. Student Edition. Matthew Bender and Company, Incorporated, 11 Penn Plaza, New York, New York 10001. 1984.

IMMIGRATION AND NATIONALITY LAW. Robert E. Juceam, Editor. Harcourt Brace Jovanovich, Incorporated 6277 Sea Harbor Drive, Orlando, Florida 32821. 1984.

IMMIGRATION AND THE JUDICIARY: LAW AND POLITICS IN BRITAIN AND AMERICA. Stephen H. Legomsky. Oxford University Press, 200 Madison Avenue, New York, New York 10016. 1987.

IMMIGRATION LAW AND PROCEDURE IN A NUTSHELL. Second Edition. David S. Weissbrodt. West Publishing Company, P.O. Box 64526, 50 West Kellogg Boulevard, St. Paul, Minnesota 55164-0526. 1989.

IMMIGRATION LAW AND REFUGEE POLICY. Arnold H. Leibowitz. Matthew Bender and Company, Incorporated, 11 Penn Plaza, New York, New York 10001. 1983- . (Periodic Supplements).

THE IMMIGRATION LAW OF THE UNITED STATES: A PRACTICAL GUIDE. George V. d'Angelo. Chapel Hill Press, P.O. Box 958, Murray Hill Station, 115 East Thirty-fourth Street, New York, New York 10156. 1985.

IMMIGRATION POLICY AND THE AMERICAN LABOR FORCE. Vernon M. Briggs, Jr. Johns Hopkins University Press, 701 West Fortieth Street, Suite 275, Baltimore, Maryland 21211. 1985.

IMMIGRATION PRIMER. Austin T. Fragomen and Steven C. Bell. Practising Law Institute, 810 Seventh Avenue, New York, New York 10019. 1985.

IMMIGRATION REFORM: A PRACTICAL GUIDE. Bureau of National Affairs, Incorporated, 1231 Twenty-fifth Street, Northwest, Washington, D.C. 20037. 1987.

IMPACT OF THE IMMIGRATION REFORM AND CONTROL ACT ON THE IMMIGRATION AND NATURALIZATION SERVICE. Rand Corporation, Institute for Civil Justice, 1700 Main Street, P.O. Box 2138, Santa Monica, California 90406. 1991.

IN DEFENSE OF THE ALIEN. Lydio F. Tomasi, Editor. Center for Migration Studies, 209 Flagg Place, Staten Island, New York 10304. 1978- .

LITIGATING THE ASYLUM CASE. Ira J. Kurzban. National Lawyers Guild, 55 Avenue of the Americas, New York, New York 10013. 1981.

MAJOR ISSUES IN IMMIGRATION LAW. David A. Martin. Federal Judicial Center, Washington, D.C. 1987.

OPEN BORDERS? CLOSED SOCIETIES?: THE ETHICAL AND POLITICAL ISSUES. Greenwood Publishing Group, Incorporated, 88 Post Road West, P.O. Box 5007, Westport, Connecticut 06881. 1988.

OPENING AND CLOSING THE DOORS: EVALUATING IMMIGRATION REFORM AND CONTROL. Frank D. Bean and Georges Vernez. University Press of America, 4720 Boston Way, Lanham, Maryland 20706. 1989.

THE PROBLEM OF IMMIGRATION. Steven Anzovin, Editor. H.W. Wilson Company, 950 University Avenue, Bronx, New York 10452. 1985.

EMIGRATION AND IMMIGRATION

THE RIGHT TO LEAVE AND RETURN IN INTERNATIONAL LAW AND PRACTICE. Hurst Hannum. Martinus Nijhoff, Kluwer Academic Publishers, 101 Philip Drive, Assinippi Park, Norwell, Massachusetts 02061. 1987. STEEL ON IMMIGRATION LAW. Richard D. Steel. Lawyers Co-Operative Publishing Company, One Graves Street, Rochester, New York 14694. 1985. (Periodic Supplements).

UNITED STATES IMMIGRATION AND REFUGEE POLICY: GLOBAL AND DOMESTIC ISSUES. Edited by Mary M. Kritz. Lexington Books, 125 Spring Street, Lexington, Massachusetts 02173. 1983.

UNITED STATES IMMIGRATION POLICY. Richard R. Hofstetter, Editor. Duke University Press, Box 6697, College Station, Durham, North Carolina 27708. 1984.

WITHOUT JUSTICE FOR ALL: THE CONSTITUTIONAL RIGHTS OF ALIENS. Elizabeth Hull. Greenwood Publishing Group, Incorporated, 88 Post Road West, P.O. Box 5007, Westport, Connecticut 06881. 1985.

DIGESTS, INDEXES, ABSTRACTS, CITATORS

DANILOV'S UNITED STATES IMMIGRATION AND NATURALIZATION LAW CITATOR. Dan P. Danilov. Butterworth Legal Publishers, 90 Stiles Road, Salem, New Hampshire 03079. 1982- . (Periodic Supplements).

PATEL'S IMMIGRATION LAW DIGEST: DECISIONS FROM 1940. Pravinchandra J. Patel. Lawyers Co-Operative Publishing Company, One Graves Street, Rochester, New York 14694. 1982- .

PATEL'S IMMIGRATION LAW DIGEST: DIGEST OF OPINIONS IN IMMIGRATION AND NATURALIZATION CASES. Pravinchandra J. Patel. Lawyers Co- Operative Publishing Company, One Graves Street, Rochester, New York 14694. 1985- .

SHEPARD'S IMMIGRATION AND NATURALIZATION CITATIONS. Shepard's/McGraw-Hill, P.O. Box 1235, Colorado Springs, Colorado 80901. 1982- . (Quarterly Supplements).

ANNUALS AND SURVEYS

ANNUAL SURVEY OF AMERICAN LAW. New York University School of Law, 137 MacDougal Street, New York, New York 10012. 1942- . Quarterly.

ANNUAL IMMIGRATION AND NATURALIZATION INSTITUTE: A COURSE HANDBOOK. Practising Law Institute, 810 Seventh Avenue, New York, New York 10019.

ANNUAL SURVEY OF AMERICAN LAW. New York University School of Law, 137 MacDougal Street, New York, New York 10012. 1942- . Quarterly.

LAW REVIEWS AND PERIODICALS

CLEARINGHOUSE REVIEW. National Clearinghouse for Legal Services, 407 South Dearborn, Suite 400, Chicago, Illinois 60605. Monthly.

GEORGETOWN IMMIGRATION LAW JOURNAL. Georgetown University Law Center, 600 New Jersey Avenue, Northwest, Washington, D.C. 20001. Biannual.

IMMIGRATION JOURNAL. American Immigration Lawyers Association, 1000 Sixteenth Street, Northwest, Washington, D.C. 20036. Quarterly.

IMMIGRATION LAW BULLETIN. National Center for Immigrant's Rights, 1544 West Eighth Street, Los Angeles, California 90017. Monthly.

INS REPORTER. United States Department of Justice, Immigration and Naturalization Service, Superintendent of Documents, United States Government Printing Office, Washington, D.C. 20402. Quarterly.

TRANSNATIONAL IMMIGRATION LAW REPORTER. International Common Law Exchange Society, P.O. Box 51, Palo Alto, California 94302. Monthly.

NEWSLETTERS AND NEWSPAPERS

ADVISOR. National Immigration, Refugee and Citizenship Forum, 220 Massachusetts Avenue, Northeast, Suite 220, Washington, D.C. 20002. Bimonthly.

AILA MONTHLY MAILING. American Immigration Lawyers Association, 1000 Sixteenth Street, Northwest, Suite 604, Washington, D.C. 20036. Monthly.

CIR REPORT. Center for Immigration Rights, 48 St. Marks Place, Fourth Floor, New York, New York 10003. Quarterly.

EPIC EVENTS. National Immigration, Refugee and Citizenship Forum, 220 Massachusetts Avenue, Northeast, Suite 220, Washington, D.C. 20002. Bimonthly.

FAIR NEWSLETTER. Federation for American Immigration Reform, 1666 Connecticut Avenue, Northwest, Suite 400, Washington, D.C. 20009. Monthly.

FEDERAL IMMIGRATION LAW REPORTER UPDATE. Washington Service Bureau, Incorporated, 655 Fifteenth Street, Northwest, Washington, D.C. 20005. Weekly.

FORUM. National Immigration, Refugee and Citizenship Forum, 220 Massachusetts Avenue, Northeast, Suite 220, Washington, D.C. 20002. Bimonthly.

THE GLOBE. Illinois State Bar Association, International and Immigration Law Section, Illinois Bar Center, Springfield, Illinois 62701. Quarterly.

IMMIGRATION BRIEFINGS. Federal Publications, Incorporated, 1120 Twentieth Street, Northwest, Washington, D.C. 20036. Monthly.

IMMIGRATION LAW AND BUSINESS NEWS. Deutsch and Salberg, 1 East Fifty-seventh Street, New York, New York 10022. Monthly.

IMMIGRATION LAW REPORT. Clark Boardman Company, Limited, 375 Hudson Street, New York, New York 10014. Monthly.

IMMIGRATION POLICY AND LAW. Buraff Publications, 1350 Connecticut Avenue, Northwest, Suite 1000, Washington, D.C. 20036. Semimonthly.

LEGALIZATION UPDATE. National Center for Immigrants' Rights, 1636 West Eighth Street, Suite 215, Los Angeles, California 90017. Monthly.

NATIONAL IMMIGRATION PROJECT NEWSLETTER. National Immigration Project of the National Lawyers Guild, 14 Beacon Street, Suite 506, Boston, Massachusetts 02108. Quarterly.

UNITED STATES IMMIGRATION NEWS. United States Immigration News, 1 Union Square, Suite 2303, Seattle, Washington 98101. Quarterly.

BIBLIOGRAPHIES

THE ADMINISTRATION OF IMMIGRATION POLICY: A BIBLIOGRAPHICAL GUIDE TO LAWS, REGULATIONS, AND ECONOMIC ACTIVITY. Vance Bibliographies, P.O. Box 229, 112 North Charter Street, Monticello, Illinois 61856. 1985.

ILLEGAL IMMIGRATION: A BIBLIOGRAPHY, 1968-1978. James W. Fox and Mary Ann Fox. Vance Bibliographies, P.O. Box 229, 112 North Charter Street, Monticello, Illinois 61856. 1978.

IMMIGRATION, ALIENS AND LAW: A SELECTED BIBLIOGRAPHY. Dittakavi Nagasankara Rao. Vance Bibliographies, P.O. Box 229, 112 North Charter Street, Monticello, Illinois 61856. 1985.

IMMIGRATION LITERATURE: ABSTRACTS OF DEMOGRAPHIC, ECONOMIC, AND POLICY STUDIES. Jeanette H. North and Susan J. Grodsky, Compilers. United States Department of Justice, Immigration and Naturalization Service. Superintendent of Documents, United States Government Printing Office, Washington, D.C. 20402. 1979.

IMMIGRATION, NATURALIZATION, AND CITIZENSHIP. Superintendent of Documents, United States Government Printing Office, Washington, D.C. 20402. 1983.

A SELECTED BIBLIOGRAPHY ON IMMIGRATION AND NATURALIZATION, 1983. Gary Hill. University of Texas School of Law, 727 East Twenty-sixth Street, Austin, Texas 78705. 1983.

STUDIES ON MIGRATION POLICY: A SELECTED BIBLIOGRAPHY. Robert Goehlert. Vance Bibliographies, P.O. Box 229, 112 North Charter Street, Monticello, Illinois 61856. 1982.

DIRECTORIES

DIRECTORY OF NONPROFIT AGENCIES THAT ASSIST PERSONS IN IMMIGRATION MATTERS. National Center for Immigrants' Rights, 1636 West Eighth Street, Suite 215, Los Angeles, California 90017. Annual.

DIRECTORY OF VOLUNTARY AGENCIES. Revised Edition. United States Department of Justice, Immigration and Naturalization Service Outreach Program. Superintendent of Documents, United States Government Printing Office, Washington, D.C. 20402. Biennial.

UNITED STATES GOVERNMENT MANUAL. Office of the Federal Register. Superintendent of Documents, United States Government Printing Office, Washington, D.C. 20402. Annual.

ASSOCIATIONS AND PROFESSIONAL SOCIETIES

AMERICAN IMMIGRATION LAWYERS ASSOCIATION. 1000 Sixteenth Street, Northwest, Suite 501, Washington, D.C. 20036. (202) 331-0046.

ASSOCIATION OF IMMIGRATION ATTORNEYS. 401 Broadway, Suite 1602, New York, New York 10013. (212) 226-3913.

CENTER FOR IMMIGRANTS' RIGHTS. 48 St. Marks Place, Fourth Floor, New York, New York 10003. (212) 505-6890.

COORDINATING COMMITTEE ON IMMIGRATION LAW. American Bar Association, 750 North Lake Shore Drive, Chicago, Illinois 60611. (312) 988-5158.

FEDERATION FOR AMERICAN IMMIGRATION REFORM. 1666 Connecticut Avenue, Northwest, Suite 400, Washington, D.C. 20009. (202) 328-7004.

NATIONAL CENTER FOR IMMIGRANTS RIGHTS. 1636 West Eighth Street, Suite 215, Los Angeles, California 90017. (213) 487-2531.

NATIONAL IMMIGRATION PROJECT OF THE NATIONAL LAWYERS GUILD. 14 Beacon Street, Suite 506, Boston, Massachusetts 02108. (617) 227-9727.

NATIONAL IMMIGRATION, REFUGEE AND CITIZENSHIP FORUM. 220 Massachusetts Avenue, Northeast, Suite 220, Washington, D.C. 20002. (202) 544-0004.

RESEARCH CENTERS, INSTITUTES, CLEARINGHOUSES

CABINET TASK FORCE ON IMMIGRATION AND REFUGEE POLICY. Executive Office of the President, Washington, D.C. 20500. (202) 633-5463.

CENTER FOR IMMIGRATION AND POPULATION STUDIES. College of Staten Island of the City University of New York, 130 Stuyvesant Place, Room 1-932, Staten Island, New York 10301. (718) 390-7946.

CENTER FOR IMMIGRATION POLICY AND REFUGEE ASSISTANCE. Georgetown University, P.O. Box 2298, Hoya Station, Washington, D.C. 20057. (202) 687-7032.

CENTER FOR IMMIGRATION RESEARCH. Temple University, Balch Institute of Ethnic Studies, 18 South Seventh Street, Philadelphia, Pennsylvania 19106. (215) 922-3454.

CENTER FOR IMMIGRATION STUDIES. 1424 Sixteenth Street, Northwest, Suite 600, Washington, D.C. 20036. (202) 328-7228.

CHURCH WORLD SERVICE IMMIGRATION AND REFUGEE PROGRAM. 475 Riverside Drive, Room 656, New York, New York 10115. (212) 870-3153.

IMMIGRATION HISTORY RESEARCH CENTER. University of Minnesota, 826 Berry Street, St. Paul, Minnesota 55114. (612) 627-4208.

EMIGRATION AND IMMIGRATION

ONLINE DATABASES

IMMIGRATION LAW AND POLICY. The Bureau of National Affairs, Incorporated, BNA ONLINE, 1231 Twenty-fifth Street, Northwest, Washington, D.C. 20037.

IMMIGRATION REFORM: A PRACTICAL GUIDE. The Bureau of National Affairs, Incorporated, BNA ONLINE, 1231 Twenty-fifth Street, Northwest, Washington, D.C. 20037.

WESTLAW IMMIGRATION LIBRARY. West Publishing Company, 50 West Kellogg Boulevard, P.O. Box 64526, St. Paul, Minnesota 55164.

STATISTICS SOURCES

IMMIGRATION AND NATIONALITY ACTS: LEGISLATIVE HISTORIES AND RELATED DOCUMENTS. James F. Bailey and Oscar M. Trelles, Editors. William S. Hein and Company, Incorporated, Hein Building, 1285 Main Street, Buffalo, New York 14209. 1979.

AUDIOVISUALS

ACKNOWLEDGEMENT AND TREATMENT OF TORTURE VICTIMS. National Practice Institute, 330 Second Avenue South, Minneapolis, Minnesota 55401. Videotape.

ASYLUM REPRESENTATION. National Practice Institute, 330 Second Avenue South, Minneapolis, Minnesota 55401. Videotape.

OTHER SOURCES

DISTRICT COURT REMEDIES IN IMMIGRATION CASES. National Immigration Project of the National Lawyers Guild, 14 Beacon Street, Suite 506, Boston, Massachusetts 02108. 1985.

THE IMMIGRATION OF ADOPTED AND PROSPECTIVE ADOPTIVE CHILDREN. United States Department of Justice, Immigration and Naturalization Service. Superintendent of Documents, United States Government Printing Office, Washington, D.C. 20402. 1984.

IMMIGRATION RAIDS ON THE WORKPLACE. National Immigration Project of the National Lawyers Guild, 14 Beacon Street, Suite 506, Boston, Massachusetts 02108. 1985.

INTRODUCTION TO IMMIGRATION LAW MATERIALS AND WHERE TO FIND THEM. 3 Legal Reference Services Quarterly 73 (1983). Legal Reference Services Quarterly. The Haworth Press, Incorporated, 10 Alice Street, Binghamton, New York 13904.

REPORT AND RECOMMENDATIONS OF THE TASK FORCE ON IRCA-RELATED DISCRIMINATION. United States Department of Justice, Washington, D.C. 1990.

RESEARCH GUIDE TO IMMIGRATION, ALIENS AND THE LAW. Scott B. Pagel. 77 Law Library Journal 465 (1984-1985). American Association of Law Libraries, 53 West Jackson Boulevard, Chicago, Illinois 60604.

UNITED STATES DEPARTMENT OF JUSTICE, IMMIGRATION AND NATURALIZATION SERVICE. 425 Eye Street, Northwest, Washington, D.C. 20536. (202) 514-2982.

U.S. IMMIGRATION LAW AND POLICY: 1952-1986: A REPORT PREPARED FOR THE USE OF THE SUBCOMMITTEE ON THE JUDICIARY, UNITED STATES SENATE. Library of Congress, Congressional Research Service. Superintendent of Documents, United States Government Printing Office, Washington, D.C. 20402. 1988.

EMINENT DOMAIN
See also: GOVERNMENT OWNERSHIP; PUBLIC LAND

STATUTES, CODES, STANDARDS, UNIFORM LAWS

MODEL EMINENT DOMAIN CODE. West Publishing Company, P.O. Box 64526, 50 West Kellogg Boulevard, St. Paul, Minnesota 55102-1611. 1976- . (Annual Supplements).

LOOSELEAF SERVICES AND REPORTERS

CONDEMNATION PROCEDURE AND TECHNIQUES--FORMS. Patrick J. Rohan and Melvin A. Reskin. Matthew Bender and Company, Incorporated, 11 Penn Plaza, New York, New York 10001. 1986- . (Biannual Supplements).

INSTITUTE ON PLANNING AND ZONING AND EMINENT DOMAIN. Matthew Bender and Company, Incorporated, 11 Penn Plaza, New York, New York 10001. 1960- . (Annual).

NICHOLS ON EMINENT DOMAIN. Third Edition. Matthew Bender and Company, Incorporated, 11 Penn Plaza, New York, New York 10001. 1956- .

HANDBOOKS, MANUALS, FORMBOOKS

MASTER GUIDE TO THE SUCCESSFUL HANDLING OF CONDEMNATION VALUATION. Henry J. Kaltenbach. Prentice-Hall, Incorporated, Route 9W, Englewood Cliffs, New Jersey 07632. 1973.

RESPONDING TO THE TAKINGS CHALLENGE: A GUIDE FOR OFFICIALS AND PLANNERS. Richard J. Roddewig. National Trust for Historic Preservation, 1776 Massachusetts Avenue, Northwest, Washington, D.C. 20036. 1989.

TEXTBOOKS AND GENERAL WORKS

EMINENT DOMAIN. Sidney Z. Searles, Chairman. Practising Law Institute, 810 Seventh Avenue, New York, New York 10019. 1982.

EMINENT DOMAIN AND LAND VALUATION LITIGATION: ALI-ABA COURSE STUDY MATERIALS. American Law Institute-American Bar Association, 4025 Chestnut Street, Philadelphia, Pennsylvania 19104. 1986.

THE FEDERAL LAW OF EMINENT DOMAIN. Jacques B. Gelin and David W. Miller. Michie Company, P.O. Box 7587, Charlottesville, Virginia 22906. 1982.

THE LAW OF EMINENT DOMAIN. Third Edition. Julius L. Sackman. Matthew Bender and Company, Incorporated, 11 Penn Plaza, New York, New York 10001. 1964- . (Annual Cumulative Supplements).

NON-TRESPASSORY TAKINGS IN EMINENT DOMAIN. William B. Stoebuck. Michie Company, P.O. Box 7587, Charlottesville, Virginia 22906. 1977.

PRIVATE PROPERTY AND THE CONSTITUTION: AN ESSAY IN PHILOSOPHY ECONOMICS AND THE LAW OF JUST COMPENSATION. Bruce A. Ackerman. Yale University Press, 302 Temple Street, New Haven, Connecticut 06520. 1978.

PROPERTY RIGHTS AND EMINENT DOMAIN. Ellen Frankel Paul. Transaction Books, Rutgers University, New Brunswick, New Jersey 08903. 1987.

REAL ESTATE VALUATION IN LITIGATION. James D. Eaton. American Institute of Real Estate Appraisers, 430 North Michigan Avenue, Chicago, Illinois 60611. 1982.

SELECTED STUDIES IN HIGHWAY LAW. John C. Vance, Editor. National Cooperative Highway Research Program, Transportation Research Board, National Research Council, 2101 Constitution Avenue, Northwest, Washington, D.C. 20418. 1976- .

STANDING GUARD: PROTECTING FOREIGN CAPITAL IN THE NINETEENTH AND TWENTIETH CENTURIES. Charles Lipson. University of California Press, 2120 Berkeley Way, Berkeley, California 94720. 1985.

TAKINGS: PRIVATE PROPERTY AND THE POWER OF EMINENT DOMAIN. Richard A. Epstein. Harvard University Press, 79 Garden Street, Cambridge, Massachusetts 02138. 1985.

A TREATISE ON THE LAW OF EMINENT DOMAIN IN THE UNITED STATES. Third Edition. John Lewis. Callaghan and Company, 155 Pfingsten Road, Deerfield, Illinois 60015. 1909.

NEWSLETTERS AND NEWSPAPERS

JUST COMPENSATION. Just Compensation, Incorporated, P.O. Box 5133, Sherman Oaks, California 91403. Monthly.

RESEARCH CENTERS, INSTITUTES, CLEARINGHOUSES

SOCIAL PHILOSOPHY AND PUBLIC POLICY. Bowling Green State University, Bowling Green, Ohio 43404. (419) 372-2536.

OTHER SOURCES

REPORT TO THE ATTORNEY GENERAL ON ECONOMIC LIBERTIES PROTECTED BY THE CONSTITUTION. United States Department of Justice, Office of Legal Policy, Washington, D.C. 1988.

EMPLOYEE FRINGE BENEFITS
See also: EMPLOYEES' COMPENSATION APPEALS BOARD; HEALTH CARE; INSURANCE, LIFE; SOCIAL SECURITY

LOOSELEAF SERVICES AND REPORTERS

EMPLOYEE BENEFIT PLANS UNDER ERISA: FEDERAL REGULATIONS. Prentice-Hall, Incorporated, Route 9W, Englewood Cliffs, New Jersey 07632. Annual.

EMPLOYEE BENEFIT PLANS UNDER TRA OF 1984. Isidore Goodman. Commerce Clearing House, Incorporated, 4025 West Peterson Avenue, Chicago, Illinois 60646. 1984.

EMPLOYEE BENEFITS AFTER THE TAX ACT OF 1984. Leon E. Irish and Thomas D. Terry, Co-Chairmen. Harcourt Brace Jovanovich, Incorporated, 6277 Sea Harbor Drive, Orlando, Florida 32821. 1984.

EMPLOYEE BENEFITS COMPLIANCE COORDINATOR. Research Institute of America, Incorporated, 90 Fifth Avenue, New York, New York 10011. 1979- . (Monthly Supplements).

EMPLOYEE BENEFITS LAW: ERISA AND BEYOND. Jeffrey D. Mamorsky. Law Journal-Seminars Press, Incorporated, 111 Eighth Avenue, New York, New York 10011. 1980- .

EMPLOYEE BENEFITS 1989: SURVEY DATA FROM BENEFIT YEAR 1988. Martin Lefkowitz. Research Center, Economic Policy Division, Chamber of Commerce of the United States, 1615 H Street, Northwest, Washington, D.C. 20062. 1989.

EMPLOYEE FRINGE BENEFITS. William E. Elwood and Warren R. Gleicher. Tax Management, Incorporated, Bureau of National Affairs, 1231 Twenty-fifth Street, Northwest, Washington, D.C. 20037. 1982- .

FRINGE BENEFITS TAX GUIDE. Commerce Clearing House, Incorporated, 4025 West Peterson Avenue, Chicago, Illinois 60646. 1985- .

PENSION AND PROFIT SHARING. Prentice-Hall, Incorporated, Route 9W, Englewood Cliffs, New Jersey 07632. 1949- .

PENSION AND PROFIT SHARING PLANS FOR SMALL AND MEDIUM SIZE BUSINESSES. Carmine V. Scudere and Kevin Moran. Panel Publishers, Incorporated, 36 West Forty-fourth Street, New York, New York 10036. 1984- .

PENSION PLAN GUIDE. Commerce Clearing House, Incorporated, 4025 West Peterson Avenue, Chicago, Illinois 60646. 1953- .

RESTRICTED PROPERTY-SECTION 83. Brookes D. Billman, Jr. Bureau of National Affairs, 1231 Twenty-fifth Street, Northwest, Washington, D.C. 20037. 1982- .

SECTION 501(C)(9) AND SELF-FUNDED EMPLOYEE BENEFITS. David S. Dunkle. Bureau of National Affairs, 1231 Twenty-fifth Street, Northwest, Washington, D.C. 20037. 1981- .

EMPLOYEE FRINGE BENEFITS

Encyclopedia of Legal Information Sources • 2nd Ed.

HANDBOOKS, MANUALS, FORMBOOKS

EMPLOYEE BENEFITS HANDBOOK. Revised Edition. Fred K. Foulkes. Research Institute of America, Incorporated, One Penn Plaza, New York, New York 10119. 1991.

ERISA AND BANKRUPTCY. Harold S. Novikoff and Richard A. Susko, Chairmen. Practising Law Institute, 810 Seventh Avenue, New York, New York 10019. 1983.

THE ERISA SOURCE MANUAL. Leo Brown. Law Journal-Seminars Press, Incorporated, 111 Eighth Avenue, New York, New York 10011. 1982- .

GUIDEBOOK TO PENSION PLANNING. Commerce Clearing House, Incorporated, 4025 West Peterson Avenue, Chicago, Illinois 60646. 1987.

THE HANDBOOK OF EMPLOYEE BENEFITS: DESIGN, FUNDING, AND ADMINISTRATION. Second Edition. Jerry S. Rosenbloom, Editor. Richard D. Irwin, Incorporated, 1818 Ridge Road, Homewood, Illinois 60430. 1988.

INTERNATIONAL HANDBOOK ON PENSIONS LAW AND SIMILAR EMPLOYEE BENEFITS. Leo Mok, Philip van Huisen and Neville Otty. Graham and Trotman, Boston, Massachusetts. 1989.

INTRODUCTION TO QUALIFIED PENSION AND PROFIT SHARING PLANS, 1986. Joseph R. Simone, Chairman. Practising Law Institute, 810 Seventh Avenue, New York, New York 10019. 1986.

PENSION AND PROFIT SHARING FORMS. Prentice-Hall, Incorporated, Route 9W, Englewood Cliffs, New Jersey 07632. 1960- .

THE PENSION ANSWER BOOK. Third Edition. Stephen J. Kross and Richard L. Keschner. Panel Publishers, Incorporated, 36 West Forty-fourth Street, New York, New York 10036. 1984- . (Annual Supplements).

PENSION PLAN FORMS. Corbel and Company, 6620 Southpoint Drive South, Jacksonville, Florida 32216. 1978- . (Periodic Supplements).

PENSION REFORM HANDBOOK: EMPLOYEE RETIREMENT INCOME SECURITY ACT OF 1974 (ERISA) AND LATER AMENDMENTS THROUGH DECEMBER 31, 1984. Martin E. Holbrook. Prentice-Hall, Incorporated, Route 9W, Englewood Cliffs, New Jersey 07632.

QUALIFIED DEFERRED COMPENSATION PLANS -- FORMS. Neil A. Mancoff and Allen Steinberg. Callaghan and Company, 155 Pfingsten Road, Deerfield, Illinois 60015. 1990.

YOUR COMPLETE GUIDE TO IRAS AND KEOGHS: THE SIMPLE, SAFE, TAX DEFERRED WAY TO FUTURE FINANCIAL SECURITY. Jack Egan. HarperCollins Publishers, 10 East Fifty-third Street, New York, New York 10022. 1982.

TEXTBOOKS AND GENERAL WORKS

ADVANCED LAW OF PENSIONS AND DEFERRED COMPENSATION: ALI-ABA COURSE OF STUDY MATERIALS. American Law Institute-American Bar Association, Committee on Continuing Professional Education, 4025 Chestnut Street, Philadelphia, Pennsylvania 19104. 1983- .

ATTORNEY'S GUIDE TO PENSION AND PROFIT SHARING PLANS. Third Edition. California Continuing Education of the Bar, 2300 Shattuck Avenue, Berkeley, California 94704. 1985- . (Periodic Supplements).

BUSINESS, WORK, AND BENEFITS: ADJUSTING TO CHANGE: AN EBRIC-ERF POLICY FORUM. Employee Benefit Research Institute, 2121 K Street, Northwest, Washington, D.C. 20037-2121. 1989.

THE CHANGING PROFILE OF PENSIONS IN AMERICA. Emily S. Andrews. Employee Benefit Research Institute, 2121 K Street, Northwest, Suite 860, Washington, D.C. 20037-2121. 1985.

COMPENSATING EMPLOYEES WITH THE LEAST TAX CONSEQUENCES. Isidore Goodman. Commerce Clearing House, Incorporated, 4025 West Peterson Avenue, Chicago, Illinois 60646. 1983.

COPING WITH THE RISING COSTS OF EMPLOYEE FRINGE BENEFITS. Isidore Goodman. Commerce Clearing House, Incorporated, 4025 West Peterson Avenue, Chicago, Illinois 60646. 1984.

EMPLOYEE BENEFITS FOR AMERICAN WORKERS. Robert Louis Clark. National Commission for Employment Policy, Washington, D.C. 1990.

EMPLOYEE BENEFITS: MERGERS AND ACQUISITIONS. Bruce Alan Miller. Practising Law Institute, 810 Seventh Avenue, New York, New York 10019. 1985.

EMPLOYEE FRINGE AND WELFARE BENEFIT PLANS: INCLUDING COVERAGE OF THE OMNIBUS BUDGET RECONCILIATION ACT OF 1989. Michael J. Canan. West Publishing Company, 50 West Kellogg Boulevard, St.Paul, Minnesota 55164. 1990.

FINANCIAL ASPECTS OF THE UNITED STATES PENSION SYSTEM. Zvi Bodie and John B. Shoven, Editors. University of Chicago Press, 5801 Ellis Avenue, Third Floor, South, Chicago, Illinois 60637. 1983.

FRINGE BENEFITS. Julian Block. Prentice-Hall Information Services, 910 Sylvan Avenue, Englewood Cliffs, New Jersey 07636. 1988.

FUNDAMENTALS OF EMPLOYEE BENEFIT PROGRAMS. Fourth Edition. Employee Benefit Research Institute, 2121 K Street, Northwest, Suite 860, Washington, D.C. 20037-2121. 1990.

ISSUES IN PENSION ECONOMICS. Zvi Bodie, John B. Shoven and David I. Wise, Editors. University of Chicago Press, 5801 Ellis Avenue, Third Floor, South, Chicago, Illinois 60637. 1987.

THE LAW OF PENSION AND PROFIT-SHARING. Russell K. Osgood. Little, Brown, and Company, 34 Beacon Street, Boston, Massachusetts 02108. 1984- . (Periodic Supplements).

PENSION AND PROFIT-SHARING. Prentice-Hall, Incorporated, Route 9W, Englewood Cliffs, New Jersey 07632. 1976- .

PENSION AND PROFIT SHARING PLANS. Sheldon M. Young. Matthew Bender and Company, Incorporated, 11 Penn Plaza, New York, New York 10001. 1977- . (Periodic Supplements).

PENSION AND PROFIT SHARING PLANS COMPLIANCE GUIDE. Carmine V. Scudere. Matthew Bender and Company, Incorporated, 11 Penn Plaza, New York, New York 10001. 1986- . (Periodic Supplements).

PENSION AND RETIREMENT PLANNING FOR SMALL BUSINESSES AND PROFESSIONALS: ALI-ABA COURSE OF STUDY MATERIALS. American Law Institute-American Bar Association, Committee on Continuing Professional Education, 4025 Chestnut Street, Philadelphia, Pennsylvania 19104. 1983.

PENSION, PROFIT-SHARING, AND OTHER DEFERRED COMPENSATION PLANS: ALI-ABA COURSE OF STUDY MATERIALS. American Law Institute-American Bar Association, Committee on Continuing Professional Education, 4025 Chestnut Street, Philadelphia, Pennsylvania 19104. 1983.

QUALIFIED DEFERRED COMPENSATION PLANS: TREATISE. Gary I. Boren and Norman P. Stein. Callaghan and Company, 155 Pfingsten Road, Deerfield, Illinois 60015. 1990.

QUALIFIED PLANS, INSURANCE, AND PROFESSIONAL CORPORATIONS: ALI-ABA COURSE OF STUDY MATERIALS. American Law Institute-American Bar Association, Committee on Continuing Professional Education, 4025 Chestnut Street, Philadelphia, Pennsylvania 19104. 1983- .

THE RESPONSIVE WORKPLACE: EMPLOYERS AND A CHANGING LABOR FORCE. Sheila B. Kamerman and Alfred J. Kahn. Columbia University Press, 562 West One Hundred Thirteenth Street, New York, New York 10025. 1988.

RETIREMENT AND WELFARE BENEFIT PLANS: A GUIDE TO UNDERSTANDING THE TAX IMPLICATIONS. Michael G. Kushner. Bureau of National Affairs, Incorporated, 1231 Twenty-fifth Street, Northwest, Washington, D.C. 20037. 1989.

RETIREMENT BENEFITS AND DIVORCE. Commerce Clearing House, Incorporated, 4025 West Peterson Avenue, Chicago, Illinois 60646. 1984.

RETIREMENT PENSIONS AND SOCIAL SECURITY. Gary S. Fields and Olivia S. Mitchell. MIT Press, 55 Hayward Street, Cambridge, Massachusetts 02142. 1985.

SECTION 401(K) PLANS. R. Theodore Benna. Prentice-Hall Information Services, 910 Sylvan Avenue, Englewood Cliffs, New Jersey 07636. 1988.

SMALL BUSINESS PENSION PLANS. Thomas J. Martin. Holt, Rinehart and Winston Publishers, Incorporated, 6277 Sea Harbor Drive, Orlando, Florida 32821. 1982.

TAX HELP FOR THE SELF-EMPLOYED. Prentice-Hall, Incorporated, Route 9W, Englewood Cliffs, New Jersey 07632. 1962.

VEBAS (VOLUNTARY EMPLOYEES' BENEFICIARY ASSOCIATIONS): EXPLAINED. Commerce Clearing House, Incorporated, 4025 West Peterson Avenue, Chicago, Illinois 60646. 1985.

DIGESTS, INDEXES, ABSTRACTS, CITATORS

EMPLOYEE BENEFITS REPORT. Research Institute of America, Incorporated, One Penn Plaza, New York, New York 10119. 1984- .

ANNUALS AND SURVEYS

EMPLOYEE BENEFITS REGULATORY UPDATE. Practising Law Institute, 810 Seventh Avenue, New York, New York 10019. 1989- .

NEWSLETTERS AND NEWSPAPERS

BENEFITS TODAY. The Bureau of National Affairs, Incorporated, 1231 Twenty-fifth Street, Northwest, Washington, D.C. 20037. Biweekly.

EBRI ISSUE BRIEF. Employee Benefits Research Institute, 2121 K Street, Northwest, Suite 600, Washington, D.C. 20037. Monthly.

EMPLOYEE BENEFITS. Illinois State Bar Association, Section on Employee Benefits, Illinois Bar Center, Springfield, Illinois 62701. Quarterly.

EMPLOYEE BENEFITS ALERT. Research Institute of America, Incorporated, 90 Fifth Avenue, New York, New York 10011. Semimonthly.

EMPLOYEE BENEFITS CONSULTANT. ProPub Incorporated, 49 Ban Syckel Lane, Wyckoff, New Jersey 07481. Monthly.

EMPLOYEE BENEFITS MANAGEMENT. Commerce Clearing House, Incorporated, 4025 West Peterson Avenue, Chicago, Illinois 60646. Bimonthly.

EMPLOYEE BENEFITS REPORT. Research Institute of America, One Penn Plaza, New York, New York 10119. Monthly.

EMPLOYERS' HEALTH BENEFITS BULLETIN. Thomson Publishing Group, 1725 K Street, Northwest, Suite 200, Washington, D.C. 20006. Monthly.

EMPLOYMENT HEALTH LAW AND BENEFITS. Employment Research Institute, Incorporated, 2568 North Clark, Suite 350, Chicago, Illinois 60614. Monthly.

ERIC EXECUTIVE REPORT. ERISA Industry Committee, 1726 M Street, Northwest, Suite 1101, Washington, D.C. 20036. Bimonthly.

LEGAL-LEGISLATURE REPORTER. International Foundation of Employee Benefit Plans, P.O. Box 69, Brookfield, Wisconsin 53008. Monthly.

THE RETIREMENT BENEFIT PLANNER. The Retirement Benefits Institute, P.O. Box 14310, Cleveland, Ohio 44114. Bimonthly.

TAXLINE. National Underwriter Company, 420 East Fourth Street, Cincinnati, Ohio 45202. Monthly.

WASHINGTON BULLETIN. Employee Benefits Research Institute, 2121 K Street, Northwest, Suite 600, Washington, D.C. 20037. Biweekly.

ASSOCIATIONS AND PROFESSIONAL SOCIETIES

AMERICAN ASSOCIATION OF PENSION ACTUARIES. 2029 K Street, Northwest, Fourth Floor, Washington, D.C. 20006. (202) 659-3620.

ASSOCIATION OF PRIVATE PENSION AND WELFARE PLANS. 1212 New York Avenue, Northwest, Suite 1250, Washington, D.C. 20005. (202) 289-6700.

CONCERNED ALLIANCE OF RESPONSIBLE EMPLOYERS. 1725 K Street, Northwest, Suite 710, Washington, D.C. 20006. (202) 872-0885.

COUNCIL ON EMPLOYEE BENEFITS. c/o Goodyear Relief Association, 1144 East Market Street, Akron, Ohio 44316. (216) 796-4008.

EMPLOYERS COUNCIL ON FLEXIBLE COMPENSATION. 927 Fifteenth Street, Northwest, Suite 1000, Washington, D.C. 20005. (202) 659-4300.

ERISA INDUSTRY COMMITTEE. 1726 M Street, Northwest, Suite 1101, Washington, D.C. 20036. (202) 833-2800.

NATIONAL COORDINATING COMMITTEE FOR MULTIEMPLOYER PLANS. 815 Sixteenth Street, Northwest, Suite 603, Washington, D.C. 20006. (202) 347-1461.

NATIONAL INSTITUTE OF PENSION ADMINISTRATORS. 145 West First Street, Suite A, Tustin, California 92680. (714) 731-3524.

PENSION RIGHTS CENTER. 1346 Connecticut Avenue, Northwest, Washington, D.C. 20036. (202) 296-3776.

SOCIETY OF PROFESSIONAL BENEFIT ADMINISTRATORS. 2033 M Street, Northwest, Suite 605, Washington, D.C. 20036. (202) 223-6413.

WOMEN'S PENSION PROJECT. 1346 Connecticut Avenue, Northwest, Washington, D.C. 20036. (202) 296-3776.

RESEARCH CENTERS, INSTITUTES, CLEARINGHOUSES

EMPLOYEE BENEFIT RESEARCH INSTITUTE. 2121 K Street, Northwest, Suite 600, Washington, D.C. 20037. (202) 659-0670.

EMPLOYMENT RESEARCH INSTITUTE, INCORPORATED. 2568 North Clark, Suite 350, Chicago, Illinois 60614. (312) 763-2801.

INSTITUTE FOR LABOR STUDIES. West Virginia University, 710 Knapp Hall, Morgantown, West Virginia 26506.

INTERNATIONAL FOUNDATION OF EMPLOYEE BENEFIT PLANS. P.O. Box 69, Brookfield, Wisconsin 53008. (414) 786-6700.

NATIONAL EMPLOYEE BENEFITS INSTITUTE. 2445 M Street, Northwest, Suite 400, Washington, D.C. 20037. (800) 558-7258.

NATIONAL EMPLOYMENT LAW PROJECT. 475 Riverside Drive, Suite 240, New York, New York 10115. (212) 870-2121.

PENSION AND WELFARE RESEARCH CENTER. Pennsylvania State University, 409F Business Administration Building, University Park, Pennsylvania 16802. (814) 865-3961.

PENSION RESEARCH COUNCIL. University of Pennsylvania, 3641 Locust Walk, Philadelphia, Pennsylvania 19104. (215) 898-7762.

THE RETIREMENT BENEFITS INSTITUTE. P.O. Box 14310, Cleveland, Ohio 44114. (216) 566-0270.

WISCONSIN RETIREMENT RESEARCH COMMITTEE. Room 316, 110 East Main Street, Madison, Wisconsin 53703. (608) 266-3019.

ONLINE DATABASES

BENEFITS TODAY. The Bureau of National Affairs, Incorporated, BNA ONLINE, 1231 Twenty-fifth Street, Northwest, Washington, D.C. 20037.

EMPLOYEE BENEFITS INFOSOURCE. International Foundation of Employee Benefit Plans, P.O. Box 69, 18700 West Bluemound Road, Brookfield, Wisconsin 53008.

HEWITT ON BENEFITS/COMPENSATION. Hewitt Associates, 100 Half Day Road, Lincolnshire, Illinois 60015.

STATISTICS SOURCES

THE HANDBOOK OF PENSION STATISTICS, 1985. Richard A. Ippolito and Walter W. Kolodrubetz, Editors. Commerce Clearing House, Incorporated, 4025 West Peterson Avenue, Chicago, Illinois 60646. 1986.

AUDIOVISUALS

PENSION LAW AND PRACTICE UPDATE. Mervin M. Wilf and Sherman P. Simmons, Planning Chairmen. American Law Institute-American Bar Association, Committee on Continuing Professional Education, 4025 Chestnut Street, Philadelphia, Pennsylvania 19104. 1985. (Videocassettes).

OTHER SOURCES

ANNUAL CONFERENCE ON EMPLOYEE BENEFITS AND EXECUTIVE COMPENSATION. Matthew Bender and Company, Incorporated, 11 Penn Plaza, New York, New York 10001. 1984- .

EMPLOYEES' COMPENSATION APPEALS BOARD
See also: LABOR DEPARTMENT

STATUTES, CODES, STANDARDS, UNIFORM LAWS

CODE OF FEDERAL REGULATIONS, TITLE 20, PART 501. Office of the Federal Register, National Archives and Records Administration. Superintendent of Documents, United States Government Printing Office, Washington, D.C. 20402. Annual. (Updated by use of monthly List of Sections Affected and daily Federal Register.)

DECISIONS OF THE EMPLOYEES' COMPENSATION APPEALS BOARD, INDEX DIGEST. United States Department of Labor, Employees' Compensation Appeals Board. Superintendent of Documents, United States Government Printing Office, Washington, D.C. 20402. Annual.

LOOSELEAF SERVICES AND REPORTERS

DECISIONS OF THE EMPLOYEES' COMPENSATION APPEALS BOARD. United States Department of Labor, Employees' Compensation Appeals Board. Superintendent of Documents, United States Government Printing Office, Washington, D.C. 20402. 1947- .

EMPLOYER AND EMPLOYEE
See: AGENCY; EMPLOYMENT LAW; LABOR AND LABOR RELATIONS; WORKERS' COMPENSATION

EMPLOYER'S LIABILITY
See: WORKERS' COMPENSATION

EMPLOYMENT DISCRIMINATION
See: DISCRIMINATION, EMPLOYMENT

EMPLOYMENT LAW
See also: DISCRIMINATION, EMPLOYMENT; DISCRIMINATION, RACE; DISCRIMINATION, SEX; EMPLOYEES' COMPENSATION APPEALS BOARD; EMPLOYEE FRINGE BENEFITS; EQUAL EMPLOYMENT OPPORTUNITY; EQUAL EMPLOYMENT OPPORTUNITY COMMISSION; LABOR AND LABOR RELATIONS

STATUTES, CODES, STANDARDS, UNIFORM LAWS

EMPLOYMENT AT WILL: A 1984 STATE-BY-STATE SURVEY. David A. Cathcart and Mark S. Dichter, Editors. National Employment Law Institute, 520 Tamalpais Drive, Suite 250, Corte Madera, California 94925. 1985.

EMPLOYMENT AT WILL: STATE LEGISLATIVE ACTIVITY. The Bureau of National Affairs, 1231 Twenty-fifth Street, Northwest, Washington, D.C. 20037. 1984.

LOOSELEAF SERVICES AND REPORTERS

EMPLOYERS' IMMIGRATION COMPLIANCE GUIDE: NEWSLETTER, COMPLIANCE REQUIREMENTS, PRIMARY SOURCE MATERIALS, FINDING AIDS, FORMS. H. Ronald Klasko. Matthew Bender and Company, Incorporated, 11 Penn Plaza, New York, New York 10001. 1987- .

EMPLOYMENT AND TRAINING REPORTER. The Bureau of National Affairs, 1231 Twenty-fifth Street, Northwest, Washington, D.C. 20037. 1969- .

EMPLOYMENT COORDINATOR. Research Institute of America, Incorporated, 90 Fifth Avenue, New York, New York. 10011. 1984- .

EMPLOYMENT DISCRIMINATION. Arthur Larson. Matthew Bender and Company, Incorporated, 11 Penn Plaza, New York, New York 10001. 1975- .

EMPLOYMENT DISCRIMINATION. Paul N. Cox. Garland Publishing, Incorporated, 136 Madison Avenue, New York, New York 10016. 1987.

FEDERAL LABOR AND EMPLOYMENT LAWS. The Bureau of National Affairs, 1231 Twenty-fifth Street, Northwest, Washington, D.C. 20037. 1985- .

INDIVIDUAL EMPLOYMENT RIGHTS CASES. Bureau of National Affairs, Incorporated, 1231 Twenty-fifth Street, Northwest, Washington, D.C. 20037. 1987- .

INVESTIGATING EMPLOYEE CONDUCT. William E. Hartsfield. Callaghan and Company, 155 Pfingsten Road, Deerfield, Illinois 60015. 1988- .

LABOR AND EMPLOYMENT LAW: COMPLIANCE AND LITIGATION. Frederick T. Golder. Callaghan and Company, 155 Pfingsten Road, Deerfield, Illinois 60015. 1986- .

LABOR LAW REPORTER. Commerce Clearing House, Incorporated, 4025 West Peterson Avenue, Chicago, Illinois 60646. 1987- .

MODERN LAW OF EMPLOYMENT CONTRACTS: FORMATION, OPERATION, AND REMEDIES FOR BREACH. Charles G. Bakaly, Jr. and Joel M. Grossman. Harcourt Brace Jovanovich, Incorporated, 6277 Sea Harbor Drive, Orlando, Florida 32821. 1983- .

RETAIL/SERVICES LABOR REPORT. The Bureau of National Affairs, 1231 Twenty-fifth Street, Northwest, Washington, D.C. 20037. 1974- .

UNJUST DISMISSAL. Lex K. Larson. Matthew Bender and Company, Incorporated, 11 Penn Plaza, New York, New York 10001. 1985- .

HANDBOOKS, MANUALS, FORMBOOKS

AMERICANS WITH DISABILITIES ACT HANDBOOK. Henry H. Perritt. John Wiley and Sons, Incorporated, 605 Third Avenue, New York, New York 10158. 1990.

EMPLOYEE HANDBOOK AND PERSONNEL POLICIES MANUAL. Second Edition. Richard J. Simmons. Castle Publications, P.O. Box 580, Van Nuys, California 91408. 1987.

EMPLOYEE PRIVACY LAW AND PRACTICE. Kurt H. Decker. John Wiley and Sons, Incorporated, 605 Third Avenue, New York, New York 10158. 1987.

EMPLOYMENT DISCRIMINATION: A CLAIMS MANUAL FOR EMPLOYEES AND MANAGERS. Andrew J. Maikovich. McFarland and Company, Incorporated, Box 611, Jefferson, North Carolina 28640. 1989.

EMPLOYMENT LAW COMPLIANCE HANDBOOK. Zachary D. Fasman and Michael J. Album. Executive Enterprises Publications Company, 22 West Twenty-first Street, New York, New York 10010-6904. 1988.

FAIR LABOR STANDARDS HANDBOOK FOR STATES, LOCAL GOVERNMENTS AND SCHOOLS. Gilbert J. Ginsburg and Daniel B. Abrahams. Thompson Publishing Group, 1725 K Street, Northwest, Suite 200, Washington, D.C. 20006. 1985.

INDIVIDUAL EMPLOYMENT LAW AND LITIGATION. Howard Specter. Michie Company, P.O. Box 7587, Charlottesville, Virginia 22906. 1989.

NEGLIGENT HIRING PRACTICE MANUAL. James A. Branch. John Wiley and Sons, Incorporated, 605 Third Avenue, New York, New York 10158. 1988.

TEXTBOOKS AND GENERAL WORKS

ADJUSTING TO AN OLDER WORK FORCE. Lois F. Copperman and Frederick D. Keast. Van Nostrand Reinhold Company, Incorporated, 115 Fifth Avenue, New York, New York 10003. 1983.

ADVANCED LABOR AND EMPLOYMENT LAW. American Law Institute-American Bar Association, Committee on Continuing Professional Education, 4025 Chestnut Street, Philadelphia, Pennsylvania 19104. 1985.

AFFIRMATIVE ACTION AND PRINCIPLES OF JUSTICE. Kathanne W. Greene. Greenwood Publishing Group, Incorporated, 88 Post Road West, P.O. Box 5007, Westport, Connecticut 06881. 1989.

AIDS IN THE WORKPLACE: LEGAL QUESTIONS AND PRACTICAL ANSWERS. William F. Banta. Lexington Books, 125 Spring Street, Lexington, Massachusetts 02173. 1988.

AIRLINE LABOR AND EMPLOYMENT LAW: A COMPREHENSIVE ANALYSIS. American Law Institute-American Bar Association, Committee on Continuing Professional Education, 4025 Chestnut Street, Philadelphia, Pennsylvania 19104. 1984.

AIRLINE LABOR LAW: THE RAILWAY LABOR ACT AND AVIATION AFTER DEREGULATION. William E. Thoms and Francis J. Dooley. Quorum Books, Greenwood Publishing Group, Incorporated, 88 Post Road West, P.O. Box 5007, Westport, Connecticut 06881. 1990.

ALCOHOL AND DRUGS: ISSUES IN THE WORKPLACE. Tia Schneider Denenberg and R.V. Denenberg. The Bureau of National Affairs, 1231 Twenty-fifth Street, Northwest, Washington, D.C. 20037. 1983.

AMERICAN LABOR POLICY: A CRITICAL APPRAISAL OF THE NATIONAL LABOR RELATIONS ACT. Bureau of National Affairs, Incorporated, 1231 Twenty-fifth Street, Northwest, Washington, D.C. 20037. 1987.

A CONFLICT OF RIGHTS: THE SUPREME COURT AND AFFIRMATIVE ACTION. Melvin I. Urofsky. Scribner Educational Publishers, 866 Third Avenue, New York, New York 10022. 1991.

CURRENT TRENDS AND DEVELOPMENTS IN LABOR AND EMPLOYEE RELATIONS LAW. Jay W. Waks. Practicing Law Institute, 810 Seventh Avenue, New York, New York 10019. 1982.

DEFENDING WORKERS' COMPENSATION AND EMPLOYEES' LIABILITY CASES. Fred L. Bardenwerper and Donald J. Hirsch, Editors. Defense Research Institute, 750 North Lake Shore Drive, Chicago, Illinois 60611. 1984.

THE ECONOMICS OF WORK AND PAY. Fourth Edition. Daniel S. Hamermesh and Albert Rees. HarperCollins Publishers, 10 East Fifty-third Street, New York, New York 10022. 1987.

EEO PROBLEMS AND THEIR APPLICABILITY TO GOVERNMENT CONTRACTORS. American Bar Association, Section of Public Contract Law, 750 North Lake Shore Drive, Chicago, Illinois 60611. 1982.

EMERGING EMPLOYEE RIGHTS: COURSE MANUAL. Robert F. Stewart, Jr. and Karl A. Fritton. Federal Publications, 1120 Twentieth Street, Northwest, Washington, D.C. 20036. 1985.

EMPLOYEE DISCIPLINE AND DISCHARGE. The Bureau of National Affairs, 1231 Twenty-fifth Street, Northwest, Washington, D.C. 20037. 1985.

EMPLOYEE DISMISSAL: LAW AND PRACTICE. Second Edition. Henry J. Perritt, Jr. John Wiley and Sons, Incorporated, 605 Third Avenue, New York, New York 10158. 1987.

EMPLOYEE TERMINATION: RIGHTS AND REMEDIES. William J. Holloway and Michael J. Leach. The Bureau of National Affairs, 1231 Twenty-fifth Street, Northwest, Washington, D.C. 20037. 1985.

THE EMPLOYER'S GUIDE TO AVOIDING JOB-BIAS LITIGATION: HOW TO PINPOINT AND REMEDY DISCRIMINATION BEFORE YOU ARE SUED. Peter C. Reid. Random House, Incorporated, 201 East Fiftieth Street, New York, New York 10022. 1986.

EMPLOYMENT-AT-WILL AND UNJUST DISMISSAL: THE LABOR ISSUE OF THE 80'S. Charles G. Bakaly, Jr. and William J. Isaacson, Co-chairmen. Harcourt Brace Jovanovich, Incorporated, 6277 Sea Harbor Drive, Orlando, Florida 32821. 1983.

THE EMPLOYMENT CONTRACT: RIGHTS AND DUTIES OF EMPLOYERS AND EMPLOYEES. Warren Freedman. Quorum Books, Greenwood Publishing Group, Incorporated, 88 Post Road West, P.O. Box 5007, Westport, Connecticut 06881. 1989.

EMPLOYMENT LAW. Professional Education Systems, Incorporated, 200 Spring Street, Eau Claire, Wisconsin 54702. 1984.

EMPLOYMENT LITIGATION AND ITS ALTERNATIVES. Mark S. Dichter and Paul I. Weiner, Co-chairmen. Practicing Law Institute, 810 Seventh Avenue, New York, New York 10019. 1984.

EMPLOYMENT PRACTICES. Professional Education Systems, Incorporated, 200 Spring Street, Eau Claire, Wisconsin 54702. 1984.

EMPLOYMENT PRACTICES FOR THE PROFESSIONAL FIRM. Victor Schachter and Jo Anne Dellaverson, Editors. Executive Enterprises Publications, 22 West Twenty-first Street, New York, New York 10010-6904. 1985.

FEDERAL LABOR LAWS. Seventh Edition. West Publishing Company, P.O. Box 64526, 50 West Kellogg Boulevard, St. Paul, Minnesota 55164-0526. 1986.

GOVERNING THE WORKPLACE: THE FUTURE OF LABOR AND EMPLOYMENT LAW. Paul C. Weiler. Harvard University Press, 79 Garden Street, Cambridge, Massachusetts 02138. 1990.

GOVERNMENT REGULATION OF EMPLOYMENT DISCRIMINATION: A SOURCEBOOK FOR MANAGERS. Richard Trotter and Susan Zacur. University Press of America, 4720 Boston Way, Lanham, Maryland 20706. 1986.

LABOR LAW AND BUSINESS CHANGE: THEORETICAL AND TRANSACTIONAL PERSPECTIVES. Quorum Books, Greenwood Publishing Group, Incorporated, 88 Post Road West, P.O. Box 5007, Westport, Connecticut 06881. 1988.

LABOR RELATIONS AND THE LITIGATION EXPLOSION. Robert J. Flanagan. Brookings Institution, 1775 Massachusetts Avenue, Washington, D.C. 20036. 1987.

LABOR RELATIONS: THE BASIC PROCESSES, LAW AND PRACTICE. Julius G. Getman and Bertrand B. Pogrebin. Foundation Press, 615 Merrick Avenue, Westbury, New York 11590. 1988.

LAW IN THE WORKPLACE. American Bar Association, Public Education Division, 750 North Lake Shore Drive, Chicago, Illinois 60611. 1987.

THE LAW OF THE WORKPLACE: RIGHTS OF EMPLOYERS AND EMPLOYEES. Second Edition. James W. Hunt. The Bureau of National Affairs, 1231 Twenty-fifth Street, Northwest, Washington, D.C. 20037. 1988.

LEGISLATION PROTECTING THE INDIVIDUAL EMPLOYEE. Robert N. Covington and Alvin L. Goldman. The Bureau of National Affairs, 1231 Twenty-fifth Street, Northwest, Washington, D.C. 20037. 1982.

MANAGER'S DESK BOOK ON EMPLOYMENT LAW: PRACTICAL GUIDELINES FOR PREVENTING DISCRIMINATION ON THE JOB. Deborah Batterman, Editor. Executive Enterprise Publications, 22 West Twenty-first Street, New York, New York 10010-6904. 1984.

MANAGING EMPLOYEE RIGHTS AND RESPONSIBILITIES. Chimezie A.B. Osigweh. Quorum Books, Greenwood Publishing Group, Incorporated, 88 Post Road West, P.O. Box 5007, Westport, Connecticut 06881. 1989.

PERSONNEL DIRECTOR'S LEGAL GUIDE. Steven C. Khan. Research Institute of America, Incorporated, One Penn Plaza, New York, New York 10119. 1989. (Periodic Supplements).

PERSONNEL LAW. Second Edition. Kenneth A. Sovereign. Prentice-Hall, Incorporated, Route 9W, Englewood Cliffs, New Jersey 07632. 1989.

PRACTICE AND PROCEDURE BEFORE THE NATIONAL LABOR RELATIONS BOARD. Fourth Edition. Theophil C. Kammholz. American Law Institute-American Bar Association, 4025 Chestnut Street, Philadelphia, Pennsylvania 19104. 1987.

THE RIGHTS OF EMPLOYEES: THE BASIC ACLU GUIDE TO AN EMPLOYEE'S RIGHTS. Wayne N. Outten. Bantam Books, Incorporated, 666 Fifth Avenue, New York, New York 10019. 1983.

RIGHTS V. CONSPIRACY: A SOCIOLOGICAL ESSAY ON THE HISTORY OF LABOUR LAW IN THE UNITED STATES. Anthony Woodiwiss. St. Martin's Press, 175 Fifth Avenue, New York, New York 10010. 1989.

UNJUST DISMISSAL, 1983: LITIGATING, SETTLING AND AVOIDING CLAIMS. Joseph Barbash and Jerome B. Kauf, Co-chairmen. Practicing Law Institute, 810 Seventh Avenue, New York, New York 10019. 1983.

WHO OWNS INNOVATION? THE RIGHTS AND OBLIGATIONS OF EMPLOYERS AND EMPLOYEES. Robert A. Spanner. Richard D. Irwin, Incorporated, 1818 Ridge Road, Homewood, Illinois 60430. 1984.

WORKER CAPITALISM: THE NEW INDUSTRIAL RELATIONS. Keith Bradley and Alan Gelb. MIT Press, 55 Hayward Street, Cambridge, Massachusetts 02142. 1983.

WORKERS' COMPENSATION AND EMPLOYEE PROTECTION LAWS IN A NUTSHELL. Second Edition. Jack B. Hood. West Publishing Company, 50 West Kellogg Boulevard, St.Paul, Minnesota 55164. 1989.

WORKERS' RIGHTS. Mary Gibson. Rowman and Allanheld, Division of Littlefield, Adams and Company, 81 Adams Drive, Totowa, New Jersey 07512. 1983.

YOUR RIGHTS AS AN EMPLOYEE: HOW FEDERAL LAWS AFFECT WORKERS IN PRIVATE EMPLOYMENT. Muriel E. Merkel. Vanguard Press, Incorporated, 201 East Fifieth Street, New York, New York 10022. 1985.

THE YOUTH LABOR MARKET PROBLEM: ITS NATURE, CAUSES AND CONSEQUENCES. Richard B. Freeman and David A. Wise, Editors. University of Chicago Press, 5801 Ellis Avenue, Third Floor, South, Chicago, Illinois 60637. 1982.

ENCYCLOPEDIAS AND DICTIONARIES

LABOR AND INDUSTRIAL RELATIONS: TERMS, LAWS, COURT DECISIONS, AND ARBITRATION STANDARDS. Matthew A. Kelly. Johns Hopkins University Press, 701 West Fortieth Street, Baltimore, Maryland 21211. 1987.

EMPLOYMENT LAW

DIGESTS, INDEXES, ABSTRACTS, CITATORS

EMPLOYMENT-AT-WILL REPORTER: ANNOTATED INDEX AND GUIDE TO DECISIONS, 1983-1985. Rosemary Hartigan, Editor. New England Legal Publishers, P.O. Box 48, Boston, Massachusetts 02101. 1985.

SHEPARD'S FEDERAL LABOR LAW CITATIONS. Second Edition. Shepard's/McGraw-Hill, P.O. Box 1235, Colorado Springs, Colorado 80901. 1975- . (Monthly Supplements).

ANNUALS AND SURVEYS

ANNUAL INSTITUTE ON EMPLOYMENT LAW. John J. Ross, Chairman. Practicing Law Institute, 810 Seventh Avenue, New York, New York 10019. Annual.

ANNUAL LABOR AND EMPLOYMENT LAW INSTITUTE. University of Louisville School of Law. Fred B. Rothman and Company, 10368 West Centennial Road, Littleton, Colorado 80127. Annual.

LAW REVIEWS AND PERIODICALS

ARBITRATION JOURNAL. American Arbitration Association, 140 West Fifty-first Street, New York, New York 10020. Quarterly.

FOUNDATION ACTION. National Right to Work Legal Defense and Education Foundation, 8001 Braddock Road, Suite 600, Springfield, Virginia 22160. Bimonthly.

INDUSTRIAL RELATIONS LAW JOURNAL. University of California, Room 1, Boalt Hall School of Law, Berkeley, California 94720. Quarterly.

LABOR LAW JOURNAL. Commerce Clearing House, Incorporated, 4025 West Peterson Avenue, Chicago, Illinois 60646. Monthly.

LABOR LAWYER. American Bar Association, Section of Labor and Employment Law, 750 North Lake Shore Drive, Chicago, Illinois 60611. 1982- . Quarterly.

MONTHLY LABOR REVIEW. Bureau of Labor Statistics, Department of Labor. Superintendent of Documents, United States Government Printing Office, Washington, D.C. 20402. Monthly.

NEWSLETTERS AND NEWSPAPERS

EMPLOYEE TESTING AND THE LAW. Vanguard Information Publications, P.O. Box 667, Chapel Hill, North Carolina 27514. Monthly.

EMPLOYMENT ALERT. Research Institute of America, 90 Fifth Avenue, New York, New York 10011. Biweekly.

EMPLOYMENT LAW BRIEFING. Sachnoff and Weaver, Limited, 30 South Wacker Drive, Twenty-ninth Floor, Chicago, Illinois 60606. Quarterly.

EMPLOYMENT LAW NEWS. National Employment Law Project, 475 Riverside Drive, Suite 240, New York, New York 10115. Quarterly.

EMPLOYMENT LAW UPDATE. Rutkowski and Associates, P.O. Box 15250, Evansville, Indiana 47716. Monthly.

HEALTH EMPLOYMENT LAW UPDATE. Rutkowski and Associates, P.O. Box 15250, Evansville, Indiana 47716. Monthly.

JUDGE O'BRIENS EMPLOYMENT NEWS. Winterbrook Publishing Company, P.O. Box 1106, Covina, California 91722. Monthly.

LABOR AND EMPLOYMENT LAW NEWSLETTER. American Bar Association, Labor and Employment Law Section, 750 North Lake Shore Drive, Chicago, Illinois 60611. Quarterly.

LABOR AND EMPLOYMENT LAW NEWSLETTER. Matthew Bender and Company, Incorporated, 11 Penn Plaza, New York, New York 10011. Monthly.

LABOR UPDATE. National Labor Law Center and National Lawyers Guild, 2000 P Street, Northwest, Washington, D.C. 20036. Five issues per year.

NATIONAL RIGHT TO WORK NEWSLETTER. National Right to Work Committee, 8001 Braddock Road, Springfield, Virginia 22160. Monthly.

PUBLIC EMPLOYMENT LAW NOTES. NYPER Publications, P.O. Box 662, Latham, New York 12110. Monthly.

PUBLIC EMPLOYMENT LAW REPORT. Data Research, Incorporated, P.O. Box 490, Rosemount, Minnesota 55068. Monthly.

YOU AND THE LAW. National Institute of Business Management, Incorporated, 1328 Broadway, New York, New York 10001. Semimonthly.

BIBLIOGRAPHIES

DISMISSAL OF EMPLOYEES: A SELECTIVE BIBLIOGRAPHY. Marian Dworaczek. Vance Bibliographies, P.O. Box 229, 112 North Charter Street, Monticello, Illinois 61856. 1983.

EMPLOYMENT-AT-WILL: A BRIEF CHECKLIST. Alva W. Stewart. Vance Bibliographies, P.O. Box 229, 112 North Charter Street, Monticello, Illinois 61856. 1989.

ASSOCIATIONS AND PROFESSIONAL SOCIETIES

AMERICAN BAR ASSOCIATION. Section of Labor and Employment Law, 750 North Lake Shore Drive, Chicago, Illinois 60611. (312) 988-6063.

NATIONAL EMPLOYMENT LAW PROJECT. 475 Riverside Drive, Suite 240, New York, New York 10115. (212) 870-2121.

NATIONAL RIGHT TO WORK COMMITTEE. 8001 Braddock Road, Springfield, Virginia 22160. (703) 321-9820.

RESEARCH CENTERS, INSTITUTES, CLEARINGHOUSES

NATIONAL RIGHT TO WORK LEGAL DEFENSE AND EDUCATION FOUNDATION. 8001 Braddock Road, Suite 600, Springfield, Virginia 22160. (703) 321-8510.

ONLINE DATABASES

LABOR LAW. Bureau of National Affairs, Database Publishing Unit, 1231 Twenty-fifth Street, Northwest, Washington, D.C. 20037.

LEXIS. FEDERAL LABOR LIBRARY AND EMPLOYMENT, STATE EMPLOYMENT LAW LIBRARY. Mead Data Central, 9443 Springboro Pike, P.O. Box 933, Dayton, Ohio 45401.

WESTLAW LABOR LIBRARY. West Publishing Company, P.O. Box 64526, 50 West Kellogg Boulevard, St. Paul, Minnesota 55102-1611.

STATISTICS SOURCES

HANDBOOK OF LABOR STATISTICS. United States Department of Labor, Bureau of Labor Statistics. Superintendent of Documents, United States Government Printing Office, Washington, D.C. 20402. Annual.

MONTHLY LABOR REVIEW. United States Department of Labor, Bureau of Labor Statistics. Superintendent of Documents, United States Government Printing Office, Washington, D.C. 20402. Monthly.

ENDANGERED SPECIES
See: ANIMALS; WILDLIFE

ENERGY
See also: ENERGY DEPARTMENT; FEDERAL ENERGY REGULATORY COMMISSION; NUCLEAR REGULATORY COMMISSION; OIL AND GAS; SOLAR ENERGY

LOOSELEAF SERVICES AND REPORTERS

COAL LAW AND REGULATION. Timothy M. Biddle. Matthew Bender and Company, Incorporated, 11 Penn Plaza, New York, New York 10001. 1983- . (Periodic Supplements).

ENERGY MANAGEMENT AND FEDERAL ENERGY GUIDELINES. Commerce Clearing House, Incorporated, 4025 West Peterson Avenue, Chicago, Illinois 60646. 1973- . (Weekly Supplements).

ENERGY RESOURCES TAX REPORTER. Commerce Clearing House, Incorporated, 4025 West Peterson Avenue, Chicago, Illinois 60646. 1983- . (Monthly Supplements).

ENERGY USERS REPORT. The Bureau of National Affairs, Incorporated, 1231 Twenty-fifth Street, Northwest, Washington, D.C. 20037. 1973- . (Weekly Supplements).

FEDERAL ENERGY REGULATORY COMMISSION REPORTS. Commerce Clearing House, Incorporated, 4025 West Peterson Avenue, Chicago, Illinois 60646. 1979- . (Periodic Supplements).

NUCLEAR REGULATION REPORTS. Commerce Clearing House, Incorporated, 4025 West Peterson Avenue, Chicago, Illinois 60646. 1975- . (Weekly Supplements).

TEXTBOOKS AND GENERAL WORKS

ALTERNATIVE ENERGY: THE FEDERAL ROLE. Linda E. Buck and Lee M. Goodwin. Shepard's/McGraw-Hill, P.O. Box 1235, Colorado Springs, Colorado 80901. 1982- . (Annual Supplements).

ENERGY AND NATURAL RESOURCE LAW: THE REGULATORY DIALOGUE. Alfred C. Aman, Jr. Matthew Bender and Company, Incorporated, 11 Penn Plaza, New York, New York 10001. 1983- .

ENERGY CONSERVATION: SUCCESSES AND FAILURES. John C. Sawhill and Richard Cotton, Editors. The Brookings Institution, 1775 Massachusetts Avenue, Northwest, Washington, D.C. 20036-2188. 1986.

ENERGY LAW AND POLICY. Joseph P. Tomain and James E. Hickey. Anderson Publishing Company, 2035 Reading Road, Cincinnati, Ohio 45202. 1989.

ENERGY LAW IN A NUTSHELL. Joseph P. Tomain. West Publishing Company, P.O. Box 64526, 50 West Kellogg Boulevard, St. Paul, Minnesota 55164-0526. 1981.

ENERGY--MARKETS AND REGULATION: ESSAYS IN HONOR OF M.A. ADELMAN. Morris Albert Adelman, Richard L. Gordon, Henry D. Jacoby and Martin B. Zimmerman. MIT Press, 55 Hayward Street, Cambridge, Massachusetts 02142. 1987.

ENERGY POLICY. Congressional Quarterly Incorporated, 1414 Twenty-second Street, Northwest, Washington, D.C. 20037. 1981.

ENERGY POLICY IN AMERICA SINCE 1945: A STUDY OF BUSINESS-GOVERNMENT RELATIONS. Richard H.K. Vietor. Cambridge University Press, 40 West Twentieth Street, New York, New York 10011. 1984.

FEDERAL REGULATION OF ENERGY. William F. Fox, Jr. Shepard's/McGraw-Hill, P.O. Box 1235, Colorado Springs, Colorado 80901. 1983- . (Annual Supplements).

OIL AND AMERICA'S SECURITY. The Brookings Institution, 1775 Massachusetts Avenue, Northwest, Washington, D.C. 20036-2188. 1988.

PIPELINE POLITICS: THE COMPLEX POLITICAL ECONOMY OF EAST-WEST ENERGY TRADE. Bruce W. Jentleson. Cornell University Press, 124 Roberts Place, P.O. Box 250, Ithaca, New York 14851. 1986.

THE POLITICS OF ENERGY CONSERVATION. Pietro S. Nivola. The Brookings Institution, 1775 Massachusetts Avenue, Northwest, Washington, D.C. 20036-2188. 1986.

PUBLIC UTILITIES AND THE POOR: RIGHTS AND RESPONSIBILITIES. David C. Sweet and Kathryn Wertheim Hexter. Praeger Publishers, One Madison Avenue, New York, New York 100103603. 1987.

ENERGY

DIGESTS, INDEXES, ABSTRACTS, CITATORS

FEDERAL ENERGY GUIDELINES FERC REPORTS. CUMULATIVE INDICES. United States Federal Energy Regulatory Commission. Superintendent of Documents, United States Government Printing Office, Washington, D.C. 20402. 1984- .

FEDERAL ENERGY LAW CITATIONS. Shepard's/McGraw-Hill, P.O. Box 1235, Colorado Springs, Colorado 80901. 1988.

LAW REVIEWS AND PERIODICALS

JOURNAL OF ENERGY LAW AND POLICY. University of Utah, College of Law, Salt Lake City, Utah 84112. Semiannually.

MONITOR. United States Federal Energy Regulatory Commission. Superintendent of Documents, United States Government Printing Office, Washington, D.C. 20402. Biweekly.

PUBLIC UTILITIES FORTNIGHTLY. Public Utilities Reports, Incorporated, 1700 North Moore Street, Suite 2100, Arlington, Virginia 22209. Biweekly.

NEWSLETTERS AND NEWSPAPERS

CALIFORNIA ENERGY MARKETS. News Data Corporation, P.O. Box 9157, Seattle, Washington 98109. Weekly.

CLEARING UP: NORTHWEST ENERGY MARKETS. News Data Service for Western Utilities, Box 9157, Queen Anne Station, Seattle, Washington 98109. Weekly.

CONGRESSIONAL REPORT, SCIENCE, ENERGY AND ENVIRONMENT. Malone Congressional Reports, 4301 Tujunga Avenue, Studio City, California 91604. Biweekly.

DIGEST OF ACTIVITIES OF CONGRESS. Oliphant Washington News Service, 1819 H Street, Suite 330, Northwest, Washington, D.C. 20006. Weekly.

THE ENERGY DAILY. King Publishing Group, 627 National Press Building, Washington, D.C. 20046. Daily.

ENERGY INFORMATION BULLETIN. American Bar Association, Coordinating Group on Energy Law, 1800 M Street, Northwest, Washington, D.C. 20036. Quarterly.

ENERGY REPORT. Pasha Publications, 1401 Wilson Boulevard, Suite 900, Arlington, Virginia 22209. Weekly.

ENERGY SUMMARY. Oliphant Washington News Service, 1819 H Street, Suite 330, Northwest, Washington, D.C. 20006. Weekly.

INDEPENDENT POWER REPORT. McGraw-Hill, Incorporated, 1221 Avenue of the Americas, New York, New York 10020. Biweekly.

INGAA UPDATE: MONTHLY PROFILES OF GAS PIPELINE PROCEEDINGS AT FERC. Interstate Natural Gas Association of America, 555 Thirteenth Street, Northwest, Suite 300, Washington, D.C. 20004.

Encyclopedia of Legal Information Sources • 2nd Ed.

INSIDE ENERGY WITH FEDERAL LANDS. McGraw-Hill, Incorporated, 1221 Avenue of the Americas, New York, New York 10020. Weekly.

INSIDE F.E.R.C. McGraw-Hill, Incorporated, 1221 Avenue of the Americas, New York, New York 10020. Weekly.

INSIDE N.R.C. McGraw-Hill, Incorporated, 1221 Avenue of the Americas, New York, New York 10020. Biweekly.

INTEGRATED WASTE MANAGEMENT. McGraw-Hill, Incorporated, 1221 Avenue of the Americas, New York, New York 10020. Biweekly.

NCLC ENERGY UPDATE. National Consumer Law Center, Incorporated, 11 Beacon Street, Boston, Massachusetts 02108. Bimonthly.

NEW FUELS REPORT. Inside Washington Publishers, P.O. Box 7167, Ben Franklin Station, Washington, D.C. 20044. Weekly.

OLIPHANT WASHINGTON SERVICE. Oliphant Washington News Service, 1819 H Street, Suite 330, Northwest, Suite 330, Washington, D.C. 20006. Semiweekly.

UTILITIES INDUSTRY LITIGATION REPORTER. Andrews Publications, 1646 West Chester Pike, Westtown, Pennsylvania 19395. Semimonthly.

UTILITY REPORTER - FUELS, ENERGY AND POWER. Merton Allen Associates, P.O. Box 15640, Plantation, Florida 33318. Monthly.

WESTERN ENERGY BULLETIN. Energy Law Center, University of Utah, College of Law, Salt Lake City, Utah 84112. Monthly.

BIBLIOGRAPHIES

BIBLIOGRAPHY ON ENERGY ECONOMICS. Henry N. McCarl. Vance Bibliographies, P.O. Box 229, 112 North Charter Street, Monticello, Illinois 61856. 1982.

ENERGY POLICY. Sandra C. Danforth. Vance Bibliographies, P.O. Box 229, 112 North Charter Street, Monticello, Illinois 61856. 1982.

DIRECTORIES

ENERGY RESEARCH PROGRAMS DIRECTORY. R.R. Bowker, 245 West Seventeenth Street, New York, New York 10011. 1980.

ASSOCIATIONS AND PROFESSIONAL SOCIETIES

ALTERNATIVE ENERGY RESOURCES ORGANIZATION. 44 North Last Chance Gulch, #8, Helena, Montana 59601. (406) 443-7272.

ALTERNATIVE SOURCES OF ENERGY. 107 South Central Avenue, Milaca, Minnesota 56353. (612) 983-6892.

AMERICANS FOR ENERGY INDEPENDENCE. 1629 K Street, Suite 602, Northwest, Washington, D.C. 20006. (202) 466-2105.

BIOMASS ENERGY RESEARCH ASSOCIATION. 1825 K Street, Northwest, Suite 503, Washington, D.C. 20006. (202) 785-2856.

CITIZEN/LABOR ENERGY COALITION. 1300 Connecticut Avenue, Northwest, Washington, D.C. 20036. (202) 857-5153.

CONSUMER ENERGY COUNCIL OF AMERICA RESEARCH FOUNDATION. 2000 L Street, Northwest, Suite 802, Washington, D.C. 20036. (202) 659-0404.

ENERGY CONSERVATION COALITION. 1525 New Hampshire Avenue, Northwest, Washington, D.C. 20036. (202) 745-4874.

FEDERAL ENERGY BAR ASSOCIATION. 1900 M Street, Northwest, Washington, D.C. 20036. (202) 223-5625.

FUSION POWER ASSOCIATES. 2 Professional Drive, Suite 248, Gaithersburg, Maryland 20879. (301) 258-0545.

NATIONAL ENERGY RESOURCES ORGANIZATION. Canal Center, Suite 250, Alexandria, Virginia 22314. (703) 739-8822.

NATIONAL GOVERNORS' ASSOCIATION. Energy and Environment Committee, 444 North Capitol Street, Northwest, Washington, D.C. 20001. (202) 624-5300.

NATIONAL LEAGUE OF CITIES, ENERGY PROGRAM. 1301 Pennsylvania Avenue, Northwest, Washington, D.C. 20004. (202) 626-1300.

U.S. COUNCIL FOR ENERGY AWARENESS. 1776 I Street, Northwest, Suite 400, Washington, D.C. 20006. (202) 293-0770.

U.S. ENERGY ASSOCIATION. 1620 I Street, Northwest, Suite 615, Washington, D.C. 20006. (202) 331-0415.

RESEARCH CENTERS, INSTITUTES, CLEARINGHOUSES

CENTER FOR ENERGY POLICY AND RESEARCH. New York Institute of Technology, Old Westbury, Connecticut 11568. (516) 686-7578.

ENERGY INFORMATION ADMINISTRATION. Forrestal Building, 1000 Independence Avenue, Southwest, Washington, D.C. 20585. (202) 586-8800.

ENERGY LAW CENTER. University of Utah, College of Law, Salt Lake City, Utah 84112. (801) 581-5880.

ENERGY RESEARCH/DEVELOPMENT CENTER. University of Kansas, 118 McCollum Laboratories, Lawrence, Kansas 66045. (913) 864-4079.

ENERGY RESEARCH INSTITUTE. 6850 Rattlesnake Hammock Road, Highway 951, Naples, Florida 33962. (813) 793-1922.

ENVIRONMENTAL POLICY INSTITUTE. 218 D Street, Southeast, Washington, D.C. 20003. (202) 544-2600.

GOVERNMENT LAW CENTER. University of Louisville, Louisville, Kentucky 40292. (502) 588-6482.

MISSISSIPPI LAW RESEARCH CENTER. University of Mississippi, Law Center, Room 518, University, Mississippi 38677. (601) 232-7775.

NATIONAL CONSUMER RESEARCH INSTITUTE. 1700 K Street, Northwest, Suite 1300, Washington, D.C. 20006. (202) 457-0710.

RENEWABLE FUELS INFO CENTER. Mindsight Corporation, 8 West Janss Road, Thousand Oaks, California 91360. (805) 388-3097.

RESOURCES FOR THE FUTURE. 1616 P Street, Northwest, Washington, D.C. 20036. (202) 328-5045.

ROCKY MOUNTAIN MINERAL LAW FOUNDATION. Porter Administration Building, 3rd Floor, East Eighteenth Avenue, Denver, Colorado 80220. (303) 321-8100.

SIERRA CLUB LEGAL DEFENSE FUND, INCORPORATED. 404 C Street, Northeast, Washington, D.C. 20003. (202) 547-1141.

WORLDWATCH INSTITUTE. 1776 Massachusetts Avenue, Northwest, Washington, D.C. 20036. (202) 452-1999.

ONLINE DATABASES

LEXIS, ENERGY LIBRARY. Mead Data Central, P.O. Box 933, Dayton, Ohio 45401.

WESTLAW, ENERGY AND UTILITIES LIBRARY. West Publishing Company, P.O. Box 64526, 50 West Kellogg Boulevard, St. Paul, Minnesota 55102-1611.

OTHER SOURCES

ENERGY POLICY: TIMELY REPORTS TO KEEP JOURNALISTS, SCHOLARS AND THE PUBLIC ABREAST OF DEVELOPING ISSUES, EVENTS AND TRENDS. Second Edition. Congressional Quarterly, 414 Twenty-second Street, Northwest, Washington, D.C. 20037. 1981.

ENERGY SECURITY: A REPORT TO THE PRESIDENT OF THE UNITED STATES. U.S. Department of Energy. Superintendent of Documents, United States Government Printing Office, Washington, D.C. 20402. 1987.

ENERGY USE AND THE U.S. ECONOMY. Congress of the U.S. Office of Technology Assessment. Superintendent of Documents, United States Government Printing Office, Washington, D.C. 20402. 1990.

ENERGY DEPARTMENT
See also: FEDERAL ENERGY REGULATORY COMMISSION; NUCLEAR REGULATORY COMMISSION

STATUTES, CODES, STANDARDS, UNIFORM LAWS

CODE OF FEDERAL REGULATIONS, TITLE 40. Office of the Federal Register, National Archives and Records Administration. Superintendent of Documents, United States Government Printing Office, Washington, D.C. 20402. Annual. (Updated by use of monthly List of Sections Affected and daily Federal Resister.)

ENERGY DEPARTMENT

LOOSELEAF SERVICES AND REPORTERS

SOLAR LAW REPORTER. United States Department of Energy. Superintendent of Documents, United States Government Printing Office, Washington, D.C. 20402. Bimonthly.

TEXTBOOKS AND GENERAL WORKS

DRILLING AND PRODUCTION UNDER TITLE ONE OF THE NATURAL GAS POLICY ACT. United States Department of Energy, Energy Information Administration, Office of Oil and Gas. Superintendent of Documents, United States Government Printing Office, Washington, D.C. 20402. 1984.

NATIONAL ENERGY POLICY PLAN, 1985. United States Department of Energy. Superintendent of Documents, United States Government Printing Office, Washington, D.C. 20402. 1985.

NATURAL GAS MARKET THROUGH 1990: AN ANALYSIS OF THE NATURAL GAS POLICY ACT AND SEVERAL ALTERNATIVES. United States Department of Energy, Energy Information Administration, Office of Oil and Gas. Superintendent of Documents, United States Government Printing Office, Washington, D.C. 20402. 1983.

DIGESTS, INDEXES, ABSTRACTS, CITATORS

SHEPARD'S FEDERAL ENERGY CITATIONS. Shepard's/McGraw-Hill, P.O. Box 1235, Colorado Springs, Colorado 80901. Quarterly Supplements.

SHEPARD'S UNITED STATES ADMINISTRATIVE CITATIONS. Shepard's/McGraw-Hill, P.O. Box 1235, Colorado Springs, Colorado 80901. Quarterly Supplements.

ANNUALS AND SURVEYS

ANNUAL ENERGY OUTLOOK. United States Department of Energy, Energy Information Administration, Office of Energy Markets and End Use. Superintendent of Documents, United States Government Printing Office, Washington, D.C. 20402. Annual.

ANNUAL ENERGY REVIEW. United States Department of Energy, Energy Information Administration, Office of Energy Markets and End Use. Superintendent of Documents, United States Government Printing Office, Washington, D.C. 20402. Annual.

DEPARTMENT OF ENERGY ANNUAL REPORT TO CONGRESS. United States Department of Energy. Superintendent of Documents, United States Government Printing Office, Washington, D.C. 20402. Annual.

LAW REVIEWS AND PERIODICALS

MONTHLY ENERGY REVIEW. United States Department of Energy, Energy Information Administration. Superintendent of Documents, United States Government Printing Office, Washington, D.C. 20402. Monthly.

RESEARCH CENTERS, INSTITUTES, CLEARINGHOUSES

ENERGY INFORMATION ADMINISTRATION. Forrestal Building, 1000 Independence Avenue, Southwest, Washington, D.C. 20585. (202) 586-8800.

FEDERAL ENERGY REGULATORY COMMISSION. 825 North Capitol Street, Northeast, Washington, D.C. 20426. (202) 208-1000.

UNITED STATES DEPARTMENT OF ENERGY LAW LIBRARY. 1000 Independence Avenue, Southwest, Room 6A-156, Washington, D.C. 20585. (202) 586-5575.

ONLINE DATABASES

LEXIS, ENERGY LIBRARY. Mead Data Central, P.O. Box 933, Dayton, Ohio 45401.

WESTLAW, ENERGY AND UTILITIES LIBRARY. West Publishing Company, P.O. Box 64526, 50 West Kellogg Boulevard, St. Paul, Minnesota 55164-0526.

ENFORCEMENT OF JUDGMENTS
See: JUDGMENTS

ENGINEERS AND ENGINEERING LAW

STATUTES, CODES, STANDARDS, UNIFORM LAWS

CODES AND STANDARDS. Kelly P. Reynolds and Associates, Incorporated, 1105 West Chicago Avenue, Chicago, Illinois 60622. 1980- . Monthly.

HANDBOOKS, MANUALS, FORMBOOKS

FORMS AND AGREEMENTS FOR ARCHITECTS, ENGINEERS AND CONTRACTORS. Albert Dib. Clark Boardman Callaghan, 1155 Pfingsten Road, Deerfield, Illinois 60015. 1976- .

LEGAL HANDBOOK FOR ARCHITECTS, ENGINEERS AND CONTRACTORS. Clark Boardman Callaghan, 1155 Pfingsten Road, Deerfield, Illinois 60015. 1986- .

PRACTICAL ARCHITECT-ENGINEER LAW: COURSE MANUAL. John D. Sours and W. Hensell Harris. Federal Publications, Incorporated, 1120 20th Street, N.W., Washington, D.C. 20036. 1983.

TEXTBOOKS AND GENERAL WORKS

ARCHITECTS/ENGINEER'S ROLE UNDER SUPERFUND, AND SELECTING A PROFESSIONAL LIABILITY INSURANCE POLICY. James A. Thompson and Frank J. Baltz. Public Contract Law Section, American Bar Association, 750 North Lake Shore Drive, Chicago, Illinois 60611. 1984.

ENGINEERING EVIDENCE. Second edition. Max Schwartz and Neil F. Schwartz. Shepard's/McGraw-Hill, P.O. Box 35300, Colorado Springs, Colorado 80935. 1987.

DIGESTS, INDEXES, ABSTRACTS, CITATORS

AIA BUILDING CONSTRUCTION LEGAL CITATOR. American Institute of Architects, 1735 New York Avenue, N.W., Washington, D.C. 20006.

NEWSLETTERS AND NEWSPAPERS

A/E LEGAL NEWLETTER. Victor O. Schinnerer & Company, Incorporated, 2 Wisconsin Circle, Chevy Chase, Maryland 20815. 1981- . Monthly.

CONSTRUCTION INDUSTRY LITIGATION REPORTER. Andrews Publications, 1646 West Chester Pike, Westtown, Pennsylvania 19395.

LAST WORD. American Consulting Engineers Council, 1015 15th Street, N.W., Washington, D.C. 20005. 1971- . Weekly.

LEGAL BRIEFS FOR THE CONSTRUCTION INDUSTRY. McGraw-Hill, Incorporated, 11 West 19th Street, New York, New York 10011. 1975- . Bimonthly.

BIBLIOGRAPHIES

ARCHITECTS AND ENGINEERS: ARTICLES FROM LAW JOURNALS. Mary A. Vance. Vance Bibliographies, P.O. Box 229, 112 North Charter Street, Monticello, Illinois 61856. 1986.

ENTERTAINMENT LAW
See also: AUTHORS AND PUBLISHERS; COPYRIGHT; SPORTS LAW

LOOSELEAF SERVICES AND REPORTERS

ENTERTAINMENT INDUSTRY CONTRACTS: NEGOTIATING AND DRAFTING GUIDE. Matthew Bender and Company, Incorporated, 11 Penn Plaza, New York, New York 10001. 1986- . (Periodic Supplements).

ENTERTAINMENT LAW. Melvin Simensky and Thomas Selz. Shepard's/McGraw-Hill, P.O. Box 1235, Colorado Springs, Colorado 80901. 1983- . (Annual Supplements).

LAW OF PROFESSIONAL AND AMATEUR SPORTS. Clark Boardman Company, Limited, 435 Hudson Street, New York, New York 10014. 1988- .

LINDEY ON ENTERTAINMENT PUBLISHING AND THE ARTS. Second Edition. Alexander Lindey. Clark Boardman Company, Limited, 435 Hudson Street, New York, New York 10014. 1980- .

THE MOTION PICTURE AND TELEVISION BUSINESS: CONTRACTS AND PRACTICES. Entertainment Business Publishing Company, 8530 Wilshire Boulevard, Beverly Hills, California 90211. 1985- .

HANDBOOKS, MANUALS, FORMBOOKS

ENTERTAINMENT, PUBLISHING AND THE ARTS HANDBOOK. John D. Viera and Robert Thorne. Clark Boardman Company, Limited, 435 Hudson Street, New York, New York 10014. 1989.

TEXTBOOKS AND GENERAL WORKS

AGENTS OF OPPORTUNITY: SPORTS AGENTS AND CORRUPTION IN COLLEGIATE SPORTS. Kenneth L. Shropshire. University of Pennsylvania Press, Blockley Hall, 418 Service Drive, Philadelphia, Pennsylvania 19104. 1990.

BEHIND THE SCENES: PRACTICAL ENTERTAINMENT LAW. Michael I. Rudell. Law and Business, Incorporated, 855 Valley Road, Clifton, New Jersey 07013. 1984.

THE BUSINESS AND LEGAL ASPECTS OF REPRESENTING TALENT IN THE ENTERTAINMENT INDUSTRY. University of California-Los Angeles Entertainment Symposiums, Los Angeles, California 90024. 1984.

ESSENTIALS OF AMATEUR SPORTS LAW. Glenn M. Wong. Auburn House Publishing Company, Greenwood Publishing Group, Incorporated, 88 Post Road West, P.O. Box 5007, Westport, Connecticut 06881. 1988.

FUNDAMENTALS OF SPORTS LAW. Walter T. Champion. Lawyers Cooperative Publishing Company, Aqueduct Building, Rochester, New York 14694. 1990.

INTERNATIONAL SPORTS LAW. James A.R. Nafziger. Transnational Publishers, P.O. Box 7282, Ardsley-on-Hudson, New York 10503. 1988.

LAW AND BUSINESS OF THE ENTERTAINMENT INDUSTRIES. Donald E. Biederman. Auburn House Publishing Company, Greenwood Publishing Group, Incorporated, 88 Post Road West, P.O. Box 5007, Westport, Connecticut 06881. 1987.

LEGAL LIABILITY AND RISK MANAGEMENT FOR PUBLIC AND PRIVATE ENTITIES: SPORT AND PHYSICAL EDUCATION, LEISURE SERVICES, RECREATION AND PARKS, CAMPING AND ADVENTURE ACTIVITIES. Betty Van der Smissen. Anderson Publishing Company, 2035 Reading Road, Cincinnati, Ohio 45202. 1990.

MEDICINE, SPORT AND THE LAW. Simon D.W. Payne. Blackwell Scientific Publications, Incorporated, 3 Cambridge Center, Cambridge, Massachusetts 02142. 1990.

PERFORMING ARTS MANAGEMENT AND LAW. Joseph Taubman. Law Arts Publishers, Incorporated, 159 Fifty-third Street, #14F, New York, New York 10019. 1978- .

PROFESSIONAL SPORTS AND ANTITRUST. Warren Freedman. Quorum Books, Greenwood Publishing Group, Incorporated, 88 Post Road West, P.O. Box 5007, Westport, Connecticut 06881. 1987.

REGULATING VIDEOGAMES. Martin Jaffe. American Planning Association, 1776 Massachusetts Avenue, Northwest, Washington, D.C. 20036. 1982.

THE SPORTS INDUSTRY AND COLLECTIVE BARGAINING. Second Edition. Paul D. Staudohar. ILR Press, New York State School of Industrial and Labor Relations, Cornell University, Ithaca, New York. 1989.

ENTERTAINMENT LAW

TAX AND FINANCIAL PLANNING FOR SPORTSMEN AND ENTERTAINERS. Richard Baldwin and Richard Harvey. Butterworth Legal Publishers, 90 Stiles Road, Salem, New Hampshire 03079. 1987.

ANNUALS AND SURVEYS

COUNSELING CLIENTS IN THE ENTERTAINMENT INDUSTRY. Practising Law Institute, 810 Seventh Avenue, New York, New York 10019. Annual.

LAW REVIEWS AND PERIODICALS

CARDOZO ARTS AND ENTERTAINMENT LAW JOURNAL. Benjamin N. Cardozo School of Law, Yeshiva University, 55 Fifth Avenue, New York, New York 10003. Biannual.

COLUMBIA-VLA JOURNAL OF THE LAW AND ARTS. Columbia University School of Law and the Volunteer Lawyers for the Arts, 1285 Avenue of the Americas, Suite 300, New York, New York 10019. Quarterly.

COMM/ENT: HASTINGS JOURNAL OF COMMUNICATIONS AND ENTERTAINMENT LAW. Hastings College of Law, 200 McAllister Street, San Francisco, California 94102. Quarterly.

LOYOLA ENTERTAINMENT LAW JOURNAL. Loyola Law School of Los Angeles, 1441 West Olympia Boulevard, Los Angeles, California 90015.

NEWSLETTERS AND NEWSPAPERS

THE E.A.S.L. The Florida Bar, Entertainment, Arts and Sports Law Section, 650 Apalachee Parkway, Tallahassee, Florida 32399. Quarterly.

THE ENTERTAINMENT AND SPORTS LAWYER. American Bar Association, Forum Committee on the Entertainment and Sports Industries, 750 North Lake Shore Drive, Chicago, Illinois 60611. Quarterly.

ENTERTAINMENT, ARTS AND SPORTS LAW SECTION NEWSLETTER. New York Bar Association, 1 Elk Street, Albany, New York 12207. Quarterly.

ENTERTAINMENT LAW AND FINANCE. Leader Publications, 111 Eighth Avenue, New York, New York 10011. Monthly.

ENTERTAINMENT LAW REPORTER. Entertainment Law Reporter Publishing Company, 2210 Wilshire Boulevard, Suite 311, Santa Monica, California 90403. Monthly.

ENTERTAINMENT LITIGATION REPORTER. Andrews Publications, Incorporated, 1646 West Chester Pike, Westtown, Pennsylvania 19395. Semimonthly.

BIBLIOGRAPHIES

ENTERTAINMENT AND SPORTS LAW BIBLIOGRAPHY: A COMPREHENSIVE BIBLIOGRAPHY OF LAW RELATED MATERIALS ON SPORTS, MOTION PICTURES, MUSIC AND THE RIGHT OF PUBLICITY. American Bar Association Forum Committee on the Entertainment and Sports Industries, 750 North Lake Shore Drive, Chicago, Illinois 60611. 1986.

ASSOCIATIONS AND PROFESSIONAL SOCIETIES

AMERICAN ARTS ALLIANCE. 1319 F Street, Northwest, Suite 307, Washington, D.C. 20004. (202) 737-1727.

AMERICAN COUNCIL FOR THE ARTS. 1285 Avenue of the Americas, Third Floor, Area M, New York, New York 10019. (212) 245-4510.

BLACK ENTERTAINMENT AND SPORTS LAWYERS ASSOCIATION. 111 Broadway, Seventh Floor, New York, New York 10006. (212) 587-0300.

VOLUNTEER LAWYERS FOR THE ARTS. 1285 Avenue of the Americas, Suite 300, New York, New York 10019. (212) 977-9270.

RESEARCH CENTERS, INSTITUTES, CLEARINGHOUSES

ENTERTAINMENT LAW INSTITUTE. University of Southern California Law Center and the Beverly Hills Bar Association. University of California at Los Angeles, Los Angeles, California 90024. (213) 553-6644.

LABOR HERITAGE FOUNDATION. 815 Sixteenth Street, Northwest, Suite 301, Washington, D.C. 20006. (202) 842-880.

NATIONAL ENDOWMENT FOR THE ARTS. 1100 Pennsylvania Avenue, Northwest, Washington, D.C. 20506. (202) 682-5400.

ENTRAPMENT

TEXTBOOKS AND GENERAL WORKS

ENTRAPMENT AND THE FEDERAL COURTS. Michael Callahan. U.S. Department of Justice, Federal Bureau of Investigation, Washington, D.C. 1984.

THE ENTRAPMENT DEFENSE. Paul Marcus. Michie Company, P.O. Box 7587, Charlottesville, Virginia 22906. 1989.

ENTRAPMENT IN CANADIAN CRIMINAL LAW. Michael I. Stober. Carswell Company, Limited, 2330 Midland Avenue, Ontario, Canada M1S 1P7. 1985.

AUDIOVISUALS

POLITICS OF THE ORIGINAL SIN - ENTRAPMENT, TEMPTATION, AND THE CONSTITUTION. Pacifica Tape Library, 5316 Venice Boulevard, Los Angeles, California 90019. Audiotape.

ENVIRONMENTAL LAW
See also: CHEMICAL INDUSTRY; ENERGY DEPARTMENT; ENVIRONMENTAL PROTECTION AGENCY; FORESTS AND FORESTRY; HAZARDOUS SUBSTANCES

STATUTES, CODES, STANDARDS, UNIFORM LAWS

ENVIRONMENTAL STATUTES. Government Institutes, Incorporated, 966 Hungerford Drive, Rockville, Maryland 20850. 1989.

INTERNATIONAL PROTECTION OF THE ENVIRONMENT: TREATIES AND RELATED DOCUMENTS, SECOND SERIES. Oceana Publications, 75 Main Street, Dobbs Ferry, New York 10522. 1990- .

A LEGISLATIVE HISTORY OF THE SUPERFUND AMENDMENTS AND REAUTHORIZATION ACT OF 1986 (PUBLIC LAW 99-499): TOGETHER WITH A SECTION-BY-SECTION INDEX. Superintendent of Documents, United States Government Printing Office, Washington, D.C. 20402. 1990.

SELECTED ENVIRONMENTAL LAW STATUTES. West Publishing Company, 50 West Kellogg Boulevard, St.Paul, Minnesota 55164. 1989.

LOOSELEAF SERVICES AND REPORTERS

AIR AND WATER POLLUTION CONTROL. The Bureau of National Affairs, Incorporated, 1231 Twenty-fifth Street, Northwest, Washington, D.C. 20037. 1986- . (Biweekly Supplements).

ENVIRONMENT REPORTER. The Bureau of National Affairs, Incorporated, 1231 Twenty-fifth Street, Northwest, Washington, D.C. 20037. 1970- .

ENVIRONMENTAL LAW REPORTER. Phillip D. Reed, Editor. Environmental Law Institute, 1616 P Street, Northwest, Suite 200, Washington, D.C. 20036. 1970- . (Monthly Supplements).

ENVIRONMENTAL REGULATION OF LAND USE. Linda A. Malone. Clark Boardman Company, Limited, 435 Hudson Street, New York, New York 10014. 1990- .

ENVIRONMENTAL REGULATION OF REAL PROPERTY. Nicholas A. Robinson. Law Journal Seminars-Press, Incorporated, 111 Eighth Avenue, Suite 900, New York, New York 10011. 1982- .

FEDERAL ENVIRONMENTAL REGULATION. John H. Davidson. Butterworth Legal Publishers, 90 Stiles Road, Salem, New Hampshire 03079. 1989- .

INTERNATIONAL ENVIRONMENT REPORTER. The Bureau of National Affairs, Incorporated, 1231 Twenty-fifth Street, Northwest, Washington, D.C. 20037. 1978- . (Monthly Supplements).

LAW OF ENVIRONMENTAL PROTECTION. Clark Boardman Company, Limited, 435 Hudson Street, New York, New York 10014. 1987.

MARINE POLLUTION AND THE LAW OF THE SEA. John Warren Kindt. William S. Hein and Company, 1285 Main Street, Buffalo, New York 14209. 1988- .

NEPA LAW AND LITIGATION: THE NATIONAL ENVIRONMENTAL POLICY ACT. Daniel R. Mandelker. Callaghan and Company, 155 Pfingsten Road, Deerfield, Illinois 60015. 1984- .

NOISE REGULATION REPORTER. The Bureau of National Affairs, Incorporated, 1231 Twenty-fifth Street, Northwest, Washington, D.C. 20037. 1974- . (Biweekly Supplements).

PESTICIDES GUIDE. J.J. Keller and Associates. 145 Wisconsin Avenue, Neenah, Wisconsin 54957. 1979- . (Semiannual Supplements).

SEWAGE TREATMENT CONSTRUCTION GRANTS MANUAL. The Bureau of National Affairs, Incorporated, 1231 Twenty-fifth Street, Northwest, Washington, D.C. 20037. 1976- . (Monthly Supplements).

STATE ENVIRONMENTAL LAW. Daniel P. Selmi. Clark Boardman Company, Limited, 435 Hudson Street, New York, New York 10014. 1989.

TREATISE ON ENVIRONMENTAL LAW. Frank P. Grad. Matthew Bender and Company, Incorporated, 11 Penn Plaza, New York, New York 10001. 1973- . (Annual Supplements).

HANDBOOKS, MANUALS, FORMBOOKS

THE ENVIRONMENTAL HANDBOOK FOR PROPERTY TRANSFER AND FINANCING. Michael K. Prescott and Douglas S. Brossman. Lewis Publishers, P.O. Drawer 519, 121 South Main Street, Chelsea, Michigan 48118. 1990.

ENVIRONMENTAL LAW HANDBOOK. Eleventh Edition. Government Institutes, Incorporated, 966 Hungerford Drive, Suite 24, Rockville, Maryland 20850. 1991.

GUIDE TO STATE ENVIRONMENTAL PROGRAMS. Second Edition. Deborah Hitchcock Jessup. Bureau of National Affairs, Incorporated, 1231 Twenty-fifth Street, Northwest, Washington, D.C. 20037. 1990.

GUIDE TO THE NATIONAL ENVIRONMENTAL POLICY ACT: INTERPRETATIONS, APPLICATIONS, AND COMPLIANCE. Valerie M. Fogelman. Quorum Books, Greenwood Publishing Group, Incorporated, 88 Post Road West, P.O. Box 5007, Westport, Connecticut 06881. 1990.

MANAGING NATIONAL PARK SYSTEM RESOURCES: A HANDBOOK ON LEGAL DUTIES, OPPORTUNITIES AND TOOLS. Conservation Foundation, 1250 Twenty-fourth Street, Northwest, Washington, D.C. 20037. 1990.

A PRACTICAL GUIDE TO ENVIRONMENTAL LAW. David Sive. American Law Institute-American Bar Association, 4025 Chestnut Street, Philadelphia, Pennsylvania 19104. 1987.

UNDERSTANDING U.S. AND EUROPEAN ENVIRONMENTAL LAW: A PRACTITIONER'S GUIDE. Turner T. Smith. Graham and Trotman, Norwell, Massachusetts. 1989.

WHAT TO DO WHEN THE CLIENT CALLS: A SUGGESTED CHECKLIST OF ITEMS TO BE COVERED DURING THE INITIAL CONFERENCE BETWEEN A PRACTITIONER AND A CLIENT WITH AN ENVIRONMENTAL PROBLEM. A Patrick Nucciarone. American Bar Association, Section of Natural Resources Law, 750 North Lake Shore Drive, Chicago, Illinois 60611. 1988.

TEXTBOOKS AND GENERAL WORKS

BIOTECHNOLOGY AND THE ENVIRONMENT: INTERNATIONAL REGULATION. Jeffrey N. Gibbs. Stockton Press, 15 East Twenty-sixth Street, New York, New York 10010. 1987.

CAREERS IN NATURAL RESOURCES AND ENVIRONMENTAL LAW. Percy R. Luney and William D. Henslee. American Bar Association, 750 North Lake Shore Drive, Chicago, Illinois 60611. 1987.

CITIZEN SUITS: PRIVATE ENFORCEMENT OF FEDERAL POLLUTION CONTROL LAWS. John Wiley and Sons, Incorporated, 605 Third Avenue, New York, New York 10158. 1987.

ECONOMICS OF THE ENVIRONMENT. Horst Siebert. Lexington Books, 125 Spring Street, Lexington, Massachusetts 02173. 1981.

THE ECONOMY OF THE EARTH: PHILOSOPHY, LAW, AND THE ENVIRONMENT. Mark Sagoff. Cambridge University Press, 40 West Twentieth Street, New York, New York 10011. 1988.

EFFICIENCY IN ENVIRONMENTAL REGULATION: A BENEFIT-COST ANALYSIS OF ALTERNATIVE APPROACHES. Ralph Andrew Luken. Kluwer Academic Publishers, 101 Philip Drive, Assinippi Park, Norwell, Massachusetts 02061. 1990.

ENVIRONMENT AND HEALTH. Congressional Quarterly, Incorporated. 1414 Twenty-second Street, Northwest, Washington, D.C. 20037. 1981.

ENVIRONMENT AND THE LAW. Second Edition. Irving J. Sloan. Oceana Publications, 75 Main Street, Dobbs Ferry, New York 10522. 1978.

ENVIRONMENTAL CONSULTATION. C. Wesley Morse. Praeger Publishers, One Madison Avenue, New York, New York 10010-3603. 1984.

ENVIRONMENTAL DISPUTE RESOLUTION. Lawrence S. Bacow and Michael Wheeler. Plenum Press, 233 Spring Street, New York, New York 10013. 1984.

ENVIRONMENTAL ECONOMICS AND POLICY. Paul B. Downing. Little, Brown and Company, 34 Beacon Street, Boston, Massachusetts 02108. 1984.

ENVIRONMENTAL HEALTH LAW. Sanford H. Brown and Theodore R. Forrest, Jr. Praeger Publishers, One Madison Avenue, New York, New York 10010-3603. 1984.

ENVIRONMENTAL JUSTICE. Peter S. Wenz. State University of New York Press, State University Plaza, Albany, New York 12246. 1988.

ENVIRONMENTAL LAW. Third Edition. Frank P. Grad. Matthew Bender and Company, Incorporated, 11 Penn Plaza, New York, New York 10001. 1985- .

ENVIRONMENTAL LAW. William H. Rodgers, Jr. West Publishing Company, P.O. Box 64526, 50 West Kellogg Boulevard, St. Paul, Minnesota 55164-0526. 1977. (1984 Pocket Part).

ENVIRONMENTAL LAW: AIR AND WATER. William H. Rodgers, Jr. West Publishing Company, P.O. Box 64526, 50 West Kellogg Boulevard, St. Paul, Minnesota 55164-0526. 1986.

ENVIRONMENTAL LAW IN A NUTSHELL. Second Edition. Roger W. Findley. West Publishing Company, P.O. Box 64526, 50 West Kellogg Boulevard, St. Paul, Minnesota 55164-0526. 1988.

ENVIRONMENTAL POLICY. George S. Tolley, Phillip E. Graves and Glenn C. Blomquist. Ballinger Division, HarperCollins Publishers, 10 East Fifty-third Street, New York, New York 10022. 1981-85.

ENVIRONMENTAL POLICY IN THE 1990s. Norman J. Vig and Michael E. Kraft. Congressional Quarterly, Incorporated, 1414 Twenty-second Street, Northwest, Washington, D.C. 20037. 1990.

ENVIRONMENTAL POLICY UNDER REAGAN'S EXECUTIVE ORDER: THE ROLE OF BENEFIT COST ANALYSIS. V. Kerry Smith, Editor. University of North Carolina Press, P.O. Box 2288, Chapel Hill, North Carolina 27515-2288. 1984.

ENVIRONMENTAL POLITICS AND POLICY. Second Edition. Walter A. Rosenbaum. Congressional Quarterly, Incorporated, 1414 Twenty-second Street, Northwest, Washington, D.C. 20037. 1990.

ENVIRONMENTAL PROTECTION AND SUSTAINABLE DEVELOPMENT: LEGAL PRINCIPLES AND RECOMMENDATIONS. R.D. Munro and J.G. Lammers. Martinus Nijhoff, Kluwer Academic Publishers, 101 Philip Drive, Assinippi Park, Norwell, Massachusetts 02061. 1987.

ENVIRONMENTAL PROTECTION: THE LEGAL FRAMEWORK. Frank F. Skillern. Shepard's/McGraw-Hill, P.O. Box 1235, Colorado Springs, Colorado 80901. 1981- . (Annual Supplements).

ENVIRONMENTAL RIGHTS AND REMEDIES. Victor J. Yannacone, Jr., Bernard S. Cohen and Steven G. Davison. Lawyers Cooperative Publishing Company, One Graves Street, Rochester, New York 14694. 1971- . (Periodic Supplements).

FEDERAL STATUTES ON ENVIRONMENTAL PROTECTION: REGULATION IN THE PUBLIC INTEREST. Warren Freedman. Quorum Books, Greenwood Publishing Group, Incorporated, 88 Post Road West, P.O. Box 5007, Westport, Connecticut 06881. 1987.

GREEN JUSTICE: THE ENVIRONMENT AND THE COURTS. Thomas More Hoban. Westview Press, Incorporated, 5500 Central Avenue, Boulder, Colorado 80301. 1987.

GUIDE TO FEDERAL ENVIRONMENTAL LAW. Robert V. Zener. Practising Law Institute, 810 Seventh Avenue, New York, New York 10019. 1981.

ICONS AND ALIENS: LAW, AESTHETICS, AND ENVIRONMENTAL CHANGE. John J. Costonis. University of Illinois Press, 54 East Gregory Drive, Champaign, Illinois 61820. 1989.

INTERNATIONAL ENVIRONMENTAL DIPLOMACY: THE MANAGEMENT AND RESOLUTION OF TRANSFRONTIER ENVIRONMENTAL PROBLEMS. John E. Carroll. Cambridge University Press, 40 West Twentieth Street, New York, New York 10011. 1988.

INTERNATIONAL LAW AND POLLUTION. University of Pennsylvania Press, Blockley Hall, 418 Service Drive, Philadelphia, Pennsylvania 19104. 1991.

LESSONS LEARNED IN GLOBAL ENVIRONMENTAL GOVERNANCE. Peter H. Sand. World Resources Institute, 1709 New York Avenue, Northwest, Washington, D.C. 20006. 1990.

THE LIMITS OF LAW: THE PUBLIC REGULATION OF PRIVATE POLLUTION. Peter C. Yeager. Cambridge University Press, 40 West Twentieth Street, New York, New York 10011. 1991.

MAKING BUREAUCRACIES THINK: THE ENVIRONMENTAL IMPACT STATEMENT STRATEGY OF ADMINISTRATIVE REFORM. Serge Taylor. Stanford University Press, Stanford, California 94305. 1984.

PUBLIC POLICIES FOR ENVIRONMENTAL PROTECTION. Paul R. Portney and Roger C. Dower. Resources for the Future, Incorporated, 1616 P Street, Northwest, Washington, D.C. 20036. 1990.

RESOLVING ENVIRONMENTAL REGULATORY DISPUTES. Lawrence Susskind, Lawrence S. Bacow and Michael Wheeler, Editors. Schenkman Books, Incorporated, Main Street, Rochester, Vermont 05767. 1983.

A SEASON OF SPOILS: THE REAGAN ADMINISTRATION'S ATTACK ON THE ENVIRONMENT. Jonathan Lash, Katherine Gillman and David Sheridan. Pantheon Books, 201 East Fiftieth Street, New York, New York 10022. 1984.

STATE OF THE ENVIRONMENT: AN ASSESSMENT AT MID-DECADE: A REPORT FROM THE CONSERVATION FOUNDATION. Conservation Foundation, 1250 Twenty-fourth Street, Northwest, Washington, D.C. 20037. 1984.

STATE RESPONSIBILITY AND THE MARINE ENVIRONMENT: THE RULES OF DECISION. Brian D. Smith. Oxford University Press, 200 Madison Avenue, New York, New York 10016. 1988.

TARGETING ECONOMIC INCENTIVES FOR ENVIRONMENTAL PROTECTION. Albert L. Nichols. MIT Press, 55 Hayward Street, Cambridge, Massachusetts 02142. 1984.

TOXIC SUBSTANCES CONTROLS GUIDE: FEDERAL REGULATION OF CHEMICALS IN THE ENVIRONMENT. Mary Devine Worobec. Bureau of National Affairs, Incorporated, 1231 Twenty-fifth Street, Northwest, Washington, D.C. 20037. 1989.

TRANSBOUNDARY RESOURCES LAW. Westview Press, Incorporated, 5500 Central Avenue, Boulder, Colorado 80301. 1987.

WHEN VALUES CONFLICT: ESSAYS ON ENVIRONMENTAL ANALYSIS, DISCOURSE AND DECISION. Laurence H. Tribe. Ballinger Division, HarperCollins Publishers, 10 East Fifty-third Street, New York, New York 10022. 1976.

ENCYCLOPEDIAS AND DICTIONARIES

THE ENVIRONMENTAL DICTIONARY. James J. King. Executive Enterprises Publications Company, 22 West Twenty-first Street, New York, New York 10010-6904. 1989.

ENVIRONMENTAL GLOSSARY. Fourth Edition. William Frick, Editor. Government Institutes, Incorporated, 966 Hungerford Drive, Rockville, Maryland 20850. 1986.

DIGESTS, INDEXES, ABSTRACTS, CITATORS

EPA INDEX: A KEY TO U.S. ENVIRONMENTAL PROTECTION AGENCY REPORTS AND SUPERINTENDENT OF DOCUMENTS AND NTIS NUMBERS. Cynthia E. Bower and Mary L. Rhoads, Editors. Oryx Press, 2214 North Central Avenue, Phoenix, Arizona 85004-1483. 1983.

HOFSTRA ENVIRONMENTAL LAW DIGEST: COMPILATION OF RECENT ENVIRONMENTAL CASES. Environmental Law Society of Hofstra University School of Law, Hempstead, New York. Semiannual.

LAW REVIEWS AND PERIODICALS

BOSTON COLLEGE ENVIRONMENTAL AFFAIRS LAW REVIEW. Boston College Law School, 885 Centre Street, Newton Centre, Massachusetts 02159. Quarterly.

COLUMBIA JOURNAL OF ENVIRONMENTAL LAW. Columbia University, School of Law, 435 One Hundred Sixteenth Street, New York, New York 10027. Semiannually.

ECOLOGY LAW QUARTERLY. University of California at Berkeley, Boalt Hall School of Law, Berkeley, California 94720. Quarterly.

ENVIRONMENTAL LAW. Lewis and Clark Law School, 10015 Southwest Terwilliger Boulevard, Portland, Oregon 97219. Quarterly.

HARVARD ENVIRONMENTAL LAW REVIEW. Harvard Law School, Publications Center, Cambridge, Massachusetts 02138. Semiannually.

JOURNAL OF LAND USE AND ENVIRONMENTAL LAW. Florida State University, College of Law, Tallahassee, Florida 32306. Semiannually.

LAND AND WATER LAW REVIEW. University of Wyoming, College of Law, University Station, Box 3035, Laramie, Wyoming 82071. Semiannually.

LAND USE AND ENVIRONMENTAL LAW REVIEW. Clark Boardman Company, Limited, 435 Hudson Street, New York, New York 10014. Annual.

LEGAL JOURNAL ON ENVIRONMENTAL LAW. Boston College, Environmental Affairs Law Review, 885 Centre Street, Newton, Massachusetts 02159. Quarterly.

NATURAL RESOURCES JOURNAL. University of New Mexico, School of Law, 1117 Stanford, Northeast, Albuquerque, New Mexico 87131. Quarterly.

OCEAN DEVELOPMENT AND INTERNATIONAL LAW. Crane, Russak and Company, 3 East Forty-fourth Street, New York, New York 10017. Quarterly.

PUBLIC UTILITIES FORTNIGHTLY. Public Utilities Reports, Incorporated, 1700 North Moore Street, Suite 2100, Arlington, Virginia 22209. Biweekly.

NEWSLETTERS AND NEWSPAPERS

AIR AND WATER POLLUTION CONTROL. The Bureau of National Affairs, Incorporated, 1231 Twenty-fifth Street, Northwest, Washington, D.C. 20037. Biweekly.

AIR TOXICS REPORT. Business Publishers, Incorporated, 951 Pershing Drive, Silver Spring, Maryland 20910. Monthly.

AIR/WATER POLLUTION REPORT. Business Publishers, Incorporated. 951 Pershing Drive, Silver Spring, Maryland 20910. Weekly.

AMSA LAW DIGEST. Association of Metropolitan Sewerage Agencies, 1000 Connecticut Avenue, Northwest, Suite 1006, Washington, D.C. 20036. Quarterly.

THE BACK FORTY. Land Conservation Law Institute, c/o The Land Trust Alliance, 900 Seventeenth Street, Northwest, Suite 410, Washington, D.C. 20006. Monthly.

BNA'S NATIONAL ENVIRONMENT WATCH. The Bureau of National Affairs, Incorporated, 1231 Twenty-fifth Street, Northwest, Washington, D.C. 20037. Biweekly.

BUSINESS AND THE ENVIRONMENT. Cutter Information Corporation, 1100 Massachusetts Avenue, Arlington, Massachusetts 02174. Semimonthly.

CLEAN WATER REPORT. Business Publishers, Incorporated, 951 Pershing Drive, Silver Spring, Maryland 20910. Biweekly.

COMMUNITY RIGHT-TO-KNOW NEWS. Thompson Publishing Group, 1725 K Street, Northwest, Suite 200, Washington, D.C. 20006. Semimonthly.

CONGRESSIONAL REPORT, SCIENCE, ENERGY AND ENVIRONMENT. Malone Congressional Reports, 4301 Tujunga Avenue, Studio City, California 91604. Biweekly.

THE DIGEST OF ENVIRONMENTAL LAW OF REAL PROPERTY. National Property Law Digests, Incorporated, 7200 Wisconsin Avenue, Suite 314, Bethesda, Maryland 20814. Monthly.

ECOLOGICAL ILLNESS LAW REPORT. Ecological Illness Law Report, P.O. Box 1796, Evanston, Illinois 60204. Quarterly.

ENVIRONMENT WEEK. King Communications Group, Incorporated, 627 National Press Building, Washington, D.C. 20046. Weekly.

THE ENVIRONMENTAL COUNSELOR. Business Laws, Incorporated, 11630 Chillicothe Road, Chesterland, Ohio 44026. Monthly.

ENVIRONMENTAL FORUM. Environmental Law Institute, 1616 P Street, Northwest, Second Floor, Washington, D.C. 20036. Bimonthly.

ENVIRONMENTAL HAZARDS. Prentice-Hall Law and Business, 270 Sylvan Avenue, Englewood Cliffs, New Jersey 07632. Monthly.

ENVIRONMENTAL HEALTH LETTER. Environews Incorporated, 1331 Pennsylvania Avenue, Northwest, Suite 509, Washington, D.C. 20004. 24 issues per year.

ENVIRONMENTAL LAW. American Bar Association Standing Committee on Environmental Law, 1800 M Street, Northwest, Washington, D.C. 20036. Quarterly.

ENVIRONMENTAL LAW IN NEW YORK. Berle, Kass and Case, 45 Rockefeller Plaza, New York, New York 10111. Bimonthly.

ENVIRONMENTAL LAW JOURNAL OF OHIO. Banks-Baldwin Law Publishing Company, University Center, P.O. Box 1974, Cleveland, Ohio 44106. Bimonthly.

ENVIRONMENTAL MANAGEMENT REVIEW. Government Institutes, Incorporated, 966 Hungerford Drive, Suite 24, Rockville, Maryland 20850. Quarterly.

ENVIRONMENTAL MANAGER'S COMPLIANCE ADVISOR. Business and Legal Reports, 64 Wall Street, Madison, Connecticut 06443. Semimonthly.

ENVIRONMENTAL POLICY ALERT. Inside Washington Publishers, P.O. Box 7167, Ben Franklin Station, Washington, D.C. 20044. Biweekly.

GLOBAL ENVIRONMENTAL CHANGE REPORT. Cutter Information Corporation, 1100 Massachusetts Avenue, Arlington, Massachusetts 02174. Semimonthly.

GREENHOUSE EFFECT REPORT. Business Publishers, Incorporated, 951 Pershing Drive, Silver Spring, Maryland 20910. Monthly.

GROUND WATER MONITOR. Business Publishers, Incorporated, 951 Pershing Drive, Silver Spring, Maryland 20910. Monthly.

GROUNDWATER POLLUTION NEWS. Buraff Publications, Incorporated, 1350 Connecticut Avenue, Northwest, Suite 1000, Washington, D.C. 20036. Semimonthly.

HAZARDOUS WASTE LITIGATION REPORTER. Andrews Publications, 1646 West Chester Pike, Westtown, Pennsylvania 19395. Semimonthly.

IN BRIEF. Sierra Club Legal Defense Fund, 2044 Fillmore Street, San Francisco, California 94115. Quarterly.

INDOOR POLLUTION LAW REPORT. Leader Publications, 111 Eighth Avenue, New York, New York 10011. Monthly.

INDOOR POLLUTION LITIGATION REPORTER. Andrews Publications, 1646 West Chester Pike, Westtown, Pennsylvania 19395. Semimonthly.

INDOOR POLLUTION NEWS. Buraff Publications, Incorporated, 1350 Connecticut Avenue, Northwest, Suite 1000, Washington, D.C. 20036. Semimonthly.

INSIDE EPA WEEKLY REPORT. Inside Washington Publishers, P.O. Box 7167, Ben Franklin Station, Washington, D.C. 20044. Weekly.

INSIDE EPA'S SUPERFUND REPORT. Inside Washington Publishers, P.O. Box 7167, Ben Franklin Station, Washington, D.C. 20044. Biweekly.

MASSACHUSETTS WASTE MANAGEMENT REPORT. Paradigm Newsletters, P.O. Box 1450, Cambridge, Massachusetts 02238. Monthly.

MEALEY'S LITIGATION REPORT: SUPERFUND. Mealey Publications, Incorporated, P.O. Box 446, Wayne, Pennsylvania 19087. Semimonthly.

MIDWEST ENVIRONMENTAL LAW LETTER. M. Lee Smith Publishers and Printers, 162 Fourth Avenue, North, Nashville, Tennessee 37219. Monthly.

NATIONAL ENVIRONMENTAL ENFORCEMENT JOURNAL. National Association of Attorneys-General, 444 North Capital Street, Suite 403, Washington D.C. 20001. Monthly.

NATIONAL WETLANDS NEWSLETTER. Environmental Law Institute, 1616 P Street, Northwest, Second Floor, Washington, D.C. 20036. Bimonthly.

NEW JERSEY JOURNAL OF ENVIRONMENTAL LITIGATION. McGuire Publications, 219-P Berlin Road, Cherry Hill, New Jersey 08034. Semimonthly.

N.R.D.C. NEWSLINE. Natural Resources Defense Council, 40 West Twentieth Street, New York, New York 10011. Bimonthly.

PENNSYLVANIA ENVIRONMENTAL LAW LETTER. Andrews Publications, 1646 West Chester Pike, Westtown, Pennsylvania 19395. Monthly.

PENNSYLVANIA JOURNAL OF ENVIRONMENTAL LITIGATION. McGuire Publications, P.O. Box 315, Springfield, Pennsylvania 19064. Semimonthly.

PESTICIDE AND TOXIC CHEMICAL NEWS. Food Chemical News, Incorporated, 1101 Pennsylvania Avenue, Southeast, Washington, D.C. 20003. Weekly.

REAL ESTATE/ENVIRONMENTAL LIABILITY NEWS. Buraff Publications, Incorporated, 1350 Connecticut Avenue, Northwest, Suite 1000, Washington, D.C. 20036. Semimonthly.

SUPERFUND. Pasha Publications, Incorporated, 1401 Wilson Boulevard, Suite 900, Arlington, Virginia 22209. Semimonthly.

UTILITIES INDUSTRY LITIGATION REPORTER. Andrews Publications, 1646 West Chester Pike, Westtown, Pennsylvania 19395. Semimonthly.

WASHINGTON ENVIRONMENTAL PROTECTION REPORT. Callaghan Publications, P.O. Box 3751, Washington, D.C. 20007. Semimonthly.

BIBLIOGRAPHIES

BIBLIOGRAPHY OF THE ENVIRONMENTAL LAW COLLECTION IN THE PACE UNIVERSITY SCHOOL OF LAW LIBRARY. Nicholas A. Robinson. Associated Faculty Press, 19 West Thirty-sixth Street, New York, New York 10018. 1984.

THE EFFECTIVENESS OF NEPA: REACTIONS TO ENVIRONMENTAL IMPACT REVIEW: A SELECTED BIBLIOGRAPHY. Sanford F. Cohen. Vance Bibliographies, P.O. Box 229, 112 North Charter Street, Monticello, Illinois 61856. 1980.

ENVIRONMENTAL LAW: A GUIDE TO INFORMATION SOURCES. Mortimer D. Schwartz. Gale Research, Incorporated, 835 Penobscot Building, Detroit, Michigan 48226. 1977.

ENVIRONMENTAL POLITICS: AN ANNOTATED BIBLIOGRAPHY. Arn H. Pearson and Frederick H. Buttel. Vance Bibliographies, P.O. Box 229, 112 North Charter Street, Monticello, Illinois 61856. 1984.

EPA PUBLICATIONS BIBLIOGRAPHY. National Technical Information Service, 5285 Port Royal Road, Springfield, Virginia 22161. 1977-83.

LABOR AND THE ENVIRONMENT: AN ANALYSIS OF AND ANNOTATED BIBLIOGRAPHY ON WORKPLACE ENVIRONMENTAL QUALITY IN THE UNITED STATES. Frederick H. Buttel, Charles C. Geisler and Irving W. Wiswall. Greenwood Publishing Group, Incorporated, 88 Post Road West, P.O. Box 5007, Westport, Connecticut 06881. 1984.

POLICY STUDIES ENVIRONMENTAL AFFAIRS: A SELECTED BIBLIOGRAPHY. Robert Goehlert. Vance Bibliographies, P.O. Box 229, 112 North Charter Street, Monticello, Illinois 61856. 1984.

WORLD ENVIRONMENT LAW BIBLIOGRAPHY: NON-PERIODICAL LITERATURE IN LAW AND THE SOCIAL SCIENCES PUBLISHED SINCE 1970 IN VARIOUS LANGUAGES WITH SELECTED REVIEWS AND ANNOTATIONS FROM PERIODICALS. Virginia Evans Templeton. Fred B. Rothman and Company, 10368 West Centennial Road, Littleton, Colorado 80127. 1987.

DIRECTORIES

DIRECTORY OF STATE ENVIRONMENTAL AGENCIES. Second Edition. Environmental Law Institute, 1616 P Street, Northwest, Washington, D.C. 20036. 1985.

ENVIRONMENTAL LAW INSTITUTE ASSOCIATES DIRECTORY. Environmental Law Institute, 1616 P Street, Northwest, Washington, D.C. 20036. 1984.

ASSOCIATIONS AND PROFESSIONAL SOCIETIES

EARTH FIRST! P.O. Box 5871, Tucson, Arizona 85703. (602) 622-1371.

ENVIRONMENTAL ACTION. 1525 New Hampshire Avenue, Northwest, Washington, D.C. 20036. (202) 745-4870.

ENVIRONMENTAL ACTION COALITION. 625 Broadway, Second Floor, New York, New York 10012. (212) 677-1601.

ENVIRONMENTAL COMPLIANCE INSTITUTE. Aetna Building, Suite 850, 2350 Lakeside Boulevard, Richardson, Texas 75082. (214) 644-8971.

ENVIRONMENTAL DEFENSE FUND. 257 Park Avenue, South, New York, New York 10010. (212) 505-2100.

GREENPEACE U.S.A. 1436 U Street, Northwest, Washington, D.C. 20009. (202) 462-1177.

HARVARD ENVIRONMENTAL LAW SOCIETY. Austin 201, Harvard Law School, Cambridge, Massachusetts 02138. (617) 495-3125.

NATURAL RESOURCES DEFENSE COUNCIL. 40 West Twentieth Street, New York, New York 10011. (212) 949-0049.

SIERRA CLUB. 730 Polk Street, San Francisco, California 94109. (415) 776-2211.

SIERRA CLUB LEGAL DEFENSE FUND. 2044 Fillmore Street, San Francisco, California 94115. (415) 567-6100.

STANDING COMMITTEE ON ENVIRONMENTAL LAW. American Bar Association, 1800 M Street, Northwest, Washington, D.C. 20036. (202) 331-2208.

THE WILDERNESS SOCIETY. 1400 I Street, Northwest, Washington, D.C. 20005. (202) 842-3400.

RESEARCH CENTERS, INSTITUTES, CLEARINGHOUSES

CITIZEN'S CLEARINGHOUSE FOR HAZARDOUS WASTES. P.O. Box 926, Arlington, Virginia 22216. (703) 276-7070.

CLEAN WATER FUND. c/o David Zwick, 317 Pennsylvania Avenue, Southeast, Washington, D.C. 20003. (202) 547-2312.

THE CONSERVATION FOUNDATION. 1250 Twenty-fourth Street, Northwest, Washington, D.C. 20037. (202) 293-4800.

ENVIRONMENTAL ACTION FOUNDATION. 1525 New Hampshire Avenue, Northwest, Washington, D.C. 20036. (202) 745-4870.

ENVIRONMENTAL CENTER. University of Hawaii at Manoa, 2550 Campus Road, Honolulu, Hawaii 96822. (808) 948-7361.

ENVIRONMENTAL LAW INSTITUTE. 1616 P Street, Northwest, Second Floor, Washington, D.C. 20036. (202) 328-5150.

ENVIRONMENTAL LIABILITY LAW PROGRAM. University of Houston, Law Center, 4800 Calhoun, Houston, Texas 77204. (713) 749-1393.

JOHN MUIR INSTITUTE FOR ENVIRONMENTAL STUDIES. 743 Wilson Street, Napa, California 94559. (707) 252-8333.

JOINT CENTER FOR ENVIRONMENTAL AND URBAN PROBLEMS. 220 Southeast Second Avenue, Fort Lauderdale, Florida 33301. (305) 355-5255.

KEYSTONE CENTER. P.O. Box 606, Keystone, Colorado 80435. (303) 468-5822.

MISSISSIPPI LAW RESEARCH INSTITUTE. University of Mississippi, Law Center, Room 518, University, Mississippi 38677. (601) 232-7775.

NATIONAL INSTITUTE FOR URBAN WILDLIFE. 10921 Trotting Ridge Way, Columbia, Maryland 21044. (301) 596-3311.

ROCKY MOUNTAIN MINERAL LAW FOUNDATION. Porter Administration Building, Third Floor, 7039 East Eighteenth Avenue, Denver, Colorado 80220. (303) 321-8100.

WILDERNESS INSTITUTE. University of Montana, Forestry Building, Room 207, Missoula, Montana 59812. (406) 243-5361.

ONLINE DATABASES

ASBESTOS CONTROL REPORT. Business Publishers, Incorporated, 951 Pershing Drive, Silver Spring, Maryland 20910.

BNA ENVIRONMENT DAILY. Bureau of National Affairs, Incorporated, BNA ONLINE, 1231 Twenty-fifth Street, Northwest, Washington, D.C. 20037.

ENVIROLINE. Bowker A and I Publishing, 245 West Seventeenth Street, New York, New York 10011.

ENVIRONET. ENSR Consulting and Engineering, 35 Nagog Park, Acton, Massachusetts 01720.

ENVIRONMENT REPORTER. Bureau of National Affairs, Incorporated, BNA ONLINE, 1231 Twenty-fifth Street, Northwest, Washington, D.C. 20037.

ENVIRONMENTAL HEALTH NEWS. Occupational Health Services, Incorporated, 450 Seventh Avenue, Suite 2407, New York, New York 10123.

ENVIRONMENTAL INFORMATION CENTER, INCORPORATED. Environment Information System, 48 West Thirty-eighth Street, New York, New York 10018.

ENVIRONMENTAL LAW REPORTER. Environmental Law Institute, 1616 P Street, Northwest, Suite 200, Washington, D.C. 20036.

FOCUS ON: GLOBAL CHANGE. Institute for Scientific Information, 3501 Market Street, Philadelphia, Pennsylvania 19104.

HAZARDOUS WASTE BIBLIOGRAPHIC DATA BASE. National Water Well Association, National Ground Water Information Center, 6375 Riverside Drive, Dublin, Ohio 43017.

LEXIS ENVIRONMENTAL LAW LIBRARY. Mead Data Central, P.O. Box 933, Dayton, Ohio 45401.

MEDICAL WASTE NEWS. Business Publishers, Incorporated, 951 Pershing Drive, Silver Spring, Maryland 20910.

PRESSNET ENVIRONMENTAL REPORTS. PressNet Systems, Incorporated, 400 East Pratt Street, Suite 842, Baltimore, Maryland 21202.

REPORT ON DEFENSE PLANT WASTES. Business Publishers, Incorporated, 951 Pershing Drive, Silver Spring, Maryland 20910.

SUPERFUND. Pasha Publications, 1401 Wilson Boulevard, Suite 900, Arlington, Virginia 22209.

WESTLAW ENVIRONMENTAL LAW LIBRARY. West Publishing Company, P.O. Box 64526, 50 West Kellogg Boulevard, St. Paul, Minnesota 55164-0526.

AUDIOVISUALS

ENVIRONMENTAL LAW FOR THE PRACTICING LAWYER. American Bar Association, 750 North Lake Shore Drive, Chicago, Illinois 60611. 1990. Videotape.

ENVIRONMENTAL PROTECTION AGENCY

STATUTES, CODES, STANDARDS, UNIFORM LAWS

CODE OF FEDERAL REGULATIONS, TITLE 40. Office of the Federal Register, National Archives and Records Administration. Superintendent of Documents, United States Government Printing Office, Washington, D.C. 20402. Annual. (Updated by use of monthly List of Sections Affected and daily Federal Register.)

HANDBOOKS, MANUALS, FORMBOOKS

ASBESTOS WASTE MANAGEMENT GUIDANCE: GENERATION, TRANSPORT, DISPOSAL. Environmental Protection Agency, Office of Solid Waste. Superintendent of Documents, United States Government Printing Office, Washington, D.C. 20402. 1985.

PERMIT APPLICANTS' GUIDANCE MANUAL FOR HAZARDOUS WASTE LAND TREATMENT, STORAGE, AND DISPOSAL FACILITIES, FINAL DRAFT. Arthur Day. Environmental Protection Agency, Office of Solid Waste and Emergency Response. Superintendent of Documents, United States Government Printing Office, Washington, D.C. 20402. 1984.

RESOURCE CONSERVATION AND RECOVERY ACT ORIENTATION MANUAL. Robert Knox. Environmental Protection Agency, Office of Solid Waste. Superintendent of Documents, United States Government Printing Office, Washington, D.C. 20402. 1990.

TEXTBOOKS AND GENERAL WORKS

BUREAUCRATIC POLITICS AND REGULATORY REFORM: THE EPA AND EMISSIONS TRADING. Brian J. Cook. Greenwood Publishing Group, Incorporated, 88 Post Road West, P.O. Box 5007, Westport, Connecticut 06881. 1988.

THE ENVIRONMENTAL PROTECTION AGENCY: ASKING THE WRONG QUESTIONS. Marc Karnis Landy, Marc J. Roberts and Stephen R. Thomas. Oxford University Press, 200 Madison Avenue, New York, New York 10016. 1990.

NATIONAL SURVEY OF HAZARDOUS WASTE GENERATORS AND TREATMENT, STORAGE AND DISPOSAL FACILITIES REGULATED UNDER RCRA IN 1981. Stephen Deitz. Environmental Protection Agency. Superintendent of Documents, United States Government Printing Office, Washington, D.C. 20402. 1984.

PROTECT AND ENHANCE: JURIDICAL DEMOCRACY AND THE PREVENTION OF SIGNIFICANT DETERIORATION OF AIR QUALITY. A. Stanley Meiburg. Garland Publishing, Incorporated, 136 Madison Avenue, New York, New York 10016. 1991.

QUALITY CRITERIA FOR WATER. Environmental Protection Agency, Office of Water and Hazardous Materials. Superintendent of Documents, United States Government Printing Office, Washington, D.C. 20402. 1976.

DIGESTS, INDEXES, ABSTRACTS, CITATORS

TOXIC SUBSTANCES CONTROL ACT (TSCA) CHEMICAL SUBSTANCE INVENTORY: 1985 EDITION. Environmental Protection Agency, Office of Toxic Substances. Superintendent of Documents, United States Government Printing Office, Washington, D.C. 20402. 1986.

LAW REVIEWS AND PERIODICALS

EPA JOURNAL. Environmental Protection Agency. Superintendent of Documents, United States Government Printing Office, Washington, D.C. 20402. Monthly.

RESEARCH CENTERS, INSTITUTES, CLEARINGHOUSES

UNITED STATES ENVIRONMENTAL PROTECTION AGENCY LAW LIBRARY. Waterside Mall, 401 M Street, Southwest, Washington, D.C. 20460. (202) 382-5930.

ONLINE DATABASES

LEXIS, ENVIRONMENTAL LAW LIBRARY. Mead Data Central, P.O. Box 933, Dayton, Ohio 45401.

WESTLAW, ENVIRONMENTAL LAW LIBRARY. West Publishing Company, P.O. Box 64526, 50 West Kellogg Boulevard, St. Paul, Minnesota 55164-0526.

EQUAL EMPLOYMENT OPPORTUNITY
See also: AGE DISCRIMINATION; AGED AND EMPLOYMENT; DISCRIMINATION, EMPLOYMENT; DISCRIMINATION, RACE; DISCRIMINATION, SEX; EQUAL EMPLOYMENT OPPORTUNITY COMMISSION

LOOSELEAF SERVICES AND REPORTERS

EEOC DECISIONS. Commerce Clearing House, Incorporated, 4025 West Peterson Avenue, Chicago, Illinois 60646. 1983- .

EQUAL EMPLOYMENT OPPORTUNITY

EMPLOYMENT DISCRIMINATION. Arthur Larson and Lex R. Larson. Matthew Bender and Company, Incorporated, 11 Penn Plaza, New York, New York 10001. 1975- .

THE EQUAL EMPLOYMENT COMPLIANCE MANUAL. Callaghan and Company, 155 Pfingsten Road, Deerfield, Illinois 60015. 1977- .

EQUAL EMPLOYMENT OPPORTUNITY COMPLIANCE MANUAL. Prentice-Hall, Incorporated, Route 9W, Englewood Cliffs, New Jersey 07632. 1979- .

EQUAL EMPLOYMENT OPPORTUNITY LAW. W.A. Hancock. Business Laws, Incorporated, 11630 Chillicothe Road, Chesterland, Ohio 44026. 1985- .

FAIR EMPLOYMENT PRACTICE SERVICE. The Bureau of National Affairs, Incorporated, 1231 Twenty-fifth Street, Northwest, Washington, D.C. 20037. 1964- .

MANUAL ON EMPLOYMENT DISCRIMINATION LAW AND CIVIL RIGHTS ACTIONS IN THE FEDERAL COURTS. Charles R. Richey. Clark Boardman Company, Limited, 435 Hudson Street, New York, New York 10014. 1985-

HANDBOOKS, MANUALS, FORMBOOKS

EEOC AND THE LAWS IT ENFORCES: A REFERENCE MANUAL. United States Equal Employment Opportunity Commission. Superintendent of Documents, United States Government Printing Office, Washington, D.C. 20402. 1988.

THE EMPLOYER'S GUIDE TO AVOIDING JOB-BIAS LITIGATION. Peter C. Reid. Random House, Incorporated, 201 East Fiftieth Street, New York, New York 10022. 1986.

EQUAL EMPLOYMENT OPPORTUNITY AND AFFIRMATIVE ACTION: A SOURCEBOOK FOR COURT MANAGERS. Cynthia G. Sulton and Randy P. Wolfe. National Center for State Courts, 300 Newport Avenue, Williamsburg, Virginia 23187-8798. 1982.

GOVERNMENT REGULATION OF EMPLOYMENT DISCRIMINATION: A SOURCEBOOK FOR MANAGERS. Richard Trotter and Susan P. Zacur. University Press of America, 4720 Boston Way, Lanham, Maryland 20706. 1986.

TEXTBOOKS AND GENERAL WORKS

AFFIRMATIVE ACTION AND JUSTICE: A PHILOSOPHICAL AND CONSTITUTIONAL INQUIRY. Michel Rosenfeld. Yale University Press, 302 Temple Street, New Haven, Connecticut 06520. 1991.

AFFIRMATIVE ACTION AND PRINCIPLES OF JUSTICE. Kathanne W. Greene. Greenwood Publishing Group, Incorporated, 88 Post Road West, P.O. Box 5007, Westport, Connecticut 06881. 1989.

AFFIRMATIVE ACTION AND THE CONSTITUTION. John Charles Daly. American Enterprise Institute for Public Policy Research, 1150 Seventeenth Street, Northwest, Washington, D.C. 20036. 1987.

BEHIND BAKKE: AFFIRMATIVE ACTION AND THE SUPREME COURT. Bernard Schwartz. New York University Press, 70 Washington Square South, New York, New York 10012. 1988.

THE CIVIL RIGHTS ERA: ORIGINS AND DEVELOPMENT OF NATIONAL POLICY, 1960-1972. Hugh Davis Graham. Oxford University Press, 200 Madison Avenue, New York, New York 10016. 1990.

COMPARABLE WORTH: ISSUES AND ALTERNATIVES. Second Edition. Robert Livernash. Equal Employment Advisory Council, 1015 Fifteenth Street, Northwest, Suite 1220, Washington, D.C. 20005. 1984.

COMPARABLE WORTH: NEW DIRECTIONS FOR RESEARCH. Heidi I. Hartmann, Editor. National Academy Press, 2101 Constitution Avenue, Northwest, Washington, D.C. 20418. 1985.

COMPARABLE WORTH: THE MYTH AND THE MOVEMENT. Elaine Johansen. Westview Press, 5500 Central Avenue, Boulder, Colorado 80301. 1985.

A CONFLICT OF RIGHTS: THE SUPREME COURT AND AFFIRMATIVE ACTION. Melvin I. Urofsky. Scribner Educational Publishers, 866 Third Avenue, New York, New York 10022. 1991.

CURRENT DEVELOPMENTS IN EQUAL EMPLOYMENT OPPORTUNITY LAW: APRIL 1983 CONFERENCE. Federal Bar Association, 1815 H Street, Northwest, Washington, D.C. 20006-3604. 1983.

DEFENSE OF EQUAL EMPLOYMENT OPPORTUNITY CLAIMS. Shepard's/McGraw-Hill, P.O. Box 1235, Colorado Springs, Colorado 80901. 1982- . (Periodic Supplements).

DISCRIMINATION, JOBS, AND POLITICS: THE STRUGGLE FOR EQUAL EMPLOYMENT OPPORTUNITY IN THE UNITED STATES SINCE THE NEW DEAL. Paul Burstein. University of Chicago Press, 5801 Ellis Avenue, Chicago, Illinois 60637. 1985.

EMPLOYEE SELECTION: LEGAL AND PRACTICAL ALTERNATIVES TO COMPLIANCE AND LITIGATION. Second Edition. Edward E. Potter. Equal Employment Advisory Council, 1015 Fifteenth Street, Northwest, Suite 1220, Washington, D.C. 20005. 1986.

EMPLOYMENT DISCRIMINATION LAW. Michael A. Warner and Lee E. Miller. The Bureau of National Affairs, Incorporated, 1231 Twenty-fifth Street, Northwest, Washington, D.C. 20037. 1984.

EQUAL OPPORTUNITY. Norman E. Bowie. Westview Press, Incorporated, 5500 Central Avenue, Boulder, Colorado 80301. 1988.

THE EQUAL PAY ACT: IMPLICATIONS FOR COMPARABLE WORTH. Walter Fogel. Praeger Publishers, One Madison Avenue, New York, New York 10010-3603. 1984.

EQUALITY TRANSFORMED: A QUARTER-CENTURY OF AFFIRMATIVE ACTION. Herman Belz. Transaction Books, Rutgers University, New Brunswick, New Jersey 08903. 1991.

EQUITY AND PROHIBITION OF DISCRIMINATION IN EMPLOYMENT. Roger Blanpain. Kluwer Law Book Publishers, Incorporated, 36 West Forty-fourth Street, New York, New York 10036. 1985.

FEDERAL EQUAL EMPLOYMENT OPPORTUNITY POLICY AND NUMERICAL GOALS AND TIMETABLES: AN IMPACT ASSESSMENT. J. Edward Kellough. Praeger Publishers, One Madison Avenue, New York, New York 10010-3603. 1989.

FEDERAL LAW OF EMPLOYMENT DISCRIMINATION IN A NUTSHELL. Second Edition. Mack A. Player. West Publishing Company, P.O. Box 64526, 50 West Kellogg Boulevard, St. Paul, Minnesota 55164-0526. 1981.

FEDERAL STATUTORY LAW OF EMPLOYMENT DISCRIMINATION. Charles A. Sullivan. Michie Company, P.O. Box 7587, Charlottesville, Virginia 22906. 1980- . (Periodic Supplements).

THE LAW OF EQUAL EMPLOYMENT OPPORTUNITY. Stephen N. Shulman. Research Institute of America, Incorporated, One Penn Plaza, New York, New York 10119. 1990.

MAJOR ISSUES IN THE FEDERAL LAW OF EMPLOYMENT DISCRIMINATION. George Rutherglen. Federal Judicial Center, 1520 H Street, Northwest, Washington, D.C. 20005. 1983.

MY TROUBLES ARE GOING TO HAVE TROUBLE WITH ME: EVERYDAY TRIALS AND TRIUMPHS OF WOMEN WORKERS. Karen B. Sacks and Dorothy Remy. Rutgers University Press, 109 Church Street, New Brunswick, New Jersey 08901. 1984.

PATTERN DISCOVERY: EMPLOYMENT DISCRIMINATION. Douglas Danner. Lawyers Co-Operative Publishing Company, One Graves Street, Rochester, New York 14694. 1981- . (Periodic Supplements).

PAY EQUITY AND COMPARABLE WORTH. The Bureau of National Affairs, Incorporated, 1231 Twenty-fifth Street, Northwest, Washington, D.C. 20037. 1984.

PRIMER OF EQUAL EMPLOYMENT OPPORTUNITY. Michael D. Levin-Epstein. Bureau of National Affairs, Incorporated, 1231 Twenty-fifth Street, Northwest, Washington, D.C. 20037. 1984.

SEX DISCRIMINATION IN EMPLOYMENT. William F. Pepper and Florynce R. Kennedy. Michie Company, P.O. Box 7587, Charlottesville, Virginia 22906. 1982.

STATISTICAL METHODS IN DISCRIMINATION LITIGATION. D.H. Kaye and Mikel Aickin. Marcel Dekker, Incorporated, 720 Madison Avenue, New York, New York 10016. 1986.

TITLE VII AT 20. The Bureau of National Affairs, Incorporated, 1231 Twenty-fifth Street, Northwest, Washington, D.C. 20037. 1985. (Special Supplement No. 83, October 18, 1985).

WOMEN, MINORITIES, AND UNIONS IN THE PUBLIC SECTOR. Norma Riccucci. Greenwood Publishing Group, Incorporated, 88 Post Road West, P.O. Box 5007, Westport, Connecticut 06881. 1990.

WOMEN'S WAGES AND WORK IN THE TWENTIETH CENTURY. James P. Smith and Michael P. Ward. Rand Corporation, P.O. Box 2138, Santa Monica, California 90406-2138. 1984.

WOMEN'S WORK: DEVELOPMENT AND THE DIVISION OF LABOR BY GENDER. Eleanor Leacock and Helen I. Safa. Bergin and Garvey Publishers, Incorporated, 670 Amherst Road, Granby, Massachusetts 01033. 1988.

ANNUALS AND SURVEYS

ANNUAL INSTITUTE ON EQUAL EMPLOYMENT OPPORTUNITY COMPLIANCE. Practising Law Institute, 810 Seventh Avenue, New York, New York 10019.

ANNUAL REPORT ON EQUAL EMPLOYMENT OPPORTUNITY COMMISSION. United States Equal Opportunity Employment Commission. Superintendent of Documents, United States Government Printing Office, Washington, D.C. 20402.

EQUAL OPPORTUNITY EMPLOYMENT REPORT. United States Equal Opportunity Employment Commission. Superintendent of Documents, United States Government Printing Office, Washington, D.C. 20402. Annual.

NEWSLETTERS AND NEWSPAPERS

EEO REVIEW. Executive Enterprises Publications Company, Incorporated, 22 West Twenty-first Street, New York, New York 10010. Monthly.

EQUAL EMPLOYMENT COMPLIANCE UPDATE. Callaghan and Company, 155 Pfingsten Road, Deerfield, Illinois 60015. Monthly.

FAIR EMPLOYMENT COMPLIANCE. Management Resources, Incorporated, 379 West Broadway, Fourth Floor, New York, New York 10014. Semimonthly.

FAIR EMPLOYMENT PRACTICES: SUMMARY OF LATEST DEVELOPMENTS. The Bureau of National Affairs, Incorporated, 1231 Twenty-fifth Street, Northwest, Washington, D.C. 20037. Semimonthly.

BIBLIOGRAPHIES

COMPARABLE WORK AND EQUAL PAY: A BIBLIOGRAPHY. Anthony G. White. Vance Bibliographies, P.O. Box 229, 112 North Charter Street, Monticello, Illinois 61856. 1980.

COMPARABLE WORTH. Earleen H. Cook. Vance Bibliographies, P.O. Box 229, 112 North Charter Street, Monticello, Illinois 61856. 1983.

EQUAL OPPORTUNITY IN THE WORKPLACE: A CHECKLIST 1980-1983. Dale E. Casper. Vance Bibliographies, P.O. Box 229, 112 North Charter Street, Monticello, Illinois 61856. 1984.

EQUAL PAY FOR COMPARABLE WORK: A BIBLIOGRAPHY. Marian Dworaczek. Vance Bibliographies, P.O. Box 229, 112 North Charter Street, Monticello, Illinois 61856. 1984.

DIRECTORIES

EEO POLICIES AND PROGRAMS. Personnel Policies Forum. Bureau of National Affairs, Incorporated, 1231 Twenty-fifth Street, Northwest, Washington, D.C. 20037. 1986.

EQUAL OPPORTUNITY EMPLOYMENT AND AFFIRMATIVE ACTION: A SOURCEBOOK. Floyd D. Weatherspoon. Garland Publishers, Incorporated, 136 Madison Avenue, New York, New York 10016. 1985.

ASSOCIATIONS AND PROFESSIONAL SOCIETIES

AMERICAN ASSOCIATION FOR AFFIRMATIVE ACTION. 11 East Hubbard Street, Suite 200, Chicago, Illinois 60611. (312) 329-2512.

RESEARCH CENTERS, INSTITUTES, CLEARINGHOUSES

EQUAL EMPLOYMENT ADVISORY COUNCIL. 1015 Fifteenth Street, Northwest, Washington, D.C. 20005. (202) 789-8600.

HUMAN RESOURCES INSTITUTE. University of Alabama, P.O. Box 870225, Tuscaloosa, Alabama 35487. (205) 348-8939.

NAACP LEGAL DEFENSE AND EDUCATIONAL FUND. 1275 K Street, Northwest, Washington, D.C. 20006. (202) 682-1300.

NATIONAL COMMITTEE ON PAY EQUITY. 1201 Sixteenth Street, Northwest, Washington, D.C. 20036. (202) 822-7304.

NATIONAL COUNCIL ON EMPLOYMENT POLICY. 1730 K Street, Northwest, Washington, D.C. 20006. (202) 833-2530.

NATIONAL EMPLOYMENT LAW PROJECT. 475 Riverside Drive, Suite 240, New York, New York 10115. (212) 870-2121.

NATIONAL FOUNDATION FOR THE STUDY OF EQUAL EMPLOYMENT POLICY. 1015 Fifteenth Street, Northwest, Washington, D.C. 20005. (202) 789-8685.

NATIONAL WOMEN'S LAW CENTER. 1616 P Street, Northwest, Washington, D.C. 20036. (202) 328-5160.

UNITED STATES COMMISSION ON CIVIL RIGHTS, OFFICE OF PROGRAMS, POLICY, AND RESEARCH. 1121 Vermont Avenue, Northwest, Washington, D.C. 20425. (202) 376-8582.

WOMEN EMPLOYED INSTITUTE. 22 West Monroe, Suite 1400, Chicago, Illinois 60603. (312) 782-3902.

ONLINE DATABASES

AFFIRMATIVE ACTION PLANNING GUIDE. Executive Telecon System, Incorporated, College Park North, 9585 Valparaiso Court, Indianapolis, Indiana 46268.

AFFIRMATIVE ACTION TODAY. Bureau of National Affairs, Incorporated, BNA ONLINE, 1231 Twenty-fifth Street, Northwest, Washington, D.C. 20037.

EEO POLICIES AND PROGRAMS. Bureau of National Affairs, Incorporated, BNA ONLINE, 1231 Twenty-fifth Street, Northwest, Washington, D.C. 20037.

FAIR EMPLOYMENT PRACTICES: SUMMARY OF LATEST DEVELOPMENTS. Bureau of National Affairs, Incorporated, BNA ONLINE, 1231 Twenty-fifth Street, Northwest, Washington, D.C. 20037.

STATISTICS SOURCES

EQUAL OPPORTUNITY EMPLOYMENT STATISTICS. United States Office of Personnel Management. Superintendent of Documents, United States Government Printing Office, Washington, D.C. 20402. 1978- . Annual.

OTHER SOURCES

INVESTIGATION OF CIVIL RIGHTS ENFORCEMENT BY THE EQUAL OPPORTUNITY EMPLOYMENT COMMISSION REPORT. House Committee on Education and Labor. Superintendent of Documents, United States Government Printing Office, Washington, D.C. 20402. 1986.

EQUAL EMPLOYMENT OPPORTUNITY COMMISSION

STATUTES, CODES, STANDARDS, UNIFORM LAWS

CODE OF FEDERAL REGULATIONS, TITLE 29. Office of the Federal Register, National Archives and Records Administration. Superintendent of Documents, United States Government Printing Office, Washington, D.C. 20402. Annual. (Updated by use of monthly List of Sections Affected and daily Federal Register .)

HANDBOOKS, MANUALS, FORMBOOKS

EMPLOYMENT DISCRIMINATION: A CLAIMS MANUAL FOR EMPLOYEES AND MANAGERS. Andrew J. Maikovich. McFarland and Company, Incorporated, Box 611, Jefferson, North Carolina 28640. 1989.

STATE AND LOCAL PROGRAM HANDBOOK. United States Equal Employment Opportunity Commission, Office of Program Operations, State and Local Branch, Washington, D.C. 1987.

TEXTBOOKS AND GENERAL WORKS

MAKING A RIGHT A REALITY: AN ORAL HISTORY OF THE EARLY YEARS OF THE EEOC, 1965-1972: IN CELEBRATION OF THE TWENTY-FIFTH ANNIVERSARY, JULY 2, 1990. United States Equal Employment Opportunity Commission, Washington, D.C. 1990.

RESEARCH CENTERS, INSTITUTES, CLEARINGHOUSES

UNITED STATES EQUAL EMPLOYMENT OPPORTUNITY COMMISSION LIBRARY. 1801 L Street, Northwest, Washington, D.C. 20507. (202) 665-4447.

STATISTICS SOURCES

EQUAL EMPLOYMENT OPPORTUNITY REPORT, 1981, JOB PATTERNS FOR MINORITIES AND WOMEN IN PRIVATE INDUSTRY. Equal Employment Opportunity Commission. Superintendent of Documents, United States Government Printing Office, Washington, D.C. 20402. 1984.

EQUAL PAY
See: EQUAL EMPLOYMENT OPPORTUNITY; DISCRIMINATION, SEX

EQUAL PROTECTION
See: DISCRIMINATION, EMPLOYMENT; DISCRIMINATION, HOUSING; DISCRIMINATION, RACE; DISCRIMINATION, SEX; DUE PROCESS OF LAW

EQUIPMENT LEASING
See: LEASES

EQUITY PLEADING AND PROCEDURE
See: CIVIL PROCEDURE; RESTITUTION

ESCHEAT
See: WILLS, TRUSTS AND INHERITANCE

ESTATE, INHERITANCE AND TRANSFER TAXES
See also: TAX AND ESTATE PLANNING; WILLS, TRUSTS AND INHERITANCE

STATUTES, CODES, STANDARDS, UNIFORM LAWS

FEDERAL ESTATE AND GIFT TAXES: CODE AND REGULATIONS. Commerce Clearing House, Incorporated, 4025 West Peterson Avenue, Chicago, Illinois 60646. Annual.

FEDERAL INCOME TAX CODE AND REGULATIONS. Commerce Clearing House, Incorporated, 4025 West Peterson Avenue, Chicago, Illinois 60646. Annual.

FEDERAL TAX REGULATIONS. West Publishing Company, P.O. Box 64526, 50 West Kellogg Boulevard, St. Paul, Minnesota 55164-0526. Annual.

INTERNAL REVENUE BULLETIN: CUMULATIVE BULLETIN. United States Department of Treasury, Internal Revenue Service. United States Government Printing Office, Washington, D.C. 20402. Weekly.

INTERNAL REVENUE CODE. West Publishing Company, P.O. Box 64526, 50 West Kellogg Boulevard, St. Paul, Minnesota 55164-0526. Annual.

SELECTED STATUTES ON TRUSTS AND ESTATES. John H. Langbein and Lawrence W. Waggoner. Foundation Press, 615 Merrick Avenue, Westbury, New York 11590. 1991.

LOOSELEAF SERVICES AND REPORTERS

ESTATE ADMINISTRATION AND TAX PLANNING FOR SURVIVORS. Donald S. Schindel. Garland Publishing, Incorporated, 136 Madison Avenue, New York, New York 10016. 1987.

ESTATE PLANNING LAW AND TAXATION. Second Edition. David Westfall. Research Institute of America, Incorporated, One Penn Plaza, New York, New York 10119. 1989- .

ESTATE TAX FREEZE: TOOLS AND TECHNIQUES. Douglas K. Freeman. Matthew Bender and Company, Incorporated, 11 Penn Plaza, New York, New York 10001. 1985- .

ESTATE TAX TECHNIQUES. Frank B. Appleman. Matthew Bender and Company, Incorporated, 11 Penn Plaza, New York, New York 10001. 1978- .

FEDERAL ESTATE AND GIFT TAX LETTER RULINGS. Rynd Communications, 99 Painters Mill Road, Owings Mills, Maryland 21117. 1980- .

FEDERAL ESTATE AND GIFT TAX REPORTS. Commerce Clearing House, Incorporated, 4025 West Peterson Avenue, Chicago, Illinois 60646. 1913- .

FEDERAL ESTATE AND GIFT TAX REVENUE RULINGS. Alex Solid. Rynd Communications, 99 Painters Mill Road, Owings Mills, Maryland 21117. 1977- .

FEDERAL ESTATE AND GIFT TAXATION. Fifth Edition. Richard B. Stephens. Research Institute of America, Incorporated, One Penn Plaza, New York, New York 10119. 1983- .

FEDERAL ESTATE AND GIFT TAXES. Prentice-Hall, Incorporated, Route 9W, Englewood Cliffs, New Jersey 07632. 1926- .

FEDERAL INCOME, GIFT AND ESTATE TAXATION. Alan Prigal. Matthew Bender and Company, Incorporated, 11 Penn Plaza, New York, New York 10001. 1980- .

FEDERAL INCOME, GIFT AND ESTATE TAXATION. Jacob Rabkin and Mark H. Johnson. Matthew Bender and Company, Incorporated, 11 Penn Plaza, New York, New York 10001. 1972- .

FEDERAL INCOME, GIFT AND ESTATE TREASURY REGULATIONS. George J. Jones. Matthew Bender and Company, Incorporated, 11 Penn Plaza, New York, New York 10001. 1972- .

FEDERAL TAXATION OF INCOME, ESTATES AND GIFTS. Boris I. Bittker. Research Institute of America, Incorporated, One Penn Plaza, New York, New York 10119. 1981- .

FEDERAL TAXES. Prentice-Hall, Incorporated, Route 9W, Englewood Cliffs, New Jersey 07632. 1919- .

ESTATE, INHERITANCE AND TRANSFER TAXES

INHERITANCE, ESTATE AND GIFT TAX REPORTER. Commerce Clearing House, Incorporated, 4025 West Peterson Avenue, Chicago, Illinois 60646. 1950- .

INHERITANCE, ESTATE AND GIFT TAX REPORTS: STATE. Commerce Clearing House, Incorporated, 4025 West Peterson Avenue, Chicago, Illinois 60646. Monthly.

INHERITANCE TAXES. Prentice-Hall, Incorporated, Route 9W, Englewood Cliffs, New Jersey 07632. 1974- .

LAW OF FEDERAL ESTATE AND GIFT TAXATION: CODE COMMENTARY. David T. Link and Larry D. Soderquist. Callaghan and Company, 155 Pfingsten Road, Deerfield, Illinois 60015. 1978- .

STANDARD FEDERAL TAX REPORTS. Commerce Clearing House, Incorporated, 4025 West Peterson Avenue, Chicago, Illinois 60646. 1913- .

STATE INHERITANCE TAXES (ALL STATES). Prentice-Hall, Incorporated, Route 9W, Englewood Cliffs, New Jersey 07632. 1925- .

TAX MANAGEMENT: ESTATES, GIFTS AND TRUSTS SERIES. Bureau of National Affairs, 1231 Twenty-fifth Street, Northwest, Washington, D.C. 20037. 1967- .

HANDBOOKS, MANUALS, FORMBOOKS

ADVANCED WILL DRAFTING. Michael J. Weinberger, Chairman. Practising Law Institute, 810 Seventh Avenue, New York, New York 10019. 1984.

CCH ESTATE PLANNING GUIDE: INCLUDING FINANCIAL PLANNING. Ninth Edition. Sidney Kess. Commerce Clearing House, Incorporated, 4025 West Peterson Avenue, Chicago, Illinois 60646. 1989.

THE DOW JONES-IRWIN GUIDE TO ESTATE PLANNING. Sixth Edition. William C. Clay, Jr. Richard D. Irwin, Incorporated, 1818 Ridge Road, Homewood, Illinois 60430. 1984.

ESTATE PLANNING: A BASIC GUIDE. Edward F. Sutkowski and Karl B. Kuppler. American Bar Association, Section of General Practice, 750 North Lake Shore Drive, Chicago, Illinois 60611. 1990.

ESTATE PLANNING AND DRAFTING. Regis W. Campfield. Commerce Clearing House, Incorporated, 4025 West Peterson Avenue, Chicago, Illinois 60646. 1984.

ESTATE PLANNING: COMPLETE GUIDE AND WORKBOOK. Revised Edition. Alice F. Brod. Panel Publishers, Incorporated, 36 West Forty-fourth Street, New York, New York 10036. 1984.

ESTATE PLANNING MANUAL. Charles O. Galvin. John Wiley and Sons, Incorporated, 605 Third Avenue, New York, New York 10158. 1987.

ESTATE VALUATION HANDBOOK. Lawrence W. Averill. John Wiley and Sons, Incorporated, 605 Third Avenue, New York, New York 10158. 1983.

FEDERAL ESTATE AND GIFT TAXES EXPLAINED. Commerce Clearing House, Incorporated, 4025 West Peterson Avenue, Chicago, Illinois 60646. 1988.

INTERNATIONAL TAX AND ESTATE PLANNING: A PRACTICAL GUIDE FOR MULTINATIONAL INVESTORS. Second Edition. Robert C. Lawrence. Practising Law Institute, 810 Seventh Avenue, New York, New York 10019. 1989.

PLANNING AN ESTATE: A GUIDEBOOK OF PRINCIPLES AND TECHNIQUES. Third Edition. Harold Weinstock. Shepard's/McGraw-Hill, P.O. Box 1235, Colorado Springs, Colorado 80901. 1988.

PLANNING AND DRAFTING FOR THE GENERATION-SKIPPING TRANSFER TAX. Jerold I. Horn. American Law Institute-American Bar Association, 4025 Chestnut Street, Philadelphia, Pennsylvania 19104. 1990.

POSTMORTEM ESTATE PLANNING: STRATEGIES FOR EXECUTORS AND BENEFICIARIES / ALBERT KALTER, LAWRENCE NEWMAN. Albert Kalter. Practising Law Institute, 810 Seventh Avenue, New York, New York 10019. 1989.

TEXTBOOKS AND GENERAL WORKS

AFTER DEATH TAX PLANNING: MINIMIZING TAX LIABILITIES. Jerry A. Kasner and Robert Whitman. American Law Institute-American Bar Association, 4025 Chestnut Street, Philadelphia, Pennsylvania 19104. 1990.

DISCLAIMERS IN ESTATE PLANNING: A GUIDE TO THEIR EFFECTIVE USE. Ronald A. Brand. American Bar Association, Section of Real Property, Probate and Trust Law, 750 North Lake Shore Drive, Chicago, Illinois 60611. 1990.

THE DOLLARS AND SENSE OF ESTATE PLANNING. Forest J. Bowman. Prentice-Hall, Incorporated, Route 9W, Englewood Cliffs, New Jersey 07632. 1989.

FEDERAL ESTATE AND GIFT TAXATION. Sixth Edition. Research Institute of America, Incorporated, One Penn Plaza, New York, New York 10119. 1991.

FEDERAL ESTATE AND GIFT TAXATION. Fifth Edition. Boris I. Bittker and Elias Clark. Little, Brown, and Company, 34 Beacon Street, Boston, Massachusetts 02108. 1984.

FEDERAL ESTATE AND GIFT TAXATION IN A NUTSHELL. Fourth Edition. John K. McNulty. West Publishing Company, P.O. Box 64526, 50 West Kellogg Boulevard, St. Paul, Minnesota 55164-0526. 1989.

FEDERAL TAXATION OF ESTATES, GIFTS AND TRUSTS. Fourth Edition. Barry M. Nudelman. American Law Institute, 4025 Chestnut Street, Philadelphia, Pennsylvania 19104. 1988.

FEDERAL TAXATION OF INCOME, ESTATES, AND GIFTS. Second Edition. Boris I. Bittker. Research Institute of America, Incorporated, One Penn Plaza, New York, New York 10119. 1989- .

FINANCIAL ESTATE PLANNING APPLICATIONS. Fourth Edition. Gwenda L. Cannon. The American College, 270 Bryn Mawr Avenue, Bryn Mawr, Pennsylvania 19010. 1985.

INTERNATIONAL DOUBLE TAXATION OF INHERITANCES AND GIFTS. International Fiscal Association, Editor. Kluwer Academic Publishers, 101 Philip Drive, Assinippi Park, Norwell, Massachusetts 02061. 1985.

NEW FAMILY WEALTH TRANSFER OPPORTUNITIES. Sidney Kess and Bertil Westlin. Commerce Clearing House, Incorporated, 4025 West Peterson Avenue, Chicago, Illinois 60646. 1989.

PROVISIONS OF THE INTERNAL REVENUE CODE AND TREASURY REGULATIONS PERTAINING TO THE FEDERAL TAXATION OF GIFTS, TRUSTS, AND ESTATES. Douglas A. Kahn and Lawrence W. Waggoner. Little, Brown, and Company, 34 Beacon Street, Boston, Massachusetts 02108. 1983.

READINGS IN ESTATE AND GIFT TAX PLANNING. Fourth Edition. Gwenda L. Cannon, Editor. The American College, 270 Bryn Mawr Avenue, Bryn Mawr, Pennsylvania 19010. 1985.

A SIMPLIFIED APPROACH TO PLANNING ESTATES: PROBLEMS AND SOLUTIONS. Benjamin M. Becker and Ben M. Roth. Farnsworth Publishing Company, Incorporated, 78 Randall Avenue, Rockville Center, New York, 11570. 1982.

SOPHISTICATED ESTATE PLANNING TECHNIQUES: AMERICAN LAW INSTITUTE COURSE OF STUDY MATERIALS. American Law Institute-American Bar Association, Committee on Continuing Professional Education, 4025 Chestnut Street, Philadelphia, Pennsylvania 19104. 1984.

WILLS, TRUSTS, AND ESTATES INCLUDING TAXATION AND FUTURE INTERESTS. William M. McGovern. West Publishing Company, 50 West Kellogg Boulevard, St.Paul, Minnesota 55164. 1988.

DIGESTS, INDEXES, ABSTRACTS, CITATORS

ESTATE AND GIFT TAX DIGEST. Second Edition. Michael Fair. Research Institute of America, Incorporated, One Penn Plaza, New York, New York 10119. 1989.

FEDERAL TAX ARTICLES: INCOME, ESTATE, GIFT, EXCISE, EMPLOYMENT TAXES. Commerce Clearing House, Incorporated, 4025 West Peterson Avenue, Chicago, Illinois 60646. 1969- .

FEDERAL TAXES CITATOR. Prentice-Hall, Incorporated, Route 9W, Englewood Cliffs, New Jersey 07632. 1943- .

INDEX TO FEDERAL TAX ARTICLES. Gersham Goldstein, Editor. Research Institute of America, Incorporated, One Penn Plaza, New York, New York 10119. 1981- . (Quarterly Supplements).

SHEPARD'S FEDERAL TAX CITATIONS. Shepard's/McGraw-Hill, P.O. Box 1235, Colorado Springs, Colorado 80901. 1981- .

SHEPARD'S FEDERAL TAX LOCATOR: COMPLETE INDEX TO ALL THE CURRENT SOURCES OF LAW RELATING TO FEDERAL TAXATION. Shepard's/McGraw-Hill, P.O. Box 1235, Colorado Springs, Colorado 80901. 1974- .

LAW REVIEWS AND PERIODICALS

AKRON TAX JOURNAL. Akron Law Review Editorial Board, University of Akron, School of Law, Akron, Ohio 44325. Semiannual.

ESTATE PLANNING. Research Institute of America, Incorporated, One Penn Plaza, New York, New York 10119. Bimonthly.

JOURNAL OF TAXATION. Research Institute of America, Incorporated, One Penn Plaza, New York, New York 10119. Monthly.

PROBATE AND PROPERTY. American Bar Association, 750 North Lake Shore Drive, Chicago, Illinois 60611. Bimonthly.

REAL PROPERTY, PROBATE AND TRUST JOURNAL. 665 South High Street, Columbus, Ohio 43215. Quarterly.

REVIEW OF TAXATION OF INDIVIDUALS. Research Institute of America, Incorporated, One Penn Plaza, New York, New York 10119. Quarterly.

TAX LAW REVIEW. Research Institute of America, Incorporated, One Penn Plaza, New York, New York 10119. Quarterly.

THE TAX LAWYER. American Bar Association, Section of Taxation, 750 North Lake Shore Drive, Chicago, Illinois 60611. Quarterly.

TAXATION FOR LAWYERS. Research Institute of America, Incorporated, One Penn Plaza, New York, New York 10119. Bimonthly.

TAXES: THE TAX MAGAZINE. Commerce Clearing House, Incorporated, 4025 West Peterson Avenue, Chicago, Illinois 60646. Monthly.

TRUSTS AND ESTATES, Communication Channels, Incorporated. 6285 Boarfield Road, Atlanta, Georgia 30328. Monthly.

NEWSLETTERS AND NEWSPAPERS

THE CHASE REVIEW. Chase Manhattan Bank, 1211 Avenue of the Americas, 34th Floor, New York, New York 10036. Quarterly.

ELDER LAW REPORT. Little, Brown and Company, Law Division, 34 Beacon Street, Boston, Massachusetts 02108. Monthly.

ESTATE ADMINISTRATION AND TAX PLANNING FOR THE ELDERLY AND DISABLED. Garland Law Publishing, 136 Madison Avenue, New York, New York 10016. Quarterly.

ESTATE FINANCIAL PLANNING ALERT. The Research Institute of America, Incorporated, 90 Fifth Avenue, New York, New York 10011. Monthly.

ESTATE PLANNING REVIEW. Commerce Clearing House, Incorporated, 4025 West Peterson Avenue, Chicago, Illinois 60646. Monthly.

ESTATE, INHERITANCE AND TRANSFER TAXES

FEDERAL TAXES TAX BULLETIN. Research Institute of America, Incorporated, 910 Sylvan Avenue, Englewood Cliffs, New Jersey 07632. Weekly.

INSURANCE AND TAX NEWS. Prentice-Hall Professional Newsletters, Englewood Cliffs, New Jersey 07632. Semimonthly.

TAX MANAGEMENT ESTATES, GIFTS AND TRUSTS JOURNAL. The Bureau of National Affairs, Incorporated, 1231 Twenty-fifth Street, Northwest, Washington, D.C. 20037. Bimonthly.

TAXWISE GIVING. 13 Arcadia Road, Greenwich, Connecticut 06870. Monthly.

ASSOCIATIONS AND PROFESSIONAL SOCIETIES

NATIONAL ASSOCIATION OF ESTATE PLANNING COUNCILS. 98 Dennis Drive, Lexington, Kentucky 40503. (606) 276-4659.

SECTION ON TAXATION. American Bar Association, 750 North Lake Shore Drive, Chicago, Illinois 60611. (312) 988-5158.

SECTION ON TAXATION. Association of American Law Schools, One Dupont Circle, Northwest, Suite 370, Washington, D.C. 20036. (202) 296-8851.

RESEARCH CENTERS, INSTITUTES, CLEARINGHOUSES

INSTITUTE FOR CONTINUING EDUCATION IN LAW AND TAXATION. New York University, 11 West Forty-second Street, New York, New York 10036. (212) 790-1320.

NATIONAL TAX ASSOCIATION - TAX INSTITUTE FOR AMERICA. 5310 East Main Street, Suite 104, Columbus, Ohio 43213. (614) 864-1221.

ONLINE DATABASES

LEXIS, TAX LIBRARY. Mead Data Central, P.O. Box 933, Dayton, Ohio 45401.

TAX MANAGEMENT ESTATES, GIFTS AND TRUSTS JOURNAL. Bureau of National Affairs, Incorporated, BNA ONLINE, 1231 Twenty-fifth Street, Northwest, Washington, D.C. 20037.

TAX MANAGEMENT PORTFOLIO SERIES: ESTATES, GIFTS AND TRUSTS. Bureau of National Affairs, Incorporated, BNA ONLINE, 1231 Twenty-fifth Street, Northwest, Washington, D.C. 20037.

WESTLAW, TAX LIBRARY. West Publishing Company, P.O. Box 64526, 50 West Kellogg Boulevard, St. Paul, Minnesota 55164-0526.

AUDIOVISUALS

CREATIVE ESTATE PLANNING. Owen G. Fiore and Stanford J. Schesinger. New York University Institute on Federal Taxation, Totaltape Publishing, Incorporated, 4251 Southwest Thirteenth Street, Gainesville, Florida 32608. 1987. (Audiocassette).

FEDERAL ESTATE AND GIFT TAXATION. Nathan M. Bisk and Richard M. Feldheim. Totaltape Publishing, Incorporated, 4251 Southwest Thirteenth Street, Gainesville, Florida 32608. 1987. (Audiovisual).

FEDERAL ESTATE AND GIFT TAXATION. George M. Schain. Garland Publishing, Incorporated, 136 Madison Avenue, New York, New York 10016. 1987. (Audiocassette).

ESTATES
See: ESTATE, INHERITANCE AND TRANSFER TAXES; REAL PROPERTY; WILLS, TRUSTS AND INHERITANCE

ESTOPPEL
See: ACTIONS AND DEFENSES; JUDGMENTS

ETHICS
See: LEGAL ETHICS AND MALPRACTICE; PROFESSIONAL ETHICS AND LIABILITY

EUROPEAN ECONOMIC COMMUNITY
See also: FOREIGN LAW; INTERNATIONAL AGENCIES AND ORGANIZATIONS; INTERNATIONAL TRADE; INTERNATIONAL LAW AND RELATIONS

STATUTES, CODES, STANDARDS, UNIFORM LAWS

EEC LEGISLATION AND AGREEMENTS: THE TEXTS OF LEADING REGULATIONS, DIRECTIVES, AND INTERNATIONAL AGREEMENTS. Gabriel M. Wilner and Kent S. Karlsson, editors. Transnational Juris Publications, Incorporated, P.O. Box 7282, Ardsley-on-Hudson, New York 10503. 1992.

LOOSELEAF SERVICES AND REPORTERS

BUSINESS LAW IN EUROPE. Martin Storm. Kluwer Academic Publishers, 101 Philip Drive, Assinippi Park, Norwell, Massachusetts 02061. 1990- . (Periodic Supplements).

COMMON MARKET REPORTS. Commerce Clearing House, Incorporated, 4025 West Peterson Avenue, Chicago, Illinois 60646. 1962- . (Semi-monthly Supplements).

COMPETITION LAW OF THE EUROPEAN ECONOMIC COMMUNITY. Ivo Van Bael, Jean Francois Bellis, and Julian O. Von Kalinowski. Matthew Bender & Company, Incorporated, 11 Penn Plaza, New York, New York 10001. 1988- . Periodic supplements.

COMPLETING THE INTERNAL MARKET OF THE EUROPEAN COMMUNITY: 1992 LEGISLATION. Kluwer Academic Publishers, 101 Philip Drive, Assinippi Park, Norwell, Massachusetts 02061. 1989- . (Quarterly Supplements).

EUROPEAN COMMUNITY: THE SINGLE MARKET ACT. Jane Belford. Oceana Publications, 75 Main Street, Dobbs Ferry, New York 10522. 1989- . (Periodic Supplements).

HANDBOOK ON EUROPEAN EMPLOYEE COMANAGEMENT. Walter Kolvenbach and Peter Hanau. Kluwer Law & Taxation, 6 Bigelow Street, Cambridge, Massachusetts 02139. 1987- .

THE LAW OF THE EUROPEAN ECONOMIC COMMUNITY: A COMMENTARY ON THE EEC TREATY. Hans Smit. Matthew Bender and Company, Incorporated, 11 Penn Plaza, New York, New York 10001. 1976- . (Periodic Supplements).

LAW AND PRACTICE UNDER GATT, AND OTHER TRADING AGREEMENTS: THE EUROPEAN COMMUNITY: THE SINGLE MARKET. Oceana Publications, 75 Main Street, Dobbs Ferry, New York 10522. 1990- . (Periodic Supplements).

UNITED STATES, COMMON MARKET AND INTERNATIONAL ANTITRUST: A COMPARATIVE GUIDE. Second Edition. Barry E. Hawk. Prentice-Hall, Incorporated, Route 9W, Englewood Cliffs, New Jersey 07632. 1984- . (Periodic Supplements).

HANDBOOKS, MANUALS, FORMBOOKS

COMPLETING THE INTERNAL MARKET OF THE EUROPEAN COMMUNITY: 1992 HANDBOOK. Mark Brealey and Conor Quigley. Graham & Trotman, Incorporated, 101 Philip Drive, Norwell, Massachusetts 02061 . 1989.

EUROPE WITHOUT FRONTIERS: A LAWYER'S GUIDE. Audrey Winter. Bureau of National Affairs, Incorporated, 1231 25th Street, N.W., Washington, D.C. 20037. 1989.

GERMAIN'S TRANSNATIONAL LAW RESEARCH: A GUIDE FOR ATTORNEYS. Claire M. Germain. Transnational Juris Publications, Incorporated, P.O. Box 7282, Ardsley-on-Hudson, New York 10503. 1991.

GUIDE TO WORKING IN EUROPE WITHOUT FRONTIERS. Jean-Claude Seche. Commission of the European Communities, European Community Information Service, 2100 M Street, N.W., Washington, D.C. 20037. 1988.

MERGER AND JOINT VENTURE ACTIVITIES IN THE EEC: A GUIDE TO DOING BUSINESS UNDER THE NEW REGULATIONS. Mario Siragusa. Practising Law Institute, 810 Seventh Avenue, New York, New York 10019. 1990.

SETTING UP A COMPANY IN THE EUROPEAN COMMUNITY: A COUNTRY BY COUNTRY GUIDE. Oryx Press, 2214 North Central Avenue, Phoenix, Arizona 85004. 1989.

TEXTBOOKS AND GENERAL WORKS

AIR POLLUTION CONTROL IN THE EUROPEAN COMMUNITY: IMPLEMENTATION OF THE EC DIRECTIVES IN THE TWELVE MEMBER STATES. Graham Bennett. Graham & Trotman, Incorporated, 101 Philip Drive, Norwell, Massachusetts 02061 . 1991.

THE APPLICATION OF THE COMPETITION RULES (ANTITRUST LAW) OF THE EUROPEAN ECONOMIC COMMUNITY TO ENTERPRISES AND ARRANGEMENTS EXTERNAL TO THE COMMON MARKET. Boaz Barack. Kluwer Law Book Publishers, Incorporated, 36 West Forty-fourth Street, New York, New York 10036. 1981.

BANKING IN EUROPE: THE SINGLE MARKET. Rob Dixon. Routledge, 29 West 35th Street, New York, New York 10001. 1991.

BASIC COMMUNITY CASES. Bernard Rudden. Oxford University Press, 200 Madison Avenue, New York, New York 10016. 1987.

BUSINESS LAW IN EUROPE: LEGAL, TAX, AND LABOUR ASPECTS OF BUSINESS OPERATIONS IN THE EUROPEAN COMMUNITY COUNTRIES AND SWITZERLAND. Second Edition. Kluwer Law Book Publishers, Incorporated, 36 West Forty-fourth Street, New York, New York 10036. 1990- .

COMMERCIAL AGENCY AND DISTRIBUTION AGREEMENTS: LAW AND PRACTICE IN THE MEMBER STATES OF THE EUROPEAN COMMUNITY. Guy-Martial Weijer. Graham and Trotman, Incorporated, 101 Philip Drive, Norwell, Massachusetts 02061. 1989.

COMMUNITY LEGAL ORDER. Second edition. Jean-Victor Louis. Office for Official Publications of the European Communities, UNIPUB, 4611-F Assembly Drive, Lanham, Maryland 20706. 1990.

COMPANY LAW IN THE UNITED KINGDOM AND THE EUROPEAN COMMUNITY: ITS HARMONISATION AND UNIFICATION. Frank Wooldridge. Athlone Press, 165 First Avenue, Atlantic Highlands, New Jersey. 07716. 1991.

COMPETITION LAW IN THE EUROPEAN COMMUNITIES. Commission of the European Communities. Office for Official Publications of the European Communities, UNIPUB, 4611-F Assembly Drive, Lanham, Maryland 20706. 1990.

COMPETITION LAW IN THE EUROPEAN COMMUNITY. David M. Jacobs and Sir Jack Stewart-Clark. Kogan Page Limited, 120 Pentonville Road, London N1 9JN, England. 1990.

COMPETITION LAW OF THE EEC. Ivo Van Bael, Jean Francois Bellis. Commerce Clearing House, Incorporated, 4025 West Peterson Avenue, Chicago, Illinois 60646. 1987. .

CONFLICT OF LAWS AND EUROPEAN COMMUNITY LAW: WITH SPECIAL REFERENCE TO THE COMMUNITY CONVENTIONS ON PRIVATE INTERNATIONAL LAW. Ian F. Fletcher. Elsevier Science Publishing Company, P.O. Box 882, Madison Square Station, New York, New York 10159. 1982.

CONSTITUTIONAL FUNCTIONS AND CONSTITUTIONAL PROBLEMS OF INTERNATIONAL ECONOMIC LAW: INTERNATIONAL AND DOMESTIC FOREIGN TRADE LAW AND FOREIGN TRADE POLICY IN THE UNITED STATES, THE EUROPEAN COMMUNITY AND SWITZERLAND. Ernst-Ulrich Petersmann. Westview Press, Incorporated, 5500 Central Avenue, Boulder, Colorado 80301. 1991.

CREATION OF A EUROPEAN BANKING SYSTEM: A STUDY OF ITS LEGAL AND TECHNICAL ASPECTS. Richard Cordero. Peter Lang Publishing, 62 West 45th Street, New York, New York 10036. 1990.

THE CUSTOMS LAW OF THE EUROPEAN ECONOMIC COMMUNITY. Second Edition. Dominik Lasok. Kluwer Law Book Publishers, Incorporated, 36 West Forty-fourth Street, New York, New York 10036. 1990.

DIRECT INVESTMENT TAX INITIATIVES OF THE EUROPEAN COMMUNITY. Fred C. de Hosson, editor. Kluwer Law & Taxation, 6 Bigelow Street, Cambridge, Massachusetts 02139. 1990.

DISTRIBUTORSHIP, FRANCHISING, AGENCY COMMUNITY, AND NATIONAL LAWS AND PRACTICE IN THE EEC. Roberto Baldi. Kluwer Law & Taxation, 6 Bigelow Street, Cambridge, Massachusetts 02139. 1987.

EC 1992: UPDATE ON CURRENT BUSINESS, REGULATORY AND LEGAL ISSUES. Edward M. Rozynski and Matthew Gallivan. Health Industry Manufacturers Association, 1030 15th Street, N.W., Washington, D.C. 20005. 1991.

EC GOVERNMENT PROCUREMENT: COURSE MANUAL. Jean-Pierre. Federal Publications, Incorporated, 1120 20th Street, N.W., Washington, D.C. 20036. 1991.

EEC COMPETITION LAW. D.G. Goyder. Oxford University Press, 200 Madison Avenue, New York, New York 10016. 1988.

EEC COMPETITION POLICY IN THE SINGLE MARKET. Second edition. Office for Official Publications of the European Communities, European Community Information Service, 2100 M Street, N.W., Washington, D.C. 20037. 1989.

EEC CUSTOMS LAW: LEGISLATION, CASE LAW AND EXPLANATORY TEXT ON THE CUSTOMS SYSTEM OF THE EUROPEAN ECONOMIC COMMUNITY. Patrick L. Kelley. ESC Publications Limited, Oxford, England. 1986.

EEC DIRECTIVES ON COMPANY LAW AND FINANCIAL MARKETS. Daniel D. Prentice, editor. Oxford University Press, 200 Madison Avenue, New York, New York 10016. 1991.

EEC FISHERIES LAW. Robin R. Churchill. Kluwer Academic Publishers, 101 Philip Drive, Assinippi Park, Norwell, Massachusetts 02061. 1987.

EMPLOYMENT LAW IN EUROPE. Gower Publishing Company, Old Post Road, Brookfield, Vermont 05036. 1991.

EUROPEAN AIR LAW: TEXTS AND DOCUMENTS. Ronald S. Giemulla. Kluwer Law & Taxation, 6 Bigelow Street, Cambridge, Massachusetts 02139. 1992.

THE EUROPEAN COMMUNITY AND GATT. Kluwer Law Book Publishers, Incorporated, 36 West Forty-fourth Street, New York, New York 10036. 1986.

EUROPEAN COMMUNITY LAW. William Rawlinson and Malachy P. Cornwell-Kelly. Waterlow Directories Limited, 50 Fetter Lane, London EC4A 1AA, England. 1990.

EUROPEAN COMMUNITY LAW AND INSTITUTIONS IN PERSPECTIVE: TEXT, CASES, AND READINGS. Eric Stein and Peter Hay. Bobbs-Merrill Company, Incorporated, 4300 West Sixty-second Street, Indianapolis, Indiana 46206. Defunct. 1985- .

EUROPEAN COMMUNITY LAW IN A NUTSHELL. Ralph H. Folsom. West Publishing Company, 3773 Highway 149, Eagan, Minnesota 55123. 1992.

EUROPEAN COMMUNITY LAW IN THE UNITED KINGDOM. Fourth Edition. Lawrence Collins. Butterworths, 75 Clegg Road, Markham, Ontario, Canada L3R 9Y6. 1990.

EUROPEAN COMMUNITY SEX EQUALITY LAW. Evelyn Ellis. Oxford University Press, 200 Madison Avenue, New York, New York 10016. 1991.

THE EUROPEAN COMMUNITY: THE SOCIAL DIMENSION: LABOUR MARKET POLICIES FOR 1992. Paul Teague. Kogan Page Limited, 120 Pentonville Road, London N1 9JN, England. 1989.

EUROPEAN COMPANY AND FINANCIAL LAW: EUROPEAN COMMUNITY LAW-TEXT COLLECTION. Klaus J. Hopt and E. Wymeersch. Walter de Gruyter, Incorporated, 200 Saw Mill Road, Hawthorne, New York 10532. 1991.

EUROPEAN COMPANY LAWS: A COMPARATIVE APPROACH. Robert R. Drury and Peter G. Xuereb, editors. Brookfield Publishing Company, Old Post Road, Brookfield, Vermont 05036. 1991.

EUROPEAN ECONOMIC COMMUNITY: PRODUCTS LIABILITY RULES AND ENVIRONMENTAL POLICY. Patrick E. Thieffry and G. Marc Whitehead. Practising Law Institute, 810 Seventh Avenue, New York, New York 10019. 1990.

EUROPEAN INTERNAL MARKET POLICY. Kevin Featherstone. Routledge, 29 West 35th Street, New York, New York 10001. 1988.

EXCHANGE RATES IN INTERNATIONAL LAW AND ORGANIZATION. Joseph Gold. Section of International Law and Practice, American Bar Association, 750 North Lake Shore Drive, Chicago, Illinois 60611. 1988.

EXPLOITING THE INTERNAL MARKET: COOPERATION AND COMPETITION TOWARD 1992. Pieter J. Slot and M.H. van der Woude. Kluwer Law & Taxation, 6 Bigelow Street, Cambridge, Massachusetts 02139. 1989.

THE FOUNDATIONS OF EUROPEAN COMMUNITY LAW: AN INTRODUCTION TO THE CONSTITUTIONAL AND ADMINISTRATIVE LAW OF THE EUROPEAN COMMUNITY. Second Edition. Trevor C. Hartley. Oxford University Press, 200 Madison Avenue, New York, New York 10016. 1988.

FREE MOVEMENT IN EUROPEAN COMMUNITY LAW. F. Burrows. Oxford University Press, 200 Madison Avenue, New York, New York 10016. 1987.

FREE TRADE AND COMPETITION IN THE EEC: LAW, POLICY, AND PRACTICE. Helen Papaconstantinou. Routledge, 29 West 35th Street, New York, New York 10001. 1988.

GENDER DISCRIMINATION LAW OF THE EUROPEAN COMMUNITY. Sacha Prechal and Noreen Burrows. Gower Publishing Company, Old Post Road, Brookfield, Vermont 05036. 1990.

GENDER DISCRIMINATION LAW OF THE EUROPEAN COMMUNITY. Sacha Prechal. Gower Publishing Company, Old Post Road, Brookfield, Vermont 05036. 1990.

GENERAL PRINCIPLES OF EEC LAW AND THE INDIVIDUAL. Anthony Arnull. St. Martin's Press, 175 Fifth Avenue, New York, New York 10010. 1990.

A GUIDE TO EUROPEAN COMMUNITY LAW. Fifth Edition. P.S.R.F. Mathijsen. Sweet and Maxwell Limited, South Quay Plaza, 183 Marsh Wall, London E14 9FT, England. 1990.

GUIDE TO UNITED KINGDOM AND EUROPEAN COMMUNITY COMPETITION POLICY. Nick Gardner. St. Martin's Press, 175 Fifth Avenue, New York, New York 10010. 1990.

GUIDE TO VAT IN EUROPE. Graham & Trotman, Incorporated, 101 Philip Drive, Norwell, Massachusetts 02061. 1989.

HUMAN RIGHTS AND EUROPEAN POLITICS: THE LEGAL-POLITICAL STATUS OF WORKERS IN THE EUROPEAN COMMUNITY. Fritz Fabricius. St. Martin's Press, 175 Fifth Avenue, New York, New York 10010. 1992.

INSIDE INFORMATION AND SECURITIES TRADING: A LEGAL AND ECONOMIC ANALYSIS OF THE FOUNDATIONS OF LIABILITY IN THE USA AND THE EUROPEAN COMMUNITY. Bernhard Bergmans. Graham & Trotman, Incorporated, 101 Philip Drive, Norwell, Massachusetts 02061. 1991.

INTERNATIONALISATION OF LEGAL PRACTICE: U.S. AND EUROPEAN PERSPECTIVES AND OPPORTUNITIES. Prentice Hall Law & Business, Incorporated, 270 Sylvan Avenue, Englewood Cliffs, New Jersey 07632. 1990.

INTRODUCTION TO THE LAW OF THE EUROPEAN COMMUNITIES AFTER THE COMING INTO FORCE OF THE SINGLE EUROPEAN ACT. John T. Bredima-Savopoulou and Anna Bredima-Savopoulou. Elsevier Science Publishing Company, P.O. Box 882, Madison Square Station, New York, New York 10159. 1990.

INTRODUCTION TO THE LAW OF THE EUROPEAN COMMUNITIES AFTER THE COMING INTO FORCE OF THE SINGLE EUROPEAN ACT. Second edition. Paul J. Kapteyn, Pieter V. van Themat, and Laurence W. Gormley. Kluwer Law & Taxation, 6 Bigelow Street, Cambridge, Massachusetts 02139. 1989.

AN INTRODUCTORY GUIDE TO EEC COMPETITION LAW AND PRACTICE. Fourth Edition. Valentine Korah. ESC Publications Limited, Oxford, England. 1990.

LABOUR LAW AND INDUSTRIAL RELATIONS OF THE EUROPEAN COMMUNITY. R. Blanpain. Kluwer Law Book Publishers, Incorporated, 36 West Forty-fourth Street, New York, New York 10036. 1991.

LAWYERS IN THE EUROPEAN COMMUNITY. Serge-Pierre Laguette and Patrick Latham. European Community Information Service, 2100 M Street, N.W., Washington, D.C. 20037. 1987.

LEADING CASES AND MATERIALS ON THE SOCIAL POLICY OF THE EEC. Angela Byre. Kluwer Law & Taxation, 6 Bigelow Street, Cambridge, Massachusetts 02139. 1989.

LEADING CASES ON THE LAW OF THE EUROPEAN COMMUNITIES. Fifth Edition. M. van Empel. Kluwer Law Book Publishers, Incorporated, 36 West Forty-fourth Street, New York, New York 10036. 1990.

LEASING LAW IN THE EUROPEAN COMMUNITY. Howard Rosen. Euromoney Publications, London, England. 1991.

LEGAL ASPECTS OF AGRICULTURE IN THE EUROPEAN COMMUNITY. John Anthony Usher. Oxford University Press, 200 Madison Avenue, New York, New York 10016. 1988.

LEGAL FOUNDATIONS OF THE SINGLE EUROPEAN MARKET. Nicholas Green, Trevor C. Hartley, and John A. Usher. Oxford University Press, 200 Madison Avenue, New York, New York 10016. 1991.

MERGER CONTROL IN THE EEC: A SURVEY OF EUROPEAN COMPETITION LAWS. Kluwer Law & Taxation, 6 Bigelow Street, Cambridge, Massachusetts 02139. 1988.

MERGERS AND JOINT VENTURES IN EUROPE: THE LAW AND POLICY OF THE EEC. Frank L. Fine. Graham & Trotman, Incorporated, 101 Philip Drive, Norwell, Massachusetts 02061. 1989.

MONOPOLY LAW AND MARKET: STUDIES OF EC COMPETITION WITH US AMERICAN ANTITRUST LAW AS A FRAME OF REFERENCE AND SUPPORTED BY BASIC MARKET ECONOMICS. Jens Fejo. Kluwer Law & Taxation, 6 Bigelow Street, Cambridge, Massachusetts 02139. 1990.

NEW DIRECTIONS IN EUROPEAN COMMUNITY LAW. Francis G. Snyder. Weidenfeld and Nicolson, Ten East Fifty-third Street, New York, New York 10022. 1990.

THE POLITICAL AND LEGAL FRAMEWORK OF TRADE RELATIONS BETWEEN THE EUROPEAN COMMUNITY AND EASTERN EUROPE. Martinus Nijhoff, Kluwer Academic Publishers, 101 Philip Drive, Assinippi Park, Norwell, Massachusetts 02061. 1989.

PRIVATE INTERNATIONAL LAW OF TORT AND PRODUCT LIABILITY: JURISDICTION, APPLICABLE LAW, AND EXTRATERRITORIAL PROTECTIVE MEASURES. Peter Kaye. Brookfield Publishing Company, Old Post Road, Brookfield, Vermont 05036. 1991.

PROTECTIONISM AND THE EUROPEAN COMMUNITY. Second edition. E.L.M. Volker and others, editors. Kluwer Law & Taxation, 6 Bigelow Street, Cambridge, Massachusetts 02139. 1987.

SALES TAXATION: THE CASE FOR THE VALUE ADDED TAX IN THE EUROPEAN COMMUNITY. Ben Terra. Kluwer Law & Taxation, 6 Bigelow Street, Cambridge, Massachusetts 02139. 1988.

SEX DISCRIMINATION LAW. Evelyn Ellis. Gower Publishing Company, Old Post Road, Brookfield, Vermont 05036. 1988.

SUPERVISION IN EUROPEAN COMMUNITY LAW: OBSERVANCE BY THE MEMBER STATES OF THEIR TREATY OBLIGATIONS: A TREATISE ON INTERNATIONAL AND SUPRA-NATIONAL SUPERVISION. Second Edition. H.A.H. Audretsch. Elsevier Science Publishing Company, P.O. Box 882, Madison Square Station, New York, New York 10159. 1986.

TAX COORDINATION IN THE EUROPEAN COMMUNITY. Sijbren Cnossen. Kluwer Law & Taxation, 6 Bigelow Street, Cambridge, Massachusetts 02139. 1987.

TAXATION, TRADE, AND INVESTMENT IN THE EUROPEAN COMMUNITIES. ALI- ABA Committee on Continuing Professional Education, 4025 Chestnut Street, Philadelphia, Pennsylvania 19104. 1990.

TOWARD A COMMUNITY AIR TRANSPORT POLICY: THE LEGAL DIMENSION. Pieter J. Slot and P.D. Dagtoglou. Kluwer Law & Taxation, 6 Bigelow Street, Cambridge, Massachusetts 02139. 1989.

TRANSBORDER FLOW OF PERSONAL DATA WITHIN THE EC. Adriana C. Nugter. Kluwer Law & Taxation, 6 Bigelow Street, Cambridge, Massachusetts 02139. 1990.

TRANSNATIONAL LEGAL PRACTICE IN THE EEC AND THE UNITED STATES. Linda S. Spedding. Transnational Juris Publications, Incorporated, P.O. Box 7282, Ardsley-on-Hudson, New York 10503. 1991.

TRANSPORT LAW OF THE EUROPEAN COMMUNITY. Rosa Greaves. Athlone Press, 165 First Avenue, Atlantic Highlands, New Jersey 07716. 1991.

UNITED STATES, COMMON MARKET AND INTERNATIONAL ANTITRUST: A COMPARATIVE GUIDE. Second edition. Barry E. Hawk. Prentice Hall Law & Business, Incorporated, 270 Sylvan Avenue, Englewood Cliffs, New Jersey 07632. 1984.

ENCYCLOPEDIAS AND DICTIONARIES

ENCYCLOPEDIA OF EUROPEAN COMMUNITY LAW. K.R. Simmonds. Sweet and Maxwell Limited, South Quay Plaza, 183 Marsh Wall, London E14 9FT, England. 1973- .

THE OXFORD ENCYCLOPAEDIA OF EUROPEAN COMMUNITY LAW. A.G. Toth. Oxford University Press, 200 Madison Avenue, New York, New York 10016. 1990- .

DIGESTS, INDEXES, ABSTRACTS, CITATORS

CASE SEARCH MONTHLY, EUROPEAN COMMUNITY LAW. European Law Centre, London, England. 1988- .

DIGEST OF CASE-LAW RELATING TO THE EUROPEAN COMMUNITIES: A SERIES. Office for Official Publications of the European Communities, Luxembourg.

GAZETTEER OF EUROPEAN LAW: CASE SEARCH, EUROPEAN COMMUNITY LAW, 1953-1983. European Law Centre, London, England. 1983.

LAW REVIEWS AND PERIODICALS

EUROPEAN ENVIRONMENT REVIEW: THE JOURNAL OF EUROPEAN COMMUNITY AND INTERNATIONAL ENVIRONMENTAL POLICY AND LAW. European Environment Review, Brussels, Belgium. 1986- .

NEWSLETTERS AND NEWSPAPERS

1992 M & A MONTHLY. Dixon & Company, 667 Madison Avenue, New York, New York 10019. 1989- . Monthly.

1992 -- THE EXTERNAL IMPACT OF EUROPEAN UNIFICATION. Buraff Publications, 1350 Connecticut Avenue, N.W., Washington, D.C. 20036. 1989- . Biweekly.

BUSINESS EUROPE. Julia Crawford, editor. Business International Corporation, 215 Park Avenue, New York, New York 10003. 1960- . Weekly.

CROSSLAND'S EUROPEAN ENVIRONMENTAL BULLETIN. International Environment Group, 184 Amherst Street, Amherst, New Hampshire 03031. 1990- . Bimonthly.

EUROMEDIA REGULATION. Paul Kagan Associates, Incorporated, 126 Clock Tower Place, Carmel, California 93929. 1990- . Monthly.

EUROPE 1992: LAW & STRATEGY. Leader Publications, 111 Eighth Avenue, New York, New York 10011. 1989- . Monthly.

EUROPEAN COMMUNITY LAW AND BUSINESS REPORTER. Legal-Medical Studies, Incorporated, Box 8219, Boston, Massachusetts 02114. 1990- . Semimonthly.

EUROSCOPE. Euroscope, Incorporated, 46679 Winchester Drive, Sterling, Virginia 22170. 1991- . Bimonthly.

MEALEY'S EUROPEAN ENVIRONMENTAL LAW REPORT. Mealey Publications, Incorporated, P.O. Box 446, Wayne, Pennsylvania 19087. 1990- . Bimonthly.

BIBLIOGRAPHIES

EUROPEAN COMMUNITY LAW: A SELECTIVE BIBLIOGRAPHY OF PUBLICATIONS IN ENGLISH, FRENCH AND GERMAN WITH ANNOTATIONS. Claire M. Germain. C.F. Muller, Postfach 4320, Amalienstrasse 29, D-7500 Karlsruhe 1, Germany. 1980.

ASSOCIATIONS AND PROFESSIONAL SOCIETIES

COMMISSION OF THE EUROPEAN COMMUNITIES. 200, Rue de la Loi, B- 1049 Brussels, Belgium. 2 2351111.

COUNCIL OF THE BARS AND LAW SOCIETIES OF THE EUROPEAN COMMUNITY. 40, Rue Washington, B-1050 Brussels, Belgium. 2 6404274.

RESEARCH CENTERS, INSTITUTES, CLEARINGHOUSES

CENTER FOR RESEARCH AND DOCUMENTATION ON THE EUROPEAN COMMUNITY. American University, 4400 Massachusetts Avenue, N.W., Washington, D.C. 20016. (202) 885-1984.

EUROPEAN COMMUNITY INFORMATION SERVICE. 2100 M Street, N.W., Washington, D.C. 20037. (202) 862-9500.

UNITED NATIONS ECONOMIC COMMISSION FOR EUROPE. Palais des Nations, CH-1211 Geneva 10, Switzerland. 7349825.

UNIVERSITY CENTER FOR EUROPEAN AND INTERNATIONAL RESEARCH. 38040 Grenoble, France. 76 82 55 94.

ONLINE DATABASES

ABEL. Commission of the European Communities, Office of Official Publications, 2, Rue Mercier, L-2985 Luxembourg, Luxembourg.

CELEX. Commission of the European Communities, Directorate General for Personnel and Administration, 200, Rue de la Loi, B- 1049 Brussels, Belgium.

COMEXT. Commission of the European Communities, Statistical Office of the European Communities, Batiment Jean Monnet, B.P. 1907, Rue Alcide de Gasperi, L-2920 Luxembourg, Luxembourg.

CRONOS. Commission of the European Communities, Statistical Office of the European Communities, Batiment Jean Monnet, B.P. 1907, Rue Alcide de Gasperi, L-2920 Luxembourg, Luxembourg.

DUNS EUROPA. Dun & Bradstreet Europe Limited, Holmers Farm Way, High Wycombe, Bucks. HP12 4UL, England.

EURO ABSTRACTS. Commission of the European Communities, Directorate for Telecommunications, Information Industries and Innovation, Batiment Jean Monnet, B.P. 1907, Rue Alcide de Gasperi, L-2920 Luxembourg, Luxembourg.

EUROPEAN COMMUNITY LIBRARY AUTOMATED SYSTEM (ECLAS). Commission of the European Communities, Directorate General for Personnel and Administration, 200, Rue de la Loi, B-1049 Brussels, Belgium.

INFO 92. Commission of the European Communities, Directorate General for Personnel and Administration, 200, Rue de la Loi, B- 1049 Brussels, Belgium.

LEXIS UNITED KINGDOM AND COMMONWEALTH LEGAL LIBRARIES. Mead Data Central, Incorporated, 9393 Springboro Pike, Dayton, Ohio 45401. (513) 865-6800.

STATISTICS SOURCES

STATISTICAL OFFICE OF THE EUROPEAN COMMUNITIES. Batiment Jean Monnet, L-2920 Kirchberg, Luxembourg. 43013107.

OTHER SOURCES

EC 1992: A COMMERCE DEPARTMENT ANALYSIS OF EUROPEAN COMMUNITY DIRECTIVES. Debra L. Miller, editor. International Trade Commission, U.S. Department of Commerce, U.S. Government Printing Office, Washington, D.C. 20402. 1990.

EUTHANASIA
See also: MEDICAL JURISPRUDENCE

TEXTBOOKS AND GENERAL WORKS

ABATING TREATMENT WITH CRITICALLY ILL PATIENTS: ETHICAL AND LEGAL LIMITS TO THE MEDICAL PROLONGATION OF LIFE. Robert F. Weir. Oxford University Press, 200 Madison Avenue, New York, New York 10016. 1989.

BENEFICENT EUTHANASIA. Marvin Kohl, Editor. Prometheus Books, 700 East Amherst Street, Buffalo, New York 14215. 1975.

CHOOSING LIFE OR DEATH: A GUIDE FOR PATIENTS, FAMILIES, AND PROFESSIONALS. William J. Winslade and Judith W. Ross. Free Press, 866 Third Avenue, New York, New York 10022. 1986.

THE CONSUMER'S GUIDE TO DEATH, DYING AND BEREAVEMENT. Roger R. Shipley. ETC Publications, 700 East Vereda del Sur, Palm Springs, California 92262. 1982.

THE DEATH DECISION. Leonard J. Nelson. Servant Publications, 840 Airport Boulevard, Ann Arbor, Michigan 48107. 1984.

DEATH, DYING, AND EUTHANASIA. Dennis J. Horan and David Mall, Editors. Greenwood Publishing Group, Incorporated, 88 Post Road West, Westport, Connecticut 06881. 1980.

DECIDING TO FOREGO LIFE-SUSTAINING TREATMENT: A REPORT ON THE ETHICAL, MEDICAL, AND LEGAL ISSUES IN TREATMENT DECISIONS. Superintendent of Documents, United States Government Printing Office, Washington, D.C. 20402. 1983.

DECISION MAKING AND THE DEFECTIVE NEWBORN. Chester A. Swinyard. Charles C. Thomas Publishers, 2600 South First Street, Springfield, Illinois 62794-9265. 1978.

THE END OF LIFE: EUTHANASIA AND MORALITY. James Rachels. Oxford University Press, 200 Madison Avenue, New York, New York 10016. 1986.

THE ETHICS OF DELIBERATE DEATH. Eike-Henner W. Kluge. Associated Faculty Press, 19 West Thirty-sixth Street, New York, New York 10018. 1981.

EUTHANASIA. A. Carmi, Editor. Springer-Verlag New York, Incorporated, 175 Fifth Avenue, New York, New York 10010. 1984.

EUTHANASIA AND RELIGION: A SURVEY OF THE ATTITUDES OF WORLD RELIGIONS TO THE RIGHT-TO-DIE. Gerald A. Larue. Hemlock Society, P.O. Box 11830, Eugene, Oregon 97440. 1985.

EUTHANASIA AND THE NEWBORN: CONFLICTS REGARDING SAVING LIVES. Reidel Publishing Company, 101 Philip Drive, Norwell, Massachusetts 02061. 1987.

EUTHANASIA: MERCY OR MURDER? La Verne Miley. Randall House Publications, 114 Bush Road, P.O. Box 17306, Nashville, Tennessee 37217. 1981.

EUTHANASIA

EUTHANASIA: OR, MEDICAL TREATMENT IN AID OF AN EASY DEATH. William Munk. Ayer Company Publishers, Incorporated, 50 Northwestern Drive, P.O. Box 958, Salem, New Hampshire 03079. 1977 reprint of 1887 edition.

EUTHANASIA: SPIRITUAL, MEDICAL AND LEGAL ISSUES IN TERMINAL HEALTH CARE. Beth Spring. Multnomah Press, 10209 Southeast Division Street, Portland, Oregon 97266. 1988.

EUTHANASIA: TOWARD AN ETHICAL SOCIAL POLICY. David C. Thomasma and Glenn C. Graber. Continuum Publishing Corporation, 370 Lexington Avenue, New York, New York 10017. 1990.

FREEDOM TO DIE: MORAL AND LEGAL ASPECTS OF EUTHANASIA. Second Edition. Ruth O. Russell. Human Sciences Press, Incorporated, 233 Spring Street, New York, New York 10013. 1977.

LIFE AND DEATH WITH LIBERTY AND JUSTICE: A CONTRIBUTION TO THE EUTHANASIA DEBATE. Germain Grisez and Joseph M. Boyle, Jr. University of Notre Dame Press, P.O. Box L, Notre Dame, Indiana 46556. 1980.

MEDICAL POWER AND MEDICAL ETHICS. Jan H. Van Den Berg. W.W. Norton and Company, Incorporated, 500 Fifth Avenue, New York, New York 10110. 1978.

MEDICAL RESPONSIBILITY: PATERNALISM, INFORMED CONSENT, AND EUTHANASIA. Wade L. Robinson and Michael Pritchard, Editors. The Humana Press, P.O. Box 2148, Clifton, New Jersey 07015. 1979.

SELECTIVE NONTREATMENT OF HANDICAPPED NEWBORNS: MORAL DILEMMAS IN NEONATAL MEDICINE. Robert F. Weir. Oxford University Press, 200 Madison Avenue, New York, New York 10016. 1984.

SOCIETY FOR THE RIGHT TO DIE: HANDBOOKS OF ENACTED LAWS. Society for the Right to Die, Incorporated, 250 West Fifty-seventh Street, New York, New York 10107. 1981.

SUICIDE AND EUTHANASIA: HISTORICAL AND CONTEMPORARY THEMES. Baruch A. Brody. Kluwer Academic Publishers, 101 Philip Drive, Assinippi Park, Norwell, Massachusetts 02061. 1989.

SUICIDE AND EUTHANASIA: THE RIGHTS OF PERSONHOOD. Samuel E. Wallace and Albin Eser. University of Tennessee Press, 293 Communications Building, Knoxville, Tennessee 37996-0325. 1981.

THINKING CLEARLY ABOUT DEATH. Jay F. Rosenberg. Prentice-Hall, Incorporated, Route 9W, Englewood Cliffs, New Jersey 07632. 1983.

TO DIE OR NOT TO DIE?: CROSS-DISCIPLINARY, CULTURAL, AND LEGAL PERSPECTIVES ON THE RIGHT TO CHOOSE DEATH. Arthur S. Berger and Joyce Berger. Praeger Publishers, One Madison Avenue, New York, New York 10010-3603. 1990.

TO TREAT OR NOT TO TREAT: A WORKING DOCUMENT FOR MAKING CRITICAL LIFE DECISIONS. J. Stuart Showalter and Brian L. Andrew. Catholic Health Association of the United States, 4455 Woodson Road, St. Louis, Missouri. 63134-0889. 1984.

BIBLIOGRAPHIES

EUTHANASIA AND THE RIGHT TO DIE: THE MEDICAL AND LEGAL VIEWPOINT. Earleen H. Cook. Vance Bibliographies, P.O. Box 229, 112 North Charter Street, Monticello, Illinois 61856. 1982.

EUTHANASIA CONTROVERSY, EIGHTEEN TWELVE TO NINETEEN SEVENTY-FOUR: A BIBLIOGRAPHY WITH SELECT ANNOTATIONS. Charles W. Triche and Diane Triche. Whitston Publishing Company, Incorporated, P.O. Box 958, Troy, New York 12181. 1975.

ASSOCIATIONS AND PROFESSIONAL SOCIETIES

AMERICANS UNITED FOR LIFE. 343 South Dearborn, Suite 1804, Chicago, Illinois 60604. (312) 786-9494.

CENTER FOR THE RIGHTS OF THE TERMINALLY ILL. 2319 Eighteenth Street, South, Fargo, North Dakota 58103. (701) 237-5667.

CONCERN FOR DYING. 250 West Fifty-seventh Street, New York, New York 10107. (212) 246-6962.

HEMLOCK SOCIETY. P.O. Box 11830, Eugene, Oregon 97440. (503) 342-5748.

HUMAN LIFE FOUNDATION. 150 East Thirty-fifth Street, Room 840, New York, New York 10016. (212) 685-5210.

SOCIETY FOR THE RIGHT TO DIE. 250 West Fifty-seventh Street, New York, New York 10107. (212) 246-6973.

RESEARCH CENTERS, INSTITUTES, CLEARINGHOUSES

CENTER FOR BIOETHICS. Clinical Research Institute of Montreal, 110 Pine Avenue West, Montreal, PQ, Canada H2W 1R7. (514) 987-5615.

CENTER FOR HEALTH ETHICS AND POLICY. University of Colorado-Denver, 1200 Larimer Street, Campus Box 133, Denver, Colorado 80204. (303) 556-4837.

HUMAN LIFE CENTER. University of Steubenville, Steubenville, Ohio 43952. (614) 282-9953.

KENNEDY INSTITUTE OF ETHICS. Georgetown University, Washington, D.C. 20057. (202) 687-6774.

ONLINE DATABASES

BIOETHICSLINE. Georgetown University, Kennedy Institute of Ethics, Center for Bioethics, Washington, D.C. 20057.

EVICTION
See: LANDLORD AND TENANT

EVIDENCE

See also: CIVIL PROCEDURE; CONFESSIONS; CONFIDENTIAL COMMUNICATIONS; CRIMINAL PROCEDURE; CROSS-EXAMINATION; DISCOVERY; EAVESDROPPING; LIE DETECTORS AND DETECTION; PHOTOGRAPHS AND PHOTOGRAPHY; WITNESSES

STATUTES, CODES, STANDARDS, UNIFORM LAWS

FEDERAL RULES OF EVIDENCE FOR UNITED STATES COURTS AND MAGISTRATES. West Publishing Company, P.O. Box 64526, 50 West Kellogg Boulevard, St. Paul, Minnesota 55164-0526. 1990. (Annual).

FEDERAL RULES OF EVIDENCE: LEGISLATIVE HISTORIES AND RELATED DOCUMENTS. James F. Bailey, III and Oscar M. Trelles, II. Hein and Company, 1285 Main Street, Buffalo, New York 14209. 1980.

UNIFORM ABSENCE AS EVIDENCE OF DEATH AND ABSENTEE'S PROPERTY ACT. Uniform Laws Annotated Pocket. West Publishing Company, P.O. Box 64526, 50 West Kellogg Boulevard, St. Paul, Minnesota 55164-0526. 1985- . (Annual Supplements).

UNIFORM AUDIO-VISUAL DEPOSITION ACT. Uniform Laws Annotated Pocket Part. West Publishing Company, P.O. Box 64526, 50 West Kellogg Boulevard, St. Paul, Minnesota 55164-0526. 1985- . (Annual Supplements).

UNIFORM FASCIMILE SIGNATURES OF PUBLIC OFFICIALS ACT. Uniform Laws Annotated. West Publishing Company, P.O. Box 64526, 50 West Kellogg Boulevard, St. Paul, Minnesota 55164-0526. 1985- . (Annual Supplements).

UNIFORM PERPETRATION OF TESTIMONY ACT. Uniform Laws Annotated. West Publishing Company, P.O. Box 64526, 50 West Kellogg Boulevard, St. Paul, Minnesota 55164-0526. 1985- . (Annual Supplements).

UNIFORM PHOTOGRAPHIC COPIES OF BUSINESS PUBLIC RECORDS AS EVIDENCE ACT. Uniform Laws Annotated. West Publishing Company, P.O. Box 64526, 50 West Kellogg Boulevard, St. Paul, Minnesota 55164-0526. 1985- . (Annual Supplements).

UNIFORM PRESERVATION OF PRIVATE BUSINESS RECORDS ACT. Uniform Laws Annotated. West Publishing Company, P.O. Box 64526, 50 West Kellogg Boulevard, St. Paul, Minnesota 55164-0526. 1985- . (Annual Supplements).

UNIFORM RECOGNITION OF ACKNOWLEDGMENTS ACT. Uniform Laws Annotated. West Publishing Company, P.O. Box 64526, 50 West Kellogg Boulevard, St. Paul, Minnesota 55164-0526. 1985- . (Annual Supplements).

UNIFORM RULES OF EVIDENCE. Uniform Laws Annotated. West Publishing Company, P.O. Box 64526, 50 West Kellogg Boulevard, St. Paul, Minnesota 55164-0526. 1985- . (Annual Supplements).

LOOSELEAF SERVICES AND REPORTERS

THE DEMONSTRATIVE EVIDENCE SOURCEBOOK. Douglas Filter. Staffort Hart Publishing Company, 5860 South Curtice, Littleton, Colorado 80120. 1985- . (Periodic Supplements).

DOCUMENTARY EVIDENCE. Asley S. Lipson. Matthew Bender and Company, Incorporated, 11 Penn Plaza, New York, New York 10001. 1986- . (Periodic Supplements).

EYEWITNESS IDENTIFICATION: LEGAL AND PRACTICAL PROBLEMS. 2nd Edition. Nathan R. Sobel. Clark Boardman Company, Limited, 435 Hudson Street, New York, New York 10014. 1981- . (Annual Supplements).

FEDERAL COURTROOM EVIDENCE. Joseph W. Cotchett and Arnold B. Elkind. Parker and Son, Publications, Incorporated, P.O. Box 60001, Los Angeles, California 90060. 1987- . (Annual Supplements).

FEDERAL EVIDENCE FOUNDATIONS. Murl A. Larkin. Butterworth Legal Publishers, 90 Stiles Road, Salem, New Hampshire 03079. 1988- . (Annual Supplements).

FEDERAL EVIDENCE PRACTICE GUIDE. Joseph M. McLauglin. Matthew Bender and Company, Incorporated, 11 Penn Plaza, New York, New York 10001. 1989- . (Annual Supplements).

FEDERAL RULES DECISIONS. West Publishing Company, P.O. Box 64526, 50 West Kellogg Boulevard, St. Paul, Minnesota 55164-0526. 1941- .

FEDERAL RULES OF EVIDENCE. 2nd Edition. Paul F. Rothstein. Clark Boardman Company, Limited, 435 Hudson Street, New York, New York 10014. 1978- . (Annual Supplements).

FEDERAL RULES OF EVIDENCE SERVICE. Pike and Fisher, Editors. Callaghan and Company, 155 Pfingsten Road, Deerfield, Illinois 60015. 1983- . (Monthly Supplements).

FEDERAL TESTIMONIAL PRIVILEGES. Murl A. Larkin. Clark Boardman Company, Limited, 435 Hudson Street, New York, New York 10014. 1982- . (Annual Supplements).

FEDERAL TRIAL EVIDENCE. Mark A. Dombroff. James Publishing, Incorporated, 3520 Cadillac Avenue, Suite E, Costa Mesa, California 92626. 1986- . (Periodic Supplements).

FEDERAL TRIAL EVIDENCE. Charles Wagner. Butterworth Legal Publishers, 90 Stiles Road, Salem, New Hampshire 03079. 1984- . (Quarterly Supplements).

MODERN VISUAL EVIDENCE. Gregory P. Joseph. Law Journal Seminars-Press, Incorporated, 111 Eighth Avenue, Suite 900, New York, New York 10011. 1984- . (Periodic Supplements).

PROVING FEDERAL CRIMES. U.S. Department of Justice. Superintendent of Documents, U.S. Government Printing Office, Washington, D.C. 20402. 1980- . (Periodic Supplements).

QUALIFYING AND ATTACKING EXPERT WITNESSES. Robert C. Clifford. James Publishing, Incorporated, 3520 Cadillac Avenue, Suite E, Costa Mesa, California 92626. 1988- . (Annual Supplements).

EVIDENCE

TANGIBLE EVIDENCE: HOW TO USE EXHIBITS AT TRIAL. 2nd Edition. Deanne C. Siemer. Prentice Hall, Law and Business, Incorporated, 910 Sylvan Avenue, Englewood Cliffs, New Jersey 07632. 1989- . (Periodic Supplements).

TRIAL EVIDENCE FOUNDATIONS. John A. Taratino and James R. Nanko. James Publishing, Incorporated, 3520 Cadillac Avenue, Suite E, Costa Mesa, California 92626. 1986- . (Annual Supplements).

TRIAL HEARSAY: OBJECTIONS AND EXCEPTIONS. Mark A. Dombroff. James Publishing, Incorporated, 3520 Cadillac Avenue, Suite E, Costa Mesa, California 92626. 1984- . (Annual Supplements).

TRIAL OBJECTIONS. Mark A. Dombroff. James Publishing, Incorporated, 3520 Cadillac Avenue, Suite E, Costa Mesa, California 92626. 1985- . (Annual Supplements).

UNCHARGED MISCONDUCT EVIDENCE. Edward J. Imwinkelried. Matthew Bender and Company, Incorporated, 11 Penn Plaza, New York, New York 10001. 1984- . (Periodic Supplements).

WEINSTEIN'S EVIDENCE MANUAL. Honorable Jack B. Weinstein and Margaret A. Berger. Matthew Bender and Company, Incorporated, 11 Penn Plaza, New York, New York 10001. 1987- . (Periodic Supplments).

WEINSTEIN'S EVIDENCE UNITED STATES COURT RULES. Honorable Jack B. Weinstein and Margaret A. Berger. Matthew Bender and Company, Incorporated, 11 Penn Plaza, New York, New York 10001. 1975- . (Semiannual Supplements).

HANDBOOKS, MANUALS, FORMBOOKS

FEDERAL RULES OF EVIDENCE MANUAL. Fifth Edition. Stephen A. Saltzburg and Kenneth R. Redden. Michie/Bobbs-Merrill Law Publishing Company, P.O. Box 7587, Charlottesville, Virginia 22906. 1990- . (Annual Supplements).

HANDBOOK OF FEDERAL EVIDENCE. Third Edition. Michael H. Graham. West Publishing Company, 50 West Kellogg Boulevard, St. Paul, Minnesota 55164. 1991.

HANDBOOK ON BASIC TRIAL EVIDENCE. Second Edition. Joseph M. Pellicciotti. University Press of America, 4720 Boston Way, Lanham, Maryland 20706. 1988.

HEARSAY: A PRACTICAL GUIDE THROUGHT THE THICKET. Irving Younger. Prentice-Hall Law and Business, Incorporated, Route 9W, Englewood Cliffs, New Jersey 07632.

THE HEARSAY HANDBOOK: THE HEARSAY RULE AND ITS EXCEPTIONS. Second edition. Shepard's/McGraw-Hill, P.O. Box 1235, Colorado Springs, Colorado 80901. 1984- . (Annual Supplements).

MILITARY RULES OF EVIDENCE MANUAL. Second edition. Stephen A Saltzburg. Michie/Bobbs-Merrill Law Publishing Company, P.O. Box 7587, Charlottesville, Virginia 22906. 1986- . (Annual Supplements).

MODERN STATE AND FEDERAL EVIDENCE: A COMPREHENSIVE REFERENCE TEXT. Michael H. Graham. National Institute for Trial Advocacy, Notre Dame Law School, Notre Dame, Indiana 46556. 1989.

TRIAL HANDBOOK. Second Edition. Kent Sinclair. Practising Law Institute, 810 Seventh Avenue, New York, New York 10019. 1990.

TEXTBOOKS AND GENERAL WORKS

ACME'S PLAINTIFF'S PROOF OF A PRIMA FACIE CASE. Patricia A. Groble. Callaghan and Company, 155 Pfingsten Road, Deerfield, Illinois 60015. 1986- .

ADVANCED LITIGATION SKILLS USING VIDEO. Practising Law Institute, 810 Seventh Avenue, New York, New York 10019. 1987.

AMERICAN JURISPRUDENCE PROOF OF FACTS, THIRD SERIES. Lawyers Co-Operative Publishing Company, One Graves Street, Rochester, New York 14694. 1973- . (Annual Supplements).

BANKRUPTCY EVIDENCE MANUAL. Barry Russell. West Publishing Company, 50 West Kellogg Boulevard, St. Paul, Minnesota 55164. 1990.

BASIC PROBLEMS OF EVIDENCE. Sixth Edition. Michael M. Martin. American Law Institute-American Bar Association, 4025 Chestnut Street, Philadelphia, Pennsylvania 19104. 1988.

CONSTRUCTION ENGINEERING EVIDENCE. Loren W. Peters. John Wiley and Sons, Incorporated, 605 Third Avenue, New York, New York 10158. 1989.

COPING WITH PSYCHIATRIC AND PSYCHOLOGICAL TESTIMONY. Fourth Edition. Jay Ziskin. Law and Psychology Press, P.O. Box 24219, Los Angeles, California 90024. 1988.

COURTROOM CRIMINAL EVIDENCE. Michie Company, P.O. Box 7587, Charlottesville, Virginia 22906. 1987.

CRIMINAL EVIDENCE. Fourth Edition. John C. Klotter. Anderson Publishing Company, P.O. Box 1576, Cincinnati, Ohio 45201. 1987.

DESTRUCTION OF EVIDENCE. Jamie S. Gorelick, Stephen Marzen and Lawrence Solum. John Wiley and Sons, Incorporated, 605 Third Avenue, New York, New York 10158. 1989.

DISCOVERY. Mark A. Dombroff. Kluwer Academic Publishers, 101 Philip Drive, Assinippi Park, Norwell, Massachusetts 02061 1986.

ENGINEERING EVIDENCE. Second Edition. Max Schwartz. Shepard's/McGraw-Hill, P.O. Box 1235, Colorado Springs, Colorado 80901.

EVIDENCE: COMMON LAW AND FEDERAL RULES OF EVIDENCE. Paul R. Rice. Matthew Bender and Company, Incorporated, 11 Penn Plaza, New York, New York 10001. 1987.

EVIDENCE: COMMON SENSE AND COMMON LAW. John MacArthur Maguire. West Publishing Company, 50 West Kellogg Boulevard, St. Paul, Minnesota 55164. 1990 reprint of 1947 edition.

EVIDENCE: HOW AND WHEN TO USE THE RULES TO WIN CASES. Edward T. Wright. Prentice-Hall, Incorporated, Route 9W, Englewood Cliffs, New Jersey 07632. 1990.

EVIDENCE IN AMERICA: THE FEDERAL RULES IN THE STATES. Gregory P. Joseph. Michie Company, P.O. Box 7587, Charlottesville, Virginia 22906. 1987- .

EVIDENCE IN ARBITRATION. Second Edition. Bureau of National Affairs, Incorporated, 1231 Twenty-fifth Street, Northwest, Washington, D.C. 20037. 1987.

EVIDENCE IN NEGLIGENCE CASES. Eighth edition. Charles Kramer and Daniel Kramer. Practising Law Institute, 810 Seventh Avenue, New York, New York 10019. 1987.

EVIDENCE IN TRIALS AT COMMON LAW (WIGMORE ON EVIDENCE). John Henry Wigmore. Little, Brown and Company, 34 Beacon Street, Boston, Massachusetts 02106. 1961- . (Periodic Supplements).

EVIDENCE: MAKING THE RECORD. Jon R. Waltz and John Kaplan. Foundation Press, P.O. Box 64056, Textbook Department, St. Paul, Minnesota 55164-0056. 1982.

EVIDENCE SCIENTIFIC IN CRIMINAL LAW CASES. Third edition. Andre A. Moenssens, Fred E. Inbau, and James Starrs. Foundation Press, P.O. Box 64056, Textbook Department, St. Paul, Minnesota 55164-0056. 1986.

EVIDENCE, STATE AND FEDERAL RULES IN A NUTSHELL. Second edition. Paul Rothstein. West Publishing Company, P.O. Box 64526, 50 West Kellogg Boulevard, St. Paul, Minnesota 55164-0526. 1981.

EVIDENTIARY FOUNDATIONS. Second Edition. Edward J. Imwinkelried. Michie Company, P.O. Box 7587, Charlottesville, Virginia 22906. 1989.

EVIDENTIARY TRIAL OBJECTIONS, WITH CASE ILLUSTRATIONS. George B. Rickter. National Judicial College, University of Nevada, Judicial College Building, Reno, Nevada 89557. 1984.

EXPERT EVIDENCE: INTERPRETING SCIENCE IN THE LAW. Roger Smith and Brian Wynne. Routledge, Chapman and Hall, Incorporated, 29 West 35th Street, New York, New York 10001.

EXPERT WITNESS CHECKLISTS. Douglas Danner. Lawyers Co-Operative Publishing Company, One Graves Street, Rochester, New York 14694. 1983- . (Periodic Supplements).

FEDERAL CRIMINAL TRIAL EVIDENCE. John C. O'Brien. Practising Law Institute, 810 Seventh Avenue, New York, New York 10019. 1989.

FEDERAL EVIDENCE. David W. Louisell and Christopher B. Mueller. Lawyers Co-Operative Publishing Company, One Graves Street, Rochester, New York 14694. 1981- . (Annual Supplements).

FEDERAL EVIDENCE. Glen Weissenberger. Anderson Publishing Company, 2035 Reading Road, Cincinnati, Ohio 45202. 1987.

FEDERAL PRACTICE AND PROCEDURE. Charles Alan Wright and Kenneth W. Graham, Jr. West Publishing Company, P.O. Box 64526, 50 West Kellogg Boulevard, St. Paul, Minnesota 55164-0526. 1969- . Annual Supplements.

FEDERAL RULES OF EVIDENCE IN A NUTSHELL. Second edition. Michael H. Graham. West Publishing Company, P.O. Box 64526, 50 West Kellogg Boulevard, St. Paul, Minnesota 55164-0526. 1987.

FEDERAL RULES OF EVIDENCE: A FRESH REVIEW AND EVALUATION. Section on Criminal Justice, Committee on Rules of Criminal Procedure and Evidence, American Bar Association, 750 North Lake Shore Drive, Chicago, Illinois 60611. 1987.

FEDERAL RULES OF EVIDENCE MANUAL. Fifth Edition. Stephen A. Saltzburg and Kenneth R. Redden. Michie Company, P.O. Box 7587, Charlottesville, Virginia 22906. 1990- . (Annual Supplements).

GENETICS IN THE COURTS. Henry M. Butzel. Edwin Mellen Press, P.O. Box 450, Lewiston, New York 14092. 1987.

INTRODUCTION TO CRIMINAL EVIDENCE. Third Edition. John R. Waltz. Nelson-Hall, Incorporated, 111 North Canal Street, Chicago, Illinois 60606. 1991.

AN INTRODUCTION TO THE LAW OF EVIDENCE. Second edition. Graham C. Lilly. West Publishing Company, P.O. Box 64526, 50 West Kellogg Boulevard, St. Paul, Minnesota 55164-0526. 1987.

JONES ON EVIDENCE, CIVIL AND CRIMINAL. Spencer A. Gard. Lawyers Co-Operative Publishing Company, One Graves Street, Rochester, New York 14694. 1972- . (Periodic Supplements).

LAW OF EVIDENCE FOR CRIMINAL JUSTICE PROFESSIONALS. Third Edition. Irving J. Klein. West Publishing Company, P.O. Box 64526, 50 West Kellogg Boulevard, St. Paul, Minnesota 55164-0526. 1989.

MAKING TRIAL OBJECTIONS. James F. McCarthy, Sr. John Wiley and Sons, Incorporated, 605 Third Avenue, New York, New York 10158. 1986.

MCCORMICK ON EVIDENCE. Third edition. Edward W. Cleary. West Publishing Company, P.O. Box 64526, 50 West Kellogg Boulevard, St. Paul, Minnesota 55164-0526. 1984- . (1987 Pocket Supplement).

THE METHODS OF ATTACKING SCIENTIFIC EVIDENCE. Edward J. Imwinkelried. Michie Company, P.O. Box 7587, Charlottesville, Virginia 22906. 1982- . (Periodic Supplements).

PRACTICAL GUIDE TO FEDERAL EVIDENCE: OBJECTIONS, RESPONSES, RULES, AND PRACTICE COMMENTARY. Anthony J. Bocchino and David A. Sonenshein. National Institute for Trial Advocacy, Notre Dame Law School, Notre Dame, Indiana 46556. 1988.

PRINCIPLES OF EVIDENCE. Irving Younger and Michael Goldsmith. National Practice Institute, 510 First Avenue, North, Suite 205, Minneapolis, Minnesota 55403. 1984.

PRIVILEGED COMMUNICATIONS AS A BRANCH OF LEGAL EVIDENCE. John F. Hageman. Fred B. Rothman and Company, 10368 West Centennial Road, Littleton, Colorado 80127. 1983.

PROBABILITY AND INFERENCE IN THE LAW OF EVIDENCE: LIMITS OF BAYESIANISM. Kluwer Academic Publishers, 101 Philip Drive, Assinippi Park, Norwell, Massachusetts 02061. 1988.

PSYCHIATRIC AND PSYCHOLOGICAL EVIDENCE. Daniel W. Shuman. Shepard's/McGraw-Hill, P.O. Box 1235, Colorado Springs, Colorado 80901. 1986- .

PSYCHOLOGICAL METHODS IN CRIMINAL INVESTIGATION AND EVIDENCE. David C. Raskin. Springer Publishing Company, Incorporated, 536 Broadway, New York, New York 10012.

PSYCHOLOGY OF EVIDENCE AND TRIAL PROCEDURE. Saul M. Kassin, Editor. Sage Publications, P.O. Box 6944, San Mateo, California 94403. 1985.

SCIENTIFIC EVIDENCE. Paul C. Imwinkelried. Michie Company, P.O. Box 7587, Charlottesville, Virginia 22906. 1986- . (Periodic Supplements).

SOCIAL SCIENCE IN COURT: MOBILIZING EXPERTS IN THE DESEGREGATION CASES. Mark A. Chesler. University of Wisconsin Press, 114 North Murray Street, Madison, Wisconsin 53715. 1988.

SPONSORSHIP STRATEGY: EVIDENTIARY TACTICS FOR WINNING JURY TRIALS. Robert H. Klonoff and Paul L. Colby. Michie Company, P.O. Box 7587, Charlottesville, Virginia 22906. 1990.

STRATEGIC USE OF CIRCUMSTANTIAL EVIDENCE. John F. Romano. Kluwer Academic Publishers, 101 Philip Drive, Assinippi Park, Norwell, Massachusetts 02061. 1986.

STRATEGIC USE OF SCIENTIFIC EVIDENCE. Kluwer Academic Publishers, 101 Philip Drive, Assinippi Park, Norwell, Massachusetts 02061. 1988.

TRIAL EVIDENCE AND TECHNIQUES IN FEDERAL AND STATE COURTS: A CLINICAL STUDY OF RECENT DEVELOPMENTS. American Law Institute-American Bar Association, 4025 Chestnut Street, Philadelphia, Pennsylvania 19104. 1989.

TRIAL OF THE EXPERT: A STUDY OF EXPERT EVIDENCE AND FORENSIC EXPERTS. Ian R. Freckelton. Oxford University Press, 200 Madison Avenue, New York, New York 10016. 1987.

WHARTON'S CRIMINAL EVIDENCE. Fourteenth Edition. Charles E. Torcia. Lawyers Cooperative Publishing Company, 50 East Broad Street, Rochester, New York 14694. 1985-1987.

DIGESTS, INDEXES, ABSTRACTS, CITATORS

SHEPARD'S UNITED STATES CITATIONS. STATUTES AND COURT RULES. Shepard's/McGraw-Hill, P.O. Box 1235, Colorado Springs, Colorado 80901. (Monthly Supplements).

NEWSLETTERS AND NEWSPAPERS

THE EXPERT AND THE LAW. National Forensic Center, 17 Temple Terrace, Lawrenceville, New Jersey 08648. 1981- . Bimonthly.

EXPERT EVIDENCE REPORTER. Shepard's/McGraw-Hill, P.O. Box 1235, Colorado Springs, Colorado 80901. 1989- . Monthly.

THE EXPERT WITNESS JOURNAL. Seak, Incorporated, P.O. Box 590, Falmouth, Massachusetts 02541. 1989- .

FEDERAL RULES OF EVIDENCE NEWS. John R. Schmertz, Jr., Editor. Callaghan and Company, 155 Pfingsten Road, Deerfield, Illinois 60015. 1975- . Monthly.

ASSOCIATIONS AND PROFESSIONAL SOCIETIES

AALS SECTION ON EVIDENCE. Association of American Law Schools, Suite 370, One Dupont Circle, Washington, D.C. 20036.

RESEARCH CENTERS, INSTITUTES, CLEARINGHOUSES

NATIONAL INSTITUTE FOR TRIAL ADVOCACY. Notre Dame Law School, Notre Dame, Indiana 46556.

NATIONAL JUDICIAL COLLEGE. Judicial College Building, University of Nevada, Reno, Nevada 89557.

STATISTICS SOURCES

STATISTICAL EVIDENCE IN LITIGATION: METHODOLOGY, PROCEDURE, AND PRACTICE. David W. Barnes and John M. Conley. Little, Brown and Company, 34 Beacon Street, Boston, Massachusetts 02106. 1986.

STATISTICAL METHODS IN DISCRIMINATION LITIGATION. D. H. Kaye and Mikel Aickin. Marcel Dekker, Incorporated, 270 Madison Avenue, New York, New York 10016. 1986.

STATISTICAL REASONING IN LAW AND SOCIAL POLICY. Joseph L. Gastwirth. Academic Press, Incorporated, 1250 6th Avenue, San Diego, California 92101.

STATISTICS AND THE LAW. Morris H. DeGroot, Stephen E. Fienberg, and Joseph B. Kadane, editors. John Wiley and Sons, Incorporated, 605 Third Avenue, New York, New York 10158. 1986- .

STATISTICS IN LITIGATION: PRACTICAL APPLICATIONS FOR LAWYERS. Richard A. Wehmhoefer. Shepard's/McGraw-Hill, P.O. Box 1235, Colorado Springs, Colorado 80901. 1985.

STATISTICS AS PROOF: FUNDAMENTALS OF QUANTITATIVE EVIDENCE. David W. Barnes. Little, Brown and Company, 34 Beacon Street, Boston, Massachusetts 02106. 1983.

EVIDENCE

AUDIOVISUALS

THE ART OF ADVOCACY: EXPERT WITNESSES. National Institute for Trial Advocacy, American Bar Association Videolaw Seminars, American Bar Association, 750 North Lake Shore Drive, Chicago, Illinois 60611. 1988. 10 Videotapes.

THE ART OF CROSS-EXAMINATION: A LECTURE BY IRVING YOUNGER. Section of Litigation. American Bar Association Videolaw Seminars, American Bar Association, 750 North Lake Shore Drive, Chicago, Illinois 60611. 1975. 2 Videotapes.

BASIC CONCEPTS OF EVIDENCE: LECTURES BY IRVING YOUNGER. National Institute for Trial Advocacy, American Bar Association Videolaw Seminars, American Bar Association, 750 North Lake Shore Drive, Chicago, Illinois 60611. 1975. 15 Videotapes.

CREDIBILITY AND CROSS-EXAMINATION: A LECTURE BY IRVING YOUNGER. Irving Younger. Professional Education Group, Hopkins, Minnesota. 55343. 1986. 2 Videotapes.

DEVELOPING AND USING TANGIBLE EVIDENCE. National Institute for Trial Advocacy, American Bar Association Videolaw Seminars, American Bar Association, 750 North Lake Shore Drive, Chicago, Illinois 60611. 1985. 2 Videotapes.

DIRECT AND CROSS EXAMINATION. National Institute for Trial Advocacy, Notre Dame Law School, Notre Dame, Indiana 46556. 1976-77. 8 Videotapes.

EVERYTHING YOU ALWAYS WANTED TO KNOW ABOUT HEARSAY, BUT WERE AFRAID TO ASK. American Bar Association Section of Litigation, American Bar Association Videolaw Seminars, American Bar Association, 750 North Lake Shore Drive, Chicago, Illinois 60611. 1976. 2 Videotapes.

EVIDENCE UPDATE. National Institute for Trial Advocacy, American Bar Association Videolaw Seminars, American Bar Association, 750 North Lake Shore Drive, Chicago, Illinois 60611. 1980. 3 Videotapes.

EXHIBIT SERIES. National Institute for Trial Advocacy, American Bar Association Videolaw Seminars, American Bar Association, 750 North Lake Shore Drive, Chicago, Illinois 60611. 1979. 5 Videotapes.

EXPERT WITNESSES. Irving Younger. Professional Education Group, Hopkins, Minnesota. 55343. 1986. 2 Videotapes.

EXPERT WITNESSES. National Institute for Trial Advocacy, Notre Dame Law School, Notre Dame, Indiana 46556. 1977- 1980. 8 Videotapes.

EXPERTS: LAW OF EVIDENCE. National Institute for Trial Advocacy, American Bar Association Videolaw Seminars, American Bar Association, 750 North Lake Shore Drive, Chicago, Illinois 60611. 1980. 2 Videotapes.

HEARSAY. Irving Younger. Professional Education Group, Hopkins, Minnesota. 55343. 1986. 2 Videotapes.

THE INTRODUCTION AND USE OF DEMONSTRATIVE EVIDENCE. National Institute for Trial Advocacy. American Bar Association Videolaw Seminars, American Bar Association, 750 North Lake Shore Drive, Chicago, Illinois 60611. 1983. 1 Videotape.

LASER DISC TECHNOLOGY IN THE COURTROOM. National Institute for Trial Advocacy, Notre Dame Law School, Notre Dame, Indiana 46556. 1990. Videotape.

LAYING THE FOUNDATION FOR EXHIBITS AND WITNESSES AT TRIAL. National Institute for Trial Advocacy, American Bar Association Videolaw Seminars, American Bar Association, 750 North Lake Shore Drive, Chicago, Illinois 60611. 1983. 1 Videotape.

MASTERING THE ART OF CROSS EXAMINATION. National Institute for Trial Advocacy, American Bar Association Videolaw Seminars, American Bar Association, 750 North Lake Shore Drive, Chicago, Illinois 60611. 11 Videotapes.

PERSUASIVE EXPERT TESTIMONY. National Institute for Trial Advocacy, Notre Dame Law School, Notre Dame, Indiana 46556. 1990. 2 Videotapes.

PRESENTING DOCUMENTARY AND DEMONSTRATIVE EVIDENCE EFFECTIVELY. California Continuing Education of the Bar. Distributed by Division of Professional Education, American Bar Association, 750 North Lake Shore Drive, Chicago, Illinois 60611. Videocassette.

PRINCIPLES OF EXAMINATION. National Institute for Trial Advocacy. American Bar Association Videolaw Seminars, American Bar Association, 750 North Lake Shore Drive, Chicago, Illinois 60611. 1978. 2 Videotapes.

SCIENTIFIC EVIDENCE. Irving Younger. Professional Education Group, Hopkins, Minnesota. 55343. 1986. 2 Videotapes.

THE TEN COMMANDMENTS OF CROSS-EXAMINATION. American Bar Association Videolaw Seminars, American Bar Association, 750 North Lake Shore Drive, Chicago, Illinois 60611. 1988. 1 Videotape.

TESTIMONY OF EXPERT WITNESSES UNDER THE FEDERAL RULES OF EVIDENCE. National Institute for Trial Advocacy. American Bar Association Videolaw Seminars, American Bar Association, 750 North Lake Shore Drive, Chicago, Illinois 60611. 1988. 1 Videotape.

TRIAL EVIDENCE -- MAKING AND MEETING OBJECTIONS. National Institute for Trial Advocacy, Notre Dame Law School, Notre Dame, Indiana 46556. 1991. Videotape.

USING FINANCIAL EXPERTS IN BUSINESS LITIGATION. National Institute for Trial Advocacy, Notre Dame Law School, Notre Dame, Indiana 46556. 1988. Videotape.

COMPUTER-ASSISTED LEGAL INSTRUCTION

BEST EVIDENCE RULE AND AUTHENTICATION. Robert W. Peterson. Center for Computer-Assisted Legal Instruction, 229 19th Street, South, Minneapolis, Minnesota 55455. Computer program.

BREW V. HARRIS I, II AND III. Interactive Video Library, Harvard Law School, Educational Technology Department, 18 Everett Street, Cambridge, Massachusetts 02138. Interactive videodisc.

CALIFORNIA AND FEDERAL BEST EVIDENCE RULES AND AUTHENTICATION RULES. Robert W. Peterson. Center for Computer-Assisted Instruction, 229 Nineteenth Avenue South, University of Minnesota, Minneapolis, Minnesota 55455. Machine-readable computer file.

CHARACTER EVIDENCE UNDER FEDERAL RULES. Roger Park. Center for Computer-Assisted Legal Instruction, 229 Nineteenth Avenue South, University of Minnesota, Minneapolis, Minnesota 55455. Machine-readable computer file.

COMPUTER GAME OBJECTION! TransMedia Productions,Incorporated, c/o Center for Computer-Assisted Instruction, 229 19th Avenue South, University of Minnesota, Minneapolis, Minnesota 55455. Machine- readable computer file.

CONCEPT OF HEARSAY. Roger Park. Center for Computer-Assisted Legal Instruction, 229 Nineteenth Avenue South, University of Minnesota, Minneapolis, Minnesota 55455. Machine-readable computer file.

DAVIS V. JACOBY. Center for Computer-Assisted Instruction, 229 Nineteenth Avenue South, University of Minnesota, Minneapolis, Minnesota 55455. Interactive videodisc.

EASERLY V. LETWIN. Center for Computer-Assisted Instruction, 229 Nineteenth Avenue South, University of Minnesota, Minneapolis, Minnesota 55455. Interactive videodisc.

EVIDENCE. Charles R. Nesson. National Practice Institute, 330 Second Avenue South, Minneapolis, Minnesota 55401. Videotape.

EVIDENCE FOR THE TRIAL LAWYER. Faust F. Rossi. National Practice Institute, 330 Second Avenue South, Minneapolis, Minnesota 55401. Videotape.

EVIDENCE OBJECTIONS. Roger W. Kirst. Center for Computer- Assisted Legal Instruction, 229 Nineteenth Avenue South, University of Minnesota, Minneapolis, Minnesota 55455. Interactive videodisc program.

EVIDENTIARY FOUNDATIONS ILLUSTRATED. CLE Group, 274 Willow Road, Menlo Park, California 94025. Interactive videodisc.

EXPERT AND OPINION EVIDENCE. Ronald L. Carlson. Center for Computer-Assisted Legal Instruction, 229 19th Street, South, Minneapolis, Minnesota 55455. Computer program.

FRANCIS V. SPINDLER. Interactive Video Library, Harvard Law School, Educational Technology Department, 18 Everett Street, Cambridge, Massachusetts 02138. Interactive videodisc.

HEARSAY FROM SQUARE ONE: THE DEFINITION OF HEARSAY. Roger Park. Center for Computer-Assisted Legal Instruction, 229 Nineteenth Avenue South, University of Minnesota, Minneapolis, Minnesota 55455. Machine-readable computer file.

THE HEARSAY RULE AND ITS EXCEPTIONS. Roger C. Park. Center for Computer-Assisted Legal Instruction, 229 Nineteenth Avenue South, University of Minnesota, Minneapolis, Minnesota 55455. Machine-readable computer file.

IMPEACHMENT AND REHABILITATION OF WITNESSES. Roger Park. Center for Computer-Assisted Legal Instruction, 229 19th Street, South, Minneapolis, Minnesota 55455. Computer program.

INTERACTIVE VIDEO LIBRARY. Interactive Video Project, Harvard University Law School, Langdell Hall, Cambridge, Massachusetts 02138. 1987- . (Various lessons deal with evidence).

OLCOTT V. OLCOTT. Center for Computer-Assisted Instruction, 229 19th Avenue South, University of Minnesota, Minneapolis, Minnesota 55455. Interactive videodisc.

ORTIZ V. FLEISHMAN I, II AND III. Center for Computer-Assisted Instruction, 229 19th Avenue South, University of Minnesota, Minneapolis, Minnesota 55455. Interactive videodisc.

SEARCH AND SEIZURE. Center for Computer-Assisted Instruction, 229 19th Avenue South, University of Minnesota, Minneapolis, Minnesota 55455. Interactive videodisc.

SETTLING CASES FASTER WITH VIDEO EVIDENCE. National Practice Institute, 330 Second Avenue South, Minneapolis, Minnesota 55401. Videotape.

STATE V. GILBERT. Center for Computer-Assisted Instruction, 229 19th Avenue South, University of Minnesota, Minneapolis, Minnesota 55455. Interactive videodisc.

STATE V. RODGERS. Center for Computer-Assisted Instruction, 229 19th Avenue South, University of Minnesota, Minneapolis, Minnesota 55455. Interactive videodisc.

STATE V. WILLIAMS I & II. Center for Computer-Assisted Instruction, 229 19th Avenue South, University of Minnesota, Minneapolis, Minnesota 55455. Interactive videodisc.

SURVEY OF EVIDENCE--CIVIL PROCEDURE VERSION. Roger C. Park and Douglas D. McFarland. Center for Computer-Assisted Instruction, 229 19th Avenue South, University of Minnesota, Minneapolis, Minnesota 55455. Machine-readable data file.

SURVEY OF EVIDENCE-EVIDENCE VERSION. Roger C. Park. Center for Computer-Assisted Instruction, 229 19th Avenue South, University of Minnesota, Minneapolis, Minnesota 55455. Machine-readable computer file.

TRIAL EVIDENCE AND CROSS-EXAMINATION SKILLS. CLE Group, 274 Willow Road, Menlo Park, California 94025. Interactive videodisc.

TRIAL EVIDENCE AND DIRECT EXAMINATION SKILLS. CLE Group, 274 Willow Road, Menlo Park, California 94025. Interactive videodisc.

TRIAL SKILLS ILLUSTRATED I AND II. CLE Group, 274 Willow Road, Menlo Park, California 94025. Interactive videodisc.

YOU BE THE JUDGE. CLE Group, 274 Willow Road, Menlo Park, California 94025. Interactive videodisc.

EXCISE TAXES

See also: SALES AND USE TAXES; TAX LEGISLATION AND POLICY

STATUTES, CODES, STANDARDS, UNIFORM LAWS

FEDERAL INCOME TAX CODE AND REGULATIONS. Commerce Clearing House, Incorporated, 4025 West Peterson Avenue, Chicago, Illinois 60646. Annual.

FEDERAL TAX REGULATIONS. West Publishing Company, P.O. Box 64526, 50 West Kellogg Boulevard, St. Paul, Minnesota 55164-0526. Annual.

INTERNAL REVENUE BULLETIN: CUMULATIVE BULLETIN. United States Department of Treasury, Internal Revenue Service. United States Government Printing Office, Washington, D.C. 20402. Weekly.

INTERNAL REVENUE CODE. West Publishing Company, P.O. Box 64526, 50 West Kellogg Boulevard, St. Paul, Minnesota 55164-0526. Annual.

LOOSELEAF SERVICES AND REPORTERS

EXCISE TAXES. Prentice-Hall, Incorporated, Route 9W, Englewood Cliffs, New Jersey 07632. 1965- .

FEDERAL EXCISE TAX REPORTER: CODE, REGULATIONS, RULINGS, DECISIONS. Commerce Clearing House, Incorporated, 4025 West Peterson Avenue, Chicago, Illinois 60646. 1966- .

FEDERAL TAXES. Prentice-Hall, Incorporated, Route 9W, Englewood Cliffs, New Jersey 07632. 1919- .

STANDARD FEDERAL TAX REPORTS. Commerce Clearing House, Incorporated, 4025 West Peterson Avenue, Chicago, Illinois 60646. 1913- .

UNITED STATES EXCISE TAX GUIDE. Commerce Clearing House, Incorporated, 4025 West Peterson Avenue, Chicago, Illinois 60646. (Annual).

HANDBOOKS, MANUALS, FORMBOOKS

MANUAL RELATING TO FEDERAL EXCISE TAXES ON PETROLEUM PRODUCTS. Eighth Edition. American Petroleum Institute, 1220 L Street, Northwest, Washington, D.C. 20005. 1984.

DIGESTS, INDEXES, ABSTRACTS, CITATORS

FEDERAL TAX ARTICLES: INCOME, ESTATE, GIFT, EXCISE, EMPLOYMENT TAXES. Commerce Clearing House, Incorporated, 4025 West Peterson Avenue, Chicago, Illinois 60646. 1969- .

FEDERAL TAX VALUATION DIGEST: BUSINESS INTERESTS AND BUSINESS ENTERPRISES. John A. Bishop and Arthur H. Rosenbloom. Research Institute of America, Incorporated, One Penn Plaza, New York, New York 10119. 1979- .

FEDERAL TAXES CITATOR. Prentice-Hall, Incorporated, Route 9W, Englewood Cliffs, New Jersey 07632. 1943- .

INDEX TO FEDERAL TAX ARTICLES. Gersham Goldstein, Editor. Research Institute of America, Incorporated, One Penn Plaza, New York, New York 10119. 1975- . (Quarterly Supplements).

SHEPARD'S FEDERAL TAX CITATIONS. Shepard's/McGraw-Hill, P.O. Box 1235, Colorado Springs, Colorado 80901. 1981- . (Monthly Supplements).

SHEPARD'S FEDERAL TAX LOCATOR: COMPLETE INDEX TO ALL THE CURRENT SOURCES OF LAW RELATING TO FEDERAL TAXATION. Shepard's/McGraw-Hill, P.O. Box 1235, Colorado Springs, Colorado 80901. 1974- .

ANNUALS AND SURVEYS

A COMPENDIUM OF STATE STATUTES AND INTERNATIONAL TREATIES IN TRUST AND ESTATE LAW: REFERENCE AND REFERRAL GUIDE FOR PRACTICING ATTORNEYS. M. Henner. Quorum Books, 88 Post Road West, P.O. Box 5007, Westport, Connecticut 06881. 1985.

SCHEDULE OF PRESENT FEDERAL EXCISE TAXES (AS OF JANUARY 1, 1990). United States Congress, Joint Committee on Taxation. Superintendent of Documents, United States Government Printing Office, Washington, D.C. 20402. 1990.

LAW REVIEWS AND PERIODICALS

JOURNAL OF TAXATION. Research Institute of America, Incorporated, One Penn Plaza, New York, New York 10119. Monthly.

TAX LAW REVIEW. Research Institute of America, Incorporated, One Penn Plaza, New York, New York 10119. Quarterly.

THE TAX LAWYER. American Bar Association, Section on Taxation, 750 North Lake Shore Drive, Chicago, Illinois 60611. Quarterly.

TAXATION FOR LAWYERS. Research Institute of America, Incorporated, One Penn Plaza, New York, New York 10119. Bimonthly.

TAXES: THE TAX MAGAZINE. Commerce Clearing House, Incorporated, 4025 West Peterson Avenue, Chicago, Illinois 60646. Monthly.

VIRGINIA TAX REVIEW. Virginia Tax Review Association, University of Virginia, School of Law, Charlottesville, Virginia 22901. Semiannual.

ASSOCIATIONS AND PROFESSIONAL SOCIETIES

SECTION ON TAXATION. American Bar Association, 750 North Lake Shore Drive, Chicago, Illinois 60611. (312) 988-5158.

SECTION ON TAXATION. Association of American Law Schools, One Dupont Circle, Northwest, Suite 370, Washington, D.C. 20036. (202) 296-8851.

EXCISE TAXES

RESEARCH CENTERS, INSTITUTES, CLEARINGHOUSES

INSTITUTES FOR CONTINUING EDUCATION IN LAW AND TAXATION. New York University, 11 West Forty-second Street, New York, New York 10036. (212) 790-1320.

NATIONAL TAX ASSOCIATION - TAX INSTITUTE FOR AMERICA. 5310 East Main Street, Suite 104, Columbus, Ohio 43213. (614) 864-1221.

UNIVERSITY OF SOUTHERN CALIFORNIA INSTITUTE ON FEDERAL TAXATION. Law Center, University Park Campus, Los Angeles, California 90089-0071. (213) 740-2646.

ONLINE DATABASES

LEXIS, TAX LIBRARY. Mead Data Central, P.O. Box 933, Dayton, Ohio 45401.

WESTLAW, TAX LIBRARY. West Publishing Company, P.O. Box 64526, 50 West Kellogg Boulevard, St. Paul, Minnesota 55164-0526.

EXECUTION
See: CAPITAL PUNISHMENT; JUDGMENTS

EXECUTIVE POWER
See also: PRESIDENT (UNITED STATES)

STATUTES, CODES, STANDARDS, UNIFORM LAWS

CODE OF FEDERAL REGULATIONS, TITLE 3, THE EXECUTIVE. Office of the Federal Register, National Archives and Records Administration, Superintendent of Documents, United States Government Printing Office, Washington, D.C. 20402. Annual. (Updated by use of monthly *List of Section Affected* and daily *Federal Register*.

CODIFICATION OF PRESIDENTIAL PROCLAMATIONS AND EXECUTIVE ORDERS. General Services Administration, National Archives and Records Service, Office of the Federal Register. Superintendent of Documents, United States Government Printing Office, Washington, D.C. 20402. (Irregular).

THE EXECUTIVE REORGANIZATION ACT: A SOURCE OF PROPOSALS FOR RENEWAL AND MODIFICATION. American Enterprise Institute for Public Policy Research, 1150 Seventeenth Street, Northwest, Washington, D.C. 20036. 1977.

TEXTBOOKS AND GENERAL WORKS

ALL THINGS TO ALL MEN: THE FALSE PROMISE OF THE MODERN AMERICAN PRESIDENCY. Godfrey Hodgson. Simon and Schuster, Incorporated, 1230 Avenue of the Americas, New York, New York 10020. 1980.

ANALYZING THE PRESIDENCY. Robert E. DiClerico. Dushkin Publishing Group, Incorporated, Sluice Dock, Guilford, Connecticut 06437. 1985.

Encyclopedia of Legal Information Sources • 2nd Ed.

BIG BUSINESS AND PRESIDENTIAL POWER: FROM FDR TO REAGAN. Kim McQuaid. William Morrow and Company, Incorporated, 105 Madison Avenue, New York, New York 10016. 1982.

CONFLICT OR CODETERMINATION?: CONGRESS, THE PRESIDENT, AND THE POWER TO MAKE WAR. Marc E. Smyrl. Ballinger Division, HarperCollins Publishers, 10 East Fifty-third Street, New York, New York 10022. 1988.

CONGRESS AND THE PRESIDENCY. Fourth Edition. Nelson W. Polsby. Prentice-Hall, Incorporated, Route 9W, Englewood Cliffs, New Jersey 07632. 1986.

CONGRESS, THE PRESIDENCY, AND AMERICAN FOREIGN POLICY. John Spanier and Joseph Nogee, Editors. Pergamon Press, Incorporated, Maxwell House, Fairview Park, Elmsford, New York 10523. 1981.

CONGRESS, THE PRESIDENT, AND FOREIGN POLICY. Steven P. Soper, Editor. American Bar Association, Standing Committee on Law and National Security, 1800 M Street, Northwest, Washington, D.C. 20036. 1984.

CONGRESSIONAL GOVERNMENT: A STUDY IN AMERICAN POLITICS. Woodrow Wilson and Walter Lippman. Johns Hopkins University Press, 701 West Fortieth Street, Suite 275, Baltimore, Maryland 21211. 1981 Reprint.

THE CONSTITUTION AND THE AMERICAN PRESIDENCY. Martin L. Fausold and Alan Shank. State University of New York Press, State University Plaza, Albany, New York 12246. 1991.

THE DILEMMAS OF PRESIDENTIAL LEADERSHIP: OF CARETAKERS AND KINGS. Francis P. Kessler. Prentice-Hall, Incorporated, Route 9W, Englewood Cliffs, New Jersey 07632. 1982.

EXECUTIVE AGREEMENTS AND PRESIDENTIAL POWER IN FOREIGN POLICY. Lawrence Margolis. Praeger Publishers, One Madison Avenue, New York, New York 10010-3603. 1985.

THE EXECUTIVE VETO. Chester James Antieau. Oceana Publications, 75 Main Street, Dobbs Ferry, New York 10522. 1988.

THE FETTERED PRESIDENCY: LEGAL CONSTRAINTS ON THE EXECUTIVE BRANCH. L. Gordon Crovitz and Jeremy A. Rabkin. American Enterprise Institute for Public Policy Research, 1150 Seventeenth Street, Northwest, Washington, D.C. 20036. 1989.

FIRST USE OF NUCLEAR WEAPONS: UNDER THE CONSTITUTION, WHO DECIDES? Greenwood Publishing Group, Incorporated, 88 Post Road West, P.O. Box 5007, Westport, Connecticut 06881. 1987.

GOVERNMENT FROM REFLECTION TO CHOICE: CONSTITUTIONAL ESSAYS ON WAR, FOREIGN RELATIONS, AND FEDERALISM. Charles Lofgren. Oxford University Press, 200 Madison Avenue, New York, New York 10016. 1986.

THE ILLUSION OF PRESIDENTIAL GOVERNMENT. Hugh Heclo and Lester M. Salamon, Editors. Westview Press, 5500 Central Avenue, Boulder, Colorado 80301. 1981.

THE IMPOSSIBLE PRESIDENCY: ILLUSIONS AND REALITIES OF EXECUTIVE POWER. Harold M. Barger. Scott Foresman and Company, 1900 East Lake Avenue, Glenview, Illinois 60025. 1984.

THE LAW OF PRESIDENTIAL POWER: CASES AND MATERIALS. Peter M. Shane and Harold H. Bruff. Carolina Academic Press, P.O. Box 51879, Durham, North Carolina 27717. 1988.

THE MAKING OF INTERNATIONAL AGREEMENTS: CONGRESS CONFRONTS THE EXECUTIVE. Loch K. Johnson. New York University Press, 70 Washington Square, South, New York, New York 10012. 1985.

POLITICS AND THE OVAL OFFICE: TOWARDS PRESIDENTIAL GOVERNANCE. Arnold J. Meltsner, Editor. Transaction Books, Rutgers-The State University of New Jersey, New Brunswick, New Jersey 08903. 1981.

THE POWER OF THE PRESIDENCY: CONCEPTS AND CONTROVERSY. Third Edition. Robert S. Hirschfield, Editor. Aldine de Gruyter, 200 Saw Mill River Road, Hawthorne, New York 10532. 1982.

THE PRESIDENCY AND INFORMATION POLICY. Harold C. Relyea. Center for the Study of the Presidency, 208 East Seventy-fifth Street, New York, New York 10021. 1981.

THE PRESIDENCY IN THE CONSTITUTIONAL ORDER. Joseph M. Bessette and Jeffrey Tulis, Editors. Louisiana State University Press, Highland Road, Baton Rouge, Louisiana 70893. 1981.

THE PRESIDENT AND THE PUBLIC PHILOSOPHY. Kenneth W. Thompson. Louisiana State University Press, Highland Road, Baton Rouge, Louisiana 70893. 1981.

THE PRESIDENT, CONGRESS, AND THE CONSTITUTION: POWER AND LEGITIMACY IN AMERICAN POLITICS. Christopher H. Pyle and Richard M. Pious. Free Press, 866 Third Avenue, New York, New York 10022. 1984.

THE PRESIDENT, THE CONGRESS, AND FOREIGN POLICY. Kenneth Rush. University Press of America, 4720 Boston Way, Lanham, Maryland 20706. 1986.

THE PRESIDENT: OFFICE AND POWERS, 1787-1984: HISTORY AND ANALYSIS OF PRACTICE AND OPINION. Fifth Edition. Randall W. Bland. New York University Press, 70 Washington Square South, New York, New York 10012. 1984.

PRESIDENTIAL POWER. Arthur Selwyn Miller. West Publishing Company, P.O. Box 64526, 50 West Kellogg Boulevard, St. Paul, Minnesota 55164-0526. 1977.

PRESIDENTIAL POWER AND ACCOUNTABILITY: TOWARD A NEW CONSTITUTION. Charles M. Hardin. University of Chicago Press, 5801 Ellis Avenue, Chicago, Illinois 60637. 1975.

PRESIDENTIAL POWER IN A NUTSHELL. Arthur Selwyn Miller. West Publishing Company, P.O. Box 64526, 50 West Kellogg Boulevard, St. Paul, Minnesota 55164-0526. 1977.

PRESIDENTIAL POWER IN THE UNITED STATES. Raymond Tatalovich and Byron W. Daynes. Brooks/Cole Publishing Company, 511 Forest Lodge Road, Pacific Grove, California 93950. 1984.

PRESIDENTIAL POWER: THE POLITICS OF LEADERSHIP FROM FDR TO CARTER. Richard E. Neustadt. John Wiley and Sons, Incorporated, 605 Third Avenue, New York, New York 10158. 1980.

PRESIDENTS AND POLITICS: THE LIMITS OF POWER. Charles Funderburk. Brooks/Cole Publishing Company, 511 Forest Lodge Road, Pacific Grove, California 93950. 1982.

THE SUPREME COURT, THE CONSTITUTION, AND PRESIDENTIAL POWER. Michael A. Genovese. University Press of America, 4720 Boston Way, Lanham, Maryland 20706. 1980.

THE TETHERED PRESIDENCY: A STUDY OF NEW CONGRESSIONAL RESTRAINTS ON PRESIDENTIAL POWER AND THEIR EFFECT ON AMERICA'S ABILITY TO CONDUCT AN EFFECTIVE FOREIGN POLICY. Thomas M. Franck, Editor. New York University Press, 70 Washington Square, New York, New York 10012. 1981.

TRUMAN AND THE STEEL SEIZURE CASE: THE LIMITS OF PRESIDENTIAL POWER. Maeva Marcus. Columbia University Press, 562 West One Hundred Thirteenth Street, New York, New York 10025. 1977.

WAR, FOREIGN AFFAIRS, AND CONSTITUTIONAL POWER, 1829-1901. Henry Bartholomew Cox. Ballinger Division, HarperCollins Publishers, 10 East Fifty-third Street, New York, New York 10022. 1984.

LAW REVIEWS AND PERIODICALS

PRESIDENTIAL STUDIES QUARTERLY. Center for the Study of the Presidency, 208 East Seventy-fifth Street, New York, New York 10021. Quarterly.

BIOGRAPHICAL SOURCES

GOVERNOR REAGAN, GOVERNOR BROWN: A SOCIOLOGY OF EXECUTIVE POWER. Gary G. Hamilton and Nicole W. Biggart. Columbia University Press, 562 West One Hundred Thirteenth Street, New York, New York 10025. 1984.

RESEARCH CENTERS, INSTITUTES, CLEARINGHOUSES

CENTER FOR THE STUDY OF THE PRESIDENCY. 208 East Seventy-fifth Street, New York, New York 10021. (212) 249-1200.

LEAGUE OF WOMEN VOTERS EDUCATION FUND. 1730 M Street, Northwest, Washington, D.C. 20036. (202) 429-1965.

WHITE BURKETT MILLER CENTER OF PUBLIC AFFAIRS. University of Virginia, Box 5106, Charlottesville, Virginia 22905. (804) 924-7236.

EXECUTORS AND ADMINISTRATORS
See: WILLS, TRUSTS AND INHERITANCE

EXPATRIATION AND DEPORTATION
See: CITIZENS AND CITIZENSHIP; EMIGRATION AND IMMIGRATION

EXPERT WITNESSES
See: TRIAL PRACTICE; WITNESSES

EXPLOSIVES
See: FIRES AND FIRE PREVENTION; HAZARDOUS SUBSTANCES

EXPORT AND IMPORT
See also: CUSTOMS SERVICE; INTERNATIONAL TRADE ADMINISTRATION; INTERNATIONAL TRADE COMMISSION

STATUTES, CODES, STANDARDS, UNIFORM LAWS

OVERVIEW AND COMPILATION OF U.S. TRADE STATUTES: INCLUDING ECONOMIC DATA. Superintendent of Documents, United States Government Printing Office, Washington, D.C. 20402. 1991.

LOOSELEAF SERVICES AND REPORTERS

ANTIDUMPING AND COUNTERVAILING DUTY LAWS. Joseph E. Pattison. Clark Boardman Company, Limited, 435 Hudson Street, New York, New York 10014. 1984- .

CHINA HAND: INVESTING, LICENSING, AND TRADING CONDITIONS TODAY. Business International Corporation, 1 Dag Hammerskjold Plaza, New York, New York 10017. 1981- . (Monthly Supplements).

COMMERCIAL, BUSINESS AND TRADE LAWS OF THE WORLD. Kenneth R. Simmonds, Editor. Oceana Publications, 75 Main Street, Dobbs Ferry, New York 10522. 1981- .

CUSTOMS LAW AND ADMINISTRATION. Third Edition. Ruth Sturm. Oceana Publications, 75 Main Street, Dobbs Ferry, New York 10522. 1982- .

CUSTOMS REGULATIONS OF THE UNITED STATES. United States Customs Service. Superintendent of Documents, United States Government Printing Office, Washington, D.C. 20402. (Periodic Supplements). 1932- .

EXPORT ADMINISTRATION REGULATIONS. Superintendent of Documents, United States Government Printing Office, Washington, D.C. 20402. 1978- . (Kept up to date by Export Administration Bulletin).

EXPORT CONTROLS IN THE UNITED STATES. John R. Liebman, Robert L. Johnson and Raner H. Meyer. Prentice-Hall, Incorporated, Route 9W, Englewood Cliffs, New Jersey 07632. 1985- .

EXPORT SHIPPING MANUAL. Bureau of National Affairs, Incorporated, 1231 Twenty-fifth Street, Northwest, Washington, D.C. 20037. 1947- .

EXPORT TRADING COMPANY ACT OF 1982. W.A. Hancock. Business Laws, Incorporated, 11630 Chillicothe Road, Chesterland, Ohio 44026. 1983- . (Periodic Supplements).

FEDERAL REGULATION OF INTERNATIONAL BUSINESS. Stuart S. Malawer. William S. Hein and Company, Incorporated, Hein Building, 1285 Main Street, Buffalo, New York 14209. 1980- .

FED-TRACK GUIDE TO ANTIDUMPING FINDINGS AND ORDERS. Fed-Track Publications, 810 Eighteenth Street, Northwest, Washington, D.C. 20006. 1983- .

FED-TRACK GUIDE TO COUNTERVAILING DUTY CASES. Fed-Track Publications, 810 Eighteenth Street, Northwest, Washington, D.C. 20006. 1984- .

FED-TRACK GUIDE TO INTERNATIONAL TRADE RULES. Fed-Track Publications, 810 Eighteenth Street, Northwest, Washington, D.C. 20006. 1984- .

FINANCING FOREIGN OPERATIONS. Business International Corporation, 1 Dag Hammerskjold Plaza, New York, New York 10017. 1957- .

GUIDE TO ANTIDUMPING AND COUNTERVAILING DUTIES AND OTHER UNFAIR IMPORT LAWS. Business Laws, Incorporated, 11630 Chillicothe Road, Chesterland, Ohio 44026. 1983- .

GUIDE TO INTERNATIONAL COMMERCE LAW. Paul H. Vishny. Shepard's/McGraw-Hill, P.O. Box 1235, Colorado Springs, Colorado 80901. 1981- .

HISTORY OF THE TARIFF SCHEDULES OF THE UNITED STATES ANNOTATED. United States International Trade Commission. Superintendent of Documents, United States Government Printing Office, Washington, D.C. 20402. 1981- .

INTERNATIONAL BOYCOTTS. W.A. Hancock. Business Laws, Incorporated, 11630 Chillicothe Road, Chesterland, Ohio 44026. 1978- .

INTERNATIONAL BUSINESS PLANNING: LAW AND TAXATION--UNITED STATES. William P. Streng and J.W. Salacuse. Matthew Bender and Company, Incorporated, 11 Penn Plaza, New York, New York 10001. 1982- .

INTERNATIONAL TRADE REPORTER. Bureau of National Affairs, Incorporated, 1231 Twenty-fifth Street, Northwest, Washington, D.C. 20037. 1984- .

INVESTING, LICENSING AND TRADING CONDITIONS ABROAD. Business International Corporation, 1 Dag Hammerskjold Plaza, New York, New York 10017. 1955- .

INVESTMENT LAWS OF THE WORLD: THE DEVELOPING NATIONS. Oceana Publications, 75 Main Street, Dobbs Ferry, New York 10522. 1973- .

LAW AND PRACTICE OF UNITED STATES REGULATION OF INTERNATIONAL TRADE. Oceana Publications, 75 Main Street, Dobbs Ferry, New York 10522. 1987- .

THE LAW OF TRANSNATIONAL BUSINESS TRANSACTIONS. Ved P. Nada. Clark Boardman Company, Limited, 435 Hudson Street, New York, New York 10014. 1981- .

THE LEGAL ASPECTS OF EXPORTING: AN INTRODUCTION. Federal Bar Association, 1815 H Street, Northwest, Washington, D.C. 20006. 1984- .

TARIFF SCHEDULES OF THE UNITED STATES ANNOTATED. United States International Trade Commission. Superintendent of Documents, United States Government Printing Office, Washington, D.C. 20402. 1981- .

TAX-FREE TRADE ZONES OF THE WORLD. Walter Diamond and Dorothy B. Diamond. Matthew Bender and Company, Incorporated, 11 Penn Plaza, New York, New York 10001. 1977- .

TRANSNATIONAL ECONOMIC AND MONETARY LAW. Leonard Lazar, Editor. Oceana Publications, 75 Main Street, Dobbs Ferry, New York 10522. 1978- .

UNITED STATES COURT OF INTERNATIONAL TRADE RULES AND ANNOTATION SERVICE. Rules Service Company, 7658 Standish Place, Rockville, Maryland 20855. 1984- .

UNITED STATES CUSTOMS AND INTERNATIONAL TRADE GUIDE. Peter Buck Feller, Editor. Matthew Bender and Company, Incorporated, 11 Penn Plaza, New York, New York 10001. 1979- .

UNITED STATES INTERNATIONAL TRADE REPORTS. New series. Edward S. Newman and Eugene M. Wypski, Editors. Oceana Publications, 75 Main Street, Dobbs Ferry, New York 10522. 1986- .

HANDBOOKS, MANUALS, FORMBOOKS

A BASIC GUIDE TO EXPORTING. Fourth Edition. United States Department of Commerce, International Trade Administration. Superintendent of Documents, United States Government Printing Office, Washington, D.C. 20402. 1986.

COPING WITH UNITED STATES EXPORT CONTROLS: A COURSE HANDBOOK. Practising Law Institute, 810 Seventh Avenue, New York, New York 10019. 1991.

DEVELOPING AN EXPORT TRADE BUSINESS. Practising Law Institute, 810 Seventh Avenue, New York, New York 10019. 1988.

EUROPE: AN EXPORTER'S HANDBOOK. Paul Jenner. Facts on File, Incorporated, 460 Park Avenue, South, New York, New York 10016. 1981.

EXPORT ADMINISTRATION REGULATIONS. United States Department of Commerce, Office of Export Administration. Superintendent of Documents, United States Government Printing Office, Washington, D.C. 20402. Annual. (Irregular Supplements).

FOREIGN COMMERCE HANDBOOK. Chamber of Commerce of the United States, 1615 H Street, Northwest, Washington, D.C. 20062. Issued every four or five years.

FOREIGN IMPORT AND EXCHANGE CONTROLS AND COMMON MARKET MANUAL. Bureau of National Affairs, Incorporated, 1231 Twenty-fifth Street, Northwest, Washington, D.C. 20037. Weekly.

FOREIGN TRADE AND INVESTMENT: A LEGAL GUIDE. Thomas F. Clasen. Callaghan and Company, 155 Pfingsten Road, Deerfield, Illinois 60015. 1987.

IMPORT PRACTICE. David Serko. Practising Law Institute, 810 Seventh Avenue, New York, New York 10019. 1985.

THE LEGAL ENVIRONMENT OF INTERNATIONAL BUSINESS: A GUIDE FOR UNITED STATES FIRMS. Don Alan Evans. McFarland and Company, Incorporated, Box 611, Jefferson, North Carolina 28640. 1990.

PENETRATING INTERNATIONAL MARKETS: FROM SALES AND LICENSINGS TO SUBSIDIARIES AND ACQUISITIONS. Kluwer Law Book Publishers, Incorporated, 36 West Forty-fourth Street, New York, New York 10036. 1991.

TEXTBOOKS AND GENERAL WORKS

AGGRESSIVE UNILATERALISM: AMERICA'S 301 TRADE POLICY AND THE WORLD TRADING SYSTEM. Jagdish N. Bhagwati. University of Michigan Press, P.O. Box 1104, 839 Greene Street, Ann Arbor, Michigan 48106. 1990.

THE ANTIDUMPING AND COUNTERVAILING DUTY LAWS: KEY LEGAL AND POLICY ISSUES: A COMPILATION OF ARTICLES. Judith Hippler Bello. American Bar Association, Section of International Law and Practice, 1800 M Street, Northwest, Washington, D.C. 20036. 1987.

ARBITRATION IN INTERNATIONAL TRADE. Rene David. Kluwer Academic Publishers, 101 Philip Drive, Norwell, Massachusetts 02061. 1985.

CLIVE M. SCHMITTHOFF'S SELECT ESSAYS ON INTERNATIONAL TRADE LAW. Clive Maximilian Schmitthoff. Martinus Nijhoff, Kluwer Academic Publishers, 101 Philip Drive, Assinippi Park, Norwell, Massachusetts 02061. 1988.

CURRENT LEGAL ASPECTS OF DOING BUSINESS IN THE EUROPEAN ECONOMIC COMMUNITY. American Bar Association, International Law and Practice Section, 750 North Lake Shore Drive, Chicago, Illinois 60611. 1978.

THE CUSTOMS LAW OF THE EUROPEAN ECONOMIC COMMUNITY. Second Edition. Dominik Lasok. Kluwer Law Book Publishers, Incorporated, 36 West Forty-fourth Street, New York, New York 10036. 1990.

DEVELOPING COUNTRIES IN THE GATT LEGAL SYSTEM. Robert E. Hudec. Gower Publishing Company, Old Post Road, Brookfield, Vermont 05036. 1987.

THE ECONOMICS OF EXPORT RESTRICTIONS. Jimmy Weinblatt. Westview Press, Incorporated, 5500 Central Avenue, Boulder, Colorado 10025. 1985.

THE EXPORT-IMPORT BANK: AN ECONOMIC ANALYSIS. David P. Baron. Academic Press, 1250 Sixth Avenue, San Diego, California 92101. 1983.

EXPORT-IMPORT FINANCING. Second Edition. Harrry M. Venedikian and Gerald Warfield. John Wiley and Sons, Incorporated, 605 Third Avenue, New York, New York 10158. 1986.

THE EXPORT PERFORMANCE OF THE UNITED STATES: POLITICAL, STRATEGIC, AND ECONOMIC IMPLICATIONS. Center for Strategic and International Studies. Praeger Publishers, One Madison Avenue, New York, New York 10010-3603. 1981.

FOREIGN COMMERCE AND THE ANTITRUST LAWS. Fourth Edition. Wilbur L. Fugate. Little, Brown and Company, 34 Beacon Street, Boston, Massachusetts 02108. 1991.

FOREIGN SALES CORPORATION: FINAL IRS REGULATIONS AND HOST GOVERNMENT INCENTIVES. Walter H. Diamond. Oceana Publications, 75 Main Street, Dobbs Ferry, New York 10522. 1987.

THE GATT LEGAL SYSTEM AND WORLD TRADE DIPLOMACY. Second Edition. Robert E. Hudec. Butterworth Legal Publishers, 90 Stiles Road, Salem, New Hampshire 03079. 1990.

GOING INTERNATIONAL: INTERNATIONAL TRADE FOR THE NONSPECIALIST: ALI-ABA COURSE OF STUDY MATERIALS. American Law Institute-American Bar Association, 4025 Chestnut Street, Philadelphia, Pennsylvania 19104. 1987.

INTERNATIONAL BUSINESS TRANSACTIONS IN A NUTSHELL. Third Edition. Ralph Haughwout Folsom. West Publishing Company, 50 West Kellogg Boulevard, St. Paul, Minnesota 55164. 1988.

INTERNATIONAL ECONOMIC LAW. Ignaz Seidl-Hohenveldern. Martinus Nijhoff, Kluwer Academic Publishers, 101 Philip Drive, Assinippi Park, Norwell, Massachusetts 02061. 1989.

INTERNATIONAL OPPORTUNITIES AND THE EXPORT TRADING COMPANY ACT OF 1982. Dennis Unkovic, John A. Maher and Nancy Jean LaMont. Bureau of National Affairs, Incorporated, 1231 Twenty-fifth Street, Northwest, Washington, D.C. 20037. 1984.

INTERNATIONAL PRIVATE TRADE. Second Edition. Andreas F. Lowenfeld. Matthew Bender and Company, Incorporated, 11 Penn Plaza, New York, New York 10001. 1988.

THE LAW AND POLICY OF INTERNATIONAL BUSINESS: SELECTED ISSUES: A FESTSCHRIFT FOR WILLIAM SPRAGUE BARNES. William Sprague Barnes. University Press of America, 4720 Boston Way, Lanham, Maryland 20706. 1991.

THE LAW OF GRAY AND COUNTERFEIT GOODS. Practising Law Institute, 810 Seventh Avenue, New York, New York 10019. 1987.

THE LEGAL AND ECONOMIC ASPECTS OF GRAY MARKET GOODS. Seth E. Lipner. Quorum Books, Greenwood Publishing Group, Incorporated, 88 Post Road West, P.O. Box 5007, Westport, Connecticut 06881. 1990.

LEGAL ASPECTS OF INTRODUCING PRODUCTS TO THE UNITED STATES MARKET. John Richards and Robert Alpert. Kluwer Law Book Publishers, Incorporated, 36 West Forty-fourth Street, New York, New York 10036. 1988.

LEGAL ASPECTS OF TRADE AND INVESTMENT IN THE SOVIET UNION AND EASTERN EUROPE. Practising Law Institute, 810 Seventh Avenue, New York, New York 10019. 1990- .

LEGAL STRUCTURE OF INTERNATIONAL TEXTILE TRADE. Henry R. Zheng. Quorum Books, Greenwood Publishing Group, Incorporated, 88 Post Road West, P.O. Box 5007, Westport, Connecticut 06881. 1988.

LETTERMAN'S LAW OF PRIVATE INTERNATIONAL BUSINESS. G. Gregory Letterman. Lawyers Cooperative Publishing Company, Aqueduct Building, Rochester, New York 14694. 1990.

THE MAKING OF INTERNATIONAL AGREEMENTS: CONGRESS CONFRONTS THE EXECUTIVE. Loch K. Johnson. New York University Press, 70 Washington Square South, New York, New York 10012. 1985.

A MANUAL FOR EXPORTING ELECTRONIC PRODUCTS OVERSEAS. Flora Lacchia. Ballinger Division, HarperCollins Publishers, 10 East Fifty-third Street, New York, New York 10022. 1985.

THE NEW GATT ROUND OF MULTILATERAL TRADE NEGOTIATIONS: LEGAL AND ECONOMIC PROBLEMS. Kluwer Law Book Publishers, Incorporated, 36 West Forty-fourth Street, New York, New York 10036. 1988.

THE NEW TRADE LAW: OMNIBUS TRADE AND COMPETITIVENESS ACT OF 1988. Practising Law Institute, 810 Seventh Avenue, New York, New York 10019. 1988- . Annual.

PROBLEMS IN INTERNATIONAL TRADE POLICY: THE LAWYER'S PERSPECTIVE. American Bar Association, 750 North Lake Shore Drive, Chicago, Illinois 60611. 1984.

THE TRADE AGREEMENTS PROGRAM OF THE UNITED STATES: ANNUAL REPORTS OF THE PRESIDENT, 1957-1985. William S. Hein and Company, 1285 Main Street, Buffalo, New York 14209. 1989.

TRADE CONTROLS FOR POLITICAL ENDS. Second Edition. Andreas Lowenfeld. Matthew Bender and Company, Incorporated, 11 Penn Plaza, New York, New York 10001. 1987.

TRADE LAW AND POLICY INSTITUTE. Practising Law Institute, 810 Seventh Avenue, New York, New York 10019. 1989.

UNITED STATES FOREIGN TRADE LAW. Bruce E. Clubb. Little, Brown and Company, 34 Beacon Street, Boston, Massachusetts 02108. 1991.

U.S. STRATEGIC TRADE: AN EXPORT CONTROL SYSTEM FOR THE 1990'S. John Heinz. Westview Press, Incorporated, 5500 Central Avenue, Boulder, Colorado 80301. 1991.

ENCYCLOPEDIAS AND DICTIONARIES

ENCYCLOPEDIA OF INTERNATIONAL COMMERCE. William J. Miller. Cornell Maritime Press, Incorporated, P.O. Box 456, Centreville, Maryland 21617. 1985.

EXPORTERS ENCYCLOPEDIA. Dun and Bradstreet, Incorporated, 299 Park Avenue, New York, New York 10171. Annual.

TERMS OF TRADE: THE LANGUAGE OF INTERNATIONAL TRADE POLICY, LAW, AND DIPLOMACY. Thomas F. O'Herron. International Advisory Services Group, Washington, D.C. 1990.

ANNUALS AND SURVEYS

ANNUAL REPORT ON EXCHANGE RESTRICTIONS. International Monetary Fund, 700 Nineteenth Street, Northwest, Washington, D.C. 20431.

YEARBOOK OF INTERNATIONAL TRADE STATISTICS. United Nations Publishing Service, Room DC2-0853, New York, New York 10017. Annual.

LAW REVIEWS AND PERIODICALS

AMERICAN IMPORT/EXPORT BULLETIN. North American Publishing Company, 401 North Broad Street, Philadelphia, Pennsylvania 19108. Monthly.

EXPORT ADMINISTRATION BULLETIN. Office of Export Administration, United States Department of Commerce. Superintendent of Documents, United States Government Printing Office, Washington, D.C. 20402. Monthly.

JOURNAL OF WORLD TRADE LAW. P.O. Box 93, 1211 Geneve 11, Switzerland. Six issues per year.

LAW AND POLICY IN INTERNATIONAL BUSINESS. Georgetown University Law Center, 600 New Jersey Avenue, Northwest, Washington, D.C. 20001. Quarterly.

NEWSLETTERS AND NEWSPAPERS

BUSINESS INTERNATIONAL. Business International Corporation, 1 Dag Hammerskjold Plaza, New York, New York 10017. Weekly.

CUSTOMS RECORD. International Business Reports, Incorporated, P.O. Box 1009, Falls Church, Virginia 22041. Weekly.

IMPORT DAILY. Journal of Commerce, 110 Wall Street, New York, New York 10005. Daily.

INTERNATIONAL LETTER. Federal Reserve Bank of Chicago, 230 South LaSalle Street, P.O. Box 834, Chicago, Illinois 60604. Monthly.

INTERNATIONAL TRADE ALERT. American Association of Exporters and Importers, 11 West Forty-second Street, New York, New York 10036. Weekly.

INTERNATIONAL TRADE MONTHLY. American Association of Exporters and Importers, 11 West Forty-second Street, New York, New York 10036. Monthly.

INTERNATIONAL TRADE REPORTER CURRENT REPORTS. Bureau of National Affairs, Incorporated, 1231 Twenty-fifth Street, Northwest, Washington, D.C. 20037. Weekly.

JOURNAL OF COMMERCE IMPORT BULLETIN. Journal of Commerce, 110 Wall Street, New York, New York 10005. Weekly.

WASHINGTON INTERNATIONAL BUSINESS REPORT. International Business Government Counsellors, 818 Connecticut Avenue, Northwest, 12th Floor, Washington, D.C. 20006. Monthly.

WASHINGTON TARIFF AND TRADE LETTER. Gilston Communications Group, P.O. Box 467, Washington, D.C. 20044. Weekly.

WORLD TRADE BULLETIN. International Business Division, New York Chamber of Commerce and Industry, 200 Madison Avenue, New York, New York 10016. Biweekly.

BIBLIOGRAPHIES

A COLLECTION OF BIBLIOGRAPHIC AND RESEARCH RESOURCES: INTERNATIONAL LAW BIBLIOGRAPHY. Oceana Publications, 75 Main Street, Dobbs Ferry, New York 10522. 1984.

EXPORT BIBLIOGRAPHY: A GUIDE TO PUBLICATIONS ON THE MECHANICS OF EXPORTING. United States Department of Commerce, International Trade Administration. Superintendent of Documents, United States Government Printing Office, Washington, D.C. 20402. 1983.

DIRECTORIES

AMERICAN IMPORTERS ASSOCIATION MEMBERSHIP DIRECTORY. 11 West Forty-second Street, New York, New York 10036. Biennial.

AMERICAN REGISTER OF EXPORTERS AND IMPORTERS. One Penn Plaza, 250 West Thirty-fourth Street, New York, New York 10119. Annual.

ANGLO AMERICAN TRADE DIRECTORY. American Chamber of Commerce, United Kingdom, 75 Brook Street, London, England W1Y 2EB. Biennial.

CUSTOM HOUSE GUIDE. North American Publishing Company, 401 North Broad Street, Philadelphia, Pennsylvania 19108. Annual.

DIRECTORY OF UNITED STATES IMPORTERS. Journal of Commerce, 110 Wall Street, New York, New York 10005. Biennial.

EXPORT TRADING COMPANIES: CONTRACT FACILITATION SERVICE DIRECTORY. United States Department of Commerce, International Trade Association. Superintendent of Documents, United States Government Printing Office, Washington, D.C. 20402. 1984.

EXPORTERS DIRECTORY/UNITED STATES BUYING GUIDE. Journal of Commerce, 110 Wall Street, New York, New York 10005. Biennial.

FOREIGN TRADE MARKETPLACE. Gale Research, Incorporated, 835 Penobscot Building, Detroit, Michigan 48226. 1977.

INTERNATIONAL INTERTRADE INDEX OF NEW IMPORTED PRODUCTS. Box 636, Federal Square, Newark, New Jersey 07101. Monthly.

ASSOCIATIONS AND PROFESSIONAL SOCIETIES

AMERICAN ASSOCIATION OF EXPORTERS AND IMPORTERS. 11 West Forty-second Street, New York, New York 10036. (212) 944-2230.

AMERICAN LEAGUE FOR EXPORTS AND SECURITY ASSISTANCE. 122 C Street, Northwest, Suite 740, Washington, D.C. 20001. (202) 783-0051.

COMMITTEE FOR SMALL BUSINESS EXPORTS. P.O. Box 6, Aspen, Colorado 81612. (303) 925-7567.

COUNCIL FOR EXPORT TRADING COMPANIES. 1200 Nineteenth Street, Northwest, Suite 605, Washington, D.C. 20036. (202) 861-4705.

NATIONAL ASSOCIATION OF EXPORT COMPANIES. 17 Battery Place, Suite 1425, New York, New York 10004. (516) 561-6209.

TRADE RELATIONS COUNCIL OF THE UNITED STATES. c/o Stewart Trade Data, 808 Seventeenth Street, Northwest, Suite 850, Washington, D.C. 20036. (202) 785-4194.

RESEARCH CENTERS, INSTITUTES, CLEARINGHOUSES

DEAN RUSK CENTER FOR INTERNATIONAL AND COMPARATIVE LAW. University of Georgia, Atlanta, Georgia 30602. (404) 542-7875.

DIVISION OF BUSINESS AND ECONOMIC RESEARCH. University of New Orleans, New Orleans, Louisiana 70148. (504) 286-6248.

INTERNATIONAL LAW INSTITUTE. 1615 New Hampshire Avenue, Northwest, Washington, D.C. 20009. (202) 483-7979.

INTERNATIONAL LEGAL STUDIES PROGRAM. Harvard University, 1557 Massachusetts Avenue, Cambridge, Massachusetts 02138. (617) 495-3117.

INTERNATIONAL TAX PROGRAM. Harvard University, 400 Pound Hall, Cambridge, Massachusetts 02138. (617) 495-4406.

WORLD TRADE EDUCATION CENTER. Cleveland State University, 1983 East Twenty-fourth Street, Cleveland, Ohio 44115. (216) 687-3786.

ONLINE DATABASES

THE EXPORTER. Trade Data Reports, Incorporated, 6 West Thirty-seventh Street, New York, New York 10018.

INTERNATIONAL ECONOMIC LAW DOCUMENTS. American Society of International Law, International Economic Law Interest Group, 2223 Massachusetts Avenue, Northwest, Washington, D.C. 20008.

LEXIS, INTERNATIONAL TRADE LIBRARY. Mead Data Central, P.O. Box 933, Dayton, Ohio 45401.

PTS, INTERNATIONAL TIME SERIES. Predicasts, Incorporated, 11001 Cedar Avenue, Cleveland, Ohio 44106.

WESTLAW, INTERNATIONAL LAW LIBRARY. West Publishing Company, P.O. Box 64526, 50 West Kellogg Boulevard, St. Paul, Minnesota 55164.

STATISTICS SOURCES

SUMMARY OF UNITED STATES EXPORT AND IMPORT MERCHANDISE TRADE. United States Department of Commerce, Bureau of the Census. Superintendent of Documents, United States Government Printing Office, Washington, D.C. 20402. Monthly.

UNITED STATES AIRBORNE EXPORTS AND GENERAL IMPORTS. United States Department of Commerce, Bureau of the Census. Superintendent of Documents, United States Government Printing Office, Washington, D.C. 20402. Monthly.

UNITED STATES SCHEDULE E COMMODITY GROUPINGS: COMMODITY BY COUNTRY. United States Department of Commerce, Bureau of the Census. Superintendent of Documents, United States Government Printing Office, Washington, D.C. 20402. Monthly.

EXPROPRIATION
See: EMINENT DOMAIN; GOVERNMENT OWNERSHIP

EXTRADITION AND ASYLUM
See: EMIGRATION AND IMMIGRATION

EXTRATERRITORIALITY
See: INTERNATIONAL LAW AND RELATIONS

F

FAIR EMPLOYMENT PRACTICES

See also: AGE DISCRIMINATION; AGED AND EMPLOYMENT; DISCRIMINATION, EMPLOYMENT; DISCRIMINATION, RACE; DISCRIMINATION, SEX; EQUAL EMPLOYMENT OPPORTUNITY; EQUAL EMPLOYMENT OPPORTUNITY COMMISSION; LABOR AND LABOR RELATIONS

STATUTES, CODES, STANDARDS, UNIFORM LAWS

CIVIL RIGHTS AND EMPLOYMENT DISCRIMINATION LAW: SELECTED STATUTES AND REGULATIONS. Theodore Eisenberg. Michie Company, P.O. Box 7587, Charlottesville, Virginia 22906. 1991.

LOOSELEAF SERVICES AND REPORTERS

EMPLOYMENT DISCRIMINATION: LAW AND LITIGATION. Merrick T. Rossein. Clark Boardman Company, Limited, 435 Hudson Street, New York, New York 10014. 1990.

EMPLOYMENT LAW CHECKLISTS AND FORMS. Andrew J. Ruzicho and Louis A. Jacobs. Clark Boardman Company, Limited, 435 Hudson Street, New York, New York 10014. 1991.

EMPLOYMENT LAW DESKBOOK. Shawe and Rosenthal. Matthew Bender and Company, Incorporated, 11 Penn Plaza, New York, New York 10001. 1989.

EMPLOYMENT PRACTICES DECISIONS. Commerce Clearing House, Incorporated, 4025 West Peterson Avenue, Chicago, Illinois 60646. 1971- .

FAIR EMPLOYMENT PRACTICE CASES. Bureau of National Affairs, Incorporated, 1231 Twenty-fifth Street, Northwest, Washington, D.C. 20037. 1969- .

FAIR EMPLOYMENT PRACTICE SERVICE. Bureau of National Affairs, Incorporated, 1231 Twenty-fifth Street, Northwest, Washington, D.C. 20037. 1964.

FEDERAL EMPLOYMENT RELATIONS MANUAL. Bureau of National Affairs, Incorporated, 1231 Twenty-fifth Street, Northwest, Washington, D.C. 20037. 1987- .

INDIVIDUAL EMPLOYMENT RIGHTS. Bureau of National Affairs, Incorporated, 1231 Twenty-fifth Street, Northwest, Washington, D.C. 20037. 1986- .

MANUAL ON EMPLOYMENT DISCRIMINATION AND CIVIL RIGHTS ACTIONS IN THE FEDERAL COURTS. Attorney's Edition. Charles R. Richey. Kluwer Law Book Publishers, Incorporated, 36 West Forty-fourth Street, New York, New York 10036. 1988. (Revised Edition).

MANUAL ON EMPLOYMENT DISCRIMINATION LAW AND CIVIL RIGHTS ACTIONS IN THE FEDERAL COURTS. Charles R. Richey. Clark Boardman Company, Limited, 435 Hudson Street, New York, New York 10014. 1988.

SEX-BASED EMPLOYMENT DISCRIMINATION. Susan M. Omilian and Jean P. Kamp. Callaghan and Company, 155 Pfingsten Road, Deerfield, Illinois 60015. 1990.

USE OF STATISTICS IN EQUAL EMPLOYMENT OPPORTUNITY LITIGATION. Walter B. Connelly, Jr., David W. Peterson and Michael J. Connolly. Law Journal Seminars-Press, 111 Eighth Avenue, New York, New York 10011. 1980- .

HANDBOOKS, MANUALS, FORMBOOKS

AGE DISCRIMINATION: A LEGAL AND PRACTICAL GUIDE FOR EMPLOYERS. Stephen S. Rappoport. Bureau of National Affairs, Incorporated, 1231 Twenty-fifth Street, Northwest, Washington, D.C. 20037. 1989.

THE EEO PRIMER FOR MANAGERS AND SUPERVISORS. Molly Vaux. Executive Enterprises Publications Company, 22 West Twenty-first Street, New York, New York 10010-6904. 1988.

EMPLOYMENT DISCRIMINATION: A CLAIMS MANUAL FOR EMPLOYEES AND MANAGERS. Andrew J. Maikovich and Michele D. Brown. McFarland and Company, Incorporated, Box 611, Jefferson, North Carolina 28640. 1989.

MANAGING EQUALLY AND LEGALLY: A PRACTICAL BUSINESS GUIDE TO PREVENTING DISCRIMINATION COMPLAINTS AND TERMINATION LAWSUITS. Lynne Curry-Swann. McFarland and Company, Incorporated, Box 611, Jefferson, North Carolina 28640. 1990.

PRIMER ON EQUAL EMPLOYMENT OPPORTUNITY. Fifth Edition. Nancy J. Sedmak and Michael D. Levin-Epstein. Bureau of National Affairs, Incorporated, 1231 Twenty-fifth Street, Northwest, Washington, D.C. 20037. 1991.

FAIR EMPLOYMENT PRACTICES

TEXTBOOKS AND GENERAL WORKS

AFFIRMATIVE ACTION AND PRINCIPLES OF JUSTICE. Kathanne W. Greene. Greenwood Publishing Group, Incorporated, 88 Post Road West, P.O. Box 5007, Westport, Connecticut 06881. 1989.

AGE DISCRIMINATION IN EMPLOYMENT LAW. Second Edition. Joseph E. Kalet. Bureau of National Affairs, Incorporated, 1231 Twenty-fifth Street, Northwest, Washington, D.C. 20037. 1990.

DISABILITY DISCRIMINATION IN EMPLOYMENT. John J. Coleman. Clark Boardman Company, Limited, 435 Hudson Street, New York, New York 10014. 1991.

EMPLOYMENT DISCRIMINATION. Paul N. Cox. Garland Publishing, Incorporated, 136 Madison Avenue, New York, New York 10016. 1987.

EMPLOYMENT DISCRIMINATION. Second Edition. Charles A. Sullivan, Michael J. Zimmer and Richard F. Richards. Little, Brown and Company, 34 Beacon Street, Boston, Massachusetts 02108. 1988.

EMPLOYMENT DISCRIMINATION AND CIVIL RIGHTS ACTIONS IN THE FEDERAL COURTS. American Law Institute-American Bar Association Committee on Continuing Professional Education, 4025 Chestnut Street, Philadelphia, Pennsylvania 19104. 1986.

EMPLOYMENT DISCRIMINATION LAW. Barbara Lindemann Schlei and Paul Grossman. Bureau of National Affairs, Incorporated, 1231 Twenty-fifth Street, Northwest, Washington, D.C. 20037. 1983- . (Periodic Supplements).

EMPLOYMENT DISCRIMINATION LAW. Second Edition. Lee M. Modjeska. Lawyers Cooperative Publishing Company, Aqueduct Building, Rochester, New York 14694. 1988.

EMPLOYMENT DISCRIMINATION LAW: CASES AND MATERIALS. Third Edition. Arthur B. Smith, Charles B. Craver and Leroy D. Clark. Michie Company, P.O. Box 7587, Charlottesville, Virginia 22906. 1988.

EMPLOYMENT DISCRIMINATION LITIGATION. Andrew J. Ruzicho, Louis A. Jacobs and Louis M. Thrasher. Anderson Publishing Company, 2035 Reading Road, Cincinnati, Ohio 45202. 1989.

EQUAL EMPLOYMENT OPPORTUNITY. Michal R. Belknap. Garland Publishing, Incorporated, 136 Madison Avenue, New York, New York 10016. 1991.

EQUAL EMPLOYMENT OPPORTUNITY LAW. Second Edition. David P. Twomey. South-Western Publishing Company, 5101 Madison Road, Cincinnati, Ohio 45227. 1990.

EUROPEAN COMMUNITY SEX EQUALITY LAW. Evelyn Ellis. Oxford University Press, 200 Madison Avenue, New York, New York 10016. 1991.

FAIR EMPLOYMENT LITIGATION: PROVING AND DEFENDING A TITLE VII CASE. Second Edition. Susan R. Agid. Practising Law Institute, 810 Seventh Avenue, New York, New York 10019. 1979.

FEDERAL LAW OF EMPLOYMENT DISCRIMINATION IN A NUTSHELL. Third Edition. Mack A. Player. West Publishing Company, 50 West Kellogg Boulevard, St. Paul, Minnesota 55164. 1992.

FORBIDDEN GROUNDS: THE CASE AGAINST EMPLOYMENT DISCRIMINATION LAWS. Richard Allen Epstein. Harvard University Press, 79 Garden Street, Cambridge, Massachusetts 02138. 1992.

A GUIDE TO FEDERAL SECTOR EQUAL EMPLOYMENT LAW AND PRACTICE: 1979-1990. Third Edition. Ernest C. Hadley. Dewey Publications, Incorporated, P.O. Box 3423, Arlington, Virginia 22203. 1990.

INVISIBLE VICTIMS: WHITE MALES AND THE CRISIS OF AFFIRMATIVE ACTION. Frederick R. Lynch. Praeger Publishers, One Madison Avenue, New York, New York 10010-3603. 1991.

THE LAW OF EQUAL EMPLOYMENT OPPORTUNITY. Stephen N. Shulman and Charles F. Abernathy. Research Institute of America, Incorporated, One Penn Plaza, New York, New York 10119. 1990.

THE LAW OF SEX DISCRIMINATION. J. Ralph Lindgren and Nadine Taub. West Publishing Company, 50 West Kellogg Boulevard, St. Paul, Minnesota 55164. 1988.

LITIGATION, COURTS, AND WOMEN WORKERS. Karen J. Maschke. Praeger Publishers, One Madison Avenue, New York, New York 10010-3603. 1989.

MAJOR ISSUES IN THE FEDERAL LAW OF EMPLOYMENT DISCRIMINATION. Second Edition. George Rutherglen. Federal Judicial Center, 1520 H Street, Northwest, Washington, D.C. 20005. 1987.

NEW APPROACHES TO ECONOMIC AND SOCIAL ANALYSES OF DISCRIMINATION. Richard R. Cornwall and Phanindra V. Wunnava. Praeger Publishers, One Madison Avenue, New York, New York 10010-3603. 1991.

OPPORTUNITIES DENIED, OPPORTUNITIES DIMINISHED: RACIAL DISCRIMINATION IN HIRING. Margery Austin Turner, Michael Fix and Raymond J. Struyk. Urban Institute Press, University Press of America, 4720 Boston Way, Lanham, Maryland 20706. 1991.

THE POLITICAL ECONOMY OF ETHNIC DISCRIMINATION AND AFFIRMATIVE ACTION: A COMPARATIVE PERSPECTIVE. Michael L. Wyzan. Praeger Publishers, One Madison Avenue, New York, New York 10010-3603. 1990.

PRIMER OF EQUAL EMPLOYMENT OPPORTUNITY. Third Edition. Michael D. Levin-Epstein. Bureau of National Affairs, Incorporated, 1231 Twenty-fifth Street, Northwest, Washington, D.C. 20037. 1984.

RACISM AND JUSTICE: THE CASE FOR AFFIRMATIVE ACTION. Gertrude Ezorsky. Cornell University Press, 124 Roberts Place, Ithaca, New York 14850. 1991.

REMEDIES IN EMPLOYMENT DISCRIMINATION LAW. Robert Belton. John Wiley and Sons, Incorporated, 605 Third Avenue, New York, New York 10158. 1992.

SEEDTIME FOR THE MODERN CIVIL RIGHTS MOVEMENT: THE PRESIDENT'S COMMITTEE ON FAIR EMPLOYMENT PRACTICE, 1941-1946. Merl Elwyn Reed. Louisiana State University Press, Highland Road, Baton Rouge, Louisiana 70893. 1991.

SEX, RACE, AND THE LAW: LEGISLATING FOR EQUALITY. Jeanne Gregory. Sage Publications, 2455 Teller Road, Newbury Park, California 91320. 1987.

WORKING WOMEN AND THE LAW: EQUALITY AND DISCRIMINATION IN THEORY AND PRACTICE. Anne E. Morris and Susan M. Nott. Routledge, Chapman & Hall, 29 West Thirty-fifth Street, New York, New York 10001. 1990.

DIGESTS, INDEXES, ABSTRACTS, CITATORS

FAIR EMPLOYMENT PRACTICE CASES: CUMULATIVE DIGEST AND INDEX. Bureau of National Affairs, Incorporated, 1231 Twenty-fifth Street, Northwest, Washington, D.C. 20037. 1976- .

SHEPARD'S FEDERAL LABOR LAW CITATIONS. Shepard's/McGraw-Hill, P.O. Box 1235, Colorado Springs, Colorado 80901. (Monthly Supplements).

NEWSLETTERS AND NEWSPAPERS

EEO REVIEW. Executive Enterprises Publications Company, Incorporated, 22 West Twenty-first Street, New York, New York 10010. Monthly.

EQUAL EMPLOYMENT COMPLIANCE UPDATE. Callaghan and Company, 155 Pfingsten Road, Deerfield, Illinois 60015. Monthly.

FAIR EMPLOYMENT COMPLIANCE. Management Resources, Incorporated, 379 West Broadway, 4th Floor, New York, New York 10014. Semimonthly.

FAIR EMPLOYMENT PRACTICES GUIDELINES. The Bureau of Business Practice, Incorporated, 24 Rope Ferry Road, Waterford, Connecticut 06386. Monthly.

FAIR EMPLOYMENT PRACTICES: SUMMARY OF LATEST DEVELOPMENTS. The Bureau of National Affairs, Incorporated, 1231 Twenty-fifth Street, Northwest, Washington, D.C. 20037. Biweekly.

FAIR EMPLOYMENT REPORT. Business Publishers, Incorporated, 951 Pershing Drive, Silver Spring, Maryland 20910. Biweekly.

BIBLIOGRAPHIES

AFFIRMATIVE ACTION AND MINORITIES: A BIBLIOGRAPHY. Marian Dworaczek. Vance Bibliographies, P.O. Box 229, 112 North Charter Street, Monticello, Illinois 61856. 1988.

ASSOCIATIONS AND PROFESSIONAL SOCIETIES

SECTION ON LABOR AND EMPLOYMENT LAW. American Bar Association, 750 North Lake Shore Drive, Chicago, Illinois 60611. (312) 988-5158.

RESEARCH CENTERS, INSTITUTES, CLEARINGHOUSES

EQUAL EMMPLOYMENT OPPORTUNITY COMMISSION LIBRARY. 1801 L Street, Northwest, Washington, D.C. 20507. (202) 663-4264.

ONLINE DATABASES

FAIR EMPLOYMENT PRACTICES: SUMMARY OF LATEST DEVELOPMENTS. Bureau of National Affairs, Incorporated, BNA ONLINE, 1231 Twenty-fifth Street, Northwest, Washington, D.C. 20037.

FAIR TRIAL, RIGHT TO
See also: DUE PROCESS OF LAW; FREEDOM OF PRESS

TEXTBOOKS AND GENERAL WORKS

MURDER, COURTS, AND THE PRESS: ISSUES IN FREE PRESS/FAIR TRIAL. Peter E. Kane. Southern Illinois University Press, P.O. Box 3697, Carbondale, Illinois 62902-3697. 1986.

NEWS OF CRIME: COURTS AND PRESS IN CONFLICT. J. Edward Gerald. Greenwood Publishing Group, Incorporated, 88 Post Road West, P.O. Box 5007, Westport, Connecticut 06881. 1983.

ASSOCIATIONS AND PROFESSIONAL SOCIETIES

COMMISSION FOR INTERNATIONAL DUE PROCESS OF LAW. 105 West Adams Street, Chicago, Illinois 60603. (312) 782-1946.

FAMILY LAW
See also: ABORTION; ADOPTION; BIRTH CONTROL; CHILD ABUSE AND NEGLECT; CHILD CUSTODY; CHILDREN; COHABITATION; COMMUNITY PROPERTY; DISPUTE RESOLUTION; DIVORCE, SEPARATION AND MARRIAGE; FAMILY VIOLENCE; FOSTER CARE

STATUTES, CODES, STANDARDS, UNIFORM LAWS

UNIFORM ACT ON PATERNITY. National Conference on Uniform Laws. Uniform Laws Annotated. West Publishing Company, P.O. Box 64526, 50 West Kellogg Boulevard, St. Paul, Minnesota 55164-0526. 1979- . (Annual Supplements).

UNIFORM CIVIL LIABILITY FOR SUPPORT ACT. National Conference on Uniform Laws. Uniform Laws Annotated. West Publishing Company, P.O. Box 64526, 50 West Kellogg Boulevard, St. Paul, Minnesota 55164-0526. 1976- . (Annual Supplements).

UNIFORM PARENTAGE ACT. National Conference on Uniform Laws. Uniform Laws Annotated. West Publishing Company, P.O. Box 64526, 50 West Kellogg Boulevard, St. Paul, Minnesota 55164-0526. 1979- . (Annual Supplements).

FAMILY LAW

UNIFORM PRE-MARITAL AGREEMENT ACT. National Conference on Uniform Laws. Uniform Laws Annotated. West Publishing Company, P.O. Box 64526, 50 West Kellogg Boulevard, St. Paul, Minnesota 55164-0526. 1979- . (Annual Supplements).

UNIFORM RECIPROCAL ENFORCEMENT OF SUPPORT ACT -- 1950 ACT. National Conference on Uniform Laws. Uniform Laws Annotated. West Publishing Company, P.O. Box 64526, 50 West Kellogg Boulevard, St. Paul, Minnesota 55164-0526. 1979- . (Annual Supplements).

LOOSELEAF SERVICES AND REPORTERS

CONTEMPORARY FAMILY LAW: PRINCIPLES, POLICY, AND PRACTICE. Lynn D. Wardle. Callaghan and Company, 155 Pfingsten Road, Deerfield, Illinois 60015. 1988.

FAMILY LAW AND PRACTICE. Arnold H. Rutkin, Editor. Matthew Bender and Company, Incorporated, 11 Penn Plaza, New York, New York 10001. 1985- .

THE FAMILY LAW REPORTER. Bureau of National Affairs, Incorporated, 1231 Twenty-fifth Street, Northwest, Washington, D.C. 20037. 1974- .

FAMILY LAW TAX GUIDE. Commerce Clearing House, Incorporated, 4025 West Peterson Avenue, Chicago, Illinois 60646. 1985- .

HANDBOOKS, MANUALS, FORMBOOKS

EVERYWOMAN'S LEGAL GUIDE: PROTECTING YOUR RIGHTS AT HOME, THE WORKPLACE, AND IN THE MARKETPLACE. Barbara A. Burnett, Editor. Doubleday and Company, Incorporated, 666 Fifth Avenue, New York, New York 10103. 1985.

FAMILY LAW HANDBOOK. Joel Kolko, Editor. Bureau of National Affairs, Incorporated, 1231 Twenty-fifth Street, Northwest, Washington, D.C. 20037. 1985.

HANDBOOK OF FAMILY LAW. Lester Wallman and Lawrence J. Schwarz. Prentice-Hall, Incorporated, 113 Sylvan Avenue, Englewood Cliffs, New Jersey 07632. 1989.

HOT TIPS FROM THE EXPERTS: GREAT IDEAS FOR IMPROVING YOUR FAMILY LAW PRACTICE. American Bar Association, Section of Family Law, 750 North Lake Shore Drive, Chicago, Illinois 60611. 1988.

STATE-BY-STATE GUIDE TO WOMEN'S LEGAL RIGHTS. National Organization of Women/Legal Defense and Education Fund and Dr. Renee Cherow-O'Heary. Shepard's/McGraw-Hill, P.O. Box 1235, Colorado Springs, Colorado 80901. 1987.

TEXTBOOKS AND GENERAL WORKS

AMERICAN FAMILY LAW IN TRANSITION. Walter O. Weyrauch and Sanford N. Katz. Bureau of National Affairs, Incorporated, 1231 Twenty-fifth Street, Northwest, Washington, D.C. 20037. 1983.

DOMESTIC TORTS: FAMILY VIOLENCE, CONFLICT, AND SEXUAL ABUSE. Leonard Karp. Shepard's/McGraw-Hill, P.O. Box 1235, Colorado Springs, Colorado 80901. 1989.

Encyclopedia of Legal Information Sources • 2nd Ed.

FAMILY AND STATE: THE PHILOSOPHY OF FAMILY LAW. Laurence D. Houlgate. Rowman and Littlefield Publishers, Incorporated, 8705 Bollman Place, Savage, Maryland 20763. 1988.

FAMILY LAW IN A NUTSHELL. Second Edition. Harry D. Krause. West Publishing Company, P.O. Box 64526, 50 West Kellogg Boulevard, St. Paul, Minnesota 55164-0526. 1986.

FAMILY MEDIATION PRACTICE. John Lemmon. Free Press, 866 Third Avenue, New York, New York 10022. 1985.

FEDERAL REGULATION OF FAMILY LAW. Kenneth L. Redden. Michie/Bobbs-Merrill Law Publishing, P.O. Box 7587, Charlottesville, Virginia 22906-7582. 1982.

JOSEPHSON'S ESSENTIAL PRINCIPLES OF FAMILY LAW. Marc Perlin. Center for Creative Education Services, Herbert Legal Series, 2060 Huntington Drive, Number 4, San Marino, California 91108. 1984.

THE LAW OF DOMESTIC RELATIONS IN THE UNITED STATES. Student Edition, Second Edition. Homer Harrison Clark. West Publishing Company, P.O. Box 64526, 50 West Kellogg Boulevard, St. Paul, Minnesota 55164-0526. 1988.

THE LEGAL GUIDE FOR THE FAMILY. Donald L. Very. J.G. Ferguson Publishing Company, 200 West Monroe, Suite 250, Chicago, Illinois 60606. 1992.

MARRIAGE AND FAMILY LAW: HISTORICAL, CONSTITUTIONAL AND PRACTICAL PERSPECTIVES. Peter J. Riga. Associated Faculty Press, 19 West Thirty-sixth Street, New York, New York 10018. 1985.

OPTIONS FOR ALL AGES: FAMILY DISPUTE RESOLUTION. American Bar Association, Standing Committee on Dispute Resolution, Division for Public Services, Governmental Affairs and Public Services Group, 1800 M Street, Northwest, Washington, D.C. 20036. 1990.

READINGS IN FAMILY LAW: DIVORCE AND ITS CONSEQUENCES. Frederica K. Lombard. Foundation Press, 615 Merrick Avenue, Westbury, New York 11590. 1990.

THE RESOLUTION OF FAMILY CONFLICT: COMPARATIVE LEGAL PERSPECTIVES. John M. Eekelaar and Sanford N. Katz, Editors. Butterworth and Company, Limited, 2265 Midland Avenue, Scarborogh, Ontario M1P 451, Canada. 1984.

SMITH'S REVIEW OF FAMILY LAW. Second Edition. Myron G. Hill, Jr. West Publishing Company, P.O. Box 64526, 50 West Kellogg Boulevard, St. Paul, Minnesota 55164-0526. 1981.

SUPPORT PRACTICE HANDBOOK: PREPARATION, NEGOTIATION, TRIAL. Neil Hurowitz. Mitchie Company, P.O. Box 7587, Charlottesville, Virginia 22906-7582. 1985. (With Supplements).

SUPREME COURT AND THE AMERICAN FAMILY: IDEOLOGY AND ISSUES. Eva R. Rubin. Greenwood Publishing Group, Incorporated, 88 Post Road West, P.O. Box 5007, Westport, Connecticut 06881. 1986.

THE TRANSFORMATION OF FAMILY LAW: STATE, LAW, AND FAMILY IN THE UNITED STATES AND WESTERN EUROPE. Mary Ann Glendon. University of Chicago Press, 5801 Ellis Avenue, Chicago, Illinois 60637. 1989.

ENCYCLOPEDIAS AND DICTIONARIES

FAMILY LEGAL GUIDE: A COMPLETE ENCYCLOPEDIA OF LAW FOR THE LAYMAN. Readers Digest Editors. Random House Publicity, 201 East Fiftieth Street, New York, New York 10022. 1981.

THE GUIDE TO AMERICAN LAW: EVERYONE'S LEGAL ENCYLCOPEDIA. West Publishing Company, P.O. Box 64526, 50 West Kellogg Boulevard, St. Paul, Minnesota 55164-0526. 1983- .

DIGESTS, INDEXES, ABSTRACTS, CITATORS

JUVENILE AND FAMILY LAW DIGEST. National Council of Juvenile and Family Court Judges, University of Nevada, P.O. Box 8970, Reno, Nevada 89557. Monthly.

ANNUALS AND SURVEYS

FAMILY STUDIES REVIEW YEARBOOK. Sage Publications, Incorporated, 2455 Teller Road, Newbury Park, California 91320. 1983- . (Annual).

SUBJECT COMPILATION OF STATE LAWS, 1985-1988: RESEARCH GUIDE AND ANNOTATED BIBLIOGRAPHY. Cheryl Nyberg and Carol Boast. C. Boast and C. Nyberg, 716 West Indiana Avenue, Urbana, Illinois 61801-4836. 1989.

LAW REVIEWS AND PERIODICALS

FAMILY ADVOCATE. American Bar Association, 750 North Lake Shore Drive, Chicago, Illinois 60611. Quarterly.

FAMILY AND CONCILIATION COURTS REVIEW. Association of Family and Conciliation Courts, c/o Ann Milne, 329 West Wilson, Madison, Wisconsin 53703. Semiannually.

FAMILY LAW QUARTERLY. American Bar Association, 750 North Lake Shore Drive, Chicago, Illinois 60611. Quarterly.

JOURNAL OF FAMILY LAW. University of Louisville, 2301 South Third Street, Louisville, Kentucky 40292. Quarterly.

JOURNAL OF THE AMERICAN ACADEMY OF MATRIMONIAL LAWYERS. American Academy of Matrimonial Lawyers, 20 North Michigan Avenue, Suite 540, Chicago, Illinois 60602. Semiannual.

JUVENILE AND FAMILY COURT JOURNAL. National Council of Juvenile and Family Court Judges, Judicial College Building, University of Nevada, Reno, Nevada 89507. Quarterly.

MEDIATION QUARTERLY. Academy of Family Mediators, P.O. Box 10501, Eugene, Oregon 97440. Quarterly.

NEWSLETTERS AND NEWSPAPERS

AAML NEWSLETTER. American Academy of Matrimonial Lawyers, 20 North Michigan Avenue, Sutie 540, Chicago, Illinois 60602. Monthly.

ACTION ALERT. American Association of University Women, 111 Sixteenth Street, Northwest, Washington, D.C. 20036. Monthly.

AFCC NEWSLETTER. Association of Family and Conciliation Courts, c/o Ann Milne, 329 West Wilson, Madison, Wisconsin 53703. Quarterly.

FAMILY LAW. Illinois State Bar Association, Illinois Bar Center, Springfield, Illinois 62701. Quarterly.

THE FAMILY LAW COMMENTATOR. The Florida Bar, 650 Apalachee Parkway, Tallahassee, Florida 32399. Quarterly.

FAMILY LAW NEWS. State Bar of California, 555 Franklin Street, San Francisco, California 94102. Quarterly.

FAMILY LAW REPORTER. The Bureau of National Affairs, Incorporated, 1231 Twenty-fifth Street, Northwest, Washington, D.C. 20037. Weekly.

FAMILY LAW REVIEW. New York State Bar Association, 1 Elk Street, Albany, New York 12207. Quarterly.

JUVENILE AND FAMILY COURT NEWSLETTER. National Council of Juvenile and Family Court Judges, P.O. Box 8970, Reno, Nevada 89507. Bimonthly.

JUVENILE AND FAMILY LAW DIGEST. National Council of Juvenile and Family Court Judges, P.O. Box 8970, Reno, Nevada 89507. Monthly.

THE LIBERATOR. Men's Rights Association, Route 6, Forest Lake, Minnesota 55025. Monthly.

THE NATIONAL REPORT ON WORK AND FAMILY. Buraff Publications, 1350 Connecticut Avenue, Northwest, Suite 1000, Washington, D.C. 20036. Semimonthly.

NCOWFL NEWSLETTER. National Center on Women and Family Law, Room 402, 799 Broadway, New York, New York 10003. Bimonthly.

NCSEA NEWSLETTER. National Child Support Enforcement Association, 444 North Capitol Street, Northwest, Suite 613, Washington, D.C. 20001. Bimonthly.

THE WOMEN'S ADVOCATE. National Center on Women and Family Law, 799 Broadway, New York, New York 10003. Bimonthly.

BIBLIOGRAPHIES

PARENT-CHILD RELATIONSHIP IN THE LAW: RECENT ACTIONS AND CASES, 1980-1985. Dale E. Casper. Vance Bibliographies, P.O. Box 229, 112 North Charter Street, Monticello, Illinois 61856. 1985.

ASSOCIATIONS AND PROFESSIONAL SOCIETIES

ACADEMY OF FAMILY MEDIATORS. P.O. Box 10501, Eugene, Oregon 97440. (503) 345-1205.

FAMILY LAW

AMERICAN ACADEMY OF MATRIMONIAL LAWYERS. 20 North Michigan Avenue, Suite 540, Chicago, Illinois 60602. (312) 263-6477.

ASSOCIATION OF FAMILY AND CONILIATION COURTS. c/o Ann Milne, 329 West Wilson, Madison, Wisconsin 53703. (608) 251-4001.

FAMILY LAW PROJECT. NOW Legal Defense and Education Fund, 99 Hudson Street, 12th Floor, New York, New York 10013. (212) 925-6635.

FAMILY LAW SECTION. American Bar Association, 750 North Lake Shore Drive, Chicago, Illinois 60611. (312) 988-5584.

JOINT CUSTODY ASSOCIATION. 10606 Wilking Avenue, Los Angeles, California 90024. (213) 475-5352.

MEN'S RIGHTS ASSOCIATION. Route 6, Forest Lake, Minnesota 55025. (612) 464-7663.

NATIONAL CHILD SUPPORT ENFORCEMENT ASSOCIATION. 444 North Capitol Street, Northwest, Suite 613, Washington, D.C. 20001. (202) 624-8180.

PARENTS AND CHILDREN'S EQUALITY. 1816 Florida Avenue, Palm Harbor, Florida 34683. (813) 787-3875.

SECTION ON FAMILY AND JUVENILE LAW. American Association of Law Schools, 1 Dupont Circle, Northwest, Washington, D.C. 20009. (202) 296-8851.

RESEARCH CENTERS, INSTITUTES, CLEARINGHOUSES

ALABAMA LAW INSTITUTE. P.O. Box 1425, Tuscaloosa, Alabama 35486. (205) 348-7411.

FAMILY LAW RESEARCH FOUNDATION. 5242 West North Avenue, Chicago, Illinois 60639. (312) 637-3037.

NATIONAL CENTER ON WOMEN AND FAMILY LAW. 799 Broadway, Room 402, New York, New York 10003. (212) 674-8200.

NATIONAL COUNCIL OF JUVENILE AND FAMILY COURT JUDGES. P.O. Box 8970, Reno, Nevada 89507. (702) 784-6012.

NORTH CAROLINA CENTER FOR LAWS AFFECTING WOMEN, INCORPORATED. 1111 Broodstown Avenue, Winston-Salem, North Carolina 27101. (919) 722-0098.

ONLINE DATABASES

FAMILY RESOURCES. National Council on Family Relations, Family Resource and Referral Center, 1910 West Country Road B, Suite 147, St. Paul, Minnesota 55113.

FROM THE STATE CAPITOLS: WOMEN AND THE LAW. Wakeman/Walworth, Incorporated, 300 North Washington Street, Suite 204, Alexandria, Virginia 22314.

THE NATIONAL REPORT ON WORK AND FAMILY. Bureau of National Affairs, Incorporated, BNA ONLINE, 1231 Twenty-fifth Street, Northwest, Washington, D.C. 20037.

WESTLAW FAMILY LAW LIBRARY. West Publishing Company, 50 West Kellogg Boulevard, P.O. Box 64526, St. Paul, Minnesota 55164.

AUDIOVISUALS

PREPARING AND TRYING A CHILD CUSTODY CASE. American Bar Association, 750 North Lake Shore Drive, Chicago, Illinois 60611. 1981. Videotape.

REPRESENTING THE STATE IN CHILD ABUSE AND NEGLECT PROCEEDINGS. American Bar Association, 750 North Lake Shore Drive, Chicago, Illinois 60611. 1981. Videotape.

UNMARRIEDS LIVING TOGETHER. American Bar Association, 750 North Lake Shore Drive, Chicago, Illinois 60611. 1978. Videotape.

COMPUTER-ASSISTED LEGAL INSTRUCTION

OLCOTT V. OLCOTT. Center for Computer-Assisted Instruction, 229 19th Avenue South, University of Minnesota, Minneapolis, Minnesota 55455. Interactive videodisc.

OTHER SOURCES

GOVERNING THE HEARTH: LAW AND THE FAMILY IN THE NINETEENTH CENTURY. Michael Grossberg. University of North Carolina Press, P.O. Box 2288, 116 South Boundary Street, Chapel Hill, North Carolina 27515-2288. 1988.

JUSTICE, EQUAL OPPORTUNITY AND THE FAMILY. James S. Fishkin. Yale University Press, 302 Temple Street, New Haven, Connecticut 06520. 1983.

MANAGEMENT OF A FAMILY LAW PRACTICE. American Bar Association, 750 North Lake Shore Drive, Chicago, Illinois 60611. 1981.

FAMILY VIOLENCE
See also: CHILD ABUSE AND NEGLECT; DISPUTE RESOLUTION; FAMILY LAW

LOOSELEAF SERVICES AND REPORTERS

ARNOLD H. RUTKIN. Matthew Bender and Company, Incorporated, 11 Penn Plaza, New York, New York 10001. 1985- .

DOMESTIC VIOLENCE CASES: SKILLS AND STRATEGIES. Maryland Institute for Continuing Professional Education of Lawyers, Incorporated, 520 West Fayette Street, Baltimore, Maryland 21201. 1987.

HANDBOOKS, MANUALS, FORMBOOKS

MARITAL AND PARENTAL TORTS: A GUIDE TO CAUSES OF ACTION, ARGUMENTS AND DAMAGES. American Bar Association, Section of Family Law, 750 North Lake Shore Drive, Chicago, Illinois 60611. 1990.

WORKING WITH VIOLENT FAMILIES: A GUIDE FOR CLINICAL AND LEGAL PRACTITIONERS. Frank G. Bolton. Sage Publications, 2455 Teller Road, Newbury Park, California 91320. 1987.

TEXTBOOKS AND GENERAL WORKS

ATTORNEY GENERAL'S TASK FORCE ON FAMILY VIOLENCE: FINAL REPORT, SEPTEMBER 1984. Attorney General's Task Force, United States Department of Justice. Superintendent of Documents, United States Government Printing Office, Washington, D.C. 20402. 1984.

THE BATTERED WOMAN SYNDROME. Lenore E. Walker. Springer Publishing Company, 536 Broadway, New York, New York 10012. 1984.

CONFRONTING DOMESTIC VIOLENCE: A GUIDE FOR CRIMINAL JUSTICE AGENCIES. Gail A. Goolkasian. United States Department of Justice, National Institute of Justice, Office of Communication and Research Utilization. Superintendent of Documents, United States Government Printing Office, Washington, D.C. 20402. 1986.

CRIME AND THE FAMILY. Alan J. Lincoln, Editor. Charles C. Thomas, Publishers, 2600 South First Street, Springfield, Illinois 62794-9265. 1985.

DOMESTIC TORTS: FAMILY VIOLENCE, CONFLICT, AND SEXUAL ABUSE. Leonard Karp. Shepard's/McGraw-Hill, P.O. Box 1235, Colorado Springs, Colorado 80901. 1989.

DOMESTIC TYRANNY: THE MAKING OF SOCIAL POLICY AGAINST FAMILY VIOLENCE FROM COLONIAL TIMES TO THE PRESENT. Elizabeth Hafkin Pleck. Oxford University Press, 200 Madison Avenue, New York, New York 10016. 1987.

DOMESTIC VIOLENCE CASES: SKILLS AND STRATEGIES. House of Ruth Domestic Violence Legal Clinic. The Maryland Institute for Continuing Professional Education for Lawyers, Incorporated, 520 West Fayette Street, Baltimore, Maryland 21201. 1987.

DOMESTIC VIOLENCE ON TRIAL: PSYCHOLOGICAL AND LEGAL DIMENSIONS OF FAMILY VIOLENCE. Daniel J. Sonkin, Editor. Springer Publishing Company, Incorporated, 536 Broadway, New York, New York 10012. 1987.

FAMILY VIOLENCE. Second Edition. Richard J. Gelles. Sage Publications, 2455 Teller Road, Newbury Park, California 91320. 1987.

FAMILY VIOLENCE. University of Chicago Press, 5801 Ellis Avenue, Chicago, Illinois 60637. 1989.

FAMILY VIOLENCE: RESEARCH AND PUBLIC POLICY ISSUES. AEI Press, University Press of America, 4720 Boston Way, Lanham, Maryland 20706. 1990.

INTIMATE INTRUSIONS: WOMEN'S EXPERIENCES OF MALE VIOLENCE. Routledge and Kegan Paul, 29 West Thirty-fifth Street, New York, New York 10001. 1984.

INTIMATE VIOLENCE: A STUDY OF INJUSTICE. Julie Blackman. Columbia University Press, 562 West One Hundred Thirteenth Street, New York, New York 10025. 1989.

INTIMATE VIOLENCE IN FAMILIES. Second Edition. Richard J. Gelles and Claire Pedrick Cornell. Sage Publications, Incorporated, 2455 Teller Road, Newbury, California 91320. 1990.

NAMING THE VIOLENCE: SPEAKING OUT ABOUT LESBIAN BATTERING. Kerry Lobel, Editor. Seal Press-Feminist, 3131 Western Avenue, Number 410, Seattle, Washington 98121-1028. 1986.

VIOLENCE AGAINST WOMEN IN THE FAMILY. Jane Frances Connors. United Nations Publishing Service, Room DC2-0853, New York, New York 10017. 1989.

VIOLENCE IN THE HOME: INTERDISCIPLINARY PERSPECTIVES. Mary Lystad. Brunner/Mazel, Incorporated, 19 Union Square West, New York, New York 10003. 1986.

WOMEN ABUSE: FACTS REPLACING MYTHS. Lewis Okun. State University of New York Press, State University Plaza, Albany, New York 12246. 1986.

LAW REVIEWS AND PERIODICALS

JOURNAL OF FAMILY VIOLENCE. Plenum Publishing Corporation, 233 Spring Street, New York, New York 10013-1578. Quarterly.

RESPONSE TO THE VICTIMIZATION OF WOMEN AND CHILDREN. Center for Women Policy Studies, 2000 P Street, Northwest, Suite 508, Washington, D.C. 20036. Quarterly.

NEWSLETTERS AND NEWSPAPERS

EMERGE NEWSLETTER. Emerge, 280 Green Street, Second Floor, Cambridge, Massachusetts 02139. Quarterly.

EXCHANGE. National Woman Abuse Prevention Project, 2000 P Street, Northwest, Suite 508, Washington, D.C. 20036. Quarterly.

FRIENDS. House of Ruth, 501 H Street, Northeast, Washington, D.C. 20002. Quarterly.

NCCAFU NEWSLETTER. National Council on Child Abuse and Family Violence, 1155 Connecticut Avenue, Northwest, Suite 300, Washington, D.C. 20036. Quarterly.

NETWORK NEWSLETTER. Batterers Anonymous, 1269 Northeast Street, San Bernadino, California 92405. Quarterly.

RECAP NEWSLETTER. National Assault Prevention Center, P.O. Box 02005, Columbus, Ohio 43202. Quarterly.

VOICE. National Coalition Against Domestic Violence, P.O. Box 34103, Washington, D.C. 20043. Quarterly.

THE WOMAN'S ADVOCATE. National Center on Women and Family Law, 799 Broadway, Room 402, New York, New York 10003. Bimonthly.

FAMILY VIOLENCE

BIBLIOGRAPHIES

BATTERED WIVES: A COMPREHENSIVE ANNOTATED BIBLIOGRAPHY OF ARTICLES, BOOKS AND STATUTES IN THE UNITED STATES OF AMERICA. Nathan Aaron Rosen. National Center on Women and Family Law, 799 Broadway, Room 402, New York, New York 10003. 1988.

VIOLENCE IN THE FAMILY: AN ANNOTATED BIBLIOGRAPHY. Elizabeth Kemmer. Garland Publishing, Incorporated, 136 Madison Avenue, New York, New York 10016. 1984.

DIRECTORIES

SHELTERING BATTERED WOMEN: A NATIONAL STUDY AND SERVICE GUIDE. Albert R. Roberts. Springer Publishing Company, 536 Broadway, New York, New York 10012. 1981.

BIOGRAPHICAL SOURCES

THE POISON TREE: A TRUE STORY OF FAMILY TERROR. Alan Prendergast. Avon Books, 105 Madison Avenue, New York, New York 10016. 1987.

ASSOCIATIONS AND PROFESSIONAL SOCIETIES

AWARD NETWORK. 8000 East Prentice Avenue, D-1, Englewood, Colorado 80111. (303) 220-1707.

BATTERERS ANONYMOUS. 1269 Northeast Street, San Bernadino, California 92405. (714) 355-1100.

EMERGE: A MEN'S COUNSELING SERVICE ON DOMESTIC VIOLENCE. 280 Green Street, Second Floor, Cambridge, Massachusetts 02139. (617) 547-9870.

NATIONAL ASSAULT PREVENTION CENTER. P.O. Box 02005, Columbus, Ohio 43202. (614) 291-2540.

NATIONAL COUNCIL ON CHILD ABUSE AND FAMILY VIOLENCE. 1155 Connecticut Avenue, Northwest, Suite 300, Washington, D.C. 20036. (202) 429-6695.

NATIONAL COALITION AGAINST DOMESTIC VIOLENCE. P.O. Box 34103, Washington, D.C. 20043. (202) 638-6388.

NATIONAL WOMAN ABUSE PREVENTION PROJECT. 2000 P Street, Northwest, Suite 508, Washington, D.C. 20036. (202) 857-0216.

TASK FORCE ON FAMILIES IN CRISES. 4004 Hillsboro Road, Suite 223B, Nashville, Tennessee 37215. (615) 383-4575.

RESEARCH CENTERS, INSTITUTES, CLEARINGHOUSES

ADMINISTRATION FOR CHILDREN, YOUTH, FAMILIES. Health and Human Services Department, National Center on Child Abuse and Neglect, 330 C Street, Southwest, Washington, D.C. 20013. (202) 245-0586.

BOULDER INSTITUTE OF BEHAVIORAL SCIENCE. University of Colorado, Boulder, Colorado 80309. (303) 492-6991.

CENTER FOR RESEARCH ON AGRESSION. Syracuse University, 805 South Crouse Avenue, Syracuse, New York 13244. (315) 443-9641.

CENTER FOR THE STUDY OF WOMEN. University of California, Los Angeles, 236A Kinsey Hall, 405 Hilgard Avenue, Los Angeles, California 90024. (213) 825-0590.

CENTER FOR WOMEN POLICY STUDIES. 2000 P Street, Northwest, Suite 508, Washington, D.C. 20036. (202) 872-1770.

CHILD WELFARE LEAGUE OF AMERICA. 440 First Street, Northwest, Suite 310, Washington, D.C. 20001. (202) 638-2952.

CRIME CONTROL INSTITUTE AND CRIME CONTROL RESEARCH FOUNDATION. 1063 Thomas Jefferson Street, Northwest, Washington, D.C. 20007. (202) 337-2700.

ELIZABETH WISNER SOCIAL WELFARE RESEARCH CENTER FOR FAMILIES AND CHILDREN. Tulane University, School of Social Work, New Orleans, Louisiana 70118. (504) 865-5314.

FAMILY RESEARCH LABORATORY. University of New Hampshire, 128 Horton Social Science Center, Durham, New Hampshire 03824. (603) 862-1888.

HOUSE OF RUTH. 501 H Street, Northeast, Washington, D.C. 20002. (202) 547-6173.

ILLUSION THEATER. 528 Hennepin Avenue, Suite 704, Minneapolis, Minnesota 55403. (612) 339-4944.

MARRIAGE COUNCIL AT PHILADELPHIA. 4025 Chestnut Street, Second Floor, Philadelphia, Pennsylvania 19104. (215) 382-6680.

NATIONAL CENTER ON WOMEN AND FAMILY LAW. 799 Broadway, Room 402, New York, New York 10003. (212) 674-8200.

NATIONAL LEGAL RESOURCE CENTER FOR CHILD ADVOCACY AND PROTECTION. American Bar Association, 1800 M Street, Northwest, Washington, D.C. 20036. (202) 331-2200.

OREGON SOCIAL LEARNING CENTER, INCORPORATED. 207 East Fifth Avenue, Suite 202, Eugene, Oregon 97401. (503) 485-2711.

PROGRAM OF POLICY RESEARCH ON WOMEN AND FAMILIES. Urban Institute, 2100 M Street, Northest, Washington, D.C. 20037. (202) 833-7200.

SCHOOL OF JUSTICE STUDIES. Arizona State University, Tempe, Arizona 85287. (602) 965-7682.

SOCIAL AND INDIVIDUAL RESPONSIBILITY PROJECT. American Enterprise Institute for Public Policy Research, 1150 Seventeenth Street, Northwest, Washington, D.C. 20036. (202) 862-5800.

UNIVERSITY CENTER FOR THE CHILD AND FAMILY. University of Michigan, 1007 East Huron Street, Ann Arbor, Michigan 48104. (313) 764-9466.

STATISTICS SOURCES

CRIMINAL VICTIMIZATION IN THE UNITED STATES. United States Department of Justice, Annual Report. Superintendent of Documents, United States Government Printing Office, Washington, D.C. 20402. Annual.

FARMS AND FARMING
See: AGRICULTURE

FEDERAL AID
See also: FEDERAL AID TO EDUCATION; GRANTS-IN-AID

LOOSELEAF SERVICES AND REPORTERS

FEDERAL FUNDING GUIDE. Charles E. Edwards, Editor. Government Information Services, 1611 Kent Street, Suite 508, Arlington, Virginia 22209. 1977- .

FEDERAL GRANTS AND COOPERATIVE AGREEMENTS--LAW, POLICY, AND PRACTICE. Richard B. Cappalli. Callaghan and Company, 155 Pfingsten Road, Deerfield, Illinois 60015. 1983- .

HANDBOOKS, MANUALS, FORMBOOKS

FEDERAL AID TO STATES. United States Department of Commerce, Census Bureau. Superintendent of Documents, United States Government Printing Office, Washington, D.C. 20402. Annual.

GRANTS FOR LIBRARIES: A GUIDE TO PUBLIC AND PRIVATE FUNDING PROGRAMS AND PROPOSAL WRITING TECHNIQUES. Second Edition. Libraries Unlimited, Incorporated, P.O. Box 3988, Englewood, Colorado 80155-3988. 1986.

TEXTBOOKS AND GENERAL WORKS

A CHILDREN'S DEFENSE BUDGET: AN ANALYSIS OF THE PRESIDENT'S FY 1986 BUDGET AND CHILDREN. Children's Defense Fund, 122 C Street, Northwest, Washington, D.C. 20001. 1985.

DECENTRALIZING URBAN POLICY: STUDIES IN COMMUNITY DEVELOPMENT. Paul R. Dommel and others. Brookings Institution, 1775 Massachusetts Avenue, Northwest, Washington, D.C. 20036-2188. 1982.

DEVOLUTION OF FEDERAL AID HIGHWAY PROGRAMS: CASES IN STATE-LOCAL RELATIONS AND ISSUES IN STATE LAW. Michael A. Pagano. Advisory Commission on Intergovernmental Relations, 1111 Twentieth Street, Northwest, Suite 2000, Washington, D.C. 20575. 1988.

THE EVOLUTION OF A PROBLEMATIC PARTNERSHIP: THE FEDS AND HIGHER EDUCATION. Advisory Commission on Inter-govermental Relations, 1111 Twentieth Street, Northwest, Suite 2000, Washington, D.C. 20575. 1981.

FEDERAL AID TO BIG CITIES: THE POLITICS OF DEPENDENCE. James W. Fossett. Brookings Institution, 1775 Massachusetts Avenue, Northwest, Washington, D.C. 20036-2188. 1983.

FEDERAL AID TO CRIMINAL JUSTICE: RHETORIC, RESULTS, LESSONS. John K. Hudzik and others. National Criminal Justice Association, 444 North Capitol Street, Northwest, Washington, D.C. 20001. 1982.

GOVERNING URBAN AMERICA: A POLICY FOCUS. Bryan D. Jones. Scott Foresman and Company. 1900 East Lake Avenue, Glenview, Illinois 60025.

GRANTS FOR THE ARTS. Virginia White. Public Service Materials Center, 111 North Central Avenue, Hartsdale, New York 10530. 1981.

THE ILLUSORY GROWTH IN FEDERAL GRANTS-IN-AID TO CITIES. National League of Cities, 1301 Pennsylvania Avenue, Northwest, Washington, D.C. 20004. 1981.

A NATION OF CITIES: THE FEDERAL GOVERNMENT AND URBAN AMERICA 1933-1965. Mark I. Gelfand. Oxford University Press, 200 Madison Avenue, New York, New York 10016. 1975.

THE NEW DEAL FOR ARTISTS. R. McKinzie. Princeton University Press, 41 Williams Street, Princeton, New Jersey 08540. 1973.

PATRONS DESPITE THEMSELVES: TAXPAYERS AND ARTS POLICY. Alan L. Feld, Michael O'Hare and J. Mark Davidson. New York University Press, 70 Washington Square, New York, New York 10012. 1983.

THE REAGAN BLOCK GRANTS: WHAT HAVE WE LEARNED? George E. Peterson and others. Urban Institute Press, 2100 M Street, Northwest, Washington, D.C. 20037. 1986.

THE REGULATION OF AMERICAN FEDERALISM. Donald F. Kettl. Lousiana State University Press, Highland Road, Baton Rouge, Lousiana 70893. 1983.

SCIENCE POLICY FROM FORD TO REAGAN: CHANGE AND CONTINUITY. Claude E. Barfield. American Enterprise Institute for Public Policy Research, 1150 Seventeenth Street, Northwest, Washington, D.C. 20036. 1982.

THE STATES AND DISTRESSED COMMUNITIES: STATE PROGRAMS TO AID DISTRESSED COMMUNITIES. Mark L. Matulef. Advisory Commission on Intergovernmental Relations. 1111 Connecticut Avenue, Northwest, Suite 2000, Washington, D.C. 20575. 1985.

THE SUBSIDIZED MUSE. D. Netzer. Cambridge University Press, 40 West Twentieth, New York, New York 10011. 1978.

SUBSIDIZED PUBLIC TRANSPORT AND THE DEMAND FOR TRAVEL. Bailey Goodwin and others. Gower Publishing Company, Old Post Road, Brookfield, Vermont 05036. 1983.

FEDERAL AID

THE SUPREME COURT AND PUBLIC FUNDS FOR RELIGIOUS SCHOOLS: THE BURGER YEARS, 1969-1986. Joseph E. Bryson. McFarland and Company, Incorporated, Box 611, Jefferson, North Carolina 28640. 1990.

LAW REVIEWS AND PERIODICALS

INTERGOVERNMENTAL PERSPECTIVE. Advisory Commission on Intergovernmental Relations, 1111 Connecticut Avenue, Northwest, Washington, D.C. 20036. Quarterly.

NEWSLETTERS AND NEWSPAPERS

COMMUNITY DEVELOPMENT DIGEST. CD Publications, 8204 Fenton Street, Silver Spring, Maryland 20910. Semimonthly.

FEDERAL ASSISTANCE MONITOR. CD Publications, 8204 Fenton Street, Silver Spring, Maryland 20910. Semimonthly.

FEDERAL GRANTS AND CONTRACTS WEEKLY. Capitol Publications, Incorporated, 1101 King Street, Suite 444, Alexandria, Virginia 22314. Weekly.

FROM THE STATE CAPITOLS: FEDERAL ACTION AFFECTING THE STATES. Wakeman/Walworth, Incorporated, 300 North Washington Street, Suite 204, Alexandria, Virginia 22314. Semimonthly.

DIRECTORIES

THE CATALOG OF FEDERAL DOMESTIC ASSISTANCE. United States General Services Administration. Superintendent of Documents, United States Government Printing Office, Washington, D.C. 20402. Annual.

ASSOCIATIONS AND PROFESSIONAL SOCIETIES

COUNCIL OF STATE GOVERNMENTS. 444 North Capitol Street, Northwest, Washington, D.C. 20001. (202) 624-5460.

NATIONAL ASSOCIATION OF COUNTIES. 440 First Street, Northwest, Washington, D.C. 20001. (202) 393-6226.

NATIONAL GOVERNOR'S ASSOCIATION. 444 North Capitol Street, Northwest, Washington, D.C. 20001. (202) 624-5300.

NATIONAL LEAGUE OF CITIES. 1301 Pennsylvania Avenue, Northwest, Washington, D.C. 20004. (202) 626-3000.

UNITED STATES CONFERENCE OF MAYORS. 1620 Eye Street, Northwest, Washington, D.C. 20006. (202) 293-7330.

RESEARCH CENTERS, INSTITUTES, CLEARINGHOUSES

ACADEMY FOR STATE AND LOCAL GOVERNMENT. 444 North Capitol Street, Northwest, Washington, D.C. 20001.

ADVISORY COMMISSION ON INTERGOVERNMENTAL RELATIONS LIBRARY. 1111 Twentieth Street, Northwest, Washington, D.C. 20575.

CENTER FOR LEGAL STUDIES ON INTERGOVERNMENTAL RELATIONS. Tulane University, 6801 Freret Street, Room 109, New Orleans, Louisiana 70118. (504) 865-5995.

EDWIN F. JAECKLE CENTER FOR STATE AND LOCAL GOVERNMENT LAW. State University of New York at Buffalo, 422 O'Brien Hall, Amherst, New York 14260. (716) 636-2072.

GOVERNMENT FINANCE RESEARCH CENTER. 1750 K Street, Northwest, Washington, D.C. 20036. (202) 429-2750.

MUNICIPAL RESEARCH AND SERVICES CENTER OF WASHINGTON. 10517 Northeast Thirty-eighth Place, Kirkland, Washington 98033. (206) 827-4334.

NATIONAL CONFERENCE OF STATE LEGISLATURES. 444 North Capitol Street, Northwest, Washington, D.C. 20001.

POLICY RESEARCH INSTITUTE. University of Texas at Austin, LBJ School of Public Affairs, Drawer Y, University Station, Austin, Texas 78713. (512) 471-4962.

FEDERAL AID TO EDUCATION

STATUTES, CODES, STANDARDS, UNIFORM LAWS

A COMPILATION OF FEDERAL EDUCATION LAWS ... AS AMENDED THROUGH DECEMBER 31, 1990: PREPARED FOR THE USE OF THE COMMITTEE ON EDUCATION AND LABOR, HOUSE OF REPRESENTATIVES, ONE HUNDRED SECOND CONGRESS, FIRST SESSION. Superintendent of Documents, United States Government Printing Office, Washington, D.C. 20402. 1991.

LOOSELEAF SERVICES AND REPORTERS

CHAPTER I HANDBOOK. Education Funding Research Council, 1611 North Kent Street, Suite 508, Arlington, Virginia 22209. 1971- .

FEDERAL GRANTS AND COOPERATIVE AGREEMENTS--LAW, POLICY, AND PRACTICE. Richard B. Cappalli. Callaghan and Company, 155 Pfingsten Road, Deerfield, Illinois 60015. 1983- .

FEDERAL GRANTS MANAGEMENT HANDBOOK. Kathleen Dunten. Grants Management Advisory Service, 1725 K Street, Northwest, Washington, D.C. 20006. 1978- .

HANDBOOKS, MANUALS, FORMBOOKS

HANDBOOK FOR EDUCATIONAL FUND RAISING: A GUIDE TO SUCCESSFUL PRINCIPLES AND PRACTICES FOR COLLEGES, UNIVERSITIES AND SCHOOLS. Francis C. Pray, Editor. Books on Demand, 300 North Zeeb, Ann Arbor, Michigan 48106-1346. 1981.

SCHOOL LOAN PROGRAM GUIDE. National Association of Independent Schools, 75 Federal Street, Boston, Massachusetts 02110. 1984.

URBAN FUNDING GUIDE: SOURCES OF FUNDS FOR URBAN PROGRAMS AT COLLEGES AND UNIVERSITIES. American Association of State Colleges and Universities, Office of Urban Affairs, 1 Dupont Circle, Suite 700, Northwest, Washington, D.C. 20036. 1983.

TEXTBOOKS AND GENERAL WORKS

THE CHANGING GOVERNMENT OF EDUCATION. Stewart Rauson and John Tomlinson, Editors. Allen and Unwin, Incorporated, P.O. Box 442, Concord, Massachusetts 01742. 1986.

FEDERAL BLOCK GRANTS TO EDUCATION. E. Cohn, Editor. Pergamon Press, Incorporated, Maxwell House, Fairview Park, Elmsford, New York 10523. 1986.

THE INTERACTION OF FEDERAL AND RELATED STATE EDUCATION PROGRAMS. Mary T. Moore. Educational Testing Service, Education Policy Research Institute, Rosedale Road, Princeton, New Jersey 08541. 1983.

INTERGOVERNMENTALIZING THE CLASSROOM: FEDERAL INVOLVEMENT IN ELEMENTARY AND SECONDARY EDUCATION. Advisory Commission On Intergovernmental Relations, 1111 Twentieth Street, Northwest, Suite 2000, Washington, D.C. 20575. 1981.

THE LIMITS OF REFORM: POLITICS AND FEDERAL AID TO EDUCATION 1937-1950. Gilbert E. Smith. Garland Publishing, Incorporated, 136 Madison Avenue, New York, New York 10016. 1981.

PRIVATE EDUCATION AND PUBLIC POLICY: STUDIES IN CHOICE AND PUBLIC POLICY. Daniel C. Levy, Editor. Oxford University Press, 200 Madison Avenue, New York, New York 10016. 1986.

PROBLEMS CONCERNING EDUCATION VOUCHER PROPOSALS AND ISSUES RELATED TO CHOICE. Superintendent of Documents, United States Government Printing Office, Washington, D.C. 20402. 1990.

SCHOLARS, DOLLARS AND BUREAUCRATS. Chester E. Finn. The Brookings Institution, 1775 Massachusetts Avenue, Northwest, Washington, D.C. 20036-2188. 1978.

SUBSIDIES TO HIGHER EDUCATION: THE ISSUES. Howard P. Tuckman and Edward L. Whalen, Editors. Praeger Publications, One Madison Avenue, New York, New York 10010-3603. 1980.

THE SUPREME COURT AND PUBLIC FUNDS FOR RELIGIOUS SCHOOLS: THE BURGER YEARS, 1969-1986. Joseph E. Bryson. McFarland and Company, Incorporated, Box 611, Jefferson, North Carolina 28640. 1990.

THE UNCERTAIN TRIUMPH: FEDERAL EDUCATION POLICY IN THE KENNEDY AND JOHNSON YEARS. Hugh D. Graham. University of North Carolina Press, P.O. Box 2288, Chapel Hill, North Carolina 27515-2288. 1984.

ANNUALS AND SURVEYS

GUIDE TO FEDERAL FUNDING FOR EDUCATION. Mary M. Strump, Editor. Education Funding Research Council, 1611 North Kent Street, Suite 508, Arlington, Virginia 22209. 1975- .

NEWSLETTERS AND NEWSPAPERS

CHRONICLE OF HIGHER EDUCATION. 1255 Twenty-third Street, Northwest, Washington, D.C. 20036. Weekly.

FEDERAL GRANTS AND CONTRACTS WEEKLY. Capitol Publications, Incorporated, 1101 King Street, Suite 444, Alexandria, Virginia 22314. Weekly.

DIRECTORIES

AMERICAN EDUCATION--GUIDE TO DEPARTMENT OF EDUCATION PROGRAMS ISSUE. Department of Education. Superintendent of Documents, United States Government Printing Office, Washington, D.C. 20402. Annual.

BUREAU OF INDIAN AFFAIRS HIGHER EDUCATION GRANT PROGRAM. Office of Indian Education Programs, Bureau of Indian Affairs, Department of the Interior. Superintendent of Documents, United States Government Printing Office, Washington, D.C. 20402. Annual.

CFAE CORPORATE HANDBOOK OF AID-TO-EDUCATION PROGRAMS. Council for Financial Aid to Education. 680 Fifth Avenue, New York, New York 10019. Biennial.

DIRECTORY OF FEDERAL AID FOR EDUCATION. Ready Reference Press, P.O. Box 5169, Santa Monica, California 90405. 1982.

DIRECTORY OF FINANCIAL AIDS FOR WOMEN, (1991-1992). Gail A. Schlachter. Reference Service Press, 1100 Industrial Road, Suite 9, San Carlos, California 94070. 1991.

GUIDE TO FEDERAL ASSISTANCE (Education). Wellborn Associates, Incorporated, 262 Grady Drive, Rock Hill, South Carolina 29732. Monthly.

ASSOCIATIONS AND PROFESSIONAL SOCIETIES

COUNCIL FOR ADVANCEMENT AND SUPPORT OF EDUCATION. 11 Dupont Circle, Northwest, Washington, D.C. 20036. (202) 328-5900.

NATIONAL ASSOCIATION FOR EQUAL OPPORTUNITY IN HIGHER EDUCATION. 400 Twelfth Street, Northeast, Washington, D.C. 20002. (202) 543-9111.

NATIONAL ASSOCIATION FOR THE ADVANCEMENT OF COLORED PEOPLE. 1025 Vermont Avenue, Northwest, Washington, D.C. 20005. (202) 638-2269.

NATIONAL ASSOCIATION FOR THE EDUCATION OF YOUNG CHILDREN. 1834 Connecticut Avenue, Northwest, Washington, D.C. 20009. (202) 232-8777.

FEDERAL AID TO EDUCATION

NATIONAL EDUCATION ASSOCIATION. 1201 Sixteenth Street, Northwest, Washington, D.C. 20036. (202) 822-7400.

NATIONAL ENDOWMENT FOR THE ARTS AND HUMANITIES. 1100 Pennsylvania Avenue, Northwest, Washington, D.C. 20506. (202) 682-5400.

NATIONAL SCIENCE FOUNDATION. Research Career Development, 1800 G Street, Washington, D.C. 20550. (202) 357-9859.

PUBLIC EDUCATION FUND NETWORK. 600 Grant Street, Suite 4444, Pittsburgh, Pennsylvania 15219. (412) 391-3235.

RESEARCH CENTERS, INSTITUTES, CLEARINGHOUSES

CARNEGIE FOUNDATION FOR THE ADVANCEMENT OF TEACHING. 5 Ivy Lane, Princeton, New Jersey 08540. (609) 452-1780.

CENTER FOR LAW AND EDUCATION. 236 Massachusetts Avenue, Northeast, Washington, D.C. 20002. (202) 546-5300.

DIVISION OF EDUCATIONAL POLICY RESEARCH. Educational Testing Service, Princeton, New Jersey 08541. (609) 734-5694.

EDUCATION COMMISSION OF THE STATES. 444 North Capitol Street, Northwest, Washington, D.C. 20001. (202) 624-5838.

EDUCATIONAL RESOURCES INFORMATION CENTER. United States Department of Education, 2440 Research Boulevard, Suite 400, Rockville, Maryland 20850. (301) 258-5500.

THE FOUNDATION CENTER LIBRARY. 1001 Connecticut Avenue, Northwest, Washington, D.C. 20036. (202) 331-1400.

INSTITUTE FOR EDUCATIONAL LEADERSHIP. 1001 Connecticut Avenue, Northwest, Washington, D.C. 20036. (202) 822-8405.

ONLINE DATABASES

ERIC. United States Department of Education, Educational Resources Information Center, 2440 Research Boulevard, Suite 400, Rockville, Maryland 20850.

STATISTICS SOURCES

THE BUDGET OF THE UNITED STATES GOVERNMENT. Executive Office of the President, Office of Management and Budget. Superintendent of Documents, United States Government Printing Office, Washington, D.C. 20402. Annual.

DIGEST OF EDUCATION STATISTICS. United States Department of Education. Superintendent of Documents, United States Government Printing Office, Washington, D.C. 20402. Annual.

FEDERAL SUPPORT TO UNIVERSITIES, COLLEGES, AND SELECTED NONPROFIT INSTITUTIONS. United States National Science Foundation, 1800 G Street, Northwest, Washington, D.C. 20550. Annual.

REVENUES AND EXPENDITURES FOR PUBLIC ELEMENTARY AND SECONDARY EDUCATION. United States Department of Education. Superintendent of Documents, United States Government Printing Office, Washington, D.C. 20402. Annual.

FEDERAL AVIATION ADMINISTRATION
See also: NATIONAL TRANSPORTATION SAFETY BOARD; TRANSPORTATION DEPARTMENT

STATUTES, CODES, STANDARDS, UNIFORM LAWS

FEDERAL AVIATION REGULATIONS. Transportation Department, Federal Aviation Administration. Superintendent of Documents, United States Government Printing Office, Washington, D.C. 20402. Irregular. (Issued in individual parts).

UNITED STATES STANDARD FOR TERMINAL INSTRUMENT PROCEDURES (TERPS). Transportation Department, Federal Aviation Administration and Coast Guard, and Defense Department, Army, Navy, and Air Force. Superintendent of Documents, United States Government Printing Office, Washington, D.C. 20402. Irregular. (Issued in individual chapters).

RESEARCH CENTERS, INSTITUTES, CLEARINGHOUSES

FEDERAL AVIATION ADMINISTRATION LIBRARY. United States Department of Transportation, Federal Aviation Administration, 800 Independence Avenue, Southwest, Washington, D.C. 20591. (202) 267-3484.

ONLINE DATABASES

FAA DATA BASE. Comp Comm, Incorporated, Information Services Division, Station House, Fourth Floor, 900 Hadden Avenue, Collingswood, New Jersey 08108.

FEDERAL BUREAU OF INVESTIGATION

HANDBOOKS, MANUALS, FORMBOOKS

HANDBOOK OF FORENSIC SCIENCE. Justice Department, Federal Bureau of Investigation. Gordon Press Publishers, P.O. Box 459, Bowling Green Station, New York, New York 10004. 1991.

TEXTBOOKS AND GENERAL WORKS

THE BOSS: J. EDGAR HOOVER AND THE GREAT AMERICAN INQUISITION. Athan G. Theoharis. Temple University Press, 1601 North Broad Street, University Services Building, Philadelphia, Pennsylvania 19122. 1988.

PROCEEDINGS OF A FORENSIC SCIENCE SYMPOSIUM ON THE ANALYSIS OF SEXUAL ASSAULT EVIDENCE, JULY 6-8, 1983. Justice Department, Federal Bureau of Investigation, Forensic Science Research and Training Center, Laboratory Division, FBI Acadamy. Superintendent of Documents, United States Government Printing Office, Washington, D.C. 20402. 1985.

SCIENCE OF FINGERPRINTS: CLASSIFICATION AND USES. Justice Department, Federal Bureau of Investigation. Superintendent of Documents, United States Government Printing Office, Washington, D.C. 20402. 1985.

BIOGRAPHICAL SOURCES

SECRECY AND POWER: THE LIFE OF J. EDGAR HOOVER. Richard Gid Powers. Free Press, 866 Third Avenue, New York, New York 10022. 1987.

STATISTICS SOURCES

CRIME IN THE UNITED STATES. Justice Department, Federal Bureau of Investigation. Superintendent of Documents, United States Government Printing Office, Washington, D.C. 20402. Annual.

FEDERAL COMMUNICATIONS COMMISSION

STATUTES, CODES, STANDARDS, UNIFORM LAWS

CODE OF FEDERAL REGULATIONS, TITLE 47. Office of the Federal Register, National Archives and Records Administration. Superintendent of Documents, United States Government Printing Office, Washington, D.C. 20402. Annual. (Updated by use of monthly List of Sections Affected and daily Federal Register).

COMMUNICATIONS ACT OF 1934, AS AMENDED, AND OTHER SELECTED PROVISIONS OF LAW. Federal Communications Commission. Superintendent of Documents, United States Government Printing Office, Washington, D.C. 20402. 1983- .

LOOSELEAF SERVICES AND REPORTERS

FEDERAL COMMUNICATIONS COMMISSION REPORTS. Superintendent of Documents, United States Government Printing Office, Washington, D.C. 20402. 1934- .

FEDERAL COMMUNICATIONS COMMISSION RULES AND REGULATIONS. Federal Communications Commission. Superintendent of Documents, United States Government Printing Office, Washington, D.C. 20402. Irregular.

MEDIA LAW REPORTER. Bureau of National Affairs, 1231 Twenty-fifth Street, Northwest, Washington, D.C. 20037. 1977- .

PIKE AND FISCHER RADIO REGULATION, SECOND SERIES. John W. Willis and Henry G. Fischer. Pike and Fischer, Incorporated, 4550 Montgomery Avenue, Suite 433N, Bethesda, Maryland 20814. 1967- .

TEXTBOOKS AND GENERAL WORKS

FCC: THE UPS AND DOWNS OF RADIO-TV REGULATION. William Ray. Iowa State University Press, 2121 South State Avenue, Ames, Iowa 50010. 1990.

DIGESTS, INDEXES, ABSTRACTS, CITATORS

SHEPARD'S UNITED STATES ADMINISTRATIVE CITATIONS. Shepard's/McGraw-Hill, P.O. Box 1235, Colorado Springs, Colorado 80901. Bimonthly.

ANNUALS AND SURVEYS

FEDERAL COMMUNICATIONS COMMISSION ANNUAL REPORT. Federal Communications Commission. Superintendent of Documents, United States Government Printing Office, Washington, D.C. 20402. Annual.

ASSOCIATIONS AND PROFESSIONAL SOCIETIES

FEDERAL COMMUNICATIONS BAR ASSOCIATION. P.O. Box 34434, Bethesda, Maryland 20817. (301) 299-7299.

RESEARCH CENTERS, INSTITUTES, CLEARINGHOUSES

UNITED STATES FEDERAL COMMUNICATIONS COMMISSION LIBRARY. 1919 M Street, Northwest, Room 639, Washington, D.C. 20554. (202) 632-7100.

ONLINE DATABASES

LEXIS, FEDERAL COMMUNICATIONS LIBRARY. Mead Data Central, P.O. Box 933, Dayton, Ohio 45401.

WESTLAW, COMMUNICATIONS LIBRARY. West Publishing Company, P.O. Box 64526, 50 West Kellogg Boulevard, St. Paul, Minnesota 55164-0526.

FEDERAL CONTRACTS
See: GOVERNMENT CONTRACTS

FEDERAL COURTS
See also: ADMINISTRATIVE OFFICE OF THE UNITED STATES COURTS; CIRCUIT COURTS OF APPEAL (UNITED STATES); COURTS; DISTRICT COURTS (UNITED STATES); FEDERAL JUDICIAL CENTER; SUPREME COURT (UNITED STATES)

STATUTES, CODES, STANDARDS, UNIFORM LAWS

FEDERAL CIVIL PROCEDURE AND RULES. West Publishing Company, P.O. Box 64526, 50 West Kellogg Boulevard, St. Paul, Minnesota 55164-0526. Annual.

FEDERAL PROCEDURE RULES SERVICE. Lawyers Cooperative Publishing Company, Aqueduct Building, Rochester, New York 14694. Annual.

JUDICIARY AND JUDICIAL PROCEDURE, FEDERAL RULES OF CIVIL PROCEDURE, FEDERAL RULES OF APPELLATE PROCEDURE AND FEDERAL COURT RULES. United States Code, Title 28 and Title 28 Appendices. Superintendent of Documents, United States Government Printing Office, Washington, D.C. 20402. Annual Supplements,

JUDICIARY AND JUDICIAL PROCEDURE, FEDERAL RULES OF CIVIL PROCEDURE, FEDERAL RULES OF APPELLATE PROCEDURE AND FEDERAL COURT RULES. United States Code Annotated, Title 28 and Title 28 Appendices. West Publishing Company, P.O. Box 64526, 50 West Kellogg Boulevard, St. Paul, Minnesota 55164-0526. Annual Supplements.

JUDICIARY AND JUDICIAL PROCEDURE, FEDERAL RULES OF CIVIL PROCEDURE, FEDERAL RULES OF APPELLATE PROCEDURE AND FEDERAL COURT RULES. United States Code Service, Title 28 and Court Rules volumes. Lawyers Cooperative Publishing Company, Aqueduct Building, Rochester, New York 14694. Annual Supplements.

MOORE'S FEDERAL PRACTICE: RULES PAMPHLET. James William Moore, Kathleen D. Harper and Linda J. Folkman. Matthew Bender and Company, Incorporated, 11 Penn Plaza, New York, New York 10001. 1984.

RULES OF CIVIL PROCEDURE FOR THE UNITED STATES DISTRICT COURTS: PRACTICE COMMENTS. Thomas A. Coyne. Clark Boardman Company, Limited, 435 Hudson Street, New York, New York 10014. 1983. (Annual Supplements).

HANDBOOKS, MANUALS, FORMBOOKS

FEDERAL TRIAL HANDBOOK, SECOND EDITION. Robert S. Hunter. Lawyers Cooperative Publishing Company, Aqueduct Building, Rochester, New York 14694. 1984. (With Supplements).

GUIDE TO THE FEDERAL COURTS: AN INTRODUCTION TO THE FEDERAL COURTS AND THEIR OPERATION: INCLUDES EXPLANATION OF HOW A CASE IS LITIGATED. Want Publishing Company, 1511 K Street, Northwest, Washington, D.C. 20005. 1984.

WEST'S FEDERAL PRACTICE MANUAL. Marlin M. Volz. West Publishing Company, P.O. Box 64526, 50 West Kellogg Boulevard, St. Paul, Minnesota 55164-0526. 1983. (Supplemented).

TEXTBOOKS AND GENERAL WORKS

CONGRESS AND THE COURTS: A LEGISLATIVE HISTORY, 1978-1984: DOCUMENTS AND MATERIALS REGARDING THE CREATION, STRUCTURE, AND ORGANIZATION OF FEDERAL COURTS AND THE FEDERAL JUDICIARY. Bernard D. Reames, Jr. William S. Hein and Company, Incorporated, Hein Building, 1285 Main Street, Buffalo, New York 14209. 1985- .

A DATABASE MANAGEMENT SYSTEM FOR THE FEDERAL COURTS. Jack R. Buchanan, Richard D. Fennell and Hanan Samet. Association for Computing Machinery, 11 West Forty-second Street, New York, New York 10036. 1984.

THE FEDERAL COURTS. Robert A. Carp and Robert Stidham. Congressional Quarterly, Incorporated, 1414 Twenty-second Street, Northwest, Washington, D.C. 20037. 1990.

THE FEDERAL COURTS AS A POLITICAL SYSTEM. Third Edition. Sheldon Goldman and Thomas P. Jahnige. HarperCollins Publishers, 10 East Fifty-third Street, New York, New York 10022. 1985.

THE FEDERAL COURTS: CRISIS AND REFORM. Richard A. Posner. Harvard University Press, 79 Garden Street, Cambridge, Massachusetts 02138. 1985.

FEDERAL JURISDICTION. Erwin Chemerinsky. Little, Brown and Company, 34 Beacon Street, Boston, Massachusetts 02108. 1989.

FEDERAL JURISDICTION IN A NUTSHELL. Third Edition. David P. Currie. West Publishing Company, 50 West Kellogg Boulevard, St. Paul, Minnesota 55164. 1990.

FEDERAL STANDARDS OF REVIEW. S.A. Childress. John Wiley and Sons, Incorporated, 605 Third Avenue, New York, New York 10158. 1986.

HISTORY OF THE FEDERAL COURTS. Erwin C. Surrency. Oceana Publications, 75 Main Street, Dobbs Ferry, New York 10522. 1987.

THE LAW OF FEDERAL COURTS HANDBOOK. Fourth Edition. Charles A. Wright. West Publishing Company, P.O. Box 64526, 50 West Kellogg Boulevard, St. Paul, Minnesota 55164-0526. 1983.

MOTIONS IN FEDERAL COURT, CIVIL PRACTICE. Shepard's/McGraw-Hill, P.O. Box 1235, Colorado Springs, Colorado 80901. 1982.

PREPARING A UNITED STATES COURT FOR AUTOMATION. Gordon Bermant. Federal Judicial Center, Dolley Madison House, 1520 H Street, Northwest, Washington, D.C. 20005. 1985.

RESTRUCTURING JUSTICE: THE INNOVATIONS OF THE NINTH CIRCUIT AND THE FUTURE OF THE FEDERAL COURTS. Arthur D. Hellman. Cornell University Press, 124 Roberts Place, Ithaca, New York 14850. 1990.

REWRITING THE HISTORY OF THE JUDICIARY ACT OF 1789: EXPOSING MYTHS, CHALLENGING PREMISES, AND USING NEW EVIDENCE. Wilfred J. Ritz and Wythe Holt. University of Oklahoma Press, 105 Asp Avenue, Norman, Oklahoma 73019. 1990.

ANNUALS AND SURVEYS

ANNUAL REPORTS OF THE DIRECTOR OF THE ADMINISTRATIVE OFFICE OF THE UNITED STATES COURTS. Administrative Office of the United States Courts. Superintendent of Documents, United States Government Printing Office, Washington, D.C. 20402. Annual.

REPORT OF THE PROCEEDINGS OF THE JUDICIAL CONFERENCE OF THE UNITED STATES. Administrative Office of the United States Courts. Superintendent of Documents, United States Government Printing Office, Washington, D.C. 20402. Annual.

Encyclopedia of Legal Information Sources • 2nd Ed. FEDERAL ENERGY REGULATORY COMMISSION

NEWSLETTERS AND NEWSPAPERS

COURT OF APPEALS FOR THE THIRD CIRCUIT NEWSLETTER. American Bar Association, Litigation Section, 750 North Lake Shore Drive, Chicago, Illinois 60611. Bimonthly.

COURT REVIEW. American Judges Association, 300 Newport Avenue, Williamsburg, Virginia 23187. Quarterly.

FEDERAL TRIAL NEWS. American Bar Association, 750 North Lake Shore Drive, Chicago, Illinois 60611. Quarterly.

PARASCOPE. American Bar Association, 750 North Lake Shore Drive, Chicago, Illinois 60611. Quarterly.

THE THIRD BRANCH: BULLETIN OF THE FEDERAL COURTS. Federal Judicial Center, 1250 H Street, Northwest, Washington, D.C. 20005. Monthly.

BIBLIOGRAPHIES

CONGESTION IN THE U.S. COURT SYSTEM: A BRIEF BIBLIOGRAPHY. Alva W. Stewart. Vance Bibliographies, P.O. Box 229, 112 North Charter Street, Monticello, Illinois 61856. 1984.

COURT ADMINISTRATION: MONOGRAPHS. Mary Vance. Vance Bibliographies, P.O. Box 229, 112 North Charter Street, Monticello, Illinois 61856. 1983.

DIRECTORIES

THE AMERICAN BENCH: JUDGES OF THE NATION. Reginald Bishop Forster and Associates, 3287 Ramos Circle, Sacramento, California 95827. Biennial.

FEDERAL JUDICIARY ALMANAC. W. Stuart Dornette and Robert R. Cross. John Wiley and Sons, Incorporated, 605 Third Avenue, New York, New York 10158. 1986.

UNITED STATES COURT DIRECTORY. Administrative Office of the United States Courts. Superintendent of Documents, United States Government Printing Office, Washington, D.C. 20402. Semiannual.

WANT'S FEDERAL-STATE COURT DIRECTORY. Want Publishing Company, 1511 K Street, Northwest, Washington, D.C. 20005. Annual.

BIOGRAPHICAL SOURCES

ALMANAC OF THE FEDERAL JUDICIARY: PROFILES OF ALL ACTIVE UNITED STATES DISTRICT JUDGES. Lawletters, Incorporated. 332 South Michigan Avenue, Suite 1460, Chicago, Illinois 60604. Semiannual.

BIOGRAPHICAL DICTIONARY OF THE FEDERAL JUDICIARY. Harold Chase, Samuel Krislov, Keith O. Boyum and Jerry N. Clark. Gale Research, Incorporated, 825 Penobscot Building, Detroit, Michigan 48226. 1976. (Retrospective).

ASSOCIATIONS AND PROFESSIONAL SOCIETIES

COMMITTEE ON FEDERAL JUDICIAL IMPROVEMENTS. American Bar Association, 750 North Lake Shore Drive, Chicago, Illinois 60611. (312) 988-5158.

COMMITTEE ON FEDERAL JUDICIARY. American Bar Association, 750 North Lake Shore Drive, Chicago, Illinois 60611. (312) 988-5158.

RESEARCH CENTERS, INSTITUTES, CLEARINGHOUSES

ADMINISTRATIVE OFFICE OF THE UNITED STATES COURTS LIBRARY. 811 Vermont Avenue, Northwest, Washington, D.C. 20544. (202) 786-7138.

FEDERAL JUDICIAL CENTER LIBRARY. Dolley Madison House, 1520 H Street, Northwest, Washington, D.C. 20005. (202) 633-6011.

ONLINE DATABASES

LEXIS, GENERAL FEDERAL LIBRARY. Mead Data Central. 9393 Springboro Pike, P.O. Box 933, Dayton, Ohio 45401.

WESTLAW, FEDERAL DATABASES. West Publishing Company, P.O. Box 64526, 50 West Kellogg Boulevard, St. Paul, Minnesota 55164-0526.

STATISTICS SOURCES

FEDERAL COURT MANAGEMENT STATISTICS. Administrative Office of the United States Courts. Superintendent of Documents, United States Government Printing Office, Washington, D.C. 20402. Annual.

COMPUTER-ASSISTED LEGAL INSTRUCTION

ANALYSIS OF A DIVERSITY JURISDICTION CASE. Roger C. Park and Douglas D. McFarland. Center for Computer-Assisted Instruction, 229 19th Avenue South, University of Minnesota, Minneapolis, Minnesota 55455. Machine-readable computer file.

ELEVENTH AMENDMENT. Suzanna Sherry. Center for Computer-Assisted Instruction, 229 19th Avenue South, University of Minnesota, Minneapolis, Minnesota 55455. Machine-readable computer file.

FEDERAL HABEAS CORPUS. Suzanna Sherry. Center for Computer- Assisted Instruction, 229 19th Avenue South, University of Minnesota, Minneapolis, Minnesota 55455. Machine-readable computer file.

OTHER SOURCES

REPORT OF THE FEDERAL COURTS STUDY COMMITTEE. Judicial Conference of the United States, Federal Courts Study Committee, Philadelphia, Pennsylvania. 1990.

THE UNITED STATES COURTS: THEIR JURISDICTION AND WORK. Administrative Office of the United States Courts, Washington, D.C. 20544. 1989.

FEDERAL ENERGY REGULATORY COMMISSION

See also: ENERGY DEPARTMENT

FEDERAL ENERGY REGULATORY COMMISSION

STATUTES, CODES, STANDARDS, UNIFORM LAWS

CODE OF FEDERAL REGULATIONS, TITLE 18. Office of the Federal Register, National Archives and Records Administration. Superintendent of Documents, United States Government Printing Office, Washington, D.C. 20402. Annual. (Updated by use of monthly List of Sections Affected and daily Federal Register).

LOOSELEAF SERVICES AND REPORTERS

FEDERAL ENERGY REGULATORY COMMISSION REPORTER. Commerce Clearing House, Incorporated, 4025 West Peterson Avenue, Chicago, Illinois 60646. 1979- .

FERC PRACTICE AND PROCEDURE MANUAL. Stephen A. Herman. Federal Programs Advisory Service, Washington, D.C. 1982.

HEARING PROCESS STATUS REPORT, DATA FOR DECISIONS. Energy Department, Federal Energy Regulatory Commission. Superintendent of Documents, United States Government Printing Office, Washington, D.C. 20402. Monthly.

PUBLIC UTILITIES REPORTS: FOURTH SERIES. Books on Demand, 300 North Zeeb Road, Ann Arbor, Michigan 48106-1346. 1986.

UTILITIES LAW REPORTER. Commerce Clearing House, Incorporated, 4025 West Peterson Avenue, Chicago, Illinois 60646. 1977- .

HANDBOOKS, MANUALS, FORMBOOKS

FEDERAL ENERGY REGULATORY COMMISSION PRODUCER MANUAL: A MANUAL OF INSTRUCTIONS PREPARED BY THE FERC STAFF FOR PRODUCER COMPLIANCE WITH THE PROVISIONS OF THE NATURAL GAS POLICY ACT OF 1978. Energy Department, Federal Energy Regulatory Commission. Superintendent of Documents, United States Government Printing Office, Washington, D.C. 20402. 1979- .

DIGESTS, INDEXES, ABSTRACTS, CITATORS

PUR DIGEST, THIRD SERIES. Public Utilities Reports, Incorporated, 2111 Wilson Boulevard, Suite 200, Arlington, Virginia 22201. 1975- .

SHEPARD'S FEDERAL ENERGY LAW CITATIONS. Shepard's/McGraw-Hill, P.O. Box 1235, Colorado Springs, Colorado 80901. Quarterly.

SHEPARD'S UNITED STATES ADMINISTRATIVE CITATIONS. Shepard's/McGraw-Hill, P.O. Box 1235, Colorado Springs, Colorado 80901. Bimonthly.

ANNUALS AND SURVEYS

FEDERAL ENERGY REGULATORY COMMISSION ANNUAL REPORT. Energy Department, Federal Energy Regulatory Commission. Superintendent of Documents, United States Government Printing Office, Washington, D.C. 20402. Annual.

NEWSLETTERS AND NEWSPAPERS

ENERGY SUMMARY. Oliphant Washington News Service, 1819 H Street, Northwest, Suite 330, Washington, D.C. 20006. Weekly.

INSIDE F.E.R.C. McGraw-Hill, Incorporated, 1221 Avenue of the Americas, New York, New York 10020. Weekly.

ASSOCIATIONS AND PROFESSIONAL SOCIETIES

FEDERAL ENERGY BAR ASSOCIATION. c/o Lorna Wilson, 1900 M Street, Northwest, Washington D.C. 20036. (202) 223-5625.

ONLINE DATABASES

LEXIS, ENERGY LIBRARY. Mead Data Central, P.O. Box 933, Dayton, Ohio 45401.

WESTLAW, ENERGY AND UTILITIES LIBRARY. West Publishing Company, P.O. Box 64526, 50 West Kellogg Boulevard, St. Paul, Minnesota 55164-0526.

FEDERAL JUDICIAL CENTER

HANDBOOKS, MANUALS, FORMBOOKS

HANDBOOK ON JURY USE IN THE FEDERAL DISTRICT COURTS. Jody George. Federal Judicial Center, 1520 H Street, Northwest, Washington, D.C. 20005. 1989.

JUDICIAL WRITING MANUAL. Federal Judicial Center, 1520 H Street, Northwest, Washington, D.C. 20005. 1991.

LAW CLERK HANDBOOK: A HANDBOOK FOR LAW CLERKS TO FEDERAL JUDGES. Alvin B. Rubin and Laura B. Bartell. Federal Judicial Center, 1520 H Street, Northwest, Washington, D.C. 20005. 1989. (Revised).

MANUAL ON EMPLOYMENT DISCRIMINATION LAW AND CIVIL RIGHTS ACTIONS IN THE FEDERAL COURTS. Charles R. Richey. Mitchie Company, P.O. Box 7587, Charlottesville, Virginia 22906-7582. 1988.

MANUAL ON RECURRING PROBLEMS IN CRIMINAL TRIALS. Third Edition. Donald S. Voorhees. Federal Judicial Center, 1520 H Street, Northwest, Washington, D.C. 20005. 1990.

A PRACTICAL GUIDE TO REVISION OF LOCAL COURT RULES. Jeanne Johnson Bowden. Federal Judicial Center, 1520 H Street, Northwest, Washington, D.C. 20005. 1988.

TEXTBOOKS AND GENERAL WORKS

DECIDING CASES WITHOUT ARGUMENT: AN EXAMINATION OF FOUR COURTS OF APPEALS. Joe S. Cecil. Federal Judicial Center, 1520 H Street, Northwest, Washington, D.C. 20005. 1987.

DISABILITY APPEALS IN SOCIAL SECURITY PROGRAMS. Lance Liebman. Federal Judicial Center, 1520 H Street, Northwest, Washington, D.C. 20005. 1985.

AN EMPIRICAL STUDY OF RULE 11 SANCTIONS. Saul M. Kassin. Federal Judicial Center, 1520 H Street, Northwest, Washington, D.C. 20005. 1985.

THE FEDERAL APPELLATE JUDICIARY IN THE TWENTY-FIRST CENTURY. Cynthia Harrison and Russell R. Wheeler. Federal Judicial Center, 1520 H Street, Northwest, Washington, D.C. 20005. 1989.

"FRAUD" AND CIVIL LIABILITY UNDER THE FEDERAL SECURITIES LAW. Louis Loss. Federal Judicial Center, 1520 H Street, Northwest, Washington, D.C. 20005. 1983.

ILLUSTRATIVE RULES GOVERNING COMPLAINTS OF JUDICIAL MISCONDUCT AND DISABILITY: WITH COMMENTARY. J. Browning, C. Seitz and C. Clark. Federal Judicial Center, 1520 H Street, Northwest, Washington, D.C. 20005. 1986.

IMPACT OF THE FEDERAL DRUG AFTERCARE PROGRAM. James B. Eaglin. Federal Judicial Center, 1520 H Street, Northwest, Washington, D.C. 20005. 1986.

MAJOR ISSUES IN IMMIGRATION LAW. David A. Martin. Federal Judicial Center, 1520 H Street, Northwest, Washington, D.C. 20005. 1986.

MAJOR ISSUES IN THE FEDERAL LAW OF EMPLOYMENT DISCRIMINATION. George Rutherglen. Federal Judicial Center, 1520 H Street, Northwest, Washington, D.C. 20005. 1983.

MANAGING APPEALS IN FEDERAL COURTS. Federal Judicial Center, 1520 H Street, Northwest, Washington, D.C. 20005. 1988.

OBSERVATION AND STUDY IN THE FEDERAL DISTRICT COURTS. Julie Horney. Federal Judicial Center, 1520 H Street, Northwest, Washington, D.C. 20005. 1985.

A PRIMER ON THE JURISDICTION OF THE UNITED STATES COURTS OF APPEALS. Thomas E. Baker. Federal Judicial Center, 1520 H Street, Northwest, Washington, D.C. 20005. 1989.

THE ROLES OF MAGISTRATES IN FEDERAL DISTRICT COURTS. Carroll Seron. Federal Judicial Center, 1520 H Street, Northwest, Washington, D.C. 20005. 1983.

THE ROLES OF MAGISTRATES: NINE CASE STUDIES. Carroll Seron. Federal Judicial Center, 1520 H Street, Northwest, Washington, D.C. 20005. 1985.

SETTLEMENT STRATEGIES FOR FEDERAL DISTRICT JUDGES. D. Marie Provine. Federal Judicial Center, 1520 H Street, Northwest, Washington, D.C. 20005. 1986.

NEWSLETTERS AND NEWSPAPERS

THE THIRD BRANCH: BULLETIN OF THE FEDERAL COURTS. Federal Judicial Center, 1520 H Street, Northwest, Washington, D.C. 20005. 1986. Monthly.

RESEARCH CENTERS, INSTITUTES, CLEARINGHOUSES

FEDERAL JUDICIAL CENTER LIBRARY. 1520 H Street, Northwest, Washington, D.C. 20005. (202) 633-6011.

OTHER SOURCES

FEDERAL COURTS AND WHAT THEY DO. Federal Judicial Center, 1520 H Street, Northwest, Washington, D.C. 20005. 1987.

WELCOME TO THE FEDERAL COURT. Federal Judicial Center, 1520 H Street, Northwest, Washington, D.C. 20005. 1987.

FEDERAL JURISDICTION
See: JURISDICTION

FEDERAL LABOR RELATIONS AUTHORITY
See also: LABOR DEPARTMENT; NATIONAL LABOR RELATIONS BOARD

STATUTES, CODES, STANDARDS, UNIFORM LAWS

CODE OF FEDERAL REGULATIONS, TITLE 5. Office of the Federal Register, National Archives and Records Administration. Superintendent of Documents, United States Government Printing Office, Washington, D.C. 20402. Annual. (Updated by use of monthly List of Sections Affected and daily Federal Register).

LOOSELEAF SERVICES AND REPORTERS

DECISIONS OF THE FEDERAL LABOR RELATIONS AUTHORITY. Superintendent of Documents, United States Government Printing Office, Washington, D.C. 20402. 1979- .

FEDERAL SERVICE IMPASSES PANEL RELEASES. Superintendent of Documents, United States Government Printing Office, Washington, D.C. 20402. 1970- .

HANDBOOKS, MANUALS, FORMBOOKS

GUIDE TO THE FEDERAL SERVICE LABOR MANAGEMENT RELATIONS STATUTE. Federal Labor Relations Authority. Superintendent of Documents, United States Government Printing Office, Washington, D.C. 20402. 1990.

TEXTBOOKS AND GENERAL WORKS

THE FEDERAL GOVERNMENT AS EMPLOYER: THE FEDERAL LABOR RELATIONS AUTHORITY AND THE PATCO CHALLENGE. Herbert Roof Northrup. University of Pennsylvania, The Wharton School, Industrial Research Unit, 37733 Spruce Street, Philadelphia, Pennsylvania 19104. 1988.

GRIEVANCE ARBITRATION IN THE FEDERAL SERVICE. Dennis K. Reischl and Ralph Russell Smith. Federal Personnel Management Institute, Huntsville, Alabama. 1987.

A GUIDE TO FEDERAL LABOR RELATIONS AUTHORITY LAW AND PRACTICE, 1979-1988. Second Edition. Peter B. Broida. Dewey Publications, Incorporated, P.O. Box 3423, Arlington, Virginia 22203. 1988.

FEDERAL LABOR RELATIONS AUTHORITY

DIGESTS, INDEXES, ABSTRACTS, CITATORS

SHEPARD'S FEDERAL LABOR LAW CITATIONS. Shepard's/McGraw-Hill, P.O. Box 1235, Colorado Springs, Colorado 80901. Monthly.

STAFF DRAFT SUBJECT MATTER INDEX OF THE DECISIONS OF THE FEDERAL LABOR RELATIONS AUTHORITY. Federal Labor Relations Authority, Office of Case Management, 500 C Street, Southwest, Washington, D.C. 20424. 1987.

ANNUALS AND SURVEYS

REPORT ON CASE HANDLING DEVELOPMENTS OF THE OFFICE OF THE GENERAL COUNSEL. Federal Labor Relations Authority, Office of the General Counsel. Superintendent of Documents, United States Government Printing Office, Washington, D.C. 20402. Annual.

RESEARCH CENTERS, INSTITUTES, CLEARINGHOUSES

UNITED STATES FEDERAL LABOR RELATIONS AUTHORITY LIBRARY, 500 C Street, Southwest, Room 234, Washington, D.C. 20424. (202) 382-0748.

ONLINE DATABASES

LEXIS, FEDERAL LABOR LIBRARY. Mead Data Central, P.O. Box 933, Dayton, Ohio 45401.

WESTLAW, LABOR LIBRARY. West Publishing Company, P.O. Box 64526, 50 West Kellogg Boulevard, St. Paul, Minnesota 55164-0526.

FEDERAL MARITIME COMMISSION

STATUTES, CODES, STANDARDS, UNIFORM LAWS

CODE OF FEDERAL REGULATIONS, TITLE 46. Office of the Federal Register, National Archives and Records Administration. Superintendent of Documents, United States Government Printing Office, Washington, D.C. 20402. Annual. (Updated by use of monthly List of Sections Affected and daily Federal Register).

LOOSELEAF SERVICES AND REPORTERS

FEDERAL MARITIME COMMISSION REPORTS. Superintendent of Documents, United States Government Printing Office, Washington, D.C. 20402. 1947- .

DIGESTS, INDEXES, ABSTRACTS, CITATORS

SHEPARD'S UNITED STATES ADMINISTRATIVE CITATIONS. Shepard's/McGraw-Hill, P.O. Box 1235, Colorado Springs, Colorado 80901. Bimonthly.

RESEARCH CENTERS, INSTITUTES, CLEARINGHOUSES

UNITED STATES FEDERAL MARITIME COMMISSION LIBRARY. 1100 L Street, Northwest, Room 1139, Washington, D.C. 20573. (202) 523-5707.

ONLINE DATABASES

LEXIS, FEDERAL ADMIRALTY LIBRARY. Mead Data Central, P.O. Box 933, Dayton, Ohio 45401.

WESTLAW, ADMIRALTY LIBRARY. West Publishing Company, P.O. Box 64526, 50 West Kellogg Boulevard, St. Paul, Minnesota 55164-0526.

FEDERAL MINE SAFETY AND HEALTH REVIEW COMMISSISON
See also: LABOR DEPARTMENT; OCCUPATIONAL SAFETY AND HEALTH ADMINISTRATION; OCCUPATIONAL SAFETY AND HEALTH REVIEW COMMISSION

STATUTES, CODES, STANDARDS, UNIFORM LAWS

CODE OF FEDERAL REGULATIONS, TITLE 29. Office of the Federal Register, National Archives and Records Administration. Superintendent of Documents, United States Government Printing Office, Washington, D.C. 20402. Annual. (Updated by use of monthly List of Sections Affected and daily Federal Register).

LOOSELEAF SERVICES AND REPORTERS

FEDERAL MINE SAFETY AND HEALTH REVIEW COMMISSION DECISIONS. Superintendent of Documents, United States Government Printing Office, Washington, D.C. 20402. 1979- .

HANDBOOKS, MANUALS, FORMBOOKS

SURFACE COAL MINING SAFETY RULE HANDBOOK. National Safety Council, 444 North Michigan Avenue, Chicago, Illinois 60611. 1989.

TEXTBOOKS AND GENERAL WORKS

REGULATING DANGER: THE STRUGGLE FOR MINE SAFETY IN THE ROCKY MOUNTAIN COAL INDUSTRY. James Whiteside. University of Nebraska Press, 901 North Seventeenth Street, Lincoln, Nebraska 68588. 1990.

BIBLIOGRAPHIES

REVIEW OF RECENT RESEARCH ON ORGANIZATIONAL AND BEHAVIORAL FACTORS ASSOCIATED WITH MINE SAFETY. Robert H. Peters. United States Department of the Interior, Bureau of Mines, 2401 E Street, Northwest, Washington, D.C. 20241. 1989.

FEDERAL RESERVE BOARD

STATUTES, CODES, STANDARDS, UNIFORM LAWS

CODE OF FEDERAL REGULATIONS, TITLE 12. Office of the Federal Register, National Archives and Records Administration. Superintendent of Documents, United States Government Printing Office, Washington, D.C. 20402. Annual. (Updated by use of monthly List of Sections Affected and daily Federal Register).

THE FEDERAL RESERVE ACT, AND OTHER STATUTORY PROVISIONS AFFECTING THE FEDERAL RESERVE SYSTEM. Federal Reserve Board. Publications Services, Mail Stop 138, Board of Governors of the Federal Reserve System, Washington, D.C. 20551. 1986.

MICHIE ON BANKS AND BANKING: REGULATIONS OF THE BOARD OF GOVERNORS OF THE FEDERAL RESERVE SYSTEM. Michie/Bobbs-Merrill, The Michie Company, P.O. Box 7587, Charlottesville, Virginia 22906-7582. Annual.

REGULATIONS OF THE BOARD OF GOVERNORS OF THE FEDERAL RESERVE SYSTEM. Federal Reserve Board. Publications Services, Mail Stop 138, Board of Governors of the Federal Reserve System, Washington, D.C. 20551. Annual.

HANDBOOKS, MANUALS, FORMBOOKS

FEDERAL RESERVE REGULATORY SERVICE. Federal Reserve Board. Publications Services, Mail Stop 138, Board of Governors of the Federal Reserve System, Washington, D.C. 20551. Monthly. (Includes Consumer and Community Affairs Handbook, Monetary Policy and Reserve Requirements Handbook, and Securities Credit Transactions Handbook).

WRITING IN STYLE AT THE FEDERAL RESERVE. Federal Reserve Board. Publications Services, Mail Stop 138, Board of Governors of the Federal Reserve System, Washington, D.C. 20551. 1984.

TEXTBOOKS AND GENERAL WORKS

ANTITRUST LAWS, JUSTICE DEPARTMENT GUIDELINES, AND THE LIMITS OF CONCENTRATION IN LOCAL BANKING MARKETS. James Burke. Federal Reserve Board. Publications Services, Mail Stop 138, Board of Governors of the Federal Reserve System, Washington, D.C. 20551. 1984.

THE FEDERAL RESERVE SYSTEM - PURPOSES AND FUNCTIONS. AMS Press Incorporated, 56 East Thirteenth Street, New York, New York 10003. Reprint of 1939 edition.

THE IMPLICATIONS FOR BANK MERGER POLICY OF FINANCIAL DEREGULATION, INTERSTATE BANKING, AND FINANCIAL SUPERMARKETS. Stephen A. Rhoades. Publications Services, Mail Stop 138, Board of Governors of the Federal Reserve System, Washington, D.C. 20551. 1984.

SECRETS OF THE TEMPLE: HOW THE FEDERAL RESERVE RUNS THE COUNTRY. William Greider. Simon and Schuster, Incorporated, 1230 Avenue of the Americas, New York, New York 10020. 1987.

ANNUALS AND SURVEYS

ANNUAL REPORT. Federal Reserve Board. Publications Services, Mail Stop 138, Board of Governors of the Federal Reserve System, Washington, D.C. 20551. Annual.

LAW REVIEWS AND PERIODICALS

FEDERAL RESERVE BULLETIN. Federal Reserve Board. Publications Services, Mail Stop 138, Board of Governors of the Federal Reserve System, Washington, D.C. 20551. Monthly.

NEWSLETTERS AND NEWSPAPERS

ACTIONS OF THE BOARD: APPLICATIONS AND REPORTS RECEIVED. Federal Reserve Board. Publications Services, Mail Stop 138, Board of Governors of the Federal Reserve System, Washington, D.C. 20551. Weekly.

RESEARCH CENTERS, INSTITUTES, CLEARINGHOUSES

FEDERAL RESERVE BOARD LAW LIBRARY. Twentieth and Constitution Avenue, Northwest, B1066, Washington, D.C. 20551. (202) 452-3000.

ONLINE DATABASES

LEXIS, BANKING LIBRARY. Mead Data Central, P.O. Box 933, Dayton, Ohio 45401.

WESTLAW, FINANCIAL SERVICES LIBRARY. West Publishing Company, P.O. Box 64526, 50 West Kellogg Boulevard, St. Paul, Minnesota 55164-0526.

STATISTICS SOURCES

ANNUAL STATISTICAL DIGEST. Federal Reserve Board. Publications Services, Mail Stop 138, Board of Governors of the Federal Reserve System, Washington, D.C. 20551. Annual.

FEDERAL TRADE COMMISSION
See also: COMMERCE DEPARTMENT

STATUTES, CODES, STANDARDS, UNIFORM LAWS

CODE OF FEDERAL REGULATIONS, TITLE 16. Office of the Federal Register, National Archives and Records Administration. Superintendent of Documents, United States Government Printing Office, Washington, D.C. 20402. Annual. (Updated by use of monthly List of Sections Affected and daily Federal Register).

LOOSELEAF SERVICES AND REPORTERS

FEDERAL TRADE COMMISSION DECISIONS. Superintendent of Documents, United States Government Printing Office, Washington, D.C. 20402. 1915- .

FEDERAL TRADE COMMISSION

HANDBOOKS, MANUALS, FORMBOOKS

COMPLYING WITH THE LAW: HOW TO ADVERTISE CONSUMER CREDIT. Federal Trade Commission. Superintendent of Documents, United States Government Printing Office, Washington, D.C. 20402. 1983.

WRITING READABLE WARRANTIES. Allen Hile and Nancy Sachs. Federal Trade Commission, Division of Warranty Practices and Office of Consumer and Business Education. Superintendent of Documents, United States Government Printing Office, Washington, D.C. 20402. 1983.

TEXTBOOKS AND GENERAL WORKS

ANTITRUST AND THE TRIUMPH OF ECONOMICS: INSTITUTIONS, EXPERTISE, AND POLICY CHANGE. Marc Allen Eisner. University of North Carolina Press, P.O. Box 2288, 116 South Boundary Street, Chapel Hill, North Carolina 27515-2288. 1991.

CONSUMERS, COMMISSIONS, AND CONGRESS: LAW, THEORY, AND THE FEDERAL TRADE COMMISSION, 1968-1985. Bernice Rothman Hasin. Transaction Books, Rutgers University, New Brunswick, New Jersey 08903. 1987.

THE ECONOMIST AS REFORMER: REVAMPING THE FTC, 1981-1985. James Clifford Miller. American Enterprise Institute for Public Policy Research, 1150 Seventeenth Street, Northwest, Washington, D.C. 20036. 1989.

THE FTC LEGAL PROGRAM. Federal Trade Commission, Pennsylvania Avenue at Sixth Street, Northwest, Washington, D.C. 20580. 1990.

A GUIDE TO THE FEDERAL TRADE COMMISSION. Federal Trade Commission, Pennsylvania Avenue at Sixth Street, Northwest, Washington, D.C. 20580. 1987.

MARKETING AND ADVERTISING REGULATION: THE FEDERAL TRADE COMMISSION IN THE 1990S. Patrick E. Murphy and William L. Wilkie. University of Notre Dame Press, Notre Dame, Indiana 46556. 1990.

PUBLIC CHOICE AND REGULATION: A VIEW FROM INSIDE THE FEDERAL TRADE COMMISSION. Robert J. Mackay, James Clifford Miller and Bruce Yandle. Hoover Institution Press, Stanford, California. 1987.

DIGESTS, INDEXES, ABSTRACTS, CITATORS

SHEPARD'S UNITED STATES ADMINISTRATIVE CITATIONS. Shepard's/McGraw-Hill, P.O. Box 1235, Colorado Springs, Colorado 80901. Bimonthly.

RESEARCH CENTERS, INSTITUTES, CLEARINGHOUSES

UNITED STATES FEDERAL TRADE COMMISSION LIBRARY. Sixth and Pennsylvania Avenue, Northwest, Room 630, Washington, D.C. 20580. (202) 326-2395.

ONLINE DATABASES

LEXIS, BANKING LIBRARY. Mead Data Central, P.O. Box 933, Dayton, Ohio 45401.

LEXIS, FEDERAL TRADE REGULATION LIBRARY. Mead Data Central, P.O. Box 933, Dayton, Ohio 45401.

WESTLAW, ANTITRUST AND BUSINESS REGULATIONS LIBRARY. West Publishing Company, P.O. Box 64526, 50 West Kellogg Boulevard, St. Paul, Minnesota 55164-0526.

FEDERALISM
See also: CONSTITUTIONAL HISTORY; CONSTITUTIONS

TEXTBOOKS AND GENERAL WORKS

AMERICAN FEDERALISM: A VIEW FROM THE STATES. Third Edition. Daniel J. Elazar. HarperCollins Publishers, 10 East Fifty-third Street, New York, New York 10022. 1984.

AMERICAN FEDERALISM: COMPETITION AMONG GOVERNMENTS. Thomas R. Dye. Lexington Books, 125 Spring Street, Lexington, Massachusetts 02173. 1990.

AMERICAN INTERGOVERNMENTAL RELATIONS: FOUNDATIONS, PERSPECTIVES AND ISSUES. Laurence J. O'Toole, Jr. Congressional Quarterly, Incorporated, 1414 Twenty-second Street, Northwest, Washington, D.C. 20037. 1985.

ANTITRUST FEDERALISM: THE ROLE OF STATE LAW. American Bar Association, Section of Antitrust Law, 750 North Lake Shore Drive, Chicago, Illinois 60611. 1988.

COMPARATIVE CONSTITUTIONAL FEDERALISM: EUROPE AND AMERICA. Mark V. Tushnet. Greenwood Publishing Group, Incorporated, 88 Post Road West, P.O. Box 5007, Westport, Connecticut 06881. 1990.

CONSTITUTIONAL FEDERALISM IN A NUTSHELL. Second Edition. David E. Engdahl. West Publishing Company, P.O. Box 64526, 50 West Kellogg Boulevard, St. Paul, Minnesota 55164-0526. 1987.

THE COSTS OF FEDERALISM: IN HONOR OF JAMES W. FESTER. Robert T. Golembiewski and Aaron Wildavsky. Transaction Books, Rutgers University, New Brunswick, New Jersey 08903. 1984.

EMERGING CONFLICTS IN THE DOCTRINE OF FEDERALISM: THE INTERGOVERNMENTAL PREDICAMENT. James C. Smith. University Press of America, 4720 Boston Way, Lanham, Maryland 20706. 1984.

EXPLORING FEDERALISM. Daniel J. Elazar. University of Alabama Press, P.O. Box 870380, Tuscaloosa, Alabama 35487. 1986.

FEDERALISM AND EUROPEAN UNION: POLITICAL IDEAS, INFLUENCES, AND STRATEGIES IN THE EUROPEAN COMMUNITY, 1972-1987. Michael Burgess. Routledge, Chapman & Hall, 29 West Thirty-fifth Street, New York, New York 10001. 1989.

FEDERALISM AND FEDERATION. Preston King. Johns Hopkins University Press, 701 West Fortieth Street, Suite 275, Baltimore, Maryland 21211-2190. 1983.

FEDERALISM AND INTERGOVERNMENTAL RELATIONS. Deil S. Wright. American Society for Public Administration. 1120 G Street, Northwest, Suite 500, Washington, D.C. 20005. 1984.

FEDERALISM AND INTERNATIONAL RELATIONS: THE ROLE OF SUBNATIONAL UNITS. Hans J. Michelmann and Panayotis Soldatos. Oxford University Press, 200 Madison Avenue, New York, New York 10016. 1990.

FEDERALISM AND REGULATION. Jerry L. Mashaw and Susan Rose-Ackerman. Center for Law and Economics Studies, Columbia University School of Law, Box A17, 435 West One Hundred Sixteenth Street, New York, New York 10027. 1983.

FEDERALISM AS A DEMOCRATIC PROCESS. Ezra Pound and others. Zenger Publishing Company, P.O. Box 42026, Washington, D.C. 20015. Reprint of 1942 edition.

FEDERALISM: THE FOUNDER'S DESIGN. Raoul Berger. University of Oklahoma Press, 1005 Asp Avenue, Norman, Oklahoma 73019. 1987.

FEDERALISM: THE POLITICS OF INTERGOVERNMENTAL RELATIONS. David C. Nice. St. Martin's Press, Incorporated, 175 Fifth Avenue, New York, New York 10010. 1986.

THE GROWTH OF FEDERAL POWER IN AMERICAN HISTORY. Rhodri Jeffreys-Jones and Bruce Collins. Northern Illinois University Press, Williston, 320A, De Kalb, Illinois 60115. 1983.

HOW FEDERAL IS THE CONSTITUTION? Robert A. Goldwin and William A. Schambra, Editors. American Enterprise Institute for Public Policy Research, 1150 Seventeenth Street, Northwest, Washington, D.C. 20036. 1987.

MODERN FEDERALISM: AN ANALYTICAL APPROACH. Peter W. House and Wilbur A. Steger. Lexington Books, 125 Spring Stree, Lexington, Massachusetts 02173. 1982.

THE NEW DEAL AND THE STATES: FEDERALISM IN TRANSITION. James T. Patterson. Greenwood Publishing Group, Incorporated, 88 Post Road West, P.O. Box 5007, Westport, Connecticut 06881. 1981, c1969

THE ORIGINS OF THE FEDERAL REPUBLIC: JURISDICTIONAL CONTROVERSIES IN THE U.S. 1775-1787. Peter S. Onuf. University of Pennsylvania Press, 418 Service Drive, Blockley Hall, Thirteenth Floor, Philadelphia, Pennsylvania 19104. 1983.

THE POLITICAL THEORY OF A COMPOUND REPUBLIC: DESIGNING THE AMERICAN EXPERIMENT. Second Edition. Vincent Ostrom. University of Nebraska Press, 901 North Seventeenth Street, Lincoln, Nebraska 68588-0520. 1987.

PUBLIC POLICY AND FEDERALISM: ISSUES IN STATE AND LOCAL POLITICS. Jeffrey Henig. St. Martin's Press, 175 Fifth Avenue, New York, New York 10010. 1985.

THE ROLE OF STATE SUPREME COURTS IN THE NEW JUDICIAL FEDERALISM. Susan P. Fino. Greenwood Publishing Group, Incorporated, 88 Post Road West, P.O. Box 5007, Westport, Connecticut 06881. 1987.

THE STATES RIGHTS DEBATE: ANTI-FEDERALISM AND THE CONSTITUTION. Second Edition. Alpheus T. Mason. Oxford University Press, 200 Madison Avenue, New York, New York 10016. 1972.

STATES' RIGHTS UNDER FEDERAL CONSTITUTIONS. Chester James Antieau. Oceana Publications, Incorporated, 75 Main Street, Dobbs Ferry, New York 10522. 1984.

THE UNITED STATES FEDERAL SYSTEM: LEGAL INTEGRATION IN THE AMERICAN EXPERIENCE. Peter Hay and Ronald D. Rotunda. Oceana Publications, Incorporated, 75 Main Street, Dobbs Ferry, New York 10522. 1982.

WHEN FEDERALISM WORKS. Paul E. Peterson, Barry G. Rabe and Kenneth K. Wong. Brookings Institution, 1775 Massachusetts Avenue, Northwest, Washington, D.C. 20036-2188. 1987.

LAW REVIEWS AND PERIODICALS

DIRECTIVES. New Federalist Party, 760 Lilian Way, Suite 15, Los Angeles, California 90038. Monthly.

HARVARD JOURNAL OF LAW AND PUBLIC POLICY. Harvard Society for Law and Public Policy, Incorporated, Harvard Law School, Cambridge, Massachusetts 02138. Three issues per year.

INTERGOVERNMENTAL PERSPECTIVE. Advisory Commission on Intergovernmental Relations, 1111 Twentieth Street, Northwest, Washington, D.C. 20575. Quarterly.

PUBLIUS. Center for the Study of Federalism, Temple University, Broad and Oxford Streets, Philadelphia, Pennsylvania 19122. Quarterly.

WORLD FEDERALIST. World Federalist Association, P.O. Box 15250, Washington, D.C. 20003. Quarterly.

NEWSLETTERS AND NEWSPAPERS

FEDERALIST CAUCUS ANNUAL REPORT. Federal Caucus, P.O. Box 19482, Portland, Oregon 97219. Annual.

THE FEDERALIST PAPER. Federalist Society for Law and Public Policy Studies, 1700 K Street, Northwest, Suite 901, Washington, D.C. 20006. Quarterly.

NEW FEDERALIST PAPERS. New Federalist Party, 760 Lilian Way, Suite 15, Los Angeles, California 90038. Weekly.

NFP NEWSLETTER. New Federalist Party, 760 Lilian Way, Suite 15, Los Angeles, California 90038. Biweekly.

BIBLIOGRAPHIES

STRENGTHENING THE UNITED NATIONS: A BIBLIOGRAPHY ON UNITED NATIONS REFORM AND WORLD FEDERALISM. Joseph Preston Baratta. Greenwood Publishing Group, Incorporated, 88 Post Road West, P.O. Box 5007, Westport, Connecticut 06881. 1987.

ASSOCIATIONS AND PROFESSIONAL SOCIETIES

FEDERALIST CAUCUS. P.O. Box 19480, Portland, Oregon 97219. (503) 292-4586.

FEDERALIST SOCIETY FOR LAW AND PUBLIC POLICY STUDIES. 1700 K Street, Northwest, Suite 901, Washington, D.C. 20006. (202) 822-8138.

NEW FEDERALIST PARTY. 760 Lilian Way, Suite 15, Los Angeles, California 90038. (213) 464-5468.

WORLD FEDERALIST ASSOCIATION. P.O. Box 15250, Washington, D.C. 20003. (202) 546-3950.

RESEARCH CENTERS, INSTITUTES, CLEARINGHOUSES

CENTER FOR ENTERPRISING. Southern Methodist University, Edwin L. Cox School of Business, Dallas, Texas 75275. (214) 692-3326.

CENTER FOR THE STUDY OF FEDERALISM. Temple University, Gladfelten Hall, Room 1019, Philadelphia, Pennsylvania 19122. (215) 787-1480.

INSTITUTE OF GOVERNMENTAL STUDIES. University of California, Berkeley, Berkeley, California 94720. (415) 642-6722.

PUBLIC CHOICE CENTER. George Mason University, St. George's Hall, 4400 University Drive, Fairfax, Virginia 22030. (703) 323-3774.

FEES
See: LAWYERS' FEES

FICTION
See: LEGAL PROFESSION IN FICTION

FIDUCIARY RELATIONSHIP
See: GUARDIAN AND WARD; WILLS, TRUSTS AND INHERITANCE

FINANCE
See: CREDIT; LOANS; MORTGAGES; PUBLIC FINANCE

FINANCIAL RESPONSIBILITY LAWS
See: INSURANCE, MOTOR VEHICLE AND AVIATION

FIREARMS AND BALLISTICS
See also: ALCHOHOL, TOBACCO AND FIREARMS BUREAU

STATUTES, CODES, STANDARDS, UNIFORM LAWS

CODE OF FEDERAL REGULATIONS TITLE 27. General Services Administration, Office of the Federal Register. Superintendent of Documents, United States Government Printing Office, Washington, D.C. 20402. 1982.

STATE LAWS AND PUBLISHED ORDINANCES. Treasury Department, Bureau of Alcohol, Tobacco and Firearms. Superintendent of Documents, United States Government Printing Office, Washington, D.C. 20402. 1982.

LOOSELEAF SERVICES AND REPORTERS

FIREARMS LITIGATION REPORTER. Foundation for Handgun Education, 100 Maryland Avenue, Northeast, Washington, D.C. 20002. 1983. (Quarterly).

HANDBOOKS, MANUALS, FORMBOOKS

THE NEW HANDBOOK OF HANDGUNNING. Paul B. Weston. Charles C. Thomas, Publishers, 2600 South First Street, Springfield, Illinois 62794-9265. 1980.

ORGANIZING FOR HANDGUN CONTROL: A CITIZEN'S MANUAL. National Coalition to Ban Handguns, 100 Maryland Avenue, Northeast, Washington, D.C. 20002. 1985.

YOUR GUIDE TO FEDERAL FIREARMS REGULATION 1984-1985. Treasury Department, Bureau of Alcohol, Tobacco, and Firearms. Superintendent of Documents, United States Government Printing Office, Washington, D.C. 20402. 1984.

TEXTBOOKS AND GENERAL WORKS

THE CITIZEN'S GUIDE TO GUN CONTROL. Franklin E. Zimring and Gordon Hawkins. Macmillan Publishing Company, Incorporated, 866 Third Avenue, New York, New York 10022. 1987.

FIREARMS AND VIOLENCE: ISSUES OF PUBLIC POLICY. Don B. Kates, Jr. Pacific Institute on Public Policy Research Series. Ballinger Division, HarperCollins Publishers, 10 East Fifty-third Street, New York, New York 10022. 1984.

GUN CONTROL: ISSUES AND ANSWERS. David Lester. Charles C. Thomas, Publishers, 2600 South First Street, Springfield, Illinois 62794-9265. 1984.

GUN CONTROL: RESTRICTING RIGHTS OR PROTECTING PEOPLE? Mark A. Siegel, Editor. Information Aids, Incorporated, 1401 Windy Meadow Drive, Plano, Texas 75023. 1991.

GUNS DON'T DIE--PEOPLE DO: THE PROS, THE CONS, THE FACTS. Pete Shields. Arbor House Publishing Company, 1350 Avenue of the Americas, New York, New York 10019. 1981.

HANDGUN RETENTION SYSTEM. James W. Lindell. Calibre Press, Incorporated, 666 Dundee Road, Suite 1607, Northbrook, Illinois 60062-2727. 1982.

INTRUDER IN YOUR HOME: HOW TO DEFEND YOURSELF LEGALLY WITH A FIREARM. Ronald L. Cruit. Stein and Day, Scarborough House, P.O. Box 459, Chelsea, Michigan 48118. 1983.

THE ISSUE OF GUN CONTROL. Thomas Draper. H.W. Wilson, 950 University Avenue, Bronx, New York 10452. 1981.

ORIGINS AND DEVELOPMENT OF THE SECOND AMENDMENT. David T. Hardy. Blacksmith Corporation, P.O. Box 1752, Chino Valley, Arizona 86323. 1986.

PRACTICAL HANDGUN BALLISTICS. M. Williams. Charles C. Thomas, Publishers, 2600 South First Street, Springfield, Illinois 62794-9265. 1980.

THE PRIVILEGE TO KEEP AND BEAR ARMS: THE SECOND AMENDMENT AND ITS INTERPRETATION. Warren Freedman. Quorum Books, Greenwood Publishing Group, Incorporated, 88 Post Road West, P.O. Box 5007, Westport, Connecticut 06881. 1989.

PROJECT IDENTIFICATION: A STUDY OF HANDGUNS USED IN CRIMES. National Coalition to Ban Handguns and Bureau of Alcohol, Tobacco, and Firearms, United States Department of the Treasury. National Coalition to Ban Handguns, 100 Maryland Avenue, Northeast, Washington, D.C. 20002. 1984.

THE RIGHT TO KEEP AND BEAR ARMS. Earl R. Kruschke. Charles C. Thomas, Publishers, 2600 South First Street, Springfield, Illinois 62794-9265. 1985.

THE RIGHT TO KEEP AND BEAR ARMS: A PRESENTATION OF BOTH SIDES. Gordon Press, Publications, P.O. Box 459, Bowling Green Station, New York, New York 10004. 1986.

THE RIGHTS OF GUN OWNERS. Alan Gottleib. Gordon Press, Publishers, P.O. Box 459, Bowling Green Station, New York, New York 10004. 1986.

THAT EVERY MAN BE ARMED: THE EVOLUTION OF A CONSTITUTIONAL RIGHT. Stephen P. Halbrook. Liberty Tree Press, 134 Ninety-eighth Avenue, Oakland, California 94603. 1988.

DIGESTS, INDEXES, ABSTRACTS, CITATORS

LAW ENFORCEMENT HANDGUN DIGEST. Third Edition. Jack Lewis. DBI Books, Incorporated, 4092 Commercial Avenue, Northbrook, Illinois 60062. 1980.

ANNUALS AND SURVEYS

ARMED AND CONSIDERED DANGEROUS: A SURVEY OF FELONS AND THEIR FIREARMS. James D. Wright and Peter H. Rossi. Aldine de Gruyter, 200 Saw Mill River Road, Hawthorne, New York 10532. 1986.

LAW REVIEWS AND PERIODICALS

AMERICAN HUNTER. National Rifle Association of America, 1600 Rhode Island Avenue, Northwest, Washington, D.C. 20036. Monthly.

AMERICAN RIFLEMAN. National Rifle Association of America, 1600 Rhode Island Avenue, Northwest, Washington, D.C. 20036. Monthly.

BUREAU OF ALCOHOL TOBACCO AND FIREARMS QUARTERLY BULLETIN. Treasury Department, Bureau of Alcohol, Tobacco and Firearms, Superintendent of Documents, United States Government Printing Office, Washington, D.C. 20402. Quarterly.

INSIGHTS. National Rifle Association of America, 1600 Rhode Island Avenue, Northwest, Washington, D.C. 20036. Monthly.

NEWSLETTERS AND NEWSPAPERS

ARMS CONTROL TODAY NEWSLETTER. Arms Control Association, 11 Dupont Circle, Northwest, Washington, D.C. 20036. Monthly.

THE BANNER. National Coalition to Ban Handguns, 100 Maryland Avenue, Northeast, Washington, D.C. 20002. Quarterly.

FIREARMS LITIGATION REPORTER NEWSLETTER. Educational Fund to End Handgun Violence, Box 72, 110 Maryland Avenue, Northeast, Washington, D.C. 20002. Quarterly.

HANDGUN CONTROL PROGRESS REPORT. Handgun Control, Incorporated, 1225 I Street, Northwest, Suite 1100, Washington, D.C. 20005. Quarterly.

HANDGUN CONTROL -- WASHINGTON REPORT. Handgun Control, Incorporated, 1225 I Street, Northwest, Suite 1100, Washington, D.C. 20005. Quarterly.

NRACTION. National Rifle Association of America, 1600 Rhode Island Avenue, Northwest, Washington, D.C. 20036. Bimonthly.

POINT BLANK. Citizens Committee For The Right To Keep And Bear Arms. Liberty Park, 12500 Northeast, Ten Place, Bellevue, Washington 98005. Monthly.

BIBLIOGRAPHIES

GUN CONTROL: A BRIEF HISTORICAL-LEGAL OVERVIEW: A BIBLIOGRAPHY. Robert J. Nissinbaum. Tarlton Law Library, University of Texas School of Law, 727 East Twenty-sixth Street, Austin, Texas 78705-5799. 1983.

GUN CONTROL AND THE SECOND AMENDMENT. Earleen H. Cook and Joseph L. Cook. Vance Bibliographies, P.O. Box 229, 112 North Charter Street, Monticello, Illinois 61856. 1980.

WEAPONS CRIME AND VIOLENCE IN AMERICA AN ANNOTATED BIBLIOGRAPHY. James D. Wright. Justice Department, National Institute of Justice. Superintendent of Documents, United States Government Printing Office, Washington, D.C. 20402. 1981.

ASSOCIATIONS AND PROFESSIONAL SOCIETIES

ARMS CONTROL ASSOCIATION, 11 Dupont Circle, Northwest, Suite 250, Washington, D.C. 20036. (202) 797-4626.

CENTER TO PREVENT HANDGUN VIOLENCE. 1225 I Street, Northwest, Suite 1100, Washington, D.C. 20005. (202) 289-7319.

FIREARMS AND BALLISTICS

CITIZENS COMMITTEE FOR THE RIGHT TO KEEP AND BEAR ARMS. Liberty Park, 12500 Northeast, Tenth Place, Bellevue, Washington 98005. (206) 454-4911.

EDUCATIONAL FUND TO END HANDGUN VIOLENCE. Box 72, 110 Maryland Avenue, Northeast, Washington, D.C. 20002. (202) 544-7227.

GUN OWNERS, INCORPORATED. 5457 Diablo Drive, Suite One, Sacramento, California 95842. (916) 349-1812.

HANDGUN CONTROL, INCORPORATED. 1225 I Street, Northwest, Suite 1100, Washington, D.C. 20005. (202) 898-0792.

NATIONAL CAMPAIGN TO SAVE THE ABM TREATY. 1601 Connecticut Avenue, Northwest, Suite 704, Washington, D.C. 20009. (202) 939-5770.

NATIONAL COALITION TO BAN HANDGUNS. 100 Maryland Avenue, Northeast, Washington, D.C. 20002. (202) 544-7190.

NATIONAL RIFLE ASSOCIATION OF AMERICA. 1600 Rhode Island Avenue, Northwest, Washington, D.C. 20036. (202) 828-6000.

SECOND AMENDMENT FOUNDATION. James Madison Building, 12500 Northeast Tenth Place, Bellevue, Washington 98005. (202) 454-7012.

RESEARCH CENTERS, INSTITUTES, CLEARINGHOUSES

FIREARMS RESEARCH AND IDENTIFICATION ASSOCIATION. 17524 Coliuna Road, Suite 360, Rowland Heights, California 91748. (714) 598-8919.

HAROLD McCRACKEN RESEARCH LIBRARY. P.O. Box 1000, Cody, Wyoming 82414. (307) 587-4771.

OTHER SOURCES

GUN CONTROL. Philip J. Cook and D. Richards, Editors. American Academy of Political and Social Science, 3937 Chestnut Street, Philadelphia, Pennsylvania 19104. 1986.

RIGHT TO KEEP AND BEAR ARMS REPORT. Senate Committee on the Judiciary, Subcommittee on the Constitution. Superintendent of Documents, United States Government Printing Office, Washington, D.C. 20402. 1982.

FIRES AND FIRE PREVENTION
See also: INSURANCE, PROPERTY

STATUTES, CODES, STANDARDS, UNIFORM LAWS

THE BOCA BASIC FIRE PREVENTION CODE. Building Officials Conference of America, 1313 East Sixtieth Street, Chicago, Illinois 60637. 1981- . (Periodic Supplements).

FIRE-RELATED CODES, LAWS AND ORDINANCES. Vince H. Clet. Glencoe Publishing Company, 15319 Chatsworth Street, Mission Hills, California 91345. 1978.

NATIONAL FIRE CODES: A COMPILATION OF NFPA CODES, STANDARDS, RECOMMENDED PRACTICES AND MANUALS. National Fire Protection Association, One Batterymarch Park, Quincy, Massachusetts 02269-9101. 1986- . (Periodic Supplements).

UNIFORM FIRE CODE STANDARDS. International Conference of Building Officials, Western Fire Chiefs Association, 5360 South Workman Mill Road, Whittier, California 90601. 1985.

LOOSELEAF SERVICES AND REPORTERS

INSURANCE LAW REPORTS--FIRE AND CASUALTY. Commerce Clearing House, Incorporated, 4025 West Peterson Avenue, Chicago, Illinois 60646. 1929- .

HANDBOOKS, MANUALS, FORMBOOKS

CONDUCTING FIRE INSPECTIONS: A GUIDEBOOK FOR FIELD USE. National Fire Protection Association, One Batterymarch Park, Quincy, Massachusetts 02269-9101. 1989.

FIRE LITIGATION HANDBOOK. National Fire Protection Association, One Batterymarch Park, Quincy, Massachusetts 02269-9101. 1979- . (Periodic Supplements).

FIRE PROTECTION HANDBOOK. Seventeenth Edition. National Fire Protection Association, One Batterymarch Park, Quincy, Massachusetts 02269-9101. 1986.

LIFE SAFETY CODE HANDBOOK. Third Edition. James K. Lathrop, Editor. National Fire Protection Association, One Batterymarch Park, Quincy, Massachusetts 02269-9101. 1985.

NFPA GUIDE TO OSHA FIRE PROTECTION REGULATIONS. Third Edition. National Fire Protection Association, One Batterymarch Park, Quincy, Massachusetts 02269-9101. 1977- . (Periodic Supplements).

TEXTBOOKS AND GENERAL WORKS

FIRE PROTECTION THROUGH MODERN BUILDING CODES. Fifth Edition. Delbert F. Boring, James C. Spence and Walter G. Wells. American Iron and Steel Institute, 1133 Fifteenth Street, Northwest, Washington, D.C. 20005. 1981.

INTRODUCTION TO FIRE PREVENTION LAW. Donna L. Rosenbauer. National Fire Protection Association, One Batterymarch Park, Quincy, Massachusetts 02269-9101. 1978.

KIRK'S FIRE INVESTIGATION. Third Edition. John D. DeHaan. PH Press, MIT Branch, P.O. Box 195, Cambridge, Massachusetts 02139. 1990.

PHYSICAL AND TECHNICAL ASPECTS OF FIRE AND ARSON INVESTIGATION. John R. Carroll. Charles C. Thomas, Publishers, 2600 South First Street, Springfield, Illinois 62794-9265. 1983.

ENCYCLOPEDIAS AND DICTIONARIES

FIRE SCIENCES DICTIONARY. B.W. Kuvshinoff. John Wiley and Sons, Incorporated, 605 Third Avenue, New York, New York 10158. 1977.

ANNUALS AND SURVEYS

NATIONAL FIRE CODES. National Fire Protection Association, One Batterymarch Park, Quincy, Massachusetts 02269-9101. Annual.

NATIONAL FIRE PROTECTION ASSOCIATION YEARBOOK AND COMMITTEE LIST. National Fire Protection Association, One Batterymarch Park, Quincy, Massachusetts 02269-9101. Annual.

LAW REVIEWS AND PERIODICALS

FIRE AND ARSON INVESTIGATOR. International Association of Arson Investigators, 5428 Del Maria Way, Suite 201, P.O. Box 91119, Louisville, Kentucky 40291. Quarterly.

FIRE CHIEF. 40 Huron Street, Chicago, Illinois 60611. Monthly.

FIRE COMMAND. National Fire Protection Association, One Batterymarch Park, Quincy, Massachusetts 02269. Monthly.

FIRE ENGINEERING. Technical Publishing Corporation, 875 Third Avenue, New York, New York 10022. Monthly.

FIRE INTERNATIONAL: THE JOURNAL OF THE WORLD'S FIRE PROTECTION SERVICES. UNISAF Publications, Limited, Queensway House, 2 Queensway, Redhill, Surrey, England RH1 125. Bimonthly.

FIRE JOURNAL. National Fire Protection Association, One Batterymarch Park, Quincy, Massachusetts 02269. Bimonthly.

FIRE MARSHALS' BULLETIN. Fire Marshals' Association of North America, One Batterymarch Park, Quincy, Massachusetts 02269. Quarterly.

FIRE NEWS. National Fire Protection Association, One Batterymarch Park, Quincy, Massachusetts 02269. Monthly.

FIRE STATION DIGEST. North American Fireman's Association, 6830 Northeast Twenty-sixth Street, Seattle, Washington 98115. Bimonthly.

FIRE TECHNOLOGY. National Fire Protection Association, One Batterymarch Park, Quincy, Massachusetts 02269. Quarterly.

IFPA PHOTOGRAPHY JOURNAL. International Fire Prevention Association, P.O. Box 8337, Rolling Meadows, Illinois 60008. Quarterly.

INTERNATIONAL FIRE CHIEF. International Association of Fire Chiefs, 1329 Eighteenth Street, Northwest, Washington, D.C. 20036. Monthly.

NEWSLETTERS AND NEWSPAPERS

ARSON REPORTER. American Bar Association, 750 North Lake Shore Drive, Chicago, Illinois 60611. Monthly.

FIREHOUSE LAWYER MONTHLY NEWSLETTER. Quinlan Publishing Company, 23 Drydock Avenue, Boston, Massachusetts 02210. Monthly.

IAFC ON SCENE. International Association of Fire Chiefs, 1329 Eighteenth Street, Northwest, Washington, D.C. 20036. Semimonthly.

INTERNATIONAL FIRE FIGHTER. International Association of Fire Fighters, 1750 New York Avenue, Northwest, Washington, D.C. 20006. Bimonthly.

BIBLIOGRAPHIES

DIRECTORY OF FIRE RESEARCH IN THE UNITED STATES. Eighth Edition. National Academy of Sciences, National Research Council, Committee on Fire Research, 2101 Constitution Avenue, Northwest, Washington, D.C. 20418. 1978.

FIRE PROTECTION IN OFFICE BUILDINGS. David Kent Ballast. Vance Bibliographies, P.O. Box 229, 112 North Charter Street, Monticello, Illinois 61856. 1987.

FIREPROOF BUILDING. Mary A. Vance. Vance Bibliographies, P.O. Box 229, 112 North Charter Street, Monticello, Illinois 61856. 1988.

DIRECTORIES

FIRE PROTECTION REFERENCE DIRECTORY. National Fire Protection Association, One Batterymarch Park, Quincy, Massachusetts 02269-9101. Annual.

FIRE RESEARCH SPECIALISTS: A DIRECTORY. National Bureau of Standards, Commerce Department. Superintendent of Documents, United States Government Printing Office, Washington, D.C. 20402. Irregular.

ASSOCIATIONS AND PROFESSIONAL SOCIETIES

BUILDING OFFICIALS AND CODE ADMINISTRATORS INTERNATIONAL. 4051 West Flossmoor Road, Country Club Hills, Illinois 60477. (708) 799-2300.

FIRE MARSHALS ASSOCIATION OF NORTH AMERICA. One Batterymarch Park, Quincy, Massachusetts 02269. (617) 770-0700.

INTERNATIONAL ASSOCIATION OF ARSON INVESTIGATORS. 5428 Del Maria Way, Suite 201, P.O. Box 91119, Louisville, Kentucky 40291. (502) 491-7482.

INTERNATIONAL ASSOCIATION OF FIRE CHIEFS. 1329 Eighteenth Street, Northwest, Washington, D.C. 20036. (202) 833-3420.

INTERNATIONAL ASSOCIATION OF FIRE FIGHTERS. 1750 New York Avenue, Northwest, Washington, D.C. 20006. (202) 737-8484.

INTERNATIONAL FIRE PHOTOGRAPHERS ASSOCIATION. P.O. Box 8337, Rolling Meadows, Illinois 60008. (708) 394-5835.

NATIONAL ARSON PREVENTION AND ACTION COALITION. c/o Urban Educational Systems, P.O. Box 1146, Jamaica Plain, Massachusetts 02130. (617) 522-7118.

NATIONAL FIRE PROTECTION ASSOCIATION. One Batterymarch Park, Quincy, Massachusetts 02269. (617) 770-3000.

FIRES AND FIRE PREVENTION

RESEARCH CENTERS, INSTITUTES, CLEARINGHOUSES

CENTER FOR FIRE SAFETY STUDIES. Worcester Polytechnic Institute, 100 Institute Road, Worcester, Massachusetts 01609. (508) 831-5593.

FIRE INFORMATION RESEARCH AND EDUCATION CENTER. 100 Capitol Square Building, 550 Cedar Street, St. Paul, Minnesota 55101. (612) 296-6516.

FIRE SCIENCE INSTITUTE. John Jay College of Criminal Justice of CUNY, 899 Tenth Avenue, Room 633, New York, New York 10019. (212) 237-8650.

INSTITUTE FOR ADVANCED SAFETY STUDIES. 5950 West Touhy Avenue, Niles, Illinois 60648. (708) 647-1101.

ITT RESEARCH INSTITUTE. 10 West Thirty-fifth Street, Chicago, Illinois 60616. (312) 567-4000.

NATIONAL FIRE PROTECTION RESEARCH FOUNDATION. One Batterymarch Park, Quincy, Massachusetts 02269. (617) 770-3000.

UNITED STATES FIRE ADMINISTRATION, OFFICE OF FIRE DATA AND ANALYSIS. Emmitsburg, Maryland 21727. (301) 447-1272.

UNITED STATES NATIONAL INSTITUTE OF STANDARDS AND TECHNOLOGY, CENTER FOR FIRE RESEARCH. Building 224, Room A252, Gaithersburg, Maryland 20899. (301) 975-6862.

ONLINE DATABASES

FIRE INCIDENT DATA ORGANIZATION SYSTEM. National Fire Protection Association, Fire Analysis and Research Division, One Batterymarch Park, Quincy, Massachusetts 02269.

FIRE SERVICE INVENTORY. National Fire Protection Association, Fire Analysis and Research Division, One Batterymarch Park, Quincy, Massachusetts 02269.

FIREDOC. United States National Institute of Standards and Technology, Center for Fire Research, Building 224, Room A252, Gaithersburg, Maryland 20899.

NATIONAL FIRE EXPERIENCE SURVEY. National Fire Protection Association, Fire Analysis and Research Division, One Batterymarch Park, Quincy, Massachusetts 02269.

NATIONAL FIRE INCIDENT REPORTING SURVEY. United States Fire Administration, Office of Fire Data and Analysis, Emmitsburg, Maryland 21727.

STATISTICS SOURCES

BEST'S AGGREGATES AND AVERAGES. A.M. Best Company, Ambest Road, Oldwick, New Jersey 08858. Annual.

INSURANCE FACTS. Insurance Information Institute, 110 Williams Street, New York, New York 10038. Annual.

STATISTICAL BULLETIN. Metropolitan Life Insurance Company, One Madison Avenue, New York, New York 10010. Bimonthly.

OTHER SOURCES

MASTER INDEX TO NATIONAL FIRE CODES. National Fire Protection Association, One Batterymarch Park, Quincy, Massachusetts 02269-9101. 1987- . Annual.

FISH AND FISHING
See also: LAW OF THE SEA; WILDLIFE

STATUTES, CODES, STANDARDS, UNIFORM LAWS

CODE OF FEDERAL REGULATIONS, TITLE 50, WILDLIFE AND FISHERIES. National Archives and Records Administration. Superintendent of Documents, United States Government Printing Office, Washington, D.C. 20402. Annual.

LOOSELEAF SERVICES AND REPORTERS

MARINE FISHERIES MANAGEMENT REPORTER. Gary Knight, Editor. Jonathan Publishing Company, 3604 Pinnacle Road, Austin, Texas 78746-7417. 1982- .

TEXTBOOKS AND GENERAL WORKS

COASTAL STATE REQUIREMENTS FOR FOREIGN FISHING (Revised Second Edition). Gerald K. Moore. Unipub, 4611-F Assembly Drive, Lanham, Maryland 20706-4391. 1986.

DISPUTED WATERS: NATIVE AMERICANS AND THE GREAT LAKES FISHERY. Robert Doherty. University Press of Kentucky, 663 South Limestone Street, Lexington, Kentucky 40506-0336. 1990.

EEC FISHERIES LAW. R.R. Churchill. Martinus Nijhoff, Kluwer Academic Publishers, 101 Philip Drive, Assinippi Park, Norwell, Massachusetts 02061. 1987.

THE FISH FEUD: THE U.S. AND CANADIAN BOUNDARY DISPUTE. David L. Vander Zwaag. Lexington Books, 125 Spring Street, Lexington, Massachusetts 02173. 1983.

FISHERIES FOR THE FUTURE: RESTRUCTURING THE GOVERNMENT-INDUSTRY PARTNERSHIP: NATIONAL OCEAN GOALS AND OBJECTIVES FOR THE 1980'S. National Advisory Committee on Oceans and Atmosphere. Superintendent of Documents, United States Government Printing Office, Washington, D.C. 20402. 1982.

THE FISHERIES REGIME OF THE EXCLUSIVE ECONOMIC ZONE. Mohamed Dahmani. Martinus Nijhoff, Kluwer Academic Publishers, 101 Philip Drive, Assinippi Park, Norwell, Massachusetts 02061. 1987.

IN SEARCH OF A COMMON FISHERIES POLICY. John Farnell and James Elles. Gower Publishing Company, Old Post Road, Brookfield, Vermont 05036. 1984.

INDUSTRY IN TROUBLE: THE FEDERAL GOVERNMENT AND THE NEW ENGLAND FISHERIES. Margaret Dewer. Temple University Press, 1601 North Broad, Philadelphia, Pennsylvania 19122. 1983.

INTERNATIONAL CONTROL OF SEA RESOURCES. Second Edition. Shigeru Oda. Martinus Nijhoff, Kluwer Academic Publishers, 101 Philip Drive, Assinippi Park, Norwell, Massachusetts 02061. 1989.

THE INTERNATIONAL LAW OF FISHERIES: A FRAMEWORK FOR POLICY-ORIENTED INQUIRIES. Douglas M. Johnston. Kluwer Academic Publishers, 101 Philip Drive, Assinippi Park, Norwell, Massachusetts 02061. 1987.

INTERNATIONAL TRADE IN FISH PRODUCTS: EFFECTS OF THE 200-MILE LIMITS. Organization for Economic Cooperation and Development, 2001 L Street, Northwest, Suite 700, Washington, D.C. 20036. 1982.

MANAGING THE SEA'S LIVING RESOURCES: LEGAL AND POLITICAL ASPECTS OF HIGH SEAS FISHERIES. H. Gary Knight. Lexington Books, 125 Spring Street, Lexington, Massachusetts 02173. 1977.

OCEAN AND COASTAL LAW. Richard G. Hildreth and Ralph W. Johnson. Prentice-Hall, Incorporated, 113 Sylvan Avenue, Englewood Cliffs, New Jersey 07632. 1983.

PROHIBITIVE POLICY: IMPLEMENTING THE FEDERAL ENDANGERED SPECIES ACT. Steven Lewis Yaffee. MIT Press, 55 Hayward Street, Cambridge, Massachusetts 02142. 1982.

THE REGIME FOR THE EXPLOITATION OF TRANSBOUNDARY MARINE FISHERIES RESOURCES: THE UNITED NATIONS LAW OF THE SEA CONVENTION COOPERATION BETWEEN STATES. Ellen Hey. Martinus Nijhoff, Kluwer Academic Publishers, 101 Philip Drive, Assinippi Park, Norwell, Massachusetts 02061. 1989.

RIGHTS BASED FISHING. NATO Advanced Research Workshop on Scientific Foundations for Rights Based Fishing, Kluwer Academic Publishers, 101 Philip Drive, Assinippi Park, Norwell, Massachusetts 02061. 1989.

NEWSLETTERS AND NEWSPAPERS

ANADROMOUS FISH LAW MEMO. Natural Resources Law Institute, Lewis and Clark School of Law, 10015 Southwest Terilliger Boulevard, Portland, Oregon 97219. Quarterly.

LOUISIANA COASTAL LAW. Sea Grant Legal Program, 170 Law Center, Louisiana State University, Baton Rouge, Louisiana 70803. Quarterly.

OCEAN LAW MEMO. Oregon State University, Corvallis, Oregon 97331. Bimonthly.

DIRECTORIES

AMERICAN FISHERIES DIRECTORY AND REFERENCE BOOK. National Fisherman, 21 Elm Street, Camden, Maine 04843. 1982.

CURRENT FEDERAL AID RESEARCH REPORT--FISH. Division of Federal Aid, United States Fish and Wildlife Service, Interior Department. Superintendent of Documents, United States Government Printing Office, Washington, D.C. 20402. Annual.

INTERNATIONAL DIRECTORY OF FISH TECHNOLOGY INSTITUTES. Department of Fisheries, Food and Agriculture Organization of the United Nations, Via delle Terme di Caracalla, 1-00100, Rome, Italy. 1984.

LIST OF FISHERY COOPERATIVES IN THE UNITED STATES. National Marine Fisheries Service, National Oceanic and Atmospheric Administration. Superintendent of Documents, United States Government Printing Office, Washington, D.C. 20402. Annual.

LIST OF NATIONAL FISH HATCHERIES AND FISHING ASSISTANCE STATIONS. United States Fish and Wildlife Service, Interior Department. Superintendent of Documents, United States Government Printing Office, Washington, D.C. 20402. Annual.

NAFO LIST OF FISHING VESSELS. North Atlantic Fisheries Organization, Box 638, Dartmouth, Nova Scotia B2Y 3Y9, Canada. Annual.

BIOGRAPHICAL SOURCES

WHO'S WHO IN THE FISH INDUSTRY. Urner Barry Publications, Incorporated, Box 389, Toms River, New Jersey 08753. Annual.

ASSOCIATIONS AND PROFESSIONAL SOCIETIES

AMERICAN FISHERIES SOCIETY. 5410 Grosvenor Lane, Suite 110, Bethesda, Maryland 20814. (301) 897-8616.

ATLANTIC STATES MARINE FISHERIES COMMISSION. 1400 Sixteenth Street, Northwest, Suite 310, Washington, D.C. 20036. (202) 387-5330.

INTERNATIONAL ASSOCIATION OF FISH AND WILDLIFE AGENCIES. 444 North Capitol Street, Northwest, Suite 534, Washington, D.C. 20001. (202) 624-7890.

INTERNATIONAL GAME FISH ASSOCIATION. 3000 East Las Olas Boulevard, Ft. Lauderdale, Florida 33316. (305) 467-0161.

NATIONAL FISH AND WILDLIFE FOUNDATION. United States Department of the Interior, 1849 C Street, Northwest, Washington, D.C. 20240. (202) 208-3040.

NATIONAL FISHERIES INSTITUTE. 2000 M Street, Northwest, Suite 580, Washington, D.C. 20036. (202) 296-5090.

PACIFIC MARINE FISHERIES COMMISSION. 2000 Southwest First Avenue, Portland, Oregon 97201. (503) 326-7025.

SPORT FISHING INSTITUTE. 1010 Massachusetts Avenue, Northwest, Suite 100, Washington, D.C. 20001. (202) 898-0770.

UNITED STATES TUNA FOUNDATION. 1101 Seventeenth Street, Northwest, Suite 609, Washington, D.C. 20036. (202) 857-0610.

RESEARCH CENTERS, INSTITUTES, CLEARINGHOUSES

AQUATIC RESEARCH INSTITUTE. 2242 Davis Court, Hayward, California 94545. (415) 785-2216.

FISH AND FISHING

CENTER FOR ENVIRONMENTAL EDUCATION. 1725 DeSales Street, Northwest, Washington, D.C. 20036. (202) 429-5609.

CENTER FOR OCEANS LAW AND POLICY. University of Virginia, School of Law, Charlottesville, Virginia 22901. (804) 924-7441.

COASTAL FISHERIES INSTITUTE. Louisiana State University, Center for Wetland Resources, Baton Rouge, Louisiana 70803. (504) 388-6734.

INSTITUTE FOR FISHERIES RESEARCH. 212 Museums Annex, Ann Arbor, Michigan 48109. (313) 663-3554.

INSTITUTE OF FISHERIES ANALYSIS. Simon Fraser University, Burnaby, BC, Canada V5A 1S6. (604) 291-4893.

LAW OF THE SEA INSTITUTE. Richardson School of Law, 2515 Dole Street, Room 208, Honolulu, Hawaii 96822. (808) 948-6750.

MARINE LAW INSTITUTE. University of Southern Maine, 246 Deering Avenue, Portland, Maine 04102. (207) 780-4474.

MARINE POLICY CENTER. Crowell House, Woods Hole Oceanographic Institution, Woods Hole, Massachusetts 02543. (617) 548-1400.

NATIONAL FISHERIES EDUCATION AND RESEARCH FOUNDATION. 2000 M Street, Northwest, Washington, D.C. 20036. (202) 296-5090.

OCEAN AND COASTAL LAW CENTER. University of Oregon, Law School, Eugene, Oregon 97403. (503) 686-3845.

OCEANIC SOCIETY. 1536 Sixteenth Street, Northwest, Washington, D.C. 20036. (202) 328-0098.

SPORT FISHERY RESEARCH PROGRAM. 1010 Massachusetts Avenue, Northwest, Suite 100, Washingotn, D.C. 20001. (202) 898-0770.

TROUT UNLIMITED. 501 Church Street, Northeast, Vienna, Virginia 22180. (703) 281-1100.

ONLINE DATABASES

ASFIS REGISTER OF INTERNATIONAL ACTIVITIES IN MARINE AFFAIRS. Fisheries Resources and Environment Division, Food and Agriculture Organization of the United Nations. Via Delle Terme di Caracella, 1-00100 Rome, Italy.

FISHERY STATISTICS DATA BASE. United States Fish and Wildlife Service, Fisheries Statistics Division. NOAA-F/REI, Silver Spring, Maryland 20910.

GULF STATES MARINE FISHERIES COMMISSION. Gulf Coast Research Laboratory. Menhaden Information Data Bank, P.O. Box 726, Ocean Springs, Mississippi 39564.

OCEANIC ABSTRACTS. Cambridge Scientific Abstracts. 7200 Wisconsin Boulevard, Bethesda, Maryland 20814.

SEA GRANT NETWORK. National Sea Grant Depository. Pell Library Building, University of Rhode Island, Bay Campus, Narragansett, Rhode Island 02882.

UNITED STATES FISH AND WILDLIFE REFERENCE SERVICE. United States Fish and Wildlife Service. The Maxima Corporation, 5430 Grovesnor Lane, Suite 110, Bethesda, Maryland 20814.

WILDLIFE AND FISH WORLDWIDE. United States Fish and Wildlife Service. Department of the Interior, 1849 C Street, Northwest, Washington, D.C. 20240.

STATIS TICS SOURCES

WILDLIFE STATISTICS. United States Department of Agriculture, Forest Service. Superintendent of Documents, United States Government Printing Office, Washington, D.C. 20402.

FIXTURES
See: LANDLORD AND TENANT; REAL PROPERTY

FLAMMABLE SUBSTANCES
See: FIRES AND FIRE PREVENTION; HAZARDOUS SUBSTANCES

FOOD AND DRUG ADMINISTRATION

STATUTES, CODES, STANDARDS, UNIFORM LAWS

CODE OF FEDERAL REGULATIONS, TITLE 21. Office of the Federal Register, National Archives and Records Administration. Superintendent of Documents, United States Government Printing Office, Washington, D.C. 20402. Annual. (Updated by use of monthly List of Sections Affected and daily Federal Register).

FEDERAL FOOD, DRUG AND COSMETIC ACT, AS AMENDED AND RELATED LAWS. United States Health and Human Services Department, Food and Drug Administration. Superintendent of Documents, United States Government Printing Office, Washington, D.C. 20402. 1990.

REQUIREMENTS OF LAWS AND REGULATIONS ENFORCED BY THE UNITED STATES FOOD AND DRUG ADMINISTRATION. United States Health and Human Services Department, Food and Drug Administration. Superintendent of Documents, United States Government Printing Office, Washington, D.C. 20402. 1984.

HANDBOOKS, MANUALS, FORMBOOKS

EVERYTHING YOU ALWAYS WANTED TO KNOW ABOUT THE MEDICAL DEVICE AMENDMENT AND WEREN'T AFRAID TO ASK. United States Health and Human Services Department, Food and Drug Administration, Center for Devices and Radiological Health. Superintendent of Documents, United States Government Printing Office, Washington, D.C. 20402, 1984

IMPORT/EXPORT OF MEDICAL DEVICES: A WORKSHOP MANUAL. Darlene M. Greathouse. United States Health and Human Services Department, Food and Drug Administration, Center for Devices and Radiological Health, Division of Small Manufacturers Assistance, Office of Training and Assistance. Superintendent of Documents, United States Government Printing Office, Washington, D.C. 20402. 1983.

INVESTIGATIONAL DEVICE EXEMPTIONS, REGULATORY REQUIREMENTS FOR MEDICAL DEVICES. United States Health and Human Services Department, Food and Drug Administration, Center for Devices and Radiological Health, Division of Small Manufacturers Assistance, Office of Training and Assistance. Superintendent of Documents, United States Government Printing Office, Washington, D.C. 20402. 1984.

LABELING REGULATORY REQUIREMENTS FOR MEDICAL DEVICES. United States Health and Human Services Department, Food and Drug Administration, Center for Devices and Radiological Health, Division of Small Manufacturers Assistance, Office of Training and Assistance. Superintendent of Documents, United States Government Printing Office, Washington, D.C. 20402. 1986.

PREMARKET NOTIFICATION: 510(k) REGULATORY REQUIREMENTS FOR MEDICAL DEVICES. United States Health and Human Services Department, Food and Drug Administration, Center for Devices and Radiological Health, Division of Small Manufacturers Assistance, Office of Training and Assistance. Superintendent of Documents, United States Government Printing Office, Washington, D.C. 20402. 1986.

REGISTRATION AND LISTING: REGULATORY REQUIREMENTS FOR MEDICAL DEVICES. United States Health and Human Services Department, Food and Drug Administration, Center for Devices and Radiological Health, Division of Small Manufacturers Assistance, Office of Training and Assistance. Superintendent of Documents, United States Government Printing Office, Washington, D.C. 20402. 1983.

TEXTBOOKS AND GENERAL WORKS

PURE FOOD: SECURING THE FEDERAL FOOD AND DRUGS ACT OF 1906. James Harvey Young. Princeton University Press, 41 William Street, Princeton, New Jersey 08540. 1989.

SAFETY FIRST: PROTECTING AMERICA'S FOOD SUPPLY. United States Department of Health and Human Services, Public Health Service, Food and Drug Administration, 5600 Fishers Lane, Rockville, Maryland 20857. 1988.

DIRECTORIES

NATIONAL DRUG CODE DIRECTORY, 1985. United States Health and Human Services Department, Food and Drug Administration, National Center for Drugs and Biologics, Drug Listing Branch. Superintendent of Documents, United States Government Printing Office, Washington, D.C. 20402. 1985.

FOOD LAWS
See also: ADVERTISING; AGRICULTURE DEPARTMENT; DRUG LAWS; FOOD AND DRUG ADMINISTRATION; HAZARDOUS SUBSTANCES; HOTELS, RESTAURANTS, ETC.; PRODUCTS LIABILITY AND SAFETY

STATUTES, CODES, STANDARDS, UNIFORM LAWS

CODE OF FEDERAL REGULATIONS, TITLE 21. Office of the Federal Register, National Archives and Records Administration. Superintendent of Documents, United States Government Printing Office, Washington, D.C. 20402. Annual. (Updated monthly by the List of Sections Affected, and daily by the Federal Register).

A LEGISLATIVE HISTORY OF THE FEDERAL FOOD, DRUG, AND COSMETIC ACT AND ITS AMENDMENTS (34 volumes). United States Department of Health and Human Services, Food and Drug Administration. Superintendent of Documents, United States Government Printing Office, Washington, D.C. 20402. 1979.

UNITED STATES FOOD LAWS, REGULATIONS, AND STANDARDS (Second Edition). Y.H. Hui. John Wiley and Sons, Incorporated, 605 Third Avenue, New York, New York 10158. 1986.

LOOSELEAF SERVICES AND REPORTERS

FDA COMPLIANCE POLICY GUIDES MANUAL. National Technical Information Service, 5285 Post Royal Road, Springfield, Virginia 22161. 1981- .

FOOD AND DRUG ADMINISTRATION. James T. O'Reilly. Shepard's/McGraw-Hill, P.O. Box 1235, Colorado Springs, Colorado 80901. 1983- .

FOOD AND DRUG COSMETIC LAW REPORTER. Commerce Clearing House, Incorporated, 4025 West Peterson Avenue, Chicago, Illinois 60646. 1963- .

HANDBOOKS, MANUALS, FORMBOOKS

FOOD LAW HANDBOOK. H.W. Schultz. AVI Publishing Company, Incorporated, 115 Fifth Avenue, New York, New York 10003-1004. 1981.

INTERNATIONAL FOOD REGULATION HANDBOOK: POLICY, SCIENCE, LAW. Roger D. Middlekauff and Philippe Shubik. Marcel Dekker, 720 Madison Avenue, New York, New York 10016. 1989.

TEXTBOOKS AND GENERAL WORKS

ALTERED HARVEST: AGRICULTURE GENETICS, AND THE FATE OF THE WORLD'S FOOD SUPPLY. Jack Doyle. Viking Penguin, Incorporated, 375 Hudson Street, New York, New York 10014. 1985.

CONSUMER PROTECTION LEGISLATION AND THE U.S. FOOD INDUSTRY. Melvin Hinich and Richard Staelin. Pergamon Press, Incorporated, Maxwell House, Fairview Park, Elmsford, New York 10523. 1980.

EATING CLEAN: FOOD SAFETY AND THE CHEMICAL HARVEST. Ralph Nader and Michael Fortun, Editors. Center for the Study of Responsive Law, P.O. Box 19367, Washington, D.C. 20036. 1982.

FAIR PLAY IN THE MARKETPLACE: THE FIRST BATTLE FOR PURE FOOD AND DRUGS. Mitchell Okun. Northern Illinois University Press, Williston, 320A, Dekalb, Illinois 60115. 1986.

FEEDING HUNGRY PEOPLE: RULEMAKING IN THE FOOD STAMP PROGRAM. Jeffrey M. Berry. Rutgers University Press, 109 Church Street, New Brunswick, New Jersey 08901. 1984.

FOOD AND DRUG COMPLIANCE: MINIMIZING PRODUCT LIABILITY EXPOSURE. George M. Burditt and Russell D. Munves, Co-chairmen. Practising Law Institute, 810 Seventh Avenue, New York, New York 10019. 1984.

GOOD TO EAT: RIDDLES OF FOOD AND CULTURE. Marvin Harris. Simon and Schuster, Incorporated, 1230 Avenue of the Americas, New York, New York 10020. 1985.

THE ORGANIZATION AND PERFORMANCE OF THE U.S. FOOD SYSTEM. Bruce W. Marion. Free Press, 866 Third, New York, New York 10022. 1985.

PURE FOOD: SECURING THE FEDERAL FOOD AND DRUGS ACT OF 1906. James Harvey Young. Princeton University Press, 41 William Street, Princeton, New Jersey 08540. 1989.

THE RIGHT TO FOOD. P. Alston and K. Tomasevski, Editors. Kluwer Academic Publishing, 101 Philip Drive, Assinippi Park, Norwell, Massachusetts 02061. 1984.

SAFETY FIRST: PROTECTING AMERICA'S FOOD SUPPLY. United States Department of Health and Human Services, Public Health Service, Food and Drug Administration, 5600 Fishers Lane, Rockville, Maryland 20857. 1988.

LAW REVIEWS AND PERIODICALS

FOOD AND AGRICULTURAL LEGISLATION. Food and Agricultural Organization of the United Nations. Unipub, Box 433, Murray Hill Station, New York, New York 10157. Quarterly.

FOOD, DRUG, COSMETIC LAW JOURNAL. Food and Drug Law Institute, 1000 Vermont Avenue, Northwest, Suite 1200, Washington, D.C. 20005. Bimonthly.

NEWSLETTERS AND NEWSPAPERS

FDLI UPDATE. Food and Drug Law Institute, 1000 Vermont Avenue, Northwest, Suite 1200, Washington, D.C. 20005. Bimonthly.

FOOD AND DRUG LAW REPORT. Food and Drug Law Institute, 1000 Vermont Avenue, Northwest, Suite 1200, Washington, D.C. 20005. Monthly.

THE FOOD AND DRUG LETTER. Washington Business Information, Incorporated, 1117 North Nineteenth Street, Arlington, Virginia 22209. Semimonthly.

THE FOOD AND FIBER LETTER. Webster Communications Corporation, P.O. Box 9153, Arlington, Virginia 22209. Weekly.

FOOD CHEMICAL NEWS. Food Chemical News, Incorporated, 1101 Pennsylvania Avenue, Sooutheast, Washington, D.C. 20003. Weekly.

FOOD DRUG AND COSMETIC LAW SECTION NEWSLETTER. New York State Bar Association, One Elk Street, Albany, New York 12207. Quarterly.

THE GMP LETTER. Washington Business Information, Incorporated, 1117 North Nineteenth Street, Arlington, Virginia 22209. Monthly.

INFORMATION LETTER. National Food Processors Association, 1401 New York Avenue, Northwest, Suite 400, Washington, D.C. 20005. Monthly.

NUTRITION LEGISLATION NEWS. Nutrition Legislation Services, P.O. Box 75035, Washington, D.C. 20013. Monthly.

WASHINGTON BEVERAGE INSIGHT. George Wells and Associates, Incorporated, 1120 Connecticut Avenue, Northwest, Suite 270, Washington, D.C. 20036. Semimonthly.

BIBLIOGRAPHIES

FOOD BIBLIOGRAPHY: REFERENCES TO REPORTS AND OTHER DOCUMENTS. United States General Accounting Office, 441 G Street, Northwest, Washington, D.C. 20548. Annual.

RESOURCES FOR FOOD CO-OPS: A BIBLIOGRAPHY. National Consumer Cooperative Bank, 1630 Connecticut Avenue, Northwest, Washington, D.C. 20009. 1983.

ASSOCIATIONS AND PROFESSIONAL SOCIETIES

AMERICANS FOR SAFE FOOD. 1501 Sixteenth Street, Northwest, Washington, D.C. 20036. (202) 332-9110.

ASSOCIATION OF FOOD AND DRUG OFFICIALS. P.O. Box 3425, York, Pennsylvania 17402. (717) 757-2888.

ASSOCIATION OF FOOD INDUSTRIES. 177 Main Street, P.O. Box 776, Matawan, New Jersey 07747. (201) 583-3188.

INTERNATIONAL FOODSERVICE MANUFACTURERS ASSOCIATION. 321 North Clark Street, Suite 2900, Chicago, Illinois 60610. (312) 644-8989.

NATIONAL FOOD PROCESSORS ASSOCIATION. 1401 New York Avenue, Northwest, Fourth Floor, Washington, D.C. 20005. (202) 639-5900.

RESEARCH CENTERS, INSTITUTES, CLEARINGHOUSES

CENTER FOR SCIENCE IN THE PUBLIC INTEREST. 1501 Sixteenth Street, Northwest, Washington, D.C. 20036. (202) 332-9110.

COMMUNITY NUTRITION INSTITUTE. 2001 S Street, Northwest, Washington, D.C. 20009. (202) 462-4700.

FOOD AND AGRICULTURAL ORGANIZATION OF THE UNITED NATIONS LIBRARY. Liaison Office for North America, 1001 Twenty-second Street, Northwest, Washington, D.C. 20437. (202) 653-2402.

FOOD AND DRUG LAW INSTITUTE. 1000 Vermont Avenue, Northwest, Suite 1200, Washington, D.C. 20005. (202) 371-1420.

FOOD MARKETING INSTITUTE LIBRARY. 1750 K Street, Northwest, Washington, D.C. 20006. (202) 452-8444.

FOOD PROCESSORS INSTITUTE. 1401 New York Avenue, Northwest, Suite 400, Washington, D.C. 20005. (202) 393-0890.

FOOD RESEARCH AND ACTION CENTER, INCORPORATED. 1319 F Street, Northwest, Suite 500, Washington, D.C. 20004. (202) 393-5060.

FOOD RESEARCH INSTITUTE. Stanford University, Stanford, California 94305. (415) 723-3941.

INSTITUTE FOR FOOD AND DEVELOPMENT POLICY. Food First, 145 Ninth Street, San Francisco, California 94103. (415) 864-8555.

INTERNATIONAL FOOD INFORMATION COUNCIL. 1100 Connecticut Avenue, Northwest, Suite 430, Washington, D.C. 20036. (202) 296-6540.

INTERNATIONAL FOOD POLICY RESEARCH INSTITUTE. 1776 Massachusetts Avenue, Northwest, Washington, D.C. 20036. (202) 862-5600.

INTERNATIONAL LIFE SCIENCES INSTITUTE/NUTRITION FOUNDATION. 1126 Sixteenth Street, Northwest, Washington, D.C. 20036. (202) 659-0074.

NATIONAL CENTER FOR FOOD AND AGRICULTURAL POLICY. Resources for the Future, 1616 P Street, Northwest, Washington, D.C. 20036. (202) 328-5082.

PUBLIC VOICE FOR FOOD AND HEALTH POLICY. 1001 Connecticut Avenue, Northwest, Washington, D.C. 20036. (202) 659-5930.

WORLDWATCH INSTITUTE. 1776 Massachusetts Avenue, Northwest, Washington, D.C. 20036. (202) 452-1999.

FORECLOSURES
See also: MORTGAGES

LOOSELEAF SERVICES AND REPORTERS

INS AND OUTS OF FORECLOSURE. Michael Yarnell and Burt Apker. State Bar of Arizona, 363 North First Avenue, Phoenix, Arizona 85003. 1984- . (Periodic Supplements).

THE LAW OF DISTRESSED REAL ESTATE: FORECLOSURE, WORKOUTS, PROCEDURES. Baxter Dunaway. Clark Boardman Company, Limited, 435 Hudson Street, New York, New York 10014. 1985- .

MORTGAGE FORECLOSURES. John S. Goodland and others. Continuing Legal Education for Wisconsin, University of Wisconsin-Extension, 905 University Avenue, Madison, Wisconsin 53706. 1980- . (Periodic Supplements).

MORTGAGES AND MORTGAGE FORECLOSURE IN NEW YORK. D. Kirk Drussel and Mary Anne Foran. Callaghan and Company, 155 Pfingsten Road, Deerfield, Illinois 60015. 1982- . (Periodic Supplements).

NEW JERSEY MORTGAGE FORECLOSURE HANDBOOK. Leonard B. Zucker and Sanford J. Becker. New Jersey Institute of Continuing Legal Education, One Constitution Square, New Brunswick, New Jersey 08901. 1983- .

TEXTBOOKS AND GENERAL WORKS

DISPOSITION OF REPOSSESSED COLLATERAL UNDER THE UNIFORM COMMERCIAL CODE. Christine A. Ferris. John Wiley and Sons, Incorporated, 605 Third Avenue, New York, New York 10158. 1990.

DISTRESSED PROPERTY HANDBOOK: A NATIONAL GUIDE FOR INVESTORS. Gene Sherman. Sherbart Publishing Company, P.O. Box 5107, Cedar Rapids, Iowa 52406-5107. 1984.

FORECLOSURE LAW MANUAL. State Bar of California, 555 Franklin Street, San Francisco, California 94102. 1984.

GOLDMINING IN FORECLOSURE PROPERTIES. Second Edition. Val Cabot; Patricia C. Golomb, Editor. Impact Publishers, Incorporated, P.O. Box 1094, San Luis Obispo, California 93406. 1982.

HOW TO STOP FORECLOSURE. Hal Morris. Beaufort Books, 226 West Twenty-sixth Street, New York, New York 10001. 1983.

MODERN MORTGAGE LAW PRACTICE. Second Edition. R. Kratovil and R. Werner. Prentice-Hall, Incorporated, 113 Sylvan Avenue, Englewood Cliffs, New Jersey 07632. 1981.

MORTGAGES, LIENS AND FORECLOSURES. New Hampshire Bar Association Continuing Legal Education, 18 Centre Street, Concord, New Hampshire 03301. 1986.

NEWSLETTERS AND NEWSPAPERS

FORECLOSURE LAW BULLETIN. Quinlan Publishing Company, 23 Drydock Avenue, Boston, Massachusetts 02110. Monthly.

FOREIGN AFFAIRS
See: INTERNATIONAL LAW AND RELATIONS

FOREIGN CORPORATIONS
See: CORPORATIONS, FOREIGN AND MULTINATIONAL; INTERNATIONAL TRADE

FOREIGN INVESTMENTS
See: INTERNATIONAL TRADE

FOREIGN LAW

GENERAL

AMERICAN FOREIGN LAW ASSOCIATION. c/o Richard E. Lutringer, Whitman and Ransom, 200 Park Avenue, New York, New York 10166. (212) 351-3277.

AMERICAN JOURNAL OF COMPARATIVE LAW. American Foreign Law Association, 200 Park Avenue, New York, New York 10166. Quarterly.

AMERICAN JOURNAL OF INTERNATIONAL LAW. American Society of International Law, 2223 Massachusetts Avenue, Northwest, Washington, D.C. 20008-2864. Quarterly.

AMERICAN SOCIETY OF INTERNATIONAL LAW. 2223 Massachusetts Avenue, Northwest, Washington, D.C. 20008-2864. (202) 265-4313.

CONSTITUTIONS OF THE COUNTRIES OF THE WORLD. A.P. Blaustein and G.H. Flanz, Editors. Oceana Publications, Incorporated, 75 Main Street, Dobbs Ferry, New York 10522. 1971- .

DIGESTS OF LAWS, INTERNATIONAL SECTION. Martindale-Hubbell Law Directory, Volume Eight. Martindale-Hubbell, Incorporated, P.O. Box 1001, Summit, New Jersey 07902. Annual.

INSTITUTE OF COMPARATIVE LAW. McGill University, 3674 Peel Street, Montreal, PQ, Canada H3A 1X1. (514) 398-6646.

INTERNATIONAL LAW INSTITUTE. 1615 New Hampshire Avenue, Northwest, Washington, D.C. 20009. (202) 483-7979.

INTERNATIONAL LEGAL MATERIALS. American Society of International Law, 2223 Massachusetts Avenue, Northwest, Washington, D.C. 20008-2864. Bimonthly.

INTERNATIONAL LEGAL STUDIES PROGRAM. Harvard University, 1557 Massachusetts Avenue, Cambridge, Massachusetts 02138. (617) 495-3117.

INTERNATIONAL THIRD WORLD LEGAL STUDIES ASSOCIATION. c/o International Center for Law in Development, 777 United Nations Plaza, New York, New York 10017. (212) 687-0036.

SECTION ON INTERNATIONAL LAW AND PRACTICE. American Bar Association, 1800 M Street, Northwest, Washington, D.C. 20036. (202) 331-2239.

UNITED NATIONS LAW REPORTS. Walker and Company, 720 Fifth Avenue, New York, New York 10019. Monthly.

WASHINGTON FOREIGN LAW SOCIETY. c/o Audrey S. Winter, Secretary/Treasurer, 1775 Pennsylvania Avenue, Northwest, Washington, D. C. 20006. (202) 785-4444.

AFRICA

AFRICA AND THE DEVELOPMENT OF INTERNATIONAL LAW. Second Revised Edition. M. Nijhoff, Kluwer Academic Publishers, 101 Philip Drive, Assinippi Park, Norwell, Massachusetts 02061. 1988.

EUROPEAN EXPANSION AND LAW: THE ENCOUNTER OF EUROPEAN AND INDIGENOUS LAW IN NINETEENTH- AND TWENTIETH-CENTURY AFRICA AND ASIA. W.J. Mommsen and J.A. de Moor. St. Martin's Press, 175 Fifth Avenue, New York, New York 10010. 1991.

THE INTERNATIONAL LAW OF HUMAN RIGHTS IN AFRICA: BASIC DOCUMENTS AND ANNOTATED BIBLIOGRAPHY. M. Hamalengwa, C. Flinterman and E.V.O. Dankwa. Martinus Nijhoff, Kluwer Academic Publishers, 101 Philip Drive, Assinippi Park, Norwell, Massachusetts 02061. 1988.

INTERNATIONAL LAW OF TAKE-OVERS AND MERGERS: SOUTHERN EUROPE, AFRICA, AND THE MIDDLE EAST. H. Leigh Ffrench. Quorum Books, Greenwood Publishing Group, Incorporated, 88 Post Road West, P.O. Box 5007, Westport, Connecticut 06881. 1987.

LAW IN COLONIAL AFRICA. Kristin Mann and Richard Roberts. Heinemann Educational Books, Incorporated, 361 Hanover Street, Portsmouth, New Hampshire 03801. 1991.

LEGAL ASPECTS OF DOING BUSINESS IN AFRICA. Dennis Campbell, Editor. Kluwer Law Book Publishers, Incorporated, 36 West Forty-fourth Street, New York, New York 10036. 1992.

TITLE TO TERRITORY IN AFRICA: INTERNATIONAL LEGAL ISSUES. Malcolm N. Shaw. Clarendon Press, Oxford University Press, 200 Madison Avenue, New York, New York 10016. 1985.

ASIA AND THE PACIFIC

ARBITRATION IN ASIA AND THE PACIFIC. Kenneth R. Simmons and Sigvard Garvin. Oceana Publications, Incorporated, 75 Main Street, Dobbs Ferry, New York 10522. 1987.

ASIA INDIGENOUS LAW: INTERACTION WITH RECEIVED LAW. Masaji Chiba, Editor. KPI, Methuen, Incorporated, 29 West Thirty-fifth Street, New York, New York 10001. 1986.

COMMERCIAL ARBITRATION LAW IN ASIA AND THE PACIFIC. Kenneth R. Simmonds and Brian H.W. Hill. Oceana Publications, 75 Main Street, Dobbs Ferry, New York 10522. 1987.

CONSTITUTIONAL SYSTEMS IN LATE TWENTIETH CENTURY ASIA. Lawrence W. Beer. University of Washington Press, P.O. Box 50096, Seattle, Washington 98145-5096. 1992.

EAST ASIAN LEGAL STUDIES PROGRAM. Harvard University, Pound Hall, Room 426, Harvard University Law School, Cambridge, Massachusetts 02138. (617) 495-4629.

LAW AND THE STATE IN TRADITIONAL EAST ASIA: SIX STUDIES ON THE SOURCES OF EAST ASIAN LAW. Brian E. McKnight. University of Hawaii Press, 2840 Kolowalu Street, Honolulu, Hawaii 96822. 1987.

THE LAW OF THE SEA AND MARITIME BOUNDARY DELIMITATION IN SOUTH-EAST ASIA. Kriangsak Kittichaisaree. Oxford University Press, 200 Madison Avenue, New York, New York 10016. 1987.

LEGAL ASPECTS OF DOING BUSINESS IN ASIA AND THE PACIFIC. Dennis Campbell, Editor. Kluwer Law Book Publishers, Incorporated, 36 West Forty-fourth Street, New York, New York 10036. 1992.

AUSTRALIA AND NEW ZEALAND

AUSTRALIAN AND SOUTH PACIFIC LAW: STRUCTURE AND LEGAL MATERIALS: PAPERS AND PROCEEDINGS OF THE 8TH ANNUAL IALL COURSE ON LAW LIBRARIANSHIP, MAY 10-15, 1981. William S. Hein and Company, Incorporated, Hein Building, 1285 Main Street, Buffalo, New York 14209. 1983.

AUSTRALIAN BUSINESS LAW. Paul Stephen Latimer. CCH Australia, Limited, P.O. Box 230, North Ryde, New South Wales 2113, Australia. 1990.

AUSTRALIAN CONSTITUTIONAL LAW. Third Edition. Peter Hanks. Butterworths Pty. Limited, P.O. Box 345, North Ryde, New South Wales 2113, Australia. 1985.

BANKING LAW AND THE FINANCIAL SYSTEM IN AUSTRALIA. Second Edition. W.S. Weerasooria. Butterworths Pty. Limited, 271-273 Lane Cove Road, North Ryde, New South Wales 2113 Australia. 1988.

BUSINESS LAW OF AUSTRALIA. Sixth Edition. R.B. Vermeesch and K.E. Lindgren. Butterworths Pty. Limited, 271-273 Lane Cove Road, North Ryde, New South Wales 2113 Australia. 1990.

BUTTERWORTHS FAMILY LAW GUIDE. Butterworths of New Zealand, Limited, P.O. Box 472, 205-207 Victoria Street, Wellington, New Zealand. 1983.

CCH AUSTRALIAN COMPANY LAW AND PRACTICE. CCH Australia, Limited, P.O. Box 230, North Ryde, New South Wales 2113, Australia. 1981- .

CHESHIRE AND FIFOOT'S LAW OF CONTRACT. Fifth Edition. J.G. Starke. Butterworth Legal Publishers, 90 Stiles Road, Salem, New Hampshire 03079. 1988.

COMMERCIAL TENANCY LAW IN AUSTRALIA. Adrian J. Bradbrook and C.E. Croft. Butterworth Legal Publishers, 90 Stiles Road, Salem, New Hampshire 03079. 1990.

COMPETITION LAW AND POLICY IN AUSTRALIA. S.G. Corones. Law Book Company Limited, 44-50 Waterloo Road, North Ryde, New South Wales 2113, Australia. 1990.

COMPULSORY ACQUISITION OF LAND IN AUSTRALIA. Second Edition. Graham L. Fricke. Law Book Company, 44-50 Waterloo Road, North Ryde, New South Wales 2113, Australia. 1982.

CONSUMER CREDIT LAW IN AUSTRALIA: A COMMENTARY ON THE NEW CREDIT LEGISLATION. S.W. Cavanagh and Shenagh Barnes. Butterworths Pty. Limited, 271-273 Lane Cove Road, North Ryde, New South Wales 2113 Australia. 1988.

CONSUMER PROTECTION LAW IN AUSTRALIA. Third Edition. John Goldring, L.W. Maher and J. McKeough. Butterworths Pty. Limited, 271-273 Lane Cove Road, North Ryde, New South Wales 2113 Australia. 1987.

CONTRACT LAW IN AUSTRALIA. K.E. Lindgren, J.W. Carter and D.J. Harland. Butterworths Pty. Limited, P.O. Box 345, North Ryde, New South Wales 2113, Australia. 1986.

ENVIRONMENTAL LAW IN AUSTRALIA. Second Edition. G.M. Bates. Butterworths Pty. Limited, 271-273 Lane Cove Road, North Ryde, New South Wales 2113 Australia. 1987.

THE FAMILY AND GOVERNMENT POLICY IN NEW ZEALAND. Peggy G. Koopman-Boyden and Claudia D. Scott. Allen and Unvin, Incorporated, P.O. Box 442, Concord, Massachusetts 01742. 1984.

FAMILY LAW IN AUSTRALIA. Fourth Edition. H.A. Finlay and Rebecca J. Bailey-Harris. Butterworths Pty. Limited, 271-273 Lane Cove Road, North Ryde, New South Wales 2113 Australia. 1989.

FAMILY LAW, 1986 STYLE. P.R.H. Webb and J.G. Adams. Legal Research Foundation, Auckland, New Zealand. 1986.

FISHER ON MATRIMONIAL PROPERTY. Second Edition. R.L. Fisher. Butterworths of New Zealand, Limited, P.O. Box 472, 205-207 Victoria Street, Wellington, New Zealand. 1984.

GARROW AND ALSTON LAW OF WILLS AND ADMINISTRATION. Fifth Edition. Andrew Alston. Butterworths of New Zealand, Limited, P.O. Box 472, 205-207 Victoria Street, Wellington, New Zealand. 1984.

A GUIDE TO AUSTRALIAN LAW FOR JOURNALISTS, AUTHORS, PRINTERS, AND PUBLISHERS. Third Edition. Goeffrey Sawer. Melbourne University Press, International Specialized Book Services, 5602 Northeast Hassalo Street, Portland, Oregon 97213-3640. 1984.

GUIDEBOOK TO CONTRACT LAW IN AUSTRALIA. Second Edition. Bradford A. Caffney. CCH Australia, Limited, P.O. Box 230, North Ryde, New South Wales 2113, Australia. 1983.

GUIDEBOOK TO INSURANCE LAW IN AUSTRALIA. Second Edition. Francis Marks. CCH Australia, Limited, P.O. Box 230, North Ryde, New South Wales 2112, Australia. 1987.

GUIDEBOOK TO INSURANCE LAW IN AUSTRALIA AND NEW ZEALAND. Richard G. Thomas. CCH Australia, Limited, P.O. Box 230, North Ryde, New South Wales 2113, Australia. 1981.

GUIDEBOOK TO NEW ZEALAND COMPANIES AND SECURITIES LAW. Commerce Clearing House, P.O. Box 2378, Auckland, New Zealand. 1985.

HIGGINS AND FLETCHER THE LAW OF PARTNERSHIP IN AUSTRALIA AND NEW ZEALAND. Fifth Edition. Keith L. Fletcher. Law Book Company Limited, 44-50 Waterloo Road, North Ryde, New South Wales 2113, Australia. 1987.

INDEX TO NEW ZEALAND LEGAL WRITING AND CASES. K.A. Palmer and J.F. Northey. Legal Research Foundation, Auckland, New Zealand. 1987.

INDUSTRIAL DESIGN LAW IN AUSTRALIA AND NEW ZEALAND. Kanwal K. Puri. Butterworths of New Zealand, Limited, P.O. Box 472, 205-207 Victoria Street, Wellington, New Zealand. 1986.

INTELLECTUAL PROPERTY IN AUSTRALIA: COPYRIGHT LAW. James Lahore. Butterworths Pty. Limited, 271-273 Lane Cove Road, North Ryde, New South Wales 2113 Australia. 1988- .

INTELLECTUAL PROPERTY LAW IN NEW ZEALAND AND AUSTRALIA: PAPERS PRESENTED BY M.P. CREW, ET AL. Legal Research Foundation, Auckland, New Zealand. 1985.

INTRODUCTION TO NEW ZEALAND SALES TAX LAW. P.J. Brannigan. Commerce Clearing House, P.O. Box 2378, Auckland, New Zealand. 1984.

INTRODUCTION TO THE NEW ZEALAND LEGAL SYSTEM. Sixth Edition. R.D. Mulholland. Butterworths of New Zealand, Limited, P.O. Box 472, 205-207 Victoria Street, Wellington, New Zealand. 1985.

THE LAW AND PRACTICE OF COMPANY ACCOUNTING IN AUSTRALIA. Sixth Edition. Trevor R. Johnston, Martin O. Jager and Reginald B. Taylor. Butterworths Pty. Limited, 271-273 Lane Cove Road, North Ryde, New South Wales 2113 Australia. 1987.

LAW OF CONTRACT IN AUSTRALIA. David E. Allan and Mary E. Hiscock. CCH Australia, North Ryde, New South Wales, Australia. 1987.

LAW OF EVIDENCE IN AUSTRALIA. Peter Gillies. Legal Books, Sydney, Australia. 1987.

THE LAW OF INTELLECTUAL PROPERTY IN NEW ZEALAND: AN EXPOSITION OF THE NEW ZEALAND LAW RELATING TO TRADE MARKS, PASSING OFF, COPYRIGHT, REGISTERED DESIGNS, PATENTS, TRADE SECRETS, AND THE FAIR TRADING ACT 1986. Andrew Brown. Butterworths of New Zealand, Limited, P.O. Box 472, 205-207 Victoria Street, Wellington, New Zealand. 1989.

THE LAW OF JOURNALISM IN AUSTRALIA. Sally Walker. Law Book Company Limited, 44-50 Waterloo Road, North Ryde, New South Wales 2113, Australia. 1989.

THE LAW RELATING TO THE RESTRICTIVE TRADE PRACTICES AND MONOPOLIES, MERGERS, AND TAKE-OVERS IN NEW ZEALAND. Second Edition. John Collinge. Butterworths of New Zealand, Limited, P.O. Box 472, 205-207 Victoria Street, Wellington, New Zealand. 1982.

LEXIS, AUSTRALIAN LAW LIBRARY. Mead Data Central, P.O. Box 933, Dayton, Ohio 45401.

LEXIS, NEW ZEALAND LAW LIBRARY. Mead Data Central, P.O. Box 933, Dayton, Ohio 45401.

MEDIA LAW IN AUSTRALIA: A MANUAL. Second Edition. Mark Armstrong, Michael Blakeney and Ray Watterson. Oxford University Press, 200 Madison Avenue, New York, New York 10016. 1988.

MENTAL DISORDER AND CRIMINAL LAW IN AUSTRALIA AND NEW ZEALAND. I.G. Campbell. Butterworths of New Zealand Limited, P.O. Box 472, 205-207 Victoria Street, Wellington, New Zealand. 1988.

M.J.L. RAJANAYAGAM'S THE LAW OF NEGOTIABLE INSTRUMENTS IN AUSTRALIA. Second Edition. M.J.L. Rajanayagam and Brian Conrick. Butterworths Pty. Limited, 271-273 Lane Cove Road, North Ryde, New South Wales 2113 Australia. 1989.

NATURAL RESOURCES LAW IN AUSTRALIA: A MACRO-LEGAL SYSTEM IN OPERATION. D.E. Fisher. Law Book Company Limited, 44-50 Waterloo Road, North Ryde, New South Wales 2113, Australia. 1987.

OUTLINE OF CONTRACT LAW IN AUSTRALIA. J.W. Carter. Butterworths Pty. Limited, 271-273 Lane Cove Road, North Ryde, New South Wales 2113 Australia. 1990.

THE PRACTICE OF THE HIGH COURT AND COURT OF APPEAL OF NEW ZEALAND. Twelfth Edition. Gordon Cain. Butterworths of New Zealand, Limited, P.O. Box 472, 205-207 Victoria Street, Wellington, New Zealand. 1978.

PRINCIPLES OF THE LAW OF PARTNERSHIP. Third Edition. P.R.H. Webb and Anne Webb. Butterworths of New Zealand, Limited, P.O. Box 472, 205-207 Victoria Street, Wellington, New Zealand. 1983.

THE PROCESS OF LAW IN AUSTRALIA: INTERCULTURAL PERSPECTIVES. Greta Bird. Butterworths Pty. Limited, 271-273 Lane Cove Road, North Ryde, New South Wales 2113 Australia. 1988.

PRODUCT LIABILITY IN AUSTRALIA. S.W. Cavanagh and C.S. Phegan. Butterworths Pty. Limited, P.O. Box 345, North Ryde, New South Wales 2113, Australia. 1983.

THE REGULATION OF FOREIGN INVESTMENT IN AUSTRALIA. Michael Sexton and Alexander Adamovich. CCH Australia, Limited, P.O. Box 345, North Ryde, New South Wales 2113, Australia. 1981.

RYAN'S MANUAL OF THE LAW OF INCOME TAX IN AUSTRALIA. Seventh Edition. G.W. O'Grady and K.J. O'Rourke. Law Book Company Limited, 44-50 Waterloo Road, North Ryde, New South Wales 2113, Australia. 1989.

SECURITIES LAW IN NEW ZEALAND: THE TEXT OF THE SECURITIES ACT 1978 AND THE AMENDMENTS AND REGULATIONS WITH ANNOTATIONS. R.P. Darvell and R.S. Clarke. Butterworths of New Zealand, Limited, P.O. Box 472, 205-207 Victoria Street, Wellington, New Zealand. 1983.

TAXATION LAW IN AUSTRALIA. Geoffrey Lehmann and Cynthia Coleman. Butterworths Pty. Limited, 271-273 Lane Cove Road, North Ryde, New South Wales 2113 Australia. 1989.

WILL MAKING AND ADMINISTRATION OF ESTATES: A SHORT GUIDE. J.M. Power. Butterworths Pty. Limited, P.O. Box 345, North Ryde, New South Wales 2113, Australia. 1984.

BOLIVIA

DOING BUSINESS IN BOLIVIA. Price, Waterhouse, New York, New York.

A GUIDE TO THE LAW AND LEGAL LITERATURE OF BOLIVIA. Helen L. Clagett. Gordon Press, P.O. Box 459, Bowling Green Station, New York, New York 10004. 1977.

BRAZIL

LEGAL ASPECTS OF DOING BUSINESS IN LATIN AMERICA: MEXICO, BRAZIL, ARGENTINA, CHILE, AND THE ANDEAN COMMON MARKET COUNTRIES. Practising Law Institute, 810 Seventh Avenue, New York, New York 10019. 1980.

CANADA

ADVOCACY IN CHILD WELFARE CASES: A PRACTITIONER'S GUIDE. William J. Sammon. Carswell Company, 2330 Midland Avenue, Agincourt, Ontario, Canada M1S 1P7. 1985.

THE AGREEMENTS BETWEEN THE UNITED STATES OF AMERICA AND CANADA RELATIVE TO THE TRANS-ALASKA/TRANS-CANADA NATURAL GAS PIPELINE. Leslie E. Lobaugh, Jr. World Peace Through Law Center, 1000 Connecticut Avenue, Northwest, Suite 800, Washington, D.C. 20036. 1981.

THE ANNOTATED IMMIGRATION ACT OF CANADA. Second Edition. Frank N. Marroco and Henry M. Goslett. Carswell Company, 2330 Midland Avenue, Agincourt, Ontario, Canada M1S 1P7. 1982.

AUTHORS AND PUBLISHERS: AGREEMENTS AND LEGAL ASPECTS OF PUBLISHING. Lazar Sarna. Butterworth Company, Limited. 2265 Midland Avenue, Scarborough, Ontario, Canada M1P 4S1. 1980.

BANKRUPTCY LAW IN CANADA. L.W. Houlden and C.H. Morawetz. Carswell Company, 2330 Midland Avenue, Agincourt, Ontario, Canada M1S 1P7. 1984- .

BOUNDARIES AND SURVEYS. David W. Lambden and Izaak de Rijcke. Carswell Company, 2330 Midland Avenue, Agincourt, Ontario, Canada M1S 1P7. 1985.

BROADCASTING LAW IN CANADA: FAIRNESS IN THE ADMINISTRATIVE PROCESS. Donna Soble Kaufman. Carswell Company, 2330 Midland Avenue, Agincourt, Ontario, Canada M1S 1P7. 1987.

CANADA CORPORATION MANUAL. R.A. Kingston, Editor. Richard DeBoo, Ltd., 51 Wellington Street, Toronto, Ontario, Canada M5T 1H2. 1965- .

CANADA-U.S. REPORT ON FREE TRADE. American Banker -- Bond Buyer Newsletter Division, P.O. Box 30240, Bethesda, Maryland 20814. Weekly.

CANADIAN BUILDING CONTRACTS. Third Edition. Immanuel Goldsmith. Carswell Company, 2330 Midland Avenue, Agincourt, Ontario, Canada M1S 1P7. 1983.

CANADIAN BUSINESS CORPORATIONS ACT AND REGULATION, 1984. Seventh Edition. Richard DeBoo, Ltd., 51 Wellington Street, Toronto, Ontario, Canada M5T 1H2. 1984.

THE CANADIAN CHARTER OF RIGHTS, ANNOTATED. John B. Laskin and others, Editors. Canada Law Book, Incorporated, 240 Edward Street, Aurora, Ontario, Canada L4G 3S9. 1986- .

CANADIAN FOREIGN INVESTMENT CONTROLS. Third Edition. J.A. Langford. CCH Canadian Ltd., 6 Garamond Court, Don Mills, Ontario, Canada M3C 1Z5. 1983.

CANADIAN FORMS OF WILLS. Fourth Edition. Terence Sheard, Rodney Hull and Michael M.K. Fitzpatrick. Carswell Company, 2330 Midland Avenue, Agincourt, Ontario, Canada M1S 1P7. 1982.

CANADIAN FRANCHISE GUIDE. Jerry White and Frank Zaid, Editors. Richard DeBoo, Ltd., 51 Wellington Street, Toronto, Ontario, Canada M5T 1H2. 1983- .

CANADIAN INCOME TAXATION OF TRUSTS. Second Edition. Lloyd F. Raphael. CCH Canadian Ltd., 6 Garamond Court, Don Mills, Ontario, Canada M3C 1Z5. 1982.

CANADIAN LEGAL AND LEGISLATIVE BENEFITS REPORTER. International Foundation of Employee Benefit Plans, P.O. Box 69, Brookfield, Wisconsin 53008-0069. Bimonthly.

THE CANADIAN LEGAL SYSTEM. Second Edition. Gerald L. Gall. Carswell Company, 2330 Midland Avenue, Agincourt, Ontario, Canada M1S 1P7. 1983.

CANADIAN MUNICIPAL AND PLANNING LAW. Stanley M. Makuch. Carswell Company, 2330 Midland Avenue, Agincourt, Ontario, Canada M1S 1P7. 1983.

CANADIAN TAX TREATMENT OF LOSSES. D. Bernard Morris and Janice McCart. CCH Canadian Ltd., 6 Garamond Court, Don Mills, Ontario, Canada M3C 1Z5. 1983.

CANADIAN TRADE MARKS ACT, ANNOTATED. Hughes G. Richard. Richard DeBoo, Ltd., 51 Wellington Street, Toronto, Ontario, Canada M5T 1H2. 1984. (Semiannual Supplements).

CHILD PROTECTION LAW IN CANADA. Marvin M. Bernstein. Carswell Company, 2330 Midland Avenue, Agincourt, Ontario, Canada M1S 1P7. 1990.

THE CHILD WELFARE ACT ANNOTATED. Michael D. Hartrick and Yan Arthur M. Lazor. Carswell Company, 2330 Midland Avenue, Agincourt, Ontario, Canada M1S 1P7. 1983.

COMPETITION LAW OF CANADA Gordon Kaiser and Julian O. von Kalinowski. Matthew Bender and Company, Incorporated, 11 Penn Plaza, New York, New York 10001. 1988- .

COHABITATION: THE LAW IN CANADA. Winifred H. Holland and Barbro E. Stalbecker-Pountney. Carswell Company, 2330 Midland Avenue, Agincourt, Ontario, Canada M1S 1P7. 1990.

COMPUTER TECHNOLOGY AND THE LAW IN CANADA. J. Fraser Mann. Carswell Company, 2330 Midland Avenue, Agincourt, Ontario, Canada M1S 1P7. 1987

CONSTRUCTION AND MECHANICS' LIENS IN CANADA. Fifth Edition. Douglas N. Macklem and David I. Bristow. Carswell Company, 2330 Midland Avenue, Agincourt, Ontario, Canada M1S 1P7. 1985.

CORPORATE TAXATION. Kathleen A. Lahey. Emond-Montgomery Publications, Limited, 80 Gerrard Street, East, Toronto, Ontario, Canada M5B 1G6. 1984.

CREDITOR-DEBTOR LAW IN CANADA. C.R.B. Dunlop. Carswell Company, 2330 Midland Avenue, Agincourt, Ontario, Canada M1S 1P7. 1981.

DIGESTS OF THE LAWS OF CANADA (FEDERAL) AND THE PROVINCES. Martindale-Hubbell Law Directory, Volume Eight. Martindale-Hubbell, Incorporated, P.O. Box 1001, Summit, New Jersey 07902-1001. Annual.

DRUG OFFENSES IN CANADA. Second Edition. Bruce A. MacFarlane. Canada Law Book, Incorporated, 240 Edward Street, Aurora, Ontario, Canada L4G 3S9. 1986.

EDUCATION LAW IN CANADA. A. Wayne MacKay. Emond-Montgomery Publications, 80 Gerrard Street, East, Toronto, Ontario, Canada M5B 1G6. 1984.

FEDERAL EMPLOYMENT LAW IN CANADA. M. Norman Grosman. Carswell Company, 2330 Midland Avenue, Agincourt, Ontario, Canada M1S 1P7. 1990.

FRASER'S HANDBOOK ON CANADIAN COMPANY LAW. Seventh Edition. H. Sutherland, D.B. Horsley and J.M. Edmiston, Editors. Carswell Company, 2330 Midland Avenue, Agincourt, Ontario, Canada M1S 1P7. 1985.

GOLDSMITH'S DAMAGES FOR PERSONAL INJURY AND DEATH IN CANADA. Robert C. Stonehouse, Editor. Carswell Company, 2330 Midland Avenue, Agincourt, Ontario, Canada M1S 1P7. 1985.

INJUNCTIONS: A PRACTICAL HANDBOOK. David Stockwood. Carswell Company, 2330 Midland Avenue, Agincourt, Ontario, Canada M1S 1P7. 1985.

INSURANCE LAW IN CANADA: A TREATISE ON THE PRINCIPLES OF INDEMNITY INSURANCE AS APPLIED IN THE COMMON LAW PROVINCES OF CANADA. Craig Brown and Julio Menezes. Carswell Company, 2330 Midland Avenue, Agincourt, Ontario, Canada M1S 1P7. 1982.

AN INTRODUCTION TO INTERNATIONAL LAW: CHIEFLY AS INTERPRETED AND APPLIED IN CANADA. Second Edition. S.A. Williams and A.L.C. de Mestral. Butterworths, 75 Clegg Road, Markham, Ontario, Canada L3R 9Y6. 1987.

LABOUR LAW AND INDUSTRIAL RELATIONS IN CANADA. Third Edition. H.W. Arthurs. Kluwer Academic Publishers, 101 Philip Drive, Assinippi Park, Norwell, Massachusetts 02061. 1988.

LABOUR LEGISLATION IN CANADA: A BIBLIOGRAPHY. Marian Dworaczek. Vance Bibliographies, P.O. Box 229, 112 North Charter Street, Monticello, Illinois 61856. 1989.

THE LAW AND MEDICINE IN CANADA. Second Edition. Gilbert Sharpe. Butterworths, 75 Clegg Road, Markham, Ontario, Canada L3R 9Y6. 1987.

LAW FOR SOCIAL WORKERS: A CANADIAN GUIDE. Elaine J. Vadya and Mary T. Satterfield. Carswell Company, 2330 Midland Avenue, Agincourt, Ontario, Canada M1S 1P7. 1984.

LAW LIBRARIES IN CANADA: ESSAYS TO HONOUR DIANA M. PRIESTLY. Diana M. Priestly and Joan N. Fraser. Carswell Company, 2330 Midland Avenue, Agincourt, Ontario, Canada M1S 1P7. 1988.

THE LAW OF CONTRACTS. Second Edition. S.M. Waddams. Canada Law Book, Incorporated, 240 Edward Street, Aurora, Ontario, Canada L4G 3S9. 1984.

THE LAW OF DAMAGES. S.M. Waddams. Canada Law Book, Incorporated, 240 Edward Street, Aurora, Ontario, Canada L4G 3S9. 1983.

THE LAW OF DEFAMATION IN CANADA. Raymond E. Brown. Carswell Company, 2330 Midland Avenue, Agincourt, Ontario, Canada M1S 1P7. 1987.

THE LAW OF DISMISSAL IN CANADA. Howard A. Levitt. Canada Law Book, Incorporated, 240 Edward Street, Aurora, Ontario, Canada L4G 3S9. 1985.

THE LAW OF LIBEL AND SLANDER IN CANADA. Second Edition. Jeremy S. Williams. Butterworths, 75 Clegg Road, Markham, Ontario, Canada L3R 9Y6. 1988.

THE LAW OF TORTS IN CANADA. G.H.L. Fridman. Carswell Company, 2330 Midland Avenue, Agincourt, Ontario, Canada M1S 1P7. 1989- .

LAW OF TRUSTS IN CANADA. Second Edition. D.W.M. Waters. Carswell Company, 2330 Midland Avenue, Agincourt, Ontario, Canada M1S 1P7. 1984.

THE LAW OF VENDOR AND PURCHASER: THE LAW AND PRACTICE RELATING TO CONTRACTS FOR SALE OF LAND IN THE COMMON LAW PROVINCES OF CANADA. Third Edition. J. Victor Di Castri. Carswell Company, 2330 Midland Avenue, Agincourt, Ontario, Canada M1S 1P7. 1988- .

LEGAL AID IN CANADA. Dieter Hoehne. Edwin Mellen Press, P.O. Box 450, Lewiston, New York 14092. 1989.

LEGAL ASPECTS OF DOING BUSINESS IN CANADA. Barry M. Fisher, Chairman. Practising Law Institute, 810 Seventh Avenue, New York, New York 10019. 1983.

LEGAL ASPECTS OF DOING BUSINESS IN NORTH AMERICA AND CANADA. Dennis Campbell. Kluwer Law and Taxation Publishers, Boston, Massachusetts. 1987.

LEGAL LIABILITY OF DOCTORS AND HOSPITALS IN CANADA. Second Edition. Ellen I. Picard. Carswell Company, 2330 Midland Avenue, Agincourt, Ontario, Canada M1S 1P7. 1984.

LEGAL RIGHTS IN THE CANADIAN CHARTER OF RIGHTS AND FREEDOMS: A MANUAL OF ISSUES AND SOURCES. David C. McDonald. Carswell Legal Publications, 2330 Midland Avenue, Agincourt, Ontario, Canada M1S 1P7. 1982.

MARINE INSURANCE LAW OF CANADA. Rui M. Fernandes. Butterworths, 75 Clegg Road, Markham, Ontario, Canada L3R 9Y6. 1987.

MENTAL DISABILITY AND THE LAW IN CANADA. Gerald B. Robertson. Carswell Company, 2330 Midland Avenue, Agincourt, Ontario, Canada M1S 1P7. 1987.

MENTAL HEALTH LAW IN CANADA. Harvey Savage and Carla McKague. Butterworths, 75 Clegg Road, Markham, Ontario, Canada L3R 9Y6. 1987.

MIGRATION-CANADA: A GUIDE TO TAX, LEGAL AND OTHER IMPLICATIONS OF COMING TO, INVESTING IN, AND LEAVING CANADA. H. Arnold Sherman and Jeffrey D. Sherman. Kluwer Law Book Publishers, Incorporated, 36 West Forty-Fourth Street, New York, New York 10036. 1985.

MUSICIANS AND THE LAW IN CANADA. Paul Sanderson. Carswell Company, 2330 Midland Avenue, Agincourt, Ontario, Canada M1S 1P7. 1985.

OIL AND GAS LAW IN CANADA. Alastair R. Lucas and Constance D. Hunt. Carswell Company, 2330 Midland Avenue, Agincourt, Ontario, Canada M1S 1P7. 1990.

RESTITUTION. G.H.L. Freeman and James G. McLeod. Carswell Company, 2330 Midland Avenue, Agincourt, Ontario, Canada M1S 1P7. 1982.

SEARCH AND SEIZURE IN CANADA. Winston McCalla. Canada Law Book, Incorporated, 240 Edward Street, Aurora, Ontario, Canada L4G 3S9. 1984.

SEARCH AND SEIZURE LAW IN CANADA. Scott C. Hutchison and James C. Morton. Carswell Company, 2330 Midland Avenue, Agincourt, Ontario, Canada M1S 1P7. 1991.

SPORTS AND THE LAW IN CANADA. Second Edition. John Barnes. Butterworths, 75 Clegg Road, Markham, Ontario, Canada L3R 9Y6. 1988.

THE SUPREME COURT OF CANADA HANDBOOK ON ASSESSMENT OF DAMAGES IN PERSONAL INJURY CASES. W.H.R. Charles. Carswell Company, 2330 Midland Avenue, Agincourt, Ontario, Canada M1S 1P7. 1982.

TAXATION OF FLUCTUATION INCOMES IN CANADA. Fourth Edition. Vladimir Salyzyn. CCH Canadian Ltd., 6 Garamond Court, Don Mills, Ontario, Canada M3C 1Z5. 1984.

UNITED STATES-CANADA FREE-TRADE ACT: A LEGISLATIVE HISTORY OF THE UNITED STATES-CANADA FREE-TRADE AGREEMENT IMPLEMENTATION ACT OF 1988, PUBLIC LAW 100-449. Bernard D. Reams, Jr. and Mary Ann Nelson. William S. Hein and Company, 1285 Main Street, Buffalo, New York 14209. 1990.

THE UNITED STATES/CANADA TRADE AGREEMENT. Judith Hippler Bello and Homer E. Moyer, Jr. Practising Law Institute, 810 Seventh Avenue, New York, New York 10019. 1989.

USING A LAW LIBRARY: A GUIDE FOR STUDENTS AND LAWYERS IN THE COMMON LAW PROVINCES OF CANADA. Margaret A. Banks. Carswell Company, 2330 Midland Avenue, Agincourt, Ontario, Canada M1S 1P7. 1985.

WILLIAMS AND RHODES CANADIAN LAW OF LANDLORD AND TENANT. Fifth Edition. F.W. Rhodes and Marc Casavant. Carswell Company, 2330 Midland Avenue, Agincourt, Ontario, Canada M1S 1P7. 1983.

WILSON: CHILDREN AND THE LAW. Second Edition. Jeffrey Wilson and Mary Tomlinson. Butterworth Company, Limited. 2265 Midland Avenue, Scarborough, Ontario, Canada M1P 4S1. 1986.

CHINA

BASIC PRINCIPLES OF CIVIL LAW IN CHINA. William C. Jones. M.E. Sharpe, Incorporated, 80 Business Park Drive, Armonk, New York 10504. 1989.

CHINA TRADE AGREEMENTS. Second Edition. Thomas C.W. Chiu. Taylor and Francis, Incorporated, 1990 Frost Road, Suite 101, Bristol, Pennsylvania 19007. 1988.

CHINA TRADE DOCUMENTS. Second Edition. Thomas C.W. Chiu. Taylor and Francis, Incorporated, 1990 Frost Road, Suite 101, Bristol, Pennsylvania 19007. 1988.

CHINA TRADE LAW: CODE OF THE FOREIGN TRADE LAW OF THE PEOPLE'S REPUBLIC OF CHINA. Francois De Bauw and Bernard Dewit. Bruylant, Kluwer Academic Publications, 101 Philip Drive, Assinippi Park, Norwell, Massachusetts 02061. 1982.

CHINA'S CIVIL AND COMMERCIAL LAW. Henry R. Zheng. Butterworth Legal Publishers, 90 Stiles Road, Salem, New Hampshire 03079. 1988.

CHINA'S INVESTMENT LAWS: NEW DIRECTIONS. Guiguo Wang. Butterworth and Company (Asia) Pte. Limited, 30 Robinson Road, 12-01 Tuan Sing Towers, Singapore 0104. 1988.

CHINA'S PRACTICE IN THE LAW OF THE SEA. Jeanette Greenfield. Clarendon Press, Oxford, England. 1992.

CHINESE INTELLECTUAL PROPERTY AND TECHNOLOGY TRANSFER LAW. Zheng Chengsi and Michael D. Pendleton. Sweet and Maxwell Limited, South Quay Plaza, 183 Marsh Wall, London E14 9FT, England. 1987.

CONSUMER PROTECTION IN CHINA: TRANSLATIONS, DEVELOPMENTS, AND RECOMMENDATIONS. Donald B. King and Gao Tong. Fred B. Rothman and Company, 10368 West Centennial Road, Littleton, Colorado 80127. 1991.

CONTROL OF PUBLISHING IN CHINA: PAST AND PRESENT. Chan Hok-lam. Australian National University Press, P.O. Box 1365, New York, New York 10023. 1983.

THE CRIMINAL LAW AND THE CRIMINAL PROCEDURE LAW OF THE PEOPLE'S REPUBLIC OF CHINA. Foreign Languages Press, China Books and Periodicals, Incorporated, 2929 Twenty-fourth Street, San Francisco, California 94110. 1984.

DOING BUSINESS IN CHINA: PEOPLE'S REPUBLIC OF CHINA. William P. Streng and Allen D. Wilcox. Matthew Bender and Company, Incorporated, 11 Penn Plaza, New York, New York 10001. 1990- .

ENVIRONMENTAL LAW AND POLICY IN THE PEOPLE'S REPUBLIC OF CHINA. Lester Ross and Mitchell A. Silk. Quorum Books, Greenwood Publishing Group, Incorporated, 88 Post Road West, P.O. Box 5007, Westport, Connecticut 06881. 1987.

FOREIGN TRADE, INVESTMENT, AND THE LAW IN THE PEOPLE'S REPUBLIC OF CHINA. Second Edition. Michael J. Moser and Jesse T.H. Chang. Oxford University Press, Incorporated, 200 Madison Avenue, New York, New York 10016. 1987.

A GUIDE TO THE LAWS, REGULATIONS, AND POLICIES OF THE PEOPLE'S REPUBLIC OF CHINA ON FOREIGN TRADE AND INVESTMENT. James L. Kenworthy. William S. Hein and Company, 1285 Main Street, Buffalo, New York 14209. 1989.

GUIDE TO THE PATENT LAW OF THE PEOPLE'S REPUBLIC OF CHINA. Philip Gladwin. Graham and Trotman, 13 Park Avenue, Gaithersburg, Maryland 20877. 1985.

INTELLECTUAL PROPERTY LAW IN THE PEOPLE'S REPUBLIC OF CHINA: A GUIDE TO PATENTS, TRADEMARKS AND TECHNOLOGY TRANSFER. Michael D. Pendleton. Butterworth and Company, 30 Robinson Road, 12-01 Tuan Sing Towers, Singapore 0104. 1986.

LABOR LAW IN CHINA: CHOICE AND RESPONSIBILTY. Hilary K. Josephs. Butterworth Legal Publishers, 90 Stiles Road, Salem, New Hampshire 03079. 1990.

LAW AND BUSINESS PRACTICE IN SHANGHAI. Ellen R. Eliasoph. Longman Publishing Group, 95 Church Street, White Plains, New York 10601. 1987.

LAW IN THE PEOPLE'S REPUBLIC OF CHINA: COMMENTARY, READINGS, AND MATERIALS. Ralph H. Folsom and John H. Minan. Martinus Nijhoff, Kluwer Academic Publishers, 101 Philip Drive, Assinippi Park, Norwell, Massachusetts 02061. 1989.

LEGAL ASPECTS OF DOING BUSINESS IN CHINA, 1983. Jerome A. Cohen, Chairman. Practising Law Institute, 810 Seventh Avenue, New York, New York 10019. 1983.

THE LEGAL SYSTEM AND CRIMINAL RESPONSIBILITY OF INTELLECTUALS IN THE PEOPLE'S REPUBLIC OF CHINA, 1949-1982. Carlos Wing-hung Lo. School of Law, University of Maryland, 20 North Paca Street, Baltimore, Maryland 21201. 1985. Occasional Papers.

THE LEGAL SYSTEM OF THE PEOPLE'S REPUBLIC OF CHINA: SELECTED MATERIALS IN ENGLISH. Tim J. Watts. Vance Bibliographies, P.O. Box 229, 112 North Charter Street, Monticello, Illinois 61856. 1988.

PRC LAWS FOR CHINA TRADERS AND INVESTORS. C.W. Chiu. Taylor and Francis, Incorporated, 79 Madison Avenue, Suite 1106, New York, New York 10016. 1988.

TAXATION OF FOREIGN INVESTMENT IN THE PEOPLE'S REPUBLIC OF CHINA. A.J. Easson and Li Jinyan. Kluwer Academic Publishers, 101 Philip Drive, Assinippi Park, Norwell, Massachusetts 02061. 1989.

TECHNOLOGY TRANSFER IN THE PEOPLE'S REPUBLIC OF CHINA: LAW AND PRACTICE. Richard J. Goossen. Martinus Nijhoff, Kluwer Academic Publishers, 101 Philip Drive, Assinippi Park, Norwell, Massachusetts 02061. 1987.

TRADE AND INVESTMENT OPPORTUNITIES IN CHINA: THE CURRENT COMMERCIAL AND LEGAL FRAMEWORK. Danian Zhang, Milton R. Larson and Dong Shizhong. Quorum Books, Greenwood Publishing Group, Incorporated, 88 Post Road West, P.O. Box 5007, Westport, Connecticut 06881. 1992.

EASTERN EUROPE

A CALENDAR OF SOVIET TREATIES, 1974-1980. George Ginsburgs, editor. Martinus Nijhoff, Kluwer Academic Publishers, 101 Philip Drive, Assinippi Park, Norwell, Massachusetts 02061. 1987.

COMMENTARY ON THE CZECHOSLOVAK CIVIL CODE. Theodor Jan Vondracek. Martinus Nijhoff, Kluwer Academic Publishers, 101 Philip Drive, Assinippi Park, Norwell, Massachusetts 02061. 1988.

THE IMPACT OF PERESTROIKA ON SOVIET LAW. Albert J. Schmidt, editor. Martinus Nijhoff, Kluwer Academic Publishers, 101 Philip Drive, Assinippi Park, Norwell, Massachusetts 02061. 1990.

JOINT VENTURES AND PRIVATIZATION IN EASTERN EUROPE. Monte E. Wetzler. Practising Law Institute, 810 Seventh Avenue, New York, New York 10019. 1991.

LAW AND THE GORBACHEV ERA: ESSAYS IN HONOR OF DIETRICH ANDRE LOEBER. Donald D. Barry, Georg Brunner, F.J.M. Feldbrugge and George Ginsburgs, editors. Martinus Nijhoff, Kluwer Academic Publishers, 101 Philip Drive, Assinippi Park, Norwell, Massachusetts 02061. 1988.

LEGAL ASPECTS OF TRADE AND INVESTMENT IN THE SOVIET UNION AND EASTERN EUROPE, 1990. Eugene Theroux. Practising Law Institute, 810 Seventh Avenue, New York, New York 10019. 1990.

THE POLITICAL AND LEGAL FRAMEWORK OF TRADE RELATIONS BETWEEN THE EUROPEAN COMMUNITY AND EASTERN EUROPE. Marc Maresceau, editor. Martinus Nijhoff, Kluwer Academic Publishers, 101 Philip Drive, Assinippi Park, Norwell, Massachusetts 02061. 1989.

PRIVATE INTERNATIONAL LAW: THE SOVIET APPROACH. M.M. Boguslavskii. Martinus Nijhoff, Kluwer Academic Publishers, 101 Philip Drive, Assinippi Park, Norwell, Massachusetts 02061. 1988.

SOVIET ADMINISTRATIVE LAW: THEORY AND POLICY. George Ginsburgs, Gianmaria Ajani, Ger P. Van den Berg and William B. Simons, editors. Martinus Nijhoff, Kluwer Academic Publishers, 101 Philip Drive, Assinippi Park, Norwell, Massachusetts 02061. 1989.

SOVIET CIVIL LAW. Olimpiad S. Ioffe. Martinus Nijhoff, Kluwer Academic Publishers, 101 Philip Drive, Assinippi Park, Norwell, Massachusetts 02061. 1988.

THE SOVIET ECONOMIC SYSTEM: A LEGAL ANALYSIS. Olimpiad S. Ioffe and Peter B. Maggs. Westview Press, Incorporated, 5500 Central Avenue, Boulder, Colorado 80301. 1987.

SOVIET LAW AND ECONOMY. Olimpiad S. Ioffe and Mark W. Janis, editors. Martinus Nijhoff, Kluwer Academic Publishers, 101 Philip Drive, Assinippi Park, Norwell, Massachusetts 02061. 1987.

THE SOVIET UNION AND INTERNATIONAL COOPERATION IN LEGAL MATTERS. George Ginsburgs and William B. Simons. Martinus Nijhoff, Kluwer Academic Publishers, 101 Philip Drive, Assinippi Park, Norwell, Massachusetts 02061. 1988- .

EGYPT

BUSINESS LAW IN EGYPT. Michael H. Davis. Kluwer Law Book Publishers, Incorporated, 36 West Forty-fourth Street, New York, New York 10036. 1983.

BUSINESS LAWS OF EGYPT. Translated from Arabic to English by Nicola H. Karam. Graham and Trotham, Incorporated, 13 Park Avenue, Gaithersburg, Maryland 20877. 1985- .

EUROPE

THE ABC OF COMMUNITY LAW. Second Edition. Klaus-Dieter Borchardt. Office for Official Publications of the European Communities, Commission of the European Communities, 2100 M Street, Northwest, Suite 707, Washington, D. C. 20037. 1986.

ANTIDUMPING LAW AND PRACTICE IN THE UNITED STATES AND THE EUROPEAN COMMUNITIES: A COMPARATIVE ANALYSIS. Edwin A. Vermulst. Elsevier Science Publishing Company, P.O. Box 882, Madison Square Station, New York, New York 10159. 1987.

ATLANTIC TRADE REPORT. King Publishing Group, 627 National Press Building, Washington, D.C. 20045. Semimonthly.

BANKING IN EUROPE: THE SINGLE MARKET. Rob Dixon. Routledge, Chapman & Hall, 29 West Thirty-fifth Street, New York, New York 10001. 1991.

BASIC COMMUNITY CASES. Bernard Rudden, editor. Clarendon Press, Oxford, Oxfordshire, England. 1987.

BASIC COMMUNITY LAWS. Second Edition. Bernard Rudden and Derrick Wyatt, Editors. Clarendon Press, Oxford University Press, 200 Madison Avenue, New York, New York 10016. 1986.

COMMERCIAL AGENCY AND DISTRIBUTION AGREEMENTS: LAW AND PRACTICE IN THE MEMBER STATES OF THE EUROPEAN COMMUNITY. Guy-Martial Weijer, editor. Graham and Trotman Limited, Sterling House, 66 Wilton Road, London SW1V 1DE, England. 1989.

COMMON MARKET LAW OF COMPETITION. Third Edition. Christopher Bellamy and Graham D. Child. Sweet and Maxwell Limited, South Quay Plaza, 183 Marsh Wall, London E14 9FT, England. 1987.

COMPANY LAW IN THE UNITED KINGDOM AND THE EUROPEAN COMMUNITY: ITS HARMONIZATION AND UNIFICATION. Frank Wooldridge. Athlone Press, Atlantic Highlands, New Jersey. 1991.

COMPETITION LAW OF THE EUROPEAN ECONOMIC COMMUNITY. Ivo Van Bael and Jean-Francois Bellis. Matthew Bender and Company, Incorporated, 11 Penn Plaza, New York, New York 10001. 1988- .

COMPLETING THE INTERNAL MARKET OF THE EUROPEAN COMMUNITY: 1992 HANDBOOK. Mark Brealey and Conor Quigley. Graham and Trotman Limited, Sterling House, 66 Wilton Road, London SW1V 1DE, England. 1989.

CONFLICT OF LAWS AND EUROPEAN COMMUNITY LAW: WITH SPECIAL REFERENCE TO THE COMMUNITY CONVENTIONS ON PRIVATE INTERNATIONAL LAW. Ian F. Fletcher. Elsevier Science Publishing Company, P.O. Box 882, Madison Square Station, New York, New York 10159. 1982.

CORPORATE TAXATION IN EC COUNTRIES, 1990-91. Jean-Marc Tirard. Longman Group UK Limited, Longman House, Burnt Mill, Harlow, Essex CM20 2JE, England. 1990.

THE CREATION OF A EUROPEAN BANKING SYSTEM: A STUDY OF ITS LEGAL AND TECHNICAL ASPECTS. Richard Cordero. Peter Lang Publishing, Incorporated, 62 West Forty-fifth Street, New York, New York 10036. 1990.

CROSSLAND'S EUROPEAN ENVIRONMENTAL BULLETIN. International Environment Group, 184 Amherst Street, P.O. Box 524, Amherst, New Hampshire 03031. Semimonthly.

THE CUSTOMS LAW OF THE EUROPEAN ECONOMIC COMMUNITY. Second Edition. D. Lasok. Kluwer Academic Publishers, 101 Philip Drive, Assinippi Park, Norwell, Massachusetts 02061. 1990.

THE DIRECT INVESTMENT TAX INITIATIVES OF THE EUROPEAN COMMUNITY. Fred C. de Hosson, editor. Martinus Nijhoff, Kluwer Academic Publishers, 101 Philip Drive, Assinippi Park, Norwell, Massachusetts 02061. 1990.

DIRECT PROTECTION OF INNOVATION. William Kingston, editor. Kluwer Academic Publishers, 101 Philip Drive, Assinippi Park, Norwell, Massachusetts 02061. 1987.

EASTERN EUROPEAN BUSINESS MONITOR. I.A. Ernst and Company, Incorporated, 5328 Saratoga Avenue, Chevy Chase, Maryland 20815. Monthly.

EC BANKING LAWYER. American Banker -- Bond Buyer Newsletter Division, P.O. Box 30240, Bethesda, Maryland 20814. Weekly.

EEC COMPETITION LAW. D.G. Goyder. Oxford University Press, 200 Madison Avenue, New York, New York 10016. 1988.

EEC DIRECTIVES ON COMPANY LAW AND FINANCIAL MARKETS. D.D. Prentice, editor. Oxford University Press, 200 Madison Avenue, New York, New York 10016. 1991.

EEC FISHERIES LAW. R.R. Churchill. Martinus Nijhoff, Kluwer Academic Publishers, 101 Philip Drive, Assinippi Park, Norwell, Massachusetts 02061. 1987.

EEC LEGISLATION AND AGREEMENTS: THE TEXTS OF LEADING REGULATIONS, DIRECTIVES, AND INTERNATIONAL AGREEMENTS. Gabriel M. Wilner and Kent S. Karlsson, editors. Transnational Publishers, P.O. Box 7282, Ardsley-on-Hudson, New York 10503. 1992.

EEC TREATY AND ENVIRONMENTAL PROTECTION. Ludwig Kramer. Sweet and Maxwell Limited, South Quay Plaza, 183 Marsh Wall, London E14 9FT, England. 1990.

ENCYCLOPEDIA OF EUROPEAN COMMUNITY LAW. K.R. Simmonds, Editor. Sweet and Maxwell, Matthew Bender and Company, Incorporated, 11 Penn Plaza, New York, New York 10001. 1973- .

EUROMEDIA REGULATION. Paul Kegan Associates, Incorporated, 126 Clock Tower Place, Carmel, California 93929. Monthly.

EUROPE 1992: LAW AND STRATEGY. Leader Publications, 111 Eighth Avenue, New York, New York 10011. Monthly.

EUROPE 1992: THE REPORT ON THE SINGLE EUROPEAN MARKET. Lafayette Publications, Incorporated, 1701 K Street, Northwest, Suite 805, Washington, D.C. 20006. Semimonthly.

EUROPE WITHOUT FRONTIERS: A LAWYER'S GUIDE. Audrey Winter. Bureau of National Affairs, Incorporated, 1231 Twenty-fifth Street, Northwest, Washington, D.C. 20037. 1989.

EUROPEAN AIR LAW: TEXTS AND DOCUMENTS. Elmar Giemulla and Ronald Schmid, editors. Kluwer Academic Publishers, 101 Philip Drive, Assinippi Park, Norwell, Massachusetts 02061. 1992.

EUROPEAN BANKING IN THE 1990S. Jean Dermine, editor. Blackwell Scientific Publications, Incorporated, 3 Cambridge Center, Cambridge, Massachusetts 02142. 1990.

EUROPEAN BANKING LAW: AN ANALYSIS OF COMMUNITY AND MEMBER STATE LEGISLATION. Stanley Crossick and Margie Lindsay. Financial Times Business Information, Financial Times, Limited, Minister House, Arthur Street, London EC4R 9AX, England. 1983.

EUROPEAN BUSINESS LAW: LEGAL AND ECONOMIC ANALYSES ON INTEGRATION AND HARMONIZATION. Richard M. Buxbaum and Marina Hertig, editors. Walter de Gruyter, Incorporated, 200 Saw Mill Road, Hawthorne, New York 10532. 1991.

EUROPEAN COMMUNITY LAW: A GUIDE TO COMMUNITY AND MEMBER STATE LEGISLATION. Belmont Community Law Office. Financial Times Business Information, Financial Times, Limited, Minister House, Arthur Street, London EC4R 9AX, England. 1986.

EUROPEAN COMMUNITY LAW IN A NUTSHELL. Ralph H. Folsom and Ralph Haughwout. West Publishing Company, 50 West Kellogg Boulevard, St. Paul, Minnesota 55164. 1992.

EUROPEAN COMMUNITY SEX EQUALITY LAW. Evelyn Ellis. Oxford University Press, 200 Madison Avenue, New York, New York 10016. 1991.

EUROPEAN COMPANY AND FINANCIAL LAW: EUROPEAN COMMUNITY LAW-TEXT COLLECTION. Klaus J. Hopt and Eddy Wymeersch, editors. Walter de Gruyter, Incorporated, 200 Saw Mill Road, Hawthorne, New York 10532. 1991.

EUROPEAN COMPANY LAWS: A COMPARATIVE APPROACH. Robert R. Drury and Peter G. Xuereb, editors. Dartmouth, Brookfield, Vermont. 1991.

THE EUROPEAN ECONOMIC COMMUNITY: PRODUCTS LIABILITY RULES AND ENVIRONMENTAL POLICY. Patrick E. Thieffry and G. Marc Whitehead. Practising Law Institute, 810 Seventh Avenue, New York, New York 10019. 1990.

EUROPEAN INTERNAL MARKET POLICY. Kevin Featherstone. Routledge, Chapman & Hall, 29 West Thirty-fifth Street, New York, New York 10001. 1990.

EUROPEAN LEGAL LITERATURE INFORMATION SERVICE. European Law Centre, 4 Bloomsbury Square, London WC1A 2RL, England. Ten issues yearly with annual accumulations.

EXPLOITING THE INTERNAL MARKET: CO-OPERATION AND COMPETITION TOWARD 1992. P.J. Slot and M.H. van der Woude, editors. Kluwer Academic Publishers, 101 Philip Drive, Assinippi Park, Norwell, Massachusetts 02061. 1988.

THE FOUNDATIONS OF EUROPEAN COMMUNITY LAW: AN INTRODUCTION TO THE CONSTITUTIONAL AND ADMINISTRATIVE LAW OF THE EUROPEAN COMMUNITY. Second Edition. T.C. Hartley. Clarendon Press, Oxford University Press, 200 Madison Avenue, New York, New York 10016. 1988.

FREE TRADE AND COMPETITION IN THE EEC: LAW, POLICY, AND PRACTICE. Helen Papaconstantinou. Routledge, Chapman & Hall, 29 West Thirty-fifth Street, New York, New York 10001. 1988.

GENDER DISCRIMINATION LAW OF THE EUROPEAN COMMUNITY. Sacha Prechal and Noreen Burrows. Gower Publishing Company, Old Post Road, Brookfield, Vermont 05036. 1990.

THE GENERAL PRINCIPLES OF EEC LAW AND THE INDIVIDUAL. Anthony Arnull. St. Martin's Press, 175 Fifth Avenue, New York, New York 10010. 1990.

GERMAIN'S TRANSNATIONAL LAW RESEARCH: A GUIDE FOR ATTORNEYS. Claire M. Germain. Transnational Publishers, P.O. Box 7282, Ardsley-on-Hudson, New York 10503. 1991- .

A GUIDE TO UNITED KINGDOM AND EUROPEAN COMMUNITY COMPETITION POLICY. Nick Gardner. St. Martin's Press, 175 Fifth Avenue, New York, New York 10010. 1990.

GUIDE TO VAT IN EUROPE. Price Waterhouse, Graham and Trotman Limited, Sterling House, 66 Wilton Road, London SW1V 1DE, England. 1989.

HANDBOOK ON EUROPEAN EMPLOYEE CO-MANAGEMENT. Walter Kolvenbach and Peter Hanau. Kluwer Academic Publishers, 101 Philip Drive, Assinippi Park, Norwell, Massachusetts 02061. 1987- .

HARMONIZATION OF LAWS IN THE EUROPEAN COMMUNITIES: PRODUCTS LIABILITY, CONFLICT OF LAWS, AND CORPORATION LAW: [PROCEEDINGS OF THE] FIFTH SOKOL COLLOQUIUM. Peter E. Herzog, Editor. University Press of Virginia, P.O. Box 3608, University Station, Charlottesville, Virginia 22903. 1983.

HUMAN RIGHTS AND EUROPEAN POLITICS: THE LEGAL-POLITICAL STATUS OF WORKERS IN THE EUROPEAN COMMUNITY. Fritz Fabricius. St. Martin's Press, 175 Fifth Avenue, New York, New York 10010. 1992.

INSIDE INFORMATION AND SECURITIES TRADING: A LEGAL AND ECONOMIC ANALYSIS OF THE FOUNDATIONS OF LIABILITY IN THE U.S.A. AND THE EUROPEAN COMMUNITY. Bernhard Bergmans. Kluwer Academic Publishers, 101 Philip Drive, Assinippi Park, Norwell, Massachusetts 02061. 1991.

AN INTRODUCTION TO THE LAW AND INSTITUTIONS OF THE EUROPEAN COMMUNITIES. D. Lasok and J.W. Bridge. Butterworth Legal Publishers 90 Stiles Road, Salem, New Hampshire 03079. 1982.

LABOUR LAW AND INDUSTRIAL RELATIONS OF THE EUROPEAN COMMUNITY. R. Blanpain. Kluwer Academic Publishers, 101 Philip Drive, Assinippi Park, Norwell, Massachusetts 02061. 1991.

LAW OF THE EUROPEAN COMMUNITIES. Lord Hailsham and David Vaughan, Editors. Butterworth and Company, Limited, Borough Green, Sevenoaks, Kent TN15 8PH, England. 1986.

LEADING CASES AND MATERIALS ON THE SOCIAL POLICY OF THE EEC. Angela Byre. Kluwer Academic Publishers, 101 Philip Drive, Assinippi Park, Norwell, Massachusetts 02061. 1989.

LEADING CASES ON THE LAW OF THE EUROPEAN COMMUNITIES. Fifth Edition. M. van Empel, editor. Kluwer Academic Publishers, 101 Philip Drive, Assinippi Park, Norwell, Massachusetts 02061. 1990.

LEGAL AND CONTRACTUAL LIMITATIONS TO WORKING-TIME IN THE EUROPEAN COMMUNITY MEMBER STATES. R. Blanpain, E. Kohler, editors. Kluwer Academic Publishers, 101 Philip Drive, Assinippi Park, Norwell, Massachusetts 02061. 1989.

LEGAL ASPECTS OF AGRICULTURE IN THE EUROPEAN COMMUNITY. J.A. Usher. Oxford University Press, 200 Madison Avenue, New York, New York 10016. 1988.

LEGAL ASPECTS OF DOING BUSINESS IN EUROPE. Dennis Campbell, Editor. Kluwer Law Book Publishers, Incorporated, 36 West Forty-fourth Street, New York, New York 10036. 1992.

LEGAL ASPECTS OF THE ECU. Chris Sunt. Butterworth and Company (Publishers) Limited, Borough Green, Sevenoaks, Kent TN15 8PH, England. 1989.

THE LEGAL FOUNDATIONS OF THE SINGLE EUROPEAN MARKET. Nicholas Green, Trevor C. Hartley and John A. Usher. Oxford University Press, 200 Madison Avenue, New York, New York 10016. 1991.

LEXIS, EUROPEAN COMMUNITIES FILE. Mead Data Central, P.O. Box 933, Dayton, Ohio 45401.

MEALEY'S EUROPEAN ENVIRONMENTAL LAW REPORT. Mealey Publications, Incorporated, P.O. Box 446, Wayne, Pennsylvania 19087. Semimonthly.

MERGER AND JOINT VENTURE ACTIVITIES IN THE EEC: A GUIDE TO DOING BUSINESS UNDER THE NEW REGULATIONS. Mario Siragusa. Practising Law Institute, 810 Seventh Avenue, New York, New York 10019. 1990.

MERGERS AND JOINT VENTURES IN EUROPE: THE LAW AND POLICY OF THE EEC. Frank L. Fine. Graham and Trotman Limited, Sterling House, 66 Wilton Road, London SW1V 1DE, England. 1989.

MONOPOLY LAW AND MARKET: STUDIES OF EC COMPETITION LAW WITH US AMERICAN ANTITRUST LAW AS A FRAME OF REFERENCE AND SUPPORTED BY BASIC MARKET ECONOMICS. Jens Fejo. Kluwer Academic Publishers, 101 Philip Drive, Assinippi Park, Norwell, Massachusetts 02061. 1990.

THE 1992 M AND A MONTHLY. Translink International Group, 730 Fifth Avenue, Suite 1906, New York, New York 10019. Monthly.

1992, THE CHANGING LEGAL LANDSCAPE FOR DOING BUSINESS IN EUROPE. Walter W. Oberreit. Practising Law Institute, 810 Seventh Avenue, New York, New York 10019. 1989.

1992 -- THE EXTERNAL IMPACT OF EUROPEAN UNIFICATION. Buraff Publications, 1350 Connecticut Avenue, Northwest, Suite 1000, Washington, D.C. 20036. Semimonthly.

ON LAW AND POLICY IN THE EUROPEAN COURT OF JUSTICE: A COMPARATIVE STUDY IN JUDICIAL POLICYMAKING. Hjalte Rasmussen. Martinus Nijhoff, Kluwer Academic Publishers, 101 Philip Drive, Assinipii Park, Norwell, Massachusetts 02061. 1986.

THE OXFORD ENCYCLOPAEDIA OF EUROPEAN COMMUNITY LAW. A.G. Toth. Oxford University Press, 200 Madison Avenue, New York, New York 10016. 1990- .

PRACTICING LAW IN THE EEC. Linda S. Spedding. Transnational Publishers, Incorporated, P.O. Box 7282, Ardsley-on-Hudson, New York 10503. 1986.

PROTECTIONISM AND THE EUROPEAN COMMUNITY: IMPORT RELIEF MEASURES TAKEN BY THE EUROPEAN ECONOMIC COMMUNITY AND THE MEMBER STATES, AND THE LEGAL REMEDIES AVAILABLE TO PRIVATE PARTIES. E.L.M. Volker, editor. Kluwer Academic Publishers, 101 Philip Drive, Assinippi Park, Norwell, Massachusetts 02061. 1987.

SALES TAXATION: THE CASE OF VALUE ADDED TAX IN THE EUROPEAN COMMUNITY. Ben Terra. Kluwer Academic Publishers, 101 Philip Drive, Assinippi Park, Norwell, Massachusetts 02061. 1988.

SETTING UP A COMPANY IN THE EUROPEAN COMMUNITY: A COUNTRY BY COUNTRY GUIDE. Oryx Press, 2214 North Central Avenue, Phoenix, Arizona 85004. 1989.

SOURCEBOOK OF EUROPEAN FINANCIAL AND COMMERCIAL LAW. Ann Hand and Norman Nunn-Price, editors. Woodhead-Faulkner, New York, New York. 1990- .

THE SUBSTANTIVE LAW OF THE EEC. Second Edition. Derrick Wyatt and Alan Dashwood. Sweet and Maxwell Limited, South Quay Plaza, 183 Marsh Wall, London E14 9FT, England. 1987.

TEXTBOOK ON EEC LAW. Second Edition. Josephine Steiner. Blackstone Press, BPP House, Aldine Place, 142-144 Uxbridge Road, London W12 8AA, England. 1990.

TOWARD A COMMUNITY AIR TRANSPORT POLICY: THE LEGAL DIMENSION. P.J. Slot and P.D. Dagtoglou, editors. Kluwer Academic Publishers, 101 Philip Drive, Assinippi Park, Norwell, Massachusetts 02061. 1989.

TRANSNATIONAL LEGAL PRACTICE IN THE EEC AND THE UNITED STATES. Linda S. Spedding. Transnational Publishers, P.O. Box 7282, Ardsley-on-Hudson, New York 10503. 1987.

TRANSPORT LAW OF THE EUROPEAN COMMUNITY. Rosa Greaves. Athlone, Atlantic Highlands, New Jersey. 1991.

UNDERSTANDING U.S. AND EUROPEAN ENVIRONMENTAL LAW: A PRACTITIONER'S GUIDE. Turner T. Smith, Jr. and Pascale Kromarek, editors. Graham and Trotman Limited, Sterling House, 66 Wilton Road, London SW1V 1DE, England. 1989.

WORLD ALMANAC'S LEGAL GUIDE FOR AMERICAN TRAVELERS: EUROPE. Jack D. Novik. World Almanac Publications, Ballantine Books, Random House, Incorporated, Random House Publicity, (11-6) 201 East Fiftieth Street, New York, New York 10022. 1986.

FINLAND

THE FINNISH LEGAL SYSTEM. Second Edition. Jaakko Uotila, Editor. Finnish Lawyers Publishing Company, Coronet Books, 311 Bainbridge Street, Philadelphia, Pennsylvania 19147. 1985.

LABOUR LAW AND INDUSTRIAL RELATIONS IN FINLAND. A.J. Suviranta. Kluwer Academic Publishers, 101 Philip Drive, Assinippi Park, Norwell, Massachusetts 02061. 1987.

FRANCE

CIVIL LAW I. FRANCE: A BASIC COLLECTION. Law Library Microform Consortium, P.O. Box 11033, Honolulu, Hawaii 96828. 1988.

CONSTITUTIONALISM AND HUMAN RIGHTS: AMERICA, POLAND, AND FRANCE: A BICENTENNIAL COLLOQUIUM AT THE MILLER CENTER. Kenneth W. Thompson and Rett R. Ludwikowski, editors. University Press of America, 4720 Boston Way, Lanham, Maryland 20706. 1991.

AN ENGLISH READER'S GUIDE TO THE FRENCH LEGAL SYSTEM. Martin Weston. St. Martin's Press, 175 Fifth Avenue, New York, New York 10010. 1991.

THE FRENCH CIVIL LAW: AN INSIDER'S VIEW. Christian Arias. Louisiana State University Press, Highland Road, Baton Rouge, Louisiana 70893. 1987.

A FRENCH-ENGLISH DICTIONARY OF LEGAL AND COMMERCIAL TERMS. Graham Olver. Fred B. Rothman and Company, 10368 West Centennial Road, Littleton, Colorado 80127. 1988. (Reprint)

FRENCH LAW: CONSTITUTION AND SELECTIVE LEGISLATION. Henry P. de Vries, Nina M. Galston and Regina B. Loening. Matthew Bender and Company, Incorporated, 11 Penn Plaza, New York, New York 10001. 1984- .

THE FRENCH LAW OF ARBITRATION. Jean Robert and Thomas E. Carbonneau. Matthew Bender and Company, Incorporated, 11 Penn Plaza, New York, New York 10001. 1983.

FRENCH LAW OF CONTRACT. Barry Nicholas. Butterworth and Company, Limited, Borough Green, Sevenoaks, Kent TN15 8PH, England. 1982.

LEGAL ASPECTS OF DOING BUSINESS WITH FRANCE. Claude Le Gal. Practising Law Institute, 810 Seventh Avenue, New York, New York 10019. 1987.

LEXIS, FRENCH LAW LIBRARIES. Mead Data Central, P.O. Box 933, Dayton, Ohio 45401.

A SOURCE-BOOK ON FRENCH LAW: PUBLIC LAW--CONSTITUTIONAL AND ADMINISTRATIVE LAW: PRIVATE LAW--STRUCTURE, CONTRACT. Third Edition. Sir Otto Kahn-Freund, Claudine Levy and Bernard Rudden. Oxford University Press, 200 Madison Avenue, New York, New York 10016. 1991.

WOMEN'S RIGHTS IN FRANCE. Dorothy McBride Stetson. Greenwood Publishing Group, Incorporated, 88 Post Road West, P.O. Box 5007, Westport, Connecticut 06881. 1987.

GERMANY

BASIC LITERATURE ON LAW: FEDERAL REPUBLIC OF GERMANY: A SELECTIVE BIBLIOGRAPHY. Ralph Lansky. J. Schweitzer, Transnational Publishers, Incorporated, P.O. Box 7282, Ardsley-on-Hudson, New York 10503. 1984.

COMMERCIAL ARBITRATION IN THE FEDERAL REPUBLIC OF GERMANY. Ottoarndt Glossner. Kluwer Law Book Publishers, Incorporated, 36 West Forty-fourth Street, New York, New York 10036. 1984,

A COMPARATIVE INTRODUCTION TO THE GERMAN LAW OF TORT. B.S. Markesinis. Clarendon Press, Oxford University Press, 200 Madison Avenue, New York, New York 10016. 1986.

CORPORATE ACQUISITIONS AND MERGERS IN GERMANY: A PRACTICAL GUIDE TO THE LEGAL, FINANCIAL, AND ADMINISTRATIVE IMPLICATIONS. Dieter Beinert. Graham and Trotman Limited, Sterling House, 66 Wilton Road, London SW1V 1DE, England. 1991.

FOREIGN TRADE LAW OF THE FEDERAL REPUBLIC OF GERMANY: AN INTRODUCTION TO THE FOREIGN TRADE ACT AND THE FOREIGN TRADE ORDINANCE ... Ulf R. Siebel. Fritz Knapp Verlag GmbH, Junghofstrasse 16, Postfach 111151, D-6000 Frankfurt-am-Main, Germany. 1989.

GERMAN ADMINISTRATIVE LAW IN COMMON LAW PERSPECTIVE. Pal Singh. Springer-Verlag, 175 Fifth Avenue, New York, New York 10010. 1985.

GERMAN ANTITRUST LAW: AN INTRODUCTION TO THE GERMAN ANTITRUST LAW WITH GERMAN TEXT AND SYNOPTIC ENGLISH TRANSLATION OF THE ACT AGAINST RESTRAINTS OF COMPETITION. Rudolf Mueller. Fritz Knapp, GmbH Verlag, Neue Mainzer Straae 60, 6000 Frankfurt-am-Main 1, Germany. 1984.

THE GERMAN COMPETITION LAW: LEGISLATION AND COMMENTARY. Dietrich Hoffmann and Stefan Schaub. Kluwer Law Book Publishers, Incorporated, 36 West Forty-fourth Street, New York, New York 10036. 1984.

GERMAN LAW PERTAINING TO COMPANIES WITH LIMITED LIABILITY: A SYNOPTIC TRANSLATION INCLUDING COMPREHENSIVE INTRODUCTORY COMMENTS ON THE LAWS AFFECTING THE GERMAN GMBH. Martin Peltzer and Jeremy P. Brooks. Otto Schmidt, KG Verlag, Ulmenalle 96-98, 5000 Koeln 51, Germany. 1987.

LABOUR LAW AND INDUSTRIAL RELATIONS IN THE FEDERAL REPUBLIC OF GERMANY. Manfred Weiss. Kluwer Academic Publishers, 101 Philip Drive, Assinippi Park, Norwell, Massachusetts 02061. 1987.

LAW OF MONOPOLIES: COMPETITION LAW AND PRACTICE IN THE USA, EEC, GERMANY, AND THE UK. D.M. Raybould and Alison Firth. Graham and Trotman Limited, Sterling House, 66 Wilton Road, London SW1V 1DE, England. 1991.

THE LAW RELATING TO BUSINESS TENANCIES IN GERMANY. Konrad Mohr. Fritz Knapp, GmbH Verlag, Neue Mainzer Strasse 60, 6000 Frankfurt-am-Main 1, Germany. 1985.

POLITICS AND THE LAW IN LATE NINETEENTH-CENTURY GERMANY: THE ORIGINS OF THE CIVIL CODE. Michael John. Oxford University Press, 200 Madison Avenue, New York, New York 10016. 1989.

GHANA

CRIMINAL LAW IN GHANA. P.K. Twumasi. Ghana Publishing Corporation, Private Post Bag, Terna, Ghana. 1985.

GHANA INCOME TAX LAW AND PRACTICE. P.O. Andah. Sedco Publishing Limited, P.O. Box 2051, Sedco House, Tabon Street, North Ridge, Accra, Ghana. 1987.

GHANA: THE PEOPLE, THE LAWS, THE COURTS: THE SEVENTH ANNUAL ALUMNI LECTURE OF THE UNIVERSITY OF GHANA. E.S. Aidoo. Institute of Statistical, Social, and Economic Research, University of Ghana, Ghana Universities Press, P.O. Box 4219, Accra, Ghana. 1985.

OLLENNU'S PRINCIPLES OF CUSTOMARY LAND LAW IN GHANA. Second Edition. Nii Amaa Ollennu and Gordon R. Woodman. CAL Press, Birmingham, England. 1985.

HONG KONG

COMMERCIAL, BUSINESS AND TRADE LAWS: HONG KONG. Agnes Young and Allan P.K. Reese, Editors. Oceana Publications, Incorporated, 75 Main Street, Dobbs Ferry, New York 10522. 1982- .

THE COMMON LAW SYSTEM IN CHINESE CONTEXT. Berry Fong-Chung Hsu. M.E. Sharpe, Incorporated, 80 Business Park Drive, Armonk, New York 10504. 1992.

CONSTITUTIONAL CONFRONTATION IN HONG KONG: ISSUES AND IMPLICATIONS OF THE BASIC LAW. Michael C. Davis. St. Martin's Press, 175 Fifth Avenue, New York, New York 10010. 1990.

DAMAGES FOR PERSONAL INJURIES AND FATAL ACCIDENTS IN HONG KONG: A REVIEW OF THE LAW AND A DIGEST OF THE CASES. Robyn Martin and Peter Rhodes. Butterworth and Company, Limited, Borough Green, Sevenoaks, Kent TN15 8PH, England. 1982.

FAMILY LAW IN HONG KONG. Second Edition. Leonard Pegg. Butterworth and Company, 30 Robinson Road, 12-01 Tuan Sing Towers, Singapore, 0104. 1986.

THE FUTURE OF THE LAW IN HONG KONG. Raymond Wacks, editor. Oxford University Press, 200 Madison Avenue, New York, New York 10016. 1989.

THE HONG KONG BASIC LAW: BLUEPRINT FOR STABILITY AND PROSPERITY UNDER CHINESE SOVEREIGNTY? Ming K. Chan and David J. Clark, editors. M.E. Sharpe, Incorporated, 80 Business Park Drive, Armonk, New York 10504. 1991.

HONG KONG COMPANY LAW. Vanessa Stott. Pitman Publishing Limited, 128 Long Acre, London WC2E 9AN, England. 1987.

INDUSTRIAL RELATIONS AND LAW IN HONG KONG. Second Edition. Joe England. Oxford University Press, 200 Madison Avenue, New York, New York 10016. 1989.

AN INTRODUCTION TO HONG KONG EMPLOYMENT LAW. Kevin Williams. Oxford University Press, 200 Madison Avenue, New York, New York 10016. 1990.

THE LAW IN HONG KONG, 1969-1989. Raymond Wacks, editor. Oxford University Press, 200 Madison Avenue, New York, New York 10016. 1989.

LAW OF INTELLECTUAL AND INDUSTRIAL PROPERTY IN HONG KONG: A GUIDE TO TRADE MARKS, COPYRIGHT, PATENTS, REGISTERED DESIGNS AND OTHER PROTECTED COMMERCIAL INFORMATION. Michael D. Pendleton. Butterworth and Company (Asia), 289 East Fifth Street, St. Paul, Minnesota 55101-1989. 1984.

HUNGARY

CENTRAL AND EASTERN EUROPEAN LEGAL MATERIALS. HUNGARY. United States National Technical Information Service, Springfield, Virginia. 1991- .

DISPUTES AND THE LAW. Maureen Cain and K'alm'an Kulcs'ar, Editors. European Coordination Centre for Research and Documentation in Social Sciences. Akad'emiai Kiad'o, Humanities Press International, 171 First Avenue, Atlantic Highlands, New Jersey 07716-1289. 1983.

FOREIGN INVESTMENTS IN HUNGARY; LAW AND PRACTICE. Tamas Sarkozy, editor. Lang, Budapest, Hungary. 1988.

THE LAWS OF HUNGARY. Janos M. Bak, Gyorgy Bonist and James Ross Sweeney, editors. Charles Schlacks, Jr., Publisher, Bakersfield, California. 1989-

LEGAL SOURCES AND BIBLIOGRAPHY OF HUNGARY. Mid-European Law Project, Praeger Publishers, One Madison Avenue, New York, New York 10010-3603. 1956.

NEW TRAITS OF THE DEVELOPMENT OF STATE AND LEGAL LIFE IN HUNGARY. Gyorgy Antalffy and Rezso H'arsfalvil, Editors. Hungarian Lawyers' Association, Budapest, Hungary. 1981.

PRESS LAW IN HUNGARY. Miklos K. Radvanyi. Library of Congress, Law Library, 101 Independence Avenue, Southeast, Washington, D.C. 20540. 1987.

INDIA

CONSTITUTIONAL LAW OF INDIA: A CRITICAL COMMENTARY. (Supplement). H.M. Seervai. Tripathi, Sweet and Maxwell, Limited, 11 New Fetter Lane, London EC4P 4EE, England. 1988.

DIVORCE LAW IN INDIA: INTER-SPOUSAL CONFLICTS IN RELATION TO MAINTENANCE, PROPERTY, AND CUSTODY OF CHILDREN. B.K. Sharma. Deep and Deep Publications, D-01-24 Rajouri Gdn., New Delhi 110027, India. 1989.

JURISPRUDENCE, A STUDY OF INDIAN LEGAL THEORY. Second Edition. S.N. Dhyani. Metropolitan Book Company, Asia Book Corporation of America, 45-77 One Hundred Fifty-seventh Street, Flushing, New York 11355. 1985.

LAW AND PRACTICE OF LIFE INSURANCE IN INDIA. T.S. Mann. Deep and Deep Publications, D-1-24 Rajouri Gdn., New Delhi 110027, India. 1987.

LAW AND PRACTICE OF RESTRICTIVE TRADE PRACTICES IN INDIA. M.P. Jain. Deep and Deep Publications, D-1-24 Rajouri Gdn. New Delhi 110027, India. 1987.

LAW AND SOCIAL CHANGE IN INDIA. Balbir Sahai Sinha. Deep and Deep Publications, Advent Books, Incorporated, 141 East Forty-fourth Street, Suite 511, New York, New York 10017. 1983.

LAW AND SOCIETY IN MODERN INDIA. K.D. Gaur. Deep and Deep Publications, D-1-24 Rajouri Gdn., New Delhi 110027, India. 1989.

LAW AND SOCIETY IN MODERN INDIA. Marc Galanter. Oxford University Press, 200 Madison Avenue, New York, New York 10016. 1989.

LAW OF CONSUMER PROTECTION IN INDIA. D.N. Saraf. N.M. Tripathi Pvt. Limited, 164 Shamaldas Gandhi Marg, Bombay 400002, India. 1990.

LAW OF CONTRACT IN INDIA: THE DOCTRINE OF CONSIDERATION. Amar Singh. Deep and Deep Publications, Advent Books, Incorporated, 141 East Forty-fourth Street, Suite 511, New York, New York 10017. 1985.

LAW OF MARRIAGES, MAINTENANCE, SEPARATION, AND DIVORCE IN INDIA. Second Edition. S. Krishnamurthi Aiyar. University Book Agency, Allahabad, India. 1989.

LAW OF MUNICIPALITIES AND MUNICIPAL CORPORATIONS IN INDIA. Third Edition. R. D. Agarwal. Law Publishers, P.O. Box 1077, Sardar Patel Marg, Allahabad 211001, India. 1987.

LAW OF TORTS 1976. Fourth Edition. Balbir Sahai Sinha. State Mutual Book, 521 Fifth Avenue, Seventeenth Floor, New York, New York 10175. 1981.

LAW OF TORTS: WITH EXHAUSTIVE NOTES, COMMENTS, AND CASE LAW REFERENCES. Ratanlal Ranchhoddas and Dhirajlal Keshavlal Thakore. Wadhwa Sales Corporation, Nagpur, India. 1984.

THE LEGAL PROFESSION IN COLONIAL SOUTH INDIA. John J. Paul. Oxford University Press, 200 Madison Avenue, New York, New York 10016. 1991.

MANTHA RAMAMURTI'S LAW OF WILLS IN INDIA AND PAKISTAN. Mantha Ramamurti. Law Publishers, P.O. Box 1077, Sardar Patel Marg, Allahabad 211001, India. 1988.

A MANUAL OF CIVIL LAWS, CONTAINING IMPORTANT CIVIL ACTS AND RULES. Delhi Law House, Delhi, India. 1986.

INDONESIA

INDONESIA AND THE RULE OF LAW: TWENTY YEARS OF "NEW ORDER" GOVERNMENT: A STUDY. Hans Thoolen, editor. The International Commission of Jurists and the Netherlands Institute of Human Rights (SIM), Pinter Publishers, Limited, 25 Floral Street, Covent Garden, London WCZE 9DS, England. 1987.

LEGAL PROCESS AND ECONOMIC DEVELOPMENT: A CASE STUDY OF INDONESIA. Cheryl W. Gray. World Bank, Office of the Vice President, 1818 H Street, Northwest, Washington, D.C. 20433. 1989.

TAXATION IN INDONESIA. J.S. Uppal. Gadjah Mada University Press, Sinauer Associates, Incorporated, North Main Street, Sunderland, Massachusetts 01375. 1986.

IRAQ

BUSINESS LAWS OF IRAQ. Tenth Edition. Nicola H. Karam, Translator. Graham and Trotman Limited, Sterling House, 66 Wilton Road, London SW1V 1DE, England. 1990.

THE GULF WAR OF 1980-1988: THE IRAN-IRAQ WAR IN INTERNATIONAL LEGAL PERSPECTIVE. Ige F. Dekker and Harry H.G. Post, editors. Martinus Nijhoff, Kluwer Academic Publishers, 101 Philip Drive, Assinippi Park, Norwell, Massachusetts 02061. 1992.

THE KUWAIT/IRAQ SANCTIONS: U.S. REGULATIONS IN AN INTERNATIONAL SETTING. Preston Brown. Practising Law Institute, 810 Seventh Avenue, New York, New York 10019. 1991.

IRAN

IRANIAN ASSETS LITIGATION REPORTER. Andrews Publications, 1646 West Chester Pike, Westtown, Pennsylvania 19395. Semimonthly.

MEALEY'S LITIGATION REPORT: IRANIAN CLAIMS. Mealey Publications, Incorporated, P.O. Box 446, Wayne, Pennsylvania 19087. Semimonthly.

IRELAND

ADMINISTRATIVE LAW IN IRELAND. Second Edition. David Gwynn Morgan and Gerard Hogan. Sweet and Maxwell Limited, South Quay Plaza, 183 Marsh Wall, London E14 9FT, England. 1991.

COMMERCIAL LAW IN IRELAND. Michael Forde. Butterworth and Company (Publishers) Limited, Borough Green, Sevenoaks, Kent TN15 8PH, England. 1990.

COMPANY LAW IN THE REPUBLIC OF IRELAND. Second Edition. Ronan Keane and Ronan Justice. Butterworth Legal Publishers, 90 Stiles Road, Salem, New Hampshire 03079. 1991.

COMPETITION LAWS OF UNITED KINGDOM AND REPUBLIC OF IRELAND. William Allan and Gerard Hogan. Matthew Bender and Company, Incorporated, 11 Penn Plaza, New York, New York 10001. 1988.

CONSTITUTIONAL LAW AND CONSTITUTIONAL RIGHTS IN IRELAND. Brian Doolan. Gill and Macmillan, Limited, 15-17 Eden Quay, Dublin 1, Ireland. 1984.

CONSTITUTIONAL LAW IN IRELAND. James Casey. Sweet and Maxwell, Limited, South Quay Plaza, 183 Marsh Wall, London E14 PFT, England. 1987.

CONTRACT. Second Edition. Robert Clark. Sweet and Maxwell, Limited, South Quay Plaza, 183 Marsh Wall, London E14 9FT, England. 1986.

DISMISSAL LAW IN THE REPUBLIC OF IRELAND. Mary Redmond. Incorporated Law Society of Ireland, Solicitors Building, Four Courts, Dublin 7, Ireland. 1982.

EQUITY AND THE LAW OF TRUSTS IN THE REPUBLIC OF IRELAND. Ronan Keane. Butterworth Legal Publishers, 90 Stiles Road, Salem, New Hampshire 03079. 1988.

INTRODUCTION TO LAW IN THE REPUBLIC OF IRELAND: ITS HISTORY, PRINCIPLES, ADMINISTRATION AND SUBSTANCE. Richard H. Grimes and Patrick T. Horgan. Wolfhound Press, Dufour Editions, Incorporated, Box 449, Chester Springs, Pennsylvania 19425-0449. 1981.

INVESTMENT IN THE REPUBLIC OF IRELAND. Stokes K. Crowley. S.K. Crowley, Dublin, Ireland. 1983.

IRISH COMPANY LAW, 1973-1983: A GUIDE AND HANDBOOK. B.J. Power. Gill and Macmillan, Limited, 15-17 Eden Quay, Dublin 1, Ireland. 1984.

IRISH LAND LAW. Second Edition. J.C.W. Wylie. Professional Books, Limited, 46 Milton Trading Estate, Abingdon, Oxfordshire OX14 4SY, England. 1986.

LAW AND SOCIAL POLICY: SOME CURRENT PROBLEMS IN IRISH LAW. William Duncan, Editor. Dublin University Law Journal, Dublin, Ireland. 1987.

THE LAW OF LOCAL GOVERNMENT IN THE REPUBLIC OF IRELAND. Ronan Keane. Incorporated Law Society of Ireland, Solicitors Building, Four Courts, Dublin 7, Ireland. 1982.

THE LEGAL SYSTEM OF NORTHERN IRELAND. Second Edition. Brice Dickson. SLS, Belfast, Northern Ireland. 1989.

LEXIS, IRELAND LAW LIBRARY. Mead Data Central, P.O. Box 933, Dayton, Ohio 45401.

THE LIMITATION OF ACTIONS IN THE REPUBLIC OF IRELAND. James C. Brady and Tony Kerr. Incorporated Law Society of Ireland, Solicitors Building, Four Courts, Dublin 7, Ireland. 1984.

MARRIAGE BREAKDOWN IN IRELAND: LAW AND PRACTICE. William R. Duncan and Paula E. Scully. Butterworth and Company (Publishers) Limited, Borough Green, Sevenoaks, Kent TN15 8PH, England. 1990.

POLITICAL VIOLENCE AND THE LAW IN IRELAND. Gerard Hogan and Clive Walker. St. Martin's Press, 175 Fifth Avenue, New York, New York 10010. 1989.

PRINCIPLES OF IRISH LAW. Second Edition. Brian Doolan. Gill and Macmillan, Limited, 15-17 Eden Quay, Dublin 1, Ireland. 1986.

SHATTER'S FAMILY LAW IN THE REPUBLIC OF IRELAND. Third Edition. Wolfhound Press, Dufour Editions, Incorporated, Box 449, Chester Springs, Pennsylvania 19425-0449. 1986.

A SOURCEBOOK ON PLANNING LAW IN IRELAND. Philip O'Sullivan and Katharine Shepherd. Professional Books, Limited, 46 Milton Trading Estate, Abingdon, Oxfordshire OX14 4SY, England. 1984.

SUCCESSION LAW IN IRELAND. James C. Brady. Butterworth and Company (Publishers) Limited, Borough Green, Sevenoaks, Kent TN15 8PH, England. 1989.

ISRAEL

INHERITANCE IN ISRAEL: FOR THE LAYMAN AND THE LAWYER: INCLUDING THE LAW OF SUCCESSION, 1965. Jonathan Harpaz and Myer Zaslansky, editors. Haifa Law Publishers, Haifa, Israel. 1990.

LAW AND MORALITY IN ISRAEL'S WAR WITH THE PLO. William V. O'Brien. Routledge, Chapman & Hall, 29 West Thirty-fifth Street, New York, New York 10001. 1991.

THE LAW OF THE STATE OF ISRAEL: AN INTRODUCTION. Ariel Bin-Nun. Rubin Mass, Limited, P.O. Box 990, 11 David Marcus Street, Jerusalem 91000, Israel. 1990.

THE LEGAL STATUS OF THE ARABS IN ISRAEL. David Kretzmer. Westview Press, Incorporated, 5500 Central Avenue, Boulder, Colorado 80301. 1990.

SECURITY, TERRORISM AND TORTURE: DETAINEES RIGHTS IN SOUTH AFRICA AND ISRAEL: A COMPARATIVE STUDY. Harold Rudolph. Juta and Company, P.O. Box 123, 7790 Kenwyn, South Africa. 1984.

ITALY

CIVIL LAW II. ITALY, SPAIN, PORTUGAL AND THE LOW COUNTRIES: A BASIC COLLECTION. Law Library Microform Consortium, P.O. Box 11033, Honolulu, Hawaii 96828. 1991.

THE ITALIAN LEGAL SYSTEM. G. Leroy Certoma. Butterworths, Limited, 271-273 Lane Cove Road, North Ryde, New South Wales 2113, Australia. 1985.

JAPAN

ANTIMONOPOLY LAW IN JAPAN. Second Edition. Hiroshi Iyori and Akinori Uesugi. Federal Legal Publications, 157 Chambers Street, New York, New York 10007. 1983.

DOING BUSINESS IN JAPAN. Zentaro Kitagawa, Editor. Matthew Bender and Company, Incorporated, 11 Penn Plaza, New York, New York 10001. 1985- .

FREEDOM OF EXPRESSION IN JAPAN: A STUDY IN COMPARATIVE LAW, POLITICS, AND SOCIETY. Lawrence W. Beer. Kodansha International, HarperCollins Publishers, 10 East Fifty-third Street, New York, New York 10022. 1984.

A HISTORY OF LAW IN JAPAN UNTIL 1868. Carl Steenstrup. E.J. Brill, P.O. Box 467, 24 Hudson Street, Kinderhook, New York 12106. 1991.

JAPAN BUSINESS LAW GUIDE. Barker Gosling, editor. CCH International, North Ryde, New South Wales, Australia. 1988- .

JAPANESE AMERICAN SOCIETY FOR LEGAL STUDIES. c/o Professor John O. Haley, University of Washington School of Law, Seattle, Washington 98105. (206) 623-7900.

JAPANESE LEGAL PERIODICALS: A CHECKLIST OF HOLDINGS. Takeo Nishioka, Compiler. Law Library, Library of Congress, 101 Independence Avenue, Southeast, Washington, D.C. 20540. 1982.

LAW AND SOCIAL CHANGE IN POSTWAR JAPAN. Frank K. Upham. Harvard University Press, 79 Garden Street, Cambridge, Massachusetts 02138. 1987.

LAW AND SOCIETY IN CONTEMPORARY JAPAN: AMERICAN PERSPECTIVES. John O. Haley, editor. Kendall/Hunt Publishing Company, 2460 Kerper Boulevard, Dubuque, Iowa 52001. 1988. Reprint.

LAW, LABOUR, AND SOCIETY IN JAPAN: FROM REPRESSION TO RELUCTANT RECOGNITION. Anthony Woodiwiss. Routledge, Chapman & Hall, 29 West Thirty-fifth Street, New York, New York 10001. 1991.

TOKYO BUSINESS MONTH. Buraff Publications, 1350 Connecticut Avenue, Northwest, Suite 1000, Washington, D.C. 20036. Monthly.

UNITED STATES/JAPAN COMMERCIAL LAW AND TRADE. V. Kusuda-Smick, editor. Transnational Publishers, P.O. Box 7282, Ardsley-on-Hudson, New York 10503. 1990.

LATIN AMERICA

LATIN-AMERICAN LAWS AND INSTITUTIONS. Albert S. Golbert and Yenny Nun. Praeger Publications, Incorporated, One Madison Avenue, New York, New York 10010-3603. 1982.

LATIN AMERICAN LEGAL ABBREVIATIONS: A COMPREHENSIVE SPANISH/PORTUGUESE DICTIONARY WITH ENGLISH TRANSLATIONS. Arturo L. Torres and Francisco Avalos. Greenwood Publishing Group, Incorporated, 88 Post Road West, P.O. Box 5007, Westport, Connecticut 06881. 1989.

LATIN-AMERICAN LEGAL STUDIES: A GUIDE TO BASIC RESEARCH. Frederick E. Snyder. Greenwood Publishing Group, Incorporated, 88 Post Road West, P.O. Box 5007, Westport, Connecticut 06881. 1983.

LATIN-AMERICAN SOCIETY AND LEGAL CULTURE: A BIBLIOGRAPHY. Frederick E. Snyder. Greenwood Publishing Group, Incorporated, 88 Post Road West, P.O. Box 5007, Westport, Connecticut 06881. 1985.

LATIN AMERICAN SOVEREIGN DEBT MANAGEMENT: LEGAL AND REGULATORY ASPECTS. Ralph Reisner, Emilio J. Cardenas and Antonio Mendes, editors. Inter-American Development Bank, 1300 New York Avenue, Northwest, Washington, D.C. 20577. 1990.

LEGAL ASPECTS OF DOING BUSINESS IN LATIN AMERICA. Dennis Campbell, Editor. Kluwer Law Book Publishers, Incorporated, 36 West Forty-fourth Street, New York, New York 10036. 1992. (Supplemented).

WASHINGTON REPORT. Council of the Americas, 680 Park Avenue, New York, New York 10021. Quarterly.

LEBANON

THE LEBANESE LEGAL SYSTEM. Antoine Elias El-Gemayel, Editor. International Law Institute, 1615 New Hampshire Avenue, Northwest, Washington, D. C. 20009. 1985.

MALAWI

CRIMINAL PROCEDURE AND EVIDENCE IN MALAWI. David Newman. Chancellor College Department of Law, Zomba, Malawi. 1982.

THE LAW AND LIBERTY OF MOVEMENT IN MALAWI REVISITED. M.R.E. Machika. University of Malawi, Zomba, Malawi. 1984.

LAW, CUSTOM, AND SOCIAL ORDER: THE COLONIAL EXPERIENCE IN MALAWI AND ZAMBIA. Martin Chanock. Cambridge University Press, 40 West Twentieth Street, New York, New York 10011. 1985.

MALAYSIA AND SINGAPORE

BREACHES OF TRUST IN SINGAPORE AND MALAYSIA. W.J.M. Ricquier and Stanley Yeo Meng Heong. Butterworths and Company (Asia) Pte. Limited, 30 Robinson Road, 12-01 Tuan Sing Towers, Singapore 0104. 1984.

THE COMMON LAW IN SINGAPORE AND MALAYSIA: A VOLUME OF ESSAYS MARKING THE 25TH ANNIVERSARY OF THE MALAYA LAW REVIEW, 1959-1984. A.J. Harding, Editor. Butterworths and Company (Asia) Pte. Limited, 30 Robinson Road, 12-01 Tuan Sing Towers, Singapore 0104. 1985.

CONSTRUCTION LAW IN SINGAPORE AND MALAYSIA. Nigel M. Robinson and Anthony P. Lavers. Butterworth and Company (Asia) Pte. Limited, 30 Robinson Road, 12-01 Tuan Sing Towers, Singapore 0104. 1988.

THE EMPLOYER AND THE EMPLOYEE AND THE LAW IN MALAYSIA. Dunston Ayadurai. Butterworths and Company (Asia) Pte. Limited, 30 Robinson Road, 12-01 Tuan Sing Towers, Singapore 0104. 1985.

FAMILY LAW IN SINGAPORE: CASES AND COMMENTARY ON THE WOMEN'S CHARTER AND FAMILY LAW. Leong Wai Kum. Malayan Law Journal, Limited, Butterworth and Company (Asia) Pte. Limited, 30 Robinson Road, 12-01 Tuan Sing Towers, Singapore 0104. 1990.

THE INDUSTRIAL RELATIONS LAW OF MALAYSIA. Wu Min Aun. Heinemann Educational Books, Kuala Lampur, Malaysia. 1982.

INSURANCE LAW IN SINGAPORE. Tan Lee Meng. Butterworth and Company (Asia) Pte. Limited, 30 Robinson Road, 12-01 Tuan Sing Towers, Singapore 0104. 1988.

LAND LAW IN MALAYSIA: CASES AND COMMENTARY. Teo Keang Sood and Khaw Lake Tee. Butterworth and Company (Asia) Pte. Limited, 30 Robinson Road, 12-01 Tuan Sing Towers, Singapore 0104. 1987.

MALAYSIA'S NATIONAL LANGUAGE POLICY AND THE LEGAL SYSTEM. Richard Mead. Yale University Southeast Asia Publications, Box 13A, New Haven, Connecticut 06520. 1988.

PERTONAS, ITS CORPORATE AND LEGAL STATUS. V.K. Moorthy. Malayan Law Journal, Malayan Law Publications, Kuala Lampur, Malaysia. 1983.

THE SALE AND PURCHASE OF REAL PROPERTY IN MALAYSIA. Visu Sinnadurai. Butterworths and Company (Asia) Pte., Limited, 30 Robinson Road, 12-01 Tuan Sing Towers, Singapore 0104. 1984.

SESQUICENTENNIAL CHRONOLOGICAL TABLES OF THE WRITTEN LAWS OF THE REPUBLIC OF SINGAPORE, 1834-1984. G.W. Bartholomew, Elizabeth Srinivasagam and Pascal Baylon Netto. Malayan Law Journal, Limited, Butterworth and Company (Asia) Pte. Limited, 30 Robinson Road, 12-01 Tuan Sing Towers, Singapore 0104. 1987.

SURVEY OF MALAYSIAN LAW, 1980. Professor Datuk Ahmad Ibrahim, Editor. Published for the Faculty of Law, University of Malaya, Malaya Law Journal, Sweet and Maxwell, Limited, South Quay Plaza, 183 Marsh Wall, London E14 9FT, England. 1982.

MEXICO

AN INTRODUCTION TO THE MEXICAN LEGAL SYSTEM. James E. Herget and Jorge Camil. William S. Hein and Company, Incorporated, Hein Building, 1285 Main Street, Buffalo, New York 14209. 1978.

LAW AND MARKET SOCIETY IN MEXICO. George M. Armstrong, Jr. Praeger Publishers, One Madison Avenue, New York, New York 10010-3603. 1989.

A LAYMAN'S GUIDE TO MEXICAN LAW. Alberto Mayagoitia. University of New Mexico Press, Journalism Building, Albuquerque, New Mexico 87131. 1977.

MALDEFN NEWSLETTER. Mexican-American Legal Defense and Educational Fund, 634 South Spring Street, Twelfth Floor, Los Angeles, California 90014. Quarterly.

MEXICO -- UNITED STATES LAW INSTITUTE. University of San Diego, Alcala Park, San Diego, California 92110. (619) 260-4600.

MIDDLE EAST

BUSINESS LAWS OF IRAQ. Tenth Edition. Nicola H. Karam, translator. Graham and Trotman Limited, Sterling House, 66 Wilton Road, London SW1V 1DE, England. 1990.

BUSINESS LAWS OF OMAN. Third Edition. Marjorie J. Hall, translator. Graham and Trotman Limited, Sterling House, 66 Wilton Road, London SW1V 1DE, England. 1988

THE CIVIL CODE OF THE UNITED ARAB EMIRATES: THE LAW OF CIVIL TRANSACTIONS OF THE STATE OF THE UNITED ARAB EMIRATES. James Whelan and Marjorie J. Hall, Translators. Graham and Trotman Limited, Sterling House, 66 Wilton Road, London SW1V 1DE, England. 1987.

INTERNATIONAL LAW OF TAKE-OVERS AND MERGERS: SOUTHERN EUROPE, AFRICA, AND THE MIDDLE EAST. H. Leigh Ffrench. Quorum Books, Greenwood Publishing Group, Incorporated, 88 Post Road West, P.O. Box 5007, Westport, Connecticut 06881. 1987.

LABOR LAWS IN THE MIDDLE EAST: TRADITION IN TRANSIT. David Ziskind. Litlaw Foundation, Los Angeles, California. 1990

LAW AND ISLAM IN THE MIDDLE EAST. Daisy Hilse Dwyer, Editor. Bergin and Garvey Publishers, Incorporated, Rural Route 1, Box 105, Blue Hill, Maine 04614-9721. 1990.

THE LAW OF AGENCY AND DISTRIBUTORSHIP IN THE ARAB MIDDLE EAST. S. Saleh. Graham and Trotman Limited, Sterling House, 66 Wilton Road, London SW1V 1DE, England. 1988.

LAW, PERSONALITIES, AND POLITICS OF THE MIDDLE EAST: ESSAYS IN HONOR OF MAJID KHADDURI. James Piscatori and George S. Harris, editors. Westview Press, Incorporated, 5500 Central Avenue, Boulder, Colorado 80301. 1987.

LEGAL ASPECTS OF DOING BUSINESS IN THE MIDDLE EAST. Dennis Campbell, Editor. Kluwer Law Book Publishers, Incorporated, 36 West Forty-fourth Street, New York, New York 10036. 1992.

SOCIAL LEGISLATION IN THE CONTEMPORARY MIDDLE EAST. Laurence O. Michalak and Jeswald W. Salacuse, Editors. Institute of International Studies, University of California, Berkeley, 215 Moses Hall, Berkeley, California 94720. 1986.

TOWARD AN ISLAMIC REFORMATION: CIVIL LIBERTIES, HUMAN RIGHTS, AND INTERNATIONAL LAW. Abdullahi Ahmed An-Na'im. Syracuse University Press, 1600 Jamesville Avenue, Syracuse, New York 13244-5160. 1990.

MONGOLIA

COMMERCIAL, BUSINESS, AND TRADE LAWS. THE SOVIET UNION AND MONGOLIA. Oceana Publications, 75 Main Street, Dobbs Ferry, New York 10522. 1982- .

MONGOLIAN-ENGLISH-RUSSIAN DICTIONARY OF LEGAL TERMS AND CONCEPTS. W.E. Butler and A.J. Nathanson. Kluwer Academic Publications, 101 Philip Drive, Assinippi Park, Massachusetts 02061. 1983.

NETHERLANDS

DUTCH BUSINESS LAW: LEGAL, ACCOUNTING, AND TAX ASPECTS OF DOING BUSINESS IN THE NETHERLANDS. Third Edition. Steven R. Schuit. Kluwer Academic Publishers, 101 Philip Drive, Assinippi Park, Norwell, Massachusetts 02061. 1989.

DUTCH MATRIMONIAL PROPERTY AND INHERITANCE LAW AND ITS FISCAL IMPLICATIONS. Gregor van der Burght. Kluwer Academic Publishers, 101 Philip Drive, Assinippi Park, Norwell, Massachusetts 02061. 1990.

LEGAL LANGUAGE: U.S.-DUTCH LEGAL CONCEPTS ON BUSINESS AND TAX LAW: A GLOSSARY. Marjorie J. Sinke. Kluwer Academic Publishers, 101 Philip Drive, Assinippi Park, Norwell, Massachusetts 02061. 1990.

MERGERS AND ACQUISITIONS IN THE NETHERLANDS: LEGAL AND TAX ASPECTS. Peter N. Wakkie and H. Tom van der Meer. Kluwer Academic Publishers, 101 Philip Drive, Assinippi Park, Norwell, Massachusetts 02061. 1992.

PRIVATE INTERNATIONAL LAW IN THE NETHERLANDS. Rene van Rooij and Maurice V. Polak. Kluwer Academic Publishers, 101 Philip Drive, Assinippi Park, Norwell, Massachusetts 02061. 1987.

TRANSBORDER FLOW OF PERSONAL DATA WITHIN THE EEC: A COMPARATIVE ANALYSIS OF THE PRIVACY STATUTES OF THE FEDERAL REPUBLIC OF GERMANY, FRANCE, THE UNITED KINGDOM, AND THE NETHERLANDS AND THEIR IMPACT ON THE PRIVATE SECTOR. A.C.M. Nugter. Kluwer Academic Publishers, 101 Philip Drive, Assinippi Park, Norwell, Massachusetts 02061. 1990.

NIGERIA

COMMERCIAL LAW IN NIGERIA. Okay Achike. Fourth Dimension Publishers, Enugu, Nigeria. 1985.

A CONSTITUTIONAL HISTORY OF NIGERIA. B.O. Nwabueze. Longman Publishing Group, 95 Church Street, White Plains, New York 10601. 1982.

THE COURTS AND ADMINISTRATION OF LAW IN NIGERIA. Fidelis Ejike O. Ume. Fourth Dimension Publishing Company Limited, Plot 64A, City Layout, New Haven PMB 01164, Enugu, Nigeria. 1989.

FINANCIAL AND LEGAL PUBLICATIONS OF THE NIGERIAN CAPITAL MARKETS. Olukonyinsola Ajayi. Evans Brothers, Limited, Jericho Road, P.M.B. 5164, Ibadan, Nigeria. 1984.

INTRODUCTION TO NIGERIAN COMPANY LAW. J.O. Orojo. Sweet and Maxwell, Limited, South Quay Plaza, 183 Marsh Wall, London E14 9FT, England. 1985.

NIGERIAN BUSINESS LAW. Galus Ezejiofor, C.O. Okonkwo and C.U. Illegbune. Sweet and Maxwell, Limited, South Quay Plaza, 183 Marsh Wall, London E14 9FT, England. 1982.

NIGERIAN LAW OF CONTRACT. I.E. Sagay. Sweet and Maxwell, Limited, South Quay Plaza, 183 Marsh Wall, London E14 9FT, England. 1985.

NIGERIAN LAW OF TORTS: NIGERIAN NUTSHELLS. E. Mara-Brown. Sweet and Maxwell, Limited, South Quay Plaza, 183 Marsh Wall, London E14 9FT, England. 1987.

NIGERIAN SHIPPING LAWS. Louis Nnamdi Mbanfelo, Editor. Professional Books, Limited, 46 Milton Trading Estate, Abingdon, Oxfordshire OX14 4SY. England. 1983.

PAKISTAN

THE FOREIGNERS LAWS. Masud-ul-Hassan. Khyber Law Publishers, Lahore, Pakistan. 1983.

LAW OF WRITS IN PAKISTAN. M. Farani. Lahore Law Times Publications, Lahore, Pakistan. 1990.

LEGAL AND POLITICAL STRUCTURE OF AN ISLAMIC STATE: THE IMPLICATIONS FOR IRAN AND PAKISTAN. Yahya Noori and Sayed Hassan Amin. Royston, Glasgow, Scotland. 1987.

MANTHA RAMAMURTI'S LAW OF WILLS IN INDIA AND PAKISTAN. Fourth Edition. Mantha Ramamurti. Law Publishers, P.O. Box 1077, Sardar Patel Marg, Allahabad 211001, India. 1988.

MANUAL OF FAMILY LAWS IN PAKISTAN. M. Farani. Lahore Law Times Publications, Lahore, Pakistan. 1989.

PRACTICE AND LAW OF BANKING IN PAKISTAN. Fourth Edition. Asrar H. Siddiqi. Royal Book Company, P.O. Box 7737, 232 Saddar, Cooperative Market, Abdullah Haroon Road, Karachi 3, Pakistan. 1988.

PAPUA NEW GUINEA

LAW AND SOCIAL CHANGE IN PAPUA NEW GUINEA. David Weisbrot, Abdul Paliwala and Akilagpa. Butterworths, Limited, P.O. Box 345, North Ryde, New South Wales 2113, Australia. 1982.

PHILIPPINES

COMMERCIAL LAWS OF THE PHILIPPINES. Aguedo F. Agbayani. AFA Publications, La Vista Quezon City, Philippines. 1987.

THE INTRODUCTION OF AMERICAN LAW IN THE PHILIPPINES AND PUERTO RICO, 1898-1905. Winfred Lee Thompson. University of Arkansas Press, Fayetteville, Arkansas 72701. 1989.

JUSTICES OF THE SUPREME COURT OF THE PHILIPPINES: THEIR LIVES AND OUTSTANDING DECISIONS. Victor J. Sevilla. New Day Publishers, Cellar Book Shop, 18090 Wyoming, Detroit, Michigan 48221. 1984.

LABOR STANDARDS AND WELFARE LEGISLATION. Perfecto V. Fernandez. Tala Publishing Corporation, Quezon City, Philippines. 1984.

LAW OF MASS MEDIA, 1984. Perfecto V. Fernandez. Tala Publishing Corporation, Quezon City, Philippines. 1984.

MERCANTILE LAW COMPENDIUM. Simeon M. Gopengco. Central Lawbook Publishing Corporation, Quezon City, Philippines. 1983.

THE SHAPE OF LEGAL ASPECTS OF EDUCATION IN THE PHILIPPINES TODAY. Alta Grace Q. de Gracia, Editor. Episcopal Commission on Education and Religious Instruction, Associations of Catholic Universities of the Philippines, Manila, Philippines. 1982.

A SHORT GUIDE TO PHILIPPINE TAXES. National Tax Research Center, National Economic and Development Authority, Manila, Philippines. 1982.

SOUTH AFRICA

ADMINISTRATIVE LAW. Marinus Wiechers. Butterworth Publishers, P.O. Box 792, Durban, South Africa. 1985.

BILLS OF EXCHANGE, CHEQUES, AND PROMISSORY NOTES IN SOUTH AFRICAN LAW. F.R. Malan. Butterworth Publishers, P.O. Box 792, Durban, South Africa. 1983.

BUSINESS TRANSACTIONS LAW. Robert Sharrock and Andrew Borrowdale. Juta and Company, P.O. Box 30, Regis House, Church Street, Capetown 8000, South Africa. 1986.

CANEY'S THE LAW OF SURETYSHIP IN SOUTH AFRICA. Third Edition. C.F. Forsyth. Juta and Company, P.O. Box 30, Regis House, Church Street, Capetown 8000, South Africa. 1982.

CONVEYANCING IN SOUTH AFRICA. Third Edition. R.J.M. Jones. Juta and Company, P.O. Box 30, Regis House, Church Street, Capetown 8000, South Africa. 1985.

COWEN, THE LAW OF NEGOTIABLE INSTRUMENTS IN SOUTH AFRICA. Fifth Edition. Denis V. Cowen and Leonard Gering. Juta and Company, P.O. Box 30, Regis House, Church Street, Capetown 8000, South Africa. 1985- .

DAMAGES FOR LOST INCOME. Robert J. Koch. Juta and Company, P.O. Box 30, Regis House, Church Street, Capetown 8000, South Africa. 1984.

ENGINEERING AND CONSTRUCTION LAW: WITH ILLUSTRATIONS AND CASES. P.C. Loots. Juta and Company, P.O. Box 30, Regis House, Church Street, Capetown 8000, South Africa. 1985.

FAMILY, THINGS, AND SUCCESSION: LEE AND HONORE. Second Edition. H.J. Erasmus, C.G. Van Der Merwe and A.H. Van Wyk. Butterworth Publishers, P.O. Box 792, Durban, South Africa. 1983.

A GUIDE TO POLITICAL CENSORSHIP IN SOUTH AFRICA. Louise Silver. Witwatersrand University Press, 1 Jan Smuts Avenue, 2000 Johannesburg, South Africa. 1984.

HENOCHSBERG ON THE COMPANIES ACT. Fourth Edition. Philip M. Meskin, Editor. Butterworth Publishers, P.O. Box 792, Durban, South Africa. 1985.

IN A TIME OF TROUBLE: LAW AND LIBERTY IN SOUTH AFRICA'S STATE OF EMERGENCY. Stephen Ellmann. Oxford University Press, 200 Madison Avenue, New York, New York 10016. 1991.

INTRODUCTION TO COMPANY LAW. H.S. Cilliers, M.L. Benade, J.J. Henning, D.H. Botha and E.M. de la Rey. Butterworth Publishers, P.O. Box 792, Durban, South Africa. 1985.

INTRODUCTION TO SOUTH AFRICAN LAW AND LEGAL THEORY. W.J. Hosten. Butterworth Publishers, P.O. Box 792, Durban, South Africa. 1983. (Revised Reprint).

JUDGES AT WORK: THE ROLE AND ATTITUDES OF THE SOUTH AFRICAN APPELLATE JUDICIARY, 1910-1950. Hugh Corder. Juta and Company, P.O. Box 30, Regis House, Church Street, Capetown 8000, South Africa. 1984.

KELSEY STUART'S THE NEWSPAPERMAN'S GUIDE TO THE LAW. Fourth Edition. Kelsey W. Stuart and William Lane. Butterworth Publishers, P.O. Box 792, Durban, South Africa. 1986.

LABOUR UNDER THE APARTHEID REGIME: PRACTICAL PROBLEMS AND LEGAL FRAMEWORK OF LABOUR RELATIONS IN SOUTH AFRICA. Michael Kittner, Marita Korner-Dammann and Albert Schunk. Kluwer Academic Publishers, 101 Philip Drive, Assinippi Park, Norwell, Massachusetts 02061. 1989.

LANSDOWN'S SOUTH AFRICAN LIQUOR LAW. Fifth Edition. Albert Hruger. Juta and Company, P.O. Box 30, Regis House, Church Street, Capetown 8000, South Africa. 1983.

THE LAW AND PRACTICE OF EMPLOYMENT. Second Edition. H.G. Ringrose. Juta and Company, P.O. Box 30, Regis House, Church Street, Capetown 8000, South Africa. 1983, 1976.

LAW OF COSTS. Second Edition. A.C. Cilliers. Butterworth Legal Publications, 90 Stiles Road, Salem, New Hampshire 03079. 1984.

THE LAW OF CREDIT AGREEMENTS AND HIRE-PURCHASE IN SOUTH AFRICA. Fifth Edition. M.A. Diemont and P.J. Aronstam. Juta and Company, P.O. Box 30, Regis House, Church Street, Capetown 8000, South Africa. 1982.

THE LAW OF INSOLVENCY. Second Edition. Catherine Smith. Butterworth Publishers, P.O. Box 792, Durban, South Africa. 1982.

LAW OF PARENT AND CHILD Fourth Edition. Erwin Spiro. Juta and Company, P.O. Box 30, Regis House, Church Street, Capetown 8000, South Africa. 1985.

THE LAW OF PROPERTY: SILBERBERG AND SCHOEMAN. Second Edition. J. Schoeman. Butterworth Publishers, P.O. Box 792, Durban, South Africa. 1983.

THE LAW OF SALE AND LEASE. A.J. Kerr. Butterworth Publishers, P.O. Box 792, Durban, South Africa. 1984.

THE LAW, PROCEDURE, AND CONDUCT OF MEETINGS IN SOUTH AFRICA. Fifth Edition. Arthur Lewin. Juta and Company, P.O. Box 30, Regis House, Church St., Capetown 8000, South Africa. 1985.

MACKEURTAN'S SALE OF GOODS IN SOUTH AFRICA. Fifth Edition. G.R.J. Hackwill. Juta and Company, P.O. Box 30, Regis House, Church Street, Capetown 8000, South Africa. 1984.

THE MINING AND MINERAL LAWS OF SOUTH AFRICA. Blen Lloyd, Stuart Franklin and Morris Kaplan. Butterworth Publishers, P.O. Box 792, Durban, South Africa. 1982.

MODERN BUSINESS LAW. Department Mercantile Law, University of South Africa. Butterworth Publishers, P.O. Box 792, Durban, South Africa. 1979- .

SECTIONAL TITLES, SHARE BLOCKS, AND TIME-SHARING. C.G. van der Merwe and D.W. Butler. Butterworth Publishers, P.O. Box 792, Durban, South Africa. 1985.

SECURITY, TERRORISM AND TORTURE: DETAINEES RIGHTS IN SOUTH AFRICA AND ISRAEL: A COMPARATIVE STUDY. Harold Rudolph. Juta and Company, P.O. Box 30, Regis House, Church Street, Capetown 8000, South Africa. 1984.

SOUTH AFRICA: HUMAN RIGHTS AND THE RULE OF LAW. Geoffrey Bindman, Editor. International Commission of Jurists, Pinter Publishers, 562 West One Hundred-Thirteenth Street, New York, New York 10025. 1988.

THE SOUTH AFRICAN LAW OF EVIDENCE. Third Edition. L.H. Hoffman and D. T. Zeffrett. Butterworth Publishers, P.O. Box 792, Durban, South Africa. 1981.

THE SOUTH AFRICAN LAW OF HUSBAND AND WIFE. Fifth Edition. H.R. Hahio. Juta and Company, P.O. Box 30, Regis House, Church Street, Capetown 8000, South Africa. 1985.

THE SOUTH AFRICAN LAW OF TRUSTS. Third Edition. Tony Honore. Juta and Company, P.O. Box 30, Regis House, Church Street, Capetown 8000, South Africa. 1983.

SOUTH AFRICAN MARITIME LAW AND MARINE INSURANCE: SELECTED TOPICS. Clare Dillon and J.P. van Niekerk. Butterworth Publishers, P.O. Box 792, Durban, South Africa. 1983.

SOUTH AFRICAN MERCANTILE AND COMPANY LAW. Fifth Edition. J.T.R. Gibson and R.G. Comrie. Juta and Company, P.O. Box 30, Regis House, Church Street, Capetown 8000, South Africa. 1983.

URBAN BLACK LAW. T.W. Bennett and others, Editors. Juta and Company, P.O. Box 30, Regis House, Church Street, Capetown 8000, South Africa. 1985.

WILLE'S LAW OF MORTGAGE AND PLEDGE IN SOUTH AFRICA. Third Edition. George Wille, T.J. Scott and Susan Scott. Juta and Company, Limited, P.O. Box 30, Regis House, Church Street, Cape Town 8000, South Africa. 1987.

WILLIE AND MILLIN'S MERCANTILE LAW OF SOUTH AFRICA. Eighteenth Edition. J.F. Coaker and D.T. Zeffertt, Editors. Hortors Stationery, Johannesburg, South Africa. 1984.

SOVIET UNION

BASIC DOCUMENTS ON THE SOVIET LEGAL SYSTEM. Second Edition. William E. Butler, Editor. Oceana Publications, Incorporated, 75 Main Street, Dobbs Ferry, New York 10522. 1991.

BIBLIOGRAPHY ON THE SOVIET UNION AND THE DEVELOPMENT OF THE LAW OF THE SEA. William E. Butler, Editor. Oceana Publications, Incorporated, 75 Main Street, Dobbs Ferry, New York 10522. 1985.

BUSINESS VENTURES IN EASTERN EUROPE AND THE SOVIET UNION: THE EMERGING LEGAL FRAMEWORK FOR FOREIGN INVESTMENT. David E. Birenbaum and Dimitri P. Racklin. Prentice-Hall, Incorporated, 113 Sylvan Avenue, Englewood Cliffs, New Jersey 07632. 1990- .

THE CITIZENSHIP LAW OF THE USSR. George Ginsburgs. Martinus Nijhoff Publishers, Kluwer Academic Publishers, 101 Philip Drive, Assinippi Park, Norwell, Massachusetts 02061. 1984.

CIVIL LAW AND THE PROTECTION OF PERSONAL RIGHTS IN THE USSR. Nikolai Malein. Progress Publishers, Imported Publications, Incorporated, 320 West Ohio Street, Chicago, Illinois 60610. 1985.

ENCYCLOPEDIA OF SOVIET LAW. Second Edition. F.J.M. Feldbrugge, G.P. van den Berg and William B. Simons. Martinus Nijhoff, Kluwer Academic Publishers, 101 Philip Drive, Assinippi Park, Norwell, Massachusetts 02061. 1985.

JOINT VENTURES IN THE SOVIET UNION: LAW AND PRACTICE. Eugene Theroux and Arthur L. George. Baker and McKenzie, 815 Connecticut Avenue, Northwest, Washington, D.C. 20006. 1988.

JOINT VENTURES WITH THE SOVIET UNION: LAW AND PRACTICE. Christopher Osakwe. Butterworth Legal Publishers, 90 Stiles Road, Salem, New Hampshire 03079. 1990- .

LAW AND ECONOMIC DEVELOPMENT IN THE SOVIET UNION. Reter B. Maggs, Gordon B. Smith and George Ginsburgs. Westview Press, 5500 Central Avenue, Boulder, Colorado 80301. 1982.

LAW, MORALITY AND MAN: THE SOVIET LEGAL SYSTEM IN ACTION. A. Vengerov and A. Danilevich. Progress Publishers, Imported Publications, Incorporated, 320 West Ohio Street, Chicago, Illinois 60610. 1985.

LAWYERS IN SOVIET WORKLIFE. Louise I. Shelley. Rutgers University Press, 109 Church Street, New Brunswick, New Jersey 08901. 1984.

LEGAL ASPECTS OF DOING BUSINESS IN EUROPE. Dennis Campbell, Editor. Kluwer Law Book Publishers, Incorporated, 36 West Forty-fourth Street, New York, New York 10036. 1992.

LEGAL ASPECTS OF TRADE AND INVESTMENT IN THE SOVIET UNION AND EASTERN EUROPE, 1990. Eugene Theroux. Practising Law Institute, 810 Seventh Avenue, New York, New York 10019. 1990.

MONGOLIAN-ENGLISH-RUSSIAN DICTIONARY OF LEGAL TERMS AND CONCEPTS. W.E. Butler and A.J. Nathanson. Kluwer Academic Publications, 101 Philip Drive, Assinippi Park, Norwell, Massachusetts 02061. 1983.

A NEW LOOK AT DOING BUSINESS WITH THE SOVIET UNION, 1989. Eugene Theroux. Practising Law Institute, 810 Seventh Avenue, New York, New York 10019. 1989.

THE RIGHT OF THE ACCUSED TO DEFENSE IN THE USSR. Yuri Stetsovsky. Progress Publishers, Imported Publications, Incorporated, 320 West Ohio Street, Chicago, Illinois 60610. 1982.

SOVIET BUSINESS LAW REPORT. Buraff Publications, 1350 Connecticut Avenue, Northwest, Suite 1000, Washington, D.C. 20036. Monthly.

THE SOVIET ECONOMIC SYSTEM: A LEGAL ANALYSIS. Olimpiad S. Ioffe and Peter B. Maggs. Westview Press, Incorporated, 5500 Central Avenue, Boulder, Colorado 80301. 1987.

SOVIET LAW. Second Edition. William E. Butler. Butterworth and Company, Limited, Borough Green, Sevenoaks, Kent TN15 8PH, England. 1988.

SOVIET LAW AND SOVIET REALITY. Olimpiad S. Ioffe. Martinus Nijhoff Publishers, Kluwer Academic Publishers, 101 Philip Drive, Assinippi Park, Norwell, Massachusetts 02061. 1985.

SOVIET LAW AND SOVIET SOCIETY: ETHICAL FOUNDATIONS OF THE SOVIET STRUCTURE, MECHANISM OF THE PLANNED ECONOMY, DUTIES AND RIGHTS OF THE PEASANTS AND WORKERS, RULERS AND TOILERS, THE FAMILY AND THE STATE, SOVIET JUSTICE, NATIONAL MINORITIES AND THEIR AUTONOMY, THE PEOPLE'S DEMOCRACIES AND THE SOVIET PATTERN FOR A UNITED WORLD. George C. Guins. Hyperion Press, 47 Riverside Avenue, Westport, Connecticut 06880. 1982.

SOVIET LAW IN THEORY AND PRACTICE. Olympiad S. Ioffe and Peter B. Maggs. Oceana Publications, Incorporated, 75 Main Street, Dobbs Ferry, New York 10522. 1983.

THE SOVIET LEGAL SYSTEM: THE LAW IN THE 1980s. John N. Hazard, William E. Butler and Peter B. Maggs. Parker School of Foreign and Comparative Law, Columbia University. Oceana Publications, Incorporated, 75 Main Street, Dobbs Ferry, New York 10522. 1984.

THE SOVIET UNION AND INTERNATIONAL COOPERATION IN LEGAL MATTERS. George Ginsburgs and William B. Simons. Martinus Nijhoff, Kluwer Academic Publishers, 101 Philip Drive, Assinippi Park, Norwell, Massachusetts 02061. 1988- .

THE SOVIET UNION THROUGH ITS LAWS. Leo Hecht, Editor. Praeger Publishers, One Madison Avenue, New York, New York 10010-3603. 1983.

THE STRUCTURE OF CRIMINAL PROCEDURE: LAWS AND PRACTICE OF FRANCE, THE SOVIET UNION, CHINA, AND THE UNITED STATES. Barton L. Ingraham. Greenwood Publishing Group, Incorporated, 88 Post Road West, P.O. Box 5007, Westport, Connecticut 06881. 1987.

SPAIN

BUSINESS LAW GUIDE TO SPAIN. Fabregat and Bermejo. Commerce Clearing House, Incorporated, 4025 West Peterson Avenue, Chicago, Illinois 60646. 1990.

CIVIL LAW II. ITALY, SPAIN, PORTUGAL AND THE LOW COUNTRIES: A BASIC COLLECTION. Law Library Microform Consortium, P.O. Box 11033, Honolulu, Hawaii 96828. 1991.

SPANISH BUSINESS LAW. Bernardo M. Cremades, Editor. Kluwer Law Book Publishers, Incorporated, 36 West Forty-fourth Street, New York, New York 10036. 1985.

SUDAN

ISLAMIC LAW AND SOCIETY IN THE SUDAN. Carolyn Fluehr-Lobban. Frank Cass and Company Limited, Gainsborough House, Gainsborough Road, London E11 1RS, England. 1987.

NATURAL RESOURCES DEVELOPMENT AND PROTECTION UNDER THE SUDANESE PETROLEUM LAWS. Muna Ahmed Yassin. College of Law, University of Utah, Salt Lake City, Utah 84112. 1985.

SWEDEN

ARBITRATION IN SWEDEN. Second Edition. Stockholm Chamber of Commerce, Stockholm, Sweden. 1984.

SWITZERLAND

BUSINESS LAW IN EUROPE: LEGAL, TAX, AND LABOUR ASPECTS OF BUSINESS OPERATIONS IN THE EUROPEAN COMMUNITY COUNTRIES AND SWITZERLAND. Second Edition. Kluwer Academic Publishers, 101 Philip Drive, Assinippi Park, Norwell, Massachusetts 02061. 1990- .

INTRODUCTION TO SWISS LAW. F. Dessemontet and T. Ansay. Deventer, Kluwer Law Book Publishers, Incorporated, 36 West Forty-fourth Street, New York, New York 10036. 1984.

THE TAXATION OF CORPORATIONS IN SWITZERLAND: PROFIT AND CAPITAL CASES OF THE CONFEDERATION, CANTONS, AND MUNICIPALITIES. Andre Margairaz and Roger Merkli. Deventer, Kluwer Law Book Publishers, Incorporated, 36 West Forty-fourth Street, New York, New York 10036. 1983.

TAIWAN

MARTIAL LAW IN TAIWAN: A HUMAN RIGHTS REPORT FROM THE ASIA RESOURCE CENTER AND FORMOSAN ASSOCIATION FOR HUMAN RIGHTS. Asia Resource Center, P.O. Box 15275, Washington, D. C. 20003. 1985.

TURKEY

INTRODUCTION TO TURKISH LAW. Tugrul Ansay and Don Wallace, Jr., Editors. Oceana Publications, Incorporated, 75 Main Street, Dobbs Ferry, New York 10522. 1987.

UNITED KINGDOM

BRITISH NATIONALITY LAW AND THE 1981 ACT. Laurie Fransman and Mithu Ghosh. Fourmat Publishing, 25 Bedford Row, London WC1R 4HE, England. 1982.

BUCKLEY ON THE COMPANIES ACTS. Fourteenth Edition. G. Brian Parker and Martin Buckley. Butterworth and Company, Limited, Borough Green, Sevenoaks, Kent TN15 8PH, England. 1981.

BUSINESS LAW. Stanley B. Marsh and J. Soulsby. State Mutual Book, 521 Fifth Avenue, Seventeenth Floor, New York, New York 10175. 1989.

CIVIL JURISDICTION IN SCOTLAND. A.E. Anton. W. Green and Son, St. Giles Street, Edinburgh EH1 1PU, Scotland. 1984.

CLARKE HALL AND MORRISON LAW RELATING TO CHILDREN AND YOUNG PERSONS. Tenth Edition. Margaret Booth, Brian Harris and A.H. White, Editors. Butterworth and Company, Limited, Borough Green, Sevenoaks, Kent TN15 8PH, England. 1985- .

COMPANY LAW IN THE UNITED KINGDOM AND THE EUROPEAN COMMUNITY: ITS HARMONIZATION AND UNIFICATION. Frank Wooldridge. Athlone Press, Atlantic Highlands, New Jersey. 1991.

COMPENSATION FOR CRIMINAL DAMAGE TO PROPERTY. D.S. Greer and V.A. Mitchell. SLS Legal Publications, Belfast, Northern Ireland. 1982.

COMPETITION LAWS OF UNITED KINGDOM AND REPUBLIC OF IRELAND. William Allan and Gerard Hogan. Matthew Bender and Company, Incorporated, 11 Penn Plaza, New York, New York 10001. 1988- .

COMPUTER CONTRACTS HANDBOOK: PRECEDENTS OF CONTRACTS FOR THE SALE, PURCHASE, SUPPORT, DISTRIBUTION AND LICENCE OF COMPUTERS AND COUPUTER SOFTWARE. M.T. Mich'elc Rennie. Sweet and Maxwell, Limited, South Quay Plaza, 183 Marsh Wall, London E14 9FT, England. 1985.

CONSTRUCTION LAW: LAW AND PRACTICE RELATING TO THE CONSTRUCTION INDUSTRY. Fourth Edition. John Uff. Sweet and Maxwell, Limited, South Quay Plaza, 183 Marsh Wall, London E14 9FT, England. 1985.

CONSUMER LAW FOR THE SMALL BUSINESS. Patricia Clayton. Kogan Page, Limited, 120 Petonville Road, London N1 9JN, England. 1983.

COPYRIGHT LAW IN THE UNITED KINGDOM AND THE EUROPEAN COMMUNITY. Peter Stone. Athlone Press, Atlantic Highlands, New Jersey. 1990.

DRINK/DRIVING: THE NEW LAW. Patrick Halnan. Oyex Longman, Norwich House, 11-13 Norwich Street, London EC4 1AB, England. 1984.

ENGLISH HABEAS CORPUS: LAW, HISTORY, AND POLITICS. University of California, Hastings College of the Law. Cosmos of Humanists Press, P.O. Box 11143, San Francisco, California 94101. 1984.

THE ENGLISH LEGAL SYSTEM. Seventh Edition. A.K.R. Kiralfy. Sweet and Maxwell, Limited, South Quay Plaza, 183 Marsh Wall, London E14 9FT, England. 1984.

THE ENGLISH LEGAL SYSTEM. Sixth Edition. R.J. Walker. Butterworth and Company, Limited, Borough Green, Sevenoaks, Kent TN15 8PH, England. 1985.

EUROPEAN COMMUNITY LAW IN THE UNITED KINGDOM. Fourth Edition. Lawrence Collins. Butterworth and Company, Limited, Borough Green, Sevenoaks, Kent TN15 8PH, England. 1990.

FRAUD. Anthony J. Arlidge and Jacques Parry. Waterlow Directories, Limited, 50 Fetter Lane, London EC4A 1AA, England. 1985.

GENERAL PRINCIPLES OF LAW. Third Edition. Clive R. Newton. State Mutual Book, 521 Fifth Avenue, Seventeenth Floor, New York, New York 10175. 1983.

GENERAL PRINCIPLES OF SCOTS LAW. Fourth Edition. Enid A. Marshall. W. Green and Son, St Giles Street, Edinburgh EH1 1PU, Scotland. 1982.

HOUSEMAN AND DAVIES LAW OF LIFE ASSURANCE. Tenth Edition. B.P.A. Davies. Butterworth and Company, Limited, Borough Green, Sevenoaks, Kent TN15 8PH, England. 1984.

HOUSING LAW IN NORTHERN IRELAND. Tom B. Hadden and W. David Trimble. SLS Legal Publications, Belfast, Northern Ireland. 1985.

IMMIGRATION LAW AND PRACTICE IN THE UNITED KINGDOM. Third Edition. Ian A. MacDonald and Nicholas J. Blake. Butterworth and Company, Limited, Borough Green, Sevenoaks, Kent TN15 8PH, England. 1991.

INFORMATION SOURCES IN LAW. R.G. Logan, Editor. K.G. Saur, 121 Chanlon Road, New Providence, New Jersey 07974. 1986.

INTRODUCTION TO ENGLISH LAW. Eleventh Edition. Philip S. James. State Mutual Book, 521 Fifth Avenue, Seventeenth Floor, New York, New York 10175. 1989.

INTRODUCTION TO ENGLISH LAW. Tenth Edition. William Geldart and D.C.M. Yardley. Oxford University Press, Incorporated, 200 Madison Avenue, New York, New York 10016. 1991.

AN INTRODUCTION TO THE LAW OF OBLIGATIONS. A.M. Tettenborn. Butterworth and Company, Limited, Borough Green, Sevenoaks, Kent TN15 8PH, England. 1984.

INTRODUCTION TO THE LAW OF SCOTLAND: BY W.M. GLOAG AND R. CANDLISH HENDERSON. Eighth Edition. A.B. Wilkinson and W.A. Wilson. W. Green and Son, St. Giles Street, Edinburgh EH1 1PU, Scotland. 1980.

LAW OF CLUBS: WITH A NOTE ON UNINCORPORATED ASSOCIATIONS. Sixth Edition. Longman, Incorporated, 95 Church Street, White Plains, New York 10601. 1987.

LAW OF COMPULSORY PURCHASE AND COMPENSATION. Fourth Edition. Keith Davies. Butterworth and Company, Limited, Borough Green, Sevenoaks, Kent TN15 8PH, England. 1984.

THE LAW OF HUSBAND AND WIFE IN SCOTLAND. Second Edition. Eric M. Clive. Scottish Universities Law Institute, W. Green and Son, St. Giles Street, Edinburgh EH1 1PU, Scotland. 1982.

THE LAW OF PUBLIC LEISURE SERVICES. Michael Scott. Sweet and Maxwell, Limited, South Quay Plaza, 183 Marsh Wall, London E14 9FT, England. 1985.

LEXIS, UNITED KINGDOM LAW LIBRARIES. Mead Data Central, P.O. Box 933, Dayton, Ohio 45401.

THE LICENSING OF ENTERTAINMENT IN ENGLAND AND WALES: LAW AND PRACTICE. Brian M. Gunn. Butterworth and Company, Limited, Borough Green, Sevenoaks, Kent TN15 8PH, England. 1985.

LOCAL GOVERNMENT IN SCOTLAND. George Monies. W. Green and Son, St. Giles Street, Edinburgh EH1 1PU, Scotland. 1985.

MASTERING BASIC ENGLISH LAW. William T. Major. Macmillan Education, Humanities Press International, 165 First Avenue, Atlantic Highlands, New Jersey 07716-1289. 1985.

MODERN EMPLOYMENT LAW: A GUIDE TO JOB SECURITY AND SAFETY. Sixth Edition. Michael Whincup. Heinemann, Limited, David and Charles, Incorporated, P.O. Box 257, North Pomfret, Vermont 05053. 1988.

THE MODERN ENGLISH LEGAL SYSTEM. P.F. Smith and S.H. Bailey. Sweet and Maxwell, Limited, South Quay Plaza, 183 Marsh Wall, London E14 9FT, England. 1984.

NORTHERN IRELAND SUPPLEMENT TO CROSS ON EVIDENCE. Fifth Edition. J.D. Jackson. SLS Legal Publications, Belfast, Northern Ireland. 1983.

THE PREVENTION OF TERRORISM IN BRITISH LAW. Clive Walker. Manchester University Press, St. Martin's Press, Incorporated, 175 Fifth Avenue, New York, New York 10010. 1986.

PROFESSIONAL NEGLIGENCE. Second Edition. A.M. Dundale and K.M. Stanton. Butterworth and Company, Limited, Borough Green, Sevenoaks, Kent TN15 8PH, England. 1989.

PUBLIC LAW AND DEMOCRACY IN THE UNITED KINGDOM AND THE UNITED STATES OF AMERICA. P.P. Craig. Oxford University Press, 200 Madison Avenue, New York, New York 10016. 1990.

RIGHTS IN SECURITY OVER MOVEABLES, CAUTIONARY OBLIGATIONS AND BANKRUPTCY. E.A. Marshall. W. Green and Son, St. Giles Street, Edinburgh EH1 1PU, Scotland. 1983.

SAFE TO BREATHE?: THE LEGAL AND PRACTICAL IMPLICATIONS OF WORKPLACE EXPOSURE LIMITS. David Farmer. Kingwood Publishing, Limited, 23 Kingfisher Way, Horsham, West Sussex RH12 2LT, England. 1984.

SCOTS LAW FOR JOURNALISTS. Fourth Edition. Eric M. Clive, George A. Watt and Bruce McKain. W. Green and Son, St. Giles Street, Edinburgh EH1 1PU, Scotland. 1984.

SCOTS LAW: TERMS AND EXPRESSIONS. John A. Beaton. W. Green and Son, St. Giles Street, Edinburgh EH1 1PU, Scotland. 1982.

SCOTS MERCANTILE LAW. Enid A. Marshall. W. Green and Son, St. Giles Street, Edinburgh EH1 1PU, Scotland. 1983.

UNITED KINGDOM LAW IN THE 1990S: COMPARATIVE AND COMMON LAW STUDIES FOR THE XIIITH INTERNATIONAL CONGRESS OF COMPARATIVE LAW. J.P. Gardner, Editor. United Kingdom National Committee of Comparative Law, available from: British Institute of International and Comparative Law, London, England. 1990.

UNITED KINGDOM OFFSHORE LEGISLATION GUIDE 1981. Second Edition. Harry Whitehead. Kogan Page, Limited, 120 Petonville Road, London N1 9JN, England. 1981.

THE WELSH VETO: THE WALES ACT 1978 AND THE REFERENDUM. David Foulkes, J. Barry Jones and R.A. Wilford. University of Wales Press, Cardiff, Wales. 1983.

WINDING UP COMPANIES IN NORTHERN IRELAND: A PRACTITIONERS GUIDE. John M. Hunter. Faculty of Law, Queen's University, Belfast, Northern Ireland. 1984.

VENEZUELA

VENEZUELAN LAW GOVERNING RESTRICTIVE BUSINESS PRACTICES. Gustave Brillembourg. International Law Institute, 1615 New Hampshire Avenue, Northwest, Washington, D.C. 20009-2550. 1986.

VIETNAM

THE LE CODE: LAW IN TRADITIONAL VIETNAM: A COMPARATIVE SINO-VIETNAMESE LEGAL STUDY WITH HISTORICAL-JURIDICAL ANALYSIS AND ANNOTATIONS. Nguyen Ngoc Huy and Ta Van Tai. Ohio University Press, Scott Quadrangle 220, Athens, Ohio 45701. 1987.

ZAMBIA

LAW, CUSTOM, AND SOCIAL ORDER: THE COLONIAL EXPERIENCE IN MALAWI AND ZAMBIA. Martin Chanock. Cambridge University Press, 40 West Twentieth Street, New York, New York 10011. 1985.

LAW IN ZAMBIA. Muna Ndulo, Editor. East Africa Publishing House, Northwestern University Press, 1735 Benson Avenue, Evanston, Illinois 60201. 1984.

FOREIGN RELATIONS
See: INTERNATIONAL LAW AND RELATIONS

FOREIGN TRADE
See: EXPORT AND IMPORT

FORENSIC MEDICINE
See: CORONERS AND MEDICAL EXAMINERS; MEDICAL JURISPRUDENCE AND MALPRACTICE

FORESTS AND FORESTRY
See also: AGRICULTURE DEPARTMENT; ENVIRONMENTAL PROTECTION AGENCY

STATUTES, CODES, STANDARDS, UNIFORM LAWS

THE PRINCIPAL LAWS RELATING TO FOREST SERVICE ACTIVITIES. United States Department of Agriculture, Forest Service. Superintendent of Documents, United States Government Printing Office, Washington, D.C. 20402. 1983.

LOOSELEAF SERVICES AND REPORTERS

FORESTLAND MANAGEMENT AND OPERATIONS: BUSINESS AND LEGAL PROBLEMS OF THE FOREST PRODUCTS INDUSTRY. Washington State Bar Association, 505 Madison Street, Seattle, Washington 98104. 1982.

TIMBER TRANSACTIONS. F. Gerald Burnett. Tax Management, Incorporated, 1231 Twenty-fifth Street, Northwest, Washington, D.C. 20037. 1983- .

TEXTBOOKS AND GENERAL WORKS

AMERICAN FOREST POLICY IN DEVELOPMENT. Stephen H. Spurr. University of Washington Press, P.O. Box 50096, Seattle, Washington 98145-5096. 1976.

AMERICAN FORESTRY: A HISTORY OF NATIONAL, STATE, AND PRIVATE COOPERATION. University of Nebraska Press, 901 North Seventeenth Street, Lincoln, Nebraska 68588-0520. 1985.

DECADE OF CHANGE: THE REMAKING OF FOREST SERVICE STATUTORY AUTHORITY DURING THE 1970'S. Dennis C. Le Master. Greenwood Publishing Group, Incorporated, 88 Post Road West, P.O. Box 5007, Westport, Connecticut 06881. 1984.

THE DEVELOPMENT OF FOREST LAW IN AMERICA: A HISTORICAL PRESENTATION OF THE SUCCESSIVE ENACTMENTS BY THE LEGISLATURES OF THE FORTY-EIGHT STATES OF THE AMERICAN UNION AND BY THE FEDERAL CONGRESS. J.P. Kinney. Ayer Company Publishers, Incorporated, 382 Main Street, P.O. Box 958, Salem, New Hampshire 03079. 1972. (Reprint of 1917 Edition).

THE DEVELOPMENT OF GOVERNMENTAL FOREST CONTROL IN THE UNITED STATES. Jenks Cameron. Da Capo Press, Incorporated, 233 Spring Street, New York, New York 10013. 1972. (Reprint of 1928 Edition).

FOREST POLICY. F.C. Hummel. Martinus Nijhoff/Kluwer Academic Publishers, 101 Philip Drive, Assinippi Park, Norwell, Massachusetts 02061. 1984.

THE FOREST SERVICE. Second Edition. Michael Frome. Westview Press, 5500 Central Avenue, Boulder, Colorado 80301. 1984.

FORESTLANDS: PUBLIC AND PRIVATE. Second Edition. Robert T. Deacon and M. Bruce Johnson, Editors. Pacific Institute for Public Policy Research. Ballinger Division, HarperCollins Publishers, 10 East Fifty-third Street, New York, New York 10022. 1985.

FORESTRY SECTOR INVERVENTION: THE IMPACTS OF PUBLIC REGULATION ON SOCIAL WELFARE. Roy Boyd. Iowa State University Press, 2121 South State Avenue, Ames, Iowa 50010. 1989.

INVESTMENTS IN FORESTRY: RESOURCES, LAND USE AND PUBLIC POLICY. Roger A. Sedjo. Westview Press. 5500 Central Avenue, Boulder, Colorado 80301. 1985

LEGISLATING FOR THE WILDERNESS: RARE II AND THE CALIFORNIA NATIONAL FORESTS. William D. Doron. Associated Faculty Press, Incorporated, 19 West Thirty-sixth Street, New York, New York 10018. 1986.

NEW STATE FOREST PRACTICE LAWS. National Conference of State Legislators, 1050 Seventeenth Street, Suite 2100, Denver, Colorado 80265-2101. 1980.

PRINCIPLES OF FOREST POLICY. A. Worrell. Shepard's/McGraw-Hill, P.O. Box 1235, Colorado Springs, Colorado 80901. 1970.

TAXATION OF NATURAL RESOURCES: OIL, GAS, MINERALS, AND TIMBER. Richard A. Westin. Practising Law Institute, 810 Seventh Avenue, New York, New York 10019. 1987.

DIGESTS, INDEXES, ABSTRACTS, CITATORS

DIGEST OF STATE FOREST FIRE LAWS. United States Department of Agriculture, Forest Service, Northeastern Area, State and Private Forestry. Superintendent of Documents, United States Government Printing Office, Washington, D.C. 20402. 1979.

LAW REVIEWS AND PERIODICALS

BOSTON COLLEGE ENVIRONMENTAL AFFAIRS LAW REVIEW. Boston College, 885 Centre Street, Newton Centre, Massachusetts 02159. Quarterly.

COLUMBIA JOURNAL OF ENVIRONMENTAL LAW. Columbia University, 435 West One Hundred Sixteenth Street, New York, New York 10027. Semiannually.

ECOLOGY LAW QUARTERLY. Boalt Hall School of Law, University of California at Berkeley, Berkeley, California 94720. Quarterly.

ENVIRONMENTAL LAW. Northwestern School of Law of Lewis and Clark College, 10015 Southwest Terilliger Boulevard, Portland, Oregon 97219. Quarterly.

ENVIRONMENTAL LAW REPORTER. Environmental Law Institute, 1616 P Street, Northwest, Suite 200, Washington, D.C. 20036. Monthly.

HARVARD ENVIRONMENTAL LAW REVIEW. Harvard Law School, Publications Center, Cambridge, Massachusetts 02138. Semiannually.

JOURNAL OF LAND USE AND ENVIRONMENTAL LAW. Florida State University, College of Law, Tallahassee, Florida 32306. Semiannually.

LAND AND WATER LAW REVIEW. University of Wyoming College of Law, University Station, Box 3035, Laramie, Wyoming 82071. Semiannual.

LEGAL JOURNAL OF ENVIRONMENTAL LAW. Boston College, Environmental Affairs Law Review, 885 Centre Street, Newton Centre, Massachusetts 02159. Quarterly.

NATURAL RESOURCE JOURNAL. University of New Mexico School of Law, 1117 Stanford Northeast, Albuquerque, New Mexico 87131. Quarterly.

NATURAL RESOURCES AND ENVIRONMENT. American Bar Association, Section of Natural Resources Law, 750 North Lake Shore Drive, Chicago, Illinois 60611. Quarterly.

TIMBER TAX JOURNAL. International Specialized Book Services, 5602 Northeast Hassalo Street, Portland, Oregon 97213-3640.

UCLA JOURNAL OF ENVIRONMENTAL LAW AND POLICY. UCLA School of Law, 405 Hilgard Avenue, Los Angeles, California 90024. Semiannually.

VIRGINIA JOURNAL OF NATURAL RESOURCES LAW. University of Virginia, School of Law, Charlottesville, Virginia 22901. Semiannually.

NEWSPAPERS AND NEWSLETTERS

FOREST LAND OWNER. Forest Land Owners of California, 3807 Pasadena Avenue, Suite 100, Sacramento, California 95821. Monthly.

BIBLIOGRAPHIES

FOREST TAXATION. Jeffrey C. Stier. Vance Bibliographies, P.O. Box 229, 112 North Charter Street, Monticello, Illinois 61856. 1982.

LAW, NATURAL RESOURCES AND LAND USE: THE ENVIRONMENTAL COLLECTION OF THE PAUL L. BOLEY LAW LIBRARY. Joe Stephens. Northwestern School of Law of Lewis and Clark College, 10015 Southwest Terilliger Boulevard, Portland, Oregon 97219. 1984.

LAW, POLICY, PLANNING AND ADMINISTRATION IN FORESTRY. Judith L. Schwab. Vance Bibliographies, P.O. Box 229, 112 North Charter Street, Monticello, Illinois 61856. 1982.

NATIONAL PARKS AND FORESTS: THE ADMINISTRATION OF THE NATIONAL PARK SERVICE AND FOREST SERVICE. Glenna Dunning. Vance Bibliographies, P.O. Box 229, 112 North Charter Street, Monticello, Illinois 61856. 1985.

DIRECTORIES

DIRECTORY OF URBAN AND COMMUNITY FORESTRY PROFESSIONALS IN THE UNITED STATES AND CANADA. American Forestry Association, 1516 P Street, Northwest, Washington, D.C. 20005. 1982- .

FOREST RESOURCES SYSTEMS INSTITUTE -- DIRECTORY OF FORESTRY-RELATED SOFTWARE. 201 North Pine Street, Suite 24, Florence, Alabama 35630. 1985- .

INTERNATIONAL DIRECTORY OF FORESTRY AND FOREST PRODUCT LIBRARIES. Pacific Southwest Forest and Range, Experiment Station, United States Forest Service. United States Department of Agriculture, 201 Fourteenth Street, Southwest, Washington, D.C. 20250. 1985- .

ASSOCIATIONS AND PROFESSIONAL SOCIETIES

AMERICAN FOREST COUNCIL. 1250 Connecticut Avenue, Northwest, Suite 320, Washington, D.C. 20036. (202) 463-2455.

FORESTS AND FORESTRY

AMERICAN FORESTRY ASSOCIATION. 1516 P Street, Northwest, Washington, D.C. 20005. (202) 667-3300.

ASSOCIATION OF CONSULTING FORESTERS. 5410 Grosvenor Lane, Suite 205, Bethesda, Maryland 20814. (301) 530-6795.

FOREST FARMERS ASSOCIATION. P.O. Box 95385, Atlanta, Georgia 30347. (404) 325-2954.

FOREST HISTORY SOCIETY. 701 Vickers Avenue, Durham, North Carolina 27701. (919) 682-9319.

FOREST INDUSTRIES COUNCIL. 1250 Connecticut Avenue, Northwest, Suite 320, Washington, D.C. 20036. (202) 463-2460.

NATIONAL ASSOCIATION OF STATE FORESTERS. c/o Terri Bates, Hall of States, 444 North Capitol Street, Northwest, Washington, D.C. 20001. (202) 624-5415.

SECTION OF NATURAL RESOURCES, ENERGY AND ENVIRONMENTAL LAW. American Bar Association, 750 North Lake Shore Drive, Chicago, Illinois 60611. (312) 988-5158.

SOCIETY OF AMERICAN FORESTERS. 5400 Grosvenor Lane, Bethesda, Maryland 20814. (301) 897-8720.

UNITED STATES FOREST SERVICE. United States Department of Agriculture, 201 Fourteenth Street, Southwest, Washington, D.C. 20250. (202) 447-6661.

WORLD FORESTRY CENTER. 4033 Southwest Canyon Road, Portland, Oregon 97221. (503) 228-1367.

RESEARCH CENTERS, INSTITUTES, CLEARINGHOUSES

SCIENCE FOR CITIZENS CENTER. Western Michigan University, 328 Moore Hall, Kalamazoo, Michigan 49008. (616) 387-2715.

ENVIRONMENTAL LAW INSTITUTE. 1616 P Street, Northwest, Suite 200, Washington, D.C. 20036. (202) 328-5150.

INTERNATIONAL DEVELOPMENT RESEARCH CENTRE. 250 Albert Street, P.O. Box/C.P. 8500, O Hawa, ON, Canada K1G 3H9. (613) 236-6163.

STATISTICS SOURCES

AGRICULTURE STATISTICS. United States Department of Agriculture. Superintendent of Documents, United States Government Printing Office, Washington, D.C. 20402. Annual.

NATIONAL FOREST SYSTEM. United States Department of Agriculture, 201 Fourteenth Street, Southwest, Washington, D.C. 20250. Annual.

UNPUBLISHED DATA. United States Department of Agriculture, 201 Fourteenth Street, Southwest, Washington, D.C. 20250.

WILDLIFE STATISTICS. United States Department of Agriculture, 201 Fourteenth Street, Southwest, Washington, D.C. 20250. Annual.

OTHER SOURCES

PUBLIC LAW AND POLICY: ALI-ABA COURSE OF STUDY MATERIALS. American Law Institute--American Bar Association Committee on Continuing Professional Education, 4025 Chestnut Street, Philadelphia, Pennsylvania 19104. 1984.

FORGERY
See also: COUNTERFEITING; FRAUD

TEXTBOOKS AND GENERAL WORKS

THE ART OF THE FORGER. Christopher Wright. State Mutual Book, 521 Fifth Avenue, New York, New York 10125. 1984.

CHECK FORGERS. John F. Klein and Arthur Montague. Lexington Books, 125 Spring Street, Lexington, Massachusetts 02173. 1977.

COUNTERFEITING AND FORGERY: A PRACTICAL GUIDE TO THE LAW. Roland Rowell. Butterworth Legal Publishers, 90 Stiles Road, Salem, New Hampshire 03079. 1986.

CROSS-CHECK SYSTEM FOR FORGERY AND QUESTIONED DOCUMENT EXAMINATION. Doris M. Williamson and Antoinette E. Meenach. Nelson-Hall, Publishers, 111 North Canal Street, Chicago, Illinois 60606. 1981.

FAKING IT: ART AND THE POLITICS OF FORGERY. Ian Haywood. Harvester Press, Brighton, Sussex, England. 1987.

FORGED DOCUMENTS: PROCEEDINGS OF THE 1989 HOUSTON CONFERENCE. Oak Knoll Books, 414 Delaware Street, New Castle, Delaware 19720. 1990.

THE GENUINE ARTICLE: THE MAKING AND UNMASKING OF FAKES AND FORGERIES. John F. Mills. Universe Books Incorporated, 300 Park Avenue South, New York, New York 10010. 1982.

LAW OF DISPUTED AND FORGED DOCUMENTS. J. Newton Baker. Michie Company, P.O. Box 7587, Charlottesville, Virginia 22906-7582. 1955.

QUESTIONED DOCUMENTS. Albert S. Osborn. Nelson-Hall, Publishers, 111 North Canal Street, Chicago, Illinois 60606. 1974. (Reprint of 1926 Edition).

SCIENTIFIC EXAMINATION OF QUESTIONED DOCUMENTS. O. Hilton. Elsevier Science Publishing Company, Incorporated, P.O. Box 882, Madison Square Station, New York, New York 10159. 1981.

ASSOCIATIONS AND PROFESSIONAL SOCIETIES

AMERICAN ASSOCIATION OF HANDWRITING ANALYSTS. 820 West Maple, Hinsdale, Illinois 60521. (312) 325-2266.

AMERICAN HANDWRITING ANALYSIS FOUNDATION. 1211 El Solyo Avenue, Campbell, California 95008. (408) 377-6775.

HANDWRITING ANALYSTS, INTERNATIONAL. 1504 West Twenty-ninth Street, Davenport, Iowa 52804. (319) 391-7350.

FORMS
See: LEGAL FORMS

FOSTER CARE
See also: FAMILY LAW

HANDBOOKS, MANUALS, FORMBOOKS

REASONABLE EFFORTS TO PREVENT FOSTER PLACEMENT: A GUIDE TO IMPLEMENTATION. Second Edition. Debra Ratterman. American Bar Association, 1800 M Street, Northwest, Washington, D.C. 20036. 1987.

TEXTBOOKS AND GENERAL WORKS

ADVOCATING FOR CHILDREN AND FAMILIES IN NEED OF ASSISTANCE (CINA) PROCEEDINGS. Susan P. Leviton and Larry M. Waranch. Maryland Institute for Continuing Professional Education of Lawyers, Incorporated, 520 West Fayette Street, Baltimore, Maryland 21201. 1985.

CHILDREN IN FOSTER CARE: A LONGITUDINAL INVESTIGATION. David Fanshel and Eugene B. Shinn. Columbia University Press, 562 West One Hundred Thirteenth Street, New York, New York 10025. 1978.

FOSTER CARE: CURRENT ISSUES, POLICIES, AND PRACTICES. Martha J. Cox and Roger D. Cox, Editors. ABLEX Publishing Corporation, 355 Chestnut Street, Norwood, New Jersey 07648. 1985.

FOSTER CHILDREN IN THE COURTS. Mark Hardin, Editor. Butterworth Legal Publishers, 90 Stiles Road, Salem, New Hampshire 03079. 1983.

GROUP CHILD CARE AS A FAMILY SERVICE. Alan Keith-Lucas and Clifford W. Sanford, Editors. University of North Carolina Press, P.O. Box 2288, 116 South Boundary Street, Chapel Hill, North Carolina 27515-2288. 1977.

THE KID BUSINESS, HOW IT EXPLOITS THE CHILDREN IT SHOULD HELP. Ronald B. Taylor. Houghton Mifflin Company, 1 Beacon Street, Boston, Massachusetts 02108. 1981.

THE LEGAL FRAMEWORK FOR ENDING FOSTER CARE DRIFT: A GUIDE TO EVALUATING AND IMPROVING STATE LAWS, REGULATIONS AND COURT RULES. Diane Dodson, with Mark Hardin and others. Foster Care Project, National Legal Resource Center for Child Advocacy and Protection, American Bar Association, 1800 M Street, Northwest, Washington, D.C. 20036. 1983.

LONG TERM FOSTER CARE. Janet Rowe and others. St. Martin's Press, 175 Fifth Avenue, New York, New York 10010. 1984.

THE RIGHTS OF FOSTER PARENTS. Robert M. Horowitz. American Bar Association, Young Lawyers Division, National Legal Resource Center for Child Advocacy and Protection, 1800 M Street, Northwest, Washington, D.C. 20036. 1989.

STATE CHILD WELFARE REFORM: TOWARD A FAMILY-BASED POLICY. Susan Robison and Sharon Schwoch. National Conference of State Legislatures, 1050 Seventeenth Street, Suite 2100, Denver, Colorado 80265. 1987.

ASSOCIATIONS AND PROFESSIONAL SOCIETIES

AMERICAN FOSTER CARE RESOURCES. P.O. Box 271, King George, Virginia 22485. (703) 775-7410.

CHILD WELFARE LEAGUE OF AMERICA. 440 First Street, Northwest, Washington, D.C. 20001. (202) 638-2952.

CHILDHELP U.S.A., INCORPORATED. 6463 Independence Avenue, Woodland Hills, California 91370. (818) 347-7280.

NATIONAL ASSOCIATION OF FOSTER CARE REVIEWERS. 3627 East Indian School Road, Suite 107, Phoenix, Arizona 85018. (602) 381-1601.

ORPHAN FOUNDATION OF AMERICA. 1500 Massachusetts Avenue, Northwest, Washington, D.C. 20005. (202) 861-0762.

FOUNDATIONS
See: ASSOCIATIONS AND NONPROFIT CORPORATIONS; CHARITIES

FRANCHISING

LOOSELEAF SERVICES AND REPORTERS

BUSINESS FRANCHISE GUIDE. Commerce Clearing House, Incorporated, 4025 West Peterson Avenue, Chicago, Illinois 60646. 1980- .

ESTABLISHING AND OPERATING UNDER A FRANCHISE RELATIONSHIP. Martin D. Fern. Matthew Bender and Company, Incorporated, 11 Penn Plaza, New York, New York 10001. 1986- .

FRANCHISING. Gladys Glickman. Matthew Bender and Company, Incorporated, 11 Penn Plaza, New York, New York 10001. 1969- .

FRANCHISING: REALITIES AND REMEDIES. Harold Brown. Law Journal Seminars-Press, Incorporated, 111 Eighth Avenue, New York, New York 10011. 1981- .

TEXTBOOKS AND GENERAL WORKS

COMMERCIAL AGENCY AND DISTRIBUTION AGREEMENTS: LAW AND PRACTICE IN THE MEMBER STATES OF THE EUROPEAN COMMUNITY. Graham and Trotman Limited, Sterling House, 66 Wilton Road, London SW1V 1DE, England. 1989.

FRANCHISE PROTECTION: LAWS AGAINST TERMINATION AND THE ESTABLISHMENT OF ADDITIONAL FRANCHISES. American Bar Association, 750 North Lake Shore Drive, Chicago, Illinois 60611. 1990.

FRANCHISING. William L. Siegel. John Wiley and Sons, Incorporated, 605 Third Avenue, New York, New York 10158. 1983.

FRANCHISING ADVISER. William J. Keating. Shepard's/McGraw-Hill, P.O. Box 1235, Colorado Springs, Colorado 80901. 1987.

FRANCHISING: IT'S NATURE, SCOPE, ADVANTAGES, AND DEVELOPMENT. Second Edition. Charles L. Vaughn. Lexington Books, 125 Spring Street, Lexington, Massachusetts 02173. 1979.

FRANCHISING: LEGAL AND FINANCIAL ASPECTS. Icarus Press, Incorporated, P.O. Box 1225, South Bend, Indiana 46624-1225. 1985.

FRANCHISING: REGULATION OF BUYING AND SELLING A FRANCHISE. (Corporate Practice Series). Phillip F. Zeidman and Perry C. Ausbrook. Bureau of National Affairs, 1231 Twenty-fifth Street, Northwest, Washington, D.C. 20037. 1983- . (Periodic Supplements).

INTERNATIONAL FRANCHISING: AN OVERVIEW. M. Mendelsohn, Editor. Elsevier Publishing Company, P.O. Box 882, Madison Square Station, New York, New York 10159. 1984.

REFUSALS TO DEAL AND EXCLUSIVE DISTRIBUTORSHIPS. American Bar Association, Section of Antitrust Law, 750 North Lake Shore Drive, Chicago, Illinois 60611. 1983.

ROADSIDE EMPIRES: HOW THE CHAINS FRANCHISED AMERICA. Stan Luxenberg. Viking Press, 375 Hudson Street, New York, New York 10014-3657. 1986.

UNDERSTANDING FRANCHISE CONTRACTS. David C. Hjelmfelt. Pilot Books, 103 Cooper Street, Babylon, New York 11702. 1984.

ENCYCLOPEDIAS AND DICTIONARIES

INTERNATIONAL FRANCHISING: COMMONLY USED TERMS. Alexander S. Konigsberg. International Bar Association, London, England. 1989.

ANNUALS AND SURVEYS

FORUM COMMITTEE ON FRANCHISING ANNUAL FORUM. American Bar Association, 750 North Lake Shore Drive, Chicago, Illinois 60611. Annual.

SURVEY OF FOREIGN LAWS AND REGULATIONS AFFECTING INTERNATIONAL FRANCHISING. Second edition. Philip F. Zeidman. American Bar Association, Franchising Committee, 750 North Lake Shore Drive, Chicago, Illinois 60611. 1990.

LAW REVIEWS AND PERIODICALS

FRANCHISE LAW JOURNAL. American Bar Association, Forum Committee on Franchising, 750 North Lake Shore Drive, Chicago, Illinois 60611. Quarterly.

NEWSLETTERS AND NEWSPAPERS

CABLE TV FRANCHISING. Paul Kegan Associates, Incorporated, 126 Clock Tower Place, Carmel, California 93923. Monthly.

FRANCHISE LAW JOURNAL. American Bar Association, Forum Committee on Franchising, 750 North Lake Shore Drive, Chicago, Illinois 60611. Quarterly.

FRANCHISE LEGAL DIGEST. International Franchise Association, 1350 New York Avenue, Northwest, Suite 900, Washington, D.C. 20005. Bimonthly.

THE INFO-FRANCHISE NEWSLETTER. Info Press, 728 Center Street, Box 550, Lewiston, New York 14092. Monthly.

BIBLIOGRAPHIES

FRANCHISE LAW BIBLIOGRAPHY. Section of Antitrust Law, American Bar Association, 750 North Lake Shore Drive, Chicago, Illinois 60611. 1984.

ASSOCIATIONS AND PROFESSIONAL SOCIETIES

AMERICAN FRANCHISE ASSOCIATION. 2730 Wilshire Boulevard, Suite 400 Santa Monica, California 90403. (213) 829-0841.

FRANCHISE CONSULTANTS INTERNATIONAL ASSOCIATION. 5147 South Angela Road, Memphis, Tennessee 38117. (901) 761-3085.

INTERNATIONAL FRANCHISE ASSOCIATION. 1350 New York Avenue, Northwest, Suite 900, Washington, D.C. 20005. (202) 628-8000.

NATIONAL ASSOCIATION OF FRANCHISE COMPANIES. P.O. Box 6996, Hollywood, Florida 33081. (305) 966-1530.

OTHER SOURCES

FRANCHISING IN THE U.S. ECONOMY: PROSPECTS AND PROBLEMS. Dean M. Sagar. Superintendent of Documents, United States Government Printing Office, Washington, D.C. 20402. 1990.

FRAUD
See also: COUNTERFEITING; CRIMINAL LAW; FORGERY

STATUTES, CODES, STANDARDS, UNIFORM LAWS

UNIFORM FRAUDULENT TRANSFER ACT. National Conference of Commissioners on Uniform State Laws. Uniform Laws Annotated. West Publishing Company, P.O. Box 64526, 50 West Kellogg Boulevard, St. Paul, Minnesota 55164-0526. 1984- . (Annual Supplements).

LOOSELEAF SERVICES AND REPORTERS

BUSINESS CRIME. Stanley S. Arkin. Matthew Bender and Company, Incorporated, 11 Penn Plaza, New York, New York 10001. 1981- .

FRAUDULENT BROKER-DEALER PRACTICES. Stuart C. Goldberg. American Institute for Securities Regulation, 39 Broadway, New York, New York 10014. 1978- .

GOVERNMENT CONTRACT FRAUD. Brian C. Elmer. Federal Publications, Incorporated, 1120 Twentieth Street, Northwest, Washington, D.C. 20036. 1985- .

LITIGATION AND PRACTICE UNDER RULE 10b-5. Second Edition. Arnold S. Jacobs. Clark Boardman Company, Limited, 435 Hudson Street, New York, New York 10014. 1981- .

SECURITIES FRAUD AND COMMODITIES FRAUD. Alan R. Broomberg and Lewis D. Lowenfels. Shepard's/McGraw-Hill, P.O. Box 1235, Colorado Springs, Colorado 80901. 1980- .

TEXTBOOKS AND GENERAL WORKS

CORPORATE FRAUD. Michael J. Comer. Shepard's/McGraw-Hill, P.O. Box 1235, Colorado Springs, Colorado 80901. 1985.

CORPORATE FRAUD: THE BASICS OF PREVENTION AND DETECTION. Jack Bologna. Butterworth Legal Publishers, 90 Stiles Road, Salem, New Hampshire 03079. 1984.

ELECTRONIC FUND TRANSFER SYSTEMS FRAUD: COMPUTER CRIME. Jones M. Tien, Thomas F. Rich and Michael F. Cahn. Public Systems Evaluation, Incorporated, Cambridge, Massachusetts. 1985.

ENFORCING STATE AND FEDERAL MONEY JUDGMENTS AND COMMERCIAL CLAIMS. Practising Law Institute, 810 Seventh Avenue, New York, New York 10019. 1988.

HOW TO DETECT AND PREVENT BUSINESS FRAUD. W. Steve Albrecht. Prentice-Hall, Incorporated, 113 Sylvan, Englewood Cliffs, New Jersey 07632. 1982.

THE HUTTON REPORT: A SPECIAL INVESTIGATION INTO THE CONDUCT OF E.F. HUTTON AND COMPANY, INCORPORATED THAT GAVE RISE TO THE PLEA OF GUILTY ENTERED ON MAY 2, 1985. Griffin B. Bell. King and Spaulding Law Firm, 2500 Trust Company Tower, Atlanta, Georgia 30303. 1985.

IDENTIFYING AND PROSECUTING FRAUD AND ABUSE IN STATE AND LOCAL CONTRACTING. Section on Urban, State and Local Government Law and Section of Public Contract Law, American Bar Association, 750 North Lake Shore Drive, Chicago, Illinois 60611. 1984.

LYING, CHEATING, STEALING. Gwynn Nettler. Anderson Publishing Company, 2035 Reading Road, Cincinnati, Ohio 45202. 1982.

MENS REA: STATE OF MIND DEFENSES IN CRIMINAL AND CIVIL CASES: A COURSE HANDBOOK. Practising Law Institute, 810 Seventh Avenue, New York, New York 10019. 1985.

PROFITS OF DECEIT: DISPATCHES FROM THE FRONT LINES OF FRAUD. Patricia Franklin. Heinemann, London, England. 1990.

RECOVERY OF DAMAGES FOR FRAUD. Robert L. Dunn. Lawpress, P.O. Box 596, Kentfield, California 94914. 1988.

WAYWARD CAPITALISTS: TARGET OF THE SECURITIES AND EXCHANGE COMMISSION. Susan P. Shapiro. Yale University Press, 302 Temple Street, New Haven, Connecticut 06520. 1984.

NEWSLETTERS AND NEWSPAPERS

ECONOMIC CRIME DIGEST. National District Attorneys Association, 1033 North Fairfax Street, Alexandria, Virginia 22314. Monthly.

BIBLIOGRAPHIES

FRAUD: A BIBLIOGRAPHY. Mary Vance. Vance Bibliographies, P.O. Box 229, 112 North Charter Street, Monticello, Illinois 61856. 1983.

ASSOCIATIONS AND PROFESSIONAL SOCIETIES

ALLIANCE AGAINST FRAUD IN TELEMARKETING. National Consumers League, 815 Fifteenth Street, Northwest, Suite 516, Washington, D.C. 20005. (202) 639-8140.

COMMUNICATIONS FRAUD CONTROL ASSOCIATION. 7921 Jones Branch Drive, Suite 300, McLean, Virginia 22102. (703) 848-9768.

INSURANCE CRIME PREVENTIION INSTITUTE. 15 Franklin Street, Westport, Connecticut 06880. (203) 226-6347.

NATIONAL ASSOCIATION OF CERTIFIED FRAUD EXAMINERS. 716 West Avenue, Austin, Texas 78701. (512) 478-9070.

NATIONAL CONSUMER FRAUD TASK FORCE. 1500 West Twenty-third Street, Sunset Island, No. 3, Miami Beach, Florida 33140. (305) 532-2607.

FREEDOM OF ASSEMBLY AND ASSOCIATION
See also: CIVIL RIGHTS

HANDBOOKS, MANUALS, FORMBOOKS

THE RIGHT TO PROTEST: THE BASIC ACLU GUIDE TO FREE EXPRESSION. Joel M. Gora. Southern Illinois University Press, P.O. Box 3697, Carbondale, Illinois 62902-3697. 1991.

TEXTBOOKS AND GENERAL WORKS

CIVIL LIBERTIES AND NAZIS: THE SKOKIE FREE SPEECH CONTROVERSY. James L. Gibson and Richard D. Bingham. Praeger Publications, One Madison Avenue, New York, New York 10010-3603. 1985.

THE FIRST AMENDMENT, 1791-1991: TWO HUNDRED YEARS OF FREEDOM. James E. Leahy. McFarland and Company, Incorporated, Box 611, Jefferson, North Carolina 28640. 1991.

FREEDOM OF ASSEMBLY AND ASSOCIATION

FREE SPEECH AND ASSOCIATION: THE SUPREME COURT AND FIRST AMENDMENT. Philip B. Kurland. University of Chicago Press, 5801 Ellis Avenue, Fourth Floor, Chicago, Illinois 60637. 1976.

HUMAN RIGHTS AND INTERNATIONAL ACTION: THE CASE OF FREEDOM OF ASSOCIATION. Ernst B. Haas. Stanford University Press, Stanford, California 94305-2235. 1970.

NAZIS IN SKOKIE: FREEDOM, COMMUNITY AND THE FIRST AMENDMENT. Donald A. Downs. University of Notre Dame Press, P.O. Box L, Notre Dame, Indiana 46556. 1986.

THE NEGRO AND THE FIRST AMENDMENT. Harry J. Kalven. University of Chicago Press, 5801 Ellis Avenue, Fourth Floor, Chicago, Illinois 60637. 1966.

THE RIGHT OF ASSEMBLY AND ASSOCIATION. Second Edition. M. Glenn Abernathy. University of South Carolina Press, 508 Assembly Street, Columbus, South Carolina 29208. 1981.

LAW REVIEWS AND PERIODICALS

BILL OF RIGHTS JOURNAL. National Emergency Civil Liberties Committee, 175 Fifth Avenue, Suite 814, New York, New York 10010. Annual.

CIVIL LIBERTIES. American Civil Liberties Union, 132 West Forty-third Street, New York, New York 10036. Quarterly.

CIVIL LIBERTIES ALERT. American Civil Liberties Union, 132 West Forty-third Street, New York, New York 10036. Monthly.

ASSOCIATIONS AND PROFESSIONAL SOCIETIES

ALLIANCE TO END REPRESSION. 220 South State Street, Suite 1430, Chicago, Illinois 60604. (312) 427-4064.

AMERICAN CIVIL LIBERTIES UNION. 132 West Forty-third Street, New York, New York 10036. (212) 944-9800.

AMERICAN JEWISH CONGRESS. 15 East Eighty-fourth Street, New York, New York 10028. (212) 879-4500.

CENTER FOR CONSTITUTIONAL RIGHTS. 666 Broadway, Seventh Floor, New York, New York 10012. (212) 614-6464.

NAACP LEGAL DEFENSE AND EDUCATION FUND. 99 Hudson Street, 16th Floor, New York, New York 10013. (212) 219-1900.

NATIONAL COMMITTEE AGAINST REPRESSIVE LEGISLATION. 1313 West Eighth Street, Suite 313, Los Angeles, California 90017. (213) 484-6661.

NATIONAL EMERGENCY CIVIL LIBERTIES COMMITTEE. 175 Fifth Avenue, Suite 814, New York, New York 10010. (212) 673-2040.

NATIONAL JUSTICE FOUNDATION OF AMERICA. 1617 Sixteenth Street, Sacramento, California 95814. (916) 442-0537.

PEOPLE FOR THE AMERICAN WAY. 2000 M Street, Northwest, Suite 400, Washington, D.C. 20036. (202) 467-4999.

SOUTHERN CHRISTIAN LEADERSHIP COUNCIL. 334 Auburn Avenue, Northwest, Atlanta, Georgia 30312. (404) 522-1420.

RESEARCH CENTERS, INSTITUTES, CLEARINGHOUSES

CENTER FOR APPLIED JURISPRUDENCE. Pacific Research Institute for Public Policy, 177 Post Street, Suite 500, San Francisco, California 94108. (415) 989-0833.

INSTITUTE OF BILL OF RIGHTS LAW. College of William and Mary, Marshall-Wythe School of Law, Williamsburg, Virginia 23185. (804) 221-3810.

FREEDOM OF ASSOCIATION
See: FREEDOM OF ASSEMBLY AND ASSOCIATION

FREEDOM OF INFORMATION
See also: FREEDOM OF PRESS; FREEDOM OF SPEECH; JUSTICE DEPARTMENT

LOOSELEAF SERVICES AND REPORTERS

BUSINESS INFORMATION: PROTECTION AND DISCLOSURE--THE FREEDOM OF INFORMATION ACT AND RELATED LAWS. Peter C. Hein. Law and Business, Incorporated, 855 Valley Road, Clifton, New Jersey 07013. 1983- . (Periodic Supplements).

FEDERAL INFORMATION DISCLOSURE: PROCEDURES, FORMS, AND THE LAW. Second Edition. James T. O'Reilly. Shepard's/McGraw-Hill, P.O. Box 1235, Colorado Springs, Colorado 80901. 1990. (Annual Supplements).

GOVERNMENT DISCLOSURE. Robert G. Vaughn, Editor. Prentice-Hall, Incorporated, 113 Sylvan Avenue, Englewood Cliffs, New Jersey 07632. 1979- .

GUIDEBOOK TO THE FREEDOM OF INFORMATION AND PRIVACY ACTS. Robert F. Bouchard and Justin D. Franklin. Clark Boardman Company, Limited, 435 Hudson Street, New York, New York 10014. 1986- . (Annual Supplements).

INFORMATION LAW: FREEDOM OF INFORMATION, PRIVACY, OPEN MEETINGS, OTHER ACCESS LAWS. Burt A. Braverman and Frances J. Chetwynd. Practising Law Institute, 810 Seventh Avenue, New York, New York 10019. 1985- .

PRIVACY LAW AND PRACTICE. Matthew Bender and Company, Incorporated, 11 Penn Plaza, New York, New York 10001. 1987.

HANDBOOKS, MANUALS, FORMBOOKS

FREEDOM OF INFORMATION GUIDE. Want Publishing Company, 1511 K Street, Northwest, Washington, D.C. 20005. 1984.

THE FREEDOM OF INFORMATION ACT FOR ATTORNEYS AND ACCESS PROFESSIONALS. Office of Legal Education, United States Department of Justice. Superintendent of Documents, United States Government Printing Office, Washington, D.C. 20402. 1989.

HOW TO USE THE FEDERAL FOI ACT: A PUBLICATION OF THE FOI SERVICE CENTER, A PROJECT OF THE REPORTERS COMMITTEE FOR FREEDOM OF THE PRESS. Fifth Edition. Elaine P. English, Editor. Freedom of Information Service Center, 2000 P Street, Northwest, Washington, D.C. 20036. 1985.

HOW TO USE THE FREEDOM OF INFORMATION ACT. Third Edition. Washington Researchers Publishing, 2612 P Street, Northwest, Washington, D.C. 20007. 1989.

PROTECTING THE FREEDOM TO LEARN: A CITIZEN'S GUIDE. Barbara Parker and Stefanie Weiss. People for the American Way, 2000 M Street, Northwest, Suite 400, Washington, D.C. 20036. 1983.

USING THE FREEDOM OF INFORMATION ACT: A STEP BY STEP GUIDE. American Civil Liberties Union, 132 West Forty-third Street, New York, New York 10036. 1990.

YOUR RIGHT TO GOVERNMENT INFORMATION (AN ACLU HANDBOOK). Christine M. Marwick. Southern Illinois University Press, P.O. Box 3697, Carbondale, Illinois 62902-3697. 1985.

TEXTBOOKS AND GENERAL WORKS

BUSINESS INFORMATION: PROTECTION AND DISCLOSURE, FREEDOM OF INFORMATION ACT AND RELATED LAWS. William S. Hein and Company, Incorporated, Hein Building, 1285 Main Street, Buffalo, New York 14209. 1983.

A CITIZEN'S RIGHT TO KNOW: RISK COMMUNICATION AND PUBLIC POLICY. Susan G. Hadden. Westview Press, Incorporated, 5500 Central Avenue, Boulder, Colorado 80301. 1989.

FAIR USE AND FREE INQUIRY: COPYRIGHT LAW AND THE NEW MEDIA. Second Edition. Ablex Publishing Corporation, 355 Chestnut Street, Norwood, New Jersey 07648. 1989.

FEDERAL INFORMATION IN THE ELECTRONIC AGE: POLICY ISSUES FOR THE 1990S. Toby J. McIntosh. Bureau of National Affairs, Incorporated, 1231 Twenty-fifth Street, Northwest, Washington, D.C. 20037. 1990.

FEDERAL INFORMATION POLICIES IN THE 1980S: CONFLICTS AND ISSUES. Peter Hernon. Ablex Publishing Corporation, 355 Chestnut Street, Norwood, New Jersey 07648. 1987.

THE FIRST AMENDMENT--THE CHALLENGES OF NEW TECHNOLOGY. Praeger Publishers, One Madison Avenue, New York, New York 10010-3603. 1989.

THE FIRST FREEDOM TODAY: CRITICAL ISSUES RELATING TO CENSORSHIP AND INTELLECTUAL FREEDOM. Robert B. Downs and Ralph E. McCoy. American Library Association, 50 East Huron Street, Chicago, Illinois 60611. 1984.

FREE FLOW OF INFORMATION: A NEW PARADIGM. Achal Mehra. Greenwood Publishing Group, Incorporated, 88 Post Road West, P.O. Box 5007, Westport, Connecticut 06881. 1986.

FREEDOM AT RISK: SECRECY, CENSORSHIP, AND REPRESSION IN THE 1980S. Temple University Press, 1601 North Broad Street, University Services Building, Philadelphia, Pennsylvania 19122. 1988.

FREEDOM OF INFORMATION: COURSE MANUAL. Kenneth S. Kramer. Federal Publications, 1120 Twentieth Street, Northwest, Washington, D.C. 20036. 1981.

GOVERNMENT IN THE SUNSHINE ACT: HISTORY AND RECENT ISSUES: A REPORT OF THE COMMITTEE ON GOVERNMENTAL AFFAIRS, UNITED STATES SENATE. Superintendent of Documents, United States Government Printing Office, Washington, D.C. 20402. 1989.

HOW TO GET YOUR PERSONAL FILE: THE NEW FREEDOM OF INFORMATION ACT AND PERSONAL FILES, WHAT THE ACT SAYS, HOW TO USE IT, WHERE TO GET HELP. Center for National Security Studies, 122 Maryland Avenue, Northeast, Washington, D.C. 20002. 1975.

INFORMATION LAW: FREEDOM OF INFORMATION, PRIVACY, OPEN MEETINGS, OTHER ACCESS LAWS. Burt A. Braverman, Frances J. Chetwynd. Practising Law Institute, 810 Seventh Avenue, New York, New York 10019. 1986.

INTERNATIONAL LAW GOVERNING COMMUNICATIONS AND INFORMATION: A COLLECTION OF BASIC DOCUMENTS. Edward W. Ploman. Greenwood Publishing Group, Incorporated, 88 Post Road West, P.O. Box 5007, Westport, Connecticut 06881. 1982.

LESS ACCESS TO LESS INFORMATION BY AND ABOUT THE UNITED STATES GOVERNMENT: A 1981-1987 CHRONOLOGY. American Library Association, 50 East Huron Street, Chicago, Illinois 60611. 1988.

LIBERTY DENIED: THE CURRENT RISE OF CENSORSHIP IN AMERICA. Donna A. Demac. PEN American Center, 568 Broadway, New York, New York 10012. 1988.

LITIGATION UNDER THE FEDERAL FREEDOM OF INFORMATION ACT AND PRIVACY ACT. Fifteenth Edition. Allen Adler, Editor. American Civil Liberties Union, 132 West Forty-third Street, New York, New York 10036. 1990. Annual.

MINIMUM DISCLOSURE: HOW THE PENTAGON MANIPULATES THE NEWS. Hyergeb Arthur Heise. W.W. Norton and Company, Incorporated, 500 Fifth Avenue, New York, New York 10110. 1979.

PUBLIC ACCESS TO GOVERNMENT INFORMATION: ISSUES, TRENDS, AND STRATEGIES. Peter Hernon and Charles R. McClure. Ablex Publishing Corporation, 355 Chestnut Street, Norwood, New Jersey 07648. 1988.

PUBLIC ACCESS TO INFORMATION. Andrew C. Gordon and John P. Heinz. Transaction Books, Rutgers University, New Brunswick, New Jersey 08903. 1979.

TAKING LIBERTIES: NATIONAL BARRIERS TO THE FREE FLOW OF IDEAS. Elizabeth Hull. Praeger Publishers, One Madison Avenue, New York, New York 10010-3603. 1990.

TO FREE THE MIND: LIBRARIES, TECHNOLOGY, AND INTELLECTUAL FREEDOM. Eli M. Oboler. Libraries Unlimited, Incorporated, P.O. Box 3988. Englewood, Colorado 80155-3988. 1983.

TOP SECRET/TRADE SECRET: ACCESSING AND SAFEGUARDING RESTRICTED INFORMATION. Ellis Mount and Wilda B. Newman. Neal-Schuman Publications, Incorporated, 23 Leonard Street, New York, New York 10013. 1985.

WHEN GOVERNMENT SPEAKS: POLITICS, LAW, AND GOVERNMENT EXPRESSION IN AMERICA. Mark G. Yudof. University of California Press, 2120 Berkeley Way, Berkeley, California 94720. 1983.

DIGESTS, INDEXES, ABSTRACTS, CITATORS

FREEDOM OF INFORMATION CASE LIST. Office of Information Law and Policy. Superintendent of Documents, United States Government Printing Office, Washington, D.C. 20402. Annual.

LAW REVIEWS AND PERIODICALS

FOIA UPDATE. United States Department of Justice, Office of Information Law and Policy. Superintendent of Documents, United States Government Printing Office, Washington, D.C. 20402. Monthly.

FREEDOM OF INFORMATION, PRIVACY, SUNSHINE ACTS. Law Journal Seminars-Press, 111 Eighth Avenue, Suite 900, New York, New York 10011. Annual.

NEWSLETTERS AND NEWSPAPERS

ACCESS REPORTS/FREEDOM OF INFORMATION. Access Reports, Incorporated, 417 Elmwood Avenue, Lynchburg, Virginia 25403. Semimonthly.

ANTITRUST FOIA LOG. Washington Regulatory Reporting Associates, P.O. Box 2220, Springfield, Virginia 22152. Weekly.

COALITION ON GOVERNMENT INFORMATION NEWSLETTER. American Library Association, 110 Maryland Avenue, Northeast, Washington, D.C. 20002. Quarterly.

FTC FREEDOM OF INFORMATION ACT LOG. Washington Regulatory Reporting Associates, P.O. Box 2220, Springfield, Virginia 22152. Weekly.

PRIVACY JOURNAL. Privacy Journal, P.O. Box 28577, Providence, Rhode Island 02908. Monthly.

PRIVACY TIMES. Privacy Times, Incorporated, P.O. Box 21501, Washington, D.C. 20009. Semimonthly.

BIBLIOGRAPHIES

FREEDOM OF INFORMATION: A BIBLIOGRAPHY. Mary Vance. Vance Bibliographies, P.O. Box 229, 112 North Charter Street, Monticello, Illinois 61856. 1986.

FREEDOM OF INFORMATION ACT: A COMPREHENSIVE BIBLIOGRAPHY OF LAW RELATED MATERIALS. Frank G. Houdek. Tarlton Law Library, University of Texas, 727 East Twenty-sixth Street, Austin, Texas 78705-5799. 1985.

FREEDOM OF INFORMATION ACT: LEGAL ACTIONS AND INTERPRETATION: 1980-1985. Dale E. Casper. Vance Bibliographies, P.O. Box 229, 112 North Charter Street, Monticello, Illinois 61856. 1986.

FREEDOM OF INFORMATION IN THE UNITED STATES: A BIBLIOGRAPHY. Ben Silverstein. Vance Bibliographies, P.O. Box 229, 112 North Charter Street, Monticello, Illinois 61856. 1987.

INTELLECTUAL FREEDOM AND CENSORSHIP: AN ANNOTATED BIBLIOGRAPHY. Frank W. Hoffmann. Scarecrow Press, Incorporated, 52 Liberty Street, Box 4167, Metuchen, New Jersey 08840. 1989.

DIRECTORIES

AMERICAN SOCIETY OF ACCESS PROFESSIONAL-- MEMBERSHIP DIRECTORY. American Society of Access Professionals, 7910 Woodmont Avenue, Suite 1208, Bethesda, Maryland 20814-3015. Annual.

FREEDOM OF INFORMATION CONTACTS. Washington Information Directory. Congressional Quarterly, Incorporated, 1414 Twenty-second Street, Northwest, Washington, D.C. 20037. Annual.

ASSOCIATIONS AND PROFESSIONAL SOCIETIES

COALITION ON GOVERNMENT INFORMATION. American Library Association, 110 Maryland Avenue, Northeast, Washington, D.C. 20002. (202) 547-4440.

RESEARCH CENTERS, INSTITUTES, CLEARINGHOUSES

CENTER FOR NATIONAL SECURITIES STUDIES. 122 Maryland Avenue, Northeast, Washington, D.C. 20002. (202) 544-1681.

FREEDOM OF INFORMATION CENTER. Box 858, University of Missouri, Columbia, Missouri 65205. (314) 882-4856.

FREEDOM OF INFORMATION CLEARINGHOUSE. P.O. Box 19367, Washington, D.C. 20036. (202) 785-3704.

NATIONAL CENTER FOR FREEDOM OF INFORMATION STUDIES. Loyola University of Chicago, 820 North Michigan Avenue, Chicago, Illinois 60611. (312) 670-3116.

SCHOLARS AND CITIZENS FOR FREEDOM OF INFORMATION. c/o John Anthony Scott School of Law, Rutgers University, 15 Washington, Street, Newark, New Jersey 07102. (201) 648-5687.

ONLINE DATABASES

ACCESS REPORTS. Access Reports, Incorporated, 417 Elmwood Avenue, Lynchburg, Virginia 25403.

ANTITRUST FOIA LOG. Washington Regulatory Reporting Associates, P.O. Box 2220, Springfield, Virginia 22152.

FTC FOIA LOG. Washington Regulatory Reporting Associates, P.O. Box 2220, Springfield, Virginia 22152.

FREEDOM OF PRESS
See also: CENSORSHIP; FREEDOM OF INFORMATION; FREEDOM OF SPEECH

HANDBOOKS, MANUALS, FORMBOOKS

COMMUNICATIONS LAW. James C. Goodale, Chairman. Practising Law Institute, 810 Seventh Avenue, New York, New York 10019. 1980- . Annual.

HANDBOOK OF FREE SPEECH AND FREE PRESS. Jerome A. Barron and Thomas C. Dienes. Little, Brown and Company, 34 Beacon Street, Boston, Massachusetts 02108. 1979.

THE RIGHTS OF FAIR TRIAL AND FREE PRESS: THE AMERICAN BAR ASSOCIATION STANDARDS: AN INFORMATION MANUAL FOR THE BAR, NEWS MEDIA, LAW ENFORCEMENT OFFFICIALS, AND COURTS. Lori B. Andrews. American Bar Association, 750 North Lake Shore Drive, Chicago, Illinois 60611. 1981.

TEXTBOOKS AND GENERAL WORKS

AMERICAN BROADCASTING AND THE FIRST AMENDMENT. L.A. Scot Powe. University of California Press, 2120 Berkeley Way, Berkeley, California 94720. 1987.

CABLE, TELEVISION AND THE FIRST AMENDMENT. Patrick Parsons, Free Press, 866 Third Avenue, New York, New York 10022. 1987.

A CHILLING EFFECT: THE MOUNTING THREAT OF LIBEL AND INVASION OF PRIVACY ACTIONS TO THE FIRST AMENDMENT. Lois G. Forer. W.W Norton and Company, Incorporated, 500 Fifth Avenue, New York, New York 10110. 1987.

CONGRESS SHALL MAKE NO LAW: OLIVER WENDELL HOLMES, THE FIRST AMENDMENT, AND JUDICIAL DECISION-MAKING. Jeremy Cohen. Iowa State University Press, 2121 South State Avenue, Ames, Iowa 50010. 1989.

THE COURSE OF TOLERANCE: FREEDOM OF THE PRESS IN NINETEENTH-CENTURY AMERICA. Donna Lee Dickerson. Greenwood Publishing Group, Incorporated, 88 Post Road West, P.O. Box 5007, Westport, Connecticut 06881. 1990.

EMERGENCE OF A FREE PRESS. Leonard W. Levy. Oxford University Press, 200 Madison Avenue, New York, New York 10016. 1985.

FIRST AMENDMENT AND LIBEL: THE EXPERTS LOOK AT PRINT BROADCAST AND CABLE. John R. Cooper and Bruce W. Sanford. Harcourt, Brace, Jovanovich, Incorporated, 6277 Sea Harbor Drive, Orlando, Florida 32821. 1983.

THE FIRST AMENDMENT IN A FREE SOCIETY. Jonathan Barlett. H.W. Wilson, 950 University Avenue, Bronx, New York 10452. 1979.

THE FIRST AMENDMENT RECONSIDERED: NEW PERSPECTIVES ON THE MEANING OF FREEDOM OF SPEECH AND PRESS. Bill F. Chamberlin and Charlene J. Brown, Editors. Longman, Publishing Group, 95 Church Street, White Plains, New York 10601. 1982.

THE FIRST AMENDMENT, 1791-1991: TWO HUNDRED YEARS OF FREEDOM. James E. Leahy. McFarland and Company, Incorporated, Box 611, Jefferson, North Carolina 28640. 1991.

THE FOURTH ESTATE AND THE CONSTITUTION: FREEDOM OF THE PRESS IN AMERICA. L.A. Scot Powe. University of California Press, 2120 Berkeley Way, Berkeley, California 94720. 1991.

FREEDOM FOR THE COLLEGE STUDENT PRESS: COURT CASES AND RELATED DECISIONS DEFINING THE CAMPUS FOURTH ESTATE BOUNDARIES. Louis E. Ingelhart. Greenwood Publishing Group, Incorporated, 88 Post Road West, P.O. Box 5007, Westport, Connecticut 06881. 1985.

FREEDOM OF EXPRESSION. Archibald Cox. Harvard University Press, 79 Garden Street, Cambridge, Massachusetts 02138. 1981.

FREEDOM OF EXPRESSION: PURPOSE AS LIMIT. Francis Canavan. Carolina Academic Press, P.O. Box 51879, Durham, North Carolina 27717-1879. 1986.

FREEDOM OF THE PRESS. William L. Chenery. Greenwood Publishing Group, Incorporated, 88 Post Road West, P.O. Box 5007, Westport, Connecticut 06881. 1977.

FREEDOM OF THE PRESS VERSUS PUBLIC ACCESS. Benno C. Schmidt and Aspen Program on Communications and Society. Praeger Publishers, One Madison Avenue, New York, New York 10010-3603. 1975.

FREEDOM UNDER FIRE: UNITED STATES CIVIL LIBERTIES IN TIMES OF WAR. Michael Linfield. South End Press, 116 Saint Boloph Street, Boston, Massachusetts 02115. 1990.

JUSTICE AND THE MEDIA: ISSUES AND RESEARCH. Ray Surette, Editor. Charles C. Thomas, Publishers, 2600 South First Street, Springfield, Illinois 62794-9265. 1984.

LIBEL AND THE FIRST AMENDMENT: LEGAL HISTORY AND PRACTICE IN PRINT AND BROADCASTING. Richard E. Labunski. Transaction Books, Rutgers University, New Brunswick, New Jersey 08903. 1989.

MINNESOTA RAG: THE SCANDAL SHEET THAT SHAPED THE CONSTITUTION. Fred W. Friendly. Random House Publicity, 201 East Fiftieth Street, New York, New York 10022. 1982.

NEW YORK TIMES V. SULLIVAN: THE NEXT TWENTY YEARS: A COURSE HANDBOOK. Practising Law Institute, 810 Seventh Avenue, New York, New York 10019. 1984.

PRESS FREEDOMS: A DESCRIPTIVE CALENDAR OF CONCEPTS, INTERPRETATIONS, EVENTS, AND COURT ACTIONS, FROM 4000 B.C. TO THE PRESENT. Louis E. Ingelhart. Greenwood Publishing Group, Incorporated, 88 Post Road West, P.O. Box 5007, Westport, Connecticut 06881. 1987.

PRINTERS AND PRESS FREEDOM: THE IDEOLOGY OF EARLY AMERICAN JOURNALISM. Jeffery Alan Smith. Oxford University Press, 200 Madison Avenue, New York, New York 10016. 1988.

THE SUPREME COURT ON FREEDOM OF THE PRESS: DECISIONS AND DISSENTS. William A. Hachten. Iowa State University Press, 2121 South State Avenue, Ames, Iowa 50010. 1968.

UNAMERICAN ACTIVITIES: THE CAMPAIGN AGAINST THE UNDERGROUND PRESS. Geoffrey Rips, Anne Janowitz and Nancy J. Peters, Editors. PEN American Center, 568 Broadway, New York, New York 10012. 1981.

THE WATCHDOG CONCEPT: THE PRESS AND THE COURTS IN NINETEENTH-CENTURY AMERICA. Timothy W. Gleason. Iowa State University Press, 2121 South State Avenue, Ames, Iowa 50010. 1989.

LAW REVIEWS AND PERIODICALS

NEWS MEDIA AND THE LAW. Reporters Committee for Freedom of the Press. 1735 I Street, Northwest, Suite 504, Washington, D.C. 20006. Quarterly.

NEWSLETTERS AND NEWSPAPERS

CENSORSHIP NEWS. National Coalition Against Censorship. 2 West Sixty-fourth Street, New York, New York 10023. Quarterly.

FREEDOM TO READ FOUNDATION NEWS. 50 East Huron, Chicago, Illinois 60611. Quarterly.

NEWS MEDIA UPDATE. Reporters Committee for Freedom of the Press. 1735 I Street, Northwest, Suite 504, Washington, D.C. 20006. Biweekly.

BIBLIOGRAPHIES

FREEDOM OF THE PRESS: A BIBLIOCYCLOPEDIA. A TEN YEAR SUPPLEMENT. Ralph E. McCoy. Southern Illinois University Press, P.O. Box 3697, Carbondale, Illinois 62902-3697. 1979.

FREEDOM OF THE PRESS: AN ANNOTATED BIBLIOGRAPHY. Ralph E. McCoy. Southern Illinois University Press, P.O. Box 3697, Carbondale, Illinois 62902-3697. 1968.

NEWS MEDIA AND PUBLIC POLICY: AN ANNOTATED BIBLIOGRAPHY. Joseph P. McKerns. Garland Publishing, Incorporated, 136 Madison Avenue, New York, New York 10016. 1985.

ASSOCIATIONS AND PROFESSIONAL SOCIETIES

FIRST AMENDMENT CENTER. Society of Professional Journalists, 201 National Press Building, Northwest, Washington, D.C. 20002. (202) 628-1411.

REPORTERS COMMITTEE FOR FREEDOM OF THE PRESS. 1735 I Street, Northwest, Suite 504, Washington, D.C. 20006. (202) 466-6313.

WOMEN'S INSTITUTE FOR FREEDOM OF THE PRESS. 3306 Ross Place, Northwest, Washington, D.C. 20008. (202) 966-7783.

RESEARCH CENTERS, INSTITUTES, CLEARINGHOUSES

JOHN SHORENSTEIN BARONE CENTER ON THE PRESS, POLITICS AND PUBLIC POLICY. Harvard University, 79 John F. Kennedy Street, Cambridge, Massachusetts 02138. (617) 495-8269.

INSTITUTE OF BILL OF RIGHTS LAW. College of William and Mary, Marshall-Wythe School of Law, Williamsburg, Virginia 23185. (804) 221-3810.

THE MEDIA INSTITUTE. 3017 M Street, Northwest, Washington, D.C. 20007. (202) 298-7512.

OTHER SOURCES

PRESS FREEDOMS: A DESCRIPTIVE CALENDAR OF CONCEPTS, INTERPRETATIONS, EVENTS AND COURT ACTIONS FROM 4,000 B.C. TO PRESENT. Louis Edward Ingelhart. Greenwood Publishing Group, Incorporated, 88 Post Road West, P.O. Box 5007, Westport, Connecticut 06881. 1987.

FREEDOM OF RELIGION
See: CHURCH AND STATE; RELIGION

FREEDOM OF SPEECH
See also: FREEDOM OF INFORMATION; FREEDOM OF PRESS

LOOSELEAF SERVICES AND REPORTERS

NIMMER ON FREEDOM OF SPEECH. Melville B. Nimmer. Matthew Bender and Company, Incorporated, 11 Penn Plaza, New York, New York 10001. 1984- . (Annual Supplements).

HANDBOOKS, MANUALS, FORMBOOKS

HANDBOOK OF FREE SPEECH AND FREE PRESS. Jerome A. Barron and Thomas C. Dienes. Little, Brown and Company, 34 Beacon Street, Boston, Massachusetts 02108. 1979.

THE RIGHT TO PROTEST: THE BASIC ACLU GUIDE TO FREE EXPRESSION. Joel M. Gora. Southern Illinois University Press, P.O. Box 3697, Carbondale, Illinois 62902-3697. 1991.

TEXTBOOKS AND GENERAL WORKS

ADVERTISING AND THE FIRST AMENDMENT. Michael Gartner. Priority Press Publications, 41 East Seventieth Street, New York, New York 10021. 1989.

THE BIG CHILL: NEW DANGERS TO FREE SPEECH IN AMERICA. Eve Pell. Beacon Press, c/o HarperCollins Publishers, 10 East Fifty-third Street, New York, New York, 10022. 1984.

BULWARK OF LIBERTY: THE COURTS AND THE FIRST AMENDMENT. David S. Bogen. Associated Faculty Press, Incorporated, 19 West Thirty-sixth Street, New York, New York 10018. 1985.

CABLE TELEVISION AND THE FIRST AMENDMENT. Patrick Parsons. Lexington Books, 125 Spring Street, Lexington, Massachusetts 02173. 1987.

CABLESPEECH: THE CASE FOR FIRST AMENDMENT PROTECTION. George H. Shapiro, Philip B. Kurland and James P. Mercurio. Law and Business, Incorporated, 855 Valley Road, Clifton, New Jersey 07013. 1983.

CIVIL LIBERTIES AND NAZIS: THE SKOKIE FREE-SPEECH CONTROVERSY. James L. Gibson and Richard D. Bingham. Praeger Publishers, One Madison Avenue, New York, New York 10010-3603. 1985.

THE CLOISTERED VIRTUE: FREEDOM OF SPEECH AND THE ADMINISTRATION OF JUSTICE IN THE WESTERN WORLD. Barend van Niekerk. Praeger Publishers, One Madison Avenue, New York, New York 10010-3603. 1987.

COMMUNICATION UNDER LAW. Joseph J. Hemmer, Jr. Scarecrow Press, Incorporated, 52 Liberty Street, Box 4167, Metuchen, New Jersey 08840. 1979.

CORPORATE AND COMMERCIAL FREE SPEECH: FIRST AMENDMENT PROTECTION OF EXPRESSION IN BUSINESS. Edwin P. Rome and William H. Roberts. Greenwood Publishing Group, Incorporated, 88 Post Road West, P.O. Box 5007, Westport, Connecticut 06881. 1985.

CORPORATE FIRST AMENDMENT RIGHTS AND THE SEC. Nicholas Wolfson. Quorum Books, Greenwood Publishing Group, Incorporated, 88 Post Road West, P.O. Box 5007, Westport, Connecticut 06881. 1990.

EMERGENCE OF A FREE PRESS. Leonard Williams Levy. Oxford University Press, 200 Madison Avenue, New York, New York 10016. 1985.

FIGHTING FAITHS: THE ABRAMS CASE, THE SUPREME COURT, AND FREE SPEECH. Richard Polenberg. Viking/Penguin Press, 375 Hudson Street, New York, New York 10014. 1989.

THE FIRST AMENDMENT, DEMOCRACY, AND ROMANCE. Steven H. Shiffrin. Harvard University Press, 79 Garden Street, Cambridge, Massachusetts 02138. 1990.

THE FIRST AMENDMENT: THE LEGACY OF GEORGE MASON. Daniel Shumate. University Publishing Associates, Incorporated, 4720 Boston Way, Lanham, Maryland 20706. 1987.

FREEDOM OF EXPRESSION. Archibald Cox. Harvard University Press, 79 Garden Street, Cambridge, Massachusetts 02138. 1981.

FREEDOM OF EXPRESSION: A CRITICAL ANALYSIS. Martin H. Redish. Michie/Bobbs-Merrill Law Publishing Company, P.O. Box 7587, Charlottesville, Virginia 22906-7582. 1984.

FREEDOM OF SPEECH IN THE UNITED STATES. Thomas L. Tedford. Southern Illinois University Press, P.O. Box 3697, Carbondale, Illinois 62902-3697. 1985.

FREEDOM OF SPEECH ON PRIVATE PROPERTY. Warren Freedman. Quorum Books, Greenwood Publishing Group, Incorporated, 88 Post Road West, P.O. Box 5007, Westport, Connecticut 06881. 1988.

FREEDOM, RIGHTS, AND PORNOGRAPHY: A COLLECTION OF PAPERS. Fred R. Berger and Bruce Russell. Kluwer Academic Publishers, 101 Philip Drive, Assinippi Park, Norwell, Massachusetts 02061. 1990.

THE FUTURE OF FREE SPEECH LAW. R. George Wright. Quorum Books, Greenwood Publishing Group, Incorporated, 88 Post Road West, P.O. Box 5007, Westport, Connecticut 06881. 1990.

HISTORY OF FREE SPEECH IN DECISION MAKING. Second Edition. Backes-Shields. Kendall/Hunt Publishing Company, 2460 Kerper Boulevard, Dubuque, Iowa 52001. 1989.

HUMAN LIBERTY AND FREEDOM OF SPEECH. C. Edwin Baker. Oxford University Press, 200 Madison Avenue, New York, New York 10016. 1989.

INTERPRETATIONS OF THE FIRST AMENDMENT. William W. Van Alstyne. Duke University Press, Box 6697 College Station, Durham, North Carolina 22708. 1984.

JUSTICE OLIVER WENDELL HOLMES: FREE SPEECH AND THE LIVING CONSTITUTION. H.L. Pohlman. New York University Press, 70 Washington Square South, New York, New York 10012. 1991.

LIBEL AND THE FIRST AMENDMENT: LEGAL HISTORY AND PRACTICE IN PRINT AND BROADCASTING. Richard Labunski. Transaction Books, Rutgers University, New Brunswick, New Jersey 08903. 1989.

LIBERTY DENIED: THE CURRENT RISE OF CENSORSHIP IN AMERICA. Donna A. Demac. PEN American Center, 568 Broadway, New York, New York 10012. 1988.

MORE SPEECH: DIALOGUE RIGHTS AND MODERN LIBERTY. Paul Chevigny. Temple University Press, 1601 North Broad Street, University Services Building, Philadelphia, Pennsylvania 19122. 1988.

NAZIS IN SKOKIE: FREEDOM, COMMUNITY, AND THE FIRST AMENDMENT. Donald A. Downs. University of Notre Dame Press, P.O. Box L, Notre Dame, Indiana 46556. 1986.

PERSPECTIIVES ON FREEDOM OF SPEECH: SELECTED ESSAYS FROM THE JOURNALS OF THE SPEECH COMMUNICATION ASSOCIATION. Thomas L. Tedford, John J. Makay and David L. Jamison. Southern Illinois University Press, P.O. Box 3697, Carbondale, Illinois 62902-3697. 1987.

POLITICAL TOLERANCE IN AMERICA: FREEDOM AND EQUALITY IN PUBLIC ATTITUDES. Michail Corbett. Longman, Publishing Group, 95 Church Street, White Plains, New York 10601. 1982.

THE PRINCIPLES AND PRACTICE OF FREEDOM OF SPEECH. Haig A. Bosmajian. Second Edition. University Press of America, 4720 Boston Way, Lanham, Maryland 20706. 1983.

PROTESTERS ON TRIAL: CRIMINAL JUSTICE IN THE SOUTHERN CIVIL RIGHTS AND VIETNAM ANTIWAR MOVEMENTS. Steven E. Barkan. Rutgers University Press, 109 Church Street, New Brunswick, New Jersey 08901. 1985.

REGULATING THE INTELLECTUALS: PERSPECTIVES ON ACADEMIC FREEDOM IN THE 1980'S. Craig Kaplen and Ellen Schrecker, Editors. Praeger Publishers, One Madison Avenue, New York, New York 10010-3603. 1983.

THE RIGHT TO PICKET AND THE FREEDOM OF PUBLIC DISCOURSE. John N. Whitehead. Crossway Books, 1300 Crescent Street, Wheaton, Illinois 60187. 1984.

SHAPING THE FIRST AMENDEMENT: THE DEVELOPMENT OF FREE EXPRESSION. John D. Stevens. Books on Demand, 300 North Zeeb Road, Ann Arbor, Michigan 48106-1346. 1982.

SPEECH AND LAW IN A FREE SOCIETY. Franklyn Saul Haiman. University of Chicago Press, 5801 Ellis Avenue, Chicago, Illinois 60637. 1984.

SPEECH, CRIME, AND THE USES OF LANGUAGE. Kent Greenawalt. Oxford University Press, 200 Madison Avenue, New York, New York 10016. 1989.

THE SUPREME COURT AND THE FIRST AMENDEMENT. Joseph J. Hemmer, Jr. Praeger Publishers, One Madison Avenue, New York, New York 10010-3603. 1986.

THE TOLERANT SOCIETY: FREEDOM OF SPEECH AND EXTREMIST SPEECH IN AMERICA. Lee C. Bollinger. Oxford University Press, 200 Madison Avenue, New York, New York 10016. 1989.

TOLERATION AND THE CONSTITUTION. David A. Richards. Oxford University Press, 200 Madison Avenue, New York, New York 10016. 1989.

A WORTHY TRADITION: FREEDOM OF SPEECH IN AMERICA. Harry Kalven. HarperCollins Publishers, 10 East Fifty-third Street, New York, New York 10022. 1988.

LAW REVIEWS AND PERIODICALS

BILL OF RIGHTS JOURNAL. National Emergency Civil Liberties Committee, 175 Fifth Avenue, Suite 814, New York, New York 10010. Annual.

CIVIL LIBERTIES. American Civil Liberties Union, 132 West Forty-third Street, New York, New York 10036. Quarterly.

CIVIL LIBERTIES ALERT. American Civil Liberties Union, 132 West Forty-third Street, New York, New York 10036. Monthly.

BIBLIOGRAPHIES

JUSTICE DOUGLAS AND FREEDOM OF SPEECH. Haig Bosmajian. Scarecrow Press, Incorporated, 52 Liberty Street, Box 4167, Metuchen, New Jersey 08840. 1980.

ASSOCIATIONS AND PROFESSIONAL SOCIETIES

ALLIANCE TO END REPRESSION. 220 South State Street, Suite 1430, Chicago, Illinois 60604. (312) 427-4064.

AMERICAN CIVIL LIBERTIES UNION. 132 West Forty-third Street, New York, New York 10036. (212) 944-9800.

CENTER FOR CONSTITUTIONAL RIGHTS. 666 Broadway, Seventh Floor, New York, New York 10012. (212) 614-6464.

CONSTITUTIONAL RIGHTS FOUNDATION. P.O. Box 2362, Texas City, Texas 77592. (713) 440-6549.

FREEDOM OF EXPRESSION FOUNDATION. 5220 South Marina Pacifica, Long Beach, California 90803. (213) 985-4301.

NATIONAL COMMITTEE AGAINST REPRESSIVE LEGISLATION. 1313 West Eighth Street, Suite 313, Los Angeles, California 90017. (213) 484-6661.

NATIONAL EMERGENCY CIVIL LIBERTIES COMMITTEE. 175 Fifth Avenue, Suite 814, New York, New York 10010. (212) 673-2040.

NATIONAL JUSTICE FOUNDATION OF AMERICA. 1617 Sixteenth Street, Sacramento, California 95814. (916) 442-0537.

PEOPLE FOR THE AMERICAN WAY. 2000 M Street, Northwest, Suite 400, Washington, D.C. 20036. (202) 467-4999.

RESEARCH CENTERS, INSTITUTES, CLEARINGHOUSES

AMERICAN CIVIL LIBERTIES UNION FOUNDATION. 132 West Forty-third Street, New York, New York 10036. (212) 944-9800.

CENTER FOR APPLIED JURISPRUDENCE. Pacific Research Institute for Public Policy, 177 Post Street, Suite 500, San Francisco, California 94108. (415) 989-0833.

FIRST AMENDMENT RESEARCH INSTITUTE. 821 Massachusetts Avenue, Northeast, Washington, D.C. 20002. (202) 547-4090.

INSTITUTE OF BILL OF RIGHTS LAW. College of William and Mary, Marshall-Wythe School of Law, Williamsburg, Virginia 23185. (804) 221-3810.

FREIGHT
See: TRADE REGULATION; TRANSPORTATION

FUNERALS AND BURIAL

HANDBOOKS, MANUALS, FORMBOOKS

FAMILY GUIDE TO ESTATE PLANNING, FUNERAL ARRANGEMENTS, AND SETTLING AN ESTATE AFTER DEATH. Theodore E. Hughes and David Klein. 1983.

LIFE FROM DEATH: THE ORGAN AND TISSUE DONATION AND TRANSPLANTATION SOURCE BOOK. Phillip G. Williams. P. Gaines. 1989.

MORTUARY LAW. Seventh edition. Thomas F. H. Stueve. Cincinnati Foundation for Mortuary Education, 220 Victor Parkway, Cincinnati, Ohio 45206. 1984.

TEXTBOOKS AND GENERAL WORKS

DEALING WITH DEATH: PRACTICES AND PROCEDURES. Jennifer Green and Michael Green. Chapman and Hall, New York, New York. 1991.

DEATH, DISSECTION AND THE DESTITUTE. Ruth Richardson. Routledge, 29 West 35th Street, New York, New York 10001. 1987.

DISPUTING THE DEAD: U.S. LAW ON ABORIGINAL REMAINS AND GRAVE GOODS. H. Marcus Price. University of Missouri Press, Columbia, Missouri. 1991.

STATUTORY REGULATION OF ORGAN DONATION IN THE UNITED STATES. Second edition. R. Hunter Manson. South-Eastern Organ Procurement Foundation, P.O. Box 28060, Richmond, Virginia 23228. 1986.

ASSOCIATIONS AND PROFESSIONAL SOCIETIES

AMERICAN CEMETARY ASSOCIATION. 3 Skyline Place, 5201 Leesburg Pike, Falls Church, Virginia 22041. (703) 379-5838.

NATIONAL FUNERAL DIRECTORS ASSOCIATION, 11121 West Oklahoma Avenue, Milwaukee, Wisconsin 53727. (414) 541-2500.

FUTURE INTERESTS
See: REAL PROPERTY; WILLS TRUSTS AND INHERITANCE

FUTURES
See: COMMODITY TRADING

G

GAMBLING

HANDBOOKS, MANUALS, FORMBOOKS

LIONEL SAWYER AND COLLINS NEVADA GAMING LICENSE GUIDE. Jerome J. Vallen. Lionel Sawyer and Collins, Las Vegas, Nevada. 1988.

TEXTBOOKS AND GENERAL WORKS

BOOKIES AND BETTORS: TWO HUNDRED YEARS OF GAMBLING. Richard Sasuly. New York: Holt, Rinehart and Winston, Incorporated, 6277 Sea Harbor Drive, Orlando, Florida 32821. 1982.

THE BUSINESS OF RISK: COMMERCIAL GAMBLING IN MAINSTREAM AMERICA. Vicki Abt, James F. Smith and Eugene M. Christiansen. University Press of Kansas, 2501 West Fifteenth Street, Lawrence, Kansas 66049. 1985.

GAMBLING AND THE LAW. I. Nelson Rose. Gambling Times, Incorporated, 16760 Stagg Street, Number 213, Van Nuys, California 91406. 1985.

GAMBLING TECHNOLOGY. Kier Boyd. Superintendent of Documents, United States Government Printing Office, Washington, D.C. 20402. 1981.

NATION OF GAMBLERS: AMERICA'S BILLION-DOLLAR-A-DAY HABIT. Stuart Winston and Harriet Harres. Prentice-Hall, Incorporated, 113 Sylvan Avenue, Englewood Cliffs, New Jersey 07632. 1984.

PEOPLE OF CHANCE: GAMBLING IN AMERICAN SOCIETY FROM JAMESTOWN TO LAS VEGAS. John M. Findlay. Oxford University Press, 200 Madison Avenue, New York, New York 10016. 1986.

DIRECTORIES

GAMING AND WAGERING: BUSINESS-DIRECTORY OF GAMING ESTABLISHMENTS ISSUE. BMT Publications Incorporated, 254 West Thirty-first Street, New York, New York 10001. Annual.

GAMING AROUND THE WORLD. Gambling Times Incorporated, 16760 Stagg Street, Number 213, Van Nuys, California 91406. Irregular.

ROYER'S GUIDE TO NEVADA GAMING. Casino Control Publications, 3394 Lakeside Court, Reno, Nevada 87509. 1987. Irregular.

THOROUGHBRED RACING ASSOCIATIONS OF NORTH AMERICA-DIRECTORY AND RECORD BOOK. Thoroughbred Racing Association of North America, 3000 Marcus Avenue, Suite 2W4, Lake Success, New York 11042. Annual.

ASSOCIATIONS AND PROFESSIONAL SOCIETIES

GAM-ANON INTERNATIONAL SERVICE OFFICE. P.O. Box 197, Whitestone, New York 11357. (718) 352-1671.

GAMBLERS ANONYMOUS. 3255 Wilshire Boulevard, Suite 610, Santa Monica, California 90010. (213) 386-8789.

NATIONAL ASSOCIATION OF OFF-TRACK BETTING. 700 Ellicot Street, Batavia, New York 14020. (716) 343-1423.

NATIONAL COUNCIL ON PROBLEM GAMBLING. John Jay College of Criminal Justice, 445 West Fifty-ninth Street, New York, New York 10019. (212) 765-3833.

NEVADA ASSOCIATION OF RACE AND SPORTS BOOK OPERATORS. 35-65 Central Park Circle, Suite 8, Las Vegas, Nevada 89109. (702) 731-0749.

UNITED JEWISH APPEAL-FEDERATION OF JEWISH PHILANTHROPIES OF NEW YORK, TASK FORCE ON COMPULSIVE GAMBLING. 130 East Fifty-nonth Street, New York, New York 10022. (212) 980-1000.

ONLINE DATABASES

CASINO. Chase Econometrics/Interactive Data, 150 Monument Road, Bala Cynwyd, Pennsylvania 19004.

STATISTICS SOURCES

GAMBLING AND GAMBLERS-ARRESTS. United States Department of Justice, Federal Bureau of Investigation, Ninth and Pennsylvania Avenue, Northwest, Washington, D.C. 20535. Annual.

GAME
See: WILDLIFE

GARNISHMENT
See: ATTACHMENT AND GARNISHMENT

GAS
See: OIL AND GAS

GAYS
See: SEXUAL ORIENTATION

GENERAL ACCOUNTING OFFICE
See also: COMPTROLLER GENERAL

STATUTES, CODES, STANDARDS, UNIFORM LAWS

CODE OF FEDERAL REGULATIONS, TITLE 4. Office of the Federal Register, National Archives and Records Administration. Superintendent of Documents, United States Government Printing Office, Washington, D.C. 20402. Annual. (Updated by use of monthly List of Sections Affected and daily Federal Register.)

STANDARDS FOR AUDIT OF GOVERNMENTAL ORGANIZATIONS, PROGRAMS, ACTIVITIES AND FUNCTIONS. General Accounting Office. Superintendent of Documents, United States Government Printing Office, Washington, D.C. 20402. 1981.

LOOSELEAF SERVICES AND REPORTERS

DECISIONS OF THE COMPTROLLER GENERAL OF THE UNITED STATES. General Accounting Office. Superintendent of Documents, United States Government Printing Office, Washington, D.C. 20402. 1921- .

HANDBOOKS, MANUALS, FORMBOOKS

CIVILIAN PERSONNEL LAW MANUAL. Second Edition. General Accounting Office, Office of the General Counsel. Superintendent of Documents, United States Government Printing Office, Washington, D.C. 20402. 1983- . (Supplemented).

GAO MANUAL FOR GUIDANCE OF FEDERAL AGENCIES. General Accounting Office. Superintendent of Documents, United States Government Printing Office, Washington, D.C. 20402. 1983- . (Supplemented).

POLICY AND PROCEDURES MANUAL FOR GUIDANCE OF FEDERAL AGENCIES. General Accounting Office. Superintendent of Documents, United States Government Printing Office, Washington, D.C. 20402. 1984. (Supplemented).

TEXTBOOKS AND GENERAL WORKS

PRINCIPLES OF THE FEDERAL APPROPRIATIONS LAW. General Accounting Office, Office of General Counsel. Superintendent of Documents, United States Government Printing Office, Washington, D.C. 20402. 1982.

DIGESTS, INDEXES, ABSTRACTS, CITATORS

DIGESTS OF DECISIONS OF THE COMPTROLLER GENERAL OF THE UNITED STATES. United States General Accounting Office, Office of General Counsel. Superintendent of Documents, United States Government Printing Office, Washington, D.C. 20402.

ANNUALS AND SURVEYS

GENERAL ACCOUNTING OFFICE ANNUAL REPORT. General Accounting Office. Superintendent of Documents, United States Government Printing Office, Washington, D.C. 20402. Annual.

RESEARCH CENTERS, INSTITUTES, CLEARINGHOUSES

UNITED STATES GENERAL ACCOUNTING OFFICE LAW LIBRARY. 441 G Street, Northwest, Room 7056, Washington, D.C. 20548.

GENETIC ENGINEERING
See: MEDICAL JURISPRUDENCE AND MALPRACTICE

GENOCIDE
See also: HUMAN RIGHTS; INTERNATIONAL CRIME; INTERNATIONAL LAW AND RELATIONS

TEXTBOOKS AND GENERAL WORKS

AMERICANS: HISTORY OF GENOCIDE. Yves Ternon. Caravan Books, P.O. Box 344, Delmar, New York 12054. 1981.

GENOCIDE AND HUMAN RIGHTS: A GLOBAL ANTHOLOGY. Jack N. Porter, editor. University Press of America, 4720 Boston Way, Lanham, Maryland 20706. 1982.

GENOCIDE: ITS POLITICAL USE IN THE TWENTIETH CENTURY. Leo Kuper. Yale University Press, 302 Temple Street, New Haven, Connecticut 06520. 1982.

GENOCIDE: THE HUMAN CANCER. Israel W. Charny and Chanan Rapaport. William Morrow and Company, Incorporated, 105 Madison Avenue, New York, New York 10016. 1983.

THE NAZI DOCTORS: MEDICAL KILLING AND THE PSYCHOLOGY OF GENOCIDE. Robert J. Lifton. Basic Books, 10 East Fifty-third Street, New York, New York 10022. 1988.

THE POLICIES OF GENOCIDE: JEWS AND SOVIET PRISONERS OF WAR IN NAZI GERMANY. Gerhard Hirschfeld. Allen and Unwin Incorporated, P.O. Box 442, Concord, Massachusetts 01742. 1986.

THE PREVENTION OF GENOCIDE. Leo Kuper. Yale University Press, 302 Temple Street, New Haven, Connecticut 06520. 1986.

TAKING LIVES: GENOCIDE AND STATE POWER. Third edition. Irving L. Horowitz. Transaction Books, Rutgers University, New Brunswick, New Jersey 08903. 1981.

TOWARD UNDERSTANDING AND PREVENTION OF GENOCIDE: PROCEEDINGS OF THE INTERNATIONAL CONFERENCE ON THE HOLOCAUST AND GENOCIDE. Westview Press, 5500 Central Avenue, Boulder, Colorado 80301. 1984.

THE UNITED STATES AND THE GENOCIDE CONVENTION. Lawrence J. LeBlanc. Duke University Press, Box 6697 College Station, Durham, North Carolina 27708. 1991.

BIBLIOGRAPHIES

THE MAN WHO INVENTED GENOCIDE: THE PUBLIC CAREER AND CONSEQUENCES OF RAPHAEL LEMKIN. James J. Martin. Institute for Historical Review, The Noontide Press, 1822 1/2 Newport Boulevard, Number 191, Costa Mesa, California 92627. 1984.

ASSOCIATIONS AND PROFESSIONAL SOCIETIES

AD HOC COMMITTEE ON HUMAN RIGHTS AND GENOCIDE TREATIES. Jewish Labor Committee, 25 East Twenty-first Street, New York, New York 10010. (212) 477-0707.

INSTITUTE FOR THE STUDY OF GENOCIDE. 899 Tenth Avenue, Room 623, New York, New York 10019. (212) 237-8631.

RESEARCH CENTERS, INSTITUTES, CLEARINGHOUSES

ANNE FRANK INSTITUTE OF PHILADELPHIA FOR INTERFAITH HOLOCAUST EDUCATION. P.O. Box 40119, Lafayette Building, Suite 608, Fifth and Chestnut Streets, Philadelphia, Pennsylvania 19106. (215) 625-0411.

CENTER FOR HOLOCAUST STUDIES, DOCUMENTATION AND RESEARCH. 1610 Avenue J, Brooklyn, New York 11230. (212) 388-6494.

FRED ROBERTS CRAWFORD WITNESS TO THE HOLOCAUST PROJECT. Emory University, Atlanta, Georgia 30322. (404) 329-6428.

HOLOCAUST AWARENESS INSTITUTE. University of Denver, Denver, Colorado 80208. (303) 871-3020.

INSTITUTE FOR HOLOCAUST STUDIES. City University of New York, 33 West Forty-second Street, Room 1450, New York, New York 10036. (212) 642-2183.

INSTITUTE ON THE HOLOCAUST AND GENOCIDE. P.O. Box 10311, 91102, Jerusalem, Israel (2) 720424.

JOHN JAY COLLEGE OF CRIMINAL JUSTICE OF CUNY. 899 Tenth Avenue, New York, New York 10019. (212) 237-8334.

SIMON WIESENTHAL CENTER. 9760 West Pico Boulevard, Los Angeles, California 90035. (213) 553-9036.

YAD VACHEM. Har Hazikavon, P.O. Box 3477, 91034, Jerusalem, Israel (2) 731611.

GERONTOLOGY
See: AGED AND AGING

GIFTS
See: WILLS, TRUSTS AND INHERITANCE

GOVERNMENT
See: ADMINISTRATIVE LAW; GOVERNMENT CONTRACTS; GOVERNMENT CORPORATIONS; GOVERNMENT IMMUNITY AND LIABILITY; GOVERNMENT OWNERSHIP; LOCAL GOVERNMENT; STATES

GOVERNMENT CONTRACTS
See also: COMPTROLLER GENERAL

STATUTES, CODES, STANDARDS, UNIFORM LAWS

THE ABA MODEL PROCUREMENT CODE FOR STATE AND LOCAL GOVERNMENTS: RECOMMENDED REGULATIONS. American Bar Association, Section of Public Contract Law, and Section of Urban, State and Local Government Law, 750 North Lake Shore Drive, Chicago, Illinois 60611. 1981.

ANNOTATIONS TO THE MODEL PROCUREMENT CODE FOR STATE AND LOCAL GOVERNMENTS. Louis F. DelDuca, Patrick J. Falvey and Theodore Adler. American Bar Association, Section of Urban, State and Local Government Law, 750 North Lake Shore Drive, Chicago, Illinois 60611. 1987.

CODE OF FEDERAL REGULATIONS: TITLES 41, 48. Office of the Federal Register, National Archives and Records Administration. Superintendent of Documents, U.S. Government Printing Office, Washington, D.C. 20402. Annual.

THE MODEL PROCUREMENT ORDINANCE FOR LOCAL GOVERNMENTS. American Bar Association, Section of Public Contract Law, 750 North Lake Shore Drive, Chicago, Illinois 60611. 1982.

PROCUREMENT CODE PACKAGE: THE CODE AND RECOMMENDED REGULATIONS. American Bar Association, Section of Public Contract Law, and Section of Urban, State and Local Government Law, 750 North Lake Shore Drive, Chicago, Illinois 60611. 1979-1981.

PROPOSED DEBARMENT AND SUSPENSION REFORM ACT. American Bar Association, Section of Public Contract Law, 750 North Lake Shore Drive, Chicago, Illinois 60611. 1982.

LOOSELEAF SERVICES AND REPORTERS

COMPTROLLER GENERAL'S PROCUREMENT DECISIONS. Federal Publications, 1120 Twentieth Street, Northwest, Washington, D.C. 20036. 1974- .

COST ACCOUNTING STANDARD GUIDE. Commerce Clearing House, Incorporated, 4025 West Peterson Avenue, Chicago, Illinois 60646. 1972- .

EXTRAORDINARY CONTRACTUAL RELIEF REPORTER. David V. Anthony and Carl L. Vacketta, editors. Federal Publications, Incorporated, 1120 Twentieth Street, Northwest, Washington, D.C. 20036. 1974- .

FEDERAL CONTRACTS REPORT. Bureau of National Affairs, Incorporated, 1231 Twenty-fifth Street, Northwest, Washington, D.C. 20037. 1964- . Weekly.

FEDERAL COURT PROCUREMENT DECISIONS. Federal Publications, 1120 Twentieth Street, Northwest, Washington, D.C. 20036. 1982- .

FEDERAL GRANTS AND COOPERATIVE AGREEMENTS: LAW, POLICY AND PRACTICE. Richard B. Cappalli. Callaghan and Company, 155 Pfingsten Road, Deerfield, Illinois 60015. 1982- .

GOVERNMENT CONTRACT ACCOUNTING. Second edition. James Redingfield and Louis Rosen. Federal Publications, 1120 Twentieth Street, Northwest, Washington, D.C. 20077-9519. 1985- . (Periodic Supplements).

GOVERNMENT CONTRACT COSTS. Melvin Rishe. Federal Publications, 1120 Twentieth Street, Northwest, Washington, D.C. 20036. 1983- . (Annual Supplements).

GOVERNMENT CONTRACT DISPUTES. Second edition. Peter S. Latham. Federal Publications, 1120 Twentieth Street, Northwest, Washington, D.C. 20036. 1986- . (Periodic Supplements).

GOVERNMENT CONTRACT FRAUD. Brian C. Elmer. Federal Publications, 1120 Twentieth Street, Northwest, Washington, D.C. 20036. 1985- . (Periodic Supplements).

GOVERNMENT CONTRACT GUIDEBOOK. Donald F. Arnavas and Willian Ruberry. Federal Publications, 1120 Twentieth Street, Northwest, Washington, D.C. 20036. 1986- . (Periodic Supplements).

THE GOVERNMENT CONTRACTOR DEFENSE: A FAIR DEFENSE OR THE CONTRACTOR'S SHIELD. Juanita M. Madole, editor. American Bar Association, Tort and Insurance Practice Section, 750 North Lake Shore Drive, Chicago, Illinois 60611. 1987.

GOVERNMENT CONTRACTS: CYCLOPEDIC GUIDE TO LAW ADMINISTRATION, PROCEDURE. John Cosgrove McBride. Matthew Bender and Company, Incorporated, 11 Penn Plaza, New York, New York 10001. 1962- . (Monthly Supplements).

GOVERNMENT CONTRACTS REPORTS. Commerce Clearing House, Incorporated, 4025 West Peterson Avenue, Chicago, Illinois 60646. 1941- . (Weekly Supplements).

THE LAW OF FEDERAL NEGOTIATED CONTRACT FORMATION. Andrew K. Gallagher. GCA Publications, Incorporated, 255 North Stonestreet Avenue, Rockville, Maryland 20850. 1981- . Annual.

HANDBOOKS, MANUALS, FORMBOOKS

THE ANTITRUST GOVERNMENT CONTRACTS HANDBOOK. William E. Kovacic and Joe Sims. American Bar Association, Section of Antitrust Law, 750 North Lake Shore Drive, Chicago, Illinois 60611. 1990.

ARMED SERVICES PRICING MANUAL. Commerce Clearing House, Incorporated, 4025 West Peterson Avenue, Chicago, Illinois 60646. Annual.

FEDERAL CONTRACT COMPLIANCE MANUAL. United States Department of Labor, Office of Federal Contract Compliance Programs. Superintendent of Documents, U.S. Government Printing Office, Washington, D.C. 20402. 1979- . (Periodic Supplements).

FEDERAL CONTRACT MANAGEMENT: A MANUAL FOR THE CONTRACT PROFESSIONAL. Norman A. Steiger. Matthew Bender and Company, Incorporated, 11 Penn Plaza, New York, New York 10001. 1982- . (Periodic Supplements).

FEDERAL GOVERNMENT SUBCONTRACT FORMS. Robert J. English. Callaghan and Company, 155 Pfingsten Road, Deerfield, Illinois 60015. 1983- .

FEDERAL GRATUITIES POLICIES: A CONTRACTOR GUIDE. Robrt J. Kenney and Douglas R. Duberstein. Federal Publications, Incorporated, 1120 Twentieth Street, Northwest, Washington, D.C. 20036. 1990.

GOVERNMENT CONTRACT BIDDING. Third edition. Paul A. Shoitzer. Federal Publications, 1120 Twentieth Street, Northwest, Washington, D.C. 20036. 1987.

GOVERNMENT CONTRACT LAW MANUAL: A SUMMARY AND COMPARISON OF GOVERNMENT PROCUREMENT AT THE STATE, FEDERAL, AND INTERNATIONAL LEVELS. Glenn E. Monroe. Michie/Bobbs-Merrill Law Publishing Company, P.O. Box 7587, Charlottesville, Virginia 22906-7582. 1979.

HOW TO REVIEW A FEDERAL CONTRACT AND RESEARCH FEDERAL CONTRACT LAW. James F. Nagle. American Bar Association, 750 North Lake Shore Drive, Chicago, Illinois 60611. 1990.

PRACTICAL GUIDE TO THE GATT AGREEMENT ON GOVERNMENT PROCUREMENT. General Agreement on Tariffs and Trade, Geneva, Switzerland. 1989- .

TEXTBOOKS AND GENERAL WORKS

THE ARCHITECT-ENGINEER PRIMER OF FEDERAL GOVERMENT CONTRACTING. Third edition. Federal Publications, 1120 Twentieth Street, Northwest, Washington, D.C. 20036. 1983.

CONTRACTING FOR COMMERCIAL PRODUCTS AND SERVICES. American Bar Association, Section of Criminal Justice, 1800 M Street, Northwest, Washington, D.C. 20036. 1989.

CONTRACTING WITH THE FEDERAL GOVERNMENT. Second Edition. Frank M. Alston, Franklin R. Johnson and Margaret M. Worthington. John Wiley and Sons, Incorporated, 605 Third Avenue, New York, New York 10158. 1988.

EEO PROBLEMS AND THEIR APPLICABILITY TO GOVERNMENT CONTRACTORS. American Bar Association, 750 North Lake Shore Drive, Chicago, Illinois 60611. 1982.

FEDERAL CONTRACTS, GRANTS AND ASSISTANCE. Dennis J. Riley. Shepard's/McGraw-Hill, P.O. Box 1235, Colorado Springs, Colorado 80901. 1984- . (Annual Supplements).

FEDERAL PROCUREMENT REGULATIONS: POLICY, PRACTICE, AND PROCEDURES. James F. Nagle. American Bar Association, General Practice Section, 750 North Lake Shore Drive, Chicago, Illinois 60611. 1987.

FOREIGN MILITARY SALES AND INTERNATIONAL CONTRACTING WITH GOVERNMENTS: PROBLEMS AND POTENTIAL. American Bar Association, Public Contract Law Section, 750 North Lake Shore Drive, Chicago, Illinois 60611. 1981.

FORMATION OF GOVERNMENT CONTRACTS. John Cibinic, Jr. and Ralph C. Nash, Jr. Government Contracts Program, George Washington University, 801 Twenty-second Street, Northwest, Washington, D.C. 20052.

FUNDAMENTALS OF CONTRACT LAW. Eugene W. Massengale. Quorum Books, Greenwood Publishing Group, Incorporated, 88 Post Road West, P.O. Box 5007, Westport, Connecticut 06881. 1991.

GOVERNMENT CONTRACT CHANGES. Ralph C. Nash. Federal Publications, 1120 Twentieth Street, Northwest, Washington, D.C. 20036. 1981.

GOVERNMENT CONTRACT CLAIMS. Ralph C. Nash and John Cibinic, Jr. Government Contracts Program, 801 Twenty-second Street, Northwest, Washington, D.C. 20052. 1981.

GOVERNMENT CONTRACTING MANUAL. Timothy J. Healy. Prentice-Hall, Incorporated, 113 Sylvan Avenue, Englewood Cliffs, New Jersey 07632. 1990.

GOVERNMENT CONTRACTS IN A NUTSHELL. Second Edition. W. Noel Keyes. West Publishing Company, P.O. Box 64526, 50 West Kellogg Boulevard, St. Paul, Minnesota 55164-0526. 1990.

GOVERNMENT CRACKDOWN ON WASTE, FRAUD, AND ABUSE IN DEFENSE CONTRACTS. American Bar Association, Section of Public Contract Law, 750 North Lake Shore Drive, Chicago, Illinois 60611. 1983.

HOW TO WIN GOVERNMENT CONTRACTS. Robert B. Greenly. Van Nostrand Reinhold Company, 115 Fifth Avenue, New York, New York 10003. 1983.

IDENTIFYING AND PROSECUTING FRAUD AND ABUSE IN STATE AND LOCAL CONTRACTING. American Bar Association, Section of Public Contract Law and Section of Urban, State and Local Government Law, 750 North Lake Shore Drive, Chicago, Illinois 60611. 1984.

PERSONAL CONFLICTS OF INTEREST IN GOVERNMENT CONTRACTING. James L. D'Agostino and Roger G. Darley. American Bar Association, Conflicts of Interest and Ethics Committee, 750 North Lake Shore Drive, Chicago, Illinois 60611. 1988.

THE PROTEST EXPERIENCE UNDER THE COMPETITION IN CONTRACTING ACT: A REPORT. American Bar Association, 750 North Lake Shore Drive, Chicago, Illinois 60611. 1989.

PUBLIC PROCUREMENT AND CONSTRUCTION: TOWARDS AN INTEGRATED MARKET. Second Edition. Office for Official Publications of the European Communities, Luxembourg. 1989.

RECOVERY OF INDIRECT COSTS: PRICING OF EQUITABLE ADJUSTMENTS: TERMINATIONS FOR CONVENIENCE. David G. Anderson. American Bar Association, Section of Public Contract Law, 750 North Lake Shore Drive, Chicago, Illinois 60611. 1989.

STATE AND LOCAL GOVERNMENT PROCUREMENT: DEVELOPMENTS IN LEGISLATION AND LITIGATION. Louis F. DeDuca, Patrick J. Falvey and Theodore A. Adler. American Bar Association, Section of Urban, State and Local Government Law, 750 North Lake Shore Drive, Chicago, Illinois 60611. 1986.

WINNING GOVERNMENT CONTRACTS: A COMPLETE TWENTY-SEVEN STEP GUIDE FOR SMALL BUSINESSES. Eli Chappe. Prentice-Hall, Incorporated, 113 Sylvan Avenue, Englewood Cliffs, New Jersey 07632. 1984.

ENCYCLOPEDIAS AND DICTIONARIES

KEYES ENCYCLOPEDIC DICTIONARY OF CONTRACT AND PROCUREMENT LAW: DEFINITIONS OF LEGAL TERMS AND CONCEPTS IN PRIVATE PROCUREMENT AND PUBLIC PROCUREMENT OF FEDERAL, STATE, AND LOCAL GOVERNMENTS, THEIR CONTRACTORS AND SUBCONTRACTORS. Fourth edition. W. Noel Keyes. Oceana Publications, 75 Main Street, Dobbs Ferry, New York 10522. 1987- .

DIGESTS, INDEXES, ABSTRACTS, CITATORS

ANNOTATIONS TO THE MODEL PROCUREMENT CODE FOR STATE AND LOCAL GOVERNMENTS. Louis F. Del Duca. American Bar Association, Section of Urban, State, and Local Government Law, 750 North Lake Shore Drive, Chicago, Illinois 60611. 1987.

CONTRACT APPEAL DECISIONS REPORT: MAIN CITATOR TABLE. Commerce Clearing House, Incorporated, 4025 West Peterson Avenue, Chicago, Illinois 60646. Annual.

GOVERNMENT CONTRACTS CITATOR. Federal Publications, Incorporated, 1120 Twentieth Street, Northwest, Washington, D.C. 20036. 1958- .

QUARTERLY DIGESTS OF UNPUBLISHED DECISIONS OF THE COMPTROLLER GENERAL OF THE UNITED STATES PROCUREMENT LAW. United States General Accounting Office, Office of General Counsel, Index-Digest Section. Office of Administrative Services Distribution Section, 441 G Street, Northwest, Washington, D.C. 20548. Quarterly.

GOVERNMENT CONTRACTS

ANNUALS AND SURVEYS

THE CHANGING FACE OF PUBLIC PURCHASING: THE ABA MODEL IMPLEMENTATIONS. American Bar Association, Section of Public Contract Law and Section of Urban, State and Local Government Law, 750 North Lake Shore Drive, Chicago, Illinois 60611. 1983.

DEVELOPMENTS IN GOVERNMENT CONTRACT LAW. American Bar Association, Section of Public Contract Law, 750 North Lake Shore Drive, Chicago, Illinois 60611. Annual. 1975-1982.

YEARBOOK OF PROCURMENT ARTICLES. Federal Publications, 1120 Twentieth Street, Northwest, Washington, D.C. 20036. 1961- . Annual.

LAW REVIEW S AND PERIODICALS

ADMINISTRATIVE LAW REVIEW. American Bar Association, Administrative Law Section, 750 North Lake Shore Drive, Chicago, Illinois 60611. Quarterly.

BRIEFING PAPERS. Federal Publications, Incorporated, 1120 Twentieth Street, Northwest, Washington, D.C. 20077-9519. 1963- . Monthly.

CONTRACT MANAGEMENT. National Contract Management Association, 1912 Woodford Road, Vienna, Virginia 22182. Monthly.

DEFENSE MANAGEMENT JOURNAL. Office of the Assistant Secretary of Defense, Superintendent of Documents, United States Government Printing Office, Washington, D.C. 20402. Quarterly.

THE NASH AND CIBINIC REPORT. Keiser Publications, 2828 Pennsylvania Avenue, Northwest, Washington, D.C. 20007. 1987- . Monthly.

NATIONAL CONTRACT MANAGEMENT JOURNAL. National Contract Management Association, 1912 Woodford Road, Vienna, Virginia 22182. Semiannually.

NATIONAL ESTIMATOR. National Estimating Society, 101 South Whiting Drive, Suite 313, Alexandria, Virginia 22304. Quarterly.

PUBLIC CONTRACT LAW JOURNAL. American Bar Association, Section of Public Contract Law, 750 North Lake Shore Drive, Chicago, Illinois 60611. Biannual.

NEWSLETTERS AND NEWSPAPERS

BRIEFING PAPERS. Federal Publications, Incorporated, 1120 Twentieth Street, Northwest, Washington, D.C. 20036. Monthly.

CONSTRUCTION BRIEFINGS. Federal Publications, Incorporated, 1120 Twentieth Street, Nowthwest, Washington, D.C. 20036. Monthly.

THE CONSTRUCTION CONTRACTOR. Federal Publications, Incorporated, 1120 Twentieth Street, Northwest, Washington, D.C. 20036. Semimonthly.

CONSTRUCTION LITIGATION REPORTER. Shepard's/McGraw-Hill, Incorporated, 420 North Cascade Avenue, Colorado Springs, Colorado 80903. Monthly.

CPP NEWSLETTER. Coalition for Prompt Pay, 3150 Spring Street, Fairfax, Virginia 22031. Quarterly.

DEFENSE CONTRACT LITIGATION REPORTER. Shepard's/McGraw-Hill, Incorporated, 420 Cascade Avenue, Colorado Springs, Colorado. 80903. Semimonthly.

DOLLARS AND SENSE. National Estimating Society, 101 South Whiting Street, Suite 313, Alexandria, Virginia 22304. Bimonthly.

FEDERAL ACQUISITION REPORT. Management Concepts, Incorporated, 1964 Gallows Road, Vienna, Virginia 22180. Monthly.

FEDERAL CONTRACT DISPUTES. Business Publishers, Incorporated, 951 Pershing Drive, Silver Spring, Maryland 20910. Monthly.

FEDERAL CONTRACTS REPORT. Bureau of National Affairs, Incorporated, 1231 Twenty-fifth Street, Nortwest, Washington, D.C. 20037 Weekly.

FEDERAL GRANTS AND CONTRACTS WEEKLY. Capitol Publications, Incorporated, 1101 King Street, Suite 444, Alexandria, Virginia 22314. Weekly.

GOVERNMENT CONTRACT COSTS, PRICING AND ACCOUNTING REPORT. Federal Publications, Incorporated, 1120 Twentieth Street, Northwest, Washington, D.C. 20036. Monthly.

THE GOVERNMENT CONTRACTOR. Federal Publications, 1120 Twentieth Street, Northwest, Washington, D.C. 20036. Biweekly.

HEALTH GRANTS AND CONTRACTS WEEKLY. Capitol Publications, Incorporated, 1101 King Street, Suite 444, Alexandria, Virginia. Weekly.

INSIDE THE NAVY. Inside Washington Publishers, P.O. Box 7167, Ben Franklin Station, Washington, D.C. 20044. Weekly.

INSIDE THE PENTAGON. Inside Washington Publishers, P.O. Box 7167, Ben Franklin Station, Washington, D.C. 20044. Weekly.

INTERNATIONAL PROCUREMENT COMMITTEE REPORT. American Bar Association, Public Contract Law Section, 750 North Lake Shore Drive, Chicago, Illinois 60611. Quarterly.

LAMA NEWSLETTER: WASHINGTON NOTES. Latin-American Management Association, 419 New Jersey Avenue, Southwest, Washington, D.C. 20003. Bimonthly.

MAINTENANCE CONTRACT INITIATIVES. Contract Services Association of America, 1350 New York Avenue, Northwest, Suite 200, Washington, D.C. 20005. Quarterly.

NCSFC NEWSLETTER. National Council of Small Federal Contractors, 1029 Vermont Avenue, Northwest, Suite 800, Washington, D.C. 20005. Monthly.

NEWS UPDATE. Contract Services Association of America, 1350 New York Avenue, Northwest, Suite 200, Washington, D.C. 20005. Semimonthly.

OFF THE SHELF. Coalition for Government Procurement, 1900 M Street, Northwest, Suite 400, Washington, D.C. 20036. Monthly.

PUBLIC CONTRACT NEWSLETTER. American Bar Association, Section of Public Contract Law, 750 North Lake Shore Drive, Chicago, Illinois 60611. Quarterly.

PUBLIC PROCUREMENT AND PRIVATE CONSTRUCTION NEWSLETTER. Washington Bar Association, 500 Westin Building, 2001 Sixth Avenue, Seattle, Washington 98121.

BIBLIOGRAPHIES

TRANSNATIONAL ARBITRATION AND STATE CONTRACTS: SELECTIVE BIBLIOGRAPHY. Centre for Studies and Research of the Hague Academy of International Law, Hague, Netherlands. 1987.

DIRECTORIES

CONSOLIDATED LIST OF DEBARRED, SUSPENDED AND INELIGIBLE CONTRACTORS. United States General Services Adminstration, Office of Acquisition Policy. Superintendent of Documents, United States Government Printing Office, Washington, D.C. 20402. Monthly.

GOVERNMENT CONTRACTS DIRECTORY. Government Data Publications, P.O. Box 1352, Bay City, Michigan 48706. Annual.

ASSOCIATIONS AND PROFESSIONAL SOCIETIES

AMERICAN BAR ASSOCIATION, SECTION OF PUBLIC CONTRACT LAW, 750 North Lake Shore Drive, Chicago, Illinois 60611.

COALITION FOR GOVERNMENT PROCUREMENT. 1900 M Street, Northwest, Suite 400, Washington, D.C. 20036. (202) 331-0975.

COALITION FOR PROMPT PAY. 3150 Spring Street, Fairfax, Virginia 22031. (703) 273-7200.

COMMERCIAL PRODUCT ACQUISITION TEAM. 1735 New York Avenue, Northwest, Suite 500, Washington, D.C. 20006. (202) 628-1700.

CONTRACT SERVICES ASSOCIATION OF AMERICA. 1350 New York Avenue, Northwest, Suite 200, Washington, D.C. 20005. (202) 347-0600.

NATIONAL ASSOCIATION OF GOVERNMENT SERVICE CONTRACTORS. 444 North Capitol Street, Northwest, Suite 820, Washington, D.C. 20001. (202) 628-9639.

NATIONAL CONTRACT MANAGEMENT ASSOCIATION. 1912 Woodford Road, Vienna, Virginia 22182. (703) 448-9231.

NATIONAL COUNCIL OF SMALL FEDERAL CONTRACTORS. 1029 Vermont Avenue, Northwest, Suite 800, Washington, D.C. 20005. (202) 737-2696.

NATIONAL ESTIMATING SOCIETY. 101 South Whiting Street, Suite 313, Alexandria, Virginia 22304. (703) 751-0346.

RESEARCH CENTERS, INSTITUTES, CLEARINGHOUSES

GOVERNMENT CONTRACTS PROGRAM. George Washington University, 2020 K Street, Northwest, Suite 300, Washington, D.C. 20052. (202) 994-5278.

NATIONAL INSTITUTE OF GOVERNMENTAL PURCHASING, 115 Hillwood Avenue, Falls Church, Virginia 22046. (703) 533-7300.

ONLINE DATABASES

ADVANCED MILITARY COMPUTING. Pasha Publications, Incorporated, 1401 Wilson Boulevard, Suite 900, Arlington, Virginia 22209.

BNA FEDERAL CONTRACTS DAILY. Bureau of National Affairs, Incorporated, 1231 Twenty-fifth Street, Northwest, Washington, D.C. 20037.

CBD PLUS. DRI/McGraw-Hill, Data Products Division, 24 Hartwell Avenue, Lexington, Massachusetts 02173.

COMMERCE BUSINESS DAILY. United States Department of Commerce, P.O. Box 5999, Chicago, Illinois 60680.

COMPUTER ASSISTED PRODUCT SEARCH. Southwestern Pennsylvania Regional Planning Commission, The Waterfront, 200 First Avenue, Pittsburgh, Pennsylvania 15222.

DMS/FI CONTRACT AWARDS. Forecast International Incorporated/DMS, 22 Commerce Road, Newtown, Connecticut 06470.

DMS/FI CONTRACTORS. Forecast International Incorporated/DMS, 22 Commerce Road, Newtown, Connecticut 06470.

DRI FEDERAL CONTRACT ANNOUNCEMENTS. DRI/McGraw-Hill, Data Products Division, 24 Hartwell Avenue, Lexington, Massachusetts 02173.

DRI FEDERAL CONTRACT AWARDS. DRI/McGraw-Hill, Data Products Division, 24 Hartwell Avenue, Lexington, Massachusetts 02173.

FAR ONLINE. Compusearch Corporation, Federal Systems Division, 7631 Leesburg Pike, Falls Church, Virginia 22043.

LEXIS. FEDERAL PUBLIC CONTRACTS LIBRARY. Mead Data Central, Incorporated, 9393 Springboro Pike, P.O. Box 933, Dayton, Ohio 45401.

NASA RESEARCH AND DEVELOPMENT CONTRACTS SEARCH FILE. United States National Aeronautics and Space Administration, NASA Scientific and Technical Information Facility, P.O. Box 8757, BWI Airport, Maryland 21240.

PROCUREMENT AUTOMATED SOURCE SYSTEM. United States Small Business Administration, Office of Procurement Assistance, 1441 L Street, Northwest, Washington, D.C. 20416.

WESTLAW. GOVERNMENT CONTRACTS LIBRARY. West Publishing Company, P.O. Box 64526, 50 West Kellogg Boulevard, St. Paul, Minnesota 55164-0526.

GOVERNMENT CORPORATIONS
See also: LOCAL GOVERNMENT

LOOSELEAF SERVICES AND REPORTERS

LOCAL GOVERNMENT LAW. Callaghan and Company, 155 Pfingsten Road, Deerfield, Illinois 60015. 1981- .

LOCAL GOVERNMENT LAW. Chester James Antieau, editor. Matthew Bender and Company, Incorporated, 11 Penn Plaza, New York, New York 10001. 1955- .

TEXTBOOKS AND GENERAL WORKS

ACCOUNTABILITY AND THE BUSINESS STATE: THE STRUCTURE OF FEDERAL CORPORATIONS. Francis J. Leazes. Praeger Publishers, One Madison Avenue, New York, New York 10010-3603. 1987.

CORPORATIONS IN AND UNDER INTERNATIONAL LAW. Ignaz Seidl-Hohenveldern. Grotius Publications, Cambridge, England. 1987.

LOCAL GOVERNMENT LAW IN A NUTSHELL. Third edition. David J. McCarthy. West Publishing Company, P.O. Box 64526, 50 West Kellogg Boulevard, St. Paul, Minnesota 55164-0526. 1990.

THE PUBLIC'S BUSINESS: THE POLITICS AND PRACTICES OF GOVERNMENT CORPORATIONS. Annmarie H. Walsh. MIT Press, 55 Hayward Street, Cambridge, Massachusetts 02142. 1978.

REYNOLDS' HORNBOOK ON LOCAL GOVERNMENT LAW. Osborne M. Reynolds, Jr. West Publishing Company, P.O. Box 64526, 50 West Kellogg Boulevard, St. Paul, Minnesota 55164-0526. 1982- . (1987 Supplement).

SUING FOREIGN GOVERNMENTS AND THEIR CORPORATIONS. Joseph W. Dellapenna. Bureau of National Affairs, Incorporated, 1231 Twenty-fifth Street, Northwest, Washington, D.C. 20037. 1988.

DIGESTS, INDEXES, ABSTRACTS, CITATORS

MUNICIPAL LAW COURT DECISIONS. National Institute of Municipal Law Officers, 1000 Connecticut Avenue, Northwest, Suite 902, Washington, D.C. 20036. Bimonthly.

BIBLIOGRAPHIES

GOVERNMENT CORPORATIONS, SPECIAL DISTRICTS, AND PUBLIC AUTHORITIES: THEIR ORGANIZATION AND MANAGEMENT: A SELECTED, ANNOTATED BIBLIOGRAPHY. Xenia W. Dustin. Institute of Public Administration, 55 West Forty-fourth Street, New York, New York 10036. 1985.

URBAN POLICY: A BIBLIOGRAPHY OF MATERIALS PUBLISHED 1980-1984. Mary Vance. Vance Bibliographies, P.O. Box 229, 112 North Charter Street, Monticello, Illinois 61856. 1985.

NEWSLETTERS AND PERIODICALS

THE MUNICIPAL ATTORNEY. National Institute of Municipal Law Officers, 1000 Connecticut Avenue, Northwest, Suite 902, Washington, D.C. 20036. Bimonthly.

MUNICIPAL IMMUNITY LAW BULLETIN. Quinlan Publishing Company, 23 Drydock Avenue, Boston, Massachusetts 02110. Monthly.

MUNICIPAL LAW COURT DECISIONS. National Institute of Municipal Law Officers, 1000 Connecticut Avenue, Northwest, Suite 902, Washington, D.C. 20036. Bimonthly.

MUNICIPAL LAW DOCKET. National Institute of Municipal Law Officers, 1000 Connecticut Avenue, Northwest, Suite 902, Washington, D.C. 20036. Bimonthly.

MUNICIPAL LIABILITY LITIGATION REPORTER. Andrews Publications, 1646 West Chester Pike, Westtown, Pennsylvania 19395. Semimonthly.

MUNICIPAL LITIGATION REPORTER. Stratford Publications, Incorporated, 1375 Peachtree Street, Northwest, Suite 235, Atlanta, Georgia 30367. Monthly.

MUNICIPAL ORDINANCE REVIEW. National Institute of Municipal Law Officers, 1000 Connecticut Avenue, Northwest, Suite 902, Washington, D.C. 20036. Bimonthly.

MUNICIPAL PLANNERS AND CONTRACTORS LAW BULLETIN. Quinlan Publishing Company, 23 Drydock Avenue, Boston, Massachusetts 02110. Monthly.

MUNICIPAL WORKERS LAW BULLETIN. Quinlan Publishing Company, 23 Drydock Avenue, Boston, Massachusetts 02110. Monthly.

MUNICIPALITIES IN THE UNITED STATES SUPREME COURT. National Institute of Municipal Law Officers, 1000 Connecticut Avenue, Northwest, Suite 902, Washington, D.C. 20036. Quarterly.

ASSOCIATIONS AND PROFESSIONAL SOCIETIES

INTERNATIONAL CITY MANAGEMENT ASSOCIATION. 777 North Capitol Street, Northwest, Suite 500, Washington, D.C. 20002. (202) 289-4262.

LOCAL GOVERNMENT CENTER. 2716 Ocean Park Boulevard, Suite 1062, Santa Monica, California 90405. (213) 392-0443.

NATIONAL CENTER FOR MUNICIPAL DEVELOPMENT. 1620 Eye Street, Northwest, Third Floor, Washington, D.C. 20006. (202) 429-0160.

NATIONAL INSTITUTE OF MUNICIPAL LAW OFFICERS. 1000 Connecticut Avenue, Northwest, Suite 902, Washington, D.C. 20036. (202) 466-5424.

NATIONAL LEAGUE OF CITIES. 1301 Pennsylvania Avenue, Northwest, Washington, D.C. 20004. (202) 626-3000.

RESEARCH CENTERS, INSTITUTES, CLEARINGHOUSES

COUNCIL ON MUNICIPAL PERFORMANCE. 1601 Grant Street, Suite 250, Denver, Colorado 80203. (303) 832-5615.

MUNICIPAL LEGAL STUDIES CENTER. Southwestern Legal Foundation, P.O. Box 830707, Richardson, Texas 75083. (214) 690-2370.

STATE, LOCAL AND INTER-GOVERNMENTAL CENTER. Harvard University, John F. Kennedy School of Government, 53 Church Street, Cambridge, Massachusetts 02138. (617) 495-7908.

GOVERNMENT EMPLOYEES
See: PUBLIC OFFICIALS AND EMPLOYEES

GOVERNMENT IMMUNITY AND LIABILITY

STATUTES, CODES, STANDARDS, UNIFORM LAWS

UNITED NATIONS CODIFICATION OF STATE RESPONSIBILITY. Bruno Simma and Marina Spinedi. Oceana Publications, 75 Main Street, Dobbs Ferry, New York 10522. 1987.

LOOSELEAF SERVICES AND REPORTERS

HANDLING FEDERAL TORT CLAIMS: ADMINISTRATIVE AND JUDICIAL REMEDIES. Lester S. Jayson. Matthew Bender and Company, Incorporated, 11 Penn Plaza, New York, New York 10001. 1985- .

HANDBOOKS, MANUALS, FORMBOOKS

FEDERAL TORT CLAIMS ACT LITIGATION SEMINAR. Office of Legal Education, Executive Office for the United States Attorneys, United States Department of Justice, Washington, D.C. 1990.

TEXTBOOKS AND GENERAL WORKS

ACCOUNTABILITY AND THE BUSINESS STATE: THE STRUCTURE OF FEDERAL CORPORATIONS. Frances J. Leazes, Jr. Praeger Publishers, One Madison Avenue, New York, New York 10010-3603. 1987.

ANTITRUST LAW AND LOCAL GOVERNMENT. Mark R. Lee. Greenwood Publishing Group, Incorporated, 88 Post Road, Box 5007, Westport, Connecticut 06881. 1985.

CIVIL ACTIONS AGAINST THE UNITED STATES, ITS AGENCIES, OFFICERS, AND EMPLOYEES. Shepard's/McGraw-Hill, P.O. Box 1235, Colorado Springs, Colorado 80901. 1982- . (Periodic Supplements).

THE ELEVENTH AMENDMENT AND SOVEREIGN IMMUNITY. Clyde E. Jacobs. Greenwood Publishing Group, Incorporated, 88 Post Road, P.O. Box 5007, Westport, Connecticut 06881. 1972.

THE GOVERNMENT CONTRACTOR DEFENSE: A FAIR DEFENSE OR THE CONTRACTOR'S SHIELD? Juanita M. Madole, editor. American Bar Association, Tort and Insurance Practice Section, 750 North Lake Shore Drive, Chicago, Illinois 60611. 1987.

GOVERNMENT LIABILITY AND DISASTER MITIGATION: A COMPARATIVE STUDY. James Huffman. University Press of America, 4720 Boston Way, Lanham, Maryland 20706. 1986.

HIGHWAY DESIGN LIABILITY. John L. Messina. Association of Trial Lawyers of America Education Fund, 1050 31st Street, Northwest, Washington, D.C. 2007. 1983.

HOW TO FIGHT CITY HALL, THE IRS, BANKS, CORPORATIONS, YOUR LOCAL AIPORT AND OTHER NUISANCES. Joel D. Joseph. Contemporary Books, Incorporated, 180 North Michigan Avenue, Chicago, Illinois 60601. 1983.

IMMUNITY OF FEDERAL EMPLOYEES IN PERSONAL DAMAGES ACTIONS. Larry Lee Gregg. United States Department of Justice, Civil Division. Superintendent of Documents, United States Government Printing Office, Washington, D.C. 20402. 1985.

LITIGATION WITH THE FEDERAL GOVERNMENT. Second Edition. John M. Steadman, David Schwartz and Sidney Jacoby. American Law Institute, 4025 Chestnut Street, Philadelphia, Pennsylvania 19104. 1983.

NON-CONTRACTUAL LIABILITY OF THE EUROPEAN COMMUNITIES. Kluwer Academic Publishers, 101 Philip Drive, Assinippi Park, Norwell, Massachusetts 02061. 1988.

RISK MANAGEMENT TODAY: A HOW-TO GUIDE FOR LOCAL GOVERNMENT. Natalie Wasserman and Dean Phelus, editors. International City Management Association, 1120 G Street, Northwest, Washington, D.C. 20005. 1985.

SECTION 1983, SWORD AND SHIELD: CIVIL RIGHTS VIOLATIONS AND THE LIABILITY OF URBAN, STATE AND LOCAL GOVERNMENT. Robert H. Freilich and Richard G. Carlisle. American Bar Association, 750 North Lake Shore Drive, Chicago, Illinois 60611. 1983.

THE STATE AS DEFENDANT: GOVERNMENTAL ACCOUNTABILITY AND THE REDRESS OF INDIVIDUAL GRIEVANCES. Leon Hurwitz. Greenwood Publishing Group, Incorporated, 88 Post Road, Box 5007, Westport, Connecticut 06881. 1981.

STATE IMMUNITY: SOME RECENT DEVELOPMENTS. Christoph Schreuer. Grotius Publications, Cambridge, England. 1988.

STATE RESPONSIBILITY. (International). Ian Brownlie. Clarendon Press, Oxford University Press, 200 Madison Avenue, New York, New York 10016. 1983- .

STATE RESPONSIBILITY AND THE MARINE ENVIRONMENT: THE RULES OF DECISION. Brian D. Smith. Oxford University Press, 200 Madison Avenue, New York, New York 10016. 1988.

STATE RESPONSIBILITY FOR TECHNOLOGICAL DAMAGE IN INTERNATIONAL LAW. Jan Willisch. Duncker und Humblot GmbH, Postfach 410329, Dietrich-Schaefer Weg 9, D-1000 Berlin 41, Germany. 1987.

SUING GOVERNMENT: CITIZEN REMEDIES FOR OFFICIAL WRONGS. Yale University Press, 302 Temple Street, New Haven, Connecticut 06520. 1984.

U.S. LAW OF SOVERIGN IMMUNITY. International Publications Service, Incorporated, 220 Forbes Road, Number 106, Braintree, Massachusetts 02184-2705. 1984.

DIGESTS, INDEXES, ABSTRACTS, CITATORS

U.S. COURT OF CLAIMS DIGEST 1855 TO DATE. West Publishing Company, P.O. Box 64526, 50 West Kellogg Boulevard, St. Paul, Minnesota 55164-0526. 1950- .

ANNUALS AND SURVEYS

PRESIDENT'S COUNCIL ON INTEGRITY AND EFFICIENCY: A PROGRESS REPORT TO THE PRESIDENT: EFFORTS TO PREVENT FRAUD, WASTE AND MISMANAGEMENT. Executive Office of the President of the United States. Superintendent of Documents, United States Government Printing Office, Washington, D.C. 20402. 1987- .

BIBLIOGRAPHIES

GOVERNMENT LIABILITY: MONOGRAPHS. Mary Vance. Vance Bibliographies, P.O. Box 229, 112 North Charter Street, Monticello, Illinois 61856. 1983.

OTHER SOURCES

GOVERNMENTS AT RISK: LIABILITY INSURANCE AND TORT REFORM. Advisory Commission on Intergovernmental Relations, Washington, D.C. 1987.

GOVERNMENT INFORMATION
See: FREEDOM OF INFORMATION

GOVERNMENT LIABILITY
See: GOVERNMENT IMMUNITY AND LIABILITY

GOVERNMENT OWNERSHIP

TEXTBOOKS AND GENERAL WORKS

PUBLIC ENTERPRISE: A MODERN APPROACH. Peter J. Curwen. St. Martin's Press, Incorporated, 175 Fifth Avenue, New York, New York 10010. 1986.

SANCTITY VERSUS SOVEREIGNTY: THE UNITED STATES AND THE NATIONALIZATION OF NATURAL RESOURCE INVESTMENTS. Kenneth Aaron Rodman. Columbia University Press, 562 West One Hundred Thirteenth Street, New York, New York 10025. 1988.

BIBLIOGRAPHIES

GOVERNMENT OWNERSHIP: MONOGRAPHS. Mary Vance. Vance Bibliographies, P.O. Office Box 229, 112 North Charter Street, Monticello, Illinois 61856. 1984.

OTHER SOURCES

PRIVATIZATION: TOWARD MORE EFFECTIVE GOVERNMENT: REPORT OF THE PRESIDENT'S COMMISSION ON PRIVATIZATION. Superintendent of Documents, United States Government Printing Office, Washington, D.C. 20402. 1988.

GRAND JURY
See also: JURY

STATUTES, CODES, STANDARDS, UNIFORM LAWS

ABA GRAND JURY POLICY AND MODEL ACT. Second Edition. American Bar Association, 750 North Lake Shore Drive, Chicago, Illinois 60611. 1982.

LOOSELEAF SERVICES AND REPORTERS

CORPORATE RESPONSES TO FEDERAL GRAND JURY INVESTIGATIONS. Peter F. Vaira. Matthew Bender and Company, Incorporated, 11 Penn Plaza, New York, New York 10001. 1984- .

FEDERAL GRAND JURY PRACTICE AND PROCEDURE. Paul S. Diamond. Prentice-Hall, Incorporated, 113 Sylvan Avenue, Englewood Cliffs, New Jersey 07632. 1990- .

GRAND JURY LAW AND PRACTICE. Sara Sun Beale and William C. Bryson. Callaghan and Company, 155 Pfingsten Road, Deerfield, Illinois 60015. 1986- .

REPRESENTATION OF WITNESSES BEFORE FEDERAL GRAND JURIES. Third edition. Clark Boardman Company, Limited, 435 Hudson Street, New York, New York 10014. 1985- .

HANDBOOKS, MANUALS, FORMBOOKS

ANTITRUST GRAND JURY PRACTICE MANUAL: A MANUAL OF THE ANTITRUST DIVISION OF THE U.S. DEPARTMENT OF JUSTICE: TEXT OF MANUAL WITH CCH FOREWARD. Commerce Clearing House, Incorporated, 4025 West Peterson Avenue, Chicago, Illinois 60646. 1975.

FEDERAL GRAND JURY PRACTICE MANUAL. Veta M. Carney. Superintendent of Documents, United States Government Printing Office, Washington, D.C. 20402. 1983.

HANDBOOK ON ANTITRUST GRAND JURY INVESTIGATIONS: A PROJECT OF THE CRIMINAL PRACTICE AND PROCEDURE COMMITTEE OF THE ANTITRUST SECTION OF THE AMERICAN BAR ASSOCIATION. Second Edition. Ray V. Hartwell. American Bar Association, 750 North Lake Shore Drive, Chicago, Illinois 60611. 1988.

TEXTBOOKS AND GENERAL WORKS

THE GRAND JURY: AN INSTITUTION ON TRIAL. Marvin E. Frankel. Hill and Wang, Incorporated, 19 Union Square West, New York, New York 10003. 1977.

THE GRAND JURY, THE USE AND ABUSE OF POLITICAL POWER. Leroy D. Clark. Times Books. Random House, Incorporated, 201 East Fiftieth Street, New York, New York 10022. 1975.

PARALLEL GRAND JURY AND ADMINISTRATIVE AGENCY INVESTIGATIONS. Neil A. Kaplan, et al, editors. American Bar Association, 750 North Lake Shore Drive, Chicago, Illinois 60611. 1981.

THE PEOPLE'S PANEL: THE GRAND JURY IN THE UNITED STATES. Richard D. Younger. University Press of New England, 17 Lebanon Street, Hanover, New Hampshire 03755. 1963.

PRE-INDICTMENT TACTICS IN CRIMINAL CASES. Frederick P. Hafetz. Practising Law Institute, 810 Seventh Avenue, New York, New York 10019. 1981.

THE ROLE OF THE GRAND JURY AND THE PRELIMINARY HEARING IN PRETRIAL SENTENCING. Deborah Day Emerson and Nancy L. Ames. United States Department of Justice, National Institute of Justice. Superintendent of Documents, United States Government Printing Office, Washington, D.C. 20402.

NEWSLETTERS AND NEWSPAPERS

NEWSLETTER-GRAND JURY EXCHANGE SEMINAR. American Grand Jury Federation, 1120 Fourteenth Street, Suite 5, Modesto, California 95354.

RESEARCH CENTERS, INSTITUTES, CLEARINGHOUSES

AMERICAN GRAND JURY FOUNDATION. 1120 Fourteenth Street, Suite 5, Modesto, California 95354. (209) 527-0966.

GRANTS-IN-AID

HANDBOOKS, MANUALS, FORMBOOKS

DRAFTING FEDERAL GRANT STATUTES. Administrative Conference of the United States, Office of the Chairman. Superintendent of Documents, United States Government Printing Office, Washington, D.C. 20402. 1990.

HOW TO GET GOVERNMENT GRANTS. Philip Des Marars. Public Service Materials Center, 5130 MacArthur Boulevard, Northwest, Apartment 200, Washington, D.C. 20016-3316. 1980.

91 PROVEN TIPS AND SECRETS FOR WINNING GRANT $$$. Government Information Services, 1611 Kent Street, Suite 508, Arlington, Virginia 2209. 1987.

LOOSELEAF SERVICES AND REPORTERS

CHAPTER I HANDBOOK. Mary M. Stump, editor. Education Funding Research Council, 1611 North Kent Street, Suite 508, Arlington, Virginia 22209. 1971- .

FEDERAL FUNDING GUIDE. Charles E. Edwards, editor. Government Information Services, 1611 North Kent Street, Suite 508, Arlington, Virginia 22209. 1977- .

FEDERAL GRANTS AND COOPERATIVE AGREEMENTS -- LAW, POLICY AND PRACTICE. Richard B. Cappalli. Callaghan and Company, 155 Pfingsten Road, Deerfield, Illinois 60015. 1983- .

FEDERAL GRANTS MANAGEMENT HANDBOOK. Kathlenn Dunten. Grants Management Advisory Service, 1725 K Street, Northwest, Washington, D.C. 20006. 1978- .

GUIDE TO FEDERAL FUNDING FOR EDUCATION. Mary M. Stump, editor. Education Funding Research Council, 1611 North Kent Street, Suite 508, Arlington, Virginia 2209. 1975- .

TEXTBOOKS AND GENERAL WORKS

THE CHANGING POLITICS OF FEDERAL GRANTS. Lawrence D. Brown, James W. Fossett and Kenneth T. Palmer. Brookings Institution, 1775 Massachusetts Avenue, Northwest, Washington, D.C. 20036-2188. 1984.

ESSENTIALS OF GRANT LAW PRACTICE. Paul G. Dembling and Malcolm S. Mason. American Law Institute-American Bar Association Committee on Continuing Professional Education, 4025 Chestnut Street, Philadelphia, Pennsylvania 19104. 1991.

FEDERAL AID TO BIG CITIES: THE POLITICS OF DEPENDENCE. James W. Fossett. Brookings Institution, 1775 Massachusetts Avenue, Northwest, Washington, D.C. 20036-2188. 1983.

FEDERAL CONTRACTS, GRANTS AND ASSISTANCE. Dennis J. Riley. Shepard's/McGraw-Hill, P.O. Box 1235, Colorado Springs, Colorado 80901. 1984- . (Annual Supplements).

FEDERAL FINANCIAL ASSISTANCE TO LOCAL GOVERNMENT PROJECTS. Kenneth W. Bond and George L. Consolvo. Law Journal-Seminars Press, 111 Eighth Avenue, New York, New York 10011. 1981.

FEDERAL GRANT LAW. Malcolm S. Mason, editor. American Bar Association, Section of Public Contract Law, 750 North Lake Shore Drive, Chicago, Illinois 60611. 1982.

GRANTS. Virginia White. Public Service Materials, 5130 MacArthur Boulevard, Northwest, Apartment 200, Washington, D.C. 20016-3316.

MANAGING FEDERALISM: EVOLUTION AND DEVELOPMENT OF THE GRANT-IN-AID SYSTEM. Raymond A. Shapek. Community Collaborators, P.O. Box 5429, Charlottesville, Virginia 222905. 1980.

THE NEW FEDERALISM. Second Edition. Michael D. Reagan and John G. Sanzone. Oxford University Press, 200 Madison Avenue, New York, New York 10016. 1981.

POLITICAL BENEFITS: EMPIRICAL STUDIES OF AMERICAN PUBLIC PROGRAMS. Barry S. Rundquist. Lexington Books, 125 Spring Street, Lexington, Massachusetts 02173. 1980.

THE POLITICS OF FEDERAL GRANTS. George E. Hale and Marion Lief Palley. Congressional Quarterly, Incorporated, 1414 Twenty-second Street, Northwest, Washington, D.C. 20037. 1981.

RIGHTS AND REMEDIES UNDER FEDERAL GRANTS. Richard B. Cappalli. Books on Demand, 300 North Zeeb Road, Ann Arbor, Michigan 48106-1346. 1979.

THE STATES AND DISTRESSED COMMUNITIES: STATE PROGRAMS TO AID DISTRESSED COMMUNITIES. Advisory Commission on Intergovernmental Relations, 1111 Twentieth Street, Northwest, Suite 2000, Washington, D.C. 20575. 1985.

WHEN FEDERALISM WORKS. Paul E. Peterson, Barry G. Rabe, and Kenneth W. Wong. Brookings Insitution, 1775 Massachusetts Avenue, Northwest, Washington, D.C. 20036-2188. 1987.

ANNUALS AND SURVEYS

A CATALOG OF FEDERAL GRANT-IN-AID PROGRAMS TO STATE AND LOCAL GOVERNMENTS. Albert J. Richter. Advisory Commission on Intergovernmental Relations, Washington, D.C. 1989. Annual.

NEWSLETTERS AND NEWSPAPERS

ARTS AND CULTURE FUNDING REPORT. Education Funding Research Council, 1611 North Kent Street, Arlington, Virginia 22209. Monthly.

COMMUNITY DEVELOPMENT DIGEST. CD Publications, 8204 Fenton Street, Silver Spring, Maryland 20910. Semimonthly.

EDUCATION FUNDING NEWS. Education Funding Research Council, 1611 North Kent Street, Suite 508, Arlington, Virginia 22209. Weekly.

FEDERAL ASSISTANCE MONITOR. CD Publications, 8204 Fenton Street, Silver Spring, Maryland 20910. Semimonthly.

FEDERAL GRANTS AND CONTRACTS WEEKLY. Capitol Publications, Incorporated, 1101 King Street, Suite 444, Alexandria, Virginia 22314. Weekly.

HEALTH FUNDS DEVELOPMENT LETTER. Health Resources Publishing, Brinley Plaza, 3100 Highway 138, Wall Township, New Jersey 07719. Monthly.

HEALTH GRANTS AND CONTRACTS WEEKY. Capitol Publications, Incorporated, 1101 King Street, Suite 444, Alexandria, Virginia 22314. Weekly.

MINORITY FUNDING REPORT. Government Information Services, 1611 North Kent Street, Arlington, Virginia 22209. Monthly.

PUBLIC CONTRACT NEWSLETTER. American Bar Association, Section of Public Contract Law, 750 North Lake Shore Drive, Chicago, Illinois 60611. Quarterly.

STUDENT AID NEWS. Capitol Publications, Incorporated, 1101 King Street, Suite 444, Alexandria, Virginia 22314. Biweekly.

DIRECTORIES

DIRECTORY OF FEDERAL PROGRAMS: RESOURCES FOR CORRECTIONS. Tamara Hatfield, Mario Greszes and Hildy Saizow. United States Department of Justice, National Institute of Corrections. Superintendent of Documents, United States Government Printing Office, Washington, D.C. 20402. Irregular.

A GUIDE TO GRANTS - GOVERNMENTAL AND NON-GOVERNMENTAL. Second edition. Government Research Publications, Incorporated, P.O. Box 122, Newton Centre, Massachusetts 02159.

RESEARCH CENTERS, INSTITUTES, CLEARINGHOUSES

ADVISORY COMMISSION ON INTERGOVERNMENTAL RELATIONS. 1111 Twentieth Street, Northwest, Washington, D.C. 20575. (202) 653-5540.

COUNCIL OF STATE GOVERNMENTS. 444 North Capitol Street, Northwest, Washington, D.C. 20001. (202) 624-5460.

ONLINE DATABASES

FEDERAL ASSISTANCE PROGRAMS RETRIEVAL SYSTEM. United States General Services Administration, Federal Domestic Assistance Catalog Staff, 300 Seventh Street, Southwest, Ground Floor, Washington, D.C. 20407.

FEDERAL GRANTS AND CONTRACTS WEEKLY. Capitol Publications, Incorporated, Capitol Publishers Group, P.O. Box 1453, Alexandria, Virginia 22313.

FOUNDATION DIRECTORY. The Foundation Center, 79 Fifth Avenue, New York, New York 10003.

FOUNDATION GRANTS INDEX. The Foundation Center, 79 Fifth Avenue, New York, New York 10003.

GRANTS. Oryx Press, 4041 North Central Avenue, Phoenix, Arizona 85012.

HEALTH GRANTS AND CONTRACTS WEEKLY. Capitol Publications, Incorporated, Capitol Publishing Group, P.O. Box 1453, Alexandria, Virginia 22313.

LESKO'S INFO-POWER. Information USA, Incorporated, 10335 Kensington Parkway, P.O. Box E, Kensington, Maryland 20895.

NATIONAL SCHOLARSHIP RESEARCH SERVICE DATABASE. National Scholarship Research Service, P.O. Box 2516, San Rafael, California 94912.

STUDENT AIDS NEWS. Capitol Publications, Incorporated, Capitol Publishing Group, P.O. Box 1453, Alexandria, Virginia 22313.

GUARANTY
See: SURETYSHIP AND GUARANTY

GUARDIAN AND WARD
See also: ADOPTION; CHILD CUSTODY; FAMILY LAW; FOSTER CARE

STATUTES, CODES, STANDARDS, UNIFORM LAWS

MODEL STANDARDS TO ENSURE QUALITY GUARDIANSHIP AND REPRESENTATIVE PAYEESHIP SERVICES: A REPORT. Superintendent of Documents, United States Government Printing Office, Washington, D.C. 20402. 1989.

HANDBOOKS, MANUALS, FORMBOOKS

GUARDIANSHIP OF THE ELDERLY: A PRIMER FOR ATTORNEYS. Erica Wood. American Bar Association, Commission on Legal Problems of the Elderly, and Young Lawyers Division, Committee on the Delivery of Legal Services to the Elderly, 1800 M Street, Northwest, Washington, D.C. 20036. 1990.

HANDBOOK OF GUARDIANSHIPS AND CONSERVATORSHIPS. Fourth edition. Stuart J. Faber. Lega Books, 3255 Wilshire Boulevard, Suite 1514, Los Angeles, California 90010. 1984.

TEXTBOOKS AND GENERAL WORKS

DETERMINING COMPETENCY IN GUARDIANSHIP PROCEEDINGS. Stephen J. Anderer. American Bar Association, 1800 M Street, Northwest, Washington, D.C. 20036. 1990.

THE FOUNDATIONS OF CHILD ADVOCACY: THE ROLE OF GUARDIAN AD LITEM. Bookmakers Guild, Incorporated, 1430 Florida Avenue, Suite 202, Longmont, Colorado 80501. 1986.

THE LAW OF GUARDIANSHIP. Third Edition. Oceana Publications, Incorporated, 75 Main Street, Dobbs Ferry, New York 10522. 1980.

A NEW LOOK AT GUARDIANSHIP: PROTECTIVE SERVICES THAT SUPPORT PERSONALIZED LIVING. Tony Apolloni and Thomas P. Cooke. Paul H. Brookes Publishing Company, P.O. Box 10624, Baltimore, Maryland 21285-0624. 1984.

REPRESENTATION FOR THE ABUSED AND NEGLECTED CHILD: THE GUARDIAN AND AD LITEM AND LEGAL COUNSEL: A SPECIAL REPORT. Marlene H. Alderman. National Center on Child Abuse and Neglect. Superintendent of Documents, United States Government Printing Office, Washington, D.C. 20402. 1980.

STEPS TO ENHANCE GUARDIANSHIP MONITORING. Sally Balch Hurme. American Bar Association, Commission on the Mentally Disabled and Commission on Legal Problems of the Elderly, 1800 M Street, Northwest, Washington, D.C. 20036. 1991.

NEWSLETTERS AND NEWSPAPERS

THE GUARDIAN. Guardian Association, P.O. Box 1826, Pinellas Park, Florida 34664. (813) 791-7643.

ASSOCIATIONS AND PROFESSIONAL SOCIETIES

GUARDIAN ASSOCIATION. P.O. Box 1826, Pinellas Park, Florida 34664. (813) 791-7643.

OTHER SOURCES

ABUSES IN GUARDIANSHIP OF THE ELDERLY AND INFIRM: A NATIONAL DISGRACE: A BRIEFING. Superintendent of Documents, United States Government Printing Office, Washington, D.C. 20402. 1988.

GUARDIANSHIP: AN AGENDA FOR REFORM: RECOMMENDATIONS OF THE NATIONAL GUARDIANSHIP SYMPOSIUM AND POLICY OF THE AMERICAN BAR ASSOCIATION. American Bar Association, Commission on the Mentally Disabled and Commission on Legal Problems of the Elderly, 1800 M Street, Northwest, Washington, D.C. 20036. 1989.

GUN CONTROL
See: FIREARMS AND BALLISTICS

H

HABEAS CORPUS
See also: POST CONVICTION REMEDIES

HANDBOOKS, MANUALS, FORMBOOKS

FEDERAL HABEAS CORPUS. Second edition. Ronald P. Sokol. Michie/Bobbs-Merrill Law Publishing Company, P.O. Box 7587, Charlottesville, Virginia 22906-7582. 1969.

FEDERAL HABEAS CORPUS PRACTICE AND PROCEDURE. James S. Liebman. Michie Company, P.O. Box 7587, Charlottesville, Virginia 22906. 1988.

TEXTBOOKS AND GENERAL WORKS

AMERICAN HABEAS CORPUS: LAW, HISTORY, AND POLITICS. Badshah K. Miar. Cosmos of Humanists Press, P.O. Box 11143, San Francisco, California 94101. 1984.

A CONSTITUTIONAL HISTORY OF HABEAS CORPUS. William F. Duker. Greenwood Publishing Group, Incorporated, 88 Post Road West, P.O. Box 5007, Westport, Connecticut 06881. 1980.

THE DEFENDANT'S RIGHTS TODAY. David Fellman. University of Wisconsin Press, 114 North Murray Street, Madison, Wisconsin 53706. 1976.

HABEAS CORPUS: FEDERAL REVIEW OF STATE PRISONER PETITIONS. United States Department of Justice, Bureau of Justice Statistics. Superintendent of Documents, United States Government Printing Office, Washington, D.C. 20402. 1984.

THE LAW OF HABEAS CORPUS. Second Edition. Robert J. Sharpe. Oxford University Press, 200 Madison Avenue, New York, New York 10016. 1989.

THE PRACTICE OF EXTRAORDINARY REMEDIES: HABEAS CORPUS AND THE OTHER COMMON LAW WRITS. Chester James Antieau. Oceana Publications, 75 Main Street, Dobbs Ferry, New York 10522. 1987.

STATISTICS SOURCES

HABEAS CORPUS REFORM: HEARING BEFORE THE COMMITTEE ON JUDICIARY, UNITED STATES SENATE, NINETY-NINTH CONGRESS, FIRST SESSION, ON S. 238, A BILL TO REFORM PROCEDURES FOR COLLATERAL REVIEW OF CRIMINAL JUDGMENTS AND FOR OTHER PURPOSES, OCTOBER 8, 1985. Superintendent of Documents, United States Government Printing Office, Washington, D.C. 20402. 1986.

COMPUTER-ASSISTED LEGAL INSTRUCTION

FEDERAL HABEAS CORPUS. Suzanna Sherry. Center for Computer-Assisted Instruction, 229 19th Avenue South, University of Minnesota, Minneapolis, Minnesota 55455. Machine-readable computer file.

OTHER SOURCES

IN MEMORIAM, PROFESSOR CHARLES A. THOMPSON: SYMPOSIUM, STATE PRISONER USE OF FEDERAL HABEAS CORPUS PROCEDURES. 44(2) Ohio State Law Journal 261. 1659 North High Street, Columbus, Ohio 43210-1391. 1983.

MILLIGAN CASE. Samuel Klaus. Da Capo Press, Incorporated, 233 Spring Street, New York, New York 10013. 1970.

REPORT TO THE ATTORNEY GENERAL ON FEDERAL HABEAS CORPUS REVIEW OF STATE JUDGMENTS. United States Department of Justice, Office of Legal Policy. Superintendent of Documents, United States Government Printing Office, Washington, D.C. 20402. 1988.

A TREATISE ON THE RIGHT OF PERSONAL LIBERTY AND ON THE WRIT OF HABEAS CORPUS. Rollin Carlos Hurd. Da Capo Press, Incorporated, 233 Spring Street, New York, New York 10013. 1972.

HANDICAPPED
See: MENTAL HEALTH AND DISABILITY; PHYSICALLY HANDICAPPED

HANDWRITING
See: EVIDENCE

HAZARDOUS SUBSTANCES

See also: CHEMICAL INDUSTRY; ENVIRONMENTAL LAW; ENVIRONMENTAL PROTECTION AGENCY; EQUAL EMPLOYMENT OPPORTUNITY COMMISSION; FOOD AND DRUG ADMINISTRATION; INTERIOR DEPARTMENT; NATURAL RESOURCES; OCCUPATIONAL SAFETY AND HEALTH; OCCUPATIONAL SAFETY AND HEALTH ADMINISTRATION; TRANSPORTATION DEPARTMENT

LOOSELEAF SERVICES AND REPORTERS

CHEMICAL REGULATION REPORTER. Bureau of National Affairs, Incorporated, 1231 Twenty-fifth Street, Northwest, Washington, D.C. 20037. 1977- . (Weekly Supplements).

CHEMICAL SUBSTANCE CONTROL. Bureau of National Affairs, Incorporated, 1231 Twenty-fifth Street, Northwest, Washington, D.C. 20037. 1980- . (Periodic Supplements).

ENVIRONMENTAL SPILL REPORTING PROCEDURES MANUAL. Kenneth R. Myers and Nancy B. Berenson. Morgan, Lewis and Bockius, Philadelphia, Pennsylvania. 1990.

HAZARDOUS MATERIALS TRANSPORTATION. Bureau of National Affairs, Incorporated, 1231 Twenty-fifth Street, Northwest, Washington, D.C. 20037. 1977- . (Monthly Supplements).

HAZARDOUS WASTE. Matthew Bender and Company, Incorporated, 11 Penn Plaza, New York, New York 10001. 1986- . (Periodic Supplements).

LAW OF CHEMICAL REGULATION AND HAZARDOUS WASTE. Donald W. Stever. Clark Boardman Company, Limited, 435 Hudson Street, New York, New York 10014. 1986- . (Annual Supplements).

LAW OF TOXIC TORTS: LITIGATION, DEFENSE, INSURANCE. Michael Dore. Clark Boardman Company, Limited, 435 Hudson Street, New York, New York 10014. 1987.

SPILLS AND RELEASES OF OIL AND HAZARDOUS SUBSTANCES. Prentice-Hall, Incorporated, Law and Business, 113 Sylvan Avenue, Englewood Cliffs, New Jersey 07632. 1987- . (Periodic Supplements).

TOXIC SUBSTANCES CONTROL GUIDE. J.J. Keller and Associates, Incorporated, 145 West Wisconsin Avenue, Neenah, Wisconsin 54956. 1979- . (Semiannual Supplements).

TOXICS LAW REPORTER. Bureau of National Affairs, Incorporated, 1231 Twenty-fifth Street, Northwest, Washington, D.C. 20037. 1986- . Weekly.

WORKPLACE RIGHT-TO-KNOW REPORTER. Thompson Publishing Group, 1725 K Street, Northwest, Suite 200, Washington, D.C. 20006. 1986- . (Quarterly Supplements).

HANDBOOKS, MANUALS, FORMBOOKS

ELEMENTS OF TOXICOLOGY AND CHEMICAL RISK ASSESSMENT: A HANDBOOK FOR NONSCIENTISTS, ATTORNEYS AND DECISION MAKERS. Environmental Law Institute, 1616 P Street, Northwest, Washington, D.C. 20036. 1986.

ENVIRONMENTAL LAW HANDBOOK. Eleventh Edition. J. Gordon Arbuckle. Government Institutes, Incorporated, 966 Hungerford Drive, Rockville, Maryland 20850. 1991.

HANDBOOK OF HAZARD COMMUNICATION AND OSHA REQUIREMENTS. George G. Lowry and Robert C. Lowry. Lewis Publishers, Incorporated, 121 South Main Street, P.O. Box 519, Chelsea, Michigan 48118. 1985.

HANDBOOK OF HAZARDOUS WASTE REGULATION. Second edition. Thomas Balf, editor. Business and Legal Reports, 64 Wall Street, Madison, Connecticut 06443. 1987- .

HAZARDOUS MATERIALS TRANSPORT GUIDE. Bureau of National Affairs Editoral Staff. Bureau of National Affairs, Incorporated, 1231 Twenty-fifth Street, Northwest, Washington, D.C. 20037. 1984.

HAZARDOUS WASTE REGULATION HANDBOOK: A PRACTICAL GUIDE TO RCRA AND SUPERFUND. Susan M. Briggum. Executive Enterprises, Publications Company, 22 West Twenty-first Street, New York, New York 10010-6904. 1985.

HOW TO COMPLY WITH THE OSHA HAZARD COMMUNICATION STANDARD: A COMPLETE GUIDE TO COMPLIANCE WITH OSHA WORKER RIGHT-TO-KNOW REGULATIONS. Daniel J. Young. Van Nostrand Reinhold Company, Incorporated, 115 Fifth Avenue, New York, New York 10003. 1989.

IDENTIFICATION OF RCRA-REGULATED SUBSTANCES: HOW TO DETERMINE IF YOUR COMPANY IS HANDLING A HAZARDOUS WASTE AND POSSIBLE WAYS TO SOFTEN THE BLOW. Kristina M. Woods. American Bar Association, 750 North Lake Shore Drive, Chicago, Illinois 60611. 1989.

LEGISLATIVE SOURCEBOOK ON TOXICS. David Jones and Jeffery Tryens, editors. National Center for Policy Alternatives, 2000 Florida Avenue, Northwest, Washington, D.C. 20009. 1986.

PREPARATION AND TRIAL OF A COMPLEX TOXIC CHEMICAL OR HAZARDOUS WASTE CASE. Sheila L. Birnbaun and Richard J. Phelan. Practising Law Institute, 810 Seventh Avenue, New York, New York 10019. 1984.

TOXIC SUBSTANCES CONTROLS GUIDE: FEDERAL REGULATION OF CHEMICALS IN THE ENVIRONMENT. Mary Devine Worobec. Bureau of National Affairs, Incorporated, 1231 Twenty-fifth Street, Northwest, Washington, D.C. 20037. 1989.

TOXIC TORT REFERENCE MATERIALS. Association of Trial Lawyers of America Education Fund Staff, 1050 Thirty-first Street, Northwest, Washington, D.C. 20007. 1985.

TEXTBOOKS AND GENERAL WORKS

BEYOND DUMPING: NEW STRATEGIES FOR CONTROLLING TOXIC CONTAMINATION. Bruce Piasecki, editor. Greenwood Publishing Group, Incorporated, 88 Post Road West, P.O. Box 5007, Westport, Connecticut 06881. 1984.

A CITIZEN'S RIGHT TO KNOW: RISK COMMUNICATION AND PUBLIC POLICY. Susan G. Hadden. Westview Press, Incorporated, 5500 Central Avenue, Boulder, Colorado 80301. 1989.

CONTROLLING CHEMICALS: THE POLITICS OF REGULATION IN EUROPE AND THE UNITED STATES. Ronald Brickman, Sheila Jasanoff and Thomas Ilgen. Cornell University Press, 124 Roberts Place, Ithaca, New York 14850. 1985.

CORPORATE DISCLOSURE OF ENVIRONMENTAL RISKS: U.S. AND EUROPEAN LAW. Butterworth Legal Publishers, 90 Stiles Road, Salem, New Hampshire 03079 1990.

THE DILEMMA OF TOXIC SUBSTANCE REGULATION: HOW OVERREGULATION CAUSES UNDERREGULATION AT OSHA. John M. Mendeloff. MIT Press, 55 Hayward Street, Cambridge, Massachusetts 02142. 1988.

HAZARDOUS WASTE LAW AND PRACTICE. John-Mark Stensvaag. John Wiley and Sons, Incorporated, 605 Third Avenue, New York, New York 10158. 1986- . (Annual Supplements).

HAZARDOUS WASTE MANAGEMENT. Gaynor W. Dawson. John Wiley and Sons, Incorporated, 605 Third Avenue, New York, New York 10158. 1986.

LEARNING ABOUT RISK: CONSUMER AND WORKER RESPONSES TO HAZARD INFORMATION. W. Kip Viscusi. Harvard University Press, 79 Garden Street, Cambridge, Massachusetts 02138. 1987.

THE POLITICS OF HAZARDOUS WASTE MANAGEMENT. Jane P. Lester and O. M. Bowman. Duke University Press, Box 6697, College Station, Durham, North Carolina 27708. 1983.

STATUTORY REFORM OF "TOXIC TORTS": RELIEVING LEGAL, SCIENTIFIC AND ECONOMIC BURDENS ON THE CHEMICAL VICTIM. Jeffery Trauberman. Environmental Law Institute, 1616 P Street, Northwest, Suite 200, Washington, D.C. 20036. 1983.

TOXIC SUBSTANCES CONTROLS PRIMER: FEDERAL REGULATION OF CHEMICALS IN THE ENVIRONMENT. Second Edition. Mary Devine Worobec. Bureau of National Afairs, Incorporated, 1231 Twenty-fifth Street, Northwest, Washington, D.C. 20037. 1986.

TOXIC TORT LITIGATION. Manning Gasch, Jr., Chairman. Practising Law Institute, 810 Seventh Avenue, New York, New York 10019. 1984.

TOXIC TORTS: LITGATION OF HAZARDOUS SUBSTANCE CASES. Gary Z. Nothstein. Shepard's/McGraw-Hill, P.O. Box 1235, Colorado Springs, Colorado 80901. 1984- . Annual Supplements.

TRANSFERRING HAZARDOUS TECHNOLOGIES AND SUBSTANCES: THE INTERNATIONAL LEGAL CHALLENGE. Graham and Trotman, Norwell, Massachusetts. 1989.

ENCYCLOPEDIAS AND DICTIONARIES

CHEMICAL CONTROL LEGISLATION: AN INTERNATIONAL GLOSSARY OF KEY TERMS. Organization for Economic Cooperation and Development, Publications and Development Center, 2001 L Street, Suite 1207, Washington, D.C. 20036. 1982.

DIGESTS, INDEXES, ABSTRACTS, CITATORS

INDEX TO FEDERAL HAZARDOUS WASTE REGULATIONS. McCoy and Associates, 13701 West Jewell Avenue, Suite 202, Lakewood, Colorado 80228. 1984.

SPEER'S DIGEST OF TOXIC SUBSTANCES STATE LAW, (1983-1984). Strategic Assessments, Incorporated, P.O. Box 8005-265, Boulder, Colorado 80306. Annual.

ANNUALS AND SURVEYS

HAZARD COMMUNICATION: FEDERAL/STATE RIGHT TO KNOW LAWS AS OF OCTOBER 1, 1985: TEXT AND EXPLANATION. Commerce Clearing House, Incorporated, 4025 West Peterson Avenue, Chicago, Illinois 60646. 1985.

LAW REVIEWS AND PERIODICALS

COURIER. Hazardous Materials Advisory Council, 1110 Vermont Avenue, Northwest, Suite 250, Washington, D.C. 20005. Monthly.

ECOLOGY LAW QUARTERLY. Boalt Hall School of Law, University of California at Berkeley, Berkeley, California 94720. Quarterly.

ENVIRONMENTAL FORUM. Environmental Law Institute, 1616 P Street, Northwest, Washington, D.C. 1982. Monthly.

ENVIRONMENTAL LAW. Northwestern School of Law of Lewis and Clark College, 10015 Southwest, Terwilliger Boulevard, Portland, Oregon 97219. Quarterly.

ENVIRONMENTAL LAW REPORTER. Environmental Law Institute, 1616 P Street, Suite 200, Washington, D.C. 20036. Monthly.

HARVARD ENVIRONMENTAL LAW REVIEW. Publications Center, Harvard Law School, Cambridge, Massachusetts 02138. Semiannually.

HAZARDOUS MATERIALS CONTROL MAGAZINE. Hazardous Materials Control Research Institute, 9300 Columbia Boulevard, Silver Spring, Maryland 20910. Bimonthly.

JOURNAL ON HAZARDOUS WASTE AND HAZARDOUS MATERIALS. Hazardous Materials Control Research Institute, 9300 Columbia Boulevard, Silver Spring, Maryland 20910. Quarterly.

HAZARDOUS SUBSTANCES

THE MINIMIZER. Center for Hazardous Materials Research, 320 William Pitt Way, University of Pittsburgh, Applied Research Center, Pittsburgh, Pennsylvania 15238. Quarterly.

NUCLEAR AND CHEMICAL WASTE MANAGEMENT. Pergamon Press, Maxwell House, Fairview Park, Elmsford, New York 10523. Quarterly.

TOXIC SUSTANCES JOURNAL. Executive Enterprises Publishing Company, Incorporated, 10 Columbia Circle, New York, New York 10019. Quarterly.

NEWSLETTERS AND NEWSPAPERS

AIR TOXICS REPORT. Business Publishers Incorporated, 951 Pershing Drive, Silver Spring, Maryland 20910. Monthly.

ASBESTOS ABATEMENT LITIGATION REPORTER. Andrews Publications, 1646 West Chester Pike, Westtown, Pennsylvania 19395. Monthly.

ASBESTOS ABATEMENT REPORT. Buraff Publications, 1350 Connecticut Avenue, Northwest, Suite 1000, Washington, D.C. 20036. Semimonthly.

ASBESTOS CONTROL REPORT. Business Publishers Incorporated, 951 Pershing Drive, Silver Spring, Maryland 20910. Biweekly.

ASBESTOS LITIGATION REPORTER. Andrews Publications, 1646 West Chester Pike, Westtown, Pennsylvania 19395. Semimonthly.

ASBESTOS MONITOR. Monitor Communications, P.O. Box 19976, Houston, Texas 77224. Monthly.

ASBESTOS PROPERTY LITIGATION REPORTER. Andrews Publications, 1646 West Chester Pike, Westtown, Pennsylvania 19395. Semimonthly.

CHEMICAL WASTE LITIGATION REPORTER. Law Reporters, 1519 Connecticut Avenue, Northwest, Suite 200, Washington, D.C. 20036. Monthly.

COMMUNITY RIGHT-TO-KNOW NEWS. Thompson Publishing Group, 1725 K Street, Northwest, Suite 200, Washington, D.C. 20006. Semimonthly.

ECOLOGICAL ILLNESS LAW REPORT. P.O. Box 1796, Evanston, Illinois 60204. Quarterly.

ENVIRONMENTAL HAZARDS. Prentice Hall Law and Business, 270 Sylvan Avenue, Englewood Cliffs, New Jersey 07632. Monthly.

FROM THE STATE CAPITALS--WASTE DISPOSAL AND POLLUTION CONTROL. Wakeman Walworth, Incorporated, 300 North Washington Street, Suite 204, Alexandria, Virginia 22314. Monthly.

HAZARDOUS AND SOLID WASTE MINIMAZATION AND RECYCLING REPORT. Government Institutes, Incorporated, 966 Hungerford Drive, Suite 24, Rockville, Maryland 20850. Monthly.

HARARDOUS MATERIALS TRANSPORTATION. Washington Business Information, Incorporated, 1117 North Nineteenth Street, Arlington, Virginia 22209. Semimonthly.

HAZARDOUS SUBSTANCE ADVISOR. J.J. Keller and Associates, Incorporated, 145 West Wisconsin Avenue, Neenah, Wisconsin 54956. Monthly.

HAZARDOUS WASTE AND TOXIC TORTS: LAW AND STRATEGY. Leader Publications, 111 Eighth Avenue, Suite 900, New York, New York 10011. Monthly.

HAZARDOUS WASTE LITIGATION REPORTER. Andrews Publications, 1646 West Chester Pike, Westtown, Pennsylvania 19395. Semimonthly.

HAZARDOUS WASTE NEWS. Business Publishers, Incorporated, 951 Pershing Drive, Silver Spring, Maryland 20910. Weekly.

HAZCHEM ALERT. Van Nostrand Reinhold, 115 Fifth Avenue, New York, New York 10003. Biweekly.

ILTA NEWSLETTER. Independent Liquid Terminals Association, 1133 Fifteenth Street, Northwest, Suite 204, Washington, D.C. 20005. Monthly.

INDOOR POLLUTION LAW REPORT. Leader Publications, 111 Eighth Avenue, New York, New York 10011. Monthly.

INDOOR POLLUTION LITIGATION REPORTER. Andrews Publications, 1646 West Chester Pike, Westtown, Pennsylvania 19395. Monthly.

INDOOR POLLUTION NEWS. Buraff Publications, 1350 Connecticut Avenue, Northwest, Suite 1000, Washington, D.C. 20036. Semimonthly.

INTEGRATED WASTE MANAGEMENT. McGraw-Hill Incorporated, 1221 Avenue of the Americas, New York, New York 10020. Biweekly.

OSHA COMPLIANCE ADVISOR. Business and Legal Reports, 64 Wall Street, Madison, Connecticut 06443. Semimonthly.

OSHA TRAINING BULLETIN FOR SUPERVISORS. Business and Legal Reports, 64 Wall Street, Madison, Connecticut 06443. Monthly.

RADON NEWS DIGEST. Hoosier Environmental Publishing, 8935 North Meridien Street, Suite 114, Indianapolis, Indiana 46240. Monthly.

SCAA SPILL BRIEFS. Spill Control Association of America, 400 Renaissance Center, Suite 1900, Detroit, Michigan 48243. Monthly.

TOXIC CHEMICALS LITIGATION REPORTER. Andrews Publications, 1646 West Chester Pike, Westtown, Pennsylvania 19395. Semimonthly.

TOXIC MATERIALS NEWS. Business Publishers Incorporated, 951 Pershing Drive, Silver Spring, Maryland 20910. Weekly.

TOXIC MATERIALS TRANSPORT. Business Publishers Incorporated, 951 Pershing Drive, Silver Spring, Maryland 20910. Biweekly.

TOXICS LAW REPORTER. BNA Books, 1231 Twenty-fifth Street, Washington, D.C. 20037. Weekly.

DIRECTORIES

RIGHT TO KNOW: A GUIDE TO FEDERAL AND STATE PROGRAMS. Inter/Face Associates, Incorporated, P.O. Box 431, Durham, Connecticut 06422. 1986.

ASSOCIATIONS AND PROFESSIONAL SOCIETIES

AMERICAN BAR ASSOCIATION, STANDING COMMITTEE ON ENVIRONMENTAL LAW. 750 North Lake Shore Drive, Chicago, Illinois 60611. (312) 988-5152.

CITIZENS CLEARINGHOUSE FOR HAZARDOUS WASTES. P.O. Box 926, Arlington, Virginia 22216. (703) 276-7070.

CONFERENCE ON SAFE TRANSPORTATION OF HAZARDOUS ARTICLES. c/o Lawrence W. Bierlein, 2300 N Street, Northwest, Washington, D.C. 20037. (202) 663-9245.

HAZARDOUS MATERIALS ADVISORY COUNCIL. 1110 Vermont Avenue, Northwest, Suite 290, Washington, D.C. 20005. (202) 728-1460.

HAZARDOUS WASTE FEDERATION. c/o New Mexico Hazardous Waste Management Society, Division 3314, P.O. Box 5800, Albuquerque, New Mexico 87185. (505) 846-2655.

SPILL CONTROL ASSOCIATION OF AMERICA. 400 Renaissance Center, Suite 1900, Detroit, Michigan 48243. (213) 567-0500.

RESEARCH CENTERS, INSTITUTES, CLEARINGHOUSES

BATTELLE RESEARCH CENTER. 4000 Northeast, Forty-first Street, Seattle, Washington 98105. (206) 525-3130.

CENTER FOR HAZARDOUS MATERIALS RESEARCH. 320 William Pitt Way, University of Pittsburgh, Applied Research Center, Pittsburgh, Pennsylvania 15238. (412) 826-5320.

CENTER FOR HAZARDOUS SUBSTANCE RESEARCH. Kansas State University, Durland Hall 112, Manhattan, Kansas 66506. (913) 532-5584.

CENTER FOR STUDY OF RESPONSIVE LAW. P.O. Box 19367, Washington, D.C. 20036. (202) 387-8030.

CENTER HILL SOLID AND HAZARDOUS WASTE RESEARCH LABORATORY. 5995 Center Hill Road, Cincinnati, Ohio 45224. (513) 569-7885.

COOPERATIVE INSTITUTE FOR RESEARCH IN ENVIRONMENTAL SCIENCES. University of Colorado--Boulder, Campus Box 216, Boulder, Colorado 80309. (303) 492-1143.

ENVIRONMENTAL ACTION FOUNDATION. 1525 New Hampshire Avenue, Northwest, Washington, D.C. 20036. (202) 745-4870.

ENVIRONMENTAL LAW INSTITUTE. 1616 P Street, Northwest, Suite 200, Washington, D.C. 20036. (202) 328-5150.

ENVIRONMENTAL POLICY INSTITUTE. 218 D Street, Southeast, Washington, D.C. 20003. (202) 544-2600.

ENVIRONMENTAL QUALITY LABORATORY. California Institute of Technology, 105-96, Pasadena, California 91125. (818) 356-4167.

ENVIRONMENTAL RESEARCH INSTITUTE FOR HAZARDOUS MATERIALS AND WASTES. University of Connecticut, 191 Auditorium Road, Box U 210, Storrs, Connecticut 06268. (203) 486-4015.

GEORGIA TECH RESEARCH INSTITUTE. Georgia Institute of Technology, Atlanta, Georgia 30332. (404) 894-3400.

HAZARDOUS MATERIALS CONTROL RESEARCH INSTITUTE. 9300 Columbia Boulevard, Silver Spring, Maryland 20910. (301) 587-9390.

HAZARDOUS MATERIALS MANAGEMENT AND RESOURCE RECOVERY. University of Alabama, Department of Chemical Engineering, P.O. Box 870203, Tuscaloosa, Alabama 35487. (205) 348-8401.

HAZARDOUS MATERIALS RESEARCH CENTER. Metropolitan Center for High Technology, 2727 Second Avenue, Detroit, Michigan 48201. (313) 963-0616.

HAZARDOUS SUBSTANCE MANAGEMENT RESEARCH CENTER. New Jersey Institute of Technology, Newark, New Jersey 07102. (201) 596-3233.

HAZARDOUS WASTE RESEARCH AND INFORMATION CENTER. 1808 Woodfield Drive, Savoy, Illinois 61874. (217) 333-8940.

HAZARDOUS WASTE RESEARCH CENTER. Louisiana State University, 3418 CEBA Building, Baton Rouge, Louisiana 70803. (504) 388-6770.

PACIFIC BASIN CONSORTIUM FOR HAZARDOUS WASTES. c/o East-West Center, Environmental and Policy Institute, 1777 East-West Road, Honolulu, Hawaii 96848. (808) 944-7555.

WORLD RESOURCES INSTITUTE (WRI). 1709 New York Avenue, Northwest, Suite 700, Washington, D.C. 20006. (202) 638-6300.

WORLDWATCH INSTITUTE. 1776 Massachusetts Avenue, Northwest, Washington, D.C. 20036. (202) 452-1999.

ONLINE DATABASES

CERCLIS DATABASE OF HAZARDOUS WASTE SITES. Chemical Information Systems, Incorporated, 7215 York Road, Baltimore, Maryland 21212.

ENVIROLINE. Bowker A and I Publishing, 245 West Seventeenth Street, New York, New York 10018.

ENVIRONMENT REPORTER. Bureau of National Affairs Incorporated, BNA Online, 1231 Twenty-fifth Street, Northwest, Washington, D.C. 20037.

ENVIRONMENT WEEK. King Communications Group, Incorporated, 627 National Press Building, Washington, D.C. 20045.

ENVIRONMENTAL BIBLIOGRAPHY. Environmental Studies Institute, 800 Garden Street, Suite D, Santa Barbara, California 93101.

ENVIRONMENTAL HEALTH NEWS. Occupational Health Services, Incorporated, 450 Seventh Avenue, Suite 2407, New York, New York 10123.

HAZARDOUS MATERIALS INTELLIGENCE REPORT. World Information Systems, P.O. Box 535, Cambridge, Massachusetts 02238.

HAZARDOUS SUBSTANCES DATA BANK. United States National Library of Medicine, Toxicology Information Program, 8600 Rockville Pike, Bethesda, Maryland 20894.

HAZARDOUS WASTE NEWS. Business Publishers, Incorporated, 951 Pershing Drive, Silver Spring, Maryland 20910.

REPORT ON DEFENSE PLANT WASTES. Business Publishers, Incorporated, 951 Pershing Drive, Silver Spring, Maryland 20910.

SUSPECT CHEMICALS SOURCEBOOK. Roytech Publications, Incorporated, 840 Hiuckley Road, Suite 147, Burlingame, California 94010.

TOXIC MATERIALS NEWS. Business Publishers, Incorporated, 951 Pershing Drive, Silver Spring, Maryland 20910.

TOXIC MATERIALS TRANSPORT. Business Publishers, Incorporated, 951 Pershing Drive, Silver Spring, Maryland 20910.

WASTE TREATMENT TECHNOLOGY NEWS. Business Communications Company, 25 Van Zant Street, Norwalk, Connecticut 06855.

STATISTICS SOURCES

QUALITY OF LIFE IN AMERICAN NEIGHBORHOODS: LEVELS OF AFFLUENCE, TOXIC WASTE, AND CANCER MORTALITY IN RESIDENTIAL ZIP CODE AREAS. Jay M. Gould. CEP International Company, 1 Sansome, Suite 2000, San Francisco, California 94104. 1986.

OTHER SOURCES

HEALTH ASPECTS OF THE DISPOSAL OF WASTE CHEMICALS. Joe W. Grisham, M.D., editor. Pergamon Press, Incorporated, Maxwell House, Fairview Park, Elmsford, New York 10523. 1985.

SUPERFUND STRATEGY. United States Congress, Office of Technology Assessment. Superintendent of Documents, United States Government Printing Office, Washington, D.C. 20402. 1985.

HEALTH AND HUMAN SERVICES DEPARTMENT
See also: FOOD AND DRUG ADMINISTRATION; SOCIAL SECURITY ADMINISTRATION

STATUTES, CODES, STANDARDS, UNIFORM LAWS

CODE OF FEDERAL REGULATIONS, TITLE 45. Office of the Federal Register, National Archives and Records Administration. Superintendent of Documents, United States Government Printing Office, Washington, D.C. 20402. Annual. (Updated by use of monthly List of Sections Affected and daily Federal Register.)

COMPILATION OF THE SOCIAL SECURITY LAWS, INCLUDING THE SOCIAL SECURITY ACT, AS AMENDED, AND RELATED ENACTMENTS THROUGH JANUARY 1, 1987. United States Department of Health and Human Services. Superintendent of Documents, United States Government Printing Office, Washington, D.C. 20402. 1987.

HANDBOOKS, MANUALS, FORMBOOKS

MEDICARE HOSPITAL MANUAL. Health and Human Services Department, Health Care Financing Administration. Superintendent of Documents, United States Government Printing Office, Washington, D.C. 20402. 1985. Looseleaf.

TEXTBOOKS AND GENERAL WORKS

DEINSTITUTIONALIZATION: A CROSS-PROBLEM ANALYSIS. Paul Lerman. Health and Human Services Department, National Institute of Mental Health, Division of Special Mental Health Programs. Superintendent of Documents, United States Government Printing Office, Washington, D.C. 20402. 1981.

EMPLOYEE DRUG SCREENING: DETECTION OF DRUG USE BY URINALYSIS. Micheal J. Walsh. Health and Human Services Department, Alcohol, Drug Abuse, and Mental Health Administration, National Institute on Drug Abuse. Superintendent of Documents, United States Government Printing Office, Washington, D.C. 20402. 1986.

INTERDISCIPLINARY APPROACHES TO THE PROBLEM OF DRUG ABUSE IN THE WORKPLACE: CONSENSUS SUMMARY. Micheal J. Walsh and Steven W. Gust. Health and Human Services Department, National Institute on Drug Abuse, Division of Clinical Research. Superintendent of Documents, United States Government Printing Office, Washington, D.C. 20402. 1986.

INVESTOR'S GUIDE TO HEALTH MAINTENANCE ORGANIZATIONS. Health and Human Services Department, Office of Health Maintenance Organizations, Division of Program Promotion. Superintendent of Documents, United States Government Printing Office, Washington, D.C. 20402. 1982.

PHENCYCLIDINE: AN UPDATE. Doris H. Clouet. Health and Human Services Department, Alcohol, Drug Abuse, and Mental Health Administration, National Institute on Drug Abuse. Superintendent of Documents, United States Government Printing Office, Washington, D.C. 20402. 1986.

REGISTRY OF TOXIC EFFECTS OF CHEMICAL SUBSTANCES. Richard L. Lewis and Doris V. Sweet. Health and Human Services Department, Public Health Service, Centers for Disease Control, National Institute for Occupational Safety and Health. Superintendent of Documents, United States Government Printing Office, Washington, D.C. 20402. 1985.

URINE TESTING FOR DRUGS OF ABUSE. Richard L. Hawks and Nora C. Chiang. Health and Human Services Department, Alcohol, Drug Abuse, and Mental Health Administration, National Institute on Drug Abuse, Division of Preclinical Research. Superintendent of Documents, United States Government Printing Office, Washington, D.C. 20402. 1986.

RESEARCH CENTERS, INSTITUTES, CLEARINGHOUSES

UNITED STATES DEPARTMENT OF HEALTH AND HUMAN SERVICES LIBRARY. 330 Independence Avenue, Southwest, Washington, D.C. 20201. (202) 619-3531.

HEALTH CARE
See also: AGED AND HEALTH CARE; AIDS; BIOETHICS; HEALTH AND HUMAN SERVICES DEPARTMENT; HOSPITALS; MEDICAL JURISPRUDENCE AND MALPRACTICE; MENTAL HEALTH AND DISABILITY; NURSES AND NURSING; NURSING HOMES; OCCUPATIONAL SAFETY AND HEALTH

STATUTES, CODES, STANDARDS, UNIFORM LAWS

MODEL HEALTH CARE CONSENT ACT. National Conference of Commissioners on Uniform State Laws. Uniform Laws Annotated. West Publishing Company, P.O. Box 64526, 50 West Kellogg Boulevard, St. Paul, Minnesota 55164-0526. 1976- . (Annual Supplements).

UNIFORM HEALTH CARE INFORMATION ACT. Uniform Laws Annotated. West Publishing Company, P.O. Box 64526, 50 West Kellogg Boulevard, St. Paul, Minnesota 55164-0526. 1976- . (Annual Supplements).

LOOSELEAF SERVICES AND REPORTERS

AMBULATORY SERVICES: REGULATIONS AND GUIDELINES. National Law and Health Publishing, 99 Painters Mill Road, Owings Mills, Maryland 21117. 1979- .

BIOLAW. James F. Childress, et al. University Publications of America, 4520 East West Highway, Suite 600, Bethesda, Maryland 20814. 1983- .

COMPENDIUM OF ANTITRUST HEALTH CARE CASES. Antitrust Law Section, American Bar Association, 750 North Lake Shore Drive, Chicago, Illinois 60611. 1986- .

A GUIDE TO REHABILITATION. Paul Deutsch and Horace W. Sawyer. Matthew Bender and Company, Incorporated, 11 Penn Plaza, New York, New York 10001. 1985- .

HEALTH ADMINISTRATION: LAWS, REGULATIONS AND GUIDELINES. National Law and Health Publishing, 99 Painters Mill Road, Owings Mills, Maryland 21117. 1977- .

HEALTH CARE LABOR MANUAL. Martin E. Skoler. Aspen Publishers, Incorporated, 1600 Research Boulevard, Rockville, Maryland 20850. 1974- .

HEALTH CARE LAW: A PRACTICAL GUIDE. Matthew Bender and Company, Incorporated, 11 Penn Plaza, New York, New York 10001. 1985- .

HMO LAW MANUAL. Aspen Publishers, Incorporated, 1600 Research Boulevard, Rockville, Maryland 20850. 1975- .

LABORATORY REGULATION MANUAL. Aspen Publishers, Incorporated, 1600 Research Boulevard, Rockville, Maryland 20850. 1976- .

OPERATING STANDARDS IN HEALTH CARE FACILITIES. National Law and Health Publishing, 99 Painters Mill Road, Owings Mill, Maryland 21117. 1984- .

ORGAN PROCUREMENT AND TRANSPLANTATION MANUALS: LAWS, REGULATIONS AND GUIDELINES. National Law and Health Publishing, 99 Painters Mill Road, Owings Mill, Maryland 21117. 1987- .

HANDBOOKS, MANUALS, FORMBOOKS

THE ANTITRUST HEALTH CARE HANDBOOK: TASK FORCE ON ANTITRUST COMPLIANCE PROGRAM FOR THE HEALTH CARE INDUSTRY. American Bar Association, Section of Antitrust Law, 750 North Lake Shore Drive, Chicago, Illinois 60611. 1988.

CONSENT TO TREATMENT: A PRACTICAL GUIDE. Fay A. Rozovsky. Little, Brown and Company, 34 Beacon Street, Boston, Massachusetts 02108. 1984.

HANDBOOK ON CRITICAL LIFE ISSUES. Pope John Center, 186 Forbes Road, Braintree, Massachusetts 02184. 1988.

HEALTH AND THE LAW: A HANDBOOK FOR HEALTH PROFESSIONALS. Tom Christoffel. Free Press, 866 Third Avenue, New York, New York 10022. 1985.

HEALTH CARE CONSENT MANUAL: POLICIES, LAWS, AND PROCEDURES. Second edition. Karen M. Engstrom. Catholic Health Association of the United States, 4455 Woodson Road, St. Louis, Missouri 63134-0889. 1985.

HEALTH CARE SUPERVISOR'S LEGAL GUIDE. Karen H. Henry. Aspen Publishers, Incorporated, 1600 Research Boulevard, Rockville, Maryland 20850. 1984.

LEGAL GUIDE FOR MEDICAL OFFICE MANAGERS. Marshall B. Knapp. Health Administration Press, 1021 East Huron Street, University of Michigan, Ann Arbor, Michigan 48104-9990. 1985.

TEXTBOOKS AND GENERAL WORKS

AIDS AND THE HEALTH CARE SYSTEM. Larry O. Gostin. Yale University Press, 302 Temple Street, New Haven, Connecticut 06520. 1990.

AMERICAN HEALTH CARE: REALITIES, RIGHTS, AND REFORMS. Charles J. Dougherty. Oxford University Press, 200 Madison Avenue, New York, New York 10016. 1988.

AMERICAN HEALTH LAW. George J. Annas. Little, Brown and Company, 34 Beacon Street, Boston, Massachusetts 02108. 1990.

CARE AND PUNISHMENT: THE DILEMMAS OF PRISON MEDICINE. Curtis Prout and Robert N. Ross. University of Pittsburgh Press, 127 North Bellefield Avenue, Pittsburgh, Pennsylvania 15260. 1988.

DEVELOPMENTS IN ANTITRUST HEALTH CARE LAW. American Bar Association, Section of Antitrust Law, 750 North Lake Shore Drive, Chicago, Illinois 60611. 1990.

FINANCING HEALTH CARE: ECONOMIC EFFICIENCY AND EQUITY. Steven R. Eastaugh. Auburn House Publishing Company, Greenwood Publishing Group, Incorporated, 88 Post Road West, P.O. Box 5007, Westport, Connecticut 06881. 1987.

HEALTH CARE AND THE LAW III: REPORTS ON THREE ROUND TABLE DISCUSSIONS. Michael E. Carbine. Roscoe Pound Foundation, 1050 Thirty-first Street, Northwest, Washington, D.C. 20007. 1990.

HEALTH CARE IN AMERICA: THE POLITICAL ECONOMY OF HOSPITALS AND HEALTH INSURANCE. Pacific Research Institute for Public Policy, 177 Post Street, Suite 500, San Francisco, California 94108. 1988.

HEALTH CARE ISSUES IN BLACK AMERICA: POLICIES, PROBLEMS, AND PROSPECTS. Greenwood Publishing Group, Incorporated, 88 Post Road West, P.O. Box 5007, Westport, Connecticut 06881. 1987.

HEALTH CARE LAW AND ETHICS IN A NUTSHELL. Mark A. Hall. West Publishing Company, 50 West Kellogg Boulevard, St. Paul, Minnesota 55164. 1990.

HEALTH CARE: LEGAL RESPONSES TO NEW ECONOMIC FORCES. Robert M. McNair, Jr. Practising Law Institute, 810 Seventh Avenue, New York, New York 10019. 1985.

HEALTH POLICY IN TRANSITION: A DECADE OF HEALTH POLITICS, POLICY, AND LAW. Duke University Press, Box 6697 College Station, Durham, North Carolina 27708. 1987.

LAW AND ETHICS IN HEALTH CARE. John B. McKinlay, editor. MIT Press, 55 Hayward Street, Cambridge, Massachusetts 02142. 1982.

LAW AND ETHICS IN THE MEDICAL OFFICE: INCLUDING BIOETHICAL ISSUES. Second Edition. Marcia A. Lewis and Carol D. Warden. F.A. Davis Company, 1915 Arch Street, Philadelphia, Pennsylvania 19103. 1988.

THE LAW OF HOSPITAL AND HEALTH CARE ADMINISTRATON. Second Edition. Arthur F. Southwick and Debora A. Slee. Health Administration Press, Department KW, 1021 East Huron Street, Ann Arbor, Michigan 48104. 1988.

LEGAL AND ETHICAL ASPECTS OF TREATING CRITICALLY AND TERMINALLY ILL PATIENTS. Edward A. Daudern and Douglas J. Peters, editors. Health Administration Press, 1021 East Huron Street, University of Michigan, Ann Arbor, Michigan 48109-9990. 1982.

MANAGED CARE AND ANTITRUST: THE PPO EXPERIENCE. Robert J. Enders. American Bar Association, Section of Antitrust Law, 750 North Lake Shore Drive, Chicago, Illinois 60611. 1990.

MEDICAL ETHICS AND ECONOMICS IN HEALTH CARE. Oxford University Press, 200 Madison Avenue, New York, New York 10016. 1988.

MEDICAL ETHICS AND THE ELDERLY: A CASE BOOK. Mark H. Waymack. Pluribus Press, 160 East Illinois Street, Chicago, Illinois 60611. 1988.

MEDICAL RISK MANAGEMENT: PREVENTIVE LEGAL STRATEGIES FOR HEALTH CARE PROVIDERS. Edward P. Richards, III and Katherine C. Rathbun. Aspen Publishing, Incorporated, 1600 Research Boulevard, Rockville, Maryland 20850. 1982.

MEDICARE AND EXTENDED CARE: ISSUES, PROBLEMS, AND PROSPECTS. Genrose J. Alfano. National Health Publishing, 99 Painters Mill Road, Owings Mills, Maryland 21117. 1987.

PAINFUL CHOICES: RESEARCH AND ESSAYS ON HEALTH CARE. David Mechanic. Transaction Books, Rutgers University, New Brunswick, New Jersey 08903. 1989.

RATIONING HEALTH CARE IN AMERICA: PERCEPTIONS AND PRINCIPLES OF JUSTICE. Larry R. Churchill. University of Notre Dame Press, Notre Dame, Indiana 46556. 1987.

RATIONING MEDICINE. Robert H. Blank. Columbia University Press, 562 West One Hundred Thirteenth Street, New York, New York 10025. 1988.

THE RIGHTS OF OLDER PERSONS. Second Edition. Robert N. Brown. Southern Illinois University Press, P.O. Box 3697, Carbondale, Illinois 62902-3697. 1989.

SETTING LIMITS: MEDICAL GOALS IN AN AGING SOCIETY. Daniel Callahan. Simon and Schuster, Incorporated, 1230 Avenue of the Americas, New York, New York 10020. 1987.

TOO POOR TO BE SICK: ACCESS TO MEDICAL CARE FOR THE UNINSURED. Patricia A. Butler. American Public Health Association, 1015 Fifteenth Street, Northwest, Washington, D.C. 20005. 1988.

WHERE COVERAGE ENDS: CATASTROPHIC ILLNESS AND LONG-TERM HEALTH CARE. Employee Benefit Research Institute, 2121 K Street, Northwest, Suite 600, Washington, D.C. 20037-2121. 1988.

ENCYCLOPEDIAS AND DICTIONARIES

ATTORNEY'S DICTIONARY OF MEDICINE. J. E. Schmidt. Matthew Bender and Company, Incorporated, 11 Penn Plaza, New York, New York 10001. 1962- . (Annual Supplements).

LAWYERS' MEDICAL CYCLOPEDIA. Charles J. Frankel and James G. Zimmerly, editors. Michie/Bobbs-Merrill Law Publishing, P.O. Box 7587, Charlottesville, Virginia 22906-7582. 1972- . (Periodic Supplements).

MASA: MEDICAL ACRONYMS, SYMBOLS AND ABBREVIATIONS. Betty Hamilton and Barbara Guidos, editors. Neal-Schuman Publishers, Incorporated, 23 Cornelia Street, New York, New York 10013. 1988.

DIGESTS, INDEXES, ABSTRACTS, CITATORS

LAWYER'S MEDICAL DIGEST. Callaghan and Company, 155 Pfingsten Road, Deerfield, Illinois 60015. Monthly.

SPECIALTY LAW DIGEST: HEALTH CARE. Bureau of National Affairs, Incorporated, 1231 Twenty-fifth Street, Northwest, Washington, D.C. 20037. 1979- .

NEWSLETTERS AND NEWSPAPERS

AHCA NOTES. American Health Care Association, 1201 L Street, Northwest, Washington, D.C. 20005. Semimonthly.

AIDS POLICY AND LAW. Buraff Publications, 1350 Connecticut Avenue, Northwest, Suite 1000, Washington, D.C. 20036. Semimonthly.

THE CITATION. American Medical Association, 535 North Dearborn Street, Chicago, Illinois 60610. Semimonthly.

EMERGENCY MEDICAL TECHNICIAN LEGAL BULLETIN. Med/Law Publishers, Incorporated, P.O. Box 293, Westville, New Jersey 08093. Quarterly.

EMERGENCY NURSE LEGAL BULLETIN. Med/Law Publishers, Incorporated, P.O. Box 293, Westville, New Jersey 08093. Quarterly.

EMERGENCY PHYSICIAN LEGAL BULLETIN. Med/Law Publishers, Incorporated, P.O. Box 293, Westville, New Jersey 08093. Quarterly.

THE FEDERAL HEALTH MONITOR. National Health Lawyers Association, 1620 Eye Street, Northwest, Suite 900, Washington, D.C. 20006. Monthly.

HEALTH ADVOCATE. National Health Law Program, South Cienega Boulevard, Los Angeles, California 90034. Quarterly.

HEALTH CARE NEWSLETTER. Matthew Bender and Company, Incorporated, 11 Penn Plaza, New York, New York 10001. Monthly.

HEALTH LAW BULLETIN. Institute of Government, University of North Carolina, Knapp Building, CB #3330, Chapel Hill, North Carolina 27599.

HEALTH LAW DIGEST. National Health Lawyers Association, 1620 Eye Street, Northwest, Suite 900, Washington, D.C. 20006. Monthly.

THE HEALTH LAWYER. American Bar Association, 750 North Lake Shore Drive, Chicago, Illinois 60611. Quarterly.

HEALTHCARE AND THE LAW. Reed, McClure, Moceri, Thorr and Moriarty, 3600 Columbia Center, 701 Fifth Avenue, Seattle, Washington 98104. Quarterly.

HEALTHSPAN: THE REPORT OF HEALTH BUSINESS AND LAW. Prentice Hall Law and Business, 270 Sylvan Avenue, Englewood Cliffs, New Jersey 07632. Monthly.

HOSPICE LETTER. Health Resources Publishing, Brinley Plaza, 3100 Highway 138, Wall Township, New Jersey 07719. Monthly.

INFOTRENDS: MEDICINE, LAW AND ETHICS. Univerisity of Medicine and Dentistry of New Jersey, Robert Wood Johnson Medical School, P.O. Box 896, Piscataway, New Jersey 08855. Quarterly.

MEDICINE AND HEALTH CARE WITH PERSPECTIVES. Faulkner and Gray Health Care Information Center, 1133 Fifteenth Street, Northwest, Suite 450, Washington, D.C. 20005. Weekly.

PUBLIC HEALTH LAW BULLETIN. Peters-Jenson Publishing Company, 8A East Mason Avenue, Alexandria, Virginia 22301. Semimonthly.

SPECIALTY LAW DIGEST: HEALTH CARE. Specialty Digest Publications, Incorporated, 10301 University Avenue, Northeast, Blaine, Minnesota 55433. Monthly.

THE WASHINGTON MEMO. The Alan Guttmacher Institute, 2010 Massachusetts Avenue, Northwest, Washington, D.C. 20036. Semimonthly.

LAW REVIEWS AND PERIODICALS

AMERICAN JOURNAL OF LAW AND MEDICINE. American Society of Law and Medicine, 765 Commonwealth Avenue, Sixteenth Floor, Boston, Massachusetts 02215. Quarterly.

JOURNAL OF CONTEMPORARY HEALTH LAW AND POLICY. The Columbus School of Law, 620 Michigan Avenue, Northeast, Washington, D.C. 20064. Semiannually.

JOURNAL OF HEALTH, POLITICS, POLICY AND LAW. Department of Health Administration, 6697 College Station, Box 3018, Durham, North Carolina 27710. Quarterly.

LAW, MEDICINE AND HEALTH CARE. American Society of Law and Medicine, 765 Commonwealth Avenue, Sixteenth Floor, Boston, Massachusetts 02215. Six issues per year.

LEGAL ASPECTS OF MEDICAL PRACTICE. Pharmaceutical Communications, Incorporated, 42-15 Crescent Street, Long Island City, New York 11101. Monthly.

TRAUMA. Matthew Bender. Matthew Bender and Company, Incorporated, 235 East Forty-fifth Street, New York, New York 10017. Six issues per year.

BIBLIOGRAPHIES

LEGAL ASPECTS OF HEALTH CARE FOR THE ELDERLY: AN ANNOTATED BIBLIOGRAPHY. Marshall B. Kapp. Greenwood Publishing Group, Incorporated, 88 Post Road West, P.O. Box 5007, Westport, Connecticut 06881. 1988.

A SOURCEBOOK FOR RESEARCH IN LAW AND MEDICINE. Salvatore F. Fiscina. National Law Publishing Corporation, 99 Painters Mill Road, Owings Mills, Maryland 21117. 1985.

DIRECTORIES

AMERICAN MEDICAL DIRECTORY: DIRECTORY OF PHYSICIANS IN THE UNITED STATES, PUERTO RICO, VIRGIN ISLANDS, CERTAIN PACIFIC ISLANDS AND U.S. PHYSICIANS TEMPORARILY LOCATED IN FOREIGN COUNTRIES. Twenty-eighth edition. American Medical Association, 515 North State Street, Chicago, Illinois 60610. 1982.

HEALTH CARE STANDARDS: OFFICIAL DIRECTORY. ECRI, 5200 Butler Pike, Plymouth Meeting, Pennsylvania 19462. 1989. Annual.

ASSOCIATIONS AND PROFESSIONAL SOCIETIES

AMERICAN BAR ASSOCIATION. Forum Committee on Health Law, 750 North Lake Shore Drive, Chicago, Illinois 60611. (312) 988-5000.

AMERICAN COLLEGE OF PHYSICIANS. Independence Mall West, Sixth Street at Race, Philadelphia, Pennsylvania 19106. (215) 351-2400.

AMERICAN HEALTH CARE ASSOCIATION. 1201 L Street, Northwest, Washington, D.C. 20005. (202) 842-4444.

AMERICAN MEDICAL ASSOCIATION. 535 North Dearborn Street, Chicago, Illinois 60610. (312) 645-4607.

AMERICAN SOCIETY OF LAW AND MEDICINE. 765 Commonwealth Avenue, Sixteenth Floor, Boston, Massachusetts 02215. (617) 262-4990.

ASSOCIATION OF AMERICAN PHYSICIANS. Department of Medicine, Box 8125, 660 South Euclid Avenue, Washington University Medical School, St. Louis, Missouri 63110. (314) 362-8803.

ASSOCIATION OF AMERICAN PHYSICIANS AND SURGEONS. 9203 Lake Braddock Drive, Burke, Virginia 22015. (703) 425-6300.

NATIONAL HEALTH LAWYERS ASSOCIATION. 1620 Eye Street, Northwest, Suite 900, Washington, D.C. 20006. (202) 833-1100.

RESEARCH CENTERS, INSTITUTES, CLEARINGHOUSES

THE ALAN GUTTMACHER INSTITUTE. 2010 Massachusetts Avenue, Northwest, Washington, D.C. 20036. (202) 296-4012.

CASE WESTERN RESERVE UNIVERSITY, LAW-MEDICINE CENTER. Gund Hall, Cleveland, Ohio 44106.

FAULKNER AND GRAY HEALTH CARE INFORMATION CENTER. 1133 Fifteenth Street, Northwest, Suite 450, Washington, D.C. 20005. (202) 828-4150.

NATIONAL HEALTH LAW PROGRAM. 2639 South Cienega Boulevard, Los Angeles, California 90034. (213) 204-6010.

NATIONAL LIBRARY OF MEDICINE. 8600 Rockville Pike, Bethesda, Maryland 20209.

ONLINE DATABASES

AFTERCARE INSTRUCTIONS. Micromedex, Incorporated, 600 Grant Street, Denver, Colorado 80203.

AMA/NET AP MEDICAL NEWS SERVICE. American Medical Association, 535 North Dearborn Street, Chicago, Illinois 60610, and The Associated Press, 50 Rockefeller Plaza, New York, New York 10020.

BIRTH DEFECTS INFORMATION SERVICE. Center for Birth Defects Information Services, Incorporated, Dover Medical Building, Box 1776, Dover, Massachusetts 02030.

CENTERS FOR DISEASE CONTROL INFORMATION SERVICE. U.S. Department of Health and Human Services, Public Health Service, Centers for Disease Control, Epidemiology Program Office, 1600 Clifton Road, Atlanta, Georgia 30333.

COMPREHENSIVE CARE MEDICAL LIBRARY. BRS Information Technologies, 8000 Westpark Drive, McLean, Virginia 22102.

DRI HEALTH CARE COST FORECASTING. DRI/McGraw-Hill, Data Products Division, 24 Hartwell Avenue, Lexington, Massachusetts 02173.

HEALTH CARE COMPETITION WEEK. Capitol Publications, Incorporated, Capital Publishing Group, P.O. Box 1453, Alexandria, Virginia 22313.

HEALTH CARE COSTS: WHERE'S THE BOTTOM LINE? Bureau of National Affairs, Incorporated, 1231 Twenty-fifth Street, Northwest, Washington, D.C. 20037.

HEALTH CARE INDUSTRY COMPETITIVE INTELLIGENCE TRACKING SERVICE. Strategic Intelligence Systems, Incorporated, 404 Park Avenue South, Suite 1301, New York, New York 10016.

HEALTH PLANNING AND ADMINISTRATION. National Library of Medicine, 8600 Rockville Pike, Bethesda, Maryland 20209.

HEALTHCARE EVALUATION SYSTEM. National Planning Data Corporation, P.O. Box 610, Ithaca, New York 14851.

HEALTHLAWYER. American Hospital Association, 840 North Lake Shore Drive, Chicago, Illinois 60611.

MANAGED CARE LAW OUTLOOK. Capitol Publications, Incorporated, Capitol Publishing Group, P.O. Box 1453, Alexandria, Virginia 22313.

MANAGED CARE OUTLOOK. Capitol Publications, Incorporated, Capitol Publishing Group, P.O. Box 1453, Alexandria, Virginia 22313.

MANAGED CARE REPORT. Key Communications, 4350 East West Highway, Suite 1124, Bethesda, Maryland 20814.

MEDICAL ABSTRACTS NEWSLETTER. Communi-T Publications, P.O. Box 2170, Teaneck, New Jersey 07666.

THE MEDICAL ROUNDTABLE. Michael P. Weinstein, M.D., P.O. Box 416, Hudson, New Hampshire 03051.

MEDIS. Mead Data Central, Post Office Box 933, Dayton, Ohio 45401.

MEDLINE. National Library of Medicine, 8600 Rockville Pike, Bethesda, Maryland 20209.

PHYCOM. BRS/Saunders Colleague, 555 East Lancaster Avenue, Fourth Floor, St. Davids, Pennsylvania 19087.

SURGEON GENERAL'S INFORMATION SERVICE. U.S. Public Health Service, Office of the Surgeon General, 5600 Fishers Lane, Room 1866, Rockville, Maryland 20857.

TOXLINE. National Library of Medicine, Toxicology Information Program, 8600 Rockville Pike, Bethesda, Maryland 20209.

AUDIOVISUALS

TERMINATION OF MEDICAL TREATMENT DECISIONS: LEGAL AND ETHICAL ISSUES. (2 audiocassettes). American Bar Association, Section of Real Property, Probate, and Trust Laws, 750 North Lake Shore Drive, Chicago, Illinois 60611. 1984.

OTHER SOURCES

BUILDING AN AMERICAN HEALTH SYSTEM: JOURNEY TOWARD A HEALTHY AND CARING AMERICA: A REPORT. United States Congress, House Select Committee on Aging. Superintendent of Documents, United States Government Printing Office, Washington, D.C. 20402. 1990.

FAMILY USE OF HEALTH CARE. Marvin Dicker. United States Department of Health and Human Services, Health Care Financing Administration, Office of Research and Demonstration. Superintendent of Documents, United States Government Printing Office, Washington, D.C. 20402. 1987.

THE HEALTH CARE CRISIS: A REPORT TO THE AMERICAN PEOPLE. Edward Moore Kennedy. Superintendent of Documents, United States Government Printing Office, Washington, D.C. 20402. 1990.

LIFE-SUSTAINING TECHNOLOGIES AND THE ELDERLY. Congress of the United States, Office of Technology Assessment. Superintendent of Documents, United States Government Printing Office, Washington, D.C. 20402. 1987.

HEARSAY
See: EVIDENCE

HEIRS
See: WILLS, TRUSTS AND INHERITANCE

HIGH TECHNOLOGY
See also: COMPUTERS; NATIONAL TELECOMMUNICATIONS AND INFORMATION ADMINISTRATION; SPACE LAW; TELECOMMUNICATIONS

HANDBOOKS, MANUALS, FORMBOOKS

ENGINEERING/HIGH-TECHNOLOGY STUDENT'S HANDBOOK. Peterson's Guide, Incorporated, P.O. Box 2123, Princeton, New Jersey 08543-2123. 1985.

LESKO'S NEW TECH SOURCEBOOK: A DIRECTORY TO FINDING ANSWERS IN TODAY'S TECHNOLOGY--ORIENTED WORLD. Matthew Lesko. HarperCollins Publishers, 10 East Fifty-third Street, New York, New York 10022. 1986.

TEXTBOOKS AND GENERAL WORKS

ACQUISITIONS AND MERGERS OF HIGH-TECHNOLOGY COMPANIES. Gordon K. Davidson. Practising Law Institute, 810 Seventh Avenue, New York, New York 10019. 1986.

HIGH-TECHNOLOGY POLICIES: A FIVE NATION COMPARISON. Richard R. Nelson. American Enterprise Institute for Public Policy Research, 1150 Seventeenth Street, Northwest, Washington, D.C. 20036. 1984.

NON-TARIFF BARRIERS TO HIGH-TECHNOLOGY TRADE. Robert B. Cohen, Richard W. Ferguson, and Michael F. Oppenheimer. Westview Press, Incorporated, 5500 Central Avenue, Boulder, Colorado 80301. 1985.

NONTARIFF BARRIERS: THE EFFECTS ON CORPORATE STRATEGY IN HIGH-TECHNOLOGY SECTORS. Michael F. Oppenheimer and Donna M. Tuths. Westview Press, Incorporated, 5500 Central Avenue, Boulder, Colorado 80301. 1987.

REPRESENTING THE GROWING TECHNOLOGY COMPANY: ALI-ABA COURSE OF STUDY MATERIALS. American Law Institute--American Bar Association, 4025 Chestnut Street, Philadelphia, Pennsylvania 19104. 1986.

TAX ASPECTS OF HIGH TECHNOLOGY OPERATIONS. John Wiley and Sons, Incorporated, 605 Third Avenue, New York, New York 10158. 1985- .

LAW REVIEWS AND PERIODICALS

HIGH TECHNOLOGY LAW JOURNAL. Boalt Hall School of Law, University of California, Berkeley. University of California Press, 2120 Berkeley Way, Berkeley, California 94720. 1986- . Biannual.

JOURNAL OF LAW AND TECHNOLOGY. Georgetown University Law Center, 600 New Jersey Avenue, Northwest, Washington, D.C. 20001. Semiannual.

RUTGERS COMPUTER AND TECHNOLOGY LAW JOURNAL. Rutgers Law School, 15 Washington Street, Neward, New Jersey 07102. Biannual.

SANTA CLARA COMPUTER AND HIGH-TECHNOLOGY LAW JOURNAL. University of Santa Clara School of Law, Santa Clara, California 95033. 1985- . Biannual.

TECHNOLOGY REVIEW. Massachusetts Institute of Technology Building W59, Cambridge, Massachusetts 02139. 8 issues per year.

NEWSLETTERS AND NEWSPAPERS

BULLETIN OF LAW, SCIENCE AND TECHNOLOGY. American Bar Association, 750 North Lake Shore Drive, Chicago, Illinois 60611. Bimonthly.

COURT TECHNOLOGY BULLETIN. National Center for State Courts, 300 Newport Avenue, Williamsburg, Virginia 23187. Bimonthly.

TEKBRIEFS. TEKLICON, INCORPORATED. 444 Castro Street, Suite 818, Mountain View, California 94041. Bimonthly.

HIGH TECHNOLOGY

DIRECTORIES

DIRECTORY OF PUBLIC HIGH TECHNOLOGY CORPORATIONS. American Investors, Incorporated, 311 Bainbridge Street, Philadelphia, Pennsylvania 19147. Annual.

LEADING CONSULTANTS IN TECHNOLOGY. Research Publications, 12 Lunar Drive, Drawer AB, Woodbridge, Connecticut 06525.

HIJACKING OF AIRLINERS
See: TERRORISM

HISTORIC PRESERVATION
See also: INTERIOR DEPARTMENT; ZONING AND PLANNING

LOOSELEAF SERVICES AND REPORTERS

THE FEDERAL TAX LAW OF CONSERVATION EASEMENTS. Stephen J. Small. Land Trust Exchange, 1017 Duke Street, Alexandria, Virginia 22314. 1986- .

HISTORIC PRESERVATION LAW. Matthew Bender and Company, Incorporated, 11 Penn Plaza, New York, New York 10001. 1986- . (Periodic Supplements).

INFORMATION: A PRESERVATION SOURCE BOOK. National Trust for Historic Preservation, 1776 Massachusetts Avenue, Northwest, Washington, D.C. 20036. 1979- . (Periodic Supplements).

PRESERVATION LAW REPORTER. National Trust for Historic Preservation, 1776 Massachusetts Avenue, Washington, D.C. 20036. 1982- . (Bimonthly Supplements).

HANDBOOKS, MANUALS, FORMBOOKS

A HANDBOOK ON HISTORIC PRESERVATION LAW. Christopher J. Duerksen. World Wildlife Fund, 1250 Twenty-fourth Street, Northwest, Washington, D.C. 20037. 1983.

HISTORIC AMERICA: BUILDINGS, STRUCTURES AND SITES. Historic American Buildings Survey and the Historic American Engineering Record. Superintendent of Documents, United States Government Printing Office, Washington, D.C. 20402. 1983.

RESPONDING TO THE TAKINGS CHALLENGE: A GUIDE FOR OFFICIALS AND PLANNERS. Richard J. Roddewig. National Trust for Historic Preservation, 1776 Massachusetts Avenue, Northwest, Suite 704, Washington, D.C. 20036. 1989.

TEXTBOOKS AND GENERAL WORKS

HISTORIC PRESERVATION LAW: ALI-ABA COURSE OF STUDY MATERIALS. American Law Institute-American Bar Association, 4025 Chestnut Street, Philadelphia, Pennsylvania 19104. 1983.

HISTORIC PRESERVATION LAW AND TAXATION. Tersh Boasberg, Thomas A. Coughlin and Julia H. Miller. Transnational Publishers, P.O. Box 7282, Ardsley-on-Hudson, New York 10503. 1991.

INFORMATION ON HISTORIC PRESERVATION TAX INCENTIVES: REPORT TO THE JOINT COMMITTEE ON TAXATION, CONGRESS OF THE UNITED STATES. United States General Accounting Office. Superintendent of Documents, United States Government Printing Office, Washington, D.C. 20402. 1984.

LANDMARKS PRESERVATION AND THE PROPERTY TAX: ASSESSING LANDMARK BUILDINGS FOR REAL TAXATION PURPOSES. David Listokin. Center for Urban Policy Research, Rutgers University, Kilmer Campus, Building 4051, New Brunswick, New Jersey 80903. 1982.

PREPARING A HISTORIC PRESERVATION ORDINANCE. Richard J. Roddewig, American Planning Association, 1776 Massachusetts Avenue, Northwest, Suite 704, Washington, D.C. 20036. 1983.

READINGS IN HISTORIC PRESERVATION: WHY? WHAT? HOW? Norman Williams, Junior. Center for Urban Policy Research, Transaction Books, Rutgers University, Kilmer Campus, Building 4051, New Brunswick, New Jersey 80903. 1982.

TAX INCENTIVES FOR HISTORIC PRESERVATION. Gregory E. Andrews, editor. National Trust for Historic Preservation, 1776 Massachusetts Avenue, Washington, D.C. 20036. 1980.

ANNUALS AND SURVEYS

HISTORIC PRESERVATION YEARBOOK. Adler and Adler, Incorporated, Publishers, 4550 Montgomery Avenue, Suite 705, Bethesda, Maryland 20814. 1984/1985- . Annual.

LAW REVIEWS AND PERIODICALS

AIC JOURNAL. American Institute for Conservation of Historic and Artistic Works, 1400 Sixteenth Street, Northwest, Suite 340, Washington, D.C. 20036. Semiannually.

APTI BULLETIN. Association for Preservation Technology International, P.O. Box 8178, Fredricksburg, Virginia 22404. Quarterly.

HISTORIC PRESERVATION. National Trust for Historic Preservation, 1785 Massachusetts Avenue, Northwest, Washington, D.C. 20036. Bimonthly.

LAW AND HISTORY REVIEW. Cornell Law School and the American Society of Local History. Cornell University, Ithaca, New York 14853. Biannual.

PRESERVATION FORUM. National Trust for Historic Preservation, 1785 Massachusetts Avenue, Northwest, Washington, D.C. 20036. Quarterly.

PRESERVATION LAW REPORTER. National Trust for Historic Preservation, 1785 Massachusetts Avenue, Northwest, Washington, D.C. 20036. Bimonthly.

Encyclopedia of Legal Information Sources • 2nd Ed. HOMELESSNESS

NEWSLETTERS AND NEWSPAPERS

AIC NEWSLETTER. American Institute for Conservation of Historic and Artistic Works, 1400 Sixteenth Street, Northwest, Suite 340, Washington, D.C. 20036. Bimonthly.

ALERT. Preservation Action, 1350 Connecticut Avenue, Northwest, Suite 401, Washington, D.C. 20036. Quarterly.

ASSOCIATION FOR PRESERVATION TECHNOLOGY-COMMUNIQUE. Association for Preservation Technology International P.O. Box 8178, Fredricksburg, Virginia 22404. Bimonthly.

PRESERVATION FORUM NEWSLETTER. National Trust for Historic Preservation, 1785 Massachusetts Avenue, Northwest, Washington, D.C. 20036. Bimonthly.

PRESERVATION NEWS. National Trust for Historic Preservation, 1785 Massachusetts Avenue, Northwest, Washington, D.C. 20036. Monthly.

BIBLIOGRAPHIES

ARCHITECTURAL PRESERVATION AND URBAN RENOVATION: AN ANNOTATED BIBLIOGRAPHY OF UNITED STATES CONGRESSIONAL DOCUMENTS. Richard Tubesing. Garland Publishing, Incorporated, 136 Madison Avenue, New York, New York 10016. 1982.

HISTORIC PRESERVATION PLANS: AN ANNOTATED BIBLIOGRAPHY. Anne Baggerman. Preservation Press, 1776 Massachusetts Avenue, Northwest, Washington, D.C. 20036. 1976.

DIRECTORIES

AMERICAN INSTITUTE FOR CONSERVATION OF HISTORIC AND ARTISTIC WORKS-DIRECTORY. American Institute for Conservation of Historic and Artistic Works (AIC), 1400 Sixteenth Street, Northwest, Suite 340, Washington, D.C. 20036. Biennial.

BROWN BOOK: A DIRECTORY OF PRESERVATION INFORMATION. Preservation Press, National Trust for Historic Preservation, 1776 Massachusetts Avenue, Northwest, Washington, D.C. 20036. 1983.

DIRECTORY OF HISTORIC PRESERVATION LAWYERS. National Trust for Historic Preservation, 1776 Massachusetts Avenue, Northwest, Washington, D.C. 20036. 1984- .

ENCYCLOPEDIA OF HISTORIC PLACES. Facts on File, Incorporated, 460 Park Avenue South, New York, New York 10016. 1984.

A GUIDE TO STATE HISTORIC PRESERVATION PROGRAMS. National Trust for Historic Preservation of the United States, Preservation Press, 1776 Massachusetts Avenue, Northwest, Washington, D.C. 20036. 1976.

NATIONAL REGULATIONS OF HISTORIC PLACES. National Park Service. Superintendent of Documents, United States Government Printing Office, Washington, D.C. 20402. 1979.

SOURCES OF FUNDING FOR PRESERVATION PROJECTS. Preservation League of New York State, 307 Hamilton Street, Albany, New York 12210. 1983.

ASSOCIATIONS AND PROFESSIONAL SOCIETIES

AMERICAN BAR ASSOCIATION: URBAN, STATE AND LOCAL GOVERNMENT SECTION. 750 North Lake Shore Drive, Chicago, Illinois 60611. (312) 988-5000.

AMERICAN INSTITUTE FOR CONSERVATION OF HISTORIC AND ARTISTIC WORKS. 1400 Sixteenth Street, Northwest, Suite 340, Washington, D.C. 20036. (202) 232-6636.

ARCHITECHTURAL HERITAGE FOUNDATION. Old City Hall, 45 School Street, Boston, Massachusetts 02108. (617) 523-8678.

ASSOCIATION FOR PRESERVATION TECHNOLOGY INTERNATIONAL. P.O. Box 8178, Fredricksburg, Virginia 22404. (703) 373-1621.

CONSERVATION FOUNDATION. 1250 Twenty-fourth Street, Northwest, Washington, D.C. 20037. (202) 293-4800.

NATIONAL TRUST FOR HISTORIC PRESERVATION. 1785 Massachusetts Avenue, Northwest, Washington, D.C. 20036. (202) 673-4000.

PRESERVATION ACTION. 1350 Connecticut Avenue, Northwest, Suite 401, Washington, D.C. 20036. (202) 659-0915.

RESEARCH CENTERS, INSTITUTES, CLEARINGHOUSES

HISTORICAL PRESERVATION PROGRAM. University of Nevada, Reno, 501 BB, Reno, Nevada 89557. (702) 784-6851.

INSTITUTE FOR AMERICAN RESEARCH. 300 North Los Carneros Road, Goleta, California 93117. (805) 964-3549.

AUDIOVISUALS

OVERVIEW ON HISTORIC PRESERVATION LAW. (2 audiocassettes). American Bar Association, Urban, State and Local Government Law Section, 750 North Lake Shore Drive, Chicago, Illinois 60611. 1984.

HISTORY
See: HISTORIC PRESERVATION; LEGAL HISTORY

HOMELESSNESS

HANDBOOKS, MANUALS, FORMBOOKS

AMERICAN HOMELESSNESS: A REFERENCE HANDBOOK. Mary E. Hombs. ABC-CLIO, P.O. Box 1911, Santa Barbara, California 93116. 1990.

TEXTBOOKS AND GENERAL WORKS

AMERICA'S HOMELESS: NUMBERS, CHARACTERISTICS, AND PROGRAMS THAT SERVE THEM. Martha R. Burt. University Press of America, 4720 Boston Way, Lanham, Maryland 20706. 1989.

BEYOND HOMELESSNESS: FRAMES OF REFERENCE. Benedict Giamo and Jeffrey Grunberg. University of Iowa, Iowa City, Iowa 52242. 1992.

DOWN AND OUT IN AMERICA: THE ORIGINS OF HOMELESSNESS. Peter H. Rossi. University of Chicago Press, 5801 South Ellis Avenue, Chicago, Illinois 60637. 1989.

DOWN ON THEIR LUCK: A STUDY OF HOMELESS STREET PEOPLE. David A. Snow and Leon Anderson. University of California Press, 2120 Berkeley Way, Berkeley, California 94720. 1992.

THE FACES OF HOMELESSNESS. Marjorie Hope and James Young. Lexington Books, 125 Spring Street, Lexington, Massachusetts 02173. 1986.

GIMME SHELTER: A SOCIAL HISTORY OF HOMELESSNESS IN CONTEMPORARY AMERICA. Gregg Barak. Praeger Publishers, Greenwood Publishing Group, Incorporated, 88 Post Road West, P.O. Box 5007, Westport, Connecticut 06881. 1991.

HEALTH CARE OF HOMELESS PEOPLE. Philip W. Brickner. Springer Publishing Company, 536 Broadway, New York, New York 10012. 1985.

HELPING THE HOMELESS: WHERE DO WE GO FROM HERE? John R. Belcher and Fredrick A. DiBlasio. Lexington Books, 125 Spring Street, Lexington, Massachusetts 02173. 1990.

HOMELESS FAMILIES. George Thorman. Charles C.Thomas, Publishers, 2600 South First Street, Springfield, Illinois 62794. 1988.

HOMELESS IN AMERICA. Carol L.M. Caton. Oxford University Press, 200 Madison Avenue, New York, New York 10016. 1990.

THE HOMELESS IN CONTEMPORARY SOCIETY. Richard D. Bingham, Roy E. Green and Sammis B. White. Sage Publications, P.O. Box 6944, San Mateo, California 94403. 1987.

THE HOMELESS MENTALLY ILL: A TASK FORCE REPORT OF THE AMERICAN PSYCHIATRIC ASSOCIATION. H. Richard Lamb. American Psychiatric Association, 1400 K Street, Northwest, Washington, D.C. 20005. 1984.

HOMELESSNESS: A NATIONAL PERSPECTIVE. Marjorie J. Robertson and Milton Greenblatt. 1992.

HOMELESSNESS: A PREVENTION-ORIENTED APPROACH. Rene I. Jahiel. Johns Hopkins University Press, 701 West 40th Street, Baltimore, Maryland 21211. 1992.

HOMELESSNESS AMID AFFLUENCE: STRUCTURE AND PARADOX IN THE AMERICAN POLITICAL ECONOMY. Michael H. Lang. Praeger Publishers, Greenwood Publishing Group, Incorporated, 88 Post Road West, P.O. Box 5007, Westport, Connecticut 06881. 1989.

HOMELESSNESS IN AMERICA: A FORCED MARCH TO NOWHERE. Third Edition. Mary Ellen Hombs and Mitch Snyder. Community for Creative Non-violence, 425 Second Street, Northwest, Washington, D.C. 20001. 1986.

HOMELESSNESS IN THE UNITED STATES. Jamshid A. Momeni. Greenwood Press, 88 Post Road West, Westport, Connecticut 06880. 1990.

HOUSING AND HOMELESSNESS: A FEMINIST PERSPECTIVE. Sophie Watson and Helen Austerberry. Routledge, 29 West 35th Street, New York, New York 10001. 1986.

HOUSING THE HOMELESS. Jon Erickson. Center for Urban Policy Research, New Brunswick, New Jersey. 1986.

INVENTING A NON-HOMELESS FUTURE: A PUBLIC POLICY AGENDA FOR PREVENTING HOMELESSNESS. Madeleine R. Stoner. Peter Lang Publishing, 62 West 45th Street, New York, New York 10036. 1989.

LANDSCAPES OF DESPAIR: FROM DEINSTITUTIONALIZATION TO HOMELESS. Michael J. Dear and Jennifer R. Wolch. Princeton University Press, 41 William Street, Princeton, New Jersey 08540. 1987.

NEW HOMELESS AND OLD: COMMUNITY AND THE SKID ROW HOTEL. Charles Hoch and Robert A. Slayton. Temple University Press, Broad and Oxford Streets, University Services Building, Room 305, Philadelphia, Pennsylvania 19122. 1989.

ON THE BOWERY: CONFRONTING HOMELESSNESS IN AMERICAN SOCIETY. Benedict Giamo. University of Iowa Press, Iowa City, Iowa 52242. 1989.

ON THE FRINGE: THE DISPOSSESSED IN AMERICA. Henry Miller. Lexington Books, 125 Spring Street, Lexington, Massachusetts 02173. 1991.

OVER THE EDGE: THE GROWTH OF HOMELESSNESS IN THE 1980'S. Martha R. Burt. Russell Sage Foundation, 112 East 64th Street, New York, New York 10021. 1992.

RACHEL AND HER CHILDREN: HOMELESS FAMILIES IN AMERICA. Jonathan Kozol. Crown Publishers, Incorporated, 225 Park Avenue South, New York, New York 10003. 1988.

RESPONDING TO AMERICA'S HOMELESS: PUBLIC POLICY ALTERNATIVES. F. Stevens Redburn and Terry F. Buss. Praeger Publishers, Greenwood Publishing Group, Incorporated, 88 Post Road West, P.O. Box 5007, Westport, Connecticut 06881. 1986.

THE RIGHTS OF THE HOMELESS. Robert M. Hayes. Practising Law Institute, 810 Seventh Avenue, New York, New York 10019. 1988.

THE VISIBLE POOR: HOMELESSNESS IN THE UNITED STATES. Joel Blau. Oxford University Press, 200 Madison Avenue, New York, New York 10016. 1992.

WITHOUT SHELTER: HOMELESSNESS IN THE 1980'S. Peter Henry Rossi. Priority Press Publications, 41 East Seventieth Street, New York, New York 10021. 1989.

THE WOMEN OUTSIDE: MEANINGS AND MYTHS OF HOMELESSNESS. Stephanie Golden. University of California Press, 2120 Berkeley Way, Berkeley, California 94720. 1992.

NEWSLETTERS AND NEWSPAPERS

HOUSING LAW BULLETIN. National Housing Law Project, Incorporated, 1950 Addison Street, Berkeley, California 94704.

JOURNAL OF SOCIAL DISTRESS AND THE HOMELESS. Human Sciences Press, 233 Spring Street, New York, New York 10013.

BIBLIOGRAPHIES

AMERICAN HOMELESSNESS IN THE 1980'S: A SELECTED BIBLIOGRAPHY. Anthony G. White. Vance Bibliographies, P.O. Box 229, 112 North Charter Street, Monticello, Illinois 61856. 1987.

THE HOMELESS IN AMERICA: A SELECT BIBLIOGRAPHY. Andrew Garoogian. Vance Bibliographies, P.O. Box 229, 112 North Charter Street, Monticello, Illinois 61856. 1984.

ASSOCIATIONS AND PROFESSIONAL SOCIETIES

COMMUNITY FOR CREATIVE NON-VIOLENCE. 425 2nd Street, N.W., Washington, D.C. 20001. (202) 393-4409.

NATIONAL COALITION FOR THE HOMELESS. 1621 Connecticut Avenue, N.W., Washington, D.C. 20009. (202) 265-2371.

RESEARCH CENTERS, INSTITUTES, CLEARINGHOUSES

AMERICAN AFFORDABLE HOUSING INSTITUTE. Rutgers University, P.O. Box 118, New Brunswick, New Jersey 08903. (908) 932-6812.

AMERICAN BAR ASSOCIATION REPRESENTATION OF THE HOMELESS PROJECT. 1800 M Street, N.W., Washington, D.C. 20036. (202) 3312291.

HOMELESSNESS INFORMATION EXCHANGE. 1830 Connecticut Avenue, N.W., Washington, D.C. 20009. (202) 462-7551.

NATIONAL ALLIANCE TO END HOMELESSNESS. 1518 K Street, N.W., Washington, D.C. 20005. (202) 638-1536.

NATIONAL RESOURCE CENTER ON HOMELESSNESS AND MENTAL ILLNESS. Policy Research Associates, 262 Delaware Avenue, Delmar, New York 12054. (800) 444-7415.

STATISTICS SOURCES

HOMELESSNESS IN THE UNITED STATES: DATA AND ISSUES. Jamshid A. Momeni. Praeger Publishers, Greenwood Publishing Group, Incorporated, 88 Post Road West, P.O. Box 5007, Westport, Connecticut 06881. 1990.

AUDIOVISUALS

LAWYERING TO HOUSE TO HOMELESS: CREATIVE TOOLS. American Bar Association, 750 North Lake Shore Drive, Chicago, Illinois 60611. 1990. Videotape.

OTHER SOURCES

HOMELESSNESS: A COMPLEX PROBLEM AND THE FEDERAL RESPONSE: REPORT. The Office of Homelessness, Washington, D.C. 1985.

STAFF REPORT ON HOMELESSNESS IN THE UNITED STATES. Superintendent of Documents, United States Government Printing Office, Washington, D.C. 20402. 1990.

HOMESTEAD LAW
See: REAL PROPERTY

HOMICIDE
See: MURDER; SUICIDE

HOMOSEXUALITY
See: SEXUAL ORIENTATION

HOSPITALS
See also: HEALTH CARE; MEDICAL JURISPRUDENCE AND MALPRACTICE; NURSES AND NURSING; NURSING HOMES

LOOSELEAF SERVICES AND REPORTERS

THE HEALTH CARE INDUSTRY. Michael W. Peregrine and Bernadette M. Broccolo. Commerce Clearing House, Incorporated, 4025 West Peterson Avenue, Chicago, Illinois 60646. 1988.

HEALTH CARE LAW: A PRACTICAL GUIDE. Michael G. Macdonald. Matthew Bender and Company, Incorporated, 11 Penn Plaza, New York, New York 10001. 1985- .

HOSPITAL CONTRACTS MANUAL. Aspen Publishing, Incorporated, 1600 Research Boulevard, Rockville, Maryland 20850. 1982- . (Semiannual Supplements).

HOSPITAL COST MANAGEMENT. Prentice-Hall, Incorporated, 113 Sylvan Avenue, Englewood Cliffs, New Jersey 07632. 1982- . (Monthly Supplements).

HOSPITAL LAW MANUAL, ATTORNEY'S VOLUMES. Aspen Publishing, Incorporated, 1600 Research Boulevard, Rockville, Maryland 20850 1959- (Quarterly Supplements).

HOSPITAL LIABILITY. James Walker Smith. New York Law Publishing, Company, 111 Eighth Avenue, New York, New York 10011. 1985- . (Periodic Supplements).

HOSPITALS

MEDICAL DIRECTORSHIPS REGULATIONS AND GUIDELINES. National Law and Health Publishing, 99 Painters Mill Road, Owings Mill, Maryland 21117. 1982- . (Periodic Supplements).

MEDICARE HOSPITAL MANUAL. United States Department of Health and Human Services, Health Care Financing Administration. Superintendent of Documents, United States Government Printing Office, Washington, D.C. 20402.

PROSPECTIVE PAYMENTS: LAWS, REGULATIONS, GUIDELINES, AND DECISIONS. National Health Publishing, 99 Painters Mill Road, Owings Mill, Maryland 21117. 1984- . (Periodic Supplements).

HANDBOOKS, MANUALS, FORMBOOKS

ACCREDITATION MANUAL FOR HOSPITALS. Joint Commission on Accreditation of Hospitals, Department of Publications, 875 North Michigan Avenue, Chicago, Illinois 60611. 1988.

FEDERAL REGULATION: HOSPITAL ATTORNEY'S DESK REFERENCE. American Society of Hospital Attorneys. American Hospital Association, 840 North Lake Shore Drive, Chicago, Illinois 60611. 1980.

HOSPITAL LEGAL FORMS, CHECKLISTS AND GUIDELINES. Howard S. Rowland and Beatrice L. Rowland. Aspen Publishing, Incorporated, 1600 Research Boulevard, Rockville, Maryland 20850. 1986.

TEXTBOOKS AND GENERAL WORKS

EMERGENCY CARE AND THE LAW. Marquerite R. Mancini and Alice T. Gale. Aspen Publishing, Incorporated, 1600 Research Boulevard, Rockville, Maryland 20850. 1981.

HANDLING BIRTH TRAUMA CASES. Stanley S. Schwartz and Norman D. Tucker. John Wiley and Sons, Incorporated, 605 Third Avenue, New York, New York 10158. 1991.

HEALTH CARE IN AMERICA: THE POLITICAL ECONOMY OF HOSPITALS AND HEALTH INSURANCE. Pacific Research Institute for Public Policy, 177 Post Street, Suite 500, San Francisco, California 94108. 1988.

HEALTH CARE ISSUES IN BLACK AMERICA: POLITICS, PROBLEMS AND PROSPECTS. Woodrow Jones, Jr. and Mitchell F. Rice, editors. Greenwood Publishing Group, Incorporated, Incorporated, 88 Post Road West, Box 5007, Westport, Connecticut 06881. 1987.

THE HEALTH CARE SURVIVAL CURVE: COMPETITION AND COOPERATION IN THE MARKET PLACE. Irwin Miller. Dow Jones-Irwin, Incorporated, 1818 Ridge Road, Homewood, Illinois 60403. 1984.

HOSPITAL LAW. Amnon Carmi, S. Schneider and J. Adler. Springer Publishing Company, 536 Broadway, New York, New York 10012. 1988.

HOSPITAL LIABILITY: LAW AND PRACTICE. Fifth Edition. Practising Law Institute, 810 Seventh Avenue, New York, New York 10019. 1987.

Encyclopedia of Legal Information Sources • 2nd Ed.

THE HOSPITAL MEDICAL STAFF: IT'S LEGAL RIGHTS AND RESPONSIBILITIES. William P. Isele. Charles C. Thomas, Publishers, 2600 South First Street, Springfield, Illinois 62794-9265. 1984.

THE HOSPITAL POWER EQUILIBRIUM: PHYSICIAN BEHAVIOR AND COST CONTROL. David W. Young and Richard B. Saltman. Johns Hopkins University Press, 701 West Fortieth Street, Suite 275, Baltimore, Maryland 21211-2190. 1985.

HOSPITALS IN TODAY'S HEALTH CARE MARKETPLACE. Leonard H. Gilbert. Practising Law Institute, 810 Seventh Avenue, New York, New York 10019. 1985.

THE IMPACT OF COLLECTIVE BARGAINING ON HOSPITALS. Richard U. Miller. Praeger Publishers, One Madison Avenue, New York, New York 10010-3603. 1979.

INSURANCE, REGULATION, AND HOSPITAL COSTS. Frank A. Sloan and Bruce Steinwald. Lexington Books, 125 Spring Street, Lexington, Massachusetts 02173. 1980.

ISSUES IN HOSPITAL ADMINISTRATION. John B. Mckinlay, editor. MIT Press, 55 Hayward Street, Cambridge, Massachusetts 02142. 1982.

THE LAW OF HOSPITAL AND HEALTH CARE ADMINISTRATION. Second Edition. Arthur F. Southwick and Debora A. Slee. Health Administration Press, Department KW, 1021 East Huron Street, Ann Arbor, Michigan 48104. 1988.

LEGAL IMPLICATIONS OF HOSPITAL POLICIES AND PRACTICES. Jossey-Bass, Incorporated, 350 Sansome Street, San Francisco, California 94104. 1989.

MALPRACTICE PREVENTION AND LIABILITY CONTROL FOR HOSPITALS. Second Edition. James E. Orlikoff and Audrone M. Vanagunas. American Hospital Publishing, Incorporated, 211 East Chicago Avenue, Chicago, Illinois 60611. 1988.

MEDICARE AND EXTENDED CARE: ISSUES, PROBLEMS, AND PROSPECTS. Genrose J. Alfano. National Health Publishing, 99 Painters Mill Road, Owings Mills, Maryland 21117. 1987.

MEDICOLEGAL ASPECTS OF CRITICAL CARE. Katherine Benesch. Aspen Publishing, Incorporated, 1600 Research Boulevard, Rockville, Maryland 20850. 1986.

NEW LIABILITY ASPECTS OF HOSPITAL ADMINISTRATION: ALI-ABA COURSE OF STUDY MATERIALS. Council of Medical Specialty Societies (United States) and American Law Institute, American Bar Association, Committee on Continuing Professional Education. American Law Institute, 4025 Chestnut Street, Philadelphia, Pennsylvania 19104. 1986.

PATIENTS' RIGHTS AND PROFESSIONAL PRACTICE. James J. Ziegenfuss. Van Nostrand Reinhold Company, Incorporated, 115 Fifth Avenue, New York, New York 10003. 1983.

PRIVACY AND CONFIDENTIALITY OF HEALTH CARE INFORMATION. Second Edition. Jo Anne Czecowski Bruce. American Hospital Publishing, Incorporated, 211 East Chicago Avenue, Chicago, Illinois 60611. 1988.

PROBLEMS IN HOSPITAL LAW. Sixth Edition. Robert D. Miller. Aspen Publishing, Incorporated, 1600 Research Boulevard, Rockville, Maryland 20850. 1990.

THE RIGHTS OF DOCTORS, NURSES, AND ALLIED HEALTH PROFESSIONALS: A HEALTH PRIMER. George J. Annas, Leonard H Glantz and Barbara F. Katz. Avon Books, 105 Madison Avenue, New York, New York 10016. 1981.

THE RIGHTS OF PATIENTS: THE BASIC ACLU GUIDE TO PATIENT RIGHTS. Second Edition. George J. Annas. Southern Illinois University Press, P.O. Box 3697, Carbondale, Illinois 62902-3697. 1989.

TAX MANAGEMENT FOR EXEMPT HOSPITALS. Aspen Publishing, Incorporated, 1600 Research Boulevard, Rockville, Maryland 20850. 1980.

UNCOMPENSATED HOSPITAL CARE: RIGHTS AND RESPONSIBILITIES. Frank A. Sloan, editor. James F. Blumstein and James M. Perrin. Books on Demand, 300 North Zeeb Road, Ann Arbor, Michigan 48106-1346. 1986.

ANNUALS AND SURVEYS

STATE REGULATION OF PREFERRED PROVIDER ORGANIZATIONS: A SURVEY OF STATE STATUTES. (State Legal Initiatives: Legal Development Report Series: Number Four) American Hospital Association, 840 North Lake Shore Drive, Chicago, Illinois 60611. 1984.

LAW REVIEWS AND PERIODICALS

JOURNAL OF HEALTH AND HOSPITAL LAW: A PUBLICATION OF THE AMERICAN ACADEMY OF HOSPITAL ATTORNEYS OF THE AMERICAN HOSPITAL ASSOCIATION. American Academy of Hospital Attorneys, 840 North Lake Shore Drive, Chicago, Illinois 60611. 1988.

NEWSLETTERS AND NEWSPAPERS

AMERICAN SOCIETY OF HOSPITAL ATTORNEYS NEWSLETTER. American Society of Hospital Attorneys, 840 North Lake Shore Drive, Chicago, Illinois 60611. Monthly.

EMERGENCY DEPARTMENT LAW. Buraff Publications, 1350 Connecticut Avenue, Northwest, Suite 1000, Washington, D.C. 20036. Semimonthly.

HEALTH LAW VIGIL. American Hospital Association, Office of Legal Communications, 840 North Lake Shore Drive, Chicago, Illinois 60611. Biweekly.

HOSPICE LETTER. Health Resources Publishing, Brinley Plaza, 3100 Highway 138, Wall Township, New Jersey 07719. Monthly.

HOSPITAL LAW NEWSLETTER. Aspen Publishers, Incorporated, 200 Orchard Ridge Drive, Gaithersburg, Maryland 20878. Monthly.

HOSPITAL LITIGATION REPORTER. Strafford Publications, Incorporated, 1375 Peachtree Street, Northwest, Suite 235, Atlanta, Georgia 30367. Monthly.

HOSPITAL RISK MANAGEMENT. American Health Consultants, Incorporated, 67 Peachtree Park Drive, Northeast, Atlanta, Georgia 30309. Monthly.

HOSPITAL WEEK. American Hospital Publishing Incorporated, 211 East Chicago Avenue, Suite 700, Chicago, Illinois 60611. Weekly.

MEDICAID FRAUD REPORT. National Association of Attorneys General, 444 North Capital Street, Suite 403, Washington, D.C. 20001. Monthly.

MEDICAL MALPRACTICE LAW AND STRATEGY. Leader Publications, 111 Eighth Avenue, New York, New York 10011. Monthly.

MEDICAL STAFF NEWS. American Hospital Publishing, Incorporated 211 East Chicago Avenue, Suite 700, Chicago, Illinois 60611. 1985- . Monthly.

REGAN REPORT ON HOSPITAL LAW. Medica Press Incorporated, 1231 Fleet National Bank Building, Providence, Rhode Island 02903. Monthly.

STAFF PRIVILEGES REPORT. Little Brown and Company, Law Division, 34 Beacon Street, Boston, Massachusetts 02108. Monthly.

DIRECTORIES

AMERICAN COLLEGE OF HEALTH CARE EXECUTIVES--DIRECTORY. American College of Health Care Executives, 840 North Lake Shore Drive, Suite 1103W, Chicago, Illinois 60611.

AMERICAN HOSPITAL ASSOCIATION-GUIDE TO THE HEALTH CARE FIELD. American Hospital Association, 840 North Lake Shore Drive, Chicago, Illinois 60611. Annual.

THE NHLA REGISTER. National Health Lawyers Association, 1620 I Street, Northwest, Suite 900, Washington, D.C. 20006. 1985- . Quarterly.

ASSOCIATIONS AND PROFESSIONAL SOCIETIES

AMERICAN ACADEMY OF HOSPITAL ATTORNEYS. American Hospital Association, 840 North Lake Shore Drive, Chicago, Illinois 60611. (312) 280-6601.

AMERICAN HOSPITAL ASSOCIATION. 840 North Lake Shore Drive, Chicago, Illinois 60611. (312) 280-6000.

AMERICAN MEDICAL ASSOCIATION. 515 North State Street, Chicago, Illinois 60610. (312) 645-4818.

ASSOCIATION OF HIGH MEDICARE HOSPITALS. 1015 Eighteenth Street, Northwest, Suite 900, Washington, D.C. 20026. (202) 785-9670.

NATIONAL ASSOCIATION OF CHILDREN'S HOSPITALS AND RELATED INSTITUTIONS. 401 Wythe Street, Alexandria, Virginia 22314. (703) 684-1355.

NATIONAL ASSOCIATION OF PUBLIC HOSPITALS. 1212 New York Avenue, Northwest, Suite 800, Washington, D.C. 20005. (202) 408-0223.

HOSPITALS

NATIONAL HEALTH LAWYERS ASSOCIATION. 1620 Eye Street, Northwest, Washington, D.C. 20036. (202) 833-1100.

NATIONAL HOSPICE ORGANIZATION. 1901 North Moore Street, Suite 901, Arlington, Virginia 22209. (703) 243-5900.

NATIONAL SOCIETY OF PATIENT REPRESENTATIVES OF THE AMERICAN HOSPITAL ASSOCIATION. 840 North Lake Shore Drive, Chicago, Illinois 60611. (312) 280-6000.

RESEARCH CENTERS, INSTITUTES, CLEARINGHOUSES

CENTER FOR HEALTH SERVICES EDUCATION AND RESEARCH. St. Louis University, 3525 Caroline Street, St. Louis, Missouri 63104. (314) 577-8682.

CENTER FOR NURSING RESEARCH. University of Texas at Arlington, P.O. Box 19407, Arlington, Texas 76019. (817) 273-2776.

CONNECTICUT HOSPITAL RESEARCH AND EDUCATION FOUNDATION, INCORPORATED. P.O. Box 90, 110 Barnes Road, Wallingford, Connecticut 06492. (203) 265-7611.

HEALTH SERVICES RESEARCH AND DEVELOPMENT CENTER. Johns Hopkins University, 624 North Broadway, Baltimore, Maryland 21205. (301) 955-6562.

HEALTH SYSTEMS RESEARCH DIVISION. University of Florida, Box-J-177, J. Hillis Miller Health Center, Gainesville, Florida 32610. (904) 392-2571.

HOSPITAL RESEARCH AND EDUCATION TRUST. 840 North Lake Shore Drive, Chicago, Illinois 60611. (312) 280-6000.

INSTITUTE OF CRITICAL CARE MEDICINE. 1975 Zonal Avenue, KAM 307B, Los Angeles, California 90033.

WEST VIRGINIA HOSPITAL RESEARCH AND EDUCATION FOUNDATION. 3422 Pennsylvania Avenue, Charleston, West Virginia 25302. (304) 345-9842.

ONLINE DATABASES

AMA LIBRARY INFORMATION SERVICE. American Medical Association, Division of Library and Information Management, 535 North Dearborn Street, Chicago, Illinois 60610.

AMERICAN HOSPITAL ASSOCIATION. Hospital Data Center, 840 North Lake Shore Drive, Chicago, Illinois 60611.

IMSPACT. IMS America Limited, P.O. Box 905, Plymouth Meeting, Pennsylvania 19462.

MEDIS. Mead Data Central, P.O. Box 933, Dayton, Ohio 45401.

MEDLINE. National Library of Medicine, 8600 Rockville Pike, Bethesda, Maryland 20209

NLM/NIH INFORMATION SERVICE. American Medical Association, National Library of Medicine and National Institute of Health. National Library of Medicine, 8600 Rockville Pike, Bethesda, Maryland 20209.

STATISTICS SOURCES

ANNUAL REPORT OF THE ADMINISTRATOR OF VETERANS AFFAIRS. United States Veterans Administration. Superintendent of Documents, United States Government Printing Office, Washington, D.C. 20402. Annual.

HOSPITAL STATISTICS. American Hospital Association, 840 North Lake Shore Drive, Chicago, Illinois 60611. Annual.

OTHER SOURCES

PRESIDENT'S PRIVATE SECTOR SURVEY ON COST CONTROL: REPORT ON FEDERAL HOSPITAL MANAGEMENT. (Grace Commission Report). Superintendent of Documents, United States Government Printing Office, Washington, D.C. 20402. 1983.

HOSTAGES
See: KIDNAPPING; TERRORISM

HOTELS, RESTAURANTS, ETC.
See also: ALCOHOL CONTROL AND DRINKING BEHAVIOR; ALCOHOL, TOBACCO AND FIREARMS BUREAU; FOOD LAWS

HANDBOOKS, MANUALS, FORMBOOKS

HOTEL-MOTEL LAW: A PRIMER ON INNKEEPER LIABILITY. J. Gregory Service. Charles C. Thomas Publishers, Incorporated, 2600 South First Street, Springfield, Illinois 62794- 9265. 1983.

HOTEL, RESTAURANT AND TRAVEL LAW. Third Edition. Norman G. Cournoyer and Anthony Marshall. Delmar Publishers, Incorporated, P.O. Box 15015, Two Computer Drive, West, Albany, New York 12212. 1988.

THE LAWS OF INNKEEPERS: FOR HOTELS, MOTELS, RESTAURANTS, AND CLUBS. John E. H. Sherry. Cornell University Press, 124 Roberts Place, Ithaca, New York 14850. 1981- . (Periodic Supplements.)

LEGAL ASPECTS OF FOOD SERVICE MANAGEMENT. John E. H. Sherry. National Institute for Food Service Industry, Kendall/Hunt Publishing Company, 2460 Kerper Boulevard, Dubuque, Iowa 52001. 1987.

THE NEGOTIATION AND ADMINISTRATION OF HOTEL MANAGEMENT CONTRACTS. Second edition. James J. Eyster. School of Hotel Administration, Cornell University, 327 Statler Hall, Ithaca, New York 14853. 1980.

TRAVEL AND LODGING LAW: PRINCIPLES, STATUTES AND CASES. John R. Goodwin and James M. Rovelstad. John Wiley and Sons, Incorporated, 605 Third Avenue, New York, New York 10158. 1984.

UNDERSTANDING HOTEL/MOTEL LAW. Jack P. Jefferies. Educational Institute of the American Hotel and Motel Association, 1407 South Harrison Road, P.O. Box 240, East Lansing, Michigan 48823. 1983.

LAW REVIEWS AND PERIODICALS

ALCOHOL BEVERAGE LEGAL BRIEFS. National Alcoholic Beverage Control Association, Alexandria, Virginia. 1986- . Bimonthly.

NEWSLETTERS AND NEWSPAPERS

FROM THE STATE CAPITALS: TOURIST BUSINESS PROMOTION. Wakeman Walworth, Incorporated, 300 North Washington Street, Suite 204, Alexandria, Virginia 22314. Monthly.

HOSPITALITY LAW. Masna Publications, Incorporated, 2718 Dryden Drive, Madison, Wisconsin 53704. Monthly.

NATIONAL RESTAURANT ASSOCIATION: WASHINGTON WEEKLY. National Restaurant Association, 1200 Seventeenth Street, Northwest, Washington, D.C. 20036. Weekly.

DIRECTORIES

MOBIL TRAVEL GUIDE. Mobil Oil Corporation, 3225 Gallows Road, Fairfax, Virginia 22037. Annual.

ASSOCIATIONS AND PROFESSIONAL SOCIETIES

AMERICAN HOTEL AND MOTEL ASSOCIATION. 1201 New York Avenue, Northwest, Suite 600, Washington, D.C. 20005. (202) 289-3100.

NATIONAL RESTAURANT ASSOCIATION. 1200 Seventeenth Street, Northwest, Washington, D.C. 20036. (202) 331-5900.

RESEARCH CENTERS, INSTITUTES, CLEARINGHOUSES

CENTER FOR HOSPITALITY RESEARCH AND SERVICE. Virginia Polytechnic Institute and State University, c/o Hotel, Restaurant and Institutional Management, Blacksburg, Virginia 24061. (703) 231-5515.

FAMILY AND CONSUMER SCIENCES RESEARCH INSTITUTE. Iowa State University, 126 McKay, Ames, Iowa 50011. (515) 294-5982.

HOSPITALITY, LODGING AND TRAVEL RESEARCH FOUNDATION. 1201 New York Avenue, Northwest, Washington, D.C. 20005. (202) 289-3117.

STATISTICS SOURCES

OCCUPATIONAL INJURIES AND ILLNESSES IN THE UNITED STATES BY INDUSTRY. United States Department of Labor, Bureau of Labor Statistics. Superintendent of Documents, United States Government Printing Office, Washington, D.C. 20402. Annual.

HOUSING
See also: DISCRIMINATION, HOUSING

STATUTES, CODES, STANDARDS, UNIFORM LAWS

UNIFORM HOUSING CODE. International Conference of Building Officials, 5360 South Workman Mill Road, Whittier, California 90601. 1988.

LOOSELEAF SERVICES AND REPORTERS

COOPERATIVE HOUSING LAW AND PRACTICE: FORMS. Matthew Bender and Company, Incorporated, 11 Penn Plaza, New York, New York 10001. 1967- .

FAIR HOUSING -- FAIR LENDING. Prentice Hall, Incorporated, 113 Sylvan Avenue, Englewood Cliffs, New Jersey 07632. 1985- .

HOUSING AND DEVELOPMENT REPORTER. Bureau of National Affairs, 1231 25th Street, Northwest, Washington, D.C. 20037. 1973- .

THE LAW OF REAL ESTATE FINANCING: WITH TAX ANALYSIS, PLANNING, AND FORMS. Michael T. Madison and Jeffrey R. Dwyer. Research Institute of America, Incorporated, One Penn Plaza, New York, New York 10119. 1981- .

MULTI-FAMILY HOUSING: FEDERAL PROGRAMS FOR THE PRIVATE SECTOR. James W. Jones. Law Journal-Seminars Press, Incorporated, 111 Eighth Avenue, Suite 900, New York, New York 10011. 1986- . (Periodic Supplements).

HANDBOOKS, MANUALS, FORMBOOKS

ATTORNEYS' AND LENDERS' GUIDE TO COMMON INTEREST OWNERSHIP ACTS: CONDOMINIUMS, COOPERATIVES, AND PLANNED COMMUNITIES. Dennis P. Anderson and Gurdon H. Buck. American Bar Association, Real Property, Probate and Trust Law Section, 750 North Lake Shore Drive, Chicago, Illinois 60611. 1989.

GUIDE TO FEDERAL HOUSING PROGRAMS. Second Edition. Barry G. Jacobs. Bureau of National Affairs, Incorporated, 1231 Twenty-fifth Street, Northwest, Washington, D.C. 20037. 1986.

THE SUBSIDIZED HOUSING HANDBOOK: HOW TO PROVIDE, PRESERVE AND MANAGE HOUSING FOR LOWER-INCOME PEOPLE. National Housing Law Project, 1950 Addison Street, Berkeley, California 94704. 1982.

TEXTBOOKS AND GENERAL WORKS

CRITICAL PERSPECTIVES ON HOUSING. Rachel G. Bratt, Chester Hartman and Ann Meyerson, editors. Temple University Press, 1601 North Broad Street, University Services Building, Philadelphia, Pennsylvania 19122. 1986.

DIVIDED NEIGHBORHOODS: CHANGING PATTERNS OF RACIAL SEGREGATION. Gary A. Tobin. Sage Publications, 2455 Teller Road, Newbury Park, California 91320. 1987.

ENERGY COSTS, URBAN DEVELOPMENT, AND HOUSING. Anthony Downs and Katharine L Bradbury. Brookings Institution, 1775 Massachusetts Avenue, Northwest, Washington, D.C. 20036-2188. 1984.

FAIR HOUSING: DISCRIMINATION IN REAL ESTATE, COMMUNITY DEVELOPMENT AND REVITALIZATION. James A. Kushner. Shepard's/McGraw-Hill, P.O. Box 1235, Colorado Springs, Colorado 80901. 1983- . (Annual Supplements).

THE FEDERAL GOVERNMENT AND URBAN HOUSING: IDEOLOGY AND CHANGE IN PUBLIC POLICY. R. Allen Hays. State University of New York Press, State University Plaza, Albany, New York 12246. 1985.

FEDERAL HOUSING POLICY AND PROGRAMS: PAST AND PRESENT. J. Paul Mitchell. Center for Urban Policy Research, Rutgers University, Kilmer Campus, Building 4051, New Brunswick, New Jersey 08903. 1986.

FUTURE UNITED STATES HOUSING POLICY: MEETING THE DEMOGRAPHIC CHALLENGE. Raymond J. Struyk. University Press of America, 4720 Boston Way, Lanham, Maryland 20706. 1988.

HOUSING AMERICA. The American Academy of Political and Social Science. Sage Publications, 2455 Teller Road, Newbury Park, California 91320.

HOUSING AMERICA: LEARNING FROM THE PAST, PLANNING FOR THE FUTURE. Margery Austin Turner and Veronica Reed. University Press of America, 4720 Boston Way, Lanham, Maryland 20706. 1990.

HOUSING AND COMMUNITY DEVELOPMENT: CASES AND MATERIALS. Second Edition. Charles E. Daye. Carolina Academic Press, P.O. Box 51879, Durham, North Carolina 27717. 1989.

HOUSING AND PUBLIC POLICY: A ROLE FOR MEDIATING STRUCTURES. John Ehan. Ballinger Division, HarperCollins Publishers, 10 East Fifty-Third Street, New York, New York 10022. 1981.

THE HOUSING FINANCE SYSTEM AND FEDERAL POLICY: RECENT CHANGES AND OPTIONS FOR THE FUTURE. Congress of the United States, Congressional Budget Office. Superintendent of Documents, United States Government Printing Office, Washington, D.C. 20402. 1983.

HOUSING FOR THE ELDERLY IN 2010: PROJECTIONS AND POLICY OPTIONS. Harold M. Katsura. University Press of America, 4720 Boston Way, Lanham, Maryland 20706. 1989.

HOUSING ISSUES OF THE 1990S. Praeger Publishers, One Madison Avenue, New York, New York 10010-3603. 1989.

HUD HOUSING PROGRAMS: TENANT'S RIGHTS. National Housing Law Project, 1950 Addison Street, Berkeley, California 94704. 1981.

INCLUSIONARY HOUSING PROGRAMS: POLICIES AND PRACTICES. Center for Urban Policy Research, Rutgers University, Kilmer Campus, Building 4051, New Brunswick, New Jersey 08903. 1984.

THE LAW OF CONDOMINIUMS AND COOPERATIVES. Vincent Di Lorenzo. Research Institute of America, Incorporated, One Penn Plaza, New York, New York 10119. 1990.

THE LEGACY OF JUDICIAL POLICY-MAKING: GAUTREAUX V CHICAGO HOUSING AUTHORITY: THE DECISION AND ITS IMPACTS. Elizabeth Warren. University Press of America, 4720 Boston Way, Lanham, Maryland 20706. 1988.

NEW FRONTIERS IN HOUSING TAX MANUAL: A GUIDE TO CHANGES UNDER THE TAX REFORM ACT OF 1986 AFFECTING THE DEVELOPMENT, PRESERVATION, AND EQUITY INVESTMENT IN LOW-INCOME HOUSING. National Low Income Housing Coalition, 1012 Fourteenth Street, Northwest, Suite 1500, Washington, D.C. 20005. 1987.

PATTERNS OF DEVELOPMENT. George Sternlieb. Center for Urban Policy Research, Rutgers University, Kilmer Campus, Building 4051, New Brunswick, New Jersey 08903. 1986.

A PLACE TO CALL HOME: THE CRISIS IN HOUSING FOR THE POOR. Paul A. Leonard, Cushing N. Dolbeare and Edward B. Lazere. Center on Budget and Policy Priorities: Low Income Housing Information Service, 1012 Fourteenth Street, Northwest, Suite 1500, Washington, D.C. 20005. 1989.

POLICIES FOR AFFORDABLE HOUSING: A LEGISLATOR'S GUIDE. Margaret A. Smith. Uniform Laws Annotated. West Publishing Company, P.O. Box 64526, 50 West Kellogg Boulevard, St. Paul, Minnesota 55164-0526. 1983- . (Annual Supplements).

PRESERVING HUD-ASSISTED HOUSING FOR USE BY LOW-INCOME TENANTS: AN ADVOCATE'S GUIDE. Sara Elizabeth Johnson. National Clearinghouse for Legal Services, Incorporated, 407 South Dearborn, Chicago, Illinois 60605. 1985.

RETHINKING RENTAL HOUSING. John Ingram Gilderbloom and Richard P. Appelbaum. Temple University Press, 1601 North Broad Street, University Services Building, Philadelphia, Pennsylvania 19122. 1988.

THE RIGHT TO HOUSING: A BLUEPRINT FOR HOUSING THE NATION. Dick Cluster. Institute for Policy Studies, 1601 Connecticut Avenue, Northwest, Fifth Floor, Washington, D.C. 20009. 1989.

SUBSIDIZING SHELTER: THE RELATIONSHIP BETWEEN WELFARE AND HOUSING ASSISTANCE. Sandra J. Newman. University Press of America, 4720 Boston Way, Lanham, Maryland 20706. 1988.

THE URBAN ECONOMY AND HOUSING. Ronald E. Grieson, editor. Lexington Books, 125 Spring Street, Lexington, Massachusettes 02173. 1983.

URBAN HOUSING IN THE 1980'S: MARKETS AND POLICIES. Margery Austin Turner and Raymond J. Struyk. Urban Institute Press, 2100 M Street, Northwest, Washington, D.C. 20037. 1984.

ANNUALS AND SURVEYS

THE CONVERSION OF RENTAL HOUSING TO CONDOMINIUMS AND COOPERATIVES: STATE AND LOCAL CONVERSION REGULATIONS. Division of Policy Studies, Department of Housing and Urban, Development and Office of Policy Research. Superintendent of Documents, United States Government Printing Office, Washington, D.C. 20402. 1982.

LAW REVIEWS AND PERIODICALS

THE AUTHORITY. Housing and Developement Law Institute, 1614 Twentieth Street, Northwest, Washington, D.C. 20036. 1983- . Quarterly.

LAW AND HOUSING JOURNAL. Case Western University, School of Law, Cleveland, Ohio 44106. Quarterly.

NEWSLETTERS AND NEWSPAPERS

BULLETIN. National Leased Housing Association, 2300 M Street, Northwest, Suite 260, Washington, D.C. 20037. Monthly.

CD: HOUSING REGISTER. CD Publications, 8204 Fenton Street, Silver Spring, Maryland 20910. Semimonthly.

COMMUNITY ASSOCIATION LAW REPORTER. Community Associations Institute, 1630 Duke Street, Suite 30, Alexandria, Virginia 22314. Monthly.

HELPING THE HOMELESS REPORT. CD Publications, 8204 Fenton Street, Silver Spring, Maryland 20910. Semimonthly.

HOUSING AFFAIRS LETTER. CD Publications, 8204 Fenton Street, Silver Spring, Maryland 20910. Weekly.

HOUSING COURT REPORTER CASE NOTE SERVICE. Lamb's Flight Limited, Rural Route #1, Airport Road, Box 2055, Johnson City, New York 13790. Monthly.

HOUSING LAW BULLETIN. National Housing Law Project, 1950 Addison Street, Berkeley, California 94704. Bimonthly.

HUD INFORMATION BULLETIN. American Bar Association, 1800 M Street, Northwest, Washington, D.C. 20036. Quarterly.

MANAGING HOUSING LETTER. CD Publications, 8204 Fenton Street, Silver Spring, Maryland 20910. Monthly.

WASHINGTON REPORT. Mortgage Bankers Association of America, 1125 Fifteenth Street, Northwest, Washington, D.C. 20005. Monthly.

BIBLIOGRAPHIES

DISCRIMINATION IN HOUSING. Robert E. Ansley, Jr. CPL Bibliographies, 1313 East Sixtieth Street, Merriam Center, Chicago, Illinois 60637-2897. 1985.

GOVERNMENT REGULATIONS AND THE COST OF HOUSING: A PARTIALLY ANNOTATED BIBLIOGRAPHY. Anne McGowan. CPL Bibliographies, 1313 East Sixtieth Street, Merriam Center, Chicago, Illinois 60637-2897. 1979.

HOUSING POLICY: A BIBLIOGRAPHY. Mary Vance. Vance Bibliographies, P.O. Box 229, 112 North Charter Street, Monticello, Illinois 61856. 1983.

POLICY STUDIES ON HOUSING: A SELECTED BIBLIOGRAPHY. Robert Goehlert. Vance Bibliographies, P.O. Box 229, 112 North Charter Street, Monticello, Illinois 61856. 1984.

STATE HOUSING FINANCE AGENCIES. Edward Duensing. Vance Bibliographies, P.O. Box 229, 112 North Charter Street, Monticello, Illinois 61856. 1982.

SUBSIDIZED HOUSING: A BIBLIOGRAPHY. Mary Vance. Vance Bibliographies, P.O. Box 229, 112 North Charter Street, Monticello, Illinois 61856. 1982.

DIRECTORIES

NATIONAL ASSOCIATION OF HOUSING AND REDEVELOPEMENT OFFICIALS: DIRECTORY OF LOCAL AGENCIES. National Association of Housing and Redevelopement Officials, 1320 Eighteenth Street, Northwest, Washington, D.C. 20036. Triennial.

SOCIAL SERVICE ORGANIZATIONS AND AGENCIES DIRECTORY. Gale Research, Incorporated, 835 Penobscot Building, Detroit, Michigan 48226. 1982.

ASSOCIATIONS AND PROFESSIONAL SOCIETIES

COMMUNITY ASSOCIATIONS INSTITUTE. 1630 Duke Street, Suite 30, Alexandria, Virginia 22314. (703) 548-8600.

COUNCIL FOR RURAL HOUSING AND DEVELOPMENT. 2300 M Street, Northwest, Suite 260, Washington, D.C. 20037. (202) 955-9715.

FEDERAL HOME LOAN BANK BOARD. 1700 G. Street, Northwest, Washington, D.C. 20552. (202) 906-6000.

HABITAT FOR HUMANITY INTERNATIONAL. Habitat and Church Streets, Americus, Georgia 31709. (912) 924-6935.

HOUSING ASSISTANCE COUNCIL. 1025 Vermont Avenue, Northwest, Suite 606, Washington, D.C. 20005. (202) 842-8600.

MORTGAGE BANKERS ASSOCIATION OF AMERICA. 1125 Fifthteenth Street, Northwest, Washington, D.C. 20005. (202) 861-6500.

NATIONAL COALITION FOR THE HOMELESS. 1621 Connecticut Avenue, Northwest, Suite 400, Washington, D.C. 20009. (202) 265-2371.

NATIONAL HOUSING AND REHABILITATION ASSOCIATION. 1726 Eighteenth Street, Northwest, Washington, D.C. 20009. (202) 328-9171.

NATIONAL HOUSING CONFERENCE. 1126 Sixteenth Street, Northwest, Suite 211, Washington, D.C. 20036. (202) 223-4844.

NATIONAL LEASED HOUSING ASSOCIATION. 2300 M Street, Northwest, Suite 260, Washington, D.C. 20037. (202) 785-8888.

HOUSING

NATIONAL LOW INCOME HOUSING COALITION. 1012 Fourteenth Street, Northwest, Suite 1500, Washington, D.C. 20005. (202) 662-1530.

NATIONAL MULTI-HOUSING COUNCIL. 1250 Connecticut Avenue, Northwest, Suite 620, Wasington, D.C. 20036. (202) 659-3381.

NATIONAL RURAL HOUSING COALITION. 122 C Street, Northwest, Suite 875, Washington, D.C. 20001. (202) 393-5229.

RURAL AMERICA, INCORPORATED. 725 Fifteenth Street, Northwest, Washington, D.C. 20036. (202) 628-1480.

SPECIAL COMMITTEE ON HOUSING AND URBAN DEVELOPMENT LAW, AMERICAN BAR ASSOCIATION. American Bar Association, 1800 M Street, Northwest, Washington, D.C. 20036. (202) 331-2278.

RESEARCH CENTERS, INSTITUTES, CLEARINGHOUSES

ANNE BLAINE HARRISON INSTITUTE FOR PUBLIC LAW. Georgetown University, 25 E Street, Northwest, Suite 514, Washington, D.C. 20001. (202) 662-9600.

NATIONAL HOUSING INSTITUTE. 439 Main Street, Orange, New Jersey 07050. (201) 678-3110.

NATIONAL HOUSING LAW PROJECT. 1950 Addison Street, Berkeley, California 94704. (415) 548-9400.

THE URBAN INSTITUTE PUBLIC FINANCE AND HOUSING CENTER. 2100 M Street, Northwest, Washington, D.C. 20037.

ONLINE DATABASES

CALIFORNIA PLANNING AND DEVELOPMENT REPORT. Tors Fulton Associates, 1275 Sunnycrest Avenue, Ventura, California 93003.

DODGE REAL ESTATE ANALYSIS AND PLANNING FORECAST. DRI/McGraw Hill, Data Products Division, 24 Hartwell Avenue, Lexington, Massachusetts 02173.

DRI HOUSING FORECAST. DRI/McGraw Hill, Data Products Division, 24 Hartwell Avenue, Lexington, Massachusetts 02173.

HANDSNET. HandsNet, Incorporated, 819 Pacific Avenue, Suite Z, Santa Cruz, California 95060.

HUD USER ONLINE. United States Department of Housing and Urban Development, Office of Policy Development and Research, P.O. Box 6091, Rockville, Maryland 20850.

MSA AND STATE HOUSING AND CONSTRUCTION. The WEFA Group, 150 Monument Road, Bala Cynwyd, Pennsylvania 19004.

MSA AND STATE HOUSING AND CONSTRUCTION FORECASTS. The WEFA Group, 150 Monument Road, Bala Cynwyd, Pennsylvania 19004.

WORLDWIDE PROPERTY GUIDE. Worldwide Exchange, 2501 East Cliff Drive, Santa Cruz, California 95060.

STATISTICS SOURCES

CENSUS OF HOUSING. Department of Commerce, Bureau of the Census. Superintendent of Documents, United States Government Printing Office, Washington, D.C. 20402.

OTHER SOURCES

NEW DIRECTIONS IN HOUSING AND URBAN POLICY, 1981-1989: A REVIEW OF THE ACTIVITIES AND PROGRAMS OF THE UNITED STATES DEPARTMENT OF HOUSING AND URBAN DEVELOPMENT. The Department of Housing and Urban Development, Washington, D.C. 1989.

A NEW NATIONAL HOUSING POLICY: RECOMMENDATIONS OF ORGANIZATIONS AND INDIVIDUALS CONCERNED ABOUT AFFORDABLE HOUSING IN AMERICA. Superintendent of Documents, United States Government Printing Office, Washington, D.C. 20402. 1987.

HOUSING DISCRIMINATION
See: DISCRIMINATION, HOUSING

HUMAN RIGHTS
See also: CIVIL RIGHTS AND LIBERTIES; GENOCIDE; STATE DEPARTMENT

STATUTES, CODES, STANDARDS, UNIFORM LAWS

HUMAN RIGHTS: A COMPILATION OF INTERNATIONAL INSTRUMENTS. Fifth Edition. United Nations Publishing Service, Room DC2-0853, New York, New York 10017. 1988.

INTERNATIONAL HUMAN RIGHTS INSTRUMENTS: A COMPILATION OF TREATIES, AGREEMENTS AND DECLARATIONS OF ESPECIAL INTEREST TO THE UNITED STATES. Second Edition. William S. Hein and Company, 1285 Main Street, Buffalo, New York 14209. 1990.

LOOSELEAF SERVICES AND REPORTERS

EUROPEAN HUMAN RIGHTS REPORTS. European Law Centre, Limited, London, England. 1979- .

HUMAN RIGHTS: THE INTER-AMERICAN SYSTEM. Oceana Publications, Incorporated, 75 Main Street, Dobbs Ferry, New York 10522. 1982- .

HUMAN RIGHTS: THE INTERNATIONAL PETITION SYSTEM. Oceana Publications, Incorporated, 75 Main Street, Dobbs Ferry, New York 10522. 1979- .

INTERNATIONAL HUMAN RIGHTS INSTRUMENTS. Richard B. Lillich. William S. Hein and Company, Incorporated, 1285 Main Street, Buffalo, New York 14209. 1982- .

THE REGULATION OF STATELESSNESS UNDER INTERNATIONAL AND NATIONAL LAW. Peter Mutharika, editor. Oceana Publications, Incorporated, 75 Main Street, Dobbs Ferry, New York 10522. 1979- .

HANDBOOKS, MANUALS, FORMBOOKS

AMNESTY INTERNATIONAL HANDBOOK. Hunter House, Incorporated, Publishers, P.O. Box 847, Claremont, California 91711-0847. 1991.

BASIC DOCUMENTS PERTAINING TO HUMAN RIGHTS IN THE INTER-AMERICAN SYSTEM. Organization of American States, IACHR Court, General Secretariat, Seventeenth Street and Constitution Avenue, Northwest, Washington, D.C. 20006. 1988.

FREEDOM IN THE WORLD: POLITICAL AND CIVIL LIBERTIES. 1986-1987. Raymond D. Gastil. Transaction Publishers, Rutgers University, New Brunswick, New Jersey 08903. 1980.

HUMAN RIGHTS: A REFERENCE HANDBOOK. Lucille Whalen. ABC-CLIO, P.O. Box 1911, Santa Barbara, California 93116-1911. 1989.

INTERNATIONAL HANDBOOK OF HUMAN RIGHTS. Jack Donnelly and Rhoda E. Howard. Greenwood Publishing Group, Incorporated, 88 Post Road West, P.O. Box 5007, Westport, Connecticut 06881. 1987.

THE UNITED NATIONS CONVENTION AGAINST TORTURE: A HANDBOOK ON THE CONVENTION AGAINST TORTURE AND OTHER CRUEL, INHUMAN, OR DEGRADING TREATMENT OR PUNISHMENT. J. Herman Burgers. Martinus Nijhoff, Kluwer Academic Publishers, 101 Philip Drive, Assinippi Park, Norwell, Massachusetts 02061. 1988.

TEXTBOOKS AND GENERAL WORKS

THE AGE OF RIGHTS. Louis Henkin. Columbia University Press, 562 West One Hundred Thirteenth Street, New York, New York 10025. 1990.

ASIAN PERSPECTIVES ON HUMAN RIGHTS. Claude Emerson Welch and Virginia A. Leary. Westview Press, Incorporated, 5500 Central Avenue, Boulder, Colorado 80301. 1990.

THE BATTLE OF HUMAN RIGHTS: GROSS, SYSTEMATIC VIOLATIONS AND THE INTER-AMERICAN SYSTEM. Cecilia Medina Quiroga. Martinus Nijhoff, Kluwer Academic Publishers, 101 Philip Drive, Assinippi Park, Norwell, Massachusetts 02061. 1988.

BEHIND THE DISAPPEARANCES: ARGENTINA'S DIRTY WAR AGAINST HUMAN RIGHTS AND THE UNITED NATIONS. Iain Guest. University of Pennsylvania Press, Blockley Hall, 418 Service Drive, Philadelphia, Pennsylvania 19104. 1990.

THE CONCEPT AND PRESENT STATUS OF THE INTERNATIONAL PROTECTION OF HUMAN RIGHTS: FORTY YEARS AFTER THE UNIVERSAL DECLARATION. B.G. Ramcharan. Martinus Nijhoff, Kluwer Academic Publishers, 101 Philip Drive, Assinippi Park, Norwell, Massachusetts 02061. 1989.

CRY OF THE OPPRESSED: THE HISTORY AND HOPE OF THE HUMAN RIGHTS REVOLUTION. Robert F. Drinan. HarperCollins Publishers, Ballinger Division, 10 East Fifty-third Street, New York, New York 10022. 1987.

DEFENDING CIVIL RESISTANCE UNDER INTERNATIONAL LAW. Francis Anthony Boyle. Transnational Publishers, P.O. Box 7282, Ardsley-on-Hudson, New York 10503. 1987.

THE DIPLOMACY OF HUMAN RIGHTS. David D. Newson. University Press of America, 4720 Boston Way, Lanham, Maryland 20706. 1986.

ENFORCEMENT OF HUMAN RIGHTS IN PEACE AND WAR AND THE FUTURE OF HUMANITY. Nagendra Singh. Kluwer Academic Publishers, 101 Philip Drive, Assinippi Park, Norwell, Massachusetts 02061. 1987.

ESSAYS ON HUMAN RIGHTS IN THE HELSINKI PROCESS. A. Bloed, P. van Dijk, and Martinus Nijhoff. Distributed by Kluwer Academic Publishers, 101 Philip Drive, Assinippi Park, Norwell, Massachusetts 02061. 1985.

FEDERAL COURTS AND THE INTERNATIONAL HUMAM RIGHTS PARADIGM. Kenneth C. Randall. Duke University Press, Box 6697 College Station, Durham, North Carolina 27708. 1990.

THE FINAL ACT: THE DRAMATIC, REVEALING STORY OF THE MOSCOW HELSINKI WATCH GROUP. Paul Goldberg. William Morrow and Company, 105 Madison Avenue, New York, New York 10016. 1988.

FOREIGN POLICY AND HUMAN RIGHTS: ISSUES AND RESPONSES. R.J. Vincent. Cambridge University Press, 40 West Twentieth Street, New York, New York 10011. 1986.

GROUP RIGHTS AND DISCRIMINATION IN INTERNATIONAL LAW. Natan Lerner. Martinus Nijhoff, Kluwer Academic Publishers, 101 Philip Drive, Assinippi Park, Norwell, Massachusetts 02061. 1991.

HELSINKI, HUMAN RIGHTS, AND EUROPEAN SECURITY: ANALYSIS AND DOCUMENTATION. Vojtech Mastny. Duke University Press, Box 6697, College Station, Durham, North Carolina 27708. 1986.

HUMAN RIGHTS. Ellen Frankel Paul, Jeffrey Paul, and Fred D. Miller, Jr. Basil Blackwell, Incorporated, 3 Cambridge Center, Cambridge, Massachusetts 02143. 1985.

HUMAN RIGHTS. J. Roland Pennock and John W. Chapman. New York University Press, 70 Washington Square South, New York, New York 10012. 1981.

HUMAN RIGHTS AND AMERICAN FOREIGN POLICY: THE CARTER AND REAGAN EXPERIENCES. A. Glenn Mower. Greenwood Publishing Group, Incorporated, 88 Post Road West, P.O. Box 5007, Westport, Connecticut 06881. 1987.

HUMAN RIGHTS AND DEVELOPMENT: INTERNATIONAL VIEWS. St. Martin's Press, 175 Fifth Avenue, New York, New York 10010. 1989.

HUMAN RIGHTS AND FOREIGN POLICY: PRINCIPLES AND PRACTICE. St. Martin's Press, 175 Fifth Avenue, New York, New York 10010. 1989.

HUMAN RIGHTS AND HUMANITARIAN NORMS AS CUSTOMARY LAW. Theodor Meron. Oxford University Press, 200 Madison Avenue, New York, New York 10016. 1989.

HUMAN RIGHTS AND STATE SOVEREIGNTY. Richard Falk. Holmes and Meier Publishers, Incorporated, IUB Building, 30 Irving Place, New York, New York 10003. 1984.

HUMAN RIGHTS AND THE NEW REALISM: STRATEGIC THINKING IN A NEW AGE. Michael Novak. Freedom House, 48 East 21st Street, New York, New York 10010. 1986.

HUMAN RIGHTS AND U.S. FOREIGN POLICY: BUREAUCRACY AND DIPLOMACY. Lawyers Committee for Human Rights, 330 Seventh Avenue, Tenth Floor, New York, New York 10001. 1989.

HUMAN RIGHTS AND U.S. FOREIGN POLICY: CONGRESS RECONSIDERED. David P. Forsythe. University Presses of Florida, 15 Northwest Fifteenth Street, Gainesville, Florida 32603. 1988.

HUMAN RIGHTS AND U.S. FOREIGN POLICY: LINKING SECURITY ASSISTANCE AND HUMAN RIGHTS. Eric R. Biel. Lawyers Committee for Human Rights, 330 Seventh Avenue, Tenth Floor, New York, New York 10001. 1989.

HUMAN RIGHTS AND U.S. FOREIGN POLICY: REPORT AND RECOMMENDATIONS. Lawyers Committee for Human Rights, 330 Seventh Avenue, Tenth Floor, New York, New York 10001. 1988.

HUMAN RIGHTS AND WORLD POLITICS. Second Revised Edition. David P. Forsythe. University of Nebraska Press, 901 North 17th Street, Lincoln, Nebraska 68588-0520. 1989.

HUMAN RIGHTS, ETHNICITY, AND DISCRIMINATION. Vernon Van Dyke. Greenwood Publishing Group, Incorporated, 88 Post Road West, P.O. Box 5007, Westport, Connecticut 06881. 1985.

HUMAN RIGHTS: FACT OR FANCY? Henry Babcock Veatch. Louisiana State University Press, Highland Road, Baton Rouge, Louisiana 70893. 1985.

HUMAN RIGHTS: FROM RHETORIC TO REALITY. Tom Campbell, editor. Basil Blackwell, Incorporated, 3 Cambridge Center, Cambridge, Massachusetts 02142. 1986.

HUMAN RIGHTS IN A PLURALIST WORLD: INDIVIDUALS AND COLLECTIVITIES. Meckler Corporation, 11 Ferry Lane West, Westport, Connecticut 06880. 1990.

HUMAN RIGHTS IN AFRICA: CROSS-CULTURAL PERSPECTIVES. Abd Allah Ahmad Naim and Francis Mading Deng. Brookings Institution, 1775 Massachusetts Avenue, Washington, D.C. 20036. 1990.

HUMAN RIGHTS IN IRAQ. Yale University Press, 302 Temple Street, New Haven, Connecticut 06520. 1990.

HUMAN RIGHTS IN POST-MAO CHINA. John F. Cooper, Franz Michail, and Yuan-li Wu. Westview Press, Incorporated, 5500 Central Avenue, Boulder, Colorado 80301. 1985.

HUMAN RIGHTS IN THE ISRAELI-OCCUPIED TERRITORIES, 1967-1982. Esther Rosalind Cohen. Manchester University Press, 175 Fifth Avenue, New York, New York 10010. 1988.

HUMAN RIGHTS IN THE PEOPLE'S REPUBLIC OF CHINA. Yuan-li Wu. Westview Press, Incorporated, 5500 Central Avenue, Boulder, Colorado 80301. 1988.

HUMAN RIGHTS IN THE WORLD COMMUNITY: ISSUES AND ACTION. Richard Pierre Claude and Burns H. Weston. University of Pennsylvania Press, Blockley Hall, 418 Service Drive, Philadelphia, Pennsylvania 19104. 1989.

HUMAN RIGHTS IN THE UNITED NATIONS DECLARATION. Helle Kanger, Almqvist and Wiksell, International, Rowman and Littlefield, 8705 Bollman Place, Savage, Maryland 20763. 1984.

THE HUMAN RIGHTS MOVEMENT: WESTERN VALUES AND THEOLOGICAL PERSPECTIVES. Warren Lee Holleman. Praeger Publishers, One Madison Avenue, New York, New York 10010-3603. 1987.

HUMAN RIGHTS OF ALIENS IN CONTEMPORARY INTERNATIONAL LAW. Richard B. Lillich. Manchester University Press, 175 Fifth Avenue, New York, New York 10010. 1984.

THE HUMAN RIGHTS READER. Revised Edition. Walter Laqueur and Barry M. Rubin. New American Library, 1633 Broadway, New York, New York 10019. 1990.

HUMAN RIGHTS: STATUS OF INTERNATIONAL INSTRUMENTS. United Nations Publishing Service, Room DC2-0853, New York, New York 10017. 1987.

HUMAN RIGHTS, THE HELSINKI ACCORDS, AND THE UNITED STATES: SELECTED EXECUTIVE AND CONGRESSIONAL DOCUMENTS. Igor I. Kavass, and Jacqueline P. Granier, editors. William S. Hein and Company, Incorporated, Hein Building, 1285 Main Street, Buffalo, New York 14209. 1982.

HUMAN RIGHTS TREATIES AND THE SENATE: A HISTORY OF OPPOSITION. Natalie Hevener Kaufman. University of North Carolina Press, P.O. Box 2288, 116 South Boundary Street, Chapel Hill, North Carolina 27515-2288. 1990.

HUMANITARIAN INTERVENTION: AN INQUIRY INTO LAW AND MORALITY. Fernando R. Teson. Transnational Publishers, P.O. Box 7282, Ardsley-on-Hudson, New York 10503. 1988.

INTERNATIONAL HUMAN RIGHTS IN A NUTSHELL. Thomas Buergenthal. West Publishing Company, 50 West Kellogg Boulevard, St. Paul, Minnesota 55164. 1988.

INTERNATIONAL HUMAN RIGHTS: LAW, POLICY, AND PROCESS. Frank C. Newman and David S. Weissbrodt. Anderson Publishing Company, 2035 Reading Road, Cincinnati, Ohio 45202. 1990.

INTERNATIONAL HUMAN RIGHTS: PROBLEMS OF LAW, POLICY, AND PRACTICE. Second Edition. Richard B. Lillich. Little, Brown and Company, 34 Beacon Street, Boston, Massachusetts 02108. 1991.

INTERNATIONAL HUMAN RIGHTS: UNIVERSALISM VERSUS RELATIVISM. Alison Dundes Renteln. Sage Publications, 2455 Teller Road, Newbury Park, California 91320. 1990.

THE INTERNATIONALIZATION OF HUMAN RIGHTS. David P. Forsythe. Lexington Books, 125 Spring Street, Lexington, Massachusetts 02173. 1991.

INVOKING INTERNATIONAL HUMAN RIGHTS LAW IN DOMESTIC COURTS. Richard B. Lillich. American Bar Association, Division of Public Services, 750 North Lake Shore Drive, Chicago, Illinois 60611. 1985.

THE LAWFUL RIGHTS OF MANKIND: AN INTRODUCTION TO THE INTERNATIONAL LEGAL CODE OF HUMAN RIGHTS. Paul Sieghart. Oxford University Press, 200 Madison Avenue, New York, New York 10016. 1985.

MAKING SENSE OF HUMAN RIGHTS: PHILOSOPHICAL REFLECTIONS ON THE UNIVERSAL DECLARATION OF HUMAN RIGHTS. James W. Nickel. University of California Press, 2120 Berkeley Way, Berkeley, California 94720. 1987.

NEW DIRECTIONS IN HUMAN RIGHTS. Ellen L. Lutz, Hurst Hannum and Kathryn Burke. University of Pennsylvania Press, Blockley Hall, 418 Service Drive, Philadelphia, Pennsylvania 19104. 1989.

NO DISTANT MILLENIUM: THE INTERNATIONAL LAW OF HUMAN RIGHTS. John Thomas Humphrey. UNESCO, 7 Place de Fontenoy, F-75700 Paris, France. 1989.

PHILOSOPHICAL ISSUES IN HUMAN RIGHTS: THEORIES AND APPLICATIONS. Patricia H. Werhane, A.R. Gini, David T. Ozar. Random House Publicity, 201 East Fiftieth Street, New York, New York 10022. 1986.

RETHINKING HUMAN RIGHTS: CHALLENGES FOR THEORY AND ACTION. Smitu Kothari and Harsh Sethi. New Horizon Press, P.O. Box 669, Far Hills, New Jersey 07931. 1989.

RIGHT TO ADEQUATE FOOD AS A HUMAN RIGHT. United Nations Publishing Service, Room DC2-0853, New York, New York 10017. 1989.

THE RIGHT TO LIFE IN INTERNATIONAL LAW. B. G. Ramcharan, Martinus Nijhoff. Distributed by Kluwer Academic Publishers, 101 Philip Drive, Assinippi Park, Norwell, Massachusetts 02061. 1985.

THE RIGHTS OF PEOPLES. James Crawford. Oxford University Press, 200 Madison Avenue, New York, New York 10016. 1988.

STATES OF EMERGENCY: THEIR IMPACT ON HUMAN RIGHTS: A STUDY. International Commission of Jurists, Geneva, Switzerland. 1983.

TEARS, BLOOD, AND CRIES: HUMAN RIGHTS IN AFGHANISTAN SINCE THE INVASION, 1979-1984. Jeri Laber. United States Helsinki Watch Committee, 485 Fifth Avenue, New York, New York 10017. 1984.

THE THEORY AND PRACTICE OF HUMAN RIGHTS. L.J. Macfarland. St. Martin's Press, 175 Fifth Avenue, New York, New York 10010. 1985.

UNIVERSAL HUMAN RIGHTS IN THEORY AND PRACTICE. Jack Donnelly. Cornell University Press, 124 Roberts Place, Ithaca, New York 14850. 1989.

VICTIMS OF POLITICS: THE STATE OF HUMAN RIGHTS. Kurt Glaser, and Stefan T. Possony. Columbia University Press, 562 West 113th Street, New York, New York 10025. 1979.

WITH FRIENDS LIKE THESE: THE AMERICAS WATCH REPORT ON HUMAN RIGHTS AND UNITED STATES POLICY IN LATIN AMERICA. Cynthia Brown, editor. Pantheon Books, 201 East 50th Street, New York, New York 10022. 1985.

WORLD JUSTICE? U.S. COURTS AND INTERNATIONAL HUMAN RIGHTS. Mark Gibney. Westview Press, Incorporated, 5500 Central Avenue, Boulder, Colorado 80301. 1991.

ENCYCLOPEDIAS AND DICTIONARIES

HUMAN RIGHTS TERMINOLOGY IN INTERNATIONAL LAW: A THESAURUS. Bjorn Stormorken and Leo Zwaak. Martinus Nijhoff, Kluwer Academic Publishers, 101 Philip Drive, Assinippi Park, Norwell, Massachusetts 02061. 1988.

ANNUALS AND SURVEYS

COUNTRY REPORTS ON HUMAN RIGHTS PRACTICES FOR (YEAR). Report submitted to the Committee on Foreign Relations, United States Senate and Committee on Foreign Affairs, United States House of Representatives, by the Department of State. Superintendent of Documents, United States Government Printing Office, Washington, D.C. 20402. Annual.

LAW REVIEWS AND PERIODICALS

AMNESTY INTERNATIONAL REPORT. Amnesty International of the United States of America, 322 Eighth Avenue, New York, New York 10001. Annual.

BULLETIN. Lawyers Committee for Human Rights, 330 Seventh Avenue, New York, New York 10001. Quarterly.

HARVARD HUMAN RIGHTS JOURNAL. Harvard Law School, Cambridge, Massachusetts. 1990.

HARVARD HUMAN RIGHTS YEARBOOK. Harvard Law School, Cambridge, Massachusetts. 1988-1989.

HUMAN RIGHTS. Section of Individual Rights, American Bar Association, 750 North Lake Shore Drive, Chicago, Illinois 60611. Annual.

HUMAN RIGHTS BULLETIN. International League for Human Rights, 432 Park Avenue, South, Room 1103, New York, New York 10016. Bimonthly.

HUMAN RIGHTS INTERNET REPORTER. Harvard Law School, Pound Hall, Room 401, Cambridge, Massachusetts 02138. Quarterly.

HUMAN RIGHTS LAW JOURNAL. N.P. Engel, Publisher, 3608 South Twelfth Street, Arlington, Virginia 22204. Semiannual.

HUMAN RIGHTS QUARTERLY. Johns Hopkins University Press, Journals Publishing Division, 701 West Fortieth Street, Suite 275, Baltimore, Maryland 21211. Quarterly.

JOURNAL OF INTERGROUP RELATIONS. National Association of Human Rights Workers, Broward County Human Relations Division, Government Center, Room 116, 115 South Andrews, Fort Lauderdale, Florida 33301. Quarterly.

THE LAW GROUP DOCKET. International Human Rights Law Group, 1601 Connecticut Avenue, Northwest, Suite 700, Washington, D.C. 20009. Quarterly.

LAWASIA HUMAN RIGHTS BULLETIN. The Law Association for Asia and the Pacific, 170 Phillip Street, Sydney, Australia 2000. Quarterly.

NEW YORK LAW SCHOOL HUMAN RIGHTS ANNUAL. New York Law School, New York, New York 10001. Annual.

NEW YORK LAW SCHOOL JOURNAL OF HUMAN RIGHTS. New York Law School, New York, New York. 1987- .

NEWSLETTERS AND NEWSPAPERS

AMNESTY ACTION. Amnesty International of the United States of America, 322 Eighth Avenue, New York, New York 10001. Bimonthly.

CENTER FOR THE STUDY OF HUMAN RIGHTS NEWSLETTER. 1108 International Affairs Building, Columbia University, New York, New York 10027. Quarterly.

CENTER OF CONCERN: CENTER FOCUS. 3700 Thirteenth Street, Northwest, Washington, D.C. 20017. Bimonthly.

CONGRESSIONAL HUMAN RIGHTS CAUCUS NEWSLETTER. House Annex Two, Room 552, Washington, D.C. 20515. Quarterly.

THE FIRST FREEDOM. Puebla Institute, 910 Seventeenth Street, Northwest, Suite 409, Washington, D.C. 20006. Bimonthly.

HUMAN RIGHTS WATCH. 485 Fifth Avenue, New York, New York 10017. Bimonthly.

LAWYERS COMMITTEE FOR HUMAN RIGHTS: NEWSBRIEFS. 330 Seventh Avenue, 10th Floor, North, New York, New York 10001. Quarterly.

WORLD INSIGHT. Freedom Fund, 4534 1/2 University Way, Northeast, Seattle, Washington 98105. Bimonthly.

BIBLIOGRAPHIES

HUMAN RIGHTS POLICY: A SELECTED BIBLIOGRAPHY. Robert Goehlert. Vance Bibliographies, P.O. Box 229, 112 North Charter Street, Monticello, Illinois 61856. 1984.

HUMAN RIGHTS REPORTS: AN ANNOTATED BIBLIOGRAPHY OF FACT-FINDING MISSIONS. Berth Verstappen. Bowker-Saur Limited, Borough Green, Sevenoaks, Kent TN15 8PH, England. 1987.

THE INTERNATIONAL LAW OF HUMAN RIGHTS IN AFRICA: BASIC DOCUMENTS AND ANNOTATED BIBLIOGRAPHY. Martinus Nijhoff, Kluwer Academic Publishers, 101 Philip Drive, Assinippi Park, Norwell, Massachusetts 02061. 1988.

KEYGUIDE TO INFORMATION SOURCES ON THE INTERNATIONAL PROTECTION OF HUMAN RIGHTS. John A. Andrews and W.D. Hines. Mansell Publishing Limited, Artillery House, Artillery Row, London SW1P 1RT, England. 1987.

DIRECTORIES

DIRECTORY OF CENTRAL AMERICAN ORGANIZATIONS. Central American Resource Center, Box 2327, Austin, Texas 78768. Annual.

GUIDE TO INTERNATIONAL HUMAN RIGHTS PRACTICE. Hurst Hannum. University of Pennsylvania Press, 418 Service Drive, Blockley Hall, 13th Floor, Philadelphia, Pennsylvania 19104-6097. 1983.

HUMAN RIGHTS: A DIRECTORY OF RESOURCES. Thomas P. Fenton and Mary J. Heffron. Orbis Books, Walsh Building, Maryknoll, New York 10545. 1989.

HUMAN RIGHTS DIRECTORY: LATIN AMERICA, AFRICA, ASIA. Human Rights International, Harvard Law School, Pound Hall, Room 401, Cambridge, Massachusetts 02138. 1987.

HUMAN RIGHTS DIRECTORY: WESTERN EUROPE. Human Rights International, Harvard Law School, Pound Hall, Room 401, Cambridge, Massachusetts 02138. 1982.

HUMAN RIGHTS ORGANIZATIONS AND PERIODICALS DIRECTORY. Meiklelejohn Civil Liberties Institute, 1715 Francisco Street, Berkeley, California 94703. Irregular.

NORTH AMERICAN HUMAN RIGHTS DIRECTORY. Human Rights Internet, Harvard Law School, Pound Hall, Room 401, Cambridge, Massachusetts 02138. 1984.

SOCIAL SERVICE ORGANIZATIONS AND AGENCIES DIRECTORY. Gale Research, Incorporated, 835 Penobscot Building, Detroit, Michigan 48226. 1982.

WORLD DIRECTORY OF HUMAN RIGHTS TEACHING AND RESEARCH INSTITUTIONS. UNESCO, 7 Place de Fontenoy, F-75700 Paris, France. 1988.

ASSOCIATIONS AND PROFESSIONAL SOCIETIES

AMERICAN ASSOCIATION FOR THE INTERNATIONAL COMMISSION OF JURISTS. 777 United Nations Plaza, 10th Floor, New York, New York 10017. (212) 972-0883.

AMERICAN COUNCIL FOR THE ADVANCEMENT OF HUMAN RIGHTS. 4801 Massachusetts Avenue, Northwest, Suite 400, Washington, D.C. 20016. (202) 364-8710.

AMNESTY INTERNATIONAL OF THE UNITED STATES OF AMERICA. 322 Eighth Avenue, New York, New York 10001. (212) 807-8400.

ASIA WATCH COMMITTEE. 1522 K Street, Northwest, Suite 910, Washington, D.C. 20005. (202) 371-6592.

CENTER OF CONCERN. 3700 Thirteenth Street, Northeast, Washington, D.C. 20017. (202) 635-2757.

COMMITTEE OF CONCERNED SCIENTISTS. 41 West Thirty-third Street, Suite 400, New York, New York 10001. (212) 695-2560.

CONGRESSIONAL HUMAN RIGHTS CAUCUS. House Annex Two, Room 552, Washington, D.C. 20515. (202) 226-4040.

FREEDOM FUND. 4534 1/2 University Way, Northeast, Seattle, Washington 98105. (206) 547-7644.

HUMAN RIGHTS WATCH. 485 Fifth Avenue, New York, New York 10017. (212) 972-8400.

INTER-AMERICAN COMMISSION ON HUMAN RIGHTS. 1889 F Street, Northwest, Suite LLZ, Washington, D.C. 20006. (202) 458-6007.

INTERNATIONAL HUMAN RIGHTS LAW GROUP. 1601 Connecticut Avenue, Northwest, Suite 700, Washington, D.C. 20009. (202) 232-8500.

INTERNATIONAL LEAGUE FOR HUMAN RIGHTS. 432 Park Avenue, South, Room 1103, New York, New York 10016. (212) 684-1221.

LAWYER'S COMMITTEE FOR HUMAN RIGHTS. 330 Seventh Avenue, 10th Floor, North, New York, New York 10001. (212) 629-6170.

NATIONAL ASSOCIATION OF HUMAN RIGHTS WORKERS. Broward County Human Relations Division, Government Center, Room 116, 115 South Andrews, Fort Lauderdale, Florida 33301. (305) 357-6047.

SECTION OF INDIVIDUAL RIGHTS. American Bar Association, 750 North Lake Shore Drive, Chicago, Illinois 60611. (312) 988-5000.

UNITED NATIONS COMMISSION ON HUMAN RIGHTS. United Nations Plaza, New York, New York. (212) 306-7500.

UNITED STATES HELSINKI WATCH COMMITTEE, 485 Fifth Avenue, New York, New York 10017. (212) 840-9460.

RESEARCH CENTERS, INSTITUTES, CLEARINGHOUSES

CENTER FOR THE STUDY OF HUMAN RIGHTS. 1108 International Affairs Building, Columbia University, New York, New York 10027. (212) 854-2479.

HUMAN RIGHTS ADVOCATES INTERNATIONAL. 230 Park Avenue, Suite 460, New York, New York 10169. (212) 986-5555.

HUMAN RIGHTS INTERNET. Harvard Law School, Pound Hall, Room 401, Cambridge, Massachusetts 02138. (617) 495-9924.

RESEARCH CENTER FOR RELIGION AND HUMAN RIGHTS IN CLOSED SOCIETIES. 475 Riverside Drive, Suite 448, New York, New York 10115. (212) 870-2481.

PUEBLA INSTITUTE. 910 Seventeenth Street, Northwest, Suite 409, Washington, D.C. 20006. (202) 659-3229.

ONLINE DATABASES

HRI BIBLIOGRAPHY. Human Rights Internet, Harvard Law School, Pound Hall, Room 401, Cambridge, Massachusetts 02138.

HRI ORGANIZATIONS. Human Rights Internet, Harvard Law School, Pound Hall, Room 401, Cambridge, Massachusetts 02138.

AUDIOVISUALS

ACKNOWLEDGEMENT AND TREATMENT OF TORTURE VICTIMS. National Practice Institute, 330 Second Avenue South, Minneapolis, Minnesota 55401. Videotape.

ASYLUM REPRESENTATION. National Practice Institute, 330 Second Avenue South, Minneapolis, Minnesota 55401. Videotape.

OTHER SOURCES

BASIC DOCUMENTS ON HUMAN RIGHTS. Third edition. Ian Brownlie, compiler. Oxford University Press, 200 Madison Avenue, New York, New York 10016. 1991.

HUMAN RIGHTS DOCUMENTS: COMPILATION OF DOCUMENTS PERTAINING TO HUMAN RIGHTS INSTRUMENTS; UNITED STATES LAWS ON HUMAN RIGHTS; UNITED NATIONS INSTRUMENTS IN SELECTED HUMAN RIGHTS AREAS; REGIONAL HUMAN RIGHTS INSTRUMENTS; WAR CRIMES AND INTERNATION HUMANITARIAN LAWS (LAWS OF ARMED CONFLICT); HUMAN RIGHTS BODIES ESTABLISHED BY UNITED STATES LAWS OR MULTILATERAL INSTRUMENTS. Superintendent of Documents, United States Government Printing Office, Washington, D.C. 20402. 1983.

HUMOR
See: LEGAL HUMOR

HUSBAND AND WIFE
See: COMMUNITY PROPERTY; DIVORCE, SEPARATION AND MARRIAGE; FAMILY LAW; FAMILY VIOLENCE

I

IDENTIFICATION
See: EVIDENCE; FIREARMS AND BALLISTICS

ILLEGITIMACY
See: FAMILY LAW

IMMIGRATION
See: EMIGRATION AND IMMIGRATION

IMMIGRATION AND NATURALIZATION SERVICE
See also: CITIZENS AND CITIZENSHIP; EMIGRATION AND IMMIGRATION

STATUTES, CODES, STANDARDS, UNIFORM LAWS

CODE OF FEDERAL REGULATIONS, TITLE 8. Office of the Federal Register, National Archives and Records Administration. Superintendent of Documents, United States Government Printing Office, Washington, D.C. 20402. Annual. (Updated by use of monthly List of Sections Affected and daily Federal Register .)

IMMIGRATION AND NATURALIZATION SERVICE: STUDENT AND SCHOOL REGULATIONS. Justice Department, Immigration and Naturalization Service. Superintendent of Documents, United States Government Printing Office, Washington, D.C. 20402. 1983.

LOOSELEAF SERVICES AND REPORTERS

ADMINISTRATIVE DECISIONS UNDER IMMIGRATION AND NATIONALITY LAWS OF THE UNITED STATES. Justice Department, Immigration and Naturalization Service, Board of Immigration Appeals. Superintendent of Documents, United States Government Printing Office, Washington, D.C. 20402. 1940- .

IMMIGRATION AND NATURALIZATION SERVICE CODE, OPERATIONS, INSTRUCTIONS, REGULATIONS, AND INTERPRETATIONS. Justice Department, Immigration and Naturalization Service. Superintendent of Documents, United States Government Printing Office, Washington, D.C. 20402. 1986- .

IMMIGRATION BOARD OF APPEALS, INTERIM DECISIONS. Justice Department, Board of Immigration Appeals. Superintendent of Documents, United States Government Printing Office, Washington, D.C. 20402. 1984- .

INS REPORTER. Justice Department, Immigration and Naturalization Service. Superintendent of Documents, United States Government Printing Office, Washington, D.C. 20402. 1976- . Quarterly.

TEXTBOOKS AND GENERAL WORKS

CHADHA: THE STORY OF AN EPIC CONSTITUTIONAL STRUGGLE. Barbara Hinkson Craig. University of California Press, 2120 Berkeley Way, Berkeley, California 94720. 1990.

THE IMMIGRATION AND NATURALIZATION SERVICE. Edward H. Dixon and Mark A. Galan. Chelsea House Publishers, 1974 Sproul Road, Suite 400, Broomall, Pennsylvania 19008. 1990.

IMPACT OF THE IMMIGRATION REFORM AND CONTROL ACT ON THE IMMIGRATION AND NATURALIZATION SERVICE. Jason Juffras. Program for Research on Immigration Policy. Rand Corporation, available from: University Press of America, 4720 Boston Way, Lanham, Maryland 20706. 1991.

DIGESTS, INDEXES, ABSTRACTS, CITATORS

SHEPARD'S IMMIGRATION AND NATURALIZATION CITATIONS. Shepard's/McGraw-Hill, P.O. Box 1235, Colorado Springs, Colorado 80901.

IMMUNITY
See: DIPLOMATIC PRIVILEGES AND IMMUNITY; GOVERNMENT IMMUNITY AND LIABILITY

IMPEACHMENT OF PUBLIC OFFICIALS
See: PRESIDENT (UNITED STATES); PUBLIC OFFICIALS AND EMPLOYEES

IMPLIED TRUSTS
See: WILLS, TRUSTS AND INHERITANCE

IMPORTS
See: EXPORTS AND IMPORTS

INCAPACITY
See: CHILDREN; MENTAL HEALTH AND DISABILITY; PHYSICALLY HANDICAPPED

INCOME TAX, FEDERAL
See also: INTERNAL REVENUE SERVICE; TAX LEGISLATION AND POLICY; TAX PRACTICE AND ENFORCEMENT; TAX RETURNS; TAX SHELTERS; TAXATION, STATE AND LOCAL

STATUTES, CODES, STANDARDS, UNIFORM LAWS

THE COMPLETE INTERNAL REVENUE CODE OF 1954. Prentice-Hall, Incorporated, 113 Sylvan Avenue, Englewood Cliffs, New Jersey 07632. Annual.

FEDERAL INCOME TAX CODE AND REGULATIONS. Commerce Clearing House, Incorporated, 4025 West Peterson Avenue, Chicago, Illinois 60646. Annual.

FEDERAL INCOME TAX PROJECT: INTEGRATION OF THE INDIVIDUAL AND CORPORATE INCOME TAXES: MEMORANDUM. American Law Institute-American Bar Association, 4025 Chestnut Street, Philadelphia, Pennsylvania 19104. 1990- .

FEDERAL INCOME TAX PROJECT: INTERNATIONAL ASPECTS OF UNITED STATES INCOME TAXATION: PROPOSALS ON UNITED STATES TAXATION OF FOREIGN PERSONS AND OF THE FOREIGN INCOME OF UNITED STATES PERSONS. Adopted by the American Law Institute at Washington, D.C., May 14, 1986. American Law Institute-American Bar Association, 4025 Chestnut Street, Philadelphia, Pennsylvania 19104. 1987.

FEDERAL INCOME TAX REGULATIONS. Prentice-Hall, Incorporated, 113 Sylvan Avenue, Englewood Cliffs, New Jersey 07632. Annual.

FEDERAL TAX REGULATIONS. West Publishing Company, P.O. Box 64526, 50 West Kellogg Boulevard, St. Paul, Minnesota 55164-0526. Annual.

INTERNAL REVENUE BULLETIN; CUMULATIVE BULLETIN. United States Department of Treasury, Internal Revenue Service. United States Government Printing Office, Washington, D.C. 20402. Weekly.

INTERNAL REVENUE CODE. West Publishing Company, P.O. Box 64526, 50 West Kellogg Boulevard, St. Paul, Minnesota 55164-0526. Annual.

PENSION AND EMPLOYEE BENEFITS: CODE, ERISA, REGULATIONS. Commerce Clearing House, Incorporated, 4025 West Peterson Avenue, Chicago, Illinois 60646. Annual.

RESTATEMENTS

FEDERAL INCOME TAX PROJECT: TENTATIVE DRAFT NO. 14: INTERNATIONAL ASPECTS OF UNITED STATES INCOME TAXATION. American Law Institute, 4025 Chestnut Street, Philadelphia, Pennsylvania 19104. 1986.

LOOSELEAF SERVICES AND REPORTERS

ACCOUNTING PERIODS AND METHODS. Thomas J. Purcell, III, Editor. Commerce Clearing House, Incorporated, 4025 West Peterson Avenue, Chicago, Illinois 60646. 1987- .

BENDER'S FEDERAL TAX SERVICE. Matthew Bender and Company, Incorporated, 11 Penn Plaza, New York, New York 10001. 1989- .

CORPORATE ALTERNATIVE MINIMUM TAX (AMT). Byrle M. Abbin, Stephen R. Corrick and Robert W. Hriszko. Commerce Clearing House, Incorporated, 4025 West Peterson Avenue, Chicago, Illinois 60646. 1988- .

CUMULATIVE CHANGES, 1954 CODE AND REGULATIONS. Prentice-Hall, Incorporated, 113 Sylvan Avenue, Englewood Cliffs, New Jersey 07632. 1954- .

EXECUTIVE COMPENSATION AND TAXATION COORDINATOR. Research Institute of America, Incorporated, 90 Fifth Avenue, New York, New York 10011. 1979- .

FAMILY LAW TAX GUIDE. Commerce Clearing House, Incorporated, 4025 West Peterson Avenue, Chicago, Illinois 60646. 1985- .

FEDERAL INCOME, GIFT AND ESTATE TAXATION. Jacob Rabkin and Mark H. Johnson. Matthew Bender and Company, Incorporated, 11 Penn Plaza, New York, New York 10001. 1972- .

FEDERAL INCOME, GIFT AND ESTATE TREASURY REGULATIONS. George J. Jones, et al. Matthew Bender and Company, Incorporated, 11 Penn Plaza, New York, New York 10001. 1972- .

FEDERAL INCOME TAXATION OF BANKS AND FINANCIAL INSTITUTIONS. Fifth Edition. Banking Law Journal Editorial Board. Research Institute of America, Incorporated, One Penn Plaza, New York, New York 10119. 1978- .

FEDERAL INCOME TAXATION OF CORPORATIONS AND SHAREHOLDERS: FORMS. Third Edition. Boris I. Bittker, Meade Emory and William P. Streng. Research Institute of America, Incorporated, One Penn Plaza, New York, New York 10119. 1989- .

FEDERAL INCOME TAXATION OF DEBT INSTRUMENTS. David C. Garlock. Prentice-Hall, Incorporated, 113 Sylvan Avenue, Englewood Cliffs, New Jersey 07632. 1991- .

FEDERAL INCOME TAXATION OF INDIVIDUALS. Boris I. Bittker and Martin J. McMahon, Jr. Research Institute of America, Incorporated, One Penn Plaza, New York, New York 10119. 1988.

FEDERAL INCOME TAXATION OF INVENTORIES. Leslie J. Schneider. Matthew Bender and Company, Incorporated, 11 Penn Plaza, New York, New York 10001. 1979- .

FEDERAL INCOME TAXATION OF LIFE INSURANCE COMPANIES. Richard S. Antes. Matthew Bender and Company, Incorporated, 11 Penn Plaza, New York, New York 10001. 1984- .

FEDERAL INCOME TAXATION OF LIFE INSURANCE COMPANIES. Keith A. Tucker and Dennis P. Van Mieghem. Prentice-Hall, Incorporated, 113 Sylvan Avenue, Englewood Cliffs, New Jersey 07632. 1983- .

FEDERAL INCOME TAXATION OF PASSIVE ACTIVITIES. Michael N. Jennings and Daniel R. Bolar. Research Institute of America, Incorporated, One Penn Plaza, New York, New York 10119. 1990- .

FEDERAL INCOME TAXATION OF REAL ESTATE. Gerald J. Robinson. Research Institute of America, Incorporated, One Penn Plaza, New York, New York 10119. 1988.

FEDERAL TAX ASPECTS OF BANKRUPTCY. C. Richard McQueen and Jack Crestol. Shepard's/McGraw-Hill, P.O. Box 1235, Colorado Springs, Colorado 80901. 1984- .

FEDERAL TAX COORDINATOR SECOND. Research Institute of America, Incorporated, 90 Fifth Avenue, New York, New York 10011. 1955- .

FEDERAL TAX DEDUCTIONS. Brian E. Comerford and Mason Sachs. Research Institute of America, Incorporated, One Penn Plaza, New York, New York 10119. 1983- .

FEDERAL TAX GUIDE. Commerce Clearing House, Incorporated, 4025 West Peterson Avenue, Chicago, Illinois 60646. 1917- .

FEDERAL TAX GUIDE. Jared Kaplan and John B. Truskowski. Callaghan and Company, 155 Pfingsten Road, Deerfield, Illinois 60015. 1987.

FEDERAL TAXATION OF INCOME, ESTATES, AND GIFTS. Boris I. Bittker. Research Institute of America, Incorporated, One Penn Plaza, New York, New York 10119. 1981- .

FEDERAL TAXATION OF PARTNERSHIPS AND PARTNERS. William S. McKee, William F. Nelson and Robert L. Whitmore. Research Institute of America, Incorporated, One Penn Plaza, New York, New York 10119. 1977- .

FEDERAL TAXATION OF REAL ESTATE. Allan J. Samansky and James C. Smith. Law Journal-Seminars Press, Incorporated, 111 Eighth Avenue, New York, New York 10011. 1985- .

FEDERAL TAXES. Prentice-Hall, Incorporated, 113 Sylvan Avenue, Englewood Cliffs, New Jersey 07632. 1919- .

FEDERAL TAXES AFFECTING REAL ESTATE. Ivan Faggen, et al. Matthew Bender and Company, Incorporated, 11 Penn Plaza, New York, New York 10001. 1981- .

FRINGE BENEFITS TAX GUIDE. Commerce Clearing House, Incorporated, 4025 West Peterson Avenue, Chicago, Illinois 60646. 1985- .

INCOME TAX TECHNIQUES. Alan J. Aronson. Matthew Bender and Company, Incorporated, 11 Penn Plaza, New York, New York 10001. 1965- .

INCOME TAXATION OF FOREIGN RELATED TRANSACTIONS. Rufus V. Rhoades. Matthew Bender and Company, Incorporated, 11 Penn Plaza, New York, New York 10001. 1971- .

INCOME TAXATION OF NATURAL RESOURCES. Charles W. Russell and Robert W. Bowhay. Prentice-Hall, Incorporated, 113 Sylvan Avenue, Englewood Cliffs, New Jersey 07632. 1986- .

INFORMATION RETURNS GUIDE. Commerce Clearing House, Incorporated, 4025 West Peterson Avenue, Chicago, Illinois 60646. 1987.

IRA COMPLIANCE MANUAL. Prentice-Hall, Incorporated, 113 Sylvan Avenue, Englewood Cliffs, New Jersey 07632. 1982- .

IRS LETTER RULINGS. Commerce Clearing House, Incorporated, 4025 West Peterson Avenue, Chicago, Illinois 60646. 1977- .

MERTENS CODE COMMENTARY. James J. Doheny. Callaghan and Company, 155 Pfingsten Road, Deerfield, Illinois 60015. 1981- .

MERTENS LAW OF FEDERAL TAXATION. James J. Doheny. Callaghan and Company, 155 Pfingsten Road, Deerfield, Illinois 60015. 1954- .

MULTISTATE PART-YEAR/NONRESIDENT RETURN GUIDE. Commerce Clearing House, Incorporated, 4025 West Peterson Avenue, Chicago, Illinois 60646. 1989.

PARTNERSHIP TAXATION. Third Edition. John S. Pennel and Philip F. Postlewaite. Shepard's/McGraw-Hill, P.O. Box 1235, Colorado Springs, Colorado 80901. 1981- .

PAYROLL MANAGEMENT GUIDE. Commerce Clearing House, Incorporated, 4025 West Peterson Avenue, Chicago, Illinois 60646. 1943- .

A PRACTICAL GUIDE TO THE ORIGINAL ISSUE DISCOUNT REGULATIONS. David C. Garlock. Prentice-Hall, Incorporated, 113 Sylvan Avenue, Englewood Cliffs, New Jersey 07632. 1987.

REDUCING PERSONAL INCOME TAXES: A GUIDE TO DEDUCTIONS AND CREDITS. John E. Davidian and Jacob L. Todres. Law Journal Seminars-Press, Incorporated, 111 Eighth Avenue, Suite 900, New York, New York 10011. 1988- .

STANDARD FEDERAL TAX REPORTS. Commerce Clearing House, Incorporated, 4025 West Peterson Avenue, Chicago, Illinois 60646. 1913- .

START-UP EXPENSES. George B. Javaras, Todd F. Maynes and Kent F. Wisner. Commerce Clearing House, Incorporated, 4025 West Peterson Avenue, Chicago, Illinois 60646. 1991.

TAX GUIDE. Research Institute of America, Incorporated, 90 Fifth Avenue, New York, New York 10011. 1966- .

TAX IDEAS. Research Institute of America, Incorporated, 910 Sylvan Avenue, Englewood Cliffs, New Jersey 07632. 1990.

TAX MANAGEMENT-COMPENSATION PLANNING SERIES. Bureau of National Affairs, 1231 Twenty-fifth Street, Northwest, Washington, D.C. 20037. 1982- .

TAX MANAGEMENT-ESTATES, GIFTS AND TRUSTS SERIES. Bureau of National Affairs, 1231 Twenty-fifth Street, Northwest, Washington, D.C. 20037. 1967- .

TAX MANAGEMENT-FOREIGN INCOME SERVICES. Bureau of National Affairs, 1231 Twenty-fifth Street, Northwest, Washington, D.C. 20037. 1964- .

TAX MANAGEMENT-PRIMARY SOURCES SERIES: IV. Bureau of National Affairs, 1231 Twenty-fifth Street, Northwest, Washington, D.C. 20037. 1982.

TAX MANAGEMENT-UNITED STATES INCOME SERIES. Bureau of National Affairs, 1231 Twenty-fifth Street, Northwest, Washington, D.C. 20037. 1959- .

TAX PLANNING FOR THE ALTERNATIVE MINIMUM TAX. Lance W. Rook. Matthew Bender and Company, Incorporated, 11 Penn Plaza, New York, New York 10001. 1989- .

TAX SERVICE FOR EMPLOYEE RETIREMENT PLANS. Mark A. Stephens, Limited, 10018 Colesville Road, Silver Spring, Maryland 20901. 1982- .

TAX STRATEGIES FOR SEPARATION AND DIVORCE. William J. Brown. Shepard's/McGraw-Hill, P.O. Box 1235, Colorado Springs, Colorado 80901. 1984- .

TAXATION OF FINANCIAL INSTITUTIONS. Henry W. Schmidt. Matthew Bender and Company, Incorporated, 11 Penn Plaza, New York, New York 10001. 1983- .

TAXATION OF INTELLECTUAL PROPERTY. Marvin Petry. Matthew Bender and Company, Incorporated, 11 Penn Plaza, New York, New York 10001. 1985- .

TAXATION OF PASSIVE ACTIVITIES. Neil Kimmelfield. Prentice-Hall, Incorporated, 113 Sylvan Avenue, Englewood Cliffs, New Jersey 07632. 1989- .

TAXATION OF SECURITIES TRANSACTIONS. Martin L. Fried. Matthew Bender and Company, Incorporated, 11 Penn Plaza, New York, New York 10001. 1971- .

UNITED STATES TAXATION OF INTERNATIONAL OPERATIONS. Prentice-Hall, Incorporated, 113 Sylvan Avenue, Englewood Cliffs, New Jersey 07632. 1975- .

WEST'S FEDERAL TAX GUIDE. William H. Hoffman and Dale Bandy. West Publishing Company, P.O. Box 64526, 50 West Kellogg Boulevard, St. Paul, Minnesota 55164-0526. 1984- .

HANDBOOKS, MANUALS, FORMBOOKS

BENDER'S PAYROLL TAX GUIDE. Matthew Bender and Company Incorporated, 11 Penn Plaza, New York, New York 10001. Annual.

CHILDREN AND TAXES: A PARENTS' GUIDE. Commerce Clearing House, Incorporated, 4025 West Peterson Avenue, Chicago, Illinois 60646. 1990.

CORPORATION-PARTNERSHIP-FIDUCIARY FILLED-IN TAX RETURN FORMS. Commerce Clearing House, Incorporated, 4025 West Peterson Avenue, Chicago, Illinois 60646. Annual.

DEPRECIATION AND INVESTMENT CREDIT MANUAL: EXPLAINING ALL OF THE LATEST ACRS RULES. Martin E. Holbrook and Lawrence H. MacKirdy. Prentice-Hall, Incorporated, 113 Sylvan Avenue, Englewood Cliffs, New Jersey 07632. 1985.

EDUCATOR'S INCOME TAX GUIDE: SPECIALIZING IN EDUCATIONAL DEDUCTIONS. Teachers Tax Service, P.O. Box 8809, Chico, California 95927. 1991.

ERNST AND YOUNG'S TAX SAVING STRATEGIES, 1990-1991. Peter W. Bernstein, Editor. John Wiley and Sons, Incorporated, 605 Third Avenue, New York, New York 10158. 1990.

FARM INCOME TAX MANUAL. Charles Davenport and John C. O'Byrne. Michie Company, P.O. Box 7587, Charlottesville, Virginia 22906. 1989.

FEDERAL INCOME, GIFT AND ESTATE TAXATION: DESK EDITION. Alan Prigal. Matthew Bender and Company, Incorporated, 11 Penn Plaza, New York, New York 10001. 1972. (Periodic Supplements).

FEDERAL TAX COMPLIANCE MANUAL. Commerce Clearing House, Incorporated, 4025 West Peterson Avenue, Chicago, Illinois 60646. 1985. (Periodic Supplements).

FEDERAL TAX FORMS. Commerce Clearing House, Incorporated, 4025 West Peterson Avenue, Chicago, Illinois 60646. 1987- .

FEDERAL TAX GUIDEBOOK. Matthew Bender and Company, Incorporated, 11 Penn Plaza, New York, New York 10001. 1986- .

FEDERAL TAX MANUAL. Commerce Clearing House, Incorporated, 4025 West Peterson Avenue, Chicago, Illinois 60646. Annual.

INDIVIDUALS' FILLED-IN TAX RETURN FORMS. Commerce Clearing House, Incorporated, 4025 West Peterson Avenue, Chicago, Illinois 60646. Annual.

INTERNATIONAL TAX GUIDE: U.S. INCOME TAXATION. John F. Cooper and I. Richard Gershon. Callaghan and Company, 155 Pfingsten Road, Deerfield, Illinois 60015. 1991.

KIPLINGER'S SURE WAYS TO CUT YOUR TAXES. Kevin McCormally. Kiplinger Books, 1729 H Street, Northwest, Washington, D.C. 20006. 1991. Revised for 1992.

MASTER FEDERAL TAX MANUAL. Research Institute of America, Incorporated, 90 Fifth Avenue, New York, New York 10001. Annual.

THE MCGRAW-HILL PERSONAL TAX ADVISOR. Second Edition. Cliff Roberson. McGraw-Hill Publishing Company, 1221 Avenue of the Americas, New York, New York 10020. 1992.

THE PROFESSIONAL'S TAX DESK MANUAL. Executive Reports Corporation, Subsidiary of Prentice-Hall, Incorporated, 113 Sylvan Avenue, Englewood Cliffs, New Jersey 07632. 1981. (Periodic Supplements).

A STUDENT'S GUIDE TO THE INTERNAL REVENUE CODE. Richard Gershon. Matthew Bender and Company, Incorporated, 11 Penn Plaza, New York, New York 10001. 1988.

TAX ANALYSIS AND FORMS: LEGAL CHECKLISTS. Jere D. McGaffey. Callaghan and Company, 155 Pfingsten Road, Deerfield, Illinois 60015. 1977- .

TAX MANAGEMENT. IRS FORMS. Tax Management, Incorporated, 1231 Twenty-fifth Street, Northwest, Washington, D.C. 20037. 1988- .

THE TAX PRACTICE DESKBOOK. Harrop A. Freeman and Norman D. Freeman. Research Institute of America, Incorporated, One Penn Plaza, New York, New York 10119. 1973 (Annual Supplements).

TEXTBOOKS AND GENERAL WORKS

ACCOUNTING FOR INCOME TAXES: A REVIEW OF ALTERNATIVES. Dennis R. Beresford. Financial Accounting Standards Board, High Ridge Park, P.O. Box 3821, Stamford, Connecticut 06905. 1983.

ACCOUNTING FOR INCOME TAXES: ANALYSIS AND COMMENTARY. Arthur Siegel and others. Research Institute of America, Incorporated, One Penn Plaza, New York, New York 10119. 1988.

ALTERNATIVE MINIMUM TAX. Stewart S. Karlinsky. Research Institute of America, Incorporated, 910 Sylvan Avenue, Englewood Cliffs, New Jersey 07632. 1991.

BASIC FEDERAL INCOME TAXATION. Fourth Edition. William D. Andrews. Little, Brown, and Company, 34 Beacon Street, Boston, Massachusetts 02108. 1991.

BUSINESS LAW AND TAXES: A DESK GUIDE. Roger L. Miller and Kenneth A. Burns. John Wiley and Sons, Incorporated, 605 Third Avenue, New York, New York 10158. 1984.

BUSINESS TAX DEDUCTION MASTER GUIDE: STRATEGIES FOR BUSINESS AND PROFESSIONAL PEOPLE. W. Murray Bradford and Glen B. Davis. Prentice-Hall, Incorporated, 113 Sylvan Avenue, Englewood Cliffs, New Jersey 07632. 1985.

CASES AND MATERIALS ON FUNDAMENTALS OF FEDERAL INCOME TAXATION. Seventh Edition. James J. Freeland, Stephen A. Lind and Richard B. Stephens. Foundation Press, 615 Merrick Avenue, Westbury, New York 11590. 1991.

CASES, TEXT, AND PROBLEMS ON FEDERAL INCOME TAXATION. Second Edition. Alan Gunn and Larry D. Ward. West Publishing Company, 50 West Kellogg Boulevard, St. Paul, Minnesota 55164. 1988.

COMPENSATING UNITED STATES EMPLOYEES ABROAD. Charles F. O'Connell. Matthew Bender and Company, Incorporated, 11 Penn Plaza, New York, New York 10001. 1988.

CONGRESS AND THE INCOME TAX. Barber B. Conable, Jr. and A.L. Singleton. University of Oklahoma Press, 105 Asp Avenue, Norman, Oklahoma 73019. 1989.

DEALING WITH THE NEW ACRS REGULATIONS. Mark L. Yecies, Chairman. Harcourt Brace Jovanovich, Incorporated, 6277 Sea Harbor Drive, Orlando, Florida 32821. 1984.

DIVORCE AND SEPARATION TAXATION UNDER THE 1984 TAX LAW. Carlyn S. McCaffery. Harcourt Brace Jovanovich, Incorporated, 6277 Sea Harbor Drive, Orlando, Florida 32821. 1984.

DO TAXES MATTER?: THE IMPACT OF THE TAX REFORM ACT OF 1986. Joel Slemrod, Editor. MIT Press, 55 Hayward Street, Cambridge, Massachusetts 02142. 1990.

EMPLOYEE BENEFITS AFTER THE TAX ACT OF 1984. Leon E. Irish and Thomas D. Terry, Chairmen. Harcourt Brace Jovanovich, Incorporated, 6277 Sea Harbor Drive, Orlando, Florida 32821. 1984.

ESOP: THE EMPLOYEE STOCK OWNERSHIP PLAN. Second Edition. Harry F. Weyher and Hiram Knott. Commerce Clearing House, Incorporated, 4025 West Peterson Avenue, Chicago, Illinois 60646. 1985.

ESSENTIALS OF TAXATION. Ray Sommerfeld. Addison-Wesley Publishing Company, Incorporated, Route 128, Reading, Massachusetts 01867. 1990.

EXECUTIVE COMPENSATION AND TAXATION COORDINATOR. Research Institute of America, Incorporated, 90 Fifth Avenue, New York, New York 10011. 1986.

FEDERAL INCOME TAX: A STUDENT'S GUIDE TO THE INTERNAL REVENUE CODE. Douglas A. Kahn. Foundation Press, 615 Merrick Avenue, Westbury, New York 11590. 1990.

THE FEDERAL INCOME TAX: ITS SOURCES AND APPLICATIONS. Clarence F. McCarthy and D. Larry Crumbley. Prentice-Hall, Incorporated, 113 Sylvan Avenue, Englewood Cliffs, New Jersey 07632. 1984.

FEDERAL INCOME TAX PROJECT: TENTATIVE DRAFT. American Law Institute, 4025 Chestnut Street, Philadelphia, Pennsylvania 19104. 1983.

FEDERAL INCOME TAXATION. Third Edition. David M. Hudson and Stephen A. Lind. West Publishing Company, P.O. Box 64526, 50 West Kellogg Boulevard, St. Paul, Minnesota 55164-0526. 1990.

FEDERAL INCOME TAXATION. Seventh Edition. Boris I. Bittker, William A. Klein and Lawrence M. Stone. Little, Brown, and Company, 34 Beacon Street, Boston, Massachusetts 02108. 1987.

FEDERAL INCOME TAXATION: A CONCEPTUAL APPROACH. Stephen B. Cohen. Foundation Press, 615 Merrick Avenue, Westbury, New York 11590. 1989.

FEDERAL INCOME TAXATION: A LAW STUDENT'S GUIDE TO THE LEADING CASES AND CONCEPTS. Sixth Edition. Marvin A. Chirelstein. Foundation Press, 615 Merrick Avenue, Westbury, New York 11590. 1991.

FEDERAL INCOME TAXATION OF BUSINESS ENTERPRISES. Second Edition. Bernard Wolfman. Little, Brown, and Company, 34 Beacon Street, Boston, Massachusetts 02108. 1982.

FEDERAL INCOME TAXATION OF CORPORATIONS AND SHAREHOLDERS. Fifth Edition. Boris I. Bittker and James S. Eustice. Research Institute of America, Incorporated, One Penn Plaza, New York, New York 10119. 1987.

FEDERAL INCOME TAXATION OF ESTATES AND BENEFICIARIES. M. Carr Ferguson and James F. Freeland. Little, Brown, and Company, 34 Beacon Street, Boston, Massachusetts 02108. 1970. (1984 Supplement).

FEDERAL INCOME TAXATION OF INDIVIDUALS. Fourth Edition. Patricia Ann Metzer. American Law Institute, 4025 Chestnut Street, Philadelphia, Pennsylvania 19104. 1984.

FEDERAL INCOME TAXATION OF INDIVIDUALS AND BASIC CONCEPTS IN THE TAXATION OF ALL ENTITIES. Daniel Q. Posin, Jr. West Publishing Company, P.O. Box 64526, 50 West Kellogg Boulevard, St. Paul, Minnesota 55164-0526. 1983. (Hornbook).

FEDERAL INCOME TAXATION OF INDIVIDUALS IN A NUTSHELL. Fourth Edition. John K McNulty. West Publishing Company, P.O. Box 64526, 50 West Kellogg Boulevard, St. Paul, Minnesota 55164-0526. 1988.

FEDERAL INCOME TAXATION OF PARTNERSHIPS AND CORPORATIONS. Paul R. McDaniel. Foundation Press, 615 Merrick Avenue, Westbury, New York 11590. 1991.

FEDERAL INCOME TAXATION: PRINCIPLES AND POLICIES. Second Edition. Michael J. Graetz. Foundation Press, 615 Merrick Avenue, Westbury, New York 11590. 1988.

FEDERAL INCOME TAXES OF DECEDENTS AND ESTATES. Commerce Clearing House, Incorporated, 4025 West Peterson Avenue, Chicago, Illinois 60646. 1985.

FEDERAL TAX ACCOUNTING. Stephen F. Gertzman. Research Institute of America, Incorporated, One Penn Plaza, New York, New York 10119. 1988.

FEDERAL TAX DEDUCTIONS. Brian E. Comerford and Mason J. Sachs. Research Institute of America, Incorporated, One Penn Plaza, New York, New York 10119. 1990. (Periodic Supplements).

FEDERAL TAX ELECTIONS. Michael B. Lang and Colleen A. Khoury. Research Institute of America, Incorporated, One Penn Plaza, New York, New York 10119. 1991.

FEDERAL TAXATION OF INCOME, ESTATES, AND GIFTS. Second Edition. Boris I. Bittker and Lawrence Lokken. Research Institute of America, Incorporated, One Penn Plaza, New York, New York 10119. 1989- . (Periodic Supplements).

FEDERAL TAXATION OF INSURANCE COMPANIES. Dennis P. Van Mieghem and Keith A. Tucker. Prentice-Hall, Incorporated, 113 Sylvan Avenue, Englewood Cliffs, New Jersey 07632. 1987.

FEDERAL TAXATION OF INTELLECTUAL PROPERTY TRANSFERS. Joseph E. Olson. Law Journal-Seminars Press, Incorporated, 111 Eighth Avenue, New York, New York 10011. 1986.

FEDERAL TAXATION OF INTERNATIONAL TRANSACTIONS: PRINCIPLES, PLANNING AND POLICY. Richard L. Kaplan. West Publishing Company, 50 West Kellogg Boulevard, St. Paul, Minnesota 55164. 1988.

FEDERAL TAXATION OF PARTNERS AND PARTNERSHIPS. G. Fred Streuling, James H. Boyd, and Kenneth H. Heller. Prentice-Hall, Incorporated, 113 Sylvan Avenue, Englewood Cliffs, New Jersey 07632. 1986.

FEDERAL TAXATION OF TRUSTS, GRANTORS AND BENEFICIARIES: INCOME, ESTATE, GIFT TAXATION. John L. Peschel and Edward D. Spurgeon. Research Institute of America, Incorporated, One Penn Plaza, New York, New York 10119. 1978. (Periodic Supplements).

FINAL REPORT OF THE WORLDWIDE UNITARY TAXATION WORKING GROUP: CHAIRMAN'S REPORT AND SUPPLEMENTAL VIEWS. United States Department of the Treasury, Worldwide Unitary Taxation Working Group. Superintendent of Documents, United States Government Printing Office, Washington, D.C. 20402. 1984.

FINANCIAL ACCOUNTING AND REPORTING OF INCOME TAXES. American Institute of Certified Public Accountants, 1211 Avenue of the Americas, New York, New York 10036-8755. 1982.

FUNDAMENTALS OF FEDERAL INCOME TAXATION. Boris I. Bittker. Research Institute of America, Incorporated, One Penn Plaza, New York, New York 10119. 1983.

FUNDAMENTALS OF INTERNATIONAL TAXATION: U.S. TAXATION OF FOREIGN INCOME AND FOREIGN TAXPAYERS. Boris I. Bittker and Lawrence Lokken. Research Institute of America, Incorporated, One Penn Plaza, New York, New York 10119. 1991.

HIS, HERS, OR THEIRS? FEDERAL INCOME TAXATION OF DIVORCE, PROPERTY SETTLEMENTS: EXISTING LAW, ANALYSIS AND CRITIQUE, PLANNING AND DRAFTING, RESEARCH AIDS. Commerce Clearing House, Incorporated, 4025 West Peterson Avenue, Chicago, Illinois 60646. 1983.

THE IMPACT OF TAXES ON UNITED STATES CITIZENS WORKING ABROAD. Ernest R. Larkins. UMI Research Press, Division of University Microfilms International, 300 North Zeeb Road, Ann Arbor, Michigan 48106-1346. 1983.

INCOME TAX FUNDAMENTALS. Gerald E. Whittenberg and Ray Whittington. West Publishing Company, P.O. Box 64526, 50 West Kellogg Boulevard, St. Paul, Minnesota 55164-0526. 1991.

INCOME TAXATION: ACCOUNTING METHODS AND PERIODS. George G. Bauernfeind. Shepard's/McGraw-Hill, P.O. Box 1235, Colorado Springs, Colorado 80901. 1983.

INCOME TAXATION AND INTERNATIONAL MOBILITY. Jagdish N. Bhagwati and John Douglas Wilson, Editors. MIT Press, 55 Hayward Street, Cambridge, Massachusetts 02142. 1989.

INCOME TAXATION OF ESTATES AND TRUSTS. Arthur D. Sederbaum, Chairman. Practising Law Institute, 810 Seventh Avenue, New York, New York 10019. 1990.

THE INTERNATIONAL INCOME TAX RULES OF THE UNITED STATES. Michael J. McIntyre. Butterworth Legal Publishers, 90 Stiles Road, Salem, New Hampshire 03079. 1989.

INTERNATIONAL TAXATION IN A NUTSHELL. Richard L. Doernberg. West Publishing Company, 50 West Kellogg Boulevard, St. Paul, Minnesota 55164. 1989.

INTERNATIONAL TAXATION: U.S. TAXATION OF FOREIGN TAXPAYERS AND FOREIGN INCOME. Joseph Isenberg. Little, Brown and Company, 34 Beacon Street, Boston, Massachusetts 02108. 1990.

INTRODUCTION TO FEDERAL INCOME TAXATION. William D. Popkin. Matthew Bender and Company, Incorporated, 11 Penn Plaza, New York, New York 10001. 1987.

INTRODUCTION TO UNITED STATES INTERNATIONAL TAXATION. Third Revised Edition. Paul R. McDaniel and Hugh J. Ault. Kluwer Law Book Publishers, Incorporated, 36 West Forty-fourth Street, New York, New York 10036. 1989.

LIMITS AND PROBLEMS OF TAXATION. Finn R. Forsund and Seppo Honkapohja, Editors. St. Martin's Press, Incorporated, 175 Fifth Avenue, New York, New York 10010. 1985.

THE LOGIC OF TAX: FEDERAL INCOME TAX THEORY AND POLICY. Joseph M. Dodge. West Publishing Company, 50 West Kellogg Boulevard, St. Paul, Minnesota 55164. 1989.

THE 1987 RIA TAX GUIDE. Research Institute of America, Incorporated, 90 Fifth Avenue, New York, New York 10011. 1987.

1986 FEDERAL TAX COURSE. Commerce Clearing House, Incorporated, 4025 West Peterson Avenue, Chicago, Illinois 60646. 1985.

1986 TAX GUIDE FOR COLLEGE TEACHERS AND OTHER COLLEGE PERSONNEL. Allen Bernstein. Academic Information Service, Incorporated, 1344 Ingraham Street, Northwest, P.O. Box 6296, Washington, D.C. 20015. 1985.

1986 UNITED STATES MASTER TAX GUIDE. Commerce Clearing House, Incorporated, 4025 West Peterson Avenue, Chicago, Illinois 60646. 1985.

NON-QUALIFIED DEFERRED COMPENSATION PLANS. Gerald P. Wolf, Chairman. Practising Law Institute, 810 Seventh Avenue, New York, New York 10019. 1985.

THE OPPORTUNITIES FOR OWNERS OF CLOSELY HELD COMPANIES. Marvin J. Dickman. Boardroom Books, 330 West Forty-Second Street, New York, New York 10036. 1985.

OPTIMAL INCOME TAX AND REDISTRIBUTION. Matti Tuomala. Oxford University Press, 200 Madison Avenue, New York, New York 10016. 1990.

OVERVIEW OF THE FEDERAL TAX SYSTEM: INCLUDING DATA ON TAX AND REVENUE MEASURES WITHIN THE JURISDICTION OF THE COMMITTEE ON WAYS AND MEANS, UNITED STATES HOUSE OF REPRESENTATIVES. Superintendent of Documents, United States Government Printing Office, Washington, D.C. 20402. 1990.

PARTNERSHIP TAXATION. Third Edition. Arthur B. Willis. Shepard's/McGraw-Hill, P.O. Box 1235, Colorado Springs, Colorado 80901. 1989. (Periodic Supplements).

PARTNERSHIP TAXATION: AN ADVANCED TAX PROGRAM. Hershel M. Bloom and David W. Mills, Co-chairmen. Practising Law Institute, 810 Seventh Avenue, New York, New York 10019. 1985.

PASSIVE ACTIVITY LOSS RULES: ANALYSIS, COMPLIANCE, PLANNING. Michael N. Jennings and Daniel R. Bolar. Research Institute of America, Incorporated, One Penn Plaza, New York, New York 10119. 1989.

PLANNING AND WORKING WITH THE ALTERNATIVE MINIMUM TAX. Harold S. Peckron. Commerce Clearing House, Incorporated, 4025 West Peterson Avenue, Chicago, Illinois 60646. 1989.

PRACTICAL GUIDE TO THE TAX ACT OF 1984. Law and Business, Harcourt Brace Jovanovich, Incorporated, 6277 Sea Harbor Drive, Orlando, Florida 32821. 1985.

PRINCIPLES OF FEDERAL INCOME TAXATION. Dennis J. Gaffney and Donald H. Skadden. McGraw-Hill Book Company, 1221 Avenue of the Americas, New York, New York 10020. 1984.

PROBLEMS AND MATERIALS IN FEDERAL INCOME TAXATION. Second Edition. Sanford M. Guerin and Philip F. Postlewaite. Little, Brown and Company, 34 Beacon Street, Boston, Massachusetts 02108. 1988.

QUESTIONS AND ANSWERS ON THE PENSION AND PROFIT SHARING PROVISIONS OF THE NEW TAX LAW: WITH AN EXPLANATION OF THE RETIREMENT PLAN PROVISIONS OF TEFRA. Prentice-Hall, Incorporated, 113 Sylvan Avenue, Englewood Cliffs, New Jersey 07632. 1983.

READINGS IN INCOME TAXATION. Third Edition. Donald P. Vernon. The American College, 270 Bryn Mawr Avenue, Bryn Mawr, Pennsylvania 19010. 1984.

A REVIEW OF ESSENTIALS OF TAXATION. Ray Sommerfeld. Addison-Wesley Publishing Company, Incorporated, Route 128, Reading, Massachusetts 01867. 1990.

THE RIA COMPLETE ANALYSIS OF THE 1986 TAX REFORM ACT. Research Institute of America, Incorporated, 90 Fifth Avenue, New York, New York 10011. 1986.

RIA FEDERAL TAX COURSE: INDIVIDUAL INCOME TAX. Research Institute of America. Richard D. Irwin, Incorporated, 1818 Ridge Road, Homewood, Illinois 60430. 1986.

SHIFTING THE BURDEN: THE STRUGGLE OVER GROWTH AND CORPORATE TAXATION. Cathie J. Martin. University of Chicago Press, 5801 Ellis Avenue, Chicago, Illinois 60637. 1991.

STANLEY AND KILCULLEN'S FEDERAL INCOME TAX LAW. Stephen R. Leiberg, et al. Research Institute of America, Incorporated, One Penn Plaza, New York, New York 10119. 1991.

TAX ACCOUNTING PERIODS, METHODS, AND RELATED TIMING ISSUES. Richard A. Westin and Kermit O. Keeling. Callaghan and Company, 155 Pfingsten Road, Deerfield, Illinois 60015. 1991.

TAX ASPECTS OF DIVORCE AND SEPARATION. Robert S. Taft. Law Journal-Seminars Press, Incorporated, 111 Eighth Avenue, New York, New York 10011. 1984.

TAX ASPECTS OF HIGH TECHNOLOGY OPERATIONS. Deloitte, Haskins and Sells. John Wiley and Sons, Incorporated, 605 Third Avenue, New York, New York 10158. 1985.

TAX ASPECTS OF MARITAL DISSOLUTION. Harold G. Wren, Leon Gabinst and David Calyton Carrad. Callaghan and Company, 155 Pfingsten Road, Deerfield, Illinois 60015. 1990.

TAX CONSEQUENCES OF MARRIAGE, SEPARATION AND DIVORCE. American Law Institute-American Bar Association, Committee on Continuing Professional Education, 4025 Chestnut Street, Philadelphia, Pennsylvania 19104. 1986. (1987 Supplement).

THE TAX ON ACCUMULATED EARNINGS. Commerce Clearing House, Incorporated, 4025 West Peterson Avenue, Chicago, Illinois 60646. 1986.

THE TAX REFORM ACT OF 1986: A SELECTIVE ANALYSIS. James S. Eustice, Joel D. Kuntz, Charles S. Lewis III and Thomas P. Deering. Research Institute of America, Incorporated, One Penn Plaza, New York, New York 10119. 1986.

THE TAX REFORM ACT OF 1986: ANALYSIS AND COMMENTARY. James S. Eustice and others. Research Institute of America, Incorporated, One Penn Plaza, New York, New York 10119. 1987.

TAX REFORM AND THE COST OF CAPITAL. Dale W. Jorgenson and Kun-Young Yun. Oxford University Press, 200 Madison Avenue, New York, New York 10016. 1991.

TAX REFORM: THE RICH AND THE POOR. Second Edition. Joseph A. Pechman. Brookings Institution, 1775 Massachusetts Avenue, Washington, D.C. 20036. 1989.

TAX REFORM UPDATE INCLUDING TECHNICAL CORRECTIONS. James P. Fuller. Practising Law Institute, 810 Seventh Avenue, New York, New York 10019. 1987.

TAXATION IN THE GLOBAL ECONOMY. Assaf Razin and Joel Slemrod. University of Chicago Press, 5801 Ellis Avenue, Chicago, Illinois 60637. 1990.

THE TAXATION OF CAPITAL INCOME. Alan J. Auerbach. Harvard University Press, 79 Garden Street, Cambridge, Massachusetts 02138. 1983.

THE TAXATION OF INCOME FROM CAPITAL: A COMPARATIVE STUDY OF THE UNITED STATES, THE UNITED KINGDOM, SWEDEN AND WEST GERMANY. Mervyn A. King and Don Fullerton, Editors. Books on Demand, 300 North Zeeb Road, Ann Arbor, Michigan 48106-1346. 1984.

TAXATION OF INDIVIDUAL INCOME. J. Martin Burke and Michael K. Friel. Matthew Bender and Company, Incorporated, 11 Penn Plaza, New York, New York 10001. 1988.

TAXATION OF RESIDENCE TRANSACTIONS. Janus Edward Maule. John Wiley and Sons, Incorporated, 605 Third Avenue, New York, New York 10158. 1985.

TAXATION OF SECURITIES COMMODITIES AND OPTIONS. Andrea S. Kramer. John Wiley and Sons, Incorporated, 605 Third Avenue, New York, New York 10158. 1986.

TAXES IN PARADISE: DEVELOPING BASIC INCOME TAX CONCEPTS. Richard L. Haight. Fred B. Rothman and Company, 10368 West Centennial Road, Littleton, Colorado 80127. 1990.

TAXING CHOICES: THE POLITICS OF TAX REFORM. Timothy J. Conlan, Margaret T. Wrightson and David R. Beam. Congressional Quarterly Books, 1414 Twenty-second Street, Northwest, Washington D.C. 20037. 1990.

TRAVEL AND ENTERTAINMENT DEDUCTION GUIDE: WITH ANSWERS TO 201 VITAL QUESTIONS ON HOW TO NAIL BIG CASH SAVINGS UNDER THE ALL-NEW T AND E SETUP. Executive Reports Corporation, Subsidiary of Prentice-Hall, Incorporated, 113 Sylvan Avenue, Englewood Cliffs, New Jersey 07632. 1985.

TRAVEL AND ENTERTAINMENT DEDUCTIONS AND BUSINESS CAR WRITEOFFS. Robert Trinz. Prentice-Hall, Incorporated, 113 Sylvan Avenue, Englewood Cliffs, New Jersey 07632. 1989.

UNDERSTANDING THE FEDERAL INCOME TAX: A LAWYER'S GUIDE TO THE CODE AND ITS PROVISIONS. Fred W. Peel, Jr. American Bar Association, Section of General Practice, 750 North Lake Shore Drive, Chicago, Illinois 60611. 1988.

UNTANGLING THE INCOME TAX. David F. Bradford. Harvard University Press, 79 Garden Street, Cambridge, Massachusetts 02138. 1986.

WILEY'S FEDERAL INCOME TAXATION. Dennis J. Gaffney, et al. John Wiley and Sons, Incorporated, 605 Third Avenue, New York, New York 10158. 1987.

DIGESTS, INDEXES, ABSTRACTS, CITATORS

FEDERAL TAX ARTICLES: INCOME, ESTATE, GIFT, EXCISE, EMPLOYMENT TAXES. Commerce Clearing House, Incorporated, 4025 West Peterson Avenue, Chicago, Illinois 60646. 1969- .

FEDERAL TAX VALUATION DIGEST: BUSINESS INTERESTS AND BUSINESS ENTERPRISES. John A. Bishop and Arthur H. Rosenbloom. Research Institute of America, Incorporated, One Penn Plaza, New York, New York 10119. 1979- .

FEDERAL TAXES CITATOR. Prentice-Hall, Incorporated, 113 Sylvan Avenue, Englewood Cliffs, New Jersey 07632. 1943- .

INDEX TO FEDERAL TAX ARTICLES. Gersham Goldstein, Editor. Research Institute of America, Incorporated, One Penn Plaza, New York, New York 10119. 1975- .

THE RANDOM HOUSE BOOK OF MORTGAGE AND TAX-SAVINGS TABLES. Eric Kaplan. Random House, Incorporated, 201 East Fiftieth Street, New York, New York 10022. 1990.

SHEPARD'S FEDERAL TAX CITATIONS. Shepard's/McGraw-Hill, P.O. Box 1235, Colorado Springs, Colorado 80901. 1981- .

SHEPARD'S FEDERAL TAX LOCATOR: COMPLETE INDEX TO ALL THE CURRENT SOURCES OF LAW RELATING TO FEDERAL TAXATION. Shepard's/McGraw-Hill, P.O. Box 1235, Colorado Springs, Colorado 80901. 1974- .

ANNUALS AND SURVEYS

FEDERAL TAX COURSE. Commerce Clearing House, Incorporated, 4025 West Peterson Avenue, Chicago, Illinois 60646. Annual.

FEDERAL TAX COURSE. Prentice-Hall, Incorporated, 113 Sylvan Avenue, Englewood Cliffs, New Jersey 07632. Annual.

FEDERAL TAX HANDBOOK. Prentice-Hall, Incorporated, 113 Sylvan Avenue, Englewood Cliffs, New Jersey 07632. Annual.

PROCEEDINGS OF THE INSTITUTE ON FEDERAL TAXATION, NEW YORK UNIVERSITY. Matthew Bender and Company, Incorporated, 11 Penn Plaza, New York, New York 10001. Annual.

THE RIA TAX GUIDE. Research Institute of America, Incorporated, 90 Fifth Avenue, New York, New York 10011. Annual.

THE TAX YEAR IN REVIEW. Research Institute of America, Incorporated, 90 Fifth Avenue, New York, New York 10011. Annual.

UNITED STATES MASTER TAX GUIDE. Commerce Clearing House, Incorporated, 4025 West Peterson Avenue, Chicago, Illinois 60646. Annual.

WEST'S FEDERAL TAXATION. West Publishing Company, P.O. Box 64526, 50 West Kellogg Boulevard, St. Paul, Minnesota 55164-0526. Annual.

LAW REVIEWS AND PERIODICALS

AKRON TAX JOURNAL. University of Akron, School of Law, Akron, Ohio 44325. Annually.

AMERICAN JOURNAL OF TAX POLICY. American College of Tax Counsel, University of Alabama School of Law, P.O. Box 1435, University, Alabama 35486. Annual.

BANK TAX REPORT. Research Institute of America, Incorporated, One Penn Plaza, New York, New York 10119. Monthly.

EMPLOYEE BENEFIT PLAN REVIEW. Charles B. Spenser and Associates, Incorporated, 222 West Adams, Chicago, Illinois 60606. Monthly.

ESTATE PLANNING. Research Institute of America, Incorporated, One Penn Plaza, New York, New York 10119. Bimonthly.

INTERNATIONAL TAX JOURNAL. Panel Publishers, Incorporated, 14 Plaza Road, Greenvale, New York 11548. Quarterly.

JOURNAL OF AGRICULTURAL TAXATION AND LAW. Research Institute of America, Incorporated, One Penn Plaza, New York, New York 10119. Quarterly.

JOURNAL OF CORPORATE TAXATION. Research Institute of America, Incorporated, One Penn Plaza, New York, New York 10119. Quarterly.

JOURNAL OF PENSION PLANNING AND COMPLIANCE. Panel Publishers, Incorporated, 14 Plaza Road, Greenvale, New York 11548. Quarterly.

JOURNAL OF REAL ESTATE TAXATION. Research Institute of America, Incorporated, One Penn Plaza, New York, New York 10119. Quarterly.

JOURNAL OF TAXATION. Research Institute of America, Incorporated, One Penn Plaza, New York, New York 10119. Monthly.

JOURNAL OF TAXATION OF INVESTMENTS. Research Institute of America, Incorporated, One Penn Plaza, New York, New York 10119. Quarterly.

JOURNAL OF THE AMERICAN TAXATION ASSOCIATION. American Accounting Association, Tax Section, 5727 Bessie Drive, Sarasota, Florida 33583. Semiannual.

NATIONAL TAX JOURNAL. National Tax Association, 21 East State Street, Columbus, Ohio 43215. Quarterly.

THE PRACTICAL TAX LAWYER. American Law Institute-American Bar Association, Committee on Continuing Professional Education, 4025 Chestnut Street, Philadelphia, Pennsylvania 19104. 1986- . Quarterly.

PROBATE AND PROPERTY. American Bar Association, 750 North Lake Shore Drive, Chicago, Illinois 60611. Bimonthly.

REVIEW OF TAXATION OF INDIVIDUALS. Research Institute of America, Incorporated, One Penn Plaza, New York, New York 10119. Quarterly.

TAX ADVISOR. American Institute of Certified Public Accountants, Incorporated, 1211 Avenue of the Americas, New York, New York 10036. Monthly.

TAX IDEAS. Prentice-Hall, Incorporated, Route 9W, Englewood Cliffs, New Jersey 07632. Bimonthly.

TAX LAW REVIEW. Research Institute of America, Incorporated, One Penn PLaza, New York, New York 10119. Quarterly.

THE TAX LAWYER. American Bar Association, Section of Taxation, 750 North Lake Shore Drive, Chicago, Illinois 60611. Quarterly.

THE TAX TIMES. Rosenfeld, Emmanual, Incorporated, Prentice-Hall, Information Services. 240 Firsch Court, Paramus, New Jersey 07652. Semiannually.

INCOME TAX, FEDERAL

TAXATION FOR ACCOUNTANTS. Research Institute of America, Incorporated, One Penn Plaza, New York, New York 10119. Monthly.

TAXATION FOR LAWYERS. Research Institute of America, Incorporated, One Penn Plaza, New York, New York 10119. Bimonthly.

TAXES: THE TAX MAGAZINE. Commerce Clearing House, Incorporated, 40125 West Peterson Avenue, Chicago, Illinois 60646. Monthly.

TRUSTS AND ESTATES. Communication Channels, Incorporated, 6255 Barfield Road, Atlanta, Georgia 30328. Monthly.

VIRGINIA TAX REVIEW. Virginia Tax Review Association, University of Virginia, School of Law, Charlottesville, Virginia 22901. Semiannual.

NEWSLETTERS AND NEWSPAPERS

ACCOUNTANT'S WEEKLY REPORT. Executive Reports Corporation, Subsidiary of Prentice-Hall, Incorporated, 210 Sylvan Avenue, Englewood Cliffs, New Jersey 07632. Weekly.

THE ATTORNEY - CPA. American Association of Attorneys-CPAs, 24196 Alicia Parkway, Suite K, Mission Viego, California 92691. Bimonthly.

BANK TAX REPORT. Research Institute of America, Incorporated, One Penn Plaza, New York, New York 10119. Bi-weekly.

BENDER'S FEDERAL TAX WEEK. Matthew Bender and Company, Incorporated, 11 Penn Plaza, New York, New York 10001. Weekly.

BNA'S WEEKLY TAX REPORT. Bureau of National Affairs, 1231 Twenty-fifth Street, Northwest, Washington, D.C. 20037. Weekly.

BUSINESS TAX STRATEGIST. Newsletter Management Corporation, 10076 Boca Entrada Blvd., Boca Raton, Florida 33433. Monthly.

CONSOLIDATED RETURNS TAX REPORT. Faulkner and Gray, 106 Fulton Street, New York, New York 10038. Monthly.

DAILY REPORT FOR EXECUTIVES. Bureau of National Affairs, 1231 Twenty-fifth Street, Northwest, Washington, D.C. 20037. Daily.

DAILY TAX REPORT. Bureau of National Affairs, 1231 Twenty-fifth Street, Northwest, Washington, D.C. 20037. Daily.

DOCTOR'S TAX REPORT. Executive Reports Corporation, Subsidiary of Prentice-Hall, Incorporated, 210 Sylvan Avenue, Englewood Cliffs, New Jersey 07632. Biweekly.

EXECUTIVE COMPENSATION ALERT. Research Institute of America, Incorporated, 589 Fifth Avenue, New York, New York 10017. Monthly.

EXECUTIVE'S TAX REPORT. Executive Reports Corporation, Subsidiary of Prentice-Hall, Incorporated, 210 Sylvan Avenue, Englewood Cliffs, New Jersey 07632. Monthly.

FARMERS FEDERAL TAX ALERT. Research Institute of America, Incorporated, 589 Fifth Avenue, New York, New York 10017. Monthly.

FARMER'S TAX WATCH. Commerce Clearing House, Incorporated, 4025 West Peterson Avenue, Chicago, Illinois 60646. Monthly.

FEDERAL TAXATION. Illinois State Bar Association, Illinois Bar Center, Springfield, Illinois 62701. Quarterly.

FEDERAL TAXES REPORT BULLETIN. Prentice-Hall, Incorporated, Route 9W, Englewood Cliffs, New Jersey 07632. Weekly.

FEDERAL TAXES TAX BULLETIN. Research Institute of America, Incorporated, 910 Sylvan Avenue, Englewood Cliffs, New Jersey 07632. Weekly.

HIGHLIGHTS AND DOCUMENTS. Tax Analysts, 6830 North Fairfax Drive, Arlington, Virginia 22213. Daily.

IRS AUDIT ALERT. Rosenfeld Emanuel, Incorporated, 481 Main Street, New Rochelle, New York 10801. Monthly.

IRS LITIGATION REPORTER. Litigation Reporting Service, P.O. Box 248, Chalfont, Pennsylvania 18914. Semimonthly.

IRS PRACTICE ALERT. Research Institute of America, Incorporated, One Penn Plaza, New York, New York 10119. Monthly.

KIPLINGER TAX LETTER. Kiplinger Washington Editors, Incorporated, 1729 H Street, Northwest, Wasington, D.C. 20006. Biweekly.

LAWYERS WEEKLY REPORT. Prentice-Hall, Incorporated, 113 Sylvan Avenue, Englewood Cliffs, New Jersey 07632. Weekly.

LEGISLATIVE TAX BULLETIN. The Tax Council, 1 Thomas Circle, Northwest, Suite 500, Wasington, D.C. 20005. Monthly.

LETTER RULINGS AND TECHNICAL ADVISE MEMORANDUMS. Tax Analysts, 6830, North Fairfax Drive, Arlington, Virginia 22213. Weekly.

MERTENS CURRENT TAX HIGHLIGHTS. Callaghan and Company, 3201 Old Glenview Road, Wilmette, Illinois 60091. Monthly.

PERSONAL TAX STRATEGIST. Newsletter Management Corporation, 10076 Boca Entrada Boulevard, Boca Raton, Florida 33433. Monthly.

REAL ESTATE TAX ANALYST. Federal Research Press, 65 Franklin Street, Boston, Massachusetts 02110. Monthly.

REAL ESTATE TAX DIGEST. Matthew Bender and Company, Incorporated, 235 East Forty-fifth Street, New York, New York 10017. Monthly.

SECTION OF TAXATION NEWSLETTER. American Bar Association, Taxation Section, 750 North Lake Shore Drive, Chicago, Illinois 60611. Quarterly.

TAX ADMINISTRATION NEWS. Federation of Tax Administrators, 444 North Capitol Street, Northwest, Washington D.C. 20001. Monthly.

TAX AVOIDANCE DIGEST. Commerce Clearing House, Incorporated, 4025 West Peterson Avenue, Chicago, Illinois 60646. Monthly.

TAX DAY REPORT. Commerce Clearing House, Incorporated, 4025 West Peterson Avenue, Chicago, Illinois 60646. Daily.

TAX LEGISLATIVE BULLETIN. The Tax Council, 122 C Street, Northwest, Suite 330, Washington, D.C. 20001. Bimonthly.

TAX LITERATURE REPORT. Symposia Press, P.O. Box 418, Moorestown, New Jersey 08057. 46 issues per year.

TAX MANAGEMENT WASHINGTON TAX REVIEWS. American Bar Association, 750 North Lake Shore Drive, Chicago, Illinois 60611. Monthly.

TAX MANAGEMENT WEEKLY REPORT. American Bar Association, 750 North Lake Shore Drive, Chicago, Illinois 60611. Weekly.

TAX NOTES. Tax Analysts, 6830 N. Fairfax Drive, Arlington, Virginia 22213. Weekly.

TAXBASE NEWS. Tax Analysts, 6830 North Fairfax Drive, Arlington, Virginia 22213. Bimonthly.

TAXES ON PARADE. Commerce Clearing House, Incorporated, 4025 West Peterson Avenue, Chicago, Illinois 60646. Weekly.

UNITED STATES TAX WEEK. Matthew Bender and Company, Incorporated, 235 East Forty-fifth Street, New York, New York 10017. Weekly.

WEEKLY ALERT. Research Institute of America, Incorporated, 589 Fifth Avenue, New York, New York 10017. Weekly.

BIBLIOGRAPHIES

BIBLIOGRAPHY ON TAXATION OF FOREIGN OPERATIONS AND FOREIGNERS, 1976 - 1982. Elizabeth A. Owens and Gretchen A. Hovemeyer. Harvard Law School, International Tax Program, Cambridge, Massachusetts 02138. 1983.

FLAT-RATE INCOME TAX: A SELECTED BIBLIOGRAPHY. Felix Chin. Vance Bibliographies, P.O. Box 229, 112 North Charter Street, Monticello, Illinois 61856. 1982.

INDEXING THE INCOME TAX: A SELECTED BIBLIOGRAPHY. Felix Chin. Vance Bibliographies, P.O. Box 229, 112 North Charter Street, Monticello, Illinois 61856. 1983.

THE UNITED STATES INTERNAL REVENUE SERVICE AND THE INCOME TAX: A CHRONOLOGICAL HISTORY. Janice Dee Gilbert. Vance Bibliographies, P.O. Box 229, 112 North Charter Street, Monticello, Illinois 61856. 1983.

ASSOCIATIONS AND PROFESSIONAL SOCIETIES

AMERICAN SOCIETY OF TAX PROFESSIONALS. P.O. Box 1024, Sioux Falls, South Dakota 57101. (605) 335-1185.

AMERICAN TAXATION ASSOCIATION. c/o American Accounting Association, 5717 Bessie Drive, Sarasota, Florida 34233. (813) 921-7747.

FEDERATION OF TAX ADMINISTRATORS. 444 North Capital Street, Northwest, Washington, D.C. 20001. (202) 624-5890.

NATIONAL COALITION OF IRS WHISTLE BLOWERS. P.O. Box 4283, Pocatello, Idaho 83201. (202) 546-5345.

NATIONAL TAXPAYERS UNION. 325 Pennsylvania Avenue, Southeast, Washington, D.C. 20003. (202) 543-1300.

SECTION ON TAXATION, AMERICAN BAR ASSOCIATION. 750 North Lake Shore Drive, Chicago, Illinois 60611. (312) 988-5000.

SECTION ON TAXATION, ASSOCIATION OF AMERICAN LAW SCHOOLS. One Dupont Circle, Northwest, Suite 370, Washington, D.C. 20036. (202) 296-8851.

RESEARCH CENTERS, INSTITUTES, CLEARINGHOUSES

AMERICAN BAR FOUNDATION. 750 North Lake Shore Drive, Chicago, Illinois 60611. (312) 988-6500.

AMERICAN LAW INSTITUTE. 4025 Chestnut, Philadelphia, Pennsylvania 19104. (800) 253-6397.

CENTER FOR TAX POLICY STUDIES. Purdue University, West Lafayette, Indiana 47906. (317) 494-4442.

CITIZENS FOR TAX JUSTICE. 1311 L Street, Northwest, Washington, D.C. 20005. (202) 626-3780.

INSTITUTE FOR CONTINUING EDUCATION IN LAW AND TAXATION. New York University, 11 West Forty-second Street, Room 429, New York, New York 10036. (212) 302-6199.

INSTITUTE FOR RESEARCH ON THE ECONOMICS OF TAXATION. 1331 Pennsylvania Avenue, Northwest, Suite 505, Washington, D.C. 20004. (202) 347-9570.

INSTITUTE FOR TAX ADMINISTRATION. Academy for International Training, 900 Wilshire Boulevard, Suite 624, Los Angeles, California 90017. (213) 623-1103.

INTERNATIONAL TAX PROGRAM. Harvard University, 400 Pound Hall, Cambridge, Massachusetts 02138. (617) 495-4406.

TAX ANALYSTS. 6830 North Fairfax Drive, Arlington, Virginia 22213. (703) 532-1850.

THE TAX COUNCIL. 122 C Stret, Northwest, Suite 330, Washington, D.C. 20001. (202) 822-8062.

TAX FOUNDATION, INCORPORATED. 3000 K Street, Northwest, Suite 400, Washington, D.C. 20007. (202) 822-9050.

ONLINE DATABASES

BNA TAX UPDATES. Bureau of National Affairs, BNA Online, 1231 Twenty-fifth Street, Northwest, Washington, D.C. 20037.

INCOME TAX, FEDERAL

CCH TAX DAY: FEDERAL. Commerce Clearing House, Incorporated, 4025 West Peterson Avenue, Chicago, Illinois 60646.

CHARITABLE GIVING TECHNIQUES. Charitable Giving Consultants, 44 West Broadway, Suite 303, P.O. Box 11278, Eugene, Oregon 97440.

DAILY TAX ADVANCE. Bureau of National Affairs, BNA Online, 1231 Twenty-fifth Street, Northwest, Washington, D.C. 20037.

DAILY TAX REPORT. Bureau of National Affairs, BNA Online, 1231 Twenty-fifth Street, Northwest, Washington, D.C. 20037.

IRS PUBLICATIONS. International Revenue Service, Publishing Services Branch, 1111 Constitutional Avenue, Northwest, Room 1545, Washington, D.C. 20224.

LEXIS, TAX LIBRARY. Mead Data Central, P.O. Box 933, Dayton, Ohio 45401.

PHINET-FEDTAX. Prentice-Hall Information Network, 242 Madison Avenue, 4th Floor, New York, New York 10017.

PRIVATE LETTER RULINGS. Bureau of National Affairs, BNA Online, 1231 Twenty-fifth Street, Northwest, Washington, D.C. 20037.

SALARY GROSS-UP TABLES. On-Line Researching, Incorporated, 200 Railroad Avenue, Greenwich, Connecticut 06830.

THE TAX DIRECTORY. Tax Analysts, 6830 North Fairfax Drive, Arlington, Virginia 22213.

TAX MANAGEMENT MEMORANDUM. Bureau of National Affairs, BNA Online, 1231 Twenty-fifth Street, Northwest, Washington, D.C. 20037.

TAX MANAGEMENT PORTFOLIO SERIES: U.S. INCOME. Bureau of National Affairs, BNA Online, 1231 Twenty-fifth Street, Northwest, Washington, D.C. 20037.

TAX MANAGEMENT WASHINGTON TAX REVIEW. Bureau of National Affairs, BNA Online, 1231 Twenty-fifth Street, Northwest, Washington, D.C. 20037.

TAX MANAGEMENT WEEKLY REPORT. Bureau of National Affairs, BNA Online, 1231 Twenty-fifth Street, Northwest, Washington D.C. 20037.

TAX NOTES TODAY. Tax Analysts, 6830 North Fairfax Drive, Arlington, Virginia 22213.

WESTLAW, TAX LIBRARY. West Publishing Company, P.O. Box 64526, 50 West Kellogg Boulevard, St. Paul, Minnesota 55164-0526.

AUDIOVISUALS

ANNUAL TAXATION UPDATE. Totaltape Publishing, CPE Division, Totaltape Plaza, 4251 Southwest Thirteenth Street, Gainesville, Florida 32608. Audiocassette. Annual.

AUDIO TAX REPORT: YOUR MONTHLY MAGAZINE OF TAX INFORMATION AND ANALYSIS. Totaltape Publishing, Incorporated, P.O. Box 1469, Gainesville, Florida 32605. Monthly. Audiocassette.

BASIC GUIDE TO PENSION AND PROFIT-SHARING PLANS. Willliam Brent Carper. Totaltape Publishing, CPE Division, Totaltape Plaza, 4251 Southwest Thirteenth Street, Gainesville, Florida 32608. 1987. Audiocassette.

EXECUTIVE COMPENSATION AND EMPLOYEE BENEFITS. Totaltape Publishing, CPE Division, Totaltape Plaza, Southwest Thirteenth Street, Gainesville, Florida 32608. 1987. Audiocassette.

FEDERAL TAXATION OF PARTNERSHIPS. Richard M. Feldmein. Totaltape Publishing, CPE Division, Totaltape Plaza, 4251 Southwest Thirteenth Street, Gainesville, Florida 32608. 1987. Audiocassette.

INDIVIDUAL INCOME TAX REFRESHER COURSE. Sidney Kess. Commerce Clearing House, Incorporated, 4025 West Peterson Avenue, Chicago, Illinois 60646. Annual. Audiocassettes.

INDIVIDUAL TAXATION. Totaltape Publishing, CPE Division, Totaltape Plaza, 4251 Southwest Thirteenth Street, Gainesville, Florida 32608. 1987. Audiocassette.

OVERVIEW OF FEDERAL INCOME TAXATION. Nathan M. Bisk, Richard M Feldheim and Keven M. Daly. Totaltape Publishing, Incorporated, P.O. Box 1469, Gainesville, Florida 32605. 1983.

PARTNERSHIP TAXATION: SPECIAL TOPICS. Totaltape Publishing, CPE Division, Totaltape Plaza, 4251 Southwest Thirteenth Street, Gainesville, Florida 32608. 1987. Audiocassette.

RESPONSIBILITIES OF TAX PRACTITIONERS. Totaltape Publishing, Totaltape Plaza, 4251 Southwest Thirteenth Street, Gainesville, Florida 32608. 1987. Audiocassette.

TAXATION OF THE SOPHISTICATED INVESTOR. Totaltape Publishing, CPE Division, Totaltape Plaza, 4251 Southwest Thirteenth Street, Gainesville, Florida 32608. 1987. Audiocassette.

COMPUTER-ASSISTED LEGAL INSTRUCTION

BASIC FEDERAL INCOME TAXATION. Taxjem, Incorporated, c/o Center for Computer-Assisted Instruction, 229 19th Avenue South, University of Minnesota, Minneapolis, Minnesota 55455. Machine- readable computer file.

DEDUCTIONS-CONCEPTUAL ASPECTS I AND II. Lewis D. Solomon. Center for Computer-Assisted Instruction, 229 19th Avenue South, University of Minnesota, Minneapolis, Minnesota 55455. Machine- readable computer file.

GROSS INCOME-CONCEPTUAL ASPECTS. Lewis D. Solomon. Center for Computer-Assisted Instruction, 229 19th Avenue South, University of Minnesota, Minneapolis, Minnesota 55455. Machine-readable computer file.

INTRODUCTION TO FEDERAL INCOME TAXATION. Lewis D. Solomon. Center for Computer-Assisted Instruction, 229 19th Avenue South, University of Minnesota, Minneapolis, Minnesota 55455. Machine-readable computer file.

INTRODUCTION TO FEDERAL WEALTH TRANSFER TAXATION. Lewis D. Solomon. Center for Computer-Assisted Instruction, 229 19th Avenue South, University of Minnesota, Minneapolis, Minnesota 55455. Machine-readable computer file.

PARTNERSHIP TAXATION. Taxjem, Incorporated, c/o Center for Computer-Assisted Instruction, 229 19th Avenue South, University of Minnesota, Minneapolis, Minnesota 55455. Machine-readable computer file.

INCOMPETENTS
See: GUARDIAN AND WARD

INCORPORATION
See: CORPORATIONS, FORMATION

INDEPENDENT CONTRACTORS
See: AGENCY

INDIANS OF NORTH AMERICA
See also: INTERIOR DEPARTMENT

STATUTES, CODES, STANDARDS, UNIFORM LAWS

CHEROKEE NATION CODE ANNOTATED. Equity Publishing, Main Street, Orford, New Hampshire 03777. (Supplemented).

CONSTITUTIONS AND LAWS OF THE AMERICAN INDIAN TRIBES, SERIES ONE. Scholarly Resources, Incorporated, 104 Greenhill Avenue, Wilmington, Delaware 19805-1897. 1973 (Reprint).

CONSTITUTIONS AND LAWS OF THE AMERICAN INDIAN TRIBES, SERIES TWO. Scholarly Resources, Incorporated, 104 Greenhill Avenue, Wilmington, Delaware 19805-1897. 1975 (Reprint).

EARLY AMERICAN INDIAN DOCUMENTS: TREATIES AND LAWS, 1607-1789. Alden T. Vaughan, Editor. University Press of America, 4720 Boston Way, Lanham, Maryland 20706. 1983.

NAVAJO TRIBAL CODE. Equity Publishing, Main Street, Orford, New Hampshire 03777. 1987. (Supplemented).

RIFLE, BLANKET, AND KETTLE: SELECTED INDIAN TREATIES AND LAWS. Frederick E. Hosen, Editor. McFarland and Company, Incorporated, P.O. Box 611, Jefferson, North Carolina 28640. 1985.

HANDBOOKS, MANUALS, FORMBOOKS

THE RIGHTS OF INDIANS AND TRIBES: THE BASIC ACLU GUIDE TO INDIAN AND TRIBAL RIGHTS. Second Edition. Stephen L. Pevar. Southern Illinois University Press, P.O. Box 3697, Carbondale, Illinois 62902-3697. 1992.

TEXTBOOKS AND GENERAL WORKS

THE AGGRESSIONS OF CIVILIZATION: FEDERAL INDIAN POLICY SINCE THE 1880s. Sandra L. Cadwalader and Vine Delovia, Jr., Editors. Temple University Press, 1601 North Broad Street, University Services Building, Philadelphia, Pennsylvania 19122. 1984.

THE AMERICAN INDIAN IN WESTERN LEGAL THOUGHT: THE DISCOURSES OF CONQUEST. Robert A. Williams, Jr. Oxford University Press, 200 Madison Avenue, New York, New York 10016. 1990.

AMERICAN INDIAN LAW: CASES AND MATERIALS. Third Edition. Robert N. Clinton, Nell Jessup Newton and Monroe E. Price. Michie Company, P.O. Box 7587, Charlottesville, Virginia 22906. 1991.

AMERICAN INDIAN LAW IN A NUTSHELL. Second Edition. William C. Canby, Jr., West Publishing Company, P.O. Box 64526, 50 West Kellogg Boulevard, St. Paul, Minnesota 55164-0526. 1988.

AMERICAN INDIAN POLICY. Theodore W. Taylor. Lomond Publications, Incorporated, P.O. Box 88, Mount Airy, Maryland 21771. 1983.

AMERICAN INDIAN POLICY IN THE TWENTIETH CENTURY. Vine Deloria, Jr., Editor. University of Oklahoma Press, 105 Asp Avenue, Norman, Oklahoma 73019. 1985.

AMERICAN INDIAN WATER RIGHTS AND THE LIMITS OF LAW. Lloyd Burton. University Press of Kansas, 329 Carruth, Lawrence, Kansas 66045. 1991.

AMERICAN INDIANS, AMERICAN JUSTICE. Vine Deloria, Jr., and Clifford M. Lytle. University of Texas Press, P.O. Box 7819, Austin, Texas 78713-7819. 1983.

AMERICAN INDIANS, TIME AND THE LAW: HISTORICAL RIGHTS AT THE BAR OF THE SUPREME COURT. Charles F. Wilkinson. Yale University Press, 302 Temple Street, New Haven, Connecticut 06520. 1987.

AMERICAN INDIANS, TIME AND THE LAW: NATIVE SOCIETIES IN A MODERN CONSTITUTIONAL DEMOCRACY. Charles F. Wilkinson. Yale University Press, 302 Temple Street, New Haven, Connecticut 06520. 1987.

AMERICAN PROTESTANTISM AND UNITED STATES INDIAN POLICY, 1869-1882. Robert H. Keller, Jr. University of Nebraska Press, 901 North Seventeenth Street, Lincoln, Nebraska 68588-0520. 1983.

BEHIND THE TRAIL OF BROKEN TREATIES: AN INDIAN DECLARATION OF INDEPENDENCE. University of Texas Press, P.O. Box 7819, Austin, Texas 78713-7819. 1985.

CRIMINAL JURISDICTION ALLOCATION IN INDIAN COUNTRY. Ronald B. Flowers. Associated Faculty Press, 19 West Thirty-sixth Street, New York, New York 10018. 1983.

DISPUTING THE DEAD: U.S. LAW ON ABORIGINAL REMAINS AND GRAVE GOODS. H. Marcus Price, III. University of Missouri Press, 2910 LeMone Boulevard, Columbia, Missouri 65201. 1991.

DOCUMENTS OF UNITED STATES INDIAN POLICY. Second Edition. Francis Paul Prucha, Editor. University of Nebraska Press, 901 North Seventeenth Street, Lincoln, Nebraska 68588. 1990.

THE EMBATTLED NORTHEAST: THE ELUSIVE IDEAL OF ALLIANCE IN ABENAKIEURAMERICAN RELATIONS. Kenneth M. Morrison. University of California Press, 2120 Berkeley Way, Berkeley, California 94720. 1984.

THE GREAT FATHER: THE UNITED STATES GOVERNMENT AND THE AMERICAN INDIANS. Francis P. Prucha. University of Nebraska Press, 901 North Seventeenth Street, Lincoln, Nebraska 68588-0520. 1986.

A GUIDE TO THE INDIAN TRIBES OF THE PACIFIC NORTHWEST. Robert H. Ruby and John A. Brown. University of Oklahoma Press, 105 Asp Avenue, Norman, Oklahoma 73019. 1986.

HANDBOOK OF AMERICAN INDIAN RELIGIOUS FREEDOM. Christopher Vecsey, Editor. Crossroad Publishing Company, 370 Lexington Avenue, New York, New York 10017. 1991.

THE INDIAN ARTS AND CRAFTS BOARD: AN ASPECT OF NEW DEAL INDIAN POLICY. Robert F. Schrader. University of New Mexico Press, 1720 Lomas Boulevard, Northeast, Albuquerque, New Mexico 87131. 1983.

INDIAN LAW/RACE LAW: A FIVE HUNDRED YEAR HISTORY. James E. Falkowski. Praeger Publishers, One Madison Avenue, New York, New York 10010-3603. 1992.

THE INDIAN RIGHTS ASSOCIATION: THE HERBERT WELSH YEARS, 1882-1904. Universtiy of Arizona Press, 1230 North Park, Number 102, Tuscon, Arizona 85719. 1985.

INDIAN SELF-RULE: FIRST HAND ACCOUNTS OF INDIAN-WHITE RELATIONS FROM ROOSEVELT TO REAGAN. Kenneth R. Philp, Editor. Howe Brothers, Box 6394, Salt Lake City, Utah 84106. 1986.

INDIANS, SUPERINTENDENTS, AND COUNCILS: NORTHWESTERN INDIAN POLICY, 1850-1855. Clifford E. Trafzer, Editor. University of America Press, 4720 Boston Way, Lanham, Maryland 20706. 1986.

AN IRON HAND UPON THE PEOPLE: THE LAW AGAINST THE POTLATCH ON THE NORTHWEST COAST. Douglas Cole and Ira Chaikin. University of Washington Press, P.O. Box 50096, Seattle, Washington 98145-5096. 1990.

IRREDEEMABLE AMERICA: THE INDIAN ESTATE AND LAND CLAIMS. Imre Sutton, Editor. University of New Mexico Press, 1720 Lomas Boulevard, Northeast, Albuquerque, New Mexico 87131. 1986.

LAW AND THE AMERICAN INDIAN: READINGS, NOTES AND CASES. Second Edition. Monroe E. Price and Robert Clinton. Michie/Bobbs-Merrill, The Michie Company, P.O. Box 7587, Charlottesville, Virginia 22906-7582. 1983.

LICENSE FOR EMPIRE: COLONIALISM BY TREATY IN EARLY AMERICA. University of Chicago Press, 5801 Ellis Avenue, Third Floor, South, Chicago, Illinois 60637. 1982.

MODEL COURT DEVELOPMENT PROJECT: FULL FAITH AND CREDIT FOR INDIAN COURT JUDGEMENTS. National Center for State Courts, 300 Newport Avenue, Williamsburg, Virginia 23187-8798. 1982.

THE NATIONS WITHIN: THE PAST AND FUTURE OF AMERICAN INDIAN SOVEREIGNTY. Vine Deloria, Jr. and Clifford M. Lytle. Pantheon Books, Random House, Incorporated, Random House Publicity, 201 East Fiftieth Street, New York, New York 10022. 1984.

NATIVE AMERICANS AND NIXON: PRESIDENTIAL POLITICS AND MINORITY SELF DETERMINATION, 1969-1972. Second Edition. Jack Forbes. University of California American Indians Studies Center, 3220 Campbell Hall, University of California, Los Angeles, California 90024-1548. 1984.

NATIVE AMERICANS AND PUBLIC POLICY. Fremont J. Lyden and Lyman H. Legters, Editors. University of Pittsburgh Press, 127 North Bellefield Avenue, Pittsburgh, Pennsylvania 15260. 1992.

NATIVE LAW. Jack Woodward. Carswell, Toronto, Ontario, Canada. 1989.

THE NEW AMERICAN STATE PAPERS: INDIAN AFFAIRS SUBJECT SET. Loring B. Priest, Editor. Scholarly Resources, Incorporated, 104 Greenhill Avenue, Wilmington, Delaware 19805-1897. 1973.

OF AMERICAN INDIANS, TIME AND THE LAW: HISTORICAL RIGHTS AT THE BAR OF THE SUPREME COURT. Charles F. Wilkinson. Yale University Press, 302 Temple Street, New Haven, Connecticut 06520. 1986.

PARTIAL JUSTICE: FEDERAL INDIAN LAW IN A LIBERAL CONSTITUTIONAL SYSTEM. Petra T. Shattuck and Jill Norgren. Berg, New York, New York. 1991.

THE POLITICS OF INDIAN REMOVAL: CREEK GOVERNMENT AND SOCIETY IN CRISIS. Michael D. Green. University of Nebraska Press, 901 North Seventeenth Street, Lincoln, Nebraska 68588-0520. 1985.

PURITAN JUSTICE AND THE INDIAN: WHITE MAN'S LAW IN MASSACHUSETTS, 1630-1763. Yasuhide Kawashima. University Press of New England, 17 Lebanon Street, Hanover, New Hampshire 03755. 1986.

RED POWER: THE AMERICAN INDIANS FIGHT FOR FREEDOM. Alvin M. Josephy, Jr. University of Nebraska Press, 901 North Seventeenth Street, Lincoln, Nebraska 68588-0520. 1985.

RESTITUTION: THE LAND CLAIMS OF THE MASHPEE, PASSAMAQUODDY AND PENOBSCOT INDIANS OF NEW ENGLAND. Paul Brodeur. Northeastern University Press, 360 Huntington Avenue, Huntington Plaza, Northeastern University, Boston, Massachusetts 02115. 1985.

TERMINATION AND RELOCATION: FEDERAL INDIAN POLICY, 1945-1960. Donald L. Fixico. Journalism Building, University of New Mexico Press, 1720 Lomas Boulevard, Northeast, Albuquerque, New Mexico 87131. 1990.

TREATIES ON TRIAL: THE CONTINUING CONTROVERSY OVER NORTHWEST INDIAN FISHING RIGHTS. Fay G. Cohen. University of Washington Press, P.O. Box 50096, Seattle, Washington 98145-5096. 1986.

ENCYCLOPEDIAS AND DICTIONARIES

ENCYCLOPEDIA OF NORTH AMERICAN INDIAN TRIBES. Bill Yenne. Crown Publishing, 225 Park Avenue South, New York, New York 10003. 1986.

REFERENCE ENCYCLOPEDIA OF THE AMERICAN INDIAN. Fifth Edition. Barry T. Klein, Editor. Todd Publishers, 18 North Greenbush Road, West Nyack, New York 10994. 1990.

DIGESTS, INDEXES, ABSTRACTS, CITATORS

THE AMERICAN INDIAN INDEX: A DIRECTORY OF INDIAN COUNTRY, USA. Gregory W. Frazier and Randolph J. Punley. Arrowstar Publishing, 10134 University Park Station, Denver, Colorado 80210-1034. 1985.

DIGEST OF AMERICAN INDIAN LAW: CASES AND CHRONOLOGY. H. Barry Holt and Gary Forrester. Fred B. Rothman and Company, 10368 West Centennial Road, Littleton, Colorado 80127. 1990.

LAW REVIEWS AND PERIODICALS

AMERICAN INDIAN JOURNAL. Institute for Development of Indian Law, 927 Fifteenth Street, Northwest, Washington, D.C. 20005. Quarterly.

AMERICAN INDIAN LAW REVIEW. College of Law, University of Oklahoma, 300 Timberdell Road, Norman, Oklahoma 73019. Semiannual.

NEWSLETTERS AND NEWSPAPERS

AMERICAN INDIAN COURTLINE. American Indian Court Clerks Association, 1000 Connecticut Avenue, Northwest, Washington, D.C. 20036. Bimonthly.

AMERICAN INDIAN LAW NEWSLETTER. American Indian Law Center, P.O. Box 4456, Station A, Albuquerque, New Mexico 87196. Bimonthly.

AMERICAN INDIAN LAW STUDENTS ASSOCIATION NEWSLETTER. American Indian Law Students Association, American Indian Law Center, University of New Mexico, 1117 Stanford, Northeast, Albuquerque, New Mexico 87131. Periodic.

DNA NEWSLETTER. DNA People's Legal Services, Incorporated, P.O. Box 306, Window Rock, Arizona 86515. Quarterly.

INDIAN AFFAIRS. Association on American Indian Affairs, Incorporated, 95 Madison Avenue, New York, New York 10016. Quarterly.

INDIAN COURTS NEWSLETTER. National American Indian Court Judges Association, 1000 Connecticut Avenue, Northwest, Washington, D.C. 20036. Semiannually.

INDIAN LAW REPORTER. American Indian Lawyer Training Program, 319 MacArthur Boulevard, Oakland, California 94610. Monthly.

INDIAN LAW SUPPORT CENTER REPORTER. Native American Rights Fund, 1506 Broadway, Boulder, Colorado 80302. Monthly.

LINKAGES. TCI Incorporated, 3410 Garfield Street, Northwest, Washington, D.C. 20007. Bimonthly.

NARF LEGAL REVIEW. Native American Rights Fund, 1506 Broadway, Boulder, Colorado 80302. Quarterly.

BIBLIOGRAPHIES

AMERICAN INDIAN LAND CLAIMS: A SELECTED BIBLIOGRAPHY. Joan Kuklinski. Vance Bibliographies, P.O. Box 229, 112 North Charter Street, Monticello, Illinois 61856. 1982.

AMERICAN INDIAN TRIBAL AUTONOMY AND AMERICAN SOCIETY IN THE 1980'S: A BIBLIOGRAPHY. Tim J. Watts. Vance Bibliographies, P.O. Box 229, 112 North Charter Street, Monticello, Illinois 61856. 1988.

NATIONAL INDIAN LAW LIBRARY CATALOGUE. Native American Rights Fund, 1506 Broadway, Boulder, Colorado 80302. 1973 (Annual Supplements).

NATIVE AMERICAN COLLECTION: A BIBLIOGRAPHY DESCRIBING THE MICROFICHE COLLECTION ASSEMBLED AND MARKETED BY THE LAW LIBRARY MICROFORM CONSORTIUM. Jerry Dupont. Law Library Microform Consortium, P.O. Box 11033, Honolulu, Hawaii 96828. 1990.

NATIVE PEOPLE: THEIR LEGAL STATUS, CLAIMS, AND HUMAN RIGHTS. Edward Stanek. Vance Bibliographies, P.O. Box 229, 112 North Charter Street, Monticello, Illinois 61856. 1987.

ASSOCIATIONS AND PROFESSIONAL SOCIETIES

ALL INDIAN PUEBLO COUNCIL. P.O. Box 3256, Albequerque, New Mexico 87190. (505) 881-1992.

AMERICAN INDIAN LAW CENTER. P.O. Box 4456, Station A, Albuquerque, New Mexico 87196. (505) 277-5462.

AMERICAN INDIAN LAW STUDENTS ASSOCIATION. American Indian Law Center, University of New Mexico School of Law, 1117 Stanford Drive, Northeast, Albuquerque, New Mexico 87131. (505) 277-5462.

AMERICAN INDIAN MOVEMENT. 710 Clayton Street, Suite 1, San Francisco, California 94117. (415) 566-0251.

INDIANS OF NORTH AMERICA

ASSOCIATION ON AMERICAN INDIAN AFFAIRS. 95 Madison Avenue, New York, New York 10016. (212) 689-8720.

INDIAN LAW RESOURCE CENTER. 601 E Street, Southeast, Washington, D.C. 20003. (202) 547-2800.

INDIAN RIGHTS ASSOCIATION. 1601 Market Street, Philadelphia, Pennsylvania 19103. (215) 665-4523.

INSTITUTE FOR THE DEVELOPMENT OF INDIAN LAW. Oklahoma City University, School of Law, Oklahoma City, Oklahoma 73106. (405) 521-5188.

INTERNATIONAL INDIAN TREATY COUNCIL. 710 Clayton Street, Suite 1, San Francisco, California 94117. (415) 566-0251.

NATIONAL AMERICAN INDIAN COURT JUDGES ASSOCIATION. 1000 Connecticut Avenue, Northwest, Washington, D.C. 20036. (202) 296-0685.

NATIONAL CONGRESS OF AMERICAN INDIANS. 900 Pennsylvania Avenue, Southeast, Washington, D.C. 20003. (202) 546-9404.

NATIVE AMERICAN POLICY NETWORK. Barry University, 11300 Second Avenue, Northeast, Miami, Florida 33161. (305) 758-3392.

NATIVE AMERICAN RIGHTS FUND. 1506 Broadway, Boulder, Colorado 80302. (303) 447-8760.

SECTION ON NATIVE AMERICAN RIGHTS. Association of American Law Schools, One Dupont Circle, Northwest, Washington, D.C. 20036. (202) 296-8851.

SEVENTH GENERATION FUND FOR INDIAN DEVELOPMENT. P.O. Box 10, Forestville, California 95436. (707) 887-1559.

UNITED INDIANS OF ALL TRIBES FOUNDATION. Daybreak Star Arts Center, Discovery Park, P.O. Box 99100, Seattle, Washington 98199. (206) 285-4425.

RESEARCH CENTERS, INSTITUTES, CLEARINGHOUSES

AMERICAN INDIAN LAW CENTER, INCORPORATED. University of New Mexico Law School, P.O. Box 4456-Station A, Albuquerque, New Mexico 87196. (505) 277-5462.

AMERICAN INDIAN STUDIES CENTER. University of California, Los Angeles, 3220 Campbell Hall, Los Angeles, California 90024. (213) 825-7315.

CENTER FOR NATIVE AMERICAN STUDIES. Montana State University, Bozeman, Montana 59717. (406) 994-3881.

INSTITUTE FOR THE DEVELOPMENT OF INDIAN LAW. Oklahoma City University, School of Law, 2501 North Blackwelder, Oklahoma City, Oklahoma 73106. (405) 521-5188.

NATIONAL INDIAN LAW LIBRARY. Native American Rights Fund, 1506 Broadway, Boulder, Colorado 80302. (303) 447-8760.

NATIVE AMERICAN RESEARCH AND TRAINING CENTER. Northern Arizona University, C.U. Box 5630, Institute for Human Development, Flagstaff, Arizona 86011. (602) 523-4791.

NATIVE LAW CENTRE. University of Saskatchewan, 141 Diefenbaker Centre, Saskatoon, Saskatchewan, Canada S7N 0W0. (306) 966-6189.

NORTHERN AND NATIVE STUDIES. Carleton University, Institute of Canadian Studies, Colonel By Drive, Ottawa, Ontario, Canada K15 5B6. (613) 564-2874.

INDIGENCE
See also: FEDERAL AID; LEGAL AID

TEXTBOOKS AND GENERAL WORKS

COMMON DECENCY: PROPOSALS FOR THE NEW WELFARE STATE. Alvin L. Schorr. Yale University Press, 302 Temple Street, New Haven, Connecticut 06520. 1986.

THE CONSTITUTION OF POVERTY: TOWARD A GENEALOGY OF LIBERAL GOVERNANCE. Mitchell Dean. Routledge, Chapman & Hall, 29 West Thirty-fifth Street, New York, New York 10001. 1991.

COURTS AND THE POOR. Christopher E. Smith. Nelson-Hall Publishers, 111 North Canal Street, Chicago, Illinois 60606. 1991.

AN ECONOMIC HISTORY OF THE ENGLISH POOR LAW, 1750-1850. George R. Boyer. Cambridge University Press, 40 West Twentieth Street, New York, New York 10011. 1990.

LAW AND SOCIAL WORK PRACTICE. Raymond Albert. Springer Publishing Company, Incorporated, 536 Broadway, New York, New York 10012. 1986.

LAW OF THE POOR. Arthur B. LaFrance, Milton R. Schroeder, Robert W. Bennett and William E. Boyd. West Publishing Company, P.O. Box 64526, 50 West Kellogg Boulevard, St. Paul, Minnesota 55164-0526. 1973.

LAW, RIGHTS AND THE WELFARE STATE. Denis Galligan and Charles Sampford, Editors. Longwood Publishing Group, Incorporated, 27 South Main Street, Wolfboro, New Hampshire, 03894-2069. 1986.

LEGAL SERVICES FOR THE POOR: A COMPARATIVE AND CONTEMPORARY ANALYSIS OF INTERORGANIZATIONAL POLITICS. Mark Kessler. Greenwood Publishing Group, Incorporated, 88 Post Road West, P.O. Box 5007, Westport, Connecticut 06881. 1987.

LEGAL SERVICES FOR THE POOR: TIME FOR REFORM. Douglas J. Besharov, Editor. American Enterprise Institute for Public Policy Research. AEI Press, Avilable From: University Press of America, 4720 Boston Way, Lanham, Maryland 20706. 1990.

POLITICS AND SOCIAL WELFARE POLICY IN THE UNITED STATES. Robert X. Browning. University of Tennessee Press, 293 Communications Building, Knoxville, Tennessee 37996-0325. 1986.

THE POLITICS OF POVERTY. R. N. Hadimani. South Asia Books, P.O. Box 502, Columbia, Missouri 65205. 1985.

THE POOR IN COURT: THE LEGAL SERVICES PROGRAM AND SUPREME COURT DECISION MAKING. Susan E. Lawrence. Princeton University Press, 41 William Street, Princeton, New Jersey 08540. 1990.

POVERTY AND AID. J. R. Parkinson, Editor. Saint Martin's Press, Incorporated, 175 Fifth Avenue, New York, New York 10010. 1983.

POVERTY AND POLICY IN AMERICAN HISTORY. Michael B. Katz, Edtior. Academic Press, Incorporated, 1250 Sixth Avenue, Suite 400, San Diego, California 92101. 1983.

POVERTY, JUSTICE, AND THE LAW: NEW ESSAYS ON NEEDS, RIGHTS, AND OBLIGATIONS. George R. Lucas, Jr., Editor. University Press of America, 9720 Boston Way, Lanham, Maryland 20706. 1987.

THE RIGHTS OF THE HOMELESS. Robert M. Hayes. Practising Law Institute, 810 Seventh Avenue, New York, New York 10019. 1988.

THE STIGMA OF POVERTY: A CRITIQUE OF POVERTY THEORIES AND POLICIES. Second Edition. Chaim I. Waxman. Pergamon Press, Incorporated, Maxwell House, Fairview Park, Elmsford, New York 10523. 1983.

THE URBAN HOUSING CRISIS: SOCIAL, ECONOMIC, AND LEGAL ISSUES AND PROPOSALS. Arlene Zarembka. Greenwood Publishing Group, Incorporated, 88 Post Road West, P.O. Box 5007, Westport, Connecticut 06881. 1990.

WELFARE AND POVERTY. National Center For Policy Alternatives, 2000 Florida Avenue, Northwest, Washington, D.C. 20009. 1983.

WELFARE FRAUD INVESTIGATION. Gary W. Hutton. Charles C. Thomas Publishing, 2600 South First Street, Springfield, Illinois 62794-9265. 1985.

WELFARE LAW--STRUCTURE AND ENTITLEMENT: IN A NUTSHELL. Arthur B. LaFrance. West Publishing Company, P.O. Box 64526, 50 West Kellogg Boulevard, St. Paul, Minnesota 55164-0526. 1979.

BIBLIOGRAPHIES

THE DECLINE OF LEGAL SERVICES TO THE POOR. Tim J. Watts. Vance Bibliographies, P.O. Box 229, 112 North Charter Street, Monticello, Illinois 61856. 1988.

POLICY STUDIES ON POVERTY: A SELECTED BIBLIOGRAPHY. Robert Goehlert. Vance Bibliographies, P.O. Box 229, 112 North Charter Street, Monticello, Illinois 61856. 1984.

ASSOCIATIONS AND PROFESSIONAL SOCIETIES

AMERICAN ASSOCIATION OF PUBLIC WELFARE ATTORNEYS. 810 First Street, Northeast, Suite 500, Washington, D.C. 20002. (202) 682-0100.

AMERICAN ASSOCIATION OF PUBLIC WELFARE INFORMATION SYSTEMS MANAGEMENT. 810 First Street, Northeast, Suite 500, Washington, D.C. 20002. (202) 682-0100.

AMERICAN PUBLIC WELFARE ASSOCIATION. 810 First Street, Northeast, Suite 500, Washington, D.C. 20002. (202) 682-0100.

CENTER ON SOCIAL WELFARE POLICY AND LAW. 95 Madison Avenue, New York, New York 10016. (212) 679-3709.

NAACP LEGAL DEFENSE AND EDUCATION FUND. 99 Hudson Street, 16th Floor, New York, New York 10013. (212) 219-1900.

NATIONAL ASSOCIATION OF COUNTY HUMAN SERVICES ADMINISTRATORS. c/o National Association of Counties. 440 First Street, Northwest, Washington, D.C. 20001. (202) 393-6226.

NATIONAL COALITION FOR THE HOMELESS. 1621 Connecticut Avenue, Northwest, Suite 400, Washington, D.C. 20009. (202) 265-2371.

NATIONAL COUNCIL OF LOCAL PUBLIC WELFARE ADMINISTRATORS. 810 First Street, Northeast, Suite 500, Washington, D.C. 20002. (202) 682-0100.

NATIONAL COUNCIL OF STATE HUMAN SERVICE ADMINISTRATORS. 810 First Street, Northeast, Suite 500, Washington, D.C. 20002. (202) 682-0100.

OMB WATCH. 1731 Connecticut Avenue, Northwest, Washington, D.C. 20036. (202) 234-8494.

REPRESENTATION OF THE HOMELESS. American Bar Association, 1800 M Street, Northwest, Washington, D.C. 20036. (202) 331-2291.

SOUTHERN POVERTY LAW CENTER. P.O. Box 2087, Montgomery, Alabama 36102. (205) 264-0286.

WESTERN CENTER ON LAW AND POVERTY. 3535 West Sixth Street, Los Angelos, California 90020. (213) 487-7211.

WORKING GROUP ON DOMESTIC HUNGER AND POVERTY. 475 Riverside Drive, Room 572, New York, New York 10115. (212) 870-2307.

RESEARCH CENTERS, INSTITUTES, CLEARINGHOUSES

CENTER FOR NATIONAL POLICY. 317 Massachusetts Avenue, Northeast, Washington, D.C. 20002. (202) 546-9300.

CENTER FOR POLICY RESEARCH. 1720 Emerson Street, Denver, Colorado 80218. (303) 837-1555.

DIVISION OF BEHAVIORAL SCIENCE RESEARCH. Tuskegee University, Carver Research Foundation, Fourth Floor, Carnegie Hall, Tuskegee Institute, Alabama 36088. (205) 727-8575.

INSTITUTE FOR RESEARCH IN HUMAN RESOURCES. North Carolina A & T State University, 305 Dowdy Building, Greensboro, North Carolina 27411. (919) 334-7995.

INSTITUTE FOR RESEARCH ON POVERTY. University of Wisconsin-Madison, Social Science Building, Madison, Wisconsin. 53706. (608) 262-6358.

INDIGENCE

INSTITUTE FOR SOCIAL RESEARCH. University of Michigan, 426 Thompson Street, P.O. Box 1248, Ann Arbor, Michigan 48106. (313) 764-8363.

INSTITUTE FOR SOCIOECONOMIC STUDIES. Airport Road, White Plains, New York 10604. (914) 428-7400.

IOWA URBAN COMMUNITY RESEARCH CENTER. University of Iowa, W170 Seashore Hall, Iowa City, Iowa 52242. (319) 335-2525.

WELFARE RESEARCH, INCORPORATED. 112 State Street, Albany, New York 12207. (518) 432-2576.

STATISTICS SOURCES

TWO NATIONWIDE SURVEYS: 1989 PILOT ASSESSMENTS OF THE UNMET LEGAL NEEDS OF THE POOR AND OF THE PUBLIC GENERALLY. Consortium on Legal Services and the Public. American Bar Association, 750 North Lake Shore Drive, Chicago, Illinois 60611. 1989.

COMPUTER-ASSISTED LEGAL INSTRUCTION

STATE V. RODGERS. Center for Computer-Assisted Instruction, 229 19th Avenue South, University of Minnesota, Minneapolis, Minnesota 55455. Interactive videodisc.

OTHER SOURCES

CIVIL JUSTICE: AN AGENDA FOR THE 1990's: REPORT OF THE AMERICAN BAR ASSOCIATION NATIONAL CONFERENCE ON ACCESS TO JUSTICE IN THE 1990's, NEW ORLEANS, LOUISIANA, JUNE 9-11, 1989. American Bar Association, Consortium on Legal Services and the Public, 750 North Lake Shore Drive, Chicago, Illinois 60611. 1991.

REPORT ON THE SAN ANTONIO STUDY OF LEGAL SERVICES DELIVERY SYSTEMS. American Bar Association, Special Committee on the Delivery of Legal Services, 750 North Lake Shore Drive, Chicago, Illinois 60611. 1989.

INDUSTRIAL ARBITRATION
See: LABOR ARBITRATION

INDUSTRIAL DISEASES
See: OCCUPATIONAL SAFETY AND HEALTH

INDUSTRIAL PROPERTY
See: PATENTS; TRADEMARKS AND TRADE NAMES

INDUSTRIAL RELATIONS
See: LABOR AND LABOR RELATIONS

Encyclopedia of Legal Information Sources • 2nd Ed.

INDUSTRIAL SAFETY
See: OCCUPATIONAL SAFETY AND HEALTH

INFANTS
See: CHILDREN

INFORMATION, FREEDOM
See: FREEDOM OF INFORMATION

INFORMATION STORAGE AND RETRIEVAL SYSTEM S
See: COMPUTERS; LEGAL RESEARCH

INHERITANCE
See: WILLS, TRUSTS AND INHERITANCE

INHERITANCE AND TRANSFER TAXES

COMPUTER-ASSISTED LEGAL INSTRUCTION

INTRODUCTION TO FEDERAL WEALTH TRANSFER TAXATION. Lewis D. Solomon. Center for Computer-Assisted Instruction, 229 19th Avenue South, University of Minnesota, Minneapolis, Minnesota 55455. Machine-readable computer file.

RETAINED INTERESTS-WEALTH TRANSFER TAXATION. Lewis D. Solomon. Center for Computer-Assisted Instruction, 229 19th Avenue South, University of Minnesota, Minneapolis, Minnesota 55455. Machine- readable computer file.

INITIATIVE AND REFERENDUM
See: ELECTION LAW; LEGISLATIVE HISTORY AND PROCESS

INJUNCTIONS
See: CIVIL PROCEDURE; REMEDIES

INJURIES
See: PERSONAL INJURIES; TORTS

INNS
See: HOTELS, RESTAURANTS, ETC.

INSANITY
See: MENTAL HEALTH AND DISABILITY

INSEMINATION, ARTIFICIAL
See: FAMILY LAW

INSOLVENCY
See: BANKRUPTCY

INSTRUCTIONS TO JURIES
See: JURY; STATES

INSURANCE
See also: ATTORNEY GENERAL (UNITED STATES);
INSURANCE, HEALTH AND UNEMPLOYMENT;
INSURANCE, LIABILITY; INSURANCE, LIFE;
INSURANCE, MOTOR VEHICLE AND AVIATION;
INSURANCE, PROPERTY; PREPAID LEGAL
SERVICES

STATUTES, CODES, STANDARDS, UNIFORM LAWS

NATIONAL LAW PUBLISHING. Insurance Revenue Rulings and Letter Rulings, 2 volumes. National Law Publishing Corporation, 99 Painters Mill Road, Owings Mills, Maryland 21117. 1983. (Supplemented).

UNIFORM INSURERS LIQUIDATION ACT. Uniform Laws Annotated, West Publishing Company, P.O. Box 64526, 50 West Kellogg Boulevard, St. Paul, Minnesota 55164-0526. 1986. (Annual Supplements).

LOOSELEAF SERVICES AND REPORTERS

CASUALTY INSURANCE CLAIMS: COVERAGE, INVESTIGATION, LAW. Third Edition. Pat Magarick. Clark Boardman Company, Limited, 435 Hudson Street, New York, New York 10014. 1988- .

EXCESS LIABILITY: THE LAW OF EXTRA-CONTRACTUAL LIABILITY OF INSURERS. Third Edition. Pat Magarick. Clark Boardman Company, Limited, 435 Hudson Street, New York, New York 10014. 1989.

EXCHANGE: A GUIDE TO AN ALTERNATIVE INSURANCE MARKET. Peter H. Bickford. NILS Publishing Company, Chatsworth, California. 1987-

FEDERAL INSURANCE LAWS. National Insurance Law Service, 21625 Prairie Street, Chatsworth, California 91311. 1985- .

FEDERAL INSURANCE REGULATIONS. National Insurance Law Service, 21625 Prairie Street, Chatsworth, California 91311. 1978- .

FEDERAL INSURANCE REVENUE AND LETTER RULINGS UNDER THE INTERNAL REVENUE CODE OF 1954. National Law Publishing Corporation, 99 Painters Mills Road, Owings Mills, Maryland 21117. 1982- .

FEDERAL TAXATION OF INSURANCE COMPANIES. Keith A. Tucker and Dennis P. Van Mieghem. Prentice-Hall, Incorporated, 113 Sylvan Avenue, Englewood Cliffs, New Jersey 07632. 1983- .

A GUIDE TO THE FEDERAL LAW OF BANKING AND INSURANCE. Richard M. Whiting and James E. Scott. Prentice-Hall, Incorporated, 113 Sylvan Avenue, Englewood Cliffs, New Jersey 07632. 1989.

HANDBOOK ON INSURANCE COVERAGE DISPUTES. Third Edition. Barry R. Ostrager and Thomas R. Newman. Prentice-Hall, Incorporated, 113 Sylvan Avenue, Englewood Cliffs, New Jersey 07632. 1990.

INSURING REAL PROPERTY. Stephen A. Cozen, General Editor. Matthew Bender and Company, Incorporated, 11 Penn Plaza, New York, New York 10001. 1989- .

THE LAW OF LIFE AND HEALTH INSURANCE. Bertram Harnett and Irving I. Lesnick. Matthew Bender and Company, Incorporated, 11 Penn Plaza, New York, New York 10001. 1988- .

NATIONAL INSURANCE ADVERTISING REGULATION SERVICE. The Insurance Center, Drake University, 318 West Franklin Avenue, Minneapolis, Minnesota 55404. 1974- .

UNITED STATES AND OFF-SHORE INSURANCE LAWS. National Insurance Law Service Publishing Company, 21625 Prairie Street, Chatsworth, California 91311. 1981- .

HANDBOOKS, MANUALS, FORMBOOKS

COMPLY: A COMPLETE GUIDE TO CAPTIVE INSURANCE COMPANY LAWS AND REGULATIONS. National Insurance Law Service, 21625 Prairie Street, Chatsworth, California 91311. 1987.

CONSTRUCTION INDUSTRY INSURANCE HANDBOOK. Deutsch, Kerrigan and Stiles. John Wiley and Sons, Incorporated, 605 Third Avenue, New York, New York 10158. 1991.

CONSTRUCTION SURETY AND BONDING HANDBOOK. Gordon Hunt. John Wiley and Sons, Incorporated, 605 Third Avenue, New York, New York 10158. 1991.

FIRREA: A LEGISLATIVE HISTORY AND SECTION-BY-SECTION ANALYSIS. Gregory Pulles, Robert Whitlock and James Hogg. Merrill/Magnus Publishing Corporation, One Merrill Circle, St. Paul, Minnesota 55108. 1991.

HANDBOOK ON INSURANCE COVERAGE DISPUTES. Fourth Edition. Barry R. Ostrager and Thomas R. Newman. Prentice-Hall, Incorporated, 113 Sylvan Avenue, Englewood Cliffs, New Jersey 07632. 1991.

HANDLING PROPERTY AND CASUALTY CLAIMS. Robert F. Cushman and Charles H. Stamm, Editors. John Wiley and Sons, Incorporated, 605 Third Avenue, New York, New York 10158. 1985.

HOW TO COLLECT AN INSURANCE CLAIM. Theodore Ferris, et al. New Pacific Publications, Incorporated, 4320 Coldwater Canyon Avenue, Suite 1, Studio City, California 91604-1421. 1984.

REFERENCE HANDBOOK ON INSURANCE COMPANY INSOLVENCY. Second Edition. Richard J. Marcus, Editor. American Bar Association, Tort and Insurance Practice Section, Committee on Public Regulation of Insurance Law, 750 North Lake Shore Drive, Chicago, Illinois 60611. 1989.

TEXTBOOKS AND GENERAL WORKS

AGENT'S LEGAL RESPONSIBILITY. Third Edition. Ronald T. Anderson. National Underwriter Company, 420 East Fourth Street, Cincinnati, Ohio 45202. 1991.

ANDERSON ON LIFE INSURANCE. Buist M. Anderson. Little, Brown and Company, 34 Beacon Street, Boston, Massachusetts 02108. 1991.

ANNOTATED BANKERS BLANKET BOND. Frank L. Skiller, Jr. and Harvey C. Koch, Editors. American Bar Association, 750 North Lake Shore Drive, Chicago, Illinois 60611. 1987.

BAD FAITH LITIGATION AND INSURER VS. INSURER DISPUTES. Richard D. Williams, Chairman. Practising Law Institute, 810 Seventh Avenue, New York, New York 10019. 1989.

THE BLAME GAME: INJURIES, INSURANCE, AND INJUSTICE. Jeffrey O'Connell and C. Brian Kelly. Lexington Books, 125 Spring Street, Lexington, Massachusetts 02173. 1987.

CASES, MATERIALS, AND PROBLEMS ON GENERAL PRACTICE INSURANCE LAW. Second Edition. Kenneth H. York and John W. Whelan. West Publishing Company, 50 West Kellogg Boulevard, St. Paul, Minnesota 55164. 1988.

COUCH CYCLOPEDIA OF INSURANCE LAW. Second Edition. Ronald A. Anderson. Lawyers Cooperative Publishing Company, Aqueduct Building, Rochester, New York 14694. 1959. (Annual Supplements).

DISTRIBUTING RISK: INSURANCE, LEGAL THEORY, AND PUBLIC POLICY. Yale University Press, 302 Temple Street, New Haven, Connecticut 06520. 1986.

THE ECONOMICS OF INSURANCE REGULATION: A CROSS-NATIONAL STUDY. Jorg Finsinger and Mark V. Pauly, Editors. State Mutual Book, 521 Fifth Avenue, Seventh Floor, New York, New York 10175. 1986.

ESSENTIAL CASES IN INSURANCE LAW. Kenneth Cannar. State Mutual Book, 521 Fifth Avenue, Seventh Floor, New York, New York 10175. 1985.

EXCESS LIABILITY: DUTIES AND RESPONSIBILITIES OF THE INSURER. Pat Magarick. Clark Boardman Company, Limited, 435 Hudson Street, New York, New York 10014. 1982. (Supplement 1985).

FEDERAL INCOME TAXATION OF LIFE INSURANCE. Donald O. Jansen. American Bar Association, Real Property, Probate, and Trust Law Section, 750 North Lake Shore Drive, Chicago, Illinois 60611. 1989.

FEDERAL LAWS IMPACTING INSURANCE ACTIVITIES OF BANKS. American Bankers Association, 1120 Connecticut Avenue, Northwest, Washington, D.C. 20036. 1984.

FIRREA: IMPLEMENTATION AND COMPLIANCE. Karen D. Shaw, James C. Sivon and Mary Johannes. Research Institute of America, Incorporated, One Penn Plaza, New York, New York 10119. 1991.

FREEDMAN'S RICHARDS ON THE LAW OF INSURANCE. Sixth Edition. Warren Freedman. Lawyers Cooperative Publishing Company, Aqueduct Building, Rochester, New York 14694. 1990.

HOW INSURANCE COMPANIES SETTLE CASES. Clinton E. Miller. James Publishing Group, Santa Ana, California. 1989.

INSOLVENCY AND SOLIDITY OF INSURANCE COMPANIES. Thomas A. Harnett. Practising Law Institute, 810 Seventh Avenue, New York, New York 10019. 1987.

INSURANCE BAD FAITH LITIGATION. William M. Shernoff and Sanford M. Gage. Matthew Bender and Company, Incorporated, 11 Penn Plaza, New York, New York 10001. 1984. (Annual Supplements).

INSURANCE CLAIMS AND DISPUTES: REPRESENTATION OF INSURANCE COMPANIES AND INSUREDS. Second Edition. A.D. Windt. Shepard's/McGraw-Hill, P.O. Box 1235, Colorado Springs, Colorado 80901. 1988.

INSURANCE COMPANY SOLVENCY: CAPITAL ADEQUACY, REGULATORY DEVELOPMENTS, AND LIABILITY ISSUES. James Corcoran. Practising Law Institute, 810 Seventh Avenue, New York, New York 10019. 1991.

INSURANCE COVERAGE DISPUTES. Thomas R. Newman and Barry R. Ostrager. Prentice-Hall, Incorporated, 113 Sylvan Avenue, Englewood Cliffs, New Jersey 07632. 1990.

INSURANCE COVERAGE OF CONSTRUCTION DISPUTES. Scott C. Turner. Shepard's/McGraw-Hill, P.O. Box 1235, Colorado Springs, Colorado 80901. 1992.

INSURANCE ENVIRONMENT AND OPERATIONS. Third Edition. R. Robert Rackley. Insurance Achievement, Incorporated, 7330 Highland Road, Baton Rouge, Louisiana 70808. 1985.

INSURANCE, EXCESS, AND REINSURANCE COVERAGE DISPUTES. Barry R. Ostrager and Thomas R. Newman. Practising Law Institute, 810 Seventh Avenue, New York, New York 10019. 1990.

INSURANCE LAW: A GUIDE TO FUNDAMENTAL PRINCIPLES, LEGAL DOCTRINES, AND COMMERCIAL PRACTICES. Robert E. Keeton and Alan I. Widiss. West Publishing Company, 50 West Kellogg Boulevard, St. Paul, Minnesota 55164. 1988.

INSURANCE LAW AND PRACTICE. John Alan Appleman and Jean Appleman. West Publishing Company, P.O. Box 64526, 50 West Kellogg Boulevard, St. Paul, Minnesota 55164-0526. 1981. (Supplemented).

INSURANCE LAW AND REGULATION: CASES AND MATERIALS. Kenneth S. Abraham. Foundation Press, 615 Merrick Avenue, Westbury, New York 11590. 1990.

INSURANCE LAW: CASES AND MATERIALS. Roger C. Henderson. Michie Company, P.O. Box 7587, Charlottesville, Virginia 22906. 1989.

INSURANCE LAW IN A NUTSHELL. Second Edition. John F. Dobbyn. West Publishing Company, P.O. Box 64526, 50 West Kellogg Boulevard, St. Paul, Minnesota 55164-0526. 1989.

INSURANCE LITIGATION AND COVERAGE ISSUES. Eugene R. Anderson, Chairman. Practising Law Institute, 810 Seventh Avenue, New York, New York 10019. 1986.

INSURANCE MARKETS: INFORMATION PROBLEMS AND REGULATION. David Lereah. State Mutual Book, 521 Fifth Avenue, New York, New York 10175. 1985.

INSURANCE: MATERIALS ON FUNDAMENTAL PRINCIPLES, LEGAL DOCTRINES, AND REGULATORY ACTS. Alan I. Widiss. West Publishing Company, 50 West Kellogg Boulevard, St. Paul, Minnesota 55164. 1989.

INSURANCE OPERATIONS BY SAVING INSTITUTIONS: AN INTRODUCTION. Harold B. Olin. United States League of Savings Institutions, 1709 New York Avenue, Northwest, Suite 801, Washington, D.C. 20006. 1985.

INSURANCE PRODUCTS UNDER THE SECURITIES LAWS: NEW REGULATORY INITIATIVES. Practising Law Institute, 810 Seventh Avenue, New York, New York 10019. 1984.

INSURING MEDICAL MALPRACTICE. Frank A. Sloan, Randall R. Bovbjerg and Penny B. Githens. Oxford University Press, 200 Madison Avenue, New York, New York 10016. 1991.

INTERNATIONAL INSURANCE: MANAGING RISK IN THE WORLD. David L. Bickelhaupt and Ran Bar-Niv. Books on Demand, 300 North Zeeb Road, Ann Arbor, Michigan 48106-1346. 1983.

INTRODUCTION TO BUSINESS INSURANCE. Dan L. Goldwasser and David W. Ichel, Co-chairmen. Practising Law Institute, 810 Seventh Avenue, New York, New York 10019. 1985.

INTRODUCTION TO INSURANCE. Second Edition. Mark S. Dorfman. Prentice-Hall, Incorporated, 113 Sylvan Avenue, Englewood Cliffs, New Jersey 07632. 1987.

LAW AND PRACTICE OF INSURANCE COMPANY INSOLVENCY REVISITED. Francine L. Semaya, Editor. American Bar Association, Committee on Public Regulation of Insurance Law, 750 North Lake Shore Drive, Chicago, Illinois 60611. 1989.

THE LAW OF INSURANCE. Third Edition. Irwin M. Taylor. Oceana Publications, Incorporated, 75 Main Street, Dobbs Ferry, New York 10522. 1983.

THE LAW OF INSURANCE CONTRACTS. Malcolm A. Clarke. Lloyd's of London Press, New York, New York. 1989.

THE LEGAL ENVIRONMENT OF INSURANCE. Third Edition. James J. Lorimer. American Institute for Property and Liability Underwriters, 720 Providence Road, Malvern, Pennsylvania 19355. 1987.

LIABILITY: PERSPECTIVES AND POLICY. Robert E. Litan and Clifford Winston, Editors. Brookings Institution, 1775 Massachusetts Avenue, Washington, D.C. 20036. 1988.

LIFE INSURANCE: INCLUDING HEALTH AND DISABILITY INSURANCE. Second Edition. Darwin B. Close. Anderson Publishing Company, 2035 Reading Road, Cincinnati, Ohio 45202. 1987.

LIFE INSURANCE PRODUCTS. Richard A. Schwartz, Catherine R. Turner and Michael D. Weinberg. American Bar Association, Real Property, Probate, and Trust Law Section, 750 North Lake Shore Drive, Chicago, Illinois 60611. 1989.

LITIGATION AND PREVENTION OF INSURER BAD FAITH. Dennis J. Wall. Shepard's/McGraw-Hill, P.O. Box 1235, Colorado Springs, Colorado 80901. 1985.

LLOYD'S, THE ILU, AND THE LONDON INSURANCE MARKET. Sol Kroll. Practising Law Institute, 810 Seventh Avenue, New York, New York 10019. 1988.

MAJOR CHANGES IN INSURANCE COMPANY INVESTMENTS, GOVERNANCE, SUBSIDIARIES, AND SEPARATE ACCOUNTS. American Law Institute-American Bar Association, Committee on Continuing Professional Education, 4025 Chestnut Street, Philadelphia, Pennsylvania 19104. 1983.

MARINE INSURANCE AND GENERAL AVERAGE IN THE UNITED STATES: AN AVERAGE ADJUSTER'S VIEWPOINT. Third Edition. Leslie J. Buglass. Cornell Maritime Press, P.O. Box 456, Centreville, Maryland 21617. 1991.

MAXIMUM RECOVERY FOR INSURANCE CLAIMANTS. James H. Hargrove. La Jolla Book Publishing Company, P.O. Box 569, La Jolla, California 92037. 1986.

PERSONAL LINES UNDERWRITING. Second Edition. G. William Glendenning and Robert B. Holton. Insurance Institute of America, Incorporated, 720 Providence Road, Malvern, Pennsylvania 19355. 1982.

THE POLITICAL ECONOMY OF REGULATION: THE CASE OF INSURANCE. Kenneth J. Meier. State University of New York Press, State University Plaza, Albany, New York 12246. 1988.

REACTIVE RISK AND RATIONAL ACTION: MANAGING MORAL HAZARD IN INSURANCE CONTRACTS. Carol A. Heimer. University of California Press, 2120 Berkeley Way, Berkeley, California 94720. 1985.

READINGS IN MULTILINE INSURANCE LAW AND OPERATIONS. Charles E. Hughes. American College, 270 Bryn Mawr Avenue, Bryn Mawr, Pennsylvania 19010. 1986.

THE REFORM OF FEDERAL DEPOSIT INSURANCE: DISCIPLINING THE GOVERNMENT AND PROTECTING TAXPAYERS. James R. Barth and R. Dan Brumbaugh, Jr., Editors. HarperCollins Publishers, 10 East Fifty-third Street, New York, New York 10022. 1992.

REINSURANCE: FUNDAMENTALS AND CURRENT ISSUES. Ruth Gastel and Sean Mooney. Insurance Information Institute, 110 William Street, New York, New York 10038. 1983.

RESPONSIBILITITES OF INSURANCE AGENTS AND BROKERS. Betram Harnett. Matthew Bender and Company, Incorporated, 11 Penn Plaza, New York, New York 10001. 1974- . (Annual Supplements).

RISK AND INSURANCE. Sixth Edition. Green and Trieschmann. South- Western Publishing Company, 5101 Madison Road, Cincinnati, Ohio 45227. 1988.

THE SELF-INSURANCE MANUAL. Claude C. Lilly, III and H. Glen Boggs. National Insurance Law Service, 21625 Prairie Street, Chatsworth, California 91311. 1984. (Supplement).

SPLIT-DOLLAR LIFE INSURANCE. Stanford A. Wynn. American Bar Association, Section of Real Property, Probate and Trust Law, 750 North Lake Shore Drive, Chicago, Illinois 60611. 1991.

THE SUICIDE CASE: INVESTIGATION AND TRIAL OF INSURANCE CLAIMS. James L. Nolan, Editor. American Bar Association, Tort and Insurance Practice Section, 750 North Lake Shore Drive, Chicago, Illinois 60611. 1988.

TAXING INSURERS: THE REVOLUTION AHEAD. Carolyn Bowers. Washington Business Information, Incorporated, 1117 North Nineteenth Street, Number 200, Arlington, Virginia 22209-1798. 1983.

STUDIES IN MODERN CHOICE-OF-LAW: TORTS, INSURANCE, LAND TITLES. Moffatt Hancock. William S. Hein and Company, Incorporated, 1285 Main Street, Buffalo, New York 14209. 1984.

UNDERSTANDING INSURANCE LAW. Robert H. Jerry, II. Matthew Bender and Company, Incorporated, 11 Penn Plaza, New York, New York 10001. 1987.

ENCYCLOPEDIAS AND DICTIONARIES

DESKBOOK ENCYCLOPEDIA OF AMERICAN INSURANCE LAW. Fifth Edition. Data Research, Incorporated, 4635 Nicols Road, Suite 100, Eagan, Minnesota 55122. 1991.

DIGESTS, INDEXES, ABSTRACTS, CITATORS

BECKER'S INSURANCE INDEX/CITATOR: A DETAILED COMPILATION OF CITATIONS COVERING THE ENTIRE RANGE OF INSURANCE LAW AS PRESENTED IN THE VARIOUS LEGAL REFERENCE WORKS, CORRELATED AS TO SUBJECT MATTER, AND ARRANGED IN A SINGLE ALPHABETICAL SERIES. Fourth Edition. Olga Becker. Index/Citator System, Incorporated, 4400 Lindell Boulevard, St. Louis, Missouri 63108. 1991.

CONSTRUCTION AND ENVIRONMENTAL INSURANCE CASE DIGESTS. John Wiley and Sons, Incorporated, 605 Third Avenue, New York, New York 10158. 1991.

INSURANCE PERIODICALS INDEX. 1985 Edition. National Insurance Law Service, 21625 Prairie Street, Chatsworth, California 91311. 1985.

SHEPARD'S INSURANCE LAW CITATIONS. Shepard's/McGraw-Hill, P.O. Box 1235, Colorado Springs, Colorado 80901. 1987.

THE TIPS INDEX OF PAPERS: AN INDEX OF PAPERS PREPARED FOR THE ABA TORT AND INSURANCE PRACTICE SECTION AND PRESENTED AT ITS MEETINGS AND THROUGH ITS PUBLICATIONS. American Bar Association, 750 North Lake Shore Drive, Chicago, Illinois 60611. 1985.

ANNUALS AND SURVEYS

THE ECONOMICS OF INSURANCE REGULATION: A CROSS-NATIONAL STUDY. Jorg Finsinger and Mark V. Pauly, Editors. State Mutual Book, 521 Fifth Avenue, New York, New York 10175. 1986.

INSURANCE RATE LITIGATION: A SURVEY OF JUDICIAL TREATMENT OF INSURANCE RATEMAKING AND INSURANCE RATE REGULATION. Judith K. Mintel. Kluwer- Nijhoff Publishing, Kluwer Academic Publishers, 101 Philip Drive, Assinippi Park, Norwell, Massachusetts 02061. 1983.

LAW REVIEWS AND PERIODICALS

FEDERATION OF INSURANCE AND CORPORATE COUNSEL QUARTERLY. Federal of Insurance and Corporate Counsel, 117 North Linn Street, Iowa City, Iowa 52440. Quarterly.

INSURANCE COUNSEL JOURNAL. International Association of Insurance Counsel, 20 North Wacker Drive, Chicago 60606. Quarterly.

INSURANCE LAW JOURNAL. Commerce Clearing House, Incorporated, 4025 West Peterson Avenue, Chicago, Illinois 60646. Monthly.

NATIONAL INSURANCE LAW REVIEW. National Insurance Law Service, 20675 Bahama Street, Chatsworth, California 91311. Quarterly.

TORT AND INSURANCE LAW JOURNAL. American Bar Association, 750 North Lake Shore Drive, Chicago, Illinois 60611. Quarterly.

NEWSLETTERS AND NEWSPAPERS

BAD FAITH LAW REPORT. Stratton Press, P.O. Box 22391, San Francisco, California 94122. Monthly.

BAD FAITH LAW UPDATE. Matthew Bender and Company, Incorporated, 11 Penn Plaza, New York, New York 10001. Monthly.

BANKS IN INSURANCE REPORT. Executive Enterprises Publications Company, Incorporated, 22 West Twenty-first Street, New York, New York 10010. Monthly.

THE CLAIMS FORUM. American Arbitration Association, 140 West Fifty-first Street, New York, New York 10020. Quarterly.

Encyclopedia of Legal Information Sources • 2nd Ed.   **INSURANCE**

COILETTER. National Conference of Insurance Legislators, P.O. Box 217, Brookfield, Wisconsin 53008. Monthly.

CORPORATE INSURANCE LAW BULLETIN. Quinlan Publishing Company, Incorporated, 23 Drydock Avenue, Boston, Massachusetts 02110. Monthly.

DEFENSE LAW JOURNAL. The Michie Company, P.O. Box 7587, Charlottesville, Virginia 22906. Bimonthly.

FEDERAL AND STATE INSURANCE WEEK. JR Publishing Incorporated, P.O. Box 6654, McLean, Virginia 22106. Weekly.

FIDELITY AND SURETY NEWS. American Bar Association, Tort and Insurance Practice Section, 750 North Lake Shore Drive, Chicago, Illinois 60611. Quarterly.

FROM THE STATE CAPITALS: INSURANCE REGULATION. Wakeman Walworth, Incorporated, 300 North Washington Street, Suite 204, Alexandria, Virginia 22314. Weekly.

INSIGHT/INSTATUS. NILS Publishing Company, 21625 Prairie Street, Chatsworth, California 91311. Monthly.

INSURANCE INDUSTRY LITIGATION REPORTER. Andrews Publications, 1646 West Chester Pike, Westtown, Pennsylvania 19395. Semimonthly.

INSURANCE INDUSTRY NEWSLETTER. Insurance Field Company, Incorporated, P.O. Box 3006, Savannah, Georgia 31402-3006. Weekly.

INSURANCE LITIGATION REPORTER. Litigation Research Group, 500 Howard Street, San Francisco, California 94107. Monthly.

INSURANCE OUTLOOK. Capitol Publications, Incorporated, 1101 King Street, Suite 444, Alexandria, Virginia 22314. Semimonthly.

THE INSURANCE TAX REVIEW. Tax Analysts, 6830 North Fairfax Drive, Arlington, Virginia 22213. Bimonthly.

JOHN LINER LETTER. Federal Research Press, 155 Federal Street, Boston, Massachusetts 02111. Monthly.

LEGAL NOTES FOR INSURANCE. Data Research, Incorporated, P.O. Box 409, Rosemount, Minnesota 55068. Monthly.

THE LEGISLATIVE REPORTER. National Association of Independent Insurers, 2600 River Road, Des Plaines, Illinois 60018. Biweekly.

LIABILITY WEEK. JR Publishing Incorporated, P.O. Box 6654, McLean, Virginia 22106. Weekly.

THE LITIGATION REPORTER. National Association of Independent Insurers, 2600 River Road, Des Plaines, Illinois 60018. Quarterly.

LLOYD'S INSURANCE INTERNATIONAL. Lloyd's of London Press, Incorporated, 611 Broadway, Suite 523, New York, New York 10012.

MEALEY'S LITIGATION REPORT: INSURANCE. Mealey Publications, P.O. Box 446, Wayne, Pennsylvania 19087. Bimonthly.

MEALEY'S LITIGATION REPORT: INSURANCE INSOLVENCY. Mealey Publications, P.O. Box 446, Wayne, Pennsylvania 19087. Semimonthly.

MEALEY'S LITIGATION REPORT: REINSURANCE. Mealey Publications, P.O. Box 446, Wayne, Pennsylvania 19087. Semimonthly.

THE NAIC NEWS. National Association of Insurance Commissioners, 120 West Twelfth Street, Suite 1100, Kansas City, Missouri 64105. Monthly.

THE REGULATORY REPORTER. National Association of Independent Insurers, 2600 River Road, Des Plaines, Illinois 60018. Quarterly.

SMART'S INSURANCE BULLETIN. Darrell Heppner. Risk Management Services, Incorporated, 154 Sunnyside Drive, Leandro, California 94577. Weekly.

TORT AND INSURANCE PLEADINGS AND BRIEF. Law Research Incorporated, 425 Brannan Street, San Francisco, California 94107. Monthly.

BIBLIOGRAPHIES

NUCLEAR HAZARDS INSURANCE: A BIBLIOGRAPHY. Mary Vance. Vance Bibliographies, P.O. Box 229, 112 North Charter Street, Monticello, Illinois 61856. 1989.

DIRECTORIES

BEST'S AGENTS GUIDE TO LIFE INSURANCE COMPANIES. A. M. Best Companies, Ambest Road, Oldwick, New Jersey 08858.

BEST'S DIRECTORY OF RECOMMENDED INSURANCE ADJUSTERS. A. M. Best Company, Ambest Road, Oldwick, New Jersey 08858. Annual.

BEST'S DIRECTORY OF RECOMMENDED INSURANCE ATTORNEYS. A. M. Best Company, Ambest Road, Oldwick, New Jersey 08858. Annual.

BEST'S INSURANCE REPORTS. A. M. Best Company, Ambest Road, Oldwick, New Jersey 08858.

BEST'S MARKET GUIDE. A. M. Best Company, Ambest Road, Oldwick, New Jersey 08858.

BLUE BOOK OF ADJUSTERS. National Association of Independent Insurance Adjusters, 222 West Adams Street, Chicago, Illinois 60606.

THE GROUP INSURANCE DIRECTORY. Benefits Research, Incorporated, 601 North Jefferson Street, Suite 201, Parispanny, New Jersey 07054.

GROUP INSURANCE STANDARD DIRECTORY. Duna Marketing Services, 48 Old Bloomfield Avenue, Mountain Lakes, New Jersey 07046.

HINE'S DIRECTORY OF INSURANCE ADJUSTERS. Hine's Legal Directory, Incorporated, P.O. Box 71, Glen Ellyn, Illinois 60138. Annual.

HINE'S INSURANCE COUNSEL. Hine's Legal Directory, Incorporated, P.O. Box 71, Glen Ellyn, Illinois 60138. Annual.

INSURANCE ALMANAC. Underwriter Printing and Publishing Company, 291 South Van Brunt Street, Englewood, New Jersey 07631. Annual.

INSURANCE BAR DIRECTORY. Bar List Publishing Company, 426 Huehl Road, Number 6B, Northbrook, Illinois 60062. Annual.

INSURANCE CONSULTANTS DIRECTORY. American Business Directories, Incorporated, American Business Lists, Incorporated, 5707 South Eighty-sixth Circle, Omaha, Nebraska 68127. Annual.

INSURANCE DIRECTORY. American Business Directories, Incorporated, American Business Lists, Incorporated, 5707 South Eighty-sixth Circle, Omaha, Nebraska 68127. Annual.

INSURANCE LEGISLATIVE FACT BOOK AND ALMANAC. Conference of Insurance Legislators, Box 217, Brookfield, Wisconsin 53005.

INSURANCE MARKET PLACE. Rough Notes Company, Incorporated, Box 564, Indianapolis, Indiana 46206. Annual.

NATIONAL INSURANCE ASSOCIATION-MEMBER ROSTER. National Insurance Association, P.O. Box 53230, Chicago, Illinois 60653-0230. 1986. Irregular.

UNDERWRITERS LIST OF TRIAL COUNSEL. Underwriters List Publishing Company, C/o Wiliam Brinker, 48 Oakland Hills, Rotunda West, Florida 33946. Annual.

WHO'S WHO IN INSURANCE. Underwriter Printing and Publishing Company, 50 East Palisade Avenue, Englewood, New Jersey 07631.

WHO'S WHO IN RISK MANAGEMENT. Underwriter Printing and Publishing Company, 50 East Palisade Avenue, Englewood, New Jersey 07631.

ASSOCIATIONS AND PROFESSIONAL SOCIETIES

AMERICAN ACADEMY OF ACTUARIES. 1720 Eye Street, Northwest, Seventh Floor, Washington, D.C. 20006. (202) 223-8196.

AMERICAN INSURANCE ASSOCIATION. 1130 Connecticut Avenue, Northwest, Suite 1000, Washington, D.C. 20036. (202) 828-7100.

ASSOCIATION OF DEFENSE TRIAL ATTORNEYS. 600 Jefferson Bank Building, Peoria, Illinois 61602. (309) 676-0400.

CAPTIVE INSURANCE COMPANIES ASSOCIATION. 205 East Forty-second Street, New York, New York 10017. (212) 687-4501.

FEDERATION OF INSURANCE AND CORPORATION COUNSEL. c/o Harrison G. Ball, 15 Ridge Road, Marblehead, Massachusetts 01945. (617) 639-0698.

HEALTH INSURANCE ASSOCIATION OF AMERICA. 1025 Connecticut Avenue, Northwest, Suite 1200, Washington, D.C. 20036. (202) 223-7780.

INDEPENDENT INSURANCE AGENTS OF AMERICA. 127 Peyton, Alexandria, Virginia 22314. (703) 683-4422.

INSURANCE CRIME PREVENTION INSTITUTE. 15 Franklin Street, Westport, Connecticut 06880. (203) 226-6347.

INTERNATIONAL ASSOCIATION FOR INSURANCE LAW IN THE UNITED STATES. c/o Life Office Management Association, 5770 Powers Ferry Road, Atlanta, Georgia 30327. (404) 951-1770.

INTERNATIONAL ASSOCIATION OF DEFENSE COUNSEL. 20 North Wacker Drive, Suite 3100, Chicago, Illinois 60606. (312) 368-1494.

NATIONAL ASSOCIATION OF INDEPENDENT INSURANCE ADJUSTERS. 300 West Washington, Suite 805, Chicago, Illinois 60606. (312) 853-0808.

NATIONAL ASSOCIATION OF INSURANCE COMMISSIONERS. 120 West Twelfth Street, Suite 1100, Kansas City, Missouri 64105. (816) 842-3600.

NATIONAL ASSOCIATION OF PUBLIC INSURANCE ADJUSTERS. 300 Water Street, Suite 400, Baltimore, Maryland 21202. (301) 539-4141.

NATIONAL CONFERENCE GROUP OF LAWYERS, INSURANCE COMPANIES AND ADJUSTERS. American Bar Association, 750 North Lake Shore Drive, Chicago, Illinois 60611. (312) 988-5000.

NATIONAL CONFERENCE OF INSURANCE LEGISLATORS. 1776 Church View Drive, P.O. Box 217, Brookfield, Wisconsin 53008. (414) 782-6669.

NATIONAL COUNCIL OF SELF-INSURERS. 10 South Riverside Plaza, Suite 1530, Chicago, Illinois 60606. (312) 454-5110.

PROFESSIONAL INSURANCE AGENTS. 400 North Washington Street, Alexandria, Virginia 22314. (703) 836-9340.

PUBLIC RISK MANAGEMENT ASSOCIATION. 1117 North Nineteenth Street, Suite 900, Arlington, Virginia 22209. (703) 528-7701.

REINSURANCE ASSOCIATION OF AMERICA. 1819 L Street, Northwest, Seventh Floor, Washington, D.C. 20036. (202) 293-3335.

RISK AND INSURANCE MANAGEMENT SOCIETY. 205 East Forty-second Street, New York, New York 10017. (212) 286-9292.

SOCIETY OF ACTUARIES. 475 North Martingale Road, Schaumberg, Illinois 60173. (312) 706-3500.

SOCIETY OF CERTIFIED INSURANCE COUNSELORS. P.O. Box 27027, Austin, Texas 78755. (512) 345-7932.

RESEARCH CENTERS, INSTITUTES, CLEARINGHOUSES

ALL-INDUSTRY RESEARCH ADVISORY COUNCIL. 1200 Harger Road, Suite 310, Oak Brook, Illinois 60521. (708) 572-1177.

AMERICAN COUNCIL OF LIFE INSURANCE. 1001 Pennsylvania Avenue, Northwest, Washington, D.C. 20004. (202) 624-2470.

CENTER FOR INSURANCE EDUCATION AND RESEARCH. University of Georgia, 206 Brooks Hall, Athens, Gerogia 30602. (404) 542-4290.

CENTER FOR INSURANCE RESEARCH. Florida State University, College of Business, Tallahassee, Florida 32306. (904) 644-4070.

CENTER FOR RESEARCH ON RISK AND INSURANCE. University of Pennsylvania, Wharton School, 3641 Locust Walk, Philadelphia, Pennsylvania 19104. (215) 898-2515.

CENTER FOR RISK MANAGEMENT AND INSURANCE RESEARCH. Georgia State University, College of Business Administration, University Plaza, Atlanta, Georgia 30303. (404) 651-4250.

HEALTH BENEFITS RESEARCH CENTER. Cornell University, 52 Vanderbilt Avenue, Room 1503, New York, New York 10017. (212) 370-7820.

HIGHWAY LOSS DATA INSTITUTE. 1005 North Glebe Road, Suite 800, Arlington, Virginia 22201. (703) 247-1600.

INSTITUTE FOR INSURANCE EDUCATION AND RESEARCH. University of Iowa, College of Business Administration, 116 International Center, Iowa City, Iowa 52242. (319) 335-2527.

INSURANCE INFORMATION INSTITUTE. 110 William Street, New York, New York 10038. (212) 669-9200.

INSURANCE INSTITUTE OF AMERICA. 720 Providence Road, Malvern, Pennsylvania 19355. (215) 644-2100.

LIFE INSURANCE MARKETING AND RESEARCH ASSOCIATION, RESEARCH DIVISION. 8 Farm Springs, Farmington, Connecticut 06032. (203) 677-0033.

PROPERTY LOSS RESEARCH BUREAU. 1501 Woodfield Road, Suite 400W, Schaumberg, Illinois 60173. (708) 330-8650.

SOCIETY OF INSURANCE RESEARCH. P.O. Box 933, Appleton, Wisconsin 54912. (414) 730-8858.

S.S. HUEBNER FOUNDATION. University of Pennsylvania, 3641 Locust Walk, Philadelphia, Pennsylvania 19104. (215) 898-7620.

ONLINE DATABASES

BUSINESS INSURANCE. Crain Communications Incorporated, 1400 Woodbridge, Detroit, Michigan 48207.

DRI U.S. INSURANCE DATA BANK. Data Resources, Incorporated, 1750 K Street, Northwest, Washington, D.C. 20006.

DUN'S UNDERWRITING GUIDE. Dun and Bradstreet Corporation, 99 Church Street, New York, New York 10007.

FEDERAL AND STATE INSURANCE WEEK. JR Publishing Incorporated, P.O. Box 6654, McLean, Virginia 22106.

FROM THE STATE CAPITALS: INSURANCE REGULATION. Wakeman Walworth, Incorporated, 300 North Washington Street, Suite 204, Alexandria, Virginia 22314.

I.I.I. DATA BASE NEWS. Insurance Information Institute, 110 William Street, New York, New York 10038.

I.I.I. DATA BASE REPORTS. Insurance Information Institute, 110 William Street, New York, New York 10038.

I.I.I. DATA BASE SEARCH. Insurance Information Institute, 110 William Street, New York, New York 10038.

IMS NEWS PLUS. Insurance Marketing Services, 1510 Eleventh Street, Santa Monica, California 90406.

IMS WEEKLY MARKETEER. Insurance Marketing Services, 1510 Eleventh Street, Santa Monica, California 90406.

INSURANCE ABSTRACTS. University Microfilms International, 300 North Zeeb Road, Ann Arbor, Michigan 48106.

INSURANCE AND RISK MANAGEMENT. Bureau of National Affairs, BNA Online, 1231 Twenty-fifth Street, Northwest, Washington, D.C. 20037.

INSURANCE INDUSTRY DATA BASE. National Association of Insurance Commissioners, 120 West Twelfth Street, Suite 1100, Kansas City, Missouri 64105.

INSURLAW. NILS Publishing Company, P.O. Box 2507, Chatsworth, California 91311.

LEXIS, INSURANCE LIBRARY. Mead Data Central, P.O. Box 933, Dayton, Ohio 45401.

LIABILITY WEEK. JR Publishing, Incorporated, P.O. Box 6654, McLean, Virginia 22106.

RIMS GOVERNMENT AFFAIRS/INDUSTRY RELATIONS. Risk and Insurance Management Society, 205 East Forty-second Street, Suite 1504, New York, New York 10017.

RIMSNET NEWS BUREAU. Risk and Insurance Management Society, 205 East Forty-second Street, Suite 1504, New York, New York 10017.

RISK MANAGEMENT DATABASE. Risk and Insurance Management Society, 205 East Forty-second Street, Suite 1504, New York, New York 10017.

STANDARD AND POOR'S INSURANCE RATING SERVICE. Standard and Poor's Corporation, 25 Broadway, New York, New York 10004.

WESTLAW, STATE INSURANCE LAW LIBRARY. West Publishing Company, P.O. Box 64526, 50 West Kellogg Boulevard, St. Paul, Minnesota 55164.

STATISTICS SOURCES

INSURANCE FACTS. Insurance Information Institute, 110 William Street, New York, New York 10038. 1983.

INSURANCE

AUDIOVISUALS

INSURANCE, EXCESS, AND REINSURANCE COVERAGE DISPUTES. Thomas R. Newman, Barry R. Ostrager, et al. Practising Law Institute, 810 Seventh Avenue, New York, New York 10019. 1984. Audiocassettes.

COMPUTER-ASSISTED LEGAL INSTRUCTION

DECISIONS ON INSURANCE. Robert E. Keeton. Center for Computer-Assisted Instruction, 229 19th Avenue South, University of Minnesota, Minneapolis, Minnesota 55455. Machine-readable computer file.

INSURANCE LAW. Robert E. Keeton. Center for Computer-Assisted Instruction, 229 19th Avenue South, University of Minnesota, Minneapolis, Minnesota 55455. Machine-readable computer file.

INSURANCE, DISABILITY
See: INSURANCE, HEALTH AND UNEMPLOYMENT

INSURANCE, HEALTH AND UNEMPLOYMENT

LOOSELEAF SERVICES AND REPORTERS

EMPLOYEE BENEFIT PLAN REVIEW RESEARCH REPORTS. Charles D. Spencer and Associates, Incorporated, 222 West Adams Street, Chicago, Illinois 60606. 1953- .

THE LAW OF LIFE AND HEALTH INSURANCE. Bertram Harnett and Irving I. Lesnick. Matthew Bender and Company, Incorporated, 11 Penn Plaza, New York, New York 10001. 1988- .

MEDICARE-MEDICAID GUIDE. Commerce Clearing House, Incorporated, 4025 West Peterson Avenue, Chicago, Illinois 60646. 1969- . Biweekly.

UNEMPLOYMENT INSURANCE - SOCIAL SECURITY: FEDERAL AND ALL STATES. Commerce Clearing House, Incorporated, 4025 West Peterson Avenue, Chicago, Illinois 60646. 1924- . Weekly.

TEXTBOOKS AND GENERAL WORKS

ATTORNEY'S GUIDE TO SOCIAL SECURITY DISABILITY CLAIMS. Kenneth F. Laritz. Shepard's/McGraw-Hill, P.O. Box 1235, Colorado Springs, Colorado 80901. 1986.

DISEASE AND THE COMPENSATION DEBATE. Jane Stapleton. Oxford University Press, Incorporated, 200 Madison Avenue, New York, New York 10016. 1986.

EMPLOYEE BENEFITS FOR SMALL BUSINESS. Jane White and Bruce Pyenson. Prentice-Hall, Incorporated, 113 Sylvan Avenue, Englewood Cliffs, New Jersey 07632. 1991.

EVALUATING INCOME REPLACEMENT FOR SHORT-TERM DISABILITY: THE ROLE OF WORKERS' COMPENSATION. Devol. Workers Compensation Research Institute, 245 First Street, Suite 402, Cambridge, Massachusetts 02141. 1985.

FEDERAL DISABILITY LAW AND PRACTICE: 1986 SUPPLEMENT. Frank S. Bloch. John Wiley and Sons, Incorporated, 605 Third Avenue, New York, New York 10158. 1986.

FEDERAL-STATE RELATIONS IN UNEMPLOYMENT INSURANCE: A BALANCE OF POWER. Murray Rubin. W. E. UpJohn Institute for Employemnt Research, 300 South Westredge Avenue, Kalamazoo, Michigan 49007-4686. 1983.

HOW TO PREPARE AND CONDUCT A SOCIAL SECURITY DISABILITY HEARING. National Clearinghouse for Legal Services, Incorporated, 407 South Dearborne, Chicago, Illinois 60605. 1985.

INSURANCE FOR UNEMPLOYMENT. Michael Beenstock and Valerie Brasse. Allen and Unwin, Incorporated, P.O. Box 442, Concord, Massachusetts 01742. 1986.

LEGAL ASPECTS OF HEALTH CARE REIMBURSEMENT. Robert J. Buchanan and James D. Minor. Aspen Publishers, 1600 Research Boulevard, Rockville, Maryland 20850. 1984.

LIFE INSURANCE: INCLUDING HEALTH AND DISABILITY INSURANCE. Second Edition. Darwin B. Close. Anderson Publishing Company, 2035 Reading Road, Cincinnati, Ohio 45202. 1987.

MEDICAL IMPROVEMENT STANDARD IN SOCIAL SECURITY AND SSI DISABILITY CASES. National Clearinghouse for Legal Services, Incorporated, 407 South Dearborne, Chicago, Illinois 60605. 1986.

MEDICAL PROOF OF SOCIAL SECURITIES DISABILITY. David A. Morton, III. West Publishing Company, P.O. Box 64526, 50 West Kellogg Boulevard, St. Paul, Minnesota 55164-0526. 1983 (1986 Supplement).

MEDICARE AND MEDICAID CLAIMS AND PROCEDURES. Second Edition. Harvey L. McCormich. West Publishing Company, P.O. Box 64526, 50 West Kellogg Boulevard, St. Paul, Minnesota 55164-0526. 1986.

MEDICARE EXPLAINED. Commerce Clearing House, Incorporated, 4025 West Peterson Avenue, Chicago, Illinois 60646. 1988.

MEDICARE POLICY: NEW DIRECTIONS FOR HEALTH AND LONG-TERM CARE. Karen Davis and Diane E. Rowland. Johns Hopkins University Press, 701 West Fortieth Street, Suite 275, Baltimore, Maryland 21211-2190. 1985.

NONMONETARY ELIGIBILITY IN STATE UNEMPLOYMENT INSURANCE PROGRAMS: LAW AND PRACTICE. Walter Corson, et al. Upjohn, W.E., Institute for Employment Research, 300 S. Westnedge Avenue, Kalamazoo, Michigan 49007-4686. 1986.

NON-PENSION BENEFITS FOR RETIRED EMPLOYEES: STUDY OF BENEFITS AND ACCOUNTING PRACTICES. Coopers and Lybrand. Financial Executives Research Foundation, 10 Madison Avenue, Box 1938, Morristown, New Jersey 07962-1938. 1985.

POLITICS AND HEALTH CARE ORGANIZATIONS: HMO'S AS FEDERAL POLICY. Brookings Institution, 1775 Massachusetts Avenue, Northwest, Washington, D.C. 20036-2188. 1983.

RETIREE HEALTH BENEFITS: FUNDING, ACCOUNTING, AND COST CONTAINMENT ISSUES. Kent A. Mason and William L. Sollee. Prentice-Hall, Incorporated, 113 Sylvan Avenue, Englewood Cliffs, New Jersey 07632. 1989.

SOCIAL SECURITY DISABILITY CLAIMS. Ronald R. Gilbert and J. Douglas Peters. Lawyers Cooperative Publishing Company, Aqueduct Building, Rochester, New York 14694. 1983. (Supplemented).

SOCIAL SECURITY DISABILITY CLAIMS. Practising Law Institute, 810 Seventh Avenue, New York, New York 10019. 1984.

SOCIAL SECURITY DISABILITY CLAIMS: PRACTICE AND PROCEDURE. Robert Francis. Callaghan and Company, 155 Pfingsten Road, Deerfield, Illinois 60015. 1990.

SOCIAL SECURITY DISABILITY CLAIMS: PRACTICE AND PROCEDURE. Don C. Keenan. Harrison Company, 3110 Crossing Park, Norcross, Georgia 30091. 1983. (Supplement 1985).

SOCIAL SECURITY DISABILITY PRACTICE. Kenneth J. Forrester. Lawyers Cooperative Publishing Company, Aqueduct Building, Rochester, New York 14694. 1985.

SOLVING THE PROBLEM OF MEDICARE. Peter Ferrara, et al. National Center for Policy Analysis, 7701 Stemmons, Suite 717, Dallas, Texas 75247. 1984.

ANNUALS AND SURVEYS

COMPARATIVE HEALTH SYSTEMS: DESCRIPTIVE ANALYSES OF FOURTEEN NATIONAL HEALTH SYSTEMS. Pennsylvania State University Press, 820 North University Drive, Suite C, Barbara Building, University Park, Pennsylvania 16802. 1984.

COMPARISON OF STATE UNEMPLOYMENT INSURANCE LAWS. United States Department of Labor, Employment and Training Administration, Unemployment Insurance Service. Superintendent of Documents, United States Government Printing Office, Washington, D.C. 20402. 1983.

ASSOCIATIONS AND PROFESSIONAL SOCIETIES

HEALTH INSURANCE ASSOCIATION OF AMERICA. 1025 Connecticut Avenue, Northwest, Suite 1200, Washington, D.C. 20036. (202) 223-7780.

INSURANCE, LIABILITY

LOOSELEAF SERVICES AND REPORTERS

EXCESS LIABILITY: THE LAW OF EXTRA-CONTRACTUAL LIABILITY OF INSURERS. Third Edition. Pat Magarick. Clark Boardman Company, Limited, 435 Hudson Street, New York, New York 10014. 1989- .

LEGAL GUIDE TO HANDLING TOXIC SUBSTANCES IN THE WORKPLACE. Lawrence P. Postol and William A. Hancock, Editor. Business Laws, Incorporated, 11630 Chillicothe Road, Chesterland, Ohio 44026. 1990- .

HANDBOOKS, MANUALS, FORMBOOKS

D & O LIABILITY HANDBOOK: LAW, SAMPLE DOCUMENTS, FORMS. Mark A. Sargent. Clark Boardman Company, Limited, 435 Hudson Street, New York, New York 10014. 1990.

TEXTBOOKS AND GENERAL WORKS

THE ARCHITECT-ENGINEER'S ROLE UNDER SUPERFUND AND SELECTING A PROFESSIONAL LIABILITY INSURANCE POLICY. American Bar Association, Public Contract Law Section, 750 North Lake Shore Drive, Chicago, Illinois 60611. 1985.

ASSESSING THE EFFECTS OF TORT REFORMS. Stephen J. Carrol with Nicholas Pace. Rand Corporation, Institute for Civil Justice, 1700 Main Street, P.O. Box 2138, Santa Monica, California 90406. 1987.

AVOIDING COMMERCIAL INSURANCE PITFALLS: A GUIDE FOR CORPORATE COUNSEL AND BUSINESSES. Jill B. Berkeley. Callaghan and Company, 155 Pfingsten Road, Deerfield, Illinois 60015. 1987.

BAD FAITH LIABILITY: A STATE-BY-STATE REVIEW. Stephen S. Ashley. Callaghan and Company, 155 Pfingsten Road, Deerfield, Illinois 60015. 1987.

THE BLAME GAME: INJURIES, INSURANCE, AND INJUSTICE. Jeffrey O'Connell and C. Brian Kelly. Lexington Books, 125 Spring Street, Lexington, Massachusetts 02173. 1987.

BUSINESS INTERRUPTION INSURANCE: ITS THEORY AND PRACTICE. Robert M. Morrison. National Underwriter Company, 420 East Fourth Street, Cincinnati, Ohio 45202. 1986.

COMMERCIAL GENERAL LIABILITY: THE NEW CLAIMS-MADE AND OCCURENCE FORMS. Third Edition. Donald S. Malecki and Arthur L. Flitner. National Underwriter Company, 420 East Fourth Street, Cincinnati, Ohio 45202. 1990.

COMMERCIAL LIABILITY RISK MANAGEMENT AND INSURANCE. Second Edition. American Institute for Property and Liability Underwriters, Incorporated, 720 Providence Road, Malvern, Pennsylvania 19355. 1986.

COMMERCIAL LIABILITY UNDERWRITING. Third Edition. Larry D. Gaunt, Numan A. Williams, and Everett D. Randall. Insurance Institute of America, 720 Providence Road, Malvern, Pennsylvania 19355. 1990.

INSURANCE, LIABILITY

COMPENSATION FOR ACCIDENTAL INJURIES IN THE UNITED STATES. EXECUTIVE SUMMARY. Deborah R. Hensler. Rand Corporation, Institute for Civil Justice, 1700 Main Street, P.O. Box 2138, Santa Monica, California 90406. 1991.

THE COMPREHENSIVE GENERAL LIABILITY POLICY: A CRITIQUE OF SELECTED PROVISIONS. American Bar Association, 750 North Lake Shore Drive, Chicago, Illinois 60611. 1985.

CORPORATE DIRECTORS AND OFFICERS LIABILITY, INSURANCE, AND RISK MANAGEMENT. Paul Cottrell and Joseph P. Monteleone, Editors. Executive Enterprises Publications Company, 22 West Twenty-first Street, New York, New York 10010-6904. 1989.

THE DEVELOPING LAW OF BUSINESS ERRORS AND OMISSIONS INSURANCE. Dennis R. Yeager. Practising Law Institute, 810 Seventh Avenue, New York, New York 10019. 1982.

DIRECTORS' AND OFFICERS' LIABILITY INSURANCE AND SELF INSURANCE: A COURSE HANDBOOK. Dan L. Goldwaser. Practising Law Institute, 810 Seventh Avenue, New York, New York 10019. 1986.

ESTIMATED LIABILITIES FOR LOSSES AND LOSS ADJUSTMENT EXPENSES. Ruth E. Salzmann. Prentice-Hall, Incorporated, 113 Sylvan Avenue, Englewood Cliffs, New Jersey 07632. 1984.

HANDLING FIDELITY AND SURETY CLAIMS. Robert F. Cushman and Charles H. Stamm, Editors. John Wiley and Sons, Incorporated, 605 Third Avenue, New York, New York 10158. 1984. (Supplemented).

HOW INSURANCE WORKS: AN INTRODUCTION TO PROPERTY AND LIABILITY INSURANCE. Barry D. Smith. Insurance Institute of Amerca, Incorporated, 720 Providence Road, Malvern, Pennsylvania 19355. 1984.

INSURING MEDICAL MALPRACTICE. Frank A. Sloan, Randall R. Bovbjerg and Penny B. Githens. Oxford University Press, 200 Madison Avenue, New York, New York 10016. 1991.

INTRODUCTION TO BUSINESS INSURANCE: LAW AND LITIGATION. Dan L. Goldwasser and David W. Ichel, Co-chairman. Practising Law Institute, 810 Seventh Avenue, New York, New York 10019. 1985.

INTRODUCTION TO COMMERCIAL INSURANCE. Sol Schreiber, Chairman. Longman, Incorporated, 19 West Forty-fourth Street, New York, New York 10036. 1986.

LAW OF CORPORATE OFFICERS AND DIRECTORS: INDEMINIFICATION AND INSURANCE. Joseph Bishop. Callaghan and Company, 155 Pfingsten Road, Deerfield, Illinois 60015. 1990.

THE LAW OF LIABILITY INSURANCE. Rowland H. Long. Matthew Bender and Company, Incorporated, 11 Penn Plaza, New York, New York 10001. 1985. (Annual Supplements).

LIABILITY IN MEDICAL PRACTICE: A REFERENCE FOR PHYSICIANS. Norman S. Blackman and Charles P. Bailey. Harwood Academic Publishers, GmbH, P.O. Box 786, New York, New York 10276. 1990.

Encyclopedia of Legal Information Sources • 2nd Ed.

LIABILITY: PERSPECTIVES AND POLICY. Robert E. Litan and Clifford Winston, Editors. Brookings Institution, 1775 Massachusetts Avenue, Washington, D.C. 20036. 1988.

LITIGATING FOR AND AGAINST THE FDIC AND THE RTC, 1991. Howard N. Cayne and Michael S. Helfer. Practising Law Institute, 810 Seventh Avenue, New York, New York 10019. 1991.

MEDIA INSURANCE AND RISK MANAGEMENT. John C. Lankenau. Longman, Incorporated, 19 West Forty-fourth Street, New York, New York 10036. 1985.

MEDIA INSURANCE: PROTECTING AGAINST HIGH JUDGMENTS, PUNITIVE DAMAGES, AND DEFENSE COSTS. John C. Landenau. Practising Law Institute, 810 Seventh Avenue, New York, New York 10019. 1983.

MEDICAL MALPRACTICE ON TRIAL. Paul C. Weiler. Harvard University Press, 79 Garden Street, Cambridge, Massachusetts 02138. 1991.

PERSONAL RISK MANAGEMENT AND INSURANCE. Third Edition. American Institute for Property and Liability Underwriters, Incorporated, 720 Providence Road, Malvern, Pennsylvania 19355. 1989.

PLANNING AND MODELING IN PROPERTY-LIABILITY INSURANCE. Kluwer-Nijhoff Publishing, Kluwer Academic Publishers, 101 Philip Drive, Assinippi Park, Norwell, Massachusetts 02061. 1984.

PROPERTY AND LIABILITY INSURANCE. Third Edition. S. S. Huebner, et al. Prentice-Hall, Incorporated, 113 Sylvan Avenue, Englewood Cliffs, New Jersey 07632. 1982.

PROPERTY-LIABILITY INSURANCE ACCOUNTING AND FINANCE. Second Edition. Terrie E. Troxel and Cormick L. Breslin. American Institute for Property and Liability Underwriters, Incorporated, 720 Province Road, Malvern, Pennsylvania 19355. 1983.

THIRD-PARTY REIMBURSEMENT OF CLINICAL SOCIAL WORKERS. Claire M. Marumoto. Hawair Legal Reference Bureau, State Capitol, Honolulu, Hawaii 96813. 1985.

NEWSLETTERS AND NEWSPAPERS

BUSINESS RISK MANAGEMENT LAW BULLETIN. Quinlan Publishing Company, Incorporated, 131 Beverly Street, Boston, Massachusetts 02114. Monthly.

LIABILITY AND INSURANCE BULLETIN. Buraff Publications, Incorporated, 1231 25th Street, Northwest, Washington, D.C. 20037. Weekly.

LIABILITY WEEK. JR Publishing, Incorporated, P.O. Box 6654, McLean, Virginia 22106. Weekly.

ASSOCIATIONS AND PROFESSIONAL SOCIETIES

AMERICAN NUCLEAR INSURERS. The Exchange, Suite 245, 270 Farmington Avenue, Farmington, Connecticut 06032. (203) 677-7305.

AMERICAN RISK AND INSURANCE ASSOCIATION. c/o David Klock, Department of Finance, College of Business, University of Central Florida, Orlando, Florida 32816. (407) 281-5567.

RESEARCH CENTERS, INSTITUTES, CLEARINGHOUSES

CENTER FOR RESEARCH ON RISK AND INSURANCE (CCR). University of Pennsylvania, Wharton School, 3641 Locust Walk, Philadelphia, Pennsylvania 19104. (215) 898-2515.

ONLINE DATABASES

LIABILITY WEEK. JR Publishing, Incorporated, P.O. Box 6654, McLean, Virginia 22106.

COMPUTER-ASSISTED LEGAL INSTRUCTION

INSURANCE LAW. Robert E. Keeton. Center for Computer-Assisted Instruction, 229 19th Avenue South, University of Minnesota, Minneapolis, Minnesota 55455. Machine-readable computer file.

LIABILITY INSURANCE. Robert E. Keeton. Center for Computer-Assisted Instruction, 229 19th Avenue South, University of Minnesota, Minneapolis, Minnesota 55455. Machine-readable computer file.

INSURANCE, LIFE

LOOSELEAF SERVICES AND REPORTERS

THE LAW OF LIFE AND HEALTH INSURANCE. Bertram Harnett and Irving I. Lesnick. Matthew Bender and Company, Incorporated, 11 Penn Plaza, New York, New York 10001. 1988- .

TEXTBOOKS AND GENERAL WORKS

ANDERSON ON LIFE INSURANCE. Buist M. Anderson. Little, Brown and Company, 34 Beacon Street, Boston, Massachusetts 02108. 1991.

CONFERENCE ON LIFE INSURANCE COMPANY PRODUCTS: CURRENT SECURITIES AND TAX ISSUES: ALI-ABA COURSE OF STUDY MATERIALS. American Law Institute-American Bar Association, Committee on Continuing Professional Education, 4025 Chestnut Street, Philadelphia, Pennsylvania 19104. 1983.

FEDERAL INCOME TAXATION OF LIFE INSURANCE. Donald O. Jansen, Laila M. Asmar, Corinne B. Kahn and Lawrence Brody. American Bar Association, Section or Real Property, Probate, and Trust Law, 750 North Lake Shore Drive, Chicago, Illinois 60611. 1989.

FEDERAL INCOME TAXATION OF LIFE INSURANCE COMPANIES. Second Edition. Ernst and Whinney. Matthew Bender and Company, Incorporated, 11 Penn Plaza, New York, New York 10001. 1986.

FEDERAL TAXATION OF LIFE INSURANCE. Sherwin P. Simmons. American Law Institute, 4025 Chestnut Street, Philadelphia, Pennsylvania 19104. 1966.

FINANCIAL AND ESTATE PLANNING WITH LIFE INSURANCE PRODUCTS: SUCCESSOR TO LIFE INSURANCE IN ESTATE PLANNING. James C. Munch. Little, Brown and Company, 34 Beacon Street, Boston, Massachusetts 02108. 1990.

THE IRREVOCABLE LIFE INSURANCE TRUST: WHEN TO USE IT, WHAT KIND TO USE, AND HOW TO AVOID THE TAX PITFALLS. Massachusetts Continuing Legal Education, 20 West Street, Boston, Massachusetts 02111. 1990.

LAW AND THE LIFE INSURANCE CONTRACT. Sixth Edition. Muriel L. Crawford and William T. Beadles. Richard D. Irwin, Incorporated, 1818 Ridge Road, Homewood, Illinois 60430. 1989.

LIFE AND HEALTH INSURANCE: PRINCIPLES AND PRACTICE. Paula Lyons. Longman Financial Services Publishers, Chicago, Illinois. 1988.

LIFE INSURANCE IN ESTATE PLANNING. James C. Munch, Jr. Little, Brown, and Company, 34 Beacon Street, Boston, Massachusetts 02108. 1981. (Annual Supplements).

LIFE INSURANCE: INCLUDING HEALTH AND DISABILITY INSURANCE. Second Edition. Darwin B. Close. Anderson Publishing Company, 2035 Reading Road, Cincinnati, Ohio 45202. 1987.

LIFE INSURANCE PRODUCTS, ILLUSTRATIONS, AND DUE DILIGENCE. Richard A. Schwartz, Catherine R. Turner and Michael D. Weinberg. American Bar Association, Section of Real Property, Probate and Trust Law, 750 North Lake Shore Drive, Chicago, Illinois 60611. 1989.

THE MISREPRESENTATION CASE IN A CHANGING LIFE AND HEALTH INSURANCE CLIMATE. American Bar Association, Tort and Insurance Practice Section, 750 North Lake Shore Drive, Chicago, Illinois 60611. 1990.

THE PECULIAR PROBLEM OF TAXING LIFE INSURANCE COMPANIES. Henry J. Aaron. Brookings Institution, 1775 Massachusetts Avenue, Northwest, Washington, D.C. 20036-2188. 1983.

RETIREMENT BENEFITS AND LIFE INSURANCE: A LAWYER'S REFERENCE (WHICH EVERY RETIREE SHOULD READ!). Edward F. Koren. Callaghan and Company, 155 Pfingsten Road, Deerfield, Illinois 60015. 1987.

SPLIT-DOLLAR LIFE INSURANCE. Stanford A. Wynn. American Bar Association, Section of Real Property, Probate and Trust Law, 750 North Lake Shore Drive, Chicago, Illinois 60611. 1991.

THE SUICIDE CASE: INVESTIGATION AND TRIAL OF INSURANCE CLAIMS. James L. Nolan, Editor. American Bar Association, Tort and Insurance Practice Section, 750 North Lake Shore Drive, Chicago, Illinois 60611. 1988.

LAW REVIEWS AND PERIODICALS

JOURNAL OF AMERICAN SOCIETY OF CHARTERED LIFE UNDERWRITERS. American Society of Chartered Life Underwriters, 270 Bryn Mawr Avenue, Bryn Mawr, Pennsylvania 19010. Bimonthly.

ASSOCIATIONS AND PROFESSIONAL SOCIETIES

AMERICAN COUNCIL OF LIFE INSURANCE. 1001 Pennsylvania Avenue, Northwest, Washington, D.C. 20004. (202) 624-2000.

THE ASSOCIATION OF LIFE INSURANCE COUNSEL. c/o Emily S. Crandall, 201 Park Avenue, South, New York, New York 10003. (212)679-1110.

NATIONAL ASSOCIATION OF BAR-RELATED TITLE INSURERS. 29 South LaSalle Street, Suite 500, Chicago, Illinois 60603. (312) 372-6791.

NATIONAL ASSOCIATION OF LIFE COMPANIES. 1455 Pennsylvania Avenue, Northwest, Suite 1250, Washington, D.C. 20004. (202) 783-6252.

NATIONAL COMMITTEE ON PROPERTY INSURANCE. 10 Winthrop Square, Boston, Massachusetts 02110. (617) 423-4620.

NATIONAL CONFERENCE GROUP OF LAWYERS AND LIFE INSURANCE COMPANIES, AMERICAN BAR ASSOCIATION. 750 North Lake Shore Drive, Chicago, Illinois 60611. (312) 988-5000.

COMPUTER-ASSISTED LEGAL INSTRUCTION

INSURANCE LAW. Robert E. Keeton. Center for Computer-Assisted Instruction, 229 19th Avenue South, University of Minnesota, Minneapolis, Minnesota 55455. Machine-readable computer file.

INSURANCE, MOTOR VEHICLE AND AVIATION

LOOSELEAF SERVICES AND REPORTERS

AUTOMOBILE LAW REPORTS - INSURANCE CASES. Commerce Clearing House, Incorporated, 4025 West Peterson Avenue, Chicago, Illinois 60646. 1966- . Weekly.

AUTOMOBILE LIABILITY INSURANCE. Second Edition. Irwin E. Schermer. Clark Boardman Company, Limited, 435 Hudson Street, New York, New York 10014. 1981.

NO-FAULT AND UNINSURED MOTORIST AUTOMOBILE INSURANCE. Matthew Bender and Company, Incorporated, 11 Penn Plaza, New York, New York 10001. 1984.

HANDBOOKS, MANUALS, FORMBOOKS

CLAIM IT YOURSELF: THE ACCIDENT VICTIM'S GUIDE TO PERSONAL INJURY CLAIMS. Michele Saadi. Pharos Books, Available From: Ballantine/Del Rey/Fawcett/Ivy Books, 201 East Fiftieth Street, New York, New York 10022. 1987.

TEXTBOOKS AND GENERAL WORKS

AVIATION INSURANCE AND REINSURANCE: LAW AND PRACTICE. Second Edition. Butterworth Legal Publications, 90 Stiles Road, Salem, New Hampshire 03079. 1987.

CAR CRASHES AND INSURANCE COMPANIES INSURANCE QUESTIONS IN AUTOMOBILE TORT LITIGATION. Massachusetts Continuing Legal Education, 20 West Street, Boston, Massachusetts 02111. 1988.

MOTOR VEHICLE NO-FAULT LAW. Josephine Y. King. John Wiley and Sons, Incorporated, 605 Third Avenue, New York, New York 10158. 1987.

NO FAULT AUTOMOBILE ACCIDENT LAW. Josephine Y. King. John Wiley and Sons, Incorporated, 605 Third Avenue, New York, New York 10158. 1987.

SELECTED REFERENCES ON NO-FAULT ARBITRATION. Laura Ferris Brown. American Arbitration Association, 140 West Fifty-first Street, New York, New York 10020. 1990.

UNINSURED AND UNDERINSURED MOTORIST COVERAGE. Second Edition. Alan I. Widiss. Anderson Publishing Company, 2035 Reading Road, Cincinnati, Ohio 45202. 1985.

ASSOCIATIONS AND PROFESSIONAL SOCIETIES

SPECIAL COMMITTEE ON AUTOMOBILE INSURANCE LEGISLATION, AMERICAN BAR ASSOCIATION. 750 North Lake Shore Drive, Chicago, Illinois 60611. (312) 988-5000.

RESEARCH CENTERS, INSTITUTES, CLEARINGHOUSES

CENTER FOR RESEARCH ON RISK AND INSURANCE. University of Pennsylvania, Wharton School, 3641 Locust Walk, Philadelphia, Pennsylvania 19104. (215) 898-2515.

HIGHWAY LOSS DATA INSTITUTE (HLDI). 1005 North Glebe Road, Suite 800, Arlington, Virginia 22201. (703) 247-1600.

COMPUTER-ASSISTED LEGAL INSTRUCTION

CAR INSURANCE. Robert E. Keeton. Center for Computer-Assisted Instruction, 229 19th Avenue South, University of Minnesota, Minneapolis, Minnesota 55455. Machine-readable computer file.

INSURANCE, PROPERTY

LOOSELEAF SERVICES AND REPORTERS

INSURING REAL PROPERTY. Stephen A. Cozen, General Editor. Matthew Bender and Company, Incorporated, 11 Penn Plaza, New York, New York 10001. 1989.

HANDBOOKS, MANUALS, FORMBOOKS

CASUALTY INVESTIGATION CHECKLISTS. Third Edition. Pat Magarick. Clark Boardman Company, Limited, 435 Hudson Street, New York, New York 10014. 1985.

HANDLING PROPERTY AND CASUALTY CLAIMS. Robert F. Cushman and Charles H. Stamm, Editors. John Wiley and Sons, Incorporated, 605 Third Avenue, New York, New York 10158. 1985.

TEXTBOOKS AND GENERAL WORKS

COMMERCIAL FIRE UNDERWRITING. National Underwriter Company, 420 East Fourth Street, Cincinnati, Ohio 45202. 1984.

HANDLING PROPERTY AND CASUALTY CLAIMS. Robert F. Cushman and Charles H. Stamm, Editors. John Wiley and Sons, Incorporated, 605 Third Avenue, New York, New York 10158. 1985.

HOW INSURANCE WORKS: AN INTRODUCTION TO PROPERTY AND LIABILITY INSURANCE. Barry D. Smith. Insurance Institute of Amerca, Incorporated, 720 Providence Road, Malvern, Pennsylvania 19355. 1984.

INSURING THE LEASE EXPOSURE. Harry F. Brooks and Donald S. Malecki. National Underwriter Company, 420 East Fourth Street, Cincinnati, Ohio 45202. 1982.

INTRODUCTION TO CLAIMS. Robert J. Prahl. Insurance Institute of America, 720 Providence Road, Malvern, Pennsylvania 19355. 1988.

LAW OF TITLE INSURANCE. Barlow D. Burke, Jr. Little, Brown, and Company, 34 Beacon Street, Boston, Massachusetts 02108. 1986. (Supplemented Annually).

PROPERTY AND LIABILITY INSURANCE. Third Edition. S. S. Huebner. Prentice-Hall, Incorporated, 113 Sylvan Avenue, Englewood Cliffs, New Jersey 07632. 1982.

PROPERTY INSURANCE. Second Edition. Robert R. Rackley. Insurance Achievement, 7330 Highland Road, Baton Rouge, Louisiana 70808. 1984.

PROPERTY INSURANCE ANNOTATIONS: FIRE AND EXTENDED COVERAGES. American Bar Association, 750 North Lake Shore Drive, Chicago, Illinois 60611. 1977. (Supplemented).

PROPERTY-LIABILITY INSURANCE ACCOUNTING AND FINANCE. Third Edition. Terrie E. Troxel and Cormick L. Breslin. American Institute for Property and Liability Underwriters, 720 Providence Road, Malvern, Pennsylvania 19355. 1990.

PROPERTY LOSS ADJUSTING. James J. Markham, Editor. Insurance Institute of America, 720 Providence Road, Malvern, Pennsylvania 19355. 1990.

REAL ESTATE AND THE RTC: A GUIDE TO ASSET PURCHASES AND CONTRACTING. Leonard A. Zax, Editor. Urban Land Institute, Washington, D.C. 1990.

STRATEGIC PLANNING AND MODELING IN PROPERTY-LIABILITY INSURANCE. David J. Cummings. Kluwer-Nijhoff Publishing, Kluwer Academic Publishers, 101 Philip Drive, Assinippi Park, Norwell, Massachusetts 02061. 1984.

TAX ASPECTS OF PROPERTY AND CASUALTY RISK MANAGEMENT. Keith C. Kakacek and W. Roy Adams, Jr. Commerce Clearing House, Incorporated, 4025 West Peterson Avenue, Chicago, Illinois 60646. 1987.

TITLE INSURANCE IN 1989. Practising Law Institute, 810 Seventh Avenue, New York, New York 10019. 1989.

TRANSPORTATION INSURANCE IN PLAIN ENGLISH. William J. Augello. Shippers National Freight Claim Council, 120 Main Street, Huntington, New York 11743. 1985.

DIGESTS, INDEXES, ABSTRACTS, CITATORS

ANNOTATIONS TO THE HOMEOWNERS' POLICY. Committee on Property Insurance Law and Insurance Practice Section, American Bar Association, 750 North Lake Shore Drive, Chicago, Illinois 60611. 1980. (Supplement 1985).

PROPERTY INSURANCE ANNOTATIONS: FIRE AND EXTENDED COVERAGES. Committee on Property Insurance Law, Section on Insurance, Negligence and Compensation Law, American Bar Association, 750 North Lake Shore Drive, Chicago, Illinois 60611. 1977. (Supplemented)

ASSOCIATIONS AND PROFESSIONAL SOCIETIES

NATIONAL COMMITTEE ON PROPERTY INSURANCE. 10 Winthrop Square, Boston, Massachusetts 02110. (617) 423-4620.

ONLINE DATABASES

INDEPENDENT INSURANCE. CompuServe Information Service, 5000 Arlington Centre Boulevard, Columbus, Ohio 43220.

AUDIOVISUALS

ARSON FOR PROFIT: THE INSURER'S DEFENSE. Tort and Insurance Practice Section, American Bar Association, 750 North Lake Shore Drive, Chicago, Illinois 60611. 1981. Videocassette.

COMPUTER-ASSISTED LEGAL INSTRUCTION

INSURABLE INTEREST IN PROPERTY. Robert E. Keeton. Center for Computer-Assisted Instruction, 229 19th Avenue South, University of Minnesota, Minneapolis, Minnesota 55455. Machine-readable computer file.

INSURANCE LAW. Robert E. Keeton. Center for Computer-Assisted Instruction, 229 19th Avenue South, University of Minnesota, Minneapolis, Minnesota 55455. Machine-readable computer file.

INSURANCE, UNEMPLOYMENT
See: INSURANCE, HEALTH AND UNEMPLOYMENT

INTEGRATION
See: SEGREGATION AND INTEGRATION

INTELLECTUAL PROPERTY
See: COPYRIGHT; LICENSING, INDUSTRIAL AND INTELLECTUAL; PATENTS; TRADEMARKS AND TRADE NAMES

INTEREST AND USURY
See: BANKS AND BANKING; CONSUMER CREDIT; CREDIT; LOANS

INTERIOR DEPARTMENT

STATUTES, CODES, STANDARDS, UNIFORM LAWS

CODE OF FEDERAL REGULATIONS, TITLES 41 & 43. Office of the Federal Register, National Archives and Records Administration. Superintendent of Documents, United States Government Printing Office, Washington, D.C. 20402. Annual. (Updated by use of monthly List of Sections Affected and daily Federal Register.)

CONSTRUCTION SAFETY STANDARDS. Interior Department, Bureau of Reclamation, Division of Safety, Engineering and Research Center. Superintendent of Documents, United States Government Printing Office, Washington, D.C. 20402. 1982- .

SECRETARY OF THE INTERIOR'S STANDARDS FOR HISTORIC PRESERVATION PROJECTS WITH GUIDELINES FOR APPLYING THE STANDARDS. Morton W. Morton and Gary L. Hume. Interior Department, National Park Service, Preservation Assistance Division. Superintendent of Documents, United States Government Printing Office, Washington, D.C. 20402. 1985.

LOOSELEAF SERVICES AND REPORTERS

DECISIONS OF THE DEPARTMENT OF THE INTERIOR. Interior Department. Superintendent of Documents, United States Government Printing Office, Washington, D.C. 20402. 1930- .

HANDBOOKS, MANUALS, FORMBOOKS

HANDBOOK OF TOXICITY OF PESTICIDES TO WILDLIFE. Rick H. Hudson. Interior Department, Fish and Wildlife Service. Superintendent of Documents, United States Government Printing Office, Washington, D.C. 20402. 1984.

INVESTIGATION OF FIRE AND EXPLOSION ACCIDENTS IN THE CHEMICAL, MINING, AND FUEL-RELATED INDUSTRIES: A MANUAL. Joseph M. Kuchta. Interior Department, Bureau of Mines. Superintendent of Documents, United States Government Printing Office, Washington, D.C. 20402. 1986.

MANUAL OF ACUTE TOXICITY: INTERPRETATION AND DATA BASE FOR 410 CHEMICALS AND 66 SPECIES OF FRESH WATER ANIMALS. Foster L. Mayer, Jr. and Mark R. Ellersieck. Interior Department, Fish and Wildlife Service. Superintendent of Documents, United States Government Printing Office, Washington, D.C. 20402. 1986.

TEXTBOOKS AND GENERAL WORKS

THE DEPARTMENT OF EVERYTHING ELSE: HIGHLIGHTS OF INTERIOR HISTORY. Robert M. Utley and Barry Mackintosh. United States Department of the Interior, Bureau of Mines, 2401 E Street, Northwest, Washington, D.C. 20241. 1988.

THE DEPARTMENT OF THE INTERIOR. Fred Clement. Chelsea House Publishers, 1974 Sproul Road, Suite 400, Broomall, Pennsylvania 19008. 1989.

REPORT OF THE SECRETARY OF THE INTERIOR UNDER THE MINING AND MINERAL POLICY ACT OF 1970. Interior Department, Bureau of Mines. Superintendent of Documents, United States Government Printing Office, Washington, D.C. 20402. 1984.

RONALD REAGAN AND THE PUBLIC LANDS: AMERICA'S CONSERVATION DEBATE, 1979-1984. C. Brant Short. Texas A & M University Press, Drawer C, Lewis Street, College Station, Texas 77843. 1989.

DIGESTS, INDEXES, ABSTRACTS, CITATORS

QUINQUENNIAL INDEX DIGEST OF THE DEPARTMENT OF THE INTERIOR. Interior Department. Superintendent of Documents, United States Government Printing Office, Washington, D.C. 20402. 1986.

SHEPARD'S UNITED STATES ADMINISTRATIVE CITATIONS. Shepard's/McGraw-Hill, P.O. Box 1235, Colorado Springs, Colorado 80901. Bimonthly.

RESEARCH CENTERS, INSTITUTES, CLEARINGHOUSES

UNITED STATES DEPARTMENT OF THE INTERIOR LIBRARY, LAW BRANCH. 1849 C Street, Northwest, Washington, D.C. 20240. (202) 208-5821.

INTERNAL REVENUE SERVICE
See also: INCOME TAX; TAX PRACTICE AND ENFORCEMENT; TAX RETURNS; TAX SHELTERS; TAXATION, STATE AND LOCAL

STATUTES, CODES, STANDARDS, UNIFORM LAWS

CODE OF FEDERAL REGULATIONS, TITLE 26. Office of the Federal Register, National Archives and Records Administration. Superintendent of Documents, United States Government Printing Office, Washington, D.C. 20402. Annual. (Updated by use of monthly List of Sections Affected and daily Federal Register.)

INTERNAL REVENUE SERVICE LOOSELEAF REGULATIONS SYSTEM, SERVICE NUMBER 1, INCOME TAX. Treasury Department, Internal Revenue Service. Superintendent of Documents, United States Government Printing Office, Washington, D.C. 20402. 1976- .

INTERNAL REVENUE SERVICE LOOSELEAF REGULATIONS SYSTEM, SERVICE NUMBER 2, ESTATE AND GIFT TAX. Treasury Department, Internal Revenue Service. Superintendent of Documents, United States Government Printing Office, Washington, D.C. 20402. 1978- .

INTERNAL REVENUE SERVICE LOOSELEAF REGULATIONS SYSTEMS, SERVICE NUMBER 3, EMPLOYMENT TAX. Treasury Department, Internal Revenue Service. Superintendent of Documents, United States Government Printing Office, Washington, D.C. 20402. 1978- .

INTERNAL REVENUE SERVICE LOOSELEAF REGULATIONS SYSTEM, SERVICE NUMBER 4, EXCISE TAXES. Treasury Department, Internal Revenue Service. Superintendent of Documents, United States Government Printing Office, Washington, D.C. 20402. 1978- .

LOOSELEAF SERVICES AND REPORTERS

INTERNAL REVENUE BULLETIN. Treasury Department, Internal Revenue Service. Superintendent of Documents, United States Government Printing Office, Washington, D.C. 20402. Weekly.

INTERNAL REVENUE CUMULATIVE BULLETIN. Treasury Department, Internal Revenue Service. Superintendent of Documents, United States Government Printing Office, Washington, D.C. 20402. Biannual.

IRS POSITIONS. Commerce Clearing House, Incorporated, 4025 West Peterson Avenue, Chicago, Illinois 60646. 1982- .

IRS PRACTICE AND PROCEDURES TAX PACKAGE. LaVaughn T. Davis. Mark A. Stephens, Ltd., 10018 Colesville Road, Silver Spring, Maryland 20901. 1977- .

IRS PUBLICATIONS. Commerce Clearing House, Incorporated, 4025 West Peterson Avenue, Chicago, Illinois 60646. 1977- .

PRIVATE LETTER RULINGS. Prentice-Hall, Incorporated, 113 Sylvan Avenue, Englewood Cliffs, New Jersey 07632. 1977- .

REPRESENTATION BEFORE THE APPEALS DIVISION OF THE IRS. Arthur H. Boelter. Callaghan and Company, 155 Pfingsten Road, Deerfield, Illinois 60015. 1990.

REPRESENTATION BEFORE THE COLLECTION DIVISION OF THE IRS. Robert E. McKenzie. Callaghan and Company, 155 Pfingsten Road, Deerfield, Illinois 60015. 1989- .

REPRESENTING THE AUDITED TAXPAYER BEFORE THE IRS. Robert E. McKenzie, Karen V. Kole and M. Kevin Outterson. Callaghan and Company, 155 Pfingsten Road, Deerfield, Illinois 60015. 1990- .

HANDBOOKS, MANUALS, FORMBOOKS

HOW TO HANDLE TAX AUDITS, REQUESTS FOR RULINGS, FRAUD CASES, AND OTHER PROCEDURES BEFORE THE IRS. Irving Schreiber and Carmine Seudere. Paladin Press, P.O. Box 1307, Boulder, Colorado 80306. 1977 (Periodic Supplements).

HOW TO PRACTICE IRS: NO TRICKS, NO MAGIC: A PROCEDURAL MANUAL FOR PRACTITIONERS. Robert S. Schriebman. Commerce Clearing House, Incorporated, 4025 West Peterson Avenue, Chicago, Illinois 60646. 1990.

INTERNAL REVENUE MANUAL, ABRIDGED AND ANNOTATED. Bryan E. Gates. Callaghan and Company, 155 Pfingsten Road, Deerfield, Illinois 60015. 1991.

INTERNAL REVENUE MANUAL: ADMINISTRATION. Commerce Clearing House, Incorporated, 4025 West Peterson Avenue, Chicago, Illinois 60646. 1973 (Periodic Supplements).

INTERNAL REVENUE MANUAL: AUDIT. Commerce Clearing House, Incorporated, 4025 West Peterson Avenue, Chicago, Illinois 60646. 1977 (Periodic Supplements).

INTERNAL REVENUE SERVICE PRACTICE AND PROCEDURE DESKBOOK. Second Edition. Practising Law Institute, 810 Seventh Avenue, New York, New York 10019. 1989.

IRS CLASSIFICATION HANDBOOK. Commerce Clearing House, Incorporated, 4025 West Peterson Avenue, Chicago, Illinois 60646. 1987.

IRS COMPLIANCE MANUAL. Prentice-Hall, Incorporated, 113 Sylvan Avenue, Englewood Cliffs, New Jersey 07632. 1982 (Monthly Supplements).

IRS PRACTICE AND PROCEDURE. Second Edition. Michael I. Saltzman. Research Institute of America, Incorporated, One Penn Plaza, New York, New York 10119. 1991.

IRS TAX COLLECTION PROCEDURES: A MANUAL FOR PRACTITIONERS. Robert S. Schriebman. Commerce Clearing House, Incorporated, 4025 West Peterson Avenue, Chicago, Illinois 60646. 1985.

OBTAINING IRS PRIVATE LETTER RULINGS: A MANUAL OF FORMS AND PROCEDURES. Gerald W. Padwe, Donald C. Wiese, and Issaac W. Zimbalist. Oceana Publications, Incorporated, 75 Main Street, Dobbs Ferry, New York 10522. 1983 (Periodic Supplements).

PACKAGE X: INFORMATIONAL COPIES OF FEDERAL TAX FORMS. Treasury Department, Internal Revenue Service. Superintendent of Documents, United States Government Printing Office, Washington, D.C. 20402. 1986.

REPRODUCIBLE FEDERAL TAX FORMS FOR USE IN LIBRARIES, INTERNAL REVENUE SERVICE TAX PUBLICATION 1132, SECTION 1. Treasury Department, Internal Revenue Service. Superintendent of Documents, United States Government Printing Office, Washington, D.C. 20402. 1986- .

TEXTBOOKS AND GENERAL WORKS

BATTLING THE IRS: A TAXPAYER'S GUIDE TO RESPONDING TO IRS NOTICES AND ASSESSMENTS. David J. Silverman. Scott, Foresman and Company, 1900 East Lake Avenue, Glenview, Illinois 60025. 1991.

FEDERAL ESTATE AND GIFT TAXES. Treasury Department, Internal Revenue Service. Superintendent of Documents, United States Government Printing Office, Washington, D.C. 20402. 1984.

INTERNAL REVENUE SERVICE STUDY OF INTERNATIONAL CASES INVOLVING SECTION 482 OF THE INTERNAL REVENUE CODE. Treasury Department, Internal Revenue Service. Superintendent of Documents, United States Government Printing Office, Washington, D.C. 20402. 1984.

THE I.R.S. AND THE FREEDOM OF INFORMATION AND PRIVACY ACTS OF 1974: THE DISCLOSURE POLICIES OF THE INTERNAL REVENUE SERVICE AND HOW TO OBTAIN DOCUMENTS FROM THEM. Marcus Farbenblum. McFarland and Company, Incorporated, Box 611, Jefferson, North Carolina 28640. 1991.

A LAW UNTO ITSELF: THE IRS AND THE ABUSE OF POWER. David Burnham. Vintage Books, New York, New York. 1989.

MASTERS OF PARADISE: ORGANIZED CRIME AND THE INTERNAL REVENUE SERVICE IN THE BAHAMAS. Alan A. Block. Transaction Books, Rutgers University, New Brunswick, New Jersey 08903. 1991.

PROCEDURE BEFORE THE INTERNAL REVENUE SERVICE. Sixth Edition. American Law Institute-American Bar Association, Committee on Continuing Professional Education, 4025 Chestnut Street, Philadelphia, Pennsylvania 19104. 1984. (Supplemented).

UNDERSTANDING IRS COMMUNICATIONS. Commerce Clearing House, Incorporated, 4025 West Peterson Avenue, Chicago, Illinois 60646. 1989.

YOU CAN PROTECT YOURSELF FROM THE IRS: THE YEAR-ROUND INSIDERS' GUIDE TO TAXES. Sandor Frankel and Robert S. Fink. Simon and Schuster, Incorporated, 1230 Avenue of the Americas, New York, New York 10020. 1988.

DIGESTS, INDEXES, ABSTRACTS, CITATORS

BULLETIN INDEX-DIGEST SYSTEM, SERVICE 1, INCOME TAX. Treasury Department, Internal Revenue Service. Superintendent of Documents, United States Government Printing Office, Washington, D.C. 20402. Annual.

BULLETIN INDEX-DIGEST SYSTEM, SERVICE 2, ESTATE AND GIFT TAX. 1984. Treasury Department, Internal Revenue Service. Superintendent of Documents, United States Government Printing Office, Washington, D.C. 20402. Annual.

BULLETIN INDEX-DIGEST SYSTEM, SERVICE 3, EMPLOYMENT TAXES. Treasury Department, Internal Revenue Service. Superintendent of Documents, United States Government Printing Office, Washington, D.C. 20402. Annual

SHEPARD'S FEDERAL TAX CITATIONS. Shepard's/McGraw-Hill, P.O. Box 1235, Colorado Springs, Colorado 80901. Bimonthly.

SHEPARD'S UNITED STATES ADMINISTRATIVE CITATIONS. Shepard's/McGraw-Hill, P.O. Box 1235, Colorado Springs, Colorado 80901. Bimonthly.

ANNUALS AND SURVEYS

INTERNAL REVENUE SERVICE ANNUAL REPORT. Treasury Department, Internal Revenue Service. Superintendent of Documents, United States Government Printing Office, Washington, D.C. 20402. Annual.

DIRECTORIES

CUMULATIVE LIST OF ORGANIZATIONS DESCRIBED IN SECTION 170(c) OF THE INTERNAL REVENUE CODE OF 1954. Treasury Department, Internal Revenue Service. Superintendent of Documents, United States Government Printing Office, Washington, D.C. 20402. 1986 (Quarterly Supplements).

RESEARCH CENTERS, INSTITUTES, CLEARINGHOUSES

UNITED STATES INTERNAL REVENUE SERVICE LIBRARY. 1111 Constitution Avenue, Northwest, Room 4324, Washington, D.C. 20224. (202) 566-4024.

ONLINE DATABASES

LEXIS, FEDERAL TAX LIBRARY. Mead Data Central, P.O. Box 933, Dayton, Ohio 45401.

WESTLAW, TAX LIBRARY. West Publishing Company, P.O. Box 64526, 50 West Kellogg Boulevard, St. Paul, Minnesota 55164-0526.

INTERNATIONAL AGENCIES AND ORGANIZATIONS

LOOSELEAF SERVICES AND REPORTERS

INTERNATIONAL ADMINISTRATION: LAW AND MANAGEMENT PRACTICES IN INTERNATIONAL ORGANISATIONS. Chris de Cooker, Editor. United Nations Institute for Training and Research. Martinus Nijhoff, Kluwer Academic Publishers, 101 Philip Drive, Assinippi Park, Norwell, Massachusetts 02061. 1990- .

TEXTBOOKS AND GENERAL WORKS

ACRONYMS AND ABBREVIATIONS COVERING THE UNITED NATIONS SYSTEM AND OTHER INTERNATIONAL ORGANIZATIONS. United Nations, 2 United Nations Plaza, Sales Section, Publishing Division, Room DCZ-853, New York, New York 10017. 1981.

BASIC DOCUMENTS OF ASIAN REGIONAL ORGANIZATIONS. Michael Hass. Oceana Publications, Incorporated, 75 Main Street, Dobbs Ferry, New York 10522. 1984.

BETWEEN TWO WORLDS: THE WORLD BANK'S NEXT DECADE. Transaction Books, Rutgers University, New Brunswick, New Jersey 08903. 1986.

CHINA AND INTERNATIONAL ORGANIZATIONS: PARTICIPATION IN NON-GOVERNMENTAL ORGANIZATIONS SINCE 1971. Gerald Chan. Oxford University Press, 200 Madison Avenue, New York, New York 10016. 1989.

DEFENDING THE WEST: A HISTORY OF NATO. William Park. Westview Press, 5500 Central Avenue, Boulder, Colorado 80301. 1986.

DOCUMENTS OF THE INTER-AMERICAN COMMISSION ON HUMAN RIGHTS, 1960-1984. Organization of American States, Seventh Street and Constitutional Avenue, Northwest, Washington, D.C. 20006. 1986.

DOCUMENTS ON INTERNATIONAL ORGANIZATION AND INTEGRATION: ANNOTATED BASIC DOCUMENTS OF INTERNATIONAL ORGANIZATIONS AND ARRANGEMENTS. Louis Sohn, Editor. Martinus Nijhoff, Kluwer Academic Publishers, 101 Philip Drive, Assinippi Park, Norwell, Massachusetts 02061. 1986.

ESSAYS ON INTERNATIONAL LAW AND ORGANIZATION. Leo Gross. Transnational Publishers, Incorporated, P. O. Box 7282, Ardsley-on-Hudson, New York 10503. 1983.

THE EVOLUTION OF THE UNITED NATIONS SYSTEM. Amos Yoder. Crane Russak, New York, New York. 1989.

THE FUTURE OF EUROPEAN DEFENCE: PROCEEDINGS OF THE SECOND INTERNATIONAL ROUND TABLE CONFERENCE OF THE NETHERLANDS ATLANTIC COMMISSION ON MAY 24 AND 25, 1985. Frans Bletz, and Rio Praaning, Editors. Kluwer Academic Publishers, 101 Philip Drive, Assinippi Park, Norwell, Massachusetts 02061. 1986.

GLOBAL ISSUES IN THE UNITED NATIONS' FRAMEWORK. Paul Taylor and A.J.R. Groom, Editors. St. Martin's Press, 175 Fifth Avenue, New York, New York 10010. 1989.

THE INTERNATIONAL CIVIL SERVICE: A STUDY OF BUREAUCRACY: INTERNATIONAL ORGANIZATIONS. Hans Mouritzen. Dartmouth, Brookfield, Vermont. 1990.

INTERNATIONAL CIVIL SERVICE: PRINCIPLES, PRACTICE AND PROSPECTS. S. L. Goel. Apt Books, Incorporated, 141 East Forty-fourth Street, Suite 511, New York, New York 10017. 1984.

INTERNATIONAL INSTITUTIONS AT WORK. Paul Taylor and A.J.R. Groom, Editors. St. Martin's Press, 175 Fifth Avenue, New York, New York 10010. 1988.

INTERNATIONAL LAW AND THE INTERNATIONAL SYSTEM. W.E. Butler, Editor. Martinus Nijhoff, Kluwer Academic Publishers, 101 Philip Drive, Assinippi Park, Norwell, Massachusetts 02061. 1987.

THE INTERNATIONAL MONETARY FUND, 1972-1978. Margaret Garritson De Vries. Books on Demand, 300 North Zeeb Road, Ann Arbor, Michigan 48106-1346. 1985.

INTERNATIONAL ORGANIZATION AND INTEGRATION: ANNOTATED BASIC DOCUMENTS AND DESCRIPTION DIRECTORY OF INTERNATIONAL ORGANIZATIONS AND ARRANGEMENTS. P. J. Kapteyn, Editor. Kluwer Academic Publishers, 101 Philip Drive, Assinippi Park, Norwell, Massachusetts 02061. 1981.

INTERNATIONAL ORGANIZATIONS. Clive Archer. Allen and Unwin, Incorporated, P.O. Box 442, Concord, Massachusetts 01742. 1983.

INTERNATIONAL ORGANIZATIONS: A COMPARATIVE APPROACH. Second Edition. Werner J. Feld and Robert S. Jordan. Praeger Publishers, One Madison Avenue, New York, New York 10010-3603. 1988.

INTERNATIONAL ORGANIZATIONS AND LAW. Ford Foundation, 320 East Forty-third Street, New York, New York 10017. 1990.

INTERNATIONAL ORGANIZATIONS: PRINCIPLES AND ISSUES. Fifth Edition. A. LeRoy Bennett. Prentice-Hall, Incorporated, 113 Sylvan, Englewood Cliffs, New Jersey 07632. 1991.

INTERNATIONAL REGIMES. Stephen D. Krasner, Editor. Cornell University Press, 124 Roberts Place, Ithaca, New York 14850. 1983.

LEGAL PROBLEMS OF INTERNATIONAL ORGANIZATIONS. Hersch Lauterpacht Memorial Lecture Series, Grotius Publications, Limited, Wind Street, Llandysuw, Dyfed SA44 4BQ, Wales. 1986.

MANAGEMENT PROBLEMS IN UNITED NATIONS ORGANIZATIONS: REFORM OR DECLINE? Yves Beigbeder. St. Martin's Press, 175 Fifth Avenue, New York, New York 10010. 1987.

THE MODERN LAW OF DIPLOMACY: EXTERNAL MISSIONS OF STATES AND INTERNATIONAL ORGANIZATIONS. Ludwik Dembinski. Martinus Nijhoff, Kluwer Academic Publishers, 101 Philip Drive, Assinippi Park, Norwell, Massachusetts 02061. 1988.

NATIONALISM AND INTERNATIONAL SOCIETY. James Mayall. Cambridge University Press, 40 West Twentieth Street, New York, New York 10011. 1990.

NETWORKS OF INDEPENDENCE: INTERNATIONAL ORGANIZATIONS AND THE GLOBAL POLITICAL SYSTEM. Second Edition. Harold K. Jacobson. Alfred A. Knopf, Incorporated, 201 East Fiftieth Street, New York, New York 10022. 1979.

NONPROLIFERATION ROLE OF THE INTERNATIONAL ATOMIC ENERGY AGENCY: A CRITICAL ASSESSMENT. Lawrence Scheinman. Resources for the Future, Incorporated, 1616 P Street, Northwest, Washington, D.C. 20036. 1985.

NONSTATE ACTORS IN INTERNATIONAL POLITICS: FROM TRANSREGIONAL TO SUBSTATE ORGANIZATIONS. Phillip Taylor. Westview Press, 5500 Central Avenue, Boulder, Colorado 80301. 1984.

THE POLITICAL ECONOMY OF INTERNATIONAL ORGANIZATIONS: A PUBLIC CHOICE APPROACH. Roland Vaubel and Thomas D. Willett, Editors. Westview Press, Incorporated, 5500 Central Avenue, Boulder, Colorado 80301. 1991.

POLITICS AND PROCESS IN THE SPECIALIZED AGENCIES OF THE UNITED NATIONS. Houshang Ameri. Gower Publishing Company, Old Post Road, Brookfield, Vermont 05036. 1982.

THE POLITICS OF INTERNATIONAL ORGANIZATIONS: PATTERNS AND INSIGHTS. Paul F. Diehl, Editor. Dorsey Press, 10 Davis Drive, Belmont, California 94002. 1989.

THE RISE OF THE INTERNATIONAL ORGANIZATION: A SHORT HISTORY. David Armstrong. Saint Martin's Press, Incorporated, 175 Fifth Avenue, New York, New York 10010. 1989.

THE SPECIALIZED AGENCIES AND THE UNITED NATIONS. Douglas Williams. Saint Martin's Press, Incorporated, 175 Fifth Avenue, New York, New York 10010. 1990.

THIRD-WORLD POLITICAL ORGANIZATIONS: A REVIEW OF DEVELOPMENTS. Second Edition. Gwyneth Williams. Humanities Press International, Incorporated, 171 First Avenue, Atlantic Highlands, New Jersey 07716-1289. 1987.

THE UN UNDER ATTACK. Jeffrey Harrod and Nico Schrijver, Editors. Gower Publishing Company, Old Post Road, Brookfield, Vermont 05036. 1988.

WHEN KNOWLEDGE IS POWER: THREE MODELS OF CHANGE IN INTERNATIONAL ORGANIZATIONS. Ernst B. Haas. University of California Press, 2120 Berkeley Way, Berkeley, California 94720. 1990.

ENCYCLOPEDIAS AND DICTIONARIES

DICTIONARY OF INTERNATIONAL RELATIONS TERMS. Department of State Library. Superintendent of Documents, United States Government Printing Office, Washington, D.C. 20402. 1987.

ENCYCLOPEDIA OF ASSOCIATIONS, VOLUME FOUR, INTERNATIONAL ORGANIZATIONS. Gale Research, Incorporated, 835 Penobscot Building, Detroit, Michigan 48226. 1987. (Annual Supplements).

EUROPEAN POLITICAL FACTS, 1918-90. Third Edition. Chris Cook and John Paxton. Facts on File, Incorporated, 460 Park Avenue South, New York, New York 10016. 1992.

THE INTERNATIONAL ORGANIZATIONS AND WORLD ORDER DICTIONARY. Sheikh Rustum Ali. ABC-CLIO, P.O. Box 1911, Santa Barbara, California 93116-1911. 1992.

WORLD ENCYCLOPEDIA OF PEACE. Ervin Laszlo and Jong Youl Yoo, Editors. Pergamon Press, Incorporated, Maxwell House, Fairview Park, Elmsford, New York 10523. 1986.

DIGESTS, INDEXES, ABSTRACTS, CITATORS

DIGEST OF LEGAL ACTIVITIES OF INTERNATIONAL ORGANIZATIONS AND OTHER INSTITUTIONS. Oceana Publications, Incorporated, 75 Main Street, Dobbs Ferry, New York 10522. 1980- .

BIBLIOGRAPHIES

INTERNATIONAL INFORMATION: DOCUMENTS, PUBLICATIONS, AND INFORMATION SYSTEMS OF INTERNATIONAL GOVERNMENTAL ORGANIZATIONS. Peter I. Hajnal, Editor. Libraries Unlimited, Incorporated, P.O. Box 3988, Englewood, Colorado 80155-3988. 1988.

INTERNATIONAL ORGANIZATIONS, 1918-1945: A GUIDE TO RESEARCH AND RESEARCH MATERIALS. Revised Edition. George W. Baer. Scholarly Resources, 104 Greenhill Avenue, Wilmington, Delaware 19805. 1991.

PEACE BY PIECES: UNITED NATIONS AGENCIES AND THEIR ROLES: A READER AND SELECTIVE BIBLIOGRAPHY. Robert N. Wells, Jr., Editor. Scarecrow Press, Incorporated, 52 Liberty Street, Box 4167, Metuchen, New Jersey 08840. 1991.

PUBLIC INTERNATIONAL LAW AND INTERNATIONAL ORGANIZATIONS: A BASIC SELECTIVE BIBLIOGRAPHY. United Nations, Sales Section, Publishing Division, New York, New York 10017. 1982.

DIRECTORIES

A GUIDE TO AFRICAN INTERNATIONAL ORGANIZATIONS. Richard Fredland. H. Zell, New York, New York. 1990.

INTERNATIONAL ECONOMIC INSTITUTIONS. Sixth Edition, Revised. M.A.G. van Meerhaeghe. Kluwer Academic Publishers, 101 Philip Drive, Assinippi Park, Norwell, Massachusetts 02061. 1991.

INTERNATIONAL ORGANIZATIONS. Second Edition. Clive Archer. Routledge, Chapman & Hall, 29 West Thirty-fifth Street, New York, New York 10001. 1992.

INTERNATIONAL ORGANIZATIONS: A DICTIONARY AND DIRECTORY. Giuseppe Schiavone. St. James Press, 233 East Ontario, Chicago, Illinois 60611. 1983.

THE SOVIET PROPAGANDA NETWORK: A DIRECTORY OF ORGANISATIONS SERVING SOVIET FOREIGN POLICY. Clive Rose. St. Martin's Press, 175 Fifth Avenue, New York, New York 10010. 1988.

YEARBOOK OF INTERNATIONAL ORGANIZATIONS. Union of International Associations. Saur Veriag, Munich. 1990/91.

BIOGRAPHICAL SOURCES

BIOGRAPHICAL DICTIONARY OF INTERNATIONALISTS. Warren F. Kuehl, Editor. Greenwood Publishing Group, Incorporated, 88 Post Road West, P.O. Box 5007, Westport, Connecticut 06881. 1983.

ONLINE DATABASES

DIRECTORY OF UNITED NATIONS SYSTEM DATABASES ON NON-GOVERNMENTAL ORGANIZATIONS. United Nations Publishing Service, Room DC2-0853, New York, New York 10017. 1988.

INTERNATIONAL AGREEMENTS
See: TREATIES AND CONVENTIONS

INTERNATIONAL ARBITRATION

See also: INTERNATIONAL COURTS AND TRIBUNALS; INTERNATIONAL LAW AND RELATIONS; TREATIES AND CONVENTIONS

LOOSELEAF SERVICES AND REPORTERS

ARBITRATION AND THE LICENSING PROCESS. Robert Goldscheider and Michael de Hass, Editors. Clark Boardman Company, Limited, 435 Hudson Street, New York, New York 10014. 1981.

INTERNATIONAL CHAMBER OF COMMERCE ARBITRATION. W. Laurence Craig, William W. Clark, and Jan Paulssou. Oceana Publications, Incorporated, 75 Main Street, Dobbs Ferry, New York 10522. 1984- .

INTERNATIONAL COMMERCIAL ARBITRATION: CASES UNDER THE NEW YORK CONVENTION. Giorgio Gaja. Oceana Publications, Incorporated, 75 Main Street, Dobbs Ferry, New York 10522. 1978- .

IRANIAN ASSETS LITIGATION REPORTER. Andrews Publications, Incorporated, 1646 West Chester Pike, Westtown, Pennsylvania 19395. 1981- .

MEALEY'S LITIGATION REPORT: IRANIAN CLAIMS. Mealey Publications, P. O. Box 446, Wayne, Pennslyvania 19087. 1984- .

SOVIET COMMERCIAL AND MARITIME ARBITRATION. William E. Butler, Editor. Oceana Publications, Incorporated, 75 Main Street, Dobbs Ferry, New York 10522. 1980- .

HANDBOOKS, MANUALS, FORMBOOKS

A GUIDE TO THE UNCITRAL MODEL LAW ON INTERNATIONAL COMMERCIAL ARBITRATION: LEGISLATIVE HISTORY AND COMMENTARY. Howard M. Holtzmann and Joseph E. Neuhaus. United Nations Commission on International Trade Law. Kluwer Law Book Publishers, Incorporated, 36 West Forty-fourth Street, New York, New York 10036. 1989.

INTERNATIONAL COMMERCIAL AGREEMENTS: A FUNCTIONAL PRIMER ON DRAFTING, NEGOTIATING, AND RESOLVING DISPUTES. William F. Fox, Jr. Kluwer Law Book Publishers, Incorporated, 36 West Forty-fourth Street, New York, New York 10036. 1988.

INTERNATIONAL COMMERCIAL ARBITRATION AND THE COURTS: A SOURCE GUIDE. Transnational Publishers, P.O. Box 7282, Ardsley-on-Hudson, New York 10503. 1989.

INTERNATIONAL COMMERCIAL ARBITRATION. REFERENCE AND FINDING TOOLS. Brian H.W. Hill. Oceana Publications, 75 Main Street, Dobbs Ferry, New York 10522. 1988.

INTERNATIONAL HANDBOOK ON COMMERCIAL ARBITRATION. Pieter Sanders, Editor. Kluwer Law Book Publishers, Incorporated, 36 West Forty-fourth Street, New York, New York 10036. 1985.

TEXTBOOKS AND GENERAL WORKS

ARBITRATION: AN ELEMENT OF INTERNATIONAL LAW. Teklewold Gebrehana. Almquist and Wiskell International, Drottninggata Box 62, S101 20 Stockholm Sweden Distributed by Esselte Documentation Center. 1984.

ARBITRATION AND CONCILIATION UNDER THE UNCITRAL RULES: A TEXTUAL ANAYLSIS. Issaak T. Dore. Martinus Nijhoff, Kluwer Academic Publishers, 101 Philip Drive, Assinippi Park, Norwell, Massachusetts 02061. 1986.

ARBITRATION AND RENEGOTIATION OF INTERNATIONAL INVESTMENT AGREEMENTS: A STUDY WITH PARTICULAR REFERENCE TO MEANS OF CONFLICT AVOIDANCE UNDER NATURAL RESOURCES INVESTMENT AGREEMENT. Peter Wolfgang. Martinus Nijhoff, Kluwer Academic Publishers, 101 Philip Drive, Assinippi Park, Norwell, Massachusetts 02061. 1986.

ARBITRATION AND STATE ENTERPRISES. Heinz Boeckstiegel. ICC Publishing Corporation, 156 Fifth Avenue, Suite 820, New York, New York 10010. 1984.

ARBITRATION IN INTERNATIONAL TRADE. Rene David. Kluwer Law Book Publishers, Incorporated, 36 West Forty-fourth Street, New York, New York 10036. 1985.

ARBITRATION LAW IN EUROPE. ICC Publishing Corporation, 156 Fifth Avenue, Suite 820, New York, New York 10010. 1985.

COMMENTARY ON THE UNCITRAL MODEL LAW ON INTERNATIONAL COMMERCIAL ARBITRATION. Aron Broches. Kluwer Law Book Publishers, Incorporated, 36 West Forty-fourth Street, New York, New York 10036. 1990.

CONTEMPORARY PROBLEMS IN INTERNATIONAL ARBITRATION. Julian D.M. Lew. Martinus Nijhoff, Kluwer Academic Publishers, 101 Philip Drive, Assinippi Park, Norwell, Massachusetts 02061. 1987.

ESSAYS ON INTERNATIONAL COMMERCIAL ARBITRATION. Petar Sarcevic. Graham and Trotman Limited, Sterling House, 66 Wilton Road, London SW1V 1DE, England. 1989.

FACT-FINDING BEFORE INTERNATIONAL TRIBUNALS. Richard B. Lillich, Editor. University of Virginia. School of Law. Transnational Publishers, P.O. Box 7282, Ardsley-on-Hudson, New York 10503. 1992.

GUIDE TO ARBITRATION; HOW TO PREVENT AND SOLVE INTERNATIONAL COMMERCIAL DISPUTES. ICC Publishing Corporation, 156 Fifth Avenue, Suite 820, New York, New York 10010. 1983.

INTERNATIONAL ARBITRATION. Thomas Oehmke. Lawyers Cooperative Publishing Company, Aqueduct Building, Rochester, New York 14694. 1990.

INTERNATIONAL ARBITRATION BETWEEN PRIVATE PARTIES AND GOVERNMENTS. Gerald Asken, Chairman. Practising Law Institute, 810 Seventh Avenue, New York, New York 10019. 1982.

THE INTERNATIONAL ARBITRATION KIT: A COMPILATION OF BASIC AND FREQUENTLY REQUESTED DOCUMENTS. Laura F. Brown. American Arbitration Association, 140 West Fifty-first Street, New York, New York 10020. 1982.

INTERNATIONAL ARBITRATION LAW. Mauro Rubino-Sammartano. Kluwer Law Book Publishers, Incorporated, 36 West Forty-fourth Street, New York, New York 10036. 1990.

INTERNATIONAL CHAMBER OF COMMERCE ARBITRATION. Second Edition. W. Laurence Craig, William W. Park and Jan Paulsson. Oceana Publications, 75 Main Street, Dobbs Ferry, New York 10522. 1990.

INTERNATIONAL COMMERCIAL ARBITRATION: RECENT DEVELOPMENTS. Emmanuel Gaillard and Robert B. von Mehren. Practising Law Institute, 810 Seventh Avenue, New York, New York 10019. 1988.

INTERNATIONAL DISPUTE SETTLEMENT. J.G. Merrills. Sweet and Maxwell, South Quay Plaza, 183 Marsh Wall, London E14 9FT, England. 1984.

INTERNATIONAL INVESTMENT DISPUTES: AVOIDANCE AND SETTLEMENT. Seymour J. Rubin and Richard W. Nelson, Editors. American Society of International Law, 2223 Massachusetts Avenue, Northwest, Washington, D.C. 20008. 1985.

INTERNATIONAL TRANSACTIONS AND CLAIMS INVOLVING GOVERNMENT PARTIES: CASE LAW OF THE IRAN-UNITED STATES CLAIMS TRIBUNAL. John A. Westberg. International Law Institute, 1615 New Hampshire Avenue, Northwest, Washington, D.C. 20009. 1991.

THE IRAN-UNITED STATES CLAIMS TRIBUNAL, 1981-1983. Seventh Sokol Colloquium. Richard B. Lillich, Editor. University Press of Virginia, P. O. Box 3608, University Station, Charlottesville, Virginia 22903. 1984.

JUDICIAL REMEDIES IN INTERNATIONAL LAW. Christine D. Gray. Oxford University Press, 200 Madison Avenue, New York, New York 10016. 1987.

PEACE THROUGH AGREEMENT: REPLACING WAR WITH NON-VIOLENT DISPUTE-RESOLUTION METHODS. Gerald Rabow. Praeger Publishers, One Madison Avenue, New York, New York 10010-3603. 1990.

PEACETIME UNILATERAL REMEDIES: AN ANALYSIS OF COUNTERMEASURES. Elizabeth Zoller. Transnational Publishers, Incorporated, P. O. Box 7282, Ardsley-on-Hudson, New York 10503. 1984.

RESOLVING TRANSNATIONAL DISPUTES THROUGH INTERNATIONAL ARBITRATION. Sixth Sokol Colloquium. Thomas E. Carbonneau, Editor. University Press of Virginia, P. O. Box 3608, University Station, Charlottesville, Virginia 22903. 1984.

A SUMMARY OF COURT DECISIONS ON INTERNATIONAL COMMERCIAL ARBITRATION. American Arbitration Association, 140 West Fifty-first Street, New York, New York 10020. 1990.

SURVEY OF INTERNATIONAL ARBITRATION SITES. American Arbitration Association, 140 West Fifty-first Street, New York, New York 10020. 1988.

SYSTEMS OF CONTROL IN INTERNATIONAL ADJUDICATION AND ARBITRATION: BREAKDOWN AND REPAIR. W. Michael Reisman. Duke University Press, Box 6697 College Station, Durham, North Carolina 27708. 1992.

THEORY AND PRACTICE OF MULTIPARTY COMMERCIAL ARBITRATION WITH SPECIAL REFERENCE TO THE UNCITRAL FRAMEWORK. Isaak I. Dore. Graham and Trotman Limited, Sterling House, 66 Wilton Road, London SW1V 1DE, England. 1990.

TRANSNATIONAL LITIGATION AND COMMERCIAL ARBITRATION: A COMPARATIVE ANALYSIS OF AMERICAN, EUROPEAN AND INTERNATIONAL LAW. Joseph Lookofsky. Transnational Publishers, P.O. Box 7282, Ardsley-on-Hudson, New York 10503. 1992.

NEWSLETTERS AND NEWSPAPERS

NEWS FROM THE ICSID. International Center for Settlement of Investment Disputes, 1818 H Street, E Building, Washington, D.C. 20433. Semiannual.

BIBLIOGRAPHIES

COLLECTION OF ICC ARBITRAL AWARDS, 1974-1985. Sigvard Jarvin and Yves Derains. International Chamber of Commerce. Kluwer Law Book Publishers, Incorporated, 36 West Forty-fourth Street, New York, New York 10036. 1990.

SURVEY OF INTERNATIONAL ARBITRATIONS, 1794-1989. Third Edition. A.M. Stuyt, Editor. Martinus Nijhoff, Kluwer Academic Publishers, 101 Philip Drive, Assinippi Park, Norwell, Massachusetts 02061. 1990.

ASSOCIATIONS AND PROFESSIONAL SOCIETIES

AMERICAN ARBITRATION ASSOCIATION. 140 West Fifty-first Street, New York, New York 10020. (212) 484-4000.

INTER-AMERICAN COMMERCIAL ARBITRATION COMMISSION. 1889 F Street, Northwest, Room LL-3, Washington, D.C. 20006. (202) 293-1455.

INTERNATIONAL CENTRE FOR SETTLEMENT OF INVESTMENT DISPUTES. 1818 H Street, Northwest, Washington, D.C. 20433. (202) 477-1234.

INTERNATIONAL CLAIMS
See: GOVERNMENT IMMUNITY AND LIABILITY

INTERNATIONAL COMMER CE
See: EXPORT AND IMPORT

INTERNATIONAL CONVENTIONS
See: TREATIES AND CONVENTIONS

INTERNATIONAL COURTS AND TRIBUNALS

STATUTES, CODES, STANDARDS, UNIFORM LAWS

A DRAFT INTERNATIONAL CRIMINAL CODE AND DRAFT STATUTE FOR AN INTERNATIONAL CRIMINAL TRIBUNAL. Second Edition. M. Cherif Bassiouni. Martinus Nijhoff, Kluwer Academic Publishers, 101 Philip Drive, Assinippi Park, Norwell, Massachusetts 02061. 1987.

TREATIES, JUDICIAL OPINIONS, RECORDS, DOCUMENTS

ACTS AND DOCUMENTS CONCERNING THE ORGANIZATION OF THE COURT. International Court of Justice, United Nations, Sales Section, Publishing Division, New York, New York 10017. Irregular.

AMERICAN INTERNATIONAL LAW CASES, 1783-1978. Francis Deak, Editor. Oceana Publications, Incorporated, 75 Main Street, Dobbs Ferry, New York 10522. 1980.

AMERICAN INTERNATIONAL LAW CASES, 1969-1979. Francis S. Ruddy, Editor. Oceana Publications, Incorporated, 75 Main Street, Dobbs Ferry, New York 10522. 1985.

DECISIONS AND REPORTS: EUROPEAN COMMISSION OF HUMAN RIGHTS. Secretariat of the European Commission of Human Rights, Council of Europe, Strasbourg, West Germany. 1975- .

DECISIONS OF INTERNATIONAL INSTITUTES BEFORE DOMESTIC COURTS. Christopher Schreuer. Oceana Publications, Incorporated, 75 Main Street, Dobbs Ferry, New York 10522. 1981.

INTER-AMERICAN COURT OF HUMAN RIGHTS; SERIES A, JUDGMENTS AND OPINIONS. Inter-American Court of Human Rights, Secretariat of the Court, San Jose, Costa Rica. 1982- .

MAIN TEXTS GOVERNING THE REGIONAL POLICY OF THE EUROPEAN COMMUNITIES. Commission of the European Communities, 2100 M Street, Northwest, Washington, D.C. 20037. 1985

PLEADINGS, ORAL ARGUMENTS AND DOCUMENTS. International Court of Justice, United Nations, Sales Section, Publishing Division, New York, New York 10017. Irregular.

REPORT OF JUDGMENTS, ADVISORY OPINIONS AND ORDERS. International Court of Justice, United Nations, Sales Section, Publishing Division, New York, New York 10017. Slip opinions and annual volumes.

REPORTS OF CASES BEFORE THE COURT. Court of Justice of the European Communities, Office for Official Publications of the European Communities, Luxembourg. 1959- .

TEXTBOOKS AND GENERAL WORKS

DOCUMENTS ON INTERNATIONAL ADMINISTRATIVE TRIBUNALS. C.F. Amerasinghe, Editor. Oxford University Press, 200 Madison Avenue, New York, New York 10016. 1989.

FACT-FINDING BEFORE INTERNATIONAL TRIBUNALS. Richard B. Lillich, Editor. University of Virginia. School of Law. Transnational Publishers, P.O. Box 7282, Ardsley-on-Hudson, New York 10503. 1992.

INTERIM MEASURES IN THE HAGUE COURT: AN ATTEMPT AT A SCRUTINY. Jerzy Sztucki. Kluwer Academic Publishers, 101 Philip Drive, Assinippi Park, Norwell, Massachusetts 02061. 1983.

THE INTERNATIONAL COURT OF JUSTICE AND SOME CONTEMPORARY PROBLEMS: ESSAYS ON INTERNATIONAL LAW. Taslim O. Elias. Kluwer Academic Publishers, 101 Philip Drive, Assinippi Park, Norwell, Massachusetts 02061. 1984.

INTERNATIONAL LAW AS APPLIED BY INTERNATIONAL COURTS AND TRIBUNALS: VOLUME IV INTERNATIONAL JUDICIAL LAW. George Schwarzenberger. Stevens, London. 1986.

THE IRAN-UNITED STATES CLAIMS TRIBUNAL, 1981-1983. Seventh Sokol Colloquium. Richard B. Lillich, Editor. University Press of Virginia, P. O. Box 3608, University Station, Charlottesville, Virginia 22903. 1984.

JUDICIAL REMEDIES IN INTERNATIONAL LAW. Christine D. Gray. Oxford University Press, 200 Madison Avenue, New York, New York 10016. 1987.

THE LAW AND PRACTICE OF THE INTERNATIONAL COURT. Second Revised Edition. Shabtai Rosenne. Kluwer Academic Publishers, 101 Philip Drive, Assinippi Park, Norwell, Massachusetts 02061. 1985.

LAW AND PROCEDURE OF THE INTERNATIONAL COURT OF JUSTICE. Sir Gerald Fitzmaurice. Grotius Publications, Limited, Wind Street, Llandysuw, Dyfed SA44 4BQ, Wales. 1986.

THE LAW OF THE INTERNATIONAL CIVIL SERVICE: AS APPLIED BY INTERNATIONAL ADMINISTRATIVE TRIBUNALS. C.F. Amerasinghe. Oxford University Press, 200 Madison Avenue, New York, New York 10016. 1988.

LITIGATING INTERNATIONAL LAW. Anthony D'Amato. Transnational Publishers, Incorporated, P.O. Box 7282, Ardsley-on-Hudson, New York 10503. 1986.

NON-APPEARANCE BEFORE THE INTERNATIONAL COURT OF JUSTICE. H. W. A. Thirlway. Cambridge University Press, 40 West Twentieth Street, New York, New York 10011. 1985.

NON-APPEARANCE BEFORE THE INTERNATIONAL COURT OF JUSTICE: FUNCTIONAL AND COMPARATIVE ANALYSIS. Jerome B. Elkind. Kluwer Academic Publishers, 101 Philip Drive, Assinippi Park, Norwell, Massachusetts 02061. 1984.

PROCEDURE IN INTERNATIONAL COURT: A COMMENTARY ON THE 1978 RULES OF THE INTERNATIONAL COURT OF JUSTICE. Shabtai Rosenne. Kluwer Academic Publishers, 101 Philip Drive, Assinippi Park, Norwell, Massachusetts 02061. 1983.

REVIVING THE WORLD COURT. Richard A. Falk. University Press of Virginia, P.O. Box 3608, University Station, Charlottesville, Virginia 22903. 1986.

THE SYSTEM FOR SETTLEMENT OF DISPUTES UNDER THE UNITED NATIONS CONVENTION ON THE LAW OF THE SEA: A DRAFTING HISTORY AND A COMMENTARY. A.O. Adede. Martinus Nijhoff, Kluwer Academic Publishers, 101 Philip Drive, Assinippi Park, Norwell, Massachusetts 02061. 1987.

SYSTEMS OF CONTROL IN INTERNATIONAL ADJUDICATION AND ARBITRATION: BREAKDOWN AND REPAIR. W. Michael Reisman. Duke University Press, Box 6697 College Station, Durham, North Carolina 27708. 1992.

THE UNITED STATES AND THE COMPULSORY JURISDICTION OF THE INTERNATIONAL COURT OF JUSTICE. Anthony Clark Arend, Editor. University Press of America, 4720 Boston Way, Lanham, Maryland 20706. 1986.

DIGESTS, INDEXES, ABSTRACTS, CITATORS

CASE-LAW OF THE WORLD BANK ADMINISTRATIVE TRIBUNAL: AN ANALYTICAL DIGEST. C.F. Amerasinghe. Oxford University Press, 200 Madison Avenue, New York, New York 10016. 1989.

BIBLIOGRAPHIES

BIBLIOGRAPHY: INTERNATIONAL COURT OF JUSTICE. United Nations, Sales Section, Publishing Division, New York, New York 10017. Annual.

INTERNATIONAL COURT OF JUSTICE: A SELECTED BIBLIOGRAPHY OF LAW REVIEW ARTICLES. Jim Milles. Vance Bibliographies, P.O. Box 229, 112 North Charter Street, Monticello, Illinois 61856. 1985.

NEWSLETTERS AND NEWSPAPERS

THE WORLD JURIST. World Peace Through Law Center, 1000 Connecticut Avenue, Suite 800, Washington, D.C. 20036. Bimonthly.

ASSOCIATIONS AND PROFESSIONAL SOCIETIES

AMERICAN ASSOCIATION FOR THE INTERNATIONAL COMMISSION OF JURISTS. 777 United Nations Plaza, Tenth Floor, New York, New York 10017. (212) 972-0883.

INTERNATIONAL CRIME
See also: CENTRAL INTELLIGENCE AGENCY; GENOCIDE; TERRORISM

STATUTES, CODES, STANDARDS, UNIFORM LAWS

A DRAFT INTERNATIONAL CRIMINAL CODE AND DRAFT STATUTE FOR AN INTERNATIONAL CRIMINAL TRIBUNAL. Second Edition, revised and updated. M. Cherif Bassiouni. Martinus Nijhoff, Kluwer Academic Publishers, 101 Philip Drive, Assinippi Park, Norwell, Massachusetts 02061. 1987.

HANDBOOKS, MANUALS, FORMBOOKS

INTERNATIONAL CRIMINAL LAW: A GUIDE TO U.S. PRACTICE AND PROCEDURE: ANTITRUST, SECURITIES, EXTRADITION, TAX, TERRORISM. Ved P. Nanda and M. Cherif Bassiouni, Editors. Practising Law Institute, 810 Seventh Avenue, New York, New York 10019. 1987.

TEXTBOOKS AND GENERAL WORKS

DEFENDING CIVIL DISOBEDIENCE UNDER INTERNATIONAL LAW. Francis A. Boyle. Transnational Publishers, Incorporated, P.O. Box 7282, Ardsley-on-Hudson, New York 10503. 1986.

GUIDE TO UNITED NATIONS CRIMINAL POLICY. Manuel Lopez-Rey. Gower Publishing Company, Old Post Road, Brookfield, Vermont 05036. 1985.

INDIVIDUAL RESPONSIBILITY IN INTERNATIONAL LAW FOR SERIOUS HUMAN RIGHTS VIOLATIONS. Lyal S. Sunga. Martinus Nijhoff, Kluwer Academic Publishers, 101 Philip Drive, Assinippi Park, Norwell, Massachusetts 02061. 1992.

INTERNATIONAL CRIMINAL LAW. M. Cherif Bassiouni, Editor. Transnational Publishers, Incorporated, P.O. Box 7282, Ardsley-on-Hudson, New York 10503. 1987.

LEGAL RESTRAINTS ON THE USE OF FORCE 40 YEARS AFTER THE UN CHARTER. A. B. Gassesse, Editor. Martinus Nijhoff, Kluwer Academic Publishers, 101 Philip Drive, Assinippi Park, Norwell, Massachusetts 02061. 1986.

NEW DIMENSIONS IN TRANSNATIONAL CRIME. Donal E. MacNamara and Phillip J. Stead. John Jay Press, 899 Tenth Avenue, New York, New York 10019. 1982.

THE NUREMBERG TRIAL AND INTERNATIONAL LAW. George Ginsburgs and V.N. Kudriavtsev. Martinus Nijhoff, Kluwer Academic Publishers, 101 Philip Drive, Assinippi Park, Norwell, Massachusetts 02061. 1990.

TERRORISM, INTERNATIONAL CRIME, AND ARMS CONTROL. Leonard J. Hippchen and Yong S. Yim. Charles C. Thomas Publishing, 2600 South First Street, Springfield, Illinois 62794-9265. 1982.

THE TOKYO WAR CRIMES TRIAL: AN INTERNATIONAL SYMPOSIUM. Chibir Hosoya et al. Kodansha International, c/o HarperCollins Publishers, 10 East Fifty-third Street, New York, New York 10022. 1986.

DIGESTS, INDEXES, ABSTRACTS, CITATORS

PEACE LAW DOCKET, 1945-1988. Ann Fagan Ginger, Editor. Meiklejohn Civil Liberties Institute, P.O. Box 673, Berkeley, California 94701. 1988.

BIBLIOGRAPHIES

WAR CRIMES, WAR CRIMINALS, AND WAR CRIMES TRIALS: AN ANNOTATED BIBLIOGRAPHY AND SOURCE BOOK. Norman E. Tutorow, Editor. Greenwood Publishing Group, Incorporated, 88 Post Road West, P. O. Box 5007, Westport, Connecticut 06881. 1986.

INTERNATIONAL CRIMINAL LAW
See: INTERNATIONAL CRIME

INTERNATIONAL JURISPRUDENCE
See: INTERNATIONAL LAW AND RELATIONS

INTERNATIONAL LAW AND RELATIONS
See also: CONFLICT OF LAWS; DIPLOMATIC PRIVILEGES AND IMMUNITY; FOREIGN LAW; GOVERNMENT IMMUNITY AND LIABILITY; HUMAN RIGHTS; INTERNATIONAL AGENCIES AND ORGANIZATIONS; INTERNATIONAL ARBITRATION; INTERNATIONAL COURTS AND TRIBUNALS; INTERNATIONAL CRIME; LAW OF THE SEA; POLITICAL CRIMES AND OFFENSES; SPACE LAW; STATE DEPARTMENT; TAXATION, INTERNATIONAL; TREATIES AND CONVENTIONS

STATUTES, CODES, STANDARDS, UNIFORM LAWS

BASIC DOCUMENTS IN INTERNATIONAL LAW AND WORLD ORDER. Second Edition. Burns H. Weston, Richard A. Falk and Anthony A. D'Amato, Editors. West Publishing Company, 50 West Kellogg Boulevard, St. Paul, Minnesota 55164. 1990.

DOCUMENTS ON THE LAWS OF WAR. Second Edition. Adam Roberts and Richard Guelff, Editors. Oxford University Press, 200 Madison Avenue, New York, New York 10016. 1989.

THE INTERNATIONAL LAW COMMISSION'S DRAFT ARTICLES ON STATE RESPONSIBILITY: PART 1, ARTICLES 1-35. Shabtai Rosenne. United Nations. International Law Commission. Martinus Nijhoff, Kluwer Academic Publishers, 101 Philip Drive, Assinippi Park, Norwell, Massachusetts 02061. 1991.

INTERNATIONAL LAW: SELECTED DOCUMENTS. Barry E. Carter and Phillip R. Trimble. Little, Brown and Company, 34 Beacon Street, Boston, Massachusetts 02108. 1991.

THE LAWS OF ARMED CONFLICTS: A COLLECTION OF CONVENTIONS, RESOLUTIONS, AND OTHER DOCUMENTS. Third Revised Edition. Dietrich Schindler and Jiri Toman. Martinus Nijhoff, Kluwer Academic Publishers, 101 Philip Drive, Assinippi Park, Norwell, Massachusetts 02061. 1988.

TREATIES, JUDICIAL OPINIONS, RECORDS, DOCUMENTS

ANARCTICA AND INTERNATIONAL LAW: A COLLECTION OF INTER-STATE AND NATIONAL DOCUMENTS. W. M. Bush. Oceana Publications, Incorporated, 75 Main Street, Dobbs Ferry, New York 10522. 1982.

INTERNATIONAL ECONOMIC INSTITUTIONS. Fourth Edition. Marcel A. G. Van Meerhaeghe. Kluwer Academic Publishers, 190 Old Derby Street, Hingham, Massachusetts 02043. 1985.

RESTATEMENTS

RESTATEMENT OF THE LAW, SECOND: FOREIGN RELATIONS LAW OF THE UNITED STATES, 1965; RESTATEMENT OF THE LAW: FOREIGN RELATIONS LAW OF THE UNITED STATES (REVISED): TENTATIVE DRAFTS NUMBERS 1-7, 1980-1986; RESTATEMENT OF THE FOREIGN RELATIONS LAW OF THE UNITED STATES, REVISED (AS APPROVED BY THE AMERICAN LAW INSTITUTE IN 1986) 1987 American Law Institute, 4025 Chestnut Street, Philadelphia, Pennsylvania 19104.

LOOSELEAF SERVICES AND REPORTERS

THE REGULATION OF INTERNATIONAL COMMERCIAL AVIATION. Stanley Rosenfield. Oceana Publications, Incorporated, 75 Main Street, Dobbs Ferry, New York 10522. 1983- .

HANDBOOKS, MANUALS, FORMBOOKS

A DIPLOMAT'S HANDBOOK OF INTERNATIONAL LAW AND PRACTICE. Third Revised Edition. S. Sen. Martinus Nijhoff, Kluwer Academic Publishers, 101 Philip Drive, Assinippi Park, Norwell, Massachusetts 02061. 1988.

GUIDE TO INTERNATIONAL LEGAL RESEARCH. THE GEORGE WASHINGTON JOURNAL OF INTERNATIONAL LAW AND ECONOMICS. Butterworth Legal Publishers, 90 Stiles Road, Salem, New Hampshire 03079. 1989.

INTERNATIONAL LEGAL RESEARCH PERSPECTIVES. Adolf Sprudzs. William S. Hein and Company, 1285 Main Street, Buffalo, New York 14209. 1988.

THE UNITED NATIONS CONVENTION AGAINST TORTURE: A HANDBOOK ON THE CONVENTION AGAINST TORTURE AND OTHER CRUEL, INHUMAN, OR DEGRADING TREATMENT OR PUNISHMENT. J. Herman Burgers and Hans Danelius. Martinus Nijhoff, Kluwer Academic Publishers, 101 Philip Drive, Assinippi Park, Norwell, Massachusetts 02061. 1988.

TEXTBOOKS AND GENERAL WORKS

ACT OF STATE AND EXTRATERRITORIAL REACH: PROBLEMS OF LAW AND POLICY. American Bar Association, Section of International Law and Practice, 750 North Lake Shore Drive, Chicago, Illinois 60611. 1983.

AFRICA AND THE DEVELOPMENT OF INTERNATIONAL LAW. Second Revised Edition. T.O. Elias and Richard Akinjide. Martinus Nijhoff, Kluwer Academic Publishers, 101 Philip Drive, Assinippi Park, Norwell, Massachusetts 02061. 1988.

THE AMERICAN CHARACTER AND FOREIGN POLICY. Michael P. Hamilton, Editor. Books on Demand, 300 North Zeeb Road, Ann Arbor, Michigan 48106-1346. 1986.

AMERICAN SECURITY IN A CHANGING WORLD: ISSUES AND CHOICES. Joseph Richard Goldman, Editor. University Press of America, 4720 Boston Way, Lanham, Maryland 20706. 1987.

ASPECTS OF THE ADMINISTRATION OF INTERNATIONAL JUSTICE. Elihu Lauterpacht. Grotius Publications, Cambridge, Connecticut. 1991.

BLUNDERING INTO DISASTER: SURVIVING THE FIRST CENTURY OF THE NUCLEAR AGE. Robert McNamara. Pantheon Books, 201 East Fiftieth Street, New York, New York 10022. 1987.

CARIBBEAN PERSPECTIVES ON INTERNATIONAL LAW AND ORGANIZATIONS. B.G. Ramcharan and L.B. Francis, Editors. Martinus Nijhoff, Kluwer Academic Publishers, 101 Philip Drive, Assinippi Park, Norwell, Massachusetts 02061. 1989.

CASES AND MATERIALS ON THE INTERNATIONAL LEGAL SYSTEM. Third Edition. Joseph Modeste Sweeney, Covey T. Oliver and Noyes E. Leech. Foundation Press, 615 Merrick Avenue, Westbury, New York 11590. 1988.

CHEMICAL WARFARE ARMS CONTROL: A FRAMEWORK FOR CONSIDERING POLICY ALTERNATIVES. Julian Perry Robinson. Taylor and Francis, Incorporated, 1990 Frost Road, Suite 101, Bristol, Pennsylvania 19007. 1985.

THE CHINA CONNECTION: UNITED STATES POLICY AND THE PEOPLE'S REPUBLIC OF CHINA. James A. Gregor. Hoover Institution Press, Stanford University, Stanford, California 94305. 1986.

CONFLICT AND PEACE IN THE MODERN INTERNATIONAL SYSTEM: A STUDY OF THE PRINCIPLES OF INTERNATIONAL ORDER. Evan Luard. State University of New York Press, State University Plaza, Albany, New York 12246. 1988.

CONTEMPORARY INTERNATIONAL LAW: A CONCISE INTRODUCTION. Second Edition. Werner Levi. Westview Press, Incorporated, 5500 Central Avenue, Boulder, Colorado 80301. 1991.

THE COURSE OF AMERICAN DIPLOMACY: FROM THE REVOLUTION TO THE PRESENT. Howard Jones. Wadsworth Publishing Co., 10 Davis Drive, Belmont, California 94002. 1988.

CURRENT ISSUES IN EUROPEAN AND INTERNATIONAL LAW: ESSAYS IN MEMORY OF FRANK DOWRICK. Robin White and Bernard Smythe, Editors. Sweet and Maxwell Limited, South Quay Plaza, 183 Marsh Wall, London E14 9FT, England. 1990.

DISPUTE SETTLEMENT IN PUBLIC INTERNATIONAL LAW: TEXTS AND MATERIALS. Karin Oellers-Frahm. Springer-Verlag New York, Incorporated, 175 Fifth Avenue, New York, New York 10010. 1985.

DOOMSDAY OR DETERRENCE. Ferenc Feher and Agnes Heller. M. E. Sharpe, Incorporated, 80 Business Park Drive, Armonk, New York 10504. 1986.

DYNAMIC MODELS OF INTERNATIONAL CONFLICT. Urs Luterbacher and Michael D. Ward. Lynne Rienner, Publishers, Incorporated, 1800 Thirtieth Street, Suite 314, Boulder, Colorado 80301. 1985.

THE DYNAMICS OF INTERNATIONAL LAW IN CONFLICT RESOLUTION. Joaquin Tacsan. Martinus Nijhoff, Kluwer Academic Publishers, 101 Philip Drive, Assinippi Park, Norwell, Massachusetts 02061. 1992.

EMPTY PROMISE: THE GROWING CASE AGAINST STAR WARS. John Tirman, Editor. Beacon Press, Incorporated, 25 Beacon Street, Boston, Massachusetts 02108. 1986.

ESSAYS ON INTERNATIONAL LAW. Stuart S. Malawer. William S. Hein and Company, Incorporated, Hein Building, 1285 Main Street, Buffalo, New York 14209. 1986.

ETHICS AND NUCLEAR ARMS: EUROPEAN AND AMERICAN PERSPECTIVES. Raymond English, Editor. Ethics and Public Policy Center, 1030 Fifteenth Street, Northwest, Suite 300, Washington, D.C. 20005. 1985.

EXPANDING THE FRONTIERS: SUPERPOWER INTERVENTION IN THE COLD WAR. Karen A. Feste. Praeger Publishers, One Madison Avenue, New York, New York 10010-3603. 1992.

FEDERAL COURTS AND THE INTERNATIONAL HUMAN RIGHTS PARADIGM. Kenneth C. Randall. Duke University Press, Box 6697 College Station, Durham, North Carolina 27708. 1990.

FORCEFUL PERSUASION: COERCIVE DIPLOMACY AS AN ALTERNATIVE TO WAR. Alexander L. George. United States Institute of Peace Press, 1550 M Street, Northwest, Suite 700, Washington, D.C. 20005. 1992.

FOREIGN NEWS AND THE NEW WORLD INFORMATION ORDER. Robert L. Stevenson, and Douglas L. Shaw, Editors. Iowa State University Press, 2121 South State Avenue, Ames, Iowa 50010. 1984.

THE FOREIGN POLICY OF NEW STATES. Peter Calvert. Saint Martin's Press, Incorporated, 175 Fifth Avenue, New York, New York 10010. 1986.

FUNDAMENTAL PERSPECTIVES ON INTERNATIONAL LAW. William R. Slomanson. West Publishing Company, 50 West Kellogg Boulevard, St. Paul, Minnesota 55164. 1990.

FURTHER STUDIES IN INTERNATIONAL LAW. F.A. Mann. Oxford University Press, 200 Madison Avenue, New York, New York 10016. 1990.

THE FUTURE OF INTERNATIONAL LAW AND AMERICAN FOREIGN POLICY. Francis Anthony Boyle. Transnational Publishers, P.O. Box 7282, Ardsley-on-Hudson, New York 10503. 1989.

THE FUTURE OF INTERNATIONAL LAW IN A MULTICULTURAL WORLD. Reno-Jean Dupuy, Editor. Kluwer Academic Publishers, 101 Philip Drive, Assinippi Park, Norwell, Massachusetts 02061. 1984.

GOOD FAITH IN INTERNATIONAL LAW. J.F. O'Connor. Dartmouth, Brookfield, Vermont. 1991.

GOVERNMENT FROM REFLECTION AND CHOICE: CONSTITUTIONAL ESSAYS ON WAR, FOREIGN RELATIONS, AND FEDERALISM. Charles A. Lofgren. Oxford University Press, Incorporated, 200 Madison Avenue, New York, New York 10016. 1986.

THE GULF WAR OF 1980-1988: THE IRAN-IRAQ WAR IN INTERNATIONAL LEGAL PERSPECTIVE. Ige F. Dekker and Harry H.G. Post, Editors. Martinus Nijhoff, Kluwer Academic Publishers, 101 Philip Drive, Assinippi Park, Norwell, Massachusetts 02061. 1992.

HISTORY, PHILOSOPHY, AND FOREIGN RELATIONS: BACKGROUND FOR THE MAKING OF FOREIGN POLICY. Louis Joseph Halle. University Press of America, 4720 Boston Way, Lanham, Maryland 20706. 1987.

HUGO GROTIUS AND INTERNATIONAL RELATIONS. Hedley Bull, Benedict Kingsbury, and Adam Roberts. Oxford University Press, 200 Madison Avenue, New York, New York 10016. 1990.

HUMAN RIGHTS OF ALIENS IN CONTEMPORARY INTERNATIONAL LAW. Richard B. Lillich. Manchester University Press, 175 Fifth Avenue, New York, New York 10010. 1985.

HUMAN RIGHTS IN INTERNATIONAL LAW: LEGAL AND POLICY ISSUES. Theodor Meron. Oxford University Press, Incorporated, 200 Madison Avenue, New York, New York 10016. 1986.

HUMAN RIGHTS IN STATES OF EMERGENCY IN INTERNATIONAL LAW. Jaime Oraa. Oxford University Press, 200 Madison Avenue, New York, New York 10016. 1992.

IN THE MIDDLE: NON-OFFICIAL MEDIATION IN VIOLENT SITUATIONS. Adam Curle. Berg Publishers, Incorporated, 165 Taber Avenue, Providence, Rhode Island 02906. 1987.

INDIVIDUAL RESPONSIBILITY IN INTERNATIONAL LAW FOR SERIOUS HUMAN RIGHTS VIOLATIONS. Lyal S. Sunga. Martinus Nijhoff, Kluwer Academic Publishers, 101 Philip Drive, Assinippi Park, Norwell, Massachusetts 02061. 1992.

INTERNATIONAL CONFLICT RESOLUTION: THEORY AND PRACTICE. Edward E. Azar and John W. Burton. Lynn Rienner Publishers, Incorporated, 1800 Thirtieth Street, Suite 314, Boulder, Colorado 80301. 1986.

INTERNATIONAL CULTURAL RELATIONS. J. M. Mitchell. Allen and Unwin, Eight Winchester Place, Winchester, Massachusetts 01890. 1986.

INTERNATIONAL DOCUMENTS FOR THE EIGHTIES: THEIR ROLE AND USE. Throdore Dimitrov and L. Marulli-Kornig, Editors. Unifo Publishers, Limited, P.O. Box 3858, Sarasota, Florida 34230. 1982.

INTERNATIONAL HUMANITARIAN LAW: THE REGULATION OF ARMED CONFLICTS. Hilaire McCoubrey. Gower Publishing Company, Old Post Road, Brookfield, Vermont 05036. 1990.

INTERNATIONAL INCIDENTS: THE LAW THAT COUNTS IN WORLD POLITICS. W. Michael Reisman and Andrew R. Willard, Editors. Princeton University Press, 41 William Street, Princeton, New Jersey 08540. 1988.

INTERNATIONAL LAW. Barry E. Carter and Phillip R. Trimble. Little, Brown and Company, 34 Beacon Street, Boston, Massachusetts 02108. 1991.

INTERNATIONAL LAW. Martti Koskenniemi, Editor. New York University Press, 70 Washington Square South, New York, New York 10012. 1971. 1992 Reprint.

INTERNATIONAL LAW. Rebecca M. M. Wallace. Sweet and Maxwell, South Quay Plaza, 183 Marsh Wall, London E14 9FT, England. 1986.

INTERNATIONAL LAW. Second Edition. Malcom H. Shaw. Grotius Publications, Limited, Wind Street, Llandysuw, Dyfed SA44 4BQ, Wales. 1986.

INTERNATIONAL LAW: A CANADIAN PERSPECTIVE. Second Edition. L.C. Green. Carswell Company, Toronto, Ontario, Canada. 1988.

INTERNATIONAL LAW AND ABORIGINAL RIGHTS. Barbara Hocking, Editor. Longwood Publishing Group, Incorporated, 27 South Main Street, Wolfbora, New Hampshire 03894-2069. 1986.

INTERNATIONAL LAW AND DEVELOPMENT. Paul de Waart, Paul Peters and Erik Denters, Editors. Martinus Nijhoff, Kluwer Academic Publishers, 101 Philip Drive, Assinippi Park, Norwell, Massachusetts 02061. 1988.

INTERNATIONAL LAW AND INTERNATIONAL SECURITY: MILITARY AND POLITICAL DIMENSIONS: A U.S.-SOVIET DIALOGUE. Paul B. Stephen, III and Boris M. Klimenko, Editors. M.E. Sharpe, Incorporated, 80 Business Park Drive, Armonk, New York 10504. 1991.

INTERNATIONAL LAW AND ITS SOURCES. Wybo P. Heere. Kluwer Law Book Publishers, Incorporated, 36 West Forty-fourth Street, New York, New York 10036. 1989.

INTERNATIONAL LAW AND THE ADMINISTRATION OF OCCUPIED TERRITORIES: TWO DECADES OF ISRAELI OCCUPATION OF THE WEST BANK AND GAZA STRIP. Emma Playfair, Editor. Oxford University Press, 200 Madison Avenue, New York, New York 10016. 1992.

INTERNATIONAL LAW AND THE USE OF FORCE BY NATIONAL LIBERATION MOVEMENTS. Heather A. Wilson. Oxford University Press, 200 Madison Avenue, New York, New York 10016. 1988.

INTERNATIONAL LAW AND WORLD ORDER: A PROBLEM-ORIENTED COURSEBOOK. Second Edition. Burns H. Weston, Richard A. Falk and Anthony D'Amato. West Publishing Company, 50 West Kellogg Boulevard, St. Paul, Minnesota 55164. 1990.

INTERNATIONAL LAW AT A TIME OF PERPLEXITY: ESSAYS IN HONOUR OF SHABTAI ROSENNE. Yoram Dinstein and Mala Tabory. Martinus Nijhoff, Kluwer Academic Publishers, 101 Philip Drive, Assinippi Park, Norwell, Massachusetts 02061. 1989.

INTERNATIONAL LAW IN A DIVIDED WORLD. Antonio Cassese. Clarendon Press, Oxford University Press, 200 Madison Avenue, New York, New York 10016. 1989.

INTERNATIONAL LAW IN THEORY AND PRACTICE. Oscar Schachter. Martinus Nijhoff, Kluwer Academic Publishers, 101 Philip Drive, Assinippi Park, Norwell, Massachusetts 02061. 1991.

THE INTERNATIONAL LAW OF ARMED CONFLICT: PERSONAL AND MATERIAL FIELDS OF APPLICATION. Edward Kwakwa. Martinus Nijhoff, Kluwer Academic Publishers, 101 Philip Drive, Assinippi Park, Norwell, Massachusetts 02061. 1992.

INTERNATIONAL LAW OF HUMAN RIGHTS. Paul Sieghart. Oxford University Press, Incorporated, 200 Madison Avenue, New York, New York 10016. 1983.

INTERNATIONAL LAW OF POLLUTION: PROTECTING THE GLOBAL ENVIRONMENT IN A WORLD OF SOVEREIGN STATES. Allen L. Springer. Greenwood Publishing Group, Incorporated, 88 Post Road West, P.O. Box 5007, Westport, Connecticut 06881. 1983.

INTERNATIONAL LAW OF STATE RESPONSIBILITY FOR INJURIES TO ALIENS. Richard B. Lilich. University Press of Virginia, P.O. Box 3608, University Station, Charlottesville, Virginia 22903. 1983.

INTERNATIONAL LAW: PROSPECT AND PROCESS. Transnational Publishers, Incorporated, P.O. Box 7282, Ardsley-on-Hudson, New York 10503. 1987.

INTERNATIONAL RESPONSIBILITY FOR ENVIRONMENTAL HARM. Francesco Francioni and Tullio Scovazzi, Editors. Graham and Trotman Limited, Available From: Kluwer Academic Publishers, 101 Philip Drive, Assinippi Park, Norwell, Massachusetts 02061. 1991.

INTERNATIONAL SECURITY AND ARMS CONTROL. Ellen Propper Mickiewicz and Roman Kolkowicz, Editors. Greenwood Publishing Group, Incorporated, 88 Post Road West, P.O. Box 5007, Westport, Connecticut 06881. 1986.

INTERVENTION IN WORLD POLITICS. Hedley Bull, Editor. Oxford University Press, Incorporated, 200 Madison Avenue, New York, New York 10016. 1988.

AN INTRODUCTION TO CONTEMPORARY INTERNATIONAL LAW: A POLICY-ORIENTED PERSPECTIVE. Lung-chu Chen. Yale University Press, 302 Temple Street, New Haven, Connecticut 06520. 1989.

AN INTRODUCTION TO INTERNATIONAL LAW. Mark W. Janis. Little, Brown and Company, 34 Beacon Street, Boston, Massachusetts 02108. 1988.

AN INTRODUCTION TO INTERNATIONAL LAW. Second Edition. Sharon A. Williams and Armand L. C. de Mestral. Butterworth Legal Publishing, Incorporated, 90 Stiles Road, Salem, New Hampshire 03079. 1986.

INVITATION TO STRUGGLE: CONGRESS, THE PRESIDENT, AND FOREIGN POLICY. Third Edition. Congressional Quarterly, Incorporated, 1414 Twenty-second Street, Northwest, Washington, D.C. 20037. 1988.

JUDICIAL SETTLEMENT OF INTERNATIONAL DISPUTES: JURISDICTION, JUSTICIABILITY, AND JUDICIAL LAW-MAKING ON THE CONTEMPORARY INTERNATIONAL COURT. Edward McWhinney. Martinus Nijhoff, Kluwer Academic Publishers, 101 Philip Drive, Assinippi Park, Norwell, Massachusetts 02061. 1991.

JUST WAR AND JIHAD: HISTORICAL AND THEORETICAL PERSPECTIVES ON WAR AND PEACE IN WESTERN AND ISLAMIC TRADITIONS. John Kelsay and James Turner Johnson, Editors. Greenwood Publishing Group, Incorporated, 88 Post Road West, P.O. Box 5007, Westport, Connecticut 06881. 1991.

JUSTIFYING INTERNATIONAL ACTS. Lea Brilmayer. Cornell University Press, 124 Roberts Place, Ithaca, New York 14850. 1989.

LAW AMONG NATIONS: AN INTRODUCTION TO PUBLIC INTERNATIONAL LAW. Sixth Revised Edition. Macmillan Publishing Company, Incorporated, 866 Third Avenue, New York, New York 10022. 1992.

LAW AND FORCE IN THE NEW INTERNATIONAL ORDER. Lori Fisler Damrosch and David J. Scheffer, Editors. Westview Press, Incorporated, 5500 Central Avenue, Boulder, Colorado 80301. 1991.

LAW, MORALITY AND THE RELATIONS OF STATES. Terry Nardin. Princeton University Press, 41 William Street, Princeton, New Jersey 08540. 1983.

THE LAWS OF WAR: BASIC DOCUMENTS ON INTERNATIONAL ARMED CONFLICT. Michael Reisman and Christos Antoniou. Vintage Books, New York, New York. 1991.

LITIGATING INTERNATIONAL LAW. Anthony D'Amato. Transnational Publishers, Incorporated, P.O. Box 7282, Ardsley-on-Hudson, New York 10503. 1986.

LOCAL REMEDIES IN INTERNATIONAL LAW. C.F. Amerasinghe. Grotius Publications, Cambridge, Connecticut. 1990.

THE LOGIC OF SURPRISE IN INTERNATIONAL CONFLICT. Alex Roberto Hybel. Free Press, 866 Third Avenue, New York, New York 10022. 1986.

MEDIATION OF CIVIL WARS. Hizkias Assefa. Westview Press, 5500 Central Avenue, Boulder, Colorado 80301. 1986.

MODERN INTERNATIONAL LAW. Second Edition. R. C. Hingorani. Oceana Publications, Incorporated, 75 Main Street, Dobbs Ferry, New York 10522. 1984.

NEGOTIATING WORLD ORDER: THE ARTISANSHIP AND ARCHITECTURE OF GLOBAL DIPLOMACY. Alan K. Henrickson, Editor. Scholarly Resources, Incorporated, 104 Greenhill Avenue, Wilmington, Delaware 19805-1897. 1986.

NEOREALISM AND ITS CRITICS. Robert O. Keohane, Editor. Columbia University Press, 562 West 113th Street, New York, New York 10025. 1986.

NUCLEAR BLACKMAIL AND NUCLEAR BALANCE. Richard K. Betts. Brookings Institution, 1775 Massachusetts Avenue, Northwest, Washington, D.C. 20036-2188. 1987.

NUCLEAR STRATEGY AND NATIONAL STYLE. Colin S. Gray. University Press of America, 4720 Boston Way, Lanham, Maryland 20706. 1986.

NUCLEAR TERRORISM: DEFINING THE THREAT. Paul Leventhal and Yonah Alexander, Editor. Pergamon Press, Incorporated, Maxwell House, Fairview Park, Elmsford, New York 10523. 1986.

NUCLEAR WEAPONS AND CONTEMPORARY INTERNATIONAL LAW. Second Edition. Nagendra Singh and Edward McWhinney. Martinus Nijhoff, Kluwer Academic Publishers, 101 Philip Drive, Assinippi Park, Norwell, Massachusetts 02061. 1989.

THE NUREMBERG TRIAL AND INTERNATIONAL LAW. George Ginsburgs and V.N. Kudriavtsev, Editors. Martinus Nijhoff, Kluwer Academic Publishers, 101 Philip Drive, Assinippi Park, Norwell, Massachusetts 02061. 1990.

ON THE LAW OF NATIONS. Daniel Patrick Moynihan. Harvard University Press, 79 Garden Street, Cambridge, Massachusetts 02138. 1990.

PEACEKEEPING IN INTERNATIONAL POLITICS. Alan James. St. Martin's Press, 175 Fifth Avenue, New York, New York 10010. 1990.

PERESTROIKA AND INTERNATIONAL LAW: CURRENT ANGLO-SOVIET APPROACHES TO INTERNATIONAL LAW. Anthony Carty and Gennady Danilenko. St. Martin's Press, 175 Fifth Avenue, New York, New York 10010. 1990.

PERMANENT SOVEREIGNTY OVER NATIONAL RESOURCES IN INTERNATIONAL LAW: PRINCIPLE AND PRACTICE. Kamal Hossain and Subrata Roy Chowdbury, Editor. Saint Martin's Press, Incorporated, 175 Fifth Avenue, New York, New York 10010. 1984.

POLITICAL CHANGE AND FOREIGN POLICIES. Gavin Boyd and Gerald W. Hopple, Editors. Saint Martin's Press, Incorporated, 175 Fifth Avenue, New York, New York 10010. 1987.

THE POWER OF LEGITIMACY AMONG NATIONS. Thomas M. Franck. Oxford University Press, 200 Madison Avenue, New York, New York 10016. 1990.

PRACTICE AND METHODS OF INTERNATIONAL LAW. Shabtai Rosenne. Oceana Publications, Incorporated, 75 Main Street, Dobbs Ferry, New York 10522. 1984.

PRINCIPLES OF PUBLIC INTERNATIONAL LAW. Fourth Edition. Ian Brownlie. Oxford University Press, Incorporated, 200 Madison Avenue, New York, New York 10016. 1990.

PRIOR CONSULTATION IN INTERNATIONAL LAW: A STUDY OF STATE PRACTICE. Frederic L. Kirgis. University Press of Virginia, P.O. Box 3608, University Station, Charlottesville, Virginia 22903. 1983.

PROHIBITION OF NUCLEAR WEAPONS: THE RELEVANCE OF INTERNATIONAL LAW. Elliott L. Meyrowitz. Transnational Publishers, P.O. Box 7282, Ardsley-on-Hudson, New York 10503. 1990.

PUBLIC INTERNATIONAL LAW. Branimir M. Jankovic. Transnational Publishers, Incorporated, P.O. Box 7282, Ardsley-on-Hudson, New York 10503. 1983.

PUBLIC INTERNATIONAL LAW IN A NUTSHELL. Second Edition. Thomas Buergenthal and Harold G. Maier. West Publishing Company, 50 West Kellogg Boulevard, St. Paul, Minnesota 55164. 1990.

REGULATING COVERT ACTION: PRACTICES, CONTEXTS, AND POLICIES OF COVERT COERCION ABROAD IN INTERNATIONAL AND AMERICAN LAW. W. Michael Reisman and James E. Baker. Yale University Press, 302 Temple Street, New Haven, Connecticut 06520. 1992.

RETHINKING THE SOURCES OF INTERNATIONAL LAW. G. J. H. Van Hoof. Kluwer Law Book Publishers, Incorporated, 36 West Forty-fourth Street, New York, New York 10036. 1983.

REVITALIZING INTERNATIONAL LAW. Richard Falk. Iowa State University Press, 2121 South State Avenue, Ames, Iowa 50010. 1989.

RIGHTS OF INDIGENOUS PEOPLES IN INTERNATIONAL LAW: WORKSHOP REPORT. University of Saskatchewan Native Law Centre, 141 Diefenbaker Centre, Saskatoon, Saskatchewan S7N 0W0, Canada. 1986.

RULES, NORMS, AND DECISIONS: ON THE CONDITIONS OF PRACTICAL AND LEGAL REASONING IN INTERNATIONAL RELATIONS AND DOMESTIC AFFAIRS. Friedrich V. Kratochwil. Cambridge University Press, 40 West Twentieth Street, New York, New York 10011. 1989.

THE SOCIOLOGY OF INTERNATIONAL RELATIONS. Marcel Merle. Berg Publishers, Incorporated, 165 Taber Avenue, Providence, Rhode Island 02906. 1987.

SOVEREIGNTY IN DISPUTE: THE FALKLANDS-MALVINAS, 1493-1982. Fritz L. Hoffman and Olga M. Hoffmann. Westview Press, 5500 Central Avenue, Boulder, Colorado 80301. 1984.

STATE IMMUNITY: AN ANALYTICAL AND PROGNOSTIC VIEW. Gamal M. Badar. Kluwer Academic Publishers, 101 Philip Drive, Assinippi Park, Norwell, Massachusetts 02061. 1984.

STRENGTHENING THE BIOLOGICAL WEAPONS CONVENTION BY CONFIDENCE-BUILDING MEASURES. Erhard Geissler, Editor. Oxford University Press, 200 Madison Avenue, New York, New York 10016. 1990.

THE STRUCTURE AND PROCESS OF INTERNATIONAL LAW: ESSAYS IN LEGAL PHILOSOPHY, DOCTRINE OF THEORY. Ronald S. MacDonald and Douglas M. Johnston, Editors. Kluwer Academic Publishers, 101 Philip Drive, Assinippi Park, Norwell, Massachusetts 02061. 1984.

THE TERRITORIAL DIMENSION OF POLITICS WITHIN, AMONG, AND ACROSS NATIONS. Ivo D. Duchacek. Westview Press, 5500 Central Avenue, Boulder, Colorado 80301. 1986.

TOWARD A LAW OF GLOBAL COMMUNICATIONS NETWORKS: THE SCIENCE AND TECHNOLOGY SECTION OF THE AMERICAN BAR ASSOCIATION. Anne W. Branscomb, Editor. Longman, Incorporated, 19 West Forty-fourth Street, New York, New York 10036. 1986.

TOWARDS A NORMATIVE THEORY OF INTERNATIONAL RELATIONS: A CRITICAL ANALYSIS OF THE PHILISOPHICAL AND METHODOLOGICAL ASSUMPTIONS. Mervyn Frost. Cambridge University Press, 40 West Twentieth Street, New York, New York 10011. 1986.

TRADITIONS OF INTERNATIONAL ETHICS. Terry Nardin and David R. Mapel, Editors. Cambridge University Press, 40 West Twentieth Street, New York, New York 10011. 1992.

TRANSFRONTIER POLLUTION AND INTERNATIONAL LAW. Kluwer Academic Publishers, 101 Philip Drive, Assinippi Park, Norwell, Massachusetts 02061. 1986.

THE TREATMENT OF PRISONERS UNDER INTERNATIONAL LAW. Nigel S. Rodley. Clarendon Press, Oxford University Press, 200 Madison Avenue, New York, New York 10016. 1987.

UNIFICATION OF LAW IN INTERNATIONAL PROTECTION OF INDUSTRIAL PROPERTY. Endre Lontai. Martinus Nijhoff, Kluwer Academic Publishers, 101 Philip Drive, Assinippi Park, Norwell, Massachusetts 02061. 1990.

UNITED STATES-ISRAELI RELATIONS. Gabriel Sheffer, Editor. Westview Press, 5500 Central Avenue, Boulder, Colorado 80301. 1986.

WAR CRIMES AND LAWS OF WAR. Second Edition. Donald A. Wells. University Press of America, 4720 Boston Way, Lanham, Maryland 20706. 1991.

THE WAR-MAKING POWERS OF THE PRESIDENT: CONSTITUTIONAL AND INTERNATIONAL LAW ASPECTS. Southern Methodist University Press, P.O. Box 415, Dallas, Texas 75275. 1982.

WAR, PEACE, AND INTERNATIONAL POLITICS. Fifth Edition. David W. Ziegler. Scott, Foresman and Company, 1900 East Lake Avenue, Glenview, Illinois 60025. 1989.

WORLD AT RISK: THE DEBATE OVER ARMS CONTROL. Dennis Menos. McFarland and Company, Incorporated, P.O. Box 611, Jefferson, North Carolina 28640. 1986.

WORLD POLITICS AND INTERNATIONAL LAW. Francis A. Boyle. Duke University Press, Box 6697 College Station, Durham, North Carolina 27708. 1985.

ENCYCLOPEDIAS AND DICTIONARIES

DICTIONARY OF INTERNATIONAL AND COMPARATIVE LAW. James R. Fox. Oceana Publications, 75 Main Street, Dobbs Ferry, New York 10522. 1992.

ENCYCLOPEDIA OF PUBLIC INTERNATIONAL LAW. Max Planck Institute for Comparative Public Law and International Law. Elsevier Science Publishing Company, P.O. Box 882, Madison Square Station, New York, New York 10159. 1981.

AN ENCYCLOPEDIC DICTIONARY OF INTERNATIONAL LAW. Clive Parry and John Grant. Oceana Publications, Incorporated, 75 Main Street, Dobbs Ferry, New York 10522. 1985.

THE INTERNATIONAL BUSINESS DICTIONARY AND REFERENCE. Lewis A. Presner. John Wiley and Sons, Incorporated, 605 Third Avenue, New York, New York 10158. 1991.

INTERNATIONAL LAW DICTIONARY. Robert L. Bledsoe and Boleslaw A. Boczek. ABC-Clio, Incorporated, P.O. Box 1911, Santa Barbara, California 93116-1911. 1987.

WORLD ENCYCLOPEDIA OF PEACE. Ervin Laszlo and Jong Youl Yoo, Editors. Pergamon Press, Incorporated, Maxwell House, Fairview Park, Elmsford, New York 10523. 1986.

DIGESTS, INDEXES, ABSTRACTS, CITATORS

DIGEST OF INTERNATIONAL LAW, 1963-1973. Marjorie M. Whitman. Superintendent of Documents, United States Government Printing Office, Washington, D.C. 20402.

DIGEST OF THE DECISIONS OF THE INTERNATIONAL COURT OF JUSTICE, 1976-1985. International Court of Justice. Springer Publishing Company, 536 Broadway, New York, New York 10012. 1990.

DIGEST OF UNITED STATES PRACTICES IN INTERNATIONAL LAW. Superintendent of Documents, United States Government Printing Office, Washington, D.C. 20402. 1973- .

SUBJECT HEADINGS FOR THE LITERATURE OF LAW AND INTERNATIONAL LAW, AND INDEX TO LC K SCHEDULES: A THESAURUS OF LAW SUBJECT TERMS. Fourth Edition. Tillie Krieger. Fred B. Rothman and Company, 10368 West Centennial Road, Littleton, Colorado 80127. 1990.

ANNUALS AND SURVEYS

ACTIVITIES OF THE UNITED NATIONS IN THE FIELD OF LAW. American Foreign Law Association, c/o Richard E. Lutringer, Whitman and Ransom, 200 Park Avenue, New York, New York 10166. Annual.

AMERICAN SOCIETY OF INTERNATIONAL LAW PROCEEDINGS. American Society of International Law, 2223 Massachusetts Avenue, Northwest, Washington, D.C. 20008. Annual.

INTERNATIONAL LAW JOURNAL. Association of Student International Law Societies, 2223 Massachusetts Avenue, Northwest, Washington, D.C. 20008. Annual.

INTERNATIONAL LAW JOURNAL. University of Notre Dame, School of Law, Notre Dame, Indiana 46556. Annual.

MICHIGAN YEARBOOK OF INTERNATIONAL LEGAL STUDIES. University of Michigan, School of Law, 1020 Greene Street, Ann Arbor, Michigan 48109-1444. Annual.

LAW REVIEWS AND PERIODICALS

AMERICAN JOURNAL OF INTERNATIONAL LAW. American Society of International Law, 2223 Massachusetts Avenue, Northwest, Washington, D.C. 20008. Quarterly.

THE AMERICAN UNIVERSITY JOURNAL OF INTERNATIONAL LAW AND POLICY. American University, Washington College of Law, 4400 Massachusetts Avenue, Northwest, Washington, D.C. 20016. 1986.

ARIZONA JOURNAL OF INTERNATIONAL AND COMPARATIVE LAW. University of Arizona School of Law, Tucson, Arizona 85721. Semiannual.

BOSTON COLLEGE INTERNATIONAL AND COMPARATIVE LAW REVIEW. Boston College, Law School, 885 Centre Street, Newton Centre, Massachusetts 02159. Semiannual.

BOSTON COLLEGE THIRD WORLD LAW JOURNAL. Boston College, Law School, 885 Centre Street, Newton Centre, Massachusetts 02159. Semiannual.

BOSTON UNIVERSITY INTERNATIONAL LAW JOURNAL. Boston University, School of Law, 765 Commonwealth Avenue, Boston, Massachusetts 02215. Biannual.

BROOKLYN JOURNAL OF INTERNATIONAL LAW. Brooklyn Law School, 250 Joralemon Street, Brooklyn, New York 11201. Semiannual.

CALIFORNIA WESTERN INTERNATIONAL LAW JOURNAL. California Western School of Law, 350 Cedar Street, San Diego, California 92101. Quarterly.

CASE WESTERN RESERVE JOURNAL OF INTERNATIONAL LAW. Case Western Reserve University, School of Law, Cleveland, Ohio 44106. Three issues per year.

COLUMBIA HUMAN RIGHTS LAW REVIEW. Columbia University, School of Law, 435 West 116th Street, New York, New York 10027. Semiannual.

COLUMBIA JOURNAL OF TRANSNATIONAL LAW. Columbia University, School of Law, 435 West 116th Street, New York, New York 10027. Three issues per year.

CORNELL INTERNATIONAL LAW JOURNAL. Cornell University Law School, Myron Taylor Hall, Ithaca, New York 14853. Semiannual.

DENVER JOURNAL OF INTERNATIONAL LAW AND POLICY. University of Denver, College of Law, Denver, Colorado 80220. Triannual.

DICKINSON JOURNAL OF INTERNATIONAL LAW AND POLICY. Dickinson School of Law, 150 South College Street, Carlisle, Pennsylvania 17013. Semiannual.

EMORY JOURNAL OF INTERNATIONAL DISPUTE RESOLUTION. Emory University School of Law, Harrta, Georgia 30322. 1986.

FORDHAM INTERNATIONAL LAW JOURNAL. Fordham University, School of Law, 140 West Sixty-second Street, New York, New York 10023. Semiannual.

GEORGE WASHINGTON JOURNAL OF INTERNATIONAL LAW AND ECONOMICS. George Washington University, National Law Center, 720 Twentieth Street, Northwest, Washington, D.C. 20052. Three issues per year.

GEORGIA JOURNAL OF INTERNATIONAL AND COMPARATIVE LAW. University of Georgia, School of Law, Athens, Georgia 30602. Semiannual.

HARVARD INTERNATIONAL LAW JOURNAL. Harvard Law School, Cambridge, Massachusetts 02138. Three issues per year.

HASTINGS INTERNATIONAL AND COMPARATIVE LAW REVIEW. University of California, Hastings College of Law, 200 McAllister Street, San Francisco, California 94102. Semimonthly.

HOUSTON JOURNAL OF INTERNATIONAL LAW. University of Houston, Law Center, 4800 Calhoun, Houston, Texas 77004. Semiannual.

HUMAN RIGHTS QUARTERLY. Johns Hopkins University Press, Journals Division, Thirty-third and Charles Street, Baltimore, Maryland 21218. Quarterly.

INTER-AMERICAN LEGAL MATERIALS. American Bar Association, Section of International Law and Practice, 750 North Lake Shore Drive, Chicago, Illinois 60611. Quarterly.

INTERNATIONAL COMMISSION OF JURISTS REVIEW. American Association for the International Commission of Jurists, 777 United Nations Plaza, New York, New York 10017. Semiannual.

INTERNATIONAL LAW JOURNAL. Loyola Law School, 1441 West Olympic Boulevard, P. O. Box 15019, Los Angeles, California 90015. Semiannual.

INTERNATIONAL LAW JOURNAL. University of Texas School of Law, 2500 Red River Street, Austin, Texas 78705. Three issues per year.

INTERNATIONAL LAW JOURNAL. University of Wisconsin, School of Law, Madison, Wisconsin 53706. Semiannual.

INTERNATIONAL LAWYER. American Bar Association, Section of International Law, 750 North Lake Shore Drive, Chicago, Illinois 60611. Quarterly.

INTERNATIONAL LEGAL MATERIALS. American Society of International Law, 2223 Massachusetts Avenue, Northwest, Washington, D.C. 20008. Bimonthly.

JOURNAL OF INTERNATIONAL AFFAIRS. Columbia University, International Affairs Building, New York, New York 10027. Semiannual.

JOURNAL OF INTERNATIONAL LAW AND ECONOMICS. George Washington University, International Law Society, National Law Center, 720 Twentieth Street, Northwest, Washington, D.C. 20052. Three issues per year.

NEW YORK UNIVERSITY JOURNAL OF INTERNATIONAL LAW AND POLITICS. New York University, School of Law, 137 MacDougal Street, New York, New York 10012. Quarterly.

NORTH CAROLINA JOURNAL OF INTERNATIONAL LAW AND COMMERCIAL REGULATION. University of North Carolina, School of Law, Chapel Hill, North Carolina 27514. Three issues per year.

NORTHWESTERN JOURNAL OF INTERNATIONAL LAW AND BUSINESS. Northwestern University, School of Law, 357 East Chicago Avenue, Chicago, Illinois 60611. Semiannual.

STANFORD JOURNAL OF INTERNATIONAL LAW. Stanford University, School of Law, Stanford, California 94305. Semiannual.

SUFFOLK TRANSNATIONAL LAW JOURNAL. Suffolk University, Law School, 41 Temple Street, Beacon Hill, Boston, Massachusetts 02114. Semiannual.

SYRACUSE JOURNAL OF INTERNATIONAL LAW AND COMMERCE. Syracuse University, College of Law, Syracuse, New York 13210. Quarterly.

VANDERBILT JOURNAL OF TRANSNATIONAL LAW. Vanderbilt University, School of Law, Nashville, Tennesee 37240. Quarterly.

VIRGINIA JOURNAL OF INTERNATIONAL LAW. University of Virginia, School of Law, Charlotteville, Virginia 22901. Quarterly.

NEWSLETTERS AND NEWSPAPERS

AMERICAN ASSOCIATION FOR THE INTERNATIONAL COMMISSION OF JURISTS NEWSLETTER. American Association for the International Commission of Jurists, 777 United Nations Plaza, New York, New York 10017. Semiannually.

AMERICAN SOCIETY OF INTERNATIONAL LAW NEWSLETTER. American Society of International Law, 2223 Massachusetts Avenue, Northwest, Washington, D.C. 20008. Bimonthly.

ASSOCIATION OF STUDENT INTERNATIONAL LAW SOCIETIES NEWSLETTER. Association of Student International Law Societies, 2223 Massachusetts Avenue, Northwest, Washingotn, D.C. 20008. Quarterly.

CENTER FOR THE STUDY OF HUMAN RIGHTS NEWSLETTER. Center for the Study of Human Rights, 704 International Affairs Building, Columbia University, New York, New York 10027. Semiannually.

IGO REPORT. United States Council for International Business, 1212 Avenue of the Americas, New York, New York 10036. Monthly.

ILSA NEWSLETTER. International Law Students Association, 2223 Massachusetts Avenue, Northwest, Washington, D.C. 20008. Quarterly.

INTER-AMERICAN BAR ASSOCIATION QUARTERLY NEWSLETTER. Inter-American Bar Association, 4801 Massachusetts Avenue, Northwest, Suite 400, Washington, D.C. 20016. Quarterly.

INTERNATIONAL LAW AND TRADE PERSPECTIVE. International Law and Trade Perspectice, P.O. Box 27495, Washington, D.C. 20038. Monthly.

INTERNATIONAL LAW NEWS. American Bar Association, Section of International Law, 750 North Lake Shore Drive, Chicago, Illinois 60611. Quarterly.

INTERNATIONAL LAWYERS NEWSLETTER. Kluwer Law and Taxation Publishers, 6 Bigelow Street, Cambridge, Massachusetts 02139. Bimonthly.

INTERNATIONAL SECURITIES REGULATION REPORT. Buraff Publications, 1350 Connecticut Avenue, Northwest, Suite 1000, Washington, D.C. 20036. Semimonthly.

IRANIAN ASSETS LITIGATION REPORTER. Andrews Publications, 1646 West Chester Pike, Westtown, Pennsylvania 19395. Semimonthly.

MEALEY'S LITIGATION REPORT: IRANIAN CLAIMS. Mealey Publications, Incorporated, P.O. Box 446, Wayne, Pennsylvania 19087. Semimonthly.

NEWSBRIEFS. Lawyers Committee for International Human Rights, 330 Seventh Avenue, Suite 10N, New York, New York 10001. Quarterly.

NEWSLETTER. American Foreign Law Association, c/o Richard Lutringer, Whitman and Ransom, 200 Park Avenue, New York, New York 10166. Annually.

UNITED NATIONS LAW REPORTS. Walker and Company, 720 Fifth Avenue, New York, New York 10019. Monthly.

THE WORLD JURIST. World Peace Through Law Center, 1000 Connecticut Avenue, Northwest, Suite 800, Washington, D.C. 20036. Bimonthly.

BIBLIOGRAPHIES

BIBLIOGRAPHY OF INTERNATIONAL HUMANITARIAN LAW, APPLICABLE IN ARMED CONFLICTS. International Committee of the Red Cross and Henry Dunant Institute, Geneva. 1980.

BIBLIOGRAPHY ON LAND-LOCKED STATES. Third Edition. Martin Ira Glassner. Martinus Nijhoff, Kluwer Academic Publishers, 101 Philip Drive, Assinippi Park, Norwell, Massachusetts 02061. 1991.

A COLLECTION OF BIBLIOGRAPHIC AND RESEARCH RESOURCES. International Law Bibliography. Oceana Publications, Incorporated, 75 Main Street, Dobbs Ferry, New York 10522. 1984- .

THE DEPARTMENT OF STATE AND AMERICAN DIPLOMACY: A BIBLIOGRPAHY. Robert U. Geohlert and Elizabeth R. Hoffmeister. Garland Publishing, Incorporated, 136 Madison Avenue, New York, New York 10016. 1986.

INTERNATIONAL LEGAL BIBLIOGRAPHY. Simeone-Marie Kleckner. Oceana Publications, Incorporated, 75 Main Street, Dobbs Ferry, New York 10522. 1983.

THE LAW OF WAR AND NEUTRALITY: A SELECTIVE ENGLISH LANGUAGE BIBLIOGRAPHY. Howard S. Levie. Oceana Publications, 75 Main Street, Dobbs Ferry, New York 10522. 1988.

PUBLIC INTERNATIONAL LAW: A GUIDE TO INFORMATION SOURCES. Elizabeth Beyerly. Mansell Publishing Limited, Artillery House, Artillery Row, London SW1P 1RT, England. 1991.

THE THIRD WORLD AND INTERNATIONAL LAW: SELECTED BIBLIOGRPAHY, 1955-1982. United Nations, Sales Department, Publishing Division, New York, New York 10017. 1983.

UNITED STATES RELATIONS WITH SOUTH AFRICA: A BIBLIOGRAPHIC RESEARCH GUIDE. Y.G.-M. Lulat. Westview Press, 5500 Central Avenue, Boulder, Colorado 80301. 1991.

WORLD BIBLIOGRAPHY OF INTERNATIONAL DOCUMENTATION. Theodore Dimitrov, Editor. Unifo Publishers, Limited, P.O. Box 3858, Sarasota, Florida 34230. 1981.

DIRECTORIES

DIRECTORY OF OPPORTUNITIES IN INTERNATIONAL LAW. John Bassett Moore Society of International Law, Charlottesville, Virginia. 1984.

KIMES INTERNATIONAL LAW DIRECTORY. Kimes International Law Directory, Limited, International Publications Service, 242 Cherry Street, Philadelphia, Pennsylvania 19106-1906. Annual.

WORLD DIRECTORY OF TEACHING AND RESEARCH INSTITUTIONS IN INTERNATIONAL LAW. Second Edition. UNESCO, 7 Place de Fontenoy, F-75700 Paris, France. 1990.

WORLDWIDE GOVERNMENT DIRECTORY. 1986 Edition. Lambert Publications, Incorporated, 2433 Eighteenth Street, Northwest, Washington, D.C. 20009. 1985.

ASSOCIATIONS AND PROFESSIONAL SOCIETIES

AMERICAN ASSOCIATION FOR THE COMPARATIVE STUDY OF LAW. c/o Honorable Edward D. Re, United States Court of International Trade, One Federal Plaza, New York, New York 10007. (212) 264-2800.

AMERICAN BAR ASSOCIATION, COMMITTEE ON LAW AND NATIONAL SECURITY. 750 North Lake Shore Drive, Chicago, Illinois 60611. (312) 988-5000.

AMERICAN BAR ASSOCIATION, COMMITTEE ON WORLD ORDER UNDER THE LAW. 750 North Lake Shore Drive, Chicago, Illinois 60611. (312) 988-5000.

AMERICAN BAR ASSOCIATION, SECTION ON INTERNATIONAL LAW AND PRACTICE. 1800 M Street, Northwest, Washington, D.C. 20036. (202) 331-2239.

AMERICAN FOREIGN LAW ASSOCIATION. c/o Richard E. Lutringer, Whitman and Ransom, 200 Park Avenue, New York, New York 10166. (212) 351-3277.

AMERICAN SOCIETY OF INTERNATIONAL LAW. 2223 Massachusetts Avenue, Northwest, Washington, D.C. 20008. (202) 265-4313.

ASSOCIATION OF AMERICAN LAW SCHOOLS, SECTION ON INTERNATIONAL LAW. One Dupont Circle, Northwest, Washington, D.C. 20036. (202) 296-8851.

COMMISSION FOR INTERNATIONAL DUE PROCESS OF LAW. 105 West Adams Street, Chicago, Illinois 60603. (312) 782-1946.

INTER-AMERICAN BAR ASSOCIATION. 1889 F Street, Northwest, Suite 450, Washington, D.C. 20006. (202) 789-2747.

INTER-AMERICAN BAR FOUNDATION. 1819 H Street, Northwest, 310 Federal Bar Building, Washington, D.C. 20006. (202) 293-1455.

INTERNATIONAL LAW STUDENTS ASSOCIATION. 2223 Massachusetts Avenue, Northwest, Washington, D.C. 20008. (202) 797-7133.

INTERNATIONAL LEGAL DEFENSE COUNSEL. 111 South Fifteenth Street, Twenty-fourth Floor, Philadelphia, Pennsylvania 19102. (215) 977-9982.

INTERNATIONAL THIRD WORLD LEGAL STUDIES ASSOCIATION. c/o International Center for Law in Development, 777 United Nations Plaza, New York, New York 10017. (212) 687-0036.

WORLD ASSOCIATION OF LAWYERS. 1000 Connecticut Avenue, Northwest, Suite 800, Washington, D.C. 20036. (202) 466-5428.

RESEARCH CENTERS AND INSTITUTES

CARTER CENTER, INCORPORATED. Emory University, One Copenhill Avenue, Atlanta, Georgia 30307. (404) 420-5100.

CENTER FOR INTERNATIONAL STUDIES. New York University, 40 Washington Square South, New York, New York 10012. (212) 998-6209.

DEAN RUSK CENTER FOR INTERNATIONAL AND COMPARATIVE LAW. University of Georgia, Athens, Georgia 30602. (404) 542-7875.

INTERNATIONAL CENTER FOR LAW IN DEVELOPMENT. 777 United Nations Plaza, New York, New York 10017. (212) 687-0036.

INTERNATIONAL LAW INSTITUTE. Georgetown University, 600 New Jersey Avenue, Northwest, Washington, D.C. 20001. (202) 662-9000.

INTERNATIONAL LAW INSTITUTE. 1920 N Street, Northwest, Washington, D.C. 20036. (202) 483-3036.

INTERNATIONAL LEGAL STUDIES PROGRAM. Cornell University, Myron Taylor Hall, Ithaca, New York 14853. (607) 255-3469.

INTERNATIONAL LEGAL STUDIES PROGRAM. Harvard University, 1557 Massachusetts Avenue, Cambridge, Massachusetts 02138. (617) 495-3117.

INTERNATIONAL LAW AND RELATIONS

MEIKLEJOHN CIVIL LIBERTIES INSTITUTE. P.O. Box 673, Berkeley, California 94701. (415) 848-0599.

NATIONAL LAW CENTER. George Washington University, 720 Twentieth Street, Northwest, Washington, D.C. 20052. (202) 994-7230.

URBAN MORGAN INSTITUTE FOR HUMAN RIGHTS. University of Cincinnati, College of Law, Cincinnati, Ohio 45221. (513) 556-0093.

WORLD PEACE THROUGH LAW CENTER. 1000 Connecticut Avenue, Northwest, Washington, D.C. 20036. (202) 466-5428.

OTHER SOURCES

AMERICAN INTERNATIONAL LAW CASES. SECOND SERIES, 1979-1989. SOURCES AND DOCUMENTS. Bernard D. Reasm, Jr. Oceana Publications, 75 Main Street, Dobbs Ferry, New York 10522. 1992.

INTERNATIONAL ORGANIZATION S
See: INTERNATIONAL AGENCIES AND ORGANIZATIONS

INTERNATIONAL TRADE
See also: COURT OF CUSTOMS AND PATENT APPEALS; EXPORT AND IMPORT; INTERNATIONAL TRADE ADMINISTRATION; INTERNATIONAL TRADE COMMISSION; JOINT VENTURES; TAXATION, INTERNATIONAL

STATUTES, CODES, STANDARDS, UNIFORM LAWS

BASIC DOCUMENTS OF INTERNATIONAL ECONOMIC LAW. Stephen Zamora and Ronald A. Brand, Editors. Commerce Clearing House, Incorporated, 4025 West Peterson Avenue, Chicago, Illinois 60646. 1990.

BASIC DOCUMENTS ON INTERNATIONAL TRADE LAW. Chia-Jui Cheng. Kluwer Academic Publishers, 101 Philip Drive, Assinippi Park, Norwell, Massachusetts 02061. 1986.

INTERNATIONAL TRADE AND INVESTMENT: SELECTED DOCUMENTS. John H. Barton. Little, Brown, and Company, 34 Beacon Street, Boston, Massachusetts 02108. 1986.

UNIFORM LAW FOR INTERNATIONAL SALES. Second Edition. John O. Honnold. Kluwer Academic Publishers, 101 Philip Drive, Assinippi Park, Norwell, Massachusetts 02061. 1991.

LOOSELEAF SERVICES AND REPORTERS

ANTIDUMPING AND COUNTERVAILING DUTY LAWS. Joseph E. Pattison. Clark Boardman Company, Limited, 435 Hudson Street, New York, New York 10014. 1984- .

CHINA HAND: INVESTING, LICENSING, AND TRADING CONDITIONS. Business International Corporation, 1 Dag Hammerskjold Plaza, New York, New York 10017. 1981- .

COMMERCIAL BUSINESS AND TRADE LAWS OF THE WORLD. Kenneth R. Simmonds, Editor. Oceana Publications, Incorporated, 75 Main Street, Dobbs Ferry, New York 10522. 1980- .

COMMERCIAL LAWS OF THE MIDDLE EAST. Allen P. K. Keesee. Oceana Publications, Incorporated, 75 Main Street, Dobbs Ferry, New York 10522. 1980- .

COMMERCIAL LAWS OF THE WORLD. Foreign Tax Law Association, Incorporated, P.O. Box 340, Alachua, Florida 32615. 1947.

CUSTOMS LAW AND ADMINISTRATION. Third Edition. Ruth Strum. Oceana Publications, Incorporated, 75 Main Street, Dobbs Ferry, New York 10522. 1982- .

DOING BUSINESS IN BRAZIL. Pinheiro Neto and Cia. Matthew Bender and Company, Incorporated, 11 Penn Plaza, New York, New York 10001. 1979- .

DOING BUSINESS IN CANADA. Matthew Bender and Company, Incorporated, 11 Penn Plaza, New York, New York 10001. 1984- .

DOING BUSINESS IN EUROPE. Commerce Clearing House, Incorporated, 4025 West Peterson Avenue, Chicago, Illinois 60646. 1972- .

DOING BUSINESS IN FRANCE. Matthew Bender and Company, Incorporated, 11 Penn Plaza, New York, New York 10001. 1983- .

DOING BUSINESS IN JAPAN. Zentaro Kitagawa. Matthew Bender and Company, Incorporated, 11 Penn Plaza, New York, New York 10001. 1980- .

DOING BUSINESS IN MEXICO. S. Theodore Reiner and Ann Reiner, Editors. Matthew Bender and Company, Incorporated, 11 Penn Plaza, New York, New York 10001. 1980- .

DOING BUSINESS IN SAUDI ARABIA AND THE ARAB GULF STATES. Nancy A. Shilling. Inter-Crescent Publishing Company, Incorporated, 12021 Nieta Drive, Garden Grove, California 92640. 1983- .

DOING BUSINESS WITH EASTERN EUROPE. Business International Corporation, 1 Dag Hammerskjold Plaza, New York, New York 10017. 1975- .

EAST-WEST TRADE COMECON LAW: AMERICAN-SOVIET TRADE. Thomas W. Hoya. Oceana Publications, Incorporated, 75 Main Street, Dobbs Ferry, New York 10522. 1984- .

EEC COMPETITION LAW. Utz Toepke. John Wiley and Sons, Incorporated, 605 Third Avenue, New York, New York 10158. 1982- .

EXPORT SHIPPING MANUAL. Bureau of National Affairs, 1231 Twenty-fifth Street, Northwest, Washington, D.C. 20037. 1947- .

EXPORT TRADING COMPANY ACT OF 1982. W. A. Hancock. Business Laws, Incorporated, 11630 Chillicothe Road, Chesterland, Ohio 44026. 1983- .

FEDERAL REGULATION OF INTERNATIONAL BUSINESS. Stuart S. Malawar. National Chamber Foundation, 1615 H Street, Northwest, Washington, D.C. 20062. 1980- .

FED-TRACK GUIDE TO ANTIDUMPING FINDINGS AND ORDERS. Fed-Track Publications, 810 Eighteenth Street, Northwest, Washington, D.C. 20006. 1983- .

FED-TRACK GUIDE TO COUNTERVAILING DUTY CASES. Fed-Track Publications, 810 Eighteenth Street, Northwest, Washington, D.C. 20006. 1984- .

FED-TRACK GUIDE TO INTERNATIONAL TRADE RULES. Fed-Track Publications, 810 Eighteenth Street, Northwest, Washington, D.C. 20006. 1984- .

FINANCING FOREIGN OPERATIONS. Business International Corporation, 1 Dag Hammerskjold Plaza, New York, New York 10017. 1957- .

GUIDE TO ANTIDUMPING AND COUNTERVAILING DUTIES AND OTHER UNFAIR IMPORT LAWS. Business Laws, Incorporated, 11630 Chillicothe Road, Chesterland, Ohio 44026. 1983- .

GUIDE TO INTERNATIONAL COMMERCE LAW. Paul H. Vishny. Shepard's/McGraw-Hill, P. O. Box 1235, Colorado Springs, Colorado 80901. 1981- .

INTERNATIONAL BOYCOTTS. W.A. Hancock. Business Laws, Incorporated, 11630 Chillicothe Road, Chesterland, Ohio 44026. 1978- .

INTERNATIONAL BUSINESS AND TRADE LAW REPORTER. 930 F. Street, Northwest, Suite 617, Washington, D.C. 20004. 1985- .

INTERNATIONAL BUSINESS PLANNING: LAW AND TAXATION. William P. Streng and J. W. Salacuse. Matthew Bender and Company, Incorporated, 11 Penn Plaza, New York, New York 10001. 1982- .

INTERNATIONAL SALES: THE UNITED NATIONS CONVENTION FOR THE INTERNATIONAL SALE OF GOODS. Nina M. Galston and Hans Smit, Editors. Matthew Bender and Company, Incorporated, 11 Penn Plaza, New York, New York 10001. 1984- .

INTERNATIONAL TRADE POLICY: A DEVELOPING-COUNTRY PERSPECTIVE. Dilip K. Das. St. Martin's Press, 175 Fifth Avenue, New York, New York 10010. 1990.

INTERNATIONAL TRADE PRACTICE. Harvey Kaye. Shepard's/McGraw-Hill, P.O. Box 1235, Colorado Springs, Colorado 80901. 1981- .

INTERNATIONAL TRADE REPORTER. Bureau of National Affairs, 1231 Twenty-fifth Street, Northwest, Washington, D.C. 20037. 1984- .

INVESTING, LICENSING AND TRADING CONDITIONS ABROAD. Business International Corporation, 1 Dag Hammerskjold Plaza, New York, New York 10017. 1955- .

LAW OF THE EUROPEAN ECONOMIC COMMUNITY - COMMENTARY ON THE EEC TREATY. Hans Smit. Matthew Bender and Company, Incorporated, 11 Penn Plaza, New York, New York 10001. 1976- .

LAW OF TRANSNATIONAL BUSINESS TRANSACTIONS. Ved P. Nanda. Clark Boardman Company, Limited, 435 Hudson Street, New York, New York 10014. 1980- .

LEGAL ASPECTS OF EXPORTING MANUAL. Federal Bar Association, 1815 H Street, Northwest, Suite 408, Washington, D.C. 20006-3604. 1984- .

PAYMENT PRACTICES IN EASTERN EUROPE. Business International Corporation, 1 Dag Hammerskjold Plaza, New York, New York 10017. 1980- .

TAX-FREE TRADE ZONES OF THE WORLD. Walter Diamond and Dorothy B. Diamond. Matthew Bender and Company, Incorporated, 11 Penn Plaza, New York, New York 10001. 1977- .

THE TRADE AND TARIFF ACT OF 1984. Stephen Lande and Craig Van Grasstek. Free Press, 866 Third Avenue, New York, New York 10022. 1986.

TRANSNATIONAL CONTRACTS: APPLICABLE LAW AND SETTLEMENT OF DISPUTES. George R. Delaume. Oceana Publications, Incorporated, 75 Main Street, Dobbs Ferry, New York 10522. 1979- .

TRANSNATIONAL ECONOMIC AND MONETARY LAW. Leonard Lazar. Oceana Publications, Incorporated, 75 Main Street, Dobbs Ferry, New York 10522. 1978- .

UNITED STATES COURT OF INTERNATIONAL TRADE-RULES. Invictus Publishing Corporation, 180 South Broadway, White Plains, New York 10605. 1980- .

UNITED STATES COURT OF INTERNATIONAL TRADE RULES AND ANNOTATION SERVICE. Rules Service Company, 7658 Standish Place, Suite 106, Rockville, Maryland 20855. 1984- .

UNITED STATES CUSTOMS AND INTERNATIONAL TRADE GUIDE. Peter B. Feller. Matthew Bender and Company, Incorporated, 11 Penn Plaza, New York, New York 10001. 1979- .

UNITED STATES INTERNATIONAL TRADE REPORTS. Edwin S. Newman and Eugene M. Wypyski. Oceana Publications, Incorporated, 75 Main Street, Dobbs Ferry, New York 10522. 1981- .

HANDBOOKS, MANUALS, FORMBOOKS

EXPORT TRADING COMPANY GUIDEBOOK. United States Department of Commerce, International Trade Administration. Superintendent of Documents, United States Government Printing Office, Washington, D.C. 20402. 1987.

EXPORTING: A PRACTICAL MANUAL FOR DEVELOPING EXPORT MARKETS AND COPING WITH FOREIGN CUSTOMS. Second Edition. Ernest Y. Maitland. International Self-Counsel Press, P.O. Box 40, Blue Ridge Summit, Pennsylvania 17294-0850. 1982.

GUIDE FOR THE PREVENTION OF INTERNATIONAL TRADE FRAUD. ICC Publishing Company, 156 Fifth Avenue, Suite 820, New York, New York 10010. 1985.

INTERNATIONAL BUSINESS AGREEMENTS: A PRACTICAL GUIDE TO THE NEGOTIATION AND FORMULATION OF AGENCY, DISTRIBUTION, AND INTELLECTUAL PROPERTY LICENSING AGREEMENTS. Patrick Hearn. Gower Publishing Company, Old Post Road, Brookfield, Vermont 05036. 1987.

INTERNATIONAL BUSINESS HANDBOOK. V.H. (Manek) Kirpalani, Editor. Haworth Press, Incorporated, 10 Alice Street, Binghamton, New York 13904. 1990.

THE LEGAL ENVIRONMENT OF INTERNATIONAL BUSINESS: A GUIDE FOR UNITED STATES FIRMS. Don Alan Evans. McFarland and Company, Incorporated, Box 611, Jefferson, North Carolina 28640. 1990.

LEGAL GUIDE TO INTERNATIONAL BUSINESS TRANSACTIONS. Philip Raworth. Carswell, Toronto, Ontario, Canada. 1991.

MANUAL FOR THE PRACTICE OF INTERNATIONAL TRADE LAW. William K. Ince and Leslie A. Glick. Federal Bar Association, 1815 H Street, Northwest, Suite 408, Washington, D.C. 20006-3604. 1984.

THE MCGRAW-HILL HANDBOOK OF GLOBAL TRADE AND INVESTMENT FINANCING. Lawrence W. Tuller. McGraw-Hill Publishing Company, 1221 Avenue of the Americas, New York, New York 10020. 1992.

MULTINATIONAL CORPORATIONS: INVESTMENTS TECHNOLOGY, TAX, LABOR, SECURITIES: EUROPEAN, NORTH AND LATIN AMERICAN PERSPECTIVES. Alain A. Levasseur and Enrique Dahl, Editors. University Press of America, 4720 Boston Way, Lanham, Maryland 20706. 1986.

TEXTBOOKS AND GENERAL WORKS

THE ABC'S OF INTERNATIONAL FINANCE: UNDERSTANDING THE TRADE AND DEBT CRISIS. James Charles Pool and Stephen C. Stamos. Free Press, 866 Third Avenue, New York, New York 10022. 1987.

AMERICAN TRADE POLITICS: SYSTEM UNDER STRESS. I. M. Destler. Institute for International Economics, 11 Dupont Circle, Northwest, Publications Department, Washington, D.C. 20036. 1986.

ANTI-DUMPING AND ANTI-SUBSIDY LAW: THE EUROPEAN COMMUNITITES. Sweet and Maxwell/International Chamber of Commerce, South Quay Plaza, 183 Marsh Wall, London E14 9FT, England. 1986.

ARBITRATION AND RENEGOTIATION OF INTERNATIONAL INVESTMENT AGREEMENTS: A STUDY WITH PARTICULAR REFERENCE TO MEANS OF CONFLICT AVOIDANCE UNDER NATURAL RESOURCES INVESTMENT AGREEMENTS. Wolfgang Peter. Martinus Nijhoff, Kluwer Academic Publishers, 101 Philip Drive, Assinippi Park, Nowell, Massachusetts 02061. 1986.

ASSESSMENT OF THE TRADE AND TARIFF ACT OF 1984. Stephen L. Lande and Craig Van Grasstek. MIT Press, 55 Hayward Street, Cambridge, Massachusetts 02142. 1984.

BARGAINING ACROSS BORDERS: HOW TO NEGOTIATE BUSINESS SUCCESSFULLY ANYWHERE IN THE WORLD. Dean Allen Foster. McGraw-Hill Publishing Company, 1221 Avenue of the Americas, New York, New York 10020. 1992.

THE BORDERLESS WORLD: POWER AND STRATEGY IN THE INTERLINKED ECONOMY. Kenichi Ohmae. HarperCollins Publishers, 10 East Fifty-third Street, New York, New York 10022. 1990.

BUILDING AN IMPORT/EXPORT BUSINESS. Kenneth D. Weiss. John Wiley and Sons, Incorporated, 605 Third Avenue, New York, New York 10158. 1991. Revised and expanded.

THE CHALLENGE OF FREE TRADE. Alan Oxley. St. Martin's Press, 175 Fifth Avenue, New York, New York 10010. 1990.

THE COMMERCE DEPARTMENT SPEAKS ON IMPORT ADMINISTRATION AND EXPORT ADMINISTRATION. Practising Law Institute, 810 Seventh Avenue, New York, New York 10019. 1984.

COMMERCIAL AND CONSUMER LAW FROM AN INTERNATIONAL PERSPECTIVE: PAPERS FROM THE CONFERENCE OF THE INTERNATIONAL ACADEMY OF COMMERCIAL AND CONSUMER LAW. Donald B. King, Editor. Fred B. Rothman and Company, 10368 West Centennial Road, Littleton, Colorado 80127. 1986.

CONFLICT AMONG NATIONS: TRADE POLICIES IN THE 1990s. Thomas R. Howell. Westview Press, Incorporated, 5500 Central Avenue, Boulder, Colorado 80301. 1992.

CONGRESS, THE EXECUTIVE BRANCH, AND SPECIAL INTERESTS: THE AMERICAN RESPONSE TO THE ARAB BOYCOTT OF ISRAEL. Kennan L. Teslik. Greenwood Publishing Group, Incorporated, 88 Post Road West, P.O. Box 5007, Westport, Connecticut 06881. 1982.

COPING WITH UNITED STATES EXPORT CONTROLS: NEW REGULATORY DEVELOPMENTS, TECHNICAL DATA CONTROLS, ENFORCEMENT AND COMPLIANCE. Evan R. Berlack, Cecil Hunt and Terrence R. Murphy, Chairmen. Practising Law Institute, 810 Seventh Avenue, New York, New York 10019. 1991.

CREATING A WORLD ECONOMY: MERCHANT CAPITAL, COLONIALISM, AND WORLD TRADE, 1400-1825. Alan K. Smith. Westview Press, Incorporated, 5500 Central Avenue, Boulder, Colorado 80301. 1991.

CURRENT LEGAL ASPECTS OF INTERNATIONAL TRADE LAW. Patrick F. Macrory and Peter O. Suchman, Editors. American Bar Association, Section of International Law and Practice. 750 North Lake Shore Drive, Chicago, Illinois 60611. 1982.

THE CUSTOMS LAW OF THE EUROPEAN ECONOMIC COMMUNITY. Second Edition. Dominik Lasok and W. Cairns. Kluwer Academic Publishers, 101 Philip Drive, Assinippi Park, Norwell, Massachusetts 02061. 1991.

THE DETERMINANTS AND CONSEQUENCES OF TRADE RESTRICTIONS IN THE UNITED STATES ECONOMY. Victor A. Canto. Praeger Publishers, Division of Holt, Rhinehart and Winston/CBS, One Madison Avenue, New York, New York 10010-3603. 1985.

DEVELOPING COUNTRIES AND THE GLOBAL TRADING SYSTEM. John Whalley. University of Michigan Press, P.O. Box 1104, 839 Greene Street, Ann Arbor, Michigan 48106. 1989.

ECONOMIC COSTS AND BENEFITS OF SUBSIDIZING WESTERN CREDITS TO THE EAST. Daniel F. Kohler. The Rand Corporation, P.O. Box 2138, Santa Monica, California 90406. 1984.

ECONOMIC DEVELOPMENT AND INTERNATIONAL TRADE. David Greenaway. St. Martin's Press, 175 Fifth Avenue, New York, New York 10010. 1988.

THE ECONOMICS OF TECHNICAL CHANGE AND INTERNATIONAL TRADE. Giovanni Dosi, Keith Pavitt and Luc Soete. New York University Press, 70 Washington Square South, New York, New York 10012. 1990.

ELEMENTS OF INTERNATIONAL TRADE AND PAYMENTS. Geoffrey Whitehead. Woodhead-Faulkner Publishers, Limited, 51 Washington Street, Dover, New Hampshire 08320. 1983.

EMERGING STANDARDS OF INTERNATIONAL TRADE AND INVESTMENT. Seymour J. Rubin, Editor. Rowman and Allanheld, Division of Littlefield, Adams and Company, 420 Boston Way, Lanham, Maryland 20706. 1984.

EMPIRICAL METHODS FOR INTERNATIONAL TRADE. Robert C. Feenstra, Editor. MIT Press, 55 Hayward Street, Cambridge, Massachusetts 02142. 1988.

ENTERPRISE AND COMPETITIVENESS: A SYSTEMS VIEW OF INTERNATIONAL BUSINESS. Mark Casson. Oxford University Press, 200 Madison Avenue, New York, New York 10016. 1990.

EXPLORING THE GLOBAL ECONOMY: EMERGING ISSUES IN TRADE AND INVESTMENT. Raymond Vernon. Center for International Affairs, Harvard University Press, 79 Garden Street, Cambridge, Massachusetts 02138. 1985.

EXPORT ACTIVITY AND STRATEGIC TRADE POLICY. Horst Krager and Klaus F. Zimmermann, Editors. Springer-Verlag New York, Incorporated, 175 Fifth Avenue, New York, New York 10010. 1992.

EXPORT CONTROLS IN THE UNITED STATES. John R. Liebman and Robert L. Johnson. Harcourt Brace Jovanovich, Incorporated, 6277 Sea Harbor Drive, Orlando, Florida 32821. 1985.

EXPORT DEVELOPMENT STRATEGIES: UNITED STATES PROMOTION POLICY. Michael R. Czinkota. Praeger Publishers, Division of Holt, Rhinehart and Winston/CBS, One Madison Avenue, New York, New York 10010-3603. 1982.

EXPORT POLICY: A GLOBAL ASSESSMENT. Michael R. Czinkota and George Tesar, Editors. Praeger Publishers, Division of Holt, Rhinehart and Winston/CBS, One Madison Avenue, New York, New York 10010-3603. 1982.

EXPORT PROMOTION: THE PUBLIC AND PRIVATE SECTOR INTERACTION. Michael R. Xzinkota, Editor. Praeger Publishers, Division of Holt, Rhinehart and Winston/CBS, One Madison Avenue, New York, New York 10010-3603. 1983.

THE EXPORT TRADING COMPANY ACT. Henry N. Schiffman, Chairman. Practising Law Institute, 810 Seventh Avenue, New York, New York 10019. 1983.

FEDERAL REGULATION OF INTERNATIONAL BUSINESS: AN ANNOTATED SOURCEBOOK OF LEGISLATION, REGULATIONS, AND TREATIES. Stuart S. Malawne. International Law Institute, 1615 New Hampshire Avenue, Northwest, Washington, D.C. 20009-2550. 1986. (Periodic Supplements).

FOREIGN COMMERCE AND THE ANTITRUST LAWS. Third Edition. Wilbur L. Fugte. Little, Brown, and Company, 34 Beacon Street, Boston, Massachusetts 02108. 1982.

FOREIGN MULTINATIONAL INVESTMENT IN THE UNITED STATES: STRUGGLE FOR INDUSTRIAL SUPREMACY. Sara L. Gordon and Francis A. Lees. Greenwood Publishing Group, Incorporated, 88 Post Road West, P.O. Box 5007, Westport, Connecticut 06881. 1986.

FOREIGN TRADE AND THE NATIONAL ECONOMY: MERCANTILIST AND CLASSICAL PERSPECTIVES. Leonard Gomes. St. Martin's Press, 175 Fifth Avenue, New York, New York 10010. 1987.

FREE TRADE BETWEEN MEXICO AND THE UNITED STATES. Sidney Weintraub. Brookings Institution, 1775 Massachusetts Avenue, Northwest, Washington, D.C. 20036-2188. 1984.

THE GLOBAL ECONOMY IN THE 90s. Bill Orr. New York University Press, 70 Washington Square South, New York, New York 10012. 1992.

THE GLOBAL FINANCIAL STRUCTURE IN TRANSITION: CONSEQUENCES FOR INTERNATIONAL TRADE AND FINANCE. Joel McClellan. Lexington Books, Division of D.C. Heath and Company, 125 Spring Street, Lexington, Massachusetts 02173. 1985.

GLOBALIZING THE GATT: THE SOVIET UNION, EAST CENTRAL EUROPE, AND THE INTERNATIONAL TRADING SYSTEM. Leah A. Haus. Brookings Institution, 1775 Massachusetts Avenue, Washington, D.C. 20036. 1992.

THE GREENING OF WORLD TRADE ISSUES. Kym Anderson and Richard Blackhurst. University of Michigan Press, P.O. Box 1104, 839 Greene Street, Ann Arbor, Michigan 48106. 1992.

GUIDE TO ANTIDUMPING AND COUNTERVAILING DUTIES AND OTHER UNFAIR IMPORT LAWS. W. A. Hancock, Editor. Business Laws, Incorporated, 11630 Chillicothe Road, Chesterland, Ohio 44026. 1983.

HAGUE-ZAGREB ESSAYS 5: ON THE LAW OF INTERNATIONAL TRADE. C.C.A. Voskuil and J. A. Wade, Editor. Martinus Nijhoff, Kluwer Academic Publishers, 101 Philip Drive, Assinippi Park, Norwell, Massachusetts 02061. 1985.

HARD BARGAINING AHEAD: UNITED STATES TRADE POLICY AND DEVELOPING COUNTRIES. Ernest H. Preeg, et al, Editors. Transaction Books, Rutgers University, New Brunswick, New Jersey 08903. 1985.

HARMONIZATION AND INTERNATIONAL TRADE. Gote Hansson. Routledge, Chapman & Hall, 29 West Thirty-fifth Street, New York, New York 10001. 1990.

IMPERFECT COMPETITION AND INTERNATIONAL COMMODITY TRADE: THEORY DYNAMICS, AND POLICY MODELLING. Montague J. Lord. Oxford University Press, 200 Madison Avenue, New York, New York 10016. 1991.

IMPERFECT COMPETITION AND INTERNATIONAL TRADE. Gene M. Grossman, Editor. MIT Press, 55 Hayward Street, Cambridge, Massachusetts 02142. 1992.

IMPLEMENTING THE TOKYO ROUND: NATIONAL CONSTITUTIONS AND INTERNATIONAL ECONOMIC RULES. John H. Jackson, Jean-Victor Louis, and Mitsuo Matsushita. University of Michigan Press, P.O. Box 1104, Ann Arbor, Michigan 48106. 1984.

IMPORT CONTROLS AND EXPORT-ORIENTED DEVELOPMENT: A REASSESSMENT OF THE SOUTH KOREAN CASE. Richard Luedde-Neurath. Westview Press, 5500 Central Avenue, Boulder, Colorado 80301. 1985.

IMPORT PRACTICE: CUSTOMS AND INTERNATIONAL TRADE LAW. David A. Serko. Practising Law Institute, 810 Seventh Avenue, New York, New York 10019. 1985.

INNOVATION AND GROWTH IN THE GLOBAL ECONOMY. Gene M. Grossman and Elhanan Helpman. MIT Press, 55 Hayward Street, Cambridge, Massachusetts 02142. 1991.

INTERNATIONAL BUSINESS AND NATIONAL JURISDICTION. A.D. Neale and M.L. Stephens. Oxford University Press, 200 Madison Avenue, New York, New York 10016. 1988.

INTERNATIONAL BUSINESS ENVIRONMENTS AND OPERATIONS. Fifth Edition. Lee H. Radebaugh, Editor. Addison-Wesley Publication Company, Incorporated, Route 128, Reading, Massachusetts 01867. 1989.

INTERNATIONAL BUSINESS LAW AND ITS ENVIRONMENT. Richard Schaffer, Beverley Earle and Filiberto Agusti. West Publishing Company, 50 West Kellogg Boulevard, St. Paul, Minnesota 55164. 1990.

INTERNATIONAL BUSINESS RESEARCH: A COMPREHENSIVE SURVEY. Peter Buckley and Michael Brooke. Basil Blackwell, Incorporated, 3 Cambridge Center, Cambridge, Massachusetts 02142. 1992.

INTERNATIONAL BUSINESS: THEORY AND PRACTICE. M. Reza Vaghefi, Steven K. Paulson and William H. Tomlinson. Taylor and Francis, Incorporated, 1990 Frost Road, Suite 101, Bristol, Pennsylvania 19007. 1991.

INTERNATIONAL BUSINESS TRANSACTIONS IN A NUTSHELL. Ralph H. Folsom, Michael Wallace Gordon and John A. Spanogle, Jr. West Publishing Company, 50 West Kellogg Boulevard, St. Paul, Minnesota 55164. 1988.

INTERNATIONAL CODES AND MULTINATIONAL BUSINESS: SETTING GUIDELINES FOR INTERNATIONAL BUSINESS OPERATIONS. John M. Kline. Greenwood Publishing Group, Incorporated, 88 Post Road West, P.O. Box 5007, Westport, Connecticut 06881. 1985.

INTERNATIONAL DIMENSIONS OF THE LEGAL ENVIRONMENT OF BUSINESS. Michael Litka. PWS-Kent Publishing Company, 20 Park Plaza, Boston, Massachusetts 02116. 1988.

INTERNATIONAL ECONOMICS AND INTERNATIONAL ECONOMIC POLICY: A READER. Philip King. McGraw-Hill Publishing Company, 1221 Avenue of the Americas, New York, New York 10020. 1990.

INTERNATIONAL HIGH-TECHNOLOGY COMPETITION. F.M. Scherer. Harvard University Press, 79 Garden Street, Cambridge, Massachusetts 02138. 1992.

INTERNATIONAL TRADE. Ali M. El-Agraa. St. Martin's Press, 175 Fifth Avenue, New York, New York 10010. 1989.

INTERNATIONAL TRADE: AN INTRODUCTION TO THEORY AND POLICY. Richard Pomfret. Basil Blackwell, Incorporated, 3 Cambridge Center, Cambridge, Massachusetts 02142. 1991.

INTERNATIONAL TRADE AND COMPETITION: CASES AND NOTES IN STRATEGY AND MANAGEMENT. David B. Yoffie. McGraw-Hill Publishing Company, 1221 Avenue of the Americas, New York, New York 10020. 1990.

INTERNATIONAL TRADE AND FINANCE: A NORTH AMERICAN PERSPECTIVE. Khosrow Fatemi, Editor. Praeger Publishers, One Madison Avenue, New York, New York 10010-3603. 1988.

INTERNATIONAL TRADE AND GLOBAL DEVELOPMENT: ESSAYS IN HONOUR OF JAGDISH BHAGWATI. Ad Koekkoek and L.B.M. Mennes, Editors. Routledge, Chapman & Hall, 29 West Thirty-fifth Street, New York, New York 10001. 1991.

INTERNATIONAL TRADE AND INVESTMENT. Sixth Edition. Franklin R. Root. South-Western Publishing Company, 5101 Madison Road, Cincinnati, Ohio 45227. 1990.

INTERNATIONAL TRADE AND INVESTMENT: REGULATING INTERNATIONAL BUSINESS. Little, Brown, and Company, 34 Beacon Street, Boston, Massachusetts 02108. 1986.

INTERNATIONAL TRADE AND TRADE POLICY. Elhanan Helpman and Assaf Razin, Editors. MIT Press, 55 Hayward Street, Cambridge, Massachusetts 02142. 1991.

INTERNATIONAL TRADE FOR THE NONSPECIALIST. Third Edition. American Law Institute, 4025 Chestnut Street, Philadelphia, Pennsylvania 19104. 1984.

INTERNATIONAL TRADE IN ENDANGERED SPECIES: A GUIDE TO CITES. David S. Favre. Martinus Nijhoff, Kluwer Academic Publishers, 101 Philip Drive, Assinippi Park, Norwell, Massachusetts 02061. 1989.

INTERNATIONAL TRADE LAW AND PRACTICE.
Julian D. M. Lew and Clive Stanbrook, Editors. Euromoney
Publications, London United Kingdom. 1983.

INTERNATIONAL TRADE POLICIES: GAINS FROM
EXCHANGE BETWEEN ECONOMICS AND
POLITICAL SCIENCE. John S. Odell and Thomas D.
Willett, Editors. University of Michigan Press, P.O. Box 1104,
839 Greene Street, Ann Arbor, Michigan 48106. 1990.

INTERNATIONAL TRADE POLICY: A
DEVELOPING-COUNTRY PERSPECTIVE. Dilip K. Das.
St. Martin's Press, 175 Fifth Avenue, New York, New York
10010. 1990.

INTERNATIONAL TRADE REGULATION: GATT,
THE UNITED STATES AND THE EUROPEAN
COMMUNITY. Second Edition. Edmond McGovern. Exeter
Globefield Press, Exeter, United Kingdom. 1986.

INTERNATIONAL TRADE: SELECTED READINGS.
Second Edition. Jagdish N. Bhagwati. MIT Press, 55
Hayward Street, Cambridge, Massachusetts 02142. 1987.

INTERNATIONAL TRADE: THEORETICAL ISSUES.
Bharat R. Hazari. New York University Press, Distributed by
Columbia University Press, 562 West One Hundred
Thirteenth Street, New York, New York 10025. 1986.

INVESTING, LICENSING, AND TRADING
CONDITIONS ABROAD. Business International
Corporation, 1 Dag Hammerskjold Plaza, New York, New
York 10017. 1983.

LAW AND ITS LIMITATIONS IN THE GATT
MULTILATERAL TRADE SYSTEM. Olivier Long.
Kluwer Academic Publishers, 101 Philip Drive, Assinippi
Park, Norwell, Massachusetts 02061. 1985.

THE LAW AND PRACTICE OF INTERNATIONAL
FINANCE. Phillip Wood. Clark Boardman Company,
Limited, 435 Hudson Street, New York, New York 10014.
1981. (Supplement 1985).

LEGAL ASPECTS OF DOING BUSINESS IN CHINA.
Jerome A. Cohen, Chairman. Practising Law Institute, 810
Seventh Avenue, New York, New York 10019. 1983.

LEGAL ASPECTS OF DOING BUSINESS WITH JAPAN.
Isaac Shapiro, Chairman. Practising Law Institute, 810
Seventh Avenue, New York, New York 10019. 1985.

LEGAL ASPECTS OF INTERNATIONAL BUSINESS
TRANSACTIONS. D. Campbell and C. Rohwer, Editors.
Elsevier-Dutton, Incorporated, 2 Park Avenue, New York,
New York 10016. 1985.

LEGAL OPINIONS IN INTERNATIONAL
TRANSACTIONS: FOREIGN LAWYERS' RESPONSE
TO US OPINION REQUESTS: REPORT OF THE
SUBCOMMITTEE ON LEGAL OPINIONS OF THE
COMMITTEE ON BANKING LAW OF THE SECTION
ON BUSINESS LAW OF THE INTERNATIONAL BAR
ASSOCIATION. Second Edition. Michael Gruson, Stephan
Hutter and Michael Kutschera. Graham and Trotman
Limited, Sterling House, 66 Wilton Road, London SW1V
1DE, England. 1989.

LETTERMAN'S LAW OF PRIVATE INTERNATIONAL
BUSINESS. G. Gregory Letterman. Lawyers Cooperative
Publishing Company, Aqueduct Building, Rochester, New
York 14694. 1990.

MONOPOLISTIC COMPETITION AND
INTERNATIONAL TRADE. Henryk Kierzkowski, Editor.
Clarendon Press, Oxford University Press, 200 Madison
Avenue, New York, New York 10016. 1989.

MULTILATERAL TRADE NEGOTIATIONS: WORLD
TRADE AFTER THE TOKYO ROUND. Leslie A. Glick.
Rowman and Allanheld, Division of Littlefield, Adams and
Company, 420 Boston Way, Lanham, Maryland 20706. 1984.

MULTINATIONAL ENTERPRISES, ECONOMIC
STRUCTURE, AND INTERNATIONAL
COMPETITIVENESS. John H. Dunning, Editor. John Wiley
and Sons, Incorporated, 605 Third Avenue, New York, New
York 10158. 1986.

NATIONAL LAWS AND INTERNATIONAL
COMMERCE: THE PROBLEM OF
EXTRATERRITORIALITY. Douglas E. Rosenthal and
William M. Knighton. Routledge and Kegan, Methuen,
Incorporated, 29 West Thirty-fifth Street, New York, New
York 10001. 1982.

NATIONAL SECURITY AND TECHNOLOGY
TRANSFER: THE STRATEGIC DIMENSIONS OF
EAST-WEST TRADE. Gary Bertsch and John R. McIntyre,
Editors. Westview Press, 5500 Central Avenue, Boulder,
Colorado 80301. 1983.

NONTARIFF BARRIERS TO HIGH TECHNOLOGY
TRADE. Robert B. Cohen. Westview Press, 5500 Central
Avenue, Boulder, Colorado 80301. 1985.

PENETRATING INTERNATIONAL MARKETS: FROM
SALES AND LICENSINGS TO SUBSIDIARIES AND
ACQUISITIONS. Dennis Campbell and Fernando Pombo,
Editors. Kluwer Law Book Publishers, Incorporated, 36 West
Forty-fourth Street, New York, New York 10036. 1991.

PERCEPTIONS AND INTERESTS: DEVELOPING
COUNTRIES AND THE INTERNATIONAL
ECONOMIC SYSTEM. Raymond G. Clemencon. Peter
Lang Publishing, Incorporated, 62 West Forty-fifth Street,
New York, New York 10036. 1990.

PERSPECTIVES ON TRADE AND DEVELOPMENT.
Anne O. Krueger. University of Chicago Press, 5801 Ellis
Avenue, Chicago, Illinois 60637. 1990.

POLITICAL ECONOMY AND INTERNATIONAL
ECONOMICS. Jagdish Bhagwati. MIT Press, 55 Hayward
Street, Cambridge, Massachusetts 02142. 1991.

THE POLITICAL ECONOMY OF UNITED STATES
TARIFFS: AN EMPIRICAL ANALYSIS. Real P.
LaVergne. Academic Press, Incorporated, 1250 Sixth Avenue,
Suite 400, San Diego, California 92101. 1983.

THE POLITICS OF ECONOMIC INTERDEPENDENCE.
Edmund Dell. St. Martin's Press, 175 Fifth Avenue, New
York, New York 10010. 1987.

POWER, PROTECTION, AND FREE TRADE:
INTERNATIONAL SOURCES OF U.S. COMMERCIAL
STRATEGY, 1887-1939. David A. Lake. Cornell University
Press, 124 Roberts Place, Ithaca, New York 14850. 1988.

THE PRACTICE OF MULTINATIONAL BANKING: MACRO-POLICY ISSUES AND KEY INTERNATIONAL CONCEPTS. Dara Khambata. Quorum Books, Imprint of Greenwood Publishing Group, Incorporated, 88 Post Road West, P.O. Box 5007, Westport, Connecticut 06881. 1986.

PROTECTION AND COMPETITION IN INTERNATIONAL TRADE: ESSAYS IN HONOR OF W.M. CORDEN. Henryk Kierzhowski. Basil Blackwell, Incorporated, 3 Cambridge Center, Cambridge, Massachusetts 02142. 1987.

PROTECTIONISM AND THE EUROPEAN COMMUNITY. Kluwer Academic Publishers, 101 Philip Drive, Assinippi Park, Norwell, Massachusetts 02061. 1988.

REGULATORY THEORY AND ITS APPLICATON TO TRADE POLICY: A STUDY OF ITC DECISION-MAKING, 1975-1985. Wendy L. Hansen. Garland Publishing, Incorporated, 136 Madison Avenue, New York, New York 10016. 1990.

RESISTING PROTECTIONISM: GLOBAL INDUSTRIES AND THE POLITICS OF INTERNATIONAL TRADE. Helen V. Milner. Princeton University Press, 41 William Street, Princeton, New Jersey 08540. 1988.

RETHINKING INTERNATIONAL TRADE. Paul R. Krugman. MIT Press, 55 Hayward Street, Cambridge, Massachusetts 02142. 1990.

SELECTED READINGS IN INTERNATIONAL TRADE. Khosrow Fatemi, Editor. Taylor and Francis, Incorporated, 1990 Frost Road, Suite 101, Bristol, Pennsylvania 19007. 1991.

SELECTIVE SAFEGUARD MEASURES IN MULTILATERAL TRADE RELATIONS: ISSUES OF PROTECTIONISM IN GATT, EUROPEAN COMMUNITY, AND UNITED STATES LAW. Marco C. Bronckers. Kluwer Law Book Publishers, Incorporated, 36 West Forty-fourth Street, New York, New York 10036. 1985.

SHIPPING IN INTERNATIONAL TRADE RELATIONS. Ademuni-Odeke. Avebury, Brookfield, Vermont. 1988.

SINO-AMERICAN ECONOMIC EXCHANGES: THE LEGAL CONTRIBUTIONS. Guiguo Wang. Praeger Publishers, Division of Holt, Rhinehart and Winston/CBS, One Madison Avenue, New York, New York 10010-3603. 1985.

STRATEGIC TRADE POLICY AND THE NEW INTERNATIONAL ECONOMICS. Paul Krugman, Editor. MIT Press, 55 Hayward Street, Cambridge, Massachusetts 02142. 1986.

SUBSIDIES IN INTERNATIONAL TRADE. Gary C. Hufbauer and Joanna Shelton-Erb. Institute for International Economics, Publications Department, Eleven Dupont Circle, Northwest, Washington, D.C. 20036. 1984.

THE THEORY OF INTERNATIONAL TRADE. James R. Markusen and James R. Melvin. HarperCollins Publishers, 10 East Fifty-third Street, New York, New York 10022. 1988.

TRADE POLICIES FOR INTERNATIONAL COMPETITIVENESS. Robert C. Feenstra, Editor. University of Chicago Press, 5801 Ellis Avenue, Chicago, Illinois 60637. 1989.

TRADE PROTECTION IN THE UNITED STATES: 31 CASE STUDIES. Gary Clyde Hufbauer. Institute for International Economics, Publications Department, 11 Dupont Circle, Northwest, Washington, D.C. 20036. 1986.

TRADE WARS AGAINST AMERICA: A HISTORY OF UNITED STATES TRADE AND MONETARY POLICY. William J. Gill. Praeger Publishers, One Madison Avenue, New York, New York 10010-3603. 1990.

TRANSFORMATIONS IN THE GLOBAL POLITICAL ECONOMY. Dennis C. Pirages and Christine Sylvester, Editors. St. Martin's Press, 175 Fifth Avenue, New York, New York 10010. 1990.

UNEQUAL TRADE: THE ECONOMICS OF DISCRIMINATORY INTERNATIONAL TRADE POLICIES. Richard Pomfret. Basil Blackwell, Incorporated, 3 Cambridge Center, Cambridge, Massachusetts 02142. 1988.

UNITED STATES IMPORT TRADE REGULATION. Eugene Rossides. Bureau of National Affairs, 1231 Twenty-fifth Street, Northwest, Washington, D.C. 20037. 1986.

UNITED STATES INTERNATIONAL TRADE LAWS. Alan M. Stowell, Editor. Bureau of National Affairs, 1231 Twenty-fifth Street, Northwest, Washington, D.C. 20037. 1985.

THE VALUATION OF GOODS FOR CUSTOMS PURPOSES. Henk De Pagter and Richard Van Raan. Kluwer Academic Publishers, 101 Philip Drive, Assinippi Park, Norwell, Massachusetts 02061. 1981.

THE WORLD ECONOMY IN PERSPECTIVE: ESSAYS ON INTERNATIONAL TRADE AND EUROPEAN INTEGRATION. Herbert Giersch. Edward Elgar, Brookfield, Vermont. 1991.

ENCYCLOPEDIAS AND DICTIONARIES

KEYWORDS IN INTERNATIONAL TRADE. Third Edition. ICC Publishing Corporation, 156 Fifth Avenue, Suite 820, New York, New York 10010. 1989.

ANNUALS AND SURVEYS

SURVEY OF THE INTERNATIONAL SALE OF GOODS. Louis Lafili, Franklin Gevurtz and Dennis Campbell, Editors. Kluwer Academic Publishers, 101 Philip Drive, Assinippi Park, Norwell, Massachusetts 02061. 1986.

UNITED NATIONS COMMISSION ON INTERNATIONAL TRADE LAW YEARBOOK. United Nations, Sales Section, Publishing Division, New York, New York 10017. 1986-1989.

WORLD TRADE ANNUAL. Walker and Company, 720 Fifth Avenue, New York, New York 10019. Annual.

LAW REVIEWS AND PERIODICALS

AMERICAN IMPORT AND EXPORT BULLETIN. North American Publishing Company, 401 North Broad Street, Philadelphia, Pennsylvania 19108. Monthly.

FOREIGN INVESTMENT LAW JOURNAL. Johns Hopkins University Press, 701 West Fortieth Street, Suite 275, Baltimore, Maryland 21211. Quarterly.

INTERNATIONAL TRADE LAW JOURNAL. University of Maryland, School of Law, 500 West Baltimore Street, Baltimore, Maryland 21201. Semiannual.

JOURNAL OF WORLD TRADE LAW. Vincent Press, London, United Kingdom. Bimonthly.

NEWSLETTERS AND NEWSPAPERS

AD/CVD RECORD. International Business Reports, Incorporated, P.O. Box 1009, Falls Church, Virginia 22041. Weekly.

CANADA - U.S. REPORT ON FREE TRADE. American Banker - Bond Buyer Newsletter, Division, P.O. Box 30240, Bethesda, Maryland 20814. Weekly.

CIT TEST CASE RECORD. International Business Reports, Incorporated, P.O. Box 1009, Falls Church, Virginia 22041. Quarterly.

CITBA NEWSLETTER. Customs and International Trade Bar Association, c/o Andrew P. Vance, Esquire, Barnes, Richardson and Colburn, 475 Park Avenue South, New York, New York 10016. Bimonthly.

CORPORATE COUNSELOR'S INTERNATIONAL ADVISOR. Business Laws, Incorporated, 11630 Chillicothe Road, Chesterland, Ohio 44026. Monthly.

EASTERN EUROPEAN BUSINESS MONITOR. I.A. Ernst and Company, Incorporated, 5328 Saratoga Avenue, Chevy Chase, Maryland 20815. Monthly.

E.D. UPDATE. United States Council for International Business, 1212 Avenue of the Americas, New York, New York 10036. Quarterly.

INSIDE UNITED STATES TRADE. Inside Washington Publishers, P. O. Box 7167, Ben Franklin Station, Washington, D.C. 20044. Weekly.

INTERNATIONAL BUSINESS REGULATION REPORT. International Reports, Incorporated, 200 Park Avenue, South, New York, New York 10003. Monthly.

INTERNATIONAL LAW AND TRADE PERSPECTIVE. International Law Perspective, P.O. Box 27495, Washington, D.C. 20038. Monthly.

INTERNATIONAL TRADE ALERT. American Association of Exporters and Importers, 11 West Forty-second Street, New York, New York 10036. Weekly.

INTERNATIONAL TRADE REPORTER CURRENT REPORTS. Bureau of National Affairs, Incorporated, 1231 Twenty-fifth Street, Northwest, Washington, D.C. 20037. Weekly.

337 NEWSLETTER. I. T. C. International Lawyers Association, 1019 Nineteenth Street, Northwest, Washington, D.C. 20036. Monthly.

TRADING PARTNERS. Ocean Publications, Incorporated, 75 Main Street, Dobbs Ferry, New York 10522. Semiannually.

UNITED STATES EXPORT WEEKLY. Bureau of National Affairs, 1231 Twenty-fifth Street, Northwest, Washington, D.C. 20037. Weekly.

UNITED STATES IMPORT WEEKLY. Bureau of National Affairs, 1231 Twenty-fifth Street, Northwest, Washington, D.C. 20037. Weekly.

WASHINGTON INTERNATIONAL BUSINESS REPORT. International Business Government Counsellors, 818 Connecticut Avenue, Northwest, Twelfth Floor, Washington, D.C. 20006. Monthly.

WASHINGTON TARIFF AND TRADE LETTER. Gilston Communications Group, P.O. Box 467, Washington, D.C. 20044. Weekly.

BIBLIOGRAPHIES

A COLLECTION OF BIBLIOGRAPHIES AND RESEARCH SOURCES: INTERNATIONAL LAW BIBLIOGRAPHY: NUMBER THREE, INTERNATIONAL TRADE LAW. Blanka Kudej. Oceana Publications, Incorporated, 75 Main Street, Dobbs Ferry, New York 10522. 1984.

DIRECTORIES

AMERICAN ASSOCIATION OF EXPORTERS AND IMPORTERS-MEMBERSHIP DIRECTORY. American Association of Exporters and Importers, 11 West Forth-second Street, New York, New York 10036. 1984.

AMERICAN EXPORT REGISTER. Thomas International Publishing Company, 5 Penn Plaza, New York, New York 10001. Annual.

AMERICAN SOCIETY OF INTERNATIONAL EXECUTIVES-ROSTER. American Society of International Executives, 18 Sentry Parkway, Suite 1, Blue Bell, Pennsylvania 19422. Annual.

CUSTOM HOUSE GUIDE (UNITED STATES). North American Publishing Company, 401 North Broad Street, Philadelphia, Pennsylvania 19108. Annual.

DIRECTORY OF UNITED STATES IMPORTERS. Journal of Commerce, 110 Wall Street, New York, New York 10005. 1985.

EXPORT TRADING COMPANIES: CONTRACT FACILITATION SERVICE DIRECTORY. United States Department of Commerce, International Trade Administration. Superintendent of Documents, United States Government Printing Office, Washington, D.C. 20402. 1984.

EXPORTERS DIRECTORY/UNITED STATES BUYING GUIDE. Journal of Commerce, 110 Wall Street, New York, New York 10005.

INTERNATIONAL TRADE

NATIONAL CUSTOMS BROKERS AND FORWARDERS ASSOCIATION OF AMERICA - MEMBERSHIP DIRECTORY. National Customs Brokers and Forwarders Association of America, One World Trade Center, Suite 1153, New York, New York 10048. 1986.

WORLD TRADE CENTERS ASSOCIATION - DIRECTORY. World Trade Centers Association, One World Trade Center, Suite 7701, New York, New York 10048.

WORLD TRADE CLUBS IN THE UNITED STATES. Chamber of Commerce of the United States of America, International Division, 1615 H Street, Northwest, Washington, D.C. 20062. 1984.

WORLD WIDE SHIPPING GUIDE. World Wide Shipping Guide, Incorporated, 77 Moehring Drive, Blauvelt, New York 10913. Annual.

ASSOCIATIONS AND PROFESSIONAL SOCIETIES

AMERICAN ASSOCIATION OF EXPORTERS AND IMPORTERS. 11 West Forty-second Street, New York, New York 10036. (212) 944-2230.

AMERICAN BAR ASSOCIATION, SECTION OF INTERNATIONAL LAW AND PRACTICE. 1800 M Street, Northwest, Washington, D.C. 20036-5886. (202) 331-2200.

AMERICAN LEAGUE FOR EXPORTS AND SECURITY ASSISTANCE. 122 C Street, Northwest, Washington, D.C. 20002. (202) 783-0051.

CUSTOMS AND INTERNATIONAL TRADE BAR ASSOCIATION. c/o Joseph F. Donohue, Jr., 26 Broadway, New York, New York 10004. (212) 269-2330.

FEDERATION OF INTERNATIONAL TRADE ASSOCIATIONS. 1851 Alexander Bell Drive, Restor, Virginia 22091. (703) 391-6106.

INTERNATIONAL TRADE COUNCIL. 1900 Mt. Vernon Avenue, P.O. Box 2478, Alexandria, Virginia 22301. (703) 548-1234.

INTERNATIONAL TRADE INSTITUTE. 25 K Street, Northeast, Washington, D.C. 20004. (202) 289-1505.

NATIONAL FOREIGN TRADE COUNCIL. 100 East Forty-second Street, New York, New York 10001. (212) 867-5630.

TRADE RELATIONS COUNCIL OF THE UNITED STATES. 808 Seventeenth Street, Northwest, Washington, D.C. 20036. (202) 785-4194.

WESTERN INTERNATIONAL TRADE GROUP. c/o Ronald A. Ingersoll, P. O. Box 29744, Phoenix, Arizona 85038. (602) 528-6546.

RESEARCH CENTERS, INSTITUTES, CLEARINGHOUSES

WORLD TRADE EDUCATION CENTER. Cleveland State University, 1983 East Twenty-fourth Street, Cleveland, Ohio 44115. (216) 687-3786.

ONLINE DATABASES

INTERNATIONAL TRADE INFORMATION SERVICE MONTHLY MONITOR. Data Resources, Incorporated, Data Products Division Headquarters, 1750 K Street, Northwest, Suite 1060, Washington, D.C. 20006.

INTERNATIONAL TRADE REPORTER. Business of National Affairs, Data Publishing Unit, 1231 Twenty-fifth Street, Northwest, Washington, D.C. 20037.

LEXIS INTERNATIONAL TRADE LIBRARY. Mead Data Central, Incorporated, 9393 Springboro Pike, P.O. Box 933, Dayton, Ohio 45401.

STATISTICS SOURCES

GUIDE TO FOREIGN TRADE STATISTICS. Bureau of the Census. Superintendent of Documents, United States Government Printing Office, Washington, D.C. 20402. Annual.

STATISTICS OF FOREIGN TRADE. Series A: Monthly Bulletin. Series B: Trade by Commodities. Country Summaries. Organization for Economic Cooperation and Development. OECD Publications Center, 1750 Pennsylvania Avenue, Northwest, Washington, D.C. 20086. Series A. Monthly. Series B. Quarterly.

WESTERN WORLD. Joseph A. Camilleri. University of Washington Press, P. O. Box 50096, Seattle, Washington 98145-5096. 1984.

YEARBOOK OF INTERNATIONAL TRADE STATISTICS. United Nations, States Section, Publishing Division, New York, New York 10017. Annual.

INTERNATIONAL TRADE ADMINISTRATION
See also: INTERNATIONAL TRADE COMMISSION

STATUTES, CODES, STANDARDS, UNIFORM LAWS

CODE OF FEDERAL REGULATIONS, TITLE 15. Office of the Federal Register, National Archives and Records Administration. Superintendent of Documents, United States Government Printing Office, Washington, D.C. 20402. Annual. (Updated by use of monthly List of Sections Affected and daily Federal Register.)

EXPORT ADMINISTRATION REGULATIONS. Commerce Department, International Trade Administration, Office of Export Administration. Superintendent of Documents, United States Government Printing Office, Washington, D.C. 20402. 1986- .

TEXTBOOKS AND GENERAL WORKS

EC 1992: A COMMERCE DEPARTMENT ANALYSIS OF EUROPEAN COMMUNITY DIRECTIVES. Prepared by the Trade Development industry specialists of the International Trade Administration. Debra L. Miller, Editor. United States Department of Commerce, International Trade Administration. Superintendent of Documents, United States Government Printing Office, Washington, D.C. 20402. 1990.

FOREIGN BUSINESS PRACTICES: MATERIAL ON PRACTICAL ASPECTS OF EXPORTING, INTERNATIONAL LICENSING AND INVESTING. Commerce Department, International Trade Administration, Office of Trade Finance. Gordon Press, Publishers, P.O. Box 459, Bowling Green Station, New York, New York 10004. 1991.

IMPORT PRACTICE: CUSTOMS AND INTERNATIONAL TRADE LAW. David Serko. Practising Law Institute, 810 Seventh Avenue, New York, New York 10019. 1991.

JOINT VENTURE AGREEMENTS IN THE PEOPLE'S REPUBLIC OF CHINA. Daniel Stein and Pomiliu Verzariu. Commerce Department, International Trade Administration. Superintendent of Documents, United States Government Printing Office, Washington, D.C. 20402. 1982.

UNDERSTANDING UNITED STATES FOREIGN TRADE DATA. Victor B. Bailey and Sara R. Bowden. Commerce Department, International Trade Administration, Office of Trade and Investment Analysis. Superintendent of Documents, United States Government Printing Office, Washington, D.C. 20402. 1985.

ANNUALS AND SURVEYS

EXPORT ADMINISTRATION ANNUAL REPORT. Commerce Department, International Trade Administration, Office of Export Administration. Superintendent of Documents, United States Government Printing Office, Washington, D.C. 20402. Annual.

ONLINE DATABASES

LEXIS, INTERNATIONAL TRADE LIBRARY. Mead Data Central, P.O. Box 933, Dayton, Ohio 45401.

INTERNATIONAL TRADE COMMISSION
See also: INTERNATIONAL TRADE ADMINISTRATION

STATUTES, CODES, STANDARDS, UNIFORM LAWS

CODE OF FEDERAL REGULATIONS, TITLE 19. Office of the Federal Register, National Archives and Records Administration. Superintendent of Documents, United States Government Printing Office, Washington, D.C. 20402. Annual. (Updated by use of monthly List of Sections Affected and daily Federal Register.)

LOOSELEAF SERVICES AND REPORTERS

COURT OF INTERNATIONAL TRADE REPORTS. Superintendent of Documents, United States Government Printing Office, Washington, D.C. 20402. 1980- .

INTERNATIONAL TRADE REPORTER DECISIONS. Bureau of National Affairs, 1231 Twenty-fifth Street, Northwest, Washington, D.C. 20037. 1980- .

HANDBOOKS, MANUALS, FORMBOOKS

A GUIDE TO THE UNCITRAL MODEL LAW ON INTERNATIONAL COMMERCIAL ARBITRATION: LEGISLATIVE HISTORY AND COMMENTARY. Howard M. Holtzmann and Joseph E. Neuhaus. Kluwer Academic Publishers, 101 Philip Drive, Assinippi Park, Norwell, Massachusetts 02061. 1989.

TEXTBOOKS AND GENERAL WORKS

COMMENTARY ON THE UNCITRAL MODEL LAW ON INTERNATIONAL COMMERCIAL ARBITRATION. Aron Broches. Kluwer Academic Publishers, 101 Philip Drive, Assinippi Park, Norwell, Massachusetts 02061. 1990.

FEDERAL UNFAIR COMPETITION ACTIONS: PRACTICE AND PROCEDURE UNDER SECTION 337 OF THE TARIFF ACT OF 1930. Donald Knox Duvall. Clark Boardman Company, Limited, 435 Hudson Street, New York, New York 10014. 1990.

REGULATORY THEORY AND ITS APPLICATION TO TRADE POLICY: A STUDY OF ITC DECISION-MAKING, 1975-1985. Wendy L. Hansen. Garland Publishing, Incorporated, 136 Madison Avenue, New York, New York 10016. 1990.

DIGESTS, INDEXES, ABSTRACTS, CITATORS

SHEPARD'S UNITED STATES ADMINISTRATIVE CITATIONS. Shepard's/McGraw-Hill, P.O. Box 1235, Colorado Srings, Colorado 80901. Bimonthly.

RESEARCH CENTERS, INSTITUTES, CLEARINGHOUSES

UNITED STATES INTERNATIONAL TRADE COMMISSION LIBRARY. 500 E Street, Southwest, Washington, D.C. 20436. (202) 252-1630.

ONLINE DATABASES

LEXIS, INTERNATIONAL TRADE LIBRARY. Mead Data Central, P.O. Box 933, Dayton, Ohio 45401.

WESTLAW, INTERNATIONAL TRANSACTIONS. West Publishing Company, P.O. Box 64526, 50 West Kellogg Boulevard, St. Paul, Minnesota 55164.

INTERPRETATION OF STATUTES
See: STATUTORY CONSTRUCTION AND DRAFTING

INTERROGATORIES
See: DISCOVERY, CIVIL; DISCOVERY, CRIMINAL

INTERSTATE AGREEMENTS
See: STATE GOVERNMENT

INTERSTATE COMMERCE
See: INTERSTATE COMMERCE COMMISSION; TRADE REGULATION; TRANSPORTATION

INTERSTATE COMMERCE COMMISSION

STATUTES, CODES, STANDARDS, UNIFORM LAWS

CODE OF FEDERAL REGULATIONS, TITLE 49. Office of the Federal Register, National Archives and Records Administration. Superintendent of Documents, United States Government Printing Office, Washington, D.C. 20402. Annual. (Updated by use of monthly List of Sections Affected and daily Federal Register.)

LOOSELEAF SERVICES AND REPORTERS

INTERSTATE COMMERCE COMMISSION REPORTS. Superintendent of Documents, United States Government Printing Office, Washington, D.C. 20402. 1887- .

INTERSTATE COMMERCE COMMISSION REPORTS, MOTOR CARRIER CASES. Interstate Commerce Commission. Superintendent of Documents, United States Government Printing Office, Washington, D.C. 20402. 1936- .

INTERSTATE COMMERCE COMMISSION VALUATION REPORTS. Superintendent of Documents, United States Government Printing Office, Washington, D.C. 20402. 1929- .

HANDBOOKS, MANUALS, FORMBOOKS

A GUIDE FOR PUBLIC PARTICIPATION IN RAIL ABANDONMENT CASES UNDER THE INTERSTATE COMMERCE ACT. Third Edition. United States Interstate Commerce Commission, Office of Public Assistance., Washington, D.C. 1990.

TEXTBOOKS AND GENERAL WORKS

THE INTERSTATE COMMERCE COMMISSION AND THE RAILROAD INDUSTRY: A HISTORY OF REGULATORY POLICY. Richard D. Stone. Praeger Publishers, One Madison Avenue, New York, New York 10010-3603. 1991.

DIGESTS, INDEXES, ABSTRACTS, CITATORS

SHEPARD'S UNITED STATES ADMINISTRATIVE CITATIONS. Shepard's/McGraw-Hill, P.O. Box 1235, Colorado Springs, Colorado 80901. Bimonthly.

ANNUALS AND SURVEYS

INTERSTATE COMMERCE COMMISSION ANNUAL REPORT. Superintendent of Documents, United States Government Printing Office, Washington, D.C. 20402. Annual.

ASSOCIATIONS AND PROFESSIONAL SOCIETIES

ASSOCIATION OF TRANSPORTATION PRACTITIONERS. 1725 K Street, Northwest, Washington D.C. 20036. (202) 466-2080.

ONLINE DATABASES

LEXIS, FEDERAL TRANSPORTATION LIBRARY. Mead Data Central, P.O. Box 933, Dayton, Ohio 45401.

INTOXICATING LIQUORS
See: ALCOHOL CONTROL AND DRINKING BEHAVIOR

INVENTIONS
See: PATENTS

INVESTMENTS
See also: SECURITIES

LOOSELEAF SERVICES AND REPORTERS

BUSINESS INVESTMENT AND TAXATION HANDBOOK. Probus Publishing Company, 118 North Linton Street, Chicago, Illinois 60606. 1989.

DEPRECIATION AND THE INVESTMENT TAX CREDIT: WITH TAX PLANNING. Matthew Bender and Company, Incorporated, 11 Penn Plaza, New York, New York 10001. 1983- .

FOREIGN TRADE AND INVESTMENT: A LEGAL GUIDE. Second Edition. Thomas F. Clasen. Butterworth Legal Publishers, 90 Stiles Road, Salem, New Hampshire 03079. 1990- .

INVESTING, LICENSING AND TRADING CONDITIONS ABROAD. Business International Corporation, One Dag Hammarskjold Plaza, New York, New York 10017. 1955- . Monthly.

INVESTMENT ADVISERS GUIDE. Investment Company Institute, 1600 M Street, Northwest, Suite 600, Washington, D.C. 20036. 1984- . Semiannual.

INVESTMENT TREATIES. International Centre for Settlement of Investment Disputes. Oceana Publications, Incorporated, 75 Main Street, Dobbs Ferry, New York 10522. 1983.

JOINT VENTURES WITH INTERNATIONAL PARTNERS. James A. Dobkin and Jeffrey A. Burt. Butterworth Legal Publishers, 90 Stiles Road, Salem, New Hampshire 03079. 1989.

NEW YORK UNIVERSITY ANNUAL CONFERENCE ON TAXATION OF INVESTMENTS. Steven S. Goldberg. Matthew Bender and Company, Incorporated, 11 Penn Plaza, New York, New York 10001. 1984- .

TAXATION OF INVESTMENTS. Lewis D. Solomon. Prentice-Hall, Incorporated, 113 Sylvan Avenue, Englewood Cliffs, New Jersey 07632. 1987- .

TAXES AND INVESTMENT IN THE MIDDLE EAST. International Bureau of Fiscal Documentation, Amsterdam, Netherlands. 1979- .

UNITED STATES PORTFOLIO INVESTMENT BY FOREIGN TAXPAYERS. Leonard Schneidman. Commerce Clearing House, Incorporated, 4025 West Peterson Avenue, Chicago, Illinois 60646. 1989- .

HANDBOOKS, MANUALS, FORMBOOKS

BUSINESS OPPORTUNITIES IN THE UNITED STATES: THE COMPLETE REFERENCE GUIDE TO PRACTICES AND PROCEDURES. Robert F. Cushman and R. Lawrence Soares, Editors. Richard D. Irwin, Incorporated, 1818 Ridge Road, Homewood, Illinois 60430. 1992.

FOREIGN INVESTMENT IN UNITED STATES REAL ESTATE: A COMPREHENSIVE GUIDE. Timothy E. Powers, Editor. American Bar Association, Section of Real Property, Probate and Trust Law, 750 North Lake Shore Drive, Chicago, Illinois 60611. 1990.

MANDATING SOCIAL PRUDENCE; A HANDBOOK FOR PENSION INVESTMENT. Micheal T. Leibig. National Center for Policy Alternatives, 2000 Florida Avenue, Northwest, Washington, D.C. 20009. 1982.

REITS 1986: A COURSE HANDBOOK. Benito M. Lopez, Jr. and Thomas R. Smith. Practising Law Institute, 810 Seventh Avenue, New York, New York 10019. 1986.

TAX SHELTERED INVESTMENTS HANDBOOK. Robert D. Haft and Peter M. Fass, et al. Clark Boardman Company, Limited, 435 Hudson Street, New York, New York 10014. 1982.

THE WOMEN'S INVESTMENT HANDBOOK. Gail Perkins and Judith Rhoades. New American Library, 1633 Broadway, New York, New York 10019. 1983.

TEXTBOOKS AND GENERAL WORKS

ALLIED HAMBRO EXPATRIATE TAX AND INVESTMENT GUIDE. Nigelk Eastway and David Young. Oyez Longman, Incorporated, 19 West Forty-fourth Street, New York, New York 10036. 1984.

ALLIED HAMBRO INVESTMENT GUIDE 1982. Michael Sayers, Editor. Oyez Longman, Incorporated, 19 West Forty-fourth Street, New York, New York 10036. 1982.

ARBITRATION AND RENEGOTIATION OF INTERNATIONAL INVESTMENT AGREEMENTS: A STUDY WITH PARTICULAR REFERENCE TO MEANS OF CONFLICT AVOIDANCE UNDER NATURAL RESOURCES INVESTMENT AGREEMENTS. Peter Wolfgang. Martinus Nijhoff, Kluwer Academic Publishers, 101 Philip Drive, Assinippi Park, Norwell, Massachusetts 02061. 1986.

BUSINESS INVESTMENT IN THE UNITED STATES: A GUIDE TO FEDERAL AND STATE INVENTIVE PROGRAMS, LAW AND RESTRICTIONS. Third Edition. Raymond J. Waldmann and Robert A. Cohn. Bureau of National Affairs, 1231 Twenty-fifth Street, Northwest, Washington, D.C. 20037. 1984.

CORPORATE TAXATION AND INVESTMENT DECISIONS. Eleanor Morgan. Gower Publishing Company, Old Post Road, Brookfield, Vermont 05036. 1986.

DEALING WITH THE NEW ACRS REGULATIONS. Mark L. Yecies, Chairman. Law and Business, Harcourt Brace Jovanovich, Incorporated, 6277 Sea Harbor Drive, Orlando, Florida 32821. 1984.

DEPRECIATION AND INVESTMENT CREDIT MANUAL: 1983 EDITION. Prentice-Hall, Incorporated, 113 Sylvan Avenue, Englewood Cliffs, New Jersey 07632. 1983.

DIFFERENCES IN TAX TREATMENT BETWEEN LOCAL AND FOREIGN INVESTORS AND EFFECTS OF INTER-NATIONAL TREATIES. Kluwer Academic Publishers, 101 Philip Drive, Assinippi Park, Norwell, Massachusetts 02061. 1978.

DIFFERENCES IN TAX TREATMENT OF FOREIGN INVESTORS: DOMESTIC SUBSIDIARIES AND DOMESTIC BRANCHES. John L. Forry, Editor. Kluwer Academic Publishers, 101 Philip Drive, Assinippi Park, Norwell, Massachusetts 02061. 1984.

DIRECT INVESTMENT AND DEVELOPMENT IN THE U.S.A. GUIDE TO INCENTIVE PROGRAMS: LAWS AND RESTRICITONS, 1980-1981. Revised Edition. Raymond J. Waldman. Kluwer Academic Publishers, 101 Philip Drive, Assinippi Park, Norwell, Massachusetts 02061. 1980.

DIRECT INVESTMENT TECHNIQUES FOR THE U.S.A. Richard Kirk and Christine Guillerm-Kirk. Kluwer Academic Publishers, 101 Philip Drive, Assinippi Park, Norwell, Massachusetts 02061. 1983.

EMERGING STANDARDS OF INTERNATIONAL TRADE AND INVESTMENT: MULTINATIONAL CODES AND CORPORATE CONDUCT. Seymour J. Rubin. Rowman and Allanheld, Division of Littlefield, Adams and Company, 420 Boston Way, Lanham, Maryland 20706. 1984.

EXPLORING THE GLOBAL ECONOMY: EMERGING ISSUES IN TRADE AND INVESTMENT. Raymond Vernon. University Press of America, 4720 Boston Way, Lanham, Maryland 20706. 1985.

FINANCE AND PROTECTION OF INVESTMENTS IN DEVELOPING COUNTRIES. Second Edition. Ingrid Detter De Lupis. Gower Publishing Company, Old Post Road, Brookfield, Vermont 05036. 1987.

FINANCIAL PRODUCTS: TAXATION, REGULATION, AND DESIGN. Andrea S. Kramer. John Wiley and Sons, Incorporated, 605 Third Avenue, New York, New York 10158. 1991.

FINANCING TRANSNATIONAL PROJECTS. Ronald F. Sullivan. Matthew Bender and Company, Incorporated, 11 Penn Plaza, New York, New York 10001. 1988.

FOREIGN DIRECT INVESTMENT IN THE 1990's: A NEW CLIMATE IN THE THIRD WORLD. Cynthia Day Wallace. Martinus Nijhoff, Kluwer Academic Publishers, 101 Philip Drive, Assinippi Park, Norwell, Massachusetts 02061. 1990.

FOREIGN DIRECT INVESTMENT IN THE UNITED STATES. Gordon Press, Publishers, P.O. Box 459, Bowling Green Station, New York, New York 10004. 1990.

FOREIGN INVESTMENT AND TAXATION. E. R. Barlow and Ira T. Wender. Harvard Law School, International Tax Program, Cambridge, Massachusetts 02138. 1955.

FOREIGN INVESTMENT IN THE PRESENT AND A NEW INTERNATIONAL ECONOMIC ORDER. Detlev Christian Dicke, Editor. Westview Press, Incorporated, 5500 Central Avenue, Boulder, Colorado 80301. 1988.

FOREIGN INVESTMENT IN THE UNITED STATES. David M. Hudson, Editor. Oceana Publications, Incorporated, 75 Main Street, Dobbs Ferry, New York 10522. 1983.

FOREIGN INVESTMENT IN THE UNITED STATES: A PRACTICAL APPROACH FOR THE 1990s. Bobbe Hirsh and Leslie J. Shreyer. Practising Law Institute, 810 Seventh Avenue, New York, New York 10019. 1990.

FOREIGN INVESTMENT IN THE UNITED STATES AFTER THE TAX REFORM ACT OF 1986. Marshall J. Langer. Practising Law Institute, 810 Seventh Avenue, New York, New York 10019. 1987.

FOREIGN INVESTMENT IN THE UNITED STATES: LAW, TAXATION, FINANCE. Marc M. Levey, Editor. John Wiley and Sons, Incorporated, 605 Third Avenue, New York, New York 10158. 1989.

FOREIGN INVESTMENT IN THE UNITED STATES, 1980: LEGAL ISSUES AND TECHNIQUES. Eugene J. Marans, et al., Editors. Shepard's/McGraw-Hill, P. O. Box 1235, Colorado Springs, Colorado 80901. 1984.

FOREIGN INVESTMENT IN THE UNITED STATES 1990. Practising Law Institute, 810 Seventh Avenue, New York, New York 10019. 1990.

FOREIGN INVESTMENT IN U. S. REAL ESTATE. Ronald S. Barak. Law and Business, Harcourt Brace Jovanovich, Incorporated, 6277 Sea Harbor Drive, Orlando, Florida 32821. 1983.

FOREIGN OWNERSHIP OF UNITED STATES FARMLAND. David N. Leband. Lexington Books, Division of D.C. Heath and Company, 125 Spring Street, Lexington, Massachusetts 02173. 1984.

FOREIGN TRADE AND INVESTMENT: A LEGAL GUIDE. Thomas F. Clasen. Callaghan and Company, 155 Pfingsten Road, Deerfield, Illinois 60015. 1987.

FOUNDATION INVESTMENT STRATEGIES: NEW POSSIBILITIES IN THE 1981 TAX LAW. J. Peter Williamson. Seven Springs Center, RD 3, Oregon Road, Mount Kisco, New York 10549. 1981.

THE GUIDE TO FOREIGN INVESTMENT IN UNITED STATES REAL ESTATE. Timothy D. Richards. Van Nostrand Reinhold Company, Incorporated, 115 Fifth Avenue, New York, New York 10003. 1983.

ILLINOIS CORPORATIONS' INVESTMENTS IN SOUTH AFRICA. Norman Watkins. Clergy and Laity Concerned, P.O. Box 1987, Decatur, Georgia 30031. 1985.

INDEXATION AND THE TAXATION OF BUSINESS AND INVESTMENT INCOME. Patrick Grady. Economic Council of Canada, Ottawa, Ontario. 1984.

INSTITUTIONAL INVESTORS: PASSIVE FIDUCIARIES TO ACTIVIST OWNERS. Dennis J. Block. Practising Law Institute, 810 Seventh Avenue, New York, New York 10019. 1990.

INTERIM REPORT ON THE INVESTMENT OF PUBLIC FUNDS BY THE NEW YORK STATE DORMITORY AUTHORITY. Commission of Investigation of the State of New York, 270 Broadway, New York, New York 10007. 1982.

THE INTERNATIONAL CENTRE FOR THE SETTLEMENT OF INVESTMENT DISPUTES. Donald V. Grede. MIT Press, 55 Hayward Street, Cambridge, Massachusetts 02142. 1979.

INTERNATIONAL EQUITY INVESTING. James R. Vertin, Editor. Dow Jones-Irwin, 1818 Ridge Road, Homewood, Illinois 60430. 1984.

INTERNATIONAL INVESTMENT. Second Edition. Andreas F. Lowenfeld. Matthew Bender and Company, Incorporated, 11 Penn Plaza, New York, New York 10001. 1982.

INTERNATIONAL INVESTMENT DISPUTES: AVOIDANCE AND SETTLEMENT. Seymour J. Rubin and Richard W. Nelson, Editors. American Society of International Law, 2223 Massachusetts Avenue, Northwest, Washington, D.C. 20008. 1985.

INTERNATIONAL JOINT VENTURES: A PRACTICAL APPROACH TO WORKING WITH FOREIGN INVESTORS IN THE UNITED STATES AND ABROAD: A CASE STUDY WITH SAMPLE DOCUMENTS. David N. Goldsweig and Roger H. Cummings, Editors. American Bar Association, Section of International Law and Practice, 750 North Lake Shore Drive, Chicago, Illinois 60611. 1990.

INTERNATIONAL PROPERTY INVESTMENT. Jesus A. Madalena. World Peace Through Law Center, 1000 Connecticut Avenue, Northwest, Suite 800, Washington, D.C. 20036. 1981.

INTERNATIONAL TAX AND ESTATE PLANNING: A PRACTICAL GUIDE FOR MULTINATIONAL INVESTORS. Second Edition. Robert C. Lawrence, III. Practising Law Institute, 810 Seventh Avenue, New York, New York 10019. 1989.

INTERNATIONAL TRADE AND INVESTMENT: REGULATING INTERNATIONAL BUSINESS. John Barton and Bart Fisher. Little, Brown, and Company, 34 Beacon Street, Boston, Massachusetts 02108. 1986.

INTERNATIONALISATION OF THE SECURITIES MARKETS: INCREASED ACCESS TO UNITED STATES CAPITAL MARKETS. Arthur Fleischer, Jr. and others. Prentice-Hall, Incorporated, 113 Sylvan Avenue, Englewood Cliffs, New Jersey 07632. 1990.

INVESTING IN DEVELOPING COUNTRIES: A GUIDE FOR EXECUTIVES. Thomas L. Brewer, et al. Free Press, 866 Third Avenue, New York, New York 10022. 1986.

INVESTING, LICENSING AND TRADING CONDITIONS ABROAD. Business International Corporation, One Dag Hammerskjold Plaza, New York, New York 10017. 1983.

INVESTMENT COMPANIES: AN INDUSTRY IN TRANSITION. Practising Law Institute, 810 Seventh Avenue, New York, New York 10019. 1983.

INVESTMENT COMPANIES: INDUSTRY RESPONSES TO NEW CONTEXTS AND CONCEPTS. Practising Law Institute, 810 Seventh Avenue, New York, New York 10019. 1985.

INVESTMENT COMPANIES 1989. Practising Law Institute, 810 Seventh Avenue, New York, New York 10019. 1989.

INVESTMENT COMPANY REGULATION AND COMPLIANCE: ALI-ABA COURSE OF STUDY MATERIALS. American Law Institute-American Bar Association, Committee on Continuing Professional Education, 4025 Chestnut Street, Philadelphia, Pennsylvania 19104. 1985.

INVESTMENT IN UNITED STATES REAL ESTATE. Carey D'Avino. Oyez Longman, Incorporated, 19 West Forty-fourth Street, New York, New York 10036. 1984.

INVESTMENT INCENTIVES AND DISINCENTIVES AND THE INTERNATIONAL INVESTMENT PROCESS. OECD Publication and Information Center. 1989.

INVESTMENT LAWS OF THE WORLD: THE DEVELOPING NATIONS. International Centre for Settlement of Investment Disputes. Oceana Publications, Incorporated, 75 Main Street, Dobbs Ferry, New York 10522. 1973. (Periodic Supplement).

INVESTMENT POLICY GUIDEBOOK FOR TRUSTEES: AN INTRODUCTION TO DRAFTING THE WRITTEN INVESTMENT STATEMENT FOR A LABOR-MANAGEMENT EMPLOYEE BENEFIT TRUST FUND. Second Edition. International Foundation of Employee Benefit Plans, P.O. Box 69, 18700 West Bluemound Road, Brookfield, Wisconsin 53008. 1981.

INVESTMENT REGULATION AROUND THE WORLD. Richard M. Hanner, et al., Editor. John Wiley and Sons, Incorporated, 605 Third Avenue, New York, New York 10158. 1983. (Annual Supplement).

INVESTMENT TREATIES. International Centre for Settlement of Investment Disputes. Oceana Publications, Incorporated, 75 Main Street, Dobbs Ferry, New York 10522. 1983. (Periodic Supplement).

INVESTMENTS AND THE LAW. Rachel S. Epstein and Paul A. Samuelson. Chelsea House Publishers, 1974 Sproul Road, Suite 400, Broomall, Pennsylvania 19008. 1988.

INVESTMENTS IN UNITED STATES REAL ESTATE FROM A EUROPEAN PERSPECTIVE. Roger Zach, Editor. P. Haupt, Bern, Switzerland. 1985.

INVESTORS LEGAL GUIDE. Second Edition. S. L. Kaufman. Oceana Publications, Incorporated, 75 Main Street, Dobbs Ferry, New York 10522. 1979.

INVESTOR'S TAX SURVIVAL GUIDE. Irving L. Blackman. Blackman Kallick Company, Limited, Certified Public Accountants, 300 South Riverside Plaza, Suite 660, Chicago, Illinois 60606. 1988.

THE J. K. LASSER GUIDE TO TAX-FREE INVESTMENTS. Simon and Schuster, Incorporated, 1230 Avenue of the Americas, New York, New York 10020. 1985.

LAND-SOMETHING OF VALUE: TAX AND POLICY ISSUES, PART II. Gene Wunderlich. Lincoln Institute of Land Policy, 26 Trowbridge Street, Cambridge, Massachusetts 02138. 1983.

LAW OF INVESTMENT MANAGEMENT. Harvey E. Bines. Research Institute of America, Incorporated, One Penn Plaza, New York, New York 10019. 1977.

THE LAW OF THE INVESTMENT MARKETS. Robert R. Pennington. Basil Blackwell, Incorporated, 3 Cambridge Center, Cambridge, Massachusetts 02142. 1990.

LEGAL ASPECTS OF INTERNATIONAL INVESTMENT. Stephen Gorove, Editor. Fred B. Rothman and Company, 10368 West Centennial Road, Littleton, Colorado 80127. 1977.

LEGAL ENVIRONMENT FOR FOREIGN DIRECT INVESTMENT IN THE UNITED STATES. Second Edition. Rudolph A. Houck, III and Nancy L. Caywood, Editors. International Law Institute, 1330 Connecticut Avenue, Northwest, Washington, D.C. 20036. 1981.

THE MODERN PRUDENT INVESTOR. Charles P. Curtis. American Law Institute, 4025 Chestnut Street, Philadelphia, Pennsylvania 19104. 1961.

THE NEW ABC'S OF THE DEPRECIATION AND INVESTMENT CREDIT. Prentice-Hall, Incorporated, 113 Sylvan Avenue, Englewood Cliffs, New Jersey 07632. 1983.

NEW DEPRECIATION AND INVESTMENT CREDIT RULES UNDER 1986 TAX REFORM. Commerce Clearing House, Incorporated, 4025 West Peterson Avenue, Chicago, Illinois 60646. 1986.

NEW INTERNATIONAL ARRANGEMENTS FOR FOREIGN DIRECT INVESTMENT. C. Fred Bergsten. MIT Press, 55 Hayward Street, Cambridge, Massachusetts 02142. 1986.

NON-RESIDENT INDIANS: INVESTMENTS AND FACILITIES, WITH TAX PLANNING. Third Edition. W. P. Ohawan. South Asia Books, P.O. Box 502, Columbia, Missouri 65205. 1984.

OIL AND GAS DRILLING FUNDS: A PRIMER FOR ATTORNEYS AND INVESTORS. Grayson C. Fox. State Bar of Texas, P. O. Box 12487, Capitol Station, Austin, Texas 78711. 1983.

PENSION PLAN INVESTMENTS: CONFRONTING TODAY'S LEGAL ISSUES. Howard Pianko and A. Richard Susko. Practising Law Institute, 810 Seventh Avenue, New York, New York 10019. 1991.

THE POLITICS OF INTERNATIONAL INVESTMENT. Earl H. Fry. Shepard's/McGraw-Hill, P.O. Box 1235, Colorado Springs, Colorado 80901. 1983.

A PRACTICAL GUIDE TO FOREIGN INVESTMENT IN THE UNITED STATES. Second Edition. John I. Forry. Bureau of National Affairs, 1231 Twenty-fifth Street, Northwest, Washington, D.C. 20037. 1983.

PROTECTION OF FOREIGN INVESTMENTS: A PRIVATE LAW STUDY OF SAFEGUARDING DEVICES IN INTERNATIONAL CRISIS SITUATIONS. Walter Kolvenbach. Kluwer Academic Publishers, 101 Philip Drive, Assinippi Park, Norwell, Massachusetts 02061. 1989.

THE REGULATION OF FOREIGN DIRECT INVESTMENT IN CANADA AND THE UNITED STATES: PROSPECTS AND CHALLENGES. Earl H. Fry and Lee H. Radebaugh. Brigham Young University, David M. Kennedy Center, Provo, Utah 84602. 1983.

REVIEW OF INVESTOR PROTECTION: A DISCUSSION DOCUMENT. Gower Publishing Company, Old Post Road, Brookfield, Vermont 05036. 1982.

RISK AND THE POLITICAL ECONOMY OF RESOURCE DEVELOPMENT. David W. Pearce. St. Martin's Press, Incorporated, 175 Fifth Avenue, New York, New York 10010. 1984.

SELECTING FINANCIAL SERVICES FOR GOVERNMENT. Girard Miller. Municipal Finance Officers Association of the United States and Canada, 180 North Michigan Avenue, Suite 800, Chicago, Illinois 60601. 1984.

SOUTHWESTERN LEGAL FOUNDATION. Private Investers Abroad. Matthew Bender and Company, Incorporated, 11 Penn Plaza, New York, New York 10001. 1983.

STRUCTURING FOREIGN INVESTMENT IN UNITED STATES REAL ESTATE. W. Donald Knight, Jr. and Richard L. Doernberg. Kluwer Academic Publishers, 101 Philip Drive, Assinippi Park, Norwell, Massachusetts 02061. 1988.

TAX FACTS ON INVESTMENTS: TAX FACTS 2. Advanced Sales Reference Service Department Editorial Staff, Editors. National Underwriter Company, 420 East Fourth Street, Cincinnati, Ohio 45202. 1983.

TAX INCENTIVES FOR INVESTMENT IN SMALL BUSINESSES. Butterworth Legal Publishers, 90 Stiles Road, Salem, New Hampshire 03079. 1984.

TAX PLANNING FOR FOREIGN INVESTORS IN THE UNITED STATES. Adam Starchild and Paul D. Brundage. Kluwer Academic Publishers, 101 Philip Drive, Assinippi Park, Norwell, Massachusetts 02061. 1983.

TAX SHELTER ALTERNATIVES: MEASURING THE RISKS. Michael N. Fitzgerald. Dow Jones-Irwin, 1818 Ridge Road, Homewood, Illinois 60430. 1985.

TAXATION OF DIRECT INVESTMENT IN THE UNITED STATES. J. F. Chown and L. Halpern. Butterworth Legal Publishers, 90 Stiles Road, Salem, New Hampshire 03079. 1980.

THIRD WORLD MULTINATIONALS: THE RISE OF FOREIGN INVESTMENT FROM DEVELOPING COUNTRIES. Louis T. Wells, Jr. MIT Press, 55 Hayward Street, Cambridge, Massachusetts 02142. 1983.

UNITED STATES INVESTMENT TREATIES: POLICY AND PRACTICE. Kenneth J. Vandevelde. Kluwer Academic Publishers, 101 Philip Drive, Assinippi Park, Norwell, Massachusetts 02061. 1991.

UNITED STATES SECURITIES AND INVESTMENT REGULATION HANDBOOK. Peter Farmery and Keith Walmsley, Editors. Graham and Trotman Limited, Sterling House, 66 Wilton Road, London SW1V 1DE, England. 1992.

UNITED STATES TAXATION OF FOREIGN INVESTMENT INCOME: ISSUES AND ARGUMENTS. Peggy B. Musgrave. International Tax Program, Harvard Law School, Cambridge, Massachusetts 02138. 1969.

VOTING BY INSTITUTIONAL INVESTORS ON CORPORATE GOVERNANCE ISSUES: 1990 PROXY SEASON. Sixth Edition. Ellen Flax. Investor Responsibility Research Center, 1755 Massachusetts Avenue, Northwest, Suite 100, Washington, D.C. 20036. 1990.

ENCYCLOPEDIAS AND DICTIONARIES

THE ENCYCLOPEDIA OF INVESTMENT TAXATION AND YEAR-ROUND PLANNING GUIDE. Kenneth J. Soderman. HarperCollins Publishers, 10 East Fifty-third Street, New York, New York 10022. 1991.

LAW REVIEWS AND PERIODICALS

THE JOURNAL OF TAXATION OF INVESTMENTS. Research Institute of America, Incorporated, One Penn Plaza, New York, New York 10119. Quarterly.

MUNICIPAL MARKET DEVELOPMENTS. Public Securities Association, 40 Broad Street, Twelfth Floor, New York, New York 10004. Quarterly.

PERSPECTIVE ON MUTUAL FUND ACTIVITY. Investment Company Institute, Suffridge Building, 1600 M Street, Northwest, Washington, D.C. 20036. Quarterly.

SECURITIES INDUSTRY TRENDS. Securities Industry Association, 120 Broadway, New York, New York 10271. Monthly.

TRENDS IN MUTUAL FUND ACTIVITY. Investment Company Institute, Suffridge Building, 1600 M Street, Northwest, Washington, D.C. 20036. Monthly.

WASHINGTON REPORT. Securities Industry Association, 120 Broadway, New York, New York 10271. Bimonthly.

NEWSLETTERS AND NEWSPAPERS

FOREIGN ACTIVITY REPORT. Securities Industry Association, 120 Broadway, New York, New York 10271. Weekly.

GOVERNMENT SECURITIES NEWSLETTER. Public Securities Association, 40 Broad Street, Twelfth Floor, New York, New York 10004. Monthly.

WASHINGTON NEWSLETTER: AN INVESTORS GUIDE TO TAX EXEMPT SECURITIES. Public Securities Association, 40 Broad Street, Twelfth Floor, New York, New York 10004. Weekly.

BIBLIOGRAPHIES

FOREIGN DIRECT INVESTMENT AND THE MULTINATIONAL ENTERPRISE: A BIBLIOGRAPHY. Cynthia Day Wallace, Editor. Martinus Nijhoff, Kluwer Academic Publishers, 101 Philip Drive, Assinippi Park, Norwell, Massachusetts 02061. 1988.

DIRECTORIES

DIRECTORY OF INCENTIVES FOR BUSINESS INVESTMENT AND DEVELOPMENT IN THE UNITED STATES: A STATE-BY-STATE GUIDE. Third Edition. National Association of State Development Agencies, 444 North Capitol Street, Northwest, Suite 611, Washington, D.C. 20001. 1991.

NATIONAL DIRECTORY OF INVESTMENT NEWSLETTERS. Idea Publishing Corporation, 55 East Alton Avenue, Yardley, Pennsylvania 19067.

NELSON'S DIRECTORY OF WALL STREET RESEARCH. W. R. Nelson and Company, 11 Elm Place, Rye, New York 10580.

ASSOCIATIONS AND PROFESSIONAL SOCIETIES

INVESTMENT COMPANY INSTITUTE. Suffridge Building, 1600 M Street, Northwest, Washington, D.C. 20036. (202) 293-7700.

PUBLIC SECURITIES ASSOCIATION. 40 Broad Street, Twelfth Floor, New York, New York 10004. (212) 809-7000.

SECURITIES INDUSTRY ASSOCIATION. 120 Broadway, New York, New York 10271. (212) 608-1500.

ONLINE DATABASES

INVESTEXT, THE BUSINESS INTELLIGENCE DATABASE. Business Research Corporation, 12 Farnsworth Street, Boston, Massachusetts 02210.

INVESTOR SERVICES. The Source, Source Telecomputing Corporation, 1616 Anderson Road, McLean, Virginia 22102.

INVESTMENTS, FOREIGN
See: CORPORATIONS, FOREIGN AND MULTINATIONAL; INTERNATIONAL TRADE

IRRIGATION
See: WATER LAW

J

JOB DISCRIMINATION
See: DISCRIMINATION, EMPLOYMENT

JOB SAFETY
See: OCCUPATIONAL SAFETY AND HEALTH

JOINT VENTURES

LOOSELEAF SERVICES AND REPORTERS

JOINT VENTURES WITH INTERNATIONAL PARTNERS. James A. Dobkin and Jeffrey A. Burt, Editors. Butterworth Legal Publishers, 90 Stiles Road, Salem, New Hampshire 03079. 1989.

JOINT VENTURES WITH THE SOVIET UNION: LAW AND PRACTICE. Christopher Osakwe. Butterworth Legal Publishers, 90 Stiles Road, Salem, New Hampshire 03079. 1990.

TRANSNATIONAL JOINT VENTURES. Peter B. Fitzpatrick. Business Laws, Incorporated, 11630 Chillicothe Road, Chesterland, Ohio 44026. 1989- .

HANDBOOKS, MANUALS, FORMBOOKS

DIRECT INVESTMENT AND JOINT VENTURES IN CHINA: A HANDBOOK FOR CORPORATE NEGOTIATORS. James E. Shapiro and others. Quorum Books, Greenwood Publishing Group, Incorporated, 88 Post Road West, P.O. Box 5007, Westport, Connecticut 06881. 1991.

A GUIDE TO HEALTH CARE JOINT VENTURES. I. Donald Snook and Edita M. Kaye. Aspen Publishers, Incorporated, 1600 Research Boulevard, Rockville, Maryland 20850. 1987.

THE HANDBOOK OF JOINT VENTURING. John D. Carter, Robert F. Cushman and C. Scott Hartz. Dow Jones-Irwin, 1818 Ridge Road, Homewood, Illinois 60430. 1988.

INTERNATIONAL JOINT VENTURES: A PRACTICAL APPROACH TO WORKING WITH FOREIGN INVESTORS IN THE UNITED STATES AND ABROAD: A CASE STUDY WITH SAMPLE DOCUMENTS. David N. Goldsweig and Roger H. Cummings, Editors. American Bar Association, Section of International Law and Practice, 750 North Lake Shore Drive, Chicago, Illinois 60611. 1990.

JOINT VENTURES: AN ACCOUNTING, TAX, AND ADMINISTRATIVE GUIDE. Joseph M. Morris. John Wiley and Sons, Incorporated, 605 Third Avenue, New York, New York 10158. 1987.

JOINT VENTURES AND CORPORATE PARTNERSHIPS: A STEP-BY-STEP GUIDE TO FORMING STRATEGIC BUSINESS ALLIANCES. Jennifer Lindsey. Probus Publishing Company, 118 North Linton Street, Chicago, Illinois 60606. 1989.

MERGER AND JOINT VENTURE ACTIVITIES IN THE EEC: A GUIDE TO DOING BUSINESS UNDER THE NEW REGULATIONS. Mario Siragusa. Practising Law Institute, 810 Seventh Avenue, New York, New York 10019. 1990.

THE PRACTICAL GUIDE TO JOINT VENTURES AND CORPORATE ALLIANCES: HOW TO FORM, HOW TO ORGANIZE, HOW TO OPERATE. Robert Porter Lynch. John Wiley and Sons, Incorporated, 605 Third Avenue, New York, New York 10158. 1989.

TEAMING UP FOR THE 90s: A GUIDE TO INTERNATIONAL JOINT VENTURES AND STRATEGIC ALLIANCES. Timothy M. Collins and Thomas L. Doorley, III. Business One Irwin, Homewood, Illinois. 1991.

TEXTBOOKS AND GENERAL WORKS

ALTERNATIVES TO INCORPORATION FOR PERSONS IN QUEST OF PROFIT: CASES AND MATERIALS ON PARTNERSHIPS, LIMITED PARTNERSHIPS, JOINT VENTURES, AND RELATED AGENCY CONCEPTS. Third Edition. Daniel William Fessler. West Publishing Company, 50 West Kellogg Boulevard, St. Paul, Minnesota 55164. 1991.

BUSINESS IN POLAND: A PRIMER AND OVERVIEW. Jack A. Barbanel and Lynda L. Maillet. Transnational Publishers, P.O. Box 7282, Ardsley-on-Hudson, New York 10503. 1991.

BUSINESS IN THE SOVIET UNION: A PRIMER AND OVERVIEW. Jack A. Barbanel and Lynda L. Maillet. Transnational Publishers, P.O. Box 7282, Ardsley-on-Hudson, New York 10503. 1991.

BUSINESS ORGANIZATIONS: PARTNERSHIPS. Gary A. Gotto, Ronald Jay Cohen and Ed Hendricks. West Publishing Company, 50 West Kellogg Boulevard, St. Paul, Minnesota 55164. 1991.

ESTABLISHING A UNITED STATES JOINT VENTURE WITH A FOREIGN PARTNER. David W. Detjen. Matthew Bender and Company, Incorporated, 11 Penn Plaza, New York, New York 10001. 1988.

ESTABLISHING JOINT VENTURES IN THE USSR. Lisen Aulin. Kluwer Academic Publishers, 101 Philip Drive, Assinippi Park, Norwell, Massachusetts 02061. 1990.

FOREIGN INVESTMENT IN CHINA UNDER THE OPEN POLICY: THE EXPERIENCE OF HONG KONG COMPANIES. John T. Thoburn and others. Gower Publishing Company, Old Post Road, Brookfield, Vermont 05036. 1990.

HOW TO STRUCTURE AND OPERATE INTERNATIONAL JOINT VENTURES. Massachusetts Continuing Legal Education, 20 West Street, Boston, Massachusetts 02111. 1990.

INDUSTRIAL COLLABORATION WITH JAPAN. Louis Turner. Routledge, Chapman & Hall, 29 West Thirty-fifth Street, New York, New York 10001. 1987.

THE INTERNATIONAL JOINT VENTURE. R. Duane Hall. Greenwood Publishing Group, Incorporated, 88 Post Road West, P.O. Box 5007, Westport, Connecticut 06881. 1984.

INTERNATIONAL JOINT VENTURES. Second Edition. James A. Dobkin, and others. Federal Publications, Incorporated, 1120 Twentieth Street, Northwest, Washington, D.C. 20036. 1988.

JOINT VENTURE PARTNER SELECTION: STRATEGIES FOR DEVELOPED COUNTRIES. J. Michael Geringer. Quorum Books, Greenwood Publishing Group, Incorporated, 88 Post Road West, P.O. Box 5007, Westport, Connecticut 06881. 1988.

JOINT VENTURE STRATEGIES AND CORPORATE INNOVATION. Sanford V. Berg, Jerome Duncan and Phillip Friedman. Oelgeschlager, Gunn and Hain, Incorporated, 245 Mirriam Street, Weston, Massachusetts 02193. 1982.

JOINT VENTURES. Terrence Maclaren. Clark Boardman Company, Limited, 435 Hudson Street, New York, New York 10014. 1985.

JOINT VENTURES AND OTHER COOPERATIVE BUSINESS ARRANGEMENTS. Michael A. Epstein, Michael S. Ostrach and Robert C. Weinbaum, Editors. Prentice-Hall, Incorporated, 113 Sylvan Avenue, Englewood Cliffs, New Jersey 07632. 1989.

JOINT VENTURES AND PRIVATIZATION IN EASTERN EUROPE. Monte E. Wetzler. Practising Law Institute, 810 Seventh Avenue, New York, New York 10019. 1991.

JOINT VENTURES BETWEEN HOSPITALS AND PHYSICIANS: A COMPETITIVE STRATEGY FOR THE HEALTHCARE MARKETPLACE. Linda A. Burns and Douglas M. Mancino. Dow Jones-Irwin, 1818 Ridge Road, Homewood, Illinois 60430. 1987.

JOINT VENTURES IN THE PEOPLE'S REPUBLIC OF CHINA: CAN CAPITALISM AND COMMUNISM COEXIST? Alfred K. Ho. Praeger Publishers, One Madison Avenue, New York, New York 10010-3603. 1990.

JOINT VENTURES IN THE PEOPLE'S REPUBLIC OF CHINA: THE CONTROL OF FOREIGN DIRECT INVESTMENT UNDER SOCIALISM. Margaret M. Pearson. Princeton University Press, 41 William Street, Princeton, New Jersey 08540. 1991.

JOINT VENTURES: STRUCTURING ALTERNATIVES. Carolyn S. Nachmias and James F. Nasuti. Shepard's/McGraw-Hill, P.O. Box 1235, Colorado Springs, Colorado 80901. 1988.

JOINT VENTURING ABROAD: A CASE STUDY. American Bar Association, Section of International Law and Practice, 750 North Lake Shore Drive, Chicago, Illinois 60611. 1984.

LEGAL ASPECTS OF JOINT VENTURES IN EASTERN EUROPE. Dennis Campbell, Editor. Kluwer Law Book Publishers, Incorporated, 36 West Forty-fourth Street, New York, New York 10036. 1981.

MERGERS AND JOINT VENTURES IN EUROPE: THE LAW AND POLICY OF THE EEC. Frank L. Fine. Graham and Trotman Limited, Sterling House, 66 Wilton Road, London SW1V 1DE, England. 1989.

MULTINATIONAL JOINT VENTURES IN DEVELOPING COUNTRIES. Paul W. Beamish. Routledge, Chapman & Hall, 29 West Thirty-fifth Street, New York, New York 10001. 1988.

REALTY JOINT VENTURES, 1985. Lewis R. Kaster and Noel W. Nellis, Co-Chairmen. Practising Law Institute, 810 Seventh Avenue, New York, New York 10019. 1985.

SOURCES OF JOINT VENTURE INFORMATION AND ASSISTANCE IN THE UNITED STATES AND EUROPE. Organization of American States, Executive Secretariat For Economic and Social Affairs, Information Service For Foreign Trade, Seventeeth Street and Constitution Avenue, Northwest, Washington, D.C. 20006. 1983.

STRATEGIES FOR JOINT VENTURES. Kathryn R. Harrigan. Lexington Books, Division of D.C. Heath and Company, 125 Spring Street, Lexington, Massachusetts 02173. 1985.

STRATEGIES FOR JOINT VENTURES IN THE PEOPLE'S REPUBLIC OF CHINA. Ike Mathur and Chen Jai-Sheng. Praeger Publishers, One Madison Avenue, New York, New York 10010-3603. 1987.

STRUCTURING REAL ESTATE JOINT VENTURES. Robert Bell. John Wiley and Sons, Incorporated, 605 Third Avenue, New York, New York 10158. 1992.

VENTURE CAPITAL FINANCING, 1990. Bruce Alan Mann. Practising Law Institute, 810 Seventh Avenue, New York, New York 10019. 1990.

ANNUALS AND SURVEYS

SECOND ANNUAL INSTITUTE: CORPORATE JOINT VENTURES. Ira M. Millstein, Chairman. Harcourt Brace Jovanovich, Incorporated, 6277 Sea Harbor Drive, Orlando, Florida 32821. 1986.

SECOND ANNUAL NEGOTIATING AND STRUCTURING JOINT VENTURES AND OTHER COOPERATIVE BUSINESS ARRANGEMENTS. Michael A. Epstein and William H. Weigel. Prentice-Hall, Incorporated, 113 Sylvan Avenue, Englewood Cliffs, New Jersey 07632. 1990.

JUDGE-MADE LAW
See: COMMON LAW

JUDGES AND JUDICIAL PROCESS
See also: ADMINISTRATION OF JUSTICE; COURTS; CRIMINAL LAW; FEDERAL JUDICIAL CENTER; JUDGMENTS

STATUTES, CODES, STANDARDS, UNIFORM LAWS

MODEL RULES OF PROFESSIONAL CONDUCT AND CODE OF JUDICIAL CONDUCT. American Bar Association, Center For Professional Responsibility, 750 North Lake Shore Drive, Chicago, Illinois 60611. 1989.

STANDARDS FOR JUDICIAL EDUCATION. American Bar Association, National Conference of State Trial Judges, 750 North Lake Shore Drive, Chicago, Illinois 60611. 1985.

STANDARDS OF PROFESSIONAL CONDUCT FOR LAWYERS AND JUDGES. Norman Redlich. Little, Brown, and Company, 34 Beacon Street, Boston, Massachusetts 02108. 1984.

LOOSELEAF SERVICES AND REPORTERS

DESKBOOK FOR CHIEF JUDGES OF UNITED STATES DISTRICT COURTS. Russell R. Wheeler. Federal Judicial Center, 1520 H Street, Northwest, Washington, D.C. 20005. 1984- .

JUDICIAL CONDUCT REPORTER. American Judicature Society, Suite 1600, 25 East Washington, Chicago, Illinois 60602. 1979- .

HANDBOOKS, MANUALS, FORMBOOKS

ELECTING JUSTICE: A HANDBOOK OF JUDICIAL ELECTION REFORMS. Sara Mathias. American Judicature Society, 25 East Washington Street, Suite 1600, Chicago, Illinois 60602. 1990.

HANDBOOK FOR JUDGES: AN ANTHOLOGY OF INSPIRATIONAL AND EDUCATIONAL READINGS. George H. Williams and Kathleen M. Sampson, Editors. American Judicature Society, Suite 1600, 25 East Washington, Chicago, Illinois 60602. 1984.

THE JUDGE'S BOOK. American Bar Association, 750 North Lake Shore Drive, Chicago, Illinois 60611. 1989.

JUDICIAL OPINION WRITING HANDBOOK. Second Edition. Joyce J. George. William S. Hein and Company, Incorporated, Hein Building, 1285 Main Street, Buffalo, New York 14209. 1986.

A MANUAL FOR MANAGING NOTORIOUS CASES. Timothy R. Murphy, Genevre Kay Loveland and G. Thomas Munsterman. National Center for State Courts, 300 Newport Avenue, Williamsburg, Virginia 23187. 1992.

TEXTBOOKS AND GENERAL WORKS

ADJUDICATING CONSTITUTIONAL ISSUES. Chester J. Antieau. Oceana Publications, Incorporated, 75 Main Street, Dobbs Ferry, New York 10522. 1985.

ALTERNATIVE FUTURES FOR THE STATE COURTS OF 2020. James A. Dator and Sharon J. Rogers. State Justice Institute. American Judicature Society, 25 East Washington Street, Suite 1600, Chicago, Illinois 60602. 1991.

AMERICAN COURT SYSTEMS: READINGS IN JUDICIAL PROCESS AND BEHAVIOR. Second Edition. Sheldon Goldman and Austin Sarat. Longman Publishing Group, 95 Church Street, White Plains, New York 10601. 1989.

THE AMERICAN JUDICIAL TRADITION: PROFILES OF LEADING AMERICAN JUDGES. G. Edward White. Oxford University Press, 200 Madison Avenue, New York, New York 10016. 1988.

THE AMERICAN JUDICIARY: CRITICAL ISSUES. Russell R. Wheeler. Sage Publications, Incorporated, 2455 Teller Road, Newbury Park, California 91320. 1982.

THE ANTAGONISTS: HUGO BLACK, FELIX FRANKFURTER AND CIVIL LIBERTIES IN MODERN AMERICA. James F. Simon. Simon and Schuster, Incorporated, 1230 Avenue of the Americas, New York, New York 10020. 1989.

APPOINTMENT OF JUDGES, THE JOHNSON PRESIDENCY. Neil D. McFeeley. University of Texas Press, P.O. Box 7819, Austin, Texas 78713-7819. 1987.

THE ART OF JUDGING. James E. Bond. Transaction Books, Rutgers University, New Brunswick, New Jersey 08903. 1987.

BATTLE FOR JUSTICE: HOW THE BORK NOMINATION SHOOK AMERICA. Ethan Bronner. Anchor Books, New York, New York. 1990.

BEYOND REPROACH: ETHICAL RESTRICTIONS ON THE EXTRAJUDICIAL ACTIVITIES OF STATE AND FEDERAL JUDGES. Steven Lubet. American Judicature Society, Suite 1600, 25 East Washington, Chicago, Illinois 60602. 1984.

BLACK ROBES, WHITE JUSTICE. Bruce Wright. L. Stuart, Secaucus, New Jersey. 1987.

BRANDEIS AND AMERICA. Nelson L. Dawson, Editor. University Press of Kentucky, 663 South Limestone Street, Lexington, Kentucky 40506-0336. 1989.

THE BURGER COURT: POLITICAL AND JUDICIAL PROFILES. Charles M. Lamb and Stephen C. Halpern. University of Illinois Press, 54 East Gregory Drive, Champaign, Illinois 61820. 1991.

A CENTURY OF JUDGING: A POLITICAL HISTORY OF THE WASHINGTON SUPREME COURT. Charles H. Sheldon. University of Washington Press, P.O. Box 50096, Seattle, Washington 98145-5096. 1988.

CLEMENT HAYNSWORTH, THE SENATE, AND THE SUPREME COURT. John P. Frank. University Press of Virginia, Charlottesville, Virginia. 1991.

COMPUTER-AIDED JUDICIAL ANALYSIS: PREDICTING, PRESCRIBING, AND ADMINISTERING. Stuart S. Nagel. Quorum Books, Greenwood Publishing Group, Incorporated, 88 Post Road West, P.O. Box 5007, Westport, Connecticut 06881. 1992.

CONGRESS SHALL MAKE NO LAW: OLIVER WENDELL HOLMES, THE FIRST AMENDMENT, AND JUDICIAL DECISION MAKING. Jeremy Cohen. Iowa State University Press, 2121 South State Avenue, Ames, Iowa 50010. 1989.

THE CONGRESSIONAL IMPEACHMENT PROCESS AND THE JUDICIARY: DOCUMENTS AND MATERIALS ON THE REMOVAL OF FEDERAL DISTRICT JUDGE HARRY E. CLAIBORNE. Bernard D. Reams, Jr. and Carol J. Gray. William S. Hein and Company, 1285 Main Street, Buffalo, New York 14209. 1987.

THE CONSTITUTION, THE COURTS, AND HUMAN RIGHTS: AN INQUIRY INTO THE LEGITIMACY OF CONSTITUTIONAL POLICY MAKING BY THE JUDICIARY. Michael J. Perry. Yale University Press, 302 Temple Street, New Haven, Connecticut 06520. 1982.

CONSTITUTIONAL FAITHS: FELIX FRANKFURTER, HUGO BLACK AND THE PROCESS OF JUDICIAL DECISION-MAKING. Mark Silverstein. Cornell University Press, 124 Roberts Place, Ithaca, New York 14850. 1984.

CONSTITUTIONAL FATE: THEORY OF THE CONSTITUTION. Phillip Bobbitt. Oxford University Press, Incorporated, 200 Madison Avenue, New York, New York 10016. 1982.

CONSTITUTIONAL LAW AND JUDICIAL POLICY MAKING. Third Edition. Joel B. Grossman and Richard S. Wells. Longman Publishing Group, 95 Church Street, White Plains, New York 10601. 1988.

A COURT DIVIDED: THE FIFTH CIRCUIT COURT OF APPEALS AND THE POLITICS OF JUDICIAL REFORM. Deborah J. Barrow and Thomas G. Walker. Yale University Press, 302 Temple Street, New Haven, Connecticut 06520. 1988.

COURTS AND JUDGES: HOW THEY WORK. Katherine J. Lee. HALT, Incorporated, 1319 F Street, Northwest, Suite 300, Washington, D.C. 20004. 1987.

COURTS AND POLITICS: THE FEDERAL JUDICIAL SYSTEM. Second Edition. Howard Ball. Prentice-Hall, Incorporated, 113 Sylvan Avenue, Englewood Cliffs, New Jersey 07632. 1987.

COURTS, CORRECTIONS, AND THE CONSTITUTION: THE IMPACT OF JUDICIAL INTERVENTION ON PRISONS AND JAILS. John J. Di Iulio, Jr. Oxford University Press, 200 Madison Avenue, New York, New York 10016. 1990.

COURTS, JUDGES, AND POLITICS: AN INTRODUCTION TO THE JUDICIAL PROCESS. Fourth Edition. Walter F. Murphy. McGraw-Hill Publishing Company, 1221 Avenue of the Americas, New York, New York 10020. 1986.

DECIDING TO DECIDE: AGENDA SETTING IN THE UNITED STATES SUPREME COURT. H.W. Perry, Jr. Harvard University Press, 79 Garden Street, Cambridge, Massachusetts 02138. 1991.

THE DIMENSIONS OF NON-LEGAL EVIDENCE IN THE AMERICAN JUDICIAL PROCESS: THE SUPREME COURT'S USE OF EXTRA-LEGAL MATERIALS IN THE TWENTIETH CENTURY. John W. Johnson. Garland Publishing, Incorporated, 136 Madison Avenue, New York, New York 10016. 1990.

DISCRETIONARY POWERS: A LEGAL STUDY OF OFFICIAL DISCRETION. Denis James Galligan. Clarendon Press, Oxford University Press, Incorporated, 200 Madison Avenue, New York, New York 10016. 1990.

DOING JUSTICE: A TRIAL JUDGE AT WORK. Robert Satter. Simon and Schuster, Incorporated, 1230 Avenue of the Americas, New York, New York 10020. 1990.

ECONOMIC LIBERTIES AND THE JUDICIARY. James A. Dorn and Henry G. Manne, Editors. George Mason University Press, Fairfax, Virginia. 1987.

ELECTING JUSTICE: THE LAW AND ETHICS OF JUDICIAL ELECTION CAMPAIGNS. Patrick M. McFadden. American Judicature Society, 25 East Washington Street, Suite 1600, Chicago, Illinois 60602. 1990.

EVALUATIVE AND EXPLANATORY LEGAL REASONING. Stuart S. Nagel. Quorum Books, Greenwood Publishing Group, Incorporated, 88 Post Road West, P.O. Box 5007, Westport, Connecticut 06881. 1992.

THE FEDERAL COURTS: CRISIS AND REFORM. Richard A. Posner. Harvard University Press, 79 Garden Street, Cambridge, Massachusetts 02138. 1985.

FEDERAL STANDARDS OF REVIEW. S. A. Childress. John Wiley and Sons, Incorporated, 605 Third Avenue, New York, New York 10158. 1986.

GOD SAVE THIS HONORABLE COURT: HOW THE CHOICE OF SUPREME COURT JUSTICES SHAPES OUR HISTORY. Laurence H. Tribe. Random House, Incorporated, Random House Publicity, (11-6) 201 East Fiftieth Street, New York, New York 10022. 1985.

THE GOOD JUDGE: REPORT OF THE TWENTIETH CENTURY FUND TASK FORCE ON FEDERAL JUDICIAL RESPONSIBILITY. Thomas E. Baker. Priority Press Publications, 41 East Seventieth Street, New York, New York 10021. 1989.

HARD JUDICIAL CHOICES: FEDERAL DISTRICT COURT JUDGES AND STATE AND LOCAL OFFICIALS. Phillip J. Cooper. Oxford University Press, 200 Madison Avenue, New York, New York 10016. 1988.

HE, TOO, SPOKE FOR DEMOCRACY: JUDGE HASTIE, WORLD WAR II, AND THE BLACK SOLDIER. Phillip McGuire. Greenwood Publishing Group, Incorporated, 88 Post Road West, P.O. Box 5007, Westport, Connecticut 06881. 1988.

HOW JUDGES REASON. Joel Levin. Peter Lang Publishing, Incorporated, 62 West Forty-fifth Street, New York, New York 10036. 1992.

HUGO L. BLACK AND THE DILEMMA OF AMERICAN LIBERALISM. Tony Freyer. Scott, Foresman and Company, 1900 East Lake Avenue, Glenview, Illinois 60025. 1990.

JOHN MARSHALL AND INTERNATIONAL LAW: STATESMAN AND CHIEF JUSTICE. Frances Howell Rudko. Greenwood Publishing Group, Incorporated, 88 Post Road West, P.O. Box 5007, Westport, Connecticut 06881. 1991.

JOHN MARSHALL'S ACHIEVEMENT: LAW, POLITICS, AND CONSTITUTIONAL INTERPRETATIONS. Thomas C. Shevory, Editor. Greenwood Publishing Group, Incorporated, 88 Post Road West, P.O. Box 5007, Westport, Connecticut 06881. 1989.

JUDGES. David Pannick. Oxford University Press, 200 Madison Avenue, New York, New York 10016. 1987.

JUDGES AND LAWYERS: THE HUMAN SIDE OF JUSTICE. Paul Wice. HarperCollins Publishers, 10 East Fifty-third Street, New York, New York 10022. 1991.

JUDGES AND THE CITIES: INTERPRETING LOCAL AUTONOMY. Gordon L. Clark. University of Chicago Press, 5801 Ellis Avenue, Third Floor, South, Chicago, Illinois 60637. 1985.

THE JUDGES CHAMBER: STORIES. Lowell B. Komie. American Bar Association, Professional Education Publications, 750 North Lake Shore Drive, Chicago, Illinois 60611. 1983.

JUDGES, LAW, AND BUSINESSMEN: AS SEEN FROM THE FINANCIAL TIMES. A. H. Hermann. Kluwer Academic Publishers, 101 Philip Drive, Assinippi Park, Norwell, Massachusetts 02061. 1983.

JUDGING. Robert E. Keeton. West Publishing Company, 50 West Kellogg Boulevard, St. Paul, Minnesota 55164. 1990.

JUDGING CREDENTIALS: NONLAWYER JUDGES AND THE POLITICS OF PROFESSIONALISM. Doris Marie Provine. University of Chicago Press, 5801 Ellis Avenue, Third Floor, South, Chicago, Illinois 60637. 1986.

JUDGING IN GOOD FAITH. Steven J. Burton. Cambridge University Press, 40 West Twentieth Street, New York, New York 10011. 1992.

JUDICIAL ACTIVISM IN COMPARATIVE PERSPECTIVE. Kenneth M. Holland. St. Martin's Press, 175 Fifth Avenue, New York, New York 10010. 1991.

THE JUDICIAL APPLICATION OF LAW. Jerzy Wroblewski. Kluwer Academic Publishers, 101 Philip Drive, Assinippi Park, Norwell, Massachusetts 02061. 1992.

JUDICIAL DECISION MAKING, SENTENCING POLICY, AND NUMERICAL GUIDANCE. Austin Lovegrove. Springer-Verlag New York, Incorporated, 175 Fifth Avenue, New York, New York 10010. 1989.

JUDICIAL DISCIPLINE AND REMOVAL IN THE UNITED STATES. Russell R. Wheller and A. Leo Levin. Federal Judicial Center, 1520 H Street, Northwest, Washington, D.C. 20005. 1987.

JUDICIAL INDEPENDENCE: THE CONTEMPORARY DEBATE. Shimon Shetreet and Jules Deschenes, Editors. Kluwer Academic Publishers, 101 Philip Drive, Assinippi Park, Norwell, Massachusetts 02061. 1985.

JUDICIAL INDISCRETION. James Whitfield Ellison. St. Martin's Press, 175 Fifth Avenue, New York, New York 10010. 1987.

JUDICIAL POLICIES: IMPLEMENTATION AND IMPACT. Charles A. Johnson and Bradley C. Canon. Congressional Quarterly, Incorporated, 1414 Twenty-second Street, Northwest, Washington, D.C. 20037. 1984.

JUDICIAL POLITICS: AN INTRODUCTION. Jerome R. Corsi. Prentice-Hall, Incorporated, 113 Sylvan Avenue, Englewood Cliffs, New Jersey 07632. 1984.

JUDICIAL PROCESS IN A NUTSHELL. Second Edition. William L. Reynolds. West Publishing Company, P.O. Box 64526, 50 West Kellogg Boulevard, St. Paul, Minnesota 55164-0526. 1991.

JUDICIAL PROCESS IN AMERICA. Robert A. Carp and Ronald Stidham. Congressional Quarterly Books, 1414 Twenty-second Street, Northwest, Washington D.C. 20037. 1989.

JUDICIAL PROCESS: LAW, COURTS, AND POLITICS IN THE UNITED STATES. David W. Neubauer. Brooks/Cole Publishing Company, 511 Forest Lodge Road, Pacific Grove, California 93950. 1991.

JUDICIAL RETIREMENT PLANS. Revised Edition. Timothy S. Pyne. American Judicature Society, Suite 1600, 25 East Washington, Chicago, Illinois 60602. 1984.

JUDICIAL REVIEW AND THE NATIONAL POLITICAL PROCESS: A FUNCTIONAL RECONSIDERATION OF THE ROLE OF THE SUPREME COURT. Jesse H. Choper. University of Chicago Press, 5801 Ellis Avenue, Third Floor, South, Chicago, Illinois 60637. 1983.

JUDICIAL ROULETTE: REPORT OF THE TWENTIETH CENTURY FUND TASK FORCE ON JUDICIAL SELECTION. Priority Press Publications, 41 East Seventieth Street, New York, New York 10021. 1988.

JUDICIAL RULEMAKING: A COMPENDIUM. Donna J. Pugh. Greenwood Publishing Group, Incorporated, 88 Post Road West, P.O. Box 5007, Westport, Connecticut 06881. 1984.

THE JUDICIARY IN AMERICAN LIFE: MAJOR HISTORICAL INTERPRETATIONS. Kermit L. Hall, Editor. Garland Publishing, Incorporated, 136 Madison Avenue, New York, New York 10016. 1987.

JUDICIARY LAW SELECTION, COMPENSATION, ETHICS, AND DISCIPLINE. Marvin Comisky and Philip C. Patterson. Quorum Books, Imprint of Greenwood Publishing Group, Incorporated, 88 Post Road West, P.O. Box 5007, Westport, Connecticut 06881. 1987.

JUSTICE AND PREDICTABILITY. Antony Cutler and David Nye. Macmillan Publishing Company, Incorporated, 866 Third Avenue, New York, New York 10022. 1983.

JUSTICE HUGO BLACK AND MODERN AMERICA. Tony Freyer. University of Alabama Press, P.O. Box 870380, Tuscaloosa, Alabama 35487. 1990.

JUSTICE OLIVER WENDELL HOLMES: FREE SPEECH AND THE LIVING CONSTITUTION. H.L. Pohlman. New York University Press, 70 Washington Square South, New York, New York 10012. 1991.

JUSTICE REHNQUIST AND THE CONSTITUTION. Sue Davis. Princeton University Press, 41 William Street, Princeton, New Jersey 08540. 1989.

JUSTICES AND PRESIDENTS: A POLITICAL HISTORY OF APPOINTMENTS TO THE SUPREME COURT. Third edition. Henry J. Abraham. Oxford University Press, 200 Madison Avenue, New York, New York 10016. 1992.

MANAGERIAL JUDGES. Judith Resnik. Rand Corporation, 1700 Main Street, Santa Monica, California 90406. 1982.

THE NATURE OF THE JUDICIAL PROCESS. Benjamin N. Cardozo. Yale University Press, 302 Temple Street, New Haven, Connecticut 06520. 1921. (1991, Reprint).

OF POWER AND RIGHT: HUGO BLACK, WILLIAM O. DOUGLAS, AND AMERICA'S CONSTITUTIONAL REVOLUTION. Howard Ball, Phillip J. Cooper. Oxford University Press, 200 Madison Avenue, New York, New York 10016. 1991.

PACKING THE COURTS: THE CONSERVATIVE CAMPAIGN TO REWRITE THE CONSTITUTION. Herman Schwartz. Scribner Educational Publishers, 866 Third Avenue, New York, New York 10022. 1988.

POLICY ARGUMENTS IN JUDICIAL DECISIONS. John Bell. Oxford University Press, Incorporated, 200 Madison Avenue, New York, New York 10016. 1983.

POLICYMAKING AND POLITICS IN THE FEDERAL DISTRICT COURTS. Robert A. Carp and C. K. Rowland. University of Tennessee Press, 293 Communications Building, Knoxville, Tennessee 37996-0325. 1983.

POLITICS, DEMOCRACY, AND THE SUPREME COURT: ESSAYS ON THE FUTURE OF CONSTITUTIONAL THEORY. Arthur S. Miller. Greenwood Publishing Group, Incorporated, 88 Post Road West, P.O. Box 5007, Westport, Connecticut 06881. 1985.

THE POLITICS OF JUDICIAL INTERPRETATION: THE FEDERAL COURTS, DEPARTMENT OF JUSTICE, AND THE CIVIL RIGHTS, 1866-1876. Robert J. Kaczorwski. Oceana Publications, Incorporated, 75 Main Street, Dobbs Ferry, New York 10522. 1985.

PRACTICES AND PROCEDURES OF STATE JUDICIAL CONDUCT ORGANIZATIONS. Judith Rosenbaum, Jeffrey M. Shaman and Katherine Levin. American Judicature Society, 25 East Washington Street, Suite 1600, Chicago, Illinois 60602. 1990.

PUBLIC ADMINISTRATION AND LAW: BENCH V. BUREAU IN THE UNITED STATES. David H. Rosenbloom. Marcel Dekker, Incorporated, 720 Madison Avenue, New York, New York 10016. 1983.

RACE VERSUS ROBE: THE DILEMMA OF BLACK JUDGES. Michael D. Smith. Associated Faculty Press, 19 West Thirty-sixth Street, New York, New York 10018. 1983.

REGULATION AND THE COURTS: THE CASE OF THE CLEAN AIR ACT. R. Shep Melnick. Brookings Institution, 1775 Massachusetts Avenue, Northwest, Washington, D.C. 20036-2188. 1983.

A REPRESENTATIVE SUPREME COURT?: THE IMPACT OF RACE, RELIGION, AND GENDER ON APPOINTMENTS. Barbara A. Perry. Greenwood Publishing Group, Incorporated, 88 Post Road West, P.O. Box 5007, Westport, Connecticut 06881. 1991.

THE ROLE OF MAGISTRATES IN FEDERAL DISTRICT COURTS. Carroll Seron. Federal Judicial Center, 1520 H Street, Northwest, Washington, D.C. 20005. 1983.

SETTLING CIVIL SUITS: LITIGATORS' VIEWS ABOUT APPROPRIATE ROLES AND EFFECTIVE TECHNIQUES FOR FEDERAL JUDGES. American Bar Association, Judicial Administration Division, 750 North Lake Shore Drive, Chicago, Illinois 60611. 1984.

THE SUPREME COURT AND ITS JUSTICES. Jesse H. Choper, Editor. American Bar Association, 750 North Lake Shore Drive, Chicago, Illinois 60611. 1987.

SUPREME COURTS AND JUDICIAL LAWMAKING: CONSTITUTIONAL TRIBUNALS AND CONSTITUTIONAL REVIEW. Edward McWhinney. Martinus Nijhofff, Kluwer Academic Publishers, 101 Philip Drive, Assinippi Park, Norwell, Massachusetts 02061. 1986.

A SURVEY OF STATE JUDICIAL FRINGE BENEFITS. American Bar Association, Judicial Administration Division, Committee on State Judicial Salaries and Compensation, 750 North Lake Shore Drive, Chicago, Illinois 60611. 1988.

TRUMAN'S COURT: A STUDY IN JUDICIAL RESTRAINT. Frances Howell Rudko. Greenwood Publishing Group, Incorporated, 88 Post Road West, P.O. Box 5007, Westport, Connecticut 06881. 1988.

VIEWS FROM THE BENCH: THE JUDICIARY AND CONSTITUTIONAL POLITICS. Mark W. Cannon and David M. O'Brien, Editors. Chatham House Publishers, P.O. Box One, Chatham, New Jersey 07928. 1985.

THE VINSON COURT ERA: THE SUPREME COURT'S CONFERENCE VOTES: DATA AND ANALYSIS. Jan Palmer. AMS Press, Incorporated, 56 East Thirteenth Street, New York, New York 10003. 1990.

WHY COURTS DON'T WORK. Richard Neely. McGraw-Hill Book Company, 1221 Avenue of the Americas, New York, New York 10020. 1983.

DIGESTS, INDEXES, ABSTRACTS, CITATORS

JUDICIAL DISCIPLINE AND DISABILITY DIGEST. Terrance V. Brooks and Tamara A. Stewart. American Judicature Society, Suite 1600, 25 East Washington, Chicago, Illinois 60602. 1980 (Periodic Supplements).

JUDICIAL EDUCATION: A GUIDE TO STATE AND NATIONAL PROGRAMS. Foundation for Women Judges. 1225 Fifteenth Street, Northwest, Washington, D.C. 20005. 1986.

JUDICIAL PROFILER: FEDERAL COURTS FOR THE DISTRICT OF COLUMBIA. Shepard's/McGraw-Hill, P.O. Box 1235, Colorado Springs, Colorado 80901. 1981- .

SHEPARD'S PROFESSIONAL AND JUDICIAL CONDUCT CITATIONS. Shepard's/McGraw-Hill, P.O. Box 1235, Colorado Springs, Colorado 80901. 1991.

LAW REVIEWS AND PERIODICALS

JUDGE. Syracuse University, College of Law, Syracuse, New York 13210. Semimonthly.

JUDGES JOURNAL. American Bar Association, Administration Division, 750 North Lake Shore Drive, Chicago, Illinois 60611. Quarterly.

JUDICATURE. American Judicature Society, Suite 1601, 25 East Washington, Chicago, Illinois 60602. Monthly.

NEWSLETTERS AND NEWSPAPERS

AJA BENCHMARK. American Judges Association, 300 Newport Avenue, Williamsburg, Virginia 23185. Quarterly.

ASSOCIATION OF ADMINISTRATIVE LAW JUDGES NEWSLETTER. c/o Ronald G. Bernoski, Henry Reuss Federal Plaza, Room 880, 310 West Wisconsin Avenue, Milwaukee, Wisconsin 53203. Bimonthly.

COUNTERBALANCE. National Association of Women Judges, 300 Newport Avenue, Williamsburg, Virginia 23187. Quarterly.

COURT REVIEWS. American Judges Association, 300 Newport Avenue, Williamsburg, Virginia 23187. Quarterly.

FEDERAL TRIAL NEWS. American Bar Association, National Conference of Federal Trial Judges, 750 North Lake Shore Drive, Chicago, Illinois 60611. Semiannually.

IJA REPORT. Institute of Judicial Administration, One Washington Square Village, New York, New York 10012. Quarterly.

JUDICIAL CONDUCT REPORTER. American Judicative Society, 25 East Washington, Suite 1600, Chicago, Illinois 60602. Quarterly.

THE JUDICIAL FORUM. Office of State Courts Administrators, Supreme Court Building, Tallahassee, Florida 32399. Monthly.

JUDICIAL LEGISLATIVE WATCH REPORT. National Legal Center for the Public Interest, 1101 17th Street, Northwest, Suite 810, Washington, D.C. 20036. Monthly.

NATIONAL CONFERENCE OF ADMINISTRATIVE LAW JUDGES NEWSLETTER. American Bar Association, National Conference of Administrative Law Judges, 750 North Lake Shore Drive, Chicago, Illinois 60611. Quarterly.

NAWJ NEWS AND ANNOUNCEMENTS. National Association of Women Judges, 300 Newport Avenue, Williamsburg, Virginia 23185. Semiannually.

SPECIAL COURT NEWS. American Bar Association, National Conference of Special Court Judges, 750 North Lake Shore Drive, Chicago, Illinois 60611. Quarterly.

STATE JUDICIARY NEWS. National Center for State Courts, 300 Newport Avenue, Williamsburg, Virginia 23185. Quarterly.

SURVEY OF JUDICIAL SALARIES. National Conference for State Courts, 300 Newport Avenue, Williamsburg, Virginia 23185. Semiannual.

THE THIRD BRANCH: BULLETIN OF THE FEDERAL COURTS. Federal Judicial Center, 1520 H Street, Northwest, Washington, D.C. 20005. Monthly.

TRIAL JUDGES NEWS. American Bar Association, National Conference of State Trial Judges, 750 North Lake Shore Drive, Chicago, Illinois 60611. Quarterly.

BIBLIOGRAPHIES

BIBLIOGRAPHY OF JUSTICE TOM C. CLARK. University of Texas, Tarlton Law Library, 727 East Twenty-sixth Street, Austin, Texas 78705-5799. 1985.

COURT SUPERVISION AND OVERSIGHT OF GOVERNMENT AGENCIES: A SELECTED BIBLIOGRAPHY. Anthony G. White. Vance Bibliographies, P.O. Box 229, 112 North Charter Street, Monticello, Illinois 61856. 1982.

JUSTICE LOUIS D. BRANDEIS: A BIBLIOGRAPHY OF WRITINGS AND OTHER MATERIALS ON THE JUSTICE. Gene Teitelbaum. Fred B. Rothman and Company, 10368 West Centennial Road, Littleton, Colorado 80127. 1988.

POLICY STUDIES ON JUDICIAL PROCESSES: A SELECTED BIBLIOGRAPHY. Robert U. Goehlert. Vance Bibliographies, P.O. Box 229, 112 North Charter Street, Monticello, Illinois 61856. 1983.

SELECTED LITERATURE ON JUDICIAL CONDUCT AND DISABILITY: AN ANNOTATED BIBLIOGRAPHY. Jane van Schaick and Kathleen M. Sampson. American Judicature Society, Suite 1600, 25 East Washington, Chicago, Illinois 60602. 1983.

UNITED STATES SUPREME COURT APPOINTMENTS, 1961-1986: A BRIEF BIBLIOGRAPHY. Alva W. Stewart. Vance Bibliographies, P.O. Box 229, 112 North Charter Street, Monticello, Illinois 61856. 1987.

DIRECTORIES

THE ALMANAC OF THE FEDERAL JUDICIARY: PROFILES OF ALL ACTIVE UNITED STATES DISTRICT COURT JUDGES. Lawletters, Incorporated, 332 South Michigan Avenue, Suite 1460, Chicago, Illinois 60604. 1984- .

THE AMERICAN BENCH: JUDGES OF THE NATION. Third Edition. Forster-Long, Incorporated, 3280 Ramos Circle, Sacramento, California 95827. Biennial.

BNA'S DIRECTORY OF STATE COURTS, JUDGES, AND CLERKS: A STATE-BY STATE LISTING. Third Edition. Kamla J. King and Judith Springberg. Bureau of National Affairs, Incorporated, 1231 Twenty-fifth Street, Northwest, Washington, D.C. 20037. Annual.

FEDERAL COURT DIRECTORY. Want Publishing Company, 1511 K Street, Northwest, Washington, D.C. 20005. Annual.

FEDERAL JUDICIARY ALMANAC. W. Stuart Dornette and Robert R. Cross. John Wiley and Sons, Incorporated, 605 Third Avenue, New York, New York 10158. Annual.

LAW AND LEGAL INFORMATION DIRECTORY. Seventh Edition. Steven Wasserman and Jacqueline Wasserman O'Brien. Gale Research, Incorporated, 835 Penobscot Building, Detroit, Michigan 48226. 1992.

UNITED STATES COURT DIRECTORY. Administration Office of the United States Courts. Superintendent of Documents, United States Government Printing Office, Washington, D.C. 20402. Semiannual.

WANT'S FEDERAL-STATE COURT DIRECTORY. Want Publishing Company, 1511 K Street, Northwest, Washington, D.C. 20005. Annual.

BIOGRAPHICAL SOURCES

ABE FORTAS: A BIOGRAPHY. Laura Kalman. Yale University Press, 302 Temple Street, New Haven, Connecticut 06520. 1990.

ALMANAC OF THE FEDERAL JUDICIARY: PROFILES AND EVALUATIONS OF ALL JUDGES OF THE UNITED STATES DISTRICT COURTS. Prentice-Hall, Incorporated, 113 Sylvan Avenue, Englewood Cliffs, New Jersey 07632. 1989- .

ALMANAC OF THE FEDERAL JUDICIARY: PROFILES OF ALL ACTIVE UNITED STATES DISTRICT JUDGES. Lawletters, Incorporated, 332 South Michigan Avenue, Suite 1460, Chicago, Illinois 60604. Semiannual.

THE AMERICAN BENCH: JUDGES OF THE NATION. Third Edition. Forster-Long, Incorporated, 3280 Ramos Circle, Sacramento, California 95827. Biennial.

BIOGRAPHICAL DICTIONARY OF THE FEDERAL JUDICIARY. Harold Chase, Samuel Krislov, Keith O. Boyum and Jerry N. Clark. Gale Research, Incorporated, 835 Penobscot Building, Detroit, Michigan 48226. 1976. (Retrospective).

BRANDEIS AND FRANKFURTER: A DUAL BIOGRAPHY. Leonard Baker. New York University Press, 70 Washington Square, South, New York, New York 10012. 1986.

A CAPACITY FOR OUTRAGE: THE JUDICIAL ODYSSEY OF J. SKELLY WEIGHT. Arthur S. Miller. Greenwood Publishing Group, Incorporated, 88 Post Road West, P.O. Box 5007, Westport, Connecticut 06881. 1984.

CARDOZO: A STUDY IN REPUTATION. Richard A. Posner. University of Chicago Press, 5801 Ellis Avenue, Chicago, Illinois 60637. 1990.

EIGHT MEN AND A LADY: PROFILES OF THE JUSTICES OF THE UNITED STATES SUPREME COURT. National Press, Incorporated, 7201 Wisconsin Avenue, Suite 720, Bethesda, Maryland 20814. 1990.

FEDERAL JUDGES AND JUSTICES: A CURRENT LISTING OF NOMINATIONS, CONFIRMATIONS, ELEVATIONS, RESIGNATIONS, RETIREMENTS. Iris J. Wildman and Mark J. Handler. Fred B. Rothman and Company, 10368 West Centennial Road, Littleton, Colorado 80127. 1987.

FORTAS: THE RISE AND RUIN OF A SUPREME COURT JUSTICE. Bruce Allen Murphy. William Morrow and Company, 105 Madison Avenue, New York, New York 10016. 1988.

GUIDE TO FEDERAL DISTRICT JUDGES: BACKGROUND, MAJOR RULINGS, AND COURTROOM STYLE. Am-Law Publishing Corporation, 205 Lexington Avenue, New York, New York 10016. Annual.

HALF BROTHER, HALF SON: THE LETTERS OF LOUIS D. BRANDEIS TO FELIX FRANKFURTER. Melvin I. Urofsky and David W. Levy, Editors. University of Oklahoma Press, 105 Asp Avenue, Norman, Oklahoma 73019. 1991.

HONORABLE JUSTICE: THE LIFE OF OLIVER WENDELL HOLMES. Sheldon M. Novick. Little, Brown and Company, 34 Beacon Street, Boston, Massachusetts 02108. 1989.

THE ICONOCLAST AS REFORMER: JEROME FRANK'S IMPACT ON AMERICAN LAW. Robert J. Glennon. Cornell University Press, 124 Roberts Place, Ithaca, New York 14850. 1985.

JOHN JAY, COLONIAL LAWYER. Herbert A. Johnson. Garland Publishing, Incorporated, 136 Madison Avenue, New York, New York 10016. 1989.

JOHN MARSHALL HARLAN: GREAT DISSENTER OF THE WARREN COURT. Tinsley E. Yarbrough. Oxford University Press, 200 Madison Avenue, New York, New York 10016. 1992.

JOHN MARSHALL HARLAN: THE LAST WHIG JUSTICE. Loren P. Beth. University Press of Kentucky, 663 South Limestone Street, Lexington, Kentucky 40506-0336. 1992.

THE JUSTICE FROM BEACON HILL: THE LIFE AND TIMES OF OLIVER WENDELL HOLMES. Liva Baker. HarperCollins Publishers, 10 East Fifty-third Street, New York, New York 10022. 1991.

LOUIS D. BRANDEIS: JUSTICE FOR THE PEOPLE. Philippa Strum. Schocken Books, New York, New York. 1984. (Reprint 1989).

MR. JUSTICE REHNQUIST, JUDICIAL ACTIVIST. Donald E. Boles. Iowa State University Press, 2121 South State Avenue, Ames, Iowa 50010. 1987-

SALMON P. CHASE: A LIFE IN POLITICS. Frederick J. Blue. Kent State University Press, 101 Franklin Hall, Kent, Ohio 44242. 1987.

SANDRA DAY O'CONNOR: JUSTICE FOR ALL. Beverly Gherman. Viking Penguin, Incorporated, 375 Hudson Street, New York, New York 10014. 1991.

THURGOOD MARSHALL: A LIFE FOR JUSTICE. Jim Haskins. Henry Holt and Company, 115 West Eighteenth Street, New York, New York 10011. 1992.

TWO JEWISH JUSTICES: OUTCASTS IN THE PROMISED LAND. Robert A. Burt. University of California Press, 2120 Berkeley Way, Berkeley, California 94720. 1988.

THE WASHINGTON HIGH BENCH: A BIOGRAPHICAL HISTORY OF THE STATE SUPREME COURT, 1889-1991. Charles H. Sheldon. Washington State University Press, Pullman, Washington 99164-5910. 1992.

WHO'S WHO IN AMERICAN LAW. Sixth Edition. Marquis Who's Who, Incorporated, 3002 Glenview Road, Wilmette, Illinois 60091. 1990.

WILLIAM WAYNE JUSTICE: A JUDICIAL BIOGRAPHY. Frank R. Kemerer. University of Texas Press, P.O. Box 7819, Austin, Texas 78713-7819. 1991.

ASSOCIATIONS AND PROFESSIONAL SOCIETIES

AMERICAN BAR ASSOCIATION, COMMISSION ON FEDERAL JUDICIAL COMPENSATION. 750 North Lake Shore Drive, Chicago, Illinois 60611. (312) 988-5000.

AMERICAN BAR ASSOCIATION, COMMITTEE ON FEDERAL JUDICIAL IMPROVEMENTS. 750 North Lake Shore Drive, Chicago, Illinois 60611. (312) 988-5000.

AMERICAN BAR ASSOCIATION, COMMITTEE ON JUDICIAL SELECTION, TENURE, AND COMPENSATION. 750 North Lake Shore Drive, Chicago, Illinois 60611. (312) 988-5000.

AMERICAN BAR ASSOCIATION, COMMITTEE ON THE FEDERAL JUDICIARY. 750 North Lake Shore Drive, Chicago, Illinois 60611. (312) 988-5000.

AMERICAN BAR ASSOCIATION, JUDICIAL ADMINISTRATION DIVISION, APPELLATE JUDGES' CONFERENCE. 750 North Lake Shore Drive, Chicago, Illinois 60611. (312) 988-5000.

AMERICAN BAR ASSOCIATION, JUDICIAL ADMINISTRATION DIVISION, NATIONAL CONFERENCE OF ADMINISTRATIVE LAW JUDGES. 750 North Lake Shore Drive, Chicago, Illinois 60611. (312) 988-5000.

AMERICAN BAR ASSOCIATION, JUDICIAL ADMINISTRATION DIVISION, NATIONAL CONFERENCE OF FEDERAL TRIAL JUDGES. 750 North Lake Shore Drive, Chicago, Illinois 60611. (312) 988-5000.

AMERICAN BAR ASSOCIATION, JUDICIAL ADMINISTRATION DIVISION, NATIONAL CONFERENCE OF SPECIAL COURT JUDGES. 750 North Lake Shore Drive, Chicago, Illinois 60611. (312) 988-5000.

AMERICAN BAR ASSOCIATION, JUDICIAL ADMINISTRATION DIVISION, NATIONAL CONFERENCE OF STATE JUDGES. 750 North Lake Shore Drive, Chicago, Illinois 60611. (312) 988-5000.

AMERICAN BAR ASSOCIATION, SPECIAL COMMITTEE ON FEDERAL JUDICIAL IMPROVEMENTS. 750 North Lake Shore Drive, Chicago, Illinois 60611. (312) 988-5000.

AMERICAN JUDGES ASSOCIATION. 300 Newport Avenue, Williamsburg, Virginia 23187. (804) 253-2000.

AMERICAN JUDICATURE SOCIETY. 25 East Washington, Suite 1606, Chicago, Illinois 60602. (312) 558-6900.

CONFERENCE OF CHIEF JUSTICES. National Center For State Courts, 300 Newport Avenue, Williamsburg, Virginia 23185. (804) 253-2000.

CONFERENCE OF SPECIAL COURT JUDGES. 750 North Lake Shore Drive, Chicago, Illinois 60611.

COUNCIL FOR COURT EXCELLENCE. 1025 Vermont Avenue, Northwest, Suite 510, Washington, D.C. 20005. (202) 783-7736.

FEDERAL ADMINISTRATIVE LAW JUDGES CONFERENCE. 424 National Lawyers Club, 1815 H Street, Northwest, Washington, D.C. 20006. (202) 357-9251.

FUND FOR MODERN COURTS. 36 West Forty-fourth Street, Room 310, New York, New York 10036. (212) 575-1577.

NATIONAL AMERICAN INDIAN COURT JUDGES ASSOCIATION. 1000 Connecticut Avenue, Northwest, Suite 401, Washington, D.C. 20036. (202) 296-0685.

NATIONAL ASSOCIATION OF WOMEN JUDGES. National Center For State Courts, 300 Newport Avenue, Williamsburg, Virginia 23185. (804) 253-2000.

NATIONAL CONFERENCE OF BANKRUPTCY JUDGES. c/o Judge George C. Paine, Customs House, Room 218, 701 Broadway, Nashville, Tennessee 37203. (615) 736-5587.

NATIONAL COUNCIL OF JUVENILE AND FAMILY COURT JUDGES. P.O. Box 8970, University of Nevada, Reno, Nevada 89507. (702) 784-6012.

NATIONAL JUDGES ASSOCIATION. 42 Little Horn Road, Westcliffe, Colorado 81252. (719) 783-2274.

RESEARCH CENTERS AND INSTITUTES

AMERICAN ACADEMY OF JUDICIAL EDUCATION. 2025 Eye Street, Northwest, Suite 903, Washington, D.C. 20006.

CENTER FOR JUDICIAL STUDIES. P.O. Box 17248, Richmond, Virginia 23229. (804) 282-1798.

FEDERAL JUDICIAL CENTER. Dolly Madison House, 1520 H Street, Northwest, Washington, D.C. 20005.

INSTITUTE FOR COURT MANAGEMENT OF THE NATIONAL CENTER FOR STATE COURTS. 1331 Seventeenth Street, Suite 402, Denver, Colorado 80202. (303) 293-3063.

INSTITUTE OF JUDICIAL ADMINISTRATION. One Washington Square Village, New York, New York 10012. (212) 998-6280.

JUDICIAL SELECTION PROJECT. Alliance For Justice, 600 New Jersey Avenue, Northwest, Washington, D.C. 20001. (202) 662-9634.

NATIONAL CENTER FOR STATE COURTS. 300 Newport Avenue, Williamsburg, Virginia 23185. (804) 253-2000.

NATIONAL JUDICIAL COLLEGE. Judicial College Building, University of Nevada, Reno, Nevada 89557. (702) 784-6747.

OTHER SOURCES

CLARENCE THOMAS--CONFRONTING THE FUTURE: SELECTIONS FROM THE SENATE CONFIRMATION HEARINGS AND PRIOR SPEECHES. United States Congress, Senate Committee on the Judiciary, Regnery Gateway. National Book Network, Lanham, Maryland. 1992.

JUDGMENTS
See also: COMMON LAW; STATES

STATUTES, CODES, STANDARDS, UNIFORM LAWS

MODEL PERIODIC PAYMENT OF JUDGMENTS ACT. National Conference of Commissioners on Uniform State Laws. Uniform Laws Annotated. West Publishing Company, P.O. Box 64526, 50 West Kellogg Boulevard, St. Paul, Minnesota 55164-0526. 1976. (Annual Supplements).

UNIFORM DECLARATORY JUDGMENTS ACT. National Conference of Commissioners on Uniform State Laws. Martindale-Hubbell Law Directory, Volume Seven. Martindale-Hubbell, Incorporated, 121 Chanlon Road, New Providence, New Jersey 07974. Annual.

UNIFORM DECLARATORY JUDGMENTS ACT. National Conference of Commissioners on Uniform State Laws. Uniform Laws Annotated. West Publishing Company, P.O. Box 64526, 50 West Kellogg Boulevard, St. Paul, Minnesota 55164-0526. 1976. (Annual Supplements).

UNIFORM ENFORCEMENT OF FOREIGN JUDGMENTS ACT. National Conference of Commissioners on Uniform State Laws. Martindale-Hubbell Law Directory, Volume Seven. Martindale-Hubbell, Incorporated, 121 Chanlon Road, New Providence, New Jersey 07904. Annual.

UNIFORM ENFORCEMENT OF FOREIGN JUDGMENTS ACT. National Conference of Commissioners on Uniform State Laws. Uniform Laws Annotated. West Publishing Company, P.O. Box 64526, 50 West Kellogg Boulevard, St. Paul, Minnesota 55164-0526. 1976. (Annual Supplement).

UNIFORM FOREIGN MONEY JUDGMENTS RECOGNITION ACT. National Conference of Commissioners on Uniform State Laws. Uniform Laws Annotated. West Publishing Company, P.O. Box 64526, 50 West Kellogg Boulevard, St. Paul, Minnesota 55164-0526. 1976. (Annual Supplements).

RESTATEMENTS

RESTATEMENT OF THE LAW OF JUDGMENTS, 1942; RESTATEMENT OF THE LAW, SECOND, JUDGMENTS, 1982. American Law Institute, 4025 Chestnut Street, Philadelphia, Pennsylvania 19104.

LOOSELEAF SERVICES AND REPORTERS

ENFORCEMENT OF MONEY JUDGMENTS ABROAD. Philip R. Weems, Editor. Matthew Bender and Company, Incorporated, 11 Penn Plaza, New York, New York 10001. 1988- .

TEXTBOOKS AND GENERAL WORKS

CIVIL JUDGMENT RECOGNITION AND THE INTEGRATION OF MULTIPLE-STATE ASSOCIATIONS: CENTRAL AMERICA, THE UNITED STATES OF AMERICA, AND THE EUROPEAN ECONOMIC COMMUNITY. Robert C. Casad. University Press of Kansas, 329 Carruth, Lawrence, Kansas 66045. 1982.

THE EEC CONVENTION ON JURISDICTION AND THE ENFORCEMENT OF JUDGMENTS. Peter Byrne. Round Hall Press, Dublin, Ireland. 1990.

ENFORCEMENT OF FOREIGN JUDGMENTS WORLDWIDE. Charles Platto. Graham and Trotman Limited, Sterling House, 66 Wilton Road, London SW1V 1DE, England. 1989.

A GUIDE TO THE CIVIL JURISDICTION AND JUDGMENTS CONVENTION. Alan Dashwood, Richard Hacon and Robin White. Kluwer Academic Publishers, 101 Philip Drive, Assinippi Park, Norwell, Massachusetts 02061. 1987.

JUDICIAL ENFORCEMENT OF INTERNATIONAL DEBT OBLIGATIONS. David M. Sassoon and Daniel D. Bradlow, Editors. International Law Institute. Distributed by University Press of America, 4720 Boston Way, Lanham, Maryland 20706. 1987.

RECOGNITION AND ENFORCEMENT OF FOREIGN JUDGMENTS IN VARIOUS FOREIGN COUNTRIES. George J. Roman. Law Library, Library of Congress. Superintendent of Documents, United States Governments Printing Office, Washington, D.C. 20402. 1984.

RES JUDICATA IN A NUTSHELL. Robert C. Casad. West Publishing Company, P.O. Box 64526, 50 West Kellogg Boulevard, St. Paul, Minnesota 55164-0526. 1976.

JUDICIAL OPINIONS
See: JUDGMENTS

JUDICIAL PROCESS
See: ADMINISTRATION OF JUSTICE; COURTS; JUDGES AND JUDICIAL PROCESS

JUDICIAL REVIEW
See: COMMON LAW; JUDGES AND JUDICIAL PROCESS; SEPARATION OF POWERS

JURISDICTION
See also: CIVIL PROCEDURE; CONFLICT OF LAWS

LOOSELEAF SERVICES AND REPORTERS

FOREIGN STATE IMMUNITY IN COMMERCIAL TRANSACTONS. Michael Wallace Gordon. Butterworth Legal Publishers, 90 Stiles Road, Salem, New Hampshire 03079. 1991- .

JURISDICTION AND FORUM SELECTION. Robert C. Casad. Callaghan and Company, 155 Pfingsten Road, Deerfield, Illinois 60015. 1988- .

HANDBOOKS, MANUALS, FORMBOOKS

A PRIMER ON THE JURISDICTION OF THE UNITED STATES COURTS OF APPEALS. Thomas E. Baker. Federal Judicial Center, 1520 H Street, Northwest, Washington, D.C. 20005. 1989.

TEXTBOOKS AND GENERAL WORKS

ABOLITION OF DIVERSITY JURISPRUDENCE: AN IDEA WHOSE TIME HAS COME? M. Caldwell Butler and John P. Frank. National Legal Center For the Public Interest, 1000 Sixteenth Street, Northtwest, Washington, D.C. 20036. 1983.

THE BUDGETARY IMPACT OF POSSIBLE CHANGES IN DIVERSITY JURISDICTION. Anthony Partridge. Federal Judicial Center, 1520 H Street, Northwest, Washington, D.C. 20005. 1988.

CASES AND MATERIALS ON FEDERAL COURTS. Eighth Edition. Charles T. McCormick, James H. Chadbourn and Charles Alan Wright. Foundation Press, 615 Merrick Avenue, Westbury, New York 11590. 1988.

FEDERAL COURTS AND THE INTERNATIONAL HUMAN RIGHTS PARADIGM. Kenneth C. Randall. Duke University Press, Box 6697 College Station, Durham, North Carolina 27708. 1990.

FEDERAL COURTS AND THE LAW OF FEDERAL-STATE RELATIONS. Second Edition. Peter W. Low and John Calvin Jeffries, Jr. Foundation Press, 615 Merrick Avenue, Westbury, New York 11590. 1989.

FEDERAL COURTS: CASES AND MATERIALS. Fourth Edition. David P. Currie. West Publishing Company, 50 West Kellogg Boulevard, St. Paul, Minnesota 55164. 1990.

THE FEDERAL COURTS IN THE POLITICAL ORDER: JUDICIAL JURISDICTION AND AMERICAN POLITICAL THEORY. Martin H. Redish. Carolina Academic Press, P.O. Box 51879, Durham, North Carolina 27717. 1991.

FEDERAL JURISDICTION. Erwin Chemerinsky. Little, Brown and Company, 34 Beacon Street, Boston, Massachusetts 02108. 1989.

FEDERAL JURISDICTION. Second Edition. Martin H. Redish. West Publishing Company, P.O. Box 64526, 50 West Kellogg Boulevard, St. Paul, Minnesota 55164-0526. 1991.

FEDERAL JURISDICTION IN A NUTSHELL. Third Edition. David P. Currie. West Publishing Company, P.O. Box 64526, 50 West Kellogg Boulevard, St. Paul, Minnesota 55164-0526. 1990.

FEDERAL JURISDICTION: POLICY AND PRACTICE: CASE AND MATERIALS. Second Edition. Howard P. Fink and Mark V. Tushnet. Michie Company, P.O. Box 7587, Charlottesville, Virginia 22906-7582. 1987.

FEDERAL JURISDICTION: TENSIONS IN THE ALLOCATION OF JUDICIAL POWER. Second Edition. Martin H. Redish. Michie Company, P.O. Box 7587, Charlottesville, Virginia 22906-7582. 1990.

A GUIDE TO THE CIVIL JURISDICTION AND JUDGMENTS CONVENTION. Alan Dashwood, Richard Hacon and Robin White. Kluwer Academic Publishers, 101 Philip Drive, Assinippi Park, Norwell, Massachusetts 02061. 1987.

HART AND WECHSLER'S THE FEDERAL COURTS AND THE FEDERAL SYSTEM. Third Edition. Henry Melvin Hart, Herbert Wechsler and Paul M. Bator. Foundation Press, 615 Merrick Avenue, Westbury, New York 11590. 1988.

INTERNATIONAL CIVIL LITIGATION IN UNITED STATES COURTS: COMMENTARY AND MATERIALS. Gary B. Born with David Westin. Kluwer Academic Publishers, 101 Philip Drive, Assinippi Park, Norwell, Massachusetts 02061. 1989.

INTERNATIONAL COMMERCIAL LITIGATION. Stephen Cromie, Peter Perry and others and William Park, Consulting Editor. Butterworth Legal Publishers, 90 Stiles Road, Salem, New Hampshire 03079. 1990.

ISSUES AND PERSPECTIVES IN CONFLICT OF LAWS. Second Edition. Gary J. Simson. Carolina Academic Press, P.O. Box 51879, Forest Hills Station, Durham, North Carolina 27717. 1991. (Supplemented).

THE JUDICIAL POWER OF THE UNITED STATES: THE ELEVENTH AMENDMENT IN AMERICAN HISTORY. John V. Orth. Oxford University Press, 200 Madison Avenue, New York, New York 10016. 1987.

JUDICIAL SETTLEMENT OF INTERNATIONAL DISPUTES: JURISDICTION, JUSTICIABILITY, AND JUDICIAL LAW-MAKING ON THE CONTEMPORARY INTERNATIONAL COURT. Edward McWhinney. Martinus Nijhoff, Kluwer Academic Publishers, 101 Philip Drive, Assinippi Park, Norwell, Massachusetts 02061. 1991.

JURISDICTION IN A NUTSHELL, STATE AND FEDERAL. Fourth Esition. Albert A. Ehronzweig, David W. Louisell, and Geoffrey C. Hazard, Jr. West Publishing Company, P.O. Box 64526, 50 West Kellogg Boulevard, St. Paul, Minnesota 55164-0526. 1980.

JURISDICTION IN CIVIL ACTIONS: TERRITORIAL BASIS AND PROCESS LIMITATIONS ON JURISPRUDENCE OF STATE AND FEDERAL COURTS. Second Edition. Robert C. Casad. Butterworth Legal Publishers, 90 Stiles Road, Salem, New Hampshire 03079. 1991.

JURISPRUDENCE FOR A FREE SOCIETY: STUDIES IN LAW, SCIENCE, AND POLICY. Harold D. Lasswell and Myres S. McDougal. Martinus Nijhoff, Kluwer Academic Publishers, 101 Philip Drive, Assinippi Park, Norwell, Massachusetts 02061. 1991.

THE LAW OF FEDERAL COURTS. Fourth Edition. Charles Alan Wright. West Publishing Company, P.O. Box 64526, 50 West Kellogg Boulevard, St. Paul, Minnesota 55164-0526. 1983. (Handbook).

LITIGATION AND INEQUALITY: FEDERAL DIVERSITY JURISDICTION IN INDUSTRIAL AMERICA, 1870-1958. Edward A. Purcell, Jr. Oxford University Press, 200 Madison Avenue, New York, New York 10016. 1992.

NATIONAL LAWS AND INTERNATIONAL COMMERCE: THE PROBLEM OF EXTRATERRITORIALITY. Douglas E. Rosenthal and William M. Knighton. Routledge and Kegan Paul, 29 West Thirty-fifth Street, New York, New York 10001. 1982.

NON-APPEARANCE BEFORE THE INTERNATIONAL COURT OF JUSTICE. H. W. A. Thirlway. Cambridge University Press, 40 West Twentieth Street, New York, New York 10011. 1985.

NON-APPEARANCE BEFORE THE INTERNATIONAL COURT OF JUSTICE: FUNCTIONAL AND COMPARATIVE ANALYSIS. Jerome B. Elkind. Kluwer Academic Publishers, 101 Philip Drive, Assinippi Park, Norwell, Massachusetts 02061. 1984.

THE QUESTION OF ARBITRABILITY: CHALLENGES TO THE ARBITRATUR'S JURISDICTION AND AUTHORITY. Mark M. Grossman. ILR Press, New York State School of Industrial Relations, Cornell University, Box 1000, Ithaca, New York 14851-0952. 1984.

REWRITING THE HISTORY OF THE JUDICIARY ACT OF 1789: EXPOSING MYTHS, CHALLENGING PREMISES, AND USING NEW EVIDENCE. Wilfred J. Ritz. University of Oklahoma Press, 105 Asp Avenue, Norman, Oklahoma 73019. 1990.

STATE IMMUNITY: AN ANALYTICAL AND PROGNOSTIC VIEW. Gamal Moursi Badr. Kluwer Academic Publishers, 101 Philip Drive, Assinippi Park, Norwell, Massachusetts 02061. 1984.

SUING FOREIGN GOVERNMENTS AND THEIR CORPORATIONS. Joseph W. Dellappenna. Bureau of National Affairs, Incorporated, 1231 Twenty-fifth Street, Northwest, Washington, D.C. 20037. 1988.

COMPUTER-ASSISTED LEGAL INSTRUCTION

ANALYSIS OF A DIVERSITY JURISDICTION CASE. Roger C. Park and Douglas D. McFarland. Center for Computer-Assisted Instruction, 229 19th Avenue South, University of Minnesota, Minneapolis, Minnesota 55455. Machine-readable computer file.

JURISDICTION AND VENUE. Roger C. Park and Douglas D. McFarland. Center for Computer-Assisted Instruction, 229 19th Avenue South, University of Minnesota, Minneapolis, Minnesota 55455. Machine- readable computer file.

OTHER SOURCES

THE JUDICIARY ACT OF 1789. David Eisenberg. National Archives and Records Administration, Eighth Street at Pennsylvania Avenue, Northwest, Washington, D.C. 20408. 1989.

REPORT TO THE ATTORNEY GENERAL ON FEDERAL HABEAS CORPUS REVIEW OF STATE JUDGMENTS. United States Department of Justice, Office of Legal Policy. Superintendent of Documents, United States Government Printing Office, Washington, D.C. 20402. 1988.

JURISDICTION, INTERNATIONAL LAW
See: INTERNATIONAL ARBITRATION;
INTERNATIONAL COURTS AND TRIBUNALS;
JURISDICTION

JURISPRUDENCE
See also: NATURAL LAW

TEXTBOOKS AND GENERAL WORKS

AMERICAN JURISPRUDENCE, 1870-1970: A HISTORY. James E. Herget. Rice University Press, P.O. Box 1892, Houston, Texas 77251. 1990.

AN ANALYSIS OF RIGHTS. S. J. Stoljar. Saint Martin's Press, Incorporated, 175 Fifth Avenue, New York, New York 10010. 1984.

THE AUTHORITATIVE AND AUTHORITARIAN. Joseph Vining. University of Chicago Press, 5801 Ellis Avenue, Third Floor, South, Chicago, Illinois 60637. 1988.

THE BATTLE OF DEMOCRACY: CONFLICT, CONSENSUS AND THE INDIVIDUAL. Barnes and Noble, HarperCollins Publishers, Incorporated, 10 East Fifty-third Street, New York, New York 10022. 1986.

BEYOND MONOPOLY: LAWYERS, STATE CRISES, AND PROFESSIONAL EMPOWERMENT. Terence C. Halliday. University of Chicago Press, 5801 Ellis Avenue, Chicago, Illinois 60637. 1987.

THE COMMON GOOD: ITS POLITICS, POLICIES AND PHILOSOPHY. Marcus G. Raskin. Routlege and Kegan Paul, 29 West Thirty-fifth Street, New York, New York 10001. 1986.

THE COMMON LAW AND ENGLISH JURISPRUDENCE, 1760-1850. Michael Lobban. Oxford University Press, 200 Madison Avenue, New York, New York 10016. 1991.

COMPARATIVE LEGAL CULTURES. Csaba Vargo. New York University Press, 70 Washington Square South, New York, New York 10012. 1992.

CONFLICTS OF LAW AND MORALITY. R. Kent Greenawalt. Oxford University Press, Incorporated, 200 Madison Avenue, New York, New York 10016. 1989.

THE CONSTITUTION, LAW, AND AMERICAN LIFE: CRITICAL ASPECTS OF THE NINETEENTH CENTURY EXPERIENCE. Donald G. Nieman. University of Georgia Press, Athens, Georgia 30602. 1992.

THE CONSTITUTIONAL BASES OF POLITICAL AND SOCIAL CHANGE IN THE UNITED STATES. Shlomo Slonim. Praeger Publishers, One Madison Avenue, New York, New York 10010-3603. 1990.

THE CRITICAL LEGAL STUDIES MOVEMENT. Roberto Mangabeira Unger. Harvard University Press, 79 Garden Street, Cambridge, Massachusetts 02138. 1986.

DANGEROUS SUPPLEMENTS: RESISTANCE AND RENEWAL IN JURISPRUDENCE. Peter Fitzpatrick. Duke University Press, Box 6697 College Station, Durham, North Carolina 27708. 1991.

THE DECLINE OF JUDICIAL REASON: DOCTRINE AND THEORY IN THE LEGAL ORDER. Nigel E. Simmonds. St. Martin's Press, Incorporated, 175 Fifth Avenue, New York, New York 10010. 1988.

THE DEMISE OF THE REASONABLE MAN: A CROSS-CULTURAL STUDY OF A LEGAL CONCEPT. Michael Saltman. Transaction Books, Rutgers University, New Brunswick, New Jersey 08903. 1991.

DESCENT INTO SUBJECTIVITY: STUDIES OF RAWLS, DWORKIN, AND UNGER IN THE CONTEXT OF MODERN THOUGHT. Cornelius F. Murphy, Jr. Longwood Academic, Wakefield, New Hampshire. 1990.

DIALECTIC OF NIHILISM: POST-STRUCTURALISM AND LAW. Gillian Rose. Basil Blackwell, 3 Cambridge Center, Cambridge, Massachusetts 02142. 1984.

THE DISORDER OF LAW: A CRITIQUE OF LEGAL THEORY. Charles Sampford. Basil Blackwell, Incorporated, 3 Cambridge Center, Cambridge, Massachusetts 02142. 1989.

THE END OF LAW? Timothy O'Hagen. Basil Blackwell, Incorporated, 3 Cambridge Center, Cambridge, Massachusetts 02142. 1985.

EQUAL JUSTICE. Eric Rakowski. Oxford University Press, 200 Madison Avenue, New York, New York 10016. 1991.

ESSAYS IN JURISPRUDENCE AND LEGAL HISTORY. John W. Salmond. Fred B. Rothman and Company, 10368 West Centennial Road, Littleton, Colorado 80127. 1891. (1987 Reprint).

ESSAYS IN JURISPRUDENCE AND PHILOSOPHY. H. L. Hart. Oxford University Press, Incorporated, 200 Madison Avenue, New York, New York 10016. 1984.

EVERYDAY JUSTICE: RESPONSIBILITY AND THE INDIVIDUAL IN JAPAN AND THE UNITED STATES. V. Lee Hamilton and Joseph Sanders. Yale University Press, 302 Temple Street, New Haven, Connecticut 06520. 1991.

FEMINISM AND THE POWER OF LAW. Carol Smart. Routledge, Chapman & Hall, 29 West Thirty-fifth Street, New York, New York 10001. 1989.

THE FORMATIVE ESSAYS OF JUSTICE HOLMES: THE MAKING OF AN AMERICAN LEGAL PHILOSOPHY. Frederic Rogers Kellogg. Greenwood Publishing Group, Incorporated, 88 Post Road West, Post Office Box 5007, Westport, Connecticut 06881. 1984.

THE FOUNDATION OF A FREE SOCIETY. Andrew R. Cecile. University of Texas Press, P.O. Box 7819, Austin, Texas 78713-7819. 1983.

GENERAL THEORY OF NORMS. Hans Kelsen. Oxford University Press, 200 Madison Avenue, New York, New York 10016. 1990.

GETTING JUSTICE AND GETTING EVEN: LEGAL CONSCIOUSNESS AMONG WORKING-CLASS AMERICANS. Sally Engle Merry. University of Chicago Press, 5801 Ellis Avenue, Chicago, Illinois 60637. 1990.

GROUNDS OF LIABILITY: AN INTRODUCTION TO THE LEGAL PHILOSOPHY OF LAW. Alan R. White. Clarendon Press, Oxford University Press, 200 Madison Avenue, New York, New York 10016. 1985.

HAYEK ON LIBERTY. Second Edition. John Gray. Basil Blackwell, Incorporated, 3 Cambridge Center, Cambridge, Massachusetts 02143. 1986.

THE HOLLOW HOPE: CAN COURTS BRING ABOUT SOCIAL CHANGE? Gerald N. Rosenberg. University of Chicago Press, 5801 Ellis Avenue, Chicago, Illinois 60637. 1991.

THE HUMAN MEASURE: SOCIAL THOUGHT IN THE WESTERN LEGAL TRADITION. Donald R. Kelley. Harvard University Press, 79 Garden Street, Cambridge, Massachusetts 02138. 1990.

INSTRUMENTALISM AND AMERICAN LEGAL THEORY. Robert S. Summers. Cornell University Press, 124 Roberts Place, Ithaca, New York 14850. 1980.

INTERPRETATION AND LEGAL THEORY. Andrei Marmor. Oxford University Press, 200 Madison Avenue, New York, New York 10016. 1992.

INTRODUCTION TO THE PROBLEMS OF LEGAL THEORY: A TRANSLATION OF THE FIRST EDITION OF THE REINE RECHTSLEHRE OR PURE THEORY OF LAW. Hans Kelsen. Oxford University Press, 200 Madison Avenue, New York, New York 10016. 1991.

AN INTRODUCTIONAL THEORY OF LAW: NEW APPROACHES TO LEGAL POSITIVISM. Neil MacCormick and Ota Weinberger. Kluwer Academic Publishers, 101 Philip Drive, Assinippi Park, Norwell, Massachusetts 02061. 1986.

AN INVITATION TO LAW AND SOCIAL SCIENCE: DESERTS, DISPUTES, AND DISTRIBUTION. Richard Lempert and Joseph Sanders, Editor. Longman, Incorporated, 19 West Forty-fourth Street, New York, New York 10036. 1986.

JOSEPH STORY AND THE COMITY OF ERRORS: A CASE STUDY IN CONFLICT OF LAWS. Alan Watson. University of Georgia Press, Athens, Georgia 30602. 1992.

JURISCULTURE. Gray Dorsey. Transaction Books, Rutgers University, New Brunswick, New Jersey 08903. 1989- .

JURISPRUDENCE: A DESCRIPTIVE AND NORMATIVE ANALYSIS OF LAW. Anthony D'Amato. Kluwer Academic Publishers, 101 Philip Drive, Assinippi Park, Norwell, Massachusetts 02061. 1984.

JURISPRUDENCE AS IDEOLOGY. Valerie Kerruish. Routledge, Chapman & Hall, 29 West Thirty-fifth Street, New York, New York 10001. 1991.

JURISPRUDENCE FOR A FREE SOCIETY: STUDIES IN LAW, SCIENCE, AND POLICY. Harold D. Lasswell and Myres S. McDougal. Martinus Nijhoff, Kluwer Academic Publishers, 101 Philip Drive, Assinippi Park, Norwell, Massachusetts 02061. 1991.

JURISPRUDENCE: UNDERSTANDING AND SHAPING LAW: CASES, READINGS, COMMENTARY. W. Michael Reisman and Aaron M. Schreiber. New Haven Press, P.O. Box 1751, New Haven, Connecticut 06511. 1987.

JURISPRUDENCE: WITH MEDICAL, LEGAL AND SCIENTIFIC SUBJECT ANALYSIS AND BIBLIOGRAPHY. Roy R. Zimmerman. ABBE Publishers Association of Washington, DC, 4111 Gallows Road, Annandale, Virginia 22003-1862. 1987.

JUSTICE. Thomas Morawetz, Editor. New York University Press, 70 Washington Square South, New York, New York 10012. 1991.

JUSTICE: INTERDISCIPLINARY PERSPECTIVES. Klaus R. Scherer. Cambridge University Press, 40 West Twentieth Street, New York, New York 10011. 1992.

JUSTICE OLIVER WENDELL HOLMES AND UTILITARIAN JURISPRUDENCE. H. L. Pohlman. Harvard University Press, 79 Garden Street, Cambridge, Massachusetts 02138. 1984.

JUSTIFYING LAW: THE DEBATE OVER FOUNDATIONS, GOALS, AND METHODS. Raymond A. Belliotti. Temple University Press, 1601 North Broad Street, University Services Building, Philadelphia, Pennsylvania 19122. 1991.

LAW AND ITS PRESUPPOSITIONS: ACTIONS, AGENTS AND RULES. S. C. Coval and J. C. Smith. Routledge and Kegan Paul, 29 West Thirty-fifth Street, New York, New York 10001. 1986.

LAW AND JUSTICE: AN INTRODUCTION. Richard A. Myren. Brooks/Cole Publishing Company, 511 Forest Lodge Road, Pacific Grove, California 93950. 1988.

LAW AND LIBERATION. Robert E. Rodes. University of Notre Dame Press, HarperCollins, Publishers, 10 East Fifty-third Street, New York, New York 10022. 1986.

LAW AND REVOLUTION: THE FORMATION OF THE WESTERN LEGAL TRADITION. Harold J. Berman. Harvard University Press, 79 Garden Street, Cambridge, Massachusetts 02138. 1983.

LAW AND SOCIETY. Third Edition. Steven Vago. Prentice-Hall, Incorporated, 113 Sylvan Avenue, Englewood Cliffs, New Jersey 07632. 1991.

LAW AND THE ORDER OF CULTURE. Robert Post, Editor. University of California Press, 2120 Berkeley Way, Berkeley, California 94720. 1991.

LAW AND THE SEARCH FOR COMMUNITY. Joel F. Handler. University of Pennsylvania Press, Blockley Hall, 418 Service Drive, Philadelphia, Pennsylvania 19104. 1990.

LAW AND THE SOCIAL SCIENCES. Leon Lipson and Stanton Wheeler, Editor. Russell Sage Foundation, HarperCollins Publishers, Incorporated, 10 East Fifty-third Street, New York, New York 10022. 1987.

LAW, CULTURE, AND VALUES: ESSAYS IN HONOR OF GRAY L. DORSEY. Sava Alexander Vojcanin, Editor. Transaction Books, Rutgers University, New Brunswick, New Jersey 08903. 1990.

LAW IN A CHANGING SOCIETY. Wolfgang Gaston Friedmann. Fred B. Rothman and Company, 10368 West Centennial Road, Littleton, Colorado 80127. 1959. (Reprint, 1988).

LAW, INSTITUTION, AND LEGAL POLITICS: FUNDAMENTAL PROBLEMS OF LEGAL THEORY AND SOCIAL PHILOSOPHY. Ota Weinberger. Kluwer Academic Publishers, 101 Philip Drive, Assinippi Park, Norwell, Massachusetts 02061. 1991.

LAW, INTERPRETATION, AND REALITY: ESSAYS IN EPISTEMOLOGY, HERMENEUTICS, AND JURISPRUDENCE. Patrick Nerhot, Editor. Kluwer Academic Publishers, 101 Philip Drive, Assinippi Park, Norwell, Massachusetts 02061. 1990.

LAW: ITS NATURE, FUNCTIONS, AND LIMITS. Third Edition. Robert S. Summers, Kevin M. Clermont, Robert A. Hillman, et al. West Publishing Company, P.O. Box 64526, 50 West Kellogg Boulevard, St. Paul, Minnesota 55164-0526. 1986.

LAW, MORALITY AND RIGHTS. M. A. Stewart. Kluwer Academic Publishers, 101 Philip Drive, Assinippi Park, Norwell, Massachusetts 02061. 1983.

LAW, ORDER, AND POWER. Second Edition. William Chambliss and Robert Seidman. Addison-Wesley Publishing Company, Route 128, Reading, Massachusetts 01867. 1982.

LAW, SOCIETY, AND CHANGE. Stephen Livingstone and John Morison, Editors. Dartmouth, Brookfield, Vermont. 1990.

THE LEGACY OF OLIVER WENDELL HOLMES, JR. Robert W. Gordon. Stanford University Press, Stanford, California 94305. 1992.

LEGAL DISCOURSE: STUDIES IN LINGUISTICS, RHETORIC, AND LEGAL ANALYSIS. Peter Goodrich. St. Martin's Press, Incorporated, 175 Fifth Avenue, New York, New York 10010. 1987.

LEGAL KNOWLEDGE AND ANALOGY: FRAGMENTS OF LEGAL EPISTEMOLOGY, HERMENEUTICS, AND LINGUISTICS. Patrick Nerhot. Kluwer Academic Publishers, 101 Philip Drive, Assinippi Park, Norwell, Massachusetts 02061. 1991.

LEGAL REALISM AND TWENTIETH-CENTURY AMERICAN JURISPRUDENCE: THE CHANGING CONSENSUS. Gary J. Aichele. Garland Publishing, Incorporated, 136 Madison Avenue, New York, New York 10016. 1990.

LEGAL SECRETS: EQUALITY AND EFFICIENCY IN THE COMMON LAW. Kim Lane Scheppele. University of Chicago Press, 5801 Ellis Avenue, Chicago, Illinois 60637. 1988.

LEGAL SOCIALIZATION: A STUDY OF NORMS AND RULES. Ellen S. Cohn and Susan O. White. Springer-Verlag New York, Incorporated, 175 Fifth Avenue, New York, New York 10010. 1990.

LEGAL THINKING: ITS LIMITS AND TENSIONS. William Read. University of Pennsylvania Press, Blockley Hall, 418 Service Drive, Philadelphia, Pennsylvania 19104. 1986.

LEGALISM: LAW, MORALS, AND POLITICAL TRIALS. Judith N. Shklar. Harvard University Press, 79 Garden Street, Cambridge, Massachusetts 02138. 1986.

LIBERTY AND JUSTICE. John Patrick Day. Routledge, Chapman and Hall, 29 West Thirty-fifth Street, New York, New York 10001. 1986.

LIBERTY, JUSTICE, AND MORALS: CONTEMPORARY VALUE CONFLICTS. Third Edition. Burton M. Leiser. Macmillan Publishing Company, Incorporated, 866 Third Avenue, New York, New York 10022. 1986.

THE LIMITS OF REASON: INDETERMINACY IN LAW, EDUCATION, AND MORALITY. John Eisenberg. Transaction Books, Rutgers University, New Brunswick, New Jersey 08903. 1992.

LITERACY, LAW, AND SOCIAL ORDER. Edward W. Stevens, Jr. Northern Illinois University Press, DeKalb, Illinois 60115. 1988.

LITIGATING MORALITY: AMERICAN LEGAL THOUGHT AND ITS ENGLISH ROOTS. Alice Fleetwood Bartee and Wayne C. Bartee. Praeger Publishers, One Madison Avenue, New York, New York 10010-3603. 1992.

LIVING LAW: THE TRANSFORMATION OF AMERICAN JURISPRUDENCE IN THE EARLY 20TH CENTURY. David M. Speak. Garland Publishing, Incorporated, 136 Madison Avenue, New York, New York 10016. 1987.

THE LOGIC OF LIBERTY. G. B. Madison. Greenwood Publishing Group, Incorporated, 88 Post Road West, P.O. Box 5007, Westport, Connecticut 06881. 1986.

MAKING ALL THE DIFFERENCE: INCLUSION, EXCLUSION, AND AMERICAN LAW. Martha Minow. Cornell University Press, 124 Roberts Place, Ithaca, New York 14850. 1990.

MAKING LAW BIND: ESSAYS LEGAL AND PHILOSOPHICAL. Tony Honore. Oxford University Press, 200 Madison Avenue, New York, New York 10016. 1987.

MARX AND JUSTICE: THE RACIAL CRITIQUE OF LIBERALISM. Allen E. Buchanan. Rowman and Allanheld, Division of Littlefield, Adams and Company, 420 Boston Way, Lanham, Maryland 20706. 1982.

A MATTER OF PRINCIPLE. Ronald M. Dworkin. Harvard University Press, 79 Garden Street, Cambridge, Massachusetts 02138. 1985.

MAX WEBER'S THEORY OF CONCEPT FORMATION: HISTORY, LAWS, IDEAL TYPES. Expanded Edition. Thomas Burger. Duke University Press, P.O. Box 6697, College Station, Durham, North Carolina 27708. 1987.

MONTESQUIEU AND HIS READER: A STUDY OF THE ESPRIT DES LOIS. Diane Kollar Monticone. University Press of America, 4720 Boston Way, Lanham, Maryland 20706. 1989.

MORAL ARGUMENT AND SOCIAL VISION IN THE COURTS: A STUDY OF TORT ACCIDENT LAW. Henry J. Steiner. University of Wisconsin Press, 114 North Murray, Madison, Wisconsin 53706. 1987.

THE MYTHOLOGY OF MODERN LAW. Peter Fitzpatrick. Routledge, Chapman & Hall, 29 West Thirty-fifth Street, New York, New York 10001. 1992.

NATURAL REASONS: PERSONALITY AND POLITY. S.L. Hurley. Oxford University Press, 200 Madison Avenue, New York, New York 10016. 1989.

THE NATURE OF THE LAW AND RELATED LEGAL WRITINGS. Robert Anthony Pascal, James Lee Babin and John William Corrington, Editors. Louisiana State University Press, Highland Road, Baton Rouge, Louisiana 70893. 1991.

NEW DIRECTIONS IN THE STUDY OF JUSTICE, LAW, AND SOCIAL CONTROL. Arizona State University. School of Justice Studies. Plenum Publishing Corporation, 233 Spring Street, New York, New York 10013. 1990.

ORDER WITHOUT LAW: HOW NEIGHBORS SETTLE DISPUTES. Robert C. Ellickson. Harvard University Press, 79 Garden Street, Cambridge, Massachusetts 02138. 1991.

PEIRCE AND LAW: ISSUES IN PRAGMATISM, LEGAL REALISM, AND SEMIOTICS. Roberta Kevelson. Peter Lang Publishing, Incorporated, 62 West Forty-fifth Street, New York, New York 10036. 1991.

A PHILOSOPHY OF FREE EXPRESSION AND ITS CONSTITUTIONAL APPLICATIONS. Robert F. Ladenson. Rowman and Allanheld, Division of Littlefield, Adams and Company, 420 Boston Way, Lanham, Maryland 20706. 1983.

PHILOSOPHY OF LAW. Fourth Edition. Joel Feinberg and Hyman Gross. Wadsworth Publishing Company, 10 Davis Drive, Belmont, California 94002. 1991.

PHILOSOPHY OF LAW: AN INTRODUCTION TO JURISPRUDENCE. Jeffrie G. Murphy and Jules L. Coleman. Westview Press, Incorporated, 5500 Central Avenue, Boulder, Colorado 80301. 1990.

THE POLITICS OF JURISPRUDENCE: A CRITICAL INTRODUCTION TO LEGAL PHILOSOPHY. Roger Cotterrell. University of Pennsylvania Press, Blockley Hall, 418 Service Drive, Philadelphia, Pennsylvania 19104. 1992.

POSTMODERN JURISPRUDENCE: THE LAW OF TEXT IN THE TEXTS OF LAW. Costas Douzinas and Ronnie Warrington with Shaun McVeigh. Routledge, Chapman & Hall, 29 West Thirty-fifth Street, New York, New York 10001. 1991.

PRAGMATISM IN LAW AND SOCIETY. Michael Brint and William Weaver. Westview Press, Incorporated, 5500 Central Avenue, Boulder, Colorado 80301. 1991.

A PRIMER IN THE SOCIOLOGY OF LAW. Dragan Milovanovic. Harrow and Heston, P.O. Box 3934 Stuyvesant Plaza, Albany, New York 12203. 1988.

PRINCIPLES OF LAW: A NORMATIVE ANALYSIS. Michael D. Bayles. D. Reidel Publishing Company, Available from: Kluwer Academic Publishers, 101 Philip Drive, Assinippi Park, Norwell, Massachusetts 02061. 1987.

THE PROBLEMS OF JURISPRUDENCE. Richard A. Posner. Harvard University Press, 79 Garden Street, Cambridge, Massachusetts 02138. 1990.

PRUDENCE AND JURISPRUDENCE: READINGS IN THE MEMORY OF LAW. Peter J. Riga. Associated Faculty Press, 19 West Thirty-sixth Street, New York, New York 10018. 1986.

READINGS IN PHILOSOPHY OF LAW. John Arthur and William Shaw, Editors. Prentice-Hall, Incorporated, 113 Sylvan Avenue, Englewood Cliffs, New Jersey 07632. 1984.

REASON IN LAW. Third Edition. Lief H. Carter. Scott, Foresman, and Company, 1900 East Lake Avenue, Glenview, Illinois 60025. 1988.

THE REPUBLIC OF CHOICE: LAW, AUTHORITY, AND CULTURE. Lawrence M. Friedman. Harvard University Press, 79 Garden Street, Cambridge, Massachusetts 02138. 1990.

REVOLUTIONARY POLITICS AND LOCKE'S TWO TREATISES OF GOVERNMENT. Richard Ashcraft. Princeton University Press, 41 William Street, Princeton, New Jersey 08540. 1986.

RIGHTS. Alan R. White. Oxford University Press, Incorporated, 200 Madison Avenue, New York, New York 10016. 1984.

THE ROLE OF COURTS IN SOCIETY. Shimon Shetreet. Martinus Nijhoff, Kluwer Academic Publishers, 101 Philip Drive, Assinippi Park, Norwell, Massachusetts 02061. 1988.

RONALD DWORKIN AND CONTEMPORARY JURISPRUDENCE. Marshall Cohen, Editor. Rowman and Allanheld, Division of Littlefield, Adams and Company, 420 Boston Way, Lanham, Maryland 20706. 1984.

RULES VERSUS RELATIONSHIPS: THE ETHNOGRAPHY OF LEGAL DISCOURSE. John M. Conley and William M. O'Barr. University of Chicago Press, 5801 Ellis Avenue, Chicago, Illinois 60637. 1990.

SEMIOTICS AND LEGAL THEORY. Bernard S. Jackson. Routledge and Kegan Paul, 29 West Thirty-fifth Street, New York, New York 10001. 1987.

A SHORT HISTORY OF LEGAL THINKING IN THE WEST. Stig Stromholm. Norstedts Foring AB, Fred B. Rothman and Company, 10368 West Centennial Road, Littleton, Colorado 80127. 1986.

A SHORT HISTORY OF WESTERN LEGAL THEORY. J.M. Kelly. Oxford University Press, 200 Madison Avenue, New York, New York 10016. 1992.

SIR HENRY MAINE: A STUDY IN VICTORIAN JURISPRUDENCE. R.C.J. Cocks. Cambridge University Press, 40 West Twentieth Street, New York, New York 10011. 1988.

SOCIAL STRUCTURE AND LAW: THEORETICAL AND EMPIRICAL PERSPECTIVES. William M. Evan. Sage Publications, 2455 Teller Road, Newbury Park, California 91320. 1990.

SOCIOLOGICAL JUSTICE. Donald Black. Oxford University Press, 200 Madison Avenue, New York, New York 10016. 1989.

SPHERES OF LIBERTY: CHANGING PERCEPTIONS OF LIBERTY IN AMERICAN CULTURE. Michael Kammen. University of Wisconsin Press, 114 North Murray Street, Madison, Wisconsin 53706. 1986.

TACTICS OF LEGAL REASONING. Pierre Schlag and David Skover. Carolina Academic Press, P.O. Box 51879, Forest Hills Station, Durham, North Carolina 27717. 1986.

A THEORY OF LAW. Phillip Soper. Harvard University Press, 79 Garden Street, Cambridge, Massachusetts 02138. 1984.

A THEORY OF RIGHTS: PERSONS UNDER LAWS, INSTITUTIONS, AND MORALS. Carl Wellman. Rowman and Allanheld, Division of Littlefield, Adams and Company, 420 Boston Way, Lanham, Maryland 20706. 1985.

THERAPEUTIC JURISPRUDENCE: THE LAW AS A THERAPEUTIC AGENT. David B. Wexler. Carolina Academic Press, P.O. Box 51879, Durham, North Carolina 27717. 1990.

TOTAL JUSTICE. Lawrence M. Friedman. Beacon Press, 25 Beacon Street, Boston, Massachusetts 02108. 1987.

THE TRANSFORMATION OF AMERICAN LAW, 1870-1960: THE CRISIS OF LEGAL ORTHODOXY. Morton J. Horwitz. Oxford University Press, 200 Madison Avenue, New York, New York 10016. 1992.

THE UNITY OF LAW AND MORALITY: A REFUTATION OF LEGAL POSITIVISM. M. J. Detmold. Routledge and Kegan Paul, 29 West Thirty-fifth Street, New York, New York 10001. 1984.

UTILITARIAN JURISPRUDENCE IN AMERICA: THE INFLUENCE OF BENTHAM AND AUSTIN ON AMERICAN LEGAL THOUGHT IN THE NINETEENTH CENTURY. Peter J. King. Garland Publishing, Incorporated, 136 Madison Avenue, New York, New York 10016. 1986.

Encyclopedia of Legal Information Sources • 2nd Ed. JURY

THE VICTORIAN ACHIEVEMENT OF SIR HENRY MAINE: A CENTENNIAL REAPPRAISAL. Alan Diamond. Cambridge University Press, 40 West Twentieth Street, New York, New York 10011. 1991.

WITTGENSTEIN AND LEGAL THEORY. Dennis M. Patterson. Westview Press, Incorporated, 5500 Central Avenue, Boulder, Colorado 80301. 1992.

DIGESTS, INDEXES, ABSTRACTS, CITATORS

JURISPRUDENCE AND CONFIDENTIALITY: INDEX OF MODERN INFORMATION. Harold P. Drummond. ABBE Publishers Association of Washington, DC, 4111 Gallows Road, Annandale, Virginia 22003-1862. 1991.

ANNUALS AND SURVEYS

OXFORD ESSAYS IN JURISPRUDENCE. THIRD SERIES. John Eekelaar and John Bell. Oxford University Press, 200 Madison Avenue, New York, New York 10016. 1987.

LAW REVIEWS AND PERIODICALS

AMERICAN JOURNAL OF JURISPRUDENCE. University of Notre Dame, School of Law, Notre Dame, Indiana 46556. Annual.

THE LEGAL STUDIES FORUM. American Legal Studies Association, Department of Legal Studies, University of Massachusetts, Amherst, Massachusetts 01003. Three issues per year.

BIBLIOGRAPHIES

CRITICAL LEGAL STUDIES AND SOCIOLOGICAL JURISPRUDENCE: SOCIAL AND CULTURAL FACTORS IN THE ADMINISTRATION OF JUSTICE. Tim J. Watts. Vance Bibliographies, P.O. Box 229, 112 North Charter Street, Monticello, Illinois 61856. 1987.

ROSCOE POUND'S SOCIOLOGICAL LIBRARY: THE FOUNDATIONS OF AMERICAN SOCIOLOGICAL JURISPRUDENCE, A BIBLIOGRAPHY. Michael R. Hill. Vance Bibliographies, P.O. Box 229, 112 North Charter Street, Monticello, Illinois 61856. 1989.

ASSOCIATIONS AND PROFESSIONAL SOCIETIES

AMERICAN SOCIETY FOR POLITICAL AND LEGAL PHILOSOPHY. c/o Professor Martin P. Golding. Philosophy Department, Duke University, Durham, North Carolina 27708. (919) 648-3838.

ASSOCIATION OF AMERICAN LAW SCHOOLS, SECTION ON JURISPRUDENCE. One Dupont Circle, Northwest, Washington, D.C. 20036. (202) 296-8851.

CENTER FOR PHILOSOPHY, LAW, CITIZENSHIP. Knapp Hall 15, State University of New York, Farmingdale, New York 11735. (516) 420-2047.

RESEARCH CENTERS, INSTITUTES, CLEARINGHOUSES

COUNCIL FOR THE STUDY OF ETHICS AND PUBLIC POLICY. Powder Maker Hall, Room 360, Flushing, New York 11367. (718) 520-7402.

INSTITUTE FOR HUMANE STUDIES. George Mason University, 4400 University Drive, Fairfax, Virginia 22030. (703) 323-1055.

JURISPRUDENCE CENTRE. Carleton University, Law Deprtment, Ottawa, Ontario, Canada K1S 5B6. (613) 564-7540.

JURY
See also: DUE PROCESS OF LAW; GRAND JURY

STATUTES, CODES, STANDARDS, UNIFORM LAWS

STANDARDS RELATING TO JUROR USE AND MANAGEMENT. American Bar Association, 750 North Lake Shore Drive, Chicago, Illinois 60611. 1983.

UNIFORM JURY SELECTION AND SERVICE ACT. Uniform Laws Annotated. West Publishing Company, P.O. Box 64526, 50 West Kellogg Boulevard, St. Paul, Minnesota 55164-0526. 1976. (Annual Supplements).

LOOSELEAF SERVICES AND REPORTERS

BAJI FORMS--CALIFORNIA JURY INSTRUCTIONS, CIVIL. Seventh Edition. California Superior Court. West Publishing Company, 50 West Kellogg Boulevard, St. Paul, Minnesota 55164. 1989- .

COLORADO JURY INSTRUCTIONS--CIVIL. Colorado Supreme Court Committee on Civil Jury Instructions. Bancroft-Whitney Company, P.O. Box 7005, San Francisco, California 94120. 1989- .

FLORIDA FORMS OF JURY INSTRUCTIONS. Matthew Bender and Company, Incorporated, 11 Penn Plaza, New York, New York 10001. 1989- .

ILLINOIS NON-PATTERN JURY INSTRUCTIONS. Second Edition. Carl L. Rowley and Jon M. Moyers. Lawyers Cooperative Publishing Company, Aqueduct Building, Rochester, New York 14694. 1991- .

ILLINOIS PATTERN JURY INSTRUCTIONS, CIVIL [IPI]. Third Edition. Illinois Supreme Court Committee on Jury Instructions in Civil Cases. West Publishing Company, 50 West Kellogg Boulevard, St. Paul, Minnesota 55164. 1990- .

INDIANA PATTERN JURY INSTRUCTIONS, CIVIL. Second Edition. Michie Company, P.O. Box 7587, Charlottesville, Virginia 22906. 1989.

INDIANA PATTERN JURY INSTRUCTIONS, CRIMINAL. Second Edition. Michie Company, P.O. Box 7587, Charlottesville, Virginia 22906. 1991.

JUROR MISCONDUCT: LAW AND LITIGATION. Lillian B. Hardwick and B. Lee Ware. Clark Boardman Company, Limited, 435 Hudson Street, New York, New York 10014. 1988- .

SAMPLE JURY INSTRUCTIONS IN CIVIL ANTITRUST CASES. American Bar Association, 750 North Lake Shore Drive, Chicago, Illinois 60611. 1987- .

VIRGINIA MODEL JURY INSTRUCTIONS, CRIMINAL. Michie Company, P.O. Box 7587, Charlottesville, Virginia 22906. 1989.

HANDBOOKS, MANUALS, FORMBOOKS

ANTITRUST CIVIL JURY INSTRUCTIONS. Section of Antitrust Law, American Bar Association, 750 North Lake Shore Drive, Chicago, Illinois 60611. 1980 (Supplement 1986).

THE ART OF SELECTING A JURY. Second Edition. Robert A. Wenke. Charles C. Thomas, Publishers, 2600 South First Street, Springfield, Illinois 62794. 1989.

CALIFORNIA JURY INSTRUCTIONS, CRIMINAL. Fifth Edition. Arnold Levin, Editor. West Publishing Company, 50 West Kellogg Boulevard, St. Paul, Minnesota 55164. 1988.

FEDERAL CRIMINAL JURY INSTRUCTIONS. Stephen H. Saltzburg and Harvey S. Perlman. The Michie Company, P.O. Box 7587, Charlottesville, Virginia 22906-7582. 1985.

FEDERAL JURY PRACTICE AND INSTRUCTIONS: CIVIL AND CRIMINAL. Third Edition. Edward J. Devitt and Charles B. Blackmar. West Publishing Company, P.O. Box 64526, 50 West Kellogg Boulevard, St. Paul, Minnesota 55164-0526. 1982 (Supplement 1985).

HANDBOOK ON ANTITRUST GRAND JURY INVESTIGATIONS: A PROJECT OF THE CRIMINAL PRACTICE AND PROCEDURE COMMITTEE OF THE ANTITRUST SECTION OF THE AMERICAN BAR ASSOCIATION. Second Edition. Ray V. Hartwell III and Christoper J. Mugel, Editors. American Bar Association, Section of Antitrust Law, Criminal Practice and Procedure Committee, 750 North Lake Shore Drive, Chicago, Illinois 60611.

HANDBOOK ON JURY USE IN THE FEDERAL DISTRICT COURTS. Jody George, Deirdre Golash and Russell Wheeler. Federal Judicial Center, 1520 H Street, Northwest, Washington, D.C. 20005. 1989.

INSTRUCTIONS FOR VIRGINIA AND WEST VIRGINIA. Third Edition. Michie Company, P.O. Box 7587, Charlottesville, Virginia 22906. 1987.

JURY ARGUMENT IN CRIMINAL CASES: A TRIAL LAWYER'S GUIDE. Ray Moses. Azimuth Press, P.O. Box 66212, Houston, Texas 77266. 1985.

JURY INSTRUCTIONS IN AUTOMOBILE NEGLIGENCE AND RELATED CASES. Graham Douthwaite. Allen Smith Company, Incorporated, 1435 North Meridian Street, Indianapolis, Indiana 46202. 1986. (1990 Supplement).

JURY INSTRUCTIONS IN INTELLECTUAL PROPERTY CASES. Duane Burton. Big Foot Press, 1720 South Bellaire Street, Suite 1100, Denver, Colorado 80222. 1980 (Supplement 1984).

JURY INSTRUCTIONS ON DAMAGES IN TORT ACTIONS. Second Edition. Graham Douthwaite. The Michie Company, P.O. Box 7587, Charlottesville, Virginia 22906-7582. 1988. (Supplement 1990).

JURY INSTRUCTIONS ON MEDICAL ISSUES. Third Edition. Graham Douthwaite and George J. Alexander. Michie Company, P.O. Box 7587, Charlottesville, Virginia 22906. 1987.

JURY INSTRUCTIONS ON PRODUCTS LIABILITY. Graham Douthwaite. Michie Company, P.O. Box 7587, Charlottesville, Virginia 22906. 1987.

JURY SELECTION: AN ATTORNEY'S GUIDE TO JURY LAW AND METHODS. V. Hale Starr and Mark McCormick. Little, Brown, and Company, 34 Beacon Street, Boston, Massachusetts 02108. 1985.

JURY SELECTION PROCEDURES IN UNITED STATES DISTRICT COURTS. Gordon Bermant. Federal Judicial Center, 1520 H Street, Northwest, Washington, D.C. 20005. 1982.

JURY SELECTION: THE LAW, ART, AND SCIENCE OF SELECTING A JURY. Second Edition. James J. Gobert and Walter E. Jordan. Shepard's/McGraw-Hill, P.O. Box 1235, Colorado Springs, Colorado 80901. 1990.

MANUAL OF MODEL JURY INSTRUCTIONS FOR THE NINTH CIRCUIT. West Publishing Company, P.O. Box 64526, 50 West Kellogg Boulevard, St. Paul, Minnesota 55164-0526. 1985.

MARYLAND CRIMINAL JURY INSTRUCTIONS AND COMMENTARY. Second Edition. David E. Aaronson. Michie Company, P.O. Box 7587, Charlottesville, Virginia 22906. 1988.

MINNESOTA JURY INSTRUCTION GUIDES, MISDEMEANOR AND GROSS MISDEMEANOR. West Publishing Company, 50 West Kellogg Boulevard, St. Paul, Minnesota 55164. 1989.

MODEL JURY INSTRUCTIONS FOR BUSINESS TORT LITIGATION: A PROJECT OF THE BUSINESS TORTS LITIGATION COMMITTEE, SUBCOMMITTEE ON JURY INSTRUCTIONS, SECTION OF LITIGATION, AMERICAN BAR ASSOCIATION. Second Edition. American Bar Association, 750 North Lake Shore Drive, Chicago, Illinois 60611. 1988.

MODERN FEDERAL JURY INSTRUCTIONS: CRIMINAL. Leonard Sand and John S. Siffert. Matthew Bender and Company, Incorporated, 11 Penn Plaza, New York, New York 10001. 1984 (Periodic Supplements).

NEW YORK FORMS OF JURY INSTRUCTION. Vincent C. Alexander. Matthew Bender and Company, Incorporated, 11 Penn Plaza, New York, New York 10001. 1992.

SAMPLE JURY INSTRUCTIONS IN CRIMINAL ANTITRUST CASES. ABA, Section of Antitrust Law. American Bar Association, 750 North Lake Shore Drive, Chicago, Illinois 60611. 1984.

TENNESSEE PATTERN JURY INSTRUCTIONS, CIVIL. Second Edition. June F. Entman. West Publishing Company, 50 West Kellogg Boulevard, St. Paul, Minnesota 55164. 1988.

TENNESSEE PATTERN JURY INSTRUCTIONS, CRIMINAL. Second Edition. Donald J. Hall. West Publishing Company, 50 West Kellogg Boulevard, St. Paul, Minnesota 55164. 1988.

TOWARD MORE ACTIVE JURIES: TAKING NOTES AND ASKING QUESTIONS. American Judicature Society, 25 East Washington Street, Suite 1600, Chicago, Illinois 60602. 1991.

VIRGINIA JURY INSTRUCTIONS. Second Edition. Emanual Emroch. West Publishing Company, 50 West Kellogg Boulevard, St. Paul, Minnesota 55164. 1990.

WASHINGTON PATTERN JURY INSTRUCTIONS. CIVIL, WPI. Third Edition. West Publishing Company, 50 West Kellogg Boulevard, St. Paul, Minnesota 55164. 1989.

A WINNING CASE: HOW TO USE PERSUASIVE COMMUNICATION TECHNIQUES FOR SUCCESSFUL TRIAL WORK. Noelle C. Nelson. Prentice-Hall, Incorporated, 113 Sylvan Avenue, Englewood Cliffs, New Jersey 07632. 1991.

TEXTBOOKS AND GENERAL WORKS

ANALYTIC JUROR RATER. Walter F. Abbott. American Law Institute-American Bar Association, 4025 Chestnut Street, Philadelphia, Pennsylvania 19104. 1987.

ANATOMY OF A JURY: THE SYSTEM ON TRIAL. Seymour Wishman. Times Books, Viking Penquin, 375 Hudson Street, New York, New York 10014-3657. 1987.

THE ART OF ADVOCACY: JURY SELECTION. Ward Wagner. Matthew Bender and Company, Incorporated, 11 Penn Plaza, New York, New York 10001. 1981 (Periodic Supplements).

CIVIL JURIES IN THE 1980s: TRENDS IN JURY TRIALS AND VERDICTS IN CALIFORNIA AND COOK COUNTY, ILLINOIS. Mark A. Peterson. Rand Corporation, Institute for Civil Justice, 1700 Main Street, P.O. Box 2138, Santa Monica, California 90406. 1987.

COMPLEX LITIGATION CONFRONTS THE JURY SYSTEM: A CASE STUDY. Arthur D. Austin. Greenwood Publishing Group, Incorporated, 88 Post Road West, P.O. Box 5007, Westport, Connecticut 06881. 1984.

THE DEBATE OVER JURY PERFORMANCE: OBSERVATIONS FROM A RECENT ASBESTOS CASE. Molly Selvin and Larry Picus. Rand Corporation, Institute for Civil Justice, 1700 Main Street, P.O. Box 2138, Santa Monica, California 90406. 1987.

FEDERAL GRAND JURY PRACTICE AND PROCEDURE. Paul S. Diamond. Prentice-Hall, Incorporated, 113 Sylvan Avenue, Englewood Cliffs, New Jersey 07632. 1990- .

INSIDE THE JUROR: THE PSYCHOLOGY OF JUROR DECISION MAKING. Reid Hastie, Editor. Cambridge University Press, 40 West Twentieth Street, New York, New York 10011. 1992.

INSIDE THE JURY. Reid Hastie. Harvard University Press, 79 Garden Street, Cambridge, Massachusetts 02138. 1984.

IN THE JURY BOX: CONTROVERSIES IN THE COURTROOM. Lawrence S. Wrightsman, Saul M. Kassin and Cynthia E. Willis. Sage Publications, 2455 Teller Road, Newbury Park, California 91320. 1987.

JUDGING THE JURY. Valerie P. Hans and Neil Vidmar. Plenum Publishing Corporation, 233 Spring Street, New York, New York 10013. 1986.

JURIES AND POLITICS. James P. Levine. Brooks/Cole Publishing Company, 511 Forest Lodge Road, Pacific Grove, California 93950. 1992.

JURIES ON TRIAL: FACES OF AMERICAN JUSTICE. Paula Diperna. W. W. Norton and Company, Incorporated, 500 Fifth Avenue, New York, New York 10110. 1984.

JURY COMPREHENSION IN COMPLEX CASES: REPORT OF THE SPECIAL COMMITTEE OF THE ABA SECTION OF LITIGATION. Daniel H. Margolis. American Bar Association, Section of Litigation, Special Committee on Jury Comprehension, 750 North Lake Shore Drive, Chicago, Illinois 60611. 1990.

THE JURY IN AMERICA. John Guinther. Facts on File, Incorporated, 460 Park Avenue South, New York, New York 10016. 1988.

JURY SELECTION. Walter E. Jordan. Shepard's/McGraw-Hill, P.O. Box 1235, Colorado Springs, Colorado 80901. 1980 (Supplement 1985).

JURY SELECTION, BODY LANGUAGE AND THE VISUAL TRIAL. James Rasicot. AB Publications, 6705 Woodedge Road, Mound, Minnesota 55364-8104. 1983.

JURY SELECTION IN CIVIL AND CRIMINAL TRIALS. Second Edition. Ann F. Ginger. Lawpress, P.O. Box 596, Kentfield, California 94914. 1984.

JURY SELECTION IN CRIMINAL TRIALS: NEW TECHNIQUES AND CONCEPTS. Ann F. Ginger. Lawpress, P.O. Box 596, Kentfield, California 94914, 1975 (Periodic Supplements).

JURY SERVICE IN LENGTHY CIVIL TRIALS. Joe S. Cecil, E. Allan Lind and Gordon Bermant. Federal Judicial Center, 1520 H Street, Northwest, Washington, D.C. 20005. 1987.

THE JURY: TECHNIQUES FOR TRIAL LAWYERS. J. R. Wing, Chairman. Practising Law Institute, 810 Seventh Avenue, New York, New York 10019. 1984.

THE JURY, TOOL OF KINGS, PALLADIUM OF LIBERTY. Second Edition. Lloyd E. Moore. Anderson Publishing Company, 2035 Reading Road, Cincinnati, Ohio 45202. 1988.

JURY TRIAL LAW AND PRACTICE. Richardson R. Lynn. John Wiley and Sons, Incorporated, 605 Third Avenue, New York, New York 10158. 1986.

JURY WORK: SYSTEMATIC TECHNIQUES. Second Edition. National Jury Project. Clark Boardman Company, Limited, 435 Hudson Street, New York, New York 10014. 1983.

MAKING JURY INSTRUCTIONS UNDERSTANDABLE. Amiram Elwork and Bruce D. Sales. Michie/Bobbs-Merrill, The Michie Company, P.O. Box 7587, Charlottesville, Virginia 22906-7582. 1982.

MAXIMIZING DAMAGES THROUGH VOIR DIRE AND SUMMATION. Thomas William Malone. Harrison Company, 3110 Crossing Park, Norcross, Georgia 30091. 1988.

MODERN CIVIL JURY SELECTION. Arne Werchick. John Wiley and Sons, Incorporated, 605 Third Avenue, New York, New York 10158. 1991.

THE PSYCHOLOGY OF THE AMERICAN JURY. Jeffrey T. Frederick. Michie Company, P.O. Box 7587, Charlottesville, Virginia 22906. 1987.

TRIAL BY JURY. Jo Kolanda and Judge Patricia Curley. Franklin Watts, Incorporated, 387 Park Avenue South, New York, New York 10016. 1988.

TRIAL PSYCHOLOGY: COMMUNICATION AND PERSUASION IN THE COURTROOM. Margaret C. Roberts. Butterworth Legal Publishers, 90 Stiles Road, Salem, New Hampshire 03079. 1987.

TWELVE GOOD MEN AND TRUE: THE CRIMINAL TRIAL JURY IN ENGLAND 1200-1800. J.S. Cockburn and Thomas A. Green, Editors. Princeton University Press, 41 William Street, Princeton, New Jersey 08540. 1988.

VERDICT ACCORDING TO CONSCIENCE: PERSPECTIVES ON THE ENGLISH CRIMINAL TRIAL JURY, 1200-1800. Thomas A. Green. University of Chicago Press, 5801 Ellis Avenue, Third Floor, South, Chicago, Illinois 60637. 1988.

WHAT MAKES JURIES LISTEN: A COMMUNICATIONS EXPERT LOOKS AT THE TRIAL. Sonya Hamlin. Harcourt Brace Jovanovich, Incorporated, 6277 Sea Harbor Drive, Orlando, Florida 32821. 1984.

WINNING JURY TRIALS: LOOKING AT THE CASE THROUGH THE EYES OF THE JURY. Massachusetts Continuing Legal Education, 20 West Street, Boston, Massachusetts 02111. 1990.

NEWSLETTERS AND NEWSPAPERS

ATLA LAW REPORTER. Association of Trial Lawyers of America, 1050 31st Street, Northwest, Washington, D.C. 20007. Monthly.

MEDICAL MALPRACTICE VERDICTS, SETTLEMENTS AND EXPERTS. Lewis Laska, 901 Church Street, Nashville, Tennessee 37203. Monthly.

NATIONAL VERDICT SURVEY. Jury Verdict Research, Incorporated, 5325-B Naiman Parkway, Solon, Ohio 44139. Weekly.

NEWSLETTER - GRAND JURY EXCHANGE SEMINAR. American Grand Jury Foundation, 1120 Fourteenth Street, Suite 5, Modesto, California 95354. Semiannually.

VERDICT REVIEWS. Jury Verdict Research, Incorporated, 5325-B Naiman Parkway, Solon, Ohio 44139. Weekly.

VERDICTS AND SETTLEMENTS. Litigation Research Group, 425 Brannon Street, San Francisco, California 94107. Monthly.

ASSOCIATIONS AND PROFESSIONAL SOCIETIES

NATIONAL JURY PROJECT. 1540 San Pablo Avenue, Ninth Floor, Oakland, California 94612. (415) 832-2583.

RESEARCH CENTERS, INSTITUTES, CLEARINGHOUSES

AMERICAN GRAND JURY FOUNDATION. 1120 Fourteenth Street, Suite 5, Modesto, California 95354. (209) 527-0966.

CENTER FOR RESPONSIVE PSYCHOLOGY. Brooklyn College of City University of New York, Brooklyn, New York 11210. (718) 780-5960.

JEFFERSON CENTER. 530 Plymouth Building, Minneapolis, Minnesota 55402. (602) 333-5300.

NATIONAL CENTER FOR STATE COURTS. 300 Newport Avenue, Williamsburg, Virginia 23187. (804) 253-2000.

AUDIOVISUALS

ADVOCACY AND THE ART OF STORYTELLING. National Institute for Trial Advocacy, Notre Dame Law School, Notre Dame, Indiana 46556. 1990. Videotape.

ART OF ADVOCACY: SELECTING AND PERSUADING THE JURY. National Institute for Trial Advocacy, Notre Dame Law School, Notre Dame, Indiana 46556. 1988. Videotape.

JURY COMPREHENSION IN COMPLEX CASES. American Bar Association, 750 North Lake Shore Drive, Chicago, Illinois 60611. 1990. Videotape.

JURY SELECTION. Irving Younger. Professional Education Systems, Incorporated, 3410 Sky Park Boulevard, Eau Claire, Wisconsin 54702. 1985. Videotape.

JURY SELECTION: A LECTURE BY CHARLES BECTON. Consortium for Professional Education, American Bar Association, 750 North Lake Shore Drive, Chicago, Illinois 60611. 1980. Videotape.

JURY SELECTION: QUESTIONS AND CHALLENGES. Consortium for Professional Education, American Bar Association, 750 North Lake Shore Drive, Chicago, Illinois 60611. 1980. Videotape.

PICKING AND PERSUADING A JURY: 1. SELECTING A JURY - DEMONSTRATION AND TECHNIQUE; 2. THE JUROR'S PERSPECTIVE; 3. CASE AND COMMUNITY ANALYSIS; 4. LANGUAGE AND COMMUNICATION; 5. PERSUADING THE JURY. Consortium for Professional Education, American Bar Association, 750 North Lake Shore Drive, Chicago, Illinois 60611. 1980. Videotape.

SYSTEMATIC JURY SELECTION TECHNIQUES: A LECTURE BY HANS ZEISEL. Consortium for Professional Education, American Bar Association, 750 North Lake Shore Drive, Chicago, Illinois 60611. 1980. Videotape.

JUSTICE DEPARTMENT
See also: ATTORNEY GENERAL (UNITED STATES); CIVIL RIGHTS COMMISSION; FEDERAL BUREAU OF INVESTIGATION; IMMIGRATION AND NATURALIZATION SERVICE

STATUTES, CODES, STANDARDS, UNIFORM LAWS

CODE OF FEDERAL REGULATIONS, TITLE 28. Office of the Federal Register, National Archives and Records Administration. Superintendent of Documents, United States Government Printing Office, Washington, D.C. 20402. Annual. (Updated by use of monthly List of Sections Affected and daily Federal Register.)

LOOSELEAF SERVICES AND REPORTERS

THE DEPARTMENT OF JUSTICE MANUAL. Prentice-Hall, Incorporated, 113 Sylvan Avenue, Englewood Cliffs, New Jersey 07632. 1987- .

OPINIONS OF THE OFFICE OF LEGAL COUNSEL OF THE UNITED STATES DEPARTMENT OF JUSTICE. Justice Department, Office of Legal Counsel. Superintendent of Documents, United States Government Printing Office, Washington, D.C. 20402. 1977- .

HANDBOOKS, MANUALS, FORMBOOKS

FEDERAL GRAND JURY PRACTICE MANUAL. Justice Department, Criminal Division, Narcotics and Dangerous Drug Section. Superintendent of Documents, United States Government Printing Office, Washington, D.C. 20402. 1983.

HANDBOOK ON THE COMPREHENSIVE CRIME CONTROL ACT OF 1984 AND OTHER CRIMINAL STATUTES ENACTED BY THE 98TH CONGRESS. Justice Department. Superintendent of Documents, United States Government Printing Office, Washington, D.C. 20402. 1984.

UNITED STATES ATTORNEYS' MANUAL TITLES 1-8. Justice Department. Superintendent of Documents, United States Government Printing Office, Washington, D.C. 20402. 1985- .

UNITED STATES ATTORNEY'S MANUAL TITLE 9, CRIMINAL DIVISION. Justice Department. Superintendent of Documents, United States Government Printing Office, Washington, D.C. 20402. 1985- .

TEXTBOOKS AND GENERAL WORKS

ADMINISTRATIVE HISTORY OF THE CIVIL RIGHTS DIVISION OF THE DEPARTMENT OF JUSTICE DURING THE JOHNSON ADMINISTRATION. Garland Publishing, Incorporated, 136 Madison Avenue, New York, New York 10016. 1991.

AGENT ORANGE: PRODUCT LIABILITY LITIGATION. Justice Department, United States Court Eastern District of New York. Superintendent of Documents, United States Government Printing Office, Washington, D.C. 20402. 1984.

ATTORNEY GENERAL'S COMMISSION ON PORNOGRAPHY, FINAL REPORT. Justice Department. Superintendent of Documents, United States Government Printing Office, Washington, D.C. 20402. 1986.

THE ATTORNEY GENERAL'S LAWYER: INSIDE THE MEESE JUSTICE DEPARTMENT. Douglas W. Kmiec. Praeger Publishers, One Madison Avenue, New York, New York 10010-3603. 1992.

BEYOND THE COURTROOM: A COMPARATIVE ANALYSIS OF MISDEMEANOR SENTENCING. Anthony J. Regona and John Paul Ryan. Justice Department. Superintendent of Documents, United States Government Printing Office, Washington, D.C. 20402. 1984.

CAPITAL PUNISHMENT 1982. Justice Department, Bureau of Justice Statistics. Superintendent of Documents, United States Government Printing Office, Washington, D.C. 20402. 1984.

CONFLICTING LOYALTIES: LAW AND POLITICS IN THE ATTORNEY GENERAL'S OFFICE, 1789-1990. Nancy V. Baker. University Press of Kansas, 329 Carruth, Lawrence, Kansas 66045. 1992.

THE DEPARTMENT OF JUSTICE. Lynne Dunn. Chelsea House Publishers, 1974 Sproul Road, Suite 400, Broomall, Pennsylvania 19008. 1989.

DETERMINATE SENTENCING AND THE CORRECTIONAL PROCESS: A STUDY OF THE IMPLEMENTATION AND IMPACT OF SENTENCING REFORM IN THREE STATES. Lynne Goodstein. Justice Department, National Institute of Justice. Superintendent of Documents, United States Government Printing Office, Washington, D.C. 20402. 1984.

EFFECTS OF EXCLUSIONARY RULE: A STUDY IN CALIFORNIA. W. Robert Burkhart. Justice Department, National Institute of Justice. Superintendent of Documents, United States Government Printing Office, Washington, D.C. 20402. 1982.

FEDERAL PROSECUTION OF ELECTION OFFENSES, FOURTH EDITION. Craig C. Donsanto. Justice Department, Criminal Division, Public Integrity Section. Superintendent of Documents, United States Government Printing Office, Washington, D.C. 20402. 1984.

A FREE BALLOT AND A FAIR COUNT: THE DEPARTMENT OF JUSTICE AND THE ENFORCEMENT OF VOTING RIGHTS IN THE SOUTH, 1877-1893. Robert M. Goldman. Garland Publishing, Incorporated, 136 Madison Avenue, New York, New York 10016. 1990.

GEODESIC NETWORK: 1987 REPORT ON COMPETITION IN THE TELEPHONE INDUSTRY. Peter W. Huber. Justice Department, Antitrust Division. Superintendent of Documents, United States Government Printing Office, Washington, D.C. 20402. 1987.

JUSTICE DEPARTMENT BRIEFS IN CRUCIAL CIVIL RIGHTS CASES. United States Department of Justice. Garland Publishing, Incorporated, 136 Madison Avenue, New York, New York 10016. 1991.

JUSTICE DEPARTMENT

JUSTICE DEPARTMENT CIVIL RIGHTS POLICIES PRIOR TO 1960: CRUCIAL DOCUMENTS FROM THE FILES OF ARTHUR BRANN CALDWELL. Arthur Brann Caldwell. Garland Publishing, Incorporated, 136 Madison Avenue, New York, New York 10016. 1991.

PUBLIC DANGER AS A FACTOR IN PRETRIAL RELEASE: A COMPARATIVE ANALYSIS OF STATE LAWS. Barbara Gottlieb. Justice Department, National Institute of Justice. Superintendent of Documents, United States Government Printing Office, Washington, D.C. 20402. 1985.

RESEARCH ON SENTENCING: THE SEARCH FOR REFORM, SUMMARY REPORT. Alfred Blumstein. Justice Department, National Institute of Justice, Panel on Sentencing Research. Superintendent of Documents, United States Government Printing Office, Washington, D.C. 20402. 1983.

ROLE OF THE GRAND JURY AND THE PRELIMINARY HEARING IN PRETRIAL SCREENING. Deborah Day Emerson. Justice Department, National Institute of Justice. Superintendent of Documents, United States Government Printing Office, Washington, D.C. 20402. 1984.

SENTENCING GUIDELINES: STRUCTURING JUDICIAL DISCRETION, ESTABLISHING A SENTENCING GUIDELINES SYSTEM. Arthur M. Getman. Justice Department, National Institute of Justice. Superintendent of Documents, United States Government Printing Office, Washington, D.C. 20402. 1982.

THE UNITED STATES DEPARTMENT OF JUSTICE AND INDIVIDUAL RIGHTS, 1937-1962. John T. Elliff. Garland Publishing, Incorporated, 136 Madison Avenue, New York, New York 10016. 1987.

VICTIM WITNESS LEGISLATION: AN OVERVIEW. John R. Anderson and Paul L. Woodward. Justice Department, Bureau of Justice Statistics. Superintendent of Documents, United States Government Printing Office, Washington, D.C. 20402. 1984.

ANNUALS AND SURVEYS

FREEDOM OF INFORMATION CASE LIST. Pamela Maida. Justice Department, Office of Information and Privacy. Superintendent of Documents, United States Government Printing Office, Washington, D.C. 20402. Annual.

RESEARCH CENTERS, INSTITUTES, CLEARINGHOUSES

UNITED STATES DEPARTMENT OF JUSTICE ANTITRUST LIBRARY. Tenth and Pennsylvania Avenue, Northwest, Room 3310, Washington, D.C. 20530. (202) 514-2512.

UNITED STATES DEPARTMENT OF JUSTICE CIVIL LIBRARY. Tenth and Pennsylvania Avenue, Northwest, Room 3344, Washington, D.C. 20530. (202) 514-3301.

UNITED STATES DEPARTMENT OF JUSTICE CIVIL RIGHTS LIBRARY. Tenth and Pennsylvania Avenue, Northwest, Room 7618, Washington, D.C. 20530. (202) 514-2151.

UNITED STATES DEPARTMENT OF JUSTICE CRIMINAL LIBRARY. 100 Federal Triangle Building, Washington, D.C. 20530. (202) 514-2601.

UNITED STATES DEPARTMENT OF JUSTICE LANDS LIBRARY. Tenth and Pennsylvania Avenue, Northwest, Room 2333, Washington, D.C. 20530. (202) 514-2701.

UNITED STATES DEPARTMENT OF JUSTICE MAIN LIBRARY. Tenth and Pennsylvania Avenue, Northwest, Room 5400, Washington, D.C. 20530. (202) 514-2133.

UNITED STATES DEPARTMENT OF JUSTICE TAX LIBRARY. Tenth and Pennsylvania Avenue, Northwest, Room 4335, Washington, D.C. 20530. (202) 307-6419.

OTHER SOURCES

DEPARTMENT OF JUSTICE INVESTIGATIVE FILES. Melvyn Dubofsky and Mark Naison. University Publications of America, 4520 East West Highway, Suite 600, Bethesda, Maryland 20814. 1989.

200th ANNIVERSARY OF THE OFFICE OF THE ATTORNEY GENERAL, 1789-1989. United States Department of Justice, Criminal Division, Tenth Street and Pennsylvania Avenue, Northwest, Washington, D.C. 20530. 1990.

JUSTICES OF THE PEACE
See: COURTS; JUDGES

JUVENILE COURTS
See: CHILDREN; COURTS; JUVENILES

JUVENILE DELINQUENCY
See: CHILDREN; CRIMINAL LAW

JUVENILES

STATUTES, CODES, STANDARDS, UNIFORM LAWS

COURT RULES TO ACHIEVE PERMANANCY FOR FOSTER CHILDREN: SAMPLE RULES AND COMMENTARY. Mark Hardin and Ann Shalleck. National Legal Resource Center for Child Advocacy and Protection, American Bar Association, 750 North Lake Shore Drive, Chicago, Illinois 60611. 1985.

UNIFORM JUVENILE COURT ACT. National Conference of Commissioners on Uniform State Laws. Uniform Laws Annotated. West Publishing Company, Post Office Box 64526, 50 West Kellogg Boulevard, St. Paul, Minnesota 55164-0526. 1976 (Annual Supplements).

LOOSELEAF SERVICES AND REPORTERS

JUVENILE LAW REPORTERS. Knehans-Miller Publications, P.O. Box 88, Warrensburg, Missouri 64093. 1979- .

NATIONAL JUVENILE LAW REPORTER. National Juvenile Law Center, 3701 Lindell Boulevard, St. Louis, Missouri 63178. 1982- .

REPRESENTING THE CHILD CLIENT. Mark I. Soler and others. Matthew Bender and Company, Incorporated, 11 Penn Plaza, New York, New York 10001. 1987- .

HANDBOOKS, MANUALS, FORMBOOKS

CLINICAL HANDBOOK OF CHILD PSYCHIATRY AND THE LAW. Diane H. Schetky and Elissa P. Benedek, Editors. Williams and Wilkins, 428 East Preston, Baltimore, Maryland 21202. 1992.

FOCUS ON TEENS IN TROUBLE: A REFERENCE HANDBOOK. Daryl Sander. ABC-CLIO, P.O. Box 1911, Santa Barbara, California 93116-1911. 1991.

HANDBOOK OF PSYCHIATRIC PRACTICE IN THE JUVENILE COURT. American Psychiatric Association, Workgroup on Psychiatric Practice in the Juvenile Court, 1400 K Street, Northwest, Washington, D.C. 20005. 1992.

JUVENILE JUSTICE: A GUIDE TO PRACTICE AND THEORY. Third Edition. Steven M. Cox and John J. Conrad. William C. Brown Group, 2460 Kerper Boulevard, Dubuque, Iowa 52001. 1991.

REASONABLE EFFORTS TO PREVENT FOSTER PLACEMENT: A GUIDE TO IMPLEMENTATION. Second Edition. Debra Ratterman, G. Diane Dodson and Mark A. Hardin. National Legal Resource Center for Child Advocacy and Protection, American Bar Association, Young Lawyers Division, 1800 M Street, Northwest, Washington, D.C. 20036. 1987.

TEXTBOOKS AND GENERAL WORKS

ABNORMAL OFFENDERS, DELINQUENCY AND THE CRIMINAL JUSTICE SYSTEM. John Gunn and David P. Farrington. Books on Demand, 300 North Zeeb Road, Ann Arbor, Michigan 48106-1346. 1982.

THE ADOLESCENT CRIMINAL: AN EXAMINATION OF TODAY'S JUVENILE OFFENDER. R. Barri Flowers. McFarland and Company, Incorporated, Box 611, Jefferson, North Carolina 28640. 1990.

AMERICAN DELINQUENCY, ITS MEANING AND CONSTRUCTION. Third Edition. LaMar T. Empey and Mark C. Stafford. Wadsworth Publishing Company, 10 Davis Drive, Belmont, California 94002. 1991.

THE AMERICAN JUVENILE JUSTICE SYSTEM. Gennaro F. Vito and Deborah G. Wilson. Sage Publications, Incorporated, 2455 Teller Road, Newbury Park, California 91320. 1985.

AT A TENDER AGE: VIOLENT YOUTH AND JUVENILE JUSTICE. Rita Kramer. Holt, Rinehart, and Winston, Incorporated, 6277 Sea Harbor Drive, Orlando, Florida 32821. 1988.

BEHIND THE BLACK ROBES: JUVENILE COURT JUDGES AND THE COURT. H. Ted Rubin. Sage Publications, Incorporated, 2455 Teller Road, Newbury Park, California 91320. 1985.

CHILD PORNOGRAPHY AND PROSTITUTION: BACKGROUND AND LEGAL ANALYSIS. Howard A. Davidson and Gregory A. Loken. National Center for Missing and Exploited Children: United States Department of Justice, National Obscenity Enforcement Unit, Tenth Street and Pennsylvania Avenue, Northwest, Washington, D.C. 20530. 1987.

CHILDREN BEFORE THE COURT: REFLECTIONS ON LEGAL ISSUES AFFECTING MINORS. Second Edition. Paul R. Kfoury. Butterworth-Heinemann, 80 Montvale Avenue, Stoneham, Massachusetts 02180. 1991.

CHILDREN IN CUSTODY. Gill Stewart and Norman Tutt. Avebury, Brookfield, Vermont. 1987.

THE CYCLE OF JUVENILE JUSTICE. Thomas J. Bernard. Oxford University Press, 200 Madison Avenue, New York, New York 10016. 1992.

DEALING WITH DELINQUENCY: AN INVESTIGATION OF JUVENILE JUSTICE. Jay S. Albanese. University Press of America, 4720 Boston Way, Lanham, Maryland 20706. 1985.

DEATH PENALTY FOR JUVENILES. Victor L. Streib. Indiana University Press, Tenth and Morton Streets, Bloomington, Indiana 47405. 1987.

DELINQUENCY AND CITIZENSHIP: RECLAIMING THE YOUNG OFFENDER, 1914-1948. Victor Bailey. Oxford University Press, 200 Madison Avenue, New York, New York 10016. 1987.

DELINQUENCY AND COMMUNITY: CREATING OPPORTUNITIES AND CONTROLS. Alden D. Miller. Sage Publications, Incorporated, 2455 Teller Road, Newbury Park, California 91320. 1985.

DELINQUENCY AND DISORDERLY BEHAVIOR. Eric H. Monkkonen, Editor. Meckler Corporation, 11 Ferry Lane West, Westport, Connecticut 06880. 1991.

DELINQUENCY AND JUSTICE. Third Edition. William E. Thornton, Jr. and Lydia Voigt. McGraw-Hill Publishing Company, 1221 Avenue of the Americas, New York, New York 10020. 1992.

DELINQUENCY AND JUVENILE CONTROL: A SOCIOLOGICAL PERSPECTIVE. William B. Waegel. Prentice-Hall, Incorporated, 113 Sylvan Avenue, Englewood Cliffs, New Jersey 07632. 1989.

DELINQUENCY IN SOCIETY: A CHILD-CENTERED APPROACH. Robert M. Regoli and John D. Hewitt. McGraw-Hill Publishing Company, 1221 Avenue of the Americas, New York, New York 10020. 1991.

DELINQUENT BEHAVIOR. Fifth Edition. Don C. Gibbons and Marvin D. Krohn. Prentice-Hall, Incorporated, 113 Sylvan Avenue, Englewood Cliffs, New Jersey 07632. 1991.

EMERGING ISSUES IN CHILD PSYCHIATRY AND THE LAW. Diane Schetky and Elissa P. Benedek, Editors. Brunner-Mazel, Incorporated, 19 Union Square West, New York, New York 10003. 1985.

EVALUATING JUVENILE JUSTICE. James R. Kluegel, Editor. Sage Publications, Incorporated, 2455 Teller Road, Newbury Park, California 91320. 1983.

FAMILY AND DELINQUENCY: RESOCIALIZING THE YOUNG OFFENDER. Ludwig L. Geismar and Katherine Wood. Human Sciences Press, Incorporated, 233 Spring Street, New York, New York 10013. 1986.

GIRLS, DELINQUENCY, AND JUVENILE JUSTICE. Meda Chesney-Lind and Randall G. Shelden. Brooks/Cole Publishing Company, 511 Forest Lodge Road, Pacific Grove, California 93950. 1992.

GROWING UP GOOD: POLICING THE BEHAVIOUR OF GIRLS IN EUROPE. Maureen Cain, Editor. Sage Publications, 2455 Teller Road, Newbury Park, California 91320. 1989.

HANDLING JUVENILE DELINQUENCY CASES. F. Lee Bailey and Henry B. Rothblatt. Lawyers Co-Operative Publishing Company, Aqueduct Building, Rochester, New York 14694. 1982. (Supplemented).

HOW THE LAW THINKS ABOUT CHILDREN. Michael King and Christine Piper. Gower Publishing Company, Old Post Road, Brookfield, Vermont 05036. 1990.

INJUSTICE FOR JUVENILES: RETHINKING THE BEST INTERESTS OF THE CHILD. Ira M. Schwartz. Lexington Books, 125 Spring Street, Lexington, Massachusetts 02173. 1989.

INSIDE A JUVENILE COURT: THE TARNISHED IDEAL OF INDIVIDUAL JUSTICE. M. A. Bortner. New York University Press. Distributed by Columbia University Press, 562 West One Hundred Thirteenth Street, New York, New York 10025. 1982.

INTRODUCTION TO JUVENILE DELINQUENCY: YOUTH AND THE LAW. James T. Carey and Patrick D. McAnany. Prentice-Hall, Incorporated, 113 Sylvan Avenue, Englewood Cliffs, New Jersey 07632. 1984.

JUVENILE CORRECTIONAL REFORM: TWO DECADES OF POLICY AND PROCEDURAL CHANGE. Edmund F. McGarrell. State University of New York Press, State University Plaza, Albany, New York 12246. 1988.

JUVENILE COURT AND COMMUNITY CORRECTIONS. Thomas G. Blumberge. University Press of America, 4720 Boston Way, Lanham, Maryland 20706. 1985.

JUVENILE COURTS IN A NUTSHELL. Third Edition. Sanford J. Fox. West Publishing Company, P.O. Box 64526, 50 West Kellogg Boulevard, St. Paul, Minnesota 55164-0526. 1984.

JUVENILE CRIMES AGAINST THE ELDERLY. Frank P. Morello. Charles C. Thomas Publishing, 2600 South First Street, Springfield, Illinois 62794-9265. 1982.

JUVENILE DELINQUENCY. Second Edition. Clemens Bartollas. Macmillan Publishing Company, Incorporated, 866 Third Avenue, New York, New York 10022. 1990.

JUVENILE DELINQUENCY. Third Edition. Martin R. Haskell and Lewis Yablonsky. Houghton-Mifflin Company, One Beacon Street, Boston, Massachusetts 02108. 1982.

JUVENILE DELINQUENCY. Third Edition. Peter C. Kratcoski and Lucille Dunn Kratcoski. Prentice-Hall, Incorporated, 113 Sylvan Avenue, Englewood Cliffs, New Jersey 07632. 1990.

JUVENILE DELINQUENCY: A BOOK OF READINGS. Fourth Edition. Rose Giallombardo. John Wiley and Sons, Incorporated, 605 Third Avenue, New York, New York 10158. 1982.

JUVENILE DELINQUENCY: A JUSTICE PERSPECTIVE. Second Edition. Ralph A. Weisheit and Robert G. Culbertson, Editors. Waveland Press, Incorporated, P.O. Box 400, Prospect Heights, Illinois 60070. 1990.

JUVENILE DELINQUENCY AND CORRECTIONS: THE GAP BETWEEN THEORY AND PRACTICE. James O. Finkenauer. Academic Press, Incorporated, 1250 Sixth Avenue, Suite 400, San Diego, California 92101. 1984.

JUVENILE DELINQUENCY AND JUVENILE JUSTICE. Joseph W. Rogers and G. Larry Mays. John Wiley and Sons, Incorporated, 605 Third Avenue, New York, New York 10158. 1987.

JUVENILE DELINQUENCY AND JUVENILE JUSTICE. Roy Lotz, Eric D. Poole, and Robert M. Regoli. McGraw-Hill Publishing Company, 1221 Avenue of the Americas, New York, New York 10020. 1985.

JUVENILE DELINQUENCY: THEORY, PRACTICE, AND LAW. Fourth Edition. Larry J. Siegel and Joseph J. Senna. West Publishing Company, 50 West Kellogg Boulevard, St. Paul, Minnesota 55164. 1991.

JUVENILE DELINQUENCY: TRENDS AND PERSPECTIVES. Michael Ruttler and Henri Giller. Guilford Publications, Incorporated, 72 Spring Street, New York, New York 10012. 1984.

JUVENILE JUSTICE. Robert W. Drowns and Karen M. Hess. West Publishing Company, 50 West Kellogg Boulevard, St. Paul, Minnesota 55164. 1990.

JUVENILE JUSTICE: AN INTRODUCTION. John T. Whitehead and Steven P. Lab. Anderson Publishing Company, 2035 Reading Road, Cincinnati, Ohio 45202. 1990.

JUVENILE JUSTICE IN AMERICA. Third Edition. Clifford E. Simonsen and Marshall S. Gordon. Macmillan Publishing Company, Incorporated, 866 Third Avenue, New York, New York 10022. 1991.

JUVENILE JUSTICE IN CONTEXT. Anne Rankin Mahoney. Northeastern University Press, 272 Huntington Plaza, 360 Huntington Avenue, Boston, Massachusetts 02115. 1987.

JUVENILE JUSTICE: POLICY, PRACTICE, AND LAW. Second Edition. H. Ted Rubin. McGraw-Hill Publishing Company, 1221 Avenue of the Americas, New York, New York 10020. 1985.

JUVENILE JUSTICE POLICY: ANALYZING TRENDS AND OUTCOMES. Scott H. Decker, Editor. Sage Publications, Incorporated, 2455 Teller Road, Newbury Park, California 91320. 1984.

JUVENILE JUSTICE REFORM: A MODEL FOR THE STATES. Ralph A. Rossum, Benedict J. Koller and Christopher P. Manfredi. American Legislative Exchange Council, 214 Massachusetts Avenue, Northeast, Suite 240, Washington, D.C. 20002. 1987.

THE JUVENILE JUSTICE SYSTEM: DELINQUENCY, PROCESSING, AND THE LAW. Dean J. Champion. Macmillan Publishing Company, Incorporated, 866 Third Avenue, New York, New York 10022. 1992.

JUVENILE JUSTICE: THE ADJUDICATORY PROCESS. Jerry L. Mershow. National Council of Juvenile and Family Court Judges, Box 8970, University of Nevada, Reno, Nevada 89557. 1982.

JUVENILE LAW AND ITS PROCESSES: CASES AND MATERIALS. Second Edition. Francis Barry McCarthy and James G. Carr. Michie Company, P.O. Box 7587, Charlottesville, Virginia 22906. 1989.

JUVENILE LAW: CASES AND COMMENTS. Second Edition. Joseph J. Senna and Larry J. Siegel. West Publishing Company, 50 West Kellogg Boulevard, St. Paul, Minnesota 55164. 1992.

THE JUVENILE OFFENDER AND THE LAW. Third Edition. Paul H. Hahn. Books on Demand, 300 North Zeeb Road, Ann Arbor, Michigan 48106-1346. 1984.

JUVENILE OFFENDERS AND THE JUVENILE JUSTICE SYSTEM. Sol Rubin. Oceana Publications, Incorporated, 75 Main Street, Dobbs Ferry, New York 10522. 1986.

JUVENILE RESPONSIBILITY AND LAW. Third edition. Linda Riekes, Steve Jenkins, and Armentha Russell. West Publishing Company, 50 West Kellogg Boulevard, St. Paul, Minnesota 55164-0526. 1990.

JUVENILES IN PROSTITUTION: FACT VS. FICTION. Laura J. Smith and Sharon B. Mitchell. R and E Publishers, P.O. Box 2008, Saratoga, California 95070-2008. 1984.

LAW ENFORCEMENT AND THE YOUTHFUL OFFENDER: DELINQUENCY AND JUVENILE JUSTICE. Fourth Edition. Edward Eldefonso. John Wiley and Sons, Incorporated, 605 Third Avenue, New York, New York 10158. 1983.

THE MANDATE FOR JUVENILE JUSTICE. Mark Harrison Moore with Thomas Bearrows. Springer-Verlag New York, Incorporated, 175 Fifth Avenue, New York, New York 10010. 1987.

THE OTHER SIDE OF DELINQUENCY. Waln K. Brown. Rutgers University Press, 101 Church Street, New Brunswick, New Jersey 08901. 1983.

PATTERNS OF JUVENILE DELINQUENCY. Howard B. Kaplan. Sage Publications, Incorporated, 2455 Teller Road, Newbury Park, California 91320. 1984.

POLICE WORK WITH JUVENILES AND THE ADMINISTRATION OF JUVENILE JUSTICE. Seventh Edition. John P. Kenney. Charles C. Thomas Publishing, 2600 South First Street, Springfield, Illinois 62794-9265. 1989.

PREVENTION AND CONTROL OF JUVENILE DELINQUENCY. Richard J. Lundman. Oxford University Press, Incorporated, 200 Madison Avenue, New York, New York 10016. 1984.

PSYCHOLOGY OF JUVENILE CRIME. Amy Lamsom. Human Sciences Press, Incorporated, 233 Spring Street, New York, New York 10013. 1982.

REHABILITATING JUVENILE JUSTICE. Charles Shireman. Columbia University Press, 562 West 113th Street, New York, New York 10025. 1989.

RIGHTS OF JUVENILES: THE JUVENILE JUSTICE SYSTEM. Second Edition. Samuel M. Davis. Clark Boardman Company, Limited, 435 Hudson Street, New York, New York 10014. 1980. (Annual Supplements).

THE ROLE OF THE COURTS IN CHILD PROTECTION. Human Resources Press, P.O. Box 24240, Los Angeles, California 90024. 1985.

THE ROLE OF THE JUVENILE COURT. Francis X. Hartmann, Editor. Springer-Verlag New York, Incorporated, 175 Fifth Avenue, New York, New York 10010. 1987.

RURAL POLICE AND RURAL YOUTH. Michael P. Roche. University Press of Virginia, P.O. Box 3608, University Station, Charlottesville, Virginia 22903. 1985.

SCARED STRAIGHT AND THE PANACEA PHENOMENON. James O. Finckenaeuer. Prentice-Hall, Incorporated, 113 Sylvan Avenue, Englewood Cliffs, New Jersey 07632. 1982.

THE SOCIOLOGY OF JUVENILE DELINQUENCY. Ronald J. Berger. Nelson-Hall Publishers, 111 North Canal Street, Chicago, Illinois 60606. 1991.

STUBBORN CHILDREN: CONTROLLING DELINQUENCY IN THE UNITED STATES, 1640-1981. John R. Sutton. University of California Press, 2120 Berkeley Way, Berkeley, California 94720. 1988.

THEORIES OF DELINQUENCY: AN EXAMINATION OF EXPLANATIONS OF DELINQUENT BEHAVIOR. Donald J. Shoemaker. Oxford University Press, Incorporated, 200 Madison Avenue, New York, New York 10016. 1990.

TRANSFERRING JUVENILES TO CRIMINAL COURTS: TRENDS AND IMPLICATIONS FOR CRIMINAL JUSTICE. Dean J. Champion and G. Larry Mays. Praeger Publishers, One Madison Avenue, New York, New York 10010-3603. 1991.

WESTERN SYSTEMS OF JUVENILE JUSTICE. Malcolm W. Klein, Editor. Sage Publications, Incorporated, 2455 Teller Road, Newbury Park, California 91320. 1984.

YOUTH VIOLENCE: PROGRAMS AND PROSPECTS. Steven J. Apter and Arnold P. Goldstein, Editors. Pergamon Press, Incorporated, Maxwell House, Fairview Park, Elmsford, New York 10523. 1986.

DIGESTS, INDEXES, ABSTRACTS, CITATORS

JUVENILE AND FAMILY LAW DIGEST. National Council of Juvenile and Family Court Judges, P.O. Box 8970, University of Nevada, Reno, Nevada 89557. Monthly.

KINDEX: AN INDEX TO PERIODICAL LITERATURE CONCERNING CHILDREN. National Center For Juvenile Justice, Research Division of National Council of Juvenile and Family Court Judges, 701 Forbes Avenue, Pittsburgh, Pennsylvania 15219. Annual.

JUVENILES

LAW REVIEWS AND PERIODICALS

CRIME AND DELINQUENCY. National Council on Crime and Delinquency, 2125 Center Avenue, Fort Lee, New Jersey 07024. Quarterly.

JOURNAL OF JUVENILE LAW. University of LaVerne, College of Law, 1950 Third Street, LaVerne, California 91750. Annual.

JUVENILE AND FAMILY COURT JOURNAL. National Council of Juvenile and Family Court Judges. P.O. Box 8978, Reno, Nevada 89507. Quarterly.

NEWSLETTERS AND NEWSPAPERS

AMERICAN BAR ASSOCIATION JUVENILE AND CHILD WELFARE LAW REPORTER. American Bar Association, National Legal Resource Center For Child Advocacy and Protection, 1800 M Street, Northwest, Washington, D.C. 20036. Monthly.

CHILD ADVOCACY AND PROTECTION NEWSLETTER. American Bar Association, 750 North Lake Shore Drive, Chicago, Illinois 60611. Semiannually.

CHILDREN'S VOICE. Child Welfare League of America, 440 First Street, Northwest, Washington, D.C. 20001. Bimonthly.

JUVENILE AND FAMILY COURT NEWSLETTER. National Council of Juvenile and Family Court Judges, P.O. Box 8978, Reno, Nevada 89507. Bimonthly.

JUVENILE AND FAMILY LAW DIGEST. National Council of Juvenile and Family Court Judges, P.O. Box 8970, Reno, Nevada 89507. Monthly.

JUVENILE JUSTICE DIGEST. Washington Crime News Services, 3918 Prosperity Avenue, Suite 318, Fairfax, Virginia 22031. Semimonthly.

JUVENILE LAW REPORTS. Krehaus-Miller Publications, P.O. Box 88, Warrensburg, Missouri 64093. Monthly.

LEGISLATIVE ALERT. Child Welfare League of America, 440 First Street, Northwest, Washington, D.C. 20001. Bimonthly.

SCHOOL CHILD CARE REPORT. Business Publishers, Incorporated, 951 Pershing Drive, Silverspring, Maryland 20910. Monthly.

YOUTH LAW NEWS. National Center for Youth Law, 1663 Mission Street, San Francisco, California 94103. Bimonthly.

BIBLIOGRAPHIES

CRIME, DELINQUENCY, AND CRIMINAL JUSTICE WITHIN THE RURAL CONTEXT: A BIBLIOGRAPHY. David P. Van Buren. Vance Bibliographies, P.O. Box 229, 112 North Charter Street, Monticello, Illinois 61856. 1985.

JUVENILE COURTS: A BIBLIOGRAPHY. Mary Vance. Vance Bibliographies, P.O. Box 229, 112 North Charter Street, Monticello, Illinois 61856. 1988.

JUVENILE DELINQUENCY: MEDICAL AND PSYCHOLOGICAL SUBJECT ANALYSIS AND RESEARCH INDEX WITH BIBLIOGRAPHY. Sylvia S. Gelstein. ABBE Publishers Association of Washington D.C., 4111 Gallows Road, Annandale, Virginia 22003-1862. 1985.

THE SERIOUS JUVENILE OFFENDERS: A SELECTED BIBLIOGRAPHY. Thomas Schrinel and Marjorie Kravitz. Aspen Publishers, Incorporated, 1600 Research Boulevard, Rockville, Maryland 20850. 1982.

DIRECTORIES

DIRECTORY OF JUDGES WITH JUVENILE/FAMILY LAW JURISDICTION. National Council of Juvenile and Family Court Judges, P.O. Box 8970, University of Nevada, Reno, Nevada 89557. Semiannual.

DIRECTORY OF JUVENILE AND ADULT CORRECTIONAL DEPARTMENTS, INSTITUTIONS, AGENCIES AND PAROLING AUTHORITIES. American Correctional Association, 8025 Laurel Lakes Court, Laurel, Maryland 20707. Annual.

NATIONAL DIRECTORY OF CHILDREN AND YOUTH SERVICES. CPR Directory Services Company, 1301 20th Street, Northwest, Washington, D.C. 20036. 1985.

ASSOCIATIONS AND PROFESSIONAL SOCIETIES

ASSOCIATION OF AMERICAN LAW SCHOOLS, SECTION ON FAMILY AND JUVENILE LAW. One Dupont Circle, Northwest, Washington, D.C. 20036. (202) 296-8851.

NATIONAL ASSOCIATION OF JUVENILE CORRECTIONAL AGENCIES. 55 Albin Road, Bow, New Hampshire 03304. (603) 271-5945.

NATIONAL COUNCIL ON CRIME AND DELINQUENCY. 77 Maiden Lane, Fourth Floor, San Francisco, California 94108. (415) 956-5651.

NATIONAL COUNCIL OF JUVENILE AND FAMILY COURT JUDGES. P.O. Box 8970, University of Nevada, Reno, Nevada 89507. (702) 784-6012.

RESEARCH CENTERS, INSTITUTES, CLEARINGHOUSES

CENTER FOR THE STUDY OF CRIME, DELINQUENCY, AND CORRECTIONS. Southern Illinois University at Carbondale, Carbondale, Illinois 62901. (618) 453-5701.

DELINQUENCY CONTROL INSTITUTE. University of Southern California, Center for the Administration of Justice, Tyler Building, 3601 South Flower Street, Los Angeles, California 90007. (213) 743-2497.

NATIONAL CENTER FOR JUVENILE JUSTICE. 701 Forbes Avenue, Pittsburgh, Pennsylvania 15219. (415) 227-6950.

NATIONAL CENTER FOR YOUTH LAW. 1663 Mission Street, 5th Floor, San Francisco, California 94103. (415) 543-3307.

STATISTICS SOURCES

CRIMINAL JUSTICE INFORMATION POLICY: JUVENILE RECORDS AND RECORDKEEPING SYSTEMS. United States Department of Justice, Criminal Division, Tenth Street and Pennsylvania Avenue, Northwest, Washington, D.C. 20530. 1988.

K

KIDNAPPING

See also: CRIMINAL LAW; FEDERAL BUREAU OF INVESTIGATION; TERRORISM

HANDBOOKS, MANUALS, FORMBOOKS

INTERNATIONAL CHILD ABDUCTIONS: A GUIDE TO APPLYING THE 1988 HAGUE CONVENTION, WITH FORMS. Gloria F. DeHart, Editor. American Bar Association, Section of Family Law, 750 North Lake Shore Drive, Chicago, Illinois 60611. 1989.

TEXTBOOKS AND GENERAL WORKS

THE CHILD SNATCHERS. Bobbi Lawrence and Olivia Taylor-Young. Charles River Books, 1 Thompson Square, P.O. Box 65, Boston, Massachusetts 02129. 1982.

CHILD SNATCHING: THE LEGAL RESPONSE TO THE ABDUCTION OF CHILDREN. Sanford N. Katz. American Bar Association, Section of Family Law, 750 North Lake Shore Drive, Chicago, Illinois 60611. 1981.

CHILDREN IN THE CROSSFIRE: THE TRAGEDY OF PARENTAL KIDNAPPING. Sally Abrahams. Macmillan Publishing Company, Incorporated, 866 Third Avenue, New York, New York 10022. 1983.

THE FACE ON THE MILK CARTON. Caroline B. Cooney. Bantam Books, 666 Fifth Avenue, New York, New York 10103. 1990.

HOSTAGE!: KIDNAPPING AND TERRORISM IN OUR TIME. L.B. Taylor, Jr. Franklin Watts, Incorporated, 387 Park Avenue South, New York, New York 10016. 1989.

INTERNATIONAL PARENTAL CHILD ABDUCTION. Third Edition. United States Department of State, Bureau of Consular Affairs, Washington, D.C. 1989.

INTERSTATE CHILD CUSTODY DISPUTES AND PARENTAL KIDNAPPING: POLICY, PRACTICE, AND LAW. Patricia M. Hoff. National Clearinghouse For Legal Services, 407 South Dearborn, Room 400, Chicago, Illinois 60605. 1982.

KIDNAP, HIJACK, AND EXTORTION: THE RESPONSE. Richard Clutterbuck. St. Martin's Press, 175 Fifth Avenue, New York, New York 10010. 1987.

KIDNAPPED!: COULD IT HAPPEN TO YOU? Elaine Scott. Franklin Watts, Incorporated, 387 Park Avenue South, New York, New York 10016. 1989.

THE LINDBERGH CASE. Jim Fisher. Rutgers University Press, 109 Church Street, New Brunswick, New Jersey 08901. 1987.

PARENTAL KIDNAPPING: A BIBLIOGRAPHY. Earlene H. Cook and Karen F. Harrell. Vance Bibliographies, P.O. Box 229, 112 North Charter Street, Monticello, Illinois 61856. 1984.

PARENTAL KIDNAPPING: HOW TO PREVENT AN ABDUCTION AND WHAT TO DO IF YOUR CHILD IS ABDUCTED. Patricia Hoff. National Legal Resource Center for Child Advocacy and Protection, American Bar Association, 750 North Lake Shore Drive, Chicago, Illinois 60611. 1985.

POLITICAL KIDNAPPING: AN INTRODUCTORY OVERVIEW. William L. Cassidy. Sycamore Island Books, Division of Paladin Enterprises, Incorporated, P.O. Box 1307, Boulder, Colorado 80306. 1978.

RANSOM KIDNAPPING IN AMERICA, 1874-1974: THE CREATION OF A CAPITAL CRIME. Ernest K. Alix. Southern Illinois University Press, P.O. Box 3697, Carbondale, Illinois 62902-3697. 1978.

STOLEN CHILDREN: HOW AND WHY PARENTS KIDNAP THEIR CHILDREN. John E. Gill. Penguin Books, Incorporated, 375 Hudson Street, New York, New York 10014. 1982.

TERRORISM AND PERSONAL PROTECTION. Brian M. Jenkins, Editor. Butterworth Legal Publishers, 90 Stiles Road, Salem, New Hampshire 03079. 1985.

ASSOCIATIONS AND PROFESSIONAL SOCIETIES

ADAM WALSH CHILD RESOURCE CENTER. 3111 South Dixie Highway, Suite 244, West Palm Beach, Florida 33405. (407) 833-9080.

AMERICAN BAR ASSOCIATION, SECTION OF FAMILY LAW. 750 North Lake Shore Drive, Chicago, Illinois 60611. (312) 988-5000.

NATIONAL LEGAL RESOURCE CENTER FOR CHILD ADVOCACY AND PROTECTION OF THE AMERICAN BAR ASSOCIATION. 750 North Lake Shore Drive, Chicago, Illinois 60611.

L

LABOR AND LABOR RELATIONS
See also: AGENCY; DISCRIMINATION, EMPLOYEMENT; EMPLOYEE FRINGE BENEFITS; EMPLOYEES COMPENSATION APPEALS BOARD; EMPLOYMENT LAW; FEDERAL LABOR RELATIONS AUTHORITY; LABOR ARBITRATION; LABOR DEPARTMENT; MERIT SYSTEMS PROTECTION BOARD; NATIONAL LABOR RELATIONS BOARD; OCCUPATIONAL SAFETY AND HEALTH

STATUTES, CODES, STANDARDS, UNIFORM LAWS

LEGISLATIVE HISTORY OF THE NATIONAL LABOR RELATIONS ACT, AS AMENDED. Superintendent of Documents, United States Government Printing Office, Washington, D.C. 20402. 1985.

LOOSELEAF SERVICES AND REPORTERS

CONSTRUCTION LABOR REPORT. Bureau of National Affairs, 1231 Twenty-fifth Street, Northwest, Washington, D.C. 20037. 1955- .

CORPORATE COUNSEL'S GUIDE TO EMPLOYEE RELATIONS LAW. Business Laws, Incorporated, 11630 Chillicothe Road, Chesterland, Ohio 44026. 1991- .

EMPLOYEE AND UNION MEMBER GUIDE TO LABOR LAW. National Lawyers Guild. Clark Boardman Company, Limited, 435 Hudson Street, New York, New York 10014. 1981- .

EMPLOYER'S GUIDE TO AUDITING PERSONNEL AND EMPLOYMENT PRACTICES. Barry A. Hartstein and William A. Hancock, Editor. Business Laws, Incorporated, 11630 Chillicothe Road, Chesterland, Ohio 44026. 1988- .

EMPLOYMENT DISPUTES: LAW AND STRATEGIES FOR REPRESENTING THE EMPLOYER. Carter K. Combe. Butterworth Legal Publishers, 90 Stiles Road, Salem, New Hampshire 03079. 1991- .

EMPLOYMENT LAW CHECKLISTS AND FORMS. Andrew J. Ruzicho and Louis A. Jacobs. Clark Boardman Company, Limited, 435 Hudson Street, New York, New York 10014. 1991.

EMPLOYMENT LAW DESKBOOK. Shawe and Rosenthal. Matthew Bender and Company, Incorporated, 11 Penn Plaza, New York, New York 10001. 1989- .

EMPLOYMENT LAW MANUAL: WRONGFUL DISMISSAL, HUMAN RIGHTS, AND EMPLOYMENT STANDARDS. John R. Sproat. Carswell Company, 2330 Midland Avenue, Agincourt, Ontario, Canada M1S 1P7. 1990- .

FEDERAL LABOR AND EMPLOYMENT LAWS. Bureau of National Affairs, 1231 Twenty-fifth Street, Northwest, Washington, D.C. 20037. 1985- .

HUMAN RESOURCES MANAGEMENT REPORTER. Stewart S. Manela and Gary S. Marx, Editors. Research Institute of America, Incorporated, One Penn Plaza, New York, New York 10119. 1987- .

INVESTIGATING EMPLOYEE CONDUCT. William E. Hartsfield. Callaghan and Company, 155 Pfingsten Road, Deerfield, Illinois 60015. 1988- .

LABOR AND EMPLOYMENT LAW: COMPLIANCE AND LITIGATION. Frederick T. Golder. Callaghan and Company, 155 Pfingsten Road, Deerfield, Illinois 60015. 1986- .

LABOR LAW. Theodore W. Kheel. Matthew Bender and Company, Incorporated, 11 Penn Plaza, New York, New York 10001. 1972- .

LABOR LAW DEVELOPMENTS. Matthew Bender and Company, Incorporated, 11 Penn Plaza, New York, New York 10001. 1964- .

LABOR LAW REPORTS: EMPLOYMENT PRACTICES. Commerce Clearing House, Incorporated, 4025 West Peterson Avenue, Chicago, Illinois 60646. 1976- .

LABOR RELATIONS GUIDE. Prentice-Hall, Incorporated, 113 Sylvan Avenue, Englewood Cliffs, New Jersey 07632. 1978- .

LABOR RELATIONS REPORTER. Bureau of National Affairs, 1231 Twenty-fifth Street, Northwest, Washington, D.C. 20037. 1937- .

NLRB ADVICE MEMORANDUM REPORTER. Labor Relations Press, P.O. Box 579, Fort Washington, Pennsylvania 19034. 1979- .

NLRB CASE HANDLING REPORTER. Commerce Clearing House, Incorporated, 4025 West Peterson Avenue, Chicago, Illinois 60646. 1976- .

LABOR AND LABOR RELATIONS

NLRB REPRESENTATION ELECTIONS: LAW, PRACTICE AND PROCEDURE. Third Edition. John D. Feerick, Henry P. Baer and Jonathan P. Arfa. Prentice-Hall, Incorporated, 113 Sylvan Avenue, Englewood Cliffs, New Jersey 07632. 1988- .

RETAIL/SERVICES LABOR REPORT. Bureau of National Affairs, 1231 Twenty-fifth Street, Northwest, Washington, D.C. 20037. 1974- .

UNION LABOR REPORT. Bureau of National Affairs, 1231 Twenty-fifth Street, Northwest, Washington, D.C. 20037. 1954- .

HANDBOOKS, MANUALS, FORMBOOKS

COLLECTIVE BARGAINING: HOW IT WORKS AND WHY: A MANUAL OF THEORY AND PRACTICE. Thomas E. Colosi. American Arbitration Association, 140 West Fifty-first Street, New York, New York 10020. 1986.

DRAFTING AND REVISING EMPLOYMENT HANDBOOKS. Kurt H. Decker and H. Thomas Felix, II. John Wiley and Sons, Incorporated, 605 Third Avenue, New York, New York 10158. 1991.

EMPLOYEE DISMISSAL LAW: FORMS AND PROCEDURES. Mark S. Dichter, et al., Editors. John Wiley and Sons, Incorporated, 605 Third Avenue, New York, New York 10158. 1986.

THE EMPLOYEE RIGHTS HANDBOOK: ANSWERS TO LEGAL QUESTIONS--FROM INTERVIEW TO PINK SLIP. Steven Mitchell Sack. Facts on File, Incorporated, 460 Park Avenue South, New York, New York 10016. 1991.

THE EMPLOYEE TERMINATION HANDBOOK. Jeffrey G. Allen, Editor. John Wiley and Sons, Incorporated, 605 Third Avenue, New York, New York 10158. 1986.

EMPLOYER'S COMPLIANCE REVIEW. Lee T. Paterson. Parker and Son Publications, Incorporated, P.O. Box 60001, Los Angeles, California 90060. 1991.

EMPLOYMENT LAW COMPLIANCE HANDBOOK. Zachary D. Fasman and Michael J. Album. Executive Enterprises Publications Company, 22 West Twenty-first Street, New York, New York 10010-6904. 1988.

EMPLOYMENT LAW MANUAL: RECRUITMENT, SELECTION, TERMINATION. Gerard P. Panaro. Research Institute of America, Incorporated, One Penn Plaza, New York, New York 10119. 1990.

FAIR LABOR STANDARDS HANDBOOK FOR STATES, LOCAL GOVERNMENTS AND SCHOOLS. Gilbert J. Ginsburg and Daniel B. Abrahams. Thomas Publishing Group, 1725 K Street, Northwest, Suite 200, Washington, D.C. 20006. 1985.

FAIR, SQUARE, AND LEGAL: SAFE HIRING, MANAGING AND FIRING PRACTICES TO KEEP YOU AND YOUR COMPANY OUT OF COURT. Donald H. Weiss. AMACOM, 135 West Fiftieth Street, New York, New York 10020. 1991.

GUIDE TO EMPLOYEE HANDBOOKS: A MODEL FOR MANAGEMENT, WITH COMMENTARY. Robert J. Nobile. Research Institute of America, Incorporated, One Penn Plaza, New York, New York 10119. 1990.

Encyclopedia of Legal Information Sources • 2nd Ed.

GUIDEBOOK TO LABOR RELATIONS. Commerce Clearing House, Incorporated, 4025 West Peterson Avenue, Chicago, Illinois 60646. Annual.

THE HUMAN RESOURCE PROBLEM-SOLVER'S HANDBOOK. Joseph D. Levesque. McGraw-Hill Publishing Company, 1221 Avenue of the Americas, New York, New York 10020. 1991.

THE LABOR AND EMPLOYMENT LAW DESK BOOK. Gordon E. Jackson. Prentice-Hall, Incorporated, 113 Sylvan Avenue, Englewood Cliffs, New Jersey 07632. 1986.

LABOR GUIDE TO LABOR LAW. Third Edition. Bruce S. Feldacker. Prentice-Hall, Incorporated, 113 Sylvan Avenue, Englewood Cliffs, New Jersey 07632. 1990.

LABOR LAW HANDBOOK. Michael Yates. South End Press, 116 Saint Boloph Street, Boston, Massachusetts 02115. 1987.

LABOR MANAGEMENT RELATIONS ACT MANUAL: A GUIDE TO EFFECTIVE LABOR RELATIONS. Stephen J. Cabot. Research Institute of America, Incorporated, One Penn Plaza, New York, New York 10119. 1978. (1985 Supplement).

MINIMUM WAGES AND OVERTIME PAY: ANSWER BOOK ON FEDERAL LAW. Commerce Clearing House, Incorporated, 4025 West Peterson Avenue, Chicago, Illinois 60646. 1985.

NATIONAL LABOR RELATIONS BOARD MANUAL. Division of Judges, National Labor Relations Board. Superintendent of Documents, United States Government Printing Office, Washington, D.C. 20402. 1984.

NEGLIGENT HIRING PRACTICE MANUAL. James A. Branch, Jr. John Wiley and Sons, Incorporated, 605 Third Avenue, New York, New York 10158. 1988.

NEGOTIATING A LABOR CONTRACT: A MANAGEMENT HANDBOOK. Charles S. Loughran. Bureau of National Affairs, 1231 Twenty-fifth Street, Northwest, Washington, D.C. 20037. 1984.

PENSION HANDBOOK FOR UNION NEGOTIATORS. Jeffrey A. MacDonald and Anne Bingham. Bureau of National Affairs, 1231 Twenty-fifth Street, Northwest, Washington, D.C. 20037. 1986.

PERSONNEL DIRECTOR'S LEGAL GUIDE. Second Edition. Steven C. Kahn. Research Institute of America, Incorporated, One Penn Plaza, New York, New York 10119. 1990.

PERSONNEL LAW ANSWER BOOK. James O. Castagnera. Panel Publishers, Incorporated, 36 West Forty-fourth Street, New York, New York 10036. 1988.

PRACTICAL LAWYER'S MANUAL ON LABOR LAW. American Law Institute-American Bar Association, Committee on Continuing Professional Education, 4025 Chestnut Street, Philadelphia, Pennsylvania 19104. 1988.

PRIMER OF LABOR RELATIONS. Twenty-fourth Edition. Bureau of National Affairs, 1231 Twenty-fifth Street, Northwest, Washington, D.C. 20037. 1989.

A PRIMER ON AMERICAN LABOR LAW. Second Edition. MIT Press, 55 Hayward Street, Cambridge, Massachusetts 02142. 1986.

YOUR RIGHTS AS AN EMPLOYEE: HOW FEDERAL LABOR LAWS PROTECT WORKERS IN PRIVATE EMPLOYMENT. Muriel E. Merkel. The Vanguard Press, 201 East Fiftieth Street, Second Floor, New York, New York 10022. 1985.

YOUR RIGHTS IN THE WORKPLACE. Dan Lacey. Nolo Press, 950 Parker Street, Berkeley, California 94710. 1991.

TEXTBOOKS AND GENERAL WORKS

ADVANCED LABOR AND EMPLOYMENT LAW. American Law Institute-American Bar Association, Committee on Continuing Professional Education, 4025 Chestnut Street, Philadelphia, Pennsylvania 19104. 1985.

ADVANCED STRATEGIES IN EMPLOYMENT LAW, 1988. Jerome B. Kauff. Practising Law Institute, 810 Seventh Avenue, New York, New York 10019. 1988.

AIDS IN THE WORKPLACE: LEGAL QUESTIONS AND PRACTICAL ANSWERS. William F. Banta. Lexington Books, 125 Spring Street, Lexington, Massachusetts 02173. 1988.

AIRLINE LABOR AND EMPLOYMENT LAW: A COMPREHENSIVE ANALYSIS. American Law Institute, 4025 Chestnut Street, Philadelphia, Pennsylvania 19104. 1984.

AIRLINE LABOR LAW: THE RAILWAY LABOR ACT AND AVIATION AFTER DEREGULATION. William E. Thoms and Frank J. Dooley. Quorum Books, Greenwood Publishing Group, Incorporated, 88 Post Road West, P.O. Box 5007, Westport, Connecticut 06881. 1990.

AMERICAN LABOR POLICY: A CRITICAL APPRAISAL OF THE NATIONAL LABOR RELATIONS ACT. Charles J. Morris, Editor. Bureau of National Affairs, 1231 Twenty-fifth Street, Northwest, Washington, D.C. 20037. 1987.

AMERICAN WORKERS, AMERICAN UNIONS, 1920-1985. Robert H. Zieger. Johns Hopkins University Press, 701 West Fortieth Street, Suite 275, Baltimore, Maryland 21211-2190. 1986.

BASICS PATTERNS IN UNION CONTRACTS. Twelfth Edition. Bureau of National Affairs, 1231 Twenty-fifth Street, Northwest, Washington, D.C. 20037. 1989.

BELATED FEUDALISM: LABOR, THE LAW, AND LIBERAL DEVELOPMENT IN THE UNITED STATES. Karen Orren. Cambridge University Press, 40 West Twentieth Street, New York, New York 10011. 1991.

BNA PLUS GUIDE TO FEDERAL LABOR LAWS. Bureau of National Affairs, Incorporated, 1231 Twenty-fifth Street, Northwest, Washington, D.C. 20037. 1988.

CASES IN COLLECTIVE BARGAINING AND INDUSTRIAL RELATIONS: A DECISIONAL APPROACH. Sixth Edition. Sterling H. Schoen and Raymond L. Hilgert. Richard D. Irwin, Incorporated, 1818 Ridge Road, Homewood, Illinois 60430. 1988.

THE CHANGING LAW OF FAIR REPRESENTATION. Jean T. McKelvey, Editor. ILR Press, New York State School of Industrial Relations, Cornell University, Box 1000, Ithaca, New York 14851-0952. 1985.

THE COLD WAR AGAINST LABOR: AN ANTHOLOGY. Ann Fagan Ginger and David Christiano, Editors. Meiklejohn Civil Liberties Institute, P.O. Box 673, Berkeley, California 94701. 1987.

COLLECTIVE BARGAINING. Third Edition. Neil W. Chamberlain and James W. Kuhn. McGraw-Hill Book Company, 1221 Avenue of the Americas, New York, New York 10020. 1985.

COLLECTIVE BARGAINING BY OBJECTIVES: A POSITIVE APPROACH. Second Edition. Reed C. Richardson. Prentice-Hall, Incorporated, 113 Sylvan Avenue, Englewood Cliffs, New Jersey 07632. 1985.

COLLECTIVE BARGAINING IN A CHANGING ENVIRONMENT. M. David Vaughn. Practising Law Institute, 810 Seventh Avenue, New York, New York 10019. 1982.

COMBINATION AND CONSPIRACY: A LEGAL HISTORY OF TRADE UNIONISM, 1721-1906. John V. Orth. Oxford University Press, 200 Madison Avenue, New York, New York 10016. 1991.

COMPARATIVE LABOR LAW AND INDUSTRIAL RELATIONS. Third Edition. Roger Blanpain, Editor. Kluwer Law Book Publishers, Incorporated, 36 West Forty-fourth Street, New York, New York 10036. 1988.

COMPARATIVE LABOUR LAW: ANGLO-SOVIET PERSPECTIVES. W. E. Butler. Gower Publishing Company, Old Post Road, Brookfield, Vermont 05036. 1987.

CONSTRUCTION LABOR RELATIONS. Arthur B. Smith. Commerce Clearing House, Incorporated, 4025 West Peterson Avenue, Chicago, Illinois 60646. 1984.

CONTEMPORARY COLLECTIVE BARGAINING. Fourth Edition. Harold W. Davey, Mario F. Bognanno and David L. Estenson. Prentice-Hall, Incorporated, 113 Sylvan Avenue, Englewood Cliffs, New Jersey 07632. 1982.

CURRENT TRENDS AND DEVELOPMENT IN LABOR AND EMPLOYEE RELATIONS LAW. Jay W. Waks. Practising Law Institute, 810 Seventh Avenue, New York, New York 10019. 1982.

THE DEVELOPING LABOR LAW: THE BOARD, THE COURTS, AND THE NATIONAL LABOR RELATIONS ACT. Second Edition. Charles J. Morris, Editor. Bureau of National Affairs, 1231 Twenty-fifth Street, Northwest, Washington, D.C. 20037. 1983. (Supplement 1985).

DISPUTE RESOLUTION: NEGOTIATION AND CONSENSUS BUILDING. John T. Dunlop. Greenwood Publishing Group, Incorporated, 88 Post Road West, P.O. Box 5007, West Port, Connecticut 06881. 1984.

THE ECONOMICS OF COLLECTIVE BARGAINING: CASE STUDIES IN THE PRIVATE SECTOR. Charles Craypo. Bureau of National Affairs, 1231 Twenty-fifth Street, Northwest, Washington, D.C. 20037. 1986.

THE ECONOMICS OF COMPARABLE WORTH. Mark Aldrich. Ballinger Publishing Company, Subsidiary of HarperCollins, Publishers, 10 East Fifty-third Street, New York, New York 10022. 1986.

THE ECONOMICS OF WAGE CONTROLS. K. Holden. Saint Martin's Press, Incorporated, 175 Fifth Avenue, New York, New York 10010. 1987.

THE ECONOMICS OF WORK AND PAY. Fourth Edition. Daniel S. Mamermesh and Albert Rees. HarperCollins Publishers, 10 East Fifty-third Street, New York, New York 10022. 1987.

EMPLOYEE PARTICIPATION AND LABOR LAW IN THE AMERICAN WORKPLACE. Raymond L. Hogler and Guillermo J. Grenier. Quorum Books, Greenwood Publishing Group, Incorporated, 88 Post Road West, P.O. Box 5007, Westport, Connecticut 06881. 1992.

EMPLOYER'S GUIDE TO STRIKE PLANNING AND PREVENTION. Mark A. Hutcheson. Practising Law Institute, 810 Seventh Avenue, New York, New York 10019. 1985.

THE EMPLOYMENT CONTRACT: RIGHTS AND DUTIES OF EMPLOYERS AND EMPLOYEES. Warren Freedman. Quorum Books, Greenwood Publishing Group, Incorporated, 88 Post Road West, P.O. Box 5007, Westport, Connecticut 06881. 1989.

EXTRATERRITORIAL EMPLOYMENT STANDARDS OF THE UNITED STATES: THE REGULATION OF THE OVERSEAS WORKPLACE. James Michael Zimmerman. Quorum Books, Greenwood Publishing Group, Incorporated, 88 Post Road West, P.O. Box 5007, Westport, Connecticut 06881. 1992.

THE FAIR LABOR ACT OF 1938. Irving J. Sloan, Editor. Oceana Publications, Incorporated, 75 Main Street, Dobbs Ferry, New York 10522. 1984.

FEDERAL LABOR LAWS. Seventh Edition. West Publishing Company, P.O. Box 64526, 50 West Kellogg Boulevard, St. Paul, Minnesota 55164-0526. 1986.

GOVERNING THE WORKPLACE: THE FUTURE OF LABOR AND EMPLOYMENT LAW. Paul C. Weiler. Harvard University Press, 79 Garden Street, Cambridge, Massachusetts 02138. 1990.

HANDLING AND PREVENTION OF FAIR REPRESENTATION AND BREACH OF LABOR CONTRACT CASES: MANAGEMENT AND UNION VIEWPOINTS. Paul I. Weiner, Chairman. Practising Law Institute, 810 Seventh Avenue, New York, New York 10019. 1985.

HAZARD COMMUNICATION-FEDERAL AND STATE RIGHT-TO-KNOW LAWS. Commerce Clearing House, Incorporated, 4025 West Peterson Avenue, Chicago, Illinois 60646. 1985.

HUMAN RIGHTS AND EUORPEAN POLITICS: THE LEGAL-POLITICAL STATUS OF WORKERS IN THE EUROPEAN COMMUNITY. Fritz Fabricius. St. Martin's Press, 175 Fifth Avenue, New York, New York 10010. 1992.

INDIVIDUAL EMPLOYMENT LAW AND LITIGATION. Howard A. Specter and Matthew W. Finkin. Michie Company, P.O. Box 7587, Charlottesville, Virginia 22906. 1989.

AN INTRODUCTION TO LABOR LAW. Michael Evan Gold. ILR Press, New York State School of Industrial and Labor Relations. Cornell University Press, 124 Roberts Place, Ithaca, New York 14850. 1989.

ISSUES IN MANAGEMENT-LABOR RELATIONS IN THE 1990'S. Stephen G. Peitchinis. Saint Martin's Press, Incorporated, 175 Fifth Avenue, New York, New York 10010. 1985.

JAPAN'S AGREEMENT IN NEGOTIATION AND ARBITRATION. Arnold M. Zack and Richard I. Bloch. Bureau of National Affairs, 1231 Twenty-fifth Street, Northwest, Washington, D.C. 20037. 1983.

LABOR AND EMPLOYMENT LAW: RESOURCE MATERIALS. Second Edition. Peter M. Panken, Editor. American Law Institute-American Bar Association, Committee on Continuing Professional Education, 4025 Chestnut Street, Philadelphia, Pennsylvania 19104. 1984.

LABOR GUIDE TO LABOR LAW. Third Edition. Bruce S. Feldacker. Reston Publishing Company, Incorporated, 113 Sylvan Avenue, Englewood Cliffs, New Jersey 07632. 1990.

LABOR GUIDE TO NEGOTIATING WAGES AND BENEFITS. Gene Daniels and Kenneth Gagala. Reston Publishing Company, Incorporated, 113 Sylvan Avenue, Englewood Cliffs, New Jersey 07632. 1985.

LABOR INJUNCTIONS. H. H. Perritt. John Wiley and Sons, Incorporated, 605 Third Avenue, New York, New York 10158. 1986.

LABOR LAW AND INDUSTRIAL RELATIONS IN THE UNITED STATES OF AMERICA. Second Edition. Albin L. Goldman. Bureau of National Affairs, 1231 Twenty-fifth Street, Northwest, Washington, D.C. 20037. 1984.

LABOR LAW AND LEGISLATION. Seventh Edition. David P. Twomey. South-Western Publishing Company, 5101 Madison Road, Cincinnati, Ohio 45227. 1986.

LABOR LAW AND THE EMPLOYMENT MARKET: FOUNDATIONS AND APPLICATIONS. Richard A. Epstein and Jeffrey Paul, Editors. Transaction Books, Rutgers University, New Brunswick, New Jersey 08093. 1985.

LABOR LAW IN A NUTSHELL. Third Edition. Douglas L. Leslie. West Publishing Company, 50 West Kellogg Boulevard, St. Paul, Minnesota 55164-0526. 1992.

LABOR LAW IN AMERICA: HISTORICAL AND CRITICAL ESSAYS. Christopher L. Tomlins and Andrew J. King. Johns Hopkins University Press, 701 West Fortieth Street, Baltimore, Maryland 21211. 1992.

LABOR RELATIONS. Seventh Edition. Arthur A. Sloane and Fred Witney. Prentice-Hall, Incorporated, 113 Sylvan Avenue, Englewood Cliffs, New Jersey 07632. 1991.

LABOR RELATIONS AND THE LITIGATION EXPLOSION. Robert J. Flanagan. Brookings Institution, 1775 Massachusetts Avenue, Washington, D.C. 20036. 1987.

LABOR RELATIONS CONSULTANTS: ISSUES, TRENDS, AND CONTROVERSIES. Bureau of National Affairs, 1231 Twenty-fifth Street, Northwest, Washington, D.C. 20037. 1985.

LABOR RELATIONS FOR THE PRACTITIONER. Walter E. Baer. McFarland and Company, Incorporated, Box 611, Jefferson, North Carolina 28640. 1989.

LABOR RELATIONS IN AN ECONOMIC RECESSION: JOB LOSSES AND CONCESSION BARGAINING. Bureau of National Affairs, 1231 Twenty-fifth Street, Northwest, Washington, D.C. 20037. 1982.

LABOR RELATIONS IN PROFESSIONAL SPORTS. Robert C. Berry, William B. Gould, IV, and Paul D. Staudohar. Greenwood Publishing Group, Incorporated, 88 Post Road West, P.O. Box 5007, Westport, Connecticut 06881. 1986.

LABOR RELATIONS LAW. Sixth Edition. Benjamin J. Taylor and Fred Witney. Prentice-Hall, Incorporated, 113 Sylvan Avenue, Englewood Cliffs, New Jersey 07632. 1992.

LABOR RELATIONS LAW: CASES AND MATERIALS. Eighth Edition. Leroy Merrifield, et al. Michie/Bobbs-Merrill, The Michie Company, P.O. Box 7587, Charlottesville, Virginia 22906-7582. 1989.

LABOR RELATIONS LAW IN CORPORATE RETRENCHMENT. Jay W. Waks, Chairman. Practising Law Institute, 810 Seventh Avenue, New York, New York 10019. 1984.

LABOR RELATIONS LAW IN THE PUBLIC SECTOR. Fourth Edition. Harry T. Edwards. The Michie Company, P.O. Box 7587, Charlottesville, Virginia 22906-7582. 1991. (1990 Supplement).

LABOR RELATIONS: LAW, PRACTICE AND POLICY. Second Edition. Julius G. Getman and John D. Blackburn. Foundation Press, Incorporated, 615 Merrick Avenue, Westbury, New York 11590. 1982. (1988 Supplement).

LABOR RELATIONS: PROCESS AND OUTCOMES. Marcus Hart Sandver. Little, Brown and Company, 34 Beacon Street, Boston, Massachusetts 02108. 1987.

LABOUR LAW AND INDUSTRIAL RELATIONS OF THE EUROPEAN COMMUNITY. R. Blanpain. Kluwer Academic Publishers, 101 Philip Drive, Assinippi Park, Norwell, Massachusetts 02061. 1991.

LAW AND THE SHAPING OF THE AMERICAN LABOR MOVEMENT. William E. Forbath. Harvard University Press, 79 Garden Street, Cambridge, Massachusetts 02138. 1991.

THE LAW OF THE WORKPLACE: RIGHTS OF EMPLOYERS AND EMPLOYEES. Second Edition. James W. Hunt. Bureau of National Affairs, Incorporated, 1231 Twenty-fifth Street, Northwest, Washington, D.C. 20037. 1988.

LEGAL PROTECTION FOR THE INDIVIDUAL EMPLOYEE. Matthew W. Finkin, Alvin L. Goldman and Clyde W. Summers. West Publishing Company, 50 West Kellogg Boulevard, St. Paul, Minnesota 55164. 1989.

MANAGING EMPLOYEE RIGHTS AND RESPONSIBILITIES. Chimezie A. B. Osigweh, Editor. Quorum Books, Greenwood Publishing Group, Incorporated, 88 Post Road West, P.O. Box 5007, Westport, Connecticut 06881. 1989.

MANAGING WORKPLACE DISPUTES FROM PREVENTION TO CURE: HUMAN RESOURCE PROFESSIONALS AND ATTORNEYS WORKING TOGETHER. American Bar Association, Section of Litigation, Division of Professional Education, 750 North Lake Shore Drive, Chicago, Illinois 60611. 1991.

MODERN LAW OF EMPLOYMENT RELATIONSHIPS. Charles G. Bakaly, Jr. and Joel M. Grossman. Prentice-Hall, Incorporated, 113 Sylvan Avenue, Englewood Cliffs, New Jersey 07632. 1989.

THE NATIONAL LABOR RELATIONS ACT OF 1935. Irving J. Sloan, Editor. Oceana Publications, Incorporated, 75 Main Street, Dobbs Ferry, New York 10522. 1984.

NLRB PRACTICE. Lee Modjeska. Lawyers Cooperative Publishing Company, Aqueduct Building, Rochester, New York 14694. 1983. (Periodic Supplements).

NLRB REGULATION OF ELECTION CONDUCT. Robert E. Williams. Industrial Research Unit, Wharton School, University of Pennsylvania, 3733 Spruce Street, Philadelphia, Pennsylvania 19104. 1985.

NLRB REPRESENTATION ELECTIONS: LAW, PRACTICE, AND PROCEDURE. John D. Feerick, Henry P. Baer and Jonathon P. Afra. Law and Business, Harcourt Brace Jovanovich, Incorporated, 6277 Sea Harbor Drive, Orlando, Florida 32821. 1985.

ORGANIZING AND THE LAW. Fourth Edition. Stephen I. Schlossberg and Judith A. Scott. Bureau of National Affairs, 1231 Twenty-fifth Street, Northwest, Washington, D.C. 20037. 1991.

PERSONNEL LAW. Second Edition. Kenneth L. Sovereign. Prentice-Hall, Incorporated, 113 Sylvan Avenue, Englewood Cliffs, New Jersey 07632. 1989.

THE PLANT CLOSURE POLICY DILEMMA: LABOR, LAW, AND BARGAINING. Wayne R. Wendling. W. E. Upjohn Insitute for Employment Research, 300 South Westnedge Avenue, Kalamazoo, Michigan 49007-4686. 1984.

PRACTICAL LABOR RELATIONS. Kenneth A. Kovach. University Press of America, 4720 Boston Way, Lanham, Maryland 20706. 1987.

THE PRACTICE OF COLLECTIVE BARGAINING. Eighth Edition. Edwin F. Beal and James P. Begin. Richard D. Irwin, Incorporated, 1818 Ridge Road, Homewood, Illinois 60430. 1989.

A PRIMER ON AMERICAN LABOR LAW. Second Edition. William B. Gould. MIT Press, 55 Hayward Street, Cambridge, Massachusetts 02142. 1986.

PROTECTING AMERICAN WORKERS: AN ASSESSMENT OF GOVERNMENT PROGRAMS. Sar A. Levitan, Peter E. Carlson and Issac Shapiro. Bureau of National Affairs, 1231 Twenty-fifth Street, Northwest, Washington, D.C. 20037. 1986.

PUBLIC SECTOR MEDIATION. Arnold M. Zack. Bureau of National Affairs, 1231 Twenty-fifth Street, Northwest, Washington, D.C. 20037. 1985.

READINGS AND CASES IN LABOR RELATIONS AND COLLECTIVE BARGAINING. James E. Martin and Timothy J. Keaveny, Editors. Addison-Wesley Publishing Company, Route 128, Reading, Massachusetts 01867. 1985.

THE RIGHT TO STRIKE IN PUBLIC EMPLOYMENT. Second Edition. Grace Sterrett and Antone Aboud. ILR Press, New York State School of Industrial Relations, Cornell University, Box 1000, Ithaca, New York 14851-0952. 1982.

THE RIGHTS OF EMPLOYEES: THE BASIC ACLU GUIDE TO AN EMPLOYEE'S RIGHTS. Wayne N. Otten. Bantam Books, Incorporated, 666 Fifth Avenue, New York, New York 10103. 1983.

RIGHTS V. CONSPIRACY: A SOCIOLOGICAL ESSAY ON THE HISTORY OF LABOUR LAW IN THE UNITED STATES. Anthony Woodiwiss. St. Martin's Press, 175 Fifth Avenue, New York, New York 10010. 1990.

THE SPORTS INDUSTRY AND COLLECTIVE BARGAINING. Second Edition. Paul D. Staudohar. ILR Press, New York State School of Industrial Relations, Cornell University, Box 1000, Ithaca, New York 14851-0952. 1989.

THE STATE AND THE UNIONS: LABOR RELATIONS, LAW AND THE ORGANIZED LABOR MOVEMENT IN AMERICA, 1880-1960. Christopher L. Tomlins. Cambridge University Press, 40 West Twentieth Street, New York, New York 10011. 1985.

STRIKES, DISPUTE PROCEDURES AND ARBITRATION. William B. Gould. Greenwood Publishing Group, Incorporated, 88 Post Road West, P.O. Box 5007, Westport, Connecticut 06881. 1985.

TEACHER STRIKES AND THE COURTS. David L. Colton and Edith E. Graber. Lexington Books, Division of D.C. Heath and Company, 125 Spring Street, Lexington, Massachusetts 02173. 1982.

UNION VIOLENCE: THE RECORD AND THE RESPONSE BY COURTS, LEGISLATURES AND THE NLRB. Armand J. Theiblot and Thomas R. Haggard. University of Pennsylvania, The Wharton School, Industrial Research Unit, 37733 Spruce Street, Philadelphia, Pennsylvania 19104. 1984.

UNIONS, WORKERS AND THE LAW. Betty W. Justice. Bureau of National Affairs, 1231 Twenty-fifth Street, Northwest, Washington, D.C. 20037. 1983.

U.S. LABOR RELATIONS LAW: HISTORICAL DEVELOPMENT. Benjamin J. Taylor and Fred Witney. Prentice-Hall, Incorporated, 113 Sylvan Avenue, Englewood Cliffs, New Jersey 07632. 1992.

VALUES AND ASSUMPTIONS IN AMERICAN LABOR LAW. James B. Atleson. University of Massachusetts Press, P.O. Box 429, Amherst, Massachusetts 01004. 1983.

VULNERABLE WORKERS: PSYCHOSOCIAL AND LEGAL ISSUES. Marilyn J. Davidson and Jill Earnshaw, Editors. John Wiley and Sons, Incorporated, 605 Third Avenue, New York, New York 10158. 1991.

WORKER CAPITALISM: THE NEW INDUSTRIAL RELATIONS. Keith Bradley and Alan Gelb. MIT Press, 55 Hayward Street, Cambridge, Massachusetts 02142. 1983.

WORKERS' COMPENSATION AND EMPLOYEE PROTECTION LAWS IN A NUTSHELL. Second Edition. Jack B. Hood, Benjamin A. Hardy, Jr. and Harold S. Lewis, Jr. West Publishing Company, 50 West Kellogg Boulevard, St. Paul, Minnesota 55164. 1990.

WORKER'S RIGHTS. Mary Gibson. Rowman and Allanheld, Division of Littlefield, Adams and Company, 420 Boston Way, Lanham, Maryland 20706. 1983.

WORKPLACE TORTS: RIGHTS AND LIABILITIES. Henry H. Perritt, Jr. John Wiley and Sons, Incorporated, 605 Third Avenue, New York, New York 10158. 1991.

YOUR RIGHTS AT WORK. Darien A. McWhirter. John Wiley and Sons, Incorporated, 605 Third Avenue, New York, New York 10158. 1989.

ENCYCLOPEDIAS AND DICTIONARIES

LABOR AND INDUSTRIAL RELATIONS: TERMS, LAWS, COURT DECISIONS, AND ARBITRATION STANDARDS. Matthew A. Kelly. Johns Hopkins University Press, 701 West Fortieth Street, Baltimore, Maryland 21211. 1987.

ROBERT'S DICTIONARY OF INDUSTRIAL RELATIONS. Third Edition. Harold S. Roberts. Industrial Relations Center of the University of Hawaii. BNA Books Distribution Center, 300 Raritan Center Parkway, Edison, New Jersey 08818. 1986.

DIGESTS, INDEXES, ABSTRACTS, CITATORS

SHEPARD'S FEDERAL LABOR LAW CASE NAMES CITATOR: A COMPILATION OF CASE NAMES AND CITATIONS OF FEDERAL LABOR CASES DECIDED FROM 1945 TO THE PRESENT. Shepard's/McGraw-Hill, P.O. Box 1235, Colorado Springs, Colorado 80901. 1989.

SHEPARD'S FEDERAL LABOR LAW CITATIONS. Second Edition. Shepard's/McGraw-Hill, P.O. Box 1235, Colorado Springs, Colorado 80901. 1987.

ANNUALS AND SURVEYS

ANNUAL LABOR AND EMPLOYMENT LAW INSTITUTE. University of Louisville School of Law. Fred B. Rothman and Company, 10368 West Centennial Road, Littleton, Colorado 80127. Annual.

LAW REVIEWS AND PERIODICALS

THE ARBITRATION JOURNAL. American Arbitration Association, 140 West Fifty-first Street, New York, New York 10020. Quarterly.

COMPARATIVE LABOR LAW. International Society for Labor Law and Social Security, United States National Branch, University of California at Los Angeles, School of Law, Los Angeles, California 90024. Quarterly.

EMPLOYMENT RELATIONS LAW JOURNAL. Executive Enterprises, Incorporated, 33 West Sixtieth Street, New York, New York 10023. Quarterly.

GOVERNMENT UNION REVIEW. Public Service Research Foundation, 8330 Old Courthouse Road, Suite 600, Vienna, Virginia 22180. Quarterly.

THE GUILD PRACTITIONERS. P.O. Box 673, Berkeley, California 94701. Quarterly.

HOFSTRA LABOR LAW FORUM. Hofstra University School of Law, Hempstead, New York 11550. Semiannual.

INDUSTRIAL AND LABOR RELATIONS REVIEW. New York State School of Industrial and Labor Relations, Cornell University Press, 124 Roberts Place, P.O. Box 250, Ithaca, New York 14851. Quarterly.

INDUSTRIAL RELATIONS. Institute of Industrtial Relations, University of California, Berkeley, California 94720. Semiannually.

INDUSTRIAL RELATIONS LAW JOURNAL. University of California, Boalt Hall, School of Law, 2120 Berkeley Way, Berkeley, California 94720. Quarterly.

JOURNAL OF COLLECTIVE NEGOTIATIONS IN THE PUBLIC SECTOR. Baywood Publishing Company, Incorporated, 120 Marine Street, Farmingdale, New York 11735. Quarterly.

LABOR LAW JOURNAL. Commerce Clearing House, Incorporated, 4025 West Peterson Avenue, Chicago, Illinois 60646. Monthly.

LABOR LAWYER. American Bar Association, Section of Labor and Employment Law, 750 North Lake Shore Drive, Chicago, Illinois 60611. Quarterly.

NEWSLETTERS AND NEWSPAPERS

BNA'S EMPLOYEE RELATIONS WEEKLY. Bureau of National Affairs, Incorporated, 1231 Twenty-fifth Street, Northwest, Washington, D.C. 20037. Weekly.

COLLECTIVE BARGAINING CONTRACT CLAUSES. Business Research Publications, Incorporated, 817 Broadway, New York, New York 10003. Semimonthly.

CONSTRUCTION LABOR REPORT. Bureau of National Affairs, Incorporated, 1231 Twenty-fifth Street, Northwest, Washington, D.C. 20037. Weekly.

DAILY LABOR REPORT. Bureau of National Affairs, 1231 Twenty-fifth Street, Northwest, Washington, D.C. 20037. Daily.

DISCIPLINE AND GRIEVANCES (BLUE COLLAR EDITION). The Bureau of Business Practice, Incorporated, 24 Rope Ferry Road, Waterford, Connecticut 06386. Monthly.

DISCIPLINE AND GRIEVANCES (GOVERNMENT EDITION). The Bureau of Business Practice, Incorporated, 24 Rope Ferry Road, Waterford, Connecticut 06386. Monthly.

EMPLOYEE RELATIONS IN ACTION. Business Research Publications, Incorporated, 817 Broadway, New York, New York 10003. Semimonthly.

EMPLOYEE TESTING AND THE LAW. Vanguard Information Publications, P.O. Box 667, Chapel Hill, North Carolina 27514. Monthly.

EMPLOYMENT ALERT. Research Institute of America, Incorporated, 90 Fifth Avenue, New York, New York 10011. Biweekly.

EMPLOYMENT LAW BRIEFING. Sachnoff and Weaver Limited, 30 South Wacker Drive, Twenty-ninth Floor, Chicago, Illinois 60606. Quarterly.

EMPLOYMENT LAW NEWS. National Employment Law Project, 475 Riverside Drive, Suite 240, New York, New York 10115. Quarterly.

EMPLOYMENT LAW UPDATE. Rutkowski and Associates, Incorporated, P.O. Box 15250, Evansville, Indiana 47716. Monthly.

FOUNDATION ACTION. National Right to Work Legal Defense Foundation, 8001 Braddock Road, Springfield, Virginia 22160. Bimonthly.

HEALTH LABOR RELATIONS REPORTS. Interwood Publications, P.O. Box 20241, Cincinnati, Ohio 45220. Semimonthly.

HUMAN RESOURCES MANAGEMENT - IDEAS AND TRENDS. Commerce Clearing House, Incorporated, 4025 West Peterson Avenue, Chicago, Illinois 60646. Biweekly.

JUDGE O'BRIENS EMPLOYMENT NEWS. Winterbrook Publishing Company, P.O. Box 1106, Covina, California 91722. Monthly.

LABOR AND EMPLOYMENT LAW NEWSLETTER. American Bar Association, Labor and Employment Law Section, 750 North Lake Shore Drive, Chicago, Illinois 60611. Quarterly.

LABOR AND EMPLOYMENT LAW NEWSLETTER. Matthew Bender and Company, Incorporated, 11 Penn Plaza, New York, New York 10001. Monthly.

LABOR AND EMPLOYMENT UPDATE. Reed, McClure, Moceri, Thorn and Morianty, 3600 Columbia Center, 701 Fifth Avenue, Seattle, Washington 98104. Quarterly.

LABOR ARBITRATION IN GOVERNMENT. American Arbitration Association, 140 West Fifty-first Street, New York, New York 10020. Monthly.

LABOR CONTRACT LAW BULLETIN. Quinlan Publishing Company, 23 Drydock Avenue, Boston, Massachusetts 02110. Monthly.

LABOR LAW PERSONNEL NOTES. NYPER Publications, P.O. Box 662, Latham, New York 12110. Monthly.

LABOR LAW REPORTS. Commerce Clearing House, Incorporated, 4025 West Peterson Avenue, Chicago, Illinois 60646. Weekly.

LABOR RELATIONS CIRCULAR. R.C. Simpson Company, P.O. Box 567, Ridgewood, New Jersey 07451. Monthly.

LABOR RELATIONS WEEK. Bureau of National Affairs, Incorporated, 1231 Twenty-fifth Street, Northwest, Washington, D.C. 20037. Weekly.

LABOR UPDATE. National Labor Law Center, and National Lawyer's Guild, 2000 P Street, Northwest, Washington, D.C. 20036. Bimonthly.

LABORWATCH. Laborwatch, Incorporated, 10050 Regency Circle, Suite 403, Omaha, Nebraska 68114. Bimonthly.

LEGAL INSIGHTS FOR MANAGERS. Bureau of Business Practice, 24 Rope Ferry Road, Waterford, Connecticut 06386. Monthly.

NATIONAL REPORT ON EMPLOYEE TERMINATIONS. Quinlan Publishing Company, Incorporated, 23 Drydock Avenue, Boston, Massachusetts 02110. Monthly.

NATIONAL RIGHT TO WORK NEWSLETTER. National Right to Work Committee, 8001 Braddock Road, Springfield, Virginia 22160. Monthly.

PERSONNEL LAW UPDATE. Borgman Associates, 321 Lennon Lane, Walnut Creek, California 94598. Monthly.

PERSONNEL MANAGERS LEGAL REPORTER. Business and Legal Reports, 64 Wall Street, Madison, Connecticut 06443. Monthly.

POLICE OFFICER GRIEVANCES BULLETIN. Quinlan Publishing Company, Incorporated, 23 Drydock Avenue, Boston, Massachusetts 02110. Monthly.

SUMMARY OF LABOR ARBITRATION AWARDS. American Arbitration Association, 140 West Fifty-first Street, New York, New York 10020. Monthly.

UNFAIR LABOR PRACTICES LAW BULLETIN. Quinlan Publishing Company, Incorporated, 23 Drydock Avenue, Boston, Massachusetts 02110. Monthly.

UNION LABOR REPORT WEEKLY NEWSLETTER. Bureau of National Affairs, Incorporated, 1231 Twenty-fifth Street, Northwest, Washington, D.C. 20037. Weekly.

UNION LABOR REPORT'S ON THE LINE. Bureau of National Affairs, Incorporated, 1231 Twenty-fifth Street, Northwest, Washington, D.C. 20037. Quarterly.

WHAT TO DO ABOUT PERSONNEL PROBLEMS. Business and Legal Reports, 64 Wall Street, Madison, Connecticut 06443. Monthly.

WHAT'S NEW IN COLLECTIVE BARGAINING NEGOTIATIONS AND CONTRACTS. Bureau of National Affairs, Incorporated, 1231 Twenty-fifth Street, Northwest, Washington, D.C. 20037. Biweekly.

WORK IN AMERICA. Buraff Publications, 1350 Connecticut Avenue, Northwest, Suite 1000, Washington, D.C. 20036. Monthly.

WORKPLACE REGULATORY REPORT. Management Resources, Incorporated, 379 West Broadway, Fourth Floor, New York, New York 10012. Monthly.

WRONGFUL DISCHARGE REPORT. Andrews Publications, 1646 West Chester Pike, Westtown, Pennsylvania 19395. Monthly.

WRONGFUL TERMINATION REPORTER. Andrews Publications, 1646 West Chester Pike, Westtown, Pennsylvania 19395. Semimonthly.

YOU AND THE LAW. National Institute of Business Management, Incorporated, 1328 Broadway, New York, New York 10001. Semimonthly.

BIBLIOGRAPHIES

COLLECTIVE BARGAINING UNITS: A SELECTIVE BIBLIOGRAPHY OF PERIODICAL ARTICLES. Marian Dworaczek. Vance Bibliographies, P.O. Box 229, 112 North Charter Street, Monticello, Illinois 61856. 1983.

EMPLOYMENT-AT-WILL. Joseph L. Cook and Earleen H. Cook. Vance Bibliographies, P.O. Box 229, 112 North Charter Street, Monticello, Illinois 61856. 1985.

LABOR CONCESSIONS IN COLLECTIVE BARGAINING: AN ARTICLE BIBLIOGRAPHY. Marian Dworaczek. Vance Bibliographies, P.O. Box 229, 112 North Charter Street, Monticello, Illinois 61856. 1984.

LABOR IN AMERICA: A HISTORICAL BIBLIOGRAPHY. ABC-Clio Information Services, Riviera Campus, 2040 Alameda Padre Serra, P.O. Box 1911, Santa Barbara, California 93116-1911. 1985.

LABOR MANAGEMENT RELATIONS IN THE PUBLIC SECTOR: AN ANNOTATED BIBLIOGRAPHY. N. Joseph Cayer and Sherry S. Dickerson. Garland Publishing, Incorporated, 136 Madison Avenue, New York, New York 10016. 1984.

LABOR RELATIONS AND COLLECTIVE BARGAINING: A BIBLIOGRAPHIC GUIDE TO DOCTORAL RESEARCH. Milden J. Fox, Jr. and Patsy C. Howard. Scarecrow Press, 52 Liberty Street, Box 4167, Metuchen, New Jersey 08840. 1983.

PLANT CLOSING LEGISLATION IN THE UNITED STATES: A BIBLIOGRAPHY. Edward Duensing. Vance Bibliographies, P.O. Box 229, 112 North Charter Street, Monticello, Illinois 61856. 1985.

PRIVACY IN THE WORKPLACE: A BIBLIOGRAPHIC SURVEY. Alva W. Stewart. Vance Bibliographies, P.O. Box 229, 112 North Charter Street, Monticello, Illinois 61856. 1987.

WORK STOPPAGES: PROTECTING THE PUBLIC AND THE WORKPLACE: LEGAL ACTIONS AND INTERPRETATIONS, 1980-1985. Vance Bibliographies, P.O. Box 229, 112 North Charter Street, Monticello, Illinois 61856. 1986.

DIRECTORIES

DIRECTORY OF UNITED STATES LABOR ORGANIZATIONS, 1990/1991. Bureau of National Affairs, 1231 Twenty-fifth Street, Northwest, Washington, D.C. 20037. 1990.

LABOR OFFICES IN THE UNITED STATES AND CANADA. Employment Standards Administration, Labor Department, Room S-3524, 200 Constitution Avneue, Northwest, Washington, D.C. 20210. 1984.

ASSOCIATIONS AND PROFESSIONAL SOCIETIES

AMERICAN BAR ASSOCIATION, SECTION OF LABOR AND EMPLOYMENT LAW. 750 North Lake Shore Drive, Chicago, Illinois 60611. (312) 988-5000.

AMERICAN FEDERATION OF LABOR AND CONGRESS OF INDUSTRIAL ORGANIZATION (AFL-CIO). 815 Sixteenth Street, Northwest, Washington, D.C. 20006. (202) 637-5000.

CONGRESS OF INDEPENDENT UNIONS. 303 Ridge Street, Alton, Illinois 62002. (618) 462-2447.

NATIONAL FEDERATION OF INDEPENDENT UNIONS. 1166 South Eleventh Street, Philadelphia, Pennsylvania 19147. (215) 336-3300.

NATIONAL LABOR MANAGEMENT FOUNDATION. 1707 L Street, Northwest, Suite 333, Washington, D.C. 20036. (202) 296-8577.

RESEARCH CENTERS, INSTITUTES, CLEARINGHOUSES

ASSOCIATION FOR UNION DEMOCRACY. YMCA Building, Room 619, 30 Third Avenue, Brooklyn, New York 11217. (718) 855-6650.

INDUSTRIAL RELATIONS RESEARCH ASSOCIATION. 7226 Social Science Building, University of Wisconsin, Madison, Wisconsin 53706. (608) 262-2762.

INSTITUTE OF INDUSTRIAL RELATIONS. University of California Press, 2521 Channing Way, Berkeley, California 94720. (415) 642-5452.

INSTITUTE OF LABOR AND INDUSTRIAL RELATIONS. Victor Vaughn Building, 1111 Catherine, University of Michigan, Ann Arbor, Michigan 48109. (313) 763-3116.

LABOR EDUCATION AND RESEARCH PROJECT. 7435 Michigan Avenue, Detroit, Michigan 48210. (313) 842-6262.

LABOR RELATIONS COUNCIL. University of Pennsylvania, Vance Hall, 3733 Spruce Street, Philadelphia, Pennsylvania 19104. (215) 898-7906.

LABOR RESEARCH ASSOCIATION. 80 East Eleventh Street, New York, New York 10003. (212) 473-1042.

NATIONAL RIGHT TO WORK LEGAL DEFENSE FOUNDATION. 8001 Braddock Road, Springfield, Virginia 22160. (703) 321-8510.

NEW YORK SCHOOL OF INDUSTRIAL RELATIONS. Cornell University, 124 Roberts Place, P.O. Box 250, Ithaca, New York 14851. (607) 255-2000.

ONLINE DATABASES

DAILY LABOR REPORT. Bureau of National Affairs, Incorporated, 1231 Twenty-fifth Street, Northwest, Washington, D.C. 20037.

DIRECTORY OF UNITED STATES LABOR ORGANIZATIONS. Bureau of National Affairs, Incorporated, 1231 Twenty-fifth Street, Northwest, Washington, D.C. 20037.

FROM THE STATE CAPITALS: LABOR RELATIONS. Wakeman Walworth, Incorporated, 300 North Washington Street, Suite 204, Alexandria, Virginia 22314.

JOB ABSENCE AND TURNOVER DATABASE. Bureau of National Affairs, Incorporated, 1231 Twenty-fifth Street, Northwest, Washington, D.C. 20037.

LABOR ARBITRATION INFORMATION SYSTEM. LRP Publications, P.O. Box 579, Fort Washington, Pennsylvania 19034.

LABOR LAW. Bureau of National Affairs, Bureau of National Affairs, Incorporated, 1231 Twenty-fifth Street, Northwest, Washington, D.C. 20037.

LABOR RELATIONS WEEK. Bureau of National Affairs, Incorporated, 1231 Twenty-fifth Street, Northwest, Washington, D.C. 20037.

LABOR STATISTICS. U.S. Bureau of Labor Statistics, 441 G Street, Northwest, Washington, D.C. 20212.

LEXIS FEDERAL LABOR LIBRARY. Mead Data Central, Incorporated, 9393 Springboro Pike, P.O. Box 933, Dayton, Ohio 45401.

UNION LABOR REPORT. Bureau of National Affairs, Incorporated, 1231 Twenty-fifth Street, Northwest, Washington, D.C. 20037.

WESTLAW LABOR AND EMPLOYMENT LIBRARY. West Publishing Company, 50 West Kellogg Boulevard, P.O. Box 64526, St. Paul, Minnesota 55164.

STATISTICS SOURCES

HANDBOOK OF LABOR STATISTICS. United States Bureau of Labor Statistics. Superintendent of Documents, United States Government Printing Office, Washington, D.C. 20402. Annual.

MONTHLY LABOR REVIEW. Bureau of Labor Statistics, Department of Labor. Superintendent of Documents, United States Government Printing Office, Washington, D.C. 20402. Monthly.

COMPUTER-ASSISTED LEGAL INSTRUCTION

RECOGNITIONAL PICKETING. Laura J. Cooper and Elaine Kumpula. Center for Computer-Assisted Instruction, 229 19th Avenue South, University of Minnesota, Minneapolis, Minnesota 55455. Machine-readable computer file.

LABOR ARBITRATION

See also: EMPLOYEES' COMPENSATION APPEALS BOARD; FEDERAL LABOR RELATIONS AUTHORITY; LABOR DEPARTMENT; NATIONAL LABOR RELATIONS BOARD

LABOR ARBITRATION

STATUTES, CODES, STANDARDS, UNIFORM LAWS

UNIFORM ARBITRATION ACT. National Conference of Commissioners on Uniform State Laws. Martindale-Hubbell Law Directory, Volume Eight. Martindale-Hubbell, Incorporated, 121 Chanlon Road, New Providence, New Jersey 07974. Annual.

UNIFORM ARBITRATION ACT. National Conference of Commissioners on Uniform State Laws. Uniform Laws Annotated. West Publishing Company, P.O. Box 64526, 50 West Kellogg Boulevard, St. Paul, Minnesota 55164-0526. 1976. (Annual Supplements).

LOOSELEAF SERVICES AND REPORTERS

LABOR ARBITRATION AWARDS. Commerce Clearing House, Incorporated, 4025 West Peterson Avenue, Chicago, Illinois 60646. 1961- .

LABOR ARBITRATION INFORMATION SYSTEM. Labor Relations Press, P.O. Box 579, Fort Washington, Pennsylvania 19034. 1982- .

LABOR ARBITRATION REPORTS. Bureau of National Affairs, 1231 Twenty-fifth Street, Northwest, Washington, D.C. 20037. 1946- .

HANDBOOKS, MANUALS, FORMBOOKS

THE ARBITRATION HANDBOOK: A GUIDE TO THE PRACTICAL AND LEGAL ISSUES IN LABOR ARBITRATION. Julius M. Steiner. Executive Enterprises Publications Company, 22 West Twenty-first Street, New York, New York 10010-6904. 1989.

FAIRWEATHER'S PRACTICE AND PROCEDURE IN LABOR ARBITRATION. Third Edition. Ray J. Schoonhoven, Editor. Bureau of National Affairs, Incorporated, 1231 Twenty-fifth Street, Northwest, Washington, D.C. 20037. 1991.

FEDERAL ARBITRATION ADVOCATE'S HANDBOOK. Al Celmer and Robert A. Creo. LRP Publications, 747 Dresher Road, Horsham, Pennsylvania 19044. 1991.

LABOR ARBITRATION: A PRACTICAL GUIDE FOR ADVOCATES. Max Zimny, William F. Dolson and Christopher A. Barreca, Editors. American Bar Association, Section of Labor and Employment Law, 750 North Lake Shore Drive, Chicago, Illinois 60611. 1990.

LABOR ARBITRATION DEVELOPMENT: A HANDBOOK. Christopher A. Barreca. Bureau of National Affairs, 1231 Twenty-fifth Street, Northwest, Washington, D.C. 20037. 1983.

TEXTBOOKS AND GENERAL WORKS

ANATOMY OF A LABOR ARBITRATION. Second Edition. Sam Kagel. Bureau of National Affairs, 1231 Twenty-fifth Street, Northwest, Washington, D.C. 20037. 1986.

ARBITRATION AND COLLECTIVE BARGAINING: CONFLICT RESOLUTION IN LABOR RELATIONS. Second Edition. Paul Prasow and Edward Peters. McGraw-Hill Book Company, 1221 Avenue of the Americas, New York, New York 10020. 1983.

BASIC DOCUMENTS ON GRIEVANCE ARBITRATION, PRIVATE SECTOR. Stephen P. Frisbee. Eastman Arbitration Library, American Arbitration Association, 140 West Fifty-first Street, New York, New York 10020. 1990.

BUSINESS ARBITRATION: WHAT YOU NEED TO KNOW. Third Edition. Robert Coulson. American Arbitration Association, 140 West Fifty-first Street, New York, New York 10020. 1986.

COLLECTIVE BARGAINING AND IMPASSE RESOLUTION IN THE PUBLIC SECTOR. David A. Dilts and William J. Walsh. Quorum Books, Greenwood Publishing Group, Incorporated, 88 Post Road West, P.O. Box 5007, Westport, Connecticut 06881. 1988.

COLLECTIVE BARGAINING AND LABOR ARBITRATION. Third Edition. Donald P. Rothschild, Leroy S. Merrifield and Charles B. Craver. Michie Company, P.O. Box 7587, Charlottesville, Virginia 22906. 1988.

DISCHARGE FOR CAUSE: ARBITRAL ENFORCEMENT UNDER THE COLLECTIVE BARGAINING AGREEMENT. Douglas H. Thompson. Praeger Publishers, One Madison Avenue, New York, New York 10010-3603. 1989.

EMPLOYER'S GUIDE TO STRIKE PLANNING AND PREVENTION. Mark A. Hutcheson, et al. Practising Law Institute, 810 Seventh Avenue, New York, New York 10019. 1985.

EMPLOYMENT, LABOR AND PENSION ARBITRATION. Thomas Oehmke. Lawyers Cooperative Publishing Company, Aqueduct Building, Rochester, New York 14694. 1989.

HOW ARBITRATION WORKS. Fourth Edition. Frank Elkouri and Edna Elkouri. Bureau of National Affairs, 1231 Twenty-fifth Street, Northwest, Washington, D.C. 20037. 1985. (Periodic Supplements).

INDUSTRIAL CONFLICT RESOLUTION IN MARKET ECONOMIES: A STUDY OF AUSTRALIA, THE FEDERAL REPUBLIC OF GERMANY, ITALY, JAPAN, AND THE USA. Second Edition. T. Hanami and R. Blanpain, Editors. Kluwer Academic Publishers, 101 Philip Drive, Assinippi Park, Norwell, Massachusetts 02061. 1989.

AN INTRODUCTION TO LABOR ARBITRATION. Charles S. LaCugna. Praeger Publishers, One Madison Avenue, New York, New York 10010-3603. 1988.

JAPAN AGREEMENT IN NEGOTIATION AND ARBITRATION. Arnold M. Zack and Richard I. Bloch. Bureau of National Affairs, 1231 Twenty-fifth Street, Northwest, Washington, D.C. 20037. 1983.

THE LABOR AGREEMENT IN NEGOTIATION AND ARBITRATION. Arnold M. Zack and Richard I. Bloch. Bureau of National Affairs, 1231 Twenty-fifth Street, Northwest, Washington, D.C. 20037. 1983.

LABOR AND EMPLOYMENT ARBITRATION. Tim Bornstein and Ann Gosline, Editors. Matthew Bender and Company, Incorporated, 11 Penn Plaza, New York, New York 10001. 1988- .

LABOR ARBITRATION ADVOCACY: EFFECTIVE TACTICS AND TECHNIQUES. Jay E. Grenig and R. Wayne Estes. Butterworth-Heinemann, 80 Montvale Avenue, Stoneham, Massachusetts 02180. 1989.

LABOR ARBITRATION IN PRACTICE. Arnold M. Zack. ILR Press, New York State School of Industrial Relations, Cornell University, Box 1000, Ithaca, New York 14851-0952. 1985.

LABOR ARBITRATION IN STATE AND LOCAL GOVERNMENT: AN EXAMINATION OF THE EXPERIENCE IN EIGHT STATES AND NEW YORK CITY. Richard A. Lester. Princeton University Press, 41 William Street, Princeton, New Jersey 08540. 1984.

LABOR ARBITRATION LAW AND PRACTICE IN A NUTSHELL. Dennis R. Nolan. West Publishing Company, P.O. Box 64526, 50 West Kellogg Boulevard, St. Paul, Minnesota 55164-0526. 1979.

LABOR ARBITRATION: THE STRATEGY OF PERSUASION. Norman Brand. Practising Law Institute, 810 Seventh Avenue, New York, New York 10019. 1987.

PRACTICE AND PROCEDURE IN LABOR ARBITRATION. Owen Fairweather. Bureau of National Affairs, 1231 Twenty-fifth Street, Northwest, Washington, D.C. 20037. 1983.

REMEDIES IN ARBITRATION. Second Edition. Marvin F. Hill, Jr. and Anthony V. Sinicropi. Bureau of National Affairs, Incorporated, 1231 Twenty-fifth Street, Northwest, Washington, D.C. 20037. 1991.

RETHINKING LABOUR-MANAGEMENT RELATIONS: THE CASE FOR ARBITRATION. Christopher J. Bruce and Jo Carby-Hall. Routledge, Chapman & Hall, 29 West Thirty-fifth Street, New York, New York 10001. 1991.

WINNING IN LABOR ARBITRATION. Walt Baer. National Textbook Company, 4255 West Touhy Avenue, Lincolnwood, Illinois 60646-1975. 1982.

WITNESSES IN ARBITRATION: SELECTION, PREPARATION, AND PRESENTATION. Edward Levin and Donald Grody. Bureau of National Affairs, Incorporated, 1231 Twenty-fifth Street, Northwest, Washington, D.C. 20037. 1987.

DIGESTS, INDEXES, ABSTRACTS, CITATORS

SHEPARD'S LABOR ARBITRATION CITATIONS. Shepard's/McGraw-Hill, P.O. Box 1235, Colorado Springs, Colorado 80901. 1989.

STEEL ARBITRATION DIGEST. John W. Willis, Editor. Pike and Fischer, Incorporated, 4550 Montgomery Avenue, Suite 433N, Bethesda, Maryland 20814. 1961.

LAW REVIEWS AND PERIODICALS

THE ARBITRATION JOURNAL. American Arbitration Association, 140 West Fifty-first Street, New York, New York 10020. Quarterly.

NEWSLETTERS AND NEWSPAPERS

LABOR ARBITRATION IN GOVERNMENT. American Arbitration Association, 140 West Fifty-first Street, New York, New York 10020. Monthly.

LAWYERS ARBITRATION LETTER. American Arbitration Association, 140 West Fifty-first Street, New York, New York 10020. Quarterly.

THE PUNCH LIST. American Arbitration Association, 140 West Fifty-first Street, New York, New York 10020. Quarterly.

SUMMARY OF LABOR ARBITRATION AWARDS. American Arbitration Association, 140 West Fifty-first Street, New York, New York 10020. Monthly.

DIRECTORIES

DIRECTORY OF LABOR ARBITRATORS. Labor Relations Press, Box 579, Fort Washington, Pennsylvania 19034. 1982.

DIRECTORY OF UNITED STATES LABOR ARBITRATORS: A GUIDE FOR FINDING AND USING LABOR ARBITRATORS. Courtney D. Gifford and William P. Hobgood. Bureau of National Affairs, 1231 Twenty-fifth Street, Northwest, Washington, D.C. 20037. 1985.

ASSOCIATIONS AND PROFESSIONAL SOCIETIES

AMERICAN ARBITRATION ASSOCIATION. American Arbitration Association, 140 West Fifty-first Street, New York, New York 10020. (212) 484-4012.

AUDIOVISUALS

LABOR ARBITRATION: THE 1987 CONFERENCE. National Practice Institute, 330 Second Avenue South, Minneapolis, Minnesota 55401. Audiotape.

LABOR ARBITRATION: THE 1988 CONFERENCE. National Practice Institute, 330 Second Avenue South, Minneapolis, Minnesota 55401. Audiotape.

LABOR ARBITRATION: THE 1989 CONFERENCE. National Practice Institute, 330 Second Avenue South, Minneapolis, Minnesota 55401. Audiotape.

LABOR ARBITRATION: THE 1989 MIDWEST CONFERENCE. National Practice Institute, 330 Second Avenue South, Minneapolis, Minnesota 55401. Audiotape.

LABOR ARBITRATION: THE 1989 SAN FRANCISCO CONFERENCE. National Practice Institute, 330 Second Avenue South, Minneapolis, Minnesota 55401. Audiotape.

LABOR ARBITRATION: THE 1990 CONFERENCE. National Practice Institute, 330 Second Avenue South, Minneapolis, Minnesota 55401. Audiotape.

LABOR DEPARTMENT

See also: EMPLOYEES' COMPENSATION APPEALS BOARD; FEDERAL LABOR RELATIONS AUTHORITY; FEDERAL MINE SAFETY AND HEALTH REVIEW COMMISSION; LABOR AND LABOR RELATIONS; MERIT SYSTEMS PROTECTION BOARD; NATIONAL LABOR RELATIONS BOARD; OCCUPATIONAL SAFETY AND HEALTH ADMINISTRATION; OCCUPATIONAL SAFETY AND HEALTH REVIEW COMMISSION

STATUTES, CODES, STANDARDS, UNIFORM LAWS

CODE OF FEDERAL REGULATIONS, TITLE 29. Office of the Federal Register, National Archives and Records Administration. Superintendent of Documents, United States Government Printing Office, Washington, D.C. 20402. Annual. (Updated by use of monthly List of Sections Affected and daily Federal Register).

SAFETY AND HEALTH STANDARDS APPLICABLE TO SURFACE METAL AND NONMETAL MINING AND MILLING OPERATIONS. Labor Department, Mine Safety and Health Administration, Metal and Nonmetal Mine Safety and Health. Superintendent of Documents, United States Government Printing Office, Washington, D.C. 20402. 1985- .

SAFETY AND HEALTH STANDARDS APPLICABLE TO UNDERGROUND METAL AND NONMETAL MINING AND MILLING OPERATIONS. Labor Department, Mine Safety and Health Administration, Metal and Nonmetal Mine Safety and Health. Superintendent of Documents, United States Government Printing Office, Washington, D.C. 20402. 1985- .

HANDBOOKS, MANUALS, FORMBOOKS

COAL MINE INSPECTION MANUAL ON PROCEDURES, ORDERS, CITATIONS AND INSPECTION REPORTS. Labor Department, Mine Safety and Health Administration, Coal Mine Safety and Health. Superintendent of Documents, United States Government Printing Office, Washington, D.C. 20402. 1983- .

DAVIS-BACON CONSTRUCTION WAGE DETERMINATION MANUAL OF OPERATIONS. Labor Department, Employment Standards Administration, Wage and Hour Division. Superintendent of Documents, United States Government Printing Office, Washington, D.C. 20402. 1986.

FEDERAL CONTRACT COMPLIANCE MANUAL. Labor Department, Employment Standards Administration, Office of Federal Contract Compliance Programs. Superintendent of Documents, United States Government Printing Office, Washington, D.C. 20402. 1979- .

GENERAL WAGE DETERMINATIONS ISSUED UNDER THE DAVIS-BACON AND RELATED ACTS. Labor Department, Employment Standards Administration, Wage and Hour Division. Superintendent of Documents, United States Government Printing Office, Washington, D.C. 20402. 1986- .

TEXTBOOKS AND GENERAL WORKS

COMPARISON OF STATE UNEMPLOYMENT INSURANCE LAWS. Labor Department, Employment and Training Administration, Unemployment Insurance Service. Superintendent of Documents, United States Government Printing Office, Washington, D.C. 20402. 1985- .

THE DEPARTMENT OF LABOR. Cheryl Cutrona. Chelsea House Publishers, 1974 Sproul Road, Suite 400, Broomall, Pennsylvania 19008. 1988.

FINAL REPORT TO CONGRESS ON AGE DISCRIMINATION IN EMPLOYMENT ACT STUDIES. Labor Department, Employment Standards Administration. Superintendent of Documents, United States Government Printing Office, Washington, D.C. 20402. 1982.

U.S. DEPARTMENT OF LABOR, THE FIRST SEVENTY-FIVE YEARS. United States. Department of Labor. Superintendent of Documents, United States Government Printing Office, Washington, D.C. 20402. 1988.

DIGESTS, INDEXES, ABSTRACTS, CITATORS

SHEPARD'S FEDERAL LABOR LAW CITATIONS. Shepard's/McGraw-Hill, P.O. Box 1235, Colorado Springs, Colorado 80901. Monthly.

LAW REVIEWS AND PERIODICALS

MONTHLY LABOR REVIEW. Labor Department, Labor Statistics Bureau. Superintendent of Documents, United States Government Printing Office, Washington, D.C. 20402. Monthly.

DIRECTORIES

BUSINESS, MANAGERIAL, AND LEGAL OCCUPATIONS. Labor Department Labor Statistics Bureau. Superintendent of Documents, United States Government Printing Office, Washington, D.C. 20402. 1986.

REGISTER OF REPORTING LABOR ORGANIZATIONS. Labor Department, Office of Labor-Management Standards. Superintendent of Documents, United States Government Printing Office, Washington, D.C. 20402. 1986.

RESEARCH CENTERS, INSTITUTES, CLEARINGHOUSES

NATIONAL LABOR RELATIONS BOARD LIBRARY. 1717 Pennsylvania Avenue, Northwest, Washington, D.C. 20570. (202) 254-7126.

UNITED STATES DEPARTMENT OF LABOR LAW LIBRARY. 200 Constitution Avenue, Northwest, Room N-2439, Washington, D.C. 20210. (202) 523-6414.

ONLINE DATABASES

LEXIS, FEDERAL LABOR LIBRARY. Mead Data Central, P.O. Box 933, Dayton, Ohio 45401.

WESTLAW, LABOR LIBRARY. West Publishing Company, P.O. Box 64526, 50 West Kellogg Boulevard, St. Paul, Minnesota 55164-0526.

STATISTICS SOURCES

HANDBOOK OF LABOR STATISTICS. Labor Department, Labor Statistics Bureau. Superintendent of Documents, United States Government Printing Office, Washington, D.C. 20402. 1989.

LABOR RELATIONS
See: LABOR AND LABOR RELATIONS

LAND USE
See: AGRICULTURE; PUBLIC LAND; ZONING AND PLANNING

LANDLORD AND TENANT

STATUTES, CODES, STANDARDS, UNIFORM LAWS

UNIFORM RESIDENTIAL LANDLORD AND TENANT ACT. National Conference of Commissioners on Uniform State Laws. Uniform Laws Annotated. West Publishing Company, P.O. Box 64526, 50 West Kellogg Boulevard, St. Paul, Minnesota 55164-0526. 1976. (Annual Supplements).

RESTATEMENTS

RESTATEMENT OF THE LAW, SECOND: PROPERTY: LANDLORD AND TENANT. American Law Institute, 4025 Chestnut Street, Philadelphia, Pennsylvania 19104. 1977.

HANDBOOKS, MANUALS, FORMBOOKS

COMMERCIAL TENANT'S LEASING TRANSACTIONS GUIDE: FORMS AND STRATEGIES. Alan D. Sugarman and Joel J. Goldberg. John Wiley and Sons, Incorporated, 605 Third Avenue, New York, New York 10158. 1991.

CURRENT LEASING LAW AND TECHNIQUES-FORMS. Patrick J. Rohan. Matthew Bender and Company, Incorporated, 11 Penn Plaza, New York, New York 10001. 1982. (Annual Supplements).

THE LANDLORD'S HANDBOOK: A COMPLETE GUIDE TO MANAGING SMALL RESIDENTIAL PROPERTIES. Daniel Goodwin and Richard Rusdorf. Longman Publishing Group, 95 Church Street, White Plains, New York 10601. 1989.

THE LANDLORD'S LAW BOOK: RIGHTS AND RESPONSIBILITIES. Third Edition. David Brown. Nolo Press, 950 Parker Street, Berkeley, California 94710. 1991.

MODERN REAL ESTATE LEASING FORMS. Jack Kusnet and Robert Lopatin. Research Institute of America, Incorporated, One Penn Plaza, New York, New York 10119. 1980. (1991 Supplement).

TENANTS' RIGHTS. Eleventh California Edition. Myron Moskovitz and Ralph Warner. Nolo Press, 950 Parker Street, Berkeley, California 94710. 1991.

TEXTBOOKS AND GENERAL WORKS

AMERICAN LAW OF LANDLORD AND TENANT. Robert S. Schoshinski. Lawyers Cooperative Publishing Company, Aqueduct Building, Rochester, New York 14694. 1980. (Periodic Supplements).

JUSTICE EVICTED. Jerome L. Reide. Access to Justice Project. American Civil Liberties Union, 132 West Forty-third Street, New York, New York 10036. 1987.

LANDLORD AND TENANT LAW. Fourth Edition. Raymond I. Korona. West Publishing Company, 50 West Kellogg Boulevard, St. Paul, Minnesota 55164. 1990.

LANDLORD AND TENANT LAW IN A NUTSHELL. Second Edition. David S. Hill. West Publishing Company, P.O. Box 64526, 50 West Kellogg Boulevard, St. Paul, Minnesota 55164-0526. 1986.

LANDLORDS AND PROPERTY: SOCIAL RELATIONS IN THE PRIVATE RENTED SECTOR. John Allen and Linda McDowell. Cambridge University Press, 40 West Twentieth Street, New York, New York 10011. 1989.

THE LANDLORD'S LAW BOOK. Second Edition. David Brown and Ralph Warner. Nolo Press, 950 Parker Street, Berkeley, California 94710. 1987.

THE LIMITS OF THE LEGAL PROCESS: A STUDY OF LANDLORDS, LAW AND CRIME. David Nelken. Academic Press, Incorporated, 1250 Sixth Avenue, Suite 400, San Diego, California 92101. 1983.

MANAGING RESIDENTIAL REAL ESTATE. Paul D. Lapides. Research Institute of America, Incorporated, One Penn Plaza, New York, New York 10119. 1985.

REAL ESTATE LAW. Second Edition. George J. Siedell, III. West Publishing Company, 50 West Kellogg Boulevard, St. Paul, Minnesota 55164. 1989.

RENTAL HOUSING IN THE 1980'S. Anthony Downs. Brookings Institution, 1775 Massachusetts Avenue, Washington, D.C. 20036-2188. 1983.

TENANTS AND THE AMERICAN DREAM: IDEOLOGY AND THE TENANT MOVEMENT. Allan D. Heskin. Praeger Publishers, Division of Holt, Rhinehart and Winston/CBS, One Madison Avenue, New York, New York 10010-3603. 1983.

LAW REVIEWS AND PERIODICALS

LAW AND HOUSING JOURNAL. Law Students Service Association, 11075 East Boulevard, Cleveland, Ohio 44016. Semi-annual.

NEWSLETTERS AND NEWSPAPERS

LANDLORD TENANT LAW BULLETIN. Quinlan Publishing Company, 131 Beverly Street, Boston, Massachusetts 02114. Monthly.

LANDLORD-TENANT RELATIONS REPORT. CD Publications, 100 Summit Building, 8555 Sixteenth Street, Silver Spring, Maryland 20910. Monthly.

COMPUTER-ASSISTED LEGAL INSTRUCTION

BREW V. HARRIS I, II AND III. Interactive Video Library, Harvard Law School, Educational Technology Department, 18 Everett Street, Cambridge, Massachusetts 02138. Interactive videodisc.

LAW ENFORCEMENT
See also: FEDERAL BUREAU OF INVESTIGATION; POLICE

HANDBOOKS, MANUALS, FORMBOOKS

A HANDBOOK OF FEDERAL POLICE AND INVESTIGATIVE AGENCIES. Donald A. Torres. Greenwood Publishing Group, Incorporated, 88 Post Road West, P.O. Box 5007, Westport, Connecticut 06881. 1985.

HANDBOOK ON ARTIFICIAL INTELLIGENCE AND EXPERT SYSTEMS IN LAW ENFORCEMENT. Edward C. Ratledge and Joan E. Jacoby. Greenwood Publishing Group, Incorporated, 88 Post Road West, P.O. Box 5007, Westport, Connecticut 06881. 1989.

THE LAW ENFORCEMENT HANDBOOK. Desmond Rowland and James Bailey. Facts on File, 460 Park Avenue, South, New York, New York 10016. 1985.

THE LAW OFFICER'S POCKET MANUAL. John G. Miles, Jr. Bureau of National Affairs, 1231 Twenty-fifth Street, Northwest, Washington, D.C. 20037. 1984.

TEXTBOOKS AND GENERAL WORKS

CHARACTER AND COPS: ETHICS IN POLICING. Edwin J. Delattre. American Enterprise Institute for Public Policy Research, Distributed by University Press of America, 4720 Boston Way, Lanham, Maryland 20706. 1989.

CIVIL LIABILITIES IN AMERICAN POLICING: A TEXT FOR LAW ENFORCEMENT PERSONNEL. Rolando V. del Carmen. Brady, Englewood Cliffs, New Jersey. 1991.

COMING TO TERMS WITH POLICING. Rod Morgan and David J. Smith, Editors. Routledge, Chapman & Hall, 29 West Thirty-fifth Street, New York, New York 10001. 1988.

COMMUNICATION AND LAW ENFORCEMENT. Dennis F. Gunderson and Robert Hopper. University Press of America, 4720 Boston Way, Lanham, Maryland 20706. 1988.

CRITICAL ISSUES IN LAW ENFORCEMENT. Fourth Edition. Harry W. More, Jr. Anderson Publishing Company, 2035 Reading Road, Cincinnati, Ohio 45202. 1985.

DISTANT JUSTICE: POLICING THE ALASKAN FRONTIER. William R. Hunt. University of Oklahoma Press, 105 Asp Avenue, Norman, Oklahoma 73019. 1987.

THE ECONOMICS OF CRIME AND LAW ENFORCEMENT. David J. Pyle. Saint Martin's Press, Incorporated, 175 Fifth Avenue, New York, New York 10010. 1984.

THE ETHICS OF LAW ENFORCEMENT AND CRIMINAL PUNISHMENT. Edward A. Malloy. University Press of America, 4720 Boston Way, Lanham, Maryland 20706. 1983.

THE FRUSTRATION OF POLICY: RESPONSES TO CRIME BY AMERICAN CITIES. Herbert Jacob. Scott, Foresman and Company, 1900 East Lake Avenue, Glenview, Illinois 60025. 1984.

HUMAN RELATIONS: LAW ENFORCEMENT IN A CHANGING COMMUNITY. Third Edition. Alan Coffey. Prentice-Hall, Incorporated, 113 Sylvan Avneue, Englewood Cliffs, New Jersey 07632. 1982.

THE IDEA OF LAW ENFORCEMENT. Carl B. Klockars. Sage Publications, Incorporated, 2455 Teller, Newbury Park, California 91320. 1985.

INTERPOL: ISSUES IN WORLD CRIME AND INTERNATIONAL CRIMINAL JUSTICE. Michael Fooner. Plenum Publishing Corporation, 233 Spring Street, New York, New York 10013. 1989.

INTERVIEWING: AN INTRODUCTION TO INTERROGATION. Charles L. Yeschke. Charles C. Thomas, Publishers, 2600 South First Street, Springfield, Illinois 62794. 1987.

INTRODUCTION TO LAW ENFORCEMENT: AN INSIDER'S VIEW. William G. Doerner. Prentice-Hall, Incorporated, 113 Sylvan Avenue, Englewood Cliffs, New Jersey 07632. 1992.

INTRODUCTION TO LAW ENFORCEMENT AND CRIMINAL JUSTICE. A.C. Germann, Frank D. Day and Robert R.J. Gallati. Charles C. Thomas Publishing, 2600 South First Street, Springfield, Illinois 62794-9265. 1988. (Revised).

INTRODUCTION TO LAW ENFORCEMENT AND CRIMINAL JUSTICE. Third Edition. Henry M. Wrobleski and Karen M. Hess. West Publishing Company, 50 West Kellogg Boulevard, St. Paul, Minnesota 55164. 1990.

THE LAW AND POLITICS OF POLICE DISCRETION. Gregory H. Williams. Greenwood Publishing Group, Incorporated, 88 Post Road West, P.O. Box 5007, Westport, Connecticut 06881. 1984.

LAW ENFORCEMENT: A HUMAN RELATIONS APPROACH. Alan R. Coffey. Prentice-Hall, Incorporated, 113 Sylvan Avenue, Englewood Cliffs, New Jersey 07632. 1990.

LAW ENFORCEMENT: AN INTRODUCTION. Richard N. Holden. Prentice-Hall, Incorporated, 113 Sylvan Avenue, Englewood Cliffs, New Jersey 07632. 1992.

LAW ENFORCEMENT: AN INTRODUCTION TO POLICE IN SOCIETY. Bruce L. Berg. Allyn and Bacon, 160 Gould Street, Needham Heights, Massachusetts 02194. 1991.

LAW ENFORCEMENT AND THE YOUTHFUL OFFENDER: DELINQUENCY AND JUVENILE JUSTICE. Fourth Edition. Edward Eldefonso. John Wiley and Sons, Incorporated, 605 Third Avenue, New York, New York 10158. 1983.

LAW ENFORCEMENT BIBLE NO. 2. Robert A. Scanlon. Editor. Stoeger Publishing Company, 55 Ruta Court, South Hackensack, New Jersey 07606. 1982.

LAW ENFORCEMENT CAREER PLANNING: A HANDBOOK DESIGNED TO PREPARE LAW ENFORCEMENT OFFICERS FOR PROMOTIONAL OPPORTUNITIES AND EXAMS, RESUME WRITING, UNDERSTANDING THE ORGANIZATION, ASSESSMENT CENTERS, ORAL INTERVIEWS, AND MORE. Thomas Mahoney. Charles C. Thomas, Publishers, 2600 South First Street, Springfield, Illinois 62794. 1989.

LAW ENFORCEMENT PLANNING: THE LIMITS OF ECONOMIC ANALYSIS. Jeffrey L. Sedgwick. Greenwood Publishing Group, Incorporated, 88 Post Road West, P.O. Box 5007, Westport, Connecticut 06881. 1984.

LAW ENFORCEMENT, THE MAKING OF A PROFESSION: A COMPREHENSIVE GUIDE FOR THE POLICE TO ACHIEVE AND SUSTAIN PROFESSIONALISM. Neal E. Trautman. Charles C. Thomas, Publishers, 2600 South First Street, Springfield, Illinois 62794. 1988.

THE LIMITS OF LAW ENFORCEMENT. Hans Zeisel. University of Chicago Press, 5801 Ellis Avenue, Third Floor, South, Chicago, Illinois 60637. 1983.

MORMONS AND COWBOYS, MOONSHINERS AND KLANSMEN: FEDERAL LAW ENFORCEMENT IN THE SOUTH AND WEST, 1870-1893. Stephen Cresswell. University of Alabama Press, P.O. Box 870380, Tuscaloosa, Alabama 35487. 1991.

ORGANIZED CRIME: CONCEPTS AND CONTROL. Second Edition. Denny F. Pace and Jimmie C. Styles. Prentice-Hall, Incorporated, 113 Sylvan Avenue, Englewood Cliffs, New Jersey 07632. 1982.

POLICE AND POLICING: CONTEMPORARY ISSUES. Dennis Jay Kenney, Editor. Praeger Publishers, One Madison Avenue, New York, New York 10010-3603. 1989.

POLICE PROFESSIONALISM: THE RENAISSANCE OF AMERICAN LAW ENFORCEMENT. Thomas J. Deakin. Charles C. Thomas, Publishers, 2600 South First Street, Springfield, Illinois 62794. 1988.

POLICING DOMESTIC VIOLENCE: WOMEN, THE LAW, AND THE STATE. Susan S.M. Edwards. Sage Publications, 2455 Teller Road, Newbury Park, California 91320. 1989.

POLICING LIBERAL SOCIETY. Steve Uglow. Oxford University Press, 200 Madison Avenue, New York, New York 10016. 1988.

POLICING MULTI-ETHNIC NEIGHBORHOODS: THE MIAMI STUDY AND FINDINGS FOR LAW ENFORCEMENT IN THE UNITED STATES. Geoffrey P. Alpert and Roger G. Dunham. Greenwood Publishing Group, Incorporated, 88 Post Road West, P.O. Box 5007, Westport, Connecticut 06881. 1988.

POLICING THE WORLD: INTERPOL AND THE POLITICS OF INTERNATIONAL POLICE CO-OPERATION. Malcolm Anderson. Oxford University Press, 200 Madison Avenue, New York, New York 10016. 1989.

THE POLITICS OF STREET CRIME: CRIMINAL PROCESS AND CULTURAL OBSESSION. Stuart A. Scheingold. Temple University Press, 1601 North Broad Street, University Services Building, Philadelphia, Pennsylvania 19122. 1991.

POWER AND RESTRAINT: THE MORAL DIMENSION OF POLICE WORK. Howard S. Cohen and Michael Feldberg. Praeger Publishers, One Madison Avenue, New York, New York 10010-3603. 1991.

PRINCIPLES OF LAW ENFORCEMENT: AN OVERVIEW OF THE JUSTICE SYSTEM. Third Edition. Edward Eldefonso. John Wiley and Sons, Incorporated, 605 Third Avenue, New York, New York 10158. 1982.

THE PSYCHOLOGICAL EFFECTS OF POLICE WORK: A PSYCHODYNAMIC APPROACH. Philip Bonifacio. Plenum Publishing Corporation, 233 Spring Street, New York, New York 10013. 1991.

RACIAL VIOLENCE AND LAW ENFORCEMENT IN THE SOUTH. Michal R. Belknap. Garland Publishing, Incorporated, 136 Madison Avenue, New York, New York 10016. 1991.

THE REBIRTH OF PRIVATE POLICING. Les Johnston. Routledge, Chapman & Hall, 29 West Thirty-fifth Street, New York, New York 10001. 1991. A RESEARCH GUIDE FOR LAW ENFORCEMENT AND THE CRIMINAL JUSTICE SYSTEM. Jack E. Whitehouse. R & E Publications, P.O. Box 2008, Saratoga, California 95070-2008. 1983.

RURAL LAW ENFORCEMENT. Allen P. Bristow. Allyn and Bacon, Incorporated, 160 Gould Street, Needham Heights, Massachusetts, 02194. 1982.

A STUDY OF LAW ENFORCEMENT: A COMPREHENSIVE STUDY OF THE WORLD'S GREATEST, YET MOST DIFFICULT, PROFESSION. Neal E. Trautman. Charles C. Thomas, Publishers, 2600 South First Street, Springfield, Illinois 62794. 1990.

THE TACTICAL EDGE: SURVIVING HIGH-RISK PATROL. Charles Remsberg. Calibre Press, 666 Dundee Road, Suite 1607, Northbrook, Illinois 60062-2727. 1986.

TELEVISION AND LAW ENFORCEMENT. Joseph Missonellie and James S. D'Angelo. Charles C. Thomas Publishing, 2600 South First Street, Springfield, Illinois 62794-9265. 1984.

TEMPERED ZEAL: A COLUMBIA LAW PROFESSOR'S YEAR ON THE STREETS WITH THE NEW YORK CITY POLICE. H. Richard Uviller. Contemporary Books, Incorporated, 180 North Michigan Avenue, Chicago, Illinois 60601. 1988.

UNDERSTANDING LAW ENFORCEMENT. Second Edition. Linda Riekes and Sharon Slane. West Publishing Company, 50 West Kellogg Boulevard, St. Paul, Minnesota 55164. 1992.

ENCYCLOPEDIAS AND DICTIONARIES

DICTIONARY OF CRIME: CRIMINAL JUSTICE, CRIMINOLOGY AND LAW ENFORCEMENT. Jay Robert Nash, Editor. Paragon House Publishers, 90 Fifth Avenue, New York, New York 10011. 1992.

LAW ENFORCEMENT

THE POLICE DICTIONARY AND ENCYCLOPEDIA. John J. Fay. Charles C. Thomas, Publishers, 2600 South First Street, Springfield, Illinois 62794. 1988.

DIGESTS, INDEXES, ABSTRACTS, CITATORS

BRIEFS OF 100 LEADING CASES IN LAW ENFORCEMENT. Rolando V. del Carmen and Jeffrey T. Walker. Anderson Publishing Company, 2035 Reading Road, Cincinnati, Ohio 45202. 1991.

LAW REVIEWS AND PERIODICALS

JOURNAL OF POLICE SCIENCE AND ADMINISTRATION. International Association of Chiefs of Police, 13 Firstfield Road, Gaithersburg, Maryland 20878. Quarterly.

POLICE TIMES MAGAZINE. American Federation of Police, 1000 Connecticut Avenue, Northwest, Washington, D.C. 20026.

NEWSLETTERS AND NEWSPAPERS

LAW ENFORCEMENT LEGAL DEFENSE MANUAL. James P. Manak, 421 Ridgewood Avenue, Glen Ellyn, Illinois 60137. Quarterly.

LAW ENFORCEMENT LEGAL REVIEW. James P. Manak, 421 Ridgewood Avenue, Glen Ellyn, Illinois 60137. Semimonthly.

LAW ENFORCEMENT PERSONNEL NOTES. NYPER Publications, P.O. Box 662, Latham, New York 12110. Monthly.

LAW OFFICER'S BULLETIN. Bureau of National Affairs, Incorporated, 1231 Twenty-fifth Street, Northwest, Washington, D.C. 20037. Biweekly.

LIABILITY REPORTER. Americans for Effective Law Enforcement, Incorporated, 5519 North Cumberland, Suite 1008, Chicago, Illinois 60656. Monthly.

NATIONAL BULLETIN ON POLICE MISCONDUCT. Quinlan Publishing Company, Incorporated, 23 Drydock Avenue, Boston, Massachusetts 02110. Biweekly.

POLICE LIABILITY REVIEW. Alpha Enterprises, P.O. Box 1013, Warrensburg, Missouri 64093. Quarterly.

SECURITY AND SPECIAL POLICE LEGAL UPDATE. Americans for Effective Law Enforcement, Incorporated, 5519 North Cumberland, Suite 1008, Chicago, Illinois 60656. Monthly.

BIBLIOGRAPHIES

A LIST OF PERSONAL COMPUTER PROGRAMS FOR PUBLIC SAFETY SERVICE AND ANALYSIS: A SELECTED BIBLIOGRAPHY. Anthony G. White. Vance Bibliographies, P.O. Box 229, 112 North Charter Street, Monticello, Illinois 61856. 1990.

POLICY STUDIES ON LAW ENFORCEMENT: A SELECTED BIBLIOGRAPHY. Robert Goehlart. Vance Bibliographies, P.O. Box 229, 112 North Charter Street, Monticello, Illinois 61856. 1983.

SPECIAL ACCESS REQUIRED: A PRACTITIONER'S GUIDE TO LAW ENFORCEMENT INTELLIGENCE LITERATURE. Henry W. Prunckun, Jr. Scarecrow Press, Incorporated, 52 Liberty Street, Box 4167, Metuchen, New Jersey 08840. 1990.

DIRECTORIES

DIRECTORY OF AUTOMATED CRIMINAL JUSTICE INFORMATION SYSTEMS. Bureau of Justice Statistics, Justice Department, Superintendent of Documents, United States Government Printing Office, Washington, D.C. 20402. 1983.

DIRECTORY OF CRIMINAL JUSTICE INFORMATION SOURCES. Fifth Edition. National Criminal Justice Reference Service, National Institute of Justice, Superintendent of Documents, United States Government Printing Office, Washington, D.C. 20402. 1984.

WHO'S WHO IN AMERICAN LAW ENFORCEMENT. Fifth Edition. Donna M. Shepherd, Editor. American Federation of Police, 3801 Biscayne Boulevard, Miami, Florida 33137. 1986. (Triennial).

WHO'S WHO IN LAW ENFORCEMENT COLLECTING AND POLICE TRAINERS. 1988 Edition. Elizabeth Dalein Alley, Editor. Who's Who in Law Enforcement Collecting and Police Trainers, P.O. Box J-4025, New Bedford, Massachusetts 02742-0366. 1988.

ASSOCIATIONS AND PROFESSIONAL SOCIETIES

AMERICAN FEDERATION OF POLICE. 1000 Connecticut Avenue, Northwest, Suite 9, Washington, D.C. 20036. (202) 293-9088.

AMERICAN SOCIETY OF LAW ENFORCEMENT TRAINERS. 9611 Four-hundredth Avenue, P.O. Box 1003, Twin Lakes, Wisconsin 53181. (414) 279-5700.

ATTORNEY GENERAL TASK FORCE ON VIOLENT CRIME. United States Department of Justice, Office of Attorney General, 633 Indiana Avenue, Northwest, Washington, D.C. 20530. (202) 307-5933.

FEDERAL LAW ENFORCEMENT OFFI56. 1981.

ADMINISTRATIVE LAW: MONOGRAPHS PUBLISHED IN THE ENGLISH LANGUAGE, 1980-1987. Mary Vance. Vance Bibliographies, P.O. Box 229, 112 North Charter Street, Monticello, Illinois 61856. 1988.

THE CODE OF FEDERAL REGULATIONS: BIBLIOGRAPHY AND GUIDE. Second Edition. Erwin C. Surrency. Oceana Publications, Incorporated, 75 Main Street, Dobbs Ferry, New York 10522. 1986.

COURT SUPERVISION AND OVERSIGHT OF GOVERNMENT AGENCIES: A SELECTED BIBLIOGRAPHY. Anthony G. White. Vance Bibliographies, P.O. Box 229, 112 North Charter Street, Monticello, Illinois 61856. 1982.

UNION LIST OF STATE ADMINISTRATIVE CODES AND REGISTERS. New England Law Library Consortium. Compiled by Donald Dunn. Western New England College, Springfield, Massachusetts 01119. 1983.

Encyclopedia of Legal Information Sources • 2nd Ed.   **LAW LIBRARIES**

DIRECTORIES

FEDERAL EXECUTIVE DIRECTORY. Nancy Cahill, Editor. Carroll Publishing Company, 1058 Thomas Jefferson Street, Northwest, Washington, D.C. 20007. Bimonthly.

FEDEersity of Wisconsin, Madison, 610 Langdon Street, Madison, Wisconsin 53706. (608) 262-3635.

POLICE EXECUTIVE RESEARCH FORUM. 2300 M Street, Northwest, Suite 910, Washington, D.C. 20037. (202) 466-7820.

POLICE FOUNDATION. 1001 Twenty-second Street, Northwest, Suite 200, Washington, D.C. 20037. (202) 833-1460.

ONLINE DATABASES

A.L.E.R.T.: A LAW ENFORCEMENT ROUNDTABLE. GE Information Services, General Electric Network for Information Exchange, 401 North Washington Boulevard, Rockville, Maryland 20850.

FROM THE STATE CAPITALS: JUSTICE POLICIES. Wakeman Walworth, 300 North Washington Street, Suite 204, Alexandria, Virginia (703) 549-8606.

LAW ENFORCEMENT AND CRIMINAL JUSTICE INFORMATION DATABASE. International Research and Evaluation, 21098 IRE Control Center, Eagan, Minnesota 55121.

LAW EXAMINATIONS

HANDBOOKS, MANUALS, FORMBOOKS

BARRON'S HOW TO PREPARE FOR THE LSAT, LAW SCHOOL ADMISSION TEST. Sixth Edition. Jerry Bobrow. Barron's Educational Series, Incorporated, 250 Wireless Boulevard, Hauppauge, New York 11788. 1991.

BLOND'S MULTISTATE QUESTIONS. Third Edition. Neil C. Blond. Sulzburger and Graham Publishing, 165 West Ninety-first Street, New York, New York 10024. 1990.

CRAM COURSE FOR THE LSAT. Second Edition. Suzee J. Vlk. Arco, New York, New York. 1990.

GRE-LSAT LOGIC WORKBOOK. Mark A. Stewart. ARCO, Distributed by Prentice-Hall, Incorporated, 113 Sylvan Avenue, Englewood Cliffs, New Jersey 07632. 1991.

HOW TO DO YOUR BEST ON LAW SCHOOL EXAMS. John Delaney. John Delaney Publications, P.O. Box 404, Bogota, New Jersey 07603. 1982.

HOW TO PASS THE BAR EXAM. J.P. Davis. William S. Hein and Company, 1285 Main Street, Buffalo, New York 14209. 1989.

HOW TO PREPARE FOR THE LSAT. Second Edition. Karl Weber. Harcourt, Brace, Jovanovich, Incorporated, 6277 Sea Harbor Drive, Orlando, Florida 32821. 1990.

INSIDE THE LSAT. 1992 Edition. Thomas O. White. Peterson's Guides, 202 Carnegie Center, P.O. Box 2123, Princeton, New Jersey 08543-2123. 1991.

SUPERCOURSE FOR THE LSAT. Second Edition. Thomas H. Martinson. ARCO, Distributed by Prentice-Hall, Incorporated, 113 Sylvan Avenue, Englewood Cliffs, New Jersey 07632. 1989.

TEXTBOOKS AND GENERAL WORKS

STUDYING LAW. Second Edition. Phillip H. Kenny. Butterworth and Company (Publishers) Limited, Borough Green, Sevenoaks, Kent TN15 8PH, England. 1991.

DIGESTS, INDEXES, ABSTRACTS, CITATORS

NATIONAL BAR EXAMINATION DIGEST. Harcourt, Brace, Jovanovich, Incorporated, 6277 Sea Harbor Drive, Orlando, Florida 32821. 1975- .

LAW REVIEWS AND PERIODICALS

BAR EXAMINER. National Conference of Bar Examiners, 333 North Michigan Avenue, Suite 1025, Chicago, Illinois 60601. 1931- .

LAW IN ART

TEXTBOOKS AND GENERAL WORKS

THE WEST COLLECTION. West Publishing Company, 50 West Kellogg Boulevard, St. Paul, Minnesota 55164. 1986.

WEST '84, ART AND THE LAW. Sheila Bennett, Editor. West Publishing Company, 50 West Kellogg Boulevard, St. Paul, Minnesota 55164. 1984.

LAW LIBRARIES

LOOSELEAF SERVICES AND REPORTERS

LEGAL RESEARCH AND LAW LIBRARY MANAGEMENT. Revised Edition. Julius J. Marke and Richard Sloane. Law Journal Seminars-Press, Incorporated, 111 Eighth Avenue, Suite 900, New York, New York 10011. 1990- .

HANDBOOKS, MANUALS, FORMBOOKS

BUILDING YOUR LAW LIBRARY: A STEP-BY-STEP GUIDE. Mickie A. Voges. American Bar Association, Section of Economics of Law Practice, 750 North Lake Shore Drive, Chicago, Illinois 60611. 1988.

GRANTS FOR LIBRARIES: A GUIDE TO PUBLIC AND PRIVATE FUNDING PROGRAMS AND PROPOSAL WRITING TECHNIQUES. Second Edition. Emmett Corry. Libraries Unlimited, P.O. Box 3988, Englewood, Colorado 80155-3988. 1986.

INSPECTING A PRISON LAW LIBRARY. Gene Teitelbaum. William W. Gaunt and Sons, Incorporated, Gaunt Building, 3011 Gulf Drive, Holmes Beach, Florida 34217-2199. 1989.

LAW LIBRARIANSHIP: A HANDBOOK. Heinz P. Mueller and Patrick E. Kehoe. Fred B. Rothman and Company, 10368 West Centennial Road, Littleton, Colorado 80127. 1983.

LAW LIBRARY FUND RAISING: A PRIMER. Gerald C. Crane. Glanville, Incorporated, 75 Main Street, Dobbs Ferry, New York 10522. 1983.

MANUAL OF LAW LIBRARIANSHIP: THE USE AND ORGANIZATION OF LEGAL LITERATURE. Elizabeth M. Moys. Knowledge Industry Publications, 701 Westchester Avenue, White Plains, New York 10604. 1987.

MANUAL OF PROCEDURES FOR PRIVATE LAW LIBRARIES. Susan K. Dyer. G.K. Hall and Company, 70 Lincoln Street, Boston, Massachusetts 02111. 1984.

WERNER'S MANUAL FOR PRISON LAW LIBRARIES. Second Edition. Arturo A. Flores. American Association of Law Libraries. Fred B. Rothman and Company, 10368 West Centennial Road, Littleton, Colorado 80127. 1990.

TEXTBOOKS AND GENERAL WORKS

BASICS OF LAW LIBRARIANSHIP. Deborah S. Panella. Haworth Press, Incorporated, 10 Alice Street, Binghamton, New York 13904. 1991.

FUNDING FOR LAW: LEGAL EDUCATION, RESEARCH AND STUDY. Karen Cantrell and Denise Wallen. Oryx Press, 2214 North Central Avenue, Phoenix, Arizona 85004. 1991.

INSURING THE LAW LIBRARY: FIRE AND DISASTER RISK MANAGEMENT. Bernard D. Reams and Erwin C. Surreney. Glanville, Incorporated, 75 Main Street, Dobbs Ferry, New York 10522. 1982.

LAW LIBRARIES IN CANADA: ESSAYS TO HONOUR DIANA M. PRIESTLY. Joan N. Fraser, Editor. Carswell Company, 2330 Midland Avenue, Agincourt, Ontario, Canada M1S 1P7. 1988.

LAW LIBRARY STAFF ORGANIZATION AND ADMINISTRATION. Martha J. Dragich and Peter C. Schanck. American Association of Law Libraries. Fred B. Rothman and Company, 10368 West Centennial Road, Littleton, Colorado 80127. 1990.

LEGAL RESEARCH AND LAW LIBRARY MANAGEMENT. Julius J. Marke and Richard Sloane. Law Journal-Seminars Press, Incorporated, 111 Eighth Avenue, Suite 900, New York, New York 10011. 1986.

MANAGEMENT OF THE ONE PERSON LIBRARY. Robert Berk. Oryx Press, 2214 North Central Avenue, Phoenix, Arizona 85004-1483. 1986.

PLANNING THE LAW LIBRARY AS A LEGAL INFORMATION CENTER. Dan F. Henke and Julius J. Marke. Glanville, Incorporated, 75 Main Street, Dobbs Ferry, New York 10522. 1985.

THE PRIVATE LAW LIBRARY IN THE HIGH-TECH ERA. Jean Strohofer and Marie Wallace. Practising Law Institute, 810 Seventh Avenue, New York, New York 10019. 1983.

PROFESSIONAL STAFFING AND JOB SECURITY IN THE ACADEMIC LAW LIBRARY. Joyce Saltalamachia and Janet Tracy. Glanville Publishers, 75 Main Street, Dobbs Ferry, New York 10522. 1988.

RARE BOOKS FOR LAW LIBRARIES. Thomas H. Reynolds. Glanville, Incorporated, 75 Main Street, Dobbs Ferry, New York 10522. 1983.

REFLECTIONS ON LAW LIBRARIANSHIP: A COLLECTION OF INTERVIEWS. Marjorie A. Garson. American Association of Law Libraries. Fred B. Rothman and Company, 10368 West Centennial Road, Littleton, Colorado 80127. 1988.

THE SPIRIT OF LAW LIBRARIANSHIP: A READER. Roy M. Mersky and Richard A. Leiter. Fred B. Rothman and Company, 10368 West Centennial Road, Littleton, Colorado 80127. 1991.

THE TWENTY-FIRST CENTURY: TECHNOLOGY'S IMPACT ON ACADEMIC RESEARCH AND LAW LIBRARIES. Betty W. Taylor, Elizabeth B. Mann and Robert J. Munro. G.K. Hall and Company, Incorporated, 70 Lincoln Street, Boston, Massachusetts 02111. 1988.

DIGESTS, INDEXES, ABSTRACTS, CITATORS

AALL ANNUAL MEETINGS: AN ANNOTATED INDEX OF THE RECORDINGS. Frank G. Houdek and Susan D. Goldner. Fred B. Rothman and Company, 10368 West Centennial Road, Littleton, Colorado 80127. 1989- .

LEGAL INFORMATION MANAGEMENT INDEX. Elyse Fox, Editor. Fox Information Consultants, Incorporated, P.O. Box 67, Newton Highlands, Massachusetts 02161. Six issues per year.

ANNUALS AND SURVEYS

CONFERENCE ON THE GLOBAL RESPONSIBILITY OF LAW LIBRARIANS: PROCEEDINGS, OCTOBER 18-21, 1989, THE UNIVERSITY OF TEXAS SCHOOL OF LAW, AUSTIN, TEXAS. David R. Burch and Stephen E. Young. Fred B. Rothman and Company, 10368 West Centennial Road, Littleton, Colorado 80127. 1990.

PROCEEDINGS OF THE CONFERENCE ON TEACHING LEGAL AND FACTUAL RESEARCH IN PRIVATE LAW LIBRARIES: APRIL 26-APRIL 29, 1990, WESTFIELD INTERNATIONAL CONFERENCE CENTER, CHANTILLY, VIRGINIA. Fred B. Rothman and Company, 10368 West Centennial Road, Littleton, Colorado 80127. 1991.

SETTING THE LEGAL INFORMATION AGENDA FOR THE YEAR 2000: BASED ON A WORKSHOP OF THE AMERICAN ASSOCIATION OF LAW LIBRARIES NATIONAL LEGAL RESOURCES COMMITTEE, WASHINGTON, D.C., OCTOBER 23-26, 1988. Mary Kathleen Price and Margaret Maes Axtmann, Editors. American Association of Law Libraries. Fred B. Rothman and Company, 10368 West Centennial Road, Littleton, Colorado 80127. 1991- .

LAW REVIEWS AND PERIODICALS

INTERNATIONAL JOURNAL OF LEGAL INFORMATION. International Association of Law Libraries, P.O. Box 5709, Washington, D.C. 20016. Three issues per year.

LAW LIBRARY JOURNAL. American Association of Law Libraries, 53 West Jackson Boulevard, Chicago, Illinois 60604. Quarterly.

LEGAL REFERENCE SERVICES QUARTERLY. Haworth Press, Incorporated, 28 East Twenty-second Street, New York, New York 10010. Quarterly.

NEWSLETTERS AND NEWSPAPERS

ACADEMIC LAW LIBRARIES SPECIAL INTEREST SECTION. American Association of Law Libraries, 53 West Jackson Boulevard, Chicago, Illinois 60604. Quarterly.

ADVANCE SHEET. Dallas Association of Law Librarians, P.O. Box 50183, Dallas, Texas 75250. Monthly.

ALLA NEWSLETTER. Atlanta Law Libraries Association, c/o Anne J. Johnson, Fisher and Phillips, 1500 Resurgers Plaza, 945 East Paces Ferry Road, Atlanta, Georgia 30326. Quarterly.

AMERICAN ASSOCIATION OF LAW LIBRARIES NEWSLETTER. American Association of Law Libraries, 53 West Jackson Boulevard, Chicago, Illinois 60604. Ten issues per year.

ASSOCIATION OF LAW LIBRARIES OF UPSTATE NEW YORK NEWSLETTER. c/o Eleanor Molnar, Supreme Court Library of Buffalo, 92 Franklin Street, Buffalo, New York 14202. Quarterly.

AUTOMATOME. American Association of Law Libraries, Automation and Scientific Developments Special Interest Section, 53 West Jackson Boulevard, Chicago, Illinois 60604. Quarterly.

AV/MICROGRAPHICS NEWSLETTER. AV/Micrographics Special Interest Section, American Association of Law Libraries, 53 West Jackson Boulevard, Chicago, Illinois 60604. Quarterly.

COUNCIL OF CALIFORNIA COUNTY LAW LIBRARIANS NEWSLETTER. c/o Coral Henning, San Francisco County Law Library, 400 Van Ness Avenue, Room 436, San Francisco, California 94102. Quarterly.

COUNTY LAW LIBRARY PROJECT BULLETIN. Minnesota State Law Library, 117 University Avenue, St. Paul, Minnesota 55159. Bimonthly.

DOCUMENTS TO THE PEOPLE. Government Documents Round Table, American Library Association, c/o Lee Decker, Distribution Manager, 8304 Tomlinson Avenue, Bethesda, Maryland 20817. Quarterly.

GPLLA NEWSLETTER. Greater Philadelphia Law Library Association, P.O. Box 335, Philadelphia, Pennsylvania 19105. Monthly.

HALL NEWS. Houston Area Law Librarians, c/o Jerry McCulley, Liddell, Sapp and Zivley, 3400 Texas Commerce Tower, 600 Travis, Houston, Texas 77002. Monthly.

THE IALL MESSENGER. International Associational Association of Law Libraries, c/o Adolf Sprudzs, University of Chicago, D'Angelo Law School Library, 1121 East Sixtieth Street, Chicago, Illinois 60637. Quarterly.

JURISDOCS. Government Documents Special Interest Section, American Association of Law Libraries, c/o Keith Buckley, Indiana University Law Library, Bloomington, Indiana 47405.

LAW BOOKS IN REVIEW. Glanville Publishers, 75 Main Street, Dobbs Ferry, New York 10522. Quarterly.

LAW LIBRARIAN'S BULLETIN BOARD. Legal Information Services, P.O. Box 67, Newton Highlands, Massachusetts 02161. Semiquarterly.

LAW LIBRARY LIGHTS. Law Librarians' Society of Washington, D.C., Incorporated, 1717 Largo Road, Upper Marlboro, Maryland 20772. Bimonthly.

LAW LINES. Law Library Association of Greater New York, c/o Linda Holmes, Brooklyn Law School, 250 Joraleman Street, Brooklyn, New York 11201. Semiquarterly.

LEGAL BIBLIOGRAPHY JOURNAL. The Legal Institute, 281 East Colorado Boulevard, Box 219, Pasadena, California 91102. Three issues per year.

LEGAL INFORMATION ALERT. United States Library Alert, 399 Fullerton, Chicago, Illinois 60614. Ten issues per year.

LEGAL INFORMATION MANAGEMENT INDEX. Legal Information Services, P.O. Box 67, Newton Highlands, Massachusetts 02161. Bimonthly.

LEGAL INFORMATION MANAGEMENT REPORTS. Legal Information Services, P.O. Box 67, Newton Highlands, Massachusetts 02161. Quarterly.

LEGAL RESEARCH JOURNAL. The Legal Institute, 281 East Colorado Boulevard, Box 219, Pasadena, California 91102. Three issues per year.

LEGAL VIDEO REVIEW. Lawrence R. Cohen Media Library, Social Law Library, 1200 Courthouse, Boston, Massachusetts 02108. Quarterly.

LISP NEWSLETTER. Legal Information Services to the Public Special Interest Section, c/o Supreme Court Library at Syracuse, 500 Court House, Syracuse, New York 13202. Quarterly.

LLAW NEWSLETTER. Law Librarians Association of Wisconsin, c/o University of Wisconsin - Madison Law Library, Madison, Wisconsin 53706. Quarterly.

LLNE NEWS. Law Librarians of New England, c/o Maria Sekula, Social Law Library, 1200 Court House, Boston, Massachusetts 02108. Quarterly.

LOQUITOR. Minnesota State Law Library, 117 University Avenue, St. Paul, Minnesota 55155. Quarterly.

MALL NEWSLETTER. Minnesota Association of Law Libraries, c/o Debbie Murtean, Briggs and Morgan, 2400 IDS Tower, Minnesota 55402. Bimonthly.

NEW ORLEANS LAW LIBRARIAN. New Orleans Association of Law Librarians, c/o Fifth Circuit Court Library, 600 Camp Street, Room 106, New Orleans, Louisiana 70130. Quarterly.

NEWSLETTER: STATE, COURT AND COUNTY LAW LIBRARIES SPECIAL INTEREST SECTION. State, Court and County Law Libraries Special Interest Section, American Association of Law Libraries, 53 West Jackson Boulevard, Chicago, Illinois 60604. Semiannual.

NJLLA BRIEF. New Jersey Law Librarians Association, c/o Robert L. Blard, New Jersey State Law Library, 185 West State Street, Trenton, New Jersey, 08625. Quarterly.

NORTHERN CALIFORNIA ASSOCIATION OF LAW LIBRARIES - NOCALL NEWS. c/o Judy Janes, University of California Law Library, Davis, California 95616. Bimonthly.

OBITER DICTA. Southern New England Law Libraries Association, c/o Connecticut State Library/Law Library at Hartford, 95 Washington Street, Hartford, Connecticut 06106. Quarterly.

OCEANA'S LAW LIBRARY NEWSLETTER. Oceana Publications, Incorporated, 75 Main Street, Dobbs Ferry, New York 10522. Monthly.

ORALL NEWSLETTER. Ohio Regional Association of Law Libraries, c/o Butler County Law Library, 141 Court Street, Hamilton, Ohio 45011. Quarterly.

PAALL NEWSLETTER. Phoenix Area Association of Law Libraries, c/o Maricopa County Law Library, 101 West Jefferson, Phoenix, Arizona 85003. Quarterly.

PLL PERSPECTIVES. Private Law Libraries Special Interest Section, American Association of Law Libraries, 53 West Jackson Boulevard, Chicago, Illinois 60604. Quarterly.

PUBLICATIONS CLEARING HOUSE BULLETIN. American Association of Law Libraries, Committee on Relations with Publishers and Dealers, 53 West Jackson Boulevard, Chicago, Illinois 60604. Three issues per year.

READER SERVICES LAW LIBRARIAN. American Association of Law Libraries, Readers' Services Special Interest Section, 53 West Jackson Boulevard, Chicago, Illinois 60604. Quarterly.

SCALL NEWSLETTER. Southern California Association of Law Libraries, c/o Carol Hyne, Unocal Corporation, 1201 West Fifth Street, Room 1142A, Los Angeles, California 90017. Quarterly.

SOUTHEASTERN LAW LIBRARIAN. Southeast Chapter of American Association of Law Libraries, c/o Rumberger, Kirk, etal, P.O. Box 1873, Orlando, Florida 32802. Quarterly.

SWALL BULLETIN. Southwestern Association of Law Libraries, c/o Lucille Fercho, Oklahoma City University Law School, Oklahoma City, Oklahoma 73106. Quarterly.

TECHNICAL SERVICES LAW LIBRARIAN. American Association of Law Libraries, Technical Services Special Interest Section, 53 West Jackson Boulevard, Chicago, Illinois 60604. Quarterly.

TRENDS IN LAW LIBRARY MANAGEMENT AND TECHNOLOGY. Fred B. Rothman and Company, 10368 West Centennial Road, Littleton, Colorado 80127. Monthly.

WESTPAC NEWS. Western Pacific Chapter of American Association of Law Libraries, c/o Boley Law Library, Northwestern School of Law, 10015 South West Terwilliger Boulevard, Portland, Oregon 97219. Quarterly.

BIBLIOGRAPHIES

LIBRARY STANDARDS: A SUBJECT BIBLIOGRAPHY WITH EMPHASIS ON LAW LIBRARY STANDARDS. Reynold Kosek and Mary Anne Royle. Vance Bibliographies, P.O. Box 229, 112 North Charter Street, Monticello, Illinois 61856. 1983.

DIRECTORIES

AMERICAN LIBRARY DIRECTORY. Jaques Cattell Press, R. R. Bowker Company, 121 Chanlon Road, New Providence, New Jersey 07974. 1991.

DIRECTORY OF FEDERAL LIBRARIES. William R. Evinger. Oryx Press, 2214 North Central Avenue, Phoenix, Arizona 85004-1483. 1992.

DIRECTORY OF GOVERNMENT DOCUMENT COLLECTIONS AND LIBRARIANS. Fifth Edition. American Library Association. Congressional Information Service, Incorporated, 4520 East-West Highway, Suite 800-DM, Bethesda, Maryland 20814-3389. 1987.

DIRECTORY OF LAW LIBRARIES. American Association of Law Libraries, 53 West Jackson Boulevard, Suite 940, Chicago, Illinois 60604. Annual.

DIRECTORY OF ONLINE DATABASES. Cuadra Associates, Incorporated, 838 Broadway, New York, New York 10003. 1985.

DIRECTORY OF SPECIAL LIBRARIES AND INFORMATION CENTERS. Gale Research, Incorporated, 835 Penobscot Building, Detroit, Michigan 48226. Biennial.

INTERNATIONAL ASSOCIATION OF LAW LIBRARIES DIRECTORY. International Association of Law Libraries. William S. Hein and Company, Incorporated, Hein Building, 1285 Main Street, Buffalo, New York 14209. 1985.

LAW AND LEGAL INFORMATION DIRECTORY. Gale Research, Incorporated, 835 Penobscot Building, Detroit, Michigan 48226. Biennial.

BIOGRAPHICAL SOURCES

AMERICAN ASSOCIATION OF LAW LIBRARIES BIOGRAPHICAL DIRECTORY. Fourth Edition. American Association of Law Libraries, 53 West Jackson Boulevard, Chicago, Illinois 60604. 1984.

ASSOCIATIONS AND PROFESSIONAL SOCIETIES

AMERICAN ASSOCIATION OF LAW LIBRARIES. 53 West Jackson Boulevard, Chicago, Illinois 60604. (312) 939-4764.

AMERICAN BAR ASSOCIATION, COMMITTEE ON FACILITIES OF THE LAW LIBRARY OF CONGRESS. 750 North Lake Shore Drive, Chicago, Illinois 60611. (312) 988-5000.

INTERNATIONAL ASSOCIATION OF LAW LIBRARIES. P.O. Box 5709, Washington, D.C. 20016.

AUDIOVISUALS

AMERICAN ASSOCIATION OF LAW LIBRARIES ANNUAL MEETING SOUND RECORDINGS. American Association of Law Libraries, Mobiltape Company, Incorporated, 1741 Gardena Avenue, Glendale, California 91204. Annual. Audiocassettes.

LAW OF THE SEA
See also: ADMIRALTY; COMMERCIAL LAW; FEDERAL MARITIME COMMISSION; FISH AND FISHING

STATUTES, CODES, STANDARDS, UNIFORM LAWS

EASTERN EUROPEAN STATES AND THE DEVELOPMENT OF THE LAW OF THE SEA. Viktor Sebek, Editor. Oceana Publications, Incorporated, 75 Main Street, Dobbs Ferry, New York 10522. 1977. (Periodic Supplements).

LATIN AMERICA AND THE DEVELOPMENT OF THE LAW OF THE SEA: REGIONAL DOCUMENTS, NATIONAL LEGISLATION. Alberto Szekely, Editor. Oceana Publications, Incorporated, 75 Main Street, Dobbs Ferry, New York 10522. 1976. (Periodic Supplements).

THE LAW OF THE SEA: ARCHIPELAGIC STATES: LEGISLATIVE HISTORY OF PART IV OF THE UNITED NATIONS CONVENTION ON THE LAW OF THE SEA. United Nations Publishing Service, Office for Ocean Affairs and the Law of the Sea. Room DC2-0853, New York, New York 10017. 1990.

THE LAW OF THE SEA: MARITIME BOUNDARY AGREEMENTS (1970-1984). United Nations Publishing Service, Office for Ocean Affairs and the Law of the Sea, Room DC2-0853, New York, New York 10017. 1987.

LAW OF THE SEA: NAVIGATION ON THE HIGH SEAS: LEGISLATIVE HISTORY OF PART VII, SECTION I (ARTICLES 87, 89, 90-94, 96-98) OF THE UNITED NATIONS CONVENTION ON THE LAW OF THE SEA. United Nations Publishing Service, Office for Ocean Affairs and the Law of the Sea, Room DC2-0853, New York, New York 10017. 1989.

THE LAW OF THE SEA: OFFICIAL TEXT OF THE UNITED NATIONS CONVENTION ON THE LAW OF THE SEA WITH ANNEXES AND INDEXES. United Nations, Sales Section, Publishing Division, Room DC2-0853, New York, New York 10017. 1983.

THE LAW OF THE SEA. REGIME OF ISLANDS: LEGISLATIVE HISTORY OF PART VIII (ARTICLE 121) OF THE UNITED NATIONS CONVENTION ON THE LAW OF THE SEA. United Nations Publishing Service, Office for Ocean Affairs and the Law of the Sea, Room DC2-0853, New York, New York 10017. 1988.

NEW DIRECTIONS IN THE LAW OF THE SEA. Kenneth R. Simmonds, Editor. Oceana Publications, Incorporated, 75 Main Street, Dobbs Ferry, New York 10522. 1983. (Periodic Supplements).

NORTH AMERICA AND ASIA-PACIFIC AND THE DEVELOPMENT OF THE SEA: TREATIES AND NATIONAL LEGISLATION. Myron H. Nordquist and Choon-Ho Park, Editor. Oceana Publications, Incorporated, 75 Main Street, Dobbs Ferry, New York 10522. 1981. (Periodic Supplements).

OCEANS POLICY STUDY SERIES. Center for Oceans Law and Policy, University of Virginia School of Law. Oceana Publications, Incorporated, 75 Main Street, Dobbs Ferry, New York 10522. 1984. (Periodic Supplements).

THIRD UNITED NATIONS CONFERENCE ON THE LAW OF THE SEA: DOCUMENTS. Renate Platzoder, Editor. Oceana Publications, Incorporated, 75 Main Street, Dobbs Ferry, New York 10522. 1982- .

WESTERN EUROPE AND THE DEVELOPMENT OF THE LAW OF THE SEA: REGIONAL DOCUMENTS, NATIONAL LEGISLATION. Francesco Durante and Walter Rodino, Editors. Oceana Publications, Incorporated, 75 Main Street, Dobbs Ferry, New York 10522. 1979. (Periodic Supplements).

HANDBOOKS, MANUALS, FORMBOOKS

A HANDBOOK ON THE NEW LAW OF THE SEA. Rene-Jean Dupuy and Daniel Vignes, Editors. Martinus Nijhoff, Kluwer Academic Publishers, 101 Philip Drive, Assinippi Park, Norwell, Massachusetts 02061. 1990.

TEXTBOOKS AND GENERAL WORKS

ARREST OF SHIPS: LAW AND PRACTICE. Christopher Hill. Lloyd's of London Press, 611 Broadway, Suite 523, New York, New York 10012. 1985. (Supplemented).

CHINA'S PRACTICE IN THE LAW OF THE SEA. Jeanette Greenfield. Clarendon Press, Oxford, England. 1992.

COMMON HERITAGE OR COMMON BURDEN?: THE UNITED STATES POSITION ON THE DEVELOPMENT OF A REGIME FOR DEEP SEA-BED MINING IN THE LAW OF THE SEA CONVENTION. Markus G. Schmidt. Oxford University Press, 200 Madison Avenue, New York, New York 10016. 1989.

CONSENSUS AND CONFRONTATION: THE UNITED STATES AND THE LAW OF THE SEA CONVENTION. Jon M. Van Dyke, Editor. Law of the Sea Institute, 2515 Dole Street, Room 208, Honolulu, Hawaii 96822. 1985.

CONTROL OF MARINE POLLUTION IN INTERNATIONAL LAW. Ramanlal Soni. Lloyds of London Press, 611 Broadway, Suite 523, New York, New York 10012. 1985.

DEEP SEA MINING AND THE LAW OF THE SEA. Alexandra M. Post. Kluwer Academic Publishers, 101 Philip Drive, Assinippi Park, Norwell, Massachusetts 02061. 1983.

DENUCLEARISATION OF THE OCEANS. R. B. Byers, Editor. Saint Martin's Press, Incorporated, 175 Fifth Avenue, New York, New York 10010. 1986.

THE EVOLUTION OF THE LAW OF THE SEA: A STUDY OF RESOURCES AND STRATEGY WITH SPECIAL REGARD TO THE POLAR REGIONS. Bo Hohnson Thertenberg. Unipub, A Xerox Publishing Company, 205 East Forty-second Street, New York, New York 10017. 1984.

IMPACTS OF THE UNITED NATIONS CONVENTION ON THE LAW OF SEA ON TUNA REGULATION. W. T. Burke. Unipub, A Xerox Publishing Company, 4611-F Assembly Drive, Lanham, Maryland 20706-4391. 1982.

INTERNATIONAL LAW OF THE SEA. D.P. O'Connell. Clarendon Press, Oxford University Press, 200 Madison Avenue, New York, New York 10016. Volume I, 1982; Volume II, 1983.

THE INTERNATIONAL LAW OF THE SEA: CASES, DOCUMENTS, AND READINGS. Gary Knight and Hungdah Chiu. Elsevier Science Publishing Company, P.O. Box 882, Madison Square Station, New York, New York 10159. 1991.

INTERNATIONALIZING THE SEABED. Roderick Ogley. Gower Publishing Company, Old Post Road, Brookfield, Vermont 05036. 1984.

LAND-LOCKED AND GEOGRAPHICALLY DISADVANTAGED STATES IN THE INTERNATIONAL LAW OF THE SEA. S.C. Vasciannie. Oxford University Press, 200 Madison Avenue, New York, New York 10016. 1990.

LANDLOCKED STATES AND THE UNCLOS REGIME. A. Mpazi Sinjela. Oceana Publications, Incorporated, 75 Main Street, Dobbs Ferry, New York 10522. 1983.

THE LAW OF THE SEA. Robin R. Churchill and A. V. Lowe. St. Martin's Press, 175 Fifth Avenue, New York, New York 10010. 1988.

THE LAW OF THE SEA: AN HISTORICAL ANALYSIS OF THE 1982 TREATY AND ITS REJECTION BY THE UNITED STATES. James B. Morell. McFarland and Company, Incorporated, Box 611, Jefferson, North Carolina 28640. 1991.

LAW OF THE SEA AND INTERNATIONAL SHIPPING: ANGLO-SOVIET POST - UNCLOS PERSPECTIVES. William E. Butler, Editor. Oceana Publications, Incorporated, 75 Main Street, Dobbs Ferry, New York 10522. 1985.

LAW OF THE SEA AND OCEAN DEVELOPMENT ISSUES IN THE PACIFIC BASIN: PROCEEDINGS, 15TH ANNUAL CONFERENCE, 1981. Edward L. Miles and Scott Allen, Editors. Law of the Sea Institute, 2515 Dole Street, Room 208, Honolulu, Hawaii 96822. 1983.

LAW OF THE SEA AND OCEAN INDUSTRY: NEW OPPORTUNITIES AND RESTRAINTS. Douglas M. Johnston and Norman G. Letalik. Law of the Sea Institute, 2515 Dole Street, Room 208, Honolulu, Hawaii 96822. 1984.

THE LAW OF THE SEA: DOCUMENTS, 1983-1989. Renate Platzoder, Editor. Preparatory Commission for the International Sea-Bed Authority and for the International Tribunal for the Law of the Sea. Oceana Publications, 75 Main Street, Dobbs Ferry, New York 10522. 1990.

LAW OF THE SEA IN A NUTSHELL. Louis B. Sohn and Kristen Gustafson. West Publishing Company, P.O. Box 64526, 50 West Kellogg Boulevard, St. Paul, Minnesota 55164-0526. 1984.

THE LAW OF THE SEA: NATIONAL LEGISLATION ON THE CONTINENTAL SHELF. United Nations Publishing Service, Office for Ocean Affairs and the Law of the Sea, Room DC2-0853, New York, New York 10017. 1989.

THE LAW OF THE SEA: PROBLEMS FROM THE EAST ASIAN PERSPECTIVE. Choon-Ho Park, Editor. Law of the Sea Institute, 2515 Dole Street, Room 208, Honolulu, Hawaii 96822. 1987.

LAW OF THE SEA: STATE PRACTICE IN ZONES OF SPECIAL JURISDICTION. Thomas A. Clingan, Editor. Law of the Sea Institute, 2515 Dole Street, Room 208, Honolulu, Hawaii 96822. 1982.

LAW OF THE SEA: UNITED STATES POLICY DILEMMA. Bernard Oxman, Editor. Institute for Contemporary Studies, 243 Kearny Street, San Francisco, California 94108. 1983.

THE LEGAL ORDER OF SEABED MINING UNDER THE LAW OF THE SEA CONVENTION. W. Hauser. Kluwer Academic Publishers, 101 Philip Drive, Assinippi Park, Norwell, Massachusetts 02061. 1983.

MARINE POLLUTION AND THE LAW OF THE SEA. John W. Kindt. William S. Hein and Company, Incorporated, Hein Building, 1285 Main Street, Buffalo, New York 14209. 1986.

MARINE SCIENTIFIC RESEARCH AND THE LAW OF SEA. Alfred H. Soons. Kluwer Academic Publishers, 101 Philip Drive, Assinippi Park, Norwell, Massachusetts 02061. 1982.

MARITIME BOUNDARY. S. P. Jagota. Kluwer Academic Publishers, 101 Philip Drive, Assinippi Park, Norwell, Massachusetts 02061. 1985.

NEGOTIATING THE LAW OF THE SEA. James K. Sebenius. Harvard University Press, 79 Garden Street, Cambridge, Massachusetts 02138. 1984.

THE NEW ORDER OF THE OCEAN: THE ADVENT OF MANAGED ENVIRONMENT. Giulio Pontecorvo, Editor. Columbia University Press, 562 West One Hundred Thirteenth Street, New York, New York 10025. 1986.

THE NORTHWEST PASSAGE: ARTIC STRAITS. Donat Pharand. Kluwer Academic Publishers, 101 Philip Drive, Assinippi Park, Norwell, Massachusetts 02061. 1984.

OCEAN USES AND THEIR REGULATION. Luc Cuyvers. John Wiley and Sons, Incorporated, 605 Third Avenue, New York, New York 10158. 1984.

ORIGIN AND DEVELOPMENT OF THE LAW OF THE SEA. R. P. Anand. Kluwer Academic Publishers, 101 Philip Drive, Assinippi Park, Norwell, Massachusetts 02061. 1983.

PERSPECTIVES ON UNITED STATES POLICY TOWARD THE LAW OF THE SEA: PRELUDE TO THE FINAL SESSION OF THE THIRD U.N. CONFERENCE ON THE LAW OF THE SEA. David D. Caron and Charles L. O. Buder. Law of the Sea Institute, 2515 Dole Street, Room 208, Honolulu, Hawaii 96822. 1985.

THE REGIME FOR THE EXPLOITATION OF TRANSBOUNDARY MARINE FISHERIES RESOURCES: THE UNITED NATIONS LAW OF THE SEA CONVENTION COOPERATION BETWEEN STATES. Ellen Hey. Martinus Nijhoff, Kluwer Academic Publishers, 101 Philip Drive, Assinippi Park, Norwell, Massachusetts 02061. 1989.

RESEARCH MANAGEMENT AND THE OCEANS: THE POLITICAL ECONOMY OF DEEP SEABED MINING. Kurt M. Shusterich. Westview Press, 5500 Central Avenue, Boulder, Colorado 80301. 1982.

THE SOVIET UNION IN ARTIC WATERS. Willy Ostreng. Law of the Sea Institute, 2515 Dole Street, Room 208, Honolulu, Hawaii 96822. 1987.

STRAITS IN INTERNATIONAL NAVIGATION: CONTEMPORARY ISSUES. Kheng-Lian Koh. Oceana Publications, Incorporated, 75 Main Street, Dobbs Ferry, New York 10522. 1982.

SUPERPOWER AT SEA: UNITED STATES OCEAN POLICY. Finn Laurensen. Greenwood Publishing Group, Incorporated, 88 Post Road, West, P.O. Box 5007, Westport, Connecticut 06881. 1983.

THE SYSTEM FOR SETTLEMENT OF DISPUTES UNDER THE UNITED NATIONS CONVENTION ON THE LAW OF THE SEA: A DRAFTING HISTORY AND A COMMENTARY. A.O. Adede. Martinus Nijhoff, Kluwer Academic Publishers, 101 Philip Drive, Assinippi Park, Norwell, Massachusetts 02061. 1987.

TO SETTLE THE OCEANS: THE LAW OF THE SEA IN PRACTICE. Clyde Sanger. University of Toronto Press, 10 St. Mary Street, Suite 700, Toronto, Ontario, Canada M4Y 2WB. 1987.

TOWARD A NEW INTERNATIONAL MARINE ORDER. Finn Laurensen. Kluwer Academic Publishers, 101 Philip Drive, Assinippi Park, Norwell, Massachusetts 02061. 1982.

THE TRANSFER OF MARINE TECHNOLOGY TO DEVELOPING NATIONS IN INTERNATIONAL LAW. Boleslaw A. Boczek. Law of the Sea Institute, 2515 Dole Street, Room 208, Honolulu, Hawaii 96822. 1982.

THE 200 MILE EXCLUSIVE ECONOMIC ZONE IN THE NEW LAW OF THE SEA. Barbara Kwiatkowska. Martinus Nijhoff, Kluwer Academic Publishers, 101 Philip Drive, Assinippi Park, Norwell, Massachusetts 02061. 1989.

THE UCTAD LINER CODE: UNITED STATES MARITIME POLICY AT THE CROSSROADS. Lawrence Juda. Westview Press, 5500 Central Avenue, Boulder, Colorado 80301. 1983.

UNITED NATIONS CONVENTIONON THE LAW OF THE SEA: A COMMENTARY. Myron H. Nordquist. Kluwer Academic Publishers, 101 Philip Drive, Assinippi Park, Norwell, Massachusetts 02061. 1985.

THE UNITED STATES AND THE LAW OF THE SEA TREATY. Steven R. David and Peter Digeser. Foreign Policy Institute, The Paul H. Nitze School of Advanced International Studies, The John Hopkins University. University Press of America, 4720 Boston Way, Lanham, Maryland 20706. 1990.

ANNUALS AND SURVEYS

THE DEVELOPING ORDER OF THE OCEANS: PROCEEDINGS OF THE EIGHTEENTH ANNUAL LAW OF THE SEA INSTITUTE CONFERENCE. Robert B. Krueger and Stefan A. Richardson, Editors. Law of the Sea Institute, 2515 Dole Street, Room 208, Honolulu, Hawaii 96822. 1986.

LAW REVIEWS AND PERIODICALS

OCEAN DEVELOPMENT AND INTERNATIONAL LAW JOURNAL. Crane, Russak and Company, Incorporated, 3 East Forty-fourth Street, New York, New York 10017. Quarterly.

OCEANS POLICY STUDY SERIES. Center for Oceans Law and Policy, University of Virginia School of Law. Oceana Publications, Incorporated, 75 Main Street, Dobbs Ferry, New York 10522. 1984. (Periodic Supplements)

NEWSLETTERS AND NEWPAPERS

OCEAN AND COASTAL LAW MEMO. Ocean and Coastal Law Center, University of Oregon Law School, Eugene, Oregon 97403. Quarterly.

OCEAN LAW LETTER. Ocean Science Services International, 663 Fifth Avenue, New York, New York 10022. Monthly.

BIBLIOGRAPHIES

BIBLIOGRAPHY ON THE SOVIET UNION AND THE DEVELOPMENT OF THE LAW OF THE SEA. William E. Butler. Oceana Publications, Incorporated, 75 Main Street, Dobbs Ferry, New York 10522. 1985.

INTERNATIONAL LAW OF THE SEA AND MARITIME AFFAIRS: A BIBLIOGRAPHY. Nikos Papadakis and Martin Glassner. Kluwer Academic Publishers, 101 Philip Drive, Assinippi Park, Norwell, Massachusetts 02061. 1980. (Supplement 1984).

LAW OF THE SEA: A SELECT BIBLIOGRAPHY. Unipub, A Xerox Publishing Company, 4611-F Assembly Drive, Lanham, Maryland 20706-4391. 1991. 1985.

THE LAW OF THE SEA: A SELECT BIBLIOGRAPHY, 1990. United Nations Publishing Service, Office for Ocean Affairs and the Law of the Sea, Room DC2-0853, New York, New York 10017. 1991.

MARITIME BOUNDARY DELIMITATION: AN ANNOTATED BIBLIOGRAPHY. Ted L. McDorman and Kenneth P. Beauchamp. Lexington Books, Division of D.C. Health and Company, 125 Spring Street, Lexington, Massachusetts 02173. 1983.

THE UNITED STATES AND THE NEW LAW OF THE SEA: TERRITORIAL CLAIMS AND SEA BED EXPLOITATION IN THE 1980'S. Tim J. Watts. Vance Bibliographies, P.O. Box 229, 112 North Charter Street, Monticello, Illinois 61856. 1987.

ASSOCIATIONS AND PROFESSIONAL SOCIETIES

ASSOCIATION OF AMERICAN LAW SCHOOLS. Section on Maritime Law, One Dupont Circle, Northwest, Washington, D.C. 20036. (202) 296-8851.

RESEARCH CENTERS, INSTITUTES, CLEARINGHOUSES

CENTER FOR OCEANS LAW AND POLICY. University of Virginia School of Law, Charlottesville, Virginia 22901. (804) 924-7441.

LAW OF THE SEA INSTITUTE. Richardson School of Law, 2515 Dole Street, Room 208, Honolulu, Hawaii 96822. (808) 948-6750.

MARINE LAW INSTITUTE. University of Southern Maine, 246 Dearing Avenue, Portland, Maine 04102. (207) 780-4474.

OCEAN AND COASTAL LAW CENTER. University of Oregon Law School, Eugene, Oregon 97403. (503) 686-3845.

LAW OFFICE MANAGEMENT
See also: LEGAL ASSISTANTS; LEGAL SECRETARIES

LOOSELEAF SERVICES AND REPORTERS

THE AUTOMATED LAW FIRM: A COMPLETE GUIDE TO SOFTWARE AND SYSTEMS. Richard L. Robbins. Prentice-Hall, Incorporated, 113 Sylvan Avenue, Englewood Cliffs, New Jersey 07632. 1989.

THE BUSINESS OF LAW: A HANDBOOK ON HOW TO MANAGE LAW FIRMS. Second Edition. Larry Smith and Emily Couric. Prentice-Hall, Incorporated, 113 Sylvan Avenue, Englewood Cliffs, New Jersey 07632. 1990.

CORPORATE COUNSEL'S MANAGERIAL GUIDE. William A. Hancock, Editor. Business Laws, Incorporated, 11630 Chillicothe Road, Chesterland, Ohio 44026. 1988- .

HANDBOOKS, MANUALS, FORMBOOKS

BASICS FOR BUYING YOUR PERSONAL COMPUTER. Perry J. Radoff. American Bar Association, Economics of Law Practice Section, 750 North Lake Shore Drive, Chicago, Illinois 60611. 1987.

THE BUSINESS OF LAW: A HANDBOOK ON HOW TO MANAGE LAW FIRMS. Emily Couric, Editor. Harcourt Brace Jovanovich, Incorporated, 6277 Sea Harbor Drive, Orlando, Florida 32821. 1984.

A BUYER'S GUIDE TO OFFICE TECHNOLOGY: PLUS TEN WAYS TO AVOID HIGH-TECH ANXIETY. AM-LAW Publishing Company, 205 Lexington Avenue, New York, New York 10016. 1984.

CHOOSING AND USING COMPUTERS TO IMPROVE YOUR LAW PRACTICE. Kline D. Strong. American Bar Association, Section of Economics of Law Practice, 750 North Lake Shore Drive, Chicago, Illinois 60611. 1983.

A COMMON SENSE GUIDE TO LAW OFFICE AUTOMATION. Sara Piovia. Prentice-Hall, Incorporated, 113 Sylvan Avenue, Englewood Cliffs, New Jersey 07632. 1984.

THE COMPUTERIZED LAWYER: A GUIDE TO THE USE OF COMPUTERS IN THE LEGAL PROFESSION. Philip Leith. Springer-Verlag, Incorporated, 175 Fifth Avenue, New York, New York 10010. 1991.

DECISION-AIDING SOFTWARE AND LEGAL DECISION-MAKING: A GUIDE TO SKILLS AND APPLICATIONS THROUGHOUT THE LAW. Stuart S. Nagel. Quorum Books, Greenwood Publishing Group, Incorporated, 88 Post Road West, P.O. Box 5007, Westport, Connecticut 06881. 1989.

DESIGNING YOUR LAW OFFICE: A GUIDE TO SPACE PLANNING, RENOVATION, AND RELOCATION. Marjorie A. Miller. American Bar Association, Section of Economics of Law Practice, 750 North Lake Shore Drive, Chicago, Illinois 60611. 1989.

THE DOW JONES-IRWIN HANDBOOK OF MICROCOMPUTER APPLICATIONS IN LAW. Ronald W. Staudt and Bernard J. Farber, Editors. Dow Jones-Irwin, 1818 Ridge Road, Homewood, Illinois 60430. 1987.

HANGING OUT A SHINGLE: AN INSIDER'S GUIDE TO STARTING YOUR OWN LAW FIRM. Harry F. Weyher. Dodd, Mead and Company, Incorporated, 71 Fifth Avenue, New York, New York 10003. 1987.

HOW TO MANAGE YOUR LAW OFFICE. Mary Ann Altman and Robert I. Weil. Matthew Bender and Company, Incorporated, 11 Penn Plaza, New York, New York 10001. 1973. (Periodic Supplements).

IMPROVING LAWYER PRODUCTIVITY: HOW TO TRAIN, MANAGE AND SUPERVISE YOUR LAWYERS. Joel Henning. Lawletters, 322 South Michigan Avenue, Suite 1460, Chicago 60604. 1985.

LAW OFFICE ECONOMICS AND MANAGEMENT MANUAL 1970-1990. Paul S. Hoffman, Editor. Callaghan and Company, 155 Pfingsten Road, Deerfield, Illinois 60015. 1990. (Periodic Supplements).

LAW OFFICE GUIDE TO SMALL COMPUTERS. Forrest D. Rhoads and John Edwards. Shepard's/McGraw-Hill, P. O. Box 1235, Colorado Springs, Colorado 80901. 1984.

LAW OFFICE SOFTWARE: ATTORNEY'S GUIDE TO SELECTION. James J. Ayres. John Wiley and Sons, Incorporated, 605 Third Avenue, New York, New York 10158. 1990.

LAW OFFICE STAFF MANUAL: MODEL POLICIES AND PROCEDURES FOR LAW OFFICE PERSONNEL. Berne Ralston. American Bar Association, Section of Economics of Law Practice, 750 North Lake Shore Drive, Chicago, Illinois 60611. 1982.

MANUAL OF IN-HOUSE TRAINING: A GUIDE FOR LAW FIRMS AND LEGAL DEPARTMENTS. Joel F. Henning and Mitch Pacelle, Editors. Lawletters, 322 South Michigan Avenue, Suite 1460, Chicago 60604. 1982.

99 QUESTIONS: A MANAGEMENT WORKBOOK DESIGNED TO PULL YOUR FIRM TOGETHER-OR SMASH IT TO SMITHEREENS. Steven Brill and David Maister. AM-LAW Publishing Corporation, 205 Lexington Avenue, New York, New York 10016. 1984.

A PLANNING WORKBOOK FOR LAW FIRM MANAGEMENT. Second Edition. William C. Cobb. American Bar Association, Section of Economics of Law Practice, 750 North Lake Shore Drive, Chicago, Illinois 60611. 1985.

THE PRACTICAL LAWYER'S LAW OFFICE MANAGEMENT MANUAL. American Law Institute-American Bar Association, Committee on Continuing Professional Education, 4025 Chestnut Street, Philadelphia, Pennsylvania 19104. 1984.

TELEPHONE EQUIPMENT FOR THE LAW OFFICE: A LAWYER'S GUIDE TO COMMUNICATION SYSTEMS. Paul S. Hoffman, Stan Bailin and Jerry W. Mills. American Bar Association, Section of Economics of Law Practice, 750 North Lake Shore Drive, Chicago, Illinois 60611. 1983.

WHAT A LAWYER NEEDS TO KNOW TO BUY AND USE A COMPUTER. Robert P. Wilkins. R. P. W. Publishing Corporation, P.O. Box 1108, Lexington, South Carolina 29072. 1984.

WORDPERFECT FOR LAWYERS: HOW TO EASILY AUTOMATE THE PRODUCTION OF DOCUMENTS IN LAW OFFICES: VERSION 5.1. Don Silver. Adams-Hall Publishing, P.O. Box 491002, Los Angeles, California 90049. 1990.

TEXTBOOKS AND GENERAL WORKS

ACCOUNTING FOR LAWYERS. Fourth Edition. E. McGruder Faris, Jr. The Michie Company, P.O. Box 7587, Charlottesville, Virginia 22906-7587. 1982.

ACCOUNTING SYSTEMS FOR LAW OFFICES. William J. Burke. Matthew Bender and Company, Incorporated, 11 Penn Plaza, New York, New York 10001. 1978. (Periodic Supplements).

ASSESSING LAWYER EVALUATION AND PARTNERSHIP DECISIONS AFTER HISHON V. KING AND SPAULDING. Stanley J. Brown, Chairman. Practising Law Institute, 810 Seventh Avenue, New York, New York 10019. 1985.

AUTOMATED LAW OFFICE SYSTEMS: A SURVEY OF TODAY'S TOOLS AND TECHNIQUES. Sidney W. Frost and James C. Dunlap. West Publishing Company, P. O. Box 64526, 50 West Kellogg Boulevard, St. Paul, Minnesota 55164-0526. 1983.

AUTOMATED LITIGATION SUPPORT: A PRACTICE INTRODUCTION. Fred M. Greguras. Bureau of National Affairs, 1231 Twenty-fifth Street, Northwest, Washington, D.C. 20037. 1984.

BUILDING YOUR FIRM WITH ASSOCIATES: A GUIDE FOR HIRING AND MANAGING NEW ATTORNEYS. Richard N. Feferman. American Bar Association, Section of Economics of Law Practice, 750 North Lake Shore Drive, Chicago, Illinois 60611. 1988.

COMPUTER POWER FOR YOUR LAW OFFICE. Daniel Remer. Sybex, Incorporated, 2021 Challenger Drive, Alameda, California 94501. 1983.

COMPUTERIZING YOUR LAW PRACTICE. American Bar Association, Section of Economics of Law Practice, 750 North Lake Shore Drive, Chicago, Illinois 60611. 1984.

COMPUTERS FOR LAWYERS: A COMPREHENSIVE GUIDE TO AUTOMATING YOUR LAW FIRM. Paul Bernstein. Association of Trial Lawyers of America, 1050 Thirty-first Street, Northwest, Washington, D.C. 20007. 1992.

COMPUTERS IN THE LAW: CONCEPTS AND APPLICATIONS. Brent D. Roper. West Publishing Company, 50 West Kellogg Boulevard, St. Paul, Minnesota 55164. 1992.

COST ACCOUNTING FOR LAW FIRMS. Robert J. Arndt and James F. Rabenhorst. American Bar Association, Section of Economics of Law Practice, 750 North Lake Shore Drive, Chicago, Illinois 60611. 1984.

FROM YELLOW PADS TO COMPUTERS: TRANSFORMING YOUR LAW PRACTICE WITH A COMPUTER. Fran Shellenberger and Kathryn M. Braeman. American Bar Association, Economics of Law Practice Section, Law Practice Management Division, Administrative procedures Committee, 750 North Lake Shore Drive, Chicago, Illinois 60611. 1987.

IMPROVING LAW FIRM PRODUCTIVITY BY ENCOURAGING LAWYERS' USE OF PERSONAL COMPUTERS. Law and Business, Harcourt Brace Jovanovich, Incorporated, 6277 Sea Harbor Drive, Orlando, Florida 32821. 1985.

IMPROVING YOUR SUMMER ASSOCIATE PROGRAM. Arnold Kanter. Lawletters, Incorporated, 332 South Michigan, Chicago, Illinois 60604. 1986.

AN INTRODUCTION TO LAW PRACTICE MANAGEMENT. Second Edition. Mary Ann Altman and Robert I. Weil. Matthew Bender and Company, Incorporated, 11 Penn Plaza, New York, New York 10001. 1987.

AN INTRODUCTION TO USING COMPUTERS IN LAW. Mary Ann Mason. West Publishing Company, P. O. Box 64526, 50 West Kellogg Boulevard, St. Paul, Minnesota 55164-0526. 1984.

LAW FIRM LIABILITY INSURANCE CRISIS: PRACTICAL APPROACHES FOR A DIFFICULT MARKET. Law and Business, Harcourt Brace Jovanovich, Incorporated, 6277 Sea Harbor Drive, Orlando, Florida 32821. 1986.

LAW OFFICE AUTOMATION AND TECHNOLOGY. Frank Arentowicz, Jr. and Ward Bower. Matthew Bender and Company, Incorporated, 11 Penn Plaza, New York, New York 10001. 1980. (Periodic Supplements).

LAW OFFICE AUTOMATION FOR PARALEGALS, ADMINISTRATORS, AND LEGAL SECRETARIES. Ashley Saunders Lipson. Prentice-Hall, Incorporated, 113 Sylvan Avenue, Englewood Cliffs, New Jersey 07632. 1989.

LAW OFFICE MANAGEMENT FOR PARALEGALS. Jonathan Lynton, Donna Masinter and Terri Mick Lyndall. Delmar Publishers, Incorporated, P.O. Box 15015, Two Computer Drive West, Albany, New York 12212. 1991.

LAW PRACTICE MANAGEMENT FOR THE SOLO AND SMALL OFFICE PRACTITIONER, 1990. Edna R.S. Alvarez. Practising Law Institute, 810 Seventh Avenue, New York, New York 10019. 1990.

LAW PRACTICE MANAGEMENT: MATERIALS AND CASES. Gary A. Munneke. West Publishing Company, 50 West Kellogg Boulevard, St. Paul, Minnesota 55164. 1991.

LEGAL KEYBOARDING: TYPEWRITERS, ELECTRONIC TYPEWRITERS AND WORD PROCESSORS. Mary Bauman and Mary Bahntge. John Wiley and Sons, Incorporated, 605 Third Avenue, New York, New York 10158. 1985.

LEGAL OFFICE ADMINISTRATION. Polly McGlew. Delmar Publishers, Incorporated, P.O. Box 15015, Two Computer Drive West, Albany, New York 12212. 1989.

LEGAL SIMULATION FOR WORD PROCESSING. Patricia A. Custer. Prentice-Hall, Incorporated, 113 Sylvan Avenue, Englewood Cliffs, New Jersey 07632. 1988.

LEGAL WORD PROCESSING EXERCISES. Sandra Muehlman-Shortt. Prentice-Hall, Incorporated, 113 Sylvan Avenue, Englewood Cliffs, New Jersey 07632. 1991.

LITIGATION SUPPORT SYSTEMS: AN ATTORNEY'S GUIDE. E. Hugh Kinney. Callaghan and Company, 155 Pfingsten Road, Deerfield, Illinois 60015. 1985.

MANAGEMENT FOR IN-HOUSE COUNSEL: TECHNIQUES, TOOLS, APPROACHES. American Bar Association, Section of Economics of Law Practice, 750 North Lake Shore Drive, Chicago, Illinois 60611. 1985.

MANAGING A LAW PRACTICE: THE HUMAN SIDE. Richard C. Reed. American Bar Association, Section of Economics of Law Practice, 750 North Lake Shore Drive, Chicago, Illinois 60611. 1988.

MANAGING FOR PROFIT: IMPROVING OR MAINTAINING YOUR BOTTOM LINE. Robert J. Arndt. American Bar Association, Section of Law Practice Management, 750 North Lake Shore Drive, Chicago, Illinois 60611. 1991.

MANAGING PARTNER 101: A PRIMER ON FIRM LEADERSHIP. Robert Michael Greene. American Bar Association, Section of Law Practice Management, 750 North Lake Shore Drive, Chicago, Illinois 60611. 1990.

MICROCOMPUTERS FOR LAWYERS. J. Stewart Schneider and Charles E. Bowen. TAB Books, Incorporated, P.O. Box 40, Blue Ridge Summit, Pennsylvania 17294-0850. 1983.

MICROCOMPUTERS FOR LEGAL PROFESSIONALS. Christina J. McClung, John A. Guerrieri, and Kenneth A. McClung, Jr. John Wiley and Sons, Incorporated, 605 Third Avenue, New York, New York 10158. 1984.

ON TRAINING ASSOCIATES. Theodore Voorhees. American Law Institute-American Bar Association, 4025 Chestnut Street, Philadelphia, Pennsylvania 19104. 1989.

OUTPLACEMENT OF LAWYERS: A GUIDE TO THE ART OF FIRING FOR LAW FIRMS AND CORPORATE LEGAL DEPARTMENTS. Vincent J. Donnelly. Innovations Press, 59 South Hayden Parkway, Hudson, Ohio 44236. 1985.

PERSONAL COMPUTERS FOR LAWYERS: AN ABA NATIONAL INSTITUTE. Chicago-Kent College of Law. American Bar Association, Division of Professional Education, 750 North Lake Shore Drive, Chicago, Illinois 60611. 1988.

PRACTICAL SYSTEMS: TIPS FOR ORGANIZING YOUR LAW OFFICE. Charles R. Coulter. American Bar Association, Section of Law Practice Management, 750 North Lake Shore Drive, Chicago, Illinois 60611. 1991.

PRACTICING LAW AND MANAGING PEOPLE: HOW TO BE SUCCESSFUL. Deborah Heller and James M. Hunt. Butterworth-Heinemann, 80 Montvale Avenue, Stoneham, Massachusetts 02180. 1988.

SIMPLIFIED ACCOUNTING SYSTEMS AND CONCEPTS FOR LAWYERS WITH A STANDARD CHART OF ACCOUNTS. Klinc D. Strong. American Bar Association, Section of Economics of Law Practice, 750 North Lake Shore Drive, Chicago, Illinois 60611. 1982.

THE SUCCESSFUL LAW FIRM: NEW APPROACHES TO STRUCTURE AND MANAGEMENT. Second Edition. Bradford W. Hildebrandt and Jack Kaufman. Prentice-Hall, Incorporated, 113 Sylvan Avenue, Englewood Cliffs, New Jersey 07632. 1988.

USING COMPUTERS IN THE LAW: AN INTRODUCTION AND PRACTICAL GUIDE. Second Edition. Mary Ann Mason. West Publishing Company, 50 West Kellogg Boulevard, St. Paul, Minnesota 55164. 1988.

WINNING WITH COMPUTERS: TRIAL PRACTICE IN THE TWENTY-FIRST CENTURY. John C. Tredennick, Jr., Editor. American Bar Association, Section of Law Practice Management, 750 North Lake Shore Drive, Chicago, Illinois 60611. 1991.

WRITING YOUR LAW FIRM NEWSLETTER, FROM START TO FINISH. Michael L. Goldblatt. Section of Economics of Law practice, American Bar Association, 750 North Lake Shore Drive, Chicago, Illinois 60611. 1987.

DIGESTS, INDEXES, ABSTRACTS, CITATORS

LEGAL INFORMATION MANAGEMENT INDEX. Elyse Fox, Editor. Fox Information Consultants, Incorporated, P. O. Box 67, Newton Highlands, Massachusetts. 02161. Bi-monthly.

ANNUALS AND SURVEYS

COMPENSATION SURVEY. Association of Legal Administrators, 175 East Hawthorn Parkway, Suite 325, Vernon Hills, Illinois 60061-1428. Annual.

LAW OFFICE MANAGEMENT: COURSE HANDBOOK. Practising Law Institute, 810 Seventh Avenue, New York, New York 10019. Annual.

LAW REVIEWS AND PERIODICALS

LAW OFFICE ECONOMICS AND MANAGEMENT. Callaghan and Company, 3201 Old Glenview Road, Wilmette, Illinois 60091. Quarterly.

LEGAL ADMINISTRATOR. Association of Legal Administrators, 1800 Pickwick Avenue, Glenview, Illinois 60025. Quarterly.

LEGAL ECONOMICS. American Bar Association, Section of Economics of Law Practice, 750 North Lake Shore Drive, Chicago, Illinois 60611. Semiquarterly.

NEWSLETTERS AND NEWSPAPERS

ACCOUNTING FOR LAW FIRMS. Leader Publications, 111 Eighth Avenue, New York, New York 10011. Monthly.

ALA NEWS. Association of Legal Administrators, 1800 Pickwick Avenue, Glenview, Illinois 60025. Eight issues per year.

ALTMAN AND WEIL REPORT TO LEGAL MANAGEMENT. Altman and Weil Publications, Incorporated, P. O. Box 472, Ardmore, Pennsylvania 19003. Monthly.

ASSOCIATION'S FORUM. The Attorneys Group, National Association of Professions and American Business Association, 292 Madison Avenue, New York, New York 10017. Quarterly.

ATTORNEYS COMPUTER REPORT. Professional Publications, 50 South Ninth Street, Suite 200, Minneapolis, Minnesota 55402. Monthly.

ATTORNEYS OFFICE MANAGEMENT REPORT. Professional Publications, Incorporated, P. O. Box 81067, Atlanta, Georgia 30366. Quarterly.

ATTORNEYS PERSONNEL REPORT. Professional Publications, Incorporated, P.O. Box 81067, Atlanta, Georgia 30366. Monthly.

COMPUTER COUNSEL. Computer Counsel, 641 West Lake Street, Suite 903, Chicago, Illinois 60606. Monthly.

THE CORPORATE COUNSELLOR. Leader Publications, Incorporated, 111 Eighth Avenue, New York, New York 10011. Monthly.

CORPORATE COUNSEL'S MANAGERIAL ADVISOR. Business Laws, Incorporated, 11630 Chillicative Road, Chesterfield, Ohio 44026. Monthly.

FINANCIAL MANAGEMENT NEWSLETTER. Association of Legal Administrators, 175 East Hawthorn Parkway, Suite 325, Vernon Hills, Illinois 60061. Quarterly.

HILDEBRANDT REPORT. Hildebrandt Incorporated, 501 Post Office Plaza, 50 Division Street, Somerville, New Jersey 08876. Bimonthly.

LAW FIRM PROFIT REPORT. Key Communications Group, 4350 East-West Highway, Suite 1124, Bethesda, Maryland 20814. Monthly.

LAW OFFICE MANAGEMENT AND ADMINISTRATION REPORT. Institute for Office Management and Administration, Incorporated. Five West Thirty-sixth Street, New York, New York 10018. Monthly.

LAW OFFICE MANAGEMENT DIGEST. Law Publications, Incorporated, 1180 South Beverly Drive, Los Angeles, California 90035. Bimonthly .

LEADER'S LEGAL TECH NEWSLETTER. Leader Publications, Incorporated, 111 Eighth Avenue, New York, New York 10011. Monthly.

MANAGEMENT AND ADMINISTRATION NEWSLETTER. Association of Legal Administrators, 175 East Hawthorn Parkway, Suite 325, Vernon Hills, Illinois 60061. Quarterly.

OF COUNSEL: THE MONTHLY LEGAL PRACTICE REPORT. Law and Business, Incorporated, Harcourt Brace Jovanovich, Incorporated, 1250 Sixth Avenue, San Diego, California 92101. Monthly.

PEOPLE TO PEOPLE. Association of Legal Administrators, 175 East Hawthorn Parkway, Suite 325, Vernon Hills, Illinois 60061. Bimonthly.

THE PROFITABLE LAWYER. Law and Business, Incorporated, Harcourt Brace Jovanovich, Incorporated, 1250 Sixth Avenue, San Diego, California 92101. Ten issues per year.

SMALL LAW OFFICE MANAGEMENT REPORT. Institute for Office Management and Administration, Incorporated, Five West Thirty-sixth Street, New York, New York 10018. Monthly.

BIBLIOGRAPHIES

A BIBLIOGRAPHY OF TECHNOLOGY FOR THE LAW FIRM: COMPUTERS AND THE LAW. Joseph J. Galin. Vance Bibliographies, P.O. Box 229, 112 North Charter Street, Monticello, Illinois 61856. 1985.

DIRECTORIES

DIRECTORY. Association of Legal Administrators, 175 East Hawthorn Parkway, Vernon Hills, Illinois 60061-1428. Annual.

FACSIMILE USER'S DIRECTORY. Facsimile User's Directory, 461 Park Avenue South, New York, New York 10016. 1989.

LOCATE: A DIRECTORY OF LAW OFFICE COMPUTER SOFTWARE. American Bar Association, Section of Economics of Law Practice, 750 North Lake Shore Drive, Chicago, Illinois 60611. 1985.

ASSOCIATIONS AND PROFESSIONAL SOCIETIES

AMERICAN BAR ASSOCIATION. Section of Economics of Law Practice, 750 North Lake Shore Drive, Chicago, Illinois 60611. (312) 988-5000.

ASSOCIATION OF LEGAL ADMINISTRATORS. 175 East Hawthorn Parkway, Suite 325, Vernon Hills, Illinois 60061. (708) 816-1212.

AUDIOVISUALS

COMPUTERS IN THE LAW OFFICE. American Bar Association, 750 North Lake Shore Drive, Chicago, Illinois 60611. 1984. Videotape.

FIVE COMPUTER APPLICATIONS FOR THE BUSY LAWYER. American Bar Association, 750 North Lake Shore Drive, Chicago, Illinois 60611. 1987. Videotape.

HOW TO COMPUTERIZE YOUR ESTATE PLANNING AND PROBATE PRACTICE. American Bar Association, 750 North Lake Shore Drive, Chicago, Illinois 60611. 1990. Videotape.

HOW TO COMPUTERIZE YOUR RESIDENTIAL REAL ESTATE PRACTICE. American Bar Association, 750 North Lake Shore Drive, Chicago, Illinois 60611. 1990. Videotape.

HOW TO USE YOUR COMPUTER TO PREPARE YOUR CASES FOR TRIAL. American Bar Association, 750 North Lake Shore Drive, Chicago, Illinois 60611. 1989. Videotape.

HOW TO SET A FAIR FEE. American Bar Association, 750 North Lake Shore Drive, Chicago, Illinois 60611. 1987. Videotape.

LITIGATION MANAGEMENT AND ORGANIZATION: THE WINNING EDGE. Mark A. Dombroff. National Practice Institute, 330 Second Avenue South, Minneapolis, Minnesota 55401. Videotape.

MANAGING YOUR LAW FIRM. American Bar Association, Consortium for Professional Education, 750 North Lake Shore Drive, Chicago, Illinois 60611. 1982. (Videotape).

STREAMLINING THE LAW OFFICE. American Bar Association, Section of Economics of Law Practice, 750 North Lake Shore Drive, Chicago, Illinois 60611. 1982. (Audiocassette).

LAW PRACTICE

See also: AMERICAN BAR ASSOCIATION; LAWYER AND CLIENT; LEGAL ASSISTANTS; LEGAL DIRECTORIES; LEGAL ETHICS AND MALPRACTICE; LEGAL SECRETARIES; STATES

STATUTES, CODES, STANDARDS, UNIFORM LAWS

RESTATEMENT OF THE LAW, THE LAW GOVERNING LAWYERS: COUNCIL DRAFT. American Law Institute-American Bar Association, 4025 Chestnut Street, Philadelphia, Pennsylvania 19104. 1989- .

SELECTED STATUTES, RULES, AND STANDARDS ON THE LEGAL PROFESSION. West Publishing Company, P.O. Box 64526, 50 West Kellogg Boulevard, St. Paul, Minnesota 55164-0526. 1990.

LOOSELEAF SERVICES AND REPORTERS

CASE ASSESSMENT AND EVALUATION. Don Howarth and Suzelle M. Smith. Callaghan and Company, 155 Pfingsten Road, Deerfield, Illinois 60015. 1989- .

REPORTER ON THE LEGAL PROFESSION. Legal-Medical Studies, Incorporated, P.O. Box 8219, JFK Station, Boston, Massachusetts 02114. 1979- .

HANDBOOKS, MANUALS, FORMBOOKS

THE ATTORNEY'S COMPLETE GUIDE TO PRACTICE DEVELOPMENT: HOW TO BUILD YOUR PRACTICE AND CAREER. Roger F. Smith and James H. Mitchell. Prentice-Hall, Incorporated, 113 Sylvan Avenue, Englewood Cliffs, New Jersey 07632. 1991.

BUSINESS LAWYERS HANDBOOK. Clifford R. Ennico. Clark Boardman Company, Limited, 435 Hudson Street, New York, New York 10014. 1991.

THE BUSINESS OF LAW: A HANDBOOK ON HOW TO MANAGE LAW FIRMS. Second Edition. Larry Smith, Editor. Prentice-Hall, Incorporated, 113 Sylvan Avenue, Englewood Cliffs, New Jersey 07632. 1990.

COMPENSATION OF ATTORNEYS: NON-LAW FIRMS. Eighth Edition. Steven Langer. Abbott, Langer and Associates, 548 First Street, Crete, Illinois 60417. 1986.

FORTY-NINE THINGS YOU NEED TO KNOW TO PRACTICE LAW. Massachusetts Continuing Legal Education, 20 West Street, Boston, Massachusetts 02111. 1989.

HANDBOOK ON SPECIALIZATION. American Bar Association, Section on Specializaton, 750 North Lake Shore Drive, Chicago, Illinois 60611. 1983.

HOW TO BUILD A SUCCESSFUL ESTATE PRACTICE. Robert S. Hunter. Lawyers Cooperative Publishing Company, Aqueduct Building, Rochester, New York 14694. 1984. (Supplemented).

HOW TO GET AND KEEP GOOD CLIENTS. Second Edition. Jay G. Foonberg. Lawyers Alert Press, Boston, Massachusetts. 1990.

HOW TO MARKET LEGAL SERVICES. Robert W. Denney. Van Nostrand Reinhold Company, Incorporated, 115 Fifth Avenue, New York, New York 10003. 1984.

HOW TO START AND BUILD A LAW PRACTICE. Third Edition. Jay G. Foonberg. American Bar Association, Law Student Division, Section of Law Practice Management, 750 North Lake Shore Drive, Chicago, Illinois 60611. 1991.

THE LAW OF LAWYERING: A HANDBOOK ON THE MODEL RULES OF PROFESSIONAL CONDUCT. Geoffrey C. Hazard, Jr. and W. William Hodes. Harcourt Brace Jovanovich, Incorporated, 6277 Sea Harbor Drive, Orlando, Florida 32821. 1985.

LAW OFFICE DESKBOOK: WITH ANNOTATED FORMS. Valera Grapp. Prentice-Hall, Incorporated, 113 Sylvan Avenue, Englewood Cliffs, New Jersey 07632. 1982.

LAWYER'S DESK BOOK. Ninth Edition. Prentice-Hall, Incorporated, 113 Sylvan Avenue, Englewood Cliffs, New Jersey 07632. 1989.

LAWYER'S DIARY AND DESK REFERENCE 1986. Arlene L. Eis, Editor. National Law Journal, New York Law Publishing Company, 111 Eighth Avenue, New York, New York 10011. 1986.

LAWYER'S REFERENCE MANUAL. Shepard's/McGraw-Hill, P.O. Box 1235, Colorado Springs, Colorado 80901. 1983. (Annual Supplements).

SHARK REPELLANT AND GOLDEN PARACHUTES: A HANDBOOK FOR THE PRACTITIONER. Robert H. Winter, Mark H. Stumpf, and Gerald L. Hawkins, Editors. Law and Business, Harcourt Brace Jovanovich, Incorporated, 6277 Sea Harbor Drive, Orlando, Florida 32821. 1983.

TEXTBOOKS AND GENERAL WORKS

ADVISE AND INVENT: THE LAWYER AS COUNSELOR-STRATEGIST AND OTHER ESSAYS. James C. Freund. Prentice-Hall, Incorporated, 113 Sylvan Avenue, Englewood Cliffs, New Jersey 07632. 1990.

ADVOCATES. David Pannick. Oxford University Press, 200 Madison Avenue, New York, New York 10016. 1992.

AMERICAN LAWYERS. Richard L. Abel. Oxford University Press, 200 Madison Avenue, New York, New York 10016. 1989.

THE AMERICAN LEGAL PROFESSION AND THE ORGANIZATIONAL SOCIETY, 1890-1930. Wayne K. Hobson. Garland Publishing, Incorporated, 136 Madison Avenue, New York, New York 10016. 1986.

ANARCHY AND ELEGANCE: CONFESSIONS OF A JOURNALIST AT YALE LAW SCHOOL. Chris Goodrich. Little, Brown and Company, 34 Beacon Street, Boston, Massachusetts 02108. 1991.

BEFORE THE LAW: AN INTRODUCTION TO THE LEGAL PROCESS. Fourth Edition. John J. Bonsignore. Houghton Mifflin Company, 1 Beacon Street, Boston, Massachusetts 02108. 1989.

BLACKS IN THE LAW: PHILADELPHIA AND THE NATION. Geraldine R. Segal. University of Pennsylvania Press, 418 Service Drive, Blockley Hall, Philadelphia, Pennsylvania 19104. 1983.

BLANCHE KNOTT'S TRULY TASTELESS LAWYER JOKES. Blanche Knott. St. Martin's Press, 175 Fifth Avenue, New York, New York 10010. 1990.

CAREER PATHS STUDY. Consortium of Northeastern Area Law Schools. Harvard Law School Press, 79 Garden Street, Cambridge, Massachusetts 02138. 1986.

COMPENSATION OF ATTORNEYS; NON-LAW FIRMS. Eighth Edition. Steven Langer. Abbott, Langer and Associates, 548 First Street, Crete, Illinois 60417. 1986.

COMPENSATION OF LEGAL AND RELATED JOBS: NON-LAW FIRMS. Thirteenth Edition. Steven Langer. Abbott, Langer and Associates, 548 First Street, Crete, Illinois 60417. 1991.

COMRADE LAWYER: INSIDE SOVIET JUSTICE IN AN ERA OF REFORM. Robert Rand. Westview Press, Incorporated, 5500 Central Avenue, Boulder, Colorado 80301. 1991.

COUNTRY LAWYERS: THE IMPACT OF CONTEXT ON PROFESSIONAL PRACTICE. Donald D. Landon. Praeger Publishers, One Madison Avenue, New York, New York 10010-3603. 1990.

DISPUTING IN AMERICA: THE LAWYER'S CHANGING ROLE. Stephen Gillers and Norman Dorsen. Little, Brown, and Company, 34 Beacon Street, Boston, Massachusetts 02106. 1985.

EXPANDING YOUR PRACTICE: THE ETHICAL RISKS. Harry J. Haynesworth. American Bar Association, Section of Economics of Law Practice, 750 North Lake Shore Drive, Chicago, Illinois 60611. 1984.

FLYING SOLO: A SURVIVAL GUIDE FOR LAWYERS. Donna M. Killoughey. American Bar Association, Section of Economics of Law Practice, 750 North Lake Shore Drive, Chicago, Illinois 60611. 1984.

FROM LAW SCHOOL TO LAW PRACTICE: THE NEW ASSOCIATES'S GUIDE. Suzanne B. O'Neill and Catherine Gerhauser Sparkman. American Law Institute-American Bar Association, 4025 Chestnut Street, Philadelphia, Pennsylvania 19104. 1989.

FULL DISCLOSURE: DO YOU REALLY WANT TO BE A LAWYER?. Susan J. Bell. American Bar Association, Young Lawyers Division, 202 Carnegie Center, P.O. Box 2123, Princeton, New Jersey 08543-2123. 1989.

GENTLEMEN OF THE BAR: LAWYERS IN COLONIAL SOUTH CAROLINA. Hoyt P. Canady. Garland Publishing, Incorporated, 136 Madison Avenue, New York, New York 10016. 1987.

THE GENTLEMEN OF THE PROFESSION: THE EMERGENCE OF LAWYERS IN MASSACHUSETTS, 1630-1810. Richard Scott Eckert. Garland Publishing, Incorporated, 136 Madison Avenue, New York, New York 10016. 1981.

HOW CAN YOU DEFEND THOSE PEOPLE? THE MAKING OF A CRIMINAL LAWYER. James S. Kunen. Random House, Incorporated, Random House Publicity, (11-6) 201 East Fiftieth Street, New York, New York 10022. 1983.

INTERNATIONALISATION OF LEGAL PRACTICE: UNITED STATES AND EUROPEAN PERSPECTIVES AND OPPORTUNITIES. Prentice-Hall, Incorporated, 113 Sylvan Avenue, Englewood Cliffs, New Jersey 07632. 1990.

INTERVIEWING, COUNSELING, AND NEGOTIATING: SKILLS FOR EFFECTIVE REPRESENTATION. Robert M. Bastress and Joseph D. Harbaugh. Little, Brown and Company, 34 Beacon Street, Boston, Massachusetts 02108. 1990.

AN INTRODUCTION TO LAW PRACTICE MANAGEMENT. Second Edition. Mary Ann Altman and Robert I. Weil. Matthew Bender and Company, Incorporated, 11 Penn Plaza, New York, New York 10001. 1987.

THE INVISIBLE BAR: THE WOMAN LAWYER IN AMERICA: 1638 TO THE PRESENT. Random House, Incorporated, Random House Publicity, (11-6) 201 East Fiftieth Street, New York, New York 10022. 1986.

KILL ALL THE LAWYERS? A USER FRIENDLY GUIDE TO WORKING WITH A LAWYER. Sloan Bashinsky. Simon and Schuster, Incorporated, 1230 Avenue of the Americas, New York, New York 10020. 1985.

THE LAW BUSINESS: A TIRED MONOPOLY. Joseph W. Bartlett. Fred B. Rothman and Company, 10368 West Centennial Road, Littleton, Colorado 80127. 1982.

LAW, DECISION-MAKING, AND MICROCOMPUTERS: CROSS-NATIONAL PERSPECTIVES. Stuart S. Nagel, Editor. Quorum Books, Greenwood Publishing Group, Incorporated, 88 Post Road West, P.O. Box 5007, Westport, Connecticut 06881. 1991.

LAW FIRM AGREEMENTS AND DISAGREEMENTS. John H. Eickemeyer. Practising Law Institute, 810 Seventh Avenue, New York, New York 10019. 1988.

LAW, LAWYERS, AND LAYMEN: MAKING SENSE OF THE AMERICAN LEGAL SYSTEM. Bertram Harnett. Harcourt Brace Jovanovich, Incorporated, 6277 Sea Harbor Drive, Orlando, Florida 32821. 1984.

LAW, POLICY AND OPTIMIZING ANALYSIS. Stuart S. Nagel. Greenwood Publishing Group, Incorporated, 88 Post Road West, P. O. Box 5007, Westport, Connecticut 06881. 1986.

LAW PRACTICE MANAGEMENT FOR THE SOLO AND SMALL OFFICE PRACTITIONER, 1990. Edna R.S. Alvarez. Practising Law Institute, 810 Seventh Avenue, New York, New York 10019. 1990.

LAW PRACTICE MANAGEMENT: MATERIALS AND CASES. Gary A. Munneke. West Publishing Company, 50 West Kellogg Boulevard, St. Paul, Minnesota 55164. 1991.

LAW PRACTICE QUALITY GUIDELINES: INCLUDING SELF-SURVEY QUESTIONNAIRES. American Law Institute-American Bar Association, Committee on Continuing Professional Education, 4025 Chestnut Street, Philadelphia, Pennsylvania 19104. 1985.

LAWYERS AND JUSTICE: AN ETHICAL STUDY. David Luban. Princeton University Press, 41 William Street, Princeton, New Jersey 08540. 1988.

LAWYERS AND THIEVES. Roy Grutman and Bill Thomas. Simon and Schuster, Incorporated, 1230 Avenue of the Americas, New York, New York 10020. 1990.

LAWYERS FOR HIRE: SALARIED PROFESSIONALS AT WORK. Eve Spangler. Yale University Press, 302 Temple Street, New Haven, Connecticut 06520. 1986.

LAWYERS' IDEALS/LAWYERS' PRACTICES: TRANSFORMATIONS IN THE AMERICAN LEGAL SYSTEM. Robert L. Nelson, David M. Trubek and Rayman L. Solomon, Editors. Cornell University Press, 124 Roberts Place, Ithaca, New York 14850. 1992.

THE LAWYER'S PROFESSIONAL INDEPENDENCE: PRESENT THREATS/FUTURE CHALLENGES. American Bar Association, Tort and Insurance Practice Section, 750 North Lake Shore Drive, Chicago, Illinois 60611. 1984.

LEARNING LAWYERS' SKILLS. Neil Gold, Karl Mackie and William Twining, Editors. Butterworth Legal Publishers, 90 Stiles Road, Salem, New Hampshire 03079. 1989.

LEGAL CLINICS: MERELY ADVERTISING LAW FIRMS? National Survey on Legal Clinics. American Bar Association, 750 North Lake Shore Drive, Chicago, Illinois 60611. 1982.

LEGAL EASE: FRESH INSIGHTS INTO LAWYERING. James C. Freund. Harcourt Brace Jovanovich, Incorporated, 6277 Sea Harbor Drive, Orlando, Florida 32821. 1984.

LEGAL EDUCATION AND LAWYER COMPETENCY. E. Gordon Gee and Donald W. Jackson. Brigham Young Universiy Press, 205 University Press Building, Provo, Utah 84602. 1983.

LEGAL EDUCATION, LAW PRACTICE, AND THE ECONOMY: A NEW ENGLAND STUDY. Thomas C. Fischer. New England Board of Higher Education. Commission on the Legal Profession and the Economy of New England. Fred B. Rothman and Company, 10368 West Centennial Road, Littleton, Colorado 80127. 1990.

LEGAL FEES AND REPRESENTATION AGREEMENTS. James W. McRae. American Bar Association, Section of Economics of Law Practice, 750 North Lake Shore Drive, Chicago, Illinois 60611. 1983.

LEGAL NEGOTIATIONS: GETTING MAXIMUM RESULTS. Mark K. Schoenfield and Rich M. Schoenfield. Shepard's/McGraw-Hill, P.O. Box 1235, Colorado Springs, Colorado 80901. 1988.

THE LEGAL PROFESSION: MAJOR HISTORICAL INTERPRETATIONS. Kermit L. Hall, Editor. Garland Publishing, Incorporated, 136 Madison Avenue, New York, New York 10016. 1987.

THE LURE OF THE LAW. Richard W. Moll. Viking Penguin, Incorporated, 375 Hudson Street, New York, New York 10014. 1990.

MALICE AFORETHOUGHT: HOW LAWYERS USE OUR SECRET RULES TO GET RICH, GET SEX, GET EVEN-- AND GET AWAY WITH IT. David W. Marston. William Morrow and Company, 105 Madison Avenue, New York, New York 10016. 1991.

MANAGING FOR PROFIT: IMPROVING OR MAINTAINING YOUR BOTTOM LINE. Robert J. Arndt. American Bar Association, Section of Law Practice Management, 750 North Lake Shore Drive, Chicago, Illinois 60611. 1991.

MARKETING YOUR LAW PRACTICE IN TODAY'S ECONOMY. Robert W. Denney. Advanced Legal Education, Hamline University School of Law, 1536 Hewitt Avenue, St. Paul, Minnesota 55104. 1984.

MARKETING YOUR PRACTICE AND EXPANDING YOUR CLIENT BASE. Michael A. West. Massachusetts Continuing Legal Education, 20 West Street, Boston, Massachusetts 02111. 1990.

MICROCOMPUTERS AS DECISION AIDS IN LAW PRACTICE. Stuart S. Nagel. Quorum Books, Greenwood Publishing Group, Incorporated, 88 Post Road West, P.O. Box 5007, Westport, Connecticut 06881. 1987.

THE MORAL, SOCIAL, AND PROFESSIONAL DUTIES OF ATTORNEYS AND SOLICITORS BY SAMUEL WARREN. Samuel Warren. Fred B. Rothman and Company, 10368 West Centennial Road, Littleton, Colorado 80127. 1870. (1991 Reprint).

MORAL VISION AND PROFESSIONAL DECISIONS: THE CHANGING VALUES OF WOMEN AND MEN LAWYERS. Rand Jack and Dana Crowley Jack. Cambridge University Press, 40 West Twentieth Street, New York, New York 10011. 1989.

MULTIDISCIPLINARY PARTNERSHIPS: NON-LEGAL BUSINESS AFFILIATES OF LAW FIRMS. Mortimer Caplin and James W. Jones. Prentice-Hall, Incorporated, 113 Sylvan Avenue, Englewood Cliffs, New Jersey 07632. 1990.

ON TRAINING ASSOCIATES. Theodore Voorhees. American Law Institute-American Bar Association, 4025 Chestnut Street, Philadelphia, Pennsylvania 19104. 1989.

ON TRIAL!: LAW, LAWYERS, AND THE LEGAL SYSTEM. Benjamin M. Becker and David L. Gibberman. Philosophical Library, New York, New York. 1987.

OUT-OF-STATE PRACTICE OF LAW: MULTISTATE AND PRO HAC VICE. Don C. Keenan. Harrison Company, 3110 Crossing Park, Norcross, Georgia 30091. 1981. (Supplement 1983).

PARTNERS WITH POWER: THE SOCIAL TRANSFORMATION OF THE LARGE LAW FIRM. Robert L. Nelson. University of California Press, 2120 Berkeley Way, Berkeley, California 94720. 1988.

POWER OF ATTORNEY: THE RISE OF THE GIANT LAW FIRMS. Mark Stevens. McGraw-Hill Book Company, 1221 Avenue of the Americas, New York, New York 10020. 1987.

PRACTICE BY FOREIGN LAWYERS IN JAPAN. Richard H. Wohl, Stuart M. Chemtob and Glen S. Fukushima. American Bar Association, Section of International Law and Practice, 750 North Lake Shore Drive, Chicago, Illinois 60611. 1989.

PRACTICING LAW IN FRONTIER CALIFORNIA. Gordon Morris Bakken. University of Nebraska Press, 901 North Seventeenth Street, Lincoln, Nebraska 68588. 1991.

A PRIMER FOR NEW CORPORATE LAWYERS: WHAT BUSINESS LAWYERS DO. Clifford R. Ennico. Clark Boardman Company, Limited, 435 Hudson Street, New York, New York 10014. 1990.

PROFESSIONAL RESPONSIBILITY IN A NUTSHELL. Second Edition. Robert H. Aronson and Donald T. Weckstein. West Publishing Company, 50 West Kellogg Boulevard, St. Paul, Minnesota 55164. 1991.

THE PROFESSIONAL SKILLS OF THE SMALL BUSINESS LAWYER. Harry J. Haynesworth. American Law Institute-American Bar Association, Committee on Continuing Professional Education, 4025 Chestnut Street, Philadelphia, Pennsylvania 19104. 1984.

PROFESSIONS AND PROFESSIONAL IDEOLOGIES IN AMERICA. Gerald L. Geison, Editor. University of North Carolina Press, P.O. Box 2288, Chapel Hill, North Carolina 27514. 1983.

PSYCHOLOGY AND THE LEGAL SYSTEM. Second Edition. Lawrence S. Wrightsman. Brooks/Cole Publishing Company, 511 Forest Lodge Road, Pacific Grove, California 93950. 1991.

THE QUALITY PURSUIT: ASSURING STANDARDS IN THE PRACTICE OF LAW. Robert J. Conroy and Robert Michael Green. Section of Law Practice Management, American Bar Association, 750 North Lake Shore Drive, Chicago, Illinois 60611. 1989.

RAINMAKING FOR LAWYERS--BRINGING IN THE BUSINESS AND KEEPING IT. Massachusetts Continuing Legal Education, 20 West Street, Boston, Massachusetts 02111. 1989.

RASCALS: THE SELLING OF THE LEGAL PROFESSION. Peter Megargee Brown. Benchmark Press, 701 Congressional Boulevard, Suite 340, Carmel, Indiana 46032. 1989.

REBELLIOUS LAWYERING: ONE CHICANO'S VISION OF PROGRESSIVE LAW PRACTICE. Gerald P. Lopez. Westview Press, Incorporated, 5500 Central Avenue, Boulder, Colorado 80301. 1992.

RECONSTRUCTING AMERICAN LAW. Bruce A. Ackerman. Harvard University Press, 79 Garden Street, Cambridge, Massachusetts 02138. 1984.

THE REGULATION OF FOREIGN LAWYERS. American Bar Association, Section of International Law and Practice, 750 North Lake Shore Drive, Chicago, Illinois 60611. 1984.

REGULATION OF LAWYERS: PROBLEMS OF LAW AND ETHICS. Stephen Gillers and Norman Dursen. Little, Brown, and Company, 34 Beacon Street, Boston, Massachusetts 02108. 1985.

REPRESENTING THE CORPORATE CLIENT: DESIGNS FOR QUALITY. Richard H. Weise. Prentice-Hall, Incorporated, 113 Sylvan Avenue, Englewood Cliffs, New Jersey 07632. 1991.

THE SOCIAL RESPONSIBILITIES OF LAWYERS: CASE STUDIES. Philip B. Heymann and Lance Liebman. Foundation Press, 615 Merrick Avenue, Westbury, New York 11590. 1988.

SURVIVING YOUR ROLE AS A LAWYER. Second Edition. David H. Barber. Spectra Publishing Company, Incorporated, P. O. Box 1403, Dillon, Colorado 80435. 1987.

TAKE THE BAR AND BEAT ME: AN IRREVERENT LOOK AT LAW SCHOOL AND CAREER CHOICES FOR PRELAWS, LAW STUDENTS, ADVANCED PARALEGALS--AND THE PEOPLE WHO ONCE LOVED THEM. Raymond L. Woodcock. Career Press, 62 Beverly Road, P.O. Box 34, Hawthorne, New Jersey 07507. 1991.

TRANSNATIONAL LEGAL PRACTICE IN THE EEC AND THE UNITED STATES. Linda S. Spedding. Transnational Publishers, P.O. Box 7282, Ardsley-on-Hudson, New York 10503. 1987.

UTOPIANISM AND THE EMERGENCE OF THE COLONIAL LEGAL PROFESSION: NEW YORK, 1664-1710, A TEST CASE. John R. Aiken. Garland Publishing, Incorporated, 136 Madison Avenue, New York, New York 10016. 1989.

LAW PRACTICE

WOMEN LAWYERS: PERSPECTIVES ON SUCCESS. Emily Covric, Editor. Law and Business, Harcourt Brace Jovanovich, Incorporated, 6277 Sea Harbor Drive, Orlando, Florida 32821. 1984.

YOUR FUTURE AS A LAWYER. Charles Z. Cohen. Rosen Publishing Group, 20 East 21st Street, New York, New York 10010. 1983.

ENCYCLOPEDIAS AND DICTIONARIES

MODERN LEGAL SYSTEMS CYCLOPEDIA. Kenneth R. Redden. William S. Hein and Company, Incorporated, Hein Building, 1285 Main Street, Buffalo, New York 14209. 1984.

ANNUALS AND SURVEYS

ANNUAL SURVEY OF AMERICAN LAW. New York University School of Law, 40 Washington Square South, New York, New York 10012. Quarterly.

LAW REVIEWS AND PERIODICALS

AMERICAN BAR ASSOCIATION JOURNAL. American Bar Association, 750 North Lake Shore Drive, Chicago, Illinois 60611. Monthly.

AMERICAN BAR FOUNDATION RESEARCH JOURNAL. American Bar Foundation, 750 North Lake Shore Drive, Chicago, Illinois 60611. Quarterly.

AMERICAN LAWYER. AM-LAW Publishing Corporation, 488 Madison Avenue, New York, New York 10022. Monthly.

BARRISTER. American Bar Association, Young Lawyers Division, 750 North Lake Shore Drive, Chicago, Illinois 60611. Quarterly.

THE COMPLEAT LAWYER. American Bar Association, Section of General Practice, 750 North Lake Shore Drive, Chicago, Illinois 60611. Quarterly.

JOURNAL OF THE LEGAL PROFESSION. University of Alabama School of Law, P. O. Box 1976, Universiy, Alabama 35486. Annual.

PRACTICAL LAWYER. American Law Institute-American Bar Association, Committee on Continuing Professional Education, 4025 Chestnut Street, Philadelphia, Pennsylvania 19104. Bimonthly.

NEWSLETTERS AND NEWSPAPERS

CLIENT UPDATE. American Bar Association, Section of General Practice, 750 North Lake Shore Drive, Chicago, Illinois 60611. Quarterly.

LAWYERS LETTER. American Bar Association, Judicial Administration Division, 750 North Lake Shore Drive, Chicago, Illinois 60611. Quarterly.

LAWYERS NEWSLETTER. Law Publications, Incorporated, 1180 South Beverly Drive, Los Angeles, California 90035. Bimonthly.

LEGAL TIMES. Legal Times, 1730 M Street, Northwest, Washington, D.C. 20036. Weekly.

NATIONAL LAW JOURNAL. Law Journal-Seminars Press, Incorporated, 111 Eighth Avenue, New York, New York 10011. Weekly.

NEW YORK LAW JOURNAL. New York Law Publishing Company, 111 Eighth Avenue, New York, New York 10011. Workdays.

OF COUNSEL; THE MONTHLY LEGAL PRACTICE REPORT. Prentice Hall Law and Business, 270 Sylvan Avenue, Englewood Cliffs, New Jersey 07632. Semimonthly.

UNITED STATES LAW NEWS. Law News Plaza, 31872 Camino Capistrano, San Juan Capistrano, California 92675. Weekly.

BIBLIOGRAPHIES

ABA CATALOG: BOOKS, PERIODICALS, PAMPHLETS AND AUDIOVISUAL MATERIALS. American Bar Association, 750 North Lake Shore Drive, Chicago, Illinois 60611. Annual.

LAWYERS AND PUBLIC ADMINISTRATORS: A SELECTED BIBLIOGRAPHY. Anthony G. White. Vance Bibliographies, P.O. Box 229, 112 North Charter Street, Monticello, Illinois 61856. 1982.

LINCOLN AS A LAWYER: AN ANNOTATED BIBLIOGRAPHY. Elizabeth W. Matthews. Southern Illinois University Press, P.O. Box 3697, Carbondale, Illinois 62902-3697. 1991.

STARTING YOUR OWN LAW PRACTICE: A BIBLIOGRAPHY. Carol Ebbinghouse. Southwestern University School of Law, 675 South Westmoreland Avenue, Los Angeles, California 90005. 1983.

BIOGRAPHICAL SOURCES

BREAKTHROUGH: WOMEN IN LAW. Betsy Covington Smith. Walker Publishing Company, Incorporated, 720 Fifth Avenue, New York, New York 10019. 1984.

CHICAGO LAWYERS: THE SOCIAL STRUCTURE OF THE BAR. John P. Heinz and Edward D. Laumann. Russell Sage Foundation, 112 East 64th Street, New York, New York 10021. 1982.

EDWARD BENNETT WILLIAMS FOR THE DEFENSE. Second Edition. Robert Pack. HarperCollins, Publishers, 10 East Fifty-third Street, New York, New York 10022. 1988.

LIONS OF THE EIGHTIES: THE INSIDE STORY OF THE POWERHOUSE LAW FIRMS. Paul Hoffman. Doubleday and Company, Incorporated, 666 Fifth Avenue, New York, New York 10103. 1982.

THE NEW HIGH PRIESTS: LAWYERS IN POST-CIVIL WAR AMERICA. Gerard W. Gawalt, Editor. Greenwood Publishing Group, Incorporated, 88 Post Road West, P.O. Box 5007, Westport, Connecticut 06881. 1984.

THE PARTNERS: INSIDE AMERICA'S MOST POWERFUL LAW FIRMS. James A. Stewart. Simon and Schuster, Incorporated, 1230 Avenue of the Americas, New York, New York 10020. 1983.

Encyclopedia of Legal Information Sources • 2nd Ed. **LAW SOCIETIES**

RIGHTS ON TRIAL: THE ODYSSEY OF A PEOPLE'S LAWYER. Arthur Kinoy. Harvard University Press, 79 Garden Street, Cambridge, Massachusetts 02138. 1983.

ASSOCIATIONS AND PROFESSIONAL SOCIETIES

AMERICAN BAR ASSOCIATION. 750 North Lake Shore Drive, Chicago, Illinois 60611. (312) 988-5000.

AMERICAN BAR ENDOWMENT. 750 North Lake Shore Drive, Chicago, Illinois 60611. (312) 988-5346.

AMERICAN BAR FOUNDATION. 750 North Lake Shore Drive, Chicago, Illinois 60611. (312) 988-6500.

AMERICAN LAWYERS AUXILIARY. 750 North Lake Shore Drive, Chicago, Illinois 60611. (312) 988-6387.

ASSOCIATION OF LEGAL ADMINISTRATORS. 175 East Hawthorn Parkway, Suite 325, Vernon Hills, Illinois 60061. (708) 816-1212.

NATIONAL ASSOCIATION OF BAR EXECUTIVES. 750 North Lake Shore Drive, Chicago, Illinois 60611. (312) 988-5346.

NATIONAL BAR ASSOCIATION. 1225 I Street, Northwest, Washington, D.C. 20001. (202) 842-3900.

NATIONAL CONFERENCE OF BAR FOUNDATIONS. 750 North Lake Shore Drive, Chicago, Illinois 60611. (312) 988-5346.

NATIONAL CONFERENCE OF BAR PRESIDENTS. 750 North Lake Shore Drive, Chicago, Illinois 60611. (312) 988-5346.

NATIONAL ORGANIZATION OF BAR COUNSEL. c/o John Berry, Attorney Grievance Commission of Maryland, 580 Taylor Avenue, Room 404, Annapolis, Maryland 21401. (301) 974-2791.

ONLINE DATABASES

ABA/NET. American Bar Association, 750 North Lake Shore Drive, Chicago, Illinois 60611.

STATISTICS SOURCES

THE LAWYER STATISTICAL REPORTS: A STATISTICAL PROFILE OF THE UNITED STATES LEGAL PROFESSION IN THE 1980'S. Barbara A. Curran. American Bar Association, 750 North Lake Shore Drive, Chicago, Illinois 60611. 1985.

AUDIOVISUALS

GETTING AND KEEPING THE CLIENTS YOU WANT. American Bar Association, 750 North Lake Shore Drive, Chicago, Illinois 60611. 1988. Videotape.

INDIVIDUAL LAWYER AND BAR ASSOCIATION ADVERTISING. American Bar Association, Commission on Advertising, 750 North Lake Shore Drive, Chicago, Illinois 60611. 1981. Videotape.

THE LEGAL SYSTEM: DOES IT WORK? American Bar Association, Young Lawyers Division, 750 North Lake Shore Drive, Chicago, Illinois 60611. 1983. Videotape.

LITIGATION MANAGEMENT AND ORGANIZATION: THE WINNING EDGE. Mark A. Dombroff. National Practice Institute, 330 Second Avenue South, Minneapolis, Minnesota 55401. Videotape.

SECRETS OF EFFECTIVE PUBLIC SPEAKING. American Bar Association, 750 North Lake Shore Drive, Chicago, Illinois 60611. 1990. Videotape.

SUCCESSFUL MARKETING FOR THE SMALL AND MEDIUM SIZE FIRM. American Bar Association, 750 North Lake Shore Drive, Chicago, Illinois 60611. 1988. Videotape.

LAW SCHOOLS
See: LEGAL EDUCATION

LAW SOCIETIES
See also: STATES

ASSOCIATIONS AND PROFESSIONAL SOCIETIES

ABA CENTER ON CHILDREN AND THE LAW (ABACCL). 1800 M Street, Northwest, Washington, D.C. 20036. (202) 331-2250.

ACADEMY OF FAMILY MEDIATORS (AFM). P.O. Box 10501, Eugene, Oregon 97440. (503) 345-1205.

AFRICAN BAR ASSOCIATION (ABA). P.O. Box 2595, Harare, Zimbabwe.

ALI-ABA COMMITTEE ON CONTINUING PROFESSIONAL EDUCATION (ALI-ABA). 4025 Chestnut Street, Philadelphia, Pennsylvania 19104. (215) 243-1600.

AMERICAN ACADEMY OF HOSPITAL ATTORNEYS (AAHA). American Hospital Association, 840 North Lake Shore Drive, Chicago, Illinois 60611. (312) 280-6601.

AMERICAN ACADEMY OF JUDICIAL EDUCATION. 2025 Eye Street, Northwest, Suite 903, Washington, D.C. 20006. (202) 775-0083.

AMERICAN ACADEMY OF MATRIMONIAL LAWYERS (AAML). 20 North Michigan Avenue, Suite 540, Chicago, Illinois 60602. (312) 263-6477.

AMERICAN ACADEMY OF MEDICAL-LEGAL ANALYSIS (AAMLA). 5122 Rossmore Drive, Las Vegas, Nevada 89110. (702) 385-6886.

AMERICAN ACADEMY OF PSYCHIATRY AND THE LAW (AAPL). 891 Park Avenue, Baltimore, Maryland 21201. (301) 539-0379.

AMERICAN AGRICULTURAL LAW ASSOCIATION (AALA). University of Arkansas, Leflar Law Center, Fayetteville, Arkansas 72701. (501) 575-7389.

AMERICAN ASSOCIATION FOR PARALEGAL EDUCATION (AAFPE). P.O. Box 40244, Overland Park, Kansas 66204. (913) 381-4458.

LAW SOCIETIES

AMERICAN ASSOCIATION FOR THE COMPARATIVE STUDY OF LAW (AACSL). c/o Honorable Edward D. Re, United States Court of International Trade, One Federal Plaza, New York, New York 10007. (212) 264-2800.

AMERICAN ASSOCIATION OF ATTORNEYS - CERTIFIED PUBLIC ACCOUNTANTS. 24196 Alicia Parkway, Suite K, Mission Viejo, California 92691. (714) 768-0336.

AMERICAN ASSOCIATION OF LAW LIBRARIES. 53 West Jackson Boulevard, Suite 940, Chicago, Illinois 60604. (312) 939-4764.

AMERICAN ASSOCIATION OF NURSE ATTORNEYS. 113 West Franklin Street, Baltimore, Maryland 21201. (301) 752-3318.

AMERICAN ASSOCIATION OF PUBLIC WELFARE ATTORNEYS. 810 First Street, Northeast, Suite 500, Washington, D.C. 20002. (202) 682-0100.

AMERICAN BANKRUPTCY INSTITUTE (ABI). 510 C Street, Northeast, Washington, D.C 20002. (202) 543-1234.

AMERICAN BAR ASSOCIATION. 750 North Lake Shore Drive, Chicago, Illinois 60611. (312) 988-5000.

- Adjunct Committee on Fair Trial/Free Press in Criminal Issues
- Commission on Advertising
- Commission on Federal Judicial Compensation
- Commission on Public Understanding About the Law
- Committee on Air and Space
- Committee on Continuing Legal Education of the Bar
- Committee on Customs Law
- Committee on Environmental Law
- Committee on Ethics and Professional Responsibility
- Committee on Federal Judiciary
- Committee on Federal Judicial Improvements
- Committee on International Law
- Committee on Judicial Selection, Tenure and Compensation
- Committee on Law and National Security
- Committee on Lawyer Referral and Information Services
- Committee on Lawyer's Professional Liability
- Committee on Lawyer's Responsibility for Client Protection
- Committee on Lawyer's Title and Guaranty Funds
- Committee on Lawyers in the Armed Forces
- Committee on Legal Aid and Indigent Defendants
- Committee on Legal Assistants
- Committee on Military Law
- Committee on Patent, Copyright and Trademark Law
- Committee on Professional Discipline
- Committee on Professional Utilization and Career Development
- Committee on Retirement of Lawyers
- Committee on Specialization
- Committee on the Mentally Disabled
- Committee on World Order Under the Law
- Consortium on Legal Services and the Public
- Consortium on Professional Competence
- Coordinating Committee on Energy Law
- Coordinating Committee on Immigration Law
- Fidelity and Surety Committee, Section of Insurance
- Forum Committee on Communications Law
- Forum Committee on Construction Industry
- Forum Committee on Franchising
- Forum Committee on Health Law
- Forum Committee on the Entertainment and Sports Industries
- Judicial Administration Division
- Judicial Administration Division, Committee on Traffic Court Program
- Judicial Administration Division, Lawyers Conference
- Judicial Administration Division, National Conference of Federal Trial Judges
- Judicial Administration Division, National Conference of Special Court Judges
- Judicial Administration Division, National Conference of State Judges
- Judicial Administration Division, National Conference of State Trial Judges
- Law Student Division
- National Conference Group of Lawyers and Collection Agencies
- National Conference Group of Lawyers and Corporate Fiduciaries
- National Conference Group of Lawyers and Environmental Design Professions
- National Conference Group of Lawyers and Life Insurance Companies
- National Conference Group of Lawyers and Realtors
- National Conference Group of Lawyers and Representatives of the Media
- National Conference Group of Lawyers, Insurance Companies and Adjusters
- Section of Corporation, Banking and Business Law
- Section of Economics of Law Practice
- Section of Family Law
- Section of General Practice
- Section of Individual Rights and Responsibilities
- Section of Insurance
- Section of Labor and Employment Law
- Section of Law and Religion
- Section of Legal Education and Admission to the Bar
- Section of Litigation
- Section of Natural Resources Law
- Section of Patent, Trademark, Probate, and Trust Law
- Section of Public Utility Law
- Section of Real Property, Probate, and Trust Law
- Section of Remedies
- Section of Science and Technology
- Section of Tort and Insurance Practice
- Section of Urban, State and Local Government
- Special Committee on Automobile Insurance Legislation
- Special Committee on Cooperation with the Newspaper Publishers Association
- Special Committee on Delivery of Legal Services
- Special Committee on Election Law and Voter Participation
- Special Committee on Evaluation of Judicial Performance
- Special Committee on Housing and Urban Development Law
- Special Committee on Implications of Model Rules
- Special Committee on Lawyers in Government
- Special Committee on Lawyers Public Service Responsibilities
- Special Committee on Public Education
- Special Committee on Youth Education and Citizenship
- Standing Committee on Legal Assistance for Military Personnel
- Standing Committee on Prepaid Legal Service
- Young Lawyers Division.

AMERICAN BAR ASSOCIATION CENTER FOR PROFESSIONAL RESPONSIBILITY (ABACPR). 750 North Lake Shore Drive, Chicago, Illinois 60611. (312) 988-5293.

AMERICAN BAR ASSOCIATION FAMILY LAW SECTION, MEDIATION AND ARBITRATION COMMITTEE (ABAFLSMAC). c/o American Bar Association, 750 North Lake Shore Drive, Chicago, Illinois 60611. (312) 988-5584.

AMERICAN BAR ASSOCIATION REPRESENTATION OF THE HOMELESS PROJECT (ABARHP). 1800 M Street, Northwest, Washington, D.C. 20036. (202) 331-2291.

AMERICAN BAR ASSOCIATION SECTION OF CRIMINAL JUSTICE (SCJ). 1800 M Street, Northwest, Second Floor, South Lobby, Washington, D.C. 20036. (202) 331-2260.

AMERICAN BAR ASSOCIATION SECTION OF INTERNATIONAL LAW AND PRACTICE (ABASILP). Second Floor, South Lobby, 1800 M Street, Northwest, Suite 450J, Washington, D.C. 20036. (202) 331-2239.

AMERICAN BAR ASSOCIATION STANDING COMMITTEE ON DISPUTE RESOLUTION (ABASCODR). 1800 M Street, Northwest, Suite 200, Washington, D.C. 20036. (202) 331-2258.

AMERICAN BAR ASSOCIATION YOUNG LAWYERS DIVISION (ABAYLD). 750 North Lake Shore Drive, Chicago, Illinois 60611. (312) 988-5000.

AMERICAN BAR ENDOWMENT. 750 North Lake Shore Drive, Chicago, Illinois 60611. (312) 988-5346.

AMERICAN BAR FOUNDATION (ABF). 750 North Lake Shore Drive, Chicago, Illinois 60611. (312) 988-6500.

AMERICAN BLIND LAWYERS ASSOCIATION. 1010 Vermont Avenue, Northwest, Suite 1100, Washington, D.C. 20005. (202) 393-3666.

AMERICAN BOARD OF TRIAL ADVOCATES. 16633 Ventura Boulevard, Suite 1015, Encino, California 91436. (818) 501-3250.

AMERICAN COLLEGE OF BANKRUPTCY. 510 C Street, Northeast, Washington, D.C. 20002. (202) 546-6725.

AMERICAN COLLEGE OF PROBATE COUNSEL. 2716 Ocean Park Boulevard, Suite 1080, Santa Monica, California 90405. (213) 450-2033.

AMERICAN COLLEGE OF TRIAL LAWYERS. 8001 Irvine Center Drive, Suite 960, Irvine, California 92718. (714) 727-3194.

AMERICAN COPYRIGHT SOCIETY. 345 West Fifty-eighth Street, New York, New York 10019. (212) 582-5705.

AMERICAN CORPORATE COUNSEL ASSOCIATION (ACCA). 1225 Connecticut Avenue, Northwest, Suite 302, Washington, D.C. 20036. (202) 296-4522.

AMERICAN CORPORATE COUNSEL INSTITUTE (ACCI). c/o American Corporate Counsel Association, 1225 Connecticut Avenue, Northwest, Suite 302, Washington, D.C. 20036 (202) 296-4522.

AMERICAN FOREIGN LAW ASSOCIATION (AFLA). c/o Richard E. Lutninger, 200 Park Avenue, Suite 1515, New York, New York 10166. (212) 351-3277.

AMERICAN IMMIGRATION LAWYERS ASSOCIATION (AILA). 1000 Sixteenth Street, Northwest, Suite 604, Washington, D.C. 20036. (202) 331-0046.

AMERICAN INTELLECTUAL PROPERTY LAW ASSOCIATION. 2001 Jefferson Davis Highway, Suite 203, Arlington, Virginia 22202. (703) 521-1680.

AMERICAN JUDGES ASSOCIATION. 300 Newport Avenue, Williamsburg, Virginia 23187. (804) 253-2000.

AMERICAN JUDICATURE SOCIETY. 25 East Washington, Suite 1600, Chicago, Illinois 60602. (312) 558-6900.

AMERICAN LAW INSTITUTE (ALI). 4025 Chestnut Street, Philadelphia, Pennsylvania 19104. (215) 243-1600.

AMERICAN LAWYERS AUXILIARY. 750 North Lake Shore Drive, Chicago, Illinois 60611. (312) 988-6387.

AMERICAN LEGAL STUDIES ASSOCIATION. c/o Law, Policy and Soceity, 305 Cushing, Northeastern University, Boston, Massachusetts 02115. (617) 437-5211.

AMERICAN SOCIETY FOR LEGAL HISTORY. c/o Professor M. del Lardon, Department of History, University of Mississippi, University, Mississippi 38677. (601) 232-7148.

AMERICAN SOCIETY FOR POLITICAL AND LEGAL PHILOSOPHY. c/o Professor Martin P. Golding, Philosophy Department, Duke University, Durham, North Carolina 27708. (919) 648-3838.

AMERICAN SOCIETY OF INTERNATIONAL LAW (ASIL). 2223 Massachusetts Avenue, Northwest, Washington, D.C. 20008. (202) 265-4313.

AMERICAN TORT REFORM ASSOCIATION (ATRA). 1212 New York Avenue, Northwest, Suite 515, Washington, D.C. 20005. (202) 682-1163.

AMERICAN TRIAL LAWYERS FOUNDATION. 1050 Thirty-first Street, Northwest, Washington, D.C. 20007. (202) 965-3500.

ARAB LAWYERS UNION (ALU). Union des Avocats Arabes (UAA), 13 Arab Lawyers' Union Street, Garden City, Cairo, Egypt. 2 3557132.

ASIA-PACIFIC LAWYERS ASSOCIATION (APLA). Korea Re-Insurance Building, Fifth Floor, 80, Soosong-Dong, Chongro-ku, Seoul, Republic of Korea. 2 7355621.

ASSOCIATION OF AMERICAN LAW SCHOOLS. One Dupont Circle, Northwest, Suite 370, Washington, D.C. 20036. (202) 296-8851.

- Section on Administration of Law Schools
- Section on Admission to Law School
- Section on Antitrust and Economic Regulation
- Section on Aviation and Space Law
- Section on Business Associations
- Section on Clinical Legal Education
- Section on Commercial and Consumer Law
- Section on Comparative Law
- Section on Conflict of Laws
- Section on Constitutional Law (State)
- Section on Contract Law
- Section on Creditors and Debtor's Rights
- Section on Criminal Justice

LAW SOCIETIES

- Section on Donative Transfers
- Section on Employment Discrimination Law
- Section on Environmental Law
- Section on Evidence
- Section on Family and Juvenile Law
- Section on Gay and Lesbian Issues
- Section on Graduate Studies
- Section on Immigration Law
- Section on Intellectual Property
- Section on International Law
- Section on International Legal Exchange
- Section on Jurisprudence
- Section on Law and Computers
- Section on Law and Economics
- Section on Law and Education
- Section on Law and Psychiatry
- Section on Law and Social Science
- Section on Legal History
- Section on Legal Writing, Reasoning and Research
- Section on Legislation
- Section on Litigation
- Section on Local Government
- Section on Maritime Law
- Section on Mass Communications Law
- Section on Minority Groups
- Section on Native American Rights
- Section on Paralegal Education
- Section on Professional Responsibility
- Section on Real Property
- Section on Sports Law
- Section on Teaching Methods
- Section on Teaching Law Outside Law Schools
- Section on Torts
- Section on Women in Legal Education

ASSOCIATION OF CONTINUING LEGAL EDUCATION ADMINISTRATORS (ACLEA). c/o American Bar Association, 750 North Lake Shore Drive, Chicago, Illinois 60611. (312) 988-6196.

ASSOCIATION OF DEFENSE TRIAL ATTORNEYS. 600 Jefferson Bank Building, Peoria, Illinois 61602. (309) 676-0400.

ASSOCIATION OF FAMILY AND CONCILIATION COURTS (AFCC). c/o Ann Milne, 329 West Wilson, Madison, Wisconsin 53703. (608) 251-4001.

ASSOCIATION OF LEGAL ADMINISTRATORS (ALA). 751 East Hawthorn Parkway, Suite 325, Vernon Hills, Illinois 60061-1428. (708) 816-1212.

ASSOCIATION OF LIFE INSURANCE COUNSEL. c/o Emily S. Crandall, 201 Park Avenue, South, New York, New York 10003. (212) 679-1110.

ASSOCIATION OF STATE MENTAL HEALTH ATTORNEYS. 1101 Kins Street, Suite 160, Alexandria, Virginia 22314. (703) 739-9333.

ASSOCIATION OF TRANSPORTATION PRACTITIONERS. 1725 K Street, Northwest, Suite 301, Washington, D.C. 20006. (202) 466-2080.

ASSOCIATION OF TRIAL LAWYERS OF AMERICA. 1050 Thirty-first Street, Northwest, Washington, D.C. 20007. (202) 965 3500.

ASSOCIATION OF UNITED STATES MEMBERS OF THE INTERNATIONAL INSTITUTE OF SPACE LAW. c/o Stephen E. Doyle, 3431 Bridget Brae, Shingle Springs, California 95682. (916) 355-6941.

THE ATTORNEYS GROUP. 292 Madison Avenue, New York, New York 10017. (212) 949-5900.

AUXILIARY OF THE DECALOGUE SOCIETY OF LAWYERS. 179 West Washington, Suite 350, Chicago, Illinois 60602. (312) 263-6493.

BLACK ENTERTAINMENT AND SPORTS LAWYERS ASSOCIATION (BESLA). 111 Broadway, Seventh Floor, New York, New York 10006. (212) 587-0300.

CENTER FOR LAW AND EDUCATION (CLE). 955 Massachusetts, Avenue, Cambridge, Massachusetts 02139. (617) 876-6611.

CENTER FOR LAW AND SOCIAL POLICY (CLASP). 1616 P Street, Northwest, Suite 350, Washington, D.C. 20036. (202) 328-5140.

CENTER FOR LAW IN THE PUBLIC INTEREST (CLIPI). 11835 West Olympic Boulevard, Suite 1155, Los Angeles, California 90064. (213) 470-3000.

CENTER FOR SEAFARERS' RIGHTS (CSR). 50 Broadway, Third Floor, New York, New York 10004. (212) 269-2710.

CENTER FOR THE STUDY OF LAW AND POLITICS (CSLP). 2962 Fillmore Street, San Francisco, California 94123. (415) 775-0791.

CHRISTIAN LAW ASSOCIATION. Box 30, Conneaut, Ohio 44030. (216) 599-8900.

CHRISTIAN LEGAL SOCIETY. P.O. Box 1492, Merrifield, Virginia 22116. (703) 642-1070.

COMMERCIAL LAW LEAGUE OF AMERICA (CLLA). 175 West Jackson Boulevard, Suite 1541, Chicago, Illinois 60604-2703. (312) 431-1305.

COMMISSION FOR INTERNATIONAL DUE PROCESS OF LAW (CIDPL). 105 West Adams Street, Chicago, Illinois 60603. (312) 782-1946.

COMMISSION ON ACCREDITATION FOR LAW ENFORCEMENT AGENCIES (CALEA). 4242B Chain Bridge Road, Fairfax, Virginia 22030. (703) 352-4225.

COMMISSION ON THE MENTALLY DISABLED (MPDLRSDB). c/o American Bar Association, 1800 M Street, Northwest, Washington, D.C. 20036. (202) 331-2240.

COMMONWEALTH LAWYERS' ASSOCIATION (CLA). c/o Law Society, 50 Chancery Lane, London WC2A ISX, England. 71 2421222.

COMPUTER LAW ASSOCIATION. 8303 Arlington Boulevard, Suite 210, Fairfax, Virginia 22031. (703) 560-7747.

CONFERENCE OF CHIEF JUSTICES. c/o National Center for State Courts, 300 Newport Avenue, Williamsburg, Virginia 23187. (804) 253-2000.

CONFERENCE ON CRITICAL LEGAL STUDIES (CCLS). c/o Alan Freeman, State University of New York-Buffalo, School of Law, John O'Brian Hall, Amherst Campus, Buffalo, New York 14260. (716) 636-3035.

CONSULAR LAW SOCIETY (CLS). 635 Madison Avenue, Eleventh Floor, New York, New York 10022. (212) 371-4900.

COUNCIL OF SCHOOL ATTORNEYS. National School Boards Association, 1680 Duke Street, Alexandria, Virginia 22314. (703) 838-6722.

COUNCIL OF THE BARS AND LAW SOCIETIES OF THE EUROPEAN COMMUNITY (CCBE). Conseil des Barreaux de la Communaute Europeenne (CCBE), 40, rue Washington, B-1050 Brussels, Belgium. 2 6404274.

COUNCIL ON LEGAL EDUCATION OPPORTUNITY (CLEO). 1800 M Street, Northwest, Suite 290, North Lobby, Washington, D.C. 20036. (202) 785-4840.

COUNCIL ON OCEAN LAW (COL). 1709 New York Avenue, Northwest, Seventh Floor, Washington, D.C. 20006. (202) 347-3766.

COUNCIL ON RELIGION AND LAW (CORAL). c/o Frank Alexander, Emory University, School of Law, Atlanta, Georgia. 30322.

CUSTOMS AND INTERNATIONAL TRADE BAR ASSOCIATION (CITBA). c/o Andrew P. Vance, 475 Park Avenue, South, New York, New York 10016. (212) 725-0200.

DECALOGUE SOCIETY OF LAWYERS. 179 West Washington Street, Suite 350, Chicago, Illinois 60602. (312) 263-6493.

DRI-DEFENSE RESEARCH AND TRIAL LAWYERS ASSOCIATION. 750 North Lake Shore Drive, Suite 500, Chicago, Illioís 60611. (312) 944-0575.

ENVIRONMENTAL LAW INSTITUTE (ELI). 1616 P Street, Northwest, Suite 200, Washington, D.C. 20036. (202) 328-5150.

EQUAL RIGHTS ADVOCATES (ERA). 1663 Mission Street, Suite 550, San Francisco, California 94103. (415) 621-0672.

EUROPEAN ASSOCIATION FOR CHINESE LAW (EACL). c/o Madame Dominique Grisay, 7, rue de l'Autorouice, boite 3, B-1070 Brussels, Belgium. 3 225239512.

FAMILY LAW COUNCIL (FLC). P.O. Box 217, Fair Lawn, New Jersey 07410.

FEDERAL ADMINISTRATIVE LAW JUDGES CONFERENCE. 429 National Lawyers Club, 1815 H Street, Northwest, Washington, D.C. 20006. (202) 357-9251.

FEDERAL BAR ASSOCIATION. 1815 H Street, Northwest, Suite 408, Washington, D.C. 20036. (202) 683-0252.

FEDERAL COMMUNICATIONS BAR ASSOCIATION (FCBA). 1150 Connecticut Avenue, Northwest, Suite 1050, Washington, D.C. 20036. (202) 833-2684.

FEDERAL ENERGY BAR ASSOCIATION. P.O. Box 34434, Bethesda, Maryland 20817. (301) 299-7299.

FEDERALIST SOCIETY FOR LAW AND PUBLIC POLICY STUDIES (FSLPPS). 1700 K Street, Northwest, Suite 901, Washington, D.C. 20006. (202) 822-8138.

FEDERATION OF INSURANCE AND CORPORATE COUNSEL. c/o Harrison G. Ball, 15 Ridge Road, Marblehead, Massachusetts 01945. (617) 639-0698.

FEDERATION OF WOMEN LAWYERS JUDICIAL SCREENING PANEL. 2000 P Street, Northwest, Suite 515, Washington, D.C. 20036. (202) 822-6644.

FELLOWS OF THE AMERICAN BAR FOUNDATION. 750 North Lake Shore Drive, Chicago, Illinois 60611. (312) 988-6606.

FIRST AMENDMENT LAWYERS ASSOCIATION (FALA). c/o Wayne Giampietro, 125 South Wacker Drive, Suite 2700, Chicago, Illinois 60606. (312) 236-0606.

FOUNDATION OF THE FEDERAL BAR ASSOCIATION (FFBA). c/o Marshall C. Gardner, 12118 Long Ridge Lane, Bowie, Maryland 20715. (301) 464-1992.

FRENCH SOCIETY FOR INTERNATIONAL LAW (FSIL). Societe Francaise pour le Droit International (SFDI), Universite R. Schuman, 1, place d'Athenes, F-67084 Strasbourg Cedex, France. 88 414265.

GUILD OF CATHOLIC LAWYERS. c/o Gregory de Sousa, 6 MacDonald Place, Scarsdale, New York 10583. (914) 723-3211.

GUILD OF ST. IVES. 1047 Amsterdam Avenue, New York, New York 10025. (212) 316-7412.

HAGUE CONFERENCE ON PRIVATE INTERNATIONAL LAW (CODIP). Conference de la Haye de Droit International Prive Scheveningseweg 6, NL-2517 KT The Hague, Netherlands. 70 3633303.

HALT - AN ORGANIZATION OF AMERICANS FOR LEGAL REFORM (HALT-ALR). 1319 F Street, Northwest, Suite 300, Washington, D.C. 20004. (202) 347-9600.

HARVARD ENVIRONMENTAL LAW SOCIETY (ELS). Harvard Law School, Austin 201, Cambridge, Massachusetts 02138. (617) 495-3125.

HISPANIC NATIONAL BAR ASSOCIATION. 1101 Fourteenth Street, Northwest, Suite 610, Washington, D.C. 20005. (202) 371-1555.

INNER CIRCLE OF ADVOCATES. 127 West Franklin Street, Tucson, Arizona 85701. (602) 622-8855.

INSTITUTE OF INTERNATIONAL LAW (IIL). Institute de Droit International (IDI), c/o M. Nicholas Valticos, 22, avenue William-Favre, CH-1207 Geneva, Switzerland. 22 7360772.

INTER-AMERICAN BAR ASSOCIATION (IABA). 1889 F Street, Northwest, Suite LL-2, Washington, D.C. 20006. (202) 789-2747.

INTER-AMERICAN BAR FOUNDATION (IABF). 310 Federal Bar Building, 1819 H Street, Northwest, Washington, D.C. 20006. (202) 293-1455.

INTERNATIONAL ACADEMY OF LEGAL MEDICINE AND SOCIAL MEDICINE. Academie Internationale de Medecine Legale et de Medecine Sociale 49A, avenue Nicolai, Boite Postale 8, B-4802 Verviers, Belgium. 87 229821.

INTERNATIONAL ACADEMY OF TRIAL LAWYERS. 4 North Second Street, Suite 175, San Jose, California 95113. (408) 275-6767.

INTERNATIONAL ASSOCIATION OF CHIEFS OF POLICE (IACP). 1110 North Glebe Road, Suite 200, Arlington, Virginia 22201. (703) 243-6500.

INTERNATIONAL ASSOCIATION OF CONSTITUTIONAL LAW (IACL). Association Internationale de Droit Constitutionnel (AIDC), c/o Pravni Falkultet, Bulevar Revolucije 67, YU-11000 Belgrade, Yugoslavia. 11 341501.

INTERNATIONAL ASSOCIATION OF DEFENSE COUNSEL. 20 North Wacker Drive, Suite 3100, Chicago, Illinois 60606. (312) 368-1494.

INTERNATIONAL ASSOCIATION OF ENTERTAINMENT LAWYERS (IAEL). Association Internationale des Avocats du Monde et des Industries du Spectacle, 250, avenue Louise, Boite Postale 31, B-1050 Brussels, Belgium. 2 6474060.

INTERNATIONAL ASSOCIATION OF JEWISH LAWYERS AND JURISTS. 30 Iben Gevirol Street, 64078 Tel Aviv, Israel. 3 210673.

INTERNATIONAL ASSOCIATION OF LAW FIRMS (IALF). P.O. Box 180, Fairfax Station, Virginia 22039. (703) 425-2500.

INTERNATIONAL BAR ASSOCIATION (IBA). Association Internationale du Barreau, 2 Harewood Place, Hanover Square, London WIR 9HB, England. 71 6291206.

INTERNATIONAL BROTHERHOOD OF POLICE OFFICERS (IBPO). 285 Dorchester Avenue, Boston, Massachusetts 02127. (617) 268-5002.

INTERNATIONAL CENTER FOR LAW IN DEVELOPMENT (ICLD). 777 United Nations Plaza, New York, New York 10017. (212) 687-0036.

INTERNATIONAL CENTER FOR MEDICINE AND LAW (ICML). 170 Forest Green, Staten Island, New York 10312. (212) 747-1755.

INTERNATIONAL COUNCIL OF ENVIRONMENTAL LAW (ICEL). Conseil International du Droit de l'Environnement Adenauerallee 214, W-5300 Bonn 1, Germany. 228 2692240.

INTERNATIONAL CRIMINAL LAW COMMISSION (ICLC). 1493 Tunnel Road, Mission Canyon Heights, Santa Barbara, California 93105. (805) 682-1449.

INTERNATIONAL FEDERATION FOR EUROPEAN LAW (FIDE). Federation International pour le Droit Europeen (FIDE), Hippokratous 33, GR-106 80 Athens, Greece. 1 3629065.

INTERNATIONAL FEDERATION OF WOMEN LAWYERS. 186 Fifth Avenue, New York, New York 10010. (212) 206-1666.

INTERNATIONAL INSTITUTE FOR THE UNIFICATION OF PRIVATE LAW (UNIDROIT). Institut International pour l'Unification du Droit Prive (UNIDROIT). Via Panisperna 28, I-00184 Rome, Italy. 6 6841372.

INTERNATIONAL LAW ASSOCIATION (ILA). Association de Droit International, Charles Clore House, 17 Russell Square, London WC1B 5DR, England. 71 3232978

INTERNATIONAL LAW INSTITUTE (ILI). 1615 New Hampshire Avenue, Northwest, Washington D.C. 20009. (202) 483-3036.

INTERNATIONAL LAW STUDENTS ASSOCIATION (ILSA). 2223 Massachusetts Avenue, Northwest, Washington, D.C. 20008-2864. (202) 265-4375.

INTERNATIONAL LEGAL DEFENSE COUNSEL. 111 South Fifteenth Street, Twenty-fourth Floor, Philadelphia, Pennsylvania 19102. (215) 977-9982.

INTERNATIONAL MARITIME COMMITTEE (CMI). Comite Maritime International (CMI), Mechelsesteenweg 203 B 6, B-2018 Antwerp, Belgium. 3 2184887.

INTERNATIONAL SOCIETY FOR MILITARY LAW AND LAW OF WAR. Scoiete Internationale de Droit Militaire et de Droit de la Guerre, c/o Auditorat General pres la Cour Militaire, Palais de Justice, B-1000 Brussels, Belgium. 2 5086611.

INTERNATIONAL SOCIETY OF BARRISTERS. 3586 East Huron River Drive, Ann Arbor, Michigan 48104. (313) 577-3993.

INTERNATIONAL SOCIETY OF FAMILY LAW (ISFL). Societe Internationale de Droit de la Famille, c/o Professor David S. Pearl, School of Law, University of East Anglia, Norwich, Norfolk, England. 603 592836.

INTERNATIONAL THIRD WORLD LEGAL STUDIES ASSOCIATION (INTWORLSA). c/o International Center For Law in Development, 777 United Nations Plaza, New York, New York 10017. (212) 687-0036.

INTERNATIONAL UNION OF POLICE ASSOCIATIONS (IUPA). 1016 Duke Street, Alexandria, Virginia 22314. (703) 549-7473.

ISLAMIC JURISPRUDENCE ACADEMY (IJA). Majma'a al-Fiqh al-Islami (IFA), P.O. Box 13719, Jeddah 21414, Saudi Arabia. 2 6609329.

JAPANESE AMERICAN SOCIETY FOR LEGAL STUDIES (JASLS). c/o Professor Daniel H. Foote, University of Washington Law School, JB-20, Seattle, Washington 98105. (206) 685-1897.

JEWISH LAWYERS GUILD. 160 Broadway, New York, New York 10038. (212) 732-3053.

JOINT CUSTODY ASSOCIATION (JCA). 10606 Wilkins Avenue, Los Angeles, California 90024. (213) 475-5352.

JUDGE ADVOCATES ASSOCIATION (JAA). 1815 H Street, Northwest, Suite 408, Washington, D.C. 20006. (202) 628-0979.

LATIN AMERICAN CONSTITUTIONAL LAW ASSOCIATION (LACLA). Asociacion Latinoamericana de Derecho Constitucional (ALDC). Avenida Santa Fe 2108, 4 A, 1123 Buenos Aires, Argentina 1 831138.

LAW AND SOCIETY ASSOCIATION (LSA). University of Massachusetts, Hampshire House, Amherst, Massachusetts 01003. (413) 545-4617.

LAW ASSOCIATION FOR ASIA AND THE PACIFIC (LAWASIA). 170 Phillip Street, Tenth Floor, Sydney, New South Wales 2000, Australia. 2 2212970.

LAW OF THE SEA INSTITUTE (LSI). Richardson School of Law, 2515 Dole Street, Room 208, University of Hawaii, Honolulu, Hawaii 96822. (808) 956-6750.

LAW SCHOOL ADMISSION COUNCIL/LAW SCHOOL ADMISSION SERVICES (LSAC/LSAS). P.O. Box 40, Newtown, Pennsylvania 18940. (215) 968-1101.

LAW STUDENT DIVISION - AMERICAN BAR ASSOCIATION (ABA/LSD). American Bar Center, 750 North Lake Shore Drive, Chicago, Illinois 60611. (312) 988-5624.

LAWYERS ALLIANCE FOR NUCLEAR ARMS CONTROL. 43 Charles Street, Suite 3, Boston, Massachusetts 02114. (617) 227-0118.

LAWYERS COMMITTEE FOR CIVIL RIGHTS UNDER LAW (LCCRUL). 1400 I Street, Northwest, Suite 400, Washington, D.C. 20005. (202) 371-1212.

LAWYERS COMMITTEE FOR HUMAN RIGHTS. 330 Seventh Avenue, Tenth Floor, North, New York, New York 10001. (212) 629-6170.

LAWYERS COMMITTEE ON NUCLEAR POLICY. 225 Lafayette Street, Room 513, New York, New York 10012. (212) 334-8044.

LAWYERS-PILOTS BAR ASSOCIATION. c/o John S. Yodice, 500 E Street, Southwest, Suite 930, Washington, D.C. 20024. (202) 863-1000.

LEGAL ASSISTANT MANAGEMENT ASSOCIATION (LAMA). Box 40129, Overland Park, Kansas 66204. (913) 381-4458.

MARITIME LAW ASSOCIATION OF THE UNITED STATES (MLA). 400 Poydris Street, New Orleans, Louisiana 70130. (504) 566-1311.

MEXICAN AMERICAN LEGAL DEFENSE AND EDUCATION FUND. 634 South Spring Street, Twelfth Floor, Los Angeles, California 90014. (213) 629-2512.

NATIONAL ADVOCATES SOCIETY. c/o Richard Puchalski, 20 North Wacker Drive, Chicago, Illinois 60606. (312) 726-3065.

NATIONAL AMERICAN INDIAN COURT JUDGES ASSOCIATION. 1000 Connecticut Avenue, Northwest, Suite 401, Washington, D.C. 20036. (202) 296-0685.

NATIONAL ASSOCIATION OF ATTORNEYS GENERAL. 444 North Capitol Street, Suite 403, Washington, D.C. 20001. (202) 628-0435.

NATIONAL ASOCIATION OF BANKRUPTCY TRUSTEES (NABT). 3008 Millwood Avenue, Columbia, South Carolina 29205. (803) 252-5646.

NATIONAL ASSOCIATION OF BAR EXECUTIVES (NABE). Division for Bar Services, 750 North Lake Shore Drive, Chicago, Illinois 60611. (312) 988-5346.

NATIONAL ASSOCIATION OF BENCH AND BAR SPOUSES. 5617 Congress Boulevard, Baton Rouge, Louisiana 70808. (504) 928-1663.

NATIONAL ASSOCIATION OF BLACK WOMEN ATTORNEYS. 3711 Macomb Street, Northwest, Second Floor, Washington, D.C. 20016. (202) 966-9693.

NATIONAL ASSOCIATION OF BOND LAWYERS. P.O. Box 397, Hinsdale, Illinois 60522. (312) 920-0160.

NATIONAL ASSOCIATION OF COLLEGE AND UNIVERSITY ATTORNEYS (NACUA). One Dupont Circle, Suite 620, Washington, D.C. 20036. (202) 833-8390.

NATIONAL ASSOCIATION OF COUNSEL FOR CHILDREN (NACC). 1205 Oneida Street, Denver, Colorado 80220. (303) 321-3963.

NATIONAL ASSOCIATION OF COUNTY CIVIL ATTORNEYS. 440 First Street, Northwest, Washington, D.C. 20001. (202) 393-6226.

NATIONAL ASSOCIATION OF CRIMINAL DEFENSE LAWYERS (NACDL). 1110 Vermont Avenue, Northwest, Suite 1150, Washington, D.C. 20005. (202) 872-8688.

NATIONAL ASSOCIATION OF JD/MBA PROFESSIONALS. c/o BU Capital, 575 Fifth Avenue Seventeenth Floor, New York, New York 10017 (212) 808-0990.

NATIONAL ASSOCIATION OF POLICE ORGANIZATIONS (NAPO). c/o Robert Scully, Detroit Police Officers Association, 6525 Lincoln, Detroit, Michigan 48202. (313) 871-0484.

NATIONAL ASSOCIATION OF RAILROAD TRIAL COUNSEL. 88 Alma Real Drive, Suite 218, Pacific Palisades, California 90272. (213) 459-7659.

NATIONAL ASSOCIATION OF SECURITIES AND COMMERCIAL LAW ATTORNEYS (NASCAT). 1300 I Street, Northwest, East Tower, Suite 480, Washington, D.C. 20005. (202) 962-3863.

NATIONAL ASSOCIATION OF WOMEN JUDGES. c/o National Center for State Courts, 300 Newport Avenue, Williamsburg, Virginia 23187. (804) 253-2000.

NATIONAL ASSOCIATION OF WOMEN LAWYERS. 750 North Lake Shore Drive, Chicago, Illinois 60611. (312) 988-6186.

NATIONAL BAR ASSOCIATION. 1225 Eleventh Street, Northwest, Washington, D.C. 20001. (202) 842-3900.

NATIONAL BLACK POLICE ASSOCIATION (NBPA). 1919 Pennsylvania Avenue, Northwest, Suite 300 Washington, D.C. 20006. (202) 457-0563.

NATIONAL BOARD OF TRIAL ADVOCACY. Suffolk University Law School, Beacon Hill, Boston, Massachusetts 02114. (617) 573-8700.

NATIONAL CENTER FOR YOUTH LAW (NCYL). 114 Sansome Street, Suite 900, San Francisco, California 94104. (415) 543-3307.

NATIONAL CENTER ON WOMEN AND FAMILY LAW (NCOWFL). 799 Broadway, Room 402, New York, New York 10003. (212) 674-8200.

NATIONAL CHAMBER LITIGATION CENTER (NCLC). 1615 H Street, Northwest, Washington, D.C. 20062. (202) 463-5337.

NATIONAL CHILD SUPPORT ENFORCEMENT ASSOCIATION (NCSEA). Hall of States, 444 N. Capitol, Northwest, Number 613, Washington, D.C. 20001. (202) 624-8180.

NATIONAL CLIENTS COUNCIL (NCC). 2617 Martha Street, Philadelphia, Pennsylvania 19125. (215) 686-2913.

NATIONAL COALITION TO ABOLISH CORPORAL PUNISHMENT (NCMESD). 155 West Main Street, Number 100-B, Columbus, Ohio 43215. (614) 221-8829.

NATIONAL COLLEGE OF DISTRICT ATTORNEYS (NCDA). University of Houston, Law Center, Houston, Texas 77204-6380. (713) 747-6232.

NATIONAL CONFERENCE OF BANKRUPTCY JUDGES. c/o Judge George C. Paine, Customs House, Room 218, 701 Broadway, Nashville, Tennessee 37203. (615) 736-5587.

NATIONAL CONFERENCE OF BAR EXAMINERS (NCBE). 333 North Michigan, Suite 1025, Chicago, Illinois 60601-4090. (312) 641-0963.

NATIONAL CONFERENCE OF BAR FOUNDATIONS (NCBF). c/o American Bar Association, Division of Bar Services, 750 North Lake Shore Drive, Chicago, Illinois 60611. (312) 988-5354.

NATIONAL CONFERENCE OF BAR PRESIDENTS (NCBP). Division for Bar Services, 750 North Lake Shore Drive, Chicago, Illinois 60611. (312) 988-5346.

NATIONAL CONFERENCE OF BLACK LAWYERS. 126 West One Hundred Nineteenth Street, New York, New York 10026. (212) 864-4000.

NATIONAL CONFERENCE OF SPECIAL COURT JUDGES (NCSCJ). 750 North Lake Shore Drive, Chicago, Illinois 60611. (312) 988-5697.

NATIONAL CONFERENCE OF WOMEN'S BAR ASSOCIATIONS (NCWBA). P.O. Box 77, Edenton, North Carolina 27932-0077. (919) 482-8202.

NATIONAL COUNCIL OF INTELLECTUAL PROPERTY LAW ASSOCIATIONS. c/o Office of Public Affaris, Crystal Plaza 2, Room 1A05, 2021 Jefferson Davis Highway, Arlington, Virginia 22202. (703) 557-3341.

NATIONAL COUNCIL OF JUVENILE AND FAMILY LAW COURT JUDGES. P.O. Box 8970, Reno, Nevada 89507. (702) 784-6012.

NATIONAL DISABLED LAW OFFICERS ASSOCIATION (NDLOA). 75 New Street, Nutley, New Jersey 07110. (201) 667-9569.

NATIONAL DISTRICT ATTORNEYS ASSOCIATION. 1033 North Fairfax Street, Suite 200, Alexandria, Virginia 22314. (703) 549-9222.

NATIONAL GAY RIGHTS ADVOCATES (NGRA). 540 Castro Street, San Francisco, California 94114. (415) 863-3624.

NATIONAL HEALTH LAW PROGRAM (NHELP). 2639 South La Cienega Boulevard, Los Angeles, California 90034. (213) 204-6010.

NATIONAL HEALTH LAWYERS ASSOCIATION (NHLA). 1620 I Street, Northwest, Suite 900, Washington, D.C. 20006. (202) 833-1100.

NATIONAL INVENTORS FOUNDATION (NIF). 345 West Cypress Street, Glendale, California 91204. (818) 246-6540.

NATIONAL JUDICIAL COLLEGE. University of Nevada, Judicial College Building, Reno, Nevada 89557. (702) 784-6747.

NATIONAL JUVENILE COURT SERVICES ASSOCIATION (NJCSA). P.O. Box 8970, University of Nevada, Reno, Nevada 89507. (702) 784-4859.

NATIONAL LAW ENFORCEMENT COUNCIL (NLEC). 1140 Connecticut Avenue, Northwest, Suite 804, Washington, D.C. 20036. (202) 223-6850.

NATIONAL LAWYERS CLUB. 1815 H Street, Northwest, Washington, D.C. 20006. (202) 638-3200.

NATIONAL LAWYERS COMMITTEE FOR SOVIET JEWRY. 10 East Fortieth Street, Suite 907, New York, New York 10016. (212) 679-6122.

NATIONAL LAWYERS GUILD. 55 Sixth Avenue, New York, New York 10013. (212) 966-5000.

NATIONAL LAWYERS GUILD - MILITARY LAW TASK FORCE (MLTF). 1168 Union, Suite 201, San Diego, California 92101. (619) 233-1701.

NATIONAL LEGAL AID AND DEFENDER ASSOCIATION. 1625 K Street, Northwest, D.C. 20006. (202) 452-0620.

NATIONAL LEGAL CENTER FOR THE PUBLIC INTEREST (NLCPI). 1000 Sixteenth Street, Northwest, Suite 301, Washington, D.C. 20036. (202) 296-1683.

NATIONAL LEGAL FOUNDATION (NLF). P.O. Box 64845, Virginia Beach, Virginia 23464. (804) 424-4242.

NATIONAL ORGANIZATION OF BAR COUNSEL (NOBC). c/o David E. Johnson, Jr., Office of Attorney Ethics, 25 West Market Street, CN 962, Trenton, New Jersey 08625. (609) 292-1011.

NATIONAL ORGANIZATION OF BAR COUNSEL. c/o John Berry, Attorney Grievance Commission of Maryland, 580 Taylor Avenue, Room 404, Annapolis, Maryland 21401. (301) 974-2791.

NATIONAL ORGANIZATION ON LEGAL PROBLEMS OF EDUCATION (NOLPE). Southwest Plaza Building, 3601 West Twenty-ninth Street, Suite 223, Topeka, Kansas 66614. (913) 273-3550.

NATIONAL POLICE OFFICERS ASSOCIATION OF AMERICA (NPOAA). 1316 Gardiner Lane, Suite 204, Louisville, Kentucky 40213. (502) 451-7550.

NATIONAL WOMEN AND THE LAW ASSOCIATION (NWLA). 1810 Sixth Street, Berkley, California 94710. (415) 704-0151.

NATURAL RIGHTS CENTER (NRC). 156 Drakes Lane, Summertown, Tennessee 38483-0090. (615) 964-3992.

OCEAN EDUCATION PROJECT (OEP). c/o Miriam Levering, Route 2, Ararat, Virginia 24053. (703) 755-3592.

ORDER OF THE COIF. c/o John A. Bauman, UCLA School of Law, 405 Hilgard Avenue, Los Angeles, California 90024. (213) 825-4739.

PACIFIC LEGAL FOUNDATION (PLF). 2700 Gateway Oaks Drive, Suite 200, Sacramento, California 95833. (916) 641-8888.

PHILIP C. JESSUP INTERNATIONAL LAW MOOT COURT COMPETITION (PCJILMCC). c/o International Law Students Association, 2223 Massachusetts Avenue, Northwest, Washington, D.C. 20008. (202) 265-4375.

PUBLIC LAW EDUCATION INSTITUTE (PLEI). 1601 Connecticut Avenue, Northwest, Suite 450, Washington, D.C. 20009. (202) 232-1400.

PUERTO RICAN BAR ASSOCIATION. 888 Brand Concourse, Suite 1-0, Bronx, New York 10451. (212) 292-8201.

PUERTO RICAN LEGAL DEFENSE AND EDUCATION FUND. 99 Hudson Street, Fourteenth Floor, New York, New York 10013. (212) 219-3360.

ROSCOE POUND FOUNDATION. 1050 Thirty-first Street, Northwest, Washington, D.C. 20007. (202) 965-3500.

SCRIBES. P.O. Box 7206, Reynolds Station, Wake Forest University School of Law, Winston-Salem, North Carolina 27109. (919) 761-5440.

SECTION OF INDIVIDUAL RIGHTS AND RESPONSIBILITIES (SIRR). c/o American Bar Association, 1800 M Street, Northwest, Suite 200, Washington, D.C. 20036. (202) 331-2279.

SELDEN SOCIETY. Langdell Hall 490, Harvard Law School, Cambridge, Massachusetts 02138. (617) 495-8279.

SERBIAN-AMERICAN BAR ASSOCIATION (SABA). c/o Deyon Ranko Brashich, 80 West Fortieth Street, Penthouse, New York, New York 10018. (212) 575-1778.

SIERRA CLUB LEGAL DEFENSE FUND (SCLDF). 2044 Fillmore Street, San Francisco, California 94115. (415) 567-6100.

SOCIETY FOR THE STUDY OF WOMEN IN LEGAL HISTORY. c/o Nancy S. Erickson, 619 Carroll Street, Brooklyn, New York 11215. (718) 783-8162.

SOCIETY OF AMERICAN LAW TEACHERS. c/o Charles R. Lawrence, School of Law, Stanford University, Palo Alto, California 94305. (415) 723-3627.

SOCIETY OF COMPARATIVE LEGISLATION. Societe de Legislation Comparee, 28, rue St.-Guillaume, F-75007 Paris, France 1 45444467.

SOUTHWESTERN LEGAL FOUNDATION (SWLF). P.O. Box 830707, Richardson, Texas 75083-0707. (214) 690-2370.

SPORTS LAWYERS ASSOCIATION (SLA). c/o REI Management Group, 2017 Lathrop Avenue, Racine, Wisconsin 53405. (414) 632-4040.

TRANSPORTATION LAWYERS ASSOCIATION. 3310 Harrison, Topeka, Kansas 66611. (913) 266-7014.

TRIAL LAWYERS FOR PUBLIC JUSTICE (TLPJ). 1625 Massachusetts Avenue, Northwest, Suite 100, Washington, D.C. 20036. (202) 797-8600.

UNION OF SOVIET LAWYERS. Soyuz Advokatov SSSR, Ulitsa Pushkinskaya 9, str 6, SU-103009 Moscow, Russia. 95 2923260.

UNITED STATES JUSTICE FOUNDATION (USJF). 2091 East Valley Parkway, Suite 1-C, Escondido, California 92027. (619) 741-8086.

VOLUNTEER LAWYERS FOR THE ARTS. 1285 Avenue of the Americas, Third Floor, New York, New York 10019. (212) 977-9270.

WASHINGTON LEGAL FOUNDATION (WLF). 1705 N Street, Northwest, Washington, D.C. 20036. (202) 857-0240.

WORLD ASSOCIATION OF JUDGES. 1000 Connecticut Avenue, Northwest, Suite 800, Washington, D.C. 20036. (202) 466-5428.

WORLD ASSOCIATION OF LAW PROFESSORS (WALP). 1000 Connecticut Avenue, Northwest, Suite 800, Washington, D.C. 20036. (202) 466-5428.

WORLD ASSOCIATION OF LAW STUDENTS (WALS). 1000 Connecticut Avenue, Northwest, Suite 800, Washington, D.C. 20036. (202) 466-5428.

WORLD ASSOCIATION OF LAWYERS (WAL). 1000 Connecticut Avenue, Northwest, Suite 800, Washington, D.C. 20036. (202) 466-5428.

LAWYER AND CLIENT

LOOSELEAF SERVICES AND REPORTERS

CASE ASSESSMENT AND EVALUATION. Don Howarth and Suzelle M. Smith. Callaghan and Company, 155 Pfingsten Road, Deerfield, Illinois 60015. 1989- .

HANDBOOKS, MANUALS, FORMBOOKS

THE PRACTICAL LAWYER'S MANUAL ON LAWYER-CLIENT RELATIONS. American Law Institute-American Bar Association, Committee on Continuing Professional Education, 4025 Chestnut Street, Philadelphia, Pennsylvania 19104. 1983.

YOU AND YOUR CLIENTS: A GUIDE TO A MORE SUCCESSFUL LAW PRACTICE THROUGH BEHAVIOR MANAGEMENT. Stanley S. Clawar. Section of General Practice, American Bar Association, 750 North Lake Shore Drive, Chicago, Illinois 60611. 1988.

TEXTBOOKS AND GENERAL WORKS

ADVISE AND INVENT: THE LAWYER AS COUNSELOR-STRATEGIST AND OTHER ESSAYS. James C. Freund. Prentice-Hall, Incorporated, 113 Sylvan Avenue, Englewood Cliffs, New Jersey 07632. 1990.

THE ATTORNEY-CLIENT PRIVILEGE AND THE WORK-PRODUCT DOCTRINE: A PROJECT OF THE TRIAL EVIDENCE COMMITTEE, SECTION OF LITIGATION. American Bar Association, 750 North Lake Shore Drive, Chicago, Illinois 60611. 1989.

CLIENTS AND LAWYERS: SECURING THE RIGHTS OF DISABLED PERSONS. Susan M. Olson. Greenwood Publishing Group, Incorporated, 88 Post Road West, P.O. Box 5007, Westport, Connecticut 06881. 1984.

COMPETENT COUNSEL: WORKING WITH LAWYERS. Denise G. Shekerjian. Dodd, Mead and Company, 71 Fifth Avenue, New York, New York 10003. 1985.

EFFECTIVE INTERVIEWING AND A PROFITABLE PRACTICE. Fred E. Jandt and Fred Edmund. Anderson Publishing Company, 2035 Reading Road, Cincinnati, Ohio 45202. 1990.

ETHICS COMPLIANCE FOR BUSINESS LAWYERS. Brooke Wunnicke. John Wiley and Sons, Incorporated, 605 Third Avenue, New York, New York 10158. 1987.

HOW TO GET AND KEEP GOOD CLIENTS. Second Edition. Jay G. Foonberg. Lawyers Alert Press, Boston, Massachusetts. 1990.

HOW TO GET THE BEST LEGAL HELP FOR YOUR BUSINESS (AT THE LOWEST POSSIBLE COST). Mead J. Hedglon. McGraw-Hill Publishing Company, 1221 Avenue of the Americas, New York, New York 10020. 1992.

HOW TO SERVE CLIENTS EFFECTIVELY. J. Harris Morgan. Hamline University, Advanced Legal Education, School of Law, 1536 Hewitt Avenue, St. Paul, Minnesota 55104. 1990.

INTERVIEWING, COUNSELING, AND NEGOTIATING: SKILLS FOR EFFECTIVE REPRESENTATION. Robert M. Bastress and Joseph D. Harbaugh. Little, Brown and Company, 34 Beacon Street, Boston, Massachusetts 02108. 1990.

KILL ALL THE LAWYERS? A USER FRIENDLY GUIDE TO WORKING WITH A LAWYER. Sloan Bashinsky. Simon and Schuster, Incorporated, 1230 Avenue of the Americas, New York, New York 10020. 1985.

LAWYERS AS COUNSELORS: A CLIENT CENTERED APPROACH. David A. Binder, Paul Bergman and Susan C. Price. West Publishing Company, 50 West Kellogg Boulevard, St. Paul, Minnesota 55164. 1991.

LEGAL INTERVIEWING AND COUNSELING IN A NUTSHELL. Second Edition. Thomas L. Shaffer and James R. Elkins. West Publishing Company, 50 West Kellogg Boulevard, St. Paul, Minnesota 55164. 1987.

LEGAL NEGOTIATION IN A NUTSHELL. Larry L. Teply. West Publishing Company, 50 West Kellogg Boulevard, St. Paul, Minnesota 55164. 1992.

LEGAL NEGOTIATION: THEORY AND APPLICATIONS. Donald G. Gifford. West Publishing Company, 50 West Kellogg Boulevard, St. Paul, Minnesota 55164. 1989.

LEGAL NEGOTIATIONS: GETTING MAXIMUM RESULTS. Mark K. Schoenfield and Rick M. Schoenfield. Shepard's/McGraw-Hill, P.O. Box 1235, Colorado Springs, Colorado 80901. 1988.

LIMITED WAIVER OF ATTORNEY-CLIENT PRIVILEGE AND WORK PRODUCT DOCTRINE IN INTERNAL CORPORATE INVESTIGATIONS: AN EMERGING CORPORATE SELF-EVALUATIVE PRIVILEGE. Nancy C. Crisman and Arthur F. Mathews. American Bar Association, 750 North Lake Shore Drive, Chicago, Illinois 60611. 1983.

PROFESSIONAL RESPONSIBILITY IN A NUTSHELL. Second Edition. Robert H. Aronson and Donald T. Weckstein. West Publishing Company, 50 West Kellogg Boulevard, St. Paul, Minnesota 55164. 1991.

REPRESENTING THE CORPORATE CLIENT: DESIGNS FOR QUALITY. Richard H. Weise. Prentice-Hall, Incorporated, 113 Sylvan Avenue, Englewood Cliffs, New Jersey 07632. 1991.

SERVING TWO MASTERS: THE LAW OF LAWYER DISQUALIFICATION. Leonard H. Gilbert and George Zadorozny. American Bar Association, 750 North Lake Shore Drive, Chicago, Illinois 60611. 1984.

THE SOCIAL RESPONSIBILITIES OF LAWYERS: CASE STUDIES. Philip B. Heymann and Lance Liebman. Foundation Press, 615 Merrick Avenue, Westbury, New York 11590. 1988.

THE TERRIBLE TRUTH ABOUT LAWYERS: HOW LAWYERS REALLY WORK AND HOW TO DEAL WITH THEM SUCCESSFULLY. Mark H. McCormack. Beech Tree Books, New York, New York. 1987.

UNANTICIPATED CLIENT PERJURY. Wayne D. Brazil. American Bar Association, 750 North Lake Shore Drive, Chicago, Illinois 60611. 1981.

USING A LAWYER-- AND WHAT TO DO IF THINGS GO WRONG: A STEP-BY-STEP GUIDE. Revised Edition. Kay Ostberg. Random House, Incorporated, 201 East Fiftieth Street, New York, New York 10022. 1990.

WHAT LAWYERS DO-- AND HOW TO MAKE THEM WORK FOR YOU. Daniel R. White. E.P. Dutton, 375 Hudson Street, New York, New York 10014. 1987.

NEWSLETTERS AND NEWSPAPERS

CLIENT COUNSELING UPDATE. American Bar Association, Young Lawyers Division, 750 North Lake Shore Drive, Chicago, Illinois 60611. Quarterly.

CLIENT UPDATE. American Bar Association, Section of General Practice, 750 North Lake Shore Drive, Chicago, Illinois 60611. Quarterly.

AUDIOVISUALS

ATTORNEY-CLIENT RELATIONS. American Bar Association, 750 North Lake Shore Drive, Chicago, Illinois 60611. 1989. Videotape.

CLIENT CONFIDENTIALITY. American Bar Association, 750 North Lake Shore Drive, Chicago, Illinois 60611. 1989. Videotape.

CONFLICTS OF INTEREST. American Bar Association, 750 North Lake Shore Drive, Chicago, Illinois 60611. 1989. Videotape.

CRIMINAL LAW: CLIENT COUNSELING COMPETITION VIDEOTAPE. American Bar Association, 750 North Lake Shore Drive, Chicago, Illinois 60611. 1986. Videotape.

ETHICAL DILEMMAS AND PROFESSIONALISM. American Bar Association, 750 North Lake Shore Drive, Chicago, Illinois 60611. 1989. Videotape.

HOW TO PREVENT LEGAL MALPRACTICE. American Bar Association, 750 North Lake Shore Drive, Chicago, Illinois 60611. 1989. Videotape.

INDEPENDENCE OF COUNSEL. American Bar Association, 750 North Lake Shore Drive, Chicago, Illinois 60611. 1989. Videotape.

PREVENTING LEGAL MALPRACTICE. American Bar Association, 750 North Lake Shore Drive, Chicago, Illinois 60611. 1987. Videotape.

COMPUTER-ASSISTED LEGAL INSTRUCTION

CLIENT INTERVIEWING SKILLS. CLE Group, 274 Willow Road, Menlo Park, California 94025. Interactive videodisc.

COMPUGRAPH V. CHANG. Interactive Video Library, Harvard Law School, Educational Technology Department, 18 Everett Street, Cambridge, Massachusetts 02138. Interactive videodisc.

DAVIS V. JACOBY. Center for Computer-Assisted Instruction, 229 19th Avenue South, University of Minnesota, Minneapolis, Minnesota 55455. Interactive videodisc.

PROFESSIONAL RESPONSIBILITY. Center for Computer-Assisted Instruction, 229 19th Avenue South, University of Minnesota, Minneapolis, Minnesota 55455. Interactive videodisc.

LAWYERS
See: ADMISSION TO THE BAR; AMERICAN BAR ASSOCIATION; LAW OFFICE MANAGEMENT;LAWPRACTICE; LAWYER AND CLIENT; LAWYER'S FEES; LEGAL AID; LEGAL ETHICS AND MALPRACTICE; LEGAL PROFESSION IN FICTION; PREPAID LEGAL SERVICE, PUBLIC PROSECUTORS

LAWYERS' FEES
See also: PREPAID LEGAL SERVICES

STATUTES, CODES, STANDARDS, UNIFORM LAWS

LEGISLATIVE HISTORY OF THE TEN DOLLAR ATTORNEY FEE LIMITATION IN CLAIMS FOR VETERANS' BENEFITS. Committee on Veterans' Affairs, United States House of Representatives, 100th Congress. Superintendent of Documents, United States Government Printing Office, Washington, D.C. 20402. 1987.

HANDBOOKS, MANUALS, FORMBOOKS

FEE AGREEMENT FORMS MANUAL. Bob Pickus. California Continuing Education of the Bar, Berkeley, California. 1989- .

HOW TO GET YOUR MONEY IN FOREIGN COUNTRIES: A SURVEY OF COURT COSTS AND LAWYER'S FEES IN 151 COUNTRIES. Ivo Greiter. Kluwer Academic Publishers, 101 Philip Drive, Assinippi Park, Norwell, Massachusetts 02061. 1988.

USING A LAWYER-- AND WHAT TO DO IF THINGS GO WRONG: A STEP-BY-STEP GUIDE. Revised Edition. Kay Ostberg. Random House, Incorporated, 201 East Fiftieth Street, New York, New York 10022. 1990.

TEXTBOOKS AND GENERAL WORKS

ATTORNEY FEE AWARDS. Herbert B. Newberg. Shepard's/McGraw-Hill, P.O. Box 1235, Colorado Springs, Colorado 80901. 1986.

ATTORNEY FEE AWARDS REPORTER. Law and Business, Incorporated, 855 Valley Road, Clifton, New Jersey 07013. 1982. (Updated).

ATTORNEY'S FEES. Stuart M. Speiser. Lawyers Cooperative Publishing Company, Aqueduct Building, Rochester, New York 14694. 1973. (Annual).

ATTORNEY'S FEES: WINNING A RECOVERY IN FEDERAL COURT. Jeffery R. Goodstein. The Michie Company, P.O. Box 7587, Charlottesville, Virginia 22906-7587. 1985.

THE BILLABLE HOUR: EXAMINING THE ALTERNATIVES. Massachusetts Continuing Legal Education, 20 West Street, Boston, Massachusetts 02111. 1990.

COMPENSATION OF ATTORNEYS: NON-LAW FIRMS. Eighth Edition. Steven Langer, Abbott, Langer and Associates, 548 First Street, Crete, Illinois 60417. 1986.

CONTROLLING LITIGATION COSTS: COST CONTROL TECHNIQUES FOR THE NINETIES. Leroy C. Richie and Deanne C. Siemer. Prentice-Hall, Incorporated, 113 Sylvan Avenue, Englewood Cliffs, New Jersey 07632. 1991.

COURT AWARDED ATTORNEY FEES. Mary F. Derfner and Arthur D. Wolf. Matthew Bender and Company, Incorporated, 11 Penn Plaza, New York, New York 10001. 1983. (Annual Supplements).

LAWYERS' FEES

COURT AWARDS OF ATTORNEYS' FEES: LITIGATING ANTITRUST, CIVIL RIGHTS, PUBLIC INTEREST, AND SECURITIES CASES. Guy T. Saperstein and Melvyn I. Weiss. Practising Law Institute, 810 Seventh Avenue, New York, New York 10019. 1987.

HOW TO SET AND COLLECT ATTORNEY FEES IN CRIMINAL CASES. American Bar Association, 750 North Lake Shore Drive, Chicago, Illinois 60611. 1985.

THE INFLUENCE OF RULES RESPECTING RECOVERY OF ATTORNEYS' FEES ON SETTLEMENT OF CIVIL CASES. John E. Shapard. Federal Judicial Center, 1520 H Street, Northwest, Washington, D.C. 20005. 1984.

LEGAL FEES AND REPRESENTATION AGREEMENTS. James W. McRae. American Bar Association, Section on Economics of Law Practice, 750 North Lake Shore Drive, Chicago, Illinois 60611. 1983.

LET'S TALK MONEY: A LAWYER'S GUIDE TO SETTING AND COLLECTING FEES. John A. Streby. Callaghan and Company, 155 Pfingsten Road, Deerfield, Illinois 60015. 1987.

PROTECTING YOURSELF AND YOUR FEE: A DEFENSE LAWYER'S PRACTICE GUIDE IN A NEW AGE OF FEDERAL LAW. American Bar Association, RICO Cases Committee, Criminal Justice Section, 750 North Lake Shore Drive, Chicago, Illinois 60611. 1990.

WHAT LAWYERS DO -- AND HOW TO MAKE THEM WORK FOR YOU. Daniel R. White. E.P. Dutton, 375 Hudson Street, New York, New York 10014. 1987.

WINNING ATTORNEY'S FEES FROM THE UNITED STATES GOVERNMENT. Joel P. Bennett. New York Law Publishers, 111 Eighth Avenue, New York, New York 10011. 1984. (Supplement 1985).

NEWSLETTERS AND NEWSPAPERS

ALTERNATIVES TO THE HIGH COST OF LITIGATION. Center for Public Resources, 366 Madison Avenue, New York, New York 10017. Monthly.

ATTORNEY FEE AWARDS REPORTER. Prentice Hall Law and Business, 270 Sylvan Avenue, Englewood Cliffs, New Jersey 07632. Bimonthly.

CLASS ACTION REPORTS. Class Action Reports, Incorporated, 4900 Massachusetts Avenue, Northwest, Suite 205, Washington, D.C. 20016. Bimonthly.

PIPELINE. Alliance for Justice, 1601 Connecticut Avenue, Northwest, Suite 600, Washington, D.C. 20009. Quarterly.

AUDIOVISUALS

HOW TO SET A FAIR FEE. American Bar Association, 750 North Lake Shore Drive, Chicago, Illinois 60611. 1987. Videotape.

LEARNING DISABLED
See: MENTAL HEALTH AND DISABILITY

LEASES
See also: AGRICULTURE; LANDLORD AND TENANT

STATUTES, CODES, STANDARDS, UNIFORM LAWS

ACCOUNTING FOR LEASES: FASB STATEMENT NUMBER 13 AS AMENDED AND INTERPRETED: INCORPORATING FASB STATEMENTS, INTERPRETATIONS, AND TECHNICAL BULLETINS ISSUED THROUGH JANUARY 1990. Financial Accounting Standards Board of the Financial Accounting Foundation, 401 Merritt, Norwalk, Connecticut 06856-5116. 1990.

UNIFORM COMMERCIAL CODE: AMENDMENTS TO ARTICLE 2A. LEASES. DRAFTED BY THE NATIONAL CONFERENCE OF COMMISSIONERS ON UNIFORM STATE LAWS AND BY IT APPROVED AND RECOMMENDED FOR ENACTMENT IN ALL THE STATES AT ITS ANNUAL CONFERENCE MEETING IN ITS NINETY-NINTH YEAR IN MILWAUKEE, WISCONSIN, JULY 13-20, 1990. American Law Institute-American Bar Association, 4025 Chestnut Street, Philadelphia, Pennsylvania 19104. 1990.

LOOSELEAF SERVICES AND REPORTERS

AUTOMOBILE LENDING AND LEASING MANUAL. Randall R. McCathren and Ronald S. Loshin. Research Institute of America, Incorporated, One Penn Plaza, New York, New York 10119. 1989- .

COMMERCIAL REAL ESTATE FORMS. Stuart M. Saft. Shepard's/McGraw-Hill, P.O. Box 1235, Colorado Springs, Colorado 80901. 1987- .

EQUIPMENT LEASING. Michael W. Berwind. Commerce Clearing House, 4025 West Peterson Avenue, Chicago, Illinois 60646. 1988- .

EQUIPMENT LEASING. Philip J. Glick. Matthew Bender and Company, Incorporated, 11 Penn Plaza, New York, New York 10001. 1987.

HANDBOOKS, MANUALS, FORMBOOKS

COMMERCIAL REAL ESTATE LEASES--FORMS. Second Edition. Mark A. Senn. John Wiley and Sons, Incorporated, 605 Third Avenue, New York, New York 10158. 1990.

COMMERCIAL REAL ESTATE LEASES: PREPARATION AND NEGOTIATION. Second Edition. Mark A. Senn. John Wiley and Sons, Incorporated, 605 Third Avenue, New York, New York 10158. 1990.

THE COMMERCIAL REAL ESTATE TENANT'S HANDBOOK: A GUIDE FOR MANAGERS, ARCHITECTS, ENGINEERS, ATTORNEYS, AND REAL ESTATE PROFESSIONALS. Alan D. Sugarman, Robert F. Cushman and Andrew D. Lipman. John Wiley and Sons, Incorporated, 605 Third Avenue, New York, New York 10158. 1987.

COMMERCIAL TENANT'S LEASING TRANSACTIONS GUIDE: FORMS AND STRATEGIES. Alan D. Sugarman and Joel J. Goldberg. John Wiley and Sons, Incorporated, 605 Third Avenue, New York, New York 10158. 1991.

A DOCUMENTARY GUIDE TO COMMERCIAL LEASING. Bernard H. Goldstein. American Law Institute-American Bar Association, Committee on Continuing Professional Education, 4025 Chestnut Street, Philadelphia, Pennsylvania 19104. 1987.

EQUIPMENT LEASING GUIDE FOR LESSEES. Albert R. McMeen, III. John Wiley and Sons, Incorporated, 605 Third Avenue, New York, New York 10158. 1990.

EQUIPMENT LEASING PARTNERSHIPS: A COMPLETE INVESTMENT GUIDE TO THE ECONOMICS, THE RISKS AND THE OPPORTUNITIES. E.F. Cudworth. Probus Publishing Company, 118 North Linton Street, Chicago, Illinois 60606. 1989.

GROUND LEASES AND LAND ACQUISITION CONTRACTS. Emanuel B. Halper. Law Journal Seminars-Press, Incorporated, 111 Eighth Avenue, Suite 900, New York, New York 10011. 1988.

HANDBOOK OF EQUIPMENT LEASING: A DEAL MAKER'S GUIDE. Richard M. Contino. AMACOM, 135 West Fiftieth Street, New York, New York 10020. 1989.

A HANDBOOK OF LEASING: TECHNIQUES AND ANALYSIS. Terry A. Isom and Sudhir P. Amembal. Petrocelli Books, 115 Fifth Avenue, New York, New York 10003. 1982.

MANAGING AND LEASING COMMERCIAL PROPERTIES: FORMS AND PROCEDURES. alan A. Alexander and Richard F. Muhlebach. John Wiley and Sons, Incorporated, 605 Third Avenue, New York, New York 10158. 1991.

THE TENANT'S LEASING HANDBOOK. Jeanne D. Newman. Dearborn Financial Publications, 520 North Dearborn Street, Chicago, Illinois 60610. 1992.

TEXTBOOKS AND GENERAL WORKS

ADVANCED ISSUES IN COMMERCIAL REAL ESTATE LEASING. American Law Institute-American Bar Association, Committee on Continuing Professional Education, 4025 Chestnut Street, Philadelphia, Pennsylvania 19104. 1984.

BASIC UCC SKILLS, 1989: ARTICLE 2A. William C. Hillman. Practising Law Institute, 810 Seventh Avenue, New York, New York 10019. 1989.

CAPITAL COST RECOVERY AND LEASING. Earl F. Davis and Caroline D. Strobel. Shepard's/McGraw-Hill, P.O. Box 1235, Colorado Springs, Colorado 80901. 1987.

COMMERCIAL GROUND LEASES. Jerome D. Whalen. Practising Law Institute, 810 Seventh Avenue, New York, New York 10019. 1988.

COMMERCIAL REAL ESTATE LEASES, 1991. Milton R. Friedman, Chairman. Practising Law Institute, 810 Seventh Avenue, New York, New York 10019. 1991.

COMMERCIAL REAL ESTATE LEASES: PREPARATION AND NEGOTIATION. Mark A. Senn. John Wiley and Sons, Incorporated, 605 Third Avenue, New York, New York 10158. 1985.

CORPORATE LEASE ANALYSIS: A GUIDE TO CONCEPTS AND EVALUATION. Bennie H. Nunnally, Jr., D. Anthony Plath and Helene W. Johns. Quorum Books, Greenwood Publishing Group, Incorporated, 88 Post Road West, P.O. Box 5007, Westport, Connecticut 06881. 1991.

CURRENT LEASING LAW AND TECHNIQUES-FORMS. Patrick Rohan. Matthew Bender and Company, Incorporated, 11 Penn Plaza, New York, New York 10001. 1982. (Annual Supplements).

DRAFTING A FAIR OFFICE LEASE. Gary Goldman. American Law Institute-American Bar Association, 4025 Chestnut Street, Philadelphia, Pennsylvania 19104. 1989.

DRAFTING AND NEGOTIATING COMMERCIAL LEASES, 1990. Joseph E. Browdy. Practising Law Institute, 810 Seventh Avenue, New York, New York 10019. 1990.

EQUIPMENT LEASING. Third Edition. Peter K. Nevitt and Frank J. Fabozzi. Dow Jones-Irwin, 1818 Ridge Road, Homewood, Illinois 60430. 1988.

FRIEDMAN ON LEASES. Third Edition. Milton R. Friedman. Practising Law Institute, 810 Seventh Avenue, New York, New York 10019. 1990.

GROUND LEASES AND LAND ACQUISITION CONTRACTS. Emanuel B. Halper. Law Journal Seminars-Press, Incorporated, 111 Eighth Avenue, Suite 900, New York, New York 10011. 1988.

HANDLING AUTOMOBILE FINANCING AND LEASING CASES. Roger D. Billings, Jr. Lawyers Cooperative Publishing Company, Aqueduct Building, Rochester, New York 14694. 1988.

LANDLORD AND TENANT LAW. Fourth Edition. Sharon Rivenson Mark and Raymond I. Korona. West Publishing Company, 50 West Kellogg Boulevard, St. Paul, Minnesota 55164. 1990.

LEASE ESCALATORS AND OTHER PASS-THROUGH CLAUSES. Revised Edition. Institute of Real Estate Management, 430 North Michigan Avenue, Chicago, Illinois 60611. 1984.

LEASE FINANCING: A WORKSHOP ON NEW TECHNIQUES FOR MUNICIPALITIES. Joseph C. Daly, Chairman. Harcourt Brace Jovanovich, Incorporated, 6277 Sea Harbor Drive, Orlando, Florida 32821. 1982.

LEASE OPTIONS AND LEASE PURCHASES. Stephen R. Mettling. Longman Group USA, Incorporated, 500 North Dearborn Street, Chicago, Illinois 60610. 1983.

THE LEASE VERSUS BUY DECISION. Harold Bierman. Prentice-Hall, Incorporated, 113 Sylvan Avenue, Englewood Cliffs, New Jersey 07632. 1982.

LEVERAGED AND SINGLE-INVESTOR LEASING, 1988. Ray Warman. Practising Law Institute, 810 Seventh Avenue, New York, New York 10019. 1988.

MAKING THE LEASE-BUY DECISION. Revised Edition. Robert E. Pritchard and Thomas J. Hindeland. AMACOM, Division of American Management Association, 135 West 50th Street, New York, New York 10020. 1984.

MANAGING AND LEASING COMMERCIAL PROPERTIES. Alan A. Alexander and Richard F. Muhlebach. John Wiley and Sons, Incorporated, 605 Third Avenue, New York, New York 10158. 1990.

MANAGING AND LEASING RESIDENTIAL PROPERTIES. Paul Lapides. John Wiley and Sons, Incorporated, 605 Third Avenue, New York, New York 10158. 1992.

MODERN REAL ESTATE LEASING FORMS. Jack Kusnet and Robert Lupatin. Research Institute of America, Incorporated, One Penn Plaza, New York, New York 10119. 1980. (Annual Supplements).

MODERN REAL ESTATE TRANSACTIONS. Fifth Edition. American Law Institute-American Bar Association, Committee on Continuing Professional Education, 4025 Chestnut Street, Philadelphia, Pennsylvania 19104. 1984.

NEGOTIATING COMMERCIAL REAL ESTATE LEASES IN A DISTRESSED MARKET. Joseph F. Browdy. Practising Law Institute, 810 Seventh Avenue, New York, New York 10019. 1991.

PETROLEUM LANDS AND LEASING. Joan Burk. Penn Well Books, P.O. Box 21288, Tulsa, Oklahoma 74121. 1983.

SALES, LEASES, AND BULK TRANSFERS. Peter A. Alces and Nathaniel Hansford. Matthew Bender and Company, Incorporated, 11 Penn Plaza, New York, New York 10001. 1989.

SHOPPING CENTER AND STORE LEASES. Emmanuel B. Halper. New York Law Publishers, 111 Eighth Avenue, New York, New York 10011. 1979. (Annual Supplements).

TAX GUIDE TO MANAGING AND LEASING COMMERCIAL PROPERTIES. Martin M. Schenkman. John Wiley and Sons, Incorporated, 605 Third Avenue, New York, New York 10158. 1991.

UNIFORM COMMERCIAL CODE. ARTICLE 2A, LEASES OF GOODS. Third Edition. James J. White and Robert S. Summers. West Publishing Company, 50 West Kellogg Boulevard, St. Paul, Minnesota 55164. 1991.

NEWSLETTERS AND NEWSPAPERS

COMMERCIAL LEASE LAW AND STRATEGY. Leader Publications, 111 Eighth Avenue, New York, New York 10011. Monthly.

COMMERCIAL LEASE LAW INSIDER. Brownstone Publishers, Incorporated, 304 Park Avenue South, New York, New York 10010. Monthly.

THE LEASING LETTER. Research Institute of America, Incorporated/Rosenfeld Launer, 15 Columbus Circle, Eighteenth Floor, New York New York 10023. Monthly.

DIRECTORIES

WORLD LEASING YEARBOOK. Hawkins Publishers, Davsell, Limited, 310 Tahitiway, Number 108, Marina del Ray, California 90291. Annual.

AUDIOVISUALS

ADVANCED ISSUES AND CASE STUDIES IN EQUIPMENT LEASING. Practising Law Institute, 810 Seventh Avenue, New York, New York 10019. 1985. Audiocassette.

BASICS OF LEASING. Practising Law Institute, 810 Seventh Avenue, New York, New York 10019. 1985. Audiocassette.

RECENT DEVELOPMENTS IN EQUIPMENT LEASING. Practising Law Institute, 810 Seventh Avenue, New York, New York 10019. 1985. Audiocassette.

LEGAL ABBREVIATIONS
See: LEGAL RESEARCH

LEGAL AID

HANDBOOKS, MANUALS, FORMBOOKS

THE RESOURCE: A PRO BONO MANUAL. Esther F. Lardent, Editor. American Bar Association, Special Committee on Lawyer's Public Service Responsibility, 750 North Lake Shore Drive, Chicago, Illinois 60611. 1983.

TEXTBOOKS AND GENERAL WORKS

COURTS AND THE POOR. Christopher E. Smith. Nelson-Hall Publishers, 111 North Canal Street, Chicago, Illinois 60606. 1991.

CRIMINAL DEFENSE SERVICES FOR THE POOR: METHODS AND PROGRAMS FOR PROVIDING LEGAL REPRESENTATION AND THE NEED FOR ADEQUATE FINANCING. American Bar Association, Standing Committe on Legal Aid and Indigent Defendants, 750 North Lake Shore Drive, Chicago, Illinois 60611. 1982.

LEGAL SERVICES CORPORATION: THE ROBBER BARONS OF THE POOR? Orrin G. Hatch. Washington Legal Foundation, 1705 N Street, Northwest, Washington, D.C. 20036. 1985.

LEGAL SERVICES FOR THE POOR: A COMPARATIVE AND CONTEMPORARY ANALYSIS OF INTERORGANIZATIONAL POLITICS. Mark Kessler. Greenwood Publishing Group, Incorporated, 88 Post Road West, P.O. Box 5007, Westport, Connecticut 06881. 1987.

LEGAL SERVICES FOR THE POOR: TIME FOR REFORM. Douglas J. Besharov, Editor. American Enterprise Institute for Public Policy Research, Distributed by University Press of America, 4720 Boston Way, Lanham, Maryland 20706. 1990.

POLICY IMPLICATIONS OF THE DELIVERY SYSTEMS STUDY OF THE LEGAL SERVICES CORPORATION: A CONSULTANT'S REPORT. Richard D. Schwartz. American Bar Association, Standing Committee on Legal Aid and Indigent Defendants, 750 North Lake Shore Drive, Chicago, Illinois 60611. 1984.

THE POOR IN COURT: THE LEGAL SERVICES PROGRAM AND SUPREME COURT DECISION MAKING. Susan E. Lawrence. Princeton University Press, 41 William Street, Princeton, New Jersey 08540. 1990.

POOR PEOPLE'S LAWYERS IN TRANSITION. Jack Katz. Rutgers University Press, 30 College Avenue, New Brunswick, New Jersey 08903. 1984.

PUBLIC INTEREST LAW GROUPS: INSTITUTIONAL PROFILES. Karen O'Connor and Lee Epstein. Greenwood Publishing Group, Incorporated, 88 Post Road West, P.O. Box 5007, Westport, Connecticut 06881. 1989.

RESEARCH ON LEGAL SERVICES FOR THE POOR AND DISADVANTAGED: LESSONS FROM THE PAST AND ISSUES FOR THE FUTURE. Bryant Garth, Editor. Disputes Processing Research Program, University of Wisconsin-Madison Law School, Madison, Wisconsin 53706. 1983.

THE RIGHT TO JUSTICE: THE POLITICAL ECONOMY OF LEGAL SERVICES IN THE UNITED STATES. Charles K. Rowley. E. Elgar Publishing Company, Brookfield, Vermont. 1991.

STANDARDS FOR PROVIDERS OF CIVIL LEGAL SERVICES TO THE POOR. American Bar Association, Standing Committee on Legal Aid and Indigent Defendants, 750 North Lake Shore Drive, Chicago, Illinois 60611. 1985.

A SWORD FOR THE CONVICTED: REPRESENTING INDIGENT DEFENDANTS ON APPEAL. David T. Wasserman. Greenwood Publishing Group, Incorporated, 88 Post Road West, P.O. Box 5007, Westport, Connecticut 06881. 1990.

ANNUALS AND SURVEYS

LEGAL AID REVIEW. Legal Aid Society of New York, 11 Park Place, New York, New York 10007. Annual.

NEWSLETTERS AND NEWSPAPERS

PRO BONO REPORT. Minnesota Justice Foundation, Incorporated, 229 Nineteenth Avenue, South, Minneapolis, Minnesota 55455. Bimonthly.

BIBLIOGRAPHIES

THE DECLINE OF LEGAL SERVICES TO THE POOR. Tim J. Watts. Vance Bibliographies, P.O. Box 229, 112 North Charter Street, Monticello, Illinois 61856. 1988.

PRIVATE ATTORNEY INVOLVEMENT IN LEGAL SERVICES TO THE POOR: BIBLIOGRAPHY OF SELECTED RESOURCE MATERIALS. American Bar Association, Private Bar Involvement Project, 750 North Lake Shore Drive, Chicago, Illinois 60611. 1985.

PUBLIC LEGAL SERVICES IN THE 1980'S. Jim Buchanan. Vance Bibliographies, P.O. Box 229, 112 North Charter Street, Monticello, Illinois 61856. 1987.

DIRECTORIES

NLADA DIRECTORY OF LEGAL AID AND DEFENDER OFFICES IN THE UNITED STATES. National Legal Aid and Defender Association, 1625 K Street, Northwest, Eighth Floor, Washington, D.C. 20006. Biennial.

ASSOCIATIONS AND PROFESSIONAL SOCIETIES

AMERICAN BAR ASSOCIATION, COMMITTEE ON LEGAL AID AND INDIGENT DEFENDANTS. 750 North Lake Shore Drive, Chicago, Illinois 60611. (312) 988-5000.

AMERICAN BAR ASSOCIATION, CONSORTIUM ON LEGAL SERVICES AND THE PUBLIC. 750 North Lake Shore Drive, Chicago, Illinois 60611. (312) 988-5000.

CENTER FOR CONSTITUTIONAL RIGHTS. 666 Broadway, Seventh Floor, New York, New York 10012. (212) 614-6464.

LAWYERS COMMITTEE FOR CIVIL RIGHTS UNDER LAW. 1400 Eye Street, Northwest, Suite 400, Washington, D.C. 20005.

MEXICAN AMERICAN LEGAL DEFENSE AND EDUCATION FUND. 634 South Spring Street, Twelfth Floor, Los Angeles, California 90014. (213) 629-2912.

NAACP LEGAL DEFENSE AND EDUCATIONAL FUND. 99 Hudson Street, Sixteenth Floor, New York, New York 10013. (212) 219-1900.

NATIONAL CLIENTS COUNCIL. 2617 Martha Street, Philadelphia, Pennsylvania 19125. (215) 686-2913.

NATIONAL LEGAL AID AND DEFENDER ASSOCIATION. 1625 K Street, Northwest, Eighth Floor, Washington, D.C. 20006. (202) 452-0620.

PUERTO RICAN LEGAL DEFENSE AND EDUCATION FUND. 99 Hudson Street, Fourteenth Floor, New York, New York 10013. (212) 219-3360.

WESTERN CENTER ON LAW AND POVERTY. 3535 West Sixth Street, Los Angeles, California. 90020. (213) 487-7211.

RESEARCH CENTERS, INSTITUTES, CLEARINGHOUSES

CENTER FOR THE STUDY OF DEMOCRATIC INSTITUTIONS. 10951 Pico Boulevard, Suite 202, Los Angeles, California 90064. (213) 474-0011.

MUNICIPAL RESEARCH AND SERVICES CENTER OF WASHINGTON. 10517 Northeast Thirty-eighth Place, Kirkland, Washington 98033. (206) 827-4334.

NATIONAL CENTER FOR IMMIGRANTS' RIGHTS, INCORPORATED. 1636 West Eighth Street, Suite 215, Los Angeles, California 90017. (213) 487-2531.

NATIONAL CLEARINGHOUSE FOR LEGAL SERVICES. 407 South Dearborn, Suite 400, Chicago, Illinois 60605. (312) 939-3830.

LEGAL AID

STATISTICS SOURCES

TWO NATIONWIDE SURVEYS: 1989 PILOT ASSESSMENTS OF THE UNMET LEGAL NEEDS OF THE POOR AND OF THE PUBLIC GENERALLY. American Bar Association, Consortium on Legal Services and the Public, 750 North Lake Shore Drive, Chicago, Illinois 60611. 1989.

OTHER SOURCES

FEDERAL PRACTICE FOR LEGAL SERVICES ATTORNEYS: DRAFT. National Legal Aid and Defender Association, 1625 K Street, Northwest, Eighth Floor, Washington, D.C. 20006. 1989.

LEGAL ASSISTANTS

HANDBOOKS, MANUALS, FORMBOOKS

HANDBOOK FOR BEGINNING LEGAL ASSISTANTS AND RECEPTIONISTS. Carl W. Salser, C. Theo. Yerian and Mark R. Salser. National Book Company, P.O. Box 8795, Portland, Oregon 97207-8795. 1989.

HOW TO FIND A JOB AS A PARALEGAL: A STEP-BY-STEP JOB SEARCH GUIDE. Second Edition. Marie Kisiel. West Publishing Company, 50 West Kellogg Boulevard, St. Paul, Minnesota 55164. 1992.

THE INDEPENDENT PARALEGAL'S HANDBOOK. Second Edition. Ralph Warner. Nolo Press, 950 Parker Street, Berkeley, California 94710. 1991.

LEGAL ASSISTANT'S HANDBOOK. Second Edition. Thomas W. Brunner, Julie P. Hamre, and Joan F. McCaffrey. Bureau of National Affairs, 1231 Twenty-fifth Street, Northwest, Washington, D.C. 20037. 1988.

LEGAL DOCUMENT PREPARATION: A GUIDE TO THE PREPARATION AND HANDLING OF LEGAL DOCUMENTS. Reed K. Bilz. Delmar Publishers, Incorporated, P.O. Box 15015, Two Computer Drive West, Albany, New York 12212. 1988.

THE LINCOLN AND DARROW WORKBOOK FOR PARALEGAL TRAINING. Second Edition. Jason A. Sokolov and Shelley G. Widoff. Paralegal Resource Center, Box 343, Boston University Station, Boston, Massachusetts 02215. 1985.

MANUAL FOR LEGAL ASSISTANTS. Second Edition. National Association of Legal Assistants. West Publishing Company, 50 West Kellogg Boulevard, St. Paul, Minnesota 55164. 1992.

OBTAINING ABA APPROVAL: A REFERENCE MANUAL FOR LEGAL ASSISTANT EDUCATORS. American Bar Association, Standing Committee on Legal Assistants, 750 North Lake Shore Drive, Chicago, Illinois 60611. 1989.

PARALEGAL HANDBOOK: THEORY, PRACTICE, AND MATERIALS. Charles P. Nemeth. Prentice-Hall, Incorporated, 113 Sylvan, Englewood Cliffs, New Jersey 07632. 1986.

PARALEGAL PRACTICE AND PROCEDURE: A PRACTICAL GUIDE FOR THE LEGAL ASSISTANT. Second Edition. Deborah E. Larbalestrier. Prentice-Hall, Incorporated, 113 Sylvan, Englewood Cliffs, New Jersey 07632. 1986.

THE PARALEGAL RESOURCE MANUAL. Charles P. Nemeth. Anderson Publishing Company, 2035 Reading Road, Cincinnati, Ohio 45202. 1989.

RESOURCE MANUAL FOR CIVIL LITIGATION FOR PARALEGALS. Elizabeth C. Richardson and Milton C. Regan, Jr. South-Western Publishing Company, 5101 Madison Road, Cincinnati, Ohio 45227. 1992.

TEXTBOOKS AND GENERAL WORKS

THE BASICS OF PARALEGAL STUDIES. David Lee Goodrich. Prentice-Hall, Incorporated, 113 Sylvan Avenue, Englewood Cliffs, New Jersey 07632. 1991.

CIVIL LITIGATION FOR THE PARALEGAL. Peggy N. Kerley, Paul A. Sukys and Joanne Banker Hames. Lawyers Cooperative Publishing Company, Aqueduct Building, Rochester, New York 14694. 1992.

CRIMINAL LAW AND PROCEDURE FOR PARALEGALS. Daniel Hall. Lawyers Cooperative Publishing Company, Aqueduct Building, Rochester, New York 14694. 1992.

ESSENTIALS OF PARALEGALISM. William P. Statsky. West Publishing Company, 50 West Kellogg Boulevard, St. Paul, Minnesota 55164. 1988.

ETHICS FOR THE LEGAL ASSISTANT. Deborah K. Orlik. Scott, Foresman, and Company, 1900 East Lake Avenue, Glenview, Illinois 60025. 1986.

FOUNDATIONS OF LAW FOR PARALEGALS: CASES, COMMENTARY, AND ETHICS. Ransford C. Pyle. Delmar Publishers, Incorporated, P.O. Box 15015, Two Computer Drive West, Albany, New York 12212. 1991.

FUNDAMENTALS OF LITIGATION FOR PARALEGALS. Thomas A. Mauet and Marlene A. Maerowitz. Little, Brown and Company, 34 Beacon Street, Boston, Massachusetts 02108. 1991.

FUNDAMENTALS OF PARALEGALISM. Second Edition. Thomas E. Eimermann. Little, Brown and Company, 34 Beacon Street, Boston, Massachusetts 02108. 1987.

A GUIDE FOR LEGAL ASSISTANTS: ROLES, RESPONSIBILITIES, SPECIALIZATIONS. Second Edition. Michele C. Gowen, Editor. Practising Law Institute, 810 Seventh Avenue, New York, New York 10019. 1991.

INTRODUCTION TO PARALEGALISM: PERSPECTIVES, PROBLEMS AND SKILLS. Fourth Edition. William P. Statsky. West Publishing Company, 50 West Kellogg Boulevard, St. Paul, Minnesota 55164. 1992.

LAW OFFICE MANAGEMENT FOR PARALEGALS. Jonathan Lynton, Donna Masinter and Terri Mick Lyndall. Delmar Publishers, Incorporated, P.O. Box 15015, Two Computer Drive West, Albany, New York 12212. 1991.

LEGAL ASSISTANTS 1984. Patricia R. Wheeler, Chairperson. Practising Law Institute, 810 Seventh Avenue, New York, New York 10019. 1984.

LEGAL RESEARCH. Charles P. Nemeth. American Institute for Paralegal Studies, Incorporated. Prentice-Hall, Incorporated, 113 Sylvan, Englewood Cliffs, New Jersey 07632. 1987.

LEGAL WRITING FOR PARALEGALS. Steve Barber. South-Western Publishing Company, 5101 Madison Road, Cincinnati, Ohio 45227. 1992.

LITIGATION, PLEADINGS, AND ARBITRATION. Charles P. Nemeth. Anderson Publishing Company, 2035 Reading Road, Cincinnati, Ohio 45202. 1990.

PARALEGAL: AN INSIDER'S GUIDE TO THE FASTEST-GROWING OCCUPATION OF THE 1990s. Barbara Bernardo. Peterson's Guides, 202 Carnegie Center, P.O. Box 2123, Princeton, New Jersey 08543-2123. 1990.

PARALEGAL CAREERS. William R. Fry. Enslow Publishers, Bloy Street and Ramsey Avenue, Box 777, Hillside, New Jersey 07205. 1986.

PARALEGAL EMPLOYMENT: FACTS AND STRATEGIES FOR THE 1990s. William P. Statsky. West Publishing Company, 50 West Kellogg Boulevard, St. Paul, Minnesota 55164. 1988.

PARALEGAL: WILLS, TRUSTS AND ESTATES. Patricia Winn Carter. D&S Publishers, Incorporated, P.O. Box 5101, Clearwater, Florida 33518. 1982. (Periodic Supplements).

PARALEGALS: PROGRESS AND PROSPECTS OF A SATELLITE OCCUPATION. Quiton Johnstone and Martin Wenglinsky. Greenwood Publishing Group, Incorporated, 88 Post Road West, P.O. Box 5007, Westport, Connecticut 06881. 1985.

THE REGULATION OF PARALEGALS: ETHICS, PROFESSIONAL RESPONSIBILITY, AND OTHER FORMS OF CONTROL. William P. Statsky. West Publishing Company, 50 West Kellogg Boulevard, St. Paul, Minnesota 55164. 1987.

WILLS, TRUSTS, AND ESTATE ADMINISTRATION FOR THE PARALEGAL. Third Edition. Dennis R. Hower. West Publishing Company, 50 West Kellogg Boulevard, St. Paul, Minnesota 55164. 1991.

WORKSHOPS FOR LEGAL ASSISTANTS 1985. Michele C. Gowan and Patricia R. Wheeler, Co-Chairpersons. Practising Law Institute, 810 Seventh Avenue, New York, New York 10019. 1985.

NEWSLETTERS AND NEWSPAPERS

THE LAMA MANAGER. Legal Assistant Management Association, P.O. Box 40129, Overland Park, Kansas 66204. Quarterly.

NATIONAL PARALEGAL REPORTER. National Federation of Paralegal Associations, Incorporated, 104 Wilmot Road, Suite 201, Deerfield, Illinois 60015. Quarterly.

THE PARALEGAL. National Paralegal Association, P.O. Box 406, Solebury, Pennsylvania 18963. Bimonthly.

THE PARALEGAL EDUCATER. American Association of Paralegal Education, P.O. Box 40244, Overland Park, Kansas 66204. Quarterly.

ASSOCIATIONS AND PROFESSIONAL SOCIETIES

AMERICAN ASSOCIATION FOR PARALEGAL EDUCATION. P.O. Box 40244, Overland Park, Kansas 66204. (913) 381-4451.

ASSOCIATION OF AMERICAN LAW SCHOOLS, SECTION OF PARALEGAL EDUCATION. Association of American Law Schools, One Dupont Circle, Northwest, Washington, D.C. 20036. (202) 296-8851.

AMERICAN BAR ASSOCIATION, COMMITTEE ON LEGAL ASSISTANTS. 750 North Lake Shore Drive, Chicago, Illinois 60611. (312) 988-5000.

INSTITUTE FOR PARALEGAL TRAINING. 1926 Arch Street, Philadelphia, Pennsylvania 19103. (215) 567-4000.

LEGAL ASSISTANT MANAGEMENT ASSOCIATION. P.O. Box 40129, Overland Park, Kansas 66204. (913) 381-4458.

NATIONAL ASSOCIATION OF LEGAL ASSISTANTS. 1601 South Main Street, Suite 300, Tulsa, Oklahoma 74119. (918) 587-6828.

NATIONAL ASSOCIATION OF PARA-LEGALS PERSONNEL. P.O. Box 8202, Northfield, Illinois 60093. (312) 973-7712.

NATIONAL FEDERATION OF PARALEGAL ASSOCIATIONS, INCORPORATED. 104 Wilmot Road, Suite 201, Deerfield, Illinois 60015. (708) 940-8800.

NATIONAL FOUNDATION FOR PROFESSIONAL LEGAL ASSISTANTS. P.O. Box 31951, Raliegh, North Carolina 27622. (919) 821-7762.

NATIONAL PARALEGAL ASSOCIATION. P.O. Box 406, Solebury, Pennsylvania 18963. (215) 297-8333.

PROFESSIONAL LEGAL ASSISTANTS. P.O. Box 31951, Raliegh, North Carolina 27622. (919) 821-7762.

LEGAL DICTIONARIES
See: LEGAL RESEARCH

LEGAL DIRECTORIES
See also: LEGAL RESEARCH

DIRECTORIES

ALLEN'S INTERNATIONAL DIRECTORY OF ENGLISH-SPEAKING ATTORNEYS. National Legal Directory Publishing Company, Incorporated, 225 West Thirty-fourth Street, New York, New York 10122-0072. 1986.

AMERICAN BANK ATTORNEYS. Capron Publishing Company, P.O. Box 711, Wellesley Hills, Massachusetts 02181. Semiannual.

AMERICAN BAR ASSOCIATION -- DIRECTORY. American Bar Association, 750 North Lake Shore Drive, Chicago, Illinois 60611. Annual.

THE AMERICAN BAR -- THE CANADIAN BAR -- THE INTERNATIONAL BAR. Forster-Long, Incorporated, 3280 Ramos Circle, Sacramento, California 95827. Annual.

THE AMERICAN BENCH: JUDGES OF THE NATION. Third Edition, 1985/1986. Forster-Long, Incorporated, 3280 Ramos Circle, Sacramento, California 95827. Biennial.

AMERICAN DIRECTORY OF COLLECTION AGENCIES AND ATTORNEYS. Service Publishing Company, Washington Building, Fifteenth and New York Avenue, Northwest, Washington, D.C. 20005. 1977- .

AMERICAN LAWYER GUIDE TO LEADING LAW FIRMS, 1984-85. Am-Law Publishing Corporation, 2 Park Avenue, New York, New York 10016. Annual.

AMERICAN LAWYERS QUARTERLY. The American Lawyers Company, 24441 Detroit Road, Suite 200, Cleveland, Ohio 44145. Semiannual. (Monthly Supplements).

ATTORNEY'S REGISTER. Attorney's Register Publishing Company, Incorporated, 101 East Redwood Street, Baltimore, Maryland 21202. Annual.

BARRON'S GUIDE TO LAW SCHOOLS. Ninth Edition. Gary A. Munneke. Barron's Educational Series, Incorporated, 250 Wireless Boulevard, Hauppauge, New York 11788. 1990.

THE BEST LAWYERS IN AMERICA. Steven Naifeh and Gregory W. Smith. Woodward/White, Incorporated, 129 First Avenue, Southwest, Aiken, South Carolina 29801. 1991.

BEST'S DIRECTORY OF RECOMMENDED INSURANCE ATTORNEYS. A. M. Best Company, Incorporated, Ambest Road, Oldwick, New Jersey 08858. Annual.

BNA'S DIRECTORY OF STATE COURTS, JUDGES, AND CLERKS: A STATE-BY-STATE LISTING. Karmia J. King and Marilyn J. Moklin. Bureau of National Affairs, 1231 Twenty-fifth Street, Northwest, Washington, D.C. 20037. 1990.

CAMPBELL'S LIST. Campbell's List, Incorporated, P.O. Box 428, 100 East Ventris Avneue, Maitland, Florida 32751. Annual.

CANADA LEGAL DIRECTORY. Richard De Boo Publishers, 81 Curiew Drive, Dow Mills, Ontario M3A 3P7 Canada. Annual.

CAREERS IN NATURAL RESOURCES AND ENVIRONMENTAL LAW. Percy R. Luney, Jr., and edited by: William D. Henslee, Gary A. Munneke and Theodore P. Orenstein. American Bar Association, 750 North Lake Shore Drive, Chicago, Illinois 60611. 1987.

CLEARING HOUSE QUARTERLY. Attorney's National Clearing House Company, P.O. Box 8688, Naples, Florida 33941. Annual.

THE COLUMBIA LIST. Columbia Directory Company, Incorporated, 2003 Jericho Turnpike, New Hyde Park, New York 11040. Semiannual.

C-R-C ATTORNEY DIRECTORY. C-R-C Law List Company, 361 Broadway, New York, New York 10013. Annual.

DECALOGUE SOCIETY OF LAWYERS -- DIRECTORY OF MEMBERS. Decalogue Society of Lawyers, 180 West Washington Street, Chicago, Illinois 60602.

DICTIONARY OF CULPRITS AND CRIMINALS. George C. Kohn. Scarecrow Press, 52 Library Street, Box 4176, Metuchen, New Jersey 08840. 1986.

THE DIRECTORY OF BANKRUPTCY ATTORNEYS. Lynn M. LoPucki and Ann T. Reilly. Thomas Redding and Associates, P.O. Box 9039, Incline Village, Nevada 89450. 1986.

DIRECTORY OF FOREIGN LAW COLLECTIONS IN SELECTED LAW LIBRARIES. Ellen G. Schaffer and Thomas R. Bruce, Editors. Fred B. Rothman and Company, 10368 West Centennial Road, Littleton, Colorado 80127. 1991.

DIRECTORY OF LAW SCHOOL DISPUTE RESOLUTION COURSES AND PROGRAMS: A DIRECTORY OF COURSES, CLINICS, PROFESSORS, KEY CONTACTS, SAMPLE COURSE DESCRIPTIONS, AND TEACHING METHODS IN DISPUTE RESOLUTION. Carl Artman, Lethaniel Pugh, Dora I. Soria, Elizabeth Kundinger Hocking and Frederick E. Woods, Editors. American Bar Association, Standing Committee on Dispute Resolution, 1800 M Street, Northwest, Washington, D.C. 20036. 1989.

DIRECTORY OF LAW TEACHERS. Association of American Law Schools. West Publishing Company, P.O. Box 64526, 50 West Kellogg Boulevard, St. Paul, Minnesota 55164-0526. Annual.

FEDERAL JUDICIARY ALMANAC. W. Stuart Dornette and Robert R. Cross. John Wiley and Sons, Incorporated, 605 Third Avenue, New York, New York 10158. Annual.

FOREIGN COUNSEL DIRECTORY. American Corporate Counsel Association, 1225 Connecticut Avenue, Northwest, Washington, D.C. 20036. 1983.

FORWARDERS LISTS OF ATTORNEYS. Forwarders List Company, Incorporated, 101 East Redwood Street, Baltimore, Maryland 21202. Annual.

FUNDING FOR LAW: LEGAL EDUCATION, RESEARCH AND STUDY. Karen Cantrell and Denise Wallen. Oryx Press, 2214 North Central Avenue, Phoenix, Arizona 85004. 1991.

THE GENERAL BAR. General Bar, Incorporated, 20545 Center Ridge Road, Cleveland, Ohio 44116. Annual.

GUIDE TO FOREIGN LAW FIRMS. American Bar Association, Section of International Law and Practice, 750 North Lake Shore Drive, Chicago, Illinois 60611. 1988.

THE GUIDE TO NEW YORK LAW FIRMS. Erwin Cherovsky. St. Martin's Press, 175 Fifth Avenue, New York, New York 10010. 1991.

INSIDE THE LAW SCHOOLS: A GUIDE BY STUDENTS FOR STUDENTS. Fifth Edition, Revised and updated. Sally F. Goldfarb and Edward A. Adams. Plume, New York, New York. 1991.

THE INSIDER'S GUIDE TO THE TOP FIFTEEN LAW SCHOOLS. Cynthia L. Cooper. Doubleday and Company, 666 Fifth Avenue, New York, New York 10103. 1990.

INTERNATIONAL DIRECTORY OF BAR ASSOCIATIONS. Betty Sikes, Editor. American Bar Association, 750 North Lake Shore Drive, Chicago, Illinois 60611. 1983.

INTERNATIONAL LAWYERS LAW LIST. International Lawyers Company, Incorporated, Box 21, Williston Park, New York 11596. Annual.

KEYGUIDE TO INFORMATION SOURCES IN PUBLIC INTEREST LAW. Jeremy Cooper. Mansell Publishing Limited, Artillery House, Artillery Row, London SW1P 1RT, England. 1991.

KIMES INTERNATIONAL LAW DIRECTORY. International Publications Service, 242 Cherry Street, Philadelphia, Pennsylvania 19106. Annual.

LAW AND BUSINESS DIRECTORY OF CORPORATE COUNSEL. Law and Business, Incorporated, Harcourt Brace Jovanovich, Publishers, 6277 Sea Harbor Drive, Orlando, Florida 32821. Annual.

LAW AND BUSINESS DIRECTORY OF MAJOR UNITED STATES LAW FIRMS, 1984-1985. Law and Business, Incorporated, Harcourt Brace Jovanovich, Publishers, 6277 Sea Harbor Drive, Orlando, Florida 32821. 1984.

LAW AND LEGAL INFORMATION DIRECTORY. Seventh Edition. Steven Wasserman and Jacqueline O'Brien, Editors. Gale Research, Incorporated, 835 Penobscot Building, Detroit, Michigan 48226. 1992.

THE LAWYER'S ALMANAC. Law and Business, Incorporated, Harcourt Brace Jovanovich, Publishers, 6277 Sea Harbor Drive, Orlando, Florida 32821. Annual.

LAWYERS AND CREDITORS SERVICE DIRECTORY. Thomas Stetler, Editor. John Wiley and Sons, Incorporated, 605 Third Avenue, New York, New York 10158. 1990.

THE LAWYER'S LIST. Law List Publishing Company, Box 768, Danbury, Connecticut 06810. Annual.

LAWYER'S REGISTER BY SPECIALTIES AND FIELDS OF LAW. Lawyer's Register Publishing Company, 30700-H Bainbridge Road, Solen, Ohio 44139. Annual.

LIST OF BANK-RECOMMENDED ATTORNEYS. Financial Publishing Division, Rand McNally and Company, 8255 North Central Park Avenue, Skokie, Illinois 60070-2970. Annual.

MARKHAM'S NEGLIGENCE COUNSEL. Markham Publishing Corporation, 219 Atlantic Street, Stanford, Connecticut 06901. Annual.

MARTINDALE-HUBBELL LAW DIRECTORY. Martindale-Hubbell, Incorporated, 121 Chanlon Road, New Providence, New Jersey 07974. Annual.

NATIONAL DIRECTORY OF CRIMINAL LAWYERS. Barry Tarlow, Editor. National Directory of Criminal Lawyers, 9119 Sunset Boulevard, Los Angeles, California 90069. 1979.

NATIONAL DIRECTORY OF LEGAL SERVICES. Robert L. Davidson, III, Editor. Prentice-Hall, Incorporated, 113 Sylvan Avenue, Englewood Cliffs, New Jersey 07632. 1989.

NATIONAL DIRECTORY OF PROSECUTING ATTORNEYS. National District Attorneys Association, 1033 North Fairfax Street, Suite 200, Alexandria, Virginia 22314. Biennial.

NATIONAL LAW JOURNAL DIRECTORY OF THE LEGAL PROFESSION. New York Law Publishing Company, 111 Eighth Avenue, New York, New York 10011. 1984. (Periodic Supplements).

NATIONAL LIST. National List, Incorporated, 142 Joralemon Street, Suite 9B, Brooklyn Heights, New York 11201. Annual.

NATIONAL TRIAL AND DEPOSITION DIRECTORY. 421 West Franklin, Boise, Idaho 83702. 1986.

NELSON'S LAW OFFICE DIRECTORY. Nelson Company, Box 309, Hopkins, Minnesota 55343. Annual.

PHI DELTA PHI INTERNATIONAL LEGAL FRATERNITY -- ALUMNI DIRECTORY. Phi Delta Phi International Legal Fraternity, 1750 North Street, Northwest, Washington, D.C. 20036. 1980. (Irregular).

PUBLIC INTEREST LAW GROUPS: INSTITUTIONAL PROFILES. Karen O'Connor and Lee Epstein. Greenwood Publishing Group, Incorporated, 88 Post Road West, P.O. Box 5007, Westport, Connecticut 06881. 1989.

RUSSELL LAW LIST. Russel Law List, P.O. Box 1067, Naples, Forida 33939. Annual.

TOP LAW SCHOOLS: THE ULTIMATE GUIDE. Bruce S. Stuart and Kim D. Stuart. Prentice-Hall, Incorporated, 113 Sylvan Avenue, Englewood Cliffs, New Jersey 07632. 1990.

UNITED STATES BAR DIRECTORY. Attorneys National Clearing House Company, Box 8688, Naples, Florida 33941. Annual.

UNITED STATES COURT DIRECTORY. Superintendent of Documents, United States Government Printing Office, Washington, D.C. 20402. Annual.

UNITED STATES LAWYERS REFERENCE DIRECTORY. Legal Directories Publishing Company, 2122 Kidwell, P.O. Box 140200, Dallas, Texas 75214. Annual.

WANT'S FEDERAL-STATE COURT DIRECTORY. Want Publishing Company, 1511 K Street, Northwest, Washington, D.C. 20005. Annual.

WASHINGTON LOBBYISTS AND LAWYERS DIRECTORY. Communications Services, Incorporated, 121 Fourth Street, Southeast, Washington, D.C. 20003. Annual.

WASHINGTON REPRESENTATIVES: LOBBYISTS, FOREIGN AGENTS, CONSULTANTS, LEGAL ADVISORS, PUBLIC AFFAIRS AND PUBLIC RELATIONS. Columbia Books, Incorporated, 1212 New York Avenue, Northwest, Suite 330, Washington, D.C. 20005. Annual.

WHO'S WHO IN AMERICAN LAW. Sixth Edition. Marquis Who's Who, Incorporated, 3002 Glenview Road, Wilmette, Illinois 60091. 1990.

WHO'S WHO IN LAW ENFORCEMENT COLLECTING AND POLICE TRAINERS. Elizabeth Dalein Alley, Editor. Who's Who in Law Enforcement Collecting and Police Trainers, P.O. Box J-4025, New Bedford, Massachusetts 02742-0366. 1988.

WORLD DIRECTORY OF TEACHING AND RESEARCH INSTITUTIONS IN INTERNATIONAL LAW. Second Edition. UNESCO, 7 Place de Fontenoy, F-75700 Paris, France. 1990.

LEGAL DRAFTING
See: LEGAL WRITING; STATUTORY CONSTRUCTION AND DRAFTING

LEGAL EDUCATION
See also: CRITICAL LEGAL STUDIES

STATUTES, CODES, STANDARDS, UNIFORM LAWS

APPROVAL OF LAW SCHOOLS: AMERICAN BAR ASSOCIATION STANDARDS AND RULES OF PROCEDURE, AS AMENDED 1987. American Bar Association, 750 North Lake Shore Drive, Chicago, Illinois 60611. 1987.

HANDBOOKS, MANUALS, FORMBOOKS

BARRON'S GUIDE TO LAW SCHOOLS. Eighth Edition. Barron's Educational Series, Incorporated, P.O. Box 8040, Wireless Boulevard, Hauppauge, New York 11788. 1988.

CLIFFS LAW SCHOOL ADMISSION TEST: PREPARATION GUIDE. Peter Z. Orton. Cliffs Notes, Incorporated, 1701 P Street, Lincoln, Nebraska 68501. 1986.

THE COMPLETE LAW SCHOOL COMPANION: HOW TO EXCEL AT AMERICA'S MOST DEMANDING POST-GRADUATE CURRICULUM. Second Edition. Jeff Deaver. John Wiley and Sons, Incorporated, 605 Third Avenue, New York, New York 10158. 1992.

FINANCING YOUR LAW SCHOOL EDUCATION. Law School Admission Council/Law School Admission Services, P.O. Box 40, Newton, Pennsylvania 18940. 1987.

HOW TO PREPARE FOR THE NEW LAW SCHOOL ADMISSIONS TEST. Stephen Miklos. Harcourt Brace Jovanovich, Incorporated, 6277 Sea Harbor Drive, Orlando, Florida 32821. 1983.

HOW TO SUCCEED IN LAW SCHOOL. Gary A. Munneke. Barron's Educational Series, Incorporated, 250 Wireless Boulevard, Hauppauge, New York 11788. 1989.

HOW TO THRIVE IN LAW SCHOOL. John D. Calamari and Joseph M. Perillo. Hook Mountain Press, 50 Rockledge Drive, Pelham Manor, New York 10803. 1984.

INSIDE THE LAW SCHOOLS: A GUIDE BY STUDENTS FOR STUDENTS. Fourth Edition. Sally F. Goldfarb. E. P. Dutton, 375 Hudson, New York, New York 10014. 1986.

LAW SCHOOL ADMISSION TEST (LSAT): PREPARATION FOR THE NEW TEST. Thomas H. Martinson and Gino Crocetti. Arco Publishing Company, One Gulf and Western Building, New York, New York 10023. 1989.

LAW STUDENTS: HOW TO GET A JOB WHEN THERE AREN'T ANY. Carolina Academic Press, P.O. Box 8795, Forest Hills Station, Durham, North Carolina 27707. 1986.

LOOKING AT LAW SCHOOL: A STUDENT GUIDE FROM THE SOCIETY OF AMERICAN LAW TEACHERS. Third Edition. Stephen Gillers, Editor. Meridian Publishing, 40 Arlington Road, Utica, New York 13501. 1990.

LOVEJOY'S SHORTCUTS AND STRATEGIES FOR THE LSAT. Second Edition. David Tajgman. Monarch Press, 15 Columbus Circle, New York, New York 10023. 1985.

LSAT: LAW SCHOOL ADMISSION TEST: A TEST PREPARATION GUIDE. Third Edition. Randolph Z. Volkell. John Wiley and Sons, Incorporated, 605 Third Avenue, New York, New York 10158. 1983.

101 TIPS FOR SCORING HIGH ON THE LSAT. Thomas Martinson. Prentice-Hall, Incorporated, 113 Sylvan Avenue, Englewood Cliffs, New Jersey 07632. 1986.

PRELAW HANDBOOK: THE OFFICIAL GUIDE TO UNITED STATES LAW SCHOOLS. Association of American Law Schools, Law School Admission Services, Incorporated, 1201 Connecticut Avenue, Northwest, Suite 800, Washington, D.C. 20036. Annual.

A STUDENT'S GUIDE TO THE STUDY OF LAW: AN INTRODUCTION. Lewis H. LaRue. Matthew Bender and Company, Incorporated, 11 Penn Plaza, New York, New York 10001. 1987.

TEXTBOOKS AND GENERAL WORKS

ABA LAWYERING SKILLS: COURSE MATERIALS, CLIENT INSTRUCTIONS. ABA Standing Committee on Continuing Legal Education of the Bar. American Bar Association, 750 North Lake Shore Drive, Chicago, Illinois 60611. 1982.

ABA LAWYERING SKILLS: INSTRUCTOR'S MANUAL. ABA Standing Committee on Continuing Legal Education of the Bar. American Bar Association, 750 North Lake Shore Drive, Chicago, Illinois 60611. 1982.

THE AMERICAN LAW SCHOOL AND THE RISE OF ADMINISTRATIVE GOVERNMENT. William C. Chase. University of Wisconsin Press, 114 North Murray Street, Madison, Wisconsin 53706. 1982.

ANARCHY AND ELEGANCE: CONFESSIONS OF A JOURNALIST AT YALE LAW SCHOOL. Chris Goodrich. Little, Brown and Company, 34 Beacon Street, Boston, Massachusetts 02108. 1991.

CAREER PATHS STUDY. Consortium of Northeastern Area Law Schools. Harvard Law School Publications Center, 79 Garden Street, Cambridge, Massachusetts 02138. 1986.

Encyclopedia of Legal Information Sources • 2nd Ed. **LEGAL EDUCATION**

CASES: A RESOURCE GUIDE FOR TEACHING ABOUT THE LAW. R. Murray Thomas and Paul U. Murray. Scott Foresman & Company, 1900 East Lake Avenue, Glenview, Illinois 60025. 1982.

THE COMPLETE LAW SCHOOL COMPANION. Jeff Deaver. John Wiley and Sons, Incorporated, 605 Third Avenue, New York, New York 10158. 1984.

COMPUTERS AND LEGAL INSTRUCTION. American Bar Association, Section of Legal Education and Admission to the Bar, 750 North Lake Shore Drive, Chicago, Illinois 60611. 1985.

CONFERENCE ON LEGAL EDUCATION IN THE 1980'S. American Bar Association, Section of Legal Education and Admission to the Bar, 750 North Lake Shore Drive, Chicago, Illinois 60611. 1982.

THE CRITICAL LEGAL STUDIES MOVEMENT. Roberto Mangabeira Unger. Harvard University Press, 79 Garden Street, Cambridge, Massachusetts 02138. 1986.

DEAN'S LIST OF RECOMMENDED READINGS FOR PRELAW AND LAW STUDENTS. Second Edition. Julios J. Marke and Edward J. Bander. Oceana Publications, Incorporated, 75 Main Street, Dobbs Ferry, New York 10522. 1984.

A DIALOGUE ABOUT LEGAL EDUCATION AS IT APPROACHES THE TWENTY-FIRST CENTURY. J. Clark Kelso. American Bar Association, Section of Legal Education and Admissions to the Bar, 750 North Lake Shore Drive, Chicago, Illinois 60611. 1987.

THE EDUCATION OF COMPETENT LAWYERS: THE AMERICAN EXPERIENCE AND RISING EXPECTATIONS IN LAW PRACTICE AND LEGAL EDUCATION. Roger C. Cramton. American Bar Association, Section on Legal Education and Admissions to the Bar, 750 North Lake Shore Drive, Chicago, Illinois 60611. 1984.

FROM LAW STUDENT TO LAWYER: A CAREER PLANNING MANUAL. Gary Munneke. American Bar Association, Law Student Division, 750 North Lake Shore Drive, Chicago, Illinois 60611. 1984.

FULL DISCLOSURE: DO YOU REALLY WANT TO BE A LAWYER?. Susan J. Bell. American Bar Association. Young Lawyers Division. Peterson's Guides, 202 Carnegie Center, P.O. Box 2123, Princeton, New Jersey 08543-2123. 1989.

FUNDING FOR LAW: LEGAL EDUCATION, RESEARCH AND STUDY. Karen Cantrell and Denise Wallen. Oryx Press, 2214 North Central Avenue, Phoenix, Arizona 85004. 1991.

THE GLADSOME LIGHT OF JURISPRUDENCE: LEARNING THE LAW IN ENGLAND AND THE UNITED STATES IN THE EIGHTEENTH AND NINETEENTH CENTURIES. Michael H. Hoeflich, Editor. Greenwood Publishing Group, Incorporated, 88 Post Road West, P.O. Box 5007, Westport, Connecticut 06881. 1988.

THE GOALS AND MISSIONS OF LAW SCHOOLS. W. Scott Van Alstyne, Jr., Joseph R. Julin and Larry D. Barnett. Peter Lang Publishing, Incorporated, 62 West Forty-fifth Street, New York, New York 10036. 1990.

INSTITUTIONS AND METHODS OF LAW: INTRODUCTORY TEACHING MATERIALS. Jack Davies and Roberta P. Lowry. West Publishing Company, P.O. Box 64526, 50 West Kellogg Boulevard, St. Paul, Minnesota 55164-0526. 1982.

INTRODUCTION TO LEGAL METHOD AND PROCESS: CASES AND MATERIALS. Second edition. Michael A. Berch, Rebecca White Berch, and Ralph S. Spritzer. West Publishing Company, 50 West Kellogg Boulevard, St. Paul, Minnesota 55164-0526. 1992.

INTRODUCTION TO THE STUDY AND PRACTICE OF LAW IN A NUTSHELL. Kenney F. Hegland. West Publishing Company, P.O. Box 64526, 50 West Kellogg Boulevard, St. Paul, Minnesota 55164-0526. 1983.

INTRODUCTION TO THE STUDY OF LAW: CASES AND MATERIALS. John Makdisi. Anderson Publishing Company, 2035 Reading Road, Cincinnati, Ohio 45202. 1990.

LAW IN THE CLASSROOM. Revised Edition. Mary J. Turner and Lynn Parisi. Social Science Education Consortium, Incorporated, 3300 Mitchell Lane, Suite 240, Boulder, Colorado 80301-2272. 1984.

LAW SCHOOL: LEGAL EDUCATION IN AMERICA FROM THE 1850'S TO THE 1980'S. Robert Stevens. University of North Carolina Press, P.O. Box 2288, 116 South Boundary Street, Chapel Hill, North Carolina 27515-2288. 1987.

LEARNING AND EVALUATION IN LAW SCHOOL. Michael S. Josephson. Association of American Law Schools, 1201 Connecticut Avenue, Suite 800, Northwest, Washington, D.C. 20036. 1984.

LEGAL EDUCATION, 2000. John P. Grant, R. Jagtenberg and K.J. Nijkerk, Editors. Avebury, Brookfield, Vermont. 1988.

LEGAL EDUCATION AND LAWYER COMPETENCY. E. Gordon Gee and Donald W. Jackson. Brigham Young University Press, 205 University Building, Provo, Utah 84602. 1983.

LEGAL INTERVIEWING AND COUNSELING IN A NUTSHELL. Thomas L. Shaffer. West Publishing Company, P.O. Box 64526, 50 West Kellogg Boulevard, St. Paul, Minnesota 55164-0526. 1987.

LEGAL REALISM AT YALE, 1927-1960. Laura Kalman. University of North Carolina Press, P.O. Box 2288, 116 South Boundary Street, Chapel Hill, North Carolia 27515-2288. 1986.

LONG-RANGE PLANNING FOR LEGAL EDUCATION IN THE UNITED STATES: A REPORT OF THE COUNCIL OF THE AMERICAN BAR ASSOCIATION, SECTION OF LEGAL EDUCATION AND ADMISSIONS TO THE BAR. American Bar Association, 750 North Lake Shore Drive, Chicago, Illinois 60611. 1987.

MAXIMIZING THE LAW SCHOOL EXPERIENCE: A COLLECTION OF ESSAYS. Michael I. Swygert and Robert Batey. Stetson University College of Law, 1401 Sixty-first Street, South, St. Petersburg, Florida 33707. 1983.

PROPERTY LAW AND LEGAL EDUCATION: ESSAYS IN HONOR OF JOHN E. CRIBBET. Peter Hay and Michael H. Hoeflich, Editors. University of Illinois Press, 54 East Gregory Drive, Champaign, Illinois 61820. 1988.

PRUDENCE AND JURISPRUDENCE: READINGS IN THE MEANING OF LAW. Peter J. Riga. Associated Faculty Press, 19 West Thirty-sixth Street, New York, New York 10018. 1985.

RECOMMENDED PUBLICATIONS FOR LEGAL RESEARCH. Oscar J. Miller and Mortimer D. Schwartz Rothman. Fred B. Rothman and Company, 10368 West Centennial Road, Littleton, Colorado 80127. 1987.

SLAYING THE LAW SCHOOL DRAGON: HOW TO SURVIVE--AND THRIVE--IN FIRST-YEAR LAW SCHOOL. Second Edition. George Roth. John Wiley and Sons, Incorporated, 605 Third Avenue, New York, New York 10158. 1991.

STUDENT EVALUATION FOR LAW TEACHING: OBSERVATIONS, RESOURCE MATERIALS, AND A PROPOSED QUESTIONNAIRE. William Roth. Association of American Law Schools, 1201 Connecticut Avenue, Suite 800, Northwest, Washington, D.C. 20036. 1983.

A STUDY OF CONTEMPORARY LAW SCHOOL CURRICULA. William B. Powers. Office of the Consultant on Legal Education to the American Bar Association. American Bar Association, 750 North Lake Shore Drive, Chicago, Illinois 60611. 1987.

STUDYING LAW. Second edition. Phillip H. Kenny. Butterworths, 75 Clegg Road, Markham, Ontario, Canada L3R 9Y6. 1991.

STUDYING LAW: AN INTRODUCTION TO LEGAL RESEARCH. J. Clark Kelso. Matthew Bender and Company, Incorporated, 11 Penn Plaza, New York, New York 10001. 1990.

THE TEACHER IN INTERNATIONAL LAW: TEACHINGS AND TEACHING. Second edition. Manfred Lachs. Martinus Nijhoff, Kluwer Academic Publishers, 101 Philip Drive, Assinippi Park, Norwell, Massachusetts 02061. 1987.

UNDERSTANDING THE LAW: A HANDBOOK ON EDUCATING THE PUBLIC. Robert S. Peck and Charles J. White, editors. American Bar Association, Commission on Public Understanding About the Law, 750 North Lake Shore Drive, Chicago, Illinois 60611. 1983.

VIDEO, A GUIDE FOR LAWYERS. Ellen J. Miller. Law-Arts Publishers, 159 West Fifty-third Street, Number 14F, New York, New York 10019. 1983.

WINNING IN LAW SCHOOL: STRESS REDUCTION. David H. Barber. Spectra Publishing Company, Incorporated, P.O. Box 1403, Dillon, Colorado 80435. 1983.

DIGESTS, INDEXES, ABSTRACTS, CITATORS

THE GREENWOOD ANNUAL ABSTRACT OF LEGAL DISSERTATIONS AND THESES. Kenneth Brown, editor. Greenwood Publishing Group, Incorporated, 88 Post Road West, P.O. Box 5007, Westport, Connecticut 06881. Annual.

INDEX TO LAW SCHOOL ALUMNI PUBLICATIONS. Mary D. Burchill. Fred B. Rothman and Company, 10368 West Centennial Road, Littleton, Colorado 80127. Semiannual.

ANNUALS AND SURVEYS

NNUAL EXAMINATIONS IN LAW. Harvard Law School, Registrar's Office, 100 Griswold Hall, Cambridge, Massachusetts 02138. 1986.

MULTISTATE BAR EXAMINATION QUESTIONS VIII. National Conference of Bar Examiners. Lucas Brothers Publishing, 909 Lowry Mall Missouri Bookstore, Columbia, Missouri 65201. 1985.

A REVIEW OF LEGAL EDUCATION IN THE UNITED STATES FALL, 1985: LAW SCHOOLS AND BAR ADMISSION REQUIREMENTS. American Bar Association, Section of Legal Education and Admission to the Bar, 750 North Lake Shore Drive, Chicago, Illinois 60611. Annual.

LAW REVIEWS AND PERIODICALS

JOURNAL OF LAW AND EDUCATION. Jefferson Law Book Company, 408 Colorado Building, 1341 G Street, Northwest, Washington, D.C. 20005. Quarterly.

JOURNAL OF LEGAL EDUCATION. Association of American Law Schools, One Dupont Circle, Northwest, Washington, D.C. 20036. Quarterly.

LAW SCHOOL JOURNAL. Legal Institute 573, South Lake Avenue, Pasadena, California 91101. Three issues per year.

THE LEGAL STUDIES FORUM. American Legal Studies Association, Department of Legal Studies, University of Massachusetts, Amherst, Massachusetts 01003. Three issues per year.

SYLLABUS. American Bar Association, Section of Legal Education and Admissions to the Bar, 750 North Lake Shore Drive, Chicago, Illinois 60611. Quarterly.

NEWSLETTERS AND NEWSPAPERS

LAWYERING SKILLS NEWS. American Bar Association, Division of Professional Education, 750 North Lake Shore Drive, Chicago, Illinois 60611.

LEGAL EDUCATION NEWSLETTER. American Bar Association, Section of Legal Education and Admissions to the Bar, 750 North Lake Shore Drive, Chicago, Illinois 60611. Quarterly.

PASSPORT TO LEGAL UNDERSTANDING. American Bar Association, Commission on Public Understanding About the Law, 750 North Lake Shore Drive, Chicago, Illinois 60611. Semiannual.

UPDATE ON LAW-RELATED EDUCATION. American Bar Association, Special Committee on Youth Education for Citizenship, 750 North Lake Shore Drive, Chicago, Illinois 60611. Three issues per year.

DIRECTORIES

ABA CATALOG: BOOKS, PERIODICALS, PAMPHLETS, AND AUDIOVISUAL MATERIALS. American Bar Association, 750 North Lake Shore Drive, Chicago, Illinois 60611. Annual.

DIRECTORY OF INTERSCHOLASTIC MOOT COURT COMPETITIONS. Moot Court Board, National Law Center, George Washington University, Washington, D.C. 20052. 1989.

DIRECTORY OF LAW SCHOOL DISPUTE RESOLUTION COURSES AND PROGRAMS: A DIRECTORY OF COURSES, CLINICS, PROFESSORS, KEY CONTACTS, SAMPLE COURSE DESCRIPTIONS, AND TEACHING METHODS IN DISPUTE RESOLUTION. Carl Artman, Lethaniel Pugh, Dora I. Soria and Elizabeth Kundinger Hocking. American Bar Association, Standing Committee on Dispute Resolution, Governmental Affairs Group/Public Services Division, 1800 M Street, Northwest, Washington, D.C. 20036. 1989.

DIRECTORY OF LAW TEACHERS. Association of American Law Schools, 1201 Connecticut Avenue, Suite 800, Northwest, Washington, D.C. 20036. Annual.

INTERNATIONAL DIRECTORY OF LEGAL SEMINARS. S. E. Engleberg, editor. International Directory of Legal Seminars, 518 Shasta Way, Mill Valley, California 94941. 1984.

LAW AND LEGAL INFORMATION DIRECTORY. Gale Research, Incorporated, 835 Penobscot Building, Detroit, Michigan 48226. Biennial.

VIDEOLAW SEMINARS 1985-1986: CATALOG OF CONTINUING LEGAL EDUCATION VIDEOTAPE PROGRAMS. American Bar Association, Consortium for Professional Education, 750 North Lake Shore Drive, Chicago, Illinois 60611. 1985.

WORLD DIRECTORY OF TEACHING AND RESEARCH INSTITUTIONS IN INTERNATIONAL LAW. Second Edition. UNESCO, 7 Place de Fontenoy, F-75700 Paris, France. 1990.

ASSOCIATIONS AND PROFESSIONAL SOCIETIES

AMERICAN BAR ASSOCIATION. 750 North Lake Shore Drive, Chicago, Illinois 60611. (312) 988-5000.

- Committee on Continuing Legal Education of the Bar.
- Committee on Lawyer Referral and Information Service.
- Law Student Division.
- Section of Legal Education and Admission to the Bar.
- Young Lawyer's Division.

AMERICAN LAW INSTITUTE. 4025 Chestnut Street, Philadelphia, Pennsylvania 19104. (215) 243-1600.

AMERICAN LAW INSTITUTE-AMERICAN BAR ASSOCIATION, Committee on Continuing Professional Education. 4025 Chestnut Street, Philadelphia, Pennsylvania 19104. (215) 243-1600.

AMERICAN LEGAL STUDIES ASSOCIATION. c/o Law, Policy and Socidety, 305 Cushing, Northeastern University, Boston, Massachusetts 02115. (617) 437-5211.

ASSOCIATION OF AMERICAN LAW SCHOOLS. Suite 307, One Dupont Circle, Northwest, Washington, D.C. 20036. (202) 296-8851.

- Section on Administration of Law Schools
- Section on Admission to Law School
- Section on Clinical Legal Education
- Section on Legal Writing, Reasoning and Research
- Section on Teaching Law Outside Law Schools
- Section on Teaching Methods
- Section on Women in Legal Education

ASSOCIATION OF CONTINUING LEGAL EDUCATION ADMINISTRATORS. c/o American Bar Association, 750 North Lake Shore Drive, Chicago, Illinois 60611. (312) 988-6196.

CENTER FOR COMPUTER-ASSISTED LEGAL INSTRUCTION. 229 Nineteenth Avenue, South, Minneapolis, Minnesota 55455. (612) 625-3419.

CONFERENCE ON CRITICAL LEGAL STUDIES. c/o Alan Freeman, School of Law, John O'Brian Hall, Amherst Campus, State University of New York, Buffalo, New York 14260. (716) 636-3035.

COUNCIL ON LEGAL EDUCATION OPPORTUNITY. Suite 290, 1800 M Street, Northwest, Washington, D.C. 20036. (202) 785-4840.

EARL WARREN LEGAL TRAINING PROGRAM. 99 Hudson Street, Suite 1600, New York, New York 10013. (212) 219-1900.

LAW SCHOOL ADMISSION SERVICES. P.O. Box 40, Newton, Pennsylvania 18940. (215) 968-1101.

NATIONAL ASSOCIATION FOR LAW PLACEMENT. 1666 Connecticut Avenue, Northwest, Suite 450, Washington, D.C. 20009. (202) 667-1666.

ORDER OF THE COIF. c/o John Bauman, UCLA School of Law, 405 Hilgard Avenue, Los Angeles, California 90024. (213) 825-4739.

PRACTICING LAW INSTITUTE. 810 Seventh Avenue, New York, New York 10019. (212) 765-5700.

SOCIETY OF AMERICAN LAW TEACHERS. c/o Charles R. Lawrence, School of Law, Stanford University, Palo Alto, California 94305. (415) 723-3627.

RESEARCH CENTERS, INSTITUTES, CLEARINGHOUSES

CALIFORNIA CENTER FOR JUDICIAL EDUCATION AND RESEARCH. 2000 Powell Street, Eighth Floor, Emeryville, California 94608. (415) 464-3828.

CENTER FOR CONTINUING PROFESSIONAL DEVELOPMENT. Louisiana State University, Room 275, Paul M. Hepert Law Center, Baton Rouge, Louisiana 70803. (504) 388-5837.

CONTINUING EDUCATION IN LAW AND TAXATION. New York University, 11 West Forty-second Street, Room 429, New York, New York 10036. (212) 790-1320.

LEGAL EDUCATION

INSTITUTE FOR CONTINUING LEGAL EDUCATION. One Constitution Square, New Brunswick, New Jersey 08901. (201) 249-5100.

INSTITUTE OF CONTINUING LEGAL EDUCATION. 1020 Greene Street, University of Michigan, Ann Arbor, Michigan 48109. (313) 764-0533.

PRACTICING LAW INSTITUTE. 810 Seventh Avenue, New York, New York 10019. (212) 765-5700.

PUBLIC LAW EDUCATION INSTITUTE. 1601 Connecticut Avenue, Northwest, Washington, D.C. 20009. (202) 232-1400.

ONLINE DATABASES

ABA/NET. American Bar Association, 750 North Lake Shore Drive, Chicago, Illinois 60611.

LEGAL ETHICS AND MALPRACTICE
See also: PROFESSIONAL ETHICS AND LIABILITY

STATUTES, CODES, STANDARDS, UNIFORM LAWS

ANNOTATED MODEL RULES OF PROFESSIONAL CONDUCT. American Bar Association, 750 North Lake Shore Drive, Chicago, Illinois 60611. 1985.

THE LEGISLATIVE HISTORY OF THE MODEL RULES OF PROFESSIONAL CONDUCT: THEIR DEVELOPMENT IN THE AMERICAN BAR ASSOCIATION HOUSE OF DELEGATES. Center for Professional Responsibility. American Bar Association, 750 North Lake Shore Drive, Chicago, Illinois 60611. 1987.

MODEL RULES OF PROFESSIONAL CONDUCT AND CODE OF JUDICIAL CONDUCT. Martindale-Hubbell, Incorporated, 121 Chanlon Road, New Providence, New Jersey 07974. Annual.

REGULATION OF LAWYERS: STATUTES AND STANDARDS WITH RECENT SUPREME COURT DECISIONS, 1991. Stephen Gillers and Roy D. Simon, Jr. Little, Brown and Company, 34 Beacon Street, Boston, Massachusetts 02108. 1991.

RESTATEMENT OF THE LAW, THE LAW GOVERNING LAWYERS. COUNCIL DRAFT. American Law Institute-American Bar Association, 4025 Chestnut Street, Philadelphia, Pennsylvania 19104. 1989- .

RULES OF PROCEDURE, AMERICAN BAR ASSOCIATION STANDING COMMITTEE ON ETHICS AND PROFESSIONAL RESPONSIBILITY. Martindale-Hubbell Law Directory, Volume Eight, Martindale-Hubbell, Incorporated, 121 Chanlon Road, New Providence, New Jersey 07974. Annual.

SELECTED STATUTES, RULES, AND STANDARDS ON THE LEGAL PROFESSION. West Publishing Company, P.O. Box 64526, 50 West Kellogg Boulevard, St. Paul, Minnesota 55164-0526. 1991.

STANDARDS OF PROFESSIONAL CONDUCT FOR LAWYERS AND JUDGES. Norman Redlich. Little, Brown, and Company, 34 Beacon Street, Boston, Massachusetts 02108. 1984.

LOOSELEAF SERVICES AND REPORTERS

ABA/BNA LAWYERS' MANUAL ON PROFESSIONAL CONDUCT. Bureau of National Affairs, 1231 Twenty-fifth Street, Northwest, Washington, D.C. 20037. 1984- .

ATTORNEY MALPRACTICE: PREVENTION AND DEFENSE. Dennis J. Horn and George W. Spellmire. Garland Publishing, Incorporated, 136 Madison Avenue, New York, New York 10016. 1985. (Periodic Supplements).

CRIMINAL DEFENSE ETHICS: LAW AND LIABILITY. John M. Burkoff. Clark Boardman Company, Limited, 435 Hudson Street, New York, New York 10014. 1991- .

FORMAL AND INFORMAL ETHICS OPINIONS. American Bar Association, Committee on Ethics and Professional Responsibility, 750 North Lake Shore Drive, Chicago, Illinois 60611. 1985.

INFORMAL ETHICS OPINIONS, VOLUMES 1 AND 2. American Bar Association, Committee on Ethics and Professional Responsibility, 750 North Lake Shore Drive, Chicago, Illinois 60611. 1975.

THE LAW OF LAWYERING: A HANDBOOK ON THE MODEL RULES OF PROFESSIONAL CONDUCT. Second Edition. Geoffrey C. Hazard, Jr. and W. William Hodes. Prentice-Hall, Incorporated, 113 Sylvan Avenue, Englewood Cliffs, New Jersey 07632. 1990- .

LEGAL MALPRACTICE REPORTER. The Michie Company, P.O. Box 7587, Charlottesville, Virginia 22906-7582. 1976- .

NATIONAL REPORTER ON LEGAL ETHICS AND PROFESSIONAL RESPONSIBILITY. University Publications of America, 4520 East West Highway, Suite 600, Bethesda, Maryland 20814. 1982- .

OPINIONS ON PROFESSIONAL ETHICS. American Bar Association, Committee on Ethics and Professional Responsibility, 750 North Lake Shore Drive, Chicago, Illinois 60611. 1967.

RECENT ETHICS OPINIONS. American Bar Association, Committee on Ethics and Professional Responsibility, 750 North Lake Shore Drive, Chicago, Illinois 60611. 1985- .

REPORTER ON THE LEGAL PROFESSION. Legal-Medical Studies, Incorporated, P.O. Box 8219, JFK Station, Boston, Massachusetts 02114. 1979- .

HANDBOOKS, MANUALS, FORMBOOKS

FEDERAL ETHICS HANDBOOK. The Michie Company, P.O. Box 7587, Charlottesville, Virginia 22906-7582. 1981. (Supplement 1984).

HANDBOOK OF PROFESSIONAL CONDUCT FOR SOLICITORS. Frances Silverman. Butterworth Legal Publishers, 90 Stiles Road, Salem, New Hampshire 03079. 1989.

HOW TO AVOID BEING SUED BY YOUR CLIENT: PREVENTION AND CURES FOR LEGAL MALPRACTICE. Thomas P. Brown. American Bar Association, Section of Economics of Law Practice, 750 North Lake Shore Drive, Chicago, Illinois 60611. 1981.

THE LAW OF LAWYERING: A HANDBOOK ON THE MODERN RULES OF PROFESSIONAL CONDUCT. Geoffrey C. Hazard, Jr. and W. William Hodes. Law and Business, Harcourt Brace Jovanovich, Incorporated, 6277 Sea Harbor Drive, Orlando, Florida 32821. 1985. (Supplements).

A LAWYER'S GUIDE TO LEGAL MALPRACTICE INSURANCE. Jo Ann Felix. American Bar Association, Standing Committee on Lawyer's Professional Liability, 750 North Lake Shore Drive, Chicago, Illinois 60611. 1988.

A PRACTICAL GUIDE TO PREVENTING LEGAL MALPRACTICE. Duke N. Stern and Jo Ann Felix-Retzke. Shepard's/McGraw-Hill, P.O. Box 1235, Colorado Springs, Colorado 80901. 1983.

TEXTBOOKS AND GENERAL WORKS

AMERICAN LAWYERS AND THEIR COMMUNITIES: ETHICS IN THE LEGAL PROFESSION. Thomas L. Shaffer and Mary M. Shaffer. University of Notre Dame Press, Notre Dame, Indiana 46556. 1991.

A CASE FOR LEGAL ETHICS: LEGAL ETHICS AS A SOURCE FOR A UNIVERSAL ETHIC. Vincent Luizzi. State University of New York Press, State University Plaza, Albany, New York 12246. 1992.

CASES AND MATERIALS ON THE PROFESSIONAL RESPONSIBILITY OF LAWYERS. John F. Sutton, Jr. and John S. Dzienkowski. West Publishing Company, 50 West Kellogg Boulevard, St. Paul, Minnesota 55164. 1989.

CHARACTERISTICS OF LEGAL MALPRACTICE: REPORT OF THE NATIONAL LEGAL MALPRACTICE DATA CENTER. William H. Gates and Sheree L. Swetin. National Legal Malpractice Data Center. American Bar Association, 750 North Lake Shore Drive, Chicago, Illinois 60611. 1989.

CONFLICTS OF INTEREST IN LEGAL REPRESENTATION. Robert J. Jossen. Practising Law Institute, 810 Seventh Avenue, New York, New York 10019. 1988.

ETHICAL PROBLEMS IN FEDERAL TAX PRACTICE. Second Edition. Bernard Wolfman and James P. Holden. The Michie Company, P.O. Box 7587, Charlottesville, Virginia 22906-7587. 1985.

ETHICS AND THE PRACTICE OF LAW. David E. Schrader. Prentice-Hall, Incorporated, 113 Sylvan Avenue, Englewood Cliffs, New Jersey 07632. 1988.

ETHICS COMPLIANCE FOR BUSINESS LAWYERS. Brooke Wunnicke. John Wiley and Sons, Incorporated, 605 Third Avenue, New York, New York 10158. 1987.

ETHICS FOR THE LEGAL ASSISTANT. Deborah K. Orlik. Scott, Foresman, and Company, 1900 East Lake Avenue, Glenview, Illinois 60025. 1986.

THE GOOD LAWYER: LAWYERS' ROLES AND LAWYERS' ETHICS. David Luban, Editor. Rowman and Allanheld, Division of Littlefield, Adams and Company, 420 Boston Way, Lanham, Maryland 20706. 1984.

THE JUDICIAL RESPONSE TO LAWYERS MISCONDUCT. American Bar Association, 750 North Lake Shore Drive, Chicago, Illinois 60611. 1984.

THE LAW AND ETHICS OF LAWYERING. Geoffrey C. Hazard, Jr. and Susan P. Koniak. Foundation Press, 615 Merrick Avenue, Westbury, New York 11590. 1990.

LAW FIRM BREAKUPS: THE LAW AND ETHICS OF GRABBING AND LEAVING. Robert W. Hillman. Little, Brown and Company, 34 Beacon Street, Boston, Massachusetts 02108. 1990.

LAWYERS AND JUSTICE: AN ETHICAL STUDY. David Luban. University of Maryland, College Park. Institute for Philosophy and Public Policy. Princeton University Press, 41 William Street, Princeton, New Jersey 08540. 1988.

LAWYERS' IDEALS/LAWYERS' PRACTICES: TRANSFORMATIONS IN THE AMERICAN LEGAL SYSTEM. Robert L. Nelson, David M. Trubek and Rayman L. Solomon. Cornell University Press, 124 Roberts Place, Ithaca, New York 14850. 1992.

LEGAL ETHICS. Kenneth Kipnis. Prentice-Hall, Incorporated, 113 Sylvan Avenue, Englewood Cliffs, New Jersey 07632. 1986.

LEGAL ETHICS: CASES AND MATERIALS. David Luban and Deborah L. Rhode. Foundation Press, 615 Merrick Avenue, Westbury, New York 11590. 1992.

LEGAL ETHICS: EVERYTHING A LAWYER NEEDS TO KNOW AND SHOULD NOT BE AFRAID TO ASK. Jonathan J. Lerner. Practising Law Institute, 810 Seventh Avenue, New York, New York 10019. 1988.

LEGAL ETHICS, 1990: WHAT EVERY LAWYER NEEDS TO KNOW. Robert J. Jossen and Jonathan J. Lerner. Practising Law Institute, 810 Seventh Avenue, New York, New York 10019. 1990.

LEGAL ETHICS: THE LAW OF PROFESSIONAL RESPONSIBILITY. Third Edition. L. Ray Patterson with Thomas B. Metzloff. Matthew Bender and Company, Incorporated, 11 Penn Plaza, New York, New York 10001. 1989.

LEGAL MALPRACTICE. Third Edition. Ronald E. Mallen and Jeffrey M. Smith. West Publishing Company, P.O. Box 64526, 50 West Kellogg Boulevard, St. Paul, Minnesota 55164-0526. 1989.

LEGAL MALPRACTICE PREVENTION AND DEFENSE. Dennis J. Horan and George W. Spellmire. Gower Publishing Company, Old Post Road, Brookfield, Vermont 05036. 1985.

THE LEGAL PROFESSION: RESPONSIBILITY AND REGULATION. Second Edition. Geoffrey C. Hazard, Jr. and Deborah L. Rhode, Editors. Foundation Press, 615 Merrick Avenue, Westbury, New York 11590. 1988.

LIBERTY, JUSTICE, AND MORALS: CONTEMPORARY VALUE CONFLICTS. Third Edition. Burton M. Leiser. Macmillan Publishing Company, Incorporated, 866 Third Avenue, New York, New York 10022. 1986.

THE LITIGATION EXPLOSION: WHAT HAPPENED WHEN AMERICA UNLEASHED THE LAWSUIT. Walter K. Olson. E.P. Dutton, 375 Hudson Street, New York, New York 10014. 1991.

MALICE AFORETHOUGHT: HOW LAWYERS USE OUR SECRET RULES TO GET RICH, GET SEX, GET EVEN-- AND GET AWAY WITH IT. David W. Marston. William Morrow and Company, 105 Madison Avenue, New York, New York 10016. 1991.

MORAL VISION AND PROFESSIONAL DECISIONS: THE CHANGING VALUES OF WOMEN AND MEN LAWYERS. Rand Jack and Dana Crowley Jack. Cambridge University Press, 40 West Twentieth Street, New York, New York 10011. 1989.

MULTIDISCIPLINARY PARTNERSHIPS: NON-LEGAL BUSINESS AFFILIATES OF LAW FIRMS. Mortimer Caplin and James W. Jones. Prentice-Hall, Incorporated, 113 Sylvan Avenue, Englewood Cliffs, New Jersey 07632. 1990.

ORGANIZING SUCCESSFUL CLIENT SEMINARS. Michael L. Goldblatt. American Bar Association, Section of Law Practice Management, 750 North Lake Shore Drive, Chicago, Illinois 60611. 1990.

PRACTICAL ISSUES OF PROFESSIONAL RESPONSIBILITY IN THE PRACTICE OF LAW. Legal-Medical Studies, Incorporated, P.O. Box 8219, JFK Station, Boston, Massachusetts 02114. 1984.

PREVENTING LEGAL MALPRACTICE. Jeffrey M. Smith and Ronald E. Mallen. West Publishing Company, 50 West Kellogg Boulevard, St. Paul, Minnesota 55164. 1989.

PROBLEMS AND MATERIALS ON PROFESSIONAL RESPONSIBILITY. Fifth Edition. Thomas D. Morgan and Ronald D. Rotunda. Foundation Press, 615 Merrick Avenue, Westbury, New York 11590. 1991.

PROBLEMS IN LEGAL ETHICS. Second Edition. Mortimer D. Schwartz and Richard C. Wydick. West Publishing Company, 50 West Kellogg Boulevard, St. Paul, Minnesota 55164. 1988.

PROBLEMS IN PROFESSIONAL RESPONSIBILITY. Third Edition. Andrew L. Kaufman. Little, Brown and Company, 34 Beacon Street, Boston, Massachusetts 02108. 1989.

PROFESSIONAL CONDUCT FOR CANADIAN LAWYERS. Beverley G. Smith. Butterworths, 75 Clegg Road, Markham, Ontario, Canada L3R 9Y6. 1989.

PROFESSIONAL LIABILITY INSURANCE COVERAGE PROBLEMS: ATTORNEYS, ACCOUNTANTS, AND INSURANCE BROKERS. David I. Ichel, Chairman. Practising Law Institute, 810 Seventh Avenue, New York, New York 10019. 1984.

PROFESSIONAL RESPONSIBILITY. Third Edition. Ronald D. Rotunda. West Publishing Company, P.O. Box 64526, 50 West Kellogg Boulevard, St. Paul, Minnesota 55164-0526. 1992.

PROFESSIONAL RESPONSIBILITY IN A NUTSHELL. Second Edition. Robert H., Aronson and Donald T. Weckstein. West Publishing Company, P.O. Box 64526, 50 West Kellogg Boulevard, St. Paul, Minnesota 55164-0526. 1991.

PROFESSIONAL RESPONSIBILITY OF THE CRIMINAL LAWYER. John Wesley Hall, Jr. Lawyers Cooperative Publishing Company, Aqueduct Building, Rochester, New York 14694. 1987.

RASCALS: THE SELLING OF THE LEGAL PROFESSION. Peter Megargee Brown. Benchmark Press, 701 Congressional Boulevard, Suite 340, Carmel, Indiana 46032. 1989.

RECENT DEVELOPMENTS IN ATTORNEY'S LIABILITY. Litigation Research Group, 500 Howard Street, San Francisco, California 94105. 1986.

REGULATION OF LAWYERS: PROBLEMS OF LAW AND ETHICS. Second Edition. Stephen Gillers and Norman Dorsen. Little, Brown and Company, 34 Beacon Street, Boston, Massachusetts 02108. 1989.

THE REGULATION OF PARALEGALS: ETHICS, PROFESSIONAL RESPONSIBILITY, AND OTHER FORMS OF CONTROL. William P. Statsky. West Publishing Company, 50 West Kellogg Boulevard, St. Paul, Minnesota 55164. 1987.

SERVING TWO MASTERS: THE LAW OF LAWYER DISQUALIFICATION. Leonard H. Gilbert. American Bar Association, Section of General Practice, 750 North Lake Shore Drive, Chicago, Illinois 60611. 1984.

THE SOCIAL RESPONSIBILITIES OF LAWYERS: CASE STUDIES. Philip B. Heymann and Lance Liebman. Foundation Press, 615 Merrick Avenue, Westbury, New York 11590. 1988.

TRIAL ETHICS. Richard H. Underwood and William H. Fortune. Little, Brown and Company, 34 Beacon Street, Boston, Massachusetts 02108. 1988.

ANNUALS AND SURVEYS

ANNUAL WORKSHOP ON LAWYER'S PROFESSIONAL RESPONSIBILITY. American Bar Association, 750 North Lake Shore Drive, Chicago, Illinois 60611. Annual.

SURVEY OF LAWYER DISCIPLINARY PROCEDURES IN THE UNITED STATES. American Bar Association, Center for Professional Responsibility, 750 North Lake Shore Drive, Chicago, Illinois 60611. 1984.

DIGESTS, INDEXES, ABSTRACTS, CITATORS

SHEPARD'S PROFESSIONAL AND JUDICIAL CONDUCT CITATIONS. Shepard's/McGraw-Hill, P.O. Box 1235, Colorado Springs, Colorado 80901. 1991.

NEWSLETTERS AND NEWSPAPERS

ATLA PROFESSIONAL NEGLIGENCE LAW REPORTER. Association of Trial Lawyers of America, 1050 Thirty-first Street, Northwest, Washington, D.C. 20007. Monthly.

LAWYER'S LIABILITY REVIEW. The Line Publishing Company, Incorporated, P.O. Box 1435, Bellevue, Washington 98009. Monthly.

LAWYER'S PROFESSIONAL LIABILITY UPDATE. American Bar Association, Standing Committee on Lawyer's Professional Liability, 750 North Lake Shore Drive, Chicago, Illinois 60611. Annual.

MALPRACTICE PREVENTION REPORTER FOR THE LEGAL PROFESSION. Duke, Nordlinger, Stern and Associates, Incorporated, 1336 Fifty-fourth Avenue, Northeast, St. Petersburg, Florida 33703. Quarterly.

THE MALPRACTICE REPORTER. Public Reporting Services, Incorporated, 496A Hudson Street, New York, New York 10014. Bimonthly.

PROFESSIONAL LIABILITY NEWSLETTER. Professional Liability Newsletter, P.O. Box 834, Berkeley, California 94701. Monthly.

PROFESSIONAL LIABILITY REPORTER. Shepard's/McGraw-Hill, Incorporated, 420 North Cascade Avenue, Colorado Springs, Colorado 80903. Monthly.

BIBLIOGRAPHIES

BIBLIOGRAPHY OF LEGAL ARTICLES, TEXTBOOKS, AND TREATISES ON PROFESSIONAL RESPONSIBILITY, 1970-1983. American Bar Association, Center for Professional Responsibility, 750 North Lake Shore Drive, Chicago, Illinois 60611. 1984.

LEGAL ETHICS: AN ANNOTATED BIBLIOGRAPHY AND RESOURCE GUIDE. Frederick A. Elliston and Jane Van Shaick. Fred B. Rothman and Company, 10368 West Centennial Road, Littleton, Colorado 80127. 1984.

DIRECTORIES

IF YOU WANT TO SUE A LAWYER-- A DIRECTORY OF LEGAL MALPRACTICE ATTORNEYS. Kay Ostberg and Theresa Meehan Rudy. Random House, Incorporated, 201 East Fiftieth Street, New York, New York 10022. 1991.

ASSOCIATIONS AND PROFESSIONAL SOCIETIES

AMERICAN BAR ASSOCIATION, 750 North Lake Shore Drive, Chicago, Illinois 60611. (312) 988-5000.

- Commission on Advertising.
- Committee on Ethics and Professional Responsibility.
- Committee on Lawyer's Professional Liability.
- Committee on Lawyer's Responsibility for Client Protection.
- Committee on Professional Discipline.
- Consortium on Professional Competence.
- Special Committee on Implementation of Model Rules.

ASSOCATION OF AMERICAN LAW SCHOOLS, SECTION ON PROFESSIONAL RESPONSIBILITY. One Dupont Circle, Northwest, Washington, D.C. 20036. (202) 296-8851.

RESEARCH CENTERS, INSTITUTES, CLEARINGHOUSES

AMERICAN BAR ASSOCIATION, CENTER FOR PROFESSIONAL RESPONSIBILITY. 750 North Lake Shore Drive, Chicago, Illinois 60611. (312) 988-5000.

ONLINE DATABASES

ABA/NET. American Bar Association, 750 North Lake Shore Drive, Chicago, Illinois 60611.

LEXIS, ABA LIBRARY. American Bar Association, Mead Data Central, Incorporated, P.O. Box 933, Dayton, Ohio 45401.

WESTLAW, ABA FILE. American Bar Association, West Publishing Company, P.O. Box 64526, 50 West Kellogg Boulevard, St. Paul, Minnesota 55164-0526.

AUDIOVISUALS

APPLYING THE MODEL RULES OF PROFESSIONAL CONDUCT. Practising Law Institute, 810 Seventh Avenue, New York, New York 10019. 1984. Videotape.

ATTORNEY-CLIENT RELATIONS. American Bar Association, 750 North Lake Shore Drive, Chicago, Illinois 60611. 1989. Videotape.

AUDIOVISUAL MATERIALS ON PROFESSIONAL RESPONSIBILITY. Roger C. Cramton and Matthew R. Carnevale. American Bar Association, Committee on Lawyer Independence and Professional Responsibility, 1800 M Street, Northwest, Washington, D.C. 20036. 1987.

CLIENT CONFIDENTIALITY. American Bar Association, 750 North Lake Shore Drive, Chicago, Illinois 60611. 1989. Videotape.

CONFLICTS OF INTEREST. American Bar Association, 750 North Lake Shore Drive, Chicago, Illinois 60611. 1989. Videotape.

ETHICAL DILEMMAS AND PROFESSIONALISM. American Bar Association, 750 North Lake Shore Drive, Chicago, Illinois 60611. 1989. Videotape.

HOW TO PREVENT LEGAL MALPRACTICE. American Bar Association, 750 North Lake Shore Drive, Chicago, Illinois 60611. 1989. Videotape.

INDEPENDENCE OF COUNSEL. American Bar Association, 750 North Lake Shore Drive, Chicago, Illinois 60611. 1989. Videotape.

LAWYER ADVERTISING: HOW FAR CAN REGULATION GO? American Bar Association, 750 North Lake Shore Drive, Chicago, Illinois 60611. 1990. Videotape.

LEGAL ADVERTISING: OF THE PEOPLE, BY THE PEOPLE, FOR THE PEOPLE. American Bar Association, 750 North Lake Shore Drive, Chicago, Illinois 60611. 1985. Videotape.

LEGAL ETHICS - APPLYING THE MODEL RULES. American Bar Association, Consortium for Professional Education, 750 North Lake Shore Drive, Chicago, Illinois 60611. 1984. Videotape.

LEGAL ETHICS AND MALPRACTICE

PREVENTING LEGAL MALPRACTICE. American Bar Association, 750 North Lake Shore Drive, Chicago, Illinois 60611. 1987. Videotape.

PROFESSIONAL RESPONSIBILITY. Center for Computer-Assisted Instruction, 229 19th Avenue South, University of Minnesota, Minneapolis, Minnesota 55455. Interactive videodisc.

UNDERSTANDING MODERN ETHICAL STANDARDS. National Institute for Trial Advocacy, Notre Dame Law School, Notre Dame, Indiana 46556. 1985. Videotape.

WHAT WENT WRONG? CONVERSATIONS WITH DISCIPLINED LAWYERS. Weil Productions, 1563 Yorkshire, Birmingham, Michigan 48008. 1985. Video Cassette.

COMPUTER-ASSISTED LEGAL INSTRUCTION

CODE OF PROFESSIONAL RESPONSIBILITY I. Kenneth R. Kirwin and Roger C. Park. Center for Computer-Assisted Instruction, 229 19th Avenue South, University of Minnesota, Minneapolis, Minnesota 55455. Machine-readable computer file.

CODE OF PROFESSIONAL RESPONSIBILITY II. Kenneth R. Kirwin and Roger C. Park. Center for Computer-Assisted Instruction, 229 19th Avenue South, University of Minnesota, Minneapolis, Minnesota 55455. Machine-readable computer file.

DECISIONS BEFORE TRIAL. Robert E. Keeton and Kenneth K. Kirwin. Center for Computer-Assisted Instruction, 229 19th Avenue South, University of Minnesota, Minneapolis, Minnesota 55455. Machine-readable computer file.

DEFENSE FUNCTION-CODE OF PROFESSIONAL RESPONSIBILITY VERSION. Kenneth K. Kirwin and Roger C. Park. Center for Computer-Assisted Instruction, 229 19th Avenue South, University of Minnesota, Minneapolis, Minnesota 55455. Machine-readable computer file.

DEFENSE FUNCTION-RULES OF PROFESSIONAL CONDUCT VERSION. Kenneth K. Kirwin and Roger C. Park. Center for Computer-Assisted Instruction, 229 19th Avenue South, University of Minnesota, Minneapolis, Minnesota 55455. Machine-readable computer file.

MODEL RULES OF PROFESSIONAL CONDUCT I: PRELIMINARY DRILL. Kenneth K. Kirwin and Roger C. Park. Center for Computer-Assisted Instruction, 229 19th Avenue South, University of Minnesota, Minneapolis, Minnesota 55455. Machine-readable computer file.

MODEL RULES OF PROFESSIONAL CONDUCT II: QUESTIONS AND PROBLEMS. Kenneth K. Kirwin and Roger C. Park. Center for Computer-Assisted Instruction, 229 19th Avenue South, University of Minnesota, Minneapolis, Minnesota 55455. Machine-readable computer file.

LEGAL FORMS

HANDBOOKS, MANUALS, FORMBOOKS

AMERICAN JURISPRUDENCE LEGAL FORMS ANNOTATED. Lawyers Cooperative Publishing Company, Aqueduct Building, Rochester, New York 14694. 1953- .

AMERICAN JURISPRUDENCE PLEADING AND PRACTICE FORMS ANNOTATED. Lawyers Cooperative Publishing Company, Aqueduct Building, Rochester, New York 14694. 1966- .

ANNOTATED TAX FORMS: PRACTICE AND PROCEDURE. Sidney I. Roberts, Sanford H. Goldberg, and Martin J. Rabinowitz. Prentice-Hall, Incorporated, 113 Sylvan Avenue, Englewood Cliffs, New Jersey 07632. 1969- .

BASIC BOOK OF BUSINESS AGREEMENTS. Arnold S. Goldstein. Enterprise Publishing Company, 725 Market Street, Wilmington, Delaware 19801. 1983- .

BASIC LEGAL FORMS, WITH COMMENTARY. Marvin T. Hyman. Research Institute of America, Incorporated, One Penn Plaza, New York, New York 10119. 1981- .

BASIC LEGAL TRANSACTIONS. Vincent DiLorenzo. Research Institute of America, Incorporated, One Penn Plaza, New York, New York 10119. 1985. (Supplements).

BENDER'S FEDERAL PRACTICE FORMS: ANNOTATIONS AND CROSS-REFERENCES TO MOORE'S FEDERAL PRACTICE. Second Edition. Louis R. Frumer, Irwin Hall, and Marvin Waxner. Matthew Bender and Company, Incorporated, 11 Penn Plaza, New York, New York 10001. 1982.

BENDER'S FORMS FOR THE CIVIL PRACTICE, WITH EXPLANATORY NOTES AND CROSS-REFERENCES. Louis R. Frumer and Oscar L. Warren. Matthew Bender and Company, Incorporated, 11 Penn Plaza, New York, New York 10001. 1976- .

BENDER'S FORMS OF DISCOVERY. Matthew Bender and Company, Incorporated, 11 Penn Plaza, New York, New York 10001. 1963- .

BUSINESS FORMS AND CONTRACTS (IN PLAIN ENGLISH) FOR CRAFTSPEOPLE. Leonard D. DuBoff. Madrona Publishers, P.O. Box 51245, Palo Alto, California 94303. 1986.

BUSINESS FORMS FROM ALI-ABA COURSE MATERIALS. American Law Institute-American Bar Association, Committee on Continuing Professional Education, 4025 Chestnut Street, Philadelphia, Pennsylvania 19104. 1983- .

BUSINESS INVESTMENT AND LOAN AGREEMENTS: FORMS AND AUTHORITIES. Herbert B. Max. Law and Business, Harcourt Brace Jovanovich, Incorporated, 6277 Sea Harbor Drive, Orlando, Florida 32821. 1985- .

CABLE TELEVISION: HANDBOOK AND FORMS. Ira C. Stein. Shepard's/McGraw-Hill, P.O. Box 1235, Colorado Springs, Colorado 80901. 1985.

COLLIER FORMS MANUAL. Third Edition. Arthur L. Moller. Matthew Bender and Company, Incorporated, 11 Penn Plaza, New York, New York 10001. 1979- .

COMPLETE BOOK OF CORPORATE FORMS. Ted Nicholas. Enterprise Publishing Company, 725 Market Street, Wilmington, Delaware 19801. 1980- .

THE COMPLETE BOOK OF LEGAL FORMS AND AGREEMENTS. Charles B. Chernofsky and Griffith G. deNoyelles, Jr. Round Lake Publishing Company, 30 Bailey Avenue, Ridgefield, Connecticut 06877. 1991.

CONDOMINIUM LAW AND PRACTICE: FORMS. Patrick J. Rohan and Melvin A. Reskin. Matthew Bender and Company, Incorporated, 11 Penn Plaza, New York, New York 10001. 1965- .

CORPORATION FORMS. Prentice-Hall, Incorporated, 113 Sylvan Avenue, Englewood Cliffs, New Jersey 07632. 1961- .

CURRENT LEASING LAW AND TECHNIQUES: FORMS. Patrick J. Rohan. Matthew Bender and Company, Incorporated, 11 Penn Plaza, New York, New York 10001. 1982- .

CURRENT LEGAL FORMS WITH TAX ANALYSIS. Jacob Rabkin and Mark H. Johnson. Matthew Bender and Company, Incorporated, 11 Penn Plaza, New York, New York 10001. 1948- .

DATA PROCESSING AGREEMENTS. W. A. Hancock, Editor. Business Laws, Incorporated, 11630 Chillicothe Road, Chesterland, Ohio 44026. 1984- .

DRAFTING THE DURABLE POWER OF ATTORNEY. Francis J. Collins, Jr. R. P. W. Publishing Company, P.O. Box 1108, Lexington, South Carolina 29072. 1984- .

DWI DEFENSE FORMS AND CHECKLISTS. John A. Tarantino. James Publishing Company, 3520 Cadillac Avenue, Costa Mesa, California 92626. 1984- .

EVERYDAY LEGAL FORMS. Irving J. Sloan. Oceana Publications, Incorporated, 75 Main Street, Dobbs Ferry, New York 10522. 1984.

FEDERAL FORMS. Royanne R. Hollins. James Publishing, 3520 Cadillac Avenue, Costa Mesa, California 92626. 1986.

FEDERAL PROCEDURAL FORMS. Lawyers Cooperative Publishing Company, Aqueduct Building, Rochester, New York 14694. 1975- .

FEDERAL SECURITIES ACT: ANALYSIS, PROCEDURE, AND FORMS. Hugh L. Soward. Matthew Bender and Company, Incorporated, 11 Penn Plaza, New York, New York 10001. 1965- .

FEDERAL TAX FORMS. Commerce Clearing House, Incorporated, 4025 West Peterson Avenue, Chicago, Illinois 60646. 1973- .

FEDERAL TAX FORMS. West Publishing Company, P.O. Box 64526, 50 West Kellogg Boulevard, St. Paul, Minnesota 55164-0526. 1982- .

FORMS AND AGREEMENTS FOR ARCHITECTS, ENGINEERS, AND CONTRACTORS. Albert Dib. Clark Boardman Company, Limited, 435 Hudson Street, New York, New York 10014. 1976- .

FORMS AND AGREEMENTS ON INTELLECTUAL PROPERTY AND INTERNATIONAL LICENSING. Third Edition. L. W. Melville. Clark Boardman Company, Limited, 435 Hudson Street, New York, New York 10014. 1979- .

FORMS AND PROCEDURES UNDER THE UNIFORM COMMERCIAL CODE. Federick M. Hart and William F. Willier. Matthew Bender and Company, Incorporated, 11 Penn Plaza, New York, New York 10001. 1963- .

FORMS OF COMMERCIAL AGREEMENTS. Herbert Schlagman. Gower Publishing Company, Old Post Road, Brookfield, Vermont 05036. 1986.

FORMS OF COMMERCIAL AGREEMENTS OF THE WORLD. Oceana Publications, Incorporated, 75 Main Street, Dobbs Ferry, New York 10522. 1984- .

HANDBOOK OF PERSONAL INJURY FORMS AND LITIGATION MATERIALS. Edward M. Swartz and Fredric A. Swartz. Lawyers Cooperative Publishing Company, Aqueduct Building, Rochester, New York 14694. 1982- .

INSTANT LEGAL FORMS: READY-TO-USE DOCUMENTS FOR ALMOST ANY OCCASION. Ralph E. Troisi. Liberty House, Blue Ridge Summit, Pennsylvania. 1989.

INTERSTATE MOTOR CARRIER FORMS MANUAL: PERMITTING, LICENSING, TAX REPORTING. J. J. Keller and Associates, P.O. Box 368, 145 West Wisconsin Avenue, Neenah, Wisconsin 54907-0368. 1976- .

LAW OFFICE DESKBOOK: WITH ANNOTATED FORMS. Valera Grapp. Prentice-Hall, Incorporated, 113 Sylvan Avenue, Englewood Cliffs, New Jersey 07632. 1982.

LEGAL CHECKLISTS AND SPECIALLY SELECTED FORMS. Benjamin M. Becker, Bernard Savin, and David M. Becker. Callaghan and Company, 155 Pfingsten Road, Deerfield, Illinois 60015. 1977- .

LEGAL FORMS FOR TRAVEL AGENTS. Jeffrey R. Miller. Merton House, Travel and Tourism Publishers, Incorporated, 2 Computer Drive, West, Albany, New York 12205.

LEGAL-WISE: SELF-HELP LEGAL FORMS FOR EVERYONE. Second Edition. Carl W. Battle. Allworth Press, 10 East Twenty-third Street, New York, New York 10010. 1991.

LIBEL LITIGATION FORMBOOK. Libel Defense Resource Center, 404 Park Avenue South, Sixteenth Floor, New York, New York 10016. 1984.

MCGAFFEY TAX ANALYSIS AND FORMS: BUSINESS TRANSACTIONS AND ESTATE PLANNING. Jere D. McGaffey. Callaghan and Company, 155 Pfingsten Road, Deerfield, Illinois 60015. 1977- .

MANUAL OF CORPORATE FORMS FOR SECURITIES PRACTICE. Arnold S. Jacobs. Clark Boardman Company, Limited, 435 Hudson Street, New York, New York 10014. 1981- .

MEDICOLEGAL FORMS WITH LEGAL ANALYSIS. American Medical Association, Office of the General Counsel, 515 North State Street, Chicago, Illinois 60610. 1982.

MODERN ACCOUNTING AND AUDITING FORMS. Paul J. Wendall. Research Institute of America, Incorporated, One Penn Plaza, New York, New York 10119. 1978- .

MODERN CONSTRUCTION AND DEVELOPMENT FORMS: WITH CHECKLISTS. James A. Douglas, Jack Kusnet and Rosa M. Koppel. Research Institute of America, Incorporated, One Penn Plaza, New York 10119. 1983- .

MODERN LEGAL FORMS. Second Edition. West Publishing Company, P.O. Box 64526, 50 West Kellogg Boulevard, St. Paul, Minnesota 55164-0526. 1982- .

MODERN PERSONNEL FORMS. Revised Edition. Deborah J. Launer and Nancy Asquith. Research Institute of America, Incorporated, One Penn Plaza, New York, New York 10119. 1983- .

MODERN REAL ESTATE ACQUISITION AND DISPOSITION FORMS WITH COMMENTARY. Jack Kusnet and Robert Lopatin. Research Institute of America, Incorporated, One Penn Plaza, New York, New York 10119. 1981- .

MODERN REAL ESTATE AND MORTGAGE FORMS SERIES. Revised Edition. Alvin L Arnold. Research Institute of America, Incorporated, One Penn Plaza, New York, New York 10119. 1978- .

MODERN REAL ESTATE LEASING FORMS. Jack Kusnet and Robert Lopatin. Research Institute of America, Incorporated, One Penn Plaza, New York, New York 10119. 1980- .

MODERN TRUST FORMS AND CHECKLISTS. Second Edition. Robert E. Parella and Joel E. Miller. Research Institute of America, Incorporated, One Penn Plaza, New York, New York 10119. 1980- .

MODERN UCC LITIGATION FORMS. Peter J. Bestos. Matthew Bender and Company, Incorporated, 11 Penn Plaza, New York, New York 10001. 1969- .

MUNICIPAL ORDINANCES: TEXTS AND FORMS. Second Edition. Byron S. Matthews. Callaghan and Company, 155 Pfingsten Road, Deerfield, Illinois 60015. 1972- .

MURPHY'S WILL CLAUSES: ANNOTATIONS AND FORMS WITH TAX EFFECTS. Joseph H. Murphy. Matthew Bender and Company, Incorporated, 11 Penn Plaza, New York, New York 10001. 1960- .

NEW ENCYCLOPEDIA OF REAL ESTATE FORMS. Jerome S. Gross. Prentice-Hall, Incorporated, 113 Sylvan Avenue, Englewood Cliffs, New Jersey 07632. 1983.

NICHOLS CYCLOPEDIA OF FEDERAL PROCEDURE FORMS. Callaghan and Company, 155 Pfingsten Road, Deerfield, Illinois 60015. 1974- .

OBTAINING IRS PRIVATE LETTER RULINGS: A MANUAL OF FORMS AND PROCEDURES. Oceana Publications, Incorporated, 75 Main Street, Dobbs Ferry, New York 10522. 1983- .

PARALEGAL'S HANDBOOK OF ANNOTATED LEGAL FORMS, CLAUSES, AND PROCEDURES. Deborah E. Larbalestrier. Prentice-Hall, Incorporated, 113 Sylvan Avenue, Englewood Cliffs, New Jersey 07632. 1982.

PATENT AND TRADEMARK FORMS: FOR APPLICATION, PROSECUTION, APPEALS, INTERFERENCES, AGREEMENTS, AND LITIGATION. Second Edition. Albert L. Jacobs. Clark Boardman Company, Limited, 435 Hudson Street, New York, New York 10014. 1977- .

PERSONAL INJURY FORMS: DISCOVERY AND SETTLEMENT. John A. Tarantino and David J. Oliviera. James Publishing Company, 3520 Cadillac Avenue, Costa Mesa, California 92626. 1985- .

PORTFOLIO OF BUSINESS FORMS, AGREEMENTS, AND CONTRACTS. Valera Grapp. Prentice-Hall, Incorporated, 113 Sylvan Avenue, Englewood Cliffs, New Jersey 07632. 1984.

PROXY STATEMENTS: STRATEGY AND FORMS. Howard E. Deutsch. University Publications of America, 4520 East West Highway, Suite 600, Bethesda, Maryland 20814. 1985- .

PURCHASER'S FORMBOOK OF CONTRACTS AND AGREEMENTS. William A. Hancock, Editor. Business Laws, Incorporated, 11630 Chillicothe Road, Chesterland, Ohio 44026. 1985- .

REAL ESTATE FINANCING FORMS MANUAL: WITH COMMENTARY. James A. Douglas and Rosa Kuppelo. Research Institute of America, Incorporated, One Penn Plaza, New York, New York 10119. 1985- .

REAL ESTATE FINANCING: TEXT, FORMS, TAX ANALYSIS. Patrick J. Rohan. Matthew Bender and Company, Incorporated, 11 Penn Plaza, New York, New York 10001. 1973- .

REAL ESTATE FORMS FROM ALI-ABA COURSE MATERIALS. American Law Institute-American Bar Association, Committee on Continuing Professional Education, 4025 Chestnut Street, Philadelphia, Pennsylvania 19104. 1983- .

SIMPLIFIED CONSUMER CREDIT FORMS. Carl Felsenfeld and Alan Siegal. Research Institute of America, Incorporated, One Penn Plaza, New York, New York 10119. 1978- .

SPECIALIZED FORMS. James W. Martin. West Publishing Company, 50 West Kellogg Boulevard, St. Paul, Minnesota 55164. 1990.

WARREN'S FORMS OF AGREEMENT. Oscar L. Warren. Matthew Bender and Company, Incorporated, 11 Penn Plaza, New York, New York 10001. 1959- .

WEST'S FEDERAL FORMS. Third Edition. West Publishing Company, P.O. Box 64526, 50 West Kellogg Boulevard, St. Paul, Minnesota 55164-0526. 1981- .

WEST'S MCKINNEY'S FORMS. West Publishing Company, P.O. Box 64526, 50 West Kellogg Boulevard, St. Paul, Minnesota 55164-0526. 1964- .

WILL FORMS AND CLAUSES. Robert A. Booth, Editor. Anderson Publishing Company, 2035 Reading Road, Cincinnati, Ohio 45202. 1984- .

TEXTBOOKS AND GENERAL WORKS

LITIGATION, PLEADINGS, AND ARBITRATION. Charles P. Nemeth. Anderson Publishing Company, 2035 Reading Road, Cincinnati, Ohio 45202. 1990.

LEGAL HISTORY

TEXTBOOKS AND GENERAL WORKS

AMBIVALENT LEGACY: A LEGAL HISTORY OF THE SOUTH. David J. Bodenhamer and James W. Ely, Jr., Editors. University Press of Mississippi, 3825 Ridgewood Road, Jackson, Mississippi 39211. 1984.

AMERICAN LAW AND THE CONSTITUTIONAL ORDER: HISTORICAL PERSPECTIVES. Lawrence M. Friedman and Harry N. Scheiber. Harvard University Press, 79 Garden Street, Cambridge, Massachusetts 02138. 1988.

AMERICAN LEGAL AND CONSTITUTIONAL HISTORY. Harold Hyman and Stuart Bruchey, Editors. Gower Publishing Company, Old Post Road, Brookfield, Vermont 05036. 1986.

AMERICAN LEGAL HISTORY: CASES AND MATERIALS. Kermit L. Hall, William M. Wiecek and Paul Finkelman. Oxford University Press, 200 Madison Avenue, New York, New York 10016. 1991.

THE AMERICAN LEGAL PROFESSION AND THE ORGANIZATIONAL SOCIETY, 1890-1930. Wayne K. Hobson. Garland Publishing, Incorporated, 136 Madison Avenue, New York, New York 10016. 1986.

THE BIRTH OF THE ENGLISH COMMON LAW. Second Edition. R.C. van Caenegem. Cambridge University Press, 40 West Twentieth Street, New York, New York 10011. 1988.

THE CHANGING LEGAL STATUS OF POLICTICAL PARTIES IN THE UNITED STATES. John W. Epperson. Garland Publishing, Incorporated, 136 Madison Avenue, New York, New York 10016. 1986.

THE COMMON LAW AND ENGLISH JURISPRUDENCE, 1760-1850. Michael Lobban. Oxford University Press, 200 Madison Avenue, New York, New York 10016. 1991.

COMPARATIVE LEGAL TRADITIONS IN A NUTSHELL. Mary A. Glendon, Michael W. Gordon, and Christopher Osakwe. West Publishing Company, P.O. Box 64526, 50 West Kellogg Boulevard, St. Paul, Minnesota 55164-0526. 1982.

CONSTITUTIONAL AND LEGAL HISTORY OF ENGLAND. M.M. Knappen. Fred B. Rothman and Company, 10368 West Centennial Road, Littleton, Colorado 80127. 1942. (1987 Reprint).

CONSTITUTIONAL HISTORY OF THE AMERICAN REVOLUTION: THE AUTHORITY OF RIGHTS. John Philip Reid. University of Wisconsin Press, 114 North Murray Street, Madison, Wisconsin 53706. 1987.

CROSS-EXAMINATIONS OF LAW AND LITERATURE: COOPER, HAWTHORNE, STOWE, AND MELVILLE. Brook Thomas. Cambridge University Press, 40 West Twentieth Street, New York, New York 10011. 1987.

THE DEVELOPMENT OF LAW IN FRONTIER CALIFORNIA: CIVIL LAW AND SOCIETY, 1850-1890. Gorden M. Bakken. Greenwood Publishing Group, Incorporated, 88 Post Road West, P.O. Box 5007, Westport, Connecticut 06881. 1985.

THE DEVELOPMENT OF LAW ON THE ROCKY MOUNTAIN FRONTIER: CIVIL LAW AND SOCIETY, 1850-1912. Gordon M. Bakken. Greenwood Publishing Group, Incorporated, 88 Post Road West, P.O. Box 5007, Westport, Connecticut 06881. 1983.

THE DISCOURSE OF LAW. Sally Humphreys, Editor. Harwood Academic Publishers, GmbH, P.O. Box 786, New York, New York 10276. 1985.

DISPUTES AND SETTLEMENTS: LAW AND HUMAN RELATIONS IN THE WEST. John Bossy, Editor. Cambridge University Press, 40 West Twentieth Street, New York, New York 10011. 1984.

DOCUMENTS OF POLITICAL FOUNDATION WRITTEN BY COLONIAL AMERICANS: FROM COVENANT TO CONSTITUTION. Donald S. Lutz, Editor. Institute for the Study of Human Issues, 322 South Sixteenth Street, Philadelphia, Pennsylvania 19102. 1986.

DOING WHAT COMES NATURALLY: CHANGE, RHJETORIC, AND THE PRACTICE OF THEORY IN LITERARY AND LEGAL STUDIES. Stanley Fish. Duke University Press, Box 6697 College Station, Durham, North Carolina 27708. 1989.

ESSAYS IN JURISPRUDENCE AND LEGAL HISTORY. John W. Salmond. Fred B. Rothman and Company, 10368 West Centennial Road, Littleton, Colorado 80127. Reprint of 1891 edition.

FAMOUS ADVOCATES AND THEIR SPEECHES: BRITISH FORENSIC ELOQUENCE, FROM LORD ERSKINE TO LORD RUSSELL OF KILLOWEN. Bernard W. Kelly. Fred B. Rothman and Company, 10368 West Centennial Road, Littleton, Colorado 80127. 1986. (Reprint).

FORM AND SUBSTANCE IN ANGLO-AMERICAN LAW: A COMPARATIVE STUDY OF LEGAL REASONING, LEGAL THEORY, AND LEGAL INSTITUTIONS. P.S. Atiyah and Robert S. Summers. Oxford University Press, 200 Madison Avenue, New York, New York 10016. 1991.

THE FORMATIVE ESSAYS OF JUSTICE HOLMES: THE MAKING OF AN AMERICAN LEGAL PHILOSOPHY. Frederic Rogers Kellogg. Greenwood Publishing Group, Incorporated, 88 Post Road West, P.O. Box 5007, Westport, Connecticut 06881. 1984.

FROM CRIMINAL LAW TO REGULATION: A HISTORICAL ANALYSIS OF HEALTH AND SAFETY LAW. Garland Publishing, Incorporated, 136 Madison Avenue, New York, New York 10016. 1986.

FUNDAMENTAL AUTHORITY IN LATE MEDIEVAL ENGLISH LAW. Norman Doe. Cambridge University Press, 40 West Twentieth Street, New York, New York 10011. 1990.

GEORGE WYTHE LAWYER, REVOLUTIONARY, JUDGE. Robert Bevier Kirtland. Garland Publishing, Incorporated, 136 Madison Avenue, New York, New York 10016. 1986.

HIGH POINTS OF LEGAL HISTORY: THE DEVELOPMENT OF BUSINESS LAW. John R. Goodwin. Publishing Horizons, Incorporated, 8233 North Via Paseo del Norte, Suite F400, Scotsdale, Arizona 85258. 1982.

HISTORICAL INTRODUCTION TO ANGL0-AMERICAN LAW IN A NUTSHELL. Third Edition. Frederick G. Kempin, Jr. West Publishing Company, 50 West Kellogg Boulevard, St. Paul, Minnesota 55164. 1990.

HISTORY AND POWER IN THE STUDY OF LAW: NEW DIRECTIONS IN LEGAL ANTHROPOLOGY. June Starr and Jane F. Collier. Cornell University Press, 124 Roberts Place, Ithaca, New York 14850. 1989.

A HISTORY OF AMERICAN LAW. Second Revised Edition. Lawrence M. Friedman. Simon and Schuster, Incorporated, 1230 Avenue of the Americas, New York, New York 10020. 1986.

A HISTORY OF LAW IN JAPAN UNTIL 1868. Carl Steenstrup. E.J. Brill, P.O. Box 467, 24 Hudson Street, Kinderhook, New York 12106. 1991.

HOW BLACKSTONE LOST THE COLONIES: ENGLISH LAW, COLONIAL LAWYERS, AND THE AMERICAN REVOLUTION. Beverly Zweiben. Garland Publishing, Incorporated, 136 Madison Avenue, New York, New York 10016. 1990.

THE HUMAN MEASURE: SOCIAL THOUGHT IN THE WESTERN LEGAL TRADITION. Donald R. Kelley. Harvard University Press, 79 Garden Street, Cambridge, Massachusetts 02138. 1990.

IDEAS AND FORCES IN SOVIET LEGAL DEVELOPMENT: A READER ON THE SOVIET STATE AND LAW. Zigurds L. Zile, Editor. Oxford University Press, 200 Madison Avenue, New York, New York 10016. 1992.

THE IDEOLOGY OF APOLITICAL POLITICS: ELITE LAWYERS' RESPONSE TO THE LEGITIMATION CRISIS OF AMERICAN CAPITALISM 1870-1929. James C. Foster. Garland Publishing, Incorporated, 136 Madison Avenue, New York, New York 10016. 1990.

INDEPENDENCE ON TRIAL: FOREIGN AFFAIRS AND THE MAKING OF THE CONSTITUTION. Second Edition. Frederick W. Marks, III. Scholarly Resources, Incorporated, 104 Greenhill Avenue, Wilmington, Delaware 19805. 1986.

AN INTRODUCTION TO ENGLISH LEGAL HISTORY. Third Edition. J.H. Baker. Butterworth-Heinemann, 80 Montvale Avenue, Stoneham, Massachusetts 02180. 1990.

JURISCULTURE. Gray Dorsey. Transaction Books, Rutgers University, New Brunswick, New Jersey 08903. 1989- .

JUSTICE DELAYED: THE RECORD OF THE JAPANESE AMERICAN INTERNMENT CASES. University Press of New England, 17 Lebanon Street, Hanover, New Hampshire 03755. 1989.

LAW AND COMMUNITY ON THE MEXICAN CALIFORNIA FRONTIER: ANGLO-AMERICAN EXPATRIATES AND THE CLASH OF LEGAL TRADITIONS, 1821-1846. David J. Langum. University of Oklahoma Press, 105 Asp Avenue, Norman, Oklahoma 73019. 1987.

LAW AND ECONOMIC GROWTH: THE LEGAL HISTORY OF THE LUMBER INDUSTRY IN WISCONSIN. James Willard Hurst. University of Wisconsin Press, 114 North Murray Street, Madison, Wisconsin 53706. 1984.

LAW AND JURISPRUDENCE IN AMERICAN HISTORY: CASES AND MATERIALS. Second Edition. Stephen B. Presser and Jamil S. Zainaldin, Editors. West Publishing Company, 50 West Kellogg Boulevard, St. Paul, Minnesota 55164. 1989.

LAW AND REVOLUTION: THE FORMATION OF THE WESTERN LEGAL TRADITION. Harold J. Berman. Harvard University Press, 79 Garden Street, Cambridge, Massachusetts 02138. 1983.

LAW AND SOCIAL PROCESS IN UNITED STATES HISTORY. James Willard Hurst. William S. Hein and Company, 1285 Main Street, Buffalo, New York 14209. 1960. (1987 Reprint).

LAW AND SOCIETY IN ENGLAND: 1750-1950. W.R. Cornish and G. de N. Clark. Sweet and Maxwell Limited, South Quay Plaza, 183 Marsh Wall, London E14 9FT, England. 1989.

LAW AND THE NATION, 1865-1912. Jonathon Lurie. Random House, Incorporated, 201 East Fiftieth Street, New York, New York 10022. 1983.

LAW, BIOLOGY, AND CULTURE: THE EVOLUTION OF LAW. Margaret Gruter and Paul Bohannon, Editors. Ross-Erickson, Incorporated, 223 Via Sevilla, Santa Barbara, California 93109. 1983.

LAW IN A CHANGING SOCIETY. W. Friedmann. Fred B. Rothman and Company, 10368 West Centennial Road, Littleton, Colorado 80127. 1959. (1988 Reprint).

THE LAW IN AMERICA, 1607-1861. William Pencak and Wythe W. Holt, Jr. New York Historical Society, New York, New York. 1989.

LAW IN ANTEBELLUM SOCIETY: LEGAL CHANGE AND ECONOMIC EXPANSION. Jamil Zainaldin. Alfred A. Knopf, Incorporated, Subdivision of Random House, Incorporated, 201 East 50th Street, New York, New York 10022. 1983.

LAW IN ART: MELVILLE'S MAJOR FICTION AND NINETEENTH-CENTURY AMERICAN LAW. Susan Weiner. Peter Lang Publishing, Incorporated, 62 West Forty-fifth Street, New York, New York 10036. 1991.

THE LAW IN CLASSICIAL ATHENS. Douglas M. MacDowell. Cornell University Press, 124 Roberts Place, Ithaca, New York 14850. 1986.

LAW IN COLONIAL AFRICA. Kristin Mann and Richard Roberts, Editors. Heinemann Educational Books, Incorporated, 361 Hanover Street, Portsmouth, New Hampshire 03801. 1991.

THE LAW IN THE WEST. David J. Langum, Editor. Sunflower University Press, 1531 Yuma, P.O. Box 1009, Manhattan, Kansas 66502-4228. 1985.

LAW IN UNITED STATES HISTORY: A TEACHER RESOURCE MANUAL. Melinda R. Smith, Editor. Social Science Education Consortium, Incorporated, 855 Broadway, Boulder, Colorado 80302. 1983.

THE LAW OF THE LAND: THE EVOLUTION OF OUR LEGAL SYSTEM. Charles Rembar. Perennial Library, New York, New York. 1989.

LAW ON THE PRAIRIE, 1830-1900. Ronald G. Klein. Gurler Heritage Association, 205 Pine Street, Dekalb, Illinois 60115. 1982.

LEGAL HISTORY: A EUROPEAN PERSPECTIVE. R.C. Van Caenegem. Hambledon Press, Rio Grande, Ohio. 1991.

LEGAL HISTORY AND COMPARATIVE LAW: ESSAYS IN HONOUR OF ALBERT KIRALFY. Richard Plender, Editor. Frank Cass and Company Limited, Gainsborough House, Gainsborough Road, London E11 1RS, England. 1990.

LEGAL HISTORY IN THE MAKING: PROCEEDINGS OF THE NINTH BRITISH LEGAL HISTORY CONFERENCE, GLASGOW, 1989. W.M. Gordon and T.D. Fergus. Hambledon Press, Rio Grande, Ohio. 1991.

THE LITERATURE OF AMERICAN LEGAL HISTORY. John P. Reid and William E. Nelson. Oceana Publications, Incorporated, 75 Main Street, Dobbs Ferry, New York 10522. 1985.

LIVING LAW: THE TRANSFORMATION OF AMERICAN JURISPRUDENCE IN THE EARLY TWENTIETH-CENTURY. David M. Speak. Garland Publishing, Incorporated, 136 Madison Avenue, New York, New York 10016. 1987.

THE MAGIC MIRROR: LAW IN AMERICAN HISTORY. Kermit L. Hall. Oxford University Press, 200 Madison Avenue, New York, New York 10016. 1989.

MAIN THEMES IN UNITED STATES CONSTITUTIONAL AND LEGAL HISTORY: MAJOR HISTORICAL ESSAYS. Kermit L. Hall. Garland Publishing, Incorporated, 136 Madison Avenue, New York, New York 10016. 1987.

MODERN CHIVALRY IN EARLY AMERICAN LAW: H.H. BRACKENRIDGE'S LEGAL THOUGHT. Madeline Sapienza. University Press of America, 4720 Boston Way, Lanham, Maryland 20706. 1991.

THE NEW RIVER: A LEGAL HISTORY. Bernard Ruddon. Oxford University Press, Incorporated, 200 Madison Avenue, New York, New York 10016. 1985.

ORDERED LIBERTY: LEGAL REFORM IN THE TWENTIETH CENTURY. Gerald L. Fetner. McGraw-Hill Publishing Company, 1221 Avenue of the Americas, New York, New York 10020. 1983.

THE ORIGINS OF MEDIEVAL JURISPRUDENCE: PAVIA AND BOLOGNA, 850-1150. Charles M. Radding. Yale University Press, 302 Temple Street, New Haven, Connecticut 06520. 1988.

OUR LADY THE COMMON LAW: AN ANGLO-AMERICAN LEGAL COMMUNITY, 1870-1930. Richard A. Cosgrove. New York University Press, Distributed by Columbia University Press, 562 West One Hundred Thirteenth Street, New York, New York 10025. 1986.

OUTGROWING DEMOCRACY: A HISTORY OF THE UNITED STATES IN THE TWENTIETH CENTURY. John Lukas. University Press of America, 4720 Boston Way, Lanham, Maryland 20706. 1986.

PATHS OF THE LAW: THE PURSUIT OF JUSTICE IN A TIME OF TRANSITION, 1960-1980. Vincent A. Carrafiello. University Press of America, 4720 Boston Way, Lanham, Maryland 20706. 1983.

PETTYFOGGERS AND VIPERS OF THE COMMONWEALTH: THE LOWER BRANCH OF THE LEGAL PROFESSION IN EARLY MODERN ENGLAND. C. W. Brooks. Cambridge University Press, 40 West Twentieth Street, New York, New York 10011. 1986.

THE PROVINCE OF LEGISLATION DETERMINED: LEGAL THEORY IN EIGHTEENTH-CENTURY BRITAIN. David Lieberman. Cambridge University Press, 40 West Twentieth Street, New York, New York 10011. 1989.

THE RATIONAL STRENGTH OF ENGLISH LAW. F.H. Lawson. Fred B. Rothman and Company, 10368 West Centennial Road, Littleton, Colorado 80127. 1951. (1988 Reprint).

REVOLUTION IN LAW: CONTRIBUTIONS TO THE DEVELOPMENT OF SOVIET LEGAL THEORY, 1917-1938. Piers Beirne. M.E. Sharpe, Incorporated, 80 Business Park Drive, Armonk, New York 10504. 1990.

REVOLUTIONARY POLITICS AND LOCKE'S TWO TREATISES OF GOVERNMENT. Richard Ashcraft. Princeton University Press, 41 William Street, Princeton, New Jersey 08540. 1986.

THE SHAPING OF NINETEENTH-CENTURY LAW: JOHN APPLETON AND RESPONSIBLE INDIVIDUALISM. David M. Gold. Greenwood Publishing Group, Incorporated, 88 Post Road West, P.O. Box 5007, Westport, Connecticut 06881. 1990.

A SHORT HISTORY OF LEGAL THINKING IN THE WEST. Stig Stromholm. Norstedts Foriag AB, Fred B. Rothman and Company, 10368 West Centennial Road, Littleton, Colorado 80127. 1986.

A SOCIAL STUDY OF LAWYERS IN MARYLAND, 1660-1775. Alan F. Day. Garland Publishing, Incorporated, 136 Madison Avenue, New York, New York 10016. 1989.

THINKING UNDER FIRE: GREAT COURTROOM LAWYERS AND THEIR IMPACT ON AMERICAN HISTORY. Daniel J. Kornstein. Dodd, Mead and Company, Incorporated, 71 Fifth Avenue, New York, New York 10003. 1987.

THOMAS JEFFERSON, LAWYER. Frank L. Dewey. University Press of Virginia, P.O. Box 3608, University Station, Charlottesville, Virginia 22903. 1986.

TRIAL BY FIRE AND WATER: THE MEDIEVAL JUDICIAL ORDEAL. Robert Bartlett. Clarendon Press, Oxford University Press, 200 Madison Avenue, New York, New York 10016. 1986.

UTILITARIAN JURISPRUDENCE IN AMERICA: THE INFLUENCE OF BENTHAM AND AUSTIN ON AMERICAN LEGAL THOUGHT IN THE NINETEENTH CENTURY. Peter J. King. Garland Publishing, Incorporated, 136 Madison Avenue, New York, New York 10016. 1986.

THE WESTERN HERITAGE AND AMERICAN VALUES: LAW, THEOLOGY, AND HISTORY. Alberto R. Coll. University Press of America, 4720 Boston Way, Lanham, Maryland 20706. 1982

WHAT SAYETH THE LAW: THE TREATMENT OF SLAVES AND FREE BLACKS IN THE STATE AND LOCAL COURTS OF TENNESSEE. Arthur F. Howington. Garland Publishing, Incorporated, 136 Madison Avenue, New York, New York 10016. 1986.

WOMEN AND THE LAW OF PROPERTY IN EARLY AMERICA. Marylynn Salmon. University of North Carolina Press, P.O. Box 2288, 116 South Boundary Street, Chapel Hill, North Carolina 27515-2288. 1986.

ENCYCLOPEDIAS AND DICTIONARIES

LAWMAKING AND LEGISLATORS IN PENNSYLVANIA: A BIOGRAPHICAL DICTIONARY. Craig W. Horle. Temple University. Center for Public Policy. University of Pennsylvania Press, Blockley Hall, 418 Service Drive, Philadelphia, Pennsylvania 19104. 1991- .

LAW REVIEWS AND PERIODICALS

THE AMERICAN JOURNAL OF LEGAL HISTORY. Temple University School of Law, 1715 North Broad Street, Philadelphia, Pennsylvania 19122. Quarterly.

JOURNAL OF LEGAL HISTORY. Frank Cass and Company, Limited, Gainsborough House, 11 Gainsborough Road, London E11 1RS England. Three Issues Per Year.

LAW AND HISTORY REVIEW. Cornell Law School, Myron Taylor Hall, Ithaca, New York 14853. Semiannual.

NEWSLETTERS AND NEWSPAPERS

ASLH NEWSLETTER. American Society for Legal History, c/o Department of History, University of Mississippi, University, Mississippi 38677. Semiannually.

BIBLIOGRAPHIES

A COMPREHENSIVE BIBLIOGRAPHY OF AMERICAN CONSTITUTIONAL AND LEGAL HISTORY, 1896-1979. Kermit L. Hall. Kraus International Publications, Route 100, Millwood, New York 10546. 1984. (1990 Supplement).

ENGLISH LEGAL HISTORY: A BIBLIOGRAPHY AND GUIDE TO THE LITERATURE. W.D. Hines. Garland Publishing, Incorporated, 136 Madison Avenue, New York, New York 10016. 1990.

ASSOCIATION AND PROFESSIONAL SOCIETIES

THE AMERICAN SOCIETY FOR LEGAL HISTORY, c/o Department of History, University of Mississippi, University, Mississippi 38677. (601) 232-7148.

ASSOCIATION OF AMERICAN LAW SCHOOLS, SECTION ON LEGAL HISTORY, Association of American Law Schools, One Dupont Circle, Northwest, Washington, D.C. 20036. (202) 296-8851.

SOCIETY FOR THE STUDY OF WOMEN IN LEGAL HISTORY. c/o Nancy S. Erickson, 619 Carroll Street, Brooklyn 11215. (718) 783-8162.

RESEARCH CENTERS, INSTITUTES, CLEARINGHOUSES

CENTER FOR RENAISSANCE AND BAROQUE STUDIES. University of Maryland, Francis Scott Key Hall, College Park, Maryland 20742. (301) 454-2740.

INSTITUTE OF MEDIEVAL CANON LAW. University of California, Berkeley, Boalt Hall, Berkeley, California 94720. (415) 642-5094.

LEGAL HUMOR

TEXTBOOKS AND GENERAL WORKS

BLANCHE KNOTT'S TRULY TASTELESS LAWYER JOKES. St. Martin's Press, 175 Fifth Avenue, New York, New York 10010. 1990.

THE CARTOON GUIDE TO LAW. Douglas Michael. HarperCollins Publishers, 10 East Fifty-third Street, New York, New York 10022. 1987.

THE CARTOON GUIDE TO THE CONSTITUTION OF THE UNITED STATES. Eric Lurio. HarperCollins Publishers, 10 East Fifty-third Street, New York, New York 10022. 1987.

A COMPENDIUM OF ODD LAWS. Susan S. Twarog. Apple-wood Books, P.O. Box 365, Bedford, Massachusetts 01730-0365. 1985.

THE COMPLETE MURPHY'S LAW: A DEFINITIVE COLLECTION. Arthur Bloch. Price Stern Sloan, Incorporated, 11150 Olympic Boulevard, Los Angeles, California 90064. 1990.

CRIME DOESN'T PAY: LAW AND ORDER JOKES. Charles Keller. Simon and Schuster, Incorporated, 1230 Avenue of the Americas, New York, New York 10020. 1989.

THE FIRST RUMPOLE OMNIBUS. John Mortimer. Penguin Books, Incorporated, 375 Hudson Street, New York, New York 10014. 1984.

THE HOWLS OF JUSTICE: COMEDY'S DAY IN COURT. Harry T. Shafer and Angie Papadakis. Harcourt, Brace, Jovanovich, Incorporated, 6277 Sea Harbor Drive, Orlando, Florida 32821. 1988.

IT'S LEGAL TO LAUGH: A COLLECTION OF HUMOR ABOUT THE LEGAL PROFESSION. Milton D. Green. Vantage Press, 516 West Thirty-Fourth Street, New York, New York 10001.

THE JUDICIAL HUMORIST: A COLLECTION OF JUDICIAL OPINIONS AND OTHER FRIVOLITIES. William L. Prosser. Fred B. Rothman and Company, 10368 West Centennial Road, Littleton, Colorado 80127. 1952. (1989 Reprint).

JURIS-JOCULAR: AN ANTHOLOGY OF MODERN AMERICAN LEGAL HUMOR. Ronald L. Brown. Fred B. Rothman and Company, 10368 West Centennial Road, Littleton, Colorado 80127. 1988.

LAW AND LAUGHTER. George A. Morton and D. Macleod Malloch. Fred B. Rothman and Company, 10368 West Centennial Road, Littleton, Colorado 80127. Reprint of 1913 edition.

LOONY LAWS: ...THAT YOU NEVER KNEW YOU WERE BREAKING, REVISED AND UPDATED. Robert Wayne Pelton and cartoons by Greg Jarnigan. Walker and Company, 720 Fifth Avenue, New York, New York 10019. 1990.

LOONY SEX LAWS: THAT YOU NEVER KNEW YOU WERE BREAKING. Robert Wayne Pelton. Walker and Company, 720 Fifth Avenue, New York, New York 10019. 1992.

NOT THE OFFICIAL LAWYER'S HANDBOOK. Kevin P. Ward. NAL Dutton, 375 Hudson Street, New York, New York 10014-3657. 1984.

THE OFFICAL LAWYER'S HANDBOOK. D. Robert White. Simon and Schuster, Incorporated, 1230 Avenue of the Americas, New York, New York 10020. 1983.

THE OXFORD BOOK OF LEGAL ANECDOTES. Michael Gilbert, Editor. Oxford University Press, Incorporated, 200 Madison Avenue, New York, New York 10016. 1989.

SUPREME FOLLY. Rodney R. Jones and Gerald F. Uelmen. W.W Norton and Company, Incorporated, 500 Fifth Avenue, New York, New York 10110. 1990.

TRIALS AND TRIBULATIONS: AN ANTHOLOGY OF APPEALING LEGAL HUMOR. Daniel R. White, Editor. Plume, New York, New York. 1991.

THE ULTIMATE LAWYERS JOKE BOOK. Larry Wilde. Bantam Books, 666 Fifth Avenue, New York, New York 10103. 1987.

WHITE'S LAW DICTIONARY. D. Robert White. Warner Books, 666 Fifth Avenue, New York, New York 10103. 1985.

WIT AND HUMOR OF BENCH AND BAR. Marshall Brown. Fred B. Rothman and Company, 10368 West Centennial Road, Littleton, Colorado 80127. 1986. (Reprint).

LAW REVIEWS AND PERIODICALS

COMMON LAW REVIEW. CapriComp, 1301 Maple Avenue, Wilmington, Delaware 19805. Quarterly.

LEGAL MALPRACTICE

See: LEGAL ETHICS AND MALPRACTICE; PROFESSIONAL ETHICS AND LIABILITY

LEGAL PROFESSION

See: AMERICAN BAR ASSOCIATIONS; LAW PRACTICE; LAWYER AND CLIENT; LEGAL ASSISTANTS; LEGAL DIRECTORIES; LEGAL ETHICS AND MALPRACTICE; LEGAL PROFESSION IN FICTION; LEGAL SECRETARIES

LEGAL PROFESSION IN FICTION

TEXTBOOKS AND GENERAL WORKS

CORAM PARIBUS: IMAGES OF THE COMMON LAWYER IN ROMANTIC AND VICTORIAN LITERATURE. E.F.J. Tucker. Citadel, The Military College of south Carolina, Charleston, South Carolina. 1986.

FAILURE OF THE WORD: THE PROTAGONIST AS LAWYER IN MODERN FICTION. Richard H. Weisberg. Yale University Press, 302 Temple Street, New Haven, Connecticut 06520. 1984.

FRANZ KAFKA'S USE OF LAW IN FICTION: A NEW INTERPRETATION OF IN DER STRAFKOLONIC, DER PROZESS, AND DAS SCHLOSS. Lida Kirchberger. Peter Lang Publishing Incorporated, 62 West Forty-fifth Street, Fourth Floor, New York, New York 10036-4202. 1986.

INTRUDER INTO EDEN: REPRESENTATIONS OF THE COMMON LAWYER IN ENGLISH LITERATURE, 1350-1750. E.F.J. Tucker. Camden House, Drawer 2025, Columbia, South Carolina 29202. 1984.

LAW AND AMERICAN LITERATURE: A COLLECTION OF ESSAYS. Carl S. Smith, John R. McWilliams, and Maxwell Bloomfield. Alfred A. Knopf, Incorporated, 201 East Fiftieth Street, New York, New York 10022. 1980.

LAW AND LETTERS IN AMERICAN CULTURE. Robert A. Ferguson. Harvard University Press, 79 Garden Street, Cambridge, Massachusetts 02138. 1984.

NOVEL VERDICTS: A GUIDE TO COURTROOM FICTION. Jon L. Breen. Scarecrow Press, Incorporated, 52 Liberty Street, Box 4167, Metuchen, New Jersey 08840. 1984.

TROLLOPE AND THE LAW. R.D. McMaster. St. Martin's Press, 175 Fifth Avenue, New York, New York 10010. 1986.

BIBLIOGRAPHIES

LEGAL NOVELS: AN ANNOTATED BIBLIOGRAPHY. Karen L. Kretschman and Judith Helburn. University of Texas, Tarlton Law Library, 727 East Twenty-sixth Street, Austin, Texas 78705-5799. 1979.

LEGAL QUOTATIONS

TEXTBOOKS AND GENERAL WORKS

A COLLECTION OF LEGAL MAXIMS IN LAW AND EQUITY: WITH ENGLISH TRANSLATIONS. S. S. Peloubet. Fred B. Rothman and Company, 10368 West Centennial Road, Littleton, Colorado 80127. 1985.

THE CYCLOPEDIC DICTIONARY OF LAW: COMPRISING THE TERMS AND PHRASES OF AMERICAN JURISPRUDENCE, INCLUDING ANCIENT AND MODERN COMMON LAW, INTERNATIONAL LAW, AND NUMEROUS SELECT TITLES FROM THE CIVIL LAW, THE FRENCH AND THE SPANISH LAW, ETC., ETC., WITH AN EXHAUSTIVE COLLECTION OF LEGAL MAXIMS. Walter A. Shumaker and George Foster Longsdorf. Fred B. Rothman and Company, 10368 West Centennial Road, Littleton, Colorado 80127. 1901. (1987 Reprint).

THE DICTIONARY OF LEGAL QUOTATIONS; OR, SELECTED DICTA OF ENGLISH CHANCELLORS AND JUDGES FROM THE EARLIEST PERIODS TO THE PRESENT. James William Norton-Kyshe. Gale Research, Incorporated, 835 Penobscot Building, Detroit, Michigan 48226. 1984.

FAMOUS ADVOCATES AND THEIR SPEECHES: BRITISH BASIC ELOQUENCE, FROM LORD ERSKINE TO LORD RUSSELL OF KILLOWEN. Fred B. Rothman and Company, 10368 West Centennial Road, Littleton, Colorado 80127. 1986. (Reprint).

THE QUOTABLE LAWYER: BEST QUOTES IN THE LAW. David Shrager and Elizabeth Frost, Editors. Facts on File, 460 Park Avenue, South, New York, New York 10016. 1989.

QUOTE IT! II: A DICTIONARY OF MEMORABLE LEGAL QUOTATIONS. Eugene C. Gerhart. William S. Hein and Company, 1285 Main Street, Buffalo, New York 14209. 1988.

LEGAL RESEARCH
See also: COMPUTERS AND LEGAL RESEARCH; LEGAL DIRECTORIES

STATUTES, CODES, STANDARDS, UNIFORM LAWS

CODE OF FEDERAL REGULATIONS. Superintendent of Documents, United States Government Printing Office, Washington, D.C. 20402. Annual. (Subject arrangement of federal administrative regulations).

FEDERAL REGISTER. Superintendent of Documents, United States Government Printing Office, Washington, D.C. 20402. Daily. (Chronological arrangement of proposed and final federal administrative regulations).

STATE CODES AND STATE ADMINISTRATIVE REGULATIONS. See topic STATES.

UNIFORM LAWS ANNOTATED. West Publishing Company, P.O. Box 64526, 50 West Kellogg Boulevard, St. Paul, Minnesota 55164-0526. Annual. (Same or similar state laws passed by a number of states).

UNITED STATES CODE. Superintendent of Documents, United States Government Printing Office, Washington, D.C. 20402. Annual Supplements. (Subject arrangement of federal laws).

UNITED STATES CODE ANNOTATED. West Publishing Company, P.O. Box 64526, 50 West Kellogg Boulevard, St. Paul, Minnesota 55164-0526. (Subject arrangement of federal laws).

UNITED STATES CODE CONGRESSIONAL AND ADMINISTRATIVE NEWS. West Publishing Company, P.O. Box 64526, 50 West Kellogg Boulevard, St. Paul, Minnesota 55164-0526. (Chronological arrangement of federal laws).

UNITED STATES CODE SERVICE. Lawyers Cooperative Publishing Company, Aqueduct Building, Rochester, New York 14694. (Subject arrangement of federal laws).

UNITED STATES STATUTES AT LARGE. Superintendent of Documents, United States Government Printing Office, Washington, D.C. 20402. Annual. (Chronological arrangement of federal laws).

RESTATEMENTS

RESTATEMENTS OF THE LAW: AGENCY, SECOND (1953); CONFLICT OF LAWS, SECOND (1971); CONTRACTS, SECOND (1981); FOREIGN RELATIONS, REVISED (1980); JUDGMENTS, SECOND (1982); RESTITUTION (1937); RESTITUTION, SECOND, TENTATIVE DRAFTS (1980-); SECURITY (1941); PROPERTY (1936-1944); PROPERTY, SECOND, LANDLORD AND TENANT (1977); PROPERTY, SECOND, DONATIVE TRANSFERS (1983); TORTS, SECOND (1965-1979); TRUSTS, SECOND (1959). American Law Institute, 4025 Chestnut Street, Philadelphia, Pennsylvania 19104. (Scholars' syntheses of the fifty states' case law).

LOOSELEAF SERVICES AND REPORTERS

AMERICAN LAW REPORTS. Lawyers Cooperative Publishing Company, Aqueduct Building, Rochester, New York 14694. (Selectively reports and elaborates upon appellate court decisions, federal and state; subject indexed by Index to Annotations).

FLORIDA LEGAL RESEARCH AND SOURCE BOOK. Niki L. Martin. D&S/Butterworths, Clearwater, Florida. 1989- .

FOREIGN LAW: CURRENT SOURCES OF CODES AND BASIC LEGISLATION IN JURISDICTIONS OF THE WORLD. Thomas H. Reynolds and Arturo A. Flores. Fred B. Rothman and Company, 10368 West Centennial Road, Littleton, Colorado 80127. 1989- .

GERMAIN'S TRANSNATIONAL LAW RESEARCH: A GUIDE FOR ATTORNEYS. Claire M. Germain. Transnational Publishers, P.O. Box 7282, Ardsley-on-Hudson, New York 10503. 1991- .

GUIDE TO STATE LEGISLATIVE AND ADMINISTRATIVE MATERIALS. Fourth Edition. Mary L. Fisher. Fred B. Rothman and Company, 10368 West Centennial Road, Littleton, Colorado 80127. 1988- .

HANDBOOK OF LEGAL RESEARCH IN MASSACHUSETTS. Margot Botsford and Ruth G. Matz. Massachusetts Continuing Legal Education, 20 West Street, Boston, Massachusetts 02111. 1988.

LEGAL LOOSELEAFS IN PRINT. Infosources Publishing, 118 West Seventy-ninth Street, New York, New York 10024. Annual. (Bibliography).

LEGAL RESEARCH AND LAW LIBRARY MANAGEMENT. Julius J. Marke and Richard Sloane. Revised Edition. Law Journal Seminars-Press, Incorporated, 111 Eighth Avenue, Suite 900, New York, New York 10011. 1990- .

NATIONAL REPORTER SYSTEM (ATLANTIC, CALIFORNIA, FEDERAL, NEW YORK, NORTH EASTERN, NORTH WESTERN, PACIFIC, SOUTH EASTERN, SOUTH WESTERN, SOUTHERN, SUPREME COURT). West Publishing Company, P.O. Box 64526, 50 West Kellogg Boulevard, St. Paul, Minnesota 55164-0526. (Reports appellate court decisions, federal and state; subject indexed by American Digest System, Regional Digests and state Digests).

SOUTH DAKOTA LEGAL RESEARCH GUIDE. Delores A. Jorgensen. William S. Hein and Company, 1285 Main Street, Buffalo, New York 14209. 1988- .

SPECIALIZED LEGAL RESEARCH. Leah F. Chanin, Editor. Little, Brown and Company, 34 Beacon Street, Boston, Massachusetts 02108. 1987- .

UNITED STATES LAW WEEK. Bureau of National Affairs, 1231 Twenty-fifth Street, Northwest, Washington, D.C. 20037. Weekly. (Reports United States Supreme Court decisions and selectively reports and abstracts other federal and state decisions).

HANDBOOKS, MANUALS, FORMBOOKS

ARIZONA LEGAL RESEARCH GUIDE. Kathy Shimpock-Vieweg and Marianne Sidorski Alcorn. William S. Hein and Company, 1285 Main Street, Buffalo, New York 14209. 1992.

BANKS ON USING A LAW LIBRARY: A CANADIAN GUIDE TO LEGAL RESEARCH. Fifth Edition. Margaret A. Banks. Carswell Company, 2330 Midland Avenue, Agincourt, Ontario, Canada M1S 1P7. 1991.

BIEBER'S CURRENT AMERICAN LEGAL CITATIONS. Second Edition. Mary Miles Prince, Editor. William S. Hein and Company, Incorporated, Hein Building, 1285 Main Street, Buffalo, New York 14209. 1986.

DOING RESEARCH IN FEDERAL COMMUNICATIONS LAW. John M. Howard. Law Library, Library of Congress, 101 Independence Avenue, Southeast, Washington, D.C. 20540. 1981.

THE FEDERAL REGISTER: WHAT IT IS AND HOW TO USE IT: A GUIDE FOR THE USER OF THE FEDERAL REGISTER, CODE OF FEDERAL REGULATIONS SYSTEM. Superintendent of Documents, United States Government Printing Office, Washington, D.C. 20402. 1986.

FEDERAL TAX RESEARCH: GUIDE TO MATERIALS AND TECHNIQUES. Third Edition. Gail Levin Richmond. Foundation Press, Incorporated, 615 Merrick Avenue, Westbury, New York 11590. 1987.

FIND THE LAW IN THE LIBRARY: A GUIDE TO LEGAL RESEARCH. John Corbin. American Library Association, 50 East Huron Street, Chicago, Illinois 60611. 1989.

FINDING THE LAW: A WORKBOOK ON LEGAL RESEARCH FOR LAYPERSONS. Al Coco. Prepared for: Bureau of Land Management, Branch of Survey and Mapping Development, Denver Service Center. William S. Hein and Company, Incorporated, Hein Building, 1285 Main Street, Buffalo, New York 14209. 1986.

FUNDAMENTALS OF LEGAL RESEARCH. J. Myron Jacobstein and Roy M. Mersky. Foundation Press, Incorporated, 615 Merrick Avenue, Westbury, New York 11590. 1990.

GRIFFITH'S GUIDE TO COMPUTER ASSISTED LEGAL RESEARCH. Cary Griffith. Anderson Publishing Company, 2035 Reading Road, Cincinnati, Ohio 45202. 1992.

GUIDE TO GEORGIA LEGAL RESEARCH AND LEGAL HISTORY. Leah F. Chanin and Suzanne L. Cassidy. Harrison Company, 3110 Crossing Park, Norcross, Georgia 30091. 1990.

GUIDE TO INTERNATIONAL LEGAL RESEARCH. Butterworth-Heinemann, 80 Montvale Avenue, Stoneham, Massachusetts 02180. 1989.

GUIDE TO STATE LEGISLATIVE MATERIALS. Fourth Edition. Mary L. Fisher. Fred B. Rothman and Company, 10368 West Centennial Road, Littleton, Colorado 80127. 1988.

HOW TO BRIEF A CASE: AN INTRODUCTION TO JURISPRUDENCE. Revised Edition. John Delaney. John Delaney Publications, P.O. Box 404, Bogota, New Jersey 07603. 1987.

HOW TO FIND THE LAW. Ninth Edition. Morris L. Cohen and Robert C. Berring. West Publishing Company, P.O. Box 64526, 50 West Kellogg Boulevard, St. Paul, Minnesota 55164-0526. 1989.

ILLINOIS LEGAL RESEARCH MANUAL. Laurel Wendt. Butterworth Legal Publishers, 90 Stiles Road, Salem, New Hampshire 03079. 1988.

INTRODUCTION TO LEGAL RESEARCH: A LAYPERSON'S GUIDE TO FINDING THE LAW. Al Coco. Want Publishing Company, 1511 K Street, Northwest, Washington, D.C. 20005. 1985.

LEGAL RESEARCH: A SELF-TEACHING GUIDE TO THE LAW LIBRARY. W. William Hodes. National Institute for Trial Advocacy, Notre Dame Law School, Notre Dame, Indiana 46556. 1988.

LEGAL RESEARCH: EFFECTIVE APPROACHES AND TECHNIQUES: A MANUAL FOR LAW OFFICE PROFESSIONALS. Melvin S. Merzon. Professional Education Systems, Incorporated, 200 Spring Street, Eau Claire, Wisconsin 54702. 1988.

LEGAL RESEARCH FOR EDUCATORS. David Lowe and Annette Jones Watters. Phi Delta Kappa Educational Foundation, Eighth and Union, Box 789, Bloomington, Indiana 47402. 1986.

LEGAL RESEARCH HANDBOOK: A GUIDE FOR STUDENTS AND LAYMEN. Robert L. Bledsoe. Kendall/Hunt Publishing Company, 2460 Kerper Boulevard, Dubuque, Iowa 52001. 1986.

LEGAL RESEARCH: HOW TO FIND AND UNDERSTAND THE LAW. Third National Edition. Stephen Elias, Susan Levinkind and Mary Randolph. Nolo Press, 950 Parker Street, Berkeley, California 94710. 1992.

LEGAL RESEARCH ILLUSTRATED: AN ABRIDGMENT OF FUNDAMENTALS OF LEGAL RESEARCH. Fifth Edition. J. Myron Jacobstein and Roy M. Mersky. Foundation Press, Incorporated, 615 Merrick Avenue, Westbury, New York 11590. 1990.

THE LEGAL RESEARCH MANUAL: A GAME PLAN FOR LEGAL RESEARCH AND ANALYSIS. Second Edition. Christopher G. Wren and Jill Robinson Wren. Adams and Ambrose Publishing, 1274 South Park Street, P.O. Box 9684, Madison, Wisconsin 53715-0684. 1988.

LOUISIANA LEGAL RESEARCH. Second Edition. Win-Shin S. Chiang. Butterworth Legal Publishers, 90 Stiles Road, Salem, New Hampshire 03079. 1990.

MICHIGAN LEGAL LITERATURE: AN ANNOTATED GUIDE. Second Edition. Richard L. Beer and Judith J. Field. William S. Hein and Company, 1285 Main Street, Buffalo, New York 14209. 1991.

NEW YORK LEGAL RESEARCH GUIDE. Ellen M. Gibson. William S. Hein and Company, 1285 Main Street, Buffalo, New York 14209. 1988.

PERSONAL LAW: A PRACTICAL LEGAL GUIDE. Robert D. Rothenberg. John Wiley and Sons, Incorporated, 605 Third Avenue, New York, New York 10158. 1984.

REPORTER SERVICES AND THEIR USE. Second Edition. Bureau of National Affairs, Incorporated, 1231 Twenty-fifth Street, Northwest, Washington, D.C. 20037. 1989.

SEARCHING THE LAW. Edward J. Bander, Frank Bae and Francis R. Doyle. Transnational Publishers, P.O. Box 7282, Ardsley-on-Hudson, New York 10503. 1987.

SOURCEBOOK OF AMERICAN STATE LEGISLATION. American Legislative Exchange Council, 214 Massachusetts Avenue, Northeast, Suite 240, Washington, D.C. 20002. Biennial.

STATE LEGISLATIVE SOURCEBOOK. Government Research Service, 701 Jackson, Room 304, Topeka, Kansas 66603. Annual.

TODAY'S TAX AND BUSINESS LAW-- AND HOW TO FIND IT. Commerce Clearing House, Incorporated, 4025 West Peterson Avenue, Chicago, Illinois 60646. 1990.

A UNIFORM SYSTEM OF CITATION. Fourteenth Edition. The Harvard Law Review Association, Gannett House, Cambridge, Massachusetts 02138. 1986. (Citation style manual).

USING AMERICAN LAW BOOKS: INCLUDING ONLINE SERVICES. Third Edition. Alfred J. Lewis. Kendall/Hunt Publishing Company, 2460 Kerper Boulevard, Dubuque, Iowa 52001. 1990.

WEST'S FEDERAL TAX RESEARCH. Second Edition. William A. Raabe, Gerald E. Whittenburg and John C. Bost. West Publishing Company, 50 West Kellogg Boulevard, St. Paul, Minnesota 55164. 1991.

TEXTBOOKS AND GENERAL WORKS

BRIEF MAKING AND THE USE OF LAW BOOKS. William M. Lile. William S. Hein and Company, 1285 Main Street, Buffalo, New York 14209. 1906. (1988 Reprint).

CASE ANALYSIS AND FUNDAMENTALS OF LEGAL WRITING. Third Edition. William P. Statsky and R. John Wernet, Jr. West Publishing Company, 50 West Kellogg Boulevard, St. Paul, Minnesota 55164. 1989.

CIVIL RICO: A RESEARCH GUIDE TO CIVIL LIABILITY FOR BUSINESS CRIMES. Peter Somers Dickinson. William S. Hein and Company, 1285 Main Street, Buffalo, New York 14209. 1989.

COMMUNICATING WITH LEGAL DATABASES: TERMS AND ABBREVIATIONS FOR THE LEGAL RESEARCHER. Anne L. McDonald, Lynda Thompson, and Mary E. Ziebarth. Neal-Schuman Publications, Incorporated, 23 Leonard Street, New York, New York 10013. 1987.

THE COMPUTERIZED LAWYER: A GUIDE TO THE USE OF COMPUTERS IN THE LEGAL PROFESSION. Philip Leith. Springer-Verlag New York, Incorporated, 175 Fifth Avenue, New York, New York 10010. 1991.

COMPUTERS, ARTIFICIAL INTELLIGANCE, AND THE LAW. Mervyn Bennun. E. Horwood, New York, New York. 1991.

CONGRESS AND LAW-MAKING: RESEARCHING THE LEGISLATIVE PROCESS. Second Edition. Robert U. Goehlert and Fenton S. Martin. ABC-CLIO, P.O. Box 1911, Santa Barbara, California 93116-1911. 1989.

CRIMINAL JUSTICE RESEARCH IN LIBRARIES: STRATEGIES AND RESOURCES. Marilyn Lutzker and Eleanor Ferrall. Greenwood Publishing Group, Incorporated, 88 Post Road West, P.O. Box 5007, Westport, Connecticut 06881. 1986.

EFFECTIVE LEGAL RESEARCH. Fourth Edition. Miles O. Price, Harry Bitner and Shirley Raissi Byseiewicz. Little, Brown, and Company, 34 Beacon Street, Boston, Massachusetts 02108. 1979.

EXHAUSTIVE LEGAL SEARCH: ILLUSTRATED. George N. Foster. William S. Hein and Company, 1285 Main Street, Buffalo, New York 14209. 1917. (1988 Reprint).

EXPERT SYSTEMS IN LAW: A JURISPRUDENTIAL INQUIRY. Richard E. Susskind. Oxford University Press, 200 Madison Avenue, New York, New York 10016. 1987.

FEDERAL TAX RESEARCH: GUIDE TO MATERIALS AND TECHNIQUES. Fourth Edition. Gail Levin Richmond. Foundation Press, 615 Merrick Avenue, Westbury, New York 11590. 1990.

FINDING THE ANSWERS TO YOUR FEDERAL TAX QUESTIONS. Commerce Clearing House, Incorporated, 4025 West Peterson Avenue, Chicago, Illinois 60646. 1990.

FINDING THE LAW: AN ABRIDGED EDITION OF HOW TO FIND THE LAW. Ninth Edition. Morris L. Cohen, Kent C. Olson and Robert C. Berring. West Publishing Company, P.O. Box 64526, 50 West Kellogg Boulevard, St. Paul, Minnesota 55164-0526. 1989.

FUNDAMENTALS OF LEGAL RESEARCH. Fifth Edition. J. Myron Jacobstein and Roy M. Mersky. Foundation Press, 615 Merrick Avenue, Westbury, New York 11590. 1990.

HANDBOOK OF LEGISLATIVE RESEARCH. Gerhard Loewenberg, Samuel C. Patterson and Malcolm E. Jewell, Editors. Harvard University Press, 79 Garden Street, Cambridge, Massachusetts 02138. 1985.

HOW TO FIND THE LAW. Ninth Edition. Morris L. Cohen and Robert C. Berring. West Publishing Company, P.O. Box 64526, 50 West Kellogg Boulevard, St. Paul, Minnesota 55164-0526. 1989.

INTERNATIONAL LEGAL RESEARCH PERSPECTIVES. Adolf Sprudzs. William S. Hein and Company, 1285 Main Street, Buffalo, New York 14209. 1988.

LAW AND LEGAL LITERATURE OF NORTH KOREA: A GUIDE. Sung Yoon Cho. Library of Congress. Far Eastern Law Division. Superintendent of Documents, United States Government Printing Office, Washington, D.C. 20402. 1988.

LAW LIBRARIES IN CANADA: ESSAYS TO HONOUR DIANA M. PRIESTLY. Joan N. Fraser, Editor. Carswell Company, 2330 Midland Avenue, Agincourt, Ontario, Canada M1S 1P7. 1988.

THE LEGAL BIBLIOGRAPHY: TRADITION, TRANSITIONS, AND TRENDS. Scott B. Pagel, Editor. Haworth Press, Incorporated, 10 Alice Street, Binghamton, New York 13904. 1989.

LEGAL PROBLEM SOLVING: ANALYSIS, RESEARCH AND WRITING. Fifth Edition. Majorie D. Rombauer. West Publishing Company, P.O. Box 64526, 50 West Kellogg Boulevard, St. Paul, Minnesota 55164-0526. 1991.

LEGAL RESEARCH. Charles P. Nemeth. Prentice-Hall, Incorporated, 113 Sylvan Avenue, Englewood Cliffs, New Jersey 07632. 1987.

LEGAL RESEARCH AND CITATION. Third Edition. Larry L. Teply. West Publishing Company, 50 West Kellogg Boulevard, St. Paul, Minnesota 55164. 1989.

LEGAL RESEARCH AND LAW LIBRARY MANAGEMENT. Julius J. Marke and Richard Sloane. New York Law Publishers, 111 Eighth Avenue, New York, New York 10011. 1986.

LEGAL RESEARCH AND WRITING: SOME STARTING POINTS. Third Edition. William P. Statsky. West Publishing Company, P.O. Box 64526, 50 West Kellogg Boulevard, St. Paul, Minnesota 55164-0526. 1986.

LEGAL RESEARCH EXERCISES TO ACCOMPANY HOW TO FIND THE LAW, EIGHTH EDITION. Second Edition. Lynn Foster and Elizabeth Slusser Kelly. West Publishing Company, P.O. Box 64526, 50 West Kellogg Boulevard, St. Paul, Minnesota 55164-0526. 1985.

LEGAL RESEARCH ILLUSTRATED: AN ABRIDGEMENT OF FUNDAMENTALS OF LEGAL RESEARCH, FIFTH EDITION. J. Myron Jacobstein and Roy M. Mersky. Foundation Press, 615 Merrick Avenue, Westbury, New York 11590. 1990.

LEGAL RESEARCH IN A NUTSHELL. Fourth Edition. Morris L. Cohen. West Publishing Company, P.O. Box 64526, 50 West Kellogg Boulevard, St. Paul, Minnesota 55164-0526. 1985.

LEGAL RESEARCH MATERIALS. Second Edition. Deborah J. Klein. Kendall/Hunt Publishing Company, 2460 Kerper Boulevard, Dubuque, Iowa 52001. 1989.

LEGAL RESEARCH, WRITING AND ADVOCACY: A SOURCEBOOK FOR STUDENTS, LAWYERS, AND PARALEGALS. Second Edition. Wesley Gilmer, Jr. Anderson Publishing Company, 2035 Reading Road, Cincinnati, Ohio 45202. 1987.

LEGAL WRITING, ANALYSIS, AND ORAL ARGUMENT. Larry L. Teply. West Publishing Company, 50 West Kellogg Boulevard, St. Paul, Minnesota 55164. 1990.

LEXIS: A LEGAL RESEARCH MANUAL. Kathleen M. Carrick. Mead Data Central, Dayton, Ohio. 1989.

THE MEXICAN LEGAL SYSTEM. Francisco A. Avalos. Greenwood Publishing Group, Incorporated, 88 Post Road West, P.O. Box 5007, Westport, Connecticut 06881. 1992.

PRACTICAL APPROACHES TO LEGAL RESEARCH. Kent C. Olson and Robert C. Berring. Haworth Press, Incorporated, 10 Alice Street, Binghamton, New York 13904. 1988.

THE PROCESS OF LEGAL RESEARCH: SUCCESSFUL STRATEGIES. Second Edition. Christina L. Kunz. Little, Brown and Company, 34 Beacon Street, Boston, Massachusetts 02108. 1989.

PROGRAMMED GUIDE TO TAX RESEARCH. Fourth Edition. Don C. Marshall, Kevin M. Misiewicz and James E. Parker. PWS-Kent Publishing Company, 20 Park Plaza, Boston, Massachusetts 02116. 1989.

PROGRAMMED MATERIALS ON LEGAL RESEARCH AND CITATION. Second Edition. Larry L. Teply. West Publishing Company, P.O. Box 64526, 50 West Kellogg Boulevard, St. Paul, Minnesota 55164-0526. 1986.

RESEARCH GUIDE, SURROGATE MOTHERHOOD. Kathleen K. Bach. William S. Hein and Company, 1285 Main Street, Buffalo, New York 14209. 1988.

RESEARCH IN FEDERAL TAXATION. Seventeenth Edition. Prentice-Hall, Incorporated, 113 Sylvan Avenue, Englewood Cliffs, New Jersey 07632. 1988.

RESEARCH METHODS AND STATISTICS: A PRIMER FOR CRIMINAL JUSTICE AND RELATED SCIENCES. Ronald J. Hy, Douglas G. Feig, and Robert M. Regoli. Anderson Publishing Company, 2035 Reading Road, Cincinnati, Ohio 45202. 1983.

RESEARCHING CONSTITUTIONAL LAW. Albert P. Melone. Scott, Foresman and Company, 1900 East Lake Avenue, Glenview, Illinois 60025. 1990.

SEARCHING THE LAW. Edward J. Bander, Frank Bae and Francis R. Doyle, Editors. Transnational Publishers, Incorporated, P.O. Box 7282, Ardsley-on-Hudson, New York 10503. 1987. (With Supplements).

SOURCES OF CONNECTICUT LAW. Shirley Bysiewicz. Butterworth-Heinemann, 80 Montvale Avenue, Stoneham, Massachusetts 02180. 1987.

STUDYING LAW. Second Edition. Phillip H. Kenny. Butterworth and Company (Publishers) Limited, Borough Green, Sevenoaks, Kent TN15 8PH, England. 1991.

STUDYING LAW: AN INTRODUCTION TO LEGAL RESEARCH. J. Clark Kelso. Matthew Bender and Company, Incorporated, 11 Penn Plaza, New York, New York 10001. 1990.

USING COMPUTERS IN THE LAW: AN INTRODUCTION AND PRACTICAL GUIDE. Second Edition. Mary Ann Mason. West Publishing Company, 50 West Kellogg Boulevard, St. Paul, Minnesota 55164. 1988.

ENCYCLOPEDIAS AND DICTIONARIES

AMERICAN JURISPRUDENCE; A MODERN COMPREHENSIVE TEXT STATEMENT OF AMERICAN LAW, STATE AND FEDERAL. Second Edition. Lawyers Cooperative Publishing Company, Aqueduct Building, Rochester, New York 14694. (Annual Supplements).

BALLENTINE'S LAW DICTIONARY. Third Edition. Lawyers Cooperative Publishing Company, Aqueduct Building, Rochester, New York 14694. 1969.

BLACKS'S LAW DICTIONARY. Sixth Abbreviated Edition. West Publishing Company, P.O. Box 64526, 50 West Kellogg Boulevard, St. Paul, Minnesota 55164-0526. 1991.

CORPUS JURIS SECONDUM: A COMPLETE RESTATEMENT OF THE ENTIRE AMERICAN LAW AS DEVELOPED BY ALL REPORTED CASES. West Publishing Company, P.O. Box 64526, 50 West Kellogg Boulevard, St. Paul, Minnesota 55164-0526. (Annual Supplements).

DICTIONARY OF LEGAL ABBREVIATIONS USED IN AMERICAN LAW BOOKS. Second Edition. Doris M. Bieber. William S. Hein and Company, Incorporated, Hein Building, 1285 Main Street, Buffalo, New York 14209. 1985.

THE GUIDE TO AMERICAN LAW: EVERYONE'S LEGAL ENCYCLOPEDIA. West Publishing Company, P.O. Box 64526, 50 West Kellogg Boulevard, St. Paul, Minnesota 55164-0526. 1985.

THE LAW DICTIONARY: GILMER'S REVISION: PRONOUNCING EDITION: A DICTIONARY OF LEGAL WORDS AND PHRASES WITH LATIN AND FRENCH MAXIMS OF THE LAW. Sixth Edition. Wesley Gilmer, Jr. Anderson Publishing Company, 2035 Reading Road, Cincinnati, Ohio 45202. 1986.

THE LAW GLOSSARY: BEING A SELECTION OF THE GREEK, LATIN, SAXON, FRENCH, NORMAN AND ITALIAN SENTENCES, PHRASES, AND MAXIMS. Ninth Edition. Thomas Tayler. Fred B. Rothman and Company, 10368 West Centennial Road, Littleton, Colorado 80127. 1986.

LEGAL THESAURUS-DICTIONARY: A RESOURCE FOR THE WRITER AND COMPUTER RESEARCHER. William Statsky. West Publishing Company, P.O. Box 64526, 50 West Kellogg Boulevard, St. Paul, Minnesota 55164-0526. 1985.

THE NEW DICTIONARY OF LEGAL TERMS. Revised Edition. Irving Shapiro. Looseleaf Law Publications, P.O. Box 42, Fresh Meadows Stations, Fresh Meadows, New York 11365. 1984.

WORDS AND PHRASES: ALL JUDICIAL CONSTRUCTIONS AND DEFINITIONS OF WORDS AND PHRASES BY THE STATE AND FEDERAL COURTS FROM THE EARLIEST TIMES, ALPHABETICALLY ARRANGED AND INDEXED. West Publishing Company, P.O. Box 64526, 50 West Kellogg Boulevard, St. Paul, Minnesota 55164-0526. (Annual Supplements).

DIGESTS, INDEXES, ABSTRACTS, CITATORS

AMERICAN DIGEST SYSTEM, UNITED STATES SUPREME COURT DIGEST, FEDERAL PRACTICE DIGEST 3D, REGIONAL DIGESTS AND STATE DIGESTS. West Publishing Company, P.O. Box 64526, 50 West Kellogg Boulevard, St. Paul, Minnesota 55164-0526. Monthly, for American Digest System; annually for others. (Indexes caselaw).

CURRENT LAW INDEX/LEGAL RESOURCE INDEX/LEGALTRAK. Information Access Company, 362 Lakeside Drive, Foster City, California 94404. Monthly. (Indexes legal periodicals).

THE GREENWOOD ANNUAL ABSTRACT OF LEGAL DISSERTATIONS AND THESES. Kenneth Brown, Editor. Greenwood Publishing Group, Incorporated, 88 Post Road West, P.O. Box 5007, Westport, Connecticut 06881. 1986.

INDEX TO ANNOTATIONS. Lawyers Cooperative Publishing Company, Aqueduct Building, Rochester, New York 14694. (Indexes caselaw and the publisher's articles elaborating upon caselaw).

INDEX TO LEGAL PERIODICALS. H. W. Wilson Company, 950 University Avenue, Bronx, New York 10452. Monthly.

SHEPARD'S CITATIONS. Shepard's/McGraw-Hill, P.O. Box 1235, Colorado Springs, Colorado 80901. (Monthly, quarterly or annually, depending upon set). (Citation index for statutory and case law).

SUBJECT GUIDE TO IAC DATABASES. Second Edition. Information Access Company, 362 Lakeside Drive, Foster City, California 94404. Monthly.

SUBJECT GUIDE TO UNITED STATES GOVERNMENT REFERENCE SOURCES. Judith Schiek Robinson. Libraries Unlimited, Incorporated, P.O. Box 3988, Englewood, Colorado 80155-3988. 1985.

ANNUALS AND SURVEYS

RESEARCH IN FEDERAL TAXATION. Prentice-Hall, Incorporated, 113 Sylvan Avenue, Englewood Cliffs, New Jersey 07632. Annual.

LAW REVIEWS AND PERIODICALS

CURRENT LAW INDEX/LEGAL RESOURCE INDEX/ LEGALTRACK. Information Access Company, 11 Davis Drive, Belmont, California 94002. Monthly.

INDEX TO LEGAL PERIODICALS. H. W. Wilson Company, 950 University Avenue, Bronx, New York 10452. Monthly.

INTERNATIONAL JOURNAL OF LEGAL INFORMATION. International Association of Law Libraries, P.O. Box 5709, Washington, D.C. 20016-1309. Bimonthly.

LAW LIBRARY JOURNAL. American Association of Law Libraries, 53 West Jackson Boulevard, Chicago, Illinois 60604. Quarterly.

LEGAL REFERENCE SERVICE QUARTERLY. Harwal Publishing Company, 330 West State Street, Media, Pennsylvania 19063. Quarterly.

NEWSLETTERS AND NEWSPAPERS

AUTO-CITE UPDATE. Lawyer's Cooperative Publishing Company, Aqueduct Building, Rochester, New York 14694. Bimonthly.

DIALOG DOCKET. Dialog Information Services, Incorporated, 3460 Hillview Avenue, Palo Alto, California 94304. Quarterly.

THE JOURNAL OF THE NEW YORK INSTITUTE OF LEGAL RESEARCH. P.O. Box 398, Yorktown Heights, New York 10598. Monthly.

LAWTALK. Lawyers Cooperative Publishing Company, Aqueduct Building, Rochester, New York 14694. Bimonthly.

LEGAL INFORMATION ALERT. Alert Publications, Incorporated, 399 West Fullerton Parkway, Chicago, Illinois 60614. Monthly.

LEGAL RESEARCH JOURNAL. The Legal Institute, 3250 Wilshire Boulevard, North, Suite 1000, Los Angeles, California 90010. Quarterly.

LEXIS BRIED. Mead Data Central, P.O. Box 933, Dayton, Ohio 45401. Bimonthly.

LEXIS UPDATE. Mead Data Central, Incorporated, 200 Park Avenue, New York, New York 10166. Monthly.

THE NOTES-UP. William S. Hein and Company, Incorporated, 1285 Main Street, Buffalo, New York 14209. Semiannually.

WEST LAW PASSWORD. West Publishing Company, 50 West Kellogg Boulevard, St. Paul, Minnesota 55164. Monthly.

BIBLIOGRAPHIES

AMERICAN LEGAL LITERATURE: A GUIDE TO SELECTED LEGAL RESOURCES. Bernard D. Reams. Libraries Unlimited, Incorporated, P.O. Box 3988, Englewood, Colorado 80155-3988. 1985.

ATTORNEY'S GUIDE TO GOVERNMENT STUDIES AND REPORTS. Bari Chase, Editor. Matthew Bender and Company, Incorporated, 11 Penn Plaza, New York, New York 10001. 1986.

THE CODE OF FEDERAL REGULATIONS: BIBLIOGRAPHY AND GUIDE. Second Edition. Erwin C. Surrency. Oceana Publications, Incorporated, 75 Main Street, Dobbs Ferry, New York 10522. 1986.

COUNSEL: CONSOLIDATED UNION SERIALS LIST. Law Librarians' Society of Washington, D.C., P.O. Box 3312, Washington, D.C. 22033. Annual.

GUIDE TO STATE LEGISLATIVE AND ADMINISTRATIVE MATERIALS. Fourth Edition. Mary L. Fisher, Editor. Fred B. Rothman and Company, 10368 West Centennial Road, Littleton, Colorado 80127. 1988.

GUIDES TO LEGAL RESEARCH AND REFERENCE SOURCES IN AMERICAN LAW: A SELECT BIBLIOGRAPHY. Tim J. Watts. Vance Bibliographies, P.O. Box 229, 112 North Charter Street, Monticello, Illinois 61856. 1987.

LAW BOOKS AND SERIALS IN PRINT. R. R. Bowker Company, 121 Chanlon Road, New Providence, New Jersey 07974. Ten issues per year; Annual Cumulation.

LAW BOOKS IN REVIEW. Glanville Publishers, Incorporated, 75 Main Street, Dobbs Ferry, New York 10522. Quarterly.

LEGAL LOOSELEAFS IN PRINT. Infosources Publishing, 140 Norma Road, Teaneck, New Jersey 07666. Annual.

LEGAL NEWSLETTERS IN PRINT. Infosources Publishing, 140 Norma Road, Teaneck, New Jersey 07666. Annual.

LEGAL PERIODICALS IN ENGLISH. Eugene M. Wypinski. Glanville Publishers, Incorporated, 75 Main Street, Dobbs Ferry, New York 10522. 1976. (Periodic Supplements).

LEGAL RESOURCE INDEX/LEGAL TRAK. Information Access Company, 11 Davis Drive, Belmont, California 94002. Monthly. (Includes indexing of major legal newspapers).

NATIONAL LEGAL BIBLIOGRAPHY. William S. Hein and Company, Incorporated, Hein Building, 1285 Main Street, Buffalo, New York 14209. Monthly.

RECOMMENDED PUBLICATIONS FOR LEGAL RESEARCH. Oscar J. Miller and Mortimer D. Schwartz. Fred B. Rothman and Company, 10368 West Centennial Road, Littleton, Colorado 80127. 1986.

SELECTIVE BIBLIOGRAPHY OF GUIDES TO RESEARCH IN FOREIGN LAW. Tim J. Watts. Vance Bibliographies, P.O. Box 229, 112 North Charter Street, Monticello, Illinois 61856. 1987.

STATE GOVERNMENT RESEARCH CHECKLIST. Council of State Governments, Iron Works Pike, P.O. Box 11910, Lexington, Kentucky 40578. Bimonthly.

SUBJECT COMPILATIONS OF STATE LAWS 1985-1988: AN ANNOTATED BIBLIOGRAPHY. Carol Boast and Cheryl Rae Nyberg. Carol Boast and Cheryl Rae Nyberg, 716 West Indiana Avenue, Urbana, Illinois 61801-4836. 1989.

LEGAL RESEARCH

ASSOCIATIONS AND PROFESSIONAL SOCIETIES

AMERICAN ASSOCIATION OF LAW LIBRARIES. 53 West Jackson Boulevard, Suite 940, Chicago, Illinois 60604. (312) 939-4764.

ASSOCIATIONS OF AMERICAN LAW SCHOOLS, SECTION ON LEGAL WRITING, RESEARCH AND REASONING. Association of American Law Schools, One Dupont Circle, Northwest, Washington, D.C. 20036. (202) 296-8851.

RESEARCH CENTERS, INSTITUTES, CLEARINGHOUSES

AMERICAN BAR FOUNDATION. 750 North Lake Shore Drive, Chicago, Illinois 60611. (312) 988-6500.

BUREAU OF LEGAL RESEARCH. University of Alabama, Box 870382, University Station, Tuscaloosa, Alabama 35487. (205) 348-5750.

AUDIOVISUALS

LEGAL RESEARCH: A SYSTEMATIC APPROACH FOR THE YOUNG LAWYER. Longman, Incorporated, 19 West Forty-fourth Street, New York, New York 10036. 1985. Videotape.

COMPUTER-ASSISTED LEGAL INSTRUCTION

CITATION FORM FOR BRIEFS AND LEGAL MEMORANDA. Daisy H. Floyd, Bertis E. Downs, IV, and Cathleen Wharton. Center for Computer- Assisted Instruction, 229 19th Avenue South, University of Minnesota, Minneapolis, Minnesota 55455. Machine-readable computer file.

LEARNING LEGAL ANALYSIS THROUGH ITS COMPONENTS. Peter J. Honigsberg. Center for Computer-Assisted Instruction, 229 19th Avenue South, University of Minnesota, Minneapolis, Minnesota 55455. Machine-readable computer file.

LEGAL-EZE. Numina Group, Incorporated, c/o Center for Computer- Assisted Instruction, 229 19th Avenue South, University of Minnesota, Minneapolis, Minnesota 55455. Machine-readable computer file.

SEEDPAD. WILMER, CUTLER & PICKERING, c/o Center for Computer- Assisted Instruction, 229 19th Avenue South, University of Minnesota, Minneapolis, Minnesota 55455. Machine-readable computer file.

LEGAL SECRETARIES

LOOSELEAF SERVICES AND REPORTERS

LEGAL SECRETARY BANKRUPTCY. Pamela I. Everett and Shary Smith. James Publishers. Santa Ana, California. 1987- .

HANDBOOKS, MANUALS, FORMBOOKS

THE COMPLETE LEGAL SECRETARIAL COURSE. Patricia A. Anreoni. Allyn and Bacon, Incorporated, Division of Esquire, Incorporated, 160 Gould Street, Needham Heights, Massachusetts, 02194. 1983.

HANDBOOK FOR BEGINNING LEGAL ASSISTANTS AND RECEPTIONISTS. Carl W. Salser, C. Theo Yerian and Mark R. Salser. National Book Company, P.O. Box 8795, Portland, Oregon 97207-8795. 1989.

HANDBOOK FOR FEDERAL JUDGES' SECRETARIES. Revised Edition. Federal Judicial Center, 1520 H Street, Northwest, D.C. 20005. 1985.

LEGAL DOCUMENTS: STEP BY STEP PREPARATION. Veronica E. Simon. Tejia Publishing Company, 5014 N. Saginaw Street, Flint, Michigan 48505. 1988.

LEGAL KEYBOARDING: TYPEWRITERS, ELECTRONIC TYPEWRITERS, AND WORD PROCESSORS. Mary Bauman and Mary Bahntge. John Wiley and Sons, Incorporated, 605 Third Avenue, New York, New York 10158. 1985.

LEGAL SECRETARIAL PROCEDURES. Third Edition. Joyce Morton. Prentice-Hall, Incorporated, 113 Sylvan Avenue, Englewood Cliffs, New Jersey 07632. 1992.

LEGAL SECRETARY FEDERAL LITIGATION. Second Edition. Lois Crawford-Hopkins and Mark A. Dombroff. James Publishing Company, 3520 Cadillac Avenue, Costa Mesa, California 92626. 1985.

LEGAL SECRETARY LOCAL FEDERAL FORMS. Roxanne R. Hollins. James Publishing Company, 3520 Cadillac Avenue, Costa Mesa, California 92626. 1986.

LEGAL SECRETARY'S HANDBOOK. Twelfth Edition. Kay Bliss, Editor. Parker and Son Publications, Incorporated, P.O. Box 9040, Carlsbad, California 92018-9040. 1985.

LEGAL SECRETARY'S STANDARD DESK BOOK. Carole A. Bruno. Prentice-Hall, Incorporated, 113 Sylvan Avenue, Englewood Cliffs, New Jersey 07632. 1987.

THE LEGAL WORD FINDER. Linnea L. Ochs. Prentice-Hall, Incorporated, 113 Sylvan Avenue, Englewood Cliffs, New Jersey 07632. 1983.

MANUAL FOR THE LAWYER'S ASSISTANT. Second Edition. West Publishing Company, 50 West Kellogg Boulevard, St. Paul, Minnesota 55164. 1988.

TEXTBOOKS AND GENERAL WORKS

THE CAREER LEGAL SECRETARY. Revised Edition. West Publishing Company, 50 West Kellogg Boulevard, St. Paul, Minnesota 55164. 1987.

LAW OFFICE TRANSCRIPTION. Debra A. Differding and Sandra Halsne. South-Western Publishing Company, 5101 Madison Road, Cincinnati, Ohio 45227. 1992.

LEGAL STUDIES, TO WIT: BASIC LEGAL TERMINOLOGY AND TRANSCRIPTION. Third Edition. Wanda Walker Roderick. South-Western Publishing Company, 5101 Madison Road, Cincinnati, Ohio 45227. 1990.

Encyclopedia of Legal Information Sources • 2nd Ed.   **LEGAL WRITING**

ENCYCLOPEDIAS AND DICTIONARIES

LEGAL SECRETARY'S ENCYCLOPEDIC DICTIONARY. Third Edition. Mary A. De Vries. French and European Publishers, Incorporated, 115 Fifth Avenue, New York, New York 10003. 1982.

WEBSTER'S NEW WORLD LEGAL WORD FINDER. Second Edition. Linnea Leedham Ochs. Prentice-Hall, Incorporated, 113 Sylvan Avenue, Englewood Cliffs, New Jersey 07632. 1987.

NEWSLETTERS AND NEWSPAPERS

DOCKET. National Association of Legal Secretaries, 2250 East Seventy-third Street, Tulsa, Oklahoma 74136. Bimonthly.

ASSOCIATIONS AND PROFESSIONAL SOCIETIES

NATIONAL ASSOCIATION OF LEGAL SECRETARIES. 2250 East Seventy-third Street, Suite 550, Tulsa, Oklahoma 74136. (918) 493-3540.

LEGAL SERVICES CORPORATION
See: FEDERAL AID; LEGAL AID

LEGAL TERMINOLOGY
See: LEGAL RESEARCH; STATUTORY CONSTRUCTION AND DRAFTING

LEGAL WRITING
See also: STATUTORY CONSTRUCTION AND DRAFTING

HANDBOOKS, MANUALS, FORMBOOKS

AUTHOR'S MANUAL FOR LAW SCHOOL PUBLICATIONS. West Publishing Company, 50 West Kellogg Boulevard, St. Paul, Minnesota 55164. 1988.

CITING AND TYPING THE LAW: A COURSE ON LEGAL CITATION AND STYLE. Second Edition. C. Edward Good. Blue Jeans Press, 707 East Jefferson Street, Charlottesville, Virginia 22901. 1987.

CURRENT LEGAL CITATIONS WITH 2,100 EXAMPLES. Doris M. Bieber, Editor. William S. Hein and Company, Incorporated, Hein Building, 1285 Main Street, Buffalo, New York 14209. 1983.

A HANDBOK OF ENGLISH USAGE: A GUIDE FOR THE BENCH AND BAR. Thomas J. Terputac. Brunswick, Route 1, Box 1A1, Lawrenceville, Virginia 23868. 1989.

JUDICIAL WRITING MANUAL. Federal Judicial Center. Superintendent of Documents, United States Government Printing Office, Washington, D.C. 20402. 1991.

A UNIFORM SYSTEM OF CITATION. Fourteenth Edition. Harvard Law Review Association, Gannet House, Cambridge, Massachusetts 02138. 1986.

TEXTBOOKS AND GENERAL WORKS

BASIC LEGAL WRITING. Pamela R. Tepper and Herbert G. Feuerhake. Glencoe, Lake Forest, Illinois. 1992.

BEYOND THE BASICS: A TEXT FOR ADVANCED LEGAL WRITING. Mary Barnard Ray and Barbara J. Cox. West Publishing Company, 50 West Kellogg Boulevard, St. Paul, Minnesota 55164. 1991.

CASE ANALYSIS AND FUNDAMENTALS OF LEGAL WRITING. Third Edition. William P. Statsky and R. John Wernet, Jr. West Publishing Company, P.O. Box 64526, 50 West Kellogg Boulevard, St. Paul, Minnesota 55164-0526. 1989.

CLEAR AND EFFECTIVE LEGAL WRITING. Veda R. Charrow and Myra K. Erhardt. Little, Brown, and Company, 34 Beacon Street, Boston, Massachusetts 02108. 1986.

CLEAR UNDERSTANDINGS: A GUIDE TO LEGAL WRITING. Ronald L. Goldfarb and James C. Raymond. Random House, Incorporated, Random House Publicity, 201 East Fiftieth Street, New York, New York 10022. 1982.

CREATIVE WRITING FOR LAWYERS. Michael H. Cohen. Carol Publishing Group, 120 Enterprise Avenue, Secaucus, New Jersey 07094. 1991.

DRAFTING LEGAL DOCUMENTS: MATERIALS AND PROBLEMS. Barbara Child. West Publishing Company, 50 West Kellogg Boulevard, St. Paul, Minnesota 55164. 1988.

DRAFTING LEGAL OPINION LETTERS. M. John Sterba, Jr., Editor. John Wiley and Sons, Incorporated, 605 Third Avenue, New York, New York 10158. 1988.

EFFECTIVE LEGAL WRITING: FOR LAW STUDENTS AND LAWYERS. Fourth Edition. Gertrude Block. Foundation Press, Incorporated, 615 Merrick Avenue, Westbury, New York 11590. 1992.

THE ELEMENTS OF LEGAL STYLE. Bryan A. Garner. Oxford University Press, 200 Madison Avenue, New York, New York 10016. 1991.

FUNDAMENTALS OF LEGAL DRAFTING. Second Edition. Reed Dickerson. Little, Brown, and Company, 34 Beacon Street, Boston, Massachusetts 02108. 1986.

INTRODUCTION TO LEGAL WRITING AND ORAL ADVOCACY. Karen K. Porter. Matthew Bender and Company, Incorporated, 11 Penn Plaza, New York, New York 10001. 1989.

JUDICIAL OPINION WRITING HANDBOOK. Second Edition. Joyce J. George. William S. Hein and Company, Incorporated, Hein Building, 1285 Main Street, Buffalo, New York 14209. 1986.

THE LAWYER'S GUIDE TO WRITING WELL. Tom Goldstein and Jethro K. Lieberman. University of California Press, 2120 Berkeley Way, Berkeley, California 94720. 1991.

LEARNING LAWYERS' SKILLS. Neil Gold, Karl Mackie and William Twining. Butterworth Legal Publishers, 90 Stiles Road, Salem, New Hampshire 03079. 1989.

LEGAL METHOD AND WRITING. Charles R. Calleros. Little, Brown and Company, 34 Beacon Street, Boston, Massachusetts 02108. 1990.

LEGAL PROBLEM SOLVING: ANALYSIS, RESEARCH AND WRITING. Fifth Edition. Majorie Dick Rombauer. West Publishing Company, P.O. Box 64526, 50 West Kellogg Boulevard, St. Paul, Minnesota 55164-0526. 1991.

LEGAL REASONING AND LEGAL WRITING: STRUCTURE, STRATEGY, AND STYLE. Richard K. Neumann, Jr. Little, Brown and Company, 34 Beacon Street, Boston, Massachusetts 02108. 1990.

LEGAL RESEARCH, WRITING AND ADVOCACY: A SOURCEBOOK FOR STUDENTS, LAWYERS, AND PARALEGALS. Second Edition. Wesley Gilmer, Jr. Anderson Publishing Company, 2035 Reading Road, Cincinnati, Ohio 45202. 1987.

LEGAL WRITING: A SYSTEMATIC APPROACH. Diana V. Pratt and Diana Volkman. West Publishing Company, 50 West Kellogg Boulevard, St. Paul, Minnesota 55164. 1989.

LEGAL WRITING, ANALYSIS, AND ORAL ARGUMENT. Larry L. Teply. West Publishing Company, 50 West Kellogg Boulevard, St. Paul, Minnesota 55164. 1990.

LEGAL WRITING FOR PARALEGALS. Steve Barber. South-Western Publishing Company, 5101 Madison Road, Cincinnati, Ohio 45227. 1992.

LEGAL WRITING--GETTING IT RIGHT AND GETTING IT WRITTEN. Mary Barnard Ray and Jill J. Ramsfield. West Publishing Company, 50 West Kellogg Boulevard, St. Paul, Minnesota 55164. 1987.

LEGAL WRITING IN A NUTSHELL. Lynn B. Squires and Margorie D. Rombauer. West Publishing Company, P.O. Box 64526, 50 West Kellogg Boulevard, St. Paul, Minnesota 55164-0526. 1982.

LEGAL WRITING MATERIALS: ASSIGNMENTS AND AUTHORITIES, 1987-1988. Deborah J. Klein. Kendall/Hunt Publishing Company, 2460 Kerper Boulevard, Dubuque, Iowa 52001. 1987.

LEGAL WRITING: SENSE AND NONSENSE. David Mellinkoff. West Publishing Company, P.O. Box 64526, 50 West Kellogg Boulevard, St. Paul, Minnesota 55164-0526. 1981.

LEGAL WRITING STYLE. Second Edition. Henry Weihofen. West Publishing Company, P.O. Box 64526, 50 West Kellogg Boulevard, St. Paul, Minnesota 55164-0526. 1980.

LEGAL WRITING: THE STRATEGY OF PERSUASION. Second Edition. Norman Brand and John O. White. St. Martin's Press, 175 Fifth Avenue, New York, New York 10010. 1988.

LINGUISTIC ASPECTS OF LEGISLATIVE EXPRESSION. Frederick Bowers. University of British Columbia Press, 6344 Memorial Road, Vancouver, British Columbia, Canada V6T 1Z2. 1989.

THE LITERATE LAWYER: LEGAL WRITING AND ORAL ADVOCACY. Second Edition. Robert B. Smith. Butterworth-Heinemann, 80 Montvale Avenue, Stoneham, Massachusetts 02180. 1991.

THE LITTLE BOOK ON LEGAL WRITING. Alan L. Dworsky. Fred B. Rothman and Company, 10368 West Centennial Road, Littleton, Colorado 80127. 1990.

MIGHTIER THAN THE SWORD: POWERFUL WRITING IN THE LEGAL PROFESSION. C. Edward Good. Blue Jeans Press, Charlottesville, Virginia. 1989.

OPINION WRITING. Ruggero J. Aldisert. West Publishing Company, 50 West Kellogg Boulevard, St. Paul, Minnesota 55164. 1990.

PLAIN AND ACCURATE STYLE IN COURT PAPERS. Irwin Alterman. American Law Institute-American Bar Association, 4025 Chestnut Street, Philadelphia, Pennsylvania 19104. 1987.

PLAIN ENGLISH FOR LAWYERS. Second Edition. Richard C. Wydick. Carolina Academic Press, P.O. Box 51879, Durham, North Carolina 27717. 1985.

PROBLEMS AND CASES FOR LEGAL WRITING. Revised Edition. Teresa G. Phelps. National Institute for Trial Advocacy, Legal Education Center, Notre Dame Law School, Notre Dame, Indiana 46556. 1990.

UNTANGLING THE LAW: STRATEGIES FOR LEGAL WRITERS. Kristin R. Woolever. Wadsworth Publishing Company, 10 Davis Drive, Belmont, California 94002. 1987.

WHEN LAWYERS WRITE. Richard H. Weisberg. Little, Brown and Company, 34 Beacon Street, Boston, Massachusetts 02108. 1987.

WINNING WORDS: A GUIDE TO PERSUASIVE WRITING FOR LAWYERS. Lucy V. Katz. Law and Business, Harcourt Brace Jovanovich, Incorporated, 6277 Sea Harbor Drive, Orlando, Florida 32821. 1985.

WRITING AND ANALYSIS IN THE LAW. Second Edition. Helene S. Shapo, Marilyn R. Walter and Elizabeth Fajans. Foundation Press, 615 Merrick Avenue, Westbury, New York 11590. 1991.

WRITING PERSUASIVE BRIEFS. Girvan Peck. Little, Brown, and Company, 34 Beacon Street, Boston, Massachusetts 02108. 1984.

ENCYCLOPEDIAS AND DICTIONARIES

A DICTIONARY OF MODERN LEGAL USAGE. Bryan A. Garner. Oxford University Press, 200 Madison Avenue, New York, New York 10016. 1987.

LAW REVIEWS AND PERIODICALS

JOURNAL OF LEGAL DRAFTING AND WRITING. Scribes, P.O. Box 7206, Reynolds Station, Wake Forest University School of Law, Winston-Salem, North Carolina 27109. Quarterly.

NEWSLETTERS AND NEWSPAPERS

LEGAL WRITING JOURNAL. The Legal Institute, 281 East Colorado, P.O. Box 219, Pasadena, California 91120. Quarterly.

THE SCRIVENES. Scribes, P.O. Box 7206, Reynolds Station, Wake Forest University School of Law, Winston-Salem, North Carolina 27109. Quarterly.

ASSOCIATIONS AND PROFESSIONAL SOCIETIES

AMERICAN ASSOCIATION OF LAW SCHOOLS, SECTION ON LEGAL WRITING, REASONING AND RESEARCH. One Dupont Circle, Northwest, Washington, D.C. 20036. (202) 296-8851.

SCRIBES. P.O. Box 7206, Reynolds Station, Wake Forest University School of Law, Winston-Salem, North Carolina 27109. (919) 761-5440.

COMPUTER-ASSISTED LEGAL INSTRUCTION

DRAFTING A COMPLAINT. Roger C. Park and Douglas D. McFarland. Center for Computer-Assisted Instruction, 229 19th Avenue South, University of Minnesota, Minneapolis, Minnesota 55455. Machine- readable computer file.

DRAFTING A CONTRACT: THE SALE OF GOODS. Scott J. Burnham. Center for Computer-Assisted Instruction, 229 19th Avenue South, University of Minnesota, Minneapolis, Minnesota 55455. Machine- readable computer file.

CITATION FORM FOR BRIEFS AND LEGAL MEMORANDA. Daisy H. Floyd, Bertis E. Downs, IV, and Cathleen Wharton. Center for Computer- Assisted Instruction, 229 19th Avenue South, University of Minnesota, Minneapolis, Minnesota 55455. Machine-readable computer file.

LEARNING LEGAL ANALYSIS THROUGH ITS COMPONENTS. Peter J. Honigsberg. Center for Computer-Assisted Instruction, 229 19th Avenue South, University of Minnesota, Minneapolis, Minnesota 55455. Machine-readable computer file.

LEGAL-EZE. Numina Group, Incorporated, c/o Center for Computer- Assisted Instruction, 229 19th Avenue South, University of Minnesota, Minneapolis, Minnesota 55455. Machine-readable computer file.

SEEDPAD. WILMER, CUTLER & PICKERING, c/o Center for Computer- Assisted Instruction, 229 19th Avenue South, University of Minnesota, Minneapolis, Minnesota 55455. Machine-readable computer file.

LEGISLATIVE HISTORY AND PROCESS
See also: CONGRESS; STATES; STATUTORY CONSTRUCTION AND DRAFTNG

HANDBOOKS, MANUALS, FORMBOOKS

CAPITOL HILL MANUAL. Second Edition. Frank Cummings. Bureau of National Affairs, 1231 Twenty-fifth Street, Northwest, Washington, D.C. 20037. 1984.

CONGRESS AND LAW-MAKING: RESEARCHING THE LEGISLATIVE PROCESS. Second Edition. Robert U. Goehlert and Fenton S. Martin. ABC-CLIO, P.O. Box 1911, Santa Barbara, California 93116-1911. 1989.

CONGRESSIONAL PUBLICATIONS: A RESEARCH GUIDE TO LEGISLATION, BUDGETS, AND TREATIES. Jerrold Zwirn. Libraries Unlimited, Incorporated, P.O. Box 3988, Englewood, Colorado 80155-3988. 1988.

GUIDE TO STATE LEGISLATIVE MATERIALS. Fourth Edition. Mary L. Fisher. Fred B. Rothman and Company, 10368 West Centennial Road, Littleton, Colorado 80127. 1988.

HANDBOOK OF LEGISLATIVE RESEARCH. Gerhard Loewenberg and Samuel C. Patterson, editors. Harvard University Press, 79 Garden Street, Cambridge, Massachusetts 02138. 1985.

A RESEARCH GUIDE TO CONGRESS: HOW TO MAKE CONGRESS WORK FOR YOU. Judith Manion, Joseph Meringolo and Robert Oaks. Private Law Librarians Special Interest Section, Law Librarians Society of Washington, D.C., P.O. Box 33112, Washington, D.C. 20033. 1985.

SOURCEBOOK OF AMERICAN STATE LEGISLATION. American Legislative Exchange Council, 214 Massachusetts Avenue, Northeast, Suite 240, Washington, D.C. 20002. Biennial.

STATE LEGISLATIVE SOURCEBOOK. Government Research Service, 701 Jackson, Topeka, Kansas 66603. Annual.

TEXTBOOKS AND GENERAL WORKS

THE AMERICAN LEGISLATIVE PROCESS: CONGRESS AND THE STATES. Seventh Edition. William J. Keefe and Morris S. Ogul. Prentice-Hall, Incorporated, 113 Sylvan Avenue, Englewood Cliffs, New Jersey 07632. 1989.

AMERICA'S LEGISLATIVE PROCESSES: CONGRESS AND THE STATES. Fred R. Harris and Paul L. Hain. Scott, Foresman and Company, 1900 East Lake Avenue, Glenview, Illinois 60025. 1983.

COMPARING LEGISLATURES. Gerhard Loewenberg and Samuel C. Patterson. University Press of America, 4720 Boston Way, Lanham, Maryland 20706. 1979. (1988 Reprint).

EMERGING INFLUENTIALS IN STATE LEGISLATURES: WOMEN, BLACKS, AND HISPANICS. Albert J. Nelson. Praeger Publishers, One Madison Avenue, New York, New York 10010-3603. 1991.

GOVERNORS AND LEGISLATURES: CONTENDING POWERS. Alan Rosenthal. Congressional Quarterly Books, 1414 Twenty-second Street, Northwest, Washington D.C. 20037. 1990.

INSIDE THE LEGISLATIVE PROCESS: THE PASSAGE OF THE FOREIGN SERVICE ACT OF 1980. William I. Bacchus. Westview Press, 5500 Central Avenue, Boulder, Colorado 80301. 1984.

KNOWLEDGE, POWER, AND THE CONGRESS. William H. Robinson and Clay H. Wellborn, Editors. Congressional Quarterly Books, 1414 Twenty-second Street, Northwest, Washington D.C. 20037. 1991.

LEGISLATIVE ANALYSIS AND DRAFTING. William P. Statsky. West Publishing Company, P.O. Box 64526, 50 West Kellogg Boulevard, St. Paul, Minnesota 55164-0526. 1984.

THE LEGISLATIVE COMMITTEE GAME: A COMPARATIVE ANALYSIS OF FIFTY STATES. Wyane L. Francis. Ohio State University Press, 1070 Carmack Road, Columbus, Ohio 43120-1002. 1989.

LEGISLATIVE LAW AND PROCESS IN A NUTSHELL. Second Edition. Jack Davies. West Publishing Company, P.O. Box 64526, 50 West Kellogg Boulevard, St. Paul, Minnesota 55164-0526. 1986.

THE LEGISLATIVE PROCESS IN THE UNITED STATES. Fourth Edition. Malcolm E. Jewell and Samuel C. Patterson. Random House, Incorporated, 201 East Fiftieth Street, New York, New York 10022. 1985.

LEGISLATIVE VETO: CONGRESSIONAL CONTROL OF REGULATION. Barbara H. Craig. Westview Press, 5500 Central Avenue, Boulder, Colorado 80301. 1984.

LEGISLATURES. Philip Norton. Oxford University Press, 200 Madison Avenue, New York, New York 10016. 1990.

LEGISLATURES IN THE POLICY PROCESS: THE DILEMMAS OF ECONOMIC POLICY. David M. Olson and Michael L. Mezey, Editors. Cambridge University Press, 40 West Twentieth Street, New York, New York 10011. 1991.

THE LOGIC OF LAWMAKING: A SPATIAL THEORY APPROACH. Gerald S. Strom. Johns Hopkins University Press, 701 West Fortieth Street, Baltimore, Maryland 21211. 1990.

MAKING THE GOVERNMENT WORK: LEGISLATIVE - EXECUTIVE REFORM. Robert E. Hunter and Wayne L. Berman, Editors. Georgetown University, Center for Strategic and International Studies, 1800 K Street, Northwest, Suite 1102, Washington, D.C. 20006. 1985.

ORIGINS OF LEGISLATIVE SOVEREIGNTY AND THE LEGISLATIVE STATE. A. London Fell. Praeger Publishers, Greenwood Publishing Group, Incorporated, 88 Post Road West, P.O. Box 5007, Westport, Connecticut 06881. 1991.

PARLIAMENTS IN THE MODERN WORLD. Philip Laundy. Gower Publishing Company, Old Post Road, Brookfield, Vermont 05036. 1989.

PARLIAMENTS IN WESTERN EUROPE. Philip Norton. Frank Cass and Company Limited, Gainsborough House, Gainsborough Road, London E11 1RS, England. 1990.

POLITICS AND THE BUDGET: THE STRUGGLE BETWEEN THE PRESIDENT AND THE CONGRESS. Howard E. Shuman. Prentice-Hall, Incorporated, 113 Sylvan Avenue, Englewood Cliffs, New Jersey 07632. 1988.

PRESIDENTS AND ASSEMBLIES: CONSTITUTIONAL DESIGN AND ELECTORAL DYNAMICS. Matthew Soberg Shugart and John M. Carey. Cambridge University Press, 40 West Twentieth Street, New York, New York 10011. 1992.

THE REFORM OF STATE LEGISLATURES AND THE CHANGING CHARACTER OF REPRESENTATION. Eugene W. Hickok, Jr. and Jeffery Leigh Sedgwick. University Press of America, 4720 Boston Way, Lanham, Maryland 20706. 1992.

REPRESENTATION AND RESPONSIBILITY: EXPLORING LEGISLATIVE ETHICS. Bruce Jennings and Daniel Callahan, editors. Plenum Publishing Corporation, 233 Spring Street, New York, New York 10013. 1985.

A SEASON OF INQUIRY: THE SENATE INTELLIGENCE INVESTIGATION. Loch K. Johnson. University Press of Kentucky, University of Kentucky, 633 South Limestone Street, Lexington, Kentucky 40506-0336. 1985.

TELEVISED LEGISLATURES: POLITICAL INFORMATION TECHNOLOGY AND PUBLIC CHOICE. W. Mark Crain and Brian L. Goff. Kluwer Academic Publishers, 101 Philip Drive, Assinippi Park, Norwell, Massachusetts 02061. 1988.

TWO INTO ONE: THE POLITICS AND PROCESSES OF NATIONAL LEGISLATIVE CAMERAL CHANGE. Lawrence D. Longley and David M. Olson, Editors. Westview Press, Incorporated, 5500 Central Avenue, Boulder, Colorado 80301. 1991.

USING AND MISUSING LEGISLATIVE HISTORY: A RE-EVALUATION OF THE STATUS OF LEGISLATIVE HISTORY IN STATUTORY INTERPRETATION. United States Department of Justice, Criminal Division, Tenth Street and Pennsylvania Avenue, Northwest, Washington, D.C. 20530. 1989.

DIGESTS, INDEXES, ABSTRACTS, CITATORS

CIS/INDEX TO PUBLICATIONS OF THE UNITED STATES CONGRESS. Congressional Information Service, Incorporated, 4520 East-West Highway, Suite 806, Bethesda, Maryland 20814-3389. Monthly. (Index to Congressional hearings and reports; includes abstracts, and is complimented by CIS/Michrofiche Library which provides full-text microfiche copies of all publications covered in CIS/Index.)

CONGRESSIONAL INDEX. Commerce Clearing House, Incorporated, 4025 West Peterson Avenue, Chicago, Illinois 60646. Weekly. (Index to bills before Congress).

CONGRESSIONAL QUARTERLY. Weekly Report. Congressional Quarterly, Incorporated, 1414 Twenty-second Street, Northwest, Washington, D.C. 20037. Weekly. (News coverage of Congress.)

CONGRESSIONAL RECORD: PROCEEDINGS AND DEBATES OF CONGRESS. Superintendent of Documents, United States Government Printing Office, Washington, D.C. 20402. Daily.

DIGEST OF PUBLIC GENERAL BILLS AND RESOLUTIONS. Legislative Reference Service, Library of Congress, Superintendent of Documents, United States Government Printing Office, Washington, D.C. 20402.

UNITED STATES CODE CONGRESSIONAL AND ADMINISTRATIVE NEWS: LEGISLATIVE HISTORY. West Publishing Company, P.O. Box 64526, 50 West Kellogg Boulevard, St. Paul, Minnesota 55164-0526. Monthly. (Selectively publishes Congressional reports.)

WEEKLY COMPILATION OF PRESIDENTIAL DOCUMENTS. Office of the Federal Register. Superintendent of Documents, United States Government Printing Office, Washington, D.C. 20402. Weekly.

ANNUALS AND SURVEYS

CONGRESSIONAL QUARTERLY ALMANAC. Congressionl Quarterly, Incorporated, 1414 Twenty-second Street, Northwest, Washington, D.C. 20037.

ICS/ANNUAL: LEGISLATIVE HISTORIES OF UNITED STATES PUBLIC LAWS. Congressional Information Service, Incorporated. 4520 East-West Highway, Suite 800, Bethesda, Maryland 20814-3389. Annual.

LAW REVIEWS AND PERIODICALS

HARVARD JOURNAL ON LEGISLATION. Harvard Legislative Reserach Bureau. Langdel Hall-196, Harvard Law School, Cambridge, Massachusetts 02138. Semiannual.

JOURNAL OF LEGISLATION. Notre Dame Law School, Notre Dame, Indiana 46556. Semiannual.

LEGISLATIVE STUDIES QUARTERLY. Comparative Legislative Research Center, 304 Schaeffer Hall, Universtiy of Iowa, Iowa City, Iowa 52242. Quarterly.

SETON HALL LEGISLATIVE JOURNAL. Seton Hall University Law Center, 1095 Raymond Boulevard, Newark, New Jersey 07102. Semiannual.

STATE LEGISLATURES. National Conference of State Legislatures, 1125 Seventeenth Street, Denver, Colorado 80202. Ten issues per year.

BIBLIOGRAPHIES

LEGISLATIVE REFERENCE CHECKLIST: THE KEY TO LEGISLATIVE HISTORIES FROM 1789-1903. Eugene Nabors. Fred B. Rothman and Company, 10368 West Centennial Road, Littleton, Colorado 80127. 1982.

RESOURCE GUIDE TO INFLUENCING STATE LEGISLATURES: AN ANNOTATED BIBLIOGRAPHY. Third Edition. Lynn Hellebust. Government Research Services, 701 Jackson, Topeka, Kansas 66603. 1991.

SOURCES OF COMPILED LEGISLATIVE HISTORIES: A BIBLIOGRPAHY OF GOVERNMENT DOCUMENTS, PERIODICAL ARTICLES, AND BOOKS, 1ST CONGRESS-94TH CONGRESS. Nancy P. Johnson. Fred B. Rothman and Company, 10368 West Centennial Road, Littleton, Colorado 80127. 1979- .

STATE BLUE BOOKS, LEGISLATIVE MANUALS, AND REFERENCE PUBLICATIONS: A SELECTIVE BIBLIOGRAPHY. Lynn Hellebust, Editor. Government Research Service, Topeka, Kansas. 1990.

STATE LEGISLATURES: A BIBLIOGRAPHY. Robert U. Goehlart and Frederick W. Musto. ABC-Clio Information Services, Riviera Campus, 2040 Alameda Padre Serra, P.O. Box 1911, Santa Barbara, California 93116-1911. 1985.

UNION LIST OF LEGISLATIVE HISTORIES: 47TH CONGRESS, 1881--101ST CONGRESS, 1990. Sixth Edition. Law Librarians, Society of Washington, D.C. Fred B. Rothman and Company, 10368 West Centennial Road, Littleton, Colorado 80127. 1991.

DIRECTORIES

BOOK OF THE STATES, SUPPLEMENT ONE: STATE ELECTIVE OFFICIALS AND THE LEGISLATURES. Council of State Governments, Iron Works Pike, P.O. Box 11910, Lexington, Kentucky 40578. Biennial.

BOOK OF THE STATES, SUPPLEMENT TWO: STATE LEGISLATIVE LEADERSHIP, COMMITTEES AND STAFF. Council of State Governments, Iron Works Pike, P.O. Box 11910, Lexington, Kentucky 40578. Biennial.

BRADDOCK'S FEDERAL-STATE-LOCAL GOVERNMENT DIRECTORY. Braddock Publications, 1001 Connecticut Avenue, Northwest, Washington, D.C. 22036. Biennial.

CONGRESSIONAL DIRECTORY. Office of the Congressional Directory, Joint Committee on Printing, United States Congress. Superintendent of Documents, United States Government Printing Office, Washington, D.C. 20402. Biennial.

CONGRESSIONAL HANDBOOK. Department of the Legislature, Chamber of Commerce of the United States, 1615 H Street, Northwest, Washington, D.C. 20062. Annual.

CONGRESSIONAL MONITOR DAILY. Congressional Quarterly, Incorporated, 1411 Twenty-second Street, Northwest, Washington, D.C. 20037. Daily. (Covers committee hearings scheduled).

CONGRESSIONAL PICTORIAL DIRECTORY. Joint Committee on Printing; United States Congress. Superintendent of Documents, United States Government Printing Office, Washington, D.C. 20402. Biennial.

CONGRESSIONAL REPRESENTATIVES NAMES AND ADDRESSES. Tyson Capitol Institute, 7735 Old Georgetown Road, Bethesda, Maryland 20814. Continously updated.

CONGRESSIONAL STAFF DIRECTORY. Congressional Staff Directory, Box 62, Mount Vernon, Virginia 22121. Annual.

CONGRESSIONAL YELLOW BOOK. Washington Monitor, Incorporated, 1301 Pennsylvania Avenue, Northwest, Washington, D.C. 20004. Quarterly.

DIRECTORY OF ELECTION OFFICIALS. Clearinghouse on Election Administration, Federal Election Commission. Superintendent of Documents, United States Government Printing Office, Washington, D.C. 20402. Annual.

DIRECTORY OF FORMER MEMBERS OF CONGRESS. United States Association of Former Members of Congress, 1755 Massachusetts Avenue, Northwest, Suite 412, Washington, D.C. 20036. 1986.

THE STATE SLATE: A GUIDE TO LEGISLATIVE PROCEDURES AND LANDMAKERS. Public Affairs Information Service, Incorporated, 521 West Forty-third Street, New York, New York 10036-4396. Annual.

UNITED STATES HOUSE OF REPRESENTATIVES TELEPHONE NUMBERS. Clerk of the House, United States House of Representatives. Superintendent of Documents, United States Government Printing Office, Washington, D.C. 20402. Annual.

LEGISLATIVE HISTORY AND PROCESS

UNITED STATES SENATE TELEPHONE DIRECTORY. United States Senate. Superintendent of Documents, United States Government Printing Office, Washington, D.C. 20402. Semiannual.

WASHINGTON INFORMATION DIRECTORY. Congressional Quarterly, Incorporated, 1414 Twenty-second, Northwest, Washington, D.C. 20037. Annual.

BIOGRAPHICAL SOURCES

ALMANAC OF AMERICAN POLITICS. National Journal, 1730 M Street, Northwest, Washington, D.C. 20036. Biennial.

KNOW YOUR CONGRESS. Capitol Publishers, Incorporated, 89 Primrose Way, Sacramento, California 95819. 1986.

POLITICS IN AMERICA: MEMBERS OF CONGRESS IN WASHINGTON AND AT HOME. Congressional Quarterly, Incorporated, 1414 Twenty-second Street, Northwest, Washington, D.C. 20037. Biennial.

ASSOCIATIONS AND PROFESSIONAL SOCIETIES

ADMINISTRATIVE ASSISTANTS ASSOCIATION OF THE UNITED STATES HOUSE OF REPRESENTATIVES. 1740 Longworth House Office Building, Washington, D.C. 20515. (202) 225-5256.

ASSOCIATION OF AMERICAN LAW SCHOOLS, SECTION ON LEGISLATION. One Dupont Circle, Washington, D.C. 20036. (202) 296-8851.

COUNCIL OF STATE GOVERNMENTS. P.O. Box 11910, Iron Works Pike, Lexington, Kentucky 40578. (606) 231-1939.

NATIONAL BLACK CAUCUS OF STATE LEGISLATORS. 206 Hall of State Building, 444 North Capitol, Northwest, Washington, D.C. 20001. (202) 624-5457.

NATIONAL CONFERENCE OF STATE LEGISLATURES. 1050 Seventeenth Street, Suite 21001, Denver, Colorado 80265. (303) 623-7800.

UNITED STATES ASSOCIATION OF FORMER MEMBERS OF CONGRESS. 1755 Massachusetts Avenue, Northwest, Suite 412, Washington, D.C. 20036. (202) 332-3532.

RESEARCH CENTERS AND INSTITUTES

COMPARATIVE LEGISLATIVE RESEARCH CENTER. 304 Schaeffer Hall, University of Iowa, Iowa City, Iowa 52242.

LEGISLATIVE DRAFTING RESEARCH FUND. Columbia University, 435 West One Hundred Sixteenth Street, New York, New York 10027. (212) 854-2685.

LEGISLATIVE OFFICE FOR RESEARCH LIAISON. P.O. Box 218, Main Capitol, Harrisburg, Pennsylvania 17120. (717) 787-8948.

LEGISLATIVE RESEARCH BUREAU. Harvard University, Harvard Law School, Hastings Hall, Cambridge, Massachusetts 02138.

Encyclopedia of Legal Information Sources • 2nd Ed.

ONLINE DATABASES

BILLCAST LEGISLATIVE FORECASTS. George Mason University, Center for Study of Public Choice, 4400 University Drive, Fairfax, Virginia 22030.

CIS. Congressional Information Service, Incorporated, 4520 East-West Highway, Bethesda, Maryland 20814.

CQ ANALYSIS. Congressional Quarterly, Incorporated, 1414 Twenty-second Street, Northwest, Washington, D.C. 20037.

CQ BILL STATUS. Congressional Quarterly, Incorporated, 1414 Twenty-second Street, Northwest, Washington, D.C. 20037.

CQ COMMITTEE REPORTS. Congressional Quarterly, Incorporated, 1414 Twenty-second Street, Northwest, Washington, D.C. 20037.

CQ CONGRESSIONAL DOCUMENTS. Congressional Quarterly, Incorporated, 1414 Twenty-second Street, Northwest, Washington, D.C. 20037.

CQ CONGRESSIONAL SCHEDULES. Congressional Quarterly, Incorporated, 1414 Twenty-second Street, Northwest, Washington, D.C. 20037.

CQ FULL TEXT OF BILLS. Congressional Quarterly, Incorporated, 1414 Twenty-second Street, Northwest, Washington, D.C. 20037.

CQ INFO. Congressional Quarterly, Incorporated, 1414 Twenty-second Street, Northwest, Washington, D.C. 20037.

CQ LEGISLATIVE ACTION. Congressional Quarterly, Incorporated, 1414 Twenty-second Street, Northwest, Washington, D.C. 20037.

CQ NEWS. Congressional Quarterly, Incorporated, 1414 Twenty-second Street, Northwest, Washington, D.C. 20037.

CQ WASHINGTON ALERT SERVICE. Congressional Quarterly, Incorporated, 1414 Twenty-second Street, Washington, D.C. 20037.

CQ WEEKLY REPORT. Congressional Quarterly, Incorporated, 1414 Twenty-second Street, Northwest, Washington, D.C. 20037.

ELSS: ELECTRONIC LEGISLATIVE SEARCH SYSTEM. Commerce Clearing House, Incorporated, 4025 West Peterson Avenue, Chicago, Illinois 60646.

LEGI-SLATE. Legi-Slate, Incorporated, 111 Massachusetts Avenue, Northwest, Washington, D.C. 20001.

LEGI-TECH. Legi-Tech Corporation, The Senator Hotel, 1121 L Street, Sacramento, California 95814.

OTHER SOURCES

STATUTORY INTERPRETATION AND THE USES OF LEGISLATIVE HISTORY: HEARING BEFORE THE SUBCOMMITTEE ON COURTS, INTELLECTUAL PROPERTY, AND THE ADMINISTRATION OF JUSTICE OF THE COMMITTEE ON THE JUDICIARY, HOUSE OF REPRESENTATIVES, ONE HUNDRED FIRST CONGRESS, SECOND SESSION, APRIL 19, 1990. Superintendent of Documents, United States Government Printing Office, Washington, D.C. 20402. 1990.

LEGISLATIVE PROCESS
See: LEGISLATIVE HISTORY AND PROCESS

LESBIANS
See: SEXUAL ORIENTATION

LETTERS OF CREDIT

STATUTES, CODES, STANDARDS, UNIFORM LAWS

UNIFORM COMMERCIAL CODE, ARTICLE FIVE, LETTERS OF CREDIT. National Conference of Commissioners on Uniform State Laws. Uniform Laws Annotated. West Publishing Company, P.O. Box 64526, 50 West Kellogg Boulevard, St. Paul, Minnesota 55164-0526. 1976. (Annual Supplements).

UNIFORM COMMERCIAL CODE, ARTICLE FIVE, LETTERS OF CREDIT. National Conference of Commissioners on Uniform State Laws. Martindale-Hubbell Law Directory, Volume Eight. Martindale-Hubbell, Incorporated, 121 Chanlon Road, New Providence, New Jersey 07974. Annual.

UNIFORM CUSTOMS AND PRACTICE FOR DOCUMENTARY CREDITS: 1974 REVISION IN FORCE AS OF OCTOBER 1, 1975. International Chamber of Commerce, 156 Fifth Avenue, Suite 820, New York, New York 10010. 1981.

LOOSELEAF SERVICES AND REPORTERS

LETTERS OF CREDIT. Burton V. McCullough. Matthew Bender and Company, Incorporated, 11 Penn Plaza, New York, New York 10001. 1987- .

HANDBOOKS, MANUALS, FORMBOOKS

LETTERS OF CREDIT GUIDEBOOK. Dominic J. Policano. Executive Education Press, 144 Liberty Street, New York, New York 10023. 1983.

A PRACTICAL GUIDE TO LETTERS OF CREDIT. Charles E. Aster and Katheryn C. Patterson, Editors. Executive Enterprises Publications Company, 22 West Twenty-first Street, New York, New York 10010-6904. 1990.

A STUDENT'S GUIDE TO SALES OF GOODS, LETTERS OF CREDIT, AND DOCUMENTS OF TITLE. Frederick M. Hart and Robert Laurence. Matthew Bender and Company, Incorporated, 11 Penn Plaza, New York, New York 10001. 1987.

TEXTBOOKS AND GENERAL WORKS

DOCUMENTARY CREDITS: UCP 1974/1983 REVISIONS COMPARED AND EXPLAINED. International Chamber of Commerce Publishing Corporation, 156 Fifth Avenue, New York, New York 10010. 1984.

INTERNATIONAL PRIVATE TRADE. Second Revised Edition. Andreas F. Lowenfeld. Matthew Bender and Company, Incorporated, 11 Penn Plaza, New York, New York 10001. 1988.

INTRODUCTION TO SECURED TRANSACTIONS AND LETTERS OF CREDIT, 1991: UCC ARTICLES 9 AND 5. William C. Hillman. Practising Law Institute, 810 Seventh Avenue, New York, New York 10019. 1991.

THE LAW OF BANKERS' COMMERCIAL CREDITS. Seventh Edition. H. C. Gutteridge and Maurice H. Megrah. Europa Publications, c/o UNIPUB, Customer Service Department, P.O. Box 1222, Ann Arbor, Michigan 48106. 1984.

THE LAW OF LETTERS OF CREDIT: COMMERCIAL AND STANDBY CREDITS. Second Edition. John F. Dolan. Research Institute of America, Incorporated, One Penn Plaza, New York, New York 10119. 1991.

LETTERS OF CREDIT. Gerald T. McLaughlin. Harcourt Brace Jovanovich, Incorporated, 6277 Sea Harbor Drive, Orlando, Florida 32821. 1985.

LETTERS OF CREDIT. Henry Harfield. American Law Institute-American Bar Association, Committee on Continuing Professional Education, 4025 Chestnut Street, Philadelphia, Pennsylvania 19104. 1979.

LETTERS OF CREDIT: ALI-ABA COURSE OF STUDY MATERIALS. American Law Institute-American Bar Association, Committee on Continuing Professional Education, 4025 Chestnut Street, Philadelphia, Pennsylvania 19104. 1985.

LETTERS OF CREDIT AND BANKERS' ACCEPTANCES, 1988. Reade Ryan, Jr., Chairman. Practising Law Institute, 810 Seventh Avenue, New York, New York 10019. 1988.

LETTERS OF CREDIT: CURRENT THINKING IN AMERICA. William C. Hillman, Editor. Butterworth-Heinemann, 80 Montvale Avenue, Stoneham, Massachusetts 02180. 1987.

LETTERS OF CREDIT UNDER INTERNATIONAL TRADE LAW: U.C.C., U.C.P., AND LAW MERCHANT. Matti Kurkela. Oceana Publications, Incorporated, 75 Main Street, Dobbs Ferry, New York 10522. 1985.

STANDBY LETTERS OF CREDIT. Brooke Wunnicke and Diane B. Wunnicke. John Wiley and Sons, Incorporated, 605 Third Avenue, New York, New York 10158. 1989.

A STUDENT'S GUIDE TO SALES, LETTERS OF CREDIT AND DOCUMENTS OF TITLE. Robert Laurence and Frederick M. Hart. Matthew Bender and Company, Incorporated, 11 Penn Plaza, New York, New York 10001. 1986.

USING LETTERS OF CREDIT: A PROMISE OF CERTAINTY IN AN UNCERTAIN WORLD? Lawrence D. Bragg. Massachusetts Continuing Legal Education, 20 West Street, Boston, Massachusetts 02111. 1991.

NEWLETTERS AND NEWSPAPERS

LETTERS OF CREDIT REPORT. Executive Enterprises Publications Company, Incorporated. 22 West Twenty-first Street, New York, New York 10010. Bimonthly.

LETTERS OF CREDIT UPDATE. Government Information Services, 1611 Kent Street, Suite 508, Arlington, Virginia 22209. Monthly.

AUDIOVISUALS

LETTERS OF CREDIT AND BANKERS' ACCEPTANCES. Practising Law Institute, 810 Seventh Avenue, New York, New York 10019. 1983. Audiocassette.

LIABILITY
See: CRIMINAL LAW; DAMAGES; GOVERNMENT IMMUNITY AND LIABILITY; PRODUCTS LIABILITY AND SAFETY; TORTS

LIABILITY INSURANCE
See: INSURANCE, LIABILITY; INSURANCE, MOTOR VEHICLE AND AVIATION

LIBEL AND SLANDER
See also: CRIMINAL LAW

STATUTES, CODES, STANDARDS, UNIFORM LAWS

LDRC 50-STATE SURVEY: CURRENT DEVELOPMENTS IN MEDIA LIBEL AND INVASION OF PRIVACY. Henry R. Kaufman, Editor. Libel Defense Resource Center, 404 Park Avenue South, Sixteenth Floor, New York, New York 10016. 1984.

LOOSELEAF SERVICES AND REPORTERS

EMPLOYEE, BUSINESS AND PROFESSIONAL DEFAMATION. Paul Alexander and Vanessa Wells. Matthew Bender and Company, Incorporated, 11 Penn Plaza, New York, New York 10001. 1990- .

LIBEL AND PRIVACY. Second Edition. Bruce W. Sanford. Prentice-Hall, Incorporated, 113 Sylvan Avenue, Englewood Cliffs, New Jersey 07632. 1991- .

HANDBOOKS, MANUALS, FORMBOOKS

THE ASSOCIATED PRESS STYLEBOOK AND LIBEL MANUAL: WITH APPENDIXES ON PHOTO CAPTIONS, FILING THE WIRE. Revised Edition. Christopher W. French, Editior. Addison-Wesley Publishing Company, Incorporated, Route 128, Reading, Massachusetts 01867. 1987.

HOW TO BULLETPROOF YOUR MANUSCRIPT. Bruce B. Henderson. Writer's Digest Books, 1507 Dana Avenue, Cincinnati, Ohio 45207. 1986.

THE JOURNALIST'S HANDBOOK ON LIBEL AND PRIVACY. Barbara Dill. Free Press, Division of Macmillan Publishing Company, Incorporated, 866 Third Avenue, New York, New York 10022. 1986.

LIBEL LITIGATION FORMBOOK. Libel Defense Resource Center, 404 Park Avenue, South, Sixteenth Floor, New York, New York 10016. 1984.

MAKE IT LEGAL. Lee Wilson. Allworth Press, 10 East Twenty-third Street, New York, New York 10010. 1990.

TEXTBOOKS AND GENERAL WORKS

ACTUAL MALICE: TWENTY-FIVE YEARS AFTER TIMES V. SULLIVAN. W. Wat Hopkins. Praeger Publishers, One Madison Avenue, New York, New York 10010-3603. 1989.

BLOOD LIBEL: THE INSIDE STORY OF GENERAL ARIEL SHARON'S HISTORY-MAKING SUIT AGAINST TIME MAGAZINE. Uri Dan. Simon and Schuster, Incorporated, 1230 Avenue of the Americas, New York, New York 10020. 1987.

A CHILLING EFFECT: THE MOUNTING THREAT OF LIBEL AND INVASION OF PRIVACY ACTIONS TO THE FIRST AMENDMENT. Lois G. Forer. W.W Norton and Company, Incorporated, 500 Fifth Avenue, New York, New York 10110. 1987.

COALS OF FIRE: THE ALTON TELEGRAPH LIBEL CASE. Thomas B. Littlewood. Southern Illinois University Press, P.O. Box 3697, Carbondale, Illinois 62902-3697. 1988.

THE COST OF LIBEL: ECONOMIC AND POLICY IMPLICATIONS. Everette E. Dennis and Eli M. Noam, Editors. Columbia University Press, 562 West One Hundred Thirteenth Street, New York, New York 10025. 1989.

DEFAMATION--LIBEL AND SLANDER. Theodore R. Kupferman, Editor. Meckler Corporation, 11 Ferry Lane West, Westport, Connecticut 06880. 1990.

ERRORS, LIES, AND LIBEL. Peter E. Kane. Southern Illinois University Press, P.O. Box 3697, Carbondale, Illinois 62902-3697. 1992.

THE FAIR REPORT PRIVILEGE. David A. Elder. Butterworth-Heinemann, 80 Montvale Avenue, Stoneham, Massachusetts 02180. 1988.

FEEDING FRENZY: HOW ATTACK JOURNALISM HAS TRANSFORMED AMERICAN POLITICS. Larry J. Sabato. Free Press, 866 Third Avenue, New York, New York 10022. 1991.

FIRST AMENDMENT AND LIBEL: THE EXPERTS LOOK AT PRINT, BROADCAST AND CABLE. R. John Cooper and Bruce W. Sanford, Co-chairmen. Harcourt Brace Jovanovich, Incorporated, 6277 Sea Harbor Drive, Orlando, Florida 32821. 1983.

GERTZ V. ROBERT WELCH, INC.: THE STORY OF A LANDMARK LIBEL CASE. Elmer Gertz. Southern Illinois University Press, P.O. Box 3697, Carbondale, Illinois 62902-3697. 1992.

THE GOLDMARK CASE: AN AMERICAN LIBEL TRIAL. William L. Dwyer. University of Washington Press, P.O. Box 50096, Seattle, Washington 98145-5096. 1984.

JERRY FALWELL V. LARRY FLYNT: THE FIRST AMENDMENT ON TRIAL. Rodney A. Smolla. University of Illinois Press, 54 East Gregory Drive, Champaign, Illinois 61820. 1990.

THE JUROR AND THE GENERAL. Patricia M. Roth. William Morrow and Company, Incorporated, 105 Madison Avenue, New York, New York 10016. 1986.

THE LAW OF DEFAMATION, PRIVACY, PUBLICITY, AND "MORAL RIGHTS": CASES AND MATERIALS ON PROTECTION OF PERSONALITY INTERESTS. Sheldon W. Halpern. Anderson Publishing Company, 2035 Reading Road, Cincinnati, Ohio 45202. 1988.

LIBEL AND PRIVACY LITIGATION. Bruce W. Sanford. Harcourt Brace Jovanovich, Incorporated, 6277 Sea Harbor Drive, Orlando, Florida 32821. 1983. (Supplements)

LIBEL AND PRIVACY: THE PREVENTION AND DEFENSE OF LITIGATION. Bruce W. Saford. Harcourt Brace Jovanovich, Incorporated, 6277 Sea Harbor Drive, Orlando, Florida 32821. 1985.

LIBEL AND THE FIRST AMENDMENT: LEGAL HISTORY AND PRACTICE IN PRINT AND BROADCASTING. Richard Labunski. Transaction Books, Rutgers University, New Brunswick, New Jersey 08903. 1989.

LIBEL LAW AND THE PRESS: MYTH AND REALITY. Randall P. Bezanson, Gilbert Cranberg and John Soloski. Free Press, 866 Third Avenue, New York, New York 10022. 1987.

THE LIBEL REVOLUTION: A NEW LOOK AT DEFAMATION AND PRIVACY. Michael F. Mayer. Law Arts Publishers, 159 West Fifty-third Street, New York, New York 10019. 1987.

MAKE NO LAW: THE SULLIVAN CASE AND THE FIRST AMENDMENT. Anthony Lewis. Random House, Incorporated, 201 East Fiftieth Street, New York, New York 10022. 1991.

A MATTER OF HONOR: GENERAL WILLIAM C. WESTMORELAND VS THE COLUMBIA BROADCASTING SYSTEM. Don Kowett. Macmillan Publishing Company, Incorporated, 866 Third Avenue, New York, New York 10022. 1984.

MEDIA INSURANCE: PROTECTING AGAINST HIGH JUDGMENTS, PUNITIVE DAMAGES, AND DEFENSE COSTS. John C. Landenau, Chairman. Practising Law Institute, 810 Seventh Avenue, New York, New York 10019. 1983.

NEW YORK TIMES VS SULLIVAN: THE NEXT TWENTY YEARS. Richard N. Winfield, Chairman. Practising Law Institute, 810 Seventh Avenue, New York, New York 10019. 1984.

POWER, PUBLICITY, AND THE ABUSE OF LIBEL LAW. Donald M. Gillmor. Oxford University Press, 200 Madison Avenue, New York, New York 10016. 1992.

THE PRACTICAL GUIDE TO LIBEL LAW. Neil J. Rosini. Praeger Publishers, One Madison Avenue, New York, New York 10010-3603. 1991.

PROTECTING THE BEST MAN: AN INTERPRETIVE HISTORY OF THE LAW OF LIBEL. Norman L. Rosenberg. University of North Carolina Press, P.O. Box 2288, 116 South Boundary Street, Chapel Hill, North Carolina 27515-2288. 1990.

RECKLESS DISREGARD: WESTMORELAND V. CBS ET AL, SHARON V. TIME. Renata Adler. Random House, Incorporated, Random House Publicity, (11-6) 201 East Fiftieth Street, New York, New York 10022. 1988.

SANFORD'S SYNOPSIS OF LIBEL AND PRIVACY. Fourth Edition. Bruce W. Sanford. Pharos Books, 200 Park Avenue, New York, New York 10166. 1991.

VIETNAM ON TRIAL: WESTMORELAND VS. CBS. Bob Brewin and Sydney Shaw. Atheneum Publishers, 866 Third Avenue, New York, New York 10022. 1987.

LAW REVIEWS AND PERIODICALS

MEDIA LAW JOURNAL. American Resource Publishing, P.O. Box 141, Pitman, New Jersey 08071. Monthly.

NEWSLETTERS AND NEWSPAPERS

LDRC BULLETIN. Libel Defense Resource Center, 404 Park Avenue, South, Sixteenth Floor, New York, New York 10016. Quarterly.

BIBLIOGRAPHIES

WESTMORELAND V. CBS: GUIDE TO THE MICROFICHE COLLECTION. Walter Schneir, Editor. Clearwater Publishing Company, New York, New York. 1987.

RESEARCH CENTERS, INSTITUTES, CLEARINGHOUSES

LIBEL DEFENSE RESOURCE CENTER. 404 Park Avenue, South, Sixteenth Floor, New York, New York 10016. (212) 889-2306.

AUDIOVISUALS

ANATOMY OF A LIBEL TRIAL: CAROL BURNETT V. NATIONAL ENQUIRER. Practising Law Institute, 810 Seventh Avenue, New York, New York 10019. 1983. Videotape.

LIBRARIES
See also: LAW LIBRARIES

LOOSELEAF SERVICES AND REPORTERS

LEGAL RESEARCH AND LAW LIBRARY MANAGEMENT. Revised Edition. Julius J. Marke and Richard Sloane. Law Journal Seminars-Press, Incorporated, 111 Eighth Avenue, Suite 900, New York, New York 10011. 1990- .

ON-SITE ACCESS GUIDE TO RLG ARCHIVAL, MANUSCRIPT, AND SPECIAL COLLECTIONS. Research Libraries Group, 1200 Villa Street, Mountain View, California 94041-1100. 1990.

HANDBOOKS, MANUALS, FORMBOOKS

BUILDING YOUR LAW LIBRARY: A STEP-BY-STEP GUIDE. Mickie A. Voges. American Bar Association, Section of Economics of Law Practice, 750 North Lake Shore Drive, Chicago, Illinois 60611. 1988.

HOW LIBRARIES COMPLY WITH THE AMERICANS WITH DISABILITIES ACT (ADA). Donald D. Foos and Nancy C. Pack, Editors. Oryx Press, 2214 North Central Avenue, Phoenix, Arizona 85004. 1992.

WERNER'S MANUAL FOR PRISON LAW LIBRARIES. Second Edition. Arturo A. Flores. Fred B. Rothman and Company, 10368 West Centennial Road, Littleton, Colorado 80127. 1990.

TEXTBOOKS AND GENERAL WORKS

AMERICAN LIBRARY LAWS. Fifth Edition. Alex Ladenson, Editor. American Library Association, 50 East Huron Street, Chicago, Illinois 60611. 1984.

BASICS OF LAW LIBRARIANSHIP. Deborah S. Panella. Haworth Press, Incorporated, 10 Alice Street, Binghamton, New York 13904. 1991.

CENSORSHIP, LIBRARIES AND THE LAW. Haig A. Bosmajian. Neal-Schuman Publishers Company, Incorporated, 23 Leonard Street, New York, New York 10013. 1983.

CONFERENCE ON THE GLOBAL RESPONSIBILITY OF LAW LIBRARIANS: PROCEEDINGS, OCTOBER 18-21, 1989, THE UNIVERSITY OF TEXAS SCHOOL OF LAW, AUSTIN, TEXAS. David R. Burch, Stephen E. Young, Editors. Fred B. Rothman and Company, 10368 West Centennial Road, Littleton, Colorado 80127. 1990.

CRIME IN THE LIBRARY: A STUDY OF PATTERNS, IMPACT AND SECURITY. Alan J. Lincoln. R.R. Bowker, 121 Chanlon Road, New Providence, New Jersey 07974. 1984.

DEFUSING CENSORSHIP: THE LIBRARIAN'S GUIDE TO HANDLING CENSORSHIP CONFLICTS. Frances M. Jones. Oryx Press, 2214 North Central Avenue, Phoenix, Arizona 85004-1483. 1983.

FEDERAL AID AND STATE LIBRARY AGENCIES: FEDERAL POLICY IMPLEMENTATION. David Shavit. Greenwood Publishing Group, Incorporated, 88 Post Road West, P.O. Box 5007, Westport, Connecticut 06881. 1985.

THE FEDERAL ROLE IN LIBRARY AND INFORMATION SERVICES. Marilyn Gell Mason. G.K. Hall and Company, 70 Lincoln Street, Boston, Massachusetts 02111. 1983.

THE FEDERAL ROLES IN SUPPORT OF ACADEMIC AND RESEARCH LIBRARIES. R. Kathleen Molz. American Library Association, 50 East Huron Street, Chicago, Illinois 60611. 1991.

FUNDING FOR LAW: LEGAL EDUCATION, RESEARCH AND STUDY. Karen Cantrell and Denise Wallen. Oryx Press, 2214 North Central Avenue, Phoenix, Arizona 85004. 1991.

INSPECTING A PRISON LAW LIBRARY. Gene Teitelbaum. William W. Gaunt and Sons, Incorporated, Gaunt Building, 3011 Gulf Drive, Holmes Beach, Florida 34217-2199. 1989.

LAW LIBRARY STAFF ORGANIZATION AND ADMINISTRATION. Martha J. Dragich and Peter C. Schanck. Fred B. Rothman and Company, 10368 West Centennial Road, Littleton, Colorado 80127. 1990.

LEGAL AND ETHICAL ISSUES IN ACQUISITIONS. Katina Strauch and Bruce Strauch, Editors. Haworth Press, Incorporated, 10 Alice Street, Binghamton, New York 13904. 1990.

LEGAL ISSUES IN PUBLIC AND SCHOOL LIBRARIES: SOME RECENT REFERENCES. John O. Christensen. Vance Bibliographies, P.O. Box 229, 112 North Charter Street, Monticello, Illinois 61856. 1990.

LIBRARY LAW AND LEGISLATION IN THE UNITED STATES. Alex Ladenson. Scarecrow Press, 52 Liberty Street, Box 4167, Metuchen, New Jersey 08840. 1982.

THE LOCAL UNION IN PUBLIC LIBRARIES. Doreen Lilore. Library Professional Publications, Shoe String Press, Incorporated, P.O. Box 4327, Hamden, Connecticut 06514. 1984.

POLICIES OF PUBLISHERS: A HANDBOOK FOR ORDER LIBRARIANS. David U. Kim and Craig A. Wilson. Scarecrow Press, Incorporated, 52 Liberty Street, Box 4167, Metuchen, New Jersey 08840. 1989.

PROCEEDINGS OF THE CONFERENCE ON TEACHING LEGAL AND FACTUAL RESEARCH IN PRIVATE LAW LIBRARIES: APRIL 26-APRIL 29, 1990, WESTFIELD INTERNATIONAL CONFERENCE CENTER, CHANTILLY, VIRGINIA. Fred B. Rothman and Company, 10368 West Centennial Road, Littleton, Colorado 80127. 1991.

PROFESSIONAL STAFFING AND JOB SECURITY IN THE ACADEMIC LAW LIBRARY. Joyce Saltalamachina and Janet Tracy. Glanville Publishers, 75 Main Street, Dobbs Ferry, New York 10522. 1988.

PUBLIC ACCESS TO GOVERNMENT INFORMATION: ISSUES, TRENDS, STRATEGIES. Peter Hernon and Charles R. McClure. Ablex Publishing Corporation, 355 Chestnut Street, Norwood, New Jersey 07648. 1988.

REFLECTIONS ON LAW LIBRARIANSHIP: A COLLECTION OF INTERVIEWS. Marjorie A. Garson and others. American Association of Law Libraries. Fred B. Rothman and Company, 10368 West Centennial Road, Littleton, Colorado 80127. 1988.

THE RIGHT TO INFORMATION: LEGAL QUESTIONS AND POLICY ISSUES. Jana Varlejs. McFarland and Company, Incorporated, P.O. Box 611, Jefferson, North Carolina 28640. 1984.

SETTING THE LEGAL INFORMATION AGENDA FOR THE YEAR 2000: BASED ON A WORKSHOP OF THE AMERICAN ASSOCIATION OF LAW LIBRARIES NATIONAL LEGAL RESOURCES COMMITTEE, WASHINGTON, D.C., OCTOBER 23-26, 1988. Mary Kathleen Price and Margaret Maes Axtmann, Editors. Fred B. Rothman and Company, 10368 West Centennial Road, Littleton, Colorado 80127. 1991- .

THE SPIRIT OF LAW LIBRARIANSHIP: A READER. Roy M. Mersky and Richard A. Leiter. Fred B. Rothman and Company, 10368 West Centennial Road, Littleton, Colorado 80127. 1991.

TO FACE THE MIND: LIBRARIES, TECHNOLOGY AND INTELLECTUAL FREEDOM. Eli M. Oboler. Libraries Unlimited, P.O. Box 3988, Englewood, Colorado 80155-3988. 1983.

THE TWENTY-FIRST CENTURY: TECHNOLOGY'S IMPACT ON ACADEMIC RESEARCH AND LAW LIBRARIES. Betty W. Taylor, Elizabeth B. Mann and Robert J. Munro. G.K. Hall and Company, Incorporated, 70 Lincoln Street, Boston, Massachusetts 02111. 1988.

DIGESTS, INDEXES, ABSTRACTS, CITATORS

AALL ANNUAL MEETINGS: AN ANNOTATED INDEX OF THE RECORDINGS. Frank G. Houdek and Susan D. Goldner. Fred B. Rothman and Company, 10368 West Centennial Road, Littleton, Colorado 80127. 1989- .

LIBRARY LITERATURE. H. W. Wilson Company, 950 University Avenue, Bronx, New York 10452. Bimonthly.

ANNUALS AND SURVEYS

ALA YEARBOOK. American Library Association, 50 East Huron Street, Chicago, Illinois 60611. 1983.

LAW REVIEWS AND PERIODICALS

AMERICAN LIBRARIES. American Library Association, 50 East Huron Street, Chicago, Illinois 60611. Monthly.

LIBRARY JOURNAL. Bowker, 205 East Forty-second Street, New York, New York 10017. Semimonthly.

WILSON LIBRARY BULLETIN. H. W. Wilson Company, 950 University Avenue, Bronx, New York 10452. Monthly.

NEWSLETTERS AND NEWSPAPERS

ALA WASHINGTON NEWSLETTER. American Library Association, 110 Maryland Avenue, Northeast, Washington, D.C. 20002. Monthly.

NEWSLETTER ON INTELLECTUAL FREEDOM. American Library Association, 50 East Huron Street, Chicago, Illinois 60611. Bimonthly.

BIBLIOGRAPHIES

ALTERNATIVE PUBLICATIONS: A GUIDE TO DIRECTORIES, INDEXES, BIBLIOGRAPHIES, AND OTHER SOURCES. Cathy Seitz Whitaker, Editor. American Library Association. Task Force on Alternatives in Print. McFarland and Company, Incorporated, Box 611, Jefferson, North Carolina 28640. 1990.

CD-ROM RESEARCH COLLECTIONS: AN EVALUATIVE GUIDE TO BIBLIOGRAPHIC AND FULL-TEXT CD-ROM DATABASES. Pat Ensor. Meckler Corporation, 11 Ferry Lane West, Westport, Connecticut 06880. 1991.

OBSCENITY, PORNOGRAPHY, AND LIBRARIES: A SELECTIVE BIBLIOGRAPHY. John O. Christensen. Vance Bibliographies, P.O. Box 229, 112 North Charter Street, Monticello, Illinois 61856. 1991.

DIRECTORIES

ALA HANDBOOK OF ORGANIZATION AND MEMBERSHIP DIRECTORY. American Library Association, 50 East Huron Street, Chicago, Illinois 60611. Annual.

AMERICAN LIBRARY DIRECTORY. R.R. Bowker, 121 Chanlon Road, New Providence, New Jersey 07974. Annual.

ASIS HANDBOOK AND DIRECTORY. American Society for Information Science, 8720 Georgia Avenue, Suite 501, Silver Spring, Maryland 20910-3602. 1985.

CD-ROM, POTENTIAL USERS, 1988-1990: A DIRECTORY OF 5,306 POTENTIAL USERS IN THE LIBRARY AND INFORMATION PROFESSIONS WITH INTENTIONS TO PURCHASE CD-ROM TECHNOLOGY IN 1988, 1989 AND BEYOND. Research Publications, Woodbridge, Connecticut. 1989.

DIRECTORY OF AUTOMATED LIBRARY SYSTEMS. Second Edition. John Corbin. Neal-Schuman Publications, Incorporated, 23 Leonard Street, New York, New York 10013. 1989.

DIRECTORY OF COMPUTER CONFERENCING IN LIBRARIES. Brian Williams. Meckler Corporation, 11 Ferry Lane West, Westport, Connecticut 06880. 1991.

DIRECTORY OF FEDERAL LIBRARIES. Second Edition. William R. Evinger, Editor. Oryx Press, 2214 North Central Avenue, Phoenix, Arizona 85004-1483. 1992.

DIRECTORY OF SPECIAL LIBRARIES AND INFORMATION CENTERS. Gale Research, Incorporated, 835 Penobscot Building, Detroit, Michigan 48226. Biennial.

DIRECTORY OF THE INTERNATIONAL ASSOCIATION OF LESBIAN AND GAY ARCHIVES AND LIBRARIES. Alan V. Miller. International Association of Lesbian and Gay Archives. Toronto, Ontario, Canada. 1987.

GOVERNMENT DEPOSITORY LIBRARIES. Joint Committee on Printing, United States Congress. Superintendent of Documents, United States Government Printing Office, Washington, D.C. 20402. 1984.

GRANTS FOR LIBRARIES: A GUIDE TO PUBLIC AND PRIVATE FUNDING PROGRAMS AND PROPOSAL WRITING TECHNIQUES. Second Edition. Emmett Corry. Libraries Unlimited, P.O. Box 3988, Englewood, Colorado 80155-3988. 1986.

INTERLIBRARY LOAN POLICIES DIRECTORY. Fourth Edition. Leslie R. Morris and Sandra Chass Morris. Neal-Schuman Publications, Incorporated, 23 Leonard Street, New York, New York 10013. 1991.

INTERNATIONAL DIRECTORY OF LIBRARIES FOR THE BLIND. Third Edition. Hiroshi Kawamura, Editor. International Federation of Library Associations and Institutions. Section of Libraries for the Blind. K.G. Saur, 245 West Seventeenth Street, New York, New York 10011. 1990.

LIBRARY COMPUTER AND TECHNOLOGY SPECIALISTS: A DIRECTORY. Barbara Desmarais and Norman Desmarais. Meckler Corporation, 11 Ferry Lane West, Westport, Connecticut 06880. 1991.

NATIONAL DIRECTORY OF EDUCATION LIBRARIES AND COLLECTIONS. Doris H. Christo. Meckler Corporation, 11 Ferry Lane West, Westport, Connecticut 06880. 1990.

WORLD DIRECTORY OF BIOLOGICAL AND MEDICAL SCIENCES LIBRARIES. Ursula H. Poland, Editor. K.G. Saur, 245 West Seventeenth Street, New York, New York 10011. 1988.

WORLD GUIDE TO SPECIAL LIBRARIES. Second Edition. K.G. Saur, 245 West Seventeenth Street, New York, New York 10011. 1990.

BIOGRAPHICAL SOURCES

BIOGRAPHICAL DIRECTORY OF NATIONAL LIBRARIANS. Frances Laverne Carroll and Philip J. Schwartz. Mansell Publishing Limited, Artillery House, Artillery Row, London SW1P 1RT, England. 1989.

WHO'S WHO IN LIBRARY AND INFORMATION SERVICES. American Library Association, 50 East Huron Street, Chicago, Illinois 60611. 1982.

ASSOCIATIONS AND PROFESSIONAL SOCIETIES

AMERICAN LIBRARY ASSOCIATION. 50 East Huron Street, Chicago, Illinois 60611. (312) 944-6780.

LIBRARY ADMINISTRATION AND MANAGEMENT ASSOCIATION. American Library Association, 50 East Huron Street, Chicago, Illinois 60611. (312) 944-6780.

SPECIAL LIBRARIES ASSOCIATION. 1700 Eighteenth Street, Northwest, Washington, D.C. 20009. (202) 234-4700.

RESEARCH CENTERS, INSTITUTES, CLEARINGHOUSES

CENTER FOR THE STUDY OF LIBRARIANSHIP. Kent State University, 314 University Library, Kent, Ohio 44242. (216) 672-2782.

CENTER FOR THE STUDY OF RURAL LIBRARIANSHIP. Clarion University of Pennsylvania, College of Library Science, Clarion, Pennsylvania 16214. (814) 226-2392.

COUNCIL ON LIBRARY RESOURCES. 1785 Massachusetts Avenue, Northwest, Suite 313, Washington, D.C. 20036. (202) 483-7474.

LIBRARY RESEARCH CENTER. University of Illinois, 410 David Kingley Hall, 1407 West Gregory Drive, Urbana, Illinois 61801. (217) 333-1980.

ONLINE DATABASES

ALANET. American Library Association, 50 East Huron Street, Chicago, Illinois 60611.

INFORMATION SCIENCE ABSTRACTS. IFI/Plenum Data Company, 302 Swann Avenue, Alexandria, Virginia 22301.

LIBRARY LITERATURE. H. W. Wilson Company, 950 University Avenue, Bronx, New York 10452.

LICENSING, INDUSTRIAL AND INTELLECTUAL
See also: COPYRIGHT; COPYRIGHT OFFICE; EXPORT AND IMPORT; LOCAL GOVERNMENT; PATENT AND TRADEMARK OFFICE; PATENTS; TRADEMARKS AND TRADE NAMES

LOOSELEAF SERVICES AND REPORTERS

MILGRIM ON LICENSING. Robert M. Milgrim. Matthew Bender and Company, Incorporated, 11 Penn Plaza, New York, New York 10001. 1990- .

TECHNOLOGY MANAGEMENT: LAW, TACTICS, FORMS. Robert Goldscheider. Clark Boardman Company, Limited, 435 Hudson Street, New York, New York 10014. 1988- .

HANDBOOKS, MANUALS, FORMBOOKS

THE BUSINESS OF INDUSTRIAL LICENSING: A PRACTICAL GUIDE TO PATENTS, KNOW-HOW, TRADEMARKS, AND INDUSTRIAL DESIGN. Second Edition. Patrick Hearn. Gower Publishing Company, Old Post Road, Brookfield, Vermont 05036. 1981.

AN EXECUTIVE'S COMPLETE GUIDE TO LICENSING. Roger A. McCaffrey and Thomas A. Meyer. Dow Jones-Irwin, 1818 Ridge Road, Homewood, Illinois 60430. 1989.

FORMS AND AGREEMENTS ON INTELLECTUAL PROPERTY AND INTERNATIONAL LICENSING. Third Edition. L. W. Melville. Clark Boardman Company, Limited, 435 Hudson Street, New York, New York 10014. 1979. (Annual Supplements).

INTERNATIONAL BUSINESS AGREEMENTS: A PRACTICAL GUIDE TO THE NEGOTIATION AND FORMULATION OF AGENCY, DISTRIBUTION, AND INTELLECTUAL PROPERTY LICENSING AGREEMENTS. Patrick Hearn. Gower Publishing Company, Old Post Road, Brookfield, Vermont 05036. 1987.

JOINT VENTURES AND CORPORATE PARTNERSHIPS: A STEP-BY-STEP GUIDE TO FORMING STRATEGIC BUSINESS ALLIANCES. Jennifer Lindsey. Probus Publishing Company, 118 North Linton Street, Chicago, Illinois 60606. 1989.

LICENSING IN FOREIGN AND DOMESTIC OPERATIONS: FORMS. Robert S. Goldscheider. Clark Boardman Company, Limited, 435 Hudson Street, New York, New York 10014. 1978. (Annual Supplements).

LICENSING LAW HANDBOOK. Brian G. Brunsuold, Editor. Clark Boardman Company, Limited, 435 Hudson Street, New York, New York 10014. 1984.

TEXTBOOKS AND GENERAL WORKS

ARBITRATION AND THE LICENSING PROCESS. Robert Goldscheider and Michael De Hass, Editors. Clark Boardman Company, Limited, 435 Hudson Street, New York, New York 10014. 1981. (Periodic Supplements).

DOMESTIC AND FOREIGN TECHNOLOGY LICENSING, 1984. Tom Arnold, Chairman. Longman, Incorporated, 19 West Forty-fourth Street, New York, New York 10036. 1984.

DRAFTING LICENSE AGREEMENTS. Michael A. Epstein, Editor. Prentice-Hall, Incorporated, 113 Sylvan Avenue, Englewood Cliffs, New Jersey 07632. 1991.

FINDING AND LICENSING NEW PRODUCTS AND TECHNOLOGY FROM THE U.S.A. John W. Morehead. Technology Search International, Incorporated, 500 East Higgins Road. Elk Grove Village, Illinois 60007-1437. 1982.

FRANCHISING AND LICENSING: TWO WAYS TO BUILD YOUR BUSINESS. Andrew J. Sherman. AMACOM, 135 West Fiftieth Street, New York, New York 10020. 1991.

FROM TECHNICAL PROFESSIONAL TO ENTREPRENEUR: A GUIDE TO INDUSTRIAL PROPERTY RIGHTS. David E. Doughtery. John Wiley and Sons, Incorporated, 605 Third Avenue, New York, New York 10158. 1986.

LAW AND BUSINESS OF LICENSING: LICENSING IN THE 1980'S. Second Edition. Robert Goldscheider and Tom Arnold, Editors. Clark Boardman Company, Limited, 435 Hudson Street, New York, New York 10014. 1983. (Annual Supplements).

THE LAW OF MERCHANDISING AND CHARACTER LICENSING. Charles W. Grimes and Gregory J. Battersby. Clark Boardman Company, Limited, 435 Hudson Street, New York, New York 10014. 1985.

LICENCE AGREEMENTS IN DEVELOPING COUNTRIES. United Centre on Transnational Corporations. United Nations Publishing Service, Room DC2-0853, New York, New York 10017. 1987.

LICENSING AGREEMENTS: PATENTS, KNOW-HOW, TRADE SECRETS, AND SOFTWARE. Kojo Yelpaala, Donald R. Worley and Dennis Campbell, Editors. Kluwer Academic Publishers, 101 Philip Drive, Assinippi Park, Norwell, Massachusetts 02061. 1988.

LICENSING IN INTERNATIONAL STRATEGY: A GUIDE FOR PLANNING AND NEGOTIATION. Farok J. Contractor. Greenwood Publishing Group, Incorporated, 88 Post Road West, P.O. Box 5007, Westport, Connecticut 06881. 1985.

MARKETING BY AGREEMENT: A CROSS-CULTURAL APPROACH TO BUSINESS NEGOTIATIONS. Second Edition. J. B. McCall and M. B. Warrington. John Wiley and Sons, Incorporated, 605 Third Avenue, New York, New York 10158. 1989.

AN OVERVIEW OF UNITED STATES EXPORT CONTROLS. L.J. Kutten and Brian C. Murphy. Kluwer Academic Publishers, 101 Philip Drive, Assinippi Park, Norwell, Massachusetts 02061. 1989.

REVERSE LICENSING: INTERNATIONAL TECHNOLOGY TRANSFER TO THE UNITED STATES. Manuchehr Shahrokhi. Praeger Publishers, One Madison Avenue, New York, New York 10010-3603. 1987.

UNDERSTANDING COMMERCIAL AND INDUSTRIAL LICENSING. Brendan Fowlston. Pergamon Press, Incorporated, Maxwell House, Fairview Park, Elmsford, New York 10523. 1984.

UNFAIR TRADE PRACTICES AND INTELLECTUAL PROPERTY. Roger E. Schechter. West Publishing Company, P.O. Box 64526, 50 West Kellogg Boulevard, St. Paul, Minnesota 55164-0526. 1986.

LAW REVIEWS AND PERIODICALS

AIPLA QUARTERLY JOURNAL. American Intellectual Property Law Association, 20001 Jefferson Davis Highway, Arlington, Virginia 22202. Quarterly.

INTELLECTUAL PROPERTY LAW REVIEW. Clark Boardman Company, Limited, 435 Hudson Street, New York, New York 10014. Annual.

NEWSLETTERS AND NEWSPAPERS

INTERNATIONAL COMPUTER LAW ADVISER. Law and Technology Press, Incorporated, P.O. Box 3780, Manhattan Beach, California 90266. Monthly.

LES NOUVELLES. Licensing Executives Society International, 1225 Elbur Avenue, Cleveland, Ohio 44107. Quarterly.

LICENSING AND ENTERTAINMENT LAW BULLETIN. Pioneer Publishing Company, 131 Beverly Street, Boston, Massachusetts 02114. Monthly.

THE LICENSING JOURNAL. GB Enterprises, P.O. Box 1169, Stanford, Connecticut 06904. Monthly.

LICENSING LAW AND BUSINESS REPORT. Clark Boardman Company, Limited, 435 Hudson Street, New York, New York 10014. Bimonthly.

THE MERCHANDISING REPORTER. Pennfair Communications, Incorporated, P.O. Box 2264, Westport, Connecticut 06880. Ten issues per year.

SOFTWARE PROTECTION. Law and Technology Press, Incorporated, P.O. Box 3780, Manhattan Beach, California 90266. Monthly.

ASSOCIATIONS AND PROFESSIONAL SOCIETIES

AMERICAN INTELLECTUAL PROPERTY LAW ASSOCIATION. 2001 Jefferson Davis Highway, Suite 203, Arlington, Virginia 22202. (703) 521-1680.

INTERNATIONAL LICENSING INDUSTRY AND MERCHANDISERS' ASSOCIATION. 350 Fifth Avenue, Suite 6210, New York, New York 10118. (212) 244-1944.

PR COMMITTEE FOR LICENSING AND REGISTRATION. 9321 Millbranch Place, Fairfax, Virginia 22031. (703) 691-2440.

SECTION ON INTELLECTUAL PROPERTY. Association of American Law Schools, One Dupont Circle, Northwest, Washington, D.C. 20036. (202) 296-8851.

LICENSING, OCCUPATIONAL
See: PROFESSIONAL ETHICS AND LIABILITY

LIE DETECTORS AND DETECTION

STATUTES, CODES, STANDARDS, UNIFORM LAWS

EMPLOYEE POLYGRAPH PROTECTION ACT OF 1988: LAW AND EXPLANATION. Commerce Clearing House, 4025 West Paterson Avenue, Chicago, Illinois 60646. 1988.

LOOSELEAF SERVICES AND REPORTERS

POLYGRAPH LAW REPORTER. American Polygraph Association, Box 8037, Chattanooga, Tennessee 37411.

HANDBOOKS, MANUALS, FORMBOOKS

THE COMPLETE POLYGRAPH HANDBOOK. Stan Abrams. Lexington Books, 125 Spring Street, Lexington, Massachusetts 02173. 1989.

TEXTBOOKS AND GENERAL WORKS

THE ACCURACY AND UTILITY OF POLYGRAPH TESTING. Norman Ansley. American Polygraph Association, Box 8037, Chattanooga, Tennessee 37411. 1984.

CREDIBILITY ASSESSMENT. John C. Yuille, Editor. Kluwer Academic Publishers, 101 Philip Drive, Assinippi Park, Norwell, Massachusetts 02061. 1989.

DRUG TESTS AND POLYGRAPHS: ESSENTIAL TOOLS OR VIOLATIONS OF PRIVACY? Daniel Jussim. Messner, New York, New York. 1987.

LIE DETECTOR USE IN THE WORKPLACE: FEDERAL AND STATE RESTRICTIONS. Gary J. Tulacz, Gary S. Mogel and Michael P. O'Toole. Prentice-Hall, Incorporated, 113 Sylvan Avenue, Englewood Cliffs, New Jersey 07632. 1988.

THE POLYGRAPH TEST: LIES, TRUTH, AND SCIENCE. Anthony Gale, Editor. Sage Publications, 2455 Teller Road, Newbury Park, California 91320. 1988.

PRE-EMPLOYMENT POLYGRAPH. Robert J. Ferguson and Chris Gugas, Sr. Charles C. Thomas Publishing, 2600 South First Street, Springfield, Illinois 62794-9265. 1984.

QUICK REFERENCE GUIDE TO POLYGRAPH ADMISSIBILITY, LICENSING LAWS, AND LIMITING LAWS. Twelfth Edition. Norman Ansley. American Polygraph Association, Box 8037, Chattanooga, Tennessee 37411. 1988.

TELLING LIES: CLUES TO DECEIT IN THE MARKETPLACE, POLITICS, AND MARRIAGE. Paul Ekman. W. W. Norton and Company, 500 Fifth Avenue, New York, New York 10110. 1991.

THEORIES AND APPLICATIONS IN THE DETECTION OF DECEPTION: A PSYCHOPHYSIOLOGICAL AND INTERNATIONAL PERSPECTIVE. Gershon Ben-Shakhar and John J. Furedy. Springer-Verlag New York, Incorporated, 175 Fifth Avenue, New York, New York 10010. 1990.

LAW REVIEWS AND PERIODICALS

AMERICAN POLYGRAPH ASSOCIATION JOURNAL. American Polygraph Association, Publications Manager, P.O. Box 1061, Severna Park, Maryland 21146. Quarterly.

NEWSLETTERS AND NEWSPAPERS

AMERICAN POLYGRAPH ASSOCIATION NEWSLETTER. American Polygraph Association, Publications Manager, P.O. Box 1061, Severna Park, Maryland 21146. Bimonthly.

BIBLIOGRAPHIES

LIE DETECTORS AND DETECTION: A SELECTED BIBLIOGRAPHY, 1985-1987. Verna Casey. Vance Bibliographies, P.O. Box 229, 112 North Charter Street, Monticello, Illinois 61856. 1988.

PRIVACY IN THE WORKPLACE: A BIBLIOGRAPHIC SURVEY. Alva W. Stewart. Vance Bibliographies, P.O. Box 229, 112 North Charter Street, Monticello, Illinois 61856. 1987.

TRUTH AND SCIENCE: A COMPREHENSIVE INDEX TO INTERNATIONAL LITERATURE ON THE DETECTION OF DECEPTION AND THE POLYGRAPH (LIE DETECTOR) TECHNIQUE. Second Edition. Norman Ansley, Frank Horvath, and Gordon Barland. American Polygraph Association, Box 8037, Chattanooga, Tennessee 37411. 1983.

ASSOCIATIONS AND PROFESSIONAL SOCIETIES

AMERICAN ASSOCIATION OF POLICE POLYGRAPHISTS. c/o Henry L. Canty, 1918 Sleepy Hollow, Pearland, Texas 77581. (713) 485-0902.

AMERICAN POLYGRAPH ASSOCIATION, Box 8037, Chattanooga, Tennessee 37411. (615) 892-3992.

RESEARCH CENTERS, INSTITUTES, CLEARINGHOUSES

AMERICAN POLYGRAPH ASSOCIATION RESEARCH CENTER. Michigan State University, 560 Baker Hall, East Lansing, Michigan 48824. (517) 355-2197.

AUDIOVISUALS

THE POLYGRAPH: DEMONSTRATION AND DISCUSSION. American Bar Association, Consortium for Professional Education, 750 North Lake Shore Drive, Chicago, Illinois 60611. 1977. Videotape.

THE POLYGRAPH: USEFUL TOOL OR DANGEROUS WEAPON. American Bar Association, Consortium for Professional Education, 750 North Lake Shore Drive, Chicago, Illinois 60611. 1977. Videotape.

SCIENTIFIC EVIDENCE: THE POLYGRAPH. American Bar Association, Consortium for Professional Education, 750 North Lake Shore Drive, Chicago, Illinois 60611. 1978. Videotape.

LIENS
See: ADMIRALTY; CONSTRUCTION INDUSTRY; MORTGAGES; SECURED TRANSACTIONS

LIFE ESTATES
See: REAL PROPERTY; WILLS, TRUSTS AND INHERITANCE

LIFE INSURANCE
See: INSURANCE, LIFE

LIMITATIONS OF ACTIONS
See: CIVIL PROCEDURE

LIQUIDATION
See also: BANKRUPTCY

LOOSELEAF SERVICES AND REPORTERS

CORPORATE LIQUIDATIONS: SECTION 331 AND RELATED PROBLEMS. David M. Flynn. Tax Management, Incorporated, Bureau of National Affairs, 1231 Twenty-fifth Street, Northwest, Washington, D.C. 20037. 1983- .

FAILING AND FAILED BUSINESSES. Gordon D. Henderson and Stuart J. Goldring. Commerce Clearing House, Incorporated, 4025 West Peterson Avenue, Chicago, Illinois 60646. 1987- .

LIQUIDATION OF SUBSIDIARIES: BASIS -- SECTION 334(B)(2). James T. O'Hara and Joseph L. Schiffhouer. Tax Management, Incorporated, Bureau of National Affairs, 1231 Twenty-fifth Street, Northwest, Washington, D.C. 20037. 1984- .

LIQUIDATION -- REINCORPORATION. Frederic A. Nicholson. Tax Management, Incorporated, Bureau of National Affairs, 1231 Twenty-fifth Street, Northwest, Washington, D.C. 20037. 1984- .

PARTIAL LIQUIDATION. Bayson L. Cook. Tax Management, Incorporated, Bureau of National Affairs, 1231 Twenty-fifth Street, Northwest, Washington, D.C. 20037. 1981- .

HANDBOOKS, MANUALS, FORMBOOKS

TAX MANUAL FOR CORPORATE LIQUIDATIONS, REDEMPTIONS, AND ESTATE PLANNING RECAPITALIZATIONS. Stanley Hagendorf. Greenwood Publishing Group, Incorporated, 88 Post Road West, P.O. Box 5007, Westport, Connecticut 06881. 1984.

TEXTBOOKS AND GENERAL WORKS

CORPORATE LIQUIDATIONS FOR THE LAWYER AND ACCOUNTANT. Fifth Edition. Howard A. Rumpf. Prentice-Hall, Incorporated, 113 Sylvan Avenue, Englewood Cliffs, New Jersey 07632. 1982.

FEDERAL INCOME TAXATION OF CORPORATE LIQUIDATIONS. Neil M. Goff. Shepard's/McGraw-Hill, P.O. Box 1235, Colorado Springs, Colorado 80901. 1984.

LIQUIDATING BANKRUPTCY: CORPORATE AND BUSINESS APPLICATIONS. Third Edition. Richard F. Broude. Bureau of National Affairs, 1231 Twenty-fifth Street, Northwest, Washington, D.C. 20037. 1987.

LIQUIDATION UNDER CHAPTER 7 OF THE BANKRUPTCY CODE. Second Edition. Walter Ray Phillips. Harrison Company, 3110 Crossing Park, Norcross, Georgia 30091. 1988.

VOLUNTARY CORPORATE LIQUIDATIONS. Ronald J. Kudla. Quorum Books, Greenwood Publishing Group, Incorporated, 88 Post Road West, P.O. Box 5007, Westport, Connecticut 06881. 1988.

LIQUOR LAWS
See: ALCOHOL CONTROL AND DRINKING BEHAVIOR

LITERARY PROPERTY
See: AUTHORS AND PUBLISHERS; COPYRIGHT

LITIGATION
See: COMPLEX LITIGATION; TRIAL PRACTICE

LOANS
See also: BANKS AND BANKING; CONSUMER CREDIT; CREDIT; MORTGAGES; PUBLIC FINANCE; SECURED TRANSACTIONS

LOOSELEAF SERVICES AND REPORTERS

BANK LOAN AGREEMENTS. Sidney S. Goldstein. Matthew Bender and Company, Incorporated, 11 Penn Plaza, New York, New York 10001. 1990- .

COMMERCIAL FINANCE GUIDE. Joseph Jude Norton, Thomas E. Gillespie and Darrel A. Rice. Matthew Bender and Company, Incorporated, 11 Penn Plaza, New York, New York 10001. 1990- .

COMMERCIAL LOAN DOCUMENTATION GUIDE. Joseph Jude Norton. Matthew Bender and Company, Incorporated, 11 Penn Plaza, New York, New York 10001. 1988- .

THE COMMUNITY REINVESTMENT ACT: POLICIES AND COMPLIANCE. Roland E. Brandel and David E. Teitelbaum. Prentice-Hall, Incorporated, 113 Sylvan Avenue, Englewood Cliffs, New Jersey 07632. 1989- .

HOME EQUITY UPDATE: A MANUAL FOR LENDERS AND LAWYERS. John H. Mancuso. Sheshunoff Information Services, Incorporated, Capitol Station, P.O. Box 13203, Austin, Texas 78711. 1989- .

SECURITIZATION OF FINANCIAL ASSETS. Jason H.P. Kravitt. Prentice-Hall, Incorporated, 113 Sylvan Avenue, Englewood Cliffs, New Jersey 07632. 1991.

STRUCTURING COMMERCIAL REAL ESTATE WORKOUTS: ALTERNATIVES TO FORECLOSURE. Stanley M. Stevens, Editor. Prentice-Hall, Incorporated, 113 Sylvan Avenue, Englewood Cliffs, New Jersey 07632. 1991.

STRUCTURING SECURED COMMERCIAL LOAN DOCUMENTS. James J. Cunningham, Richard Jay Goldstein and Matthew W. Kavanaugh. Research Institute of America, Incorporated, One Penn Plaza, New York, New York 10119. 1991- .

HANDBOOKS, MANUALS, FORMBOOKS

THE BANKER'S GUIDE TO MULTI-BANK CREDITS AND LOAN PARTICIPATIONS. Paul V. Reagon. Executive Enterprises Publications Company, 22 West Twenty-first Street, New York, New York 10010-6904. 1989.

BANKING AND COMMERCIAL LENDING LAW: RESOURCE MATERIALS. American Law Institute, 4025 Chestnut Street, Philadelphia, Pennsylvania 19104. 1983.

COMMUNITY REINVESTMENT ACT, HOME MORTGAGE DISCLOSURE ACT: REGULATORY COMPLIANCE MANUAL. Sheshunoff Information Services, Incorporated, Capitol Station, P.O. Box 13203, Austin, Texas 78711. 1989.

CONSUMER CREDIT COMPUTATION AND COMPLIANCE GUIDE WITH ANNUAL PERCENTAGE RATE TABLES. David Thorndike. Research Institute of America, Incorporated, One Penn Plaza, New York, New York 10119. 1980. (Supplement 1984).

GUIDE TO COMMERCIAL LENDING LAW. Pamela S. Gotcher. Sheshunoff Information Services, Incorporated, Capitol Station, P.O. Box 13203, Austin, Texas 78711. 1989.

GUIDE TO COMMERCIAL REAL ESTATE LOAN DOCUMENTATION. Donald E. Rapp, Jr. Prentice-Hall, Incorporated, 113 Sylvan Avenue, Englewood Cliffs, New Jersey 07632. 1990.

GUIDE TO SECURED LENDING TRANSACTIONS. Arnold B. Cohen. Research Institute of America, Incorporated, One Penn Plaza, New York, New York 10119. 1988.

HOW TO FINANCE YOUR SMALL BUSINESS WITH GOVERNMENT MONEY: SAB AND OTHER LOANS. Second Edition. Rick S. Hayes and John C. Howell. John Wiley and Sons, Incorporated, 605 Third Avenue, New York, New York 10158. 1983.

HOW TO PROFITABLY PROVIDE HOME EQUITY LINES OF CREDIT. Sheshunoff Information Services, Incorporated, Capitol Station, P.O. Box 13203, Austin, Texas 78711. 1987.

THE LENDER'S GUIDE TO CONSUMER COMPLIANCE AND ANTI-DISCRIMINATION LAWS: WITH COMPLETE COVERAGE OF THE COMMUNITY REINVESTMENT ACT, THE EQUAL CREDIT OPPORTUNITY ACT, AND THE HOME MORTGAGE DISCLOSURE ACT. Paul H. Schieber and Dennis Replansky. Probus Publishing Company, 118 North Linton Street, Chicago, Illinois 60606. 1991.

LOAN DOCUMENTATION HANDBOOK. Revised Edition. Continental Bank Educational Services Division, 231 South La Salle Street, Chicago, Illinois 60690. 1982.

A PRACTICAL GUIDE TO CONSTRUCTION LENDING. Richard Ridloff. Van Nostrand Reinhold Company, Incorporated, 115 Fifth Avenue, New York, New York 10003. 1985.

A PRACTICAL GUIDE TO HOME EQUITY LINES OF CREDIT. Gary S. Smuckler and Arthur B. Axelson. Executive Enterprises Publications Company, 22 West Twenty-first Street, New York, New York 10010-6904. 1989.

A PRACTICAL GUIDE TO THE LAW OF SECURED LENDING. Eric M. Holmes. Prentice-Hall, Incorporated, 113 Sylvan Avenue, Englewood Cliffs, New Jersey 07632. 1986.

REAL ESTATE LENDING: COMPREHENSIVE COMPLIANCE MANUAL. Robert P. Chamness and Timothy P. Meredith. American Bankers Association, 1120 Connecticut Avenue, Northwest, Washington, D.C. 20036. 1990- .

TERM LOAN HANDBOOK. John J. McCann, Editor. American Bar Association, Section of Corporation, Banking and Business Law, Law and Business, Prentice-Hall, Incorporated, 113 Sylvan Avenue, Englewood Cliffs, New Jersey 07632. 1983.

TRUTH IN LENDING: A COMPREHENSIVE GUIDE. Roland E. Brandel. Law and Business, Harcourt Brace Jovanovich, Incorporated, 6277 Sea Harbor Drive, Orlando, Florida 32821. 1985.

TRUTH-IN LENDING MANUAL: TEXT, FORMS, AND PROCEDURES FOR COMPLIANCE WITH THE FEDERAL TRUTH-IN LENDING LAW AND REGULATION Z. Sixth Edition. Ralph C. Clontz, Jr. Research Institute of America, Incorporated, One Penn Plaza, New York, New York 10119. 1991. (Updated Semianually).

TEXTBOOKS AND GENERAL WORKS

ASSET-BASED FINANCING: A TRANSACTIONAL GUIDE. Howard Ruda, Editor. Matthew Bender and Company, Incorporated, 11 Penn Plaza, New York, New York 10001. 1985. (Annual Supplements).

ASSET BASED LENDING: THE BASICS AND BEYOND. Edwin E. Smith. Massachusetts Continuing Legal Education, 20 West Street, Boston, Massachusetts 02111. 1990.

ASSET FINANCING. Michael Downey Rice. Little, Brown and Company, 34 Beacon Street, Boston, Massachusetts 02108. 1989.

BUSINESS LOAN WORKOUTS, 1988. Albert F. Reisman, Chairman. Practising Law Institute, 810 Seventh Avenue, New York, New York 10019. 1988.

COMMERCIAL FINANCE, FACTORING, AND OTHER ASSET-BASED LENDING, 1985. Peter H. Weil, Chairman. Practising Law Institute, 810 Seventh Avenue, New York, New York 10019. 1985.

COMMERCIAL LOAN DOCUMENTATION. Third Edition. William C. Hillman. Practising Law Institute, 810 Seventh Avenue, New York, New York 10019. 1990.

COMMUNITY REINVESTMENT ACT ALERT. John D. Hawke, Jr. Prentice-Hall, Incorporated, 113 Sylvan Avenue, Englewood Cliffs, New Jersey 07632. 1989.

CREATIVE REAL ESTATE FINANCING 1991. Richard J. Kane, Chairman. Practising Law Institute, 810 Seventh Avenue, New York, New York 10019. 1991.

ECONOMIC COSTS AND BENEFITS OF SUBSIDIZING WESTERN CREDITS TO THE EAST. Daniel F. Kohler. The Rand Corporation, 1700 Main Street, P.O. Box 2138, Santa Monica, California 90406. 1984.

EQUAL CREDIT OPPORTUNITY ACT. Geary Azata. National Consumer Law Center, 11 Beacon Street, Boston, MA 02108. 1988.

FIDUCIARY OBLIGATION, AGENCY, AND PARTNERSHIP: DUTIES IN ONGOING BUSINESS RELATIONSHIPS. Deborah A. DeMott. West Publishing Company, 50 West Kellogg Boulevard, St. Paul, Minnesota 55164. 1991.

HIDDEN SPENDING: THE POLITICS OF FEDERAL CREDIT PROGRAMS. Dennis S. Ippolito. University of North Carolina Press, P.O. Box 2288, Chapel Hill, North Carolina 27515-2288. 1984.

LAW OF TRUTH IN LENDING. Ralph J. Rohner and Fred H. Miller. Research Institute of America, Incorporated, One Penn Plaza, New York, New York 10119. 1984. (Supplement 1985).

THE LEGAL IMPLICATIONS OF SOVEREIGN SYNDICATED LENDING. Padazis Karamanolis. Oceana Publications, 75 Main Street, Dobbs Ferry, New York 10522. 1992.

LENDING TRANSACTIONS AND THE BANKRUPTCY ACT, 1986. Michael S. Lury, Chairman. Practising Law Institute, 810 Seventh Avenue, New York, New York 10019. 1986.

THE LIABILITY GAME: STRATEGIC PLANNING FOR REAL ESTATE LENDING. Stuart Marshall Bloch, Editor. Executive Enterprises Publications Company, 22 West Twenty-first Street, New York, New York 10010-6904. 1988.

LOAN AGREEMENTS FOR THE 90'S: EFFECTIVE DRAFTING AND NEGOTIATING. Massachusetts Continuing Legal Education, 20 West Street, Boston, Massachusetts 02111. 1990.

MODERN LENDING PRACTICES. John J. McCann, Chairman. Law and Business, Harcourt Brace Jovanovich, Incorporated, 6277 Sea Harbor Drive, Orlando, Florida 32821. 1983.

REAL ESTATE FINANCE. Second Edition. Michael R. Buchanan and Ronald D. Johnson. American Bankers Association, 1120 Connecticut Avenue, Northwest, Washington, D.C. 20036. 1988.

RESPA, TRUTH-IN LENDING, AND ECOA IN REAL ESTATE TRANSACTIONS. Second Edition. Comer Woodward Padrick, Jr. Harrison Company, 3110 Crossing Park, Norcross, Georgia 30091. 1987.

RISK ASSESSMENTS: LOAN FRAUD AND INSIDER ABUSE: A BANKWIDE ASSESSMENT OF RISKS ASSOCIATED WITH TRADITIONAL AND NONTRADITIONAL SERVICES AND NEW BUSINESS OPPORTUNITIES. American Bankers Association, 1120 Connecticut Avenue, Northwest, Washington, D.C. 20036. 1987.

STRUCTURING COMMERCIAL LOAN AGREEMENTS. Rodger Tighe. Research Institute of America, Incorporated, One Penn Plaza, New York, New York 10119. 1984.

TAXES, LOANS, AND INFLATION: HOW THE NATION'S WEALTH BECOMES MISALLOCATED. C. Eugene Steuerle. Brookings Institution, 1775 Massachusetts Avenue, Northwest, Washington, D.C. 20036-2188. 1985.

TROUBLED CONSTRUCTION LOANS: LAW AND PRACTICE. Stanley P. Sklar, Editor. John Wiley and Sons, Incorporated, 605 Third Avenue, New York, New York 10158. 1991.

TRUTH-IN-LENDING AND REGULATION Z. Dennis Replansky. American Law Institute-American Bar Association, Committee on Continuing Professional Education, 4025 Chestnut Street, Philadelphia, Pennsylvania 19104. 1984.

TRUTH-IN-LENDING IN TRANSACTION. Ernest L. Sarason. National Consumer Law Center, 11 Beacon Street, Boston, Massachusetts 02108. 1982. (Supplement 1984).

ANNUALS AND SURVEYS

FOURTH ANNUAL INSTITUTE CURRENT ISSUES IN DRAFTING COMMERCIAL BANK LOANS. H. Rodgin Cohen and Michael A. Ross. Prentice-Hall, Incorporated, 113 Sylvan Avenue, Englewood Cliffs, New Jersey 07632. 1989.

LAW REVIEWS AND PERIODICALS

COMMERCIAL LENDING REVIEW. John Colet Press, 306 Dartmouth Street, Boston, Massachusetts 02116. Quarterly.

AUDIOVISUALS

STRUCTURING UNSECURED LENDING TRANSACTIONS. Practising Law Institute, 810 Seventh Avenue, New York, New York 10019. 1984. Videotape.

LOBBYING

LOOSELEAF SERVICES AND REPORTERS

STATE LOBBYING LAWS. Elizabeth Bartz. S&FA Reporting Services, Incorporated, 1101 15th Street, Northwest, Suite 204, Washington, D.C. 20005. 1976- .

HANDBOOKS, MANUALS, FORMBOOKS

HOW TO LOBBY CONGRESS: A GUIDE FOR THE CITIZEN LOBBYIST. Donald DeKieffer. Dodd, Mead and Company, 71 Fifth Avenue, New York, New York 10003. 1981.

HOW TO WIN IN WASHINGTON: VERY PRACTICAL ADVICE ABOUT LOBBYING, THE GRASSROOTS, AND THE MEDIA. Ernest Wittenberg and Elisabeth Wittenberg. Basil Blackwell, Incorporated, 3 Cambridge Center, Cambridge, Massachusetts 02142. 1989.

LOBBYING AND GOVERNMENT RELATIONS: A GUIDE FOR EXECUTIVES. Charles S. Mack. Quorum Books, Greenwood Publishing Group, Incorporated, 88 Post Road West, P.O. Box 5007, Westport, Connecticut 06881. 1989.

LOBBYING: COURSE MANUAL. Karen Hastie Williams. Federal Publications, Incorporated, 1120 Twentieth Street, Northwest, Washington, D.C. 20036. 1984.

LOBBYING FOR FREEDOM IN THE 1980'S: A GRASS ROOTS GUIDE TO PROTECTING YOUR RIGHTS. Kenneth P. Norwick, Editor. Perigree Books, The Putnam Publishing Group, 200 Madison Avenue, New York, New York 10016. 1983.

THE LOBBYING HANDBOOK. John L. Zorack. Professional Lobbying and Consulting Center, 1111 Fourteenth Street, Northwest, Washington, DC 20005. 1990.

MANUAL FOR STATE LEGISLATIVE PROGRAMS. Second Edition. State Legislation Committee, American Institute of Certified Public Accountants, 1211 Avenue of the Americas, New York, New York 10036-8775. 1982.

TEXTBOOKS AND GENERAL WORKS

THE BEST CONGRESS MONEY CAN BUY. Philip M. Stern. Pantheon Books, 201 East Fiftieth Street, New York, New York 10022. 1988.

BUSINESS LOBBIES: THE PUBLIC GOOD AND THE BOTTOM LINE. Sar A. Levitan and Martha R. Cooper. Johns Hopkins University Press, 701 West Fortieth Street, Suite 275, Baltimore, Maryland 21211-2190. 1983.

THE CAMPAIGN FINANCE, ETHICS, AND LOBBY BLUE BOOK. James Whelan and David Johnson. Council of State Governments, Iron Works Pike, P.O. Box 11910, Lexington, Kentucky 40578. 1984.

CHARITY, ADVOCACY, AND THE LAW. Bruce R. Hopkins. John Wiley and Sons, Incorporated, 605 Third Avenue, New York, New York 10158. 1992.

COMMON CAUSE: LOBBYING IN THE PUBLIC INTEREST. Andrew S. McFarland. Chatham House Publishers, Incorporated, Box 1, Chatham, New Jersey 07928. 1984.

CORPORATE PACS AND FEDERAL CAMPAIGN FINANCING LAWS: USE OR ABUSE OF POWER? Ann B. Matasar. Greenwood Publishing Group, Incorporated, 88 Post Road West, P.O. Box 5007, Westport, Connecticut 06881. 1986.

CORPORATED GOVERNMENT RELATIONS AND LOBBYING: ALI-ABA COURSE OF STUDY MATERIALS. American Law Institute-American Bar Association, Committee on Continuing Professional Education, 4025 Chestnut Street, Philadelphia, Pennsylvania 19104. 1984.

THE CORPORATION IN POLITICS: PACS, LOBBYING LAWS, AND PUBLIC OFFICIALS. Thomas J. Schwarz, Vigo "Chip" Nielsen, Co-chairmen. Practising Law Institute, 810 Seventh Avenue, New York, New York 10019. 1983.

EFFECTIVE LOBBYING IN THE EUROPEAN COMMUNITY. James N. Gardner. Kluwer Academic Publishers, 101 Philip Drive, Assinippi Park, Norwell, Massachusetts 02061. 1991.

EFFECTIVE WASHINGTON REPRESENTATION. Stanley J. Marcuss, Editor. Law and Business, Harcourt Brace Jovanovich, Incorporated, 6277 Sea Harbor Drive, Orlando, Florida 32821. 1982.

FEDERAL LOBBYING. Jerald A. Jacobs, Editor. Bureau of National Affairs, Incorporated, 1231 Twenty-fifth Street, Northwest, Washington, D.C. 20037. 1989.

FROM THE GROUND UP: LINKING CITIZENS TO POLITICS AT COMMON CAUSE. Lawrence S. Rothenberg. Cambridge University Press, 40 West Twentieth Street, New York, New York 10011. 1992.

GAINING ACCESS: CONGRESS AND THE FARM LOBBY, 1919-1981. John Mark Hansen. University of Chicago Press, 5801 Ellis Avenue, Chicago, Illinois 60637. 1991.

HOW ORGANIZATIONS ARE REPRESENTED IN WASHINGTON: TOWARD A BROADER UNDERSTANDING OF THE SEEKING OF INFLUENCE AND OF PATTERNS OF REPRESENTATION. Lewis Anthony Dexter. University Press of America, 4720 Boston Way, Lanham, Maryland 20706. 1987.

INTEREST GROUP POLITICS IN AMERICA. Second Edition. Ronald J. Hrebenar and Ruth K. Scott. Prentice-Hall, Incorporated, 113 Sylvan Avenue, Englewood Cliffs, New Jersey 07632. 1990.

INTEREST GROUPS AND THE BUREAUCRACY: THE POLITICS OF ENERGY. John E. Chubb. Stanford University Press, Stanford, California 94305-2235. 1983.

LOBBYING AND THE LAW: A GUIDE TO FEDERAL TAX LAW LIMITATIONS ON LEGISLATIVE AND POLITICAL ACTIVITIES BY NONPROFIT ORGANIZATIONS. Second Edition. Deborah T. Ashford and Robert H. Frank. Frank and Company, McLean, Virginia. 1990.

LOBBYING CONGRESS: HOW THE SYSTEM WORKS. Bruce C. Wolpe. Congressional Quarterly Books, 1414 Twenty-second Street, Northwest, Washington D.C. 20037. 1990.

LOBBYING FOR SOCIAL CHANGE. Willard C. Richan. Haworth Press, Incorporated, 10 Alice Street, Binghamton, New York 13904. 1991.

LOBBYISTS AND LEGISLATORS: A THEORY OF POLITICAL MARKETS. Michael T. Hayes. Rutgers University Press, 109 Church Street, New Brunswick, New Jersey 08901. 1984.

LOSING BALANCE: THE DE-DEMOCRATIZATION OF AMERICA. William P. Kreml. M.E. Sharpe, Incorporated, 80 Business Park Drive, Armonk, New York 10504. 1991.

MOBILIZING INTEREST GROUPS IN AMERICA: PATRONS, PROFESSIONS, AND SOCIAL MOVEMENTS. Jack L. Walker, Jr. University of Michigan Press, P.O. Box 1104, 839 Greene Street, Ann Arbor, Michigan 48106. 1991.

MORE ACTION FOR A CHANGE. Ralph Nader and Kelley Griffin. Dembner Books, 80 Eighth Avenue, Suite 1803, New York, New York 10011. 1987.

THE NONPROFIT LOBBYING GUIDE: ADVOCATING YOUR CAUSE--AND GETTING RESULTS. Bob Smucker. Jossey-Bass, Incorporated, 350 Sansome Street, San Francisco, California 94104. 1991.

THE ORGANIZATION OF INTERESTS: INCENTIVES AND INTERNAL DYNAMICS OF POLITICAL INTEREST GROUPS. Terry M Moe. University of Chicago Press, 5801 Ellis Avenue, South, Chicago, Illinois 60637. 1988.

REGIONALISM, BUSINESS INTERESTS, AND PUBLIC POLICY. William D. Coleman and Henry J. Jacek, Editors. Sage Publications, 2455 Teller Road, Newbury Park, California 91320. 1989.

REPRESENTING GOD IN WASHINGTON: THE ROLE OF RELIGIOUS LOBBIES IN THE AMERICAN POLITY. Allen D. Hertzke. University of Tennessee Press, 293 Communications Building, Knoxville, Tennessee 37996. 1988.

SPECIAL INTEREST GROUPS IN AMERICAN POLITICS. Stephen Miller. Transaction Books, Rutgers University, New Brunswick, New Jersey 08903. 1983.

WASHINGTON AT WORK: BACK ROOMS AND CLEAN AIR. Richard E. Cohen. Research Institute of America, Incorporated, 910 Sylvan Avenue, Englewood Cliffs, New Jersey 07632. 1992.

THE WASHINGTON LOBBY. Fifth Edition. Congressional Quarterly, Incorporated, 1414 Twenty-second Street, Washington, D.C. 20037. 1987.

NEWSLETTERS AND NEWSPAPERS

PACS AND LOBBIES. Amward Publications, Incorporated. 2000 National Press Building, Washington, D.C. 20045. Semimonthly.

BIBLIOGRAPHIES

CORRIDOR GOVERNMENT: THE WASHINGTON LOBBY -- A SELECT BIBLIOGRAPHY OF PERIODICAL AND MONOGRAPH LITERATURE, 1977-1982. Nancy E. Fitch. Vance Bibliographies, P.O. Box 229, 112 North Charter Street, Monticello, Illinois 61856. 1982.

LOBBYING: A BIBLIOGRAPHY. Mary Vance. Vance Bibliographies, P.O. Box 229, 112 North Charter Street, Monticello, Illinois 61856. 1982.

RESOURCE GUIDE TO INFLUENCING STATE LEGISLATURES: AN ANNOTATED BIBLIOGRAPHY. Lynn Hellebust. Government Research Service, 701 Jackson, Topeka, Kansas 66603. 1991.

DIRECTORIES

NATIONAL DIRECTORY OF CORPORATE PUBLIC AFFAIRS. Columbia Books, Incorporated, 1212 New York Avenue, Northwest, Suite 330, Washington, D.C. 20005. Annual.

WASHINGTON LOBBYIST AND LAWYERS DIRECTORY. Sixth Edition. Paul Donovan, Editor. Communications Services, Incorporated, 121 Fouth Street, Southeast, Washington, D.C. 20003. 1986.

WASHINGTON REPRESENTATIVES: LOBBYISTS, FOREIGN AGENTS, CONSULTANTS, LEGAL ADVISORS, PUBLIC AFFAIRS AND GOVERNMENT RELATIONS. Columbia Books, Incorporated, 1212 New York Avenue, Northwest, Suite 330, Washington, D.C. 20005. Annual.

ASSOCIATIONS AND PROFESSIONAL SOCIETIES

AMERICAN LEAGUE OF LOBBYISTS. P.O. Box 30005, Alexandria, Virginia 22310. (703) 960-3011.

LOCAL GOVERNMENT
See also: TREASURY DEPARTMENT

LOOSELEAF SERVICES AND REPORTERS

LOCAL GOVERNMENT LAW. Chester J. Antieau. Matthew Bender and Company, Incorporated, 11 Penn Plaza, New York, New York 10001. 1955.

HANDBOOKS, MANUALS, FORMBOOKS

ELECTED OFFICIALS HANDBOOKS: PRACTICAL AIDS FOR BUSY LOCAL OFFICIALS. Third Edition. Susan G. Clark. International City Management Association, 1120 G Street, Northwest, Washington, D.C. 20005. 1988.

MOODY'S MUNICIPAL AND GOVERNMENT MANUAL. Moody's Investors Service, Incorporated, 99 Church Street, New York, New York 10007. Annual.

MUNICIPAL ORDINANCES: TEXT AND FORMS. Second Edition. Byron S. Matthews. Callaghan and Company, 155 Pfingsten Road, Deerfield, Illinois 60015. 1982. (Periodic Supplements).

TEXTBOOKS AND GENERAL WORKS

ANTITRUST AND LOCAL GOVERNMENT: PERSPECTIVES ON THE BOULDER DECISION. James V. Siena. Seven Locks Press, P.O. Box 27, Cabin John, Maryland 20818. 1982.

ANTITRUST LAW AND LOCAL GOVERNMENT. Mark R. Lee. Quorum Books, Imprint of Greenwood Publishing Group, Incorporated, 88 Post Road West, P.O. Box 5007, Westport, Connecticut 06881. 1985.

THE CHANGING FACE OF PUBLIC PURCHASING: THE ABA MODEL PROCUREMENT CODE AND ITS IMPLEMENTATION. American Bar Association, Section of Public Contract Law, 750 North Lake Shore Drive, Chicago, Illinois 60611. 1983.

FEDERAL CONSTITUTIONAL LAW AND LOCAL GOVERNMENT: A TREATISE FOR CITY ATTORNEYS, PUBLIC INTEREST LITIGATIONS, AND STUDENTS. M. David Gelfand. The Michie Company, P.O. Box 7587, Charlottesville, Virginia 22906-7587. 1984.

GOVERNING AT THE GRASSROOTS: STATE AND LOCAL GOVERNMENT. Second Edition. Nicholas Henry. Prentice-Hall, Incorporated, 113 Sylvan Avenue, Englewood Cliffs, New Jersey 07632. 1984.

GOVERNMENTAL STRUCTURE AND LOCAL PUBLIC FINANCE. David L. Chicoine and Norman Walzer. Oelgeschlager, Gunn and Hain, Incorporated, 245 Mirriam Street, Weston, Massachusetts 02193. 1985.

GUIDE TO MUNICIPAL OFFICIAL STATEMENTS. Joseph C. Daly. Harcourt Brace Jovanovich, Incorporated, 6277 Sea Harbor Drive, Orlando, Florida 32821. 1980. (Periodic Supplements).

HANDBOOK OF LOCAL GOVERNMENT LAW. Osborne M. Reynolds. West Publishing Company, P.O. Box 64526, 50 West Kellogg Boulevard, St. Paul, Minnesota 55164-0526. 1982. (Hornbook).

JUDGES AND THE CITIES: INTERPRETING LOCAL AUTONOMY. Gordon L. Clark. University of Chicago Press, 5801 Ellis Avenue, Third Floor, South, Chicago, Illinois 60637. 1985.

LOCAL GOVERNMENT LAW. C. Dallas Sands and Michael E. Libonatio. Callaghan and Company, 155 Pfingsten Road, Deerfield, Illinois 60015. 1981. (Annual).

LOCAL GOVERNMENT LAW: CASES AND MATERIALS. Fourth Edition. William D. Valente and David J. McCarthy. West Publishing Company, 50 West Kellogg Boulevard, St. Paul, Minnesota 55164. 1991.

LOCAL GOVERNMENT LAW IN A NUTSHELL. Third Edition. David J. McCarthy, Jr. West Publishing Company, P.O. Box 64526, 50 West Kellogg Boulevard, St. Paul, Minnesota 55164-0526. 1990.

MANAGING STATE AND LOCAL GOVERNMENT: CASES AND READINGS. Frederick S. Lane, Editor. Saint Martin's Press, Incorporated, 175 Fifth Avenue, New York, New York 10010. 1980.

ORDINANCE LAW ANNOTATIONS: A COMPREHENSIVE DIGEST OF AMERICAN CASES THAT INTERPRET OR APPLY CITY AND COUNTY ORDINANCES. Wesley H. Wisborne and J. F. Corcoran, Editors. Shepard's/McGraw-Hill, P.O. Box 1235, Colorado Springs, Colorado 80901. 1983. (Annual Supplements).

PUBLIC POLICY AND FEDERALISM: ISSUES IN STATE AND LOCAL POLITICS. Jeffrey R. Henig. Saint Martin's Press, Incorporated, 175 Fifth Avenue, New York, New York 10010. 1985.

A REVIEW OF PRIVATE APPROACHES FOR DELIVERY OF PUBLIC SERVICES. Harry P. Hatry. Urban Institute Press, 4720-A Boston Way, Lanham Way, Maryland 20706. 1983.

STATE AND LOCAL GOVERNMENT DEBT FINANCING. M. David Gelfand and Robert S. Amdursky, Editors. Callaghan and Company, 155 Pfingsten Road, Deerfield, Illinois 60015. 1990.

STATE AND LOCAL GOVERNMENT IN THE FEDERAL SYSTEM: CASES AND MATERIALS. Third Edition. Daniel R. Mandelker and Dawn Clark Netsch. The Michie Company, P.O. Box 7587, Charlottesville, Virginia 22906-7582. 1990.

STATE AND LOCAL GOVERNMENT: THE NEW BATTLEGROUND. Gerald L. Houseman. Prentice-Hall, Incorporated, 113 Sylvan Avenue, Englewood Cliffs, New Jersey 07632. 1986.

STATE AND LOCAL POLITICS: THE GREAT ENTANGLEMENT. Third Edition. Robert S. Lorch. Prentice-Hall, Incorporated, 113 Sylvan Avenue, Englewood Cliffs, New Jersey 07632. 1989.

STATE-LOCAL RELATIONS: A PARTNERSHIP APPROACH. Joseph F. Zimmerman. Praeger Publishers, One Madison Avenue, New York, New York 10110-3603. 1983.

DIGESTS, INDEXES, ABSTRACTS, CITATORS

SHEPARD'S STATE CITATORS. Shepard's/McGraw-Hill, P.O. Box 1235, Colorado Springs, Colorado 80901. Supplemented two to eight times per year depending upon state. (Cites appellate cases citing city ordinances; arranged by city).

ANNUALS AND SURVEYS

MUNICIPAL YEAR BOOK. International City Management Association, 1120 G Street, Northwest, Washington, D.C. 20005. Annual.

STATE AND LOCAL GOVERNMENT FISCAL ALMANAC. Municipal, 180 North Michigan Avenue, Suite 800, Chicago, Illinois 60601. 1982.

LAW REVIEWS AND PERIODICALS

STATE AND LOCAL GOVERNMENT REVIEW. Institute of Government, Terrell Hall, University of Georgia, Athens, Georgia 30602. Triannual.

UNIVERSITY OF DETROIT JOURNAL OF URBAN LAW. University of Detroit, School of Law, 651 East Jefferson Avenue, Detroit, Michigan 48226. Quarterly.

URBAN LAWYER. American Bar Association, Section of Urban, State and Local Government Law, 750 North Lake Shore Drive, Chicago, Illinois 60611. Quarterly.

WASHINGTON UNIVERSITY JOURNAL OF URBAN AND CONTEMPORARY LAW. Washington University, School of Law, St. Louis, Missouri 63130. Semiannual.

NEWSLETTERS AND NEWSPAPERS

CURRENT MUNICIPAL PROBLEMS. Callaghan and Company, 3201 Old Glenview Road, Wilmette, Illinois 60091. Quarterly.

FINANCING LOCAL GOVERNMENT. Government Information Sources, 1611 North Kent Street, Arlington, Virginia 22209. Semimonthly.

LOCAL GOVERNMENT LAW BULLETIN. Institute of Government, University of North Carolina, Knapp Building, CB#3330, Chapel Hill, North Carolina 27599. Quarterly.

LOCAL STATE FUNDING REPORT. Government Information Sources, 1611 North Kent Street, Arlington, Virginia 22209. Weekly.

THE MAYOR. United States Conference of Mayors, 1620 I Street, Northwest, Washington, D.C. 20006. Twenty-four issues per year.

MCQUILLAN MUNICIPAL LAW REPORT. Callaghan and Company, 3201 Old Glenview Road, Wilmette, Illinois 60091. Monthly.

MUNICIPAL IMMUNITY LAW BULLETIN. Quinlan Publishing Company, 23 Drydock Avenue, Boston, Massachusetts 02110. Monthly.

MUNICIPAL LAW COURT DECISIONS. National Institute of Municipal Law Officers, 1000 Connecticut Avenue, Northwest, Washington, D.C. 20036. Bimonthly.

MUNICIPAL LAW DOCKET. National Institute of Municipal Law Officers, 1000 Connecticut Avenue, Northwest, Washington, D.C. 20036. Bimonthly.

MUNICIPAL LITIGATION REPORTER. Legal Research Services, 810 Idylberry Road, San Rafael, California 94903. Monthly.

MUNICIPAL ORDINANCE REVIEW. National Institute of Municipal Law Officers, 1000 Connecticut Avenue, Northwest, Washington, D.C. 20036. Bimonthly.

NIMLO CONGRESSIONAL NEWS. National Institute of Municipal Law Officers, 1000 Connecticut Avenue, Northwest, Suite 902, Washington, D.C. 20036. Quarterly.

URBAN, STATE AND LOCAL LAW NEWSLETTER. American Bar Association, Section of Urban, State, and Local Government Law, 750 North Lake Shore Drive, Chicago, Illinois 60611. Three issues per year.

U.S. MAYOR. U.S. Conference of Mayors, 1620 I Street, Northwest, Washington, D.C. 20006. Semimonthly.

BIBLIOGRAPHIES

GOVERNMENT CORPORATIONS, SPECIAL DISTRICTS, AND PUBLIC AUTHORITIES: THEIR ORGANIZATION AND MANAGEMENT: A SELECTED, ANNOTATED BIBLIOGRAPHY. Xenia W. Dustin. Institute of Public Administration, Publications Office, 55 West Forty-fourth Street, New York, New York 10036. 1985.

DIRECTORIES

BRADDOCK'S FEDERAL-STATE-LOCAL GOVERNMENT DIRECTORY. Braddock Publications, 1001 Connecticut Avenue, Northwest, Suite 210, Washington, D.C. 20036. Biennial.

COMPENSATION: AN ANNUAL REPORT ON LOCAL GOVERNMENT EXECUTIVE SALARIES AND FRINGE BENEFITS. International City Management Association, 1120 G Street, Northwest, Washington, D.C. 20009. Annual.

COUNTY EXECUTIVE DIRECTORY. Carroll Publishing Company, 1058 Thomas Jefferson Street, Northwest, Washington, D.C. 20007. Semiannual.

MAYORS OF AMERICA'S PRINCIPAL CITIES. United States Conference on Mayors, 1620 I Steet, Northwest, Washington, D.C. 20006. Semiannual.

MUNICIPAL EXECUTIVE DIRECTORY. Carroll Publishing Company, 1058 Thomas Jefferson Street, Northwest, Washington, D.C. 20007. Semiannual.

STATE-LOCAL GOVERNMENT DIRECTORY. Want Publishing Company, 1511 K Street, Northwest, Washington, D.C. 20005. Annual.

STATE MUNICIPAL LEAGUE DIRECTORY. National League of Cities, 1301 Pennsylvania Avenue, Northwest, Washington, D.C. 20004. Annual.

ASSOCIATIONS AND PROFESSIONAL SOCIETIES

AMERICAN BAR ASSOCIATION, SECTION OF URBAN, STATE AND LOCAL GOVERNMENT LAW. 750 North Lake Shore Drive, Chicago, Illinois 60611. (312) 988-5000.

AMERICAN BAR ASSOCIATION, SPECIAL COMMITTEE ON HOUSING AND URBAN DEVELOPMENT LAW. 750 North Lake Shore Drive, Chicago, Illinois 60611. (312) 988-5000.

ASSOCIATION OF AMERICAN LAW SCHOOLS, SECTION ON LOCAL GOVERNMENT. One Dupont Circle, Northwest, Washington, D.C. 20036. (202) 296-8851.

NATIONAL ASSOCIATION OF COUNTIES. 440 First Street, Northwest, Washington, D.C. 20001. (202) 393-6226.

NATIONAL ASSOCIATION OF COUNTY CIVIL ATTORNEYS. 440 First Street, Northwest, Washingon, D.C. 20001. (202) 393-6226.

NATIONAL ASSOCIATION OF TOWNS AND TOWNSHIPS. 1522 K Street, Northwest, Suite 730, Washington, D.C. 20005. (202) 737-5200.

NATIONAL LEAGUE OF CITIES. 1301 Pennsylvania Avenue, Northwest, Washington, D.C. 20004. (202) 626-3000.

RESEARCH CENTERS, INSTITUTES, CLEARINGHOUSES

ACADEMY FOR STATE AND LOCAL GOVERNMENT. 444 North Capitol Street, Northwest, Suite 349, Washington, D.C. 20001. (202) 638-1445.

EDWIN F. JAECKLE CENTER FOR STATE AND LOCAL GOVERNMENT LAW. State University of New York at Buffalo, 422 O'Brian Hall, Amherst, New York 14260. (716) 636-2072.

GOVERNMENT LAW CENTER. University of Louisville, Louisville, Kentucky 40292. (502) 588-6482.

INSTITUTE OF GOVERNMENT. University of North Carolina at Chapel Hill, Knapp Building, CBB330, Chapel Hill, North Carolina 27599. (919) 966-5381.

STATISTICS SOURCES

1982 CENSUS OF GOVERNMENTS. Volume 5, Local Government in Metropolitan Areas. United States Department of Commerce, Bureau of the Census. Superintendent of Documents, United States Government Printing Office, Washington, D.C. 20402. 1985.

AUDIOVISUALS

1983-1984 ANNUAL REVIEW OF STATE, URBAN AND LOCAL GOVERNMENT LAW. American Bar Association, Section of State, Urban, and Local Government Law, 750 North Lake Shore Drive, Chicago, Illinois 60611. 1984. Audiocassette.

LOCAL TRANSIT

HANDBOOKS, MANUALS, FORMBOOKS

LOCAL OFFICIALS GUIDE TO TRANSIT FINANCIAL PLANNING. National League of Cities, 1301 Pennsylvania Avenue, Northwest, Washington, D.C. 20004. 1989.

TEXTBOOKS AND GENERAL WORKS

ACCESS TO MASS TRANSIT FOR BLIND AND VISUALLY IMPAIRED TRAVELERS. Mark M. Uslan. American Foundation for the Blind, 15 West Sixteenth Street, New York, New York 10011. 1990.

THE AUTOMOBILE AND URBAN TRANSIT: THE FORMATION OF PUBLIC POLICY IN CHICAGO, 1900-1930. Paul Barrett. Temple University Press, 1601 North Broad Street, University Services Building, Philadelphia, Pennsylvania 19122. 1983.

BUS DEREGULATION IN THE METROPOLITAN AREAS. Laurie Pickup. Avebury, Brookfield, Vermont. 1991.

CASH, TOKENS, AND TRANSFERS: A HISTORY OF URBAN MASS TRANSIT IN NORTH AMERICA. Brian J. Cudahy. Fordham University Press, University Box L, Bronx, New York 10458-5172. 1990.

CITY TRANSPORT IN DEVELOPED AND DEVELOPING COUNTRIES. Tom Rallis. St. Martin's Press, 175 Fifth Avenue, New York, New York 10010. 1988.

CRIME, FEAR, AND THE NEW YORK CITY SUBWAYS: THE ROLE OF CITIZEN ACTION. Dennis Jay Kenney. Praeger Publishers, One Madison Avenue, New York, New York 10010-3603. 1987.

THE FEDERAL ROLE IN URBAN MASS TRANSPORTATION. George M. Smerk. Indiana University Press, Tenth and Morton Streets, Bloomington, Indiana 47405. 1991.

MANAGING PUBLIC TRANSIT STRATEGICALLY: A COMPREHENSIVE APPROACH TO STRENGTHENING SERVICE AND MONITORING PERFORMANCE. Gordon J. Fielding. Jossey-Bass, Incorporated, 350 Sansome Street, San Francisco, California 94104. 1987.

MARKETING PUBLIC TRANSIT: A STRATEGIC APPROACH. Christopher H. Lovelock. Praeger Publishers, One Madison Avenue, New York, New York 10010-3603. 1987.

PRIVATE INNOVATIONS IN PUBLIC TRANSIT. John C. Weicher. American Enterprise Institute for Public Policy Research, Distributed by University Press of America, 4720 Boston Way, Lanham, Maryland 20706. 1988.

PUBLIC POLICY AND TRANSIT SYSTEM MANAGEMENT. George M. Guess. Greenwood Publishing Group, Incorporated, 88 Post Road West, P.O. Box 5007, Westport, Connecticut 06881. 1990.

PUBLIC TRANSPORTATION. Second Edition. George E. Gray and Lester A. Hoel, Editors. Prentice-Hall, Incorporated, 113 Sylvan Avenue, Englewood Cliffs, New Jersey 07632. 1992.

TRANSPORT PLANNING FOR THIRD WORLD CITIES. Harry T. Dimitriou. Routledge, Chapman & Hall, 29 West Thirty-fifth Street, New York, New York 10001. 1990.

TRANSPORTATION ECONOMICS AND PUBLIC POLICY, WITH URBAN EXTENSIONS. Alan Abouchar. Robert E. Krieger Publishing Company, Incorporated, P.O. Box 9542, Malabar, Florida 32902-9542. 1983.

UNDER THE SIDEWALKS OF NEW YORK: THE STORY OF THE GREATEST SUBWAY SYSTEM IN THE WORLD. Revised Edition. Brian J. Cudahy. S. Greene Press, Distributed by Viking Penguin, Incorporated, 375 Hudson Street, New York, New York 10014. 1988.

URBAN TRANSIT POLICY: AN ECONOMIC AND POLITICAL HISTORY. David Jones. Prentice-Hall, Incorporated, 113 Sylvan Avenue, Englewood Cliffs, New Jersey 07632. 1985.

ENCYCLOPEDIAS AND DICTIONARIES

URBAN PUBLIC TRANSPORTATION GLOSSARY. Benita H. Gray, Editor. National Research Council. Transportation Research Board. Committee on Public Transportation Planning and Development. Subcommittee on Urban Public Transportation Terms, 2101 Constitution Avenue, Northwest, Washington, D.C. 20418. 1989.

LAW REVIEWS AND PERIODICALS

TRANSIT JOURNAL. American Public Transit Association, 1225 Connecticut Avenue, Northwest, Washington, D.C. 20036. Quarterly.

TRANSPORTATION JOURNAL. American Society of Traffic and Transportation, Incorporated, 547 West Jackson Boulevard, Chicago, Illinois 60606. Quarterly.

NEWSLETTERS AND NEWSPAPERS

PASSENGER TRANSPORT. American Public Transit Association, 1225 Connecticut Avenue, Northwest, Washington, D.C. 20036. Weekly.

PUBLIC TRANSIT REPORT. Business Publishers, Box 1067, Silver Spring, Maryland 20910. Biweekly.

BIBLIOGRAPHIES

LOCAL TRANSIT, FINANCE: PUBLICATIONS, 1980-1987. Mary Vance. Vance Bibliographies, P.O. Box 229, 112 North Charter Street, Monticello, Illinois 61856. 1988.

DIRECTORIES

JANE'S URBAN TRANSPORT SYSTEMS. Jane's Publishing Incorporated, 1340 Braddock Place, Suite 300, Box 1436, Alexandria, Virginia 22314-1651. Annual.

URBAN TRANSPORTATION OFFICIALS: A GUIDE TO THE TRANSPORTATION STAFF OF THE NATION'S MAYORS. United States Conference of Mayors, 1620 I Street, Northwest, Washington, D.C. 20006. Annual.

ASSOCIATIONS AND PROFESSIONAL SOCIETIES

AMERICAN PUBLIC TRANSIT ASSOCIATION. 1201 New York Avenue, Northwest, Suite 400, Washington, D.C. 20005. (202) 898-4000.

AMERICAN SOCIETY OF TRANSPORTATION, AND LOGISTICS. P.O. Box 33095, Louisville, Kentucky 40232. (502) 451-8150.

RESEARCH CENTERS, INSTITUTES, CLEARINGHOUSES

CENTER FOR TRANSPORTATION STUDIES. Massachusetts Institute of Technology, Cambridge, Massachusetts 02139. (617) 253-5320.

INSTITUTE OF TRANSPORTATION STUDIES. University of California, Berkeley, 109 McLaughlin Hall, Berkeley, California 94720. (415) 642-3585.

TRANSPORTATION RESEARCH CENTER. College of Engineering, University of Florida, Gainesville, Florida 32611. (904) 392-0378.

URBAN TRANSPORTATION CENTER. University of Illinois at Chicago, 1033 West Van Buren Street, Chicago, Illinois 60607. (312) 996-4820.

STATISTICS SOURCES

CENSUS OF TRANSPORTATION. United States Bureau of the Census, Transportation Division. Superintendent of Documents, United States Government Printing Office, Washington, D.C. 20402. Every Five Years.

NATIONAL TRANSPORTATION STATISTICS. United States Department of Transportation, Transportation Information Division, Superintendent of Documents, United States Government Printing Office, Washington, D.C. 20402. Annual.

OTHERS SOURCES

COMMUTER, REGIONAL, AND RAIL TRANSIT: RESEARCH AND ANALYSIS. National Research Council. Transportation Research Board, 2101 Constitution Avenue, Northwest, Washington, D.C. 20418. 1988.

PUBLIC TRANSIT RESEARCH: MANAGEMENT AND PLANNING, 1991. National Research Council. Transportation Research Board, 2101 Constitution Avenue, Northwest, Washington, D.C. 20418. 1991.

PUBLIC TRANSIT RESEARCH: RAIL, BUS, AND NEW TECHNOLOGY, 1991. National Research Council. Transportation Research Board, 2101 Constitution Avenue, Northwest, Washington, D.C. 20418. 1991.

REPORT ON THE FEDERAL MASS TRANSIT POLICY: VIEWS AND RECOMMENDATIONS. Senate Committee on Banking, Housing, and Urban Affairs, Subcommittee on Housing and Urban Affairs. Superintendent of Documents, United States Government Printing Office, Washington, D.C. 20402. 1991.

RESEARCH FOR PUBLIC TRANSIT: NEW DIRECTIONS: STRATEGIC TRANSPORTATION RESEARCH STUDY: TRANSIT. Transportation Research Board, National Research Council, 2101 Constitution Avenue, Northwest, Washington, D.C. 20418. 1987.

RESEARCH IN BUS AND RAIL TRANSIT OPERATIONS. National Research Council. Transportation Research Board, 2101 Constitution Avenue, Northwest, Washington, D.C. 20418. 1989.

TRANSIT ADMINISTRATION AND PLANNING RESEARCH. National Research Council. Transportation Research Board, 2101 Constitution Avenue, Northwest, Washignton, D.C. 20418. 1989.

TRANSIT ISSUES AND RECENT ADVANCES IN PLANNING AND OPERATIONS TECHNIQUES. National Research Council. Transportation Research Board, 2101 Constitution Avenue, Northwest, Washington, D.C. 20418. 1989.

TRANSIT MANAGEMENT AND REPLACEMENT CAPITAL PLANNING. National Research Council. Transporation Research Board, 2101 Constitution Avenue, Northwest, Washington, D.C. 20418. 1988.

TRANSIT MANAGEMENT, MARKETING, AND PERFORMANCE. National Research Council. Transportation Research Board, 2101 Constitution Avenue, Northwest, Washington, D.C. 20418. 1987.

TRANSIT MARKETING: SUCCESSES AND FAILURES. Richard L. Oram. Transportation Research Board, National Research Council, 2101 Constitution Avenue, Northwest, Washington, D.C. 20418. 1987.

URBAN PUBLIC TRANSPORTATION: PLANNING AND SERVICE OPERATION ISSUES. National Research Council. Transportation Research Board, 2101 Constitution Avenue, Northwest, Washington, D.C. 20418. 1987.

URBAN PUBLIC TRANSPORTATION RESEARCH, 1990. National Research Council. Transportation Research Board, 2101 Constitution Avenue, Northwest, Washington, D.C. 20418. 1990.

LOCKOUTS
See: LABOR AND LABOR RELATIONS

LOST PROPERTY
See: PERSONAL PROPERTY

LOTTERIES
See: GAMBLING

LOYALTY OATHS
See: POLITICAL CRIMES AND OFFENSES; CONSTITUTIONAL LAW

LUMBER
See: FORESTS AND FORESTRY

M

MAGISTRATES
See: FEDERAL JUDICIAL CENTER

MALICIOUS PROSECUTION
See: TORTS

MALPRACTICE
See: LEGAL ETHICS AND MALPRACTICE; MEDICAL JURISPRUDENCE AND MALPRACTICE

MANAGEMENT-LABOR RELATIONS
See: LABOR AND LABOR RELATIONS

MANSLAUGHTER
See: MURDER

MARITIME LAW
See: ADMIRALTY; LAW OF THE SEA

MARRIAGE AND DIVORCE
See: CHILD CUSTODY; COHABITATION; COMMUNITY PROPERTY; DIVORCE, SEPARATION AND MARRIAGE; FAMILY LAW

MASTER AND SERVANT
See: AGENCY; LABOR AND LABOR RELATIONS

MATERIALMEN'S LIENS
See: CONSTRUCTION INDUSTRY

MECHANIC'S LIENS
See: CONSTRUCTION INDUSTRY

MEDIA LAW
See: FEDERAL COMMUNICATIONS COMMISSION; TELECOMMUNICATIONS; TELEVISION AND RADIO

MEDIATION
See: ARBITRATION AND AWARD; LABOR ARBITRATION

MEDICAL EXAMINERS
See: CORONERS AND MEDICAL EXAMINERS

MEDICAL JURISPRUDENCE AND MALPRACTICE
See also: BIOETHICS; CORONERS AND MEDICAL EXAMINERS; DEATH; DENTAL JURISPRUDENCE; EUTHANASIA; HEALTH CARE; HOSPITALS; MENTAL HEALTH AND DISABILITY; NURSES AND NURSING; NURSING HOMES; PERSONAL INJURIES; PROFESSIONAL ETHICS AND LIABILITY; PSYCHIATRY; PSYCHOLOGY

STATUTES, CODES, STANDARDS, UNIFORM LAWS

THE HEALTH CARE QUALITY IMPROVEMENT ACT OF 1986: A LEGISLATIVE HISTORY OF PUBLIC LAW NUMBER 99-660. Bernard D. Reams, Jr. William S. Hein and Company, 1285 Main Street, Buffalo, New York 14209. 1990.

UNIFORM ABORTION ACT. National Conference of Commissioners on Uniform State Laws. Uniform Laws Annotated. West Publishing Company, P.O. Box 64526, 50 West Kellogg Boulevard, St. Paul, Minnesota 55164-0526. 1976. (Annual Supplements).

UNIFORM ANATOMICAL GIFT ACT. National Conference of Commissioners on Uniform State Laws. Martindale-Hubbell Law Directory, Volume Seven. Martindale-Hubbell, Incorporated, 121 Chanlon Road, New Providence, New Jersey 07974. Annual.

UNIFORM ANATOMICAL GIFT ACT. National Conference of Commissioners on Uniform State Laws. Uniform Laws Annotated. West Publishing Company, P.O. Box 64526, 50 West Kellogg Boulevard, St. Paul, Minnesota 55164-0526. 1976. (Annual Supplements).

UNIFORM CONTROLLED SUBSTANCE ACT. National Conference of Commissioners on Uniform State Laws. Uniform Laws Annotated. West Publishing Company, P.O. Box 64526, 50 West Kellogg Boulevard, St. Paul, Minnesota 55164-0526. 1976. (Annual Supplements).

UNIFORM DEATH ACT. National Conference of Commissioners on Uniform State Laws. Uniform Laws Annotated. West Publishing Company, P.O. Box 64526, 50 West Kellogg Boulevard, St. Paul, Minnesota 55164-0526. 1976. (Annual Supplements).

UNIFORM DETERMINATION OF DEATH ACT. National Conference of Commissioners on Uniform State Laws. Martindale-Hubbell Law Directory, Volume Seven. Martindale-Hubbell, Incorporated, 121 Chanlon Road, New Providence, New Jersey 07974. Annual.

UNIFORM DETERMINATION OF DEATH ACT. National Conference of Commissioners on Uniform State Laws. Uniform Laws Annotated. West Publishing Company, P.O. Box 64526, 50 West Kellogg Boulevard, St. Paul, Minnesota 55164-0526. 1976. (Annual Supplements).

UNIFORM HEALTH CARE INFORMATION ACT. National Conference of Commissioners on Uniform State Laws. Uniform Laws Annotated. West Publishing Company, P.O. Box 64526, 50 West Kellogg Boulevard, St. Paul, Minnesota 55164-0526. 1976. (Annual Supplements).

UNIFORM NARCOTIC DRUG ACT. National Conference of Commissioners on Uniform State Laws. Uniform Laws Annotated. West Publishing Company, P.O. Box 64526, 50 West Kellogg Boulevard, St. Paul, Minnesota 55164-0526. 1976. (Annual Supplements).

UNIFORM PARENTAGE ACT. National Conference of Commissioners on Uniform State Laws. Uniform Laws Annotated. West Publishing Company, P.O. Box 64526, 50 West Kellogg Boulevard, St. Paul, Minnesota 55164-0526. 1976. (Annual Supplements).

UNIFORM PATERNITY ACT. National Conference of Commissioners on Uniform State Laws. Uniform Laws Annotated. West Publishing Company, P.O. Box 64526, 50 West Kellogg Boulevard, St. Paul, Minnesota 55164-0526. 1976. (Annual Supplements).

UNIFORM RIGHTS OF THE TERMINALLY ILL ACT. National Conference of Commissioners on Uniform State Laws. Uniform Laws Annotated. West Publishing Company, P.O. Box 64526, 50 West Kellogg Boulevard, St. Paul, Minnesota 55164-0526. 1976. (Annual Supplements).

LOOSELEAF SERVICES AND REPORTERS

ABDOMINAL INJURIES. Jules R. Kalisch and Harold Williams. Matthew Bender and Company, Incorporated, 11 Penn Plaza, New York, New York 10001. 1973- .

ATTORNEY'S TEXTBOOK OF MEDICINE. Third Edition. Roscoe N. Gray and Louise J. Gordy. Matthew Bender and Company, Incorporated, 11 Penn Plaza, New York, New York 10001. 1985- .

BIOLAW: A LEGAL AND ETHICAL REPORTER ON MEDICINE, HEALTH CARE, AND BIOENGINEERING. James F. Childrress, Patricia King, Karen Rothenberg, and Walter Wadlington, Editors. University Publications of America, 4520 East West Highway, Suite 600, Bethesda, Maryland 20814. 1985- .

CANCER. Arthur L. Frank and Michael D. Carlin. Matthew Bender and Company, Incorporated, 11 Penn Plaza, New York, New York 10001. 1978- .

CHEST, HEART AND LUNGS. Jules R. Kalisch and Haold Williams. Matthew Bender and Company, Incorporated, 11 Penn Plaza, New York, New York 10001. 1975- .

CROSS-EXAMINATION OF MEDICAL EXPERTS. Marshall Houts. Matthew Bender and Company, Incorporated, 11 Penn Plaza, New York, New York 10001. 1982.

DEATH. Marshall Houts. Matthew Bender and Company, Incorporated, 11 Penn Plaza, New York, New York 10001. 1966- .

THE EYE. Loring F. Chapman and Edward A. Dunlap. Matthew Bender and Company, Incorporated, 11 Penn Plaza, New York, New York 10001. 1981- .

HEAD AND BRAIN. Loring F. Chapman. Matthew Bender and Company, Incorporated, 11 Penn Plaza, New York, New York 10001. 1972- .

HIP AND THIGH. Jules R. Kalisch and Harold Williams. Matthew Bender and Company, Incorporated, 11 Penn Plaza, New York, New York 10001. 1972- .

THE KNEE AND ITS RELATED STRUCTURES. Jules R. Kalisch and Harold Willaims. Matthew Bender and Company, Incorporated, 11 Penn Plaza, New York, New York 10001. 1972- .

LANE MEDICAL LITIGATION GUIDE. Fred Lane. Callaghan and Company, 155 Pfingsten Road, Deerfield, Illinois 60015. 1981- .

LAWYER'S GUIDE TO MEDICAL PROOF. Marshall Houts. Matthew Bender and Company, Incorporated, 11 Penn Plaza, New York, New York 10001. 1966- .

LEGAL GUIDE FOR PHYSICIANS. Joseph M. Taraska. Matthew Bender and Company, Incorporated, 11 Penn Plaza, New York, New York 10001. 1987.

LITIGATING HEAD TRAUMA CASES. Arthur C. Roberts, Phillip J. Resnick, and Arthur C. Roberts. PESI Legal Publishing, 200 Spring Street, Eau Claire, Wisconsin 54702. 1989.

LITIGATING NECK AND BACK INJURIES. John A. Tarantino, David J. Oliveira and Nancy Robinson. Ford Publishers, Santa Ana, California. 1987.

THE LOW BACK. Leo Gelfand, Raoul D. Magana and R.R. Merliss. Matthew Bender and Company, Incorporated, 11 Penn Plaza, New York, New York 10001. 1962- .

MEDICAL AND HOSPITAL NEGLIGENCE. Miles J. Zaremski and Louis S. Goldstein. Callaghan and Company, 155 Pfingsten Road, Deerfield, Illinois 60015. 1988.

MEDICAL DEVICES REPORTER. Commerce Clearing House, Incorporated, 4025 West Peterson Avenue, Chicago, Illinois 60646. 1976- .

MEDICAL LIABILITY REPORTER. Litigation Research Group, 425 Brannan Street, San Francisco, California 94107. 1979- .

MEDICAL MALPRACTICE. David W. Louisell and Harold Williams. Matthew Bender and Company, Incorporated, 11 Penn Plaza, New York, New York 10001. 1960- .

MEDICAL MALPRACTICE LITIGATION REPORTER. Andrews Publications, Incorporated, 1646 West Chester Pike Westtown, Pennsylvania 19395. 1985- .

THE NECK. Leo Wolfstone, et al., Matthew Bender and Company, Incorporated, 11 Penn Plaza, New York, New York 10001. 1965- .

OB-GYN LITIGATION REPORTER. Andrews Publications, Incorporated, 1646 West Chester Pike, Westtown, Pennsylvania 19395. 1982.

PAIN AND SUFFERING. Loring F. Chapman. Matthew Bender and Company, Incorporated, 11 Penn Plaza, New York, New York 10001. 1967- .

THE PREPARATION AND TRIAL OF MEDICAL MALPRACTICE CASES. Richard E. Shandell and Patricia Smith. Law Journal Seminars-Press, Incorporated, 111 Eighth Avenue, Suite 900, New York, New York 10011. 1990.

PROFESSIONAL LIABILITY REPORTER. Litigation Research Group, 425 Brannan Street, San Francisco, California 94107. 1980-

PROVING MEDICAL DIAGNOSIS AND PROGNOSIS. Marshall Houts and Leonard Marmor. Matthew Bender and Company, Incorporated, 11 Penn Plaza, New York, New York 10001. 1970- .

PSYCHIC INJURIES. Marvin E. Lewis and Robert L. Sadoff. Matthew Bender and Company, Incorporated, 11 Penn Plaza, New York, New York 10001. 1975- .

SHOULDER AND ELBOW. Jules R. Kalisch and Harold Williams. Matthew Bender and Company, Incorporated, 11 Penn Plaza, New York, New York 10001. 1971- .

THE SKIN. Charles W. Whitmore. Matthew Bender and Company, Incorporated, 11 Penn Plaza, New York, New York 10001. 1971- .

TRAUMA: MEDICINE-ANATOMY-SURGERY. Marshall Houts. Matthew Bender and Company, Incorporated, 11 Penn Plaza, New York, New York 10001. 1959- .

HANDBOOKS, MANUALS, FORMBOOKS

AIDS LEGAL GUIDE: A PROFESSIONAL RESOURCE ON AIDS-RELATED ISSUES AND DISCRIMINATION. LAMBDA Legal Defense and Evaluation Fund, Incorporated, 666 Broadway, New York, New York 10012. 1984.

ANALYZING MEDICAL RECORDS: A METHOD FOR TRIAL LAWYERS. J. Stanley McQuade. Harrison Company, 3110 Crossing Park, Norcross, Georgia 30091. 1981. (Annual Supplements).

ATTORNEY'S MEDICAL DESKBOOK. Second Edition. Dan J. Tennenhouse. Lawyers Cooperative Publishing Company, Aqueduct Building, Rochester, New York 14694. 1983. (Annual Supplements).

ATTORNEY'S MEDICAL REFERENCE. B. Creighton, D.A. Smith, and L.A. Young. Parker and Son Publications, Incorporated, P.O. Box 60001, Los Angeles, California 90060. 1984.

BENDER'S ANATOMY CHARTS. Marshall Houts and Ted Bloodhart. Matthew Bender and Company, Incorporated, 11 Penn Plaza, New York, New York 10001. 1983.

CANCER: CAUSES AND METHODS OF TREATMENT FOR TRIAL LAWYERS. John R. McLaren. Harrison Company, 3110 Crossing Park, Norcross, Georgia 30091. 1985.

CONSENT TO TREATMENT: A PRACTICAL GUIDE. Second Edition. Fay A. Rozovsky. Little, Brown, and Company, 34 Beacon Street, Boston, Massachusetts 02108. 1989. (Supplemented).

DETERMINING DISABILITY AND PERSONAL INJURY DAMAGE: MEDICAL EVALUATION FOR TRIAL LAWYERS. J. Stanley McQuade. Harrison Company, 3110 Crossing Park, Norcross, Georgia 30091. 1984. (Supplements).

DISCOVERY IN MEDICAL MALPRACTICE, PRODUCTS LIABILITY AND PERSONAL INJURY CASES. Marc J. Bern and Steven E. North. Practising Law Institute, 810 Seventh Avenue, New York, New York 10019. 1985.

FORENSIC MEDICINE: A HANDBOOK FOR PROFESSIONALS. Alan A. Watson. Gower Publishing Company, Old Post Road, Brookfield, Vermont 05036. 1989.

GUIDES TO THE EVALUATION OF PERMANENT IMPAIRMENT. Third Edition. Alan L. Engelberg. American Medical Association, Public Affairs Group, Division of Legislative Activities, Department of State Legislation, 515 North State Street, Chicago, Illinois 60610. 1988.

HANDBOOK OF MEDICOLEGAL PRACTICE. John P.W. Varian. Butterworth-Heinemann, 80 Montvale Avenue, Stoneham, Massachusetts 02180. 1991.

HANDLING BIRTH TRAUMA CASES. Stanley S. Schwartz and Norman D. Tucker. John Wiley and Sons, Incorporated, 605 Third Avenue, New York, New York 10158. 1989.

HEAD AND NECK INJURY HANDBOOK. Lawrence J. Smith. Shepard's/McGraw-Hill, P.O. Box 1235, Colorado Springs, Colorado 80901. 1989.

HEALTH AND THE LAW: A HANDBOOK FOR HEALTH PROFESSIONALS. Tom Christoffel. Free Press, 866 Third Avenue, New York, New York 10022. 1985.

MEDICAL JURISPRUDENCE AND MALPRACTICE

HEALTH CARE CONSENT MANUAL: POLICIES, LAWS, PROCEDURES. Second Edition. Karen M. Engstrom. The Catholic Health Association, 4455 Woodson Road, St. Louis, Missouri 63134-0889. 1985.

HEALTH CARE GUIDE LAW: A PRACTICAL GUIDE. Michael G. MacDonald, Kathryn C. Meyer and Beth Essig. Matthew Bender and Company, Incorporated, 11 Penn Plaza, New York, New York 10001. 1985.

HEALTH CARE SUPERVISOR'S LEGAL GUIDE. Karen H. Henry. Aspen Publishers, Incorporated, 1600 Research Boulevard, Rockville, Maryland 20850. 1984.

JURY INSTRUCTIONS ON MEDICAL ISSUES. Third Edition. Graham Douthwaite and George J. Alexander. Michie Company, P.O. Box 7587, Charlottesville, Virginia 22906. 1987.

LEGAL GUIDE FOR MEDICAL OFFICE MANAGERS. Marshall B. Kapp. Pluribus Press, 160 East Illinois Street, Chicago, Illinois 60611. 1985.

LIABILITY IN MEDICAL PRACTICE: A REFERENCE FOR PHYSICIANS. Norman S. Blackman and Charles P. Bailey. Harwood Academic Publishers, GmbH, P.O. Box 786, New York, New York 10276. 1990.

LITIGATING MEDICAL MALPRACTICE CLAIMS: ALI-ABA COURSE OF STUDY MATERIALS. American Law Institute-American Bar Association, Committee on Continuing Professional Education, 4025 Chestnut Street, Philadelphia, Pennsylvania 19104. 1985.

MALPRACTICE: A GUIDE TO THE LEGAL RIGHTS OF DOCTORS AND PATIENTS. Donald J. Flaster. Charles Scribner's Sons, 866 Third Avenue, New York, New York 10022. 1983.

MALPRACTICE: MANAGING YOUR DEFENSE. Second Edition. Raymond M. Fish, Melvin E. Ehrhardt and Betty Fish. Medical Economic Books, 5 Paragon Drive, Montvale, New Jersey 07645. 1989.

MANN'S MEDICAL HANDBOOK FOR LITIGATION. Arnold Mann. The Michie Company, P.O. Box 7587, Charlottesville, Virginia 22906-7587. 1985.

MEDICAL INFORMATION SYSTEM FOR LAWYERS. J. Stanley McQuade. Lawyers Cooperative Publishing Company, Aqueduct Building, Rochester, New York 14694. 1989.

MEDICAL MALPRACTICE FOR TRIAL LAWYERS. Second Edition. J. Stanley McQuade. Harrison Company, 3110 Crossing Park, Norcross, Georgia 30091. 1985. (Annual Supplements).

MEDICAL MALPRACTICE - GUIDE TO MEDICAL ISSUES. Matthew Bender and Company, Incorporated, 11 Penn Plaza, New York, New York 10001. 1986.

MEDICINE IN THE COURTROOM: COURSE MANUAL. Harold L. Hirsh. Federal Publications, Incorporated, 1120 Twentieth Street, Northwest, Washington, D.C. 20036. 1984.

PATIENT CARE DECISION MAKING: A LEGAL GUIDE FOR PROVIDERS. Claire C. Obade. Clark Boardman Company, Limited, 435 Hudson Street, New York, New York 10014. 1991.

PATTERN DISCOVERY: MEDICAL MALPRACTICE. Second Edition. Douglas Danner. Lawyers Cooperative Publishing Company, Aqueduct Building, Rochester, New York 14694. 1986. (Supplements).

A PRACTICAL GUIDE TO MEDICINE AND THE LAW. J.P. Jackson. Springer-Verlag New York, Incorporated, 175 Fifth Avenue, New York, New York 10010. 1991.

A PRACTICAL GUIDE TO PREVENTING MEDICAL MALPRACTICE. Duke N. Stern and Jo Ann Felix-Reltzke. Shepard's/McGraw-Hill, P.O. Box 1235, Colorado Springs, Colorado 80901. 1983 (Annual Supplements).

THE PREPARATION AND TRIAL OF MEDICAL MALPRACTICE CASES. Richard E. Shandell. New York Law Publishing Company, 111 Eighth Avenue, New York, New York 10011. 1985. (Annual Supplements).

PREPARATION OF MEDICAL CASES FOR SETTLEMENT AND TRIAL. Lee A. Holley. Harrison Company, 3110 Crossing Park, Norcross, Georgia 30091. 1982.

RESPONSIBILITY FOR DRUG-INDUCED INJURY: A REFERENCE BOOK FOR LAWYERS, THE HEALTH PROFESSIONS, AND MANUFACTURERS. M.N. Graham Dukes and Barbara Swartz. Elsevier Science Publishing Company, P.O.Box 882, Madison Square Station, New York, New York 10159. 1988.

TESTIFYING IN COURT: A GUIDE FOR PHYSICIANS. Third Edition. Jack E. Horsley and John Carlova. Medical Economics Books, 5 Paragon Drive, Montvale, New Jersey 07645. 1988.

WIN/WIN OUTCOMES: A PHYSICIAN'S NEGOTIATING GUIDE. Seymour J. Burrows. Health Administration Press, Department KW, 1021 East Huron Street, Ann Arbor, Michigan 48104. 1984.

TEXTBOOKS AND GENERAL WORKS

ACCEPTABLE RISKS. Pascal J. Imperato and Greg Mitchell. Viking-Penguin, Incorporated, 375 Hudson, New York, New York 10014. 1985.

ADVANCED MEDICAL MALPRACTICE: ANESTHESIOLOGY, GENERAL SURGERY AND NEUROLOGY. Stephen H. Mackauf. Practising Law Institute, 810 Seventh Avenue, New York, New York 10019. 1983.

ASBESTOS: MEDICAL AND LEGAL ASPECTS. Barry Castleman. Law and Business, Harcourt Brace Jovanovich, Incorporated, 6277 Sea Harbor Drive, Orlando, Florida 32821. 1984.

BELLI FOR YOUR MALPRACTICE DEFENSE. Second Edition. Melvin M. Belli, Sr. Medical Economics Books, 680 Kinderkamack Road, Oradell, New Jersey 07649. 1989.

CAN THE CARDIAC STAND TRIAL? Meyer Texton. Hemisphere Publishing Corporation, 79 Madison Avenue, Suite 1110, New York, New York 10016. 1987.

CLINICAL TRIALS: ISSUES AND APPROACHES. Stanley H. Shapiro, Editor. Marcel Dekker, Incorporated, 270 Madison Avenue, New York, New York 10016. 1983.

THE COURTS AND THE DOCTOR. D.J. Gee and J.K. Mason. Oxford University Press, 200 Madison Avenue, New York, New York 10016. 1990.

CRIMINALISTICS: AN INTRODUCTION TO FORENSIC SCIENCE. Fourth Edition. Richard Saferstein. Prentice-Hall, Incorporated, 113 Sylvan Avenue, Englewood Cliffs, New Jersey 07632. 1990.

DECIDING FOR OTHERS: THE ETHICS OF SURROGATE DECISIONMAKING. Allen E. Buchanan and Dan W. Brock. Cambridge University Press, 40 West Twentieth Street, New York, New York 10011. 1989.

DEFENDANT: A PSYCHIATRIST ON TRIAL FOR MEDICAL MALPRACTICE: AN EPISODE IN AMERICA'S HIDDEN HEALTH CARE CRISIS. Sara C. Charles and Eugene Kennedy. Random House, Incorporated, 201 East Fiftieth Street, New York, New York 10022. 1986.

DETERMINING DISABILITY AND PERSONAL INJURY DAMAGE: MEDICAL EVALUATION FOR TRIAL LAWYERS. Second Edition. J. Stanley McQuade. Harrison Company, 3110 Crossing Park, Norcross, Georgia 30091. 1988.

DOCTOR FOR THE PROSECUTION: A FIGHTING SURGEON TAKES THE STAND. Richard Chadoff. Putnam Publishing Group, 200 Madison Avenue, New York, New YOrk 10016. 1983.

ETHICS AND REGULATION OF CLINICAL RESEARCH. Robert J. Levine. Yale University Press, 302 Temple Street, New Haven, Connecticut 06520. 1988.

EMERGENCY MEDICINE MALPRACTICE. Scott M. Lewis and Jeffrey R. McCutchen. John Wiley and Sons, Incorporated, 605 Third Avenue, New York, New York 10158.

FORENSIC DETECTION. Lionel Bender. Gloucester Press, New York, New York. 1990.

FORENSIC MEDICINE: A GUIDE TO PRINCIPLES. Third Edition. I. Gordon, H.A. Shapiro and S.D. Berson. Churchill Livingstone, Incorporated, 1560 Broadway, New York, New York 10036. 1988.

FUNDAMENTALS OF OPHTHALMIC PRACTICE: OFFICE AND RISK MANAGEMENT: ETHICS AND ECONOMICS. Stephen A. Kamenetzky. Gower Medical Publishing Limited, 101 Fifth Avenue, New York, New York 10003. 1992.

HANDLING SOFT TISSUE INJURY CASES. Stanley E. Preiser, Monty L. Preiser and Cyril H. Wecht. Kluwer Law Book Publishers, Incorporated, 36 West Forty-fourth Street, New York, New York 10036. 1987.

HEALTH CARE LAW, FORENSIC SCIENCE, AND PUBLIC POLICY. Fourth Edition. William J. Curran, Mark A. Hall and David H. Kaye. Little, Brown and Company, 34 Beacon Street, Boston, Massachusetts 02108. 1990.

HEALTH CARE: LEGAL RESPONSES TO NEW ECONOMIC FORCES. Robert M. McNair, Jr., Chariman. Practising Law Institute, 810 Seventh Avenue, New York, New York 10019. 1985.

A HISTORY AND THEORY OF INFORMED CONSENT. Ruth R. Faden and Tom L. Beauchamp. Oxford University Press, Incorporated, 200 Madison Avenue, New York, New York 10016. 1986.

INSURANCE STRATEGIES FOR PHYSICIANS. Phillip Huston. Medical Economics Books, 5 Paragon Drive, Montvale, New Jersey 07645. 1983.

JOINT VENTURES FOR HOSPITALS AND PHYSICIANS: LEGAL CONSIDERATIONS. Ross E. Stromberg. American Hospital Publishing, Incorporated, 211 East Chicago Avenue, Chicago, Illinois 60611. 1986.

JURISPRUDENCE: WITH MEDICAL, LEGAL AND SCIENTIFIC SUBJECT ANALYSIS AND BIBLIOGRAPHY. Roy R. Zimmerman. ABBE Publishers Association of Washington, DC, 4111 Gallows Road, Annandale, Virginia 22003-1862. 1987.

LAW AND ETHICS IN HEALTH CARE. John B. McKinlay, Editor. MIT Press, 55 Hayward Street, Cambridge, Massachusetts 02142. 1982.

LAW AND ETHICS IN THE MEDICAL OFFICE: INCLUDING BIOETHICAL ISSUES. Second Edition. Marcia A. Lewis and Carol D. Warden. F. A. Davis Company, 1915 Arch Street, Philadelphia, Pennsylvania 19103. 1988.

LAW, MEDICINE, AND SOCIAL JUSTICE. Larry I. Palmer. Westminster/John Knox Press, 100 Witherspoon Street, Louisville, Kentucky 40202-1396. 1989.

THE LAW OF MEDICAL MALPRACTICE IN A NUTSHELL. Second Edition. Joseph H. King, Jr. West Publishing Company, P.O. Box 64526, 50 West Kellogg Boulevard, St. Paul, Minnesota 55164-0526. 1986.

LEGAL AND ETHICAL ASPECTS OF TREATING CRITICALLY AND TERMINALLY ILL PATIENTS. Edward A. Davdera and Douglas J. Peters, Editors. Health Administration Press Perspectives, Department KW, 1021 East Huron Street, University of Michigan, Ann Arbor, Michigan 48104. 1982.

LEGAL ASPECTS OF ANAESTHESIA. J.F. Crul. Kluwer Academic Publishers, 101 Philip Drive, Assinippi Park, Norwell, Massachusetts 02061. 1989.

LEGAL ASPECTS OF HEALTH CARE ADMINISTRATION. Fourth Edition. George D. Pozgar. Aspen Publishers, Incorporated, 1600 Research Boulevard, Rockville, Maryland 20850. 1990.

LEGAL ASPECTS OF MEDICAL PRACTICE. Fourth Edition. Bernard Knight, J.F.A. Harbison, T.K. Marshall and Alan Watson. Churchill Livingstone, Incorporated, 1560 Broadway, New York, New York 10036. 1987.

LEGAL ASPECTS OF MEDICINE: INCLUDING CARDIOLOGY, PULMONARY MEDICINE, AND CRITICAL CARE MEDICINE. J.R. Vevaina, R.C. Bone and E. Kassoff. Springer-Verlag New York, Incorporated, 175 Fifth Avenue, New York, New York 10010. 1989.

LEGAL ASPECTS OF PREVENTIVE AND REHABILITATIVE EXERCISE PROGRAMS. Second Edition. David L. Herbert and William G. Herbert. Professional and Executive Reports and Publications, 4665 Douglas Circle, Northwest Canton, Ohio 44718. 1989.

LEGAL MEDICINE: LEGAL DYNAMICS OF MEDICAL ENCOUNTERS. Second Edition. C.V. Mosby Company, 11830 Westline Industrial Drive, St. Louis, Missouri 63146. 1991.

LIABILITY AND QUALITY ISSUES IN HEALTH CARE. Barry R. Furrow. West Publishing Company, 50 West Kellogg Boulevard, St. Paul, Minnesota 55164. 1991.

LITIGATING HEAD TRAUMA CASES. Arthur C. Roberts, Phillip J. Resnick and Arthur C. Roberts. John Wiley and Sons, Incorporated, 605 Third Avenue, New York, New York 10158. 1991,

MALPRACTICE DEPOSITIONS: AVOIDING THE TRAPS. Raymond M. Fish and Melvin E. Ehrhardt. Medical Economics Books, 5 paragon Drive, Montvale, New Jersey 07649. 1987.

MEDICAL ETHICS AND THE LAW. Sheila McLean. Gower Publishing Company, Old Post Road, Brookfield, Vermont 05036. 1986.

MEDICAL MALPRACTICE. David M. Harney. Allen Smith Company, Incorporated, 1435 North Meridian Street, Indianapolis, Indiana 46202. 1984.

MEDICAL MALPRACTICE. Fifth Edition. Charles Kramer and Daniel Kramer. Practising Law Institute, 810 Seventh Avenue, New York, New York 10019. 1983.

MEDICAL MALPRACTICE: A PREVENTIVE APPROACH. Willaim O. Robertson. University of Washington Press, P.O. Box 50096, Seattle, Washington 98105-5096. 1985.

MEDICAL MALPRACTICE: BASES OF LIABILITY. Michael D. McCafferty and Steven M. Meyer. Shepard's/McGraw-Hill, P.O. Box 1235, Colorado Springs, Colorado 80901. 1985.

MEDICAL MALPRACTICE FOR ATTORNEYS, PHYSICIANS, AND RISK MANAGERS. American Bar Association, Division for Professional Education, 750 North Lake Shore Drive, Chicago, Illinois 60611. 1986.

MEDICAL MALPRACTICE: HANDLING EMERGENCY MEDICINE CASES. G.M. Flick. Shepard's/McGraw-Hill, P.O. Box 1235, Colorado Springs, Colorado 80901. 1991.

MEDICAL MALPRACTICE LAW: HOW MEDICINE IS CHANGING THE LAW. Barbara U. Werthmann. Lexington Books, Division of D.C. Heath and Company, 125 Spring Street, Lexington, Massachusetts 02173. 1984.

MEDICAL MALPRACTICE LITIGATION: ART AND SCIENCE. John F. Eisberg. Mason Publishing Company, Butterworth MN, 289 East Fifth Street, St. Paul, Minnesota 55101-1989. 1982.

MEDICAL MALPRACTICE: OBSTETRIC AND NEONATAL CASES. Michael D. Volk and Melvin D. Morgan, Editors. Shepard's/McGraw-Hill, P.O. Box 1235, Colorado Springs, Colorado 80901. 1986.

MEDICAL MALPRACTICE: PHARMACY LAW. David B. Brushwood. Shepard's/McGraw-Hill, P.O. Box 1235, Colorado Springs, Colorado 80901. 1986.

MEDICAL MALPRACTICE, PSYCHIATRIC CARE. Joseph T. Smith. Shepard's/McGraw-Hill, P.O. Box 1235, Colorado Springs, Colorado 80901. 1986.

MEDICAL MALPRACTICE SOLUTIONS: SYSTEMS AND PROPOSALS FOR INJURY COMPENSATION. M. Martin Halley. Charles C. Thomas, Publishers, 2600 South First Street, Springfield, Illinois 62794. 1989.

MEDICAL MALPRACTICE: THEORY, EVIDENCE, AND PUBLIC POLICY. Patricia M. Danzon. Harvard University Press, 79 Garden Street, Cambridge, Massachusetts 02138. 1985.

MEDICAL NEGLIGENCE AND HOSPITAL LIABILITY. Association of Trial Lawyers of America Education Fund, 1050 31st Street, Northwest, Washington, D.C. 20007. 1984.

MEDICAL PRACTICE FOR TRIAL LAWYERS. Third Edition. J. Stanley McQuade. Harrison Company, 3110 Crossing Park, Norcross, Georgia 30091. 1989.

MEDICAL RESEARCH WITH CHILDREN: ETHICS, LAW, AND PRACTICE: THE REPORT OF AN INSTITUTE OF MEDICAL ETHICS WORKING GROUP ON THE ETHICS OF CLINICAL RESEARCH INVESTIGATION ON CHILDREN. Richard H. Nicholson. Oxford University Press, Incorporated, 200 Madison Avenue, New York, New York 10016. 1986.

MEDICAL RISK MANAGEMENT: PREVENTIVE LEGAL STRATEGIES FOR HEALTH CARE PROVIDERS. Edward P. Richards III and Katherine C. Rathbun. Aspen Publishers, Incorporated, 1600 Research Boulevard, Rockville, Maryland 20850. 1982.

MEDICARE AND MEDICAID CLAIMS AND PROCEDURES. Second Edition. Harvey L. McCormick. West Publishing Company, P.O. Box 64526, 50 West Kellogg Boulevard, St. Paul, Minnesota 55164-0526. 1986.

MEDICINE AND THE LAW. Neil Grauer and C. Everett Koop. Chelsea House Publishers, 1974 Sproul Road, Suite 400, Broomall, Pennsylvania 19008. 1989.

MEDICOLEGAL ASPECTS OF CRITICAL CARE. Katherine Benesch, et al. Aspen Publishers, Incorporated, 1600 Research Boulevard, Rockville, Maryland 20850. 1986.

MEDICOLEGAL EXAMINATION, EVALUATION, AND REPORT. Bernard J. Ficarra. CRC Press, Incorporated, 2000 Corporate Boulevard, Northwest, Boca Raton, Florida 33431. 1987.

MEDICOLEGAL REPORTING IN ORTHOPAEDIC TRAUMA. Michael A. Foy and Phillip S. Fagg. Churchill Livingstone, Incorporated, 1560 Broadway, New York, New York 10036. 1990.

NURSING JURISPRUDENCE. Mary Cushing. Appleton and Lange, 25 Van Zant Street, East Norwalk, Connecticut 06855. 1988.

OB/GYN MALPRACTICE. Scott M. Lewis. John Wiley and Sons, Incorporated, 605 Third Avenue, New York, New York 10158. 1989.

PRESERVING LIFE: PUBLIC POLICY AND THE LIFE NOT WORTH LIVING. Richard Sherlock. Loyola University Press, 3441 North Ashland Avenue, Chicago, Illinois 60657. 1987.

PREVENTING MALPRACTICE IN LONG-TERM CARE: STRATEGIES FOR RISK MANAGEMENT. Marshall B. Kapp. Springer Publishing Company, Incorporated, 536 Broadway, New York, New York 10012. 1987.

PROBLEMS IN HOSPITAL LAW. Sixth Edition. Aspen Publishers, Incorporated, 1600 Research Boulevard, Rockville, Maryland 20850. 1990.

PSYCHIATRIC INTERVENTIONS AND MALPRACTICE: A PRIMER FOR LIABILITY PREVENTION. Robert I. Somon. Charles C. Thomas Publishing, 2600 South First Street, Springfield, Illinois 62794-9265. 1982.

REFLECTIONS ON MEDICINE, BIOTECHNOLOGY, AND THE LAW. Zelman Cowen. University of Nebraska Press, 901 North Seventeenth Street, Lincoln, Nebraska 68588-0520. 1986.

SECURING AND USING MEDICAL EVIDENCE IN PERSONAL INJURY AND HEALTH-CARE CASES. Robert C. Strodel. Prentice-Hall, Incorporated, 113 Sylvan Avenue, Englewood Cliffs, New Jersey 07632. 1988.

THE SEXUALLY TRANSMITTED DISEASES. Charles E. Rinear. McFarland and Company, Incorporated, P.O. Box 611, Jefferson, North Carolina 28640. 1986.

STATUTE OF LIMITATIONS ON MALPRACTICE. Ale Hou Nalua. Todd and Honeywell, Incorporated, 10 Cuttermill Road, Great Neck, New York 11021. 1984.

TO DO NO HARM: DES AND THE DILEMMAS OF MODERN MEDICINE. Roberts J. Apfel and Susan M. Fisher. Yale University Press, 302 Temple Street, New Haven, Connecticut 06520. 1984.

TREATMENT CHOICES AND INFORMED CONSENT: CURRENT CONTROVERSIES IN PSYCHIATRIC MALPRACTICE LITIGATION. John Gulton Malcolm. Charles C. Thomas, Publishers, 2600 South First Street, Springfield, Illinois 62794. 1988.

UNDERSTANDING AND HANDLING THE BACK AND NECK INJURY CASE. Thomas J. Murray, Jr., and Donald W. Robertson. John Wiley and Sons, Incorporated, 605 Third Avenue, New York, New York 10158. 1991.

ENCYCLOPEDIAS AND DICTIONARIES

ATTORNEY'S DICTIONARY OF MEDICINE. J. E. Schmidt. Matthew Bender and Company, Incorporated, 11 Penn Plaza, New York, New York 10001. 1962. (Annual Supplements).

BUTTERWORTHS MEDICO-LEGAL ENCYCLOPAEDIA. J.K. Mason and R.A. McCall Smith. Butterworth and Company (Publishers) Limited, Borough Green, Sevenoaks, Kent TN15 8PH, England. 1987.

LAWYERS' MEDICAL ENCYCLOPEDIA. Charles J. Frankel and James G. Zimmerly, Editors. The Michie Company, P.O. Box 7587, Charlottesville, Virginia 22906-7587. 1989. (Annual Supplements).

MASA: MEDICAL ACRONYMS, SYMBOLS AND ABBREVIATIONS. Betty Hamilton and Barbara Guidos, editors. Neal-Schuman Publishers Company, Incorporated, 23 Leonard Street, New York, New York 10013. 1988.

MEDICOLEGAL GLOSSARY. Walter L. Scott. Medical Economics Books, 5 Paragon Drive, Montvale, New Jersey 07645. 1989.

THE SLOANE-DORLAND ANNOTATED MEDICAL-LEGAL DICTIONARY. Richard Sloane. West Publishing Company, 50 West Kellogg Boulevard, St. Paul, Minnesota 55164. 1987.

DIGESTS, INDEXES, ABSTRACTS, CITATORS

COMPREHENSIVE INDEX TO THE JOURNAL OF FORENSIC SCIENCES (1972-1986). Abel M. Dominguez. American Society for Testing and Materials, 1916 Race Street, Philadelphia, Pennsylvania 19103. 1987.

JURISPRUDENCE AND CONFIDENTIALITY: INDEX OF MODERN INFORMATION. Harold P. Drummond. ABBE Publishers Association of Washington, DC, 4111 Gallows Road, Annandale, Virginia 22003-1862. 1991.

LAWYERS' MEDICAL DIGEST. Callaghan and Company, 155 Pfingsten Road, Deerfield, Illinois 60015. Monthly.

MEDICAL MALPRACTICE DIGEST. Dean E. Snyder. Lawyers Cooperative Publishing Company, Aqueduct Building, Rochester, New York 14694. 1991.

MEDICAL MALPRACTICE: VERDICTS AND SETTLEMENTS. Litigation Research Group, 425 Brannan Street, San Francisco, California 94107. 1986.

SHEPARD'S MEDICAL MALPRACTICE CITATIONS. Shepard's/McGraw-Hill, P.O. Box 1235, Colorado Springs, Colorado 80901. 1987.

LAW REVIEWS AND PERIODICALS

AMERICAN JOURNAL OF LAW AND MEDICINE. American Society of Law and Medicine, 765 Commonwealth Avenue, Sixteenth Floor, Boston, Massachusetts 02215. Quarterly.

JOURNAL OF CONTEMPORARY HEALTH LAW AND POLICY. The Catholic University of America, Columbus School of Law, Leahy Hall, 620 Michigan Avenue, Northeast, Washington, D.C. 20064. Annual.

JOURNAL OF FORENSIC SCIENCES. ASTM Headquarters, 1916 Race Street, Philadelphia, Pennsylvania 19103. Quarterly.

JOURNAL OF HEALTH, POLITICS, POLICY AND LAW. Department of Health Administration, 6697 College Station, Box 3018, Durham, North Carolina 27710. Quarterly.

LAW, MEDICINE AND HEALTH CARE. American Society of Law and Medicine, 765 Commonwealth Avenue, Sixteenth Floor, Boston, Massachusetts 02215. Bimonthly.

MEDICAL JURISPRUDENCE AND MALPRACTICE

MEDICAL TRIAL TECHNIQUES QUARTERLY. Callaghan and Company, 3201 Old Glenview Road, Wilmette, Illinois 60091. Quarterly.

TRAUMA. Matthew Bender and Company, Incorporated, 235 East Forty-fifth Street, New York, New York 10017. Six issues per year.

NEWSLETTERS AND NEWSPAPERS

AIDS POLICY AND LAW. Bureau of National Affairs, 1231 Twenty-fifth Street, Northwest, Washington, D.C. 20037. Biweekly.

THE CITATION. American Medical Association, Office of General Counsel, 535 North Dearborn Street, Chicago, Illinois 60610. Semimonthly.

HASTINGS CENTER REPORT. Hastings Center, 255 Elm Road, Briarcliff Manor, New York 10510. Bimonthly.

HOSPTIAL LITIGATION REPORTER. Strafford Publications, Incorporated, 1375 Peachtree Street, Northwest, Suite 235, Atlanta, Georgia 30367. Monthly.

LEGAL ASPECTS OF MEDICAL PRACTICE. Shugar Publicating, Incorporated, 32 Mill Road, Westhampton Beach, New York 11978. Quarterly.

MEDICAL DEVICES, DIAGNOSTICS AND INSTRUMENTATION REPORTS. F-D-C Reports, Incorporated, 550 Friendship Boulevard, Chevy Chase, Maryland 20815. Weekly.

MEDICAL ETHICS ADVISOR. American Health Consoltants, Incorporated, 67 Peachtree Park Drive, Northeast, Atlanta, Georgia 30309. Monthly.

MEDICAL LIABILITY MONITOR. Malpractice Lifeline, Incorporated, P.O. Box 9011, Winnetka, Illinois 60093. Monthly.

MEDICAL LIABILITY REPORTER. Shepard's/McGraw-Hill, P.O. Box 1235, Colorado Springs, Colorado 80901. Monthly.

MEDICAL MALPRACTICE LAW AND SOCIETY. Leader Publications, 111 Eighth Avenue, New York, New York 10011. Monthly.

MEDICAL MALPRACTICE REPORTS. Matthew Bender and Company, Incorporated, 11 Penn Plaza, New York, New York 10001. Monthly.

MEDICAL MALPRACTICE VERDICTS, SETTLEMENTS AND EXPERTS. Lewis Laska, 901 Church Street, Nashville, Tennessee 37203. Monthly.

THE MEDICO-LEGAL ADVISOR. Health Law Research Group, Incorporated, 140 East Division Road, Health Law Plaza, Suite C-3, Oak Ridge, Tennessee 37830. Monthly.

NEWSLETTER OF BIOMEDICAL SAFETY AND STANDARDS. Quest Publishing Company, 1351 Titan Way, Brea, California 92621. Semimonthly.

REGAN REPORT ON MEDICAL LAW. Medica Press, Incorporated, 1231 Fleet National Bank Building, Providence, Rhode Island 02903. Monthly.

Encyclopedia of Legal Information Sources • 2nd Ed.

BIBLIOGRAPHIES

BIBLIOGRAPHY OF BIOETHICS. LeRoy Walters and Tamar Joy Kahn, Editors. Kennedy Institute of Ethics, Georgetown University, Washington, D.C. 20057. 1990.

LAW, MEDICINE AND HEALTH CARE: A BIBLIOGRAPHY. James T. Ziegenfuss, Jr. Facts on File, 460 Park Avenue, South, New York, New York 10016. 1984.

MALPRACTICE I: MEDICAL SUBJECT ANALYSIS AND RESEARCH GUIDE WITH BIBLIOGRAPHY. Roy R. Zimmerman. ABBE Publishers Association of Washington D.C., 4111 Gallows Road, Annandale, Virginia 22003-1862. 1984.

MALPRACTICE II: LEGISLATION AND JURISPRUDENCE WITH SUBJECT ANALYSIS AND BIBLIOGRAPHY. Roy R. Zimmerman. ABBE Publishers Association of Washington D.C., 4111 Gallows Road, Annandale, Virginia 22003-1862. 1985.

A SOURCEBOOK FOR RESEARCH IN LAW AND MEDICINE. Salvatore F. Fiscina, et al. National Law Publishing, Corporation, 428 Preston Street, Baltimore, Maryland 21202. 1985.

DIRECTORIES

ABMS COMPENDIUM OF CERTIFIED MEDICAL SPECIALISTS. American Board of Medical Specialties, One Rotary Center, Suite 805, Evanston, Illinois 60201. 1988.

AMERICAN MEDICAL DIRECTORY: DIRECTORY OF PHYSICIANS IN THE UNITED STATES, PUERTO RICO, VIRGIN ISLANDS, CERTAIN PACIFIC ISLANDS AND U.S. PHYSICIANS TEMPORARILY LOCATED IN FOREIGN COUNTRIES. Thirty-second Edition. American Medical Association, 515 North State Street, Chicago, Illinois 60610. (Irregular).

FORENSIC SERVICES DIRECTORY: THE NATIONAL REGISTER OF FORENSIC EXPERTS, LITIGATION CONSULTANTS AND LEGAL SUPPORT SPECIALISTS. Betty S. Lipscher, Editor. West Publishing Company, 50 West Kellogg Boulevard, St. paul, Minnesota 55164-0526. 1981.

UNITED STATES MEDICAL DIRECTORY. Seventh Edition. United States Medical Directory Service, Publishers, 655 Northwest One Hundred Twenty-eighth Street, Miami, Florida 33168.

ASSOCIATIONS AND PROFESSIONAL SOCIETIES

AMERICAN COLLEGE OF PHYSICIANS. Independence Mall West, Sixth Street at Race, Philadelphia, Pennsylvania 19106. (215) 351-2400.

AMERICAN HOSPITAL ASSOCIATION. 840 North Lake Shore Drive, Chicago, Illinois. 60611. (312) 280-6000.

AMERICAN MEDICAL ASSOCIATION. 515 North State Street, Chicago, Illinois 60610. (312) 464-5000.

AMERICAN SOCIETY OF LAW AND MEDICINE. 765 Commonwealth Avenue, Sixteenth Floor, Boston, Massachusetts 02215. (617) 262-4990.

ASSOCIATION OF AMERICAN PHYSICIANS. Washington University Medical School, Department of Medicine, 660 South Euclid Avenue, Box 8125, St. Louis, Missouri 63110. (314) 362-8803.

ASSOCIATION OF TRIAL LAWYERS OF AMERICA. 1050 Thirty-first Street, Northwest, Washington, D.C. 20007. (202) 965-3500.

SOCIETY OF MEDICAL JURISPRUDENCE. c/o Lea S. Singer, P.O. Box 1304, New York, New York 10008. (212) 473-0523.

RESEARCH CENTERS, INSTITUTES, CLEARINGHOUSES

AMERICAN BAR FOUNDATION. 750 North Lake Schore Drive, Chicago, Illinois 60611. (312) 988-6500.

CASE WESTERN RESERVE UNIVERSITY, LAW-MEDICINE CENTER. Gund Hall, Cleveland, Ohio 44106. (216) 368-3983.

CENTER FOR LAW AND HEALTH SCIENCES. Boston University, 765 Commonwealth Avenue, Boston, Massachusetts 02215. (617) 353-2904.

FORENSIC SCIENCES FOUNDATION, INCORPORATED. P.O. Box 669, Colorado Springs, Colorado 80901. (719) 636-1100.

INSTITUTE ON MENTAL DISABILITY AND THE LAW. National Center for State Courts, 300 New port Avenue, Williamsburg, Virginia 23187. (804) 253-2000.

ONLINE DATABASES

AMA/NET AP MEDICAL NEWS SERVICE. American Medical Association, 535 North Dearborn Street, Chicago, Illinois 60610, and The Associated Press, 50 Rockefeller Plaza, New York, New York 10021.

BIRTH DEFECTS INFORMATION SERVICE. Center for Birth Defects Information Services, Incorporated, Dover Medical Building, Box 1776, Dover, Massachusetts 02030.

CENTERS FOR DISEASE CONTROL INFORMATION SERVICE. United States Department of Health and Human Services, Public Health Service, Centers for Disease Control, Epidemiology Program Office, 1600 Clifton Road, Atlanta, Georgia 30333, and American Medical Association, 535 North Dearborn Street, Chicago, Illinois 60610.

COMPUTERIZED AIDS INFORMATION NETWORK. Los Angeles Gay and Lesbian Community Services Center, 1213 North Highland Avenue, Hollywood, California 90038.

HEALTH PLANNING AND ADMINISTRATION. National Library of Medicine, 8600 Rockville Pike, Bethesda, Maryland 20209, and American Hospital Association, 840 North Lake Shore Drive, Chicago, Illinois 60611.

HEALTHLAWYER. American Hospital Association, 840 North Lake Shore Drive, Chicago, Illinois 60611.

MEDICAL ABSTRACTS NEWSLETTER. Communi-T Publications, P.O. Box 2170, Teaneck, New Jersey 07666.

MEDLINE. National Library of Medicine, 8600 Rockville Pike, Bethesda, Maryland 20209.

PHYCOM. BRS/Saunders Colleague, 555 East Lancaster Avenue, Fourth Floor, Saint Davids, Pennsylvania 19087.

SURGEON GENERAL'S INFORMATION SERVICE. U.S. Public Health Service, Office of the Surgeon General, 5600 Fishers Lane, Room 1866, Rockville, Maryland 20857 and American Medical Association, 535 North Dearborn Street, Chicago, Illinois 60610.

TOXLINE. National Library of Medicine, Toxicology Information Program, 8600 Rockville Pike, Bethesda, Maryland 20209.

AUDIOVISUALS

BOWER AND KRAMER ON MEDICAL MALPRACTICE. Practising Law Institute, 810 Seventh Avenue, New York, New York 10019. 1983. Videotape.

BRAIN-DAMAGED INFANTS: CASE EVALUATION AND MANAGEMENT. Practising Law Institute, 810 Seventh Avenue, New York, New York 10019. 1985. Videotape.

THE RIGHT TO DIE. Produced by Norman Baxley and Associates, Incorporated. Carle Medical Communications, 510 West Main Street, Urbana, Illinois 61806 1985. Videotape.

TERMINATION OF MEDICAL TREATMENT DECISIONS: LEGAL AND ETHICAL ISSUES. American Bar Association, Section of Real Property, Probate, and Trust Law, 750 North Lake Shore Drive, Chicago, Illinois 60611. 1984. Audiocassette.

MEDICAL MALPRACTICE
See: MEDICAL JURISPRUDENCE AND MALPRACTICE

MEDICARE AND MEDICAID
See: AGED AND HEALTH CARE; HEALTH CARE; HOSPITALS; INSURANCE, HEALTH AND UNEMPLOYMENT; SOCIAL SECURITY

MENTAL HEALTH AND DISABILITY
See also: PSYCHIATRY; PSYCHOLOGY; MEDICAL JURISPRUDENCE AND MALPRACTICE

STATUTES, CODES, STANDARDS, UNIFORM LAWS

ABA CRIMINAL JUSTICE MENTAL HEALTH STANDARDS. American Bar Association, 750 North Lake Shore Drive, Chicago, Illinois 60611. 1989.

FIRST TENTATIVE DRAFT: CRIMINAL JUSTICE MENTAL HEALTH STANDARDS. American Bar Association, Standing Committee on Association Standards for Criminal Justice, 750 North Lake Shore Drive, Chicago, Illinois 60611. 1983.

A MODEL ACT REGULATING BOARD AND CARE HOMES: GUIDELINES FOR STATES. Jane Beyer, Josephine Bulkley, and Paula Hopkins. American Bar Association, 750 North Lake Shore Drive, Chicago, Illinois 60611. 1984.

MODEL INSANITY DEFENSE AND POST-TRIAL DISPOSITION ACT. National Conference of Commissioners on Uniform State Laws. Uniform Laws Annotated. West Publishing Company, P.O. Box 64526, 50 West Kellogg Boulevard, St. Paul, Minnesota 55164-0526. 1976. (Annual Supplements).

RIGHTS OF THE MENTALLY DISABLED: STATEMENTS AND STANDARDS. Hospital and Community Psychiatry Service, American Psychiatric Association, 1400 K Street, Northwest, Washington, D.C. 20005. 1982.

UNIFORM LAW COMMISSIONERS' MODEL INSANITY DEFENSE AND POST-TRIAL DISPOSTION ACT. Uniform Laws Annotated, Volume II. West Publishing Company, P.O. Box 64526, 50 West Kellogg Boulevard, St. Paul, Minnesota 55164-0526. 1974. (Annual Supplements).

HANDBOOKS, MANUALS, FORMBOOKS

HANDICAPPED REQUIREMENTS HANDBOOK. Federal Programs Advisory Service, Thompson Publishing Group, 1725 K Street Northwest, Suite 200, Washington, D.C. 20006. 1983.

THE INSANITY DEFENSE: A BIBLIOGRAPHIC RESEARCH GUIDE. D. Cheryn Picauet and Reba A. Best. Harrison Company, 3110 Crossing Park, Norcross, Georgia 30091. 1985.

LEGAL ISSUES AND GUIDELINES FOR NURSES WHO CARE FOR THE MENTALLY ILL. Joyce K. Laben and Colleen P. McLean. Slack Incorporated, 6900 Grove Road, Thorofare, New Jersey 08086-9447. 1984.

LEGAL ISSUES IN THE CARE OF PSYCHIATRIC PATIENTS: A GUIDE FOR THE MENTAL HEALTH PROFESSIONAL. Robert Sadoff. Springer Publishing Company, Incorporated, 536 Broadway, New York, New York 10012. 1982.

TEXTBOOKS AND GENERAL WORKS

BACK TO THE ASYLUM: THE FUTURE OF MENTAL HEALTH LAW IN THE UNITED STATES. Mary L. Durham and John Q. Lafond. Oxford University Press, 200 Madison Avenue, New York, New York 10016. 1992.

CHILDREN, MENTAL HEALTH, AND THE LAW. N. Dickon Reppucci, et al, Editors. Books on Demand, 300 North Zeeb Road, Ann Arbor, Michigan 48106-1346. 1984.

COMMUNITY MENTAL HEALTH CENTERS AND THE COURTS: AN EVALUATION OF COMMUNITY-BASED FORENSIC SERVICES. Gary B.Melton, Lois A. Weithorn, and Christopher Slobogin. University of Nebraska Press, 901 North 17th, Lincoln, Nebraska 68588-0520. 1985.

THE COURT OF LAST RESORT: MENTAL ILLNESS AND THE LAW. Carol A. Warren. University of Chicago Press, 5801 Ellis Avenue, Third Floor, South, Chicago, Illinois 60637. 1984.

DANGEROUS BEHAVIOR, THE LAW AND MENTAL DISORDER. Herschel Prins. Routledge, Chapman and Hall, 29 West Thirty-fifth Street, New York, New York 10001. 1986.

DECISION MAKING FOR INCOMPETENT PERSONS. Shannon M. Jordan. Charles C. Thomas, Publisher, 2600 South First Street, Springfield, Illinois 62794-9265. 1985.

DUE PROCESS IN SPECIAL EDUCATION: ON GOING TO A HEARING. Milton Budoff, Alan Orenstein and Carol Kervick. Brookline Books, P.O. Box 1046, Cambridge, Massachusetts 02238. 1988.

ESTATE AND FINANCIAL PLANNING FOR THE AGING OR INCAPACITATED CLIENT. David P. Callahan and Peter J. Strauss, Co-chairmen, Practising Law Institute, 810 Seventh Avenue, New York, New York 10019. 1990.

ETHICS AND LAW IN MENTAL HEALTH ADMINISTRATION. Walter E. Barton and Gail M. Barton. International Universities Press, Incorporated, 59 Boston Post Road, P.O. Box 1524, Madison, Connecticut 06443-1524. 1984.

FORENSIC PSYCHIATRY AND LEGAL PROTECTIONS OF THE INSANE. Second Edition. Stanley Pearlstein and Irving J. Sloan. Oceana Publications, Incorporated, 75 Main Street, Dobbs Ferry, New York 10522. 1986.

HOMELESS MENTALLY ILL: A TASK FORCE REPORT OF THE AMERICAN PSYCHIATRIC ASSOCIATION. American Psychiatric Association, 1400 K Street, Northwest, Washington, D.C. 20005. 1984.

LAW AND MENTAL HEALTH: INTERNATIONAL PERSPECTIVES. David N. Weisstub. Pergamon Press, Incorporated, Maxwell House, Fairview Park, Elmsford, New York 10523. 1990.

LAW AND THE MENTAL HEALTH SYSTEM: CIVIL AND CRIMINAL ASPECTS. Second Edition. Ralph Reisner and Christopher Slobogin. West Publishing Company, P.O. Box 64526, 50 West Kellogg Boulevard, St. Paul, Minnesota 55164-0526. 1990.

LAW, BEHAVIOR, AND MENTAL HEALTH: POLICY AND PRACTICE. Steven R. Smith and Robert G. Meyer. New York University Press, 70 Washington Square South, New York, New York 10012. 1987.

LEGAL ISSUES AND GUIDELINES FOR NURSES WHO CARE FOR THE MENTALLY ILL. Second Edition. Joyce Kemp Laben and Colleen Powell MacLean. Williams and Wilkins, 428 East Preston, Baltimore, Maryland 21202. 1989.

LEGAL ISSUES IN THE EDUCATION OF THE HANDICAPPED. Donald G. Turner, Phi Delta Kappa Educational Foundation, Eighth and Union, Box 789, Bloomington, Indiana 47402. 1983.

LEGAL ISSUES IN SPECIAL EDUCATION. Stehen B. Thomas. National Organization on Legal Problems of Education, 3601 West Twenty-ninth Street, Topeka, Kansas 66614. 1985.

LEGAL RIGHTS AND MENTAL-HEALTH CARE. Stanley S. Herrand Richart E. Wallace, Junior. Free Press, 866 Third Avenue, New York, New York 10022. 1983.

MENTAL DISABILITY LAW: A PRIMER. John Parry, Editor. Commission on the Mentally Disabled, American Bar Association, 1800 M Street, Northwest, Washington, D.C. 20036. 1988.

MENTAL DISABILITY LAW: CIVIL AND CRIMINAL. Michael L. Perlin. Michie Company, P.O. Box 7587, Charlottesville, Virginia 22906-7587. 1989.

MENTAL HEALTH AND THE LAW. Edward B. Beis. Aspen Publishers, Incorporated, 1600 Research Boulevard, Rockville, Maryland 20850. 1983.

MENTAL HEALTH LAW IN CONTEXT: DOCTOR'S ORDERS? Michael Cavadino. Gower Publishing Company, Old Post Road, Brookfield, Vermont 05036. 1989.

MENTAL HEALTH, SOCIAL POLICY AND THE LAW. Tom Butler. Macmillan Publishing Company, Incorporated, 866 Third Avenue, New York, New York 10022. 1985.

MENTAL ILLNESS: PREJUDICE, DISCRIMINATION, AND THE LAW. Tom Campbell and Christopher Heginbotham. Gower Publishing Company, Incorporated, Old Post Road, Brookfield, Vermont 05036. 1991.

MENTAL RETARDATION: ITS SOCIAL AND LEGAL CONTEXT. Stanley J. Vitello and Ronald M. Soskin. Prentice-Hall, Incorporated, 113 Sylvan Avenue, Englewood Cliffs, New Jersey 07632. 1985.

THE MENTALLY DISABLED AND THE LAW. Third Edition. Samuel Jan Brakel, John Parry and Barbara A. Weiner. American Bar Association, American Bar Foundation, 750 North Lake Shore Drive, Chicago, Illinois 60611. 1985.

MENTALLY DISORDERED OFFENDERS: PERSPECTIVES FROM LAW AND SOCIAL SCIENCE. John Monahan and Henry J. Steadman, editors. Plenum Publishing Corporation, 233 Spring Street, New York, New York 10013. 1983.

1987 LEGISLATION MENTAL HEALTH, MENTAL RETARDATION/DEVELOPMENTAL DISABILITIES, SUBSTANCE ABUSE. Martha P. King. National Conference of State Legislatures, 1050 Seventeenth Street, Suite 2100, Denver, Colorado 80265. 1988.

PATIENTS, PSYCHIATRISTS, AND LAWYERS: LAW AND THE MENTAL HEALTH SYSTEM. Raymond L. Spring, Roy B. Lacoursiere and Glen Weissenberger. Anderson Publishing Company, 2035 Reading Road, Cincinnati, Ohio 45202. 1989.

THE POLITICS OF MENTAL HEALTH LEGISLATION. Clive Unsworth. Oxford University Press, 200 Madison Avenue, New York, New York 10016. 1987.

PRIVILEGED COMMUNICATIONS IN THE MENTAL HEALTH PROFESSIONS. Samuel Knapp and Leon VandeCreek. Van Nostrand Reinhold Company, Incorporated, 115 Fifth Avenue, New York, New York 10003. 1987.

PSYCHIATRIC PATIENT RIGHTS AND PATIENT ADVOCACY: ISSUES AND EVIDENCE. Bernard L. Bloom and Shirley J. Asher, Editors. Human Sciences Press, Incorporated, 233 Spring Street, New York, New York 10013. 1982.

PSYCHOTHERAPY AND THE LAW. Louis Everstine, and Diana Sullivan Everstine, Editors. Grune and Stratton, Academic Press, Incorporated, 1250 Sixth Avenue, San Diego, California 92101. 1986.

REFUSING TREATMENT IN MENTAL HEALTH INSTITUTIONS: VALUES IN CONFLICT. A. Edward Doudera and Judith P. Swazey, editors. AUPHA Press, 1911 North Fort Myer Drive, Suite 503, Arlington, Virginia 22209. 1982.

RIGHTS AND ADVOCACY FOR RETARDED PEOPLE. Stanley S. Herr. Lexington Books, Division of D.C. Heath and Company, 125 Spring Street, Lexington, Massachusetts 02173. 1983.

SPECIAL EDUCATION IN AMERICA: ITS LEGAL AND GOVERMNENTAL FOUNDATIONS. Joseph Ballard, Bruce A. Ramirez and Frederick J. Weintraub, Editors. Council for Exceptional Children, 1920 Association Drive, Reston, Virginia 22091. 1982.

THERAPEUTIC JURISPRUDENCE: THE LAW AS A THERAPEUTIC AGENT. David B. Wexler. Carolina Academic Press, P.O. Box 51879, Durham, North Carolina 27717. 1990.

THE TRIAL OF JOHN W. HINCKLEY, JR.: A CASE STUDY IN THE INSANITY DEFENSE. Peter W. Low, John Calvin Jeffries and Richard J. Bonnie. Foundation Press, Incorporated, 615 Merrick Avenue, Westbury, New York 11590. 1986.

TRIBUNALS ON TRIAL: A STUDY OF DECISION-MAKING UNDER THE MENTAL HEALTH ACT 1983. Jill Peay. Oxford University Press, 200 Madison Avenue, New York, New York 10016. 1989.

DIGESTS, INDEXES, ABSTRACTS, CITATORS

MENTAL HEALTH COURT DIGEST. Juridical Digests Institute, 1860 Broadway, New York, New York 10003. Monthly.

LAW REVIEWS AND PERIODICALS

BEHAVIORAL SCIENCES AND THE LAW. John Wiley and Sons, Incorporated, 605 Third Avenue, New York, New York 10158. Quarterly.

NEWSLETTERS AND NEWSPAPERS

DIS/ABILITY LAW BRIEFS. American Bar Association, 1800 M Street, Northwest, Washington, D.C. 20036. Quarterly.

EDUCATION OF THE HANDICAPPED. Capital Publishing Company, 1101 King Street, Suite 444, Alexandria, Virginia 22314. Biweekly.

MENTAL AND PHYSICAL DISABILITY LAW REPORTER. American Bar Association, 1800 M Street, Northwest, Washington, D.C. 20036. Bimonthly.

MENTAL HEALTH AND DISABILITY

MENTAL HEALTH LAW NEWS. Interwood Publications, P.O. Box 20241, Cincinnati, Ohio 45220. Monthly.

MENTAL HEALTH LAW PROJECTS ACTION LINE. Mental Health Law Project, 2021 L Street Northwest, Suite 800, Washington, D.C. 20036. Bimonthly.

MENTAL HEALTH LAW REPORTER. Business Publishers, Incorporated, 951 Pershing Drive, Silver Spring, Maryland 20910. Monthly.

MENTAL HEALTH REPORTS. Business Publishers, Incorporated, 951 Pershing Drive, Silver Spring, Maryland 20910. Biweekly.

NEWSLETTER OF THE AMERICAN ACADEMY OF PSYCHIATRY AND THE LAW. 819 Park Avenue, Baltimore, Maryland 21201. Quarterly.

BIBLIOGRAPHIES

THE INSANE OR MENTALLY IMPAIRED DEFENDANT: A SELECTED BIBLIOGRAPHY. Earleen H. Cook. Vance Bibliographies, P.O. Box 229, 112 North Charter Street, Monticello, Illinois 61856. 1983.

DIRECTORIES

LEGAL RESOURCES FOR THE MENTALLY DISABLED: A DIRECTORY OF LAWYERS AND OTHER SPECIALISTS. Commission on the Mentally Disabled, American Bar Association, 1800 M Street, Northwest, Washington, D.C. 20036. 1983.

MENTAL HEALTH DIRECTORY. National Institute of Public Health. Superintendent of Documents, United States Government Printing Office, Washington, D.C. 20402. 1985.

ASSOCIATIONS AND PROFESSIONAL SOCIETIES

AMERICAN ACADEMY ON MENTAL RETARDATION. c/o Jack A. Stark, Ph.D., Creighton-Nebraska Universities, Department of Psychiatry, 2205 South Tenth Street, Omaha, Nebraska 68108. (402) 449-4783.

AMERICAN ACADEMY OF PSYCHIATRY AND THE LAW. 819 Park Avenue, Baltimore, Maryland 21201. (301) 539-0379.

AMERICAN ASSOCIATION ON MENTAL RETARDATION. 1719 Kalorama Road, Northwest, Washington, D.C. 20009. (202) 387-1968.

ASSOCIATION OF STATE MENTAL HEALTH ATTORNEYS. 1101 King Street, Suite 160, Alexandria, Virginia 22314. (703) 739-9333.

COMMISSION ON THE MENTALLY DISABLED. c/o American Bar Association, 1800 M Street, Northwest, Washington, D.C. 20036. (202) 331-2240.

MENTAL HEALTH LAW PROJECT. 1101 Fifteenth Street, Northwest, Suite 1212, Washington, D.C. 20005. (202) 467-5730.

MENTAL RETARDATION ASSOCIATION OF AMERICA. 211 East 300 South, Suite 212, Salt Lake City, Utah 84111. (801) 328-1575.

NATIONAL MENTAL HEALTH ASSOCIATION. 1021 Prince Street, Alexandria, Virginia 22314. (703) 684-7722.

RESEARCH CENTERS, INSTITUTES, CLEARINGHOUSES

CENTER FOR LAW AND HEALTH SCIENCE. Boston University, 765 Commonwealth Avenue, Boston, Massachusetts 02215. (617) 353-2904.

CENTER FOR PSYCHIATRIC REHABILITATION. Boston University, 730 Commonwealth Avenue, Boston, Massachusetts 02215. (617) 353-3549.

INSTITUTE ON MENTAL DISABILITY AND THE LAW. National Center for State Courts, 300 Newport Avenue, Williamsburg, Virginia 23187. (804) 253-2000.

NATIONAL INSTITUTE OF MENTAL HEALTH. Clinical Research Department, Health and Human Services Department, 5600 Fishers Lane, Rockville, Maryland 20857. (301) 443-3648.

ONLINE DATABASES

MENTAL HEALTH ABSTRACTS. IFI/Plenum Data Company, 302 Swann Avenue, Alexandria, Virginia 22301.

STATISTICS SOURCES

THE ALCOHOL, DRUG ABUSE, AND MENTAL HEALTH NATIONAL DATA BOOK: A REFERENCE BOOK ON THE INCIDENCE AND PREVALENCE, FACILITIES, SERVICES, UTILIZATION, PRACTITIONERS, COSTS AND FINANCING. Thomas R. Vischili, et al. United States Alcohol, Drug Abuse and Mental Health Administration. Superintendent of Documents, United States Government Printing Office, Washington, D.C. 20402.

DIAGNOSTIC AND STATISTICAL MANUAL OF MENTAL DISORDERS. Third Edition. American Psychiatric Association, Task Force on Nomenclature and Statistics, 1400 K Street, Northwest, Washington, D.C. 20005. 1987.

MENTAL ILLNESS
See: MENTAL HEALTH AND DISABILITY

MENTALLY HANDICAPPED

HANDBOOKS, MANUALS, FORMBOOKS

ISSUES IN HUMAN RIGHTS: A GUIDE FOR PARENTS, PROFESSIONALS, POLICYMAKERS, AND ALL THOSE WHO ARE CONCERNED ABOUT THE RIGHTS OF MENTALLY RETARDED AND DEVELOPMENTALLY DISABLED PEOPLE. Stanley S. Herr. Youth Adult Institute Press, 460 West 34th Street, New York, New York 10001. 1984.

LIFE SERVICES PLANNING: CREATING YOUR PROGRAM. Deborah Zuckerman. American Bar Association, Commission on the Mentally Disabled, Commission on Legal Problems of the Elderly, 1800 M Street, Northwest, Washington, D.C. 20036. 1988.

MENTAL DISABILITY LAW: A PRIMER. John Parry, Marc Lampson and Leonard Tao. Commission on the Mentally Disabled, American Bar Association, 1800 M Street, N.W., Washington, D.C. 20036. 1984.

PSYCHOLOGICAL TESTING AND ASSESSMENT OF THE MENTALLY RETARDED: A HANDBOOK. Manny Sternlicht and Lillian Martinez. Garland Publishing, Incorporated, 136 Madison Avenue, New York, New York 10016. 1985.

TEXTBOOKS AND GENERAL WORKS

AGING AND DEVELOPMENTAL DISABILITIES: ISSUES AND APPROACHES. Matthew P. Janicki and Henryk M. Wisniewski. Paul H. Brookes Publishing Company, P.O. Box 10624, Baltimore, Maryland 21285. 1985.

ETHICS AND MENTAL RETARDATION. Loretta Kopelman and John C. Moskop. Kluwer Academic Publishers, 101 Philip Drive, Assinippi Park, Norwell, Massachusetts 02061. 1984.

FEDERAL POLICY TOWARD MENTAL RETARDATION AND DEVELOPMENTAL DISABILITIES. David Braddock. Paul H. Brookes Publishing Company, P.O. Box 10624, Baltimore, Maryland 21285. 1987.

THE IMPACT OF ZONING ON GROUP HOMES FOR THE MENTALLY DISABLED: A NATIONAL SURVEY. Lester D. Steinman. American Bar Association, Section of Urban, State, and Local Government Law, 750 North Lake Shore Drive, Chicago, Illinois 60611. 1986.

LIFE SERVICES PLANNING: SUPPORT SERVICES AND ALTERNATIVES TO GUARDIANSHIP. Deborah Zuckerman and others. Commission on the Mentally Disabled and Commission on Legal Problems of the Elderly, American Bar Association, 750 North Lake Shore Drive, Chicago, Illinois 60611. 1988.

MENTAL RETARDATION: ITS SOCIAL AND LEGAL CONTEXT. Stanley J. Vitello and Ronald M. Soskin. Prentice Hall, Incorporated, 270 Sylvan Avenue, Englewood Cliffs, New Jersey 07632. 1985.

PERSPECTIVES ON A PARENT MOVEMENT: THE REVOLT OF PARENTS OF CHILDREN WITH INTELLECTUAL LIMITATIONS. Rosemary F. Dybwad. Brookline Books, P.O. Box 1046, Cambridge, Massachusetts 02238. 1990.

PSYCHOLOGICAL EVALUATION OF EXCEPTIONAL CHILDREN. Harold D. Love. Charles C.Thomas, Publishers, 2600 South First Street, Springfield, Illinois 62794. 1985.

RIGHTS AND ADVOCACY FOR RETARDED PEOPLE. Stanley S. Herr. Lexington Books, 125 Spring Street, Lexington, Massachusetts 02173. 1983.

RIGHTS OF THE MENTALLY RETARDED--DEVELOPMENTALLY DISABLED TO TREATMENT AND EDUCATION. Issam B. Amary. Charles C.Thomas, Publishers, 2600 South First Street, Springfield, Illinois 62794. 1980.

TRANSITIONS TO ADULT LIFE FOR PEOPLE WITH MENTAL RETARDATION: PRINCIPLES AND PRACTICES. Barbara L. Ludlow, Ann P. Turnbull, and Ruth Luckasson. Paul H. Brookes Publishing Company, P.O. Box 10624, Baltimore, Maryland 21285. 1988.

UNEQUAL JUSTICE? WHAT CAN HAPPEN WHEN PERSONS WITH RETARDATION OR OTHER DEVELOPMENTAL DISABILITIES ENCOUNTER THE CRIMINAL JUSTICE SYSTEM. Robert Perske. Abingdon Press, 201 Eighth Avenue, South, Nashville, Tennessee 37202. 1991.

WILLOWBROOK WARS. David J. Rothman and Sheila M. Rothman. Harper and Row, 10 East 53rd Street, New York, New York 10022. 1984.

ENCYCLOPEDIAS AND DICTIONARIES

DICTIONARY OF MENTAL HANDICAP. Mary P. Lindsey. Routledge, Chapman & Hall, 29 West Thirty-fifth Street, New York, New York 10001. 1989.

ENCYCLOPEDIA OF MENTAL AND PHYSICAL HANDICAPS. David F. Tver and Betty M. Tver. PRO-ED, Incorporated, 8700 Shoal Creek, Austin, Texas 78758. 1991.

ANNUALS AND SURVEYS

IMPACT OF ZONING ON GROUP HOMES FOR THE MENTALLY DISABLED: A NATIONAL SURVEY. Lester D. Steinman. Section of Urban, State, and Local Government Law, American Bar Association, 750 North Lake Shore Drive, Chicago, Illinois 60611. 1986.

NEWSLETTERS AND NEWSPAPERS

MENTAL AND PHYSICAL DISABILITY LAW REPORTER. American Bar Association, Commission on the Mentally Diabled, 1800 M Street, N.W., Washington, D.C. 20036. 1976- . Bimonthly.

BIBLIOGRAPHIES

DEINSTITUTIONALIZATION AND THE CARE OF THE DEVELOPMENTALLY DISABLED: A SELECT BIBLIOGRAPHY, 1961-1981. Andrew Garoogian. Vance Bibliographies, P.O. Box 229, 112 North Charter Street, Monticello, Illinois 61856. 1982.

DESIGNING FACILITIES FOR THE MENTALLY HANDICAPPED. Robert P. Bartholomew. Vance Bibliographies, P.O. Box 229, 112 North Charter Street, Monticello, Illinois 61856. 1980.

SOCIAL BEHAVIOR OF THE MENTALLY RETARDED: AN ANNOTATED BIBLIOGRAPHY. Manny Sternlicht and George Windholz. Garland Publishing, Incorporated, 136 Madison Avenue, New York, New York 10016. 1984.

MENTALLY HANDICAPPED

DIRECTORIES

LEGAL RESOURCES FOR THE MENTALLY DISABLED: A DIRECTORY OF LAWYERS AND OTHER SPECIALISTS. Commission on the Mentally Disabled, American Bar Association, 750 North Lake Shore Drive, Chicago, Illinois 60611. 1983.

ASSOCIATIONS AND PROFESSIONAL SOCIETIES

AMERICAN ASSOCIATION ON MENTAL RETARDATION. 1719 Kalorama Road, N.W., Washington, D.C. 20009. (202) 387-1968.

ASSOCIATION FOR RETARDED CITIZENS (ARC). P.O. Box 6109, Arlington, Texas 76005. (817) 640-0204.

COMMISSION ON THE MENTALLY DISABLED. c/o American Bar Association, 1800 M Street, Northwest, Washington, D.C. 20036. (202) 331-2240. (Formerly: Mental Disability Legal Resources Center).

COUNCIL FOR EXCEPTIONAL CHILDREN. ERIC Clearinghouse on Handicapped and Gifted Children, 1920 Association Drive, Reston, Virginia 22091. (703) 620-3660.

MENTAL HEALTH LAW PROJECT (MHLP). 1101 Fifteenth Street, Northwest, Suite 1212, Washington, D.C. 20005. (202) 467-5730.

MENTAL RETARDATION ASSOCIATION OF AMERICA (MRAA). 211 East 300 South, Suite 212, Salt Lake City, Utah 84111. (801) 328-1575.

RESEARCH CENTERS, INSTITUTES, CLEARINGHOUSES

AMERICAN ASSOCIATION ON MENTAL RETARDATION, 1719 Kalorama Road, Northwest, Washington, D.C. 20009. (202) 387-1968.

CENTER FOR THE STUDY OF HUMAN RIGHTS. Columbia University, 1108 International Affairs Building, New York, New York 10027. (212) 854-2479.

ERIC CLEARINGHOUSE ON HANDICAPPED AND GIFTED CHILDREN. Council for Exceptional Children, 1920 Association Drive, Reston, Virginia 22091. (703) 620-3660.

INSTITUTE FOR THE STUDY OF DEVELOPMENTAL DISABILITIES. Indiana University, 2853 East Tenth Street, Bloomington, Indiana 47405. (812) 855-6508.

INSTITUTE ON MENTAL DISABILITY AND THE LAW. 300 Newport Avenue, National Center for State Courts, Williamsburg, Virginia 23187. (804) 253-2000.

MENTAL RETARDATION RESEARCH AND HUMAN DEVELOPMENT CENTER. 300 Longwood Avenue, Boston, Massachusetts 02115. (617) 735-7046.

NATIONAL INSTITUTE ON DISABILITY AND REHABILITATION RESEARCH. 400 Maryland Avenue, Southwest, Washington, D.C. 20202-2572. (202) 732-1134.

UNITED STATES PUBLIC HEALTH SERVICE, CENTERS FOR DISEASE CONTROL, CENTER FOR ENVIRONMENTAL HEALTH AND INJURY CONTROL. Birth Defects and Developmental Disabilities Division, Mail Stop F37, 1600 Clifton Road, Northeast, Atlanta, Georgia 30333. (404) 488-4706.

UNITED STATES PUBLIC HEALTH SERVICE, NATIONAL INSTITUTES OF HEALTH, NATIONAL INSITUTE OF CHILD HEALTH AND HUMAN DEVELOPMENT CENTER FOR RESEARCH FOR MOTHERS AND CHILDREN. Mental Retardation and Developmental Disabilities Branch, Executive Plaza North, 6130 Executive Boulevard, Bethesda, Maryland 20892. (301) 496-1383.

ONLINE DATABASES

EXCEPTIONAL CHILD EDUCATION RESOURCES (ECER). Council for Exceptional Children (CEC), Department of Information Services, 1920 Association Drive, Reston, Virginia 22091.

MENTAL HEALTH ABSTRACTS. IFI/Plenum Data Corporation, 302 Swann Avenue, Alexandria, Virginia 22301.

NATIONAL REHABILITATION INFORMATION CENTER (NARIC). Macro Systems, Incorporated, 8455 Colesville Road, Suite 935, Silver Spring, Maryland 20910-3319.

OTHER SOURCES

CITIZENS WITH MENTAL RETARDATION AND THE LAW: PROCEEDINGS OF THE SECOND NATIONAL CONFERENCE ON THE LEGAL RIGHTS OF CITIZENS WITH MENTAL RETARDATION. Julius S. Cohen, Lawrence A. Kane, Jr. and Phyllis Brown. President's Committee on Mental Retardation, 330 Independence Avenue, Southwest, Washington, D.C. 20201-0001. 1986.

CITIZENS WITH MENTAL RETARDATION: EQUALITY UNDER THE LAW: REPORT TO THE PRESIDENT. President's Committee on Mental Retardation, U.S. Government Printing Office, Washington, D.C. 20402. 1987.

MERCHANDISE LICENSING
See: LICENSING, INDUSTRIAL AND INTELLECTUAL

MERCHANT MARINE
See: ADMIRALTY

MERGER
See: ANTITRUST LAW; CORPORATIONS, CONSOLIDATION AND MERGER

MERIT SYSTEMS PROTECTION BOARD

STATUTES, CODES, STANDARDS, UNIFORM LAWS

COD CODE OF FEDERAL REGULATIONS, TITLE 5. Office of the Federal Register, National Archives and Records Administration. Superintendent of Documents, United States Government Printing Office, Washington, D.C. 20402. Annual. (Updated by use of monthly List of Sections Affected and daily Federal Register.)

UNITED STATES MERIT SYSTEMS PROTECTION BOARD REPORTER. West Publishing Company, P.O. Box 64526, 50 West Kellogg Boulevard, St. Paul, Minnesota 55164-0526. 1979- .

LOOSELEAF SERVICES AND REPORTERS

DECISIONS OF THE UNITED STATES MERIT SYSTEMS PROTECTION BOARD. Merit Systems Protection Board. Superintendent of Documents, United States Government Printing Office, Washington, D.C. 20402. 1979- .

HANDBOOKS, MANUALS, FORMBOOKS

REPRESENTING THE AGENCY BEFORE THE UNITED STATES MERIT SYSTEMS PROTECTION BOARD, A HANDBOOK ON MSPB PRACTICE AND PROCEDURE. Harold J. Ashner and William C. Jackson. Office of Personnel Management, Office of Employee, Labor, and Agency Relations, Appellate Policies Division. Superintendent of Documents, United States Government Printing Office, Washington, D.C. 20402. 1984.

TEXTBOOKS AND GENERAL WORKS

BLOWING THE WHISTLE IN THE FEDERAL GOVERNMENT: A COMPARATIVE ANALYSIS OF 1980 AND 1983 SURVEY FINDINGS. Merit Systems Protection Board, Office of Merit Systems Review and Studies. Superintendent of Documents, United States Government Printing Office, Washington, D.C. 20402. 1984.

A GUIDE TO MERIT SYSTEMS PROTECTION BOARD, LAW AND PRACTICE. Seventh Edition. Peter B. Broida. Dewey Publications, Incorporated, 353 North Edison Street, Arlington, Virginia 22203. 1990.

MERIT SYSTEMS PROTECTION BOARD: RIGHTS AND REMEDIES. Robert G. Vaughn. Law Journal Seminars-Press, 111 Eighth Avenue, New York, New York 10011. 1984 (Supplemented).

POLITICAL ACTIVITY AND THE FEDERAL EMPLOYEE. Merit Systems Protection Board, Office of Special Counsel. Superintendent of Documents, United States Government Printing Office, Washington, D.C. 20402. 1984.

POLITICAL ACTIVITY AND THE STATE AND LOCAL EMPLOYEE. Merit Systems Protection Board, Office of the Special Counsel. Superintendent of Documents, United States Government Printing Office, Washington, D.C. 20402. 1984.

SEXUAL HARASSMENT IN THE FEDERAL WORKPLACE: IS IT A PROBLEM? Merit Systems Protection Board, Office of Merit Systems Review and Studies. Superintendent of Documents, United States Government Printing Office, Washington, D.C. 20402. 1981.

DIGESTS, INDEXES, ABSTRACTS, CITATORS

DIGEST. Merit Systems Protection Board, Office of the Board, Information Services Division. Superintendent of Documents, United States Government Printing Office, Washington, D.C. 20402. Monthly.

UNITED STATES MERIT SYSTEMS PROTECTION BOARD DIGEST. West Publishing Company, P.O. Box 64526, 50 West Kellogg Boulevard, St. Paul, Minnesota 55164-0526. 1979- .

ONLINE DATABASES

LEXIS, FEDERAL LABOR LIBRARY. Mead Data Central, P.O. Box 933, Dayton, Ohio 45401.

WESTLAW, LABOR LIBRARY. West Publishing Company, P.O. Box 64526, 50 West Kellogg Boulevard, St. Paul, Minnesota 55164-0526.

OTHER SOURCES

THE OFFICE OF SPECIAL COUNSEL: JUDICIAL VIEWS ON PROSECUTION OF PROHIBITED PERSONNEL PRACTICES: A REPORT TO THE PRESIDENT AND THE CONGRESS OF THE UNITED STATES. United States Merit Systems Protection Board, 1120 Vermont Avenue, Northwest, Washington, D.C. 20419. 1987.

MIGRANT LABOR
See: AGRICULTURE; AGRICULTURE DEPARTMENT; LABOR AND LABOR RELATIONS

MILITARY LAW AND SERVICE
See also: CONSCIENTIOUS OBJECTORS; DEFENSE DEPARTMENT; VETERANS

STATUTES, CODES, STANDARDS, UNIFORM LAWS

LEGISLATIVE HISTORY OF THE TEN DOLLAR ATTORNEY FEE LIMITATION IN CLAIMS FOR VETERANS' BENEFITS. United States Congress, House Committee on Veterans' Affairs. Superintendent of Documents, United States Government Printing Office, Washington, D.C. 20402. 1987.

UNIFORM CODE OF MILITARY JUSTICE. Uniform Laws Annotated. West Publishing Company, P.O. Box 64526, 50 West Kellogg Boulevard, St. Paul, Minnesota 55164-0526. 1976. (Annual Supplements).

LOOSELEAF SERVICES AND REPORTERS

MILITARY DISCHARGE UPGRADING AND INTRODUCTION TO VETERANS ADMINISTRATION LAW. David F. Addlestone. Veteran's Education Project, P.O. Box 42130, Washington, D.C. 20015. 1982- .

MILITARY LAW REPORTER. Public Law Education Institute, 1601 Connecticut Avenue, Northwest, Suite 450, Washington, D.C. 20009. 1972- .

WEST'S MILITARY JUSTICE REPORTER. West Publishing Company, P.O. Box 64526, 50 West Kellogg Boulevard, St. Paul, Minnesota 55164-0526. 1976- .

HANDBOOKS, MANUALS, FORMBOOKS

DRAFT COUNSELOR'S MANUAL. Robert A. Seeley, editor. Central Committee for Conscientious Objectors. 2208 South Street, Philadelphia, Pennsylvania 19146. 1982.

DRAFT, REGISTRATION AND THE LAW: A GUIDEBOOK. Second Edition. R. Charles Johnson. Nolo Press, 950 Parker Street, Berkeley, California 94710. 1991.

LAW FOR THE JUNIOR OFFICER. Kendall/Hunt Publishing Company, 2460 Kerper Boulevard, Dubuque, Iowa 52001. 1990.

MILITARY RULES OF EVIDENCE MANUAL. Third Edition. Stephen A. Saltzburg, Lee D. Schinasi, and David A. Schlueter. The Michie Company, P.O. Box 7587, Charlottesville, Virginia 22906-7587. 1986.

SERVICEMEMBER'S LEGAL GUIDE: EVERYTHING YOU AND YOUR FAMILY NEED TO KNOW ABOUT THE LAW. Second Edition. Jonathan P. Tomes. Stackpole Books, Cameron and Kelker Streets, P.O. Box 1831, Harrisburg, Pennsylvania 17105. 1992.

TEXTBOOKS AND GENERAL WORKS

AMERICA'S VOLUNTEER MILITARY: PROGRESS AND PROSPECTS. Martin Binkin. Brookings Institution, 1775 Massachusetts Avenue, Northwest, Washington, D.C. 20036-2188. 1984.

THE BANANA WARS: A HISTORY OF UNITED STATES MILITARY INTERVENTION IN LATIN AMERICA FROM THE SPANISH-AMERICAN WAR TO THE INVASION OF PANAMA. Ivan Musicant. Macmillan Publishing Company, Incorporated, 866 Third Avenue, New York, New York 10022. 1990.

COMPARATIVE ANALYSIS OF THE FEDERAL RULES OF CRIMINAL PROCEDURE WITH MILITARY PRACTICE AND PROCEDURE. American Bar Association, 750 North Lake Shore Drive, Chicago, Illinois 60611. Section of Criminal Justice. 1982.

CONSCRIPTS AND VOLUNTEERS: MILITARY REQUIREMENTS, SOCIAL JUSTICE, AND THE ALL-VOLUNTEER FORCE. Robert K. Fullinwider, Editor. Rowman and Allanheld, 420 Boston Way, Lanham, Maryland 20706. 1983.

ESSAYS ON THE MODERN LAW OF WAR. L. C. Green. Transnational Publishers, Incorporated, P.O. Box 7282, Ardsley-on-Hudson, New York 10503. 1985.

FIGHTING BACK: LESBIAN AND GAY DRAFT, MILITARY, AND VETERANS ISSUES. Katherine Bourdonnay. National Lawyers Guild, 55 Sixth Avenue, New York, New York 10013. 1984.

FOR THE SAKE OF EXAMPLE: CAPITAL COURTS-MARTIAL, 1914-1920. Anthony Babington. Saint Martin's Press, Incorporated, 175 Fifth Avenue, New York, New York 10010. 1984.

FOREIGN MILITARY INTERVENTION: THE DYNAMICS OF PROTRACTED CONFLICT. Ariel Levite, Bruce W. Jentleson and Larry Berman. Columbia University Press, 562 West One Hundred Thirteenth Street, New York, New York 10025. 1992.

GOVERNMENT FROM REFLECTION AND CHOICE: CONSTITUTIONAL ESSAYS ON WAR, FOREIGN RELATIONS, AND FEDERALISM. Charles A. Lofgren. Oxford University Press, Incorporated, 200 Madison Avenue, New York, New York 10016. 1986.

INTERNATIONAL LAW OF GUERRILLA WARFARE: THE GLOBAL POLITICS OF LAW-MAKING. Keith Suter. Saint Martin's Press, Incorporated, 175 Fifth Avenue, New York, New York 10010. 1984.

LEGITIMATE USE OF MILITARY FORCE AGAINST STATE-SPONSORED INTERNATIONAL TERRORISM. Richard J. Erickson. Air University Press, Superintendent of Documents, United States Government Printing Office, Washington, D.C. 20402. 1989.

MARINES AND MILITARY LAW IN VIETNAM: TRIAL BY FIRE. Gary D. Solis. United States Marine Corp. History and Museums Division. Superintendent of Documents, United States Government Printing Office, Washington, D.C. 20402. 1989.

MILITARY CRIMINAL JUSTICE: PRACTICE AND PROCEDURE. David A. Schlueter. The Michie Company, P.O. Box 7587, Charlottesville, Virginia 22906-7587. 1982. (Periodic supplements).

THE MILITARY DRAFT: SELECTED READINGS ON CONSCRIPTION. Martin Anderdson, editor. Hoover Institution Press, Stanford University, Stanford, California 94305-6010. 1982.

MILITARY LAW IN A NUTSHELL. Charles A. Shanor and Timothy P. Terrell. West Publishing Company, P.O. Box 64526, 50 West Kellogg Boulevard, St. Paul, Minnesota 55164-0526. 1980.

REGISTRATION AND THE DRAFT: PROCEEDINGS OF THE HOOVER-ROCHESTER CONFERENCE ON THE ALL-VOLUNTEER FORCE. Martin Anderson, Editor. Hoover Institution Press, Stanford University, Stanford, California 94305-6010. 1982.

RESCUING NATIONALS ABROAD THROUGH MILITARY COERCION AND INTERVENTION ON GROUNDS OF HUMANITY. Natalino Ronzitti. Kluwer Academic Publishers, 101 Philip Drive, Assinippi Park, Norwell, Massachusetts 02061. 1985.

SOCIO-LEGAL FOUNDATIONS OF CIVIL-MILITARY RELATIONS. James B. Jacobs. Transnational Publishers, Incorporated, P.O. Box 7282, Ardsley-on-Hudson, New York 10503. 1986.

A SOLDIER IS ALSO A CITIZEN: THE CONTROVERSY OVER MILITARY JUSTICE, 1917-1920. John M. Lindley. Garland Publishing, Incorporated, 136 Madison Avenue, New York, New York 10016. 1990.

THE THIRD AMENDMENT. Burnham Holmes. Silver Burdett Press, Incorporated, 190 Sylvan Avenue, Englewood Cliffs, New Jersey 07632. 1991.

THE TOKYO WAR CRIMES TRIAL: AN INTERNATIONAL SYMPOSIUM. Kodansha International, U.S.A., Limited, HarperCollins Publishers, 10 East Fifty-third Street, New York, New York 10022. 1986.

TOWARD A CONSENSUS ON MILITARY SERVICE: REPORT OF THE ATLANTIC COUNCIL WORKING GROUP ON MILITARY SERVICE. Andrew J. Goodpastor and Lloyd H. Elliot, Co-chairmen. Transaction Books, Rutgers University, New Brunswick, New Jersey 08903. 1983.

THE UNITED STATES MILITARY UNDER THE CONSTITUTION OF THE UNITED STATES, 1789-1989. Richard H. Kohn. New York University Press, 70 Washington Square South, New York, New York 10012. 1991.

WAR CRIMES AND LAWS OF WAR. Second Edition. Donald A. Wells. University Press of America, 4720 Boston Way, Lanham, Maryland 20706. 1991.

WAR, MORALITY, AND THE MILITARY PROFESSION. Second Edition. Malham M. Wakin, Editor. Westview Press, 5500 Central Avenue, Boulder, Colorado 80301. 1986.

DIGESTS, INDEXES, ABSTRACTS, CITATORS

SHEPARD'S MILITARY JUSTICE CITATIONS. Shepard's/McGraw-Hill, P.O. Box 1235, Colorado Springs, Colorado 80901. 1985.

LAW REVIEWS AND PERIODICALS

AIR FORCE LAW REVIEW. Air Force Judge Advocate General's School. Superintendent of Documents, United States Government Printing Office, Washington, D.C. 20402. Quarterly.

ARMY LAWYER. Judge Advocate General's School, Department of the Army. Superintendent of Documents, United States Government Printing Office, Washington, D.C. 20402. Monthly.

JAG JOURNAL. Office of the Judge Advocate General, Department of the Navy. Superintendent of Documents, United States Government Printing Office, Washington, D.C. 20402. Semiannual.

MILITARY LAW REPORTER. Public Law Education Institute, 1601 Connecticut Avenue, Northwest, Washington, D.C. 20009. Bimonthly.

MILITARY LAW REVIEW. Headquarters, United States Department of the Army. Superintendent of Documents, United States Government Printing Office, Washington, D.C. 20402. Quarterly.

NEWSLETTERS AND NEWSPAPERS

INSIDE THE PENTAGON. Inside Washington Publishers, P.O. Box 7167, Ben Franklin Station, Washington, D.C. 20044. Weekly.

LEGAL ASSISTANCE NEWSLETTER. American Bar Association, Standing Committee on Legal Assistance for Military Personnel, 750 North Lake Shore Drive, Chicago, Illinois 60611. Quarterly.

THE OBJECTOR. CCCO, P.O. Box 42249, San Francisco, California 94142. Bimonthly.

BIBLIOGRAPHIES

WAR CRIMES, WAR CRIMINALS, AND WAR CRIMES TRIALS: AN ANNOTATED BIBLIOGRAPHY AND SOURCE BOOK. Norman E. Tutorow, editor. Greenwood Publishing Group, Incorporated, 88 Post Road West, P.O. Box 5007, Westport, Connecticut 06881. 1986.

BIOGRAPHICAL SOURCES

LEWIS B. HERSHEY, MR. SELECTIVE SERVICE. George Q. Flynn. University of North Carolina Press, P.O. Box 2288, 116 South Boundary Street, Chapel Hill, North Carolina 27515-2288. 1985.

ASSOCIATIONS AND PROFESSIONAL SOCIETIES

COMMITTEE ON LAW AND NATIONAL SECURITY. American Bar Association, 750 North Lake Shore Drive, Chicago, Illinois 60611. (312) 988-5000.

COMMITTEE ON LAWYERS IN THE ARMED FORCES. American Bar Association, 750 North Lake Shore Drive, Chicago, Illinois 60611. (312) 988-5000.

COMMITTEE ON MILITARY LAW. American Bar Association, 750 North Lake Shore Drive, Chicago, Illinois 60611. (312) 988-5000.

JUDGE ADVOCATES ASSOCIATION. 1815 H Street, Northwest, Suite 408, Washington, D.C. 20006. (202) 628-0979.

MILITARY LAW TASK FORCE. 1168 Union, Suite 201, San Diego, California 92101. (619) 233-1701.

STANDING COMMITTEE ON LEGAL ASSISTANCE FOR MILITARY PERSONNEL. American Bar Association, 750 North Lake Shore Drive, Chicago, Illinois 60611. (312) 988-5000.

RESEARCH CENTERS, INSTITUTES, CLEARINGHOUSES

PUBLIC LAW EDUCATION INSTITUTE. 1601 Connecticut Avenue, Northwest, Washington, D.C. 20009. (202) 232-1400.

ONLINE DATABASES

LEXIS MILITARY JUSTICE LIBRARY. Mead Data Central, Incorporated, 9393 Springboro Pike, P.O. Box 933, Dayton, Ohio 45401.

WESTLAW MILITARY LAW LIBRARY. West Publishing Company, 50 West Kellogg Boulevard, P.O. Box 64526, St. Paul, Minnesota 55164.

MINING LAW

See also: ENERGY DEPARTMENT; FEDERAL MINE SAFETY AND HEALTH REVIEW COMMISSION; INTERIOR DEPARTMENT; OIL AND GAS

MINING LAW

LOOSELEAF SERVICES AND REPORTERS

AMERICAN LAW OF MINING. Second Edition. Matthew Bender and Company, Incorporated, 11 Penn Plaza, New York, New York 10001. 1984- .

COAL LAW AND REGULATION. Patrick C. McGinley and Donald H. Vish, editors. Matthew Bender and Company, Incorporated, 11 Penn Plaza, New York, New York 10001. 1983- .

GOWER FEDERAL SERVICE: MINING. Rocky Mountain Mineral Law Foundation, 7039 East Eighteenth Avenue, Denver, Colorado 80220. 1962- .

MINE SAFETY AND HEALTH REPORTER. Bureau of National Affairs, 1231 Twenty-fifth Street, Northwest, Washington, D.C. 20037. 1979- .

SURFACE MINING REPORTER. Pasha Publications, Incorporated, 1401 Wilson Boulevard, Suite 900, Arlington, Virginia 22209. 1984- .

TAXATION OF MINING OPERATIONS. Peter C. Maxwell and James L. Houghton. Matthew Bender and Company, Incorporated, 11 Penn Plaza, New York, New York 10001. 1981- .

TEXTBOOKS AND GENERAL WORKS

ANTARCTIC MINERAL EXPLOITATION: THE EMERGING LEGAL FRAMEWORK. Francisco Orrego Vicuna. Cambridge University Press, 40 West Twentieth Street, New York, New York 10011. 1988.

THE ANTARCTIC TREATY REGIME: LAW, ENVIRONMENT, AND RESOURCES. Gillian D. Triggs. British Institute of International and Comparative Law. Cambridge University Press, 40 West Twentieth Street, New York, New York 10011. 1987.

THE ANTARCTIC TREATY SYSTEM IN WORLD POLITICS. Arnfinn Jorgensen-Dahl and Willy Oestreng. St. Martin's Press, 175 Fifth Avenue, New York, New York 10010. 1991.

THE CONVENTION ON THE REGULATION OF ANTARCTIC MINERAL RESOURCE ACTIVITIES: AN ATTEMPT TO BREAK NEW GROUND. Rudiger Wolfrum. Springer-Verlag New York, Incorporated, 175 Fifth Avenue, New York, New York 10010. 1991.

ENERGY RESOURCES TAX REPORTS. David B. Cox. Commerce Clearing House, Incorporated, 4025 West Peterson Avenue, Chicago, Illinois 60646. 1983- .

INCOME TAXATION OF COAL OPERATIONS. Ahron H. Haspel and Douglas P. Sumner. Prentice-Hall, Incorporated, 113 Sylvan Avenue, Englewood Cliffs, New Jersey 07632. 1984.

LEGAL ASPECTS OF GEOLOGY. Ronald W. Tank. Plenum Publishing Corporation, 233 Spring Street, New York, New York 10013. 1983.

LEGAL PITFALLS, LAND STATUS AND THE ACQUISITION OF MINERAL RIGHTS. Second Edition. Olan Paul Matthews. Idaho Mining and Minerals Resources Research Institute, Universtiy of Idaho, Moscow, Idaho 83843. 1985.

MANAGING THE FROZEN SOUTH: THE CREATION AND EVOLUTION OF THE ANTARCTIC TREATY SYSTEM. M.J. Peterson. University of California Press, 2120 Berkeley Way, Berkeley, California 94720. 1988.

MINERAL FINANCING. Institute on Mineral Financing. Rocky Mountain Mineral Law Foundation, 7039 East Eighteenth Avenue, Denver, Colorado 80220. 1982.

MINERAL RESOURCES PERMITTING. Institute on Mineral Resources Permitting. Rocky Mountain Mineral Law Foundation, 7039 East Eighteenth Avenue, Denver, Colorado 80220. 1981.

MINERAL RIGHTS ON THE PUBLIC DOMAIN. Michael Braunstein. Anderson Publishing Company, 2035 Reading Road, Cincinnati, Ohio 45202. 1987- .

MINERAL TITLE EXAMINATION. Terry S. Maley. Mineral Land Publications, P.O. Box 1186, Boise, Idaho 83701. 1984.

MINING AND DRILLING LAW. Simon L. Goren. Oceana Publications, 75 Main Street, Dobbs Ferry, New York 10522. 1987- .

THE MINING LAW: A STUDY IN PERPETUAL MOTION. John D. Leshy. Resources for the Future, Incorporated, 1616 P Street, Northwest, Washington, D.C. 20036. 1987.

POLAR PROSPECTS: A MINERALS TREATY FOR ANTARCTICA. United States. Congress. Office of Technology Assessment. Superintendent of Documents, United States Government Printing Office, Washington, D.C. 20402. 1989.

SELF-INITIATION: THE HARDROCK MINER'S RIGHT. Thomas S. Barrett. Public Resource Foundation, 1815 H Street, Northwest, Suite 600, Washington, D.C. 20006. 1987.

RESOURCE MATERIALS: DOMESTIC TAXATION OF HARD MATERIALS. Second Edition. American Law Institute-American Bar Association, Committee on Continuing Professional Education, 4025 Chestnut Street, Philadelphia, Pennsylvania 19104. 1983.

A TREATISE ON THE AMERICAN LAW RELATING TO MINES AND MINERAL LANDS WITHIN THE PUBLIC LAND STATES AND TERRITORIES AND GOVERNING THE ACQUISITION AND ENJOYMENT OF MINING RIGHTS IN LANDS OF THE PUBLIC DOMAIN. Third Edition. Curtis H. Lindley. Fred B. Rothman and Company, 10368 West Centennial Road, Littleton, Colorado 80127. 1988. (Reprint).

DIGESTS, INDEXES, ABSTRACTS, CITATORS

DIGEST OF MINING CLAIM LAWS. Second Edition. Robert G. Pruitt, Jr., Editor. Rocky Mountain Mineral Law Foundation, Fleming Law Building, B-405, University of Colorado, Boulder, Colorado 80309. 1981.

MINERAL ECONOMICS ABSTRACTS. Atlantis Energy and Mineral Economic Services, Incorporated, 1270 Avenue of the Americas, New York, New York 10020. 1978- .

LAW REVIEWS AND PERIODICALS

AMERICAN MINING CONGRESS JOURNAL. American Mining Congress, 1920 N Street, Northwest, Suite 300, Washington, D.C. 20036. Monthly.

ENERGY LAW JOURNAL. Federal Energy Bar Association, 888 Sixteenth Street, Northwest, Suite 400, Washington, D.C. 20036. Semiannual.

MINERAL LAW INSTITUTE PROCEEDINGS. Rocky Mountain Mineral Law Foundation, Porter Administration Building, 7039 East Eighteenth Avenue, Denver, Colorado 80220. Annual.

NEWSLETTERS AND NEWSPAPERS

CASE UPDATE. Eastern Mineral Law Foundation, West Virginia University Law Center, P.O. Box 6130, Morgantown, West Virginia 26506. Quarterly.

INSIDE ENERGY WITH FEDERAL LANDS. McGraw-Hill Book Company, 1221 Avenue of the Americas, New York, New York 10020. Weekly.

MINE REGULATION REPORTER. Pasha Publications, Incorporated, 1401 Wilson Boulevard, Suite 900, Arlington, Virginia 22209. Biweekly.

MINERAL LAW. Illinois State Bar Association, Illinois Bar Center, Springfield, Illinois 62701. Quarterly.

MINERAL LAW NEWSLETTER. Rocky Mountain Mineral Law Foundation, 7039 East Eighteenth Avenue, Denver, Colorado 80220. Quarterly.

WASHINGTON CONCENTRATES. American Mining Congress, 1920 N Street, Northwest, Suite 300, Washington, D.C. 20036. Weekly.

WATER LAW NEWSLETTER. Rocky Mountain Mineral Law Foundation, Porter Administration Building, 7039 East Eighteenth Avenue, Denver, Colorado 80220. Quarterly.

BIBLIOGRAPHIES

LIST OF BUREAU OF MINING PUBLICATIONS AND ARTICLES. United States Bureau of Mines. Superintendent of Documents, United States Government Printing Office, Washington, D.C. 20402. Annual.

DIRECTORIES

E/MJ INTERNATIONAL DIRECTORY OF MINING. McGraw-Hill Book Company, 1221 Avenue of the Americas, New York, New York 10020. Annual.

HART'S ROCKY MOUNTAIN MINING DIRECTORY. Hart Publications, Incorporated, Box 1917, Denver, Colorado 80201. Annual.

MINERALS DATA SOURCE DIRECTORY. Interagency Minerals Data Working Group, Division of Minerals Information Systems, Bureau of Mines, Interior Department, 1849 C Street, Northwest, Washington, D.C. 20240. 1983.

WESTERN MINING DIRECTORY. Howell Publishing Company, P.O. Box 27561, Houston, Texas 77227. Annual.

ASSOCIATIONS AND PROFESSIONAL SOCIETIES

AMERICAN INSTITUTE OF MINING, METALLURGICAL AND PETROLEUM ENGINEERS. 345 East Forty-seventh Street, New York, New York 10017. (212) 705-7695.

AMERICAN MINING CONGRESS. 1920 N Street, Northwest, Suite 300, Washington, D.C. 20036. (202) 861-2800.

COALITION FOR RESPONSIBLE MINING LAW. 1212 Washington Street, Suite 306, Spokane, Washington 99201. (509) 328-5685.

COLORADO MINING ASSOCIATION. 1600 Broadway, Suite 1340, Denver, Colorado 80202. (303) 894-0536.

MINING AND METALLURGICAL SOCIETY OF AMERICA. 210 Post Street, Suite 1102, San Francisco, California 94108. (415) 398-6925.

NORTHWEST MINING ASSOICATION. 414 Peyton Building, Spokane, Washington 99201. (509) 624-1158.

SOCIETY FOR MINING METALLURGY, AND EXPLORATION, INCORPORATED. P.O. Box 625005, Littleton, Colorado 80162. (303) 973-9550.

UNITED MINING COUNCILS OF AMERICA. P.O. Box 460, Hinkley, California 92347. (619) 253-7561.

RESEARCH CENTERS, INSTITUTES, CLEARINGHOUSES

CENTER FOR ENERGY AND MINERAL POLICY RESEARCH. Pennsylvania State University, 204 Walker Building, University Park, Pennsylvania 16802. (814) 865-0631.

EASTERN MINERAL LAW FOUNDATION. West Virginia University Law Center, P.O. Box 6130, Morgantown, West Virginia 26506. (304) 293-2470.

NATIONAL RESOURCES LAW CENTER. University of Colorado, Boulder, Campus Box 401, Boulder, Colorado 80309. (303) 492-1288.

ROCKY MOUNTAIN MINERAL LAW FOUNDATION. Porter Administration Building, 7039 East Eighteenth Avenue, Denver, Colorado 80220. (303) 321-8100.

WATER LAW NEWSLETTER. Rocky Mountain Mineral Law Foundation, Porter Administration Building, 7039 East Eighteenth Avenue, Denver, Colorado 80220. Quarterly.

ONLINE DATABASES

COAL AGE. Maclean Hunter Publishing Corporation, Mining Information Services, 4 Stamford Forum, Stamford, Connecticut 06901.

COAL OUTLOOK. Pasha Publications, Incorporated, 1401 Wilson Boulevard, Suite 900, Arlington, Virginia 22209.

COAL WEEK. McGraw-Hill, Incorporated, 1221 Avenue of the Americas, New York, New York 10020.

COAL WEEK INTERNATIONAL. McGraw-Hill, Incorporated, 1221 Avenue of the Americas, New York, New York 10020.

ENGINEERING AND MINING JOURNAL. Maclean Hunter Publishing Corporation, Mining Information Services, 4 Stamford Forum, Stamford, Connecticut 06901.

MINESEARCH. Metals Economic Group, Limited. 1722 Fourteenth Street, Boulder, Colorado 80302.

PENN STATE COAL DATA BASE. Pennsylvania State University, Energy and Fuels Research Center, 517 Deike Building, University Park, Pennsylvania 16802.

PUBLICATIONS OF THE U.S. GEOLOGICAL SURVEY. American Geological Institute, GeoRef Information System, 4220 King Street, Alexandria, Virginia 22302.

STATISTICS SOURCES

CENSUS OF MINERAL INDUSTRIES. Bureau of the Census. Superintendent of Documents, United States Government Printing Office, Washington, D.C. 20402. Every five years.

MINERALS YEARBOOK. United States Bureau of Mines. Superintendent of Documents, United States Government Printing Office, Washington, D.C. 20402. Annual.

MINORITIES
See: CIVIL RIGHTS AND LIBERTIES; DISCRIMINATION, EDUCATION; DISCRIMINATION, EMPLOYMENT; DISCRIMINATION, HOUSING; DISCRIMINATION, RACE; SCHOOL INTEGRATION; SEGREGATION AND INTEGRATION

MINORS
See: CHILDREN

MODEL CODES
See: UNIFORM AND MODEL ACTS

MONEY AND MONETARY CONTROL
See also: FEDERAL RESERVE BOARD; TREASURY DEPARTMENT

STATUTES, CODES, STANDARDS, UNIFORM LAWS

LEGISLATION AIMED AT COMBATING INTERNATIONAL DRUG TRAFFICKING AND MONEY LAUNDERING: A STAFF REPORT. United States Congress, Senate Caucus on International Narcotics Control. Superintendent of Documents, United States Government Printing Office, Washington, D.C. 20402. 1987.

LOOSELEAF SERVICES AND REPORTERS

MONETARY POLICY AND RESERVE REQUIREMENTS HANDBOOK. Publications Section, Federal Reserve Board, Twentieth and Constitution Avenue, Northwest, Washington, D.C. 20551. 1981- .

TRANSNATIONAL ECONOMIC AND MONETARY LAW: TRANSACTIONS AND CONTRACTS. Leonard Lazar. Oceana Publications, Incorporated, 75 Main Street, Dobbs Ferry, New York 10522. 1976- .

HANDBOOKS, MANUALS, FORMBOOKS

A WORLD GUIDE TO EXCHANGE CONTROL REQUISITIONS. Philip Bentley, Editor. Euromoney Publications, Limited, Nester House, Playhouse Yard, London EC4V 5EX, United Kingdom. 1985.

TEXTBOOKS AND GENERAL WORKS

AMERICAN MONEY AND BANKING. Maxwell J. Fry and Raburn M. Williams. Books on Demand, 300 North Zeeb Road, Ann Arbor, Michigan 48106-1346. 1984.

BEYOND MONETARISM: FINDING THE ROAD TO STABLE MONEY. Marc A. Miles. Basic Books, Incorporated, 10 East Fifty-third Street, New York, New York 10022. 1984.

CONTROLLING MONEY: THE FEDERAL RESERVE AND ITS CRITICS. Ralph C. Bryant. Brookings Institution, 1775 Massachusetts Avenue, Northwest, Washington, D.C. 20036-2188. 1983.

CURRENCY FLUCTUATIONS: ACCOUNTING AND TAXING IMPLICATIONS. Second Edition. D. P. Wainman. Woodhead-Faulkner Publishers, Limited, 51 Washington Street, Dover, New Hampshire 08320. 1984.

EMERGING FINANCIAL CENTERS: LEGAL AND INSTITUTIONAL FRAMEWORK: BAHAMAS, HONG KONG, IVORY COAST, KENYA, KUWAIT, PANAMA, SINGAPORE. Robert C. Effros, editor. Books on Demand, 300 North Zeeb Road, Ann Arbor, Michigan 48106-1346. 1982.

EXCHANGE RATE POLICY. Roy Batchelor and Geoffrey E. Wood, Editors. Saint Martin's Press, Incorporated, 175 Fifth Avenue, New York, New York 10010. 1982.

THE FED: INSIDE THE FEDERAL RESERVE, THE SECRET POWER CENTER THAT CONTROLS THE AMERICAN ECONOMY. Maxwell Newton. Times Books, Random House, Incorporated, 201 East Fiftieth Street, New York, New York 10022. 1983.

FEDERAL RESERVE, MONEY, AND INTEREST RATES: THE VOLCKER YEARS AND BEYOND. Michael G. Hadjimichalakis. Praeger Publishers, One Madison Avenue, New York, New York 10010-3603. 1984.

FINANCIAL REGULATION AND MONETARY CONTROL: HISTORICAL PERSPECTIVE AND THE IMPACT OF THE 1980 ACT. Thomas Cargill and Gillian G. Garcia. Hoover Institution Press, Stanford University, Stanford, California 94305-6010. 1982.

FOREIGN EXCHANGE AND MONEY MARKETS: MANAGING FOREIGN AND DOMESTIC CURRENCY OPERATIONS. Heinz Riehl and Rita M. Rodriguez. McGraw Publishing Company, 1221 Avenue of the Americas, New York, New York 10020. 1983.

FOREIGN EXCHANGE FUTURES: A GUIDE TO INTER-NATIONAL CURRENCY TRADING. Allan M. Loosigian. Dow Jones-Irwin, 1818 Ridge Road, Homewood, Illinois 60430. 1981.

FUNDAMENTALS OF MONEY, BANKING AND FINANCIAL INSTITUTIONS. Jonas Praeger. HarperCollins Publishers, 10 East Fifty-third Street, New York, New York 10022. 1982.

GREAT AMERICAN RIP-OFF: AN INDICTMENT OF THE FEDERAL RESERVE BOARD. F. W. Maisel. Condido Press, P.O. Box 27551, Rancho Bernardo, San Diego, California 92128. 1983.

INSIDE THE FED: MAKING MONETARY POLICY. William C. Melton. Business 1 Irwin, 1818 Ridge Road, Homewood, Illinois 60430. 1984.

INTEREST RATE AND CURRENCY SWAPS. Daniel P. Cunningham, Chairman. Practising Law Institute, 810 Seventh Avenue, New York, New York 10019. 1989.

THE INTERNATIONAL MONETARY SYSTEM, 1945-1981. Robert Solomon. HarperCollins Publishers, 10 East Fifty-third Street, New York, New York 10022. 1982.

THE INTERNATIONAL MONETARY SYSTEM: A TIME OF TURBULENCE: A CONFERENCE SPONSORED BY THE AMERICAN ENTERPRISE INSTITUTE FOR PUBLIC POLICY RESEARCH. Jacob S. Dreyer, Gottfried Haberler, and Thomas D. Willett. Books on Demand, 300 North Zeeb Road, Ann Arbor, Michigan 48106-1346. 1982.

THE INTERNATIONAL MONETARY SYSTEM UNDER FLEXIBLE EXCHANGE RATES: GLOBAL, REGIONAL, AND NATIONAL: ESSAYS IN HONOR OF ROBERT TRIFFIN. Robert N. Cooper, et al, editors. Ballinger Publishing Company, Subsidiary of Harper and Row, Incorporated, 10 East Fifty-third Street, New York, New York 10022. 1982.

AN INTERNATIONAL STANDARD FOR MONETARY STABILIZATION. Ronald I. McKinnon. Institute for Industrial Economics. Distributed by Books on Demand, 300 North Zeeb Road, Ann Arbor, Michigan 48106-1346. 1984.

INVENTORIES AND FOREIGN CURRENCY TRANSLATION REQUIREMENTS. Kathleen R. Bindon. Books on Demand 300 North Zeeb Road, Ann Arbor, Michigan 48106-1346. 1983.

INVESTMENT COMPANIES: INDUSTRY RESPONSES TO NEW CONTEXTS AND CONCEPTS. Stanley J. Friedman, Chairman. Practising Law Institute, 810 Seventh Avenue, New York, New York 10019. 1983.

LAW AND INFLATION. Keith S. Rosenn. University of Pennsylvania Press, 418 Service Drive, Blockley Hall, Thirteenth Floor, Philadelphia, Pennsylvania 19104. 1982.

THE LAW OF MODERN PAYMENT SYSTEMS AND NOTES. Fred H. Miller. University of Oklahoma Press, 105 Asp Avenue, Norman, Oklahoma 73019. 1985.

THE LEGAL ASPECTS OF MONEY WITH SPECIAL REFERENCE TO COMPARATIVE PRIVATE AND PUBLIC INTERNATIONAL LAW. Fifth Edition. F.A. Mann. Clarendon Press, Oxford University Press, 200 Madison Avenue, New York, New York 10016. 1992.

MANAGING EXCHANGE RATE RISKS. ICC Publishing Corporation, 156 Fifth Avenue, Suite 820, New York, New York 10010. 1985.

THE MEASUREMENT OF MONETARY POLICY. M. Ray Perryman. Martinus Nijhoff, Kluwer Academic Publishers, 101 Philip Drive, Assinippi Park, Norwell, Massachusetts 02061. 1983.

MONETARY POLICY AND MODERN MONEY MARKETS: FIXED VERSUS MARKET-DETERMINED DEPOSIT RATES. Michael G. Hadjimachalakis. Lexington Books, Division of D.C. Heath and Company, 125 Spring Street, Lexington, Massachusetts 02173. 1982.

MONETARY POLICY AND THE FINANCIAL SYSTEM. Fifth Edition. Paul M. Horvitz and Richard A. Ward. Prentice-Hall, Incorporated, 113 Sylvan Avenue, Englewood Cliffs, New Jersey 07632. 1983.

MONETARY POLICY IN OUR TIMES: PROCEEDINGS OF THE FIRST CONFERENCE HELD BY THE INSTITUTE FOR MONETARY AND ECONOMIC POLICY OF THE BANK OF JAPAN. Albert Ando, et al, Editors. MIT Press, 55 Hayward Street, Cambridge, Massachusetts 02142. 1985.

MONETARY POLITICS: THE FEDERAL RESERVE AND THE POLITICS OF MONETARY POLICY. John T. Woolley. Cambridge University Press, 40 West Twentieth Street, New York, New York 10011. 1986.

MONETARY POWERS AND DISABILITIES OF THE UNITED STATES CONSTITUTION. Edwin Vieira. Devin-Adair Publishers, Incorporated, 6 North Water Street, Greenwich, Connecticut 06830. 1983.

MONEY. Fifth Revised Edition. Lawrence S. Ritter and William L. Silber. Basic Books, Incorporated, 10 East Fifty-third Street, New York, New York 10022. 1984.

MONEY AND MARKETS: ESSAYS. By Robert W. Clower and Donald Walker, Editor. Cambridge University Press, 40 West Twentieth Street, New York, New York 10011. 1986.

MONEY, BANKING, AND FINANCIAL MARKETS. Jan W. Elliott. West Publishing Company, P.O. Box 64526, 50 West Kellogg Boulevard, St. Paul, Minnesota 55164-0526. 1983.

MONEY, BANKING AND THE ECONOMY. Fifth Edition. John A. Cochran. Macmillan Publishing Company, Incorporated, 866 Third Avenue, New York, New York 10022. 1983.

THE MONEY BAZAARS: UNDERSTANDING THE BANKING REVOLUTION AROUND US. Martin Mayer. E. P. Dutton, Two Park Avenue, New York, New York 10016. 1984.

MONEY, CAPITAL AND FLUCTUATIONS: EARLY ESSAYS. Friedrich A. Hayek. University of Chicago Press, 5801 Ellis Avenue, Third Floor, South, Chicago, Illinois 60637. 1984.

THE MONEY MARKET. Third Edition. Marcia L. Stigum. Business 1 Irwin, 1818 Ridge Road, Homewood, Illinois 60430. 1989.

MONEY AND MONETARY CONTROL

MONEY, THE FINANCIAL SYSTEM, AND MONETARY POLICY. Fourth Edition. Thomas F. Cargill. Prentice-Hall, Incorporated, 113 Sylvan Avenue, Englewood Cliffs, New Jersey 07632. 1991.

THE MULTIPLE RESERVE CURRENCY SYSTEM AND INTERNATIONAL MONETARY REFORM. C. Fred Bergsten. Institute for International Economics, 11 Dupont Circle, Northwest, Publications Department, Washington, D.C. 20036. 1982.

POLITICAL ECONOMY OF DOMESTIC AND INTERNATIONAL MONETARY RELATIONS. Raymond E. Lombra and Willard E. Witte, Editors. Iowa State University Press, 2121 South State Avenue, Ames, Iowa 50010. 1982.

THE POLITICS OF MONETARISM: ITS HISTORICAL AND INSTITUTIONAL DEVELOPMENT. George Macesich. Rowman and Allanheld, 420 Boston Way, Lanham, Maryland 20706. 1984.

THE POWER TO COIN MONEY: THE EXERCISE OF MONETARY POWERS BY THE CONGRESS. Thomas Frederick Wilson. M.E. Sharpe, Incorporated, 80 Business Park Drive, Armonk, New York 10504. 1991.

THE RULES OF THE GAME: REFORM AND EVOLUTION IN THE INTERNATIONAL MONETARY SYSTEM. Kenneth W. Dam. University of Chicago Press, 5801 Ellis Avenue, Third Floor, South, Chicago, Illinois 60637. 1988.

THE SCOURGE OF MONETARISM. Second Edition. Nicholas Kaldor. Oxford University Press, Incorporated, 200 Madison Avenue, New York, New York 10016. 1985.

U.S. INTERNATIONAL MONETARY POLICY: MARKETS, POWER AND IDEAS AS SOURCES OF CHANGE. J. S. Odell. Princeton University Press, 41 William Street, Princeton, New Jersey 08540. 1982.

THE WARDLEY GUIDE TO WORLD MONEY AND SECURITY MARKETS. Lynette J. Kemp. Euromoney Publications, Limited, Nester House, Playhouse Yard, London EC4V 5EX. 1984.

ANNUALS AND SURVEYS

PICK'S CURRENCY YEARBOOK. Pick's Publishing Corporation, 21 West Street, New York, New York 10006. Annual.

LAW REVIEWS AND PERIODICALS

BANK CREDIT ANALYST: INVESTMENT AND BUSINESS FORECAST. BCA Publications, 170 Varick Street, New York, New York 10013. Monthly.

FEDERAL RESERVE BULLETIN. Federal Reserve System Board of Governors, Washington, D.C. 20551. Monthly.

IMF SURVEY. International Monetary Fund, Washington, D.C. 20431. Semimonthly.

JOURNAL OF MONEY, CREDIT AND BANKING. Ohio State University Press, 1050 Carmack Road, Columbus, Ohio 43210. Quarterley.

PICK'S WORLD CURRENCY REPORT. Pick's Publishing Corporation, 21 West Street, New York, New York 10006. Monthly.

BIBLIOGRAPHIES

MONETARY POLICY: MONOGRAPHS. Mary Vance. Vance Bibliographies, P.O. Box 229, 112 North Charter Street, Monticello, Illinois 61856. 1983.

DIRECTORIES

DONOGHUE'S MONEY FUND DIRECTORY. P and S Publications, Box C, Medway, Massachusetts 02053. Semiannual.

MONEY MARKET DIRECTORY. Money Market Directories, Incorporated, 818 East High Street, Charlottesville, Virginia 22902. Annual.

TREASURY DEPARTMENT TELEPHONE DIRECTORY. United States Department of the Treasury. United States Governement Printing Office, Washington, D.C. 20402. Semiannual.

ASSOCIATIONS AND PROFESSIONAL SOCIETIES

AMERICAN MONEY MANAGEMENT ASSOCIATION. 4620 FM 1960, West, Suite 550, Houston, Texas 77069. (713) 583-2800.

RESEARCH CENTERS, INSTITUTES, CLEARINGHOUSES

CENTER FOR ECONOMIC EDUCATION. Western Washington University, Parks Hall, Room 319, Bellingham, Washington 98225. (206) 676-3903.

CENTER FOR ECONOMIC POLICY ANALYSIS. 59 East Van Buren Street, Room 1716, Chicago, Illinois 60605. (312) 786-1825.

COMMITTEE FOR MONETARY RESEARCH AND EDUCATION, INCORPORATED. P.O. Box 1630, Greenwich, Connecticut 06836. (203) 661-2533.

LUDWIG VON MISES INSTITUTE. 851 Burlway Road, Suite 110, Burlingame, California 94010. (415) 579-2500.

RODNEY L. WHITE CENTER FOR FINANCIAL RESEARCH. University of Pennsylvania, 3250 Steinberg Hall, Philadelphia, Pennsylvania 19104. (215) 898-7616.

SALOMON BROTHERS CENTER FOR STUDY OF FINANCIAL INSTITUTIONS. New York University, Stern School of Business, 90 Trinity Place, New York, New York 10006. (212) 285-6100.

ONLINE DATABASES

CURRENCY WATCH. McCarthy, Crisanti and Maffie, Incorporated, Electronic Information Services, 71 Broadway, New York, New York 10006.

FEDWATCH. MMS International, 1301 Shoreway Road, Suite 300, Belmont, California 94002.

LEXIS FEDERAL BANKING LIBRARY. Mead Data Central, P.O. Box 933, Dayton, Ohio 45401.

MONEY DATA. Thomson Financial Networks, Incorporated, Market Analysis Services, 11 Farnsworth Street, Boston, Massachusetts 02210.

MONEY MARKET PRICE QUOTATION SERVICE. Market Data Systems, Incorporated, 3835 Lamar Avenue, Memphis, Tennessee 38118.

MONEY MARKET RATES. Reuters Limited, Suite 1900, Exchange Tower, 2 First Canadian Place, Toronto, Ontario M5X 1E3.

MONEY MARKETS DATA BASE. Interactive Data Corporation, Securities Products Division, 95 Hayden Avenue, Lexington, Massachusetts 02173.

MONEYWATCH. McCarthy, Crisanti and Maffei, Incorporated, 71 Broadway, New York, New York 10006.

STATISTICS SOURCES

ANNUAL REPORT OF THE SECRETARY OF THE TREASURY. United States Department of the Treasury. Superintendent of Documents, United States Government Printing Office, Washington, D.C. 20402. Annual.

CREDIT AND CAPITAL MARKETS. Bankers Trust Company, Economics Division, P.O. Box 318, Church Street Station, New York, New York 10015. Annual.

DAILY STATEMENT OF THE TREASURY. United States Department of the Treasury. Superintendent of Documents, United States Government Printing Office, Washington, D.C. 20402.

FEDERAL RESERVE BULLETIN. Board of Governors of the Federal Reserve System, Twentieth Street and Constitution Avenue, Northwest, Washington, D.C. 20551. Monthly.

TREASURY BULLETIN. United States Department of the Treasury. Superintendent of Documents, United States Government Printing Office, Washington, D.C. 20402. Monthly.

OTHER SOURCES

INTERNATIONAL MONETARY FUND STAFF PAPERS. International Monetary Fund, Office of External Relations, 700 Nineteenth Street, Northwest, Washington, D.C. 20431.

MONEY LAUNDERING

HANDBOOKS, MANUALS, FORMBOOKS

CRIMINAL REFERRAL REPORTING: A GUIDE FOR COMPLIANCE. Mary P. Johannes and Paul Kiczek. American Bankers Association, 1120 Connecticut Avenue, Northwest, Washington, D.C. 20036. 1989.

INVESTIGATION AND PROSECUTION OF ILLEGAL MONEY LANDERING: A GUIDE TO THE BANK SECRECY ACT. United States Department of Justice, Criminal Division, Tenth Street and Pennsylvania Avenue, Northwest, Washington, D.C. 20530. 1983.

TEXTBOOKS AND GENERAL WORKS

THE CASH CONNECTION: ORGANIZED CRIME, FINANCIAL INSTITUTIONS, AND MONEY LAUNDERING. United States. President's Commission on Organized Crime, Washington, D.C. 1984.

THE CRIMES OF PATRIOTS: A TRUE TALE OF DOPE, DIRTY MONEY, AND THE CIA. Jonathan Kwitny. W.W. Norton and Company, Incorporated, 500 Fifth Avenue, New York, New York 10110. 1987.

DIRTY MONEY. Larry Gurwin. Times Books/Random House, Incorporated, 201 East Fiftieth Street, New York, New York 10022. 1988.

HOT MONEY AND THE POLITICS OF DEBT. R.T. Naylor. Simon and Schuster, Incorporated, 1230 Avenue of the Americas, New York, New York 10020. 1987.

MASTERS OF PARADISE: ORGANIZED CRIME AND THE INTERNAL REVENUE SERVICE IN THE BAHAMAS. Alan A. Block. Transaction Books, Rutgers University, New Brunswick, New Jersey 08903. 1991.

THE SECRET MONEY MARKET: INSIDE THE DARK WORLD OF TAX EVASION, FINANCIAL FRAUD, INSIDER TRADING, MONEY LAUNDERING, AND CAPITAL FLIGHT. Ingo Walter. HarperCollins Publishers, 10 East Fifty-third Street, New York, New York 10022. 1990.

SWISS WHITEWASH: DRUGS, DIRTY MONEY, AND LAUNDERING BY THE SWISS BANKS. Jean Ziegler. Arcade Publishing, 141 Fifth Avenue, New York, New York 10010. 1992.

RESEARCH CENTERS, INSTITUTES, CLEARINGHOUSES

DRUG ENFORCEMENT ADMINISTRATION. Office of Intelligence, 1405 Eye Street, Northwest, Room 1013, Washington, D.C. 20537. (202) 307-8050.

OTHER SOURCES

THE CASH CONNECTION: ORGANIZED CRIME, FINANCIAL INSTITUTIONS, AND MONEY LAUNDERING. President's Commission on Organized Crime. Department of Justice, Tenth Street and Pennsylvania Avenue, Northwest, Washington, D.C. 20530. 1984.

CRIME AND SECRECY: THE USE OF OFFSHORE BANKS AND COMPANIES: REPORT. The Committee on Government Affairs, United States Senate. Superintendent of Documents, United States Government Printing Office, Washington, D.C. 20402. 1985.

DOMESTIC MONEY LAUNDERING: BANK SECRECY ACT COMPLIANCE AND ENFORCEMENT: REPORT. Permanent Subcommittee on Investigations of the Committee on Governmental Affairs, United States Senate. Superintendent of Documents, United States Government Printing Office, Washington, D.C. 20402. 1986.

DRUG MONEY LAUNDERING, BANKS AND FOREIGN POLICY: A REPORT TO THE COMMITTEE ON FOREIGN RELATIONS, UNITED STATES SENATE. The Subcommittee on Narcotics, Terrorism, International Operations. Superintendent of Documents, United States Government Printing Office, Washington, D.C. 20402. 1990.

LEGISLATION AIMED AT COMBATING INTERNATIONAL DRUG TRAFFICKING AND MONEY LAUNDERING: A STAFF REPORT. Senate Caucus on International Narcotics Control. Superintendent of Documents, United States Government Printing Office, Washington, D.C. 20402. 1987.

MONOPOLIES
See: ANTITRUST LAW

MONUMENTS
See: HISTORIC PRESERVATION; PUBLIC LAND

MORTGAGES
See also: FORECLOSURES

RESTATEMENTS

RESTATEMENT OF THE LAW, PROPERTY--SECURITY (MORTGAGES): COUNCIL DRAFT. American Law Institute-American Bar Association, 4025 Chestnut Street, Philadelphia, Pennsylvania 19104. 1990.

LOOSELEAF SERVICES AND REPORTERS

ALTERNATIVE MORTGAGE INSTRUMENTS. Peter M. Barnett and Joseph A. McKenzie. Research Institute of America, Incorporated, One Penn Plaza, New York, New York 10119. 1984- .

BERGMAN ON NEW YORK MORTGAGE FORECLOSURES. Bruce J. Bergman. Matthew Bender and Company, Incorporated, 11 Penn Plaza, New York, New York 10001. 1990.

FARM PRODUCTS FINANCING AND FILING SERVICE. Drew L. Kershen and J Thomas Hardin. Research Institute of America, Incorporated, One Penn Plaza, New York, New York 10119. 1990.

LENDING GUIDE. Secondary Lending Information Service, 1 Summit Avenue, Suite 300, Fort Worth, Texas 76102. 1983- .

MODERN REAL ESTATE AND MORTGAGE FARMS. Second Edition. Alvin L. Arnold. Research Institute of America, Incorporated, One Penn Plaza, New York, New York 10119. 1978- .

SECONDARY RESIDENTIAL MORTGAGE MARKET. Charles L. Edson. Matthew Bender and Company, Incorporated, 11 Penn Plaza, New York, New York 10001. 1984- .

SELLING GUIDE. Secondary Lending Information Service, 1 Summit Avenue, Suite 300, Fort Worth, Texas 76102. 1983- .

HANDBOOKS, MANUALS, FORMBOOKS

ADJUSTABLE RATE MORTGAGE MANUAL. American Bankers Association, 1120 Connecticut Avenue, Northwest, Washington, D.C. 20036. 1983.

THE COMPLETE RESIDENTIAL MORTGAGE MANUAL: HOW TO ORIGINATE PACKAGE AND SELL MORTGAGE LOANS IN THE SECONDARY MARKET. Bank Administration Institute, 2550 West Golf Road, Rolling Meadows, Illinois 60008. 1982.

A CONSUMER'S GUIDE TO THE MORTGAGE MAZE. R. J. Turner. Saint Martin's Press, Incorporated, 175 Fifth Avenue, New York, New York 10010. 1982.

MORTGAGE AND REAL ESTATE INVESTMENT GUIDE. Alan C. Sherman. Mortgage Real Estate Investment Guide, P.O. Box 703, Marshfield, Massachusetts 02050. 1984.

MORTGAGES AND FORECLOSURE: KNOW YOUR RIGHTS. David M. Goldenberg. Self-Counsel Press, Incorporated, 1704 North State Street, Bellingham Washington 98225. 1989.

1990-1991 MORTGAGE LOAN DISCLOSURE HANDBOOK: A STEP BY STEP GUIDE WITH FORMS. Kenneth F. Hall. Clark Boardman Company, Limited, 435 Hudson Street, New York, New York 10014. 1990.

REAL ESTATE FINANCING MANUAL: A GUIDE TO MONEY-MAKING STRATEGIES. Jack Cummings. Prentice-Hall, Incorporated, 113 Sylvan Avenue, Englewood Cliffs, New Jersey 07632. 1987.

TEXTBOOKS AND GENERAL WORKS

ADJUSTABLE RATE MORTGAGES. Jack P. Friedman and Jack C. Harris. Barron's Educational Series, Incorporated, 250 Wireless Boulevard, Hauppauge, New York 11788. 1987.

AFFORDABLE HOUSING: NEW POLICIES FOR THE HOUSING AND MORTGAGE MARKETS. Kenneth T. Rosen. Ballinger Division, HarperCollins Publishers, 10 East Fifty-third Street, New York, New York 10022. 1984- .

BANKRUPTCY CODE AND REAL ESTATE LENDER: TROUBLED REAL ESTATE LOANS AND DOCUMENTATION. Richard A. Gittin. Practising Law Institute, 810 Seventh Avenue, New York, New York 10019. 1983.

CASES AND MATERIALS ON REAL ESTATE TRANSFER, FINANCE, AND DEVELOPMENT. Third Edition. Grant S. Nelson and Dale A. Whitman. West Publishing Company, 50 West Kellogg Boulevard, St. Paul, Minnesota 55164. 1987.

COMMERCIAL REAL ESTATE FINANCING: RESOURCE MATERIALS. American Law Institute-American Bar Association, Committee on Continuing Professional Education, 4025 Chestnut Street, Philadelphia, Pennsylvania 19104. 1989.

CREATIVE REAL ESTATE FINANCING, 1991. Richard J. Kane, Chairman. Practising Law Institute, 810 Seventh Avenue, New York, New York 10019. 1991.

THE DEEDS BOOK. Mary Randolph. Nolo Press, 950 Parker Street, Berkeley, California 94710. 1987.

FEDERAL INTERVENTION IN THE MORTGAGE MARKETS: AN ANALYSIS. Douglas Hearth. UMI Research Press, 300 North Zeeb Road, Ann Arbor, Michigan 48106-1346. 1983.

FINANCING REAL ESTATE WITH SECURITIES. Mary Alice Hines. John Wiley and Sons, Incorporated, 605 Third Avenue, New York, New York 10158. 1988.

FROM MAIN STREET TO WALL STREET: MAKING MONEY IN REAL ESTATE. Frank A. Cappiello and Karel McClellan. John Wiley and Sons, Incorporated, 605 Third Avenue, New York, New York 10158. 1988.

THE HOME-MORTGAGE LAW PRIMER. Irving J. Sloan. Oceana Publications, 75 Main Street, Dobbs Ferry, New York 10522. 1988.

HOW TO BUY A HOUSE WITH NO (OR LITTLE) MONEY DOWN. Martin M. Shenkman and Warren Boroson. John Wiley and Sons, Incorporated, 605 Third Avenue, New York, New York 10158. 1989.

HOW TO BUY YOUR FIRST HOME. Peter Jones. Houghton Mifflin Company, 1 Beacon Street, Boston, Massachusetts 02108. 1990.

INTRODUCTION TO THE SECONDARY MORTGAGE MARKET: A PRIMER. Dall Benewitz. United States League of Savings Institutions, 1709 New York Avenue, Northwest, Suite 801, Chicago, Illinois 60601. 1983.

LAND TRANSACTIONS AND FINANCE. Second Edition. Grant S. Nelson and Dale A. Whitman. West Publishing Company, 50 West Kellogg Boulevard, St. Paul, Minnesota 55164. 1988.

LAW OF FEDERAL MORTGAGE DOCUMENTS. D. Barlow Burke. Little, Brown and Company, 34 Beacon Street, Boston, Massachusetts 02108. 1989.

THE LIABILITY GAME: STRATEGIC PLANNING FOR REAL ESTATE LENDING. Stuart Marshall Bloch. Executive Enterprises Publications Company, 22 West Twenty-first Street, New York, New York 10010-6904. 1988.

MAKING MORTGAGES WORK FOR YOU. Robert Irwin. McGraw-Hill Publishing Company, 1221 Avenue of the Americas, New York, New York 10020. 1987.

MANAGING RISK IN MORTGAGE PORTFOLIOS. Alex O. Williams. Quorum Books, Greenwood Publishing Group, Incorporated, 88 Post Road West, P.O. Box 5007, Westport, Connecticut 06881. 1987.

MODERN MORTGAGE LAW AND PRACTICE. Second Edition. Robert Kratovil and Raymond J. Aerner. Prentice-Hall, Incorporated, 113 Sylvan Avenue, Washington, D.C. 20006. 1981.

MORTGAGE BACKED SECURITIES: DEVELOPMENTS IN THE SECONDARY MORTGAGE MARKET. Kenneth G. Lore. Clark Boardman Company, Limited, 435 Hudson Street, New York, New York 10014. 1985.

MORTGAGE-BACKED SECURITIES: MORTGAGE PASS-THROUGH, CMDS, AND BUILDER BONDS. Rodney S. Dayan, Chairman. Practising Law Institute, 810 Seventh Avenue, New York, New York 10019. 1984.

MORTGAGE LIENS IN NEW YORK. Robert H. Bowmar. Lawyers Cooperative Publishing Company, Aqueduct Building, Rochester, New York 14694. 1990.

NEGOTIATING REAL ESTATE TRANSACTIONS. Mark A. Senn. John Wiley and Sons, Incorporated, 605 Third Avenue, New York, New York 10158. 1988.

REAL ESTATE FINANCE. Sherman J. Maisel. Harcourt, Brace, Jovanovich, Incorporated, 6277 Sea Harbor Drive, Orlando, Florida 32821. 1987.

REAL ESTATE FINANCE. Third Edition. Ronald W. Melicher and Maurice Albert Unger. South-Western Publishing Company, 5101 Madison Road, Cincinnati, Ohio 45227. 1989.

REAL ESTATE FINANCE IN A NUTSHELL. Third Edition. Jon W. Bruce. West Publishing Company, P.O. Box 64526, 50 West Kellogg Boulevard, St. Paul, Minnesota 55164-0526. 1991.

REAL ESTATE FINANCE LAW. Second Edition. Grant S. Nelson and Bole E. Whitman. West Publishing Company, P.O. Box 64526, 50 West Kellogg Boulevard, St. Paul, Minnesota 55164-0526. 1985 (Hornbook).

REAL ESTATE: INVESTMENT AND FINANCIAL STRATEGY. Peter Chinloy. Kluwer Academic Publishers, 101 Philip Drive, Assinippi Park, Norwell, Massachusetts 02061. 1988.

RESPA, TRUTH-IN-LENDING, AND ECOA IN REAL ESTATE TRANSACTIONS. Second Edition. Comer Woodward Padrick. Harrison Company, 3110 Crossing Park, Norcross, Georgia 30091. 1987.

RETAIL FINANCIAL SERVICES CURRENT DEVELOPMENTS. L. Richard Fischer. Practising Law Institute, 810 Seventh Avenue, New York, New York 10019. 1987.

SHIP AND AIRCRAFT MORTGAGES. Nigel Meeson. Lloyd's of London Press, New York, New York. 1989.

STRUCTURED MORTGAGE AND RECEIVABLE FINANCING. Rodney S.Dayan, Chairman. Practising Law Institute, 810 Seventh Avenue, New York, New York 10019. 1990.

UNDER ONE ROOF: RETAIL BANKING AND THE INTERNATIONAL MORTGAGE FINANCE REVOLUTION. Michael Ball. St. Martin's Press, 175 Fifth Avenue, New York, New York 10010. 1990.

ENCYCLOPEDIAS AND DICTIONARIES

ENCYCLOPEDIA OF MORTGAGE AND REAL ESTATE FINANCE: OVER 1,000 TERMS DEFINED, EXPLAINED, AND ILLUSTRATED. James E. Newell, Albert Santi and Chip Mitchell. Probus Publishing Company, 118 North Linton Street, Chicago, Illinois 60606. 1992.

MORTGAGES

LAW REVIEWS AND PERIODICALS

REAL ESTATE FINANCE LAW JOURNAL. Federal Research Press, 65 Franklin Street, Boston, Massachusetts 02110. Quarterly.

NEWSLETTERS AND NEWSPAPERS

CAPITAL UPDATE. Mortgage Insurance Companies of America, 805 Fifteenth Street, Northwest, Suite 1110, Washington, D.C. 20005. Bimonthly.

HOUSING AFFAIRS LETTER. CD Publications, 8204 Fenton Street, Silver Spring, Maryland 20910. Weekly.

MORTGAGE AND REAL ESTATE EXECUTIVES REPORT. Research Institute of America, Incorporated, 210 South Street, Boston, Massachusetts 02111. Semimonthly.

MORTGAGE COMMENTARY. American Banker-Bord Buyer, Newsletter Division, P.O. Box 30240, Bethesda, Maryland 20814. Monthly.

MORTGAGE MARKET INSIGHT. CD Publications, 8204 Fenton Street, Silver Spring, Maryland 20910. Weekly.

MORTGAGE MARKETPLACE. American Banker-Bord Buyer, Newsletter Division, P.O. Box 30240, Bethesda, Maryland 20814. Weekly.

NATIONAL FINANCING LAW DIGEST. National Property Law Digests, Incorporated, 7200 Wisconsin Avenue, Suite 314, Bethesda, Maryland 20814. Monthly.

SECONDARY MORTGAGE MARKET ANALYST. Research Institute of America, Incorporated, 210 South Street, Boston, Massachusetts 02111. Monthly.

WASHINGTON REPORT. Mortgage Bankers Association of America, 1125 Fifteenth Street, Northwest, Washington, D.C. 20005. Monthly.

DIRECTORIES

AMERICAN BANKER -- 300 LARGEST MORTGAGE BANKING FIRMS AND 100 LARGEST COMMERCIAL BANKS IN SERVICING OF PERMANENT MORTGAGES ISSUES. American Banker, Incorporated, One State Street Plaza, New York, New York 10004. Annual.

CRITTENDEN MORTGAGE DIRECTORY. Crittenden Financing, Incorporated, P.O. Box 128, Nevada City, California 95959. Annual.

MORTGAGE AND SALE SOURCE DIRECTORY. Novick Reports, 111 John Street, New York, New York 10038. Annual.

ASSOCIATIONS AND PROFESSIONAL SOCIETIES

MORTGAGE BANKERS ASSOCIATION OF AMERICA. 1125 Fifteenth Street, Northwest, Washington, D.C. 20005. (202) 861-6500.

MORTGAGE INSURANCE COMPANIES OF AMERICA. 805 Fifteenth Street, Northwest, Suite 1110, Washington, D.C. 20005. (202) 371-2899.

NATIONAL ASSOCIATION OF MORTGAGE BROKERS. 706 East Bell Road, Suite 101, Phoenix, Arizona 85022. (602) 992-6181.

UNITED MORTGAGE BANKERS OF AMERICA. 800 Ivy Hill Road, Philadelphia, Pennsylvania 19150. (215) 242-6060.

RESEARCH CENTERS, INSTITUTES, CLEARINGHOUSES

CREDIT RESEARCH CENTER. Purdue University, Krannort Graduate School of Management, West Lafayette, Indiana 47907. (317) 494-4380.

HOMER HOYT INSTITUTE. 1025 Thomas Jefferson Street, Northwest, Suite 500 East, Washington, D.C. 20007. (202) 342-5539.

OFFICE OF REAL ESTATE RESEARCH. University of Illinois, 304 David Kinsley Hall, 1407 West Gregory Drive, Urbana, Illinois 61801. (217) 244-0951.

ONLINE DATA BASES

THE MORTGAGE INDEX. Hale Systems, Incorporated, Remote Computing Division, 1044 Northern Boulevard, Roslyn, New York 11576.

PC MORTGAGE UPDATE. HSH Associates, 1200 Route 23, Butter, New Jersey 07405.

STATISTICS SOURCES

CREDIT AND CAPITAL MARKETS. Bankers Trust Company, Economics Division, P.O. Box 318, Church Street Station, New York, New York 10015. Annual.

FHA MONTHLY REPORT OF OPERATIONS: HOME MORTGAGE PROGRAMS. United States Department of Housing and Urban Development, Single Family Insured Branch, 451 Seventh Street, Southwest, Washington, D.C. 20410. Monthly.

SAVINGS AND HOME FINANCING SOURCE BOOK. United States Home Loan Bank Board, Washington, D.C. 20552. Annual.

MOTELS
See: HOTELS, RESTAURANTS, ETC.

MOTION PICTURES
See: COPYRIGHT; ENTERTAINMENT LAW

MOTIONS
See: CIVIL PROCEDURE

MOTOR VEHICLE ACCIDENTS
See: ACCIDENTS; MOTOR VEHICLES

MOTOR VEHICLE INSURANCE
See: INSURANCE, MOTOR VEHICLE AND AVIATION

MOTOR VEHICLES
See also: ACCIDENTS; INSURANCE, MOTOR VEHICLE AND AVIATION; NATIONAL TRANSPORTATION SAFETY BOARD; PRODUCTS LIABILITY AND SAFETY; TRANSPORTATION DEPARTMENT

STATUTES, CODES, STANDARDS, UNIFORM LAWS

UNIFORM MOTOR VEHICLE ACCIDENT REPARATIONS ACT. National Conference of Commissioners of Uniform State Laws. Uniform Laws Annotated. West Publishing Company, P.O. Box 64526, 50 West Kellogg Boulevard, St. Paul, Minnesota 55164-0526. 1976. (Annual Supplements).

UNIFORM MOTOR VEHICLE CERTIFICATE OF TITLE AND ANTITHEFT ACT. National Conference of Commissioners on Uniform State Laws. Unifrom Laws Annotated. West Publishing Company, P.O. Box 64526, 50 West Kellogg Boulevard, St. Paul, Minnesota 55164-0526. 1976. (Annual Supplements).

LOOSELEAF SERVICES AND REPORTERS

AUTOMOBILE LAW REPORTER. Commerce Clearing House, Incorporated, 4025 West Peterson Avenue, Chicago, Illinois 60646. 1973- .

HANDBOOKS, MANUALS, FORMBOOKS

ADVANCED TECHNIQUES IN AUTOMOBILE ACCIDENT LITIGATION. Neil T. Shayne, Chairman. Practising Law Institute, 810 Seventh Avenue, New York, New York 10019. 1984.

ANATOMY OF AN AUTOMOBILE ACCIDENT TRIAL. Neil T. Shayne, Chairman. Practising Law Institute, 810 Seventh Avenue, New York, New York 10019. 1985.

COMPUTER PROGRAMS FOR TRAFFIC ACCIDENT INVESTIGATIONS. Robert H. Morneau. Charles C. Thomas Publishing, 2600 South First Street, Springfield, Illinois 62794-9265. 1984.

DEFENDING DRINKING DRIVERS. Second Edition. Walter Frajola and John Tarantino. Jones Publishing Company, P.O. Box 70, Arden, North Carolina 28704. 1986.

DEFENSE OF SPEEDING, RECKLESS DRIVING AND VEHICULAR HOMICIDE CASES. James F. Campbell, P. David Fisher, and David A. Mausfield. Matthew Bender and Company, Incorporated, 11 Penn Plaza, New York, New York 10001. 1984. (Periodic Supplements).

DRIVING THE DRUNK OFF THE ROAD: A HANDBOOK FOR ACTION. Sand Golden. Quince Mill Books, 21 Quince Mill Court, Gaithersburg, Maryland 20878. 1983.

DRUNK DRIVING DEFENSE. Lawrence Taylor. Little, Brown, and Company, 34 Beacon Street, Boston, Massachusetts 02108. 1986. (Periodic Supplements).

DRUNK DRIVING: THE TRIAL WORKBOOK, THE TRIAL SOURCEBOOK, THE TRIAL NOTEBOOK. Reese I. Joye and Jim D. Lovett. Kluwer Academic Publishers, 101 Philip Drive, Assinippi Park, Massachusetts 02061. 1985.

DWI DEFENSE FORMS AND CHECKLISTS. John A. Tarantino. Jones Publishing Company, P.O. Box 70, Arden, North Carolina 28704. 1984. (Periodic Supplements).

HANDLING DRUNK DRIVING CASES. Stephen M. Brent and Sharon P. Stiller. Lawyers Cooperative Publishing Company, Aqueduct Building, Rochester, New York 14694. 1985. (With Supplements).

HOW TO DEFEND A DRUNK DRIVING CASE: A GUIDE TO PRACTICAL, PROCEDURAL AND LEGAL ASPECTS. John Henry Hingson, III. Clark Boardman Company, Limited, 435 Hudson Street, New York, New York 10014. 1987.

HOW TO IMPORT -- CONVERT -- LEGALIZE YOUR INVESTMENT AUTOMOBILE. E. A. Hunt. HIT Publications, P.O. Box 11198, Costa Mesa, California 92627. 1984.

JURY INSTRUCTIONS IN AUTOMOBILE NEGLIGENCE ACTION. Graham Douthwaite. The Michie Company, P.O. Box 7587, Charlottesville, Virginia 22906-7582. 1986.

JURY INSTRUCTIONS IN AUTOMOBILE NEGLIGENCE AND RELATED CASES. Graham Douthwaite. Aspen Publishers, Incorporated, 1600 Research Boulevard, Rockville, Maryland 20850. 1986.

KILLER ROADS: FROM CRASH TO VERDICT. Richard S. Kuhlman. The Michie Company, P.O. Box 7587, Charlottesville, Virginia 22906. 1986.

MOTOR VEHICLE ACCIDENT RECONSTRUCTION AND CAUSE ANALYSIS. Rudolf Limbert. Third Edition. The Michie Company, P.O. Box 7587, Charlottesville, Virginia 22906-7582. 1989.

MOTOR VEHICLE LAW AND PRACTICE. FORMS. Second Edition. James H. Walzer and J. Roger Conant. West Publishing Company, 50 West Kellogg Boulevard, St. Paul, Minnesota 55164. 1987.

PATTERN DISCOVERY: AUTOMOBILES. Second Edition. Douglas Danner. Lawyers Cooperative Publishing Company, Aqueduct Building, Rochester, New York 14694. 1985. (With Supplements).

SCIENTIFIC AUTOMOBILE ACCIDENT RECONSTRUCITON. George W. Lacy and Martin E. Barzelay, et al, Editors. Matthew Bender and Company, Incorporated, 11 Penn Plaza, New York, New York 10001. 1974. (Annual Supplements).

VEHICLE SIZES AND WEIGHTS MANUAL. J. J. Keller and Associates, P.O. Box 368, 145 West Wisconsin Avenue, Neenah, Wisconsin 54907-0368. 1987. (Semiannual Supplement).

WINNING MOTOR VEHICLE ACCIDENT CASES. Joseph W. Moch. Communications Research, Incorporated. 1986.

TEXTBOOKS AND GENERAL WORKS

ALCOHOL SERVER LIABILITY: A COMPILATION OF DRAM SHOP AND RELATED STATUTES AND JUDICIAL RULINGS. Sixth Edition. National Alcoholic Beverage Control Association, Incorporated, 4216 King Street, West, Alexandria, Virginia 22302. 1986.

ALCOHOL, YOUNG DRIVERS, AND TRAFFIC ACCIDENTS: EFFECTS OF MINIMUM AGE LAWS. Alexander C. Wagenaar. Free Press, 866 Third Avenue, New York, New York 10022. 1983.

AUTOMOBILE ACCIDENT COSTS AND PAYMENTS: STUDIES IN THE ECONOMICS OF INJURY PROTECTION. Alfred F. Conard. William S. Hein and Company, Incorporated, Hein Building, 1285 Main Street, Buffalo, New York 14209. 1983.

AUTOMOBILE DESIGN LIABILITY. Richard M. Goodman and The Center for Auto Safety. Second Edition. Lawyers Cooperative Publishing Company, Aqueduct Building, Rochester, New York 14694. 1983. (Supplements).

AUTOMOTIVE ENGINEERING AND LITIGATION. George A. Peters and Barbara J. Peters, Editors. John Wiley and Sons, Incorporated, 605 Third Avenue, New York, New York 10158. 1990.

BLASHFIELD'S AUTOMOBILE LAW AND PRACTICE. Thrid Edition. West Publishing Company, P.O. Box 64526, 50 West Kellogg Boulevard, St. Paul, Minnesota 55164-0526. 1977. (Periodic Supplements).

DETERRING THE DRINKING DRIVER: LEGAL POLICY AND SOCIAL CONTROL. H. Laurence Ross. Free Press, 866 Third Avenue, New York, New York 10022. 1984.

HOT CARS! AN INSIDE LOOK AT THE AUTO THEFT INDUSTRY. Marcus W. Ratledge. Paladin Press, P.O. Box 1307, Boulder, Colorado 80306. 1982.

MOTOR VEHICLE LAW AND PRACTICE. Second Edition. West Publishing Company, 50 West Kellogg Boulevard, St. Paul, Minnesota 55164. 1987.

QUESTIONS AND ANSWERS ON THE RULES OF THE ROAD. Fourth Edition. Robert J. Zaruba. Cornwell Maritime, Associated University Press, 440 Forsgate Drive, Cranbury, New Jersey 08512. 1982.

REGULATING THE AUTOMOBILE. Robert W. Crandell. Brookings Institution, 1775 Massachusetts Avenue, Northwest, Washington, D.C. 20036-2188. 1986.

SELECTED STUDIES IN HIGHWAY LAW. John C. Vance, Editor. National Cooperative Highway Research Programs, Transportation Research Board, National Research Council, 2101 Constitution Avenue, Northwest, Washington, D.C. 20418. 1976- . (Periodic Supplements).

TRAFFIC COURT PROCEDURE AND ADMINISTRATION. Second Edition. James P. Economos and David C. Steelman. American Bar Association, 750 North Lake Shore Drive, Chicago, Illinois 60611. 1982.

TRAFFIC INVESTIGATION AND ENFORCEMENT. Second Revised Edition. Donald O. Schultz and Derald D. Hunt. Custom Publishing Company, 1590 Lotus Road, Placerville, California 95667. 1990.

TRAFFIC MANAGEMENT AND COLLISION INVESTIGATION. Warren E. Clark. Prentice-Hall, Incorporated, 113 Sylvan Avenue, Englewood Cliffs, New Jersey 07632. 1982.

DIGESTS, INDEXES, ABSTRACTS, CITATORS

DIGEST OF STATE LAWS RELATING TO DRIVING WHILE UNDER THE INFLUENCE OF ALCOHOL. AIA Law Publications, 85 John Street, New York, New York 10038. 1986.

THE LEMON FILE: AN AUTO WARRANTY LITIGATION CASE REFERENCE SERVICE. Center for Auto Safety. 2001 S Street, Northwest, Suite 410, Washington, D.C. 20009. 1982. (Periodic Supplements).

NEWSLETTERS AND NEWSPAPERS

AUTOMOTIVE LITIGATION REPORTER. Andrews Publications, Incorporated, 1646 West Chester Pike, Westtown, Pennsylvania 19395. Semimonthly.

DRINKING/DRIVING LAW LETTER. Callaghan and Company, 155 Pfingsten Road, Deerfield, Illinois 60015. Bi-weekly.

HIGHWAY AND VEHICLE SAFETY REPORT. Stamler Publishing Company, P.O. Box 3367, Brandford, Connecticut 06405. Bi-weekly.

IMPACT. Center for Auto Safety, 2001 S Street, Northwest, Suite 410, Washington, D.C. 20009. Bimonthly.

LEMON TIMES. Center for Auto Safety, 2001 S Street, Northwest, Suite 410, Washington, D.C. 20009. Quarterly.

LIQUOR LIABILITY JOURNAL. Callaghan and Company, 155 Pfingsten Road, Deerfield, Illinois 60015. Bi-weekly.

NATIONAL TRAFFIC LAW NEWS. Donald H. Wallace, P.O. Box 478, Warrensburg, Missouri 64093. Monthly.

TRAFFIC LAW REPORTS. Kuehaus-Miller Publications, P.O. Box 88, Warrensburg, Missouri 64093. Monthly.

BIBLIOGRAPHIES

THE DRINKING DRIVER AND HIGHWAY SAFETY: A BIBLIOGRAPHIC SURVEY. Alva W. Stewart. Vance Bibliographies, P.O. Box 229, 112 North Charter Street, Monticello, Illinois 61856. 1983.

THE DRUNK DRIVER: A SELECTED BIBLIOGRAPHY. Earleen H. Cook. Vance Bibliographies, P.O. Box 229, 112 North Charter Street, Monticello, Illinois 61856. 1983.

DIRECTORIES

DIRECTORY OF AUTOMOTIVE CONSULTANTS. Society of Automotive Engineers, 400 Commonwealth Drive, Warrendale, Pennsylvania 15096. Annual.

ASSOCIATIONS AND PROFESSIONAL SOCIETIES

AMERICAN AUTOMOBILE ASSOCIATION. 1000 AAA Drive, Heathview, Florida 32746. (407) 444-7000.

CENTER FOR AUTO SAFETY. 2001 S Street, Northwest, Suite 410, Washington, D.C. 20009. (202) 328-7700.

MOTHERS AGAINST DRUNK DRIVING. 511 East John Carpenter Freeway, Suite 700, Irving, Texas 75062. (214) 744-6233.

NATIONAL COMMISSION AGAINST DRUNK DRIVING. 1140 Connecticut Avenue, Northwest, Suite 804, Washington, D.C. 20036. (202) 452-0130.

NATIONAL SAFETY COUNCIL. 444 North Michigan Avenue, Chicago, Illinois 60611. (312) 527-4800.

RESEARCH CENTERS, INSTITUTES, CLEARINGHOUSES

HIGHWAY SAFETY RESEARCH CENTER. University of North Carolina at Chapel Hill, CB#3430, C.T. Park, Chapel Hill, North Carolina 27599. (919) 962-2202.

NATIONAL COOPERATIVE HIGHWAY RESEARCH PROGRAM. Transportation Research Board, National Research Council, 2101 Constitution Avenue, Northwest, Washington, D.C. 20418. (202) 624-5800.

OCCUPATIONAL AND TRAFFIC SAFETY EDUCATION RESEARCH LABORATORY. Iowa State University, I.E.D. Building II, Room 122, Ames, Iowa 50011. (515) 294-5945.

PRODUCT LIABILITY RESEARCH SERVICE. Center for Auto Safety, 2001 S Street, Northwest, Suite 410, Washington, D.C. 20009. (202) 328-7700.

TEXAS TRANSPORTATION INSTITUTE. Accident Analysis Division, Texas A & M University, College Station, Texas 77843. (409) 845-8408.

TEXAS TRANSPORTATION INSTITUTE. Highway Safety Research Center, Texas A & M University, College Station, Texas 77843. (409) 845-6375.

ONLINE DATABASES

AUTONET/AUTOBASE. Access Dynamics, Incorporated, 8 Post Office Square, Acton, Massachusetts 01720.

HIGHWAY SAFETY LITERATURE SERVICE. National Academy of Sciences, National Research Council, Transportation Research Information Services, 2101 Constitution Avenue, Northwest, Washington, D.C. 20418.

NATIONAL SAFETY COUNCIL LIBRARY DATABASE. National Safety Council Library, 444 North Michigan Avenue, Chicago, Illinois 60611.

SAE GLOBAL MOBILITY DATABASE. Society of Automotive Engineers, Electronic Publishing Division, 400 Commonwealth Drive, Warrendale, Pennsylvania 15096.

TRANSPORTATION RESEARCH INFORMATION SERVICE. National Academy of Sciences, National Research Council, Transportation Research Information Services, 2101 Constitution Avenue, Northwest, Washington, D.C. 20418.

STATISTICS SOURCES

ACCIDENT FACTS. National Safety Council, Statistics Division, 444 North Michigan Avenue, Chicago, Illinois 60611. Annual.

ALCOHOL IN FATAL ACCIDENTS NATIONAL ESTIMATES -- U.S.A. EXECUTIVE SUMMARY. National Center for Statistics and Analysis, Mathematical Analysis Division, 400 Seventh Street, Southwest, Washington, D.C. 20590. Annual.

AUTOMOBILE FACTS AND FIGURES. Motor Vehicle Manufacturers of the United States, 320 New Center Building, Detroit, Michigan 48202. Annual.

DRIVING WHILE INTOXICATED. United States Department of Justice, Federal Bureau of Investigations, Ninth Street and Pennsylvania Avenue, Northwest, Washington, D.C. 20535. (Annual Report, "Crime in the United States".)

HIGHWAY STATISTICS. Federal Highway Administration, United States Department of Transportaton. Superintendent of Documents, United States Government Printing Office, Washington, D.C. 20402. Annual.

AUDIOVISUALS

VEHICLE COLLISION LITIGATION: TECHNIQUES AND EVALUATION. American Bar Association, 750 North Lake Shore Drive, Chicago, Illinois 60611. 1989. Videotape.

MOTOR VEHICLES AND DRINKING
See: ALCOHOL CONTROL AND DRINKING BEHAVIOR; MOTOR VEHICLES

MULTINATIONAL CORPORATIONS
See: CORPORATIONS, FOREIGN AND MULTINATIONAL

MULTINATIONAL LITIGATION
See: COMPLEX LITIGATION

MULTISTATE LITIGATION
See: COMPLEX LITIGATION

MUNICIPAL CORPORATIONS
See: LOCAL GOVERNMENT

MUNICIPAL COURTS
See: COURTS; LOCAL GOVERNMENT

MURDER

TEXTBOOKS AND GENERAL WORKS

ASSASSINATION: CASE STUDIES. Blythe F. Finke. Sam Har Press, Bindery Lane, Charlottesville, New York 12036. 1982.

THE BILLIONAIRE BOYS CLUB. Sue Horton. St. Martin's Press, 175 Fifth Avenue, New York, New York 10010. 1989.

CHILD HOMICIDE VICTIMS IN THE UNITED STATES. Richard Allen Henry. Lexington Books, 125 Spring Street, Lexington, Massachusetts 02173. 1982.

THE HOLLYWOOD MURDER CASEBOOK. Michael Munn. St. Martin's Press, 175 Fifth Avenue, New York, New York 10010. 1987.

THE HUMAN SIDE OF HOMICIDE. Bruce L. Danto, John Bruhns, and Austin H. Kutscher, editors. Columbia University Press, 562 West One Hundred Thirteenth Street, New York, New York 10025. 1982.

ICEMEN: THE DYNAMICS OF MURDER. Ken Levi. University Press of America, 4720 Boston Way, Lanham, Maryland 20706. 1983.

KILLING FOR PROFIT: THE SOCIAL ORGANIZATION OF FELONY HOMICIDE. Mary L. Dietz. Nelson-Hall, Publishers, 111 N. Canal Street, Chicago, Illinois 60606. 1983.

LIFE FOR DEATH. Michael Mewshaw. Avon Books, 105 Madison Avenue, New York, New York 10016. 1983.

THE MAMMOTH BOOK OF MURDER. Richard Glyn Jones. Carroll and Graf Publishers, 260 Fifth Avenue, New York, New York 10001. 1989.

THE MANNER OF MAN THAT KILLS. L. Vernon Briggs. Da Capo Press, Incorporated, 233 Spring Street, New York, New York 10013. 1983.

MURDER ALONG THE WAY: A PROSECUTOR'S PERSONAL ACCOUNT OF FIGHTING VIOLENT CRIME IN THE SUBURBS. Kenneth Gribetz and H. Paul Jeffers. Pharos Books, 200 Park Avenue, New York, New York 10166. 1989.

MURDER AMONG THE MIGHTY: CELEBRITY SLAYINGS THAT SHOCKED AMERICA. Jay R. Nash. Delacorte Press, 666 Fifth Avenue, New York, New York 10103. 1983.

MURDER, AN ANALYSIS OF ITS FORMS, CONDITIONS, AND CAUSES. Gerhard Falk and Clifford Falk. McFarland and Company, Incorporated, P.O. Box 611, Jefferson, North Carolina 28640. 1990.

MURDER, COURTS, AND THE PRESS: ISSUES IN FREE PRESS/FAIR TRIAL. Peter E. Kane. Southern Illinois University Press, P.O. Box 3697, Carbondale, Illinois 62902-3697. 1992.

MURDER INTO MANSLAUGHTER: THE DIMINISHED RESPONSIBILITY DEFENSE IN PRACTICE. Susanne Dell. Oxford University Press, Incorporated, 200 Madison Avenue, New York, New York 10016. 1984.

NOTABLE CRIME INVESTIGATIONS. William Bryan Anderson. Charles C. Thomas, Publishers, 2600 South First Street, Springfield, Illinois 62794. 1987.

ON ASSASSINATION. H. H. Cooper. Paladin Press, P.O. Box 1307, Boulder, Colorado 80306. 1984.

POLITICAL MURDER: FROM TYRANNICIDE TO TERRORISM. Franklin L. Ford. Harvard University Press, 79 Garden Street, Cambridge, Massachusetts 02138. 1985.

REPRESENTING--BATTERED WOMEN WHO KILL. Sara Lee Johann and Frank Osanka. Charles C. Thomas, Publishers, 2600 South First Street, Springfield, Illinois 62794. 1989.

THE SACCO-VANZETTI TRIAL: MURDER ONE. Doreen Rappaport. HarperCollins Publishers, 10 East Fifty-third Street, New York, New York 10022. 1992.

SERIAL KILLERS: THE GROWING MENACE. Joel Norris. Doubleday and Company, 666 Fifth Avenue, New York, New York 10103. 1988.

UNSOLVED: GREAT MYSTERIES OF THE TWENITH CENTURY. Kirk Wilson. Carroll and Graf Publishers, 260 Fifth Avenue, New York, New York 10001. 1990.

WITH MURDEROUS INTENT. Robert J. Hemming. Onyx, New York, New York. 1991.

ENCYCLOPEDIAS AND DICTIONARIES

ENCYCLOPEDIA OF ASSASSINATIONS. Carl Sifakis. Facts on File, Incorporated, 460 Park Avenue South, New York, New York 10016. 1991.

ENCYCLOPEDIA OF MODERN MURDER, 1962-1982. Colin Wilson and Donald Seaman. Putnam Publishing Group, 200 Madison Avenue, New York, New York 10016. 1983.

THE NEW MURDERERS' WHO'S WHO. J.H.H. Gaute and Robin Odell. International Polygonics, New York, New York. 1991.

WOMEN SERIAL AND MASS MURDERERS: A WORLDWIDE REFERENCE, 1580-1990. Kerry Segrave. McFarland and Company, Incorporated, Box 611, Jefferson, North Carolina 28640. 1992.

WORLD ENCYCLOPEDIA OF TWENTIETH CENTURY MURDER. Jay Robert Nash. Paragon House Publishers, 90 Fifth Avenue, New York, New York 10011. 1992.

BIBLIOGRAPHIES

HOMICIDE - A BIBLIOGRAPHY OF OVER 4,500 ITEMS. Bal K. Jerath. Pine Tree Publications, 711 Woodgate Court, Suite C-1, Augusta, Georgia 30909. 1982. (Supplement 1984).

MASS MURDER: AN ANNOTATED BIBLIOGRAPHY. Michael Newton. Garland Publishing, Incorporated, 136 Madison Avenue, New York, New York 10016. 1988.

BIOGRAPHICAL SOURCES

KILLER CLOWN: THE JOHN WAYNE GACY MURDERS. Terry Sullivan and Peter T. Maiken. Windsor Publishing Corporation, 475 Park Avenue, South, New York, New York 10016. 1991.

MANSON IN HIS OWN WORDS. Nuel Emmons. Weidenfeld and Nicolson, 10 East Fifty-third Street, New York, New York 10022. 1988.

NO EASY ANSWERS: THE TRIAL AND CONVICTION OF BRUCE CURTIS. Viking-Penguin, Incorporated, 375 Hudson Street, New York, New York 10014. 1986.

ONLINE DATABASES

CRIMINAL JUSTICE DATA DIRECTORY. University of Michigan, Inter-university Consortium for Political and Social Research, P.O. Box 1248, Ann Arbor, Michigan 48106.

CRIMINAL JUSTICE PERIODICAL INDEX. University Microfilms International, 300 North Zeeb Road, Ann Arbor, Michigan 48106.

NCJRS (NATIONAL CRIMINAL JUSTICE REFERENCE SERVICES). United States Department of Justice, National Institute of Justice, National Criminal Justice Reference Service, Box 6000, Rockville, Maryland 20850.

STATISTICS SOURCES

CRIME IN THE UNITED STATES. United States Department of Justice, Federal Bureau of Investigations, Ninth Street and Pennsylvania Avenue, Northwest, Washington, D.C. 20535. Annual.

VITAL STATISTICS OF THE UNITED STATES. United States Department of Health and Human Services, Public Health Service, 200 Independence Avenue, Southwest, Washington, D.C. 20201. Annual.

AUDIOVISUALS

CLOSING ARGUMENTS IN A MURDER CASE. American Bar Association, Consortium for Professional Education, 750 North Lake Shore Drive, Chicago, Illinois 60611. 1978. Videotape.

DIRECT AND CROSS EXAMINATION OF A PATHOLOGIST IN A MURDER CASE. American Bar Association, Consortium for Professional Education, 750 North Lake Shore Drive, Chicago, Illinois 60611. 1978. Videotape.

DIRECT AND CROSS EXAMINATION OF A PSYCHIATRIST IN A ROBBERY AND MURDER CASE. American Bar Association, Consortium for Professional Education, 750 North Lake Shore Drive, Chicago, Illinois 60611. 1978. Videotape.

MUSEUMS
See: ART

MUTUAL FUNDS
See: INVESTMENTS AND INVESTMENT COMPANIES

N

NARCOTICS
See: DRUG LAWS

NATIONAL DEFENSE
See: INTERNATIONAL LAW AND RELATIONS; MILITARY LAW AND SERVICE; POLITICAL CRIMES AND OFFENSES; PRESIDENT (UNITED STATES); TERRORISM

NATIONAL LABOR RELATIONS BOARD
See also: FEDERAL LABOR RELATIONS AUTHORITY; LABOR AND LABOR RELATIONS; LABOR ARBITRATION; LABOR DEPARTMENT

STATUTES, CODES, STANDARDS, UNIFORM LAWS

CODE OF FEDERAL REGULATIONS, TITLE 29. Office of the Federal Register, National Archives and Records Administration. Superintendent of Documents, United States Government Printing Office, Washington, D.C. 20402. Annual. (Updated by use of monthly List of Sections Affected and daily Federal Register.)

LOOSELEAF SERVICES AND REPORTERS

DECISIONS AND ORDERS OF THE NATIONAL LABOR RELATIONS BOARD. Superintendent of Documents, United States Government Printing Office, Washington, D.C. 20402. 1935- .

NLRB ELECTION REPORT. National Labor Relations Board, Division of Administration. Superintendent of Documents, United States Government Printing Office, Washington, D.C. 20402. Monthly.

NLRB REPRESENTATION ELECTIONS: LAW, PRACTICE AND PROCEDURE. Third Edition. John D. Feerick, Henry P. Baer, and Jonathon P. Arfa. Prentice-Hall, Incorporated, 113 Sylvan Avenue, Englewood Cliffs, New Jersey 07632. 1988.

HANDBOOKS, MANUALS, FORMBOOKS

NATIONAL LABOR RELATIONS BOARD CASE HANDLING MANUAL. National Labor Relations Board. Superintendent of Documents, United States Government Printing Office, Washington, D.C. 20402. 1983- .

NATIONAL LABOR RELATIONS BOARD MANUAL: DIVISION OF JUDGES. National Labor Relations Board. Superintendent of Documents, United States Government Printing Office, Washington, D.C. 20402. 1984- .

PRACTICE AND PROCEDURE BEFORE THE NATIONAL LABOR RELATIONS BOARD. Fourth Edition. Theophil C. Kammholz and Stanley R. Strauss. American Law Institute-American Bar Association, 4025 Chestnut Street, Philadelphia, Pennsylvania 19104. 1987.

TEXTBOOKS AND GENERAL WORKS

AMERICAN LABOR POLICY: A CRITICAL APPRAISAL OF THE NATIONAL LABOR RELATIONS ACT. Charles J. Morris, Editor. Bureau of National Affairs, Incorporated, 1231 Twenty-fifth Street, Northwest, Washington, D.C. 20037. 1987.

DIGESTS, INDEXES, ABSTRACTS, CITATORS

CLASSIFICATION OUTLINE WITH TOPICAL INDEX FOR DECISIONS OF THE NATIONAL LABOR RELATIONS BOARD AND RELATED COURT DECISIONS. National Labor Relations Board. Superintendent of Documents, United States Government Printing Office, Washington, D.C. 20402. 1982.

CLASSIFIED INDEX OF DECISIONS OF THE REGIONAL DIRECTORS OF THE NATIONAL LABOR RELATIONS BOARD IN REPRESENTATION PROCEEDINGS. National Labor Relations Board. Superintendent of Documents, United States Government Printing Office, Washington, D.C. 20402. Irregular.

CLASSIFIED INDEX OF DISPOSITIONS OF THE ULP CHARGES BY THE GENERAL COUNSEL OF THE NATIONAL LABOR RELATIONS BOARD: REGIONAL DIRECTORS DIMISSAL LETTERS, ADVICE MEMORANDA, APPEALS MEMORANDA. National Labor Relations Board. Superintendent of Documents, United States Government Printing Office, Washington, D.C. 20402. 1985.

CLASSIFIED INDEX OF NATIONAL LABOR RELATIONS BOARD DECISIONS AND RELATED COURT DECISIONS. National Labor Relations Board. Superintendent of Documents, United States Government Printing Office, Washington, D.C. 20402. Irregular.

SHEPARD'S FEDERAL LABOR LAW CITATIONS. Shepard's/McGraw-Hill, P.O. Box 1235, Colorado Springs, Colorado 80901. Quarterly.

NEWSLETTERS AND NEWSPAPERS

WEEKLY SUMMARY OF NLRB CASES. National Labor Relations Board, Information Branch. Superintendent of Documents, United States Government Printing Office, Washington, D.C. 20402. Weekly.

RESEARCH CENTERS, INSTITUTES, CLEARINGHOUSES

UNITED STATES NATIONAL LABOR RELATIONS BOARD LIBRARY. 1717 Pennsylvania Avenue, Northwest, Room 900, Washington, D.C. 20570. (202) 254-7126.

ONLINE DATABASES

LEXIS, FEDERAL LABOR LIBRARY. Mead Data Central, P.O. Box 933, Dayton, Ohio 45401.

WESTLAW, LABOR LIBRARY. West Publishing Company, P.O. Box 64526, 50 West Kellogg Boulevard, St. Paul, Minnesota 55164-0526.

NATIONAL PARKS
See: PARKS AND MONUMENTS

NATIONAL SECURITY
See: CENTRAL INTELLIGENCE AGENCY; INTERNATIONAL LAW AND RELATIONS; MILITARY LAW AND SERVICE; POLITICAL CRIMES AND OFFENSES; PRESIDENT (UNITED STATES); TERRORISM

NATIONAL TELECOMMUNICATIONS AND INFORMATION ADMINISTRATION

STATUTES, CODES, STANDARDS, UNIFORM LAWS

CODE OF FEDERAL REGULATIONS, TITLE 15. Office of the Federal Register, National Archives and Records Administration. Superintendent of Documents, United States Government Printing Office, Washington, D.C. 20402. Annual. (Updated by use of monthly List of Sections Affected and daily Federal Register .)

HANDBOOKS, MANUALS, FORMBOOKS

MANUAL OF REGULATIONS AND PROCEDURES FOR FEDERAL RADIO FREQUENCY MANAGEMENT. Commerce Department, National Telecommunications and Information Administration, Radio Advisory Committee. Superintendent of Documents, United States Government Printing Office, Washington, D.C. 20402. 1986- .

TEXTBOOKS AND GENERAL WORKS

ISSUES IN DOMESTIC TELECOMMUNICATIONS: DIRECTIONS FOR NATIONAL POLICY. Commerce Department, National Telecommunications and Information Administration. Superintendent of Documents, United States Government Printing Office, Washington, D.C. 20402. 1985.

ISSUES IN INFORMATION POLICY. Helen A. Shaw and Jane H. Yurow. Commerce Department, National Telecommunications and Information Administration. Superintendent of Documents, United States Government Printing Office, Washington, D.C. 20402. 1981.

NTIA TELECOM 2000: CHARTING THE COURSE FOR A NEW CENTURY. United States. National Telecommunications and Information Administration. United States Department of Commerce. Superintendent of Documents, United States Government Printing Office, Washington, D.C. 20402. 1988.

REVIEW OF NATIONAL TELECOMMUNICATIONS POLICY: A STAFF REPORT. Superintendent of Documents, United States Government Printing Office, Washington, D.C. 20402. 1990.

TELECOMMUNICATIONS IN THE AGE OF INFORMATION: THE NTIA INFRASTRUCTURE REPORT. National Telecommunication and Information Administration. United States Department of Commerce, Washington, D.C. 20230. 1991.

UNITED STATES TELECOMMUNICATIONS IN A GLOBAL ECONOMY: COMPETITIVENESS AT A CROSSROADS. United States Department of Commerce, International Trade Administration [and] National Telecommunications and Information Administration, Washington, D.C. 20230. 1990.

NATIONAL TRANSPORTATION SAFETY BOARD
See also: FEDERAL AVIATION ADMINISTRATION; TRANSPORTATION DEPARTMENT

STATUTES, CODES, STANDARDS, UNIFORM LAWS

CODE OF FEDERAL REGULATIONS, TITLE 49. Office of the Federal Register, National Archives and Records Administration. Superintendent of Documents, United States Government Printing Office, Washington, D.C. 20402. Annual. (Updated by use of monthly List of Sections Affected and daily Federal Register .)

LOOSELEAF SERVICES AND REPORTERS

NATIONAL TRANSPORTATION SAFETY BOARD DECISIONS. Superintendent of Documents, United States Government Printing Office, Washington, D.C. 20402. 1967- .

NATIONAL TRANSPORTATION SAFETY BOARD REGULATIONS. Rules Service Company, 7658 Standish Place, Suite 106, Rockville, Maryland 20855. 1973- .

NATIONAL TRANSPORTATION SAFETY BOARD REPORTER. Peter Katz Productions, 1280 Saw Mill River Road, Yonkers, New York 10710. 1983- .

NATIONAL TRANSPORTATION SAFETY BOARD REPORTS. Hawkins Publication Company, 310 Tahiti Way, Number 108, Marina Del Ray, California 90291. 1972- .

DIGESTS, INDEXES, ABSTRACTS, CITATORS

LEGAL RESEARCH DIGEST. Transportation Research Board, National Research Council, Washington, D.C. 1988- .

NATIONALITY
See: CITIZENS AND CITIZENSHIP

NATIONALIZATION OF INDUSTRY
See: EMINENT DOMAIN; GOVERNMENT OWNERSHIP

NATIVE RACES
See: INDIANS OF NORTH AMERICA

NATURAL GAS
See: OIL AND GAS

NATURAL LAW

TEXTBOOKS AND GENERAL WORKS

AN ANALYSIS OF RIGHTS. Samuel J. Stoljar. Saint Martin's Press, Incorporated, 175 Fifth Avenue, New York, New York 10010. 1984.

ANGLO-AMERICAN PHILOSOPHY OF LAW: AN INTRODUCTION TO ITS DEVELOPMENT AND OUTCOME. Beryl Harold Levy. Transaction Books, Rutgers University, New Brunswick, New Jersey 08903. 1991.

AT THE INTERSECTION OF LEGALITY AND MORALITY: HARTIAN LAW AS NATURAL LAW. Daniel W. Skubik. Peter Lang Publishing, Incorporated. 62 West Forty-fifth Street, New York, New York 10036. 1990.

CONFRONTING THE CONSTITUTION: THE CHALLENGE TO LOCKE, MONTESQUIEU, JEFFERSON, AND THE FEDERALISTS FROM UTILITARIANISM, HISTORICISM, MARXISM, FREUDIANISM, PRAGMATISM, EXISTENTIALISM. Allan Bloom and Steve J. Kautz, Editors. AEI Press, Washington, D.C. 1990.

CONTRACTING FOR PROPERTY RIGHTS. Gary D. Libecap. Cambridge University Press, 40 West Twentieth Street, New York, New York 10011. 1989.

A CRITIQUE OF THE NEW NATURAL LAW THEORY. Russell Hittinger. University of Notre Dame Press, Notre Dame, Indiana 46556. 1987.

DEFINITION AND RULE IN LEGAL THEORY: A CRITIQUE OF H.L.A. HART AND THE POSITIVIST TRADITION. Robert N. Moles. Basil Blackwell, Incorporated, 3 Cambridge Center, Cambridge, Massachusetts 02142. 1987.

THE DEVELOPMENT OF NATURALIST LEGAL THEORY. H. McCoubrey. Croom Helm, Paul H. Brookes Publishing Company, P.O. Box 10624, Baltimore, Maryland 21285. 1987.

DIALECTIC OF NIHILISM: POST-STRUCTURALISM AND THE LAW. Gillian Rose. Basil Blackwell, Incorporated, 3 Cambridge Center, Cambridge, Massachusetts 02142. 1984.

ESSAYS IN JURISPRUDENCE AND PHILOSOPHY. H. L. Hart. Oxford University Press, Incorporated, 200 Madison Avenue, New York, New York 10016. 1984.

THE FORMATIVE ESSAYS OF JUSTICE HOLMES: THE MAKING OF AN AMERICAN LEGAL PHILOSOPHY. Frederick R. Kellogg. Greenwood Publishing Group, Incorporated, 88 Post Road West, P.O. Box 5007, Westport, Connecticut 06881. 1984.

GHANDI'S PHILOSOPHY OF LAW. V.S. Hegde. Concept Publishing, P.O. Box 500, York, New York 14592. 1983.

GOOD LAW: TOWARD A RATIONAL LAWMAKING PROCESS. H.J. Boukema. Peter Lang Publishing, Incorporated, 62 West Forty-fifth Street, New York, New York 10036. 1982.

IDEAS THAT HAVE MADE US FREE. Chester James Antieau. University Press of America, 4720 Boston Way, Lanham, Maryland 20706. 1991.

INALIENABLE RIGHTS: A DEFENSE. Diana T. Meyers. Columbia University Press, 562 West One-hundred and thirteenth Street, New York, New York 10025. 1985.

LAW AND THE SOCIAL ORDER: ESSAYS IN LEGAL PHILOSOPHY. Morris Raphael Cohen. Transaction Books, Rutgers University, New Brunswick, New Jersey 08903. 1982.

LAW, MORALITY AND RIGHTS. M. A. Stewart, Editor. Kluwer Academic Publishers, 101 Philip Drive, Assinippi Park, Norwell, Massachusetts 02061. 1983.

LAW, ORDER AND POWER. Second Edition. William Chambliss and Robert Seidman. Addison-Wesley Publishing Company, Incorporated, Route 128, Reading, Massachusetts 01867. 1982.

LEGAL REASONING: SEMANTIC AND LOGICAL ANALYSIS. Jovan Brkic. Peter Lang Publishing Incorporated, 62 West Forty-fifth Street, New York, New York 10036. 1985.

LEGAL RIGHT AND SOCIAL DEMOCRACY: ESSAYS IN LEGAL AND POLITICAL PHILOSOPHY. Neil MacCormick. Oxford University Press, Incorporated, 200 Madison Avenue, New York, New York 10016. 1982.

THE LOCKEAN THEORY OF RIGHTS. A. John Simmons. Princeton University Press, 41 William Street, Princeton, New Jersey 08540. 1992.

THE MEDIEVAL TRADITION OF NATURAL LAW. Harold J. Johnson. Medieval Institute Publications, Western Michigan University, Kalamazoo, Michigan 49008-3851. 1987.

NATURAL LAW. John Finnis, Editor. New York University Press, 70 Washington Square South, New York, New York 10012. 1991.

NATURAL LAW AND HUMAN DIGNITY. Ernst Bloch. MIT Press, 55 Hayward Street, Cambridge, Massachusetts 02142. 1987.

NATURAL LAW AND JUSTICE. Lloyd L. Weinreb. Harvard University Press, 79 Garden Street, Cambridge, Massachusetts 02138. 1987.

NATURAL LAW AND NATURAL RIGHTS. John Finnis. Oxford University Press, Incorporated, 200 Madison Avenue, New York, New York 10016. 1984.

NATURAL LAW AND THE THEORY OF PROPERTY: GROTIUS TO HUME. Stephen Buckle. Oxford University Press, 200 Madison Avenue, New York, New York 10016. 1991.

NATURAL LAW AND THEOLOGY. Charles E. Curran and Richard A. McCormick, Editors. Paulist Press, 997 MacArthur Boulevard, Mahwah, New Jersey 07430. 1991.

NATURAL LAW THEORY: CONTEMPORARY ESSAYS. Robert P. George, Editor. Oxford University Press, 200 Madison Avenue, New York, New York 10016. 1992.

PHILOSOPHY OF FREE EXPRESSION AND ITS CONSTITUTIONAL APPLICATIONS. Robert F. Ladenson. Rowman and Allanheld, 420 Boston Way, Lanham, Maryland 20706. 1983.

THE PHILOSOPHY OF LAW: AN INTRODUCTION TO JURISPRUDENCE. Jeffrie G. Murphy. Rowman and Allanheld, 420 Boston Way, Lanham, Maryland 20706. 1984.

READINGS IN PHILOSOPHY OF LAW. John Arthur and William H. Shaw, Editors. Prentice-Hall, Incorporated, 113 Sylvan Avenue, Englewood Cliffs, New Jersey 07632. 1984.

REASON IN LAW. Second Edition. Lief H. Carter. Scott Foresman and Company, 1900 East Lake Avenue, Glenview, Illinois 60025. 1988.

RIGHTS. Alan R. White. Oxford University Press, Incorporated, 200 Madison Avenue, New York, New York 10016. 1984.

RIGHTS. Michael Freeden. University of Minnesota Press, 2037 University Avenue, Southeast, St. Paul, Minnesota 55414. 1991.

SWIMMING AGAINST THE CURRENT IN CONTEMPORARY PHILOSOPHY: OCCASIONAL ESSAYS AND PAPERS. Henry Babcock Veatch. Catholic University of American Press, 620 Michigan Avenue, Northeast, Washington, D.C. 20064. 1990.

A THEORY OF LAW. Philie Soper. Harvard University Press, 79 Garden Street, Cambridge, Massachusetts 02138. 1984.

A THEORY OF RIGHTS: PERSONS UNDER LAWS, INSTITUTIONS, AND MORALS. Carl Wellman. Rowman and Allanheld, 420 Boston Way, Lanham, Maryland 20706. 1985.

THOMAS HOBBES AND THE DEBATE OVER NATURAL LAW AND RELIGION. S.A. State. Garland Publishing, Incorporated, 136 Madison Avenue, New York, New York 10016. 1991.

LAW REVIEWS AND PERIODICALS

AMERICAN JOURNAL OF JURISPRUDENCE. Notre Dame School of Law, Notre Dame, Indiana 46556.

ASSOCIATIONS AND PROFESSIONAL SOCIETIES

AMERICAN SOCIETY FOR POLITICAL AND LEGAL PHILOSOPHY. c/o Professor Martin P. Golding, Philosophy Department, Duke University, Durham, North Carolina 27708. (919) 648-3838.

ASSOCIATION OF AMERICAN LAWS SCHOOLS, SECTION ON JURISPRUDENCE. One Dupont Circle, Northwest, Suite 370, Washington, D.C. 20036. (202) 296-8851.

NATIONAL LAW SOCIETY. c/o Professor Virginia Black, Philosophy and Religious Studies, Pace University, Pleasantville, New York 10570. (914) 773-3309.

NATURAL RIGHTS CENTER. 156 Drakes Lane, Summertown, Tennessee 38483. (615) 964-3992.

NATURAL RESOURCES
See also: ENERGY; ENERGY DEPARTMENT; ENVIRONMENTAL LAW; ENVIRONMENTAL PROTECTION AGENCY; FEDERAL ENERGY REGULATORY COMMISSION; HAZARDOUS SUBSTANCES; SOLAR ENERGY; WATER LAW; WILDLIFE

STATUTES, CODES, STANDARDS, UNIFORM LAWS

NATURAL RESOURCES STATUTES. Government Institutes, Incorporated, 966 Hungerford Drive, Rockville, Maryland 20850. 1991.

LOOSELEAF SERVICES AND REPORTERS

ENVIRONMENTAL AND NATURAL RESOURCES PERMITS: FEDERAL APPROVAL STANDARDS AND PROCEDURES. Robert L. Schmid. Butterworth Heinemann, 80 Montvale Avenue, Stoneham, Massachusetts 02180. 1991- .

THE FEDERAL TAX LAW OF CONSERVATION EASEMENTS. Second Edition. Stephen J. Small. Land Trust Exchange, 1017 Duke Street, Alexandria, Virginia 22314. 1990- .

PUBLIC NATURAL RESOURCES LAW. George Cameron Coggins. Clark Boardman Company, Limited, 435 Hudson Street, New York, New York 10014. 1990.

HANDBOOKS, MANUALS, FORMBOOKS

MANAGING NATIONAL PARK SYSTEM RESOURCES: A HANDBOOK ON LEGAL DUTIES, OPPORTUNITIES AND TOOLS. Michael A. Mantell, Editor. Conservation Foundation, 1250 Twenty-fourth Street, Northwest, Washington, D.C. 20037. 1990.

TEXTBOOKS AND GENERAL WORKS

THE ANTARCTIC LEGAL REGIME. Christopher C. Joyner and Sudhir K. Chopra. Martinus Nijhoff, Kluwer Academic Publishers, 101 Philip Drive, Assinippi Park, Norwell, Massachusetts 02061. 1988.

BATTLE FOR NATURAL RESOURCES. American Forestry Association, P.O. Box 2000, Washington, D.C. 20013. 1983.

CAREERS IN NATURAL RESOURCES AND ENVIRONMENTAL LAW. Percy R. Luney. American Bar Association, 750 North Lake Shore Drive, Chicago, Illinois 60611. 1987.

CURRENT ISSUES IN NATURAL RESOURCE POLICY. Paul R. Portney. Resources for the Future, Incorporated, 1616 P. Street, Northwest, Washington, D.C. 20036. 1982.

ENERGY AND NATURAL RESOURCES LAW IN A NUTSHELL. Jan G. Laitos and Joseph P. Tomain. West Publishing Company, 50 West Kellogg Boulevard, St. Paul, Minnesota 55164. 1992.

THE EVOLUTION OF NATIONAL WILDLIFE LAW. Michael J. Bean. Praeger Publishers, One Madison Avenue, New York, New York 10010-3603. 1983.

EXPLOITATION, CONSERVATION, PRESERVATION: A GEOGRAPHIC PERSPECTIVE ON NATURAL RESOURCE USE. Second Edition. Susan L. Cutter, Hilary Lambert and William H. Renwick. John Wiley and Sons, Incorporated, 605 Third Avenue, New York, New York 10158. 1991.

FEDERAL PUBLIC LAND AND RESOURCES LAW. Second Edition. George Cameron Coggins and Charles F. Wilkinson. Foundation Press, 615 Merrick Avenue, Westbury, New York 11590. 1987.

FORESTLANDS: PUBLIC AND PRIVATE. Robert T. Deacon and M. Bruce Johnson. Pacific Institute for Public Policy Research, 177 Post Street, San Francisco, California 94108. 1985.

IN FAIRNESS TO FUTURE GENERATIONS: INTERNATIONAL LAW, COMMON PATRIMONY, AND INTERGENERATIONAL EQUITY. Edith Brown Weiss. Transnational Publishers, P.O. Box 7282, Ardsley-on-Hudson, New York 10503. 1988.

INCOME TAXATION OF NATURAL RESOURCES. Charles Russell and Robert W. Bowhay. Prentice-Hall, Incorporated, 113 Sylvan Avenue, Englewood Cliffs, New Jersey 07632. 1988.

MEASURING THE SOCIAL IMPACT OF NATURAL RESOURCE POLICIES. William R. Burch, Jr. and Donald R. DeLuca. University of New Mexico Press, 1720 Lomas Boulevard, Northeast, Albuquerque, New Mexico 87131. 1984.

NATURAL RESOURCES AND THE ENVIRONMENT: THE REAGAN APPROACH. Paul Portney. Urban Institute Press, 2100 M Street, Northwest, Washington, D.C. 20037. 1984.

NATURAL RESOURCES: BUREAUCRATIC MYTHS AND ENVIRONMENTAL MANAGEMENT. Richard L. Stroup and John A. Baden. Pacific Institute For Public Policy Research, 177 Post Street, San Francisco, California 94108. 1983.

OUR COMMON LANDS: DEFENDING THE NATIONAL PARKS. David J. Simon. Island Press, 1718 Connecticut Avenue, Northwest, Suite 300, Washington, D.C. 20009. 1988.

PROTECTING INDIAN NATURAL RESOURCES: A MANUAL FOR LAWYERS REPRESENTING INDIAN TRIBES OF TRIBAL MEMBERS. Alan H. Sanders and Robert L. Otsca, Jr. Native American Rights Fund, 1506 Broadway, Boulder, Colorado 80302. 1983.

RESOURCE REGIMES: NATURAL RESOURCES AND SOCIAL INSTITUTIONS. Oran R. Young. University of California Press, 2120 Berkeley Way, Berkeley, California 94720. 1982.

RISK AND THE POLITICAL ECONOMY OF RESOURCES DEVELOPMENT. David W. Pearce, Horst Siebert and Ingo Walter. Saint Martin's Press, Incorporated, 175 Fifth Avenue, New York, New York 10010. 1984.

TAXATION OF NATURAL RESOURCES: OIL, GAS, MINERALS, AND TIMBER. Richard A. Westin and Fred F. Murray. Practising Law Institute, 810 Seventh Avenue, New York, New York 10019. 1987.

THIS TENDER AND DELICATE BUSINESS: THE PUBLIC TRUST DOCTRINE IN AMERICAN LAW AND ECONOMIC POLICY, 1789-1920. Molly Selvin. Garland Publishing, Incorporated, 136 Madison Avenue, New York, New York 10016. 1987.

TRANSBOUNDARY RESOURCES LAW. Albert E. Utton and Ludwik A. Teclaff, Editors. Westview Press, Incorporated, 5500 Central Avenue, Boulder, Colorado 80301. 1987.

WESTWARD IN EDEN: THE PUBLIC LANDS AND THE CONSERVATION MOVEMENT. William K. Wyant. University of California Press, 2120 Berkeley Way, Berkeley, California 94720. 1982.

WILDLIFE: CASES, LAWS, AND POLICY. David S. Faure. Associated Faculty Press, 19 West Thirty-sixth Street, New York, New York 10018. 1983.

DIGESTS, INDEXES, ABSTRACTS, CITATORS

SHEPARD'S FEDERAL ENERGY LAW CITATIONS. Shepard's/McGraw-Hill, P.O. Box 1235, Colorado Springs, Colorado 80901. Quarterly.

WEEKLY GOVERNMENT ABSTRACTS, NATIONAL RESOURCES AND EARTH SCIENCES. National Technical Information Services, 5285 Port Royal Road, Springfield, Virginia 22161. Weekly.

WESTERN NATURAL RESOURCE LITIGATION DIGEST. Conference of Western Attorneys General, 720 Sacramento Street, San Francisco, California 94108. Quarterly.

NATURAL RESOURCES

ANNUALS AND SURVEYS

NATURAL RESOURCES: THE YEAR IN REVIEW. American Bar Association, Section Of Natural Resources Law, 750 North Lake Shore Drive, Chicago, Illinois 60611. 1985.

NATURE AND RESOURCES: INTERNATIONAL NEWS ABOUT RESEARCH ON ENVIRONMENT, RESOURCES, AND CONSERVATION OF NATURE. Unesco, Unipub, 4611-F Assembly Drive, Lanham, Maryland 20706-4391. Quarterly.

LAW REVIEWS AND PERIODICALS

AMICUS JOURNAL. Natural Resources Defense Council, Incorporated, 122 East Forty-Second Street, New York, New York 10017. Quarterly.

LAND AND WATER LAW REVIEW. University of Wyoming College of Law, University Station, Box 3035, Laramie, Wyoming 82071. Semiannual.

NATURAL RESOURCES JOURNAL. University of New Mexico School of Law, 1117 Stanford, Northeast, Albuquerque, New Mexico 87131. Quarterly.

VIRIGINIA JOURNAL OF NATURAL RESOURCES LAW. University of Virginia School of Law, Charlottesville, Virginia 22901. Semiannual.

NEWSLETTERS AND NEWSPAPERS

THE BACK FORTY. Land Conservation Law Institute, 900 Seventeenth Street, Northwest, Suite 410, Washington, D.C. 20006. Monthly.

BRIEFINGS. National Water Well Association, 6375 Riverside Drive, Dublin, Ohio 43107. Quarterly.

CLEAN WATER REPORT. Business Publications, Incorporated, 951 Pershing Drive, Silver Spring, Maryland 20910. Biweekly.

CONSERVATION. National Wildlife Federation, 1400 Sixteenth Street, Northwest, Washington, D.C. 20036. Monthly.

MINERAL LAW NEWSLETTER. Rocky Mountain Mineral Law Foundation, 7039 East Eighteenth Avenue, Denver, Colorado 80220. Quarterly.

NATURAL RESOURCES AND ENVIRONMENT. American Bar Association, Section of Natural Resources Law, 750 North Lake Shore Drive, Chicago, Illinois 60611. Quarterly.

NATURAL RESOURCES LAW NEWSLETTER. American Bar Association, 750 North Lake Shore Drive, Chicago, Illinois 60611. Quarterly.

THE NATURAL RESOURCES TAX REVIEW. Tax Analysts, 6830 North Fairfax Drive, Arlington, Virginia 22213. Bimonthly.

NRDC NEWSLINE. Natural Resources Defense Council, Incorporated, 40 West Twentieth Street, New York, New York 10011. Quarterly.

WATER LAW NEWSLETTER. Rocky Mountain Mineral Law Foundation, 7039 East Eighteenth Avenue, Denver, Colorado 80220. (303) 321-8100. Quarterly.

BIBLIOGRAPHIES

BIBLIOGRAPHY ON TRANSNATIONAL LAW OF NATURAL RESOURCES. Martin Bartels. Kluwer Academic Publishers, 101 Philip Drive, Assinippi Park, Norwell, Massachusetts 02061. 1981.

NATURAL RESOURCES AND DEVELOPMENT: AN ANNOTATED BIBLIOGRAPHY. William James and David C. Short, Editors. William S. Hein and Company, 1285 Main Street, Buffalo, New York 14209. 1987.

VALUATION AND PROPERTY TAXATION OF EXTRACTION RESOURCES: A BIBLIOGRAPHY. Robert M. Clatanoff. International Association of Assessing Officers, 1313 East Sixtieth Street, Chicago, Illinois 60637. 1982.

DIRECTORIES

CONSERVATION DIRECTORY. National Wildlife Federation, 1400 Sixteenth Street, Northwest, Washington, D.C. 20036-2266. Annual.

ASSOCIATIONS AND PROFESSIONAL SOCIETIES

AMERICAN BAR ASSOCIATION, SECTION OF NATURAL RESOURCES LAW. 750 North Lake Shore Drive, Chicago, Illinois 60611. (312) 988-5000.

NATIONAL WILDLIFE FEDERATION. 1412 Sixteenth Street, Northwest, Washington, D.C. 20036. (202) 797-6800.

NATURAL RESOURCES COUNCIL OF AMERICA. 1015 Thirty-first Street, Northwest, Washington, D.C. 20007. (202) 333-8495.

NATURAL RESOURCES DEFENSE COUNCIL. 40 West Twentieth Street, New York, New York 10011. (212) 727-2700.

RENEWABLE NATURAL RESOURCES FOUNDATION. 5430 Grosvenor Lane, Bethesda, Maryland 20814. (301) 493-9101.

RESEARCH CENTERS, INSTITUTES, CLEARINGHOUSES

ENERGY LAW CENTER. University of Utah, College of Law, Salt Lake City, Utah 84112. (801) 581-5880.

LAND CONSERVATION LAW INSTITUTE. 900 Seventeenth Street, Northwest, Suite 410, Washington, D.C. 20006. (202) 785-1410.

NATURAL RESOURCES LAW CENTER. University of Colorado, Boulder, Campus Box 401, Boulder, Colorado 80309. (303) 492-1288.

ROCKY MOUNTAIN MINERAL LAW FOUNDATION. 7039 East Eighteenth Avenue, Denver, Colorado 80220. (303) 321-8100.

ONLINE DATABASES

ACID RAIN. Bowker A&I Publishing, 245 West Seventeenth Street, New York, New York 10011.

LEXIS ENVIRONMENTAL LAW LIBRARY. Mead Data Central, P.O. Box 933, Dayton, Ohio 45401.

NATURAL RESOURCES METABASE. National Information Services Corporation, Suite 6, Wyman Towers, 3100 St. Paul Street, Baltimore, Maryland 21218.

NATURALIZATION
See: CITIZENS AND CITIZENSHIP

NAVY
See: ADMIRALTY; MILITARY LAW AND SERVICE

NEGLIGENCE
See: ACCIDENTS; ADMIRALTY; AVIATION; MOTOR VEHICLES; PERSONAL INJURIES; PRODUCTS LIABILITY AND SAFETY; TORTS; WRONGFUL DEATH

NEGOTIABLE INSTRUMENTS
See also: LETTERS OF CREDIT

STATUTES, CODES, STANDARDS, UNIFORM LAW

UNIFORM COMMERCIAL CODE. National Conference of Commissioners on Uniform State Laws. Martindale-Hubbell Law Directory, Volume Eight. Martindale-Hubbell, Incorporated, 121 Chanlon Road, New Providence, New Jersey 07974. Annual.

UNIFORM COMMERCIAL CODE. National Conference of Commisioners on Uniform State Laws. Uniform Laws Annotated. West Publishing Company, P.O. Box 64526, 50 West Kellogg Boulevard, St. Paul, Minnesota 55164-0526. 1976. (Annual Supplements).

UNIFORM COMMERCIAL CODE CURRENT PAYMENT METHODS: COUNCIL DRAFT. Executive Office, American Law Institute-American Bar Association, 4025 Chestnut Street, Philadelphia, Pennsylvania 19104. 1989.

UNIFORM COMMERCIAL CODE: PROPOSED FINAL DRAFT, APRIL 12, 1990. National Conference of Commissioners on Uniform State Laws. American Law Institute-American Bar Association, 4025 Chestnut Street, Philadelphia, Pennsylvania 19104. 1990.

LOOSELEAF SERVICES AND REPORTERS

CHECKS, DRAFTS AND NOTES. Jeffrey B. Reitman and Harold Weisblatt. Matthew Bender and Company, Incorporated, 11 Penn Plaza, New York, New York 10001. 1984- .

COMMERCIAL PAPER AND PAYMENT SYSTEMS. William H. Lawrence. Butterworth-Heinemann, 80 Montvale Avenue, Stoneham, Massachusetts 02180. 1990- .

COMMERCIAL PAPER UNDER THE UNIFORM COMMERCIAL CODE. Frederick M. Hart and William F. Willier. Matthew Bender and Company, Incorporated, 11 Penn Plaza, New York, New York 10001. 1972- .

UNIFORM COMMERCIAL CODE REPORTING SERVICE. Callaghan and Company, 155 Pfingsten Road, Deerfield, Illinois 60015. 1965- .

HANDBOOKS, MANUALS, FORMBOOKS

ANDERSON ON THE UNIFORM COMMERCIAL CODE: LEGAL FORMS. Second Edition. Ronald A. Anderson. Lawyers Cooperative Publishing Company, Aqueduct Building, Rochester, New York 14694. 1974. (Annual Supplements).

ANDERSON ON THE UNIFORM COMMERCIAL CODE: PLEADING AND PRACTICE FORMS. Second Edition. Ronald A. Anderson. Lawyers Cooperative Publishing Company, Aqueduct Building, Rochester, New York 14694. 1977. (Annual Supplements).

COMMERCIAL PAPER AND ALTERNATIVE PAYMENT SYSTEMS. Marion W. Benfield and Peter A Alces. Matthew Bender and Company, Incorporated, 11 Penn Plaza, New York, New York 10001. 1987.

COMMERCIAL PAPER AND CHECK COLLECTION. William H. Lawrence. Butterworth-Heinemann, 80 Montvale Avenue, Stoneham, Massachusetts 02180. 1990.

EXPORT-IMPORT FINANCING. Third Edition. Harry M. Venedikian and Gerald Warfield. John Wiley and Sons, Incorporated, 605 Third Avenue, New York, New York 10158. 1991.

THE LAW OF BANK DEPOSITS, COLLECTIONS, AND CREDIT CARDS. Third Edition. Barkley Clark. Research Institute of America, Incorporated, One Penn Plaza, New York, New York 10119. 1990.

TEXTBOOKS AND GENERAL WORKS

ANDERSON ON THE UNIFORM COMMERCIAL CODE. Third Edition. Ronald A. Anderson. Lawyers Cooperative Publishing Company, Aqueduct Building, Rochester, New York 14694. 1981. (Annual Supplements).

BRADY ON BANK CHECKS. Fifth Edition. Henry J.Bailey. Research Institute of America, Incorporated, One Penn Plaza, New York, New York 10119. Three supplements per year.

COMMERCIAL PAPER. Second Edition. Robert L. Jordan and William D. Warren. Foundation Press, 615 Merrick Avenue, Westbury, New York 11590. 1987.

COMMERCIAL PAPER. Steve H. Nickles. West Publishing Company, 50 West Kellogg Boulevard, St. Paul, Minnesota 55164. 1988.

COMMERCIAL PAPER IN A NUTSHELL. Third Edition. Charles M. Weber and Richard E. Speidel. West Publishing Company, P.O. Box 64526, 50 West Kellogg Boulevard, St. Paul, Minnesota 55164-0526. 1982.

LAW OF BANK DEPOSITS, COLLECTIONS AND CREDIT CARDS. Barkley Clark. Research Institute of America, Incorporated, One Penn Plaza, New York, New York 10119. 1990.

LAW OF MODERN PAYMENT SYSTEMS AND NOTES. Fred H. Miller and Alvin C. Harrell. University of Oklahoma Press, 105 Asp Avenue, Norman, Oklahoma 73019. 1985.

MATERIALS FOR UNDERSTANDING CREDIT AND PAYMENT SYSTEMS. Steve H. Nickles, John H. Matheson and John F. Dolan. West Publishing Company, 50 West Kellogg Boulevard, St. Paul, Minnesota 55164. 1987.

NEGOTIABLE INSTRUMENTS AND THE PAYMENTS MECHANISM. Craig W. Smith. American Bankers Association, 1120 Connecticut Avenue, Northwest, Washington, D.C. 20036. 1983.

PAPER AND ELECTRONIC PAYMENTS LITIGATION: ALIABA COURSE OF STUDY. American Law Institute-American Bar Association, Committee on Continuing Professional Education, 4025 Chestnut Street, Philadelphia, Pennsylvania 19104. 1984.

PAYMENT SYSTEMS IN EUROPEAN RETAILING: A NEW DYNAMIC. Hilary Payne and Mark Wheeler. SRI International, 333 Ravenswood Avenue, Menlo Park, California 94025. 1991.

PROBLEMS AND MATERIALS ON NEGOTIABLE INSTRUMENTS. Second Edition. Douglas J. Whaley. Little, Brown and Company, 34 Beacon Street, Boston, Massachusetts 02108. 1988.

UCC SKILLS-ARTICLES 3,4,5, AND 9: COMMERCIAL PAPER, BANK DEPOSITS AND COLLECTIONS, LETTERS OF CREDIT, SECURED TRANSACTIONS. William C. Hillman, Chairman. Practising Law Institute, 810 Seventh Avenue, New York, New York 10019. 1985.

DIGESTS, INDEXES, ABSTRACTS, CITATORS

QUINN'S UNIFORM COMMERCIAL CODE COMMENTARY AND LAW DIGEST. Thomas M. Quinn. Research Institute of America, Incorporated, One Penn Plaza, New York, New York 10119. 1978. (Semi-annual Supplements).

SHEPARD'S UNIFORM COMMERCIAL CODE CITATIONS. Shepard's/McGraw-Hill, P.O. Box 1235, Colorado Springs, Colorado 80901. 1982. (Quarterly Supplements).

UNIFORM COMMERCIAL CODE: CASE DIGEST. Pike and Fischer, Incorporated, Editor. Callaghan and Company, 155 Pfingsten Road, Deerfield, Illinois 60015. 1976- .

LAW REVIEWS AND PERIODICALS

COMMERCIAL LAW JOURNAL. Commercial League of America, 222 West Adams Street, Chicago, Illinois 60606. Biweekly.

UNIFORM COMMERCIAL CODE LAW JOURNAL. Research Institute of America, Incorporated, One Penn Plaza, New York, New York 10119. Quarterly.

NEWSLETTERS AND NEWSPAPERS

COMMODITIES LAW LETTER. Commodities Law Press Associates, 900 Third Avenue, New York, New York 10022. Monthly.

COMMODITIES LITIGATION REPORTER. Andrews Publications, 1646 West Chester Pike, Westtown, Pennsylvania 19395. Semimonthly.

UNIFORM COMMERCIAL CODE LAW LETTER. Research Institute of America, One Penn Plaza, New York, New York 10119. Monthly.

BIBLIOGRAPHIES

NEGOTIABLE ORDER OF WITHDRAWAL (NOW) ACCOUNTS: A SELECTED BIBLIOGRAPHY, 1978-1981. Felix Chin. Vance Bibliographies, P.O. Box 229, 112 North Charter Street, Monticello, Illinois 61856. 1982.

ASSOCIATIONS AND PROFESSIONAL SOCIETIES

AMERICAN BAR ASSOCIATION, SECTION ON BUSINESS LAW. 750 North Lake Shore Drive, Chicago, Illinois 60611. (312) 988-5000.

NEGOTIATION
See: ARBITRATION AND AWARD; COMPROMISE AND SETTLEMENT; DISPUTE RESOLUTION; INTERNATIONAL ARBITRATION; LABOR ARBITRATION

NEWSPAPERS
See also: FREEDOM OF PRESS; FREEDOM OF SPEECH; TELEVISION AND RADIO

LOOSELEAF SERVICES AND REPORTERS

MEDIA LAW REPORTER. Bureau of National Affairs, 1231 Twenty-fifth Street, Northwest, Washington, D.C. 20037. 1977- .

THE PUBLISHING LAW HANDBOOK. E. Gabriel Perle and John Taylor Williams. Prentice-Hall, Incorporated, 113 Sylvan Avenue, Englewood Cliffs, New Jersey 07632. 1988- .

HANDBOOKS, MANUALS, FORMBOOKS

BOOK PUBLISHERS' LEGAL GUIDE. Second edition. Leonard D. DuBoff. Fred B. Rothman and Company, 10368 West Centennial Road, Littleton, Colorado 80127. 1991.

MEDIA LAW: A LEGAL HANDBOOK FOR WORKING JOURNALIST. Katherine M. Galvin. Nolo Press, 950 Parker Street, Berkeley, California 94710. 1984.

TEXTBOOKS AND GENERAL WORKS

ACTUAL MALICE: TWENTY-FIVE YEARS AFTER TIMES V. SULLIVAN. W. Wat Hopkins. Praeger Publishers, One Madison Avenue, New York, New York 10010-3603. 1989.

AMERICAN BROADCASTING AND THE FIRST AMENDMENT. Lucas A. Powe, Jr. University of California Press, 2120 Berkeley Way, Berkeley, California 94720. 1987.

COMMUNICATIONS LAW, 1990. James C. Goodale, Chairman. Practising Law Institute, 810 Seventh Avenue, New York, New York 10019. 1990.

THE COST OF LIBEL: ECONOMIC AND POLICY IMPLICATIONS. Everette E. Dennis and Eli M. Noam. Columbia University Press, 562 West One Hundred Thirteenth Street, New York, New York 10025. 1989.

THE ECONOMICS AND REGULATION OF UNITED STATES NEWSPAPERS. Stephen Lacy and Todd F. Simon. Ablex Publishing Corporation, 355 Chestnut Street, Norwood, New Jersey 07648. 1992.

ESSENTIAL PRINCIPLES OF COMMUNICATIONS LAW. Donald E. Lively. Praeger Publishers, One Madison Avenue, New York, New York 10010-3603. 1992.

THE FIRST AMENDMENT AND THE FIFTH ESTATE: REGULATION OF ELECTRONIC MASS MEDIA. Second edition. T. Barton Carter, Marc A. Franklin, and Jay B. Wright. Foundation Press, 615 Merrick Avenue, Westbury, New York 11590. 1989.

THE FIRST AMENDMENT AND THE FOURTH ESTATE: THE LAW OF MASS MEDIA. T. Barton Carter, Marc A. Franklin, and Jay B. Wright. Foundation Press, 615 Merrick Avenue, Westbury, New York 11590. 1991.

FOREIGN NEWS AND THE NEW WORLD INFORMATION ORDER. Robert L. Stevenson and Donald L. Shaw, editors. Iowa State University Press, 2121 South State Avenue, Ames, Iowa 50010. 1984.

FREEDOM AND ETHICS IN THE PRESS. Julian Adams. Rosen Publishing Group, 29 East Twenty-first Street, New York, New York 10010. 1983.

FREEDOM FOR THE COLLEGE STUDENT PRESS: COURT CASES AND RELATED DECISIONS DEFINING THE CAMPUS FOURTH ESTATE BOUNDARIES. Louis E. Ingelhart. Greenwood Publishing Group, Incorporated, 88 Post Road West, P.O. Box 5007, Westport, Connecticut 06881. 1985.

FREEDOM OF THE PRESS. J. Edward Evans. Lerner Publications Company, Minneapolis, Minnesota. 1990.

FREEDOM, TECHNOLOGY, AND THE FIRST AMENDMENT. Jonathan Emord. Pacific Research Institute for Public Policy, 177 Post Street, San Francisco, California 94108. 1991.

THE FREEDOM TO PUBLISH. Haig A. Bosmajian. Neal-Schuman Publications, Incorporated, 23 Leonard Street, New York, New York 10013. 1989.

GOVERNING THE PRESS: MEDIA FREEDOM IN THE UNITED STATES AND GREAT BRITAIN. Deborah Holmes. Westview Press, 5500 Central Avenue, Boulder, Colorado 80301. 1986.

IMAGES OF A FREE PRESS. Lee C. Bollinger. University of Chicago Press, 5801 Ellis Avenue, Chicago, Illinois 60637. 1991.

THE LAW (IN PLAIN ENGLISH) FOR WRITERS. Leonard D. DuBoff. John Wiley and Sons, Incorporated, 605 Third Avenue, New York, New York 10158. 1992.

LAW OF MASS COMMUNICATIONS: FREEDOM AND CONTROL OF PRINT AND BROADCAST MEDIA. Sixth Edition. Harold Nelson and Dwight L. Teeter, Jr. Foundation Press, Incorporated, 615 Merrick Avenue, Westbury, New York 11590. 1989.

THE LAW OF PUBLIC COMMUNICATION. Second edition. Kent R. Middleton and Bill F. Chamberlin. Longman Publishing Group, 95 Church Street, White Plains, New York 10601. 1991.

LIBEL LAW AND THE PRESS: MYTH AND REALITY. Free Press, 866 Third Avenue, New York, New York 10022. 1987.

LINDEY ON ENTERTAINMENT, PUBLISHING AND THE ARTS: AGREEMENTS AND THE LAW. Second Edition. Alexander Lindey. Clark Boardman Company, Limited, 435 Hudson Street, New York, New York 10014. 1982. (Annual Supplements).

MAKE NO LAW: THE SULLIVAN CASE AND THE FIRST AMENDMENT. Anthony Lewis. Random House, Incorporated, 201 East Fiftieth Street, New York, New York 10022. 1991.

MASS COMMUNICATIONS LAW IN A NUTSHELL. Third Edition. Harvey L. Zuckman and Martin J. Gaynes. West Publishing Company, P.O. Box 64526, 50 West Kellogg Boulevard, St. Paul, Minnesota 55164-0526. 1988.

MASS MEDIA AND THE SUPREME COURT: THE LEGACY OF THE WARREN YEARS. Revised Fourth Edition. Kenneth S. Devol, editor. Hastings House Publishers, Incorporated, 141 Halsted Avenue, Mamaroneck, New York 10543. 1990.

MASS MEDIA LAW. Don R. Pember. Fifth Edition. William C. Brown Company, 2460 Kerper Boulevard, Dubuque, Iowa 52001. 1990.

MASS MEDIA LAW AND REGULATION. Fifth edition. William E. Francois. Iowa State University Press, 2121 South State Avenue, Ames, Iowa 50010. 1990.

MEDIA LAW. Second edition. Ralph L. Holsinger. McGraw-Hill Publishing Company, 1221 Avenue of the Americas, New York, New York 10020. 1991.

MODERN COMMUNICATIONS LAW. Donald E. Lively. Praeger Publishers, One Madison Avenue, New York, New York 10010-3603. 1991.

NEWS OF CRIME: COURTS AND PRESS IN CONFLICT. J. Edward Gerald. Greenwood Publishing Group, Incorporated, 88 Post Road West, P.O. Box 5007, Westport, Connecticut 06881. 1983.

NEWSMAKING IN THE TRIAL COURTS. Robert E. Drechsel. Longman, Incorporated, 19 West Forty-fourth Street, New York, New York 10036. 1983.

NEWSPAPERS AND THE ANTITRUST LAWS. S. Chesterfield Oppenheim and Carrington Shields. The Michie Company, P.O. Box 7587, Charlottesville, Virginia 22906-7582. 1981.

THE OTHER GOVERNMENT: POWER AND THE WASHINGTON MEDIA. William L. Rivers. Universe Books, Incorporated, 381 Park Avenue South, New York, New York 10016. 1982.

POWER, PUBLICITY, AND THE ABUSE OF LIBEL LAW. Donald M. Gillmor. Oxford University Press, 200 Madison Avenue, New York, New York 10016. 1992.

THE PRESS AND AMERICA: AN INTERPRETIVE HISTORY OF THE MASS MEDIA. Sixth Edition. Edward Emery and Michael Emery. Prentice-Hall, Incorporated, 113 Sylvan Avenue, Englewood Cliffs, New Jersey 07632. 1988.

PRESS CONTROL AROUND THE WORLD. Jane L. Curry and Joan R. Dassin, Editors. Praeger Publishers, One Madison Avenue, New York, New York 10010-3603. 1982.

PRESS LAW IN MODERN DEMOCRACIES: A COMPARATIVE APPROACH. Pnina Lahav, Editor. Longman, Incorporated, 19 West Forty-fourth Street, New York, New York 10036. 1985.

PRESS VERSUS GOVERNMENT: CONSTITUTIONAL ISSUES. Donald J. Rogers. Messner, Julian, 190 Sylvan Avenue, Englewood Cliffs, New Jersey 07632. 1986.

PRINTERS AND PRESS FREEDOM: THE IDEOLOGY OF EARLY AMERICAN JOURNALISM. Jeffery A. Smith. Oxford University Press, 200 Madison Avenue, New York, New York 10016. 1988.

RIGHTS AND LIABILITIES OF PUBLISHERS, BROADCASTERS AND REPORTERS. Slade R. Metcalf. Shepard's/McGraw-Hill, P.O. Box 1235, Colorado Springs, Colorado 80901. 1982. (Annual Supplements).

THE SHAPING OF THE FIRST AMENDMENT, 1791 TO THE PRESENT. Paul L. Murphy. Oxford University Press, 200 Madison Avenue, New York, New York 10016. 1992.

STUDENT PUBLICATIONS: LEGALITIES, GOVERNANCE, AND OPERATION. Louis Edward Ingelhart. Iowa State University Press, 2121 South State Avenue, Ames, Iowa 50010. 1992.

SUING THE PRESS. Rodney A. Smolla. Oxford University Press, Incorporated, 200 Madison Avenue, New York, New York 10016. 1987.

THE WAR AGAINST THE PRESS: POLITICS, PRESSURE AND INTIMIDATION IN THE 80'S. Peter Stoler. Dodd, Mead and Company, 71 Fifth Avenue, New York, New York 10003. 1987.

ENCYCLOPEDIAS AND DICTIONARIES

WORLD PRESS ENCYCLOPEDIA. George T. Kurian, editor. Facts on File, 460 Park Avenue, South, New York, New York 10016. 1982.

DIGESTS, INDEXES, ABSTRACTS, CITATORS

NATIONAL NEWSPAPER INDEX. Information Access Corporation, 362 Lakeside Drive, Foster City, California 94404. Monthly. (Microfilm).

NEW YORK TIMES INDEX. New York Times Company, 229 West Forty-third Street, New York, New York 10036. Semimonthly.

NEWSPAPER INDEX. Bell and Howell, The Indexing Center, Micro Photo Division, Old Mansfield Road, Wooster, Ohio 44691. Four issues per year.

NEWSPAPER INDEXES: A LOCATION AND SUBJECT GUIDE FOR RESEARCHERS. Scarecrow Press, Incorporated, 52 Liberty Street, Box 4167, Metuchen, New Jersey 08840. 1977- .

LAW REVIEWS AND PERIODICALS

AMERICAN SOCIETY OF NEWSPAPER EDITORS-BULLETIN. P.O. Box 17004, Washington, D.C. 20041. Bimonthly.

INTERNATIONAL MEDIA LAW. Oyez Longman, 212 Colgate Avenue, Kensington, California 94707. 1982- .

NEWS MEDIA AND THE LAW. Reporters Committee for Freedom of the Press, 800 Eighteenth Street, Northwest, Suite 300, Washington, D.C. 20006. Quarterly.

NEWSLETTERS AND NEWSPAPERS

EDITORS EXCHANGE. American Society of Newspaper Editors, P.O. Box 17004, Washington, D.C. 20041. Monthly.

MEDIA LAW NOTES. University of Wisconsin, School of Journalism and Mass Communication, Madison, Wisconsin 53706. Quarterly.

MEDIA LAWLETTER. Law Letter Publishing, 963 Parkside Place, Cincinnati, Ohio 45202. Monthly.

NEWS MEDIA UPDATE. Reporter Committee for Freedom of the Press, 800 Eighteenth Street, Northwest, Suite 300, Washington, D.C. 20006. Biweekly.

NRC NEWSLETTER. Newspaper Research Council, 1000 Two Ruan Center, 601 Locust Street, Des Moines, Iowa 50309. Bimonthly.

BIBLIOGRAPHIES

NEWS MEDIA AND PUBLIC POLICY: AN ANNOTATED BIBLIOGRAPHY. Joseph P. McKerns. Garland Publishing, Incorporated, 136 Madison Avenue, New York, New York 10016. 1985.

DIRECTORIES

EDITOR AND PUBLISHER INTERNATIONAL YEAR BOOK. Editor and Publisher Company, Incorporated, 11 West Nineteenth Street, New York 10011. Annual.

NATIONAL DIRECTORY OF WEEKLY NEWSPAPERS. National Newspaper Association, 1627 K Street, Northwest, Suite 400, Washington, D.C. 20006. Annual.

ASSOCIATIONS AND PROFESSIONAL SOCIETIES

AMERICAN BAR ASSOCIATION, NATIONAL CONFERENCE GROUP ON LAWYERS AND REPRESENTATIVES OF THE MEDIA. 750 North Lake Shore Drive, Chicago, Illinois 60611. (312) 988-5000.

AMERICAN BAR ASSOCIATION, SPECIAL COMMITTEE ON COOPERATION WITH THE AMERICAN NEWSPAPER PUBLISHERS ASSOCIATION. 750 North Lake Shore Drive, Chicago, Illinois 60611. (312) 988-5000.

AMERICAN SOCIETY OF NEWSPAPER EDITORS. P.O. Box 17004, Washington, D.C. 20041. (703) 648-1144.

ASSOCIATION OF AMERICAN LAW SCHOOLS, SECTION ON MASS COMMUNICATIONS LAW. One Dupont Circle, Northwest, Washington, D.C. 20036. (202) 296-8851.

FIRST AMENDMENT LAWYERS ASSOCIATION. c/o Wayne Giampietro, 125 South Wacker Drive, Suite 2700, Chicago, Illinois 60606. (312) 236-0606.

NATIONAL NEWSPAPER ASSOCIATION. 1627 K Street, Northwest, Suite 400, Washington, D.C. 20006. (202) 455-7200.

NATIONAL PRESS CLUB. 1228 National Press Building, 529 Fourteenth Street, Northwest, Washington, D.C. 20045. (202) 662-7500.

REPORTERS COMMITTEE FOR FREEDOM OF THE PRESS. 1735 Eye Street, Northwest, Suite 504, Washington, D.C. 20006. (202) 466-6312.

WOMEN'S INSTITUTE FOR FREEDOM OF THE PRESS. 3306 Ross Place, Northwest, Washington, D.C. 20008. (202) 966-7783.

RESEARCH CENTERS, INSTITUTES, CLEARINGHOUSES

COMMUNICATION RESEARCH CENTER. University of Florida, Gainesville, Florida 32611. (904) 392-6660.

NEW DIRECTIONS FOR NEWS. University of Missouri, Columbia, School of Journalism, Box 838, Columbia, Missouri 65205. (314) 882-1110.

NEWSPAPER RESEARCH COUNCIL. 1000 Two Ruan Center, 601 Locust Street, Des Moines, Iowa 50309. (515) 245-3828.

ONLINE DATA BASES

BURRELLE'S BROADCAST DATABASE. Burrelle's Information Services, 75 East Northfield Road, Livingston, New Jersey 07039.

COMPUTER ANALYZED NEWSPAPER DATA ON-LINE. Newspaper Advertising Bureau, Incorporated, 1180 Sixth Avenue, New York, New York 10036.

GALE DIRECTORY OF PUBLICATIONS AND BROADCAST MEDIA. Gale Research, Incorporated, 835 Penobscot Building, Detroit, Michigan 48226.

THE INFORMATION BANK. New York Times Information Bank Services, Incorporated, 1719A Mount Pleasant Office Park, Route 10, Parsippany, New Jersey 07054.

THE INFORMATION BANK ABSTRACTS. The New York Times Index Department, 229 West Forty-Third Street, New York, New York 10036.

INFOTRAC. Information Access Corporation, 362 Lakeside Drive, Foster City, California 94404.

JOURNALISM FORUM. CompuServe Information Services, 5000 Arlington Centre Boulevard, P.O. Box 20212, Columbus, Ohio 43220.

NATIONAL NEWSPAPER INDEX. Information Access Corporation, 362 Lakeside Drive, Foster City, California 94404.

NEWSPAPER INDEX. Bell and Howell, Publications System Division, Old Mansfield Road, Wooster, Ohio 44691.

READERS GUIDE ABSTRACTS. H.W. Wilson Company, 950 University Avenue, Bronx, New York 10452.

READERS GUIDE TO PERIODICAL LITERATURE. H.W. Wilson Company, 950 University Avenue, Bronx, New York 10452.

UNITED STATES NEWSPAPER PROGRAM DATABASE. United States Foundation of the Arts and the Humanities, National Endowment for the Humanities, Office of Preservation, 1100 Pennsylvania Avenue, Northwest, Washington, D.C. 20506.

VU/TEXT INFORMATION SERVICES, INCORPORATED. 1211 Chestnut Street, Philadelphia, Pennsylvania 19107.

STATISTICS SOURCES

NEWSPAPER CIRCULATION ANALYSIS. Standard Rate and Data Service, Incorporated, 3004 Glenview Road, Wilmette, Illinois 60091. Annual.

NOISE
See: ENVIRONMENTAL LAW

NONPROFIT CORPORATIONS
See: ASSOCIATIONS AND NONPROFIT CORPORATIONS

NOTARIES PUBLIC

HANDBOOKS, MANUALS, FORMBOOKS

ANDERSON'S MANUAL FOR NOTARIES PUBLIC. Sixth edition. Wesley Gilmer. Anderson Publishing Company, 2035 Reading Road, Cincinnati, Ohio 45202. 1991.

HOW TO BECOME A NOTARY PUBLIC IN FIVE STATES. Second edition. Daniel I. Barness. Duane Publishers, New York, New York. 1987.

TEXTBOOKS AND GENERAL WORKS

LAW OF NOTARIES PUBLIC. Second revised editon. Lawrence G. Greene, Dusan J. Djonovichy, and Robert Sperry. Oceana Publications, Incorporated, 75 Main Street, Dobbs Ferry, New York 10522. 1967.

NOTARY HOME STUDY COURSE. National Notary Association, 8236 Remmet Avenue, P.O. Box 7184, Canoga Park, California 91304. 1985.

NOTARY PUBLIC PRACTICES AND GLOSSARY. Raymond C. Rothman. National Notary Association, 8236 Remmet Avenue, P.O. Box 7184, Canoga Park, California 91304. 1978.

UNDERSTANDING UNIVERSAL NOTARY CERTIFICATES. Raymond C. Rothman, compiler. National Notary Association, 8236 Remmet Avenue, P.O. Box 7184, Canoga Park, California 91304. 1980.

NEWSLETTERS AND NEWSPAPERS

AMERICAN NOTARY. American Society of Notaries, 918 16th Street, N.W., Washington, D.C. 20006. 1966- . Bimonthly.

NOTARY VIEWPOINT. National Notary Association, 8236 Remmet Avenue, P.O. Box 7184, Canoga Park, California 91304. 1973- . Bimonthly.

ASSOCIATIONS AND PROFESSIONAL SOCIETIES

AMERICAN SOCIETY OF NOTARIES. 918 16th Street, N.W., Washington, D.C. 20006. (202) 955-6162.

NATIONAL NOTARY ASSOCIATION. 8236 Remmet Avenue, P.O. Box 7184, Canoga Park, California 91304. (818) 713-4000.

NUCLEAR ENERGY
See also: ENERGY; ENERGY DEPARTMENT; FEDERAL ENERGY REGULATORY COMMISSION; NUCLEAR REGULATORY COMMISSION

STATUTES, CODES, STANDARDS, UNIFORM LAWS

COMPILATION OF SELECTED ENERGY-RELATED LEGISLATION. United States Congress, House Committee on Energy and Commerce. Superintendent of Documents, United States Government Printing Office, Washington, D.C. 20402. 1987- .

LOOSELEAF SERVICES AND REPORTERS

NUCLEAR REGULATION REPORTER. Commerce Clearing House, Incorporated, 4025 West Peterson Avenue, Chicago, Illinois 60646. 1975- .

TEXTBOOKS AND GENERAL WORKS

CONTROLLING THE ATOM: THE BEGINNINGS OF NUCLEAR REGULATION, 1946-1962. George T. Mazuzan and J. Samuel Walker. University of California Press, 2120 Berkeley Way, Berkeley, California 94720. 1985.

ENERGY LAW IN A NUTSHELL. Joseph P. Tomain. West Publishing Company, P.O. Box 64526, 50 West Kellogg Boulevard, St. Paul, Minnesota 55164-0526. 1981.

FOREVERMORE: NUCLEAR WASTE IN AMERICA. Donald L. Barlett and James B. Steele. William W. Norton and Company, Incorporated, 500 Fifth Avenue, New York, New York 10110. 1986.

INSURING NUCLEAR POWER: LIABILITY, SAFETY AND ECONOMIC EFFICIENCY. William C. Wood. JAI Press, Incorporated, 55 Old Post Road, Number 2, P.O. Box 1678, Greenwich, Connecticut 06830. 1983.

NUCLEAR ENERGY LAW AFTER CHERNOBYL. Peter Cameron, Leigh Hancher and Wolfgang Kuhn. Graham and Trotman, Boston, Massachusetts. 1988.

NUCLEAR ERA, ITS HISTORY, ITS IMPLICATIONS. Carl G. Jacobson. Oelgeschlager, Gunn and Hain, Incorporated, 245 Mirriam Street, Weston, Massachusetts 02193. 1982.

NUCLEAR LITIGATION, 1984. Thomas W. Evans, Chairman. Practising Law Institute, 810 Seventh Avenue, New York, New York 10019. 1984.

NUCLEAR NON-PROLIFERATION AND GLOBAL SECURITY. David Dewitt, Editor. Saint Martin's Press, Incorporated, 175 Fifth Avenue, New York, New York 10010. 1987.

NUCLEAR POWER AND PUBLIC POLICY: THE SOCIAL AND ETHICAL PROBLEMS OF FISSION TECHNOLOGY. Second Edition. Kristin S. Shrader-Frenchette. Kluwer Academic Publishers, 101 Philip Drive, Assinippi Park, Norwell, Massachusetts 02061. 1983.

NUCLEAR POWER: ASSESSING AND MANAGING HAZARDOUS TECHNOLOGY. Martin J. Pasqualetti and K. David Pijawka, Editors. Westview Press, 5500 Central Avenue, Boulder, Colorado 80301. 1984.

NUCLEAR POWER: BOTH SIDES: THE BEST ARGUMENTS FOR AND AGAINST THE MOST CONTROVERSIAL TECH-NOLOGY. Michio Kaku and Jennifer Trainer. William W. Norton and Company, Incorporated, 500 Fifth Avenue, New York, New York 10110. 1983.

NUCLEAR POWER TRANSFORMATION. Joseph P. Tomain. Indiana University Press, Tenth and Morton Streets, Bloomington, Indiana 47405. 1987.

THE STATE AND NUCLEAR POWER: CONFLICT AND CONTEST IN THE WESTERN WORLD. Joseph A. Camilleri. University of Washington Press, P.O. Box 50096, Seattle, Washington 98145-5096. 1984.

TERRORISM IN THE UNITED STATES AND THE POTENTIAL THREAT TO NUCLEAR FACILITIES. Bruce Hoffman. The Rand Corporation, 1700 Main Street, P.O. Box 2138, Santa Monica, California 90406. 1986.

TOO HOT TO HANDLE?: SOCIAL POLICY ISSUES IN THE MANAGEMENT OF RADIOACTIVE WASTES. Charles A. Walker, Leroy C. Gould, and Edward J. Woodhouse, Editors. Yale University Press, 302 Temple Street, New Haven, Connecticut 06520. 1983.

WHOOPS!/ WPPSS: WASHINGTON PUBLIC POWER SUPPLY SYSTEM NUCLEAR PLANTS. David Myhra. McFarland and Company, Incorporated, P.O. Box 611, Jefferson, North Carolina 28640. 1984.

LAW REVIEWS AND PERIODICALS

ATOMIC ENERGY LAW JOURNAL. Research Institute of America, Incorporated, One Penn Plaza, New York, New York 10119. Quarterly.

JOURNAL OF ENERGY LAW AND POLICY. University of Utah, College of Law, Salt Lake City, Utah 84112. Semiannual.

NUCLEAR AND CHEMICAL WASTE MANAGEMENT. Pergamon Press, Incorporated, Maxwell House, Fairview Park, Elmsford, New York 10523. Quarterly.

NEWSLETTERS AND NEWSPAPERS

ATOMIC ENERGY CLEARINGHOUSE. Congressional Information Bureau, Incorporated, 1325 G Street, Northwest, Washington, D.C. 20005. Weekly.

CHEMICAL WASTE LITIGATION REPORTER. Law Reporters, 1519 Connecticut Avenue, Northwest, Suite 200, Washington, D.C. 20036. Monthly.

INSIDE N.R.C. McGraw-Hill, Incorporated, 1221 Avenue of the Americas, New York, New York 10020. Biweekly.

NUCLEAR LICENSING REPORTS. Central Publishing Company, P.O. Box 10866, Rockville, Maryland 20849. Monthly.

NUCLEAR WASTE NEWS. Business Publishers, Incorporated, 951 Pershing Drive, Silver Spring, Maryland 20910. Weekly.

UTILITIES INDUSTRY LITIGATION REPORTER. Andrews Publications, 1646 West Chester Pike, Westtown, Pennsylvania 13935. Semimonthly.

WASHINGTON ATOMIC ENERGY REPORT. Reynolds Publishing Company, Incorporated, P.O. Box 738, Glen Echo, Maryland 20812. Biweekly.

BIBLIOGRAPHIES

ENVIRONMENTAL HAZARDS, RADIOACTIVE MATERIALS AND WASTES: BIBLIOGRAPHY. E. Willard Miller and Ruby M. Miller. Vance Bibliographies, P.O. Box 229, 112 North Charter Street, Monticello, Illinois 61856. 1985.

NUCLEAR ENERGY AND PUBLIC SAFETY. Michael R. Gabriel. CPL Bibliographies, 1313 East Sixtieth Street, Merriam Center, Chicago, Illinois 60637-2897. 1982.

PRICE-ANDERSON ACT: A BIBLIOGRAPHY OF PRIMARY AND SECONDARY SOURCES. Wallis D. Hoffsis and Martha J. Birchfield. Vance Bibliographies, P.O. Box 229, 112 North Charter Street, Monticello, Illinois 61856. 1990.

DIRECTORIES

AMERICAN NUCLEAR SOCIETY MEMBERSHIP LIST. American Nuclear Society, 555 North Kensington Avenue, LaGrange Park, Illinois 60525. Annual.

CURRENT MEMBERSHIP OF THE JOINT COMMITTEE ON ATOMIC ENERGY: MEMBERSHIP, PUBLICATIONS, AND OTHER PERTINENT INFORMATION. United States Congress, Joint Committee on Atomic Energy, Capitol Building, Washington, D.C. 20510. Annual.

DIRECTORY OF NUCLEAR REACTORS. International Atomic Energy Agency. Available from Unipub, Incorporated, 4611-F Assembly Drive, Lanham, Maryland 20706-4391. Irregular.

ASSOCIATIONS AND PROFESSIONAL SOCIETIES

AMERICAN NUCLEAR ENERGY COUNCIL. 410 First Street, Southeast, Washington, D.C. 20003. (202) 484-2670.

EDUCATIONAL FOUNDATION FOR NUCLEAR SCIENCE. 6042 South Kimbark, Chicago, Illinois 60637. (312) 702-2555.

FEDERAL ENERGY BAR ASSOCIATION. c/o Lorna Wilson, 1900 M Street, Northwest, Suite 620, Washington, D.C. 20036. (202) 223-5625.

NUCLEAR INFORMATION AND RESOURCE SERVICE. 1424 Sixteenth Street, Northwest, Suite 601, Washington, D.C. 20036. (202) 328-0002.

NUKEWATCH. P.O. Box 2658, Madison, Wisconsin 53701. (608) 256-4146.

OAK RIDGE ASSOCIATED UNIVERSITIES. P.O. Box 117, Oak Ridge, Tennessee 37831. (615) 576-3300.

UNION OF CONCERNED SCIENTISTS. 26 Church Street, Cambridge, Massachusetts 02238. (617) 547-5552.

UNITED STATES COUNCIL FOR ENERGY AWARENESS. 1776 Eye Street, Northwest, Suite 400, Washington, D.C. 20006. (202) 293-0770.

RESEARCH CENTERS, INSTITUTES, CLEARINGHOUSES

BROOKHAVEN NATIONAL LABORATORY. Upton, Long Island, New York 11973. (516) 282-2123.

ENVIRONMENTAL POLICY INSTITUTE. 218 D Street, Southeast, Washington, D.C. 20003. (202) 544-2600.

INSTITUTE OF NUCLEAR SCIENCE AND ENGINEERING. Oregon State University, Radiation Center-A100, Corvalis, Oregon 97331. (502) 737-2341.

LOS ALAMOS NATIONAL LABORATORY. P.O. Box 1663, Los Alamos, New Mexico 87545. (505) 667-5061.

MICHIGAN MEMORIAL-PHOENIX PROJECT. University of Michigan, Phoenix Memorial Laboratory, North Campus, Ann Arbor, Michigan 48109. (313) 764-6213.

NATURAL RESOURCES DEFENSE COUNCIL. 40 West Twentieth Street, Suite 300, New York, New York 10011. (212) 727-2700.

NUCLEAR FUEL CYCLE RESEARCH PROGRAM. University of Arizona, Department of Nuclear and Energy Engineering, Tucson, Arizona 85721. (602) 626-4985.

NUCLEAR ENERGY

POWER INFORMATION CENTER. Interagency Advanced Power Group, 1400 Eye Street, Northwest, Suite 600, Washington, D.C. 10005. (202) 842-7600.

PUBLIC CITIZEN CRITICAL MASS ENERGY PROJECT. 215 Pennsylvania Avenue, Southeast, Washington, D.C. 20003. (202) 546-4996.

ONLINE DATA BASES

INSIDE N.R.C. McGraw-Hill, Incorporated, 1221 Avenue of the Americas, New York, New York 10020.

NUCLEAR FUEL. McGaw-Hill, Incorporated, 1221 Avenue of the Americas, New York, New York 10020.

NUCLEAR SAFETY INFORMATION CENTER. Oak Ridge National Laboratory, Nuclear Safety Information Center, P.O. Box Y, Oak Ridge Tennessee, 37830.

NUCLEAR SCIENCE ABSTRACTS: NUCLEAR SCIENCE ABSTRACTS II. United States Department of Energy, Office of Scientific and Technical Information, P.O. Box 62, Oak Ridge, Tennessee 37831.

NUCLEAR WASTE NEWS. Business Publishers, Incorporated, 951 Pershing Drive, Silver Spring, Maryland 20910.

NUCLEONICS WEEK. McGraw-Hill, Incorporated, 1221 Avenue of the Americas, New York, New York 10020.

NUCLEAR REGULATORY COMMISSION
See also: ENERGY DEPARTMENT

STATUTES, CODES, STANDARDS, UNIFORM LAWS

CODE OF FEDERAL REGULATIONS, TITLE 10. Office of the Federal Register, National Archives and Records Administration. Superintendent of Documents, United States Government Printing Office, Washington, D.C. 20402. Annual. (Updated by use of monthly List of Sections Affected and daily Federal Register .)

LOOSELEAF SERVICES AND REPORTERS

NUCLEAR REGULATION REPORTS. Commerce Clearing House, Incorporated, 4025 West Peterson Avenue, Chicago, Illinois 60646. 1975- .

NUCLEAR REGULATORY COMMISSION ISSUANCES, OPINIONS AND DECISIONS OF THE NUCLEAR REGULATORY COMMISSION WITH SELECTED ORDERS. Nuclear Regulatory Commission. Superintendent of Documents, United States Government Printing Office, Washington, D.C. 20402. Monthly.

TEXTBOOKS AND GENERAL WORKS

SEABROOK AND THE NUCLEAR REGULATORY COMMISSION: THE LICENSING OF A NUCLEAR POWER PLANT. Donald W. Stever. University Press of New England, Seventeen Lebanon Street, Hanover, New Hampshire 03755. 1980.

Encyclopedia of Legal Information Sources • 2nd Ed.

DIGESTS, INDEXES, ABSTRACTS, CITATORS

SAFEGUARDS SUMMARY EVENTS LIST. Nuclear Regulatory Commission. Superintendent of Documents, United States Government Printing Office, Washington, D.C. 20402. 1983. (Semiannual Supplements).

LAW REVIEWS AND PERIODICALS

ENFORCEMENT ACTIONS: SIGNIFICANT ACTIONS RESOLVED. Nuclear Regulatory Commission. Superintendent of Documents, United States Government Printing Office, Washington, D.C. 20402. Quarterly.

LICENSED FUEL FACILITY STATUS REPORT. Nuclear Regulatory Commission. Superintendent of Documents, United States Government Printing Office, Washington, D.C. 20402. Semiannual.

LICENSEE, CONTRACTOR AND VENDOR INSPECTION STATUS REPORT. Nuclear Regulatory Commission. Superintendent of Documents, United States Government Printing Office, Washington, D.C. 20402. Quarterly.

NRC REGULATORY AGENDA. Nuclear Regulatory Commission. Superintendent of Documents, United States Government Printing Office, Washington, D.C. 20402. Quarterly.

OPERATING REACTORS LICENSING ACTIONS SUMMARY. Nuclear Regulatory Commission. Superintendent of Documents, United States Government Printing Office, Washington, D.C. 20402. Monthly.

POWER REACTOR EVENTS. Nuclear Regulatory Commission. Superintendent of Documents, United States Government Printing Office, Washington, D.C. 20402. Bimonthly.

REGULATORY AND TECHNICAL REPORTS. Nuclear Regulatory Commission. Superintendent of Documents, United States Government Printing Office, Washington, D.C. 20402. Quarterly.

REPORT TO CONGRESS ON ABNORMAL OCCURRENCES. Nuclear Regulatory Commission. Superintendent of Documents, United States Government Printing Office, Washington, D.C. 20402. Quarterly.

TOPICAL REPORT REVIEW STATUS. Nuclear Regulatory Commission. Superintendent of Documents, United States Government Printing Office, Washington, D.C. 20402. Semiannual.

UNITED STATES NUCLEAR REGULATORY COMMISSION. Nuclear Regulatory Commission. Superintendent of Documents, United States Government Printing Office, Washington, D.C. 20402.

UNRESOLVED SAFETY ISSUES SUMMARY. Nuclear Regulatory Commission. Superintendent of Documents, United States Government Printing Office, Washington, D.C. 20402. Quarterly.

NEWSLETTERS AND NEWSPAPERS

INSIDE N.R.C. McGraw-Hill Publishing Company, 1221 Avenue of the Americas, New York, New York 10020.

UNITED STATES NUCLEAR REGULATORY COMMISSION'S NEWS RELEASES. Nuclear Regulatory Commission. Superintendent of Documents, United States Government Printing Office, Washington, D.C. 20402. Weekly.

WEEKLY INFORMATION REPORT. Nuclear Regulatory Commission. Superintendent of Documents, United States Government Printing Office, Washington, D.C. 20402. Weekly.

RESEARCH CENTERS, INSTITUTES, CLEARINGHOUSES

UNITED STATES NUCLEAR REGULATORY COMMISSION LAW LIBRARY. 7735 Old Georgetown Road, Room 9110, Washington, D.C. 20814. (301) 492-0240.

ONLINE DATABASES

INSIDE N.R.C. McGraw-Hill Publishing Company, 1221 Avenue of the Americas, New York, New York 10020.

LEXIS, ENERGY LIBRARY. Mead Data Central, P.O. Box 933, Dayton, Ohio 45401.

WESTLAW, ENERGY AND UTILITIES LIBRARY. West Publishing Company, P.O. Box 64526, 50 West Kellogg Boulevard, St. Paul, Minnesota 55164-0526.

NUISANCE
See: TORTS

NURSES AND NURSING
See also: AGED AND HEALTH CARE; HEALTH CARE; HOSPITALS; MEDICAL JURISPRUDENCE AND MALPRACTICE; NURSING HOMES

STATUTES, CODES, STANDARDS, UNIFORM LAWS

SUGGESTED STATE LEGISLATION NURSING PRACTICE ACT, NURSING DISCIPLINARY DIVERSION ACT, PRESCRIPTIVE AUTHORITY ACT. American Nurses' Association. Cabinet on Nursing Practice, 2420 Pershing Road, Kansas City, Missouri 64108. 1990.

LOOSELEAF SERVICES AND REPORTERS

DIRECTOR OF NURSING MANUAL: FEDERAL REGULATIONS AND GUIDELINES. Mark L. Kander and Kenneth May. National Law and Health Publishing Corporations, 99 Painters Mill Road, Owing Mills, Maryland 21117. 1980- .

NURSING CASE LAW REPORTER. Elizabeth Hogue. National Law Publishing Corporation, 99 Painters Mill Road, Owing Mills, Maryland 21117. 1983- .

PROFESSIONAL LIABILITY REPORTER. Litigation Research Group, P.O. Box 77903, San Francisco, California 94107. 1985- .

HANDBOOKS, MANUALS, FORMBOOKS

THE LAW AND LIABILITY: A GUIDE FOR NURSES. Second Edition. Janine Fiesta. John Wiley and Sons, Incorporated, 605 Third Avenue, New York, New York 10158. 1988.

LEGAL ISSUES IN NURSING: A SOURCE BOOK FOR PRACTICE. Ginny Wacker Guido. Appleton and Lange, 25 Van Zant Street, East Norwalk, Connecticut 06855. 1988.

THE NURSE'S LEGAL ADVISOR: YOUR GUIDE TO LEGALLY SAFE PRACTICE. Arnold S. Goldstein, Sue Perdew and Susan S. Pruitt. J.B. Lippincott Company, East Washington Square, Philadelphia, Pennsylvania 19105. 1989.

NURSE'S LEGAL HANDBOOK. Reginia D. Ford. Springhouse Corporation, 1111 Bethlehem Pike, Springhouse, Pennsylvania 19477. 1985.

NURSING ADMINISTRATION AND LAW MANUAL. Karen Henry, Editor. Aspen Publishers, Incorporated, 1600 Research Boulevard, Rockville, Maryland 20850. 1985.

TEXTBOOKS AND GENERAL WORKS

ETHICAL AND LEGAL ASPECTS OF NURSING. Joseph T. Catalano and Susan Griffin. Springhouse Corporation, 1111 Bethlehem Pike, Springhouse, Pennsylvania 19477. 1991.

ETHICAL DILEMMAS AND NURSING PRACTICE. Second Edition. Anne J. Davis and Mila A. Aroskar. Appleton and Lange, 25 Van Zant Street, East Norwalk, Connecticut 06855. 1991.

THE LAW AND LIABILITY: A GUIDE FOR NURSES. Second Edition. Janine Fiesta. Delmar Publishers, Incorporated, P.O. Box 15015, Two Computer Drive West, Albany, New York 12212. 1988.

LEGAL ACCOUNTABILITY IN THE NURSING PROCESS. Second Edition. Irene A. Murchison, Thomas S. Nichols, and Rachel Hanson. C. V. Mosby and Company, 11830 Westline Industrial Drive, St. Louis, Missouri 63146. 1982.

THE LEGAL DIMENSIONS OF NURSING PRACTICE. Laverne R. Rocereto and Cynthia M. Maleski. Springer Publishing Company, Incorporated, 536 Broadway, New York, New York 10012. 1982.

LEGAL ISSUES AND GUIDELINES FOR NURSES WHO CARE FOR THE MENTALLY ILL. Joyce K. Laben and Colleen P. MacLean. Slack Incorporated, 6900 Grove Road, Thorofare, New Jersey 08086-9447. 1984.

LEGAL ISSUES FOR NURSE EDUCATORS. Ellen K. Murphy. Professional Education Systems, Incorporated, 200 Spring Street, Eau Claire, Wisconsin 54702. 1987.

LEGAL ISSUES IN NURSING. Cynthia E. Northrop and Mary E. Kelly. C.V. Mosby Company, 11830 Westline Industrial Drive, St. Louis, Missouri 63146. 1987.

LEGAL ISSUES IN SUPERVISING NURSES. Third Edition. J. Michael Kota and Jeanne M. Martoglio. PESI Legal Publishing, 200 Spring Street, Eau Claire, Wisconsin 54702. 1991.

NURSES AND NURSING

MALPRACTICE AND LIABILITY IN CLINICAL OBSTETRICAL NURSING. Sarah D. Cohn. Aspen Publishers, Incorporated, 1600 Research Boulevard, Rockville, Maryland 20850. 1990.

THE NURSE ANESTHETIST AND THE LAW. Mary J. Mannino. Grune and Statton. Curtis Center, Independence Square, West, Philadelphia, Pennsylvania 19106-3399. 1982.

THE NURSE MANAGER AND THE LAW. Carmelle Pellerin Cournoyer. Aspen Publishers, Incorporated, 1600 Research Boulevard, Rockville, Maryland 20850. 1989.

THE NURSE'S LIABILITY FOR MALPRACTICE: A PROGRAMMED COURSE. Fourth Edition. Eli P. Bernzweig. Shepard's/McGraw-Hill, P.O. Box 1235, Colorado Springs, Colorado 80901. 1987.

NURSING AND THE LAW. Fourth Edition. Ann M. Rhodes and Robert D. Miller. Aspen Systems Corporation, 1600 Research Boulevard, Rockville, Maryland 20850. 1984.

NURSING AND THE LAW. Third Edition. Sheryl A. Feutz and Sue Dill Calloway. Professional Education Systems, Incorporated, 200 Spring Street, Eau Claire, Wisconsin 54702. 1989.

NURSING JURISPRUDENCE. Mary Cushing. Appleton and Lange, 25 Van Zant Street, East Norwalk, Connecticut 06855. 1988.

REGULATING BIRTHS: MIDWIVES, MEDICINE, AND THE LAW. Raymond G. DeVries. Temple University Press, 1601 North Broad Street, Student Services Building, Philadelphia, Pennsylvania 19122. 1985.

LAW REVIEWS AND PERIODICALS

JOURNAL OF CONTEMPORARY HEALTH LAW AND POLICY. The Catholic University of America, Columbus School of Law, 620 Michigan Avenue, Northeast, Washington, D.C. 20064. Annual.

NEWSLETTERS AND NEWSPAPERS

EMERGENCY NURSE LEGAL BULLETIN. Med/Law Publishers, Incorporated, P.O. Box 293, Westville, New Jersey 08093. Quarterly.

LEGISLATIVE NETWORK FOR NURSES. Business Publshers, Incorporated, 951 Pershing Drive, Silver Spring, Maryland 20910. Biweekly.

REGAN REPORT ON NURSING LAW. Medica Press, Incorporated, 1231 Fleet National Bank Building, Providence, Rhode Island 02903. Monthly.

DIRECTORIES

THE AMERICAN ASSOCIATION OF NURSE ATTORNEYS, 1985 MEMBERSHIP DIRECTORY. Second Edition. 720 Light Street, Baltimore, Maryland 21230-3816. 1985.

NATIONAL NURSING DIRECTORY. Kenneth E. Lawrence and Howard S. Rowland, Editors. Aspen Publishers, Incorporated, 1600 Research Boulevard, Rockville, Maryland 20850. 1982.

ASSOCIATIONS AND PROFESSIONAL SOCIETIES

AMERICAN ASSOCIATION OF LEGAL NURSE CONSULTANTS. P.O. Box 2822, San Diego, California 92112. (619) 699-2587.

AMERICAN ASSOCIATION OF NURSE ATTORNEYS. 113 West Franklin Street, Baltimore, Maryland 21201. (301) 752-3318.

AMERICAN NURSES ASSOCIATION. 2420 Pershing Road, Kansas City, Missouri 64108. (816) 474-5720.

AMERICAN NURSES' FOUNDATION. 600 Maryland Avenue, Southwest, Suite 100 West, Washington D.C. 20024-2571. (202) 554-4444.

FEDERATION OF NURSES AND HEALTH PROFESSIONALS. 555 New Jersey Avenue, Northwest, Washington, D.C. 20001. (202) 879-4491.

RESEARCH CENTERS, INSTITUTES, CLEARINGHOUSES

CENTER FOR NURSING AND HEALTH SERVICES RESEARCH. University of Maryland, 655 West Lombard Street, Baltimore, Maryland 21201. (301) 328-7848.

CENTER FOR NURSING RESEARCH. Ohio State University, 1585 Neil Avenue, Columbus, Ohio 43210. (614) 292-9292.

CENTER FOR NURSING RESEARCH. University of Michigan, 400 North Ingalls, Room 4457, Ann Arbor, Michigan 48109. (313) 764-9554.

CENTER FOR NURSING RESEARCH. University of Texas at Arlington, P.O. Box 19407, Arlington, Texas 76019. (817) 273-2776.

CENTER FOR NURSING RESEARCH AND EVALUATION. University of Wisconsin, Milwaukee, P.O. Box 413, 1909 East Hartford Avenue, Milwaukee, Wisconsin 53201. (414) 229-5647.

DEPARTMENT OF NURSING RESEARCH AND EDUCATION. City of Hope National Medical Center, 1500 East Duarte Road, Duarte, California 91010. (213) 359-8111.

ONLINE DATABASES

NURSING AND ALLIED HEALTH DATABASE. Cinahl Corporation, 1509 Wilson Terrace, P.O. Box 871, Glendale, California 91209.

NURSING HOMES
See also: HEALTH CARE; HOSPITALS; MEDICAL JURISPRUDENCE AND MALPRACTICE

LOOSELEAF SERVICES AND REPORTERS

PROFESSIONAL LIABILITY REPORTER. Litigation Research Group, P.O. Box 77903, San Francisco, California 94107. 1980- .

REAL ESTATE DEVELOPMENT: LONG-TERM CARE AND RETIREMENT FACILITIES. Thomas C. Fox. Matthew Bender and Company, Incorporated, 11 Penn Plaza, New York, New York 10001. 1989- .

HANDBOOKS, MANUALS, FORMBOOKS

LONG-TERM CARE AND THE LAW: A LEGAL GUIDE FOR HEALTH CARE PROFESSIONALS. George D. Pozgar. Aspen Publishers, Incorporated, 1600 Research Boulevard, Rockville, Maryland 20850. 1992.

TEXTBOOKS AND GENERAL WORKS

LEGAL ASPECTS OF HOME HEALTH CARE. William D. Cabin and James C. Pyles. Aspen Publishers, Incorporated, 1600 Research Boulevard, Rockville, Maryland 20850. 1988.

NURSING HOMES AND THE LAW: STATE REGULATION AND PRIVATE LITIGATION. Sandra H. Johnson, Nicholas P. Terry, and Michael A. Wolff. Harrison Company, 3110 Crossing Park, Norcross, Georgia 30091. 1985.

PREVENTING MALPRACTICE IN LONG-TERM CARE: STRATEGIES FOR RISK MANAGEMENT. Marshall B. Kapp. Springer Publishing Company, 536 Broadway, New York, New York 10012. 1987.

RESOLVING GRIEVANCES IN THE NURSING HOME: A STUDY OF THE OMBUDSMAN PROGRAM. Abraham Monk, Lenard W. Kaye, and Howard Litwin. Columbia University Press, 562 West 113th Street, New York, New York 10025. 1984.

NEWSLETTERS AND NEWSPAPERS

AHCA NOTES. American Health Care Association, 1201 L Street, Northwest, Washington, D.C. 20005. Semimonthly.

NURSING HOME LAW LETTER. National Senior Citizens Law Center, 1424 Sixteenth Street, Northwest, Suite 300, Washington, D.C. 20036. Monthly.

DIRECTORIES

DIRECTORY OF NURSING HOMES. Oryx Press, 2214 North Central, Phoenix, Arizona 85004-1483. 1984.

NURSING HOME DIRECTORY. American Business Directories, Incorporated, 5639 South Eighty-sixth Circle, Omaha, Nebraska 68127. Annual.

ASSOCIATIONS AND PROFESSIONAL SOCIETIES

AMERICAN ASSOCIATION OF HOMES FOR THE AGING. 1129 Twentieth Street, Northwest, Suite 400, Washington, D.C. 20036. (202) 296-5960.

AMERICAN COLLEGE OF NURSING HOME ADMINISTRATORS. 325 South Patrick Street, Alexandria, Virginia 22314. (703) 549-5822.

AMERICAN HEALTH CARE ASSOCIATION. 1201 L Street, Northwest, Washington, D.C. 20005. (202) 842-4444.

NURSING HOME ADVISORY AND RESEARCH COUNCIL. P.O. Box 18820, Cleveland Heights, Ohio 44118. (216) 321-0403.

NURSING HOME INFORMATION SERVICE. c/o National Council of Senior Citizens, 925 Fifteenth Street, Northwest, Washington, D.C. 20005. (202) 347-8800.

RESEARCH CENTERS, INSTITUTES, CLEARINGHOUSES

SONDEREGGER RESEARCH CENTER. University of Wisconsin, Madison, School of Pharmacy, 425 North Charter Street, Madison, Wisconsin 53706. (608) 263-9664.

O

OBSCENITY

See also: ATTORNEY GENERAL (UNITED STATES); JUSTICE DEPARTMENT

LOOSELEAF SERVICES AND REPORTERS

NATIONAL DECENCY REPORTER. Children's Legal Foundation, 2845 East Camelback Road, Suite 740, Phoenix, Arizona 85016. Bimonthly. 1965- .

HANDBOOKS, MANUALS, FORMBOOKS

THE PREPARATION AND TRIAL OF AN OBSCENITY CASE: A GUIDE FOR THE PROSECUTING ATTORNEY: CDL PROSECUTOR'S MANUAL. Second Edition. Children's Legal Foundation, 2845 East Camelback Road, Suite 740, Phoenix, Arizona. 1988.

SOURCEBOOK ON PORNOGRAPHY. Franklin Mark Osanka and Sara Lee Johann. Lexington Books, 125 Spring Street, Lexington, Massachusetts 02173. 1989.

TEXTBOOKS AND GENERAL WORKS

FEMINISM AND PORNOGRAPHY. Ronald J. Berger, Patricia Searles and Charles E. Cottle. Praeger Publishers, One Madison Avenue, New York, New York 10010-3603. 1991.

FOR ADULT USERS ONLY: THE DILEMMA OF VIOLENT PORNOGRAPHY. Susan Gubar and Joan Hoff, Editors. Indiana University Press, Tenth and Morton Streets, Bloomington, Indiana 47405. 1989.

FREEDOM AND TABOO: PORNOGRAPHY AND THE POLITICS OF A SELF DIVIDED. Richard S. Randall. University of California Press, 2120 Berkeley Way, Berkeley, California 94720. 1989.

GIRLS LEAN BACK EVERYWHERE: THE LAW OF OBSCENITY AND THE ASSAULT ON GENIUS. Edward DeGrazia. Random House, Incorporated, 201 East Fiftieth Street, New York, New York 10022. 1992.

THE INFLUENCE OF PORNOGRAPHY ON BEHAVIOR. Maurice Yaffe and Edward C. Nelson, Editors. Academic Press, Incorporated, 1250 Sixth Avenue, San Diego, California 92101. 1983.

THE NEW POLITICS OF PORNOGRAPHY. Donald Alexander Downs. University of Chicago Press, 5801 Ellis Avenue, Chicago, Illinois 60637. 1989.

THE POLITICS OF OBSCENITY: GROUP LITIGATION IN A TIME OF LEGAL CHANGE. Joseph F. Kobylka. Greenwood Publishing Group, Incorporated, 88 Post Road West, P.O. Box 5007, Westport, Connecticut 06881. 1991.

PORNOGRAPHY AND CENSORSHIP. David Copp and Susan Wendell, Editors. Prometheus Books, 700 East Amherst Street, Buffalo, New York 14215. 1982.

PORNOGRAPHY AND CIVIL RIGHTS: A NEW DAY FOR WOMEN'S EQUALITY. Andrea Dworkin and Catharine A. MacKinnon. Organizing Against Pornography, 734 East Lake Street, Minneapolis, Minnesota 55407. 1988.

PORNOGRAPHY IN A FREE SOCIETY. Gordon Hawkins and Franklin E. Zimring. Cambridge University Press, 40 West Twentieth Street, New York, New York 10011. 1988.

PORNOGRAPHY, OBSCENITY AND THE LAW. Lester A. Sobel, Editor. Facts on File, Incorporated, 460 Park Avenue South, New York, New York 10016. 1979.

THE UNITED STATES OF AMERICA VERSES ONE BOOK ENTITLED ULYSSES BY JAMES JOYCE: DOCUMENTS AND COMMENTARY: 50-YEAR RETROSPECTIVE. Michael Moscato and Leslie Leblanc, Editors. Greenwood Publishing Group, Incorporated, 88 Post Road West, P.O. Box 5007, Westport, Connecticut 06881. 1984.

DIGESTS, INDEXES, ABSTRACTS, CITATORS

BRIEF BANK INDEX. National Obscenity Law Center, 475 Riverside Drive, New York, New York 10115.

LAW REVIEWS AND PERIODICALS

BACKLASH TIMES. Feminists Fighting Pornography, P.O. Box 6731, Yorkville Station, New York, New York 10128. Annual.

NEWSLETTERS AND NEWSPAPERS

MORALITY IN MEDIA NEWSLETTER. Morality in Media, 475 Riverside Drive, New York, New York 10115. Bimonthly.

OBSCENITY LAW BULLETIN. National Obscenity Law Center, 475 Riverside Drive, New York, New York 10115. Bimonthly.

WAVAW NEWSLETTER. Women Against Violence Against Women, 543 North Fairfax Avenue, Los Angeles, California 90036. Quarterly.

OBSCENITY

WOMEN AGAINST PORNOGRAPHY--NEWSREPORT. Women Against Pornography, 358 West Forty-seventh Street, New York, New York 10036. Quarterly.

BIBLIOGRAPHIES

FEMINISTS, PORNOGRAPHY AND THE LAW: AN ANNOTATED BIBLIOGRAPHY OF CONFLICT, 1970-1986. Betty-Carol Sellen and Patricia A. Young. Library Professional Publications, Hamden, Connecticut. 1987.

OBSCENITY, PORNOGRAPHY, AND LIBRARIES: A SELECTIVE BIBLIOGRAPHY. John O. Christensen. Vance Bibliographies, P.O. Box 229, 112 North Charter Street, Monticello, Illinois 61856. 1991.

ASSOCIATIONS AND PROFESSIONAL SOCIETIES

CITIZENS FOR MEDIA RESPONSIBILITY WITHOUT LAW. P.O. Box 398, Oak Ridge, North Carolina 27310. (408) 427-2858.

CRUSADE FOR DECENCY. c/o Mrs. Billie Lasker, Cathedral Towers, 325 North Newstead Avenue, St. Louis, Missouri 63108. (314) 644-0354.

FEMINISTS FIGHTING PORNOGRAPHY. P.O. Box 6731, Yorkville Station, New York, New York 10128. (212) 410-5182.

MORALITY IN MEDIA. 475 Riverside Drive, New York, New York 10115. (212) 870-3222.

WOMEN AGAINST PORNOGRAPHY. 358 West Forty-seventh Street, New York, New York 10036. (212) 307-5055.

WOMEN AGAINST VIOLENCE AGAINST WOMEN. 543 North Fairfax Avenue, Los Angeles, California 90036. (213) 658-8350.

RESEARCH CENTERS, INSTITUTES, CLEARINGHOUSES

NATIONAL OBSCENITY LAW CENTER. 475 Riverside Drive, New York, New York 10115. (212) 870-3222.

TARLTON LAW LIBRARY. University of Texas at Austin, 727 East Twenty-sixth Street, Austin, Texas 78705. (Maintains limited access collection of materials that have been the subject of obscenity litigation). (512) 471-7726.

OCCUPATIONAL DISEASES
See: OCCUPATIONAL SAFETY AND HEALTH

OCCUPATIONAL SAFETY AND HEALTH
See also: EMPLOYEES' COMPENSATION APPEALS BOARD; FEDERAL MINE SAFETY AND HEALTH REVIEW COMMISSION; HAZARDOUS SUBSTANCES; LABOR DEPARTMENT; OCCUPATIONAL SAFETY AND HEALTH ADMINISTRATION; OCCUPATIONAL SAFETY AND HEALTH REVIEW COMMISSION

STATUTES, CODES, STANDARDS, UNIFORM LAWS

CHEMICAL GUIDE TO THE OSHA HAZARD COMMUNICATION STANDARD. Kenneth B. Clansky, Editor. Roytech Publications, 7910 Woodmont Avenue, Suite 907, Bethesda, Maryland 20814. 1986.

OCCUPATIONAL SAFETY AND HEALTH STANDARDS FOR GENERAL INDUSTRY (29 CFR PART 1910): WITH AMENDMENTS AS OF JUNE 1, 1984: INCLUDING 29 CFR PART 1990, CARCINOGEN POLICY AND MODEL STANDARDS. Commerce Clearing House, Incorporated, 4025 West Peterson Avenue, Chicago, Illinois 60646. 1986.

OCCUPATIONAL SAFETY AND HEALTH STANDARDS FOR THE CONSTRUCTION INDUSTRY: (29 CFR PART 1926): WITH AMENDMENTS AS OF AUGUST 31, 1986. Commerce Clearing House, Incorporated, 4025 West Peterson Avenue, Chicago, Illinois 60646. 1986.

LOOSELEAF SERVICES AND REPORTERS

EMPLOYMENT SAFETY AND HEALTH GUIDE. Commerce Clearing House, Incorporated, 4025 West Peterson Avenue, Chicago, Illinois 60646. 1971- .

HOW TO CONDUCT SAFETY AND HEALTH AUDITS. Business and Legal Reports, Incorporated, 64 Wall Street, Madison, Connecticut 06443. 1991- .

JOB SAFETY AND HEALTH. Bureau of National Affairs, 1231 Twenty-fifth Street, Northwest, Washington, D.C. 20037. 1981- .

LABOR RELATIONS GUIDE WITH OSHA. Prentice-Hall, Incorporated, 113 Sylvan Avenue, Englewood Cliffs, New Jersey 07632. 1977- .

LEGAL GUIDE TO HANDLING TOXIC SUBSTANCES IN THE WORKPLACE. Lawrence P. Postol and William A. Hancock. Business Laws, Incorporated, 11630 Chillicothe Road, Chesterland, Ohio 44026. 1990- .

MINE SAFETY AND HEALTH REPORTER. Bureau of National Affairs, 1231 Twenty-fifth Street, Northwest, Washington, D.C. 20037. 1979- .

OCCUPATIONAL EXPOSURE GUIDE. J.J. Keller and Associates, P.O. Box 368, 145 West Wisconsin Avenue, Neenah, Wisconsin 54907-0368. 1985- .

OCCUPATIONAL SAFETY AND HEALTH ADMINISTRATION COMPLIANCE GUIDE. Commerce Clearing House, Incorporated, 4025 West Peterson Avenue, Chicago, Illinois 60646. 1977- .

OCCUPATIONAL SAFETY AND HEALTH REPORTER. Bureau of National Affairs, 1231 Twenty-fifth Street, Northwest, Washington, D.C. 20037. 1971- .

HANDBOOKS, MANUALS, FORMBOOKS

GENERAL INDUSTRY STANDARDS AND INTERPRETATIONS. United States Department of Labor, Occupational Health and Safety Administration. Superintendent of Documents, United States Government Printing Office, Washington, D.C. 20402. 1985.

HAZARD COMMUNICATION HANDBOOK: A RIGHT-TO-KNOW COMPLIANCE GUIDE. Craig A. Moyer and Michael A. Francis. Clark Boardman Company, Limited, 435 Hudson Street, New York, New York 10014. 1991.

HAZARD COMMUNICATIONS GUIDE: FEDERAL AND STATE RIGHT TO KNOW STANDARDS. J. J. Keller and Associates, 145 West Wisconsin Avenue, Neenah, Wisconsin 54907-0368. 1985.

HOW TO MANAGE WORKPLACE DERIVED HAZARDS AND AVOID LIABILITY. Charleston C.K. Wang. Noyes Publications, 120 Mill Road, Park Ridge, New Jersey 07656. 1987.

LOWRYS' HANDBOOK OF RIGHT-TO-KNOW AND EMERGENCY PLANNING: HANDBOOK OF COMPLIANCE FOR WORKER AND COMMUNITY, OSHA, EPA, AND THE STATES. George G. Lowry and Robert C. Lowry. Lewis Publishers, P.O. Drawer 519, 121 South Main Street, Chelsea, Michigan 48118. 1988.

OSHA FIELD OPERATIONS MANUAL. Second Edition. Government Institutes, Incorporated, 966 Hungerford Drive, Rockville, Maryland 20850. 1987.

OSHA HANDBOOK. Second Edition. Robert D. Moran. Government Institutes, Incorporated, 966 Hungerford Drive, Rockville, Maryland 20850. 1989.

A PRACTICAL GUIDE TO THE OCCUPATIONAL SAFETY AND HEALTH ACT. Walter B. Connolly Junior and Donald R. Crowell. Law Journal-Seminars Press, Incorporated, 111 Eighth Avenue, Suite 900, New York, New York 10011. 1982. (Periodic Supplements).

PRIMER ON OCCUPATIONAL SAFETY AND HEALTH. Fred Blosser. Bureau of National Affairs, Incorporated, 1231 Twenty-fifth Street, Northwest, Washington, D.C. 20037. 1992.

SAFETY PROGRAM ADMINISTRATION FOR ENGINEERS AND MANAGERS: A RESOURCE GUIDE FOR ESTABLISHING AND EVALUATING SAFETY PROGRAMS. Ted S. Ferry. Charles C. Thomas Publishing Company, 2600 South First Street, Springfield, Illinois, 62794-9265. 1984.

A WORKER'S GUIDE TO RIGHT TO KNOW ABOUT HAZARDS IN THE WORKPLACE. Marianne Parker Brown. University of California, Institute of Industrial Relations, Publications Center, 1001 Gayley Avenue, Second Floor, Los Angeles, California 90024-1478. 1987.

TEXTBOOKS AND GENERAL WORKS

CORPORATE DISCLOSURE OF ENVIRONMENTAL RISKS: U.S. AND EUROPEAN LAW. Michael S. Baram and Daniel G. Partan, Editors. Butterworth-Heinemann, 80 Montvale Avenue, Stoneham, Massachusetts 02180. 1990.

CRIMES AGAINST HEALTH AND SAFETY. Second Edition. Nancy Frank. Harrow and Heston, P.O. Box 3934, Stuyvesant Plaza, Albany, New York 12203. 1990.

ENVIRONMENTAL PROBLEMS ON THE JOBSITE. Inez Smith Reid and Judah Lifschitz. Federal Publications, 1120 Twentieth Street, Northwest, Washington, D.C. 20036. 1990.

HEARING CONSERVATION IN INDUSTRY. Alan S. Feldman and Charles I. Grimes. Krieger Publishing Company, Incorporated, P.O. Box 9542, Malabar, Florida 32902-9542. 1989.

THE LAW AND OCCUPATIONAL INJURY, DISEASE, AND DEATH. Warren Freedman. Quorum Books, Greenwood Publishing Group, Incorporated, 88 Post Road West, P.O. Box 5007, Westport, Connecticut 06881. 1990.

MEDICAL SCREENING AND THE EMPLOYEE HEALTH COST CRISIS. Mark A. Rothstein. Bureau of National Affairs, Incorporated, 1231 Twenty-fifth Street, Northwest, Washington, D.C. 20037. 1989.

OCCUPATIONAL SAFETY AND HEALTH ACT. Roscoe B. Hogan and R. Ben Hogan III, Editors. Matthew Bender and Company, Incorporated, 11 Penn Plaza, New York, New York 10001. 1984. (Annual Supplements).

OCCUPATIONAL SAFETY AND HEALTH ACT: HISTORY, LAW AND POLICY. Benjamin Minty. Bureau of National Affairs, 1231 Twenty-fifth Street, Northwest, Washington, D.C. 20037. 1984.

OCCUPATIONAL SAFETY AND HEALTH LAW. Third Edition. Mark A. Rothstein. West Publishing Company, 50 West Kellogg Boulevard, St. Paul, Minnesota 55164. 1990.

OCCUPATIONAL SAFETY AND HEALTH LAW. Stephen A. Bokat and Horace A. Thompson. Bureau of National Affairs, Incorporated, 1231 Twenty-fifth Street, Northwest, Washington, D.C. 20037. 1988.

OSHA 1988. Horace A. Thompson. Practising Law Institute, 810 Seventh Avenue, New York, New York 10019. 1988.

PERSONAL HEARING PROTECTION IN INDUSTRY. P.W. Alberti, Editor. Raven Press Publishers, 1185 Avenue of the Americas, New York, New York 10036. 1982.

REFORMING THE WORKPLACE: A STUDY OF SELF-REGULATION IN OCCUPATIONAL SAFETY. Joseph V. Rees. University of Pennsylvania Press, Blockley Hall, 418 Service Drive, Philadelphia, Pennsylvania 19104. 1988.

RISK BY CHOICE: REGULATING HEALTH AND SAFETY IN THE WORKPLACE. W. Kip Viscusi. Harvard University Press, 79 Garden Street, Cambridge, Massachusetts 02138. 1983.

STRESS IN THE WORKPLACE: COSTS, LIABILITY, AND PREVENTION. Bureau of National Affairs, Incorporated, 1231 Twenty-fifth Street, Northwest, Washington, D.C. 20037. 1987.

TECHNOLOGY, LAW, AND THE WORKING ENVIRONMENT. Nicholas Askounes Ashford and Charles C. Caldart. Van Nostrand Reinhold Company, Incorporated, 115 Fifth Avenue, New York, New York 10003. 1991.

WE OFFER OURSELVES AS EVIDENCE: TOWARD WORKERS' CONTROL OF OCCUPATIONAL HEALTH. Bennett M. Judkins. Greenwood Publishing Group, Incorporated, 88 Post Road West, P.O. Box 5007, Westport, Connecticut 06881. 1986.

OCCUPATIONAL SAFETY AND HEALTH

WORKERS' COMPENSATION AND WORKPLACE SAFETY: SOME LESSONS FROM ECONOMIC THEORY. Richard B. Vector, Linda Cohen, and Charles Phelps. Random House, Incorporated, 201 East Fiftieth Street, New York, New York 10022. 1982.

ENCYCLOPEDIAS AND DICTIONARIES

ENCYCLOPEDIA OF OCCUPATIONAL HEALTH AND SAFETY. Third Edition. International Labor Office, Sales Section, Suite 330 NOS, 1750 New York Avenue, Northwest, Washington, D.C. 20006. 1989.

DIGESTS, INDEXES, ABSTRACTS, CITATORS

SHEPARDS' FEDERAL OCCUPATIONAL SAFETY AND HEALTH CITATIONS. Shepard's/McGraw-Hill, P.O. Box 1235, Colorado Springs, Colorado 80901. 1981- .

NEWSLETTERS AND NEWSPAPERS

CONSTRUCTION INJURY LIABILITY MONTHLY. Business Publishers Incorporated, 951 Pershing Drive, Silver Spring, Maryland 20910. Monthly.

EMPLOYMENT SAFETY AND HEALTH GUIDE (SUMMARY). Commerce Clearing House, Incorporated, 4025 West Peterson Avenue, Chicago, Illinois 60646. Weekly.

INDUSTRIAL HEALTH AND HAZARDS UPDATE. Merton Allen Associates, P.O. Box 15640, Plantation, Florida 33318. Monthly.

INDUSTRIAL NEGLIGENCE LAW BULLETIN. Quinlan Publishing Company, Incorporated, 131 Beverly Street, Boston Massachusetts 02114. Monthly.

JOB SAFETY CONSULTANT. Business Research Publications, Incorporated, 817 Broadway, New York, New York 10003. Monthly.

OCCUPATIONAL HEALTH AND SAFETY LETTER. Business Publishers, Incorporated, 951 Pershing Drive, Silver Spring, Maryland 20910. Biweekly.

OSHA COMPLIANCE ADVISOR. Business and Legal Reports, 64 Wall Street, Madison, Connecticut 06443. Semimonthly.

OSHA TRAINING BULLETIN FOR SUPERVISORS. Business and Legal Reports, 64 Wall Street, Madison, Connecticut 06443. Monthly.

ASSOCIATIONS AND PROFESSIONAL SOCIETIES

INDUSTRIAL HEALTH FOUNDATION. 34 Penn Circle, West, Pittsburgh, Pennsylvania 15206. (412) 363-6600.

SOCIETY FOR OCCUPATIONAL AND ENVIRONMENTAL HEALTH. P.O. Box 42360, Washington, D.C. 20015. (202) 797-8666.

WOMEN'S OCCUPATIONAL HEALTH RESOURCE CENTER. 117 St. Johns Place, Brooklyn, New York 11217. (718) 230-8822.

OCCUPATIONAL SAFETY AND HEALTH ADMINISTRATION
See also: FEDERAL MINE SAFETY AND HEALTH REVIEW COMMISSION; OCCUPATIONAL SAFETY AND HEALTH REVIEW COMMISSION

STATUTES, CODES, STANDARDS, UNIFORM LAWS

CODE OF FEDERAL REGULATIONS, TITLE 29. Office of the Federal Register, National Archives and Records Administration. Superintendent of Documents, United States Government Printing Office, Washington, D.C. 20402. Annual. (Updated by use of monthly List of Sections Affected and daily Federal Register).

OCCUPATIONAL SAFETY AND HEALTH, VOLUME ONE, GENERAL INDUSTRY STANDARDS AND INTERPRETATIONS. Labor Department, Occupational Safety and Health Administration. Superintendent of Documents, United States Government Printing Office, Washington, D.C. 20402. 1977- .

OCCUPATIONAL SAFETY AND HEALTH, VOLUME TWO, MARITIME STANDARDS AND INTERPRETATIONS. Labor Department, Occupational Safety and Health Administration. Superintendent of Documents, United States Government Printing Office, Washington, D.C. 20402. 1985- .

OCCUPATIONAL SAFETY AND HEALTH, VOLUME THREE, CONSTRUCTION INDUSTRY STANDARDS AND INTERPRETATIONS. Labor Department, Occupational Safety and Health Administration. Superintendent of Documents, United States Government Printing Office, Washington, D.C. 20402. 1980- .

OCCUPATIONAL SAFETY AND HEALTH, VOLUME FOUR, OTHER REGULATIONS AND PROCEDURES. Labor Department, Occupational Safety and Health Administration. Superintendent of Documents, United States Government Printing Office, Washington, D.C. 20402. 1984- .

OCCUPATIONAL SAFETY AND HEALTH, VOLUME SIX, INDUSTRIAL HYGIENE TECHNICAL MANUAL. Labor Department, Occupational Safety and Health Administration. Superintendent of Documents, United States Government Printing Office, Washington, D.C. 20402. 1980- .

LOOSELEAF SERVICES AND REPORTERS

OCCUPATIONAL SAFETY AND HEALTH CASES. Bureau of National Affairs, 1231 Twenty-fifth Street, Northwest, Washington, D.C. 20037. 1974- .

OCCUPATIONAL SAFETY AND HEALTH DECISIONS. Commerce Clearing House, Incorporated, 4025 West Peterson Avenue, Chicago, Illinois 60646. 1973- .

HANDBOOKS, MANUALS, FORMBOOKS

CHEMICAL HAZARD COMMUNICATION GUIDEBOOK: OSHA, EPA, AND DOT REQUIREMENTS. Second Edition. Andrew B. Waldo and Richard C. Hinds. Executive Enterprises Publications Company, 22 West Twenty-first Street, New York, New York 10010-6904. 1991.

HAZARDOUS WASTE INSPECTION REFERENCE MANUAL. Labor Department, Occupational Safety and Health Administration. Superintendent of Documents, United States Government Printing Office, Washington, D.C. 20402. 1986.

OCCUPATIONAL SAFETY AND HEALTH VOLUME FIVE, FIELD OPERATIONS MANUAL. Labor Department, Occupational Safety and Health Administration. Superintendent of Documents, United States Government Printing Office, Washington, D.C. 20402. 1974- .

PRIMER ON OCCUPATIONAL SAFETY AND HEALTH. Fred Blosser. Bureau of National Affairs, Incorporated, 1231 Twenty-fifth Street, Northwest, Washington, D.C. 20037. 1992.

NEWSLETTERS AND NEWSPAPERS

OSHA COMPLIANCE ADVISOR. Business and Legal Reports, 64 Wall Street, Madison, Connecticut 06443. Semimonthly.

OSHA TRAINING BULLETIN FOR SUPERVISORS. Business and Legal Reports, 64 Wall Street, Madison, Connecticut 06443. Monthly.

OCCUPATIONAL SAFETY AND HEALTH REVIEW COMMISSION
See also: FEDERAL MINE SAFETY AND HEALTH REVIEW COMMITTEE; LABOR DEPARTMENT; OCCUPATIONAL SAFETY AND HEALTH ADMINISTRATION

STATUTES, CODES, STANDARDS, UNIFORM LAWS

CODE OF FEDERAL REGULATIONS, TITLE 29. Office of the Federal Register, National Archives and Records Administration. Superintendent of Documents, United States Government Printing Office, Washington, D.C. 20402. Annual. (Updated by use of monthly List of Sections Affected and daily Federal Register .)

LOOSELEAF SERVICES AND REPORTERS

OCCUPATIONAL SAFETY AND HEALTH CASES. Bureau of National Affairs, 1231 Twenty-fifth Street, Northwest, Washington, D.C. 20037. 1974- .

OCCUPATIONAL SAFETY AND HEALTH DECISIONS. Commerce Clearing House, Incorporated, 4025 West Peterson Avenue, Chicago, Illinois 60646. 1973- .

OCCUPATIONAL SAFETY AND HEALTH REVIEW COMMISSION, ADMINISTRATIVE LAW JUDGE AND COMMISSION DECISIONS, OSAHRC REPORTS. Occupational Safety and Health Review Commission. Superintendent of Documents, United States Government Printing Office, Washington, D.C. 20402. Monthly. (Michrofiche).

HANDBOOKS, MANUALS, FORMBOOKS

PRIMER ON OCCUPATIONAL SAFETY AND HEALTH. Fred Blosser. Bureau of National Affairs, Incorporated, 1231 Twenty-fifth Street, Northwest, Washington, D.C. 20037. 1992.

DIGESTS, INDEXES, ABSTRACTS, CITATORS

SHEPARD'S FEDERAL OCCUPATIONAL SAFETY AND HEALTH CITATIONS. Shepard's/McGraw-Hill, P.O. Box 1235, Colorado Springs, Colorado 80901. Quarterly.

RESEARCH CENTERS, INSTITUTES, CLEARINGHOUSES

OCCUPATIONAL SAFETY AND HEALTH REVIEW COMMISSION LIBRARY. 1825 K Street, Northwest, Room 400, Washington, D.C. 20006. (202) 634-7933.

ONLINE DATABASES

WESTLAW, LABOR LIBRARY. West Publishing Company, P.O. Box 64526, 50 West Kellogg Boulevard, St. Paul, Minnesota 55164-0526.

OCCUPATIONS
See: OCCUPATIONAL SAFETY AND HEALTH; PROFESSIONAL ETHICS AND LIABILITY

OFFICE OF PERSONNEL MANAGEMENT
See also: PUBLIC OFFICIALS AND EMPLOYEES

STATUTES, CODES, STANDARDS, UNIFORM LAWS

CODE OF FEDERAL REGULATIONS, TITLE 5. Office of the Federal Register, National Archives and Records Administration. Superintendent of Documents, United States Government Printing Office, Washington, D.C. 20402. Annual. (Updated by use of monthly List of Sections Affected and daily Federal Register .)

POSITION CLASSIFICATION STANDARDS FOR POSITIONS UNDER THE GENERAL SCHEDULE CLASSIFICATION SYSTEM. Office of Personnel Management. Superintendent of Documents, United States Government Printing Office, Washington, D.C. 20402. Looseleaf.

HANDBOOKS, MANUALS, FORMBOOKS

FEDERAL PERSONNEL MANUAL. Office of Personnel Management. Superintendent of Documents, United States Government Printing Office, Washington, D.C. 20402. Looseleaf.

HANDBOOK OF REASONABLE ACCOMODATION. Office of Personnel Management, Office of Affirmative Employment Programs, Office of Selective Placement Programs. Superintendent of Documents, United States Government Printing Office, Washington, D.C. 20402. 1980.

REPRESENTING THE AGENCY BEFORE THE UNITED STATES MERIT SYSTEMS PROTECTION BOARD, A HANDBOOK ON MSPB PRACTICE AND PROCEDURE. Harold J. Ashner and William C. Jackson. Office of Personnel Management, Office of Employee, Labor, and Agency Relations, Appellate Policies Division. Superintendent of Documents, United States Government Printing Office, Washington, D.C. 20402. 1984.

DIGESTS, INDEXES, ABSTRACTS, CITATORS

DIGEST OF SIGNIFICANT CLASSIFICATION DECISIONS AND OPINIONS. Office of Personnel Management. Superintendent of Documents, United States Government Printing Office, Washington, D.C. 20402. Three issues per year.

STATISTICS SOURCES

UNION RECOGNITION IN THE FEDERAL GOVERNMENT: STATISTICAL SUMMARY, SUMMARY REPORTS WITHIN AGENCIES, LISTINGS WITHIN AGENCIES OF EXCLUSIVE RECOGNITIONS AND AGREEMENTS AS OF JANUARY, 1985. Office of Personnel Management, Office of Policy and Communications, Office of Employee, Labor and Agency Relations. Superintendent of Documents, United States Government Printing Office, Washington, D.C. 20402. 1985.

OTHER SOURCES

ATTRACTING AND SELECTING QUALITY APPLICANTS FOR FEDERAL EMPLOYMENT: A REPORT TO THE PRESIDENT AND THE CONGRESS OF THE UNITED STATES. United States Merit Systems Protection Board, 1120 Vermont Avenue, Northwest, Washington, D.C. 20419. 1990.

OPM'S CLASSIFICATION AND QUALIFICATION SYSTEMS: A RENEWED EMPHASIS, A CHANGING PERSPECTIVE: A REPORT TO THE PRESIDENT AND THE CONGRESS OF THE UNITED STATES. United States Merit Systems Protection Board, 1120 Vermont Avenue, Northwest, Washington, D.C. 20419. 1989.

OFFICERS
See: CORPORATIONS, OFFICERS AND DIRECTORS; PUBLIC OFFICIALS AND EMPLOYEES

OIL AND GAS
See also: ENERGY; ENERGY DEPARTMENT; ENVIRONMENTAL LAW; ENVIRONMENTAL PROTECTION AGENCY; FEDERAL ENERGY REGULATORY COMMISSION; MINES AND MINERALS

STATUTES, CODES, STANDARDS, UNIFORM LAWS

SUMMARY OF STATE STATUTES AND REGULATIONS FOR OIL AND GAS PRODUCTION. Interstate Oil Compact Commission, P.O. Box 53127, Oklahoma City, Oklahoma 73152. 1979. (Annual Supplements).

LOOSELEAF SERVICES AND REPORTERS

FEDERAL INCOME TAXATION OF OIL AND GAS INVESTMENTS. Second Edition. Alexander Jay Bruen, Willard B. Taylor and Erik M. Jensen. Research Institute of America, Incorporated, One Penn Plaza, New York, New York 10119. 1989- .

FEDERAL TAXATION OF OIL AND GAS TRANSACTIONS. Robert Polevoi and Leland E. Fiske. Matthew Bender and Company, Incorporated, 11 Penn Plaza, New York, New York 10001. 1988- .

LOUISIANA OIL AND GAS LAW. Luther L. McDougal, III. Butterworth Legal Publishers, 90 Stiles Road, Salem, New Hampshire 03079. 1988- .

NATURAL GAS CONTRACT. Edward W. Hergerer, John F. Douglas and Peter G. Esposito. Federal Programs Advisory Service, Thompson Publishing Group, 1725 K Street, Northwest, Suite 200, Washington, D.C. 20006. 1984- .

NATURAL GAS POLICY ACT INFORMATION SERVICE. Marcie McCory. Federal Programs Advisory Service, Thompson Publishing Group, 1725 K Street, Northwest, Suite 200, Washington, D.C. 20006. 1980- .

OIL AND GAS LAW: THE NORTH SEA EXPLOITATION. Kenneth R. Simmonds. Oceana Publications, 75 Main Street, Dobbs Ferry, New York 10522. 1988- .

OIL AND GAS REPORTER. Matthew Bender and Company, Incorporated, 11 Penn Plaza, New York, New York 10001. 1952- .

TEXAS LAW OF OIL AND GAS. Ernest E. Smith and Jacqueline Lang Weaver. Butterworth Legal Publishers, 90 Stiles Road, Salem, New Hampshire 03079. 1989- .

HANDBOOKS, MANUALS, FORMBOOKS

BUYING AND SELLING GAS: A PRACTICAL GUIDE FOR OPERATORS, NON-OPERATORS, AND ROYALTY OWNERS. Paul Strohl. Executive Enterprises Publications Company, 22 West Twenty-first Street, New York, New York 10010-6904. 1989.

HANDBOOK ON GAS CONTRACTS. Thomas G. Johnson. Institute for Energy Development, Incorporated (Defunct). 1982.

NATURAL GAS HANDBOOK. Marcie McCrory. Federal Programs Advisory Service, Thompson Publishing Group, 1725 K Street, Northwest, Suite 200, Washingotn, D.C. 20006. 1982. (Monthly Supplements).

NATURAL GAS REGULATION HANDBOOK. Richard J. Pierce, Editor. Executive Enterprises Publications Company, 22 West Twenty-first Street, New York, New York 10010-6904. 1980. (Periodic Supplements).

NATURAL GAS REGULATIONS HANDBOOK. Second Edition. Phillip G. Lookadoo. Government Institutes, Incorporated, 966 Hungerford Drive, Rockville, Maryland 20850. 1988.

OIL AND GAS DRILLING PROGRAMS: PREPARING DOCUMENTATION. Clifford A. Wright. Clark Boardman Company, Limited, 435 Hudson Street, New York, New York 10014. 1985.

OIL POLLUTION DESKBOOK. Environmental Law Reporter, Environmental Law Institute, 1616 P Street, Northwest, Suite 200, Washington, D.C. 20036. 1991.

PETROLEUM LAW GUIDE. W. P. Winston. Elsevier Science Publishing Company, Incorporated, P.O. Box 882, Madison Square Station, New York, New York 10159. 1985.

TEXTBOOKS AND GENERAL WORKS

AN ANALYSIS AND EVALUATION OF RULES AND POLICIES GOVERNING OCS OPERATIONS. Douglas V. Fant. American Bar Association, Section of Natural Resources, Energy, and Environmental Law, 750 North Lake Shore Drive, Chicago, Illinois 60611. 1990.

ARTHUR YOUNG'S OIL AND GAS: FEDERAL INCOME TAXATION. James L. Houghton, Editor. Commerce Clearing House, Incorporated, 4025 West Peterson Avenue, Chicago, Illinois 60646. 1987.

CASES AND MATERIALS ON THE FEDERAL INCOME TAXATION OF OIL AND GAS AND NATURAL RESOURCES TRANSACTIONS. Peter C. Maxfield, James L. Houghton and James R. Gaar. Foundation Press, 615 Merrick Avenue, Westbury, New York 11590. 1990.

CASES AND MATERIALS ON THE LAW OF OIL AND GAS. Fifth Edition. Howard R. Williams. Foundation Press, 615 Merrick Avenue, Westbury, New York 11590. 1987.

THE CONTROL OF OIL POLLUTION. J. Wardley-Smith. Graham and Trotman Limited, Sterling House, 66 Wilton Road, London, SW1V 1DE, England. 1983.

THE COURTS' VIEW OF REGULATION AT THE FEDERAL ENERGY REGULATORY COMMISSION. David W. Miller. Norland Press, P.O. Box 1187, Springfield, Virginia 22151-0187. 1988.

DRAFTING NATURAL GAS CONTRACTS AFTER ORDER 436: THE PRODUCER'S PERSPECTIVE. Robert A. Luettgen. American Bar Association, Section of Natural Resources, Energy, and Environmental Law, 750 North Lake Shore Drive, Chicago, Illinois 60611. 1989.

ENERGY LAW IN A NUTSHELL. Joseph P. Tomain. West Publishing Company, P.O. Box 64526, 50 West Kellogg Boulevard, St. Paul, Minnesota 55164-0526. 1981.

FEDERAL AND STATE REGULATION OF OIL AND GAS EXPLORATION AND DEVELOPMENT ACTIVITIES ON THE OUTER CONTINENTAL SHELF. Teresa Hooks and Thomas McCloskey, Editors. Institute for Energy Development, Incorporated (Defunct). 1983.

FEDERAL INCOME TAXATION OF OIL AND GAS INVESTMENTS. Second Edition. Alexander J. Bruen and W. B. Taylor. Research Institute of America, Incorporated, One Penn Plaza, New York, New York 10119. 1989. (Annual Supplements).

FEDERAL OIL AND GAS LEASING AND OPERATIONS -- ONSHORE. Craig R. Carver, Editor. Institute for Energy Development, Incorporated (Defunct). 1983.

FEDERAL TAXATION OF OIL AND GAS TRANSACTIONS. Cecil L. Smith and Guy W. Anderson, Jr. Matthew Bender and Company, Incorporated, 11 Penn Plaza, New York, New York 10001. 1982. (Annual Supplements).

FUNDAMENTALS OF OIL AND GAS LAW TAXATION. John S. Lowe, Editor. Institute for Energy Development, Incorporated, (Defunt). 1984.

HAZARDOUS WASTE LAWS: REGULATIONS AND TAXES FOR THE U.S. PETROLEUM REFINING INDUSTRY. David E. Fenster. PennWell Books, P.O. Box 21288, Tulsa, Oklahoma 74121. 1990.

THE LAW OF OIL AND GAS. Third Edition. Richard W. Hemingway. West Publishing Company, 50 West Kellogg Boulevard, St. Paul, Minnesota 55164. 1991. (Hornbook).

THE LAW OF OIL AND GAS LEASES. Second Edition. Earl A. Brown. Matthew Bender and Company, Incorporated, 11 Penn Plaza, New York, New York 10001. 1967. (Annual Supplements).

MEDITERRANEAN CONTINENTAL SHELF: DELIMITATIONS AND REGIMES: INTERNATIONAL AND LEGAL SOURCES. Umberto Leanza, Luigi Sico and Maria Clelia Ciciriello, Editors. Oceana Publications, 75 Main Street, Dobbs Ferry, New York 10522. 1988.

NATURAL GAS: CURRENT FEDERAL AND STATE DEVELOPMENTS. William A. Mogel and James E. Mann. Executive Enterprises Publications Company, 22 West Twenty-first Street, New York, New York 10010-6904. 1987.

OFFSHORE LANDS: OIL AND GAS LEASING AND CONSERVATION ON THE OUTER CONTINENTAL SHELF. Walter J. Mead. Pacific Research Institute for Public Policy Research, 177 Post Street, San Francisco, California 94108. 1985.

OIL AND GAS AGREEMENTS. Rocky Mountain Mineral Law Foundation, Fleming Law Building, Campus Box 405, University of Colorado, Boulder, Colorado 80309. 1983.

OIL AND GAS CONSERVATION LAW AND PRACTICE. Rocky Mountain Mineral Law Foundation, Fleming Law Building, Campus Box 405, University of Colorado, Boulder, Colorado 80309. 1985.

OIL AND GAS FINANCINGS: CURRENT PRACTICE AND ANTICIPATED DEVELOPMENTS. Lawrence C. Tondel, Chairman. Practising Law Institute, 810 Seventh Avenue, New York, New York 10019. 1983.

THE OIL AND GAS INDUSTRY AND THE BANKRUPTCY LAWS. Alan Gover, Chairman. Longman, Incorporated, 19 West Forty-fourth Street, New York, New York 10036. 1985.

OIL AND GAS LAW. Howard R. Williams and Charles J. Meyers. Matthew Bender and Company, Incorporated, 11 Penn Plaza, New York, New York 10001. 1973. (Annual Supplements).

OIL AND GAS LAW IN A NUTSHELL. Second Edition. John S. Lowe. West Publishing Company, 50 West Kellogg Boulevard, St. Paul, Minnesota 55164. 1988.

OIL AND GAS TITLE EXAMINATION. George J. Morganthaler, Chairman. Practising Law Institute, 810 Seventh Avenue, New York, New York 10019. 1982.

OIL COMPANIES IN THE INTERNATIONAL SYSTEM. Third Edition. Louis Turner. Allen S. Unwin, Incorporated, 8 Winchester Place, Winchester, Massachusetts 01890. 1983.

PETROLEUM COMPANY OPERATIONS AND AGREEMENTS IN THE DEVELOPING COUNTRIES. Raymond F. Mikesell. Resources of the Future, Incorporated, 1616 P Street, Northwest, Washington, D.C. 20036. 1984.

PETROLEUM LANDS AND LEASING. Joan Burk. PennWell Books, P.O. Box 21288, Tulsa, Oklahoma 74121. 1983.

PROBLEMS AND PITFALLS IN EXPLORATION AGREEMENTS. Lewis G. Mosburg, Editor. Institute for Energy Development, Incorporated (Defunct). 1983.

PROTECTING OIL AND GAS LIEN AND SECURITY INTERESTS: USE OF MEMORANDUM OF OPERATING AGREEMENT AND FINANCING STATEMENT. Andrew B. Derman. American Bar Association, Section of Natural Resources Law, 750 North Lake Shore Drive, Chicago, Illinois 60611.

REGULATION OF THE GAS INDUSTRY. American Gas Association, Matthew Bender and Company, Incorporated, 11 Penn Plaza, New York, New York 10001. 1981. (Periodic Supplements).

WORLDWIDE CONCESSION CONTRACTS AND PETROLEUM LEGISLATION. Gordon H. Barrows. PennWell Books, P.O. Box 21288, Tulsa, Oklahoma 74121. 1983.

ENCYCLOPEDIAS AND DICTIONARIES

INTERNATIONAL PETROLEUM ENCYCLOPEDIA. PennWell Books, P.O. Box 21288, Tulsa, Oklahoma 74121. Annual.

LANDMAN'S ENCYCLOPEDIA. Third Edition. Robert L. Hankinson and Robert L. Hankinson, Jr. Gulf Publishing Company, P.O. Box 2608, Houston, Texas 77252. 1988.

OIL AND GAS TERMS: ANNOTATED MANUAL OF LEGAL ENGINEERING TAX WORDS AND PHRASES. Seventh Edition. Howard R. Williams and Charles J. Meyers. Matthew Bender and Company, Incorporated, 11 Penn Plaza, New York, New York 10001. 1987.

DIGESTS, INDEXES, ABSTRACTS, CITATORS

DIGEST OF STATE INSPECTION LAWS -- PETROLEUM PRODUCTS. Fourth Edition. American Petroleum Institute, 1220 L Street, Northwest, Washington, D.C. 20005. 1985.

SHEPARD'S FEDERAL ENERGY LAW CITATIONS. Shepard's/McGraw-Hill, P.O. Box 1235, Colorado Springs, Colorado 80901. 1982- .

ANNUALS AND SURVEYS

OIL AND GAS ACCOUNTING: SOUTHWESTERN LEGAL FOUNDATION. Institute on Oil and Gas Accounting. Matthew Bender and Company, Incorporated, 11 Penn Plaza, New York, New York 10001. Annual.

PROCEEDINGS OF THE ANNUAL INSTITUTE ON OIL AND GAS LAW AND TAXATION. Institute on Oil and Gas Law and Taxation. Matthew Bender and Company, Incorporated, 11 Penn Plaza, New York, New York 10001. Annual.

LAW REVIEWS AND PERIODICALS

ENERGY LAW JOURNAL. Federal Energy Bar Association, 1615 L Street, Northwest, Washington, D.C. 20036. Semiannual.

JOURNAL OF ENERGY LAW AND POLICY. University of Utah, College of Law, Salt Lake City, Utah 84112. Semiannual.

OIL AND GAS JOURNAL. PennWell Books, P.O. Box 21288, Tulsa, Oklahoma 74121. Weekly.

OIL AND GAS LAW AND TAX QUARTERLY. Matthew Bender and Company, Incorporated, 235 East Forty-fifth Street, New York, New York 10017. Quarterly.

NEWSLETTERS AND NEWSPAPERS

CASE UPDATE. Eastern Mineral Law Foundation, West Virginia University Law Center, P.O. Box 6130, Morgantown, West Virginia 26506. Quarterly.

ENERGY DAILY. King Publishing Group, 915 Fifteenth Street, Northwest, Washington, D.C. 20005. Daily.

INGAA UPDATE: MONTHLY PROFILES OF GAS PIPELINE PROCEEDINGS AT FERC. Interstate Natural Gas Association of America, 555 Thirteenth Street, Northwest, Suite 300 West, Washington, D.C. 20004. Monthly.

INSIDE ENERGY WITH FEDERAL LANDS. McGraw-Hill Book Company, 1221 Avenue of the Americas, New York, New York 10020. Weekly.

INSIDE F.E.R.C. McGraw-Hill Book Company, 1221 Avenue of the Americas, New York, New York 10020. Weekly.

INSIDE F.E.R.C.'S GAS MARKET REPORT. McGraw-Hill Book Company, 1221 Avenue of the Americas, New York, New York 10020. Biweekly.

MINERAL LAW NEWSLETTER. Rocky Mountain Mineral Law Foundation, 7039 East Eighteenth Avenue, Denver, Colorado 80220. Quarterly.

OIL AND GAS TAX ALERT. Research Institute of America, Incorporated, 589 Fifth Avenue, New York, New York 10017. Monthly.

OIL SPILL INTELLEGENCE REPORT. Cutter Information Report, 1000 Massachusetts Avenue, Arlington, Massachusetts 02174. Weekly.

OLIPHANT WASHINGTON SERVICE. Oliphant Washington News Service, 1819 H Street, Suite 330, Northwest, Washington, D.C. 20006. Semiweekly.

PETROLEUM TAXATION/LEGISLATION REPORT. Barrows Company, Incorporated, 116 East Sixty-sixth Street, New York, New York 10021. Bimonthly.

UNITED STATES OIL WEEK. Capitol Publications, 1101 King Street, Suite 444, Alexandria, Virginia 22314. Weekly.

UTILITY REPORTER -- FUELS, ENERGY AND POWER. Merten Allen Associates, P.O. Box 9136, Schenectady, New York 12309. Monthly.

WASHINGTON REPORT. Interstate Natural Gas Association of America, 555 Thirteenth Street, Northwest, Suite 300 West, Washington, D.C. 20004. Weekly.

BIBLIOGRAPHIES

ARAB OIL: A BIBLIOGRAPHY OF MATERIALS IN THE LIBRARY OF CONGRESS. George D. Selim. Superintendent of Documents, United States Government Printing Office, Washington, D.C. 20402. 1983.

NATURAL GAS PRICE DEREGULATION: A SELECTED BIBLIOGRAPHY. Anthony G. White. Vance Bibliographies, P.O. Box 229, 112 North Charter Street, Monticello, Illinois 61856. 1984.

DIRECTORIES

BROWN'S DIRECTORY OF NORTH AMERICAN AND INTERNATIONAL GAS COMPANIES. Energy Publications, Incorporated, Division of Harcourt Brace Jovanovich, Incorporated, 6277 Sea Harbor Drive, Orlando, Florida 32821. Annual.

INTERSTATE OIL COMPACT COMMISSION AND STATE OIL AND GAS AGENCIES -- DIRECTORY. Interstate Oil Compact Commission, Box 53127, Oklahoma City, Oklahoma 73152. Annual.

OIL AND GAS DIRECTORY. Geophysical Directory, Incorporated, 2200 Welch Avenue, Houston, Texas 77019. Annual.

OIL AND GAS STOCKS HANDBOOK. Standard and Poor's Corporation, 25 Broadway, New York, New York 10004. Semiannual.

OIL INDUSTRY U.S.A. Oil Daily, Incorporated, Subsidiary of Whitney Communications Corporation, 1401 New York Avenue, Northwest, Suite 500, Washington D.C. 20005. Annual.

U.S.A. OIL INDUSTRY DIRECTORY. PennWell Books, P.O. Box 21288, Tulsa, Oklahoma 74121. Annual.

WHOLE WORLD OIL DIRECTORY. Whole World Publishing, Incorporated, P.O. Box 665, Deerfield, Illinois 60015. Annual.

BIOGRAPHICAL SOURCES

FINANCIAL TIMES WHO'S WHO IN WORLD OIL AND GAS. Longman, Incorporated, 19 West Forty-forth Street, New York, New York 10036. 1982. Irregular.

ASSOCIATIONS AND PROFESSIONAL SOCIETIES

AMERICAN GAS ASSOCIATION. 1515 Wilson Boulevard, Arlington, Virginia 22209. (703) 841-8400.

AMERICAN PUBLIC GAS ASSOCIATION. P.O. Box 1426, Vienna, Virginia 22183. (703) 281-2910.

ASSOCIATION OF OIL PIPE LINES. 1725 K Street, Northwest, Suite 1205, Washington, D.C. 20006. (202) 331-8228.

FEDERAL ENERGY BAR ASSOCIATION. c/o Lorna Wilson, 1900 M Street, Northwest, Suite 620, Washington, D.C. 20036. (202) 223-5625.

GAS PROCESSORS ASSOCIATION. 6526 East Sixtieth Street, Tulsa, Oklahoma 74145. (918) 493-3872.

GAS PROCESSORS SUPPLIERS ASSOCIATION. 6526 East Sixtieth Street, Tulsa, Oklahoma 74145. (918) 493-3872.

INDEPENDENT PETROLEUM ASSOCIATION OF AMERICA. 1101 Sixteenth Street, Northwest, Washington, D.C. 20036. (202) 857-4722.

INTERSTATE MINING COMPACT COMMISSION. 459B Carlisle Drive, Herndon, Virginia 22070. (703) 709-8654.

INTERSTATE NATURAL GAS ASSOCIATION OF AMERICA. 555 Thirteenth Avenue, Northwest, Suite 300 West, Washington, D.C. 20004. (202) 626-3200.

INTERSTATE OIL COMPACT COMMISSION. P.O. Box 53127, Oklahoma City, Oklahoma 73152. (405) 525-3556.

LIAISON COMMITTEE OF COOPERATING OIL AND GAS ASSOCIATIONS 105 South Broadway, Suite 800, Wichita, Kansas 67202. (316) 263-7297.

NATIONAL PETROLEUM COUNCIL. 1625 K Street, Northwest, Suite 600, Washington, D.C. 20006. (202) 393-6100.

NATIONAL PETROLEUM REFINERS ASSOCIATION. 1899 L Street, Northwest, Suite 1000, Washington, D.C. 20036. (202) 457-0480.

NATIONAL PROPANE GAS ASSOCIATION. 1600 Eisenhower Lane, Lisle, Illinois 60532. (708) 515-0600.

PETROLEUM MARKETERS ASSOCIATION OF AMERICA. 1120 Vermont Avenue, Northwest, Suite 1130, Washington, D.C. 20005. (202) 331-1198.

RESEARCH CENTERS, INSTITUTES, CLEARINGHOUSES

AMERICAN PETROLEUM INSTITUTE. 1220 L Street, Northwest, Washington, D.C. 20005. (202) 682-8000.

COORDINATING RESEARCH COUNCIL. 219 Perimeter Center Parkway, Suite 400, Atlanta, Georgia 30346. (404) 396-3400.

EASTERN MINERAL LAW FOUNDATION. West Virginia University Law Center, P.O. Box 6130, Mogantown, West Virginia 26506. (304) 293-2470.

ENERGY LAW CENTER. University of Utah, College of Law, Salt Lake City, Utah 84112. (801) 581-5880.

GAS RESEARCH INSTITUTE. 8600 West Bryn Mawr Avenue, Chicago, Illinois 60631. (312) 399-8100.

INTERNATIONAL OIL AND GAS EDUCATIONAL CENTER. Southwestern Legal Foundation, P.O. Box 830707, Richardson, Texas 75083. (214) 690-2370.

PETROLEUM RESEARCH CENTER. School of Petroleum and Geological Engineering, University of Oklahoma, Norman, Oklahoma 73019.

ROCKY MOUNTAIN MINERAL LAW INSTITUTE. Porter Administration Building, 7039 East Eighteenth Avenue, Denver, Colorado 80220. (303) 321-8100.

ONLINE DATABASES

ENERGY DATABASE. Newport Associates, Limited, 7400 East Orchard Road, Suite 320, Englewood, Colorado 80111.

INTERNATIONAL PETROLEUM ANNUAL. United States Department of Energy, 100 Independence Avenue, Southwest, Washington, D.C. 20588.

LEXIS FEDERAL ENERGY LIBRARY. Mead Data Central, P.O. Box 933, Dayton, Ohio 45401.

MONTHLY ENERGY REVIEW. United States Department of Energy, Energy Information Administration, 1000 Independence Avenue, Southwest, Washington, D.C. 20585.

OIL AND GAS JOURNAL ENERGY DATABASE. PennWell Publishing Company, 1421 South Sheridan Road, Box 1260, Tulsa, Oklahoma 74101.

PERMIT DATA ONLINE. Petroleum Information Corporation, 4100 East Dry Creek Road, Littleton, Colorado 80122.

THE PETROLEUM DATA SYSTEM. Energy Resources Institute, University of Oklahoma Information Systems Programs, P.O. Box 3030, Norman, Oklahoma 73070.

PRODUCTION DATA ON-LINE. Petroleum Information, PI On-Line Services, P.O. Box 2612, Denver, Colorado 80201.

STATE ACTION REPORTER: NATURAL GAS AND ELECTRIC POWER. Regulatory Information Service, Congressional Information Service, Incorporated, 4520 East-West Highway, Suite 800, Bethesda, Maryland 20814.

TULSA. Petroleum Abstracts, University of Tulsa, 600 South College, Tulsa, Oklahoma 74104.

UNITED STATES OIL AND GAS FILE. Petroleum Information, Production Data Services Division, 4150 Westhermer Road, P.O. Box 1702, Houston, Texas 77251.

UTILITY REPORTER -- FUELS, ENERGY AND POWER. Merton Allen Associates, P.O. Box 9136, Schenectady, New York 12309.

STATISTICS SOURCES

ANNUAL OIL AND GAS STATISTICS. Organization for Economic Cooperation and Development. Bernan Associates, 9730/E George Palmer Highway, Lanham, Maryland 20706. Annual.

BASIC PETROLEUM DATA BOOK. American Petroleum Institute, 1220 L Street, Northwest, Washington, D.C. 20005. Quarterly.

MONTHLY ENERGY REVIEW. Energy Information Office. Superintendent of Document, United States Government Printing Office, Washington, D.C. 20402. Monthly.

STATISTICAL BULLETIN. American Petroleum Institute, 1220 L Street, Northwest, Washington, D.C. 20005. Weekly.

OPEN MEETINGS
See: FREEDOM OF INFORMATION

OPINIONS, JUDICIAL
See: JUDGMENTS

ORGANIZED CRIME

LOOSELEAF SERVICES AND REPORTERS

CIVIL RICO. David B. Smith and Terrance G. Reed. Matthew Bender and Company, Incorporated, 11 Penn Plaza, New York, New York 10001. 1987- .

RICO: CIVIL AND CRIMINAL LAW AND STRATEGY. Jed S. Rakoff and Howard W. Goldstein, Editors. Law Journal Seminars-Press, Incorporated, 111 Eighth Avenue, Suite 900, New York, New York 10011. 1989- .

RICO IN BUSINESS AND COMMERICAL LITIGATION. Kevin P. Roddy. Shepard's/McGraw-Hill, P.O. Box 1235, Colorado Springs, Colorado 80901. 1991- .

HANDBOOKS, MANUALS, FORMBOOKS

CIVIL RICO: A MANUAL FOR FEDERAL PROSECUTORS. Diane B. de Forest. United States Department of Justice. Criminal Division. Organized Crime and Racketeering Section, Tenth Street and Pennsylvania Avenue, Northwest, Washington, D.C. 20530. 1988.

CIVIL RICO PRACTICE: CAUSES OF ACTION. Harold Brown, Editor. John Wiley and Sons, Incorporated, 605 Third Avenue, New York, New York 10158. 1991.

RACKETEER INFLUENCED AND CORRUPT ORGANIZATIONS (RICO): A MANUAL FOR FEDERAL PROSECUTORS. Second Edition. United States Department of Justice, Criminal Division, Organized Crime and Racketeering Section. Superintendent of Documents, United States Government Printing Office, Washington, D.C. 20402. 1988.

TEXTBOOKS AND GENERAL WORKS

BLOOD AND POWER: ORGANIZED CRIME IN TWENTIETH-CENTURY AMERICA. Stephen R. Fox. William Morrow and Company, 105 Madison Avenue, New York, New York 10016. 1989.

THE BUSINESS OF CRIME: A DOCUMENTARY STUDY OF ORGANIZED CRIME IN THE AMERICAN ECONOMY. Alan A. Block. Westview Press, Incorporated, 5500 Central Avenue, Boulder, Colorado 80301. 1991.

CIVIL RICO. Patricia M. Hynes, Chairperson. Practising Law Institute, 810 Seventh Avenue, New York, New York 10019. 1991.

CIVIL RICO LITIGATION VS. ARBITRATION, ALI-ABA COURSE OF STUDY MATERIALS. American Law Institute-American Bar Association, 4025 Chestnut Street, Philadelphia, Pennsylvania 19104. 1988.

THE CONTAINMENT OF ORGANIZED CRIME. Herbert Edelhertz, Roland J. Cole, and Bonnie Berk. Lexington Books, Division of D.C. Heath and Company, 125 Spring Street, Lexington, Massachusetts 02173. 1984.

CORPORATION OF CORRUPTION: A SYSTEMATIC STUDY OF ORGANIZED CRIME. David L. Herbert and Howard Tritt. Charles C. Thomas Publishing, 2600 South First Street, Springfield, Illinois 62794-9265. 1984.

CRIME, CRUSADES, AND CORRUPTION: PROHIBITIONS IN THE UNITED STATES, 1900-1987. Michael Woodiwiss. Barnes and Noble Books, 10 East Fifty-third Street, New York, New York 10022. 1988.

THE CRIMINAL ELITE: PROFESSIONAL AND ORGANIZED CRIME. Howard Abadinsky. Greenwood Publishing Group, Incorporated, 88 Post Road West, P.O. Box 5007, Westport, Connecticut 06881. 1983.

THE CROOKED LADDER: GANGSTERS, ETHNICITY, AND THE AMERICAN DREAM. James M. O'Kane. Transaction Books, Rutgers University, New Brunswick, New Jersey 08903. 1992.

DISORGANIZED CRIME: THE ECONOMICS OF THE VISIBLE HAND. Peter Reuter. MIT Press, 55 Hayward Street, Cambridge, Massachusetts 02142. 1983.

INTERNATIONAL PERSPECTIVES ON ORGANIZED CRIME. Jane Rae Buckwalter, Editor. Office of International Criminal Justice, University of Illinois at Chicago, Chicago, Illinois. 1990.

MASTERS OF PARADISE: ORGANIZED CRIME AND THE INTERNAL REVENUE SERVICE IN THE BAHAMAS. Alan A. Block. Transaction Books, Rutgers University, New Brunswick, New Jersey 08903. 1991.

MEASURING THE EFFECTIVENESS OF ORGANIZED CRIME CONTROL EFFORTS. Michael D. Maltz. University of Illinois at Chicago, Office of International Criminal Justice, Chicago, Illinois. 1990.

OCTOPUS: THE LONG REACH OF THE INTERNATIONAL SICILIAN MAFIA. Claire Sterling. W.W Norton and Company, Incorporated, 500 Fifth Avenue, New York, New York 10110. 1990.

ORGANIZED CRIME. Third Edition. Howard Abadinsky. Nelson-Hall Publishing, 111 North Canal Street, Chicago, Illinois 60606. 1990.

ORGANIZED CRIME: A GLOBAL PERSPECTIVE. Robert J. Kelly, Editor. Rowman and Allanheld, 420 Boston Way, Lanham, Maryland 20706. 1986.

ORGANIZED CRIME: CONCEPTS AND CONTROL. Second Edition. Denny F. Pace and Jimmie C. Styles. Prentice-Hall, Incorporated, 113 Sylvan Avenue, Englewood Cliffs, New Jersey 07632. 1982.

ORGANIZED CRIME: CRIME CONTROL VS. CIVIL LIBERTIES. Robert P. Rhodes. Random House, Incorporated, Random House Publicity, 201 East Fiftieth Street, New York, New York 10022. 1984.

ORGANIZED CRIME IN AMERICA. Second Edition. Jay Albanese. Anderson Publishing Company, 2035 Reading Road, Cincinnati, Ohio 45202. 1989.

ORGANIZED CRIMES. Nicholas Van Hoffman. HarperCollins Publishers, 10 East Fifty-third Street, New York, New York 10022. 1984.

PERSPECTIVES ON ORGANIZING CRIME: ESSAYS IN OPPOSITION. Alan A. Block. Kluwer Academic Publishers, 101 Philip Drive, Assinippi Park, Norwell, Massachusetts 02061. 1991.

REPORT OF THE AD HOC CIVIL RICO TASK FORCE. Section of Corporation, Banking and Business Law, American Bar Association, 750 North Lake Shore Boulevard, Chicago, Illinois 60611. 1985.

RICO STRATEGIES. John C. Fricano. Buraff Publications, 1231 Twenty-fifth Street, Northwest, Washington, D.C. 20037. 1986.

DIGESTS, INDEXES, ABSTRACTS, CITATORS

ORGANIZED CRIME DIGEST. Washington Crime News Services, 7043 Wimsatt Road, Springfield, Virginia 22151. Monthly.

NEWSLETTERS AND NEWPAPERS

CIVIL RICO LITIGATION REPORTER. Andrews Publications, 1646 West Chester Pike, Westtown, Pennsylvania 19395. Monthly.

CIVIL RICO REPORT. Buraff Publications, Incorporated, 1350 Connecticut Avenue, Northwest, Suite 1000, Washington, D.C. 20037. Weekly.

RICO LAW REPORTER. Law Reporters, 1519 Connecticut Avenue, Northwest, Suite 200, Washington, D.C. 20036. Monthly.

BIBLIOGRAPHIES

A GUIDE TO THE LITERATURE ON ORGANIZED CRIME: AN ANNOTATED BIBLIOGRAPHY COVERING THE YEARS 1967-1981. Eugene Doleschal, Anne Newton, and William Hickey. Council on Crime and Delinquency, 411 Hackensack Avenue, Hackensack, New Jersey 07601. 1981.

ORGANIZED CRIME: A SELECTIVE CHECKLIST. Curtis C. Jones and Alva W. Stewart. Vance Bibliographies, P.O. Box 229, 112 North Charter Street, Monticello, Illinois 61856. 1982.

ORGANIZED CRIME AND ITS DIMENSIONS. Carol Ann Martin. Vance Bibliographies, P.O. Box 229, 112 North Charter Street, Monticello, Illinois 61856. 1981.

ORGANIZED CRIME

ASSOCIATION AND PROFESSIONAL SOCIETIES

AMERICAN BAR ASSOCIATION, SECTION OF CORPORATION, BANKING AND BUSINESS LAW, CRIMINAL LAW COMMITTEE. 750 North Lake Shore Drive, Chicago, Illinois 60611. (312) 988-5000.

INTERNATIONAL ASSOCIATION FOR THE STUDY OF ORGANIZED CRIME. c/o Fredrick Martens, Pennsylvania Crime Commission, 1100 East Hector Street, Conshohocken, Pennsylvania 19428. (215) 834-1164.

STATISTICS SOURCES

UNITED STATES DEPARTMENT OF JUSTICE, BUREAU OF JUSTICE STATISTICS. 633 Indiana Avenue, Northwest, Washington, D.C. 20531.

AUDIOVISUALS

CIVIL RICO. Practising Law Institute, 810 Seventh Avenue, New York, New York 10019. 1984. Audiocassettes.

P

PARALEGALS
See: LEGAL ASSISTANTS

PARDON
See: CRIMINAL LAW; PRESIDENT (UNITED STATES); PROBATION AND PAROLE; REHABILITATION OF OFFENDERS

PARENT AND CHILD
See: ADOPTION; CHILD ABUSE AND NEGLECT; CHILD CUSTODY; CHILDREN; FAMILY LAW; GUARDIAN AND WARD

PARKS AND MONUMENTS
See: HISTORIC PRESERVATION; PUBLIC LAND

PAROLE
See: CRIMINAL LAW; PROBATION AND PAROLE; REHABILITATION OF OFFENDERS

PARTITION
See: REAL PROPERTY

PARTNERSHIP
See also: AGENCY; BANKRUPTCY; JOINT VENTURES

STATUTES, CODES, STANDARDS, UNIFORM LAWS

CORPORATION, PARTNERSHIP, AND SECURITIES LAW; SELECTED STATUTES, RULES, AND FORMS. Larry D. Soderquist and A.A. Sommer, Jr. Michie Company, P.O. Box 7587, Charlottesville, Virginia 22906. 1991.

SELECTED CORPORATION AND PARTNERSHIP STATUTES, RULES, AND FORMS. West Publishing Company, 50 West Kellogg Boulevard, St. Paul, Minnesota 55164. 1989.

UNIFORM LIMITED PARTNERSHIP ACT. Uniform Laws Annotated. West Publishing Company, P.O. Box 64526, 50 West Kellogg Boulevard, St. Paul, Minnesota 55164-0526. 1976 (Annual Supplements).

UNIFORM PARTNERSHIP ACT. Uniform Laws Annotated. West Publishing Company, P.O. Box 64526, 50 West Kellogg Boulevard, St. Paul, Minnesota 55164-0526. 1976 (Annual Supplements).

LOOSELEAF SERVICES AND REPORTERS

BROMBERG AND RIBSTEIN ON PARTNERSHIP. Alan R. Bromberg, Larry E. Ribstein, and Judson A. Crane. Little, Brown and Company, 34 Beacon Street, Boston, Massachusetts 02108. 1988- .

THE DELAWARE LAW OF CORPORATIONS AND BUSINESS ORGANIZATIONS: TEXT, FORMS, LAW. Second Edition. R. Franklin Balotti and Jesse A. Finkelstein. Prentice-Hall, Incorporated, 113 Sylvan Avenue, Englewood Cliffs, New Jersey 07632. 1990- .

DISPOSITION OF PARTNERSHIP INTERESTS: SALES AND EXCHANGES. John B. Palmer III. Tax Management, Incorporated, Bureau of National Affairs, 1231 Twenty-fifth Street, Northwest, Washington, D.C. 20037. 1983- . (Tax Management Portfolio 237-2nd).

FEDERAL TAXATION OF PARTNERSHIPS AND PARTNERS. Second Edition. William S. McKee, William F. Nelson and Robert L. Whitmire. Research Institute of America, Incorporated, One Penn Plaza, New York, New York 10119. 1990- .

LIMITED PARTNERSHIP PROFILES. Impact Partnership Services. Commerce Clearing House, 4025 West Peterson Avenue, Chicago, Illinois 60646. 1986- .

PARTNERSHIP BASIS AND BASIS ADJUSTMENTS. Bruce Hallmark. Tax Management, Incorporated, Bureau of National Affairs, 1231 Twenty-fifth Street, Northwest, Washington, D.C. 20037. 1982- . (Tax Management Portfolio 277-2nd).

PARTNERSHIP TAX PRACTICE MANUAL. Evelyn Brody, Bruce K. Benesh, and M. Kevin Bryant. Panel Publishers, Incorporated, 36 West Forty-fourth Street, New York, New York 10036. 1989- .

PARTNERSHIP TAX REPORTER. Charles R. Levun. Commerce Clearing House, Incorporated, 4025 West Peterson Avenue, Chicago, Illinois 60646. 1988- .

PARTNERSHIP TAXATION. Fourth Edition. Arthur B. Willis, John S. Pennell, and Philip F. Postlewaite. Shepard's/McGraw-Hill, P.O. Box 1235, Colorado Springs, Colorado 80901. 1989- .

PARTNERSHIPS: TAXABLE INCOME AND DISTRIBUTIVE SHARES. Joseph D. Ament. Tax Management, Incorporated, Bureau of National Affairs, 1231 Twenty-fifth Street, Northwest, Washington, D.C. 20037. 1982- . (Tax Management Portfolio 282-2nd).

PREPARING THE FEDERAL PARTNERSHIP RETURN. Second Edition. Ted D. Englebrecht and Ernest D. Fiore. Matthew Bender and Company, Incorporated, 11 Penn Plaza, New York, New York 10001. 1987- .

SECURITIES AND PARTNERSHIP LAW FOR MLPs AND OTHER INVESTMENT LIMITED PARTNERSHIPS. Linda A. Wertheimer. Clark Boardman Co., Limited, 435 Hudson Street, New York, New York 10014. 1988- .

STATE LIMITED PARTNERSHIP LAWS: PRACTICE GUIDES, ANNOTATIONS, STATUTES, FORMS. Michael A. Bamberger and Joseph J. Basile, Jr. Prentice-Hall, Incorporated, 113 Sylvan Avenue, Englewood Cliffs, New Jersey 07632. 1987- .

TAXATION OF PARTNERSHIPS. John R. Bonn. Callaghan and Company, 155 Pfingsten Road, Deerfield, Illinois 60015. 1987- .

HANDBOOKS, MANUALS, FORMBOOKS

THE ACCOUNTANT'S GUIDE TO CORPORATION, PARTNERSHIP, AND AGENCY LAW. Sidney M. Wolf. Greenwood Publishing Group, Incorporated, 88 Post Road West, P.O. Box 5007, Westport, Connecticut 06881. 1989.

BUSINESS FORMS FROM ALI-ABA COURSE MATERIALS. American Law Institute-American Bar Association, Committee on Continuing Professional Education, 4025 Chestnut Street, Philadelphia, Pennsylvania 19104. 1983.

THE COMPLETE PARTNERSHIP MANUAL AND GUIDE WITH TAX, FINANCIAL, AND MANAGERIAL STRATEGIES. Daniel L. McKnight, Jr. Prentice-Hall, Incorporated, 113 Sylvan Avenue, Englewood Cliffs, New Jersey 07632. 1982.

THE DRAFTING OF PARTNERSHIP AGREEMENTS. Marlin M. Volz, C. Christopher Trower, and Debbie F. Reiss. American Law Institute-American Bar Association, Committee on Continuing Professional Education, 4025 Chestnut Street, Philadelphia, Pennsylvania 19104. 1986.

FEDERAL PARTNERSHIP TAXATION: A GUIDE TO THE LEADING CASES, STATUTES, AND REGULATIONS. Carter G. Bishop and Jennifer J. S. Brooks. West Publishing Company, 50 West Kellogg Boulevard, St. Paul, Minnesota 55164. 1990.

HOW TO EVALUATE REAL ESTATE PARTNERSHIP. Robert A. Stanger. 1129 Broad Street, P.O. Box 7490, Shrewsbury, New Jersey 07702. 1986.

ORGANIZATIONAL DOCUMENTS: A GUIDE FOR PARTNERSHIPS AND PROFESSIONAL CORPORATIONS. Mark F. Murray. American Institute of Certified Public Accountants, 1211 Avenue of the Americas, New York, New York 10036- 8775. 1990.

PARTNERSHIP AND S CORPORATION: TAX PLANNING GUIDE. Bruce K. Benesh and M. Kevin Bryant. Panel Publishers, Incorporated, 36 West Forty-fourth Street, New York, New York 10036. 1990.

PARTNERSHIP AND S CORPORATION: YEAR-END TAX PLANNING GUIDE. Bruce K. Benesh and M. Kevin Bryant. Panel Publishers, Incorporated, 36 West Forty-fourth Street, New York, New York 10036. 1990.

THE PARTNERSHIP BOOK: HOW TO WRITE YOUR OWN SMALL BUSINESS PARTNERSHIP AGREEMENT. Fourth Edition. Denis Clifford and Ralph Warner. Nolo Press, 950 Parker Street, Berkeley, California 94710. 1991.

PARTNERSHIP LAW ADVISER. Claire Moore Dickerson. Practising Law Institute, 810 Seventh Avenue, New York, New York 10019. 1991.

PARTNERSHIP TAXATION HANDBOOK. M. Jill Lockwood Martin. Prentice- Hall, Incorporated, 113 Sylvan Avenue, Englewood Cliffs, New Jersey 07632. 1989.

SELECTED CORPORATION AND PARTNERSHIP STATUTES, RULES AND FORMS. West Publishing Company, P.O. Box 64526, 50 West Kellogg Boulevard, St. Paul, Minnesota 55164-0526. 1991.

TEXTBOOKS AND GENERAL WORKS

AGENCY AND PARTNERSHIP: CASES, MATERIALS, AND PROBLEMS. Third Edition. J. Dennis Hynes. Michie Company, P.O. Box 7587, Charlottesville, Virginia 22906. 1989.

AGENCY-PARTNERSHIP IN A NUTSHELL. Roscoe T. Steffen. West Publishing Company, P.O. Box 64526, 50 West Kellogg Boulevard, St. Paul, Minnesota 55164-0526. 1977.

ALLOCATING PARTNERSHIP TAX BENEFITS UNDER THE NEW TREASURY REGULATIONS. William S. McKee and Robert L. Whitmire, Co-chairmen. Law and Business, Harcourt Brace Jovanovich, Incorporated, 6277 Sea Harbor Drive, Orlando, Florida 32821. 1983.

BUSINESS ORGANIZATIONS; PARTNERSHIPS. Gary A. Gotto, Ronald Jay Cohen and Ed Hendricks. West Publishing Company, 50 West Kellogg Boulevard, St. Paul, Minnesota 55164-0526. 1991.

CASES AND MATERIALS ON FUNDAMENTALS OF PARTNERSHIP TAXATION. Third Edition. Stephen A. Lind. Foundation Press, 615 Merrick Avenue, Westbury, New York 11590. 1991.

CORPORATE AND PARTNERSHIP TAXATION. Stephen Schwarz and Daniel J. Lathrope. West Publishing Company, 50 West Kellogg Boulevard, St. Paul, Minnesota 55164-0526. 1991.

ESSENTIALS OF PARTNERSHIP TAXATION. Paul R. Erickson. Prentice-Hall, Incorporated, 113 Sylvan Avenue, Englewood Cliffs, New Jersey 07632. 1989.

ESTABLISHING A UNITED STATES JOINT VENTURE WITH A FOREIGN PARTNER. David W. Detjen. Matthew Bender and Company, Incorporated, 11 Penn Plaza, New York, New York 10001. 1988.

FEDERAL INCOME TAXATION OF CORPORATE ENTERPRISE. Third Edition. Bernard Wolfman. Little, Brown and Company, 34 Beacon Street, Boston, Massachusetts 02108. 1990.

FEDERAL TAXATION OF CORPORATIONS, PARTNERSHIPS, AND THEIR OWNERS. William C. Holmes. Commerce Clearing House, Incorporated, 4025 West Peterson Avenue, Chicago, Illinois 60646. 1989.

FEDERAL TAXATION OF PARTNERS AND PARTNERSHIPS. Second Edition. G. Fred Streuling, James H. Boyd, and Kenneth H. Heller. Prentice-Hall, Incorporated, 113 Sylvan Avenue, Englewood Cliffs, New Jersey 07632. 1992.

FIDUCIARY OBLIGATION, AGENCY, AND PARTNERSHIP: DUTIES IN ONGOING BUSINESS RELATIONSHIPS. Deborah A. DeMott. West Publishing Company, 50 West Kellogg Boulevard, St. Paul, Minnesota 55164. 1991.

HANDBOOK ON THE LAW OF AGENCY AND PARTNERSHIP. Harold G. Reuschlein and William A. Gregory. West Publishing Company, P.O. Box 64526, 50 West Kellogg Boulevard, St. Paul, Minnesota 55164-0526. 1979 (Supplement 1981). (Hornbook).

HOW TO DO TAX PLANNING FOR PARTNERSHIPS. Jerold A. Friedland. Matthew Bender and Company, Incorporated, 11 Penn Plaza, New York, New York 10001. 1990.

THE HUSBAND AND WIFE BUSINESS PARTNERSHIP: WHAT THE LAW SAYS. Derrick and Margot Owles. Graham and Trotman, Boston, Massachusetts. 1989.

INTRODUCTION TO AGENCY AND PARTNERSHIP. J. S. Covington, Jr. J. Marshall Publishing Company, Houston, Texas. 1987.

AN INTRODUCTION TO AGENCY AND PARTNERSHIP. Melvin Aron Eisenberg. Foundation Press, 615 Merrick Avenue, Westbury, New York 11590. 1987.

LAW FIRM PARTNERSHIP AGREEMENTS. Bradford W. Hildebrandt and Jack Kaufman. Prentice-Hall, Incorporated, 113 Sylvan Avenue, Englewood Cliffs, New Jersey 07632. 1989.

THE LAW OF AGENCY AND PARTNERSHIP. Second Edition. Harold Gill Reuschlein and William A. Gregory. West Publishing Company, 50 West Kellogg Boulevard, St. Paul, Minnesota 55164. 1990.

THE LAW OF BUSINESS ORGANIZATIONS. Third Edition. John E. Moye. West Publishing Company, 50 West Kellogg Boulevard, St. Paul, Minnesota 55164. 1989.

LEGAL ASPECTS OF THE MANAGEMENT PROCESS. Fourth Edition. Fredrick G. Kempin, Jeremy L. Wiesen, and John W. Bagby. West Publishing Company, 50 West Kellogg Boulevard, St. Paul, Minnesota 55164. 1990.

LITIGATING LIMITED PARTNERS' SECURITIES ACTIONS. Jeffrey J. Scott. Practising Law Institute, 810 Seventh Avenue, New York, New York 10019. 1990.

MULTIDISCIPLINARY PARTNERSHIPS; NON-LEGAL BUSINESS AFFILIATES OF LAW FIRMS. Mortimer Maxwell Caplin and James W. Jones. Prentice-Hall, Incorporated, 113 Sylvan Avenue, Englewood Cliffs, New Jersey 07632. 1990.

PARTNER AND PARTNERSHIP BANKRUPTCY. Ralph C. Anzivino. John Wiley and Sons, Incorporated, 605 Third Avenue, New York, New York 10158. 1987.

PARTNERSHIP INCOME TAXATION. Alan Gunn. Foundation Press, 615 Merrick Avenue, Westbury, New York 11590. 1991.

PARTNERSHIPS IN TROUBLE. George W. Coleman and John H. Small. Prentice-Hall, Incorporated, 113 Sylvan Avenue, Englewood Cliffs, New Jersey 07632. 1991.

PARTNERSHIPS: UPA, ULPA, SECURITIES, TAXATION, AND BANKRUPTCY: RESOURCE MATERIALS. American Law Institute-American Bar Association, Committee on Continuing Professional Education, 4025 Chestnut Street, Philadelphia, Pennsylvania 19104. 1987.

REAL ESTATE LIMITED PARTNERSHIPS. Third Edition. Theodore S. Lynn, Harry F. Goldberg, and Michael Hirschfeld. John Wiley and Sons, Incorporated, 605 Third Avenue, New York, New York 10158. 1991.

REAL ESTATE LIMITED PARTNERSHIPS: A GUIDE FOR PROFITS. Hal Katersky and Klara Katersky. Prentice-Hall, Incorporated, 113 Sylvan Avenue, Englewood Cliffs, New Jersey 07632. 1989.

ENCYCLOPEDIAS AND DICTIONARIES

THE PARTNERSHIP ALMANAC: A SOURCEBOOK OF FINANCIAL DATA, TRENDS, AND PERFORMANCE RATIOS. Leo Troy. Prentice-Hall, Incorporated, 113 Sylvan Avenue, Englewood Cliffs, New Jersey 07632. 1989.

DIGESTS, INDEXES, ABSTRACTS, CITATORS

PARTNERSHIP TAX DIGEST; INCLUDING COVERAGE OF S CORPORATIONS. Second Edition. Bruce A. Furst, Daniel E. Feld, and James A. Douglas. Research Institute of America, Incorporated, One Penn Plaza, New York, New York 10119. 1991.

ANNUALS AND SURVEYS

MODERN TECHNIQUES IN STRUCTURING PARTNERSHIP AGREEMENTS: SIXTH ANNUAL INSTITUTE. Michael J. Halloran and Phillip L. Mann. Prentice-Hall, Incorporated, 113 Sylvan Avenue, Englewood Cliffs, New Jersey 07632. 1989.

LAW REVIEWS AND PERIODICAL S

JOURNAL OF PARTNERSHIP TAXATION. Research Institute of America, Incorporated, One Penn Plaza, New York, New York 10119. Quarterly.

PARTNERSHIP

NEWSLETTERS AND NEWSPAPERS

PARTNER'S REPORT-A BRIEF FOR LAW FIRM OWNERS. Institute of Management and Administration, Incorporated, 29 West Thirty-fifth Street, Fifth Floor, New York, New York 10001. Monthly.

RESEARCH CENTERS, INSTITUTES, CLEARINGHOUSES

INSTITUTE OF MANAGEMENT AND ADMINISTRATION, INCORPORATED. 29 West Thirty-fifth Street, Fifth Floor, New York, New York, 10001. (212) 244-0360.

COMPUTER-ASSISTED LEGAL INSTRUCTION

PARTNERSHIP TAXATION. Taxjem, Incorporated, c/o Center for Computer-Assisted Instruction, 229 19th Avenue South, University of Minnesota, Minneapolis, Minnesota 55455. Machine-readable computer file.

PATENT AND TRADEMARK OFFICE
See also: COURT OF CUSTOMS AND PATENT APPEALS

STATUTES, CODES, STANDARDS, UNIFORM LAWS

CODE OF FEDERAL REGULATIONS, TITLE 37. Office of the Federal Register, National Archives and Records Administration. Superintendent of Documents, United States Government Printing Office, Washington, D.C. 20402. Annual. (Updated by use of monthly List of Sections Affected and daily Federal Register.)

LOOSELEAF SERVICES AND REPORTERS

DECISIONS OF THE COMMISSIONER OF PATENTS. Superintendent of Documents, United States Government Printing Office, Washington, D.C. 20402. 1896- .

OFFICIAL GAZETTE OF THE UNITED STATES PATENT OFFICE. Superintendent of Documents, United States Government Printing Office, Washington, D.C. 20402. 1872- .

UNITED STATES PATENTS QUARTERLY, SECOND SERIES. Bureau of National Affairs, 1231 Twenty-fifth Street, Northwest, Washington, D.C. 20037. 1929- .

HANDBOOKS, MANUALS, FORMBOOKS

MANUAL OF PATENT EXAMINING PROCEDURE. Fifth Edition. Commerce Department, Patent and Trademark Office. Superintendent of Documents, United States Government Printing Office, Washington, D.C. 20402. 1983- .

TRADEMARK MANUAL OF EXAMINING PROCEDURE. Commerce Department, Patent and Trademark Office. Superintendent of Documents, United States Government Printing Office, Washington, D.C. 20402. 1974- .

TEXTBOOKS AND GENERAL WORKS

PATENTS AND THE FEDERAL CIRCUIT. Second Edition. Robert L. Harmon. Bureau of National Affairs, Incorporated, 1231 Twenty-fifth Street, Northwest, Washington, D.C. 20037. 1991.

THE STORY OF THE U.S. PATENT AND TRADEMARK OFFICE. United States Department of Commerce, Patent and Trademark Office. Superintendent of Documents, United States Government Printing Office, Washington, D.C. 20402. 1988.

DIGESTS, INDEXES, ABSTRACTS, CITATORS

CONSOLIDATED LISTING OF OFFICIAL GAZETTE NOTICES: REGARDING PATENT AND TRADEMARK OFFICE PRACTICES AND PROCEDURES. Commerce Department, Patent and Trademark Office. Superintendent of Documents, United States Government Printing Office, Washington, D.C. 20402. 1987.

SHEPARD'S UNITED STATES PATENTS AND TRADEMARKS CITATIONS. Shepard's/McGraw-Hill, P.O. Box 1235, Colorado Springs, Colorado 80901. Bimonthly.

DIRECTORIES

ATTORNEYS AND AGENTS REGISTERED TO PRACTICE BEFORE THE UNITED STATES PATENT AND TRADEMARK OFFICE. Commerce Department, Patent and Trademark Office. Superintendent of Documents, United States Government Printing Office, Washington, D.C. 20402. Annual.

RESEARCH CENTERS, INSTITUTES, CLEARINGHOUSES

TRADEMARK SEARCH LIBRARY. Patent and Trademark Office, Crystal Park, Arlington, Virginia 22202. (703) 557-3281.

ONLINE DATABASES

LEXIS, FEDERAL PATENT, TRADEMARK, AND COPYRIGHT LIBRARY. Mead Data Central, P.O. Box 933, Dayton, Ohio 45401.

WESTLAW, COPYRIGHT LIBRARY. West Publishing Company, P.O. Box 64526, 50 West Kellogg Boulevard, St. Paul, Minnesota 55164-0526.

WESTLAW, PATENTS LIBRARY. West Publishing Company, P.O. Box 64526, 50 West Kellogg Boulevard, St. Paul, Minnesota 55164-0526.

PATENTS
See also: COURT OF CUSTOMS AND PATENT APPEALS; PATENT AND TRADEMARK OFFICE; TRADE SECRETS

STATUTES, CODES, STANDARDS, UNIFORM LAWS

THE LEGISLATIVE HISTORY OF THE DRUG PRICE COMPETITION AND PATENT TERM RESTORATION ACT OF 1984. Allan M. Fox and Alan R. Bennett. Food and Drug Law Institute, 1000 Vermont Avenue, Washington, D.C. 20005. 1987.

LOOSELEAF SERVICES AND REPORTERS

COMPUTER SOFTWARE PROTECTION LAW. Cary H. Sherman, Hamish R. Sandison, and Marc D. Guren. Bureau of National Affairs, Incorporated, 1231 Twenty-fifth Street, Northwest, Washington, D.C. 20037. 1989- .

COMPUTER SOFTWARE: PROTECTION, LIABILITY, LAW, FORMS. L.J. Kutten. Clark Boardman Company, Limited, 435 Hudson Street, New York, New York 10014. 1987- .

PATENT LAW PROSPECTIVES. Second Edition. Donald R. Dunner. Matthew Bender and Company, Incorporated, 11 Penn Plaza, New York, New York 10001. 1982- .

PATENT OFFICE RULES AND PRACTICE. Lester Horwitz. Matthew Bender and Company, Incorporated, 11 Penn Plaza, New York, New York 10001. 1971- .

PATENT, TRADEMARK AND COPYRIGHT JOURNAL. Bureau of National Affairs, 1231 Twenty-fifth Street, Northwest, Washington, D.C. 20037. 1970- .

PATENTS: A TREATISE ON THE LAW OF PATENTABILITY, VALIDITY AND INFRINGEMENT. Donald S. Chisum. Matthew Bender and Company, Incorporated, 11 Penn Plaza, New York, New York 10001. 1978- .

PATENTS THROUGHOUT THE WORLD. Third Edition. Anne Marie Greene, Editor. Trade Activities Incorporated, 435 Hudson Street, New York, New York 10014. 1985- .

SCOTT ON COMPUTER LAW. Second Edition. Michael D. Scott. Prentice-Hall, Incorporated, 113 Sylvan Avenue, Englewood Cliffs, New Jersey 07632. 1991- .

UNITED STATES PATENTS QUARTERLY. Bureau of National Affairs, 1231 Twenty-fifth Street, Northwest, Washington, D.C. 20037. 1929- .

WORLD PATENT LAW AND PRACTICE: PATENT STATUTES, REGULATIONS, AND TREATIES. John P. Sinnott. Matthew Bender and Company, Incorporated, 11 Penn Plaza, New York, New York 10001. 1974- .

HANDBOOKS, MANUALS, FORMBOOKS

BIOTECHNOLOGY PATENTS: A BUSINESS MANAGER'S LEGAL GUIDE. Bureau of National Affairs, Incorporated, 1231 Twenty-fifth Street, Northwest, Washington, D.C. 20037. 1989.

THE BUSINESS OF INDUSTRIAL LICENSING: A PRACTICAL GUIDE TO PATENTS, KNOW-HOW, TRADEMARKS AND INDUSTRIAL DESIGN. Second Edition. Patrick Hearn. Gower Publishing Company, Old Post Road, Brookfield, Vermont 05036. 1986.

DRAFTING PATENT LICENSE AGREEMENTS. Third Edition. Harry R. Mayers. Bureau of National Affairs, 1231 Twenty-fifth Street, Northwest, Washington, D.C. 20037. 1991.

HOW TO PREPARE PATENT APPLICATIONS: A SELF-STUDY COURSEBOOK USING ACTUAL INVENTIONS. John R. Flanagan. Patent Educational Publications, P.O. Box 13129, Boulder, Colorado 80306-4309. 1983.

INVENTING AND PATENTING SOURCEBOOK: HOW TO SELL AND PROTECT YOUR IDEAS. Richard C. Levy and Robert J. Huffman. Gale Research, Incorporated, 835 Penobscot Building, Detroit, Michigan 48226. 1990.

THE INVENTOR'S DESKTOP COMPANION: A GUIDE TO SUCCESSFULLY MARKETING AND PROTECTING YOUR IDEAS. Richard C. Levy. Gale Research, Incorporated, 835 Penobscot Building, Detroit, Michigan 48226. 1991.

THE INVENTOR'S HANDBOOK. Armand G. Winfield. Prentice-Hall, Incorporated, 113 Sylvan Avenue, Englewood Cliffs, New Jersey 07632. 1990.

THE INVENTOR'S HANDBOOK: HOW TO DEVELOP, PROTECT, AND MARKET YOUR INVENTION. Second Edition. Robert Park. Betterway Publications, Incorporated, White Hall, Virginia 22987. 1990.

LEGAL CASE FOR YOUR SOFTWARE: A STEP-BY-STEP GUIDE FOR COMPUTER SOFTWARE WRITERS. Addison-Wesley Publishing Company, Incorporated, Route 128, Reading, Massachusetts 01867. 1982.

MANUAL OF CLASSIFICATION. United States Patent Office. Superintendent of Documents, United States Government Printing Office, Washington, D.C. 20402. 1984.

MANUAL OF PATENT EXAMINING PROCEDURE. United States Patent Office. Superintendent of Documents, United States Government Printing Office, Washington, D.C. 20402. 1984.

1985-1986 PATENT LAW HANDBOOK. C. Bruce Hamburg. Clark Boardman Company, Limited, 435 Hudson Street, New York, New York 10014. 1985.

THE PATENT BOOK: HOW TO PATENT YOUR WORK IN THE UNITED STATES. David Pressman. Nolo Press, 950 Parker Street, Berkeley, California 94710. 1985.

PATENT SMART: A COMPLETE GUIDE TO DEVELOPING, PROTECTING, AND SELLING YOUR INVENTION. Robert A. Seemann. Prentice-Hall, Incorporated, 113 Sylvan Avenue, Englewood Cliffs, New Jersey 07632. 1987.

PATENTABILITY OF COMPUTER SOFTWARE: AN INTERNATIONAL GUIDE TO THE PROTECTION OF COMPUTER RELATED INVENTIONS. Henri Hanneman. Kluwer Law and Taxation, Kluwer Law Book Publishers, Incorporated, 36 West Forty-fourth Street, New York, New York 10036. 1985.

PATENTING IN THE BIOLOGICAL SCIENCES: A PRACTICAL GUIDE FOR RESEARCH SCIENTISTS IN BIOTECHNOLOGY AND THE PHARMACEUTICAL AND AGROCHEMICAL INDUSTRIES. John Wiley and Sons, Incorporated, 605 Third Avenue, New York, New York 10158. 1982.

PATENTING MANUAL. Second Edition. Alan M. Hale. SPI, Incorporated, 1051 Clinton Street, Buffalo, New York 14206. 1983.

PATENTING OF LIFE FORMS. David W. Plant, Niels J. Reimers, and Norton D. Zinder, Editors. Cold Spring Harbor Laboratory, P.O. Box 100, Cold Spring Harbor, New York 11724. 1982.

PATENTS: A BASIC GUIDE TO PATENTING IN BIOTECHNOLOGY. R. S. Crespi. Cambridge University Press, 40 West Twentieth Street, New York, New York 10011. 1988.

SOFTWARE OWNERSHIP/CONFIDENTIALITY FORMS: A COLLECTION OF EMPLOYEE AND CONSULTANT SOFTWARE OWNERSHIP/CONFIDENTIALITY FORMS. Paul Hoffman, Chairman. American Bar Association, Section of Patent, Trademark and Copyright Law, 750 North Lake Shore Drive, Chicago, Illinois 60611. 1984.

UNDERSTANDING CHEMICAL PATENTS: A GUIDE FOR THE INVENTOR. Second Edition. John T. Maynard and Howard M. Peters. American Chemical Society, 1155 Sixteenth Street, Northwest, Washington, D.C. 20036. 1991.

WHAT THE GENERAL PRACTITIONERS SHOULD KNOW ABOUT PATENT LAW AND PRACTICE. Fourth Edition. Arthur H. Seidel. American Law Institute-American Bar Association, Committee on Continuing Professional Education, 4025 Chestnut Street, Philadelphia, Pennsylvania 19104. 1984.

TEXTBOOKS AND GENERAL WORKS

BIOTECHNOLOGY AND THE LAW. Iver P. Cooper. Clark Boardman Company, Limited, 435 Hudson Street, New York, New York 10014. 1982. (Annual Supplements).

COURT OF APPEALS FOR THE FEDERAL CIRCUIT-PRACTICE AND PROCEDURE: APPEAL AND REVIEW OF PATENT AND TRADEMARK CASES. Revised Edition. Donald R. Dunner and Charles L. Gholz. Matthew Bender and Company, Incorporated, 11 Penn Plaza, New York, New York 10001. 1985. (Periodic Supplements).

CURRENT DEVELOPMENTS IN PATENT LAW, 1985. Jack C. Goldstein, Chairman. Practising Law Institute, 810 Seventh Avenue, New York, New York 10019. 1985.

DESIGNS AND UTILITY MODELS THROUGHOUT THE WORLD. Anne M. Greene, Editor. Trade Activities, Incorporated, 435 Hudson Street, New York, New York 10014. 1983.

DOMESTIC AND FOREIGN TECHNOLOGY LICENSING, 1984. Tom Arnold, Chairman. Practising Law Institute, 810 Seventh Avenue, New York, New York 10019. 1984.

ELECTRONIC AND COMPUTER PATENT LAW. Robert Greene Sterne. Practising Law Institute, 810 Seventh Avenue, New York, New York 10019. 1990.

FOREIGN PATENT LITIGATION. Samson Helfgott and Michael N. Meller, Co-chairmen. Practising Law Institute, 810 Seventh Avenue, New York, New York 10019. 1983.

INTELLECTUAL PROPERTY: PATENTS, TRADEMARKS, AND COPYRIGHT IN A NUTSHELL. Second Edition. Arthur R. Miller and Michael H. Davis. West Publishing Company, P.O. Box 64526, 50 West Kellogg Boulevard, St. Paul, Minnesota 55164-0526. 1990.

INTELLECTUAL PROPERTY RIGHTS IN BIOTECHNOLOGY WORLDWIDE. Stephen A. Bent. Stockton Press, 15 East Twenty-sixth Street, New York, New York 10010. 1987.

LAW AND THE SOFTWARE MARKETER. Frederick L. Cooper, III. Prentice- Hall, Incorporated, 113 Sylvan Avenue, Englewood Cliffs, New Jersey 07632. 1988.

LEARNED HAND ON PATENT LAW. Paul H. Blaustein. Pineridge Publishing House, P.O. Box 289 Gedney, White Plains, New York 10605. 1983.

LIPSCOMB'S WALKER ON PATENTS. Third Edition. Ernest B. Lipscomb, III. Lawyers Cooperative Publishing Company, Aqueduct Building, Rochester, New York 14694. 1984. (Supplements).

MATERIALS AND CASES ON PATENT INTERFERENCE. Maurice H. Klitzman. Bureau of National Affairs, 1231 Twenty-fifth Street, Northwest, Washington, D.C. 20037. 1982.

PATENT AND TRADEMARK TACTICS AND PRACTICE. Second Edition. David A. Burge. John Wiley and Sons, Incorporated, 605 Third Avenue, New York, New York 10158. 1984.

PATENT ANTITRUST, 1982. David Bender, Chairman. Practising Law Institute, 810 Seventh Avenue, New York, New York 10019. 1982.

PATENT INTERFERENCE: LAW AND PRACTICE. Maurice H. Klitzman. Practising Law Institute, 810 Seventh Avenue, New York, New York 10019. 1984.

PATENT LAW FUNDAMENTALS. Second Edition. Peter D. Rosenberg. Clark Boardman Company, Limited, 435 Hudson Street, New York, New York 10014. 1980. (Annual Supplements).

PATENT LICENSING TRANSACTIONS. Harold Einhorn. Matthew Bender and Company, Incorporated, 11 Penn Plaza, New York, New York 10001. 1968. (Annual Supplements).

PATENT LITIGATION. Donald R. Dunner, Chairman. Practising Law Institute, 810 Seventh Avenue, New York, New York 10019. 1989.

PATENT LITIGATION: PROCEDURE AND TACTICS. Robert A. White. Matthew Bender and Company, Incorporated, 11 Penn Plaza, New York, New York 10001. 1971. (Annual Supplements).

PATENT PENDING: TODAY'S INVENTORS AND THEIR INVENTIONS. Richard L. Gausewitz. Alson Publishing Company, 931 Santiago Street, Santa Ana, California 92701. 1984.

PATENT PRACTICE. Irving Kayton, Editor. Patent Resources Institute, 2100 Pennsylvania Avenue, Northwest 20006. 1985.

PATENT PROTECTION FOR COMPUTER SOFTWARE: THE NEW SAFEGUARD. Michael S. Keplinger and Ronald S. Laurie. Prentice-Hall, Incorporated, 113 Sylvan Avenue, Englewood Cliffs, New Jersey 07632. 1989.

PATENT, TRADEMARK, AND COPYRIGHT LAWS. Jeffrey M. Samuels, Editor. Bureau of National Affairs, 1231 Twenty-fifth Street, Northwest, Washington, D.C. 20037. 1989.

PATENTS AND TECHNICAL DATA. Ralph C. Nash, Jr., and Leonard Rawicz. Government Contracts Program Academic Center, George Washington University, 2020 K Street, Northwest, Suite 210, Washington, D.C. 20052. 1983.

PATENTS FOR CHEMISTS. Phillip W. Grubb. Oxford University Press, Incorporated, 200 Madison Avenue, New York, New York 10016. 1982.

PATENTS PENDING: THE EVOLUTION OF ARTIFACTS. Henry Petroski. Alfred A. Knopf, Incorporated, 201 East Fiftieth Street, New York, New York 10022. 1992.

PRODUCT COUNTERFEITING: REMEDIES. David A. Gerber, Chairman. Practising Law Institute, 810 Seventh Avenue, New York, New York 10019. 1984.

PROTECTING BIOTECHNOLOGY INVENTIONS: A GUIDE FOR SCIENTISTS. Roman Saliwanchik. Science Tech Publishers, 701 Ridge Street, Madison, Wisconsin 53705. 1988.

PROTECTING YOUR PROPRIETARY RIGHTS IN THE COMPUTER AND HIGH TECHNOLOGY INDUSTRIES. Tobey B. Marzouk. Computer Society Press, Los Angeles, California. 1988.

THE PROTECTION OF COMPUTER SOFTWARE: ITS TECHNOLOGY AND APPLICATIONS. Second Edition. Derrick Grover. Cambridge University Press, 40 West Twentieth Street, New York, New York 10011. 1991.

ROLE OF PATENTS IN SCI-TECH LIBRARIES. Ellis Mount, Editor. Haworth Press Incorporated, 10 Alice Street, Binghamton, New York 13904. 1982.

TECHNOLOGY LICENSING. Tom Arnold and Thomas F. Smegal, Jr. Co-chairmen. Practising Law Institute, 810 Seventh Avenue, New York, New York 10019. 1982.

TRENDS IN BIOTECHNOLOGY AND CHEMICAL PATENT LAW. Nels T. Lippert and George M. Gould, Co-chairmen. Practising Law Institute, 810 Seventh Avenue, New York, New York 10019. 1985.

TRENDS IN BIOTECHNOLOGY AND CHEMICAL PATENT PRACTICE, 1989. Nels T. Lippert. Practising Law Institute, 810 Seventh Avenue, New York, New York 10019. 1989.

ENCYCLOPEDIAS AND DICTIONARIES

ATTORNEY'S DICTIONARY OF PATENT CLAIMS. Irwin M. Aisenberg. Matthew Bender and Company, Incorporated, 11 Penn Plaza, New York, New York 10001. 1985.

DIGESTS, INDEXES, ABSTRACTS, CITATORS

DECISIONS AND DEVELOPMENTS. Decisions and Developments Publishing Company, P.O. Box 342, Wayland, Massachusetts 01778. Bimonthly.

DIGEST OF COMMERCIAL LAWS OF THE WORLD: PATENTS AND TRADEMARKS. Oceana Publications, Incorporated, 75 Main Street, Dobbs Ferry, New York 10522. 1980- .

INDEX OF PATENTS ISSUED FROM PATENT OFFICE. United States Patent Office. Superintendent of Documents, United States Government Printing Office, Washington, D.C. 20402. Annual

PATENT DIGEST. Gas Appliance Manufacturers Association, 1901 North Moore Street, Suite 1100, Arlington, Virginia 22209. Monthly.

SHEPARD'S UNITED STATES PATENTS AND TRADEMARK CITATIONS. Shepard's/McGraw-Hill, P.O. Box 1235, Colorado Springs, Colorado 80901. 1968- .

WORLD PATENT INDEX. Derwent Publications Limited, Rochdale House, 138 Theobalds Road, London WC1X 8RP, England. Weekly.

ANNUALS AND SURVEYS

INTERNATIONAL PATENT LITIGATION: A COUNTRY BY COUNTRY ANALYSIS. Bureau of National Affairs, 1231 Twenty-fifth Street, Northwest, Washington, D.C. 20037. 1983- .

PATENT COOPERATION TREATY AND REGULATIONS. Rules Service Company, 7658 Standish Place, Suite 106, Rockville, Maryland 20855. 1981- .

PATENT LAW ANNUAL. Matthew Bender and Company, Incorporated, 11 Penn Plaza, New York, New York 10001. Annual.

LAW REVIEWS AND PERIODICALS

JOURNAL OF THE PATENT OFFICE SOCIETY. Patent Office Society, 104 Academy Avenue, Federalsburg, Maryland 21632. Monthly.

PATENT AND TRADEMARK REVIEW. Trade Activities, Incorporated, 435 Hudson Street, New York, New York 10014. Monthly.

NEWSLETTERS AND NEWSPAPERS

AIPLA BULLETIN. American Intellectual Property Law Association, 2001 Jefferson Davis Highway, Suite 203, Arlington, Virginia 22202.

BIOTECHNOLOGY NEWSWATCH. Shepard's/McGraw-Hill, P.O. Box 1235, Colorado Springs, Colorado 80901. Semimonthly

BNA'S PATENT, TRADEMARK AND COPYRIGHT JOURNAL. Bureau of National Affairs, Incorporated, 1231 Twenty-fifth Street, Washington, D.C. 20037. Weekly.

COMPUTER INDUSTRY LITIGATION REPORTER. Andrews Publications, 1646 West Chester Pike, Westtown, Pennsylvania 19395. Semimonthly

COMPUTER LAW STRATEGIST. Leader Publications. Monthly.

DECISIONS AND DEVELOPMENTS. Decisions and Developments Publishing Company, P.O. Box 342, Wayland, Massachusetts 01778. Bimonthly.

GRIMES AND BATTERS BY REPORT. GB Enterprises, P.O. Box 1169, Stamford, Connecticut 06904. Monthly

INTELLECTUAL PROPERTY FRAUD REPORTER. International Business Reports and Covington and Burling, P.O. Box 27376, Washington, D. C. 20038. Semimonthly.

INTELLECTUAL PROPERTY NOTES. National Patent Council, 2001 Jefferson Davis Highway, Suite 301, Arlington, Virginia 22202. Monthly.

THE JOURNAL OF PROPRIETARY RIGHTS. Prentice-Hall, Incorporated, 113 Sylvan Avenue, Englewood Cliffs, New Jersey 07632. Monthly.

LITALENT. Research Publications, Rapid Patent Service, P.O. Box 2527, Eads Station, Arlington, Virginia 22202. Monthly.

MEDICAL DEVICE PATENTS LETTER. Washington Business Information, Incorporated, 1117 North Nineteenth Street, Suite 200, Arlington, Virginia 22209. Monthly

NATIONAL COUNCIL OF INTELLECTUAL PROPERTY LAW ASSOCIATIONS NEWSLETTER. c/o David Powsner, Lahive and Cockfield, 60 State Street, Suite 510, Boston, Massachusetts 02109. Quarterly.

NYPTC BULLETIN. GB Enterprises, P.O. Box 1169, Stamford, Connecticut 06904. Bimonthly.

PATENT OFFICE PROFESSIONAL ASSOCIATION NEWSLETTER. Patent Office Professional Association, P.O. Box 2745, Arlington, Virginia 22202. Monthly.

PTC NEWSLETTER. American Bar Association, Section of Patent, Trademark and Copyright Law, 750 North Lake Shore Drive, Chicago, Illinois 60611. Quarterly.

SOFTWARE PROTECTION. Law and Technology Press, P.O. Box 3280, Manhattan Beach, California 90266. Monthly.

UNITED STATES PATENT OFFICE OFFICIAL GAZETTE. United States Patent Office. Superintendent of Documents, United States Government Printing Office, Washington, D.C. 20402. Weekly.

WORLD TECHNOLOGY PATENT LICENSING GAZETTE. Techni Research Association, Incorporated, Professional Center Building, 41 Easton Road, Willow Grove, Pennsylvania 19090. Bimonthly.

BIBLIOGRAPHIES

INFORMATION SOURCES IN PATENTS. Charles P. Auger. Bowker-Saur Limited, Borough Green, Sevenoaks, Kent TN15 8PH, England. 1992.

DIRECTORIES

ATTORNEYS AND AGENTS REGISTERED TO PRACTICE BEFORE UNITED STATES PATENT OFFICE. Superintendent of Documents, United States Government Printing Office, Washington, D.C. 20402. Annual.

CATALOG OF GOVERNMENT PATENTS: INVENTIONS AVAILABLE FOR LICENSING TO U.S. BUSINESSES. Center for the Utilization of Federal Technology, National Technical Information Service, Commerce Department, 5285 Port Royal Road, Springield, Virginia 22161. Annual.

CONCORDANCE, UNITED STATES PATENT CLASSIFICATION TO INTERNATIONAL PATENT CLASSIFICATION. United States Department of Commerce, Patent and Trademark Office, Washington, D.C. 20402. 1990

ASSOCIATIONS AND PROFESSIONAL SOCIETIES

AMERICAN BAR ASSOCIATION, SECTION OF PATENT, TRADEMARK AND COPYRIGHT LAW. 750 North Lake Shore Drive, Chicago, Illinois 60611. (312) 985-5000.

AMERICAN INTELLECTUAL PROPERTY LAW ASSOCIATION. 2001 Jefferson Davis Highway, Suite 203, Arlington, Virginia 22202. (703) 521-1680.

INTERNATIONAL FEDERATION OF INDUSTRIAL PROPERTY ATTORNEYS. Holbeinstrasse 36-38, CH 4051 Basel, Switzerland 61-239953.

INTERNATIONAL PATENT AND TRADEMARK ASSOCIATION. 33 West Monroe, Chicago, Illinois 60603. (312) 641-1500.

INTELLECTUAL PROPERTY OWNERS. 1255 Twenty-third Street, Northwest, Suite 850, Washington, D. C. 20037. (202) 466-2396.

NATIONAL COUNCIL OF INTELLECTUAL PROPERTY LAW ASSOCIATIONS. c/o Office of Public Affairs, U. S. Patent and Trademark Office, 2021 Jefferson Davis Highway, Room 1A05, Arlington, Virginia 22202. (703) 557-3341.

NATIONAL PATENT COUNCIL. 2121 Crystal Drive, Suite 704, Two Crystal Park, Arlington, Virginia 22202. (703) 521-1669.

PATENT AND TRADEMARK OFFICE SOCIETY. P.O. Box 2089. Arlington, Virginia 22202. (703) 557-6511.

RESEARCH CENTERS, INSTITUTES, CLEARINGHOUSES

PTC RESEARCH FOUNDATION. Franklin Pierce Law Center, 2 White Street, Concord, New Hampshire 03301. (603) 228-1541.

ONLINE DATABASES

BIOPATENTS. BIOSIS, 2100 Arch Street, Philadelphia, Pennsylvania 19103.

BNA PATENT, TRADEMARK, AND COPYRIGHT DAILY. BNA ONLINE. Bureau of National Affairs, Incorporated, 1231 Twenty-fifth Street, Northwest, Washington, D.C. 20037.

BNA'S PATENT, TRADEMARK, AND COPYRIGHT JOURNAL. BNA ONLINE. Bureau of National Affairs, Incorporated, 1231 Twenty-fifth Street, Northwest, Washington, D.C. 20037.

CLAIMS/U.S. PATENT ABSTRACTS. IFI/Plenum Data Corporation, 302 Swann Avenue, Alexandria, Virginia 22301.

LEXIS, FEDERAL PATENT, TRADEMARK AND COPYRIGHT LIBRARY. Mead Data Central, P.O. Box 933, Dayton, Ohio 45401.

LEXPAT. Mead Data Central. P.O. Box 933, Dayton, Ohio 45401.

LITALERT. Research Publications, Incorporated, 12 Lunar Drive, Woodbridge, Connecticut 06525.

PATDATA. BRS Information Technologies, 8000 Westpark Drive, McLean, Virginia 22102.

PATENT FAMILY SERVICE/PATENT RESEARCH SERVICE. Patent Documentation Center. INPADOC, Sales Department, Mollwaldplatz 4, 1040 Vienna Austria.

PATENT STATUS FILE. Research Publications, Incorporated, Rapid Patent Services, 1921 Jefferson Davis Highway, Suite 1821-D, Arlington, Virginia 22202.

PATLAW. Bureau of National Affairs, Data Base Publishing Unit, 1231 Twenty-fifth Street, Northwest, Washington, D.C. 20037.

PATSEARCH. Pergamon Infoline, Incorporated, 1340 Old Chain Bridge Road, McLean, Virginia 22101.

UNITED STATES PATENT. Derwent, Incorporated, 1313 Dolley Madison Boulevard, Suite 303, McLean, Virginia 22101.

UNITED STATES PATENT CLASSIFICATION SYSTEM. United States Patent and Trademark Office, Office of Electronic Data Conversion and Dissemination, Office of the Director, Crystal Park 2, Suite 1100B, Washington, D.C. 20231.

WESTLAW, INTELLECTUAL PROPERTY LIBRARY. West Publishing Company, P.O. Box 64526, 50 West Kellogg Boulevard, St. Paul, Minnesota 55164-0526.

STATISTICS SOURCES

ANNUAL REPORT. Commissioner of Patents. United States Patent Office. Superintendent of Documents, United States Government Printing Office, Washington, D.C. 20402.

PATERNITY
See: FAMILY LAW

PEACE OFFICERS
See: LAW ENFORCEMENT; POLICE

PENOLOGY
See: PRISONS AND PRISONERS

PENSIONS
See: EMPLOYEE FRINGE BENEFITS; INSURANCE, LIFE; SOCIAL SECURITY

PERFORMING ARTS
See: ENTERTAINMENT LAW

PERJURY
See: CRIMINAL LAW

PERSONAL INJURIES
See also: MEDICAL JURISPRUDENCE AND MALPRACTICE

LOOSELEAF SERVICES AND REPORTERS

ENGINEERING FOR THE PERSONAL INJURY ATTORNEY; THEORY, EXPERTS, EVIDENCE: LEGAL MATERIALS AND PRACTICE COMMENTARIES. Ira S. Kuperstein and Neil L. Salters. Matthew Bender and Company, Incorporated, 11 Penn Plaza, New York, New York 10001. 1991- .

DAMAGES IN TORT ACTIONS. Marilyn Minzer. Matthew Bender and Company, Incorporated, 11 Penn Plaza, New York, New York 10001. 1982- .

HANDLING MOTOR VEHICLE ACCIDENT CASES: FORMS. John L. Messina. Callaghan and Company, 155 Pfingsten Road, Deerfield, Illinois 60015. 1990- .

HANDLING OCCUPATIONAL DISEASE CASES. Frederick M. Baron. Callaghan and Company, 155 Pfingsten Road, Deerfield, Illinois 60015. 1989- .

LITIGATING HEAD TRAUMA CASES. Arthur C. Roberts and Phillip J. Resnick. PESI Legal Publishing, 200 Spring Street, Eau Claire, Wisconsin 54702. 1989- .

NATIONAL VERDICT SURVEY. M. E. Lurie, Editor. Jury Verdict Research, Incorporated, 30700H Bainbridge Road, Solon, Ohio 44139-2291. 1983- .

PERSONAL INJURY: ACTIONS, DEFENSES, DAMAGES. Louis R. Frumer. Matthew Bender and Company, Incorporated, 11 Penn Plaza, New York, New York 10001. 1957- .

PERSONAL INJURY DEFENSE REPORTER. Mark A. Dombroff. Matthew Bender and Company, Incorporated, 11 Penn Plaza, New York, New York 10001. 1985- .

PERSONAL INJURY DEFENSE TECHNIQUES. Mark A. Dombroff. Matthew Bender and Company, Incorporated, 11 Penn Plaza, New York, New York 10001. 1987- .

PERSONAL INJURY: SUCCESSFUL LITIGATION TECHNIQUES. Joseph Kelner. Matthew Bender and Company, Incorporated, 11 Penn Plaza, New York, New York 10001. 1970- .

PERSONAL INJURY VALUATION HANDBOOKS. Marci E. Lurie, Editor. Jury Verdict Research, Incorporated, 30700H Bainbridge Road, Solon, Ohio 44139-2291. 1959- .

HANDBOOKS, MANUALS, FORMBOOKS

ABDOMINAL INJURIES. Jules R. Kalisch and Harold Williams. Matthew Bender and Company, Incorporated, 11 Penn Plaza, New York, New York 10001. 1974. (Annual Supplements).

ANATOMY OF A PERSONAL INJURY TRIAL, 1982. Neil T. Shayne, Chairman. Practising Law Institute, 810 Seventh Avenue, New York, New York 10019. 1982.

BETTER, EARLIER SETTLEMENTS THROUGH ECONOMIC LEVERAGE. Philip J. Hermann. Jury Verdict Research, Incorporated, 30700 Bainbridge Road, Solon, Ohio 44139-2291. 1989.

CANCER. Arthur L. Frank and Michael D. Carlin. Matthew Bender and Company, Incorporated, 11 Penn Plaza, New York, New York 10001. 1978. (Annual Supplements).

CHEST, HEART AND LUNGS. Jules R. Kalisch and Harold Williams. Matthew Bender and Company, Incorporated, 11 Penn Plaza, New York, New York 10001. 1975. (Annual Supplements).

CLAIM IT YOURSELF: THE ACCIDENT VICTIM'S GUIDE TO PERSONAL INJURY CLAIMS. Michele Saadi. Pharos Books. Distributed by Ballantine Books, 201 East Fiftieth Street, New York, New York 10022. 1987.

THE COMPLETE PERSONAL INJURY PRACTICE MANUAL. Al J. Cone and Verne Lawyer. Prentice-Hall, Incorporated, 113 Sylvan Avenue, Englewood Cliffs, New Jersey 07632. 1983.

DEATH. Marshall Houts. Matthew Bender and Company, Incorporated, 11 Penn Plaza, New York, New York 10001. 1966. (Annual Supplements).

THE DEFENSE LAWYER'S TRIAL HANDBOOK: SUCCESSFUL COURTROOM STRATEGIES FOR DEFENDING PERSONAL INJURY AND MALPRACTICE CASES. James B. Rosenblum. Executive Reports Corporation, Subsidiary of Prentice-Hall, Incorporated, 113 Sylvan Avenue, Englewood Cliffs, New Jersey 07632. 1984.

THE EYE. Loring F. Chapman. AMS Press, Incorporated, 56 East Thirteenth Street, New York, New York 10003. 1981. (Annual Supplements).

HANDBOOK OF PERSONAL INJURY FORMS AND LITIGATION MATERIALS. Edward M. Swartz and Fredric A. Swartz. Lawyers Cooperative Publishing Company, Aqueduct Building, Rochester, New York 14694. 1983. (Supplements).

HANDLING INJURIES TO THE NECK AND BACK: SOFT TISSUE, DISC, AND SPINAL CORD. Thomas J. Murray Jr. and Joe C. Savage, Chairmen. Practising Law Institute, 810 Seventh Avenue, New York, New York 10019. 1984.

HANDLING SOFT TISSUE INJURY CASES. Stanley E. Preiser and Monty L. Preiser. Michie Company, P.O. Box 7587, Charlottesville, Virginia 22906-7587. 1987. (Supplements).

HEAD AND BRAIN. Loring F. Chapman. Matthew Bender and Company, Incorporated, 11 Penn Plaza, New York, New York 10001. 1972. (Annual Supplements).

HEAD AND NECK INJURY HANDBOOK. Lawrence J. Smith. Shepard's/McGraw-Hill, P.O. Box 1235, Colorado Springs, Colorado 80901. 1989.

HIP AND THIGH. Jules R. Kalisch and Harold Williams. Matthew Bender and Company, Incorporated, 11 Penn Plaza, New York, New York 10001. 1972. (Annual Supplements).

HOW TO SETTLE FOR TOP DOLLAR. Stephan H. Peskin. Michie Company, P.O. Box 7587, Charlottesville, Virginia 22906. 1989.

INJURED?: HOW TO GET EVERY DOLLAR YOU DESERVE. Philip J. Hermann. Jury Verdict Research, Incorporated, 30700 Bainbridge Road, Solon, Ohio 44139-2291. 1990.

THE JACOBY AND MEYERS PRACTICAL GUIDE TO PERSONAL INJURY. Gail J. Koff. Simon and Schuster, Incorporated, 1230 Avenue of the Americas, New York, New York 10020. 1991.

THE KNEE AND RELATED STRUCTURES. Jules R. Kalisch and Harold Williams. Matthew Bender and Company, Incorporated, 11 Penn Plaza, New York, New York 10001. 1972. (Annual Supplements).

THE LOW BACK. Leo Gelfand, Rauol D. Magana, and R. R. Merliss. Matthew Bender and Company, Incorporated, 11 Penn Plaza, New York, New York 10001. 1962. (Annual Supplements).

THE NECK. Leo Wolfstone. Matthew Bender and Company, Incorporated, 11 Penn Plaza, New York, New York 10001. 1965. (Annual Supplements).

PAIN AND SUFFERING. Loring F. Chapman. Matthew Bender and Company, Incorporated, 11 Penn Plaza, New York, New York 10001. 1967. (Annual Supplements).

PERSONAL INJURY DESKBOOK. Matthew Bender and Company, Incorporated, 11 Penn Plaza, New York, New York 10001. 1982. (Annual Supplements).

PERSONAL INJURY FORMS: DISCOVERY AND SETTLEMENT. John A. Tarantino and David Oliveira. James Publishing Incorporated, P.O. Box 25202, Santa Ana, California 92799.

PERSONAL INJURY TRIAL HANDBOOK. John A. Tarantino and David J. Oliveira. John Wiley and Sons, Incorporated, 605 Third Avenue, New York, New York 10158. 1989.

PSYCHIC INJURIES. Marvin E. Lewis and Robert Sudoff. Matthew Bender and Company, Incorporated, 11 Penn Plaza, New York, New York 10001. 1975. (Annual Supplements).

SHOULDER AND ELBOW. Jules R. Kalisch and Harold Williams. Matthew Bender and Company, Incorporated, 11 Penn Plaza, New York, New York 10001. 1970. (Annual Supplements).

THE SKIN. Charles W. Whitmore. Matthew Bender and Company, Incorporated, 11 Penn Plaza, New York, New York 10001. 1971. (Annual Supplements).

TRAUMA. Marshall Houts. Matthew Bender and Company, Incorporated, 11 Penn Plaza, New York, New York 10001. 1959. (Annual Supplements).

TRAUMATIC MEDICINE AND SURGERY FOR THE ATTORNEY. Matthew Bender and Company, Incorporated, 11 Penn Plaza, New York, New York 10001. 1975. (Annual Supplements).

WHAT'S IT WORTH? A GUIDE TO CURRENT PERSONAL INJURY AWARDS AND SETTLEMENTS. Robert Harley, Mary Ann Mager, and Frederick Smith. Michie Company, P.O. Box 7587, Charlottesville, Virginia 22906-7587. 1985.

TEXTBOOKS AND GENERAL WORKS

ANATOMY OF A PERSONAL INJURY LAWSUIT. Third Edition. James S. Rogers. ATLA Press, Washington, D.C. 1991.

AUTOMATED TELLER MACHINE CRIME: ARE BANKS LIABLE FOR PERSONAL INJURIES? Pamela Samuels. William S. Hein and Company, 1285 Main Street, Buffalo, New York 14209. 1990.

BASIC PERSONAL INJURY TRIAL PRACTICE. Neil T. Shayne. Practising Law Institute, 810 Seventh Avenue, New York, New York 10019. 1988.

THE BLAME GAME: INJURIES, INSURANCE AND INJUSTICE. Jeffrey O'Connell and C. Brian Kelly. Lexington Books, Division of D.C. Heath and Company, 125 Spring Street, Lexington, Massachusetts 02173. 1987.

CROSS-EXAMINATION OF MEDICAL EXPERTS. Marshall Houts. Matthew Bender and Company, Incorporated, 11 Penn Plaza, New York, New York 10001. 1982.

DAMAGES FOR PERSONAL INJURIES AND DEATH. Eighth Edition. John Munkman. Butterworths, 75 Clegg Road, Markham, Ontario, Canada L3R 9Y6. 1989.

DEFENDING A PERSONAL INJURY CASE, 1990. Neil T. Shayne and Joan A. Berk. Practising Law Institute, 810 Seventh Avenue, New York, New York 10019. 1990.

DEPOSITIONS, EXPERT WITNESSES, AND DEMONSTRATIVE EVIDENCE IN PERSONAL INJURY CASES. David G. Miller, Chairman. Practising Law Institute, 810 Seventh Avenue, New York, New York 10019. 1985.

DETERMINING DISABILITY AND PERSONAL INJURY DAMAGE: MEDICAL EVALUATION FOR TRIAL LAWYERS. Second Edition. J. Stanley McQuade. Harrison Company, 3110 Crossing Park, Norcross, Georgia 30091. 1988.

DETERMINING ECONOMIC LOSS IN INJURY AND DEATH CASES. William Gary Baker and Michael K. Seck. Shepard's/McGraw-Hill, P.O. Box 1235, Colorado Springs, Colorado 80901. 1987.

DISCOVERY IN MEDICAL MALPRACTICE, PRODUCTS LIABILITY AND PERSONAL INJURY CASES. Marc J. Bern and Steven E. North, Chairmen. Practising Law Institute, 810 Seventh Avenue, New York, New York 10019. 1985.

DOING AWAY WITH PERSONAL INJURY LAW: NEW COMPENSATION MECHANISMS FOR VICTIMS, CONSUMERS, AND BUSINESS. Stephen D. Sugarman. Greenwood Press, 88 Post Road West, P.O. Box 5007, Westport, Connecticut 06881. 1989.

ENVIRONMENTAL ACCIDENTS: PERSONAL INJURY AND PUBLIC RESPONSIBILITY. Richard H. Gaskins. Temple University Press, 1601 North Broad Street, University Services Building, Philadelphia, Pennsylvania 19122. 1989.

EVALUATING AND SETTLING PERSONAL INJURY CLAIMS. George M. Gold. PESI Legal Publishing, 200 Spring Street, Eau Claire, Wisconsin 54702. 1991.

FEDERAL TAX ASPECTS OF INJURY, DAMAGE, AND LOSS. Lawrence A. Frolik. BNA Books, 1231 Twenty-fifth Street, Washington, D.C. 20037. 1987.

HANDLING SOFT TISSUE INJURY CASES. Stanley E. Preiser and Monty L. Preiser. Kluwer Law Book Publishers, Incorporated, 36 West Forty-fourth Street, New York, New York 10036. 1987.

HARD BARGAINING: OUT OF COURT SETTLEMENT IN PERSONAL INJURY ACTIONS. Hazel Genn. Oxford University Press, 200 Madison Avenue, New York, New York 10016. 1987.

JURY INSTRUCTIONS ON MEDICAL ISSUES. Third Edition. Graham Douthwaite and George J. Alexander. Michie Company, P.O. Box 7587, Charlottesville, Virginia 22906. 1987.

THE LAW OF MARITIME PERSONAL INJURIES. Fourth Edition. Martin J. Norris. Lawyers Cooperative Publishing Company, Aqueduct Building, Rochester, New York 14694. 1990.

LITIGATING HEAD TRAUMA CASES. Arthur C. Roberts and Phillip J. Resnick. John Wiley and Sons, Incorporated, 605 Third Avenue, New York, New York 10158. 1989.

NEGOTIATING SETTLEMENTS IN PERSONAL INJURY CASES. Neil T. Shayne and Jack L. Slobodin, Co-Chairmen. Practising Law Institute, 810 Seventh Avenue, New York, New York 10019. 1984.

PERSONAL INJURY AND PRODUCT LIABILITY LITIGATION. Howard R. Reiss. Prentice-Hall, Incorporated, 113 Sylvan Avenue, Englewood Cliffs, New Jersey 07632. 1987.

PERSONAL INJURY DAMAGES: LAW AND PRACTICE. Edward C. Martin. John Wiley and Sons, Incorporated, 605 Third Avenue, New York, New York 10158. 1990.

PERSONAL INJURY PRACTICE: TECHNIQUE AND TECHNOLOGY. Lawrence S. Charfoos and David W. Christensen. Lawyers Cooperative Publishing Company, Aqueduct Building, Rochester, New York 14694. 1986. (Supplements)

PERSONAL INJURY PRACTICE: TORTS--INSURANCE. J. Kent Miller and Suzanne Lambdin. West Publishing Company, 50 West Kellogg Boulevard, St. Paul, Minnesota 55164. 1989.

PLAINTIFF'S PERSONAL INJURY NEGOTIATION STRATEGIES. Richard G. Halpern. John Wiley and Sons, Incorporated, 605 Third Avenue, New York, New York 10158. 1991.

PREPARING PERSONAL INJURY CASES FOR TRIAL. David G. Miller, Chairman. Practising Law Institute, 810 Seventh Avenue, New York, New York 10019. 1984.

THE PROSECUTION AND DEFENSE OF THE MULTI-MILLION DOLLAR PERSONAL INJURY CASE. Steven E. North and Marc J. Bern. Practising Law Institute, 810 Seventh Avenue, New York, New York 10019. 1988.

PROVING AND DEFENDING AGAINST DAMAGES IN CATASTROPHIC INJURY CASES. David B. Baum and Robert L. Conason, Co-Chairmen. Practising Law Institute, 810 Seventh Avenue, New York, New York 10019. 1983.

PSYCHIATRIC ASPECTS OF PERSONAL INJURY CLAIMS. George Mendelson. Charles C. Thomas, Publishers, 2600 South First Street, Springfield, Illinois 62794. 1988.

RECOVERING FOR PSYCHOLOGICAL INJURIES. Second Edition. William A. Barton, Christine M. Griffith, and Arnett J. Holloway. ATLA Press, Washington, D.C. 1990.

SECURING AND USING MEDICAL EVIDENCE IN PERSONAL INJURY AND HEALTH-CARE CASES. Robert C. Strodel. Prentice-Hall, Incorporated, 113 Sylvan Avenue, Englewood Cliffs, New Jersey 07632. 1988.

SETTLEMENTS INCLUDING DEFERRED PAYMENTS. Robert J. Lichtenstein, Chairman. Practising Law Institute, 810 Seventh Avenue, New York, New York 10019. 1984.

STRUCTURED SETTLEMENTS. Paul J. Lesti, Brent B. Danninger and Robert W. Johnson. Lawyers Cooperative Publishing Company, Aqueduct Building, Rochester, New York 14694. 1986. (Annual Supplements).

SYSTEMATIC SETTLEMENTS. Second Edition. Sanford W. Hornwood. Lawyers Cooperative/Bancroft-Whitney Publishing Company, Aqueduct Building, Rochester, New York 14694. 1986. (Supplements)

TACTICAL DECISIONS IN A PERSONAL INJURY CASE. Paul L. Stritmatter and Arnett J. Holloway. Association of Trial Lawyers of America, 1050 Thirty-first Street, Northwest, Washington, D.C. 20007. 1988.

TAKING AND DEFENDING DEPOSITIONS IN PERSONAL INJURY CASES. David G. Miller, Chairman. Practising Law Institute, 810 Seventh Avenue, New York, New York 10019. 1983.

THERMOGRAPHY AND PERSONAL INJURY LITIGATION. S. D. Hodge. John Wiley and Sons, Incorporated, 605 Third Avenue, New York, New York 10158. 1987.

TORT AND INJURY LAW. Marshall S. Shapo. Matthew Bender and Company, Incorporated, 11 Penn Plaza, New York, New York 10001. 1990.

TORTS, PERSONAL INJURY LITIGATION. Second Edition. William P. Statsky. West Publishing Company, 50 West Kellogg Boulevard, St. Paul, Minnesota 55164. 1990.

UNDERSTANDING AND HANDLING THE BACK AND NECK INJURY CASE. Thomas J. Murray, Jr. and Donald W. Robertson. PESI Legal Publishing, 200 Spring Street, Eau Claire, Wisconsin 54702. 1990.

ENCYCLOPEDIAS AND DICTIONARIES

CYCLOPEDIA OF TRIAL PRACTICE: PROOF OF TRAUMATIC INJURIES. Third Edition. Sydney C. Schweitzer. Lawyers Cooperative Publishing Company, Aqueduct Building, Rochester, New York 14694. 1983. (Supplements).

JVR CONCISE PERSONAL INJURY MEDICAL DICTIONARY. Third Edition. Marci E. Lurie. Jury Verdict Research, Incorporated, 30700H Bainbridge Road, Solon, Ohio 44139-2291. 1986.

NEWSLETTERS AND NEWSPAPERS

GENERAL AVIATION ACCIDENT REPORT. Andrews Publications, 1646 West Chester Pike, Westtown, Pennsylvania 19395. Weekly.

LONGSHORE NEWSLETTER AND CHRONICLE OF MARITIME INJURY LAW. 15 Fowler Court, Suite 100, San Rafael, California 94903. Monthly.

MARITIME PERSONAL INJURY REPORT. Marine Advisory Services, Incorporated, 10 Signal Road, Stamford, Connecticut 60902. Monthly.

MIB UPDATE. Marine Index Bureau, Incorporated, 44 East Thirty-second Street, P.O. Box 1964, New York, New York 10156. Bimonthly.

PERSONAL INJURY DEFENSE NEWSLETTER. Matthew Bender and Company, Incorporated, 11 Penn Plaza, New York, New York 10001. Monthly.

PERSONAL INJURY NEWSLETTER. Matthew Bender and Company, Incorporated, 11 Penn Plaza, New York, New York 10001. Biweekly.

PERSONAL INJURY RESEARCHER. Research Group, Incorporated, P.O. Box 7187, Charlottesville, Virginia 22906. Monthly.

VERDICT REVIEWS. Jury Verdict Research, Incorporated, 30700 Bainbridge Road, Suite H, Solon, Ohio 44139. Weekly.

VERDICTS AND SETTLEMENTS. Litigation Research Group, 425 Brannon Street, San Francisco, California 94107. Monthly.

VERDICTS, SETTLEMENTS AND TACTICS. Shepard's/McGraw-Hill, P.O. Box 1235, Colorado Springs, Colorado 80901. Monthly.

WEST'S PERSONAL INJURY NEWS. West Publishing Company, P.O. Box 64526, 50 West Kellogg Boulevard, St. Paul, Minnesota 55164. Biweekly.

ASSOCIATIONS AND PROFESSIONAL SOCIETIES

AMERICAN TORT REFORM ASSOCIATION. 1212 New York Avenue, Northwest, Suite 515, Washington, D.C. 20005. (202) 682-1163.

ASSOCIATION OF TRIAL LAW OF AMERICA. 1050 Thirty-first Street, Northwest, Washington, D.C. 20007. (202) 965-3500.

DRI-DEFENSE RESEARCH AND TRIAL LAWYERS ASSOCIATION. 750 North Lake Shore Drive, Suite 5000, Chicago, Illinois 60611. (312) 944-0575.

RESEARCH CENTERS, INSTITUTES, CLEARINGHOUSES

AMERICAN LAW INSTITUTE. 4025 Chestnut, Philadelphia, Pennsylvania 19104. (800) 253-6397.

DEFENSE RESEARCH INSTITUTE. 750 North Lake Shore Drive, Suite 5000, Chicago, Illinois 60611. (312) 944-0575.

LAW AND ECONOMICS CENTER. George Mason University, School of Law, 3401 North Fairfax Drive, Arlington, Virginia 22201. (703) 841-7171.

AUDIOVISUALS

DIRECT AND CROSS-EXAMINATION OF A MEDICAL RECORDS CUSTODIAN IN A PERSONAL INJURY CASE. Consortium for Professional Education, American Bar Association, 750 North Lake Shore Drive, Chcago, Illinois 60611. 1978. Videotape.

EXPERT MEDICAL WITNESS: DIRECT AND CROSS-EXAMINATION IN A PERSONAL INJURY CASE. Consortium for Professional Education, American Bar Association, 750 North Lake Shore Drive, Chicago, Illinois 60611. 1979. Videotape.

TRIAL OF A PERSONAL INJURY CASE. Consortium for Professional Education, American Bar Association, 750 North Lake Shore Drive, Chicago, Illinois 60611. 1980. Videotape.

OTHER SOURCES

COMPENSATION FOR ACCIDENTAL INJURIES IN THE UNITED STATES. Deborah R. Hensler. Rand Corporation, Institute for Civil Justice, 1700 Main Street, P.O. Box 2138, Santa Monica, California 90406. 1991.

PERSONAL PROPERTY

STATUTES, CODES, STANDARDS, UNIFORM LAWS

UNIFORM DISPOSITION OF UNCLAIMED PROPERTY ACT. National Conference of Commissioners on Uniform State Laws. Martindale-Hubbell Law Directory, Volume Eight. Martindale-Hubbell, Incorporated, 121 Chanlon Road, New Providence, New Jersey 07974. Annual.

UNIFORM DISPOSITION OF UNCLAIMED PROPERTY ACT. National Conference of Commissioners on Uniform State Laws. Uniform Laws Annotated. West Publishing Company, P.O. Box 64526, 50 West Kellogg Boulevard, St. Paul, Minnesota 55164-0526. (Annual Supplements).

TEXTBOOKS AND GENERAL WORKS

AMERICAN LAW OF PROPERTY. A. James Casner, Editor. Little, Brown, and Company, 34 Beacon Street, Boston, Massachusetts 02108. 1952. (Supplement 1977).

BASIC UCC SKILLS, 1989: ARTICLE 2A. William C. Hillman. Practising Law Institute, 810 Seventh Avenue, New York, New York 10019. 1989.

CASES, PROBLEMS, AND MATERIALS ON SECURITY INTERESTS IN PERSONAL PROPERTY. Second Edition. Douglas G. Baird and Thomas H. Jackson. Foundation Press, 615 Merrick Avenue, Westbury, New York 11590. 1987.

ENFORCING SECURITY INTERESTS IN PERSONAL PROPERTY: HERE'S HOW AND WHEN TO DO IT. Andrea A. Wirum. Regents of the University of California, Berkeley, California. 1990.

THE LAW OF PERSONAL PROPERTY. Third Edition. Ray Andrews Brown. Callaghan and Company, 155 Pfingsten Road, Deerfield, Illinois 60015. 1975.

THE LAW OF PROPERTY, LAWYER'S EDITION. Roger A. Cunningham, William B. Stoebuck and Dale A. Whitman. West Publishing Company, P.O. Box 64526, 50 West Kellogg Boulevard, St. Paul, Minnesota 55164-0526. 1984.

LEASES OF GOODS: ARTICLE 2A OF THE UNIFORM COMMERCIAL CODE, FEBRUARY 16-17, 1989, SCOTTSDALE, ARIZONA, ALI-ABA COURSE OF STUDY MATERIALS. American Law Institute-American Bar Association, 4025 Chestnut Street, Philadelphia, Pennsylvania 19104. 1989.

PERSONAL PROPERTY IN A NUTSHELL. D. Barlow Burke. West Publishing Company, P.O. Box 64526, 50 West Kellogg Boulevard, St. Paul, Minnesota 55164-0526. 1983.

PRINCIPLES OF THE LAW OF PROPERTY. Second Edition. John E. Cribbet. Foundation Press, Incorporated, 615 Merrick Avenue, Westbury, New York 11590. 1975.

SECURITY INTERESTS IN PERSONAL PROPERTY: CASES, NOTES, AND MATERIALS. Douglas K. Newell. Butterworth Legal Publishers, 90 Stiles Road, Salem, New Hampshire 03079. 1987.

SURVEY OF THE LAW OF PROPERTY. Third Edition. Ralph E. Boyer. West Publishing Company, P.O. Box 64526, 50 West Kellogg Boulevard, St. Paul, Minnesota 55164-0526. 1981.

UNIFORM COMMERCIAL CODE: ARTICLE 2A, LEASES OF GOODS. Third Edition. James J. White and Robert S. Summers. West Publishing Company, 50 West Kellogg Boulevard, St. Paul, Minnesota 55164. 1991.

PHARMACISTS AND PHARMACY
See also: DRUG LAWS; FOOD AND DRUG ADMINISTRATION

LOOSELEAF SERVICES AND REPORTERS

PHARMACEUTICAL LITIGATION REPORTER. Andrews Publications, Incorporated, 1646 West Chester Pike, Westtown, Pennsylvania 19395. 1975- .

HANDBOOKS, MANUALS, FORMBOOKS

DRUG PRODUCT LIABILITY. Marden G. Dixon. Matthew Bender and Company, Incorporated, 11 Penn Plaza, New York, New York 10001. 1974. (Annual Supplements).

PHYSICIAN'S DESK REFERENCE: PDR. Medical Economics Books, 5 Paragon Drive, Montvale, New Jersey 07645. Annual.

TEXTBOOKS AND GENERAL WORKS

CORPORATE CRIME IN THE PHARMACEUTICAL INDUSTRY. John Braithwaite. Routledge and Degan Paul, Limited, 25 West Thirty-fifth Street, New York, New York 10001-2291. 1984.

DRUGS IN LITIGATION: DAMAGE AWARDS INVOLVING PRESCRIPTION AND NONPRESCRIPTION DRUGS. Richard M. Patterson and Robert E. Robinson. Allen Smith Company, Incorporated, 1435 North Meridian Street, Indianapolis, Indiana 46202. 1991.

MEDICAL MALPRACTICE: PHARMACY LAW. David B. Brushwook. Shepard's/McGraw-Hill, P.O. Box 1235, Colorado Springs, Colorado 80901. 1986.

PHARMACY AND THE LAW. Second Edition. Carl T. DeMarco. Aspen Publishers, Incorporated, 1600 Research Boulevard, Rockville, Maryland 20850. 1984.

PHARMACY PRACTICE FOR TRIAL LAWYERS. L. Edward Hickman. Harrison Company, 3110 Crossing Park, Norcross, Georgia 30091. 1981. (Supplement 1985).

ENCYCLOPEDIAS AND DICTIONARIES

ENCYCLOPEDIA OF PHARMACEUTICAL TECHNOLOGY. James Swarbrick and James C. Boylan. Marcel Dekker, 720 Madison Avenue, New York, New York 10016. 1988- .

PHARMACEUTICAL MANUFACTURING ENCYCLOPEDIA. Second Edition. Marshall Sittig. Noyes Publications, 120 Mill Road, Park Ridge, New Jersey 07656. 1988.

PHARMACEUTICAL WORD BOOK. Second Edition. Barbara De Lorenzo. Springhouse Corporation, 1111 Bethlehem Pike, Springhouse, Pennsylvania 19477. 1992.

DIGESTS, INDEXES, ABSTRACTS, CITATORS

PHARMACY LAW DIGEST. Joseph L. Fink, Editor. Harwal Publishing Company, 605 Third Avenue, New York, New York 10158. 1985.

LAW REVIEWS AND PERIODICALS

AMERICAN PHARMACY. American Pharmaceutical Association, 2215 Constitution Avenue, Northwest, Washington, D.C. 20037. Monthly.

CONTEMPORARY DRUG PROBLEMS. Federal Legal Publications, Incorporated, 95 Morton Street, New York, New York 10014. Quarterly.

LEGAL ASPECTS OF PHARMACY PRACTICE. Professional Communications Associates, 625 North Michigan Avenue, Chicago, Illinois 60611. Eight issues per year.

REGULATORY TOXICOLOGY AND PHARMACOLOGY. Academic Press, 111 Fifth Avenue, New York, New York 10003. Quarterly.

NEWSLETTERS AND NEWSPAPERS

NABP NEWSLETTER. National Association of Boards of Pharmacy, One East Wacker Drive, Suite 2210, Chicago, Illinois 60601. Monthly.

PHARMACY WEEKLY. American Pharmaceutical Association, 2215 Constitution Avenue, Northwest, Washington, D.C. 20037. Weekly.

BIBLIOGRAPHIES

DRUG INFORMATION: A GUIDE TO CURRENT RESOURCES. Bonnie Snow. Medical Library Association, 6 North Michigan Avenue, Suite 300, Chicago, Illinois 60602. 1989.

INFORMATION SOURCES IN PHARMACEUTICALS. W.R. Pickering. Bowker-Saur Limited, Borough Green, Sevenoaks, Kent TN15 8PH, England. 1990.

KEYGUIDE TO INFORMATION SOURCES IN PHARMACY. Barry Strickland-Hodge, Michael H. Jepson, and Bruce J. Reid. Mansell Publishing Limited, Artillery House, Artillery Row, London SW1P 1RT, England. 1989.

PHARMACY LAW BIBLIOGRAPHY. Henry B. Hine. Vance Bibliographies, P.O. Box 229, 112 North Charter Street, Monticello, Illinois 61856. 1982.

DIRECTORIES

PHARMACEUTICAL MANUFACTURERS OF THE UNITED STATES. Fourth Edition. D.J. De Renzo. Noyes Publications, 120 Mill Road, Park Ridge, New Jersey 07656. 1987.

ASSOCIATIONS AND PROFESSIONAL SOCIETIES

AMERICAN ASSOCIATION OF COLLEGES OF PHARMACY. 1426 Prince Street, Alexandria, Virginia 22314. (703) 739-2330.

AMERICAN COLLEGE OF CLINICAL PHARMACOLOGY. 175 Stafford Avenue, Suite 1, Wayne, Pennsylvania 19087. (215) 687-771.

AMERICAN COLLEGE OF CLINICAL PHARMACY. 3101 Broadway Street, Suite 380, Kansas City, Missouri 64111. (816) 531-2177.

AMERICAN PHARMACEUTICAL ASSOCIATION. 2215 Constitution Avenue, Northwest, Washington, D.C. 20037. (202) 628-4410.

AMERICAN SOCIETY OF CONSULTANT PHARMACISTS. 2300 Ninth Street South, Suite 515, Arlington, Virginia 22204. (703) 920-8492.

AMERICAN SOCIETY OF HOSPITAL PHARMACISTS. 4630 Montgomery Avenue, Bethesda, Maryland 20814. (301) 657-3000.

NATIONAL ASSOCIATION OF PHARMACEUTICAL MANUFACTURERS. 747 Third Avenue, New York, New York 10017. (212) 838-3720.

PHARMACEUTICAL MANUFACTURERS ASSOCIATION. 1100 Fifteenth Street, Northwest, Washington, D.C. 20005. (202) 635-3400.

RESEARCH CENTERS, INSTITUTES, CLEARINGHOUSES

AMERICAN INSTITUTE OF THE HISTORY OF PHARMACY. Pharmacy Building, Madison, Wisconsin 53706. (608) 262-5378.

CENTER FOR COMPUTER APPLICATIONS IN PHARMACY. University of Florida, Seagle Building, Suite 408, 408 West University Avenue, Gainesville, Florida 32601. (904) 392-9259.

RESEARCH AND EDUCATIONAL FOUNDATION. American Society of Hospital Pharmacists, 4630 Montgomery Avenue, Bethesda, Maryland 20814. (301) 657-3000.

UNIT IN LAW AND PHARMACY. Temple University, Temple Law School, 1719 North Broad Street, Philadelphia, Pennsylvania 19122. (215) 787-1278.

UPJOHN CENTER FOR CLINICAL PHARMACOLOGY. Medical Center, University of Michigan, Ann Arbor, Michigan 48109. (313) 764-9121.

ONLINE DATABASES

DRUG INFORMATION FULLTEXT. American Society of Hospital Pharmacists, 4630 Montgomery Avenue, Bethesda, Maryland 20814.

STATISTICS SOURCES

ANNUAL SURVEY REPORT. Pharmaceutical Manufacturers Association, 1100 Fifteenth Street, Northwest, Washington, D.C. 20005. Annual.

PHILOSOPHY OF LAW
See: JURISPRUDENCE; NATURAL LAW

PHOTOGRAPHS AND PHOTOGRAPHY

STATUTES, CODES, STANDARDS, UNIFORM LAWS

UNIFORM PHOTOGRAPHIC COPIES OF BUSINESS RECORDS AS EVIDENCE ACT. National Conference of Commissioners on Uniform State Laws. Martindale-Hubbell Law Directory, Volume Eight. Martindale-Hubbell, 121 Chanlon Road, New Providence, New Jersey 07974. Annual.

UNIFORM PHOTOGRAPHIC COPIES OF BUSINESS RECORDS AS EVIDENCE ACT. National Conference of Commissioners on Uniform State Laws. Uniform Laws Annotated. West Publishing Company, P.O. Box 64526, 50 West Kellogg Boulevard, St. Paul, Minnesota 55164-0526. 1976. (Annual Supplements).

HANDBOOKS, MANUALS, FORMBOOKS

THE PHOTOGRAPHER'S BUSINESS AND LEGAL HANDBOOK. Leonard D. DuBoff. Images Press, P.O. Box 756, Sebastopol, California 95472. Defunct. 1989.

TEXTBOOKS AND GENERAL WORKS

FORENSIC PHOTOGRAPHY. John E. Duckworth. Charles C. Thomas Publishing, 2600 South First Street, Springfield, Illinois 62794-9265. 1983.

POLICE PHOTOGRAPHY. Second Edition. Sam J. Sansone. Anderson Publishing Company, 2035 Reading Road, Cincinnati, Ohio 45202. 1987.

THE PRACTICAL METHODOLOGY OF FORENSIC PHOTOGRAPHY. David R. Redsicker. Elsevier Science Publishing Company, P.O. Box 882, Madison Square Station, New York, New York 10159. 1991.

BIBLIOGRAPHIES

CAMERAS IN THE COURTROOM: A SELECTED BIBLIOGRAPHY. Anthony G. White. Vance Bibliographies, P.O. Box 229, 112 North Charter Street, Monticello, Illinois 61856. 1988.

ASSOCIATIONS AND PROFESSIONAL SOCIETIES

EVIDENCE PHOTOGRAPHERS INTERNATIONAL COUNCIL. 600 Main Street, Honesdale, Pennsylvania 18431. (717) 253-5450.

PHYSICALLY HANDICAPPED

STATUTES, CODES, STANDARDS, UNIFORM LAWS

UNIFORM DUTIES TO DISABLED PERSONS ACT. National Conference of Commissioners on Uniform State Laws. Uniform Laws Annotated. West Publishing Company, P.O. Box 64526, 50 West Kellogg Boulevard, St. Paul, Minnesota 55164-0526. 1976. (Annual Supplements).

LOOSELEAF SERVICES AND REPORTERS

EDUCATION FOR THE HANDICAPPED LAW REPORT. CRR Publishing Company, 421 King Street, P.O. Box 1905, Alexandria, Virginia 22313. 1979- .

MENTAL AND PHYSICAL DISABILITY LAW REPORTER. Commission on the Mentally Disabled, American Bar Association, 750 North Lake Shore Drive, Chicago, Illinois 60611. 1984- .

HANDBOOKS, MANUALS, FORMBOOKS

AMERICANS WITH DISABILITIES ACT HANDBOOK. Second Edition. Henry H. Perritt, Jr. John Wiley and Sons, Incorporated, 605 Third Avenue, New York, New York 10158. 1991.

THE ARTS AND 504: A 504 HANDBOOK FOR ACCESSIBLE ARTS PROGRAMMING. National Endowment for the Arts. Superintendent of Documents, United States Government Printing Office, Washington, D.C. 20402. 1987.

HANDICAPPED REQUIREMENTS HANDBOOK. Federal Programs Advisory Service, Thompson Publishing Group, 1725 K Street, Northwest, Suite 200, Washington, D.C. 20006. 1983.

MANUAL FOR LITIGATION: RIGHTS OF DISABLED PEOPLE: SOCIAL CHANGE THROUGH LITIGATION AND RELATED ATTORNEY FEE QUESTIONS. Stanley Fleischman and Sam Rosenwein. Southwestern University School of Law, 675 South Westmoreland Avenue, Los Angeles, California 90005. 1984.

TEXTBOOKS AND GENERAL WORKS

DISABILITY. A. Carmi, E. Chigier and S. Schneider, Editors. Springer-Verlag New York, Incorporated, 175 Fifth Avenue, New York, New York 10010. 1984.

DISABILITY AS A SOCIAL CONSTRUCT: LEGISLATIVE ROOTS. Claire H. Liachowitz. University of Pennsylvania Press, Blockley Hall, 418 Service Drive, Philadelphia, Pennsylvania 19104. 1988.

DISABILITY RIGHTS MANDATES: FEDERAL AND STATE COMPLIANCE WITH EMPLOYMENT PROTECTIONS AND ARCHITECTURAL BARRIER REMOVAL. Stephen L. Percy. Advisory Commission on Intergovernmental Relations, Washington, D.C. 1989.

FROM GOOD WILL TO CIVIL RIGHTS: TRANSFORMING FEDERAL DISABILITY POLICY. Richard K. Scotch. Temple University Press, University Services Building, 1601 North Broad Street, Philadelphia, Pennsylvania 19122. 1985.

INSTITUTIONAL DISABILITY: THE SAGA OF TRANSPORTATION POLICY FOR THE DISABLED. Robert A. Katzmann. Brookings Institution, 1775 Massachusetts Avenue, Northwest, Washington, D.C. 20036-2188. 1986.

LEGAL AND POLITICAL ISSUES IN SPECIAL EDUCATION. James J. Cremins. Charles C. Thomas Publishing, 2600 South First Street, Springfield, Illinois 62794-9265. 1983.

LEGAL RIGHTS OF HEARING-IMPAIRED PEOPLE. Fourth Edition. Gallaudet University Press, 800 Florida Avenue, Northeast, Washington, D.C. 20002-3645. 1991.

RIGHTS OF PHYSICALLY HANDICAPPED PERSONS. Laura F. Rothstein. Shepard's/McGraw-Hill, P.O. Box 1235, Colorado Springs, Colorado 80901. 1984. (Annual Supplements).

ENCYCLOPEDIAS AND DICTIONARIES

ENCYCLOPEDIA OF MENTAL AND PHYSICAL HANDICAPS. David F. Tver and Betty M. Tver. Special Child Publications, P.O. Box 33548, Seattle, Washington 98133. 1989.

LAW REVIEWS AND PERIODICALS

JOURNAL OF CONTEMPORARY HEALTH LAW AND POLICY. The Catholic University of America, Columbus School of Law, 620 Michigan Avenue, Northeast, Washington, D.C. 20064. Annual.

NEWSLETTERS AND NEWSPAPERS

DISABILITY ADVOCATES BULLETIN. Pike Institute for the Handicapped, c/o Boston University School of Law, 765 Commonwealth Avenue, Boston, Massachusetts 02215. Bimonthly.

EDUCATION OF THE HANDICAPPED. Capitol Publications, Incorporated, 1300 North Seventeenth Street, Arlington, Virginia 22209. Biweekly.

MENTAL AND PHYSICAL DISABILITY LAW REPORTER. American Bar Association, 750 North Lake Shore Drive, Chicago, Illinois 60611. Bimonthly.

REPORT ON DISABILITY PROGRAMS. Business Publishers, Incorporated, 951 Pershing Drive, Silver Spring, Maryland 20910. Biweekly.

SPECIAL EDUCATION AND THE HANDICAPPED. Data Research, Incorporated, P.O. Box 409, Rosemount, Minnesota 55068. Monthly.

BIBLIOGRAPHIES

ARCHITECTURE OF ACCESSIBILITY: PLANNING FOR THE DISABLED, A PARTIALLY ANNOTATED BIBLIOGRAPHY. Glenna Dunning. Vance Bibliographies, P.O. Box 229, 112 North Charter Street, Monticello, Illinois 61856. 1989.

DESIGN FOR THE PHYSCIALLY DISABLED. David Kent Ballast. Vance Bibliographies, P.O. Box 229, 112 North Charter Street, Monticello, Illinois 61856. 1988.

PHYSICALLY DISABLED WOMEN AND NEW DIRECTIONS IN PUBLIC POLICY, 1977- 1987. Mary Jo Deegan. Vance Bibliographies, P.O. Box 229, 112 North Charter Street, Monticello, Illinois 61856. 1987.

A READER'S GUIDE FOR PARENTS OF CHILDREN WITH MENTAL, PHYSICAL, OR EMOTIONAL DISABILITIES. Third Edition. Cory Moore. Woodbine House, 10400 Connecticut Avenue, Suite 512, Kensington, Maryland 20895. 1990.

DIRECTORIES

DIRECTORY OF COLLEGE FACILITIES AND SERVICES FOR PEOPLE WITH DISABILITIES. Third Edition. Carol H. Thomas and James L. Thomas. Oryx Press, 2214 North Central Avenue, Phoenix, Arizona 85004. 1991.

HANDICAPPED FUNDING DIRECTORY: A GUIDE TO SOURCES OF FUNDING IN THE UNITED STATES FOR HANDICAPPED PROGRAMS AND SERVICES: 1984-1985. Fourth Edition. Research Grant Guides, Box 1214, Loxahatchee, Florida 33470 Biennial.

ASSOCIATIONS AND PROFESSIONAL SOCIETIES

CONGRESS OF ORGANIZATIONS OF THE PHYSICALLY HANDICAPPED. 16630 Beverly, Tinley Park, Illinois 60477. (312) 532-3566.

DIVISION FOR THE PHYSICALLY HANDICAPPED. c/o Council for Exceptional Children, 1920 Association Drive, Reston, Virginia 22091. (703) 620- 3660.

SPECIAL INTEREST GROUP FOR COMPUTERS AND THE PHYSICALLY HANDICAPPED. c/o Association for Computing Machinery, 11 West Forty-second Street, New York, New York 10036. (212) 869-7440.

RESEARCH CENTERS, INSTITUTES, CLEARINGHOUSES

WORLD INSTITUTE ON DISABILITY. 510 Sixteenth Street, Oakland, California 94612. (415) 763-4100.

PHYSICIANS
See: MEDICAL JURISPRUDENCE AND MALPRACTICE

PICKETING
See: FREEDOM OF ASSEMBLY; FREEDOM OF SPEECH; LABOR AND LABOR RELATIONS

PIPELINES
See: OIL AND GAS

PLANNED PARENTHOOD
See: BIRTH CONTROL

PLANNING
See: ZONING AND PLANNING

PLEADING
See: CIVIL PROCEDURE; LEGAL FORMS

POISONS
See: HAZARDOUS SUBSTANCES

POLICE
See also: LAW ENFORCEMENT

LOOSELEAF SERVICES AND REPORTERS

LAW OFFICER'S BULLETIN. Bureau of National Affairs, 1231 Twenty-fifth Street, Northwest, Washington, D.C. 20037. 1976- .

LIABILITY REPORTER. Americans for Effective Law Enforcement, Incorporated, 5519 North Cumberland, Number 1008, Chicago, Illinois 60656-1471. 1972- .

POLICE MISCONDUCT AND CIVIL RIGHTS LAW REPORT. Clark Boardman Company, Limited, 435 Hudson Street, New York, New York 10014. 1983- .

POLICE MISCONDUCT: LAW AND LITIGATION. Michael Avery and David Rudovsky. Clark Boardman Company, Limited, 435 Hudson Street, New York, New York 10014. 1980- .

HANDBOOKS, MANUALS, FORMBOOKS

CRIMINAL LAW FOR POLICE OFFICERS. Fifth Edition. Neil C. Chamelin and Kenneth R. Evans. Prentice-Hall, Incorporated, 113 Sylvan Avenue, Englewood Cliffs, New Jersey 07632. 1991.

HANDBOOK OF FEDERAL POLICE AND INVESTIGATIVE AGENCIES. Donald A. Torres. Greenwood Publishing Group, Incorporated, 88 Post Road West, P.O. Box 5007, Westport, Connecticut 06881. 1985.

HANDBOOK ON ARTIFICIAL INTELLIGENCE AND EXPERT SYSTEMS IN LAW ENFORCEMENT. Edward C. Ratledge and Joan E. Jacoby. Greenwood Publishing Group, Incorporated, 88 Post Road West, P.O. Box 5007, Westport, Connecticut 06881. 1989.

LAW ENFORCEMENT CAREER PLANNING: A HANDBOOK DESIGNED TO PREPARE LAW ENFORCEMENT OFFICERS FOR PROMOTIONAL OPPORTUNITIES AND EXAMS, RESUME WRITING, UNDERSTANDING THE ORGANIZATION, ASSESSMENT CENTERS, ORAL INTERVIEWS, AND MORE. Thomas Mahoney. Charles C. Thomas, Publishers, 2600 South First Street, Springfield, Illinois 62794. 1989.

LAW ENFORCEMENT, THE MAKING OF A PROFESSION: A COMPREHENSIVE GUIDE FOR THE POLICE TO ACHIEVE AND SUSTAIN PROFESSIONALISM. Neal E. Trautman. Charles C. Thomas, Publishers, 2600 South First Street, Springfield, Illinois 62794. 1988.

PLAINCLOTHES AND OFF-DUTY OFFICER SURVIVAL: A GUIDE TO SURVIVAL FOR PLAINCLOTHES OFFICERS, UNDERCOVER OFFICERS, AND OFF-DUTY POLICE OFFICERS. John Charles Cheek and Tony Lesce. Charles C. Thomas, Publishers, 2600 South First Street, Springfield, Illinois 62794. 1988.

POLICE

PRACTICAL LEGAL GUIDELINES FOR THE PRIVATE SECURITY OFFICER: THE ESSENTIAL CONSEQUENCES OF THE LAWS REGARDING PRIVATE SECURITY AND THE AFFECTIVE SOCIAL TRENDS OF TODAY. John L. Coleman. Charles C. Thomas, Publishers, 2600 South First Street, Springfield, Illinois 62794. 1990.

TEXTBOOKS AND GENERAL WORKS

THE BADGE AND THE BULLET: POLICE USE OF DEADLY FORCE. Peter Scharf and Arnold Binder. Praeger Publishers, One Madison Avenue, New York, New York 10010-3603. 1983.

BLACK POLICE, WHITE SOCIETY. Stephen Leinen. New York University Press, Distributed by Columbia University Press, 70 Washington Square South, New York, New York 10012. 1985.

CIVIL LIABILITIES IN AMERICAN POLICING: A TEXT FOR LAW ENFORCEMENT PERSONNEL. Rolando V. del Carmen. Brady, Englewood Cliffs, New Jersey. 1991.

CONTROL IN THE POLICE ORGANIZATION. Maurice Punch, Editor. MIT Press, 55 Hayward Street, Cambridge, Massachusetts 02142. 1983.

CRIME CONTROL: THE USE AND MISUSE OF POLICE RESOURCES. David J. Farmer. Plenum Publishing Corporation, 233 Spring Street, New York, New York 10013. 1984.

CRIMINAL LAW FOR POLICE OFFICERS. Fourth Edition. Neil C. Chamelin and Kenneth R. Evans. Prentice-Hall, Incorporated, 113 Sylvan Avenue, Englewood Cliffs, New Jersey 07632. 1987.

CRIMINAL PROCEDURE FOR LAW ENFORCEMENT PERSONNEL. Rolando V. Del Carmen. Brooks/Cole Publishing Company, Wadsworth Publishing, 10 Davis Drive, Belmont, California 94002. 1987.

HUMAN RELATIONS AND POLICE WORK. Second Edition. Larry S. Miller and Michael C. Braswell. Waveland Press, Incorporated, P.O. Box 400, Prospect Heights, Illinois 60070. 1988.

THE IDEA OF POLICE. Carl B. Klockars. Sage Publications, Incorporated, 2455 Teller Road, Newbury Park, California 91320. 1985.

INTERPOL: ISSUES IN WORLD CRIME AND INTERNATIONAL CRIMINAL JUSTICE. Michael Fooner. Plenum Publishing Corporation, 233 Spring Street, New York, New York 10013. 1989.

INTRODUCTION TO LAW ENFORCEMENT: AN INSIDER'S VIEW. William G. Doerner. Prentice-Hall, Incorporated, 113 Sylvan Avenue, Englewood Cliffs, New Jersey 07632. 1992.

LAW ENFORCEMENT: AN INTRODUCTION. Richard N. Holden. Prentice-Hall, Incorporated, 113 Sylvan Avenue, Englewood Cliffs, New Jersey 07632. 1992.

LAW ENFORCEMENT: AN INTRODUCTION TO POLICE IN SOCIETY. Bruce L. Berg. Allyn and Bacon, 160 Gould Street, Needham Heights, Massachusetts 02194. 1991.

MEDICAL REFERENCE GUIDEBOOK OF CRIME AND CRIME RESEARCH. Sandra K. Reggs. ABBE Publishers Association of Washington D.C., 4111 Gallows Road, Annandale, Virginia 22003-1862. 1985.

MORAL ISSUES IN POLICE WORK. Frederick Elliston and Michael Feldberg, Editors. Rowman and Allanheld, 420 Boston Way, Lanham, Maryland 20706. 1985.

POLICE AND POLICING: CONTEMPORARY ISSUES. Dennis Jay Kenney. Praeger Publishers, One Madison Avenue, New York, New York 10010-3603. 1989.

THE POLICE AND PRETRIAL RELEASE. Floyd Feeney. Lexington Books, Division of D.C. Heath and Company, 125 Spring Street, Lexington, Massachusetts 02173. 1982.

THE POLICE AND SOCIETY: AN ENVIRONMENT FOR COLLABORATION AND CONFRONTATION. Thomas A. Johnson, Gordon Misner and Lee P. Brown. Prentice-Hall, Incorporated, 113 Sylvan Avenue, Englewood Cliffs, New Jersey 07632. 1981.

THE POLICE AS THE DEFENDANT. Donald O. Schultz. Charles C. Thomas Publishing, 2600 South First Street, Springfield, Illinois 62794-9265. 1984.

THE POLICE: AUTONOMY AND CONSENT. Michael Brogden. Academy Press, Incorporated, 5037 North Academy Boulevard, Colorado Springs, Colorado 80918. 1983.

POLICE CIVIL LIABILITY. Isidore Silver. Matthew Bender and Company, Incorporated, 11 Penn Plaza, New York, New York 10001. 1986.

POLICE CIVIL LIABILITY. Leonard Territo, Editor. Hanrow Press, P.O. Box 847, Del Mar, California 92014. 1984.

POLICE-COMMUNITY RELATIONS AND THE ADMINISTRATION OF JUSTICE. Third Edition. Pamela D. Mayhall. PH Press, P.O. Box 195, Cambridge, Massachusetts 02139. 1985.

POLICE INTELLIGENCE SYSTEMS IN CRIME CONTROL: MAINTAINING A DELICATE BALANCE IN A LIBERAL DEMOCRACY. Justin J. Dintino and Frederick T. Martens. Charles C. Thomas Publishing, 2600 South First Street, Springfield, Illinois 62794-9265. 1983.

POLICE LEADERSHIP IN AMERICA: CRISIS AND OPPORTUNITY. William A. Gellner, Editor. Praeger Publishers, One Madison Avenue, New York, New York 10010-3603. 1985.

THE POLICE PERSONNEL SYSTEM. Calvin J. Swank and James A. Cosner. PH Press, P.O. Box 195, Cambridge, Massachusetts 02139. 1983.

POLICE, PRISON, AND PUNISHMENT: MAJOR HISTORICAL INTERPRETATIONS. Kermit L. Hall. Garland Publishing, Incorporated, 136 Madison Avenue, New York, New York 10016. 1987.

POLICE PROFESSIONALISM: THE RENAISSANCE OF AMERICAN LAW ENFORCEMENT. Thomas J. Deakin. Charles C. Thomas, Publishers, 2600 South First Street, Springfield, Illinois 62794. 1988.

THE POLICE WITNESS: EFFECTIVENESS IN THE COURTROOM. Michael W. Whitaker. Charles C. Thomas Publishing, 2600 South First Street, Springfield, Illinois 62794-9265. 1985.

POLICING LIBERAL SOCIETY. Steve Uglow. Oxford University Press, 200 Madison Avenue, New York, New York 10016. 1988.

POLICING MULTI-ETHNIC NEIGHBORHOODS: THE MIAMI STUDY AND FINDINGS FOR LAW ENFORCEMENT IN THE UNITED STATES. Geoffrey P. Alpert and Roger G. Dunham. Greenwood Publishing Group, Incorporated, 88 Post Road West, P.O. Box 5007, Westport, Connecticut 06881. 1988.

POLICING THE WORLD: INTERPOL AND THE POLITICS OF INTERNATIONAL POLICE CO-OPERATION. Malcolm Anderson. Oxford University Press, 200 Madison Avenue, New York, New York 10016. 1989.

THE POLITICS OF STREET CRIME: CRIMINAL PROCESS AND CULTURAL OBSESSION. Stuart A. Scheingold. Temple University Press, 1601 North Broad Street, University Services Building, Philadelphia, Pennsylvania 19122. 1991.

POWER AND RESTRAINT: THE MORAL DIMENSION OF POLICE WORK. Howard S. Cohen and Michael Feldberg. Praeger Publishers, One Madison Avenue, New York, New York 10010-3603. 1991.

PRINCIPLES OF LAW ENFORCEMENT: AN OVERVIEW OF THE JUSTICE SYSTEM. Third Edition. Edward Eldefonso, Alan Coffey and Richard C. Grace. John Wiley and Sons, Incorporated, 605 Third Avenue, New York, New York 10158. 1982.

THE PSYCHOLOGICAL EFFECTS OF POLICE WORK: A PSYCHODYNAMIC APPROACH. Philip Bonifacio. Plenum Publishing Corporation, 233 Spring Street, New York, New York 10013. 1991.

THE PUBLIC AND THE POLICE: A PARTNERSHIP IN PROTECTION. Earl M. Sweeney. Charles C. Thomas Publishing, 2600 South First Street, Springfield, Illinois 62794-9265. 1982.

PUBLIC POLICY AND POLICE DISCRETION: PROCESSES OF DECRIMINALIZATION. David E. Aaronson, C. Thomas Diennes and Michael C. Musheno. Clark Boardman Company, Limited, 435 Hudson Street, New York, New York 10014. 1984.

STREET COPS. Jill Freedman. HarperCollins Publishers, Incorporated, 10 East Fifty-third Street, New York, New York 10022. 1981.

A STUDY OF LAW ENFORCEMENT: A COMPREHENSIVE STUDY OF THE WORLD'S GREATEST, YET MOST DIFFICULT, PROFESSION. Neal E. Trautman. Charles C. Thomas, Publishers, 2600 South First Street, Springfield, Illinois 62794. 1990.

TEMPERED ZEAL: A COLUMBIA LAW PROFESSOR'S YEAR ON THE STREETS WITH THE NEW YORK CITY POLICE. H. Richard Uviller. Contemporary Books, Incorporated, 180 North Michigan Avenue, Chicago, Illinois 60601. 1988.

ENCYCLOPEDIAS AND DICTIONARIES

THE ENCYCLOPEDIA OF POLICE SCIENCE. William G. Bailey. Garland Publishing, Incorporated, 136 Madison Avenue, New York, New York 10016. 1989.

THE POLICE DICTIONARY AND ENCYCLOPEDIA. John J. Fay. Charles C. Thomas, Publishers, 2600 South First Street, Springfield, Illinois 62794. 1988.

WORLD ENCYCLOPEDIA OF POLICE FORCES AND PENAL SYSTEMS. George Thomas Kurian. Facts on File, Incorporated, 460 Park Avenue South, New York, New York 10016. 1988.

LAW REVIEWS AND PERIODICALS

CRIMINAL JUSTICE ETHICS. John Jay College of Criminal Justice, Institute for Criminal Justice Ethics, 444 West Fifty-sixth Street, New York, New York 10019. Semiannual.

LAW ENFORCEMENT LEGAL REVIEW. International Association of Chiefs of Police, Eleven Firstfield Road, Gaithersburg, Maryland 20760. Monthly.

LAW ENFORCEMENT MISCONDUCT BULLETIN. Quinlan Publishing Company, 131 Beverly Street, Boston, Massachusetts 02114. Monthly.

POLICE OFFICER/EMPLOYEE RIGHTS BULLETIN. Quinlan Publishing Company, 131 Beverly Street, Boston, Massachusetts 02114. Monthly.

POLICE TIMES MAGAZINE. American Federation of Police, 1100 Northeast, 125th Street, North Miami, Florida 33161. Bimonthly.

NEWSLETTERS AND NEWSPAPERS

LAW ENFORCEMENT LEGAL DEFENSE MANUAL. James P. Manak, 421 Ridgewood Avenue, Glen Ellyn, Illinois 60137. Quarterly.

LAW ENFORCEMENT LEGAL REVIEW. James P. Manak, 421 Ridgewood Avenue, Glen Ellyn, Illinois 60137. Bimonthly.

LAW OFFICER'S BULLETIN. Bureau of National Affairs, Incorporated, 1231 Twenty-fifth Street, Washington, D.C. 20037. Biweekly.

LEGAL POINTS. International Association of Chiefs of Police, Thirteen Firstfield Road, Gaithersburg, Maryland 20879. Monthly.

LIABILITY REPORTER. Americans for Effective Law Enforcement, Incorporated, 5519 North Cumberland, Suite 1008, Chicago, Illinois 60656. Monthly.

NATIONAL BULLETIN ON POLICE MISCONDUCT. Quinlan Publishing Company, Incorporated, 23 Drydock Avenue, Boston, Massachusetts 02110. Monthly.

POLICE LIABILITY REVIEWS. Alpha Enterprises, P.O. Box 1013, Warrensburg, Missouri 64093. Quarterly.

POLICE MISCONDUCT AND CIVIL RIGHTS LAW REPORT. Clark Boardman Company, Limited, 435 Hudson Street, New York, New York 10014. Bimonthly.

SECURITY AND SPECIAL POLICE LEGAL UPDATE. Americans for Effective Law Enforcement, Incorporated, 5519 North Cumberland, Suite 1008, Chicago, Illinois 60656. Monthly.

BIBLIOGRAPHIES

ASSAULTS AGAINST POLICE: A BIBLIOGRAPHY. Marguerite J. Hunt. Vance Bibliographies, P.O. Box 229, 112 North Charter Street, Monticello, Illinois 61856. 1989.

CAMPUS POLICING: A SELECTED BIBLIOGRAPHY. Verna Casey. Vance Bibliographies, P.O. Box 229, 112 North Charter Street, Monticello, Illinois 61856. 1989.

LAWMEN IN SCARLET: AN ANNOTATED GUIDE TO ROYAL CANADIAN MOUNTED POLICE IN PRINT AND PERFORMANCE. Bernard A. Drew. Scarecrow Press, Incorporated, 52 Liberty Street, Box 4167, Metuchen, New Jersey 08840. 1990.

POLICE, FIREFIGHTER, AND PARAMEDIC STRESS: AN ANNOTATED BIBLIOGRAPHY. John J. Miletich. Greenwood Publishing Group, Incorporated, 88 Post Road West, P.O. Box 5007, Westport, Connecticut 06881. 1990.

POLICE MANAGEMENT--ACADEMY TRAINING: A SELECTED BIBLIOGRAPHY. Anthony G. White. Vance Bibliographies, P.O. Box 229, 112 North Charter Street, Monticello, Illinois 61856. 1988.

POLICE MANAGEMENT--RECRUIT SCREENING: A SELECTED BIBLIOGRAPHY. Anthony G. White. Vance Bibliographies, P.O. Box 229, 112 North Charter Street, Monticello, Illinois 61856. 1988.

POLICE MANAGEMENT--STRESS MANAGEMENT: A SELECTED BIBLIOGRAPHY. Anthony G. White. Vance Bibliographies, P.O. Box 229, 112 North Charter Street, Monticello, Illinois 61856. 1988.

POLICE PROFESSIONALIZATION: ACCREDITATION, A SELECTED BIBLIOGRAPHY. Anthony G. White. Vance Bibliographies, P.O. Box 229, 112 North Charter Street, Monticello, Illinois 61856. 1988.

A SELECT BIBLIOGRAPHY ON SECURITY GUARDS AND OTHER PRIVATE POLICE. Tim J. Watts. Vance Bibliographies, P.O. Box 229, 112 North Charter Street, Monticello, Illinois 61856. 1991.

DIRECTORIES

CAREERS IN LAW ENFORCEMENT AND SECURITY. Paul Cohen and Shari Cohen. Rosen Publishing Group, 20 East Twenty-first Street, New York, New York 10010. 1990.

LAW ENFORCEMENT CAREERS: A COMPLETE GUIDE FROM APPLICATION TO EMPLOYMENT. Ron Stern. Lawman Press, P.O. Box 1468, Mt. Shasta, California 96067. 1988.

WHO'S WHO IN AMERICAN LAW ENFORCEMENT. National Association of Chiefs of Police, 1100 Northeast, 125th Street, North Miami, Florida 33161. Biennial.

WHO'S WHO IN LAW ENFORCEMENT COLLECTING AND POLICE TRAINERS. Elizabeth Dalein Alley. Who's Who in Law Enforcement Collecting and Police Trainers, P.O. Box J-4025, New Bedford, Massachusetts 02742-0366. 1988.

ASSOCIATIONS AND PROFESSIONAL SOCIETIES

AFRO-AMERICAN POLICE LEAGUE. P.O. Box 49122, Chicago, Illinois 60649. (312) 753-9454.

AMERICAN FEDERATION OF POLICE. 1000 Connecticut Avenue, Northwest, Suite 9, Washington, D.C. 20036. (202) 293-9088.

INTERNATIONAL ASSOCIATION OF CHIEFS OF POLICE. 1110 North Glebe Road, Suite 200, Arlington, Virginia 22201. (703) 243-6500.

NATIONAL ASSOCIATION OF POLICE ORGANIZATIONS. c/o Robert Scully, Detroit Police Officers Association, 6525 Lincoln, Detroit, Michigan 48202. (313) 871-0484.

NATIONAL BLACK POLICE ASSOCIATION. 1919 Pennsylvania Avenue, Northwest, Suite 300, Washington, D.C. 20006. (202) 457-0563.

RESEARCH CENTERS, INSTITUTES, CLEARINGHOUSES

LAW ENFORCEMENT EDUCATION AND TRAINING CENTER. University of Wisconsin, Madison, 610 Langdon Street, Madison, Wisconsin 53706. (608) 262-3635.

POLICE EXECUTIVE RESEARCH FORUM. 2300 M Street, Northwest, Suite 910, Washington, D.C. 20037. (202) 466-7820.

POLICE FOUNDATION. 1001 Twenty-second Street, Northwest, Suite 200, Washington, D.C. 20037. (202) 833-1460.

ONLINE DATABASES

LAW ENFORCEMENT AND CRIMINAL JUSTICE INFORMATION DATABASE. International Research and Evaluation, 21098 IRE Control Center, Eagan, Minnesota 55121.

STATISTICS SOURCES

CRIME IN THE UNITED STATES: UNIFORM CRIME REPORTS. United States Department of Justice, Federal Bureau of Investigation. Superintendent of Documents, United States Government Printing Office, Washington, D.C. 20402. Annual.

POLICE MAGISTRATES
See: POLICE

POLICE POWER
See: CONSTITUTIONAL LAW; POLICE

POLITICAL CRIMES AND OFFENSES
See also: CENTRAL INTELLIGENCE AGENCY; TERRORISM

TEXTBOOKS AND GENERAL WORKS

BLOOD JUSTICE: THE LYNCHING OF MACK CHARLES PARKER. Howard Smead. Oxford University Press, Incorporated, 200 Madison Avenue, New York, New York 10016. 1988.

CRIME IN CITY POLITICS. Anne Heinz, Herbert Jacob and Robert L. Lineberry, Editors. Longman, Incorporated, 19 West Forty-fourth Street, New York, New York 10036. 1983.

CRIMES OF OBEDIENCE: TOWARD A SOCIAL PSYCHOLOGY OF AUTHORITY AND RESPONSIBILITY. Herbert C. Kelman and V. Lee Hamilton. Yale University Press, 302 Temple Street, New Haven, Connecticut 06520. 1989.

DEFENDING CIVIL RESISTANCE UNDER INTERNATIONAL LAW. Francis A. Boyle. Transnational Publishers, Incorporated, P.O. Box 7282, Ardsley-on-Hudson, New York 10503. 1987.

THE FEDERAL LOYALTY-SECURITY PROGRAM: THE NEED FOR REFORM. Guenter Lewsy. Books on Demand, 300 North Zeeb Road, Ann Arbor, Michigan 48106-1346. 1983.

THE FUTURE OF POLITICAL VIOLENCE: DESTABILIZATION, DISORDER, AND TERRORISM. Richard Clutterbuck. Saint Martin's Press, Incorporated, 175 Fifth Avenue, New York, New York 10010. 1986.

THE GREAT RED MENACE: UNITED STATES PROSECUTION OF AMERICAN COMMUNISTS, 1947-1952. Greenwood Publishing Group, Incorporated, 88 Post Road West, P.O. Box 5007, Westport, Connecticut 06881. 1984.

HOOVER AND THE UN-AMERICANS: THE FBI, HUAC, AND THE RED MENACE. Kenneth O'Reilly. Temple University Press, 1601 North Broad Street, University Services Building, Philadelphia, Pennsylvania 19122. 1983.

IN THE MIDDLE: NON-OFFICIAL MEDIATION IN VIOLENT SITUATIONS. Adam Curle. Saint Martin's Press, Incorporated, 175 Fifth Avenue, New York, New York 10010. 1987.

LEGALISM: LAW, MORALS, AND POLITICAL TRIALS. Judith N. Shklar. Berg Publishers, Incorporated, 165 Taber Avenue, Providence, Rhode Island 02906. 1986.

POLITICAL CRIMINALITY: THE DEFIANCE AND DEFENSE OF AUTHORITY. Austin T. Turk. Sage Publications, Incorporated, 2455 Teller Road, Newbury Park, California 91320. 1982.

POLITICAL KILLINGS BY GOVERNMENTS: AN AMNESTY INTERNATIONAL REPORT. Gordon Press, P.O. Box 459, Bowling Green Station, New York, New York 10004. 1991.

POLITICAL TRIALS IN ANCIENT GREECE. Richard A. Bauman. Routledge, Chapman & Hall, 29 West Thirty-fifth Street, New York, New York 10001. 1990.

POLITICAL TRIALS IN HISTORY: FROM ANTIQUITY TO THE PRESENT. Ron Christenson. Transaction Books, Rutgers University, New Brunswick, New Jersey 08903. 1991.

POLITICAL VIOLENCE AND TERROR: MOTIFS AND MOTIVATIONS. Peter H. Merkl. University of California Press, 2120 Berkeley Way, Berkeley, California 94720. 1986.

REASONABLE DOUBT: AN INVESTIGATION INTO THE ASSASSINATION OF JOHN F. KENNEDY. Henry Hurt. Holt, Rinehart and Winston Publishers, Incorporated, 6277 Sea Harbor Drive, Orlando, Florida 32821. 1987.

SPYING ON AMERICA: THE FBI'S DOMESTIC COUNTERINTELLIGENCE PROGRAM. James Kirkpatrick Davis. Praeger Publishers, One Madison Avenue, New York, New York 10010-3603. 1992.

THE TREATMENT OF PRISONERS UNDER INTERNATIONAL LAW. Nigel S. Rodley. Clarendon Press, Oxford University Press, Incorporated, 200 Madison Avenue, New York, New York 10016. 1986.

THE TREE OF LIBERTY: A DOCUMENTARY HISTORY OF REBELLION AND POLITICAL CRIME IN AMERICA. Nicholas N. Kittrie and Eldon D. Wedlock, Jr., Editors. Johns Hopkins University Press, 701 West Fortieth Street, Suite 275, Baltimore, Maryland 21211-2190. 1986.

BIBLIOGRAPHIES

CRIMINAL INTELLIGENCE AND SECURITY INTELLIGENCE: A SELECTIVE BIBLIOGRAPHY. A. Stuart Farson and Catherine J. Matthews. University of Toronto, Centre of Criminology, John P. Robarts Research Library, Room 8001, 130 St. George Street, Toronto, Ontario, Canada M5S 1A1. 1990.

POLITICAL CRIMES AND OFFENSES: MONOGRAPHS. Mary Vance. Vance Bibliographies, P.O. Box 229, 112 North Charter Street, Monticello, Illinois 61856. 1987.

OTHER SOURCES

FEDERAL BUREAU OF INVESTIGATION CONFIDENTIAL FILES. THE J. EDGAR HOOVER OFFICIAL AND CONFIDENTIAL FILE. Athan Theoharis and Martin Paul Schipper. University Publications of America, 4520 East West Highway, Suite 600, Bethesda, Maryland 20814. 1990.

POLITICAL OFFENSES
See: POLITICAL CRIMES AND OFFENSES

POLITICS
See: ELECTION LAW; LOBBYING

POLLUTION
See: ENVIRONMENTAL LAW

POOR PEOPLE
See: INDIGENCE; LEGAL AID

PORNOGRAPHY
See: OBSCENITY

POST-CONVICTION REMEDIES
See also: HABEAS CORPUS; SENTENCING

STATUTES, CODES, STANDARDS, UNIFORM LAWS

STANDARDS FOR CRIMINAL JUSTICE. Second Edition. Standing Committee on Association Standards for Criminal Justice, American Bar Association. Little, Brown, and Company, 34 Beacon Street, Boston, Massachusetts 02108. 1982. (Periodic Supplements).

UNIFORM POST-CONVICTION PROCEDURE ACT. Uniform Laws Annotated. West Publishing Company, P.O. Box 64526, 50 West Kellogg Boulevard, St. Paul, Minnesota 55164-0526. 1976. (Annual Supplements).

HANDBOOKS, MANUALS, FORMBOOKS

POST-CONVICTION REMEDIES: A SELF-HELP MANUAL. Daniel E. Manville and George N. Brezna. Oceana Publications, Incorporated, 75 Main Street, Dobbs Ferry, New York 10522. 1988.

TEXTBOOKS AND GENERAL WORKS

FEDERAL AND STATE POST-CONVICTION REMEDIES AND RELIEF. Second Edition. Donald E. Wilkes, Jr. Harrison Company, 3110 Crossing Park, Norcross, Georgia 30091. 1987.

THE LAW AND PROCESS OF POST CONVICTION REMEDIES: CASES AND MATERIALS. Ira P. Robbins. West Publishing Company, P.O. Box 64526, 50 West Kellogg Boulevard, St. Paul, Minnesota 55164-0526. 1982.

ASSOCIATIONS AND PROFESSIONAL SOCIETIES

STANDING COMMITTEE ON ASSOCIATION STANDARDS FOR CRIMINAL JUSTICE. American Bar Association, 750 North Lake Shore Drive, Chicago, Illinois 60611. (312) 988-5000.

POVERTY LAW
See: INDIGENCE

PRACTICE OF LAW
See: ADMISSION TO THE BAR; LAW OFFICE MANAGEMENT; LAW PRACTICE; LAWYER AND CLIENT; LAWYERS' FEES; LEGAL ETHICS AND MALPRACTICE; LEGAL FORMS; LEGAL PROFESSION IN FICTION; PREPAID LEGAL SERVICES

PRECEDENT, JUDICIAL
See: JUDGMENTS

PREPAID LEGAL SERVICES

HANDBOOKS, MANUALS, FORMBOOKS

A LAWYER'S GUIDE TO PREPAID LEGAL SERVICES: A HANDBOOK FOR THE SMALL FIRM. Alec M. Schwartz, David A. Baker, and Samuel J. Pasquarelli. American Bar Association, 750 North Lake Shore Drive, Chicago, Illinois 60611. 1988.

TEXTBOOKS AND GENERAL WORKS

THE API GUIDE TO PREPAID LEGAL SERVICES: THE INSIDERS' VIEW. American Prepaid Legal Services Institute, 750 North Lake Shore Drive, Chicago, Illinois 60611. 1984.

REPORT ON THE SAN ANTONIO STUDY OF LEGAL SERVICES DELIVERY SYSTEMS. American Bar Association, 750 North Lake Shore Drive, Chicago, Illinois 60611. 1989.

NEWSLETTERS AND NEWSPAPERS

AMERICAN PREPAID LEGAL SERVICES INSTITUTE NEWSBRIEFS. American Prepaid Legal Services Institute, 750 North Lake Shore Drive, Chicago, Illinois 60611. Monthly.

ASSOCIATIONS AND PROFESSIONAL SOCIETIES

AMERICAN BAR ASSOCIATION, SPECIAL COMMITTEE ON PREPAID LEGAL SERVICES, 750 North Lake Shore Drive, Chicago, Illinois 60611. (312) 988-5000.

RESEARCH CENTERS, INSTITUTES, CLEARINGHOUSES

AMERICAN PREPAID LEGAL SERVICES INSTITUTE. 750 North Lake Shore Drive, Chicago, Illinois 60611. (312) 988-5751.

PRE-MARITAL AGREEMENTS
See: FAMILY LAW

PRETRIAL PROCEDURE
See: CIVIL PROCEDURE; CRIMINAL PROCEDURE; TRIAL PRACTICE

PRESIDENT (UNITED STATES)
See also: EXECUTIVE POWER

STATUTES, CODES, STANDARDS, UNIFORM LAWS

CODE OF FEDERAL REGULATIONS, TITLE 3. Office Of The Federal Register, National Archives and Records Administration. Superintendent of Documents, United States Government Printing Office, Washington, D.C. 20402. Annual. (Updated by use of monthly List of Sections Affected and daily Federal Register.)

CODIFICATION OF PRESIDENTIAL PROCLAMATIONS AND EXECUTIVE ORDERS, JANUARY 20, 1961-JANUARY 20, 1985. Office of the Federal Register, National Archives and Records Administration. Superintendent of Documents, United States Government Printing Office, Washington, D.C. 20402. 1985.

PUBLIC PAPERS OF THE PRESIDENTS OF THE UNITED STATES. Office of the Federal Register, National Archives and Records Administration. Superintendent of Documents, United States Government Printing Office, Washington, D.C. 20402. Annual.

WEEKLY COMPILATION OF PRESIDENTIAL DOCUMENTS. Office of the Federal Register, National Archives and Records Administration. Superintendent of Documents, United States Government Printing Office, Washington, D.C. 20402. Weekly.

TEXTBOOKS AND GENERAL WORKS

AFTER THE PEOPLE VOTE: STEPS IN CHOOSING THE PRESIDENT. Walter Burns, Editor. American Enterprise Institute of Public Policy Research, 1150 Seventeenth Street, Northwest, Washington, D.C. 20036. 1984.

THE AMERICAN PRESIDENCY. B. I. Page and M. P. Petracca. McGraw-Hill Book Company, 1221 Avenue of the Americas, New York, New York 10020. 1983.

THE AMERICAN PRESIDENCY: A POLICY PERSPECTIVE FROM READINGS AND DOCUMENTS. David C. Kozak and Kenneth N. Ciboski, Editors. Nelson-Hall, Incorporated, 111 North Canal Street, Chicago, Illinois 60606. 1985.

AMERICAN PRESIDENTS AND THE PRESIDENCY. Marcus Cunliffe. Houghton Mifflin Company, 1 Beacon Street, Boston, Massachusetts 02108. 1986.

AMERICA'S UNELECTED GOVERNMENT: APPOINTING THE PRESIDENT'S TEAM. John W. Macy, et al. Ballinger Publishing Company, Subsidiary of HarperCollins, Incorporated, 10 East Fifty-third Street, New York, New York 10022. 1983.

THE ASSUMPTION OF POWER: PRESIDENTIAL TRANSITIONS FROM EISENHOWER THROUGH REAGAN. Carl M. Brauer. Oxford University Press, Incorporated, 200 Madison Avenue, New York, New York 10016. 1986.

BOTH ENDS OF THE AVENUE: THE PRESIDENCY, THE EXECUTIVE BRANCH AND CONGRESS IN THE 1980S. Anthony King, Editor. American Enterprise Institute of Public Policy Research, 1150 17th Street, N.W., Washington, D.C. 20036. 1983.

CANDIDATES EIGHTY-FOUR. Congressional Quarterly, Incorporated, 1414 22nd Street, Northwest, Washington, D.C. 20037. 1984.

CHIEF OF STATE: TWENTY-FIVE YEARS OF MANAGING THE PRESIDENCY: CONTRIBUTIONS. Samuel Kernell and Samuel L. Popkin. University of California Press, 2120 Berkeley Way, Berkeley, California 94720. 1986.

CHOOSING THE PRESIDENT: A COMPLETE GUIDE TO UNDERSTANDING THE PRESIDENTIAL ELECTION PROCESS. League of Women Voters Education Fund. Schocken Books, Incorporated, 201 East Fiftieth Street, New York, New York 10022. 1984.

CONGRESS AND THE PRESIDENCY. Fourth Edition. Nelson W. Polsby. Prentice-Hall, Incorporated, 113 Sylvan Avenue, Englewood Cliffs, New Jersey 07632. 1986.

CONGRESS, THE PRESIDENT AND FOREIGN POLICY. American Bar Association Standing Committee on Law and National Security. American Bar Association, 750 North Lake Shore Drive, Chicago, Illinois 60611. 1984.

CONSTITUTIONAL CONFLICTS BETWEEN CONGRESS AND THE PRESIDENT. Third Edition. Louis Fisher. University Press of Kansas, 329 Carruth, Lawrence, Kansas 66045. 1991.

CONTROLLING REGULATORY SPRAWL: PRESIDENTIAL STRATEGIES FROM NIXON TO REAGAN. Howard Ball. Greenwood Publishing Group, Incorporated, 88 Post Road West, P.O. Box 5007, Westport, Connecticut 06881. 1984.

A DOMESTIC POLICY FORMATION: PRESIDENTIAL-CONGRESSIONAL PARTNERSHIP? Steven A. Shull. Greenwood Publishing Group, Incorporated, 88 Post Road West, P.O. Box 5007, Westport, Connecticut 06881. 1983.

THE ELECTORAL COLLEGE ABOLITION OR REFORM: VIEWS OF THE U.S. CONGRESS. Harold J. Nufer. Exposition Press of America, Incorporated, 1701 Blount Road, Pompano Beach, Florida 33069. 1985.

EVERY FOUR YEARS: THE AMERICAN PRESIDENCY. Revised Edition. Smithsonian Books, 955 L'Enfant Plaza, Room 2100, Southwest, Washington, D.C. 20560. 1984.

FUTURE PRESIDENTS: A BRIEFING BOOK FOR COMING CHANGES IN PRESIDENTIAL NOMINATING AND RESULTING CHANGES IN POLITICS AND THE AMERICAN PRESIDENCY. Laurence G. Kraus. Rovi Publications, Inc., P.O. Box 259, Belvedere, California 94920. 1984.

HISTORY OF AMERICAN PRESIDENTIAL ELECTIONS 1972-1984. Arthur Schlesinger Jr., Editor. Chelsea House Publishers, 1974 Sproul Road, Suite 400, Broomall, Pennsylvania 19008. 1985.

THE IMPOSSIBLE PRESIDENCY: ILLUSIONS AND REALITIES OF PRESIDENTIAL POWER. Harold M. Barger. Scott, Foresman and Company, 1900 East Lake Avenue, Glenview, Illinois 60025. 1984.

THE INAUGURAL ADDRESSES OF THE PRESIDENTS OF THE UNITED STATES. Michael J. Lax, Editor. American Inheritance Press, P.O. Box 484, Linwood, New Jersey 08221-0584. 1985.

KEEPING FAITH: MEMOIRS OF A PRESIDENT: JIMMY CARTER. Bantam Books, Incorporated, 666 Fifth Avenue, New York, New York 10103. 1983.

KENNEDY. Reg Gadney. Henry Holt and Company, 115 West Eighteenth Street, New York, New York 10011. 1983.

THE LEADERSHIP QUESTION: THE PRESIDENCY AND THE AMERICAN SYSTEM. Bert A. Rockman. Praeger Publishers, One Madison Avenue, New York, New York 10010-3603. 1985.

LIBERALISM AND ITS CHALLENGERS: F.D.R. TO REAGAN. Alonzo L. Hamby. Oxford University Press, Incorporated, 200 Madison Avenue, New York, New York 10016. 1984.

MANAGING THE PRESIDENCY: CARTER, REAGAN AND THE SEARCH FOR EXECUTIVE HARMONY. Colin Campbell. University of Pittsburgh Press, 127 North Bellefield Avenue, Pittsburgh, Pennsylvania 15260. 1986.

THE MASS MEDIA AND ELECTION CAMPAIGNS. Richard A. Joslyn. Random House, Incorporated, 201 East Fiftieth Street, New York, New York 10022. 1984.

MODERN PRESIDENTS AND THE PRESIDENCY. Marc Lande, Editor. Free Press, 866 Third Avenue, New York, New York 10022. 1984.

THE NEWS STRATEGIES OF PRESIDENTIAL CAMPAIGNS. Christopher F. Atherton. Lexington Books, Division of D.C. Heath and Company, 125 Spring Street, Lexington, Massachusetts 02173. 1984.

NONE OF THE ABOVE, WHY PRESIDENTS FAIL AND WHAT CAN BE DONE ABOUT IT. Robert Shogan. New American Library, 1633 Broadway, New York, New York 10019. 1983.

NOMINATION POLITICS: PARTY ACTIVISTS AND PRESIDENTIAL CHOICE. Alan I. Abramowitz and Walter J. Stone. Praeger Publishers, One Madison Avenue, New York, New York 10010-3603. 1984.

PACKAGING THE PRESIDENCY: A HISTORY AND CRITICISM OF PRESIDENTIAL CAMPAIGNS. Kathleen L. Jamieson. Oxford University Press, Incorporated, 200 Madison Avenue, New York, New York 10016. 1992.

PAPERS ON PRESIDENTIAL DISABILITY AND THE TWENTY-FIFTH AMENDMENT, BY SIX MEDICAL, LEGAL, AND POLITICAL AUTHORITIES. Kenneth W. Thompson. University Press of America, 4720 Boston Way, Lanham, Maryland 20706. 1988.

PARTIES AND ELECTIONS IN THE UNITED STATES. John A. Crittenden. Prentice-Hall, Incorporated, 113 Sylvan Avenue, Englewood Cliffs, New Jersey 07632. 1982.

THE PERSONAL PRESIDENT: POWER INVESTED, PROMISE UNFULFILLED. Theodore J. Lowi. Cornell University Press, 124 Roberts Place, Ithaca, New York 14850. 1985.

POLITICAL PERSUASION IN PRESIDENTIAL CAMPAIGNS. L. Patrick Develin. Transaction Books, Rutgers University, New Brunswick, New Jersey 08903. 1986.

THE POLITICAL PRESIDENCY: PRACTICE OF LEADERSHIP FROM KENNEDY TO REAGAN. Barbara Kellerman. Oxford University Press, Incorporated, 200 Madison Avenue, New York, New York 10016. 1986.

THE POLITICS OF THE PRESIDENCY. R. A. Watson and N. C. Thomas. Congressional Quarterly Books, 1414 Twenty-second Street, Northwest, Washington, D.C. 20037. 1987.

THE PRESIDENCY AND PUBLIC POLICY: THE FOUR ARENAS OF PRESIDENTIAL POWER. Robert J. Spitzer. University of Alabama Press, P.O. Box 870380, Tuscaloosa, Alabama 35487. 1983.

THE PRESIDENCY AND THE POLITICAL SYSTEM. Third Edition. Michael Nelson, Editor. Congressional Quarterly, Incorporated, 1414 22nd Street, Northwest, Washington, D.C. 20037. 1990.

THE PRESIDENT AND PUBLIC POLICY MAKING. George C. Edwards, et al, Editors. University of Pittsburgh Press, 127 North Bellefield Avenue, Pittsburgh, Pennsylvania 15260. 1985.

THE PRESIDENT, CONGRESS AND THE CONSTITUTION: POWER AND LEGITIMACY IN AMERICAN POLITICS. Christopher H. Pyle and Richard M. Pious. Free Press, Division of Macmillan Publishing Company, Incorporated, 866 Third Avenue, New York, New York 10022. 1984.

THE PRESIDENTIAL BRANCH. John Hart. Pergamon Press, Incorporated, Maxwell House, Fairview Park, Elmsford, New York 10523. 1987.

PRESIDENTIAL CAMPAIGN POLITICS: COALITION STRATEGIES AND CITIZEN RESPONSE. Third Edition. John S. Kessel. Brooks/Cole Publishing Company, 511 Forest Lodge Road, Pacific Grove, California 93924. 1988.

PRESIDENTIAL CAMPAIGNS. Paul F. Boller. Oxford University Press, Incorporated, 200 Madison Avenue, New York, New York 10016. 1984.

THE PRESIDENTIAL CHARACTER: PREDICTING PERFORMANCE IN THE WHITE HOUSE. James D. Barker. Prentice-Hall, Incorporated, 113 Sylvan Avenue, Englewood Cliffs, New Jersey 07632. 1985.

THE PRESIDENTIAL CONTEST: WITH A GUIDE TO THE 1984 RACE. Richard A. Watson. Macmillan Publishing Company, Incorporated, 866 Third Avenue, New York, New York 10022. 1984.

THE PRESIDENTIAL ELECTION AND TRANSITION 1980-1981. Paul L. David and David H. Everson, Editors. Southern Illinois University Press, P.O. Box 3697, Carbondale, Illinois 62902-3697. 1983.

PRESIDENTIAL ELECTIONS AND AMERICAN POLITICS: VOTERS, CANDIDATES AND CAMPAIGNS SINCE 1952. Fifth Edition. Herbert Asher. Brooks/Cole Publishing Company, 511 Forest Lodge Road, Pacific Grove, California 93924. 1991.

PRESIDENTIAL ELECTIONS SINCE 1789. Fifth Edition. Congressional Quarterly, Incorporated, 1414 Twenty-second Street, Northwest, Washington, D.C. 20037. 1991.

PRESIDENTIAL ELECTIONS: STRATEGIES OF AMERICAN ELECTORAL POLITICS. Nelson W. Polsby and Aaron Wildavsky. Charles Scribner and Sons, 866 Third Avenue, New York, New York 10022. 1984.

PRESIDENTIAL LEADERSHIP: POLITICS AND POLICY MAKING. George C. Edwards III and Stephen J. Wayne. Saint Martin's Press, Incorporated, 175 Fifth Avenue, New York, New York 10010. 1990.

THE PRESIDENTIAL NOMINATING PROCESS: BROADENING AND NARROWING THE DEBATE. Kenneth W. Thompson, Editor. University Press of America, 4720 Boston Way, Lanham, Maryland 20706. 1984.

THE PRESIDENTIAL NOMINATING PROCESS: CONSTITUTIONAL, ECONOMIC AND POLITICAL ISSUES. University Press of America, 4720 Boston Way, Lanham, Maryland 20706. 1984.

PRESIDENTIAL PARTIES. John S. Kessel. Dorsey Press, 10 Davis Drive, Belmont, California 94002. 1984.

THE PRESIDENTIAL QUOTIENT. Wayne S. Kurzeja. Chicago Review Press, 814 North Franklin Street, Chicago, Illinois 60610. 1984.

THE PRESIDENT'S AGENDA: DOMESTIC POLICY CHOICE FROM KENNEDY TO RONALD REAGAN. Paul C. Light. Johns Hopkins University Press, 701 West Fortieth Street, Suite 275, Baltimore, Maryland 21211-2190. 1991.

PRESIDENTS AND PROMISES: FROM CAMPAIGN PLEDGE TO PRESIDENTIAL PERFORMANCE. Jeff Fishel. Congressional Quarterly, Incorporated, 1414 Twenty-second Street, Northwest, Washington, D. C. 20037. 1985.

PRESIDENTS AND THE PUBLIC. Congressional Quarterly Books, 1414 Twenty- second Street, Northwest, Washington D.C. 20037. 1990.

THE PRESIDENTS AND THEIR PARTIES: LEADERSHIP OR NEGLECT? Robert Harmel, Editor. Praeger Publishers, One Madison Avenue, New York, New York 10010-3603. 1983.

THE PRESIDENTS OF THE UNITED STATES OF AMERICA. Eleventh Edition. Frank Freidel and Frank Burt. White House Historical Association, 740 Jackson Place, Northwest, Washington, D.C. 20503. 1987.

PRESIDENTS, POLITICS AND POLICY. Erwin C. Hargrove and Michael Nelson. Johns Hopkins University Press, 701 West Fortieth Street, Suite 275, Baltimore, Maryland 21211-2190. 1984.

PROBLEMS WITH THE PRESIDENCY: A TEXT WITH READINGS. Barbara Hinckley. Scott, Foresman and Company, 1900 East Lake Avenue, Glenview, Illinois 60025. 1985.

A PROGRAM FOR REFORM: A FINAL REPORT OF THE COMMISSION ON NATIONAL ELECTIONS. Robert E. Hunter. Center for Strategic and International Studies, 1800 K Street, Northwest, Washington, D.C. 20006. 1986.

PROMISES AND PERFORMANCE: PRESIDENTIAL CAMPAIGNS AS POLICY PREDICTORS. Michael G. Krukones. University Press of America, 4720 Boston Way, Lanham, Maryland 20706. 1984.

THE ROAD TO THE WHITE HOUSE: THE POLITICS OF PRESIDENTIAL ELECTIONS. Third Edition. Stephen J. Wayne. Saint Martin's Press, Incorporated, 175 Fifth Avenue, New York, New York 10010. 1987.

ROOSEVELT TO REAGAN: A REPORTER'S ENCOUNTERS WITH NINE PRESIDENTS. Hedley Donovan. HarperCollins Publishers, Incorporated, 10 East Fifty-third Street, New York, New York 10022. 1987.

SELECTING THE PRESIDENT: THE NOMINATING PROCESS IN TRANSITION. Howard L. Reiter. University of Pennsylvania Press, Blockley Hall, 418 Service Drive, Philadelphia, Pennsylvania 19104. 1985

SYMPOSIUM ON PRESIDENTIAL POLICY MAKING. George Edwards, et al, Editors. Policy Studies Organization, University of Illinois, 361 Lincoln Hall, 702 South Wright Street, Urbana, Illinois 61801. 1984.

THREE PRESS SECRETARIES ON THE PRESIDENCY: JODY POWELL, GEORGE REEDY, JERRY TERHORST. Jody Powell, et al. University Press of America, 4720 Boston Way, Lanham, Maryland 20706. 1984.

THE TRUMAN SCANDALS AND THE POLITICS OF MORALITY. Andrew J. Dunar. University of Missouri Press, 2910 LeMone Boulevard, Columbia, Missouri 65201. 1984.

UNINFORMED CHOICE: THE FAILURE OF THE NEW PRESIDENTIAL NOMINATING SYSTEM. Scott Keeter and Cliff Zukin. Praeger Publishers, One Madison Avenue, New York, New York 10010-3603. 1983.

VERBAL STYLE AND THE PRESIDENCY: COMPUTER ASSISTED ANALYSIS OF PERSUASION. Roderick P. Hart. Academy Press, 5037 North Academy Boulevard, Colorado Springs, Colorado 80918. 1984.

THE WHITE HOUSE PRESS ON THE PRESIDENCY: NEWS MANAGEMENT AND CO-OPTION. Frank Cormier and James Deakin. University Press of America, 4720 Boston Way, Lanham, Maryland 20706. 1983.

ENCYCLOPEDIAS AND DICTIONARIES

ALMANAC OF AMERICAN PRESIDENTS, FROM 1789 TO THE PRESENT: AN ORIGINAL COMPENDIUM OF FACTS AND ANECDOTES ABOUT POLITICS AND THE PRESIDENCY IN THE UNITED STATES OF AMERICA. Thomas L. Connelly and Michael D. Senecal. Facts on File, Incorporated, 460 Park Avenue South, New York, New York 10016. 1991.

THE BULLY PULPIT: QUOTATIONS FROM AMERICA'S PRESIDENTS. Elizabeth Frost. Facts on File, Incorporated, 460 Park Avenue South, New York, New York 10016. 1988.

THE PRESIDENTS OF THE UNITED STATES: A HISTORY OF THE PRESIDENTS OF THE UNITED STATES, WITH AN ENCYCLOPEDIC SUPPLEMENT ON THE OFFICE AND POWERS OF THE PRESIDENCY, CHRONOLOGIES, AND RECORDS OF PRESIDENTIAL ELECTIONS. John and Alice Durant. Gache Publishing Company, Incorporated, 1013 East Twenty-sixth Street, Hialeah, Florida 33013. Defunct. 1987.

THE WORLD ALMANAC OF PRESIDENTIAL CAMPAIGNS. Eileen Shields-West. World Almanac, New York, New York. 1992.

THE WORLD ALMANAC OF PRESIDENTIAL FACTS. Lu Ann Paletta and Fred L. Worth. World Almanac. Distributed by Ballantine Books, 201 East Fiftieth Street, New York, New York 10022. 1988.

WORLD BOOK OF AMERICA'S PRESIDENTS. World Book, Incorporated, 510 Merchandise Mart Plaza, Chicago, Illinois 60654. 1989.

DIGESTS, INDEXES, ABSTRACTS, CITATORS

THE CUMULATED INDEXES TO THE PUBLIC PAPERS OF THE PRESIDENTS OF THE UNITED STATES: DWIGHT D. EISENHOWER, 1953-1961. Kraus International Publications, Route 100, Millwood, New York 10546. 1978.

THE CUMULATED INDEXES TO THE PUBLIC PAPERS OF THE PRESIDENTS OF THE UNITED STATES: GERALD R. FORD, 1974-1977. Kraus International Publications, Route 100, Millwood, New York 10546. 1980.

THE CUMULATED INDEXES TO THE PUBLIC PAPERS OF THE PRESIDENTS OF THE UNITED STATES: HARRY S. TRUMAN, 1945-1953. Kraus International Publications, Route 100, Millwood, New York 10546. 1979.

THE CUMULATED INDEXES TO THE PUBLIC PAPERS OF THE PRESIDENTS OF THE UNITED STATES: HERBERT HOOVER, 1929-1933. Kraus International Publications, Route 100, Millwood, New York 10546. 1979.

THE CUMULATED INDEXES TO THE PUBLIC PAPERS OF THE PRESIDENTS OF THE UNITED STATES: JIMMY CARTER, 1977-1981. Kraus International Publications, Route 100, Millwood, New York 10546. 1983.

THE CUMULATED INDEXES TO THE PUBLIC PAPERS OF THE PRESIDENTS OF THE UNITED STATES: JOHN F. KENNEDY, 1961-1963. Kraus International Publications, Route 100, Millwood, New York 10546. 1977.

THE CUMULATED INDEXES TO THE PUBLIC PAPERS OF THE PRESIDENTS OF THE UNITED STATES: LYNDON B. JOHNSON, 1963-1969. Kraus International Publications, Route 100, Millwood, New York 10546. 1978.

THE CUMULATED INDEXES TO THE PUBLIC PAPERS OF THE PRESIDENTS OF THE UNITED STATES: RICHARD M. NIXON, 1969-1974. Kraus International Publications, Route 100, Millwood, New York 10546. 1978.

THE PRESIDENCY: A RESEARCH GUIDE. Robert U. Goehlert and Fenton S. Martin. ABC-Clio Information Services, P.O. Box 1911, Santa Barbara, California 93116-1911. 1985.

SHEPARD'S CODE OF FEDERAL REGULATIONS CITATIONS. Shepard's/McGraw-Hill, P.O. Box 1235, Colorado Springs, Colorado 80901. Bimonthly.

THE WATERGATE INVESTIGATION INDEX: SENATE SELECT COMMITTEE HEARINGS AND REPORTS ON PRESIDENTIAL ACTIVITIES. Hedda Garza. Scholarly Resources, Incorporated, 104 Greenhill Avenue, Wilmington, Delaware 19805. 1982.

LAW REVIEWS AND PERIODICALS

PRESIDENTIAL STUDIES QUARTERLY. Center for the Study of the Presidency, 208 East Seventy-fifth Street, New York, New York 10021. Quarterly.

NEWSLETTERS AND NEWSPAPERS

WHITE HOUSE WEEKLY. Feistritzer Publications, 1901 Pennsylvania Avenue, Northwest, Washington, D. C. 20006. Weekly.

BIBLIOGRAPHIES

THE AMERICAN ELECTORATE: A HISTORICAL BIBLIOGRAPHY. ABC-Clio Information Services, P.O. Box 1911, Santa Barbara, California 93116-1911. 1984.

AMERICAN PRESIDENCY: A GUIDE TO INFORMATION SOURCES. Kenneth E. Davison, Editor. Gale Research, Incorporated, 835 Penobscot Building, Detroit, Michigan 48226. 1983.

AMERICAN PRESIDENTS: A BIBLIOGRAPHY. Fenton S. Martin and Robert U. Goehlert. Congressional Quarterly Books, 1414 Twenty-second Street, Northwest, Washington D.C. 20037. 1987.

THE AMERICAN PRESIDENTS: AN ANNOTATED BIBLIGRAPHY. Norman S. Cohen. Salem Press, Incorporated, P.O. Box 1097, Englewood Cliffs, New Jersey 07632. 1989.

GUBERNATORIAL AND PRESIDENTIAL TRANSITIONS: AN ANNOTATED BIBLIOGRAPHY AND RESOURCE GUIDE. James S. Bowman and Ronald L. Monet. Garland Publishing, Incorporated, 136 Madison Avenue, New York, New York 10016. 1988.

GUIDE TO PRESIDENTIAL ADVISORY COMMISSIONS, 1973-1981. Steven D. Zink. Chadwyck-Healey, Incorporated, 1101 King Street, Alexandria, Virginia 22314. 1987.

THE PEOPLE'S VOICE: AN ANNOTATED BIBLIOGRAPHY OF AMERICAN PRESIDENTIAL CAMPAIGN NEWSPAPERS, 1828-1984. William Miles. Greenwood Publishing Group, Incorporated, 88 Post Road West, P.O. Box 5007, Westport, Connecticut 06881. 1987.

PRESIDENTIAL LIBRARIES AND COLLECTIONS. Fritz Veit. Greenwood Publishing Group, Incorporated, 88 Post Road West, P.O. Box 5007, Westport, Connecticut 06881. 1987.

RECORDS OF THE PRESIDENCY: PRESIDENTIAL PAPERS AND LIBRARIES FROM WASHINGTON TO REAGAN. Frank L. Schick, Renee Schick, and Mark Carroll. Oryx Press, 2214 North Central Avenue, Phoenix, Arizona 85004. 1989.

DIRECTORIES

FEDERAL YELLOW BOOK: A DIRECTORY OF THE FEDERAL DEPARTMENTS AND AGENCIES. Monitor Publishing Company, 104 Fifth Avenue, Second Floor, New York, New York 10011. Quarterly.

BIOGRAPHICAL SOURCES

THE AMERICAN PRESIDENTS BIOGRAPHIES OF THE CHIEF EXECUTIVES FROM WASHINGTON TO BUSH. David C. Whitney and Robin Vaughn Whitney. Prentice-Hall, Incorporated, 113 Sylvan Avenue, Englewood Cliffs, New Jersey 07632. 1990.

FACTS ABOUT THE PRESIDENTS: A COMPILATION OF BIOGRAPHICAL AND HISTORICAL INFORMATION. Joseph Nathan Kane. H.W. Wilson Company, 950 University Avenue, Bronx, New York 10452. 1989.

LETTERS HOME. Harry S. Truman and Monte M. Poen. Putnam Publishing Group, 200 Madison Avenue, New York, New York 10016. 1984.

OUR COUNTRY'S PRESIDENTS. Frank Freidel. National Geographic Society, Seventeenth and M Streets, Northwest, Washington, D.C. 20036. 1992.

THE PRESIDENTS. James H. Charleton, Robert G. Ferris, and Lewis L. Gould. National Archives and Records Administration, Eighth Street at Pennsylvania Avenue, Northwest, Washington, D.C. 20408. 1992.

READERS AND COLLECTORS GUIDE TO THE BIOGRAPHIES OF THE AMERICAN PRESIDENTS. American Political Biography, 39 Boggs Hill Road, Newtown, Connecticut 06470. 1988- .

ASSOCIATIONS AND PROFESSIONAL SOCIETIES

DEMOCRATIC NATIONAL COMMITTEE. 430 South Capitol Street, Southeast, Washington, D.C. 20003. (202) 863-8000.

REPUBLICAN NATIONAL COMMITTEE. 310 First Street, Southeast, Washington, D.C. 20003. (202) 863-8500.

RESEARCH CENTERS, INSTITUTES, CLEARINGHOUSES

CENTER FOR THE STUDY OF THE PRESIDENCY. 208 East Seventy-fifth Street, New York, New York 10021. (212) 249-1200.

DWIGHT D. EISENHOWER LIBRARY. Southeast Fourth Street, Abilene, Kansas 67410. (913) 263-4751.

FRANKLIN D. ROOSEVELT LIBRARY. 259 Albany Post Road, Hyde Park, New York 12538. (914) 229-8114.

GERALD R. FORD LIBRARY. 1000 Beal Avenue, Ann Arbor, Michigan 48109. (313) 668-2218.

HARRY S. TRUMAN LIBRARY. 1200 North McKay, Independence, Missouri 64050. (816) 833-1400.

HERBERT HOOVER LIBRARY. Parkside Drive, P.O. Box 488, West Branch, Iowa 52358. (319) 643-5301.

HERBERT HOOVER PRESIDENTIAL LIBRARY ASSOCIATION. P.O. Box 696, West Branch, Iowa 52358. (319) 643-5327.

JIMMY CARTER LIBRARY. One Copenhill Avenue, Atlanta, Georgia 30307. (404) 331-3942.

JOHN F. KENNEDY LIBRARY. Columbia Point, Boston, Massachusetts 02125. (617) 929-4500.

LYNDON B. JOHNSON LIBRARY. 2313 Red River Street, Austin, Texas 78705. (512) 482-5137.

NIXON PRESIDENTIAL MATERIALS STAFF. 845 South Pickett Street, Alexandria, Virginia 22304. (703) 756-6498.

OFFICE OF PRESIDENTIAL LIBRARIES. National Archives and Records Administration, Eighth Street and Pennsylvania Avenue, Northwest, Washington, D.C. 20408. (202) 501-5700.

REAGAN PRESIDENTIAL MATERIALS STAFF. 9055 Exposition Drive, Los Angeles, California 90034. (213) 215-2125.

RUTHERFORD B. HAYES PRESIDENTIAL CENTER. Spiegel Grove, Fremont, Ohio 43420. (419) 332-2081.

WHITE BURKETT MILLER CENTER OF PUBLIC AFFAIRS. University of Virginia, Box 5106, Charlottesville, Virginia 22905. (804) 924-7236.

WHITE HOUSE LAW LIBRARY. Old Executive Office Building, Room 528, Washington, D.C. 20500. (202) 395-3397.

ONLINE DATABASES

FEDERAL ELECTION COMMISSION DIRECT ACCESS PROGRAM. Federal Election Commission, Freedom of Information Officer, 1325 K Street, Northwest, Washington, D.C. 20463.

LEXIS, GENERAL FEDERAL LIBRARY, PRESIDENTIAL DOCUMENTS FILE. Mead Data Central, P.O. Box 933, Dayton, Ohio 45401.

PACS AND LOBBIES. Newsnet, Incorporated, 945 Haverford Road, Bryn Mawr, Pennsylvania 19010.

WESTLAW, GENERAL FEDERAL LIBRARY, PRESIDENTIAL DOCUMENTS FILE. West Publishing Company, P.O. Box 64526, 50 West Kellogg Boulevard, St. Paul, Minnesota 55164-0526.

STATISTICS SOURCES

AMERICA AT THE POLLS 2: A HANDBOOK OF AMERICAN PRESIDENTIAL ELECTION STATISTICS, 1968-1984. Richard M. Scammon and Alice V. McGillivray. Congressional Quarterly Books, 1414 Twenty-second Street, Northwest, Washington D.C. 20037. 1988.

THE PURSUIT OF THE WHITE HOUSE: A HANDBOOK OF PRESIDENTIAL ELECTION STATISTICS AND HISTORY. G. Scott Thomas. Greenwood Publishing Group, Incorporated, 88 Post Road West, P.O. Box 5007, Westport, Connecticut 06881. 1987.

OTHER SOURCES

MY FELLOW AMERICANS: PRESIDENTIAL ADDRESSES THAT SHAPED HISTORY. James C. Humes. Praeger Publishers, One Madison Avenue, New York, New York 10010-3603. 1992.

SPEECHES OF THE AMERICAN PRESIDENTS. Janet Podell and Steven Anzovin. H.W. Wilson Company, 950 University Avenue, Bronx, New York 10452. 1988.

PRICE REGULATION
See: CONSUMER PROTECTION

PRINCIPAL AND AGENT
See: AGENCY

PRISONS AND PRISONERS
See also: REHABILITATION OF OFFENDERS

STATUTES, CODES, STANDARDS, UNIFORM LAWS

MODEL CORRECTIONAL RULES AND REGULATIONS. American Correctional Association, 8025 Laurel Lakes Court, Laurel, Maryland 20707. 1979.

MODEL SENTENCING AND CORRECTIONS ACT. National Conference of Commissioners on Uniform State Laws. Uniform Laws Annotated. West Publishing Company, P.O. Box 64526, 50 West Kellogg Boulevard, St. Paul, Minnesota 55164-0526. 1976. (Annual Supplements).

UNIFORM ACT ON STATUS OF CONVICTED PERSONS. National Conference of Commissioners on Uniform State Laws. Uniform Laws Annotated. West Publishing Company, P.O. Box 64526, 50 West Kellogg Boulevard, St. Paul, Minnesota 55164-0526. 1976. (Annual Supplements).

UNIFORM RENDITION OF PRISONERS AS WITNESSES IN CRIMINAL PROCEEDINGS ACT. National Conference of Commissioners on Uniform State Laws. Uniform Laws Annotated. West Publishing Company, P.O. Box 64526, 50 West Kellogg Boulevard, St. Paul, Minnesota 55164-0526. 1976. (Annual Supplements).

HANDBOOKS, MANUALS, FORMBOOKS

CORRECTIONAL OFFICER'S RESEARCH GUIDE. American Correctional Association, 8025 Laurel Lakes Court, Laurel, Maryland 20707. 1989.

LEGAL RESPONSIBILITY AND AUTHORITY OF COR- RECTIONAL OFFICERS: A HANDBOOK ON COURTS, JUDICIAL DECISIONS, AND CONSTITUTIONAL REQUIREMENTS. American Correctional Association, 8025 Laurel Lakes Court, Laurel, Maryland 20707. 1987.

POST-CONVICTION REMEDIES: A SELF-HELP MANUAL. Daniel E. Manville and George N. Brezna. Oceana Publications, 75 Main Street, Dobbs Ferry, New York 10522. 1988.

PRISONER'S SELF-HELP LITIGATION MANUAL. Revised Second Edition. Daniel E. Manville. Oceana Publications, Incorporated, 75 Main Street, Dobbs Ferry, New York 10522. 1983.

PROVIDING LEGAL SERVICES FOR PRISONERS: A TOOL FOR CORRECTIONAL ADMINISTRATORS. American Correctional Association, 8025 Laurel Lakes Court, Laurel, Maryland 20707. 1982.

THE RIGHTS OF PRISONERS: A COMPREHENSIVE GUIDE TO THE LEGAL RIGHTS OF PRISONERS UNDER CURRENT LAW. Fourth Revised Edition. David Rudovsky, Alvin J. Bronstein and Edward I. Koren. Southern Illinois University Press, P.O. Box 3697, Carbondale, Illinois 62902-3697. 1988.

THE RIGHTS OF PRISONERS: THE BASIC ACLU GUIDE TO PRISONERS' RIGHTS. David Rudovsky. Southern Illinois University Press, P.O. Box 3697, Carbondale, Illinois 62902-3697. 1988.

TEXTBOOKS AND GENERAL WORKS

CASES AND MATERIALS ON THE LAW OF SENTENCING, CORRECTIONS, AND PRISONERS' RIGHTS. Fourth Edition. Sheldon Krantz and Lynn S. Branham. West Publishing Company, 50 West Kellogg Boulevard, St. Paul, Minnesota 55164. 1991.

CONSTITUTIONAL RIGHTS OF PRISONERS. Fourth Edition. John W. Palmer. Anderson Publishing Company, 2035 Reading Road, Cincinnati, Ohio 45202. 1991.

CORRECTIONAL TREATMENT: THEORY AND PRACTICE. Clemens Bartollas. Prentice-Hall, Incorporated, 113 Sylvan Avenue, Englewood Cliffs, New Jersey 07632. 1985.

COURTS, CORRECTIONS, AND THE CONSTITUTION: THE IMPACT OF JUDICIAL INTERVENTION ON PRISONS AND JAILS. John J. DiIulio, Jr. Oxford University Press, 200 Madison Avenue, New York, New York 10016. 1990

DESIGN GUIDE FOR SECURE ADULT CORRECTIONAL FACILITIES. Association of Correctional Officers, 1474 Willow Avenue, Des Plaines, Illinois 60016. 1983.

DETERMINATE SENTENCING AND IMPRISONMENT: A FAILURE OF REFORM. Lynne Goodstein and John Hepburn. Anderson Publishing Company, 2035 Reading Road, Cincinnati, Ohio 45202. 1985.

IMPRISONMENT: THE LEGAL STATUS AND RIGHTS OF PRISONERS. G.D. Treverton-Jones. Sweet and Maxwell Limited, South Quay Plaza, 183 Marsh Wall, London E14 9FT, England. 1989.

INSPECTING A PRISON LAW LIBRARY. Gene Teitelbaum. William W. Gaunt and Sons, Incorporated, Gaunt Building, 3011 Gulf Drive, Holmes Beach, Florida 34217-2199. 1989.

THE JOINT: LANGUAGE AND CULTURE IN A MAXIMUM SECURITY PRISON. Inez Cardozo-Freeman. Charles C. Thomas Publishing, 2600 South First Street, Springfield, Illinois 62794-9265. 1984.

THE LAW OF CORRECTIONS AND PRISONERS' RIGHTS IN A NUTSHELL. Third Edition. Sheldon Krantz. West Publishing Company, P.O. Box 64526, 50 West Kellogg Boulevard, St. Paul, Minnesota 55164-0526. 1988.

THE LEGAL DIMENSIONS OF PRIVATE INCARCERATION. Ira P. Robbins. American Bar Association, 1800 M Street, Northwest, Washington, D.C. 20036. 1988.

THE LEGAL ISSUES OF FEMALE INMATES. Katherine Gabel. Smith College Publications, College Hall 32, Northampton, Massachusetts 01063. 1982.

MEN BEHIND BARS: SEXUAL EXPLOITATION IN PRISON. Wayne S. Wooden and Jay Parker. Plenum Press, 233 Spring Street, New York, New York 10013-1578. 1982.

NEW PERSPECTIVES ON PRISONS AND IMPRISONMENT. James B. Jacobs, Cornell University Press, 124 Roberts Place, Ithaca, New York 14850. 1982.

ORGANIZATIONAL AND RACIAL CONFLICT IN MAXIMUM SECURITY PRISONS. James G. Fox. Lexington Books, Division of D.C. Heath and Company, 125 Spring Street, Lexington, Massachusetts 02173. 1982.

OUTCOMES AND COSTS OF A PRERELEASE SYSTEM. David E. Duffee, Kevin N. Wright, and Peter B. Meyer. Oelgeschlager, Gunn and Hain, Incorporated, 245 Mirriam Street, Weston, Massachusetts 02193. 1983.

THE PAINS OF IMPRISONMENT. Robert Johnson and Hans Toch, Editors. Waveland Press, Incorporated, P.O. Box 4001, Prospect Heights, Illinois 60070. 1988.

PARTIAL JUSTICE: WOMEN IN STATE PRISONS, 1800-1935. Nicole Hahn Rafter. Northeastern University Press, 272 Huntington Plaza, 360 Huntington Avenue, Northeastern University, Boston, Massachusetts 02115. 1985.

THE PRISON ORDEAL. Gary L. Webb. Coker Publishing House, 625 North Riverside Drive, Grapevine, Texas 76051. 1984.

PRISON SLAVERY. Barbara Esposito, et al. Committee to Abolish Prison Slavery, P.O. Box 3207, Washington, D.C. 20010. 1982.

PRISONER LITIGATION: THE PARADOX OF THE JAILHOUSE LAWYER. Jim Thomas. Rowman and Littlefield Publishers, Incorporated, 8705 Bollman Place, Savage, Maryland 20763. 1988

PRISONERS AND THE LAW. Ira Robbins. Clark Boardman Company, Limited, 435 Hudson Street, New York, New York 10014. 1985. (Supplemented).

PRISONERS' RIGHTS IN AMERICA. Barbara B. Knight and Stephen T. Early, Jr. Nelson-Hall, Incorporated, 111 North Canal Street, Chicago, Illinois 60606. 1986.

PRISONERS' RIGHTS IN ENGLAND AND THE UNITED STATES. A.J. Fowles. Avebury, Brookfield, USA. 1989.

PRISONS AND PRISONERS: HISTORICAL DOCUMENTS. Sol Chaneles, Editor. Haworth Press, Incorporated, 10 Alice Street, Binghamton, New York 13904. 1985.

PRISONS AND THE PROCESS OF JUSTICE. Andrew Rutherford. Oxford University Press, Incorporated, 200 Madison Avenue, New York, New York 10016. 1986.

THE PRIVATE SECTOR INVOLVEMENT IN PRISON-BASED BUSINESSES: A NATIONAL ASSESSMENT. George E. Sexton. National Institute of Justice, Superintendent of Documents, United States Government Printing Office, Washington, D.C. 20402. 1985.

RIGHTS OF PRISONERS. James J. Gobert and Neil P. Cohen. Shepard's/McGraw-Hill, P.O. Box 1235, Colorado Springs, Colorado 80901. 1981. (Annual Supplements).

SANCTIONS-SYSTEMS IN THE MEMBER-STATES OF THE COUNCIL OF EUROPE. Anton M. van Kalmthout and Peter J.P. Tak. Kluwer Law Book Publishers, Incorporated, 36 West Forty-fourth Street, New York, New York 10036. 1988- .

SOCIAL SKILLS IN PRISON AND THE COMMUNITY: PROBLEM-SOLVING FOR OFFENDERS. Phillip Priestly. Routledge and Kegan Paul, Limited, 29 West Thirty-fifth Street, New York, New York 10001-2291. 1984.

STATE CONSTITUTIONS AND CRIMINAL JUSTICE. Barry Latzer. Greenwood Press, 88 Post Road West, P.O. Box 5007, Westport, Connecticut 06881. 1991.

THE TREATMENT OF PRISONERS UNDER INTERNATIONAL LAW. Nigel S. Rodley. Oxford University Press, 200 Madison Avenue, New York, New York 10016. 1987.

THE TURKEY SHOOT: TRACKING DOWN THE ATTICA COVER-UP. Malcolm Bell. Random House, Incorporated, Random House Publicity, (11-6) 201 East Fiftieth Street, New York, New York 10022. 1986.

UNITED STATES PRISON LAW: SENTENCING TO PRISON, PRISON CONDITIONS, AND RELEASE: THE COURT DECISIONS. Sol Rubin. Oceana Publications, Incorporated, 75 Main Street, Dobbs Ferry, New York 10522. 1975. (Supplemented).

WERNER'S MANUAL FOR PRISON LAW LIBRARIES. Second Edition. Arturo A. Flores. Fred B. Rothman and Company, 10368 West Centennial Road, Littleton, Colorado 80127. 1990.

DIGESTS, INDEXES, ABSTRACTS, CITATORS

CORRECTIONS COMPENDIUM. Contact Center, Incorporated, P.O. Box 81826, Lincoln, Nebraska 68501. 1976- .

CORRECTIONS DIGEST. Washington Crime News Services, 7620 Little Creek Turnpike, Suite 400, Annandale, Virginia 22003. 1969- .

CRIMINAL JUSTICE PERIODICAL INDEX. University Microfilms, International, 300 North Zeeb Road, Ann Arbor, Michigan 48106-1346. Annual.

LAW REVIEWS AND PERIODICALS

NEW ENGLAND JOURNAL ON CRIMINAL AND CIVIL CONFINEMENT. New England School of Law, 154 Stuart Street, Boston, Massachusetts 02116. Semiannual.

NEWSLETTERS AND NEWSPAPERS

CORRECTIONS COMPENDIUM. Contact Center, Incorporated, P.O. Box 81826, Lincoln, Nebraska 68501. Monthly.

CORRECTIONS DIGEST. Washington Crime News Services, 3918 Prosperity Avenue, Suite 318, Fairfax, Virginia 22031. Biweekly.

DETENTION REPORTER. CRS Incorporated, P.O. Box 234, Kents Hill, Maine 04349. Monthly.

THE FORTUNE NEWS. Fortune Society, 39 West Nineteenth Street, New York, New York 10011. Quarterly.

JAIL AND PRISONER LAW BULLETIN. Americans for Effective Law Enforcement, Incorporated, 5519 North Cumberland, Suite 1008, Chicago, Illinois 60656. Monthly.

JAIL LAW BULLETIN. Institute of Government, University of North Carolina, Knapp Building, CB# 3330, Chapel Hill, North Carolina 27599. Quarterly.

NATIONAL PRISON PROJECT JOURNAL. National Prison Project, 1875 Connecticut Avenue, Northwest, Suite 410, Washington, D.C. 20009. Quarterly.

ON THE LINE. American Correctional Association, 8025 Laurel Lakes Court, Laurel, Maryland 20707. Quarterly.

BIBLIOGRAPHIES

JAILS AND PRISONS: A BIBLIOGRAPHY (ARCHITECTURE SERIES). Mary A. Vance. Vance Bibliographies, P.O. Box 229, 112 North Charter Street, Monticello, Illinois 61856. 1986.

DIRECTORIES

DIRECTORY OF CORRECTIONAL INSTITUTIONS AND AGENCIES. American Correctional Association, 8025 Laurel Lakes Court, Laurel, Maryland 20707. 1986.

DIRECTORY OF JUVENILE AND ADULT CORRECTIONAL DEPARTMENTS, INSTITUTIONS, AGENCIES, AND PAROLING AUTHORITIES. American Correctional Association, 8025 Laurel Lakes Court, Laurel, Maryland 20707. Annual.

NATIONAL DIRECTORY OF LAW ENFORCEMENT ADMINISTRATORS AND CORRECTIONAL INSTITUTIONS. National Police and Sheriffs Information Bureau, 152 West Wisconsin Avenue, Milwaukee, Wisconsin 53203. Annual.

NATIONAL JAIL AND ADULT DETENTION DIRECTORY. American Correctional Association, 8025 Laurel Lakes Court, Laurel, Maryland 20707. Biennial.

THE NATIONAL PRISON DIRECTORY: A PRISON REFORM ORGANIZATIONAL AND RESOURCE DIRECTORY. Third Edition. Mary L. Bundy and Alice Bell, Editors. Urban Information Interpreters, Incorporated, P.O. Box AH, College Park, Maryland 20740. 1984.

PRISONER'S ASSISTANCE DIRECTORY. Sixth Edition. National Prison Project of the American Civil Liberties Union, 1875 Connecticut Avenue, Northwest, Suite 410, Washington, D.C. 20009. 1985. Annual.

ASSOCIATIONS AND PROFESSIONAL SOCIETIES

AMERICAN BAR ASSOCIATION, CRIMINAL JUSTICE SECTION, COMMITTEE ON PRISON AND JAIL PROBLEMS. American Bar Association, 750 North Lake Shore Drive, Chicago, Illinois 60611. (312) 988-5000.

AMERICAN CORRECTIONAL ASSOCIATION. 8025 Laurel Lakes Road, Laurel, Maryland 20707. (301) 206-5100.

AMERICANS FOR EFFECTIVE LAW ENFORCEMENT, INCORPORATED. 5519 North Cumberland Avenue, Suite 1008, Chicago, Illinois 60656. (312) 763- 2800.

FORTUNE SOCIETY. 39 West Nineteenth Street, 7th Floor, New York, New York. 10011. (212) 206-7070.

NATIONAL PRISON PROJECT. 1875 Connecticut Avenue, Northwest, Suite 410, Washington, D.C. 20009. (202) 234-4830.

PRISONER'S RIGHTS UNION. 1909 Sixth Street, Sacramento, California 95814. (916) 441-4214.

ONLINE DATABASES

CRIMINAL JUSTICE DATA DIRECTORY. University of Michigan, Inter-University Consortium for Political and Social Research, P.O. Box 1248, Ann Arbor, Michigan 48106.

CRIMINAL JUSTICE PERIODICAL INDEX. University Microfilms, International, 300 North Zeeb Road, Ann Arbor, Michigan 48106.

LAW ENFORCEMENT AND CRIMINAL JUSTICE INFORMATION DATABASE. International Research and Evaluation, 21908 IRE Control Center, Eagan, Minnesota 55121.

NATIONAL CRIMINAL JUSTICE REFERENCE SERVICE. U.S. Department of Justice, National Institute of Justice, National Criminal Justice Reference Service, Box 6000, Rockville, Maryland 20850.

STATISTICS SOURCES

BUREAU OF JUSTICE STATISTICS MAILING LISTS. National Criminal Justice Reference Service, User Services Department Two, Box 6000, Rockville, Maryland 20850.

JUSTICE STATISTICS CLEARINGHOUSE. National Institute of Justice/National Criminal Justice Reference Service, Box 6000, Rockville, Maryland 20850.

MONDAY MORNING HIGHLIGHTS. Federal Bureau of Prisons, Department of Justice, Tenth Street and Constitution Avenue, Northwest, Washington, D.C. 20530. Weekly.

AUDIOVISUALS

CORRECTIONS AND THE PRIVATE SECTOR: FAD OR FUTURE? National Institute of Justice, National Criminal Justice Reference Service, Box 6000, Rockville, Maryland 20850. Videocassette.

PRIVACY, RIGHT OF
See also: COMPUTER CRIMES; EAVESDROPPING

STATUTES, CODES, STANDARDS, UNIFORM LAWS

COMPILATION OF STATE AND FEDERAL PRIVACY LAWS. Robert E. Smith. Privacy Journal, Box 28577, Providence, Rhode Island 02908. 1988.

EMPLOYEE POLYGRAPH PROTECTION ACT OF 1988: LAW AND EXPLANATION. Commerce Clearing House, Incorporated, 4025 West Peterson Avenue, Chicago, Illinois 60646. 1988.

LOOSELEAF SERVICES AND REPORTERS

EMPLOYMENT SCREENING. Lex K. Larson. Matthew Bender and Company, Incorporated, 11 Penn Plaza, New York, New York 10001. 1988- .

PRIVACY LAW AND PRACTICE. George B. Trubow and Jay M. Cohen. Matthew Bender and Company, Incorporated, 11 Penn Plaza, New York, New York 10001. 1987- .

THE RIGHTS OF PUBLICITY AND PRIVACY. J. Thomas McCarthy. Clark Boardman Company, Limited, 435 Hudson Street, New York, New York 10014. 1987- .

HANDBOOKS, MANUALS, FORMBOOKS

A CITIZEN'S GUIDE ON USING THE FREEDOM OF INFORMATION ACT AND THE PRIVACY ACT OF 1974 TO REQUEST GOVERNMENT RECORDS. United States Congress. House Committee on Government Operations. Superintendent of Documents, United States Government Printing Office, Washington, D.C. 20402. 1989.

THE COMPLETE GUIDE TO FINANCIAL PRIVACY. Fourth Edition. Mark Skousen. Simon and Schuster, Incorporated, 1230 Avenue of the Americas, New York, New York 10020. 1983.

FREEDOM OF INFORMATION GUIDE. Revised Edition. Want Publishing Company, 1511 K Street, Northwest, Washington, D.C. 20005. 1984.

GUIDEBOOK TO THE FREEDOM OF INFORMATION AND PRIVACY ACTS. Second Edition. Robert F. Bouchard and Justin D. Franklin, Editors. Clark Boardman Company, Limited, 435 Hudson Street, New York, New York 10014. 1986.

THE INDIVIDUAL EMPLOYMENT RIGHTS PRIMER. Kurt H. Decker. Baywood Publishing Company, Incorporated, 26 Austin Avenue, Amityville, New York 11701. 1991.

THE LAW OF FINANCIAL PRIVACY: A COMPLIANCE GUIDE. L. R. Fischer. Research Institute of America, Incorporated, One Penn Plaza, New York, New York 10119. 1983. (Supplemented).

THE PHILOSPHICAL DIMENSIONS OF PRIVACY: AN ANTHROPOLOGY. Ferdinand D. Schoeman, Editor. Cambridge University Press, 40 West Twentieth Street, New York, New York 10011. 1984.

PRIVACY IN THE WORKPLACE: A GUIDE FOR HUMAN RESOURCE MANAGERS. Jon D. Bible and Darien A. McWhirter. Quorum Books, Greenwood Publishing Group, Incorporated, 88 Post Road West, P.O. Box 5007, Westport, Connecticut 06881. 1990.

YOUR RIGHT TO PRIVACY: A BASIC GUIDE TO LEGAL RIGHTS IN AN INFORMATION SOCIETY. Second Edition. Evan Hendricks, Trudy Hayden, and Jack D. Novick. Southern Illinois University Press, P.O. Box 3697, Carbondale, Illinois 62902-3697. 1990.

TEXTBOOKS AND GENERAL WORKS

AIDS: TESTING AND PRIVACY. Martin Gunderson, David J. Mayo, and Frank S. Rhame. University of Utah Press, 101 U.U.P., Salt Lake City, Utah 84112. 1989.

BUSINESS INFORMATION: PROTECTION, DISCLOSURE, FREEDOM OF INFORMATION ACT AND RELATED LAWS. Peter C. Hein. Harcourt Brace Jovanovich, Incorporated, 6277 Sea Harbor Drive, Orlando, Florida 32821. (Annual Supplements).

CARD-CARRYING AMERICANS: PRIVACY, SECURITY, AND THE NATIONAL ID CARD DEBATE. Joseph W. Eaton. Rowman and Allanheld, 420 Boston Way, Lanham, Maryland 20706. 1986.

DISCLOSURE OF INFORMATION AND EMPLOYEE REPORTING. Roger Hussey and Arthur Marsh. Gower Publishing Company, Old Post Road, Brookfield, Vermont 05036. 1984.

DRUG TESTS AND POLYGRAPHS: ESSENTIAL TOOLS OR VIOLATIONS OF PRIVACY? Daniel Jussim. Messner, New York, New York. 1987.

DRUGS AND ALCOHOL IN THE WORKPLACE: TESTING AND PRIVACY. Craig M. Cornish. Callaghan and Company, 155 Pfingsten Road, Deerfield, Illinois 60015. 1988.

GOVERNMENT DISCLOSURE. Robert G. Vaughn. Prentice-Hall, Incorporated, 113 Sylvan Avenue, Englewood Cliffs, New Jersey 07632. 1979. (Annual Supplements).

THE HIDDEN POLITICS OF THE WIRE TAPPING INDUSTRY: WASHINGTON TO LONDON. Morton S. Bromfield. American Privacy Foundation, Wellesley Hills, Massachusetts. 1991.

IMAGE ETHICS: THE MORAL RIGHTS OF SUBJECTS IN PHOTOGRAPHS, FILM, AND TELEVISION. Larry Gross, John Stuart Katz, and Jay Ruby. Oxford University Press, 200 Madison Avenue, New York, New York 10016. 1988.

THE INFORMATION GAME: ETHICAL ISSUES IN A MICROCHIP WORLD. Geoffrey Brown. Humanities Press International, Incorporated, 171 First Avenue, Atlantic Highlands, New Jersey 07716-1289. 1990.

THE JOURNALIST'S HANDBOOK ON LIBEL AND PRIVACY. Barbara Dill. Free Press, Division of Macmillan Publishing Company, Incorporated, 866 Third Avenue, New York, New York 10022. 1986.

THE LAW OF PRIVACY. David A. Elder. Lawyers Cooperative Publishing Company, Aqueduct Building, Rochester, New York 14694. 1991.

LIBEL AND PRIVACY. Second Edition. Bruce W. Sanford. Prentice-Hall, Incorporated, 113 Sylvan Avenue, Englewood Cliffs, New Jersey 07632. 1991.

LIE DETECTOR USE IN THE WORKPLACE: FEDERAL AND STATE RESTRICTIONS. Gary J. Tulacz, Gary S. Mogel, and Michael P. O'Toole. Prentice-Hall, Incorporated, 113 Sylvan Avenue, Englewood Cliffs, New Jersey 07632. 1988.

NOBODY'S BUSINESS: PARADOXES OF PRIVACY. Alida Brill. Addison-Wesley Publishing Company, Incorporated, Route 128, Reading, Massachusetts 01867. 1990.

PERSONAL INFORMATION: PRIVACY AND THE LAW. Raymond Wacks. Oxford University Press, 200 Madison Avenue, New York, New York 10016. 1989.

PRIVACY AND CONFIDENTIALITY OF HEALTH CARE INFORMATION. Second Edition. Jo Anne Czecowski Bruce. American Hospital Publishing, Incorporated, 211 East Chicago Avenue, Chicago, Illinois 60611. 1988.

PRIVACY AND PUBLICITY. Theodore R. Kupferman. Meckler Corporation, 11 Ferry Lane West, Westport, Connecticut 06880. 1990.

PRIVACY AND SOCIAL FREEDOM. Ferdinand David Schoeman. Cambridge University Press, 40 West Twentieth Street, New York, New York 10011. 1992.

PRIVACY IN A PUBLIC SOCIETY: HUMAN RIGHTS IN CONFLICT. Richard F. Hixson. Oxford University Press, 200 Madison Avenue, New York, New York 10016. 1987.

PRIVACY IN AMERICA: IS YOUR PRIVATE LIFE IN THE PUBLIC EYE? David F. Linowes. University of Illinois Press, 54 East Gregory Drive, Champaign, Illinois 61820. 1989.

PRIVACY: STUDIES IN SOCIAL AND CULTURAL HISTORY. Barrington Moore, Jr. M. E. Sharpe, Incorporated, 80 Business Park Drive, Armonk, New York 10504. 1984.

PRIVATE RIGHTS, PUBLIC WRONGS: THE COMPUTER AND PERSONAL PRIVACY. Michael Rogers Rubin. Ablex Publishing Corporation, 355 Chestnut Street, Norwood, New Jersey 07648. 1988.

PROTECTING PRIVACY IN SURVEILLANCE SOCIETIES: THE FEDERAL REPUBLIC OF GERMANY, SWEDEN, FRANCE, CANADA, AND THE UNITED STATES. David H. Flaherty. University of North Carolina Press, P.O. Box 2288, 116 South Boundary Street, Chapel Hill, North Carolina 27515-2288. 1989.

REGULATING PRIVACY: DATA PROTECTION AND PUBLIC POLICY IN EUROPE AND THE UNITED STATES. Colin J. Bennett. Cornell University Press, 124 Roberts Place, Ithaca, New York 14850. 1992.

THE RIGHT OF PRIVACY IN THE COMPUTER AGE. Warren Freedman. Quorum Books, Imprint of Greenwood Publishing Group, Incorporated, 88 Post Road West, P.O. Box 5007, Westport, Connecticut 06881. 1987.

THE RIGHT TO PRIVACY. Stephen Goode. Franklin Watts, Incorporated, 387 Park Avenue South, New York, New York 10016. 1983.

THE RIGHT TO PRIVACY: GAYS, LESBIANS, AND THE CONSTITUTION. Vincent J. Samar. Temple University Press, 1601 North Broad Street, University Services Building, Philadelphia, Pennsylvania 19122. 1991.

THE RISE OF THE COMPUTER STATE. David Burnham. Vintage Book Company, Box 16182, Elway Station, St. Paul, Minnesota 55116. 1984.

SANFORD'S SYNOPSIS OF LIBEL AND PRIVACY. Fourth Edition. Bruce W. Sanford. Pharos Books, 200 Park Avenue, New York, New York 10166. 1991.

SECURITY IN COMPUTING. Charles P. Pfleeger. Prentice-Hall, Incorporated, 113 Sylvan Avenue, Englewood Cliffs, New Jersey 07632. 1989.

SEX CRIME IN THE NEWS. Keith Soothill and Sylvia Walby. Routledge, Chapman & Hall, 29 West Thirty-fifth Street, New York, New York 10001. 1991.

UNDERSTANDING THE BUCKLEY AMENDMENT. Stephen Sivulich. College Placement Council, Incorporated, 62 Highland Avenue, Bethlehem, Pennsylvania 18017. 1988.

UNEASY ACCESS: PRIVACY FOR WOMEN IN A FREE SOCIETY. Anita L. Allen. Rowman and Littlefield Publishers, Incorporated, 8705 Bollman Place, Savage, Maryland 20763. 1988.

WORKPLACE PRIVACY: EMPLOYEE TESTING, SURVEILLANCE, WRONGFUL DISCHARGE, AND OTHER AREAS OF VULNERABILITY. Second Edition. Ira Michael Shepard, Robert L. Duston, and Karen S. Russell. Bureau of National Affairs, Incorporated, 1231 Twenty-fifth Street, Northwest, Washington, D.C. 20037. 1989.

YOUR RIGHT TO PRIVACY. Dorothy and Thomas Hoobler. Franklin Watts, Incorporated, 387 Park Avenue South, New York, New York 10016. 1986.

NEWSLETTERS AND NEWSPAPERS

LDRC BULLETIN. Libel Defense Resource Center, 404 Park Avenue, New York, New York 10016. Quarterly.

MEDIA LAWLETTER. Law Letter Publishing, 963 Parkeside Place, Cincinnati, Ohio 45202. Monthly.

PRIVACY JOURNAL. Privacy Journal, P.O. Box 15300, Washington, D.C. 20003. Monthly.

PRIVACY TIMES. Privacy Times, Incorporated, 2354 Champlain Street, Northwest, Washington, D.C. 20009. Bi-weekly.

BIBLIOGRAPHIES

CONFIDENTIALITY IN THE USE OF LIBRARY MATERIALS: A BIBLIOGRAPHY. Tim J. Watts. Vance Bibliographies, P.O. Box 229, 112 North Charter Street, Monticello, Illinois 61856. 1989.

CONFIDENTIALITY, PRIVACY: A SELECTED BIBLIOGRAPHY. Anthony G. White. Vance Bibliographies, P.O. Box 229, 112 North Charter Street, Monticello, Illinois 61856. 1982.

PRIVACY AND DATA PROTECTION: AN INTERNATIONAL BIBLIOGRAPHY. David H. Flaherty, Editor. G. K. Hall and Company, Incorporated, 70 Lincoln Street, Boston, Massachusetts 02111. 1984.

PRIVACY IN THE WORKPLACE: A BIBLIOGRAPHIC SURVEY. Alva W. Stewart. Vance Bibliographies, P.O. Box 229, 112 North Charter Street, Monticello, Illinois 61856. 1987.

SEARCH AND SEIZURE IN SCHOOL. Earleen H. Cook. Vance Bibliographies, P.O. Box 229, 112 North Charter Street, Monticello, Illinois 61856. 1987.

A SELECTED BIBLIOGRAPHY ON WORKPLACE PRIVACY. Tim J. Watts. Vance Bibliographies, P.O. Box 229, 112 North Charter Street, Monticello, Illinois 61856. 1991.

OTHER SOURCES

CRIMINAL JUSTICE INFORMATION POLICY: PUBLIC ACCESS TO CRIMINAL HISTORY RECORD INFORMATION. Robert R. Belair. United States Department of Justice, Bureau of Justice Statistics, Tenth Street and Pennsylvania Avenue, Northwest, Washington, D.C. 20530. 1988.

PRIVATE INTERNATIONAL LAW AND RELATIONS
See: CONFLICT OF LAWS

PRIVILEGED COMMUNICATIONS
See: CONFIDENTIAL COMMUNICATIONS

PRIVILEGES AND IMMUNITIES
See: DIPLOMATIC PRIVILEGES AND IMMUNITIES; GOVERNMENT IMMUNITY AND LIABILITY

PROBATE LAW AND PRACTICE
See: WILLS, TRUSTS AND INHERITANCE

PROBATION AND PAROLE
See also: ADMINISTRATIVE OFFICE OF THE UNITED STATES COURTS; CRIMINAL LAW; REHABILITATION OF OFFENDERS

LOOSELEAF SERVICES AND REPORTERS

PROBATION AND PAROLE LAW REPORTS. Knehans-Miller Publications, P.O. Box 88, Warrensburg, Missouri 64093. 1980- .

HANDBOOKS, MANUALS, FORMBOOKS

FROM THE INSIDE OUT: A PAROLE PLANNING MANUAL. Jim Niemeier and David R. Werner. Interstate Printers and Publishers, Incorporated, P.O. Box 50, 19 North Jackson Street, Danville, Illinois 61834-0050. 1991.

HOW AND WHERE TO FIND THE FACTS: RESEARCHING CORRECTIONS INCLUDING PROBATION AND PAROLE. Jack E. Whitehouse. R & E Publishers, P.O. Box 2008, Saratoga, California 95070-2008. 1983.

TEXTBOOKS AND GENERAL WORKS

COMMUNITY SUPERVISION FOR OFFENDERS: A NEW MODEL OF PROBATION. Philip Whitehead. Avebury, Brookfield, USA. 1990.

CONTROLLING THE OFFENDER IN THE COMMUNITY: REFORMING THE COMMUNITY SUPERVISION FUNCTION. Todd R. Clear and Vincent O'Cleary. Lexington Books, Division of D.C. Heath and Company, 125 Spring Street, Lexington, Massachusetts 02173. 1983.

CRIME, CRIMINAL JUSTICE, AND THE PROBATION SERVICE. Robert Harris. Tavistock Publications, Limited, Routledge, Chapman and Hall, Incorporated, 29 West Thirty-Fifth Street, New York, New York 10001. 1991.

DECISION MAKING IN CRIMINAL JUSTICE: TOWARD THE RATIONAL EXERCISE OF DISCRETION. Second Edition. Michael R. Gottfredson and Don M. Gottfredson. Plenum Publishing Corporation, 233 Spring Street, New York, New York 10013. 1988.

FELONY PROBATION: PROBLEMS AND PROSPECTS. Dean J. Champion. Praeger Publishers, One Madison Avenue, New York, New York 10010-3603. 1988.

INTERMEDIATE PUNISHMENTS: INTENSIVE SUPERVISION, HOME CONFINEMENT, AND ELECTRONIC SURVEILLANCE. Belinda R. McCarthy. Criminal Justice Press, Monsey, New York. 1987.

THE LAW OF PROBATION AND PAROLE. Neil P. Cohen and James J. Gobert. Shepard's/McGraw Hill, P.O. Box 1235, Colorado Springs, Colorado 80901. 1983. (Annual Supplements).

PAROLE: A CRITICAL ANALYSIS. Gray Cavender. Kennikat Press, 90 South Bayles Avenue, Port Washington, New York 11050. 1982.

PROBATION AND JUSTICE: RECONSIDERATION OF MISSION. Patrick D. McAnany, Doug Thomson and David Fogel, Editors. Oelgeschlager, Gunn, and Hain, Incorporated, 245 Mirriam Street, Weston, Massachusetts 02193. 1984.

PROBATION AND PAROLE. Rodney J. Henningson. Harcourt Brace Jovanovich, Incorporated, 6277 Sea Harbor Drive, Orlando, Florida 32821. 1981.

PROBATION AND PAROLE: THEORY AND PRACTICE. Fourth Edition. Howard Abadinsky. Prentice-Hall, Incorporated, 113 Sylvan Avenue, Englewood Cliffs, New Jersey 07632. 1991.

PROBATION AND PAROLE: CRIME CONTROL IN THE COMMUNITY. John O. Smykla. Macmillan Publishing Company, Incorporated, 866 Third Avenue, New York, New York 10022. 1984.

PROBATION AND PAROLE IN AMERICA. Harry E. Allen, et al. Free Press, Division of Macmillan Publishing Company, Incorporated, 866 Third Avenue, New York, New York 10022. 1985.

PROBATION AND PAROLE IN PRACTICE. Second Edition. Steven D. Dillingham, Reid H. Montgomery, Jr., and Richard W. Tabor. Anderson Publishing Company, 2035 Reading Road, Cincinnati, Ohio 45202. 1990.

PROBATION AND THE COMMUNITY: A PRACTICE AND POLICY READER. John Harding. Tavistock Publications, Limited, Routledge, Chapman and Hall, Incorporated, 29 West Thirty-Fifth Street, New York, New York 10001. 1987.

PROBATION AS AN ALTERNATIVE TO CUSTODY: A CASE STUDY. Peter Raynor. Avebury, Brookfield, Vermont. 1988.

PROBATION CASEWORK: THE CONVERGENCE OF THEORY WITH PRACTICE. Joan Luxenberg. University Press of America, 4720 Boston Way, Lanham, Maryland 20706. 1983.

PROBATION, PAROLE AND COMMUNITY CORRECTIONS. Third Edition. Robert M. Carter, Daniel Glaser and Leslie T. Wilkins, Editors. John Wiley and Sons, Incorporated, 605 Third Avenue, New York, New York 10158. 1985.

PROBATION, PAROLE AND COMMUNITY CORRECTIONS. Lawrence F. Travis, Editor. Waveland Press, Incorporated, P.O. Box 400, Prospect Heights, Illinois 60070. 1985.

PROBATION, TEMPORARY RELEASE SCHEMES, AND RECONVICTION: THEORY AND PRACTICE. Philip Whitehead, Neill Turver, and Jim Wheatley. Avebury, Brookfield, Vermont. 1991.

PUNISHMENT WITHOUT WALLS: COMMUNITY SERVICE SENTENCES IN NEW YORK CITY. Douglas McDonald. Rutgers University Press, 109 Church Street, New Brunswick, New Jersey 08901. 1986.

SCREWING THE SYSTEM AND MAKING IT WORK: JUVENILE JUSTICE IN THE NO- FAULT SOCIETY. Mark D. Jacobs. University of Chicago Press, 5801 Ellis Avenue, Chicago, Illinois 60637. 1990.

LAW REVIEWS AND PERIODICALS

FEDERAL PROBATION. Administrative Office of the United States Courts. Superintendent of Documents, United States Government Printing Office, Washington, D.C. 20402. Quarterly.

NEWSLETTERS AND NEWSPAPERS

FEDERAL PROBATION OFFICERS ASSOCIATION NEWSLETTER. Federal Probation Officers Association, Room 2417, U.S. Court House, Phoenix, Arizona, 85025. Quarterly.

PERSPECTIVES. American Probation and Parole Association, P.O. Box 13253, Albany, New York 12212. Quarterly.

PPCAA NEWLETTER. Probation and Parole Compact Administrators Association, c/o Council of State Governments, P.O. Box 11910, Lexington, Kentucky 40578. Quarterly.

PROBATION AND PAROLE LAW REPORTS. Knehaus-Miller Publications, P.O. Box 88, Warrensburg, Missouri 64093. Monthly.

BIBLIOGRAPHIES

PAROLE: A BIBLIOGRAPHY. Mary Vance. Vance Bibliographies, P.O. Box 229, 112 North Charter Street, Monticello, Illinois 61856. 1988.

PROBATION: A BIBLIOGRAPHY. Mary Vance. Vance Bibliographies, P.O. Box 229, 112 North Charter Street, Monticello, Illinois 61856. 1988.

DIRECTORIES

PROBATION AND PAROLE DIRECTORY: UNITED STATES AND CANADA. American Correctional Association, 8025 Laurel Lakes Court, Laurel, Maryland 20707. Irregular.

ASSOCIATIONS AND PROFESSIONAL SOCIETIES

AMERICAN PROBATION AND PAROLE ASSOCIATION, c/o Council of State Governments, P.O. Box 11910, Lexington, Kentucky 40578. (606) 231-1919.

FEDERAL PROBATION OFFICERS ASSOCIATION, c/o Tommaso D. Rendino, P.O. Box 8165, Savannah, Georgia 31412. (912) 944-4355.

PROBATION AND PAROLE COMPACT ADMINISTRATORS ASSOCIATION. c/o Council of State Governments, P.O. Box 11910, Lexington, Kentucky 40578. (606) 231-1920.

STATISTICS SOURCES

FELONS SENTENCED TO PROBATION IN STATE COURTS, 1986. John M. Dawson. United States Department of Justice, Office of Justice Statistics, Tenth Street and Pennsylvania Avenue, Northwest, Washington, D.C. 20530. 1990.

PEOPLE IN THE UNITED STATES. Parolees-Number. United States Department of Justice, Bureau of Justice Statistics, 633 Indiana Avenue, Northwest, Washington, D.C. 20531. Annual.

OTHER SOURCES

REPORT ON PENAL INSTITUTIONS, PROBATION, AND PAROLE. National Commission on Law Observance and Enforcement. Garland Publishing, Incorporated, 136 Madison Avenue, New York, New York 10016. 1987.

PROCESS SERVICE
See: CIVIL PROCEDURE

PRODUCTS LIABILITY AND SAFETY
See also: CONSUMER PRODUCT SAFETY COMMISSION; FOOD AND DRUG ADMINISTRATION

LOOSELEAF SERVICES AND REPORTERS

CONSUMER LIABILITY SAFETY GUIDE. Commerce Clearing House, Incorporated, 4025 West Peterson Avenue, Chicago, Illinois 60646. 1972- .

PRODUCT LIABILITY. John S. Allee. Law Journal-Seminars Press, Incorporated, 111 Eighth Avenue, New York, New York 10011. 1984- .

PRODUCT LIABILITY: CASES AND TRENDS. Victor E. Schwartz. Prentice-Hall, Incorporated, 113 Sylvan Avenue, Englewood Cliffs, New Jersey 07632. 1987- .

PRODUCT LIABILITY TRENDS. National Legal Research Group, Incorporated, 2421 Ivy Road, Charlottesville, Virginia 22906. 1977- .

PRODUCT SAFETY AND LIABILITY REPORTER. Bureau of National Affairs, 1231 Twenty-fifth Street, Northwest, Washington, D.C. 20037. 1973- .

PRODUCTS LIABILITY LITIGATION: CASE EVALUATION. Susan E. Loggans. Callaghan and Company, 155 Pfingsten Road, Deerfield, Illinois 60015. 1988- .

PRODUCTS LIABILITY LITIGATION: PRETRIAL PRACTICE. James A. Lowe. Callaghan and Company, 155 Pfingsten Road, Deerfield, Illinois 60015. 1988- .

PRODUCTS LIABILITY LITIGATION: TRIAL STRATEGY AND PROCEDURE. Bob Gibbins and A. Russell Smith. Callaghan and Company, 155 Pfingsten Road, Deerfield, Illinois 60015. 1988.

PRODUCTS LIABILITY PRACTICE GUIDE. John F. Vargo. Matthew Bender and Company, Incorporated, 11 Penn Plaza, New York, New York 10001. 1988- .

PRODUCTS LIABILITY REPORTER. Commerce Clearing House, Incorporated, 4025 West Peterson Avenue, Chicago, Illinois 60646. 1974- .

HANDBOOKS, MANUALS, FORMBOOKS

DISCOVERY IN MEDICAL MALPRACTICE, PRODUCTS LIABILITY AND PERSONAL INJURY CASES. Marc J. Bern and Steven E. North, Co-chairmen. Practicing Law Institute, 810 Seventh Avenue, New York, New York 10019. 1985.

DRUGS IN LITIGATION: DAMAGE AWARDS INVOLVING PRESCRIPTION AND NON-PRESCRIPTION DRUGS. Richard M. Patterson and Robert E. Robinson. Michie Company, P.O. Box 7587, Charlottesville, Virginia 22906-7587. 1991.

FOOD AND DRUG COMPLIANCES: MINIMIZING PRODUCT LIABILITY EXPOSURE. George M. Burditt and Russell D. Munves, Co-chairmen. Practising Law Institute, 810 Seventh Avenue, New York, New York 10019. 1984.

HANDLING PRODUCTS LIABILITY CASES. Professional Educational Systems, 200 Spring Street, Eau Claire, Wisconsin 54702. 1984.

HOW TO AVOID PRODUCTS LIABILITY LAWSUITS AND DAMAGES: PRACTICAL GUIDELINES FOR ENGINEERS AND MANUFACTURERS. Charles E. Witherall. Noyes Data Corporation, 120 Mill Road, Park Ridge, New Jersey 07656. 1986.

PATTERN DISCOVERY: PRODUCTS LIABILITY. Second Edition. Douglas Danner. Lawyers Cooperative Publishing Company, Aqueduct Building, Rochester, New York 14694. 1985. (Supplements)

PREPARATION OF A PRODUCTS LIABILITY CASE. Scott Baldwin, Francis H. Hare, Jr. and Francis E. McGovern. Little, Brown and Company, 34 Beacon Street, Boston, Massachusetts 02108. 1981 (Annual Supplements).

PREPARING PRODUCTS LIABILITY CASES. Terrence F. Kiely. John Wiley and Sons, Incorporated, 605 Third Avenue, New York, New York 10158. 1986.

PRODUCT LIABILITY: A MANUAL OF PRACTICE IN SELECTED NATIONS. Hans- Ulrich Stucki and Peter R. Attenburger. Oceana Publications, Incorporated, 75 Main Street, Dobbs Ferry, New York 10522. 1981 (Periodic Supplements).

THE PRODUCT LIABILITY HANDBOOK: PREVENTION, RISK, CONSEQUENCE, AND FORENSICS OF PRODUCT FAILURE. Sam Brown, Iain LeMay, Justin Sweet, and Alvin Weinstein. Van Nostrand Reinhold Company, Incorporated, 115 Fifth Avenue, New York, New York 10003. 1990.

PRODUCT LIABILITY IN THE UNITED STATES: A PRIMER FOR MANUFACTURERS AND THEIR EMPLOYEES. Perkins Coie, Seattle, Washington. 1991.

PRODUCT LIABILITY LITIGATION. Edward L. Birnbaum, et al. Practising Law Institute, 810 Seventh Avenue, New York, New York 10019. 1983.

PRODUCT LIABILITY OF MANUFACTURERS: PREVENTION AND DEFENSE: 1985. Kenneth Ross and Barbara Wanbel, Chairpersons. Practising Law Institute, 810 Seventh Avenue, New York, New York 10019. 1988.

PRODUCT LIABILITY: WARNINGS, INSTRUCTIONS, AND RECALLS. Richard J. Phelan and Kenneth Ross. Practising Law Institute, 810 Seventh Avenue, New York, New York 10019. 1989.

PRODUCTS DESIGN LITIGATION. Malcolm E. Wheeler, Chairman. Practising Law Institute, 810 Seventh Avenue, New York, New York 10019. 1982.

PRODUCTS LIABILITY FOR CORPORATE COUNSELS, CONTROLLERS, AND PRODUCT SAFETY EXECUTIVES. Van Nostrand Reinhold, Incorporated, 115 Fifth Avenue, New York, New York 10003. 1984.

PRODUCTS LIABILITY LAW: A GUIDE FOR MANAGERS. Michael Whincup. Gower Publishing Company, Old Post Road, Brookfield, Vermont 05036. 1985.

PRODUCTS LIABILITY: VERDICTS AND SETTLEMENTS. Litigation Research Group, 500 Howard Street, San Francisco, California 94105. 1986.

TEXTBOOKS AND GENERAL WORKS

AGENT ORANGE ON TRIAL: MASS TOXIC DISASTERS IN THE COURTS. Peter H. Schuck. Harvard University Press, 79 Garden Street, Cambridge, Massachusetts 02138. 1987.

AMERICAN LAW OF PRODUCTS LIABILITY. Third Edition. Robert D. Hursh and Henry J. Bailey. Lawyers Cooperative Publishing Company, Aqueduct Building, Rochester, New York 14694. 1990. (Annual Supplements).

AUTOMOTIVE ENGINEERING AND LITIGATION. George A. Peters and Barbara J. Peters. John Wiley and Sons, Incorporated, 605 Third Avenue, New York, New York 10158. 1991.

BENDING THE LAW: THE STORY OF THE DALKON SHIELD BANKRUPTCY. Richard B. Sobol. University of Chicago Press, 5801 Ellis Avenue, Chicago, Illinois 60637. 1991.

CONFIDENTIALITY ORDERS. Francis H. Hare, Jr., James L. Gilbert, and William H. Remine. John Wiley and Sons, Incorporated, 605 Third Avenue, New York, New York 10158. 1988.

CONSUMER PRODUCTS: GOVERNMENT REGULATION AND PRODUCT LIABILITY. Kenneth Ross and Michael A. Brown. Practising Law Institute, 810 Seventh Avenue, New York, New York 10019. 1984.

CORPORATE CRIME UNDER ATTACK: THE FORD PINTO CASE AND BEYOND. Francis T. Cullen, William J. Maakestad, and Gray Cavender. Anderson Publishing Company, 2035 Reading Road, Cincinnati, Ohio 45202. 1987.

CRASHWORTHINESS. Arthur H. Bryant. Association of Trial Lawyers of America, 1050 Thirty-first Street, Northwest, Washington, D.C. 20007. 1989.

DISCOVERY, EVIDENCE, AND TACTICS IN THE TRIAL OF A PRODUCTS LIABILITY LAWSUIT. Vincent S. Walkowiak. Matthew Bender and Company, Incorporated, 11 Penn Plaza, New York, New York 10001. 1987.

DRUG AND MEDICAL DEVICE LITIGATION. Henry R. Simon. Practising Law Institute, 810 Seventh Avenue, New York, New York 10019. 1989.

DRUG PRODUCT LIABILITY. Marden G. Dixon. Matthew Bender and Company, Incorporated, 11 Penn Plaza, New York, New York 10001. 1974 (Annual Supplements).

EEC STRICT LIABILITY IN 1992: THE NEW PRODUCT LIABILITY RULES. Patrick E. Thieffry and G. Marc Whitehead. Practising Law Institute, 810 Seventh Avenue, New York, New York 10019. 1989.

EFFECTIVE COORDINATION OF MULTIPLE PRODUCT LIABILITY LITIGATION. Ronald Lawrence, Fredric C. Nelson, and Richard A. Rothman. Practising Law Institute, 810 Seventh Avenue, New York, New York 10019. 1988.

THE EUROPEAN ECONOMIC COMMUNITY: PRODUCTS LIABILITY RULES AND ENVIRONMENTAL POLICY. Patrick E. Thieffry and G. Marc Whitehead. Practising Law Institute, 810 Seventh Avenue, New York, New York 10019. 1990.

EVIDENCE AND TACTICS IN THE PRODUCTS LIABILITY CASE. Vincent S. Walkowink. Matthew Bender and Company, Incorporated, 11 Penn Plaza, New York, New York 10001. 1985.

FIREARMS LITIGATION: LAW, SCIENCE, AND PRACTICE. Windle Turley and James E. Rooks. Shepard's/McGraw-Hill, P.O. Box 1235, Colorado Springs, Colorado 80901. 1988.

FOREIGN PLAINTIFFS IN PRODUCT LIABILITY ACTIONS: THE DEFENSE OF FORUM NON CONVENIENS. Warren Freedman. Quorum Books, Greenwood Publishing Group, Incorporated, 88 Post Road West, P.O. Box 5007, Westport, Connecticut 06881. 1988.

HAZARDOUS WASTE, TOXIC TORT, AND PRODUCTS LIABILITY INSURANCE PROBLEMS. Irene A. Sullivan. Practising Law Institute, 810 Seventh Avenue, New York, New York 10019. 1987.

JANNER'S COMPLETE PRODUCT LIABILITY: INCORPORATING PETER MADGE ON PRODUCT LIABILITY INSURANCE. Greville Janner and Peter Madge. Gower Publishing Company, Old Post Road, Brookfield, Vermont 05036. 1988.

JURY INSTRUCTIONS ON PRODUCTS LIABILITY. Graham Douthwaite. Michie Company, P.O. Box 7587, Charlottesville, Virginia 22906. 1987.

LAW OF PRODUCT WARRANTIES. Barkley Clark and Christopher Smith. Research Institute of America, Incorporated, One Penn Plaza, New York, New York 10119. 1984. (Supplemented)

THE LAW OF PRODUCTS LIABILITY. Second Edition. Marshall S. Shapo. Butterworth Legal Publishers, 90 Stiles Road, Salem, New Hampshire 03079. 1990.

THE LIABILITY MAZE: THE IMPACT OF LIABILITY LAW ON SAFETY AND INNOVATION. Peter W. Huber and Robert E. Litan. Brookings Institution, 1775 Massachusetts Avenue, Washington, D.C. 20036. 1991.

THE LIMITS OF LITIGATION: THE DALKON SHIELD CONTROVERSY. Ronald J. Bacigal. Carolina Academic Press, P.O. Box 51879, Durham, North Carolina 27717. 1990.

MEDICAL PRODUCTS LIABILITY AND PREVENTIVE LAW. American Law Institute, 4025 Chestnut Street, Philadelphia, Pennsylvania 19104. 1984.

PERSONAL INJURY AND PRODUCT LIABILITY LITIGATION. Howard R. Reiss. Prentice-Hall, Incorporated, 113 Sylvan Avenue, Englewood Cliffs, New Jersey 07632. 1987.

THE PRICE OF A LIFE. Tom Reilly. Fred B. Rothman and Company, 10368 West Centennial Road, Littleton, Colorado 80127. 1986.

PRIVATE INTERNATIONAL LAW OF TORT AND PRODUCT LIABILITY: JURISDICTION, APPLICABLE LAW, AND EXTRATERRITORIAL PROTECTIVE MEASURES. Peter Kaye. Avebury, Brookfield, Vermont. 1991.

PRODUCT DEFECTS AND HAZARDS: LITIGATION AND REGULATORY STRATEGIES. James T. O'Reilly. John Wiley and Sons, Incorporated, 605 Third Avenue, New York, New York 10158. 1987.

PRODUCT LIABILITY ACTIONS BY FOREIGN PLAINTIFFS IN THE UNITED STATES. Warren Freedman. Kluwer Academic Publishers, 101 Philip Drive, Assinippi Park, Norwell, Massachusetts 02061. 1988.

PRODUCT LIABILITY AND QUALITY. Society of Automotive Engineers, 400 Commonwealth Drive, Warrendale, Pennsylvania 15096. 1984.

PRODUCT LIABILITY: DESIGN AND MANUFACTURING. Lewis Bass. Fred B. Rothman and Company, 10368 West Centennial Road, Littleton, Colorado 80127. 1986.

THE PRODUCT LIABILITY MESS: HOW BUSINESS CAN BE RESCUED FROM THE POLITICS OF STATE COURTS. Richard Neely. Free Press, 866 Third Avenue, New York, New York 10022. 1988.

PRODUCT LIABILITY: PREVENTION, PRACTICE, AND PROCESS IN EUROPE AND THE UNITED STATES. Rudolph Hulsenbek and Dennis Campbell. Kluwer Law Book Publishers, Incorporated, 36 West Forty-fourth Street, New York, New York 10036. 1989.

PRODUCTS LIABILITY. Louis R. Frumer and Melvin I. Friedman. Matthew Bender and Company, Incorporated, 11 Penn Plaza, New York, New York 10001. 1960 (Annual Supplements).

PRODUCTS LIABILITY. Second Edition. M. Stuart Madden. West Publishing Company, 50 West Kellogg Boulevard, St. Paul, Minnesota 55164. 1988.

PRODUCTS LIABILITY AND SAFETY: CASES AND MATERIALS. Second Edition. W. Page Keeton. Foundation Press, 615 Merrick Avenue, Westbury, New York 11590. 1989.

PRODUCTS LIABILITY: CASES AND MATERIALS. David A. Fischer and William Powers, Jr. West Publishing Company, 50 West Kellogg Boulevard, St. Paul, Minnesota 55164. 1988.

PRODUCTS LIABILITY FOR THE GENERAL PRACTITIONER. Paul Sherman. Shepard's/McGraw-Hill, P.O. Box 1235, Colorado Springs, Colorado 80901. 1981. (Annual Supplements).

PRODUCTS LIABILITY IN A NUTSHELL. Third Edition. Jerry J. Phillips and Dix W. Noel. West Publishing Company, P.O. Box 64526, 50 West Kellogg Boulevard, St. Paul, Minnesota 55164-0526. 1988.

PRODUCTS LIABILITY: PHARMACEUTICAL DRUG CASES. Donald E. Vinson and Alexander H. Slaughter. Shepard's/McGraw-Hill, P.O. Box 1235, Colorado Springs, Colorado 80901. 1988.

PRODUCTS LIABILITY: PROBLEMS AND PROCESS. James A. Henderson, Jr. and Aaron D. Twerski. Little, Brown and Company, 34 Beacon Street, Boston, Massachusetts 02108. 1987.

PRODUCTS LIABILITY: THE A.L.I.-A.B.A. COURSE OF STUDY MATERIALS. The American Law Institute, 4025 Chestnut Street, Philadelphia, Pennsylvania 19104. 1984.

PRODUCTS LIABILITY--THE DUTY TO WARN. James M. Campbell, Richard L. Edwards, and Donald J. Hirsch. Defense Research Institute, 750 North Lake Shore Drive, Suite 500, Chicago, Illinois 60611. 1989.

PRODUCTS LIABILITY: THE FIRST 25 YEARS. Jeffrey R. White, Editor. Association of Trial Lawyers of America Education Fund, 1050 Thirty-first Street, Northwest, Washington, D.C. 20007. 1983.

REFORMING PRODUCTS LIABILITY. W. Kip Viscusi. Harvard University Press, 79 Garden Street, Cambridge, Massachusetts 02138. 1991.

REGULATING CONSUMER PRODUCT SAFETY. W. Kip Viscusi. American Enterprise Institute for Public Policy Research, 1150 Seventeenth Street, Northwest, Washington, D.C. 20036. 1984.

SAFE PRODUCT DESIGN IN LAW, MANAGEMENT, AND ENGINEERING. Herman R. Heideklang. Marcel Dekker, 720 Madison Avenue, New York, New York 10016. 1991.

SAFETY AND HEALTH FOR ENGINEERS. Roger L. Brauer. Van Nostrand Reinhold Company, Incorporated, 115 Fifth Avenue, New York, New York 10003. 1990.

SLAUGHTER BY PRODUCT: WINNING THE PRODUCTS LIABILITY CASE. Edward M. Swartz. Michie Company, P.O. Box 7587, Charlottesville, Virginia 22906-7587. 1986. (Supplements)

SWARTZ HAZARDOUS PRODUCTS LITIGATION. Second Edition. Edward M. Swartz. Lawyers Cooperative Publishing Company, Aqueduct Building, Rochester, New York 14694. 1988.

TOXIC TORTS AND PRODUCT LIABILITY: CHANGING TACTICS FOR CHANGING TIMES. Michael A. Brown. Bureau of National Affairs, Incorporated, 1231 Twenty-fifth Street, Northwest, Washington, D.C. 20037. 1989.

WARRANTY LAW IN TORT AND CONTRACT ACTIONS. Ora Fred Harris, Jr. and Alphonse M. Squillante. John Wiley and Sons, Incorporated, 605 Third Avenue, New York, New York 10158. 1989.

WHAT EVERY ENGINEER SHOULD KNOW ABOUT MATERIAL AND COMPONENT FAILURE, FAILURE ANALYSIS, AND LITIGATION. Lawrence E. Murr. Marcel Dekker, 720 Madison Avenue, New York, New York 10016. 1987.

DIGESTS, INDEXES, ABSTRACTS, CITATORS

SHEPARD'S PRODUCTS LIABILITY CITATIONS. Shepard's/McGraw Hill, P.O. Box 1235, Colorado Springs, Colorado 80901. Quarterly.

ANNUALS AND SURVEYS

PERSONAL INJURY AND PRODUCTS LIABILITY SYMPOSIUM. Vincent S. Walkowiak, Matthew Bender and Company, Incorporated, 11 Penn Plaza, New York, New York 10001. 1988.

LAW REVIEWS AND PERIODICALS

JOURNAL OF PRODUCTS LAW. Symposia Press, P.O. Box 418, Moorestown, New Jersey 08057. Quarterly.

THE JOURNAL OF PRODUCTS LIABILITY. Pergamon Press, Incorporated, Maxwell House, Fairview Park, Elmsford, New York 10523. Quarterly.

NEWSLETTERS AND NEWSPAPERS

ATLA PRODUCTS LIABILITY LAW REPORTER. Association of Trial Lawyers of America, 1050 Thirty-first Street, Northwest, Washington, D.C. 20007. Monthly.

AUTOMOTIVE LITIGATION REPORTER. Andrews Publications, 1646 West Chester Pike, Westtown, Pennsylvania 19395. Semimonthly.

AVIATION LITIGATION REPORTER. Andrews Publications, 1646 West Chester Pike, Westtown, Pennsylvania 19395. Semimonthly.

DES LITIGATION REPORTER. Andrews Publications, 1646 West Chester Pike, Westtown, Pennsylvania 19395. Semimonthly.

DRUG PRODUCT LIABILITY REPORTER. Matthew Bender and Company, Incorporated, 11 Penn Plaza, New York, New York 10001. Monthly.

LEADER'S PRODUCT LIABILITY TRENDS. National Legal Research Group, Incorporated, 2421 Ivy Road, Charlottesville, Virginia 22906. Monthly.

PRODUCT LIABILITY AND RECALL ALERT. 1112 Washington Street, Glenview, Illinois 60025. Semimonthly.

PRODUCT SAFETY LETTER. Washington Business Information, Incorporated, 1117 North Nineteenth Street, Arlington, Virginia 22209. Weekly.

BIBLIOGRAPHIES

THE PHARMACEUTICAL INDUSTRY: REGULATION AND LIABILITY. Tim J. Watts. Vance Bibliographies, P.O. Box 229, 112 North Charter Street, Monticello, Illinois 61856. 1988.

ASSOCIATIONS AND PROFESSIONAL SOCIETIES

ASSOCIATION OF TRIAL LAWYERS OF AMERICA. 1050 Thirty-first Street, Northwest, Washington, D.C. 20007. (202) 965-3500.

COALITION FOR UNIFORM PRODUCT LIABILITY LAW. 1023 Fifteenth Street, Northwest, Seventh Floor, Washington, D.C. 20005. (202) 289-1780.

NATIONAL SAFETY COUNCIL. 444 North Michigan Avenue, Chicago, Illinois 60611. (312) 527-4800.

PRODUCT LIABILITY ALLIANCE. c/o National Association of Wholesaler-Distributors, 1725 K Street, Northwest, Suite 710, Washington, D.C. 20006. (202) 872-0885.

PRODUCT LIABILITY PREVENTION AND DEFENSE. 7297 Lee Highway, Suite 10, Falls Church, Virginia 22042. (703) 533-0251.

SPECIAL COMMITTEE FOR WORKPLACE PRODUCT LIABILITY REFORM. Federal Ban Building, 1815 H Street, Northwest, Suite 800, Washington, D.C. 20006. (202) 955-4500.

RESEARCH CENTERS, INSTITUTES, CLEARINGHOUSES

AMERICAN LAW INSTITUTE. 4025 Chestnut, Philadelphia, Pennsylvania 19104. (800) 253-6397.

INSTITUTE FOR ADVANCED SAFETY STUDIES. 5950 West Touhy Avenue, Niles, Illinois 60648. (708) 647-1101.

INSTITUTE FOR INJURY REDUCTION. P.O. Box 375, Dunkirk, Maryland 20754. (301) 855-4440.

PRODUCT LIABILITY RESEARCH SERVICE. Center for Auto Safety, 2001 S Street, Northwest, Suite 410, Washington, D.C. 20009. (202) 328-7700.

AUDIOVISUALS

DIRECT AND CROSS-EXAMINATION OF PLAINTIFF'S EXPERT ENGINEERING WITNESS IN A PRODUCTS LIABILITY CASE. American Bar Association, Consortium for Professional Education, 750 North Lake Shore Drive, Chicago, Illinois 60611. 1979. (Videotape).

PRODUCTS LIABILITY LAW: A BOTTLING PLANT ACCIDENT. National Practice Institute, 330 Second Avenue South, Minneapolis, Minnesota 55401. Videotape.

PRODUCTS LIABILITY LAW: AN AUTOMOBILE DEFECT. National Practice Institute, 330 Second Avenue South, Minneapolis, Minnesota 55401. Videotape.

PRODUCTS LIABILITY LAW: AN EXPLODING LAMP CASE. National Practice Institute, 330 Second Avenue South, Minneapolis, Minnesota 55401. Videotape.

PRODUCTS LIABILITY LAW: CIRCULAR SAW ACCIDENT. National Practice Institute, 330 Second Avenue South, Minneapolis, Minnesota 55401. Audiotape.

PRODUCTS LIABILITY LAW: DRUG LITIGATION. National Practice Institute, 330 Second Avenue South, Minneapolis, Minnesota 55401. Audiotape.

PRODUCTS LIABILITY LAW: LAWN MOWER ACCIDENT. National Practice Institute, 330 Second Avenue South, Minneapolis, Minnesota 55401. Audiotape.

PRODUCTS LIABILITY LAW: MOTORCYCLE ACCELERATOR PROBLEM. National Practice Institute, 330 Second Avenue South, Minneapolis, Minnesota 55401. Audiotape.

TRIAL TECHNIQUES: A PRODUCTS LIABILITY CASE. American Bar Association, Consortium for Professional Education, 750 North Lake Shore Drive, Chicago, Illinois 60611. 1979. (Videotape).

PROFESSIONAL CORPORATIONS

LOOSELEAF SERVICES AND REPORTERS

HOW TO SAVE TAXES AND INCREASE YOUR WEALTH WITH A PROFESSIONAL CORPORATION. Irving Schreiber, Editor. Panel Publishers, Incorporated, 36 West Forty-fourth Street, New York, New York 10036. 1970- .

PROFESSIONAL CORPORATION GUIDE: ORGANIZATION, ADMINISTRATION, TERMINATION, EMPLOYEE BENEFITS, FORMS AND LAWS. Prentice-Hall, Incorporated, 113 Sylvan Avenue, Englewood, New Jersey 07632. 1982- .

PROFESSIONAL CORPORATIONS HANDBOOK. Commerce Clearing House, Incorporated, 4025 West Peterson Avenue, Chicago, Illinois 60646. 1973- .

PROFESSIONAL'S TAX DESK MANUAL. Prentice-Hall, Incorporated, 113 Sylvan Avenue, Englewood Cliffs, New Jersey 07632. 1987- .

HANDBOOKS, MANUALS, FORMBOOKS

THE CALIFORNIA PROFESSIONAL CORPORATION HANDBOOK. Fourth Edition. Anthony Mancuso. Nolo Press, 950 Parker Street, Berkeley, California 94710. 1990.

ORGANIZATIONAL DOCUMENTS: A GUIDE FOR PARTNERSHIPS AND PROFESSIONAL CORPORATIONS. Mark F. Murray. American Institute of Certified Public Accountants, 1211 Avenue of the Americas, New York, New York 10036-8775. 1990.

A PHYSICIAN'S GUIDE TO PROFESSIONAL CORPORATIONS. Alton C. Ward and Roberta Casper Watson. American Medical Association, Public Affairs Group, Division of Legislative Activities, Department of State Legislation, 515 North State Street, Chicago, Illinois 60610. 1989.

RESEARCH GUIDE TO PROFESSIONAL CORPORATE LAW. Peter Aitelli and Debra M. Dietrich. William S. Hein and Company, Incorporated, Hein Building, 1285 Main Street, Buffalo, New York 14209. 1985.

TEXTBOOKS AND GENERAL WORKS

EMPLOYMENT PRACTICES FOR THE PROFESSIONAL FIRM. Victor Schacter and Jo Anne Dellaverson, Editors. Executive Enterprises Publications Company, 22 West Twenty-first Street, New York, New York 10010-6904. 1985.

INCORPORATION AND ALTERNATIVES FOR LAWYERS AND CPA'S AFTER TEFRA. American Law Institute-American Bar Association, Committee on Continuing Professional Education, 4025 Chestnut Street, Philadelphia, Pennsylvania 19104. 1984.

PROFESSIONAL CORPORATIONS AND ASSOCIATIONS. Barrien C. Eaton, Jr. Matthew Bender and Company, Incorporated, 11 Penn Plaza, New York, New York 10001. 1970.

PROFESSIONAL CORPORATIONS AND SMALL BUSINESSES AFTER THE REFORM ACT OF 1984. Stephen H. Paley, Chairman. Practising Law Institute, 810 Seventh Avenue, New York, New York 10019. 1984.

QUALIFIED PLANS, PCS, AND WELFARE BENEFITS: ALI-ABA COURSE OF STUDY MATERIALS. American Law Institute-American Bar Association, 4025 Chestnut Street, Philadelphia, Pennsylvania 19104. 1991.

TAX AND BENEFIT PLANNING FOR PERSONAL SERVICE BUSINESSES. Dennis C. Reardon and Edward A. Stoeber. American Society of CLU, P.O. Box 59, Bryn Mawr, Pennsylvania 19010. 1983.

PROFESSIONAL ETHICS AND LIABILITY
See also: LEGAL ETHICS AND MALPRACTICE; MEDICAL JURISPRUDENCE AND MALPRACTICE

STATUTES, CODES, STANDARDS, UNIFORM LAWS

CODES OF PROFESSIONAL RESPONSIBILITY. Second Edition. Rena A. Gorlin, Editor. Bureau of National Affairs, 1231 Twenty-fifth Street, Northwest, Washington, D.C. 20037. 1990.

LOOSELEAF SERVICES AND REPORTERS

PROFESSIONAL LIABILITY REPORTER. Litigation Research Group, P.O. Box 77903, San Francisco, California 94107. 1985- .

HANDBOOKS, MANUALS, FORMBOOKS

ACCOUNTING ETHICS: A PRACTICAL GUIDE FOR PROFESSIONALS. Philip G. Cottell, Jr. and Terry M. Perlin. Quorum Books, Greenwood Publishing Group, Incorporated, 88 Post Road West, P.O. Box 5007, Westport, Connecticut 06881. 1990.

BUSINESS CRIMES: A GUIDEBOOK FOR CORPORATE AND DEFENSE COUNSEL. Jeffrey Glekel, Editor. Practising Law Institute, 810 Seventh Avenue, New York, New York 10019. 1982.

FIFTY WAYS TO AVOID MALPRACTICE: A GUIDEBOOK FOR MENTAL HEALTH PROFESSIONALS. Robert Henley Woody. Professional Resource Exchange, Incorporated, 635 South Orange Avenue, Suite 4-5, Sarasota, Florida 34236. 1988.

TEXTBOOKS AND GENERAL WORKS

BUSINESS ETHICS: READINGS AND CASES IN CORPORATE MORALITY. Second Edition. W. Michael Hoffman and Jennifer M. Moore. McGraw-Hill Book Company, 1221 Avenue of the Americas, New York, New York 10020. 1989.

CASEBOOK ON ETHICAL PRINCIPLES OF PSYCHOLOGISTS. American Psychological Association, 1200 Seventeenth Street, Northwest, Washington, D.C. 20036. 1987.

CLERGY MALPRACTICE. Robert W. McNamin. William S. Hein and Company, Incorporated, Hein Building, 1285 Main Street, Buffalo, New York 14209. 1986.

CORPORATE INTELLIGENCE AND ESPIONAGE: A BLUEPRINT FOR EXECUTIVE DECISION MAKING. Richard Eells and Peter Nehemkis. Free Press, 866 Third Avenue, New York, New York 10022. 1984.

ESSAYS ON ETHICS IN BUSINESS AND THE PROFESSIONS. Jack N. Behrman. Prentice-Hall, Incorporated, 113 Sylvan Avenue, Englewood Cliffs, New Jersey 07632. 1988.

ETHICAL AND LEGAL ISSUES IN SCHOOL COUNSELING. Wayne C. Huey and Theodore P. Remley, Jr. American School Counselor Association, 5999 Stevenson Avenue, Alexandria, Virginia 22304. 1988.

ETHICAL CHALLENGES IN LIBRARIANSHIP. Robert Hauptman. Oryx Press, 2214 North Central Avenue, Phoenix, Arizona 85004. 1988.

ETHICAL CONDUCT AND THE PROFESSIONAL'S DILEMMA: CHOOSING BETWEEN SERVICE AND SUCCESS. Banks McDowell. Quorum Books, Greenwood Publishing Group, Incorporated, 88 Post Road West, P.O. Box 5007, Westport, Connecticut 06881. 1991.

ETHICAL DILEMMAS FOR ACADEMIC PROFESSIONALS. Stephen L. Payne and Bruce H. Charnov. Charles C. Thomas Publishers, 2600 South First Street, Springfield, Illinois 62794. 1987.

ETHICAL DILEMMAS IN SOCIAL SERVICE. Second Edition. Frederic G. Reamer. Columbia University Press, 562 West One Hundred Thirteenth Street, New York, New York 10025. 1990.

ETHICAL ISSUES IN BUSINESS. Second Edition. Thomas Donaldson and Patricia H. Werhance, Editors. Prentice-Hall, Incorporated, 113 Sylvan Avenue, Englewood Cliffs, New Jersey 07632. 1983.

ETHICAL ISSUES IN COUNSELING. Ronald H. Stein. Prometheus Books, 700 East Amherst Street, Buffalo, New York 14215. 1990.

ETHICAL ISSUES IN PROFESSIONAL LIFE. Joan C. Callahan. Oxford University Press, 200 Madison Avenue, New York, New York 10016. 1988.

ETHICAL ISSUES IN THE PROFESSIONS. Peter Y. Windt. Prentice-Hall, Incorporated, 113 Sylvan Avenue, Englewood Cliffs, New Jersey 07632. 1989.

ETHICAL, LEGAL, AND PROFESSIONAL ISSUES IN THE PRACTICE OF MARRIAGE AND FAMILY THERAPY. Charles H. Huber and Leroy G. Baruth. Merrill Publishing Company, P.O. Box 508, Columbus, Ohio 43216. 1987.

ETHICS AND ARCHITECTS IN THE U.S. AND ENGLAND: A SELECTED BIBLIOGRAPHY. Anthony G. White. Vance Bibliographies, P.O. Box 229, 112 North Charter Street, Monticello, Illinois 61856. 1987.

ETHICS AND PROFESSIONALISM. John H. Kultgen. University of Pennsylvania Press, Blockley Hall, 418 Service Drive, Philadelphia, Pennsylvania 19104. 1988.

ETHICS AND THE MANAGEMENT OF COMPUTER TECHNOLOGY: PROCEEDINGS OF THE FOURTH CONFERENCE ON BUSINESS ETHICS. W. Michael Hoffman and Jennifer Mills Moore, Editors. Oelgeschlager, Gunn and Hain, Incorporated, 245 Mirriam Street, Weston, Massachusetts 02193. 1982.

ETHICS AND THE PROFESSIONS. David Appelbaum and Sarah Verone Lawton. Prentice-Hall, Incorporated, 113 Sylvan Avenue, Englewood Cliffs, New Jersey 07632. 1990.

ETHICS IN MINISTRY: A GUIDE FOR THE PROFESSIONAL. Walter E. Wiest and Elwyn A. Smith. Fortress Press, Minneapolis, Minnesota. 1990.

ETHICS IN PSYCHOTHERAPY AND COUNSELING: A PRACTICAL GUIDE FOR PSYCHOLOGISTS. Kenneth S. Pope and Melba J. T. Vasquez. Jossey-Bass, Incorporated, 350 Sansome Street, San Francisco, California 94104. 1991.

ETHICS IN THE FINANCIAL MARKETPLACE. John L. Casey. Scudder, New York, New York. 1988.

ETHICS OF AN ARTIFICIAL PERSON: LOST RESPONSIBILITY IN PROFESSIONS AND ORGANIZATIONS. Elizabeth Hankins Wolgast. Stanford University Press, Stanford, California 94305. 1992.

THE ETHICS OF SCHOOL ADMINISTRATION. Kenneth A. Strike, Emil J. Haller, and Jonas F. Soltis. Teachers College Press, New York, New York. 1988.

ETHICS, TRUST, AND THE PROFESSIONS: PHILOSOPHICAL AND CULTURAL ASPECTS. Edmund D. Pellegrino, Robert M. Veatch, and John P. Langan. Georgetown University Press, Intercultural Center, Room 111, Washington, D.C. 20057. 1991.

GUIDE TO ETHICAL PRACTICE IN PSYCHOTHERAPY. Andrew Thompson. John Wiley and Sons, Incorporated, 605 Third Avenue, New York, New York 10158. 1990.

ISSUES AND ETHICS IN THE HELPING PROFESSIONS. Fourth Edition. Gerald Corey, Marianne Schneider Corey, and Patrick Callanan. Brooks/Cole Publishing Company, 511 Forest Lodge Road, Pacific Grove, California 93950. 1992.

LAW AND SOCIAL WORK PRACTICE. Raymond Albert. Springer Publishing Company, Incorporated, 536 Broadway, New York, New York 10012. 1986.

THE LAW OF PROFESSIONAL LICENSING AND CERTIFICATION. Randolph P. Reaves. Pubications for Professionals, P.O. Box 13579 Charlotte, North Carolina 28211. 1984.

MORAL EXPERTISE: STUDIES IN PRACTICAL AND PROFESSIONAL ETHICS. Don MacNiven. Routledge, Chapman & Hall, 29 West Thirty-fifth Street, New York, New York 10001. 1990.

THE MORAL FOUNDATIONS OF PROFESSIONAL ETHICS. Alan H. Goldman. Rowman and Allanheld, 420 Boston Way, Lanham, Maryland 20706. 1980.

PASTORAL ETHICS: PROFESSIONAL RESPONSIBILITIES OF THE CLERGY. Gaylord B. Noyce. Abingdon Press, P.O. Box 801, 201 Eighth Avenue South, Nashville, Tennessee 37202. 1988.

POLICIES AND PERSONS: A CASEBOOK IN BUSINESS ETHICS. John B. Matthews and Kenneth E. Goodpaster. McGraw-Hill Book Company, 1221 Avenue of the Americas, New York, New York 10020. 1985.

PROFESSIONAL ETHICS. Second Edition. Michael D. Bayles. Wadsworth Publishing Company, 10 Davis Drive, Belmont, California 94002. 1989.

PROFESSIONAL ETHICS AND RESPONSIBILITY: THE NEW MODEL RULES IN A CHANGING LEGAL PROFESSION: ALI-ABA COURSE OF STUDY MATERIALS. American Law Institute-American Bar Association, 4025 Chestnut Street, Philadelphia, Pennsylvania 19104. 1991.

PROFESSIONAL ETHICS IN CONTEXT: INSTITUTIONS, IMAGES, AND EMPATHY. Eric Mount, Jr. Westminster/John Knox Press, 100 Witherspoon Street, Louisville, Kentucky 40202-1396. 1990.

PROFESSIONAL ETHICS IN NURSING. Joyce E. Thompson and Henry O. Thompson. Krieger Publishing Company, Incorporated, P.O. Box 9542, Malabar, Florida 32902. 1990.

PROFESSIONAL ETHICS IN UNIVERSITY ADMINISTRATION. Ronald H. Stein and Carlotta Baca, Editors. Jossey-Bass, Incorporated, 350 Sansome Street, San Francisco, California 94104. 1981.

PROFITS AND PROFESSIONS: ESSAYS IN BUSINESS AND PROFESSIONAL ETHICS. Wade L. Robinson, Editor. The Humana Press, P.O. Box 2148, Clifton, New Jersey 07015. 1983.

REAL ESTATE ETHICS. Second Edition. William H. Pivar. Real Estate Education Company, Chicago, Illinois. 1989.

THE RESPONSIBLE ADMINISTRATOR: AN APPROACH TO ETHICS FOR THE ADMINISTRATIVE ROLE. Third Edition. Terry L. Cooper. Jossey-Bass, Incorporated, 350 Sansome Street, San Francisco, California 94104. 1990.

REVOCATION OF PROFESSIONAL LICENSES BY GOVERNMENTAL AGENCIES. William O. Morris. The Michie Company, P.O. Box 7587, Charlottesville, Virginia 22906-7582. 1984.

TILL DEATH DO US PART: BENDIX VS. MARTIN MARIETTA. Hope Lampert. Harcourt Brace Jovanovich, Incorporated, 6277 Sea Harbor Drive, Orlando, Florida 32821. 1983.

VETERINARY ETHICS. Jerrold Tannenbaum. Williams and Wilkins, 428 East Preston, Baltimore, Maryland 21202. 1989.

LAW REVIEWS AND PERIODICALS

PROFESSIONAL LIABILITY TODAY. Lloyd's of London, 817 Broadway, New York, New York 10003. 1986- .

NEWSLETTERS AND NEWSPAPERS

CLEAR NEWS. Clearinghouse on Licensure, Enforcement and Regulation, Iron Works Pike, P.O. Box 11910, Lexington, Kentucky 40578. Bimonthly.

BIBLIOGRAPHIES

ETHICS AND THE PROFESSOR: AN ANNOTATED BIBLIOGRAPHY, 1970-1985. Mark Youngblood Herring. Garland Publishing, Incorporated, 136 Madison Avenue, New York, New York 10016. 1988.

ETHICS OF INFORMATION SCIENCE. Tim J. Watts. Vance Bibliographies, P.O. Box 229, 112 North Charter Street, Monticello, Illinois 61856. 1987.

OCCUPATIONAL LICENSING AND REGULATION: A BIBLIPOGRAPHY. Council of State Government, Iron Works Pike, P.O. Box 11910, Lexington, Kentucky 40578. 1983.

PROFESSIONAL DISSENT: AN ANOTATED BIBLIOGRAPHY AND RESOURCE GUIDE. James S. Bowman, Frederick A. Elliston and Paula Lockhart. Garland Publishing, Incorporated, 136 Madison Avenue, New York, New York 10016. 1984.

PUBLIC RELATIONS AND ETHICS: A BIBLIOGRAPHY. John P. Ferre and Shirley C. Willihnganz. G.K. Hall and Company, Incorporated, 70 Lincoln Street, Boston, Massachusetts 02111. 1991.

DIRECTORIES

PROFESSIONAL CODES OF CONDUCT IN THE UNITED KINGDOM: A DIRECTORY. Nigel G. E. Harris. Mansell Publishing Limited, Artillery House, Artillery Row, London SW1P 1RT, England. 1989.

PROFESSIONAL ETHICS AND LIABILITY

ASSOCIATIONS AND PROFESSIONAL SOCIETIES

COMMITTEE ON PROFESSIONAL ETHICS, RIGHTS, AND FREEDOM. c/o American Political Science Association, 1527 New Hampshire Avenue, Northwest, Washington, D.C. 20036. (202) 483-2512.

RESEARCH CENTERS, INSTITUTES, CLEARINGHOUSES

CENTER FOR APPLIED PHILOSOPHY AND ETHICS IN THE PROFESSIONS. University of Florida, 243 Dover Hall, Gainesville, Florida 32611. (904) 392-2084.

CENTER FOR THE STUDY OF ETHICS IN THE PROFESSIONS. Illinois Institute of Technology, 3101 South Dearborn Street, 166 LS, Chicago, Illinois 60616. (312) 567-3017.

OLSSON CENTER FOR APPLIED ETHICS. University of Virginia, Dandeu School, P.O. Box 6550, Charlottesville, Virginia 22906. (804) 924-0935.

POYNTER CENTER. Indiana University, 410 North Park Avenue, Bloomington, Indiana 47408. (812) 855-0261.

AUDIOVISUALS

ATTORNEY-CLIENT RELATIONS. American Bar Association, 750 North Lake Shore Drive, Chicago, Illinois 60611. 1989. Videotape.

CLIENT CONFIDENTIALITY. American Bar Association, 750 North Lake Shore Drive, Chicago, Illinois 60611. 1989. Videotape.

CONFLICTS OF INTEREST. American Bar Association, 750 North Lake Shore Drive, Chicago, Illinois 60611. 1989. Videotape.

ETHICAL DILEMMAS AND PROFESSIONALISM. American Bar Association, 750 North Lake Shore Drive, Chicago, Illinois 60611. 1989. Videotape.

HOW TO PREVENT LEGAL MALPRACTICE. American Bar Association, 750 North Lake Shore Drive, Chicago, Illinois 60611. 1989. Videotape.

INDEPENDENCE OF COUNSEL. American Bar Association, 750 North Lake Shore Drive, Chicago, Illinois 60611. 1989. Videotape.

LAWYER ADVERTISING: HOW FAR CAN REGULATION GO? American Bar Association, 750 North Lake Shore Drive, Chicago, Illinois 60611. 1990. Videotape.

LEGAL ADVERTISING: OF THE PEOPLE, BY THE PEOPLE, FOR THE PEOPLE. American Bar Association, 750 North Lake Shore Drive, Chicago, Illinois 60611. 1985. Videotape.

PREVENTING LEGAL MALPRACTICE. American Bar Association, 750 North Lake Shore Drive, Chicago, Illinois 60611. 1987. Videotape.

PROFESSIONAL RESPONSIBILITY. Center for Computer-Assisted Instruction, 229 19th Avenue South, University of Minnesota, Minneapolis, Minnesota 55455. Interactive videodisc.

UNDERSTANDING MODERN ETHICAL STANDARDS. National Institute for Trial Advocacy, Notre Dame Law School, Notre Dame, Indiana 46556. 1985. Videotape.

COMPUTER-ASSISTED LEGAL INSTRUCTION

CODE OF PROFESSIONAL RESPONSIBILITY I. Kenneth R. Kirwin and Roger C. Park. Center for Computer-Assisted Instruction, 229 19th Avenue South, University of Minnesota, Minneapolis, Minnesota 55455. Machine-readable computer file.

CODE OF PROFESSIONAL RESPONSIBILITY II. Kenneth R. Kirwin and Roger C. Park. Center for Computer-Assisted Instruction, 229 19th Avenue South, University of Minnesota, Minneapolis, Minnesota 55455. Machine-readable computer file.

DECISIONS BEFORE TRIAL. Robert E. Keeton and Kenneth K. Kirwin. Center for Computer-Assisted Instruction, 229 19th Avenue South, University of Minnesota, Minneapolis, Minnesota 55455. Machine-readable computer file.

DEFENSE FUNCTION-CODE OF PROFESSIONAL RESPONSIBILITY VERSION. Kenneth K. Kirwin and Roger C. Park. Center for Computer-Assisted Instruction, 229 19th Avenue South, University of Minnesota, Minneapolis, Minnesota 55455. Machine-readable computer file.

DEFENSE FUNCTION-RULES OF PROFESSIONAL CONDUCT VERSION. Kenneth K. Kirwin and Roger C. Park. Center for Computer-Assisted Instruction, 229 19th Avenue South, University of Minnesota, Minneapolis, Minnesota 55455. Machine-readable computer file.

MODEL RULES OF PROFESSIONAL CONDUCT I: PRELIMINARY DRILL. Kenneth K. Kirwin and Roger C. Park. Center for Computer-Assisted Instruction, 229 19th Avenue South, University of Minnesota, Minneapolis, Minnesota 55455. Machine-readable computer file.

MODEL RULES OF PROFESSIONAL CONDUCT II: QUESTIONS AND PROBLEMS. Kenneth K. Kirwin and Roger C. Park. Center for Computer-Assisted Instruction, 229 19th Avenue South, University of Minnesota, Minneapolis, Minnesota 55455. Machine-readable computer file.

PROFIT-SHARING
See: EMPLOYEE FRINGE BENEFITS

PROPERTY
See: PERSONAL PROPERTY; PUBLIC LAND; REAL PROPERTY; TIME-SHARE PROPERTY

PROSECUTING ATTORNEYS
See: PUBLIC PROSECUTERS

PROSTITUTION
See also: CRIMINAL LAW

HANDBOOKS, MANUALS, FORMBOOKS

THE LEGAL WHOREHOUSE OWNER'S HANDBOOK. Chuck Princer. Charlton House Publishing, P.O. Box 2474, Newport Beach, California 92663. 1984.

JUVENILE PROSTITUTION: A RESOURCE MANUAL. Bruce Fisher et al. Urban and Rural Systems Associates, China Basin, Suite 6600, San Francisco, California 94107. 1982.

TEXTBOOKS AND GENERAL WORKS

AIDS, DRUGS, AND PROSTITUTION. Martin Plant. Tavistock Publications, Limited, Routledge, Chapman and Hall, Incorporated, 29 West Thirty-fifth Street, New York, New York 10001. 1990.

CHILD PORNOGRAPHY AND PROSTITUTION: BACKGROUND AND LEGAL ANALYSIS. Howard A. Davidson and Gregory A. Loken. National Center for Missing and Exploited Children, 2101 Wilson Boulevard, Suite 550, Arlington, Virginia 22201. 1987.

CHILDREN ENSLAVED. Roger Sawyer. Routledge, Chapman & Hall, 29 West Thirty-fifth Street, New York, New York 10001. 1988.

CITY OF EROS: NEW YORK CITY, PROSTITUTION, AND THE COMMERCIALIZATION OF SEX, 1820-1920. Timothy J. Gilfoyle. W.W. Norton and Company, Incorporated, 500 Fifth Avenue, New York, New York 10110. 1992.

PROSTITUTION, DRUGS, GAMBLING, AND ORGANIZED CRIME. Eric H. Monkkonen. K.G. Saur, 245 West Seventeenth Street, New York, New York 10011. 1992.

RED LIGHTS OUT: A LEGAL HISTORY OF PROSTITUTION, DISORDERLY HOUSES, AND VICE DISTRICTS, 1870-1917. Thomas C. Mackey. Garland Publishing, Incorporated, 136 Madison Avenue, New York, New York 10016. 1987.

SEXUAL COERCION: A SOURCEBOOK ON ITS NATURE, CAUSES, AND PREVENTION. Elizabeth Grauerholz and Mary Koralewski. Lexington Books, 125 Spring Street, Lexington, Massachusetts 02173. 1991.

UNEASY VIRTUE: THE POLITICS OF PROSTITUTION AND THE AMERICAN REFORM TRADITION. Barbara Meil Hobson. University of Chicago Press, 5801 Ellis Avenue, Chicago, Illinois 60637. 1990.

WHITE SLAVERY: MYTH, IDEOLOGY, AND AMERICAN LAW. Frederick K. Grittner. Garland Publishing, Incorporated, 136 Madison Avenue, New York, New York 10016. 1990.

WOMEN AND PROSTITUTION: A SOCIAL HISTORY. Vern Bullough and Bonnie Bullough. Prometheus Books, 700 East Amherst Street, Buffalo, New York 14215. 1987.

WORKING WOMEN: THE SUBTERRANEAN WORLD OF STREET PROSTITUTION. Arlene Carmen and Howard Moody. HarperCollins Publishers, Incorporated, 10 East Fifty-third Street, New York, New York 10022. 1985.

BIBLIOGRAPHIES

PROSTITUTES IN MEDICAL LITERATURE: AN ANNOTATED BIBLIOGRAPHY. Sachi Sri Kantha. Greenwood Publishing Group, Incorporated, 88 Post Road West, P.O. Box 5007, Westport, Connecticut 06881. 1991.

ASSOCIATIONS AND PROFESSIONAL SOCIETIES

NATIONAL TASK FORCE ON PROSTITUTION. 333 Valencia Street, Suite 101, San Francisco, California 94103. (415) 558-0450.

PROXIMATE CAUSE
See: TORTS

PSYCHIATRY
See also: MEDICAL JURISPRUDENCE AND MALPRACTICE; MENTAL HEALTH AND DISABILITY

LOOSELEAF SERVICES AND REPORTERS

PROFESSIONAL LIABILITY REPORTER. Litigation Research Group, P.O. Box 77903, San Francisco, California 94107. 1985- .

HANDBOOKS, MANUALS, FORMBOOKS

CLINICAL HANDBOOK OF PSYCHIATRY AND THE LAW. Second Edition. Paul S. Appelbaum and Thomas G. Gutheil. Williams and Wilkins, 428 East Preston, Baltimore, Maryland 21202. 1991.

CONCISE GUIDE TO LEGAL ISSUES IN PSYCHIATRIC PRACTICE. Robert I. Simon. American Psychiatric Press, Incorporated, 1400 K Street, Northwest, Washington, D.C. 20005. 1992.

HANDBOOK OF PSYCHIATRY AND THE LAW. Ebrahim J. Kermani. Year Book Medical Publishers, Incorporated, 200 North LaSalle Street, Chicago, Illinois 60601. 1989.

PSYCHIATRY IN THE EVERYDAY PRACTICE OF LAW: A LAWYER'S MANUAL FOR CASE PREPARATION AND TRIAL. Second Edition, Martin Blinder. Lawyers Cooperative Publishing Company, Aqueduct Building, Rochester, New York 14694. 1982. (Supplemented).

PSYCHOLOGICAL EVALUATIONS FOR THE COURTS: A HANDBOOK FOR MENTAL HEALTH PROFESSIONALS AND LAWYERS. Gary B. Melton. Guilford Publications, Incorporated, 72 Spring Street, New York, New York 10012. 1987.

TEXTBOOKS AND GENERAL WORKS

THE CHRONIC PSYCHIATRIC PATIENT IN THE COMMUNITY: PRINCIPLES OF TREATMENT. Ivan Barofsky and Richard Budson, Editors. Robert B. Luce, Incorporated, 195 McGregor Street, Manchester, New Hampshire 03102. 1983.

CLINICAL PSYCHIATRY AND THE LAW. Second Edition. Robert I. Simon. American Psychiatric Press, 1400 K Street, Northwest, Washington, D.C. 20005. 1991.

CONCISE GUIDE TO CLINICAL PSYCHIATRY AND THE LAW. Robert I. Simon. American Psychiatric Press, Incorporated, 1400 K Street, Northwest, Washington, D.C. 20005. 1988.

COPING WITH PSYCHIATRIC AND PSYCHOLOGICAL TESTIMONY. Fourth Edition. Jay Ziskin. Law and Psychology Press. P.O. Box 24219, Los Angeles, California 90024. 1991.

CRITICAL ISSUES IN AMERICAN PSYCHIATRY AND THE LAW. Richard Rosner, Editor. Plenum Publishing Corporation, 233 Spring Street, New York, New York 10013. 1985.

DANGEROUS: PROBABILIITY, PREDICTION AND PUBLIC POLICY. Christopher D. Webster, Mark H. Ben-Aron, and Stephen J. Hucker, Editors. Cambridge University Press, 40 West Twentieth Street, New York, New York 10011. 1985.

DEFENDANT, A PSYCHIATRIST ON TRIAL FOR MEDICAL MALPRACTICE: AN EPISODE IN AMERICA'S HIDDEN HEALTH CARE CRISIS. Sara C. Charles and Eugene Kennedy. Free Press, Division of Macmillan Publishing Company, Incorporated, 866 Third Avenue, New York, New York 10022. 1985.

EMERGING ISSUES IN CHILD PSYCHIATRY AND THE LAW. Elisa P. Benedek and Diane H. Schetky, Editors. Brunner/Mazel Publishers, 19 Union Square W., New York, New York 10003. 1985.

FORENSIC PSYCHIATRY. Joseph T. Smith. West Publishing Company, P.O. Box 64526, 50 West Kellogg Boulevard, St. Paul, Minnesota 55164-0526. 1983.

ISSUES IN FORENSIC PSYCHIATRY: INSANITY DEFENSE, HOSPITALIZATION OF ADULTS, MODEL CIVIL COMMITTMENT LAW, SENTENCING PROCESS, CHILD CUSTODY CONSULTATION. Books on Demand, 300 North Zeeb Road, Ann Arbor, Michigan 48106-1346. 1984.

LAW AND MENTAL HEALTH: INTERNATIONAL PERSPECTIVES. David N. Weisstub. Pergamon Press, Incorporated, Maxwell House, Fairview Park, Elmsford, New York 10523. 1990.

LAW AND PSYCHIATRY: RETHINKING THE RELATIONSHIP. Michael S. Moore. Cambridge University Press, 40 West Twentieth Street, New York, New York 10011. 1984.

LAW FOR THE PSYCHOTHERAPIST. Robert G. Meyer, E. Rhett Landis, and J. Ray Hays. W.W Norton and Company, Incorporated, 500 Fifth Avenue, New York, New York 10110. 1988.

LAW, PSYCHIATRY AND MORALITY: ESSAYS AND ANALYSIS. Alan A. Stone. Books on Demand, 300 North Zeeb Road, Ann Arbor, Michigan 48106-1346. 1984.

MAN, MIND AND MORALITY: THE ETHICS OF BEHAVIORAL CONTROL. Ruth Macklin. Prentice-Hall, Incorporated, 113 Sylvan Avenue, Englewood Cliffs, New Jersey 07632. 1982.

MEDICAL MALPRACTICE, PSYCHIATRIC CARE. Joseph T. Smith. Shepard's/McGraw-Hill, P.O. Box 1235, Colorado Springs, Colorado 80901. 1986.

THE MENTAL HEALTH PROFESSIONAL AND LEGAL SYSTEM. Brunner/Mazel, Incorporated, 19 Union Square West, New York, New York 10003. 1991.

PRIVILEGED COMMUNICATIONS IN THE MENTAL HEALTH PROFESSIONS. Samuel Knapp and Leon VandeCreek. Van Nostrand Reinhold Company, Incorporated, 115 Fifth Avenue, New York, New York 10003. 1987.

PSYCHIATRIC AND PSYCHOLOGICAL EVIDENCE. Daniel W. Shuman. Shepard's/McGraw-Hill, P.O. Box 1235, Colorado Springs, Colorado 80901. 1986.

THE PSYCHIATRIC HOSPITAL AND THE FAMILY. Henry T. Harbin, Editor. Robert B. Luce, Incorporated, 195 McGregor Street, Manchester, New Hampshire 03102. 1982.

PSYCHIATRIC INTERVENTION AND MALPRACTICE: A PRIMER FOR LIABILITY PREVENTION. Robert I. Simon. Charles C. Thomas Publishing, 2600 South First Street, Springfield, Illinois 62794-9265. 1982.

PSYCHIATRIC MALPRACTICE: CASES AND COMMENTS FOR CLINICIANS. Robert L. Sadoff and Robert I. Simon. American Psychiatric Press, Incorporated, 1400 K Street, Northwest, Washington, D.C. 20005. 1991.

PSYCHIATRIC MALPRACTICE: LIABILITY OF MENTAL HEALTH PROFESSIONALS. Jeffrey D. Robertson. John Wiley and Sons, Incorporated, 605 Third Avenue, New York, New York 10158. 1988.

PSYCHIATRIC PATIENT RIGHTS AND PATIENT ADVOCACY: ISSUES AND EVIDENCE. Bernard L. Bloom and Shirley J. Asher, Editors. Human Sciences Press, Incorporated, 233 Spring Street, New York, New York 10013. 1982.

PSYCHIATRY AND THE LAW OF INSANITY. Second Edition. Stanley Pearlstein. Oceana Publications, Incorporated, 75 Main Street, Dobbs Ferry, New York 10522. 1986.

PSYCHIATRY, HUMAN RIGHTS, AND THE LAW. Martin Roth and Robert Bluglass, Editors. Cambridge University Press, 40 West Twentieth Street, New York, New York 10011. 1985.

PSYCHIATRY, LAW AND ETHICS. A. Carmi and S. Schneider, Editors. Springer-Verlag New York, Incorporated, 175 Fifth Avenue, New York, New York 10010. 1986.

PSYCHOANALYTIC PSYCHIATRY FOR LAWYERS. Daniel B. Gesensway. American Law Institute-American Bar Association, Committee on Continuing Professional Education, 4025 Chestnut Street, Philadelphia, Pennsylvania 19104. 1982.

THE PSYCHOTHERAPIST'S DUTY TO WARN OR PROTECT. Alan R. Felthous. Charles C. Thomas, Publishers, 2600 South First Street, Springfield, Illinois 62794. 1989.

PSYCHOTHERAPY AND THE LAW. Louis Everstine and Diana Sullivan Everstine. Academic Press, Incorporated, 1250 Sixth Avenue, San Diego, California 92101. 1986.

TREATMENT CHOICES AND INFORMED CONSENT: CURRENT CONTROVERSIES IN PSYCHIATRIC MALPRACTICE LITIGATION. John Gulton Malcolm. Charles C. Thomas, Publishers, 2600 South First Street, Springfield, Illinois 62794. 1988.

LAW REVIEWS AND PERIODICALS

AMERICAN ACADEMY OF PSYCHIATRY AND THE LAW BULLETIN. American Academy of Psychiatry and the Law, 1211 Cathedral Street, Baltimore, Maryland 21201. Quarterly.

INTERNATIONAL JOURNAL OF LAW AND PSYCHIATRY. Pergamon Press, Incorporated, Maxwell House, Fairview Park, Elmsford, New York 10523. Quarterly.

JOURNAL OF PSYCHIATRY AND LAW. Federal Legal Publications, Inc, 95 Morton Street, New York, New York. Quarterly.

NEWSLETTERS AND NEWSPAPERS

AMERICAN ACADEMY OF PSYCHIATRY AND LAW NEWSLETTER. American Academy of Psychiatry and Law, 1211 Cathedral Street, Baltimore, Maryland 21201. Three issues per year.

DIRECTORIES

AMERICAN PSYCHIATRIC ASSOCIATION MEMBERSHIP DIRECTORY. American Psychiatric Association, 1400 K Street, Northwest, Washington, D.C. 20005. Bi-Annual.

ASSOCIATIONS AND PROFESSIONAL SOCIETIES

AMERICAN ACADEMY OF PSYCHIATRY AND THE LAW. 891 Park Avenue, Baltimore, Maryland 21201. (301) 539-0379.

AMERICAN PSYCHIATRIC ASSOCIATION. 1400 K Street, Northwest, Washington, D.C. 20005. (202) 682-6000.

ASSOCIATIONS OF AMERICAN LAW SCHOOLS. One Dupont Circle, Northwest, Suite 370, Washington, D.C. 20036. (202) 296-8851.

PSYCHOLOGY
See also: MEDICAL JURISPRUDENCE AND MALPRACTICE; MENTAL HEALTH AND DISABILITY

LOOSELEAF SERVICES AND REPORTERS

PROFESSIONAL LIABILITY REPORTER. Andrews Publications, Incorporated, 1646 West Chester Pike, Westtown, Pennsylvania 19395. 1985- .

HANDBOOKS, MANUALS, FORMBOOKS

HANDBOOK OF PSYCHOLOGY AND LAW. D. Kagehiro and W. Laufer. Springer-Verlag New York, Incorporated, 175 Fifth Avenue, New York, New York 10010. 1991.

PSYCHOLOGICAL EVALUATIONS FOR THE COURTS: A HANDBOOK FOR MENTAL HEALTH PROFESSIONALS AND LAWYERS. Gary B. Melton. Guilford Publications, Incorporated, 72 Spring Street, New York, New York 10012. 1987.

TEXTBOOKS AND GENERAL WORKS

BEHAVIORAL SCIENTISTS IN COURTS AND CORRECTIONS. James T. Ziegenfuss, Jr. Van Nostrand Reinhold, Company, Incorporated, 115 Fifth Avenue, New York, New York 10003. 1985.

COMMUNICATION IN THE LEGAL PROCESS. Ronald J. Malton. Holt, Rinehart, and Winston, Incorporated, 6277 Sea Harbor Drive, Orlando, Florida 32821. 1988.

COPING WITH PSYCHIATRIC AND PSYCHOLOGICAL TESTIMONY. Fourth Edition. Jay Ziskin. Law and Psychology Press, P.O. Box 24219, Los Angeles, California 90024. 1991.

COURTROOM PSYCHOLOGY FOR TRIAL LAWYERS. Thomas Sannito and Peter J. McGovern. John Wiley and Sons, Incorporated, 605 Third Avenue, New York, New York 10158. 1985.

ETHICAL AND LEGAL ISSUES IN COUNSELLING AND PSYCHOTHERAPY. Second Edition. William H. Van Hoose and Jeffrey A. Kottler. Jossey-Bass Incorporated, 350 Sansome Street, San Francisco, California 94104. 1985.

EVALUATING CHILDREN FOR THE COURTS USING PSYCHOLOGICAL TESTS. Stanley Kissel and Nelson W. Freeling. Charles C. Thomas, Publishers, 2600 South First Street, Springfield, Illinois 62794. 1990.

EYEWITNESS TESTIMONY: PSYCHOLOGICAL PERSPECTIVES. Gary L. Wells, Editor. Cambridge University Press, 40 West Twentieth Street, New York, New York 10011. 1984.

FORENSIC PSYCHOLOGY: A PRIMER FOR LEGAL AND MENTAL HEALTH PROFESSIONALS. R. Keith Green and Arlene B. Schaefer. Charles C. Thomas Publishing, 2600 South First Street, Springfield, Illinois 62794-9265. 1984.

IMPACT OF SOCIAL PSYCHOLOGY ON PROCEDURAL JUSTICE. Martin F. Kaplan, Editor. Charles C. Thomas Publishing, 2600 South First Street, Springfield, Illinois 62794-9265. 1986.

LAW IN PRACTICE: APPLICATIONS OF PSYCHOLOGY TO LEGAL DECISION MAKING AND LEGAL SKILLS. Sally M. A. Lloyd-Bostock. Routledge, Chapman & Hall, 29 West Thirty-fifth Street, New York, New York 10001. 1988.

LAWYERS ON PSYCHOLOGY AND PSYCHOLOGISTS ON LAW. Peter J. van Koppen, Dick J. Hessing, and Grat van den Heuvel. Swets North America, Incorporated, P.O. Box 517, Berwyn, Pennsylvania 19312. 1988.

LEGAL LIABILITY IN PSYCHOTHERAPY. Benjamin M. Schutz. Jossey-Bass, Incorporated, 350 Sansome Street, San Francisco, California 94104. 1982.

PSYCHIATRIC AND PSYCHOLOGICAL EVIDENCE. Daniel W. Shuman. Shepard's/McGraw-Hill, P.O. Box 1235, Colorado Springs, Colorado 80901. 1986.

PSYCHOLOGICAL CONSULTATION IN THE COURTROOM. Michael T. Nietzel and Ronald C. Dillehay. Pergamon Press, Incorporated, Maxwell House, Fairview Park, Elmsford, New York 10523. 1986.

THE PSYCHOLOGICAL EFFECTS OF POLICE WORK: A PSYCHODYNAMIC APPROACH. Philip Bonifacio. Plenum Publishing Corporation, 233 Spring Street, New York, New York 10013. 1991.

PSYCHOLOGIST AS EXPERT WITNESS. Theodore H. Blau. John Wiley and Sons, Incorporated, 605 Third Avenue, New York, New York 10158. 1984.

PSYCHOLOGY AND AMERICAN LAW. Curt R. Bartol. Wadsworth Publishing Company, 10 Davis Drive, Belmont, California 94002. 1983.

PSYCHOLOGY AND LAW: TOPICS FROM AN INTERNATIONAL CONFERENCE. Dave J. Muller, Editor. John Wiley and Sons, Incorporated, 605 Third Avenue, New York, New York 10158. 1984.

PSYCHOLOGY AND THE LAW. James C. Scheirer and Barbara L. Hammonds, Editors. American Psychological Association, 1200 Seventeenth Street, Northwest, Washington, D.C. 20036. 1983.

PSYCHOLOGY AND THE LEGAL SYSTEM. Second Edition. Lawrence Samuel Wrightsman. Brooks/Cole Publishing Company, Wadsworth Publishing Companing, 10 Davis Drive, Belmont, California 94002. 1991.

PSYCHOLOGY IN AND OUT OF COURT: A CRITICAL EXAMINATION OF LEGAL PSYCHOLOGY. Michael King. Pergammon Press, Incorporated, Maxwell House, Fairview Park, Elmsford, New York 10523. 1986.

PSYCHOLOGY IN THE COMMON CAUSE. B. R. Bugelski. Praeger Publishers, One Madison Avenue, New York, New York 10010-3603. 1989.

PSYCHOLOGY OF LAW: INTEGRATIONS AND APPLICATIONS. Irwin A. Horowitz and Thomas E. Willging. Scott Foresman and Company, 1900 East Lake Avenue, Glenview, Illinois 60025. 1984.

PSYCHOLOGY OF THE COURTROOM. Norbert L. Kerr and Robert M. Bray, Editors. Academic Press, Incorporated, 1250 Sixth Avenue, Suite 400, San Diego, California 92101. 1981.

PSYCHOTHERAPY AND THE LAW. Louis Everstine and Diana Sullivan Everstine, Editors. Gurne and Stratton, Academic Press, Incorporated, 1250 Sixth Avenue, San Diego, California 92101. 1986.

THE REASONING CRIMINAL: RATIONAL CHOICE PERSPECTIVES ON OFFENDING. Derek B. Cornish and Ronald V. Clarke, Editors. Springer-Verlag New York, Incorporated, 175 Fifth Avenue, New York, New York 10010. 1986.

THE ROLE OF COMMUNICATION IN THE PRACTICE OF LAW. Dirk Cameron Gibson. University Press of America, 4720 Boston Way, Lanham, Maryland 20706. 1992.

SOCIAL PSYCHOLOGY IN COURT. Michael J. Saks. Krieger Publishing Company, P.O. Box 9542, Malabar, Florida 32902-9542. 1979. (Reprinted 1986).

THE SOCIAL PSYCHOLOGY OF PROCEDURAL JUSTICE. E. Allan Lind and Tom R. Tyler. Plenum Publishing Corporation, 233 Spring Street, New York, New York 10013. 1988.

LAW REVIEWS AND PERIODICALS

BEHAVIORAL SCIENCES AND THE LAW. Van Nostrand Reinhold Company, Incorporated, 135 West Fiftieth Street, New York, New York 10020. Quarterly.

JOURNAL OF LAW AND HUMAN BEHAVIOR. American Psychology-Law Society, Plenum Publishing Corporation, 233 Spring Street, New York, New York 10013. Quarterly.

LAW AND PSYCHOLOGY REVIEW. University of Alabama, P.O. Box 1435, University, Alabama 35486. Annual.

NEWSLETTERS AND NEWSPAPERS

AMERICAN PSYCHOLOGY-LAW NEWSLETTER. American Psychology-Law Society, c/o Stephen J. Morse, University of Southern California Law Center, University Park, Los Angeles, California 90007. Quarterly.

DIRECTORIES

AMERICAN PSYCHOLOGICAL ASSOCIATION MEMBERSHIP REGISTER. American Psychological Association, 1200 Seventeenth Street, Northwest, Washington, D.C. 20036.

BIOGRAPHICAL SOURCES

AMERICAN PSYCHOLOGICAL ASSOCIATION DIRECTORY. American Psychological Association, 1200 Seventeenth Street, Northwest, Washington, D.C. 20036.

ASSOCIATIONS AND PROFESSIONAL SOCIETIES

AMERICAN PSYCHOLOGICAL ASSOCIATION. 1200 Seventeenth Street, Northwest, Washington, D.C. 20036. (202) 955-7600.

AMERICAN PSYCHOLOGY-LAW SOCIETY. c/o Dr. Tom Grisso, University of Massachusetts, Medical Center, Department of Psychology, 55 Lake Avenue North, Worcester, Massachusetts 01655. (508) 856-3625.

ASSOCIATION OF AMERICAN LAW SCHOOLS, SECTION ON LAW AND SOCIAL SCIENCES. One Dupont Circle, Northwest, Suite 370, Washington, D.C. 20036. (202) 296-8851.

RESEARCH CENTERS, INSTITUTES, CLEARINGHOUSES

CENTER FOR RESPONSIVE PSYCHOLOGY. Brooklyn College of City University of New York, Brooklyn, New York 11210. (718) 780-5960.

ONLINE DATABASES

PSYCINFO. American Psychological Association. 1400 North Uhle Street, Arlington, Virginia 22201.

PUBLIC ADMINISTRATION
See also: ADMINISTRATIVE LAW

HANDBOOKS, MANUALS, FORMBOOKS

HANDBOOK OF COMPARATIVE AND DEVELOPMENT PUBLIC ADMINISTRATION. Ali Farazmand. Marcel Dekker, 720 Madison Avenue, New York, New York 10016. 1991.

HANDBOOK OF PUBLIC ADMINISTRATION. James L. Perry. Jossey-Bass, Incorporated, 350 Sansome Street, San Francisco, California 94104. 1989.

HANDBOOK OF PUBLIC ADMINISTRATION. Jack Rabin, W. Bartley Hildreth, and Gerald J. Miller. Marcel Dekker, 720 Madison Avenue, New York, New York 10016. 1989.

PUBLIC ADMINISTRATION DESK BOOK. James R. Coleman and Robert E. Dugan. Government Research Publications, P.O. Box 122, Newton, Massachusetts 02159. 1990.

PUBLIC ADMINISTRATION RESEARCH GUIDE. Virginia R. Cherry and Marc Holzer. Garland Publishing, Incorporated, 136 Madison Avenue, New York, New York 10016. 1992

STRATEGIC MANAGEMENT OF PUBLIC AND THIRD SECTOR ORGANIZATIONS: A HANDBOOK FOR LEADERS. Paul C. Nutt and Robert W. Backoff. Jossey- Bass, Incorporated, 350 Sansome Street, San Francisco, California 94104. 1992.

TEXTBOOKS AND GENERAL WORKS

THE ADMINISTRATIVE STATE: A STUDY OF THE POLITICAL THEORY OF AMERICAN PUBLIC ADMINISTRATION. Second Edition. Dwight Waldo. Holmes and Meier Publishers, Incorporated, 30 Irving Place, IUB Building, New York, New York 10003. 1984.

AMERICAN BUREAUCRACY: PUBLIC CHOICE AND PUBLIC LAW. Glen O. Robinson. University of Michigan Press, P.O. Box 1104, 839 Greene Street, Ann Arbor, Michigan 48106. 1991.

AMERICAN PUBLIC ADMINISTRATION: CONCEPTS AND CASES. Fourth Edition Carl E. Lutrin and Allen K. Settle. West Publishing Company, 50 West Kellogg Boulevard, St. Paul, Minnesota 55164. 1991.

THE CASE FOR JUSTICE: STRENGTHENING DECISION MAKING AND POLICY IN PUBLIC ADMINISTRATION. Gerald M. Pops and Thomas J. Pavlak. Jossey-Bass, Incorporated, 350 Sansome Street, San Francisco, California 94104. 1991.

CHANGE AND DECAY: PUBLIC ADMINISTRATION IN THE 1990S. Howard Elcock. Longman Publishing Group, 95 Church Street, White Plains, New York 10601. 1991.

CITIZEN PARTICIPATION IN PUBLIC DECISION MAKING. Jack De Sario and Stuart Langton, Editors. Greenwood Publishing Group, Incorporated, 88 Post Road West, P.O. Box 5007, Westport, Connecticut 06881. 1987.

CLASSICS OF PUBLIC ADMINISTRATION. Second Edition. Jay M. Shafritz and Albert C. Hyde. Dorsey Press, 10 Davis Drive, Belmont, California 94002. 1987.

CONTEMPORARY PUBLIC ADMINISTRATION. Dennis Palumbo and Steven Maynard-Moody. Longman Publishing Group, 95 Church Street, White Plains, New York 10601. 1991.

THE CRAFT OF PUBLIC ADMINISTRATION. Fourth Edition. George Berkley. Allyn and Bacon, Incorporated, William C. Brown Group, 2460 Kerper Boulevard, Dubuque, Iowa 52001. 1984.

CRITICAL CORNERSTONES OF PUBLIC ADMINISTRATION. Phillip Schorr, Editor. Oelgeschlager, Gunn and Hain, Incorporated, 245 Mirriam Street, Weston, Massachusetts 02193. 1985.

CURRENT ISSUES IN PUBLIC ADMINISTRATION. Fourth Edition. Frederick S. Lane, Editor. Saint Martin's Press, Incorporated, 175 Fifth Avenue, New York, New York 10010. 1990.

ETHICAL FRONTIERS IN PUBLIC MANAGEMENT: SEEKING NEW STRATEGIES FOR RESOLVING ETHICAL DILEMMAS. James S. Bowman. Jossey-Bass, Incorporated, 350 Sansome Street, San Francisco, California 94104. 1991.

THE ETHICS OF PUBLIC SERVICE: RESOLVING MORAL DILEMMAS IN PUBLIC ORGANIZATIONS. Kathryn G. Denhardt. Greenwood Publishing Group, Incorporated, 88 Post Road West, P.O. Box 5007, Westport, Connecticut 06881. 1988.

GUIDE TO ADMINISTRATIVE SERVICES IN GOVERNMENT. Donald B. Tweedy. Associated Faculty Press, 19 West Thirty-sixth Street, New York, New York 10018. 1985.

INNOVATION IN THE PUBLIC SECTOR. Richard L. Merritt and Anna J. Merritt. Sage Publications, Incorporated, 2455 Teller Road, Newbury Park, California 91320. 1984.

THE INTELLECTUAL CRISIS IN AMERICAN PUBLIC ADMINISTRATION. Second Edition. Vincent Ostrom. University of Alabama Press, P.O. Box 870380, Tuscaloosa, Alabama 35487. 1989.

THE LEGAL FOUNDATIONS OF PUBLIC ADMINISTRATION. Second Edition. Donald D. Barry and Howard R. Whitcomb. West Publishing Company, 50 West Kellogg Boulevard, St. Paul, Minnesota 55164. 1987.

MAKING PUBLIC POLICY: FROM CONFLICT TO RESOLUTION. Larry N. Gerston. Scott, Foresman and Company, 1900 East Lake Avenue, Glenview, Illinois 60025. 1983.

MANAGEMENT ANALYSIS IN PUBLIC ORGANIZATIONS: HISTORY, CONCEPTS, AND TECHNIQUES. Ray Oman. Quorum Books, Greenwood Publishing Group, Incorporated, 88 Post Road West, P.O. Box 5007, Westport, Connecticut 06881. 1992.

MODERN PUBLIC ADMINISTRATION. Seventh Edition. Felix A. Nigro and Lloyd G. Nigro. HarperCollins Publishers, Incorporated, 10 East Fifty-third Street, New York, New York 10022. 1988.

NEW DIRECTIONS IN PUBLIC ADMINISTRATION. Barry Bozeman and Jeffrey Straussman, Editors. Brooks/Cole Publishing Company, 511 Forest Lodge Road, Pacific Grove, California 93950. 1984.

PARALLEL SYSTEMS: REDUNDANCY IN GOVERNMENT. Jonathon B. Bendor. University of California Press, 2120 Berkeley Way, Berkeley, California 94720. 1985.

POLITICS AND PUBLIC MANAGEMENT: AN INTRODUCTION. Robert E. Crew. West Publishing Company, 50 West Kellogg Boulevard, St. Paul, Minnesota 55164. 1992.

THE POLITICS OF THE ADMINISTRATIVE PROCESS. James W. Fesler and Donald F. Kettl. Chatham House Publishers, Incorporated, P.O. Box 1, Chatham, New Jersey 07928. 1991.

PREFACE TO PUBLIC ADMINISTRATION: A SEARCH FOR THEMES AND DIRECTION. Richard J. Stillman, II. St. Martin's Press, 175 Fifth Avenue, New York, New York 10010. 1991.

PROPOSITION THIRTEEN AND ITS CONSEQUENCES FOR PUBLIC MANAGEMENT. Selma J. Mushkin. University Press of America. 4720 Boston Way, Lanham, Maryland 20706. 1984.

PUBLIC ADMINISTRATION. Second Edition. Jeffrey D. Straussman. Longman Publishing Group, 95 Church Street, White Plains, New York 10601. 1990.

PUBLIC ADMINISTRATION: A COMPARATIVE PERSPECTIVE. Fourth Edition. Ferrel Heady. Marcel Dekker, 720 Madison Avenue, New York, New York 10016. 1991.

PUBLIC ADMINISTRATION: A MANAGEMENT APPROACH. Donald Klinger. Houghton Mifflin Company, 1 Beacon Street, Boston, Massachusetts 02108. 1983.

PUBLIC ADMINISTRATION: A REALISTIC REINTERPRETATION OF CONTEMPORARY PUBLIC MANAGEMENT. Allan W. Lerner and John Wanat. Prentice-Hall, Incorporated, 113 Sylvan Avenue, Englewood Cliffs, New Jersey 07632. 1992.

PUBLIC ADMINISTRATION AND LAW. Bench v. Burcau in the United States. By David H. Rosenblum. Marcel Dekker, Incorporated, 720 Madison Avenue, New York, New York 10016. 1983.

PUBLIC ADMINISTRATION AND PUBLIC AFFAIRS. Fifth Edition. Nicholas L. Henry. Prentice-Hall, Incorporated, 113 Sylvan Avenue, Englewood Cliffs, New Jersey 07632. 1989.

PUBLIC ADMISTRATION IN RURAL AREAS AND SMALL JURISDICTIONS: A GUIDE TO THE LITERATURE. Beth W. Honadle. Garland Publishing, Incorporated, 136 Madison Avenue, New York, New York 10016. 1983.

PUBLIC ADMINISTRATION IN THE UNITED STATES. David Schuman and Dick W. Olufs, III. D.C. Heath and Company, 125 Spring Street, Lexington, Massachusetts 02173. 1988.

PUBLIC ADMINISTRATION: THE STATE OF THE DISCIPLINE. Naomi B. Lynn and Aaron Wildavsky. Chatham House Publishers, Incorporated, P.O. Box 1, Chatham, New Jersey 07928. 1990.

PUBLIC ADMINISTRATION: THE WORK OF GOVERNMENT. Charles R. Barton and William L. Chappell. Scott, Foresman and Company, 1900 East Lake Avenue, Glenview, Illinois 60025. 1985.

THE PUBLIC ADMINISTRATOR AND THE COURTS. John C. Pine and Patricia A. Hollander. Resource Publications, Incorporated, P.O. Box 9267, Asheville, North Carolina 28815. 1985.

PUBLIC LAW AND PUBLIC ADMINISTRATION. Second Edition. Phillip J. Cooper. Mayfield Publishing Company, 1240 Villa Street, Mountain View, California 94041. 1988.

PUBLIC MANAGEMENT IN A DEMOCRATIC SOCIETY. Robert B. Reich. Prentice-Hall, Incorporated, 113 Sylvan Avenue, Englewood Cliffs, New Jersey 07632. 1990.

PUBLIC MANAGEMENT SYSTEMS: MONITORING AND MANAGING GOVERNMENT PERFORMANCE. James E. Swiss. Prentice-Hall, Incorporated, 113 Sylvan Avenue, Englewood Cliffs, New Jersey 07632. 1991.

PUBLIC SECTOR MANAGEMENT. Marcia Lynn Whicker and Todd W. Areson. Praeger Publishers, One Madison Avenue, New York, New York 10010-3603. 1990.

PUBLIC SECTOR MANAGEMENT, SYSTEMS AND ETHICS. Louis C. Gawthrop. Books on Demand, 300 North Zeeb Road, Ann Arbor, Michigan 48106-1346. 1984.

READINGS IN PUBLIC ADMINISTRATION: INSTITUTIONS, PROCESSES, BEHAVIOR, POLICY. Fourth Edition. Robert T. Golembieski and Frank Gibson. Houghton Mifflin Company, 1 Beacon Street, Boston, Massachusetts 02108. 1983.

RESEARCH METHODS FOR PUBLIC ADMINISTRATORS. Elizabethann O'Sullivan and Gary R. Rassel. Longman Publishing Group, 95 Church Street, White Plains, New York 10601. 1989.

THE STATE OF PUBLIC BUREAUCRACY. Larry B. Hill. M.E. Sharpe, Incorporated, 80 Business Park Drive, Armonk, New York 10504. 1992.

UNDERSTANDING AND MANAGING PUBLIC ORGANIZATIONS. Hal G. Rainey. Jossey-Bass, Incorporated, 350 Sansome Street, San Francisco, California 94104. 1991.

ENCYCLOPEDIAS AND DICTIONARIES

THE FACTS ON FILE DICTIONARY OF PUBLIC ADMINISTRATION. Jay M. Shafritz. Facts on File, Subsidiary of Commerce Clearing House, 460 Park Avenue South, New York, New York 10016. 1986.

THE PUBLIC ADMINISTRATION DICTIONARY. Second Edition. R. Chandler and J. Plano. ABC-CLIO, P.O. Box 1911, Santa Barbara, California 93116-1911. 1988.

LAW REVIEWS AND PERIODICALS

PUBLIC ADMINISTRATION REVIEW. American Society for Public Administration, 1225 Connecticut Avenue, Northwest, Washington, D.C. 20036. Bi-monthly.

NEWSLETTERS AND NEWSPAPERS

THE PUBLIC ADMINISTRATOR AND THE COURTS. Research Publications, Incorporated, P.O. Box 9267, Asheville, North Carolina 28815. Quarterly.

BIBLIOGRAPHIES

AMERICAN PUBLIC ADMINISTRATION: A BIBLIOGRAPHICAL GUIDE TO THE LITERATURE. Gerald E. Caiden. Garland Publishing, Incorporated, 136 Madison Avenue, New York, New York 10016. 1984.

THE BUREAUCRATIC STATE: AN ANOTATED BIBLIOGRAPHY. Robert D. Miewald. Garland Publishing, Incorporated, 136 Madison Avenue, New York, New York 10016. 1983.

COMPARATIVE PUBLIC ADMINISTRATION: AN ANNOTATED BIBLIOGRAPHY. Mark W. Huddleston. Garland Publishing, Incorporated, 136 Madison Avenue, New York, New York 10016. 1984.

LAWYERS AS PUBLIC ADMINISTRATORS: A SELECTED BIBLIOGRAPHY. Anthony G. White. Vance Bibliographies, P.O. Box 229, 112 North Charter Street, Monticello, Illinois 61856. 1982.

LEADERSHIP STYLES IN THE PUBLIC AND PRIVATE SECTORS: A SELECTIVE BIBLIOGRAPHY. Jay Marme. Vance Bibliographies, P.O. Box 229, 112 North Charter Street, Monticello, Illinois 61856. 1988.

PUBLIC ADMINISTRATION AND DECISION-AIDING SOFTWARE: IMPROVING PROCEDURE AND SUBSTANCE. Stuart Nagel. Greenwood Publishing Group, Incorporated, 88 Post Road West, P.O. Box 5007, Westport, Connecticut 06881. 1990.

PUBLIC ADMINISTRATION DECISION-MAKING IN THE PUBLIC SECTOR. Joseph C. Santora and Diane Fitzsimmons. Vance Bibliographies, P.O. Box 229, 112 North Charter Street, Monticello, Illinois 61856. 1983.

PUBLIC ADMINISTRATION: THE LAST TWENTY-FIVE YEARS. Keith M. Henderson. Vance Bibliographies, P.O. Box 229, 112 North Charter Street, Monticello, Illinois 61856. 1984.

PUBLIC POLICY AND DECISION-MAKING: JOURNAL ARTICLES, 1983-1987. Dale E. Casper. Vance Bibliographies, P.O. Box 229, 112 North Charter Street, Monticello, Illinois 61856. 1988.

A SOURCE LIST OF PERSONAL COMPUTER PROGRAMS ON RESEARCH AND STATISTICAL ANALYSIS FOR PUBLIC ADMINISTRATION: A SELECTED BIBLIOGRAPHY. Anthony G. White. Vance Bibliographies, P.O. Box 229, 112 North Charter Street, Monticello, Illinois 61856. 1991.

ASSOCIATIONS AND PROFESSIONAL SOCIETIES

AMERICAN SOCIETY FOR PUBLIC ADMINISTRATION. 1120 G Street, Northwest, Suite 500, Washington, D.C. 20005. (202) 393-7878.

NATIONAL ACADEMY OF PUBLIC ADMINISTRATION. 1120 G Street, Northwest, Suite 540, Washington, D.C. 20005. (202) 347-3190.

NATIONAL FORUM FOR BLACK PUBLIC ADMINISTRATORS. 1301 Pennsylvania Avenue, Northwest, Suite 801, Washington, D.C. 20004. (202) 626-4900.

SECTION FOR WOMEN IN PUBLIC ADMINISTRATION. 1120 G Street, Northwest, Suite 500, Washington, D.C. 20005. (202) 393-7878.

RESEARCH CENTERS, INSTITUTES, CLEARINGHOUSES

BUREAU OF PUBLIC ADMINISTRATION. University of Maine, 25 North Stevens Hall, Ororo, Maine 04469. (207) 581-4136.

CENTER FOR PUBLIC AFFAIRS AND ADMINISTRATION. University of Utah, 2120 Annex Building, Salt Lake City, Utah 84112. (801) 581-6491.

DEPARTMENT OF PUBLIC ADMINISTRATION. Pennsylvania State University, 205 Burrowes Building, University Park, Pennsylvania 16802. (814) 865-2536.

INSTITUTE OF PUBLIC ADMINISTRATION. 55 West Forty-fourth Street, New York, New York 10036. (212) 730-5486.

PUBLIC ADMINISTRATION CENTER. San Diego State University, PSFA 100, San Diego, California 82182. (619) 265-6084.

PUBLIC ADMINISTRATION INSTITUTE. Louisiana State University, 3171 CEBA, Baton Rouge, Louisiana 70803. (504) 388-6743.

STATISTICS SOURCES

APPLIED STATISTICS FOR PUBLIC ADMINISTRATION. Kenneth J. Meier and Jeffrey L. Brudney. Brooks/Cole Publishing Company, 511 Forest Lodge Road, Pacific Grove, California 93950. 1987.

STATISTICAL ANALYSIS FOR PUBLIC AND NONPROFIT MANAGERS. Leanna Stiefel. Praeger Publishers, One Madison Avenue, New York, New York 10010-3603. 1990.

PUBLIC ASSISTANCE
See: FEDERAL AID; INDIGENCE

PUBLIC CONTRACTS
See: GOVERNMENT CONTRACTS

PUBLIC CORPORATIONS
See: GOVERNMENT CORPORATIONS; LOCAL GOVERNMENT

PUBLIC DEBTS
See: PUBLIC FINANCE

PUBLIC DEFENDERS
See: LEGAL AID

PUBLIC EMPLOYEES
See: PUBLIC OFFICIALS AND EMPLOYEES

PUBLIC FINANCE
See also: MONEY AND MONETARY CONTROL; TREASURY DEPARTMENT

LOOSELEAF SERVICES AND REPORTERS

GOVERNMENT ACCOUNTING AND FINANCIAL REPORTING MANUAL. William J. Raftery. Research Institute of America, Incorporated, One Penn Plaza, New York, New York 10119. 1991- .

HANDBOOKS, MANUALS, FORMBOOKS

ACCOUNTING AND BUDGETING IN PUBLIC AND NONPROFIT ORGANIZATIONS: A MANAGER'S GUIDE. C. William Garner. Jossey-Bass, Incorporated, 350 Sansome Street, San Francisco, California 94104. 1991.

FINANCIAL HANDBOOK FOR MAYORS AND CITY MANAGERS. Second Edition. Terry N. Clark. Van Nostrand Reinhold Company, Incorporated, 115 Fifth Avenue, New York, New York 10003. 1985.

HANDBOOK OF GOVERNMENTAL ACCOUNTING AND FINANCE. Nicholas G. Apostolou and D. Larry Crumbley. John Wiley and Sons, Incorporated, 605 Third Avenue, New York, New York 10158. 1988.

HANDBOOK ON PUBLIC BUDGETING AND FINANCIAL MANAGEMENT. Jack Rabin and Thomas D. Lynch. Marcel Dekker, Incorporated, 720 Madison Avenue, New York, New York 10016. 1983.

TEXTBOOKS AND GENERAL WORKS

ACCOUNTING AND FINANCIAL REPORTING FOR GOVERNMENTAL AND NONPROFIT ORGANIZATIONS: BASIC CONCEPTS. Robert W. Ingram, Russell J. Petersen, and Susan Work Martin. McGraw-Hill Publishing Company, 1221 Avenue of the Americas, New York, New York 10020. 1991.

ACCOUNTING FOR GOVERNMENTAL AND NONPROFIT ENTITIES. Ninth Edition. Leon E. Hay and Earl R. Wilson. Dow Jones-Irwin, 1818 Ridge Road, Homewood, Illinois 60430. 1992.

APPLYING GOVERNMENT AUDITING STANDARDS. Mortimer A. Dittenhofer. Matthew Bender and Company, Incorporated, 11 Penn Plaza, New York, New York 10001. 1990.

ECONOMIC CONSEQUENCES OF GOVERNMENT DEFICITS. Laurence H. Meyer, Editor. Kluwer Academic Publishers, 101 Philip Drive, Assinippi Park, Norwell, Massachusetts 02061. 1983.

ECONOMICS OF STATE AND LOCAL GOVERNMENT. Henry J. Raimondo. Praeger Publishers, One Madison Avenue, New York, New York 10010-3603. 1991.

ECONOMICS OF THE PUBLIC SECTOR. Second Edition. Joseph E. Stiglitz. W.W. Norton and Company, Incorporated, 500 Fifth Avenue, New York, New York 10110. 1988.

FEDERAL BUDGET AND FINANCIAL MANAGEMENT REFORM. Thomas D. Lynch. Quorum Books, Greenwood Publishing Group, Incorporated, 88 Post Road West, P.O. Box 5007, Westport, Connecticut 06881. 1991.

FINANCING STATE AND LOCAL GOVERNMENT IN THE 1980'S. Roy W. Bahl. Oxford University Press, Incorporated, 200 Madison Avenue, New York, New York 10016. 1984.

FOURTH ANNUAL INSTITUTE ON MUNICIPAL FINANCE. Robert S. Amdursky, Chairman. Practising Law Institute, 810 Seventh Avenue, New York, New York 10019. 1985.

GOVERNMENT FINANCIAL MANAGEMENT THEORY. Gerald J. Miller. Marcel Dekker, 720 Madison Avenue, New York, New York 10016. 1991.

GOVERNMENTAL AND NONPROFIT ACCOUNTING: THEORY AND PRACTICE. Patricia P. Douglas. Harcourt, Brace, Jovanovich, Incorporated, 6277 Sea Harbor Drive, Orlando, Florida 32821. 1991.

GOVERNMENTAL STRUCTURE AND LOCAL PUBLIC FINANCE. David L. Chicoine and Norman Walzer. Oelgeschlager, Gunn and Hain, Incorporated, 245 Mirriam Street, Weston, Massachusetts 02193. 1985.

MANAGING PUBLIC MONEY: AN INTRODUCTION TO PUBLIC FINANCE AND BUDGETING. David Swain. University Press of America, 4720 Boston Way, Lanham, Maryland 20706. 1987.

MODERN PUBLIC FINANCE. Fifth Edition. Bernard P. Herber. Richard D. Irwin, Incorporated, 1818 Ridge Road, Homewood, Illinois 60430. 1983.

THE MUNICIPAL MONEY CHASE: THE POLITICS OF LOCAL GOVERNMENT FINANCE. Alberta Sbragia, Editor. Westview Press, 5500 Central Avenue, Boulder, Colorado 80301. 1983.

PERSPECTIVES ON LOCAL PUBLIC FINANCE AND PUBLIC POLICY. Jai Press, Incorporated, 55 Old Post Road, Number 2, P.O. Box 1678, Greenwich, Connecticut 06830. 1988.

PRINCIPLES OF PUBLIC FINANCE. J. Ronnie Davis and Charles W. Meyer. Prentice-Hall, Incorporated, 113 Sylvan Avenue, Englewood Cliffs, New Jersey 07632. 1983.

PUBLIC BUDGETING AND FINANCE. Third Edition. Robert T. Golembieski and Jack Rabin. Marcel Dekker, Incorporated, 720 Madison Avenue, New York, New York 10016. 1983.

PUBLIC FINANCE. J. Richard Aronson. McGraw-Hill Book Company, 1221 Avenue of the Americas, New York, New York 10020. 1985.

PUBLIC FINANCE. Third Edition. Harvey S. Rosen. Richard D. Irwin, Incorporated, 1818 Ridge Road, Homewood, Illinois 60430. 1992.

PUBLIC FINANCE: A CONTEMPORARY APPLICATION OF THEORY TO POLICY. Third Edition. David N. Hyman. Dryden Press, CBS College Publishing, 383 Madison Avenue, New York, New York 10017. 1990.

PUBLIC FINANCE AND THE POLITICAL PROCESS. Randall G. Holcombe. Southern Illinois University Press, P.O. Box 3697, Carbondale, Illinois 62902-3697. 1983.

PUBLIC FINANCE IN THEORY AND PRACTICE. Fifth Edition. Richard A. Musgrave and Peggy B. Musgrave. McGraw-Hill Publishing Company, 1221 Avenue of the Americas, New York, New York 10020. 1989.

PUBLIC FINANCE: REVENUES AND EXPENDITURES IN A DEMOCRATIC SOCIETY. Richard E. Wagner. Little, Brown, and Company, 34 Beacon Street, Boston, Massachusetts 02108. 1983.

THE PUBLIC FINANCES: AN INTRODUCTORY TEXTBOOK. Sixth Edition. James M. Buchanan and Marilyn R. Flowers. Dow Jones-Irwin, 1818 Ridge Road, Homewood, Illinois 60430. 1987.

PUBLIC SECTOR AUDITING: FEDERAL, STATE AND LOCAL GOVERNMENT UNITS. Second Edition. Cornelius E. Tierney. Commerce Clearing House, Incorporated, 4025 West Peterson Avenue, Chicago, Illinois 60646. 1983.

STATE AND LOCAL GOVERNMENT DEBT FINANCING. M. David Gelfand and Robert S. Amdursky. Callaghan and Company, 155 Pfingsten Road, Deerfield, Illinois 60015. 1990.

STATE AND LOCAL PUBLIC FINANCE. Ronald C. Fisher. Scott, Foresman and Company, 1900 East Lake Avenue, Glenview, Illinois 60025. 1988.

STATE AND LOCAL TAXATION AND FINANCE IN A NUTSHELL. M. David Gelfand and Peter W. Salsich. West Publishing Company, P.O. Box 64526, 50 West Kellogg Boulevard, St. Paul, Minnesota 55164-0526. 1985.

THE THEORY OF PUBLIC CHOICE. James M. Buchanan and Robert D. Tollison. University of Michigan Press, 839 Greene Street, Ann Arbor, Michigan 48106. 1984.

WORKING WITH THE GAO: COURSE MANUAL. Michael A. Hordell and Ronald J. Berger. Federal Publications, 1120 Twentieth Street, Northwest, Washington, D.C. 20036. 1988.

LAW REVIEWS AND PERIODICALS

PUBLIC FINANCE QUARTERLY. Sage Publications, Incorporated, 275 South Beverly Drive, Beverly Hills, California 90212. Quarterly.

BIBLIOGRAPHIES

PUBLIC BUDGETING AND FINANCIAL MANAGEMENT: AN ANNOTATED BIBLIOGRAPHY. Jack Rabin. Garland Publishing, Incorporated, 136 Madison Avenue, New York, New York 10016. 1991.

PUBLIC FINANCE: AN INFORMATION SOURCEBOOK. Marion B. Marshall. Oryx Press, 2214 North Central Avenue, Phoenix, Arizona 85004. 1987.

STATE FINANCE: A BIBLIOGRAPHY. Mary Vance. Vance Bibliographies, P.O. Box 229, 112 North Charter Street, Monticello, Illinois 61856. 1983.

RESEARCH CENTERS, INSTITUTES, CLEARINGHOUSES

GOVERNMENT FINANCE RESEARCH CENTERS. 1750 K Street, Northwest, Suite 200, Washington, D.C. 20006. (202) 429-2750.

STATISTICS SOURCES

CENSUS OF GOVERNMENTS: GOVERNMENTAL FINANCE. U.S. Bureau of the Census. Superintendent of Documents, United States Government Printing Office, Washington, D.C. 20402. Every Five Years.

FACTS AND FIGURES ON GOVERNMENT FINANCE. Tax Foundation, 470 L Street, Ensart Plaza, Southwest, Suite 112, Washington, D.C. 20024. Biennial.

PUBLIC HEALTH
See: HEALTH CARE

PUBLIC HOUSING
See: HOUSING

PUBLIC LAND
See also: EMINENT DOMAIN; GOVERNMENT OWNERSHIP; INTERIOR DEPARTMENT

HANDBOOKS, MANUALS, FORMBOOKS

RESERVED WATER RIGHTS SETTLEMENT MANUAL. Peter W. Sly. Island Press, 1718 Connecticut Avenue, Northwest, Suite 300, Washington, D.C. 20009. 1988.

TEXTBOOKS AND GENERAL WORKS

THE ADMINISTRATIVE PRESIDENCY REVISITED: PUBLIC LANDS, THE BLM, AND THE REAGAN REVOLUTION. Robert F. Durant. State University of New York Press, State University Plaza, Albany, New York 12246. 1992.

THE AMERICAN WILDERNESS AND ITS FUTURE: CONSERVATION VERSUS USE. Edward F. Dolan. Franklin Watts, Incorporated, 387 Park Avenue, South, New York, New York 10016. 1992.

ECONOMIC EFFECTS OF WESTERN FEDERAL LAND USE RESTRICTIONS ON U.S. COAL MARKETS. William D. Watson. United States Geological Survey, Reston, Virginia. 1991.

FEDERAL LANDS POLICY. Phillip O. Foss. Greenwood Publishing Group, Incorporated, 88 Post Road West, P.O. Box 5007, Westport, Connecticut 06881. 1987.

FEDERAL PUBLIC LAND AND RESOURCES LAW. Second Edition. George Cameron Coggins and Charles F. Wilkinson. Foundation Press, 615 Merrick Avenue, Westbury, New York 11590. 1987.

THE LAND OFFICE BUSINESS: THE SETTLEMENT AND ADMINISTRATION OF AMERICAN PUBLIC LANDS, 1789-1837. Malcolm J. Rohrbough. Wadsworth Publishing Company, 10 Davis Drive, Belmont, California 94002. 1990.

LIFE, LIBERTY, AND THE PURSUIT OF LAND: THE PLUNDER OF EARLY AMERICA. Daniel M. Friedenberg. Prometheus Books, 700 East Amherst Street, Buffalo, New York 14215. 1992.

MINERAL RIGHTS ON THE PUBLIC DOMAIN. Michael Braunstein. Anderson Publishing Company, 2035 Reading Road, Cincinnati, Ohio 45202. 1987.

MULTIPLE-USE MANAGEMENT: THE ECONOMICS OF PUBLIC FORESTLANDS. Michael D. Bowes and John V. Krutilla. Resources for the Future, Incorporated, 1616 P Street, Northwest, Washington, D.C. 20036. 1989.

OPPORTUNITY AND CHALLENGE: THE STORY OF BLM. James Muhn and Hanson R. Stuart. United States Department of the Interior, Bureau of Land Management. Superintendent of Documents, United States Government Printing Office, Washington, D.C. 20402. 1988.

PRIVATE RIGHTS AND PUBLIC LAND. Phillip N. Truluck, Editor. Heritage Foundation, 214 Massachusetts Avenue, Northeast, Washington, D.C. 20002. 1983.

PUBLIC LAND LAW AND POLICY. American Law Institute-American Bar Association, Committee on Continuing Professional Education, 4025 Chestnut Street, Philadelphia, Pennsylvania 19104. 1984.

PUBLIC LAND LAW AND PROCEDURE. Ernest C. Baynard III. John Wiley and Sons, Incorporated, 605 Third Avenue, New York, New York 10158. 1986.

PUBLIC LANDS AND THE UNITED STATES ECONOMY: BALANCING CONSERVATION AND DEVELOPMENT. George M. Johnston and Peter M. Emerson. Westview Press, 5500 Central Avenue, Boulder, Colorado 80301. 1984.

PUBLIC LANDS CONFLICT AND RESOLUTION: MANAGING NATIONAL FOREST DISPUTES. Julia M. Wondolleck. Plenum Publishing Corporation, 233 Spring Street, New York, New York 10013. 1988.

THE PUBLIC LANDS IN JACKSONIAN POLITICS. Daniel Feller. University of Wisconsin Press, 114 North Murray Street, Madison, Wisconsin 53706. 1984.

RETHINKING THE FEDERAL LANDS. Sterling Brubaker, Editor. Resources for the Future, Incorporated, 1616 P Street, Northwest, Washington, D.C. 20036. 1984.

RONALD REAGAN AND THE PUBLIC LANDS: AMERICA'S CONSERVATION DEBATE, 1979-1984. C. Brant Short. Texas A & M University Press, Drawer C, Lewis Street, College Station, Texas 77843. 1989.

THIS LAND IS YOUR LAND: THE STRUGGLE TO SAVE AMERICA'S PUBLIC LANDS. Bernard Shanks. Sierra Club Books, Random House Incorporated, Distribution Center, 400 Hahn Road, Westminster, Maryland 21157. 1984.

TOWARD A FEDERAL LAND INFORMATION SYSTEM: EXPERIENCES AND ISSUES. James A. Sturdevant. United States Geological Survey. Superintendent of Documents, United States Government Printing Office, Washington, D.C. 20402. 1988.

A TREATISE ON THE AMERICAN LAW RELATING TO MINES AND MINERAL LANDS WITHIN THE PUBLIC LAND STATES AND TERRITORIES AND GOVERNING THE ACQUISITION AND ENJOYMENT OF MINING RIGHTS IN LANDS OF THE PUBLIC DOMAIN. Third Edition. Curtis H. Lindley. Fred B. Rothman and Company, 10368 West Centennial Road, Littleton, Colorado 80127. 1988. (Reprint).

WESTERN PUBLIC LANDS: THE MANAGEMENT OF NATURAL RESOURCES IN A TIME OF DECLINING FEUDALISM. John G. Francis and Richard Ganzel, Editors. Rowman and Allanheld, 420 Boston Way, Lanham, Maryland 20706. 1984.

WILDERNESS PRESERVATION AND THE SAGEBRUSH REBELLIONS. William L. Graf. Rowman and Littlefield Publishers, Incorporated, 8705 Bollman Place, Savage, Maryland 20763. 1990.

DIGESTS, INDEXES, ABSTRACTS, CITATORS

PUBLIC LAND AND REESOURCES LAW DIGEST. Rocky Mountain Mineral Law Foundation, University of Colorado, Fleming Law Building, Boulder, Colorado 80309. Semiannual.

LAW REVIEWS AND PERIODICALS

PUBLIC LAND LAW REVIEW. University of Montana School of Law, Missoula, Montana 59812. Annual.

NEWSLETTERS AND NEWSPAPERS

IN BRIEF. Sierra Club Legal Defense Fund, 2044 Fillmore Street, San Francisco, California 94115. Quarterly.

SIERRA CLUB NATIONAL NEWS REPORT. Sierra Club, 530 Bush Street, San Francisco, California 94108. Weekly.

BIBLIOGRAPHIES

PUBLIC LANDS: A BIBLIOGRAPHY. Mary Vance. Vance Bibliographies, P.O. Box 229, 112 North Charter Street, Monticello, Illinois 61856. 1983.

PUBLIC POLICY REGULATING PUBLIC LANDS: JOURNAL ARTICLES, 1983-1988. Dale E. Casper. Vance Bibliographies, P.O. Box 229, 112 North Charter Street, Monticello, Illinois 61856. 1989.

ASSOCIATIONS AND PROFESSIONAL SOCIETIES

ASSOCIATION OF NATIONAL GRASSLANDS. Box 1028, Hettinger, North Dakota 58639. (701) 567-4300.

OUTDOORS UNLIMITED. P.O. Box 373, Kaysville, Utah 84037. (801) 544-0960.

PUBLIC LANDS COUNCIL. 1301 Pennsylvania Avenue, Northwest, Suite 300, Washington, D.C. 20004. (202) 347-5355.

SIERRA CLUB. 730 Polk Street, San Francisco, California 94109. (415) 776-2211.

SIERRA CLUB LEGAL DEFENSE FUND. 2044 Fillmore Street, San Francisco, California 94115. (415) 567-6100.

TRUST FOR PUBLIC LAND. 116 New Montgomery Street, Fourth Floor, San Francisco, California 94105. (415) 495-4014.

STATISTICS SOURCES

PUBLIC LAND STATISTICS. Department of the Interior, Bureau of Land Management. Superintendent of Documents, United States Government Printing Office, Washington, D.C. 20402. Annual.

PUBLIC LEGAL SERVICES
See: LEGAL AID

PUBLIC MEETINGS
See: FREEDOM OF ASSEMBLY AND ASSOCIATION; FREEDOM OF INFORMATION

PUBLIC OFFICIALS AND EMPLOYEES
See also: CIVIL SERVICE; MERIT SYSTEMS PROTECTION BOARD; OFFICE OF PERSONNEL MANAGEMENT; STATE DEPARTMENT

LOOSELEAF SERVICES AND REPORTERS

DISCIPLINE AND GRIEVANCES. Bureau of Business Practice, 24 Rope Ferry Road, Waterford, Connecticut 06386. 1978- .

ETHICS IN GOVERNMENT REPORTER. Washington Service Bureau, Incorporated, 655 Fifteenth Street, Northwest, Washington, D.C. 20005. 1980- .

FEDERAL PAY AND BENEFITS REPORTER. Labor Relations Press, P.O. Box 579, Fort Washington, Pennsylvania 19034. 1985- .

GOVERNMENT EMPLOYEE RELATIONS REPORT. Bureau of National Affairs, 1231 Twenty-fifth Street, Northwest, Washington, D.C. 20037. 1963- .

MERIT SYSTEMS PROTECTION BOARD SERVICE. Hawkins Publishing Company, Incorporated, 310 Tahiti Way, Number 108, Marina Del Rey, California 90291. 1984- .

NATIONAL PUBLIC EMPLOYMENT REPORTER. Labor Relations Press, P.O. Box 579, Fort Washington, Pennsylvania 19034. 1979- .

PUBLIC EMPLOYEE BARGAINING. Commerce Clearing House, Incorporated, 4025 West Peterson Avenue, Chicago, Illinois 60646. 1977- .

PUBLIC EMPLOYEE LABOR LAW. Daniel P. Sullivan. Anderson Publishing Company, 2035 Reading Road, Cincinnati, Ohio 45202. 1969- .

PUBLIC EMPLOYEE LAW BULLETIN. Quinlan Press, 131 Beverly Street, Boston, Massachusetts 02115. 1984- .

PUBLIC PERSONEL ADMINISTRATION - POLICIES AND PRACTICES FOR PERSONEL. Prentice-Hall Information Services, 113 Sylvan Avenue, Englewood Cliffs, New Jersey 07632. 1973- .

PUBLIC OFFICIALS AND EMPLOYEES

TEXTBOOKS AND GENERAL WORKS

IMPOSSIBLE JOBS IN PUBLIC MANAGEMENT. Erwin C. Hargrove and John C. Glidewell. University Press of Kansas, 329 Carruth, Lawrence, Kansas 66045. 1990

MERIT SYSTEMS PROTECTION BOARD: RIGHTS AND REMEDIES. Robert G. Vaughn. Law Journal Seminars-Press, 111 Eighth Avenue, New York, New York 10011. 1984.

PERSONAL LIABILITY OF PUBLIC OFFICIALS UNDER FEDERAL LAW. Fourth Edition. Paul T. Hardy and J. Devereux Weeks. Carl Vinson School of Government, University of Georgia, Terrell Hall, Athens, Georgia 30602. 1988.

PUBLIC EMPLOYEES, UNIONS AND THE EROSION OF CIVIC TRUST: A STUDY OF SAN FRANCISCO IN THE 1970'S. Randolph H. Boehm and Dan C. Heldman. Greenwood Publishing Group, Incorporated, 88 Post Road West, P.O. Box 5007, Westport, Connecticut 06881. 1982.

PUBLIC PERSONNEL ADMINISTRATION, LABOR - MANAGEMENT RELATIONS. Prentice-Hall, Incorporated, 113 Sylvan Avenue, Englewood Cliffs, New Jersey 07632. 1973.

PUBLIC SERVICE ACCOUNTABILITY: A COMPARATIVE PERSPECTIVE. Joseph G. Jabbra and O. P. Dwivedi. Kumarian Press, Incorporated, 630 Oakwood Avenue, Suite 119, West Hartford, Connecticut 06110-1529. 1989.

NEWSLETTERS AND NEWSPAPERS

WEEKLY FEDERAL EMPLOYEES' NEWS DIGEST. Federal Employees' News Digest Incorporated, 510 North Washington Street, Suite 200, Falls Church, Virginia 22046. Weekly.

BIBLIOGRAPHIES

LABOR MANAGEMENT RELATIONS IN THE PUBLIC SECTOR: AN ANOTATED BIBLIOGRAPHY. N. Joseph Cayer and Sherry S. Dickerson. Garland Publishing, Incorporated, 136 Madison Avenue, New York, New York 10016. 1984.

PUBLIC SECTOR EMPLOYMENT: GENERAL ISSUES AND TRENDS, JOURNAL ARTICLES, 1982-1988. Dale E. Casper. Vance Bibliographies, P.O. Box 229, 112 North Charter Street, Monticello, Illinois 61856. 1989.

PUBLIC PROPERTY
See: PUBLIC LAND

PUBLIC PROSECUTORS

STATUTES, CODES, STANDARDS, UNIFORM LAWS

NATIONAL PROSECUTION STANDARDS. Second Edition. National District Attorneys Association, 1033 North Fairfax Street, Alexandria, Virginia 22314. 1991.

LOOSELEAF SERVICES AND REPORTERS

PROSECUTORIAL MISCONDUCT. Bennet L. Gershman. Clark Boardman Company, Limited, 435 Hudson Street, New York, New York 10014. 1985- .

HANDBOOKS, MANUALS, FORMBOOKS

CASEWEIGHTING SYSTEMS FOR PROSECUTORS: GUIDELINES AND PROCEDURES. Joan Jacoby. United States Department of Justice. Superintendent of Documents, United States Government Printing Office, Washington, D.C. 20402. 1987.

NARCOTICS PROSECUTOR'S TRAINING MANUAL. New York (State) Office of the Special Narcotics Prosecutor, 80 Centre Street, New York, New York 10013. 1990.

TEXTBOOKS AND GENERAL WORKS

INVESTIGATING AND PROSECUTING DRUG OFFENSES. American Prosecutors Research Institute, 1033 North Fairfax Street, Suite 200, Alexandria, Virginia 22314. 1989.

THE PROSECUTOR IN AMERICA'S COURTS AND THE CRIMINAL JUSTICE SYSTEM. David W. Neubauer. Brooks/Cole Publishing Company, 511 Forest Lodge Road, Pacific Grove, California 93950. 1984.

PROSECUTORIAL MISCONDUCT. Bennett L. Gershman. Clark Boardman Company, Limited, 435 Hudson Street, New York, New York 10014. 1984. (Annual Supplements).

PROSECUTORIAL MISCONDUCT: LAW, PROCEDURE, FORMS. Joseph F. Lawless. Michie Company, P.O. Box 7587, Charlottesville, Virginia 22906-7587. 1985. (Supplements).

THE PROSECUTORS: INSIDE THE OFFICES OF THE GOVERNMENT'S MOST POWERFUL LAWYERS. James B. Stewart. Simon and Schuster, Incorporated, 1230 Avenue of the Americas, New York, New York 10020. 1987.

PROSECUTOR'S REACH: LEGAL ISSUES AND THE NEW RELIGIONS. William C. Shepard. Crossroad Publishing Company, 575 Lexington Avenue, New York, New York 10022. 1982.

LAW REVIEWS AND PERIODICALS

THE PROSECUTOR. National District Attorney's Association, 708 Pendleton Street, Alexandria, Virginia 22314. Bi-monthly.

BIBLIOGRAPHIES

BIBLIOGRAPHIC GUIDE FOR PROSECUTORS. National College of Distric Attorneys, University of Houston, Law Center, Houston, Texas 77204-6380. (Annual).

DIRECTORIES

NATIONAL DIRECTORY OF PROSECUTING ATTORNEYS. National District Attorneys Association, 1033 North Fairfax Street, Suite 200, Alexandria, Virginia 22314. Biennial.

ASSOCIATIONS AND PROFESSIONAL SOCIETIES

NATIONAL ASSOCIATION OF COUNTY CIVIL ATTORNEYS. c/o National Association of Counties, 440 First Street, Northwest, Washington, D.C. 20001. (202) 393-6226.

NATIONAL COLLEGE OF DISTRICT ATTORNEYS. University of Houston, Law Center, Houston, Texas 77204. (713) 747-6232.

NATIONAL DISTRICT ATTORNEYS ASSOCIATION. 1033 North Fairfax Street, Suite 200, Alexandria, Virginia 22314. (703) 549-9222.

PUBLIC RECORDS
See: FREEDOM OF INFORMATION

PUBLIC UTILITIES
See also: ENERGY; FEDERAL ENERGY REGULATORY COMMISSION; LOCAL GOVERNMENT; OIL AND GAS

LOOSELEAF SERVICES AND REPORTERS

LAW OF INDEPENDENT POWER: DEVELOPMENT, COGENERATION, UTILITY REGULATION. Steven Ferrey. Clark Boardman Company, Limited, 435 Hudson Street, New York, New York 10014. 1989.

PUBLIC UTILITIES REPORTS. Fourth Series. Public Utilities Reports, Incorporated, 2111 Wilson Boulevard, Suite 200, Arlington, Virginia 22201. 1974- .

STATE ACTION REPORTER: GAS AND ELECTRIC. Regula- tory Information Service, 4520 East-West Highway, Bethesda, Maryland 20814. 1984- .

UTILITIES LAW REPORTER. Commerce Clearing House, Incorporated, 4025 West Peterson Avenue, Chicago, Illinois 60646. 1965- .

TEXTBOOKS AND GENERAL WORKS

AMERICAN ELECTRIC UTILITIES: PAST, PRESENT, AND FUTURE. Second Edition. Leonard Hyman. Public Utilities Reports, Incorporated, 2111 Wilson Boulevard, Suite 200, Arlington, Virginia 22201. 1985.

AMERICA'S ELECTRIC UTILITIES: UNDER SEIGE AND IN TRANSITION. Scott Fenn. Praeger Publishers, One Madison Avenue, New York, New York 10010-3603. 1984.

DEREGULATION: APPRAISAL BEFORE THE FACT. Thomas G. Gies and Werner Sichel, Editors. University of Michigan, Division of Research, Graduate School of Business Administration, Ann Arbor, Michigan 48109-1234. 1982.

THE DIMMING OF AMERICA: THE REAL COSTS OF ELECTRIC UTILITY REGULATORY FAILURE. Peter Navarro. Ballinger Division, HarperCollins, Incorporated, 10 East Fifty-third Street, New York, New York 10022. 1985.

ELECTRIC POWER: DEREGULATION AND THE PUBLIC INTREST. John C. Moorhouse. Public Policy Research, 177 Post Street, San Francisco, California 94108. 1986.

MARKETS FOR POWER: AN ANALYSIS OF ELECTRIC UTILITY DEREGULATION. Paul L. Joskow and Richard Schmalensee. MIT Press, 55 Hayward Street, Cambridge, Massachusetts 02142. 1988.

NATURAL MONOPOLY REGULATION: PRINCIPLES AND PRACTICE. Sanford V. Berg and John Tschirhart. Cambridge University Press, 40 West Twentieth Street, New York, New York 10011. 1988.

THE POLITICS OF PUBLIC UTILITY REGULATION. William T. Gormley Jr., University of Pittsburgh Press, 127 North Bellefield Avenue, Pittsburgh, Pennsylvania 15260. 1983.

PRICE LEVEL REGULATION FOR DIVERSIFIED PUBLIC UTILITIES: AN ASSESSMENT. Jordan Jay Hillman and Ronald R. Braeutigam. Kluwer Academic Publishers, 101 Philip Drive, Assinippi Park, Norwell, Massachusetts 02061. 1989.

PROJECT FINANCING 1990: POWER GENERATION, WASTE RECOVERY, AND OTHER FACILITIES. Robert Thornton Smith, Chairman. Practising Law Institute, 810 Seventh Avenue, New York, New York 10019. 1987.

PUBLIC UTILITIES: REGULATION, MANAGEMENT AND OWNERSHIP. Martin T. Farris and Roy J. Sampson. Waveland Press, Incorporated, P.O. Box 400, Prospect Heights, Illinois 60070. 1984.

RATE-MAKING TRENDS IN THE 1980S: READINGS AND RATE CASE REPORTS FROM PUBLIC UTILITIES FORTNIGHTLY, 1978-1988. Bruce W. Radford. Public Utilities Reports, Incorporated, 2111 Wilson Boulevard, Suite 200, Arlington, Virginia 22201. 1988.

REFORMING THE REGULATION OF ELECTRIC UTILITIES: PRIORITIES FOR THE 1980'S. Richard L. Gordon, Lexington Books, 125 Spring Street, Lexington, Massachusetts 02173. 1982.

REGULATED INDUSTRIES IN A NUTSHELL. Second Edition. Ernest Gellhorn and Richard J. Pierce, Jr. West Publishing Company, 50 West Kellogg Boulevard, St. Paul, Minnesota 55164. 1987.

REGULATING UTILITIES WITH MANAGEMENT INCENTIVES: A STRATEGY FOR IMPROVED PERFORMANCE. Kurt A. Strasser and Mark F. Kohler. Quorum Books, Greenwood Publishing Group, Incorporated, 88 Post Road West, P.O. Box 5007, Westport, Connecticut 06881. 1989.

THE REGULATION OF PUBLIC UTILITIES: THEORY AND PRACTICE. Second Edition. Charles F. Phillips, Jr. Public Utilities Reports, Incorporated, 2111 Wilson Boulevard, Suite 200, Arlington, Virginia 22201. 1988.

REGULATORY FINANCE: FINANCIAL FOUNDATIONS OF RATE OF RETURN REGULATION. Howard E. Thompson. Kluwer Academic Publishers, 101 Philip Drive, Assinippi Park, Norwell, Massachusetts 02061. 1991.

PUBLIC UTILITIES

REGULATORY INTERVENTIONISM IN THE UTILITY INDUSTRY: FAIRNESS, EFFICIENCY, AND THE PURSUIT OF ENERGY CONSERVATION. Barbara R. Barkovich. Quorum Books, Greenwood Publishing Group, Incorporated, 88 Post Road West, P.O. Box 5007, Westport, Connecticut 06881. 1989.

DIGESTS, INDEXES, ABSTRACTS, CITATORS

PUBLIC UTILITIES REPORT DIGEST. Third Series. Public Utilities Reports, Incorporated, 2111 Wilson Boulevard, Suite 200, Arlington, Virginia 22201. 1983- .

SHEPARD'S FEDERAL ENERGY LAW CITATIONS. Shepard's/McGraw-Hill, P.O. Box 1235, Colorado Springs, Colorado 80901. 1982- .

ANNUALS AND SURVEYS

SURVEY OF PENDING STATE LEGISLATION PERTAINING TO UTILITY REGULATION. Paul Rodgers and Michael Foley. National Association of Regulatory Utility Commissioners, P.O. Box 684, 1102 Interstate Commerce Commission Building, Constitution Avenue and Twelfth Street, Northwest, Washington, D.C. 20044-0864. 1984.

LAW REVIEWS AND PERIODICALS

PUBLIC UTILITIES FORTNIGHTLY. Public Utilities Reports, Incorporated, 1828 L Street, Northwest, Washington, D.C. 20036. Bi-weekly.

NEWSLETTERS AND NEWSPAPERS

EEI WASHINGTON LETTER. Edison Electric Institute, 1111 Nineteenth Street, Northwest, Washington, D.C. 20036. Weekly.

NARUC BULLETIN. National Association of Regulatory Utility Commissioners, 1102 ICC Building, P.O. Box 684, Washington, D.C. 20044. Weekly.

NRECA/APPA LEGAL REPORTING SERVICE. National Rural Electric Cooperative Association, 1800 Massachusetts Avenue, Northwest, Washington, D.C. 20036. Monthly.

UTILITY SECTION NEWSLETTER. American Bar Association, Section on Public Utililty Law, 750 North Lake Shore Drive, Chicago, Illinois 60611. Quarterly.

BIBLIOGRAPHIES

PUBLIC UTILITIES: AN ANNOTATED GUIDE TO INFORMATION SOURCES. Anne C. Roess. Scarecrow Press, Incorporated, 52 Liberty Street, Box 4167, Metuchen, New Jersey 08840. 1991.

PUBLIC UTILITIES LAW ANTHOLOGY. Fred C. Cooper, Editor. International Library Book Publishers, Incorporated, 101 Lake Forest Boulevard, Suite 270, Gaithersburg, Maryland 20877. 1991.

REGULATION OF PUBLIC UTILITIES: LAW AND LEGISLATION, JOURNAL ARTICLES, 1983-1988. Dale E. Casper. Vance Bibliographies, P.O. Box 229, 112 North Charter Street, Monticello, Illinois 61856. 1989.

DIRECTORIES

MOODY'S PUBLIC UTILITY MANUAL. Moody's Investors Service, Incorporated, 99 Church Street, New York, New York 10007. Annual.

ASSOCIATIONS AND PROFESSIONAL SOCIETIES

AMERICAN BAR ASSOCIATION, SECTION OF PUBLIC UTILITY LAW. 750 North Lake Shore Drive, Chicago, Illinois 60611. (312) 988-5000.

NATIONAL ASSOCIATION OF REGULATORY UTILITY COMMISSIONERS. 1102 ICC Building, Washington, D.C. 20044. (202) 898-2200.

NATIONAL ASSOCIATION OF STATE UTILITY CONSUMER ADVOCATES. 1101 Fourteenth Street, Northwest, Suite 808, Washington, D.C. 20005. (202) 727-3908.

UTILITY COMMUNICATORS INTERNATIONAL. c/o Robert Janko, 5050 Quorum Drive, Suite 243, Dallas, Texas 75240. (214) 404-9249.

RESEARCH CENTERS, INSTITUTES, CLEARINGHOUSES

EDISON ELECTRIC INSTITUTE. 1111 Nineteenth Street, Northwest, Washington, D.C. 20036. (202) 778-6400.

INSTITUTES OF PUBLIC UTILITIES. Michigan State University, 113 Olds Hall, East Lansing, Michigan 48824. (517) 355-1876.

NATIONAL REGULATORY RESEARCH INSTITUTE. Ohio State University, 1080 Carmack Road, Columbus, Ohio 43210. (614) 292-9404.

PUBLIC UTILITY RESEARCH CENTER. College of Business Administration, University of Florida, 361 Business Building, Gainesville, Florida 32611. (904) 392-6148.

WISCONSIN PUBLIC UTILITY INSTITUTE. University of Wisconsin, Madison, Graduate School of Business, 1155 Observatory Drive, Madison, Wisconsin 53706. (608) 263-4180.

ONLINE DATABASES

FROM THE STATE CAPITALS: PUBLIC UTILITIES. Wakeman Walwonth, Incorporated, 300 North Washington Street, Suite 204, Alexandria, Virginia 22314.

LEXIS PUBLIC UTILITIES LAW LIBRARY. Mead Data Central. P.O Box 933, Dayton, Ohio 45401.

PUBLIC UTILITIES REPORTS. Public Utilities Reports, Incorporated, 2111 Wilson Boulevard, Suite 200, Arlington, Virginia 22201.

UTILITY REPORTER-FUELS, ENERGY AND POWER. Merton Allen Associates, P.O. Box 9136, Schenectady, New York 12309.

WESTLAW ENERGY LIBRARY. West Publishing Company, 50 West Kellogg Boulevard, St. Paul, Minnesota 55164.

STATISTICS SOURCES

STANDARD AND POOR'S INDUSTRY SURVEYS. Standard and Poor's Corporation, 25 Broadway, New York, New York 10004. Weekly.

PUBLIC WELFARE
See: FEDERAL AID; INDIGENCE

PUBLISHERS AND AUTHORS
See: AUTHORS AND PUBLISHERS; COPYRIGHT

PUNISHMENT
See also: CAPITAL PUNISHMENT

HANDBOOKS, MANUALS, FORMBOOKS

THE UNITED NATIONS CONVENTION AGAINST TORTURE: A HANDBOOK ON THE CONVENTION AGAINST TORTURE AND OTHER CRUEL, INHUMAN, OR DEGRADING TREATMENT OR PUNISHMENT. J. Herman Burgers and Hans Danelius. Kluwer Academic Publishers, 101 Philip Drive, Assinippi Park, Norwell, Massachusetts 02061. 1988.

TEXTBOOKS AND GENERAL WORKS

BLAME AND PUNISHMENT: ESSAYS IN THE CRIMINAL LAW. Sanford H. Kadish. Macmillan Publishing Company, Incorporated, 866 Third Avenue, New York, New York 10022. 1987.

THE BROTHEL BOY, AND OTHER PARABLES OF THE LAW. Norval Morris. Oxford University Press, 200 Madison Avenue, New York, New York 10016. 1992.

CRIME, GUILT, AND PUNISHMENT: A PHILOSOPHICAL INTRODUCTION. C. L. Ten. Oxford University Press, 200 Madison Avenue, New York, New York 10016. 1987.

JUST AND PAINFUL: THE CASE FOR CORPORAL PUNISHMENT IN CRIMINAL JUSTICE. Graeme Newman. Macmillan Publishing Company, Incorporated, 866 Third Avenue, New York, New York 10022. 1983.

JUSTIFYING LEGAL PUNISHMENT. Igor Primorac. Humanities Press International, Incorporated, 171 First Avenue, Atlantic Highlands, New Jersey 07716-1289. 1989.

LITIGATING MORALITY: AMERICAN LEGAL THOUGHT AND ITS ENGLISH ROOTS. Alice Fleetwood Bartee and Wayne C. Bartee. Praeger Publishers, One Madison Avenue, New York, New York 10010-3603. 1992.

MAKING GOOD: PRISONS, PUNISHMENT AND BEYOND. Martin Wright. Humanities Press International, Incorporated, 171 First Avenue, Atlantic Highlands, New Jersey 07716-1289. 1982.

POLICE, PRISON, AND PUNISHMENT: MAJOR HISTORICAL INTERPRETATIONS. Kermit L. Hall. Garland Publishing, Incorporated, 136 Madison Avenue, New York, New York 10016. 1987.

THE POWER TO PUNISH: CONTEMPORARY PENALTY AND SOCIAL ANALYSIS. David Garland and Peter Young, Editors. Humanities Press International, Incorporated, 171 First Avenue, Atlantic Highlands, New Jersey 07716-1289. 1983.

PRISON ON TRIAL: A CRITICAL ASSESSMENT. Thomas Mathiesen. Sage Publications, 2455 Teller Road, Newbury Park, California 91320. 1990.

THE PUBLIC INTEREST ON CRIME AND PUNISHMENT. Nathan Glazer, Editor. University Press of America, 4720 Boston Way, Lanham, Maryland 20706. 1984.

PUNISHING CRIMINALS: CONCERNING A VERY OLD AND PAINFUL QUESTION. Ernest van den Haag. University Press of America, 4720 Boston Way, Lanham, Maryland 20706. 1991.

PUNISHMENT: A PHILOSOPHICAL AND CRIMINOLOGICAL INQUIRY. Phillip Bean. Basil Blackwell, Incorporated, 3 Cambridge Center, Cambridge, Massachusetts 02142. 1981.

PUNISHMENT AND MODERN SOCIETY: A STUDY IN SOCIAL THEORY. David Garland. Oxford University Press, 200 Madison Avenue, New York, New York 10016. 1990.

PUNISHMENT AND PENAL DISCIPLINE: ESSAYS ON THE PRISON AND THE PRISONER'S MOVEMENT. Second Edition. Tony Platt and Paul Takagi. Crime and Social Justice Associates, 2701 Folsom, San Francisco, California 94140. 1982.

PUNISHMENT AND RESTITUTION: A RESTITUTIONARY APPROACH TO CRIME AND THE CRIMINAL. Charles F. Abel and Frank H. Marsh. Greenwood Publishing Group, Incorporated, 88 Post Road West, P.O. Box 5007, Westport, Connecticut 06881. 1984.

PUNISHMENT AND WELFARE: A HISTORY OF PENAL STRATEGIES. David Garland. Gower Publishing Company, Old Post Road, Brookfield, Vermont 05036. 1987.

PUNISHMENT BEFORE TRIAL: AN ORGANIZATION PERSPECTIVE OF FELONY BAIL PROCESSES. Roy B. Fleming. Longman, Incorporated, 19 West Forty-fourth Street, New York, New York 10036. 1983.

REFORM AND PUNISHMENT: ESSAYS ON CRIMINAL SENTENCING. Michael Tonry and Franklin E. Zimring, Editors. University of Chicago Press, 5801 Ellis Avenue, Chicago, Illinois 60637. 1983.

SANCTIONS-SYSTEMS IN THE MEMBER-STATES OF THE COUNCIL OF EUROPE. Anton M. van Kalmthout and Peter J. P. Tak. Kluwer Law Book Publishers, Incorporated, 36 West Forty-fourth Street, New York, New York 10036. 1988.

THE URGINGS OF CONSCIENCE: A THEORY OF PUNISHMENT. Jacob Adler. Temple University Press, 1601 North Broad Street, University Services Building, Philadelphia, Pennsylvania 19122. 1991.

VISIONS OF SOCIAL CONTROL: CRIME, PUNISHMENT AND CLASSIFICATION. Stanley Cohen. Polity Press, Basil Blackwell Incorporated, 3 Cambridge Center, Cambridge, Massachusetts 02142. 1985.

WHY PEOPLE OBEY THE LAW. Tom R. Tyler. Yale University Press, 302 Temple Street, New Haven, Connecticut 06520. 1990.

WHY PUNISH? Nigel Walker. Oxford University Press, 200 Madison Avenue, New York, New York 10016. 1991.

BIBLIOGRAPHIES

CRIME AND PUNISHMENT IN AMERICA: A HISTORICAL BIBLIOGRAPHY. ABC-Clio Information Services, P.O. Box 1911, Santa Barbara, California 93116-1911. 1984.

Q

QUASI-CONTRACT
See: RESTITUTION

QUOTATIONS
See: LEGAL QUOTATIONS

R

RACE DISCRIMINATION
See: DISCRIMINATION, RACE

RACKETEERING
See: ORGANIZED CRIME

RADIO
See: TELEVISION AND RADIO

RAILROADS
See also: TRANSPORTATION

STATUTES, CODES, STANDARDS, UNIFORM LAWS

THE RAILWAY LABOR ACT OF 1926: A LEGISLATIVE HISTORY. Michael H. Campbell and Edward C. Brewer, III. American Bar Association, Section of Labor and Employment Law, 750 North Lake Shore Drive, Chicago, Illinois 60611. 1988.

LOOSELEAF SERVICES AND REPORTERS

FEDERAL CARRIERS REPORTER. Commerce Clearing House, Incorporated, 4025 West Peterson Avenue, Chicago, Illinois 60646. 1962- .

INTERSTATE COMMERCE COMMISSION REPORTS. Superintendent of Documents, United States Government Printing Office, Washington, D.C. 20402. 1887-1984.

INTERSTATE COMMERCE COMMISSION REPORTS, SECOND SERIES. Superintendent of Documents, United States Government Printing Office, Washington, D.C. 20402. Forthcoming.

NATIONAL RAILROAD ADJUSTMENT BOARD. Superintendent of Documents, United States Government Printing Office, Washington, D.C. 20402. 1934- .

RAIL CARRIER SERVICE. Hawkins Publishing Company, 310 Tahiti Way, Number 108, Marina Del Rey, California 90291. 1927- .

RAIL DEREGULATION ACT MONITOR. Traffic Service Corporation, 424 West Thirty-third Street, New York, New York 10001. 1980- .

HANDBOOKS, MANUALS, FORMBOOKS

A GUIDE FOR PUBLIC PARTICIPATION IN RAIL ABANDONMENT CASES UNDER THE INTERSTATE COMMERCE ACT. Third Edition. Interstate Commerce Commission, Office of Public Assistance, Washington, D.C. 1990.

GUIDELINES FOR STATE REGULATION OF RAIL CARRIERS UNDER THE STAGGERS RAIL ACT OF 1980. National Association of Regulatory Utility Commissioners, P.O. Box 684, 1102 Interstate Commerce Commission Building, Constitution Avenue and Twelfth Streets, Northwest, Washington, D.C. 20044-0864. 1981.

TEXTBOOKS AND GENERAL WORKS

AIR AND RAIL LABOR RELATIONS: A JUDICIAL HISTORY OF THE RAILWAY LABOR ACT. John W. Gohman, editor. Kendall/Hunt Publishing Company, 2460 Kerper Boulevard, Dubuque, Iowa 52001. 1979.

FREIGHT TRANSPORT REGULATION: EQUITY, EFFICIENCY AND COMPETITION IN THE RAIL AND TRUCKING INDUSTRIES. Ann F. Friedlaender and Richard H. Spady. MIT Press, 55 Hayward Street, Cambridge, Massachusetts 02142. 1981.

HISTORY OF RAILROAD ACCIDENTS, SAFETY PRECAUTIONS AND OPERATING PRACTICES. Second Edition. Robert B. Shaw. Northern Press, 18 Cedar Street, Potsdam, New York 13676. 1978.

THE INTERSTATE COMMERCE COMMISSION AND THE RAILROAD INDUSTRY: A HISTORY OF REGULATORY POLICY. Richard D. Stone, Praeger Publishers, One Madison Avenue, New York, New York 10010. 1991.

RAILROADS AND LAND GRANT POLICY: A STUDY OF GOVERNMENT INTERVENTION. Loyld J. Mercer. Academy Press, 5037 North Academy Boulevard, Colorado Springs, Colorado 80918. 1982.

THE THEORY OF CONTESTABLE MARKETS: APPLICATIONS TO REGULATORY AND ANTITRUST PROBLEMS IN THE RAIL INDUSTRY. William B. Tye. Greenwood Publishing Group, Incorporated, 88 Post Road West, P.O. Box 5007, Westport, Connecticut 06881. 1990.

ENCYCLOPEDIAS AND DICTIONARIES

A DICTIONARY OF RAILROAD TERMS. W.E. Wood. P.O. Box 143, Belen, New Mexico 87002. 1990.

RAILROADS

THE DICTIONARY OF RAILWAY TRACK TERMS. Christopher F. Schulte. RCON Services, P.O. Box 153, Philadelphia, Pennsylvania 19152. 1989.

LAW REVIEWS AND PERIODICALS

RAILWAY AGE. Railway Age, P.O. Box 530, Bristol, Connecticut 06010. Monthly.

NEWSLETTERS AND NEWSPAPERS

NARP NEWS. National Association of Railroad Passengers, 236 Massachusetts Avenue, Northeast, Suite 603, Washington, D.C. 20002. Monthly

NARUC BULLETIN. National Association of Regulatory Utility Commissioners, P.O. Box 684, 1102 Interstate Commerce Commission Building, Constitution Avenue and Twelfth Streets, Northwest, Washington, D.C. 20423. Weekly.

RAIL NEWS UPDATE. Association of American Railroads, 50 F Street, Northwest, Washington, D.C. 20001-1564. Biweekly.

SPEEDLINES. High Speed Rail Association, 206 Valley Court, Suite 800, Pittsburgh, Pennsylvania 15237. Monthly.

UNITED STATES RAIL NEWS. Business Publishers, Incorporated, 951 Pershing Drive, Silver Spring, Maryland 20910. Biweekly.

BIBLIOGRAPHIES

RECREATIONAL REUSE OF ABANDONED RAILROAD RIGHTS-OF-WAYS: A BIBLIOGRAPHY AND TECHNICAL RESOURCE GUIDE FOR PLANNERS. Gregory P. Ames. Council of Planning Librarians, 1313 East Sixtieth Street, Chicago, Illinois 60637-2897. 1981.

DIRECTORIES

RAILROAD NAMES: A DIRECTORY OF COMMON CARRIER RAILROADS OPERATING IN THE UNITED STATES, 1826-1989. William D. Edson. William D. Edson, 10820 Gainsborough Road, Potomac, Maryland 20854. 1989.

WHO'S WHO IN RAILROADING AND RAIL TRANSIT. Twentieth Edition. National Railway Publication Company, 424 West Thirty-third Street, Eleventh Floor, New York, New York 10001. 1985 (Irregular).

ASSOCIATIONS AND PROFESSIONAL SOCIETIES

AMERICAN COUNCIL OF RAILROAD WOMEN. c/o Melody A. Sheahan, CSX Transportation, 500 Water Street, Jacksonville, Florida 32202. (904) 359-7466.

ASSOCIATION OF AMERICAN RAILROADS. American Railroads Building, Fifty F Street, Northwest, Washington, D.C. 20001. (202) 639-2100.

HIGH SPEED RAIL ASSOCIATION. 206 Valley Court, Suite 800, Pittsburgh, Pennsylvania 15237. (412) 364-9306.

NATIONAL ASSOCIATION OF RAILROAD PASSENGERS. 236 Massachusetts Avenue, Northeast, Suite 603, Washington, D.C. 20002. (202) 546-1550.

NATIONAL ASSOCIATION OF RAILROAD TRIAL COUNSEL. 88 Allina Real Drive, Suite 218, Pacific Palisades, California 90272. (213) 459-7659.

NATIONAL ASSOCIATION OF RAILWAY BUSINESS WOMEN. c/o Jane Sebeczek, 2060 Charlton Avenue, Suite 201, West St. Paul, Minnesota 55118. (612) 450-7310.

NATIONAL ASSOCIATION OF REGULATORY UTILITY COMMISSIONERS. P.O. Box 684, 1102 Interstate Commerce Commission Building, Constitution Avenue and Twelfth Streets, Northwest, Washington, D.C. 20423. (202) 898-2200.

NATIONAL INDUSTRIAL TRANSPORTATION LEAGUE. 1090 Vermont Avenue, Northwest, Suite 410, Washington, D.C. 20005. (202) 842-3870.

NATIONAL RAILWAY LABOR CONFERENCE. 1901 L Street, Northwest, Suite 500, Washington, D.C. 20036. (202) 862-7200.

SENATE RAIL CAUCUS. 154 Russell Senate Office Buiding, Washington, D.C. 20510. (202) 224-2000.

RESEARCH CENTERS, INSTITUTES, CLEARINGHOUSES

AMERICAN RAILWAY CAR INSTITUTE. Building Five, 19900 Governor's Drive, Suite 10, Olympia Fields, Illinois 60461. (312) 747-0511.

ASSOCIATION OF AMERICAN RAILROADS RESEARCH AND TEST DEPARTMENT. 50 F Street, Northwest, Washington, D.C. 20001. (202) 639-2250.

RAIL SYSTEMS CENTER. Mellon Institute, Carnagie-Mellon University, 4400 Fifth Avenue, Pittsburg, Pennsylvania 15213. (412) 268-2960.

ONLINE DATABASES

RAILROAD MILEMAKER. Rand McNally-TDM, Incorporated, 8255 North Central Park Avenue, Skokie, Illinois 60076.

RAILROAD RESEARCH INFORMATION SERVICE. National Academy of Sciences, National Research Council, 2101 Constitution Avenue, Northwest, Washington, D.C. 20418.

TRIS. Transportation Research Board, National Academy of Sciences, 2101 Constitution Avenue, Northwest, Washington, D.C. 20418.

UNITED STATES RAIL NEWS. Business Publishers, Incorporated, 951 Pershing Drive, Silver Spring, Maryland 20910-4464.

STATISTICS SOURCES

ANNUAL REPORT. United States Interstate Commerce Commission. Twelfth and Constitution Streets, Northwest, Washington, D.C. 20423.

TRANSPORTATION STATISTICS IN THE UNITED STATES. United States Interstate Commerce Commission. Twelfth and Constitution Streets, Northwest, Washington, D.C. 20423.

RAPE
See also: SEX CRIMES

HANDBOOKS, MANUALS, FORMBOOKS

HOW TO CONVICT A RAPIST. Joy S. Eyman. Stein and Day, Scarborough House, Briarcliff Manor, New York 10510. 1982.

PROSECUTION AND DEFENSE OF SEX CRIMES. B. Anthony Morosco. Matthew Bender and Company, Incorporated, 11 Penn Plaza, New York, New York 10001. 1976 (Annual Supplements).

RAPE AND SEXUAL ASSAULT III: A RESEARCH HANDBOOK. Ann Wolbert Burgess. Garland Publishing, Incorporated, 136 Madison Avenue, New York, New York 10016. 1991.

RAPE CRISIS INTERVENTION HANDBOOK: A GUIDE FOR VICTIM CARE. Sharon L. McCombie. Plenum Publishing Corporation, 233 Spring Street, New York, New York 10013. 1980.

RAPE-VICTIMS, OFFENDERS AND TREATMENT WITH MEDICAL SUBJECT ANALYSIS AND RESEARCH GUIDE. John C. Bartone. American Health Research Institute. ABBE Publishers Association of Washington, D.C., 4111 Gallows Road, Annandale, Virginia 22003-1862. 1984.

TEXTBOOKS AND GENERAL WORKS

ACQUAINTANCE RAPE: THE HIDDEN CRIME. Andrea Parrot and Laurie Bechhofer. John Wiley and Sons, Incorporated, 605 Third Avenue, New York, New York 10158. 1991.

CRIMES OF VIOLENCE: VOLUME TWO: RAPE AND OTHER SEX CRIMES. F. Lee Bailey and Henry B. Rothblatt. Lawyers Co-Operative Publishing Company, Aqueduct Building, Rochester, New York 14694. 1973 (Annual Supplements).

DEFINING RAPE. Linda Brookover Bourque. Duke University Press, Box 6697 College Station, Durham, North Carolina 27708. 1989.

THE FACTS ABOUT RAPE. JoAnn Bren Guernsey. Crestwood House, Incorporated, c/o Macmillan Publishing Company, 866 Third Avenue, New York, New York 10022. 1990.

THE FEMALE FEAR: THE SOCIAL COST OF RAPE. Margaret T. Gordon and Stephanie Riger. University of Illinois Press, 54 East Gregory Drive, Champaign, Illinois 61820. 1989.

FOUR THEORIES OF RAPE IN AMERICAN SOCIETY: A STATE-LEVEL ANALYSIS. Larry Baron and Murray A. Straus. Yale University Press, 302 Temple Street, New Haven, Connecticut 06520. 1989.

FRATERNITY GANG RAPE: SEX, BROTHERHOOD, AND PRIVILEGE ON CAMPUS. Peggy Reeves Sanday. New York University Press, 70 Washington Square South, New York, New York 10012. 1990.

INTIMATE INTRUSIONS: WOMEN'S EXPERIENCES OF MALE VIOLENCE. Elizabeth A. Stanko. Routledge and Kegan Paul, 29 West Thirty-fifth Street, New York, New York 10001. 1985.

JURORS AND RAPE: A STUDY IN PSYCHOLOGY AND LAW. Hubert S. Feild and Leigh B. Bienen. Lexington Books, Division of D.C. Health and Company, 125 Spring Street, Lexington, Massachusetts 02173. 1980.

LICENSE TO RAPE: SEXUAL ABUSE OF WIVES. David Finkelhor and Kersti Yllo. Free Press, 866 Third Avenue, New York, New York 10022. 1987.

PRACTICAL ASPECTS OF RAPE INVESTIGATION: A MULTIDISCIPLINARY APPROACH. Robert R. Hazelwood and Ann Wolbert Burgess. Elsevier Science Publishing Company, P.O. Box 882, Madison Square Station, New York, New York 10159. 1987.

RAPE AND CRIMINAL JUSTICE: THE SOCIAL CONSTRUCTION OF SEXUAL ASSAULT. Gary D. LaFree. Wadsworth Publishing Company, 10 Davis Drive, Belmont, California 94002. 1989.

RAPE AND THE LIMITS OF LAW REFORM. Jeane C. Marsh, Alison Geist and Nathan Caplan. Auburn House Publishing Company, Greenwood Publishing Group, Incorporated, 88 Post Road West, P.O. Box 5007, Westport, Connecticut 06881. 1982.

RAPE IN MARRIAGE. Diana E. H. Russell. Indiana University Press, Tenth and Morton Streets, Bloomington, Indiana 47405. 1990.

REAL RAPE. Susan Estrich. Harvard University Press, 79 Garden Street, Cambridge, Massachusetts 02138. 1987.

THE SECOND RAPE. Nancy C. Gamble and Lee Madigan. Lexington Books, 125 Spring Street, Lexington, Massachusetts 02173. 1991.

UNDERSTANDING SEXUAL VIOLENCE: A STUDY OF CONVICTED RAPISTS. Diana Scully. Unwin Hyman, Incorporated, 8 Winchester Place, Winchester, Massachusetts 01890. 1990.

VIOLENCE IN DATING RELATIONSHIPS: EMERGING SOCIAL ISSUES. Maureen A. Pirog-Good and Jan E. Stets. Praeger Publishers, One Madison Avenue, New York, New York 10010. 1989.

THE VOICES OF RAPE. Janet Bode. Franklin Watts, Incorporated, 387 Park Avenue South, New York, New York 10016. 1990.

LAW REVIEWS AND PERIODICALS

AEGIS: MAGAZINE ON ENDING VIOLENCE AGAINST WOMEN. Feminist Alliance Against Rape, P.O. Box 21033, Washington, D.C. 20009. Quarterly.

NEWSLETTERS AND NEWSPAPERS

NATIONAL CLEARINGHOUSE ON MARITAL AND DATE RAPE: NEWSLETTER. 2325 Oak Street, Berkeley, California 94708. Quarterly.

NATIONAL COALITION AGAINST SEXUAL ASSAULT: NEWSLETTER. 2428 Ontario Road, Northwest, Washington, D.C. 20009. Quarterly.

BIBLIOGRAPHIES

RAPE: A BIBLIOGRAPHY. Joan Nordquist. Reference and Research Services, 511 Lincoln Street, Santa Cruz, California 95060. 1990.

DIRECTORIES

NATIONAL DIRECTORY: RAPE PREVENTION AND TREATMENT SOURCES. National Center for Prevention and Control of Rape. Superintendent of Documents, United States Government Printing Office, Washington, D.C. 20402. 1981.

PUBLIC AND PRIVATE SOURCES OF FUNDING FOR SEXUAL ASSAULT TREATMENT PROGRAMS. National Center for Prevention and Control of Rape. Superintendent of Documents, United States Government Printing Office, Washington, D.C. 20402. 1981.

SEXUAL ASSAULT AND CHILD SEXUAL ABUSE: A NATIONAL DIRECTORY OF VICTIM/SURVIVOR SERVICES AND PREVENTION PROGRAMS. Linda Webster. Oryx Press, 2214 North Central Avenue, Phoenix, Arizona 85004. 1989.

SURVIVING SEXUAL ASSAULT. Rochel Grossman. Saint Martin's Press, Incorporated, 175 Fifth Avenue, New York, New York 10010. 1983.

WOMEN HELPING WOMEN: A STATE-BY-STATE DIRECTORY OF SERVICES. Women's Action Alliance, 370 Lexington Avenue, New York, New York 10014. 1981.

RESEARCH CENTERS, INSTITUTES, CLEARINGHOUSES

CENTER FOR THE STUDY OF WOMEN. University of California, Los Angeles, 236A Kinsey Hall, 405 Hiljard Avenue, Los Angeles, California 90024. (213) 825-0590.

FEMINIST ALLIANCE AGAINST RAPE. P.O. Box 21033, Washington, D.C. 20009. (202) 882-1615.

INSTITUTE FOR THE STUDY OF SEXUAL ASSAULT. 403 Ashbury Street, San Francisco, California 94116. (415) 861-2048.

MARRIAGE COUNCIL OF PHILADELPHIA. 4025 Chestnut Street, Second Floor, Philadelphia, Pennsylvania 19104. (215) 382-6680.

NATIONAL CLEARINGHOUSE ON MARITAL AND DATE RAPE. 2325 Oak Street, Berkeley, California 94708. (415) 548-1770.

NATIONAL COALITION AGAINST SEXUAL ASSAULT. 2428 Ontario Road, Northwest, Washington, D.C. 20009. (202) 483-7165.

PEOPLE AGAINST RAPE. P.O. Box 160, Chicago, Illinois 60635. (312) 745-1025.

SEXUAL DISORDERS CLINIC. Johns Hopkins University, Meyer Building, Room 101, Johns Hopkins Hospital, 600 North Wolfe Street, Baltimore, Maryland 21205. (301) 955-6292.

ONLINE DATABASES

NCJRS (NATIONAL CRIMINAL JUSTICE REFERENCE SERVICE). United States Department of Justice, National Institute of Justice, National Criminal Justice Reference Service, Box 6000, Rockville, Maryland 20850.

STATISTICS SOURCES

CRIME IN THE UNITED STATES. United States Department of Justice, Federal Bureau of Investigation, Ninth Street and Pennsylvania Avenue, Northwest, Washington, D.C. 20535.

CRIMINAL VICTIMIZATION IN THE UNITED STATES. United States Department of Justice, Bureau of Justice Statistics, 633 Indiana Avenue, Northwest, Washington, D.C. 20531.

FEMALE VICTIMS OF VIOLENT CRIMES. Caroline Wolf Harlow. United States Department of Justice, Bureau of Justice Statistics, Tenth Street and Pennsylvania Avenue, Northwest, Washington, D.C. 20530. 1991.

AUDIOVISUALS

COMPARATIVE CROSS-EXAMINATION OF A RAPE VICTIM. Consortium for Professional Education, American Bar Association, 750 North Lake Shore Drive, Chicago, Illinois 60611. 1976 Videotape.

DIRECT AND CROSS EXAMINATION OF A RAPE VICTIM. Consortium for Professional Education, American Bar Association, 750 North Lake Shore Drive, Chicago, Illinois 60611. 1976. Videotape.

DIRECT AND CROSS EXAMINATION OF THE DEFENDANT IN A RAPE CASE. Consortium for Professional Education, American Bar Association, 750 North Lake Shore Drive, Chicago, Illinois 60611. 1977. Videotape.

REAL ESTATE BUSINESS
See: REAL PROPERTY

REAL PROPERTY
See also: AGRICULTURE; COMMUNITY PROPERTY; CONDOMINIUM AND COOPERATIVE BUILDINGS; FORECLOSURES; HISTORIC PRESERVATION; HOUSING; LANDLORD AND TENANT; REAL PROPERTY TAXATION; TIME-SHARE PROPERTY; ZONING AND PLANNING

REAL PROPERTY

STATUTES, CODES, STANDARDS, UNIFORM LAWS

MODEL LAND SALES PRACTICES ACT. National Conference of Commissioners on Uniform State Laws. Uniform Laws Annotated. West Publishing Company, P.O. Box 64526, 50 West Kellogg Boulevard, St. Paul, Minnesota 55164-0526. 1976. (Annual Supplemants).

MODEL LAND SALES PRACTICES ACT. National Conference of Commissioners on Uniform State Laws. Martindale-Hubbell Law Directory, Volume Eight. Martindale-Hubbell, Incorporated, 121 Chanlon Road, New Providence, New Jersey 07974. (Annual Supplements).

MODEL REAL ESTATE COOPERATIVES ACT. National Conference of Commissioners on Uniform State Laws. Uniform Laws Anotated. West Publishing Company, P.O. Box 64526, 50 West Kellogg Boulevard, St. Paul, Minnesota 55164-0526. 1976. (Annual Supplements).

UNIFORM LAND SECURITY INTEREST ACT. National Conference of Commissioners on Uniform State Laws. Uniform Laws Annotated. West Publishing Company, P.O. Box 64526, 50 West Kellogg Boulevard, St. Paul, Minnesota 55164-0526. 1976. (Annual Supplements).

UNIFORM LAND TRANSACTIONS ACT. National Conference of Commissioners on Uniform State Laws. Uniform Laws Annotated. West Publishing Company, P.O. Box 64526, 50 West Kellogg Boulevard, St. Paul, Minnesota 55164-0526. 1978. (Annual Supplements).

RESTATEMENTS

RESTATEMENT OF THE LAW OF PROPERTY. American Law Institute, 4025 Chestnut Street, Philadelphia, Pennsylvania 19104. 1936-1944. (Annual Supplements).

RESTATEMENT OF THE LAW, PROPERTY--SECURITY (MORTGAGES). American Bar Association, 750 North Lake Shore Drive, Chicago, Illinois 60611. 1990.

RESTATEMENT OF THE LAW SECOND: PROPERTY: DONATIVE TRANSFERS. American Law Institute, 4025 Chestnut Street, Philadelphia, Pennsylvania 19104. 1990. (Annual Supplements).

RESTATEMENT OF THE LAW SECOND: PROPERTY: LANDLORD AND TENANT. American Law Institute, 4025 Chestnut Street, Philadelphia, Pennsylvania 19104. 1977. (Annual Supplements).

LOOSELEAF SERVICES AND REPORTERS

HOMES AND TAXES. Harry L. Gutman. Commerce Clearing House, Incorporated, 4025 West Peterson Avenue, Chicago, Illinois 60646. 1989- .

REAL ESTATE DEVELOPMENT: BUSINESS, COMMERCIAL, INDUSTRIAL, AND MAJOR RESIDENTIAL PROPERTIES. Eugene J. Morris and Nyal D. Deems. Matthew Bender and Company, Incorporated, 11 Penn Plaza, New York, New York 10001. 1987- .

REAL ESTATE GUIDE. Prentice-Hall, Incorporated, 113 Sylvan Avenue, Englewood Cliffs, New Jersey 07632. Monthly.

REAL ESTATE INVESTMENT PLANNING. Prentice-Hall, Incorporated, 113 Sylvan Avenue, Englewood Cliffs, New Jersey 07632. Monthly.

TAX ASPECTS OF REAL ESTATE INVESTMENTS: A PRACTICAL GUIDE FOR STRUCTURING REAL ESTATE TRANSACTIONS. Peter M. Fass. Clark Boardman Company, Limited, 435 Hudson Street, New York, New York 10014. 1988- .

HANDBOOKS, MANUALS, FORMBOOKS

COMPLETE REAL ESTATE EXCHANGE AND ACQUISITION HANDBOOK. Joseph E. Kearsley. Prentice-Hall, Incorporated, 113 Sylvan Avenue, Englewood Cliffs, New Jersey 07632. 1982.

COMPLYING WITH FIRPTA: A MANUAL OF FORMS. Richard M. Fijolek and Timothy E. Powers. American Bar Association, Real Property, Probate and Trust Law Section, 750 North Lake Shore Drive, Chicago, Illinois 60611. 1989.

CONTRACTS AND CONVEYANCES OF REAL PROPERTY. Fourth Edition. Milton R. Friedman. Practising Law Institute, 810 Seventh Avenue, New York, New York 10019. 1984. (1988 Supplement).

MCGRAW-HILL REAL ESTATE HANDBOOK. Robert Irwin, Editor. McGraw-Hill Book Company, 1221 Avenue of the Americas, New York, New York 10020. 1984.

MODERN REAL ESTATE ACQUISITION AND DISPOSITION FORMS. Jack Kusnet. Research Institute of America, Incorporated, One Penn Plaza, New York, New York 10119. 1981. (Annual Supplements).

MODERN REAL ESTATE AND MORTGAGE FORMS. Alvin L. Arnold. Research Institute of America, Incorporated, One Penn Plaza, New York, New York 10119. 1979. (Annual Supplements).

MODERN REAL ESTATE LEASING FORMS. Jack Kusnet. Research Institute of America, Incorporated, One Penn Plaza, New York, New York 10119. 1980. (Annual Supplements).

NEW ENCYCLOPEDIA OF REAL ESTATE FORMS. Jerome S. Gross. Prentice-Hall, Incorporated, 113 Sylvan Avenue, Englewood Cliffs, New Jersey 07632. 1983.

REAL ESTATE AND THE BANKRUPTCY CODE: STRUCTURING AND DOCUMENTING NEW DEALS, WORKOUTS AND BANKRUPTCIES. Richard A. Gitlin, Chairman. Practising Law Institute, 810 Seventh Avenue, New York, New York 10019. 1985.

REAL ESTATE FINANCING FORMS MANUAL: WITH COMUNITY. James A. Douglas and Rosa Koppel. Research Institute of America, Incorporated, One Penn Plaza, New York, New York 10119. 1985.

REAL ESTATE INVESTORS COMPLETE HANDBOOK. Martin J. Miles. Prentice-Hall, Incorporated, 113 Sylvan Avenue, Englewood Cliffs, New Jersey 07632. 1982.

REAL ESTATE INVESTOR'S DESKBOOK. Alvin L. Arnold and Daniel E. Feld. Research Institute of America, Incorporated, One Penn Plaza, New York, New York 10119. 1987.

REAL ESTATE REVIEW PORTFOLIOS (SERIES). Research Institute of America, Incorporated, One Penn Plaza, New York, New York 10119. (Periodic Revisions).

REAL ESTATE SYNDICATION HANDBOOK: A HOW TO GUIDE FOR LAWYERS, ACCOUNTANTS, AND TAX SHELTER PROFESSIONALS. Peter M. Fass and Robert J. Taft. Clark Boardman Company, Limited, 435 Hudson Street, New York, New York 10014. 1985.

REAL ESTATE SYNDICATION MANUAL: INVESTMENT, TAX AND MARKETING STRATEGIES. Alvin L. Arnold. Research Institute of America, Incorporated, One Penn Plaza, New York, New York 10119. 1984. (1991 Supplement).

TEXTBOOKS AND GENERAL WORKS

AMERICAN LAW OF PROPERTY. Richard R. Powell and Patrick J. Rohan. Matthew Bender and Company, Incorporated, 11 Penn Plaza, New York, New York 10001. 1949. (Semiannual Supplements).

ANALYZING COMMERCIAL AND MULTI-FAMILY REAL ESTATE TRANSACTIONS. Julian R. Kossow. Practising Law Institute, 810 Seventh Avenue, New York, New York 10019. 1982.

BOUNDARY CONTROL AND LEGAL PRINCIPLES. Third Edition. Curtis M. Brown, Walter G. Robillard and Donald A. Wilson. John Wiley and Sons, Incorporated, 605 Third Avenue, New York, New York 10158. 1986.

CASES AND MATERIALS ON MORTGAGES AND REAL ESTATE FINANCE. James Cooper-Hill and Martin J. Greenberg. The Michie Company, P.O. Box 7587, Charlottesville, Virginia 22906-7587. 1982.

CASES AND MATERIALS ON REAL ESTATE TRANSFER, FINANCE, AND DEVELOPMENT. Third Edition. Grant S. Nelson and Dale A. Whitman. West Publishing Company, 50 West Kellogg Boulevard, St. Paul, Minnesota 55164. 1987.

COLLIER REAL ESTATE TRANSACTIONS AND THE BANKRUPTCY CODE. Laurence D. Cherkis. Matthew Bender and Company, Incorporated, 11 Penn Plaza, New York, New York 10001. 1984. (Annual Supplements).

COMMERCIAL REAL ESTATE LEASES, 1991. Milton R. Friedman, Chairman. Practising Law Institute, 810 Seventh Avenue, New York, New York 10019. 1991.

COMMERCIAL REAL ESTATE LEASES: PREPARATION AND NEGOTIATION. Mark A. Senn. John Wiley and Sons, Incorporated, 605 Third Avenue, New York, New York 10158. 1990.

CONTEMPORARY REAL ESTATE: THEORY AND PRACTICE. Gaylon E. Green and Michael D. Farrell. Dryden Press, 465 South Lincoln Drive, Troy, Missouri 63379. 1983.

CREATIVE REAL ESTATE FINANCING, 1991. Richard J. Kane, Chairman. Practising Law Institute, 810 Seventh Avenue, New York, New York 10019. 1991.

CREDIT RESTRUCTURING: REAL ESTATE AND CORPORATE LOAN WORKOUTS. Michael L. Cook and Elihu Fier. Harcourt Brace Jovanovich, Incorporated, 6277 Sea Harbor Drive, Orlando, Florida 32821. 1982.

EFFECTS OF SECURITIES REGULATION ON REAL ESTATE TRANSACTIONS. American Law Institute-American Bar Association, Committee on Continuing Professional Education, 4025 Chestnut Street, Philadelphia, Pennsylvania 19104. 1983.

ENVIRONMENTAL REGULATION OF REAL PROPERTY. Nicholas A. Robinson. Law Journal-Seminars Press, Incorporated, 111 Eighth Avenue, New York, New York 10011. 1986. (Periodic Supplements).

FEDERAL REGULATION OF REAL ESTATE. Second Edition. Paul Barrow. Research Institute of America, Incorporated, One Penn Plaza, New York, New York 10119. 1983.

FEDERAL TAXATION OF REAL ESTATE. Alan J. Samansky and James C. Smith, Law Journal-Seminars Press, Incorporated, 111 Eighth Avenue, New York, New York 10011. 1985. (Periodic Supplements).

THE FIRPTA MANUAL: COMPLIANCE AND PLANNING GUIDE TO THE FOREIGN INVESTMENT IN REAL PROPERTY TAX ACT: EXPLANATION AND FORMS. Charles D. Rubin. Research Institute of America, 910 Sylvan Avenue, Englewood Cliffs, New Jersey 07632. 1990.

FOREIGN INVESTMENT IN THE UNITED STATES: LAW, TAXATION, FINANCE. Marc M. Levey. John Wiley and Sons, Incorporated, 605 Third Avenue, New York, New York 10158. 1989.

FOREIGN INVESTMENT IN U.S. REAL ESTATE. Professional Education Systems, Incorporated, 200 Spring Street, Eau Claire, Wisconsin 54702. 1984.

FOREIGN INVESTMENT IN U.S. REAL ESTATE: A COMPREHENSIVE GUIDE. Timothy E. Powers. American Bar Association, Section of Real Property, Probate and Trust Law, 750 North Lake Shore Drive, Chicago, Illinois 60611. 1990.

FUTURE INTERESTS IN A NUTSHELL. Lawrence W. Waggoner. West Publishing Company, P.O. Box 64526, 50 West Kellogg Boulevard, St. Paul, Minnesota 55164-0526. 1980.

HANDBOOK OF THE LAW OF FUTURE INTERESTS. Second Edition. Lewis M. Simes. West Publishing Company, P.O. Box 64526, 50 West Kellogg Boulevard, St. Paul, Minnesota 55164-0526. 1966. (Hornbook).

HANDBOOK OF THE LAW OF REAL PROPERTY. Third Edition. William E. Burby. West Publishing Company, P.O. Box 64526, 50 West Kellogg Boulevard, St. Paul, Minnesota 55164-0526. 1965. (Hornbook).

HOW TO MAKE MONEY IN REAL ESTATE WITH GOVERNMENT LOANS AND PROGRAMS. Albert J. Lowry. Simon and Schuster, Incorporated, 1230 Avenue of the Americas, New York, New York 10020. 1985.

HOW TO SYNDICATE REAL ESTATE. Alan Parisse. Research Institute of America, Incorporated, One Penn Plaza, New York, New York 10119. 1982.

THE IMPACT OF ENVIRONMENTAL CONTROLS ON REAL ESTATE DEVELOPMENT. Joel H. Sachs, Chairman. Practising Law Institute, 810 Seventh Avenue, New York, New York 10019. 1984.

INTRODUCTION TO REAL ESTATE LAW. Third Edition. Charles S. Coit. Real Estate Education Company, Chicago, Illinois. 1989.

INTRODUCTION TO THE LAW OF REAL PROPERTY. Cornelius J. Moynihan. West Publishing Company, P.O. Box 64526, 50 West Kellogg Boulevard, St. Paul, Minnesota 55164-0526. 1962.

LAND LAW AND REAL PROPERTY IN AMERICAN HISTORY: MAJOR HISTORICAL INTERPRETATIONS. Kermit L. Hall. Garland Publishing, Incorporated, 136 Madison Avenue, New York, New York 10016. 1987.

LAND OWNERSHIP AND USE. Third Edition. Curtis J. Berger. Little, Brown, and Company, 34 Beacon Street, Boston, Massachusetts 02108. 1983.

THE LAW OF DISTRESSED REAL ESTATE FINANCING: FORECLOSURES, WORKOUTS, PROCEDURES. Baxter Dunaway. Clark Boardman Company, Limited, 435 Hudson Street, New York, New York 10014. 1985. (Annual Supplements).

THE LAW OF PROPERTY, LAWYER'S EDITION. Roger A. Cunningham, Dale A. Whitman and William B. Stoebuck. West Publishing Company, P.O. Box 64526, 50 West Kellogg Boulevard, St. Paul, Minnesota 55164-0526. 1984. (Hornbook).

LAW OF REAL ESTATE BROKERS. D. Barlow Burke. Little, Brown, and Company, 34 Beacon Street, Boston, Massachusetts 02108. 1982. (Supplement 1984).

THE LAW OF REAL ESTATE BUSINESS. Fifth Edition. William B. French and Harold F. Lusk. Richard D. Irwin, Incorporated, 1818 Ridge Road, Homewood, Illinois 60430. 1984.

THE LAW OF REAL ESTATE FINANCING: WITH TAX ANALYSIS, PLANNING AND FORMS. Michael T. Madison and Jeffrey R. Dwyer. Research Institute of America, Incorporated, One Penn Plaza, New York, New York 10119. 1981. (Semiannual Supplements).

THE LAW OF REAL PROPERTY. Richard R. Powell and Patrick J. Rohan. Matthew Bender and Company, Incorporated, 11 Penn Plaza, New York, New York 10001. 1949. (Semiannual Supplements).

LAW OF TITLE INSURANCE. D. Barlow Burke. Little, Brown, and Company, 34 Beacon Street, Boston, Massachusetts 02108. 1986.

LAWYERS AND THE MAKING OF ENGLISH LAND LAW, 1832-1940. J. Stuart Anderson. Oxford University Press, 200 Madison Avenue, New York, New York 10016. 1992.

LEGAL AND UNDERWRITING RISKS IN REAL ESTATE FINANCING. Robert M. Zinman, Chairman. Practising Law Institute, 810 Seventh Avenue, New York, New York 10019. 1982.

LEGAL MALPRACTICE AND THE REAL ESTATE PRACTITIONER. Thomas W. Hyland, Chairman. Practising Law Institute, 810 Seventh Avenue, New York, New York 10019. 1985.

MODERN REAL ESTATE PRACTICE. Twelfth Edition. Fillmore W. Galaty, Wellington J. Allaway, and Robert C. Klye. Real Estate Education Company, 500 North Dearborn Street, Chicago, Illinois 60610. 1991.

MODERN REAL ESTATE TRANSACTIONS. Sixth Edition. American Law Institute-American Bar Association, Committee on Continuing Professional Education, 4025 Chestnut Street, Philadelphia, Pennsylvania 19104. 1985.

PRACTICAL REAL ESTATE IN THE 80'S: LEGAL, TAX AND BUSINESS STRATEGIES. Second Edition. Robert K. Lifton. Harcourt Brace Jovanovich, Incorporated, 6277 Sea Harbor Drive, Orlando, Florida 32821. 1983.

PRINCIPLES OF REAL ESTATE LAW. Daniel P. McLoughlin. McGraw-Hill Publishing Company, 1221 Avenue of the Americas, New York, New York 10020. 1992.

PRIVATE REAL ESTATE SYNDICATIONS. Michael Constas and Richard D. Harroch. Law Journal-Seminars Press, Incorporated, 111 Eighth Avenue, New York, New York 10011. 1983. (Annual Supplements).

PROPERTY. Andrew Reeve. Humanities Press International, Incorporated, 171 First Avenue, Atlantic Highlands, New Jersey 07716-1289. 1986.

PROSECUTION AND DEFENSE OF FORFEITURE CASES. David B. Smith. Matthew Bender and Company, Incorporated, 11 Penn Plaza, New York, New York 10001. 1985.

PROTECTING YOUR SALES COMMISSION: PROFESSIONAL LIABILITY IN REAL ESTATE. Ronald Friedman and Benjamin N. Henszey. Real Estate Education Company, 500 North Dearborn Street, Chicago, Illinois 60610. 1985.

REAL ESTATE. James B. Kau and C.F. Sirmans. McGraw-Hill Book Company, 1221 Avenue of the Americas, New York, New York 10020. 1985.

REAL ESTATE: AN INTRODUCTION TO THE PROFESSION. Fifth Edition. Bruce M. Harwood and Charles J. Jacobus. PH Press, MIT Branch, P.O. Box 195, Cambridge, Massachusetts 02139. 1990.

REAL ESTATE AND THE BANKRUPTCY CODE. Richard A. Gitlin, Chairman. Practising Law Institute, 810 Seventh Avenue, New York, New York 10019. 1985.

REAL ESTATE AND THE LAW. Robert N. Corley, Peter J. Shedd, and Charles F. Floyd. Random House, Incorporated, McGraw-Hill Publishing Company, 1221 Avenue of the Americas, New York, New York 10020. 1982.

REAL ESTATE AND THE RTC: A GUIDE TO ASSET PURCHASES AND CONTRACTING. Leonard A. Zax. Urban Land Institute, Washington, D.C. 1990.

REAL ESTATE ASPECTS OF THE 1984 TAX ACT. Bruce S. Lane, Editor. Bureau of National Affairs, 1231 Twenty-fifth Street, Northwest, Washington, D.C. 20037. 1985.

REAL ESTATE BANKRUPTCY AND WORKOUTS: A PRACTICAL PERSPECTIVE. Anthony B. Kuklin and Paul E. Roberts, Editors. American Bar Association, Section of Real Property, Probate and Trust Law, 750 North Lake Shore Drive, Chicago, Illinois 60611. 1983.

REAL ESTATE BROKERAGE LAW AND PRACTICE. Patrick J. Rohan and Bernard H. Goldstein. Matthew Bender and Company, Incorporated, 11 Penn Plaza, New York, New York 10001. 1985. (Periodic Supplements).

REAL ESTATE DEVELOPING AND CONSTRUCTION FINANCING. Charles Zalaznick, Chairman. Practising Law Institute, 810 Seventh Avenue, New York, New York 10019. 1984.

THE REAL ESTATE DEVELOPMENT PROCESS: DRAFTING AND NEGOTIATING TECHNIQUES. Gregory W. Hummel and James M. Barkley. Prentice-Hall Law and Business Publishers, Incorporated, 855 Valley Road, Clifton, New Jersey 07013. 1989.

REAL ESTATE EXCHANGES. David W. Walters. John Wiley and Sons, Incorporated, 605 Third Avenue, New York, New York 10158. 1982.

REAL ESTATE FINANCE AND TAXATION: STRUCTURING COMPLEX TRANSACTIONS. Robert L. Nessen. John Wiley and Sons, Incorporated, 605 Third Avenue, New York, New York 10158. 1990.

REAL ESTATE FINANCE IN A NUTSHELL. Second Edition. Jon W. Bruce. West Publishing Company, P.O. Box 64526, 50 West Kellogg Boulevard, St. Paul, Minnesota 55164-0526. 1985.

REAL ESTATE FINANCE LAW. Second Edition. Grant S. Nelson and Dale A. Whitman. West Publishing Company, P.O. Box 64526, 50 West Kellogg Boulevard, St. Paul, Minnesota 55164-0526. 1985. (Hornbook).

REAL ESTATE FINANCING: TEXT, FORMS, ANALYSIS. Patrick J. Rohan. Matthew Bender and Company, Incorporated, 11 Penn Plaza, New York, New York 10001. 1973. (Semiannual Supplements).

REAL ESTATE FUNDAMENTALS. Third Edition. Wade E. Gaddy, Jr. and Robert E. Hart. Real Estate Education Company, 500 North Dearborn Street, Chicago, Illinois 60610. 1989.

REAL ESTATE INVESTMENT AND TAXATION. Fourth Edition. Roger H. Allen. PH Press, MIT Branch, P.O. Box 195, Cambridge, Massachusetts 02139. 1990.

REAL ESTATE LAW. Third Edition. William Atteberry, Karl G. Pearson and Michael P. Litka. John Wiley and Sons, Incorporated, 605 Third Avenue, New York, New York 10158. 1984.

REAL ESTATE LAW. Third Edition. Mirianne M. Jennings. PWS-Kent Publishing Company, 20 Park Plaza, Boston, Massachusetts 02116. 1992.

REAL ESTATE LAW. Ninth Edition. Robert Kratovil and Raymond J. Werner. Prentice-Hall, Incorporated, 113 Sylvan Avenue, Englewood Cliffs, New Jersey 07632. 1988.

REAL ESTATE LAW. Second Edition. George J. Siedel, III. West Publishing Company, 50 West Kellogg Boulevard, St. Paul, Minnesota 55164. 1989.

REAL ESTATE LAW AND PRACTICE. Caspar F. Cowan. West Publishing Company, 50 West Kellogg Boulevard, St. Paul, Minnesota 55164. 1990.

REAL ESTATE LIMITED PARTNERSHIPS. Second Edition. Theodore S. Lynn and Harry F. Goldberg. John Wiley and Sons, Incorporated, 605 Third Avenue, New York, New York 10158. 1983. (Supplement 1985).

REAL ESTATE PRINCIPLES. Robert H. Plattner. Harcourt Brace Jovanovich, Incorporated, 6277 Sea Harbor Drive, Orlando, Florida 32821. 1984.

REAL ESTATE PRINCIPLES AND PRACTICES. Fifth Edition. Edmund F. Ficek, Thomas P. Henderson, and Ross H. Johnson. Merrill Publishing Company, P.O. Box 508, Columbus, Ohio 43216. 1990.

REAL ESTATE SYNDICATION: TAX, SECURITIES AND BUSINESS ASPECTS. Stephen P. Jarchow. John Wiley and Sons, Incorporated, 605 Third Avenue, New York, New York 10158. 1985.

REAL ESTATE SYNDICATIONS. Patrick J. Rohan and B. Harrison Frankel. Matthew Bender and Company, Incorporated, 11 Penn Plaza, New York, New York 10001. 1985. (Periodic Supplements).

REAL ESTATE SYNDICATIONS AND LIMITED PARTNERSHIPS. Professional Education Systems, Incorporated, 200 Spring Street, Eau Claire, Wisconsin 54702. 1984.

REAL ESTATE TRANSACTIONS. Ray E. Poplett. West Publishing Company, 50 West Kellogg Boulevard, St. Paul, Minnesota 55164. 1990.

REAL ESTATE VALUATION IN LITIGATION. James D. Eaton. American Institute of Real Estate Appraisers, 430 North Michigan Avenue, Chicago, Illinois 60611. 1982.

REAL PROPERTY IN A NUTSHELL. Second Edition. Roger Bernhardt. West Publishing Company, P.O. Box 64526, 50 West Kellogg Boulevard, St. Paul, Minnesota 55164-0526. 1981.

REHABILITATING OLDER AND HISTORIC BUILDINGS: LAW, TAXATION, STRATEGIES. Stephen L. Kass, Judith M. LaBelle and David A. Hansell. John Wiley and Sons, Incorporated, 605 Third Avenue, New York, New York 10158. 1990.

SELLING REAL ESTATE INVESTMENTS ON LAND CONTRACT. Charles W. McMullen. Books on Demand, 300 North Zeeb Road, Ann Arbor, Michigan 48106-1346. 1982.

SHOPPING CENTER DEVELOPMENT. Donald H. Siskind, Chairman. Practising Law Institute, 810 Seventh Avenue, New York, New York 10019. 1985.

SOPHISTICATED TAX PLANNING FOR REAL ESTATE TRANSACTIONS. Sanford C. Presant and Leslie H. Loffman. Practising Law Institute, 810 Seventh Avenue, New York, New York 10019. 1988.

STRUCTURING FOREIGN INVESTMENT IN U.S. REAL ESTATE. Second Edition. W. Donald Knight, Jr. and Richard L. Doernberg. Kluwer Law Book Publishers, Incorporated, 36 West Forty-fourth Street, New York, New York 10036. 1988.

STRUCTURING REAL ESTATE INVESTMENTS IN THE MID-EIGHTIES: TRANSACTIONS IN TRANSITION. American Bar Association, Section of Real Property, Probate and Trust Law, 750 North Lake Shore Drive, Chicago, Illinois 60611. 1985.

SUCCESSFUL REAL ESTATE SALES AGREEMENTS: HOW TO PREPARE CONTRACTS FOR THE SALE AND EXCHANGE OF HOMES, INCOME PROPERTY AND MOBILEHOMES. Fourth Edition. Erik Jorgensen. Axiom Press Publications, P.O. Box L, San Rafael, California 94913. 1988.

SURVEY OF THE LAW OF PROPERTY. Third Edition. Ralph E. Boyer. West Publishing Company, P.O. Box 64526, 50 West Kellogg Boulevard, St. Paul, Minnesota 55164-0526. 1981.

TITLE INSURANCE IN CURRENT TRANSACTIONS. James M. Pedowitz, Chairman. Practising Law Institute, 810 Seventh Avenue, New York, New York 10019. 1983.

THE VALUATION OF REAL ESTATE. Third Edition. Alfred A. Ring and James H. Boykin. Prentice-Hall, Incorporated, 113 Sylvan Avenue, Englewood Cliffs, New Jersey 07632. 1986.

VESTED RIGHTS: BALANCING PUBLIC AND PRIVATE DEVELOPMENT EXPECTATIONS. Charles L. Sieman. Urban Land Institute, 625 Indiana Avenue, Northwest, Washington, D.C. 20004. 1982.

ENCYCLOPEDIAS AND DICTIONARIES

THE DICTIONARY OF REAL ESTATE APPRAISAL. Second Edition. American Institute of Real Estate Appraisers, Chicago, Illinois. 1989.

DICTIONARY OF REAL ESTATE TERMS. Second Revised Edition. Jack P. Friedman, Jack C. Harris, and J. Bruce Lindeman. Barron's Educational Series, Incorporated, 250 Wireless Boulevard, Hauppauge, New York 11788. 1987.

ENCYCLOPEDIA OF MORTGAGE AND REAL ESTATE FINANCE: OVER 1,000 TERMS DEFINED, EXPLAINED, AND ILLUSTRATED. James Newell, Albert Santi, and Chip Mitchell. Probus Publishing Company, 118 North Linton Street, Chicago, Illinois 60606. 1992.

ENCYCLOPEDIA OF REAL ESTATE TERMS. Damien Abbott. Gower Publishing Company, Old Post Road, Brookfield, Vermont 05036. 1987.

HANDBOOK OF REAL ESTATE TERMS. Dennis S. Tosh, Jr. Prentice-Hall, Incorporated, 113 Sylvan Avenue, Englewood Cliffs, New Jersey 07632. 1991.

THE LANGUAGE OF REAL ESTATE. Third Edition. John W. Reilly. Real Estate Education Company, Chicago, Illinois. 1989.

NEW ENCYCLOPEDIA OF REAL ESTATE FORMS. Jerome S. Gross. Prentice-Hall, Incorporated, 113 Sylvan Avenue, Englewood Cliffs, New Jersey 07632. 1983.

PORTABLE DICTIONARY OF REAL ESTATE TERMINOLOGY. Irving Marcus. Branden Press, Incorporated, P.O. Box 843, 17 Station Street, Brookline Village, Boston, Massachusetts 02147. 1983.

THE PRENTICE-HALL REAL ESTATE INVESTOR'S ENCYCLOPEDIA. Frank J. Blankenship. Prentice-Hall, Incorporated, 113 Sylvan Avenue, Englewood Cliffs, New Jersey 07632. 1989.

REAL ESTATE DICTIONARY. Third Edition. John Talamo. Financial Publishing Company, 82 Brookline Avenue, Boston, Massachusetts 02215. 1984.

DIGESTS, INDEXES, ABSTRACTS, CITATORS

NATIONAL PROPERTY LAW DIGESTS. 7900 Wisconsin Avenue, Suite 200, Bethesda, Maryalnd 20814. Monthly.

REAL ESTATE LAW DIGEST. Third Edition. James A. Douglas, Patrick J. Hamill, and Eileen R. Pollock. Research Institute of America, Incorporated, One Penn Plaza, New York, New York 10119. 1990. Monthly.

REAL ESTATE TAX DIGEST. Second Edition. James A. Douglas and Daniel E. Feld. Research Institute of America, Incorporated, One Penn Plaza, New York, New York 10119. 1990.

REAL ESTATE TAX DIGEST. Matthew Bender and Company, Incorporated, 11 Penn Plaza, New York, New York 10001. Monthly.

LAW REVIEWS AND PERIODICALS

THE PRACTICAL REAL ESTATE LAWYER. American Law Institute-American Bar Association, Committee on Continuing Professional Education, 4025 Chestnut Street, Philadelphia, Pennsylvania 19104. Bimonthly.

PROBATE AND PROPERTY. American Bar Association, Section of Real Property, Probate and Trust Law, 750 North Lake Shore Drive, Chicago, Illinois 60611. Bimonthly.

REAL ESTATE FINANCE LAW JOURNAL. Federal Research Press, 65 Franklin Street, Boston, Massachusetts 02110. Quarterly.

REAL ESTATE LAW JOURNAL. Research Institute of America, Incorporated, 210 South Street, Boston, Massachusetts 02111. Quarterly.

REAL ESTATE REVIEW. Research Institute of America, Incorporated, 210 South Street, Boston, Massachusetts 02111. Quarterly.

REAL PROPERTY, PROBATE AND TRUST LAW JOURNAL. American Bar Association, Section of Real Property, Probate and Trust Law, 750 North Lake Shore Drive, Chicago, Illinois 60611. Quarterly.

NEWSLETTERS AND NEWSPAPERS

ASBESTOS PROPERTY LITIGATION REPORTER. Andrews Publications, 1646 West Chester Pike, Westtown, Pennsylvania 19395. Semimonthly.

COMMERICAL LEASE LAW INSIDER. Brownstowne Publishers, Incorporated, 304 Park Avenue South, New York, New York 10010. Monthly.

COMMERICAL LEASING LAW AND STRATEGY. Leader Publications, 111 Eighth Avenue, New York, New York 10011. Monthly.

COMMUNITY ASSOCIATION LAW REPORTER. Community Associations Institute, 1423 Powhatan Street, Suite 7, Alexandria, Virginia 22314. Monthly.

THE DIGEST OF ENIVRONMENTAL LAW OF REAL PROPERTY. National Property Law Digests, Incorporated, 7200 Wisconsin Avenue, Suite 314, Bethesda, Maryland 20814. Monthly.

DISTRESSED BUSINESS AND REAL ESTATE NEWSLETTER. Westlake Professional Publications, Incorporated, 31304 Via Colinas, Suite 110, Westlake Village, California 91362. Bimonthly.

DISTRESSED REAL ESTATE LAW ALERT. Clark Boardman Company, Limited, 435 Hudson Street, New York, New York 10014. Monthly.

FORECLOSURE LAW BULLETIN. Quinlan Publishing Company, 23 Drydock Avenue, Boston, Massachusetts 02110. Monthly.

LAWYERS TITLE GUARANTY FUNDS NEWS. American Bar Association, Standing Committee on Lawyers Title Guaranty Funds, 750 North Lake Shore Drive, Chicago, Illinois 60611. Semiannually.

NATIONAL PROPERTY LAW DIGEST. National Property Law Digest, Incorporated, 2200 Wisconsin Avenue, Suite 314, Bethesda, Maryland 20814. Monthly.

PROFESSIONAL LIABILITY REPORTER. Andrews Publications, Incorporated, P.O. Box 200, Edgemont, Pennsylvania 19028. Monthly.

REAL ESTATE ADVISORY. Sachnoff and Weaver, Limited, 30 South Wacker Drive, Suite 2900, Chicago, Illinois 60606. Quarterly.

REAL ESTATE CLOSINGS LAW BULLETIN. Quinlan Publishing Company, 23 Drydock Avenue, Boston, Massachusetts 02110. Monthly.

REAL ESTATE LAW REPORT. Research Institute of America, Incorporated, 210 South Street, Boston, Massachusetts 02111. Monthly.

REAL ESTATE SECURITIES AND CAPITAL MARKETS. Leader Publications, Incorporated, 111 Eighth Avenue, New York, New York 10011. Monthly.

REAL ESTATE TAX ANALYST. Federal Research Press, 65 Franklin Street, Boston, Massachusetts 02110. Monthly.

REAL ESTATE TAX PLANNING NEWSLETTER. Taxplan, Incorporated, Suite 651, 440 Brickell Avenue, Miami, Florida 33131. Quarterly.

TIMESHARING LAW REPORTER. Land Development Institute, Limited, 1300 N Street, Northwest, Washington, D.C. 20005. Bimonthly.

TITLE NEWS. American Land Title Association, 1828 L Street, Northwest, Washington, D.C. 20036. Monthly.

BIBLIOGRAPHIES

BIBLIOGRAPHY OF APPRAISAL LITERATURE, 1981-1986. W. Lee Minnerly and Jamie Kosky. American Institute of Real Estate Appraisers, Chicago, Illinois. 1987.

INTERNATIONAL REAL ESTATE VALUATION, INVESTMENT, AND DEVELOPMENT: A SELECT BIBLIOGRAPHY. Valerie J. Nurcombe. Greenwood Publishing Group, Incorporated, 88 Post Road West, P.O. Box 5007, Westport, Connecticut 06881. 1987.

REAL ESTATE BOOKS AND PERIODICALS IN PRINT. John R. Johnsich. Real Estate Publishing Company, P.O. Box 41177, Sacramento, California 95841. 1988 (Supplements).

SOURCES OF PROPERTY MARKET INFORMATION: A BIBLIOGRAPHY OF PRACTICE-BASED MARKET RESEARCH AND INDICES. Douglas Scarrett. Gower Publishing Company, Old Post Road, Brookfield, Vermont 05036. 1988.

DIRECTORIES

NATIONAL REAL ESTATE INVESTOR DIRECTORY. Communication Channels, Incorporated, 6255 Barfield Road, Atlanta, Georgia 30328. Annual.

NATIONAL ROSTER OF REALTORS DIRECTORY. Stamats Publishing Company, 427 6th Avenue, Southeast, Cedar Rapids, Iowa 52406. Annual.

BIOGRAPHICAL SOURCES

WHO'S WHO IN REAL ESTATE. Grey House Publishing, Incorporated, Pocket Knife Square, Lakeville, Connecticut 06039. 1983.

ASSOCIATIONS AND PROFESSIONAL SOCIETIES

AMERICAN BAR ASSOCIATION, COMMITTEE ON LAWYERS TITLE GUARANTY FUNDS. American Bar Association, 750 North Lake Shore Drive, Chicago, Illinois 60611. (312) 988-5000.

AMERICAN BAR ASSOCIATION, NATIONAL CONFERENCE GROUP OF LAWYERS AND REALTORS. American Bar Association, 750 North Lake Shore Drive, Chicago, Illinois 60611. (312) 988-5000.

AMERICAN BAR ASSOCIATION, SECTION OF REAL PROPERTY PROBATE AND TRUST LAW. American Bar Association, 750 North Lake Shore Drive, Chicago, Illinois 60611. (312) 988-5000.

AMERICAN LAND TITLE ASSOCIATION. 1828 L Street, Northwest, Suite 705, Washington, D.C. 20036. (202) 296-3671.

ASSOCIATION OF AMERICAN LAW SCHOOLS, SECTION ON REAL PROPERTY. Association of American Law Schools, One Dupont Circle, Northwest, Washington, D.C. 20036. (202) 296-8851.

NATIONAL ASSOCIATION OF REAL ESTATE BROKERS. 1629 K Street, Northwest, Number 3, Suite 605, Washington, D.C. 20006. (202) 785-4477

NATIONAL ASSOCIATION OF REALTORS. 430 North Michigan Avenue, Chicago, Illinois 60611. (312) 329-8200.

RESEARCH CENTERS, INSTITUTES, CLEARINGHOUSES

HOMER HOYT CENTER FOR LAND ECONOMICS AND REAL ESTATE. Florida State University, 361 Bellamy Building, Tallahassee, Florida 32306. (904) 644-2870.

INSTITUTE OF REAL ESTATE MANAGEMENT. 430 North Michigan Avenue, Chicago, Illinois 60611. (312) 329-6000.

REAL ESTATE RESEARCH CENTER. University of Florida, College of Business Administration, Gainsville, Florida 32611. (904) 392-0157.

ONLINE DATABASES

REAL ESTATE INFORMATION NETWORK. Real Estate Information Network, Incorporated, P.O. Box 257, Nyack, New York 10960.

REAL ESTATE INVESTING LETTER. Harcourt Brace Jovanovich, Newsletter Bureau, Incorporated, 545 Fifth Avenue, New York, New York 10017.

WEST LAW REAL PROPERTY LIBRARY. West Publishing Company, 50 West Kellog Boulevard, St. Paul, Minnesota 55164-0526.

STATISTICS SOURCES

UNITED STATES HOUSING MARKETS. Advance Mortgage Corporation and Citicorp Real Estate, Incorporated, USHM Circulation Department, 406 City National Bank Building, Detroit, Michigan 48226. Quarterly.

AUDIOVISUALS

CONTRACTS FOR THE SALE OF COMMERCIAL PROPERTIES. American Bar Association, Section of Real Property, Probate and Trust Law, 750 North Lake Shore Drive, Chicago, Illinois 60611. 1983. Audiocassette.

HOW TO COMPUTERIZE YOUR RESIDENTIAL REAL ESTATE PRACTICE. American Bar Association, 750 North Lake Shore Drive, Chicago, Illinois 60611. 1990. Videotape.

INSURING REAL ESTATE: 1.OWNERS, LENDERS, TENANTS, MORTGAGES; 2.DURING CONSTRUCTION. American Bar Association, Section of Tort and Insurance Practice, 750 North Lake Shore Drive, Chicago, Illinois 60611. 1983. Audiocassette

PURCHASE AND SALE OF COMMERCIAL REAL ESTATE. American Bar Association, 750 North Lake Shore Drive, Chicago, Illinois 60611. 1988. Videotape.

REAL ESTATE BANKRUPTCY CASSETTE PROGRAM. American Bar Association, Section of Real Property, Probate and Trust Law, 750 North Lake Shore Drive, Chicago, Illinois 60611. 1983. Audiocassette.

REPRESENTING REAL ESTATE INTERESTS IN BANKRUPTCY REORGANIZATIONS. American Bar Association, 750 North Lake Shore Drive, Chicago, Illinois 60611. 1990. Videotape.

SALES AND LEASEBACK TRANSACTIONS/ASSIGNMENT AND SUBLETTING CLAUSES. American Bar Association, Section of Real Property, Probate, and Trust Law. 750 North Lake Shore Drive, Chicago, Illinois 60611. 1984. Audiocassette.

TITLE INSURANCE IN 1984. Practising Law Institute, 810 Seventh Avenue, New York, New York 10019. 1984. Audiocassette.

WHAT EVERY LAWYER SHOULD KNOW ABOUT THE BASICS OF REAL ESTATE APPRAISAL: AN ECONOMIC AND LITIGATION ANALYSIS. American Bar Association, Section of Real Property, Probate, and Trust Law. 750 North Lake Shore Drive, Chicago, Illinois 60611. 1984. Audiocassette.

COMPUTER-ASSISTED LEGAL INSTRUCTION

BREW V. HARRIS I, II AND III. Interactive Video Library, Harvard Law School, Educational Technology Department, 18 Everett Street, Cambridge, Massachusetts 02138. Interactive videodisc.

DAVIS V. JACOBY. Center for Computer-Assisted Instruction, 229 19th Avenue South, University of Minnesota, Minneapolis, Minnesota 55455. Interactive videodisc.

EASERLY V. LETWIN. Center for Computer-Assisted Instruction, 229 19th Avenue South, University of Minnesota, Minneapolis, Minnesota 55455. Interactive videodisc.

HAWKINS I & II. Center for Computer-Assisted Instruction, 229 19th Avenue South, University of Minnesota, Minneapolis, Minnesota 55455. Interactive videodisc.

PROBLEMS IN PROPERTY LAW SERIES. John A. Humbach. Center for Computer-Assisted Instruction, 229 19th Avenue South, University of Minnesota, Minneapolis, Minnesota 55455. Machine-readable computer file.

REAL PROPERTY TAXATION
See also: ESTATE INHERITANCE AND TRANSFER TAXES; TAX AND ESTATE PLANNING; TAX PRACTICE AND ENFORCEMENT; TAX LEGISLATION AND POLICY

STATUTES, CODES, STANDARDS, UNIFORM LAWS

FEDERAL INCOME TAX CODE AND REGULATIONS. Commerce Clearing House, Incorporated, 4025 West Peterson Avenue, Chicago, Illinois 60646. Annual.

FEDERAL TAX REGULATIONS. West Publishing Company, P.O. Box 64526, 50 West Kellogg Boulevard, St. Paul, Minnesota 55164-0526. Annual.

INTERNAL REVENUE BULLETIN: CUMMULATIVE BULLETIN. United States Department of Treasury, Internal Revenue Service. Superintendent of Documents, United States Government Printing Office, Washington, D.C. 20402. Weekly.

INTERNAL REVENUE CODE. West Publishing Company, P.O. Box 64526, 50 West Kellogg Boulevard, St. Paul, Minnesota 55164-0526. Annual.

REAL PROPERTY TAXATION

LOOSELEAF SERVICES AND REPORTERS

FEDERAL INCOME TAXATION OF REAL ESTATE: TEXT, FORMS, AND TAX PLANNING IDEAS. Gerald J. Robinson. Research Institute of America, Incorporated, One Penn Plaza, New York, New York 10119. 1984- .

FEDERAL TAXES. Prentice-Hall, Incorporated, 113 Sylvan Avenue, Englewood Cliffs, New Jersey 07632. 1919- .

FEDERAL TAXES AFFECTING REAL ESTATE. Fifth Edition. Ivan Faggen. Matthew Bender and Company, Incorporated, 11 Penn Plaza, New York, New York 10001. 1981- .

INCOME TAXATION OF NATURAL RESOURCES. Charles W. Russell and Robert W. Bowhay. Prentice-Hall, Incorporated, 113 Sylvan Avenue, Englewood Cliffs, New Jersey 07632. 1988.

PROPERTY TAXES. Prentice-Hall, Incorporated, 113 Sylvan Avenue, Englewood Cliffs, New Jersey 07632. 1925- .

REAL ESTATE FINANCING: TEXT, FORMS, TAX ANALYSIS. Patrick J. Rohan. Matthew Bender and Company, Incorporated, 11 Penn Plaza, New York, New York 10001. 1973- .

REAL ESTATE TAX APPEALS. Patrick J. Rohan. Matthew Bender and Company, Incorporated, 11 Penn Plaza, New York, New York 10001. 1984- .

REAL ESTATE TAX PLANNING FORMS. J. Scott Morris. Little, Brown, and Company, 34 Beacon Street, Boston, Massachusetts 02108. 1981- .

STANDARD FEDERAL TAX REPORTS. Commerce Clearing House, Incorporated, 4025 West Peterson Avenue, Chicago, Illinois 60646. 1913- .

TAX MANAGEMENT: REAL ESTATE SERIES. Bureau of National Affairs, 1231 Twenty-fifth Street, Northwest, Washington, D.C. 20037. 1984- .

TAXATION OF REAL ESTATE DISPOSITIONS. Sanford M. Guerin. Shepard's/McGraw-Hill, P.O. Box 1235, Colorado Springs, Colorado 80901. 1982- .

TAXATION OF REAL ESTATE IN THE UNITED STATES: ITS OWNERSHIP, SALE OR EXCHANGE, AND INHERITANCE, INCLUDING 1981 TAX LAW CHANGES. Thomas A. Bodden. Real Estate Education Company, 500 North Dearborn Street, Chicago, Illinois 60610. 1982- .

HANDBOOKS, MANUALS, FORMBOOKS

DEPRECIATION AND INVESTMENT CREDIT MANUAL: EXPLAINING ALL OF THE LATEST ACRS RULES. Martin E. Holbrook and Lawrence H. MacKirdy. Prentice-Hall, Incorporated, 113 Sylvan Avenue, Englewood Cliffs, New Jersey 07632. 1985.

REAL ESTATE SYNDICATION TAX HANDBOOK. Peter M. Fass, Robert J. Haft, Leslie H. Hoffman and Sanford C. Presant. Clark Boardman Company, Limited, 435 Hudson Street, New York, New York 10014. 1986.

TEXTBOOKS AND GENERAL WORKS

DEALING WITH THE NEW ACRS REGULATIONS. Mark L. Yecies, Chairman. Harcourt Brace Jovanovich, Incorporated, 6277 Sea Harbor Drive, Orlando, Florida 32821. 1984.

FEDERAL INCOME TAXATION OF REAL ESTATE: TEXT, FORMS AND TAX PLANNING IDEAS. Fifth Edition. Gerald J. Robinson. Research Institute of America, Incorporated, One Penn Plaza, New York, New York 10119. 1988. (Periodic Supplements).

FEDERAL REGULATION OF REAL ESTATE. Paul Barron. Research Institute of America, Incorporated, One Penn Plaza, New York, New York 10119. 1983. (Periodic Supplements).

FEDERAL TAXATION OF REAL ESTATE. Allan J. Samansky and James Charles Smith. The New York Law Publishing Company, 111 Eighth Avenue, New York, New York 10011. 1985. (Periodic Supplements.)

HOW TO LOWER YOUR PROPERTY TAXES. R. Harry Koenig. Simon and Schuster, Incorporated, 1230 Avenue of the Americas, New York, New York 10020. 1991.

AN INTRODUCTION TO THE ASSESSMENT PROFESSION. International Association of Assessing Officers, 1313 East Sixtieth Street, Chicago, Illinois 60637. 1987.

PROPERTY TAXES AND HOUSE VALUES: THE THEORY AND ESTIMATION OF INTRAJURISDICTIONAL PROPERTY TAX CAPITALIZATION. John Yinger. Academic Press, Boston, Massachusetts. 1988.

REAL ESTATE AFTER TAX REFORM: A GUIDE FOR INVESTORS. Martin M. Shenkman. John Wiley and Sons, Incorporated, 605 Third Avenue, New York, New York 10158. 1987.

REAL ESTATE INVESTMENT AND TAXATION. Fourth Edition. Stephen D. Messner. Prentice-Hall, Incorporated, 113 Sylvan Avenue, Englewood Cliffs, New Jersey 07632. 1991.

REAL ESTATE INVESTMENT STRATEGY. Third Edition. Roger H. Allen. South-Western Publishing Company, 5101 Madison Road, Cincinnati, Ohio 45227. 1989.

REAL ESTATE INVESTMENT VEHICLES: EMERGING FINANCIAL TECHNIQUES AFTER THE TAX REFORM ACT. Robert Thornton Smith, Chairman. Practising Law Institute, 810 Seventh Avenue, New York, New York 10019.

REAL ESTATE SYNDICATION UNDER THE NEW TAX LAWS. Michael Beckman. The Real Estate Institute, New York University School of Continuing Legal Education, New York University Midtown Center, 11 West Forty-second Street, New York, New York 10036. 1987.

REAL ESTATE TAX PROBLEMS, II. Gary E. Friedman. American Institute of Certified Public Accountants, 1211 Avenue of the Americas, New York, New York 10036-8775. 1985.

REAL ESTATE TAXES: THE BASICS PLANNING FOR DEPRECIATION AND INVESTMENT TAX CREDITS. Martin M. Shenkman. International Council of Shopping Centers, 665 Fifth Avenue, New York, New York 10022. 1984.

SAVE THOUSANDS ON YOUR PROPERTY TAXES! Henry W. Willen and Richard B. Stockton. Research Institute of America, Englewood Cliffs, New Jersey 07632. 1991.

SPECIAL UPDATE: THE TAX REFORM ACT OF 1986. Peter Fass, Robert J. Haft, Leslie H. Loffman and Sanford C. Presant. Research Institute of America, Incorporated, One Penn Plaza, New York, New York 10119. 1986.

STRUCTURING REAL ESTATE TRANSACTIONS UNDER THE 1986 TAX REFORM PROPOSALS. Sanford C. Pressant and Leslie H. Hoffman. The Real Estate Institute, New York University School of Continuing Legal Education, New York University Midtown Center, 11 West Forty-second Street, New York, New York 10036. 1987.

TAX ASPECTS OF REAL ESTATE TRANSACTIONS. Massachusetts Continuing Legal Education, 20 West Street, Boston, Massachusetts 02111. 1984.

TAX CONSEQUENCES OF FOREIGN INVESTMENT IN AND MORTGAGES ON UNITED STATES REAL PROPERTY. Michael Hirshfeld. The Real Estate Institute, New York University School of Continuing Legal Education, New York University Midtown Center, 11 West Forty-second Street, New York, New York 10036. 1987.

TAX CONSEQUENCES OF MORTGAGE-BACKED SECURITIES. Michael Hirshfeld. The Real Estate Institute, New York University School of Continuing Legal Education, New York University Midtown Center, 11 West Forty-second Street, New York, New York 10036. 1987.

TAX REFORM AND REAL ESTATE. James R. Follain, Editor. Urban Institute Press, 2100 M Street, Northwest, Washington, D.C. 20037. 1986.

THE TOTAL REAL ESTATE TAX PLANNER. Martin M. Shenkman. John Wiley and Sons, Incorporated, 605 Third Avenue, New York, New York 10158. 1988.

UNDERSTANDING THE INCOME TAX ASPECTS OF REAL ESTATE TRANSACTIONS. Sanford C. Pressant and Leslie H. Hoffman. The Real Estate Institute, New York University School of Continuing Legal Education, New York University Midtown Center, 11 West Forty-second Street, New York, New York 10036. 1987.

DIGESTS, INDEXES, ABSTRACTS, CITATORS

FEDERAL TAX ARTICLES: INCOME, ESTATE, GIFT, EXCISE, EMPLOYMENT TAXES. Commerce Clearing House, Incorporated, 4025 West Peterson Avenue, Chicago, Illinois 60646. 1969- .

FEDERAL TAXES CITATOR. Prentice-Hall, Incorporated, 113 Sylvan Avenue, Englewood Cliffs, New Jersey 07632. 1943- .

INDEX TO FEDERAL TAX ARTICLES. Gersham Goldstein, Editor. Research Institute of America, Incorporated, One Penn Plaza, New York, New York 10119. 1975- .

SHEPARD'S FEDERAL TAX CITATIONS. Shepard's/McGraw-Hill, P.O. Box 1235, Colorado Springs, Colorado 80901. 1981- .

SHEPARD'S FEDERAL TAX LOCATOR: COMPLETE GUIDE TO ALL THE CURRENT SOURCES OF LAW RELATING TO FEDERAL TAXATION. Shepard's/McGraw-Hill, P.O. Box 1235, Colorado Springs, Colorado 80901. 1974- .

LAW REVIEWS AND PERIODICALS

JOURNAL OF REAL ESTATE TAXATION. Research Institute of America, Incorporated, 210 South Street, Boston, Massachusetts 02111. Quarterly.

JOURNAL OF TAXATION. Research Institute of America, Incorporated, 210 South Street, Boston, Massachusetts 02111. Monthly.

THE PRACTICAL REAL ESTATE LAWYER. American Law Institute-American Bar Association, Committee on Continuing Professional Education, 4025 Chestnut Street, Philadelphia, Pennsylvania 19104. Six issues per year.

REAL ESTATE ACCOUNTING AND TAXATION. Research Institute of America, Incorporated, 210 South Street, Boston, Massachusetts 02111. Quarterly.

REAL ESTATE LAW JOURNAL. Research Institute of America, Incorporated, 210 South Street, Boston, Massachusetts 02111. Quarterly.

REAL ESTATE REVIEW. Research Institute of America, Incorporated, 210 South Street, Boston, Massachusetts 02111. Quarterly.

REAL ESTATE TAX ANALYST. Federal Research Press, 65 Franklin Street, Boston, Massachusetts 02110. Monthly.

REAL PROPERTY PROBATE AND TRUST JOURNAL. American Bar Association, Section of Real Property, Probate and Trust Law, 750 North Lake Shore Drive, Chicago, Illinois 60611. Quarterly.

THE TAX LAWYER. American Bar Association, Section of Taxation, 750 North Lake Shore Drive, Chicago, Illinois 60611. Quarterly.

TAX LAW REVIEW. Research Institute of America, Incorporated, 210 South Street, Boston, Massachusetts 02111. Quarterly.

TAXATION FOR LAWYERS. Research Institute of America, Incorporated, 210 South Street, Boston, Massachusetts 02111. Bimonthly.

TAXES: THE TAX MAGAZINE. Commerce Clearing House, Incorporated, 4025 West Peterson Avenue, Chicago, Illinois 60646. Monthly.

VIRGINIA TAX REVIEW. Virginia Tax Review Associaiton, University of Virginia, School of Law, Charlottersville, Virginia 22901. Semiannual.

NEWSLETTERS AND NEWSPAPERS

FROM THE STATE CAPITOLS: TAXES: PROPERTY. Wakeman Walworth, Incorporated, P.O. Box 1939, New Haven, Connecticut 06509. Weekly.

LAVENTHAL AND HORWATH REAL ESTATE NEWSLETTER. Laventhal and Horwath National Real Estate Department, 919 Third Avenue, New York, New York 10022. Three issues per year.

THE REAL ESTATE SYNDICATOR NEWSLETTER. Don Augustine and Walter A. Turner, Jr., Editors. The New York Law Publishing Company, 111 Eighth Avenue, New York, New York 10011. Monthly.

REAL ESTATE TAX DIGEST. Matthew Bender and Company, Incorporated, 235 East Forty-fifth Street, New York, New York 10017. Monthly.

REAL ESTATE TAX IDEAS. Research Institute of America, Incorporated, 210 South Street, Boston, Massachusetts 02111. Monthly.

TAX ANSWERS FOR REAL ESTATE PROFESSIONALS. Pro Pub Incorporated, 49 Van Syckel Lane, Wyckoff, New Jersey 07481. Monthly.

TAX DAY REPORT: A DAILY DIGEST OF FEDERAL AND STATE TAX DEVELOPMENTS. Commerce Clearing House, Incorporated, 4025 West Peterson Avenue, Chicago, Illinois 60646. Daily.

TAX MANAGEMENT REAL ESTATE JOURNAL. Bureau of National Affairs, Incorporated, 1231 Twenty-fifth Street, Northwest, Washington, D.C. 20037. Monthly.

UNITED STATES REAL ESTATE WEEK. Research Institute of America, Incorporated, 210 South Street, Boston, Massachusetts 02111. Weekly.

BIBLIOGRAPHIES

CREATING HOUSING INCENTIVES THROUGH PROPERTY TAX RELIEF: A BIBLIOGRAPHY. Lorna Peterson. Vance Bibliographies, P.O. Box 229, 112 North Charter Street, Monticello, Illinois 61856. 1988.

PUBLIC ADMINISTRATION OF PRIVATE PROPERTY TAXATION: LAWS AND LEGISLATION, JOURNAL ARTICLES, 1982-1988. Dale E. Casper. Vance Bibliographies, P.O. Box 229, 112 North Charter Street, Monticello, Illinois 61856. 1989.

ASSOCIATIONS AND PROFESSIONAL SOCIETIES

SECTION ON TAXATION, AMERICAN BAR ASSOCIATION. 750 North Lake Shore Drive, Chicago, Illinois 60611. (312) 988-5000.

SECTION ON TAXATION, ASSOCIATION OF AMERICAN LAW SCHOOLS. One Dupont Circle, Northwest, Suite 370, Washington, D.C. 20036. (202) 296-8851.

RESEARCH CENTERS, INSTITUTES, CLEARINGHOUSES

CENTER FOR THE STUDY OF ECONOMICS. 2000 Century Plaza, Suite 238, Columbia, Maryland 21044. (301) 740-1177.

INSTITUTE OF PROPERTY TAXATION. 888 Seventeenth Street, Northwest, Suite 1150, Washington, D.C. 20006. (202) 452-1213.

INTERNATIONAL COUNCIL OF SHOPPING CENTERS. 665 Fifth Avenue, New York, New York 10022. (212) 421-8181.

ONLINE DATABASES

LEXIS, TAX LIBRARY. Mead Data Control, P.O. Box 933, Dayton, Ohio 45401.

WESTLAW, TAX LIBRARY. West Publishing Company, P.O. Box 64526, 50 West Kellogg Boulevard, St. Paul, Minnesota 55164-0526.

AUDIOVISUALS

REAL ESTATE AND TAX SHELTERS AFTER THE TAX REFORM ACT OF 1986. Sidney Kess. Commerce Clearing House, Incorporated, 4025 West Peterson Avenue, Chicago, Illinois 60646. 1986. Audiocassette.

REAL ESTATE SYNDICATIONS, TAX PROBLEMS AND OPPORTUNITIES. Michael P. Oshatz and E. Paul Lipperman. New York University Institute on Federal Taxation, Totaltape Publishing, Incorporated, 4251 Southwest Thirteenth Street, Gainesville, Florida 32608. 1987.

REAL ESTATE TRANSACTIONS. Robert C. Livsey, Chairman. Law and Business, Prentice-Hall, Incorporated, Route 9W, Englewood Cliffs, New Jersey 07632. 1987. Audiocassette.

WHAT TO TELL REAL ESTATE CLIENTS ABOUT THE TAX REFORM ACT OF 1986. Harvey N. Shapiro. Prentice-Hall, Incorporated, Route 9W, Englewood Cliffs, New Jersey 07632. 1986. Audiocassette.

RECIDIVISM
See: REHABILITATION OF OFFENDERS

RECORDS
See: EVIDENCE; FREEDOM OF INFORMATION

REFERENDUM
See: ELECTION LAW; LEGISLATIVE HISTORY AND PROCESS

REFUGEES
See: EMIGRATION AND IMMIGRATION

REGIONAL PLANNING
See: ZONING AND PLANNING

REHABILITATION OF OFFENDERS
See also: PROBATION AND PAROLE

TEXTBOOKS AND GENERAL WORKS

AMERICA'S PRISONS: OPPOSING VIEWPOINTS. Fifth Edition. Stacey L. Tipp. Greenhaven Press, Incorporated, P.O. Box 289009, San Diego, California 92128-9009. 1991.

BEYOND PUNISHMENT: A NEW VIEW ON THE REHABILITATION OF CRIMINAL OFFENDERS. Edgardo Rotman. Greenwood Publishing Group, Incorporated, 88 Post Road West, P.O. Box 5007, Westport, Connecticut 06881. 1990.

THE CAUSES AND CURES OF CRIMINALITY. Hans J. Eysenck and Gisli H. Gudjonsson. Plenum Publishing Corporation, 233 Spring Street, New York, New York 10013. 1989.

CRIME, SHAME, AND REINTEGRATION. John Braithwaite. Cambridge University Press, 40 West Twentieth Street, New York, New York 10011. 1989.

DANGEROUSNESS: PROBABILITY AND PREDICTION, PSYCHIATRY AND PUBLIC POLICY. Christopher D. Webster, Mark H. Ben-Aron and Stephen J. Hucker, Editors. Cambridge University Press, 40 West Twentieth Street, New York, New York 10011. 1985.

DETERMINATE SENTENCING AND IMPRISONMENT: A FAILURE OF REFORM. Lynne Goodstein and John Hepburn. Anderson Publishing Company, 2035 Reading Road, Cinncinati, Ohio 45202. 1985.

FROM CRIME TO REHABILITATION. M. J. A. Glickman. Gower Publishing Company, Old Post Road, Brookfield, Vermont 05036. 1983.

INSIDE THE CRIMINAL MIND. Stanton E. Samenow. Times Books, 201 East Fiftieth Street, New York, New York 10022. 1984

JUSTICE FOR VICTIMS AND OFFENDERS: A RESTORATIVE RESPONSE TO CRIME. Martin Wright. Open University Press, c/o Taylor and Francis Group, 1900 Frost Road, Suite 101, Bristol, Pennsylvania 19007. 1991.

JUSTICE THROUGH PUNISHMENT: A CRITIQUE OF THE JUSTICE MODEL OF CORRECTIONS. Barbara Hudson. St. Martin's Press, 175 Fifth Avenue, New York, New York 10010. 1987.

NEITHER ANGELS NOR THIEVES: STUDIES IN DEINSTITUTIONALIZATION OF STATUS OFFENDERS. Joel F. Handler and Julie Zatz, Editors. National Academy Press, 2101 Constitution Avenue, Northwest, Washington, D.C. 20418. 1982.

OUTCOMES AND COSTS OF A PRE-RELEASE SYSTEM. David E. Duffee, Kevin N. Wright, and Peter B. Meyer. Oelgeschlager, Gunn and Hain, Incorporated, 245 Mirriam Street, Weston, Massachusetts 02193. 1983.

THE PARADOX OF CONTROL: PAROLE SUPERVISION OF YOUTHFUL OFFENDERS. Patrick G. Jackson. Praeger Publishers, One Madison Avenue, New York, New York 10010-3603. 1983.

PAST OR FUTURE CRIMES: DESERVEDNESS AND DANGEROUSNESS IN THE SENTENCING OF CRIMINALS. Andrew Von Hirsch. Rutgers University Press, 109 Church Street, New Brunswick, New Jersey 08901. 1987.

REAFFIRMING REHABILITATION. Francis T. Cullen and Karen E. Gilbert. Anderson Publishing Company, 2035 Reading Road, Cincinnati, Ohio 45202. 1982.

THE REFORM OF PRISONERS, 1830-1900. William James Forsythe. St. Martin's Press, 175 Fifth Avenue, New York, New York 10010. 1987.

RETHINKING CRIMINIOLOGY. Harold E. Pepinsky, Editor. Sage Publications, Incorporated, 2455 Teller Road, Newbury Park, California 91320. 1982.

SOCIAL SKILLS IN PRISON AND THE COMMUNITY: PROBLEM-SOLVING FOR OFFENDERS. Phillip Priestly. Routledge and Kegan Paul, Limited, 29 West Thirty-fifth Street, New York, New York 10001. 1984.

TREATING THE CRIMINAL OFFENDER. Third Edition. Alexander B. Smith and Louis Berlin. Plenum Publishing Corporation, 233 Spring Street, New York, New York 10013. 1988.

NEWSLETTERS AND NEWSPAPERS

ASSOCIATION OF PAROLING AUTHORITIES NEWSLETTER. Association of Paroling Authorities, c/o Secretariat, Sam Houston University, Huntsville, Texas 77341. Quarterly.

PERSPECTIVES. c/o Council of State Governments, P.O. Box 11910, Lexington, Kentucky 40578. (606) 252-2291. Quarterly.

PPCAA NEWSLETTER. Probation and Parole Compact Administrators Association, c/o Council of State Governments, P.O. Box 11910-1910, Lexington, Kentucky 40578. Quarterly.

PROBATION AND PAROLE LAW REPORTS. Knehaus-Miller Publications, P.O. Box 88, Warrensburg, Missouri 64093. Monthly.

BIBLIOGRAPHIES

REHABILITATION OF CRIMINALS: A BIBLIOGRAPHY. Mary A. Vance. Vance Bibliographies, P.O. Box 229, 112 North Charter Street, Monticello, Illinois 61856. 1988.

ASSOCIATIONS AND PROFESSIONAL SOCIETIES

AMERICAN PROBATION AND PAROLE ASSOCIATION. c/o Council of State Governments, P.O. Box 11910, Lexington, Kentucky 40578. (606) 252-2291.

ASSOCIATION OF PAROLING AUTHORITIES INTERNATIONAL. c/o Robert Gittens, Route Point Place, 2743 Wormwood Street, Boston, Massachusetts 02110. (617) 727-3271.

OFFENDER REHABILITATION DIVISION OF THE PUBLIC DEFENDER SERVICE. 451 Indiana Avenue, Northwest, Washington, D.C. 20001. (202) 628-1200.

VOLUNTEERS IN PREVENTION, PROBATION, PRISONS. 527 North Main Street, Royal Oak, Michigan 48067. (313) 398-8550.

STATISTICS SOURCES

PAROLE IN THE UNITED STATES. United States Department of Justice, Bureau of Justice Statistics, 633 Indiana Avenue Northwest, Washington, D.C. 20531. Annual.

RELIGION

LOOSELEAF SERVICES AND REPORTERS

RELIGIOUS FREEDOM REPORTER. Center for Law and Religious Freedom, 4208 Evergreen Lane, Suite 222, Annandale, Virginia 22003. 1981- .

HANDBOOKS, MANUALS, FORMBOOKS

HANDBOOK OF DENOMINATIONS IN THE UNITED STATES. Ninth Edition. Frank S. Mead and Samuel S. Hill. Abingdon Press, P.O. Box 801, 201 Eighth Avenue South, Nashville, Tennessee 37202. 1990.

TEXTBOOKS AND GENERAL WORKS

ADAM AND EVE. Russell Kirk, Editor. University Press of America, Center for Judicial Studies, 4720 Boston Way, Lanham, Maryland 20706. 1986.

ASCENDING LIABILITY IN RELIGIOUS AND OTHER NONPROFIT ORGANIZATIONS. Edward McGlynn Gaffney, Jr. Mercer University Press, 1400 Coleman Avenue, Macon, Georgia 31207. 1986.

BOUNDARIES DIMLY PERCEIVED: LAW, RELIGION, EDUCATION, AND THE COMMON GOOD. Christopher F. Mooney. University of Notre Dame Press, Notre Dame, Indiana 46556. 1990.

CHURCH DISCIPLINE AND THE COURTS. Lynn R. Buzzard and Thomas S. Brandon, Jr. Tyndale House Publishers, Incorporated, P.O. Box 80, 336 Gundersen Drive, Wheaton, Illinois 60189. 1987.

CLASSROOMS IN CRISIS: PARENTS' RIGHTS AND THE PUBLIC SCHOOL. Arnold Burron, John Eidamoe and Dean Turner. Accent Books, P.O. Box 15337, Lakewood Station, Denver, Colorado 80215. 1986.

CLERGY MALPRACTICE. Robert W. McMenanmin. William S. Hein and Company, Incorporated, Hein Building, 1285 Main Street, Buffalo, New York 14209. 1986.

CLERGY MALPRACTICE. H. Newton Malony. Westminster Press, 100 Witherspoon Street, Louisville, Kentucky 40202-1396. 1986.

CULTS, CULTURE, AND THE LAW: PERSPECTIVES ON NEW RELIGIOUS MOVEMENTS. Thomas Robbins, William C. Shephard and James McBride, Editors. Scholars Press, P.O. Box 15288, Decatur, Georgia 30333. 1985.

THE DECEMBER DILEMMA: CHRISTMAS IN AMERICAN PUBLIC LIFE. Albert J. Menendez. Americans United for Separation of Church and State, 8120 Fenton Street, Silver Spring, Maryland 20910. Defunct. 1988.

THE ESTABLISHMENT CLAUSE: RELIGION AND THE FIRST AMENDMENT. Leonard W. Levy. Macmillan Publishing Company, Incorporated, 866 Third Avenue, New York, New York 10022. 1989.

THE FIRST AMENDMENT. Philip A. Klinkner. Silver Burdett Press, Englewood Cliffs, New Jersey. 1991.

THE FIRST AMENDMENT, 1791-1991: TWO HUNDRED YEARS OF FREEDOM. James E. Leahy. McFarland and Company, Incorporated, Box 611, Jefferson, North Carolina 28640. 1991.

THE FIRST AMENDMENT BOOK. Robert J. Wagman and Burl Osborne. World Almanac, New York, New York. 1991.

FIRST AMENDMENT: CASES, COMMENTS, QUESTIONS. Steven H. Shiffrin and Jesse H. Choper. West Publishing Company, 50 West Kellogg Boulevard, St. Paul, Minnesota 55164. 1991.

FREEDOM OF RELIGION. Haig A. Bosmajian. Neal-Schuman Publications, Incorporated, 23 Leonard Street, New York, New York 10013. 1987.

FREEDOM OF RELIGION IN AMERICA: HISTORICAL ROOTS, PHILOSOPHICAL CONCEPTS, AND CONTEMPORARY PROBLEMS. Henry B. Clark, II, Editor. Transaction Books, Rutgers University, New Brunswick, New Jersey 08903. 1982.

GOD'S COUNTRY: A CASE AGAINST THEOCRACY. Sandy Rapp. Haworth Press, Incorporated, 10 Alice Street, Binghamton, New York 13904. 1991.

IDEAS THAT HAVE MADE US FREE. Chester James Antieau. University Press of America, 4720 Boston Way, Lanham, Maryland 20706. 1991.

IN CELEBRATION: AN AMERICAN JEWISH PERSPECTIVE ON THE BICENTENNIAL OF THE UNITED STATES CONSTITUTION. Kerry M Olitzky. University Press of America, 4720 Boston Way, Lanham, Maryland 20706. 1989.

LAW AND RELIGION. Timothy L. Fort. McFarland and Company, Incorporated, P.O. Box 611, Jefferson, North Carolina 28640. 1987.

LEGAL PROBLEMS 0F RELIGIOUS AND PRIVATE SCHOOLS. Ralph D. Mawdsley. National Organization on Legal Problems of Education, Southwest Plaza Building, 3601 West Twenty-ninth Street, Topeka, Kansas 66614. 1989.

MORALITY, SEX, AND THE CONSTITUTION: A CHRISTIAN PERSPECTIVE ON THE POWER OF GOVERNMENT TO REGULATE PRIVATE SEXUAL CONDUCT BETWEEN CONSENTING ADULTS. G. Sidney Buchanan. University Press of America, 4720 Boston Way, Lanham, Maryland 20706. 1985.

A NATION DEDICATED TO RELIGIOUS LIBERTY: THE CONSTITUTIONAL HERITAGE OF THE RELIGION CLAUSES. Arlin M. Adams and Charles J. Emmerich. University of Pennsylvania Press, Blockley Hall, 418 Service Drive, Philadelphia, Pennsylvania 19104. 1990.

ORIGINAL INTENT: CHIEF JUSTICE REHNQUIST AND THE COURSE OF AMERICAN CHURCH-STATE RELATIONS. Derek Davis and Leo Pfeffer. Prometheus Books, 700 East Amherst Street, Buffalo, New York 14215. 1991.

THE PLEDGE: THE PLEDGE OF ALLEGIANCE, SCHOOLS AND THE SUPREME COURT. D. Neven Mallak and Joel D. Joseph. National Press, Incorporated, 7201 Wisconsin Avenue, Suite 720, Bethesda, Maryland 20814. 1989.

THE PRINCIPLES OF CANON LAW. Hubert S. Box. Greenwood Publishing Group, Incorporated, 88 Post Road West, P.O. Box 5007, Westport, Connecticut 06881. 1986. (Reprint).

PROSECTOR'S REACH: LEGAL ISSUES AND THE NEW RELIGIONS. William C. Shepard. Crossroad Publishing Company, 575 Lexington Avenue, New York, New York 10022. 1983.

PUBLIC PRAYER AND THE CONSTITUTION: A CASE STUDY IN CONSTITUTIONAL INTERPRETATION. Rodney K. Smith. Scholarly Resources, Incorporated, 104 Greenhill Avenue, Wilmington, Delaware 19805. 1987.

RELIGION IN THE PUBLIC REALM. David Tracy. Crossroad Publishing Company, 370 Lexington Avenue, New York, New York 10017. 1987.

RELIGION, LAW, AND THE GROWTH OF CONSTITUTIONAL THOUGHT, 1150-1650. Brian Tierney. Cambridge University Press, 40 West Twentieth Street, New York, New York 10011. 1982.

RELIGION, MORALITY, AND THE LAW. J. Roland Pennock and John W. Chapman. New York University Press, 70 Washington Square South, New York, New York 10012. 1988.

RELIGIOUS LIBERTY AND THE SECULAR STATE: THE CONSTITUTIONAL CONTEXT. John M. Swomley. Prometheus Books, 700 East Amherst Street, Buffalo, New York 14215. 1986.

THE SHAPING OF THE FIRST AMENDMENT, 1791 TO THE PRESENT. Paul L. Murphy. Oxford University Press, 200 Madison Avenue, New York, New York 10016. 1992.

WALL OF CONTROVERSY: CHURCH-STATE CONFLICT IN AMERICA: THE JUSTICES AND THEIR OPINIONS. Francis Graham Lee. R. E. Krieger Publishing Company, Incorporated, P.O. Box 9542, Malabar, Florida 32902-9542. 1986.

THE WEIGHTIER MATTERS OF THE LAW: ESSAYS ON LAW AND RELIGION: A TRIBUTE TO HAROLD J. BERMAN. John Witte, Jr. and Frank S. Alexander. Scholars Press, P.O. Box 15288, Decatur, Georgia 30333. 1988.

ENCYCLOPEDIAS AND DICTIONARIES

A DICTIONARY OF COMPARATIVE RELIGION. S.G.F. Brandon. Scribner Educational Publishers, 866 Third Avenue, New York, New York 10022. 1987.

DICTIONARY OF RELIGION AND PHILOSOPHY. Geddes MacGregor. Paragon House Publishers, 90 Fifth Avenue, New York, New York 10011. 1989.

ENCYCLOPEDIA OF AMERICAN RELIGIONS: A COMPREHENSIVE STUDY OF THE MAJOR RELIGIOUS GROUPS IN THE UNITED STATES. J. Gordon Melton. Triumph Books, New York, New York. 1991.

THE PERENNIAL DICTIONARY OF WORLD RELIGIONS. Keith Crim, Roger A. Bullard, and Larry D. Shinn. Harper and Row, San Francisco, California. 1981.

NEWSLETTERS AND NEWSPAPERS

ADL LAW REPORT. Anti-Defamation League of B'nai Brith, 823 United Nations Plaza, New York, New York 10017. Quarterly.

RELIGIOUS FREEDOM REPORTER. Center for Law and Religious Freedom, P.O. Box 505, Buies Creek, North Carolina 27506. Monthly.

BIBLIOGRAPHIES

ONLINE SEARCHING IN RELIGION INDEXES. Julie M. Hurd. American Theological Library Association, 820 Church Street, Third Floor, Evanston, Illinois 60201. 1989.

REFERENCE WORKS FOR THEOLOGICAL RESEARCH: AN ANNOTATED SELECTIVE BIBLIOGRAPHICAL GUIDE. Third Edition. Robert J. Kepple and John R. Muether. University Press of America, 4720 Boston Way, Lanham, Maryland 20706. 1992.

RELIGION AND AMERICAN LIFE: RESOURCES. Anne T. Fraker. University of Illinois Press, 54 East Gregory Drive, Champaign, Illinois 61820. 1989.

RELIGION AND POLITICS IN THE 1980'S: A SELECTIVE BIBLIOGRAPHY. Clarence Chisholm and Alva W. Stewart. Vance Bibliographies, P.O. Box 229, 112 North Charter Street, Monticello, Illinois 61856. 1987.

RELIGION JOURNALS AND SERIALS: AN ANALYTICAL GUIDE. Eugene C. Fieg, Jr. Greenwood Publishing Group, Incorporated, 88 Post Road West, P.O. Box 5007, Westport, Connecticut 06881. 1988.

A SCHOLAR'S GUIDE TO ACADEMIC JOURNALS IN RELIGION. James Dawsey. Scarecrow Press, Incorporated, 52 Liberty Street, P.O. Box 4167, Metuchen, New Jersey 08840. 1988.

THE SOCIOLOGY OF RELIGION: AN ORGANIZATIONAL BIBLIOGRAPHY. Anthony J. Blasi and Michael W. Cuneo. Garland Publishing, Incorporated, 136 Madison Avenue, New York, New York 10016. 1990.

DIRECTORIES

DIRECTORY OF DEPARTMENTS AND PROGRAMS OF RELIGIOUS STUDIES IN NORTH AMERICA. Watson E. Mills. Mercer University, Council of Societies for the Study of Religion, Macon, Georgia 31207. 1987.

DIRECTORY OF FACULTY OF DEPARMENTS AND PROGRAMS OF RELIGIOUS STUDIES IN NORTH AMERICA. Watson E. Mills. Council of Societies for the Study of Religion, Macon, Georgia. 1992.

A DIRECTORY OF RELIGIOUS AND PARARELIGIOUS BODIES AND ORGANIZATIONS IN THE UNITED STATES. James V. Geisendorfer. Edwin Mellen Press, P.O. Box 450, Lewiston, New York 14092. 1989.

GUIDE TO SCHOOLS AND DEPARTMENTS OF RELIGION AND SEMINARIES IN THE UNITED STATES AND CANADA: DEGREE PROGRAMS IN RELIGIOUS STUDIES. Macmillan Publishing Company, Incorporated, 866 Third Avenue, New York, New York 10022. 1987.

INTERFAITH DIRECTORY. Francis Clark. International Religious Foundation, New York, New York. 1987.

RELIGIOUS BODIES IN THE UNITED STATES: A DIRECTORY. J. Gordon Melton. Garland Publishing, Incorporated, 136 Madison Avenue, New York, New York 10016. 1992.

REMAINDERS
See: REAL PROPERTY; WILLS, TRUSTS AND INHERITANCE

REMEDIES

HANDBOOKS, MANUALS, FORMBOOKS

POST CONVICTION REMEDIES: SELF-HELP MANUAL. Daniel E. Manville and George N. Brezna. Oceana Publications, 75 Main Street, Dobbs Ferry, New York 10522. 1988.

TEXTBOOKS AND GENERAL WORKS

ACTIONS AND REMEDIES. Charles E. Friend. Callaghan and Company, 155 Pfingsten Road, Deerfield, Illinois 60015. 1985.

CASES AND MATERIALS ON REMEDIES. Fifth Edition. Kenneth H. York, John A. Bauman, and Doug Rendleman. West Publishing Company, 50 West Kellogg Boulevard, St. Paul, Minnesota 55164. 1992.

CASES AND PROBLEMS ON REMEDIES. Elaine W. Shoben and William Murray Tabb. Foundation Press, 615 Merrick Avenue, Westbury, New York 11590. 1989.

CONTRACT REMEDIES IN A NUTSHELL. Jane M. Friedman. West Publishing Company, P.O. Box 64526, 50 West Kellogg Boulevard, St. Paul, Minnesota 55164-0526. 1981.

THE DEATH OF THE IRREPARABLE INJURY RULE. Douglas Laycock. Oxford University Press, 200 Madison Avenue, New York, New York 10016. 1991.

HANDBOOK ON THE LAW OF REMEDIES. Dan B. Dobbs. West Publishing Company, P.O. Box 64526, 50 West Kellogg Boulevard, St. Paul, Minnesota 55164-0526. 1973. (Hornbook).

JUDICIAL REMEDIES IN INTERNATIONAL LAW. Christine D. Gray. Oxford University Press, 200 Madison Avenue, New York, New York 10016. 1987.

REMEDIES: DAMAGES, EQUITY, AND RESTITUTION. Second Edition. Robert S. Thompson and John A. Sebert, Jr. Matthew Bender and Company, Incorporated, 11 Penn Plaza, New York, New York 10001. 1989.

REMEDIES FOR BREACH BY SELLERS AND BUYERS UNDER THE UNIFORM COMMERCIAL CODE. Melvin D. Kraft, Chairman. Practising Law Institute, 810 Seventh Avenue, New York, New York 10019. 1984.

REMEDIES IN A NUTSHELL. Second Edition. John F. O'Connell. West Publishing Company, 50 West Kellogg Boulevard, St. Paul, Minnesota 55164-0526. 1984.

REMEDIES IN EMPLOYMENT DISCRIMINATION LAW. Robert Belton. John Wiley and Sons, Incorporated, 605 Third Avenue, New York, New York 10158. 1992.

REMEDIES: PUBLIC AND PRIVATE. David Schoenbrod. West Publishing Company, 50 West Kellogg Boulevard, St. Paul, Minnesota 55164. 1990.

RIGHTS AND REMEDIES UNDER U.C.C. ARTICLE 2. Harold Greenberg. John Wiley and Sons, Incorporated, 605 Third Avenue, New York, New York 10158. 1987.

RIGHTS, WRONGS, AND REMEDIES: SECTION 1983 AND CONSTITUTIONAL RIGHTS VINDICATION. Robert L. Spurrier. Associated Faculty Press, 19 West Thirty-sixth Street, New York, New York 10018. 1986.

ASSOCIATIONS AND PROFESSIONAL SOCIETIES

ASSOCIATION OF AMERICAN LAW SCHOOLS, SECTION ON REMEDIES. One Dupont Circle, Northwest, Suite 370, Washington, D.C. 20036. (202) 296-8851.

COMPUTER-ASSISTED LEGAL INSTRUCTION

COMPUGRAPH V. CHANG. Interactive Video Library, Harvard Law School, Educational Technology Department, 18 Everett Street, Cambridge, Massachusetts 02138. Interactive videodisc.

REMOVAL OF CAUSES
See: CIVIL PROCEDURE

RENT AND RENT CONTROL
See: LANDLORD AND TENANT

RENVOI
See: CONFLICT OF LAWS

REORGANIZATION, CORPORATE
See: BANKRUPTCY

RES JUDICATA
See: CIVIL PROCEDURE; JUDGMENTS

RESIDENCE
See: JURISDICTION

RESTATEMENTS

RESTATEMENTS

RESTATEMENT OF THE LAW OF AGENCY, 1933; RESTATEMENT OF THE LAW, SECOND: AGENCY, 1958. American Law Institute, 4025 Chestnut Street, Philadelphia, Pennsylvania 19104.

RESTATEMENT OF THE LAW OF CONFLICT OF LAWS, 1934; RESTATEMENT OF THE LAW, SECOND: CONFLICT OF LAWS, 1981. American Law Institute, 4025 Chestnut Street, Philadelphia, Pennsylvania 19104.

RESTATEMENT OF THE LAW OF CONTRACTS, 1936; RESTATEMENT OF THE LAW, SECOND: CONTRACTS, 1981. American Law Institute, 4025 Chestnut Street, Philadelphia, Pennsylvania 19104.

RESTATEMENT OF THE LAW OF JUDGMENTS, 1942; RESTATEMENT OF THE LAW, SECOND: JUDGMENTS, 1982. American Law Institute, 4025 Chestnut Street, Philadelphia, Pennsylvania 19104.

RESTATEMENT OF THE LAW OF PROPERTY, 1936-1944; RESTATEMENT OF THE LAW, SECOND: PROPERTY: LANDLORD AND TENANT, 1977: RESTATEMENT OF THE LAW, SECOND: PROPERTY: DONATIVE TRANSFERS, 1983. American Law Institute, 4025 Chestnut Street, Philadelphia, Pennsylvania 19104.

RESTATEMENT OF THE LAW OF RESTITUTION, 1937; RESTATEMENT OF THE LAW, SECOND: RESTITUTION: TENTATIVE DRAFTS NUMBERS 1- , 1980- . American Law Institute, 4025 Chestnut Street, Philadelphia, Pennsylvania 19104.

RESTATEMENT OF THE LAW OF SECURITY, 1941. American Law Institute, 4025 Chestnut Street, Philadelphia, Pennsylvania 19104.

RESTATEMENT OF THE LAW OF TORTS, 1936-1942; RESTATEMENT OF THE LAW, SECOND: TORTS, 1965-1979. American Law Institute, 4025 Chestnut Street, Philadelphia, Pennsylvania 19104.

RESTATEMENT OF THE LAW, SECOND: FOREIGN RELATIONS LAW OF THE UNITED STATES, 1965; RESTATEMENT OF THE LAW: FOREIGN RELATIONS LAW OF THE UNITED STATES (REVISED): TENTATIVE DRAFTS NUMBERS 1-6, 1980-1985; RESTATEMENT OF THE FOREIGN RELATIONS LAW OF THE UNITED STATES, REVISED (AS APPROVED BY THE AMERICAN LAW INSTITUTE IN 1986) 1987. American Law Institute, 4025 Chestnut Street, Philadelphia, Pennsylvania 19104.

RESTATEMENT OF THE LAW, SECOND: TRUSTS, 1959. American Law Institute, 4025 Chestnut Street, Philadelphia, Pennsylvania 19104.

DIGESTS, INDEXES, ABSTRACTS, CITATORS

RESTATEMENT IN THE COURTS. American Law Institute, 4025 Chestnut Street, Philadelphia, Pennsylvania 19104. 1945 (Periodic Supplements).

RESTATEMENT OF THE LAW, SECOND: CONFLICT OF LAWS: APPENDIX. American Law Institute, 4025 Chestnut Street, Philadelphia, Pennsylvania 19104. 1971 (Annual Supplements).

RESTATEMENT OF THE LAW, SECOND: CONTRACTS: APPENDIX. American Law Institute, 4025 Chestnut Street, Philadelphia, Pennsylvania 19104. 1983. (Annual Supplements).

RESTATEMENT OF THE LAW, SECOND: JUDGMENTS: APPENDIX. American Law Institute, 4025 Chestnut Street, Philadelphia, Pennsylvania 19104. 1982 (Annual Supplements).

RESTATEMENT OF THE LAW, SECOND: TORTS: APPENDIX. American Law Institute, 4025 Chestnut Street, Philadelphia, Pennsylvania 19104. 1989. (Annual Supplements).

SHEPARD'S RESTATEMENT OF THE LAW CITATIONS. Shepard's/McGraw-Hill, P.O. Box 1235, Colorado Springs, Colorado 80901. 1976 (Quarterly Supplements).

ANNUALS AND SURVEYS

RESTATEMENT OF THE LAW, THIRD: FOREIGN RELATIONS OF THE UNITED STATES, THIRD, 1989. American Law Institute, 4025 Chestnut Street, Philadelphia, Pennsylvania 19104.

ASSOCIATIONS AND PROFESSIONAL SOCIETIES

AMERICAN LAW INSTITUTE. 4025 Chestnut Street, Philadelphia, Pennsylvania 19104. (215) 243-1600.

RESTAURANTS
See: HOTELS, RESTAURANTS , ETC.

RESTITUTION

RESTATEMENTS

RESTATEMENT OF THE LAW OF RESTITUTION, 1937; RESTATEMENT OF THE LAW, SECOND: RESTITUTION: TENTATIVE DRAFTS NUMBERS 1- , 1980- . American Law Institute, 4025 Chestnut Street, Philadelphia, Pennsylvania 19104.

RESTITUTION

TEXTBOOKS AND GENERAL WORKS

ESSAYS ON THE LAW OF RESTITUTION. Andrew S. Burrows. Oxford University Press, 200 Madison Avenue, New York, New York 10016. 1991.

INTRODUCTION TO CONTRACTS AND RESTITUTION FOR PARALEGALS. Martin A. Frey and Terry H. Bitting. West Publishing Company, 50 West Kellogg Boulevard, St. Paul, Minnesota 55164. 1988.

AN INTRODUCTION TO THE LAW OF RESTITUTION. Peter Birks. Clarendon Press, New York, New York. 1989.

THE LAW OF RESTITUTION. George E. Palmer. Little, Brown, and Company, 34 Beacon Street, Boston, Massachusetts 02108. 1978. (1982 Supplement).

PUNISHMENT AND RESTITUTION: A RESTITUTIONARY APPROACH TO CRIME AND THE CRIMINAL. Charles F. Abel and Frank H. Marsh. Greenwood Publishing Group, Incorporated, 88 Post Road West, P.O. Box 5007, Westport, Connecticut 06881. 1984.

REMEDIES: DAMAGES, EQUITY, AND RESTITUTION. Second Edition. Robert S. Thompson and John A. Sebert, Jr. Matthew Bender and Company, Incorporated, 11 Penn Plaza, New York, New York 10001. 1989.

TORTS AND COMPENSATION - PERSONAL ACCOUNTABILITY AND SOCIAL RESPONSIBILITY FOR INJURY. Dan B. Dobbs. West Publishing Company, P.O. Box 64526, 50 West Kellogg Boulevard, St. Paul, Minnesota 55164-0526. 1985.

THE USE AND ABUSE OF UNJUST ENRICHMENT: ESSAYS ON THE LAW OF RESTITUTION. J. Beatson. Oxford University Press, 200 Madison Avenue, New York, New York 10016. 1991.

THE WEALTH OF RACES: THE PRESENT VALUE OF BENEFITS FROM PAST INJUSTICES. Richard F. America. Greenwood Publishing Group, Incorporated, 88 Post Road West, P.O. Box 5007, Westport, Connecticut 06881. 1990.

RESTRAINT OF TRADE
See: ANTITRUST LAW

RESTRAINTS ON ALIENATION
See: REAL PROPERTY

RESTRICTIVE COVENANTS
See: CONTRACTS; REAL PROPERTY

RESULTING TRUSTS
See: WILLS, TRUSTS AND INHERITANCE

RETARDATION
See: MENTAL HEALTH AND DISABILITY

RETIREMENT COMMUNITIES
See: AGED AND AGING; AGED AND RETIREMENT

RETIREMENT INCOME
See: SOCIAL SECURITY

REVENUE SHARING
See: FEDERAL AID

REVERSIONS
See: REAL PROPERTY

RIGHT OF ASSEMBLY
See: FREEDOM OF ASSEMBLY AND ASSOCIATION

RIGHT OF PRIVACY
See: PRIVACY, RIGHT OF

RIGHT TO COUNSEL
See: DUE PROCESS OF LAW

RIGHT TO DIE
See: DEATH; EUTHANASIA; MEDICAL JURISPRUDENCE AND MALPRACTICE

RIGHT TO FAIR TRIAL
See: DUE PROCESS OF LAW

RIGHT TO LIFE
See: ABORTION; EUTHANASIA

RIGHT TO TRIAL BY JURY
See: DUE PROCESS OF LAW; JURY

RIGHT TO WORK
See: LABOR AND LABOR RELATIONS

RIOTS
See: CRIMINAL LAW

RIPARIAN RIGHTS
See: WATER LAW

ROMAN LAW
See also: CIVIL LAW

TEXTBOOKS AND GENERAL WORKS

THE CHARACTER AND INFLUENCE OF THE ROMAN CIVIL LAW: HISTORICAL ESSAYS. Peter Stein. Hambledon Press, Ronceverte, West Virginia. 1988.

EARLY ROMAN LAW: THE REGAL PERIOD. E.C. Clark. Fred B. Rothman and Company, 10368 West Centennial Road, Littleton, Colorado 80127. 1987. (Reprint)

THE ELEMENTS OF ROMAN LAW. Fourth Edition. R. W. Leo. Sweet and Maxwell, South Quay Plaza, 183 Marsh Wall, London, England E14 9FT. 1986.

EQUITY IN ROMAN LAW: LECTURES DELIVERED IN THE UNIVERSITY OF LONDON AT THE REQUEST OF THE FACULTY OF LAWS. W. W. Buckland. Fred B. Rothman and Company, 10368 West Centennial Road, Littleton, Colorado 80127. 1983.

THE EVOLUTION OF THE ROMAN LAW: FROM BEFORE THE TWELVE TABLES TO THE CORPUS JURIS. Charles Sumner Lobingier. Fred B. Rothman and Company, 10368 West Centennial Road, Littleton, Colorado 80127. 1987. (Reprint)

THE HISTORY AND PRINCIPLES OF THE CIVIL LAW OF ROME: AN AID TO THE STUDY OF SCIENTIFIC AND COMPARATIVE JURISPRUDENCE. Sheldon Amos. Fred B. Rothman and Company, 10368 West Centennial Road, Littleton, Colorado 80127. 1987. (Reprint)

INTRODUCTION TO ROMAN LAW. Ph. J. Thomas. Kluwer Law Book Publishers, Incorporated, 36 West Forty-fourth Street, New York, New York 10036. 1986.

LAW AND LIFE IN ROME: 90 B.C. TO A.D. 212. J. A. Crook. Cornell University Press, 124 Roberts Place, Ithaca, New York 14850. 1984.

LAWYERS IN ROMAN REPUBLICAN POLITICS: A STUDY OF THE ROMAN JURISTS IN THEIR POLITICAL SETTING, 316-82 B.C. Richard A. Bauman. C. H. Bech'sche, Verlagsbushandlung Oscar Beck, Wikelmster. 9, 8000 Munich 40, Germany. 1983.

NEW PERSPECTIVES IN THE ROMAN LAW OF PROPERTY: ESSAYS FOR BARRY NICHOLAS. Peter Birks. Oxford University Press, 200 Madison Avenue, New York, New York 10016. 1989.

PROBLEMS OF THE ROMAN CRIMINAL LAW. James Leigh Strachan-Davidson. Fred B. Rothman and Company, 10368 West Centennial Road, Littleton, Colorado 80127. 1991.

THE RISE OF THE ROMAN JURIST: STUDIES IN CICERO'S PRO CARCINA. Bruce W. Frier. Princeton University Press, 41 William Street, Princeton, New Jersey 08540. 1985.

ROMAN LAW AND COMPARATIVE LAW. Alan Watson. University of Georgia Press, Athens, Georgia 30602. 1991.

THE ROMAN LAW OF TRUSTS. David Johnston. Clarendon Press. 1989.

STUDIES IN ROMAN PRIVATE LAW. Alan Watson. Hambledon Press, Rio Grande, Ohio. 1991.

A SUMMARY OF THE ROMAN CIVIL LAW: ILLUSTRATED BY COMMENTARIES ON AND PARALLELS FROM THE MOSAIC, CANON, MOHAMMEDAN, ENGLISH, AND FOREIGN LAW. Patrick Mac Chombaich De Colquhoun. Fred B. Rothman and Company, 10368 West Centennial Road, Littleton, Colorado 80127. 1988. (Reprint)

A TEXT-BOOK OF ROMAN LAW FROM AUGUSTUS TO JUSTINIAN. Third Edition. William Warwick Buckland and Peter Stein. Cambridge University Press, 40 West Twentieth Street, New York, New York 10011. 1975.

S

SAFETY LAWS
See: CONSUMER PROTECTION; DRUG LAWS; FIRES AND FIRE PROTECTION; FOOD LAWS; HAZARDOUS SUBSTANCES; OCCUPATIONAL SAFETY AND HEALTH; PRODUCTS LIABILITY AND SAFETY

SALES
See: COMMERCIAL LAW; SECURED TRANSACTIONS

SALES AND USE TAXES
See also: EXCISE TAXES; TAX LEGISLATION AND POLICY

LOOSELEAF SERVICES AND REPORTERS

ABA SALES AND USE TAX HANDBOOK. D. Michael Young and John T. Piper. American Bar Association, Section of Taxation, 750 North Lake Shore Drive, Chicago, Illinois 60611. 1988- .

ALL-STATE SALES TAX REPORTER. Commerce Clearing House, Incorporated, 4025 West Peterson Avenue, Chicago, Illinois 60646. 1976- .

SALES TAXES. Prentice-Hall, Incorporated, 113 Sylvan Avenue, Englewood Cliffs, New Jersey 07632. 1925- .

TEXTBOOKS AND GENERAL WORKS

PRENTICE-HALL'S GUIDE TO SALES AND USE TAXES. Prentice-Hall, Incorporated, 113 Sylvan Avenue, Englewood Cliffs, New Jersey 07632. 1988.

SALES TAXATION: CRITICAL ISSUES IN POLICY AND ADMINISTRATION. William F. Fox. Praeger Publishers, One Madison Avenue, New York, New York 10010. 1992.

SALES TAXATION: STATE AND LOCAL STRUCTURE AND ADMINISTRATION. John F. Due and John L. Mikesell. Johns Hopkins University Press, 701 West Fortieth Street, Suite 275, Baltimore, Maryland 21211-2190. 1983.

SALES TAXATION: THE CASE OF VALUE ADDED TAX IN THE EUROPEAN COMMUNITY. Ben Terra. Kluwer Law Book Publishers, Incorporated, 36 West Forty-fourth Street, New York, New York 10036. 1988.

TAX GUIDE FOR SALES REPRESENTATIVES. Commerce Clearing House, Incorporated, 4025 West Peterson Avenue, Chicago, Illinois 60646. 1982.

UNDERSTANDING AND MANAGING SALES AND USE TAX. Robert J. Fields. Commerce Clearing House, Incorporated, 4025 West Peterson Avenue, Chicago, Illinois 60646. 1991.

SALVAGE
See: ADMIRALTY

SAVINGS AND LOAN ASSOCIATIONS
See: BANKS AND BANKING

SCHOOL INTEGRATION
See also: DISCRIMINATION, EDUCATION; EDUCATION DEPARTMENT; SEGREGATION AND INTEGRATION

LOOSELEAF SERVICES AND REPORTERS

NOLPE SCHOOL LAW REPORTER. National Organization on Legal Problems of Education, Southwest Plaza Building, 3601 West Thirty-ninth Street, Topeka, Kansas 66614. Monthly.

SCHOOL LAW REGISTER. Cynthia Carter. Capitol Publications, Incorporated, 101 King Street, Suite 444, Alexandria, Virginia 22314. 1977- .

HANDBOOKS, MANUALS, FORMBOOKS

DESEGREGATING PUBLIC SCHOOLS: A HANDBOOK FOR LOCAL OFFICIALS. David R. Morgan, Robert E. England and Diana Laverents. University of Oklahoma Press, 105 Asp Avenue, Norman, Oklahoma 73019. 1982.

TEXTBOOKS AND GENERAL WORKS

BEYOND BUSING: INSIDE THE CHALLENGE TO URBAN SEGREGATION. Paul R. Dimond. University of Michigan Press, P. O. Box 1104, Ann Arbor, Michigan 48106. 1985.

BLACK AND WHITE IN SCHOOL: TRUST, TENSION, OR TOLERANCE? Janet Ward Schofield. Teachers College Press, New York, New York. 1989.

BLACK EDUCATION: A QUEST FOR EQUITY AND EXCELLENCE. Willy DeMarcell Smith and Eva Wells Chunn. Transaction Books, Rutgers University, New Brunswick, New Jersey 08903. 1989.

BLACK-WHITE CONTACT IN SCHOOLS: ITS SOCIAL AND ACADEMIC EFFECTS. Martin Patchen. Purdue University Press, South Campus Courts-D, Building B, West Lafayette, Indiana 47907. 1982.

BOSTON AGAINST BUSING: RACE, CLASS, AND ETHNICITY IN THE 1960S AND 1970S. Ronald P. Formisano. University of North Carolina Press, P.O. Box 2288, 116 South Boundary Street, Chapel Hill, North Carolina 27515-2288. 1991.

THE BOSTON SCHOOL INTEGRATION DISPUTE: SOCIAL CHANGE AND LEGAL MANEUVERS. Brian J. Sheehan. Books on Demand, 300 North Zeeb Road, Ann Arbor, Michigan 48106-1346. 1984.

THE BURDEN OF BROWN: THIRTY YEARS OF SCHOOL DESEGREGATION. Raymond Wolters. University of Tennessee Press, 293 Communications Building, Knoxville, Tennessee 37996-0325. 1984.

THE CARROT OR THE STICK FOR SCHOOL DESEGREGATION POLICY: MAGNET SCHOOLS OR FORCED BUSING. Christine H. Rossell. Temple University Press, 1601 North Broad Street, University Services Building, Philadelphia, Pennsylvania 19122. 1990.

THE CONSEQUENCES OF SCHOOL DESEGREGATION. Christine H. Rossell and Willis D. Hawley, editors. Temple University Press, 1601 North Broad Street, University Services Building, Philadelphia, Pennsylvania 19122. 1983.

THE COURT VS. CONGRESS: PRAYER, BUSING, AND ABORTION. Edward Keynes and Randall K. Miller. Duke University Press, P.O. Box 6697 College Station, Durham, North Carolina 27708. 1989.

DESEGREGATING BIG CITY SCHOOLS: STRATEGIES, OUTCOMES, AND IMPACTS. Robert E. England and David R. Morgan. Associated Faculty Press, 19 West Thirty-sixth Street, New York, New York 10018. 1985.

DESEGREGATION AND THE LAW: THE MEANING AND EFFECT OF THE SCHOOL SEGREGATION CASES. Albert P. Blaustein and Clarence C. Ferguson, Jr. Fred B. Rothman and Company, 10368 West Centennial Road, Littleton, Colorado 80127. 1985.

DESEGREGATION IN AMERICAN SCHOOLS: COMPARATIVE INTERVENTION STRATEGIES. Brian L. Fife. Praeger Publishers, One Madison Avenue, New York, New York 10010. 1992.

THE DREAM LONG DEFERRED. Frye Gaillard. University of North Carolina Press, P.O. Box 2288, 116 South Boundary Street, Chapel Hill, North Carolina 27515-2288. 1988.

FROM LITTLE ROCK TO BOSTON. The History of School Desegregation. George R. Metcalf. Greenwood Publishing Group, Incorporated, 88 Post Road West, P. O. Box 5007, Westport, Connecticut 06881. 1983.

LIBERTY'S CHOSEN HOME: THE POLITICS OF VIOLENCE IN BOSTON. Second Edition. Alan Lupo. Beacon Press, 25 Beacon Street, Boston, Massachusetts 02108. 1988.

THE NEW AMERICAN DILEMMA: LIBERAL DEMOCRACY AND SCHOOL DESEGREGATION. Jennifer L. Hochschild. Yale University Press, 302 Temple Street, New Haven, Connecticut 06520. 1984.

RACIAL POLITICS IN LITTLE ROCK, 1954-1964. Irving J. Spitzberg, Jr. Garland Publishing, Incorporated, 136 Madison Avenue, New York, New York 10016. 1987.

SCHOOL DESEGREGATION PLANS THAT WORK. Charles Vert Willie. Greenwood Publishing Group, Incorporated, 88 Post Road West, P. O. Box 5007, Westport, Connecticut 06881. 1984.

SCHOOL DESEGREGATION RESEARCH: NEW DIRECTIONS IN SITUATIONAL ANALYSIS. Jeffrey Preger, Douglas Longshore, and Melvin Seeman. Plenum Publishing Corporation, 233 Spring Street, New York, New York 10013. 1986.

SCHOOLS ON TRIAL: AN INSIDE ACCOUNT OF THE BOSTON DESEGREGATION CASE. Robert A. Dentler and Marvin B. Scott. University Press of America, 4720 Boston Way, Lanham, Maryland 20706. 1984.

A SEMBLANCE OF JUSTICE: SCHOOL DESEGREGATION AND THE PURSUIT OF ORDER IN URBAN AMERICA. Daniel J. Monti. University of Missouri Press, 2910 LeMone Boulevard, Columbia, Missouri 65201. 1985.

THE STRUGGLE FOR EQUAL EDUCATION. Paul Finkelman. Garland Publishing, Incorporated, 136 Madison Avenue, New York, New York 10016. 1992- .

THE STRUGGLE FOR EQUAL EDUCATION. Clarence Lusane. Franklin Watts, Incorporated, 387 Park Avenue South, New York, New York 10016. 1992.

THIRTY YEARS AFTER BROWN. Jennifer L. Hochschild. Joint Center for Political and Economic Studies, 1301 Pennsylvania Avenue, Northwest, Suite 400, Washington, D.C. 20004. 1985.

ANNUALS AND SURVEYS

SCHOOL LAW UPDATE. National Organization on Legal Problems of Education, Southwest Plaza Building, 3601 West Twenty-ninth Street, Topeka, Kansas 66614. Annual.

LAW REVIEWS AND PERIODICALS

EDUCATION LAW BULLETIN. Center for Law and Education, Gutman Library, 6 Appian Way, Cambridge, Massachusetts 02138. Semiannually.

JOURNAL OF LAW AND EDUCATION. University of South Carolina, Law School, Columbia, South Carolina 29208. Quarterly.

NEWSLETTERS AND NEWSPAPERS

INQUIRY AND ANALYSIS. National School Board Association, 1680 Duke Street, Alexandria, Virginia 22314. Bimonthly.

NOLPE NOTES. National Organization on Legal Problems of Education, Southwest Plaza Building, 3601 West Twenty-ninth Street, Suite 223, Topeka, Kansas 66614. Monthly.

NOLPE SCHOOL LAW REPORTER. National Organization on Legal Problems of Education, Southwest Plaza Building, 3601 West Twenty-ninth Street, Suite 223, Topeka, Kansas 66614. Monthly.

SCHOOL LAW BULLETIN. Quinlan Publishing Company, 131 Beverly Street, Boston, Massachusetts 02114. Monthly.

SCHOOL LAW BULLETIN. University of North Carolina, Institute of Government, Knapp Building CB# 3330, Chapel Hill, North Carolina 27599. Quarterly.

SCHOOL LAW NEWS. Capitol Publications, Incorporated, 1101 King Street, Suite 444, Alexandria, Virginia 22314. Biweekly.

SCHOOL LAW NEWSLETTER. P.O. Box 199, Rauser, Texas 76470. Quarterly.

SCHOOL LAWYER. Education Information Services, Incorporated, P. O. Box 1231, Alexandria, Virginia 22313. Biweekly.

THE SCHOOLS AND THE COURTS. College Administration Publications, Incorporated, P.O. Box 8492, Asheville, North Carolina 28814. Quarterly.

A WORD ON. National School Boards Association, 1680 Duke Street, Alexandria, Virginia 22314. Bimonthly.

YOUR SCHOOL AND THE LAW. Professional Publications, 50 South Ninth Street, Suite 200, Minneapolis, Minnesota 55402. Monthly.

BIBLIOGRAPHIES

DESEGREGATION POLICIES AND THE OPERATION OF PUBLIC SCHOOLS: A CHECKLIST, 1982-1987. Dale E. Casper. Vance Bibliographies, P.O. Box 229, 112 North Charter Street, Monticello, Illinois 61856. 1987.

ASSOCIATIONS AND PROFESSIONAL SOCIETIES

CENTER FOR LAW AND EDUCATION. Gutman Library, Third Floor, 6 Appian Way, Cambridge, Massachusetts 02138. (617) 495-4666.

FUND FOR AN OPEN SOCIETY. 311 South Juniper Street, Suite 400, Philadelphia, Pennsylvania 19107. (215) 735-6915.

NATIONAL ASSOCIATION FOR EQUAL EDUCATIONAL OPPORTUNITIES. 2181 Brigden Road, Pasadena, California 91104. (714) 625-6607.

NATIONAL COALITION FOR QUALITY INTEGRATED EDUCATION, 1201 Sixteenth Street, Northwest, Suite 424, Washington, D.C. 20036. (202) 822-7708.

NATIONAL COALITION OF ADVOCATES FOR STUDENTS. 100 Boylston Street, Suite 737, Boston, Massachusetts 02116. (617) 357-8507.

NATIONAL NEIGHBORS. 2000 M Street, Northwest, Suite 400, Washington, D.C. 20036. (202) 785-4836.

NATIONAL ORGANIZATION ON LEGAL PROBLEMS OF EDUCATION, 3601 West Twenty-ninth Street, Suite 223, Topeka, Kansas 66614. (913) 273-3550.

RESEARCH CENTERS, INSTITUTES, CLEARINGHOUSES

CENTER FOR THE STUDY OF METROPOLITAN PROBLEMS IN EDUCATION. University of Missouri - Kansas City, 5100 Rockhill Road, Kansas City, Missouri 64110. (816) 276-2251.

HORACE MANN BOND CENTER FOR EQUAL EDUCATION, Library Tower, University of Massachusetts, Amherst, Massachusetts 01003. (413) 545-0327.

INSTITUTE OF GOVERNMENT. University of North Carolina, Knapp Building, CB# 3330, Chapel Hill, North Carolina 27599. (919) 966-4119.

INSTITUTE ON DESEGREGATION. North Carolina Central University, 214 Taylor Education Building, Durham, North Carolina 27707. (919) 560-6367.

INTERCULTURAL DEVELOPMENT RESEARCH ASSOCIATION. 5835 Callaghan Road, Suite 350, San Antonio, Texas 78228. (512) 684-8180.

STATISTICS SOURCES

DIGEST OF EDUCATION STATISTICS. United States Department of Education, 400 Maryland Avenue, Southwest, Washington, D.C. 20202. Annual.

SCHOOL VIOLENCE AND DISCIPLINE

LOOSELEAF SERVICES AND REPORTERS

NOLPE SCHOOL LAW REPORTER. National Organization on Legal Problems of Education, Southwest Plaza Building, 3601 West Twenty-ninth Street, Topeka, Kansas 66614. Monthly.

HANDBOOKS, MANUALS, FORMBOOKS

SCHOOL DISCIPLINE AND STUDENT RIGHTS: AN ADVOCATES MANUAL. Paul Weckstein. Center for Law and Education, 955 Massachusetts Avenue, Cambridge, Massachusetts 02139. 1982.

SCHOOL DISCIPLINE GUIDEBOOK: THEORY INTO PRACTICE. Frank A. Johns, Robert H. MacNaughton, and Nancy G. Karabinus. Allyn and Bacon, 160 Gould Street, Needham Heights, Massachusetts 02194. 1989.

SCHOOL VIOLENCE AND DISCIPLINE

TEXTBOOKS AND GENERAL WORKS

BIGOTRY AND VIOLENCE ON AMERICAN COLLEGE CAMPUSES. United States Commission on Civil Rights, 1121 Vermont Avenue, Northwest, Washington, D.C. 20425. 1990.

DISRUPTIVE SCHOOL BEHAVIOR: CLASS, RACE, AND CULTURE. Judith Lynne Hanna. Holmes and Meier Publishers, IUB Building, 30 Irving Place, New York, New York 10003. 1988.

EDUCATION AND MEDIATION: EXPLORING THE ALTERNATIVES. Prudence B. Kestner, Kim Unyong, and Judy Devonshire. American Bar Association, Standing Committee on Dispute Resolution, 1800 M Street, Northwest, Washington, D.C. 20036. 1988.

THE LAW OF SCHOOLS, STUDENTS AND TEACHERS IN A NUTSHELL. Kern Alexander and M. David Alexander. West Publishing Company, P. O. Box 64526, 50 West Kellogg Boulevard, St. Paul, Minnesota 55164-0526. 1984.

THE LURKING EVIL: RACIAL AND ETHNIC CONFLICT ON THE COLLEGE CAMPUS. Robert Hively. American Association of State Colleges and Universities, One Dupont Circle, Suite 700, Washington, D.C. 20036. 1990.

MEDIATION IN THE SCHOOLS: AN EVALUATION OF THE WAKEFIELD PILOT PEER-MEDIATION PROGRAM IN TUCSON, ARIZONA. M. Melissa McCormick. American Bar Association, Standing Committee on Dispute Resolution, 1800 M Street, Northwest, Washington, D.C. 20036. 1988.

READING, WRITING, AND THE HICKORY STICK: THE APPALLING STORY OF PHYSICAL AND PSYCHOLOGICAL ABUSE IN AMERICAN SCHOOLS. Irwin A. Hyman. Lexington Books, 125 Spring Street, Lexington, Massachusetts 02173. 1990.

SCHOOL DISCIPLINE: ORDER AND AUTONOMY. Ellen J. Hollingsworth and Henry S. Lufler. Praeger Publications, One Madison Avenue, New York, New York 10010-3603. 1984.

STUDENT DISCIPLINE STRATEGIES: RESEARCH AND PRACTICE. Oliver C. Moles. State University of New York Press, State University Plaza, Albany, New York 12246. 1990.

VIOLENCE, VALUES AND JUSTICE IN THE SCHOOLS. Rodger W. Bybee and E. Gordon Gee. Allyn and Bacon, Incorporated, 160 Gould Street, Needham Heights, Massachusetts 02194. 1982.

ANNUALS AND SURVEYS

JUDICIAL RULINGS, STATE STATUTES, AND STATE ADMINISTRATIVE REGULATIONS DEALING WITH THE USE OF CORPORAL PUNISHMENT IN PUBLIC SCHOOLS. Ronald A. Paquet. R and E Publishers, P. O. Box 2008, Saratoga, California 95070-2008. 1982.

SCHOOL LAW UPDATE. National Organization on Legal Problems of Education, 5401 Southwest Seventh Avenue, Topeka, Kansas 66606. Monthly.

NEWSLETTERS AND NEWSPAPERS

NOLPE NOTES. National Organization on Legal Problems of Education, 3601 West Twenty-ninth Street, Topeka, Kansas 66614. Monthly.

SCHOOL LAW BULLETIN. Quinlan Publishing Company, 131 Beverly Street, Boston, Massachusetts 02114. Monthly.

SCHOOL LAW BULLETIN. University of North Carolina, Institute of Government, Knapp Building CB# 3330, Chapel Hill, North Carolina 27599. Quarterly.

SCHOOL LAW NEWS. Capitol Publications, Incorporated, 1101 King Street, Suite 444, Alexandria, Virginia 22314. Biweekly.

SCHOOL LAWYER. Education Information Services, Incorporated, P. O. Box 1231, Alexandria, Virginia 22313. Biweekly.

THE SCHOOLS AND THE COURTS. College Administration Publications, Incorporated, P.O. Box 8492, Asheville, North Carolina 28814. Quarterly.

ASSOCIATIONS AND PROFESSIONAL SOCIETIES

CENTER FOR LAW AND EDUCATION. Gutman Library, Third Floor, 6 Appian Way, Cambridge, Massachusetts 02138. (617) 495-4666.

NATIONAL ORGANIZATION ON LEGAL PROBLEMS OF EDUCATION, 3601 West Twenty-ninth Street, Topeka, Kansas 66614. (913) 273-3550.

RESEARCH CENTERS, INSTITUTES, CLEARINGHOUSES

CENTER FOR THE STUDY OF METROPOLITAN PROBLEMS IN EDUCATION. University of Missouri, Kansas City, 5100 Rockhill Road, Kansas City, Missouri 64110. (816) 276-2251.

SCHOOLS
See: EDUCATION; MENTAL HEALTH AND DISABILITY; SCHOOL INTEGRATION; SCHOOL VIOLENCE AND DISCIPLINE

SCIENCE

STATUTES, CODES, STANDARDS, UNIFORM LAWS

COMPILATION OF PUBLIC LAWS REPORTED BY THE COMMITTEE ON SCIENCE, SPACE, AND TECHNOLOGY, 1958-1988. REPORT TO THE COMMITTEE ON SCIENCE, SPACE, AND TECHOLOGY, U.S. HOUSE OF REPRESENTATIVES, ONE HUNDREDTH CONGRESS, SECOND SESSION. Superintendent of Documents, United States Government Printing Office, Washington, D.C. 20402. 1989- .

THE FEDERAL LAW OF SCIENCE AND TECHNOLOGY, 1954-1984: A COLLECTION OF LAWS, LEGISLATIVE HISTORIES, AND ADMINISTRATIVE MATERIALS DOCUMENTING THE HISTORY OF FEDERAL SCIENCE POLICY. Bernard D. Reams, Jr. William S. Hein and Company, 1285 Main Street, Buffalo, New York 14209. 1987.

LOOSELEAF SERVICES AND REPORTERS

BIOETHICS REPORTER: ETHICAL AND LEGAL ISSUES IN MEDICINE, HEALTH CARE ADMINISTRATION, AND HUMAN EXPERIMENTATION. James F. Childress, et al., Editors. University Publications of America, 4520 East West Highway, Suite 600, Bethesda, Maryland 20814. 1983- .

BIOTECHNOLOGY AND THE LAW. Iver P. Cooper. Clark Boardman Company, Limited, 435 Hudson Street, New York, New York 10014. 1982- .

TECHNOLOGY MANAGEMENT: LAW, TACTICS, FORMS. Robert Goldscheider. Clark Boardman Company, Limited, 435 Hudson Street, New York, New York 10014. 1988- .

HANDBOOKS, MANUALS, FORMBOOKS

HANDBOOK ON ARTIFICIAL INTELLIGENCE AND EXPERT SYSTEMS IN LAW ENFORCEMENT. Edward C. Ratledge and Joan E. Jacoby. Greenwood Publishing Group, Incorporated, 88 Post Road West, P.O. Box 5007, Westport, Connecticut 06881. 1989.

TEXTBOOKS AND GENERAL WORKS

CONTEMPORARY BIOMATERIALS: MATERIAL AND HOST RESPONSE, CLINICAL APPLICATIONS, NEW TECHNOLOGY AND LEGAL ASPECTS. John W. Boretos and Murray Eden, Editors. Noyes Data Corporation, 120 Mill Road, Park Ridge, New Jersey 07656. 1984.

EMPTY PROMISE: THE GROWING CASE AGAINST STAR WARS. The Union of Concerned Scientists. Beacon Press, Incorporated, 25 Beacon Street, Boston, Massachusetts 02108. 1986.

FETAL DIAGNOSIS AND THERAPY: SCIENCE, ETHICS, AND THE LAW. Mark I. Evans. J. B. Lippincott Company, East Washington Square, Philadelphia, Pennsylvania 19105. 1989.

FUNDAMENTALS OF COMPUTER-HIGH TECHNOLOGY LAW. James V. Vergari and Virginia V. Shue. American Law Institute-American Bar Association, Committee on Continuing Professional Education, 4025 Chestnut Street, Philadelphia, Pennsylvania 19104. 1990.

HARNESSING SCIENCE FOR ENVIRONMENTAL REGULATION. John D. Graham. Praeger Publishers, One Madison Avenue, New York, New York 10010. 1991.

INTERNATIONAL TECHNOLOGY JOINT VENTURES IN THE COUNTRIES OF THE PACIFIC RIM. James A. Dobkin. Butterworth Legal Publishers, 90 Stiles Road, Salem, New Hampshire 03079. 1988.

INTERNATIONAL TECHNOLOGY TRANSFER FOR PROFIT. Dennis Campbell and Mark Abell. Kluwer Law Book Publishers, Incorporated, 36 West Forty-fourth Street, New York, New York 10036. 1992.

LAW AND HIGH-TECHNOLOGY INNOVATION. Aryeh S. Friedman. Butterworth Legal Publishers, 90 Stiles Road, Salem, New Hampshire 03079. 1989.

LAW AND SCIENCE IN COLLABORATION: RESOLVING REGULATORY ISSUES OF SCIENCE AND TECHNOLOGY. J. D. Nyhart and Milton M. Carrow. Lexington Books, Division of D.C. Heath and Company, 125 Spring Street, Lexington, Massachusetts 02173. 1983.

LEGAL ASPECTS OF THE TRANSFER OF TECHOLOGY TO DEVELOPING COUNTRIES. Michael Blakeney. ESC Publications, Oxford. 1989.

LEGAL ISSUES IN BIOTECHNOLOGY AND HUMAN REPRODUCTION: ARTIFICIAL CONCEPTION AND MODERN GENETICS. Warren Freedman. Quorum Books, Greenwood Publishing Group, Incorporated, 88 Post Road West, P.O. Box 5007, Westport, Connecticut 06881. 1991.

THE POLITICAL ECONOMY OF INTERNATIONAL TECHNOLOGY TRANSFER. John R. McIntyre and Daniel S. Papp, Editors. Quorum Books, Imprint of Greenwood Publishing Group, Incorporated, 88 Post Road West, P.O. Box 5007, Westport, Connecticut 06881. 1986.

POLITICS AND THE RESTRAINT OF SCIENCE. Leonard A. Cole. Rowman and Allanheld, 420 Boston Way, Lanham, Maryland 20706. 1983.

SCIENCE AND LAW: AN ESSENTIAL ALLIANCE. William A. Thomas, Editor. Westview Press, 5500 Central Avenue, Boulder, Colorado 80301. 1983.

SCIENCE AND TECHNOLOGY POLICY IN THE 1980'S AND BEYOND. Phillip Gummett, Michael Gibbons, and Bhalchandra Udgaonkar, Editors. Longman Incorporated, 19 West Forty-fourth Street, New York, New York 10036. 1984.

SCIENCE POLICY, ETHICS, AND ECONOMIC METHODOLOGY. Kristin S. Shrader-Frechette. Kluwer Academic Publications, 101 Philip Drive, Assinippi Park, Norwell, Massachusetts 20261. 1984.

SCIENCE, TECHNOLOGY, AND THE FIRST AMENDMENT: SPECIAL REPORT. Congress of the United States, Office of Technology Assessment. Superintendent of Documents, United States Government Printing Office, Washington, D.C. 20402. 1987.

SCIENTIFIC EVIDENCE IN CRIMINAL CASES. Third Edition. Andre A. Moenssens, Fred E. Inbau and James Starrs. Foundation Press, Incorporated, 615 Merrick Avenue, Westbury, New York 11590. 1986.

SOCIAL SCIENCE, LAW, AND PUBLIC POLICY. Stuart S. Nagel and Lisa A. Bievenue. University Press of America, 4720 Boston Way, Lanham, Maryland 20706. 1992.

TECHNOLOGY CONTROL, COMPETITION AND NATIONAL SECURITY: CONFLICT AND CONSENSUS. Bernard L. Seward, Jr., Editor. University Press of America, 4720 Boston Way, Lanham, Maryland 20706. 1987.

TECHNOLOGY, LAW, AND THE WORKING ENVIRONMENT. Nicholas A. Ashford and Charles C. Caldart. Van Nostrand Reinhold Company, Incorporated, 115 Fifth Avenue, New York, New York 10003. 1991.

TECHNOLOGY TRANSFER: AN EXECUTIVE GUIDE. R. Duane Hall. Random House, Incorporated, 201 East Fiftieth Street, New York, New York 10022. 1987.

THE TWENTY-FIRST CENTURY: TECHNOLOGY'S IMPACT ON ACADEMIC RESEARCH AND LAW LIBRARIES. Betty W. Taylor, Elizabeth B. Mann, and Robert J. Munro. G. K. Hall and Company, Incorporated, 70 Lincoln Street, Boston, Massachusetts 02111. 1988.

WHAT PROCESS IS DUE? COURTS AND SCIENCE-POLICY DISPUTES. David M. O'Brien. Russell Sage Foundation, 112 East Sixty-fourth Street, New York, New York 10021. 1987.

THE WORLD OF SCIENCE AND THE RULE OF THE LAW: A STUDY OF THE OBSERVANCE AND VIOLATIONS OF THE HUMAN RIGHTS OF SCIENTISTS IN THE PARTICIPATING STATES OF THE HELSINKI ACCORDS. John M. Ziman. Oxford University Press, Incorporated, 200 Madison Avenue, New York, New York 10016. 1986.

ENCYCLOPEDIAS AND DICTIONARIES

MCGRAW-HILL ENCYCLOPEDIA OF SCIENCE AND TECHNOLOGY, 5TH EDITION. Shepard's/McGraw-Hill, P.O. Box 1235, Colorado Springs, Colorado 80901. 1982.

LAW REVIEWS AND PERIODICALS

JOURNAL OF FORENSIC SCIENCES. American Academy of Forensic Sciences, 225 South Academy Blvd., Suite 201, Colorado Springs, Colorado 80910. Quarterly.

JURIMETRICS: JOURNAL OF LAW, SCIENCE, AND TECHNOLOGY. Section of Science and Technology, American Bar Association, 750 North Lake Shore Drive, Chicago, Illinois 60611. Quarterly.

NEWSLETTERS AND NEWSPAPERS

BULLETIN OF LAW, SCIENCE, AND TECHNOLOGY. American Bar Association, Section of Science and Technology, 750 North Lake Shore Drive, Chicago, Illinois 60611. Bimonthly.

RESEARCH CENTERS, INSTITUTES, CLEARINGHOUSES

NATIONAL INSTITUTE FOR SCIENCE, LAW, AND PUBLIC POLICY. 1424 Sixteenth Street, Suite 105, Washington, D.C. 20036. (202) 462-8800.

ONLINE DATABASES

SCISEARCH. Institute for Scientific Information, 3501 Market Street, Philadelphia, Pennsylvania 19104.

SEAMEN
See: ADMIRALTY

SEARCH AND SEIZURE

STATUTES, CODES, STANDARDS, UNIFORM LAWS

GUIDELINES FOR THE ISSUANCE OF SEARCH WARRANTS. American Bar Association, Section of Criminal Justice, 750 North Lake Shore Drive, Chicago, Illinois 60611. 20036. 1990.

LOOSELEAF SERVICES AND REPORTERS

NEW YORK SUPPRESSION MANUAL: ARREST, SEARCH AND SEIZURE, CONFESSION, IDENTIFICATION. Lewis R. Katz and Jay Shapiro. Matthew Bender and Company, Incorporated, 11 Penn Plaza, New York, New York 10001. 1991.

SEARCH WARRANT LAW DESKBOOK. John M. Burkoff. Clark Boardman Company, Limited, 435 Hudson Street, New York, New York 10014. 1987.

WARRANTLESS SEARCH LAW DESKBOOK. Paul R. Joseph. Clark Boardman Company, Limited, 435 Hudson Street, New York, New York 10014. 1991- .

HANDBOOKS, MANUALS, FORMBOOKS

CHECKLISTS FOR SEARCHES AND SEIZURES IN PUBLIC SCHOOLS. Jon M. Van Dyke and Melvin M. Sakurai. Clark Boardman Company, Limited, 435 Hudson Street, New York, New York 10014. 1992.

SEARCH AND SEIZURE CHECKLISTS. Michelle G. Hermann. Clark Boardman Company, Limited, 435 Hudson Street, New York, New York 10014. 1991.

SEARCH AND SEIZURE HANDBOOK. Fourth Edition. Donallis Rutledge. Custom Publishing Company, 1590 Lotus Road, Placerville, California 95667. 1990.

TEXTBOOKS AND GENERAL WORKS

BRIEFS OF 100 LEADING CASES IN LAW ENFORCEMENT. Rolando V. del Carmen and Jeffrey T. Walker. Anderson Publishing Company, 2035 Reading Road, Cincinnati, Ohio 45202. 1991.

CRIMINAL PROCEDURE: CONSTITUTIONAL CONSTRAINTS ON INVESTIGATION AND PROOF. Welsh S. White and James J. Tomkovicz. Matthew Bender and Company, Incorporated, 11 Penn Plaza, New York, New York 10001. 1990.

ENFORCING THE FOURTH AMENDMENT: A JURIS-PRUDENTIAL HISTORY. Bradford P. Wilson. Garland Publishing, Incorporated, 136 Madison Avenue, New York, New York 10016. 1986.

THE FOURTH AMENDMENT. Paula A. Franklin. Silver Burdett Press, Incorporated, 190 Sylvan Avenue, Englewood Cliffs, New Jersey 07632. 1991.

THE HISTORY AND DEVELOPMENT OF THE FOURTH AMENDMENT TO THE UNITED STATES CONSTITUTION. Nelson Bernard Lasson. AMS Press, Incorporated, 56 East Thirteenth Street, New York, New York 10003. 1988.

SEARCH AND SEIZURE. John W. Hall, Jr. Lawyers Co-Operative Publishing Company, Aqueduct Building, Rochester, New York 14694. 1982. (Periodic Supplements).

SEARCH AND SEIZURE: A TREATISE ON THE FOURTH AMENDMENT. Second Edition. Wayne R. LaFave. West Publishing Company, P.O. Box 64526, 50 West Kellogg Boulevard, St. Paul, Minnesota 55164-0526. 1987. (Annual Supplements).

SEARCH AND SEIZURE: CONSTITUTIONAL AND COMMON LAW. Polyvios G. Polyviou. Duckworth Publishing Company, Sheridan House, Incorporated, 145 Palisade Street, Dobbs Ferry, New York 10522. 1982.

SEARCHES AND SEIZURES, ARRESTS AND CONFESSIONS. Second Edition. Clark Boardman Company, Limited, 435 Hudson Street, New York, New York 10014. 1980. (Annual Supplements).

LAW REVIEWS AND PERIODICALS

SEARCH AND SEIZURE BULLETIN. Quinlan Publishing Company, 131 Beverly Street, Boston, Massachusettes 02114. Monthly.

SEARCH AND SEIZURE LAW REPORT. Clark Boardman Company, Limited, 435 Hudson Street, New York, New York 10014. Monthly.

BIBLIOGRAPHIES

SEARCH AND SEIZURE IN SCHOOL. Earleen H. Cook. Vance Bibliographies, P.O. Box 229, 112 North Charter Street, Monticello, Illinois 61856. 1987.

DIRECTORIES

A NETWORK OF KNOWLEDGE: DIRECTORY OF CRIMINAL INFORMATION SOURCES. Fifth Edition. National Institute of Justice. Superintendent of Documents, United States Government Printing Office, Washington, D.C. 20402. 1984.

RESEARCH CENTERS, INSTITUTES, CLEARINGHOUSES

CRIMINAL JUSTICE CENTER. 899 Tenth Avenue, Suite 636, New York, New York 10019. (212) 247-1600.

INSTITUTE OF CRIMINAL LAW AND PROCEDURE. Georgetown University. 600 New Jersey Avenue, Northwest, Washington, D.C. 20001. (202) 662-9070.

STATISTICS SOURCES

CRIMINAL JUSTICE STATISTICS ASSOCIATION, 444 North Capitol Street, Northwest, Suite 606, Washington, D.C. 20001.

COMPUTER-ASSISTED LEGAL INSTRUCTION

SEARCH AND SEIZURE. Center for Computer-Assisted Instruction, 229 19th Avenue South, University of Minnesota, Minneapolis, Minnesota 55455. Interactive videodisc.

OTHER SOURCES

REPORT TO THE ATTORNEY GENERAL ON THE SEARCH AND SEIZURE EXCLUSIONARY RULE. United States Department of Justice, Office of Legal Policy. Superintendent of Documents, United States Government Printing Office, Washington, D.C. 20402. 1988.

SEAS
See: ADMIRALTY; LAW OF THE SEA

SECTION 1983
See: CIVIL RIGHTS AND LIBERTIES; CIVIL RIGHTS COMMISSION

SECURED TRANSACTIONS
See also: SURETYSHIP AND GUARANTY

STATUTES, CODES, STANDARDS, UNIFORM LAWS

UNIFORM COMMERCIAL CODE, ARTICLE 9, UNIFORM LAWS ANNOTATED. West Publishing Company, P.O. Box 64526, 50 West Kellogg Boulevard, St. Paul, Minnesota 55164-0526. 1976. (Annual Supplements).

RESTATEMENTS

RESTATEMENT OF THE LAW, PROPERTY SECURITY (MORTGAGES): COUNCIL DRAFT. American Law Institute-American Bar Association, 4025 Chestnut Street, Philadelphia, Pennsylvania 19104. 1990- .

LOOSELEAF SERVICES AND REPORTERS

COMMERCIAL FINANCE GUIDE. Joseph Jude Norton, Thomas E. Gillespie, and Darrel A. Rice. Matthew Bender and Company, Incorporated, 11 Penn Plaza, New York, New York 10001. 1990- .

DOCUMENTING SECURED TRANSACTIONS: PROBLEM AVOIDANCE AND EFFECTIVE DRAFTING. William C. Hillman. Practising Law Institute, 810 Seventh Avenue, New York, New York 10019. 1987- .

THE LAW AND PRACTICE OF SECURED TRANSACTIONS: WORKING WITH ARTICLE 9. Richard F. Duncan and William H. Lyons. Law Journal Seminars-Press, Incorporated, 111 Eighth Avenue, Suite 900, New York, New York 10011. 1987- .

SECURED TRANSACTIONS GUIDE. Commerce Clearing House, Incorporated, 4025 West Peterson Avenue, Chicago, Illinois 60646. 1969- .

SECURITIZATION: ASSET-BACKED AND MORTGAGE-BACKED SECURITIES. Ronald S. Borod. Butterworth Legal Publishers, 90 Stiles Road, Salem, New Hampshire 03079. 1991- .

STRUCTURING SECURED COMMERCIAL LOAN DOCUMENTS. James J. Cunningham, Richard Jay Goldstein, and Matthew W. Kavanaugh. Research Institute of America, Incorporated, One Penn Plaza, New York, New York 10119. 1991- .

HANDBOOKS, MANUALS, FORMBOOKS

BASIC GUIDE TO SECURED TRANSACTIONS UNDER THE UNIFORM COMMERCIAL CODE. Brian N. Siegal. Associated Faculty Press, 90 South Bayles Avenue, Port Washington, New York 11050. 1985.

GUIDE TO SECURED LENDING TRANSACTIONS. Arnold B. Cohen. Research Institute of America, Incorporated, One Penn Plaza, New York, New York 10119. 1988.

GUIDEBOOK TO SECURITY INTERESTS IN PERSONAL PROPERTY. Second Edition. Eldon H. Reiley. Clark Boardman Company, Limited, 435 Hudson Street, New York, New York 10014. 1986.

LAWYER'S BASIC GUIDE TO SECURED TRANSACTIONS. Donald W. Baker. American Law Institute-American Bar Association, Committee on Continuing Professional Education, 4025 Chestnut Street, Philadelphia, Pennsylvania 19104. 1983.

A PRACTICAL GUIDE TO THE LAW OF SECURED LENDING. Eric M. Holmes and Peter J. Shedd. Prentice-Hall, Incorporated, 113 Sylvan Avenue, Englewood Cliffs, New Jersey 07632. 1986.

TEXTBOOKS AND GENERAL WORKS

ASSET FINANCING. Michael Downey Rice. Little, Brown and Company, 34 Beacon Street, Boston, Massachusetts 02108. 1989.

CASES, PROBLEMS, AND MATERIALS ON SECURITY INTERESTS IN PERSONAL PROPERTY. Second Edition. Douglas G. Baird and Thomas H. Jackson. Foundation Press, 615 Merrick Avenue, Westbury, New York 11590. 1987.

DISPOSITION OF REPOSSESSED COLLATERAL UNDER THE UNIFORM COMMERCIAL CODE. Christine A. Ferris and Bennett H. Goldstein. John Wiley and Sons, Incorporated, 605 Third Avenue, New York, New York 10158. 1990.

ENFORCING SECURED CLAIMS. David G. Epstein, Chairman. Practising Law Institute, 810 Seventh Avenue, New York, New York 10019. 1983.

ENFORCING SECURED CLAIMS. Ronald M. Martin. Professional Education Systems, Incorporated, 200 Sprint Street, Eau Claire, Wisconsin 54702. 1984.

HANDBOOK ON SECURED TRANSACTIONS UNDER THE UNIFORM COMMERCIAL CODE. Second Edition. Ray D. Henson. West Publishing Company, P. O. Box 64526, 50 West Kellogg Boulevard, St. Paul, Minnesota 55164-0526. 1979. (Hornbook).

LAW OF SECURED TRANSACTIONS UNDER THE UNIFORM COMMERCIAL CODE. Second Edition. Barkley Clark. Research Institute of America, Incorporated, One Penn Plaza, New York, New York 10119. 1988. (Supplements).

PROBLEMS AND MATERIALS ON SECURED TRANSACTIONS. Robert J. Nordstrom, John E. Murray, Jr., and Albert L. Clovis. West Publishing Company, 50 West Kellogg Boulevard, St. Paul, Minnesota 55164. 1987.

PROBLEMS AND MATERIALS ON SECURED TRANSACTIONS. Second Edition. Douglas J. Whaley. Little, Brown and Company, 34 Beacon Street, Boston, Massachusetts 02108. 1989.

PROBLEMS AND MATERIALS ON SECURED TRANSACTIONS UNDER THE UNIFORM COMMERCIAL CODE. Louis F. Del Duca, Egon Guttman, and Alphonse M. Squillante. Anderson Publishing Company, 2035 Reading Road, Cincinnati, Ohio 45202. 1992.

PROTECTING THE REAL ESTATE LENDER: WORKOUT, BANKRUPTCY, AND FINANCING STRATEGIES. Richard A. Gitlin and Lawrence D. Cherkis. Practising Law Institute, 810 Seventh Avenue, New York, New York 10019. 1988.

REPRESENTING THE SECURED CREDITOR IN CHAPTER 11 CASES. Patrick A. Murphy. Practising Law Institute, 810 Seventh Avenue, New York, New York 10019. 1991.

THE SECURED CREDITOR IN COURT: CURRENT PROBLEMS. William C. Hillman, Chairman. Practising Law Institute, 810 Seventh Avenue, New York, New York 10019. 1984.

SECURED CREDITORS AND LESSORS UNDER THE BANKRUPTCY REFORM ACT, 1990. Patrick A. Murphy, Chairman. Practising Law Institute, 810 Seventh Avenue, New York, New York 10019. 1990.

SECURED TRANSACTIONS. Robert M. Lloyd. Matthew Bender and Company, Incorporated, 11 Penn Plaza, New York, New York 10001. 1988.

SECURED TRANSACTIONS IN A NUTSHELL. Third Edition. Henry J. Bailey III and Richard B. Hagedorn. West Publishing Company, P.O. Box 64526, 50 West Kellogg Boulevard, St. Paul, Minnesota 55164-0526. 1988.

SECURED TRANSACTIONS IN PERSONAL PROPERTY. Second Edition. Robert L. Jordan and William D. Warren. Foundation Press, 615 Merrick Avenue, Westbury, New York 11590. 1987.

SECURITY INTERESTS IN PERSONAL PROPERTY: CASES, NOTES, AND MATERIALS. Douglas K. Newell. Butterworth Legal Publishers, 90 Stiles Road, Salem, New Hampshire 03079. 1987.

USING SET-OFF AS SECURITY: A COMPARATIVE SURVEY FOR PRACTITIONERS. Francis W. Neate. Graham and Trotman Limited, Sterling House, 66 Wilton Road, London SW1V 1DE, England. 1990.

AUDIOVISUALS

ENFORCING SECURED CLAIMS. Practising Law Institute, 810 Seventh Avenue, New York, New York 10019. 1983. (Videotape).

THE SECURED CREDITOR IN COURT: CURRENT PROBLEMS. Practising Law Institute, 810 Seventh Avenue, New York, New York 10019. 1984. (Audiocassette).

SECURITIES

STATUTES, CODES, STANDARDS, UNIFORM LAWS

FEDERAL SECURITIES CODE ADOPTED BY THE AMERICAN LAW INSTITUTE. American Law Institute, 4025 Chestnut Street, Philadelphia, Pennsylvania 19104. 1980. (Supplement 1981).

FEDERAL SECURITIES LAWS: LEGISLATIVE HISTORY, 1983-1987 SUPPLEMENT. BNA Books, 1231 Twenty-fifth Street, Washington, D.C. 20037. 1988.

GOVERNMENT SECURITIES LAW: A LEGISLATIVE HISTORY OF THE GOVERNMENT SECURITIES ACT OF 1986. Bernard D. Reams, Jr. and Carol J. Gray. William S. Hein and Company, 1285 Main Street, Buffalo, New York 14209. 1989.

INSIDER TRADING AND SECURITIES FRAUD: A LEGISLATIVE HISTORY OF THE INSIDER TRADING AND SECURITIES FRAUD ENFORCEMENT ACT OF 1988. Bernard D. Reams, Jr. William S. Hein and Company, 1285 Main Street, Buffalo, New York 14209. 1989.

INSIDER TRADING AND THE LAW: A LEGISLATIVE HISTORY OF THE INSIDER TRADING SANCTIONS ACT OF 1984. Bernard D. Reams, Jr. William S. Hein and Company, 1285 Main Street, Buffalo, New York 14209. 1989.

SELECTED STATUTES, RULES AND FORMS UNDER THE FEDERAL SECURITIES LAWS. Compiled by Richard W. Jennings and Harold Marsh, Jr. Foundation Press, Incorporated, 615 Merrick Avenue, Westbury, New York 11590. 1990.

UNIFORM ACT FOR SIMPLIFICATION OF FIDUCIARY SECURITY TRANSFERS. Uniform Laws Annotated. West Publishing Company, P. O. Box 64526, 50 West Kellogg Boulevard, St. Paul, Minnesota 55164-0526. 1976 (Annual Supplements).

UNIFORM SECURITIES ACT. Uniform Laws Annotated. West Publishing Company, P.O. Box 64526, 50 West Kellogg Boulevard, St. Paul, Minnesota 55164-0526. 1976 (Annual Supplements).

LOOSELEAF SERVICES AND REPORTERS

BLUE SKY LAW REPORTER. Commerce Clearing House, Incorporated, 4025 West Peterson Avenue, Chicago, Illinois 60646. 1964- .

CIVIL LIABILITIES: ENFORCEMENT AND LITIGATION UNDER THE 1933 ACT. J. William Hicks. Clark Boardman Company, Limited, 435 Hudson Street, New York, New York 10014. 1989- .

FEDERAL SECURITIES LAW REPORTER. Commerce Clearing House, Incorporated, 4025 West Peterson Avenue, Chicago, Illinois 60646. 1964- .

INSIDER TRADING: REGULATION, ENFORCEMENT, AND PREVENTION. Donald C. Langevoort. Clark Boardman Company, Limited, 435 Hudson Street, New York, New York 10014. 1991- .

THE REGULATION OF CORPORATE DISCLOSURE. J. Robert Brown, Jr. Prentice-Hall, Incorporated, 113 Sylvan Avenue, Englewood Cliffs, New Jersey 07632. 1989- .

REGULATION OF INVESTMENT ADVISERS. Thomas P. Lemke and Gerald T. Lins. Clark Boardman Company, Limited, 435 Hudson Street, New York, New York 10014. 1991.

SEC ACCOUNTING AND REPORTING UPDATE SERVICE. Research Institute of America, Incorporated, One Penn Plaza, New York, New York 10119. 1985- .

SEC ACCOUNTING RULES. Commerce Clearing House, Incorporated, 4025 West Peterson Avenue, Chicago, Illinois 60646. 1982- .

SEC ENFORCEMENT REPORTER. Washington Service Bureau, 655 Fifteenth Street, Northwest, Washington, D.C. 20005. 1982- .

SECTION 16 OF THE SECURITIES EXCHANGE ACT. Arnold S. Jacobs. Clark Boardman Company, Limited, 435 Hudson Street, New York, New York 10014. 1989- .

SECURITIES AND PARTNERSHIP LAW FOR MLPS AND OTHER INVESTMENT LIMITED PARTNERSHIPS. Linda A. Wertheimer. Clark Boardman Company, Limited, 435 Hudson Street, New York, New York 10014. 1988- .

SECURITIES REGULATION. Prentice-Hall, Incorporated, 113 Sylvan Avenue, Englewood Cliffs, New Jersey 07632. 1935- .

SECURITIES REGULATION AND LAW REPORT. Bureau of National Affairs, 1231 Twenty-fifth Street, Northwest, Washington, D.C. 20037. 1969- .

SECURITIES REGULATION GUIDE. Prentice-Hall, Incorporated, 113 Sylvan Avenue, Englewood Cliffs, New Jersey 07632. 1935- .

SECURITIZATION: ASSET-BACKED AND MORTGAGE-BACKED SECURITIES. Ronald S. Borod. Butterworth Legal Publishers, 90 Stiles Road, Salem, New Hampshire 03079. 1991- .

SECURITY AND COMMODITY DEALERS. Mark Rachleff, Mark Fichtenbaum, and Herman M. Schneider. Commerce Clearing House, Incorporated, 4025 West Peterson Avenue, Chicago, Illinois 60646. 1987- .

SECURITY AND COMMODITY INVESTORS. Herman M. Schneider and Jack Crestol. Commerce Clearing House, Incorporated, 4025 West Peterson Avenue, Chicago, Illinois 60646. 1990- .

HANDBOOKS, MANUALS, FORMBOOKS

DONNELLY SEC HANDBOOK. Bruce J. McWhirter, Editor. R. R. Donnelly, Financial Printing Division, 350 East Twenty-Second Street, Chicago, Illinois 60616. 1982.

THE FEDERAL SECURITIES ACT: ANALYSIS, PROCEDURES, FORMS. Hugh L. Sowards. Matthew Bender and Company, Incorporated, 11 Penn Plaza, New York, New York 10001. 1965 (Periodic Supplements).

GOING PUBLIC HANDBOOK. Harold S. Bloomenthal. Clark Boardman Company, Limited, 435 Hudson Street, New York, New York 10014. 1986.

GOVERNMENT SECURITIES COMPLIANCE GUIDE. Commerce Clearing House, Incorporated, 4025 West Peterson Avenue, Chicago, Illinois 60646. 1987.

MANUAL OF CORPORATE FORMS FOR SECURITIES PRACTICE. Arnold S. Jacobs. Clark Boardman Company, Limited, 435 Hudson Street, New York, New York 10014. 1981.

MOODY'S INVESTMENT MANUAL. Moody's Investors Service, Incorporated, 99 Church Street, New York, New York 10007. 1985.

A PRACTICAL GUIDE TO SECTION 16: REPORTING AND COMPLIANCE. Amy L. Goodman. Prentice-Hall, Incorporated, 113 Sylvan Avenue, Englewood Cliffs, New Jersey 07632. 1991.

THE PRIVATE OFFERING HANDBOOK. Michael J. Halloran, Robert V. Gunderson, and Keith J. Mendelson. Prentice-Hall, Incorporated, 113 Sylvan Avenue, Englewood Cliffs, New Jersey 07632. 1989.

QUICK PRIVATE OFFERING EXEMPTION COMPLIANCE GUIDE: STATE BY STATE. Sheldon B. Chernove and Ann E. Grossman. Shelcor Publishing, Incorporated, 4634 Van Nuys Boulevard, Sherman Oaks, California 91403. 1985- .

SECURITIES DEALERS MANUAL. National Association of Securities Dealers. Commerce Clearing House, Incorporated, 4025 West Peterson Avenue, Chicago, Illinois 60646. 1967- .

SECURITIES LAW COMPLIANCE: A GUIDE FOR BROKERS, DEALERS, AND INVESTORS. Allan H. Pessin. Dow Jones-Irwin, 1818 Ridge Road, Homewood, Illinois 60430. 1990.

SECURITIES LAW HANDBOOK. Harold S. Bloomenthal. Commerce Clearing House, Incorporated, 4025 West Peterson Avenue, Chicago, Illinois 60646. 1990.

SECURITIES LAW HANDBOOK FOR FINANCIAL PLANNERS. William M. Prifti. Clark Boardman Company, Limited, 435 Hudson Street, New York, New York 10014. 1991.

SECURITIES REGULATION FORMS. Ronald M. Shapiro, et al. Clark Boardman Company, Limited, 435 Hudson Street, New York, New York 10014. 1975. (Annual Supplements).

SECURITIES REGULATION HANDBOOK. Charles P. Young Company, 75 Varick Street, New York, New York 10013. 1983. (Annual Supplements).

TAKEOVERS: ATTACK AND SURVIVAL, A STRATEGIST'S MANUAL. Ralph C. Ferrara, Meredith M. Brown, John H. Hall, and Jonathan E. Richman. Butterworth Legal Publishers, 90 Stiles Road, Salem, New Hampshire 03079. 1987.

U.S. SECURITIES AND INVESTMENT REGULATION HANDBOOK. Peter Farmery and Keith Walmsley. Graham and Trotman Limited, Sterling House, 66 Wilton Road, London SW1V 1DE, England. 1992.

TEXTBOOKS AND GENERAL WORKS

ADVANCED WORKSHOP ON PROBLEMS IN SECURITIES DISCLOSURES. Alan K. Austin. Practising Law Institute, 810 Seventh Avenue, New York, New York 10019. 1990.

ANALYSIS OF KEY SEC NO-ACTION LETTERS. Robert J. Haft. Clark Boardman Company, Limited, 435 Hudson Street, New York, New York 10014. 1987.

BLUE SKY LAW. Joseph C. Long. Clark Boardman Company, Limited, 435 Hudson Street, New York, New York 10014. 1985.

BLUE SKY LAWS: A SATELLITE PROGRAM. Jack H. Halperin and Hugh H. Makens, co-chairmen. Practising Law Institute, 810 Seventh Avenue, New York, New York 10019. 1985.

BLUE SKY PRACTICE FOR PUBLIC AND PRIVATE LIMITED OFFERINGS. Peter M. Fass and Derek A. Wittner. Clark Boardman Company, Limited, 435 Hudson Street, New York, New York 10014. 1988.

BLUE SKY REGULATION. Hugh L. Sowards and Neil H. Hirsch. Matthew Bender and Company, Incorporated, 11 Penn Plaza, New York, New York 10001. 1977 (Supplement 1984).

BROKER-DEALERS 1985: REGULATION AND LITIGATION. John F. Peloso, Chairman. Practising Law Institute, 810 Seventh Avenue, New York, New York 10019. 1985.

CAPITAL FORMATIONS: PRIVATE AND PUBLIC FINANCINGS. Larry W. Sonsini, Chairman. Practising Law Institute, 810 Seventh Avenue, New York, New York 10019. 1984.

CORPORATE ANTI-TAKEOVER DEFENSES: THE POISON PILL DEVICE. Paul W. Richter. Clark Boardman Company, Limited, 435 Hudson Street, New York, New York 10014. 1987.

CORPORATE FINANCE AND THE SECURITIES LAWS. Charles J. Johnson, Jr. Prentice-Hall, Incorporated, 113 Sylvan Avenue, Englewood Cliffs, New Jersey 07632. 1990.

THE CORPORATE LAW OF BANKS: REGULATION OF CORPORATE AND SECURITIES ACTIVITIES OF DEPOSITORY INSTITUTIONS. Michael P. Malloy. Little, Brown and Company, 34 Beacon Street, Boston, Massachusetts 02108. 1988.

CREATIVE FINANCING IN THE 1980'S. Peter H. Darrow and Ricardo A. Mestress, Jr., co-chairmen. Practising Law Institute, 810 Seventh Avenue, New York, New York 10019. 1983.

ECONOMICS OF CORPORATION LAW AND SECURITIES REGULATION. Richard A. Posner and Kenneth Scott. Little, Brown, and Company, 34 Beacon Street, Boston, Massachusetts 02108. 1981.

EXEMPTED TRANSACTIONS UNDER THE SECURITIES ACT OF 1933. J. William Hicks. Clark Boardman Company, Limited, 435 Hudson Street, New York, New York 10014. 1979. (Annual Revisions).

THE FEDERAL SECURITIES CODE AND CORPORATE DISCLOSURE. William H. Painter. Michie/Bobbs-Merrill, The Michie Company, P.O. Box 7587, Charlottesville, Virginia 22906-7582. 1979 (Periodic Supplements).

THE FEDERAL SECURITIES EXCHANGE ACT OF 1934. Edward N. Gadsby. Matthew Bender and Company, Incorporated, 11 Penn Plaza, New York, New York 10001. 1967. (Periodic Supplements).

FEDERAL SECURITIES LAW AND ACCOUNTING. Gray John Previts and Alfred R. Roberts, Editors. Garland Publishing, Incorporated, 136 Madison Avenue, New York, New York 10016. 1986.

THE FEDERAL SECURITIES LAWS: LEGISLATIVE HISTORY, 1933-1982. Federal Bar Association. Bureau of National Affairs, 1231 Twenty-fifth Street, Northwest, Washington, D.C. 20037. 1983.

FINANCIAL PRODUCTS: TAXATION, REGULATION, AND DESIGN. Andrea S. Kramer. John Wiley and Sons, Incorporated, 605 Third Avenue, New York, New York 10158. 1991.

FUNDAMENTALS OF SECURITIES REGULATION. Second Edition. Louis Loss. Little, Brown and Company, 34 Beacon Street, Boston, Massachusetts 02108. 1987. (Periodic Supplements).

FUNDAMENTALS OF THE SECURITIES INDUSTRY. Allan H. Pessin. New York Institute of Finance, 70 Pine Street, New York, New York 10270. 1986.

HOW TO PREPARE AN INITIAL PUBLIC OFFERING, 1987. Candace K. Beinecke. Practising Law Institute, 810 Seventh Avenue, New York, New York 10019. 1987.

INSIDE INFORMATION AND SECURITIES TRADING: A LEGAL AND ECONOMIC ANALYSIS OF THE FOUNDATIONS OF LIABILITY IN THE U.S.A. AND THE EUROPEAN COMMUNITY. Bernhard Bergmans. Graham and Trotman Limited, Sterling House, 66 Wilton Road, London SW1V 1DE, England. 1991.

INSIDER TRADING: COPING WITH THE USE AND ABUSE OF MARKET SENSITIVE INFORMATION. Harvey L. Pitt, Chairman. Law and Business, Harcourt Brace Jovanovich, Incorporated, 6277 Sea Harbor Drive, Orlando, Florida 32821. 1985.

INSURANCE PRODUCTS UNDER THE SECURITIES LAWS: NEW REGULATORY INITIATIVES. Gary E. Hughes and Paul J. Mason, co-chairmen. Practising Law Institute, 810 Seventh Avenue, New York, New York 10019. 1985.

INTERNATIONAL CAPITAL MARKETS AND SECURITIES REGULATION. Harold S. Bloomenthal, Editor. Clark Boardman Company, Limited, 435 Hudson Street, New York, New York 10014. 1982 (Periodic Supplements).

INTERNATIONAL SECURITIES LAW AND PRACTICE. J. Michael Robinson, Editor. Euromoney Publications, Limited, Nestor House, Playhouse Yard, London ECHV 5EX, UK. 1985.

INTERNATIONAL SECURITIES MARKETS: MERGING OF THE EUROMARKET AND UNITED STATES MARKET. Law and Business, Harcourt Brace Jovanovich, Incorporated, 6277 Sea Harbor Drive, Orlando, Florida 32821. 1985.

INTERNATIONAL SECURITIES MARKETS, 1990. Ralph C. Ferrara and Michael Mann. Practising Law Institute, 810 Seventh Avenue, New York, New York 10019. 1990.

INTERNATIONALIZATION OF THE SECURITIES MARKETS: INCREASED ACCESS TO U.S. CAPITAL MARKETS. Arthur Fleischer, Jr. Prentice-Hall, Incorporated, 113 Sylvan Avenue, Englewood Cliffs, New Jersey 07632. 1990.

INTRODUCTION TO SECURITIES FILINGS UNDER THE 1933 AND 1934 ACTS. Practising Law Institute, 810 Seventh Avenue, New York, New York 10019. 1986.

INTRODUCTION TO THE SECURITIES INDUSTRY CODES. Second Edition. Robert Baxt, Editor. Butterworth Legal Publishers, 90 Stiles Road, Salem, New Hampshire 03079. 1982.

INTRODUCTION TO THE TAXATION OF FINANCIAL INSTRUMENTS: FEDERAL INCOME TAXATION OF CAPITAL TRANSACTIONS IN SECURITIES, STRADDLES, OPTIONS, AND FUTURES. Henry D. Shereff. American Law Institute-American Bar Association, Committee on Continuing Professional Education, 4025 Chestnut Street, Philadelphia, Pennsylvania 19104. 1990.

ISRAELS AND GUTTMAN'S MODERN SECURITIES TRANSFERS. Egon Guttman. Research Institute of America, Incorporated, One Penn Plaza, New York, New York 10119. 1971 (Periodic Supplements).

THE LAW OF SECURITIES REGULATION. Second Edition. Thomas L. Hazen. West Publishing Company, P.O. Box 64526, 50 West Kellogg Boulevard, St. Paul, Minnesota 55164-0526. 1990.

LEGAL CAPITAL: BEING A CONCISE PRACTICAL EXPOSITION WITH ILLUSTRATIVE EXAMPLES. Third Edition. Bayless Manning and James J. Hanks, Jr. Foundation Press, 615 Merrick Avenue, Westbury, New York 11590. 1990.

LIMITED OFFERING EXEMPTIONS: REGULATION. D. J. William Hicks. Clark Boardman Company, Limited, 435 Hudson Street, New York, New York 10014. 1987.

LITIGATING LIMITED PARTNERS' SECURITIES ACTIONS. Jeffrey J. Scott. Practising Law Institute, 810 Seventh Avenue, New York, New York 10019. 1990.

LITIGATION PRACTICE UNDER RULE 106-5. Second Edition. Arnold S. Jacobs. Clark Boardman Company, Limited, 435 Hudson Street, New York, New York 10014. 1981 (Periodic Supplements).

MECHANICS OF UNDERWRITING, 1990. Practising Law Institute, 810 Seventh Avenue, New York, New York 10019. 1990.

MERGERS AND ACQUISITIONS IN THE 1980S: ATTACK AND SURVIVAL. Ralph C. Ferrara. Practising Law Institute, 810 Seventh Avenue, New York, New York 10019. 1987.

NEW DIMENSIONS IN SECURITIES LITIGATION. American Law Institute-American Bar Association, Committee on Continuing Professional Education, 4025 Chestnut Street, Philadelphia, Pennsylvania 19104. 1985.

OPINION LETTERS IN SECURITIES MATTERS: TEXTS, CLAUSES, LAW. Arnold S. Jacobs. Clark Boardman Company, Limited, 435 Hudson Street, New York, New York 10014. 1980 (Periodic Supplements).

PATTERN DISCOVERY, SECURITIES. Douglas Danner. Lawyers Co-Operative Publishing Company, Aqueduct Building, Rochester, New York 14694. 1982.

PREPARATION OF ANNUAL DISCLOSURE DOCUMENTS, 1989. Klaus Eppler, Chairman. Practising Law Institute, 810 Seventh Avenue, New York, New York 10019. 1989.

PRIVATE AND SMALL BUSINESS OFFERINGS. Dan L. Goldwasser, Chairman. Practising Law Institute, 810 Seventh Avenue, New York, New York 10019. 1982.

PRIVATE PLACEMENTS AND RESTRICTED SECURITIES. Stuart C. Goldberg. Clark Boardman Company, Limited, 435 Hudson Street, New York, New York 10014. 1982 (Periodic Supplements).

PRIVATE PLACEMENTS: CURRENT DEVELOPMENTS IN PRIVATE FINANCINGS. Practising Law Institute, 810 Seventh Avenue, New York, New York 10019. 1990.

PROXY CONTESTS, INSTITUTIONAL INVESTOR INITIATIVES, MANAGEMENT RESPONSES; 1990. Klaus Eppler and Thomas Gilroy. Practising Law Institute, 810 Seventh Avenue, New York, New York 10019. 1990.

THE PROXY MACHINERY: SOLICITATIONS AND CONTESTS INVOLVING CORPORATE CONTROL ISSUES. Klaus Eppler and Thomas Gilroy. Practising Law Institute, 810 Seventh Avenue, New York, New York 10019. 1988.

RAISING CAPITAL: PRIVATE PLACEMENT FORMS AND TECHNIQUES. Second Edition. Robert L. Frome and Herbert B. Max. PH Press, MIT Branch, P.O. Box 195, Cambridge, Massachusetts 02139. 1989 (Periodic Supplements).

REDEEMING FALLEN BROKERS: MANAGING THE AFTERMATH OF BROKER-DEALER ENFORCEMENT PROCEEDINGS. Ralph C. Ferrara and Gregory S. Crespi. Butterworth Legal Publishers, 90 Stiles Road, Salem, New Hampshire 03079. 1988.

REGULATION BY PROSECUTION: THE SECURITIES EXCHANGE COMMISSION VS. CORPORATE AMERICA. Roberta S. Karmel. Simon and Schuster, Incorporated, 1230 Avenue of the Americas, New York, New York 10020. 1982.

RESPONSIBILITIES OF CORPORATE OFFICERS AND DIRECTORS UNDER FEDERAL SECURITIES LAWS. Fourth Edition. Commerce Clearing House, Incorporated, 4025 West Peterson Avenue, Chicago, Illinois 60646. 1991.

SEC SECTION 16 RULES. Richard R. Howe and Gloria W. Nusbacher. Practising Law Institute, 810 Seventh Avenue, New York, New York 10019. 1991.

SECURITIES AND FEDERAL CORPORATE LAW. Harold Bloomenthal, Editor. Clark Boardman Company, Limited, 435 Hudson Street, New York, New York 10014. 1972 (Periodic Supplements).

SECURITIES FILINGS: REVIEW AND UPDATE, 1990. Peter E. Yeager, Chairman. Practising Law Institute, 810 Seventh Avenue, New York, New York 10019. 1990.

SECURITIES FRAUD AND COMMODITIES FRAUD. Alan R. Bromberg and Lewis D. Lowenfels. Shepard's/McGraw-Hill, P.O. Box 1235, Colorado Springs, Colorado 80901. 1980 (Periodic Supplements).

SECURITIES LITIGATION: PROSECUTION AND DEFENSE STRATEGIES. Bruce G. Vanyo and Edward J. Yadowitz, co-chairmen. Practising Law Institute, 810 Seventh Avenue, New York, New York 10019. 1985.

SECURITIES MARKETS. Kenneth D. Garbade. McGraw-Hill Book Company, 1221 Avenue of the Americas, New York, New York 10020. 1982.

SECURITIES, PUBLIC, AND PRIVATE OFFERINGS. Revised edition. William M. Prifti. Callaghan and Company, 155 Pfingsten Road, Deerfield, Illinois 60015. 1990.

SECURITIES REGULATION IN A NUTSHELL. Third Edition. David L. Ratner. West Publishing Company, P.O. Box 64526, 50 West Kellogg Boulevard, St. Paul, Minnesota 55164-0526. 1988.

SECURITIES REGULATION: LIABILITIES AND REMEDIES. Marc I. Steinberg. Law Journal-Seminars Press, Incorporated, 111 Eighth Avenue, New York, New York 10011. 1984.

SECURITIES REGULATION OF BANKS AND THRIFTS IN THE 1990'S. Melanie L. Fein and Neal S. McCoy. Practising Law Institute, 810 Seventh Avenue, New York, New York 10019. 1990.

SECURITIES REGULATION OF BANKS AND THRIFTS, 1991. Melanie L. Fien and Neal S. McCoy. Practising Law Institute, 810 Seventh Avenue, New York, New York 10019. 1991.

SECURITIES TRANSFER: PRINCIPLES AND PROCEDURES. Fourth edition. Martin Torosian. New York Institute of Finance, 2 Broadway, New York, New York 10004. 1982.

SECURITY LITIGATIONS AND RELATED MATTERS. Donald O. Schultz and Gregory J. Service, Editors. Charles C. Thomas Publishing, 2600 South First Street, Springfield, Illinois 62794-9265. 1982.

SELECTED PROBLEMS IN THE INTITIAL PUBLIC OFFERING FOR HIGH-TECH COMPANIES. Michael G. Wolfson, Chairman. Practising Law Institute, 810 Seventh Avenue, New York, New York 10019. 1984.

THE SEPARATION OF COMMERCIAL AND INVESTMENT BANKING: THE GLASS-STEAGALL ACT REVISITED AND RECONSIDERED. George J. Benston. Oxford University Press, 200 Madison Avenue, New York, New York 10016. 1990.

SHAREHOLDER LITIGATION. Roger J. Magnuson. Callaghan and Company, 155 Pfingsten Road, Deerfield, Illinois 60015. 1981 (Periodic Supplement).

STATE REGULATION OF CAPITAL FORMATION AND SECURITIES TRANSACTIONS. Dan L. Goldwasser and Hugh H., Makens, co-chairmen. Practising Law Institute, 810 Seventh Avenue, New York, New York 10019. 1983.

STOCKBROKER SUPERVISION: MANAGING STOCKBROKERS AND SURVIVING SANCTIONS. Ralph C. Ferrara, David W. Rivkin, and Gregory S. Crespi. Butterworth Legal Publishers, 90 Stiles Road, Salem, New Hampshire 03079. 1989.

TAX PLANNING FOR SECURITIES AND OPTIONS TRANSACTIONS. Rolf Auster. Commerce Clearing House, Incorporated, 4025 West Peterson Avenue, Chicago, Illinois 60646. 1988.

TAXATION OF SECURITIES, COMMODITIES, AND OPTIONS. Andrea S. Kramer. John Wiley and Sons, Incorporated, 605 Third Avenue, New York, New York 10158. 1986. (With Supplements).

TRANSFER OF STOCK. Sixth edition. Mark S. Rhodes. Lawyers Co-Operative Publishing Company, Aqueduct Building, Rochester, New York 14694. 1985. (With Supplements).

U.S. REGULATION OF THE INTERNATIONAL SECURITIES MARKET: A GUIDE FOR DOMESTIC AND FOREIGN ISSUERS AND INTERMEDIARIES. Edward F. Greene. Prentice-Hall, Incorporated, 113 Sylvan Avenue, Englewood Cliffs, New Jersey 07632. 1991.

VALUES IN THE MARKETPLACE: THE AMERICAN STOCK MARKET UNDER FEDERAL SECURITIES LAW. James Burk. Walter de Gruyter, Incorporated, 200 Saw Mill Road, Hawthorne, New York 10532. 1988.

VENTURE CAPITAL AND PUBLIC OFFERING NEGOTIATION. Michael J. Halloran, Lee F. Benton, and Jesse R. Lovejoy, Editors. Law and Business, Harcourt Brace Jovanovich, Incorporated, 6277 Sea Harbor Drive, Orlando, Florida 32821. 1983. (Periodic Supplements).

VENTURE CAPITAL: LAW, BUSINESS STRATEGIES, AND INVESTMENT PLANNING. Joseph W. Bartlett. John Wiley and Sons, Incorporated, 605 Third Avenue, New York, New York 10158. 1988.

WAYWARD CAPITALISTS: TARGET OF THE SECURITIES AND EXCHANGE COMMISSION. Susan P. Shapiro. Yale University Press, 302 Temple Street, New Haven, Connecticut 06520. 1984.

ENCYCLOPEDIAS AND DICTIONARIES

INTERNATIONAL DICTIONARY OF THE SECURITIES INDUSTRIES. Stuart P. Valentine. Nichols Publishing Company, 11 Harts Lane, Suite I, East Brunswick, New Jersey 08816. 1985.

WORDS OF WALL STREET: 2,000 INVESTMENT TERMS DEFINED. Allan H. Pessin and Joseph A. Ross. Dow Jones-Irwin, 1818 Ridge Road, Homewood, Illinois 60430. 1983.

DIGESTS, INDEXES, ABSTRACTS, CITATORS

BUSINESS PERIODICALS INDEX. H. W. Wilson Co., 950 University Avenue, Bronx, New York 10452. Monthly.

F & S INDEX OF CORPORATIONS AND INDUSTRIES. Predicasts, Incorporated, 11001 Cedar Avenue, Cleveland, Ohio 44106. Weekly.

SHEPARD'S SECURITIES LAW LOCATOR: STATE AND FEDERAL. Shepard's/McGraw-Hill, P.O. Box 1235, Colorado Springs, Colorado 80901. 1977-- .

WALL STREET JOURNAL INDEX. 22 Cortlandt Street, New York, New York 10007. Monthly.

ANNUALS AND SURVEYS

ELEVENTH ANNUAL INSTITUTE, PROXY STATEMENTS, ANNUAL MEETINGS, AND DISCLOSURE DOCUMENTS. Michael J. Halloran. Prentice-Hall, Incorporated, 113 Sylvan Avenue, Englewood Cliffs, New Jersey 07632. 1989.

SECURITIES INDUSTRY YEARBOOK. Securities Industry Association, 120 Broadway, New York, New York 10271. Annual.

SECURITIES LAW REVIEW. Clark Boardman Company, Limited, 435 Hudson Street, New York, New York 10014. Annual.

LAW REVIEWS AND PERIODICALS

HOW TO BUY AND SELL SECURITIES IN THE INTERNATIONAL MARKETPLACE. Commerce Clearing House, Incorporated, 4025 West Peterson Avenue, Chicago, Illinois 60646. Monthly.

SECURITIES AND COMMODITIES REGULATION. Standard & Poor's Corporation, 25 Broadway, New York, New York 10004. Semimonthly.

SECURITIES AND FEDERAL CORPORATE LAW REPORT. Clark Boardman Company, Limited, 435 Hudson Street, New York, New York 10014. Monthly.

SECURITIES LAW REVIEW. Clark Boardman Company, Limited, 435 Hudson Street, New York, New York 10014. Annual.

SECURITIES REGULATION LAW JOURNAL. Research Institute of America, Incorporated, One Penn Plaza, New York, New York 10119. Quarterly.

SECURITIES WEEK. McGraw-Hill Book Company, 1221 Avenue of the Americas, New York, New York 10020. Weekly.

NEWSLETTERS AND NEWSPAPERS

THE BANK DIGEST. Washington Service Bureau, Incorporated, 655 Fifteenth Street, Northwest, Washington, D.C. 20005. Daily.

BOWNE DIGEST FOR CFO'S AND INVESTMENT BANKERS. Brumbers Publications, 124 Harvard Street, Brookline, Massachusetts 02146. Monthly.

BOWNE DIGEST FOR CORPORATE AND SECURITIES LAWYERS. Brumbers Publications, 124 Harvard Street, Brookline, Massachusetts 02146. Monthly.

COMMODITIES LAW LETTER. Commodities Law Press Associates, 900 Third Avenue, New York, New York 10022. Monthly.

FEDERAL SECURITIES LAW REPORTS (SUMMARY). Commerce Clearing House, Incorporated, 4025 West Peterson Avenue, Chicago, Illinois 60646. Weekly.

INTERNATIONAL SECURITIES REGULATION REPORT. Buraff Publications, 1350 Connecticut Avenue, Northwest, Suite 1000, Washington, D.C. 20036. Semimonthly.

MORTGAGE BACKED SECURITIES LETTER. Investment Dealers' Digest, Incorporated, 2 World Trade Center, Eighteenth Floor, New York, New York 10048. Weekly.

MSRB REPORTS. Municipal Securities Rulemaking Board, 1818 N Street, Northwest, Suite 800, Washington, D.C. 20036. Quarterly.

NASD NOTICE TO MEMBERS. National Association of Securities Dealers, Incorporated, 1735 K Street, Northwest, Washington, D.C. 20006. Irregular.

QUARTERLY NEWSLETTER OF THE NATIONAL ASSOCIATION OF BOND LAWYERS. National Association of Bond Lawyers, P.O. Box 397, Hinsdale, Illinois 60522. Quarterly.

THE REVIEW OF SECURITIES AND COMMODITIES REGULATION. Standard & Poor's Corporation, 25 Broadway, New York, New York 10004. Semimonthly.

SAC AWARD REPORTER. Securities Arbitration Commentator, P.O. Box 112, Maplewood, New Jersey 07040. Monthly.

SEC ACCOUNTING AND REPORTING UPDATE SERVICE. Research Institute of America, Incorporated, One Penn Plaza, New York, New York 10119. Irregular.

SEC ACCOUNTING REPORT. Research Institute of America, Incorporated, One Penn Plaza, New York, New York 10119. Monthly.

SEC DOCKET. Commerce Clearing House, Incorporated, 4025 West Peterson Avenue, Chicago, Illinois 60646. Weekly.

SEC FLASH. Prentice-Hall, Incorporated, 113 Sylvan Avenue, Englewood Cliffs, New Jersey 07632. Daily.

SEC NEWS DIGEST. Superintendent of Documents, United States Government Printing Office, Washington, D.C. 20402. Daily.

SEC TODAY. Washington Service Bureau, 655 Fifteenth Street, Northwest, Washington, D.C. 20005. Daily.

SECURITIES AND FEDERAL CORPORATE LAW REPORT. Clark Boardman Company, Limited, 435 Hudson Street, New York, New York 10014. Monthly.

SECURITIES CLASS ACTION ALERT. Investors Research Bureau, 400 Union Avenue, Cresskill, New Jersey 07626. Monthly.

SECURITIES INSIDER TRADING LITIGATION REPORTER. Andrews Publications, 1646 West Chester Pike, Westtown, Pennsylvania 19395. Semimonthly.

SECURITIES REGULATION LAW AND REPORT. Bureau of National Affairs, Incorporated, 1231 Twenty-fifth Street, Northwest, Washington, D.C. 20037. Weekly.

WASHINGTON REGULATORY REPORT. Clark Boardman Company, Limited, 435 Hudson Street, New York, New York 10014. Monthly.

DIRECTORIES

NELSON'S NATIONAL DIRECTORY OF WALL STREET RESEARCH. Thomas Nelson Publishers, P. O. Box 141000, Nelson Place at Elm Hill Pike, Nashville, Tennessee 37214-1000. Annual.

SEC FILING COMPANIES: A LIST OF COMPANIES FILING REPORTS WITH THE SECURITIES AND EXCHANGE COMMISSION. Disclosure Information Group, 5161 River Road, Bethesda, Maryland 20816. Annual.

SECURITY DEALERS OF NORTH AMERICA. Standard and Poor's Corporation, 25 Broadway, New York, New York 10004. Semi-annual.

SHEPARD'S FEDERAL SECURITIES LAW CITATIONS. Commerce Clearing House, Incorporated, 4025 West Peterson Avenue, Chicago, Illinois 60646. 1990.

ASSOCIATIONS AND PROFESSIONAL SOCIETIES

AMERICAN BAR ASSOCIATION, SECTION OF CORPORATION BANKING AND BUSINESS LAW, COMMITTEE ON FEDERAL REGULATION OF SECURITIES. American Bar Association, 750 North Lake Shore Drive, Chicago, Illinois 60611. (312) 988-5000.

AMERICAN STOCK EXCHANGE. 86 Trinity Place, New York, New York 10006. (212) 306-1000.

COUNCIL OF INSTITUTIONAL INVESTORS. 1420 Sixteenth Street, Northwest, Suite 405, Washington, D.C. 20036. (202) 745-0800.

INVESTMENT COUNSEL ASSOCIATION OF AMERICA. 20 Exchange Place, New York, New York 10005. (212) 344-0999.

NATIONAL ASSOCIATION OF BOND ATTORNEYS. P.O. Box 397, Hinsdale, Illinois 60522. (312) 920-0160.

NATIONAL ASSOCIATION OF OTC COMPANIES. 1707 L Street, Northwest, Suite 950, Washington, D. C. 20036. (202) 785-9200.

NATIONAL ASSOCIATION OF SECURITIES DEALERS. 1735 K Street, Northwest, Washington, D.C. 20006. (202) 728-8000.

NEW YORK STOCK EXCHANGE. 11 Wall Street, New York, New York 10005. (212) 656-3000.

NORTH AMERICAN SECURITIES ADMINISTRATION ASSOCIATION. 555 New Jersey Avenue, Northwest, Suite 750, Washington, D. C. 20001. (202) 737-0900.

Encyclopedia of Legal Information Sources • 2nd Ed. **SECURITIES AND EXCHANGE COMMISSION**

PUBLIC SECURITIES ADMINISTRATION. 40 Broad Street, Twelfth Floor, New York, New York 10004. (212) 809-7000.

SECURITIES INDUSTRY ASSOCIATION. 120 Broadway, New York, New York 10271. (212) 608-1500.

SECURITY TRADERS ASSOCIATION. One World Trade Center, Suite 4511, New York, New York 10048. (212) 524-0484.

RESEARCH CENTERS, INSTITUTES, CLEARINGHOUSES

INVESTMENT COMPANY INSTITUTE. 1600 M Street, Northwest, Suite 600, Washington, D. C. 20036. (202) 293-7700.

INVESTOR RESPONSIBILITY RESEARCH CENTER, INCORPORATED. 1755 Massachusetts Avenue, Northwest, Suite 600, Washington, D. C. 20036. (202) 939-6500.

ONLINE DATABASES

BNA SECURITIES LAW DAILY. Bureau of National Affairs, Incorporated, 1231 Twenty-fifth Street, Northwest, Washington, D.C. 20037.

CCH BLUE SKY LAW REPORTER. Commerce Clearing House, Incorporated, 4025 West Peterson Avenue, Chicago, Illinois 60646.

LEXIS FEDERAL SECURITIES LIBRARY. Mead Data Central, P. O. Box 933, Dayton, Ohio 45401.

LEXIS STATE SECURITIES LIBRARY. Mead Data Central, P.O. Box 933, Dayton, Ohio 45401.

SEC ONLINE. 200 E. 23rd Street, New York, New York 10010.

SECURITIES LAW ADVANCE. Bureau of National Affairs, 1231 Twenty-fifth Street, Northwest, Washington, D.C. 20037.

SECURITY MARKET DATA. Interactive Data Corporation, Securities Product Division, 303 Wyman Street, Waltham, Massachusetts 02254.

WESTLAW SECURITIES AND BLUE SKY LAWS LIBRARY. West Publishing Company, P.O. Box 64526, 50 West Kellogg Boulevard, St. Paul, Minnesota 55164-0526.

STATISTICS SOURCES

BARRON'S. Dow Jones and Company, 22 Cortland Street, New York, New York 10007. Weekly.

FINANCIAL WEEKLY. Media General, Incorporate, P. O. Box 26565, Richmond, Virginia 23261. Weekly.

OFFICIAL SUMMARY OF SECURITY TRANSACTIONS AND HOLDINGS. Securities and Exchange Commission. Superintendent of Documents, United States Government Printing Office, Washington, D.C. 20402. Monthly.

SEC MONTHLY STATISTICAL REVIEW. Securities and Exchange Commission, United States Government Printing Office, Washington, D.C. 20402. Monthly.

STANDARD AND POOR'S TRADE AND SECURITIES STATISTICS. Standard and Poor's Corporation, 25 Broadway, New York, New York 10004. Monthly.

UNITED STATES SECURITIES AND EXCHANGE COMMISSION ANNUAL REPORT. Superintendent of Documents, United States Government Printing Office, Washington D.C. 20402. Annual.

AUDIOVISUALS

BLUE SKY LAWS: STATE REGULATION OF SECURITIES. Practising Law Institute, 810 Seventh Avenue, New York, New York 10019. 1984. Audiocassette.

FEDERAL SECURITIES LAW: INTRODUCTION AND REVIEW. Robert C. Clark. National Practice Institute, 330 Second Avenue South, Minneapolis, Minnesota 55401. Audiotape.

INSIDE INFORMATION: AN OVERVIEW FOR COUNSELING. Practising Law Institute, 810 Seventh Avenue, New York, New York 10019. 1984. Videotape.

MECHANICS OF UNDERWRITING. Practising Law Institute, 810 Seventh Avenue, New York, New York 10019. 1983. Videotape.

MORTGAGE BACKED SECURITIES: MORTGAGE PASS-THROUGHS, CMO'S, AND BUILDER BONDS. Practising Law Institute, 810 Seventh Avenue, New York, New York 10019. 1984. Videotape.

OPINIONS OF COUNSEL. Practising Law Institute, 810 Seventh Avenue, New York, New York 10019. 1984. Videotape.

COMPUTER-ASSISTED LEGAL INSTRUCTION

SMALL ISSUES EXEMPTIONS. Thomas L. Hazen. Center for Computer- Assisted Instruction, 229 19th Avenue South, University of Minnesota, Minneapolis, Minnesota 55455. Machine-readable computer file.

SECURITIES AND EXCHANGE COMMISSION
See also: COMMODITY FUTURES TRADING COMMISSION

STATUTES, CODES, STANDARDS, UNIFORM LAWS

CODE OF FEDERAL REGULATIONS, TITLE 17. Office of the Federal Register, National Archives and Records Administration. Superintendent of Documents, United States Government Printing Office, Washington, D.C. 20402. Annual. (Updated by use of monthly List of Sections Affected and daily Federal Register.)

LOOSELEAF SERVICES AND REPORTERS

OFFICIAL SUMMARY OF SECURITY TRANSACTIONS AND HOLDINGS. Securities and Exchange Commission. Superintendent of Documents, United States Government Printing Office, Washington, D.C. 20402. Monthly.

SECURITIES AND EXCHANGE COMMISSION DECISIONS AND REPORTS. Superintendent of Documents, United States Government Printing Office, Washington, D.C. 20402. 1934- .

TEXTBOOKS AND GENERAL WORKS

EAGLE ON THE STREET: BASED ON THE PULITZER PRIZE-WINNING ACCOUNT OF THE SEC'S BATTLE WITH WALL STREET. David A. Vise and Steve Coll. Scribner Educational Publishers, 866 Third Avenue, New York, New York 10022. 1991.

AN INTRODUCTION TO THE SEC. Fifth Edition. K. Fred Skousen. South-Western Publishing Company, 5101 Madison Road, Cincinnati, Ohio 45227. 1991.

THE SECURITIES AND EXCHANGE COMMISSION. Philip Koslow. Chelsea House Publishers, 1974 Sproul Road, Suite 400, Broomall, Pennsylvania 19008. 1990.

DIGESTS, INDEXES, ABSTRACTS, CITATORS

SHEPARD'S UNITED STATES ADMINISTRATIVE CITATIONS. Shepard's/McGraw-Hill, P.O. Box 1235, Colorado Springs, Colorado 80901. Bimonthly.

ANNUALS AND SURVEYS

SECURITIES AND EXCHANGE COMMISSION ANNUAL REPORT. Securities and Exchange Commission. Superintendent of Documents, United States Government Printing Office, Washington, D.C. 20402. Annual.

DIRECTORIES

DIRECTORY OF COMPANIES REQUIRED TO FILE ANNUAL REPORTS WITH THE SECURITIES AND EXCHANGE COMMISSION UNDER THE SECURITIES EXCHANGE ACT OF 1934. Securities and Exchange Commission. Superintendent of Documents, United States Government Printing Office, Washington, D.C. 20402. Annual.

RESEARCH CENTERS, INSTITUTES, CLEARINGHOUSES

UNITED STATES SECURITIES AND EXCHANGE COMMISSION LIBRARY. 450 Fifth Street, Northwest, Washington, D.C. 20549. (202) 272-2618.

STATISTICS SOURCES

SEC MONTHLY STATISTICAL REVIEW. Securities and Exchange Commission. Superintendent of Documents, United States Government Printing Office, Washington, D.C. 20402. Monthly.

ONLINE DATABASES

LEXIS FEDERAL SECURITIES LIBRARY. Mead Data Central, P.O. Box 933, Dayton, Ohio 45401.

WESTLAW SECURITIES AND BLUE SKY REPORTER LIBRARY. West Publishing Company, P.O. Box 64526, 50 West Kellogg Boulevard, St. Paul, Minnesota 55164-0526.

SEGREGATION AND INTEGRATION
See also: DISCRIMINATION, EDUCATION; DISCRIMINATION, HOUSING; DISCRIMINATION, RACE; SCHOOL INTEGRATION

TEXTBOOKS AND GENERAL WORKS

THE AGE OF JIM CROW: SEGREGATION IN THE SOUTH FROM THE END OF RECONSTRUCTION TO THE GREAT DEPRESSION. Paul Finkelman. Garland Publishing, Incorporated, 136 Madison Avenue, New York, New York 10016. 1992.

APARTHEID IN AMERICA: AN HISTORICAL AND LEGAL ANALYSIS OF CONTEMPORARY RACIAL SEGREGATION IN THE UNITED STATES. James A. Kushner. Associated Faculty Press, 19 West Thirty-sixth Street, New York, New York 10018. 1980.

DESEGREGATING AMERICA'S COLLEGES AND UNIVERSITIES: TITLE VI REGULATION OF HIGHER EDUCATION. John B. Williams, III. Teachers College Press, New York, New York. 1988.

DESEGREGATION OF PUBLIC TRANSPORTATION, FACILITIES, AND PROGRAMS. Garland Publishing, Incorporated, 136 Madison Avenue, New York, New York 10016. 1991.

ETHNIC SEGREGATION IN THE CITIES. Ceri Peach, Vaughan Robinson, and Susan Smith, Editors. University of Georgia Press, Terrell Hall, Athens, Georgia 30602. 1981.

JOURNEY FROM JIM CROW: THE DESEGRATION OF SOUTHERN TRANSIT. Catherine A. Barnes. Columbia University Press, 562 West 113th Street, New York, New York 10025. 1983.

MARTIN LUTHER KING, JR., AND THE FREEDOM MOVEMENT. Lillie Patterson. Facts on File, Incorporated, 460 Park Avenue South, New York, New York 10016. 1989.

THE NAACP'S LEGAL STRATEGY AGAINST SEGREGATED EDUCATION, 1925-1950. Mark Tushnet. University of North Carolina Press, P.O. Box 2288, 116 South Boundary Street, Chapel Hill, North Carolina 27515-2288. 1987.

THE PLESSY CASE: A LEGAL-HISTORICAL INTERPRETATION. Charles A. Lofgren. Oxford University Press, 200 Madison Avenue, New York, New York 10016. 1987.

PROJECT CLEAR: SOCIAL RESEARCH AND THE DESEGREGATION OF THE UNITED STATES ARMY. Leo Bogart. Transaction Books, Rutgers University, New Brunswick, New Jersey 08903. 1992. (Reprint).

RACE AND SCHOOLING IN THE SOUTH, 1880-1950: AN ECONOMIC HISTORY. Robert A. Margo. University of Chicago Press, 5801 Ellis Avenue, Chicago, Illinois 60637. 1990.

SEGREGATION AND INTERGRATION, 1930-1990. Paul Finkelman. Garland Publishing, Incorporated, 136 Madison Avenue, New York, New York 10016. 1992.

SEX SEGREGATION IN THE WORKPLACE: TRENDS, EXPLANATIONS, REMEDIES. Barbara F. Reskin, Editor. National Academy Press, 2101 Constitution Avenue, Washington, D.C. 20418. 1984.

SOCIAL SCIENCE IN COURT: MOBILIZING EXPERTS IN THE SCHOOL DESEGREGATION CASES. Mark A. Chesler, Joseph Sanders, and Debra S. Kalmuss. University of Wisconsin Press, 114 North Murray, Madison, Wisconsin 53706. 1988.

STRATEGIES FOR EFFECTIVE DESEGREGATION: LESSONS FROM RESEARCH. Willis D. Hawley, et al. Lexington Books, Division of D.C. Heath and Company, 125 Spring Street, Lexington, Massachusetts 02173. 1983.

THE STRUGGLE FOR EQUAL EDUCATION. Paul Finkelman. Garland Publishing, Incorporated, 136 Madison Avenue, New York, New York 10016. 1992.

THE STRUGGLE FOR EQUAL EDUCATION. Clarence Lusane. Franklin Watts, Incorporated, 387 Park Avenue South, New York, New York 10016. 1992.

SWANN'S WAY: THE SCHOOL BUSING CASE AND THE SUPREME COURT. Bernard Schwartz. Oxford University Press, Incorporated, 200 Madison Avenue, New York, New York 10016. 1986.

LAW REVIEWS AND PERIODICALS

BLACK LAW JOURNAL. University of California, Los Angeles, School of Law, Room 2125C, Los Angeles, California 90024.

BIOGRAPHICAL SOURCES

THE AUTOBIOGRAPHY OF ROSA PARKS. James Haskins. Dial Books, 375 Hudson Street, New York, New York 10014. 1990.

ASSOCIATIONS AND PROFESSIONAL SOCIETIES

FUND FOR AN OPEN SOCIETY. 311 South Juniper Street, Suite 400, Philadelphia, Pennsylvania 19107. (215) 735-6915.

NATIONAL NEIGHBORS. 2000 M Street, Northwest, Suite 400, Washington, D.C. 20036. (202) 785-4836.

NATIONAL URBAN LEAGUE. 500 East Sixty-second Street, New York, New York 10021. (212) 310-9000.

RESEARCH CENTERS, INSTITUTES, CLEARINGHOUSES

CENTER FOR THE STUDY OF METROPOLITAN PROBLEMS IN EDUCATION. University of Missouri, Kansas City, 5100 Rockhill Road, Kansas City, Missouri 64110. (816) 276-2251.

INSTITUTE ON DESEGREGATION. North Carolina Central University, 214 Taylor Education Building, Durham, North Carolina 27707. (919) 560-6367.

INTERCULTURAL DEVELOPMENT RESEARCH ASSOCIATON. 5835 Callaghan Road, Suite 350, San Antonio, Texas 78228. (512) 684-8180.

SELECTIVE SERVICE
See: MILITARY LAW AND SERVICE

SELF INCRIMINATION
See: CRIMINAL PROCEDURE

SENIOR CITIZENS
See: AGED AND AGING

SENTENCING
See also: ADMINISTRATIVE OFFICE OF THE UNITED STATES COURTS; JUSTICE DEPARTMENT

STATUTES, CODES, STANDARDS, UNIFORM LAWS

SENTENCING GUIDELINES AND POLICY STATEMENTS. United States Sentencing Commission. Superintendent of Documents, United States Government Printing Office, Washington, D.C. 20402. 1988.

STANDARDS FOR CRIMINAL JUSTICE: SENTENCING ALTERNATIVES AND PROCEDURES. Second Edition. American Bar Association, Standing Committee on Association Standards for Criminal Justice and Task Force on Sentencing Alternatives and Review. Little, Brown and Company, 34 Beacon Street, Boston, Massachusetts 02108. 1982.

LOOSELEAF SERVICES AND REPORTERS

FEDERAL SENTENCING MANUAL. Gerald S. McFadden, Judy C. Clarke, and Jeffrey L. Staniels. Matthew Bender and Company, Incorporated, 11 Penn Plaza, New York, New York 10001. 1989- .

PRACTICE UNDER THE NEW FEDERAL SENTENCING GUIDELINES. Second Edition. Phylis Skloot Bamberger and David J. Gottlieb. Prentice-Hall, Incorporated, 113 Sylvan Avenue, Englewood Cliffs, New Jersey 07632. 1990.

SENTENCING DEFENSE MANUAL: ADVOCACY/PRACTICE/PROCEDURE. Marcia G. Shein. Clark Boardman Company, Limited, 435 Hudson Street, New York, New York 10014. 1988- .

HANDBOOKS, MANUALS, FORMBOOKS

ALTERNATIVE SENTENCING: A PRACTITIONER'S GUIDE. Andrew R. Klein. Anderson Publishing Company, 2035 Reading Road, Cincinnati, Ohio 45202. 1988.

CAPITAL CASE SENTENCING: HOW TO PROTECT YOUR CLIENT. Ursula Bentele. American Bar Association, Section of Criminal Justice, 1800 M Street, Northwest, Washington, D.C. 20036. 1988.

FEDERAL SENTENCING AND FORFEITURE GUIDE. Second Edition. Roger W. Haines, Jr. Del Mar Legal Publications, Del Mar, California. 1990.

FEDERAL SENTENCING GUIDELINES HANDBOOK: TEXT, ANALYSIS, CASE DIGESTS. Shepard's/McGraw-Hill, P.O. Box 1235, Colorado Springs, Colorado 80901. 1990.

GUIDELINES MANUAL: INCORPORATING GUIDELINE AMENDMENTS EFFECTIVE NOVEMBER 1, 1990. United States Sentencing Commission, 1331 Pennsylvania Avenue, Northwest, Suite 1400, Washington, D.C. 20004. 1990.

TEXTBOOKS AND GENERAL WORKS

BETWEEN PRISON AND PROBATION: INTERMEDIATE PUNISHMENTS IN A RATIONAL SENTENCING SYSTEM. Norval Morris and Michael Tonry. Oxford University Press, 200 Madison Avenue, New York, New York 10016. 1990.

CRIMINAL SENTENCING IN THREE NINETEENTH-CENTURY CITIES: SOCIAL HISTORY OF PUNISHMENT IN NEW YORK, BOSTON, AND PHILADELPHIA 1830-1880. William Francis Kuntz, II. Garland Publishing, Incorporated, 136 Madison Avenue, New York, New York 10016. 1988.

DANGEROUSNESS: PROBABILITY AND PREDICTION, PSYCHIATRY AND PUBLIC POLICY. Christopher D. Webster, Mark H. Ben-Aron and Stephen J. Hucker, Editors. Cambridge University Press, 40 West Twentieth Street, New York, New York 10011. 1985.

DECISION MAKING IN CRIMINAL JUSTICE: TOWARD THE RATIONAL EXERCISE OF DISCRETION. Second Edition. Michael R. Gottfredson and Don M. Gottfredson. Plenum Publishing Corporation, 233 Spring Street, New York, New York 10013. 1988.

DETERMINATE SENTENCING AND IMPRISONMENT: A FAILURE OF REFORM. Lynne Goodstein and John Hepburn. Anderson Publishing Company, 2035 Reading Road, Cincinnati, Ohio 45202. 1985.

EXPANDING OPTIONS FOR CRIMINAL SENTENCING. Joan Petersilia. Rand Corporation, Institute for Civil Justice, 1700 Main Street, P.O. Box 2138, Santa Monica, California 90406. 1987.

FEDERAL SENTENCING GUIDELINES. Kenneth R. Feinberg. Practising Law Institute, 810 Seventh Avenue, New York, New York 10019. 1987.

FEDERAL SENTENCING LAW AND PRACTICE. Thomas W. Hutchison and David Yellen. West Publishing Company, 50 West Kellogg Boulevard, St. Paul, Minnesota 55164. 1989.

HOME CONFINEMENT: AN EVOLVING SANCTION IN THE FEDERAL CRIMINAL JUSTICE SYSTEM. Paul J. Hofer and Barbara Stone Meierhoefer. Federal Judicial Center, Washington, D.C. 1987.

THE IMPACT OF SENTENCING REFORM: FROM INDETERMINATE TO DETERMINATE SENTENCING. John D. Hewitt and Todd R. Clear. University Press of America, 4720 Boston Way, Lanham, Maryland 20706. 1983.

ISSUES IN FORENSIC PSYCHIATRY: INSANITY DEFENSE, HOSPITALIZATION OF ADULTS, MODEL CIVIL COMMITMENT LAW, SENTENCING PROCESS, CHILD CUSTODY CONSULTATION. Books on Demand, 300 North Zeeb Road, Ann Arbor, Michigan 48106-1346. 1984.

JUDICIAL DECISION MAKING, SENTENCING POLICY, AND NUMERICAL GUIDANCE. Austin Lovegrove. Springer-Verlag New York, Incorporated, 175 Fifth Avenue, New York, New York 10010. 1989.

LAW OF SENTENCING. Arthur W. Campbell. Lawyers Co-Operative Publishing Company, Aqueduct Building, Rochester, New York 14694. 1978. (Supplements).

MAGISTRATES AT WORK: SENTENCING AND SOCIAL STRUCTURE. Sheila Brown. Open University Press, c/o Taylor and Francis Group, 1900 Frost Road, Suite 101, Bristol, Pennsylvania 19007. 1991.

NATIONAL CONFERENCE ON SENTENCING ADVOCACY. Charles J. Ogletree. Practising Law Institute, 810 Seventh Avenue, New York, New York 10019. 1989.

PAST OR FUTURE CRIMES: DESERVEDNESS AND DANGEROUSNESS IN THE SENTENCING OF CRIMINALS. Andrew Von Hirsch. Rutgers University Press, 109 Church Street, New Brunswick, New Jersey 08901. 1987.

PREDICTING CRIMINAL JUSTICE OUTCOMES: WHAT MATTERS? Stephen P. Klein. Rand Corporation, Institute for Civil Justice, 1700 Main Street, P.O. Box 2138, Santa Monica, California 90406. 1991.

PUBLIC ATTITUDES TO SENTENCING: SURVEYS FROM FIVE COUNTRIES. Nigel Walker and Mike Hough. Gower Publishing Company, Old Post Road, Brookfield, Vermont 05036. 1988.

RACIAL EQUITY IN SENTENCING. Stephen P. Klein, Susan Turner, and Joan Petersilia. Rand Corporation, Institute for Civil Justice, 1700 Main Street, P.O. Box 2138, Santa Monica, California 90406. 1988.

REFORM AND PUNISHMENT: ESSAYS ON CRIMINAL SENTENCING. Michael H. Tonry and Franklin E. Zimring, Editors. University of Chicago Press, 5801 Ellis Avenue, Third Floor, South, Chicago, Illinois 60637. 1983.

RESEARCH ON SENTENCING: THE SEARCH FOR REFORM. Alfred Blumstein, et al., Editors. National Academy Press, 2101 Constitution Avenue, Washington, D.C. 20418. 1983.

SENTENCING BY MATHEMATICS: AN EVALUATION OF THE EARLY ATTEMPTS TO DEVELOP AND IMPLEMENT SENTENCING GUIDELINES. William D. Rich. National Center for State Courts, 300 Newport Avenue, Williamsburg, Virginia 23187-8798. 1982.

THE SENTENCING COMMISSION AND ITS GUIDELINES. Andrew von Hirsch, Kay A. Knapp, and Michael Tonry. Northeastern University Press, 272 Huntington Plaza, 360 Huntington Avenue, Boston, Massachusetts 02115. 1987.

SENTENCING OPTIONS OF FEDERAL DISTRICT COURT JUDGES. Anthony Partridge, Alan J. Chaset, and William B. Elridge. United States Federal Judicial Center, 1520 H Street, Northwest, Washington, D.C. 20005. 1983.

SENTENCING REFORM: EXPERIMENTS IN REDUCING DISPARITY. Martin L. Forst, Editor. Books on Demand, 300 North Zeeb Road, Ann Arbor, Michigan 48106-1346. 1982.

SENTENCING YOUNG PEOPLE: THE EFFECTS OF THE CRIMINAL JUSTICE ACT OF 1982. Elizabeth Burney. Gower Publishing Company, Old Post Road, Brookfield, Vermont 05036. 1985.

SITTING IN JUDGMENT: THE SENTENCING OF WHITE-COLLAR CRIMINALS. Stanton Wheeler, Kenneth Mann, and Austin Sarat. Yale University Press, 302 Temple Street, New Haven, Connecticut 06520. 1988.

THE SOCIAL CONTEXTS OF CRIMINAL SENTENCING. Martha A. Myers and Susette M. Talarico. Springer-Verlag New York, Incorporated, 175 Fifth Avenue, New York, New York 10010. 1987.

UNMASKING THE MAGISTRATES: THE CUSTODY OR NOT DECISION IN SENTENCING YOUNG OFFENDERS. Howard Parker, Maggie Sumner, and Graham Jarvis. Open University Press, c/o Taylor and Francis Group, 1900 Frost Road, Suite 101, Bristol, Pennsylvania 19007. 1989.

THE U.S. SENTENCING GUIDELINES: IMPLICATIONS FOR CRIMINAL JUSTICE. Dean J. Champion. Praeger Publishers, One Madison Avenue, New York, New York 10010. 1989.

WHO GOES TO PRISON? James Austin and John Irwin. National Conference on Crime and Deliquency, San Francisco, California. 1990.

BIBLIOGRAPHIES

PERSPECTIVES ON DETERMINATE SENTENCING: A SELECTIVE BIBLIOGRAPHY. W. Donald Pointer and Cindy Rosenstein. National Institute of Justice. Superintendent of Documents, United States Government Printing Office, Washington, D.C. 20402. 1982.

RECENT ARTICLES ON SENTENCING ISSUES: ANNOTATED BIBLIOGRAPHY. United States Sentencing Project, 1156 Fifteenth Street, Northwest, Suite 520, Washington, D.C. 20005. 1988.

ASSOCIATIONS AND PROFESSIONAL SOCIETIES

AMERICAN BAR ASSOCIATION, STANDING COMMITTEE ON ASSOCIATION STANDARDS FOR CRIMINAL JUSTICE, TASK FORCE ON SENTENCING ALTERNATIVES AND REVIEW. American Bar Association, 750 North Lake Shore Drive, Chicago, Illinois 60611. (312) 988-5000.

THE SENTENCING PROJECT. 918 F Street, Northwest, Suite 501, Washington, D. C. 20005. (202) 628-0871.

RESEARCH CENTERS, INSTITUTES, CLEARINGHOUSES

NATIONAL INSTITUTE FOR SENTENCING ALTERNATIVES. Brandeis University, Heller Graduate School, Room 326, Waltham, Massachusetts 02254. (617) 736-3980.

OTHER SOURCES

UNITED STATES SENTENCING COMMISSION: UNPUBLISHED PUBLIC HEARINGS, 1986. William S. Hein and Company, 1285 Main Street, Buffalo, New York 14209. 1988.

SEPARATION, MARITAL
See: FAMILY LAW

SEPARATION OF POWERS
See also: JUDGES AND JUDICIAL PROCESS

TEXTBOOKS AND GENERAL WORKS

THE ANATOMY OF A CONSTITUTIONAL LAW CASE; YOUNGSTOWN SHEET AND TUBE COMPANY VERSUS SAWYER, THE STEEL SEIZURE DECISION. Alan F. Westin. Columbia University Press, 562 West One Hundred Thirteenth Street, New York, New York 10025. 1990.

CONGRESS AND THE PRESIDENCY. Fourth Edition. Nelson W. Polsby. Prentice-Hall, Incorporated, 113 Sylvan Avenue, Englewood Cliffs, New Jersey 07632. 1986.

CONGRESS AND THE SEPARATION OF POWERS. John L. Fitzgerald. Praeger Publishers, One Madison Avenue, New York, New York 10010-3603. 1985.

THE CONSTITUTION IN CONFLICT. Robert A. Burt. Belknap Press, Cambridge, Massachusetts. 1992.

CONSTITUTIONAL CONFLICTS BETWEEN CONGRESS AND THE PRESIDENT. Third Edition. Louis Fisher. University Press of Kansas, 329 Carruth, Lawrence, Kansas 66045. 1991.

CONSTITUTIONAL DIPLOMACY. Michael J. Glennon. Princeton University Press, 41 William Street, Princeton, New Jersey 08540. 1990.

CONSTITUTIONAL INTERPRETATION. POWERS OF GOVERNMENT. Fifth Edition. Craig R. Ducat and Harold W. Chase. West Publishing Company, 50 West Kellogg Boulevard, St. Paul, Minnesota 55164. 1992.

CONSTITUTIONAL REFORM IN AMERICA: ESSAYS ON THE SEPARATION OF POWERS. Charles M. Hardin. Iowa State University Press, 2121 South State Avenue, Ames, Iowa 50010. 1989.

DIVIDED DEMOCRACY: COOPERATION AND CONFLICT BETWEEN THE PRESIDENT AND CONGRESS. James A. Thurber. CQ Press, Washington, D.C. 1991.

ESSAYS ON THE HISTORY AND MEANING OF CHECKS AND BALANCES. Epaminondas P. Panagopoulow. University Press of America, 4720 Boston Way, Lanham, Maryland 20706. 1986.

FOREIGN AFFAIRS AND THE U.S. CONSTITUTION. Louis Henkin, Michael J. Glennon, and William D. Rogers. Transnational Publishers, P.O. Box 7282, Ardsley-on-Hudson, New York 10503. 1990.

GOVERNANCE II: THE PRESIDENCY, THE CONGRESS, AND THE CONSTITUTION: DEADLOCK OR BALANCE OF POWERS? Kenneth W. Thompson. University Press of America, 4720 Boston Way, Lanham, Maryland 20706. 1991.

THE IMPERIAL CONGRESS: CRISIS IN THE SEPARATION OF POWERS. Gordon S. Jones and John A. Marini. Pharos Books, 200 Park Avenue, New York, New York 10166. 1988.

INDEPENDENT JUSTICE: THE FEDERAL SPECIAL PROSECUTOR IN AMERICAN POLITICS. Katy Jean Harriger. University Press of Kansas, 329 Carruth, Lawrence, Kansas 66045. 1992.

JUDGES AND LEGISLATORS: TOWARD INSTITUTIONAL COMITY. Robert A. Katzmann. Brookings Institution, 1775 Massachusetts Avenue, Washington, D.C. 20036. 1988.

THE LOGIC OF AMERICAN GOVERNMENT: APPLYING THE CONSTITUTION TO THE CONTEMPORARY WORLD. Daniel L. Feldman. William Morrow and Company, 105 Madison Avenue, New York, New York 10016. 1990.

MARBURY V. MADISON AND JUDICIAL REVIEW. Robert Lowry Clinton. University Press of Kansas, 329 Carruth, Lawrence, Kansas 66045. 1989.

THE MEANING OF THE CONSTITUTION: AN INTERDISCIPLINARY STUDY OF LEGAL THEORY. Gary C. Leeds. Associated Faculty Press, 19 West Thirty-sixth Street, New York, New York 10018. 1985.

THE NATIONAL SECURITY CONSTITUTION: SHARING POWER AFTER THE IRAN-CONTRA AFFAIR. Harold Hongju Koh. Yale University Press, 302 Temple Street, New Haven, Connecticut 06520. 1990.

POLITICS AND THE BUDGET: THE STRUGGLE BETWEEN THE PRESIDENT AND THE CONGRESS. Third Edition. Howard E. Schuman. Prentice-Hall, Incorporated, 113 Sylvan Avenue, Englewood Cliffs, New Jersey 07632. 1992.

THE POLITICS OF SHARED POWER: CONGRESS AND THE EXECUTIVE. Second Edition. Louis Fisher. CQ Press, Washington, D.C. 1987.

THE PRESIDENCY AND THE CONSTITUTIONAL SYSTEM. Kenneth W. Thompson. University Press of America, 4720 Boston Way, Lanham, Maryland 20706. 1989.

PRESIDENTIAL ACCOUNTABILITY: NEW AND RECURRING PROBLEMS. John Orman. Greenwood Publishing Group, Incorporated, 88 Post Road West, P.O. Box 5007, Westport, Connecticut 06881. 1990.

PRESIDENTS AND ASSEMBLIES: CONSTITUTIONAL DESIGN AND ELECTORAL DYNAMICS. Matthew Soberg Shugart and John M. Carey. Cambridge University Press, 40 West Twentieth Street, New York, New York 10011. 1992.

SEPARATION OF POWERS: DOES IT STILL WORK? Robert Goldwyn and Arthur Kaufman, Editors. American Enterprise Institute for Public Policy Research, 1150 Seventeenth Street, Northwest, Washington, D.C. 20036. 1986.

SEPARATION OF POWERS IN THE AMERICAN POLITICAL SYSTEM. Barbara B. Knight. George Mason University Press, Fairfax, Virginia. 1989.

THE SUPREME COURT AND JUDICIAL CHOICE: THE ROLE OF PROVISIONAL REVIEW IN A DEMOCRARY. Paul R. Dimond. University of Michigan Press, P.O. Box 1104, 839 Greene Street, Ann Arbor, Michigan 48106. 1989.

THE SUPREME COURT AND CONSTITUTIONAL DEMOCRACY. John Agresto. Cornell University Press, 124 Roberts Place, P.O. Box 250, Ithaca, New York 14850. 1984.

WE HAVE A DUTY: THE SUPREME COURT AND THE WATERGATE TAPES LITIGATION. Howard Ball. Greenwood Publishing Group, Incorporated, 88 Post Road West, P.O. Box 5007, Westport, Connecticut 06881. 1990.

BIBLIOGRAPHIES

SEPARATION OF POWERS: MONOGRAPHS. Mary Vance. Vance Bibliographies, P.O. Box 229, 112 North Charter Street, Monticello, Illinois 61856. 1987.

SERVICE OF PROCESS
See: CIVIL PROCEDURE

SERVITUDES
See: REAL PROPERTY

SETTLEMENT
See: ARBITRATION AND AWARD; COMPROMISE AND SETTLEMENT

SET-OFF AND COUNTERCLAIMS
See: DAMAGES

SEX CRIMES
See also: CRIMINAL LAW; PROSTITUTION; RAPE; SEXUAL ORIENTATION

HANDBOOKS, MANUALS, FORMBOOKS

LAWS AGAINST SEXUAL AND DOMESTIC VIOLENCE: A CONCISE GUIDE FOR CLERGY AND LAITY. Mary S. Winters. Pilgrim Press, New York, New York. 1988.

THE SEXUAL EXPLOITATION OF CHILDREN: A PRACTICAL GUIDE TO ASSESSMENT, INVESTIGATION, AND INTERVENTION. Seth L. Goldstein. Elsevier Science Publishing Company, P.O. Box 882, Madison Square Station, New York, New York 10159. 1987.

TEXTBOOKS AND GENERAL WORKS

THE AGE OF SEX CRIME. Jane Caputi. Bowling Green State University Popular Press, 838 East Wooster Street, Bowling Green, Ohio 43403. 1987.

THE AMERICANIZATION OF SEX. Edwin M. Schur. Temple University Press, 1601 North Broad Street, University Services Building, Philadelphia, Pennsylvania 19122. 1988.

THE LUST TO KILL: A FEMINIST INVESTIGATION OF SEXUAL MURDER. Deborah Cameron and Elizabeth Frazer. New York University Press, 70 Washington Square South, New York, New York 10012. 1987.

OVEREXPOSED: TREATING SEXUAL PERVERSION IN AMERICA. Sylvere Lotringer. Pantheon Books, 201 East Fiftieth Street, New York, New York 10022. 1988.

THE PROSECUTION AND DEFENSE OF SEX CRIMES. B. Anthony Morosco. Matthew Bender and Company, Incorporated, 11 Penn Plaza, New York, New York 10001. 1976 (Annual Supplements).

RAPE AND REPRESENTATION. Lynn A. Higgins and Brenda R. Silver. Columbia University Press, 562 West One Hundred Thirteenth Street, New York, New York 10025. 1991.

SEX CRIMES. Ronald M. Holmes. Sage Publications, 2455 Teller Road, Newbury Park, California 91320. 1991.

SEX CRIMES INVESTIGATION: A MAJOR CASE APPROACH. R. H. Morneau, Jr. Charles C. Thomas Publishing, 2600 South First Street, Springfield, Illinois 62794-9265. 1983.

SEX CRIMES INVESTIGATION: A PRACTICAL MANUAL. Burt Rapp. Loompanics Unlimited, P.O. Box 1197, Port Townsend, Washington 98368. 1988.

SEX MURDER AND SEX AGGRESSION: PHENOMENOLOGY, PSYCHOPATHOLOGY, PSYCHODYNAMICS, AND PROGNOSIS. Eugene Revitch and Louis B. Schlesinger. Charles C. Thomas, Publishers, 2600 South First Street, Springfield, Illinois 62794. 1989.

SEX OFFENSE: MEDICAL AND PSYCHOLOGICAL SUBJECT ANALYSIS WITH BIBLIOGRAPHY. Harold Pietre Drummond. ABBE Publishers Association of Washington, DC, 4111 Gallows Road, Annandale, Virginia 22003. 1987.

SEXUAL ABUSE, CAUSES, CONSEQUENCES AND TREATMENT OF INCESTUOUS AND PEDOPHILIC ACTS. Adele Mayer. Learning Publications, Incorporated, 5351 Gulf Drive, Holmes Beach, Florida 34218. 1985.

SEXUAL ASSAULT AMONG ADOLESCENTS. Suzanne B. Ageton. Free Press, 866 Third Avenue, New York, New York 10022. 1983.

SEXUAL COERCION: A SOURCEBOOK ON ITS NATURE, CAUSES, AND PREVENTION. Elizabeth Grauerholz and Mary Koralewski. Lexington Books, 125 Spring Street, Lexington, Massachusetts 02173. 1991.

SEXUAL CRIMES AND CONFRONTATIONS: A STUDY OF VICTIMS AND OFFENDERS. D.J. West. Gower Publishing Company, Old Post Road, Brookfield, Vermont 05036. 1987.

SEXUAL HOMICIDE: PATTERNS AND MOTIVES. Robert K. Ressler, Ann W. Burgess, and John E. Douglas. Lexington Books, 125 Spring Street, Lexington, Massachusetts 02173. 1988.

THE SEXUAL OFFENDER AND THE CRIMINAL JUSTICE SYSTEM. Ronald M. Holmes. Charles C. Thomas Publishing, 2600 South First Street, Springfield, Illinois 62794-9265. 1983.

SURVIVING SEXUAL VIOLENCE. Liz Kelly. University of Minnesota Press, 2037 University Avenue, Southeast, St. Paul, Minnesota 55414. 1988.

BIBLIOGRAPHIES

DISABILITY, SEXUALITY, AND ABUSE: ANNOTATED BIBLIOGRAPHY. Dick Sobsey. Paul H. Brookes Publishing Company, Incorporated, P.O. Box 10624, Baltimore, Maryland 21285. 1991.

LITERATURE REVIEW OF SEXUAL ABUSE. Diane DePanfilis. National Center on Child Abuse and Neglect. Superintendent of Documents, United States Government Printing Office, Washington, D.C. 20402. 1987.

RESEARCH CENTERS, INSTITUTES, CLEARINGHOUSES

RESEARCH DATA ARCHIVE OF SEXUAL BEHAVIOR. Kinsey Institute for Research in Sex, Gender, and Reproductive Information Services, Morrison Hall, Fourth Floor, Indiana University, Bloomington, Indiana 47405.

SEX DISCRIMINATION
See: DISCRIMINATION, SEX

SEXUAL HARASSMENT

HANDBOOKS, MANUALS, FORMBOOKS

ACADEMIC AND WORKPLACE SEXUAL HARASSMENT: A RESOURCE MANUAL. Michele Antoinette Paludi and Richard B. Barickman. State University of New York Press, State University Plaza, Albany, New York 12246. 1991.

RAPE, INCEST, AND SEXUAL HARASSMENT: A GUIDE FOR HELPING SURVIVORS. Kathryn Quina and Nancy L. Carlson. Praeger Publishers, One Madison Avenue, New York, New York 10010. 1989.

SEXUAL COERCION: A SOURCEBOOK ON ITS NATURE, CAUSES, AND PREVENTION. Elizabeth Grauerholz and Mary Koralewski. Lexington Books, 125 Spring Street, Lexington, Massachusetts 02173. 1991.

SEXUAL HARASSMENT: HOW TO KEEP YOUR COMPANY OUT OF COURT. Kenneth L. Lloyd. Institute for Management, 14 Plaza Road, Greenvale, New York 11548. 1989.

SEXUAL HARASSMENT IN THE WORKPLACE: A GUIDE TO THE LAW. Third edition. Ralph H. Baxter, Jr and Lynne C. Hermle. Executive Enterprises Publications Co., 22 West 21st Street, New York, New York 10010. 1989.

TEXTBOOKS AND GENERAL WORKS

CORPORATE AFFAIRS: NEPOTISM, OFFICE ROMANCE, AND SEXUAL HARASSMENT. Bureau of National Affairs, Incorporated, 1231 25th Street, N.W., Washington, D.C. 20037. 1988.

CORPORATE ATTRACTIONS: AN INSIDE ACCOUNT OF SEXUAL HARASSMENT WITH THE NEW SEXUAL RULES FOR MEN AND WOMEN ON THE JOB. Kathleen Neville. Acropolis Books, 11741 Bowman Greene Drive, Reston, Virginia 22090. 1990.

INTENT VS. IMPACT: HOW TO EFFECTIVELY MANAGE SEXUAL HARASSMENT INVESTIGATIONS. Stephen F. Anderson, Trisha Brinkman, and James W. Mercer, Sr. Bureau of National Affairs, Incorporated, 1231 Twenty-fifth Street, Northwest, Washington, D.C. 20037. 1989.

IVORY POWER: SEXUAL HARASSMENT ON CAMPUS. Michele A. Paludi. State University of New York Press, State University Plaza, Albany, New York 12246. 1990.

THE LECHEROUS PROFESSOR: SEXUAL HARASSMENT ON CAMPUS. Second Edition. Billie Wright Dziech and Linda Weiner. University of Illinois Press, 54 East Gregory Drive, Champaign, Illinois 61820. 1990.

SEX AND THE WORKPLACE. Barbara A. Gutek. Jossey-Bass, 350 Sansome Street, San Francisco, California 94104. 1985.

SEXUAL COERCION: A SOURCEBOOK ON ITS NATURE, CAUSES, AND PREVENTION. Elizabeth Grauerholz and Mary Koralewski. Lexington Books, 125 Spring Street, Lexington, Massachusetts 02173. 1991.

SEXUAL EXPLOITATION: RAPE, CHILD SEXUAL ABUSE, AND WORKPLACE HARASSMENT. Diana E.H. Russell. Sage Publications, P.O. Box 6944, San Mateo, California 94403. 1984.

SEXUAL HARASSMENT: EMPLOYER POLICIES AND PROBLEMS. Bureau of National Affairs, Incorporated, 1231 Twenty-fifth Street, Northwest, Washington, D.C. 20037. 1987.

SEXUAL HARASSMENT: HOW TO KEEP YOUR COMPANY OUT OF COURT. Kenneth L. Lloyd. Institute for Management, 14 Plaza Road, Greenvale, New York 11548. 1989.

SEXUAL HARASSMENT IN EMPLOYMENT. Susan M. Omilian. Callaghan and Company, 155 Pfingsten Road, Deerfield, Illinois 60015. 1987.

SEXUAL HARASSMENT IN EMPLOYMENT LAW. Barbara Lindemann Schlei and David D. Kadue. Bureau of National Affairs, Incorporated, 1231 Twenty-fifth Street, Northwest, Washington, D.C. 20037. 1992.

SEXUAL HARASSMENT IN THE WORKPLACE. Arjun P. Aggarwal. Butterworth Legal Publishers, 90 Stiles Road, Salem, New Hampshire 03079. 1987.

SEXUAL HARASSMENT IN THE WORKPLACE. Richard D. Wayne and others. Massachusetts Continuing Legal Education-New England Law Institute, Incorporated, 20 West Street, Boston, Massachusetts 02111. 1991.

SEXUAL HARASSMENT IN THE WORKPLACE: HOW TO PREVENT, INVESTIGATE, AND RESOLVE PROBLEMS IN YOUR ORGANIZATION. Ellen J. Wagner. American Management Association,. 1992.

SEXUAL HARASSMENT IN THE WORKPLACE: LAW AND PRACTICE. Alba Conte. John Wiley and Sons, Incorporated, 605 Third Avenue, New York, New York 10158. 1990.

SEXUAL HARASSMENT ON THE JOB: HOW TO AVOID THE WORKING WOMAN'S NIGHTMARE. Constance Backhouse and Leah Cohen. Prentice Hall Incorporated, 270 Sylvan Avenue, Englewood Cliffs, New Jersey 07632. 1981.

SEXUAL HARASSMENT: THE ISSUES AND THE LAW. American Bankers Association, 1120 Connecticut Avenue, N.W., Washington, D.C. 20036. 1982.

SURVIVING SEXUAL VIOLENCE. Liz Kelly. University of Minnesota Press, 2037 University Avenue, Southeast, St. Paul, Minnesota 55414. 1988.

VULNERABLE WORKERS: PSYCHOSOCIAL AND LEGAL ISSUES. Marilyn J. Davidson and Jill Earnshaw. John Wiley and Sons, Incorporated, 605 Third Avenue, New York, New York 10158. 1991.

NEWSLETTERS AND NEWSPAPERS

SEXUAL HARASSMENT AND DISCRIMINATION IN THE WORKPLACE. Nu-Tec Publishing, Incorporated, 4715 Strack Road, Houston, Texas 77069. 1990- . Monthly.

DIRECTORIES

SEXUAL HARASSMENT: A GUIDE TO RESOURCES. M. Dawn McCaghy. G.K. Hall. 1985.

BIBLIOGRAPHIES

SEXUAL HARASSMENT OF WOMEN IN THE WORKPLACE: A BIBLIOGRAPHY. Alan V. Miller. Vance Bibliographies, P.O. Box 229, 112 North Charter Street, Monticello, Illinois 61856. 1981.

SEXUAL HARASSMENT ON THE JOB. Earleen H. Cook and Joseph L. Cook. Vance Bibliographies, P.O. Box 229, 112 North Charter Street, Monticello, Illinois 61856. 1980.

ASSOCIATIONS AND PROFESSIONAL SOCIETIES

ASSOCIATION FOR THE SEXUALLY HARASSED. P.O. Box 27235, Philadelphia, Pennsylvania 19118. (215) 952-8037.

RESEARCH CENTERS, INSTITUTES, CLEARINGHOUSES

LEGAL ADVOCATES FOR WOMEN. 320 Clement, San Francisco, California 94118.

PROJECT ON THE STATUS AND EDUCATION OF WOMEN. (202) 387-1300.

SEXUAL ORIENTATION
See also: SEX CRIMES

HANDBOOKS, MANUALS, FORMBOOKS

HOMOSEXUAL CONDUCT AND THE LAW. Irving J. Sloan. Oceana Publications, 75 Main Street, Dobbs Ferry, New York 10522. 1987.

A LEGAL GUIDE FOR LESBIAN AND GAY COUPLES. Sixth Edition. Denis Clifford and Hayden Curry. Sixth Edition. Nolo Press, 950 Parker Street, Berkeley, California 94710. 1991.

THE RIGHTS OF LESBIANS AND GAY MEN: THE BASIC ACLU GUIDE TO A GAY PERSON'S RIGHTS. Third Edition. Nan D. Hunter, Sherryl E. Michaelson, and Thomas B. Stoddard. Southern Illinois University Press, P.O. Box 3697, Carbondale, Illinois 62902-3697. 1992.

TEXTBOOKS AND GENERAL WORKS

ANTI-GAY LEGISLATION: AN ATTEMPT TO SANCTION INEQUALITY? Rosalyn Richter. Lambda Legal Defense and Education Fund, 666 Broadway, New York, New York 10012. 1985.

FIGHTING BACK: LESBIAN AND GAY DRAFT, MILITARY, AND VETERANS' ISSUES. National Lawyers Guild, 55 Sixth Avenue, New York, New York 10013. 1984.

GAYS AND THE LAW. Paul Crane. Pluto Press, P.O. Box 442, Concord, Massachusetts 01742. 1982.

GAYS/JUSTICE: A STUDY OF ETHICS, SOCIETY, AND LAW. Richard D. Mohr. Columbia University Press, 562 West One Hundred Thirteenth Street, New York, New York 10025. 1988.

HOMOPHOBIA: AN OVERVIEW. John P. DeCecco, Editor. The Haworth Press, Incorporated, 10 Alice Street, Binghamton, New York 13904. 1984.

HOMOSEXUAL CONDUCT AND THE LAW: THE LEGAL STANDING OF GAYS AND LESBIANS. Irving J. Sloan. Oceana Publications, Incorporated, 75 Main Street, Dobbs Ferry, New York 10522. 1987.

LEGALIZING HOMOSEXUAL CONDUCT: THE ROLE OF THE SUPREME COURT IN THE GAY RIGHTS MOVEMENT. Charles Rice. Center for Judicial Studies, P.O. Box 17248, Richmond, Virginia 23226. 1984.

MORALITY, SEX, AND THE CONSTITUTION: A CHRISTIAN PERSPECTIVE ON THE POWER OF GOVERNMENT TO REGULATE PRIVATE SEXUAL CONDUCT BETWEEN CONSENTING ADULTS. G. Sidney Buchanan. University Press of America, 4720 Boston Way, Lanham, Maryland 20706. 1985.

PEERS, QUEERS, AND COMMONS: THE STRUGGLE FOR GAY LAW REFORM FROM 1950 TO THE PRESENT. Stephen Jeffrey-Poulter. Routledge, Chapman & Hall, 29 West Thirty-fifth Street, New York, New York 10001. 1991.

PRISON HOMOSEXUALITY: MYTH AND REALITY. Alice Propper. Lexington Books, Division of D.C. Heath and Company, 125 Spring Street, Lexington, Massachusetts 02173. 1981.

THE RIGHT TO PRIVACY: GAYS, LESBIANS, AND THE CONSTITUTION. Vincent J. Samar. Temple University Press, 1601 North Broad Street, University Services Building, Philadelphia, Pennsylvania 19122. 1991.

THE RIGHTS OF GAY PEOPLE. Thomas B. Stoddard, et al. Southern Illinois University Press, P.O. Box 3697, Carbondale, Illinois 62902-3697. 1983.

SEXUAL ORIENTATION AND THE LAW. Roberta Achtenberg, Editor. Clark Boardman Company, Limited, 435 Hudson Street, New York, New York 10014. 1985 (Periodic Supplements).

SEXUAL ORIENTATION AND THE LAW. Harvard University Press, 79 Garden Street, Cambridge, Massachusetts 02138. 1990.

SEXUAL POLITICS, SEXUAL COMMUNITIES: THE MAKING OF A HOMOSEXUAL MINORITY IN THE UNITED STATES 1940-1970. John D'Emilio. University of Chicago Press, 5801 Ellis Avenue, Chicago, Illinois 60637. 1984.

SOCIETY AND THE HOMOSEXUAL. Gordon Westwood. Greenwood Publishing Group, Incorporated, 88 Post Road West, P.O. Box 5007, Westport, Connecticut 06881. 1985.

DIGESTS, INDEXES, ABSTRACTS, CITATORS

ALTERNATIVE PRESS INDEX. Alternative Press Center, Incorporated, P.O. Box 33109, Baltimore, Maryland 21218. Quarterly.

LAW REVIEWS AND PERIODICALS

THE ADVOCATE. The Advocate, 22761 Pacific Coast Highway, 8991, Suite 2341, Malibu, California 90265. Biweekly.

JOURNAL OF HOMOSEXUALITY. The Haworth Press, Incorporated, 28 East Twenty-second Street, New York, New York 10010. Quarterly.

SEXUAL ORIENTATION

NEWSLETTERS AND NEWSPAPERS

LAMBDA UPDATE. Lambda Legal Defense and Education Fund, Incorporated, 666 Broadway, New York, New York 10012. Quarterly.

LESBIAN/GAY LAW NOTES. Bar Association for Human Rights, P.O. Box 1899, Grand Central Station, New York, New York 10163. Monthly.

NATIONAL GAY RIGHTS ADVOCATES NEWSLETTER. National Gay Rights Advocates, 540 Castro Street, San Francisco, California 94114. Quarterly.

NATIONAL GAY RIGHTS ADVOCATES UPDATE. National Gay Rights Advocates, 540 Castro Street, San Francisco, California 94114. Monthly.

ASSOCIATIONS AND PROFESSIONAL SOCIETIES

AMERICAN LIBRARY ASSOCIATION, GAY AND LESBIAN TASK FORCE. 50 East Huron, Chicago, Illinois 60610. (312) 944-7280.

ASSOCIATION OF AMERICAN LAW SCHOOLS, SECTION ON GAY AND LESBIAN ISSUES. Association of American Law Schools, One Dupont Circle, Northwest, Washington, D.C. 20036. (202) 296-8851.

BAR ASSOCIATION FOR HUMAN RIGHTS. P.O. Box 1899, Grand Central Station, New York, New York 10163. (212) 431-2156.

FUND FOR HUMAN DIGNITY. 666 Broadway, Fourth Floor, New York, New York 10012. (212) 529-1600.

GAY MEDIA TASK FORCE. 421 South Van Ness Avenue, Suite 33, Los Angeles, California 90020. (213) 251-9903.

HUMAN RIGHTS CAMPAIGN FUND. 1012 Fourteenth Street, Northwest, Suite 600, Washington, D.C. 20005. (202) 628-4160.

LAMBDA LEGAL DEFENSE AND EDUCATION FUND, INCORPORATED. 666 Broadway, New York, New York 10012. (212) 995-8585.

NATIONAL COMMITTEE FOR SEXUAL CIVIL LIBERTIES. 19 Olden Lane, Princeton, New Jersey 08940. (609) 924-1950.

NATIONAL GAY AND LESBIAN TASK FORCE. 1517 U Street, Northwest, Washington, D. C. 20009. (202) 332-6483.

NATIONAL GAY RIGHTS ADVOCATES. 540 Castro Street, San Francisco, California 94114. (415) 863-3624.

TANGENT GROUP. 115 Monroe Street, Bossier City, Louisiana 71111. (318) 742-4709.

RESEARCH CENTERS, INSTITUTES, CLEARINGHOUSES

CENTER FOR RESEARCH AND EDUCATION IN SEXUALITY. San Francisco State University, Psychology Building, Room 502, San Francisco, California 94132. (415) 338-1137.

HOMOSEXUAL INFORMATION CENTER. 115 Monroe, Bossier City, Louisiana 71111. (318) 742-4709.

INSTITUTE OF SOCIAL ETHICS. One Gold Street, Suite 22-ABC, Hartford, Connecticut 06103. (203) 547-1281.

LESBIAN AND GAY STUDIES CENTER. Yale University, Department of History, P.O. Box 2585, Yale Station, New Haven, Connecticut 06520. (203) 432-1370.

MEDIA FUND FOR HUMAN RIGHTS. P.O. Box 8185, Universal City, California 91608. (818) 902-1476.

SEXUAL PREFERENCE
See: SEXUAL ORIENTATION

SHAREHOLDERS
See: CORPORATIONS; SECURITIES

SHIPPING
See: TRANSPORTATION

SHIPS AND BOATS
See: ADMIRALTY

SLANDER
See: LIBEL AND SLANDER

SLAVERY
See also: DISCRIMINATION, RACE

STATUTES, CODES, STANDARDS, UNIFORM LAWS

STATE SLAVERY STATUTES. Paul Finkelman. UPA Academic Editions, Frederick, Maryland. 1989.

STATUTES ON SLAVERY: THE PAMPHLET LITERATURE. Paul Finkelman. Garland Publishing, Incorporated, 136 Madison Avenue, New York, New York 10016. 1988.

TEXTBOOKS AND GENERAL WORKS

ABOLITIONISTS IN NORTHERN COURTS: THE PAMPHLET LITERATURE. Paul Finkelman. Garland Publishing, Incorporated, 136 Madison Avenue, New York, New York 10016. 1988.

THE AFRICAN SLAVE TRADE AND AMERICAN COURTS: THE PAMPHLET LITERATURE. Paul Finkelman. Garland Publishing, Incorporated, 136 Madison Avenue, New York, New York 10016. 1988.

AMERICAN SLAVERY AND AFTER. George Olshausen. Olema Press, P.O. Box 26481, Custom House Station, San Francisco, California 94126. 1983.

THE ANTI-SLAVERY APPEAL: AMERICAN ABOLITIONISM AFTER 1830. Ronald G. Walters. W.W. Norton and Company, Incorporated 500 Fifth Avenue New York, New York 10110. 1984.

THE BLACK LAWS IN THE OLD NORTHWEST: A DOCUMENTARY HISTORY. Stephen Middleton. Greenwood Publishing Group, Incorporated, 88 Post Road West, P.O. Box 5007, Westport, Connecticut 06881. 1992.

THE CONSTITUTION AND RACE. Donald E. Lively. Praeger Publishers, One Madison Avenue, New York, New York 10010. 1992.

THE CRIMINAL LAW OF SLAVERY AND FREEDOM, 1800-1868. Daniel J. Flanigan. Garland Publishing, Incorporated, 136 Madison Avenue, New York, New York 10016. 1987.

THE FOURTEENTH AMENDMENT AND THE BILL OF RIGHTS. Raoul Berger. University of Oklahoma Press, 105 Asp Avenue, Norman, Oklahoma 73019. 1989.

FREE BLACKS, SLAVES, AND SLAVEOWNERS IN CIVIL AND CRIMINAL COURTS: THE PAMPHLET LITERATURE. Paul Finkelman. Garland Publishing, Incorporated, 136 Madison Avenue, New York, New York 10016. 1988.

FUGITIVE SLAVES AND AMERICAN COURTS: THE PAMPHLET LITERATURE. Paul Finkelman. Garland Publishing, Incorporated, 136 Madison Avenue, New York, New York 10016. 1988.

THE LAND OF FREEDOM AND BONDAGE: A CASEBOOK. Paul Finklaman. Oceana Publications, Incorporated, 75 Main Street, Dobbs Ferry, New York 10522. 1985.

THE LAW OF AMERICAN SLAVERY: MAJOR HISTORICAL INTERPRETATIONS. Kermit L. Hall. Garland Publishing, Incorporated, 136 Madison Avenue, New York, New York 10016. 1987.

LAW, THE CONSTITUTION, AND SLAVERY. Paul Finkelman. Garland Publishing, Incorporated, 136 Madison Avenue, New York, New York 10016. 1989.

PRISON SLAVERY. Barbara Esposito and Lee Wood, Editors. Committee to Abolish Prison Slavery, P. O. Box 3207, Washington, D.C. 20010. 1982.

ROMAN SLAVE LAW. Alan Watson. Johns Hopkins University Press, 701 West Fortieth Street, Baltimore, Maryland 21211. 1987.

THE RULING RACE: A HISTORY OF AMERICAN SLAVEHOLDERS. James Oakes. Vin/Random House, Incorporated, 201 East Fiftieth Street, New York, New York 10022. 1983.

SLAVE AND CITIZEN. Frank Tannenbaum. Beacon Press, 25 Beacon Street, Boston, Massachusetts 02108. 1992.

SLAVE LAW IN THE AMERICAS. Alan Watson. University of Georgia Press, Athens, Georgia 30602. 1989.

SLAVE REBELS, ABOLITIONISTS, AND SOUTHERN COURTS: THE PAMPHLET LITERATURE. Paul Finkelman. Garland Publishing, Incorporated, 136 Madison Avenue, New York, New York 10016. 1988.

SLAVERY AND ABORTION: HISTORY REPENTS. J.C. Wilke. Hayes Publishing Company, Incorporated, 6304 Hamilton Avenue, Cincinnati, Ohio 45224. 1984.

SLAVERY AND ITS CONSEQUENCES: THE CONSTITUTION, EQUALITY, AND RACE. Robert A. Goldwin and Art Kaufman. American Enterprise Institute for Public Policy Research, 1150 Seventeenth Street, Northwest, Washington, D.C. 20036. 1988.

SLAVERY AND RACE IN AMERICAN POPULAR CULTURE. William L. Van De Burg. University of Wisconsin Press, 114 North Murray Street, Madison, Wisconsin 53706. 1984.

SLAVERY, LAW AND POLITICS: THE DRED SCOTT CASE IN HISTORICAL PERSPECTIVE. Don E. Fehrenbacher. Oxford University Press, Incorporated, 200 Madison Avenue, New York, New York 10016. 1981.

SOUTHERN SLAVES IN FREE STATE COURTS: THE PAMPHLET LITERATURE. Paul Finkelman. Garland Publishing, Incorporated, 136 Madison Avenue, New York, New York 10016. 1988.

WHAT GOD HATH WROUGHT: THE EMBODIMENT OF FREEDOM IN THE THIRTEENTH AMENDMENT. George H. Hoemann. Garland Publishing, Incorporated, 136 Madison Avenue, New York, New York 10016. 1987.

WHITE SERVITUDE IN COLONIAL AMERICA: AN ECONOMIC ANALYSIS. David Galenson. Cambridge University Press, 40 West Twentieth Street, New York, New York 10011. 1984.

ENCYCLOPEDIAS AND DICTIONARIES

DICTIONARY OF AFRO-AMERICAN SLAVERY. Randall M. Miller and John David Smith. Greenwood Publishing Group, Incorporated, 88 Post Road West, P.O. Box 5007, Westport, Connecticut 06881. 1988.

BIBLIOGRAPHIES

SLAVERY IN THE COURTROOM: AN ANNOTATED BIBLIOGRAPHY OF AMERICAN CASES. Paul Finkleman. Library of Congress. Superintendent of Documents, United States Government Printing Office, Washington, D.C. 20402. 1985.

BIOGRAPHICAL SOURCES

THE MIND OF FREDERICK DOUGLASS. Waldo E. Martin, Junior. University of North Carolina Press, P. O. Box 2288, 116 South Boundary Street, Chapel Hill, North Carolina 27515-2288. 1986.

SMALL BUSINESS

STATUTES, CODES, STANDARDS, UNIFORM LAWS

SELECTED DOCUMENTS PERTAINING TO THE WOMEN'S BUSINESS OWNERSHIP ACT OF 1988. United States Congress, Committee on Small Business. Superintendent of Documents, United States Government Printing Office, Washington, D.C. 20402. 1988.

LOOSELEAF SERVICES AND REPORTERS

ADVISING SMALL BUSINESSES. Steven C. Alberty. Callaghan and Company, 155 Pfingsten Road, Deerfield, Illinois 60015. 1989- .

SMALL BUSINESS PLANNING. John C. Wisdom. Callaghan and Company, 155 Pfingsten Road, Deerfield, Illinois 60015. 1990- .

SMALL BUSINESS TAX CONTROL. Capital Publications, 89 Primrose Way, Sacramento, California 95819. 1974- .

SMALL BUSINESS TAX PLANNER. Research Institute of America, Incorporated, 90 Fifth Avenue, New York, New York 10011. 1984- .

TAX PLANNING FOR SMALL BUSINESSES. John C. Wisdom. Clark Boardman Company, Limited, 435 Hudson Street, New York, New York 10014. 1991.

HANDBOOKS, MANUALS, FORMBOOKS

THE ATTORNEY'S HANDBOOK ON SMALL BUSINESS REORGANIZATION UNDER CHAPTER 11. John Harvey Williamson. Argyle Publishing Company, 1955 Hoyt Street, Lakewood, Colorado 80215. 1988.

THE BUSINESSPERSON'S LEGAL ADVISOR. Cliff Roberson. Tab Books, Incorporated, P.O. Box 40, Blue Ridge Summit, Pennsylvania 17294-0850. 1986.

THE COMPLETE BOOK OF SMALL BUSINESS LEGAL FORMS. Daniel Sitarz. Nova Publishing Company, 1103 West College Street, Carbondale, Illinois 62901. 1991.

ENCYCLOPEDIA OF SMALL BUSINESS RESOURCES. David E. Gumpert and Jeffry A. Timmons. HarperCollins Publishers, Incorporated, 10 East Fifty-third Street, New York, New York 10022. 1984.

GUIDE TO MARKETING LAW: WHAT EVERY SELLER SHOULD KNOW. Richard M. Steuer. Law and Business, Harcourt Brace Jovanovich, Incorporated, 6277 Sea Harbor Drive, Orlando, Florida 32821. 1986.

HANDBOOK ON THE LAW OF SMALL BUSINESS ENTERPRISES. Third Edition. John H. Williamson. Argyle Publishing Company, 1955 Hoyt Street, Lakewood, Colorado 80215. 1990.

HANDBOOKS FOR SMALL BUSINESS: A SURVEY OF SMALL BUSINESS PROGRAMS OF THE FEDERAL GOVERNMENT. Fifth Edition. Committee on Small Business, United States Senate, Superintendent of Documents, United States Government Printing Office, Washington, D.C. 20402. 1984.

HOW TO KEEP YOUR COMPANY OUT OF COURT: THE PRACTICAL LEGAL GUIDE FOR GROWING BUSINESSES. Paul A. Allen, Editor. Prentice-Hall, Incorporated, 113 Sylvan Avenue, Englewood Cliffs, New Jersey 07632. 1984.

HOW TO PROCEED IN BUSINESS LEGALLY: THE ENTREPENEUR'S PREVENTIVE LAW GUIDE. Stanley G. Jackson. Prentice-Hall, Incorporated, 113 Sylvan Avenue, Englewood Cliffs, New Jersey 07632. 1984.

INCORPORATING: A GUIDE FOR SMALL BUSINESS OWNERS. Carolyn M. Vella and John McGonagle, Junior. American Management Associations, 135 West Fiftieth Street, New York, New York 10020.

THE INSIDER'S GUIDE TO CONTRACTING WITH THE FEDERAL GOVERNMENT. Richard L. Porterfield. John Wiley and Sons, Incorporated, 605 Third Avenue, New York, New York 10158. 1992.

J.K. LASSER'S LEGAL FORMS FOR SMALLER BUSINESSES. Arnold S. Goldstein. J.K. Lasser Tax Institute, New York, New York. 1988.

LAWYERS' AND ACCOUNTANTS' GUIDE TO PURCHASE AND SALE OF A SMALL BUSINESS: BUSINESS PLANNING, LAW TAXATION, ACCOUNTING. Willard D. Horwich. Prentice-Hall, Incorporated, 113 Sylvan Avenue, Englewood Cliffs, New Jersey 07632. 1989.

LAYMAN'S GUIDE TO LEGAL INVESTMENT DOCUMENTATION. Third Edition. Stephen M. Goodman. National Association of Small Business Investment Companies, 1156 Fifteenth Street, Northwest, Washington, D.C. 20005. 1987.

LEGAL HANDBOOK FOR SMALL BUSINESS. Marc J. Lane. AMACOM, 135 West Fiftieth Street, New York, New York 10020. 1989.

LEGAL MASTER GUIDE FOR SMALL BUSINESS. Fred S. Steingold. Prentice-Hall, Incorporated, 113 Sylvan Avenue, Englewood Cliffs, New Jersey 07632. 1983.

MAIL ORDER LEGAL MANUAL: FEDERAL AND STATE LAWS THAT YOU MUST KNOW. Second Edition. Erwin J. Keup. Oasis Press, 720 South Hillview, Milpitas, California 95035. 1990.

PURCHASE AND SALE OF SMALL BUSINESSES. FORMS. Second Edition. Marc J. Lane. John Wiley and Sons, Incorporated, 605 Third Avenue, New York, New York 10158. 1991.

SETTING UP IN BUSINESS: AN INFORMATION GUIDE. Ray Prytherch and Suzanne Stanley. Gower Publishing Company, Old Post Road, Brookfield, Vermont 05036. 1989.

SMALL BUSINESS: AN INFORMATION SOURCEBOOK. Cynthia C. Ryans. Oryx Press, 2214 North Central Avenue, Phoenix, Arizona 85004. 1987.

SMALL BUSINESS LEGAL ADVISOR. Second Edition. William A. Hancock. Shepard's/McGraw-Hill, P.O. Box 1235, Colorado Springs, Colorado 80901. 1992.

SMALL BUSINESS LEGAL HANDBOOK. Robert Friedman. Enterprise Publishing Company, 725 Market Street, Wilmington, Delaware 19801. 1985.

THE SMALL BUSINESS LEGAL PROBLEM SOLVER. Arnold S. Goldstein. Van Nostrand Reinhold Company, Incorporated, 115 Fifth Avenue, New York, New York 10003. 1984.

SMALL BUSINESS SOURCEBOOK: A GUIDE TO THE INFORMATION SERVICES AND SOURCES PROVIDED TO SMALL BUSINESSES BY ASSOCIATIONS, CONSULTANTS, EDUCATIONAL PROGRAMS, FRANCHISERS, GOVERNMENT AGENCIES (FEDERAL, STATE, AND LOCAL), REFERENCE WORKS, STATISTICIANS, SUPPLIERS, TRADE SHOWS, AND VENTURE CAPITAL FIRMS. Carol Schwartz, Editor. Gale Research, Incorporated, 835 Penobscot Building, Detroit, Michigan 48226. 1992.

TEXTBOOKS AND GENERAL WORKS

ABA'S SMALL BUSINESS BANKERS. Solon J. Candage. American Bankers Association, 1120 Connecticut Avenue, Northwest, Washington, D.C. 20036. 1988.

BUSINESS LAW: PRINCIPLES AND CASES. Second Edition. Daniel V. Davidson, et al. Kent Publishing Company, Division of Wadsworth Incorporated, 20 Park Plaza, Boston, Massachusetts 02116. 1987.

BUSINESS START-UP PRACTICE. Dana Shilling. Prentice-Hall, Incorporated, 113 Sylvan Avenue, Englewood Cliffs, New Jersey 07632. 1987.

BUSINESS TRANSFERS: AN ACCOUNTANT'S AND ATTORNEY'S GUIDE. Arnold S. Goldstein. John Wiley and Sons, Incorporated, 605 Third Avenue, New York, New York 10158. 1985.

BUYING, SELLING, STARTING A BUSINESS. Ray L. Gustafson. GHC Business Books, 4214 North Post Road, Omaha, Nebraska 68112. 1982.

COMPREHENSIVE BUSINESS LAW: PRINCIPLES AND CASES. Daniel V. Davidson, et al. Kent Publishing Company, Division of Wadsworth Incorporated, 20 Park Plaza, Boston, Massachusetts 02116. 1987.

EMPLOYEE BENEFITS FOR SMALL BUSINESS. Jane White and Bruce Pyenson. Prentice-Hall, Incorporated, 113 Sylvan Avenue, Englewood Cliffs, New Jersey 07632. 1991.

EXECUTIVE COMPENSATION STRATEGIES: FOR SMALL AND MEDIUM SIZE BUSINESSES. Paul C. Stein and Lewis Schier. Panel Publishers, 36 West Forty-fourth Street, New York, New York 10036. 1985.

FUNDAMENTALS OF THE LEGAL ENVIRONMENT OF BUSINESS. Robert N. Corley and O. Lee Reed. Shepard's/McGraw-Hill, P.O. Box 1235, Colorado Springs, Colorado 80901. 1986.

HOW TO FINANCE YOUR SMALL BUSINESS WITH GOVERNMENT MONEY: SNA AND OTHER LOANS. Second Edition. Rick S. Hayes and John C. Howell. John Wiley and Sons, Incorporated, 605 Third Avenue, New York, New York 10158. 1983.

INSIDE THE FAMILY-HELD BUSINESS: A PRACTICAL GUIDE FOR ENTREPRENEURS AND THEIR ADVISORS. Law and Business, Harcourt Brace Jovanovich, Incorporated, 6277 Sea Harbor Drive, Orlando, Florida 32821. 1986.

INTRODUCTION TO BASIC LEGAL PRINCIPLES. Fourth Edition. Benjamin N. Henszey, Barry Lee Myers and Reed T. Phalan. Kendall/Hunt Publishing Company, 2460 Kerper Boulevard, Dubuque, Iowa 52001. 1989.

INTRODUCTION TO BUSINESS INSURANCE: LAW AND LITIGATION. Dan L. Goldwasser and David W. Ichel, co-chairmen. Practising Law Institute, 810 Seventh Avenue, New York, New York 10019. 1985.

KEYS TO BUYING AND SELLING A BUSINESS. Steven A. Fox. Barron's Educational Series, Incorporated, 250 Wireless Boulevard, Hauppauge, New York 11788. 1991.

LAW AND BUSINESS. Second Edition. Lawrence S. Clark and Peter D. Kinder. Shepard's/McGraw-Hill, P. O. Box 1235, Colorado Springs, Colorado 80901. 1988.

THE LAW (IN PLAIN ENGLISH) FOR SMALL BUSINESSES. Second Edition. Leonard D. DuBoff. John Wiley and Sons, Incorporated, 605 Third Avenue, New York, New York 10158. 1991.

THE MCGRAW-HILL SMALL BUSINESS TAX ADVISOR: UNDERSTANDING THE TAX LAW. Second Edition. Cliff Roberson. McGraw-Hill Publishing Company, 1221 Avenue of the Americas, New York, New York 10020. 1992.

1985 LIMITED OFFERING EXEMPTIONS: REGULATION D. J. William Hicks. Clark Boardman Company, Limited, 435 Hudson Street, New York, New York 10014. 1987.

PRACTICAL BUSINESS LAW. Second Edition. John J. Moran. Prentice-Hall, Incorporated, 113 Sylvan Avenue, Englewood Cliffs, New Jersey 07632. 1989.

THE PROFESSIONAL SKILLS OF THE SMALL BUSINESS LAWYER. Harry J. Haynsworth. American Law Institute-American Bar Association, Committee on Continuing Professional Education, 4025 Chestnut Street, Philadelphia, Pennsylvania 19104. 1984.

PURCHASE AND SALE OF SMALL BUSINESSES: TAX AND LEGAL ASPECTS. Second Edition. Marc J. Lane. John Wiley and Sons, Incorporated, 605 Third Avenue, New York, New York 10158. 1991 (With Supplements).

REGULATION D OFFERINGS OF LIMITED PARTNERSHIPS AND CORPORATE CAPITAL RAISING. American Law Institute-American Bar Association, Committee on Continuing Professional Education, 4025 Chestnut Street, Philadelphia, Pennsylvania 19104. 1985.

SELECTING THE FORM OF A SMALL BUSINESS ENTITY. Harry J. Haynsworth. American Law Institute-American Bar Association, Committee on Continuing Professional Education, 4025 Chestnut Street, Philadelphia, Pennsylvania 19104. 1985. (1988 Supplement).

SMALL BUSINESS FINANCING: FEDERAL ASSISTANCE AND CONTRACTS. Shepard's/McGraw-Hill, P.O. Box 1235, Colorado Springs, Colorado 80901. 1983.

SMALL BUSINESS IN A REGULATED ECONOMY: ISSUES AND POLICY IMPLICATIONS. Richard J. Judd, William T. Greenwood, and Fred W. Becker. Quorum Books, Greenwood Publishing Group, Incorporated, 88 Post Road West, P.O. Box 5007, Westport, Connecticut 06881. 1988.

SMALL BUSINESS REPRESENTATION: LANDING, DEVELOPING, AND SERVICING SMALL BUSINESS CLIENTS: STUDY MATERIALS. American Law Institute-American Bar Association, Committee on Continuing Professional Education. 4025 Chestnut Street, Philadelphia, Pennsylvania 19104. 1989.

START-UP COMPANIES: PLANNING, FINANCING, AND OPERATING THE SUCCESSFUL BUSINESS. Richard D. Harrock, Editor. Law Journal-Seminars Press, Incorporated, 111 Eighth Avenue, New York, New York 10011. 1985.

TAXATION FOR SMALL BUSINESS. Second Edition. Marc J. Lane. John Wiley and Sons, Incorporated, 605 Third Avenue, New York, New York 10158. 1983.

TAXES, FINANCIAL POLICY, AND SMALL BUSINESS. Theodore E. Day. Free Press, 866 Third Avenue, New York, New York 10022. 1985.

TECHNOLOGY LICENSING AND THE SMALL FIRM. Julian Lowe and Nick Crawford, Editors. Gower Publishing Company, Old Post Road, Brookfield, Vermont 05036. 1984.

VALUING SMALL BUSINESS AND PROFESSIONAL PRACTICES. Shannon Pratt. Dow Jones-Irwin, 1818 Ridge Road, Homewood, Illinois 60430. 1985.

VENTURE CAPITAL AND PUBLIC OFFERING NEGOTIATION. Michael J. Halloran, Lee F. Benton and Jesse R. Lovejoy. Law and Business, Harcourt Brace Jovanovich, Incorporated, 6277 Sea Harbor Drive, Orlando, Florida 32821. 1983 (Periodic Supplements).

VENTURE CAPITAL AND SMALL BUSINESS FINANCINGS. Robert J. Haft. Clark Boardman Company, Limited, 435 Hudson Street, New York, New York 10014. 1984.

VENTURE CAPITAL: LAW, BUSINESS STRATEGIES, AND INVESTMENT PLANNING. Joseph W. Bartlett. John Wiley and Sons, Incorporated, 605 Third Avenue, New York, New York 10158. 1988.

LAW REVIEWS AND PERIODICALS

AMERICAN JOURNAL OF SMALL BUSINESS. University of Baltimore, Baltimore, Maryland 21201. Quarterly.

NEWSLETTERS AND NEWSPAPERS

THE BUSINESS ACTION NETWORK: WASHINGTON WATCH. Chamber of Commerce of the United States, 1615 H Street, Northwest, Washington, D.C. 20062. Monthly.

THE BUSINESS COUNCIL. National Chamber Litigation Center, 1615 H Street, Northwest, Washington, D.C. 20062. Quarterly.

BUSINESS LAW MEMO. American Bar Association, Section of Corporation, Banking and Business Law, 750 North Lake Shore Drive, Chicago, Illinois 60611. Bimonthly.

BUSINESS STRATEGIES BULLETIN. Commerce Clearing House, Incorporated, 4025 West Peterson Avenue, Chicago, Illinois 60646. Monthly.

BUSINESS TAX STRATEGIST. Newsletter Management Corporation, 10076 Boca Entrada Boulevard, Boca Raton, Florida 33433. Monthly.

CONGRESSIONAL ACTION. Chamber of Commerce of the United States, 1615 H Street, Northwest, Washington, D.C. 20062. Biweekly.

THE FEDERAL REGISTER DIGEST. The Institute for Management, Incorporated, IFM Building, Old Saybrook, Connecticut 06475. Semimonthly.

NASBIC NEWS. National Association of Small Business Investment Companies, 1156 Fifteenth Street, Northwest, Suite 1101, Washington, D.C. 20005. Semimonthly.

SMALL BUSINESS COUNSELOR. Callaghan and Company, 3201 Old Glenview Road, Wilmette, Illinois 60091. Monthly.

SMALL BUSINESS LEGAL REPORT. Business Laws Incorporated, 8228 Mayfield Road, Chesterland, Ohio 44026. Monthly.

SMALL BUSINESS REPORT. Small Business Monitoring and Research Company, Incorporated, 497 Lighthouse Avenue, Monterey, California 93940. Monthly.

YOUR BUSINESS AND THE LAW. Business Research Publications, Incorporated, 817 Broadway, New York, New York 10003. Semimonthly.

BIBLIOGRAPHIES

NONPROFIT CORPORATIONS AND COMPETITION BETWEEN THE FOR-PROFIT SECTOR: AN ANNOTATED BIBLIOGRAPHY. Lorna Peterson. Vance Bibliographies, P.O. Box 229, 112 North Charter Street, Monticello, Illinois 61856. 1988.

DIRECTORIES

DIRECTORY OF BUSINESS, TRADE, AND PUBLIC POLICY ORGANIZATIONS. Office of Advocacy, Small Business Administration, Commerce Department, 409 Third Street, Northwest, Washington, D.C. 20416. 1983.

THE STATES AND SMALL BUSINESS: PROGRAMS AND ACTIVITIES. Office of Advocacy, Small Business Administration, Superintendent of Documents, United States Government Printing Office, Washington, D.C. 20402. 1989.

ASSOCIATIONS AND PROFESSIONAL SOCIETIES

AMERICAN FEDERATION OF SMALL BUSINESS. 407 South Dearborn Street, Chicago, Illinois 60605. (312) 427-0207.

NATIONAL ASSOCIATION OF SMALL BUSINESS INVESTMENT COMPANIES. 323 West Eighth Street, 5501 Lucas Place, Kansas City, Missouri 64105. (816) 374-6708.

NATIONAL SMALL BUSINESS UNITED. 1155 Fifteenth Street, Northwest, Suite 710, Washington, D.C. 20005. (202) 293-8830.

SMALL BUSINESS ASSISTANCE CENTER. 554 Main Street, P. O. Box 1441, Worcester, Massachusetts 01601. (508) 756-3513.

SMALL BUSINESS COUNCIL OF AMERICA. 4800 Hamden Lane, Seventh Floor, Bethesda, Maryland 20814. (301) 656-7603.

SMALL BUSINESS FOUNDATION OF AMERICA. 20 Park Plaza, Suite 438, Boston, Massachusetts 02116. (617) 350-5096.

SMALL BUSINESS LEGISLATIVE COUNCIL. 1156 Fifteenth Street, Northwest, Suite 510, Washington, D. C. 20005. (202) 639-8500.

SMALL BUSINESS NETWORK. P. O. Box 30149, Baltimore, Maryland 21270. (301) 581-1373.

SMALL BUSINESS SERVICE BUREAU. 554 Main Street, P. O. Box 1441, Worcester, Massachusetts 01601. (508) 756-3513.

RESEARCH CENTERS, INSTITUTES, CLEARINGHOUSES

SMALL BUSINESS DEVELOPMENT CENTER. Lehigh University, 301 Broadway, Bethlehem, Pennsylvania 18015. (215) 758-3980.

SMALL BUSINESS DEVELOPMENT CENTER, University of South Florida, College of Business Administration, Tampa, Florida 33620. (813) 974-4274.

SMALL BUSINESS INSTITUTE. Shippensburg University, Shippen Hall, Shippensburg, Pennsylvania 17257. (717) 532-1430.

SMALL BUSINESS RESEARCH INSTITUTE. State University of New York at Albany, School of Business, Albany, New York 12222. (518) 442-4914.

ONLINE DATABASES

SMALL BUSINESS REPORTS. Stevens Features, 15 Breckinridge Road, Chappaqua, New York 10514.

THE SMALL BUSINESS TAX REVIEW. Hooksett Publishing, Incorporated, P.O. Box 895, Melville, New York 11747.

SMALL CLAIMS COURTS

HANDBOOKS, MANUALS, FORMBOOKS

EVERYBODY'S GUIDE TO SMALL CLAIMS COURT. Fifth Edition. Ralph E. Warner. Nolo Press, 950 Parker Street, Berkeley, California 94710. 1991.

THE JACOBY AND MEYERS GUIDE TO SMALL CLAIMS LITIGATION. Gail J. Koff. Henry Holt and Company, 115 West Eighteenth Street, New York, New York 10011. 1991.

SMALL CLAIMS COURT. Second Edition. Paul Hasse and Chip Greenwood. HALT--An Organization of Americans for Slave Reform, Suite 319, 201 Massachusetts Avenue, Northeast, Washington, D.C. 20002. 1983.

SMALL CLAIMS COURT: MAKING YOUR WAY THROUGH THE SYSTEM, A STEP-BY-STEP GUIDE. Theresa Meehan Rudy. Random House, Incorporated, 201 East Fiftieth Street, New York, New York 10022. 1990.

SMALL CLAIMS COURT WITHOUT A LAWYER. Wanda Kelsea Wilber. Sourcebooks Trade, P.O. Box 372, Naperville, Illinois 60566. 1991.

SMALL CLAIMS FORM GUIDE BOOK. Emmanuel A. Rissman, Editor. National Conference of Special Court Judges. American Bar Association, 750 North Lake Shore Drive, Chicago, Illinois 60611. 1982.

TEXTBOOKS AND GENERAL WORKS

INEXPENSIVE JUSTICE: SELF-REPRESENTATION IN THE SMALL CLAIMS COURT. Forty-third Edition. Robert L. Spurrier. Associated Faculty Press, 19 West Thirty-sixth Street, New York, New York 10018. 1986.

SMALL CLAIMS COURTS: A COMPARATIVE STUDY. Christopher J. Whelan. Oxford University Press, 200 Madison Avenue, New York, New York 10016. 1990.

SMOG
See: ENVIRONMENTAL LAW

SOCIAL SCIENCE

TEXTBOOKS AND GENERAL WORKS

AMERICAN CULTURAL PLURALISM AND LAW. Jill Norgren and Serena Nanda. Praeger Publishers, One Madison Avenue, New York, New York 10010. 1988.

BEHAVIORAL SCIENTISTS IN COURTS AND CORRECTIONS. James T. Ziegenfuss, Jr. Van Nostrand Reinhold Company, Incorporated, 115 Fifth Avenue, New York, New York 10003. 1985.

BOUNDARIES DIMLY PERCEIVED: LAW, RELIGION, EDUCATION, AND THE COMMON GOOD. Christopher F. Mooney. University of Notre Dame Press, Notre Dame, Indiana 46556. 1990.

ETHICAL ISSUES IN SOCIAL SCIENCE RESEARCH. Tom L. Beauchamp and Ruth Faden, Editors. Johns Hopkins University Press, 701 West Fortieth Street, Suite 275, Baltimore, Maryland 21211-2190. 1982.

IMPACT OF SOCIAL PSYCHOLOGY ON PROCEDURAL JUSTICE. Martin F. Kaplan, Editor. Charles C. Thomas Publishing, 2600 South First Street, Springfield, Illinois 62794-9265. 1986.

AN INVITATION TO LAW AND SOCIAL SCIENCE: DESERT, DISPUTES, AND DISTRIBUTION. Richard Lempert and Joseph Sanders. Longman, Incorporated, 19 West Forty-fourth Street, New York, New York 10036. 1986.

JUSTICE: VIEWS FROM THE SOCIAL SCIENCE. Ronald L. Cohen, Editor. Plenum Publishing Corporation, 233 Spring Street, New York, New York 10013. 1986.

LAW AND THE SOCIAL SCIENCES. Leon Lipson and Stanton Wheeler, Editors. Sage Publications, 2455 Teller Road, Newbury Park, California 91320. 1987.

LAW, SOCIAL SCIENCE, AND CRIMINAL THEORY. Jerome Hall. Fred B. Rothman and Company, 10368 West Centennial Road, Littleton, Colorado 80127. 1982.

MICROECONOMIC CONCEPTS FOR ATTORNEYS: A REFERENCE GUIDE. Wayne C. Curtis. Quorum Books, Imprint of Greenwood Publishing Group, Incorporated, 88 Post Road West, P.O. Box 5007, Westport, Connecticut 06881. 1984.

MORALITY, POLITICS, AND LAW: A BICENTENNIAL ESSAY. Michael J. Perry. Oxford University Press, 200 Madison Avenue, New York, New York 10016. 1989.

SOCIAL RESEARCH IN THE JUDICIAL PROCESS: CASES, READINGS AND TEXT. Wallace D. Loh. Russell Sage Foundation, 112 East Sixty-fourth Street, New York, New York 10021. 1984.

SOCIAL SCIENCE IN COURT: MOBILIZING EXPERTS IN THE SCHOOL DESEGREGATION CASES. Mark A. Chesler, Joseph Sanders, and Debra S. Kalmuss. University of Wisconsin Press, 114 North Murray, Madison, Wisconsin 53706. 1988.

SOCIAL SCIENCE IN LAW: CASES AND MATERIALS. Second Edition. John Monahan and Laurens Walker. Foundation Press, 615 Merrick Avenue, Westbury, New York 11590. 1989.

SOCIAL SCIENCE IN THE COURTROOM: STATISTICAL TECHNIQUES AND RESEARCH METHODS FOR WINNING CLASS-ACTION SUITS. James W. Loewen. Lexington Books, D.C. Heath and Company, 125 Spring Street, Lexington, Massachusetts 02173. 1982.

SOCIAL SCIENCE, LAW, AND PUBLIC POLICY. Stuart S. Nagel and Lisa A. Bievenue. University Press of America, 4720 Boston Way, Lanham, Maryland 20706. 1992.

SOCIAL SCIENCE METHODS FOR LITIGATION. Donald E. Vinson and Philip K. Anthony. Michie/Bobbs-Merrill, The Michie Company, P. O. Box 7587, Charlottesville, Virginia 22906-7582. 1985.

SOCIAL SCIENCE METHODS IN THE LEGAL PROCESS. Noreen L. Channels. Rowman and Allenheld, 420 Boston Way, Lanham, Maryland 20706. 1985.

STATISTICAL CONCEPTS FOR ATTORNEYS: A REFERENCE GUIDE. Wayne C. Curtis. Qurum Books, Imprint of Greenwood Publishing Group, Incorporated, 88 Post Road West, P.O. Box 5007, Westport, Connecticut 06881. 1983

STATISTICAL METHODS IN DISCRIMINATION LITIGATION. D. H. Kaye and Mikel Aickin, Editors. Marcel Dekker, Incorporated, 720 Madison Avenue, New York, New York 10016. 1986.

LAW REVIEWS AND PERIODICALS

BEHAVIORAL SCIENCES AND THE LAW. Van Nostrand Reinhold Company, Incorporated, 135 West 50th Street, New York, New York 10020. Quarterly.

INTERNATIONAL JOURNAL OF THE SOCIOLOGY OF THE LAW. Academic Press Incorporated, 111 Fifth Avenue, New York, New York 10003. Quarterly.

NEW YORK UNIVERSITY REVIEW OF LAW AND SOCIAL CHANGE. 249 Sullivan Street, New York, New York 10012. Three issues per year.

RESEARCH IN LAW, DEVIANCE, AND SOCIAL CONTROL. Jai Press, Incorporated, 36 Sherwood Place, Greenwich, Connecticut 06836. Annual.

NEWSLETTERS AND NEWSPAPERS

CLS NEWSLETTER OF THE CONFERENCE ON CRITICAL LEGAL STUDIES. SUNY- Buffalo Law School, O'Brian Hall, Buffalo, New York 14260. Annual.

LAWS AND SOCIETY NEWSLETTER. Law and Society Association, c/o Professor Ronald Pipkin, University of Massachusetts, Amherst, Massachusetts 01003. Quarterly.

ASSOCIATIONS AND PROFESSIONAL SOCIETIES

AMERICAN ACADEMY OF POLITICAL AND SOCIAL SCIENCE. 3937 Chestnut Street, Philadelphia, Pennsylvania 19104. (215) 386-4594.

ASSOCIATION OF AMERICAN LAW SCHOOLS, Section on Law and Social Sciences. Association of American Law Schools, One Dupont Circle, Northwest, Washington, D.C. 20036. (202) 296-8851.

CONSORTIUM OF SOCIAL SCIENCE ASSOCIATIONS, 1522 K Street, Northwest, Suite 836, Washington, D.C. 20005. (202) 842-3525.

LAW AND SOCIETY ASSOCIATION, University of Massachusetts, Hampshire House, Amherst, Massachusetts 01003. (413) 545-4617.

NATIONAL INSTITUTE OF SOCIAL SCIENCES. 30 Rockefeller Plaza, Suite 4528, New York, New York 10112. (212) 223-1330.

SOCIAL SCIENCE RESEARCH COUNCIL, 605 Third Avenue, New York, New York 10158. (212) 661-0280.

RESEARCH CENTERS, INSTITUTES, CLEARINGHOUSES

INSTITUTE FOR SOCIAL SCIENCE RESEARCH. University of California at Los Angeles, 405 Hilgard Avenue, Los Angeles, California 90024. (213) 825-0711.

NORC: A SOCIAL SCIENCE RESEARCH CENTER. 1155 East Sixtieth Street, Chicago, Illinois 60637. (312) 702-1200.

SOCIAL SCIENCE WORKING GROUP. University of North Carolina at Charlotte, Department of Psychology, 4042 Colvard, Charlotte, North Carolina 28223. (704) 547-4758.

ONLINE DATABASES

SOCIAL SCIENCES INDEX. H. W. Wilson Company, 950 University Avenue, Bronx, New York 10452.

SOCIAL SCISEARCH. Institute for Scientific Information, 3501 Market Street, Philadelphia, Pennsylvania 19104.

SOCIAL SECURITY
See also: SOCIAL SECURITY ADMINISTRATION; INSURANCE, HEALTH AND UNEMPLOYMENT

STATUTES, CODES, STANDARDS, UNIFORM LAWS

THE PROFESSIONAL STANDARDS REVIEW ACT: A LEGISLATIVE HISTORY OF TITLE XI OF THE SOCIAL SECURITY AMENDMENTS OF 1972. Bernard D. Reams, Jr. William S. Hein and Company, 1285 Main Street, Buffalo, New York 14209. 1990.

LOOSELEAF SERVICES AND REPORTERS

SOCIAL SECURITY COORDINATOR. Research Institute of America, Incorporated, 90 Fifth Avenue, New York, New York 10011. 1984- .

SOCIAL SECURITY LAW AND PRACTICE. Michael A. Rosenhouse and Melvin C. Cole. Lawyers Cooperative Publishing Company, Aqueduct Building, Rochester, New York 14694. 1987.

UNEMPLOYMENT INSURANCE REPORTER. Commerce Clearing House, Incorporated, 4025 West Peterson Avenue, Chicago, Illinois 60646. 1934- .

WEST'S SOCIAL SECURITY REPORTING SERVICE. West Publishing Company, P.O. Box 64526, 50 West Kellogg Boulevard, St. Paul, Minnesota 55164-0526. 1983- .

HANDBOOKS, MANUALS, FORMBOOKS

ADVOCATE'S GUIDE TO SURVIVING THE SSI SYSTEM. Barbara E. LyBarger and Neil Onerheim. Massachusetts Poverty Law Center, 69 Canal Street, Boston, Massachusetts 02114. 1985.

ATTORNEY'S GUIDE TO SOCIAL SECURITY DISABILITY CLAIMS. Kenneth F. Laritz. Shepard's/McGraw-Hill, P.O. Box 1235, Colorado Springs, Colorado 80901. 1986.

CHECKS AND BALANCES IN SOCIAL SECURITY: SYMPOSIUM IN HONOR OF ROBERT J. MYERS. Yung-Ping Chen and George F. Rohrlich, Editors. University Press of America, 4720 Boston Way, Lanham, Maryland 20706.

THE COMPLETE SOCIAL SECURITY HANDBOOK. Bryce Webster and Robert L. Perry. Dodd, Mead and Company, 71 Fifth Avenue, New York, New York 10003. 1983.

INTERNATIONAL HANDBOOK ON OLD-AGE INSURANCE. Martin B. Tracy and Fred C. Pampel. Greenwood Publishing Group, Incorporated, 88 Post Road West, P.O. Box 5007, Westport, Connecticut 06881. 1991.

KEYS TO UNDERSTANDING SOCIAL SECURITY BENEFITS. Thomas L. Dickens and D. Larry Crumbley. Barron's Educational Series, Incorporated, 250 Wireless Boulevard, Hauppauge, New York 11788. 1991.

PHASING OUT SOCIAL SECURITY: A CRITIQUE OF RADICAL REFORM PROPOSALS. Charles W. Meyer. Lexington Books, Division of D.C. Heath and Company, 125 Spring Street, Lexington, Massachusetts 02173. 1987.

PROTECT YOUR SOCIAL SECURITY, PENSION, AND MEDICARE BENEFITS. Tom and Nancy Biracree. Contemporary Books, Incorporated, 180 North Michigan Avenue, Chicago, Illinois 60601. 1991.

SOCIAL SECURITY AFTER FIFTY: SUCCESSES AND FAILURES. Edward D. Berkowitz. Greenwood Publishing Group, Incorporated, 88 Post Road West, P.O. Box 5007, Westport, Connecticut 06881. 1987.

SOCIAL SECURITY CLAIMS AND PROCEDURES. Fourth Edition. Harvey L. McCormick. West Publishing Company, P.O. Box 64526, 50 West Kellogg Boulevard, St. Paul, Minnesota 55164-0526. 1991.

SOCIAL SECURITY DISABILITY CLAIMS. Peter Martin, Chairman. Practising Law Institute, 810 Seventh Avenue, New York, New York 10019. 1984.

SOCIAL SECURITY DISABILITY CLAIMS. Ronald R. Gilbert and J.D. Peters. Lawyers Co-Operative Publishing Company, Aqueduct Building, Rochester, New York 14694. 1983. (Annual Supplements).

SOCIAL SECURITY DISABILITY CLAIMS: PRACTICE AND PROCEDURE. Robert E. Francis. Callaghan and Company, 155 Pfingsten Road, Deerfield, Illinois 60015. 1990. (Annual Supplements).

SOCIAL SECURITY DISABILITY CLAIMS: PRACTICE AND PROCEDURE. Second Edition. Don C. Keenan and Patricia A. Lucas. Harrison Company, 3110 Crossing Park, Norcross, Georgia 30091. 1988.

SOCIAL SECURITY DISABILITY PRACTICE. Kenneth J. Forrester. James Publishing, Incorporated, P.O. Box 25202, Santa Ana, California 92799. 1985.

SOCIAL SECURITY HANDBOOK: RETIREMENT INSURANCE, SURVIVORS INSURANCE, DISABILITY INSURANCE, HEALTH INSURANCE, SUPPLEMENTAL SECURITY INCOME, BLACK LUNG BENEFITS, PUBLIC ASSISTANCE. Tenth edition. Department of Health and Human Services, Social Security Administration. Superintendent of Documents, United States Government Printing Office, Washington, D.C. 20402. 1988.

SOCIAL SECURITY MANUAL. William W. Thomas III, Editor. National Underwriter Company, 420 East Fourth Street, Cincinnati, Ohio 45202. 1978- .

SOCIAL SECURITY, MEDICARE, AND PENSIONS: THE SOURCEBOOK FOR OLDER AMERICANS. Fifth Edition. Joseph L. Matthews. Nolo Press, 950 Parker Street, Berkeley, California 94710. 1990.

SOCIAL SECURITY PRACTICE GUIDE. National Organization of Social Security Claimant's Representatives. Matthew Bender and Company, Incorporated, 11 Penn Plaza, New York, New York 10001. 1984. (Annual Supplements).

TRIAL OF A SOCIAL SECURITY DISABILITY CASE. Marvin Schwartz. Social Security Disability Foundation, P.O. Box 418, New Paltz, New York 12561. 1983 (Annual Supplements).

TEXTBOOKS AND GENERAL WORKS

BUREAUCRATIC JUSTICE: MANAGING SOCIAL SECURITY DISABILITY CLAIMS. Jerry L. Mashaw. Yale University Press, 302 Temple Street, New Haven, Connecticut 06520. 1985.

CAN AMERICA AFFORD TO GROW OLD? PAYING FOR SOCIAL SECURITY. Henry J. Aaron, Barry P. Bosworth, and Gary T. Burtless. Brookings Institution, 1775 Massachusetts Avenue, Washington, D.C. 20036. 1989.

ECONOMIC EFFECTS OF SOCIAL SECURITY. Henry J. Aaron. Brookings Institution, 1775 Massachusetts Avenue, Northwest, Washington, D.C. 20036-2188. 1982.

THE ECONOMICS OF SOCIAL SECURITY. Andrew Dilnot and Ian Walker. Oxford University Press, 200 Madison Avenue, New York, New York 10016. 1989.

EVELINE M. BURNS AND THE AMERICAN SOCIAL SECURITY SYSTEM, 1935-1960. Linda R. Wolf Jones. Garland Publishing, Incorporated, 136 Madison Avenue, New York, New York 10016. 1991.

FEDERAL SOCIAL SECURITY. Arthur Abraham. American Law Institute, 4025 Chestnut Street, Philadelphia, Pennsylvania 19104. 1979.

INCOME REDISTRIBUTION AND THE SOCIAL SECURITY PROGRAM. Nancy Wolff. UMI Research Press, Ann Arbor, Michigan. 1987.

NO LONGER DISABLED: THE FEDERAL COURTS AND THE POLITICS OF SOCIAL SECURITY DISABILITY. Susan Gluck Mezey. Greenwood Publishing Group, Incorporated, 88 Post Road West, P.O. Box 5007, Westport, Connecticut 06881. 1988.

OLD AGE IN THE WELFARE STATE: THE POLITICAL ECONOMY OF PUBLIC PENSIONS. John Myles. University Press of Kansas, 329 Carruth, Lawrence, Kansas 66045. 1989.

REAPPRAISING SOCIAL SECURITY: TOWARD AN ALTERNATIVE SYSTEM. Jeffrey D. Dunn. Lyndon B. Johnson School of Public Affairs, University of Texas at Austin, Drawer DY, University Station, Austin, Texas 78712. 1982.

RETIREMENT, PENSIONS, AND SOCIAL SECURITY. Gary S. Fields and Olivia S. Mitchell. MIT Press, 55 Hayward Street, Cambridge, Massachusetts 02142. 1985.

SOCIAL INSURANCE AND ECONOMIC SECURITY. Fourth Edition. George E. Rejda. Prentice-Hall, Incorporated, 113 Sylvan Avenue, Englewood Cliffs, New Jersey 07632. 1991.

SOCIAL SECURITY: A CRITIQUE OF RADICAL REFORM PROPOSALS. Charles W. Meyer. Lexington Books, 125 Spring Street, Lexington, Massachusetts 02173. 1987.

SOCIAL SECURITY AFTER FIFTY: SUCCESSES AND FAILURES. Edward D. Berkowitz. Greenwood Publishing Group, Incorporated, 88 Post Road West, P.O. Box 5007, Westport, Connecticut 06881. 1987.

SOCIAL SECURITY AND PRIVATE PENSIONS: PROVIDING FOR RETIREMENT IN THE TWENTY-FIRST CENTURY. Susan M. Wachter. Lexington Books, 125 Spring Street, Lexington, Massachusetts 02173. 1988.

SOCIAL SECURITY AT THE CROSSROADS: PUBLIC OPINION AND PUBLIC POLICY. Charles M. Brain. Garland Publishing, Incorporated, 136 Madison Avenue, New York, New York 10016. 1991.

SOCIAL SECURITY: BEYOND THE RHETORIC OF CRISIS. Theodore R. Marmor and Jerry L. Mashaw. Princeton University Press, 41 William Street, Princeton, New Jersey 08540. 1988.

SOCIAL SECURITY DISABILITY CLAIMS, 1987. Eileen Kaufman. Practising Law Institute, 810 Seventh Avenue, New York, New York 10019. 1987.

SOCIAL SECURITY LAW. Georgia Institute of Continuing Legal Education, University of Georgia, Athens, Georgia 30602. 1984.

THE SOCIAL SECURITY SYSTEM. Dorothy Hoobler and Thomas Hoobler. Watts, Franklin, Incorporated, 387 Park Avenue, South, New York, New York 10016. 1982.

SOCIAL SECURITY, THE FIRST HALF-CENTURY. Gerald D. Nash, Noel H. Pugach, and Richard F. Tomasson. University of New Mexico Press, 1720 Lomas Boulevard, Northeast, Albuquerque, New Mexico 87131. 1988.

SOCIAL SECURITY: THE SYSTEM THAT WORKS. Merton C. Bernstein and Joan Brodshaug Bernstein. Basic Books, Incorporated, 10 East Fifty-third Street, New York, New York 10022. 1988.

THE TRANSFORMATION OF OLD AGE SECURITY: CLASS AND POLITICS IN THE AMERICAN WELFARE STATE. Jill Quadagno. University of Chicago Press, 5801 Ellis Avenue, Chicago, Illinois 60637. 1988.

WOMEN AND SOCIAL WELFARE: A FEMINIST ANAYLSIS. Dorothy C. Miller. Praeger Publishers, One Madison Avenue, New York, New York 10010. 1990.

WORK, HEALTH, AND INCOME AMONG THE ELDERLY. Gary Burtless, Editor. Brookings Institution, 1775 Massachusetts Avenue, Washington, D.C. 20036. 1987.

BIBLIOGRAPHIES

FOUR DECADES OF INTERNATIONAL SOCIAL SECURITY RESEARCH: A BIBLIOGRAPHY OF STUDIES BY THE SOCIAL SECURITY ADMINISTRATION 1937-1980. Lois Copeland and Frank B. McArdle. United States Department of Health and Human Services, Social Security Administration, Office of Policy Research and Statistics. Superintendent of Documents, United States Government Printing Office, Washington, D.C. 20402. 1981.

SOCIAL SECURITY, ITS DEVELOPMENT FROM ROOSEVELT TO REAGAN. Alva W. Stewart. Vance Bibliographies, P.O. Box 229, 112 North Charter Street, Monticello, Illinois 61856. 1982.

ASSOCIATIONS AND PROFESSIONAL SOCIETIES

NATIONAL ACADEMY OF SOCIAL INSURANCE. 505 Capitol Court, Northeast, Suite 300, Washington, D.C. 20002. (202) 547-9592.

NATIONAL COMMITTEE TO PRESERVE SOCIAL SECURITY AND MEDICARE, 2000 K Street, Northwest, Suite 800, Washington, D.C. 20006. (202) 822-9459.

NATIONAL ORGANIZATION OF SOCIAL SECURITY CLAIMANT'S REPRESENTATIVES. 19 East Central Avenue, Second Floor, Pearl River, New York 10965. (914) 735-8812.

RESEARCH CENTERS, INSTITUTES, CLEARINGHOUSES

MICHIGAN HEALTH AND SOCIAL SECURITY RESEARCH INSTITUTE. 8000 East Jefferson Avenue, Detroit, Michigan 48214. (313) 926-5320.

ONLINE DATABASES

SOCIAL SECURITY. United States Department of Health and Human Services, Social Security Administration, Office of Information, 6401 Security Boulevard, Baltimore, Maryland 21235.

STATISTICS SOURCES

SOCIAL SECURITY BULLETIN. United States Social Security Administration. Superintendent of Documents, United States Government Printing Office, Washington, D.C. 20402. Monthly.

AUDIOVISUALS

SOCIAL SECURITY DISABILITY CLAIMS. Practising Law Institute, 810 Seventh Avenue, New York, New York 10019. 1984. Audiocassette.

SOCIAL SECURITY ADMINISTRATION

STATUTES, CODES, STANDARDS, UNIFORM LAWS

CODE OF FEDERAL REGULATIONS, TITLE 20. Office of the Federal Register, National Archives and Records Administration. Superintendent of Documents, United States Government Printing Office, Washington, D.C. 20402. Annual. (Updated by use of monthly List of Sections Affected and daily Federal Register.)

LOOSELEAF SERVICES AND REPORTERS

SOCIAL SECURITY RULINGS ON FEDERAL OLD-AGE, SURVIVORS, DISABILITY, SUPPLEMENTAL SECURITY INCOME, AND BLACK LUNG BENEFIT. Health and Human Services Department, Social Security Administration, Office of Policy. Superintendent of Documents, United States Government Printing Office, Washington, D.C. 20402. Quarterly with Annual Cummulative Editions.

HANDBOOKS, MANUALS, FORMBOOKS

SOCIAL SECURITY CLAIMS AND PROCEDURES. Fourth Edition. Harvey L. McCormick. West Publishing Company, 50 West Kellogg Boulevard, St. Paul, Minnesota 55164. 1991.

SOCIAL SECURITY HANDBOOK. Tenth Edition. Health and Human Services Department, Social Security Administration. Superintendent of Documents, United States Government Printing Office, Washington, D.C. 20402. 1988.

TEXTBOOKS AND GENERAL WORKS

AGENCY UNDER STRESS: THE SOCIAL SECURITY ADMINISTRATION IN AMERICAN GOVERNMENT. Martha Derthick. Brookings Institution, 1775 Massachusetts Avenue, Washington, D.C. 20036. 1990.

IRS AND SOCIAL SECURITY MAGNETIC MEDIA FILING REQUIREMENTS: A PRACTICAL GUIDE TO THE NEW RULES. Esther Roditti Schachter and Anne Elizabeth Fontaine. Research Institute of America, Incorporated, 910 Sylvan Avenue, Englewood Cliffs, New Jersey 07632. 1987.

NO LONGER DISABLED: THE FEDERAL COURTS AND THE POLITICS OF SOCIAL SECURITY DISABILITY. Susan Gluck Mezey. Greenwood Publishing Group, Incorporated, 88 Post Road West, P.O. Box 5007, Westport, Connecticut 06881. 1988.

SOCIAL WELFARE
See: INDIGENCE

SOCIETIES
See: ASSOCIATIONS AND NONPROFIT CORPORATIONS; LAW SOCIETIES

SOLAR ENERGY
See also: ENERGY DEPARTMENT

STATUTES, CODES, STANDARDS, UNIFORM LAWS

UNIFORM SOLAR ENERGY CODE. International Association of Plumbing and Mechanical Officials, 20001 Walnut Drive, South, Walnut, California 91789. 1988.

SOLAR ENERGY

TEXTBOOKS AND GENERAL WORKS

LEGAL ASPECTS OF SOLAR ENERGY. John H. Minan and William H. Lawrence, Editors. Lexington Books, Division of D.C. Heath and Company, 125 Spring Street, Lexington, Massachusetts 02173. 1981.

SOLAR RESOURCES. Roland L. Hulstrom. MIT Press, 55 Hayward Street, Cambridge, Massachusetts 02142. 1989.

ENCYCLOPEDIAS AND DICTIONARIES

SOLAR ENERGY DICTIONARY. V. Daniel Hunt. Industrial Press, 200 Madison Avenue, New York, New York 10016. 1982.

BIBLIOGRAPHIES

LEGAL ASPECTS OF RESIDENTIAL SOLAR ACCESS: A BIBLIOGRAPHY. Deborah Brown. Vance Bibliographies, P.O. Box 229, 112 North Charter Street, Monticello, Illinois 61856. 1982.

SOLAR HOME PLANNING: A BIBLIOGRAPHY AND A GUIDE. Steven D. Atkinson. Scarecrow Press, Incorporated, 52 Liberty Street, Box 4167, Metuchen, New Jersey 08840. 1988.

DIRECTORIES

SOLAR ELECTRICITY: A DIRECTORY OF THE U.S. PHOTOVOLTAIC INDUSTRY. Solar Energy Industries Association, 777 North Capitol Street, Northeast, Suite 805, Washington, D.C. 22202. 1989.

SOLDIERS
See: MILITARY LAW AND SERVICE; VETERANS

SOLICITORS
See: ADMISSION TO THE BAR; LAW OFFICE MANAGEMENT; LAW PRACTICE; LAWYER AND CLIENT; LAWYER'S FEES; LEGAL ETHICS AND MALPRACTICE; LEGAL PROFESSION IN FICTION; PREPAID LEGAL SERVICES

SOVEREIGNTY
See: GOVERNMENT IMMUNITY AND LIABILITY; INTERNATIONAL LAW AND RELATIONS

SPACE LAW
See also: HIGH TECHNOLOGY INDUSTRIES

STATUTES, CODES, STANDARDS, UNIFORM LAWS

COMPILATION OF PUBLIC LAWS REPORTED BY THE COMMITTEE ON SCIENCE, SPACE, AND TECHNOLOGY, 1958-1988. United States Congress, Committee on Science, Space, and Technology. Superintendent of Documents, United States Government Printing Office, Washington, D.C. 20402. 1989.

HANDBOOKS, MANUALS, FORMBOOKS

MANUAL OF SPACE LAW. Nandasiri Jasentuliyana and Roy S. Lee, Editors. Oceana Publications, Incorporated, 75 Main Street, Dobbs Ferry, New York 10522. 1979.

TEXTBOOKS AND GENERAL WORKS

AEROSPACE LAW: TELECOMMUNICATIONS SATELLITES. Nicholas M. Matte. Butterworth and Company, Limited, 75 Clegg Road, Markham, Ontario L6G 1A1 Canada. 1982.

AMERICAN SPACE LAW: INTERNATIONAL AND DOMESTIC. Nathan C. Goldman. Iowa State University Press, 2121 South State Avenue, Ames, Iowa 50010. 1988.

ASPECTS OF SPACE LAW. E. R. Van Bogaert. Kluwer Law and Taxation, 36 West Forty-fourth Street, New York, New York 10036. 1985.

DEVELOPMENTS IN SPACE LAW: ISSUES AND POLICIES. Stephen Gorove. Martinus Nijhoff, Kluwer Academic Publishers, 101 Philip Drive, Assinippi Park, Norwell, Massachusetts 02061. 1991.

INTERNATIONAL LAW OF SATELLITE REMOTE SENSING AND OUTER SPACE. Charles C. Okolie. Kendall/Hunt Publishing Company, 2460 Kerper Boulevard, Dubuque, Iowa 52001. 1989.

INTERNATIONAL SPACE LAW. Gennady Zhukow and Yuri Kolosov. Praeger Publishers, One Madison Avenue, New York, New York 10010-3603. 1984.

LAW AND POLICY IN THE SPACE STATIONS' ERA. Andrew J. Young. Martinus Nijhoff, Kluwer Academic Publishers, 101 Philip Drive, Assinippi Park, Norwell, Massachusetts 02061. 1989.

THE LAW AND REGULATION OF INTERNATIONAL SPACE COMMUNICATION. Rita Lauria White and Harold M. White, Jr. Artech House, Incorporated, 685 Canton Street, Norwood, Massachusetts 02062. 1988.

LAW AND SECURITY IN OUTER SPACE. Standing Committee on Law and National Security, American Bar Association, 750 North Lake Shore Drive, Chicago, Illinois 60611. 1983.

THE LEGALITY OF SPACE MILITARIZATION. B. A. Hurwitz. Elsevier Science Publishing Company, Incorporated, P.O. Box 882, Madison Square Station, New York 10159. 1986.

THE MODERN INTERNATIONAL LAW OF OUTER SPACE. Carl Q. Christol. Pergamon Press, Incorporated, Maxwell House, Fairview Park, Elmsford, New York 10523. 1982.

Encyclopedia of Legal Information Sources • 2nd Ed.

OUTER SPACE: NEW CHALLENGES TO LAW AND POLICY. J.E. Fawcett. Clarendon Press, Oxford University Press, 200 Madison Avenue, New York, New York 10016. 1984.

OUTER SPACE: PROBLEMS OF LAW AND POLICY. Glenn H. Reynolds and Robert P. Merges. Westview Press, Incorporated, 5500 Central Avenue, Boulder, Colorado 80301. 1989.

PEACEFUL AND NON-PEACEFUL USES OF SPACE: PROBLEMS OF DEFINITION FOR THE PREVENTION OF AN ARMS RACE. Bhupendra Jasani. Taylor and Francis, Incorporated, 1990 Frost Road, Suite 101, Bristol, Pennsylvania 19007. 1991.

PRINCIPLES OF OUTER SPACE LAW IN HINDSIGHT. Henri A. Wassenbergh. Martinus Nijhoff, Kluwer Academic Publishers, 101 Philip Drive, Assinippi Park, Norwell, Massachusetts 02061. 1991.

SPACE ACTIVITIES AND EMERGING INTERNATIONAL LAW. Nicholas M. Matte, Editor. McGill Institute of Air and Space Law, McGill University, 3690 Peel Street, Montreal, Quebec, Canada H3A 1W9. 1984.

SPACE DEBRIS: LEGAL AND POLICY IMPLICATIONS. Howard A. Baker. Martinus Nijhoff, Kluwer Academic Publishers, 101 Philip Drive, Assinippi Park, Norwell, Massachusetts 02061. 1989.

SPACE LAW. Necia H. Apfel. Franklin Watts, Incorporated, 387 Park Avenue South, New York, New York 10016. 1988.

SPACE LAW IN THE UNITED NATIONS. Marietta Benko et al. Kluwer Academic Publishers, 101 Philip Drive, Assinippi Park, Norwell, Massachusetts 02061. 1985.

SPACE LAW - NATIONAL AND INTERNATIONAL REGULATIONS. Stephen Gorove, Editor. Oceana Publications, Incorporated, 75 Main Street, Dobbs Ferry, New York 10522. 1980 (Periodic Supplements).

SPACE LAW: PAST, PRESENT, AND FUTURE. Carl Quimby Christol. Kluwer Academic Publishers, 101 Philip Drive, Assinippi Park, Norwell, Massachusetts 02061. 1991.

SPACE POLICY: AN INTRODUCTION. Nathan C. Goldman. Iowa State University Press, 2121 South State Avenue, Ames, Iowa 50010. 1992.

THE UNITED STATES AND THE DIRECT BROADCAST SATELLITE: THE POLITICS OF INTERNATIONAL BROADCASTING IN SPACE. Sara Fletcher Luther. Oxford University Press, 200 Madison Avenue, New York, New York 10016. 1988.

LAW REVIEWS AND PERIODICALS

ANNALS OF AIR AND SPACE LAW. McGill Institute of Air and Space Law, 3690 Peel Street, Montreal, Quebec, Canada H3A 1W9. Annual.

HIGH TECHNOLOGY LAW JOURNAL. University of California, Berkeley, Boalt Hall, Berkeley, California 94720. Semiannual.

JOURNAL OF SPACE LAW. University of Mississippi, Law Center, University, Mississippi 38677. Semiannual.

NORTHROP UNIVERSITY LAW JOURNAL OF AEROSPACE, ENERGY, AND THE ENVIRONMENT. Northrop University School of Law, Arbor Vitae Boulevard, Inglewood, California 90306. Annual.

NEWSLETTERS AND NEWSPAPERS

SPACE COMMERCE BULLETIN. Warren Publishing, Incorporated, 2115 Ward Court, Northwest, Washington, D.C. 20037. Biweekly.

ASSOCIATIONS AND PROFESSIONAL SOCIETIES

AMERICAN BAR ASSOCIATION, COMMITTEE ON AIR AND SPACE LAW. American Bar Association, 750 North Lake Shore Drive, Chicago, Illinois 60611. (312) 988-5000.

ASSOCIATION OF AMERICAN LAW SCHOOLS, SECTION ON AVIATION AND SPACE LAW. Association of American Law Schools, One Dupont Circle, Northwest, Washington, D.C. 20036. (202) 296-8851.

ASSOCIATION OF UNITED STATES MEMBERS OF THE INTERNATIONAL INSTITUTE OF SPACE LAW. c/o Stephen E. Doyle, 3431 Bridget Brae, Shingle Springs, California 95682. (916) 355-6941.

RESEARCH CENTERS, INSTITUTES, CLEARINGHOUSES

CENTER FOR SPACE AND GEOSCIENCES POLICY. University of Colorado at Boulder, Campus Box 361, Boulder, Colorado 80309. (303) 492-1171.

CENTRE OF AIR AND SPACE LAW. McGill University, 3690 Peel Street, Montreal, PQ H3A 1W9 Canada. (514) 398-3544.

SPECIAL EDUCATION
See: MENTAL HEALTH AND DISABILITY; PHYSICALLY HANDICAPPED

SPECIFIC PERFORMANCE
See: CONTRACTS

SPEEDY TRIAL, RIGHT TO
See: DUE PROCESS OF LAW

SPORTS LAW

LOOSELEAF SERVICES AND REPORTERS

LAW OF PROFESSIONAL AND AMATEUR SPORTS. Gary A. Uberstine and Richard J. Grad. Clark Boardman Company, Limited, 435 Hudson Street, New York, New York 10014. 1988- .

SPORTS LAW

HANDBOOKS, MANUALS, FORMBOOKS

COVERING ALL THE BASES: A COMPREHENSIVE RESEARCH GUIDE TO SPORTS LAW. Second Edition. Gary S. Uberstine. W.S. Hein and Company, Incorporated, 1285 Main Street, Buffalo, New York 14209. 1988.

REPRESENTING PROFESSIONAL ATHLETES AND TEAMS, 1990. Philip R. Hochberg and Martin E. Blackman, Co-chairmen. Practising Law Institute, 810 Seventh Avenue, New York, New York 10019. 1990.

SPORTS LAW STUDY GUIDE. Stephen C. Jeffries. Human Kinetics Publications, P.O. Box 5076, Champaign, Illinois 61825-5076. 1985.

SPORTS OFFICIATING: A LEGAL GUIDE. Alan S. Goldberger. Leisure Press, P.O. Box 5076, Champaign, Illinois 61825-5076. 1984.

TEXTBOOKS AND GENERAL WORKS

AGENTS OF OPPORTUNITY: SPORTS AGENTS AND CORRUPTION IN COLLEGIATE SPORTS. Kenneth L. Shropshire. University of Pennsylvania Press, Blockley Hall, 418 Service Drive, Philadelphia, Pennsylvania 19104. 1990.

AQUATIC INJURIES: EVALUATION AND STRATEGY. Ronald R. Gilbert and Christine M. Griffith. ATLA Press, Washington, D.C. 1990.

THE BUSINESS OF PROFESSIONAL SPORTS. Paul D. Staudohar and James A. Mangan. University of Illinois Press, 54 East Gregory Drive, Champaign, Illinois 61820. 1991.

CAREERS IN SPORTS LAW. Kenneth L. Shropshire, William D. Henslee, and Sara Vlajcic. American Bar Association, Law Student Division, Standing Committee on Professional Utilization and Career Development. 750 North Lake Shore Drive, Chicago, Illinois 60611. 1990.

ESSENTIALS OF AMATEUR SPORTS LAW. Glenn M. Wong. Auburn House Publishing Company, Greenwood Publishing Group, Incorporated, 88 Post Road West, P.O. Box 5007, Westport, Connecticut 06881. 1988.

FUNDAMENTALS OF SPORTS LAW. Walter T. Champion, Jr. Lawyers Cooperative Publishing Company, Aqueduct Building, Rochester, New York 14694. 1990.

INTERNATIONAL SPORTS LAW. James A.R. Nafziger. Transnational Publishers, P.O. Box 7282, Ardsley-on-Hudson, New York 10503. 1988.

LABOR RELATIONS IN PROFESSIONAL SPORTS. Robert C. Berry, William B. Gould, and Paul D. Staudohar. Auburn House Publishing Company, Greenwood Publishing Group, Incorporated, 88 Post Road West, P.O. Box 5007, Westport, Connecticut 06881. 1986.

LAW AND AMATEUR SPORTS. Ronald J. Waicukauski, Editor. Indiana University Press, 10th and Morton Streets, Bloomington, Indiana 47405. 1983.

LAW AND BUSINESS OF SPORTS INDUSTRIES. Robert C. Berry and Glen M. Wong. Auburn House Publishing Company, Greenwood Publishing Group, Incorporated, 88 Post Road West, P.O. Box 5007, Westport, Connecticut 06881. 1985.

LAW FOR PHYSICAL EDUCATORS AND COACHES. Second Edition. Gary Nygaard and Thomas H. Boone. Publishing Horizons, 8233 North Via Paseo del Norte, Suite F400, Scottsdale, Arizona 85258. 1989.

LAW IN SPORT AND PHYSICAL ACTIVITY. Annie Clement. Benchmark Press, 701 Congressional Boulevard, Suite 340, Carmel, Indiana 46032. 1988.

LAW IN SPORTS: LIABILITY CASES IN MANAGEMENT AND ADMINISTRATION. Bernard Patrick Maloy. Benchmark Press, 701 Congressional Boulevard, Suite 340, Carmel, Indiana 46032. 1988.

THE LAW OF SPORTS. John C. Weistart and Cym H. Lowell. Michie/Bobbs-Merrill, The Michie Company, P.O. Box 7587, Charlottesville, Virginia 22906-7582. 1979 (Annual Supplements).

LEGAL LIABILITY AND RISK MANAGEMENT FOR PUBLIC AND PRIVATE ENTITIES: SPORT AND PHYSICAL EDUCATION, LEISURE SERVICES, RECREATION AND PARKS, CAMPING AND ADVENTURE ACTIVITIES. Betty Van Der Smissen. Anderson Publishing Company, 2035 Reading Road, Cincinnati, Ohio 45202. 1990.

MARTIAL ARTS AND THE LAW. Karl J. Duff. Ohara Publications, Incorporated, 1813 Victory Place, P.O. Box 7728, Burbank, California 91510-7728.

PRODUCTS LIABILITY: RECREATION AND SPORTS EQUIPMENT. Jeffrey D. Wittenberg. Law Journal-Seminars Press, Incorporated, 111 Eighth Avenue, New York, New York 10011. 1985.

PROFESSIONAL SPORTS AND ANTITRUST. Warren Freedman. Quorum Books, Greenwood Publishing Group, Incorporated, 88 Post Road West, P.O. Box 5007, Westport, Connecticut 06881. 1987.

SPORTS AND LAW: CONTEMPORARY ISSUES. Herb Appenzeller, Editor. The Michie Company, P.O. Box 7587, Charlottesville, Virginia 22906-7587. 1985.

SPORTS AND RECREATIONAL INJURIES. Jeffrey K. Riffer. Shepard's/McGraw-Hill, P.O. Box 1235, Colorado Springs, Colorado 80901. 1985.

THE SPORTS INDUSTRY AND COLLECTIVE BARGAINING. Paul D. Staudohar. ILR Press, New York State School of Industrial and Labor Relations, Cornell University, Ithaca, New York 14851-0952. 1989.

SPORTS LAW. George W. Schubert. West Publishing Company, P. O. Box 64526, 50 West Kellogg Boulevard, St. Paul, Minnesota 55164-0526. 1986.

SPORTS LAW: CASES AND MATERIALS. Ray Yasser, James R. McCurdy, and C. Peter Goplerud. Anderson Publishing Company, 2035 Reading Road, Cincinnati, Ohio 45202. 1990.

SPORTS LAW FOR EDUCATIONAL INSTITUTIONS. Steven C. Wade and Robert D. Hay. Quorum Books, Greenwood Publishing Group, Incorporated, 88 Post Road West, P.O. Box 5007, Westport, Connecticut 06881. 1988.

SUCCESSFUL SPORTS MANAGEMENT. Guy Lewis and Herb Appenzeller, Editors. Michie/Bobbs-Merrill, The Michie Company, P.O. Box 7587, Charlottesville, Virginia 22906-7587. 1985.

TORTS AND SPORTS: LEGAL LIABILITY IN PROFESSIONAL AND AMATEUR ATHLETICS. Raymond L. Yasser. Quorum Books, Imprint of Greenwood Publishing Group, Incorporated, 88 Post Road West, P.O. Box 5007, Westport, Connecticut 06881. 1985.

YOU'RE THE JUDGE! HOW TO UNDERSTAND SPORTS, TORTS AND COURTS. John M. Fotiades. Edgeworth and North Books, P.O. Box 812, West Side Station, Worcester, Massachusetts 01602. 1989.

LAW REVIEWS AND PERIODICALS

JOURNAL OF COPYRIGHT, ENTERTAINMENT, AND SPORTS LAW. Tennessee Bar Association, Copyright, Entertainment, and Sports Law Section, 3622 West End Avenue, Nashville, Tennessee 37205. Three issues per year.

NEWSLETTERS AND NEWSPAPERS

ATHLETIC DIRECTOR AND COACH PROFESSIONAL PUBLICATIONS, 50 South Ninth Street, Suite 200, Minneapolis, Minnesota 55402. Monthly.

ENTERTAINMENT AND SPORTS LAWYER. American Bar Association, Forum Committee on the Entertainment and Sports Industries. American Bar Association, 750 North Lake Shore Drive, Chicago, Illinois 60611. Quarterly.

ENTERTAINMENT LAW AND FINANCE. Leader Publications, Incorporated, 111 Eighth Avenue, New York, New York 10011. Monthly.

ENTERTAINMENT LAW REPORTER. Entertainment Law Reporter Publishing Company, 2210 Wilshire Boulevard, Suite 311, Santa Monica, California 90403. Monthly.

SPORTS AND THE LAW. Constitutional Rights Foundation, 601 South Kingsley Avenue, Los Angeles, California 90005. Quarterly.

THE SPORTS MEDICINE STANDARDS AND MALPRACTICE REPORTER. Professional Reports Corporation, 4571 Stephen Circle, Northwest, Canton, Ohio 44718. Quarterly.

THE SPORTS, PARK AND RECREATION LAW REPORTER. Professional Reports Corporation, 4571 Stephen Circle, Northwest, Canton, Ohio 44718. Quarterly.

WASHINGTON LETTER. American Ski Foundation, 207 Constitution Avenue, Northeast, Washington, D.C. 20002. Monthly.

BIBLIOGRAPHIES

COVERING ALL THE BASES: A COMPREHENSIVE RESEARCH GUIDE TO SPORTS LAW. Second Edition. Gary A. Uberstine, Lloyd C. Bronstein, and Richard J. Grad. William S. Hein and Company, 1285 Main Street, Buffalo, New York 14209. 1988.

SPORTS AND THE LAW: A SELECTED BIBLIOGRAPHY. Dittakaui Nagasankara Rao. Vance Bibliographies, P.O. Box 229, 112 North Charter Street, Monticello, Illinois 61856. 1984.

SPORTS LAW AND LEGISLATION: AN ANNOTATED BIBLIOGRAPHY. John Hladczuk. Greenwood Publishing Group, Incorporated, 88 Post Road West, P.O. Box 5007, Westport, Connecticut 06881. 1991.

ASSOCIATIONS AND PROFESSIONAL SOCIETIES

AMERICAN BAR ASSOCIATION. Forum Committee on Entertainment and Sports Industries, 750 North Lake Shore Drive, Chicago, Illinois 60611. (312) 988-5000.

ASSOCIATION OF AMERICAN LAW SCHOOLS. Section on Sports Law, One Dupont Circle, Northwest, Washington, D.C. 20036. (202) 296-8851.

SPORTS LAWYERS ASSOCIATION. c/o REI Management Group, 2017 Lathrop Avenue, Racine, Wisconsin 53405. (414) 632-8855.

STANDING TO SUE
See: CIVIL PROCEDURE

STARE DECISIS
See: JUDGMENT AND JUDICIAL OPINIONS

STATE COURTS
See also: COURTS; STATES

STATUTES, CODES, STANDARDS, UNIFORM LAWS

STANDARDS RELATING TO APPELLATE DELAY REDUCTION. Ben F. Overton. American Bar Association, 750 North Lake Shore Drive, Chicago, Illinois 60611. 1988.

STANDARDS RELATING TO COURT ORGANIZATION. American Bar Association, 750 North Lake Shore Drive, Chicago, Illinois 60611. 1990.

STANDARDS RELATING TO TRIAL COURTS AS AMENDED, 1976 AND 1987. American Bar Association, Committee on Standards of Judicial Administration, 750 North Lake Shore Drive, Chicago, Illinois 60611. 1987.

HANDBOOKS, MANUALS, FORMBOOKS

EQUAL EMPLOYMENT OPPORTUNITY AND AFFIRMATIVE ACTION: A SOURCEBOOK FOR COURT MANAGERS. National Center for State Courts, 300 Newport Avenue, Williamsburg, Virginia 23187-8798. 1982.

A GUIDE TO COURT RECORDS MANAGEMENT. Thomas G. Dibble. National Center for State Courts, 300 Newport Avenue, Williamsburg, Virginia 23187-8798. 1986.

OFFICER SURVIVAL MANUAL. Second Edition. Devallis Rutledge. Custom Publishing Company, 1590 Lotus Road, Placerville, California 95667. 1988.

REASONABLE EFFORTS: A MANUAL FOR JUDGES. Debra Ratterman. American Bar Association, Young Lawyers Division, 750 North Lake Shore Drive, Chicago, Illinois 60611. 1987.

TEXTBOOKS AND GENERAL WORKS

ADMINISTRATIVE AGENCIES AND THE COURTS. Frank E. Cooper. William S. Hein and Company, Incorporated, Hein Building, 1285 Main Street, Buffalo, New York 14209. 1982.

ADOPTION INFORMATION IMPROVEMENT FEASIBILITY STUDY: FINAL REPORT. National Center for State Courts, 300 Newport Avenue, Williamsburg, Virginia 23187-8798. 1986.

ALTERNATIVE FUTURES FOR THE STATE COURTS OF 2020. James A. Dator and Sharon J. Rogers. State Justice Institute, Chicago, Illinois. 1991.

AMERICAN COURT MANAGEMENT: THEORIES AND PRACTICES. David J. Saari. Greenwood Publishing Group, Incorporated, 88 Post Road West, P.O. Box 5007, Westport, Connecticut 06881. 1982.

AMERICAN COURT SYSTEMS: READINGS IN JUDICIAL PROCESS AND BEHAVIOR. Second Edition. Sheldon Goldman and Austin Sarat. Longman Publishing Group, 95 Church Street, White Plains, New York 10601. 1989.

THE AMERICAN COURTS: A CRITICAL ASSESSMENT. John B. Gates and Charles A. Johnson. Congressional Quarterly Books, 1414 Twenty-second Street, Northwest, Washington D.C. 20037. 1991.

AMERICAN COURTS: PROCESS AND POLICY. Second Edition. Lawrence Baum. Houghton Mifflin Company, 1 Beacon Street, Boston, Massachusetts 02108. 1990.

AMERICAN JUDICIAL POLITICS. Harry P. Stumpf. Harcourt, Brace, Jovanovich, Incorporated, 6277 Sea Harbor Drive, Orlando, Florida 32821. 1988.

THE AMERICAN JUDICIARY. Simon E. Baldwin. Fred B. Rothman and Company, 10368 West Centennial Road, Littleton, Colorado 80127. 1991. (Reprint).

THE AMERICAN JUDICIARY: CRITICAL ISSUES. A. Leo Levin and Russel R. Wheeler, Editors. Sage Publications, Incorporated, 2455 Teller Road, Newbury Park, California 91320. 1982.

AMERICAN LAW ENFORCEMENT: POLICE, COURTS, CORRECTIONS. Third Edition. Folley. Allyn and Bacon, Incorporated, 160 Gould Street, Needham Heights, Massachusetts, 02194. 1985.

AMERICA'S COURTS AND THE CRIMINAL JUSTICE SYSTEM. Fourth Edition. David W. Neubauer. Brooks/Cole Publishing Company, 511 Forest Lodge Road, Pacific Grove, California 93950. 1992.

APPELLATE COURT CASELOADS: HISTORICAL TRENDS WITH CASELOAD STATISTICS APPENDED. National Center for State Courts, 300 Newport Avenue, Williamsburg, Virginia 23187-8798. 1983.

ASSESSING THE NEED FOR JUDICIAL RESOURCES: GUIDELINES FOR A NEW PROCESS: PRELIMINARY DRAFT. National Center for State Courts, 300 Newport Avenue, Williamsburg, Virginia 23187-8798. 1983.

ATTACKING LITIGATION COSTS AND DELAY: PROJECT REPORTS AND RESEARCH FINDINGS SUPPORTING THE FINAL REPORT OF THE ACTION COMMISSION TO REDUCE COURT COSTS AND DELAY. American Bar Association, Action Commission to Reduce Court Costs and Delay, 750 North Lake Shore Drive, Chicago, Illinois 60611. 1984.

AUTOMATED INFORMATION SYSTEMS: IMPLEMENTATION GUIDELINES. State Judicial Information Systems Project. National Center for State Courts, 300 Newport Avenue, Williamsburg, Virginia 23187-8798. 1983.

THE BILINGUAL COURTROOM: COURT INTERPRETERS IN THE JUDICIAL PROCESS. Susan Berk-Seligson. University of Chicago Press, 5801 Ellis Avenue, Chicago, Illinois 60637. 1990.

THE BUSINESS OF STATE TRIAL COURTS. Victor E. Flango, et al. National Center for State Courts, 300 Newport Avenue, Williamsburg, Virginia 23187-8798. 1983.

CAUSAL ANALYSIS OF THE RELATIONSHIP BETWEEN LEARNING DISABILITIES AND JUVENILE DELINQUENCY. National Center for State Courts, 300 Newport Avenue, Williamsburg, Virginia 23187-8798. 1984.

THE COMPUTER IN THE COURT. Alistar Kelman and Richard Sizer. Gower Publishing Company, Old Post Road, Brookfield, Vermont 05036. 1982.

CONFLICT, COURTS, AND TRIALS. Third Edition. Linda Riekes, Dolores B. Malcolm, and Michael A. Wolff. West Publishing Company, 50 West Kellogg Boulevard, St. Paul, Minnesota 55164. 1991.

THE CONTOURS OF JUSTICE: COMMUNITIES AND THEIR COURTS. James Eisenstein, Roy B. Flemming, and Peter F. Nardulli. Little, Brown and Company, 34 Beacon Street, Boston, Massachusetts 02108. 1988.

COSTS OF THE CIVIL JUSTICE SYSTEM: COURT EXPENDITURES FOR VARIOUS TYPES OF CIVIL CASES. James S. Kaklik, et al. The Rand Corporation, P.O. Box 2138, Santa Monica, California 90406. 1983.

COUNTY COURT PRACTICE 1989. R. C. L. Gregory and D. E. Peck, Editors. Butterworth Legal Publishers, 90 Stiles Road, Salem, New Hampshire 03079. 1989.

THE COUNTY COURTHOUSES OF THE UNITED STATES. B. Lowry, Editor. Princeton University Press, 41 William Street, Princeton, New Jersey 08540. 1982.

THE COURT AND PUBLIC POLICY. Robert H. Birkby. Congressional Quarterly, Incorporated, 1414 Twenty-second Street, Northwest, Washington D.C. 20037. 1983.

COURT AWARDED ATTORNEY FEES. Matthew Bender and Company, Incorporated, 11 Penn Plaza, New York, New York 10001. 1983.

COURT CASE MANAGEMENT INFORMATION SYSTEMS MANUAL: WITH MODEL DATA ELEMENTS. Mary Louise Clifford and Lynn A. Jensen. National Center for State Courts, 300 Newport Avenue, Williamsburg, Virginia 23187-8798. 1983.

COURT REFORM ON TRIAL: WHY SIMPLE SOLUTIONS FAIL. Malcolm M. Feeley. Basic Books, Incorporated, 10 East Fifty-third Street, New York, New York 10022. 1984.

COURT SELECTION: STUDENT LITIGATION IN STATE AND FEDERAL COURTS. National Center for State Courts, 300 Newport Avenue, Williamsburg, Virginia 23187-8798. 1982.

COURTROOM SURVIVAL: THE OFFICER'S GUIDE TO BETTER TESTIMONY. Second Edition. Devallis Rutledge. Custom Publishing Company, 1590 Lotus Road, Placerville, California 95667. 1989.

COURTS: A COMPARATIVE AND POLITICAL ANALYSIS. Martin Shapiro. University of Chicago Press, 5801 Ellis Avenue, South, Chicago, Illinois 60637. 1986.

COURTS: A FULCRUM OF THE JUSTICE SYSTEM. Second Edition. Random House, Incorporated, 201 East Fiftieth Street, New York, New York 10022. 1984.

COURTS AND CORRECTIONAL INSTITUTIONS. Superintendent of Documents, United States Government Printing Office, Washington, D.C. 20402. 1983.

COURTS AND POLITICS: THE FEDERAL JUDICIAL SYSTEM. Second Edition. Howard Ball. Prentice-Hall, Incorporated, 113 Sylvan Avenue, Englewood Cliffs, New Jersey 07632. 1987.

COURTS AND THE POOR. Christopher E. Smith. Nelson-Hall Publishers, 111 North Canal Street, Chicago, Illinois 60606. 1991.

THE COURTS IN AMERICAN LIFE: MAJOR HISTORICAL INTERPRETATIONS. Kermit L. Hall. Garland Publishing, Incorporated, 136 Madison Avenue, New York, New York 10016. 1987.

COURTS IN AMERICAN POLITICS: READINGS AND INTRODUCTORY ESSAYS. Henry R. Glick. McGraw-Hill Publishing Company, 1221 Avenue of the Americas, New York, New York 10020. 1990.

COURTS, JUDGES AND POLITICS: AN INTRODUCTION TO THE JUDICIAL PROCESS. Fourth Edition. McGraw-Hill Publishing Company, 1221 Avenue of the Americas, New York, New York 10020. 1986.

COURTS, POLITICS, AND JUSTICE. Second Edition. Henry R. Glick. McGraw-Hill Publishing Company, 1221 Avenue of the Americas, New York, New York 10020. 1988.

THE CRIMINAL COURTS: STRUCTURES, PERSONNEL, AND PROCESSES. N. Gary Holten and Lawson L. Lamar. McGraw-Hill Publishing Company, 1221 Avenue of the Americas, New York, New York 10020. 1991.

CURBING THE COURTS: THE CONSTITUTION AND THE LIMITS OF JUDICIAL POWER. Gary L. McDowell. Louisiana State University Press, Highland Road, Baton Rouge, Louisiana 70893. 1988.

DISORDER IN THE COURT: GREAT FRACTURED MOMENTS IN COURTROOM HISTORY. Charles M. Sevilla. W.W. Norton and Company, Incorporated, 500 Fifth Avenue, New York, New York 10110. 1992.

DOMESTIC PROCEEDINGS IN MAGISTRATES' COURTS. Sixth Edition. S. M. Gerlis. Oyez Longman, Incorporated, 19 West Forty-fourth Street, New York, New York 10036. 1982.

EMPIRICAL THEORIES ABOUT COURTS. Keith O. Boyum and Lynn Mather. Longman, Incorporated, 19 West Forty-fourth Street, New York, New York 10036. 1983.

EXPLAINING THE COURTS: MATERIALS AND SOURCES. American Bar Association, 750 North Lake Shore Drive, Chicago, Illinois 60611. 1983.

FRIENDS OF THE COURT: LAWYERS AS SUPPLEMENTAL JUDICIAL RESOURCES. Alexander B. Aikman, Mary E. Elsner, and Frederick G. Miller. National Center for State Courts, 300 Newport Avenue, Williamsburg, Virginia 23187. 1987.

THE HOLLOW HOPE: CAN COURTS BRING ABOUT SOCIAL CHANGE? Gerald N. Rosenberg. University of Chicago Press, 5801 Ellis Avenue, Chicago, Illinois 60637. 1991.

IMPLEMENTING DELAY REDUCTION AND DELAY PREVENTION PROGRAMS IN URBAN TRIAL COURTS: PRELIMINARY FINDINGS FROM CURRENT RESEARCH. National Center for State Courts, 300 Newport Avenue, Williamsburg, Virginia 23187-8798. 1985.

INSANITY DEFENSE AND ITS ALTERNATIVES: A GUIDE FOR POLICYMAKERS. National Center for State Courts, 300 Newport Avenue, Williamsburg, Virginia 23187-8798. 1984.

AN INTRODUCTION TO COURT INTERPRETING: THEORY AND PRACTICE. Elena M. de Jongh. University Press of America, 4720 Boston Way, Lanham, Maryland 20706. 1992.

JUDICIAL JEOPARDY: WHEN BUSINESS COLLIDES WITH THE COURTS. Richard McNeely. Addison-Wesley, Publishing Company, Incorporated, Route 128, Reading, Massachusetts 01867. 1986.

JUDICIAL PROCESS IN AMERICA. Robert A. Carp and Ronald Stidham. Congressional Quarterly Books, 1414 Twenty-second Street, Northwest, Washington D.C. 20037. 1989.

JUDICIAL PROCESS: LAW, COURTS, AND POLITICS IN THE UNITED STATES. David W. Neubauer. Brooks/Cole Publishing Company, 511 Forest Lodge Road, Pacific Grove, California 93950. 1991.

JUDICIAL RULEMAKING: A COMPENDIUM. Second Edition. Chris Korbakes, et al. University Publications of America, Incorporated, 4520 East West Highway, Suite 600, Bethesda, Maryland 20814. 1983.

THE JUDICIARY AND THE PEOPLE. Frederick N. Judson. Fred B. Rothman and Company, 10368 West Centennial Road, Littleton, Colorado 80127. 1982.

JUSTICE IN AMERICA: COURTS, LAWYERS AND THE JUDICIAL PROCESS. Fourth Edition. Herbert Jacob. Little, Brown, and Company, 34 Beacon Street, Boston, Massachusetts 02108. 1984.

LAWYERS, COURTS, AND PROFESSIONALISM: THE AGENDA FOR REFORM. Rudolph J. Gerber. Greenwood Publishing Group, Incorporated, 88 Post Road West, P.O. Box 5007, Westport, Connecticut 06881. 1989.

LEADING THE WAY: A HISTORY OF THE MASSACHUSETTS GENERAL COURT 1629 - 1980. Cornelius Dalton, el al. Connolly Secretary of the Commonwealth, State House, Room 340, Boston, Massachusetts 02133. 1984.

LEGAL BREAKDOWN: 40 WAYS TO FIX OUR LEGAL SYSTEM. Stephen Elias. Nolo Press, 950 Parker Street, Berkeley, California 94710. 1990.

MAGISTRATES' COURT GUIDE, 1985: ANTHONY AND BERRYMAN. Butterworth Legal Publishers, 90 Stiles Road, Salem, New Hampshire 03079. 1985.

MANAGERIAL JUDGES. Judith Resnik. The Rand Corporation, P.O. Box 2138, Santa Monica, California 90406. 1982.

MANAGING TO REDUCE DELAY: AN ABRIDGED VERSION. National Center for State Courts, 300 Newport Avenue, Williamsburg, Virginia 23187-8798. 1985.

MEDIA IN THE COURTS. Charlotte A. Carter. National Center for State Courts, 300 Newport Avenue, Williamsburg, Virginia 23187-8798. 1981.

MODELS OF COURT MANAGEMENT. Donald Dahlin. Associated Faculty Press, 19 West Thirty-sixth Street, New York, New York 10018. 1985.

MONEY AND JUSTICE: WHO OWNS THE COURTS? Lois G. Forer. W.W. Norton and Company, Incorporated, 500 Fifth Avenue, New York, New York 10110. 1986.

ON TRIAL: AMERICA'S COURTS AND THEIR TREATMENT OF SEXUALLY ABUSED CHILDREN. Second Edition. Billie Wright Dziech and Charles B. Schudson. Beacon Press, 25 Beacon Street, Boston, Massachusetts 02108. 1991.

THE PACE OF LITIGATION: CONFERENCE PROCEEDINGS. Jane W. Alder. Random House, Incorporated, Random House Publicity, (11-6) 201 East Fiftieth Street, New York, New York 10022. 1982.

THE POLITICS OF JUDICIAL REFORM. Philip L. Dubois, Editor. Lexington Books, Division of D.C. Heath and Company, 125 Spring Street, Lexington, Massachusetts 02173. 1982.

THE POLITICS OF STATE COURTS. Harry P. Stumpf and John H. Culver. Longman Publishing Group, 95 Church Street, White Plains, New York 10601. 1991.

PREPARING A UNITED STATES COURT FOR AUTOMATION. Gordon Bermant. Federal Judicial Center, 1520 H Street, Northwest, Washington D.C. 20005. 1985.

PRESS AND MEDIA ACCESS TO THE CRIMINAL COURTROOM. Warren Freedman. Quorum Books, Greenwood Publishing Group, Incorporated, 88 Post Road West, P.O. Box 5007, Westport, Connecticut 06881. 1988.

PRETRIAL REIMBURSEMENT PROGRAM. National Center for State Courts, 300 Newport Avenue, Williamsburg, Virginia 23187-8798. 1982.

THE PRODUCT LIABILITY MESS: HOW BUSINESS CAN BE RESCUED FROM THE POLITICS OF STATE COURTS. Richard Neely. Free Press, 866 Third Avenue, New York, New York 10022. 1988.

PROGRAMS FOR IMPROVING THE IMAGE OF THE JUDICIARY. National Center for State Courts, 300 Newport Avenue, Williamsburg, Virginia 23187-8798. 1984.

PROVISIONAL SUBSTANTIVE AND PROCEDURE GUIDELINES FOR INVOLUNTARY CIVIL COMMITMENT. National Center for State Courts, 300 Newport Avenue, Williamsburg, Virginia 23187-8798. 1982.

THE PUBLIC ADMINISTRATOR AND THE COURTS: BASIC CASE BOOK. John C. Pine and Patricia A. Hollander. Research Publications, Incorporated, 12 Lunar Drive, Drawer AB, Woodbridge, Connecticut 06525. 1985.

A REEVALUATION OF THE CIVIL APPEALS MANAGEMENT PLAN. Anthony Partridge and E. Allan Lind. United States Federal Judicial Center, 1520 H Street, Northwest, Washington, D.C. 20005. 1983.

REPORT WITH FINDINGS AND RECOMMENDATIONS TO THE CONFERENCE OF CHIEF JUSTICES FROM ITS TASK FORCE ON LAWYER COMPETENCE. National Center for State Courts, 300 Newport Avenue, Williamsburg, Virginia 23187-8798. 1982.

REPORTS OF THE PROCEEDINGS OF THE JUDICIAL CONFERENCE OF THE UNITED STATES 1985. Administrative Office of the United States Courts. Superintendent of Documents, United States Government Printing Office, Washington, D.C. 20402. 1985.

THE ROLE OF STATE SUPREME COURTS IN THE NEW JUDICIAL FEDERALISM. Susan P. Fino. Greenwood Publishing Group, Incorporated, 88 Post Road West, P.O. Box 5007, Westport, Connecticut 06881. 1987.

SEARCH WARRANT PROCESS: PRECONCEPTIONS, PERCEPTIONS, AND PRACTICES. National Center for State Courts, 300 Newport Avenue, Williamsburg, Virginia 23187-8798. 1985.

SHADOW JUSTICE: THE IDEOLOGY AND INSTITUTIONALIZATION OF ALTERNATIVES TO COURT. Christine B. Harrington. Greenwood Publishing Group, Incorporated, 88 Post Road West, P.O. Box 5007, Westport, Connecticut 06881. 1985.

STATE CONSTITUTIONS AND CRIMINAL JUSTICE. Barry Latzer. Greenwood Press, 88 Post Road West, P.O. Box 5007, Westport, Connecticut 06881. 1991.

STATE COURT PERSPECTIVE ON CASE MANAGEMENT IN THE UNITED STATES TAX COURT. National Center for State Courts, 300 Newport Avenue, Williamsburg, Virginia 23187-8798. 1985.

STATE SUPREME COURTS IN STATE AND NATION. G. Alan Tarr and Mary Cornelia Aldis Porter. Yale University Press, 302 Temple Street, New Haven, Connecticut 06520. 1988.

STRUCTURING JUSTICE: THE IMPLICATIONS OF COURT UNIFICATION REFORMS: POLICY SUMMARY. Thomas A Henderson and C. M. Kerwin. United States Department of Justice, Superintendent of Documents, United States Government Printing Office, Washington, D.C. 20402. 1984.

TREATISE ON THE ORGANIZATION, JURISDICTION AND PRACTICE OF THE COURTS OF THE UNITED STATES TO WHICH IS ADDED AN APPENDIX. Fourth Edition. Alfred Conkling. William W. Gaunt and Sons, Incorporated, 3011 Gulf Drive, Holmes Beach, Florida 34217-2199. 1987.

THE TRIAL: A PROCEDURAL DESCRIPTION AND CASE STUDY. Howard Myers and Jan Pudlow. West Publishing Company, 50 West Kellogg Boulevard, St. Paul, Minnesota 55164. 1991.

TRIAL COURT PERFORMANCE STANDARDS WITH COMMENTARY: A JOINT PROJECT OF THE NATIONAL CENTER FOR STATE COURTS AND THE BUREAU OF JUSTICE ASSISTANCE, UNITED STATES DEPARTMENT OF JUSTICE. National Center for State Courts, 300 Newport Avenue, Williamsburg, Virginia 23187. 1990.

TRIAL COURT REVIEW OF VERDICTS: A NATIONAL SURVEY. National Center for State Courts, 300 Newport Avenue, Williamsburg, Virginia 23187-8798. 1982.

VICTIMS, WITNESSES, AND COURTS. National Center for State Courts, 300 Newport Avenue, Williamsburg, Virginia 23187-8798. 1986.

ENCYCLOPEDIAS AND DICTIONARIES

STATE COURT MODEL STATISTICAL DICTIONARY, 1989 A JOINT EFFORT OF THE CONFERENCE OF STATE COURT ADMINISTRATORS AND THE NATIONAL CENTER FOR STATE COURTS. National Center for State Courts, 300 Newport Avenue, Williamsburg, Virginia 23187. 1989.

LAW REVIEWS AND PERIODICALS

COURT REVIEW, QUARTERLY. American Judges Association, 300 Newport Avenue, Williamsburg, Virginia 23187-8798. Quarterly.

JUDICATURE. American Judicature Society, 25 East Washington Street, Chicago, Illinois 60602. Bimonthly.

JUSTICE SYSTEM JOURNAL. Institute for Court Management of The National Center for State Court, 1624 Market Street, Suite 210, Denver, Colorado 80202. Three issues per year.

JUVENILE AND FAMILY COURT JOURNAL. National Council of Juvenile and Family Court Judges, P.O. Box 8978, University of Nevada, Reno, Nevada 89507. Quarterly.

STATE COURT JOURNAL. National Center for State Courts, 300 Newport Avenue, Williamsburg, Virginia 23187-8798. Annual.

NEWSLETTERS AND NEWSPAPERS

AJA BENCHMARK. American Judges Association, 300 Newport Avenue, Williamsburg, Virginia 23187-8798. Quarterly.

CITATIONS. Court Interpreters and Translators Association, P.O. Box 406, Peck Slip Station, New York, New York 10272. Quarterly.

CITIZENS' FORUM ON THE COURTS. American Judicature Society, 25 East Washington Street, Sixteenth Floor, Chicago, Illinois 60602. Quarterly.

COURT IMPROVEMENT BULLETIN. American Judicature Society, 12 East Washington Street, Suite 1600, Chicago, Illinois 60602. Semiannual.

THE COURT MANAGER. National Association for Court Management, 300 Newport Avenue, Williamsburg, Virginia 23187. Quarterly.

IJA REPORT. Institute of Judicial Administration. One Washington Square Village, New York, New York 10012. Quarterly.

JUVENILE AND FAMILY COURT NEWSLETTER. National Council of Juvenile and Family Court Judges, P.O. Box 8978, University of Nevada, Reno, Nevada 89507. Bimonthly.

NATIONAL CENTER FOR STATE COURTS REPORT. National Center for State Courts, 300 Newport Avenue, Williamsburg, Virginia 23187. Monthly.

THE NATIONAL SHORTHAND REPORTER. National Shorthand Reporters Association, 118 Park Street, Southeast, Vienna, Virginia 22180. Monthly.

NJC NEWSLETTER. National Judicial College, Judicial College Building, University of Nevada, Reno, Nevada 89557. Quarterly.

SPECIAL COURT NEWS. American Bar Association, National Conference of Special Court Judges, 750 North Lake Shore Drive, Chicago, Illinois 60611. Quarterly.

BIBLIOGRAPHIES

CAMERAS AND THE COURTS. Karen F. Harrell. Vance Bibliographies, P.O. Box 229, 112 North Charter Street, Monticello, Illinois 61856. 1981.

CONGESTION IN THE UNITED STATES COURT SYSTEM: A BRIEF BIBLIOGRAPHY. Alva W. Stewart. Vance Bibliographies, P.O. Box 229, 112 North Charter Street, Monticello, Illinois 61856. 1984.

COURT ADMINISTRATION: MONOGRAPHS. Mary Vance. Vance Bibliographies, P.O. Box 229, 112 North Charter Street, Monticello, Illinois 61856. 1983.

JUVENILE COURTS: A BIBLIOGRAPHY. Mary Vance. Vance Bibliographies, P.O. Box 229, 112 North Charter Street, Monticello, Illinois 61856. 1988.

STATE COURTS

DIRECTORIES

THE AMERICAN BENCH AND BAR. Forster-Long, Incorporated, 3280 Ramos Circle, Sacramento, California 95827. Biennial.

BNA'S DIRECTORY OF STATE COURTS, JUDGES, AND CLERKS: A STATE-BY-STATE LISTING. Third Edition. Kamla J. King and Judith Springberg. Bureau of National Affairs, 1231 Twenty-fifth Street, Northwest, Washington, D.C. 20037. 1990.

CONFERENCE OF CHIEF JUSTICES - ROSTER. Conference of Chief Justices, National Center for State Courts, 300 Newport Avenue, Williamsburg, Virginia 23187-8798. Continuously updated.

DIRECTORY OF JUDGES WITH JUVENILE/FAMILY LAW JURISDICTION. National Council of Juvenile and Family Court Judges, P.O. Box 8970, University of Nevada, Reno, Nevada 89557. Biennial.

NATIONAL DIRECTORY OF COURT MANAGEMENT PERSONNEL. School of Justice, American University, Massachusetts and Nebraska Avenues, Washington, D.C. 20016. 1982- .

NATIONAL JUSTICE AGENCY LIST. Bureau of Justice Statistics, Department of Justice, 633 Indiana Avenue, Northwest, Washington, D.C. 20531. (Database).

NATIONAL TRIAL AND DEPOSITION DIRECTORY. National Trial and Deposition Directory, 421 West Franklin, Boise, Idaho 83702. 1986.

WHO'S WHO IN AMERICAN LAW. Marquis Who's Who, Incorporated, 3002 Glenview Road, Wilmette, Illinois 60091. Biennial.

BIOGRAPHICAL SOURCES

THE AMERICAN BENCH AND BAR. Forster-Long, Incorporated, 3280 Ramos Circle, Sacramento, California 95827. Biennial.

CONFERENCE OF CHIEF JUSTICES - ROSTER. Conference of Chief Justices, National Center for State Courts, 300 Newport Avenue, Williamsburg, Virginia 23187-8798. Continuously updated.

DIRECTORY OF JUDGES WITH JUVENILE/FAMILY LAW JURISDICTION. National Council of Juvenile and Family Court Judges, P.O. Box 8970, University of Nevada, Reno, Nevada 89557. Biennial.

NATIONAL DIRECTORY OF COURT MANAGEMENT PERSONNEL. School of Justice, American University, Massachusetts and Nebraska Avenues, Washington, D.C. 20016. 1982- .

NATIONAL TRIAL AND DEPOSITION DIRECTORY. National Trial and Deposition Directory, 421 West Franklin, Boise, Idaho 83702. 1986.

WHO'S WHO IN AMERICAN LAW. Marquis Who's Who, Incorporated, 3002 Glenview Road, Wilmette, Illinois 60091. Biennial.

ASSOCIATIONS AND PROFESSIONAL SOCIETIES

AMERICAN JUDGES ASSOCIATION. 300 Newport Avenue, Williamsburg, Virginia 23187. (804) 253-2000.

AMERICAN JUDICATURE SOCIETY. 25 East Washington Street, Suite 1600, Chicago, Illinois 60602. (312) 558-6900.

CONFERENCE OF CHIEF JUSTICES. National Center for State Courts, 300 Newport Avenue, Williamsburg, Virginia 23187. (804) 253-2000.

JUDICIAL ADMINISTRATION DIVISION, AMERICAN BAR ASSOCIATION. 750 North Lake Shore Drive, Chicago, Illinois 60611. (312) 988-5000.

- Appellate Judges' Conference - Committee on Traffic Court Program - Lawyers Conference - National Conference of Special Court Judges - National Conference of State Court Judges

NATIONAL ASSOCIATION OF JUDICIARY INTERPRETERS AND TRANSLATORS. 815 East Fourteenth Street, Suite 6B, Brooklyn, New York 11230. (718) 434-0636.

NATIONAL CENTER FOR STATE COURTS. 300 Newport Avenue, Williamsburg, Virginia 23187. (804) 253-2000.

- Conference of State Court Administrators - National Association for Court Management - National Conference of Appellate Court Clerks

NATIONAL COUNCIL OF JUVENILE AND FAMILY COURT JUDGES. P.O. Box 8970, University of Nevada, Reno, Nevada 89557. (702) 784-6012.

NATIONAL JUDGES ASSOCIATION. 42 Little Horn Road, Westcliffe, Colorado 81252. (719) 783-2274.

NATIONAL JUDICIAL COLLEGE. Judicial College Building, University of Nevada, Reno, Nevada 89557. (702) 784-6747.

NATIONAL JUDICIAL EDUCATION PROGRAM TO PROMOTE EQUALITY FOR WOMEN AND MEN IN THE COURTS. 99 Hudson Street, Twelfth Floor, New York, New York 10013. (212) 925-6635.

NATIONAL SHORTHAND REPORTERS ASSOCIATION. 118 Park Street, Southeast, Vienna, Virginia 22180. (703) 281-4677.

RESEARCH CENTERS, INSTITUTES, CLEARINGHOUSES

INSTITUTE FOR COURT MANAGEMENT OF THE NATIONAL CENTER FOR STATE COURTS. 1331 Seventeenth Street, Suite 402, Denver, Colorado 80202. (303) 293-3063.

INSTITUTE OF JUDICIAL ADMINISTRATION. One Washington Square Village, New York, New York 10012. (212) 998-6280.

ONLINE DATABASES

NATIONAL JUSTICE AGENCY LIST. Bureau of Justice Statistics, Department of Justice, Washington, D.C. 20531.

OTHER SOURCES

INTERMEDIATE APPELLATE COURTS: IMPROVING CASE PROCESSING: FINAL REPORT. Joy A. Chapper and Roger A. Hanson. National Center for State Courts, 300 Newport Avenue, Williamsburg, Virginia 23187. 1990.

STATE DEPARTMENT
See also: PUBLIC OFFICIALS AND EMPLOYEES

STATUTES, CODES, STANDARDS, UNIFORM LAWS

CODE OF FEDERAL REGULATIONS, TITLE 22. Office of the Federal Register, National Archives and Records Administration. Superintendent of Documents, United States Government Printing Office, Washington, D.C. 20402. Annual. (Updated by use of monthly List of Sections Affected and daily Federal Register.)

STANDARDIZED REGULATIONS (GOVERNMENT CIVILIANS, FOREIGN AREAS). State Department. Superintendent of Documents, United States Government Printing Office, Washington, D.C. 20402. Thirteen issues per year.

TREATIES AND OTHER INTERNATIONAL ACTS SERIES. State Department. Superintendent of Documents, United States Government Printing Office, Washington, D.C. 20402.

TREATIES IN FORCE, A LIST OF TREATIES AND OTHER INTERNATIONAL AGREEMENTS OF THE UNITED STATES. State Department, Office of the Legal Advisor, Treaty Affairs Staff. Superintendent of Documents, United States Govern- ment Printing Office, Washington, D.C. 20402. Annual.

UNITED STATES TREATIES AND OTHER INTERNATIONAL AGREEMENTS. State Department. Superintendent of Documents, United States Government Printing Office, Washington, D.C. 20402. 1950- .

TEXTBOOKS AND GENERAL WORKS

ATLAS OF UNITED STATES FOREIGN RELATIONS. Harry Young. Gordon Press, P.O. Box 459, Bowling Green Station, New York, New York 10004. 1990.

THE DEPARTMENT OF STATE. Carl F. Bartz. Chelsea House Publishers, 1974 Sproul Road, Suite 400, Broomall, Pennsylvania 19008. 1989.

GUIDE TO DOING BUSINESS WITH THE DEPARTMENT OF STATE. State Department, Bureau of Management, Office of Small and Disadvantaged Business Utilization. Superintendent of Documents, United States Government Printing Office, Washington, D.C. 20402. 1988.

HUMAN RIGHTS REPORT, 1982. Juanita Adams. State Department, Bureau of Public Affairs, Office of Communication, Editorial Division. Superintendent of Documents, United States Government Printing Office, Washington, D.C. 20402. 1983.

OF MICE, CAGES, AND CHEESE: FOREIGN ASSESSMENT AND THE FOREIGN SERVICE PERSONNEL SYSTEM. Susan J. Irving. Garland Publishing, Incorporated, 136 Madison Avenue, New York, New York 10016. 1988.

ENCYCLOPEDIAS AND DICTIONARIES

DICTIONARY OF INTERNATIONAL RELATIONS TERMS. State Department, Library. Superintendent of Documents, United States Government Printing Office, Washington, D.C. 20402. 1987.

DIGESTS, INDEXES, ABSTRACTS, CITATORS

DIGEST OF UNITED STATES PRACTICE IN INTERNATIONAL LAW. Martin Lloyd Nash. State Department, Office of the Legal Advisor. Superintendent of Documents, United States Government Printing Office, Washington, D.C. 20402. 1983.

LAW REVIEWS AND PERIODICALS

DEPARTMENT OF STATE BULLETIN: THE OFFICIAL MONTHLY RECORD OF UNITED STATES FOREIGN POLICY. State Department, Bureau of Public Affairs. Superintendent of Documents, United States Government Printing Office, Washington, D.C. 20402. Monthly.

STATE. State Department. Superintendent of Documents, United States Government Printing Office, Washington, D.C. 20402. Monthly.

RESEARCH CENTERS, INSTITUTES, CLEARINGHOUSES

UNITED STATES DEPARTMENT OF STATE, OFFICE OF LEGAL ADVISOR LAW LIBRARY. 2201 C Street, Northwest, Washington, D.C. 20520. (202) 647-4130.

ONLINE DATABASES

LEXIS, GENERAL FEDERAL, DEPARTMENT OF STATE BULLETIN FILE. Mead Data Central, P.O. Box 933, Dayton, Ohio 45401.

OTHER SOURCES

POST WORLD WAR II FOREIGN POLICY PLANNING: STATE DEPARTMENT RECORDS OF HARLEY A. NOTTER, 1939-1945. Harley A. Notter. Congressional Information Service, 4520 East-West Highway, Suite 800, Bethesda, Maryland 20814. 1987.

RECORDS OF THE U.S. DEPARTMENT OF STATE RELATING TO COMMERCIAL RELATIONS BETWEEN THE UNITED STATES AND RUSSIA/THE SOVIET UNION, 1910- 1949. Scholarly Resources, 104 Greenhill Avenue, Wilmington, Delaware 19805. 1987. (Microfilm).

RECORDS OF THE U.S. DEPARTMENT OF STATE RELATING TO POLITICAL RELATIONS BETWEEN THE UNITED STATES AND JAPAN, 1940-1954. Scholarly Resources, 104 Greenhill Avenue, Wilmington, Delaware 19805. 1987. (Microfilm).

RECORDS OF THE U.S. DEPARTMENT OF STATE RELATING TO THE INTERNAL AFFAIRS OF ALBANIA, 1950-1954. Scholarly Resources, 104 Greenhill Avenue, Wilmington, Delaware 19805. 1987. (Microfilm).

RECORDS OF THE U.S. DEPARTMENT OF STATE RELATING TO THE INTERNAL AFFAIRS OF AUSTRIA, 1945-1954. Scholarly Resources, 104 Greenhill Avenue, Wilmington, Delaware 19805. 1987. (Microfilm).

RECORDS OF THE U.S. DEPARTMENT OF STATE RELATING TO THE INTERNAL AFFAIRS OF BULGARIA, 1945-1954. Scholarly Resources, 104 Greenhill Avenue, Wilmington, Delaware 19805. 1987. (Microfilm).

RECORDS OF THE U.S. DEPARTMENT OF STATE RELATING TO THE INTERNAL AFFAIRS OF FINLAND, 1945-1949. Scholarly Resources, 104 Greenhill Avenue, Wilmington, Delaware 19805. 1987. (Microfilm)

RECORDS OF THE U.S. DEPARTMENT OF STATE RELATING TO THE INTERNAL AFFAIRS OF HUNGARY, 1945-1949. Scholarly Resources, 104 Greenhill Avenue, Wilmington, Delaware 19805. 1987. (Microfilm).

RECORDS OF THE U.S. DEPARTMENT OF STATE RELATING TO THE INTERNAL AFFAIRS OF THE RUSSIAN ZONE (EAST GERMANY), 1950-1954. Scholarly Resources, 104 Greenhill Avenue, Wilmington, Delaware 19805. 1987. (Microfilm).

STATE GOVERNMENT
See also: LOCAL GOVERNMENT; STATES; TREASURY DEPARTMENT

HANDBOOKS, MANUALS, FORMBOOKS

FACTS ABOUT THE STATES. Joseph Nathan Kane, Steven Anzovin, and Janet Podell. H.W. Wilson Company, 950 University Avenue, Bronx, New York 10452. 1989.

GUIDE TO STATE LEGISLATIVE AND ADMINISTRATIVE MATERIALS. Fourth Edition. Mary L. Fisher. Fred B. Rothman and Company, 10368 West Centennial Road, Littleton, Colorado 80127. 1988.

HANDBOOK OF STATE LEGISLATIVE LEADERS. State Legislative Leaders Foundation, 250 Boylston Street, Boston, Massachusetts 02116. Annual.

NATIONAL ASSOCIATION OF SECRETARIES OF STATE HANDBOOK. Council of State Governments, Iron Works Pike, P.O. Box 11910, Lexington, Kentucky 40578. Annual.

SOURCE BOOK FOR AMERICAN STATE LEGISLATION. American Legislative Exchange Council, 214 Massachusetts Avenue, Northeast, Suite 240, Washington, DC 20002. Biennial.

STATE LEGISLATIVE SOURCEBOOK. Government Research Service, 701 Jackson, Topeka, Kansas 66603. Annual.

TEXTBOOKS AND GENERAL WORKS

AMERICAN FEDERALISM: A VIEW FROM THE STATES. Daniel J. Elazar. HarperCollins Publishers, Incorporated, 10 East Fifty-third Street, New York, New York 10022. 1984.

AMERICAN STATES AND CITIES. Virginia Gray and Peter Eisinger. HarperCollins Publishers, 10 East Fifty-third Street, New York, New York 10022. 1991.

CAMPAIGN FINANCE, ETHICS AND LOBBY BLUE BOOK. Council of State Governments, Iron Works Pike, P.O. Box 11910, Lexington, Kentucky 40578. 1984.

COMPARING THE STATES AND COMMUNITIES: POLITICS, GOVERNMENT, AND POLICY IN THE UNITED STATES. Norman R. Luttbeg. HarperCollins Publishers, 10 East Fifty-third Street, New York, New York 10022. 1992.

THE CONSTITUTION IN STATE POLITICS: FROM THE CALLING OF THE CONSTITUTIONAL CONVENTION TO THE FIRST FEDERAL ELECTIONS. Steven R. Boyd. Garland Publishing, Incorporated, 136 Madison Avenue, New York, New York 10016. 1990.

DEMOCRATIC GOVERNANCE IN AMERICAN STATES AND CITIES. Kim Quaile and Kenneth R. Mladenka. Brooks/Cole Publishing Company, 511 Forest Lodge Road, Pacific Grove, California 93950. 1992.

GOVERNING AT THE GRASS ROOTS: STATE AND LOCAL GOVERNMENT. Second Edition. Nicholas L. Henry. Prentice-Hall, Incorporated, 113 Sylvan Avenue, Englewood Cliffs, New Jersey 07632. 1984.

GOVERNING STATES AND COMMUNITIES: ORGANIZING FOR POPULAR RULE. John G. Grumm and Russell D. Murphy. Prentice-Hall, Incorporated, 113 Sylvan Avenue, Englewood Cliffs, New Jersey 07632. 1991.

THE GOVERNORS AND THE NEW FEDERALISM. Marshall Kaplan and Sue O'Brien. Westview Press, Incorporated, 5500 Central Avenue, Boulder, Colorado 80301. 1991.

GUBERNATORIAL LEADERSHIP AND STATE POLICY. Eric B. Herzik and Brent W. Brown. Greenwood Publishing Group, Incorporated, 88 Post Road West, P.O. Box 5007, Westport, Connecticut 06881. 1991.

MODEL LEGISLATION FOR THE STATES, 1984-1985. Mark Bohannon and Lee Webb, Editors. Conference on Alternative State and Local Policies, 2000 Florida Avenue, Northwest, Washington, DC 20009. 1984.

POLITICS AND POLICY IN STATES AND COMMUNITIES. Fourth Edition. John J. Harrigan. HarperCollins Publishers, 10 East Fifty-third Street, New York, New York 10022. 1991.

POLITICS IN STATES AND COMMUNITIES. Seventh Edition. Thomas R. Dye. Prentice-Hall, Incorporated, 113 Sylvan Avenue, Englewood Cliffs, New Jersey 07632. 1991.

THE POLITICS OF STATE AND LOCAL GOVERNMENT LAW DEBATED: READINGS IN ACCOUNTABILITY, RESPONSIVENESS AND EFFICIENCY. Herbert M. Levine. Prentice-Hall, Incorporated, 113 Sylvan Avenue, Englewood Cliffs, New Jersey 07632. 1985.

THE POLITICS OF SUBNATIONAL GOVERNANCE. Second Edition. Deirdre A. Zimmerman and Joseph F. Zimmerman. University Press of America, 4720 Boston Way, Lanham, Maryland 20706. 1991.

POLITICS, POLICY, AND MANAGEMENT IN THE AMERICAN STATES. Dennis L. Dresang and James J. Gosling. Longman Publishing Group, 95 Church Street, White Plains, New York 10601. 1989.

REPRESENTATION IN STATE LEGISLATURES. Malcolm E. Jewell. University Press of Kentucky, University of Kentucky, 633 Limestone Street, Lexington, Kentucky 40506-0336. 1982.

STATE AND COMMUNITY GOVERNMENT IN THE FEDERAL SYSTEM. Charles Press and Kenneth VerBerg. Macmillan Publishing Company, Incorporated, 866 Third Avenue, New York, New York 10022. 1983.

STATE AND COMMUNITY GOVERNMENTS IN A DYNAMIC FEDERAL SYSTEM. Third Edition. Charles Press and Kenneth VerBurg. HarperCollins Publishers, 10 East Fifty-third Street, New York, New York 10022. 1991.

STATE AND LOCAL GOVERNMENT. Ann O'M. Bowman and Richard C. Kearney. Houghton Mifflin Company, 1 Beacon Street, Boston, Massachusetts 02108. 1990.

STATE AND LOCAL GOVERNMENT DEBT FINANCING. M. David Gelfand, Editor. Callaghan and Company, 155 Pfingsten Road, Deerfield, Illinois 60015. 1990.

STATE AND LOCAL GOVERNMENT IN A CHANGING SOCIETY. Second Edition. Richard D. Bingham and David Hedge. McGraw-Hill Publishing Company, 1221 Avenue of the Americas, New York, New York 10020. 1991.

STATE AND LOCAL GOVERNMENT IN A FEDERAL SYSTEM: CASES AND MATERIALS. Daniel R. Mandelker. Michie/Bobbs-Merrill, The Michie Company, P.O. Box 7587, Charlottesville, Virginia 22906-7582. 1990.

STATE AND LOCAL GOVERNMENT: POLITICS AND PUBLIC POLICIES. Fourth Edition. David C. Saffell. McGraw-Hill Publishing Company, 1221 Avenue of the Americas, New York, New York 10020. 1989.

STATE AND LOCAL GOVERNMENT: THE THIRD CENTURY OF FEDERALISM. Richard H. Leach and Timothy G. O'Rourke. Prentice-Hall, Incorporated, 113 Sylvan Avenue, Englewood Cliffs, New Jersey 07632. 1988.

STATE AND LOCAL POLITICS. Charles R. Adrian and Michael R. Fine. Lyceum Books, Incorporated, 59 East Van Buren, Suite 810, Chicago, Illinois 60605. 1991.

STATE AND LOCAL POLITICS. Sixth Edition. David R. Berman. William C. Brown Group, 2460 Kerper Boulevard, Dubuque, Iowa 52001. 1991.

STATE AND LOCAL POLITICS: A POLITICAL ECONOMY APPROACH. William A. Schultze. West Publishing Company, 50 West Kellogg Boulevard, St. Paul, Minnesota 55164. 1988.

STATE AND LOCAL POLITICS: FUNDAMENTALS AND PERSPECTIVES. Michael Engel. Saint Martin's Press, Incorporated, 175 Fifth Avenue, New York, New York 10010. 1984.

STATE AND LOCAL POLITICS: GOVERNMENT BY THE PEOPLE. Sixth Edition. James MacGregor Burns, J.W. Peltason, and Thomas E. Cronin. Prentice-Hall, Incorporated, 113 Sylvan Avenue, Englewood Cliffs, New Jersey 07632. 1990.

STATE AND LOCAL POLITICS: THE GREAT ENTANGLEMENT. Fourth Edition. Robert S. Lorch. Prentice-Hall, Incorporated, 113 Sylvan Avenue, Englewood Cliffs, New Jersey 07632. 1992.

STATE AND LOCAL POLITICS: THE INDIVIDUAL AND THE GOVERNMENTS. W.B. Stouffer, Cynthia Opheim, and Susan Bland Day. HarperCollins Publishers, 10 East Fifty-third Street, New York, New York 10022. 1991.

THE STATE OF THE STATE. Carl E. Van Horn. Congressional Quarterly Books, 1414 Twenty-second Street, Northwest, Washington D.C. 20037. 1989.

ENCYCLOPEDIAS AND DICTIONARIES

THE STATE AND LOCAL GOVERNMENT POLITICAL DICTIONARY. Jeffrey M. Elliot and Sheikh R. Ali. ABC-CLIO, P.O. Box 1911, Santa Barbara, California 93116-1911. 1988.

LAW REVIEWS AND PERIODICALS

STATE AND LOCAL GOVERNMENT REVIEW. Carl Vinson Institute of Government, Terrell Hall, University of Georgia, Athens, Georgia 30602. Triannual.

STATE GOVERNMENT. Council of State Governments, Iron Works Pike, P.O. Box 11910, Lexington, Kentucky 40578. Quarterly.

STATE LEGISLATURES. National Conference of State Legislatures, 1125 17th Street, Suite 1500, Denver, Colorado 80202. Monthly.

NEWSLETTERS AND NEWSPAPERS

A-G REPORT. National Association of Attorneys General, 444 North Capitol Street, Washington, D.C. 20001. Monthly.

BACKGROUNDERS. Council of State Governments, P. O. Box 11910, Iron Works Pike, Lexington, Kentucky 40578. Monthly.

CAPITAL IDEAS. National Governors' Association, Hall of States, 444 North Capitol Street, Northwest, Washington, D.C. 20001. Monthly.

CAPITOL TO CAPITOL NEWSLETTER. National Conference of State Legislatures, 1125 17th Street, Suite 1500, Denver, Colorado 80202. Semi-monthly.

FROM THE STATE CAPITALS--FEDERAL ACTION AFFECTING THE STATES. Wakeman Walworth, Incorporated, P.O. Box 1939, New Haven, Connecticut 06509. Twenty issues per year.

FROM THE STATE CAPITALS--GENERAL TRENDS. Wakeman Walworth, Incorporated, P.O. Box 1939, New Haven, Connecticut 06509. Weekly.

GOVERNORS' WEEKLY BULLETIN. National Governors' Association, 444 North Capitol Street, Northwest, Washington, D.C. 20001. Weekly.

STATE GOVERNMENT NEWS. Council of State Governments, Iron Works Pike, P.O. Box 11910, Lexington, Kentucky 40578. Monthly.

URBAN, STATE AND LOCAL LAW NEWSLETTER. American Bar Association, Section of Urban, State and Local Law, 750 North Lake Shore Drive, Chicago, Illinois 60611. Quarterly.

BIBLIOGRAPHIES

AMERICAN STATE LEGISLATORS: PAY AND PERQUISITES, A BRIEF CHECKLIST. Alva W. Stewart. Vance Bibliographies, P.O. Box 229, 112 North Charter Street, Monticello, Illinois 61856. 1984.

GOVERNMENT INFOSTRUCTURES: A GUIDE TO THE NETWORKS OF INFORMATION RESOURCES AND TECHNOLOGIES AT FEDERAL, STATE, AND LOCAL LEVELS. Karen B. Levitan. Greenwood Publishing Group, Incorporated, 88 Post Road West, P.O. Box 5007, Westport, Connecticut 06881. 1987.

RESOURCE GUIDE TO INFLUENCING STATE LEGISLATURES: ANNOTATED BIBLIOGRAPHY. Third Edition. Lynn Hellebust. Government Research Service, 701 Jackson, Topeka 66603. 1991.

SELECTING AND ORGANIZING STATE GOVERNMENT PUBLICATIONS. Margaret T. Lane. American Library Association, 50 East Huron Street, Chicago, Illinois 60611. 1987.

STATE BLUE BOOKS, LEGISLATIVE MANUALS, AND REFERENCE PUBLICATIONS: A SELECTED BIBLIOGRAPHY. Council of State Governments, Iron Works Pike, P.O. Box 11910, Lexington, Kentucky 40578. 1990.

STATE BLUE BOOKS, LEGISLATIVE MANUALS, AND REFERENCE PUBLICATIONS: A SELECTIVE BIBLIOGRAPHY. Lynn Hellebust. Government Research Service, Topeka, Kansas. 1990.

STATE DOCUMENT CHECKLISTS: A HISTORICAL BIBLIOGRAPHY. Susan L. Dow. William S. Hein and Company, 1285 Main Street, Buffalo, New York 14209. 1990.

STATE GOVERNMENT RESEARCH CHECKLIST. Council of State Governments, Iron Works Pike, P.O. Box 11910, Lexington, Kentucky 40578. Bimonthly.

STATE LEGISLATURES: A BIBLIOGRAPHY. Robert U. Goehlert and Frederick W. Musto. ABC-Clio Information Services, P.O. Box 1911, Santa Barbara, California 93116-1911. 1985.

DIRECTORIES

BOOK OF THE STATES. Council of State Governments, Iron Works Pike, P.O. Box 11910, Lexington, Kentucky 40578. Biennial.

BOOK OF THE STATES, SUPPLEMENT ONE: STATE ELECTIVE OFFICIALS AND THE LEGISLATURES. Council of State Governments, Iron Works Pike, P.O. Box 11910, Lexington, Kentucky 40578. Biennial.

BOOK OF THE STATES, SUPPLEMENT THREE: STATE ADMINISTRATIVE OFFICIALS CLASSIFIED BY FUNCTION. Council of State Governments, Iron Works Pike, P.O. Box 11910, Lexington, Kentucky 40578. Biennial.

BOOK OF THE STATES, SUPPLEMENT TWO: STATE LEGISLATIVE LEADERSHIP, COMMITTEES, AND STAFF. Council of State Governments, Iron Works Pike, P.O. Box 11910, Lexington, Kentucky 40578. Biennial.

BRADDOCK'S FEDERAL-STATE-LOCAL GOVERNMENT DIRECTORY. Braddock Communication, Incorporated, 1001 Connecticut Avenue, Northwest, Washington, D.C. 22036. Biennial.

DIRECTORY OF ATTORNEYS GENERAL OF THE STATES AND OTHER JURISDICTIONS. National Association of Attorneys General, 444 North Capitol Street, Northwest, Washington, D.C. 20001. Biennial.

DIRECTORY OF ELECTION OFFICIALS. National Clearinghouse on Election Administration, Federal Election Commission. Superintendent of Documents, United States Government Printing Office, Washington, D.C. 20402. Annual.

GOVERNORS OF AMERICAN STATES, COMMONWEALTHS, TERRITORIES. National Governors' Association, Hall of States, 444 North Capitol, Northwest, Washington, D.C. 20001. Annual.

INTERSTATE COMPACTS AND AGENCIES. Council of State Governments, Iron Works Pike, P.O. Box 11910, Lexington, Kentucky 40578. 1983.

NATIONAL DIRECTORY OF STATE AGENCIES. National Standards Association, 5161 River Road, Bethesda, Maryland 20816. Annual.

STATE EXECUTIVE DIRECTORY. Carroll Publishing Company, 1058 Thomas Jefferson Street, Northwest, Washington, D.C. 20007. Three times a year.

STATE INFORMATION BOOK. Geraldine U. Jones and Leonard P. Hirsch, Editors. Infax, Incorporated, 450 Maple Avenue East, Suite 212, Vienna, Virginia 22180. 1985.

THE STATE SLATE: A GUIDE TO LEGISLATIVE PROCEDURES AND LAWMAKERS. Public Affairs Information Service, Incorporated, 521 West Forty-third Street, New York, New York 10036-4396. Annual.

ASSOCIATIONS AND PROFESSIONAL SOCIETIES

AMERICAN BAR ASSOCIATION, SECTION OF URBAN, STATE, AND LOCAL GOVERNMENT. American Bar Association, 750 North Lake Shore Drive, Chicago, Illinois 60611. (312) 988-5000.

AMERICAN LEGISLATIVE EXCHANGE COUNCIL. 214 Massachusetts Avenue, Northeast, Suite 400, Washington, DC 20002.

COUNCIL OF STATE GOVERNMENTS, Iron Works Pike, P.O. Box 11910, Lexington, Kentucky 40578. (606) 231-1939.

LOCAL GOVERNMENT CENTER. 2716 Ocean Park Boulevard, Suite 1062, Santa Monica, California 90405. (213) 392-0443.

NATIONAL ASSOCIATION OF ATTORNEY'S GENERAL. 444 North Capitol Street, Northwest, Washington, D.C. 20001. (202) 628-0435.

NATIONAL BLACK CAUCUS OF STATE LEGISLATORS. Hall of States Building, 444 North Capitol Street, Northwest, Suite 206, Washington, D.C. 20001. (202) 624-5457.

NATIONAL CONFERENCE OF COMMISSIONERS ON UNIFORM STATE LAWS. 676 North St. Clair, Suite 1700, Chicago, Illinois 60611. (312) 915-0195.

NATIONAL CONFERENCE OF LIEUTENANT GOVERNORS. Council of State Governments, Iron Works Pike, P.O. Box 11910, Lexington, Kentucky 40578. (606) 231-1813.

NATIONAL CONFERENCE OF STATE LEGISLATURES. 1050 Seventeenth Street, Suite 2100, Denver, Colorado 80265. (303) 623-7800.

NATIONAL GOVERNORS' ASSOCIATION. Hall of States Building, 444 North Capitol Street, Northwest, Washington, D.C. 20001. (202) 624-5300.

WOMEN EXECUTIVES IN STATE GOVERNMENT. 2000 M Street, Northwest, Suite 730, Washington, D.C. 20036. (202) 293-7006.

RESEARCH CENTERS, INSTITUTES, CLEARINGHOUSES

ACADEMY FOR STATE AND LOCAL GOVERNMENT. Hall of States Building, 444 North Capitol Street, Northwest, Suite 349, Washington, D.C. 20001. (202) 638-1445.

CENTER FOR LOCAL AND STATE GOVERNMENTS. Shippensburg University, Horton Hall, Shippensburg, Pennsylvania 17257. (717) 532-1502.

EDWIN F. JAECKLE CENTER FOR STATE AND LOCAL GOVERNMENT LAW. State University of New York at Buffalo, 422 O'Brian Hall, Amherst, New York 14260. (716) 636-2072.

GOVERNMENT LAW CENTER. University of Louisville, Louisville, Kentucky 40292. (502)588-6482.

LEGISLATIVE DRAFTING RESEARCH FUND. Columbia University, 435 West One Hundred Sixteenth Street, New York, New York 10027. (212) 854-2685.

STATE GOVERNMENT AFFAIRS COUNCIL. 1001 Connecticut Avenue, Northwest, Suite 800, Washington, D.C. 20036. (202) 659-7605.

ONLINE DATABASES

LEXIS STATES LIBRARY. Mead Data Central, P.O. Box 933, Dayton, Ohio 45401.

STATE NET 50--STATE LEGISLATIVE REPORTING. Information for Public Affairs, Incorporated, 1900 Fourteenth Street, Sacramento, California 95814.

STATE NET 50--STATE REGULATORY REPORTING. Information for Public Affairs, Incorporated, 1900 Fourteenth Street, Sacramento, California 95814.

WESTLAW, STATE LAW LIBRARY. West Publishing Company, 50 West Kellogg Boulevard, St. Paul, Minnesota 55164.

STATE LAW COMPILATIONS
See also: STATES

STATUTES, CODES, STANDARDS, UNIFORM LAWS

A COMPENDIUM OF STATE STATUTES AND INTERNATIONAL TREATIES IN TRUST AND ESTATE LAW: REFERENCE AND REFERRAL GUIDE FOR PRACTICING ATTORNEYS. Quorum Books, Imprint of Greenwood Publishing Group, Incorporated, 88 Post Road West, P. O. Box 5007, Westport, Connecticut 06881. 1985.

CONSTITUTIONS OF THE UNITED STATES: NATIONAL AND STATE. Second Edition. Legislative Drafting Research Fund of Columbia University, Oceana Publications, Incorporated, 75 Main Street, Dobbs Ferry, New York 10522. 1985. (Periodic Supplements).

INTERSTATE COMPACTS AND AGENCIES. Council of State Governments, Iron Works Pike, P.O. Box 11910, Lexington, Kentucky 40578. 1983.

SOURCES AND DOCUMENTS OF UNITED STATES CONSTITUTIONS. Second Series. William F. Swindler, Editor. Oceana Publications, Incorporated, 75 Main Street, Dobbs Ferry, New York 10522. 1982.

UNIFORM LAWS ANNOTATED. West Publishing Company, P. O. Box 64526, 50 West Kellogg Boulevard, St. Paul, Minnesota 55164-0526. 1969. (Annual Supplements).

LOOSELEAF SERVICES AND REPORTERS

MULTISTATE CORPORATE INCOME TAX GUIDE. Commerce Clearing House, Incorporated, 4025 West Peterson Avenue, Chicago, Illinois 60646. 1985- .

SIGNIFICANT STATE TAX DEVELOPMENTS. Prentice-Hall, Incorporated, 113 Sylvan Avenue, Englewood Cliffs, New Jersey 07632. Annual.

STATE TAX GUIDE. Commerce Clearing House, Incorporated, 4025 West Peterson Avenue, Chicago, Illinois 60646. 1937.

STATE LAW COMPILATIONS

HANDBOOKS, MANUALS, FORMBOOKS

WEST'S LEGAL DESK REFERENCE. William P. Statsky. West Publishing Company, 50 West Kellogg Boulevard, St. Paul, Minnesota 55164. 1991.

TEXTBOOKS AND GENERAL WORKS

BRIEFS OF 100 LEADING CASES IN LAW ENFORCEMENT. Rolando V. del Carmen and Jeffrey T. Walker. Anderson Publishing Company, 2035 Reading Road, Cincinnati, Ohio 45202. 1991.

CRIMINAL LAW FOR POLICE OFFICERS. Fifth Edition. Neil C. Chamelin and Kenneth R. Evans. Prentice-Hall, Incorporated, 113 Sylvan Avenue, Englewood Cliffs, New Jersey 07632. 1991.

ENCYCLOPEDIAS AND DICTIONARIES

DESKBOOK ENCYCLOPEDIA OF AMERICAN INSURANCE LAW. Fifth Edition. Data Research, Incorporated, 4635 Nicols Road, Suite 100, Eagan, Minnesota 55122. 1991.

DIGESTS, INDEXES, ABSTRACTS, CITATORS

CONSTRUCTION AND ENVIRONMENTAL INSURANCE CASE DIGESTS. Richard L. Seabolt. John Wiley and Sons, Incorporated, 605 Third Avenue, New York, New York 10158. 1991.

CONSTRUCTION LAW DIGESTS. James Acret. Shepard's/McGraw-Hill, P.O. Box 1235, Colorado Springs, Colorado 80901. 1990.

DIGEST OF STATE INSPECTION LAWS--PETROLEUM PRODUCTS. Fourth Edition. American Petroleum Institute, 2101 L Street, Northwest, Washington, DC 20005. 1985.

INDEX TO LEGAL BOOKS. R.R. Bowker Company, 121 Chanlon Road, New Providence, New Jersey 07974. 1988.

MARTINDALE-HUBBELL LAW DIRECTORY, VOLUME SEVEN. Martindale-Hubbell, Incorporated, 121 Chanlon Road, New Providence, New Jersey 07974. Annual.

MODERN HEALTH CARE LAW DIGEST: ALL THE CASES, ALL THE COURTS. Specialty Digest Publications, Blaine, Minnesota. 1988.

SHEPARD'S LAWYERS REFERENCE MANUAL. Shepard's/McGraw-Hill, P.O. Box 1235, Colorado Springs, Colorado 80901. 1983 (Annual Supplements).

ANNUALS AND SURVEYS

ALL STATES TAX HANDBOOK. Prentice-Hall, Incorporated, 113 Sylvan Avenue, Englewood Cliffs, New Jersey 07632. Annual.

STATE TAX HANDBOOK. Commerce Clearing House, Incorporated, 4025 West Peterson Avenue, Chicago, Illinois 60646. Annual.

BIBLIOGRAPHIES

HEIN'S STATE REPORT CHECKLIST. Keith Wiese. American Association of Law Libraries. William S. Hein and Company, 1285 Main Street, Buffalo, New York 14209. 1988.

SUBJECT COMPILATIONS OF STATE LAWS 1979-1983: RESEARCH GUIDE AND ANNOTATED BIBLIOGRAPHY. Cheryl R. Nyberg and Carol Boast. Quorum Books, Imprint of Greenwood Publishing Group, Incorporated, 88 Post Road West, P.O. Box 5007, Westport, Connecticut 06881. 1984.

SUBJECT COMPILATIONS OF STATE LAWS 1983-1985: AN ANNOTATED BIBLIOGRAPHY. Cheryl R. Nyberg. Carol Boast and Cheryl Nyberg, 716 West Indiana Avenue, Urbana, Illinois 61801-4836. 1986.

SUBJECT COMPILATIONS OF STATE LAWS: RESEARCH GUIDE AND ANNOTATED BIBLIOGRAPHY. Lynn Foster and Carol Boast. Quorum Books, Imprint of Greenwood Publishing Group, Incorporated, 88 Post Road West, P.O. Box 5007, Westport, Connecticut 06881. 1981.

ASSOCIATIONS AND PROFESSIONAL SOCIETIES

NATIONAL CONFERENCE OF COMMISSIONERS ON UNIFORM STATE LAWS. 676 North St. Clair, Suite 1700, Chicago, Illinois 60611. (312) 915-0195.

STATELESS PERSONS
See: CITIZENS AND CITIZENSHIP; EMIGRATION AND IMMIGRATION

STATES--ALABAMA

STATUTES, CODES, STANDARDS, UNIFORM LAWS

ACTS OF ALABAMA. Brown Printing Company, 2734 Gunter Park Drive West, Montgomery, Alabama 36109. 1949- .

ALABAMA ADMINISTRATIVE CODE. Legislative Reference Service, Administrative Procedure Division, 11 South Union Street, Montgomery, Alabama 36130. 1985- .

ALABAMA ADMINISTRATIVE MONTHLY. Legislative Reference Service, Administrative Procedure Division, Suite 100, State Capitol, 750 Washington Avenue, Montgomery, Alabama 36130. 1982- . (Monthly).

ALABAMA CRIMINAL CODE. Michie Company, P.O. Box 7587, Charlottesville, Virginia 22906-7587. 1985- . (Title 13A of the Code of Alabama). (Annual Supplements).

CODE OF ALABAMA. Michie Company, P.O. Box 7587, Charlottesville, Virginia 22906-7587. 1975- . (Annual Supplements).

LOOSELEAF SERVICES AND REPORTERS

ALABAMA APPELLATE COURT REPORTS. West Publishing Company, P.O. Box 64526, 50 West Kellogg Boulevard, St. Paul, Minnesota 55164-0526. 1910-1976. (Alabama Court of Civil Appeals).

ALABAMA REPORTS. West Publishing Company, P.O. Box 64526, 50 West Kellogg Boulevard, St. Paul, Minnesota 55164-0526. 1840-1975. (Alabama Supreme Court).

ALABAMA RULES ANNOTATED. Michie Company, P.O. Box 7587, Charlottesville, Virginia 22906-7587. Annual.

ALABAMA RULES OF CIVIL PROCEDURE ANNOTATED. Second Edition. (Alabama Practice Series). Champ Lyons, Jr. West Publishing Company, P.O. Box 64526, 50 West Kellogg Boulevard, St. Paul, Minnesota 55164-0526. 1986- . (Periodic Supplements).

ALABAMA RULES OF COURT. West Publishing Company, P.O. Box 64526, 50 West Kellogg Boulevard, St. Paul, Minnesota 55164-0526. Annual.

SOUTHERN REPORTER. West Publishing Company, P.O. Box 64526, 50 West Kellogg Boulevard, St. Paul, Minnesota 55164-0526. 1887- .

ATTORNEY GENERAL OPINIONS

ATTORNEY GENERAL REPORTS AND OPINIONS. Legislative Reference Service. 11 South Union Street, Montgomery, Alabama 36130. Irregular.

QUARTERLY REPORT OF THE ATTORNEY GENERAL OF ALABAMA (1935). Attorney General's Office, Montgomery, Alabama. Also Available On Microfilm: Trans-Media Publications, Condyne--The Oceana Group, Division of Oceana Publications, 75 Main Street, Dobbs Ferry, New York 10522. 1882-1980. Microfiche: William S. Hein and Company, Incorporated, Hein Building, 1285 Main Street, Buffalo, New York 14209. 1981- . Also available on Lexis: January 1977- .

ETHICS OPINIONS, CODES, RULES

CODE OF PROFESSIONMAL RESPOSIBILITY OF THE ALABAMA STATE BAR. Alabama State Bar, 1019 South Perry Street, Montgomery, Alabama 36104. 1986. (Includes Rules Of Disciplinary Enforcement and Ethical Considerations. Ethics Opinions for Alabama are issued by the General Counsel's office of the Alabama State Bar. These opinions are not published in full-text. Selected abstacts are published in the ABA/BNA Lawyers' Manual and in the Alabama Lawyer . For further information concerning these opinions, or to obtain full-text opinions, contact Vivian Freeman, Alabama State Bar, 1019 South Perry Street, Montgomery, Alabama 36104. 205-269-1514.

ETHICS COMMISSION ADVISORY OPINIONS. Legislative Reference Service. 11 South Union Street, Montgomery, Alabama 36130. Irregular.

JURY INSTRUCTIONS

ALABAMA JURY INSTRUCTIONS WITH FORMS. Walter B. Jones. West Publishing Company, P.O. Box 64526, 50 West Kellogg Boulevard, St. Paul, Minnesota 55164-0526. 1953- . (Periodic Supplements). (Civil and Criminal Jury Forms).

ALABAMA PATTERN JURY INSTRUCTIONS: CIVIL. Alabama Pattern Jury Instruction Committee. Lawyers Co-Operative Company, Aqueduct Building, Rochester, New York 14694. 1974- . (Periodic Supplements).

ALABAMA PATTERN JURY INSTRUCTIONS: CRIMINAL. Developed by the Alabama Bar Institute for Continuing Legal Education in Cooperation with the Alabama Circuit Judges Association and the Administrative Office of the Courts. Alabama Bar Institute for Continuing Legal Education, P.O. Box 870384, Tuscaloosa, Alabama 35487. 1980- . (Periodic Supplements).

PROPOSED PATTERN JURY INSTRUCTIONS FOR USE IN THE GUILT STAGE OF CAPITAL CASES TRIED UNDER ACT NUMBER 81-178. Alabama Bar Institute for Continuing Legal Education, P.O. Box 870384, Tuscaloosa, Alabama 39487. October, 1982.

DIGESTS, INDEXES, ABSTRACTS, CITATORS

ALABAMA ADVANCE ANNOTATION SERVICE. Michie Company, P.O. Box 7587, Charlottesville, Virginia 22906-7587. 1984- .

ALABAMA DIGEST. West Publishing Company, P.O. Box 64526, 50 West Kellogg Boulevard, St. Paul, Minnesota 55164-0526. (Annual Supplements).

SHEPARD'S ALABAMA CITATIONS. Shepard's/McGraw-Hill, P.O. Box 1235, Colorado Springs, Colorado 80901. 1972- . (Six Supplements Per Year).

SHEPARD'S SOUTHERN REPORTER CITATIONS. Shepard's/ McGraw-Hill, P.O. Box 1235, Colorado Springs, Colorado 80901. 1907- . (Monthly Supplements).

SOUTHERN DIGEST. West Publishing Company, P. O. Box 64526, 50 West Kellogg Boulevard, St. Paul, Minnesota 55164-0526. 1933- . (Annual Supplements).

LAW REVIEWS AND PERIODICALS

ALABAMA LAW REVIEW. University of Alabama School of Law, Tuscaloosa, Alabama 35487. (Quarterly).

ALABAMA LAWYER. Alabama State Bar, 415 Dexter Avenue, P.O. Box 671, Montgomery, Alabama 36104. (Seven issues per year).

ALABAMA TRIAL LAWYER'S JOURNAL. Alabama Trial Lawyer's Association, 328 Dexter Avenue, Montgomery, Alabama 36104. (Irregular).

BIRMINGHAM BAR BULLETIN. Birmingham Bar Association, 109 North 20th Street, Second Floor, Birmingham, Alabama 35203. (Quarterly).

CUMBERLAND-SAMFORD LAW REVIEW. Cumberland School of Law of Samford University. Samford University, Box 2268, 800 Lakeshore Drive, Birmingham, Alabama 35229. 1975- . (Three Issues Per Year).

MOBILE BAR ASSOCIATION MONTHLY BULLETIN. Mobile Bar Association, P.O. Drawer 2005, Mobile Alabama 36652. (Monthly).

NEWSLETTERS AND NEWSPAPERS

ALABAMA EMPLOYMENT LAW LETTER. M. Lee Smith Publishers and Printers, 162 Fourth Avenue North, Nashville, Tennessee 37219. Monthly.

ASSOCIATIONS AND PROFESSIONAL SOCIETIES

ALABAMA BAR ASSOCIATION, 415 Dexter Avenue, P.O. Box 671, Montgomery Alabama 36101. (205) 269-1515.

ALABAMA BAR INSTITUTE FOR CONTINUING LEGAL EDUCATION. P.O. Box 870384, Tuscaloosa, Alabama 35487. (205) 348-6230.

ALABAMA LAW INSTITUTE. P.O. Box 1425, University, Alabama 35486. (205) 348-7411.

BIRMINGHAM BAR ASSOCIATION, 109 North Twentieth Street, Second Floor, Birmingham, Alabama 35203. (205) 251-8006.

LAWYER REFERRAL SERVICE. Alabama Bar Association, P.O. Box 671, Montgomery, Alabama 36101. (205) 269-1515.

LEGAL SERVICES CORPORATION OF ALABAMA. 207 Montgomery Street, 900 Bell Building, Montgomery, Alabama 36104. (205) 832-4570.

MOBILE BAR ASSOCIATION, P.O. Drawer 2005, Mobile, Alabama 36652. (205) 433-9790.

STATE LAW LIBRARY. 445 Dexter Avenue, Judicial Building, Montgomery, Alabama 36130. (205) 261-4347.

DIRECTORIES

ALABAMA BAR DIRECTORY. The Desk Book Committee of the Alabama State Bar Association, P.O. Box 671, Montgomery, Alabama 36101. 1985- .

ALABAMA DIRECTORY. Brown Printing Company, 2734 Gunter Park Drive West, Montgomery, Alabama 36109. (Every Four Years). (State Departments and Agencies, the Judiciary, and Legislators).

ALABAMA GOVERNMENT MANUAL. Alabama Law Institute, Box 1425, Law Center, Room 3261, University, Alabama 35486. (Quadrennial). (State Executives and Regulatory Agencies, State Functions and Legislative and Judicial Branches).

ALABAMA LEGAL DIRECTORY. Legal Directories Publishing Company, 2122 Kidwell Street, P.O. Box 140200, Dallas, Texas 75214-0200. (Annual).

DIRECTORY OF MUNICIPAL OFFICIALS. Alabama League of Municipalities, 535 Adams Avenue, Montgomery, Alabama 36102. 1986- . (Irregular).

OTHER SOURCES

ALABAMA APPELLATE PRACTICE. Alabama Bar Association, P.O. Box 671, Montgomery, Alabama 36101. 1980.

ALABAMA BUSINESS CORPORATION HANDBOOK. Alabama Bar Association, P.O. Box 671, Montgomery, Alabama 36101. 1980.

ALABAMA CIVIL PRACTICE FORMS. Michie Company, P.O. Box 7587, Charlottesville, Virginia 22906-7587. 1986.

ALABAMA CRIMINAL TRIAL PRACTICE. Second Edition. N. Chiarkas. Harrison Company, 3110 Crossing Park, Norcross, Georgia 30091. 1987.

ALABAMA DIVORCE, ALIMONY, AND CHILD CUSTODY. Second Edition. R. McCurley and P. Davis. Harrison Company, 3110 Crossing Park, Norcross, Georgia 30091. 1986.

ALABAMA EVIDENCE. W. Schroeder and others. Harrison Company, 3110 Crossing Park, Norcross, Georgia 30091. 1987.

ALABAMA LAW OF DAMAGES. Second Edition. C. Gamble. Harrison Company, 3110 Crossing Park, Norcross, Georgia 30091. 1988.

ALABAMA LEGAL FORMS ANNOTATED. R. Smith. Harrison Company, 3110 Crossing Park, Norcross, Georgia 30091. 1967- .

ALABAMA LIMITATIONS OF ACTIONS AND NOTICE PROVISIONS. T. Hoff. Harrison Company, 3110 Crossing Park, Norcross, Georgia 30091. 1984.

ALABAMA REAL ESTATE HANDBOOK. Fourth Edition. Robert L. McCurley, Jr. and Penny A. Davis. Michie Company, P.O. Box 7587, Charlottesville, Virginia 22906-7587. 1984- .

ALABAMA TORTS CASE FINDER. A. Howell. Michie Company, P.O. Box 7587, Charlottesville, Virginia 22906-7587. 1984.

HOW TO ADMINISTER ESTATES IN ALABAMA. Second Edition. Alabama Bar Association, P.O. Box 671, Montgomery, Alabama 36101. 1988.

MARITAL LAW. Alabama Bar Association, P.O. Box 671, Montgomery, Alabama 36101. 1976.

MCELROY'S ALABAMA EVIDENCE. Third Edition. C. Gamble. Samford Univerity Press, Birmingham, Alabama. 1987.

WILLIAM'S ALABAMA EDIDENCE. R. Williams. Michie Company, P.O. Box 7587, Charlottesville, Virginia 22906-7587. 1967.

STATES--ALASKA

STATUTES, CODES, STANDARDS, UNIFORM LAWS

ALASKA ADMINISTRATIVE CODE. The Lieutenant Governor's Office. Book Publishing Company, 201 Westlace Avenue, North, Seattle, Washington 98109. 1973- . (Quarterly Supplements).

ALASKA ADMINISTRATIVE JOURNAL. Office of the Lieutenant Governor, Pouch AA, Juneau, Alaska 99811. (Biweekly).

ALASKA ADVANCED ANNOTATION SERVICE. Michie Company, P.O. Box 7587, Charlottesville, Virginia 22906-7587. 1984- .

ALASKA LEGISLATIVE REPORT. Legislative Reporting Service. 1958- .

ALASKA REGISTER QUARTERLY. Lieutenant Governor's Office. Book Publishing Company, 201 Westlace Avenue, North, Seattle, Washington 98109. (Quarterly).

ALASKA STATUTES ANNOTATED. Alaska Legislative Council. Michie Company, P.O. Box 7587, Charlottesville, Virginia 22906-7587. 1962- .

SESSION LAWS, STATE OF ALASKA, (NUMBER) LEGISLATURE, (YEAR). Microfiche: William S. Hein and Company, Incorporated, Hein Building, 1285 Main Street, Buffalo, New York 14209. 1913- . (Title Varies).

LOOSELEAF SERVICES AND REPORTERS

ALASKA CASE NOTES. Pleiades Research Group. 1983- .

ALASKA REPORTER. West Publishing Company, P.O. Box 64526, 50 West Kellogg Boulevard, St. Paul, Minnesota 55164-0526. 1960- .

PACIFIC REPORTER. First and Second Series. West Publishing Company, P.O. Box 64526, 50 West Kellogg Boulevard, St. Paul, Minnesota 55164-0526. 1883- .

ATTORNEY GENERAL OPINIONS

ATTORNEY GENERAL REPORTS AND OPINIONS: ALASKA. Microfilm. Trans-Media Publications, Condyne--The Oceana Group, Division of Oceana Publications, 75 Main Street, Dobbs Ferry, New York 10522. 1917-1968. Microfiche. William S. Hein and Company, Incorporated, Hein Building, 1285 Main Street, Buffalo, New York 14209. 1969- . Lexis: January 1977- . Westlaw: 1977- .

FORMAL AND INFORMAL OPINIONS OF THE ATTORNEY GENERAL OF ALASKA. State Publishing and Distribution center, P.O. Box G, Juneau, Alaska 94811. 1959- . Microfiche (Also available on Lexis: 1977- ; Westlaw 1977-).

INFORMAL OPINIONS OF THE OFFICE OF THE ATTORNEY GENERAL. Department of Law, P.O. Box K, Juneau, Alaska 99811. 1973- .

OPINIONS OF THE ATTORNEY. Department of Law, P.O. Box K, Juneau, Alaska 99811. 1959- .

ETHICS OPINIONS, CODES, RULES

ALASKA CODE OF PROFESSIONAL RESPONSIBILITY and the RULES OF DISCIPLINARY ENFORCMENT are published in the ALASKA RULES OF COURT.

ALASKA COURT RULES. West Publishing Company, 50 West Kellogg Boulevard, St. Paul, Minnesota 55164. 1970- .

ALASKA ETHICS OPINIONS. Published in full-text in the Alaska Bar Rag . 1968- . Abstacts of opinions are published in the ABA/BNA Lawyers' Reference Manual (Ethics Opiion Volume). For further information concerning these opinions, contact the Disciplinary Counsel of the Alaska Bar Association, P.O. Box 100279, Anchorage, Alaska 99510. 907-272-7469.

ALASKA RULES OF COURT (Official Edition). Book Publishing Company, 201 Westlake Avenue, North, Seattle, Washington 98109. 1963- . (Periodic Supplements).

JURY INSTRUCTIONS

ALASKA CIVIL PATTERN JURY INSTRUCTION. Alaska Bar Association, P.O. Box 100279, Anchorage, Alaska 99510. 1984.

ALASKA PATTERN JURY INSTRUCTIONS (CRIMINAL). Alaska Committee on Pattern Jury Instructions (Criminal). Alaska Court System, Office of the Administrative Director, 303 K Street, Anchorage, Alaska 99501. 1980- . (Periodic Supplements).

DIGESTS, INDEXES, ABSTRACTS, CITATORS

ALASKA DIGEST. West Publishing Company, P.O. Box 64526, 50 West Kellogg Boulevard, St. Paul, Minnesota 55164-0526. 1969- . (Annual Supplements).

PACIFIC DIGEST. First and Second Series. West Publishing Company, P.O. Box 64526, 50 West Kellogg Boulevard, St. Paul, Minnesota 55164-0526. 1932- . (Annual Supplements).

SHEPARD'S ALASKA CITATIONS. Shepard's/McGraw-Hill, P.O. Box 1235, Colorado Springs, Colorado 80901. 1983- . (Three pamphlets per year).

SHEPARD'S PACIFIC REPORTER CITATIONS. Shepard's/ McGraw-Hill, P.O. Box 1235, Colorado Springs, Colorado 80901. (Monthly Supplements).

LAW REVIEWS AND PERIODICALS

ALASKA BAR BRIEF. Alaska Bar Brief, P.O.Box 279, Anchorage, Alaska 99510. 1963-1978. (Monthly).

THE ALASKA BAR RAG. Alaska Bar Association, P.O. Box 100279, Anchorage, Alaska 99510. 1978- . (Monthly).

ALASKA LAW REVIEW. Duke University School of Law, Durham, North Carolina 27706. (Biannual). (Formerly U.C. Alaska Law Review).

NEWSLETTERS AND NEWSPAPERS

JURY VERDICTS NORTHWEST/ALASKA. Jury Verdict Northwest, P.O. Box 1165, Seattle, Washington 98111. Bimonthly.

LEGISLATIVE REPORTING SERVICE. P.O. Box 1376, Juneau, Alaska 99802. Biweekly.

ASSOCIATIONS AND PROFESSIONAL SOCIETIES

ALASKA BAR ASSOCIATION, P.O. Box 100279, Anchorage, Alaska 99510. (907) 272-7469.

LAWYER REFERRAL SERVICE. Alaska Bar Association, P.O. Box 100279, Anchorage, Alaska 99510. (907) 272-7469.

DIRECTORIES

ALASKA DIRECTORY OF ATTORNEYS. Todd Communication, 203 West Fifteenth Avenue, Suite 102, Anchorage, Alaska 99501. (Annual).

ALASKA MUNICIPAL OFFICIALS DIRECTORY. Alaska Municipal League, 217 Second Street, Suite 200, Juneau, Alaska 99801. (Annual).

OTHER SOURCES

ALASKA CORPORATION MANUAL. W. Walker. That New Publishing Company, 1525 Eielson Street, Fairbanks, Alaska 99701. 1977.

ALASKA LEGAL AND LAW RELATED PUBLICATIONS. A. Ruzicka. American Associaton of Law Libraries, 53 West Jackson Boulevard, Suite 940, Chicago, Illinois 60604. 1986.

ALASKA MINERAL DEVELOPMENT. Rocky Mountain Mineral Law Foundation, 7039 East Eighteenth Avenue, Denver, Colorado 80220. 1978.

CONFLICTS OF LAW: A N0RTHWEST PERSPECTIVE. J. Natziger. Butterworth Legal Publishers, 90 Stiles Road, Salem, New Hampshire 03079. 1985.

STATES--ARIZONA

STATUTES, CODES, STANDARDS, UNIFORM LAWS

ARIZONA ADMINISTRATIVE CODE. Office of the Secretary of State, State Capitol, West Wing, Suite 706, Phoenix, Arizona 1975- .

ARIZONA ADMINISTRATIVE DIGEST. Director of Publications, Office of the Secretary of State, State Capitol, West Wing, Suite 706, Phoenix, Arizona 85007. (Monthly).

ARIZONA ADMINISTRATIVE REGISTER. Office of the Secretary of State, State Capitol, West Wing, Suite 706, Phoenix Arizona 85007. (Monthly). (Semiannual index issued in June and December).

ARIZONA LEGISLATIVE SERVICE. West Publishing Company, P.O. Box 64526, 50 West Kellogg Boulevard, St. Paul, Minnesota 55164-0526. (Irregular).

ARIZONA REVISED STATUTES ANNOTATED. West Publishing Company, P.O. Box 64526, 50 West Kellogg Boulevard, St. Paul, Minnesota 55164-0526. 1984- . (Annual Supplement).

STATE OF ARIZONA OFFICIAL COMPILATION ADMINISTRATIVE CODES AND REGULATIONS. Department of State, State Capitol, Phoenix, Arizona 85007. 1975- . (Looseleaf). (Periodic Supplements).

LOOSELEAF SERVICES AND REPORTERS

ARIZONA ADVANCE REPORTS. Code * Company, P.O. Box 1471, Provo, Utah 84603. Biweekly.

ARIZONA REPORTS. West Publishing Company, P.O. Box 64526, 50 West Kellogg Boulevard, St. Paul, Minnesota 55164-0526. 1866- .

PACIFIC REPORTER. First and Second Series. West Publishing Company, P.O. Box 64526, 50 West Kellogg Boulevard, St. Paul, Minnesota 55164-0526. 1884- .

ATTORNEY GENERAL OPINIONS

ARIZONA STATE ATTORNEY GENERAL REPORTS. Microfilm. Trans-Media Publications, Condyne--The Oceana Group, Division of Oceana Publications, 75 Main Street, Dobbs Ferry, New York 10522. 1978-1983. Microfiche: William S. Hein and Company, Incorporated, Hein Building, 1285 Main Street, Buffalo, New York 14209. 1983- . Also available on Lexis: January, 1977; Westlaw: 1977.

ETHICS OPINIONS, CODES, RULES

ARIZONA ETHICS OPINIONS. Issued by the Committee on the Rules of Professional Conduct, State Bar of Arizona, 363 North First Avenue, Phoenix, Arizona 85003. 1980- . (For further information concerning these opinions contact Regina Williams at the State Bar of Arizona, 602-252-4804).

ARIZONA RULES OF COURT: STATE AND FEDERAL. West Publishing Company, P.O. Box 64526, 50 West Kellogg Boulevard, St. Paul, Minnesota 55164-0526. (Annual). (Also in Arizona Revised Statutes Volume 16, 17 and 17A). 1984- . (Annual Supplements).

1984 SPECIAL PAMPHLET, ARIZONA RULES OF THE SUPREME COURT, RULES OF PROFESSIONAL CONDUCT (Effective Febuary 1, 1985). West Publishing Company, P.O. Box 64526, 50 West Kellogg Boulevard, St. Paul, Minnesota 55164-0526. 1984.

JURY INSTRUCTIONS

RECOMMENDED ARIZONA JURY INSTRUCTIONS (CIVIL AND CRIMINAL). Arizona Supreme Court Committee on Uniform Instructions. State Bar of Arizona, 363 North First Avenue, Phoenix, Arizona 85003. 1974- . (Periodic Supplements).

RECOMMENDED ARIZONA JURY INSTRUCTIONS (CRIMINAL). Arizona Supreme Court Committee on Uniform Instructions (Criminal). State Bar of Arizona, 363 North First Avenue, Phoenix, Arizona 85003. 1980- . (Periodic Supplements).

DIGESTS, INDEXES, ABSTRACTS, CITATORS

ARIZONA DIGEST. West Publishing Company, P.O. Box 64526, 50 West Kellogg Boulevard, St. Paul, Minnesota 55164-0526. 1978- . (Annual Supplements).

PACIFIC DIGEST. First and Second Series. West Publishing Company, P.O. Box 64526, 50 West Kellogg Boulevard, St. Paul, Minnesota 55164-0526. 1932- . (Annual Supplements).

SHEPARD'S ARIZONA CITATIONS. Shepard's/McGraw-Hill, P.O. Box 1235, Colorado Springs, Colorado 80901. 1919- . (Periodic Supplements).

SHEPARD'S PACIFIC REPORTER CITATIONS. Shepard's/McGraw-Hill, P.O. Box 1235, Colorado Springs, Colorado 80901. (Monthly Supplements).

LAW REVIEWS AND PERIODICALS

ARIZONA BAR BRIEFS. State Bar of Arizona, 363 North First Avenue, Phoenix, Arizona 85003. (Monthly).

ARIZONA BAR JOURNAL. State Bar of Arizona, 363 North First Avenue, Phoenix, Arizona 85003. (Bimonthly).

ARIZONA LAW REVIEW. University of Arizona College of Law, Tucson, Arizona 85721. (Quarterly).

ARIZONA STATE LAW JOURNAL. Arizona State University College of Law, Tempe, Arizona 85287. (Quarterly).

ARIZONA STATE UNIVERSITY LAW FORUM. Arizona State University College of Law, Tempe, Arizona 85287. (Semiannual)

NEWSLETTERS AND NEWSPAPERS

ARIZONA ENVIRONMENTAL LAW LETTER. M. Lee Smith Publishers and Printers, 162 Fourth Avenue North, Nashville, Tennessee 37219. Monthly.

ARIZONA LEGISLATIVE REPORT. Arizona News Service, Incorporated, 14 North Eighteenth Avenue, Phoenix, Arizona 85007. Daily when in session.

PAALL NEWS. Phoenix Area Association of Law Libraries, c/o Maricopa County Law Library, 101 West Jefferson, Phoenix, Arizona 85003. Quarterly.

ASSOCIATIONS AND PROFESSIONAL SOCIETIES

MARICOPA COUNTY BAR ASSOCIATION, 333 West Roosevelt, Suite 604, Phoenix, Arizona 85003. (602) 257-4200.

STATE BAR OF ARIZONA, 363 North First Avenue, Phoenix, Arizona 85003. (602) 252-4804.

DIRECTORIES

LOCAL GOVERNMENT DIRECTORY (ARIZONA). League of Arizona Cities and Towns, 1820 West Washington Street, Phoenix, Arizona 85007. (Semiannual).

OTHER SOURCES

ARIZONA AGENCY HANDBOOK. Office of the Attorney General, 1275 West Washington, Phoenix, Arizona 85007. 1981- .

ARIZONA APPELLATE HANDBOOK. State Bar of Arizona, 363 North First Avenue, Phoenix, Arizona 85003. 1978- .

ARIZONA CIVIL TRIAL PRACTICE. C. Smith. West Publishing Company, 50 West Kellogg Boulevard, St. Paul, Minnesota 55164. 1986.

ARIZONA COURTROOM EVIDENCE MANUAL. Second Edition. C. McClennen, Editor. State Bar of Arizona, 363 North First Avenue, Phoenix, Arizona 85003. 1988- .

ARIZONA LAND USE LAW. D. Jorden and M. House. State Bar of Arizona, 363 North First Avenue, Phoenix, Arizona 85003. 1988.

ARIZONA LAW OF EVIDENCE. Second Edition. M. Udall. West Publishing Company, 50 West Kellogg Boulevard, St. Paul, Minnesota 55164. 1982.

ARIZONA LEGAL FORMS: DOMESTIC RELATIONS. J. Wolf. West Publishing Company, 50 West Kellogg Boulevard, St. Paul, Minnesota 55164. 1988.

ARIZONA PRACTICE MANUAL. D. Nix, Editor. State Bar of Arizona, 363 North First Avenue, Phoenix, Arizona 85003. 1985.

ARIZONA PROBATE. T. Wiley. Bancroft-Whitney Company, P.O. Box 7005, San Francisco, California 94120. 1980- .

ARIZONA REAL ESTATE PRACTICE. Second Editon. C. Rambo, Editor. State Bar of Arizona, 363 North First Avenue, Phoenix, Arizona 85003. 1982- .

SURVEY OF ARIZONA STATE LEGAL AND LAW RELATED DOCUMENTS. R. Teenstra and others. American Association of Law Libraries, 53 West Jackson Boulevard, Suite 940, Chicago, Illinois 60604. 1984.

STATES--ARKANSAS

STATUTES, CODES, STANDARDS, UNIFORM LAWS

ACTS OF ARKANSAS. The Hurley Company, Camden, Arkansas 71701. 1960.

ACTS OF THE GENERAL ASSEMBLY. Secretary of State, Accounting Division, Capitol Building, Little Rock, Arkansas 72201-1094. 1837- .

ARKANSAS ADVANCE LEGISLATIVE SERVICE. Michie Company, P.O. Box 7587, Charlottesville, Virginia 22906-7587. 1982- .

ARKANSAS CODES OF 1987 ANNOTATED. Michie Company, P. O. Box 7587, Charlottesville, Virginia 22906-7587. 1947- . (Annual Supplements).

ARKANSAS REGISTER. Secretary of State. Arkansas Register Division, Capitol Building, Room 010, Little Rock, Arkansas 72201-1094. 1977- . (Monthly). (Cummulative Index published quarterly with an annual Cummulative in June).

LOOSELEAF SERVICES AND REPORTERS

ARKANSAS APPELLATE REPORTS. State of Arkansas. The Hurley Company, Camden, Arkansas 71701. 1981- . (Bound with Arkansas Reports).

ARKANSAS CASES. West Publishing Company, P.O. Box 64526, 50 West Kellogg Boulevard, St. Paul, Minnesota 55164-0526. 1886- . (Arkansas Supreme Court; Arkansas Court of Appeals 1979-).

ARKANSAS LAW REPORTER. Democrat Printing and Lithographing Company, Little Rock, Arkansas 72201. 1911-1916. (Sixty-three Volumes).

ARKANSAS REPORTS. Arkansas Supreme Court, Published by the State of Arkansas, Little Rock, Arkansas 72201. 1837- .

SOUTHWESTERN REPORTER. (First and Second Series). West Publishing Company, P.O. Box 64526, 50 West Kellogg Boulevard, St. Paul, Minnesota 55164-0526. 1886- . (Arkansas Supreme Court; Arkansas Court of Appeals 1979-).

ATTORNEY GENERAL OPINIONS

ARKANSAS STATE ATTORNEY GENERAL OPINIONS. These are published individually by the office of the Attorney General Of Arkansas, 201 East Markham Street, Little Rock, Arkansas 72201. Also available on Lexis: January 1977-; Westlaw: 1977- .

DIGEST OF DECISIONS. Office of the Attorney General, 201 East Markham Street, Little Rock, Arkansas 72201. 1980- .

ETHICS OPINIONS, CODES, RULES

ARKANSAS COURT RULES ANNOTATED. Michie/Bobbs-Merrill Law Publishing Company, P.O. Box 7587, Charlottesville, Virginia 22906-7587. (Annual). (Also in Arkansas Statutes Annotated, Volume 3A).

ARKANSAS PROFESSIONAL AND JUDICIAL ETHICS. Howard W. Brill. Darby Printing Company, 715 West Whitehall Street, Southwest, Atlanta, Georgia 30310. 1986.

LOCAL COURT RULES. Arkansas Bar Association, 400 West Markham, Little Rock, Arkansas 72201. 1983- .

JURY INSTRUCTIONS

ARKANSAS MODEL JURY INSTRUCTIONS: CIVIL. Second Edition. Arkansas Supreme Court Committee on Jury Instructions. West Publishing Company, P.O. Box 64526, 50 West Kellogg Boulevard, St. Paul, Minnesota 55164-0526. 1974- . (Periodic Supplements).

ARKANSAS MODEL JURY INSTRUCTIONS: CRIMINAL. Arkansas Supreme Court Committee on Criminal Jury Instructions. Michie Company, P.O. Box 7587, Charlottesville, Virginia 22906-7587. 1979- . (Periodic Supplements).

DIGESTS, INDEXES, ABSTRACTS, CITATORS

ARKANSAS DIGEST. West Publishing Company, P.O. Box 64526, 50 West Kellogg Boulevard, St. Paul, Minnesota 55164-0526. 1970- . (Annual Supplements).

SHEPARD'S ARKANSAS CITATIONS. Shepard's/McGraw-Hill, P.O. Box 1235, Colorado Springs, Colorado 80901. 1915- . (Periodic Supplements).

SHEPARD'S SOUTHWESTERN REPORTER CITATIONS. Shepard's/McGraw-Hill, P.O. Box 1235, Colorado Springs, Colorado 80901. (Monthly Supplements).

SOUTH WEST DIGEST. West Publishing Company, 50 West Kellogg Boulevard, St. Paul, Minnesota 55164. 1937- .

LAW REVIEWS AND PERIODICALS

ARKANSAS BAR ASSOCIATION NEWS BULLETIN. Arkansas Bar Association. 400 West Markham, Little Rock, Arkansas 72201. (Monthly).

ARKANSAS LAW NOTES: Reports to the Arkansas Bar. University of Arkansas School of Law, Waterman Hall, Fayetteville, Arkansas 72701. (Annually).

ARKANSAS LAW REVIEW. University of Arkansas School of Law, Waterman Hall, Fayetteville, Arkansas 72701. (Quarterly).

ARKANSAS LAWYER. Arkansas Bar Association, 400 West Markham, Little Rock, Arkansas 72201. (Quarterly).

NEWSLETTERS AND NEWSPAPERS

ADMINISTRATION LAW LETTER. Arkansas Trial Lawyers Association, Administration Law Division, 400 West Capitol, Suite 2648, Little Rock, Arkansas 72201. Quarterly.

ARKANSAS BAR ASSOCIATION NEWSBULLETIN. Arkansas Bar Association, 400 West Mankhaur, Little Rock, Arkansas 72201. Quarterly.

ARKANSAS CAPITOL REPORT. Arkansas State Chambers of Commerce and Associated Industries of Arkansas, P.O. Box 3645, Little Rock, Arkansas 72203. Weekly when in session.

ARKANSAS DAILY LEGISLATIVE DIGEST. Arkansas Legislative Digest, Incorporated, 1401 West Sixth Street, Little Rock, Arkansas 72201. Daily when in session.

THE ARKANSAS LEGISLATIVE REPORT. Legislative Reports, Incorporated, P.O. Box 1304, Little Rock, Arkansas 72203. Daily when in session.

ATLA ADVOCATE. Arkansas Trial Lawyers Association, Administration Law Division, 400 West Capitol, Suite 2648, Little Rock, Arkansas 72201. Quarterly.

ATLA DOCKET. Arkansas Trial Lawyers Association, Administration Law Division, 400 West Capitol, Suite 2648, Little Rock, Arkansas 72201. Quarterly.

FAMILY LAW SECTION NEWSLETTER. Arkansas Bar Association, 400 West Mankhaur, Little Rock, Arkansas 72201. Quarterly.

INTERIM LEGISLATIVE REPORTING SERVICE. Arkansas Legislative Digest, Incorporated, 1401 West Sixth Street, Little Rock, Arkansas 72201. Weekly.

LEGISLATIVE BULLETIN. Arkansas Trial Lawyers Association, Administration Law Division, 400 West Capitol, Suite 2648, Little Rock, Arkansas 72201. Weekly when in session.

LEGISLATIVE NEWSLETTER. Arkansas Bar Association, 400 West Markham, Little Rock, Arkansas 72201. Weekly when in session.

WORKERS COMP LETTER. Arkansas Law Letter, Incorporated, P.O. Box 1304, Little Rock, Arkansas 72203. Monthly.

ASSOCIATIONS AND PROFESSIONAL SOCIETIES

ARKANSAS BAR ASSOCIATION, 400 West Markham, Little Rock, Arkansas 72201. (501) 375-4605.

DIRECTORIES

ARKANSAS LEGAL DIRECTORY. Legal Directories Publishing Company, 2122 Kidwell, P.O. Box 140200, Dallas, Texas 75214-0200. (Annual).

ARKANSAS STATE DIRECTORY. Heritage Publishing Company, 4100 Heritage Drive, North Little Rock, Arkansas 72117. (Biennial).

DIRECTORY OF ARKANSAS MUNICIPAL OFFICIALS. Arkansas Municipal League, Second and Willow Streets, North Little Rock, Arkansas 72115. (Annual).

OTHER SOURCES

ARKANSAS CIVIL PRACTICE AND PROCEDURE. D. Newbern. Harrison Company, 3110 Crossing Park, Norcross, Georgia 30091. 1985.

ARKANSAS FORM BOOK. R. Wright. Arkansas Bar Association, 400 West Markham, Little Rock, Arkansas 72201. 1988- .

ARKANSAS LAW OF DAMAGES. H. Brill. Harrison Company, 3110 Crossing Park, Norcross, Georgia 30091. 1984.

ARKANSAS LEGAL BIBLIOGRAPHY: DOCUMENTS AND SELECTED COMMERCIAL TITLES. L. Foster. American Association of Law Libraries, 53 West Jackson Boulevard, Suite 940, Chicago, Illinois 60604. 1988.

ARKANSAS SENIOR CITIZENS' HANDBOOK: A LEGAL GUIDE. Third Edition. Arkansas Bar Association, 400 West Markham, Little Rock, Arkansas 72201. 1984.

ARKANSAS WRONGFUL DEATH ACTIONS. O. Harris. Harrison Company, 3110 Crossing Park, Norcross, Georgia 30091. 1984.

CRIMINAL LAW HANDBOOK. Arkansas Bar Association, 400 West Markham, Little Rock, Arkansas 72201. 1985- .

TRIAL HANDBOOK FOR ARKANSAS LAWYERS. J. Hill. Lawyers Cooperative Publishing Company, Aqueduct Building, Rochester, New York 14694. 1986.

STATES--CALIFORNIA

STATUTES, CODES, STANDARDS, UNIFORM LAWS

CALIFORNIA ADMINISTRATIVE CODE. Office of Administrative Hearings, Department of General Services. Distributed by State of California, Documents Section, P.O. Box 20191, Sacramento, California 95820. 1945- . (Weekly Supplements). (Also available on Microfiche from University Microfilms, Incorporated, 1977).

CALIFORNIA ADMINISTRATIVE NOTICE REGISTER. Office of Administrative Hearings, Department of General Services, North Highlands, California 95660. (Weekly).

DEERING'S ANNOTATED CALIFORNIA CODE. Lawyers Co-Operative Company, Aqueduct Building, Rochester, New York 14694. 1957- . (Annual Supplements).

DEERING'S CALIFORNIA GENERAL LAWS ANNOTATED. Bancroft-Whitney Company, P.O. Box 7005, San Francisco, California 94120. 1960- .

STATE ADMINISTRATIVE MANUAL (SAM). California Department of Finance, Sacramento, California 94244. 1953- .

STATUTES OF CALIFORNIA. Office of Procurement, Publications Section, Department of General Services, State of California, P. O. Box 1015, North Highlands, California 95660. 1849- .

WEST'S ANNOTATED CALIFORNIA CODE. West Publishing Company, P. O. Box 64526, 50 West Kellogg Boulevard, St. Paul, Minnesota 55164-0526. 1981- . (Annual Supplements).

WEST'S CALIFORNIA LEGISLATIVE SERVICE. West Publishing Company, P.O. Box 64526, 50 West Kellogg Boulevard, St. Paul, Minnesota 55164-0526. (Irregular Supplements).

LOOSELEAF SERVICES AND REPORTERS

CALIFORNIA APPELLATE DECISIONS. Recorder Printing and Publishing Company, 28 Montgomery Street, San Francisco, California 94104. 1905-1940.

CALIFORNIA APPELLATE REPORTS. (First through Third Series). Lawyers Co-Operative Company, Aqueduct Building, Rochester, New York 14694. 1905- .

CALIFORNIA DECISIONS. The Recorder Printing and Publishing Company, 28 Montgomery Street, San Francisco, California 94104. 1890-1941.

CALIFORNIA REPORTS. (First through Third Series). Lawyers Co-Operative Company, Aqueduct Building, Rochester, New York 14694. 1851- .

CALIFORNIA TAX REPORTER: STATE AND LOCAL. Commerce Clearing House, Incorporated, 4025 West Peterson Avenue, Chicago, Illinois 60646. 1948- . (Periodic Supplements).

PACIFIC REPORTER. (First and Second Series). West Publishing Company, P.O. Box 64526, 50 West Kellogg Boulevard, St. Paul, Minnesota 55164-0526. 1883- . (California Supreme Court, Court of Appeals, and Appellate Department of the Superior Court).

PRENTICE-HALL CALIFORNIA STATE AND LOCAL TAX SERVICE. Prentice-Hall, Incorporated, 113 Sylvan Avenue, Englewood Cliffs, New Jersey 07632. (Looseleaf). (Periodic Supplements).

WEST'S CALIFORNIA REPORTER. West Publishing Company, P.O. Box 64526, 50 West Kellogg Boulevard, St. Paul, Minnesota 55164-0526. 1959- .

ATTORNEY GENERAL OPINIONS

OPINIONS OF THE ATTORNEY GENERAL OF CALIFORNIA. Matthew Bender and Company, Incorporated, 11 Penn Plaza, New York, New York 10001. 1943- . (Monthly Supplements). (Also published in the California Compendium on Professional Responsibility). Microfilm. Trans-Media Publications, Condyne--The Oceana Group, Division of Oceana Publications, 75 Main Street, Dobbs Ferry, New York 10522. Microfiche. William S. Hein and Company, Incorporated, Hein Building, 1285 Main Street, Buffalo, New York 14209. Also available on Lexis: January 1977-; Westlaw: 1977- .

REPORT OF THE ATTORNEY GENERAL OF THE STATE OF CALIFORNIA. California Office of the Attorney General, P.O. Box 942, Sacramento, California 94249. 1850- .

ETHICS OPINIONS, CODES, RULES

CALIFORNIA COMPENDIUM ON PROFESSIONAL RESPONSIBILITY. Paul W. Vapnek, Editor. State Bar of California, 555 Franklin Street, San Francisco, California 94102. 1983- . (Contains Code of Professional Responsibility and Disciplinary Rules and Ethics Opinion). For further information concerning California Ethics Opinions, contact The State Bar of California; Office of Investigations, 1230 West Third Street, Los Angeles, California 90017. (800-843-9053) in Southern California. Or, in Northern California, contact the State Bar of California, Office of Investigations, 555 Franklin Street, San Francisco, California 94102.

LOS ANGELES ETHICS OPINIONS. Full text published in Ethics Opinions , Committee on Legal Ethics, Los Angeles County Bar Association, P. O. Box 55020, Los Angeles, California 90055. 1968- . Full text also published in the L.A. Daily Journal , 210 South Spring Street, Los Angeles, California 90012. (Daily).

MODEL CODE OF PROFESSIONAL RESPONSIBILITY, AND OTHER SELECTED STANDARDS INCLUDING CALIFORNIA RULES ON PROFESSIONAL RESPONSIBILITY. Thomas D. Morgan and Ronald D. Rotunda. Foundation Press Incorporated, 615 Merrick Avenue, Westbury, New York 11590. (Annual).

SAN DIEGO ETHICS OPINIONS. Full text published in Compendium on Professional Responsibility . State Bar of California, 555 Franklin Street, San Francisco, California 94102. 1983- .

SAN FRANCISCO ETHICS OPINIONS. Full text published in Compendium on Professional Responsibility . State Bar of California, 555 Franklin Street, San Francisco, California 94102. 1983- .

COURT RULES

WEST'S CALIFORNIA RULES OF COURT: STATE AND FEDERAL. West Publishing Company, P.O. Box 64526, 50 West Kellogg Boulevard, St. Paul, Minnesota 55164-0526. (Annual). (Also published in West's Annotated California Code , Volume 23 Part 1 and 2).

JURY INSTRUCTIONS

CALIFORNIA JURY INSTRUCTIONS--CIVIL: BOOK OF APPROVED JURY INSTRUCTIONS (BAJI). Seventh Edition. Compiled and Edited by Charles A. Loring. West Publishing Company, P.O. Box 64526, 50 West Kellogg Boulevard, St. Paul, Minnesota 55164-0526. 1986- . (Biennial Supplements).

CALIFORNIA JURY INSTRUCTIONS--CRIMINAL. Fifth Revised Edition. West Publishing Company, P.O. Box 64526, 50 West Kellogg Boulevard, St. Paul, Minnesota 55164-0526. 1988- . (Annual Supplements).

DIGESTS, INDEXES, ABSTRACTS, CITATORS

CALIFORNIA CITATOR GUIDE, OVERRULED AND DISAPPROVED CASES. Lawyers Co-Operative Company, Aqueduct Building, Rochester, New York 14694. 1975- . (Annual Supplements).

CALIFORNIA DIGEST. First and Second Series. West Publishing Company, P.O. Box 64526, 50 West Kellogg Boulevard, St. Paul, Minnesota 55164-0526. 1951- . (Annual Supplement).

CALIFORNIA DIGEST OF OFFICIAL REPORTS. (Third Series). Lawyers Co-Operative Company, Aqueduct Building, Rochester, New York 14694. 1975- .

CALIFORNIA SUBSEQUENT HISTORY TABLE. Second Edition. West Publishing Company, P.O. Box 64526, 50 West Kellogg Boulevard, St. Paul, Minnesota 55164-0526. 1934- . (Periodic Supplements).

NEW CALIFORNIA DIGEST (First and Second Series). Lawyers Co-Operative Company, Aqueduct Building, Rochester, New York 14694. 1930-1972.

PACIFIC DIGEST. West Publishing Company, P.O. Box 64526, 50 West Kellogg Boulevard, St. Paul, Minnesota 55164-0526. 1932- . (Annual Supplements).

SHEPARD'S CALIFORNIA CASE NAMES CITATOR. Shepard's/McGraw-Hill, P.O. Box 1235, Colorado Springs, Colorado 80901. (Periodic Supplements).

SHEPARD'S CALIFORNIA CITATIONS. Shepard's/McGraw-Hill, P.O. Box 1235, Colorado Springs, Colorado 80901. (Eight issues per year).

SHEPARD'S PACIFIC REPORTER CITATIONS. Shepard's/McGraw-Hill, P.O. Box 1235, Colorado Springs, Colorado 80901. (Periodic Supplements).

WEEKLY LAW DIGEST. Weekly Law Journals, 210 South Spring Street, Los Angeles, California 90054. 1936- . (Weekly).

ENCYCLOPEDIAS AND DICTIONARIES

CALIFORNIA JURISPRUDENCE. Third Edition. Lawyers Co-Operative Company, Aqueduct Building, Rochester, New York 14694. 1972- . (Annual Supplements).

WITKIN SUMMARY OF CALIFORNIA LAW. Ninth Edition. B. E. Witkin. Lawyers Co-Operative Company, Aqueduct Building, Rochester, New York 14694. 1987- . (Annual Supplements).

LAW REVIEWS AND PERIODICALS

BERKELEY'S WOMEN'S LAW JOURNAL. Boalt Hall School of Law, University of California - Berkeley, Berkeley, California 94720. (Annual).

CALIFORNIA LAW REVIEW. Boalt Hall School of Law. University of California Press, 2120 Berkeley Way, Berkeley California 94720. (Six Issues per Year).

CALIFORNIA LAWYER. State Bar of California, 555 Franklin Street, San Francisco, California 94102-4498. (Monthly).

THE CALIFORNIA REGULATORY LAW REPORTER. Center for Public Interest Law, University of San Diego School of Law, Alcala Park, San Diego, California 92110. 1981- . (Quartely).

CALIFORNIA WESTERN INTERNATIONAL LAW JOURNAL. Californina Western School of Law, 350 Cedar Street, San Diego, California 92101. (Biannual).

CALIFORNIA WESTERN LAW REVIEW. California Western School of Law, 350 Cedar Street, San Diego, California 92101. (Biannual).

FORUM. California Trial Lawyers Association, 1820 Twelfth Street, Third Floor, Sacramento, California 95814. 1979- . (Formerly the CTLA News).

GLENDALE LAW REVIEW. Glendale University, College of Law, 220 North Glendale Avenue, Glendale, California 91206. (Biannual).

GOLDEN GATE UNIVERSITY LAW REVIEW. Golden Gate University School of Law, 536 Mission Street, San Francisco, California 94105. (Three Issues per Year).

HASTINGS CONSTITUTIONAL LAW QUARTERLY. University of California, Hastings College of Law, 200 McAllister Street, San Francisco, California 94102-4978. (Quarterly).

HASTINGS INTERNATIONAL AND COMPARATIVE LAW REVIEW. University of California, Hastings College of Law, 200 McAllister Street, San Francisco, California 94102-4978. (Three Issues per Year).

HASTINGS LAW JOURNAL. University of California, Hastings College of Law, 200 McAllister Street, San Francisco, California 94102-4978. (Six Isues per Year).

JOURNAL OF THE BEVERLY HILLS BAR ASSOCIATION. Beverly Hills Bar Association, 300 South Beverly Hills Drive, Suite 201, Beverly Hills, California 90212. (Six Issues per Year).

LOS ANGELES LAWYER. Los Angeles County Bar Association, P. O. Box 55020, Los Angeles, California 90055. (Monthly except Combined July-August Issue).

LOYOLA OF LOS ANGELES INTERNATIONAL AND COMPARATIVE LAW JOURNAL. Loyola of Los Angeles School of Law, 1441 West Olympic Boulevard, Los Angeles, California 90015-3980. (Three Issues per Year).

LOYOLA OF LOS ANGELES LAW REVIEW. Loyola of Los Angeles School of Law, 1441 West Olympic Boulevard, Los Angeles, California 90015-3980. (Quarterly).

NORTHRUP UNIVERSITY LAW JOURNAL OF AEROSPACE, BUSINESS AND TAXATION. Northrup University, 5800 West Arbor Vitae Street, Los Angeles, California 90045. (Annual).

ORANGE COUNTY BAR ASSOCIATION BULLETIN. Orange County Bar Association, 601 Civic Drive West, Santa Ana, California 92701-4002. (Monthly).

PACIFIC LAW REVIEW. University of the Pacific, McGeorge School of Law, 3200 Fifth Avenue, Sacramento, California. 95817. (Quarterly).

PEPPERDINE LAW REVIEW. Pepperdine University, 24255 Pacific Coast Highway, Malibu, California 90265. (Quarterly).

SAN DIEGO LAW REVIEW. University of San Diego School of Law, San Diego, California 92110. (Five Issues per Year).

SANTA CLARA COMPUTER AND HIGH TECHNOLOGY LAW JOURNAL. School of Law, Santa Clara University, Santa Clara, California 95053. (Biannual).

SANTA CLARA LAW REVIEW. School of Law, Santa Clara University, Santa Clara, California 95053. (Quarterly).

SOUTHERN CALIFORNIA LAW REVIEW. Gould School of Law, University of Southern California, University Park, Los Angeles, California 90089-0071. (Six Issues per Year).

SOUTHWESTERN UNIVERSITY LAW REVIEW. Southwestern University School of Law, 675 South Westmoreland Avenue, Los Angeles, California 90005. (Quarterly).

STANFORD JOURNAL OF INTERNATIONAL LAW. Stanford University School of Law, Stanford, California 94305. (Biannual).

STANFORD LAW REVIEW. Stanford University School of Law, Crown Quadrangle, Stanford, California 94305. (Six Issues per Year).

UCLA LAW REVIEW. School of Law, University of California-Los Angeles, 405 Hilgard Avenue, Los Angeles, California 90024. (Six issues per year).

UCLA PACIFIC BASIN LAW JOURNAL. School of Law, University of California-Los Angeles, 405 Hilgard Avenue, Los Angeles, California 90024. (Quarterly).

UNIVERSITY OF CALIFORNIA-DAVIS LAW REVIEW. University of California--Davis, Martin Luther King Hall, Davis, California 95616. (Quarterly).

UNIVERSITY OF SAN FRANCISCO LAW REVIEW. University of San Francisco School of Law, Kandrick Hall, 2130 Fulton Street, San Francisco, California, 94117. (Quarterly).

WESTERN STATE UNIVERSITY LAW REVIEW. Western State University Law School, 1111 North State College Boulevard, Fullerton, California 92631. (Biannual).

NEWSLETTERS AND NEWSPAPERS

BARCLAY'S CALIFORNIA ADVANCE CITATOR. Barclay's Law Publishers, 400 Oyster Point Boulevard, Suite 500, South San Francisco, California 94080. Monthly.

THE BOTTOM LINE. State Bar of California, Law Practice Management Section, 555 Franklin Street, San Francisco, California 94102. Bimonthly.

BUSINESS LAW NEWS. State Bar of California, Law Practice Management Section, 555 Franklin Street, San Francisco, California 94102. Quarterly.

CALIFORNIA BUSINESS LAW PRACTITIONER. California Continuing Education of the Bar, 2300 Shattuck Avenue, Berkeley, California 94704. Quarterly.

CALIFORNIA BUSINESS LAW REPORTER. California Continuing Education of the Bar, 2300 Shattuck Avenue, Berkeley, California 94704. Bimonthly.

CALIFORNIA CRIMINAL DEFENSE PRACTICE REPORTER. Matthew Bender and Company, Incorporated, 11 Penn Plaza, New York, New York 10001. Monthly.

CALIFORNIA EMPLOYMENT LAW LETTER. M. Lee Smith Publishers and Printers, 162 Fourth Avenue North, Nashville, Tennessee 37219.

CALIFORNIA FAMILY LAW FIRST ALERT. California Family Law Report, Incorporated, 107 Caledonia Street, Sausalito, California 94965. Weekly.

CALIFORNIA FAMILY LAW MONTHLY. Matthew Bender and Company, Incorporated, 11 Penn Plaza, New York, New York 10001. Monthly.

CALIFORNIA FAMILY LAW REPORT. California Family Law Report, Incorporated, 107 Caledonia Street, Sausalito, California 94965. Monthly.

CALIFORNIA/FEDERAL PERSONNEL LAW UPDATE. Borgman Associates, 321 Lennon Lane, Walnut Creek, California 94598. Monthly.

CALIFORNIA IN PRINT. Government Research, 815 North La Brea Avenue, Suite 197, Inglewood, California 90302. Bimonthly.

CALIFORNIA INSURANCE LAW AND REGULATION REPORTER. Shepard's/McGraw-Hill, P.O. Box 1235, Colorado Springs, Colorado 80901. Monthly.

CALIFORNIA INSURANCE LAW REPORT. Data Research, Incorporated, P.O. Box 490, Rosewood, Minnesota 55068. Monthly.

CALIFORNIA INTERNATIONAL LAW NEWSLETTER. State Bar of California, International Law Section, 555 Franklin Street, San Francisco, California 94102. Quarterly.

CALIFORNIA LABOR AND EMPLOYMENT LAW QUARTERLY. State Bar of California, Labor and Employment Section, 555 Franklin Street, San Francisco, California 94102. Quarterly.

CALIFORNIA LITIGATION. State Bar of California, Litigation Section, 555 Franklin Street, San Francisco, California 94102. Quarterly.

CALIFORNIA PUBLIC FINANCE. American Banker-Bond Buyer, Newsletter Division, P.O. Box 30240, Bethesda, Maryland 20814. Weekly.

CALIFORNIA REAL ESTATE REPORTER. Matthew Bender and Company, Incorporated, 11 Penn Plaza, New York, New York 10001. Monthly.

CALIFORNIA REGULATORY LAW REPORTER. Center for Public Interest Law, University of San Diego School of Law, Alcala Park, San Diego, California 92110. Quarterly.

CALIFORNIA SCHOOL LAW DIGEST. Whittaker Newsletters, 313 South Avenue, Fanwood, New Jersey 07023. Monthly.

CALIFORNIA TORT REPORTER. Shepard's/McGraw-Hill, P.O. Box 1235, Colorado Springs, Colorado 80901. Monthly.

CIVIL LITIGATION REPORTER. California Continuing Education of the Bar, 2300 Shattuck Avenue, Berkeley, California 94704. Bimonthly.

DAILY RECORDER. Daily Journal Company, 1115 H Street, Sacramento, California 95814. (Daily except Saturday and Sunday). (916-444-2355) (Publishes full text of all opinions of all California Appellate Courts and Courts of Appeal, the United States Court of Appeals for the 9th District and the California Supreme Court). (Formerly: Sacramento Legal Press).

ESTATE PLANNING AND CALIFORNIA PROBATE REPORTER. California Continuing Education of the Bar, 2300 Shattuck Avenue, Berkeley, California 94704. Bimonthly.

LOS ANGELES DAILY JOURNAL. 210 South Spring Street, Los Angeles, California 90054. (Daily except Saturdays and Sundays). (213-625-2141)

PREVIEWS OF CALIFORNIA SUPREME COURT CASES. Barclay's Law Publishers, 400 Oyster Point Boulevard, Suite 500, South San Francisco, California 94080. Monthly.

SAN FRANCISCO BANNER DAILY JOURNAL. P.O. Box 11296, San Francisco, California 94101. 1987- . (Daily except Saturdays and Sundays). (415-558-9888). (Publishes full text of all opinions of the United States Supreme Court, United States Court of Appeals for the 9th Circuit, California Supreme Court, and all California Courts of Appeal. Also publishes summaries of cases).

SPIDELL'S CALIFORNIA TAXLETTER. Spidell Publishing, Incorporated, 1110 North Gilbert, Anaheim, California 92801. Monthly.

TRI-SERVICE WEEKLY JURY VERDICT REPORTS. Tri-Service, 205 South Broadway, Suite 718, Los Angeles, California 90012. Weekly.

FORMBOOKS

CAL FORMS: LEGAL AND BUSINESS. Lawyers Co-Operative Company, Aqueduct Building, Rochester, New York 14694. 1985- . (Periodic Supplements).

CALIFORNIA CIVIL LITIGATION FORMS MANUAL. California Continuing Education of the Bar, 2300 Shattuck Avenue, Berkeley, California 94704. 1980- .

CALIFORNIA CRIMINAL FORMS & INSTRUCTIONS. Edward A. Rucker and Mark E. Overland. Lawyers Co-Operative Company, Aqueduct Building, Rochester, New York 14694. 1983- . (Periodic Supplements).

CALIFORNIA FORMS OF PLEADING AND PRACTICE. Matthew Bender and Company, Incorporated, 11 Penn Plaza, New York, New York 10001. 1964- . (Periodic Supplements).

CALIFORNIA JUDICIAL COUNCIL FORMS MANUAL. California Continuing Education of the Bar, 2300 Shattuck Avenue, Berkeley, California 94704. 1981- . (Periodic Supplements).

CALIFORNIA LEGAL FORMS--TRANSACTION GUIDE. Don J. Badger, et al. Matthew Bender and Company, Incorporated, 11 Penn Plaza, New York, New York 10001. 1968- . (Periodic Supplements).

CALIFORNIA PLEADING AND PRACTICE FORMS. Callaghan and Company, 155 Pfingsten Road, Deerfield, Illinois 60015. 1987- . (Periodic Supplements).

CALIFORNIA REAL ESTATE FORMS AND COMMENTARIES. Robert Cheatham and Robert E. Merritt, Jr. Prentice-Hall, Incorporated, 113 Sylvan Avenue, Englewood Cliffs, New Jersey 07632. 1984- . (Annual Supplements).

CALIFORNIA TAXATION FORMS MANUAL. Matthew Bender and Company, Incorporated, 11 Penn Plaza, New York, New York 10001. 1984- . (Periodic Supplements).

OWEN'S CALIFORNIA FORMS AND PROCEDURE. W.B. Owens. Parker and Son Publications, P.O. Box 60001, Los Angeles, California 90060. 1982- . (Six volume looseleaf).

WEST'S ANNOTATED CALIFORNIA CODES JUDICIAL COUNCIL FORMS. (To Accompany Volume 23 of West's Annotated California Codes). West Publishing Company, P.O. Box 64526, 50 West Kellogg Boulevard, St. Paul, Minnesota 55164-0526. 1954- . (Annual).

WEST'S CALIFORNIA CODE FORMS WITH PRACTICE COMMENTARIES. Second Edition. David H. Adams, Katherine L. Dealy, and Brian C. Foster. West Publishing Company, P.O. Box 64526, 50 West Kellogg Boulevard, St. Paul, Minnesota 55164-0526. 1977- . (Periodic Supplements).

PRACTICE MANUALS

BUSINESS LAWYER. Rofert C. Fellmeth and Ralph H. Folsom. Butterwoth Legal Publishers, 90 Stiles Road, Suite 100, Echelon II, Salem, New Hampshire 03079. 1981.

CALIFORNIA ATTORNEY PRACTICE. Matthew Bender and Company, Incorporated, 11 Penn Plaza, New York, New York 10001. (Three Volume Looseleaf). 1986- . (Periodic Supplements).

CALIFORNIA CORPORATE PRACTICE GUIDE. Second Edition. Morgan D. King and Marissa Banez. Lawpress Corporation, P.O. Box 596, Kentfield, California 94914. 1983- . (Annual Supplements).

CALIFORNIA CRIMINAL LAW. Second Edition. B.E. Witkin. Lawyers Cooperative Publishing Company, Aqueduct Building, Rochester, New York 14694. 1988- . (Annual Supplements).

CALIFORNIA DEATH PENALTY DEFENSE MANUAL. California Attorneys for Criminal Justice. California Public Defenders Association, Sacramento, California. 1986- . (Periodic Supplements).

CALIFORNIA EVIDENCE. Third Edition. B.E. Witkin. Lawyers Co-Operative Company, Aqueduct Building, Rochester, New York 14694. 1986- . (Annual Supplements).

CALIFORNIA JUVENILE COURT PRACTICE. California Continuing Education of the Bar, 2300 Shattuck Avenue, Berkeley, California 94704. 1981- . (Periodic Supplements).

CALIFORNIA PRACTICE. Third Edition. West Publishing Company, P.O. Box 64526, 50 West Kellogg Boulevard, St. Paul, Minnesota 55164-0526. 1981- . (Annual Supplements).

CALIFORNIA PRACTICE GUIDE: FAMILY LAW. William P. Hogoboom Donald B. King, Michael Asimov, Editors. The Rutter Group, Encino, California 91316. 1985.

CALIFORNIA PROCEDURE. Third Edition. B.E. Witkin. Lawyers Co-Operative Company, Aqueduct Building, Rochester, New York 14694. 1985- . (Annual Supplements).

CALIFORNIA REGULATORY LAW AND PRACTICE: A REFERENCE TEXT FOR BUSINESS LAWYERS. Robert C. Fellmeth and Ralph H. Folsom. Butterworth Legal Publishers, 90 Stiles Road, Salem, New Hampshire 03079. 1981.

CALIFORNIA SUPERIOR COURT CRIMINAL TRIAL JUDGES' DESKBOOK: 1986 EDITION. Ronald M. George. West Publishing Company, P.O. Box 64526, 50 West Kellogg Boulevard, St. Paul, Minnesota 55164-0526. 1985- . (Annual).

CALIFORNIA TORTS. Neil M. Levy, Michael M. Golden and Leonard Sacks. Matthew Bender and Company, Incorporated, 11 Penn Plaza, New York, New York 10001. (Six Volume Looseleaf). 1985- . (Periodic Supplements).

MARSH'S CALIFORNIA CORPORATION LAW. Second Edition. Harold Marsh, Jr. Law and Business, Incorporated, 855 Valley Road, Clifton, New Jersey 07013. (Looseleaf). 1981- . (Annual Supplements).

MODERN CALIFORNIA DISCOVERY. Third Edition. James E. Hogan. Lawyers Co-Operative Company, Aqueduct Building, Rochester, New York 14694. 1981- . (Annual Supplements).

ORGANIZING CORPORATIONS IN CALIFORNIA. Second Edition. Edward D. Giacomini, John O. Hargrove and Margaret Shulenberger. California Continuing Education of the Bar, 2300 Shattuck Avenue, Berkeley, California 94704. 1983- . (Periodic Supplements).

REAL ESTATE LAW IN CALIFORNIA. Seventh Edition. Arthur G. Bowman and W.D. Milligan. Prentice-Hall, Incorporated, 113 Sylvan Avenue, Englewood Cliffs, New Jersey 07632. 1986- .

TRIAL HANDBOOK FOR CALIFORNIA LAWYERS. Second Edition. Johnathan M. Purver, et al. Lawyers Co-Operative Company, Aqueduct Building, Rochester, New York 14694. 1987- . (Annual Supplements).

MANUALS AND RESEARCH GUIDES

ALMANAC OF CALIFORNIA GOVERNMENT AND POLITICS. California Journal Press, 1714 Capitol Avenue, Sacramento, California 95814. (Biennial).

CALIFORNIA LAW GUIDE. Second Edition. Dan Henke. Parker and Son Publications, Incorporated, P.O. Box 60001, Los Angeles, California 90060. 1976- . (1984 Supplements).

CALIFORNIA PARALEGAL'S GUIDE. Third Revised Edition. Zella Mack. Parker and Son Publications, Incorporated, P.O. Box 60001, Los Angeles, California 90060. 1991.

GUIDE TO CALIFORNIA GOVERNMENT. Thirteenth Edition. League of Women Voters of California. League of Women Voters, 942 Market Street, Sacramento, California 94102. 1986.

RESEARCH IN CALIFORNIA LAW. Second Edition. Myron Fink. Fred O. Dennis and Company, Incorporated, William S. Hein and Company, Incorporated, Hein Building, 1285 Main Street, Buffalo, New York 14209. 1964.

ASSOCIATIONS AND PROFESSIONAL SOCIETIES

BAR ASSOCIATION OF SAN FRANCISCO, 685 Market Street, Suite 700, San Francisco, California 94105. (415) 764-1600.

BAR OF CALIFORNIA. 555 Franklin Street, San Francisco, California 94102. (415) 561-8200.

BEVERLY HILLS BAR ASSOCIATION, 300 South Beverly Hills Drive, Suite 201, Beverly Hills, California 90212. (213) 553-6644.

CALIFORNIA TRIAL LAWYERS ASSOCIATION. 1820 Twelfth Street, Third Floor, Sacramento, California 95814.

FRESNO COUNTY BAR ASSOCIATION, 420 T.W. Patterson Building, Fresno, California 93721.

LONG BEACH BAR ASSOCIATION, 11 Golden Shore, Number 230, Long Beach, California 90802.

LOS ANGELES COUNTY BAR ASSOCIATION, 617 South Olive Street, Los Angeles, California 90014. (213) 627-2727.

MARIN COUNTY BAR ASSOCIATION, 1010 B Street, Suite 419, San Rafael, California 94901.

ORANGE COUNTY BAR ASSOCIATION, 601 Civic Center Drive West, Santa Ana, California 92701-4002. (714) 541-6222.

SACRAMENTO BAR ASSOCIATION, 910 H Street, Sacramento, California 95814.

SAN DIEGO COUNTY BAR ASSOCIATION, 1434 Fifth Avenue, San Diego, California 92101. (619) 231-0781.

SANTA BARBARA COUNTY BAR ASSOCIATION, 1111 Garden Street, Suite 106, Santa Barbara, California 93101.

SANTA CLARA COUNTY BAR ASSOCIATION, 2001 Gateway Place, Suite 220 West, San Jose, California 95110. (408) 288-8840.

SANTA MONICA BAR ASSOCIATION, 225 Santa Monica Boulevard, Number 906, Santa Monica, California 90401.

DIRECTORIES

ATTORNEY'S DIRECTORY (San Diego County, California). Transcript Publishing Company, 861 Sixth Avenue, San Diego, California 92101. (Annual).

ATTORNEY'S DIRECTORY OF SERVICES AND INFORMATION. California Continuing Education of the Bar, 2300 Shattuck Avenue, Berkeley, California 94704. (Annual).

CALIFORNIA AND NEVADA LSC LEGAL SERVICES PROGRAMS DIRECTORY. Western Center on Law and Poverty, 3535 West Sixth Street, Suite 200, Los Angeles, California 90020. (Annual).

CALIFORNIA JOURNAL ALMANAC OF STATE GOVERNMENT AND POLITICS. California Journal Press, 1714 Capitol Avenue, Sacramento, California 95814. (Bienniel).

CALIFORNIA JOURNAL ROSTER AND GOVERNMENT GUIDE. California Journal Press, 1714 Capitol Avenue, Sacramento, California 95814. (Annual).

CALIFORNIA LEGAL DIRECTORY (Including Arizona and Hawaii). Legal Directories Publishing Company, P.O. Box 140200, Dallas, Texas 75214-0200. (Annual).

CALIFORNIA LEGAL EXPERTS DIRECTORY. Summit University Press, Box A, Livingston, Montana 59047-1390. 1986.

DIRECTORY OF CALIFORNIA CORPORATE COUNSEL. State Bar Publications Fulfillment, Department M-121, 144 Townsend Avenue, San Francisco, California 94107. 1985.

GUIDE TO STATE SERVICES (California). California Department of General Services, Box 1015, North Highlands, California 95660. 1982.

LEGAL SERVICES FOR THE DISABLED IN CALIFORNIA - A DIRECTORY. Standing Committee on Legal Rights of Disabled Persons, Legal Services Section, State Bar of California, 555 Franklin Street, San Francisco, California 94102. (Irregular).

UNITED STATES GOVERNMENT OFFICES IN CALIFORNIA: A DIRECTORY. California Institute of Public Affairs, P.O. Box 189040, Sacramento, California 95818. (Irregular).

OTHER SOURCES

RULES REGULATING ADMISSION TO PRACTICE LAW IN CALIFORNIA. State Bar of California, Committee of Bar Examiners, San Francisco, California 94102. (Irregular).

WHERE TO PRACTICE LAW IN CALIFORNIA: STATISTICS ON LAWYERS' WORK. California Continuing Education of the Bar, 2300 Shattuck Avenue, Berkeley, California 94704. 1976.

STATES--COLORADO

STATUTES, CODES, STANDARDS, UNIFORM LAWS

CODE OF COLORADO REGULATIONS. Public Records Corporation, 1666 Lafayette Street, Denver, Colorado 80206. 1977- . (Monthly Supplements).

COLORADO REGISTER. Public Records Corporation, 1666 Lafayette Street, Denver, Colorado 80206. 1978- . (Monthly).

COLORADO REVISED STATUTES. Secretary of State of Colorado. Bradford Publishing Company, 1743 Wazee Street, Denver, Colorado 80202. 1973- . (Annual Supplements).

SESSION LAWS OF COLORADO. Bradford Publishing Company, 1743 Wazee Street, Denver, Colorado 80202. 1879- . (Annual). (Also available on Microfiche).

LOOSELEAF SERVICES AND REPORTERS

COLORADO COURT OF APPEALS REPORTS. Golden Bell Press, 2403 Champa Street, Denver, Colorado 80205. (Volume 1-44). 1891-1980. (Current Official Source: Pacific Reporter, 2nd Series).

COLORADO REPORTER. West Publishing Company, P.O. Box 64526, 50 West Kellogg Boulevard, St. Paul, Minnesota 55164-0526. 1891- . (Colorado Supreme Court and Colorado Court of Appeals).

COLORADO REPORTS. Golden Bell Press, 2403 Champa Street, Denver, Colorado 80205. (Volume 1-200). 1911-1980. (Colorado Supreme Court; Current Official Source: Pacific Reporter, 2nd Series).

PACIFIC REPORTER (First and Second Series) West Publishing Company, P.O. Box 64526, 50 West Kellogg Boulevard, St. Paul, Minnesota 55164-0526. 1883- . (Colorado Supreme Court and Colorado Court of Appeals).

ATTORNEY GENERAL OPINIONS

COLORADO STATE ATTORNEY GENERAL REPORTS AND OPINIONS. Microfilm. Trans-Media Publications, Condyne--The Oceana Group, Division of Oceana Publications, 75 Main Street, Dobbs Ferry, New York 10522. 1887-1966. Microfiche. William S. Hein and Company, Incorporated, Hein Building, 1285 Main Street, Buffalo, New York 14209. 1967- . Also available on Lexis: 1975-; Westlaw: 1977- . Not available in Hard Copy except for opinions on Administrative Rules.

ETHICS OPINIONS, CODES, RULES

COLORADO ETHICS OPINIONS DESKBOOK. Third Edition. Subcommittee of the Ethics Commission of the Colorado Bar. Continuing Legal Education in Colorado, Incorporated. University of Denver Law Center, Huchingson Hall, 1895 Quebec, Denver, Colorado 80200. 1983. (Colorado Ethics Opinions Also Published in The Colorado Lawyer). (For further information concerning ethics opinions, contact the Colorado Supreme Court Grievance Committee, Dominion Plaza Building, 600 Seventeenth Street, Suite 500 South,Denver, Colorado 80202. 303-893-3393).

COURT RULES

COLORADO CIVIL RULES ANNOTATED. Second Edition. R. Hardaway. West Publishing Company, 50 West Kellogg Boulevard, St. Paul, Minnesota 55164. 1985.

COLORADO COURT RULES ANNOTATED. Michie Company, P.O. Box 7587, Charlottesville, Virginia 22906-7587. 1984- . (Periodic Supplements).

COLORADO LOCAL COURT RULES. Colorado Legal Publishing Company, 1360 South Clarkson, Denver, Colorado 80209. 1978- . (Semiannual Supplements).

COLORADO RULES OF COURT. West Publishing Company, P.O. Box 64526, 50 West Kellogg Boulevard, St. Paul, Minnesota 55164-0526. (Annual).

COLORADO RULES OF EVIDENCE ANNOTATED. Second Edition. E. Jacobson and A. Bucholtz. Colorado Legal Publishing Company, 1360 South Clarkson, Suite 300, Denver, Colorado 80209. 1985- .

JURY INSTRUCTIONS

COLORADO JURY INSTRUCTIONS: CIVIL. Second Edition. Colorado Supreme Court Committee on Civil Jury Instructions. Lawyers Co-Operative Company, Aqueduct Building, Rochester, New York 14694. 1980- . (Annual Supplements).

COLORADO JURY INSTRUCTIONS: CRIMINAL. Revised. Colorado Supreme Court Committee on Criminal Jury Instructions. West Publishing Company, P.O. Box 64526, 50 West Kellogg Boulevard, St. Paul, Minnesota 55164-0526. 1983- .

DIGESTS, INDEXES, ABSTRACTS, CITATORS

COLORADO DIGEST. West Publishing Company, P.O. Box 64526, 50 West Kellogg Boulevard, St. Paul, Minnesota 55164-0526. 1978- . (Annual Supplements).

PACIFIC DIGEST. West Publishing Company, P.O. Box 64526, 50 West Kellogg Boulevard, St. Paul, Minnesota 55164-0526. 1932- . (Annual Supplements).

SHEPARD'S COLORADO CITATIONS. Shepard's/McGraw-Hill, P.O. Box 1235, Colorado Springs, Colorado 80901. (Bimonthly).

SHEPARD'S PACIFIC REPORTER CITATIONS. West Publishing Company, P.O. Box 64526, 50 West Kellogg Boulevard, St. Paul, Minnesota 55164-0526. (Monthly Supplements).

LAW REVIEWS AND PERIODICALS

THE COLORADO LAWYER. Colorado Bar Association, 1900 Grant Street, Suite 950, Denver, Colorado 80203-4309. Monthly.

DENVER JOURNAL OF INTERNATIONAL LAW AND POLICY. University of Denver College of Law, 7039 East Eighteenth Avenue, Denver, Colorado 80220. Quarterly.

DENVER UNIVERSITY LAW REVIEW. University of Denver College of Law, 7039 East Eighteenth Avenue, Denver, Colorado 80220. Quarterly.

ON THE RECORD. 1125 Seventeenth Street, Suite 1940, Denver, Colorado 80202. 1986- . Weekly.

TRANSPORTATION LAW JOURNAL. University of Denver College of Law, 7039 East 18th Avenue, Denver, Colorado 80220. 1969- . Annual.

UNIVERSITY OF COLORADO LAW REVIEW. University of Colorado School of Law, Fleming Building, Boulder, Colorado 80309. Quarterly.

NEWSLETTERS AND NEWSPAPERS

CAPITOLINE. Colorado Association of Commerce and Industry, 1776 Lincoln Street, Suite 1200, Denver, Colorado 80203. Weekly when in session.

COLORADO LEGISLATIVE DIGEST. Shoemaker, Wham, and Krisor, 1666 South University Boulevard, Denver, Colorado 80210. Daily when in session.

THE DOCKET. Denver Bar Association, 1900 Grant Street, Suite 950, Denver, Colorado 80203. Monthly.

JURY VERDICT REPORTER OF COLORADO. Jury Verdict Reporter of Colorado, 7396 South Garfield Court, Littleton, Colorado 80122. Bimonthly.

FORMBOOKS

COLORADO CORPORATE FORMS. D. Erickson. Callaghan and Company, 155 Pfingsten Road, Deerfield, Illinois 60015. 1984.

COLORADO ESTATE PLANNING FORMS BOOK. Third Edition. Continuing Legal Education in Colorado, Incorporated. University of Denver Law Center, Huchingson Hall, 1895 Quebec, Denver, Colorado 80200. 1983- . (Periodic Supplements).

PRACTICE MATERIALS

COLORADO ESTATE PLANNING. Third Edition. William S. Huff, Editor. Continuing Legal Education in Colorado, Incorporated, University of Denver Law Center, Huchingson Hall, 1895 Quebec, Denver, Colorado 80220. 1984- . (Periodic Supplements).

COLORADO ESTATE STATUTES: WILLS, ESTATES, TRUSTS AND TAXES. Colorado Bar Association, Probate and Trust Section, Continuing Legal Education in Colorado, University of Denver Law Center, Huchingson Hall, 1895 Quebec, Denver, Colorado 80220. 1980- . (Periodic Supplements).

COLORADO METHODS OF PRACTICE. Third Edition. C. Krendl. West Publishing Company, 50 West Kellogg Boulevard, St. Paul, Minnesota 55164. 1983.

COLORADO REAL ESTATE TRANSACTIONS. Owen L. Oliver. Bancroft-Whitney Company, P.O. Box 7005, San Francisco, California 94120. 1985- . (Annual Supplements).

HANDBOOK OF COLORADO FAMILY LAW. Susan W. Wicher. Continuing Legal Education in Colorado, Incorporated, University of Denver Law Center, Huchingson Hall, 1895 Quebec, Denver, Colorado 80220. 1982- . (Periodic Supplements).

RESEARCH GUIDES

COLORADO LEGAL RESOURCES: AN ANNOTATED BIBLIOGRAPHY. Compiled by Gary Alexander, David Burrows, Barbara Rainwater and Susan Weinstein. 16 Colorado Lawyer 1795 (October,1987), Colorado Bar Association, 1900 Grant Street, Suite 950, Denver, Colorado 80203-4309.

ASSOCIATIONS AND PROFESSIONAL SOCIETIES

BOULDER COUNTY BAR ASSOCIATION, 1942 Broadway, Suite 210, Boulder, Colorado 80302.

COLORADO BAR ASSOCIATION, 1900 Grant Street, Suite 950, Denver, Colorado 80203-4309. (303) 860-1112.

DENVER BAR ASSOCIATION, 1900 Grant Street, Suite 950, Denver, Colorado 80203-4309. (303) 860-1112.

EL PASO COUNTY BAR ASSOCIATION, 121 East Pike Peak Avenue, Number 326, Colorado Springs, Colorado 80903.

DIRECTORIES

COLORADO GENERAL ASSEMBLY DIRECTORY. Colorado General Assembly, State Capitol, Denver, Colorado 80203. (Annual).

COLORADO LEGISLATIVE DIRECTORY. Colorado Press Association, 1336 Glenarm Place, Denver, Colorado 80204. (Biennial).

DAILY JOURNAL LEGAL AND FINANCIAL DIRECTORY. The Daily Journal, McGraw-Hill, 101 University Boulevard, Denver, Colorado 80206. (Biennial).

DIRECTORY OF MUNICIPAL AND COUNTY OFFICIALS IN COLORADO. Colorado Municipal League, 1660 Lincoln, Suite 2100, Denver, Colorado 80264. (Annual)

MOUNTAIN STATES LEGAL DIRECTORY. Legal Directories Publishing Company, 2122 Kidwell Street, P.O. Box 140200, Dallas, Texas 75214-0200. (Annual). (Colorado, Idaho, Montana, New Mexico, Utah, and Wyoming).

OTHER SOURCES

CLOSELY HELD CORPORATIONS. C. Krendl. Continuing Education in Colorado, Incorporated, University of Denver Law Center, Hutchingson Hall, 1895 Quebec, Denver, Colorado 80200. 1981- .

COLORADO APPELLATE HANDBOOK. Andrew M. Low, Editor. Continuing Legal Education in Colorado, Incorporated, University of Denver Law Center, Huchingson Hall, 1895 Quebec, Denver, Colorado 80200. 1984- . (Annual Supplements).

COLORADO LAW ANNOTATED. B. Pringle. Bancroft-Whitney Company, P.O. Box 7005, San Francisco, California 94120. 1984.

STATUTORY TIME LIMITATIONS: COLORADO. Butterworths, 75 Clegg Road, Markham, Ontario, Canada L3R 9Y6. 1981- .

STATES--CONNECTICUT

STATUTES, CODES, STANDARDS, UNIFORM LAWS

CONNECTICUT GENERAL STATUTES ANNOTATED. West Publishing Company, P.O. Box 64526, 50 West Kellogg Boulevard, St. Paul, Minnesota 55164-0526. 1960- . (Annual Supplements).

CONNECTICUT LEGISLATIVE SERVICE. West Publishing Company, P.O. Box 64526, 50 West Kellogg Boulevard, St. Paul, Minnesota 55164-0526. (Periodic Supplements).

CONNECTICUT PUBLIC AND SPECIAL ACTS. Office of the Secretary of State, 30 Trinity Street, Hartford, Connecticut 06106. 1971- .

GENERAL STATUTES OF CONNECTICUT. Office of the Secretary of State, 30 Trinity Street, Hartford, Connecticut 06106. 1866- .

REGULATIONS OF CONNECTICUT STATE AGENCIES. Commission on Official Legal Publications, 111 Phoenix, Enfield, Connecticut 06082. 1962- . (Semiannual Supplements).

LOOSELEAF SERVICES AND REPORTERS

ATLANTIC REPORTER. (Frist and Second Series). West Publishing Company, P.O. Box 64526, 50 West Kellogg Boulevard, St. Paul, Minnesota 55164-0526. 1885- . (Connecticut Supreme Court, Circuit Court, and Superior Court).

CONNECTICUT REPORTER. West Publishing Company, P.O. Box 64526, 50 West Kellogg Boulevard, St. Paul, Minnesota 55164-0526. (Volume 1-481). 1885-1984. (Connecticut Supreme Court, Circuit Court, and Superior Court).

CONNECTICUT REPORTS. Commission on Official Legal Publications, 111 Phoenix, Enfield, Connecticut 06082. 1814- .

CONNECTICUT SUPPLEMENT. Commission on Official Legal Publications, 111 Phoenix, Enfield, Connecticut 06082. 1935- . (Court of Common Pleas, Circuit Court, and Superior Court).

ATTORNEY GENERAL OPINIONS

CONNECTICUT ATTORNEY GENERAL REPORTS AND OPINIONS. Microfilm. Trans-Media Publications, Condyne--The Oceana Group, Division of Oceana Publications, 75 Main Street, Dobbs Ferry, New York 10522. 1899-1968. Microfiche. William S. Hein and Company, Incorporated, Hein Building, 1285 Main Street, Buffalo, New York 14209. 1968- . (Current Opinions published in Connecticut Law Journal). Office of the Attorney General, 30 Trinity Street, Harford, Connecticut 06106. 1899- . Biennial.

ETHICS OPINIONS, CODES, RULES

CODE OF PROFESSIONAL RESPONSIBILITY AND CODE OF JUDICIAL CONDUCT. Published in Connecticut Practice Book Annotated , Second Edition. West Publishing Company, P.O. Box 64526, 50 West Kellogg Boulevard, St. Paul, Minnesota 55164-0526. 1979- . (Periodic Supplements).

INFORMAL OPINIONS. Connecticut Bar Association, 101 Corporate Place, Rocky Hill, Connecticut 06067. 1982- .

LAWYERS' DIARY. Connecticut Bar Association Continuing Legal Education, 101 Corporate Place, Rocky Hill, Connecticut 06067. 1984.

COURT RULES

CONNECTICUT RULES OF COURT. West Publishing Company, P.O. Box 64526, 50 West Kellogg Boulevard, St. Paul, Minnesota 55164-0526. (Annual). (Also published in Connecticut Statutes Annotated, Volume 23).

CONNECTICUT SUPERIOR COURT CRIMINAL RULES. L. Orland. West Publishing Company, 50 West Kellogg Boulevard, St. Paul, Minnesota 55164. 1986.

CONNECTICUT SUPERIOR COURT FORMS. J. Kaye and W. Effron. West Publishing Company, 50 West Kellogg Boulevard, St. Paul, Minnesota 55164. 1979.

CONNECTICUT SUPREME AND APPELLATE COURT RULES AND FORMS. Ninth Edition. W. Moller and W. Horton. West Publishing Company, P.O. Box 64526, 50 West Kellogg Boulevard, St. Paul, Minnesota 55164-0526. 1987.

CONNECTICUT SUPREME COURT CIVIL RULES. M. Moller and W. Horton. West Publishing Company, 50 West Kellogg Boulevard, St. Paul, Minnesota 55164. 1979.

RULES AND FORMS: PRACTICE BOOK ANNOTATED. West Publishing Company, 50 West Kellogg Boulevard, St. Paul, Minnesota 55164. 1987.

JURY INSTRUCTIONS

CONNECTICUT CRIMINAL JURY INSTRUCTIONS. D. Borland and L. Orland. West Publishing Company, P.O. Box 64526, 50 West Kellogg Boulevard, St. Paul, Minnesota 55164-0526. 1986. (Periodic Supplements).

CONNECTICUT JURY INSTRUCTIONS. Third Edition. Douglas B. Wright, John J. Daly, and David B. Havanich. Atlantic Law Book Company, 150 Hartford Avenue, Wetherfield, Connecticut 06109. 1981- . (Periodic Supplements).

DIGESTS, INDEXES, ABSTRACTS, CITATORS

ATLANTIC DIGEST. (First and Second Series). West Publishing Company, P.O. Box 64526, 50 West Kellogg Boulevard, St. Paul, Minnesota 55164-0526. 1949- . (Annual Supplements).

CONNECTICUT DIGEST. West Publishing Company, P.O. Box 64526, 50 West Kellogg Boulevard, St. Paul, Minnesota 55164-0526. 1950- . (Annual Supplements). (Covers 1764-).

CONNECTICUT FAMILY LAW CITATIONS. Butterworth Legal Publishers, 90 Stiles Road, Salem, New Hampshire 03079. 1985- .

SHEPARD'S ATLANTIC REPORTER CITATORS. Shepard's/McGraw-Hill, P.O. Box 1235, Colorado Springs, Colorado 80901. (Monthly Supplements).

SHEPARD'S CONNECTICUT CITATIONS. Shepard's/McGraw-Hill, P.O. Box 1235, Colorado Springs, Colorado 80901. 1962- . Six pamphlets per year.

LAW REVIEWS AND PERIODICALS

CONNECTICUT BAR JOURNAL. Connecticut Bar Association, 101 Corporate Place, Rocky Hill, Connecticut 06067. (Six Issues per Year).

CONNECTICUT JOURNAL OF INTERNATIONAL LAW. University of Connecticut School of Law, 65 Elizabeth Street, Hartford, Connecticut 06105. (Semiannual).

CONNECTICUT LAW REVIEW. Connecticut Law Review Association, University of Connecticut School of Law, 65 Elizabeth Street, Hartford, Connecticutt 06105. (Quarterly).

CONNECTICUT LAWYER. Connecticut Bar Association, 101 Corporate Place, Rocky Hill, Connecticut 06067. (Monthly).

UNIVERSITY OF BRIDGEPORT LAW REVIEW. University of Bridgeport School of Law, 303 University Avenue, Bridgeport, Connecticut 06601. (Biannual).

YALE LAW JOURNAL. Yale University Press, 302 Temple Street, New Haven, Connecticut 06520.

NEWSLETTERS AND NEWSPAPERS

CONNECTICUT FAMILY LAW JOURNAL. Butterworth Legal Publishers, 90 Stiles Road, Salem, New Hampshire 03079. Bimonthly.

CONNECTICUT LAW JOURNAL. (Weekly). (Decisions of the Connecticut Supreme Court, Superior Court, Attorney General Opinions, and Agency Regulations).

CONNECTICUT REAL ESTATE LAW JOURNAL. Butterworth Legal Publishers, 90 Stiles Road, Salem, New Hampshire 03079. Bimonthly.

CONNECTICUT WORKER'S COMPENSATION REVIEW OPINIONS. Butterworth Legal Publishers, 90 Stiles Road, Salem, New Hampshire 03079. Quarterly.

THE MASSACHUSETTS, CONNECTICUT, RHODE ISLAND VERDICT REPORTER. Judicial Advisory Services, Incorporated, P.O. Box 99704, 3309 College Drive, Louisville, Kentucky 40299. Monthly.

FORMBOOKS

CONNECTICUT LEGAL FORMS. Douglas B. Wright. Atlantic Law Book Company, 150 Hartford Avenue, Wethersfield, Connecticut 06109. 1958- . (Periodic Supplements).

CONNECTICUT PRACTICE BOOK ANNOTATED. Second Edition. West Publishing Company, P.O. Box 64526, 50 West Kellogg Boulevard, St. Paul, Minnesota 55164-0526. 1979- . (Periodic Supplements).

PRACTICE MATERIALS

BASIC CORPORATE PRACTICE. Connecticut Bar Association, 101 Corporate Place, Rocky Hill, Connecticut 06067. 1980.

CONNECTICUT APPELLATE PRACTICE AND PROCEDURE. Civil Justice section, Connecticut Bar Association Continuing Legal Education, 101 Corporate Place, Rocky Hill, Connecticut 06067. 1985.

CONNECTICUT CIVIL PROCEDURE. Second Edition. Edward L. Stephenson. Atlantic Law Book Company, 150 Hartford Avenue, Wethersfield, Connecticut 06109. 1970- . (Annual Supplements).

CONNECTICUT CRIMINAL PROCEDURE. Paul Spinella. Atlantic Law Book Company, 150 Hartford Avenue, Wethersfield, Connecticut 06109. 1985- . (Periodic Supplements).

CONNECTICUT ESTATE PRACTICE. G. Wilhelm. Lawyers Cooperative Publishing Company, Aqueduct Building, Rochester, New York 14694. 1971- .

CONNECTICUT LAWYERS BASIC PRACTICE MANUAL. Connecticut Bar Association, 101 Corporate Place, Rocky Hill, Connecticut 06067. 1970- .

CONNECTICUT PRACTICE. Ninth Edition. W. Moller and W. Horton. West Publishing Company, P.O. Box 64526, 50 West Kellogg Boulevard, St. Paul, Minnesota 55164-0526. 1985. (Annual Supplements). (Connecticut Supreme Court and Appellate Court Rules and Forms).

CONNECTICUT PRACTICE BOOK. Commission on Official Legal Publications. Atlantic Law Book Company, 150 Hartford Avenue, Wethersfield, Connecticut 06109. 1978- . (Periodic Supplements).

CONNECTICUT TRIAL PRACTICE. J. Fitzgerald and R. Yules. West Publishing Company, 50 West Kellogg Boulevard, St. Paul, Minnesota 55164. 1987.

HANDBOOK OF CONNECTICUT EVIDENCE. Second Edition. C. Tait. Little, Brown and Company, 34 Beacon Street, Boston, Massachusetts 02108. 1988.

ASSOCIATIONS AND PROFESSIONAL SOCIETIES

CONNECTICUT BAR ASSOCIATION, 101 Corporate Place, Rocky Hill, Connecticut 06067. (203) 721-0025.

GREATER BRIDGEPORT BAR ASSOCIATION, 955 Main Street, Bridgeport, Connecticut 06604.

HARTFORD COUNTY BAR ASSOCIATION, INCORPORATED, 61 Hungerford Street, Hartford, Connecticut 06106.

NEW HAVEN BAR ASSOCIATION, P.O. Box 1441, 205 Church Street, New Haven, Connecticut 60506.

DIRECTORIES

CONNECTICUT GUIDE TO LEGISLATIVE SERVICES. Connecticut General Assembly, State Capitol, Hartford, Connecticut 06106. (Annual).

CONNECTICUT MUNICIPLE DIRECTORY. Connecticut Conference of Municipalities, 956 Chapel Street, New Haven, Connecticut 06510. (Annual).

STATE OF CONNECTICUT REGISTER AND MANUAL. Connecticut Secretary of State, 30 Trinity Street, Room 129, Hartford, Connecticut 06106. (Annual).

OTHER SOURCES

CONNECTICUT REAL PROPERTY LAW. R. Anderson. Atlantic Law Book Company, 150 Hartford Avenue, Wethersfield, Connecticut 06109. 1984.

CONNECTICUT STATE LEGAL DOCUMENTS: A SELECTIVE BIBLIOGRAPHY. D. Voisinet and others. American Association of Law Libraries, 53 West Jackson Boulevard, Suite 940, Chicago, Illinois 60604. 1985.

SOURCES OF CONNECTICUT LAW. S. Bysiewicz. Butterworth Legal Publishers, 90 Stiles Road, Salem, New Hampshire 03079. 1987.

STATES--DELAWARE

STATUTES, CODES, STANDARDS, UNIFORM LAWS

DELAWARE CODE ANNOTATED. Michie Company, P.O. Box 7587, Charlottesville, Virginia 22906-7587. 1974- . (Annual Supplements).

GENERAL CORPORATION LAW OF THE STATE OF DELAWARE. Michie/Bobbs-Merrill Law Publishing Company, P.O. Box 7587, Charlottesville, Virginia 22906-7587. (Annual).

LAWS OF DELAWARE. Microfilm. University Microfilms. Microfiche. William S. Hein and Company, Incorporated, Hein Building, 1285 Main Street, Buffalo, New York 14209.

No Administrative Codes or Regulations are published. Call Agencies for Regulations.

COURT REPORTERS

ATLANTIC REPORTER (First and Second Series). West Publishing Company, P.O. Box 64526, 50 West Kellogg Boulevard, St. Paul, Minnesota 55164-0526. 1886- . (Delaware Supreme Court, Court of Chancery, Superior Court, and other Courts of Delaware).

DELAWARE CHANCERY REPORTS. T. and J. W. Johnson Company. 1814-1833. (Current Official Sources: Atlantic Reporter and West's Delaware Reporter).

DELAWARE REPORTER. West Publishing Company, P.O. Box 64526, 50 West Kellogg Boulevard, St. Paul, Minnesota 55164-0526. 1969- .

DELAWARE REPORTS. Law Book Publishers. 1832-1966. (Delaware Supreme Court). (Current Official Source: Atlantic Reporter, Second Series and West's Delaware Reporter).

ETHICS OPINIONS, CODES, RULES

DELAWARE ADVISORY ETHICS OPINIONS. Issued by the Ethics Committee of the Delaware State Bar Association. These opinions are not published, but abstracts of them are published in the ABA Lawyer's Manual on Professional Conduct (Ethics Opinions Volume). For further information concerning these opinions, contact the Delaware State Bar Association, 706 Market Street Mall, Wilmington, Delaware 19801. 302-571-8703.

RULES ON PROFESSIONAL CONDUCT and RULES OF THE BOARD ON PROFESSIONAL RESPONSIBILITY are published in Volume 16 of the Delaware Code Annotated . (Rules Volume).

COURT RULES

DELAWARE COURT RULES. Contained in Volume 16 and 17, Delaware Code Annotated. Michie Company, P.O. Box 7587, Charlottesville, Virginia 22906-7587. 1974- . (Annual Supplements).

SUPREME COURT RULES OF THE STATE OF DELAWARE. Michie Company, P.O. Box 7587, Charlottesville, Virginia 22906-7587. (Annual).

DIGESTS, INDEXES, ABSTRACTS, CITATORS

ATLANTIC DIGEST. (First and Second Series). West Publishing Company, P.O. Box 64526, 50 West Kellogg Boulevard, St. Paul, Minnesota 55164-0526. 1948- . (Annual Supplements).

STATES--DELAWARE

DELAWARE DISTRICT DIGEST. Delaware District Digest, Sawyer And Akin Publishing Company, Delaware Trust Building, P.O. Box 112, Wilmington, Delaware 19899. (Monthly).

SHEPARD'S ATLANTIC REPORTER CITATIONS. Shepard's/McGraw-Hill, P.O. Box 1235, Colorado Springs, Colorado 80901. (Monthly).

SHEPARD'S DELAWARE CITATIONS. Shepard's/McGraw-Hill, P.O. Box 1235, Colorado Springs, Colorado 80901. (Three Pamphlets Per Year).

LAW REVIEWS AND PERIODICALS

DELAWARE JOURNAL OF CORPORATE LAW. Delaware Law School of Widener University, Concord Pike, P.O. Box 7475, Wilmington, Delaware 19803. (Quarterly).

DELAWARE LAWYER. Delaware Bar Foundation, 25 Public Building, Eleventh and King Street, Wilmington, Delaware 19801. 1982- . (Semiannual).

NEWSLETTERS AND NEWSPAPERS

THE DELAWARE CORPORATE LAW REPORTER. Legal Communications, Limited, 1617 John F. Kennedy Boulevard, Suite 1245, Philadelphia, Pennsylvania 19103. Monthly.

DELAWARE CORPORATE LITIGATION REPORTER. Andrews Publications, 1646 West Chester Pike, Westtown, Pennsylvania 19395. Semimonthly.

DELAWARE CORPORATION LAW UPDATE--ATTORNEYS EDITION. Corporate Law Center of Delaware, Incorporated, 1300 North Market Street, P. O. Box 2325, Wilmington, Delaware 19899. Monthly.

DELAWARE DISTRICT DIGEST. Delaware District Digest, 1600 Manufacturers Hanover Building, P.O. Box 966, Wilmington, Delaware 19899. Monthly.

MONDAY MORNING. Delaware State Chamber of Commerce, One Commerce Center, Suite 200, Wilmington, Delaware 19801. Weekly while in session.

FORMBOOKS

DELAWARE LAW OF CORPORATIONS AND BUSINESS ORGANIZATIONS: TEXT, FORMS, LAW. R. Franklin Balotti and Jessie A. Finkelstein. Law and Business, Incorporated, 855 Valley Road, Clifton, New Jersey 07013. 1986- . (Four Volume Looseleaf). (Periodic Supplements).

ASSOCIATIONS AND PROFESSIONAL SOCIETIES

CORPORATE LAW CENTER OF DELAWARE. 1300 North Market Street, Wilmington, Delaware 19801. (302) 429-9315.

DELAWARE STATE BAR ASSOCIATION, 706 Market Street Mall, Wilmington, Delaware 19801. (302) 658-5278.

Encyclopedia of Legal Information Sources • 2nd Ed.

DIRECTORIES

DELAWARE LEGISLATIVE ROSTER. Delaware State Chamber of Commerce, One Commerce Center, Suite 200, Wilmington, Delaware 19801. (Biennial).

VIRGINIAS, MARYLAND, DELAWARE, AND DISTRICT OF COLUMBIA LEGAL DIRECTORY. Legal Directories Publishing Company, 2122 Kidwell, P. O. Box 140200, Dallas, Texas 75214-0200. (Annual).

OTHER SOURCES

DELAWARE BUSINESS KIT FOR STARTING AND EXISTING BUSINESSES. L. Barrientos. Simon and Schuster, Incorporated, 1230 Avenue of the Americas, New York, New York 10020. 1983.

THE DELAWARE CORPORATION. A. Sparks. Bureau of National Affairs, Incorporated, 1231 Twenty-fifth Street, Northwest, Washington, D.C. 20037. 1978- .

DELAWARE GENERAL CORPORATION LAW: A COMMENTARY AND ANALYSIS. Ernest L. Folk. Little, Brown and Company, 34 Beacon Street, Boston, Massachusetts 02108. 1972- . (Periodic Supplements).

DELAWARE LANDLORD-TENANT HANDBOOK. D. Harris. Michie Company, P.O. Box 7587, Charlottesville, Virginia 22906-7587. 1980- .

DELAWARE LAW FOR CORPORATE LAWYERS. Practising Law Institute, 810 Seventh Avenue, New York, New York 10017. 1985.

STATES--DISTRICT OF COLUMBIA

STATUTES, CODES, STANDARDS, UNIFORM LAWS

DISTRICT OF COLUMBIA ADVANCE ANNOTATION SERVICE. Michie Company, P.O. Box 7587, Charlottesville, Virginia 22906-7587. (Three Issues per Year).

DISTRICT OF COLUMBIA CODE ANNOTATED. Michie Company, P.O. Box 7587, Charlottesville, Virginia 22906-7587. 1981- . (Annual Supplements).

DISTRICT OF COLUMBIA MUNICIPAL REGULATIONS (DCMR). D.C. Office of Documents, Room 523, District Building, 1350 Pennsylvania Avenue Northwest, Washington, D.C 20004. 1983- . (Periodic Supplements). (Formerly The District of Columbia Rules and Regulations - DCRR).

DISTRICT OF COLUMBIA REGISTER. D.C. Office of Documents, Room 523, District Building, 1350 Pennsylvania Avenue Northwest, Washington, D.C. 20004. (Weekly).

DISTRICT OF COLUMBIA STATUTES AT LARGE. Compiled and distributed by the D.C. Office of Documents, Room 523, District Building, 1350 Pennsylvania Avenue Northwest, Washington, D.C. 20004. 1975- . (Annual).

LOOSELEAF SERVICES AND REPORTERS

ATLANTIC REPORTER. (First and Second Series). West Publishing Company, P.O. Box 64526, 50 West Kellogg Boulevard, St. Paul, Minnesota 55164-0526. 1886- .

DAILY WASHINGTON LAW REPORTER. Washington Law Reporter Company, 1625 Eye Street Northwest, Washington, D.C. 20006. (Daily except Saturdays, Sundays, and Holidays).

U.S. COURT OF APPEALS FOR THE D.C. CIRCUIT REPORTS. West Publishing Company, P.O. Box 64526, 50 West Kellogg Boulevard, St. Paul, Minnesota 55164-0526. 1901- .

ETHICS OPINIONS, CODES, RULES

CODE OF PROFESSIONAL RESPONSIBILITY AND OPINIONS OF THE D.C. BAR LEGAL ETHICS COMMITTEE. District of Columbia Bar, 1707 L Street, Northwest, Sixth Floor, Washington, D.C. 20036-4201. 1983- . Looseleaf. (Periodic Supplements). (Opinions Number 1 through 116 of the District of Columbia Bar, Committee on Legal Ethics). For further information concerning these opinions, contact the D.C. Bar Legal Ethics Committee, Building A, Room 127, 515 Fifth Street, N. W., Washington, D. C. 20001. (202-638-1501).

DISTRICT OF COLUMBIA COURT OF APPEALS; BOARD ON PROFESSIONAL RESPONSIBILITY, DISCIPLINARY DIGEST. Board on Professional Responsibility, 515 Fifth Street, Northwest, Room 127, Washington, D.C. 20001. 1986- . (Biannual Supplements).

COURT RULES

DISTRICT OF COLUMBIA COURT RULES ANNOTATED. Michie Company, P.O. Box 7587, Charlottesville, Virginia 22906-7587. (Two Volumes). (Annual).

DISTRICT OF COLUMBIA COURT RULES SERVICE. Rules Service Company, 7658 Standish Place, Suite 106, Rockville, Maryland 20855. 1973- . (Periodic Supplements).

LEGAL TIMES OF WASHINGTON D.C. CIRCUIT HANDBOOK. Law and Business, Incorporated, 855 Valley Road, Clifton, New Jersey 07013. 1980- . (Periodic Supplements). (Includes Rules for the United States Court of Appeals for the D.C. Circuit, the District Court for D.C., the United States Court of Claims, and the Tax Court).

JURY INSTRUCTIONS

CRIMINAL JURY INSTRUCTIONS FOR THE DISTRICT OF COLUMBIA. Fourth Edition. Young Lawyers Section, Bar Association of the District of Columbia, 1707 L Street, Northwest, Sixth Floor, Washington, D.C. 20036-4201. 1978. (Periodic Supplements).

STANDARDIZED CIVIL JURY INSTRUCTIONS FOR THE DISTRICT OF COLUMBIA. Revised Edition. Revised by the Young Lawyers Section, Bar Association of the District of Columbia, 1707 L Street, Northwest, Sixth Floor, Washington, D.C. 20036-4201. 1981- . (Periodic Supplements).

DIGESTS, INDEXES, ABSTRACTS, CITATORS

ATLANTIC DIGEST. (First and Second Series). West Publishing Company, P.O. Box 64526, 50 West Kellogg Boulevard, St. Paul, Minnesota 55164-0526. 1948- . (Annual Supplements).

DISTRICT OF COLUMBIA CASEFINDER: TORTS. Second Edition. Jacob A. Stein. Callaghan and Company, 155 Pfingsten Road, Deerfield, Illinois 60015. 1977- . (Periodic Supplements).

DISTRICT OF COLUMBIA CITATOR SERVICE. Rules Service Company, 7658 Stadish Place, Suite 106, Rockville, Maryland 20855. 1976- . (Periodic Supplements). (Covers Citations for D.C. Superior Court Rules).

DISTRICT OF COLUMBIA DIGEST. West Publishing Company, P.O. Box 64526, 50 West Kellogg Boulevard, St. Paul, Minnesota 55164-0526. 1962- . (Annual Supplements).

DISTRICT OF COLUMBIA ESTATES, TRUSTS, AND PROBATE LAW DIGEST. N. Fax, Editor. Bar Association of the District of Columbia, 1819 H Street, Twelfth Floor, Northwest, Washington, D.C. 20006. 1981- .

SHEPARD'S ATLANTIC REPORTER CITATIONS. Shepard's/McGraw-Hill, P.O. Box 1235, Colorado Springs, Colorado 80901. (Monthly Supplements).

SHEPARD'S DISTRICT OF COLUMBIA CITATIONS. Shepard's/McGraw-Hill, P.O. Box 1235, Colorado Springs, Colorado 80901. (Six Pamphlets Per Year).

ENCYCLOPEDIAS AND DICTIONARIES

DISTRICT OF COLUMBIA CODE ENCYCLOPEDIA. West Publishing Company, P.O. Box 64526, 50 West Kellogg Boulevard, St. Paul, Minnesota 55164-0526. 1966-1979. (Upkeep Discontinued 1980).

LAW REVIEWS AND PERIODICALS

THE ADMINISTRATIVE LAW JOURNAL OF THE AMERICAN UNIVERSITY. Washington College of Law, The American University, 4400 Massachusetts Avenue, Northwest, Washington, D.C. 20016. (Semiannual).

AMERICAN CRIMINAL LAW REVIEW. Georgetown University Law Center, 600 New Jersey Avenue, Northwest, Washington, D.C. 20001. (Quarterly).

THE AMERICAN UNIVERSITY JOURNAL OF INTERNATIONAL LAW AND POLICY. Washington College of Law, The American University, 4400 Massachusetts Avenue, Washington, D.C. 20016. (Semiannual).

THE AMERICAN UNIVERSITY LAW REVIEW. Washington College of Law, The American University, 4400 Massachusetts Avenue, Northwest, Washington, D.C. 20016. (Quarterly).

THE CATHOLIC UNIVERSITY LAW REVIEW. The Catholic University of America, Columbus School of Law, Leahy Hall, 620 Michigan Avenue, Northeast, Washington, D.C. 20064. Quarterly.

GEORGE WASHINGTON JOURNAL OF INTERNATIONAL LAW AND ECONOMICS. National Law Center of the George Washington University, 716 Twentieth Street, Northwest, Washington, D.C. 20052. (Quarterly).

GEORGE WASHINGTON LAW REVIEW. National Law Center of the George Washington University, 716 Twentieth Street, Northwest, Washington, D.C. 20052. Quarterly.

GEORGETOWN IMMIGRATION LAW JOURNAL. Georgetown University Law Center, 600 New Jersey Avenue, Northwest, Washington, D.C. 20001. Quarterly.

GEORGETOWN JOURNAL OF LEGAL ETHICS. Georgetown University Law Center, 600 New Jersey Avenue, Northwest, Washington, D.C. 20001. (Three issues per year).

GEORGETOWN LAW JOURNAL. Georgetown University Law Center, 600 New Jersey Avenue, Northwest, Washington, D.C. 20001. (Six issues per year).

HOWARD LAW JOURNAL. Howard University School of Law, 2900 Van Ness Street, Northwest, Washington, D.C. 20008. (Quarterly).

THE JOURNAL OF CONTEMPORARY HEALTH AND LAW POLICY. The Catholic University of America, Columbus School of Law, Leahy Hall, 620 Michigan Avenue, Northeast, Washington, D.C. 20064. Annual.

JOURNAL OF LAW AND TECHNOLOGY. Georgetown University Law Center, 600 New Jersey Avenue, Northwest, Washington, D.C. 20001. (Semiannual).

LAW AND POLICY IN INTERNATIONAL BUSINESS. Georgetown University Law Center, 600 New Jersey Avenue, Northwest, Washington, D.C. 20001. (Quarterly).

THE WASHINGTON LAWYER. District of Columbia Bar, 1707 L Street Northwest, Washington, D.C. 20036. Monthly.

NEWSLETTERS AND NEWSPAPERS

COURT EXCELLENCE. Council for Court Excellence, 1025 Vermont Avenue, Northwest, Suite 1510, Washington, D.C. 20005. Quarterly.

DAILY WASHINGTON LAW REPORTER. Washington Law Reporter Company, 1625 E Street, Northwest, Suite 814, Washington, D.C. 20006. Weekdays.

DC CIRCUIT REVIEW. Barclays Law Publishers, 400 Oyster Point Boulevard, Suite 500, South San Francisco, California 94080. Biweekly.

DISTRICT COUNCIL JOURNAL. Patrick Publishing Company, 1742 Massachusetts Avenue, Southeast, Washington, D.C. 20003. Monthly.

DISTRICT OF COLUMBIA REAL ESTATE REPORTER. Land Development Institute, Limited, 1300 N Street, Northwest, Washington, D.C. 20005. Monthly.

LAW LIBRARY LIGHTS. Law Librarian's Society of Washington, D.C., Incorporated, 1717 Largo Road, Upper Marlboro, Maryland 20772. Bimonthly.

LEGAL TIMES, 1730 M Street Northwest, Washington, D.C. 20036. (Weekly except last weeks in August and September).

METRO VERDICTS MONTHLY. Judicial Advisory Services, Incorporated, P.O. Box 99704, 3309 College Drive, Louisville, Kentucky 40299. Monthly.

FORMBOOKS

DISTRICT OF COLUMBIA PRACTICE FORMS. Flaherty. West Publishing Company, P.O. Box 64526, 50 West Kellogg Boulevard, St. Paul, Minnesota 55164-0526. 1949- . (Periodic Updates).

LEGAL TIMES OF WASHINGTON D.C. CIRCUIT HANDBOOK. Diana Huffman, Editor. Law and Business, Incorporated, 855 Valley Road, Clifton, New Jersey 07013. 1980- . (Periodic Supplements).

WILL AND TESTAMENTARY TRUST FORMS. Second Edition. District of Columbia Bar, 1707 L Street, Northwest, Sixth Floor, Washington, D.C. 20036. 1982.

PRACTICE MATERIALS

APPELLATE PRACTICE MANUAL FOR THE DISTRICT OF COLUMBIA COURT OF APPEALS. Charles L. Reischel, Editor. Bar Association of the District of Columbia, Young Lawyers Section, 1707 L Street, Northwest, Sixth Floor, Washington, D.C. 20036-4201. 1985.

CRIMINAL PRACTICE INSTITUTE TRIAL MANUAL. Young Lawyers Section, Bar Association of the District of Columbia and the Public Defender Service for the District of Columbia, 1707 L Street, Northwest, Sixth Floor, Washington, D.C. 20036-4201. (Annual).

LANDLORD AND TENANT LAW IN THE DISTRICT OF COLUMBIA. Julian Karpoff. Potomac Law Publishing Company, 111 South Patrick Street, Alexandria, Virginia. 1977.

REALLY REPRESENTING TENANTS IN THE DISTRICT OF COLUMBIA. D.C. Law Students in Court, 419 Seventh Street, Northwest, Washington, D.C. 1983.

MANUALS AND RESEARCH GUIDES

DISTRICT OF COLUMBIA ADMINISTRATIVE PROCEDURE MANUAL. Revised Edition. Prepared by the District of Columbia Law Revision Commission, Colorado Building, 1341 G Street Northwest, Suite 510, Washington, D.C. 20005. 1985.

THE DISTRICT OF COLUMBIA PRACTICE MANUAL. District of Columbia Bar Association, 1707 L Street, Northwest, Sixth Floor, Washington, D.C. 20036. 1987- .

MERSCH PROBATE COURT PRACTICE IN THE DISTRICT OF COLUMBIA. Second Edition. West Publishing Company, P.O. Box 64526, 50 West Kellogg Boulevard, St. Paul, Minnesota 55164-0526. 1952- . (Periodic Supplements).

SELECTED INFORMATION SOURCES FOR THE DISTRICT OF COLUMBIA. Second Edition. Carolyn Ahern. American Association of Law Libraries, 53 West Jackson Boulevard, Suite 940, Chicago, Illinois. 60604. 1986.

TRIAL MANUAL. Bar Association of the District of Columbia, 1819 H Street, Northwest, Twelfth Floor, Washington, D.C. 20006. 1982.

WORKER'S COMPENSATION MANUAL. E. May. District of Columbia Bar, 1707 L Street, Northwest, Sixth Floor, Washington, D.C. 20036. 1984.

ASSOCIATIONS AND PROFESSIONAL SOCIETIES

BAR ASSOCIATION OF THE DISTRICT OF COLUMBIA, 1707 L Street, Northwest, Sixth Floor, Washington, D.C. 20036-4201. (202) 223-1480.

DISTRICT OF COLUMBIA BAR, 1707 L Street, Northwest, Sixth Floor, Washington, D.C. 20036. (202) 331-3883.

DISTRICT OF COLUMBIA BAR LAWYER REFERRAL AND INFORMATION SERVICE, 1707 L Street, Northwest, Washington, D.C. 20036. (202) 331-4365.

WOMEN'S BAR ASSOCIATION OF THE DISTRICT OF COLUMBIA, 1819 H Street, Northwest, Washington, D.C. 20036. (202) 785-1940.

DIRECTORIES

DISTRICT OF COLUMBIA BAR--LAWYER'S DIRECTORY. District of Columbia Bar, 1707 L Street, Northwest, Washington, D.C. 20036. (Annual).

JUDICIAL PROFILER: FEDERAL COURTS FOR THE DISTRICT OF COLUMBIA. Shepard's/McGraw-Hill, P.O. Box 1235, Colorado Springs, Colorado 80901. 1981- . (Periodic Supplements).

METROPOLITAN LEGAL DIRECTORY. Metropolitan Washington Council of Governments, 1875 Eye Street Northwest, Suite 200, Washington, D.C. 20000. Annual.

ORGANIZATION HANDBOOK FOR THE DISTRICT OF COLUMBIA GOVERNMENT. Office of Budget and Management Systems, Executive Office of the Mayor. District of Columbia Office of Documents, Room 523, District Building, 1350 Pennsylvania Avenue, Washington, D.C. 20004. 1977. (New Edition Expected 1987).

VIRGINIA, MARYLAND, DELAWARE AND DISTRICT OF COLUMBIA LEGAL DIRECTORY. Legal Directories Publishing Company, 2122 Kidwell, P.O. Box 140200, Dallas, Texas 75214-0200. (Annual).

WASHINGTON: A COMPREHENSIVE DIRECTORY OF THE KEY INSTITUTIONS AND LEADERS OF THE NATIONAL CAPITOL AREA. Columbia Books, Incorporated, 1212 New York Avenue, Northwest, Suite 330, Washington, D.C. 20005. (Annual).

WASHINGTON LOBBYISTS AND LAWYERS DIRECTORY. Communications Services, Incorporated, 121 Fourth Street Southeast, Washington, D.C. 20003. 1986- . (Irregular).

WASHINGTON, THE GOVERNMENT, AND THE PEOPLE. Office of Policy and Program Evaluation, District of Columbia Executive Office of the Mayor, 1350 Pennsylvania Avenue Northwest, Room 412, Washington, D.C. 20004. (Annual). (Free). (District of Columbia Elected Officials).

OTHER SOURCES

D.C. CASE FINDER: TORTS. Second Edition. J. Stein. Callaghan and Company, 155 Pfingsten Road, Deerfield, Illinois 60015. 1977- .

JUVENILE LAW AND PRACTICE IN THE DISTRICT OF COLUMBIA. W. Mlyniec and J. Copacino. District of Columbia Bar, 1707 L Street, Northwest, Sixth Floor, Washington, D.C. 20036. 1988.

MEDICAL MALPRACTICE AND HEALTH CARE LAW IN THE DISTRICT OF COLUMBIA. J. Montedonico. Butterworth Legal Publishers, 90 Stiles Road, Salem, New Hampshire 03079. 1988.

STATES--FLORIDA

STATUTES, CODES, STANDARDS, UNIFORM LAWS

FLORIDA ADMINISTRATIVE CODE ANNOTATED. Florida Department of State. Harrison Company, Publisher, 3110 Crossing Park, P.O. Box 7500, Norcross, Georgia 30091-7500. 1986- . (Monthly Supplements).

FLORIDA ADMINISTRATIVE WEEKLY. Secretary of State. Elections Division, State Capitol, Tallahassee, Florida 32304. 1975- . (Weekly).

FLORIDA SESSION LAW SERVICE. West Publishing Company, P.O. Box 64526, 50 West Kellogg Boulevard, St. Paul, Minnesota 55164-0526. (Irregular).

FLORIDA STATUTES. Official Edition. State of Florida, Law Book Distribution Office, Room LL14, The Capitol, Tallahassee, Florida 32301. (Biennial).

FLORIDA STATUTES ANNOTATED. Harrison Company, Publisher, 3110 Crossing Park, P.O. Box 7500, Norcross, Georgia 30091-7500. 1943- . (Annual Supplements).

FLORIDA STATUTES ANNOTATED. West Publishing Company, P.O. Box 64526, 50 West Kellogg Boulevard, St. Paul, Minnesota 55164-0526. 1943- . (Annual Supplements).

LOOSELEAF SERVICES AND REPORTERS

FLORIDA REPORTS. Tribune Publishing Company, Incorporated, 18 Okner Parkway, Livingston, New Jersey 07039. (Florida Supreme Court). (Current Official Source: West's Florida Cases, Southern Reporter, and Florida Supplement). (Publisher Varies).

FLORIDA SUPPLEMENT (First and Second Series). Lawyers Co-Operative Company, Aqueduct Building, Rochester, New York 14694. 1952- . (Florida Circuit Courts, County Courts, and the Public Service Commission). (Publisher Varies).

SOUTHERN REPORTER (First and Second Series). West Publishing Company, P.O. Box 64526, 50 West Kellogg Boulevard, St. Paul, Minnesota 55164-0526. 2887- . (Florida Supreme Court and the District Court of Appeal).

WEST'S FLORIDA CASES. West Publishing Company, P.O. Box 64526, 50 West Kellogg Boulevard, St. Paul, Minnesota 55164-0526. 1948- .

STATES--FLORIDA — *Encyclopedia of Legal Information Sources • 2nd Ed.*

ATTORNEY GENERAL OPINIONS

ANNUAL REPORT OF THE ATTORNEY GENERAL. State of Florida, Office of the Attorney General, The Capitol, Tallahassee, Florida 32301. (Annual). (Includes Attorney General Opinions and Annual Report). Also available on Lexis: 1977-; Westlaw 1977- .

ETHICS OPINIONS, CODES, RULES

FLORIDA CODE OF PROFESSIONAL RESPONSIBILITY AND CODE OF JUDICIAL CONDUCT AND FLORIDA BYLAWS. Published in the Florida Bar Journal--Directory Issue . The Florida Bar, 650 Appalachee Parkway, Tallahassee, Florida 32399-2300. (Annual--September).

SELECTED OPINIONS OF THE COMMITTEE ON PROFESSIONAL ETHICS OF THE FLORIDA BAR. The Florida Bar, 650 Apalachee Parkway, Tallahassee, Florida 32399-2300. 1969- . (Irregular). (Opinions also published in Florida Bar News). For further information concerning these opinins, contact the Florida Bar Committee on Professional Ethics, 650 Appalachee Parkway, Tallahassee, Florida 32399-3200. (904-222-5286).

COURT RULES

FLORIDA CRIMINAL RULES AND PRACTICE. Second Edition. The Florida Bar, 650 Apalachee Parkway, Tallahassee, Florida 32399-3200. 1979- . (Periodic Supplements).

FLORIDA JURISPRUDENCE RULES OF PRACTICE. Lawyers Co-Operative Company, Aqueduct Building, Rochester, New York 14694. 1970- . (Annual Supplements).

FLORIDA RULES OF COURT SERVICE. D and S Publishers, Incorporated, P.O. Box 5105, Clearwater, Florida 34618-5105. 1972- . (Annual Supplements).

FLORIDA RULES OF COURT: STATE AND FEDERAL. Desk Copy. West Publishing Company, P.O. Box 64526, 50 West Kellogg Boulevard, St. Paul, Minnesota 55164-0526. (Annual).

FLORIDA STATUTES ANNOTATED: RULES. Harrison Company, Publisher, 3110 Crossing Park, P.O. Box 7500, Norcross, Georgia 30091-7500. 1985. (Volumes 30 - 33). (Annual Supplements).

JURY INSTRUCTIONS

FLORIDA JURY INSTRUCTIONS. James R. Richardson. West Publishing Company, P.O. Box 64526, 50 West Kellogg Boulevard, St. Paul, Minnesota 55164-0526. 1954- . (Periodic Supplements).

FLORIDA STANDARD JURY INSTRUCTION IN CIVIL CASES. Second Edition. Committee for Standard Jury Instructions in Civil Cases, The Florida Bar, 650 Appalachee Parkway, Tallahassee, Florida 32399-2300. 1986- . (Periodic Supplements).

FLORIDA STANDARD JURY INSTRUCTIONS IN CRIMINAL CASES. Second Edition. Committee on Standard Jury Instructions in Criminal Cases, The Florida Bar, 650 Appalachee Parkway, Tallahassee, Florida 32399-2300. 1981- . (Periodic Supplements).

DIGESTS, INDEXES, ABSTRACTS, CITATORS

FLORIDA BAR CASE SUMMARY SERVICE. The Florida Bar, 650 Appalachee Parkway, Tallahassee, Florida 32399-2300. (Weekly).

FLORIDA DIGESTIVE-INDEX. Harrison Company, 3110 Crossing Park, Norcross, Georgia 30091. (Annual Supplements).

FLORIDA JURY VERDICT REPORTER. Florida Legal Periodicals, Incorporated, 1333 North Adams Street, Tallahassee, Florida 32303. 1981- . (Monthly).

FLORIDA LAW FINDER. West Publishing Company, 50 West Kellogg Boulevard, St. Paul, Minnesota 55164. (Annual Supplements).

FLORIDA SUPPLEMENT DIGEST. Lawyers Cooperative Publishing Company, Aqueduct Building, Rochester, New York 14694. 1985. (Annual Supplements).

SOUTHERN DIGEST. West Publishing Company, P.O. Box 64526, 50 West Kellogg Boulevard, St. Paul, Minnesota 55164-0526. 1809- . (Annual Supplements).

SHEPARD'S FLORIDA CITATIONS. Shepard's/McGraw-Hill, P.O. Box 1235, Colorado Springs, Colorado 80901. 1914- . (Eight Pamphlets Per Year).

SHEPARD'S SOUTHERN REPORTER CITATIONS. Shepard's/McGraw-Hill, P.O. Box 1235, Colorado Springs, Colorado 80901. 1907- . (Monthly Supplements).

WEST'S FLORIDA DIGEST (First and Second Series). West Publishing Company, P.O. Box 64526, 50 West Kellogg Boulevard, St. Paul, Minnesota 55164-0526. (Annual Supplements).

ENCYCLOPEDIAS AND DICTIONARIES

FLORIDA JURISPRUDENCE 2d. Lawyers Co-Operative Company, Aqueduct Building, Rochester, New York 14694. 1977- . (Annual Supplements).

LAW REVIEWS AND PERIODICALS

FLORIDA INTERNATIONAL LAW JOURNAL. Holland Law Center, University of Florida, Gainesville, Florida 32611. (Biannual).

FLORIDA STATE UNIVERSITY LAW REVIEW. Florida State University College of Law, Tallahassee, Florida 32306. (Quarterly).

NOVA LAW REVIEW. Nova University Center for the Study of Law, 3100 Southwest Ninth Avenue, Fort Lauderdale, Florida 33315. Quarterly.

STETSON LAW REVIEW. Stetson University College of Law, 1401 Sixty-first Street South, St. Petersburg, Florida 33707. Quarterly.

UNIVERSITY OF MIAMI INTER-AMERICAN LAW REVIEW. University of Miami School of Law, P.O. Box 248087, Coral Gables, Florida 33124. Semiannual.

UNIVERSITY OF MIAMI LAW REVIEW. University of Miami School of Law, 460 Law Library, Coral Gables, Florida 33124. Bimonthly.

STATES--FLORIDA

NEWSLETTERS AND NEWSPAPERS

FLORIDA BANKRUPTCY CASENOTES. The Florida Bar, 650 Appalachee Parkway, Tallahassee, Florida 32399. Monthly.

THE FLORIDA BAR CASE SUMMARY SERVICE. The Florida Bar, 650 Appalachee Parkway, Tallahassee, Florida 32399. Weekly.

FLORIDA BAR JOURNAL. The Florida Bar, 650 Appalachee Parkway, Tallahassee, Florida 32399. Monthly.

FLORIDA BAR NEWS. The Florida Bar, 600 Apalachee Parkway, Tallahassee, Florida 32301. 1981- . (Semimonthly).

FLORIDA EMPLOYMENT LAW LETTER. M. Lee Smith Publishers and Printers, 162 Fourth Avenue North, Nashville, Tennessee 37219. Monthly.

FLORIDA ENVIRONMENTAL AND LAND USE LETTER. M. Lee Smith Publishers and Printers, 162 Fourth Avenue North, Nashville, Tennessee 37219. Monthly.

FLORIDA GENERAL PRACTICE JOURNAL. The Florida Bar, 650 Appalachee Parkway, Tallahassee, Florida 32399. Quarterly.

FLORIDA JURY VERDICT REPORTER. Florida Legal Periodicals, Incorporated, 1333 North Adams Street, Tallahassee, Florida 32303. Monthly.

THE FLORIDA LAW WEEKLY. Judicial and Administrative Research Associates, Incorporated, 1327 North Adams Street, Tallahassee, Florida 32303. Weekly.

FLORIDA LEGISLATIVE REPORTERS. Florida Legislative Reporters, Incorporated, P.O. Box 745, Tallahassee, Florida 32302. Semiweekly.

FLORIDA PUBLIC FINANCE. American Banker-Bond Buyer, Newsletter Division, P.O. Box 30240, Bethesda, Maryland 20814. Weekly.

FLORIDA TORTS REPORTER. Matthew Bender and Company, Incorporated, 11 Penn Plaza, New York, New York 10001. Monthly.

FORMBOOKS

BENDER'S FLORIDA FORMS--PLEADINGS. Matthew Bender and Company, Incorporated, 11 Penn Plaza, New York, New York 10001. 1968- . (Semiannual Supplements).

FLORIDA JURY FORMS: LEGAL AND BUSINESS. Lawyers Co-Operative Company, Aqueduct Building, Rochester, New York 14694. 1975- . (Annual Supplements).

FLORIDA UNIFORM COMMERCIAL CODE FORMS. Revised. Jarret C. Oeltjen. West Publishing Company, P.O. Box 64526, 50 West Kellogg Boulevard, St. Paul, Minnesota 55164-0526. 1982- . (Periodic Supplements).

HARRISON'S SUPPLEMENTAL FLORIDA PLEADINGS, PRACTICE AND FORMS ANNOTATED. Second Edition. Harrison Company, Publisher, 3110 Crossing Park, P.O. Box 7500, Norcross, Georgia 30091-7500. 1984- . (Annual Supplements). (Twelve Volume Looseleaf).

PRACTICE MATERIALS

FLORIDA ADMINISTRATIVE PRACTICE MANUAL. D and S Publishers, Incorporated, 2030 Calumet Street, P.O. Box 5105, Clearwater, Florida 34618-5105. 1979- . (Periodic Supplements).

FLORIDA ANTI-FENCING AND RICO ACTS. The Florida Bar, 650 Apalachee Parkway, Tallahassee, Florida 32399-2300. 1982- . (Periodic Supplements).

FLORIDA APPELLATE PRACTICE MANUAL. Arthur A. England, Jr. and Simon Tobias. D and S Publishers, Incorporated, P.O. Box 5105, Clearwater, Florida 34618-5105. 1979- . (Quarterly Supplements).

FLORIDA CIVIL TRIAL PRACTICE. Third Edition. The Florida Bar, 650 Appalachee Parkway, Tallahassee, Florida 32399-2300. 1984- . (Periodic Supplements).

FLORIDA CONDOMINIUM LAW AND PRACTICE. M. Hyman Shapiro. Matthew Bender and Company, Incorporated, 11 Penn Plaza, New York, New York 10001. 1986- . (Periodic Supplements).

FLORIDA CONDOMINIUM LAW MANUAL. Douglas S. Mc Gregen. D and S Publishers Incorporated, 2030 Calumet Street, P.O. Box 5105, Clearwater, Florida 34618-5105. 1980- . (Quarterly Supplements).

FLORIDA CONSTRUCTION LAW MANUAL. L. Leiby. Shepard's/McGraw-Hill, P.O. Box 1235, Colorado Springs, Colorado 80901. 1981. (Annual Supplements).

FLORIDA CONSUMER LAW MANUAL. T. Tennyson. D and S Publishers, Incorporated, 2030 Calumet Street, P.O. Box 5105, Clearwater, Florida 34618-5105. 1977- . (Annual Supplements).

FLORIDA CORPORATIONS. Howard P. Ross. Lawyers Co-Operative Company, Aqueduct Building, Rochester, New York 14694. 1980- . (Annual Supplement).

FLORIDA CORPORATIONS - LAWS AND PRACTICE. Larry J. Hoffman, et al. Matthew Bender and Company, Incorporated, 11 Penn Plaza, New York, New York 10001. 1985- . (Periodic Supplements).

FLORIDA CORPORATIONS MANUAL. Michael W. Gordon. D and S Publishers, Incorporated, 2030 Calumet Street, P.O. Box 5150, Clearwater, Florida 34618-5105. 1975- . (Bimonthly Supplements).

FLORIDA CREDITOR'S RIGHTS MANUAL. Stephen B. Rakusin. D and S Publishers, Incorporated, 2030 Calumet Street, P.O. Box 5150, Clearwater, Florida 34618-5105. 1975- . (Quarterly Supplements).

FLORIDA CRIMINAL DISCOVERY AND PRE-TRIAL MOTIONS MANUAL. John F. Yetter. D and S Publishers, Incorporated, 2030 Calumet Street, P.O. Box 5150, Clearwater, Florida 34618-5105. 1979- . (Quarterly Supplements).

FLORIDA CRIMINAL PROCEDURE. Thomas A. Bratten. Lawyers Co-Operative Company, Aqueduct Building, Rochester, New York 14694. 1981- . (Annual Supplements).

FLORIDA CRIMINAL PROCEDURE SERVICE. John F. Yetter. D and S Publishers, Incorporated, 2030 Calumet Street, P.O. Box 5105, Clearwater, Florida 34618-5105. 1980- . (Quarterly Supplements).

FLORIDA ESTATES PRACTICE GUIDE. (Revised Edition). Thomas A. Thomas. Matthew Bender and Company, Incorporated, 11 Penn Plaza, New York, New York 10001. 1978- . (Annual Supplements).

FLORIDA EVIDENCE MANUAL. Kenneth B. Hughes. D and S Publishers, Incorporated, 2030 Calumet Street, P.O. Box 5105, Clearwater, Florida 34618-5105. 1982- . (Quarterly Supplements).

FLORIDA FAMILY LAW. Brenda Abrams. Matthew Bender and Company, Incorporated, 11 Penn Plaza, New York, New York 10001. 1986- . (Periodic Supplements).

FLORIDA FAMILY LAW PRACTICE MANUAL. Gerald Schackow. D and S Publishers, Incorporated, 2030 Calumet Street, P.O. Box 5105, Clearwater, Florida 34618-5105. 1976- . (Quarterly Supplements).

FLORIDA LAWYER'S GUIDE. William H. Namack and W. McKinley Smiley, Jr. Callaghan and Company, 155 Pfingsten Road, Deerfield, Illinois 60015. 1984- . (Periodic Supplements).

FLORIDA MOTOR VEHICLE LIABILITY LAW. Marcia MacConnell. D and S Publishers, Incorporated, 2030 Calumet Street, P.O. Box 5105, Clearwater, Florida 34618-5105. 1981- . (Quarterly Supplements).

FLORIDA NEGLIGENCE LAW. Marcia MacConnell. D and S Publishers, Incorporated, 2030 Calumet Street, P.O. Box 5105, Clearwater, Florida 34618-5105. 1986- . (Semiannual Supplements).

FLORIDA PROBATE CODE MANUAL. David T. Smith. D and S Publishers, Incorporated, 2030 Calumet Street, P.O. Box 5105, Clearwater, Florida 34618-5105. 1975- . (Quarterly Supplements).

FLORIDA PROCEEDINGS AFTER DISSOLUTION OF MARRIAGE. The Florida Bar, 650 Appalachee Parkway, Tallahasee, Florida 32399-2300. 1983- . (Periodic Supplements).

FLORIDA PUBLIC EMPLOYEE REPORTER. LRP Publications, An Axon Group Company, 747 Dresher Road, Hrosham, Pennsylvania 19044. 1975- . (Periodic Supplements).

FLORIDA REAL ESTATE. Jonathan L. Alpert. Lawyers Co-Operative/Bancroft-Whitney Company, Aqueduct Building, Rochester, New York 14694. 1982- . (Annual Supplements).

FLORIDA REAL ESTATE HANDBOOK. J. Kenneth Ballinger. Michie/Bobbs-Merrill Law Publishing Company, P.O. Box 7587, Charlottesville, Virginia 22906-7587. 1979.

FLORIDA REAL ESTATE TRANSACTIONS. Ralph E. Boyer. Matthew Bender and Company, Incorporated, 11 Penn Plaza, New York, New York 10001. 1959- . (Annual Supplements).

FLORIDA REAL ESTATE TRANSACTIONS. Paul C. Gibson. D and S Publishers, Incorporated, 2030 Calumet Street, P.O. Box 5105, Clearwater, Florida 34618-5105. 1982- . (Quarterly Supplements).

FLORIDA RESIDENTIAL LANDLORD TENANT LAW MANUAL. James C. Hauser. D and S Publishers, Incorporated, 2030 Calumet Street, P.O. Box 5105, Clearwater, Florida 34618-5105. 1983- . (Quarterly Supplements).

FLORIDA STATE AND LOCAL TAXATION. Millard W. Clark, Jr. D and S Publishers, Incorporated, 2030 Calumet Street, P.O. Box 5105, Clearwater, Florida 34618-5105. 1983- . (Semiannual Supplements).

FLORIDA TAX SERVICE. David M. Hudson. Matthew Bender and Company, Incorporated, 11 Penn Plaza, New York, New York 10001. 1985- . (Annual Supplements).

FLORIDA TRAFFIC AND D.U.I. PRACTICE MANUAL. Richard A. Schwartz. D and S Publishers, Incorporated, 2030 Calumet Street, P.O. Box 5105, Clearwater, Florida 34618-5105. 1980- . (Semiannual Supplements).

FLORIDA WORKMEN'S COMPENSATION MANUAL. Elizabeth Hapner. D and S Publishers, Incorporated, 2030 Calumet Street, P.O. Box 5105, Clearwater, Florida 34618-5105. 1979- . (Quarterly Supplements).

FLORIDA ZONING LAW MANUAL. Lloyd Davidson and Marcia MacConnell. D and S Publishers, Incorporated, 2030 Calumet Street, P.O. Box 5105, Clearwater, Florida 34618-5105. 1980- . (Quarterly Supplements).

IMMIGRATION LAW AND PRACTICE IN FLORIDA. Florida Bar, 650 Apalachee Parkway, Tallahassee, Florida 32399. 1983.

TRIAL HANDBOOK FOR FLORIDA LAWYERS. W. Hicks. Lawyers Cooperative Publishing Company, Aqueduct Building, Rochester, New York 14694. 1970. (Periodic Supplements).

MANUALS AND RESEARCH GUIDES

GUIDE TO FLORIDA LEGAL RESEARCH. Second Edition. Gail G. Reinertsen and Richard L. Brown. Florida Bar Continuing Legal Education Department, 650 Apalachee Parkway, Tallahassee, Florida 32399-2300. 1986.

RESEARCH IN FLORIDA LAW. Second Revised Edition. Harriet L. French. Oceana Publications, Incorporated, 75 Main Street, Dobbs Ferry, New York 10522. 1965.

ASSOCIATIONS AND PROFESSIONAL SOCIETIES

THE FLORIDA BAR, 650 Appalachee Parkway, Tallahassee, Florida 32399-2300. (904) 561-5600.

DIRECTORIES

DIRECTORY OF FLORIDA GOVERNMENT. Elections Division, Florida Department of State, State Capitol, Tallahassee, Florida 32301. (Irregular). (Free).

FLORIDA BAR JOURNAL--DIRECTORY ISSUE. The Florida Bar, 650 Apalachee Parkway, Tallahassee, Florida 32399-2300. (Annual--September).

OFFICIALS OF FLORIDA MUNICIPALITIES. Florida League of Cities, 201 West Park Avenue, Tallahassee, Florida 32302. (Annual).

OTHER SOURCES

BASIC ESTATE PLANNING IN FLORIDA. The Florida Bar, 650 Appalachee Parkway, Tallahassee, Florida 32399. 1980.

COMPARATIVE NEGLIGENCE AND CONTRIBUTION IN FLORIDA. Second Edition. The Florida Bar, 650 Appalachee Parkway, Tallahassee, Florida 32399. 1982.

ENVIRONMENTAL REGULATION AND LITIGATION IN FLORIDA. The Florida Bar, 650 Appalachee Parkway, Tallahassee, Florida 32399. 1981.

FLORIDA AGRICULTURAL LAW. J. Wershow. D and S Publishers, Incorporated, 2030 Calumet Street, P.O. Box 5105, Clearwater, Florida 33618-5105. 1981- . (Annual Supplements).

FLORIDA CORPORATION SYSTEM. J. Martin. West Publishing Company, 50 West Kellogg Boulevard, St. Paul, Minnesota 55164. 1984.

FLORIDA DAMAGES. J. Alpert. Harrison Company, 3110 Crossing Park, Norcross, Georgia 30091. 1978. (Annual Supplements).

FLORIDA EVIDENCE. Second Edition. C. Ernhardt. West Publishing Company, 50 West Kellogg Boulevard, St. Paul, Minnesota 55164. 1984.

FLORIDA EVIDENCE. Second Edition. S. Gard. Lawyers Cooperative Publishing Company, Aqueduct Building, Rochester, New York 14694. 1982.

FLORIDA REAL PROPERTY LAW. J. Van Doren. Harrison Company, 3110 Crossing Park, Norcross, Georgia 30091. 1984.

FLORIDA DISSOLUTION OF MARRIAGE. Second Edition. The Florida Bar, 650 Appalachee Parkway, Tallahassee, Florida 32399. 1984- . (Annual Supplements).

STATES--GEORGIA

STATUTES, CODES, STANDARDS, UNIFORM LAWS

ADVANCE ANNOTATION SERVICE--GEORGIA. Michie Company, P.O. Box 7587, Charlottesville, Virginia 22906-7587. (Three Pamphlets per Year).

GEORGIA CODE ANNOTATED. Harrison Company, Publisher, 3110 Crossing Park, P.O. Box 7500, Norcross, Georgia 30091-7500. 1936- . (Annual Supplements).

OFFICIAL CODE OF GEORGIA ANNOTATED. Michie Company, P.O. Box 7587, Charlottesville, Virginia 22906-7587. (Official Edition). 1982- . (Annual Supplements).

OFFICIAL COMPILATION OF RULES AND REGULATIONS OF THE STATE OF GEORGIA. Secretary of State, Administrative Procedure Division, Room 205E, 166 Pryor Street Southwest, Atlanta, Georgia 30303. 1972- . (Monthly Updates).

LOOSELEAF SERVICES AND REPORTERS

GEORGIA APPEALS REPORTS. Darby Printing Company, 715 West Whitehall Street, Southwest, Atlanta, Georgia 30310. 1907- . (Quarterly). (Georgia Court of Appeals).

GEORGIA APPELLATE REPORTER. Georgia State Library, 301 Judicial Building, Atlanta, Georgia 30334. 1930- . (Georgia Court of Appeals).

GEORGIA CASES. West Publishing Company, P.O. Box 64526, 50 West Kellogg Boulevard, St. Paul, Minnesota 55164-0526. 1939- . (Georgia Supreme Court and Court of Appeals).

GEORGIA REPORTS. Georgia State Library, 301 Judicial Building, Atlanta, Georgia 30334. 1846- . (Georgia Supreme Court).

SOUTHEASTERN REPORTER. (First and Second Series). West Publishing Company, P.O. Box 64526, 50 West Kellogg Boulevard, St. Paul, Minnesota 55164-0526. 1887- . (Georgia Supreme Court and Court of Appeals).

ATTORNEY GENERAL OPINIONS

OPINIONS OF THE ATTORNEY GENERAL. Department of Law, 104 Judicial Building, Atlanta, Georgia 30334. (Annual). Also available on Lexis: January 1976-; Westlaw: 1977- .

ETHICS OPINIONS, CODES, RULES

GEORGIA ADVISORY ETHICS OPINIONS are issued by the State Disciplinary Board of the State Bar of Georgia. Proposed advisory opinions are published in the Georgia State Bar News . Abstracts of the official advisory opinions are published in the State Bar of Georgia Handbook and in the ABA/BNA Lawyers' Reference Manual . For further information concerning these opinions, or for copies of full text opinions, contact the state Disciplinary Board, State Bar of Georgia, The Hurt Building, 50 Hurt Plaza, Atlanta, Georgia 30303. (404-527-8700).

STATE BAR OF GEORGIA HANDBOOK. State Bar of Georgia, The Hurt Building, 50 Hurt Plaza, Atlanta, Georgia 30303. (Annual). (Includes Standards of Professional Responsibility rules, procedures and synopses of advisory opinions).

COURT RULES

GEORGIA COURT RULES, STATE AND FEDERAL. West Publishing Company, P.O. Box 64526, 50 West Kellogg Boulevard, St. Paul, Minnesota 55164-0526. 1987. (Annual).

GEORGIA RULES OF COURT ANNOTATED. Michie Company, P.O. Box 7587, Charlottesville, Virginia 22906-7587. (Annual).

STATES--GEORGIA

JURY INSTRUCTIONS

REQUESTS TO CHARGE: CIVIL AND CRIMINAL CASES. Harrison Company, Publisher, 3110 Crossing Park, P.O. Box 7500, Norcross, Georgia 30091-7500. 1985- .

REQUESTS TO CHARGE IN CIVIL CASES: THE LAW IN GEORGIA. John Hood Ridley and Randy Norton. Harrison Company, Publisher, 3110 Crossing Park, P.O. Box 7500, Norcross, Georgia 30091-7500. 1977- .

REQUESTS TO CHARGE IN CRIMINAL CASES: THE LAW IN GEORGIA. Harrison Company, Publisher, 3110 Crossing Park, P.O. Box 7500, Norcross, Georgia 30091-7500. 1978- . (Periodic Supplements).

SUGGESTED PATTERN JURY INSTRUCTIONS--VOLUME I: CIVIL CASES. Second Edition. Council of Superior Court Judges of Georgia, University of Georgia, Carl Vinson Institute of Government, Terrell Hall, Athens, Georgia 30602. 1984- . (Periodic Supplements).

SUGGESTED PATTERN JURY INSTRUCTIONS--VOLUME II: CRIMINAL CASES. Second Edition. Council of Superior Court Judges of Georgia, University of Georgia, Carl Vinson Institute, Terrell Hall, Athens, Georgia 30602. 1984- . (Periodic Supplements).

DIGESTS, INDEXES, ABSTRACTS, CITATORS

DIGESTIVE INDEX. Harrison Company, Publisher, 3110 Crossing Park, P.O. Box 7500, Norcross, Georgia 30091-7500. 1976- . (Index to Georgia Reports and Georgia Appeal Reports).

GEORGIA DIGEST. (First and Second Series). West Publishing Company, P.O. Box 64526, 50 West Kellogg Boulevard, St. Paul, Minnesota 55164-0526. 1986- . (Annual Supplements).

SHEPARD'S GEORGIA CITATIONS. Shepard's/McGraw-Hill, P.O. Box 1235, Colorado Springs, Colorado 80901. (Eight Pamphlets Per Year).

SHEPARD'S SOUTH EASTERN REPORTER CITATIONS. Shepard's/McGraw-Hill, P.O. Box 1235, Colorado Springs, Colorado 80901. 1921- . (Monthly Supplements).

SOUTHEAST DIGEST. (First and Second Series). West Publishing Company, P.O. Box 64526, 50 West Kellogg Boulevard, St. Paul, Minnesota 55164-0526. (Annual Supplements). 1935- .

ENCYCLOPEDIAS AND DICTIONARIES

ENCYCLOPEDIA OF GEORGIA LAW. Harrison Company, Publisher, 3110 Crossing Park, P.O. Box 7500, Norcross, Georgia 30091-7500. 1960- . (Annual Supplements).

LAW REVIEWS AND PERIODICALS

ATLANTA LAWYER. Atlanta Bar Association, Equitable Building, Suite 606, Atlanta, Georgia 30303. (Bimonthly).

Encyclopedia of Legal Information Sources • 2nd Ed.

EMORY LAW JOURNAL. Emory University School of Law, 1722 North Decatur Road, Atlanta, Georgia 30322. (Quarterly).

GEORGIA JOURNAL OF INTERNATIONAL AND COMPARATIVE LAW. University of Georgia, School of Law, Athens, Georgia 30602. (At Least Three Times per Year).

GEORGIA LAW REVIEW. University of Georgia, School of Law, Athens, Georgia 30602. (Quarterly).

GEORGIA STATE BAR JOURNAL. State Bar of Georgia, 800 The Hurt Building, Atlanta, Georgia 30303. (Quarterly).

GEORGIA STATE BAR NEWS. State Bar of Georgia, 800 The Hurt Building, Atlanta, Georgia 30303. (Bimonthly).

GEORGIA STATE UNIVERSITY BAR REVIEW. Georgia State University College of Law, Box 492, University Plaza, Atlanta, Georgia 30303-3098. (Biannual).

MERCER LAW REVIEW. Mercer University, Walter F. George School of Law, Macon, Georgia 31207. (Quarterly).

NEWSLETTERS AND NEWSPAPERS

ALLA NEWSLETTER. Atlantic Law Libraries Association, c/o Anne J. Johnson, Fisher and Phillips, 1500 Resurgers Plaza, 945 East Paces Ferry Road, Atlanta, Georgia 30326. Quarterly.

GEORGIA EMPLOYMENT LAW LETTER. M. Lee Smith Publishers and Printers, 162 Fourth Avenue North, Nashville, Tennessee 37219. Monthly.

GEORGIA ENVIRONMENTAL LAW LETTER. M. Lee Smith Publishers and Printers, 162 Fourth Avenue North, Nashville, Tennessee 37219. Monthly.

GEORGIA LAW LETTER. M. Lee Smith Publishers and Printers, 162 Fourth Avenue North, Nashville, Tennessee 37219. Weekly.

GEORGIA REAL ESTATE LAW LETTER. M. Lee Smith Publishers and Printers, 162 Fourth Avenue North, Nashville, Tennessee 37219. Monthly.

GEORGIA REAL ESTATE LAW LETTER-BROKERS EDITION. M. Lee Smith Publishers and Printers, 162 Fourth Avenue North, Nashville, Tennessee 37219. Monthly.

THE GEORGIA TRIAL REPORTER. Judicial Advisory Services, Incorporated, P.O. Box 99704, 3309 College Drive, Louisville, Kentucky 40299. Monthly.

LEGISLATIVE NEWSLETTER. League of Women Voters of Georgia, 100 Edgewood Avenue, Northeast, Suite 1010, Atlanta, Georgia 30303. Weekly when in session.

FORMBOOKS

CIVIL PLEADING AND PRACTICE FORMS. Harrison Company, Publisher, 3110 Crossing Park, P.O. Box 7500, Norcross, Georgia 30091-7500. 1985- . (Annual Supplements).

GEORGIA CRIMINAL TRIAL PRACTICE FORMS. Second Edition. William W. Daniel. Harrison Company, Publisher, P.O. Box 7500, Norcross, Georgia 30091-7500. 1987- . (Annual Supplements).

PRACTICE MATERIALS

ADMISSABILITY OF EVIDENCE IN CIVIL CASES: A MANUAL FOR GEORGIA LAWYERS. R. Herman and M. McLaughlin. Harrison Company, 3110 Crossing Park, Norcross, Georgia 30091. 1984.

BANKRUPTCY: A GEORGIA LAW PRACTICE SYSTEM. William E. Anderson and W. Stephen Scott. Michie Company, P.O. Box 7587, Charlottesville, Virginia 22906-7587. 1984- . (Periodic Supplements). (Looseleaf).

COLLECTIONS: A GEORGIA LAW PRACTICE SYSTEM. J. Glover and W. Anderson. Michie Company, P.O. Box 7587, Charlottesville, Virginia 22906-7587. 1984.

DAVIS AND SHULMAN'S GEORGIA PRACTICE AND PROCEDURE. Fifth Edition. Richard C. Ruskel and Jean M. McIntosh. Harrison Company, Publisher, 3110 Crossing Park, P.O. Box 7500, Norcross, Georgia 30091-7500. 1986- . (Periodic Supplements).

DOMESTIC RELATIONS: A GEORGIA LAW PRACTICE SYSTEM. A. Smith. Michie Company, P.O. Box 7587, Charlottesville, Virginia 22906-7587. 1987.

GEORGIA COMMERCIAL PRACTICE. Gerald L. Kock. Michie Company, P.O. Box 7587, Charlottesville, Virginia 22906-7587. 1982- . (Periodic Supplements).

GEORGIA CORPORATIONS. Douglas MacGregor. Lawyers Co-Operative Company, Aqueduct Building, Rochester, New York 14694. 1985- . (Semiannual Supplements).

GEORGIA CRIMINAL TRIAL PRACTICE. William W. Daniel. Harrison Company, Publisher, 3110 Crossing Park, P.O. Box 7500, Norcross, Georgia 30091-7500. 1986.

GEORGIA DIVORCE. Barry G. McGough. Lawyers Co-Operative Company, Aqueduct Building, Rochester, New York 14694. 1981- . (Annual Supplements).

GEORGIA DIVORCE, ALIMONY, AND CHILD CUSTODY. Third Edition. Dan E. McConaughey. Harrison Company, Publisher, 3110 Crossing Park, P.O. Box 7500, Norcross, Georgia 30091-7500. 1986.

GEORGIA FAMILY LAW MANUAL. Anita Butler. D and S Publishers, Incorporated, P.O. Box 5105, Clearwater, Florida 34618-5105. 1985- . (Semiannual Supplements).

GEORGIA HANDBOOK ON CRIMINAL EVIDENCE. William W. Daniel. Harrison Company, Publisher, P.O. Box 7500, Norcross, Georgia 30091-7500. 1986- . (Periodic Supplements).

GEORGIA MAGISTRATE COURT HANDBOOK. J. Warren. Harrison Company, 3110 Crossing Park, Norcross, Georgia 30091. 1984.

GEORGIA PROBATE. Robert E. Hall and Brent Jackson, Jr. Lawyers Co-Operative Company, Aqueduct Building, Rochester, New York 14694. 1981- . (Annual Supplements).

GEORGIA PROBATE MANUAL. E. Hapner. Butterworth Legal Publishers, 90 Stiles Road, Salem, New Hampshire 03079. 1986.

REAL ESTATE: A GEORGIA LAW PRACTICE SYSTEM. Wesley B. Warren, Jr. Michie Company, P.O. Box 7587, Charlottesville, Virginia 22906-7587. 1983- . (Periodic Supplements). (Includes Forms).

THE RULE AGAINST PERPETUITIES IN GEORGIA. Vernon F. Chaffin. Michie Company, P.O. Box 7587, Charlottesville, Virginia 22906-7587. 1984- . (Periodic Supplements).

TRIAL HANDBOOK FOR GEORGIA LAWYERS. Jack Kleiner. Lawyers Co-Operative Company, Aqueduct Building, Rochester, New York 14694. 1974- . (Annual Supplements).

MANUALS AND RESEARCH GUIDES

REFERENCE GUIDE TO GEORGIA LEGAL HISTORY AND LEGAL RESEARCH. Leah Chanin. Michie Company, P.O. Box 7587, Charlottesville, Virginia 22906-7587. 1980- . (Periodic Supplements).

ASSOCIATIONS AND PROFESSIONAL SOCIETIES

ATLANTA BAR ASSOCIATION, 100 Peachtree Street, Northwest, Atlanta, Georgia 30303. (405) 521-0781.

STATE BAR OF GEORGIA, 800 The Hurt Building, 50 Hurt Plaza, Atlanta, Georgia 30303. (404) 527-8700.

DIRECTORIES

DIRECTORY OF GEORGIA MUNICIPAL OFICIALS. Georgia Municipal Association, 201 Pryor Street, Atlanta, Georgia 30303. (Annual).

GEORGIA LEGAL DIRECTORY. Legal Directories Publishing Company, 2122 Kidwell, P.O. Box 140200, Dallas, Texas 75214-0200. (Annual).

GEORGIA OFFICIAL DIRECTORY OF UNITED STATES CONGRESSMEN, STATE AND COUNTY OFFICERS. Elections Division, Georgia Secretary of State, State Capitol, Room 110, Atlanta, Georgia 30334. (Irregular). (Free).

STATE BAR DIRECTORY. State Bar of Georgia, The Hurt Building, 50 Hurt Plaza, Atlanta, Georgia 30303. (Annual). (Includes Bar Committees and Standards of Professional Responsibility).

OTHER SOURCES

ADDITIONAL STUDIES IN GEORGIA LOCAL GOVERNMENT LAW. R. Sentell. Michie Company, P.O. Box 7587, Charlottesville, Virginia 22906-7587. 1983.

COBB AND ELDRIDGE GEORGIA LAW OF DAMAGES. Second Edition. Harrison Company, 3110 Crossing Park, Norcross, Georgia 30091. 1984.

CRIMINAL OFFENSES IN GEORGIA. P. Kurtz. Harrison Company, 3110 Crossing Park, Norcross, Georgia 30091. 1980.

GEORGIA REAL ESTATE LAW AND PROCEDURE. Second Edition. G. Pindar. Harrison Company, 3110 Crossing Park, Norcross, Georgia 30091. 1979.

GOVERNMENTAL ETHICS AND CONFLICTS OF INTEREST IN GEORGIA. K. McVay and others. Michie Company, P.O. Box 7587, Charlottesville, Virginia 22906-7587. 1980.

STATES--HAWAII

STATUTES, CODES, STANDARDS, UNIFORM LAWS

HAWAII ADMINISTRATIVE RULES DRAFTING MANUAL. Second Edition. Ken H. Takayama. Legislative Reference Bureau, State Capital, Honolulu, Hawaii 96813. 1984.

HAWAII REVISED STATUTES. Legislative Reference Bureau, Revisor of Statutes, State Capitol, Honolulu, Hawaii 96813. 1968- . (Annual Supplements). (Title Varies).

SESSION LAWS OF HAWAII. Legislative Reference Bureau, Revisor of Statutes, State Capitol, Honolulu, Hawaii 96813. 1959- . (Semiannual).

LOOSELEAF SERVICES AND REPORTERS

HAWAII APPELLATE REPORTS. West Publishing Company, P.O. Box 64526, 50 West Kellogg Boulevard, St. Paul, Minnesota 55164-0526. 1981- . (Hawaii Intermediate Court of Appeals).

HAWAII REPORTS. Supreme Court of Hawaii, Supreme Court Law Library, P.O. Box 779, Honolulu, Hawaii 96808. 1847- .

PACIFIC REPORTER (First and Second Series). West Publishing Company, P.O. Box 64526, 50 West Kellogg Boulevard, St. Paul, Minnesota 55164-0526. (Hawaii Supreme Court and Court of Appeals). 1931- .

ATTORNEY GENERAL OPINIONS

HAWAII OPINIONS OF THE ATTORNEY GENERAL. Office of the Attorney General, State Capitol, Honolulu, Hawaii 98613. (Also available on Lexis: January 1977-; Westlaw: January 1977-).

ETHICS OPINIONS, CODES, RULES

HAWAII CODE OF PROFESSIONAL RESPONSIBILITY and the DISCIPLINARY RULES are published in the Hawaii Code of Professional Responsibility. Clerk's Office, Supreme Court of Hawaii, P.O. Box 2560, Honolulu, Hawaii 96804. 1974- .

HAWAII ETHICS OPINIONS. Ethics opinions for Hawaii are issued by the Disciplinary Board of the Hawaiian Supreme Court and are not formally published by the State. Opinions are availabe on Lexis: January 1977-; Westlaw 1977- . For further information concerning these opinions or for copies, contact the Office of Disciplinary Counsel, 1164 Bishop Street, Suite 600, Honolulu, Hawaii 96813. 808-521-4591.

COURT RULES

HAWAII COURT RULES. West Publishing Company, 50 West Kellogg Boulevard, St. Paul, Minnesota 55164. 1980.

RULES OF COURT. Supreme Court Law Library, P.O. Box 779, Honolulu, Hawaii 96808. 1972- . (Periodic Supplements).

JURY INSTRUCTIONS

HAWAII STANDARD JURY INSTRUCTIONS--CRIMINAL. Hawaii Supreme Court Law Library, P.O. Box 779, Honolulu, Hawaii 96808. 1966- .

DIGESTS, INDEXES, ABSTRACTS, CITATORS

HAWAII DIGEST. West Publishing Company, P.O. Box 64526, 50 West Kellogg Boulevard, St. Paul, Minnesota 55164-0526. 1967- . (Periodic Supplements).

PACIFIC DIGEST. West Publishing Company, P.O. Box 64526, 50 West Kellogg Boulevard, St. Paul, Minnesota 55164-0526. 1932- . (Annual Supplements).

SHEPARD'S HAWAII CITATIONS. Shepard's/McGraw-Hill, P.O. Box 1235, Colorado Springs, Colorado 80901. (Quarterly Supplements).

SHEPARD'S PACIFIC REPORTER CITATIONS. Shepard's/McGraw-Hill, P.O. Box 1235, Colorado Springs, Colorado 80901. (Monthly Supplements).

LAW REVIEWS AND PERIODICALS

HAWAII BAR JOURNAL. Hawaii State Bar Association, P.O. Box 26, Honolulu, Hawaii 96810. (Semi-annual).

HAWAII BAR NEWS. Hawaii State Bar Association, Fifth Floor, Pauahi Tower, 1001 Bishop Street, Honolulu, Hawaii 96813. (Monthly).

HAWAII LAW JOURNAL. Hawaii State Bar Association, Fifth Floor, Pauahi Tower, 1001 Bishop Street, Honolulu, Hawaii 98613. (Biannual).

NEWSLETTERS AND NEWSPAPERS

HAWAII BAR NEWS. Hawaii State Bar Association, P.O. Box 26, Honolulu, Hawaii 96810. Monthly.

LEGISLATIVE TAX BILL SERVICE. Tax Foundation of Hawaii, 220 South King Street, Suite 680, Honolulu, Hawaii 96813. Weekly when in session.

TAX TOPICS. Tax Foundation of Hawaii, 220 South King Street, Suite 680, Honolulu, Hawaii 96813. Quarterly.

PRACTICE MATERIALS

HAWAII ADOPTION MANUAL. Hawaii Institute for Continuing Legal Education, University of Hawaii School of Law, 2525 Dole Street, Honolulu, Hawaii 96822. 1984- . (Looseleaf). (Periodic Supplements).

HAWAII APPELLATE HANDBOOK. Hawaii Institute for Continuing Legal Education, University of Hawaii School of Law, 2525 Dole Street, Honolulu, Hawaii 96822. (Looseleaf). 1985- . (Periodic Supplements).

HAWAII COLLECTION MANUAL. Hawaii Institute for Continuing Legal Education, University of Hawaii School of Law, 2525 Dole Street, Honolulu, Hawaii 96822. 1979- . (Looseleaf). (Periodic Supplements).

HAWAII CONVEYANCE MANUAL. Hawaii Institute for Continuing Legal Education, University of Hawaii, School of Law, 2525 Dole Street, Honolulu, Hawaii 96822. 1979.

HAWAII DIVORCE MANUAL: A COOPERATIVE EFFORT. Second Edition. Robert LeClair. Hawaii Institute for Continuing Legal Education, University of Hawaii School of Law, 2525 Dole Street, Honolulu, Hawaii 96822. 1984- . (Periodic Supplements).

HAWAII PROBATE MANUAL. Hawaii Institute for Continuing Legal Education, University of Hawaii School of Law, 2525 Dole Street, Honolulu, Hawaii 96822. 1977- . (Periodic Supplements).

TAXES OF HAWAII. R. Bock. Crossroads Press, Incorporated, Box 833, Honolulu, Hawaii 96808. 1977.

ASSOCIATIONS AND PROFESSIONAL SOCIETIES

HAWAII BAR ASSOCIATION, 1001 Bishop Street, Suite 950, Honolulu, Hawaii 96813. (808) 537-1868.

DIRECTORIES

GUIDE TO GOVERNMENT IN HAWAII--DIRECTORY OF STATE, COUNTY AND FEDERAL OFFICIALS. Hawaii Legislative Reference Bureau, State Capitol, Honolulu, Hawaii 96813. 1984- . (Annual Supplements).

HAWAII STATE BAR ASSOCIATION DIRECTORY. Crossroads Press, Incorporated, P.O. Box 833, Honolulu, Hawaii 96808. (Annual).

STATES--IDAHO

STATUTES, CODES, STANDARDS, UNIFORM LAWS

IDAHO CODE. Michie Company, P.O. Box 7587, Charlottesville, Virginia 22906-7587. 1947- . (Annual Supplements).

SESSION LAWS OF THE STATE OF IDAHO. Secretary of State, Room 203, State Capitol Building, 700 West Jefferson Street, Boise, Idaho 83720. 1891- .

LOOSELEAF SERVICES AND REPORTERS

IDAHO REPORTS. West Publishing Company, P.O. Box 64526, 50 West Kellogg Boulevard, St. Paul, Minnesota 55164-0526. (Covers Idaho Supreme Court and Court of Appeals). 1866- .

PACIFIC REPORTER. (First and Second Series). West Publishing Company, P.O. Box 64526, 50 West Kellogg Boulevard, St. Paul, Minnesota 55164-0526. 1881- .

ATTORNEY GENERAL OPINIONS

IDAHO ATTORNEY GENERAL'S OPINIONS AND ANNUAL REPORT. Office of the Attorney General, State House, Room 210, Boise, Idaho 83720. 1972- . Also available on Lexis: January 1977-; Westlaw: 1977- .

ETHICS OPINIONS, CODES, RULES

IDAHO STATE BAR DESKBOOK. Idaho State Bar, P.O. Box 895, Boise, Idaho 83701. (Annual). (Includes Code of Professional Responsibility , Disciplinary Rules and Summary of Ethics Opinions). Some advisory ethics opinions are published in The Advocate . For further information concerning Idaho ethics opinions, or for full text opinions, contact the Bar Counsel of the Idaho State Bar. (208-342-8956).

COURT RULES

IDAHO COURT RULES. Michie Company, P.O. Box 7587, Charlottesville, Virginia 22906-7587. 1980- . (Annual Supplements).

IDAHO COURT RULES. West Publishing Company, P.O. Box 64526, 50 West Kellogg Boulevard, St. Paul, Minnesota 55164-0526. (Annual).

JURY INSTRUCTIONS

IDAHO JURY INSTRUCTIONS. Idaho Pattern Jury Instructions Committee. Idaho State Bar, P.O. Box 895, Boise, Idaho 83701. 1982- . (Periodic Supplements).

DIGESTS, INDEXES, ABSTRACTS, CITATORS

IDAHO DIGEST. West Publishing Company, P.O. Box 64526, 50 West Kellogg Boulevard, St. Paul, Minnesota 55164-0526. 1938- . (Annual Supplements).

PACIFIC DIGEST. West Publishing Company, P.O. Box 64526, 50 West Kellogg Boulevard, St. Paul, Minnesota 55164-0526. 1932- . (Annual Supplements).

SHEPARD'S IDAHO CITATIONS. Shepard's/McGraw-Hill, P.O. Box 1235, Colorado Springs, Colorado 80901. (Quarterly Supplements).

SHEPARD'S PACIFIC REPORTER CITATIONS. Shepard's/McGraw-Hill, P.O. Box 1235, Colorado Springs, Colorado 80901. (Monthly supplements).

LAW REVIEWS AND PERIODICALS

THE ADVOCATE. Idaho State Bar, P.O. Box 895, Boise, Idaho 83701. (Monthly).

IDAHO LAW REVIEW. University of Idaho, College of Law, Rayborn Street, Moscow, Idaho 83843. (Three Issues per Year).

NEWSLETTERS AND NEWSPAPERS

THE ADVOCATE. The Idaho State Bar, 204 West State Street, Boise, Idaho 83701. Monthly.

STATES--IDAHO

IDAHO BANKRUPTCY COURT REPORT. Goller Publishing Corporation, P.O. Box 2576, Boise, Idaho 83701. Irregular.

IDAHO COURT OF APPEALS REPORT. Goller Publishing Corporation, P.O. Box 2576, Boise, Idaho 83701. Semimonthly.

IDAHO LEGISLATIVE REPORT. Goller Publishing Corporation, P.O. Box 2576, Boise, Idaho 83701. Daily when in session.

IDAHO SUPREME COURT REPORT. Goller Publishing Corporation, P.O. Box 2576, Boise, Idaho 83701. Irregular.

JURY VERDICTS NORTHWEST. Jury Verdicts Northwest, P.O. Box 1165, Seattle, Washington 98111. Monthly.

WEEKLY IDAHO LEGISLATIVE REPORT. Goller Publishing Corporation, P.O. Box 2576, Boise, Idaho 83701. Biweekly when in session.

PRACTICE MATERIALS

IDAHO APPELLATE HANDBOOK. Idaho Law Foundation, P.O. Box 895, Boise, Idaho 83701. 1985- . (Periodic Supplements).

IDAHO ESTATE PLANNING DESKBOOK. E. Ahreus. Idaho Law Foundation, P.O. Box 895, Boise, Idaho 83701. 1983- . (Periodic Supplements).

IDAHO FAMILY LAW HANDBOOK. P. Buser, Editor. Idaho Law Foundation, P.O. Box 895, Boise, Idaho 83701. 1981- . (Periodic Supplements).

IDAHO PRE-TRIAL CIVIL PROCEDURE. Craig Lewis. Idaho Law Foundation, P.O. Box 895, Boise, Idaho 83701. 1977- . (Periodic Supplements).

ASSOCIATIONS AND PROFESSIONAL SOCIETIES

IDAHO BAR ASSOCIOATION, 205 West State, Boise, Idaho 83702. (208) 342-8958.

IDAHO LAW FOUNDATION, P.O. Box 895, Boise, Idaho 83701. (208) 342-8958.

DIRECTORIES

DIRECTORY OF IDAHO GOVERNMENT OFFICIALS. Association of Idaho Cities, 3314 Grace Street, Boise, Idaho 83703. (Annual).

MOUNTAIN STATE LEGAL DIRECTORY. Legal Directories Publishing Company, 2122 Kidwell, P.O. Box 140200, Dallas, Texas 75214-0200. (Annual). (Colorado, Idaho, Montana, New Mexico, Utah, and Wyoming).

OTHER SOURCES

COMMUNITY PROPERTY LAW OF IDAHO. Idaho Law Foundation, P.O. Box 895, Boise, Idaho 83701. 1982.

IDAHO PROBATE SYSTEM BOOK. Idaho Law Foundation, P.O. Box 895, Boise, Idaho 83701. 1977.

STATES--ILLINOIS

STATUTES, CODES, STANDARDS, UNIFORM LAWS

ILLINOIS LEGISLATIVE SERVICE. West Publishing Company, P.O. Box 64526, 50 West Kellogg Boulevard, St. Paul, Minnesota 55164-0526. (Irregular).

ILLINOIS REVISED STATUTES. West Publishing Company, P.O. Box 64526, 50 West Kellogg Boulevard, St. Paul, Minnesota 55164-0526. 1937- . (Publisher Varies).

SMITH-HURD ILLINOIS ANNOTATED STATUTES. West Publishing Company, P.O. Box 64526, 50 West Kellogg Boulevard, St. Paul, Minnesota 55164-0526. 1934- . (Annual Supplements).

ILLINOIS ADMINISTRATIVE CODE. Secratary of State, State House, Room 213, Springfield, Illinois 62756. 1985- . (Periodic Updates).

ILLINOIS REGISTER. Secretary of State, State House, Room 213, Springfield, Illinois 62756. 1977- . (Weekly).

LOOSELEAF SERVICES AND REPORTERS

ILLINOIS APPELLATE COURT REPORTS. (First through Third Series). Pantagraph Printing and Stationary Company, Legal Division, P.O. Box 1406, Bloomington, Illinois 61702. 1877- .

ILLINOIS COURT OF CLAIMS REPORTS. Pantagraph Printing and Stationery Company, Legal Division, P.O. Box 1406, Bloomington, Illinois 61702. 1889- .

ILLINOIS COURTS BULLETIN. Illinois State Bar Association, Publications Department, Illinois Bar Center, 424 South Second Street, Springfield, Illinois 62701. (Monthly).

ILLINOIS DECISIONS. West Publishing Company, P.O. Box 64526, 50 West Kellogg Boulevard, St. Paul, Minnesota 55164-0526. 1976- . (Illinois Supreme Court and Illinois Appellate Court).

ILLINOIS REPORTS. (First and Second Series). Pantagraph Printing and Stationary Company, Legal Division, P.O. Box 1406, Bloomington, Illinois 61702. 1819- . (Illinois Supreme Court).

NORTHEASTERN REPORTER. (First and Second Series). West Publishing Company, P.O. Box 64526, 50 West Kellogg Boulevard, St. Paul, Minnesota 55164-0526. 1885- . (Illinois Supreme Court and Illinois Appellate Court).

HANDBOOKS, MANUALS, FORMBOOKS

CALLAGHAN'S ILLINOIS LEGAL FORMS WITH TAX NOTES. Callaghan and Company, 155 Pfingsten Road, Deerfield, Illinois 60015. 1982.

ILLINOIS UNIFORM COMMERCIAL CODE FORMS. W. Davenport. West Publishing Company, 50 West Kellogg Boulevard, St. Paul, Minnesota 55164. 1967- .

ATTORNEY GENERAL REPORTS

ILLINOIS ATTORNEY GENERAL'S REPORT FOR THE BIENNIAL. Attorney General's Office, Springfield, Illinois 62756. 1913- . (Biennial). (Title Varies). (Also available in Lexis: January 1977-; Westlaw: 1977-).

ETHICS OPINIONS, CODES, RULES

ATTORNEY CONDUCT, 1985. Janet L. Bassitt. Illinois Institute for Continuing Legal Education, 2395 West Jefferson Street, Springfield, Illinois 62702. 1985- . (Periodic Supplements).

CODE OF PROFESSIONAL RESPONSIBILITY ANNOTATED (ILLINOIS). J. Michael Kirtley. Illinois Institute for Continuing Legal Education, 2395 West Jefferson Street, Springfield, Illinois 62702. 1978.

ILLINOIS STATE BAR ASSOCIATION OPINIONS ON PROFESSIONAL ETHICS (OPINIONS NUMBER 101 - 687). Illinois State Bar Association, Illinois Bar Center, 424 South Second Street, Springfield, Illinois 62701. (217-525-1760). 1980.

ILLINOIS STATE BAR ASSOCIATION OPINIONS ON PROFESSIONAL ETHICS (OPINIONS NUMBER 644 - 874). Volume Two. Illinois State Bar Association, Illinois Bar Center, 424 South Second Street, Springfield, Illinois 62701. (All full text ethics opinions are also published in the Illinois Bar Journal . Abstracts of the opinions are published in the ABA/BNA Lawyers' Manual on Professional Conduct). 1984.

RULES OF THE SUPREME COURT OF ILLINOIS: ADMISSION, REGISTRATION, PROFESSIONAL RESPONSIBILTY, AND DISCIPLINE OF ATTORNEYS. Attorney Registration and Disciplinary Commission of the Supreme Court of Illinois, Suite 1900, 203 North Wabash Avenue, Chicago, Illinois 60601. 1987. (Includes Code of Professional Responsibility and the Disciplinary Rules). For further information concerning professional conduct of attorneys, contact the Commission at (312-346-0690) in Chicago and Northern Illinois. Or, in Central and Southern Illinois, 1 Old North Capital Plaza, Suite 345, Springfield, Illinois, 62701, (217-525-1760 or 800-252-8048).

COURT RULES

ILLINOIS CODE OF CIVIL PROCEDURE AND COURT RULES. West Publishing Company, P.O. Box 64526, 50 West Kellogg Boulevard, St. Paul, Minnesota 55164-0526. (Annual).

ILLINOIS COURT RULE BOOK. Fourth Edition. Walter B. Vande Werken. Law Bulletin Publishing Company, 415 North State Street, Chicago, Illinois 60610. 1985- . (Periodic Supplements).

ILLINOIS LAW FINDERS. West Publishing Company, 50 West Kellogg Boulevard, St. Paul, Minnesota 55164. Annual.

ILLINOIS RULES AND PRACTICE HANDBOOK. Second Edition. Pantograph Printing and Stationery Company, Legal Division, P.O. Box 1406, Bloomington, Illinois 61702. 1982. (Periodic Supplement).

JURY INSTRUCTIONS

ILLINOIS PATTERN JURY INSTRUCTIONS: CIVIL. Second Edition. Illinois Supreme Court Committee on Jury Instructions in Civil Cases. West Publishing Company, P.O. Box 64526, 50 West Kellogg Boulevard, St. Paul, Minnesota 55164-0526. 1971- . (Periodic Supplements).

ILLINOIS PATTERN JURY INSTRUCTIONS: CRIMINAL. Second Edition. Illinois Supreme Court Committee on Pattern Jury Instructions in Criminal Cases. West Publishing Company, P.O. Box 64526, 50 West Kellogg Boulevard, St. Paul, Minnesota 55164-0526. 1981- . (Periodic Supplements).

DIGESTS, INDEXES, ABSTRACTS, CITATORS

CALLAGHAN'S ILLINOIS DIGEST. (First through Third Edition). Callaghan and Company, 155 Pfingsten Road, Deerfield, Illinois 60015. 1922- . (Annual Supplements).

ILLINOIS DIGEST. (First and Second Edition). West Publishing Company, P.O. Box 64526, 50 West Kellogg Boulevard, St. Paul, Minnesota 55164-0526. 1982- . (Annual Supplements).

ILLINOIS LAW FINDER. West Publishing Company, P.O. Box 64526, 50 West Kellogg Boulevard, St. Paul, Minnesota 55164-0526. Annual.

ILLINOIS LAW LOCATOR. Shepard's/McGraw-Hill, P.O. Box 1235, Colorado Springs, Colorado 80901. 1972- . (Periodic Supplements).

NORTHEASTERN DIGEST. West Publishing Company, P.O. Box 64526, 50 West Kellogg Boulevard, St. Paul, Minnesota 55164-0526. 1933- . (Annual Supplements).

SHEPARD'S ILLINOIS CITATIONS. Shepard's/McGraw-Hill, P.O. Box 1235, Colorado Springs, Colorado 80901. (Eight pamphlets per year).

SHEPARD'S NORTHEASTERN REPORTER CITATIONS. Shepard's/McGraw-Hill, P.O. Box 1235, Colorado Springs, Colorado 80901. (Monthly Supplements).

ENCYCLOPEDIAS AND DICTIONARIES

ILLINOIS LAW AND PRACTICE: THE MODERN ENCYCLOPEDIA OF ILLINOIS LAW. West Publishing Company, P.O. Box 64526, 50 West Kellogg Boulevard, St. Paul, Minnesota 55164-0526. 1953- . (Annual Supplements).

LEGAL NEWSPAPERS

CHICAGO DAILY LAW BULLETIN. Law Bulletin Publishing Company, 415 North State Street, Chicago, Illinois 60610-4674. 1854- . (Daily except Saturday and Sunday).

LAW REVIEWS AND PERIODICALS

CHICAGO BAR RECORD. Chicago Bar Association, 29 South LaSalle Street, Suite 1040, Chicago, Illinois 60603. Bimonthly.

CHICAGO-KENT LAW REVIEW. Chicago-Kent College of Law, 77 South Walker Drive, Chicago, Illinois 60606. (Quarterly).

DEPAUL LAW REVIEW. DePaul University College of Law, 25 East Jackson Boulevard, Chicago, Illinois 60604. (Quarterly).

ILLINOIS BAR JOURNAL. Illinois Bar Center, 424 South Second Street, Springfield, Illinois 62701. (Monthly).

JOHN MARSHALL LAW REVIEW. John Marshall Law School, 315 South Plymoth Court, Chicago, Illinois 60604. (Quarterly).

LOYOLA UNIVERSITY OF CHICAGO LAW JOURNAL. Loyola University School of Law, 1 East Pearson Street, Chicago, Illinois 60611. (Quarterly).

NORTHERN ILLINOIS UNIVERSITY LAW REVIEW. Northern Illinois University College of Law, DeKalb, Illinois 60115-2854. (Biannual).

NORTHWESTERN UNIVERSITY LAW REVIEW. Northwestern University, School of Law, 357 East Chicago Avenue, Chicago, Illinois 60611. Bimonthly.

UNIVERSITY OF CHICAGO LAW REVIEW. University of Chicago Law School, 1111 East Sixtieth Street, Chicago, Illinois 60637. (Quarterly).

UNIVERSITY OF ILLINOIS LAW REVIEW. University of Illinois at Urbana-Champaign, College of Law, 76 Law Building, 504 East Pennsylvania Avenue, Champaign, Illinois 61820. (Quarterly).

NEWSLETTERS AND NEWSPAPERS

COOK COUNTY FINANCIAL MALPRACTICE SUIT FILING LIST. Cook County Jury Verdict Reporter, 77 West Washington, Room 1110, Chicago, Illinois 60602. Monthly.

COOK COUNTY JURY VERDICT REPORTER. Cook County Jury Verdict Reporter, 77 West Washington, Room 1110, Chicago, Illinois 60602. Weekly.

COOK COUNTY MEDICAL MALPRACTICE SUIT FILING LIST. Cook County Jury Verdict Reporter, 77 West Washington, Room 1110, Chicago, Illinois 60602. Monthly.

COOK COUNTY PRODUCT LIABILITY SUIT FILING LIST. Cook County Jury Verdict Reporter, 77 West Washington, Room 1110, Chicago, Illinois 60602. Monthly.

THE GOVERNOR'S ACTION REPORT. State Capital Information Service, Incorporated, 516 East Monroe, Springfield, Illinois 62701. Semiweekly during July, August, and September.

ILLINOIS COURTS BULLETIN. Illinois State Bar Association, Illinois Bar Center, Springfield, Illinois 62701. Monthly.

ILLINOIS EMPLOYMENT LAW LETTER. M. Lee Smith Publisher and Printer, 162 Fourth Avenue North, Nashville, Tennessee 37219. Monthly.

ILLINOIS FAMILY LAW REPORT. Illinois Family Law Report, Incorporated, 77 West Washington Street, Suite 1717, Chicago, Illinois 60602. Monthly.

ILLINOIS JURY VERDICTS REPORTER. Illinois Jury Verdicts Reporter, 77 West Washington, Room 1110, Chicago, Illinois 60602. Monthly.

VIEW FROM SPRINGFIELD. State Capital Information Service, Incorporated, 516 East Monroe, Springfield, Illinois 62701. Weekly.

FORMBOOKS

CALLAGHAN'S ILLINOIS CIVIL PRACTICE FORMS. Roland Klinge. Callaghan and Company, 155 Pfingsten Road, Deerfield, Illinois 60015. 1975- . (Annual Supplements).

ILLINOIS FORMS: LEGAL AND BUSINESS. Lawyers Co-Operative Company, Aqueduct Building, Rochester, New York 14694. 1975- . (Annual Supplements).

NICHOLS ILLINOIS CIVIL PRACTICE WITH FORMS. Clark A. Nichols. Callaghan and Company, 155 Pfingsten Road, Deerfield, Illinois 60015. 1940- . (Annual Supplements).

PRACTICE MATERIALS

CALLAGHAN'S ILLINOIS CRIMINAL LAW. Ralph J. Moore. Callaghan and Company, 155 Pfingsten Road, Deerfield, Illinois 60015. 1966.

CALLAGHAN'S ILLINOIS CRIMINAL PROCEDURE. Ralph J. Moore. Callaghan and Company, 155 Pfingsten Raod, Deerfield, Illinois 60015. 1971- . (Periodic Supplements).

CALLAGHAN'S ILLINOIS EVIDENCE: CIVIL AND CRIMINAL. H. B. Clark. Callaghan and Company, 155 Pfingsten Road, Deerfield, Illinois 60015. 1964- . (Periodic Supplements).

CLEARY AND GRAHAM'S HANDBOOK OF ILLINOIS EVIDENCE. Fourth Edition. Little, Brown and Company, 34 Beacon Street, Boston, Massachusetts 02108. 1984- . (Periodic Supplements). 1970- .

ILLINOIS CIVIL TRIAL EVIDENCE. Illinois Institute for Continuing Legal Education, 2395 West Jefferson Street, Springfield, Illinois 62702. 1983- . (Periodic Supplement).

ILLINOIS LAWYER'S MANUAL. Third Edition. B. Becker. Callaghan and Company, 155 Pfingsten Road, Deerfield, Illinois 60015. 1975- . (Periodic Supplement).

ILLINOIS PRODUCT LIABILITY PRACTICE. Illinois Institute for Continuing Legal Education, 2395 West Jefferson Street, Springfield, Illinois 62702. 1980.

ESTATE PLANNING AND ADMINISTRATION IN ILLINOIS. Second Edition. Robert S. Hunter. Lawyers Co-Operative Company, Aqueduct Building, Rochester, New York 14694. 1970- . (Periodic Supplements).

HORNER, PROBATE PRACTICE AND ESTATES, WITH FORMS. Fourth Edition. Henry Clay Horner. Callaghan and Company, 155 Pfingsten Road, Deerfield, Illinois 60015. 1976- . (Periodic Supplements).

HOW TO FORM YOUR OWN ILLINOIS CORPORATION BEFORE THE INC. DRIES! Third Edition. Phil Williams. The P. Gaines Company, 33 South Taylor, P.O. Box 2253, Oak Park, Illinois 60303. 1990.

ILLINOIS CIVIL DISCOVERY PRACTICE. Illinois Institute for Continuing Legal Education, 2395 West Jefferson Street, Springfield, Illinois 62702. 1983- . (Periodic Supplements).

ILLINOIS CIVIL PRACTICE. Illinois Institute for Continuing Legal Education, 2395 West Jefferson Street, Springfield, Illinois 62702. 1987- . (Periodic Supplements).

THE ILLINOIS CORPORATION SYSTEM. Linscott R. Hanson. Illinois Institute for Continuing Legal Education, 2395 West Jefferson Street, Springfield, Illinois 62702. 1980.

ILLINOIS CRIMINAL LAW: A SURVEY OF CRIMES AND DEFENSES. John F. Decker. Butterworth Legal Publishers, 90 Stiles Road, Salem, New Hampshire 03079. 1991.

ILLINOIS CRIMINAL PRACTICE. Illinois Institute for Continuing Legal Education, 2395 West Jefferson Street, Springfield, Illinois 62702. 1981- . (Periodic Supplements).

ILLINOIS EVIDENCE MANUAL. Second Edition. Spencer A. Gard. Lawyers Co-Operative Company, Aqueduct Building, Rochester, New York 14694. 1979- . (Periodic Supplements).

ILLINOIS LAW AND PRACTICE. West Publishing Company, P.O. Box 64526, 50 West Kellogg Boulevard, St. Paul, Minnesota 55164-0526. 1957- . (Annual Supplements).

ILLINOIS REAL ESTATE. Solomon Gutstein. Lawyers Co-Operative Company, Aqueduct Building, Rochester, New York 14694. 1983- . (Periodic Supplements).

ILLINOIS RULES AND PRACTICE HANDBOOK. Second Edition. Pantagraph Printing and Stationary Company, Legal Division, P.O. Box 1406, Bloomington, Illinois 61702. 1982- . (Quarterly Supplements).

ILLINOIS TORT LAW AND PRACTICE. Jerome Mirza and Jean Appleman. Lawyers Co-Operative Company, Aqueduct Building, Rochester, New York 14694. 1974- . (Periodic Supplements).

THE LAW OF MEDICAL PRACTICE IN ILLINOIS. Theodore R. LeBang and Eugene W. Basanter. Lawyers Co-Operative Company, Aqueduct Building, Rochester, New York 14694. 1986- . (Periodic Supplements).

NICHOL'S ILLINOIS CIVIL PRACTICE WITH FORMS. Revised Edition. Mary Anne Foran, Marvin Owen Meier, and Judity A. Wade. Callaghan and Company, 155 Pfingsten Road, Deerfield, Illinois 60015. 1984- . (Annual Supplements).

TRIAL HANDBOOK FOR ILLINOIS LAWYERS. Fifth Edition. Robert S. Hunter. Lawyers Co-Operative Company, Aqueduct Building, Rochester, New York 14694. 1983- . (Annual Supplements).

MANUALS AND RESEARCH GUIDES

ILLINOIS LEGAL RESEARCH SOURCEBOOK. Roger F. Jacobs, et al. Illinois Institute for Continuing Legal Education, 2395 West Jefferson Street, Springfield, Illinois 62702. 1977.

RESEARCH IN ILLINOIS LAW. Bernita J. Davies and Francis J. Rooney. Oceana Publications, Incorporated, 75 Main Street, Dobbs Ferry, New York 10522. 1954.

ASSOCIATIONS AND PROFESSIONAL SOCIETIES

CHICAGO BAR ASSOCIATION, 29 South LaSalle Street, Suite 1040, Chicago, Illinois 60603.

CHICAGO COUNCIL OF LAWYERS, 220 South State Street, Room 800, Chicago, Illinois 60604.

ILLINOIS STATE BAR ASSOCIATION, Illinois Bar Center, Springfield, Illinois 62701.

DIRECTORIES

DIRECTORY OF STATE OFFICIALS--ILLINOIS. Illinois Legislative Research Unit, Stratton Building, Number 107, Springfield, Illinois 62706. (Annual).

HANDBOOK OF ILLINOIS GOVERNMENT. Illinois Secretary of State, State House, Room 213, Springfield, Illinois 62756. (Biennial).

ILLINOIS BLUEBOOK. Illinois Secretary of State, State House, Room 213, Springfield, Illinois 62756. (Biennial).

ILLINOIS LEGAL DIRECTORY. Legal Directories Publishing Company, 2122 Kidwell, P.O. Box 140200, Dallas, Texas 75214-0200. (Annual).

ILLINOIS MUNICIPAL DIRECTORY. Illinois Municipal League, 1220 South Seventh Street, Springfield, Illinois 62703. (Biennial).

ILLINOIS STATE OFFICERS. Illinois State Board of Elections, 1020 South Spring Street, Springfield, Illinois 62704. (Biennial).

OTHER SOURCES

ILLINOIS ESTATE ADMINISTRATION. Illinois Institute for Continuing Legal Education, 2395 West Jefferson Street, Springfield, Illinois 62702. 1981- . (Periodic Supplement).

ILLINOIS NATURAL RESOURCES LAW. R. Beck. Butterworth Legal Publishers, 90 Stiles Road, Salem, New Hampshire 03079. 1985. (Annual Supplement).

ILLINOIS TORT LAW. M. Polelle. Butterworth Legal Publishers, 90 Stiles Road, Salem, New Hampshire 03079. 1986. (Annual Supplement).

KENOE ON LAND TRUSTS. Illinois Institute for Continuing Legal Education, 2395 West Jefferson Street, Springfield, Illinois 62702. 1981- . (Periodic Supplement).

STATES--INDIANA

STATUTES, CODES, STANDARDS, UNIFORM LAWS

BURN'S INDIANA STATUTES ANNOTATED. Michie Company, P.O. Box 7587, Charlottesville, Virginia 22906-7587. 1972- . (Annual Supplements).

INDIANA ACTS. Legislative Services Agency, Room 302, State House, 200 Washington Street, Indianapolis, Indiana 46204. (Annual).

INDIANA ACTS. Legislative Services Agency, Room 302, State House, 200 Washington Street, Indianapolis, Indiana 46204. Annual.

INDIANA ADMINISTRATIVE CODE. Indiana Legislative Council, Banks-Baldwin Law Publishing Company, P.O. Box 1974, Cleveland, Ohio 44106. 1984- . (Annual Supplements).

INDIANA ADVANCE ANNOTATION SERVICE. Michie Company, P.O. Box 7587, Charlottesville, Virginia 22906-7587. (Three pamphlets per Year).

INDIANA CODE. Indiana Legislative Council, Legislative Service Agency, Room 302, State House, Indianapolis, Indiana 46204. 1976- . (Annual Supplements).

INDIANA REGISTER. Legislative Services Agency, State House, Indianapolis, Indiana 46204. (Monthly).

WEST'S ANNOTATED INDIANA CODE. West Publishing Company, P.O. Box 64526, 50 West Kellogg Boulevard, St. Paul, Minnesota 55164-0526. 1970- . (Annual Supplements).

WEST'S INDIANA LEGISLATIVE SERVICE. West Publishing Company, P.O. Box 64526, 50 West Kellogg Boulevard, St. Paul, Minnesota 55164-0526. 1976- . (Irregular Supplements).

LOOSELEAF SERVICES AND REPORTERS

INDIANA CASES. West Publishing Company, P.O. Box 64526, 50 West Kellogg Boulevard, St. Paul, Minnesota 55164-0526. 1885- . (Supreme Court and Court of Appeals).

INDIANA COURT OF APPEALS REPORTS. Western Newspaper Publishing Company, 1891-1979. (Formerly: Indiana Appellate Court Reports). (Current source is Indiana Cases or Northeastern Reporter).

INDIANA REPORTS. Secretary of State. 1848-1981. (Current official source is Indiana Cases or Northeastern Reporter).

NORTHEASTERN REPORTER (First and Second Series). West Publishing Company, P.O. Box 64526, 50 West Kellogg Boulevard, St. Paul, Minnesota 55164-0526. 1885- . (Indiana Supreme Court and Court of Appeals).

ATTORNEY GENERAL OPINIONS

ANNUAL REPORT AND OFFICIAL OPINIONS OF THE ATTORNEY GENERAL OF INDIANA. Office of the Attorney General, State House, Room 219, Indianapolis, Indiana 46204. (Irregular). (Also published in the Indiana Register and Digested in West's Indiana Digest). Also available on Lexis: February 1977- .

ETHICS OPINIONS, CODES, RULES

Indiana Disciplinary Rules are published in Burns Indiana Statutes Annotated, Court Rules (Volume 1). 1972- . (Annual Supplements).

Indiana State Bar Ethics Opinions are published in Res Gestae. Abstracts of these opinions are published in the ABA/BNA Lawyer's Manual on Professional Conduct. For further information concerning these opinions, contact the Indiana State Bar Association, 230 East Ohio Street, Indianapolis, Indiana 46204. (317-639-5465).

COURT RULES

INDIANA RULES OF COURT. West Publishing Company, P.O. Box 64526, 50 West Kellogg Boulevard, St. Paul, Minnesota 55164-0526. (Annual). (Also published in the Indiana Code, Titles 34 and 35).

INDIANA RULES OF PROCEDURE ANNOTATED. Second Edition. William F. Harvey. West Publishing Company, P.O. Box 64526, 50 West Kellogg Boulevard, St. Paul, Minnesota 55164-0526. 1967- . (Annual Supplements).

JURY INSTRUCTIONS

INDIANA PATTERN JURY INSTRUCTIONS-CIVIL. Michie Company, P.O. Box 7587, Charlottesville, Virginia 22906-7587-7587. 1968- . (Periodic Supplements)

INDIANA PATTERN JURY INSTRUCTIONS-CRIMINAL. Michie Company, P.O. Box 7587, Charlottesville, Virginia 22906-7587-7587. 1980- . (Periodic Supplements).

DIGESTS, INDEXES, ABSTRACTS, CITATORS

INDIANA DIGEST. West Publishing Company, P.O. Box 64526, 50 West Kellogg Boulevard, St. Paul, Minnesota 55164-0526. 1954- . (Annual Supplements). (Includes digest of Attorney General Opinions).

NORTHEASTERN DIGEST. West Publishing Company, P.O. Box 64526, 50 West Kellogg Boulevard, St. Paul, Minnesota 55164-0526. 1933- . (Annual Supplements).

SHEPARD'S INDIANA CITATIONS. Shepard's/McGraw-Hill, P.O. Box 1235, Colorado Springs, Colorado 80901. (Eight pamphlets per year).

SHEPARD'S NORTHEASTERN REPORTER CITATIONS. Shepard's/McGraw-Hill, P.O. Box 1235, Colorado Springs, Colorado 80901. (Monthly Supplements).

ENCYCLOPEDIAS AND DICTIONARIES

INDIANA LAW ENCYCLOPEDIA. West Publishing Company, P.O. Box 64526, 50 West Kellogg Boulevard, St. Paul, Minnesota 55164-0526. 1957- . (Annual Supplements).

LAW REVIEWS AND PERIODICALS

INDIANA LAW JOURNAL. Indiana University School of Law, Bloomington Law Annex II, Bloomington, Indiana 47405. (Quarterly).

INDIANA LAW REVIEW. Indiana University School of Law, 735 West New York Street, Indianapolis, Indiana 46202. (Quarterly).

NOTRE DAME JOURNAL OF LAW, ETHICS, AND PUBLIC POLICY. Thomas J. White Center on Law and Government, Notre Dame Law School, Notre Dame, Indiana 46556. (Quarterly).

NOTRE DAME LAW REVIEW. Notre Dame Law School, University of Notre Dame, P.O. Box 988, Notre Dame, Indiana 46556. (Five Issues per Year).

RES GESTAE. Indiana State Bar Association, 230 East Ohio Street, Indianapolis, Indiana 46204. (Monthly).

VALPARISO UNIVERSITY LAW REVIEW. Valpariso University School of Law, Valpariso, Indiana 46383. (Three Issues per Year).

THE WEEKLY BULLETIN. Indianapolis Bar Association, One Indiana Square, Indianapolis, Indiana 46204. (Weekly).

NEWSLETTERS AND NEWSPAPERS

ADDENDUM. Indiana State Bar Association, 230 East Ohio Street, Indianapolis, Indiana 46204. Bimonthly.

INDIANA LAW REPORTER. Law Reporter Company, 209 Michigan Avenue, Crystal Falls, Michigan 49920.

INDIANA LEGISLATIVE INSIGHT. The Insight Group, P.O. Box 383, Noblesville, Indiana 46060. Weekly.

FORMBOOKS

ANNOTATED FORMS FOR INDIANA PLEADING AND PRACTICE IN CIVIL ACTIONS AND SPECIAL PROCEEDINGS. Third Edition. Joseph W. Thompson. Bobbs-Merrill Company, Incorporated, 4300 West Sixty-second Street, Indianapolis, Indiana 46206. 1962- . (Periodic Supplements).

INDIANA FORMS OF PLEADING AND PRACTICE. Charles A. Thompson and Judith Shaw Hostetler. Matthew Bender and Company, Incorporated, 11 Penn Plaza, New York, New York 10001. 1972- . (Annual Supplements).

INDIANA LEGAL BUSINESS FORMS. C. Peeples. West Publishing Company, 50 West Kellogg Boulevard, St. Paul, Minnesota 55164. 1967- . (Periodic Supplement).

INDIANA PROCEDURAL FORMS. W. Harvey and others. West Publishing Company, 50 West Kellogg Boulevard, St. Paul, Minnesota 55164. 1973- . (Periodic Supplements).

INDIANA UNIFORM COMMERCIAL CODE FORMS. D. Johnson. West Publishing Company, 50 West Kellogg Boulevard, St. Paul, Minnesota 55164. 1986- . (Periodic Supplement).

THOMPSON'S INDIANA FORMS. Third Edition. H. Grube. Michie Company, P.O. Box 7587, Charlottesville, Virginia 22906-7587. 1961- . (Periodic Supplement).

PRACTICE MATERIALS

APPELLATE PRACTICE. Indiana Continuing Legal Education Forum, 230 East Ohio Street, Suite 202, Indianapolis, Indiana 46204. 1983.

HENRY'S PROBATE LAW AND PRACTICE. Seventh Edition. John S. Grimes. Michie Company, P.O. Box 7587, Charlottesville, Virginia 22906-7587. 1978- . (Annual Supplements).

INDIANA APPELLATE PRACTICE AND PROCEDURE. Arch N. Bobbitt. Michie Company, P.O. Box 7587, Charlottesville, Virginia 22906-7587. 1972- . (Periodic Supplements).

INDIANA APPELLATE PROCEDURE. B. Bagni. West Publishing Company, 50 West Kellogg Boulevard, St. Paul, Minnesota 55164. 1979- . (Annual Supplement).

INDIANA CORPORATE PRACTICE MANUAL. Louis R. Richey. Michie Company, P.O. Box 7587, Charlottesville, Virginia 22906-7587. 1983- . (Periodic Supplements).

INDIANA PRACTICE. West Publishing Company, P.O. Box 64526, 50 West Kellogg Boulevard, St. Paul, Minnesota 55164-0526. 1967- . (Annual Supplements).

INDIANA SMALL CLAIMS. Robert Glen Witinger. Michie Company, P.O. Box 7587, Charlottesville, Virginia 22906-7587. 1980.

INDIANA TRIAL EVIDENCE MANUAL. J. Alexander Tanford and Richard M. Quinlan. Michie Company, P.O. Box 7587, Charlottesville, Virginia 22906-7587. 1982- . (Periodic Supplements).

INDIANA TRIAL NOTEBOOK. Indiana Continuing Legal Education Forum, 230 East Ohio Street, Suite 202, Indianapolis, Indiana 46204. 1985.

THE LAW OF EVIDENCE IN INDIANA. Marshall J. Seidman. Michie Company, P.O. Box 7587, Charlottesville, Virginia 22906-7587. 1977.

TRIAL HANDBOOK FOR INDIANA LAWYERS. Terrance L. Smith. Lawyers Co-Operative Company, Aqueduct Building, Rochester, New York 14694. 1982- . (Annual Supplements).

MANUALS AND RESEARCH GUIDES

AN INTRODUCTION TO INDIANA STATE PUBLICATIONS FOR THE LAW LIBRARIAN. Linda K. Fariss and Keith A. Buckley. American Association of Law Libraries, 53 West Jackson Boulevard, Room 703, Chicago, Illinois 60604. 1982.

ASSOCIATIONS AND PROFESSIONAL SOCIETIES

INDIANA BAR ASSOCIATION, 230 East Ohio Street, Sixth Floor, Indianapolis, Indiana 46204. (317) 639-5465.

INDIANAPOLIS BAR ASSOCIATION, One Indiana Square, Indianapolis, Indiana 46204. (317) 632-8240.

DIRECTORIES

INDIANA GENERAL ASSEMBLY LEGISLATIVE DIRECTORY. Indiana State Chamber of Commerce, One North Capitol, Suite 200, Indianapolis, Indiana 46204. (Biennial).

INDIANA LEGAL DIRECTORY. Legal Directories Publishing Company, 2122 Kidwell Street, P.O. Box 140200. Dallas, Texas 75214-0200. (Annual).

ROSTER OF INDIANA CITY AND TOWN OFFICIALS. Indiana Association of Cities and Towns, 150 Market Street, Suite 600, Indianapolis, Indiana 46204. (Every Four Years).

STATES--INDIANA

ROSTER OF STATE AND LOCAL OFFICIALS OF THE STATE OF INDIANA. Indiana State Board of Accounts, State Office Building, Room 912, Indianapolis, Indiana 46204. (Annual).

OTHER SOURCES

EUBANKS INDIANA CRIMINAL LAW. Third Edition. F. Symmes. Michie Company, P.O. Box 7587, Charlottesville, Virginia 22906-7587. 1956- . (Periodic Supplements).

INDIANA EVIDENCE. R. Miller. West Publishing Company, 50 West Kellogg Boulevard, St. Paul, Minnesota 55164. 1984- . (Annual Supplement).

THE LAW OF EVIDENCE IN INDIANA. M. Seielman. Michie Company, P.O. Box 7587, Charlottesville, Virginia 22906-7587. 1977- . (Periodic Supplement).

STATES--IOWA

STATUTES, CODES, STANDARDS, UNIFORM LAWS

ACTS OF THE GENERAL ASSEMBLY OF IOWA. State Printing Office, State Capitol, Des Moine, Iowa 50309. 1843- . (Annual).

CODE OF IOWA. State Printing Office, State Capitol, Des Moine, Iowa 50309. 1924- . (Biennial).

IOWA ADMINISTRATIVE BULLETIN. State Printing Office, State Capitol, Des Noine, Iowa 50309. (Biweekly).

IOWA ADMINISTRATIVE CODE. State of Iowa. State Printing Office, State Capitol, Des Moine, Iowa 50309. 1975- .

IOWA CODE ANNOTATED. West Publishing Company, P.O. Box 64526, 50 West Kellogg Boulevard, St. Paul, Minnesota 55164-0526. 1949- . (Annual Supplements).

WEST'S IOWA LEGISLATIVE SERVICE. West Publishing Company, P.O. Box 64526, 50 West Kellogg Boulevard, St. Paul, Minnesota 55164-0526. (Irregular).

LOOSELEAF SERVICES AND REPORTERS

IOWA REPORTS. State Printing Office, State Capitol, Des Moine, Iowa 50309. 1855-1968. (Iowa Supreme Court). (Current Official Source: Northwestern Reporter).

NORTHWESTERN REPORTER (First and Second Series). West Publishing Company, P.O. Box 64526, 50 West Kellogg Boulevard, St. Paul, Minnesota 55164-0526. 1878- . (Iowa Supreme Court and Court of Appeals).

ATTORNEY GENERAL OPINIONS

ATTORNEY GENERAL OPINIONS. State Printing Office, State Capitol, Des Moine, Iowa 50309. (Biennial). (Lexis: January 1977-).

ETHICS OPINIONS, CODES, RULES

FORMAL OPINIONS OF THE COMMISSION ON PROFESSIONAL ETHICS AND CONDUCT OF THE IOWA STATE BAR ASSOCIATION. Iowa State Bar Association, 1101 Fleming Building, Des Moines, Iowa 50309. 1965- . (Annual Supplements). Full text opinions are also published in the News Bulletin of the Iowa State Bar Association; Abstracts of the opinions are published in the ABA/BNA Lawyer's Reference Manual. For further information concerning these opinions, contact the Ethics Administrator, Iowa State Bar Association, 1101 Fleming Building. Des Moines, Iowa 50309. (515-243-3179). "Iowa Code of Professional Responsibility" is published in the Iowa Court Rules and in Iowa Code Annotated (Chapter 603).

COURT RULES

IOWA COURT RULES. Second Edition. State Printing Office, State Capitol, Des Moines, Iowa 50309. 1981- . (Also published in Iowa Code Annotated, Volume 58).

IOWA RULES OF COURT. West Publishing Company, P.O. Box 64526, 50 West Kellogg Boulevard, St. Paul, Minnesota 55164-0526. (Annual).

JURY INSTRUCTIONS

IOWA UNIFORM JURY INSTRUCTIONS ANNOTATED. Special Committee on Uniform Court Instructions. Iowa State Bar Association, 1101 Fleming Building, Des Moines, Iowa 50309. 1978- . (Semiannual Supplements). (Vol. 1-Civil Instructions; Vol. 2-Criminal Instructions).

DIGESTS, INDEXES, ABSTRACTS, CITATORS

IOWA DIGEST. West Publishing Company, P.O. Box 64526, 50 West Kellogg Boulevard, St. Paul, Minnesota 55164-0526. 1941- . (Annual Supplements).

IOWA DIGEST. Callaghan and Company, 155 Pfingsten Road, Deerfield, Illinois 60015. (Annual Supplements).

NORTHWESTERN DIGEST. (First and Second Series). West Publishing Company, P.O. Box 64526, 50 West Kellogg Boulevard, St. Paul, Minnesota 55164-0526. 1944- . (Annual Supplements).

SHEPARD'S IOWA CITATIONS. Shepard's/McGraw-Hill, P.O. Box 1235, Colorado Springs, Colorado 80901. (Eight pamphlets per year).

SHEPARD'S NORTHWESTERN REPORTER CITATIONS. Shepard's/McGraw-Hill, P.O. Box 1235, Colorado Springs, Colorado 80901. (Monthly Supplements).

LAW REVIEWS AND PERIODICALS

DRAKE LAW REVIEW. Drake University Law School, Des Moines, Iowa 50311. (Quarterly).

IOWA LAW REVIEW. University of Iowa, College of Law, Iowa City, Iowa 52242. (Five issues per year).

NEWS BULLETIN OF THE IOWA STATE BAR ASSOCIATION. Iowa State Bar Association, 1101 Fleming Building, Des Moines, Iowa 50309. (Monthly).

NEWSLETTERS AND NEWSPAPERS

IOWA LEGISLATIVE NEWS SERVICE. Iowa Legislative News Service, P.O. Box 8370, Des Moines, Iowa 50301. Semiweekly.

MIDWEST ENVIRONMENTAL LAW LETTER. M. Lee Smith Publishers and Printers, 162 Fourth Avenue North, Nashville, Tennessee 37219. Monthly.

NEWS BULLETIN. Iowa State Bar Assocaition, 1101 Fleming Building, Des Moines, Iowa 50309. Monthly.

FORMBOOKS

IOWA CIVIL PROCEDURE FORMS. M. Smith. West Publishing Company, 50 West Kellogg Boulevard, St. Paul, Minnesota 55164. 1984- . (Annual Supplements).

IOWA LEGAL FORMS--COMMERCIAL REAL ESTATE. Dennis A. Dietz. Butterworth Legal Publishers, 90 Stiles Road, Salem, New Hampshire 03079. 1983- . (Periodic Supplements).

IOWA LEGAL FORMS--CORPORATIONS. Hugh Field. Butterworth Legal Publishers, 90 Stiles Road, Salem, New Hampshire 03079. 1983- . (Periodic Supplements).

IOWA LEGAL FORMS--CRIMINAL LAW. Peter W. Burger and Kermit Dunahoo. Butterworth Legal Publishers, 90 Stiles Road, Salem, New Hampshire 03079. 1983- . (Periodic Supplements).

IOWA LEGAL FORMS--FAMILY LAW. Terry D. Parsons. Butterworth Legal Publishers, 90 Stiles Road, Salem, New Hampshire 03079. 1984- . (Periodic Supplements).

IOWA LEGAL FORMS--PERSONAL INJURY. Max E. Kirk. Butterworth Legal Publishers, 90 Stiles Road, Salem, New Hampshire 03079. 1983- . (Periodic Supplements).

IOWA LEGAL FORMS--PROBATE. Thomas Lawler. Butterworth Legal Publishers, 90 Stiles Road, Salem, New Hampshire 03079. 1984- . (Periodic Supplements).

IOWA LEGAL FORMS--RESIDENTIAL REAL ESTATE. David Dunakey. Butterworth Legal Publishers, 90 Stiles Road, Salem, New Hampshire 03079. 1983- . (Periodic Supplements).

IOWA LEGAL FORMS--WORKER'S COMPENSATION. Dennis L. Hanssen. Butterworth Legal Publishers, 90 Stiles Road, Salem, New Hampshire 03079. 1983- . (Periodic Supplements).

PRACTICE MATERIALS

IOWA BANKRUPTCY. Robert S. Oppold. Butterworth Legal Publishers, 90 Stiles Road, Salem, New Hampshire 03079. 1984- . (Periodic Supplements).

IOWA CRIMINAL LAW AND PROCEDURE. Second Edition. J. Yeager and R. Carlson. West Publishing Company, 50 West Kellogg Boulevard, St. Paul, Minnesota 55164. 1979- . (Annual Supplements).

IOWA MATRIMONIAL LAW. Daniel L. Bray. Butterworth Legal Publishers, 90 Stiles Road, Salem, New Hampshire 03079. 1986- . (Periodic Supplements).

IOWA METHODS OF PRACTICE. Second Edition. M. Voltz and others. West Publishing Company, 50 West Kellogg Boulevard, St. Paul, Minnesota 55164. 1976- . (Annual Supplement).

IOWA PRACTICE. Callaghan and Company, 155 Pfingsten Road, Deerfield, Illinois 60015. 1983- . (Periodic Supplements).

IOWA PROBATE. Second Edition. D. McCarthy. Callaghan and Company, 155 Pfingsten Road, Deerfield, Illinois 60015. 1964- . (Periodic Supplements).

IOWA WORKERS' COMPENSATION LAW AND PRACTICE. J. Lawyer. Harrison Company, 3110 Crossing Park, Norcross, Georgia 30091. 1984- . (Annual Supplement).

MARSHALL'S IOWA TITLE: OPINIONS AND STANDARDS. Second Edition. George F. Madsen. Michie/Bobbs-Merrill Law Publishing Company, P.O. Box 7587, Charlottesville, Virginia 22906-7587. 1978- . (Periodic Supplements).

PERSONAL INJURY VERDICT SURVEY: IOWA EDITION. Jury Verdict Research, Incorporated, 30700H Bainbridge Road, Solon, Ohio 44139-2291. (Annual).

MANUALS AND RESEARCH GUIDES

UNDERSTANDING IOWA LAW. Lisa Bartusek, Deborah T. Craig and Ellen K. Curry, Editors. Iowa Center for Law-Related Education, Iowa Department of Public Instruction, Des Moines, Iowa 1984.

ASSOCIATIONS AND PROFESSIONAL SOCIETIES

IOWA STATE BAR ASSOCIATION, 1101 Fleming Building, Des Moines, Iowa 50309. (515) 243-3179.

WOODBURY COUNTY BAR ASSOCIATION, Woodbury County Courthouse, Sixth Floor, Sioux City, Iowa 51101. (712) 279-6609.

DIRECTORIES

DIRECTORY OF IOWA MUNICIPALITIES. League of Iowa Municipalities, 900 Des Moines Street, Suite 100, Des Moines, Iowa 50309. (Biennial).

IOWA LEGAL DIRECTORY. Legal Directories Publishing Company, 2122 Kidwell Street, P.O. Box 140200, Dallas, Texas 75214-0200. (Annual).

IOWA OFFICIAL DIRECTORY OF STATE AND COUNTY OFFICERS. Iowa Secretary of State, State House, Des Moines, Iowa 50319. (Biennial).

IOWA OFFICIAL REGISTER. Iowa Secretary of State, State House, Des Moines, Iowa 50309. (Biennial).

OFFICIAL DIRECTORY OF THE LEGISLATURE: STATE OF IOWA. Iowa General Assembly, State House, Des Moines, Iowa 50319. (Annual).

OTHER SOURCES

IOWA BUSINESS ORGANIZATIONS. Second Edition. E. Haynes. West Publishing Company, 50 West Kellogg Boulevard, St. Paul, Minnesota 55164. 1985- . (Periodic Supplement).

IOWA REAL ESTATE MORTGAGES FORECLOSURE. J. Sullivan. Harrison Company, 3110 Crossing Park, Norcross, Georgia 30091. 1983- . (Periodic Supplement).

STATES--KANSAS

STATUTES, CODES, STANDARDS, UNIFORM LAWS

KANSAS ADMINISTRATIVE LAW WITH FEDERAL REFERENCES. David L. Ryan. Kansas Bar Association, 1200 Harrison, P.O. Box 1037, Topeka, Kansas 66601. 1985- . (Periodic Supplements).

KANSAS ADMINISTRATIVE REGULATIONS. Office of the Revisor of Statutes, Department of Administration, Division of Printing, Topeka, Kansas 66612. 1965- . (Annual Supplements).

KANSAS CODE OF CIVIL PROCEDURE ANNOTATED. Second Edition. Lawyers Co-Operative Company, Aqueduct Building, Rochester, New York 14694. 1979- . (Annual Supplements).

KANSAS REGISTER. Kansas Secretary of State, State Capitol, Topeka, Kansas 66612. 1982- . (Weekly).

KANSAS STATUTES ANNOTATED. (Official). Office of the Revisor of Statutes of Kansas, Department of Administration, Division of Printing, Topeka, Kansas 66612. (Annual Supplements).

LAWS OF KANSAS. Secretary of State, State House, Topeka, Kansas 66612. 1855- . (Annual).

VERNON'S KANSAS STATUTES ANNOTATED. West Publishing Company, P.O. Box 64526, 50 West Kellogg Boulevard, St. Paul, Minnesota 55164-0526. 1963- . (Annual Supplements). (Publisher Varies).

LOOSELEAF SERVICES AND REPORTERS

KANSAS CASES. West Publishing Company, P.O. Box 64526, 50 West Kellogg Boulevard, St. Paul, Minnesota 55164-0526. 1968- . (Kansas Supreme Court and Court of Appeals).

KANSAS COURT OF APPEALS REPORTS. (Second Series). Kansas Court of Appeals, Topeka, Kansas 66612. 1977- .

KANSAS REPORTS. Kansas Department of Administration, Division of Printing, Topeka, Kansas 66612. 1862- . (Kansas Supreme Court).

PACIFIC REPORTER (First and Second Series). West Publishing Company, P.O. Box 64526, 50 West Kellogg Boulevard, St. Paul, Minnesota 55164-0526. 1931- . (Kansas Supreme Court and Court of Appeals).

ATTORNEY GENERAL OPINIONS

OPINIONS OF THE ATTORNEY GENERAL. Office of the Attorney General, 301 West Tenth Street, Kansas Judicial Center, Second Floor, Topeka, Kansas 66612. 1957- . (Annual). (Also available on Lexis: January 1977- .)

ETHICS OPINIONS, CODES, RULES

DISCIPLINARY RULES OF THE SUPREME COURT OF KANSAS, RELATING TO DISCIPLINE OF ATTORNEYS. Office of the Disciplinary Administrator, Kansas Judicial Center, Room 278, 301 West Tenth Street, Topeka, Kansas 66612. 1985. (Revised edition expected January 1988).

Ethics Opinions of the Kansas Bar Association are not published except for occasional inclusions in the Think Ethics column of the Journal of the Kansas Bar Association. Opinions are furnished only to members of the Kansas Bar Association upon request. For further information concerning Kansas Ethics Opinions, contact the Kansas Bar Association, 1200 Harrison Street, P.O. Box 1037, Topeka, Kansas 66601, or the Disciplinary Administrator, The Supreme Court of Kansas, Kansas Judicial Center, Room 278, 301 West Tenth Street, Topeka, Kansas 66612. (913-296-2486).

COURT RULES

KANSAS COURT RULES AND PROCEDURE. West Publishing Company, P.O. Box 64526, 50 West Kellogg Boulevard, St. Paul, Minnesota 55164-0526. (Annual).

JURY INSTRUCTIONS

PATTERN INSTRUCTIONS FOR KANSAS--CIVIL. Second Edition. Committee on Kansas Pattern Jury Instructions, Kansas Judicial Council. Lawyers Co-Operative Company, Aqueduct Building, Rochester, New York 14694. 1977- . (Periodic Supplements).

PATTERN INSTRUCTIONS FOR KANSAS--CRIMINAL. Second Edition. R.R. Sanders. Kansas Judicial Council Advisory Committee on Criminal Jury Instructions. Kansas Judicial Council, Topeka, Kansas. 1982.

DIGESTS, INDEXES, ABSTRACTS, CITATORS

KANSAS DIGEST. West Publishing Company, P.O. Box 64526, 50 West Kellogg Boulevard, St. Paul, Minnesota 55164-0526. 1932- . (Annual Supplements).

PACIFIC DIGEST. West Publishing Company, P.O. Box 64526, 50 West Kellogg Boulevard, St. Paul, Minnesota 55164-0526. 1932- . (Annual Supplements).

SHEPARD'S KANSAS CITATIONS. Shepard's/McGraw-Hill, P.O. Box 1235, Colorado Springs, Colorado 80901. (Eight pamphlets per year).

SHEPARD'S PACIFIC REPORTER CITATIONS. Shepard's/McGraw-Hill, P.O. Box 1235, Colorado Springs, Colorado 80901. (Monthly Supplements).

LAW REVIEWS AND PERIODICALS

JOURNAL OF THE KANSAS BAR ASSOCIATION. The Kansas Bar Association, 1200 Harrison, P.O. Box 1037, Topeka, Kansas 66601. (Nine issues per Year).

UNIVERSITY OF KANSAS LAW REVIEW. University of Kansas School of Law, 510 Green Hall, Laurence, Kansas 66045. (Quarterly).

WASHBURN LAW REVIEW. School of Law, Washburn University of Topeka, Topeka, Kansas 66621. (Three issues per year).

FORMBOOKS

VERNON'S KANSAS FORMS ANNOTATED: CODE OF CIVIL PROCEDURE WITH PRACTICE COMMENTARIES. E. Hatcher. West Publishing Company, 50 West Kellogg Boulevard, St. Paul, Minnesota 55164. 1963. (Annual Supplements).

VERNON'S KANSAS FORMS ANNOTATED: UNIFORM COMMERICAL CODE WITH PRACTICE COMMENTARIES. J. Howe and D. Dale. West Publishing Company, 50 West Kellogg Boulevard, St. Paul, Minnesota 55164. 1981. (Annual Supplements).

PRACTICE MATERIALS

KANSAS ADMINISTRATIVE LAW WITH FEDERAL REFERENCES. D. Ryan. Kansas Bar Association, 1200 Harrison Street, P.O. Box 1037, Topeka, Kansas 66601. 1982- . (Periodic Supplements).

KANSAS APPELLATE PRACTICE. Jerome Harman, Editor. Kansas Bar Association, 1200 Harrison, P.O. Box 1037, Topeka, Kansas 66601. 1987- . (Periodic Supplements).

KANSAS ATTORNEY'S PRACTICE MANUAL. Douglas Country Legal Aid Society, Kansas Bar Association, 1200 Harrison, P.O. Box 1037, Topeka, Kansas 66601. 1988- . (Periodic Supplements).

KANSAS BANKRUPTCY HANDBOOK. Second Edition. Kansas Bar Association, 1200 Harrison, P.O. Box 1037, Topeka, Kansas 66601. 1982- . (Periodic Supplements).

KANSAS CORPORATION LAW AND PRACTICE (INCLUDING TAX ASPECTS). Third Edition. J. Logan and others. Kansas Bar Association, 1200 Harrison, P.O. Box 1037, Topeka, Kansas 66601. 1978- . (Periodic Supplements).

KANSAS CRIMINAL LAW HANDBOOK. M. Barbara. Kansas Bar Association, 1200 Harrison, P.O. Box 1037, Topeka, Kansas 66601. 1978- . (Periodic Supplements).

KANSAS ESTATE ADMINISTRATION. Fifth Edition. James K. Logan, Editor. Kansas Bar Association, 1200 Harrison, P.O. Box 1037, Topeka, Kansas 66601. 1986- .

KANSAS FAMILY LAW HANDBOOK. Linda Henry Elrod. Kansas Bar Association, 1200 Harrison, P.O. Box 1037, Topeka, Kansas 66601. 1983- . (Periodic Supplements).

KANSAS LAW OF SALES UNDER THE UNIFORM COMMERCIAL CODE. Paul B. Rasor. Kansas Bar Association, 1200 Harrison, P.O. Box 1037, Topeka, Kansas 66601. 1981- . (Periodic Supplements).

KANSAS OIL AND GAS HANDBOOK. David E. Pierce. Kansas Bar Association, 1200 Harrison, P.O. Box 1037, Topeka, Kansas 66601. 1986- . (Periodic Supplements).

KANSAS REAL ESTATE PRACTICE AND PROCEDURE HANDBOOK. Revised Edition. Kansas Bar Association, 1200 Harrison, P.O. Box 1037, Topeka, Kansas 66601. 1985- . (Periodic Supplements).

KANSAS STATUTES OF LIMITATIONS AND TIME STANDARDS HANDBOOK. C. McNeil, Editor. Kansas Bar Association, 1200 Harrison, P.O. Box 1037, Topeka, Kansas 66601. 1988.

DIRECTORIES

DIRECTORY OF COUNTY OFFICERS OF KANSAS. Kansas Secretary of State, State Capitol, Second Floor, Topeka, Kansas 66612. (Annual).

DIRECTORY OF THE KANSAS BAR. Kansas Bar Association, 1200 Harrison, P.O. Box 1037, Topeka, Kansas 66601. Biannual.

KANSAS DIRECTORY. Kansas Secretary of State, Secretary of State, State Capitol, Second Floor, Topeka, Kansas 66612. (Biennial).

KANSAS LEGAL DIRECTORY. Legal Directories Publishing Company, 2122 Kidwell Street, P.O. Box 140200, Dallas, Texas 75214-0200. (Annual).

LEGISLATIVE DIRECTORY. Kansas Secretary of State, State Capitol, Second Floor, Topeka, Kansas 66612. (Annual).

ASSOCIATIONS AND PROFESSIONAL SOCIETIES

KANSAS BAR ASSOCIATION, 1200 Harrison, P.O. Box 1037, Topeka, Kansas 66601. (913) 234-5696.

THE LAWYERS ASSOCIATION OF KANSAS CITY, 8026 Brookside Circle, Kansas City, Kansas 66109.

TOPEKA BAR ASSOCIATION, 500 South Kansas, Suite A, P.O. Box 1399, Topeka, Kansas 66601.

WICHITA BAR ASSOCIATION, 225 North Market Street, Suite 210, Wichita, Kansas 67202.

OTHER SOURCES

A GUIDE TO KANSAS LEGAL RESEARCH. F. Snyder. Kansas Bar Association, 1200 Harrison, P.O. Box 1037, Topeka, Kansas 66601. 1986.

KANSAS STATE DOCUMENTS FOR LAW LIBRARIES. M. Wisneski. American Association of Law Libraries, 53 West Jackson Boulevard, Suite 940, Chicago, Illinois 60604. 1984.

STATES--KENTUCKY

STATES--KENTUCKY

STATUTES, CODES, STANDARDS, UNIFORM LAWS

ADMINISTRATIVE REGISTER OF KENTUCKY. Legislative Research Commission, Room 300, State Capitol, Frankfort, Kentucky 40601. 1974- . (Monthly).

BALDWIN'S KENTUCKY REVISED STATUTES ANNOTATED. Banks-Baldwin Publishing Company, University Center, P.O. Box 1974, Cleveland, Ohio 44106. 1969- . (Periodic Supplements).

KENTUCKY ADMINISTRATIVE REGULATION SERVICE. Legislative Research Commission, Room 300, State Capitol, Frankfort, Kentucky 40601. 1975- . (Annual).

KENTUCKY REVISED STATUTES ANNOTATED. Michie Company, P.O. Box 7587, Charlottesville, Virginia 22906-7587. 1973- . (Annual Supplements).

LOOSELEAF SERVICES AND REPORTERS

KENTUCKY DECISIONS. West Publishing Company, P.O. Box 64526, 50 West Kellogg Boulevard, St. Paul, Minnesota 55164-0526. 1886- . (Kentucky Supreme Court and Court of Appeals).

KENTUCKY REPORTS. (Kentucky Court of Appeals). 1785-1951. (Current source is the Southwestern Reporter).

SOUTHWESTERN REPORTER. West Publishing Company, P.O. Box 64526, 50 West Kellogg Boulevard, St. Paul, Minnesota 55164-0526. 1886- . (Kentucky Supreme Court and Court of Appeals).

ATTORNEY GENERAL OPINIONS

ATTORNEY GENERAL OPINIONS AND REPORTS. Published upon request by the Kentucky Attorney General's Office, Banks-Baldwin Publishing Company, University Center, P.O. Box 1974, Cleveland, Ohio 44106. 1968- .

COURT RULES

KENTUCKY COURT RULES. Rules Service Company, 7658 Standish Place, Rockville, Maryland 20855. 1979- . (Periodic Supplements).

KENTUCKY RULES OF CIVIL PROCEDURE ANNOTATED. W. Bertelsman. West Publishing Company, 50 West Kellogg Boulevard, St. Paul, Minnesota 55164. (Annual Supplement).

KENTUCKY RULES OF COURT. West Publishing Company, 50 West Kellogg Boulevard, St. Paul, Minnesota 55164. Annual.

KENTUCKY RULES OF COURT ANNOTATED. Michie Company, P.O. Box 7587, Charlottesville, Virginia 22906-7587. (Annual).

JURY INSTRUCTIONS

KENTUCKY INSTRUCTIONS TO JURIES. Fourth Edition. Robert Booth. Anderson Publishing Company, 2035 Reading Road, Cincinnati, Ohio 45202. 1989.

PALMORE'S KENTUCKY INSTRUCTIONS TO JURIES: A REVISION OF STANLEY. Anderson Publishing Company, 2035 Reading Road, Cincinatti, Ohio 45202. 1975- . (Periodic Supplements).

DIGESTS, INDEXES, ABSTRACTS, CITATORS

KENTUCKY DIGEST. (First and Second Series). West Publishing Company, P.O. Box 64526, 50 West Kellogg Boulevard, St. Paul, Minnesota 55164-0526. (Annual Supplements).

SHEPARD'S KENTUCKY CITATIONS. Shepard's/McGraw-Hill, P.O. Box 1235, Colorado Springs, Colorado 80901. (Six issues per year).

SHEPARD'S SOUTHWESTERN REPORTER CITATIONS. Shepard's/McGraw-Hill, P.O. Box 1235, Colorado Springs, Colorado 80901. (Monthly Supplements).

ENCYCLOPEDIAS AND DICTIONARIES

KENTUCKY JURISPRUDENCE. Lawyers Co-Operative Company, Aqueduct Building, Rochester, New York 14694. (Periodic Supplements). 1985- . (Annual Supplements).

LAW REVIEWS AND PERIODICALS

KENTUCKY BENCH AND BAR. West Main at Kentucky River, Frankfort, Kentucky 40601. (Quarterly).

KENTUCKY LAW JOURNAL. University of Kentucky, Lexington, Kentucky 40506. (Quarterly).

LOUISVILLE LAWYER. Louisville Bar Association, 717 West Main Street, Suite 200, Louisville, Kentucky 40202. (Quarterly).

NORTHERN KENTUCKY LAW REVIEW. Northern Kentucky University, Highland Heights, Kentucky 41706. (Three Issues per Year).

FORMBOOKS

CADWELL'S KENTUCKY FORM BOOK. Fourth Edition. M. Volte and others. Anderson Publishing Company, 2035 Reading Road, Cincinnati, Ohio 45202. 1989.

KENTUCKY LEGAL FORMS. Wesley Gilmer, Jr. Banks-Baldwin Publishing Company, University Center, P.O. Box 1974, Cleveland, Ohio 44106. 1975- . (Periodic Supplements).

PRACTICE MATERIALS

ANDERSON'S KENTUCKY CORPORATION RECORD BOOK. Anderson Publishing Company, 2035 Reading Road, Cincinnati, Ohio 45202. 1989.

BALDWIN'S KENTUCKY PRACTICE: TEXT AND FORMS. Banks-Baldwin Publishing Company, University Center, P.O. Box 1974, Cleveland, Ohio 44106. 1980- . (Periodic Supplements).

KENTUCKY APPELLATE HANDBOOK. Kentucky Bar Foundation, Banks-Baldwin Publishing Company, University Center, P.O. Box 1974, Cleveland, Ohio 44106. 1985- . (Periodic Supplements).

KENTUCKY COLLECTIONS. W. Mapother. Lawyers Cooperative Publishing Company, Aqueduct Building, Rochester, New York 14694. 1981- . (Annual Supplement).

KENTUCKY CRIMINAL PRACTICE AND PROCEDURE. T. Fitzgerald. West Publishing Company, 50 West Kellogg Boulevard, St. Paul, Minnesota 55164. 1978- . (Annual Supplements).

THE KENTUCKY EVIDENCE LAW HANDBOOK. Second Edition. Robert G. Lawson. Michie Company, P.O. Box 7587, Charlottesville, Virginia 22906-7587. 1984- . (Periodic Supplements).

KENTUCKY METHODS OF PRACTICE. J. Richarson. West Publishing Company, 50 West Kellogg Boulevard, St. Paul, Minnesota 55164. 1968- . (Annual Supplements).

KENTUCKY PROBATE AND PROCEDURE WITH FORMS. J. Merrit. West Publishing Company, 50 West Kellogg Boulevard, St. Paul, Minnesota 55164. 1984. (Periodic Supplements).

KENTUCKY PROBATE METHODS. Randolph Noe. Michie Company, P.O. Box 7587, Charlottesville, Virginia 22906-7587. 1976- . (Periodic Supplements).

KENTUCKY TORT LAW: DEFAMATION AND THE RIGHT OF PRIVACY. David A. Elder. Michie Company, P.O. Box 7587, Charlottesville, Virginia 22906-7587. 1983- . (Periodic Supplements).

TRIAL HANDBOOK FOR KENTUCKY LAWYERS. T. Osborne. Lawyers Cooperative Publishing Company, Aqueduct Building, Rochester, New York 14694. 1984- . (Periodic Supplements).

MANUALS AND RESEARCH GUIDES

GUIDE TO KENTUCKY LEGAL RESEARCH: A STATE BIBLIOGRAPHY. Wesley Gilmer. Kentucky State Law Library, Room 200, State Capitol, Frankfort, Kentucky 40601-3489. 1979.

INDEX TO KENTUCKY LEGAL HISTORY. E. Lockwood. Kentucky State Law Library, Room 200, State Capitol, Frankfort, Kentucky 40601. 1983.

ASSOCIATIONS AND PROFESSIONAL SOCIETIES

KENTUCKY BAR ASSOCIATION. West Main at Kentucky River, Frankfort, Kentucky 40601. (502) 564-3795

LOUISVILLE BAR ASSOCIATION. 717 Main Street, Suite 200, Louisville, Kentucky 40202. (502) 583-5314.

DIRECTORIES

KENTUCKY LEGAL DIRECTORY. Legal Directories Publishing Company, 2122 Kidwell Street, P.O. Box 140200, Dallas, Texas 75214-0200. (Annual).

KENTUCKY MUNICIPAL LEAGUE DIRECTORY. Kentucky Municipal League, Box 22736, Lexington, Kentucky 40522. (Biennial).

STATE DIRECTORY OF KENTUCKY. Directories, Incorporated, Box 187, Pewee Valley, Kentucky 40056. (Annual).

OTHER SOURCES

KENTUCKY DIVORCE. R. Revell. Lawyers Cooperative Publishing Company, Aqueduct Building, Rochester, New York 14694. 1982- . (Periodic Supplements).

KENTUCKY DOMESTIC RELATIONS LAW. L. Graham and J. Keller. Banks-Baldwin Publishing Company, P.O. Box 1974, Cleveland, Ohio 44106. 1982- . (Periodic Supplements).

KENTUCKY FAMILY LAW. Second Edition. R. Petrilli. Anderson Publishing Company, 2035 Reading Road, Cincinnati, Ohio 45202. 1988.

KENTUCKY PROBATE. W. Schmitt. Lawyers Cooperative Publishing Company, Aqueduct Building, Rochester, New York 14694. 1980- . (Annual Supplements).

PRODUCTS LIABILITY: THE LAW IN KENTUCKY. R. Eades. Harrison Company, 3110 Crossing Park, Norcross, Georgia 30091. 1981.

THE UNIFORM COMMERICAL CODE OF KENTUCKY. D. Leibson. Michie Company, P.O. Box 7587, Charlottesville, Virginia 22906-7587. 1983- . (Annual Supplements).

STATES--LOUISIANA

STATUTES, CODES, STANDARDS, UNIFORM LAWS

LOUISIANA ADMINISTRATIVE CODE. Office of the State Register, P.O. Box 94095, Baton Rouge, Louisiana 70804-9095. (Annual Supplements).

LOUISIANA REGISTER. Division of Administration, Office of the State Register, P.O. Box 94095, Baton Rouge, Louisiana 70804-9095. 1989. Monthly.

LOUISIANA SESSION LAW SERVICE. West Publishing Company, P.O. Box 64526, 50 West Kellogg Boulevard, St. Paul, Minnesota 55164-0526.

LOUISIANA CIVIL CODE ANNOTATED. West Publishing Company, P.O. Box 64526, 50 West Kellogg Boulevard, St. Paul, Minnesota 55164-0526. (Annual Supplements).

LOUISIANA CODE OF CIVIL PROCEDURE ANNOTATED. West Publishing Company, P.O. Box 64526, 50 West Kellogg Boulevard, St. Paul, Minnesota 55164-0526. (Annual).

STATE OF LOUISIANA: ACTS OF THE LEGISLATURE. State of Louisiana, Section of States, Office of Publications, P.O. Box 94125, Baton Rouge, Louisiana 70804. 1812- .

WEST'S LOUISIANA CODE OF CRIMINAL PROCEDURE. West Publishing Company, P.O. Box 64526, 50 West Kellogg Boulevard, St. Paul, Minnesota 55164-0526. (Annual).

WEST'S LOUISIANA REVISED STATUTES. West Publishing Company, P.O. Box 64526, 50 West Kellogg Boulevard, St. Paul, Minnesota 55164-0526. (Annual Supplements).

STATES--LOUISIANA

LOOSELEAF SERVICES AND REPORTERS

LOUISIANA REPORTS. West Publishing Company, P.O. Box 64526, 50 West Kellogg Boulevard, St. Paul, Minnesota 55164-0526. Volume 1-263. 1901-1972. (Louisiana Supreme Court). (Current Offical Source: West's Louisiana Cases and The Southern Reporter).

SOUTHERN REPORTER. (First and Second Series). West Publishing Company, P.O. Box 64526, 50 West Kellogg Boulevard, St. Paul, Minnesota 55164-0526. 1887- . (Louisiana Supreme Court and Court of Appeals).

WEST'S LOUISIANA CASES. West Publishing Company, P.O. Box 64526, 50 West Kellogg Boulevard, St. Paul, Minnesota 55164-0526. 1966- . (Louisiana Supreme Court and Court of Appeals).

ATTORNEY GENERAL OPINIONS

OPINIONS OF THE ATTORNEY GENERAL OF THE STATE OF LOUISIANA. Office of the Attorney General, P.O. Box 44005, Baton Rouge, Louisiana 70804. 1853- . Lexis: January 1977- . Westlaw: January 1977- .

ETHICS OPINIONS, CODES, RULES

ATTORNEYS DESK BOOK. Louisiana State Bar Association, 210 O'Keefe Avenue, Suite 600, New Orleans, Louisiana 70112. 1968- . (Periodic Supplements). (Includes Code of Professional Responsibilities, Disciplinary Rules and Ethics Opinions). (Disciplinary Rules are also published in Volume 21A of the Louisiana Statutes Annotated, Chapter 4, Article 15 of the Articles of Incorporation of the Louisiana State Bar Association. Full text of the Ethics opinions for Louisiana are published in the Louisiana Bar Journal and in the Attorney's Desk Book. For further information concerning these opinions, contact the Executive Counsel, Louisiana State Bar Association, Suite 600, 210 O'Keefe Avenue, New Orleans, Louisiana 70012. (504-566-1600).

COURT RULES

LOUISIANA RULES OF COURT: STATE AND FEDERAL. West Publishing Company, P.O. Box 64526, 50 West Kellogg Boulevard, St. Paul, Minnesota 55164-0526. (Annual). (Also in Louisiana Revised Statutes Volume 8).

RULES OF SUPREME COURT OF LOUISIANA. West Publishing Company, 50 West Kellogg Boulevard, St. Paul, Minnesota 55164. 1973- . (Periodic Supplement).

JURY INSTRUCTIONS

LOUISIANA JURY INSTRUCTIONS--CIVIL. H. Alston Johnson. Paul M. Herbert Law Center Publications Institute, Baton Rouge, Louisiana 70803-1012. 1980.

LOUISIANA JURY INSTRUCTIONS--CRIMINAL. Cheney C. Joseph, Jr. Paul M. Herbert Law Center Publications Institute, Baton Rouge, Louisiana 70803-1012. 1980.

Encyclopedia of Legal Information Sources • 2nd Ed.

DIGESTS, INDEXES, ABSTRACTS, CITATORS

LOUISIANA DIGEST. (First and Second Series). West Publishing Company, P.O. Box 64526, 50 West Kellogg Boulevard, St. Paul, Minnesota 55164-0526. (Annual Supplements).

LOUISIANA DIGEST. Michie Company, P.O. Box 7587, Charlottesville, Virginia 22906-7587. 1973- . (Annual Supplements).

SHEPARD'S LOUISIANA CITATIONS. Shepard's/McGraw-Hill, P.O. Box 1235, Colorado Springs, Colorado 80901. (Eight issues per year).

SHEPARD'S SOUTHERN REPORTER CITATIONS. Shepard's/ McGraw-Hill, P.O. Box 1235, Colorado Springs, Colorado 80901. (Monthly Supplements).

SOUTHERN DIGEST. West Publishing Company, P.O. Box 64526, 50 West Kellogg Boulevard, St. Paul, Minnesota 55164-0526. (Annual Supplements).

LAW REVIEWS AND PERIODICALS

LOUISIANA LAW EXAMINER. University of Louisville School of Law. Belknap Campus, Louisville, Kentucky 40292. (Monthly).

LOUISIANA LAW REVIEW. Louisiana State University, Paul M. Herbert Law Center, Baton Rouge, Louisiana 70803-1012. Bimonthly.

LOUISIANA STATE BAR JOURNAL. Louisiana State Bar Association, 210 O'Keefe Avenue, Suite 600, New Orleans, Louisiana 70112. (Bimonthly).

LOYOLA LAW REVIEW. School of Law, Loyola University, New Orleans, Louisiana 70118. (Quarterly).

NEWSLETTERS AND NEWSPAPERS

DAILY LEGISLATIVE REPORT. Legiscon, P.O. Box 1643, Baton Rouge, Louisiana 70821. Daily when in session.

LOUISIANA CIVIL LAW AND PROCEDURE NEWSLETTER. Frank L. Maraist, 330 Sunset Boulevard, Baton Rouge, Louisiana 70808. Semimonthly.

LOUISIANA COASTAL LAW. Sea Grant Legal Program, 170 Law Center, Louisiana State University, Baton Rouge, Louisiana 70803. Quarterly.

THE LOUISIANA UNITED STATES DISTRICT COURT NEWSLETTER. Louisiana Esquire Incorporated, P.O. Box 52887, New Orleans, Louisiana 70152. Monthly.

NEW ORLEANS LAW LIBRARIAN. New Orleans Association of Law Librarians, c/o Fifth Circuit Court Library, 600 Camp Street, Room 106, New Orleans, Louisiana 70130. Quarterly.

PAR LEGISLATIVE BULLETIN. Public Affairs Research Council of Louisana, Incorporated, 4664 Jamestown, Suite 300, Baton Rouge, Louisiana 70808. Weekly when in session.

WEEKLY REVIEW. Louisiana New Bureau, P.O. Box 44212, Baton Rouge, Louisiana 70804. Weekly.

Encyclopedia of Legal Information Sources • 2nd Ed. STATES--MAINE

WEEKLY STATEHOUSE REPORT. Legiscon, P.O. Box 1643, Baton Rouge, Louisiana 70821. Weekly.

FORMBOOKS

LOUISIANA CIVIL PRACTICE FORMS. Roger M. Denton. Lawyers Co-Operative Company, Aqueduct Building, Rochester, New York 14694. 1985- . (Annual Supplements).

PRACTICE MATERIALS

LOUISIANA APPELLATE PRACTICE HANDBOOK. Roger A. Stetter, William V. Redmann, and Rutledge C. Clement, Jr. Lawyers Co-Operative Company, Aqueduct Building, Rochester, New York 14694. 1986- . (Periodic Supplements).

LOUISIANA CIVIL LAW TREATISE SERIES. West Publishing Company, 50 West Kellogg Boulevard, St. Paul, Minnesota 55164. (Periodic Supplements).

LOUISIANA CORPORATIONS. James A. Holliday, Jr. and Rick Norman. Lawyers Co-Operative Company, Aqueduct Building, Rochester, New York 14694. 1983- . (Annual Supplements).

LOUISIANA DIVORCE. Robert C. Lowe. Lawyers Co-Operative Company, Aqueduct Building, Rochester, New York 14694. 1984- . (Annual Supplements).

LOUISIANA EVIDENCE LAW. George W. Pugh. Michie/Bobbs-Merrill Law Publishing Company, P.O. Box 7587, Charlottesville, Virginia 22906-7587. 1974- . (Periodic Supplements).

LOUISIANA WRONGFUL DEATH. Thomas J. Andre, Jr. Butterworth Legal Publishers, 90 Stiles Road, Salem, New Hampshire 03079. (Periodic Supplements).

PRECIS IN CONVENTIONAL OBLIGATIONS. A. Levasseur. Michie Company, P.O. Box 7587, Charlottesville, Virginia 22906-7587. 1980. (Periodic Supplements).

PROPOSED LOUISIANA CODE OF EVIDENCE. Louisana State Law Institute. West Publishing Company, 50 West Kellogg Boulevard, St. Paul, Minnesota 55164. 1986.

TRIAL HANDBOOK FOR LOUISIANA LAWYERS. Eldon E. Fallon. Lawyers Co-Operative Company, Aqueduct Building, Rochester, New York 14694. 1981- . (Annual Supplements).

MANUALS AND RESEARCH GUIDES

BIBLIOGRAPHY OF BASIC MATERIALS FOR A LOUISIANA LAW LIBRARY. D. Naylor. Louisana State University, Paul M. Herbert Law Center, Library, Baton Rouge, Louisiana 70803. 1979.

LOUISIANA LEGAL DOCUMENTS AND RELATED PUBLICATIONS: A SELECTED ANNOTATED BIBLIOGRAPHY. C. Cornoil and M. Herbert. American Association of Law Libraries, 53 West Jackson Boulevard, Suite 940, Chicago, Illinois 60604. 1984.

LOUISIANA LEGAL RESEARCH. W. Chiang. Butterworth Legal Publishers, 90 Stiles Road, Salem, New Hampshire 03079. 1985.

LOUISIANA LEGAL RESEARCH MANUAL. Louisiana State University Law School, Institute of Continuing Legal Education, Baton Rouge, Louisiana 70803. 1972.

ASSOCIATIONS AND PROFESSIONAL SOCIETIES

BATON ROUGE BAR ASSOCIATION, Government Building, 222 St. Louis Street, Suite 738, Baton, Rouge, Louisiana 70801.

LOUISIANA BAR ASSOCIATION, 210 O'Keefe Avenue, Suite 600, New Orleans, Louisiana 70112. (504) 566-1600.

NEW ORLEANS BAR ASSOCIATION, Suite 310, 336 Camp Street, New Orleans, Louisiana 70130.

SHREVEPORT BAR ASSOCIATION, 500 Caddo Parish Courthouse, P.O. Box 470, Shreveport, Louisiana 71162.

DIRECTORIES

CITIZEN'S GUIDE TO THE LOUISIANA LEGISLATURE. Public Affairs Research Council of Louisiana, Box 3118, Baton Rouge, Louisiana 70821. (Quadrennial).

DIRECTORY OF LOUISIANA MUNICIPAL OFFICIALS. Louisiana Municipal Association, Box 4327, Baton Rouge, Louisiana 70821. (Irregular).

LOUISIANA ALMANAC. Pelican Publishing Company, 1101 Monroe Street, Gretna, Louisiana 70053. (Irregular).

LOUISIANA LEGAL DIRECTORY. Legal Directories Publishing Company, 2122 Kidwell Street, P.O. Box 140200, Dallas, Texas 75214-0200. (Annual).

STATE OF LOUISIANA ROSTER OF OFFICIALS. Louisiana Secretary of State, P.O. Box 94125, Baton Rouge, Louisiana 70804. (Irregular).

STATES--MAINE

STATUTES, CODES, STANDARDS, UNIFORM LAWS

CODE OF MAINE RULES. Weil and Firth, Incorporated, Two Central Plaza, Augusta, Maine 04330. 1986- . (Periodic Supplements). (N. B. This is a selective, not a complete set of regulations).

LAWS OF THE STATE OF MAINE. J. S. McCarthy Company, Incorporated, Augusta, Maine. (Title and Publisher Varies).

MAINE LEGISLATIVE SERVICE. West Publishing Company, P.O. Box 64526, 50 West Kellogg Boulevard, St. Paul, Minnesota 55164-0526. (Irregular Pamphlets).

MAINE REVISED STATUTES ANNOTATED. West Publishing Company, P.O. Box 64526, 50 West Kellogg Boulevard, St. Paul, Minnesota 55164-0526. 1979- . (Annual Supplements).

STATES--MAINE

LOOSELEAF SERVICES AND REPORTERS

ATLANTIC REPORTER (First and Second Series). West Publishing Company, P.O. Box 64526, 50 West Kellogg Boulevard, St. Paul, Minnesota 55164-0526. 1885- . (Maine Supreme Judicial Court).

MAINE REPORTER. West Publishing Company, P.O. Box 64526, 50 West Kellogg Boulevard, St. Paul, Minnesota 55164-0526. 1966- .

MAINE REPORTS. Maine Supreme Judicial Court, Portland, Maine. 1820-1965. (Supreme Court). (Current Official Source: Maine Reporter and Atlantic Reporter). (Publisher Varies).

ATTORNEY GENERAL OPINIONS

REPORT OF THE ATTORNEY GENERAL. Department of the Attorney General. 1890- . Hardcopy ceased publication in 1972. (Titles varies). Available on Lexis: January 1984- .

ETHICS OPINIONS, RULES, CODES

MAINE MANUAL ON PROFESSIONAL RESPONSIBILITY. Board of Overseers of the Bar. Tower Publishing Company, 34 Diamond Street, P.O. Box 7220, Portland, Maine 04112. 1986- . (Periodic Supplements). (Contains Maine Bar Rules and Advisory Ethics Opinions). For further information concerning Professional Responsibility in Maine, contact the Maine Board of Overseers of the Bar, P.O. Box 1820, Augusta, Maine 04330. (207-623-1121).

COURT RULES

MAINE RULES OF COURT. West Publishing Company, P.O. Box 64526, 50 West Kellogg Boulevard, St. Paul, Minnesota 55164-0526. (Annual).

JURY INSTRUCTIONS

MANUAL OF JURY PROCEDURES AND INSTRUCTIONS FOR MAINE. Judge Donald G. Alexander. Maine Trial Lawyers Association, Box 428, Augusta, Maine 04330. 1985- .

DIGESTS, INDEXES, ABSTRACTS, CITATORS

ATLANTIC DIGEST (First and Second Series). West Publishing Company, P.O. Box 64526, 50 West Kellogg Boulevard, St. Paul, Minnesota 55164-0526. 1949- . (Annual Supplements).

MAINE KEY NUMBER DIGEST. West Publishing Company, P.O. Box 64526, 50 West Kellogg Boulevard, St. Paul, Minnesota 55164-0526. 1967- . (Annual Supplements).

SHEPARD'S ATLANTIC CITATIONS. Shepard's/McGraw-Hill, P.O. Box 1235, Colorado Springs, Colorado 80901. (Monthly Supplements).

SHEPARD'S MAINE CITATIONS. Shepard's/McGraw-Hill, P.O. Box 1235, Colorado Springs, Colorado 80901. (Quarterly Supplements).

LAW REVIEWS AND PERIODICALS

MAINE BAR BULLETIN. Maine State Bar Association, P.O. Box 788, Augusta, Maine. (Six Issues per Year).

MAINE LAW REVIEW. University of Maine School of Law, 246 Deering Avenue, Portland, Maine 04102. (Semiannual).

PRACTICE MATERIALS

APPELATE ADVOCACY. Maine Bar Association, P.O. Box 788, Augusta, Maine 04330. 1981

MAINE ADMINISTRATIVE PROCEDURE. Butterworth Legal Publishers, 90 Stiles Road, Salem, New Hampshire 03079. 1985- . (Periodic Supplements).

MAINE CIVIL PRACTICE, RULES AND CIVIL PROCEDURE. R. Field. West Publishing Company, 50 West Kellogg Boulevard, St. Paul, Minnesota 55164. 1982- . (Annual Supplements).

MAINE CIVIL REMEDIES. A. Horton and P. Mcbehee. Tower Publishing Company, 34 Diamond Street, Portland, Maine 04112. 1988.

MAINE CRIMINAL PRACTICE. David P. Cluchey and Michael D. Seitzinger. Tower Publisheing Company, 34 Diamond Street, P.O. Box 7220, Portland, Maine 04112. 1985- . (Periodic Updates).

MAINE MANUAL ON PROFESSIONAL RESPONSIBILITY. Board of Overseers of the Bar, Tower Publishing Company, 34 Diamond Street, P.O. Box 7220, Portland, Maine 04112. 1986- . (Periodic Supplements).

MAINE PROBATE MANUAL. James E. Mitchell. Tower Publishing Group, 34 Diamond Street, P.O. Box 7220, Portland, Maine 04112. 1983- . (Periodic Supplements).

MAINE WORKERS COMPENSATION ACT: PRACTICE AND PROCEDURE. C. Devoe. Tower Publishing Group, 34 Diamond Street, Portland, Maine 04112. 1983.

ASSOCIATIONS AND PROFESSIONAL SOCIETIES

MAINE BAR ASSOCIATION, 124 State Street, P.O. Box 788, Augusta, Maine 04330. (207) 662-7523.

MAINE TRIAL LAWYERS ASSOCIATION, Box 428, Augusta, Maine 04330.

DIRECTORIES

LEGISLATURE, SENATE, AND HOUSE REGISTERS, STATE OF MAINE. Clerk of the House, Maine State Legislature, State House, Augusta, Maine 04333. (Biennial).

MAINE BAR DIRECTORY. Tower Publishing Company, 34 Diamond Street, P.O. Box 7220, Portland, Maine 04112. (Annual).

MAINE REGISTER. Tower Publishing Company, 34 Diamond Street, P.O. Box 7220, Portland, Maine 04112. (Annual).

MUNICIPAL DIRECTORY (MAINE). Maine Municipal Association, Community Drive, Augusta, Maine 04330. (Annual).

STATE AND COUNTY OFFICES. Maine State Secretary of State, State House, Augusta, Maine 04330. (Biennial).

OTHER SOURCES

MAINE LEGAL RESEARCH GUIDE. W. Wells. Tower Publishing Company, 34 Diamond Street, P.O. Box 7220, Portland, Maine 04112. 1989.

CORPORATION LAW. Maine Bar Association, P.O. Box 788, Augusta, Maine 04330. 1981- . (Periodic Supplements).

PROBATE LAW. Maine Bar Association, P.O. Box 788, Augusta, Maine 04330. 1982- . (Periodic Supplements).

PRODUCTS LIABILITY. Maine Bar Association, P.O. Box 788, Augusta, Maine 04330. 190- . (Periodic Supplements).

STATES--MARYLAND

STATUTES, CODES, STANDARDS, UNIFORM LAWS

ANNOTATED CODE OF MARYLAND. Michie Company, P.O. Box 7587, Charlottesville, Virginia 22906-7587. 1981- . (Annual Supplements).

CODE OF MARYLAND REGULATIONS. Office of the Secretary of State, Division of State Documents, Box 802, Annapolis, Maryland 21404. 1973- .

LAWS OF THE STATE OF MARYLAND. State Department of Legislative Reference, 90 State Circle, Annapolis, Maryland 21401.

MARYLAND ADVANCE CODE SERVICE. Michie Company, P.O. Box 7587, Charlottesville, Virginia 22906-7587. 1985- . (Three Pamphlets per Year).

MARYLAND REGISTER. Office of the Secretary of State, Division of State Documents, Box 802, Annapolis, Maryland 21402. (Biweekly).

LOOSELEAF SERVICES AND REPORTERS

ATLANTIC REPORTER. (First and Second Series). West Publishing Company, P.O. Box 64526, 50 West Kellogg Boulevard, St. Paul, Minnesota 55164-0526. (Maryland Court of Appeals and Court of Special Appeals).

MARYLAND ANTITRUST REPORTER. James K. Archibald, et al. Maryland Institute for Continuing Professional Education of Lawyers, Incorporated, 520 West Fayette Street, Baltimore, Maryland 21201. 1981- . (Periodic Supplements).

MARYLAND APPELLATE REPORTS. West Publishing Company, P.O. Box 64526, 50 West Kellogg Boulevard, St. Paul, Minnesota 55164-0526. 1962- . (Maryland Court of Special Appeals).

MARYLAND CASES ON DISCRIMINATION. Maryland State Bar Association, Section of Labor Law MCHR Digest Subcommittee, 520 West Fayette Street, Baltimore, Maryland 21201. 1986- . (Periodic Supplements).

MARYLAND REPORTS. West Publishing Company, P.O. Box 64526, 50 West Kellogg Boulevard, St. Paul, Minnesota 55164-0526. 1851- . (Maryland Court of Appeals).

MARYLAND RULES DECISIONS. Young Lawyers Section of Maryland, State Bar Association. Maryland Institute for Continuing Professional Education of Lawyers, Incorporated, 520 West Fayette Street, Baltimore, Maryland 21201. 1987- . (Periodic Supplements).

MARYLAND STATE BOARD OF CONTRACT APPEALS DECISIONS. Maryland State Board of Contract Appeals. Maryland Institute for Continuing Professional Education of Lawyers, Incorporated, 520 West Fayette Street, Baltimore, Maryland 21201. 1986- . (Periodic Supplements).

ATTORNEY GENERAL OPINIONS

ANNUAL REPORT AND OFFICIAL OPINIONS OF THE ATTORNEY GENERAL OF MARYLAND. Office of the Attorney General, Calvert and Fayette Streets, Baltimore, Maryland 21202. (Annual). Available on Lexis: January 1977- . Westlaw: 1977- .

ETHICS OPINIONS, CODES, RULES

MARYLAND LAWYER'S RULES ON PROFESSIONAL CONDUCT, are published in Maryland Rules (Volume Two). Michie Company, P.O. Box 7587, Charlottesville, Virginia 22906-7587. (Annual).

OPINIONS ON ETHICS AND PROFESSIONAL RESPONSIBILITY. Arthur W. Machen, Editor. Maryland State Bar Association, Committee on Ethics, 520 West Fayette Street, Baltimore, Maryland 21201. 1976- . (Missing numbers are unpublished). Selected opinions are published in the Maryland State Bar Journal. For further information concerning these opinions, contact the Maryland State Bar Association, 520 West Fayette Street, Baltimore, Maryland 21201. 301-685-7878.

COURT RULES

MARYLAND COURT RULES. Rules Service Company, 7658 Standish Place, Suite 106, Rockville, Maryland 20855. 1966- . (Periodic Supplements).

MARYLAND DISTRICT RULES. Rules Service Company, 7658 Standish Place, Rockville, Maryland 20855. 1971- . (Periodic Supplements).

MARYLAND RULES COMMENTARY. Paul V. Niemeyer and Linda M. Richards. Michie/Bobbs-Merrill Law Publishing Company, P.O. Box 7587, Charlottesville, Virginia 22906-7587. 1984- . (Periodic Supplements).

MARYLAND RULES OF PROCEDURE. Michie Company, P.O. Box 7587, Charlottesville, Virginia 22906-7587. 1985- . (Annual). (Issued as part of the Annotated Code).

JURY INSTRUCTIONS

MARYLAND CIVIL PATTERN JURY INSTRUCTIONS, Second Edition. Maryland State Bar Association, Incorporated, Committee on Civil Pattern Jury Instructions, Maryland Institute for Continuing Professional Education of Lawyers, 520 West Fayette Street, Baltimore, Maryland 21201. 1984- .

MARYLAND CRIMINAL JURY INSTRUCTIONS AND COMMENTARY. Second Edition. David E. Aaronson and Joan Gordon. Michie/Bobbs-Merrill Law Publishing Company, P.O. Box 7587, Charlottesville, Virginia 22906-7587. 1988.

MARYLAND CRIMINAL PATTERN JURY INSTRUCTIONS. Maryland State Bar Association, Committee on Criminal Pattern Jury Instructions. Maryland Institute for Continuing Professional Education of Lawyers, Incorporated, 520 West Fayette Street, Baltimore, Maryland 21201. 1987- . (Periodic Supplements).

DIGESTS, INDEXES, ABSTRACTS, CITATORS

ATLANTIC DIGEST, (First and Second Series). West Publishing Company, P.O. Box 64526, 50 West Kellogg Boulevard, St. Paul, Minnesota 55164-0526. 1949- . (Annual Supplements).

MARYLAND DIGEST. West Publishing Company, P.O. Box 64526, 50 West Kellogg Boulevard, St. Paul, Minnesota 55164-0526. 1981- . (Annual Supplements).

SHEPARD'S ATLANTIC REPORTER CITATIONS. Shepard's/McGraw-Hill, P.O. Box 1235, Colorado Springs, Colorado 80901. (Monthly Supplements).

SHEPARD'S MARYLAND CITATIONS. Shepard's/McGraw-Hill, P.O. Box 1235, Colorado Springs, Colorado 80901. (Eight pamphlets per year).

ENCYCLOPEDIAS AND DICTIONARIES

MARYLAND LAW ENCYCLOPEDIA. West Publishing Company, P.O. Box 64526, 50 West Kellogg Boulevard, St. Paul, Minnesota 55164-0526. 1961- . (Annual Supplements).

LAW REVIEWS AND PERIODICALS

MARYLAND BAR JOURNAL. Maryland State Bar Association, 520 West Fayette Street, Baltimore, Maryland 21201. (Monthly).

MARYLAND LAW REVIEW. University of Maryland School of Law, 500 West Baltimore Street, Baltimore, Maryland 21201. (Quarterly).

UNIVERSITY OF BALTIMORE LAW REVIEW. University of Baltimore Law Center, 1420 North Charles Street, Baltimore, Maryland 21201. (Three Issues per Year).

NEWSLETTERS AND NEWSPAPERS

THE DAILY RECORD: BUSINESS AND LEGAL NEWS OF MARYLAND. 11 East Saratoga Street, Baltimore, Maryland 21202. (Daily, Monday through Saturday).

MARYLAND EMPLOYMENT LAW LETTER. M. Lee Smith Publishers and Printers, 162 Fourth Avenue North, Nashville, Tennessee 37219. Monthly.

MARYLAND REAL ESTATE COMMISSION DECISIONS. Cable, McDaniel, Bowie, and Bord, 1 North Charles Street, Suite 1300, Baltimore, Maryland 21201. Quarterly.

METRO VERDICTS MONTHLY. Judicial Advisory Services, Incorporated, P.O. Box 99704, 3309 College Drive, Louisiville, Kentucky 40299. Monthly.

NEWSLETTER OF THE BAR ASSOCIATION OF MONTGOMERY COUNTY. Bar Association of Montgomery County, 27 West Jefferson Street, Rockville, Maryland 20850. Monthly.

REPORT FROM STATE CIRCLE. League of Women Voters of Maryland, 200 Duke of Gloucester Street, Annapolis, Maryland 21401. Semimonthly.

FORMBOOKS

MARYLAND CIVIL PROCEDURE FORMS. G. Liebmann. West Publishing Company, 50 West Kellogg Boulevard, St. Paul, Minnesota 55164. 1984. (Periodic Supplements).

MARYLAND CIVIL PROCEDURE FORMS: PRACTICE. Robert D. Klein and Edward S. Digges. Aspen Publishers, Incorporated, 1600 Research Boulevard, Rockville, Maryland 20850. 1984- . (Annual Supplements).

MARYLAND CORPORATE FORMS: PRACTICE. Aspen Publishers, Incorporated, 1600 Research Boulevard, Rockville, Maryland 20850. 1976- . (Annual Supplements).

MARYLAND DOMESTIC RELATIONS FORMS AND PRACTICE. Ann Turnbull and Joseph Wase. Aspen Publishers, Incorporated, 1600 Research Boulevard, Rockville, Maryland 20850. 1979- . (Annual Supplements).

MARYLAND ESTATE PLANNING, WILL DRAFTING, AND ESTATE ADMINISTRATION FORMS: PRACTICE. Al Barr and McDonald Plant. Aspen Publishers, Incorporated, 1600 Research Boulevard, Rockville, Maryland 20850. 1982- . (Annual Supplements).

MARYLAND PRACTICE FORMS. P. Junghans. Young Lawyers Section of the Bar Association of Baltimore. Maryland Institute for Continuing Professional Education of Lawyers, Incorporated, 520 West Fayette Street, Baltimore, Maryland 21201. 1984- . (Periodic Supplements).

MARYLAND REAL ESTATE FORMS: PRACTICE. Russell R. Reno, Jr. and W.E. Simmons, Jr. Aspen Publishers, Incorporated, 1600 Research Boulevard, Rockville, Maryland 20850. 1983- . (Annual Supplements).

PRACTICE MATERIALS

GORDON ON MARYLAND FORECLOSURES. Second Edition. Alexander Gordon. Maryland Institute for Continuing Professional Education of Lawyers, Incorporated, 520 West Fayette Street, Baltimore, Maryland 21201. 1985- . (Periodic Supplements).

GUIDE TO MARYLAND NEGLIGENCE CASES. Charles O. Fisher and Richard C. Murray. Michie Company, P.O. Box 7587, Charlottesville, Virginia 22906-7587. 1982- . (Periodic Supplements).

GUIDE TO MARYLAND ZONING DECISIONS. Second Edition. Stanley D. Abrams. Michie Company, P.O. Box 7587, Charlottesville, Virginia 22906-7587. 1984. (Periodic Supplements).

INTRODUCTION TO MARYLAND CIVIL LITIGATION. C. Brown. Michie Company, P.O. Box 7587, Charlottesville, Virginia 22906-7587. 1982. (Annual Supplements).

MARYLAND APPELLATE PRACTICE HANDBOOK. Paul M. Sandler, Editor. Maryland Institute for Continuing Professional Education of Lawyers, Incorporated, 520 West Fayette Street, Baltimore, Maryland 21201. (Two Volume) 1977- . (Periodic Supplements).

MARYLAND CRIMINAL LAW: PRACTICE AND PROCEDURE. Richard P. Gilbert and Claude E. Moylan, Jr. Michie Company, P.O. Box 7587, Charlottesville, Virginia 22906-7587. 1983- . (Periodic Supplements).

MARYLAND DISTRICT COURT PRACTICE. G. Liebmann. West Publishing Company, 50 West Kellogg Boulevard, St. Paul, Minnesota 55164.

THE MARYLAND EMPLOYER'S GUIDE TO LABOR AND EMPLOYMENT LAW. John G. Kruchko and Lawrence E. Dube, Jr. Michie Company, P.O. Box 7587, Charlottesville, Virginia 22906-7587. 1984- . (Looseleaf). (Periodic Supplements).

MARYLAND LANDLORD-TENANT LAW, PRACTICE AND PROCEDURE. Douglas M. Bregman and Gary G. Everngam. Michie Company, P.O. Box 7587, Charlottesville, Virginia 22906-7587. 1983- . (Periodic Supplements).

MARYLAND LAWYERS MANUAL. Maryland State Bar Association, 520 West Fayette Street, Baltimore, Maryland 21201. Biannual.

MARYLAND PRACTICE. George W. Liebmann. West Publishing Company, P.O. Box 64526, 50 West Kellogg Boulevard, St. Paul, Minnesota 55164-0526. 1976- . (Periodic Supplements).

MARYLAND TORT LAW HANDBOOK. Richard P. Gilbert, Paul T. Gilbert, and Richard J. Gilbert. Michie Company, P.O. Box 7587, Charlottesville, Virginia 22906-7587. 1985- (Periodic Supplements).

POE'S PLEADING AND PRACTICE. Sixth Edition. Harry M. Sachs, Jr. Michie Company, P.O. Box 7587, Charlottesville, Virginia 22906-7587. 1970- . (Periodic Supplements).

PRACTICE MANUAL FOR THE MARYLAND LAWYERS. Maryland State Bar, 520 West Fayette Street, Baltimore, Maryland 21122. 1979- . (Periodic Supplement).

TRIAL HANDBOOK FOR MARYLAND LAWYERS. Lawyers Co-Operative Company, Aqueduct Building, Rochester, New York 14694. 1986- . (Periodic supplements).

WORKMEN'S COMPENSATION IN MARYLAND. Second Edition. Maurice J. Pressman. Michie Company, P.O. Box 7587, Charlottesville, Virginia 22906-7587. 1977- . (Periodic Supplements).

MANUALS AND RESEARCH GUIDES

AN INTRODUCTION TO MARYLAND STATE PUBLICATIONS FOR THE LAW LIBRARIAN. Compile for the AALL Seventy-fourth Annual Meeting, by Lynda C. Davis. American Association of Law Libraries, 53 West Jackson Boulevard, Chicago, Illinois 60604. 1981.

MARYLAND APPELLATE PRACTICE HANDBOOK. Paul M. Sandler, Editor. Maryland Institute for Continuing Professional Education of Lawyers, Incorporated, 520 West Fayette Street, Baltimore, Maryland 21201. 1977- . (Periodic Supplements).

MARYLAND SENTENCING GUIDELINE MANUAL. Administrative Office of the Courts. Maryland Institute for Continuing Professional Education of Lawyers, Incorporated, 520 West Fayette Street, Baltimore, Maryland 21201. 1983- . (Periodic Supplements).

MARYLAND TRIAL JUDGES BENCHBOOK. Administratvie Office of the Courts. Maryland Institute for Continuing Professional Education of Lawyers, Incorporated, 520 West Fayette Street, Baltimore, Maryland 21201. 1986- (Periodic Supplements).

ASSOCIATIONS AND PROFESSIONAL SOCIETIES

BALTIMORE COUNTY BAR ASSOCIATION, 100 County Courts Building, 110 County Courts Building, 401 Basely Avenue, Towson, Maryland 21204.

BAR ASSOCIATION OF BALTIMORE CITY. 111 North Calvert Street, Baltimore, Maryland 21202. (301) 539-5936

THE BAR ASSOCIATION OF CARROLL COUNTY, 188 East Main Street, P.O. Box 389, Westminster, Maryland 21157-0389.

THE BAR ASSOCIATION OF MONTGOMERY COUNTY, 27 West Jefferson Street, Rockville, Maryland 20850.

MARYLAND BAR ASSOCIATION, 520 West Fayette Street, Baltimore, Maryland 21122. (301) 685-7878

PRINCE GEORGE'S COUNTY BAR ASSOCIATION, INCORPORATED, Bowie Building, Second Floor, 5302 East Court Drive, Upper Marlbaro, Maryland 20772.

DIRECTORIES

DIRECTORY OF MARYLAND PUBLIC OFFICIALS. Maryland Municipal League, 1212 West Street, Annapolis, Maryland 21401. (Annual).

MARYLAND GENERAL ASSEMBLY LEGISLATIVE DIRECTORY. Maryland Chamber of Commerce, 60 West Street, Annapolis, Maryland 21401. (Annual).

MARYLAND MANUAL. Archives Division, Hall of Records Commission, Department of General Services, P.O. Box 828, Annapolis, Maryland 21404. (Biennial).

STATES--MARYLAND (continued)

VIRGINIAS, MARYLAND, DELAWARE, AND DISTRCIT OF COLUMBIA LEGAL DIRECTORY. Legal Directories Publishing Company, 2122 Kidwell Street, P.O. Box 140200, Dallas, Texas 75214-0200. (Annual).

OTHER SOURCES

AN INTRODUCTION TO MARYLAND STATE PUBLICATIONS FOR THE LAW LIBRARIAN. L. Davis. American Association of Law Libraries, 53 West Jackson Boulevard, Suite 940, Chicago, Illinois 60604. 1981.

MARYLAND DIVORCE AND SEPARATION LAW. J. Alexander. Maryland Institute for Continuing Education for Lawyers, Incorporated, 520 West Fayette Street, Baltimore, Maryland 21201. 1982.

MARYLAND EVIDENCE. G. McLain. West Publishing Company, 50 West Kellogg Boulevard, St. Paul, Minnesota 55164. 1987.

MARYLAND TORT DAMAGES. Maryland Institute for Continuing Education for Lawyers, Incorporated, 520 West Fayette Street, Baltimore, Maryland 21201. 1979.

SUGGESTED MINIMUM STANDARDS LAW COLLECTION MARYLAND CIRCUIT COURT LIBRARIES: COLLECTION CONTENT. Maryland State Bar, 520 West Fayette Street, Baltimore, Maryland 21122. 1984.

STATES--MASSACHUSETTS

STATUTES, CODES, STANDARDS, UNIFORM LAWS

ACTS AND RESOLVES OF MASSACHUSETTS. Secretary of State, Bookstore, Room 116, State House, Boston, Massachusetts 02133. (Annual).

ADVANCE LEGISLATIVE SERVICE FOR THE ANNOTATED LAWS OF MASSACHUSETTS. Lawyers Co-Operative Company, Aqueduct Building, Rochester, New York 14694.(Periodic Supplements).

ANNOTATED LAWS OF MASSACHUSETTS. Lawyers Co-Operative Company, Aqueduct Building, Rochester, New York 14694. 1932- . (Annual Supplements).

CODE OF MASSACHUSETTS REGULATIONS. Office of the Secretary of the State, Bookstore, Room 116 State House, Boston, Massachusetts 02133. 1980- . (Also available in microfiche from University Microfilm. 1980).

MASSACHUSETTS GENERAL LAWS ANNOTATED. West Publishing Company, P.O. Box 64526, 50 West Kellogg Boulevard, St. Paul, Minnesota 55164-0526. 1958- . (Annual Supplements).

MASSACHUSETTS REGISTER. Office of the Secretary of the State, Room 116, State House, Boston, Massachusetts 02133. 1976- . (Weekly).

WEST'S MASSACHUSETTS LEGISLATIVE SERVICE. West Publishing Company, P.O. Box 64526, 50 West Kellogg Boulevard, St. Paul, Minnesota 55164-0526. 1978-, (Irregular).

LOOSELEAF SERVICES AND REPORTERS

MASSACHUSETTS APPEALS COURT REPORTS. Bateman and Slade, Incorporated, 45 Broad Street, Boston, Massachusetts. 1972- . (Massachusetts Appeals Court). (Publisher varies).

MASSACHUSETTS APPELLATE DECISIONS. Wilson-Hill Company, Boston, Massachusetts. 1942-1978. (Massachusetts Appellate Division of the District Court).

MASSACHUSETTS APPELLATE TAX BOARD REPORTER. Butterworth Legal Publishers, 90 Stiles Road, Salem, New Hampshire 03079. 1981- .

MASSACHUSETTS DECISIONS. West Publishing Company, P.O. Box 64526, 50 West Kellogg Boulevard, St. Paul, Minnesota 55164-0526. 1884- . (Massachusetts Supreme Judicial Court and Appeals Court).

MASSACHUSETTS REPORTS. Bateman and Slade, Incorporated, 45 Broad Street, Boston, Massachusetts. 1804- . (Massachusetts Supreme Court).

NORTHEASTERN REPORTER, (First and Second Series). West Publishing Company, P.O. Box 64526, 50 West Kellogg Boulevard, St. Paul, Minnesota 55164-0526. 1884- . (Massachusetts Supreme Court and Appeals Court).

REPORTS OF THE MASSACHUSETTS APPELLATE DIVISION. Lawyer's Weekly Publications, 30 Court Square, Boston, Massachusetts 02108. (Massachusetts District Court and Boston Municipal Court).

ATTORNEY GENERAL OPINIONS

OFFICIAL OPINIONS OF THE ATTORNEY GENERAL OF THE COMMONWEALTH OF MASSACHUSETTS. Attorney Generals Office. 1891- . Also available on Lexis: 1977-; Westlaw: 1977- .

ETHICS OPINIONS, CODES, RULES

MASSACHUSETTS ATTORNEY DISCIPLINE REPORTS: DECISIONS OF THE SUPREME JUDICIAL COURT OF MASSACHUSETTS. Board of Bar Overseers, Butterworth Legal Publishers, 90 Stiles Road, Salem, New Hampshire 03079. 1974- .

OPINIONS OF THE ETHICS COMMITTEE OF THE MASSACHUSETTS BAR ASSOCIATION. Massachusetts Bar Association, 20 West Street, Boston, Massachusetts 02111.

STATE ETHICS COMMISSION ENFORCEMENT ACTIONS, ADVISORY OPINIONS. Massachusetts State Ethics Commission, 1 Ashburton Place, Sixth Floor, Boston, Massachusetts 02108. 1983- . (Annual).

COURT RULES

MASSACHUSETTS COURT RULES. Published in Annotated Laws of Massachusetts, Rules Volumes 43a, 43b, 43c. Lawyers Co-Operative Company, Aqueduct Building, Rochester, New York 14694. (Annual Supplements).

MASSACHUSETTS RULES OF COURT: STATE AND FEDERAL. West Publishing Company, P.O. Box 64526, 50 West Kellogg Boulevard, St. Paul, Minnesota 55164-0526. (Annual).

JURY INSTRUCTIONS

JURY TRIAL MANUAL FOR CRIMINAL OFFENSES TRIED IN THE DISTRICT COURT. (Third Edition). Massachusetts District Court, Committee on Juries of Six. District Court Department of the Trial Court, Holyoke Building, Holyoke Square, Salem, Massachusetts 01970. 1985- .

DIGESTS, INDEXES, ABSTRACTS, CITATORS

MASSACHUSETTS DIGEST. (First and Second Series). West Publishing Company, P.O. Box 64526, 50 West Kellogg Boulevard, St. Paul, Minnesota 55164-0526. (Annual Supplements).

NORTHEASTERN DIGEST. West Publishing Company, P.O. Box 64526, 50 West Kellogg Boulevard, St. Paul, Minnesota 55164-0526. 1933- .

SHEPARD'S MASSACHUSETTS CITATIONS. Shepard's/McGraw-Hill, P.O. Box 1235, Colorado Springs, Colorado 80901. (Eight pamphlets per year).

SHEPARD'S NORTHEASTERN REPORTER CITATIONS. Shepard's/McGraw-Hill, P.O. Box 1235, Colorado Springs, Colorado 80901. (Monthly Supplements).

LAW REVIEWS AND PERIODICALS

BOSTON COLLEGE ENVIRONMENTAL AFFAIRS LAW REVIEW. Boston College Law School, 885 Centre Street, Newton Centre, Boston, Massachusetts 02159. (Quarterly).

BOSTON COLLEGE INTERNATIONAL AND COMPARATIVE LAW REVIEW. Boston College Law School, 885 Centre Street, Newton Centre, Boston, Massachusetts 02159. (Semiannual).

BOSTON COLLEGE LAW REVIEW. Boston College Law School, 885 Centre Street, Newton Centre, Boston, Massachusetts 02519. (Five Issues per Year).

BOSTON UNIVERSITY INTERNATIONAL LAW JOURNAL. Boston University School of Law, 765 Commonwealth Avenue, Boston, Massachusetts 02215. (Semiannual).

BOSTON UNIVERSITY LAW REVIEW. Boston University School of Law, 765 Commonwealth Avenue, Boston, Massachusetts 02215. (Five Issues per Year).

HARVARD CIVIL RIGHTS-CIVIL LIBERTIES LAW REVIEW. Harvard Law School, Cambridge, Massachusetts 02138. (Semiannual).

HARVARD ENVIRONMENTAL LAW REVIEW. Harvard Law School, Cambridge Massachusetts 02138. (Semiannual).

HARVARD INTERNATIONAL LAW JOURNAL. Harvard Law School, Cambridge, Massachusetts 02138. (Semiannual).

HARVARD JOURNAL OF LAW AND PUBLIC POLICY. Harvard Law School, Cambridge, Massachusetts 02138. (Three Issues per Year).

HARVARD JOURNAL ON LEGISLATION. Harvard Law School, Cambridge, Massachusetts 02138. (Biannual).

HARVARD LAW REVIEW. Harvard Law School, Cambridge, Massachusetts 02138. (Eight Issues per Year).

MASSACHUSETTS LAW REVIEW. Massachusetts Bar Association, 20 West Street, Boston Massachusetts 02111. (Quarterly).

NEW ENGLAND JOURNAL OF CRIMINAL AND CIVIL CONFINEMENT. New England Journal on Criminal and Civil Confinement, 154 Stuart Street, Boston, Massachusetts 02116. (Semiannual). (Former Title: New England Journal on Prison Law).

NEW ENGLAND LAW REVIEW. New England Law Review, 154 Stuart Street, Boston, Massachusetts 02116. (Quarterly).

SUFFOLK UNIVERSITY LAW REVIEW AND TRANSNATIONAL LAW JOURNAL. Suffolk University Law School, 41 Temple Street, Boston, Massachusetts 02114. (Quarterly).

WESTERN NEW ENGLAND LAW REVIEW. Western New England College School of Law, 1215 Wilbraham Road, Springfield, Massachusetts 01119. (Semiannual).

NEWSLETTERS AND NEWSPAPERS

MASSACHUSETTS APPELLATE TAX BOARD REPORTER. Butterworth Legal Publishers, 90 Stiles Road, Salem, New Hampshire 03079. Quarterly.

THE MASSACHUSETTS, CONNECTICUT, RHODE ISLAND VERDICT REPORTER. Judicial Advisory Services, Incorporated, P.O. Box 99704, 3309 College Drive, Louisville, Kentucky 40299. Monthly.

MASSACHUSETTS EMPLOYMENT LAW LETTER. M. Lee Smith Publishers and Printers, 162 Fourth Avenue North, Nashville, Tennessee 37219. Monthly.

MASSACHUSETTS LAWYERS WEEKLY. 30 Court Street, Boston, Massachusetts 02108. (Weekly).

MASSACHUSETTS UPDATE. West Publishing Company, 50 West Kellogg Boulevard, St. Paul, Minnesota 55164. Quarterly.

MASSACHUSETTS WASTE MANAGEMENT REPORT. Paradigim Newsletters, P.O. Box 1450, Cambridge, Massachusetts 02238. Monthly.

WEST'S MASSACHUSETTS UPDATE. West Publishing Company, 50 West Kellogg Boulevard, St. Paul, Minnesota 55164. Semimonthly.

FORMBOOKS

MASSACHUSETTS PLEADINGS AND PRACTICE--FORMS AND COMMENTARY. Edward M. Swartz, et al. Matthew Bender and Company, Incorporated, 11 Penn Plaza, New York, New York 10001. 1974- . (Periodic Supplements).

MASSACHUSETTS STANDARDIZED CIVIL PRACTICE FORMS. Paul G. Garrity and James A. Frieden. Little, Brown and Company, 34 Beacon Street, Boston, Massachusetts 02108. 1986- . (Annual Supplements).

PRACTICE MATERIALS

BENCH BOOK FOR PROCEEDINGS IN THE DISTRICT COURT. Second Edition. Mel L. Greenberg. Second Edition. Massachusetts Continuing Legal Education, Incorporated, 20 West Street, Boston, Massachusetts 02111-1219. (Looseleaf). 1983- .

EMPLOYMENT IN MASSACHUSETTS: A GUIDE TO EMPLOYMENT PRACTICES AND REGULATIONS. Emily K. Cheslow. Butterworth Legal Publishers, 90 Stiles Road, Salem, New Hampshire 03079. (Looseleaf). 1984- . (Periodic Supplements).

FAMILY LAW GUIDEBOOK: A HANDBOOK WITH FORMS. Edward M. Ginsburg. Butterworth Legal Publishers, 90 Stiles Road, Salem, New Hampshire 03079. 1985.

FUNDAMENTALS OF ESTATE PLANNING AND ADMINISTRATION. Massachusetts Continuing Legal Education, Incorporated, 20 West Street, Boston, Massachusetts 02111-1219. 1985.

HANDBOOK OF MASSACHUSETTS EVIDENCE. Fifth Edition. P. Liacos. Little, Brown and Company, 34 Beacon Street, Boston, Massachusetts 02108. 1981.

HANDBOOK OF MASSACHUSETTS FAMILY LAW. Second Edition. Gerald D. McLellan. Lawyer's Weekly Publications, 30 Court Square, Boston, Massachusetts 02108. 1982- . (Periodic Supplements).

MASSACHUSETTS CONSTRUCTION LAW. Fifth Edition. James J. Myers and Christopher L. Noble. Professional Education Systems, 200 Spring Street, P.O. Box 1428, Eau Claire, Wisconsin 54702. 1985.

MASSACHUSETTS CORPORATION LAW: WITH FEDERAL TAX ANALYSIS. James W. Smith and Zolman Cavitch. Matthew Bender and Company, Incorporated, 11 Penn Plaza, New York, New York 10001. (Looseleaf). 1963- .

THE MASSACHUSETTS CRIMINAL LAW: A DISTRICT COURT PROSECUTOR'S GUIDE. Fifth Edition. Richard G. Stearns. Massachusetts Prosecustor's Guide, Dedham, Massachusetts. (Looseleaf) 1983- .

MASSACHUSETTS DIVORCE PRACTICE AND PROCEDURE. Haskell C. Freedman, Editor. Massachusetts Continuing Legal Education, Incorporated, 20 West Street, Boston, Massachusetts 02111-1219. 1981- . (Annual).

MASSACHUSETTS FAMILY LAW ACTIONS: HANDBOOK ON MASSACHUSETTS DOMESTIC RELATIONS ACTIONS BASED ON AND ILLUSTRATED BY THE REPORTED CASE LAW. Charles P. Kindregan. Legal Medical Studies, Boston, Massachusetts. 1985- . (Periodic Supplements).

MASSACHUSETTS FAMILY LAW MANUAL. Haskell C. Freedman. Massachusetts Continuing Legal Education, Incorporated, 20 West Street, Boston, Massachusetts 02111-1219. 1985- . (Biennial).

MASSACHUSETTS MANUAL FOR THE GENERAL COURT. Massachusetts General Court, State House, Boston, Massachusetts 02133. (Biennial).

MASSACHUSETTS PRACTICE SERIES. West Publishing Company, P.O. Box 64526, 50 West Kellogg Boulevard, St. Paul, Minnesota 55164-0526. 1967- . (Annual Supplements).

MASSACHUSETTS PROBATE MANUAL. Joseph P. Warner and H.S. Reynolds. Massachusetts Continuing Legal Education, Incorporated, 20 West Street, Boston, Massachusetts 02111-1219. 1981- . (Periodic Supplements).

MASSACHUSETTS REAL ESTATE. Robert L. Mazelli. Lawyers Co-Operative Company, Aqueduct Building, Rochester, New York 14694. (Looseleaf). 1983- . (Periodic Supplements).

MOTIONS, DISCOVERY, AND NEGOTIATED AGREEMENTS. Massachusetts Continuing Legal Education, Incorporated, 20 West Street, Boston, Massachusetts 02111-1219. 1984.

SUPERIOR COURT CIVIL PRACTICE. Massachusetts Continuing Legal Education, Incorporated, 20 West Street, Boston, Massachusetts 02111-1219. 1981.

YOUR RIGHTS ON THE JOB: A PRACTICAL GUIDE TO EMPLOYMENT LAWS IN MASSACHUSETTS. Robert M. Schwartz; Illustrated by David Fichter. First Edition. Labor Guild of Boston, 761 Harrison Avenue, Boston, Massachusetts 02118. 1987.

MANUALS AND RESEARCH GUIDES

HANDBOOK OF LEGAL RESEARCH IN MASSACHUSETTS. Margaret Botsford and Ruth G. Matz, Editors. Massachusetts Continuing Legal Education, 20 West Street, Boston, Massachusetts 02111-1219. 1982- .

MASSACHUSETTS LAW FINDER: A NEW TOPICAL REFERENCE GUIDE FOR CO-ORDINATED RESEARCH PROVIDING COMPREHENSIVE REFERENCES TO THE FOLLOWING WEST PUBLICATIONS: MASSACHUSETTS GENERAL LAWS ANNOTATED, MASSACHUSETTS DIGEST, MASSACHUSETTS PRACTICE SERIES, UNITED STATES CODE ANNOTATED, CORPUS JURIS SECUNDUM, FEDERAL PUBLICATIONS, KEY NUMBER PUBLICATIONS, TEXTS AND TREATISES. West Publishing Company, P.O. Box 64526, 50 West Kellogg Boulevard, St. Paul, Minnesota 55164-0526. (Annual).

ASSOCIATIONS AND PROFESSIONAL SOCIETIES

BAR ASSOCIATION OF NORFOLK COUNTY, 1354 Hancock Street, Suite 300, Quincy, Massachusetts 02169.

BOSTON BAR ASSOCIATION, 16 Beacon Street, Boston, Massachusetts 02108. (617) 742-0615.

HAMPDEN COUNTY BAR ASSOCIATION, 50 State Street, Room 137, Springfield, Massachusetts 01103.

MASSACHUSETTS BAR ASSOCIATION, 20 West Street, Boston, Massachusetts 02111. (617) 542-3602.

MIDDLESEX COUNTY BAR ASSOCIATION, 40 Thorndike Street, Cambridge, Massachusetts 02141.

WORCESTER COUNTY BAR ASSOCIATION, 19 Norwich Street, Worcester, Massachusetts 01608.

DIRECTORIES

CITIZENS' GUIDE TO STATE SERVICES: A SELECTIVE LISTING OF GOVERNMENTAL AGENCIES AND PROGRAMS. Citizen Information Service. Massachusetts Secretary of State, State Street, Room 1611, Boston, Massachusetts 02133. (Irregular).

DIRECTORY OF MASSACHUSETTS LEGISLATORS AND OTHER ELECTED OFFICIALS. Associated Industries of Massachusetts, 462 Boylston Street, Boston, Massachusetts 02116. (Biennial).

LAWYER REFERRAL SERVICE RESOURCE DIRECTORY. Third Edition. Massachusetts Bar Association, 20 West Street, Boston, Massachusetts 02111-1219. (Looseleaf). 1982- .

MASSACHUSETTS LEGISLATIVE DIRECTORY. Massachusetts Taxpayers Foundation, 60 Temple Place, Boston, Massachusetts 02111. (Biennial).

MASSACHUSETTS MUNICIPAL DIRECTORY. Massachusetts Municipal Association, 131 Tremont Street, Fourth Floor, Boston, Massachusetts 02111. (Annual).

OTHER SOURCES

ADMINISTRATIVE LAW. Massachusetts Continuing Legal Education, 44 School Street, Boston, Massachusetts 02108. 1982.

ESTATE TAXATION. B. Rosales and A. Bove. Callaghan and Company, 155 Pfingsten Road, Deerfield, Illinois 60015. 1980.

HANDBOOK OF LEGAL RESEARCH IN MASSACHUSETTS. M. Botsford and R. Matz, Editors. Massachusetts Continuing Legal Education, 44 School Street, Boston, Massachusetts 02108. 1988.

JUVENILE DELINQUENCY. Massachusetts Continuing Legal Education, 44 School Street, Boston, Massachusetts 02108. 1982- . (Periodic Supplements).

MASSACHUSETTS CORPORATIONS. D. Muir. Lawyers Cooperative Publishing Company, Aqueduct Building, Rochester, New York 14694. 1981- . (Annual Supplements).

MASSACHUSETTS CRIMINAL LAW. Second Edition. J. Nolan and B. Henry. West Publishing Company, 50 West Kellogg Boulevard, St. Paul, Minnesota 55164. 1988- . (Annual Supplements).

MASSACHUSETTS DOMESTIC RELATIONS. J. Harvery and others. Lawyers Cooperative Publishing Company, Aqueduct Building, Rochester, New York 14694. 1982- . (Periodic Supplements).

PUBLIC EMPLOYEE COLLECTIVE BARGAINING IN MASSACHUSETTS: AN ANNOTATED INDEX. Rosemary Hartigan, Editor. Massachusetts Labor Relations Reporter. 1985.

STATES--MICHIGAN

STATUTES, CODES, STANDARDS, UNIFORM LAWS

MICHIGAN ADMINISTRATIVE CODE. Department of Management and Budget, Office Services Division, P.O. Box 30026, Lansing, Michigan 48909. 1979- .

MICHIGAN COMPILED LAWS. Department of Management and Budget, Office Services Division, P.O. Box 30026, Lansing, Michigan 48909. 1970- . (Annual Supplements).

MICHIGAN COMPILED LAWS ANNOTATED. West Publishing Company, P.O. Box 64526, 50 West Kellogg Boulevard, St. Paul, Minnesota 55164-0526. (Annual Supplements).

MICHIGAN LEGISLATIVE SERVICE. West Publishing Company, P.O. Box 64526, 50 West Kellogg Boulevard, St. Paul, Minnesota 55164-0526. (Irregular pamphlets).

MICHIGAN REGISTER. Department of Management and Budget, Office Services Division, P.O. Box 30026, Lansing, Michigan 48909. (Weekly).

MICHIGAN STATUTES ANNOTATED. Callaghan and Company, 155 Pfingsten Road, Deerfield, Illinois 60015. 1936- . (Annual Supplements).

LOOSELEAF SERVICES AND REPORTERS

MICHIGAN APPEALS REPORTS. Lawyers Co-Operative Company, Aqueduct Building, Rochester, New York 14694. 1965- .

MICHIGAN REPORTER. West Publishing Company, P.O. Box 64526, 50 West Kellogg Boulevard, St. Paul, Minnesota 55164-0526. 1941- .

MICHIGAN REPORTS. Lawyers Cooperative Publishing Company, Aqueduct Building, Rochester, New York 14694. 1949- .

NORTHWESTERN REPORTER. (First and Second Series). West Publishing Company, P.O. Box 64526, 50 West Kellogg Boulevard, St. Paul, Minnesota 55164-0526. 1879- .

ATTORNEY GENERAL OPINIONS

BIENNIAL REPORT OF THE ATTORNEY GENERAL. Office of the Attorney General, 525 West Ottawa, Law Building, Lansing, Michigan 48913. 1883- . Also available on Lexis: January, 1977-; Westlaw: 1977- .

ETHICS OPINIONS, CODES, RULES

Code of Professional Responsibility is published in WEST'S MICHIGAN COURT RULES (Annual). MICHIGAN BAR JOURNAL; SPECIAL SUPPLEMENT, VOLUME 63, NUMBER 5A. Prepared by the Committee on Professional and Judicial Ethics of the State Bar of Michigan, 306 Townsend Street, Lansing, Michigan 48933. For further information concerning these opinions contact the State Bar of Michigan 517-372-9030. (Opinions issued since 1984 are published in monthly issues of Michigan Bar Journal). See annual index (December) under subject heading "ETHICS".

PROFESSIONAL AND JUDICIAL ETHICS. Prepared by the Committee on Professional and Judicial Ethics of the State Bar of Michigan, 306 Townsend Street, Lansing, Michigan 48933. 1984. (Michigan Bar Journal, Special Supplement: Volume 63, Number 5A).

COURT RULES

CALLAGHAN'S MICHIGAN PLEADING AND PRACTICE. Rules Volume Second Edition (1985 revision). Callaghan and Company, 155 Pfingsten Road, Deerfield, Illinois 60015. 1985- . (Annual Supplements).

COURT RULES OF MICHIGAN SERVICE. Second Edition. Michigan Institute of Continuing Legal Education, Hutching Hall, Ann Arbor, Michigan 48109. 1985- . (Periodic Supplements).

MICHIGAN COURT RULES ANNOTATED. West Publishing Company, P.O. Box 64526, 50 West Kellogg Boulevard, St. Paul, Minnesota 55164-0526. 1962- . (Annual Supplements).

MICHIGAN COURT RULES PRACTICE. Third Edition. James A. Martin, Robert Dean, and Robert B. Webster. West Publishing Company, P.O. Box 64526, 50 West Kellogg Boulevard, St. Paul, Minnesota 55164-0526. 1985- . (Periodic Supplements).

MICHIGAN RULES OF COURT. West Publishing Company, P.O. Box 64526, 50 West Kellogg Boulevard, St. Paul, Minnesota 55164-0526. (Annual Supplements).

JURY INSTRUCTIONS

MICHIGAN CRIMINAL JURY INSTRUCTIONS. State Bar Special Committee on Standard Criminal Jury Instructions. Institute for Continuing Legal Education, 1020 Greene Street, Ann Arbor, Michigan 48109-1444. 1977- . (Periodic Supplements).

MICHIGAN STANDARD JURY INSTRUCTIONS: CIVIL. Michigan Supreme Court Committee on Standard Jury Instructions. Institute for Continuing Legal Education, 1020 Greene Street, Ann Arbor, Michigan 48109-1444. 1981- . (Annual Supplements).

DIGESTS, INDEXES, ABSTRACTS, CITATORS

MICHIGAN ANTITRUST DIGEST: FEDERAL AND STATE. Institute for Continuing Legal Education, 1020 Greene Street, Ann Arbor, Michigan 48109-1444. (Looseleaf). 1975- . (Annual Supplements).

MICHIGAN DIGEST. Callaghan and Company, 155 Pfingsten Road, Deerfield, Illinois 60015. 1920- . (Annual Supplements).

MICHIGAN DIGEST. West Publishing Company, P.O. Box 64526, 50 West Kellogg Boulevard, St. Paul, Minnesota 55164-0526. 1938- . (Annual Supplements).

NORTHWESTERN DIGEST. (First and Second Series). West Publishing Company, P.O. Box 64526, 50 West Kellogg Boulevard, St. Paul, Minnesota 55164-0526. 1944- . (Annual Supplements).

SHEPARD'S MICHIGAN CITATIONS. Shepard's/McGraw-Hill, P.O. Box 1235, Colorado Springs, Colorado 80901. (Eight pamphlets per year).

SHEPARD'S NORTHWESTERN REPORTER CITATIONS. Shepard's/McGraw-Hill, P.O. Box 1235, Colorado Springs, Colorado 80901. (Monthly Supplements).

ENCYCLOPEDIAS AND DICTIONARIES

MICHIGAN CIVIL JURISPRUDENCE. Callaghan and Company, 155 Pfingsten Road, Deerfield, Illinois 60015. 1957- . (Annual Supplements).

MICHIGAN LAW AND PRACTICE ENCYCLOPEDIA. West Publishing Company, P.O. Box 64526, 50 West Kellogg Boulevard, St. Paul, Minnesota 55164-0526. 1955- . (Annual Supplements).

LAW REVIEWS AND PERIODICALS

COOLEY LAW REVIEW. Thomas M. Cooley Law School, P.O. Box 13038, 217 South Capital Avenue, Lansing, Michigan 48901. (Three issues per year).

MICHIGAN BAR JOURNAL. State Bar of Michigan, 306 Townsend Street, Lansing, Michigan 48933-2083. (Monthly).

MICHIGAN LAW REVIEW. University of Michigan Law School, Ann Arbor, Michigan 48109-1215. (Eight issues per year).

MICHIGAN TAX LAW JOURNAL. State Bar of Michigan, Taxation Section, Detroit, Michigan 48226. (Quarterly).

UNIVERSITY OF DETROIT LAW REVIEW. University of Detroit Law School, 651 East Jefferson Avenue, Detroit, Michigan 48226. (Quarterly).

UNIVERSITY OF MICHIGAN JOURNAL OF LAW REFORM. University of Michigan Law School, S-324 Legal Research Building, Ann Arbor, Michigan 48109. (Quarterly). (Formerly: Journal of Law Reform).

WAYNE LAW REVIEW. Wayne State University Law School, 468 West Ferry Street, Detroit, Michigan 48202. (Quarterly).

NEWSLETTERS AND NEWSPAPERS

MCA NEWS. The Dale Corporation, 2684 Industrial Row, Troy, Michigan 48084. Bimonthly.

MICHIGAN EMPLOYMENT LAW LETTER. M. Lee Smith Publishers and Printers, 162 Fourth Avenue North, Nashville, Tennessee 37219. Monthly.

MICHIGAN ENVIRONMENTAL LAW LETTER. M. Lee Smith Publishers and Printers, 162 Fourth Avenue North, Nashville, Tennessee 37219. Monthly.

MICHIGAN REPORT. Gongwer News Service, Incorporated, 630 Michigan National Tower, Lansing, Michigan 48933. Daily.

THE MICHIGAN TRIAL REPORTER. Judicial Advisory Services, Incorporated, P.O. Box 99704, 3309 College Drive, Louisville, Kentucky 40299. Monthly.

MIRS LEGISLATIVE REPORT/CAPITOL CAPSULE/PUBLIC ACTS SERVICE. Michigan Information and Research Service, Incorporated, 421 West Ionia, Lansing, Michigan 48933. Daily.

FORMBOOKS

MICHIGAN CIVIL PROCEDURE MANUAL WITH FORMS. Second Edition. J. Soave. West Publishing Company, 50 West Kellogg Boulevard, St. Paul, Minnesota 55164. 1985. (Periodic Supplements).

MICHIGAN REAL ESTATE FORMBOOK. Ralph Jossman. Institute for Continuing Legal Education, 1020 Greene Street, Ann Arbor, Michigan 48109-1444. 1982- . (Periodic Supplements).

MICHIGAN UNIFORM COMMERCIAL CODE FORMS. R. Steinheimer. West Publishing Company, 50 West Kellogg Boulevard, St. Paul, Minnesota 55164. 1969. (Periodic Supplements).

PRACTICE MATERIALS

COMPARATIVE NEGLIGENCE IN MICHIGAN. Thomas Koeunke. Institute for Continuing Legal Education, 1020 Greene Street, Ann Arbor, Michigan 48109-1444. 1981- . (Periodic Supplements).

MICHIGAN ADMINISTRATIVE LAW. Institute for Continuing Legal Education, 1020 Greene Street, Ann Arbor, Michigan 48109-1444. 1981- . (Annual Supplements).

MICHIGAN APPELLATE HANDBOOK. Carl L. Gromek, et al. Institute for Continuing Legal Education, 1020 Greene Street, Ann Arbor, Michigan 48109-1444. 1985- .

MICHIGAN CORPORATION LAW WITH FEDERAL TAX ANALYSIS. Robert M. Schmidt and Zolman Cavitch. Matthew Bender and Company, Incorporated, 11 Penn Plaza, New York, New York 10001. 1963- . (Annual Supplements).

MICHIGAN COURTROOM EVIDENCE. Michael D. Wade and Jennifer J. Storm. Institute for Continuing Legal Education, 1020 Greene Street, Ann Arbor, Michigan 48109-1444. (Looseleaf). 1985- .

MICHIGAN CRIMINAL LAW AND PROCEDURE, WITH FORMS. Second Edition. Glenn C. Gillespie. Callaghan and Company, 155 Pfingsten Road, Deerfield, Illinois 60015. 1978- .

MICHIGAN DIVORCE. David E. Eason. Lawyers Co-Operative Company, Aqueduct Building, Rochester, New York 14694. 1981- . (Annual Supplements).

MICHIGAN DIVORCE MANUAL. Thomas Oehmke. West Publishing Company, 50 West Kellogg Boulevard, St. Paul, Minnesota 55164. 1986.

MICHIGAN FAMILY LAW. Norman Robbins, et al. Institute for Continuing Legal Education, 1020 Greene Street, Ann Arbor, Michigan 48109-1444. 1987- . (Annual Supplements).

MICHIGAN LAWYER'S MANUAL. Roger A. Needham. Callaghan and Company, 155 Pfingsten Road, Deerfield, Illinois 60015. 1964- . (Annual Supplements).

MICHIGAN PRACTICE. West Publishing Company, P.O. Box 64526, 50 West Kellogg Boulevard, St. Paul, Minnesota 55164-0526. 1954- . (Annual Supplements).

MICHIGAN PROBATE. Leonard Edelman. Lawyers Co-Operative Company, Aqueduct Building, Rochester, New York 14694. 1979- . (Annual Supplement).

MICHIGAN RESIDENTIAL LANDLORD-TENANT LAW. Michigan Legal Services, 220 Bagley Avenue, Suite 900, Detroit, Michigan 48226-1498. 1983- . (Irregular Supplements).

MICHIGAN TORTS. Elmer E. White. Lawyers Co-Operative Company, Aqueduct Building, Rochester, New York 14694. 1984- . (Annual Supplements).

TRIAL HANDBOOK FOR MICHIGAN LAWYERS. Harry M. Philo. Lawyers Co-Operative Company, Aqueduct Building, Rochester, New York 14694. 1973- . (Annual Supplements).

MANUALS AND RESEARCH GUIDES

AN ANNOTATED GUIDE TO THE LEGAL LITERATURE OF MICHIGAN. Richard L. Beer. Fitzsimmons Sales, P.O. Box 612, Adams Road, Rochester, Michigan 48063. 1973- .

LEGAL RESEARCH GUIDE FOR MICHIGAN LIBRARIES. Michigan Association of Law Libraries, Detroit, Michigan.

ASSOCIATONS AND PROFESSIONAL SOCIETIES

DETROIT BAR ASSOCIATION, 2380 Penobscot Building, Detroit Michigan 48226. (313) 961-6120.

GENESEE COUNTY BAR ASSOCIATION, 653 South Saginaw Street, Suite 216, Flint, Michigan 48502.

INGHAM COUNTY BAR ASSOCIATION, Room 9, Second Floor, City Hall, Lansing, Michigan 48933.

KALAMAZOO COUNTY BAR ASSOCIATION, 227 West Michigan Avenue, Kalamazoo, Michigan 49007.

MACOMB COUNTY BAR ASSOCIATION, Macomb County Court House Building, Room 437, Mount Clemens, Michigan 48403.

OAKLAND COUNTY BAR ASSOCIATION, 1220 North Telegraph, Suite 532, Pontiac, Michigan 48053. (313) 338-2100.

STATE BAR OF MICHIGAN, 306 Townsend Street, Lansing, Michigan 48933. (517) 373-3773.

DIRECTORIES

DIRECTORY OF MICHIGAN MUNICIPAL OFFICERS. Michigan Municipal League, Box 1487, Ann Arbor, Michigan 48106. (Semiannual).

ELECTIVE AND APPOINTIVE STATE OFFICERS (MICHIGAN). Michigan Department of Management and Budget, Office Services Division, 7461 Crowner Drive, P.O. Box 30026, Lansing, Michigan 48909. (Biennial).

MICHIGAN ASSOCIATIONS DIRECTORY. Second Edition. Michigan Library Association, 1000 Long Boulevard, Suite 1, Lansing, Michigan 48911. 1987.

MICHIGAN BAR JOURNAL: DIRECTORY ISSUE. State Bar of Michigan, 306 Townsend Street, Lansing, Michigan 48933. (Annual: April Issue).

MICHIGAN MANUAL. Department of Management and Budget, Office Services Division, 7461 Crowner Drive, P.O. Box 30026, Lansing, Michigan 48909. (Biennial).

STATES--MINNESOTA

STATUTES, CODES, STANDARDS, UNIFORM LAWS

MINNESOTA RULES, 1983: INCLUDING ADMINISTRATIVE RULES OF STATE AGENCIES. Revisor of Statutes, State Capitol Building, St. Paul, Minnesota 55155. 1984- . (Periodic Supplements).

MINNESOTA SESSION LAW SERVICE. West Publishing Company, P.O. Box 64526, 50 West Kellogg Boulevard, St. Paul, Minnesota 55164-0526. (Irregular Supplements).

MINNESOTA STATUTES. Document Division, Department of Administration, 117 University Avenue, St. Paul, Minnesota 55155. 1851- .

MINNESOTA STATUTES ANNOTATED. West Publishing Company, P.O. Box 64526, 50 West Kellogg Boulevard, St. Paul, Minnesota 55164-0526. 1946- . (Annual Supplements).

LOOSELEAF SERVICES AND REPORTERS

MINNESOTA REPORTER. West Publishing Company, P.O. Box 64526, 50 West Kellogg Boulevard, St. Paul, Minnesota 55164-0526. 1978- .

MINNESOTA REPORTS. 1851-1977. (Current Official Source: Northwestern Reporter).

MINNESOTA TAX REPORTER. Commerce Clearing House, Incorporated, 4025 West Peterson Avenue, Chicago, Illinois 60646. (Looseleaf). 1982- .

NORTHWESTERN REPORTER. (First and Second Series). West Publishing Company, P.O. Box 64526, 50 West Kellogg Boulevard, St. Paul, Minnesota 55164-0526. 1879- .

ATTORNEY GENERAL OPINIONS

OPINIONS OF THE ATTORNEY GENERAL OF THE STATE OF MINNESOTA. Office of the Attorney General, State Capitol Building, St. Paul, Minnesota 55155. 1858- . (Title and publisher varies). Also avialable on Lexis: January, 1977-; Westlaw: 1977- .

ETHICS OPINIONS, CODES, RULES

Advisory Ethics Opinions are occasionally issued by the Lawyers Professional Responsibility Board and are published in Bench and Bar. The January 1985 issue includes a compilation of these opinions. For further information concerning these opinions, contact the Office of Lawyers Professional Responsibility, 520 Lafayette Road, First Floor, St. Paul, Minnesota 55155. 612-296-3952.

Minnesota Rules of Professional Conduct (adopted June 1985) and the Rules on Lawyers Professional Responsibility are published in Minnesota Rules of Court and in Minnesota Statutes (Rules Volume).

COURT RULES

APPELLATE RULES ANNOTATED. Second Edition. Edward Magnunson. West Publishing Company, 50 West Kellogg Boulevard, St. Paul, Minnesota 55164. 1985.

MINNESOTA COURT RULES. Published in Minnesota Statutes Annotated, Volumes 48-52. West Publishing Company, P.O. Box 64526, 50 West Kellogg Boulevard, St. Paul, Minnesota 55164-0526. 1980- . (Annual Supplements).

MINNESOTA RULES, 1985: INCLUDING ADMINISTRATIVE RULES OF STATE AGENCIES ADOPTED AS OF APRIL 8, 1985. Office of the Revisor of Statutes, State Capitol Building, St. Paul, Minnesota 55155. 1985- . (Periodic Supplements).

MINNESOTA RULES OF CIVIL PROCEDURE ANNOTATED. Second Edition. David F. Herr and Roger S. Haydock. West Publishing Company, P.O. Box 64526, 50 West Kellogg Boulevard, St. Paul, Minnesota 55164-0526. 1985- . (Periodic Supplements).

MINNESOTA RULES OF COURT: STATE AND FEDERAL. West Publishing Company, P.O. Box 64526, 50 West Kellogg Boulevard, St. Paul, Minnesota 55164-0526. (Annual).

RULES OF APPELLATE PROCEDURE IN MINNESOTA COURTS. Minnesota Continuing Legal Education, 310 Minnesota State Bank Building, 200 South Robert Street, St. Paul, Minnesota 55107. 1983.

JURY INSTRUCTIONS

MINNESOTA JURY INSTRUCTION GUIDES: CIVIL. Third Edition. West Publishing Company, P.O. Box 64526, 50 West Kellogg Boulevard, St. Paul, Minnesota 55164-0526. 1987- . (Periodic Supplements).

MINNESOTA JURY INSTRUCTION GUIDES: CRIMINAL. Second Edition. Minnesota District Judges Association, Committee on Criminal Jury Instruction Guides. West Publishing Company, P.O. Box 64526, 50 West Kellogg Boulevard, St. Paul, Minnesota 55164-0526. 1985- . (Periodic Supplements).

DIGESTS, INDEXES, ABSTRACTS, CITATORS

MINNESOTA DIGEST. West Publishing Company, P.O. Box 64526, 50 West Kellogg Boulevard, St. Paul, Minnesota 55164-0526. 1942- . (Annual Supplements).

NORTHWESTERN DIGEST. (First and Second Series). West Publishing Company, P.O. Box 64526, 50 West Kellogg Boulevard, St. Paul, Minnesota 55164-0526. 1932- . (Annual Supplements).

SHEPARD'S MINNESOTA CITATIONS. Shepard's/McGraw-Hill, P.O. Box 1235, Colorado Springs, Colorado 80901. (Quarterly Pamphlets).

SHEPARD'S NORTHWESTERN REPORTER CITATIONS. Shepard's/McGraw-Hill, P.O. Box 1235, Colorado Springs, Colorado 80901. (Monthly Supplements).

LAW REVIEWS AND PERIODICALS

CONSTITUTIONAL COMMENTARY. University of Minnesota Law School, 229 Nineteenth Avenue South, Minneapolis, Minnesota 55455. 1984- . (Semiannual).

HAMLINE LAW REVIEW. Hamline University School of Law, 1536 Hewitt Avenue, St. Paul, Minnesota 55104. (Semiannual).

MINNESOTA LAW REVIEW. University of Minnesota Law School, 229 Nineteenth Avenue South, Minneapolis, Minnesota 55455. (Six issues per year).

WILLIAM MITCHELL LAW REVIEW. William Mitchell College of Law, 875 Summit Avenue, St. Paul, Minnesota 55105. (Quarterly).

NEWSLETTERS AND NEWSPAPERS

COUNTY LAW LIBRARY PROJECT BULLETIN. Minnesota State Law Library, 177 University Avenue, St. Paul, Minnesota 55155. Bimonthly.

LEGAL ADVISORY. Worker's Compensation Reinsurance Association, 400 North Robert Street, Suite 900, St. Paul, Minnesota 55101. As needed.

LOQUITUR. Minnesota State Law Library, 177 University Avenue, St. Paul, Minnesota 55155. Quarterly.

MALL NEWSLETTER. Minnesota Association of Law Libraries, c/o Debbie Munteau, Briggs and Morgan, 2400 IDS Tower, Minneapolis, Minnesota 55402. Bimonthly.

MINNESOTA FAMILY LAW JOURNAL. Butterworth Legal Publishers, 90 Stiles Road, Salem, New Hampshire 03079. Bimonthly.

THE MINNESOTA GOVERNMENT REPORT. Minnesota Government Report, P.O. Box 441, Willernie, Minnesota 55090. Bimonthly.

THE MINNESOTA REAL ESTATE LAW JOURNAL. Butterworth Legal Publishers, 90 Stiles Road, Salem, New Hampshire 03079. Bimonthly.

FORMBOOKS

CORPORATIONS. Minnesota Continuing Legal Education and the Corporation, Banking and Business Law Section of the Minnesota State Bar Association. Minnesota Continuing Legal Education, 310 Minnesota Bank Building, 200 South Robert Street, St. Paul, Minnesota 55107. 1984.

DEBTORS' AND CREDITORS' FORMBOOK. Minnesota Continuing Legal Education, 310 Minnesota Bank Building, 200 South Robert Street, St. Paul, Minnesota 55107. 1983.

THE DESK MANUAL: CHECKLISTS, WORKSHEETS AND FORMS. Eighth Edition. John T. Wendt, Editor. Minnesota Continuing Legal Education, 310 Minnesota Bank Building, 200 South Robert Street, St. Paul, Minnesota 55107. 1983.

MINNESOTA LEGAL FORMS--BANKRUPTCY. Butterworth Legal Publishers, 90 Stiles Road, Salem, New Hampshire 03079. 1981- . (Periodic Supplements).

MINNESOTA LEGAL FORMS--COMMERCIAL REAL ESTATE. Second Edition. John M. Miller. Butterworth Legal Publishers, 90 Stiles Road, Salem, New Hampshire 03079. 1982- . (Periodic Supplements).

MINNESOTA LEGAL FORMS--CREDITORS' REMEDIES. Thomas F. Miller. Butterworth Legal Publishers, 90 Stiles Road, Salem, New Hampshire 03079. 1981- . (Periodic Supplements).

MINNESOTA LEGAL FORMS--CRIMINAL LAW. Rick E. Mattox. Butterworth Legal Publishers, 90 Stiles Road, Salem, New Hampshire 03079. 1981- . (Periodic Supplements).

MINNESOTA LEGAL FORMS--FAMILY LAW. Daniels W. McLean. Butterworth Legal Publishers, 90 Stiles Road, Salem, New Hampshire 03079. 1981- . (Annual Supplements).

MINNESOTA LEGAL FORMS--LAW OFFICE SYSTEMS. Robert Newell. Butterworth Legal Publishers, 90 Stiles Road, Salem, New Hampshire 03079. 1981- . (Periodic Supplements).

MINNESOTA LEGAL FORMS--PERSONAL INJURY. Gary Stoneking. Butterworth Legal Publishers, 90 Stiles Road, Salem, New Hampshire 03079. 1981- . (Periodic Supplements).

MINNESOTA LEGAL FORMS--PROBATE. Jeffery Hucek. Butterworth Legal Publishers, 90 Stiles Road, Salem, New Hampshire 03079. 1981- . (Periodic Supplements).

MINNESOTA LEGAL FORMS--RESIDENTIAL REAL ESTATE. Second Edition. Kathleen Roer. Butterworth Legal Publishers, 90 Stiles Road, Salem, New Hampshire 021802471. 1982- . (Periodic Supplements).

PRACTICE MATERIALS

CRIMINAL APPEALS IN MINNESOTA. Michael F. Crommet and Gregory A. Gaut. Butterworth Legal Publishers, 90 Stiles Road, Salem, New Hampshire 03079. 1984- . (Periodic Supplements).

EMPLOYMENT IN MINNESOTA. M.G. Sautter. Butterworth Legal Publishers, 90 Stiles Road, Salem, New Hampshire 03079. 1982- . (Periodic Supplements).

EMPLOYMENT LAW HANDBOOK. Minnesota Continuing Legal Education, 310 Minnesota State Bank Building, 200 South Robert Street, St. Paul, Minnesota 55107. 1986.

FUNDAMENTALS OF MARITAL DISSOLUTION PRACTICE: PLEADINGS AND FORMS GUIDE. Sponsored by the Family Law Section, Minnesota State Bar Association, Minnesota Supreme Court Office of Continuing Education for State Court Personnel and Minnesota Continuing Legal Education. Minnesota Continuing Legal Education, 310 Minnesota State Bank Building, 200 South Robert Street, St. Paul, Minnesota 55107. 1985.

THE JUVENILE COURT HANDBOOK: A PRACTIONER'S GUIDE TO JUVENILE COURT PRACTICE IN MINNESOTA. Wright S. Walling. Butterworth Legal Publishers, 90 Stiles Road, Salem, New Hampshire 03079. 1984- . (Periodic Supplements).

JUVENILE LAW AND PRACTICE. John O. Sonsteng and Robert Scott, with Donald W. Niles. West Publishing Company, P.O. Box 64526, 50 West Kellogg Boulevard, St. Paul, Minnesota 55164-0526. 1985- . (Volume 12 and 13 of Minnesota Practice).

MINNESOTA COLLECTIONS. Andrew Zlimer. Lawyers Cooperative Publishing Company, Aqueduct Building, Rochester, New York 14694. 1979.

MINNESOTA CORPORATE LAW. Minnesota Institute of Legal Education, 29 South Fifth Street, Minneapolis, Minnesota 55402. 1985.

MINNESOTA CORPORATIONS PRACTICE MANUAL. Bert Black, Editor. Butterworth Legal Publishers, 90 Stiles Road, Salem, New Hampshire 03079. 1986- . (Periodic Supplements).

MINNESOTA CRIMINAL PRETRIAL PRACTICE AND PROCEDURE. Mark Peterson, et al. Butterworth Legal Publishers, 90 Stiles Road, Salem, New Hampshire 03079. 1986- . (Periodic Supplements).

MINNESOTA DISSOLUTION. William Haugh. Lawyers Cooperative Publishing Company, Aqueduct Building, Rochester, New York 14694. 1979- . (Periodic Supplements).

MINNESOTA EVIDENCE. Peter Thompson. West Publishing Company, 50 West Kellogg Boulevard, St. Paul, Minnesota 55164. 1979.

MINNESOTA FAMILY LAW PRACTICE MANUAL. Neil Davidson, Editor. Butterworth Legal Publishers, 90 Stiles Road, Salem, New Hampshire 03079. 1985- . (Periodic Supplements).

MINNESOTA JUVENILE LAW AND PRACTICE. John Sonsterg. West Publishing Company, 50 West Kellogg Boulevard, St. Paul, Minnesota 55164. 1985.

MINNESOTA METHODS OF PRACTICE. Louis Arthur. West Publishing Company, 50 West Kellogg Boulevard, St. Paul, Minnesota 55164. 1975.

MINNESOTA PRACTICE HANDBOOK. Minnesota Continuing Legal Education, 310 Minnesota State Bank Building, 200 South Robert Street, St. Paul, Minnesota 55107. 1984- .

MINNESOTA PROBATE LAW DIGEST. Butterworth Legal Publishers, 90 Stiles Road, Salem, New Hampshire 03079. 1982- . (Periodic Supplements).

MINNESOTA REAL ESTATE LAW DIGEST. Robert J. Deike, et al. Butterworth Legal Publishers, 90 Stiles Road, Salem, New Hampshire 03079. 1983- . (Periodic Supplements).

MINNESOTA REAL ESTATE LAW PRACTICE MANUAL. Neil Davidson, Editor. Butterworth Legal Publishers, 90 Stiles Road, Salem, New Hampshire 03079. 1985- . (Periodic Supplements).

MINNESOTA TRIAL EVIDENCE HANDBOOK. Bertrand Poritsky. Butterworth Legal Publishers, 90 Stiles Road, Salem, New Hampshire 03079. 1987- . (Periodic Supplements).

WORKERS' COMPENSATION. Minnesota Institute of Legal Education, 29 South Fifth Street, Minneapolis, Minnesota 55402. 1985.

ASSOCIATIONS AND PROFESSIONAL SOCIETIES

ELEVENTH DISTRICT BAR ASSOCIATION, 802 Torrey Building, Duluth, Minnesota 55802.

HENNEPIN COUNTY BAR ASSOCIATION, 430 Marquette Avenue, Suite 402, Minneapolis, Minnesota 55401. (612) 340-0022.

MINNESOTA INSTITUTE OF LEGAL EDUCATIONS, 29 South Fifth Street, Minneapolis, Minnesota 55402.

MINNESOTA STATE BAR ASSOCIATION, 430 Marquette Avenue, Suite 403, Minneapolis, Minnesota 55401. (612) 333-1183.

RAMSEY COUNTY BAR ASSOCIATION, West 952 First National Bank Building, 332 Minnesota Street, St. Paul, Minneosta 55101.

DIRECTORIES

DIRECTORY OF MINNESOTA CITY OFFICIALS. League of Minnesota Cities, 183 University Avenue, East Saint Paul, Minnesota 55101. (Annual).

MINNESOTA LEGAL DIRECTORY. Legal Directories Publishing Company, 2122 Kidwell Street, P.O. Box 140200, Dallas, Texas 75214-0200. (Annual).

MINNESOTA LEGISLATIVE MANUAL. Election and Legislative Manual Division, Minnesota Secretary of State, State Office Building, Number 180, St. Paul, Minnesota 55155. (Biennial).

OFFICIAL DIRECTORY OF THE MINNESOTA LEGISLATURE. Secretary of State, Minnesota Legislature, State Capitol, Room 231, St. Paul, Minnesota 55155. (Biennial).

STATE OF MINNESOTA DIRECTORY OF LICENSES AND PERMITS. Bureau of Business Licenses, Minnesota Department of Energy, Planning and Development, 480 Cedar Street, St. Paul, Minnesota 55101. (Annual).

OTHER SOURCES

THE IMPACT OF THE MINNESOTA SENTENCING GUIDELINES: THREE YEAR EVALUATION. Minnesota Sentencing Commission, Seventh and Robert Streets, St. Paul, Minnesota 55107. 1984.

MINNESOTA SENTENCING GUIDELINES AND COMMENTARY. Minnesota Sentencing Commission, Seventh and Robert Streets, St. Paul, Minnesota 55101. 1984.

STATES--MISSISSIPPI

STATUTES, CODES, STANDARDS, UNIFORM LAWS

GENERAL LAWS OF MISSISSIPPI. Office of the Secretary of State, New Capitol, Jackson, Mississippi 39205. 1871?- .

MISSISSIPPI CODE ANNOTATED. Harrison Company Publishers, 3110 Crossing Park, P.O. Box 7500, Norcross, Georgia 30071. 1972- . (Annual Supplements).

No Administrative Code or Register is published for Mississippi.

LOOSELEAF SERVICES AND REPORTERS

MISSISSIPPI CASES. West Publishing Company, P.O. Box 64526, 50 West Kellogg Boulevard, St. Paul, Minnesota 55164-0526. 1966- . (Mississippi Supreme Court).

MISSISSIPPI REPORTS. 1818-1966. Tucker Printing House, Jackson, Mississippi. (Mississippi Supreme Court). (Current source is Mississippi Cases or Southern Reporter).

SOUTHERN REPORTER. (First and Second Series). West Publishing Company, P.O. Box 64526, 50 West Kellogg Boulevard, St. Paul, Minnesota 55164-0526. 1886- . (Mississippi Supreme Court).

ATTORNEY GENERAL OPINIONS

BIENNIAL REPORT OF THE ATTORNEY GENERAL OF THE STATE OF MISSISSIPPI. Office of the Attorney General, Gartin Justice Building, Jackson, Mississippi 39205. Also available on Lexis: January 1975-; Westlaw: January 1975- .

ETHICS OPINIONS, CODES, RULES

CODE OF PROFESSIONAL RESPONSIBILITY OF THE MISSISSIPPI STATE BAR; CODE OF JUDICIAL CONDUCT ADOPTED BY MISSISSIPPI CONFERENCE OF JUDGES; ADVISORY ETHICS OPINIONS OF THE MISSISSIPPI STATE BAR. Mississippi State Bar, 620 North State Street, P.O. Box 2168, Jackson, Mississippi 39205. 1983. For further information concerning Mississippi Ethics Opinions, contact the Mississippi State Bar, 620 North State Street, P.O. Box 2168, Jackson, Mississippi 39205. 609-948-4471.

RULES OF DISCIPLINE FOR THE MISSISSIPPI STATE BAR. Mississippi State Bar Association, 620 North State Street, P.O. Box 2168, Jackson, Mississippi 39205. 1984.

COURT RULES

MISSISSIPPI RULES OF COURT. West Publishing Company, P.O. Box 64526, 50 West Kellogg Boulevard, St. Paul, Minnesota 55164-0526. 1983- . (Annual).

JURY INSTRUCTIONS

MISSISSIPPI MODEL JURY INSTRUCTIONS: CIVIL AND CRIMINAL. West Publishing Company, P.O. Box 64526, 50 West Kellogg Boulevard, St. Paul, Minnesota 55164-0526. 1977- .

DIGESTS, INDEXES, ABSTRACTS, CITATORS

MISSISSIPPI DIGEST. West Publishing Company, P.O. Box 64526, 50 West Kellogg Boulevard, St. Paul, Minnesota 55164-0526. 1936- . (Annual Supplements).

SHEPARD'S MISSISSIPPI CITATIONS. Shepard's/McGraw-Hill, P.O. Box 1235, Colorado Springs, Colorado 80901. (Six pamphlets per year).

SHEPARD'S SOUTHERN REPORTER CITATIONS. Shepard's/ McGraw-Hill, P.O. Box 1235, Colorado Springs, Colorado 80901. (Monthly Supplements).

SOUTHERN DIGEST. West Publishing Company, P.O. Box 64526, 50 West Kellogg Boulevard, St. Paul, Minnesota 55164-0526. 1938- . (Annual Supplements).

LAW REVIEWS AND PERIODICALS

MISSISSIPPI COLLEGE LAW REVIEW. Mississippi College School of Law, 151 East Griffith Street, Jackson, Mississippi 39201. (Semiannual).

MISSISSIPPI LAW JOURNAL. University of Mississippi School of Law, P.O. Box 849, University, Mississippi 38677. (Three issues per year).

THE MISSISSIPPI LAWYER. Mississippi State Bar Association, 620 North State Street, P.O. Box 2168, Jackson, Mississippi 39225. (Bimonthly).

NEWSLETTERS AND NEWSPAPERS

DAILY LEGISLATIVE REPORT. Mississippi Economic Council, P.O. Box 23276, Jackson, Mississippi 39225. Daily when in session.

FACTUAL REPORTING SERVICE. Factual Reporting Service, P.O. Box 1243, Jackson, Mississippi 39205. Daily when in session.

FORMBOOKS

MISSISSIPPI CIVIL TRIAL PRACTICE FORMS. Louis Fondren. Harrison Company Publishers, 3110 Crossing Park, P.O. Box 7500, Norcross, Georgia 30071. 1983.

PRACTICE MATERIALS

MISSISSIPPI CORPORATIONS--FORMATION AND OPERATION: WITH FORMS. William S. Painter. Harrison Company, Publisher, 3110 Crossing Park, Norcross, Georgia 30071. 1983.

MISSISSIPPI EVIDENCE. M. Carolyn Ellis and Parham H. Williams, Jr. Harrison Company Publishers, 3110 Crossing Park, Norcross, Georgia 30071. 1983.

PRODUCTS LIABILITY: THE LAW IN MISSISSIPPI. Joan Witherberg. Harrison Company, 3110 Crossing Park, Norcross, Georgia 30091. 1982.

SUMMARY OF MISSISSIPPI LAW. L. Guart. Lawyers Cooperative Publishing Company, Aqueduct Building, Rochester, New York 14694. 1969.

TRIAL HANDBOOK FOR MISSISSIPPI LAWYERS. Stanford Young. Lawyers Co-Operative Company, Aqueduct Building, Rochester, New York 14694. 1986- . (Periodic Supplements).

MANUALS AND RESEARCH GUIDES

MISSISSIPPI LEGAL RESEARCH BIBLIOGRAPHY. Chester S. Bunnell and Thomas M. Steele. University of Mississippi Law Library, University of Mississippi, University, Mississippi 38677. 1983.

ASSOCIATIONS AND PROFESSIONAL SOCIETIES

HINDS COUNTY BAR ASSOCIATION, P.O. Box 12314, Jackson, Mississippi 39211.

MISSISSIPPI STATE BAR ASSOCIATION, 643 North State Street, P.O. Box 2168, Jackson, Mississippi 39202. (601) 948-4471.

DIRECTORIES

DIRECTORY OF MISSISSIPPI ELECTIVE OFFICIALS. Mississippi Secretary of State, Box 136, Jackson, Mississippi 39205. 1984. (Quadrennial).

MISSISSIPPI LEGAL DIRECTORY. Legal Directories Publishing Company, 2122 Kidwell Street, P.O. Box 140200, Dallas, Texas 75214-0200. (Annual).

MISSISSIPPI LEGISLATURE HANDBOOK. Mississippi Legislature, State Capitol, Jackson, Mississippi 39215. 1985. (Irregular).

MISSISSIPPI MUNICIPAL DIRECTORY. Mississippi Municipal Association, 230 Barefield Complex, Jackson, Mississippi 39202. 1985. (Quadrennial).

MISSISSIPPI OFFICIAL AND STATISTICAL REGISTER. Mississippi Secretary of State, Box 136, Jackson, Mississippi 39205. 1984. (Discontinued).

STATES--MISSOURI

STATUTES, CODES, STANDARDS, UNIFORM LAWS

LAWS OF MISSOURI. Secretary of State, Capital Building, Jefferson City, Missouri 65101. 1820- . Annual.

MISSOURI CODE OF STATE REGULATIONS, ANNOTATED. Office of the Secretary of State, State Capitol, Jefferson City, Missouri 65101. 1977- . (Semiannual Supplements).

MISSOURI LEGISLATIVE SERVICE. West Publishing Company, P.O. Box 64526, 50 West Kellogg Boulevard, St. Paul, Minnesota 55164-0526. (Irregular Pamphlets).

MISSOURI REGISTER. Office of the Secretary of State, State Capitol, Jefferson City, Missouri 65101. (Monthly).

MISSOURI REVISED STATUTES. Committee on Legislative Research, 117A State Capital, Jefferson City, Missouri 65101. 1835- .

VERNON'S ANNOTATED MISSOURI STATUTES. West Publishing Company, P.O. Box 64526, 50 West Kellogg Boulevard, St. Paul, Minnesota 55164-0526. (Annual Supplements).

LOOSELEAF SERVICES AND REPORTERS

MISSOURI APPEALS REPORTS. (Missouri Court of Appeals). 1876-1952. (Current Official Source: Southwestern Reporter or Missouri Decisions).

MISSOURI DECISIONS. West Publishing Company, P.O. Box 64526, 50 West Kellogg Boulevard, St. Paul, Minnesota 55164-0526. 1886- . (Missouri Supreme Court and Court of Appeals).

MISSOURI REPORTS. E.W. Stephens Publishing Company, Columbia, Missouri 65201. 1821-1956. (Missouri Supreme Court). (Current official source: Southwestern Reporter)

MISSOURI TAX REPORTER. Commerce Clearing House, Incorporated, 4025 West Peterson Avenue, Chicago, Illinois 60646. 1981- . (looseleaf).

SOUTHWESTERN REPORTER. (First and Second Series). West Publishing Company, P.O. Box 64526, 50 West Kellogg Boulevard, St. Paul, Minnesota 55164-0526. 1886- . (Missouri Supreme Court and Court of Appeals).

HANDBOOKS, MANUALS, FORMBOOKS

MISSOURI CORPORATE AND PARTNERSHIP FORMS HANDBOOK. University of Missouri at Kansas City Continuing Legal Education, 5100 Rockhill Road, Kansas City, Missouri 64110. 1985- . (Periodic Supplements).

MISSOURI FAMILY LAW FORMBOOK. Jack Cochran, Editor. University of Missouri at Kansas City, Continuing Legal Education, 5100 Rockhill Road, Kansas City, Missouri 64110. 1985- . (Periodic Supplements).

MISSOURI PROBATE FORMS MANUAL. John A. Borron, Jr. West Publishing Company, P.O. Box 64526, 50 West Kellogg Boulevard, St. Paul, Minnesota 55164-0526. 1985- . (Periodic Supplements).

MISSOURI PROCEDURAL FORMS. Charles Wheaton. West Publishing Company, 50 West Kellogg Boulevard, St. Paul, Minnesota 55164. 1986.

MISSOURI UNIFORM COMMERCIAL CODE FORMS. Robert Duesenberg. West Publishing Company, 50 West Kellogg Boulevard, St. Paul, Minnesota 55164. 1966.

POSTMORTEM TAXES: FORMS AND PLANNING. Missouri Bar Association, 326 Monroe, P.O. Box 119, Jefferson City, Missouri 63103.

ATTORNEY GENERAL OPINIONS

MISSOURI ATTORNEY GENERAL OPINIONS. Office of the Attorney General, Supreme Court Building, P.O. Box 899, Jefferson City, Missouri 65102. (Also available on Lexis: January 1977- . Westlaw: 1977- .)

ETHICS OPINIONS, CODES, RULES

MISSOURI ADVISORY COMMITTEE OPINIONS. Advisory Committee, Missouri Bar Association, Continuing Legal Education, P.O. Box 119, Jefferson City, Missouri 65102. 1985- . (Periodic Supplements). (Formal Opinions are published in the Journal of the Missouri Bar). For further information concerning these opinions, contact the Missouri Bar Association (314-635-4128).

Rules of Professional Conduct for Missouri (Rule 4) are published in Missouri Rules of Court: State and Federal. West Publishing Company, P.O. Box 64526, 50 West Kellogg Boulevard, St. Paul, Minnesota 55164-0526. (Annual).

COURT RULES

MISSOURI CIVIL RULES PRACTICE. Charles Wheaton. West Publishing Company, 50 West Kellogg Boulevard, St. Paul, Minnesota 55164. 1976.

MISSOURI RULES OF COURT: STATE AND FEDERAL. West Publishing Company, P.O. Box 64526, 50 West Kellogg Boulevard, St. Paul, Minnesota 55164-0526. (Annual).

VERNON'S ANNOTATED MISSOURI RULES. West Publishing Company, 50 West Kellogg Boulevard, St. Paul, Minnesota 55164. (Annual).

JURY INSTRUCTIONS

MISSOURI APPROVED CHANGES: CRIMINAL. Missouri Supreme Court Committee of Jury Instructions. Missouri Supreme Court Publications, P.O. Box 448, Jefferson City, Missouri 65102. 1979- . (Periodic Supplements).

MISSOURI APPROVED JURY INSTRUCTIONS: CIVIL. Third Edition. West Publishing Company, P.O. Box 64526, 50 West Kellogg Boulevard, St. Paul, Minnesota 55164-0526. 1981- . (Periodic Supplements).

MISSOURI APPROVED JURY INSTRUCTIONS: CRIMINAL. Third Edition. Missouri Supreme Court Committee on Jury Instructions. Missouri Supreme Court Publications, P.O. Box 448, Jefferson City, Missouri 65102. 1987- . (Periodic Supplements).

DIGESTS, INDEXES, ABSTRACTS, CITATORS

MISSOURI DIGEST. Second Edition. West Publishing Company, P.O. Box 64526, 50 West Kellogg Boulevard, St. Paul, Minnesota 55164-0526. 1983- . (Annual Supplements).

MISSOURI LAW FINDER. West Publishing Company, 50 West Kellogg Boulevard, St. Paul, Minnesota 55164. 1986.

SHEPARD'S MISSOURI CITATIONS. Shepard's/McGraw-Hill, P.O. Box 1235, Colorado Springs, Colorado 80901. (Eight supplements per year).

SHEPARD'S SOUTHWESTERN REPORTER CITATIONS. Shepard's/McGraw-Hill, P.O. Box 1235, Colorado Springs, Colorado 80901. (Monthly Supplements).

SOUTH WESTERN DIGEST. West Publishing Company, 50 West Kellogg Boulevard, St. Paul, Minnesota 55164. (Annual Supplements).

LAW REVIEWS AND PERIODICALS

THE JOURNAL OF THE MISSOURI BAR, 326 Monroe, P.O. Box 119, Jefferson City, Missouri 65102. (Eight issues per year).

MISSOURI BAR BULLETIN. Missouri Bar Association, 326 Monroe, P.O. Box 119, Jefferson City, Missouri 65102. (Quarterly).

MISSOURI LAW REVIEW. University of Missouri School of Law, Ninth and Conly Streets, Columbia, Missouri 65211. (Quarterly).

ST. LOUIS UNIVERSITY LAW JOURNAL. St. Louis University School of Law, 3700 Lindell Boulevard, St. Louis, Missouri 63108. (Quarterly).

UMKC LAW REVIEW. University of Missouri-Kansas City School of Law, 5100 Rockhill Road, Kansas City, Missouri 64110. (Quarterly).

WASHINGTON UNIVERSITY LAW QUARTERLY. Washington University School of Law, St. Louis, Missouri 63130. (Quarterly).

PRACTICE MATERIALS

MISSOURI ADMINISTRATIVE LAW. Missouri Bar Association, P.O. Box 119, Jefferson City, Missouri 65102. 1979.

MISSOURI ADMINISTRATIVE PRACTICE AND PROCEDURE. A. Neely. West Publishing Company, 50 West Kellogg Boulevard, St. Paul, Minnesota 55164. 1987.

MISSOURI APPELLATE PRACTICE AND EXTRAORDINARY REMEDIES. Third Edition. Missouri Bar Association, 326 Monroe, P.O. Box 119, Jefferson City, Missouri 65102. 1981.

MISSOURI CIVIL PROCEDURE. Missouri Bar Association, P.O. Box 119, Jefferson City, Missouri 65102. (Looseleaf). 1983- . (Periodic Supplements).

MISSOURI CIVIL TRIAL PRACTICE. Second Edition. Missouri Bar Association, 326 Monroe, P.O. Box 119, Jefferson City, Missouri 65102. 1988.

MISSOURI CRIMINAL PRACTICE AND PROCEDURE. William Knox. West Publishing Company, 50 West Kellogg Boulevard, St. Paul, Minnesota 55164. 1985.

MISSOURI EVIDENCE. Spencer A. Gard. Lawyers Co-Operative Company, Aqueduct Building, Rochester, New York 14694. 1985- . (Periodic Supplements).

MISSOURI EVIDENCE. Third Edition. Missouri Bar Association, P.O. Box 119, Jefferson City, Missouri 65102. 1983.

MISSOURI EXECUTIONS ON MONEY JUDGEMENTS. Walter Henning. Harrison Company, 3110 Crossing Park, Norcross, Georgia 30091. 1984.

MISSOURI FAMILY LAW. Fourth Edition. Missouri Bar Association, P.O. Box 119, Jefferson City, Missouri 65102. 1988.

MISSOURI FARM LAW. Missouri Bar Association, P.O. Box 119, Jefferson City, Missouri 65102. 1983.

MISSOURI JURISDICTIARY VENUE AND LIMITATIONS. Charles Wheaton. West Publishing Company, 50 West Kellogg Boulevard, St. Paul, Minnesota 5164. 1965.

MISSOURI LAWYERS GUIDE. Charles Chase McCarter and Beverly J. Greenley. Callaghan and Company, 155 Pfingsten Road, Deerfield, Illinois 60015. (Looseleaf). 1984- . (Periodic Supplements).

MISSOURI LOCAL GOVERNMENT LAW. Second Edition. Missouri Bar Association, P.O. Box 119, Jefferson City, Missouri 65102. 1988. 1986.

MISSOURI METHODS OF PRACTICE. Michael Volz. West Publishing Company, 50 West Kellogg Boulevard, St. Paul, Minnesota 55164. 1986.

MISSOURI PRACTICE. Second Edition. West Publishing Company, P.O. Box 64526, 50 West Kellogg Boulevard, St. Paul, Minnesota 55164-0526. 1966- . (Annual Supplements).

MISSOURI PROBATE. Francis M. Nevins, Jr. Harrison Company, Publisher, 3110 Crossing Park, Norcross, Georgia 30071. 1983.

MISSOURI PROBATE CODE MANUAL. Francis Hanna. West Publishing Company, 50 West Kellogg Boulevard, St. Paul, Minnesota 55164. 1986.

MISSOURI PRODUCTS LIABILITY. Donald B. King. Harrison Company, Publisher, 3110 Crossing Park, Norcross, Georgia 30071. 1983.

MISSOURI REAL ESTATE PRACTICE. Third Edition. Missouri Bar Association, P.O. Box 119, Jefferson City, Missouri 65102. 1986.

MISSOURI TORT LAW. Missouri Bar Association, P.O. Box 119, Jefferson City, Missouri 65102. 1978.

MISSOURI WORKER'S COMPENSATION. Jerry Kenter. Lawyers Co-Operative Company, Aqueduct Building, Rochester, New York 14694. 1984- . (Annual Supplements).

MISSOURI WORKERS' COMPENSATION: LAW AND PRACTICE. Timothy J. Heinsz. Harrison Company, Publisher, 3110 Crossing Park, Norcross, Georgia 30071. 1984.

POSSESSORY ESTATES, FUTURE INTERESTS AND CONVEYANCES IN MISSOURI. William Eckhardt. West Publishing Company, 50 West Kellogg Boulevard, St. Paul, Minnesota 55164. 1986.

REAL ESTATE LAW. Theodore H. Hellmuth. West Publishing Company, P.O. Box 64526, 50 West Kellogg Boulevard, St. Paul, Minnesota 55164-0526. 1985- . (Annual Supplements). (Volume Eighteen of Missouri Practice).

TRIAL HANDBOOK FOR MISSOURI LAWYERS. William J. Turley. Lawyers Co-Operative Company, Aqueduct Building, Rochester, New York 14694. 1985- . (Periodic Supplements).

MANUALS AND RESEARCH GUIDES

A LAW LIBRARIAN'S INTRODUCTION TO MISSOURI STATE PUBLICATIONS. American Association of Law Libraries, 53 West Jackson Boulevard, Suite 703, Chicago, Illinois 60604. 1980.

MISSOURI LAW FINDER. West Publishing Company, P.O. Box 64526, 50 West Kellogg Boulevard, St. Paul, Minnesota 55164-0526. 1983- . (Annual).

ASSOCIATIONS AND PROFESSIONAL SOCIETIES

BAR ASSOCIATION OF METROPOLITAN ST. LOUIS, One Mercantile Center, Suite 3600, St. Louis, Missouri 63101. (314) 421-4134.

GREENE COUNTY BAR ASSOCIATION, 333 Park Central East, Suite 418, Springfield, Missouri 65806.

THE KANSAS CITY METROPOLITAN BAR ASSOCIATION, 818 Grand Avenue, Kansas City, Missouri 64106. (816) 474-4322.

THE LAWYER'S ASSOCIATION OF KANSAS CITY, 127 West 10th Street, Suite 632, Kansas City, Missouri 64105.

THE LAWYER'S ASSOCIATION OF ST. LOUIS, 1221 Locust Street, Suite 405, St. Louis, Missouri 63103.

MISSOURI BAR ASSOCIATION, P.O. Box 119, Jefferson City, Missouri 65102. (314) 635-4128.

ST. LOUIS COUNTY BAR ASSOCIATION, 7701 Forsyth, Suite 1353, Clayton, Missouri 63105.

DIRECTORIES

DIRECTORY TO THE MISSOURI JUDICIAL DEPARTMENT. State Courts Administrator's Office, Jefferson City, Missouri 65101. (Semiannual).

MISSOURI LEGAL DIRECTORY. Legal Directories Publishing Company, 2122 Kidwell Street, P.O. Box 140200, Dallas, Texas 75214-0200. (Annual).

MISSOURI LEGISLATIVE DIRECTORY. Missouri Chamber of Commerce, 428 East Capitol Avenue, Jefferson City, Missouri 65102. (Biennial).

MISSOURI MUNICIPAL OFFICIALS DIRECTORY. Missouri Municipal League, 1913 William Street, Jefferson City, Missouri 65101. (Annual).

OFFICIAL MANUAL--STATE OF MISSOURI. Missouri Secretary of State, State Capitol, Room 209, Jefferson City, Missouri 65101. (Biennial).

ROSTER OF STATE, DISTRICT, AND COUNTY, OFFICERS OF THE STATE OF MISSOURI. Missouri Secretary of State, State Capital, Room 209, Jefferson City, Missouri 65101. (Biennial).

STATES--MONTANA

STATUTES, CODES, STANDARDS, UNIFORM LAWS

ADMINISTRATIVE RULES OF MONTANA. Secretary of State, 202 Capitol Building, Helena, Montana 59620. 1979- .

LAWS OF MONTANA. Montana Legislative Council, State Capital, Room 138, Helena, Montana 59620. 1889- . (Titles and imprint varies).

A LEGISLATOR'S HANDBOOK. Third Edition. Paul Vernon, Editor. Montana Legislative Council, State Capital, Room 138, Helena, Montana 59620. 1984.

MONTANA ADMINISTRATIVE REGISTER. Secretary of State, 202 Capitol Building, Helena, Montana 59620. (Biweekly).

MONTANA CODE ANNOTATED. Montana Legislative Council, Room 138, State Capitol, Helena, Montana 59620. (Completely Replaced Every Two Years).

LOOSELEAF SERVICES AND REPORTERS

MONTANA REPORTS. State Reporter Publishing Company, Helena, Montana 59620. 1868- . (Publisher varies).

PACIFIC REPORTER. (First and Second Series). West Publishing Company, P.O. Box 64526, 50 West Kellogg Boulevard, St. Paul, Minnesota 55164-0526. 1882- .

ATTORNEY GENERAL OPINIONS

OPINIONS OF THE ATTORNEY GENERAL. Office of the Attorney Generals, Justice Building, Helena, Missouri 59620. (Also Available on Lexis: February 1977-; Westlaw: 1977- .)

ETHICS OPINIONS, CODES, RULES

A List of Montana Advisory Ethics Opinions is published in the Montana Lawyer. For Further information concerning these opinions, contact the State Bar of Montana, P.O. Box 577, Helena, Montana 59624. (406-442-7660).

Rules of Professional Conduct for Montana are published in the Montana Lawyers Desk Book and Directory. State Bar of Montana, P.O. Box 577, Helena, Montan 59624.

COURT RULES

MONTANA RULES OF COURT. West Publishing Company, P.O. Box 64526, 50 West Kellogg Boulevard, St. Paul, Minnesota 55164-0526. 1987- . (Annual).

JURY INSTRUCTIONS

MONTANA CRIMINAL JURY INSTRUCTIONS. District Court Planning Committee, State Bar of Montana, P.O. Box 577, Helena, Montana 59604. 1983.

MONTANA PATTERN INSTRUCTIONS (CIVIL). State Bar of Montana, P.O. Box 577, Helena, Montana 59624. 1987- . (Periodic Supplements).

DIGESTS, INDEXES, ABSTRACTS, CITATORS

MONTANA DIGEST. West Publishing Company, P.O. Box 64526, 50 West Kellogg Boulevard, St. Paul, Minnesota 55164-0526. 1938- . (Annual Supplements).

PACIFIC DIGEST. West Publishing Company, P.O. Box 64526, 50 West Kellogg Boulevard, St. Paul, Minnesota 55164-0526. 1932- . (Annual Supplements).

SHEPARD'S MONTANA CITATIONS. Shepard's/McGraw-Hill, P.O. Box 1235, Colorado Springs, Colorado 80901. (Quarterly Supplements).

SHEPARD'S PACIFIC REPORTER CITATIONS. Shepard's/ McGraw-Hill, P.O. Box 1235, Colorado Springs, Colorado 80901. (Monthly Supplements).

LAW REVIEWS AND PERIODICALS

MONTANA LAW REVIEW. University of Montana School of Law, Missoula, Montana 59812-1201. (Semiannual).

MONTANA LAWYER. State Bar of Montana, P.O. Box 577, Helena, Montana 59624. 1985- . (Monthly).

NEWSLETTERS AND NEWSPAPERS

LEGISLATIVE BULLETIN. Montana Chamber of Commerce, 2030 Eleventh Avenue, Helena, Montana 59601.

LEGISLATIVE SERVICE. Montana Chamber of Commerce, 2030 Eleventh Avenue, Helena, Montana 59601.

MONTANA BANKRUPTCY REPORTS. Montana Law Week, 515 North Sanders, Helena, Montana 59601. Monthly.

MONTANA FEDERAL REPORTS. Montana Law Week, 515 North Sanders, Helena, Montana 59601. Monthly.

MONTANA LAW WEEK. Montana Law Week, 515 North Sanders, Helena, Montana 59601. Weekly.

MONTANA SUPREME COURT PREVIEWS. Montana Law Week, 515 North Sanders, Helena, Montana 59601. Monthly.

PRACTICE MATERIALS

MARRIAGE AND DIVORCE HANDBOOK. Judith McAllister. State Bar of Montana, P.O. Box 577, Helena, Montana 59624. 1984.

MONTANA ADMINISTRATIVE PROCEDURES HANDBOOK. Robert Tippy. State Bar of Montana, P.O. Box 577, Helena, Montana 59624. 1984.

MONTANA LAWYER'S RULE BOOK. State Bar of Montana, P.O. Box 577, Helena, Montana 59624. 1977- . (Annual Supplements).

MONTANA PROBATE PROCEDURE. State Bar of Montana, P.O. Box 577, Helena, Montana 59624. 1983- . (Periodic Supplements).

WORKER'S COMPENSATION MANUAL. State Bar of Montana, P.O. Box 4669, Helena, Montana 59604. 1985- . (Periodic Supplements).

STATES--MONTANA

ASSOCIATIONS AND PROFESSIONAL SOCIETIES

MONTANA BAR ASSOCIATION. 46 North Last Chance Gulch, Suite 2A, P.O. Box 577, Helena, Montana 59624. (406) 442-7660

DIRECTORIES

LAWMAKERS OF MONTANA. State and Local Government Relations, Anaconda Company/Atlantic Richfield Company, 2030 11th Avenue, Suite 22, Helena, Montana 59601. (Biennial).

LAWYER'S DESKBOOK AND DIRECTORY. State Bar of Montana, P.O. Box 4669, Helena, Montana 59604. (Annual).

MONTANA STATE AND COUNTY ELECTED OFFICIALS. Montana Secretary of State, State Capitol, Helena, Montana 59620. (Biennial).

MONTANA STATE GOVERNMENT TELEPHONE DIRECTORY. Communications Division, Montana Department of Administration, Sam W. Mitchell Building, Helena, Montana 59601. (Annual).

MOUNTAIN STATES LEGAL DIRECTORY. Legal Directories Publishing Company, 2122 Kidwell Street, P.O. Box 140200, Dallas, Texas 75214-0200. (Annual). (Colorado, Idaho, Montana, New Mexico, Utah, Wyoming).

OFFICIAL ROSTER OF THE MONTANA LEGISLATURE. Montana Secretary of State, State Capitol, Helena, Montana 59620. (Biennial).

STATES--NEBRASKA

STATUTES, CODES, STANDARDS, UNIFORM LAWS

LAWS OF NEBRASKA. State of Nebraska, Legislative Council Bureau. Available from the Court Administrator's Office, Room 1214, Capitol Building, Lincoln, Nebraska 68509. 1864- .

NEBRASKA ADMINISTRATIVE RULES AND REGULATIONS. Office of the Secretary of State, Rules and Regulations Division, Room 343, Capitol Building, Lincoln, Nebraska 68509. 1980- . (Monthly updates) (34 volumes).

REVISED STATUTES OF NEBRASKA. Nebraska Revisor of Statutes, Room 1010, State Capitol, Lincoln, Nebraska 68509. 1983- . (Annual Supplements).

LOOSELEAF SERVICES AND REPORTERS

NEBRASKA REPORTS. Court Administrators Office, Room 1214, Capitol Building, Lincoln, Nebraska 68509. 1860- .

NEBRASKA TAX REPORTER. Commerce Clearing House, Incorporated, 4025 West Peterson Avenue, Chicago, Illinois 60646. 1982- .

NORTHWESTERN REPORTER. (First and Second Series). West Publishing Company, P.O. Box 64526, 50 West Kellogg Boulevard, St. Paul, Minnesota 55164-0526. 1879- .

HANDBOOKS, MANUALS, FORMBOOKS

NEBRASKA LEGAL FORMS--BANKRUPTCY. John Minahan. Butterworth Legal Publishers, 90 Stiles Road, Salem, New Hampshire 03079. 1982- . (Periodic Supplements).

NEBRASKA LEGAL FORMS--COMMERCIAL REAL ESTATE. Peter Vaughn. Butterworth Legal Publishers, 90 Stiles Road, Salem, New Hampshire 03079. 1981- . (Periodic Supplements).

NEBRASKA LEGAL FORMS--CREDITOR'S REMEDIES. Arlen Langvardt. Butterworth Legal Publishers, 90 Stiles Road, Salem, New Hampshire 03079. 1982- . (Periodic Supplements).

NEBRASKA LEGAL FORMS--CRIMINAL LAW. Donald Fiedler. Butterworth Legal Publishers, 90 Stiles Road, Salem, New Hampshire 03079. 1982- . (Periodic Supplements).

NEBRASKA LEGAL FORMS--FAMILY LAW. Elizabeth S. Borchers. Butterworth Legal Publishers, 90 Stiles Road, Salem, New Hampshire 03079. 1982- . (Periodic Supplements).

NEBRASKA LEGAL FORMS--LAW OFFICE SYSTEMS. Robert Newell. Butterworth Legal Publishers, 90 Stiles Road, Salem, New Hampshire 03079. 1981- (Periodic Supplements).

NEBRASKA LEGAL FORMS--PERSONAL INJURY. John J, Higgins. Butterworth Legal Publishers, 90 Stiles Road, Salem, New Hampshire 03079. 1981- . (Periodic Supplements).

NEBRASKA LEGAL FORMS--RESIDENTIAL REAL ESTATE. Norman Wright. Butterworth Legal Publishers, 90 Stiles Road, Salem, New Hampshire 03079. 1982- . (Periodic Supplements).

NEBRASKA LEGAL FORMS--WORKMEN'S COMPENSATION. Michael Carvel. Butterworth Legal Publishers, 90 Stiles Road, Salem, New Hampshire 03079. 1981- . (Periodic Supplements).

NEBRASKA LEGAL RESEARCH AND REFERENCE MANUAL. Paul F. Hill. Butterworth Legal Publishers, 90 Stiles Road, Salem, New Hampshire 03079. 1983.

NEBRASKA PRACTICE METHODS AND FORMS. W. Moore. West Publishing Company, 50 West Kellogg Boulevard, St. Paul, Minnesota 55164. 1969- . (Periodic Supplements).

NEBRASKA UNIFORM COMMERCIAL CODE FORMS. W. Moore. West Publishing Company, 50 West Kellogg Boulevard, St. Paul, Minnesota 55164. 1965- . (Periodic Supplements).

ATTORNEY GENERAL OPINIONS

REPORT OF THE ATTORNEY GENERAL OF THE STATE OF NEBRASKA FOR THE (NUMBER) LEGISLATURE. Office of the Attorney General, Room 2115, State Capitol, Lincoln, Nebraska 68509. 1878- . (Also available on Westlaw: 1977- .)

ETHICS OPINIONS, CODES, RULES

NEBRASKA LAWYER'S DESK BOOK. Advisory Committee of the Nebraska State Bar Association, 635 South 14th Street, Lincoln, Nebraska 68508. (Includes Code of Professional Responsibility, Disciplinary Rules, and Ethics Opinions). For further information concerning these opinions, contact the Counsel for Discipline, Nebraska State Bar Association, P.O. Box 81809, Lincoln, Nebraska 68501. (402-475-7091).

COURT RULES

NEBRASKA RULES OF COURT. West Publishing Company, P.O. Box 64526, 50 West Kellogg Boulevard, St. Paul, Minnesota 55164-0526. (Annual).

REVISED RULES OF THE SUPREME COURT OF NEBRASKA. Clerk of the Supreme Court, Supreme Court Building, Room 2413, Lincoln, Nebraska 68509.

JURY INSTRUCTIONS

NEBRASKA JURY INSTRUCTIONS (Civil and Criminal). Nebraska Supreme Court, Committee on Pattern Jury Instructions. West Publishing Company, P.O. Box 64526, 50 West Kellogg Boulevard, St. Paul, Minnesota 55164-0526. 1969- .

DIGESTS, INDEXES, ABSTRACTS, CITATORS

NEBRASKA DIGEST. West Publishing Company, P.O. Box 64526, 50 West Kellogg Boulevard, St. Paul, Minnesota 55164-0526. 1855- . (Annual Supplements).

NORTHWESTERN DIGEST. (First and Second Series). West Publishing Company, P.O. Box 64526, 50 West Kellogg Boulevard, St. Paul, Minnesota 55164-0526. 1944- . (Annual Supplements).

SHEPARD'S NEBRASKA CITATIONS. Shepard's/McGraw-Hill, P.O. Box 1235, Colorado Springs, Colorado 80901. (Quarterly Supplements).

SHEPARD'S NORTHWESTERN REPORTER CITATIONS. Shepard's/McGraw-Hill, P.O. Box 1235, Colorado Springs, Colorado 80901. (Monthly Supplements).

LAW REVIEWS AND PERIODICALS

CREIGHTON LAW REVIEW. Creighton University School of Law, 2200 California Street, Omaha, Nebraska 68178. (Quarterly).

NEBRASKA LAW REVIEW. University of Nebraska College of Law, East Campus, Lincoln, Nebraska 68583-0903. (Quarterly).

NEWSLETTER AND NEWSPAPERS

LEGISLATIVE REPORT. Nebraska Chamber of Commerce and Industry, P.O. Box 95128, Lincoln, Nebraska 68509. Weekly when in session.

NSBA NEWS. Nebraska State Bar Assocation, P.O. Box 81809, Lincoln, Nebraska 68501. Bimonthly.

ASSOCIATIONS AND PROFESSIONAL SOCIETIES

NEBRASKA STATE BAR ASSOCIATION, 635 South Fourteenth Street, Lincoln, Nebraska 68508. (402) 475-7091.

OMAHA BAR ASSOCIATION, 2133 California, Omaha, Nebraska 68178.

DIRECTORIES

DIRECTORY OF MEMBERSHIP COMMITTEES AND EMPLOYEES OF THE NEBRASKA LEGISLATURE. Clerk of the Nebraska Legislature, State Capitol, Lincoln, Nebraska 68509. (Annual).

GUIDE TO NEBRASKA STATE AGENCIES. Nebraska Publications Clearinghouse, 1420 P Street, Lincoln, Nebraska 68508. 1985. (Irregular).

NEBRASKA BLUE BOOK. Nebraska Legislative Council, Box 94814, State House Station, Lincoln, Nebraska 68509. 1984. (Triennial).

NEBRASKA DIRECTORY OF MUNICIPAL OFFICIALS. League of Nebraska Municipalities, 1335 L Street, Lincoln, Nebraska 68508. (Annual).

NEBRASKA LEGAL DIRECTORY. Legal Directories Publishing Company, 2122 Kidwell Street, P.O. Box 140200, Dallas, Texas 75214-0200. (Annual).

NEBRASKA STATE GOVERNMENT DIRECTORY. Division of Communications, Nebraska Department of Administration Services, 1800 North 33rd Street, Lincoln, Nebraska 68501. (Annual).

STATES--NEVADA

STATUTES, CODES, STANDARDS, UNIFORM LAWS

NEVADA ADMINISTRATIVE CODE. Legislative Counsel Bureau, 401 South Carson Street, Carson City, Nevada 89710.

NEVADA REVISED STATUTES (Official Edition). Legislative Counsel Bureau, 401 South Carson Street, Carson City, Nevada 89710. 1957- . (As of 1987 the official edition will be annotated).

NEVADA REVISED STATUTES ANNOTATED. Michie Company, P.O. Box 7587, Charlottesville, Virginia 22906-7587. 1986- . (Annual Supplements).

STATUTES OF NEVADA. Legislative Counsel Bureau, 401 South Carson Street, Carson City, Nevada 89710.

LOOSELEAF SERVICES AND REPORTERS

NEVADA REPORTS. Legislative Counsel Bureau, 401 South Carson Street, Carson City, Nevada 89710. 1865- .

NEVADA TAX REPORTER. Commerce Clearing House, Incorporated, 4025 West Peterson Avenue, Chicago, Illinois 60646. 1982- .

PACIFIC REPORTER. (First and Second Series). West Publishing Company, P.O. Box 64526, 50 West Kellogg Boulevard, St. Paul, Minnesota 55164-0526. 1882- .

STATES--NEVADA

ATTORNEY GENERAL OPINIONS

OFFICIAL OPINIONS OF THE ATTORNEY GENERAL. Office of the Attorney General, State Printing Office, Capitol Complex, Carson City, Nevada 89710. (Also available on Lexis: January 1977-; Westlaw: 1977- .)

ETHICS OPINIONS, CODES, RULES

Nevada Ethics Opinions are issued by the Committee on Ethics and Professional Responsibiltity of the State Bar of Nevada. Some opinions are published in Inter-Alia (Bar Journal). Abstracts are published in ABA/BNA Lawyers' Manual on Professional Conduct. For further information concerning these opinions, contact the State Bar of Nevada, 603 East Bridger, Las Vegas, Nevada 89101. (702-382-0502.)

COURT RULES

NEVADA CIVIL RULES HANDBOOK. State Bar of Nevada, 603 East Bridger, Las Vegas, Nevada 89101. (Annual).

NEVADA COURT RULES ANNOTATED. Michie Company, P.O. Box 7587, Charlottesville, Virginia 22906-7587. (Annual). (Also published in the first volume of the Nevada Revised Statutes).

JURY INSTRUCTIONS

NEVADA PATTERN CIVIL JURY INSTRUCTIONS. State Bar of Nevada, 603 East Bridger, Las Vegas, Nevada 89101. 1966- . (Biennial Supplements).

NEVADA PATTERN JURY INSTRUCTIONS. Michie Company, P.O. Box 7587, Chalottesville, Virginia 22906-7587. 1986- .

DIGESTS, INDEXES, ABSTRACTS, CITATORS

NEVADA DIGEST. Legislative Counsel, State of Nevada, Carson City, Nevada. 1977- . (Looseleaf). (New edition expected in 1988).

PACIFIC DIGEST. (1st and 2nd series). West Publishing Company, P.O. Box 64526, 50 West Kellogg Boulevard, St. Paul, Minnesota 55164-0526. (Annual Supplements).

SHEPARD'S NEVADA CITATIONS. Shepard's/McGraw-Hill, P.O. Box 1235, Colorado Springs, Colorado 80901. (Quarterly Supplements).

SHEPARD'S PACIFIC REPORTER CITATIONS. Shepard's/McGraw-Hill, P.O. Box 1235, Colorado Springs, Colorado 80901. (Monthly Supplements).

LAW REVIEWS AND PERIODICALS

INTER ALIA. State Bar of Nevada, 603 East Bridger, Las Vegas, Nevada 89101. (Bimonthly).

PRACTICE MATERIALS

NEVADA CIVIL PRACTICE MANUAL. State Bar of Nevada. Michie Company, P.O. Box 7587, Charlottesville, Virginia 22906-7587. 1986- .

Encyclopedia of Legal Information Sources • 2nd Ed.

BAR ASSOCIATIONS

BAR ASSOCIATION OF NEVADA. 295 Holcomb Avenue, Suite 2, Reno, Nevada 89502. (702) 329-4100.

CLARK COUNTY BAR ASSOCIATION, P.O. Box 657, Las Vegas, Nevada 89125. (702) 387-6011.

STATE BAR OF NEVADA, 603 East Bridger, Las Vegas, Nevada 89101. (702) 382-2200.

WASHOE COUNTY BAR ASSOCIATION, P.O. Box 1548, Reno, Nevada 89505. (702) 323-7631.

DIRECTORIES

CALIFORNIA AND NEVADA LSC LEGAL SERVICES PROGRAMS DIRECTORY. Western Center on Law and Poverty, 3535 West Sixth Street, Los Angeles, California 90020. (Annual).

LEGISLATIVE MANUAL-STATE OF NEVADA. Nevada Legislative Council Bureau, Legislative Building, Carson City, Nevada 89710. (Biennial).

ROSTER OF PUBLIC OFFICIALS OF THE STATE OF NEVADA. Research Division, Legislative Council Bureau, Legislative Building, Carson City, Nevada 89710. (Biennial).

STATES--NEW HAMPSHIRE

STATUTES, CODES, STANDARDS, UNIFORM LAWS

NEW HAMPSHIRE CODE OF ADMINISTRATIVE RULES ANNOTATED. Equity Publishing Corporation, Rural Route Number 1, Box 3, Orford, New Hampshire 03777. 1984- .

NEW HAMPSHIRE REVISED STATUTES ANNOTATED. Equity Publishing Corporation, Rural Route Number 1, Box 3, Orford, New Hampshire 03777. 1955- . (Annual Supplements).

NEW HAMPSHIRE RULEMAKING REGISTER. Office of Legislative Services, Administrative Rules Division, Room 115, State House, Concord, New Hampshire 03301. 1980- .

SESSION LAWS OF THE STATE OF NEW HAMPSHIRE. Director of Legislative Services, State House, Concord, New Hampshire 03301.

LOOSELEAF SERVICES AND REPORTERS

ATLANTIC REPORTER. (First and Second Series). West Publishing Company, P.O. Box 64526, 50 West Kellogg Boulevard, St. Paul, Minnesota 55164-0526. 1886- .

NEW HAMPSHIRE REPORTS. Equity Publishing Corporation, Rural Route Number 1, Box 3, Orford, New Hampshire 03777. 1816- .

ATTORNEY GENERAL OPINIONS

Attorney General Opinions are not published but are filed in the New Hampshire State Law Library. (Available on Lexis: January 1977-; Westlaw: 1977- .)

ETHICS OPINIONS, CODES, RULES

Full text of formal ethics opinions are issued by the New Hampshire State Bar Association and are published in the New Hampshire Law Weekly. Abstracts of both formal and informal opinions are published in the ABA/BNA Lawyers' Manual on Professional Conduct. For further information concerning these opinions, contact the New Hampshire State Bar Association, 18 Centre Street, Concord, New Hampshire 03301. (603-224-6942).

NEW HAMPSHIRE LAW WEEKLY. New Hampshire Bar Association, 18 Centre Street, Concord, New Hampshire 03301. 1980- . (Weekly). (Publishes full text of Formal Ethics Opinions.)

NEW HAMPSHIRE SUPREME COURT RULES. New Hampshire Bar Association, 18 Centre Street, Concord, New Hampshire 03301. 1986. (Includes Rules of Professional Conduct).

COURT RULES

NEW HAMPSHIRE COURT RULES ANNOTATED. Equity Publishing Corporation, Rural Route Number 1, Box 3, Orford, New Hampshire 03777. 1985- . (Two volume looseleaf). (Includes Rules of Professional Conduct).

JURY INSTRUCTIONS

NEW HAMPSHIRE CIVIL JURY INSTRUCTIONS (TENTATIVE DRAFT). New Hampshire Bar Association, 18 Centre Street, Concord, New Hampshire 03301. (January 1, 1987).

NEW HAMPSHIRE CRIMINAL JURY INSTRUCTIONS. New Hampshire Bar Association, 18 Centre Street, Concord, New Hampshire 03301. 1983- . (Periodic Supplements).

DIGESTS, INDEXES, ABSTRACTS, CITATORS

ATLANTIC DIGEST. (First and Second Series). West Publishing Company, P.O. Box 64526, 50 West Kellogg Boulevard, St. Paul, Minnesota 55164-0526. 1949- . (Annual Supplements).

NEW HAMPSHIRE DIGEST. West Publishing Company, P.O. Box 64526, 50 West Kellogg Boulevard, St. Paul, Minnesota 55164-0526. 1951- . (Annual Supplements).

SHEPARD'S ATLANTIC REPORTER CITATIONS. Shepard's/McGraw-Hill, P.O. Box 1235, Colorado Springs, Colorado 80901. (Monthly Supplements).

SHEPARD'S NEW HAMPSHIRE CITATIONS. Shepard's/McGraw-Hill, P.O. Box 1235, Colorado Springs, Colorado 80901. (Quarterly Supplements).

LAW REVIEWS AND PERIODICALS

NEW HAMPSHIRE BAR JOURNAL. New Hampshire Bar Association, 18 Centre Street, Concord, New Hampshire 03301. (Quarterly).

NEW HAMPSHIRE LAW WEEKLY. New Hampshire State Bar Association, 18 Centre Street, Concord, New Hampshire 03301.

NEWSLETTERS AND NEWSPAPERS

INDEX TO RECENT NEW HAMPSHIRE CASES. Douglas H. Adamson, P.O. Box 41, First New Hampshire Bank Building, Franklin, New Hampshire 03235. Monthly.

NEW HAMPSHIRE SUPREME COURT REPORTER. Hale Ridge Publishing, P.O. Box 370, Windham, New Hampshire, 03087. Irregular.

PRACTICE MATERIALS

ADMINISTRATIVE LAW. New Hampshire Bar Association, Continuing Legal Education, 18 Centre Street, Concord, New Hampshire 03301. 1983.

ADVANCED ESTATE PLANNING. New Hampshire Bar Association, Continuing Legal Education, 18 Centre Street, Concord, New Hampshire 03301. 1980.

APPELLATE ADVOCACY. New Hampshire Bar Association, Continuing Legal Education, 18 Centre Street, Concord, New Hampshire 03301. 1985.

CIVIL PRACTICE AND PROCEDURE. Richard Wiebusch. Equity Publishing Corporation, Rural Route Number 1, Box 3, Orford, New Hampshire 03777. 1984- .

CRIMINAL PRACTICE. New Hampshire Bar Association, Continuing Legal Education, 18 Centre Street, Concord, New Hampshire 03301. 1983.

FUNDAMENTALS OF PROBATE ADMINISTRATION. New Hampshire Bar Association, 18 Centre Street, Concord, New Hampshire 03301. 1986.

THE LAW OF WORKERS' COMPENSATION. New Hampshire Bar Association, Continuing Legal Education. Michie/Bobbs-Merrill Law Publishing Company, P.O. Box 7587, Charlottesville, Virginia 22906-7587. 1985.

NEW HAMPSHIRE DISTRICT COURT PROCEDURE. New Hampshire Bar Association, 18 Centre Street, Concord, New Hampshire 03301. 1985.

NEW HAMPSHIRE PRACTICE. Equity Publishing Corporation, Rural Route Number 1, Box 3, Orford, New Hampshire 03777. 1980- . (Periodic Supplements).

NEW HAMPSHIRE PRACTICE AND PROCEDURE HANDBOOK. New Hampshire Bar Association, 18 Centre Street, Concord, New Hampshire 03301. 1985.

PERSONAL INJURY PRACTICE. New Hampshire Bar Association, Continuing Legal Education, 18 Centre Street, Concord, New Hampshire 03301. 1989.

PRODUCTS LIABILITY PRACTICE. New Hampshire Bar Association, Continuing Legal Education, 18 Centre Street, Concord, New Hampshire 03301. 1985.

TORT LIABILITY. New Hampshire Bar Association, Continuing Legal Education, 18 Centre Street, Concord, New Hampshire 03301. 1981.

TRUSTS FOR THE YOUNG AND THE ELDERLY. New Hampshire Bar Association, Continuing Legal Education, 18 Centre Street, Concord, New Hampshire 03301. 1985.

STATES--NEW HAMPSHIRE

ASSOCIATIONS AND PROFESSIONAL SOCIETIES

NEW HAMPSHIRE BAR ASSOCIATION, 18 Centre Street, Concord, New Hampshire 03301. (603) 224-6942

DIRECTORIES

DIRECTORY OF MUNICIPAL OFFICIALS (NEW HAMPSHIRE). New Hampshire Municipal Association, 105 Loudon Road, Concord, New Hampshire 03301. (Annual).

MANUAL FOR THE USE OF THE GENERAL COURT OF NEW HAMPSHIRE (THE BLACK BOOK). New Hampshire General Court, State House, Room 317, Concord, New Hampshire 03301. (Biennial).

NEW HAMPSHIRE REGISTER. Tower Publishing Company, 34 Diamond Street, P.O. Box 7220, Portland, Maine 04112. (Annual).

STATE OF NEW HAMPSHIRE MANUAL FOR THE GENERAL COURT (THE RED BOOK). New Hampshire Secretary of State, State House, Room 204, Concord, New Hampshire 03301. (Biennial).

STATES--NEW JERSEY

STATUTES, CODES, STANDARDS, UNIFORM LAWS

LAWS OF NEW JERSEY. State of New Jersey, Leagal Documents Distribution Center, Room 35, Basement, State House Annex, CN068, Trenton, New Jersey 08625.

NEW JERSEY ADMINISTRATIVE CODE. Administrative Publications, Office of Administrative Law, CN 301, Trenton, New Jersey 08625. 1982- .

NEW JERSEY REGISTER. Administrative Publications, Office of Administrative Law, CN 301, Trenton, New Jersey 08625. 1969- . (Biweekly).

NEW JERSEY STATUTES ANNOTATED. West Publishing Company, P.O. Box 64526, 50 West Kellogg Boulevard, St. Paul, Minnesota 55164-0526. 1938- . (Annual Supplements).

LOOSELEAF SERVICES AND REPORTERS

ATLANTIC REPORTER. (First and Second Series). West Publishing Company, P.O. Box 64526, 50 West Kellogg Boulevard, St. Paul, Minnesota 55164-0526. 1885- .

NEW JERSEY EQUITY REPORTS. State of New Jersey. Soney and Sage, Newark, New Jersey 1830-1948. (Publisher varies).

NEW JERSEY LAW REPORTS. State of New Jersey. 1790-1948. (New Jersey Supreme Court and Superior Court). Available on microfilm from Oceana/Trans Media.

NEW JERSEY MISCELLANEOUS REPORTS (Unofficial). Soney and Sage Publishers, Newark, New Jersey. Available on microfilm from Oceana/Trans Media. 1923-1949. (Reported unpublished decisions).

Encyclopedia of Legal Information Sources • 2nd Ed.

NEW JERSEY REPORTS. West Publishing Company, P.O. Box 64526, 50 West Kellogg Boulevard, St. Paul, Minnesota 55164-0526. 1948- .

NEW JERSEY SUPERIOR COURT REPORTS. West Publishing Company, P.O. Box 64526, 50 West Kellogg Boulevard, St. Paul, Minnesota 55164-0526. 1948- .

NEW JERSEY TAX COURT REPORTS. West Publishing Company, P.O. Box 64526, 50 West Kellogg Boulevard, St. Paul, Minnesota 55164-0526. 1979- .

HANDBOOKS, MANUALS, FORMBOOKS

A GUIDE TO NEW JERSEY LEGAL BIBLIOGRAPHIES AND LEGAL HISTORY. Cameron Allen. Fred B. Rothman and Company, 10368 West Centennial Road, Littleton, Colorado 80127. 1984.

NEW JERSEY FORMS: LEGAL AND BUSINESS. Lawyers Co-Operative Company, Aqueduct Building, Rochester, New York 14694. 1975- . (Annual Supplements).

NEW JERSEY LAW WITH FORMS. Matthew Bender and Company, Incorporated, 11 Penn Plaza, New York, New York 10001. 1948- .

NEW JERSEY LEGAL RESEARCH HANDBOOK. Paul Axel-Lute. New Jersey Institute for Continuing Legal Education, 15 Washington Street, Newark, New Jersey 07102. 1984.

NEW JERSEY LEGAL SECRETARY'S HANDBOOK. Revised edition. New Jersey Association of Legal Secretaries, Michie/Bobbs-Merrill Law Publishing Company, P.O. Box 7587, Charlottesville, Virginia 22906-7587. 1984- . (Periodic Supplements).

NEW JERSEY PRACTICE FORMS. Martin Blacker. West Publishing Company, 50 West Kellogg Boulevard, St. Paul, Minnesota 55164. 1980.

WEST'S NEW JERSEY DIGEST 2D LAW FINDER. West Publishing Company, P.O. Box 64526, 50 West Kellogg Boulevard, St. Paul, Minnesota 55164-0526. (Annual).

ATTORNEY GENERAL OPINIONS

FORMAL OPINIONS OF THE ATTORNEY GENERAL OF NEW JERSEY. Office of the Attorney General. Compiled by the Attorney General's Library, Hughes Justice Complex, 6th Floor, Trenton, New Jersey 08625. 1949- . (No subscriptions available. Last bound volume is 1978-1984). (Available on Lexis: January 1977-; Westlaw: 1977- .)

ETHICS OPINIONS, CODES, AND RULES

OPINIONS OF THE NEW JERSEY SUPREME COURT ADVISORY COMMITTEE ON PROFESSIONAL ETHICS. New Jersey Institute for Continuing Legal Education, 15 Washington Street, Newark, New Jersey 07102-3105. 1983- .

COURT RULES

NEW JERSEY COURT RULES ANNOTATED. Third Edition. West Publishing Company, 50 West Kellogg Boulevard, St. Paul, Minnesota 55164. 1971. (Annual Supplements).

RULES GOVERNING THE COURTS OF THE STATE OF NEW JERSEY. West Publishing Company, P.O. Box 64526, 50 West Kellogg Boulevard, St. Paul, Minnesota 55164-0526. (Annual).

RULES GOVERNING THE COURTS OF THE STATE OF NEW JERSEY, WITH CORRECTIONS AND ANNOTATIONS. Sylvia B. Pressler. Gann Law Books, 1180 Raymond Boulevard, Newark, New Jersey 07102. (Annual). (Also published in looseleaf edition).

JURY INSTRUCTIONS

MODEL JURY CHARGES-CIVIL. Second Edition. New Jersey Supreme Court, Committee on Model Jury Charges, New Jersey State Bar Association and New Jersey Institute for Continuing Legal Education, 15 Washington Street, Newark, New Jersey 07102-3105. 1983- .

MODEL JURY CHARGES-CRIMINAL. Second Edition. New Jersey Supreme Court, Committee on Model Jury Charges, New Jersey State Bar Association and New Jersey Institute for Continuing Legal Education, 15 Washington Street, Newark, New Jersey 07102-3105. 1983- .

DIGESTS, INDEXES, ABSTRACTS, CITATORS

ATLANTIC DIGEST. (First and Second Series). West Publishing Company, P.O. Box 64526, 50 West Kellogg Boulevard, St. Paul, Minnesota 55164-0526. 1949- . (Annual Supplements).

NEW JERSEY DIGEST. (First and Second Series). West Publishing Company, P.O. Box 64526, 50 West Kellogg Boulevard, St. Paul, Minnesota 55164-0526. 1954- . (Annual Supplements).

SHEPARD'S ATLANTIC REPORTER CITATIONS. Shepard's/McGraw-Hill, P.O. Box 1235, Colorado Springs, Colorado 80901. (Monthly Supplements).

SHEPARD'S NEW JERSEY CITATIONS. Shepard's/McGraw-Hill, P.O. Box 1235, Colorado Springs, Colorado 80901. (Eight pamphlets per year).

LAW REVIEWS AND PERIODICALS

ADVOCATE. New Jersey State Bar, 172 West State Street, Trenton, New Jersey 08608. (Monthly).

NEW JERSEY LAWYER. New Jersey State Bar, 172 West State Street, Trenton, New Jersey 08608. (Quarterly).

RUTGERS COMPUTER AND TECHNOLOGY LAW JOURNAL. Rutgers Law School, 15 Washington Street, Newark, New Jersey 07102. (Biannual).

RUTGERS LAW JOURNAL. Rutgers School of Law--Camden, Fifth and Pennsylvania Streets, Camden, New Jersey 08102. (Quarterly).

RUTGERS LAW REVIEW. Rutgers University School of Law, 15 Washington Street, Newark, New Jersey 07102. (Quarterly).

NEWSLETTERS AND NEWSPAPERS

CASINO LAW SECTION NEWSLETTER. New Jersey State Bar Association, One Constitution Square, New Brunswick, New Jersey 08901. Semiannually.

THE GP GAZETTE. New Jersey State Bar Association, One Constitution Square, New Brunswick, New Jersey 08901. Quarterly.

NEW JERSEY EDUCATION LAW REPORT. Whittaker Newsletters, 313 South Avenue, Fanwood, New Jersey 07023. Monthly.

NEW JERSEY FAMILY LAWYER. New Jersey State Bar Association, One Constitution Square, New Brunswick, New Jersey 08901. Bimonthly.

NEW JERSEY JOURNAL OF ENVIRONMENTAL LITIGATION. McGuire Publications, 219-P Berlin Road, Cherry Hill, New Jersey 08034. Semimonthly.

NEW JERSEY JURY VERDICTS REVIEW AND ANALYSIS. Jury Verdicts Review Publications, Incorporated, 24 Commerce Street, Suite 1722, Newark, New Jersey 07102. Monthly.

NEW JERSEY LAW JOURNAL. American Lawyer Newspaper Group, 238 Mulberry Street, P.O. Box 20081, Newark, New Jersey 07101-6081. (Weekly).

NEW JERSEY LEGISLATIVE NEWS. New Jersey Ligislative News, P.O. Box 412, Trenton, New Jersey 08603. Daily when in session.

PRACTICE MATERIALS

ALTERNATIVE ADJUDICATION: AN EVALUATION OF THE NEW JERSEY AUTOMOBILE ARBITRATION PROGRAM. Rard Corporation, 2100 M Street, Northwest, Washington, D.C. 20037. 1988.

CRIMINAL LAWS OF NEW JERSEY. Third Edition. Frank G. Schlosser. Lawyers Co-Operative Company, Aqueduct Building, Rochester, New York 14694. 1970- . (Periodic Supplements).

NEW JERSEY ABSTRACTS AND TITLES. Third Edition. M. Liegerman. West Publishing Company, 50 West Kellogg Boulevard, St. Paul, Minnesota 55164. 1966.

NEW JERSEY CLOSE CORPORATIONS. Robert A. Kessler. Callaghan and Company, 155 Pfingsten Road, Deerfield, Illinois 60015. 1970- . (Annual Supplements).

NEW JERSEY CRIMINAL PRACTICE AND PROCEDURE. Second Edition. West Publishing Company, 50 West Kellogg Boulevard, St. Paul, Minnesota 55164. 1980.

NEW JERSEY MARRIAGE, DIVORCE, AND SEPERATION. P. Silverman. West Publishing Company, 50 West Kellogg Boulevard, St. Paul, Minnesota 55164. 1963.

NEW JERSEY PRACTICE. West Publishing Company, P.O. Box 64526, 50 West Kellogg Boulevard, St. Paul, Minnesota 55164-0526. 1949- . (Periodic Supplements). (Publisher varies).

NEW JERSEY WILLS AND ADMINISTRATION. Third Edition. A. Clapp. West Publishing Company, 50 West Kellogg Boulevard, St. Paul, Minnesota 55164. 1984.

TRIAL HANDBOOK FOR NEW JERSEY LAWYERS. J. Freeman. Lawyers Cooperative Publishing Company, Aqueduct Building, Rochester, New York 14694. 1972.

ASSOCIATIONS AND PROFESSIONAL SOCIETIES

BERGEN COUNTY BAR ASSOCIATION, 61 Hudson Street, Hackensack, New Jersey 07601.

CAMDEN COUNTY BAR ASSOCIATION, Heritage Bank Building, Broadway and Cooper Streets, P.O. Box 1027, Camden, New Jersey 08101.

ESSEX COUNTY BAR ASSOCIATION, Gateway One, Sixteenth Floor, Newark, New Jersey 07102. (201) 622-6207.

HUDSON COUNTY BAR ASSOCIATION, 285 Magnolia Avenue, Jersey City, New Jersey 07306.

MERCER COUNTY BAR ASSOCIATION, Mercer County Court House, P.O. Box 8068, Trenton, New Jersey 08650.

MIDDLESEX COUNTY BAR ASSOCIATION, Court House, Second Floor, John F. Kennedy Square, New Brunswick, New Jersey 08901.

MONMOUTH BAR ASSOCIATION, Court House, Freehold, New Jersey 07728.

MORRIS COUNTY BAR ASSOCIATION, 10 Park Place, Room 306, Morristown, New Jersey 07960.

NEW JERSEY BAR ASSOCIATION, 1 Constitution Square, New Brunswick, New Jersey 08901. (201) 249-5000.

OCEAN COUNTY BAR ASSOCIATION, Ocean County Courthouse, P.O. Box 381, Toms River, New Jersey 08753.

PASSAIC COUNTY BAR ASSOCIATION, Court House, Hamilton Street, Patterson, New Jersey 07505.

DIRECTORIES

FOREIGN LANGUAGES DIRECTORY (NEW JERSEY ATTORNEYS). New Jersey Bar Association, 172 West State Street, Trenton, New Jersey 08608. (Biennial).

LAWYER'S DIARY AND MANUAL INCLUDING BAR DIRECTORY OF NEW JERSEY. Lawyer's Diary, P.O. Box 1214, Newark, New Jersey 07101-11214. (Annual).

LEGISLATORS AND GOVERNMENT OFFICIALS IN THE TRI-STATE AREA. Greater Philadelphia Chamber of Commerce, Broad and Chestnut Streets, Philadelphia, Pennsylvania 19107. (Biennial).

MANUAL FOR THE LEGISLATURE OF NEW JERSEY (FITZGERALD'S). Edward J. Mullin, Box 2150, Trenton, New Jersey 08608. (Annual).

NEW JERSEY LEAGUE OF MUNICIPALITIES DIRECTORY. New Jersey State League of Municipalities, 407 West State Street, Trenton, New Jersey 08618. (Annual).

NEW JERSEY LEGISLATURE: ROSTER OF MEMBERS. Office of Legislative Services, Public Information Unit, State House Annex, CN-068, Trenton, New Jersey 08625. (Biennial with Irregular Updates).

OFFICIAL DIRECTORY OF THE STATE OF NEW JERSEY. New Jersey Department of State, State House, CN-300, Trenton, New Jersey 08625. (Annual).

STATES--NEW MEXICO

STATUTES, CODES, STANDARDS, UNIFORM LAWS

LAWS OF NEW MEXICO. State Compilation Committee. Michie Company, P.O. Box 7587, Charlottesville, Virginia 22906-7587. 1912- . Annual.

NEW MEXICO ADVANCE ANNOTATION AND RULES SERVICE. Michie Company, P.O. Box 7587, Charlottesville, Virginia 22906-7587. 1985- . (Three pamphlets per year).

NEW MEXICO STATUTES ANNOTATED. Michie Company, P.O. Box 7587, Charlottesville, Virginia 22906-7587. 1978- . (Annual Supplements).

No New Mexico Administrative Code or Register is published. Administrative Regulations can be obtained by contacting the appropriate state agency.

LOOSELEAF SERVICES AND REPORTERS

NEW MEXICO REPORTS. West Publishing Company, P.O. Box 64526, 50 West Kellogg Boulevard, St. Paul, Minnesota 55164-0526. 1852- . (New Mexico Supreme Court and Court of Appeals). (Published by West since 1933).

NEW MEXICO TAX REPORTER. Commerce Clearing House, Incorporated, 4025 West Peterson Avenue, Chicago, Illinois 60646. 1981- .

PACIFIC REPORTER. (First and Second Series). West Publishing Company, P.O. Box 64526, 50 West Kellogg Boulevard, St. Paul, Minnesota 55164-0526. 1883- . (New Mexico Supreme Court and Court of Appeals).

ATTORNEY GENERAL OPINIONS

REPORT OF THE ATTORNEY GENERAL OF NEW MEXICO. Microfiche. Office of the Attorney General, Department of Justice, State Capitok, Santa Fe, New Mexico 87503. Lexis: January 1977-; Westlaw, 1977- .

ETHICS OPINIONS, CODES, RULES

ADVISORY OPINIONS. Issued by the State Bar of New Mexico Advisory Opinions Committee, State Bar of New Mexico, P.O. Box 25883, Albuquerque, New Mexico 87125. 1983- . (Some opinions are published in the BAR BULLETIN. Abstracts are published in the ABN/BNA *Lawyers' Manual on Professional Conduct.* For further information concerning these opinions, contact the State Bar of New Mexico, P.O. Box 25883, Albuquerque, New Mexico 87125. (505) 842-5781.

Encyclopedia of Legal Information Sources • 2nd Ed.   STATES--NEW MEXICO

CODE OF JUDICIAL CONDUCT. Published in the *New Mexico Statutes Annotated*, Volume 2, Chapter 15 of the Judicial Volumes. 1985- . (Annual Supplements).

Code of Professional Responsibility and the Disciplinary Rules are published in *New Mexico Statutes Annotated* volume two (Judicial).

COURT RULES

NEW MEXICO ADVANCE ANNOTATION AND RULES SERVICE. Michie/Bobbs-Merrill Law Publishing Company, P.O. Box 7587, Charlottesville, Virginia 22906-7587. (Three Pamphlets per Year).

NEW MEXICO COURT RULES. West Publishing Company, P.O. Box 64526, 50 West Kellogg Boulevard, St. Paul, Minnesota 55164-0526. (Annual).

NEW MEXICO LOCAL AND FEDERAL RULES HANDBOOK. Institute of Public Law. Butterworth Legal Publishers, 90 Stiles Road, Salem, New Hampshire 03079. 1978- . (Periodic Supplements).

JURY INSTRUCTIONS

NEW MEXICO UNIFORM JURY INSTRUCTIONS CIVIL. West Publishing Company, 50 West Kellogg Boulevard, St. Paul, Minnesota 55164. 1966- .

NEW MEXICO UNIFORM JURY INSTRUCTIONS--CRIMINAL. Published in New Mexico Statutes Annotated, Pamphlet: Judicial 19. Michie Company, P.O. Box 7587, Charlottesville, Virginia 22906-7587. 1982- . (Annual Supplements).

UNIFORM JURY INSTRUCTIONS--CIVIL. New Mexico Supreme Court, Uniform Jury Instructions Civil Committee. Michie/Bobbs-Merrill Law Publishing Company, P.O. Box 7587, Charlottesville, Virginia 22906-7587. 1980- . (Periodic Supplements).

DIGESTS, INDEXES, ABSTRACTS, CITATORS

NEW MEXICO DIGEST. West Publishing Company, P.O. Box 64526, 50 West Kellogg Boulevard, St. Paul, Minnesota 55164-0526. 1948- . 1932- . (Annual Supplements).

PACIFIC DIGEST. (First and Second Series). West Publishing Company, P.O. Box 64526, 50 West Kellogg Boulevard, St. Paul, Minnesota 55164-0526. (Annual Supplements).

SHEPARD'S NEW MEXICO CITATIONS. Shepard's/McGraw-Hill, P.O. Box 1235, Colorado Springs, Colorado 80901. (Three supplements a year).

SHEPARD'S PACIFIC REPORTER CITATIONS. Shepard's/McGraw-Hill, P.O. Box 1235, Colorado Springs, Colorado 80901. (Monthly Supplements).

LAW REVIEWS AND PERIODICALS

NEW MEXICO LAW REVIEW. University of New Mexico School of Law, 1117 Stanford Drive, Northeast, Albuquerque, New Mexico 87131. (Three issues per year).

STATE BAR OF NEW MEXICO BULLETIN and ADVANCE OPINIONS. State Bar of New Mexico, P.O. Box 25883, Albuquerque, New Mexico 87125. (Weekly). Formerly NEWS AND VIEWS.

NEWSLETTERS AND NEWSPAPERS

MILLS CAPITOL OBSERVER. Mills Capitol Observer, P.O. Box 5141, Santa Fe, New Mexico 87502. Weekly.

NEW MEXICO REAL ESTATE LAW REPORTER. Butterworth Legal Publishers, 90 Stiles Road, Salem, New Hampshire 03079.

STATE BAR OF NEW MEXICO--BAR BULLETIN. State Bar of New Mexico, P.O. Box 25883, Albuquerque, New Mexico 87125.

FORMBOOKS

LITIGATION SERIES. New Mexico Trial Lawyers' Association, P.O. Box 301, Albuquerque, New Mexico 87103. 1985- . (Periodic Supplements).

PRACTICE MATERIALS

NEW MEXICO APPELLATE PRACTICE MANUAL. Mark B. Thompson. Butterworth Legal Publishers, 90 Stiles Road, Salem, New Hampshire 03079. 1978- . (Periodic Supplements).

NEW MEXICO COLLECTIONS MANUAL. Marion Matthews. Butterworth Legal Publishers, 90 Stiles Road, Salem, New Hampshire 03079. 1980- . (Periodic Supplements).

NEW MEXICO DIVORCE MANUAL. David H. Kelsey, et al. Butterworth Legal Publishers, 90 Stiles Road, Salem, New Hampshire 03079. 1978- . (Periodic Supplements).

NEW MEXICO DOMESTIC RELATIONS MANUAL; DIVORCE SYSTEM. B. Shapiro. State Bar of New Mexico, 1117 Stamford, Northeast, Albuqueque, New Mexico 87130.

NEW MEXICO ESTATE ADMINISTRATION SYSTEM. R. Ramo. State Bar of New Mexico, 1117 Stamford, Northeast, Albuqueque, New Mexico 87130. 1980.

NEW MEXICO PROBATE MANUAL. William N. Henderson. Butterworth Legal Publishers, 90 Stiles Road, Salem, New Hampshire 03079. 1978- . (Periodic Supplements).

NEW MEXICO RULES OF EVIDENCE TREATISE. Second Edition. John Wentworth and Murl A. Larkin. Butterworth Legal Publishers, 90 Stiles Road, Salem, New Hampshire 03079. 1986- . (Periodic Supplements).

SEARCH AND SEIZURE OUTLINES OF FEDERAL AND NEW MEXICO LAW. Second Edition. M. Hermann. State Bar of New Mexico, 1117 Stamford, Northeast, Albuqueque, New Mexico 87130. 1983.

MANUALS AND RESEARCH GUIDES

GUIDE TO NEW MEXICO STATE PUBLICATIONS. Compiled by Patricia D. Wagner. University of New Mexico School of Law, 1117 Stanford Drive, Norteast, Albuquerque, New Mexico. 87131. 1983.

STATES--NEW MEXICO

MANUAL FOR EFFECTIVE NEW MEXICO LEGAL RESEARCH. University of New Mexico Press, 1720 Lomas Boulevard, Northeast, Albuquerque, New Mexico 87131. 1955.

NEW MEXICO MANUAL. Legislative Council Service, Room 334, State Capitol, Sante Fe, New Mexico 87503. (Annual).

ASSOCIATIONS AND PROFESSIONAL SOCIETIES

ALBUQUERQUE BAR ASSOCIATION, 1210 First Interstate Building, Fourth and Gold, Southwest, Albuquerque, New Mexico 87102.

NEW MEXICO TRIAL LAWYERS ASSOCIATION, P.O. Box 301, Albuquerque, New Mexico 87103. (505) 243-6003.

STATE BAR OF NEW MEXICO, P.O. Box 25883, Albuquerque, New Mexico 87130. (505) 842-6132.

DIRECTORIES

DIRECTORY OF MUNICIPAL OFFICIALS OF NEW MEXICO. New Mexico Municipal League, Box 846, Sante Fe, New Mexico 87501. (Annual).

DIRECTORY OF THE NEW MEXICO BENCH AND BAR. State Bar of New Mexico, P.O. Box 25883, Albuquerque, New Mexico 87125. (Annual).

MOUNTAIN STATES LEGAL DIRECTORY. Legal Directories Publishing Company, 2122 Kidwell Street, P.O. Box 140200, Dallas, Texas 75214-0200. (Annual). (Colorado, Idaho, Montana, New Mexico, Utah, Wyoming).

OFFICIAL NEW MEXICO BLUE BOOK. New Mexico Secretary of State, State Capitol, Sante Fe, New Mexico 87503. (Biennial).

ROSTER OF THE STATE OF NEW MEXICO--ELECTIVE STATE, LEGISLATIVE, DISTRICT, AND COUNTY OFFICIALS. New Mexico Secretary of State, Executive/Legislative Building, Room 400, Sante Fe, New Mexico 87503. (Biennial).

STATES--NEW YORK

STATUTES, CODES, STANDARDS, UNIFORM LAWS

LAWS OF THE STATE OF NEW YORK. State of New York, Albany, New York. (Official Edition of Session Laws). 1777- . (Title and Imprint Varies).

MCKINNEY'S CONSOLIDATED LAWS OF NEW YORK ANNOTATED. West Publishing Company, P.O. Box 64526, 50 West Kellogg Boulevard, St. Paul, Minnesota 55164-0526. 1916- . (Annual Supplements).

MCKINNEY'S SESSION LAWS OF NEW YORK. West Publishing Company, P.O. Box 64526, 50 West Kellogg Boulevard, St. Paul, Minnesota 55164-0526. 1951- . (Periodic Supplements).

NEW YORK CONSOLIDATED LAWS. (Unannotated). Michie Company, P.O. Box 7587, Charlottesville, Virginia 22906-7587. 1987- . (Eight paperback pamphlets replaced annually).

NEW YORK CONSOLIDATED LAWS SERVICE. (Code). Lawyers Co-Operative Company, Aqueduct Building, Rochester, New York 14694. 1976- .

NEW YORK CONSOLIDATED LAWS SERVICE: SESSION LAWS. Lawyers Co-Operative Company, Aqueduct Building, Rochester, New York 14694. 1976- . (Annual Supplements).

NEW YORK STATE REGISTER. New York State Department of State, 162 Washington Avenue, Albany, New York 12231. 1979- . Weekly. (Supercedes New York State Bulletin).

OFFICIAL COMPILATION OF CODES, RULES AND REGULATIONS. New York State Department of State, printed by Lenz and Riecker, One Columbia Place, Albany, New York 12207. 1960- .

OFFICIAL NEW YORK LAW REPORTS: ADVANCE SHEETS OF THE OFFICIAL REPORTS. Lawyers Co-Operative Company, Aqueduct Building, Rochester, New York 14694. 1981- . (Imprint varies). (Advance Sheets of the Court of Appeals, Appellate Division, The Supreme Court and the Miscellaneous Reports).

LOOSELEAF SERVICES AND REPORTERS

APPELLATE DIVISION REPORTS. (First and Second Series). Williams Press, Incorporated, Box 4025, Patroon Station, Albany, New York 12204. 1896- . (Supreme Court, Appellate Division). (Title and imprint varies).

NEW YORK MISCELLANEOUS REPORTS. (First and Second editions). Williams Press, Incorporated, Box 4025, Patroon Station, Albany, New York 12204. 1893- . (Title and imprint varies).

NEW YORK REPORTS. (First and Second Series). Williams Press, Incorporated, Box 4025, Patroon Station, Albany, New York 12204. 1847- . (Title and imprint varies).

NEW YORK SUPPLEMENT. (1st and 2nd Series). West Publishing Company, P.O. Box 64526, 50 West Kellogg Boulevard, St. Paul, Minnesota 55164-0526. 1888- . (Court of Appeals and other miscellaneous lower courts).

NORTHEASTERN REPORTER. (First and Second Series). West Publishing Company, P.O. Box 64526, 50 West Kellogg Boulevard, St. Paul, Minnesota 55164-0526. 1888- . (Court of Appeals and other miscellaneous lower courts).

ATTORNEY GENERAL OPINIONS

ANNUAL REPORT OF THE ATTORNEY GENERAL. New York State Department of Law, 162 Washington Avenue, Albany, New York 12231. 1889-1958. (Includes formal opinions of the Attorney General). (Imprint varies).

OPINIONS OF THE NEW YORK STATE ATTORNEY GENERAL. New York State Department of Law, Lenz and Rieckert, Albany, New York. 1959- (Imprint vaires). (Also available on Lexis: January 1977-; Westlaw: 1977-).

ETHICS OPINIONS, CODES, RULES

COMMITTEE OF PROFESSIONAL ETHICS OPINIONS. Oceana Publications, Incorporated, 75 Main Street, Dobbs Ferry, New York 10522. 1980- . (Five Volumes). (Includes opinion number one (1923) through opinion number 894 (1978)). (Volume 1 includes Code of Ethics; New York Ethics Opinions also published in the New York State Bar Journal).

OPINIONS OF THE COMMITTEES ON PROFESSIONAL ETHICS OF THE ASSOCIATION OF THE BAR OF NEW YORK AND THE NEW YORK COUNTY LAWYERS' ASSOCIATION. Oceana Publications, 75 Main Street, Dobbs Ferry, New York 10522. (Includes Ethics Opinion number 1 (1923) through number 445 (1955). 1980.

Selected New York Ethics Opinions also published in the New York State Bar Journal and in the New York Law Journal (newspaper). Abstracts of opinions issued by the New York State Bar Association, Monroe County Bar Association, Bar Association of Nassau County, Suffolk County Bar Association, Queens County Bar Association, Association of the Bar of the City of New York, New York County Lawyers' Association, and the New York Women's Bar Association are published in the ABA/BNA Lawyers' Manual on Professional Conduct . For further information concerning these opinions, contact the appropriate Bar Association. (See heading Bar Associations for this state).

COURT RULES

INDIVIDUAL RULES AND PROCEDURES OF JUDGES IN THE UNITED STATES DISTRICT COURTS FOR THE SOUTHERN AND EASTERN DISTRICTS OF NEW YORK. Committee on Federal Courts, New York State Bar Association, 1 Elk Street, Albany, New York 12207. 1983.

MCKINNEY'S NEW YORK RULES OF COURT: STATE AND FEDERAL. West Publishing Company, P.O. Box 64526, 50 West Kellogg Boulevard, St. Paul, Minnesota 55164-0526. Annual. (Also published in various volumes of the Code).

RULES OF THE U.S. COURTS IN NEW YORK. Clark Boardman Company, Limited, 435 Hudson Street, New York, New York 10014. 1984- .

JURY INSTRUCTIONS

CHARGES TO THE JURY AND REQUESTS TO CHARGE IN A CRIMINAL CASE IN NEW YORK. Revised edition. Budd G. Goodman. Callaghan and Company, 155 Pfingsten Road, Deerfield, Illinois 60015. 1983- . (Two volume looseleaf).

CRIMINAL JURY INSTRUCTIONS--MISDEMEANORS. Committee on Criminal Jury Instructions, New York Office of the Court Administrator. 1978.

NEW YORK PATTERN JURY INSTRUCTIONS--CIVIL. Second edition. Association of Justices of the Supreme Court of the State of New York, Committee on Pattern Jury Instructions. Lawyers Co-Operative Company, Aqueduct Building, Rochester, New York 14694. 1974- .

DIGESTS, INDEXES, ABSTRACTS, CITATORS

NEW YORK CITY LAW DIGEST. Gould Publications, 199/300 State Street, Binghamton, New York 13901. (Annual Supplements).

NEW YORK CIVIL MOTION CITATOR. Seventh Edition. National Attorneys' Publications, P.O. Box 150, East Setauket, New York 11733. (Annual with Three Supplements per Year).

NEW YORK CRIMINAL CASE CITATOR. Second Edition. Charles E. vonSchmidt. National Attorneys' Publications, P.O. Box 150, East Setauket, New York 11733. (Three Supplements per Year).

NORTHEASTERN DIGEST. West Publishing Company, P.O. Box 64526, 50 West Kellogg Boulevard, St. Paul, Minnesota 55164-0526. 1933- . (Annual Supplements).

SHEPARD'S NEW YORK COURT OF APPEALS CITATIONS. Shepard's/McGraw-Hill, P.O. Box 1235, Colorado Springs, Colorado 80901. (Eight supplements per year).

SHEPARD'S NEW YORK MISCELLANEOUS CITATIONS. Shepard's/McGraw-Hill, P.O. Box 1235, Colorado Springs, Colorado 80901. (Eight supplements per year).

SHEPARD'S NEW YORK STATUTE CITATIONS. Shepard's/McGraw-Hill, P.O. Box 1235, Colorado Springs, Colorado 80901. (Eight pamphlets per year).

SHEPARD'S NEW YORK SUPPLEMENT CITATIONS. Shepard's/McGraw-Hill, P.O. Box 1235, Colorado Springs, Colorado 80901. (Eight pamphlets per year).

SHEPARD'S NEW YORK SUPREME COURT CITATIONS. Shepard's/McGraw-Hill, P.O. Box 1235, Colorado Springs, Colorado 80901. (Eight supplements per year).

SHEPARD'S NORTHEASTERN REPORTER CITATIONS. Shepard's/McGraw-Hill, P.O. Box 1235, Colorado Springs, Colorado 80901. (Monthly Supplements).

WEST'S NEW YORK DIGEST. (First through Third Series). West Publishing Company, P.O. Box 64526, 50 West Kellogg Boulevard, St. Paul, Minnesota 55164-0526. (Annual Supplements). (Title and imprint varies).

ENCYCLOPEDIAS AND DICTIONARIES

ENCYCLOPEDIA OF NEW YORK LAW. West Publishing Company, 50 West Kellogg Boulevard, St. Paul, Minnesota 55164. (Annual Supplements).

NEW YORK JURISPRUDENCE. (1st and 2nd Series.) Lawyers Co-Operative Company, Aqueduct Building, Rochester, New York 14694. 1958- . (Annual Supplements).

LAW REVIEWS AND PERIODICALS

ALBANY LAW REVIEW, Albany Law School of Union University, Editorial Office, 80 New Scotland Avenue, Albany, New York 12208. (Quarterly).

BROOKLYN JOURNAL OF INTERNATIONAL LAW. Brooklyn Law School, 250 Juralemon Street, Brooklyn, New York 11201. (Biannual).

BROOKLYN LAW REVIEW. Brooklyn Law School, 250 Joralemon Street, Brooklyn, New York 11201. (Quarterly).

BUFFALO LAW REVIEW. State University of New York at Buffalo, Amherst Campus, Buffalo, New York 14260. (Triennial).

CARDOZO ARTS AND ENTERTAINMENT JOURNAL. Editorial Office, 55 Fifth Avenue, Room 121, New York, New York 10003. (Biannual).

CARDOZO LAW REVIEW. Editorial Office, 55 Fifth Avenue, New York, New York 10003. (Bimonthly).

COLUMBIA BUSINESS LAW REVIEW. Columbia University School of Law, 435 West 116th Street, New York, New York 10027. (Triennial).

COLUMBIA HUMAN RIGHTS LAW REVIEW. Columbia University School of Law, 435 West 116th Street, New York, New York 10027. (Biannual).

COLUMBIA JOURNAL OF ENVIRONMENTAL LAW. Columbia School of Law, Box B-28, 435 West 116th Street, New York, New York 10027. (Biannual).

COLUMBIA JOURNAL OF LAW AND SOCIAL PROBLEMS. Columbia University School of Law, Box D-27, 435 West 116th Street, New York, New York 10027. (Quarterly).

COLUMBIA JOURNAL OF TRANSNATIONAL LAW. Columbia University School of Law, 435 West 116th Street, New York, New York 10027. (Three issues per year).

COLUMBIA LAW REVIEW. Columbia Law Review Association, Inc., Columbia School of Law, 435 West 116th Street, New York, New York 10027. (Eight Times per Year).

COLUMBIA--VLA JOURNAL OF LAW AND THE ARTS. Columbia University School of Law and Volunteer Lawyers for the Arts, 435 West 116th Street, New York, New York 10027. (Quarterly).

CORNELL LAW REVIEW. Cornell Law School, Myron Taylor Hall, Ithaca, New York 14853-4901. (Six issues per year).

FORDHAM INTERNATIONAL LAW JOURNAL. Editorial Office, Lincoln Center, 140 West 62nd Street, New York, New York 10023. (Triennial).

FORDHAM LAW REVIEW. Lincoln Center, 140 West 62nd Street, New York, New York 10023. (Bimonthly).

FORDHAM URBAN LAW JOURNAL. Fordham University School of Law, 140 West 62nd Street, New York, New York 10023. (Quarterly).

LAW AND HISTORY REVIEW. Cornell Law School. Myron Taylor Hall, Ithaca, New York 14853-4901. 1983- . Semiannual.

NEW YORK LAW SCHOOL HUMAN RIGHTS ANNUAL. New York Law School, 57 Worth Street, New York, New York 10013-2960. (Annual).

NEW YORK LAW SCHOOL JOURNAL OF INTERNATIONAL AND COMPARATIVE LAW. New York Law School, 57 Worth Street, New York, New York. 10013-2960. (Three issues per year).

NEW YORK LAW SCHOOL LAW REVIEW. New York Law School, 57 Worth Street, New York, New York 10013. (Quarterly).

NEW YORK STATE BAR JOURNAL. New York State Bar Association, One Elk Street, Albany, New York 12207. (Eight issues per year).

NEW YORK UNIVERSITY JOURNAL OF INTERNATIONAL LAW AND POLITICS. New York University School of Law, 110 West Third Street, New York, New York 10012. (Six issues per year).

NEW YORK UNIVERSITY LAW REVIEW. New York Law Review, 719 Broadway, Fifth Floor, New York, New York 10003. (Bimonthly).

NEW YORK UNIVERSITY REVIEW OF LAW AND SOCIAL CHANGE. New York University School of Law, 110 West Third Street, New York, New York 10012. (Quarterly).

PACE ENVIRONMENTAL LAW REVIEW. Pace University School of Law, 78 North Broadway, White Plains, New York 10603. (Biannual).

PACE LAW REVIEW. Pace University School of Law, 78 North Broadway, White Plains, New York 10603. (Quarterly).

RECORD OF THE ASSOCIATION OF THE BAR OF THE CITY OF NEW YORK. The Association of the Bar of New York, 42 West 44th Street, New York, New York 10036. (Six issues per year).

ST. JOHN'S UNIVERSITY LAW REVIEW. St. John's Law Review, Frombes Hall, Grand Central and Utopia Parkway, Jamaica, New York 11439. (Quarterly).

NEWSLETTERS AND NEWSPAPERS

BARCLAY'S NEW YORK ADVANCE CITATOR. Barclay's Law Publishers, 400 Oyster Point Boulevard, Suite 500, South San Francisco, California 94080. Monthly.

THE BRODER NEW YORK TORT REPORTER. Shepard's/McGraw-Hill, P.O. Box 1235, Colorado Springs, Colorado 80901. Monthly.

ENVIRONMENTAL LAW IN NEW YORK. Berle, Kass and Case, 45 Rockefeller Plaza, New York, New York 10111. Bimonthly.

44TH STREET NOTES. Association of the Bar of the City of New York, 42 West Forth-fourth Street, New York, New York 10036.

INSIDE NEW YORK TAXES. Corporate Tax Publishers, Incorporated, Box 261, Leonia, New Jersey 07605. Monthly.

N.Y. COUNTY LAWYER. New York County Lawyer's Association, 14 Vesey Street, New York, New York 10007.

NEW YORK APARTMENT LAW INSIDER. Brownstone Publishers, Incorporated, 304 Park Avenue South, New York, New York 10010. Monthly.

NEW YORK CLASS ACTION DIGEST. New York State Bar Association, One Elk Street, Albany, New York 12207. Semiannually.

NEW YORK DEFENDER DIGEST. New York Defender Digest, 295 Main Street, Buffalo, New York 14203. Biweekly.

NEW YORK EDUCATION LAW REPORT. Whittaker Newsletters, 313 South Avenue, Fanwood, New Jersey 07023. Monthly.

NEW YORK INTERNATIONAL LAW REVIEW. New York State Bar Association, One Elk Street, Albany, New York 12207. Semiannually.

NEW YORK JURY VERDICT REPORTER. The New York Jury Verdict Reporter, Incorporated, 577 Main Street, Islip, New York 11751. Quarterly.

NEW YORK LAW JOURNAL: THE OFFICIAL LAW PAPER FOR THE FIRST AND SECOND JUDICIAL DEPARTMENTS. New York Law Publishing Company, 111 Eighth Avenue, New York, New York 10011. (Daily except Saturdays and Sundays).

NEW YORK NEGLIGENCE REPORTER. Matthew Bender and Company, Incorporated, 11 Penn Plaza, New York, New York 10001. Monthly.

NEW YORK REAL ESTATE LAW REPORTER. Leader Publications, 111 Eighth Avenue, New York, New York 10011. Monthly.

WEST'S NEW YORK UPDATE. West Publishing Company, 50 West Kellogg Boulevard, St. Paul, Minnesota 55164. Semimonthly.

FORMBOOKS

BENDER'S FORMS FOR THE CIVIL PRACTICE. Louis R. Frumer, et al. Matthew Bender and Company, Incorporated, 11 Penn Plaza, New York, New York 10001. 1963- . (Semiannual Supplement).

BENDER'S FORMS OF PLEADING OF THE STATE OF NEW YORK. Matthew Bender and Company, Incorporated, 11 Penn Plaza, New York, New York 10001. 1946- .

BILLS OF PARTICULARS IN NEW YORK. Revised Edition. Benita Greenfield, Editor. Callaghan and Company, 155 Pfingsten Road, Deerfield, Illinois 60015. 1984- . (Annual Supplement).

MEDINA'S BOSTWICK. Fifth Edition. Matthew Bender and Company, Incorporated, 11 Penn Plaza, New York, New York 10001. 1949- . (Semiannual Supplement).

NEW YORK CIVIL PRACTICE. Matthew Bender and Company, Incorporated, 11 Penn Plaza, New York, New York 10001. 1963- . (Biannual Supplements).

NEW YORK COURT FORMS. Eugene W. Salisbury. Gould Publications, 199/300 State Street, Binghamton, New York 13901. 1977- . (Periodic Supplements).

NEW YORK FAMILY LAW REPORTER. New York Family Law Reporter, Garden City, New York. (Forty-eight issues per year).

NEW YORK FORMS: LEGAL AND BUSINESS. Lawyer's Co-Operative Publishing Company, Aqueduct Building, Rochester, New York 14694. 1985- . (Periodic Supplements).

WEST'S MCKINNEY'S NEW YORK FORMS. West Publishing Company, P.O. Box 64526, 50 West Kellogg Boulevard, St. Paul, Minnesota 55164-0526. 1946- .

PRACTICE MATERIALS

BOARDMAN'S NEW YORK FAMILY LAW, WITH FORMS. Elliot L. Biskind, Clark Boardman Company, Limited, 435 Hudson Street, New York, New York 10014. 1981- . (Periodic Supplements).

CALLAGHAN'S CRIMINAL LAW IN NEW YORK. Third Edition. Callaghan and Company, 155 Pfingsten Road, Deerfield, Illinois 60015. 1984- .

NEW YORK APPELLATE PRACTICE. Thomas R. Newman. Matthew Bender and Company, Incorporated, 11 Penn Plaza, New York, New York 10001. 1985- . (Periodic Supplements).

NEW YORK CIVIL PRACTICE. Matthew Bender and Company, Incorporated, 11 Penn Plaza, New York, New York 10001. 1963- . (Included in CPLR Set).

NEW YORK CIVIL PRACTICE AND PROCEDURE. Louis A. Kass. Gould Publications, 199/300 State Street, Binghamton, New York 13901. 1982- . (Periodic Supplements).

NEW YORK CRIMINAL LAW HANDBOOK. Gould Publications, 199/300 State Street, Binghamton, New York 13901. 1967- . (Annual Supplement).

NEW YORK CRIMINAL PRACTICE. Marvin E. Waxner, et al. Matthew Bender and Company, Incorporated, 11 Penn Plaza, New York, New York 10001. 1973- . (Periodic Supplements).

NEW YORK ESTATE ADMINISTRATION. Margaret V. Turano and C. Raymond Radigan. West Publishing Company, P.O. Box 64526, 50 West Kellogg Boulevard, St. Paul, Minnesota 55164-0526. 1986.

NEW YORK ESTATES PRACTICE GUIDE. Fourth edition. John Tarbox. Lawyers Co-Operative Company, Aqueduct Building, Rochester, New York 14694. 1984. (With Supplements).

NEW YORK FAMILY LAW HANDBOOK, 1985-1986. Gould Publications, 199/300 State Street, Binghamton, New York 13901. 1985- . (Annual Supplements).

NEW YORK LANDLORD AND TENANT. (Second Edition). Lawyers Co-Operative Company, Aqueduct Building, Rochester, New York 14694. 1971- .

NEW YORK MATRIMONIAL LAW AND PRACTICE. Timothy M. Tippins. Callaghan and Company, 155 Pfingsten Road, Deerfield, Illinois 60015. 1986- . (Periodic Supplements).

NEW YORK PRACTICE GUIDE: PROBATE AND ESTATE ADMINISTRATION. Joseph T. Arenson, et al. Matthew Bender and Company, Incorporated, 11 Penn Plaza, New York, New York 10001. 1985- . (Periodic Supplements).

NEW YORK PRACTICE GUIDE: REAL ESTATE. Eugene J. Morris, et al. Matthew Bender and Company, Incorporated, 11 Penn Plaza, New York, New York 10001. 1985- . (Periodic Supplements).

NEW YORK PRODUCTS LIABILITY. Michael Weinburger. Callaghan and Company, 155 Pfingsten Road, Deerfield, Illinois 60015. 1982- . (Periodic Supplements).

NEW YORK WILLS. Louis A. Kass. Gould Publications, 199/300 State Street, Binghamton, New York 13901. 1979- . (Periodic Supplements).

NEW YORK ZONING AND LAW PRACTICE. Third Edition. Robert M. Anderson, Lawyers Co-Operative Company, Aqueduct Building, Rochester, New York 14694. 1984- . (Annual Supplements).

TRIAL HANDBOOK FOR NEW YORK LAWYERS. Second Edition. Aaron J. Broder. Lawyers Co-Operative Company, Aqueduct Building, Rochester, New York 14694. 1986- . (Annual Supplements).

WHAT EVERY LANDLORD AND TENANT SHOULD KNOW. Adele Bernhard and Diane P. Adler, Editors. Citizen's Housing and Planning Council, 20 West 40th Street, New York, New York. 1985- .

MANUALS AND RESEARCH GUIDES

NEW YORK LEGAL DOCUMENTS: A SELECTIVE ANNOTATED BIBLIOGRAPHY. Susan L. Dow and Karen L. Spencer. Charles B. Sears Legal Information Center, State University of New York at Buffalo, Buffalo, New York 14260. 1985.

NEW YORK LEGAL RESEARCH GUIDE. Ellen M. Gibson. William S. Hein and Company, Incorporated, hein Building, 1285 Main Street, Buffalo, New York 14209. 1988.

SHEPARD'S NEW YORK LAW LOCATOR. Shepard's/McGraw-Hill, P.O. Box 1235, Colorado Springs, Colorado 80901. (Annual).

SOURCES OF PUBLISHED AND UNPUBLISHED ADMINISTRATIVE OPINIONS IN NEW YORK. Robert A. Carter. Albany Legislative and Governmental Services, New York State Library, Cultural Education Center, Madison Avenue, Albany, New York 12230. 1985.

ASSOCIATIONS AND PROFESSIONAL SOCIETIES

ALBANY COUNTY BAR ASSOCIATION, Albany County Court House, Room 315, Albany, New York 12207.

ASSOCIATION OF THE BAR OF THE CITY OF NEW YORK, 42 West 44th Street, New York, New York 10036. (212) 382-6600.

BAR ASSOCIATION--ERIE COUNTY, 1758 Statler Building, Buffalo, New York 14202.

BAR ASSOCIATION FOR HUMAN RIGHTS OF GREATER NEW YORK, P.O. Box 1899, Grand Central Station, New York, New York 10163.

BAR ASSOCIATION OF NASSAU COUNTY, 15th and West Streets, Mineola, New York 11501.

BRONX COUNTY BAR ASSOCIATION, 851 Grand Concourse, New York, New York 10451.

BROOME COUNTY BAR ASSOCIATION, 30 Fayette Street, Binghamton, New York 13901.

DUTCHESS COUNTY BAR ASSOCIATION, P.O. Box 4865, Poughkeepsie, New York 12602.

MONROE COUNTY BAR ASSOCIATION, 1125 First Federal Plaza, Rochester, New York 14614.

THE NASSAU LAWYERS' ASSOCIATION OF LONG ISLAND, INCORPORATED, 1140 Franklin Avenue, Garden City, New York 11530.

NEW YORK BAR ASSOCIATION, One Elk Street, Albany, New York 12207. (518) 463-3200.

NEW YORK COUNTY LAWYERS ASSOCIATION, 14 Vesey Street, New York, New York 10007. (212) 267-6646.

NEW YORK STATE TRIAL LAWYERS ASSOCIATION INCORPORATED, 132 Nassau Street, New York, New York 10038. (212) 349-5890.

ONADAGA COUNTY BAR ASSOCIATION, 505 State Tower Building, Syracuse, New York 13202.

ONEIDA COUNTY BAR ASSOCIATION, 303 Mayro Building, Utica, New York 13501.

ORANGE COUNTY BAR ASSOCIATION, 210 Main Street, P.O. Box 88, Gosher, New York 10924.

QUEENS COUNTY BAR ASSOCIATION, 90-35 148th Street, Jamaica, New York 11435.

RICHMOND COUNTY BAR ASSOCIATION, 1111 Victory Boulevard, Staten Island, New York 10301.

ROCKLAND COUNTY BAR ASSOCIATION, P.O. Box 371, 60 South Main Street, New York, New York 10956.

SUFFOLK COUNTY BAR ASSOCIATION, 4175 Veteran's Memorial Highway, Suite 406, Ronkonkoma, New York 11779.

WESTCHESTER COUNTY BAR ASSOCIATION, 199 Main Street, Suite 800, White Plains, New York 10601.

DIRECTORIES

CRIME VICTIM'S AID [NEW JERSEY, NEW YORK, PENNSYLVANIA; SOME NATIONAL]. Bloom Books Incorporated, 1020 Broad Street, Newark, New Jersey 07102. 1983.

DIRECTORY OF PERMITS [STATE OF NEW YORK]. New York State Office of Business Permits and Regulatory Assistance, A.E. Smith State Office Building, 17th Floor, Albany, New York 12225. 1984- . (Irregular).

DIRECTORY OF STATE AGENCIES [NEW YORK]. Division of Information Services, New York State Department of State, 162 Washington Avenue, Albany, New York 12231. (Annual).

EMPIRE STATE REPORT--NEW YORK LEGISLATIVE COMMITTEES REFERENCE ISSUE. New York State Legislative Institute, 17 Lexington Avenue, New York, New York 10010. (Annual).

GREENBOOK: OFFICIAL DIRECTORY OF THE CITY OF NEW YORK. Citybooks, City of New York Department of General Services, Municipal Building, Room 2223, New York, New York 10007. (Annual).

NEW YORK RED BOOK. Williams Press, Incorporated, Box 4025, Patroon Station, Albany, New York 12204. (Biennial).

NEW YORK STATE DIRECTORY: WHO'S REALLY WHO IN GOVERNMENT, POLITICS, BUSINESS. Empire State Report, Incorporated, 17 Lexington Avenue, New York, New York 10010. 1986.

NEW YORK STATE LEGISLATIVE MANUAL. Division of Information Services, New York State Department of State, 162 Washington Avenue, Albany, New York 12231. 1984. (Triennial).

STATES--NORTH CAROLINA

STATUTES, CODES, STANDARDS, UNIFORM LAWS

ADVANCE LEGISLATIVE SERVICE TO THE GENERAL STATUTES OF NORTH CAROLINA. Michie Company, P.O. Box 7587, Charlottesville, Virginia 22906-7587 (Irregular).

GENERAL STATUTES OF NORTH CAROLINA. Michie Company, P.O. Box 7587, Charlottesville, Virginia 22906-7587. 1944- . (Annual Supplements).

NORTH CAROLINA ADVANCE ANNOTATION SERVICE. Michie Company, P.O. Box 7587, Charlottesville, Virginia 22906-7587. (Three Pamphlets per Year).

NORTH CAROLINA ADMINISTRATIVE CODE. Office of Administrative Hearings, P.O. Drawer 11666, Raleigh, North Carolina. 27604. (1981 through October 1987 published in fiche only. Beginning November 1987 it will be published in paper volumes). (Biannual).

NORTH CAROLINA REGISTER. Office of Administrative Hearings, P.O. Drawer 11666, Raleigh, North Carolina 27604. 1986- . (Monthly).

SESSION LAWS OF NORTH CAROLINA. Secretary of State, Publications Department, 116 West Jones Street, Raleigh, North Carolina 27603. (Biennial).

LOOSELEAF SERVICES AND REPORTERS

NORTH CAROLINA COURT OF APPEALS REPORTS. Administrative Office of the Courts, Justice Building, Raleigh, North Carolina 27602. 1968- .

NORTH CAROLINA REPORTER. West Publishing Company, P.O. Box 64526, 50 West Kellogg Boulevard, St. Paul, Minnesota 55164-0526. 1939- . (North Carolina Supreme Court and Court of Appeals).

NORTH CAROLINA REPORTS. Administrative Office of the Courts, Justice Building, Raleigh, North Carolina 27602. (North Carolina Supreme Court). 1778- .

NORTH CAROLINA TAX REPORTER. Commerce Clearing House, Incorporated, 4025 West Peterson Avenue, Chicago, Illinois 60646. 1982- . (Periodic Supplements).

SOUTHEASTERN REPORTER. (First and Second Series). West Publishing Company, P.O. Box 64526, 50 West Kellogg Boulevard, St. Paul, Minnesota 55164-0526. 1887- . (North Carolina Supreme Court and Court of Appeals).

ATTORNEY GENERAL OPINIONS

BIENNIAL REPORT OF THE ATTORNEY GENERAL OF THE STATE OF NORTH CAROLINA. Department of Justice, Administrative Procedure Section, P.O. Box 629, Raleigh, North Carolina 27602. 1778- . (Also available on Lexis: January 1977-; Westlaw: 1977- .)

ETHICS OPINIONS, CODES, RULES

THE NORTH CAROLINA RULES OF PROFESSIONAL CONDUCT (The Green Book). North Carolina Bar Association, P.O. Box 12806, Raleigh, North Carolina 27605. 1985- . Volume three (1985) replaces volumes one and two. This volume contains the Code of Professional Responsibility, the Disciplinary Rules, and Ethics Opinions. Prior to publication in this volume, Ethics Opinions are also published in the NORTH CAROLINA STATE BAR NEWSLETTER. Abstracts are published in the ABA/BNA Lawyers' Manual on Professional Conduct . For further information concerning the Ethics Opinions, contact the North Carolina State Bar, 208 Fayetteville Street Mall, P.O. Box 25908, Raleigh, North Carolina 27611. (919-828-4620.)

COURT RULES

NORTH CAROLINA RULES ANNOTATED. Michie Company, P.O. Box 7587, Charlottesville, Virginia 22906-7587. 1985- . (Annual Supplements).

NORTH CAROLINA RULES OF COURT. West Publishing Company, P.O. Box 64526, 50 West Kellogg Boulevard, St. Paul, Minnesota 55164-0526. 1973- . (Annual).

JURY INSTRUCTIONS

NORTH CAROLINA PATTERN JURY INSTRUCTIONS FOR CIVIL CASES. North Carolina Conference of Superior Court Judges, Committee on Pattern Jury Instructions. North Carolina State Bar Association, 208 Fayetteville Street Mall, P.O. Box 25850, Raleigh, North Carolina 27611. 1970- . (Annual Supplements).

NORTH CAROLINA PATTERN JURY INSTRUCTIONS FOR CRIMINAL CASES. North Carolina Conference of Superior Court Judges, Committee on Pattern Jury Instructions. North Carolina Conference of Superior Court Judges, North Carolina. 1970- . (Annual Supplements).

DIGESTS, INDEXES, ABSTRACTS, CITATORS

SHEPARD'S NORTH CAROLINA CITATIONS. Shepard's/McGraw-Hill, P.O. Box 1235, Colorado Springs, Colorado 80901. (Eight supplements per year).

SHEPARD'S SOUTHEASTERN REPORTER CITATIONS. Shepard's/McGraw-Hill, P.O. Box 1235, Colorado Springs, Colorado 80901. (Monthly Supplements).

SOUTH EASTERN DIGEST. (First and Second Series). West Publishing Company, P.O. Box 64526, 50 West Kellogg Boulevard, St. Paul, Minnesota 55164-0526. 1935- . (Annual Supplements).

STRONG'S NORTH CAROLINA INDEX THIRD. Lawyers Co-Operative Company, Aqueduct Building, Rochester, New York 14694. 1976- . (Annual Supplements).

WEST'S NORTH CAROLINA DIGEST. West Publishing Company, P.O. Box 64526, 50 West Kellogg Boulevard, St. Paul, Minnesota 55164-0526. 1937- . (Annual Supplements).

LAW REVIEWS AND PERIODICALS

DUKE LAW JOURNAL. Duke University School of Law, Durham, North Carolina 27706. (Six issues per year).

NORTH CAROLINA JOURNAL OF INTERNATIONAL LAW AND COMMERCIAL REGULATIONS. University of North Carolina School of Law, Chapel Hill, North Carolina 27514. (Three Issues per Year).

NORTH CAROLINA LAW REVIEW. University of North Carolina School of Law, Van Hecke-Wettach Building, Chapel Hill, North Carolina 27514. (Six Issues per Year).

NORTH CAROLINA STATE BAR QUARTERLY. North Carolina State Bar, 208 Fayetteville Street, P.O. Box 25908, Raleigh, North Carolina 27611. (Quarterly).

WAKE FOREST LAW REVIEW. Wake Forest University School of Law, P.O. Box 7206, Winston-Salem, North Carolina 27109-7206. (Quarterly)

NEWSLETTERS AND NEWSPAPERS

BAR NOTES. North Carolina Bar Association, 1312 Annapolis Drive, Raliegh, North Carolina 27608. Bimonthly.

THE DAILY BULLETIN. Institute of Government, CB#3330, Knapp Building, University of North Carolina at Chapel Hill, Chapel Hill, North Carolina 27599. Irregular.

LEGAL TIDES: A NEWSLETTER FOR CURRENT EVENTS IN NORTH CAROLINA COASTAL AND OCEAN LAW. University of North Carolina Sea Grant College Program, Box 8605, NCSU, Raliegh, North Carolina 27695. Quarterly.

NORTH CAROLINA BAR NEWSLETTER, 208 Fayette Street Mall, P.O. Box 25850, Raleigh, North Carolina 27611. (Quarterly).

NORTH CAROLINA ENVIRONMENTAL LAW LETTER. M. Lee Smith Publishers and Printers, 162 Fourth Avenue North, Nashville, Tennessee 37219. Monthly.

NORTH CAROLINA LAW MONITOR. State Capital Services, Incorporated, P.O. Box 28046, Raliegh, North Carolina 27611. Semimonthly.

WEEKLY STATUS REPORT. Institute of Government, CB#3330, Knapp Building, University of North Carolina at Chapel Hill, Chapel Hill, North Carolina 27599. Irregular.

FORMBOOKS

DOUGLAS' FORMS: A COMPREHENSIVE AND ACCURATE COMPILATION OF LEGAL AND BUSINESS FORMS FOR USE IN THE STATE OF NORTH CAROLINA. Third Edition. R.D. Douglas. Michie Company, P.O. Box 7587, Charlottesville, Virginia 22906-7587. 1983- . (Periodic Supplements).

THORP'S NORTH CAROLINA TRIAL PRACTICE FORMS: A PRACTICAL COMPILATION OF TRIAL PRACTICE FORMS ARRANGED IN THE ORDER OF THE NORTH CAROLINA RULES OF CIVIL PROCEDURE. Second Edition. William L. Thorp. Harrison Company, Publisher, 3110 Crossing Park, Norcross, Georgia 30071. 1984.

PRACTICE MATERIALS

THE ADMINISTRATION OF DECEDENT'S ESTATES IN NORTH CAROLINA. John Paul Huggard. Michie/Bobbs-Merrill Law Publishing Company, P.O. Box 7587, Charlottesville, Virginia 22906-7587. 1985- . (Periodic Supplements).

ADMISSABILITY OF EVIDENCE IN NORTH CAROLINA. A. Fox. Harrison Company, 3110 Crossing Park, Norcross, Georgia 30071. 1988.

BRANDIS ON NORTH CAROLINA EVIDENCE. Second Revised Edition. Henry Brandis, Jr. Michie Company, P.O. Box 7587, Charlottesville, Virginia 22906-7587. 1982- . (Periodic Supplements).

BUSINESS ENTITIES: A NORTH CAROLINA LAW PRACTICE SYSTEM. Dudley Humphrey and George H. Gilliam. Michie Company, P.O. Box 7587, Charlottesville, Virginia 22906-7587. 1984- . (Periodic Supplements).

COLLECTIONS: A NORTH CAROLINA LAW PRACTICE SYSTEM. Marion G. Follin, Norman B. Smith, and John A. Dusenbury, Jr. Michie Company, P.O. Box 7587, Charlottesville, Virginia 22906-7587. 1984- . (Periodic Supplements).

DOMESTIC RELATIONS: A NORTH CAROLINA LAW PRACTICE SYSTEM. Martha E. Johnston, Michael K. Curtis, Charles A. Lloyd, John R. Kernodle, Jr. and Norman B. Smith. Michie Company, P.O. Box 7587, Charlottesville, Virginia 22906-7587. 1984- . (Periodic Supplements).

DRAFTING DOMESTIC AGREEMENTS AND ORDERS. North Carolina Bar Foundation, 1312 Annapolis Drive, Raliegh, North Carolina 27605. 1986- . (Periodic Supplements).

EQUITABLE DISTRIBUTION. North Carolina Bar Foundation, 1312 Annapolis Drive, Raleigh, North Carolina 27605. 1985- . (Periodic Supplements).

NORTH CAROLINA APPELLATE HANDBOOK. J. Reid Potter. Michie Company, P.O. Box 7587, Charlottesville, Virginia 22906-7587. 1978.

NORTH CAROLINA ASSOCIATION OF LEGAL SECRETARIES STATE HANDBOOK. Michie Company, P.O. Box 7587, Charlottesville, Virginia 22906-7587. 1984- . (Periodic Supplements).

NORTH CAROLINA CIVIL NEGOTIATIONS AND SETTLEMENTS MANUAL. Douglas B. Abrams, et al. Wake Forest School of Law, Continuing Legal Education, P.O. Box 7206, Reynolds Station, Winston-Salem, North Carolina 27109-7206. 1985.

NORTH CAROLINA CRIMINAL LAW AND PROCEDURE. Michie Company, P.O. Box 7587, Charlottesville, Virginia 22906-7587. 1982- . (Biannual).

NORTH CAROLINA CRIMINAL TRIAL PRACTICE. Second Edition. Ronald M. Price. Harrison Company, Publisher, 3110 Crossing Park, Norcross, Georgia 30071. 1985.

NORTH CAROLINA FAMILY LAW. Fourth Edition. Robert E. Lee. Michie Company, P.O. Box 7587, Charlottesville, Virginia 22906-7587. 1979- . (Periodic Supplements).

NORTH CAROLINA FAMILY LAW PRACTICE HANDBOOK. Revised Edition. Walter W. Baker, Jr., et al. Wake Forest University School of Law, Continuing Legal Education, P.O. Box 7206, Reynolds Station, Winston-Salem, North Carolina 27109-7206. 1984- . (Periodic Supplements).

NORTH CAROLINA METHODS OF PRACTICE. West Publishing Company, 50 West Kellogg Boulevard, St. Paul, Minnesota 55164. 1985.

NORTH CAROLINA REAL ESTATE TITLE SEARCHES. Harrison Company, 3110 Crossing Park, Norcross, Georgia 30091. 1982.

NORTH CAROLINA SECURITY INTERESTS. Richard A. Lord and Charles C. Lewis. Michie Company, P.O. Box 7587, Charlottesville, Virginia 22906-7587. 1985- . (Periodic Supplements).

NORTH CAROLINA TRIAL EVIDENCE MANUAL. Anthony J. Bocchino and J. Alexander Tanford. Michie Company, P.O. Box 7587, Charlottesville, Virginia 22906-7587. 1976- . (Annual Supplements).

NORTH CAROLINA WORKER'S COMPENSATION MANUAL. Michael J. Anderson, et al. Wake Forest School of Law, Wake Forest University, Winston-Salem, North Carolina 27109-7206. 1986.

REAL PROPERTY LITIGATION: WHAT TO DO WHEN THINGS GO WRONG. North Carolina Bar Association, P.O. Box 12806, Raleigh, North Carolina 27605. 1985- . (Periodic Supplements).

SUING IN NORTH CAROLINA SMALL CLAIMS COURT: A PRACTICAL GUIDE. David A. Guth. Michie Company, P.O. Box 7587, Charlottesville, Virginia 22906-7587. 1983.

WEBSTER'S REAL ESTATE LAW IN NORTH CAROLINA. Revised Edition. Patrick K. Hetrick. Michie Company, P.O. Box 7587, Charlottesville, Virginia 22906-7587. 1981- . (Periodic Supplements).

MANUALS AND RESEARCH GUIDES

GUIDE TO NORTH CAROLINA LEGAL RESEARCH. Igor Kavass and Bruce Christensen. William S. Hein and Company, Incorporated, Hein Building, 1285 Main Street, Buffalo, New York 14209. 1973.

ASSOCIATIONS AND PROFESSIONAL SOCIETIES

GREENSBORO BAR ASSOCIATION, P.O. Box 1825, Greensboro, N.C. 27402.

MECKLENBURG COUNTY BAR. Law Building, Suite 100, 730 East Trade Street, Charlotte, North Carolina 28202.

NORTH CAROLINA BAR ASSOCIATION, 1312 Annapolis Drive, Raleigh, North Carolina 27608. (919) 828-0561.

NORTH CAROLINA STATE BAR ASSOCIATION, 208 Fayetteville Street Mall, P.O. Box 25850, Raleigh, North Carolina 27611. (919) 828-4620.

WADE COUNTY BAR ASSOCIATION, P.O. Box 10625, Raleigh, North Carolina 27605.

DIRECTORIES

DIRECTORY OF COUNTY AND STATE OFFICIALS. Secretary of State, Publications Department, 116 West Jones Street, Raleigh, North Carolina 27603. (Annual).

DIRECTORY OF NORTH CAROLINA MUNICIPAL OFFICIALS. North Carolina League of Municipalities, Box 3069, Raleigh, North Carolina 27602. (Annual).

NORTH CAROLINA GENERAL ASSEMBLY - HOUSE OF REPRESENTATIVES RULES - DIRECTORY. North Carolina General Assembly, Raleigh, North Carolina 27611. (Biennial).

NORTH CAROLINA LEGAL DIRECTORY. Legal Directories Publishing Company, 2122 Kidwell Street, P.O. Box 140200, Dallas, Texas 75214-0200. (Annual).

NORTH CAROLINA MANUAL. North Carolina Secretary of State, 300 N. Salsbury, Room 302, Raleigh, North Carolina 27611. 1986.

STATES --NORTH DAKOTA

STATUTES, CODES, STANDARDS, UNIFORM LAWS

LAWS OF NORTH DAKOTA. Secretary of State, State Capitol, Bismark, North Dakota 58505. 1889- . (Biennial).

NORTH DAKOTA ADMINISTRATIVE CODE. North Dakota Legislative Council. Available from the Secretary of State, Bismark, North Dakota 58505. 1978- . (Periodic Supplements). (No register published).

NORTH DAKOTA CENTURY CODE ANNOTATED. Michie/Bobbs-Merrill Law Publishing Company, P.O. Box 7587, Charlottesville, Virginia 22906-7587. 1959- . (Periodic Supplements).

LOOSELEAF SERVICES AND REPORTERS

NORTH DAKOTA REPORTS. Lawyers Co-operative Publishers Company, Acqueduct Building, Rochester, New York, New York 14694. 1890-1953. (Current Official Source: NORTHWESTERN REPORTER). (Imprint varies).

STATES -- NORTH DAKOTA

NORTHWESTERN REPORTER. (First and Second Series). West Publishing Company, P.O. Box 64526, 50 West Kellogg Boulevard, St. Paul, Minnesota 55164-0526. 1879- . (Supreme Court).

ATTORNEY GENERAL OPINIONS

OPINIONS OF THE ATTORNEY GENERAL OF NORTH DAKOTA. Office of the Attorney General, State Capitol, Bismark, North Dakota 58505. 1889- . (Also available on Lexis: January 1977-; Westlaw: 1977- .)

ETHICS OPINIONS, CODES, RULES

North Dakota Code of Professional Responsibility and Rules of Disciplinary Procedure are published in North Dakota Court Rules (Desk Copy). West Publishing Company, P.O. Box 64526, 50 West Kellogg Boulevard, St. Paul, Minnesota 55164-0526. Annual. (N.B. North Dakota adopted a new model code, North Dakota Rules of Professional Conduct, in July 1987. These rules will be in effect as of January 1, 1988.)

North Dakota Ethics Opinions are issued by the Ethics Committee of the State Bar of North Dakota and are published in The Gavel, State Bar Association of North Dakota, Box 2136, Bismark, North Dakota 58501 (Monthly except August). For further information concerning these opinions, contact the State Bar Association at (701-255-1404) or the Disciplinary Board of the Supreme Court, P.O. Box 2297, Bismark, North Dakota 58502. (701-224-3348.)

COURT RULES

NORTH DAKOTA RULES OF COURT. West Publishing Company, P.O. Box 64526, 50 West Kellogg Boulevard, St. Paul, Minnesota 55164-0526. (Annual). (Also published in North Dakota Century Code Annotated, Volume 5B).

JURY INSTRUCTIONS

NORTH DAKOTA JURY INSTRUCTIONS - CRIMINAL. State Bar Association of North Dakota, P.O. Box 2136, Bismark, North Dakota 58502. 1986- . (Periodic Supplements).

NORTH DAKOTA PATTERN JURY INSTRUCTIONS - CIVIL. State Bar Association of North Dakota, P.O. Box 2136, Bismark, North Dakota 58502. 1986- . (Periodic Supplements).

DIGESTS, INDEXES, ABSTRACTS, CITATORS

DAKOTA DIGEST. West Publishing Company, P.O. Box 64526, 50 West Kellogg Boulevard, St. Paul, Minnesota 55164-0526. 1942- . (Annual Supplements).

NORTHWESTERN DIGEST. West Publishing Company, P.O. Box 64526, 50 West Kellogg Boulevard, St. Paul, Minnesota 55164-0526. 1944- . (Annual Supplements).

SHEPARD'S NORTH DAKOTA CITATIONS. Shepard's/McGraw-Hill, P.O. Box 1235, Colorado Springs, Colorado 80901. (Quarterly Supplements).

SHEPARD'S NORTHWESTERN REPORTER CITATIONS. Shepard's/McGraw-Hill, P.O. Box 1235, Colorado Springs, Colorado 80901. (Monthly Supplements).

LAW REVIEWS AND PERIODICALS

THE GAVEL, P.O. Box 2136, Bismark, North Dakota 58502. (Monthly except August).

NORTH DAKOTA LAW REVIEW. University of North Dakota School of Law, Grand Forks, North Dakota 58201. (Quarterly).

ASSOCIATIONS AND PROFESSIONAL SOCIETIES

BAR ASSOCIATION OF NORTH DAKOTA, 515 East Broadway, Suite 101, Bismark, North Dakota 58501. (701) 255-1404.

DIRECTORIES

DIRECTORY - LAWYERS, JUDGES [NORTH DAKOTA]. State Bar Board of North Dakota, State Capitol, Bismark, North Dakota 58505. (Annual).

DIRECTORY OF FEDERAL, STATE, COUNTY, CITY AND SPECIAL DISTRICT OFFICIALS IN NORTH DAKOTA. North Dakota Bureau of Governmental Affairs, University of North Dakota, Grand Forks, North Dakota 58201. (Annual).

DIRECTORY OF NORTH DAKOTA CITY OFFICIALS. North Dakota League of Cities, Box 2235, Bismark, North Dakota 58502. (Biennial).

NORTH DAKOTA AND SOUTH DAKOTA LEGAL DIRECTORY. Legal Directories Publishing Company, 2122 Kidwell Street, P.O. Box 140200, Dallas, Texas 75214-0200. (Annual).

NORTH DAKOTA BLUE BOOK. Secretary of State, State Capitol, Bismark, North Dakota 58505. (Biennial).

STRUCTURE OF THE STATE: A COMPENDIUM OF NORTH DAKOTA AGENCIES, BOARDS, COMMISSIONS, AND INSTITUTIONS. North Dakota State Library, Liberty Memorial Building, Bismark, North Dakota 58505. (Irregular).

STATES--OHIO

STATUTES, CODES, STANDARDS, UNIFORM LAWS

BALDWIN'S OHIO LEGISLATIVE SERVICE. Banks-Baldwin Publishing Company, University Center, P.O. Box 1974, Cleveland, Ohio 44106. 1971- .

OHIO ADMINISTRATIVE CODE. Banks-Baldwin Publishing Company, University Center, P.O. Box 1974, Cleveland, Ohio 44106. 1977- .

OHIO MONTHLY RECORD. Banks-Baldwin Publishing Company, University Center, P.O. Box 1974, Cleveland, Ohio 44106. 1977- . (Monthly).

OHIO REVISED CODE ANNOTATED. Banks-Baldwin Publishing Company, University Center, P.O. Box 1974, Cleveland, Ohio 44106. 1982- . (Annual Supplements).

PAGE'S OHIO REVISED CODE ANNOTATED. Anderson Publishing Company, 2035 Reading Road, Cincinnati, Ohio 45202. 1953- . (Annual Supplements).

PAGE'S OHIO REVISED CODE ANNOTATED LEGISLATIVE BULLETIN. Anderson Publishing Company, 2035 Reading Road, Cincinnati, Ohio 45202. (Five issues per year).

LOOSELEAF SERVICES AND REPORTERS

BALDWIN'S OHIO TAX SERVICE. Maryann B. Gall. Banks-Baldwin Publishing Company, University Center, P.O. Box 1974, Cleveland, Ohio 44106. 1978- . (Quarterly Supplements).

NORTHWESTERN REPORTER. (First and Second Series). West Publishing Company, P.O. Box 64526, 50 West Kellogg Boulevard, St. Paul, Minnesota 55164-0526. 1879- .

OHIO APPELLATE REPORTS. Law Abstract Publishing Company, 33 West Eleventh Street, Columbus, Ohio 43201. 1913- . (Court of Appeals).

OHIO CASES. West Publishing Company, P.O. Box 64526, 50 West Kellogg Boulevard, St. Paul, Minnesota 55164-0526. 1943- . (Supreme Court and Court of Appeals).

OHIO MISCELLANEOUS REPORTS. Law Abstract Publishing Company, 33 West Eleventh Street, Columbus, Ohio 43201. 1965- . (Miscellaneous Lower Courts).

OHIO NISI PRIUS REPORTS. Ohio Law Reporter Company. 1894-1934. (Superior Court, Court of Common Pleas, Probate and Municipal Courts).

OHIO OFFICIAL REPORTS (NEW SERIES). Anderson Publishing Company, 2035 Reading Road, Cincinnati, Ohio 45202. 1982- . (Supreme Court and Court of Appeals).

OHIO OPINIONS. Anderson Publishing Company, 2035 Reading Road, Cincinnati, Ohio 45202. 1934-1982. (Miscellaneous Ohio Courts).

OHIO STATE BAR ASSOCIATION REPORT. Ohio State Bar Association, 33 West Eleventh Avenue, Columbus, Ohio 43201. 1981- . (Weekly).

OHIO STATE REPORTS. (First and Second Series). Law Abstract Publishing Company, 33 West Eleventh Street, Columbus, Ohio 43201. 1852-1982.

OHIO STATE REPORTS. (Third Series). (Bound with Appellate Reports Third Series and Miscellaneous Reports Second Series in one volume. Published under title Ohio Official Reports).

STATE AND LOCAL TAXES: OHIO. Prentice-Hall, Incorporated, 113 Sylvan Avenue, Englewood Cliffs, New Jersey 07632. (looseleaf). (Weekly Supplements).

ATTORNEY GENERAL OPINIONS

OPINIONS OF THE ATTORNEY GENERAL OF OHIO FOR THE PERIOD [DATE]. Banks-Baldwin Publishing Company, University Center, P.O. Box 1974, Cleveland, Ohio 44106. (Quarterly Supplements). (Also available on: Lexis: January 1977-; Westlaw: 1977- .)

ETHICS OPINIONS, CODES, RULES

Ohio Code of Professional Responsibility and Disciplinary Rules are published in RULES FOR THE GOVERNMENT OF THE BAR, RULES FOR THE GOVERNMENT OF THE JUDICIARY, CODE OF PROFESSIONAL RESPONSIBILITY AND CODE OF JUDICIAL CONDUCT. Ohio Legal Center Institute, 33 West 11th Avenue, 3rd Floor, Columbus, Ohio 43201. (614-421-2500.)

Ohio Ethics Opinions are issued by the Legal Ethics and Professional Conduct Committee, Opinions Subcommittee. These Opinions are not published in full text. Abstracts, however, are published in the ABA/BNA Lawyers' Manual on Professional Conduct . For further information concerning these opinions, contact the Ohio State Bar Association, 33 West 11th Avenue, Columbus, Ohio 43201. (614-421-2121.)

PROFESSIONAL RESPONSIBILITY IN OHIO. Thomas R. Swisher, Editor. Ohio State Bar Association, 33 West 11th Avenue, Columbus, Ohio 43201. 1981.

COURT RULES

OHIO RULES OF CIVIL PROCEDURE ANNOTATED. West Publishing Company, 50 West Kellogg Boulevard, St. Paul, Minnesota 55164. 1970. (Annual Supplements).

OHIO RULES OF COURT, STATE AND FEDERAL. West Publishing Company, 50 West Kellogg Boulevard, St. Paul, Minnesota 55164. (Annual).

RULES GOVERNING THE COURTS OF OHIO: INCLUDING LATEST AMENDMENTS THROUGH JULY [YEAR] AND INTERNAL OPERATING PROCEDURES, SIXTH CIRCUIT COURT OF APPEALS. Anderson Publishing Company, 2035 Reading Road, Cincinnati, Ohio 45202. (Annual).

JURY INSTRUCTIONS

OHIO JURY INSTRUCTIONS: A COLLECTION OF STANDARD JURY INSTRUCTIONS IN CIVIL AND CRIMINAL CASES. Anderson Publishing Company, 646 Main Street, Cincinnati, Ohio 45201. 1983- . (Annual Supplements).

DIGESTS, INDEXES, ABSTRACTS, CITATORS

NORTHWESTERN DIGEST. West Publishing Company, P.O. Box 64526, 50 West Kellogg Boulevard, St. Paul, Minnesota 55164-0526. 1944- . (Annual Supplements).

OHIO DIGEST. West Publishing Company, P.O. Box 64526, 50 West Kellogg Boulevard, St. Paul, Minnesota 55164-0526. 1949- . (Annual Supplements).

SHEPARD'S NORTHWESTERN REPORTER CITATIONS. Shepard's/McGraw-Hill, P.O. Box 1235, Colorado Springs, Colorado 80901. (Monthly Supplements).

SHEPARD'S OHIO CITATIONS. Shepard's/McGraw-Hill, P.O. Box 1235, Colorado Springs, Colorado 80901. (Eight supplements per year).

STATES--OHIO

ENCYCLOPEDIAS AND DICTIONARIES

OHIO JURISPRUDENCE THIRD. Lawyers Co-Operative Company, Aqueduct Building, Rochester, New York 14694. 1977- . (Annual Supplements).

LAW REVIEWS AND PERIODICALS

AKRON LAW REVIEW. University of Akron School of Law, Akron, Ohio 44325. (Quarterly).

CAPITAL UNIVERSITY LAW REVIEW. Capital University, 2199 East Main Street, Columbus, Ohio 43209. (Quarterly).

CASE WESTERN RESERVE LAW REVIEW. Case Western Reserve School of Law, 11075 East Boulevard, Cleveland, Ohio 44106. (Quarterly).

CLEVELAND BAR JOURNAL. Bar Association of Greater Cleveland, Second Floor, 118 St. Clair Avenue, Cleveland, Ohio 44114. 1968- . (Monthly).

CLEVELAND STATE LAW REVIEW. Cleveland-Marshall College of Law, Cleveland State University, Cleveland, Ohio 44115. (Quarterly).

OHIO NORTHERN UNIVERSITY LAW REVIEW. Ohio Northern University Law School, 525 South Main Street, Ada, Ohio 45810. (Quarterly).

OHIO STATE BAR ASSOCIATION REPORT. Ohio State Bar Association, 33 West Eleventh Avenue, Columbus, Ohio 43201. (Weekly).

OHIO STATE JOURNAL ON DISPUTE RESOLUTION. Ohio State University College of Law, 1659 North High Street, Columbus, Ohio 43210-1306. (Biennial).

OHIO STATE LAW JOURNAL. Ohio State University College of Law, 1659 North High Street, Columbus, Ohio 43210. (Quarterly).

UNIVERSITY OF CINCINNATI LAW REVIEW. University of Cincinnati College of Law, Room 300, Taft Hall, Cincinnati, Ohio 45221. (Quarterly).

UNIVERSITY OF DAYTON LAW REVIEW. University of Dayton School of Law, 300 College Park, Dayton, Ohio 45469. (Three issues per year).

UNIVERSITY OF TOLEDO LAW REVIEW. University of Toledo College of Law, Toledo, Ohio 44209. (Quarterly).

NEWSLETTERS AND NEWSPAPERS

CRIMINAL LAW JOURNAL OF OHIO. Banks-Baldwin Law Publishing Company, University Center, P.O. Box 1974, Cleveland, Ohio 44106. Bimonthly.

DOMESTIC RELATIONS JOURNAL OF OHIO. Banks-Baldwin Law Publishing Company, University Center, P.O. Box 1974, Cleveland, Ohio 44106. Bimonthly.

ENVIRONMENTAL LAW JOURNAL OF OHIO. Banks-Baldwin Law Publishing Company, University Center, P.O. Box 1974, Cleveland, Ohio 44106. Bimonthly.

HEALTH LAW JOURNAL OF OHIO. Banks-Baldwin Law Publishing Company, University Center, P.O. Box 1974, Cleveland, Ohio 44106. Bimonthly.

OHIO CIVIL PRACTICE JOURNAL. Banks-Baldwin Law Publishing Company, University Center, P.O. Box 1974, Cleveland, Ohio 44106. Bimonthly.

OHIO DISTRICT COURT REVIEW. Advocates Research, Incorporated, 3620 North High Street, Columbus, Ohio 43214. Monthly.

OHIO EMPLOYMENT LAW LETTER. M. Lee Smith Publishers and Printers, 162 Fourth Avenue North, Nashville, Tennessee 37219. Monthly.

OHIO REPORT. Gorgwer News Service, Incorporated, 175 South Third Street, Suite 230, Columbus, Ohio 43215. Daily.

THE OHIO TRIAL REPORTER. Judicial Advisory Services, Incorporated, P.O. Box 99704, 3309 College Drive, Louisville, Kentucky 40299.

WORKERS' COMPENSATION JOURNAL OF OHIO. Banks-Baldwin Law Publishing Company, University Center, P.O. Box 1974, Cleveland, Ohio 44106. Bimonthly.

FORMBOOKS

BALDWIN'S OHIO LEGAL FORMS. Steven J. Eagle, Editor. Banks-Baldwin Publishing Company, University Center, P.O. Box 1974, Cleveland, Ohio 44106. 1973- . (Biennial Supplements).

COUSE'S OHIO FORMBOOK. Sixth Edition. Glen Weissenberger, Editor. Anderson Publishing Company, 2035 Reading Road, Cincinnati, Ohio 45202. 1984- . (Periodic Supplements).

OHIO CIVIL PRACTICE WITH FORMS. Anderson Publishing Company, 2035 Reading Road, Cincinnati, Ohio 45202. 1970- . (Periodic Supplements).

OHIO FORMS: LEGAL AND BUSINESS. Lawyers Co-Operative Company, Aqueduct Building, Rochester, New York 14694. 1971- . (Annual Supplements).

OHIO FORMS OF PLEADING AND PRACTICE. Matthew Bender and Company, Incorporated, 11 Penn Plaza, New York, New York 10001. 1970- . (Periodic Supplements).

OHIO TRANSACTION GUIDE -- LEGAL FORMS. Zolman Cavitch and Robert M. Nelson, Editors. Matthew Bender and Company, Incorporated, 11 Penn Plaza, New York, New York 10001. 1975- . (Periodic Supplements).

PRACTICE MATERIALS

ANDERSON'S OHIO EVIDENCE: CIVIL AND CRIMINAL. Josiah H. Blackmore and Glen Weissenberger. Anderson Publishing Company, 2035 Reading Road, Cincinnati, Ohio 45202. 1980- . (Annual Supplements).

BALDWIN'S OHIO DOMESTIC RELATIONS LAW: TEXT, FORMS, LAW & RULES. James T. Flaherty, Editor. Banks-Baldwin Publishing Company, University Center, P.O. Box 1974, Cleveland, Ohio 44106. 1984- . (Annual Supplements).

BALDWIN'S OHIO TAX LAW AND RULES. Third Edition. Banks-Baldwin Publishing Company, University Center, P.O. Box 1974, Cleveland, Ohio 44106. 1976- . (Annual Supplements).

EMPLOYMENT IN OHIO. M.G. Sautter. Butterworth Legal Publishers, 90 Stiles Road, Salem, New Hampshire 02180. 1984- . (Periodic Supplements).

EXPANDING LIABILITY IN THE WORKPLACE. Ohio Legal Center Institute, 33 West 11th Avenue, Columbus, Ohio 43201. 1985.

OHIO ADMINISTRATIVE LAW. Administrative Law Committee, Ohio State Bar Association. Banks-Baldwin Publishing Company, University Center, P.O. Box 1974, Cleveland, Ohio 44106. 1985- . (Annual Supplements).

OHIO APPELLATE PRACTICE. Alba L. Whiteside. Banks-Baldwin Publishing Company, P.O. Box 1974, Cleveland, Ohio 44106. 1974- . (Annual Supplements).

OHIO BANK LAW AND REGULATIONS MANUAL. Third Edition. Susan Barnes Collins. Banks-Baldwin Publishing Company, P.O. Box 1974, Cleveland, Ohio 44106. 1978- . (Annual Supplements).

OHIO CIVIL PRACTICE. Sidney B. Jacoby. Banks-Baldwin Publishing Company, University Center, P.O. Box 1974, Cleveland, Ohio 44106. 1970- . (Annual Supplements).

OHIO CIVIL PRACTICE WITH FORMS. John C. McCormack, et al. Anderson Publishing Company, 2035 Reading Road, Cincinnati, Ohio 45202. 1972- . (Annual Supplements).

OHIO CIVIL TRIAL PRACTICE FORMS. Joseph W. Shea. Harrison Company, Publisher, 3110 Crossing Park, Norcross, Georgia 30071. 1984- .

OHIO COMMERCIAL AND CONSUMER LAW. W. Tabac. West Publishing Company, 50 West Kellogg Boulevard, St. Paul, Minnesota 55164. 1981.

OHIO CORPORATION LAW. Jason C. Blackford. Banks-Baldwin Publishing Company, University Center, P.O. Box 1974, Cleveland, Ohio 44106. 1978- . (Annual Supplements).

OHIO CORPORATION LAW WITH FEDERAL TAX ANALYSIS. Zolman Cavitch. Matthew Bender and Company, Incorporated, 11 Penn Plaza, New York, New York 10001. 1961- . (Annual Supplements).

OHIO CORPORATIONS. John P. Beavers. Lawyers Co-Operative Company, Aqueduct Building, Rochester, New York 14694. 1980- . (Annual Supplements).

OHIO CRIMINAL LAW AND PRACTICE. Oliver C. Schroeder and Lewis R. Katz. Banks-Baldwin Publishing Company, University Center, P.O. Box 1974, Cleveland, Ohio 44106. 1974- . (Annual Supplements).

OHIO CRIMINAL PRACTICE AND PROCEDURE. Kenneth L. Aplin, et al. Anderson Publishing Company, 2035 Reading Road, Cincinnati, Ohio 45202. 1973- . (Annual Supplements).

OHIO EVIDENCE MANUAL. Paul C. Giannelli. Banks-Baldwin Publishing Company, University Center, P.O. Box 1974, Cleveland, Ohio 44106. 1982- . (Annual Supplements).

OHIO FAMILY LAW. J. Milligan. West Publishing Company, 50 West Kellogg Boulevard, St. Paul, Minnesota 55164. 1975.

OHIO LANDLORD TENANT LAW. Second Edition. Frederic White. Banks-Baldwin Publishing Company, University Center, P.O. Box 1974, Cleveland, Ohio 44106. 1990.

OHIO MANUAL OF PROCEDURE. Frank C. Leyshon. Anderson Publishing Company, 2035 Reading Road, Cincinnati, Ohio 45202. 1976- . (Semi-monthly Supplements).

OHIO PRACTICE. West Publishing Company, P.O. Box 64526, 50 West Kellogg Boulevard, St. Paul, Minnesota 55164-0526. 1981- . (Fourteen Volumes). (Annual Supplements).

OHIO PROBATE. Daniel F. Carmack. Lawyers Co-Operative Company, Aqueduct Building, Rochester, New York 14694. 1979- . (Annual Supplements).

OHIO PROBATE LAW. Angela G. Carlin and Richard W. Schwartz. Banks-Baldwin Publishing Company, University Center, P.O. Box 1974, Cleveland, Ohio 44106. 1978- . (Annual Supplements).

OHIO PROBATE PRACTICE. Chase M. Davies. Anderson Publishing Company, 2035 Reading Road, Cincinnati, Ohio 45202. 1973- . (Annual Supplements).

OHIO REAL ESTATE LAW AND PRACTICE. Robert L. Hausser and W.R. van Aken. Banks-Baldwin Publishing Company, University Center, P.O. Box 1974, Cleveland, Ohio 44106. 1985- . (Annual Supplements).

OHIO SAVINGS AND LOAN LAWS. Revised Edition. Anderson Publishing Company, 2035 Reading Road, Cincinnati, Ohio 45202. 1984- . (Annual Supplements).

OHIO WILL DRAFTING. Ohio Legal Center Institute, 33 West 11th Avenue, Columbus, Ohio 43201. 1985.

OHIO WORKERS' COMPENSATION CLAIMS. Jeffery V. Nackley. Lawyers Co-Operative Company, Aqueduct Building, Rochester, New York 14694. 1982- . (Annual Supplements).

PRODUCT LIABILITY. Ohio Legal Center Institute, 33 West Eleventh Avenue, Columbus, Ohio 43201. 1981.

TRIAL HANDBOOK FOR OHIO LAWYERS. Second Edition. Richard M. Markus. Lawyers Co-Operative Company, Aqueduct Building, Rochester, New York 14694. 1982- . (Annual Supplements).

WRONGFUL DEATH. Ohio Legal Center Institute, 33 West Eleventh Avenue, Columbus, Ohio 43201. 1982.

MANUALS AND RESEARCH GUIDES

A GUIDE TO LEGISLATIVE HISTORY IN OHIO. David M. Gold. Ohio Legislative Service Commission, (Information Bulletin. Ohio Legislative Service Commission, 1985-1.) Columbus, Ohio. February 1985.

STATES--OHIO

OHIO LEGAL RESOURCES: AN ANNOTATED BIBLIOGRAPHY AND GUIDE. Ohio Library Association and Ohio Regional Association of Law Libraries Joint Task Force on Public Access to Legal Information, 67 Jefferson Avenue, Suite 409, Columbus, Ohio 43215. 1982.

ASSOCIATIONS AND PROFESSIONAL SOCIETIES

AKRON BAR ASSOCIATION, 90 South High Street, Akron, Ohio 44308.

BAR ASSOCIATION OF GREATER CLEVELAND, Second Floor, 118 St. Clair Avenue, Mall Building, Cleveland, Ohio 44114. (216) 696-3525.

CINCINNATI BAR ASSOCIATION, 35 East Seventh Street, Eighth Floor, Cincinnati, Ohio 45202. (513) 381-8213.

COLUMBUS BAR ASSOCIATION, 40 South Third Street, Sixth Floor, Columbus, Ohio 43215. (614) 221-4112.

CUYAHOGA COUNTY BAR ASSOCIATION, 850 Euclid Avenue Number 715, Cleveland, Ohio 44114. (216) 621-5112.

DAYTON BAR ASSOCIATION, 1700 Hulman Building, Dayton, Ohio 45402.

MAHONING COUNTY BAR ASSOCIATION, Court House - Third Floor, Youngstown, Ohio 44503.

OHIO BAR ASSOCIATION, 33 West Eleventh Avenue, Columbus, Ohio 43201. (614) 421-2121.

STARK COUNTY BAR ASSOCIATION, 309 Ameritrust Building, Canton, Ohio 44702.

TOLEDO BAR ASSOCIATION, 311 North Superior, Toledo, Ohio 43604.

TRUMBULL COUNTY BAR ASSOCIATION, P.O. Box 4222, Warren, Ohio 44482.

DIRECTORIES

OFFICIAL ROSTER OF FEDERAL, STATE, AND COUNTY OFFICERS AND DEPARTMENTAL INFORMATION [OHIO]. Ohio Secretary of State, 30 East Board Street, Fourteenth Floor, Columbus, Ohio 43216. (Biennial).

OHIO GENERAL ASSEMBLY - ROSTER OF MEMBERS, OFFICERS, AND EMPLOYEES. Ohio General Assembly State House, Columbus, Ohio 43215. (Irregular).

OHIO LEGAL DIRECTORY. Legal Directories Publishing Company, 2122 Kidwell Street, Dallas, Texas 75214-0200. (Annual).

OHIO ROSTER OF MUNICIPAL AND TOWNSHIP OFFICERS AND MEMBERS OF BOARDS OF EDUCATION. Ohio Secretary of State, 30 East Board Street, Fourteenth Floor, Columbus, Ohio 43216. (Biennial).

STATES--OKLAHOMA

Encyclopedia of Legal Information Sources • 2nd Ed.

STATUTES, CODES, STANDARDS, UNIFORM LAWS

OKLAHOMA ADVANCE ANNOTATION SERVICE. West Publishing Company, P.O. Box 64526, 50 West Kellogg Boulevard, St. Paul, Minnesota 55164-0526. (Semiannual Pamphlets.)

OKLAHOMA REGISTER. Legislative Reference Department of Libraries, State Capitol, 200 North Eighth Street, Oklahoma City, Oklahoma 73105. 1983- . Monthly. (Supercedes the Oklahoma Gazette).

OKLAHOMA SESSION LAW SERVICE. West Publishing Company, P.O. Box 64526, 50 West Kellogg Boulevard, St. Paul, Minnesota 55164-0526. (Irregular pamphlets).

OKLAHOMA SESSION LAWS. West Publishing Company, P.O. Box 64526, 50 West Kellogg Boulevard, St. Paul, Minnesota 55164-0526. Annual. Also available on Microform. William S. Hein, Microform Division, 1285 Main Street, Buffalo, New York 14209. 1985. (Annual).

OKLAHOMA STATUTES (Official edition). West Publishing Company, P.O. Box 64526, 50 West Kellogg Boulevard, St. Paul, Minnesota 55164-0526. 1971- . (Annual Supplements).

OKLAHOMA STATUTES ANNOTATED. West Publishing Company, P.O. Box 64526, 50 West Kellogg Boulevard, St. Paul, Minnesota 55164-0526. 1951- . (Annual Supplements).

LOOSELEAF SERVICES AND REPORTERS

OKLAHOMA CRIMINAL REPORTS. Warden Company, Oklahoma City, Oklahoma. 1908-1953. (Court of Criminal Appeals).

OKLAHOMA DECISIONS. West Publishing Company, P.O. Box 64526, 50 West Kellogg Boulevard, St. Paul, Minnesota 55164-0526. 1931- . (Supreme Court, Court of Appeals, and Court of Criminal Appeals) (Current official sources in Pacific Reporter).

OKLAHOMA REPORTS. Harlow Publishing Company, Oklahoma City, Oklahoma. 1890-1953. (Supreme Court) (Current official source is Pacific Reporter).

PACIFIC REPORTER. (First and second series). West Publishing Company, P.O. Box 64526, 50 West Kellogg Boulevard, St. Paul, Minnesota 55164-0526. 1890- . (Supreme Court, Court of Appeals, and Court of Criminal Appeals).

ATTORNEY GENERAL OPINIONS

OPINIONS OF THE ATTORNEY GENERAL. Office of the Attorney General, State Capitol, Oklahoma City, Oklahoma 73105. 1968- . Irregular. Also available on microform. William S. Hein, Microform Division, 1285 Main Street, Buffalo, New York 14209. 1985. Available on Lexis: January 1977-).

ETHICS OPINIONS, CODES, RULES

Oklahoma Code of Professional Responsibility is published in Oklahoma Statutes , volume 5, chapter 1, appendix 3. 1981- . (Annual Supplements).

Oklahoma Disciplinary Rules are published in Oklahoma Statutes, volume 5, chapter 1, appendix 1a.

Oklahoma Ethics Opinions are issued by the Professional Responsibility Commission of the Oklahoma Bar Association and are published in the Oklahoma Bar Journal. For decisions covering the years ( ) see volumes 411-413 and 523-526 of the Pacific Reporter. Abstracts are published in the ABA/BNA Lawyers' Manual on Professional Conduct. For further information concerning these opinions, contact the General Counsel of the Oklahoma Bar Center, 1901 North Lincoln Boulevard, P.O. Box 53036, Oklahoma City, Oklahoma 73152; telephone: 405-524-2365.

COURT RULES

OKLAHOMA COURT RULES AND PROCEDURE: STATE AND FEDERAL. West Publishing Company, P.O. Box 64526, 50 West Kellogg Boulevard, St. Paul, Minnesota 55164-0526. (Annual).

JURY INSTRUCTIONS

OKLAHOMA UNIFORM JURY INSTRUCTIONS, CIVIL. Oklahoma Supreme Court Committee for Uniform Civil Instructions, Oklahoma Bar Association, P.O. Box 53036, Oklahoma City, Oklahoma 73152. 1983- . (Periodic Supplements).

OKLAHOMA UNIFORM JURY INSTRUCTIONS, CRIMINAL. Commission on Oklahoma Uniform Jury Instructions (Criminal). Oklahoma Center for Criminal Justice, Norman, Oklahoma. 1981- . (Periodic Supplements).

DIGESTS, INDEXES, ABSTRACTS, CITATORS

OKLAHOMA DIGEST. West Publishing Company, P.O. Eox 64526, 50 West Kellogg Boulevard, St. Paul, Minnesota 55164-0526. 1974- . (Annual Supplements).

PACIFIC DIGEST. West Publishing Company, P.O. Box 64526, 50 West Kellogg Boulevard, St. Paul, Minnesota 55164-0526. 1932- . (Annual Supplements).

SHEPARD'S OKLAHOMA CITATIONS. Shepard's/McGraw-Hill, P.O. Box 1235, Colorado Springs, Colorado 80901. (Six supplements per year.)

SHEPARD'S PACIFIC REPORTER CITATIONS. Shepard's/McGraw-Hill, P.O. Box 1235, Colorado Springs, Colorado 80901. (Monthly Supplements).

LAW REVIEWS AND PEIODICALS

OKLAHOMA BAR JOURNAL. Oklahoma Bar Association, P.O. Box 53036, Oklahoma City, Oklahoma 73152. Weekly.

OKLAHOMA CITY UNIVERSITY LAW REVIEW. Oklahoma City University School of law, 2501 North Blackwelder, Oklahoma City, Oklahoma 73106. Three issues per year.

OKLAHOMA LAW REVIEW. University of Oklahoma College of Law, 300 West Timbedell Road, Norman, Oklahoma 73019. Quarterly.

TULSA LAW JOURNAL. University of Tulsa College of Law, 3120 East Fourth Place, Tulsa, Oklahoma 74104. Quarterly.

NEWSLETTERS AND NEWSPAPERS

DAILY LEGISLATIVE REPORTER. Oklahoma Business News Company, 605 Northwest Thirteenth Street, Suite C, Oklahoma City, Oklahoma 73101. Daily.

OKLAHOMA ENERGY-ENVIRONMENTAL REPORT. Oklahoma Business News Company, 605 Northwest Thirteenth Street, Suite C, Oklahoma City, Oklahoma 73101. Daily.

OKLAHOMA INSURANCE REPORTER. Oklahoma Business News Company, 605 Northwest Thirteenth Street, Suite C, Oklahoma City, Oklahoma 73101. Daily.

OKLAHOMA LIQUOR REPORT. Oklahoma Business News Company, 605 Northwest Thirteenth Street, Suite C, Oklahoma City, Oklahoma 73101. Daily.

THE OKLAHOMA OIL REPORTER. Oklahoma Business News Company, 605 Northwest Thirteenth Street, Suite C, Oklahoma City, Oklahoma 73101. Daily.

WEEKLY REVIEW. Oklahoma Business News Company, 605 Northwest Thirteenth Street, Suite C, Oklahoma City, Oklahoma 73101. Daily.

PRACTICE MATERIALS

ADMINISTRATION OF ESTATES. Oklahoma Bar Association, 1901 North Lincoln, Oklahoma City, Oklahoma 73105. 1983.

BASIC WORKER'S COMPENSATION. Oklahoma Bar Association, 1901 North Lincoln, Oklahoma City, Oklahoma 73105. 1984.

OKLAHOMA APPELLATE ADVOCACY. Oklahoma Bar Association, 1901 North Lincoln, Oklahoma City, Oklahoma 73105. 1983.

OKLAHOMA BAR ASSOCIATION DESK MANUAL. Oklahoma Bar Association, P.O. Box 53036, Oklahoma City, Oklahoma 73152. 1986.

OKLAHOMA EVIDENCE. Leo H. Whinery. West Publishing Company, P.O. Box 64526, 50 West Kellogg Boulevard, St. Paul, Minnesota 55164-0526. 1985- .

MANUALS AND RESEARCH GUIDES

OKLAHOMA LEGAL AND LAW RELATED DOCUMENTS AND PUBLICATIONS: A SELECTED BIBLIOGRAPHY. Christine Corcos. University of Oklahoma Law Center Library, American Association of Law Libraries, Government Documents, SIS, 53 West Jackson Boulevard, Suite 703, Chicago, Illinois 60604. 1983.

ASSOCIATIONS AND PROFESSIONAL SOCIETIES

OKLAHOMA BAR ASSOCIATION, 1901 North Lincoln, Oklahoma City, Oklahoma 73105. (405) 524-2365.

OKLAHOMA COUNTY BAR ASSOCIATION, 500 West Main, Suite 100, Oklahoma City, Oklahoma 73102. (405) 236-8421.

TULSA COUNTY BAR ASSOCIATION, 1446 South Boston, Tulsa, Oklahoma 74119. (918) 584-5243.

DIRECTORIES

DIRECTORY OF OKLAHOMA. Oklahoma Department of Libraries, 200 Northeast Eighteenth Street, Oklahoma City, Oklahoma 73105. Biennial. (Summer of odd years).

DIRECTORY OF OKLAHOMA'S CITY AND TOWN OFFICIALS. Oklahoma Municipal League, 201 Northeast Twenty-third Street, Oklahoma City, Oklahoma 73105. Annual. (July)

OKLAHOMA LEGAL DIRECTORY. Legal Directories Publishing Company, 2122 Kidwell, P.O. Box 140200, Dallas, Texas 75214-0200. Annual. (November)

OKLAHOMA LEGISLATIVE DIRECTORY. Oklahoma Press Service Incorporated, 3501 North Lincoln Boulevard, Oklahoma City, Oklahoma 73105. Biennial. (December of even years).

OKLAHOMA STATE AGENCIES. Legislative Reference Division, Oklahoma Department of Libraries, 200 Northeast Eighteenth Street, Oklahoma City, Oklahoma 73105. Annual. (Fall)

ROSTER OF OKLAHOMA: STATE AND COUNTY OFFICERS. Oklahoma State Election Board, State Capitol, Room 3B, Oklahoma City, Oklahoma 73105. Biennial. (December of even years).

WHO IS WHO IN THE OKLAHOMA LEGISLATURE. Legislative Reference Division, Oklahoma Department of Libraries, 200 Northeast Eighteenth Street, Oklahoma City, Oklahoma 73105. Biennial. (December of even years).

STATES--OREGON

STATUTES, CODES, STANDARDS, UNIFORM LAWS

ADMINISTRATIVE RULES BULLETIN. Secretary of State, Administrative Rules Section, Room 136, State Capitol, Salem, Oregon 97310. Biweekly.

OREGON ADMINISTRATIVE RULES COMPILATION. Secretary of State, Administrative Rules Division, Room 136, State Capitol, Salem, Oregon 97310. 1983- . (Monthly Supplements).

OREGON LAWS. (Session Laws). Oregon Legislative Assembly. Available from Legislative Counsel Committee S101, State Capitol, Salem, Oregon 97310-0630. Biannual.

OREGON REVISED STATUTES. (Official edition). Legislative Counsel Committee, State Capitol, Salem, Oregon 97310. 1953- . (Periodic Supplements).

OREGON REVISED STATUTES. Butterworth Legal Publishers, 90 Stiles Road, Salem, New Hampshire 03079. 1986- . (Periodic Supplements).

LOOSELEAF SERVICES AND REPORTERS

OREGON CASES. West Publishing Company, P.O. Box 64526, 50 West Kellogg Boulevard, St. Paul, Minnesota 55164-0526. 1966- . (Supreme Court and Court of Appeals).

OREGON REPORTS. Office of the State Court Administrator, Publication Section, Supreme Court Building, Salem, Oregon 97310. 1853- . (Supreme Court).

OREGON REPORTS--COURT OF APPEALS. State Court Administrator, Publication Section, Supreme Court Building, Salem, Oregon 97310. 1969- .

OREGON TAX REPORTS. Secretary of State, Room 136, State Capitol, Salem, Oregon 97310. 1962- .

PACIFIC REPORTER. (First and second series). West Publishing Company, P.O. Box 64526, 50 West Kellogg Boulevard, St. Paul, Minnesota 55164-0526. 1883- . (Supreme Court and Court of Appeals).

ATTORNEY GENERAL OPINIONS

OPINIONS OF THE ATTORNEY GENERAL OF THE STATE OF OREGON. Office of the Attorney General, Justice Department, State Office Building, Salem, Oregon 97310. (Also available on Lexis: July 1976- .).

ETHICS OPINIONS, CODES, RULES

PROFESSIONAL RESPONSIBILITY MANUAL. Board of Governors of the Oregon State Bar, Oregon State Bar, 5200 Southwest Meadows Road, P.O. Box 1689, Lake Oswego, Oregon 97035-0889. 1985. (Includes Ethical Code, Disciplinary Rules, Discipline Board Citations and Oregon Legal Ethics Opinions). Abstracts of opinions are published in the ABA/BNA Lawyer's Manual on Professional Conduct. For further information concerning Ethics opinions, contact the Board of Governors of the Oregon State Bar at: (503-620-0222).

COURT RULES

LOCAL RULES OF THE CIRCUIT AND DISTRICT COURTS, OREGON. Butterworth Legal Publishers, 90 Stiles Road, Salem, New Hampshire 03079. 1981- . (Periodic Supplements).

OREGON RULES OF COURT. (Desk copy) West Publishing Company, P.O. Box 64526, 50 West Kellogg Boulevard, St. Paul, Minnesota 55164-0526. Annual.

JURY INSTRUCTIONS

OREGON JURY INSTRUCTIONS FOR CIVIL CASES. Oregon State Bar, Committee on Uniform Civil Jury Instructions. Oregon State Bar, 5200 S.W. Meadows Road, P.O. Box 1689, Lake Oswego, Oregon 97035-0889. 1984- . (Periodic Supplements).

OREGON JURY INSTRUCTIONS FOR CRIMINAL CASES. Oregon State Bar, Committee on Uniform Criminal Jury Instructions. Oregon State Bar, 5200 S.W. Meadows Road, P.O. Box 1689, Lake Oswego, Oregon 97035-0889. 1984- . (Periodic Supplements).

DIGESTS, INDEXES, ABSTRACTS, CITATORS

OREGON DIGEST. West Publishing Company, P.O. Box 64526, 50 West Kellogg Boulevard, St. Paul, Minnesota 55164-0526. 1961- . (Annual Supplements).

PACIFIC DIGEST. West Publishing Company, P.O. Box 64526, 50 West Kellogg Boulevard, St. Paul, Minnesota 55164-0526. 1932- . (Annual Supplements).

SHEPARD'S OREGON CITATIONS. Shepard's/McGraw-Hill, P.O. Box 1235, Colorado Springs, Colorado 80901. (Bimonthly Supplements).

SHEPARD'S PACIFIC REPORTER CITATIONS. Shepard's/McGraw-Hill, P.O. Box 1235, Colorado Springs, Colorado 80901. (Monthly Supplements).

LAW REVIEWS AND PERIODICALS

OREGON LAW REVIEW. School of Law, University of Oregon, Eugene, Oregon 97403. Quarterly.

OREGON STATE BAR BULLETIN. Oregon State Bar, 1776 Southwest Madison Street, Portland, Oregon 97205. 1941- . Monthly.

WILLAMETTE LAW REVIEW. Willamette University College of Law, 250 Winter Street Southeast, Salem, Oregon 97301. Quarterly.

NEWSLETTERS AND NEWSPAPERS

BARCLAY'S OREGON ADVANCE CITATOR. Barclay's Law Publishers, 400 Oyster Point Boulevard, Suite 500, South San Francisco, California 94080. Monthly.

THE CRIMINAL LAW NEWSLETTER. Oregon Criminal Defense Lawyers Association, 44 West Broadway, Suite 403, Eugene, Oregon 97401. Monthly.

THE OREGON DEFENSE ATTORNEY. Oregon Criminal Defense Lawyers Association, 44 West Broadway, Suite 403, Eugene, Oregon 97401. Bimonthly.

FORMBOOKS

CRIMINAL LAW FORMBOOK. Oregon Criminal Defense Lawyers Association, 7 East Broadway, Eugene, Oregon 97401. 1982- . (Periodic Supplements).

PRACTICE MATERIALS

ADMINISTERING OREGON ESTATES. James Perry, editor. Oregon State Bar, 5200 S.W. Meadows Road, P.O. Box 1689, Lake Oswego, Oregon 97035-0889. 1977- . (Periodic Supplements).

ATTORNEY GENERAL'S ADMINISTRATIVE LAW MANUAL AND MODEL RULES OF PROCEDURE. State of Oregon, Department of Justice, State Office Building, Salem, Oregon 97310. 1983.

CIVIL LITIGATION MANUAL. Second edition. Randolph Foster and J. Webb, editors. Oregon State Bar, 5200 S.W. Meadows Road, P.O. Box 1689, Lake Oswego, Oregon 97035-0889. 1982- . (Periodic Supplements).

CIVIL PLEADING AND PRACTICE. Oregon State Bar, 5200 S.W. Meadows Road, P.O. Box 1689, Lake Oswego, Oregon 97035-0889. 1985- . (Periodic Supplemnts).

CREDITOR'S RIGHTS AND REMEDIES. Jerome Shann and N. Wapnick, editors. Oregon State Bar, 5200 Southwest Meadows Road, P.O. Box 1689, Lake Oswego, Oregon 97035-0889. 1978- . (Periodic Supplements).

CRIMINAL LAW. William Snouffer, editor. Revised edition. Oregon State Bar, 5200 Southwest Meadows Road, P.O. Box 1689, Lake Oswego, Oregon 97035-0889. 1977- . (Periodic Supplements).

EMPLOYMENT IN OREGON. Joan Smith Lawrence. Butterworth Legal Publishers, 90 Stiles Road, Salem, New Hampshire 03079. 1982- . (Periodic Supplements).

FAMILY LAW. Richard Baldwin, et al., editors. Oregon State Bar, 5200 S.W. Meadows Road, P.O. Box 1689, Lake Oswego, Oregon 97035-0889. 1983- . (Periodic Supplements).

JURISDICTION AND SUMMONS IN OREGON. Fredrick R. Merrill. Butterworth Legal Publishers, 90 Stiles Road, Salem, New Hampshire 03079. 1986- . (Periodic Supplements).

LAND USE. James Mattis, et al. Oregon State Bar, 5200 S.W. Meadows Road, P.O. Box 1689, Lake Oswego, Oregon 97035-0889. 1982- . (Periodic Supplements).

OREGON DEBTOR-CREDITOR LAW. Brian A. Blum. Butterworth Legal Publishers, 90 Stiles Road, Salem, New Hampshire 03079. 1991.

THE TRIAL NOTEBOOK. Oregon Criminal Defense Lawyers Association, 7 East Broadway, Eugene, Oregon 97401. 1984- . (Periodic Supplements).

WORKER'S COMPENSATION--OREGON. Oregon State Bar, 5200 Southwest Meadows Road, P.O. Box 1689, Lake Oswego, Oregon 97035-0889. 1984- . (Looseleaf).

MANUALS AND RESEARCH GUIDES

BIBLIOGRAPHY OF LAW RELATED OREGON DOCUMENTS. Lesley Ann Buhman, et al. American Association of Law Libraries, Government SIS Section, 53 West Jackson Boulevard, Chicago, Illinois 60604. 1984.

ASSOCIATIONS AND PROFESSIONAL SOCIETIES

LANE COUNTY BAR ASSOCIATION, 200 Forum Building, 777 High Street, Eugene, Oregon 97401.

MULTNOMAH BAR ASSOCIATION, 711 Southwest Adler, Suite 311, Portland, Oregon 97205. (503) 222-3275.

OREGON BAR ASSOCIATION, 5200 Southwest Meadows Road, P.O. Box 1689, Lake Oswego, Oregon 97035-0889. (503) 620-0222.

OREGON CRIMINAL DEFENSE LAWYERS ASSOCIATION, 7 East Broadway, Eugene, Oregon 97401.

STATES--OREGON

DIRECTORIES

OREGON AND WASHINGTON LEGAL DIRECTORY [INCLUDING ALASKA]. Legal Directories Publishing Company, 2122 Kidwell Street, P.O. Box 140200, Dallas, Texas 75214-0200. Annual. (March).

OREGON BLUE BOOK. Oregon Secretary of State, State Capitol, Room 136, Salem, Oregon 97310. Biennial. (Spring of odd years).

STATES--PENNSYLVANIA

STATUTES, CODES, STANDARDS, UNIFORM LAWS

LAWS OF THE GENERAL ASSEMBLY OF THE COMMON-WEALTH OF PENNSYLVANIA. State Book Store, P.O. Box 1365, 10th and Market Streets, Harrisburg, Pennsylvania 17120. Annual.

PENNSYLVANIA BULLETIN. Legislative Reference Bureau, Main Capitol, Harrisburg, Pennsylvania 17120. Weekly.

PENNSYLVANIA CODE. (Administrative Code). Fry Communications, Incorporated, 800 West Church Road, Mechanicsburg, Pennsylvania 17055-3198. 1970- . (Quarterly Supplements).

PENNSYLVANIA LEGISLATIVE SERVICE. West Publishing Company, P.O. Box 64526, 50 West Kellogg Boulevard, St. Paul, Minnesota 55164-0526. (Irregular).

PURDON'S PENNSYLVANIA STATUTES ANNOTATED. West Publishing Company, P.O. Box 64526, 50 West Kellogg Boulevard, St. Paul, Minnesota 55164-0526. 1930- . (Annual Supplements).

LOOSELEAF SERVICES AND REPORTERS

ATLANTIC REPORTER. (First and second series). West Publishing Company, P.O. Box 64526, 50 West Kellogg Boulevard, St. Paul, Minnesota 55164-0526. 1885- . (Supreme Court, Superior Court, and Commonwealth Court).

LACKAWANNA JURIST. Lackawanna Bar Association, Lackawanna County Court House, Scranton, Pennsylvania 18503. 1888- . (Contains decisions of the courts of Lackawanna County and other county courts in Pennsylvania).

PENNSYLVANIA COMMONWEALTH COURT REPORTS. Murrelle Printing Company, Sayre, Pennsylvania 1970- .

PENNSYLVANIA COUNTY COURT REPORTS. T. and J.W. Johnson, Philadelphia, Pennsylvania. 1885-1921. (Pennsylvania lower courts).

PENNSYLVANIA DISTRICT AND COUNTY REPORTS. (First through third series). The Legal Intelligencer, Philadelphia, Pennsylvania 1921- . (Pennsylvania lower courts).

PENNSYLVANIA REPORTER. West Publishing Company, P.O. Box 64526, 50 West Kellogg Boulevard, St. Paul, Minnesota 55164-0526. 1939- . (Supreme Court, Superior Court, and Commonwealth Court).

PENNSYLVANIA STATE REPORTS. West Publishing Company, P.O. Box 64526, 50 West Kellogg Boulevard, St. Paul, Minnesota 55164-0526. 1845- .

PENNSYLVANIA SUPERIOR COURT REPORTS. West Publishing Company, P.O. Box 64526, 50 West Kellogg Boulevard, St. Paul, Minnesota 55164-0526. 1895- .

PENNSYLVANIA TAX REPORTER. Commerce Clearing House, Incorporated, 4025 West Peterson Avenue, Chicago, Illinois 60646. (Looseleaf).

PENNSYLVANIA TAX SERVICE. Matthew Bender and Company, Incorporated, 11 Penn Plaza, New York, New York 10001. 1986- . (Periodic Supplements).

ATTORNEY GENERAL OPINIONS

OFFICIAL OPINIONS OF THE ATTORNEY GENERAL OF PENNSYLVANIA FOR THE YEARS... Office of the Attorney General, 1525 Strawberry Square, Harrisburg, Pennsylvania 17120. Only single copies available. (Also available on Lexis and Westlaw: 1977- .)

ETHICS OPINIONS, CODES, RULES

ALLEGHENEY COUNTY BAR ASSOCIATION: ETHICS OPINIONS. Pittsburgh Legal Journal. 920 City-County Building, Pittsburgh, Pennsylvania 15219.

OPINIONS OF THE PHILADELPHIA ASSOCIATION PROFESSIONAL GUIDANCE COMMITTEE. Philadelphia Bar Association, 1 Reading Center, Philadelphia, Pennsylvania 19107. 1983. For further information concerning Pennsylvania ethics opinions contact the Committee on Legal Ethics and Professional Resposibility of the Pennsylvania Bar Association, (717) 238-6715.

COURT RULES

PENNSYLVANIA CONSOLIDATED RULES. Rules Service Company, 7658 Standish Place, Rockville, Maryland 20855. 1972- . (Periodic Supplements).

PENNSYLVANIA RULES OF COURT: STATE AND FEDERAL. West Publishing Company, P.O. Box 64526, 50 West Kellogg Boulevard, St. Paul, Minnesota 55164-0526. Annual.

JURY INSTRUCTIONS

PENNSYLVANIA SUGGESTED STANDARD CIVIL JURY INSTRUCTIONS. Pennsylvania Bar Institute, P.O. Box 1027, Harrisburg, Pennsylvania 17108. 1981- . (Periodic Supplements).

DIGESTS, INDEXES, ABSTRACTS, CITATORS

ATLANTIC DIGEST. (First and second series). West Publishing Company, P.O. Box 64526, 50 West Kellogg Boulevard, St. Paul, Minnesota 55164-0526. 1930- . (Annual Supplements).

PENNSYLVANIA CRIMINAL LAW DIGEST. Gould Publications, 199 State Street, Binghamton, New York 13901. (Periodic Supplements).

PENNSYLVANIA DIGEST. (First and second series). West Publishing Company, P.O. Box 64526, 50 West Kellogg Boulevard, St. Paul, Minnesota 55164-0526. 1938- . (Annual Supplements).

SHEPARD'S ATLANTIC REPORTER CITATIONS. Shepard's/ McGraw-Hill, P.O. Box 1235, Colorado Springs, Colorado 80901. (Monthly Supplements).

SHEPARD'S PENNSYLVANIA CITATIONS. Shepard's/ McGraw-Hill, P.O. Box 1235, Colorado Springs, Colorado 80901. (Eight supplements per year).

ENCYCLOPEDIAS AND DICTIONARIES

PENNSYLVANIA LAW ENCYCLOPEDIA. West Publishing Company, P.O. Box 64526, 50 West Kellogg Boulevard, St. Paul, Minnesota 55164-0526. 1957- . (Annual Supplements). (Publisher varies).

LAW REVIEWS AND PERIODICALS

DICKINSON JOURNAL OF INTERNATIONAL LAW. Dickinson School of Law, 150 South College Street, Carliste, Pennsylvania 17013. Semiannual.

DICKINSON LAW REVIEW. Dickinson School of Law, 150 South College Street, Carlisle, Pennsylvania 17012. Quarterly.

DUQUESNE LAW REVIEW. Duquesne University School of Law, 900 Locust Street, Pittsburgh, Pennsylvania 15282. Quarterly.

PENNSYLVANIA BAR ASSOCIATION QUARTERLY. P.O. Box 186, Harrisburg, Pennsylvania 17108. Quarterly. (January, April, July, and October).

THE PENNSYLVANIA LAWYER. Pennsylvania Bar Association, P.O. Box 186, Harrisburg, Pennsylvania 17108. Eight issues per year.

THE PENNSYLVANIA RESEARCHER. National Legal Research Group, Incorporated, 2421 Ivy Road, Charlotesville, Virginia 22906-7587. Monthly.

TEMPLE LAW QUARTERLY. Temple University School of Law, 1719 North Broad Street, Philadelphia, Pennsylvania 19122. Quarterly.

UNIVERSITY OF PENNSYLVANIA LAW REVIEW. University of Pennsylvania Law School, 3400 Chestnut Street, Philadelphia, Pennsylvania 19104. Six issues per year.

UNIVERSITY OF PITTSBURGH LAW REVIEW. University of Pittsburgh School of Law, Pittsburgh, Pennsylvania 15260. Quarterly.

VILLANOVA LAW REVIEW. Villanova University School of Law, Villanova, Pennsylvania 19085. Five issues per year.

NEWSLETTERS AND NEWSPAPERS

BARCLAY'S PENNSYLVANIA ADVANCE CITATOR. Barclay's Law Publishers, 400 Oyster Point Boulevard, Suite 500, South San Francisco, California 94080. Monthly.

COMMONWEALTH REGISTER. 51st Associates, 216 Briggs Street, Harrisburg, Pennsylvania 17102. Weekly.

THE GENERAL PRACTICE PRIMER. Pennsylvania Bar Association, 100 South Street, Harrisburg, Pennsylvania 17108. Quarterly.

PENNSYLVANIA FAMILY LAWYER. Pennsylvania Bar Association, 100 South Street, Harrisburg, Pennsylvania 17108. Bimonthly.

PENNSYLVANIA JURY REVIEW AND ANAYLSIS. Jury Verdict Review Publications, Incorporated, 24 Commerce Street, Suite 1722, Newark, New Jersey 07102. Monthly.

PENNSYLVANIA LAW JOURNAL-REPORTS. Tenth and Spring Garden Streets, Philadelphia, Pennsylvania 19123. (Forty-eight issues per year).

REAL PROPERTY, PROBATE AND TRUST LAW NEWSLETTER. Pennsylvania Bar Association, 100 South Street, Harrisburg, Pennsylvania 17108. Semiannually.

FORMBOOKS

DUNLAP-HANNA, PENNSYLVANIA FORMS. Matthew Bender and Company, Incorporated, 11 Penn Plaza, New York, New York 10001. 1948-1975.

PENNSYLVANIA CIVIL PRACTICE, RULES AND FORMS. R. Anderson. West Publishing Company, 50 West Kellogg Boulevard, St. Paul, Minnesota 55164. (Annual).

PENNSYLVANIA TRANSACTION GUIDE--LEGAL FORMS. Matthew Bender and Company, Incorporated, 11 Penn Plaza, New York, New York 10001. 1974-1977.

PURDON'S PENNSYLVANIA FORMS. Ronald A. Anderson. West Publishing Company, P.O. Box 64526, 50 West Kellogg Boulevard, St. Paul, Minnesota 55164-0526. 1973- . (Periodic Supplements).

PRACTICE MATERIALS

FAMILY LAW MANUAL--PENNSYLVANIA. William D. Paton and William C. Stanley. Hanford Publishing Company, 1284 Wheatland Avenue, Lancaster, Pennsylvania 17603. 1984- . (Periodic Supplement).

LADNER ON CONVEYANCING IN PENNSYLVANIA. Fourth edition. George T. Bisel Company, 710 South Washington Square, Philadelphia, Pennsylvania 19106. 1979- . (Periodic Supplements).

LAW OF WILLS IN PENNSYLVANIA: DRAFTING, INTERPRETING, CONTESTING WITH FORMS. J. Brooke Aker. George T. Bisel Company, 710 South Washington Square, Philadelphia, Pennsylvania 19106. 1983- . (Annual Supplements).

LAW OF ZONING IN PENNSYLVANIA. Robert M. Anderson. Lawyers Co-Operative Company, Aqueduct Building, Rochester, New York 14694. 1982- . (Annual Supplements).

NO FAULT DIVORCE IN PENNSYLVANIA: WHAT EVERYONE SHOULD KNOW ABOUT DIVORCE. Samuel K. Gates and Mark David Frankel. George Shumway, RD 7, Box 388B, York, Pennsylvania 17402 1983.

PENNSYLVANIA APPELLATE PRACTICE. G. Ronald Darlington, Kevin J. McKeon, Donald R. Schuckers, and Kristen W. Brown. Lawyers Co-Operative Company, Aqueduct Building, Rochester, New York 14694. 1986- . (Annual Supplements).

PENNSYLVANIA ARRESTS, SEARCHES, AND SEIZURES. Robert B. Harper. Harrison Company, 3110 Crossing Park, Norcross, Georgia 30071. 1983- . (Periodic Supplements).

PENNSYLVANIA CIVIL PRACTICE. West Publishing Company, P.O. Box 64526, 50 West Kellogg Boulevard, St. Paul, Minnesota 55164-0526.

PENNSYLVANIA CRIMINAL PRACTICE. Richard S. Wasserbly. Callaghan and Company, 155 Pfingsten Road, Deerfield, Illinois 60015. 1981- . (Periodic Supplements).

PENNSYLVANIA DIVORCE CODE. Norman Perlberger. George T. Bisel Company, 710 South Washington Square, Philadelphia, Pennsylvania 19106. 1980- . (Annual Supplements).

PENNSYLVANIA ESTATE PLANNING AND DRAFTING. J. B. Aker. George T. Bisel Company, 710 South Washington Square, Philadelphia, Pennsylvania 19106. 1969- . (Annual Supplements).

PENNSYLVANIA ESTATE PRACTICE. Nancy Rothkopf and Gilbert M. Cantor. Lawyers Co-Operative Company, Aqueduct Building, Rochester, New York 14694. 1980- . (Annual Supplements).

PENNSYLVANIA EVIDENCE: OBJECTIONS AND RESPONSES. Mark S. Greenberg and Anthony J. Bocchino. Michie Company, P.O. Box 7587, Charlottesville, Virginia 22906-7587. 1983.

PENNSYLVANIA FAMILY LAW. Albert Momjian and Norman Perlberger. George T. Bisel Company, 710 South Washington Square, Philadelphia, Pennsylvania 19106. 1978- . (Periodic Supplements).

PENNSYLVANIA FIDUCIARY GUIDE: A HANDBOOK FOR EXECUTORS AND ADMINISTRATORS. Fourth revised edition. M. Paul Smith, Richard L. Grossman, and J. L. Hollinger. George T. Bisel Company, 710 South Washington Square, Philadelphia, Pennsylvania 19106. 1983- . (Periodic Supplements).

PENNSYLVANIA GUIDE TO CRIMINAL PRACTICE AND PROCEDURE. Theodore L. Reimel. George T. Bisel Company, 710 South Washington Square, Philadelphia, Pennsylvania 19106. 1969- . (Annual Supplements).

PENNSYLVANIA INHERITANCE AND ESTATE TAX. Second edition. Richard Grossman and M. Paul Smith. George T. Bisel Company, 710 South Washington Square, Philadelphia, Pennsylvania 19106. 1986- . (Annual Supplements).

PENNSYLVANIA JUVENILE DELINQUENCY PRACTICE AND PROCEDURE. Francis B. McCarthy. Harrison Company, 3110 Crossing Park, Norcross, Georgia 30071. 1984.

PENNSYLVANIA MARRIAGE, DIVORCE, CUSTODY, PROPERTY, AND SUPPORT. Joseph B. Kelly. Harrison Company, 3110 Crossing Park, Norcross, Georgia 30071. 1985.

PENNSYLVANIA MATRIMONIAL PRACTICE. Jack A. Rounick. Lawyers Co-Operative Company, Aqueduct Building, Rochester, New York 14694. 1982- . (Annual Supplements).

PENNSYLVANIA REAL ESTATE. Emil L. Iannelli and Lynne P. Iannelli. Lawyers Co-Operative Company, Aqueduct Building, Rochester, New York 14694. 1984- . (Annual Supplements).

PENNSYLVANIA TRIAL GUIDE. Second revised edition. Stephen M. Feldman. George T. Bisel Company, 710 South Washington Square, Philadelphia, Pennsylvania 19106. 1987- . (Periodic Supplements).

PENNSYLVANIA WORKMEN'S COMPENSATION, INJURY, AND DISEASE LAWS. Alexander F. Barbieri. George T. Bisel Company, 710 South Washington Square, Philadelphia, Pennsylvania 19106. 1975- . (Periodic Supplements).

PROBATE, ESTATES, AND FIDUCIARIES CODE ANNOTATED: WITH FORMS. J. Brooke Aker. George T. Bisel Company, 710 South Washington Square, Philadelphia, Pennsylvania 19106. 1975- . (Annual Supplements).

STANDARD PENNSYLVANIA PRACTICE. Second edition. Lawyers Co-Operative Company, Aqueduct Building, Rochester, New York 14694.

STERN'S TRICKETT ON LANDLORD AND TENANT IN PENNSYLVANIA. M. Stern. George T. Bisel Company, 710 South Washington Square, Philadelphia, Pennsylvania 19106. 1973- . (Periodic Supplements).

TRIAL HANDBOOK FOR PENNSYLVANIA LAWYERS. Jack Kleiner and Edwin P. Rome. Lawyers Co-Operative Company, Aqueduct Building, Rochester, New York 14694. 1980- . (Annual Supplements).

TROUTMAN'S PENNSYLVANIA INJURY VERDICTS. George T. Bisel Company, 710 South Washington Square, Philadelphia, Pennsylvania 19106. 1969- . (Annual Supplements).

WORKER'S COMPENSATION REPORTER--PENNSYLVANIA. LRP Publications, P.O. Box 980, 747 Dresher Road, Horsham, Pennsylvania 19044-0980. 1987- . (Monthly Supplements).

MANUALS AND RESEARCH GUIDES

AN INTRODUCTION TO PENNSYLVANIA STATE PUBLICATIONS FOR THE LAW LIBRARIAN. Compiled by Joel Fishman, American Association of Law Libraries, 53 West Jackson Boulevard, Suite 703, Chicago, Illinois 60604. 1985.

RESEARCH IN PENNSYLVANIA LAW. Second edition. Edwin C. Surrency. Oceana Publications, 75 Main Street, Dobbs Ferry, New York 10522. 1965.

ASSOCIATIONS AND PROFESSIONAL SOCIETIES

ALLEGHENY COUNTY BAR ASSOCIATION, 420 Grant Building, Pittsburg, Pennsylvania 15219. (412) 261-6161.

BAR ASSOCIATION OF LEHIGH COUNTY, Old Lehigh County Courthouse, Fifth and Hamilton Streets, Allentown, Pennsylvania 18105.

BERKO COUNTY BAR ASSOCIATION, 544 Court Street, P.O. Box 1058, Reading, Pennsylvania 19603.

BUCKO COUNTY BAR ASSOCIATION, 135 East State Street, P.O. Box 511, Doylestown, Pennsylvania 18901.

CHESTER COUNTY BAR ASSOCIATION, 15 West Gay Street, Westchester, Pennsylvania 19380.

CRAWFORD COUNTY BAR ASSOCIATION, Crawford County Courthouse, Meadville, Pennsylvania 16335.

DAUPIN COUNTY BAR ASSOCIATION, 213 North Front Street, Harrisburg, Pennsylvania 17101.

DELAWARE COUNTY BAR ASSOCIATION, Front and Lemon Streets, P.O. BOX 466, Media, Pennsylvania 19063.

ERIE COUNTY BAR ASSOCIATION, 501 Sassafras Street, Erie, Pennsylvania 16507.

LACKAWANNA BAR ASSOCIATION, Lackawanna County Courthouse, Scranton, Pennsylvania 18503. (703) 963-6712.

LANCASTER BAR ASSOCIATION, 11 Duke Street, Lancaster, Pennsylvania 17602.

MONTGOMERY BAR ASSOCIATION, 100 W. Airy Street, P.O. Box 268, Norristown, Pennsylvania 19404.

PENNSYLVANIA BAR ASSOCIATION, P.O. Box 186, 100 South Street, Harrisburg, Pennsylvania 17108. (717) 238-6715.

PHILADELPHIA BAR ASSOCIATION, One Reading Center, Philadelphia, Pennsylvania 19107. (215) 238-6300.

WESTMORELAND BAR ASSOCIATION, Courthouse-Mezzanine Floor, Greenburg, Pennsylvania 15601.

YORK COUNTY BAR ASSOCIATION, York County Courthouse, York, Pennsylvania 17401.

DIRECTORIES

CRIME VICTIM'S AID [NEW JERSEY, NEW YORK, AND PENNSYLVANIA; SOME NATIONAL]. Bloom Books, Incorporated, 1020 Broad Street, Newark, New Jersey 07102.

DIRECTORY OF STATE PUBLICATIONS [PENNSYLVANIA]. Pennsylvania Department of General Services, Records Center, Harrisburg, Pennsylvania 17125.

LEGAL DIRECTORY OF METROPOLITAN PHILADELPHIA. Packard Press, Tenth and Spring Garden Streets, Philadelphia, Pennsylvania 19123. Annual. (March)

LEGISLATORS AND GOVERNMENT OFFICIALS IN THE DELAWARE VALLEY TRI-STATE AREA. Greater Philadelphia Chamber of Commerce, Broad and Chestnut Streets, Philadelphia, Pennsylvania 19107. Biennial. (Odd years)

PENNSYLVANIA LAWYERS DIRECTORY. Pennsylvania Bar Association, P.O. Box 1027, Harrisburg, Pennsylvania 17108. Annual.

PENNSYLVANIA LEAGUE OF CITIES--DIRECTORY. Pennsylvania League of Cities, 2608 North Third Street, Harrisburg, Pennsylvania 17710. Annual. (Spring)

PENNSYLVANIA LEGAL DIRECTORY. Legal Directories Publishing Company, 2122 Kidwell, P.O. Box 140200, Dallas, Texas 75214-0200. Annual. (March)

PENNSYLVANIA MANUAL. Pennsylvania Department of General Services, North Office Building, Room 515, Harrisburg, Pennsylvania 17125. Biennial. (Fall of odd years).

PENNSYLVANIA MUNICIPAL YEARBOOK. Pennsylvania State Association of Boroughs, 2941 North Front Street, Harrisburg, Pennsylvania 17110. Annual. (June)

PENNSYLVANIA SENATE LEGISLATIVE DIRECTORY. Secretary of the Senate, Pennsylvania Legislature, State Capitol, Room 462, Harrisburg, Pennsylvania 17120. Biennial. (Summer of odd years).

PROFESSIONAL AND OCCUPATIONAL PRACTICE REQUREMENTS [PENNSYLVANIA]. Division of Planning Studies, Pennsylvania Commonwealth Educational System, Pennsylvania State University, University Park, Pennsylvania 16802. 1985.

STATES--RHODE ISLAND

STATUTES, CODES, STANDARDS, UNIFORM LAWS

GENERAL LAWS OF RHODE ISLAND. Office of the Secretary of State. Michie Company, P.O. Box 7587, Charlottesville, Virginia 22906-7587. 1956- . (Annual Supplements).

No Administrative Code or Register is published. Copies of Regulations are available at the Archives. An Administrative Code and Register are expected to begin publication in 1988.

RHODE ISLAND ADVANCE ANNOTATION SERVICE. Michie Company, P.O. Box 7587, Charlottesville, Virginia 22906-7587. 1985- . (Three pamphlets per year).

RHODE ISLAND PUBLIC LAWS. General Assembly of Rhode Island. Documents Distribution Center, Room 38, State House, Providence, Rhode Island 02903.

LOOSELEAF SERVICES AND REPORTERS

ATLANTIC REPORTER. (First and second series). West Publishing Company, P.O. Box 64526, 50 West Kellogg Boulevard, St. Paul, Minnesota 55164-0526. 1886- .

RHODE ISLAND REPORTER. West Publishing Company, P.O. Box 64526, 50 West Kellogg Boulevard, St. Paul, Minnesota 55164-0526. 1987- .

RHODE ISLAND REPORTS. Loshin Publishing Company. 1828-1983.

ATTORNEY GENERAL OPINIONS

RHODE ISLAND ATTORNEY GENERAL OPINIONS. Office of the Attorney General, 72 Pine Street, Providence, Rhode Island. (Subscriptions not available). (Not available on Lexis or Westlaw).

STATES--RHODE ISLAND

COURT RULES

RHODE ISLAND COURT RULES (Included in Rhode Island General Law , Volume 2-B). 1984- . (Annual Supplements).

DIGESTS, INDEXES, ABSTRACTS, CITATORS

ATLANTIC DIGEST. (First and Second Series). West Publishing Company, P.O. Box 64526, 50 West Kellogg Boulevard, St. Paul, Minnesota 55164-0526. 1949- . (Annual Supplements).

RHODE ISLAND DIGEST. West Publishing Company, P.O. Box 64526, 50 West Kellogg Boulevard, St. Paul, Minnesota 55164-0526. 1964- . (Annual Supplements).

SHEPARD'S ATLANTIC REPORTER CITATIONS. Shepard's/ McGraw-Hill, P.O. Box 1235, Colorado Springs, Colorado 80901. (Monthly Supplements).

SHEPARD'S RHODE ISLAND CITATIONS. Shepard's/ McGraw-Hill, P.O. Box 1235, Colorado Springs, Colorado 80901. (Quarterly Supplements).

LAW REVIEWS AND PERIODICALS

RHODE ISLAND BAR JOURNAL. Rhode Island Bar Journal, 91 Friendship Street, Providence, Rhode Island 02903. Monthly.

NEWSLETTERS AND NEWSPAPERS

THE MASSACHUSETTS, CONNECTICUT, RHODE ISLAND VERDICT REPORTER. Judicial Advisory Services, Incorporated, P.O. Box 99704, 3309 College Drive, Louisville, Kentucky 40299. Monthly.

FORMBOOKS

HANDBOOK OF RHODE ISLAND PROBATE FORMS. Third edition. Rhode Island Law Institute, P.O. Box 1425, Providence, Rhode Island 02901. 1985- . (Periodic Supplements).

DIRECTORIES

DIRECTORY OF LOCAL GOVERNMENT OFFICIALS IN RHODE ISLAND. Division of Local Government Assistance, Rhode Island Department of Administration, 275 Westminster Mall, Providence, Rhode Island 02903. Annual. (January)

JOURNAL-BULLETIN RHODE ISLAND ALMANAC. Providence Journal Company, 75 Fountain Street, Providence, Rhode Island 02902. Annual. (January)

RHODE ISLAND MANUAL. Rhode Island Secretary of State, State House, Room 291, Providence, Rhode Island 02903. Biennial. (January of even years).

ASSOCIATIONS AND PROFESSIONAL SOCIETIES

RHODE ISLAND BAR ASSOCIATION, 91 Friendship Street, Providence, Rhode Island 02903. (401) 421-5740.

STATES--SOUTH CAROLINA

STATUTES, CODES, STANDARDS, UNIFORM LAWS

CODE OF LAWS OF SOUTH CAROLINA ANNOTATED. Lawyers Co-Operative Company, Aqueduct Building, Rochester, New York 14694. 1976- . (Annual Supplements).

SOUTH CAROLINA RULES AND REGULATIONS. Lawyers Co-Operative Company, Aqueduct Building, Rochester, New York 14694. 1976- . (Issued as part of Code of Laws).

SOUTH CAROLINA STATE REGISTER. Legislative Council, State House, Columbia, South Carolina 29211. Monthly.

STATUTES AT LARGE OF SOUTH CAROLINA. (ACTS AND JOINT RESOLUTIONS OF THE GENERAL ASSEMBLY OF THE STATE OF SOUTH CAROLINA). Microform. William S. Hein, Microform Division, 1285 Main Street, Buffalo, New York 14209. Annual.

LOOSELEAF SERVICES AND REPORTERS

SOUTH CAROLINA REPORTS. R. L. Bryan Company, P.O. Box 368, Columbia, South Carolina 29202. 1868- .

SOUTH EASTERN REPORTER. West Publishing Company, P.O. Box 64526, 50 West Kellogg Boulevard, St. Paul, Minnesota 55164-0526. 1886- .

ATTORNEY GENERAL OPINIONS

ANNUAL REPORT AND OFFICIAL OPINIONS OF THE ATTORNEY GENERAL OF THE STATE OF SOUTH CAROLINA. Office of the Attorney General, P.O. Box 11549, Columbia, South Carolina 29211. Annual. Also Available on Lexis, January 1959- .

ETHICS OPINIONS, CODES, RULES

ADVISORY OPINIONS OF THE STATE OF SOUTH CAROLINA STATE ETHICS COMMISSION. South Carolina Bar Continuing Legal Education Division, P.O. Box 608, Columbia, South Carolina 29202-0608. 1977- . (Annual Supplements). (These are prospective, non-binding opinions).

Code of Professional Responsibility and Disciplinary Rules are published in The Lawyer's Deskbook , issued by the South Carolina Bar, P.O. Box 608, Columbia, South Carolina 29202-0608. Annual Supplements.

SOUTH CAROLINA ETHICS OPINIONS. Opinions are published in The Transcript . For further information contact the Ethics Advisory Committee of the South Carolina Bar, P.O. Box 608, Columbia, South Carolina 29202-0608. (803) 799-6653.

COURT RULES

SOUTH CAROLINA COURT RULES. Lawyers Co-Operative Company, Aqueduct Building, Rochester, New York 14694. 1976- . (Annual Supplements). (Also Published in volume 22 of Code of Laws of South Carolina 1976-).

SOUTH CAROLINA RULES OF COURT. West Publishing Company, P.O. Box 64526, 50 West Kellogg Boulevard, St. Paul, Minnesota 55164-0526.

JURY INSTRUCTIONS

Jury instructions for South Carolina are not published.

DIGESTS, INDEXES, ABSTRACTS, CITATORS

SHEPARD'S SOUTH CAROLINA CITATIONS. Shepard's/ McGraw-Hill, P.O. Box 1235, Colorado Springs, Colorado 80901. (Bimonthly Supplements).

SHEPARD'S SOUTH EASTERN REPORTER CITATIONS. Shepard's/McGraw-Hill, P.O. Box 1235, Colorado Springs, Colorado 80901. (Monthly Supplements).

SOUTHEASTERN DIGEST. West Publishing Company, P.O. Box 64526, 50 West Kellogg Boulevard, St. Paul, Minnesota 55164-0526. (Annual Supplements).

WEST'S SOUTH CAROLINA DIGEST. West Publishing Company, P.O. Box 64526, 50 West Kellogg Boulevard, St. Paul, Minnesota 55164-0526. (Annual Supplements).

LAW REVIEWS AND PERIODICALS

SOUTH CAROLINA LAW REVIEW. University of South Carolina School of Law, Columbia, South Carolina 29208. Quarterly.

THE TRANSCRIPT. South Carolina Bar, P.O. Box 11039, Columbia, South Carolina 29211. Monthly.

NEWSLETTERS AND NEWSPAPERS

THE SOUTH CAROLINA APPELLATE DIGEST. National Legal Research Group, Incorporated, 2421 Ivy Road, Charlottesville, Virginia 22906-7587. Biweekly.

PRACTICE MATERIALS

BANKRUPTCY PROCEDURE IN THE DISTRICT OF SOUTH CAROLINA. G. Levy. South Carolina Bar Association, 950 Taylor Street, Columbia, South Carolina 29201. 1982- .

CODE PLEADING. Second Edition. South Carolina Bar Association, 950 Taylor Street, Columbia, South Carolina 29201. 1984.

DRAFTING WILLS AND TRUSTS AGREEMENTS IN SOUTH CAROLINA. Robert P. Wilkens. South Carolina Bar, P.O. Box 608, Columbia, South Carolina 29202-0608. 1982- .

SOUTH CAROLINA LAW AND PRACTICE. South Carolina Bar Association, 950 Taylor Street, Columbia, South Carolina 29201. 1984.

MANUALS AND RESEARCH GUIDES

SOUTH CAROLINA LEGAL RESEARCH HANDBOOK. Robin K. Mills and Jon S. Shultz. William S. Hein and Company, 1285 Main Street, Buffalo, New York 14209. 1976.

SOUTH CAROLINA LEGISLATIVE MANUAL. Clerk, House of Representatives, State House, Columbia, South Carolina 29211. Annual.

ASSOCIATIONS AND PROFESSIONAL SOCIETIES

CHARLESTON COUNTY BAR ASSOCIATION, 100 Broad Street, Charleston, South Carolina 29401.

RICHLAND COUNTY BAR ASSOCIATION, P.O. Box 394, Columbia, South Carolina 29202.

SOUTH CAROLINA BAR, 950 Taylor Street, Columbia, South Carolina 29201. (803) 799-6653.

DIRECTORIES

DIRECTORY OF MUNICIPAL OFFICIALS [SOUTH CAROLINA]. Municipal Associaltion of South Carolina, P.O. Box 11558, Columbia, South Carolina 29211. Annual. (January)

SOUTH CAROLINA LEGAL DIRECTORY. Legal Directories Publishing Company, 2122 Kidwell Street, P.O. Box 140200, Dallas, Texas 75214-0200. Annual. (March)

SOUTH CAROLINA LEGISLATIVE MANUAL. South Carolina House of Representatives, P.O. Box 11867, Columbia, South Carolina 29211. Annual. (January)

STATES --SOUTH DAKOTA

STATUTES, CODES, STANDARDS, UNIFORM LAWS

ADMINISTRATIVE RULES OF SOUTH DAKOTA. South Dakota Code Commission, South Dakota Bureau of Administration, 500 East Capitol, Pierre, South Dakota 57501.

SESSION LAWS OF SOUTH DAKOTA. South Dakota Code Commission, South Dakota Bureau of Administration, Pierre, South Dakota 57501. Annual.

SOUTH DAKOTA CODIFIED LAWS ANNOTATED. Michie Company, P.O. Box 7587, Charlottesville, Virginia 22906-7587. 1978- . (Annual Supplements).

SOUTH DAKOTA REGISTER. South Dakota Code Commission, South Dakota Bureau of Administration, 500 East Capitol, Pierre, South Dakota 57501. Weekly.

LOOSELEAF SERVICES AND REPORTERS

NORTH WESTERN REPORTER. (First and Second Series). West Publishing Company, P.O. Box 64526, 50 West Kellogg Boulevard, St. Paul, Minnesota 55164-0526. 1890- .

SOUTH DAKOTA REPORTS. 1890-1976. State Publishing Company, Pierre, South Dakota 57501. (Current official source is the North Western Reporter).

STATES --SOUTH DAKOTA

ATTORNEY GENERAL OPINIONS

BIENNIAL REPORT OF THE ATTORNEY GENERAL OF THE STATE OF SOUTH DAKOTA. Office of the Attorney General, East Capitol, Pierre, South Dakota 57501. (Also available on Microform. William S. Hein, Microform Division, 1285 Main Street, Buffalo, New York 14209). (Also available on Lexis: 1977.)

ETHICS OPINIONS, CODES, RULES

Code of Professional Responsibility and Disciplinary Rules are published in Chapter 16-18 of the South Dakota Codified Laws.

Ethics Opinions are issued by the Ethics Committee of the State Bar of South Dakota and are occasionally published in the State Bar Newsletter. For further information concerning these opinions, contact the State Bar of South Dakota, 222 East Captial, Pierre, South Dakota 57501. (605-224-7554.)

COURT RULES

South Dakota Court Rules are published in various volumes of the South Dakota Codified Laws.

JURY INSTRUCTIONS

SOUTH DAKOTA PATTERN JURY INSTRUCTIONS, CIVIL. State Bar of South Dakota, Committee on Pattern Jury Instructions. 222 East Capital, Pierre, South Dakota 57501. 1986- . (Annual Supplements).

SOUTH DAKOTA PATTERN JURY INSTRUCTIONS: CRIMINAL. State Bar of South Dakota, 222 East Capital, Pierre, South Dakota 57501. 1986- . (Annual Supplements).

DIGESTS, INDEXES, ABSTRACTS, CITATORS

NORTH WESTERN DIGEST. West Publishing Company, P.O. Box 64526, 50 West Kellogg Boulevard, St. Paul, Minnesota 55164-0526. 1944- . (Annual Supplements).

SHEPARD'S NORTH WESTERN REPORTER CITATIONS. Shepard's/McGraw-Hill, P.O. Box 1235, Colorado Springs, Colorado 80901. (Monthly Supplements.)

SHEPARD'S SOUTH DAKOTA CITATIONS. Shepard's/McGraw-Hill, P.O. Box 1235, Colorado Springs, Colorado 80901. (Quarterly Supplements).

SOUTH DAKOTA DIGEST. West Publishing Company, P.O. Box 64526, 50 West Kellogg Boulevard, St. Paul, Minnesota 55164-0526. 1867- . (Annual Supplements).

LAW REVIEWS AND PERIODICALS

SOUTH DAKOTA LAW REVIEW. University of South Dakota School of Law, Vermillion, South Dakota 57069. Three issues per year.

STATE BAR NEWSLETTER. 222 East Capital, Pierre, South Dakota 57501. Monthly.

Encyclopedia of Legal Information Sources • 2nd Ed.

NEWSLETTERS AND NEWSPAPERS

NEWSLETTER: THE STATE BAR OF SOUTH DAKOTA. State Bar of South Dakota, 222 East Capitol, Pierre, South Dakota 57501. Monthly.

PRACTICE MATERIALS

CONSUMER'S GUIDE TO SOUTH DAKOTA LAW. South Dakota Bar Association, 222 East Capitol, Pierre, South Dakota 57501. 1986.

SOUTH DAKOTA TRIBAL COURT HANDBOOK. South Dakota Bar Association, 222 East Capitol, Pierre, South Dakota 57501. 1987.

ASSOCIATIONS AND PROFESSIONAL SOCIETIES

SOUTH DAKOTA BAR ASSOCIATION, 222 East Capitol, Pierre, South Dakota 57501. (605) 224-7554.

DIRECTORIES

DIRECTORY OF MUNICIPAL OFFICIALS [SOUTH DAKOTA]. South Dakota Municipal League, 214 East Capitol, Pierre, South Dakota 57501. Annual. (July)

DIRECTORY OF SOUTH DAKOTA COUNTY OFFICIALS. South Dakota Association of County Commissioners, 214 East Capitol, Pierre, South Dakota 57501. Biennial. (January of odd years).

NORTH DAKOTA AND SOUTH DAKOTA LEGAL DIRECTORY. Legal Directories Publishing Company, 2122 Kidwell Street, P.O. Box 140200, Dallas, Texas 75214-0200. Annual.

SOUTH DAKOTA LEGISLATIVE MANUAL. South Dakota Bureau of Administration, Capitol Building Annex, Pierre, South Dakota 57501. Biennial. (Fall of odd years).

STATES--TENNESSEE

STATUTES, CODES, STANDARDS, UNIFORM LAWS

ADVANCE LEGISLATIVE SERVICE TO THE TENNESSEE CODE ANNOTATED. Michie Company, P.O. Box 7587, Charlottesville, Virginia 22906-7587. Irregular.

OFFICIAL COMPILATION-RULES AND REGULATIONS OF THE STATE OF TENNESSEE. Secretary of State, Administrative Procedures Division, Capitol Hill Building, Nashville, Tennessee 37219. 1978- . (Periodic Supplements).

PRIVATE ACTS OF THE STATE OF TENNESSEE. Microform. William S. Hein, Microform Division, 1285 Main Street, Buffalo, New York 14209.

PUBLIC ACTS OF THE STATE OF TENNESSEE. Microform. William S. Hein, Microform Division, 1285 Main Street, Buffalo, New York 14209.

TENNESSEE ADMINISTRATIVE REGISTER. Secretary of State, Division of Publications, Polk State Office Building, Suite 500, Capitol Hill Building, Nashville, Tennessee 37219. Monthly.

TENNESSEE ADVANCE ANNOTATION SERVICE. Michie Company, P.O. Box 7587, Charlottesville, Virginia 22906-7587. 1985- . (Three pamphlets a year).

TENNESSEE CODE ANNOTATED. Michie Company, P.O. Box 7587, Charlottesville, Virginia 22906-7587. 1955- . (Annual Supplements).

TENNESSEE RULES OF CIVIL PROCEDURE ANNOTATED. West Publishing Company, 50 West Kellogg Boulevard, St. Paul, Minnesota 55164. 1970. (Periodic Supplements).

LOOSELEAF SERVICES AND REPORTERS

SOUTHWESTERN REPORTER. (First and second series). West Publishing Company, P.O. Box 64526, 50 West Kellogg Boulevard, St. Paul, Minnesota 55164-0526. 1886- . (Supreme Court, Court of Appeals, Court of Chancery Appeals, and Court of Criminal Appeals).

STATE AND LOCAL TAX SERVICE: TENNESSEE. Prentice-Hall, Incorporated, 113 Sylvan Avenue, Englewood Cliffs, New Jersey 07632. (Looseleaf).

TENNESSEE DECISIONS. West Publishing Company, P.O. Box 64526, 50 West Kellogg Boulevard, St. Paul, Minnesota 55164-0526. 1886- . (Supreme Court and Court of Appeals).

TENNESSEE REPORTS. Rich Printing Company, Nashville, Tennessee. 1791-1972. (Current official source is Southwestern Reporter).

ATTORNEY GENERAL OPINIONS

TENNESSEE ATTORNEY GENERAL OPINIONS. Office of the Attorney General, 450 James Robertson Parkway, Nashville, Tennessee 37219. (Monthly Supplements).

ETHICS OPINIONS AND RULES

Code of Professional Responsibility and Disciplinary Rules are published in Tennessee Rules of Court , West Publishing Company, P.O. Box 64526, 50 West Kellogg Boulevard, St. Paul, Minnesota 55164-0526. Annual.

Ethics Opinions are issued by the Board of Professional Responsibility of the Supreme Court of Tennessee and are not officially published in full-text. Abstracts of opinions are published in the ABA/BNA Lawyer's Manual on Professional Conduct . For further information concerning these opinions, contact the Tennessee Bar Association, 3622 West End Avenue, Nashville, Tennessee 37205. (615-383-7421.)

COURT RULES

TENNESSEE COURT RULES ANNOTATED. Michie/Bobbs-Merrill Law Publishing Company, P.O. Box 7587, Charlottesville, Virginia 22906-7587. Annual.

TENNESSEE RULES OF CIVIL PROCEDURE ANNOTATED. West Publishing Company, P.O. Box 64526, 50 West Kellogg Boulevard, St. Paul, Minnesota 55164-0526. 1970. (Periodic Supplements).

TENNESSEE RULES OF COURT. West Publishing Company, P.O. Box 64526, 50 West Kellogg Boulevard, St. Paul, Minnesota 55164-0526. Annual.

JURY INSTRUCTIONS

TENNESSEE PATTERN JURY INSTRUCTIONS, CIVIL. Judicial Conference, Committee on Pattern Jury Instuctions (Civil). West Publishing Company, P.O. Box 64526, 50 West Kellogg Boulevard, St. Paul, Minnesota 55164-0526. 1979- . (Periodic Supplements).

TENNESSEE PATTERN JURY INSTRUCTIONS, CRIMINAL. Tennessee Judicial Conference, Committee on Pattern Jury Instructions (Criminal). West Publishing Company, P.O. Box 64526, 50 West Kellogg Boulevard, St. Paul, Minnesota 55164-0526. 1980- . (Periodic Supplements).

DIGESTS, INDEXES, ABSTRACTS, CITATORS

MICHIE'S DIGEST OF TENNESSEE REPORTS. Michie Company, P.O. Box 7587, Charlottesville, Virginia 22906-7587. (Annual Supplements).

SHEPARD'S SOUTHWESTERN REPORTER CITATIONS. Shepard's/McGraw-Hill, P.O. Box 1235, Colorado Springs, Colorado 80901. (Monthly Supplements).

SHEPARD'S TENNESSEE CITATIONS. Shepard's/McGraw-Hill, P.O. Box 1235, Colorado Springs, Colorado 80901. (Bimonthly Supplements).

TENNESSEE DIGEST. (First and second series). West Publishing Company, P.O. Box 64526, 50 West Kellogg Boulevard, St. Paul, Minnesota 55164-0526. 1947- . (Annual Supplements).

ENCYCLOPEDIAS AND DICTIONARIES

TENNESSEE JURISPRUDENCE. Michie Company, P.O. Box 7587, Charlottesville, Virginia 22906-7587. 1982- . (Annual Supplements).

LAW REVIEWS AND PERIODICALS

MEMPHIS STATE UNIVERSITY LAW REVIEW. Cecil C. Humphrey's School of Law, Memphis State University, Memphis, Tennessee 38152. Quarterly.

TENNESSEE BAR JOURNAL. Tennessee Bar Association, 3622 West End Avenue, Nashville, Tennessee 37205. Six issues per year.

TENNESSEE LAW REVIEW. University of Tennessee College of Law, 1505 West Cumberland Avenue, Knoxville, Tennessee 37996-1800. Quarterly.

VANDERBILT JOURNAL OF TRANSNATIONAL LAW. Vanderbilt University School of Law, Nashville, Tennessee 37240. Five issues per year.

VANDERBILT LAW REVIEW. Vanderbilt University School of Law, Nashville, Tennessee 37204. Six issues per year.

NEWSLETTERS AND NEWSPAPERS

TENNESSEE ATTORNEYS MEMO. Lee Smith Publishers and Printer, 162 Fourth Avenue North, Nashville, Tennessee 37219. Weekly. (Reports selected cases from all Tennessee Courts and opinions of the Attorney General).

TENNESSEE BANKRUPTCY SERVICE. M. Lee Smith Publishers and Printers, 162 Fourth Avenue North, Nashville, Tennessee 37219. Monthly.

TENNESSEE EMPLOYMENT LAW UPDATE. M. Lee Smith Publishers and Printers, 162 Fourth Avenue North, Nashville, Tennessee 37219. Monthly.

TENNESSEE ENVIRONMENTAL LAW LETTER. M. Lee Smith Publishers and Printers, 162 Fourth Avenue North, Nashville, Tennessee 37219. Monthly.

TENNESSEE FAMILY LAW LETTER. M. Lee Smith Publishers and Printers, 162 Fourth Avenue North, Nashville, Tennessee 37219. Monthly.

TENNESSEE LEGISLATION SERVICE. M. Lee Smith Publishers and Printers, 162 Fourth Avenue North, Nashville, Tennessee 37219. Biweekly.

TENNESSEE LITIGATION REPORTER. Lewis Laska, 901 Church Street, Nashville, Tennessee 37203. Bimonthly.

TENNESSEE MEDICO-LEGAL REPORTER. Lewis Laska, 901 Church Street, Nashville, Tennessee 37203. Monthly.

FORMBOOKS

GORE'S FORMS FOR TENNESSEE ANNOTATED. Third Edition. Thomas P. Gore. Michie Company, P.O. Box 7587, Charlottesville, Virginia 22906-7587. 1970-1972.

TENNESSEE CIVIL PROCEDURE FORMS. Walter Bigham. West Publishing Company, 50 West Kellogg Boulevard, St. Paul, Minnesota 55164. 1977. (Periodic Supplements).

TENNESSEE CRIMINAL PRACTICE FORMS. Joe B. Jones. Harrison Publishing Company, 3110 Crossing Park, Norcross, Georgia 30071. 1983- . (Periodic Supplements).

TENNESSEE UNIFORM COMMERCIAL CODE FORMS. West Publishing Company, 50 West Kellogg Boulevard, St. Paul, Minnesota 55164. 1987. (Periodic Supplements).

PRACTICE MATERIALS

CRIMINAL PRACTICE AND PROCEDURE. David Louis Raybin. West Publishing Company, P.O. Box 64526, 50 West Kellogg Boulevard, St. Paul, Minnesota 55164-0526. 1984- .

GIBSON'S SUITS IN CHANCERY. Sixth Edition. W. Inman. Michie Company, P.O. Box 7587, Charlottesville, Virginia 22906-7587. 1982.

PRITCHARD ON THE LAW OF WILLS AND ADMINISTRATION OF ESTATES. Fourth edition. Harry Phillips and Jack W. Robinson. Michie Company, P.O. Box 7587, Charlottesville, Virginia 22906-7587. 1983- . (Periodic Supplements).

PRODUCTS LIABILITY: THE LAW IN TENNESSEE. B. Finbers. Harrison Company, 3110 Crossing Park, Norcross, Georgia 30091. 1979.

TENNESSEE ADOPTION AUTHORITIES WITH FORMS. B. Trimble. Michie Company, P.O. Box 7587, Charlottesville, Virginia 22906-7587. 1966. (Periodic Supplements).

TENNESSEE CIRCUIT COURT PRACTICE. Lawrence A. Pivnick. The Harrison Company, 3110 Crossing Park, Norcross, Georgia 30071. 1986.

TENNESSEE CORPORATIONS. Ronald Lee Gilman. Lawyers Co-Operative Company, Aqueduct Building, Rochester, New York 14694. 1980- . (Annual Supplements).

TENNESSEE DIVORCE, ALIMONY, AND CHILD CUSTODY, WITH FORMS. W. W. Garrett. The Harrison Company, 3110 Crossing Park, Norcross, Georgia 30071. 1984.

TENNESSEE LAW OF EVIDENCE. Donald F. Paine. Michie/Bobbs-Merrill Law Publishing Company, P.O. Box 7587, Charlottesville, Virginia 22906-7587. 1974- . (Periodic Supplements).

TENNESSEE PROBATE. Albert W. Secor. Lawyers Co-Operative Company, Aqueduct Building, Rochester, New York 14694. 1980- . (Annual Supplements).

TENNESSEE WORKER'S COMPENSATION: PRACTICE AND PROCEDURE WITH FORMS. Thomas A. Reynolds. The Harrison Company, 3110 Crossing Park, Norcross, Georgia 30071. 1984.

TRIAL HANDBOOK FOR TENNESSEE LAWYERS. Robert E. Burch. Lawyers Co-Operative Company, Aqueduct Building, Rochester, New York 14694. 1980- . (Annual Supplements).

MANUALS AND RESEARCH GUIDES

TENNESSEE LEGAL RESEARCH HANDBOOK. Lewis Laska. William S. Hein and Company, Incorporated, 1285 Main Street, Hein Building, Buffalo, New York 14209. 1977.

WEST'S TENNESSEE DIGEST SECOND LAW FINDER. West Publishing Company, P.O. Box 64526, 50 West Kellogg Boulevard, St. Paul, Minnesota 55164-0526. 1987- . (Annual).

ASSOCIATIONS AND PROFESSIONAL SOCIETIES

CHATTANOOGA BAR ASSOCIATION, 151 West MacLellan Building, Chattanooga, Tennessee 37402.

KNOXVILLE BAR ASSOCIATION, 531 Gay Street, Suite 1025, Knoxville, Tennessee 37901.

MEMPHIS AND SHELLY COUNTY BAR ASSOCIATION, 302 Shelly County Courthouse, Memphis, Tennessee 38103. (901) 527-7041.

NASHVILLE BAR ASSOCIATION, 316 Stahlman Building, Nashville, Tennessee 37201.

TENNESSEE BAR ASSOCIATION, 3622 West End Avenue, Nashville, Tennessee 37205. (615) 383-7421.

DIRECTORIES

DIRECTORY OF TENNESSEE MUNICIPAL OFFICIALS. Municipal Technical Advisory Service, 891 Twentieth Street, University of Tennessee, Knoxville, Tennessee 37996. Annual. (September)

MEMBERS OF THE TENNESSEE LEGISLATURE. Office of Legislative Services, Tennessee Legislative Council, State Capitol, G3, Nashville, Tennessee 37219. Biennial. (January of odd years).

TENNESSEE BLUE BOOK. Tennessee Secretary of State, State Capitol Building, First Floor, Nashville, Tennessee 37219. Biennial. (November of odd years).

TENNESSEE LEGAL DIRECTORY. Legal Directories Publishing Company, 2122 Kidwell Street, P.O. Box 140200, Dallas, Texas 75214-0200. Annual. (August)

STATES--TEXAS

STATUTES, CODES, STANDARDS, UNIFORM LAWS

GENERAL AND SPECIAL LAWS OF THE STATE OF TEXAS. Secretary of State, P.O. Box 12887, Austin, Texas 78711. Bienniel.

OFFICIAL TEXAS ADMINISTRATIVE CODE: ANNOTATED. Approved by the Secretary of State of Texas. Hart Information Systems, 7970 Shoal Creek Boulevard, Austin, Texas 78758. 1985- . (Quarterly Supplements).

TEXAS REGISTER. Office of the Secretary of State, 201 East Fourteenth Street, P.O. Box 13824, Austin, Texas 78711. Two issues per week.

TEXAS SESSION LAW SERVICE. West Publishing Company, P.O. Box 64526, 50 West Kellogg Boulevard, St. Paul, Minnesota 55164-0526. Irregular.

VERNON'S TEXAS CODE ANNOTATED. West Publishing Company, P.O. Box 64526, 50 West Kellogg Boulevard, St. Paul, Minnesota 55164-0526. (Annual Supplements).

LOOSELEAF SERVICES AND REPORTERS

MICHIE'S TEXAS TORT REPORTER. Michie Company, P.O. Box 7587, Charlottesville, Virginia 22906-7587. 1984- . Monthly Supplements.

SOUTHWESTERN REPORTER. (First and second series). West Publishing Company, P.O. Box 64526, 50 West Kellogg Boulevard, St. Paul, Minnesota 55164-0526. 1982- . (Supreme Court, Court of Appeals, and Court of Criminal Appeals). 1887- .

TEXAS CRIMINAL REPORTS. Texas Court of Criminal Appeals. Gilbert Book Company, St. Louis, Missouri. 1876-1963.

TEXAS REPORTS. 1846-1963. (Supreme Court). (Current souce is the Southwestern Reporter).

ATTORNEY GENERAL OPINIONS

INDEX TO THE OPINIONS OF THE ATTORNEY GENERAL OF TEXAS. Attorney General of Texas, P.O. Box 12548, Austin, Texas 78711-2548. Annual. (Opinions are issued individually but are not bound. For additional information concerning these opinions or for copies, contact the Opinions Committee Division, Attorney General of Texas, 512-463-2110). (Available on Lexis and Westlaw: 1977- .)

ETHICS OPINIONS, CODES, RULES

Code of Professional Responsibility and Disciplinary Rules are published in *Vernon's Civil Statutes* , volume 1a. West Publishing Company, P.O. Box 64526, 50 West Kellogg Boulevard, St. Paul, Minnesota 55164-0526. (Annual Supplements).

TEXAS LAWYER'S PROFESSIONAL ETHICS. Young Lawyer's Association, Committee on Professional Ethics. State Bar of Texas, P.O. Box 12487, Capitol Station, Austin, Texas 78711. 1979- . (Periodic Supplements). Abstracts of ethics opinions are published in the *ABA/BNA Lawyer's Manual on Professional Responsibility* . For further information concerning ethics opinions, contact the Professional Ethics Committee, State Bar of Texas, Box 12487, Capitol Station, Austin, Texas 78711. (512-463-1463).

COURT RULES

LOCAL RULES IN THE DISTRICT COURTS OF TEXAS. S. Steves. Butterworth Legal Publishers, 90 Stiles Road, Salem, New Hampshire 03079. Biennial.

TEXAS RULES OF COURT: STATE AND FEDERAL. (Desk copy) West Publishing Company, P.O. Box 64526, 50 West Kellogg Boulevard, St. Paul, Minnesota 55164-0526. Annual.

JURY INSTRUCTIONS

JURY CHARGES FOR TEXAS CRIMINAL PRACTICE, WITH INDICTMENTS AND INFORMATION. Revised edition. Paul J. McClung. McClung Law Books, Fort Worth, Texas. 1985.

JURY ISSUE SUBMISSION. State Bar of Texas, P.O. Box 12487, Capitol Station, Austin, Texas 78711. 1985.

MANUAL OF REVERSIBLE ERRORS IN TEXAS CRIMINAL CASES. Second edition. Fred Erisman. Texas Law Book Publishers, Incorporated, P.O. Box 18069, Fort Worth, Texas 76118. 1975.

TEXAS CRIMINAL PATTERN JURY CHARGES. State Bar of Texas, Committee on Criminal Pattern Jury Charges. State Bar of Texas, P.O. Box 12487, Capitol Station, Austin, Texas 78711. 1975- .

TEXAS PATTERN JURY CHARGES. State Bar of Texas, Committee on Pattern Jury Charges. State Bar of Texas, P.O. Box 12487, Capitol Station, Austin, Texas 78711. 1969-1982.

DIGESTS, INDEXES, ABSTRACTS, CITATORS

SHEPARD'S SOUTHWESTERN REPORTER CITATIONS. Shepard's/McGraw-Hill, P.O. Box 1235, Colorado Springs, Colorado 80901. (Monthly Supplements).

SHEPARD'S TEXAS CITATIONS. Shepard's/McGraw-Hill, P.O. Box 1235, Colorado Springs, Colorado 80901. (Eight supplements per year).

TEXAS DIGEST. (First and Second Series). West Publishing Company, P.O. Box 64526, 50 West Kellogg Boulevard, St. Paul, Minnesota 55164-0526. 1935- . (Annual Supplements).

TEXAS FAMILY LAW DIGEST. Michie Company, P.O. Box 7587, Charlottesville, Virginia 22906-7587. 1984- . Quarterly.

THE TEXAS LAWYER. Butterworth Legal Publishers, 90 Stiles Road, Salem, New Hampshire 03079. 1985- . (Includes digests of very recent decisions handed down by the Texas Supreme Court, Court of Criminal Appeals, and other Courts of Appeal). Weekly.

TEXAS LAWYERS' CRIMINAL DIGEST. State Bar of Texas, P.O. Box 12487, Capitol Station, Austin, Texas 78711. 1982- .

ENCYCLOPEDIAS AND DICTIONARIES

TEXAS JURISPRUDENCE. (First through third series). Bancroft-Whitney Company, P.O. Box 7005, San Francisco, California 94120-7005. 1929- . (Annual Supplements).

LAW REVIEWS AND PERIODICALS

BAYLOR. Baylor University School of Law, Baylor University, P.O. Box 6262, Waco, Texas 76706. Quarterly.

HOUSTON LAW REVIEW. Houston Law Review, Incorporated, Room 25, University of Houston Law Center, University Park, Houston, Texas 77004. Five issues per year.

LETTER OF THE LAW. Texas Real Estate Research Center, College Station, Texas 1986- . Quarterly.

SAINT MARY'S LAW JOURNAL. Saint Mary's School of Law, One Camina Santa Maria, San Antonio, Texas 78284-0400. Quarterly.

SOUTH TEXAS LAW REVIEW. South Texas College of Law, 1303 San Jacincto, Houston, Texas 77002. Three issues per year.

TEXAS BAR JOURNAL. State Bar of Texas, P.O. Box 12487, Capitol Station, Austin, Texas 78711. (Monthly except August).

TEXAS INTERNATIONAL LAW JOURNAL. University of Texas at Austin School of Law, Incorporated, 727 East Twenty-sixth Street, Austin, Texas 78705. Three issues per year.

TEXAS LAW REVIEW. The University of Texas at Austin School of Law Publishers, Incorporated, 727 East Twenty-sixth Street, Austin, Texas 78705. Seven issues per year.

TEXAS LAWYERS WEEKLY NEWSLETTER. State Bar of Texas, P.O. Box 12487, Capitol Station, Austin, Texas 78711. Fifty issues per year.

TEXAS TECHNICAL UNIVERSITY LAW REVIEW. Texas Technical University School of Law, Lubbock, Texas 79409-0004. Four issues per year.

THURGOOD MARSHALL LAW REVIEW. 3100 Cleburne Avenue, Box 45, Houston, Texas 77004. Biannual.

NEWSLETTERS AND NEWSPAPERS

AUSTIN REPORT. Report Publications, P.O. Box 12368, Austin, Texas 78711. Weekly.

CAPITOL UPDATE. Texas State Directory Press, Incorporated, Box 12186, Capitol Station, Austin, Texas 78711. Biweekly.

TEXAS EVIDENCE REPORTER. Butterworth Legal Publishers, 90 Stiles Road, Salem, New Hampshire 03079. Bimonthly.

TEXAS LAWYERS' CIVIL DIGEST. State Bar of Texas, P.O. Box 12487, Austin, Texas 78711. Weekly.

TEXAS LAWYERS CRIMINAL DIGEST. State Bar of Texas, P.O. Box 12487, Austin, Texas 78711. Weekly.

TEXAS OIL AND GAS LAW JOURNAL. Butterworth Legal Publishers, 90 Stiles Road, Salem, New Hampshire 03079. Bimonthly.

TEXAS SUPREME COURT INDEX. Texas Court Information Service, 6030 Rose, Houston, Texas 77007. Bimonthly when in session.

TEXAS TORTS UPDATE. Matthew Bender and Company, Incorporated, 11 Penn Plaza, New York, New York 10001. Monthly.

WATER RESOURCES REPORT. RPC Publications, Incorporated, 3200 Red River, Suite 302, Austin, Texas 78705. Semimonthly.

WEST'S TEXAS LEGAL UPDATE. West Publishing Company, 50 West Kellogg Boulevard, St. Paul, Minnesota 55164. Biweekly.

WORKERS COMPENSATION REPORT. RPC Publications, Incorporated, 3200 Red River, Suite 302, Austin, Texas 78705. Monthly.

FORMBOOKS

FAMILY LAW. Thomas J. Purdom, W. F. Elliot, Editors. West Publishing Company, P.O. Box 64526, 50 West Kellogg Boulevard, St. Paul, Minnesota 55164-0526. 1984- . (Annual Supplements). (Volume 16 of West's Legal Forms).

LEGAL FORM MANUAL FOR REAL ESTATE TRANSACTIONS. Revised edition. A project of the Legal Forms Committee of the State Bar of Texas. State Bar of Texas, P.O. Box 12487, Capitol Station, Austin, Texas 78711. 1986- . (Periodic Supplements).

TEXAS CRIMINAL DEFENSE FORMS ANNOTATED: STATE AND FEDERAL TRIAL, APPELLATE AND ANCILLARY. W. V. Dunnam, Jr. Knowles Law Book Publishers, P.O. Box 911004, Fort Worth, Texas 76111. 1984- .

TEXAS CRIMINAL FORMS ANNOTATED. Eighth edition. Sam A. Willson and Thomas D. Blackwell. West Publishing Company, P.O. Box 64526, 50 West Kellogg Boulevard, St. Paul, Minnesota 55164-0526. 1977- .

Encyclopedia of Legal Information Sources • 2nd Ed.   STATES--TEXAS

TEXAS LEGAL PRATICE FORMS. Callaghan and Company, 155 Pfingsten Road, Deerfield, Illinois 60015. 1982- . (Annual Supplements).

TEXAS PERSONAL INJURY FORMS. Ruth Tone. Butterworth Legal Publishers, 90 Stiles Road, Salem, New Hampshire 03079. 1984.

TEXAS TRANSACTION GUIDE-LEGAL FORMS. Matthew Bender and Company, Incorporated, 11 Penn Plaza, New York, New York 10001. 1972- . (Annual Supplements).

VERNON'S TEXAS CODE FORMS ANNOTATED. West Publishing Company, P.O. Box 64526, 50 West Kellogg Boulevard, St. Paul, Minnesota 55164-0526. 1968- . (Periodic Supplements).

WEST'S TEXAS FORMS. West Publishing Company, P.O. Box 64526, 50 West Kellogg Boulevard, St. Paul, Minnesota 55164-0526. 1977- . (Annual Supplements).

PRACTICE MATERIALS

BLACK'S TEXAS EVIDENCE MANUAL. Thomas Black. Callaghan and Company, 155 Pfingsten Road, Deerfield, Illinois 60015. 1985- . (Periodic Supplements).

CIVIL LIBERTIES AT WORK: WHAT EVERYONE WHO LOOKS FOR A JOB, HAS ONE, OR LOSES ONE NEEDS TO KNOW ABOUT TEXAS AND FEDERAL LAW GOVERNING RIGHTS IN THE WORKPLACE AND IN THE JOB MARKET. Texas Civil Liberties Union, 600 Seventh Street, Austin, Texas 78701. 1985.

CRIMINAL EVIDENCE TRIAL MANUAL FOR TEXAS LAWYERS. Murl A. Larkin. Butterworth Legal Publishers, 90 Stiles Road, Salem, New Hampshire 03079. 1984.

EMPLOYMENT IN TEXAS: A GUIDE TO EMPLOYMENT PRACTICES AND REGULATIONS. Mark S. Sunners. Butterworth Legal Publishers, 90 Stiles Road, Salem, New Hampshire 03079. 1984- . (Periodic Supplements).

FAMILY LAW: TEXAS PRACTICE AND PROCEDURE. Matthew Bender and Company, Incorporated, 11 Penn Plaza, New York, New York 10001. 1982- . (Periodic Supplements).

FORMING, OPERATING, AND DISSOLVING THE TEXAS CORPORATION. State Bar of Texas, P.O. Box 12487, Capitol Station, Austin, Texas 78711. 1984.

HOW TO DO YOUR DIVORCE IN TEXAS. Second edition. Charles E. Sherman and Jim Simons. Nolo Press, 950 Parker Street, Berkeley, California 94710. 1986.

JUVENILE LAW AND PRACTICE. Thomas S. Morgan. West Publishing Company, P.O. Box 64526, 50 West Kellogg Boulevard, St. Paul, Minnesota 55164-0526. 1985- . (Annual Supplements). (Volume 29 of Texas Practice).

THE LAW OF TEXAS MEDICAL MALPRACTICE. Second edition. Jim M. Perdue. Houston Law Review, University of Houston Law Center, 4800 Calhoun, Houston, Texas 77004. 1985.

NONPROFIT ORGANIZATIONS (TEXAS). Second edition. University of Houston Law Foundation, Continuing Legal Education. 1986.

TEXAS ADMINISTRATIVE PRACTICE AND PROCEDURE. State Bar of Texas, P.O. Box 12487, Capitol Station, Austin, Texas 78711. 1985.

TEXAS BUSINESS ORGANIZATIONS. R. Hamilton. West Publishing Company, 50 West Kellogg Boulevard, St. Paul, Minnesota 55164. 1973. (Periodic Supplements).

TEXAS CIVIL PROCEDURE: PRETRIAL LITIGATION. Second edition. William V. Dorsaneo III and David Crump. Matthew Bender and Company, Incorporated, 11 Penn Plaza, New York, New York 10001. 1983- . (Periodic Supplements).

TEXAS CIVIL TRIAL HANDBOOK. Fred Misko and Harlow L. Sprouse. State Bar of Texas, P.O. Box 12487, Capitol Station, Austin, Texas 78711. 1984- . (Periodic Supplements).

TEXAS COLLECTIONS MANUAL. Fiman A. Hickey, Jr. State Bar of Texas, P.O. Box 12487, Capitol Station, Austin, Texas 78711. 1980- . (Periodic Supplements).

TEXAS CONDOMINIUM LAW. Butterworth Legal Publishers, 90 Stiles Road, Salem, New Hampshire 03079. 1983- . (Periodic Supplements).

TEXAS CONSUMER LAW REPORTER. Matthew Bender and Company, Incorporated, 11 Penn Plaza, New York, New York 10001. Monthly.

TEXAS CORPORATION LAW. Sheldon Pfeffer. Butterworth Legal Publishers, 90 Stiles Road, Salem, New Hampshire 03079. 1981- . (Periodic Supplements).

TEXAS CORPORATIONS-LAW AND PRACTICE. Barbara B. Aldave, et al. Matthew Bender and Company, Incorporated, 11 Penn Plaza, New York, New York 10001. 1984- . (Annual Supplements).

TEXAS COURTROOM EVIDENCE. Phillip D. Hardberger. Parker and Son Publications, P.O. Box 9040, Carlsbad, California 92018-9040. 1986- . (Periodic Supplements).

TEXAS CRIMINAL LAW. Butterworth Legal Publishers, 90 Stiles Road, Salem, New Hampshire 03079.

TEXAS CRIMINAL PRACTICE GUIDE. Marvin O. Teague. Matthew Bender and Company, Incorporated, 11 Penn Plaza, New York, New York 10001. 1979- . (Periodic Supplements).

TEXAS CRIMINAL PROCEDURE. Robert O. Dawson and George E. Dix. Matthew Bender and Company, Incorporated, 11 Penn Plaza, New York, New York 10001. 1984- . (Periodic Supplements).

TEXAS DEPOSITIONS: DEDICATED TO TRIAL LAWYERS. James Branton and Jim D. Lovett. Knowles Law Book Publishers, P.O. Box 911004, Fort Worth, Texas 1984- .

TEXAS DRUNK DRIVING LAW. J. G. Trichler and Peter Lewis. Butterworth Legal Publishers, 90 Stiles Road, Salem, New Hampshire 03079. 1984. (Periodic Supplements).

TEXAS EVIDENCE REPORTER. Butterworth Legal Publishers, 90 Stiles Road, Salem, New Hampshire 03079. Bimonthly.

STATES--TEXAS

TEXAS FAMILY LAW MANUAL. Butterworth Legal Publishers, 90 Stiles Road, Salem, New Hampshire 03079. 1982- . (Periodic Supplements).

TEXAS FAMILY LAW PRACTICE MANUAL. State Bar of Texas, P.O. Box 12487, Capitol Station, Austin, Texas 78711. 1984- . (Periodic Supplements).

TEXAS FAMILY LAW REPORTER. Matthew Bender and Company, Incorporated, 11 Penn Plaza, New York, New York 10001. 1983- . Monthly.

TEXAS FORECLOSURE LAW AND PRACTICE. W. M. Baggett. Shepard's/McGraw-Hill, P.O. Box 1235, Colorado Springs, Colorado 80901. 1984- . (Periodic Supplements).

TEXAS GUARDIANSHIP MANUAL. State Bar of Texas, P.O. Box 12487, Capitol Station, Austin, Texas 78711. 1983- . (Periodic Supplements).

TEXAS HEALTH LAW REPORTER. Butterworth Legal Publishers, 90 Stiles Road, Salem, New Hampshire 03079. 1984- . Bimonthly.

TEXAS LAWYERS' GUIDE. Jeremy C. Wicker and Daniel H. Benson. Callaghan and Company, 155 Pfingsten Road, Deerfield, Illinois 60015. 1980- . (Periodic Supplements).

THE TEXAS LEGAL SYSTEM FOR CHILD PROTECTION: A MANUAL FOR SOCIAL WORKERS AND LAWYERS. Enrique H. Pena. Butterworth Legal Publishers, 90 Stiles Road, Salem, New Hampshire 03079. 1983.

TEXAS LITIGATION GUIDE. William V. Dorsanea III, et al. Matthew Bender and Company, Incorporated, 11 Penn Plaza, New York, New York 10001. 1977- . (Annual Supplements).

TEXAS MATRIMONIAL PROPERTY LAW. Joseph W. McKnight and William A. Reppy, Jr. Michie Company, P.O. Box 7587, Charlottesville, Virginia 22906-7587. 1983.

TEXAS MUNICIPAL ZONING LAW. John Mixon. Butterworth Legal Publishers, 90 Stiles Road, Salem, New Hampshire 03079. 1984- . (Periodic Supplements).

TEXAS PERSONAL INJURY FORMS. Ruth Tone. Butterworth Legal Publishers, 90 Stiles Road, Salem, New Hampshire 03079. 1984- . (Periodic Supplements).

TEXAS PRACTICE. West Publishing Company, P.O. Box 64526, 50 West Kellogg Boulevard, St. Paul, Minnesota 55164-0526. (Imprint varies). (Annual Supplements).

TEXAS PROBATE CODE MANUAL. Butterworth Legal Publishers, 90 Stiles Road, Salem, New Hampshire 03079. 1984- . (Periodic Supplements).

TEXAS REAL ESTATE LAW. Fifth edition. Charles J. Jacobus. Reston Publishing Company, Prentice-Hall, Incorporated, 113 Sylvan Avenue, Englewood Cliffs, New Jersey 07632. 1989.

TEXAS REAL ESTATE LAW REPORTER. Butterworth Legal Publishers, 90 Stiles Road, Salem, New Hampshire 03079. 1985- . Six issues per year.

Encyclopedia of Legal Information Sources • 2nd Ed.

TEXAS RULES OF EVIDENCE MANUAL. Hulen D. Wendorf and David A. Schlueter. Michie Company, P.O. Box 7587, Charlottesville, Virginia 22906-7587. 1983- . (Periodic Supplements).

TEXAS TAX SERVICE. Larry D. Crumbley, et al. Matthew Bender and Company, Incorporated, 11 Penn Plaza, New York, New York 10001. 1985- . (Monthly Supplements).

TEXAS WORKERS' COMPENSATION TRIAL MANUAL. Parker and Son Publications, P.O. Box 9040, Carlsbad, California 92018-9040. 1984- . (Periodic Supplements).

MANUALS AND RESEARCH GUIDES

ADVANCED LEGAL RESEARCH: CREATIVE RESOURCES TODAY AND TOMORROW. University of Texas at Austin School of Law, 2500 Red River Street, Austin, Texas 78705. 1985.

GUIDE TO LEGISLATIVE INFORMATION. Prepared by the Staff of the Texas Legislative Council. P.O. Box 12128, Capitol Station, Austin, Texas 78711. 1984.

REFERENCE GUIDE TO TEXAS LAW AND LEGAL HISTORY: SOURCES AND DOCUMENTATION. Second Edition. Butterworth Legal Publishers, 90 Stiles Road, Salem, New Hampshire 03079. 1987.

TEXAS LEGISLATIVE HISTORY: A MANUAL OF SOURCES. Legislative Reference Library, P.O. Box 12488, Capitol Station, Austin, Texas 78711. 1980.

TEXAS LEGISLATIVE HISTORY AND ADMINISTRATIVE AGENCY CITATION GUIDE. Texas Technical University School of Law, Lubbock, Texas 79409-1037. 1986.

ASSOCIATIONS AND PROFESSIONAL SOCIETIES

DALLAS BAR ASSOCIATION, 2101 Ross Avenue, Dallas, Texas 75201. (214) 969-7066.

EL PASO BAR ASSOCIATION, 511 East San Antonio, Room 530, El Paso, Texas 79901.

HOUSTON BAR ASSOCIATION, 707 Travis, Suite 1300, Houston, Texas 77002. (713) 222-1441.

JEFFERSON COUNTY BAR ASSOCIATION, 1001 Pearl Street, Room 328, Beaumont, Texas 77701.

NORTHEAST TEXAS BAR ASSOCIATION, P.O. Box 7, Mount Pleasant, Texas 75455.

NUECES COUNTY BAR ASSOCIATION, 901 Leopard, Suite 312, Corpus Christi, Texas 78401.

TARRANT COUNTY BAR ASSOCIATION, 2015 The Texas Building, Fort Worth, Texas 76102.

TEXAS BAR ASSOCIATION, 1414 Colorado, P.O. Box 12487, Austin, Texas 78701. (512) 475-1463.

TEXAS CIVIL LIBERTIES UNION, 600 West Seventh Street, Austin, Texas 78701.

TRAVIS COUNTY BAR ASSOCIATION, 507 West Eleventh, Austin, Texas 78701.

DIRECTORIES

DIRECTORY OF TEXAS CITY OFFICIALS. Texas Municipal League, Southwest Tower, Number 1020, Austin, Texas 78701. Annual. (July)

HANDBOOK OF GOVERNMENTS IN TEXAS. Texas Advisory Commission on Intergovernmental Relations, P.O. Box 13206, Capitol Station, Austin, Texas 78711. (Updated continuously).

LEGISLATIVE DIRECTORY [NORTH-CENTRAL TEXAS]. North Central Texas Council of Governments, Drawer GOG, Arlington, Texas 76005. Biennial. (November of even years).

REGIONAL COUNCILS IN TEXAS: REPORT AND DIRECTORY. Texas Governors Office of Budget and Planning, Box 13561, Austin, Texas 78701. Annual. (November)

TEXAS ALMANAC (AND STATE INDUSTRIAL GUIDE) [NO COMPANIES]. Communications Center, Dallas Morning News, Dallas, Texas 75265. Biennial. (October of odd years).

TEXAS LEGAL DIRECTORY. Legal Directories Publishing Company, 2122 Kidwell Street, P.O. Box 140200, Dallas, Texas 75214-0200. Annual.

TEXAS LEGISLATIVE HANDBOOK. Legislative Associates, Box 12186, Austin, Texas 78711. Biennial. (January of odd years).

TEXAS STATE DIRECTORY. Texas State Directory, Incorporated, 1800 Nueces Street, Austin, Texas 78701. Annual. (January).

STATES--UTAH

STATUTES, CODES, STANDARDS, UNIFORM LAWS

ADMINISTRATIVE RULES OF THE STATE OF UTAH. Utah State Archives, State Capitol, Salt Lake City, Utah 84114.

LAWS OF UTAH. Utah State Archives, State Capitol, Salt Lake City, Utah 84114. Biennial. Also available in microform from William S. Hein, Microform Division, 1285 Main Street, Buffalo, New York 14209.

STATE OF UTAH BULLETIN. Utah State Archives, State Capitol, Salt Lake City, Utah 84114. Semimonthly.

UTAH ADMINISTRATIVE RULE MAKING BULLETIN. Utah State Archives, State Capitol, Salt Lake City, Utah 84114.

UTAH ADVANCE CODE SERVICE. Michie Company, P.O. Box 7587, Charlottesville, Virginia 22906-7587. 1986- . (Irregular).

UTAH CODE ANNOTATED. Michie Company, P.O. Box 7587, Charlottesville, Virginia 22906-7587. 1953- . (Annual Supplements).

LOOSELEAF SERVICES AND REPORTERS

PACIFIC REPORTER. (First and second series). West Publishing Company, P.O. Box 64526, 50 West Kellogg Boulevard, St. Paul, Minnesota 55164-0526. 1881- .

UTAH ADVANCE REPORTS. Code * Company, P.O. Box 1471, Provo, Utah 84603. Biweekly.

UTAH REPORTER. West Publishing Company, P.O. Box 64526, 50 West Kellogg Boulevard, St. Paul, Minnesota 55164-0526. 1974- .

UTAH REPORTS. (First and Second Series). West Publishing Company, P.O. Box 64526, 50 West Kellogg Boulevard, St. Paul, Minnesota 55164-0526. 1855-1974. (Publisher varies) (Current official source is the Pacific Reporter).

ATTORNEY GENERAL OPINIONS

BIENNIAL REPORT OF THE ATTORNEY GENERAL TO THE GOVERNOR OF THE STATE OF UTAH FOR THE BIENNIAL PERIOD ENDING... Attorney General's Office, State Capitol, Salt Lake City, Utah 84114. Biennial.

ETHICS OPINIONS, CODES, RULES

DESKBOOK. Utah State Bar Association, 645 South Two-hundred East, Salt Lake City, Utah 84111. (Annual).

PROCEDURES OF DISIPLINE OF THE UTAH STATE BAR. Utah State Bar, 425 East First South, Salt Lake City, Utah 84111. 1985.

REVISED RULES OF PROFESSIONAL CONDUCT OF THE UTAH STATE BAR: ADOPTED MAY 28, 1936 AND APPROVED BY THE SUPREME COURT OF THE STATE OF UTAH MARCH 1, 1937, AND AMENDED IN 1977, MAY 7, 1982 AND SEPTEMBER 16, 1985. Utah State Bar, 425 East First South, Salt Lake City, Utah 84111. 1985. (Proposed revisions of July 1987 published in Utah Advanced Reports).

UTAH ETHICS OPINIONS are issued by the Utah State Bar, Office of Bar Counsel. 425 East First South, Salt Lake City, Utah 84111. These opinions are not formally published. Abstracts are published in the ABA/BNA Lawyer's Manual on Professional Conduct. For further information, contact the Office of Bar Counsel. 801-662-9054.

COURT RULES

UTAH COURT RULES ANNOTATED. Michie Company, P.O. Box 7587, Charlottesville, Virginia 22906-7587. Annual. (Issued as a supplement to Utah Code Annotated).

UTAH RULES OF APPELLATE PROCEDURE. Utah State Bar, 425 East First South, Salt Lake City, Utah 84111. 1984- . (Periodic Supplements).

UTAH RULES OF CIVIL PROCEDURE. Utah State Bar Association, 645 South Two-hundred East, Salt Lake City, Utah 84111. (Periodic Supplements).

STATES--UTAH

JURY INSTRUCTIONS

JURY INSTRUCTION FORMS FOR UTAH. Utah State Bar Association, Committee on Standardized Instructions. Utah State Bar, 645 South Two-hundred East, Salt Lake City, Utah 84111. 1957.

DIGESTS, INDEXES, ABSTRACTS, CITATORS

PACIFIC DIGEST. (1st and 2nd series). West Publishing Company, P.O. Box 64526, 50 West Kellogg Boulevard, St. Paul, Minnesota 55164-0526. 1932- . (Annual Supplements).

SHEPARD'S PACIFIC REPORTER CITATIONS. Shepard's/McGraw-Hill, P.O. Box 1235, Colorado Springs, Colorado 80901. (Monthly Supplements).

SHEPARD'S UTAH CITATIONS. Shepard's/McGraw-Hill, P.O. Box 1235, Colorado Springs, Colorado 80901. (Quarterly Supplements).

UTAH DIGEST. West Publishing Company, P.O. Box 64526, 50 West Kellogg Boulevard, St. Paul, Minnesota 55164. (Annual).

LEGAL REVIEWS AND PERIODICALS

BRIGHAM YOUNG UNIVERSITY JOURNAL OF LEGAL STUDIES. J. Rueben Clark Law School, Room 453, Provo, Utah 84602.

BRIGHAM YOUNG UNIVERSITY LAW REVIEW. Brigham Young University School of Law, Room 453, Provo, Utah 84602. (Quarterly).

UTAH BAR JOURNAL. Utah State Bar, 425 East First South, Salt Lake City, Utah 84111. (Quarterly).

UTAH BAR LETTER. Utah State Bar, 425 East First South, Salt Lake City, Utah 84111. (Monthly).

UTAH LAW REVIEW. University of Utah College of Law, 325 University Street, Salt Lake City, Utah 84112. (Quarterly).

UTAH LAWYER ALERT. Code * Company, P.O. Box 1471, Provo, Utah 84603. 1986- .

FORMBOOKS

WILL AND TRUST FORMS. Zions First National Bank, Salt Lake City, Utah 1986.

PRACTICE MANUALS

STATUTORY TIME LIMITATIONS; UTAH. Butterworth Legal Publishers, 90 Stiles Road, Salem, New Hampshire 03079. 1981- . (Periodic Supplements).

UTAH CIVIL PROCEDURE. David A. Thomas. Utah Civil Procedure, P.O. Box 703, Provo, Utah 84601. 1980- . (Periodic Supplements).

UTAH ENVIRONMENTAL LAND USE PERMIT MANUAL. Utah State Bar, 425 East First South, Salt Lake City, Utah 84111. 1986- . (Biennial Supplements).

UTAH PROBATE SYSTEMS. Utah State Bar, 425 East First South, Salt Lake City, Utah 84111. 1977.

UTAH REMEDIES GUIDE. University of Utah College of Law, 325 University Street, Salt Lake City, Utah 84112. 1985- .

UTAH WOMEN AND THE LAW: A RESOURCE HANDBOOK. Utah's Governor's Commission on the Status of Women, Books on Demand, 300 North Zeeb Road, Ann Arbor, Michigan 48106-1346. 1987.

MANUALS AND RESEARCH GUIDES

UTAH UNDER COVER: CHECKLIST OF UTAH STATE AGENCY PUBLICATIONS. Utah State Library Division, 2150 South 300 West, Salt Lake City, Utah 84114. 1984- .

ASSOCIATIONS AND PROFESSIONAL SOCIETIES

UTAH BAR ASSOCIATION. 645 South Two-hundred East, Salt Lake City, Utah 84111. (801) 531-9077.

DIRECTORIES

MOUNTAIN STATES LEGAL DIRECTORY [COLORADO, IDAHO, MONTANA, NEW MEXICO, UTAH, WYOMING]. Legal Directories Publishing Company, 2122 Kidwell, P.O. Box 140200, Dallas, Texas 75214-0200. (Annual).

UTAH LEGISLATIVE ROSTER. Legislative Operations Committee, Utah State Legislature, State Capitol, Salt Lake City, Utah 84114. (Latest edition December 1985).

UTAH OFFICIAL ROSTER. Division of Archives, Utah Department of Administrative Services, State Capitol Building, Room 28, Salt Lake City, Utah 84114. Biennial. (July of odd years).

STATES--VERMONT

STATUTES, CODES, STANDARDS, UNIFORM LAWS

LAWS OF VERMONT. Law and Documents Unit, Department of Libraries, 111 State Street, Montpelier, Vermont 05602. (Annual).

THE REGULATIONS OF VERMONT. Office of the Secretary of State, Pavillion Office Building, 109 State Street, Montpelier, Vermont 05602. 1984- .

VERMONT ADMINISTRATIVE PROCEDURES BULLETIN. Office of the Secretary of State, Pavillion Office Building, 109 State Street, Montpelier, Vermont 05602. (Quarterly).

VERMONT ADMINISTRATIVE PROCEDURES COMPILATION. (Replaced by Regulations of Vermont).

VERMONT STATUTES ANNOTATED. Equity Publishing Company, Rural Route Number 1, P.O. Box 3, Orford, New Hampshire 03777. 1959- . (Annual Supplements).

LOOSELEAF SERVICES AND REPORTERS

ATLANTIC REPORTER. (First and Second Series). West Publishing Company, P.O. Box 64526, 50 West Kellogg Boulevard, St. Paul, Minnesota 55164-0526. 1886- .

VERMONT REPORTS. Equity Publishing Company, Rural Route Number 1, P.O. Box 3, Orford, New Hampshire 03777. 1826- .

DIGESTS, INDEXES, ABSTRACTS, CITATORS

ATLANTIC DIGEST. (First and Second Series). West Publishing Company, P.O. Box 64526, 50 West Kellogg Boulevard, St. Paul, Minnesota 55164-0526. (Annual Supplements).

SHEPARD'S ATLANTIC REPORTER CITATIONS. Shepard's/McGraw-Hill, P.O. Box 1235, Colorado Springs, Colorado 80901. (Monthly Supplements).

SHEPARD'S VERMONT CITATIONS. Shepard's/McGraw-Hill, P.O. Box 1235, Colorado Springs, Colorado 80901. (Quarterly).

VERMONT DIGEST. West Publishing Company, P.O. Box 64526, 50 West Kellogg Boulevard, St. Paul, Minnesota 55164-0526. (Annual Supplements).

ATTORNEY GENERAL OPINIONS

VERMONT ATTORNEY GENERAL REPORTS AND OPINIONS. Office of the Attorney General, Law and Documents Unit, Department of Libraries, 111 State Street, Montpelier, Vermont 05602. Biennial.

ETHICS OPINIONS AND RULES

Ethics Opinions are issued by the Committee on Professional Responsibility of the Vermont Bar Association. Opinions are published in the *Vermont Bar Journal*. Abstracts are published in the *ABA/BNA Lawyers' Manual on Professional Conduct*. For further information concerning these opinions, contact the Committee at P.O. Box 100, Montpelier, Vermont 65602. 802-223-2020.

COURT RULES

VERMONT COURT RULES ANNOTATED. Equity Publishing Company, Rural Route Number 1, P.O. Box 3, Orford, New Hampshire 03777. 1981- . (Semiannual Supplements).

LAW REVIEWS AND PERIODICALS

VERMONT LAW REVIEW. Vermont Law School, South Royalton, Vermont 05068. (Semiannual).

NEWSLETTERS AND NEWSPAPERS

VERMONT BAR JOURNAL AND LAW DIGEST. Vermont Bar Association, P.O. Box 100, Montpelier, Vermont 05602. Bimonthly.

PRACTICE MATERIALS

CRIMINAL LAW. Vermont Bar Association, P.O. Box 100, Montpelier, Vermont 05602. 1985.

DOMESTIC RELATIONS. Vermont Bar Association, P.O. Box 100, Montpelier, Vermont 05602. 1985.

ESTATE PLANNING AND PROBATE PRACTICE. Vermont Bar Association, P.O. Box 100, Montpelier, Vermont 05602. 1985.

RESIDENTIAL REAL ESTATE. Vermont Bar Association, P.O. Box 100, Montpelier, Vermont 05602. 1985.

SMALL BUSINESS. Vermont Bar Association, P.O. Box 100, Montpelier, Vermont 05602. 1985.

BAR ASSOCIATIONS

VERMONT BAR ASSOCIATION, P.O. Box 100, Montpelier, Vermont 05602. (802) 223-2020.

STATES--VIRGINIA

STATUTES, CODES, STANDARDS, UNIFORM LAWS

ACTS OF THE GENERAL ASSEMBLY OF THE COMMONWEALTH OF VIRGINIA. Secretary of the Commonwealth, Ninth Street Office Building, Richmond, Virginia 23219. (Annual).

CODE OF VIRGINIA ANNOTATED. Michie Company, P.O. Box 7587, Charlottesville, Virginia 22906-7587. 1950- . (Annual Supplements).

VIRGINIA REGISTER OF REGULATIONS. Virginia Code Commission, P.O. Box 3-AG, Richmond, Virginia 23208. 1984- . Biweekly. (No Administrative Code published).

LOOSELEAF SERVICES AND REPORTERS

SOUTH EASTERN REPORTER. (Supreme Court of Appeals). West Publishing Company, P.O. Box 64526, 50 West Kellogg Boulevard, St. Paul, Minnesota 55164-0526. 1887- .

STATE AND LOCAL TAXES, VIRGINIA. Prentice-Hall, Incorporated, 113 Sylvan Avenue, Englewood Cliffs, New Jersey 07632. (Looseleaf).

VIRGINIA CIRCUIT COURT OPINIONS. Dietz Press, Inc., 109 East Cary Street, Richmond, Virginia 23219. 1985- .

VIRGINIA REPORTS. (Virginia Supreme Court of Appeals). Darby Printing Company, Atlanta, Georgia. 1790- .

VIRGINIA TAX REPORTER. Commerce Clearing House, Incorporated, 4025 West Peterson Avenue, Chicago, Illinois 60646. (Looseleaf).

ATTORNEY GENERAL REPORTS

OPINIONS OF THE ATTORNEY GENERAL AND REPORT TO THE GOVERNOR OF VIRGINIA. Microform. William S. Hein, Microform Division, 1285 Main Street, Buffalo, New York 14209. Annual.

ETHICS OPINIONS, CODES, RULES

VIRGINIA STATE BAR PROFESSIONAL HANDBOOK. Virginia State Bar. Michie Company, P.O. Box 7587, Charlottesville, Virginia 22906-7587. 1983. For further information concerning these opinions, contact the Virginia State Bar Council. (804) 786-2061.

COURT RULES

RULES OF THE UNITED STATES BANKRUPTCY COURT FOR THE EASTERN DISTRICT OF VIRGINIA. Michie Company, P.O. Box 7587, Charlottesville, Virginia 22906-7587. 1985- . (Periodic Supplements).

VIRGINIA RULES ANNOTATED. Michie Company, P.O. Box 7587, Charlottesville, Virginia 22906-7587. Annual.

JURY INSTRUCTIONS

INSTRUCTIONS FOR VIRGINIA AND WEST VIRGINIA. Second edition. Michie Company, P.O. Box 7587, Charlottesville, Virginia 22906-7587. 1962- . (Periodic Supplements).

VIRGINIA JURY INSTRUCTIONS. M. R. Doubles. West Publishing Company, P.O. Box 64526, 50 West Kellogg Boulevard, St. Paul, Minnesota 55164-0526. 1964- . (Periodic Supplements).

VIRGINIA MODEL JURY INSTRUCTIONS: CIVIL. Model Jury Instructions Committee. Michie Company, P.O. Box 7587, Charlottesville, Virginia 22906-7587. 1984- . (Annual Supplements).

VIRGINIA MODEL JURY INSTRUCTIONS CRIMINAL. Model Jury Instructions Committee. Michie Company, P.O. Box 7587, Charlottesville, Virginia 22906-7587. 1985- . (Periodic Supplements).

DIGESTS, INDEXES, ABSTRACTS, CITATORS

SHEPARD'S SOUTH EASTERN REPORTER CITATIONS. Shepard's/McGraw-Hill, P.O. Box 1235, Colorado Springs, Colorado 80901. (Monthly Supplements).

SHEPARD'S VIRGINIA CITATIONS. Shepard's/McGraw-Hill, P.O. Box 1235, Colorado Springs, Colorado 80901. (Six issues per year).

SOUTH EASTERN DIGEST. West Publishing Company, P.O. Box 64526, 50 West Kellogg Boulevard, St. Paul, Minnesota 55164-0526. 1935- . (Annual Supplements).

VIRGINIA AND WEST VIRGINIA DIGEST. West Publishing Company, P.O. Box 64526, 50 West Kellogg Boulevard, St. Paul, Minnesota 55164-0526. (Annual Supplements).

VIRGINIA CRIMINAL LAW CASE FINDER. Joseph M. Clarke, II. Michie Company, P.O. Box 7587, Charlottesville, Virginia 22906-7587. 1987- . (Periodic Supplements).

VIRGINIA DOMESTIC RELATIONS CASE FINDER. Brien A. Roche. Michie Company, P.O. Box 7587, Charlottesville, Virginia 22906-7587. 1986- . (Periodic Supplements).

VIRGINIA TORTS CASE FINDER. Brien A, Roche. Michie Company, P.O. Box 7587, Charlottesville, Virginia 22906-7587. 1984- . (Periodic Supplements).

ENCYCLOPEDIAS AND DICTIONARIES

MICHIE'S JURISPRUDENCE OF VIRGINIA AND WEST VIRGINIA. Michie Company, P.O. Box 7587, Charlottesville, Virginia 22906-7587. 1974- . (Annual Supplements).

LAW REVIEWS AND PERIODICALS

GEORGE MASON LAW REVIEW. George Mason University School of Law, 3401 North Fairfax Drive, Arlington, Virginia 22201. Semiannual.

RICHMOND LAW REVIEW. University of Richmond Law Review, T. C. Williams School of Law, University of Richmond, Richmond, Virginia 23173. Five issues per year.

THE VIRGINIA BAR ASSOCIATION JOURNAL. Virginia State Bar Association, 701 East Franklin Street, Suite 708, Richmond, Virginia 23219. Quarterly.

THE VIRGINIA BAR NEWS. Virginia State Bar Association, 700 East Main Street, Suite 1622, Richmond, Virginia 23219. Monthly.

VIRGINIA JOURNAL OF INTERNATIONAL LAW. University of Virginia School of Law, Charlottesville, Virginia 22901. Quarterly.

VIRGINIA JOURNAL OF NATURAL RESOURCES LAW. University of Virginia School of Law, Charlottesville, Virginia 22901. Semiannual.

VIRGINIA LAW REVIEW. University of Virginia School of Law, Charlottesville, Virginia 22901. Eight issues per year.

VIRGINIA TAX LAW REIVEW. University of Virginia School of Law, Charlottesville, Virginia 22901. Quarterly.

WASHINGTON AND LEE LAW REVIEW. Washington and Lee University School of Law, Lewis Hall, Lexington, Virginia 24450. Quarterly.

WILLIAM AND MARY LAW REVIEW. College of William and Mary, Marshall-Wythe School of Law, Williamsburg, Virginia 23185. Five issues per year.

NEWSLETTER AND NEWSPAPERS

METRO VERDICTS MONTHLY. Judicial Advisory Services, Incorporated, P.O. Box 99704. 3309 College Drive, Louisville, Kentucky 40299. Monthly.

VIRGINIA EMPLOYMENT LAW LETTER. M. Lee Smith Publishers and Printers, 162 Fourth Avenue North, Nashville, Tennessee 37219. Monthly.

FORMBOOKS

HANDBOOK FOR LEGAL SECRETARIES IN VIRGINIA. Second edition. Virginia Association of Legal Secretaries. Michie Company, P.O. Box 7587, Charlottesville, Virginia 22906-7587. 1980- . (Periodic Supplements).

VIRGINIA BOOK OF FORMS. Barbara G. Gallo, et al. Michie Company, P.O. Box 7587, Charlottesville, Virginia 22906-7587. 1978- . (Periodic Supplements).

PRACTICE MATERIALS

ADMINISTRATION OF ESTATES: A VIRGINIA LAW PRACTICE SYSTEM (INCLUDES FORMS). Lucius H, Bracey, Jr. and Walter R. Rogers, Jr. Michie Company, P.O. Box 7587, Charlottesville, Virginia 22906-7587. 1984- . (Periodic Supplements).

APPELLATE LITIGATION: A VIRGINIA LAW PRACTICE SYSTEM. Randolph W. Church, Jr. Michie Company, P.O. Box 7587, Charlottesville, Virginia 22906-7587. 1983- . (Periodic Supplements).

BANKRUPTCY: A VIRGINIA LAW PRACTICE SYSTEM. Replacement edition. W. S. Scott. Michie Company, P.O. Box 7587, Charlottesville, Virginia 22906-7587. 1982- . (Periodic Supplements).

BUSINESS ENTITIES: VIRGINIA LAW PRACTICE SYSTEM. George H. Gillman. Michie Company, P.O. Box 7587, Charlottesville, Virginia 22906-7587. 1982- . (Periodic Supplements).

COLLECTIONS: A VIRGINIA LAW PRACTICE SYSTEM. Robert A. Pustilnik and Arthur F. Samuel. Michie Company, P.O. Box 7587, Charlottesville, Virginia 22906-7587. 1982- . (Periodic Supplements).

CRIMINAL PRACTICE: A VIRGINIA LAW PRACTICE SYSTEM. John C. Lowe. Michie Company, P.O. Box 7587, Charlottesville, Virginia 22906-7587. 1984- . (Periodic Supplements).

DOMESTIC RELATIONS: A VIRGINIA LAW PRACTICE SYSTEM (INCLUDES FORMS). L. L. Bean. Michie Company, P.O. Box 7587, Charlottesville, Virginia 22906-7587. 1982- . (Periodic Supplements).

ENFORCEMENTS OF JUDGEMENTS AND LIENS IN VIRGINIA. Doug Rendleman. Michie Company, P.O. Box 7587, Charlottesville, Virginia 22906-7587. 1982- . (Periodic Supplements).

HANDBOOK ON VIRGINIA CIVIL PROCEDURE. W. H. Bryson. Michie Company, P.O. Box 7587, Charlottesville, Virginia 22906-7587. 1983- . (Periodic Supplements).

HARRISON ON WILLS AND ADMINISTRATION FOR VIRGINIA AND WEST VIRGINIA. Third edition. George P. Smith, Jr. Michie Company, P.O. Box 7587, Charlottesville, Virginia 22906-7587. 1985- . (Periodic Supplements).

HOW TO GET A DIVORCE: A PRACTICAL HANDBOOK FOR RESIDENTS OF THE DISTRICT OF COLUMBIA, MARYLAND, AND VIRGINIA WHO ARE CONTEMPLATING SEPARATION AND DIVORCE. Third edition. Sandra Kalenik. Washington Book Trading Company, P.O. Box 1676, Arlington, Virginia 22210. 1991.

JUVENILE JUSTICE IN VIRGINIA. Michael F. Clayton and Preston T. Scott. Michie Company, P.O. Box 7587, Charlottesville, Virginia 22906-7587. 1982- . (Periodic Supplements).

THE LAW OF EVIDENCE IN VIRGINIA. Second edition. Charles E. Friend. Michie Company, P.O. Box 7587, Charlottesville, Virginia 22906-7587. 1983- . (Periodic Supplements).

REAL ESTATE: A VIRGINIA LAW PRACTICE SYSTEM (INCLUDES FORMS). Donald L. Wetherington and William W. Terry, III. Michie Company, P.O. Box 7587, Charlottesville, Virginia 22906-7587. 1986- . (Periodic Supplements).

SOURCES OF PROOF ON PREPARING A LAWSUIT--STATE AND FEDERAL. Andre Moenssens, editor. Joint Committee on Continuing Legal Education. University of Virginia School of Law, Charlottesville, Virginia 22901. 1981- . (Periodic Supplements).

TITLE EXECUTOR IN VIRGINIA. Sidney F. Parham, Jr. Michie Company, P.O. Box 7587, Charlottesville, Virginia 22906-7587. 1965.

TRIAL HANDBOOK FOR VIRGINIA LAWYERS. Craig D. Johnston. Lawyers Co-Operative Company, Aqueduct Building, Rochester, New York 14694. 1986- . (Annual Supplements).

VIRGINIA ADMINISTRATIVE LAW AND PRACTICE. Second edition. Charles J. Midkiff and Michael Maupin, editors. Joint Committee for Continuing Legal Education, University of Virginia School of Law, Charlottesville, Virginia 22901. 1986- . (Periodic Supplements).

VIRGINIA CIVIL PROCEDURE. T. M. Boyd, Edward Graves, and Leigh B. Middleditch, Jr. 1982- . Michie Company, P.O. Box 7587, Charlottesville, Virginia 22906-7587. (Periodic Supplements).

VIRGINIA CRIMINAL PROCEDURE. Ronald J. Bacigal. Harrison Company, 3110 Crossing Park, Norcross, Georgia 30071. 1983- . (Periodic Supplements).

THE VIRGINIA LAWYER: A BASIC PRACTICE HANDBOOK. Joseph R, Mayes, editor. Michie Company, P.O. Box 7587, Charlottesville, Virginia 22906-7587. 1979- . (Periodic Supplements).

VIRGINIA LAWYERS DESKBOOK. Michie Company, P.O. Box 7587, Charlottesville, Virginia 22906-7587. 1983. (Periodic Supplements).

VIRGINIA PRACTICE. West Publishing Company, P.O. Box 64526, 50 West Kellogg Boulevard, St. Paul, Minnesota 55164-0526. 1964- . (Annual Supplements).

VIRGINIA PROBATE HANDBOOK: WITH FORMS. David C. Dorset and Frank O. Brown, Jr. Harrison Company, 3110 Crossing Park, Norcross, Georgia 30071. 1984.

VIRGINIA REAL ESTATE CLOSINGS: WITH FORMS. W. W. Berryhill. Harrison Company, 3110 Crossing Park, Norcross, Georgia 30071.

VIRGINIA RELATIONS HANDBOOK. Margaret F. Brinig and David M. White. Michie Company, P.O. Box 7587, Charlottesville, Virginia 22906-7587. 1985- . (Periodic Supplements).

WILLS: A VIRGINIA LAW PRACTICE SYSTEM. Lucius H. Bracey, Jr. and Walter R. Rogers. 1982- . Michie Company, P.O. Box 7587, Charlottesville, Virginia 22906-7587. (Periodic Supplements).

MANUALS AND RESEARCH GUIDES

A LAW LIBRARIAN'S INTRODUCTION TO VIRGINIA STATE PUBLICATIONS. Margaret Aycock, et al. American Association of Law Libraries, 53 West Jackson Boulevard, Chicago, Illinois 60604.

LAYMAN'S GUIDE TO VIRGINIA LAW. N. J. Bailes, et al. Michie Company, P.O. Box 7587, Charlottesville, Virginia 22906-7587. 1977.

ASSOCIATIONS AND PROFESSIONAL SOCIETIES

ALEXANDRIA BAR ASSOCIATION, 520 King Street. Room 202, Alexandria, Virginia 22314.

ARLINGTON COUNTY BAR ASSOCIATION, 1400 North Court House Road, Room 501, Arlington, Viginia 22201.

BAR ASSOCIATION OF THE CITY OF RICHMOND, 710 Mutual Building, Richmond, Virginia 23219.

FAIRFAX BAR ASSOCIATION, 4110 Chain Bridge Road, Fairfax, Virginia 22030. (703) 246-2472.

NORFOLK AND DARTMOUTH BAR ASSOCIATION, 1105 Virginia National Bank, Norfolk, Virginia 23510.

THE VIRGINIA BAR ASSOCIATION, 701 East Franklin Street, Suite 1515, Richmond, Virginia 23219. (804) 664-0041

VIRGINIA BEACH BAR ASSOCIATION, Municipal Center, Virginia Beach, Virginia 23456.

VIRGINIA STATE BAR ASSOCIATION, 801 East Main Street, Suite 100, Richmond, Virginia 23219. (804) 786-2061.

DIRECTORIES

COMMONWEALTH OF VIRGINIA TELEPHONE DIRECTORY. State Controlled Telephone System, Virginia Administrative Department of Telecommunications, 805 East Broad Street, Suite 700, Richmond, Virginia 23219. Annual. (January)

MANUAL OF THE SENATE AND HOUSE OF DELEGATES [VIRGINIA]. General Assembly of Virginia, State Capitol, Richmond, Virginia 23219. Biennial. (February of even years).

NORTHERN VIRGINIA LEGAL DIRECTORY. New Town Publications, 11734 Bowman Green Drive, Reston, Virginia 22090. 1983- . Annual.

STATE OF THE JUDICIARY REPORT [VIRGINIA]. Executive Secretaries Office, Virginia Supreme Court, 100 North Ninth Street, Third Floor, Richmond, Virginia 23219. Annual. (Summer)

VIRGINIA, MARYLAND, DELAWARE, DISTRICT OF COLUMBIA LEGAL DIRECTORY. Legal Directories Publishing Company, 2122 Kidwell Street, P.O. Box 140200, Dallas, Texas 75214-0200. Annual. (March).

VIRGINIA MUNICIPAL LEAGUE DIRECTORY. Virginia Municipal League, P.O. Box 12164, Richmond, Virginia 23241. Biennial. (December of even years).

VIRGINIA RECORD--DIRECTORY OF VIRGINIA OFFICIALS ISSUE. Virginia Publisher's Wing, Drawer 2-Y, Richmond, Virginia 23205. Annual.

STATES --WASHINGTON

STATUTES, CODES, STANDARDS, UNIFORM LAWS

REVISED CODE OF WASHINGTON. Book Publishing Company, 201 Westlake Avenue North, Seattle, Washington 98109. 1950- . (Annual Supplements).

REVISED CODE OF WASHINGTON ANNOTATED. West Publishing Company, P.O. Box 64526, 50 West Kellogg Boulevard, St. Paul, Minnesota 55164-0526. 1962- . (Annual Supplements).

SESSION LAWS OF THE STATE OF WASHINGTON. Microform. William S. Hein and Company, Incorporated, Hein Building, 1285 Main Street, Buffalo, New York 14209. Annual.

WASHINGTON ADMINISTRATIVE CODE. Office of Code Revisor, Legislative Building, M.S. AS-15, Olympia, Washington 98504. 1977- . (Recompiled every three years).

WASHINGTON LEGISLATIVE SERVICE. West Publishing Company, P.O. Box 64526, 50 West Kellogg Boulevard, St. Paul, Minnesota 55164-0526. Irregular.

WASHINGTON STATE REGISTER. Office of Code Revisor, Legislative Building, M.S. AS-15, Olympia, Washington 98504. 1978- . Biweekly.

LOOSELEAF SERVICES AND REPORTERS

PACIFIC REPORTER. (First and Second series). West Publishing Company, P.O. Box 64526, 50 West Kellogg Boulevard, St. Paul, Minnesota 55164-0526. 1880- . (Supreme Court and Court of Appeals).

WASHINGTON APPELLATE REPORTS. Supreme Court of Washington, State Law Reports Office, Highway Licenses Building, Fifth Floor, M.S. AV-11, Olympia, Washington 98504. 1969- .

WASHINGTON REPORTER. West Publishing Company, P.O. Box 64526, 50 West Kellogg Boulevard, St. Paul, Minnesota 55164-0526. 1969- . (Supreme Court and Court of Appeals).

WASHINGTON REPORTS. (First and Second series). Supreme Court of Washington, State Law Reports Office, Highway Licenses Building, Fifth Floor, M.S. AV-11, Olympia, Washington, 98504. 1889- . (Supreme Court).

WASHINGTON TERRITORY REPORTS. State Law Reports Office, Highway Licenses Building, Fifth Floor, M.S. AV-11, Olympia, Washington, 98504. 1854-1888.

ATTORNEY GENERAL OPINIONS

OFFICE OF THE ATTORNEY GENERAL OPINIONS FOR ... Office of the Attorney General, Licences Building, Olympia, Washington 98504. 1892- . (Title and Frequency varies).

ETHICS OPINIONS, CODES, RULES

LEGAL MALPRACTICE. Washington State Bar Association, 500 Westin Building, 2001 Sixth Avenue, Seattle, Washington 98121-2599. 1985. For further information concerning these opinions, contact Code of Professional Responsibility Committee, Washington State Bar Association, (206) 622-6054.

RESOURCES. Washington State Bar Association, 500 Westin Building, 2001 Sixth Avenue, Seattle, Washington 98121-2599. Volume 1, Number 1, 1987- . Annual. (Includes Ethics Opinions, Bar Rules, Rules of Professional Conduct, Rules for Lawyer's Discipline, Directory of Attorneys and Court Directory). For further information concerning Professional Ethics, The Code of Professional Responsibility Committee, Washington State Association, 206-488-0441.

COURT RULES

LOCAL RULES FOR THE SUPERIOR COURT: WASHINGTON STATE. Butterworth Legal Publishers, 90 Stiles Road, Salem, New Hampshire 03079. 1981- . (Periodic Supplements).

OFFICIAL RULES OF COURT (1988), as of September 1, 1987. State Law Reports Office, Reporter of Decisions M.S. AV-11, Olympia, Washington 1983- . (Includes Disciplinary Rules). (Annual).

RULES FOR THE WESTERN DISTRICT OF WASHINGTON. Book Publishing Company, 201 Westlake Avenue North, Seattle, Washington 98109.

WASHINGTON COURT RULES. West Publishing Company, P.O. Box 64526, 50 West Kellogg Boulevard, St. Paul, Minnesota 55164-0526. Annual.

WASHINGTON COURT RULES ANNOTATED. Lawyers Co-Operative Company, Aqueduct Building, Rochester, New York 14694. 1977- . (Annual Supplements). (Three looseleaf volumes).

WASHINGTON RULES OF COURT ANNOTATED. Book Publishing Company, 201 Westlake Avenue North, Seattle, Washington 98109. 1974- . (Biannual Supplements).

JURY INSTRUCTIONS

WASHINGTON PATTERN JURY INSTRUCTIONS, CIVIL. Washington Supreme Court, Committee on Jury Instructions. West Publishing Company, P.O. Box 64526, 50 West Kellogg Boulevard, St. Paul, Minnesota 55164-0526. 1980- . (1984 Supplement). (Volume 6 of Washington Practice).

WASHINGTON PATTERN JURY INSTRUCTIONS, CRIMINAL. Washington Supreme Court, Committee on Jury Instructions. West Publishing Company, P.O. Box 64526, 50 West Kellogg Boulevard, St. Paul, Minnesota 55164-0526. 1977- . (1986 Supplementary). (Volume 11 of Washington Practice).

WASHINGTON PATTERN JURY INSTRUCTIONS FOR USE IN COMPARATIVE NEGLIGENCE CASES. Washington State Bar Association, 500 Westin Building, 2001 Sixth Avenue, Seattle, Washington 98121-2599. 1974.

DIGESTS, INDEXES, ABSTRACTS, CITATORS

PACIFIC DIGEST. (First and Second series). West Publishing Company, P.O. Box 64526, 50 West Kellogg Boulevard, St. Paul, Minnesota 55164-0526. 1933- .(Annual Supplements).

SHEPARD'S PACIFIC REPORTER CITATIONS. Shepard's/McGraw-Hill, P.O. Box 1235, Colorado Springs, Colorado 80901. (Monthly Supplements).

SHEPARD'S WASHINGTON CITATIONS. Shepard's/McGraw-Hill, P.O. Box 1235, Colorado Springs, Colorado 80901. (Eight Supplements per year).

WASHINGTON DIGEST, SECOND. West Publishing Company, P.O. Box 64526, 50 West Kellogg Boulevard, St. Paul, Minnesota 55164-0526. (Annual Supplements).

LAW REVIEWS AND PERIODICALS

GONZAGA LAW REVIEW. Gonzaga University School of Law, Spokane, Washington 99258. (Triannual).

UNIVERSITY OF PUGET SOUND LAW REVIEW. University of Puget Sound School of Law, 950 Broadway Plaza, Tacoma, Washington 98402. (Quarterly).

WASHINGTON LAW REVIEW. University of Washington School of Law, 1100 Northeast Campus Parkway, University of Washington, JB-20, Seattle, Washington 98105. Quarterly.

WASHINGTON STATE BAR NEWS. Washington State Bar Association, 500 Westin Building, 2001 Sixth Avenue, Seattle, Washington 98121-2599. (Monthly).

NEWSLETTERS AND NEWSPAPERS

ENVIRONMENTAL AND LAND USE LAW. Washington State Bar Association, 500 Westin Building, 2001 Sixth Avenue, Seattle, Washington 98121. Quarterly.

INTERNATIONAL LAW AND PRACTICE NEWSLETTERS. Washington State Bar Association, 500 Westin Building, 2001 Sixth Avenue, Seattle, Washington 98121. Quarterly.

JURY VERDICTS NORTHWEST. Jury Verdicts Northwest, P.O. Box 1165, Seattle, Washington 98111. Monthly.

NORTHWEST ARBITRATIONS. Jury Verdicts Northwest, P.O. Box 1165, Seattle, Washington 98111. Monthly.

WASHINGTON INSURANCE LAW LETTER. Reed, McClure, Moceri, Thorn and Moriarty, 701 Fifth Avenue, Seattle, Washington 98104. Monthly.

WASHINGTON TAX DECISIONS. Butterworth Legal Publishers, 90 Stiles Road, Salem, New Hampshire 03079. Irregular.

STATES --WASHINGTON

FORMBOOKS

CRIMINAL PRACTICE AND PROCEDURE, WITH FORMS. Royce A. Fergison, Jr. West Publishing Company, P.O. Box 64526, 50 West Kellogg Boulevard, St. Paul, Minnesota 55164-0526. 1984- . (Annual Supplements). (Washington Practice volumes 12 and 13).

WASHINGTON CIVIL PROCEDURE FORMS. Second Edition. M. Barbier. West Publishing Company, 50 West Kellogg Boulevard, St. Paul, Minnesota 55164. 1987.

WASHINGTON METHODS OF PRACTICE WITH FORMS. Second Edition. V. Towne. West Publishing Company, 50 West Kellogg Boulevard, St. Paul, Minnesota 55164. 1976. (Periodic Supplements).

WASHINGTON UNIFORM COMMERCIAL CODE FORMS. Walter Shattuck. West Publishing Company, 50 West Kellogg Boulevard, St. Paul, Minnesota 55164. 1967. (Periodic Supplements).

PRACTICE MATERIALS

ADVISING WASHINGTON BUSINESS. Washington State Bar Association, 500 Westin Building, 2001 Sixth Avenue, Seattle, Washington 98121-2599. 1986.

ANNUAL ESTATE PLANNING SEMINAR. Washington State Bar Association, 500 Westin Building, 2001 Sixth Avenue, Seattle, Washington 98121-2599. Annual.

CIVIL PROCEDURE BEFORE TRIAL DESKBOOK. Washington State Bar Association, 500 Westin Building, 2001 Sixth Avenue, Seattle, Washington 98121-2599. 1981- . (Annual Supplements).

COLLECTION OF JUDGMENTS IN WASHINGTON. Washington State Bar Association, 500 Westin Building, 2001 Sixth Avenue, Seattle, Washington 98121-2599. 1985.

COMMERCIAL REAL ESTATE. Washington State Bar Association, 500 Westin Building, 2001 Sixth Avenue, Seattle, Washington 98121-2599. 1984.

COMMUNITY PROPERTY DESKBOOK. Washington State Bar Association, 500 Westin Building, 2001 Sixth Avenue, Seattle, Washington 98121-2599. 1977- . (Periodic Supplements).

CONFLICT OF LAWS: A NORTHWEST PERSPECTIVE. James A. R. Nafziger. Butterworth Legal Publishers, 90 Stiles Road, Salem, New Hampshire 03079. 1985.

CREATIVE ESTATE PLANNING. Washington State Bar Association, 500 Westin Building, 2001 Sixth Avenue, Seattle, Washington 98121-2599. 1985.

EMPLOYMENT IN WASHINGTON STATE: A GUIDE TO LAWS REGULATING EMPLOYERS AND EMPLOYEES. Revised Edition. Michael Killeen. Butterworth Legal Publishers, 90 Stiles Road, Salem, New Hampshire 03079. 1990.

ESTATE AND TRUST LITIGATION. Washington State Bar Association, 500 Westin Building, 2001 Sixth Avenue, Seattle, Washington 98121-2599. 1985.

LAND USE DAMAGES AND REMEDIES: THEORIES, PROOF, AND STRATEGIC CONSIDERATIONS. Washington State Bar Association, 500 Westin Building, 2001 Sixth Avenue, Seattle, Washington 98121-2599. 1986.

THE LAW OF EVIDENCE IN WASHINGTON. Robert Aronson. Butterworth Legal Publishers, 90 Stiles Road, Salem, New Hampshire 03079. 1986- . (Periodic Supplements).

MORE EFFECTIVE TRIAL PRACTICE: THE PERSPECTIVE OF BENCH AND BAR. Washington State Bar Association, 500 Westin Building, 2001 Sixth Avenue, Seattle, Washington 98121-2599. 1986.

NATURAL DISASTERS: SELECTED PROBLEMS AND IMPLICATIONS. Washington State Bar Association, 500 Westin Building, 2001 Sixth Avenue, Seattle, Washington 98121-2599. 1980.

POST MARITAL DISSOLUTION PROCEEDINGS. Washington State Bar Association, 500 Westin Building, 2001 Sixth Avenue, Seattle, Washington 98121-2599. 1984.

SOCIAL SECURITY DISABILITY PRACTICE. Washington State Bar Association, 500 Westin Building, 2001 Sixth Avenue, Seattle, Washington 98121-2599. 1984.

STRATEGIES AND TECHNIQUES IN CRIMINAL DEFENSE. Second edition. Butterworth Legal Publishers, 90 Stiles Road, Salem, New Hampshire 03079. 1983- . (Periodic Supplements).

SUCCESSFUL LITIGATION OF ANTITRUST AND COMMERCIAL CASES. Washington State Bar Association, 500 Westin Building, 2001 Sixth Avenue, Seattle, Washington 98121-2599. 1982.

TORTS AND PRODUCTS LIABILITY PRACTICE: UPDATE ON THE 1981 ACT. Washington State Bar Association, 500 Westin Building, 2001 Sixth Avenue, Seattle, Washington 98121-2599. 1984.

WASHINGTON APPELLATE PRACTICE HANDBOOK. Washington State Bar Association, 500 Westin Building, 2001 Sixth Avenue, Seattle, Washington 98121-2599. 1980- . (Periodic Supplements).

WASHINGTON COMMERCIAL LAW DESKBOOK. Washington State Bar Association, 500 Westin Building, 2001 Sixth Avenue, Seattle, Washington 98121-2599. 1983- . (Periodic Supplements).

WASHINGTON PARTNERSHIP LAW AND PRACTICE HANDBOOK. Washington State Bar Association, 500 Westin Building, 2001 Sixth Avenue, Seattle, Washington 98121-2599. 1984.

WASHINGTON PRACTICE. West Publishing Company, P.O. Box 64526, 50 West Kellogg Boulevard, St. Paul, Minnesota 55164-0526.

WASHINGTON PROBATE PRACTICE PROCEDURE AND TAX MANUALS. Robert S. Mucklestone. Book Publishing Company, 201 Westlake Avenue North, Seattle, Washington 98109. 1983- . (Annual Supplements).

WASHINGTON PUBLIC EMPLOYMENT RELATIONS REPORTER. Book Publishing Company, 201 Westlake Avenue North, Seattle, Washington 98109. 1976- . (Monthly Supplements).

Encyclopedia of Legal Information Sources • 2nd Ed. STATES--WEST VIRGINIA

WASHINGTON REAL PROPERTY DESKBOOK. Second edition. Washington State Bar Association, 500 Westin Building, 2001 Sixth Avenue, Seattle, Washington 98121-2599. 1986- . (Periodic Supplements).

WORKMEN'S COMPENSATION UPDATE. Washington State Bar Association, 500 Westin Building, 2001 Sixth Avenue, Seattle, Washington 98121-2599. 1984.

MANUALS AND RESEARCH GUIDES

LEGAL RESEARCH GUIDE. Marion Gallagher. University of Washington Law School Library, 1100 Northeast Campus Parkway, JB-20, Seattle, Washington 98105. 1980.

WASHINGTON STATE LAW-RELATED PUBLICATIONS: A SELECTIVE BIBLIOGRAPHY WITH COMMENTARY. Scott F. Burson. Prepared for presentation at the Government Documents SIS Program, 77th Annual Meeting, San Diego, 1984. American Association of Law Libraries, 53 West Jackson Boulevard, Room 703, Chicago, Illinois 60604. 1984.

ASSOCIATIONS AND PROFESSIONAL SOCIETIES

SEATTLE-KING COUNTY BAR ASSOCIATION, 320 Central Building, Seattle, Washington 98104. (206) 624-9365.

SPOKANE BAR ASSOCIATION, West 1116 Broadway, Spokane, Washington 99260.

TACOMA-PIERRE COUNTY BAR ASSOCIATION, 930 Tacoma Avenue South, Room 240, Tacoma, Washington 98402.

WASHINGTON BAR ASSOCIATION, 500 Westin Building, 2001 Sixth Avenue, Seattle, Washington 98121-2599. (206) 448-0441.

DIRECTORIES

A CITIZEN'S GUIDE TO THE COURTS IN WASHINGTON REGION. Office of the Administrator for the Courts, Sixth Floor, Licences Building, Olympia, Washington 98504. 1990.

DIRECTORY OF COUNTY OFFICIALS IN WASHINGTON STATE. Washington Association of County Officials, 206 Tenth Avenue Southeast, Olympia, Washington 98501. Annual.

LEGISLATIVE MANUAL, STATE OF WASHINGTON. Washington Legislature, State Capitol, Olympia, Washington 98504. Biennial. (Spring of odd years).

OFFICIALS OF WASHINGTON CITIES. Municipal Research and Services Center of Washington, 4719 Brooklyn Avenue, Northeast, Seattle, Washington 98105. Biennial. (March of even years).

OREGON AND WASHINGTON LEGAL DIRECTORY [INCLUDING ALASKA]. Legal Directories Publishing Company, 2122 Kidwell, P.O. Box 140200, Dallas, Texas 75214-0200. Annual. (March)

RESOURCES. Washington State Bar Association, 500 Westin Building, 2001 Sixth Avenue, Seattle, Washington 98121-2599. 1987- . Annual. (Contains Directory of Washington Attorneys).

WASHINGTON LEGISLATURE-PICTORIAL DIRECTORY. Washington Legislature, State Capitol, Olympia, Washington 98504. Biennial. (Odd years)

WASHINGTON STATE YEARBOOK. Secretary of State, Legislative Building, Olympia, Washington, 98504. Annual.

OTHER SOURCES

SENTENCING IN WASHINGTON: A LEGAL ANALYSIS OF THE SENTENCING REFORM ACT OF 1981. David Boerner. Butterworth Legal Publishers, 90 Stiles Road, Salem, New Hampshire 03079. 1985.

WASHINGTON ASSOCIATION FOR LEGAL SECRETARIES' HANDBOOK. Book Publishing Company, 201 Westlake Avenue North, Seattle, Washington 98109.

STATES--WEST VIRGINIA

STATUTES, CODES, STANDARDS, UNIFORM LAWS

ACTS OF THE LEGISLATURE OF WEST VIRGINIA. Department of Finance and Administration, 200 Morris Street, Charleston, West Virginia 25301. Annual.

ADMINISTRATIVE LAW IN WEST VIRGINIA. Alfred S. Neely, IV. Michie Company, P.O. Box 7587, Charlottesville, Virginia 22906-7587. 1982.

WEST VIRGINIA ADVANCE ANNOTATION SERVICE. Michie Company, P.O. Box 7587, Charlottesville, Virginia 22906-7587. (Three pamphlets per year).

WEST VIRGINIA ADVANCE CODE SERVICE. Michie Company, P.O. Box 7587, Charlottesville, Virginia 22906-7587. (Irregular pamphlets).

WEST VIRGINIA ADMINISTRATIVE CODE, ANNOTATED. West Virginia Business Publishing Corporation, 1614 Washington Street, East, P.O. Box 5173, Charleston, West Virginia 25361. 1984- . (Periodic Supplements).

WEST VIRGINIA CODE ANNOTATED. Michie Company, P.O. Box 7587, Charlottesville, Virginia 22906-7587. 1966- (Annual Supplements).

WEST VIRGINIA REGISTER. West Virginia Business Publishing Corporation, 1614 Washington Street, East, P.O. Box 5173, Charleston, West Virginia 25361.

LOOSELEAF SERVICES AND REPORTERS

SOUTH EASTERN REPORTER. West Publishing Company, P.O. Box 64526, 50 West Kellogg Boulevard, St. Paul, Minnesota 55164-0526. 1886- . (Supreme Court of Appeals).

WEST VIRGINIA REPORTS. Department of Finance and Administration, 200 Morris Street, Charleston, West Virginia 25301. 1863- . (Supreme Court of Appeals).

STATES--WEST VIRGINIA

ATTORNEY GENERAL OPINIONS

WEST VIRGINIA ATTORNEY GENERAL REPORTS AND OPINIONS. Departments of Finance and Administration, 200 Morris Street, Charleston, West Virginia 25301. Biennial.

ETHICS OPINIONS, CODES, RULES

West Virginia Ethics Opinions are issued by the West Virginia State Bar Ethics Committee and are published in its CLE Bulletin. Abstracts of these opinions are published in the *ABA/BNA Lawyers' Manual on Professional Conduct*. For further information concerning these opinions, contact the Committee at E-400 State Capitol, Charleston, West Virginia 25305. 304-346-8414.

COURT RULES

WEST VIRGINIA RULES ANNOTATED. Michie Company, P.O. Box 7587, Charlottesville, Virginia 22906-7587. Annual. (Also published in Volume One of the West Virginia Code).

JURY INSTRUCTIONS

INSTRUCTIONS FOR VIRGINIA AND WEST VIRGINIA. Second edition. Earl L. Abbott and Erwin S. Solomon. Michie Company, P.O. Box 7587, Charlottesville, Virginia 22906-7587. 1962- . (Periodic Supplements).

DIGESTS, INDEXES, ABSTRACTS, CITATORS

SHEPARD'S SOUTHEASTERN REPORTER CITATIONS. Shepard's/McGraw-Hill, P.O. Box 1235, Colorado Springs, Colorado 80901. (Monthly Supplements).

SHEPARD'S WEST VIRGINIA CITATIONS. Shepard's/McGraw-Hill, P.O. Box 1235, Colorado Springs, Colorado 80901. (Quarterly Supplements).

SOUTH EASTERN DIGEST. West Publishing Company, P.O. Box 64526, 50 West Kellogg Boulevard, St. Paul, Minnesota 55164-0526. 1935- . (Monthly Supplements).

VIRGINIA AND WEST VIRGINIA DIGEST. West Publishing Company, P.O. Box 64526, 50 West Kellogg Boulevard, St. Paul, Minnesota 55164-0526. 1943- .(Annual Supplements).

ENCYCLOPEDIAS AND DICTIONARIES

MICHIE'S JURISPRUDENCE OF VIRGINIA AND WEST VIRGINIA. Michie Company, P.O. Box 7587, Charlottesville, Virginia 22906-7587. 1974- . (Annual Supplements).

LAW REVIEWS AND PERIODICALS

CLE BULLETIN. West Virginia State Bar, E-400, State Capitol, Charleston, West Virginia 25305.

WEST VIRGINIA LAW REVIEW. West Virginia University Law Center, P.O. Box 6130, Morgantown, West Virginia 26506-6130. (Quarterly).

WEST VIRGINIA STATE BAR JOURNAL. West Virginia State Bar, E-404, State Capitol, Charleston, West Virginia 25414. (Quarterly).

PRACTICE MATERIALS

ADMINISTRATIVE LAW IN WEST VIRGINIA. Michie Company, P.O. Box 7587, Charlottesville, Virginia 22906-7587. 1982. (Periodic Supplements).

BURK'S PLEADING AND PRACTICE. Fourth edition. T. M. Boyd and W. W. Koontz. Michie Company, P.O. Box 7587, Charlottesville, Virginia 22906-7587. 1961- . (Periodic Supplements).

HANDBOOK ON EVIDENCE FOR WEST VIRGINIA LAWYERS. Second edition. Franklin D. Cleckley. Michie Company, P.O. Box 7587, Charlottesville, Virginia 22906-7587. 1986- . (Periodic Supplements).

HANDBOOK ON WEST VIRGINIA CRIMINAL PROCEDURE. Franklin D. Cleckley. Michie Company, P.O. Box 7587, Charlottesville, Virginia 22906-7587. 1985- . (Periodic Supplements).

HARRISON ON WILLS AND ADMINISTRATION FOR VIRGINIA AND WEST VIRGINIA. Third edition. George P. Smith, Jr. Michie Company, P.O. Box 7587, Charlottesville, Virginia 22906-7587. 1985- . (Periodic Supplements).

THE LAW OF COAL, OIL AND GAS IN WEST VIRGINIA AND VIRGINIA. R. T. Donley. Michie Company, P.O. Box 7587, Charlottesville, Virginia 22906-7587. 1951- . (Periodic Supplements).

THE LAW OF DOMESTIC RELATIONS IN WEST VIRGINIA. William O. Morris. Michie Company, P.O. Box 7587, Charlottesville, Virginia 22906-7587. 1973- . (Periodic Supplements).

MODERN CIVIL PRACTICE IN WEST VRIGINIA. Dale P. Olsen. Michie Company, P.O. Box 7587, Charlottesville, Virginia 22906-7587. 1984- . (Periodic Supplements).

VIRGINIA AND WEST VIRGINIA LIABILITY. Robert I. Stevenson. Harrison Company, 3110 Crossing Park, Norcross, Georgia 30071. 1983- . (Periodic Supplements).

VIRGINIA AND WEST VIRGINIA WRONGFUL DEATH ACTIONS. Peter N. Swisher. Harrison Company, 3110 Crossing Park, Norcross, Georgia 30071. 1985- . (Periodic Supplements).

WEST VIRGINIA OIL AND GAS LAW. Larry L. Skeen. Michie Company, P.O. Box 7587, Charlottesville, Virginia 22906-7587. 1984- . (Periodic Supplements). (Includes forms).

WEST VIRGINIA PRACTICE HANDBOOK. Second edition. Duke N. Stern and Karen G. Sampson. Michie Company, P.O. Box 7587, Charlottesville, Virginia 22906-7587. 1977- . (Periodic Supplements).

ASSOCIATIONS AND PROFESSIONAL SOCIETIES

WEST VIRGINIA BAR ASSOCIATION, 100 Capitol Street, Charleston, West Virginia 25301. (304) 342-1474.

WEST VIRGINIA STATE BAR. E-400 State Capitol, Charleston, West Virginia 25305. (304) 346-8414.

WEST VIRGINIA TRIAL LAWYERS ASSOCIATION. P.O. Box 3968, Charleston, West Virginia 25339. (304) 344-0692.

DIRECTORIES

DIRECTORY OF STATE OFFICIALS: WEST VIRGINIA. West Virginia House of Delegates, State Capitol, Charleston, West Virginia 25305. Biennial. (Odd years)

MANUAL OF THE SENATE AND HOUSE OF DELEGATES [WEST VIRGINIA]. West Virginia House of Delegates, State Capitol, Charlston, Virginia 25305. Biennial. (January of odd years).

VIRGINIA, MARYLAND, DELAWARE, AND DISTRICT OF COLUMBIA LEGAL DIRECTORIES. Legal Directories Publishing Company, 2122 Kidwell Street, P.O. Box 140200, Dallas, Texas 75214-0200. Annual. (March)

WEST VIRGINIA BLUE BOOK. Clerk of the Senate, West Virginia Legislature, State Capitol, Room 215M, Charlston, West Virginia 25305. Annual.

STATES--WISCONSIN

STATUTES, CODES, STANDARDS, UNIFORM LAWS

LAWS OF WISCONSIN. Document Sales and Distributions, Department of Administration, 202 South Thornton Avenue, Madison, Wisconsin 53702. Biennial.

WISCONSIN ADMINISTRATIVE CODE. Document Sales and Distribution, Department of Administration, 202 South Thornton Avenue, Madison, Wisconsin 53702. 1974- . (Monthly Supplements).

WISCONSIN ADMINISTRATIVE REGISTER. Revisor of Statutes, Documents Sales and Distribution, Department of Administration, 202 South Thornton Avenue, Madison, Wisconsin 53702. 1956- . (Semimonthly).

WISCONSIN LEGISLATIVE SERVICE. West Publishing Company, P.O. Box 64526, 50 West Kellogg Boulevard, St. Paul, Minnesota 55164-0526. 1957- .

WISCONSIN STATUTES ANNOTATED. West Publishing Company, P.O. Box 64526, 50 West Kellogg Boulevard, St. Paul, Minnesota 55164-0526. 1957- . (Annual Supplements).

LOOSELEAF SERVICES AND REPORTERS

NORTHWESTERN REPORTER. (First and Second Series). West Publishing Company, P.O. Box 64526, 50 West Kellogg Boulevard, St. Paul, Minnesota 55164-0526. 1879- . (Supreme Court and Court of Appeals).

WISCONSIN REPORTER. West Publishing Company, P.O. Box 64526, 50 West Kellogg Boulevard, St. Paul, Minnesota 55164-0526. 1941- .

WISCONSIN REPORTS. Callaghan and Company, 155 Pfingsten Road, Deerfield, Illinois 60015. (Supreme Court and Court of Appeals) (Title and imprint varies).

ATTORNEY GENERAL OPINIONS

OPINIONS OF THE ATTORNEY GENERAL OF THE STATE OF WISCONSIN. Office of the Attorney General. Document Sales and Distribution, Department of Administration, 202 South Thornton Avenue, Madison, Wisconsin 53702. (Also available on Lexis: January 1977- .)

ETHICS OPINIONS, CODES, RULES

ETHICS AND PROFESSIONAL RESPONSIBILITY: A HANDBOOK FOR WISCONSIN LAWYERS. Keith J. Kaap. State Bar of Wisconsin, ATS-CLE, 402 West Wilson Street, Madison, Wisconsin 53707. 1986- . (Includes Code of Professional Responsibility and Ethics Opinions). Ethics opinions are also published in full text in the Wisconsin Bar Bulletin . Abstracts are published in the ABA/BNA Lawyer's Manual on Professional Conduct . For further information concerning these opinions, contact the State Bar Committee on Professional Ethics, P.O. Box 7158, Madison, Wisconsin 53707-7158. 608-257-3838.

COURT RULES

WISCONSIN COURT RULES AND PROCEDURE: STATE AND FEDERAL. West Publishing Company, P.O. Box 64526, 50 West Kellogg Boulevard, St. Paul, Minnesota 55164-0526. (Annual).

WISCONSIN SUPREME COURT RULES AS ADOPTED BY THE SUPREME COURT. Callaghan and Company, 155 Pfingsten Road, Deerfield, Illinois 60015. 1986- . (Annual Supplements).

JURY INSTRUCTIONS

WISCONSIN JURY INSTRUCTIONS--CIVIL. Wisconsin Judicial Conference, Civil Jury Instructions Committee. University of Wisconsin, Extension Law Department, 905 University Avenue, Suite 309 Madison, Wisconsin 53715. 1981- . (Annual Supplements).

WISCONSIN JURY INSTRUCTIONS--CRIMINAL. Wisconsin Criminal Jury Instructions Committee. University of Wisconsin, Extension Law Departments, 905 University Avenue, Suite 309, Madison, Wisconsin 53715. 1980- . (Quarterly Supplements).

DIGESTS, INDEXES, ABSTRACTS, CITATORS

NORTHWESTERN DIGEST. West Publishing Company, P.O. Box 64526, 50 West Kellogg Boulevard, St. Paul, Minnesota 55164-0526. 1944- . (Annual Supplements).

SHEPARD'S NORTHWESTERN REPORTER CITATIONS. Shepard's/McGraw-Hill, P.O. Box 1235, Colorado Springs, Colorado 80901. (Monthly Supplements).

SHEPARD'S WISCONSIN CITATIONS. Shepard's/McGraw-Hill, P.O. Box 1235, Colorado Springs, Colorado 80901. (Eight supplements per year).

WISCONSIN DIGEST. Callaghan and Company, 155 Pfingsten Road, Deerfield, Illinois 60015. (Annual Supplements).

WISCONSIN DIGEST. West Publishing Company, P.O. Box 64526, 50 West Kellogg Boulevard, St. Paul, Minnesota 55164-0526. (Annual Supplements).

LAW REVIEWS AND PERIODICALS

MARQUETTE LAW REVIEW. Marquette University Law School, 1103 West Wisconsin Avenue, Milwaukee, Wisconsin 53233. (Quarterly).

WISCONSIN BAR BULLETIN. State Bar of Wisconsin, ATS-CLE, 402 West Wilson Street, Madison, Wisconsin 53707. (Monthly).

WISCONSIN INTERNATIONAL LAW JOURNAL. University of Wisconsin Law School, 975 Beacon Mall, Madison, Wisconsin 53706. (Annual).

WISCONSIN LAW REVIEW. University of Wisconsin Law School, 975 Beacon Mall, Madison, Wisconsin 53706. (Bimonthly).

WISCONSIN STUDENT BAR JOURNAL. University of Wisconsin Law School, Room 41602, 975 Beacon Mall, Madison, Wisconsin 53706. Annual.

WISCONSIN WOMEN'S LAW JOURNAL. University of Wisconsin Law School, 975 Beacon Mall, Madison, Wisconsin 53706. Annual.

NEWSLETTERS AND NEWSPAPERS

COMPLETE LEGISLATIVE SERVICE. Wisconsin Taxpayers Alliance, 335 West Wilson Street, Madison, Wisconsin 53703. Weekly when in session.

CRIMINAL LAW NEWS. State Bar of Wisconsin, 402 West Wilson Street, Madison, Wisconsin 53703. Quarterly.

ENVIRONMENTAL LAW NEWS. State Bar of Wisconsin, 402 West Wilson Street, Madison, Wisconsin 53703. Quarterly.

GP NEWS. State Bar of Wisconsin, 402 West Wilson Street, Madison, Wisconsin 53703. Quarterly.

LITIGATION NEWS. State Bar of Wisconsin, 402 West Wilson Street, Madison, Wisconsin 53703. Biweekly.

WISCONSIN BAR NEWSLETTER. State Bar of Wisconsin, 402 West Wilson Street, Madison, Wisconsin 53703. Monthly.

WISCONSIN BAR TAX NEWS. State Bar of Wisconsin, 402 West Wilson Street, Madison, Wisconsin 53703. Quarterly.

WISCONSIN JOURNAL OF FAMILY LAW. State Bar of Wisconsin, 402 West Wilson Street, Madison, Wisconsin 53703. Quarterly.

WISCONSIN LAW REPORTER. Law Reporter Company, 209 Michigan Avenue, Crystal Falls, Michigan 49920. Semimonthly.

YOUR WISCONSIN GOVERNMENT. Wisconsin Taxpayers Alliance, 335 West Wilson Street, Madison, Wisconsin 53703. Weekly when in session.

FORMBOOKS

LEASE DRAFTING PRACTICE AND FORMS. State Bar of Wisconsin, ATS-CLE, 402 West Wilson Street, Madison, Wisconsin 53707. 1981- .

WISCONSIN CIVIL PRACTICE FORMS. Callaghan and Company, 155 Pfingsten Road, Deerfield, Illinois 60015. 1970- . (Periodic Supplements).

WISCONSIN CIVIL PROCEDURE FORMS. W. Harvey. West Publishing Company, 50 West Kellogg Boulevard, St. Paul, Minnesota 55164. 1976. (Periodic Supplements).

WISCONSIN LEGAL FORMS--COMMERCIAL REAL ESTATE. Vicky H. Speck. Butterworth Legal Publishers, 90 Stiles Road, Salem, New Hampshire 03079. 1983- . (Periodic Supplements).

WISCONSIN LEGAL FORMS--LAW OFFICE SYSTEMS. Robert L. Newell. Butterworth Legal Publishers, 90 Stiles Road, Salem, New Hampshire 03079. 1983- . (Periodic Supplements)

WISCONSIN PROBATE SYSTEM FORMS AND PROCEDURES HANDBOOK. State Bar of Wisconsin, ATS-CLE, 402 West Wilson Street, Madison, Wisconsin 53707. 1981- . (Periodic Supplements).

PRACTICE MATERIALS

ANNUAL SURVEY OF WISCONSIN LAW. State Bar of Wisconsin, 402 West Wilson Street, Madison, Wisconsin 53707. (Annual).

APPELLATE PRACTICE AND PROCEDURE IN WISCONSIN. State Bar of Wisconsin, 402 West Wilson Street, Madison, Wisconsin 53707. 1986- .

EMPLOYMENT IN WISCONSIN. M. G. Sautter. Butterworth Legal Publishers, 90 Stiles Road, Salem, New Hampshire 03079. 1983- . (Periodic Supplements).

FAMILY LAW--DOMESTIC RELATIONS. Leander J. Foley. State Bar of Wisconsin, ATS-CLE, 402 West Wilson Street, Madison, Wisconsin 53707. 1985- . (Annual Supplements).

THE LAW OF DAMAGES IN WISCONSIN. State Bar of Wisconsin, 402 West Wilson Street, Madison, Wisconsin 53707. 1988- .

THE LAWYER'S BASIC CORPORATE PRACTICE MANUAL. State Bar of Wisconsin, 402 West Wilson Street, Madison, Wisconsin 53707. 1985- .

MARITAL PROPERTY LAW IN WISCONSIN. Keith Christiansen, et al. State Bar of Wisconsin, ATS-CLE, 402 West Wilson Street, Madison, Wisconsin 53707. 1984- . (Periodic Supplements).

PERSONAL INJURY LITIGATION SYSTEM. James A. Drill. State Bar of Wisconsin, ATS-CLE, 402 West Wilson Street, Madison, Wisconsin 53707. 1979- . (Periodic Supplements).

SECURITIES LAW HANDBOOK FOR THE WISCONSIN PRACTITIONER. Joseph P. Hildebrandt, editor. State Bar of Wisconsin, ATS-CLE, 402 West Wilson Street, Madison, Wisconsin 53707. 1983- . (Annual Supplements).

SYSTEM BOOK FOR FAMILY LAW: A FORMS AND PROCEDURES HANDBOOK FOR DIVORCE. State Bar of Wisconsin, ATS-CLE, 402 West Wilson Street, Madison, Wisconsin 53707. 1988- .

WISCONSIN APPELLATE PRACTICE. R. Martineau. State Bar of Wisconsin, ATS-CLE, 402 West Wilson Street, Madison, Wisconsin 53707. 1978- .

WISCONSIN COLLECTIONS. Lawyers Co-Operative Company, Aqueduct Building, Rochester, New York 14694. 1977- . (Annual Supplements).

WISCONSIN CORPORATIONS. Lawyers Co-Operative Company, Aqueduct Building, Rochester, New York 14694. 1980- . (Annual Supplements).

WISCONSIN CRIMINAL DEFENSE MANUAL. Patrick J. Devitt. State Bar of Wisconsin, ATS-CLE, 402 West Wilson Street, Madison, Wisconsin 53707. 1981- . (Periodic Supplements).

WISCONSIN DIVORCE. K. Richard Olsen. Lawyers Co-Operative Company, Aqueduct Building, Rochester, New York 14694. 1979- . (Annual Supplements).

WISCONSIN INHERITANCE ESTATE AND GIFT HANDBOOK. Continuing Legal Education for Wisconsin, University of Wisconsin Extention, 905 University Avenue, Suite 309, Madison, Wisconsin 53715. 1982- .

WISCONSIN JUDICIAL BENCHBOOKS. Second edition. (Three Volumes). State Bar of Wisconsin, ATS-CLE, 402 West Wilson Street, Madison, Wisconsin 53707. 1984- . (Annual Supplements).

WISCONSIN JUVENILE COURT PRACTICE. M. Melli. State Bar of Wisconsin, ATS-CLE, 402 West Wilson Street, Madison, Wisconsin 53707. 1983.

WISCONSIN METHODS OF PRACTICE. West Publishing Company, P.O. Box 64526, 50 West Kellogg Boulevard, St. Paul, Minnesota 55164-0526. 1949- . (Annual Supplements).

WISCONSIN PROBATE LAW AND PRACTICE. Seventh edition. James B. MacDonald. Callaghan and Company, 155 Pfingsten Road, Deerfield, Illinois 60015. 1972- . (Annual Supplements).

WISCONSIN REAL ESTATE. Martin J. Greenberg. Lawyers Co-Operative Company, Aqueduct Building, Rochester, New York 14694. 1982- . (Annual Supplements).

WISCONSIN RULES OF EVIDENCE: A COURTROOM HANDBOOK. State Bar of Wisconsin, ATS-CLE, 402 West Wilson Street, Madison, Wisconsin 53707. 1984- . (Annual Supplements).

WORKER'S COMPENSATION HANDBOOK. John D. Neal. State Bar of Wisconsin, ATS-CLE, 402 West Wilson Street, Madison, Wisconsin 53707. 1983- . (Biennial Supplements).

MANUALS AND RESEARCH GUIDES

LEGAL RESEARCH IN WISCONSIN. Richard A. Danner. University of Wisconsin Extention, Department of Law, Suite 309, 905 University Avenue, Madison, Wisconsin 53715. 1980.

WISCONSIN LEGAL RESEARCH GUIDE. Second edition. William Knudson. University of Wisconsin Extension, Department of Law, Suite 309, 905 University Avenue, Madison, Wisconsin 53715. 1972.

ASSOCIATIONS AND PROFESSIONAL SOCIETIES

DANE COUNTY BAR ASSOCIATION, 217 South Hamilton Street, Suite 501, Madison, Wisconsin 53703.

MILWAUKEE BAR ASSOCIATION, INCORPORATED, 605 East Wisconsin Avenue, Milwaukee, Wisconsin 53202. (414) 274-6760.

STATE BAR OF WISCONSIN, 402 West Wilson Street, Madison, Wisconsin 53707. (608) 257-3838.

DIRECTORIES

DIRECTORY OF LEGISLATIVE COMMITTEES [WISCONSIN]. Wisconsin Legislative Council, State Capitol, Room 147N, Madison, Wisconsin 53702. (Semiannual).

LAWYER TO LAWYER DIRECTORY. State Bar of Wisconsin, ATS-CLE, 402 West Wilson Street, Madison, Wisconsin 53707. 1983- . (Annual). (Issued as part of Wisconsin Bar Bulletin, number 7).

WISCONSIN BLUE BOOK. Wisconsin Legislative Reference Bureau, State Capitol, Room 201N, Madison, Wisconsin 53702. Biennial. (Fall of odd years).

WISCONSIN BRIEFS--WISCONSIN OFFICERS ISSUE. Wisconsin Legislative Bureau, State Capitol, Room 201N, Madison, Wisconsin 53702. Biennial. (December of even years).

WISCONSIN LEGAL DIRECTORY. Legal Directories Publishing Company, 2122 Kidwell Street, P.O. Box 140200, Dallas, Texas 75214-0200. (Annual--July).

WISCONSIN LEGISLATIVE DIRECTORY. Wisconsin Association of Manufacturers and Commerce, 30 West Mifflin Street, Number 302, Madison, Wisconsin 53703. Biennial. (February of odd years).

WISCONSIN MUNICIPAL DIRECTORY. League of Wisconsin Municipalities, 122 West Washington Avenue, Madison, Wisconsin 53703. Annual. (June).

STATES--WYOMING

STATUTES, CODES, STANDARDS, UNIFORM LAWS

INDEX TO ADMINISTRATIVE RULES AND REGULATIONS OF WYOMING STATE AGENCIES. Office of the Secretary of State, Capitol Building, Cheyenne, Wyoming 82002. 1983- .

SESSION LAWS OF WYOMING. Office of the Secretary of State, Capital Building, Cheyenne, Wyoming 82002. Annual.

WYOMING ADVANCE ANNOTATION SERVICE. Michie Company, P.O. Box 7587, Charlottesville, Virginia 22906-7587. 1984-1985. (Three pamphlets a year).

WYOMING STATUTES ANNOTATED. Michie Company, P.O. Box 7587, Charlottesville, Virginia 22906-7587. 1977- . (Annual Supplements).

STATES--WYOMING

LOOSELEAF SERVICES AND REPORTERS

PACIFIC REPORTER. (First and Second Series). West Publishing Company, P.O. Box 64526, 50 West Kellogg Boulevard, St. Paul, Minnesota 55164-0526. 1883- .

WYOMING REPORTER. West Publishing Company, P.O. Box 64526, 50 West Kellogg Boulevard, St. Paul, Minnesota 55164-0526. 1959- .

WYOMING REPORTS. Prairie Publishing Company, 303 South Wolcott Street, Casper, Wyoming 82602. 1870-1959. (Current official source is the Pacific Reporter).

ATTORNEY GENERAL OPINIONS

OPINIONS OF THE ATTORNEY GENERAL OF WYOMING. Office of the Attorney General, 210 Capitol Building, Cheyenne, Wyoming 82002. 1940- . (Quadrennial).

COURT RULES

WYOMING COURT RULES ANNOTATED. Michie Company, P.O. Box 7587, Charlottesville, Virginia 22906-7587. 1983- . (Periodic Supplements).

JURY INSTRUCTIONS

PATTERN JURY INSTRUCTIONS-NEGLIGENCE. Wyoming State Bar, Committee on Pattern Jury Instructions. Wyoming State Bar, 211 Central Avenue, P.O. Box 109, Cheyenne, Wyoming 82003-0109. 1963.

WYOMING PATTERN JURY INSTRUCTIONS. Wyoming State Bar, Committee on Pattern Jury Instructions. Wyoming State Bar, 211 Central Avenue, P.O. Box 109, Cheyenne, Wyoming 82003-0109. 1963.

WYOMING PATTERN JURY INSTRUCTIONS, CRIMINAL. Wyoming Pattern Jury Instructions Committee, University of Wyoming, College of Law, Laramie, Wyoming 82071. 1978.

DIGESTS, INDEXES, ABSTRACTS, CITATORS

PACIFIC DIGEST. (1st and 2nd series). West Publishing Company, P.O. Box 64526, 50 West Kellogg Boulevard, St. Paul, Minnesota 55164-0526. 1933- .

SHEPARD'S PACIFIC REPORTER CITATIONS. Shepard's/ McGraw-Hill, P.O. Box 1235, Colorado Springs, Colorado 80901. (Monthly Supplements).

SHEPARD'S WYOMING CITATIONS. Shepard's/McGraw-Hill, P.O. Box 1235, Colorado Springs, Colorado 80901. (Semi-annual Supplements).

WYOMING DIGEST. West Publishing Company, 50 West Kellogg Boulevard, St. Paul, Minnesota 55164. 1933- .

LAW REVIEWS AND PERIODICALS

WYOMING LAWYER. Wyoming State Bar, 211 Central Avenue, P.O. Box, Cheyenne, Wyoming 82003-0109. (Bi-monthly).

NEWSLETTERS AND NEWSPAPERS

THE WYOMING LAWYER. The Wyoming State Bar Association, P.O. Box 109, Cheyenne, Wyoming 82003. Bimonthly.

PRACTICE MATERIALS

CRIMINAL PRACTICE MANUAL. F. Chapman. Wyoming Public Defender Program, 1712 Carey, Second Floor, Cheyenne, Wyoming 82002. 1979.

CRIMINIAL PROCEDURE IN WYOMING COURTS. Wyoming State Bar, 211 Central Avenue, P.O. Box 109, Cheyenne, Wyoming 82003. Biennial.

WYOMING LOCAL GOVERNMENT LAW. E. George Rudolph. Wyoming State Bar, 211 Central Avenue, P.O. Box 109, Cheyenne, Wyoming 82003-0109.

MANUALS AND RESEARCH GUIDES

WYOMING STATE LEGAL DOCUMENTS: AN ANNOTATED BIBLIOGRAPHY. Compiled by Nancy S. Greene. American Association of Law Libraries, 53 West Jackson Boulevard, Chicago, Illinois 60604. 1985.

ASSOCIATIONS AND PROFESSIONAL SOCIETIES

WYOMING STATE BAR. 500 Rodell Avenue, Cheyenne, Wyoming 82001. (307) 632-9061.

DIRECTORIES

LAWMAKERS OF WYOMING. Wyoming Trucking Association, 109 Rancho Road, Casper, Wyoming 82602. Biennial. (January of odd years).

MUNICIPAL/COUNTY EXECUTIVE DIRECTORY. Carrol Publishing Company, 1058 Thomas Jefferson Street, Northwest, Washington, D. C. 20007. Annual. (Winter)

OFFICIAL MUNICIPAL ROSTER [WYOMING]. Wyoming Association of Municipalities, Box 2535, Cheyenne, Wyoming 82003. (Annual--March).

WYOMING OFFICIAL DIRECTORY. Wyoming Secretary of State, State Capitol, Cheyenne, Wyoming 82002. (Annual--Spring).

STATES' RIGHTS
See: STATE GOVERNMENT

STATUTES
See: LEGISLATIVE HISTORY AND PROCESS; STATE LAW COMPILATIONS; STATES; STATUTORY CONSTRUCTION AND DRAFTING

STATUTES OF LIMITATION
See: CIVIL PROCEDURE

STATUTORY CONSTRUCTION AND DRAFTING
See also: LEGAL WRITING

STATUTES, CODES, STANDARDS, UNIFORM LAWS

MODEL STATUTORY CONSTRUCTION ACT. Uniform Laws Annotated. West Publishing Company, P.O. Box 64526, 50 West Kellogg Boulevard, St. Paul, Minnesota 55164-0526. 1976. (Annual Supplements).

TEXTBOOKS AND GENERAL WORKS

A COMMON LAW FOR THE AGE OF STATUTES. Guido Calabresi. Harvard University Press, 79 Garden Street, Cambridge, Massachusetts 02138. 1982.

DEALING WITH STATUTES. James W. Hurst. Columbia University Press, 562 West 113th Street, New York, New York 10025. 1981.

DRAFTING LEGISLATION AND RULES IN PLAIN ENGLISH. Robert J. Martineau. West Publishing Company, 50 West Kellogg Boulevard, St. Paul, Minnesota 55164. 1991.

THE INTERPRETATION AND APPLICATION OF STATUTES. Reed Dickerson. Little, Brown and Company, 34 Beacon Street, Boston, Massachusetts 02108. 1975.

INTERPRETING LAW AND LITERATURE: A HERMENEUTIC READER. Sanford Levinson and Steven Mailloux. Northwestern University Press, 625 Colfax Street, Evanston, Illinois 60201. 1988.

INTERPRETING STATUTES: A COMPARATIVE STUDY. D. Neil MacCormick and Robert S. Summers. Aldershot, Brookfield, Vermont. 1991.

LEGAL REALISM AND TWENTIETH-CENTURY AMERICAN JURISPREDENCE: THE CHANGING CONSENSUS. Gary J. Aichele. Garland Publishing, Incorporated, 136 Madison Avenue, New York, New York 10016. 1990.

MAKING ALL THE DIFFERENCE: INCLUSION, EXCLUSION, AND AMERICAN LAW. Martha Minow. Cornell University Press, 124 Roberts Place, Ithaca, New York 14850. 1990.

ON THE INTERPRETATION OF STATUTES. Sir Peter Benson Maxwell. Fred B. Rothman and Company, 10368 West Centennial Road, Littleton, Colorado 80127. 1991. (Reprint).

REASON IN LAW. Third Edition. Lief H. Carter. Scott, Foresman and Company, 1900 East Lake Avenue, Glenview, Illinois 60025. 1988.

STATUTES AND STATUTORY CONSTRUCTION: A REVISION OF SUTHERLAND STATUTORY CONSTRUCTION. Fourth Edition. C. Dallas Sands. Callaghan and Company, 155 Pfingsten Road, Deerfield, Illinois 60015. 1985. (Annual Supplements).

USING AND MISUSING LEGISLATIVE HISTORY: A RE-EVALUATION OF THE STATUS OF LEGISLATIVE HISTORY IN STATUTORY INTERPRETATION. United States Department of Justice, Office of Legal Policy. 1989.

ASSOCIATIONS AND PROFESSIONAL SOCIETIES

ASSOCIATION OF AMERICAN LAW SCHOOLS, SECTION ON LEGISLATION. Association of American Law Schools, One Dupont Circle, Northwest, Washington, D.C. 20036. (202) 296-8851.

RESEARCH CENTERS AND INSTITUTES

HARVARD LEGISLATIVE RESEARCH BUREAU. Harvard University Law School, Austin 209, Cambridge, Massachusetts 02138. (617) 495-4431.

LEGISLATIVE DRAFTING AND RESEARCH FUND. Columbia University, 435 West One Hundred Sixteenth Street, New York, New York 10027. (212) 854-2685.

STERILIZATION

TEXTBOOKS AND GENERAL WORKS

FERTILITY CONTROL: NEW TECHNIQUES, NEW POLICY ISSUES. Robert H. Blank. Greenwood Publishing Group, Incorporated, 88 Post Road West, P.O. Box 5007, Westport, Connecticut 06881. 1991.

THE LAW GOVERNING ABORTION, CONTRACEPTION AND STERILIZATION. Irving J. Sloan. Oceana Publications, 75 Main Street, Dobbs Ferry, New York 10522. 1988.

MENTAL RETARDATION AND STERILIZATION: A PROBLEM OF COMPETENCY AND PATERNALISM. Ruth Macklin and Willard Gaylin, Editors. Plenum Publishing Corporation, 233 Spring Street, New York, New York 10013. 1981.

POPULATION CONTROL POLITICS: WOMEN, STERILIZATION AND REPRODUCTIVE CHOICE. Thomas M. Shapiro. Temple University Press, North Broad Street, University Services Building, Philadelphia, Pennsylvania 19122. 1985.

SEXUALITY, LAW, AND THE DEVELOPMENTALLY DISABLED PERSON: LEGAL AND CLINICAL ASPECTS OF MARRIAGE, PARENTHOOD, AND STERILIZATION. Sarah F. Haavik and Karl A. Menninger II. Paul H. Brookes, Publishers, P.O. Box 10624, Baltimore, Maryland 21285-0624. 1981.

THE SURGICAL SOLUTION: A HISTORY OF INVOLUNTARY STERILIZATION IN THE UNITED STATES. Philip R. Reilly. Johns Hopkins University Press, 701 West Fortieth Street, Baltimore, Maryland 21211. 1991.

ASSOCIATIONS AND PROFESSIONAL SOCIETIES

ASSOCIATION FOR VOLUNTARY SURGICAL CONTRACEPTION. 122 East Forty-Second Street, New York, New York 10168. (212) 351-2500.

STOCKS
See: SECURITIES

STRICT LIABILITY
See: PRODUCTS LIABILITY AND SAFETY; TORTS

STRIKES
See: LABOR AND LABOR RELATIONS

STUDY OF LAW
See: LEGAL EDUCATION

SUBVERSIVE ACTIVITIES
See: POLITICAL CRIMES AND OFFENSES; TERRORISM

SUCCESSION
See: WILLS, TRUSTS AND INHERITANCE

SUICIDE
See also: CRIMINAL LAW

TEXTBOOKS AND GENERAL WORKS

COLLEGE STUDENT SUICIDE. Leighton C. Whitaker and Richard E. Slimak. Haworth Press, Incorporated, 10 Alice Street, Binghamton, New York 13904. 1990.

THE ECONOMY AND SUICIDE: ECONOMIC PERSPECTIVES ON SUICIDE. David Lester and Bijou Yang. AMS Press, Incorporated, 56 East Thirteenth Street, New York, New York 10003. 1992.

ETHICAL ISSUES IN SUICIDE. Margaret P. Battin. Prentice-Hall, Incorporated, 113 Sylvan Avenue, Englewood Cliffs, New Jersey 07632. 1982.

LIFE SPAN PERSPECTIVES OF SUICIDE: TIME-LINES IN THE SUICIDE PROCESS. Antoon A. Leenaars. Plenum Publishing Corporation, 233 Spring Street, New York, New York 10013. 1991.

PSYCHOTHERAPY WITH HIGH-RISK CLIENTS: LEGAL AND PROFESSIONAL STANDARDS. Richard L. Bednar. Brooks/Cole Publishing Company, 511 Forest Lodge Road, Pacific Grove, California 93950. 1991.

SUICIDE AMONG THE ELDERLY IN LONG-TERM CARE FACILITIES. Nancy J. Osgood, Barbara A. Brant, and Aaron Lipman. Greenwood Publishing Group, Incorporated, 88 Post Road West, P.O. Box 5007, Westport, Connecticut 06881. 1991.

SUICIDE AND EUTHANASIA: THE RIGHTS OF PERSONHOOD. Samuel E. Wallace and Albin Eser, editors. University of Tennessee Press, 293 Communications Building, Knoxville, Tennessee 37996-0325. 1981.

THE SUICIDE CASE: INVESTIGATION AND TRIAL OF INSURANCE CLAIMS. James L. Nolan. American Bar Association, Tort and Insurance Practice Section, 750 North Lake Shore Drive, Chicago, Illinois 60611. 1988.

YOUTH SUICIDE: WHAT THE EDUCATOR SHOULD KNOW. Eleanor C. Guetzloe. Council for Exceptional Children, 1920 Association Drive, Reston, Virginia 22091. 1989.

ENCYCLOPEDIAS AND DICTIONARIES

THE ENCYCLOPEDIA OF SUICIDE. Glen Evans and Norman L. Farberow. Facts on File, Incorporated, 460 Park Avenue South, New York, New York 10016. 1988.

BIBLIOGRAPHIES

SUICIDE. Stephen A. Flanders and Mary Lou Cass. Facts on File, Incorporated, 460 Park Avenue South, New York, New York 10016. 1991.

DIRECTORIES

DIRECTORY OF SUICIDE PREVENTION/ CRISIS INTERVENTION AGENCIES IN THE UNITED STATES. American Association of Suicidology, 2459 South Ash, Denver, Colorado 80222.

BIOGRAPHICAL SOURCES

BY HER OWN HAND: MEMOIRS OF A SUICIDE'S DAUGHTER. Signe Hammer. Vintage Books, New York, New York. 1992.

ASSOCIATIONS AND PROFESSIONAL SOCIETIES

AMERICAN ASSOCIATION OF SUICIDOLOGY. 2459 South Ash, Denver, Colorado 80222. (303) 692-0985.

NATIONAL COMMITTEE ON YOUTH SUICIDE PREVENTION. 825 Washington Street, Norwood, Massachusetss 02062. (617) 769-5686.

SAMARITANS. 500 Commonwealth Avenue, Kenmore Square, Boston, Massachusetts 02215. (617) 247-0220.

RESEARCH CENTERS, INSTITUTES, CLEARINGHOUSES

CENTER FOR THE STUDY OF SUICIDE AND LIFE THREATENING BEHAVIOR. University of South Carolina at Columbia, 228 Callcott Building, Columbia, South Carolina 29208. (803) 777-6870.

SUICIDE PREVENTION CENTER. 626 South Kingsley Drive, Los Angeles, California 90005. (213) 385-37552.

ONLINE DATABASES

SUICIDE INFORMATION AND EDUCATION. Suicide Information and Education Center, 1615 Tenth Avenue, Southwest, Suite 201, Calgary, AB, Canada T3C 0J7.

SUMMARY PROCEEDINGS
See: CIVIL PROCEDURE

SUNSET LEGISLATION
See: ADMINISTRATIVE LAW

SUPPORT OF DEPENDANTS
See: FAMILY LAW

SUPREME COURT (UNITED STATES)
See also: ADMINISTRATIVE OFFICE OF THE UNITED STATES COURTS; COURTS; FEDERAL COURTS

STATUTES, CODES, STANDARDS, UNIFORM LAWS

RULES OF THE SUPREME COURT OF THE UNITED STATES. In Digest of United States Supreme Court Reports, Lawyers' Edition, Volume 17. Lawyers Co-Operative Publishing Company, Aqueduct Building, Rochester, New York 14694. 1974 (Annual Supplements).

RULES OF THE SUPREME COURT OF THE UNITED STATES. In Supreme Court Practice. Sixth Edition. Robert L. Stern, Eugene Fressman, Stephan M. Shapiro. Bureau of National Affairs, 1231 Twenty-fifth Street, Northwest, Washington, D.C. 20037. 1986.

RULES OF THE SUPREME COURT OF THE UNITED STATES. In the United States Code, Title 28 Appendix. Superintendent of Documents, United States Government Printing Office, Washington, D.C. 20402. 1983 (Annual Supplements).

RULES OF THE SUPREME COURT OF THE UNITED STATES. In United States Code Annotated, Title 28 Appendix. West Publishing Company, P.O. Box 64526, 50 West Kellogg Boulevard, St. Paul, Minnesota 55164-0526. 1984 (Annual Supplements).

LOOSELEAF SERVICES AND REPORTERS

SUPREME COURT REPORTER. West Publishing Company, P.O. Box 64526, 50 West Kellogg Boulevard, St. Paul, Minnesota 55164-0526. 1883- .

UNITED STATES LAW WEEK. Bureau of National Affairs, 1231 Twenty-fifth Street, Northwest, Washington, D.C. 20037. Weekly.

UNITED STATES REPORTS. Superintendent of Documents, United States Government Printing Office, Washington, D.C. 20402. 1790- .

UNITED STATES SUPREME COURT BULLETIN. Commerce Clearing House, Incorporated, 4025 West Peterson Avenue, Chicago, Illinois 60646. Daily.

UNITED STATES SUPREME COURT REPORTS, LAWYER'S EDITION AND UNITED STATES SUPREME COURT REPORTS, LAWYER'S EDITION SECOND SERIES. Lawyers Co-Operative Publishing Company, Aqueduct Building, Rochester, New York 14694. 1882- .

HANDBOOKS, MANUALS, FORMBOOKS

CONGRESSIONAL QUARTERLY'S GUIDE TO THE U.S. SUPREME COURT. Second Edition. Elder Witt. Congressional Quarterly Books, 1414 Twenty-second Street, Northwest, Washington D.C. 20037. 1990.

HOW TO RESEARCH THE SUPREME COURT. Fenton S. Martin and Robert U. Goehlert. Congressional Quarterly Books, 1414 Twenty-second Street, Northwest, Washington D.C. 20037. 1992.

A REFERENCE GUIDE TO THE UNITED STATES SUPREME COURT. Stephen P. Elliot, Editor. Facts on File, 460 Park Avenue, South, New York, New York 10016. 1986.

SUPREME COURT PRACTICE. Sixth Edition. Robert L. Stern, Eugene Gressman, Stephen M. Shapiro. Bureau of National Affairs, 1231 Twenty-fifth Street, Northwest, Washington, D.C. 20037. 1986.

UNITED STATES SUPREME COURT MANUAL. Joseph M. Kadans. Legal Press Service, Incorporated, 5010 North Ridge Club Drive, Las Vegas, Nevada 89103. 1984.

TEXTBOOKS AND GENERAL WORKS

THE ASCENT OF PRAGMATISM: THE BURGER COURT IN ACTION. Bernard Schwartz. Addison-Wesley Publishing Company, Incorporated, Route 128, Reading, Massachusetts 01867. 1990.

BATTLE FOR JUSTICE: HOW THE BORK NOMINATION SHOOK AMERICA. Ethan Bronner. W.W Norton and Company, Incorporated, 500 Fifth Avenue, New York, New York 10110. 1989.

BEFORE THE CIVIL RIGHTS REVOLUTION: THE OLD COURT AND INDIVIDUAL RIGHTS. John Braeman. Greenwood Publishing Group, Incorporated, 88 Post Road West, P.O. Box 5007, Westport, Connecticut 06881. 1988.

THE BURGER COURT: POLITICAL AND JUDICIAL PROFILES. Charles M. Lamb and Stephen C. Halpern. University of Illinois Press, 54 East Gregory Drive, Champaign, Illinois 61820. 1991.

THE BURGER COURT: THE COUNTERREVOLUTION THAT WASN'T. Vincent Blasi, Editor. Yale University Press, 302 Temple Street, New Haven, Connecticut 06520. 1986.

THE BURGER YEARS: RIGHTS AND WRONGS IN THE SUPREME COURT, 1969-1986. Herman Schwartz. Penguin Books, 375 Hudson Street, New York, New York 10014. 1988.

CASES LOST, CASES WON: THE SUPREME COURT AND THE JUDICIAL PROCESS. Alice F. Bartee. Saint Martin's Press, Incorporated, 175 Fifth Avenue, New York, New York 10010. 1984.

CHIEF JUSTICE: LEADERSHIP AND THE SUPREME COURT. Robert J. Steamer. University of South Carolina Press, Columbia, South Carolina 29208. 1986.

CLEMENT HAYNSWORTH, THE SENATE, AND THE SUPREME COURT. John P. Frank. University of Virginia Press, Charlottesville, Virginia. 1991.

COHENS V. VIRGINIA (1821): THE SUPREME COURT AND STATE RIGHTS: A REEVALUATION OF INFLUENCES AND IMPACTS. W. Ray Luce. Garland Publishing, Incorporated, 136 Madison Avenue, New York, New York 10016. 1990.

CONGRESS SHALL MAKE NO LAW: OLIVER WENDELL HOLMES, THE FIRST AMENDMENT, AND JUDICIAL DECISION MAKING. Jeremy Cohen. Iowa State University Press, 2121 South State Avenue, Ames, Iowa 50010. 1989.

THE CONSERVATIVE COURT 1910-1930. Norman Bindler. Associated Faculty Press, 19 West Thirty-sixth Street, New York, New York 10018. 1986.

THE CONSTITUTION IN THE SUPREME COURT: THE SECOND CENTURY, 1888-1986. David P. Currie. University of Chicago Press, 5801 Ellis Avenue, Chicago, Illinois 60637. 1990.

CONTEMPORARY CONSTITUTIONAL LAWMAKING: THE SUPREME COURT AND THE ART OF POLITICS. Lief H. Carter. Pergamon Press, Incorporated, Maxwell House, Fairview Park, Elmsford, New York 10523. 1985.

THE CONTINUITY OF CHANGE: THE SUPREME COURT AND INDIVIDUAL LIBERTIES, 1953-1986. Melvin I. Urofsky. Wadsworth Publishing Company, 10 Davis Drive, Belmont, California 94002. 1991.

THE COURAGE OF THEIR CONVICTIONS: SIXTEEN AMERICANS WHO FOUGHT THEIR WAY TO THE SUPREME COURT. Peter Irons. Penguin Books, 375 Hudson Street, New York, New York 10014. 1990.

THE COURT AND THE AMERICAN CRISES, 1930-1952. Robert Mayer. Associated Faculty Press, 19 West Thirty-sixth Street, New York, New York 10018. 1987.

THE COURT AND THE CONSTITUTION. Archibald Cox. Houghton Mifflin Company, 1 Beacon Street, Boston, Massachusetts 02108. 1987.

THE COURT VS. CONGRESS: PRAYER, BUSING, AND ABORTION. Edward Keynes and Randall K. Miller. Duke University Press, Box 6697 College Station, Durham, North Carolina 27708. 1989.

DECIDING TO DECIDE: AGENDA SETTING IN THE UNITED STATES SUPREME COURT. H.W. Perry, Jr. Harvard University Press, 79 Garden Street, Cambridge, Massachusetts 02138. 1991.

DECISION MAKING IN THE SUPREME COURT OF THE UNITED STATES: A POLITICAL AND BEHAVIORAL VIEW. Joseph F. Menez. University Press of America, 4720 Boston Way, Lanham, Maryland 20706. 1984.

THE DIMENSIONS OF NON-LEGAL EVIDENCE IN THE AMERICAN JUDICIAL PROCESS: THE SUPREME COURT'S USE OF EXTRA-LEGAL MATERIALS IN THE TWENTIETH CENTURY. John W. Johnson. Garland Publishing, Incorporated, 136 Madison Avenue, New York, New York 10016. 1990.

DOCUMENTARY HISTORY OF THE SUPREME COURT OF THE UNITED STATES, 1789-1800. Volume 1. Maeva Marcus and James R. Perry, Editors. Columbia University Press, 562 West 113th Street, New York, New York 10025. 1990.

EIGHT MEN AND A LADY: PROFILES OF THE JUSTICES OF THE U.S. SUPREME COURT. National Press, Incorporated, 7201 Wisconsin Avenue, Suite 720, Bethesda, Maryland 20814. 1990.

THE EMBATTLED CONSTITUTION: VITAL FRAMEWORK OR CONVENIENT SYMBOL? Adoph H. Grundman, Editor. Krieger Publishing Company, Incorporated, P.O. Box 9542, Malarbar, Florida 32902-9542. 1986.

EQUAL JUSTICE UNDER LAW: THE SUPREME COURT IN AMERICAN LIFE. Fifth Edition. Mary A. Harrell and Burnett Anderson. National Geographic Society, Seventh and M Streets, Northwest, Washington, D.C. 20036. 1988.

AN ESSENTIAL SAFEGUARD: ESSAYS ON THE UNITED STATES SUPREME COURT AND ITS JUSTICES. D. Grier Stephenson, Jr. Greenwood Publishing Group, Incorporated, 88 Post Road West, P.O. Box 5007, Westport, Connecticut 06881. 1991.

GOD SAVE THIS HONORABLE COURT: HOW THE CHOICE OF SUPREME COURT JUSTICES SHAPES OUR HISTORY. Lawrence Tribe. NAC Dutton, 375 Hudson Street, New York, New York 10014-3657. 1985

HISTORY OF THE SUPREME COURT OF THE UNITED STATES: VOLUME 1, ANTECEDENTS AND BEGINNINGS TO 1801; VOLUME 2, FOUNDATIONS OF POWER: JOHN MARSHALL, 1801-1815; VOLUME 5, THE TANEY PERIOD, 1836-1864; VOLUME 6, RECONSTRUCTION AND REUNION, 1864-1868; VOLUME 9, THE JUDICIARY AND RESPONSIBLE GOVERNMENT, 1910-1921. Macmillan Publishing Company, Incorporated, 866 Third Avenue, New York, New York 10022. 1971- .

INSIDE THE WARREN COURT. Bernard Schwartz and Stephan Lesher. Doubleday and Company, Incorporated, 666 Fifth Avenue, New York, New York 10103. 1983.

THE INTELLIGIBLE CONSTITUTION: THE SUPREME COURT'S OBLIGATION TO MAINTAIN THE CONSTITUTION AS SOMETHING WE THE PEOPLE CAN UNDERSTAND. Joseph Goldstein. Oxford University Press, 200 Madison Avenue, New York, New York 10016. 1992.

INTO THE THIRD CENTURY. THE SUPREME COURT. Richard B. Bernstein and Jerome Agel. Walker and Company, 720 Fifth Avenue, New York, New York 10019. 1989.

THE JUDICIAL RESPONSE TO THE NEW DEAL: THE UNITED STATES SUPREME COURT AND ECONOMIC REGULATION, 1934-1936. Richard A. Maidment. Manchester University Press. Distributed by St. Martin's Press, 175 Fifth Avenue, New York, New York 10010. 1992.

THE JUDICIARY: THE SUPREME COURT IN THE GOVERNMENTAL PROCESS. Eighth Edition. William C. Brown Group, 2460 Kerper Boulevard, Dubuque, Iowa 52001. 1991.

JUSTICE FOR ALL? THE RICH AND POOR IN SUPREME COURT HISTORY, 1790-1990. Russell W. Galloway. Carolina Academic Press, P.O. Box 51879, Durham, North Carolina 27717. 1991.

JUSTICE OLIVER WENDELL HOLMES: FREE SPEECH AND THE LIVING CONSTITUTION. H.L. Pohlman. New York University Press, 70 Washington Square South, New York, New York 10012. 1991.

JUSTICES AND PRESIDENTS: A POLITICAL HISTORY OF APPOINTMENTS TO THE SUPREME COURT. Third Edition. Henry J. Abraham. Oxford University Press, 200 Madison Avenue, New York, New York 10016. 1992.

THE LEAST DANGEROUS BRANCH: THE SUPREME COURT AT THE BAR OF POLITICS. Second Edition. Alexander M. Bickel. Yale University Press, 302 Temple Street, New Haven, Connecticut 06520. 1986.

LIBERTY UNDER LAW: THE SUPREME COURT IN AMERICAN LIFE. William M. Wiecek. Johns Hopkins University Press, 701 West Fortieth Street, Baltimore, Maryland 21211. 1988.

LIMITS OF JUDICIAL POWER: THE SUPREME COURT IN AMERICAN POLITICS. William Lasser. University of North Carolina Press, P.O. Box 2288, 116 South Boundary Street, Chapel Hill, North Carolina 27515-2288. 1988.

THE MARSHALL COURT, 1801-1835. Adrienne Siegel. Associated Faculty Press, 19 West Thirty-sixth Street, New York, New York 10018. 1987.

THE MARSHALL COURT AND CULTURAL CHANGE, 1815-1835. G. Edward White and Gerald Gunther. Oxford University Press, 200 Madison Avenue, New York, New York 10016. 1991.

MR. JUSTICE REHNQUIST, JUDICIAL ACTIVIST. Donald E. Boles. Iowa State University Press, 2121 South State Avenue, Ames, Iowa 50010. 1987.

MR. JUSTICE THOMPSON AND THE CONSTITUTION. Donald Malcolm Roper. Garland Publishing, Incorporated, 136 Madison Avenue, New York, New York 10016. 1987.

NEITHER CONSERVATIVE NOR LIBERAL: THE BURGER COURT ON CIVIL RIGHTS AND LIBERTIES. Francis G. Lee, Editor. Robert E. Kreiger Publishing Company, Incorporated. P.O. Box 9542, Malabar, Florida 32902-9542. 1983.

NINE MEN: A POLITICAL HISTORY OF THE SUPREME COURT FROM 1790 TO 1955. Fred Rodell. Fred B. Rothman and Company, 10368 West Centennial Road, Littleton, Colorado 80127. 1988. (Reprint).

ORIGINAL INTENT AND THE FRAMERS' CONSTITUTION. Leonard W. Levy. Macmillan Publishing Company, Incorporated, 866 Third Avenue, New York, New York 10022. 1988.

ORIGINAL INTENT: CHIEF JUSTICE REHNQUIST AND THE COURSE OF AMERICAN CHURCH-STATE RELATIONS. Derek Davis. Prometheus Books, 700 East Amherst Street, Buffalo, New York 14215. 1991.

A POLITICAL HISTORY OF APPOINTMENTS TO THE SUPREME COURT. Henry J. Abraham. Oxford University Press, Incorporated, 200 Madison Avenue, New York, New York 10016.

POLITICS, DEMOCRACY, AND THE SUPREME COURT: ESSAYS ON THE FRONTIER OF CONSTITUTIONAL THEORY. Arthur S. Miller. Greenwood Publishing Group, Incorporated, 88 Post Road West, P.O. Box 5007, Westport, Connecticut 06881. 1985.

PUBLIC OPINION AND THE SUPREME COURT. Thomas R. Marshall. Unwin Hyman, Incorporated, 8 Winchester Place, Winchester, Massachusetts 01890. 1989.

REACTION AND ACCOMMODATION: THE UNITED STATES SUPREME COURT AND POLITICAL CONFLICT, 1809-1835. Dwight Wiley Jessup. Garland Publishing, Incorporated, 136 Madison Avenue, New York, New York 10016. 1987.

THE RECONSTRUCTION COURT, 1864-1888. Robert Fridlington. Associated Faculty Press, 19 West Thirty-sixth Street, New York, New York 10018. 1987.

REDEFINING THE FIRST FREEDOM: THE SUPREME COURT AND THE CONSOLIDATION OF STATE POWER, 1980-1990. Gregg Ivers. Transaction Books, Rutgers University, New Brunswick, New Jersey 08903. 1992.

REDEFINING THE SUPREME COURT'S ROLE: A THEORY OF MANAGING THE FEDERAL JUDICIAL PROCESS. Samuel Estreicher. Yale University Press, 302 Temple Street, New Haven, Connecticut 06520. 1988.

REPRESENTATION RIGHTS AND THE BURGER YEARS. Nancy Maveety. University of Michigan Press, P.O. Box 1104, 839 Greene Street, Ann Arbor, Michigan 48106. 1991.

A REPRESENTATIVE SUPREME COURT? THE IMPACT OF RACE, RELIGION, AND GENDER ON APPOINTMENTS. Barbara A. Perry. Greenwood Publishing Group, Incorporated, 88 Post Road West, P.O. Box 5007, Westport, Connecticut 06881. 1991.

THE RICH AND THE POOR IN SUPREME COURT HISTORY, 1790-1982. Russell Galloway. Paradigm Press, 127 Greenbrae Boardwalk, Greenbrae, California 94904. 1982.

SANDRA DAY O'CONNOR: JUSTICE FOR ALL. Beverly Gherman and Robert Masheris. Viking Penguin, Incorporated, 375 Hudson Street, New York, New York 10014. 1991.

THE SOLICITOR GENERAL: THE POLITICS OF LAW. Rebecca Mae Salokar. Temple University Press, 1601 North Broad Street, University Services Building, Philadelphia, Pennsylvania 19122. 1992.

STORM CENTER: THE SUPREME COURT IN AMERICAN POLITICS. Second Edition. David M. O'Brien. W. W. Norton and Company, Incorporated, 500 Fifth Avenue, New York, New York 10110. 1990.

STUDIES IN U.S. SUPREME COURT BEHAVIOR. Harold J. Spaeth and Saul Brenner. Garland Publishing, Incorporated, 136 Madison Avenue, New York, New York 10016. 1990.

THE SUPREME COURT. Fourth Edition. Lawrence Baum. Congressional Quarterly Books, 1414 Twenty-second Street, Northwest, Washington D.C. 20037. 1991.

SUPREME COURT ACTIVISM AND RESTRAINT. Stephen C. Halpern and Charles M. Lamb, Editors. Lexington Books, Division of D.C. Heath and Company, 125 Spring Street, Lexington, Massachusetts 02173. 1982.

THE SUPREME COURT AND CONSTITUTIONAL DEMOCRACY. John Agresto. Cornell University Press, 124 Roberts Place, Ithaca, New York 14850. 1984.

THE SUPREME COURT AND INDIVIDUAL RIGHTS. Second Edition. Elder Witt. Congressional Quarterly Books, 1414 Twenty-second Street, Northwest, Washington D.C. 20037. 1988.

THE SUPREME COURT AND ITS JUSTICES. Jesse H. Choper. American Bar Association, 750 North Lake Shore Drive, Chicago, Illinois 60611. 1987.

THE SUPREME COURT AND JUDICIAL CHOICE: THE ROLE OF PROVISIONAL REVIEW IN A DEMOCRARY. Paul R. Dimond. University of Michigan Press, P.O. Box 1104, 839 Greene Street, Ann Arbor, Michigan 48106. 1989.

SUPREME COURT AND PARTISAN REALIGNMENT: A MACRO- AND MICROLEVEL PERSPECTIVE. John B. Gates. Westview Press, Incorporated, 5500 Central Avenue, Boulder, Colorado 80301. 1991.

THE SUPREME COURT AND PUBLIC FUNDS FOR RELIGIOUS SCHOOLS: THE BURGER YEARS, 1969-1986. Joseph E. Bryson and Samuel H. Houston, Jr. McFarland and Company, Incorporated, Box 611, Jefferson, North Carolina 28640. 1990.

THE SUPREME COURT AND THE AMERICAN FAMILY: IDEOLOGY AND ISSUES. Eva R. Rubin. Greenwood Publishing Group, Incorporated, 88 Post Road West, P.O. Box 5007, Westport, Connecticut 06881. 1986.

SUPREME COURT AND THE CONSTITUTION: READINGS IN AMERICAN CONSTITUTIONAL HISTORY. Third Edition. Stanley Kutler, Editor. W. W. Norton Press and Company, Incorporated, 500 Fifth Avenue, New York, New York 10110. 1990.

THE SUPREME COURT AND THE DECLINE OF CONSTITUTIONAL ASPIRATION. Gary J. Jacobsohn. Rowman and Allanheld, 4270 Boston Way, Lanham, Maryland 20706. 1986

THE SUPREME COURT AT WORK. Congressional Quarterly Books, 1414 Twenty- second Street, Northwest, Washington D.C. 20037. 1990.

THE SUPREME COURT: HOW IT WAS, HOW IT IS. William H. Rehnquist. Quill, New York, New York. 1989.

THE SUPREME COURT IN THE FEDERAL JUDICIAL SYSTEM. Third Edition. Stephen L. Wasby. Nelson-Hall Publishers, 111 North Canal Street, Chicago, Illinois 60606. 1988.

THE SUPREME COURT IN UNITED STATES HISTORY. Charles Warren. Fred B. Rothman and Company, 10368 West Centennial Road, Littleton, Colorado 80127. 1987. (Reprint).

SUPREME COURT POLICY MAKING AND CONSTITUTIONAL LAW. S. Sidney Ulmer. Shepard's/McGraw-Hill, P.O. Box 1235, Colorado Springs, Colorado 80901. 1985.

THE SUPREME COURT'S CONSTITUTION. Bernard H. Siegan. Transaction Books, Rutgers University Press, 30 College Avenue, New Brunswick, New Jersey 08903. 1987.

SUPREMELY POLITICAL: THE ROLE OF IDEOLOGY AND PRESIDENTIAL MANAGEMENT IN UNSUCCESSFUL SUPREME COURT NOMINATIONS. John Massaro. State University of New York Press, State University Plaza, Albany, New York 12246. 1990.

SWANN'S WAY: THE SCHOOL BUSING CASE AND THE SUPREME COURT. Bernard Schwartz. Oxford University Press, Incorporated, 200 Madison Avenue, New York, New York 10016. 1986.

THE TANEY COURT, 1837-1864. Martin Siegel. Associated Faculty Press, 19 West Thirty-sixth Street, New York, New York 10018. 1987.

THURGOOD MARSHALL: A LIFE FOR JUSTICE. James Haskins. Henry Holt and Company, 115 West Eighteenth Street, New York, New York 10011. 1992.

THE TRANSFORMATION OF THE SUPREME COURT'S AGENDA: FROM THE NEW DEAL TO THE REAGAN ADMINISTRATION. Richard L. Pacele, Jr. Westview Press, Incorporated, 5500 Central Avenue, Boulder, Colorado 80301. 1991.

TRUMAN'S COURT: A STUDY IN JUDICIAL RESTRAINT. Frances Howell Rudko. Greenwood Publishing Group, Incorporated, 88 Post Road West, P.O. Box 5007, Westport, Connecticut 06881. 1988.

TURNING RIGHT: THE MAKING OF THE REHNQUIST SUPREME COURT. David G. Savage. John Wiley and Sons, Incorporated, 605 Third Avenue, New York, New York 10158. 1992.

UNDERSTANDING SUPREME COURT OPINIONS. Tyll R. van Geel. Longman Publishing Group, 95 Church Street, White Plains, New York 10601. 1991.

THE U.S. CONSTITUTION AND THE SUPREME COURT. Steven Anzovin and Janet Podell. H.W. Wilson Company, 950 University Avenue, Bronx, New York 10452. 1988.

THE UNITED STATES SUPREME COURT: FACT, EVIDENCE AND LAW. Steven R. Schlesinger. University Press of America, 4720 Boston Way, Lanham, Maryland 20706. 1983.

THE UNITED STATES SUPREME COURT: LAWMAKING IN THE THIRD BRANCH OF GOVERNMENT. William C. Louthan. Prentice-Hall, Incorporated, 113 Sylvan Avenue, Englewood Cliffs, New Jersey 07632. 1991.

THE VINSON COURT ERA: THE SUPREME COURT'S CONFERENCE VOTES: DATA AND ANALYSIS. Jan Palmer. AMS Press, Incorporated, 56 East Thirteenth Street, New York, New York 10003. 1990.

WALL OF CONTROVERSY: CHURCH-STATE CONFLICT IN AMERICA: THE JUSTICES AND THEIR OPINIONS. Francis Graham Lee. Krieger Publishing Company, Incorporated, P.O. Box 9542, Malabar, Florida 32902-9542. 1986.

THE WARREN COURT, 1953-1969. Arnold S. Rice. Associated Faculty Press, 19 West Thirty-sixth Street, New York, New York 10018. 1987.

ANNUALS AND REVIEWS

SUPREME COURT ECONOMIC REVIEW. Law and Economics Center of Emory University. Macmillan Publishing Company, Incorporated, 866 Third Avenue, New York, New York 10022. Annual.

SUPREME COURT HISTORICAL SOCIETY YEARBOOK. Supreme Court Historical Society, 111 Second Street, Northeast, Washington, D.C. 20002. Annual.

SUPREME COURT REVIEW. University of Chicago Press, 5801 Ellis Avenue, Third Floor, South, Chicago, Illinois 60637. Annual.

NEWSLETTERS AND NEWSPAPERS

PREVIEW OF UNITED STATES SUPREME COURT CASES. American Bar Association, Public Education Division, 750 North Lake Shore Drive, Chicago, Illinois 60611. Thirty-three issues per year.

SUPREME COURT BULLETIN. Hale Ridge Publishing, P.O. Box 370, Windham, New Hampshire 03087. Semimonthly.

SUPREME COURT HISTORICAL SOCIETY QUARTERLY. Supreme Court Historical Society, 111 Second Street, Northeast, Washington, D.C. 20002. Quarterly.

SUPREME COURT RECORD. Hale Ridge Publishing, P.O. Box 370, Windham, New Hampshire 03087. Weekly.

SUPREME COURT RESEARCHER. National Legal Research Group, Incorporated, 2421 Ivy Road, Charlottesville, Virginia 22906-7587. Monthly.

BIBLIOGRAPHIES

BIBLIOGRAPHY OF JUSTICE TOM C. CLARK. University of Texas, Tarleton Law Library, 727 East 26th Street, Austin Texas 78705-5799.

LOCATION GUIDE TO THE MANUSCRIPTS OF SUPREME COURT JUSTICES. Revised Edition. Adrienne DeVergie and Mary Kate Kell. University of Texas, Tarleton Law Library, 727 East Twenty-sixth Street, Austin, Texas 78705-5799. 1981.

PERSONAL PAPERS OF SUPREME COURT JUSTICES: A DESCRIPTIVE GUIDE. Alexandra K. Wigdor. Garland Publishing, Incorporated, 136 Madison Avenue, New York, New York 10016. 1986.

THE SUPREME COURT AND THE AMERICAN REPUBLIC: AN ANNOTATED BIBLIOGRAPHY. D. Grier Stephenson, Junior. Garland Publishing, Incorporated, 136 Madison Avenue, New York, New York 10016. 1981.

THE U.S. SUPREME COURT: A BIBLIOGRAPHY. Fenton S. Martin and Robert U. Goehlert. Congressional Quarterly Books, 1414 Twenty-second Street, Northwest, Washington D.C. 20037. 1990.

U.S. SUPREME COURT APPOINTMENTS, 1961-1986: A BRIEF BIBLIOGRAPHY. Alva W. Stewart. Vance Bibliographies, P.O. Box 229, 112 North Charter Street, Monticello, Illinois 61856. 1987.

BIOGRAPHICAL SOURCES

THE BRANDEIS-FRANKFURTER CONNECTION: THE SECRET POLITICAL ACTIVITIES OF TWO SUPREME COURT JUSTICES. Bruce A. Murphy. Oxford University Press, Incorporated, 200 Madison Avenue, New York, New York 10016. 1982.

THE BURGER COURT, 1968-1984. Arthur Galub. Associated Faculty Press, 19 West Thirty-sixth Street, New York, New York 10018. 1985.

THE FULLER COURT, 1888-1910. Howard B. Furer. Associated Faculty Press, 19 West Thirty-sixth Street, New York, New York 10018. 1985.

THE MARSHALL COURT, 1801-1835. Adrienne Siegal. Associated Faculty Press, 19 West Thirty-sixth Street, New York, New York 10018. 1985.

THE MEMOIRS OF HUGO L. BLACK AND ELIZABETH BLACK. Hugo L. Black. Random House, Incorporated, Random House Publicity, (11-6) 201 East Fiftieth Street, New York, New York 10022. 1986.

SUPER CHIEF; EARL WARREN AND HIS SUPREME COURT: A JUDICIAL BIOGRAPHY. Bernard Schwartz. New York University Press, Distributed by Columbia University Press, 562 West One-Hundred Thirteenth Street, New York, New York 10025. 1983.

SUPREME COURT JUSTICE JOSEPH STORY: STATESMAN OF THE OLD REPUBLIC. R. Kent Newmyer. University of North Carolina Press, P.O. Box 2288, Chapel Hill, North Carolina 27515-2288. 1986.

ASSOCIATIONS AND PROFESSIONAL SOCIETIES

SUPREME COURT HISTORICAL SOCIETY. 111 Second Street, Northeast, Washington, D.C. 20002. (202) 543-0400.

SUPREME COURT WATCH. 72 Fifth Avenue, New York, New York 10011. (212) 242-8400.

RESEARCH CENTERS, INSTITUTES, CLEARINGHOUSES

UNITED STATES SUPREME COURT LIBRARY. 1 First Street, Northwest, Washington, D.C. 20543. (202) 479-3177.

ONLINE DATABASES

LEXIS, GENERAL FEDERAL LIBRARY. Mead Data Central, P.O. Box 933, Dayton, Ohio 45401.

WESTLAW, ALLFEDS LIBRARY. West Publishing Company, P.O. Box 64526, 50 West Kellogg Boulevard, St. Paul, Minnesota 55164-0526.

SUPREME COURT (UNITED STATES)

STATISTICS SOURCES

CLERK'S OFFICE, UNITED STATES SUPREME COURT BUILDING, One First Street, Northeast, Washington, D.C. 20543. Unpublished Data.

AUDIOVISUALS

SUPREME COURT. American Bar Association, 750 North Lake Shore Drive, Chicago, Illinois 60611. Young Lawyers Division. 1979. Videotape.

SURETY AND GUARANTY
See also: SECURED TRANSACTIONS

TEXTBOOKS AND GENERAL WORKS

COMMERCIAL LIABILITY UNDERWRITING. Third Edition. Larry D. Gaunt, Numan A. Williams and Everett D. Randall. Insurance Institute of America, Incorporated, 720 Providence Road, Malvern, Pennsylvania 19355. 1990.

CREATING AND ENFORCING CORPORATE GUARANTEES: WILL THE LENDER GET THE BENEFITS IT EXPECTS? Miriam H. Kanter and Alan W. Beloff. Massachusetts Continuing Legal Education, 20 West Street, Boston, Massachusetts 02111. 1991.

INTERNATIONAL AND DOMESTIC GUARANTIES AND OTHER COLLATERAL ASSURANCES OF PERFORMANCE. William C. Hillman. Practising Law Institute, 810 Seventh Avenue, New York, New York 10019. 1989.

ENCYCLOPEDIAS AND DICTIONARIES

GLOSSARY OF SURETYSHIP AND RELATED DISCIPLINES. Thomas C. Schleifer, et al., Editors. Construction Management Associates, P.O. Box 2287R, Morristown, New Jersey 07960. 1981.

NEWSLETTERS AND NEWSPAPERS

FIDELITY AND SURETY NEWS. The Michie Company, P.O. Box 7587, Charlottesville, Virginia 22906-7587. Quarterly.

BIBLIOGRAPHIES

FIDELITY SURETY LAW BIBLIOGRAPHY, 1946-1978. Fidelity and Surety Law Committee, Section of Insurance, Negligence and Compensation Law, American Bar Association, 750 North Lake Shore Drive, Chicago, Illinois 60611. 1980.

SURETY LAW TOPICAL INDEX AND BIBLIOGRAPHY. American Bar Association, Fidelity and Surety Law Committee, 750 North Lake Shore Drive, Chicago, Illinois 60611. 1987.

ASSOCIATIONS AND PROFESSIONAL SOCIETIES

AMERICAN SURETY ASSOCIATION. 1029 Vermont Avenue, Northwest, Suite 800, Washington, D.C. 20005. (202) 737-2696.

FIDELITY AND SURETY LAW COMMITTEE, SECTION OF TORT AND INSURANCE PRACTICE. American Bar Association, 750 North Lake Shore Drive, Chicago, Illinois 60611. (312) 988-5000.

SURGEONS
See: MEDICAL JURISPRUDENCE AND MALPRACTICE

SURROGATE MOTHERHOOD
See: FAMILY LAW

SURVIVAL OF ACTIONS
See: WRONGFUL DEATH

T

TAVERNS
See: ALCOHOL CONTROL AND DRINKING BEHAVIOR; HOTELS, RESTAURANTS, ETC.

TAX
See: CORPORATIONS, TAXATION; ESTATE, INHERITANCE AND TRANSFER TAXES; EXCISE TAXES; INCOME TAX, FEDERAL; INTERNAL REVENUE SERVICE; REAL PROPERTY TAXATION; SALES AND USE TAXES; TAX AND ESTATE PLANNING; TAX COURT; TAX EXEMPT ORGANIZATIONS; TAX LEGISLATION AND POLICY; TAX PRACTICE AND ENFORCEMENT; TAX RETURNS; TAX SHELTERS; TAXATION, INTERNATIONAL; TAXATION, STATE AND LOCAL

TAX AND ESTATE PLANNING
See also: ESTATE, INHERITANCE AND TRANSFER TAXES; TAX PRACTICE AND ENFORCEMENT; TAX SHELTERS

STATUTES, CODES, STANDARDS, UNIFORM LAWS

FEDERAL INCOME TAX CODE AND REGULATIONS. Commerce Clearing House, Incorporated, 4025 West Peterson Avenue, Chicago, Illinois 60646. Annual.

FEDERAL TAX REGULATIONS. West Publishing Company, P.O. Box 64526, 50 West Kellogg Boulevard, St. Paul, Minnesota 55164-0526. Annual.

INTERNAL REVENUE BULLETIN: CUMULATIVE BULLETIN. United States Department of Treasury, Internal Revenue Service. United States Government Printing Office, Washington, D.C. 20402. Weekly.

INTERNAL REVENUE CODE. West Publishing Company, P.O. Box 64526, 50 West Kellogg Boulevard, St. Paul, Minnesota 55164-0526. Annual.

LOOSELEAF SERVICES AND REPORTERS

AUTOMATIC TAX PLANNER. Irving S. Schreiber. Panel Publishers, Incorporated, 36 Forty-fourth Street, New York, New York 10036. 1985- .

BUSINESS STRATEGIES. Sidney Kess and B. Weslin. Commerce Clearing House, Incorporated, 4025 West Peterson Avenue, Chicago, Illinois 60646. 1983- .

THE CLOSELY HELD CORPORATION: TAX, FINANCIAL AND ESTATE PLANNING. Irving S. Schreiber and Jonathon Skiba. Panel Publishers, Incorporated, 36 Forty-fourth Street, New York, New York 10036. 1983- .

ESTATE PLANNING. Research Institute of America, Incorporated, One Penn Plaza, New York, New York 10119. 1980- .

ESTATE PLANNING. Fifth Edition. A. James Casner and Austin W. Scott. Little, Brown, and Company, 34 Beacon Street, Boston, Massachusetts 02108. 1983- .

ESTATE PLANNING AND TAXATION COORDINATOR. Research Institute of America, Incorporated, 90 Fifth Avenue, New York, New York 10011. 1978- .

ESTATE PLANNING: COMPLETE GUIDE AND WORKBOOK. Alice F. Brod. Panel Publishers, Incorporated, 36 Forty-fourth Street, New York, New York 10036. 1984- .

ESTATE PLANNING: FORMS, PRACTICE AND TAX ANALYSIS. Gerald S. Susman. Law Journal-Seminars Press, Incorporated, 111 Eighth Avenue, Suite 900, New York, New York 10011. 1980- .

ESTATE PLANNING LAW AND TAXATION. Second Edition. David Westfall. Research Institute of America, Incorporated, One Penn Plaza, New York, New York 10119. 1989- .

ESTATE PLANNING SIMPLIFIED. Doug H. Moy and D.C. Johnson. Professional Education Systems, Incorporated, 200 Spring Street, Eau Claire, Wisconsin 54702. 1989- .

ESTATE TAX FREEZE: TOOLS AND TECHNIQUES. Douglas R. Freeman. Matthew Bender and Company, Incorporated, 11 Penn Plaza, New York, New York 10001. 1985- .

ESTATE TAX TECHNIQUES. Frank B. Appleman. Matthew Bender and Company, Incorporated, 11 Penn Plaza, New York, New York 10001. 1955- .

FAMILY LAW TAX GUIDE. Commerce Clearing House, Incorporated, 4025 West Peterson Avanue, Chicago, Illinois 60646. 1985.

FAMILY TAX PLANNING. Ralph S. Rice and Terence R. Rice. Matthew Bender and Company, Incorporated, 11 Penn Plaza, New York, New York 10001. 1960- .

FEDERAL TAXES. Prentice-Hall, Incorporated, 113 Sylvan Avenue, Englewood Cliffs, New Jersey 07632. 1919- .

FINANCIAL AND ESTATE PLANNING. Sidney Kress and Robert Whitman. Commerce Clearing House, Incorporated, 4025 West Peterson Avenue, Chicago, Illinois 60646. 1980- .

FUTURE INTEREST AND ESTATE PLANNING. William Schwartz, Anderson Publishing Company, 2035 Reading Road, Cincinnati, Ohio 45202. 1965. (1985 Supplement).

HANDBOOK OF TAX AND FINANCIAL PLANNING FOR DIVORCE AND SEPARATION. Alan S. Zipp. Prentice-Hall, Incorporated, 113 Sylvan Avenue, Englewood Cliffs, New Jersey 07632. 1985.

HOW TO PLAN FOR TAX SAVINGS IN REAL ESTATE TRANSACTIONS. Irving S. Schreiber and J. P. Sullivan. Panel Publishers, Incorporated, 36 Forty-fourth Street, New York, New York 10036. 1969- .

HOW TO SAVE TAXES AND INCREASE YOUR WEALTH WITH A PROFESSIONAL CORPORATION. Irving S. Schreiber, Editor. Panel Publishers, Incorporated, 36 Forty-fourth Street, New York, New York 10036. 1977- .

HOW TO SAVE TIME AND TAXES IN HANDLING ESTATES: A BOOK ON FEDERAL ESTATE AND INCOME TAXES. Second Edition. John A. Clark. Matthew Bender and Company, Incorporated, 11 Penn Plaza, New York, New York 10001. 1983- .

INTERNATIONAL BUSINESS PLANNING: LAW AND TAXATION (UNITED STATES). William P. Streng and Jeswald W. Salacuse. Matthew Bender and Company, Incorporated, 11 Penn Plaza, New York, New York 10001. 1982- .

INTERNATIONAL TAX PLANNING MANUAL. Commerce Clearing House, Incorporated, 4025 West Peterson Avenue, Chicago, Illinois 60646. 1986.

MODERN ESTATE PLANNING. Ernest D. Fiore, Jr., et al. Matthew Bender and Company, Incorporated, 11 Penn Plaza, New York, New York 10001. 1981- .

MODERN TAX PLANNING CHECKLISTS. Revised Edition. Ronald L. Bleich and Hal W. Mandel. Research Institute of America, Incorporated, One Penn Plaza, New York, New York 10119. 1985- .

MURPHY'S WILL CLAUSES: ANNOTATIONS AND FORMS WITH TAX EFFECTS. Joseph H. Murphy. Matthew Bender and Company, Incorporated, 11 Penn Plaza, New York, New York 10001. 1960- .

PERSONAL TAX PLANNING FOR PROFESSIONALS AND OWNERS OF SMALL BUSINESSES. California Continuing Education of the Bar, 2300 Shattuck Avenue, Berkeley, California 94704. 1983- .

REAL ESTATE INVESTMENTS: TAX AND FINANCIAL PLANNING. Richard M. Horwood and Steven Jay Katz. Panel Publishers, Incorporated, 36 Forty-fourth Street, New York, New York 10036. 1985.

REAL ESTATE TRANSACTIONS: TAX PLANNING AND CONSEQUENCES. Second Edition. Mark Lee Levine. West Publishing Company, P.O. Box 64526, 50 West Kellogg Boulevard, St. Paul, Minnesota 55164-0526. 1976- .

STANDARD FEDERAL TAX REPORTS. Commerce Clearing House, Incorporated, 4025 West Peterson Avenue, Chicago, Illinois 60646. 1913- .

SUCCESSFUL ESTATE PLANNING: IDEAS AND METHODS. Prentice-Hall, Incorporated, 113 Sylvan Avenue, Englewood Cliffs, New Jersey 07632. 1968- .

TAX, ESTATE AND FINANCIAL PLANNING FOR THE ELDERLY. John J. Regan. Matthew Bender and Company, Incorporated, 11 Penn Plaza, New York, New York 10001. 1985- .

TAX MANAGEMENT: COMPENSATION PLANNING SERIES. Bureau of National Affairs, 1231 Twenty-fifth Street, Northwest, Washington, D.C. 20037. 1982- .

TAX MANAGEMENT: ESTATE GIFTS AND TRUST PORTFOLIO SERIES. Bureau of National Affairs, 1231 Twenty-fifth Street, Northwest, Washington, D.C. 20037. 1967- .

TAX PLANNING. Prentice-Hall, Incorporated, 113 Sylvan Avenue, Englewood Cliffs, New Jersey 07632. 1954- .

TAX PLANNING FOR CORPORATIONS AND SHAREHOLDERS. Zolman Cavitch. Matthew Bender and Company, Incorporated, 11 Penn Plaza, New York, New York 10001. 1981- .

TAX PLANNING FOR DISPOSITIONS OF BUSINESS INTERESTS. Theodore Ness and William F. Indoe. Research Institute of America, Incorporated, One Penn Plaza, New York, New York 10119. 1985- .

TAX PLANNING FOR FAMILY WEALTH TRANSFERS: ANALYSIS WITH FORMS. Second Edition. Howard M. Zaritsky. Research Institute of America, Incorporated, One Penn Plaza, New York, New York 10119. 1991- .

TAX PLANNING FOR PROFESSIONALS. Harold I. Apolinsky. Research Institute of America, Incorporated, One Penn Plaza, New York, New York 10119. 1985- .

TAX PLANNING FORMS FOR BUSINESSES AND INDIVIDUALS. Dennis I. Belcher, Jerome D. Carr, Robert B. Curran and Derek L. Smith. Research Institute of America, Incorporated, One Penn Plaza, New York, New York 10119. 1985- .

TAX PLANNING STRATEGIES. Lewis D. Solomon and Susan Flax Posner. Callaghan and Company, 155 Pfingsten Road, Deerfield, Illinois 60015. 1985- .

TAXATION OF INTELLECTUAL PROPERTY: TAX PLANNING GUIDE. Marvin Petry. Matthew Bender and Company, Incorporated, 11 Penn Plaza, New York, New York 10001. 1985- .

WG & L ESTATE PLANNING AND ADMINISTRATION SERVICE. Robert Whitman. Research Institute of America, Incorporated, One Penn Plaza, New York, New York 10119. 1989- .

HANDBOOKS, MANUALS, FORMBOOKS

CCH ESTATE PLANNING GUIDE, INCLUDING FINANCIAL PLANNING. Sixth Edition. Sidney Kess and Bertil Westin. Commerce Clearing House, Incorporated, 4025 West Peterson Avenue, Chicago, Illinois 60646. 1987.

THE ESSENTIAL GUIDE TO WILLS, ESTATES, TRUSTS, AND DEATH TAXES. Alex J. Soled. American Association of Retired Persons. Scott, Foresman and Company, 1900 East Lake Avenue, Glenview, Illinois 60025. 1988.

ESTATE PLANNER'S HANDBOOK. Fourth Edition. James F. Farr and Jackson W. Wright, Jr. Little, Brown, and Company, 34 Beacon Street, Boston, Massachusetts 02108. 1985.

THE ESTATE PLANNING GUIDE. Martin M. Shenkman. John Wiley and Sons, Incorporated, 605 Third Avenue, New York, New York 10158. 1991.

ESTATE PLANNING MANUAL. Charles O. Galvin. John Wiley and Sons, Incorporated, 605 Third Avenue, New York, New York 10158. 1987.

ESTATE PLANNING MANUAL FOR TRUST OFFICERS. Roy M. Adams. American Bankers Association, 1120 Connecticut Ave., Northwest, Washington, D.C. 20036. 1982.

FINANCIAL PLANNER'S GUIDE TO ESTATE PLANNING. Third Edition. Paul J. Lochray. Prentice-Hall, Incorporated, 113 Sylvan Avenue, Englewood Cliffs, New Jersey 07632. 1991.

THE HANDBOOK OF ESTATE PLANNING. D. Larry Crumbley. Dow Jones-Irwin, 1818 Ridge Road, Homewood, Illinois 60430. 1988.

HANDBOOK OF ESTATE PLANNING. Robert A. Esperti and Renno L. Peterson. McGraw-Hill Book Company, 1221 Avenue of the Americas, New York, New York 10020. 1988.

THE HANDBOOK OF FARM AND RANCH ESTATE PLANNING. Jin G. Polson. Prentice-Hall, Incorporated, 113 Sylvan Avenue, Englewood Cliffs, New Jersey 07632. 1982.

INSTRUMENT AND FORMS SUPPLEMENT TO ESTATE PLANNING AND DRAFTING. Regis W. Campfield. Commerce Clearing House, Incorporated, 4025 West Peterson Avenue, Chicago, Illinois 60646. 1985.

INTERNATIONAL TAX AND ESTATE PLANNING: A PRACTICAL GUIDE FOR MULTINATIONAL INVESTORS. Second Edition. Robert C. Lawrence, III. Practising Law Institute, 810 Seventh Avenue, New York, New York 10019. 1989.

INTERNATIONAL TAX PLANNERS MANUAL. Allan Cinnamon, Managing Editor. Commerce Clearing House, Incorporated, 4025 West Peterson Avenue, Chicago, Illinois 60646. 1984.

KEEPING YOUR MONEY: HOW TO AVOID TAXES AND PROBATE THROUGH ESTATE PLANNING. Charles K. Plotnick and Stephan R. Leimberg. John Wiley and Sons, Incorporated, 605 Third Avenue, New York, New York 10158. 1987.

MURPHY'S WILL CLAUSES: ANNOTATIONS AND FORMS WITH TAX EFFECTS. National Edition. Joseph H. Murphy, et al. Matthew Bender and Company, Incorporated, 11 Penn Plaza, New York, New York 10001. 1960. (Semiannual Supplements).

PERSONAL FINANCIAL PLANNING: THE ADVISER'S GUIDE. Rolf Auster. Commerce Clearing House, Incorporated, 4025 West Peterson Avenue, Chicago, Illinois 60646. 1989.

PLANNING AN ESTATE: A GUIDEBOOK OF PRINCIPLES AND TECHNIQUES. Harold Weinstock. Shepard's/McGraw-Hill, P.O. Box 1235, Colorado Springs, Colorado 80901. 1988.

TAX MANUAL FOR CORPORATE LIQUIDATIONS, REDEMPTIONS, AND ESTATE PLANNING RECAPITALIZATIONS. Stanley Hagendorf. Garland Publishing, Incorporated, 136 Madison Avenue, New York, New York 10016. 1984.

TAX PLANNING FOR CORPORATIONS AND SHAREHOLDERS: FORMS. Zolman Cavitch. Matthew Bender and Company, Incorporated, 11 Penn Plaza, New York, New York 10001. 1985. (Periodic Supplements).

TAX PLANNING FORMS FOR BUSINESSES AND INDIVIDUALS. Research Institute of America, Incorporated, One Penn Plaza, New York, New York 10119. 1985.

THE TOOLS AND TECHNIQUES OF ESTATE PLANNING. Eighth Edition. Stephan R. Leimberg. National Underwriter Company, 420 East Fourth Street, Cincinnati, Ohio 45202. 1990.

YOU CAN'T TAKE IT WITH YOU: A STEP-BY-STEP PERSONALIZED APPROACH TO YOUR WILL TO AVOID PROBATE AND ESTATE TAXES. David C. Larsen. Vintage Books, New York, New York. 1988.

TEXTBOOKS AND GENERAL WORKS

ADVANCED WILL DRAFTING. Michael J. Weinberger, Chairman. Practising Law Institute, 810 Seventh Avenue, New York, New York 10019. 1984.

AFTER DEATH TAX PLANNING: MINIMIZING TAX LIABILITIES. Jerry A. Kasner and Robert Whitman. American Law Institute-American Bar Association, 4025 Chestnut Street, Philadelphia, Pennsylvania 19104. 1990.

BASIC ESTATE PLANNING UNDER THE NEW TAX LAW. Jeffrey A. Lowin. Practising Law Institute, 810 Seventh Avenue, New York, New York 10019. 1991.

BUSINESS DECISIONS AND THE FEDERAL TAXING SYSTEM: A SIMPLIFIED GUIDE FOR MANAGERS. John L. Kramer and Sandra S. Kramer. John Wiley and Sons, Incorporated, 605 Third Avenue, New York, New York 10158. 1985.

THE CLOSELY HELD CORPORATION DESKBOOK: 1986 TAX PLANNING UPDATE. Panel Publishers, Incorporated, 36 Forty-fourth Street, New York, New York 10036. 1986.

TAX AND ESTATE PLANNING

CLOSELY HELD CORPORATIONS IN BUSINESS AND ESTATE PLANNING. Edwin T. Hood, Sheldon F. Kurtz, and John D. Shors. Little, Brown, and Company, 34 Beacon Street, Boston, Massachusetts 02108. 1982. (Periodic Supplements).

CONTEMPORARY ESTATE PLANNING: TEXT AND PROBLEMS. John R. Price. Little, Brown, and Company, 34 Beacon Street, Boston, Massachusetts 02108. 1982.

COURSE MATERIALS ON LIFETIME AND TESTAMENTARY ESTATE PLANNING. Fourth Edition. Edward M. David and Maurice D. Lee. American Law Institute-American Bar Association, Committee on Continuing Professional Education, 4025 Chestnut Street, Philadelphia, Pennsylvania 19104. 1982.

COURSE OF STUDY MATERIALS: POSTMORTEM PLANNING AND ESTATE ADMINISTRATION. American Law Institute-American Bar Association, Committee on Continuing Professional Education, 4025 Chestnut Street, Philadelphia, Pennsylvania 19104. 1986.

CURRENT ESTATE AND TAX PLANNING PROBLEMS. Advanced Legal Education, Hamline University School of Law, 1536 Hewitt Avenue, St. Paul, Minnesota 55104. 1983.

DEPRECIATION AND THE INVESTMENT TAX CREDIT WITH TAX PLANNING. John T. Del Negro and Harvey Levenson. Matthew Bender and Company, Incorporated, 11 Penn Plaza, New York, New York 10001. 1983. (Periodic Supplements).

THE DOLLARS AND SENSE OF ESTATE PLANNING. Forest J. Bowman. Prentice- Hall, Incorporated, 113 Sylvan Avenue, Englewood Cliffs, New Jersey 07632. 1989.

ESTATE AND FINANCIAL PLANNING FOR THE AGING OR INCAPACITATED CLIENT: A COURSE HANDBOOK. David P. Callaghan and Peter J. Strauss, Co-chairmen. Practising Law Institute, 810 Seventh Avenue, New York, New York 10019. 1990.

ESTATE AND FINANCIAL PLANNING FOR THE CLOSELY HELD BUSINESS. Practising Law Institute, 810 Seventh Avenue, New York, New York 10019. 1983.

ESTATE FREEZES UNDER SECTION 2036(C): ANALYSIS, PLANNING, DRAFTING: SPECIAL REPORT. Howard M. Zaritsky. Research Institute of America, Incorporated, One Penn Plaza, New York, New York 10119. 1990.

ESTATE PLANNING. Gerald S. Susman. The New York Law Publishing Company, 111 Eighth Avenue, New York, New York 10011. 1977. (Periodic Supplements).

ESTATE PLANNING. Third Edition. Jerome A. Manning. Practising Law Institute, 810 Seventh Avenue, New York, New York 10019. 1989.

ESTATE PLANNING AFTER THE ECONOMIC RECOVERY ACT OF 1981: A TAX MANAGEMENT PLANNING MANUAL. William P. Streng and Phyllis K. Bywaters. Bureau of National Affairs, Incorporated, 1231 Twenty-fifth Street, Northwest, Washington, D.C. 20037. 1982.

ESTATE PLANNING AFTER THE REAGAN TAX CUT. Peter E. Lippett. Reston Publishing Company, Incorporated, 113 Sylvan Avenue, Englewood Cliffs, New Jersey 07632. 1982.

ESTATE PLANNING AND DRAFTING. Regis W. Campfield. Commerce Clearing House, Incorporated, 4025 West Peterson Avenue, Chicago, Illinois 60646. 1984.

ESTATE PLANNING AND EMPLOYER BENEFITS. Massachusetts Continuing Legal Education, Incorporated, 20 West Street, Boston, Massachusetts 02111. 1983.

ESTATE PLANNING FOR FAMILY LAWYERS. Massachusetts Continuing Legal Education, Incorporated, 20 West Street, Boston, Massachusetts 02111. 1984.

ESTATE PLANNING FOR FARMERS AND RANCHERS. Second Edition. Donald H. Kelley and David A. Ludtke. Shepard's/McGraw-Hill, P.O. Box 1235, Colorado Springs, Colorado 80901. 1986.

ESTATE PLANNING FOR INTERESTS IN A CLOSELY HELD BUSINESS. American Law Institute-American Bar Association, Committee on Continuing Professional Education, 4025 Chestnut Street, Philadelphia, Pennsylvania 19104. 1982.

ESTATE PLANNING FOR MEDICAID COVERAGE OF NURSING HOMES AND LONG TERM HEALTH CARE. Massachusetts Continuing Legal Education, Incorporated, 20 West Street, Boston, Massachusetts 02111. 1983.

ESTATE PLANNING FOR THE ELDERLY CLIENT. Sanford J. Schlesinger. John Wiley and Sons, Incorporated, 605 Third Avenue, New York, New York 10158. 1984.

ESTATE PLANNING FOR THE GENERAL PRACTITIONER: ESTATES UNDER $500,000. Massachusetts Continuing Legal Education, Incorporated, 20 West Street, Boston, Massachusetts 02111. 1983.

ESTATE PLANNING FOR THE HIGHLY PAID EXECUTIVE WITH LITTLE OR NO INHERITED WEALTH. Massachusetts Continuing Legal Education, 20 West Street, Boston, Massachusetts 02111. 1984.

ESTATE PLANNING IN DEPTH: ALI-ABA COURSE OF STUDY MATERIALS. American Law Institute-American Bar Association, Committee on Continuing Professional Education, 4025 Chestnut Street, Philadelphia, Pennsylvania 19104. 1987.

ESTATE PLANNING IN DEPTH: RESOURCE MATERIALS. American Law Institute, 4025 Chestnut Street, Philadelphia, Pennsylvania 19104. 1984.

ESTATE PLANNING IN THE '80s. Revised Edition. D. Larry Crumbley and Edward E. Milam. Books on Demand, 300 North Zeeb Road, Ann Arbor, Michigan 48106-1346. 1982.

ESTATE PLANNING LAW AND TAXATION. David Westfall. Research Institute of America, Incorporated, One Penn Plaza, New York, New York 10119. 1989. (Supplements).

ESTATE PLANNING SIMPLIFIED. Doug H. Moy. John Wiley and Sons, Incorporated, 605 Third Avenue, New York, New York 10158. 1989.

ESTATE PLANNING STRATEGIES FOR PHYSICIANS. Lawrence Farber. Medical Economics Books, 5 Paragon Drive, Montvale, New Jersey 07645. 1986.

ESTATE PLANNING: THE NEW GOLDEN OPPORTUNITES. Robert S. Holzman. Boardroom Books, Division of Boardman Reports, Incorporated, 330 West Forty-second Street, New York, New York 10036. 1985.

FAMILY ESTATE PLANNING GUIDE. Third Edition. Frederick K. Hoops. Lawyers Co-Operative Publishing Company, Aqueduct Building, Rochester, New York 14694. 1982. (Supplements).

FAMILY GUIDE TO ESTATE PLANNING, FUNERAL ARRANGEMENTS, AND SETTLING AN ESTATE AFTER DEATH. Theodore E. Hughes and David Klein. Scribner Book Company, 866 Third Avenue, New York, New York 10022. 1983.

FAMILY SECURITY THROUGH ESTATE PLANNING. Second Edition. Arnold D. Kahn. McGraw-Hill Book Company, 1221 Avenue of the Americas, New York, New York 10020. 1984.

FARM ESTATE AND BUSINESS PLANNING. Tenth Edition. Neil E. Harl. Century Communications, Incorporated, 6201 Howard Street, Niles, Illinois 60648. 1988.

FEDERAL TAXATION OF TRUSTS, GRANTORS, AND BENEFICIARIES: INCOME, ESTATE, GIFT, GENERATION-SKIPPING TRANSFER. Second Edition. John L. Peschel and Edward D. Spurgeon. Research Institute of America, Incorporated, One Penn Plaza, New York, New York 10119. 1989.

FINANCIAL AND ESTATE PLANNING APPLICATIONS. Fourth Edition. Gwenda L. Cannon. The American College, 270 Bryn Mawr Avenue, Bryn Mawr, Pennsylvania 19010. 1985.

FINANCIAL AND ESTATE PLANNING WITH LIFE INSURANCE PRODUCTS: SUCCESSOR TO LIFE INSURANCE IN ESTATE PLANNING. James C. Munch. Little, Brown and Company, 34 Beacon Street, Boston, Massachusetts 02108. 1990.

FINANCIAL PLANNER'S GUIDE TO ESTATE PLANNING. Paul J. Lochray. Prentice-Hall, Incorporated, 113 Sylvan Avenue, Englewood Cliffs, New Jersey 07632. 1989.

FUNDAMENTAL CONCEPTS OF ESTATE PLANNING. Seymour Levine, Chairman. Practising Law Institute, 810 Seventh Avenue, New York, New York 10019. 1984.

FUNDAMENTALS OF ESTATE PLANNING UNDER THE NEW TAX LAW. Jeffrey A. Lowin. Practising Law Institute, 810 Seventh Avenue, New York, New York 10019. 1989.

GROWING COMPANIES: TAX AND BUSINESS PLANNING FOR THE '80S. American Law Institute, 4025 Chestnut Street, Philadelphia, Pennsylvania 19104. 1983.

INCOME SHIFTING AFTER TAX REFORM. William A. Raabe, Karen J. Boucher and Rick J. Taylor. Prentice-Hall, Incorporated, 113 Sylvan Avenue, Englewood Cliffs, New Jersey 07632. 1988.

INSTITUTE ON ESTATE PLANNING. Matthew Bender and Company, Incorporated, 11 Penn Plaza, New York, New York 10001. 1980- .

INTERNATIONAL ESTATE PLANNING. William H. Newton, III. Shepard's/McGraw-Hill, P.O. Box 1235, Colorado Springs, Colorado 80901. 1981. (Annual Supplements).

INTRODUCTION TO ESTATE PLANNING IN A NUTSHELL. Third Edition. Robert J. Lynn. West Publishing Company, P.O. Box 64526, 50 West Kellogg Boulevard, St. Paul, Minnesota 55164-0526. 1983.

LIFE INSURANCE IN ESTATE PLANNING. James C. Munch, Jr. Little, Brown, and Company, 34 Beacon Street, Boston, Massachusetts 02108. 1981.

LIFETIME AND TESTAMENTARY ESTATE PLANNING. Tenth Edition. William Parsons and Harrison Tweed. American Law Institute-American Bar Association, 4025 Chestnut Street, Philadelphia, Pennsylvania 19104. 1988.

MARITAL DEDUCTION PLANNING AFTER ERTA. Massachusetts Continuing Legal Education, 20 West Street, Boston, Massachusetts 02111. 1984.

MULTISTATE AND MUTINATIONAL ESTATE PLANNING. Jeffrey A. Schoenblum. Little, Brown, and Company, 34 Beacon Street, Boston, Massachusetts 02108. 1982.

NON-QUALIFIED DEFERRED COMPENSATION PLANS. Gerald P. Wolf. Practising Law Institute, 810 Seventh Avenue, New York, New York 10019. 1989.

THE NORRIS CASE AND BENEFIT PLANNING. Howard J. Golden, Chairman. Practising Law Institute, 810 Seventh Avenue, New York, New York 10019. 1983.

PAUL STROSSEL'S QUICK AND EASY GUIDE TO TAX MANAGEMENT FOR 1985-86. Paul Stressels. Dow Jones-Irwin, 1818 Ridge Road, Homewood, Illinois 60430. 1986.

PERSONAL TAX PLANNING FOR PROFESSIONALS AND OWNERS OF SMALL BUSINESSES. California Continuing Education of the Bar, 2300 Shattuck Avenue, Berkeley, California 94704. 1983. (1990 Supplement).

PLAN TERMINATION: ASSET OR LIABILITY? A. Richard Susko. Practising Law Institute, 810 Seventh Avenue, New York, New York 10019. 1984.

PLANNING AN ESTATE: A GUIDEBOOK OF PRINCIPLES AND TECHNIQUES. Third Edition. Harold Weinstock. Shepard's/McGraw-Hill, P.O. Box 1235, Colorado Springs, Colorado 80901. 1988.

THE PLANNING AND ADMINISTRATION OF A LARGE ESTATE, 1986. Reginald C. Kechler, III. Practising Law Institute, 810 Seventh Avenue, New York, New York 10019. 1986.

PLANNING AND DRAFTING FOR THE MARITAL DEDUCTION. Linda B. Hirschon. Practising Law Institute, 810 Seventh Avenue, New York, New York 10019. 1982.

PLANNING FOR THE SECOND MARRIAGE. Massachusetts Continuing Legal Education, Incorporated, 20 West Street, Boston, Massachusetts 02111. 1984.

PLANNING FOR YOUR RETIREMENT: IRA'S AND KEOGH PLANS. Commerce Clearing House, Incorporated, 4025 West Peterson Avenue, Chicago, Illinois 60646. 1987.

PLANNING TECHNIQUES FOR LARGE ESTATES. American Law Institute, 4025 Chestnut Street, Philadelphia, Pennsylvania 19104. 1985.

PORTFOLIO OF ESTATE PLANNING TOOLS. Allen P. Appel. Prentice-Hall, Incorporated, 113 Sylvan Avenue, Englewood Cliffs, New Jersey 07632. 1983.

POST-MORTEM PLANNING AND ESTATE ADMINISTRATION: ALI-ABA COURSE OF STUDY MATERIALS. American Law Institute-American Bar Association, Committee on Continuing Professional Education, 4025 Chestnut Street, Philadelphia, Pennsylvania 19104. 1987.

POST MORTEM TAX PLANNING AND PROBLEMS AFTER ERTA: THE COMPLETE PICTURE. American Bar Association, Real Property, Probate and Trust Law Section, 750 North Lake Shore Drive, Chicago, Illinois 60611. 1982.

PRACTICAL INTERNATIONAL TAX PLANNING. Third Edition. Marshall J. Langer. Practising Law Institute, 810 Seventh Avenue, New York, New York 10019. 1986. (Supplements).

READINGS IN ESTATE AND GIFT TAX PLANNING. Fourth Edition. Gwenda L. Cannon. The American College, 270 Bryn Mawr Avenue, Bryn Mawr, Pennslyvania 19010. 1985.

RETIREMENT BENEFITS AND LIFE INSURANCE: A LAWYER'S REFERENCE (WHICH EVERY RETIREE SHOULD READ!). Edward F. Koren. Callaghan and Company, 155 Pfingsten Road, Deerfield, Illinois 60015. 1987.

ROBINSON'S ESTATE PLANNING: FORMS, PRACTICE AND TAX ANALYSIS. Gerald J. Robinson and Sanford J. Schlesinger. Law Journal-Seminars Press, Incorporated, 111 Eighth Avenue, New York, New York 10011. 1980. (Periodic Supplements).

SELECTING THE FORM OF A SMALL BUSINESS ENTITY. American Law Institute-American Bar Association, Committee on Continuing Professional Education, 4025 Chestnut Street, Philadelphia, Pennsylvania 19104. 1985. (1988 Supplement).

SELF-DIRECTED IRA'S FOR THE ACTIVE INVESTOR. Peter D. Heerwagen. Probus Publishing Company, Incorporated, 118 North Linton Street, Chicago, Illinois 60606. 1986.

SIXTEENTH ANNUAL ESTATE PLANNING INSTITUTE: A COURSE HANDBOOK. Practising Law Institute, 810 Seventh Avenue, New York, New York 10019. 1985.

SOPHISTICATED ESTATE PLANNING TECHNIQUES: ALI-ABA COURSE OF STUDY MATERIALS. American Law Institute, 4025 Chestnut Street, Philadelphia, Pennsylvania 19104. 1984.

TAX AND BUSINESS PLANNING FOR THE EIGHTIES: ALI-ABA COURSE OF STUDY MATERIALS. American Law Institute-American Bar Association, Committee on Continuing Professional Education, 4025 Chestnut Street, Philadelphia, Pennsylvania 19104. 1986.

TAX AND ESTATE PLANNING WITH CLOSELY HELD CORPORATIONS. Waldo G. Rothenberg. Lawyers Co-Operative Publishing Company, Aqueduct Building, Rochester, New York 14694. 1981. (Supplements).

TAX EFFECTIVE TOTAL COMPENSATION: USING 401(K) AND 125 PLANS: A COURSE HANDBOOK. Practising Law Institute, 810 Seventh Avenue, New York, New York 10019. 1985.

TAX GUIDE FOR ACQUIRING, MAINTAINING, AND DISPOSING OF BUSINESS EQUIPMENT. Philip R. Fink. Prentice-Hall, Incorporated, 113 Sylvan Avenue, Englewood Cliffs, New Jersey 07632. 1982.

TAX PLANNING FOR BUSINESS START-UPS. California Continuing Education of the Bar, 2300 Shattuck Avenue, Berkeley, California 94704. 1985.

TAX PLANNING FOR EXECUTIVE COMPENSATION. Harvey L. Frutkin. Matthew Bender and Company, Incorporated, 11 Penn Plaza, New York, New York 10001. 1983. (Periodic Supplements).

TAX PLANNING FOR FAMILY WEALTH TRANSFERS: ANALYSIS WITH FORMS. Howard M. Zaritsky. Research Institute of America, Incorporated, One Penn Plaza, New York, New York 10119. 1991. (with Supplements).

TAX PLANNING FOR HIGHLY COMPENSATED INDIVIDUALS. Second Edition. Robert E. Madden. Research Institute of America, Incorporated, One Penn Plaza, New York, New York 10119. 1989.

TAX PLANNING FOR INVESTORS: THE EIGHTIES GUIDE TO SECURITIES AND COMMODITIES INVESTMENTS AND TAX SHELTERS. Jack Crestal and Herman M. Schneider. Commerce Clearing House, Incorporated, 4025 West Peterson Avenue, Chicago, Illinois 60646. 1988.

TAX PLANNING FOR PROFESSIONALS. Harold I. Apolinsky. Research Institute of America, Incorporated, One Penn Plaza, New York, New York 10119. 1985.

TAX PLANNING OF REAL ESTATE. Paul E. Anderson. American Law Institute-American Bar Association, Committee on Continuing Professional Education, 4025 Chestnut Street, Philadelphia, Pennsylvania 19104. 1977. (1982 Supplement).

TAX PLANNING STRATEGIES. Lewis D. Solomon and Susan Flax Posner. Callaghan and Company, 155 Pfingsten Road, Deerfield, Illinois 60015. 1990.

TAX PLANNING TECHNIQUES FOR THE CLOSELY HELD CORPORATION. Second Edition. The National Underwriter Company, 420 East Fourth Street, Cincinnati, Ohio 45202. 1985.

TAX REFORM 1986: ANALYSIS AND PLANNING. Arthur and Company. Matthew Bender and Company, Incorporated, 11 Penn Plaza, New York, New York 10001. 1986.

TAX STRATEGY FOR PHYSICIANS. Third Edition. Lawrence Farber. Medical Economics Books, 5 Paragon Drive, Montvale, New Jersey 07645. 1986.

THY WILL BE DONE: A GUIDE TO WILLS, TAXATION, AND ESTATE PLANNING FOR OLDER PERSONS. Eugene J. Daly. Prometheus Books, 700 East Amherst Street, Buffalo, New York 14215. 1990.

THE TOOLS AND TECHNIQUES OF ESTATE PLANNING. Eighth Edition. The National Underwriter Company, 420 East Fourth Street, Cincinnati, Ohio 45202. 1990.

USE OF LIFETIME GIVING IN ESTATE PLANNING. Massachusetts Continuing Legal Education, Incorporated, 20 West Street, Boston, Massachusetts 02111. 1982.

USE OF QUALIFIED AND NON-QUALIFIED BENEFIT PLANS IN ESTATE PLANNING. Massachusetts Continuing Legal Education, Incorporated, 20 West Street Boston, Massachusetts 02111. 1982.

USE OF TRUSTS IN ESTATE PLANNING. Malcolm A. Moore. Practising Law Institute, 810 Seventh Avenue, New York, New York 10019. 1985.

WILL AND TRUST DRAFTING AND ESTATE DRAFTING: WITH FORMS. Randy Spiro. Lega-Books, Division of Charing Cross Publishing Company, 3255 Wilshire Boulevard, Suite 1514, Los Angeles, California 90010. 1985.

WILLS, TRUSTS, AND ESTATE PLANNING: LAW AND TAXATION, CASES AND MATERIALS. Joseph M. Dodge. West Publishing Company, 50 West Kellogg Boulevard, St. Paul, Minnesota 55164-0526. 1988.

ENCYCLOPEDIAS AND DICTIONARIES

ENCYCLOPEDIA OF ESTATE PLANNING. Second Edition. Robert J. Holzman. Boardroom Books, 330 West Forty-Second Street, New York, New York 10036. 1985.

DIGESTS, INDEXES, ABSTRACTS, CITATORS

FEDERAL TAX ARTICLES: INCOME, ESTATE, GIFT, EXCISE, EMPLOYMENT TAXES. Commerce Clearing House, Incorporated, 4025 West Peterson Avenue, Chicago, Illinois 60646. 1969- .

FEDERAL TAXES CITATOR. Prentice-Hall, Incorporated, 113 Sylvan Avenue, Englewood Cliffs, New Jersey 07632. 1943.

INDEX TO FEDERAL TAX ARTICLES. Gersham Goldstein, Editor. Research Institute of America, Incorporated, One Penn Plaza, New York, New York 10119. 1976.

SHEPARD'S FEDERAL TAX CITATIONS. Shepard's/McGraw-Hill, P.O. Box 1235, Colorado Springs, Colorado 80901. 1981- .

SHEPARD'S FEDERAL TAX LOCATOR: COMPLETE INDEX TO ALL THE CURRENT SOURCES OF LAW RELATING TO FEDERAL TAXATION. Shepard's/McGraw-Hill, P. O. Box 1235, Colorado Springs, Colorado 80901. 1974- .

ANNUALS AND SURVEYS

CCH ESTATE PLANNING GUIDE, INCLUDING FINANCIAL PLANNING. Sidney Kess and Bertil Westlin. Commerce Clearing House, Incorporated, 4025 West Peterson Avenue, Chicago, Illinois 60646. Annual.

ESTATE PLANNING INSTITUTE. Practising Law Institute, 810 Seventh Avenue, New York, New York 10019. Annual.

MAJOR TAX PLANNING. Institute on Federal Taxation, University of Southern California. Matthew Bender and Company, Incorporated, 11 Penn Plaza, New York, New York 10001. Annual.

PHILIP E. HECKERLING INSTITUTE ON ESTATE PLANNING. John T. Gaubaty, Editor. University of Miami Law Center. Matthew Bender and Company, Incorporated, 11 Penn Plaza, New York, New York 10001. Annual.

UNIVERSITY OF SOUTHERN CALIFORNIA TAX INSTITUTE. Law Center, University Park, Los Angeles, California 90089-0071. Annual.

LAW REVIEWS AND PERIODICALS

AKRON TAX JOURNAL. University of Akron School of Law, Akron, Ohio 44325. Annual.

ESTATE PLANNERS QUARTERLY. Farnsworth Publishing Company, 78 Randall Avenue, Rockville Center, New York, New York 11570. Quarterly.

ESTATE PLANNING. Research Institute of America, Incorporated, One Penn Plaza, New York, New York 10119. Monthly.

JOURNAL OF STATE TAXATION. Panel Publishers, Incorporated, 14 Plaza Road, Greenvale, New York 11548. Quarterly.

JOURNAL OF TAXATION. Research Institute of America, Incorporated, One Penn Plaza, New York, New York 10119. Monthly.

PROBATE AND PROPERTY. American Bar Association, 750 North Lake Shore Drive, Chicago, Illinois 60611. Bimonthly.

REVIEW OF TAXATION OF INDIVIDUALS. Research Institute of America, Incorporated, One Penn Plaza, New York, New York 10119. Quarterly.

THE TAX ADVISER. American Institute of Certified Public Accountants, 1211 Avenue of the Americas, New York, New York 10036. Monthly.

TAX LAW REVIEW. Research Institute of America, Incorporated, One Penn Plaza, New York, New York 10119. Quarterly.

THE TAX LAWYER. American Bar Association, 750 North Lake Shore Drive, Chicago, Illinois 60611.

TAX AND ESTATE PLANNING

TAXATION FOR LAWYERS. Research Institute of America, Incorporated, One Penn Plaza, New York, New York 10119. Bimonthly.

TAXES: THE TAX MAGAZINE. Commerce Clearing House, Incorporated, 4025 West Peterson Avenue, Chicago, Illinois 60646. Monthly.

TRUSTS AND ESTATES. Communication Channels, Incorporated, 6255 Barfield Road, Atlanta, Georgia 30328. Monthly.

VIRGINIA TAX REVIEW. Virginia Tax Review Association, University of Virginia, School of Law, Charlottesville, Virginia 22901. Semiannual.

NEWSLETTERS AND NEWSPAPERS

THE CHASE REVIEW. Chase Manhattan Bank, 1211 Avenue of the Americas, Thirty-fourth Floor, New York, New York 10036. Quarterly.

ESTATE ADMINISTRATION AND TAX PLANNING FOR THE ELDERLY AND DISABLED. Garland Law Publishing, Incorporated, 136 Madison Avenue, New York, New York 10016. Quarterly.

ESTATE FINANCIAL PLANNERS ALERT. Research Institute of America, Incorporated, 80 Fifth Avenue, New York, New York 10011. Monthly.

ESTATE PLANNING REVIEW. Commerce Clearing House, Incorporated, 4025 West Peterson Avenue, Chicago, Illinois 60646. Monthly.

INSURANCE AND TAX NEWS. Prentice-Hall Professional Newsletters, Englewood Cliffs, New Jersey 07632. Biweekly.

TAX, FINANCIAL AND ESTATE PLANNING FOR THE OWNER OF THE CLOSELY HELD CORPORATION. Panel Publishers, Incorporated, 36 Forty-fourth Street, New York, New York 10036. Monthly.

TAX MANAGEMENT ESTATES, GIFTS, AND TRUSTS JOURNAL. Bureau of National Affairs, Incorporated, 1231 Twenty-fifth Street, Northwest, Washington, D.C. 20037. Bimonthly.

TAXWISE GIVING. Taxwise Giving, 13 Arcadia Road, Old Greenwich, Connecticut 06870. Monthly.

ASSOCIATIONS AND PROFESSIONAL SOCIETIES

SECTION ON TAXATION, AMERICAN BAR ASSOCIATION. 750 North Lake Shore Drive, Chicago, Illinois 60611. (312) 988-5000.

SECTION ON TAXATION, ASSOCIATION OF AMERICAN LAW SCHOOLS. One Dupont Circle, Northwest, Suite 370, Washington D.C. 20036. (202) 296-8851.

RESEARCH CENTERS, INSTITUTES, CLEARINGHOUSES

INSTITUTE FOR CONTINUING EDUCATION IN LAW AND TAXATION. New York University, 11 West Forty-second Street, Room 429, New York, New York 10036. (212) 790-1320.

NATIONAL TAX ASSOCIATION-TAX INSTITUTE OF AMERICA. 5310 East Main Street, Suite 104, Columbus, Ohio 43213. (614) 864-1221.

TAX FOUNDATION. 470 L'Enfant, Southwest, Suite 7112, Washington, D.C. 20024. (202) 863-5454.

ONLINE DATABASES

LEXIS FEDERAL TAX LIBRARY. Mead Data Central, P.O. Box 933, Dayton, Ohio 45401.

LEXIS STATE TAX LIBRARY. Mead Data Central, P.O. Box 933, Dayton, Ohio 45401.

TAX MANAGEMENT ESTATES, GIFTS, AND TRUSTS JOURNAL. Bureau of National Affairs, Incorporated, 1231 Twenty-fifth Street, Northwest, Washington, D.C. 20037.

TAX MANAGEMENT PORTFOLIO SERIES: ESTATES, GIFTS, AND TRUSTS. Bureau of National Affairs, Incorporated, 1231 Twenty-fifth Street, Northwest, Washington, D.C. 20037.

WESTLAW, TAXATION LIBRARY. West Publishing Company, P.O. Box 64526, 50 West Kellogg Boulevard, St. Paul, Minnesota 55164-0526.

AUDIOVISUALS

THE AUDIO ESTATE PLANNER. American Law Institute-American Bar Association, Committee on Continuing Professional Education, 4025 Chestnut Street, Philadelphia, Pennsylvania 19104. 1984. Audiocassette.

CHOICE OF BUSINESS ENTITY AFTER THE TAX REFORM ACT OF 1986. American Law Institute-American Bar Association, Committee on Continuing Professional Education, 4025 Chestnut Street, Philadelphia, Pennsylvania 19104. 1987. Videocassette.

CORPORATE TAX PLANNING. T. Milton Kupfer and Stanford H. Goldberg. New York University Institute on Federal Taxation, Totaltape Publishers Incorporated, P.O. Box 1469, Gainesville, Florida 32605. 1987. Audiocassette.

ESTATE PLANNING COURSE. Sixth Edition. Sidney Kess. Commerce Clearing House, Incorporated, 4025 West Peterson Avenue, Chicago, Illinois 60646. 1984. Audiocassette.

ESTATE PLANNING FOR AND DISTRIBUTION OF EMPLOYEE BENEFITS AFTER 1986 TAX REFORM. Alex M. Brucker. California Continuing Education of the Bar, 2300 Shattuck Avenue, Berkeley, California 84704. 1987. Audiocassette.

A GUIDE TO CORPORATE TAX PLANNING. Sixth Edition. Commerce Clearing House, Incorporated, 4025 West Peterson Avenue, Chicago, Illinois 60646. 1984. Audiocassette.

INDIVIDUAL TAXATION. Francis M. Gaffrey and Mark B. Brumbaugh. New York University Institute on Taxation, Totaltape Publishing, Incorporated, 4251 Southwest Thirteenth Street, Gainesville, Florida 32608. 1987. Audiocassette.

Encyclopedia of Legal Information Sources • 2nd Ed.   **TAX COURT**

POST-MORTEM TAX PLANNING AFTER ERTA. American Bar Association, Real Property, Probate and Trust Law Section, 750 North Lake Shore Drive, Chicago, Illinois 60611. 1983. Videocassette.

TAX PLANNING AFTER THE TAX REFORM ACT OF 1986: A TWO-PART VIDEO PANEL DISCUSSION. Gerald W. Padwe and John L. Withers. Commerce Clearing House, Incorporated, 4025 West Peterson Avenue, Chicago, Illinois 60646. 1986. Videocassette.

TAX PROBLEMS OF CLOSELY HELD CORPORATIONS. Richard M. Feldheim. New York University Institute on Taxation, Totaltape Publishing, Incorporated, 4251 Southwest Thirteenth Street, Gainesville, Florida 32608. 1987. Audiocassette.

TAXATION OF THE SOPHISTICATED INVESTOR. Alex Weinberg. New York University Institute on Taxation, Totaltape Publishing, Incorporated, 4251 Southwest Thirteenth Street, Gainesville, Florida 32608. 1987. Audiocassette.

TRANSFERRING CONTROL OF THE FAMILY BUSINESS. Irving L. Blackman. Commerce Clearing House, Incorporated, 4025 West Peterson Avenue, Chicago, Illinois 60646. 1985. Audiocassette.

TRUST AND GIFT TECHNIQUES FOR FINANCING CHILDREN'S EDUCATION: ALI-ABA VIDEO LAW REVIEW STUDY MATERIALS. American Law Institute-American Bar Association, Committee on Continuing Professional Education, 4025 Chestnut Street, Philadelphia, Pennsylvania 19104. 1986. Videocassette.

TAX COURT
See also: TAX LEGISLATION AND POLICY; TAX PRACTICE AND ENFORCEMENT

STATUTES, CODES, STANDARDS, UNIFORM LAWS

RULES OF PRACTICE AND PROCEDURE OF THE UNITED STATES TAX COURT: EFFECTIVE JANUARY 16, 1984, WITH ADDITIONS AND AMENDMENTS THROUGH SEPTEMBER 7, 1983 AND OCTOBER 15, 1984. Superintendent of Documents, United States Government Printing Office, Washington, D.C. 20402. 1983.

LOOSELEAF SERVICES AND REPORTERS

AMERICAN FEDERAL TAX REPORTS. Prentice-Hall, Incorporated, 113 Sylvan Avenue, Englewood Cliffs, New Jersey 07632. 1958- .

REPORTS OF THE UNITED STATES TAX COURT. Superintendent of Documents, United States Government Printing Office, Washington, D.C. 20402. 1942-

TAX COURT MEMORANDUM DECISIONS. Commerce Clearing House, Incorporated, 4025 West Peterson Avenue, Chicago, Illinois 60646. 1942- .

TAX COURT MEMORANDUM DECISIONS. Prentice-Hall, Incorporated, 113 Sylvan Avenue, Englewood Cliffs, New Jersey 07632. 1942- .

TAX COURT MEMORANDUM DECISIONS. Superintendent of Documents, United States Government Printing Office, Washington, D.C. 20402. 1942- .

TAX COURT REPORTER. Commerce Clearing House, Incorporated, 4025 West Peterson Avenue, Chicago, Illinois 60646. 1942- .

TAX COURT REPORTS. Prentice-Hall, Incorporated, 113 Sylvan Avenue, Englewood Cliffs, New Jersey 07632. 1942- .

HANDBOOKS, MANUALS, FORMBOOKS

HOW TO HANDLE A TAX CONTROVERSY AT THE TAX COURT: ALI-ABA COURSE STUDY MATERIALS. American Law Institute-American Bar Association, Committee on Continuing Professional Education, 4025 Chestnut Street, Philadelphia, Pennsylvania 19104. 1983.

HOW TO HANDLE AND WIN A FEDERAL TAX APPEAL: A COMPLETE GUIDE FOR THE TAX PROFESSIONAL. Robert C. Carlson. Prentice-Hall, Incorporated, 113 Sylvan Avenue, Englewood Cliffs, New Jersey 07632. 1988.

TAX COURT PRACTICE. Seventh Edition. Marshall W. Taylor. American Law Institute-American Bar Association, 4025 Chestnut Street, Philadelphia, Pennsylvania 19104. 1990.

WHEN YOU GO TO TAX COURT: PROCEDURE AND PRACTICE. Twenty-fourth Edition. Commerce Clearing House, Incorporated, 4025 West Peterson Avenue, Chicago, Illinois 60646. 1986.

TEXTBOOKS AND GENERAL WORKS

TAX PROCEDURE AND TAX FRAUD IN A NUTSHELL. Patricia T. Morgan. West Publishing Company, 50 West Kellogg Boulevard, St. Paul, Minnesota 55164-0526. 1990.

LAW REVIEWS AND PERIODICALS

UNITED STATES TAX COURT. Superintendent of Documents, United States Government Printing Office, Washington, D.C. 20402. Monthly.

DIRECTORIES

TAX PROCEDURE DIGEST. Daniel E. Feld and Michael I. Saltzman. Research Institute of America, Incorporated, One Penn Plaza, New York, New York 10119. 1990.

ONLINE DATABASES

LEXIS FEDERAL TAX LIBRARY. Mead Data Central, P.O. Box 933, Dayton, Ohio 45401.

LEXIS STATE TAX LIBRARY. Mead Data Central, P.O. Box 933, Dayton, Ohio 45401.

WESTLAW, TAXATION LIBRARY. West Publishing Company, P.O. Box 64526, 50 West Kellogg Boulevard, St. Paul, Minnesota 55164-0526.

TAX EXEMPT ORGANIZATIONS
See also: ASSOCIATIONS AND NON-PROFIT CORPORATIONS; CORPORATIONS, TAXATION

STATUTES, CODES, STANDARDS, UNIFORM LAWS

FEDERAL INCOME TAX CODE AND REGULATIONS. Commerce Clearing House, Incorporated, 4025 West Peterson Avenue, Chicago, Illinois 60646. Annual.

FEDERAL TAX REGULATIONS. West Publishing Company, P.O. Box 64526, 50 West Kellogg Boulevard, St. Paul, Minnesota 55164-0526. Annual.

INTERNAL REVENUE BULLETIN; CUMULATIVE BULLETIN. United States Department of Treasury, Internal Revenue Service. United States Government Printing Office, Washington, D.C. 20402. Weekly.

INTERNAL REVENUE CODE. West Publishing Company, P.O. Box 64526, 50 West Kellogg Boulevard, St. Paul, Minnesota 55164-0526. Annual.

LOOSELEAF SERVICES AND REPORTERS

FEDERAL TAXES. Prentice-Hall, Incorporated, 113 Sylvan Avenue, Englewood Cliffs, New Jersey 07632. 1919- .

RETIREMENT AND BENEFIT PLANNING: STRATEGY AND DESIGN FOR BUSINESSES AND TAX EXEMPT ORGANIZATIONS. Randolph M. Goodman. Butterworth Legal Publishers, 90 Stiles Road, Salem, New Hampshire 03079. 1991 - .

STANDARD FEDERAL TAX REPORTS. Commerce Clearing House, Incorporated, 4025 West Peterson Avenue, Chicago, Illinois 60646. 1913- .

TAX-EXEMPT ORGANIZATIONS. Prentice-Hall, Incorporated, 113 Sylvan Avenue, Englewood Cliffs, New Jersey 07632. 1973- .

HANDBOOKS, MANUALS, FORMBOOKS

PROTECTING YOUR ORGANIZATION'S TAX-EXEMPT STATUS: A GUIDE FOR NONPROFIT MANAGERS. Mark Bookman. Jossey-Bass, Incorporated, 350 Sansome Street, San Francisco, California 94104. 1992.

QUALIFYING AS A NONPROFIT, TAX-EXEMPT ORGANIZATION: A GUIDE FOR ATTORNEYS, ACCOUNTANTS, AND EXECUTIVE MANAGEMENT. Robert N. Sughrue and Michelle L. Kopnski. Quorum Books, Greenwood Publishing Group, Incorporated, 88 Post Road West, P.O. Box 5007, Westport, Connecticut 06881. 1991.

TAX AND FINANCIAL PLANNING FOR TAX-EXEMPT ORGANIZATIONS: FORMS, CHECKLISTS, PROCEDURES. Jody Blazek. John Wiley and Sons, Incorporated, 605 Third Avenue, New York, New York 10158. 1990.

TEXTBOOKS AND GENERAL WORKS

COUNSELING TAX-EXEMPT CHARITABLE ORGANIZATIONS. Boyd J. Black, David D. Watts and J. Patrick Waley. California Continuing Education of the Bar, 2300 Shattuck Avenue, Berkeley, California 94704. 1985.

THE LAW OF TAX-EXEMPT ORGANIZATIONS. Fifth Edition. Bruce R. Hopkins. John Wiley and Sons, Incorporated, 605 Third Avenue, New York, New York 10158. 1987.

NONPRIVATE FOUNDATIONS: A TAX GUIDE FOR CHARITABLE ORGANIZATIONS. David Ross Gray. Shepard's/McGraw-Hill, P.O. Box 1235, Colorado Springs, Colorado 80901. 1978. (Annual Supplements).

PLANNING TAX-EXEMPT ORGANIZATIONS. Robert J. Desiderio and Scott Taylor. Shepard's/McGraw-Hill, P.O. Box 1235, Colorado Springs, Colorado 80901. 1986. (Annual Supplements).

PRESERVING A TRADITION OF SERVICE: REFLECTIONS ON THE TAX-EXEMPT STATUS OF NOT-FOR-PROFIT HEALTHCARE INSTITUTIONS. J. David Seay. Catholic Health Association of the United States, 4455 Woodson Road, St. Louis, Missouri 63134-0889.

TAX-EXEMPT CHARITABLE ORGANIZATIONS. Third Edition. Paul E. Treusch. American Law Institute-American Bar Association, 4025 Chestnut Street, Philadelphia, Pennsylvania 19104. 1988.

TAX-EXEMPT FINANCING OF NON-GOVERNMENTAL PROJECTS. Henry S. Klaiman and Richard Chirls, co-Chairmen. Practising Law Institute, 810 Seventh Avenue, New York, New York 10019. 1983.

TAX-EXEMPT ORGANIZATIONS. E.C. Lashbrooke, Jr. Quorum Books, Imprint of Greenwood Publishing Group, Incorporated, 88 Post Road West, P.O. Box 5007, Westport, Connecticut 06881. 1985.

DIGESTS, INDEXES, ABSTRACTS, CITATORS

FEDERAL TAX ARTICLES: INCOME, ESTATE, GIFT, EXCISE, EMPLOYMENT TAXES. Commerce Clearing House, Incorporated, 4025 West Peterson Avenue, Chicago, Illinois 60646. 1969.

FEDERAL TAXES CITATOR. Prentice-Hall, Incorporated, 113 Sylvan Avenue, Englewood Cliffs, New Jersey 07632. 1943- .

INDEX TO FEDERAL TAX ARTICLES. Gersham Goldstein, Editor. Research Institute of America, Incorporated, One Penn Plaza, New York, New York 10119. 1975- .

SHEPARD'S FEDERAL TAX CITATIONS. Shepard's/McGraw-Hill, P.O. Box 1235, Colorado Springs, Colorado 80901. 1981- .

SHEPARD'S FEDERAL TAX LOCATOR: COMPLETE INDEX TO ALL THE CURRENT SOURCES OF LAW RELATING TO FEDERAL TAXATION. Shepard's/McGraw-Hill, P.O. Box 1235, Colorado Springs, Colorado 80901. 1974- .

ANNUALS AND SURVEYS

CONFERENCE ON CHARITABLE FOUNDATIONS. New York University. Matthew Bender and Company, Incorporated, 11 Penn Plaza, New York, New York 10001. Biennial.

LAW REVIEWS AND PERIODICALS

JOURNAL OF TAXATION. Research Institute of America, Incorporated, One Penn Plaza, New York, New York 10119. Monthly.

REVIEW OF TAXATION OF INDIVIDUALS. Research Institute of America, Incorporated, One Penn Plaza, New York, New York 10119. Quarterly.

TAX LAW REVIEW. Research Institute of America, Incorporated, One Penn Plaza, New York, New York 10119. Quarterly.

THE TAX LAWYER. American Bar Association, Section of Taxation, 750 North Lake Shore Drive, Chicago, Illinois 60611. Quarterly.

TAXATION FOR LAWYERS. Research Institute of America, Incorporated, One Penn Plaza, New York, New York 10119. Bimonthly.

TAXES: THE TAX MAGAZINE. Commerce Clearing House, Incorporated, 4025 West Peterson Avenue, Chicago, Illinois 60646. Monthly.

VIRGINIA TAX REVIEW. Virginia Tax Review Association, University of Virginia, School of Law, Charlottesville, Virginia 22901. Semiannual.

NEWSLETTERS AND NEWSPAPERS

NON-PROFIT ORGANIZATION TAX LETTER. Organization Management, Incorporated, 13231 Pleasantview Lane, Fairfax, Virginia 22033. Monthly.

ASSOCIATIONS AND PROFESSIONAL SOCIETIES

SECTION ON TAXATION, AMERICAN BAR ASSOCIATION. 750 North Lake Shore Drive, Chicago, Illinois 60611. (312) 988-5000.

SECTION ON TAXATION, ASSOCIATION OF AMERICAN LAW SCHOOLS. One Dupont Circle, Northwest, Suite 370, Washington D.C. 20005. (202) 296-8851.

RESEARCH CENTERS, INSTITUTES, CLEARINGHOUSES

INSTITUTE FOR CONTINUING EDUCATION IN LAW AND TAXATION. New York University, 11 West Forty-second Street, Room 429, New York, New York 10036. (212) 790-1320.

NATIONAL TAX ASSOCIATION-TAX INSTITUTE OF AMERICA. 5310 East Main Street, Suite 104, Columbia, Ohio 43213. (614) 864-1221.

TAX FOUNDATION. 470 L'Enfant, Southwest, Suite 7112, Washington, D.C. 20024. (202) 863-5454.

ONLINE DATABASES

LEXIS FEDERAL TAX LIBRARY. Mead Data Central, P.O. Box 933, Dayton, Ohio 45401.

LEXIS STATE TAX LIBRARY. Mead Data Central, P.O. Box 933, Dayton, Ohio 45401.

WESTLAW, TAXATION LIBRARY. West Publishing Company, P.O. Box 64526, 50 West Kellogg Boulevard, St. Paul, Minnesota 55164-0526.

TAX LEGISLATION AND POLICY

STATUTES, CODES, STANDARDS, UNIFORM LAWS

FEDERAL INCOME TAX CODE AND REGULATIONS. Commerce Clearing House, Incorporated, 4025 West Peterson Avenue, Chicago, Illinois 60646. Annual.

FEDERAL TAX REGULATIONS. West Publishing Company, P.O. Box 64526, 50 West Kellogg Boulevard, St. Paul, Minnesota 55164-0526. Annual.

INTERNAL REVENUE BULLETIN; CUMULATIVE BULLETIN. United States Department of Treasury, Internal Revenue Service. United States Government Printing Office, Washington, D.C. 20402. Weekly.

INTERNAL REVENUE CODE. West Publishing Company, P.O. Box 64526, 50 West Kellogg Boulevard, St. Paul, Minnesota 55164-0526. Annual.

MODEL DOUBLE TAXATION CONVENTION ON ESTATES AND INHERITANCES AND ON GIFTS: REPORT OF THE OECD COMMITTEE ON FISCAL AFFAIRS. Organization for Economic Cooperation and Development, 200 L Street, Northwest, Suite 700, Washington, D.C 20036. 1983.

LOOSELEAF SERVICES AND REPORTERS

FEDERAL TAXES. Prentice-Hall, Incorporated, 113 Sylvan Avenue, Englewood Cliffs, New Jersey 07632. 1919- .

STANDARD FEDERAL TAX REPORTS. Commerce Clearing House, Incorporated, 4025 West Peterson Avenue, Chicago, Illinois 60646. 1913- .

TEXTBOOKS AND GENERAL WORKS

THE COMPLETE INTERNAL REVENUE CODE. January 1987 Edition. Research Institute of America, Incorporated, 90 Fifth Avenue, New York, New York 10011. 1987.

ECONOMIC RECOVERY TAX ACT OF 1981. American Law Institute-American Bar Association, Committee on Continuing Professional Education, 4025 Chestnut Street, Philadelphia, Pennsylvania 19104. 1981.

THE EFFECTS OF TAXATION ON CAPITAL ACCUMULATION. Martin Feldstein, Editor. University of Chicago Press, 5801 Ellis Avenue, Third Floor, South, Chicago, Illinois 60637. 1987.

EMPLOYEE BENEFITS LEGISLATION. Max J. Schwartz and Joseph Simone. Practising Law Institute, 810 Seventh Avenue, New York, New York 10019. 1984.

EXPLANATION OF THE TAX REFORM ACT OF 1986. Commerce Clearing House, Incorporated, 4025 West Peterson Avenue, Chicago, Illinois 60646. 1986.

FEDERAL ESTATE AND GIFT TAX PROJECT: STUDY ON GENERATION- SKIPPING TRANSFERS UNDER THE FEDERAL ESTATE TAX. American Law Institute, 4025 Chestnut Street, Philadelphia, Pennsylvania 19104. 1984.

FEDERAL INCOME TAX PROJECT: OFFICIAL DRAFT. American Law Institute, 4025 Chestnut Street, Philadelphia, Pennsylvania 19104. 1985.

FEDERAL INCOME TAXATION: PRINCIPLES AND POLICIES. Second Edition. Michael J. Graetz. Foundation Press, 615 Merrick Avenue, Westbury, New York 11590. 1988.

FEDERAL POLICY AND THE MOBILITY OF OLDER HOMEOWNERS: THE EFFECTS OF ONE-TIME CAPITAL GAINS EXCLUSION (ISR RESEARCH SERIES). Sandra J. Newman and James Reschousky. Institute for Social Research, University of Michigan, Box 1248, Ann Arbor, Michigan 48106-1248. 1985.

FEDERAL TAX POLICY. Fifth Edition. Joseph A. Pechman. The Brookings Institute, 1775 Massachusetts Avenue, Northwest, Washington, D.C. 20036-2188. 1987.

FEDERAL TAX POLICY AND CHARITABLE GIVING. Charles T. Clotfelter. University of Chicago Press, 5801 Ellis Avenue, Third Floor, South, Chicago, Illinois 60637. 1985.

THE GROWTH EXPERIMENT: HOW THE NEW TAX POLICY IS TRANSFORMING THE U.S. ECONOMY. Lawrence Lindsey. Basic Books, Incorporated, 10 East Fifty-third Street, New York, New York 10022. 1990.

THE INCOME TAX AND THE PROGRESSIVE ERA. John D. Buenker. Garland Publishing, Incorporated, 136 Madison Avenue, New York, New York 10016. 1985.

INCOME TAX COMPLIANCE: A REPORT OF THE ABA SECTION OF TAXATION INVITATIONAL CONFERENCE ON INCOME TAX COMPLIANCE. American Bar Association, 750 North Lake Shore Drive, Chicago, Illinois 60611. 1983.

THE LOGIC OF TAX: FEDERAL INCOME TAX THEORY AND POLICY. Joseph M. Dodge. West Publishing Company, 50 West Kellogg Boulevard, St. Paul, Minnesota 55164-0526. 1989.

MAKING TAX CHOICES. Joseph J. Minarik. Urban Institute Press, 2100 M Street, Northwest, Washington, D.C. 20037. 1985.

MONETARY POLICY, TAXATION, AND INTERNATIONAL INVESTMENT STRATEGY. Victor A. Canto and Arthur B. Laffer. Quorum Books, Greenwood Publishing Group, Incorporated, 88 Post Road West, P.O. Box 5007, Westport, Connecticut 06881. 1990.

OPTIMAL INCOME TAX AND REDISTRIBUTION. Matti Tuomala. Oxford University Press, 200 Madison Avenue, New York, New York 10016. 1990.

PAPERS OF JOHN F. KENNEDY, PRESIDENTIAL PAPERS, PRESIDENT'S OFFICE FILE: PRESIDENTIAL RECORDINGS, TRANSCRIPTS: TAX CUT PROPOSALS. John F. Kennedy Library, Columbia Point, Boston Massachusetts 02125. 1983.

PERSONAL INCOME TAX SYSTEMS UNDER CHANGING ECONOMIC CONDITIONS. Organization for Economic Cooperation and Development, Publications and Information Center, 200 L Street, Northwest, Suite 700, Washington, D.C. 20036. 1986.

POLITICAL ORIGINS OF THE UNITED STATES INCOME TAX. Jerold L. Waltman. University Press of Mississippi, 3825 Ridgewood Road, Jackson, Mississippi 39211. 1985.

THE POLITICS AND DEVELOPMENT OF THE FEDERAL INCOME TAX. John F. Witte. University of Wisconsin Press, 114 North Murray Street, Madison, Wisconsin 53706. 1986.

PRENTICE-HALL'S 1986 SIGNIFICANT STATE TAX DEVELOPMENTS. Ernst and Whinney. Prentice-Hall, Incorporated, 113 Sylvan Avenue, Englewood Cliffs, New Jersey 07632. 1987.

RESEARCH AND PUBLICATION IN VALUE: ADDED TAXATION, A COMPREHENSIVE BACKGROUND AND COMPILATION. Robert P. Crum. Vance Bibliographies, P.O. Box 229, 112 North Charter Street, Monticello, Illinois 61856. 1984.

THE RIA COMPLETE ANALYSIS OF THE 1986 TAX REFORM ACT. Research Institute of America, Incorporated, 90 Fifth Avenue, New York, New York 10011. 1986.

SOCIAL SECURITY: PROSPECTS FOR REAL REFORM. Peter J. Ferrara, Editor. Cato Institute, 224 Second Street, Southeast, Washington, D.C. 20003. 1985.

SPECIAL UPDATE: THE TAX REFORM ACT OF 1986. Peter M Fass, Robert J. Haft, Leslie H. Loffman and Sanford C. Presant. Clark Boardman Company, Limited, 435 Hudson Street, New York, New York 10014. 1986.

TAX ASPECTS OF HIGH TECHNOLOGY OPERATIONS. Deloitte, Haskins and Sells. John Wiley and Sons, Incorporated, 605 Third Avenue, New York, New York 10158. 1985.

TAX CREDITS AND INTERGOVERNMENTAL FISCAL RELATIONS. James Ackley Maxwell. Greenwood Publishing Group, Incorporated, 88 Post Road West, P.O. Box 5007, Westport, Connecticut 06881. 1987.

TAX EXPENDITURES. Stanley S. Surrey and Paul R. McDaniel. Harvard University Press, 79 Garden Street, Cambridge, Massachusetts 02138. 1985.

TAX POLICY AND CORPORATE CONCENTRATION. Alan L. Feld. Lexington Books, Division of D.C. Heath and Company, 125 Spring Street, Lexington, Massachusetts 02173. 1982.

TAX POLICY AND ECONOMIC DEVELOPMENT. Richard M. Bird. Johns Hopkins University Press, 701 West Fortieth Street, Baltimore, Maryland 21211. 1992.

TAX POLICY IN THE TWENTY-FIRST CENTURY. Herbert Stein. John Wiley and Sons, Incorporated, 605 Third Avenue, New York, New York 10158. 1988.

TAX REFORM ACT OF 1986. Practising Law Institute. 810 Seventh Avenue, New York, New York 10019. 1987.

THE TAX REFORM ACT OF 1986: AN ALI-ABA COUSE OF STUDY. Stegan P. Trecker, Planning Chairman. American Law Institute-American Bar Association, Committee on Continuing Professional Education, 4025 Chestnut Street, Philadelphia, Pennsylvania 19104. 1986.

TAX REFORM ACT OF 1986: ANALYSIS AND COMMENTARY. James S. Eustice, Joel D. Kuntz, Charles S. Lewe and Thomas P. Deering. Research Institute of America, Incorporated, One Penn Plaza, New York, New York 10119. 1987.

TAX REFORM ACT OF 1986, LAW AND CONTROLLING COMMITTEE REPORTS. Commerce Clearing House, Incorporated, 4025 West Peterson Avenue, Chicago, Illinois 60646. 1986.

TAX REFORM AND REAL ESTATE. James R. Follain, Editor. Urban Institute Press, 2100 M Street, Northwest, Washington, D.C. 20037. 1986.

TAX REFORM AND THE UNITED STATES ECONOMY. Joseph A. Pechman and Henry J. Aaron, Editors. The Brookings Institute, 1775 Massachusetts Avenue, Northwest, Washington, D.C. 20036-2188. 1987.

TAX REVOLT: THE BATTLE FOR THE CONSTITUTION. Martin A. Larson. Devin-Adair Publications, 6-N Water Street, Greenwich, Connecticut 06830. 1985.

TAXATION, INFLATION AND INTEREST RATES. Books on Demand, 300 North Zeeb Road, Ann Arbor, Michigan 48106-1346. 1984.

TAXING INSURERS: THE REVOLUTION AHEAD. Carolyn Bowers. Washington Business Information, Incorporated, 1117 North Nineteenth Street, Number 200, Arlington, Virginia 22209-1798. 1983.

TRANSFER SPENDING, TAXES, AND THE AMERICAN WELFARE STATE. Wallace C. Peterson. Kluwer Academic Publishers, 101 Philip Drive, Assinippi Park, Norwell, Massachusetts 02061. 1991.

U.S. FOREIGN TAX POLICY: AMERICA'S BERLIN WALL. Institute for Research on the Economics of Taxation. University Press of America, 4720 Boston Way, Lanham, Maryland 20706. 1991.

U.S. INTERNATIONAL TAX POLICY FOR A GLOBAL ENONOMY. Robert Allen Ragland. National Chamber Foundation, 1615 H Street, Northwest, Washington, D.C. 20062. 1991.

UNITED STATES TAXES AND TAX POLICY. David G. Davies. Cambridge University Press, 40 Twentieth Street, New York, New York 10011. 1986.

WORLD TAX REFORM: A PROGRESS REPORT. Joseph A. Pechman. Brookings Institution, 1775 Massachusetts Avenue, Washington, D.C. 20036. 1988.

DIGESTS, INDEXES, ABSTRACTS, CITATORS

FEDERAL TAX ARTICLES: INCOME, ESTATE, GIFT, EXCISE, EMPLOYMENT TAXES. Commerce Clearing House, Incorporated, 4025 West Peterson Avenue, Chicago, Illinois 60646. 1969- .

FEDERAL TAXES CITATOR. Prentice-Hall, Incorporated, 113 Sylvan Avenue, Englewood Cliffs, New Jersey 07632. 1943- .

INDEX TO FEDERAL TAX ARTICLES. Gersham Goldstein, Editor. Research Institute of America, Incorporated, One Penn Plaza, New York, New York 10119. 1975- .

SHEPARD'S FEDERAL TAX CITATIONS. Shepard's/McGraw-Hill, P.O. Box 1235, Colorado Springs, Colorado 80901. 1981- .

SHEPARD'S FEDERAL TAX LOCATOR: COMPLETE INDEX TO ALL THE CURRENT SOURCES OF LAW RELATING TO FEDERAL TAXATION. Shepard's/McGraw-Hill, P. O. Box 1235, Colorado Springs, Colorado 80901. 1974- .

LAW REVIEWS AND PERIODICALS

JOURNAL OF TAXATION. Research Institute of America, Incorporated, One Penn Plaza, New York, New York 10119. Monthly.

TAX LAW REVIEW. Research Institute of America, Incorporated, One Penn Plaza, New York, New York 10119. Quarterly.

THE TAX LAWYER. American Bar Association, Section of Taxation, 750 North Lake Shore Drive, Chicago, Illinois 60611. Quarterly.

TAXATION FOR LAWYERS. Research Institute of America, Incorporated, One Penn Plaza, New York, New York 10119. Bimonthly.

TAXES: THE TAX MAGAZINE. Commerce Clearing House, Incorporated, 4025 West Peterson Avenue, Chicago, Illinois 60646. Monthly.

VIRGINIA TAX REVIEW. Virginia Tax Review Association, University of Virginia, School of Law, Charlottesville, Virginia 22901. Semiannual.

NEWSLETTERS AND NEWSPAPERS

DIGEST OF ACTIVITIES OF CONGRESS. Oliphan and Washington News Service, 1819 H Street, Northwest, Suite 330, Washington, D.C. 20006. Weekly.

PEOPLE AND TAXES. Public Citizens Congress Watch, 215 Pennsylvania Avenue, Southeast, Washington, D.C. 20003. Monthly.

TAX LEGISLATIVE BULLETIN. The Tax Council, 122 C Street, Northwest, Suite 330, Washington, D.C. 20001. Bimonthly.

WEEKLY ALERT. Research Institute of America, Incorporated, 90 Fifth Avenue, New York, New York 10011. Weekly.

TAX LEGISLATION AND POLICY

BIBLIOGRAPHIES

TAX POLICY IN THE UNITED STATES: A SELECTIVE BIBLIOGRAPHY WITH ANNOTATIONS 1960-84. Howard A. Hood, Editor. Alyne Queens Massey Law Library, Vanderbilt University, Nashville, Tennessee 37212. 1985.

ASSOCIATIONS AND PROFESSIONAL SOCIETIES

SECTION ON TAXATION, AMERICAN BAR ASSOCIATION. 750 North Lake Shore Drive, Chicago, Illinois 60611. (312) 988-5000.

SECTION ON TAXATION, ASSOCIATION OF AMERICAN LAW SCHOOLS. One Dupont Circle, Northwest, Suite 370, Washington, D.C. 20036. (202) 296-8851.

RESEARCH CENTERS, INSTITUTES, CLEARINGHOUSES

INSTITUTE FOR CONTINUING EDUCATION IN LAW AND TAXATION. New York University, 11 West Forty-second Street, Room 429, New York, New York 10036. (212) 790-1320.

NATIONAL TAX ASSOCIATION-TAX INSTITUTE OF AMERICA. 5310 East Main Street, Suite 104, Columbus, Ohio 43213. (614) 864-1221.

TAX FOUNDATION. 470 L'Enfant, Southwest, Suite 7112, Washington, D.C. 20024. (202) 863-5454.

ONLINE DATABASES

LEXIS FEDERAL TAX LIBRARY. Mead Data Central, P.O. Box 933, Dayton, Ohio 45401.

LEXIS STATE TAX LIBRARY. Mead Data Central, P.O. Box 933, Dayton, Ohio 45401.

TAX MANAGEMENT WEEKLY REPORT. Bureau of National Affairs, Incorporated, 1231 Twenty-fifth Street, Northwest, Washington, D.C. 20037.

WESTLAW, TAXATION LIBRARY. West Publishing Company, P.O. Box 64526, 50 West Kellogg Boulevard, St. Paul, Minnesota 55164-0526.

AUDIOVISUALS

THE TAX ACT OF 1984: AN EXPLANATION AND ANALYSIS. Sidney Kess. Commerce Clearing House, Incorporated, 4025 West Peterson Avenue, Chicago, Illinois 60646. 1984. Audiocassette.

THE TAX REFORM ACT OF 1986: AN EXPLANATION AND ANALYSIS INCLUDING PLANNING STRATEGIES. Sidney Kess. Commerce Clearing House, Incorporated, 4025 West Peterson Avenue, Chicago, Illinois 60646. 1986.

TAX PRACTICE AND ENFORCEMENT
See also: INTERNAL REVENUE SERVICE; TAX RETURNS; TAX SHELTERS; TAXATION, INTERNATIONAL

STATUTES, CODES, STANDARDS, UNIFORM LAWS

FEDERAL INCOME TAX CODE OF 1954. Prentice-Hall, Incorporated, 113 Sylvan Avenue, Englewood Cliffs, New Jersey 07632. Annual.

FEDERAL TAX REGULATIONS. West Publishing Company, P.O. Box 64526, 50 West Kellogg Boulevard, St. Paul, Minnesota 55164-0526. Annual.

INTERNAL REVENUE BULLETIN; CUMULATIVE BULLETIN. United States Department of Treasury, Internal Revenue Service. United States Government Printing Office, Washington, D.C. 20402. Weekly.

INTERNAL REVENUE CODE. West Publishing Company, P.O. Box 64526, 50 West Kellogg Boulevard, St. Paul, Minnesota 55164-0526. Annual.

LOOSELEAF SERVICES AND REPORTERS

FEDERAL TAX GUIDE. Prentice-Hall, Incorporated, 113 Sylvan Avenue, Englewood Cliffs, New Jersey 07632. 1931- .

FEDERAL TAX REGULATIONS. Research Institute of America, Incorporated, 113 Sylvan Avenue, Englewood Cliffs, New Jersey 07632. 1990- .

FEDERAL TAXES. Prentice-Hall, Incorporated, 113 Sylvan Avenue, Englewood Cliffs, New Jersey 07632. 1919- .

IRS POSITIONS. Commerce Clearing House, Incorporated, 4025 West Peterson Avenue, Chicago, Illinois 60646. 1982- .

IRS PRACTICE AND PROCEDURES TAX PACKAGE. LaVaughn T. Davis. Mark A. Stephens, Limited, 10018 Colesville Road, Silver Spring, Maryland 20901. 1977- .

IRS PUBLICATIONS. Commerce Clearing House, Incorporated, 4025 West Peterson Avenue, Chicago, Illinois 60646. 1977- .

MCGAFFEY TAX ANALYSIS AND FORMS: BUSINESS TRANSACTIONS AND ESTATE PLANNING. Jere D. McGaffey. Callaghan and Company, 155 Pfingsten Road, Deerfield, Illinois 60015. 1977- .

PRIVATE LETTER RULINGS. Prentice-Hall, Incorporated, 113 Sylvan Avenue, Englewood Cliffs, New Jersey 07632. 1977- .

STANDARD FEDERAL TAX REPORTS. Commerce Clearing House, Incorporated, 4025 West Peterson Avenue, Chicago, Illinois 60646. 1913- .

STANDARDS OF TAX PRACTICE. Bernard Wolfman, James P. Holden, and Kenneth L. Harris. Commerce Clearing House, Incorporated, 4025 West Peterson Avenue, Chicago, Illinois 60646. 1991- .

STATE TAX CASES REPORTS. Commerce Clearing House, Incorporated, 4025 West Peterson Avenue, Chicago, Illinois 60646. 1948- .

TAX ACCOUNTING. Durwood L. Alkire. Matthew Bender and Company, Incorporated, 11 Penn Plaza, New York, New York 10001. 1983- .

TAX ACTION COORDINATOR. Research Institute of America, Incorporated, 90 Fifth Avenue, New York, New York 10011. 1970- .

TAX COURT. Prentice-Hall, Incorporated, 113 Sylvan Avenue, Englewood Cliffs, New Jersey 07632. 1921- .

TAX COURT REPORTS. Commerce Clearing House, Incorporated, 4025 West Peterson Avenue, Chicago, Illinois 60646. 1924- .

TAX MANAGEMENT: PRIMARY SOURCES: SERIES IV. Bureau of National Affairs, 1231 Twenty-fifth Street, Northwest, Washington, D.C. 20037. 1982- .

HANDBOOKS, MANUALS, FORMBOOKS

ANNOTATED TAX FORMS: PRACTICE AND PROCEDURE. Sidney I. Roberts. Prentice-Hall, Incorporated, 113 Sylvan Avenue, Englewood Cliffs, New Jersey 07632. 1969. (Bimonthly Supplements).

AUDIT-PROOFING YOUR RETURN. Jack Warren Wade. Macmillan Publishing Company, Incorporated, 866 Third Avenue, New York, New York 10022. 1986.

BATTLING THE IRS: A TAXPAYER'S GUIDE TO RESPONDING TO IRS NOTICES AND ASSESSMENTS. David J. Silverman. Scott Foresman and Company, 1900 East Lake Avenue, Glenview, Illinois 60025. 1991.

BENDER'S TAX RETURN MANUAL. Matthew Bender and Company, Incorporated, 11 Penn Plaza, New York, New York 10001. Annual.

CURRENT LEGAL FORMS WITH TAX ANALYSIS. Jacob Rabkin and Mark H. Johnson. Matthew Bender and Company, Incorporated, 11 Penn Plaza, New York, New York 10001. 1985. (Quarterly Supplements).

EXAMINATION TAX SHELTERS HANDBOOK. Prentice-Hall, Incorporated, 113 Sylvan Avenue, Englewood Cliffs, New Jersey 07632. 1985.

FEDERAL REVENUE FORMS. Prentice-Hall, Incorporated, 113 Sylvan Avenue, Englewood Cliffs, New Jersey 07632. 1974. (Periodic Supplements).

FEDERAL TAX AND RELATED FORMS. Tax Form Library, 518 West Main Street, Louisville, Kentucky 40202. 1984. (Periodic Supplements).

FEDERAL TAX FORMS. Commerce Clearing House, Incorporated, 4025 West Peterson Avenue, Chicago, Illinois 60646. 1973. (Periodic Supplements).

FEDERAL TAX MANUAL. Commerce Clearing House, Incorporated, 4025 West Peterson Avenue, Chicago, Illinois 60646. 1987.

FEDERAL TAXATION PRACTICE AND PROCEDURE. Second Edition. Robert E. Meldman and Thomas E. Mountin. Commerce Clearing House, Incorporated, 4025 West Peterson Avenue, Chicago, Illinois 60646. 1986.

HOW TO HANDLE TAX AUDITS, REQUESTS FOR RULINGS, FRAUD CASES, AND OTHER PROCEDURES BEFORE THE IRS. Irving Schreiber and Carmine Seudere, Editors. Paladin Press, P.O. Box 1307, Boulder, Colorado 80306. 1977. (Periodic Supplements).

HOW TO PRACTICE IRS NO TRICKS, NO MAGIC: A PROCEDURAL MANUAL FOR PRACTITIONERS. Robert S. Schriebman. Commerce Clearing House, Incorporated, 4025 West Peterson Avenue, Chicago, Illinois 60646. 1990.

HOW TO SAVE TIME AND TAXES IN HANDLING ESTATES. John A. Clark. Matthew Bender and Company, Incorporated, 11 Penn Plaza, New York, New York 10001. 1979. (Annual Supplements).

HOW TO SAVE TIME AND TAXES PREPARING FIDUCIARY INCOME TAX RETURNS, FEDERAL AND STATE. Second Edition. Stowell Rounds and Joseph J. O'Connell. Matthew Bender and Company, Incorporated, 11 Penn Plaza, New York, New York 10001. 1985. (Annual Supplements).

HOW TO SAVE TIME AND TAXES PREPARING THE FEDERAL PARTNERSHIP RETURN. Ernest D. Fiore, Jr. Matthew Bender and Company, Incorporated, 11 Penn Plaza, New York, New York 10001. 1985. (Periodic Supplements).

INTERNAL REVENUE MANUAL, ABRIDGED AND ANNOTATED. Bryan E. Gates. Callaghan and Company, 155 Pfingsten Road, Deerfield, Illinois 60015. 1991.

INTERNAL REVENUE MANUAL: ADMINISTRATION. Commerce Clearing House, Incorporated, 4025 West Peterson Avenue, Chicago, Illinois 60646. 1973. (Periodic Supplements).

INTERNAL REVENUE MANUAL: AUDIT. Commerce Clearing House, Incorporated, 4025 West Peterson Avenue, Chicago, Illinois 60646. 1977. (Periodic Supplements).

INTERNAL REVENUE SERVICE PRACTICE AND PROCEDURE DESKBOOK. Second Edition. Ira L. Shafiroff. Practising Law Institute, 810 Seventh Avenue, New York, New York 10019. 1989.

THE IRA HANDBOOK: A COMPLETE GUIDE. Michael P. Pancheri and David H. Flynn. New Century Publishers, Incorporated, Rural Route 1, Box 384C, Route 173 West, Hampton, New Jersey 08827. 1985.

IRS CLASSIFICATION HANDBOOK. Commerce Clearing House, Incorporated, 4025 West Peterson Avenue, Chicago, Illinois 60646. 1987.

IRS COMPLIANCE MANUAL. Prentice-Hall, Incorporated, 113 Sylvan Avenue, Englewood Cliffs, New Jersey 07632. 1982. (Monthly Supplements).

IRS TAX COLLECTION PROCEDURES: A MANUAL FOR PRACTITIONERS. Second Edition. Robert S. Schriebman. Commerce Clearing House, Incorporated, 4025 West Peterson Avenue, Chicago, Illinois 60646. 1988.

NATIONAL TAX TRAINING SCHOOL MASTER FORMS FILE. National Tax Training School, P.O. Box 382, Monsey, New York 10952. 1986- .

OBTAINING IRS PRIVATE LETTER RULINGS: A MANUAL OF FORMS AND PROCEDURES. Gerald W. Padwe, Donald C. Wiese and Isaac W. Zimbalist. Oceana Publications, Incorporated, 75 Main Street, Dobbs Ferry, New York 10522. 1983. (Periodic Supplements).

TAX ASPECTS OF DIVORCE AND SEPARATION. Robert S. Taft. Law Journal-Seminars Press, Incorporated, 111 Eighth Avenue, New York, New York 10011. 1984. (Periodic Supplements).

TAX PRACTICE DESKBOOK. Harrop A. Freeman and Norman D. Freeman. Research Institute of America, Incorporated, One Penn Plaza, New York, New York 10119. 1973. (Annual Supplements).

TAX PRACTICE HANDBOOK. Frank M. Burke, Jr. and Buford Berry. Prentice-Hall, Incorporated, 113 Sylvan Avenue, Englewood Cliffs, New Jersey 07632. 1985.

TEXTBOOKS AND GENERAL WORKS

THE ASSESSMENT AND COLLECTION OF TAX FROM NON-RESIDENTS. International Fiscal Association, Editor. Kluwer Academic Publishers, 101 Philip Drive, Assinippi Park, Norwell, Massachusetts 02061. 1985.

AUDIT-PROOFING YOUR RETURN. Jack Warren Wade. Macmillan Publishing Company, Incorporated, 866 Third Avenue, New York, New York 10022. 1986.

CRIMINAL AND CIVIL TAX FRAUD: LAW, PRACTICE, PROCEDURE. Darrell McGowen, et al. Kluwer Law Book Publishers, Incorporated, 36 West Forty-fourth Street, New York, New York 10036. 1986. (Supplement 1991).

FAMILY LAW AND PRACTICE. Arnold H. Rutkin, General Editor. Matthew Bender and Company, Incorporated, 11 Penn Plaza, New York, New York 10001. 1985. (Periodical Supplements).

FAMILY TAX PLANNING. Ralph S. Rice. Matthew Bender and Company, Incorporated, 11 Penn Plaza, New York, New York 10001. 1960. (Annual Supplements).

FEDERAL INCOME TAX PROCEDURES. Dale Bandy and Randy Swad. Prentice-Hall, Incorporated, 113 Sylvan Avenue, Englewood Cliffs, New Jersey 07632. 1983.

FEDERAL TAX EXAMINATIONS: PROCEDURES, PRACTICE, PLANNING. Michael Muroney. John Wiley and Sons, Incorporated, 605 Third Avenue, New York, New York 10158. 1985.

FEDERAL TAX LIENS. Third Edition. William T. Plumb, Harry Shapiro and Joseph Kovner. American Law Institute-American Bar Association, Committee on Continuing Professional Education, 4025 Chestnut Street, Philadelphia, Pennsylvania 19104. 1972. (1981 Supplement).

FEDERAL TAX PRACTICE. Laurence F. Casey. Callaghan and Company, 155 Pfingsten Road, Deerfield, Illinois 60015. 1955. (Annual).

FEDERAL TAXATION: PRACTICE AND PROCEDURE. Third Edition. Robert E. Meldman and Thomas E. Mountin. Commerce Clearing House, Incorporated, 4025 West Peterson Avenue, Chicago, Illinois 60646. 1988.

FINANCIAL AND CRIMINAL SANCTIONS FOR NONCOMPLIANCES WITH THE INTERNAL REVENUE CODE: ALI-ABA COURSE OF STUDY MATERIALS. American Law Institute-American Bar Association, Committee on Continuing Professional Education, 4025 Chestnut Street, Philadelphia, Pennsylvania 19104. 1987.

FLEXIBLE COMPENSATION PLANS: CASH OR DEFERRED (401K) AND CAFETERIA (125) ARRANGEMENTS. James P. Klein, Chairman. Practising Law Institute, 810 Seventh Avenue, New York, New York 10019. 1984.

GROWING COMPANIES: TAX AND BUSINESS PLANNING FOR THE '80S. American Law Institute, 4025 Chestnut Street, Philadelphia, Pennsylvania 19104. 1983.

HANDLING FEDERAL ESTATE AND GIFT TAXES. Fourth Edition. Joseph Rasch. Lawyers Co-Operative Publishing Company, Aqueduct Building, Rochester, New York 14694. 1984. (with Supplements).

HOW THE TAXPAYER BILL OF RIGHTS AFFECTS YOU. CCH Tax Law Editors. Commerce Clearing House, Incorporated, 4025 West Peterson Avenue, Chicago, Illinois 60646. 1988.

IRS PRACTICE AND PROCEDURE. Second Edition. Michael I. Saltzman. Research Institute of America, Incorporated, One Penn Plaza, New York, New York 10119. 1991.

A LAW UNTO ITSELF: POWER, POLITICS, AND THE IRS. David Burnham. Random House, Incorporated, 201 East Fiftieth Street, New York, New York 10022. 1989.

A LAWYER'S GUIDE TO INTERNATIONAL BUSINESS TRANSACTIONS: UNITED STATES TAXATION OF INTERNATIONAL BUSINESS TRANSACTIONS. Second Edition. American Law Institute-American Bar Association, Committee on Continuing Professional Education, 4025 Chestnut Street, Philadelphia, Pennsylvania 19104. 1982.

LITIGATION OF FEDERAL TAX CONTROVERSIES. Gerald Burnett and Gerald A. Kafka. Shepard's/McGraw-Hill, P.O. Box 1235, Colorado Springs, Colorado 80901. 1986.

MANAGING AN ESTATE PLANNING PRACTICE: CLIENT COMMUNICATION AND AUTOMATIC DRAFTING. Third Edition. Irving Kellogg. California Continuing Education of the Bar, 2300 Shattuck Avenue, Berkeley, California 94704. 1982.

A PRACTICAL GUIDE TO TAX SHELTER LITIGATION. Edward Brodsky. Law Journal-Seminars Press, Incorporated, 111 Eighth Avenue, New York, New York 10011. 1985.

PROCEDURE BEFORE THE INTERNAL REVENUE SERVICE. Sixth Edition. American Law Institute-American Bar Association, Committee on Continuing Professional Education, 4025 Chestnut Street, Philadelphia, Pennsylvania 19104. 1984. (Periodic Supplements).

PROFITABLE WILLS AND ESTATES PRACTICE UNDER THE ALL-NEW TAX LAW SETUP. Third Edition. J. Brooke Aker and Robert Shimer. Executive Reports Corporation, Subsidiary of Prentice-Hall, Incorporated, 113 Sylvan Avenue, Englewood Cliffs, New Jersey 07632. 1982. (Periodic Supplements).

PROTECTING YOUR BUSINESS FROM THE IRS. Robert S. Schriebman. Dow Jones-Irwin, 1818 Ridge Road, Homewood, Illinois 60430. 1987.

REPRESENTING THE BANKRUPT TAXPAYER. Arthur H. Boelter. Callaghan and Company, 155 Pfingsten Road, Deerfield, Illinois 60015. 1991.

SAVING TIME AND TAXES IN PLANNING AND PREPARING ESTATE, GIFT AND FIDUCIARY RETURNS. George M. Schain. Gower Publishing Company, Old Post Road, Brookfield, Vermont 05036. 1985.

TAX ASPECTS OF BUYING AND SELLING CORPORATE BUSINESSES. J. Clifton Fleming. Shepard's/McGraw-Hill, P.O. Box 1235, Colorado Springs, Colorado 80901. 1984.

TAX ASPECTS OF DIVORCE AND SEPARATION. Robert S. Taft. Law Journal-Seminars Press, Incorporated, 111 Eighth Avenue, New York, New York 10011. 1984. (Periodic Supplements).

THE TAX AUDIT ANSWER BOOK. Panel Publishers, Incorporated, 36 Forty-fourth Street, New York, New York 10036. 1985.

TAX AUDIT GUIDELINES FOR INTERNAL REVENUE EXAMINERS: AS ISSUED BY THE INTERNAL REVENUE SERVICE, APRIL 23, 1985. Prentice-Hall, Incorporated, 113 Sylvan Avenue, Englewood Cliffs, New Jersey 07632. 1985.

TAX COMPLIANCE AFTER TEFRA: DEALING WITH THE NEW REPORTING REQUIREMENTS AND PENALTIES. Arthur H. Kroll. Practising Law Institute, 810 Seventh Avenue, New York, New York 10019. 1983.

TAX COURT PRACTICE. Seventh Edition. Marc J. Winter and Brian J. Seery. American Law Institute-American Bar Association, Committee on Continuing Professional Education, 4025 Chestnut Street, Philadelphia, Pennsylvania 19104. 1990.

TAX FRAUD: AUDITS, INVESTIGATIONS, PROSECUTIONS. Robert S. Fink. Matthew Bender and Company, Incorporated, 11 Penn Plaza, New York, New York 10001. 1980. (Annual Supplements).

TAX POLICY AND ECONOMIC DEVELOPMENT. Richard M. Bird. Johns Hopkins University Press, 701 West Fortieth Street, Baltimore, Maryland 21211. 1992.

TAX PROCEDURE AND TAX FRAUD: CASES AND MATERIALS. Third Edition. Marvin J. Garbis, Patricia T. Morgan, and Ronald B. Rubin. West Publishing Company, 50 West Kellogg Boulevard, St. Paul, Minnesota 55164-0526. 1991.

TAX RETURN PREPARER'S LIABILITY: GUIDELINES FOR PROFESSIONAL RESPONSIBILITIES. Jules Ritholz and Barry J. London. Prentice-Hall, Incorporated, 113 Sylvan Avenue, Englewood Cliffs, New Jersey 07632. 1985.

TAX STRATEGIES: MAKING THE RIGHT DECISION. Rolf Auster. Commerce Clearing House, Incorporated, 4025 West Peterson Avenue, Chicago, Illinois 60646. 1983.

UNDERSTANDING IRS COMMUNICATIONS. CCH Tax Law Editors. Commerce Clearing House, Incorporated, 4025 West Peterson Avenue, Chicago, Illinois 60646. 1989.

WHEN YOU GO TO THE TAX COURT: PROCEDURE AND PRACTICE. Twenty-fourth Edition. Commerce Clearing House, Incorporated, 4025 West Peterson Avenue, Chicago, Illinois 60646. 1986.

DIGESTS, INDEXES, ABSTRACTS, CITATORS

FEDERAL TAX ARTICLES: INCOME, ESTATE, GIFT, EXCISE, EMPLOYMENT TAXES. Commerce Clearing House, Incorporated, 4025 West Peterson Avenue, Chicago, Illinois 60646. 1969- .

FEDERAL TAXES CITATOR. Prentice-Hall, Incorporated, 113 Sylvan Avenue, Englewood Cliffs, New Jersey 07632. 1943- .

INDEX TO FEDERAL TAX ARTICLES. Gersham Goldstein, Editor. Research Institute of America, Incorporated, One Penn Plaza, New York, New York 10119. 1976.

SHEPARD'S FEDERAL TAX CITATIONS. Shepard's/McGraw-Hill, P.O. Box 1235, Colorado Springs, Colorado 80901. 1981- .

SHEPARD'S FEDERAL TAX LOCATOR: COMPLETE INDEX TO ALL THE CURRENT SOURCES OF LAW RELATING TO FEDERAL TAXATION. Shepard's/McGraw-Hill, P.O. Box 1235, Colorado Springs, Colorado 80901. 1974- .

ANNUALS AND SURVEYS

FEDERAL TAX COMPLIANCE REPORTER. Commerce Clearing House, Incorporated, 4025 West Peterson Avenue, Chicago, Illinois 60646. Annual.

LAW REVIEWS AND PERIODICALS

JOURNAL OF TAXATION. Research Institute of America, Incorporated, One Penn Plaza, New York, New York 10119. Monthly.

THE PRACTICAL TAX LAWYER. American Law Institute-American Bar Association, Committee on Continuing Professional Education, 4025 Chestnut Street, Philadelphia, Pennsylvania 19104. Quarterly.

TAX LAW REVIEW. Research Institute of America, Incorporated, One Penn Plaza, New York, New York 10119. Quarterly.

THE TAX LAWYER. American Bar Association, Section of Taxation, 750 North Lake Shore Drive, Chicago, Illinois 60611. Quarterly.

TAXATION FOR LAWYERS. Research Institute of America, Incorporated, One Penn Plaza, New York, New York 10119. Bimonthly.

TAXES: THE TAX MAGAZINE. Commerce Clearing House, Incorporated, 4025 West Peterson Avenue, Chicago, Illinois 60646. Monthly.

VIRGINIA TAX REVIEW. Virginia Tax Review Association, University of Virginia, School of Law, Charlottesville, Virginia 22901. Semiannual.

NEWSLETTERS AND NEWSPAPERS

BNA'S WEEKLY TAX REPORT. Bureau of National Affairs, 1231 Twenty-fifth Street, Northwest, Washington, D.C. 20037. Weekly.

BRENNAN REPORTS. Brennan Reports, Incorporated, P.O. Box 882, Valley Forge, Pennsylvania 19482. Monthly.

DAILY TAX REPORT. Bureau of National Affairs, 1231 Twenty-fifth Street, Northwest, Washington, D.C. 20037. Daily.

INTERNAL REVENUE BULLETIN; CUMULATIVE BULLETIN. United States Department of Treasury, Internal Revenue Service. United States Government Printing Office, Washington, D.C. 20402. Weekly.

IRS AUDIT ALERT. Rosenfeld Emanuel, Incorporated, 481 Main Street, New Rochelle, New York 10801. Monthly.

IRS PRACTICE ALERT. Research Institute of America, Incorporated, One Penn Plaza, New York, New York 10119. Monthly.

KESS TAX PRACTICE REPORT. Research Institute of America, Incorporated, One Penn Plaza, New York, New York 10119. Monthly.

SECTION OF TAXATION NEWSLETTER. American Bar Association, Taxation Section, 750 North Lake Shore Drive, Chicago, Illinois 60611. Quarterly.

TAX ADMINISTRATIVE NEWS. Federation of Tax Administrators, 444 North Capital Street, Northwest, Washington, D.C. 20001. Monthly.

TAX AVOIDANCE DIGEST. Euler Enterprises, Incorporated, 4853 Cordell Avenue, Bethesda, Maryland 20814. Monthly.

TAX DAY REPORT. Commerce Clearing House, Incorporated, 4025 West Peterson Avenue, Chicago, Illinois 60646. Daily.

TAX LITERATURE REPORT. Symposia Press, P.O. Box 418, Moorestown, New Jersey 08057. 46 Issues per year.

UNITED STATES TAX WEEK. Matthew Bender and Company, Incorporated, 589 East Forty-fifth Street, New York, New York 10001. Weekly.

DIRECTORIES

TAX PROCEDURE DIGEST. Daniel E. Feld and Michael I. Saltzman. Warren, Gorham, and Lamont, Incorporated, One Penn Plaza, New York, New York 10119. 1990.

ASSOCIATIONS AND PROFESSIONAL SOCIETIES

COMMISSION ON TAXPAYER COMPLIANCE, AMERICAN BAR ASSOCIATION. 750 North Lake Shore Drive, Chicago, Illinois 60611. (312) 988-5000.

SECTION ON TAXATION, AMERICAN BAR ASSOCIATION. 750 North Lake Shore Drive, Chicago, Illinois 60611. (312) 988-5000.

SECTION ON TAXATION, ASSOCIATION OF AMERICAN LAW SCHOOLS. One Dupont Circle, Northwest, Suite 370, Washington, D.C. 20036. (202) 296-8851.

RESEARCH CENTERS, INSTITUTES, CLEARINGHOUSES

INSTITUTE FOR CONTINUING EDUCATION IN LAW AND TAXATION. New York University, 11 West Forty-second Street, Room 429, New York, New York 10036. (212) 790-1320.

NATIONAL TAX ASSOCIATION-TAX INSTITUTES OF AMERICA. 5310 East Main Street, Suite 104, Columbus, Ohio 43213. (614) 864-1221.

TAX FOUNDATION. 470 L'Enfant, Southwest, Suite 7112, Washington, D.C. 20024. (202) 863-5454.

ONLINE DATABASES

LEXIS FEDERAL TAX LIBRARY. Mead Data Central, P.O. Box 933, Dayton, Ohio 45401.

LEXIS STATE TAX LIBRARY. Mead Data Central, P.O. Box 933, Dayton, Ohio 45401.

WESTLAW, TAXATION LIBRARY. West Publishing Company, P.O. Box 64526, 50 West Kellogg Boulevard, St. Paul, Minnesota 55164-0526.

AUDIOVISUALS

CRIMINAL TAX FRAUD CONFERENCE. Bureau of National Affairs, 1231 Twenty-fifth Street, Northwest, Washington, D.C. 20037. Annual. Audiocassette.

INS AND OUTS OF IRS PRACTICE AND PROCEDURE. George M. Schain. Commerce Clearing House, Incorporated, 4025 West Peterson Avenue, Chicago, Illinois 60646. 1985. Audiocassette.

RESPONSIBILITIES OF TAX PRACTITIONERS. Mortimer M. Caplin and Leslie Shapiro. New York University Institute on Federal Taxation, Totaltape Publishing, Incorporated, 4521 Southwest Thirteenth Street, Gainesville, Florida 32608. 1987. Audiocassette.

TAX FRAUD. American Bar Association, 750 North Lake Shore Drive, Chicago, Illinois 60611. 1987. Videotape.

TAX RETURNS
See also: INTERNAL REVENUE SERVICE; TAX SHELTERS

STATUTES, CODES, STANDARDS, UNIFORM LAWS

FEDERAL INCOME TAX CODE AND REGULATIONS. Commerce Clearing House, Incorporated, 4025 West Peterson Avenue, Chicago, Illinois 60646. Annual.

FEDERAL TAX REGULATIONS. West Publishing Company, P.O. Box 64526, 50 West Kellogg Boulevard, St. Paul, Minnesota 55164-0526. Annual.

INTERNAL REVENUE BULLETIN; CUMULATIVE BULLETIN. United States Department of Treasury, Internal Revenue Service. United States Government Printing Office, Washington, D.C. 20402. Weekly.

INTERNAL REVENUE CODE. West Publishing Company, P.O. Box 64526, 50 West Kellogg Boulevard, St. Paul, Minnesota 55164-0526. Annual.

LOOSELEAF SERVICES AND REPORTERS

FEDERAL TAXES. Prentice-Hall, Incorporated, 113 Sylvan Avenue, Englewood Cliffs, New Jersey 07632. 1919- .

INFORMATION RETURNS GUIDE. CCH Tax Law Editors. Commerce Clearing House, Incorporated, 4025 West Peterson Avenue, Chicago, Illinois 60646. 1987- .

INTEREST AND DIVIDENDS: WITHOLDING, INFORMATION RETURNS. Commerce Clearing House, Incorporated, 4025 West Peterson Avenue, Chicago, Illinois 60646. 1982- .

STANDARD FEDERAL TAX REPORTS. Commerce Clearing House, Incorporated, 4025 West Peterson Avenue, Chicago, Illinois 60646. 1913- .

TAX PREPARER LIABILITY. Illinois Institute of Continuing Legal Education, 2395 West Jefferson Street, Springfield, Illinois 62702. 1981- .

TAX PREPARERS LIABILITY SERVICE. Research Institute of America, Incorporated, 90 Fifth Avenue, New York, New York 10011. 1977- .

HANDBOOKS, MANUALS, FORMBOOKS

THE BANK INCOME TAX RETURN MANUAL: WITH SPECIMEN FILLED-IN 1983 RETURNS. Robert M. Dolgin and Winn Booth. Research Institute of America, Incorporated, One Penn Plaza, New York, New York 10119. 1984.

BENDER'S TAX RETURN MANUAL FOR 1987. Ernest D. Fiorce, Jr., Susan Z. Frayman and Stephan L. Gillan. Matthew Bender and Company, Incorporated, 11 Penn Plaza, New York, New York 10001. 1987.

THE CONSOLIDATED TAX RETURN: PRINCIPLES, PRACTICE, PLANNING. Fourth Edition. Jack Crestol, Kevin H. Hennessey, and Anthony P. Rua. Research Institute of America, Incorporated, One Penn Plaza, New York, New York 10119. 1990. (Annual Supplements).

CONSOLIDATED TAX RETURNS: A TREATISE ON THE LAW OF CONSOLIDATED FEDERAL INCOME TAX RETURNS. Third Edition. Fred W. Pool, Jr. Callaghan and Company, 155 Pfingsten Road, Deerfield, Illinois 60015. 1990. (Periodic Supplements).

CONSOLIDATED TAX RETURNS 1985: A COURSE HANDBOOK. Practising Law Institute, 810 Seventh Avenue, New York, New York 10019. 1985.

ESTATE, GIFT, TRUST AND FIDUCIARY TAX RETURNS: PLANNING AND PREPARATION: 1987 EDITION. George M. Schain. Garland Publishing, Incorporated, 136 Madison Avenue, New York, New York 10016. 1987.

FEDERAL INCOME TAX SPECIMEN RETURNS: CORPORATION, PARTNERSHIP, AND FIDUCIARY. Prentice-Hall, Incorporated, 113 Sylvan Avenue, Englewood Cliffs, New Jersey 07632. 1984.

FEDERAL INCOME TAX SPECIMEN RETURNS: INDIVIDUAL: HOW TO SAVE TIME AND MONEY IN FILING YOUR 1982 PERSONAL TAX RETURN. Prentice-Hall, Incorporated, 113 Sylvan Avenue, Englewood Cliffs, New Jersey 07632. 1983.

FEDERAL TAX AND RELATED FORMS. Tax Form Library, 518 West Main Street, Louisville, Kentucky 40202. 1984. (Periodic Supplements).

FEDERAL TAX FORMS. Commerce Clearing House, Incorporated, 4025 West Peterson Avenue, Chicago, Illinois 60646. 1973. (Periodic Supplements).

FEDERAL TAX MANUAL. Commerce Clearing House, Incorporated, 4025 West Peterson Avenue, Chicago, Illinois 60646. (Annual Supplements).

HOW TO SAVE TIME AND TAXES IN HANDLING ESTATES. Second Edition. Matthew Bender and Company, Incorporated, 11 Penn Plaza, New York, New York 10001. 1979 (Annual Supplements).

HOW TO SAVE TIME AND TAXES PREPARING FIDUCIARY INCOME TAX RETURNS. Second Edition. Stowell Rounds and Joseph J. O'Connell. Matthew Bender and Company, Incorporated, 11 Penn Plaza, New York, New York 10001. 1985 (Annual Supplements).

ISSUES, DEVELOPMENTS AND OPPORTUNITIES IN CONSOLIDATED RETURNS. Lawrence M. Axelrod. Touche Ross Seminar and Conference Division, P.O. Box 22189, Washington, D.C. 20033-0189. 1987.

1986 TAX GUIDE FOR COLLEGE TEACHERS AND OTHER COLLEGE PERSONNEL. Academic Information Service, Incorporated, P.O. Box 929, College Park, Maryland 20740. 1986.

PREPARATION OF THE FIDUCIARY INCOME TAX RETURN, 1989. Samuel H. Laitman, Chairman. Practising Law Institute, 810 Seventh Avenue, New York, New York 10019. 1989.

PREPARING THE FEDERAL PARTNERSHIP RETURN. Second Edition Ted D. Englebrecht, Bruce K. Benesh, Betty R. Jackson, and Rodger A. Bolling. Matthew Bender and Company, Incorporated, 11 Penn Plaza, New York, New York 10001. 1987.

RIA'S TAX RETURN LIBRARY. Research Institute of America, Incorporated, 90 Fifth Avenue, New York, New York 10011. 1987.

SAVING TIME AND TAXES IN PLANNING AND PREPARING ESTATE, TRUST, AND FIDUCIARY RETURNS. George M. Schain. Gower Publishing Company, Old Post Road, Brookfield, Vermont 05036. 1984.

STOCK VALUES AND DIVIDENDS FOR 1987 TAX PURPOSES: GENERAL EDITION. Commerce Clearing House, Incorporated, 4025 West Peterson Avenue, Chicago, Illinois 60646. 1987.

TAX RETURN PREPARER'S LIABILITY: GUIDELINES FOR PROFESSIONAL RESPONSIBILITIES. Jules Ritholz and Barry J. London. Prentice-Hall, Incorporated, 113 Sylvan Avenue, Englewood Cliffs, New Jersey 07632. 1985.

1040 PREPARATION: 1988 EDITION. Sidney Kess and Ben Eisenberg. Commerce Clearing House, Incorporated, 4025 West Peterson Avenue, Chicago, Illinois 60646. 1988.

TEXTBOOKS AND GENERAL WORKS

AMERICAN BAR ASSOCIATION COMMISSION ON TAXPAYER COMPLIANCE REPORT AND RECOMMENDATONS, JULY 1987. American Bar Association, 750 North Lake Shore Drive, Chicago, Illinois 60611. 1987.

AUDIT-PROOF YOUR TAX RETURN. Jack Warren Wade, Jr. New American Library, 1633 Broadway, New York, New York 10019. 1987.

FEDERAL INCOME TAXATION: 1990 TAX RETURNS, 1991 TAX PLANNING. Harold Q. Langenderfer. South-Western Publishing Company, 5101 Madison Road, Cincinnati, Ohio 45227. 1991.

HOW TO PREPARE FOR A MEETING WITH YOUR TAX PROFESSIONAL. Thomas W. Moffitt. Scott, Foresman and Company, 1900 East Lake Avenue, Glenview, Illinois 60025. 1990.

INCOME TAX FUNDAMENTALS FOR 1990 TAX RETURNS. James F. Hopson, Dale W. Spradling, and Kent W. Meyer. Dow Jones-Irwin, 1818 Ridge Road, Homewood, Illinois 60430. 1991.

LAVENTHOL AND HORWATH SMALL BUSINESS TAX PREPARATION BOOK. Albert B. Ellentuck. Avon Books, 105 Madison Avenue, New York, New York 10016. 1989.

1990 TAX RETURN PRATICE PROBLEMS FOR CORPORATIONS, S CORPORATIONS, AND PARTNERSHIPS. Marguerite R. Hutton. Dow Jones-Irwin, 1818 Ridge Road, Homewood, Illinois 60430. 1991.

PREPARING THE 1120 RETURN. Joseph R. Oliver. Prentice-Hall, Incorporated, 113 Sylvan Avenue, Englewood Cliffs, New Jersey 07632. 1990.

PREPARING THE 1040 RETURN. Franklyn E. Lee, Lawrence B. Berkowitz, and Thomas Lechowicz. Prentice-Hall, Incorporated, 113 Sylvan Avenue, Englewood Cliffs, New Jersey 07632. 1990.

SPROUSE'S HOW TO SURVIVE A TAX AUDIT: WHAT TO DO BEFORE AND AFTER YOU HEAR FROM THE IRS. Mary L. Sprouse. Penguin Books, 375 Hudson Street, New York, New York 10014. 1988.

THE USE OF COMPUTERS IN TAX RETURN PREPARATION. American Institute of Certified Public Accountants, 1211 Avenue of the Americas, New York, New York 10036-8775. 1987.

DIGESTS, INDEXES, ABSTRACTS, CITATORS

FEDERAL TAX ARTICLES: INCOME, ESTATE, GIFT, EXCISE, EMPLOYMENT TAXES. Commerce Clearing House, Incorporated, 4025 West Peterson Avenue, Chicago, Illinois 60646. 1969- .

FEDERAL TAXES CITATOR. Prentice-Hall, Incorporated, 113 Sylvan Avenue, Englewood Cliffs, New Jersey 07632. 1943- .

INDEX TO FEDERAL TAX ARTICLES. Gersham Goldstein, Editor. Research Institute of America, Incorporated, One Penn Plaza, New York, New York 10119. 1975- .

SHEPARD'S FEDERAL TAX CITATIONS. Shepard's/McGraw-Hill, P.O. Box 1235, Colorado Springs, Colorado 80901. 1981- .

SHEPARD'S FEDERAL TAX LOCATOR: COMPLETE INDEX TO ALL THE CURRENT SOURCES OF LAW RELATING TO FEDERAL TAXATION. Shepard's/McGraw-Hill, P.O. Box 1235, Colorado Springs, Colorado 80901. 1974- .

LAW REVIEWS AND PERIODICALS

JOURNAL OF TAXATION. Research Institute of America, Incorporated, One Penn Plaza, New York, New York 10119. Monthly.

REVIEW OF TAXATION OF INDIVIDUALS. Research Institute of America, Incorporated, One Penn Plaza, New York, New York 10119. Quarterly.

TAX LAW REVIEW. Research Institute of America, Incorporated, One Penn Plaza, New York, New York 10119. Quarterly.

THE TAX LAWYER. American Bar Association, Section of Taxation, 750 North Lake Shore Drive, Chicago, Illinois 60611. Quarterly.

TAXATION FOR LAWYERS. Research Institute of America, Incorporated, One Penn Plaza, New York, New York 10119. Bimonthly.

TAXES: THE TAX MAGAZINE. Commerce Clearing House, Incorporated, 4025 West Peterson Avenue, Chicago, Illinois 60646. Monthly.

VIRGINIA TAX REVIEW. Virginia Tax Review Association, University of Virginia, School of Law, Charlottesville, Virginia 22901. Semiannual.

NEWSLETTERS AND NEWSPAPERS

CONSOLIDATED RETURNS TAX REPORT. Faulkner and Gray, 106 Fulton Street, New York, New York 10038. Monthly.

Encyclopedia of Legal Information Sources • 2nd Ed.   TAX SHELTERS

ASSOCIATIONS AND PROFESSIONAL SOCIETIES

SECTION ON TAXATION, AMERICAN BAR ASSOCIAITON. 750 North Lake Shore Drive, Chicago, Illinois 60611. (312) 988-5000.

SECTION ON TAXATION, ASSOCIATION OF AMERICAN LAW SCHOOLS. One Dupont Circle, Northwest, Suite 370, Washington D.C. 20036. (202) 296-8851.

RESEARCH CENTERS, INSTITUTES, CLEARINGHOUSES

INSTITUTE FOR CONTINUING EDUCATION IN LAW AND TAXATION. New York University, 11 West Forty-second Street, Room 429, New York, New York 10036. (202) 790-1320.

NATIONAL TAX ASSOCIATION-TAX INSTITUTE OF AMERICA. 5310 East Main Street, Suite 104, Columbus, Ohio 43213. (614) 864-1221.

TAX FOUNDATION. 470 L'Enfant, Southwest, Suite 7112, Washington, D.C. 20024. (202) 863-5454.

ONLINE DATABASES

LEXIS FEDERAL TAX LIBRARY. Mead Data Central, P.O. Box 933, Dayton, Ohio 45401.

LEXIS STATE TAX LIBRARY. Mead Data Central, P.O. Box 933, Dayton, Ohio 45401.

WESTLAW, TAXATION LIBRARY. West Publishing Company, P.O. Box 64526, 50 West Kellogg Boulevard, St. Paul, Minnesota 55164-0526.

AUDIOVISUALS

PREPARERS LIABILITY. Third Edition. George M. Schain. Commerce Clearing House, Incorporated, 4025 West Peterson Avenue, Chicago, Illinois 60646. 1985. Audiocassette.

RESPONSIBILITIES OF TAX PRACTITIONERS. Mortimer M. Caplin and Leslie Shapiro. New York University Institute on Federal Taxation, Totaltape Publishing, Incorporated, 4521 Southwest Thirteenth Street, Gainesville, Florida 32608. 1987. Audiocassette.

COMPUTER-ASSISTED LEGAL INSTRUCTION

WEST'S FEDERAL TAXATION. TAX RETURN PREPARATION WITH TURBOTAX V. 7.01. Sam A. Hicks, David M. Maloney, and ChipSoft, Inc. West Publishing Company, 50 West Kellogg Boulevard, St. Paul, Minnesota 55164-0526. 1990.

TAX SHELTERS
See also: INTERNAL REVENUE SERVICE

STATUTES, CODES, STANDARDS, UNIFORM LAWS

FEDERAL INCOME TAX CODE AND REGULATIONS. Commerce Clearing House, Incorporated, 4025 West Peterson Avenue, Chicago, Illinois 60646.

FEDERAL TAX REGULATIONS. West Publishing Company, P.O. Box 64526, 50 West Kellogg Boulevard, St. Paul, Minnesota 55164-0526. Annual.

INTERNAL REVENUE BULLETIN; CUMMULATIVE BULLETIN. United States Department of Treasury, Internal Revenue Service. United States Government Printing Office, Washington D.C. 20402. Weekly.

INTERNAL REVENUE CODE. West Publishing Company, P.O. Box 64526, 50 West Kellogg Boulevard, St. Paul, Minnesota 55164-0526. Annual.

LOOSELEAF SERVICES AND REPORTERS

FEDERAL TAX PLANNING. Richard A. Westin. Shepard's/McGraw-Hill, P.O. Box 1235, Colorado Springs, Colorado 80901. 1990- .

FEDERAL TAX SHELTER LETTER RULINGS. National Law and Health Publishing 99 Painters Mill Road, Owings Mills, Maryland 21117. 1981- .

FEDERAL TAX SHELTER REVENUE RULINGS. National Law and Health Publishing, 99 Painters Mill Road, Owings Mills, Maryland 21117. 1980- .

FEDERAL TAXES. Prentice-Hall, Incorporated, 113 Sylvan Avenue, Englewood Cliffs, New Jersey 07632. 1919- .

HOW TO USE TAX SHELTERS TODAY. Revised Edition. Irving Schreiber and Joseph P. Sullivan, Editors. Paladin Press, P.O. Box 1307, Boulder, Colorado 80306. 1980- .

STANDARD FEDERAL TAX REPORTS. Commerce Clearing House, Incorporated, 4025 West Peterson Avenue, Chicago, Illinois 60646. 1913- .

TAX ASPECTS OF REAL ESTATE INVESTMENTS: A PRACTICAL GUIDE FOR STRUCTURING REAL ESTATE TRANSACTIONS. Peter M. Fass. Clark Boardman Company, Limited, 435 Hudson Street, New York, New York 10014. 1988- .

TAX HAVENS OF THE WORLD. Walter H. Diamond and D. B. Diamond. Matthew Bender and Company, Incorporated, 11 Penn Plaza, New York, New York 10001. 1974- .

TAX SHELTERED INVESTMENTS. Third Edition. Robert J. Haft and Peter M. Fass. Boardroom Books, 330 West Forty-Second Street, New York, New York 10036. 1981- .

TAXATION OF PASSIVE ACTIVITIES. Neil Kimmelfield. Prentice-Hall, Incorporated, 113 Sylvan Avenue, Englewood Cliffs, New Jersey 07632. 1989- .

HANDBOOKS, MANUALS, FORMBOOKS

THE CROSS-OVER POINT: A GUIDE FOR TAX SHELTER OWNERS. John Pritchard. Varick Financial Press, P.O. Box 8652, Sommerville, New Jersey 08876. 1988.

EXAMINATION TAX SHELTER HANDBOOK. Prentice-Hall, Incorporated, 113 Sylvan Avenue, Englewood Cliffs, New Jersey 07632. 1985.

HOW TO TURN YOUR CLOSELY HELD CORPORATION INTO A PERSONAL TAX SHELTER. Second Edition. Irving L. Blackman. Commerce Clearing House, Incorporated, 4025 West Peterson Avenue, Chicago, Illinois 60646. 1985.

THE NEW GUIDE TO TAX SHELTERED INVESTMENTS: HOW TO EVALUATE AND BUY TAX-FAVORED INVESTMENTS THAT PERFORM. G. Timothy Haight and John C. Chanoski. Probus Publishing Company, Incorporated, 118 North Linton, Chicago, Illinois 60606. 1986.

A PRACTICAL GUIDE TO TAX SHELTER LITIGATION. Edward Brodsky. New York Law Publishing Company, 111 Eighth Avenue, New York, New York 10011. 1985.

REAL ESTATE TAX SHELTER TECHNIQUES: EXPLANATION AND PRACTICAL GUIDE. Jack Kusnet. Research Institute of America, Incorporated, One Penn Plaza, New York, New York 10119. 1982.

TAX HAVEN INVESTING: A GUIDE TO OFFSHORE BANKING AND INVESTMENT OPPORTUNITIES. Richard B. Miller. Probus Publishing Company, 118 North Linton Street, Chicago, Illinois 60606. 1988.

TAX SHELTERED INVESTMENTS HANDBOOK. Robert J. Haft, Peter M Fass, et al. Clark Boardman Company, Limited, 435 Hudson Street, New York, New York 10014. Annual.

TAX SHELTERS: A GUIDE FOR INVESTORS AND THEIR ADVISORS. Revised Edition. Robert E. Swanson. Dow Jones-Irwin, 1818 Ridge Road, Homewood, Illinois 60430. 1985.

YEAR-END TAX PLANNING MANUAL, 1984. Albert B. Ellentuck, Editor. Research Institute of America, Incorporated, One Penn Plaza, New York, New York 10119. 1984.

TEXTBOOKS AND GENERAL WORKS

ESTATE PLANNING AND PASSIVE LOSSES. Pace University Tax Institute Tax Planning Seminar. Lubin School of Business Administration, Department of Taxation, New York, New York. 1989.

INVESTMENT LIMITED PARTNERSHIPS AND OTHER PASS-THROUGH VEHICLES. Robert J. Haft and Peter M. Fass. Clark Boardman Company, Limited, 435 Hudson Street, New York, New York 10014. 1987.

MIDDLE INCOME TAX PLANNING AND SHELTERS. Richard A. Westin. Shepard's/McGraw-Hill, P.O. Box 1235, Colorado Springs, Colorado 80901. 1982. (Periodic Supplements).

PALS: WORKING WITH THE PASSIVE ACTIVITY LOSS RULES: '89 UPDATE, NEW ACTIVITY REGULATIONS. CCH Tax Law Editors. Commerce Clearing House, Incorporated, 4025 West Peterson Avenue, Chicago, Illinois 60646. 1989.

PASSIVE ACTIVITY LOSS RULES: ANAYLSIS, COMPLIANCE, PLANNING. Michael N. Jennings and Daniel R. Bolar. Research Institute of America, Incorporated, One Penn Plaza, New York, New York 10119. 1989.

PASSIVE ACTIVITY RULES: LAW AND TAX PLANNING STRATEGIES. Ronald D. Saake, Michael J. Novogradac, and Eric J. Fortenbach. John Wiley and Sons, Incorporated, 605 Third Avenue, New York, New York 10158. 1991.

THE REAL ESTATE IRA. John J. Scavuzzo. Dodd, Mead and Company, Incorporated, 71 Fifth Avenue, New York, New York 10003. 1987.

THE SINGLE SOLUTION: A TAXPAYER'S GUIDE TO SHELTERING MORE OF THE $20,000, $50,000, OR $100,000 YOU MAKE AS A SINGLE PERSON. Mary Jean Parson. Facts on File, Incorporated, 460 Park Avenue South, New York, New York 10016. 1987.

SPECIAL UPDATE: THE TAX REFORM ACT OF 1986. Peter M. Fass, Robert J. Haft, Leslie M. Loffman and Sanford C. Presant. Clark Boardman Company, Limited, 435 Hudson Street, New York, New York 10014. 1986.

TAX-DEFERRED INVESTING: USING PRE-TAX DOLLARS FOR AFTER-TAX PROFIT. Michael C. Thomsett. John Wiley and Sons, Incorporated, 605 Third Avenue, New York, New York 10158. 1991.

TAX SHELTER: ADVANCED PLANNING TECHNIQUES. Alan S. Rosenberg. Practising Law Institute, 810 Seventh Avenue, New York, New York 10019. 1985.

TAX SHELTERS IN TROUBLE: PRIVATE AND PUBLIC LITIGATION: A COURSE HANDBOOK. Practising Law Institute, 810 Seventh Avenue, New York, New York 10019. 1985.

DIGESTS, INDEXES, ABSTRACTS, CITATORS

FEDERAL TAX ARTICLES: INCOME, ESTATE, GIFT, EXCISE, EMPLOYMENT TAXES. Commerce Clearing House, Incorporated, 4025 West Peterson Avenue, Chicago, Illinois 60646. 1969- .

FEDERAL TAXES CITATOR. Prentice-Hall, Incorporated, 113 Sylvan Avenue, Englewood Cliffs, New Jersey 07632. 1943- .

INDEX TO FEDERAL TAX ARTICLES. Gersham Goldstein, Editor. Research Institute of America, Incorporated, One Penn Plaza, New York, New York 10119. 1975- .

SHEPARD'S FEDERAL TAX CITATIONS. Shepard's/McGraw-Hill, P.O. Box 1235, Colorado Springs, Colorado 80901. 1981- .

SHEPARD'S FEDERAL TAX LOCATOR: COMPLETE GUIDE TO ALL THE CURRENT SOURCES OF LAW RELATING TO FEDERAL TAXATION. Shepard's/McGraw-Hill, P.O. Box 1235, Colorado Springs, Colorado 80901. 1974- .

LAW REVIEWS AND PERIODICALS

JOURNAL OF TAXATION. Research Institute of America, Incorporated, One Penn Plaza, New York, New York 10119. Monthly.

TAX LAW REVIEW. Research Institute of America, Incorporated, One Penn Plaza, New York, New York 10119. Quarterly.

THE TAX LAWYER. American Bar Association, Section of Taxation, 750 North Lake Shore Drive, Chicago, Illinois 60611. Quarterly.

TAXATION FOR LAWYERS. Research Institute of America, Incorporated, One Penn Plaza, New York, New York 10119. Bimonthly.

TAXES: THE TAX MAGAZINE. Commerce Clearing House, Incorporated, 4025 West Peterson Avenue, Chicago, Illinois 60646. Monthly.

VIRGINIA LAW REVIEW. Virginia Tax Review Association, University Virginia, School of Law, Charlottesville, Virginia 22901. Semiannual.

NEWSLETTERS AND NEWSPAPERS

TAX PLANNING REVIEW. Commerce Clearing House, Incorporated, 4025 West Peterson Avenue, Chicago, Illinois 60646. Monthly.

TAX SHELTER ADVISOR. Callaghan and Company, 3201 Old Glenview Road, Wilmette, Illinois 60091. Monthly.

TAX SHELTER ANALYST. Tax Reports Newsletter Associates, 10076 Boca Entrada Boulevard, Boca Raton, Florida 33433. Monthly.

TAX SHELTER INSIDER. Tax Reports Newsletter Associates, 10076 Boca Entrada Boulevard, Boca Raton, Florida 33433. Monthly.

TAX SHELTERED INVESTMENTS LAW REPORT. Robert J. Haft and Peter M. Fass. Clark Boardman Company, Limited, 435 Hudson Street, New York, New York 10014. Eight issues per year.

ASSOCIATIONS AND PROFESSIONAL SOCIETIES

SECTION ON TAXATION, AMERICAN BAR ASSOCIATION. 750 North Lake Shore Drive, Chicago, Illinois 60611. (312) 988-5000.

SECTION ON TAXATION, ASSOCIATION OF AMERICAN LAW SCHOOLS. One Dupont Circle, Northwest, Suite 370, Washington, D.C. 20036. (202) 296-8851.

RESEARCH CENTERS, INSTITUTES, CLEARINGHOUSES

INSTITUTE FOR CONTINUING EDUCATION IN LAW AND TAXATION. New York University, 11 West Forty-second Street, Room 429, New York, New York 10036. (212) 790-1320.

NATIONAL TAX ASSOCIATION-TAX INSTITUTE OF AMERICA. 5310 East Main Street, Suite 104, Columbus, Ohio 43213. (614) 864-1221.

TAX FOUNDATION. 470 L'Enfant, Southwest, Suite 7112, Washington, D.C. 20024. (202) 863-5454.

ONLINE DATABASES

LEXIS FEDERAL TAX LIBRARY. Mead Data Central, P.O. Box 933, Dayton, Ohio 45401.

LEXIS STATE TAX LIBRARY. Mead Data Central, P.O. Box 933, Dayton, Ohio 45401.

WESTLAW, TAXATION LIBRARY. West Publishing Company, P.O. Box 64526, 50 West Kellogg Boulevard, St. Paul, Minnesota 55164-0526.

AUDIOVISUALS

TAXATION OF THE SOPHISTICATED INVESTOR. Alex Weinberg. New York University Institute on Federal Taxation, Totaltape Publishing, Incorporated, 4521 Southwest Thirteenth Street, Gainesville, Florida 32608. 1987. Audiocassette.

TAXATION
See: CORPORATIONS, TAXATION; ESTATE, INHERITANCE AND TRANSFER TAXES; EXCISE TAXES; INCOME TAX, FEDERAL; INTERNAL REVENUE SERVICE; REAL PROPERTY TAXATION; SALES AND USE TAXES; TAX AND ESTATE PLANNING; TAX COURT; TAX EXEMPT ORGANIZATIONS; TAX LEGISLATION AND POLICY; TAX PRACTICE AND ENFORCEMENT; TAX RETURNS; TAX SHELTERS; TAXATION, INTERNATIONAL; TAXATION, STATE AND LOCAL

TAXATION, INTERNATIONAL
See also: TAX LEGISLATION AND POLICY

STATUTES, CODES, STANDARDS, UNIFORM LAWS

FEDERAL INCOME TAX CODE AND REGULATIONS. Commerce Clearing House, Incorporated, 4025 West Peterson Avenue, Chicago, Illinois 60646. Annual.

FEDERAL INCOME TAX PROJECT: INTERNATIONAL ASPECTS OF UNITED STATES INCOME TAXATION, PROPOSALS ON UNITED STATES TAXATION OF FOREIGN PERSONS AND OF THE FOREIGN INCOME OF UNITED STATES PERSONS. American Law Institute-American Bar Association, 4025 Chestnut Street, Philadelphia, Pennsylvania 19104. 1987.

FEDERAL TAX REGULATIONS. West Publishing Company, P.O. Box 64526, 50 West Kellogg Boulevard, St. Paul, Minnesota 55164-0526. Annual.

INTERNAL REVENUE BULLETIN; CUMULATIVE BULLETIN. United States Department of Treasury, Internal Revenue Service.Superintendent of Documents, United States Government Printing Office, Washington, D.C. 20402. Weekly.

INTERNAL REVENUE CODE. West Publishing Company, P.O. Box 64526, 50 West Kellogg Boulevard, St. Paul, Minnesota 55164-0526. Annual.

MODEL DOUBLE TAXATION CONVENTION ON ESTATES AND INHERITANCES AND ON GIFTS: REPORT OF THE OECD COMMITTEE ON FISCAL AFFAIRS. Organization for Economic Cooperation and Development, 2001 L Street, Northwest, Suite 700, Washington, D.C. 20036. 1983.

LOOSELEAF SERVICES AND REPORTERS

FEDERAL TAXES. Prentice-Hall, Incorporated, 113 Sylvan Avenue, Englewood Cliffs, New Jersey 07632. 1919- .

FOREIGN TAX AND TRADE BRIEFS. Walter M. Diamond. Matthew Bender and Company, Incorporated, 11 Penn Plaza, New York, New York 10001. 1982- .

INTERNATIONAL WITHOLDING TAX TREATY GUIDE. Walter H. Diamond. Matthew Bender and Company, Incorporated, 11 Penn Plaza, New York, New York 10001. 1975- .

STANDARD FEDERAL TAX REPORTS. Commerce Clearing House, Incorporated, 4025 West Peterson Avenue, Chicago, Illinois 60646. 1913- .

TAX LAWS OF THE WORLD. Foreign Tax Law Association, Incorporated, P.O. Box 340, Alachua, Florida 32615. 1974.

TAX TREATIES. Commerce Clearing House, Incorporated, 4025 West Peterson Avenue, Chicago, Illinois 60646. 1952- .

TAX TREATIES. Prentice-Hall, Incorporated, 113 Sylvan Avenue, Englewood Cliffs, New Jersey 07632. 1969- .

UNITED STATES TAXATION OF INTERNATIONAL OPERATIONS. Prentice Hall, Incorporated, 113 Sylvan Avenue, Englewood Cliffs, New Jersey 07632. 1975- .

HANDBOOKS, MANUALS, FORMBOOKS

INTERNATIONAL TAX AND ESTATE PLANNING: A PRACTICAL GUIDE FOR MULTINATIONAL INVESTORS. Second Edition. Robert C. Lawrence, III. Practising Law Institute, 810 Seventh Avenue, New York, New York 10019. 1989.

INTERNATIONAL TAX GUIDE: U.S. INCOME TAXATION. John F. Cooper and I. Richard Gershon. Callaghan and Company, 155 Pfingsten Road, Deerfield, Illinois 60015. 1991.

A REFERENCE GUIDE TO INTERNATIONAL TAXATION: PROFITING FROM YOUR INTERNATIONAL OPERATIONS. Michel W.E. Glautier and Frederick W. Bassinger. Lexington Books, 125 Spring Street, Lexington, Massachusetts 02173. 1987.

TEXTBOOKS AND GENERAL WORKS

THE ASSESSMENT AND COLLECTION OF TAX FROM NON-RESIDENTS. International Fiscal Association, Editor. Kluwer Academic Publishers, 101 Philip Drive, Assinippi Park, Norwell, Massachusetts 02061. 1985.

EFFECTIVE TAX STRATEGIES FOR INTERNATIONAL CORPORATE ACQUISITIONS. Philip J. Cooke. Kluwer Law Book Publishers, Incorporated, 36 West Forty-fourth Street, New York, New York 10036. 1989.

FEDERAL TAXATION OF INTERNATIONAL TRANSACTIONS: PRINCIPLES, PLANNING, AND POLICY. Richard L. Kaplan. West Publishing Company, 50 West Kellogg Boulevard, St. Paul, Minnesota 55164-0526. 1988.

FUNDAMENTALS OF INTERNATIONAL TAXATION: U.S. TAXATION OF FOREIGN INCOME AND FOREIGN TAXPAYERS. Boris I. Bittker and Lawrence Lokken. Warren, Gorham, and Lamont, Incorporated, One Penn Plaza, New York, New York 10119. 1991.

INTERNATIONAL COMPETITIVENESS AND THE TAXATION OF FOREIGN SOURCE INCOME. Robert A. Ragland. National Chamber Foundation, 1615 H Street, Northwest, Washington, D.C. 20062. 1991.

THE INTERNATIONAL INCOME TAX RULES OF THE UNITED STATES. Michael J. McIntyre. Butterworth Legal Publishers, 90 Stiles Raod, Salem, New Hampshire 03079. 1989.

INTERNATIONAL JURIDICAL DOUBLE TAXATION OF INCOME. Manuel Pires. Kluwer Law Book Publishers, Incorporated, 36 West Forty-fourth Street, New York, New York 10036. 1989.

INTERNATIONAL TAX PLANNING AFTER THE TAX REFORM ACT OF 1986. Jon Bischell, Robert F. Hudson, Jr., and John C. Klotsche. Matthew Bender and Company, Incorporated, 11 Penn Plaza, New York, New York 10001. 1989.

INTERNATIONAL TAX PLANNING FOR THE U.S. MULTINATIONAL CORPORATION. Alan W. Granwell. Practising Law Institute, 810 Seventh Avenue, New York, New York 10019. 1988.

INTERNATIONAL TAXATION: ALI-ABA COURSE OF STUDY MATERIALS. American Law Institute-American Bar Association, 4025 Chestnut Street, Philadelphia, Pennsylvania 19104. 1988.

INTERNATIONAL TAXATION IN A NUTSHELL. Richard L. Doernberg. West Publishing Company, 50 West Kellogg Boulevard, St. Paul, Minnesota 55164-0526. 1989.

INTERNATIONAL TAXATION IN AN INTEGRATED WORLD. Jacob A. Frenkel, Assaf Razin, and Efraim Sadka. MIT Press, 55 Hayward Street, Cambridge, Massachusetts 02142. 1991.

INTERNATIONAL TAXATION: U.S. TAXATION OF FOREIGN TAXPAYERS AND FOREIGN INCOME. Joseph Isenbergh. Little, Brown and Company, 34 Beacon Street, Boston, Massachusetts 02108. 1990.

INTRODUCTION TO UNITED STATES INTERNATIONAL TAXATION. Third Edition. Paul R. McDaniel and Hugh J. Ault. Kluwer Law Book Publishers, Incorporated, 36 West Forty-fourth Street, New York, New York 10036. 1989.

THE JURISDICTION TO TAX IN INTERNATIONAL LAW: THEORY AND PRACTICE OF LEGISLATIVE FISCAL JURISDICTION. Rutsel Silvestre J. Martha. Kluwer Law Book Publishers, Incorporated, 36 West Forty-fourth Street, New York, New York 10036. 1989.

A LAWYER'S GUIDE TO INTERNATIONAL BUSINESS TRANSACTIONS: UNITED STATES TAXATION OF INTERNATIONAL BUSINESS TRANSACTIONS. Second Edition. American Law Institute, 4025 Chestnut Street, Philadelphia, Pennsylvania 19104.

THE NEW CANADA: UNITED STATES TAX TREATY AND OTHER KEY DEVELOPMENTS IN INTERNATIONAL TAXATION. Insight Educational Services, 100 University Avenue, Suite 503, Toronto, MSJ IV6, Canada. 1984.

NONDISCRIMINATION IN INTERNATIONAL TAX LAW. K. Van Raad, Editor. Kluwer Academic Publishers, 101 Philip Drive, Assinippi Park, Norwell, Massachusetts 02061. 1986.

TAXATION OF INTERNATIONAL EXECUTIVES. Deloitte, Haskins and Sells, Editor. Kluwer Academic Publishers, 101 Philip Drive, Assinippi Park, Norwell, Massachusetts 02061. 1985.

U.S. INCOME TAXATION OF FOREIGN GOVERNMENTS, INTERNATIONAL ORGANIZATIONS AND THEIR EMPLOYEES. Brett R. Dick, C. Jean Ryan, and Stephen P. Jarchow. Tax Management, 1231 Twenty-fifth Street, Northwest, Washington, D.C. 20037. 1990.

U.S. INTERNATIONAL TAX POLICY FOR A GLOBAL ECONOMY. Robert Allen Ragland. National Chamber Foundation, 1615 H Street, Northwest, Washington, D.C. 20062. 1991.

DIGESTS, INDEXES, ABSTRACTS, CITATORS

FEDERAL TAX ARTICLES: INCOME, ESTATE, GIFT, EXCISE, EMPLOYMENT TAXES. Commerce Clearing House, Incorporated, 4025 West Peterson Avenue, Chicago, Illinois 60646. 1969- .

FEDERAL TAXES CITATOR. Prentice-Hall, Incorporated, 113 Sylvan Avenue, Englewood Cliffs, New Jersey 07632. 1943- .

INDEX TO FEDERAL TAX ARTICLES. Gersham Goldstein, Editor. Research Institute of America, Incorporated, One Penn Plaza, New York, New York 10119. 1975- .

SHEPARD'S FEDERAL TAX CITATIONS. Shepard's/McGraw-Hill, P.O. Box 1235, Colorado Springs, Colorado 80901. 1981- .

SHEPARD'S FEDERAL TAX LOCATOR: COMPLETE INDEX TO ALL THE CURRENT SOURCES OF LAW RELATING TO FEDERAL TAXATION. Shepard's/McGraw-Hill, P.O. Box 1235, Colorado Springs, Colorado 80901. 1974- .

ANNUALS AND SURVEYS

TAX SYSTEMS OF AFRICA, ASIA, AND THE MIDDLE EAST: A GUIDE FOR BUSINESS AND THE PROFESSIONS. C. J. Platt. Gower Publishing Company, Old Post Road, Brookfield, Vermont 05036. 1982.

TAX SYSTEMS OF WESTERN EUROPE: A GUIDE FOR BUSINESS AND THE PROFESSIONS. Third Edition. C. J. Platt. Gower Publishing Company, Old Post Road, Brookfield, Vermont 05036. 1985.

LAW REVIEWS AND PERIODICALS

INTERNATIONAL TAX JOURNAL. Panel Publishers, Incorporated, 36 Forty-fourth Street, New York, New York 10036. Quarterly.

JOURNAL OF TAXATION. Research Institute of America, Incorporated, One Penn Plaza, New York, New York 10119. Monthly.

TAX LAW REVIEW. Research Institute of America, Incorporated, One Penn Plaza, New York, New York 10119. Quarterly.

THE TAX LAWYER. American Bar Association, Section of Taxation, 750 North Lake Shore Drive, Chicago, Illinois 60611. Quarterly.

TAXES: THE TAX MAGAZINE. Commerce Clearing House, Incorporated, 4025 West Peterson Avenue, Chicago, Illinois 60646. Bimonthly.

VIRGINIA TAX REVIEW. Virginia Tax Review Association, University of Virginia, School of Law, Charlottesville, Virginia 22901. Semiannual.

ASSOCIATIONS AND PROFESSIONAL SOCIETIES

SECTION ON TAXATION, AMERICAN BAR ASSOCIATION. 750 North Lake Shore Drive, Chicago, Illinois 60611. (312) 988-5000.

SECTION ON TAXATION, ASSOCIATION OF AMERICAN LAW SCHOOLS. One Dupont Circle, Northwest, Washington, D.C. 20036. (202) 296-8851.

RESEARCH CENTERS, INSTITUTES, CLEARINGHOUSES

INSTITUTE FOR CONTINUING EDUCATION IN LAW AND TAXATION. New York University, 11 West Forty-second Street, Room 429, New York, New York 10036. (212) 790-1320.

NATIONAL TAX ASSOCIATION-TAX INSTITUTE OF AMERICA. 5310 East Main Street, Suite 104, Columbus, Ohio 43213. (614) 864-1221.

TAX FOUNDATION. 470 L'Enfant, Southwest, Suite 7112, Washington, D.C. 20024. (202) 863-5454.

ONLINE DATABASES

LEXIS FEDERAL TAX LIBRARY. Mead Data Central, P.O. Box 933, Dayton, Ohio 45401.

TAXATION, INTERNATIONAL

TAX MANAGEMENT INTERNATIONAL JOURNAL. Bureau of National Affairs, Incorporated, 1231 Twenty-fifth Street, Northwest, Washington, D.C. 20037.

TAX NOTES INTERNATIONAL. Tax Analysts, 6830 North Fairfax Drive, Arlington, Virginia 22213.

WESTLAW, TAXATION LIBRARY. West Publishing Company, P.O. Box 64526, 50 West Kellogg Boulevard, St. Paul, Minnesota 55164-0526.

TAXATION, STATE AND LOCAL

See also: CORPORATIONS, TAXATION; ESTATE, INHERITANCE AND TRANSFER TAXES; EXCISE TAXES; INCOME TAX, FEDERAL; INTERNAL REVENUE SERVICE; REAL PROPERTY TAXATION; SALES AND USE TAXES; TAX AND ESTATE PLANNING; TAX COURT; TAX LEGISLATION AND POLICY; TAX PRACTICE AND ENFORCEMENT; TAX RETURNS

LOOSELEAF SERVICES AND REPORTERS

ALL STATES TAX GUIDE. Prentice-Hall, Incorporated, 113 Sylvan Avenue, Englewood Cliffs, New Jersey 07632. 1960- .

ESTATE PLANNING: INHERITANCE AND TRANSFER TAXES. Prentice-Hall, Incorporated, 113 Sylvan Avenue, Englewood Cliffs, New Jersey 07632. 1925.

RIA'S STATE TAX ACTION. CENTRAL REGION. Research Institute of America, Incorporated, 90 Fifth Avenue, New York, New York 10011. 1986.

RIA'S STATE TAX ACTION. EASTERN REGION. Research Institute of America, Incorporated, 90 Fifth Avenue, New York, New York 10011. 1986.

RIA'S STATE TAX ACTION. NORTHEAST REGION. Research Institute of America, Incorporated, 90 Fifth Avenue, New York, New York 10011. 1986.

RIA'S STATE TAX ACTION. SOUTHERN REGION. Research Institute of America, Incorporated, 90 Fifth Avenue, New York, New York 10011. 1986.

RIA'S STATE TAX ACTION. SOUTHWEST REGION. Research Institute of America, Incorporated, 90 Fifth Avenue, New York, New York 10011. 1986.

RIA'S STATE TAX ACTION. WESTERN REGION. Research Institute of America, Incorporated, 90 Fifth Avenue, New York, New York 10011. 1986.

STATE AND LOCAL TAXES. Prentice-Hall, Incorporated, 113 Sylvan Avenue, Englewood Cliffs, New Jersey 07632. 1925- .

STATE INCOME TAXES. Prentice Hall, Incorporated, 113 Sylvan Avenue, Englewood Cliffs, New Jersey 07632. 1925- .

STATE TAX ACTION COORDINATOR. Research Institute of America, Incorporated, 90 Fifth Avenue, New York, New York 10011. 1982- .

STATE TAX GUIDE. Second Edition. Commerce Clearing House, Incorporated, 4025 West Peterson Avenue, Chicago, Illinois 60646. 1985- .

HANDBOOKS, MANUALS, FORMBOOKS

ALL STATES TAX HANDBOOK, 1989. Prentice-Hall, Incorporated, 113 Sylvan Avenue, Englewood Cliffs, New Jersey 07632. 1989.

STATE PERSONAL INCOME TAX FORMS. Commerce Clearing House, Incorporated, 4025 West Peterson Avenue, Chicago, Illinois 60646. 1977- .

STATE TAX FORMS: CORPORATE. Tax Form Library, 518 West Main Street, Louisville, Kentucky 40202. 1985.

STATE TAX FORMS: INDIVIDUAL. Tax Form Library, 518 West Main Street, Louisville, Kentucky 40202. 1985.

STATE TAX FORMS: PARTNERSHIP AND FIDUCIARY. Tax Form Library, 518 West Main Street, Louisville, Kentucky 40202. 1985.

STATE TAX HANDBOOK, AS OF OCTOBER 1, 1989. CCH Tax Law Editors, Commerce Clearing House, Incorporated, 4025 West Peterson Avenue, Chicago, Illinois 60646. 1989.

TEXTBOOKS AND GENERAL WORKS

LOCAL GOVERNMENT TAX AUTHORITY AND USE. John H. Bowman and John L. Mikesell. National League of Cities, 1301 Pennsylvania Avenue, Northwest, Washington, D.C. 20004. 1987.

A LOOK AT STATE AND LOCAL TAX POLICIES: PAST TRENDS AND FUTURE PROSPECTS. Frederick D. Stocker. Lincoln Institute of Land Policy, 26 Trowbridge Street, Cambridge, Massachusetts 02138. 1991.

STATE AND LOCAL TAXATION AND FINANCE IN A NUTSHELL. M. David Gelfand and Peter W. Salsich. West Publishing Company, P.O. Box 64526, 50 West Kellogg Boulevard, St. Paul, Minnesota 55164-0526. 1985.

STATE AND LOCAL TAXATION: CASES AND MATERIALS. Fifth Edition. Jerome R. Hellerstein and Walter Hellerstein. West Publishing Company, 50 West Kellogg Boulevard, St. Paul, Minnesota 55164-0526. 1988.

STATE TAXATION: CORPORATE INCOME AND FRANCHISE TAXES. Jerome R. Hellerstein. Research Institute of America, Incorporated, One Penn Plaza, New York, New York 10119. 1983. (Periodic Supplements).

STATE TAXATION OF BANK AND THRIFT INSTITUTIONS. Second Edition. American Bar Association, Section of Taxation, 750 North Lake Shore Drive, Chicago, Illinois 60611. 1983.

YOUR CITY'S 1040: FEDERAL TAX REFORM AND MUNICIPALITIES. Larry C. Ledebur, Susan Gutchess, Diana Day, and Douglas Peterson. National League of Cities, 1301 Pennsylvania Avenue, Northwest, Washington, D.C. 20004. 1987.

Encyclopedia of Legal Information Sources • 2nd Ed. **TELECOMMUNICATIONS**

ANNUALS AND SURVEYS

INTERSTATE TAX REPORT. Interstate Tax Press, 250 East 39th Street - 6A, New York, New York 10016. 1981- . Monthly.

SIGNIFICANT STATE TAX DEVELOPMENTS. Philip M. Tatarowicz. Prentice-Hall, Incorporated, 113 Sylvan Avenue, Englewood Cliffs, New Jersey 07632. Annual.

STUDIES IN TAXATION, PUBLIC FINANCE AND RELATED SUBJECTS. Fund for Public Policy Research, 1730 Rhode Island Avenue, Northwest, Washington, D.C. 20005. 1977.

TAX FACT BOOK. Research Institute of America, Incorporated, One Penn Plaza, New York, New York 10119. Annual.

LAW REVIEWS AND PERIODICALS

JOURNAL OF STATE TAXATION. Panel Publishers, Incorporated, 14 Plaza Road, Greenvale, New York 11548. Quarterly.

NEWSLETTERS AND NEWSPAPERS

FROM THE STATE CAPITALS: TAXATION AND REVENUE. Wakeman Walworth, Incorporated, P.O. Box 1939, New Haven, Connecticut 06509. Weekly.

INTERSTATE TAX REPORT. Interstate Tax Press, Incorporated, 26 Veasey Street, Suite 401, New York, New York 10007. Monthly.

STATE AND LOCAL TAX AND REVENUE REPORT. CD Publications, 100 Summit Building, 8555 Sixteenth Street, Silver Spring, Maryland 20910. Semi-monthly.

STATE TAX ACTION COORDINATOR RETURN PREPARER'S ALERT. Research Institute of America, Incorporated, 589 Fifth Avenue, New York, New York 10017. Monthly.

STATE TAX CASES REPORT. Commerce Clearing House, Incorporated, 4025 West Peterson Avenue, Chicago, Illinois 60646. Monthly.

STATE TAX REVIEW. Commerce Clearing House, Incorporated, 4025 West Peterson Avenue, Chicago, Illinois 60646. Weekly.

TAX ADMINISTRATION NEWS. Federation of Tax Administrators, 444 North Capital Street, Northwest, Washington, D.C. 20001. Monthly.

ASSOCIATIONS AND PROFESSIONAL SOCIETIES

SECTION OF TAXATION. American Bar Association, 750 North Lake Shore Drive, Chicago, Illinois 60611. (312) 988-5000.

SECTION ON TAXATION, ASSOCIATION OF AMERICAN LAW SCHOOLS. One Dupont Circle, Northwest, Washington, D.C. 20036. (202) 296-8851.

RESEARCH CENTERS, INSTITUTES, CLEARINGHOUSES

CENTER FOR LOCAL TAX RESEARCH. Henry George School, 5 East Forty-fourth Street, New York, New York 10017. (212) 697-9880.

INSTITUTE FOR CONTINUING EDUCATION IN LAW AND TAXATION. New York University, 11 West Forty-second Street, Room 429, New York, New York 10036. (212) 790-1320.

NATIONAL TAX ASSOCIATION-TAX INSTITUTE OF AMERICA. 5310 East Main Street, Suite 104, Columbus, Ohio 43213. (614) 864-1221.

TAX FOUNDATION. 470 L'Enfant, Southwest, Suite 7112, Washington, D.C. 20024. (202) 863-5454.

STATISTICS SOURCES

STATE GOVERNMENT TAX COLLECTIONS. United States Department of Commerce, Census Bureau, United States Government Printing Office, Washington, D.C. 20402. Annual.

ONLINE DATABASES

CCH STATE TAX WEEK. Commerce Clearing House, Incorporated, 4025 West Peterson Avenue, Chicago, Illinois 60646.

LEXIS STATE TAX LIBRARY. Mead Data Central, P.O. Box 933, Dayton, Ohio 45401.

TEACHERS
See: EDUCATION; SCHOOL INTEGRATION; SCHOOL VIOLENCE AND DISCIPLINE

TELECOMMUNICATIONS
See also: FEDERAL COMMUNICATIONS COMMISSION; HIGH TECHNOLOGY INDUSTRIES; NATIONAL TELECOMMUNICATIONS AND INFORMATION ADMINISTRATION; TELEVISION AND RADIO

STATUTES, CODES, STANDARDS, UNIFORM LAWS

THE CABLE COMMUNICATIONS POLICY ACT OF 1984. Jay E. Ricks and Richard E. Wiley, Chairmen. Law and Business, Harcourt Brace Jovanovich, Incorporated, 6277 Sea Harbor Drive, Orlando, Florida 32821. 1985.

COMPILATION OF THE COMMUNICATIONS ACT OF 1934 AND RELATED PROVISIONS OF LAW. United States Congress, House Committee on Energy and Commerce. Superintendent of Documents, United States Government Printing Office, Washington, D.C. 20402. 1988.

INTERNATIONAL LAW GOVERNING COMMUNICATIONS AND INFORMATION: A COLLECTION OF DOCUMENTS. Edward W. Ploman, Editor. Greenwood Publishing Group, Incorporated, 88 Post Road West, P.O. Box 5007, Westport, Connecticut 06881. 1982.

A LEGISLATIVE HISTORY OF THE COMMUNICATIONS ACT OF 1934. Max D. Paglin. Oxford University Press, 200 Madison Avenue, New York, New York 10016. 1989.

MODEL TELECOMMUNICATIONS SERVICE RULES. National Association of Regulatory Utility Commissioners, P.O. Box 684, 1102 Interstate Commerce Commission Building, Constitution Avenue and Twelfth Street, Northwest, Washington, D.C. 20044-0864. 1984.

LOOSELEAF SERVICES AND REPORTERS

COMMUNICATIONS COMMON CARRIER DECISIONS. Federal Publications, Incorporated, 1120 Twentieth Street, Northwest, Washington, D.C. 20036. 1986.

MEDIA LAW REPORTER. Bureau of National Affairs. 1231 Twenty-fifth Street, Northwest, Washington, D.C. 20037. 1977- .

PIKE AND FISCHER RADIO REGULATION, SECOND SERIES. John W. Willis and Henry G. Fischer. Pike and Fischer, Incorporated, 4550 Montgomery Avenue, Suite 433N, Bethesda, Maryland 20814. 1967- .

STATE ACTION REPORTER: TELECOMMUNICATIONS. Regulatory Information Service 4520 East-West Highway, Bethesda, Maryland 20814. 1985- .

TELECOMMUNICATIONS REGULATORY MONITOR. David A. Irwin. Phillips Publishing, Incorporated, 7811 Montrose Road, Potomac, Maryland 20854. 1987- .

HANDBOOKS, MANUALS, FORMBOOKS

COMMUNICATIONS PRACTICE: THE TRANSACTIONAL SIDE. Federal Communications Bar Association. American Bar Association, 750 North Lake Shore Drive, Chicago, Illinois 60611. 1987.

DOING RESEARCH IN FEDERAL COMMUNICATIONS LAW. John M. Howard. Law Library, Library of Congress, 101 Independence Avenue, Southeast, Washington, D.C. 20540. 1981.

HOW TO FIND INFORMATION ABOUT COMPANIES IN THE TELECOMMUNICATIONS, DATA PROCESSING, AND OFFICE AUTOMATION INDUSTRIES. Washington Researchers Publishing, 2612 P Street, Northwest, Washington, D.C. 20007. 1987.

A PRACTICAL GUIDE TO THE CABLE COMMUNICATIONS POLICY ACT OF 1984. George R. Borsari, Jr. and Gary L. Christensen, Co-Chairmen. Practising Law Institute, 810 Seventh Avenue, New York, New York 10019. 1985.

THE TELECOMMUNICATIONS DEREGULATION SOURCEBOOK. Stuart N. Brotman. Artech House, Incorporated, 685 Canton Street, Norwood, Massachusetts 02062. 1987.

TEXTBOOKS AND GENERAL WORKS

THE BIRTH OF ELECTRONIC PUBLISHING: LEGAL AND ECONOMIC ISSUES IN TELEPHONE, CABLE, AND OVER-THE-AIR-TEXT AND VIDEOTEXT. Richard M. Neustadt. Knowledge Industry Publications, Incorporated, 701 Westchester Avenue, White Plains, New York. 1982.

CABLE TELEVISION AND OTHER NONBROADCAST VIDEO: LAW AND POLICY. Daniel L. Brenner and Monroe E. Price. Clark Boardman Company, Limited, 435 Hudson Street, New York, New York 10014. 1986.

COMMUNICATIONS DEREGULATION: THE UNLEASHING OF AMERICA'S COMMUNICATION. Jeremy Tunstall. Blackwell, Basil, Publishers, 3 Cambridge Center, Cambridge, Massachusetts 02142. 1986.

THE DEAL OF THE CENTURY: THE BREAK UP OF AT&T. Steve Coll. Atheneum Publishers, 866 Third Avenue, New York, New York 10022. 1986.

THE DEREGULATION OF INTERNATIONAL TELECOMMUNICATIONS. Ronald S. Eward. Books on Demand, 300 North Zeeb Road, Ann Arbor, Michigan 48106-1346. 1985.

DISCONNECTING BELL: THE IMPACT OF THE AT&T DIVESTITURE. Harry M. Shooshan, Editor. Pergamon Press, Incorporated, Maxwell House, Fairview Park, Elmsford, New York 10523. 1984.

THE ELECTRONIC MEDIA AND THE TRANSFORMATION OF LAW. M. Ethan Katsh. Oxford University Press, 200 Madison Avenue, New York, New York 10016. 1989.

ESSENTIAL PRINCIPLES OF COMMUNICATIONS LAW. Donald E. Lively. Praeger Publishers, One Madison Avenue, New York, New York 10010. 1992.

FREEDOM, TECHNOLOGY, AND THE FIRST AMENDMENT. Jonathan Emord. Pacific Research Institute for Public Policy, 177 Post Street, San Francisco, California 94108. 1991.

INTERNATIONAL BROADCASTING BY SATELLITE: ISSUES OF REGULATION, BARRIERS TO COMMUNICATION. Jon T. Powell. Greenwood Publishing Group, Incorporated, 88 Post Road West, P.O. Box 5007, Westport, Connecticut 06881. 1985.

INTERNATIONAL REGULATION OF SATELLITE COMMUNICATION. Milton L. Smith. Martinus Nijhoff, Kluwer Academic Publishers, 101 Philip Drive, Assinippi Park, Norwell, Massachusetts 02061. 1990.

ISSUES IN INTERNATIONAL TELECOMMUNICATIONS: GOVERNMENT REGULATION OF COMSAT. Leland L. Johnson. Rand Corporation, 1700 Main Street, P.O. Box 2138, Santa Monica, California 90406. 1987.

ISSUES IN INTERNATIONAL TELECOMMUNICATIONS POLICY: A SOURCEBOOK. Jane H. Yurow, Editor. George Washington University, Center for Telecommunications Studies, 2130 H Street, Northwest, Room W1, Washington, D.C. 20052. 1983.

THE LAW AND REGULATION OF INTERNATIONAL SPACE COMMUNICATION. Rita Lauria White and Harold M. White, Jr. Artech House, Incorporated, 685 Canton Street, Norwood, Massachusetts 02062. 1988.

LAW AND SPACE TELECOMMUNICATIONS. Francis Lyall. Gower Publishing Company, Old Post Road, Brookfield, Vermont 05036. 1989.

LAW OF INTERNATIONAL TELECOMMUNICATIONS IN THE UNITED STATES. Stephen R. Barnett, Michael Botein, and Eli M. Noam. Nomos Verlagsgesellschaft mbH und Co. KG, Postfach 610, Waldseestrasse 3-5, D-7570 Baden-Baden, Germany. 1988.

LAW OF MASS COMMUNICATIONS: FREEDOM AND CONTROL OF PRINT AND BROADCAST MEDIA. Harold L. Nelson, Dwight L. Teeter, Jr., and Don R. Le Duc. Foundation Press, 615 Merrick Avenue, Westbury, New York 11590. 1989.

LEGAL ASPECTS OF IMPLEMENTING INTERNATIONAL TELECOMMUNICATION LINKS: INSTITUTIONS, REGULATIONS, AND INSTRUMENTS. Jan M. Smits. Martinus Nijhoff, Kluwer Academic Publishers, 101 Philip Drive, Assinippi Park, Norwell, Massachusetts 02061. 1991.

MASS COMMUNICATION LAW: CASES AND COMMENT. Fifth Edition. Donald M. Gillmor. West Publishing Company, 50 West Kellogg Boulevard, St. Paul, Minnesota 55164-0526. 1990.

MASS MEDIA AND THE SUPREME COURT: THE LEGACY OF THE WARREN YEARS. Fourth Edition. Kenneth S. Devol. Hastings House Publishers, Incorporated, 141 Halstead Avenue, Mamaroneck, New York 10543. 1990.

MODERN COMMUNICATIONS LAW. Donald E. Lively. Praeger Publishers, One Madison Avenue, New York, New York 10010. 1991.

NEGOTIATING TELECOMMUNICATIONS CONTRACTS: BUSINESS AND LEGAL ASPECTS. Henry D. Levine and David R. Anderson, Co-Chairmen. Law and Business, Harcourt Brace Jovanovich, Incorporated, 6277 Sea Harbor Drive, Orlando, Florida 32821. 1985.

THE NEW TELECOMMUNICATIONS ERA AFTER THE AT&T DIVESTITURE: THE TRANSITION TO FULL COMPETITION. Practising Law Institute, 810 Seventh Avenue, New York, New York 10019. 1985.

THE NEW TELECOMMUNICATIONS MARKETPLACE. John E. Bryson and Richard E. Wiley, Co-chairman. Harcourt Brace Jovanovich, Incorporated, 6277 Sea Harbor Drive, Orlando, Florida 32821. 1983.

THE POLITICAL ECONOMY OF INTERNATIONAL TECHNOLOGY TRANSFER. John R. McIntyre and Daniel S. Papp, Editors. Quorum Books, Imprint of Greenwood Publishing Group, Incorporated, 88 Post Road West, P.O. Box 5007, Westport, Connecticut 06881. 1986.

REGULATION OF TRANSNATIONAL COMMUNICATIONS (MICHIGAN YEARBOOK OF INTERNATIONAL LEGAL STUDIES). Clark Boardman Company, Limited, 435 Hudson Street, New York, New York 10014. 1984.

A SLIPPERY SLOPE: THE LONG ROAD TO THE BREAKUP OF AT&T. Fred W. Henck and Bernard Strassburg. Greenwood Publishing Group, Incorporated, 88 Post Road West, P.O. Box 5007, Westport, Connecticut 06881. 1988.

TECHNOLOGIES OF FREEDOM. Ithiel de Sola Pool. Belknap Press of Harvard University Press, 79 Garden Street, Cambridge, Massachusetts 02138. 1983.

TECHNOLOGY CONTROL, COMPETITION, AND NATIONAL SECURITY: CONFLICT AND CONSENSUS: PROCEEDINGS FROM THE FOURTH ANNUAL SEMINAR OF THE CENTER FOR LAW AND NATIONAL SECURITY AT CHARLOTTESVILLE, VIRGINIA, ON OCTOBER 17-19, 1985. Bernard L. Seward, Jr., Editor. University Press of America, 4720 Boston Way, Lanham, Maryland 20706. 1987.

TELECOM DEREGULATION. Andrew D. Lipman. Telephony Publishing Corporation, 55 East Jackson Boulevard, Chicago, Illinois 60604. 1987.

TELECOMMUNICATIONS AMERICA: MARKETS WITHOUT BOUNDARIES. Manley R. Irwin. Quorum Books, Imprint of Greenwood Publishing Group, Incorporated, 88 Post Road West, P.O. Box 5007, Westport, Connecticut 06881. 1984.

TELECOMMUNICATIONS AND THE LAW: AN ANTHOLOGY. Walter Sapronov. Computer Science Press, 41 Madison Avenue, New York, New York 10010-3546. 1988.

TELECOMMUNICATIONS IN CRISIS: THE FIRST AMENDMENT, TECHNOLOGY, AND DEREGULATION. Edwin Diamond, Norman Sandler, and Milton Mueller. Cato Institute, 224 Second Street, Southeast, Washington, D.C. 20003. 1983.

TELECOMMUNICATIONS IN THE POST-DIVESTITURE ERA: ESSAYS IN HONOR OF JASPER N. DORSEY AND BEN T. WIGGINS. Albert L. Danielsen and David R. Kamerschen, Editors. Free Press, 866 Third Avenue, New York, New York 10022. 1986.

TELECOMMUNICATIONS LAW AND PRACTICE. Collin D. Long. Sweet and Maxwell Limited, South Quay Plaza, 183 Marsh Wall, London E14 9FT, England. 1988.

TELECOMMUNICATIONS: POLICY AND REGULATION IN THE NEW ADMINISTRATION. Richard E. Wiley. Practising Law Institute, 810 Seventh Avenue, New York, New York 10019. 1988.

TELECOMMUNICATIONS POLICY FOR THE 1990'S AND BEYOND: NEW MARKETS, TECHNOLOGY AND GLOBAL COMPETITIVE TREND. Walter G. Bolter, Editor. M.E. Sharpe, Incorporated, 80 Business Park Drive, Armonk, New York 10504. 1990.

TELECOMMUNICATIONS REGULATION AND DEREGULATION IN INDUSTRIALIZED DEMOCRACIES. M. S. Snow. Elsevier Science, P.O. Box 882, Madison Square Station, New York 10159. 1986.

TELECOMMUNICATIONS REGULATION TODAY AND TOMORROW. Eli M. Noam, Editor. Harcourt Brace Jovanovich, Incorporated, 6277 Sea Harbor Drive, Orlando, Florida 32821. 1984.

TOWARD A LAW OF GLOBAL COMMUNICATIONS NETWORKS: THE SCIENCE AND TECHNOLOGY SECTION OF THE AMERICAN BAR ASSOCIATION. Anne W. Branscomb. Longman, Incorporated, 19 West Forty-fourth Street, New York, New York 10036. 1986.

WIRING THE CONSTITUTION: THE NEW MEDIA IN AN INFORMATION AGE. Media Institute, 3017 M Street, Northwest, Washington, D.C. 20007. 1987.

ENCYCLOPEDIAS AND DICTIONARIES

COMMUNICATIONS STANDARD DICTIONARY. Second Edition. Martin H. Weik. Van Nostrand Reinhold Company, Incorporated, 115 Fifth Avenue, New York, New York 10003. 1989.

DATA AND COMPUTER COMMUNICATIONS: TERMS, DEFINITIONS, AND ABBREVIATIONS. Gilbert Held. John Wiley and Sons, Incorporated, 605 Third Avenue, New York, New York 10158. 1989.

DICTIONARY OF TELECOMMUNICATION. S. J. Aries. Butterworth Legal Publishers, 90 Stiles Road, Salem, New Hampshire 03079. 1981.

ENCYCLOPEDIA OF TELECOMMUNICATIONS. Robert A. Meyers. Academic Press, Incorporated, 1250 Sixth Avenue, San Diego, California 92101. 1989.

THE FACTS ON FILE DICTIONARY OF TELE-COMMUNICATIONS. Updated and revised. John Graham and Sue J. Lowe. Facts on File, Incorporated, 460 Park Avenue South, New York, New York 10016. 1991.

THE FROEHLICH/KENT ENCYCLOPEDIA OF TELECOMMUNICATIONS. Fritz E. Froehlich and Allen Kent. Marcel Dekker, 720 Madison Avenue, New York, New York 10016. 1991.

INFORMATION TECHNOLOGY ATLAS--EUROPE. J.C.P. Bus, Wedgwood and Company, Limited. Distributed by Elsevier Science Publishing Company, P.O. Box 882, Madison Square Station, New York, New York 10159. 1987.

VAN NOSTRAND REINHOLD DICTIONARY OF INFORMATION TECHNOLOGY. Third Edition. Dennis Longley and Michael Shain. Van Nostrand Reinhold Company, Incorporated, 115 Fifth Avenue, New York, New York 10003. 1989.

ANNUALS AND SURVEYS

SATELLITE REGULATORY COMPENDIUM. Christine A. Meagher. Phillips Publishing, 7811 Montrose Road, Potomac, Maryland 20854. 1985.

LAW REVIEWS AND PERIODICALS

COMM/ENT: A JOURNAL OF COMMUNICATIONS AND ENTERTAINMENT LAW. Hastings College of Law, 200 McAllister Street, San Francisco, California 94102. Six issues per year.

COMMUNICATIONS AND THE LAW. Meckler Publishing, 520 Riverside Avenue, Westport, Connecticut 06880. Quarterly.

COMMUNICATIONS LAWYER. Forum Committee on Communications Law, American Bar Association, 750 North Lake Shore Drive, Chicago, Illinois 60611. Quarterly.

FEDERAL COMMUNICATIONS LAW JOURNAL. University of California at Los Angeles School of Law and Federal Communications Bar Association, 405 Hilgard Avenue, Los Angeles, California 90024. Three issues per year.

INTERNATIONAL MEDIA LAW. Oyez Longman, Lamb's Conduit Street, London WCIN 3NJ. Monthly.

TELEMATICS: THE NATIONAL JOURNAL OF COMMUNICATIONS BUSINESS AND REGULATION. P.O. Box 6407, Duluth, Minnesota 55806. Monthly.

TELEPHONY. Telephony Publishing Corporation, 55 East Jackson, Chicago, Illinois 60604. Weekly.

NEWSLETTERS AND NEWSPAPERS

COMMON CARRIER WEEK. Television Digest, Incorporated, 1836 Jefferson Place, Northwest, Washington, D.C. 20036. 1984. Weekly.

COMMUNICATIONS DAILY. Televison Digest, Incorporated, 1836 Jefferson Place, Northwest, Washington, D.C. 20036. Daily.

COMMUNICATIONS LAWYER. ABA Forum Committee on Communications Law. American Bar Association, 750 North Lake Shore Drive, Chicago, Illinois 60611. Quarterly.

COMMUNICATIONS WEEK. CMP Publications, Incorporated, 600 Community Drive, Manhasset, New York 11030. Weekly.

CONGRESSIONAL REPORT ON COMMUNICATIONS. News Media Publishing, 1117 North Nineteenth Street, Arlington, Virginia 22209-1798. Semimonthly.

FCC WEEK. Telecom Publishing Group, Capitol Publications, Incorporated, 1300 North Seventeenth Street, Arlington, Virginia 22209. Weekly.

INDUSTRIAL COMMUNICATIONS. Phillips Publishing, Incorporated, 7811 Montrose Road, Potomac, Maryland 20854. Weekly.

INTERNATIONAL COMMUNICATIONS NEWS. Dawson-Butwick Publishers, 1001 Connecticut Avenue, Northwest, Washington, D.C. 20036. Biweekly.

SATELLITE NEWS. Phillips Publishing, Incorporated, 7811 Montrose Road, Potomac, Maryland 20854. Weekly.

SATELLITE WEEK. Warren Publishing, Incorporated, 2115 Ward Court, Northwest, Washington, D.C. 20037. Weekly.

STATE TELEPHONE REGULATION REPORT. Capital Publications, Incorporated, 1300 North Seventeenth Street, Arlington, Virginia 22209. Biweekly.

TELECOMMUNICATIONS ALERT. Management Telecommunications Publishing, 1 Park Avenue, New York, New York 10016. Monthly.

TELECOMMUNICATIONS REPORTS. Telecommunications Reports, 1036 National Press Building, Washington, D.C. 20045. Weekly.

TELECOMMUNICATIONS REPORTS INTERNATIONAL. Business Research Publications, Incorporated, 1036 National Press Building, Washington, D.C. 20045. Semimonthly.

TELECOMMUNICATIONS WEEK. Business Research Publications, Incorporated, 817 Broadway, New York, New York 10003. Weekly.

TELEPHONE NEWS. Phillips Publishing, Incorporated, 7811 Montrose Road, Potomac, Maryland 20854. Weekly.

THE WASHINGTON WEEKLY REPORT. Organization for Protection and Advancement of Small Telephone Companies, 2000 K Street, Suite 205, Washington, D.C. 20006. Weekly.

BIBLIOGRAPHIES

A BIBLIOGRAPHY OF TELECOMMUNICATIONS AND SOCIO-ECONOMIC DEVELOPMENT. Heather E. Hudson. Artech House, Incorporated, 685 Canton Street, Norwood, Massachusetts 02062. 1988.

IMPACT OF THE NEW TELECOMMUNICATIONS TECHNOLOGIES ON URBAN STRUCTURE: A SELECTIVE, ANNOTATED BIBLIGRAPHY. James Joseph Sanchez. Vance Bibliographies, P.O. Box 229, 112 North Charter Street, Monticello, Illinois 61856. 1987.

IMPLICATIONS OF DEREGULATION ON THE PUBLIC ADMINISTRATION OF THE FEDERAL COMMUNICATIONS COMMISSION, 1981-1987: AN ANNOTATED BIBLIOGRAPHY. Donald J. Jung, Jr. Vance Bibliographies, P.O. Box 229, 112 North Charter Street, Monticello, Illinois 61856. 1989.

INTERNATIONAL LAW. Edward Reiter. Oceana Publications, Incorporated, 75 Main Street, Dobbs Ferry, New York 10522. 1984.

THE SOCIAL CONTEXT OF THE NEW INFORMATION AND COMMUNICATION TECHNOLOGIES: A BIBLIOGRAPHY. Elia Zureik and Dianne Hartling. Peter Lang Publishing, Incorporated, 62 West Forty-fifth Street, New York, New York 10036. 1987.

TELECOMMUNICATION ECONOMICS AND INTERNATIONAL REGULATORY POLICY: AN ANNOTATED BIBLIOGRAPHY. Marcellus S. Snow and Meheroo Jussawalla. Greenwood Publishing Group, Incorporated, 88 Post Road West, P.O. Box 5007, Westport, Connecticut 06881. 1986.

DIRECTORIES

DICTIONARY OF COMPUTERS, INFORMATION PROCESSING, AND TELECOMMUNICATIONS. Second Edition. Jerry M. Rosenberg. John Wiley and Sons, Incorporated, 605 Third Avenue, New York, New York 10158. 1987.

FACSIMILE USERS' DIRECTORY. 461 Park Avenue South, New York, New York 10016. 1989.

NORTH AMERICAN TELECOMMUNICATIONS SOURCEBOOK. North American Telecommunications Association, 2000 M Street, Northwest, Suite 550, Washington, D.C. 20036. Annual.

TELECOMMUNICATIONS SYSTEMS AND SERVICES DIRECTORY. Martin Conners, Editor. Gale Research, Incorporated, 835 Penobscot Building, Detroit, Michigan 48226. 1985.

ASSOCIATIONS AND PROFESSIONAL SOCIETIES

AMERICAN BAR ASSOCIATION, FORUM COMMITTEE ON COMMUNICATIONS LAW. 750 North Lake Shore Drive, Chicago, Illinois 60611. (312) 988-5000.

AMERICAN BAR ASSOCIATION, SECTION ON SCIENCE AND TECHNOLOGY. 750 North Lake Shore Drive, Chicago, Illinois 60611. (312) 988-5000.

ASSOCIATION OF AMERICAN LAW SCHOOLS, SECTION ON MASS COMMUNICATION LAW. Association of American Law Schools, One Dupont Circle, Northwest, Washington, D.C. 20036. (202) 296-8851.

COMMUNICATIONS COMMITTEE, NATIONAL ASSOCIATION OF REGULATORY UTILITY COMMISSIONERS. P.O. Box 684, 1102 Interstate Commerce Commission Building, Washington, D.C. 20044. (202) 898-2200.

FEDERAL COMMUNICATIONS BAR ASSOCIATION. 1150 Connecticut Avenue, Northwest, Suite 1050, Washington, D.C. 20036. (202) 833-2684.

NORTH AMERICAN TELECOMMUNICATIONS ASSOCIATION. 2000 M Street, Northwest, Suite 550, Washington, D.C. 20036. (202) 296-9800.

RESEARCH CENTERS, INSTITUTES, CLEARINGHOUSES

TELECOMMUNICATIONS RESEARCH AND ACTION CENTER. P.O. Box 12038, Washington, D.C. 20005. (202) 462-2250.

ONLINE DATABASES

COMMON CARRIER WEEK. Warren Publishing, Incorporated, 2115 Ward Court, Northwest, Washington, D.C. 20037.

COMMUNICATIONS DAILY. Warren Publishing, Incorporated, 2115 Ward Court, Northwest, Washington, D.C. 20037.

TELECOMMUNICATIONS. Bowker A and I Publishing, 245 West Seventeenth Street, New York, New York 10011.

TELECOMMUNICATIONS ALERT. United Communications Group, 4550 Montgomery Avenue, Suite 700N, Bethesda, Maryland 20814.

TELEPHONES
See: TELECOMMUNICATIONS

TELEVISON AND RADIO
See also: FEDERAL COMMUNICATIONS COMMISSION; NATIONAL TELECOMMUNICATIONS AND INFORMATION AGENCY; TELECOMMUNICATIONS

LOOSELEAF SERVICES AND REPORTERS

ALL ABOUT CABLE: LEGAL AND BUSINESS ASPECTS OF CABLE AND PAY TELEVISION. Morton I. Hamburg. Law Journal-Seminars Press, Incorporated, 111 Eighth Avenue, New York, New York 10011. 1983- .

LINDEY ON ENTERTAINMENT, PUBLISHING, AND THE ARTS: AGREEMENTS AND THE LAW. Second Edition. Alexander Lindey. Clark Boardman Company, Limited, 435 Hudson Street, New York, New York 10014. 1980- .

MEDIA LAW REPORTER. Bureau of National Affairs, 1231 Twenty-fifth Street, Northwest, Washington, D.C. 20037. 1977- .

PIKE AND FISCHER RADIO REGULATION, SECOND SERIES. John W. Willis and Henry G. Fischer, Editors. Pike and Fischer, Incorporated, 4550 Montgomery Avenue, Suite 433N, Bethesda, Maryland 20814. 1967- .

PIKE AND FISCHER'S PRIVATE RADIO RULES SERVICE. Jeffrey Tobias and Michael M. Eisenstadt. Pike and Fischer, Incorporated, 4550 Montgomery Avenue, Suite 433N, Bethesda, Maryland 20814. 1987- .

RIGHTS AND LIABILITIES OF PUBLISHERS, BROADCASTERS, AND REPORTERS. Slade R. Metcalf. Shepard's/McGraw-Hill, P.O. Box 1235, Colorado Springs, Colorado 80901. 1982- .

HANDBOOKS, MANUALS, FORMBOOKS

THE BROADCASTERS SURVIVAL GUIDE: A HANDBOOK OF FCC RULES AND REGULATIONS FOR RADIO AND TV STATIONS. Jack W. Whitley and Gregg P. Skall. Scripps Howard Books, New York, New York. 1988.

CABLE TELEVISION: A REFERENCE GUIDE TO INFORMATION. Ronald Garay. Greenwood Publishing Group, Incorporated, 88 Post Road West, P.O. Box 5007, Westport, Connecticut 06881. 1988.

CABLE TELEVISION: HANDBOOK AND FORMS. Ira C. Stein. Shepard's/McGraw-Hill, P.O. Box 1235, Colorado Springs, Colorado 80901. 1985.

MEDIA ABUSES: RIGHTS AND REMEDIES--A GUIDE TO LEGAL REMEDIES. The Media Institute, 3017 M Street, Northwest, Washington, D.C. 20007. 1983.

PRACTICAL GUIDE TO THE CABLE COMMUNICATIONS POLICY ACT OF 1984. George R. Borsari, Jr. and Gary L. Christensen, co-Chairmen. Practising Law Institute, 810 Seventh Avenue, New York, New York 10019. 1985.

RADIO: A REFERENCE GUIDE. Thomas Allen Greenfield. Greenwood Publishing Group, Incorporated, 88 Post Road West, P.O. Box 5007, Westport, Connecticut 06881. 1989.

VIDEO CASSETTES: PRODUCTION, DISTRIBUTION, AND PROGRAMMING FOR THE VCR MARKETPLACE. E. Gabriel Perle and Jeffrey L. Squires, co-Chairmen. Practising Law Institute, 810 Seventh Avenue, New York, New York 10019. 1985.

TEXTBOOKS AND GENERAL WORKS

AN ANALYSIS OF THE FEDERAL COMMUNICATIONS COMMISSION GROUP OWNERSHIP RULES. Stanley M. Besen. The Rand Corporation, 1700 Main Street, P.O. Box 2138, Santa Monica, California 90406. 1984

BROADCAST/CABLE REGULATION. Marvin R. Bensman. University Press of America, 4720 Boston Way, Lanham, Maryland 20706. 1990.

BROADCAST FAIRNESS: DOCTRINE, PRACTICE, PROSPECTS: A REAPPRAISAL OF THE FAIRNESS DOCTRINE AND EQUAL TIME RULE. Ford Rowan. Longman, Incorporated, 19 West Forty-fourth Street, New York, New York 10036. 1984.

BROADCAST LAW AND REGULATION. John R. Bittner. Prentice-Hall, Incorporated, 113 Sylvan Avenue, Englewood Cliffs, New Jersey 07632. 1982.

BROADCAST LAW AND REGULATION. R. Terry Elmore. Tab Books, Incorporated, P.O. Box 40, Blue Ridge Summit, Pennsylvania 17294-0850. 1982.

BROADCAST REGULATION: SELECTED CASES AND DECISIONS. Second Edition. University Press of America, 4720 Boston Way, Lanham, Maryland 20706. 1985.

BROADCASTING AND TELECOMMUNICATIONS: AN INTRODUCTION. Third Edition. John R. Bittner. Prentice-Hall, Incorporated, 113 Sylvan Avenue, Englewood Cliffs, New Jersey 07632. 1991.

CABLE TELEVISION. William Grant. Reston Publishing Company, Incorporated, 113 Sylvan Avenue, Englewood Cliffs, New Jersey 07632. 1983.

CABLE TELEVISION: AN UNNATURAL MONOPOLY. Clint Bolick. Cato Institute, 224 Second Street, Southeast, Washington, D.C. 20003. 1984.

CABLE TELEVISION AND OTHER NONBROADCAST VIDEO: LAW AND POLICY. Daniel L. Brenner and Monroe E. Price. Clark Boardman Company, Limited, 435 Hudson Street, New York, New York 10014. 1986.

CABLE TELEVISION AND THE FIRST AMENDMENT. Patrick Parsons. Lexington Books, 125 Spring Street, Lexington, Massachusetts 02173. 1987.

CABLE TELEVISION: MEDIA AND COPYRIGHT LAW ASPECTS. Herman Jehoram, Editor. Kluwer Academic Publishers, 101 Philip Drive, Assinippi Park, Norwell, Massachusetts 02061. 1982.

CABLE TELEVISION: RETROSPECTIVE AND PROSPECTIVE. Gary L. Christensen, Chairman. Practising Law Institute, 810 Seventh Avenue, New York, New York 10019. 1985.

CONGRESSIONAL TELEVISION: A LEGISLATIVE HISTORY. Ronald Garay. Greenwood Publishing Group, Incorporated, 88 Post Road West, P.O. Box 5007, Westport, Connecticut 06881. 1984.

CURRENT DEVELOPMENTS IN TV AND RADIO. Richard S. Rodin, Chairman. Practising Law Institute, 810 Seventh Avenue, New York, New York 10019.

DOCUMENTS OF AMERICAN BROADCASTING. Fourth Edition. Frank J. Kahn, Editor. Prentice-Hall, Incorporated, 113 Sylvan Avenue, Englewood Cliffs, New Jersey 07632. 1984.

FCC: THE UPS AND DOWNS OF RADIO-TV REGULATION. William B. Ray. Iowa State University Press, 2121 South State Avenue, Ames, Iowa 50010. 1990.

THE FIRST AMENDMENT AND THE FIFTH ESTATE: REGULATION OF ELECTRONIC MASS MEDIA. Second Edition. T. Barton Carter, Marc A. Franklin, and Jay B. Wright. Foundation Press, 615 Merrick Avenue, Westbury, New York 11590. 1989.

LAW OF MASS COMMUNICATIONS: FREEDOM AND CONTROL OF PRINT AND BROADCAST MEDIA. Sixth Edition. Harold L. Nelson and Dwight L. Teeter. Foundation Press, 615 Merrick Avenue, Westbury, New York 11590. 1989.

MASS COMMUNICATIONS LAW IN A NUTSHELL. Third Edition. Harry L. Zuckman. West Publishing Company, P.O. Box 64526, 50 West Kellogg Boulevard, St. Paul, Minnesota 55164-0526. 1988.

MASS MEDIA LAW AND REGULATION. Fifth Edition. William E. Francois. Iowa State University Press, 2121 South State Avenue, Ames, Iowa 50010. 1990.

MEDIA INSURANCE AND RISK MANAGEMENT, 1985. John C. Lankenau, Chairman. Practising Law Institute, 810 Seventh Avenue, New York, New York 10019. 1985.

NEW PROGRAM OPPORTUNITIES IN THE ELECTRONIC MEDIA. George H. Shapiro, Chairman. Practising Law Institute, 810 Seventh Avenue, New York, New York 10019. 1983.

NEWS OF CRIME: COURTS AND PRESS IN CONFLICT. J. Edward Gerald. Quorum Books, Imprint of Greenwood Publishing Group, Incorporated, 88 Post Road West, P.O. Box 5007, Westport, Connecticut 06881. 1983.

PRIME-TIME TELEVISION: CONTENT AND CONTROL. Second Edition. Muriel G. Cantor and Joel M. Cantor. Sage Publications, 2455 Teller Road, Newbury Park, California 91320. 1991.

PUBLIC INTEREST AND THE BUSINESS OF BROADCASTING: THE BROADCAST INDUSTRY LOOKS AT ITSELF. Jon T. Powell and Wally Gair Powell. Quorum Books, Greenwood Publishing Group, Incorporated, 88 Post Road West, P.O. Box 5007, Westport, Connecticut 06881. 1988.

RECKLESS DISREGARD: WESTMORELAND V. CBS ET AL, SHARON V. TIME. Renata Adler. Random House, Incorporated, Random House Publicity, (11-6) 201 East Fiftieth Street, New York, New York 10022. 1988.

REGULATION OF THE ELECTRONIC MASS MEDIA: LAW AND POLICY FOR RADIO, TELEVISION, CABLE, AND THE NEW VIDEO TECHNOLOGIES. Second Edition. Douglas H. Ginsburg, Michael Botein, and Mark D. Director. West Publishing Company, 50 West Kellogg Boulevard, St. Paul, Minnesota 55164-0526. 1991.

RIGHTS AND LIABILITIES OF PUBLISHERS, BROADCASTERS, AND REPORTERS. Slade R. Metcalf. Shepard's/ McGraw-Hill, P.O. Box 1235, Colorado Springs, Colorado 80901. 1982. (Periodic Supplements).

SHOW BUSINESS LAW: MOTION PICTURES, TELEVISION, VIDEO. Peter Muller. Quorum Books, Greenwood Publishing Group, Incorporated, 88 Post Road West, P.O. Box 5007, Westport, Connecticut 06881. 1991.

TELEVISION PIRACY. Anthony F. LoFrisco, Chairman. Practising Law Institute, 810 Seventh Avenue, New York, New York 10019. 1985.

TELEVISION'S GUARDIANS: THE FCC AND THE POLITICS OF PROGRAMMING, 1958-1967. James L. Baughman. University of Tennessee Press, 293 Communications Building, Knoxville, Tennessee 37996-0325. 1985.

TO SEE THE WORLD: THE GLOBAL DIMENSION IN INTERNATIONAL DIRECT TELEVISION BROADCASTING BY SATELLITE. M. LeSueur Stewart. Martinus Nijhoff, Kluwer Academic Publishers, 101 Philip Drive, Assinippi Park, Norwell, Massachusetts 02061. 1990.

TOTAL TELEVISION: A COMPREHENSIVE GUIDE TO PROGRAMMING FROM 1948 TO THE PRESENT. Third Edition. Alex McNeil. Penguin Books, 375 Hudson Street, New York, New York 10014. 1991.

THE UNITED STATES AND THE DIRECT BROADCAST SATELLITE: THE POLITICS OF INTERNATIONAL BROADCASTING IN SPACE. Sara Fletcher Luther. Oxford University Press, 200 Madison Avenue, New York, New York 10016. 1988.

ENCYCLOPEDIAS AND DICTIONARIES

BROADCAST COMMUNICATIONS DICTIONARY. Third Edition. Lincoln Diamant, Editor. Greenwood Publishing Group, Incorporated, 88 Post Road West, P.O. Box 5007, Westport, Connecticut 06881. 1991.

JONES DICTIONARY OF CABLE TELEVISION TERMINOLOGY: INCLUDING RELATED COMPUTER AND SATELLITE DEFINITIONS. Third Edition. Glenn R. Jones. Jones 21st Century, Englewood, Colorado. 1988.

THE NEW VIDEO ENCYCLOPEDIA. Larry Langman and Joseph A. Molinari. Garland Publishing, Incorporated, 136 Madison Avenue, New York, New York 10016. 1990.

THE TELEVISION INDUSTRY: A HISTORICAL DICTIONARY. Anthony Slide. Greenwood Publishing Group, Incorporated, 88 Post Road West, P.O. Box 5007, Westport, Connecticut 06881. 1991.

THE TV ENCYCLOPEDIA. David Inman. Perigee Books, New York, New York. 1991.

LAW REVIEWS AND PERIODICALS

COMMENT: HASTINGS JOURNAL OF COMMUNICATIONS AND ENTERTAINMENT LAW. Hastings College of Law, 200 McAllister Street, San Francisco, California 94102. Six issues per year.

COMMUNICATIONS AND THE LAW. Meckler Publishing, 520 Riverside Avenue, Westport, Connecticut 06880. Quarterly.

FEDERAL COMMUNICATIONS LAW JOURNAL. University of California at Los Angeles School of Law and Federal Communications Bar Association, 405 Hilgard Avenue, Los Angeles, California 90024. Three issues per year.

INTERNATIONAL MEDIA LAW. Oyez Longman, 21/27 Lamb's Conduit Street, London WEIN 3NJ UK. Monthly.

JOURNAL OF BROADCASTING AND ELECTRONICS MEDIA. Broadcast Education Association, 1771 N Street, Northwest, Washington, D.C. 20036. Quarterly.

NEWS MEDIA AND THE LAW. The Reporters Committee for Freedom of the Press, 1750 Pennsylvania Avenue, Northwest, Washington, D.C. 20006. Six issues per year.

NEWSLETTERS AND NEWSPAPERS

COMMUNICATIONS DAILY. Television Digest, Incorporated, 1836 Jefferson Place, Northwest, Washington, D.C. 20045. Daily.

COMMUNICATIONS LAWYER. American Bar Association, 750 North Lake Shore Drive, Chicago, Illinois 60611. Quarterly.

FCC WEEK. Telecom Publishing Group, Capitol Publications, Incorporated, 1300 North Seventeenth Street, Arlington, Virginia 22209. Weekly.

PUBLIC BROADCASTING REPORT. Television Digest, Incorporated, 1836 Jefferson Place, Northwest, Washington, D.C. 20045. Bi-weekly.

SATELLITE WEEK. Television Digest, Incorporated, 1836 Jefferson Place, Northwest, Washington, D.C. 20045. Weekly.

TELEVISION DIGEST. Television Digest, Incorporated, 1836 Jefferson Place, Northwest, Washington, D.C. 20045. Weekly.

VIDEO WEEK. Television Digest, Incorporated, 1836 Jefferson Place, Northwest, Washington, D.C. 20045. Weekly.

BIBLIOGRAPHIES

FILM, TELEVISION, AND VIDEO PERIODICALS: A COMPREHENSIVE ANNOTATED LIST. Katherine Loughney. Garland Publishing, Incorporated, 136 Madison Avenue, New York, New York 10016. 1991.

HIGH DEFINITION TELEVISION: A BIBLIOGRAPHY. William Saffady. Meckler Corporation, 11 Ferry Lane West, Westport, Connecticut 06880. 1990.

NEWS MEDIA AND PUBLIC POLICY: AN ANNOTATED BIBLIOGRAPHY. James P. McKerns. Garland Publishing, Incorporated, 136 Madison Avenue, New York, New York 10016. 1985.

RADIO BROADCASTING FROM 1920 TO 1990: AN ANNOTATED BIBLIOGRAPHY. Diane Foxhill Carothers. Garland Publishing, Incorporated, 136 Madison Avenue, New York, New York 10016. 1991.

RADIO DE-REGULATION: A SELECTED BIBLIOGRAPHY. Felix Chin. Vance Bibliographies, P.O. Box 229, 112 North Charter Street, Monticello, Illinois 61856. 1982.

RADIO RESEARCH: AN ANNOTATED BIBLIOGRAPHY, 1975-1988. Second Edition. Josephine Langham and Janine Chrichley. Avebury, Brookfield, Vermont. 1989.

REGULATION OF CHILDREN'S TELEVISION: A SELECTED BIBLIOGRAPHY ON THE DEBATE OVER PUBLIC POLICY. Tim J. Watts. Vance Bibliographies, P.O. Box 229, 112 North Charter Street, Monticello, Illinois 61856. 1987.

REGULATION OF SEX ON CABLE TELEVISION: A SELECTED BIBLIOGRAPHY. Anthony G. White. Vance Bibliographies, P.O. Box 229, 112 North Charter Street, Monticello, Illinois 61856. 1988.

TELEVISION AND ETHICS: A BIBLIOGRAPHY. Thomas W. Cooper, Robert Sullivan, Christopher Weir, and Peter Medaglia. G.K. Hall and Company, Incorporated, 70 Lincoln Street, Boston, Massachusetts 02111. 1988.

TELEVISION DEREGULATION. Linda D. Lewis. Vance Bibliographies, P.O. Box 229, 112 North Charter Street, Monticello, Illinois 61856. 1986.

DIRECTORIES

THE AMERICAN FILM INSTITUTE GUIDE TO COLLEGE COURSES IN FILM AND TELEVISION. Eighth Edition. William James Horrigan. American Film Institute. Distributed by Prentice-Hall, Incorporated, 113 Sylvan Avenue, Englewood Cliffs, New Jersey 07632. 1990.

INDEX TO THE ANNENBERG TELEVISION SCRIPT ARCHIVE. Sharon Black and Elizabeth Sue Moersh. Annenberg School of Communications. Oryx Press, 2214 North Central Avenue, Phoenix, Arizona 85004. 1990.

INTERNATIONAL DIRECTORY OF FILM AND TV DOCUMENTATION CENTRES. Third Edition. Frances Thorpe. St. James Press, 233 East Ontario, Chicago, Illinois 60611. 1988.

BIOGRAPHICAL SOURCES

INTERNATIONAL TELEVISION ALMANAC. Quigley Publishing Company. Practising Law Institute, 810 Seventh Avenue, New York, New York 10019. Annual.

ASSOCIATIONS AND PROFESSIONAL SOCIETIES

FEDERAL COMMUNICATIONS BAR ASSOCIATION, 1150 Connecticut Avenue, Northwest, Suite 1050, Washington, D.C. 20036. (202) 833-2684.

FIRST AMENDMENT LAWYERS ASSOCIATION, c/o Wayne Giampietro, 125 South Wacker Drive, Suite 2700, Chicago, Illinois 60606. (312) 236-0606.

NATIONAL CONFERENCE ON LAWYERS AND REPRESENTATIVES OF THE MEDIA, AMERICAN BAR ASSOCIATION. 750 North Lake Shore Drive, Chicago, Illinois 60611. (312) 988-5000.

SECTION ON MASS COMMUNICATIONS LAW, ASSOCIATION OF AMERICAN LAW SCHOOLS. Association of American Law Schools, One Dupont Circle, Northwest, Washington, D.C. 20036. (202) 296-8851.

RESEARCH CENTERS, INSTITUTES, CLEARINGHOUSES

CENTER FOR RESEARCH ON THE INFLUENCES OF TELEVISION ON CHILDREN. University of Kansas, Department of Human Development, Lawrence, Kansas 66045. (913) 841-4646.

FILM AND TELEVISION DOCUMENTATION CENTER. State University of New York at Albany, Rich 390C, 1400 Washington Avenue, Albany, New York 12222. (518) 442-5745.

NATIONAL COALITION ON TELEVISION VIOLENCE. P.O. Box 2157, Champaign, Illinois 61820. (217) 384-1920.

STATISTICS SOURCES

STATISTICAL TRENDS IN BROADCASTING. John Blair Company, 717 Fifth Avenue, New York, New York 10022. Annual.

T.V. BROADCAST FINANCIAL DATA. Federal Communications Commission, 1919 M Street, Northwest, Washington, D.C. 20554. Annual.

TENANCY
See: LANDLORD AND TENANT

TENDER OFFERS
See: CORPORATIONS, CONSOLIDATION AND MERGER

TERMINOLOGY
See: LEGAL RESEARCH; STATUTORY CONSTRUCTION AND DRAFTING

TERRITORIAL WATERS
See: LAW OF THE SEA

TERRORISM
See also: INTERNATIONAL CRIME; POLITICAL CRIMES AND OFFENSES

STATUTES, CODES, STANDARDS, UNIFORM LAWS

INTERNATIONAL TERRORISM: A COMPILATION OF MAJOR LAWS, TREATIES, AGREEMENTS, AND EXECUTIVE DOCUMENTS. United States Congress, House Committee on Foreign Affairs. Superintendent of Documents, United States Government Printing Office, Washington, D.C. 20402. 1991.

TRANSNATIONAL TERRORISM, CONVENTIONS AND COMMENTARY: A COMPILATION OF TREATIES, AGREEMENTS AND DECLARATIONS OF SPECIAL INTERESTS. Richard B. Lillich, Editor. The Michie Company, P.O. Box 7587, Charlottesville, Virginia 22906-7587. 1982.

HANDBOOKS, MANUALS, FORMBOOKS

A GUIDE TO UNITED NATIONS CRIMINAL POLICY. Manuel Lopez-Rey. Gower Publishing Company, Old Post Road, Brookfield, Vermont 05036. 1985.

INTERNATIONAL TERRORISM--AN ANNOTATED BIBLIOGRAPHY AND RESEARCH GUIDE. Augustus R. Norton and Martin H. Greenberg. West Publishing Company, P.O. Box 64526, 50 West Kellogg Boulevard, St. Paul, Minnesota 55164-0526. 1980.

PRIME TARGET: SECURITY MEASURES FOR THE EXECUTIVE AT HOME AND ABROAD. Bruce L. Danto. Charles Press Publishers, Incorporated, P.O. Box 15715, Philadelphia, Pennsylvania 19103. 1990.

TEXTBOOKS AND GENERAL WORKS

BEST LAID PLANS: THE INSIDE STORY OF AMERICA'S WAR AGAINST TERRORISM. David C. Martin and John Walcott. Simon and Schuster, Incorporated, 1230 Avenue of the Americas, New York, New York 10020. 1989.

BEYOND THE IRAN-CONTRA CRISIS: THE SHAPE OF U.S. ANTI-TERRORISM POLICY IN THE POST-REAGAN ERA. Neil C. Livingstone and Terrell E. Arnold. Lexington Books, 125 Spring Street, Lexington, Massachusetts 02173. 1988.

COMBATING THE TERRORISTS: DEMOCRATIC RESPONSES TO POLITICAL VIOLENCE. H. H. Tucker. Facts on File, Incorporated, 460 Park Avenue South, New York, New York 10016. 1988.

CONSTITUTIONS IN CRISIS: POLITICAL VIOLENCE AND THE RULE OF LAW. John E. Finn. Oxford University Press, 200 Madison Avenue, New York, New York 10016. 1991.

THE FALL OF PAN AM 103: INSIDE THE LOCKERBIE INVESTIGATION. Steven Emerson and Brian Duffy. Putnam Publishing Group, 200 Madison Avenue, New York, New York 10016. 1990.

FIGHTING BACK: WINNING THE WAR AGAINST TERRORISM. Neil C. Livingstone and Terrell E. Arnold. Free Press, 866 Third Avenue, New York, New York 10022. 1985.

THE FUTURE OF POLITICAL VIOLENCE: DESTABILIZATION, DISORDER, AND TERRORISM. Richard Clutterbuck. Saint Martin's Press, Incorporated, 175 Fifth Avenue, New York, New York 10010. 1986.

IN THE MIDDLE: NON-OFFICIAL MEDIATION IN VIOLENT SITUATIONS. Adam Curle. Berg Publishers, Incorporated, 165 Taber Avenue, Providence, Rhode Island 02906. 1987.

INTERNATIONAL TERRORISM: HOW NATIONS RESPOND TO TERRORISTS. William L. Waugh, Jr. Documentary Publications, 106 Kenan Street, Chapel Hill, North Carolina 27514. 1982.

LEGAL ASPECTS OF INTERNATIONAL TERRORISM. Alona E. Evans and John F. Murphy. American Society of International Law, 2223 Massachusetts Avenue, Northwest, Washington, D.C. 20008-2864. 1980.

LEGAL RESPONSES TO INTERNATIONAL TERRORISM: U.S. PROCEDURAL ASPECTS. M. Cherif Bassiouni. Martinus Nijhoff, Kluwer Academic Publishers, 101 Philip Drive, Assinippi Park, Norwell, Massachusetts 02061. 1988.

LEGISLATIVE RESPONSES TO TERRORISM. Yonah Alexander and Allan Nanes, Editors. Kluwer Academic Publishers, 101 Philip Drive, Assinippi Park, Norwell, Massachusetts 02061. 1986.

LEGITIMATE USE OF MILITARY FORCE AGAINST STATE-SPONSORED INTERNATIONAL TERRORISM. Richard J. Erickson. Air University Press. Superintendent of Documents, United States Government Printing Office, Washington, D.C. 20402. 1989.

MARITIME TERRORISM AND INTERNATIONAL LAW. Natalino Ronzitti. Martinus Nijhoff, Kluwer Academic Publishers, 101 Philip Drive, Assinippi Park, Norwell, Massachusetts 02061. 1990.

MEDIA COVERAGE OF TERRORISM: METHODS OF DIFFUSION. A. Odasuo Alali and Kenoye Kelvin Eke. Sage Publications, 2455 Teller Road, Newbury Park, California 91320. 1991.

MISPERCEIVING THE TERRORIST THREAT. Jeffrey D. Simon. Rand Corporation, Institute for Civil Justice, 1700 Main Street, P.O. Box 2138, Santa Monica, California 90406. 1987.

PERSPECTIVES ON TERRORISM. Lawrence Zelic Freedman and Yonah Alexander, Editors. Scholarly Resources, Incorporated, 104 Greenhill Avenue, Wilmington, Delaware 19805. 1983.

A POLITICAL ORGANIZATION APPROACH TO TRANSNATIONAL TERRORISM. Kent Layne Oots. Greenwood Publishing Group, Incorporated, 88 Post Road West, P.O. Box 5007, Westport, Connecticut 06881. 1986.

POLITICAL TERRORISM: A NEW GUIDE TO ACTORS, AUTHORS, CONCEPTS, DATA BASES, THEORIES, AND LITERATURE. Alex P. Schmid, Albert J. Jongman, and Michael Stohl. Transaction Books, Rutgers University, New Brunswick, New Jersey 08903. 1988.

POLITICAL VIOLENCE AND TERROR: MOTIFS AND MOTIVATIONS. Peter H. Merkl. University of California Press, 2120 Berkeley Way, Berkeley, California 94720. 1986.

RECENT TRENDS AND FUTURE PROSPECTS OF TERRORISM IN THE UNITED STATES. Bruce Hoffman. Rand Corporation, Institute for Civil Justice, 1700 Main Street, P.O. Box 2138, Santa Monica, California 90406. 1988.

TALES OF TERROR: TELEVISION NEWS AND THE CONSTRUCTION OF THE TERRORIST THREAT. Bethami A. Dobkin. Praeger Publishers, One Madison Avenue, New York, New York 10010. 1992.

TERRORISM AND CRIMINAL JUSTICE: AN INTERNATIONAL PERSPECTIVE. Ronald D. Crelinsten, Danielle LaBerge-Altmejd and Denis Szabo. Lexington Books, Division of D.C. Heath and Company, 125 Spring Street, Lexington, Massachusetts 02173. 1978.

TERRORISM AND DEMOCRACY. Stansfield Turner. Houghton Mifflin Company, 1 Beacon Street, Boston, Massachusetts 02108. 1991.

TERRORISM AND THE AMERICAN RESPONSE. Alvin H. Buckelew. MIRA Academic Press, P.O. Box 4334, Civic Center Branch, San Rafael, California 94913. 1984.

TERRORISM IN THE UNITED STATES AND THE POTENTIAL THREAT TO NUCLEAR FACILITIES. Bruce Hoffman. The Rand Corporation, 1700 Main Street, Santa Monica, California 90406. 1986.

TERRORISM, POLITICAL VIOLENCE AND WORLD ORDER. Henry H. Han, Editor. University Press of America, 4720 Boston Way, Lanham, Maryland 20706. 1984.

TERRORISM: PRAGMATIC INTERNATIONAL DETERRENCE AND COOPERATION. Richard Allan. Institute for East-West Security Studies. Distributed by Westview Press, Incorporated, 5500 Central Avenue, Boulder, Colorado 80301. 1990.

TERRORISM, THE MEDIA AND THE LAW. Abraham H. Miller, Editor. Transnational Publishers, Incorporated, P.O. Box 7282, Ardsley-on-Hudson, New York 10503. 1982.

TERRORISM: U.S. STRATEGY, AND REAGAN POLICIES. Marc A. Celmer. Greenwood Publishing Group, Incorporated, 88 Post Road West, P.O. Box 5007, Westport, Connecticut 06881. 1987.

TERRORIST ORGANIZATIONS IN THE UNITED STATES: AN ANALYSIS OF ISSUES, ORGANIZATIONS, TACTICS, AND RESPONSES. Wayman C. Mullins. Charles C. Thomas, Publishers, 2600 South First Street, Springfield, Illinois 62794. 1988.

TRANSNATIONAL TERRORISM, CONVENTIONS AND COMMENTARY: A COMPILATION OF TREATIES, AGREEMENTS, AND DECLARATIONS OF SPECIAL INTEREST TO THE UNITED STATES. Richard B. Lillich, Editor. The Michie Company, P.O. Box 7587, Charlottesville, Virginia 22906-7587. 1982.

THE WAR AGAINST THE TERRORISTS: HOW TO WIN IT. Gayle Rivers. Charter Books, imprint of Berkeley Publishers, 200 Madison Avenue, New York, New York 10016. 1989.

ENCYCLOPEDIAS AND DICTIONARIES

ENCYCLOPEDIA OF TERRORISM AND POLITICAL VIOLENCE. John Richard Thackrah. Routledge and Kegan Paul, London, England. 1987.

BIBLIOGRAPHIES

A BIBLIOGRAPHY OF INTERNATIONAL TERRORISM. Amos Lakos. Westview Press, 5500 Central Avenue, Boulder, Colorado 80301. 1986.

GLOBAL TERRORISM: A HISTORICAL BIBLIOGRAPHY. Suzanne Robitaille Ontiveros, Editor. ABC-Clio, Box 1911, Santa Barbara, California 93116-1911. 1986.

TERRORISM, 1980-1987: A SELECTIVELY ANNOTATED BIBLIOGRAPHY. Edward F. Mickolus and Peter A. Flemming. Greenwood Publishing Group, Incorporated, 88 Post Road West, P.O. Box 5007, Westport, Connecticut 06881. 1988.

TERRORISM, 1980-1990: A BIBLIOGRAPHY. Amos Lakos. Westview Press, Incorporated, 5500 Central Avenue, Boulder, Colorado 80301. 1991.

TERRORISM IN THE UNITED STATES AND EUROPE, 1800-1959: AN ANNOTATED BIBLIOGRAPHY. Michael Newton and Judy Ann Newton. Garland Publishing, Incorporated, 136 Madison Avenue, New York, New York 10016. 1988.

VIOLENCE AND TERROR IN THE MASS MEDIA: AN ANNOTATED BIBLIOGRAPHY. Nancy Signorielli and George Gerbner. Greenwood Publishing Group, Incorporated, 88 Post Road West, P.O. Box 5007, Westport, Connecticut 06881. 1988.

DIRECTORIES

THE DIRECTORY OF INTERNATIONAL TERRORISM. George Rosie. Paragon House Publishers, 90 Fifth Street, New York, New York 10011. 1987.

RESEARCH CENTERS, INSTITUTES, CLEARINGHOUSES

INSTITUTE FOR STUDIES IN INTERNATIONAL TERRORISM. State University of New York, Oreonta, New York 13820. (607) 431-3709.

INSTITUTE OF STRATEGIC STUDIES ON TERRORISM. P.O. Box 3372, Early, Texas 76803. (915) 646-8674.

ONLINE DATABASES

COUNTER-TERRORISM SECURITY INTELLIGENCE. Interests Limited, 8512 Cedar Street, Silver Springs, Maryland 20910.

RIGKUET. The Ackerman Group, 1666 Kennedy Causeway, Suite 700, Miami Beach, Florida 33141.

TERRORISM DATABASE. Business Risks International, Incorporated, Risk Assessment International Service, 1600 Wilson Boulevard, Suite 901, Arlington, Virginia 22209.

THEATRES
See: ENTERTAINMENT LAW

TIME-SHARE PROPERTY

STATUTES, CODES, STANDARDS, UNIFORM LAWS

UNIFORM LAW COMMISSIONERS' MODEL REAL ESTATE TIME-SHARE ACT, UNIFORM LAWS ANNOTATED. West Publishing Company, P.O. Box 64526, 50 West Kellogg Boulevard, St. Paul, Minnesota 55164-0526. 1976. (Annual Supplements).

LOOSELEAF SERVICES AND REPORTERS

TIMESHARING IN THE U.S. Douglas S. MacGregor. D and S Publishers, P.O. Box 5105, Clearwater, Florida 34618-5105. 1989.

TIMESHARING LAW REPORTER. Land Development Institute, Limited, 1300 N Street, Northwest, Washington, D.C. 20005. 1981- .

HANDBOOKS, MANUALS, FORMBOOKS

THE LEGAL ASPECTS OF REAL ESTATE TIME SHARING. William B. Ingersoll, Chairman. Practising Law Institute, 810 Seventh Avenue, New York, New York 10019. 1982.

TEXTBOOKS AND GENERAL WORKS

INTERNATIONAL TIMESHARING. Second Edition. James Edmonds. Services to Lawyers, Limited, Carswell Company, Limited, 145 Adelaide Street, Toronto, Ontario, M5H 3H4. 1986.

THE LAW AND BUSINESS OF TIME SHARE RESORTS. Mark E. Henze. Clark Boardman Company, Limited, 435 Hudson Street, New York, New York 10014. 1982. (Periodic Supplements).

THE LEGAL ASPECTS OF REAL ESTATE TIME-SHARING. William B. Ingersoll, Chairman. Practising Law Institute, 810 Seventh Avenue, New York, New York 10019. 1982.

ASSOCIATIONS AND PROFESSIONAL SOCIETIES

INTERNATIONAL FOUNDATION FOR TIMESHARING. 1220 L Street, Northwest, Washington, D.C. 20005. (202) 371-6700.

NATIONAL TIMESHARING COUNCIL. c/o American Land Development Association, 1220 L Street, Northwest, Washington, D.C. 20005. (202) 371-6700.

TITLE TO LAND
See: REAL PROPERTY

TORT CLAIM ACT
See: GOVERNMENT IMMUNITY AND LIABILITY

TORTS

See also: ACCIDENTS; ADMIRALTY; AVIATION ACCIDENTS; GOVERNMENT IMMUNITY AND LIABILITY; HAZARDOUS SUBSTANCES; PERSONAL INJURIES; PRODUCTS LIABILITY AND SAFETY; WRONGFUL DEATH

STATUTES, CODES, STANDARDS, UNIFORM LAWS

COMPENSATION AND LIABILITY FOR PRODUCT AND PROCESS INJURIES: PROPOSED FINAL REPORT, COUNCIL DRAFT. American Law Institute-American Bar Association, 4025 Chestnut Street, Philadelphia, Pennsylvania 19104. 1990- .

COMPENSATION AND LIABILITY FOR PRODUCT AND PROCESS INJURIES: FINAL REPORT, PRELIMARY DRAFT NUMBER 3 (AUGUST 15, 1990). American Law Institute-American Bar Association, 4025 Chestnut Street, Philadelphia, Pennsylvania 19104. 1990.

UNIFORM COMPARATIVE FAULT ACT. National Conference of Commissioners on Uniform State Laws. Uniform Laws Annotated. West Publishing Company, P.O. Box 64526, 50 West Kellogg Boulevard, St. Paul, Minnesota 55164-0526. 1976 (Annual Supplement).

UNIFORM CONTRIBUTION AMONG TORTFEASORS ACT. National Conference of Commissioners on Uniform State Laws. Uniform Laws Annotated. West Publishing Company, P.O. Box 64526, 50 West Kellogg Boulevard, St. Paul, Minnesota 55164-0526. 1976. (Annual Supplements).

UNIFORM SINGLE PUBLICATION ACT. National Conference of Commissioners on Uniform State Laws. Uniform Laws Annotated. West Publishing Company, P.O. Box 64526, 50 West Kellogg Boulevard, St. Paul, Minnesota 55164-0526. 1976. (Annual Supplements).

RESTATEMENTS

RESTATEMENT OF THE LAW, SECOND: TORTS. American Law Institute, 4025 Chestnut Street, Philadelphia, Pennsylvania 19104. 1965-1979.

RESTATEMENT OF THE LAW, SECOND: TORTS: APPENDIX. American Law Institute, 4025 Chestnut Street, Philadelphia, Pennsylvania 19104. 1966-1982. (Annual Supplement).

LOOSELEAF SERVICES AND REPORTERS

THE BUSINESS TORT OF FRAUD AND MISREPRESENTATION. Warren Freedman. Butterworth Legal Publishers, 90 Stiles Road, Salem New Hampshire 03079. 1989- .

DAMAGES IN TORT ACTIONS. Marilyn Minzer, Editor. Matthew Bender and Company, Incorporated, 11 Penn Plaza, New York, New York 10001. 1982- .

ENVIRONMENTAL DUE DILIGENCE: THE COMPLETE RESOURCE GUIDE FOR REAL ESTATE LENDERS, BUYERS, SELLERS, AND ATTORNEYS. James P. O'Brien and William Harris Frank. Bureau of National Affairs, Incorporated, 1231 Twenty-fifth Street, Northwest, Washington, D.C. 20037. 1989- .

A GUIDE TO TOXIC TORTS. Margie Tyler Searcy. Matthew Bender and Company, Incorporated, 11 Penn Plaza, New York, New York 10001. 1987- .

HANDLING OCCUPATIONAL DISEASE CASES. Frederick M. Baron. Callaghan and Company, 155 Pfingsten Road, Deerfield, Illinois 60015. 1989- .

LAW OF TOXIC TORTS: LITIGATION, DEFENSE, INSURANCE. Michael Dore. Clark Boardman Company, Limited, 435 Hudson Street, New York, New York 10014. 1987- .

LENDER LIABILITY. A. Barry Cappello and Frances E. Komoroske. Parker and Son Publications, Incorporated, P.O. Box 60001, Los Angeles, California 90060. 1987- .

MANAGING ENVIRONMENTAL RISK: REAL ESTATE AND BUSINESS TRANSACTIONS. Jennifer L. Machlin and Tomme R. Young. Clark Boardman Company, Limited, 435 Hudson Street, New York, New York 10014. 1988- .

MEDICAL AND HOSPITAL NEGLIGENCE. Miles J. Zaremski and Louis S. Goldstein. Callaghan and Company, 155 Pfingsten Road, Deerfield, Illinois 60015. 1988.

MODERN TORT LAW: LIABILITY AND LITIGATION. J.D. Lee, Barry A. Lindahl, and James A. Dooley. Callaghan and Company, 155 Pfingsten Road, Deerfield, Illinois 60015. 1988- .

NEGLIGENCE COMPENSATION CASES ANNOTATED. Fourth Series. Callaghan and Company, 155 Pfingsten Road, Deerfield, Illinois 60015. 1968- .

THE PREPARATION AND TRIAL OF MEDICAL MALPRACTICE CASES. Richard E. Shandell and Patricia Smith. Law Journal Seminars-Press, Incorporated, 111 Eighth Avenue, Suite 900, New York, New York 10011. 1990- .

VICTIMS' RIGHTS: LAW AND LITIGATION. Frank Carrington and James A. Rapp. Matthew Bender and Company, Incorporated, 11 Penn Plaza, New York, New York 10001. 1989- .

HANDBOOKS, MANUALS, FORMBOOKS

COMPARATIVE NEGLIGENCE MANUAL. Revised Edition. John J. Palmer and Stephen M. Flanagan. Callaghan and Company, 155 Pfingsten Road, Deerfield, Illinois 60015. 1986-1990.

THE ENVIRONMENT LITIGATION DESKBOOK. Kathleen A. Touby, Kenneth J. Smith, and Jame T. O'Reilly. Executive Enterprises Publications Company, 22 West Twenty-first Street, New York, New York 10010-6904. 1989.

ENVIRONMENTAL DUE DILIGENCE HANDBOOK. Second Edition. Government Institutes, Incorporated, 966 Hungerford Drive, Rockville, Maryland 20850. 1991.

JURY INSTRUCTIONS ON DAMAGES IN TORT ACTIONS. Second Edition. Graham Douthwaite. Michie Company, P.O. Box 7587, Charlottesville, Virginia 22906. 1988.

MARTIAL AND PARENTAL TORTS: A GUIDE TO CAUSES OF ACTION, ARGUMENTS, AND DAMAGES. American Bar Association, Section of Family Law, 750 North Lake Shore Drive, Chicago, Illinois 60611. 1990.

MODEL JURY INSTRUCTIONS FOR BUSINESS TORT LITIGATION: A PROJECT OF THE BUSINESS TORTS LITIGATION COMMITTEE, SUBCOMMITTEE ON JURY INSTRUCTIONS, SECTION OF LITIGATION, AMERICAN BAR ASSOCIATION. Second Edition. American Bar Association, 750 North Lake Shore Drive, Chicago, Illinois 60611. 1988.

MUNICIPAL LIABILITY LAW AND PRACTICE: FORMS. Vincent R. Fontana. John Wiley and Sons, Incorporated, 605 Third Avenue, New York, New York 10158. 1991.

NEGLIGENCE LITIGATION HANDBOOK: FEDERAL AND STATE. Mark A. Dombroff, Patricia K. Gilmore and Juanita M. Madole. John Wiley and Sons, Incorporated, 605 Third Avenue, New York, New York 10158. 1986.

TOXIC TORT LITIGATION HANDBOOK: A STEP-BY-STEP GUIDE WITH FORMS. Michael Dore. Clark Boardman Company, Limited, 435 Hudson Street, New York, New York 10014. 1988.

TEXTBOOKS AND GENERAL WORKS

AMERICAN LAW OF TORTS. Stuart M. Speiser, Charles F. Krause, and Alfred W. Gans. Lawyers Co-Operative Publishing Company, Aqueduct Building, Rochester, New York 14694. 1983. (Periodic Supplements).

THE AMERICAN TORT PROCESS. John G. Fleming. Oxford University Press, Incorporated, 200 Madison Avenue, New York, New York 10016. 1990.

ASSESSING THE EFFECTS OF TORT REFORMS. Stephen J. Carroll and Nicholas Pace. Rand Corporation, Institute for Civil Justice, 1700 Main Street, P.O. Box 2138, Santa Monica, California 90406. 1987.

AUTOMATED TELLER MACHINE CRIME: ARE BANKS LIABLE FOR PERSONAL INJURIES? Pamela Samuels. William S. Hein and Company, 1285 Main Street, Buffalo, New York 14209. 1990.

BAD FAITH LIABILITY: A STATE-BY-STATE REVIEW. Stephen S. Ashley. Callaghan and Company, 155 Pfingsten Road, Deerfield, Illinois 60015. 1987.

CAUSES OF ACTION. Shepard's Editorial Staff. Shepard's/McGraw-Hill, P.O. Box 1235, Colorado Springs, Colorado 80901. 1983. (Supplement 1984).

THE COMPACT GUIDE TO TORT LAW: A CIVILIZED APPROACH TO THE LAW. Jefferson Hane Weaver. West Publishing Company, 50 West Kellogg Boulevard, St. Paul, Minnesota 55164-0526. 1990.

COMPARATIVE NEGLIGENCE. L Larson, et al. Matthew Bender and Company, Incorporated, 11 Penn Plaza, New York, New York 10001. 1984.

COMPARATIVE NEGLIGENCE. Second Edition. Victor E. Schwartz. The Michie Company, P.O. Box 7587, Charlottesville, Virginia 22906-7587. 1986.

COMPARATIVE NEGLIGENCE DEFENSE TACTICS. James C. McConnell. John Wiley and Sons, Incorporated, 605 Third Avenue, New York, New York 10158. 1985.

COMPENSATION FOR ACCIDENTAL INJURIES IN THE UNITED STATES. Deborah R. Hensler. Rand Corporation, 1700 Main Street, P.O. Box 2138, Santa Monica, California 90406. 1991.

COSTS OF THE CIVIL JUSTICE SYSTEM: COURT EXPENDITURES FOR PROCESSING TORT CASES. James S. Kakalik and Abby Eisenhtat Robyn. The Rand Corporation, 1700 Main Street, Santa Monica, California 90406. 1982.

DOMESTIC TORTS: FAMILY VIOLENCE, CONFLICT, AND SEXUAL ABUSE. Leonard Karp and Cheryl L. Karp. Shepard's/McGraw-Hill, P.O. Box 1235, Colorado Springs, Colorado 80901. 1989.

ECONOMIC ANALYSIS OF ACCIDENT LAW. Steven Shavell. Harvard University Press, 79 Garden Street, Cambridge, Massachusetts 02138. 1987.

THE ECONOMIC STRUCTURE OF TORT LAW. William M. Landes and Richard A. Posner. Harvard University Press, 79 Garden Street, Cambridge, Massachusetts 02138. 1987.

ENVIRONMENTAL AND TOXIC TORT CLAIMS: INSURANCE COVERAGE IN 1990 AND BEYOND. Richard D. Williams. Practising Law Institute, 810 Seventh Avenue, New York, New York 10019. 1990.

EVIDENCE IN NEGLIGENCE CASES. Eighth Edition. Charles Kramer. Practising Law Institute, 810 Seventh Avenue, New York, New York 10019. 1987.

EXTRACONTRACTUAL DAMAGES. John R. Groves, Editor. Tort and Insurance Practice Section, American Bar Association, 750 North Lake Shore Drive, Chicago, Illinois 60611. 1983.

GOOD FAITH-BAD FAITH LITIGATION. Terry O. Tottenham. Fulbright and Jaworski, Austin, Texas. 1988.

THE GREAT HARTFORD CIRCUS FIRE: CREATIVE SETTLEMENT OF MASS DISASTERS. Henry S. Cohn and David Bollier. Yale University Press, 302 Temple Street, New Haven, Connecticut 06520. 1991.

HANDLING BIRTH TRAUMA CASES. Stanley S. Schwartz and Norman D. Tucker. John Wiley and Sons, Incorporated, 605 Third Avenue, New York, New York 10158. 1989.

HANDLING FEDERAL TORT CLAIMS: ADMINISTRATIVE AND JUDICIAL REMEDIES. Jayson S. Lester. Matthew Bender and Company, Incorporated, 11 Penn Plaza, New York, New York 10001. 1984.

HAZARDOUS WASTES AND TOXIC TORTS: LAW AND STRATEGY. Leader Publications, 111 Eighth Avenue, New York, New York 10111. 1985.

JURY INSTRUCTIONS ON DAMAGES AND TORT ACTIONS. Second Edition. Graham Douthwaite. Michie Company, P.O. Box 7587, Charlottesville, Virginia 22906-7587. 1988. (Supplement 1990).

THE LAW OF TORTS. Second Edition. Fowler V. Harper, Fleming James, Jr. and Oscar S. Gray. Little, Brown, and Company, 34 Beacon Street, Boston, Massachusetts 02108. 1986.

LEGAL LIABILITY AND RISK MANAGEMENT FOR PUBLIC AND PRIVATE ENTITIES: SPORT AND PHYSICAL EDUCATION, LEISURE SERVICES, RECREATION AND PARKS, CAMPING AND ADVENTURE ACITIVITIES. Betty Van Der Smissen. Anderson Publishing Company, 2035 Reading Road, Cincinnati, Ohio 45202. 1990.

THE LIABILITY MAZE: THE IMPACT OF LIABILITY LAW ON SAFETY AND INNOVATION. Peter W. Huber and Robert E. Litan. Brookings Institution, 1775 Massachusetts Avenue, Washington, D.C. 20036. 1991.

LIABILITY OF SCHOOL OFFICIALS AND ADMINISTRATORS FOR CIVIL RIGHTS TORTS. Richard S. Vacca and H. C. Hudgins, Jr. The Michie Company, P.O. Box 7587, Charlottesville, Virginia 22906-7587. 1982.

LIABILITY: PERSPECTIVES AND POLICY. Robert E. Litan and Clifford Winston. Brookings Institution, 1775 Massachusetts Avenue, Washington, D.C. 20036. 1988.

LIABILITY: THE LEGAL REVOLUTION AND ITS CONSEQUENCES. Peter W. Huber. Basic Books, Incorporated, 10 East Fifty-third Street, New York, New York 10022. 1988.

LITIGATING HAZARDOUS HIGHWAY CLAIMS. James A. Branch, Jr., Cynthia A. Fry, and Mary E. Lebeck. John Wiley and Sons, Incorporated, 605 Third Avenue, New York, New York 10158. 1990.

MALPRACTICE IN THE EMERGENCY ROOM. Stephen H. Mackauf. Practising Law Institute, 810 Seventh Avenue, New York, New York 10019. 1988.

MALPRACTICE PREVENTION AND LIABILITY CONTROL FOR HOSPITALS. Second Edition. James E. Orlikoff and Audrone M. Vanagunas. American Hospital Publishing, Incorporated, 211 East Chicago Avenue, Chicago, Illinois 60611. 1988.

MANAGEMENT OF MASS TORT LITIGATION. Lawrence H. Curtis and Edward D. Tanenhaus, Co-Chairmen. Practising Law Institute, 810 Seventh Avenue, New York, New York 10019. 1983.

MEDICOLEGAL ASPECTS OF CRITICAL CARE. Katherine Beneach, et al., Editor. Aspen Publishers, Incorporated, 1600 Research Boulevard, Rockville, Maryland 20850. 1986.

MODERN TORT LAW: LIABILITY AND LITIGATION. James A. Dooley. Callaghan and Company, 155 Pfingsten Road, Deerfield, Illinois 60015. 1977. (Periodic Supplements).

MODERN TORT LIABILITY: RECOVERY IN THE '90S. Terrence F. Kiely. John Wiley and Sons, Incorporated, 605 Third Avenue, New York, New York 10158. 1990.

MORAL ARGUMENT AND SOCIAL VISION IN THE COURTS: A STUDY OF TORT ACCIDENT LAW. Henry J. Steiner. University of Wisconsin Press, 114 North Murray, Madison, Wisconsin 53706. 1987.

MUNICIPAL LIABILITY: LAW AND PRACTICE. Vincent R. Fontana. John Wiley and Sons, Incorporated, 605 Third Avenue, New York, New York 10158. 1990.

PERSPECTIVES ON TORT LAW. Third Edition. Robert L. Rabin. Little, Brown and Company, 34 Beacon Street, Boston, Massachusetts 02108. 1990.

PREPARING A TOXIC TORT CASE FOR TRIAL, 1991. G. Marc Whitehead. Practising Law Institute, 810 Seventh Avenue, New York, New York 10019. 1991.

PROSSER AND KEETON ON THE LAW OF TORTS. Fifth Edition. W. Page Keeton, Dan B. Dobbs, Robert E. Keeton, and David G. Owen. West Publishing Company, P.O. Box 64526, 50 West Kellogg Boulevard, St. Paul, Minnesota 55164-0526. 1984. (Hornbook).

PUNITIVE DAMAGES IN BAD FAITH CASES. Fourth Edition. John C. McCarthy. Lawpress Corporation, P.O. Box 596, Kentfield, California 94914. 1987.

RECOVERY OF DAMAGES FOR FRAUD. Robert L. Dunn. Lawpress, P.O. Box 596, Kentfield, California 94914. 1988.

TORT AND INJURY LAW. Marshall S. Shapo. Matthew Bender and Company, Incorporated, 11 Penn Plaza, New York, New York 10001. 1990.

TORT LAW. Second Edition. Robert Force, Daniel Jay Baum, and Judith Lass Elting. South-Western Publishing Company, 5101 Madison Road, Cincinnati, Ohio 45227. 1988.

TORT LAW. Ernest J. Weinrib. New York University Press, 70 Washington Square South, New York, New York 10012. 1991.

TORT LAW. Allen P. Wilkinson and Edward Barker. West Publishing Company, 50 West Kellogg Boulevard, St. Paul, Minnesota 55164-0526. 1991.

TORT LAW AND ECONOMIC INTERESTS. Peter Cane. Oxford University Press, Incorporated, 200 Madison Avenue, New York, New York 10016. 1991.

TORT LAW AND THE PUBLIC INTEREST: COMPETITION, INNOVATION, AND CONSUMER WELFARE. Peter H. Schuck. W. W. Norton and Company, Incorporated, 500 Fifth Avenue, New York, New York 10110. 1991.

TORT LAW: CASES AND ECONOMIC ANALYSIS. Richard A. Posner. Little, Brown and Company, 34 Beacon Street, Boston, Massachusetts 02108. 1982.

TORT LAW: CASES, MATERIALS, PROBLEMS. Jerry J. Phillips. Michie Company, P.O. Box 7587, Charlottesville, Virginia 22906. 1991.

TORT LAW FOR LEGAL ASSISTANTS: A PRACTICAL GUIDE. Linda L. Edwards and J. Stanley Edwards. West Publishing Company, 50 West Kellogg Boulevard, St. Paul, Minnesota 55164-0526. 1992.

TORT LAW IN AMERICAN HISTORY: MAJOR HISTORICAL INTERPRETATIONS. Kermit L. Hall. Garland Publishing, Incorporated, 136 Madison Avenue, New York, New York 10016. 1987.

TORTS. Edward J. Kionka. West Publishing Company, 50 West Kellogg Boulevard, St. Paul, Minnesota 55164-0526. 1988.

TORTS AND SPORTS: LEGAL LIABILITY IN PROFESSIONAL AND AMATEUR ATHLETICS. Raymond L. Yasser. Greenwood Publishing Group, Incorporated, 88 Post Road West, P.O. Box 5007, Westport, Connecticut 06881. 1985.

TORTS IN A NUTSHELL. Second Edition. Edward J. Kionka. West Publishing Company, 50 West Kellogg Boulevard, St. Paul, Minnesota 55164-0526. 1992.

TORTS, PERSONAL INJURY LITIGATION. Second Edition. William P. Statsky. West Publishing Company, 50 West Kellogg Boulevard, St. Paul, Minnesota 55164-0526. 1990.

TOWARDS A JURISPRUDENCE OF INJURY. American Bar Association, Special Committee on the Tort Liability System. American Bar Association, 750 North Lake Shore Drive, Chicago, Illinois 60611. 1984.

TOXIC TORT LITIGATION. Edward Greer, Warren Freedman, and Stephanie Levin. Rosenfeld Launer Publications, New York, New York. 1989.

TOXIC TORT LITIGATION: A PRIMER IN MANAGEMENT. Pennsylvania Bar Institute, P.O. Box 1027, Harrisburg, Pennsylvania 17108. 1983.

TOXIC TORTS: LITIGATION OF HAZARDOUS SUBSTANCES CASES. Gary Z. Nothstein. Shepard's/McGraw-Hill, P.O. Box 1235, Colorado Springs, Colorado 80901. (Periodic Supplements).

TRENDS IN TORT LITIGATION: THE STORY BEHIND THE STATISTICS. Deborah R. Hensler. Rand Corporation, Institute for Civil Justice, 1700 Main Street, P.O. Box 2138, Santa Monica, California 90406. 1987.

WHO SHOULD BE LIABLE? A GUIDE TO POLICY DEALING WITH RISK. Committee for Economic Development, 1700 K Street, Northwest, Washington, D.C. 20006. 1989.

DIGESTS, INDEXES, ABSTRACTS, CITATORS

MEDICAL MALPRACTICE DIGEST. Dean E. Snyder. Lawyers Cooperative Publishing Company, Aqueduct Building, Rochester, New York 14694. 1991.

LAW REVIEWS AND PERIODICALS

THE BRIEF. American Bar Association, Section on Tort and Insurance Practice, 750 North Lake Shore Drive, Chicago, Illinois 60611. Quarterly.

DEFENSE LAW JOURNAL. The Michie Company, P.O. Box 7587, Charlottesville, Virginia 22906. Quarterly.

FOR THE DEFENSE. Defense Research Institute, 750 North Lake Shore Drive, Suite 500, Chicago, Illinois 60611. Monthly.

LITIGATION. American Bar Association, 750 North Lake Shore Drive, Chicago, Illinois 60611. Quarterly.

TORT AND INSURANCE JOURNAL. Section of Tort and Insurance Practice, American Bar Association, 750 North Lake Shore Drive, Chicago, Illinois 60611. Quarterly.

NEWSLETTERS AND NEWSPAPERS

ATLA LAW REPORTER. Association of Trial Lawyers of America, 1050 Thirty-first Street, Northwest, Washington, D.C. 20007. (Monthly).

THE BUSINESS TORTS REPORTER. Business Torts Research, Incorporated, Lenox Hill Station, P.O. Box 1093, New York, New York 10021. Monthly.

HAZARDOUS WASTE AND TOXIC TORTS LAW AND STRATEGY. Leader Publications, 111 Eighth Avenue, New York, New York 10111. Monthly.

INSURANCE ANTITRUST AND TORT REFERUM REPORT. Mealey Publications, P.O. Box 446, Wayne, Pennsylvania 19087. Semimonthly.

THE REFORMER. American Tort Reform Association, 1212 New York Avenue, Northwest, Suite 515, Washington, D.C. 20005. Monthly.

THE TORT HOT LINE. Jury Verdicts Weekly, Incorporated, 738 Montecito Center, Santa Rosa, California 95409. Monthly.

DIRECTORIES

MARKHAM'S NEGLIGENCE COUNSEL. Markham Publishing Corporation, 219 Atlantic Street, Stamford, Connecticut 06901. 1956- .

ASSOCIATIONS AND PROFESSIONAL SOCIETIES

AMERICAN BAR ASSOCIATION, SECTION OF TORT AND INSURANCE PRACTICE. 750 North Lake Shore Drive, Chicago, Illinois 60611. (312) 988-5000.

AMERICAN TORT REFORM ASSOCIATION. 1212 New York Avenue, Northwest, Suite 515, Washington, D.C. 20005. (212) 682-1163.

ASSOCIATION OF AMERICAN LAW SCHOOLS, SECTION ON TORTS. One Dupont Circle, Northwest, Washington, D.C. 20036. (202) 296-8851.

AUDIOVISUALS

MEDIATION: SIMULATION OF A PERSONAL INJURY CASE. National Practice Institute, 330 Second Avenue South, Minneapolis, Minnesota 55401. Videotape.

PRODUCTS LIABILITY LAW: A BOTTLING PLANT ACCIDENT. National Practice Institute, 330 Second Avenue South, Minneapolis, Minnesota 55401. Videotape.

PRODUCTS LIABILITY LAW: AN AUTOMOBILE DEFECT. National Practice Institute, 330 Second Avenue South, Minneapolis, Minnesota 55401. Videotape.

PRODUCTS LIABILITY LAW: AN EXPLODING LAMP CASE. National Practice Institute, 330 Second Avenue South, Minneapolis, Minnesota 55401. Videotape.

PRODUCTS LIABILITY LAW: CIRCULAR SAW ACCIDENT. National Practice Institute, 330 Second Avenue South, Minneapolis, Minnesota 55401. Audiotape.

PRODUCTS LIABILITY LAW: DRUG LITIGATION. National Practice Institute, 330 Second Avenue South, Minneapolis, Minnesota 55401. Audiotape.

PRODUCTS LIABILITY LAW: LAWN MOWER ACCIDENT. National Practice Institute, 330 Second Avenue South, Minneapolis, Minnesota 55401. Audiotape.

PRODUCTS LIABILITY LAW: MOTORCYCLE ACCELERATOR PROBLEM. National Practice Institute, 330 Second Avenue South, Minneapolis, Minnesota 55401. Audiotape.

COMPUTER-ASSISTED LEGAL INSTRUCTION

FRANCIS V. SPINDLER. Interactive Video Library, Harvard Law School, Educational Technology Department, 18 Everett Street, Cambridge, Massachusetts 02138. Interactive videodisc.

INTENT ONE: THE USE OF INTENT IN TORT. Robert E. Keeton. Center for Computer-Assisted Instruction, 229 19th Avenue South, University of Minnesota, Minneapolis, Minnesota 55455. Machine-readable computer file.

INTENT TWO: COMPUTER-AIDED TORT EXERCISES. Robert E. Keeton. Center for Computer-Assisted Instruction, 229 19th Avenue South, University of Minnesota, Minneapolis, Minnesota 55455. Machine-readable computer file.

ORTIZ V. FLEISHMAN I, II AND III. Center for Computer-Assisted Instruction, 229 19th Avenue South, University of Minnesota, Minneapolis, Minnesota 55455. Interactive videodisc.

SPRAGUE CASE: CHILD INJURY IN TORT LAW. Robert E. Keeton. Center for Computer-Assisted Instruction, 229 19th Avenue South, University of Minnesota, Minneapolis, Minnesota 55455. Machine-readable computer file.

TOWN GOVERNMENT
See: LOCAL GOVERNMENT

TOXIC SUBSTANCES
See: HAZARDOUS SUBSTANCES

TRADE
See: COMMERCIAL LAW; TRADE REGULATION

TRADE AND PROFESSIONAL ASSOCIATIONS
See: ASSOCIATIONS AND NONPROFIT CORPORATIONS

TRADE REGULATION
See also: ANTITRUST LAW; COMMERCE DEPARTMENT; COMMERCIAL LAW; COMMODITY FUTURES TRADING COMMISSION; EXPORT AND IMPORT; FEDERAL TRADE COMMISSION; INTERNATIONAL TRADE ADMINISTRATION; INTERNATIONAL TRADE COMMISSION; INTERSTATE COMMERCE COMMISSION; SECURITIES AND EXCHANGE COMMISSION

RESTATEMENTS

UNIFORM DECEPTIVE TRADE PRACTICES ACT. Uniform Laws Annotated. West Publishing Company, P.O. Box 64526, 50 West Kellogg Boulevard, St. Paul, Minnesota 55164-0526. 1976 (Annual Supplement).

LOOSELEAF SERVICES AND REPORTERS

ANTITRUST AND TRADE REGULATION REPORT. Bureau of National Affairs, 1231 Twenty-fifth Street, Northwest, Washington, D.C. 20037. 1961- .

TRADE REGULATION REPORTS. Commerce Clearing House, Incorporated, 4025 West Peterson Avenue, Chicago, Illinois 60646. 1961- .

HANDBOOKS, MANUALS, FORMBOOKS

FEDERAL TRADE COMMISSION. Stephanie W. Kanwit. Shepard's/McGraw-Hill, P.O. Box 1235, Colorado Springs, Colorado 80901. 1979. (Periodic Supplements).

GOVERNMENT REGULATION OF BUSINESS: AN INFORMATION SOURCEBOOK. Robert Goehlert and Nels Gunderson. Oryx Press, 2214 North Central Avenue, Phoenix, Arizona 85004. 1987.

PRACTICAL LAWYER'S MANUAL. American Law Institute- American Bar Association Committee on Continuing Professional Education, 4025 Chestnut Street, Philadelphia, Pennsylvania 19104. 1985.

TEXTBOOKS AND GENERAL WORKS

ANTITRUST AND THE TRIUMPH OF ECONOMICS: INSTITUTIONS, EXPERTISE, AND POLICY CHANGE. Marc Allen Eisner. University of North Carolina Press, P.O. Box 2288, 116 South Boundary Street, Chapel Hill, North Carolina 27515-2288. 1991.

ANTITRUST LAWS AND TRADE REGULATION. Matthew Bender and Company, Incorporated, 11 Penn Plaza, New York, New York 10001. 1983- .

ANTITRUST PENALTY REFORM: AN ECONOMIC ANALYSIS. William Breit and Kenneth G. Elzinga. American Enterprise Institute for Public Policy Research, 1150 Seventeenth Street, Northwest, Washington, D.C. 20036. 1986.

BUSINESS AND GOVERNMENT. Joseph Frese and Jacob Judd Editors. Sleepy Hollow Press, 150 White Plains Road, Tarrytown, New York 10591. 1985.

BUSINESS AND ITS LEGAL ENVIRONMENT. Third Edition. Thomas W. Dunfee, Janice R. Bellace, and David Barrett Cohen. Prentice-Hall, Incorporated, 113 Sylvan Avenue, Englewood Cliffs, New Jersey 07632. 1992.

BUSINESS LAW AND THE REGULATION OF BUSINESS. Third Edition. Len Young Smith, Richard A. Mann and Barry S. Roberts. West Publishing Company, P.O. Box 64526, 50 West Kellogg Boulevard, St. Paul, Minnesota 55164-0526. 1990.

COMMERCIAL, BUSINESS AND TRADE LAWS: THE UNITED STATES. Joseph J. Norton. Oceana Publications Incorporated, 75 Main Street, Dobbs Ferry, New York 10522. 1983- .

THE CONSTITUTION AND THE ECONOMY: OBJECTIVE THEORY AND CRITICAL COMMENTARY. Michael Conant. University of Oklahoma Press, 105 Asp Avenue, Norman, Oklahoma 73019. 1991.

THE COST OF DOING BUSINESS: LEGAL AND REGULATORY ISSUES IN THE UNITED STATES AND ABROAD. Peter Chinloy. Praeger Publishers, One Madison Avenue, New York, New York 10010. 1989.

DISMANTLING AMERICA: THE RUSH TO DEREGULATE. Susan J. Tolchin and Martin Tolchin. Oxford University Press, 200 Madison Avenue, New York, New York 10016. 1985.

ECONOMIC LAW AND ECONOMIC GROWTH: ANTITRUST, REGULATION, AND THE AMERICAN GROWTH SYSTEM. George E. Garvey and Gerald J. Garvey. Praeger Publishers, One Madison Avenue, New York, New York 10010. 1990.

THE ECONOMICS OF REGULATION: PRINCIPLES AND INSTITUTIONS. Alfred E. Kahn. MIT Press, 55 Hayward Street, Cambridge, Massachusetts 02142. 1988.

THE FEDERAL TRADE COMMISSION. Pamela B. Stuart. Chelsea House Publishers, 1974 Sproul Road, Suite 400, Broomall, Pennsylvania 19008. 1991.

INDUSTRY REGULATION AND THE PERFORMANCE OF THE AMERICAN ECONOMY. Paul W. MacAvoy. W. W. Norton and Company, Incorporated, 500 Fifth Avenue, New York, New York 10110. 1992.

ISSUES AFTER A CENTURY OF FEDERAL COMPETITION POLICY. Robert L. Wills, Julie A. Caswell, and John D. Culbertson. Lexington Books, 125 Spring Street, Lexington, Massachusetts 02173. 1987.

LAW AND MARKETS IN UNITED STATES HISTORY: DIFFERENT MODES OF BARGAINING AMONG INTERESTS. James W. Hurst. University of Wisconsin Press, 114 North Murray Street, Madison, Wisconsin 53706. 1982.

THE LAW OF BUSINESS AND COMMERCE: MAJOR HISTORICAL INTERPRETATIONS. Kermit L. Hall. Garland Publishing, Incorporated, 136 Madison Avenue, New York, New York 10016. 1987.

THE LEGAL AND ETHICAL ENVIRONMENT OF BUSINESS. Edwin W. Tucker and Jan W. Henkel. Richard D. Irwin, Incorporated, 1818 Ridge Road, Homewood, Illinois 60430. 1991.

THE LEGAL ENVIRONMENT OF BUSINESS. Second Edition. Edward J. Conry, Gerald R. Ferrera and Karla H. Fox. Allyn and Bacon, 160 Gould Street, Needham Heights, Massachusetts 02194. 1990.

THE LEGAL ENVIRONMENT OF BUSINESS. Robert Prentice and John R. Allison. Dryden Press, 465 South Lincoln Drive, Troy, Missouri 63379. 1990.

THE LEGAL ENVIRONMENT OF BUSINESS: REGULATORY LAW AND CONRACTS. Douglas Whitman, John William Gergacz, and Murry Levin. McGraw-Hill Publishing Company, 1221 Avenue of the Americas, New York, New York 10020. 1992.

REBUILDING AMERICA: THE CASE FOR ECONOMIC REGULATION. Frederick C. Thayer. Praeger Publishers, One Madison Avenue, New York, New York 10010-3603. 1984.

REFORMING FEDERAL REGULATION. Robert E. Litan and William D. Nordhaus. Yale University Press, 302 Temple Street, New Haven, Connecticut 06520. 1983.

REGULATING BIG BUSINESS: ANTITRUST IN GREAT BRITAIN AND AMERICA, 1880 TO 1990. Tony Freyer. Cambridge University Press, 40 West Twentieth Street, New York, New York 10011. 1992.

REGULATION AND ITS REFORM. Stephen G. Breyer. Harvard University Press, 79 Garden Street, Cambridge, Massachusetts 02138. 1982.

REGULATION OF BUSINESS ENTERPRISE IN THE U.S.A. Joseph J. Norton. Oceana Publications Incorporated, 75 Main Street, Dobbs Ferry, New York 10522. 1983- .

REGULATORY POLICY AND PRACTICES: REGULATING BETTER AND REGULATING LESS. Fred Thompson and L. R. Jones. Praeger Publishers, One Madison Avenue, New York, New York 10010-3603. 1982.

REVOLT AGAINST REGULATION: THE RISE AND PAUSE OF THE CONSUMER MOVEMENT. Michael Pertschuk. University of California Press, 2120 Berkeley Way, Berkeley, California 94720. 1982.

UNFAIR TRADE PRACTICES IN A NUTSHELL. Second Edition. Charles R. McManis. West Publishing Company, P.O. Box 64526, 50 West Kellogg Boulevard, St. Paul, Minnesota 55164-0526. 1988.

WEST'S LEGAL ENVIRONMENT OF BUSINESS: TEXT, CASES, ETHICAL, AND REGULATORY ISSUES. Frank B. Cross and Roger LeRoy Miller. West Publishing Company, 50 West Kellogg Boulevard, St. Paul, Minnesota 55164-0526. 1991.

NEWSLETTERS AND NEWSPAPERS

ANTITRUST AND TRADE REGULATION REPORT. Bureau of National Affairs, Incorporated, 1231 Twenty-fifth Street, Northwest, Washington, D.C. 20037. Weekly.

FTC FREEDOM OF INFORMATION ACT LOG. Washington Regulatory Reporting Associates, P.O. Box 2220, Springfield, Virginia 22152. Weekly.

FTC WATCH. Washington Regulatory Reporting Association, P.O. Box 2220, Springfield, Virginia 22152. Twenty-two issues per year.

BIBLIOGRAPHIES

A BIBLIOGRAPHY ON ANTITRUST AND TRADE REGULATION SOURCES. Revised Edition. Margie Knott. Federal Trade Commission, Sixth Street and Pennsylvania Avenues, Northwest, Washington, D.C. 20580. 1985.

DIRECTORIES

NATIONAL TRADE AND PROFESSIONAL ASSOCIATIONS OF THE UNITED STATES. John J. Russell, Editor. Columbia Books, Incorporated, 1212 New York Avenue, Northwest, Suite 330, Washington, D.C. 20005. 1991.

BIOGRAPHICAL SOURCES

PROPHETS OF REGULATION: CHARLES FRANCIS ADAMS, LOUIS D. BRANDEIS, JAMES M. LANDIS, ALFRED E. KAHN. Thomas K. McCraw. Harvard University Press, 79 Garden Street, Cambridge, Massachusetts 02138. 1984.

ASSOCIATIONS AND PROFESSIONAL SOCIETIES

AMERICAN BAR ASSOCIATION, SECTION ON ANTITRUST. 750 North Lake Shore Drive, Chicago, Illinois 60611. (312) 988-5000.

ASSOCIATION OF AMERICAN LAW SCHOOLS, SECTION ON ANTITRUST AND ECONOMIC REGULATION. One Dupont Circle, Northwest, Washington, D.C. 20036. (202) 296-8851.

RESEARCH CENTERS, INSTITUTES, CLEARINGHOUSES

CENTER FOR RESEARCH IN REGULATED INDUSTRIES. Rutgers University, Graduate School of Management, 180 University Avenue, Newark, New Jersey 07102. (201) 648-5049.

CENTER FOR THE STUDY OF REGULATED INDUSTRY. Georgia State University, Department of Finance, University Plaza, Atlanta, Georgia 30303. (404) 651-2628.

NATIONAL REGULATORY RESEARCH INSTITUTE. Ohio State University, 1080 Carwack Road, Columbus, Ohio 43210. (614) 292-9404.

ONLINE DATABASES

LEXIS TRADE REGULATION LIBRARY. Mead Data Central, P.O. Box 933, Dayton, Ohio 45401.

TRADE SECRETS
See also: PATENTS

STATUTES, CODES, STANDARDS, UNIFORM LAWS

UNIFORM TRADE SECRETS ACT. National Conference of Commissioners on Uniform State Laws. Uniform Laws Annotated. West Publishing Company, P.O. Box 64526, 50 West Kellogg Boulevard, St. Paul, Minnesota 55164-0526. 1976 (Annual Supplements).

LOOSELEAF SERVICES AND REPORTERS

CORPORATE COUNSEL'S GUIDE TO PROTECTING TRADE SECRETS. William A. Hancock. Business Laws, Incorporated, 8228 Mayfield Road, Chesterland, Ohio 44026. 1987.

PREVENTION AND PROSECUTION OF COMPUTER AND HIGH TECHNOLOGY CRIME. Stanley S. Arkin. Matthew Bender and Company, Incorporated, 11 Penn Plaza, New York, New York 10001. 1988- .

TRADE SECRET LAW REPORTER. James H. Pooley, Editor. Law and Technology Press, P.O. Box 3280, Manhattan Beach, California 90266. 1985- .

UNITED STATES PATENTS QUARTERLY: REPORT OF CASES RELATING TO PATENTS, TRADEMARKS AND COPYRIGHT. Bureau of National Affairs, 1231 Twenty-fifth Street, Northwest, Washington, D.C. 20037. 1929- .

HANDBOOKS, MANUALS, FORMBOOKS

THE EXECUTIVE'S GUIDE TO PROTECTING PROPRIETARY BUSINESS INFORMATION AND TRADE SECRETS. James H. A. Pooley. Probus Publishing Company, 118 North Linton Street, Chicago, Illinois 60606. 1987.

TRADE SECRETS: A GUIDE TO PROTECTING PROPRIETARY BUSINESS INFORMATION. James H. A. Pooley. American Management Association, 135 West Fiftieth Street, New York, New York 10020. 1989.

THE TRADE SECRETS HANDBOOK: STRATEGIES AND TECHNIQUES FOR SAFEGUARDING CORPORATE INFORMATION. Dennis Unkovic. Prentice-Hall, Incorporated, 113 Sylvan Avenue, Englewood Cliffs, New Jersey 07632. 1985.

TEXTBOOKS AND GENERAL WORKS

CORPORATE INTELLIGENCE AND ESPIONAGE: A BLUEPRINT FOR EXECUTIVE DECISION MAKING. Richard Eells and Peter Nehemkis. Free Press, 866 Third Avenue, New York, New York 10022. 1984.

ENTREPENEURSHIP, PRODUCTIVITY, AND THE FREEDOM OF INFORMATION ACT: PROTECTING CIRCUM-STANTIALLY RELEVANT BUSINESS INFORMATION. William L. Casey Jr., John E. Marthinsen, and Laurence S. Moss. Lexington Books, Division of D.C. Heath and Company, 125 Spring Street, Lexington, Massachusetts 02173. 1983.

HOW COMPETITORS LEARN YOUR COMPANY'S SECRETS. Leila K. Kight. Washington Researchers Publishing, 2612 P Street, Northwest, Washington, D.C. 20007. 1990.

LAW AND HIGH-TECHNOLOGY INNOVATION. Aryeh S. Friedman. Butterworth Legal Publishers, 90 Stiles Road, Salem, New Hampshire 03079. 1989.

PROTECTING TRADE SECRETS. Laurence H. Pretty, Chairman. Practising Law Institute, 810 Seventh Avenue, New York, New York 10019. 1985

PROTECTING TRADE SECRETS UNDER SARA TITLE III. James T. O'Reilly. Executive Enterprises Publications Company, 22 West Twenty-first Street, New York, New York 10010-6904. 1988.

PROTECTING WORKPLACE SECRETS: MANAGERS'S GUIDE TO CONFIDENTIALITY AND THE RIGHT TO KNOW. James T. O'Reilly. Executive Enterprise Publications, 22 West Twenty-first Street, New York, New York 10010-6904. 1985.

PROTECTING YOUR BUSINESS SECRETS. Michael Saunders. Nichols Publishing Company, 11 Harts Lane, Suite 1, East Brunswick, New Jersey 08816. 1985.

RESTRAINT OF TRADE AND BUSINESS SECRETS: LAW AND PRACTICE. Second Edition. Simon Mehigan and David Griffiths. Longman Publishing Group, 95 Church Street, White Plains, New York 10601. 1991.

RIGHTS IN TECHNICAL DATA AND PATENTS: COURSE MANUAL. Federal Publications, 1120 Twentieth Street, Northwest, Washington, D.C. 20036. 1989.

TOP SECRET/TRADE SECRET: ACCESSING AND SAFEGUARDING RESTRICTED INFORMATION. Ellis Mount. Neal-Schuman Publishers Company, Incorporated, 23 Leonard Street, New York, New York 10013. 1985.

TRADE SECRET LITIGATION. Steven J. Stein, Chairman. Practising Law Institute, 810 Seventh Avenue, New York, New York 10019. 1985.

TRADE SECRETS. Roger M. Milgrim. The Michie Company, P.O. Box 7587, Charlottesville, Virginia 22906-7587. 1967 (Supplement 1984).

TRADE SECRETS AND RESTRICTIVE COVENANTS IN EMPLOYMENT AND SALE-OF-BUSINESS AGREEMENTS. American Law Institute- American Bar Association, Committee on Continuing Education, 4025 Chestnut Street, Philadelphia, Pennsylvania 19104. 1983.

TRADE SECRETS: HOW TO PROTECT YOUR IDEAS AND ASSETS. James Pooley. Osborne/McGraw Hill, 2600 Tenth Street, Berkeley, California 94710. 1982.

TRADE SECRETS LAW. Melvin F. Jager. Clark Boardman Company, Limited, 435 Hudson Street, New York, New York 10014. 1985.

TRADE SECRETS: PROTECTION AND REMEDIES. Roy E. Hofer. Bureau of National Affairs, 1231 Twenty-fifth Street, Northwest, Washington, D.C. 20037. 1985.

WHAT THE GENERAL PRACTITIONER SHOULD KNOW ABOUT TRADE SECRETS AND EMPLOYMENT AGREEMENTS. Second Edition. Arthur H. Seidel. American Law Institute-American Bar Association, Committee on Continuing Education, 4025 Chestnut Street, Philadelphia, Pennsylvania 19104. 1984.

LAW REVIEWS AND PERIODICALS

TRADE SECRET LAW REPORTER. Law and Technology Press, P.O. Box 3280, Manhattan Beach, California 90266. Monthly.

BIBLIOGRAPHIES

INDUSTRIAL ESPIONAGE AND TRADE SECRETS: AN INTERNATIONAL BIBLIOGRAPHY. Martin H. Sable. The Haworth Press, Incorporated, 10 Alice Street, New York, New York 13904. 1985.

ONLINE DATABASES

TRADE SECRETS, MATTHEW BENDER REFERENCE LIBRARY. The Michie Company, P.O. Box 7587, Charlottesville, Virginia 22906.

TRADE UNIONS
See: LABOR AND LABOR RELATIONS

TRADEMARKS AND TRADE NAMES

RESTATEMENTS

RESTATEMENT OF THE LAW, UNFAIR COMPETITION: COUNCIL DRAFT. American Law Institute-American Bar Association, 4025 Chestnut Street, Philadelphia, Pennsylvania 19104. 1989.

LOOSELEAF SERVICES AND REPORTERS

BNA'S PATENT, TRADEMARK AND COPYRIGHT JOURNAL. Bureau of National Affairs, 1231 Twenty-fifth Street, Northwest, Washington, D.C. 20037. 1970- .

THE LAW OF UNFAIR COMPETITION, TRADEMARKS AND MONOPOLIES. Fourth Edition. Callaghan and Company, 155 Pfingsten Road, Deerfield, Illinois 60015. 1981- .

PATENT, TRADEMARK, AND COPYRIGHT REGULATIONS. James D. Crowne. Bureau of National Affairs, Incorporated, 1231 Twenty-fifth Street, Northwest, Washington, D.C. 20037. 1991- .

STATE TRADEMARK AND UNFAIR COMPETITION LAW. Miles J. Alexander. United States Trademark Association, 6 East Forty-fifth Street, New York, New York 10017. 1988- .

TRADEMARK ADMINISTRATION: A GUIDE FOR PARALEGALS, ADMINISTRATORS, AND ATTORNEYS. Glenn Spencer Bacal. United States Trademark Association, 6 East Forty-fifth Street, New York, New York 10017. 1990- .

TRADEMARK REGISTRATION PRACTICE. James E. Hawes. Clark Boardman Company, Limited, 435 Hudson Street, New York, New York 10014. 1987- .

TRADEMARKS THROUGHOUT THE WORLD. Anne Marie Greene, Editor. Third Edition. Clark Boardman Company, Limited, 435 Hudson Street, New York, New York 10014. 1979- .

UNITED STATES PATENTS QUARTERLY: REPORT OF CASES RELATING TO PATENTS, TRADEMARKS AND COPYRIGHT. Bureau of National Affairs, 1231 Twenty-fifth Street, Northwest, Washington, D.C. 20037. 1929- .

HANDBOOKS, MANUALS, FORMBOOKS

HOW TO HANDLE BASIC COPYRIGHT AND TRADEMARK PROBLEMS. Richard Dannay. Practising Law Institute, 810 Seventh Avenue, New York, New York 10019. 1989.

HOW TO PROTECT YOUR BUSINESS, PROFESSIONAL, AND BRAND NAMES. David A. Weinstein. John Wiley and Sons, Incorporated, 605 Third Avenue, New York, New York 10158. 1991.

LITIGATING COPYRIGHT, TRADEMARK AND UNFAIR COMPETITION CASES, 1984. Robert G. Sugarman, Chairman. Practising Law Institute, 810 Seventh Avenue, New York, New York 10019. 1990.

MAKE IT LEGAL. Lee Wilson. Allworth Press, 10 East Twenty-third Street, New York, New York 10010. 1990.

1984-85 TRADEMARK LAW HANDBOOK. Clark Boardman Company, Limited, 435 Hudson Street, New York, New York 10014. 1985.

A PRACTICAL GUIDE TO COPYRIGHTS AND TRADEMARKS. Frank H. Andorka. World Almanac. Distributed by St. Martin's Press, 175 Fifth Avenue, New York, New York 10010. 1989.

TRADEMARK LAW: A PRACTITIONER'S GUIDE. Siegrun D. Kane. Practising Law Institute, 810 Seventh Avenue, New York, New York 10019. 1987.

TRADEMARK LAW PRACTICE FORMS. Barry Kramer and Allen D. Brufsky. Clark Boardman Company, Limited, 435 Hudson Street, New York, New York 10014. 1986.

TEXTBOOKS AND GENERAL WORKS

THE BUSINESS OF INDUSTRIAL LICENSING: A PRACTICAL GUIDE TO PATENTS, KNOW-HOW, TRADEMARKS, AND INDUSTRIAL DESIGN. Second Edition. Patrick Hearn. Gower Publishing Company, Old Post Road, Brookfield, Vermont 05036. 1986.

INTELLECTUAL PROPERTIES AND THE PROTECTION OF FICTIONAL CHARACTERS: COPYRIGHT, TRADEMARK, OR UNFAIR COMPETITION? Dorothy J. Howell. Quorum Books, Greenwood Publishing Group, Incorporated, 88 Post Road West, P.O. Box 5007, Westport, Connecticut 06881. 1990.

INTELLECTUAL PROPERTY: PATENTS, TRADEMARKS, AND COPYRIGHT IN A NUTSHELL. Arthur R. Miller and Michael H. Davis. West Publishing Company, P.O. Box 64526, 50 West Kellogg Boulevard, St. Paul, Minnesota 55164-0526. 1990.

INTENT-TO-USE TRADEMARK PRACTICE. Phillip H. Smith. Bureau of National Affairs, Incorporated, 1231 Twenty-fifth Street, Northwest, Washington, D.C. 20037. 1991.

INTRODUCTION TO COPYRIGHT AND TRADEMARK LAW. Richard Dannay. Practising Law Institute, 810 Seventh Avenue, New York, New York 10019. 1987.

THE LAW OF GRAY AND COUNTERFEIT GOODS. David Bender and David Gerber. Practising Law Institute, 810 Seventh Avenue, New York, New York 10019. 1987.

LITIGATING COPYRIGHT, TRADEMARK, AND UNFAIR COMPETITION CASES, 1990. Robert G. Sugarman, Chairman. Practising Law Institute, 810 Seventh Avenue, New York, New York 10019. 1990.

PATENT, TRADEMARK AND COPYRIGHT LAWS. Jeffrey M. Samuels, Editor. Bureau of National Affairs, 1231 Twenty-fifth Street, Northwest, Washington, D.C. 20037. 1989.

PREPARING AND PROVING SURVEY RESEARCH IN TRADEMARK LITIGATION. Robert C. Sorensen. United States Trademark Association, 6 East Forty-fifth Street, New York, New York 10017. 1990.

PRODUCT COUNTERFEITING REMEDIES. David A Gerber, Chairman. Practising Law Institute, 810 Seventh Avenue, New York, New York 10019. 1984.

THE PROTECTION OF CORPORATE NAMES: A COUNTRY BY COUNTRY SURVEY. United States Trademark Association. Clark Boardman Company, Limited, 435 Hudson Street, New York, New York 10014. 1982.

THE STORY OF THE U.S. PATENT AND TRADEMARK OFFICE. United States Department of Commerce, Patent and Trademark Office. Superintendent of Documents, United States Government Printing Office, Washington, D.C. 20402. 1988.

TRADEMARK LITIGATION: PRAGMATIC TACTICS AND TECHNIQUES OF WINNING. Miles J. Alexander, Chairman. Practising Law Institute, 810 Seventh Avenue, New York, New York 10019. 1984.

TRADEMARK PROTECTION AND PRACTICE. Jerome Gilson. The Michie Company, P.O. Box 7587, Charlottesville, Virginia 22906-7587. 1974 (Supplement 1985).

TRADEMARKS. Beverly W. Pattishall and David Craig Hilliard. Matthew Bender and Company, Incorporated, 11 Penn Plaza, New York, New York 10001. 1987.

TRADEMARKS AND UNFAIR COMPETITION. Second Edition. J. Thomas McCarthy. Lawyers Co-Operative Publishing Company, Aqueduct Building, Rochester, New York 14694. 1984. (Periodic Supplements).

NEWSLETTERS AND NEWSPAPERS

BNA'S PATENT, TRADEMARK, AND COPYRIGHT JOURNAL. Bureau of National Affairs, Incorporated, 1231 Twenty-fifth Street, Northwest, Washington, D.C. 20037. Weekly.

COPIAT NEWSLETTER. Coalition to Preserve the Integrity of American Trademarks, 1201 Pennsylvania Avenue, Northwest, Washington, D.C. 20044. Semiannually.

THE JOURNAL OF PROPRIETARY RIGHTS. Prentice-Hall Law and Business, Incorporated, 113 Sylvan Avenue, Englewood Cliffs, New Jersey 07632. Monthly.

NYPTC BULLETIN. GB Enterprises, P.O. Box 1169, Stanford, Connecticut 06904. Bimonthly.

PTC NEWSLETTER. American Bar Association, 750 North Lake Shore Drive, Chicago, Illinois 60611. Quarterly.

ENCYCLOPEDIAS AND DICTIONARIES

DICTIONARY OF TRADE NAME ORIGINS. Adrian Room. Routledge and Kegan Paul, Limited, 29 West Thirty-fifth Street, New York, New York 10001. 1990.

LAW REVIEWS AND PERIODICALS

OFFICIAL GAZETTE OF THE UNITED STATES PATENT AND TRADEMARK OFFICE: TRADEMARKS. United States Government Printing Office, Washington, D.C. 20402. Weekly.

PATENT AND TRADEMARK REVIEW. Trade Activities, Incorporated, 435 Hudson Street, New York, New York 10014. Monthly.

TRADEMARK REPORTER. United States Trademark Association, 6 East Forty-fifth Street, New York, New York 10017. Bimonthly.

BIBLIOGRAPHIES

PATENTS AND TRADEMARKS: A BIBLIOGRAPHY OF MATERIALS AVAILABLE FOR SELECTION. Michele McKnelly and Johanna Johnson. Patent Depository Library Association, Springfield, Virginia. 1989.

DIRECTORIES

BRANDS AND THEIR COMPANIES. Susan Stetler. Gale Research, Incorporated, 835 Penobscot Building, Detroit, Michigan 48226. Annual.

BRANDS AND THEIR COMPANIES SUPPLEMENT. Susan Stetler. Gale Research, Incorporated, 835 Penobscot Building, Detroit, Michigan 48226. Annual.

A DIGEST OF THE LAW OF TRADE-MARKS AND UNFAIR TRADE. Norman F. Hesseltine. Fred B. Rothman and Company, 10368 West Centennial Road, Littleton, Colorado 80127. 1991. (Reprint).

PRODUCTS COMPARISON MANUAL FOR TRADEMARK USERS: COVERING U.S. PATENTS QUARTERLY, VOLUMES 1-231, 1929-1986. Francis M. Pinckney. Bureau of National Affairs, Incorporated, 1231 Twenty-fifth Street, Northwest, Washington, D.C. 20037. 1988.

SHEPARD'S UNITED STATES PATENTS AND TRADEMARKS CITATIONS. Second Edition. Shepard's/McGraw-Hill Publishing Company, 1221 Avenue of the Americas, New York, New York 10020. 1988.

TRADEMARK REGISTER OF THE UNITED STATES. Trademark Register, National Press Building, Washington, D.C. 20045. Annual.

ASSOCIATIONS AND PROFESSIONAL SOCIETIES

AMERICAN BAR ASSOCIATION, SECTION OF PATENT, TRADEMARK, AND COPYRIGHT LAW. 750 North Lake Shore Drive, Chicago, Illinois 60611. (312) 988-5000.

COALITION TO PRESERVE THE INTEGRITY OF AMERICAN TRADEMARKS. 1201 Pennsylvania Avenue, Northwest, Washington, D.C. 20044. (703) 759-3377.

INTERNATIONAL PATENT AND TRADEMARK ASSOCIATION. 33 West Monroe, Chicago, Illinois 60603. (312) 641-1800.

TRADEMARK SOCIETY. P.O. Box 2631, Eads Station, Arlington, Virginia 22202. (703) 557-3277.

UNITED STATES TRADEMARK ASSOCIATION. 6 East Forty-fifth Street, New York, New York 10017. (212) 986-5880.

ONLINE DATABASES

BNA'S PATENT, TRADEMARK, AND COPYRIGHT DAILY. Bureau of National Affairs, Incorporated, 1231 Twenty-fifth Street, Northwest, Washington, D.C. 20037.

COMO-MARK U.S. ONLINE. Compu-Mark U.S., 7201 Wisconsin Avenue, Bethesda, Maryland 20814.

LEXIS FEDERAL PATENT, TRADEMARK AND COPYRIGHT LIBRARY. Mead Data Central, P.O. Box 933, Dayton, Ohio 45401.

PATENT, TRADEMARK AND COPYRIGHT JOURNAL. Bureau of National Affairs, 1231 Twenty-fifth Street, Northwest, Washington, D.C. 20037.

PATLAW. BNA ONLINE. Bureau of National Affairs, 1231 Twenty-fifth Street, Northwest, Washington, D.C. 20037.

THOMAS REGISTER. Thomas Publishing Company, Thomas Online, One Penn Plaza, 250 West Thirty-fourth Street, New York, New York 10119.

TRADE NAMES DATABASE. Gale Research, Incorporated, 835 Penobscot Building, Detroit, Michigan 48226.

TRADEMARK PROTECTION AND PRACTICE, MATTHEW BENDER REFERENCE LIBRARY. Matthew Bender and Company, Incorporated, 11 Penn Plaza, New York, New York 10001.

TRADEMARKSCAN-STATE. Thomson and Thomson, 500 Victory Road, North Quincy, Massachusetts 02171.

TRADEMARKSCAN-FEDERAL. Thomson and Thomson, 500 Victory Road, North Quincy, Massachusetts 02171.

WESTLAW INTELLECTUAL PROPERTY LIBRARY. West Publishing Company, 50 West Kellogg Boulevard, St. Paul, Minnesota 55164-0526.

AUDIOVISUALS

LITIGATING COPYRIGHT, TRADEMARK AND UNFAIR COMPETITION CASES, 1984. Robert G. Sugarman, Chairman. Practising Law Institute, 810 Seventh Avenue, New York, New York 10019. 1984. Audiocassettes.

TRAFFIC
See: MOTOR VEHICLES

TRANSNATIONAL LITIGATION
See: CONFLICT OF LAWS

TRANSPORTATION
See also: ADMIRALTY; AVIATION; INTERSTATE COMMERCE COMMISSION; LOCAL TRANSIT; MOTOR VEHICLES; NATIONAL TRANSPORTATION SAFETY BOARD; RAILROADS; TRADE REGULATION; TRANSPORTATION DEPARTMENT; TRAVEL AGENCY

LOOSELEAF SERVICES AND REPORTERS

FEDERAL CARRIERS REPORTS. Commerce Clearing House, Incorporated, 4025 West Peterson Avenue, Chicago, Illinois 60646. 1937- .

FREIGHT CLAIMS MANUAL. J. J. Keller and Associates, P.O. Box 368, 145 West Wisconsin Avenue, Neenah, Wisconsin 54907-0368. 1979- .

SHIPPING REGULATION. Pike and Fischer, Incorporated, 4550 Montgomery Avenue, Suite 433N, Bethesda, Maryland 20814. 1961- .

STATE HAZARDOUS MATERIALS MANUAL: STATE REQUIREMENTS FOR SHIPPING AND TRANSPORTATION. J.J. Keller and Associates, Incorporated, P.O. Box 368, 145 West Wisconsin Avenue, Neenah, Wisconsin 54907-0368. 1990- .

STATE MOTOR CARRIER GUIDE. Commerce Clearing House, Incorporated, 4025 West Peterson Avenue, Chicago, Illinois 60646. 1940- .

TRANSPORTATION ANTITRUST REPORT. Priority Reports, Incorporated, 1411 K Street, Northwest, Washington, D.C. 20005. 1983- .

HANDBOOKS, MANUALS, FORMBOOKS

EMERGENCY AND TRIP PERMIT HANDBOOK: OPERATING PERMIT INFORMATION FOR INTERSTATE TRUCKING OPERATIONS IN THE UNITED STATES AND CANADA. J. J. Keller and Associates, P.O. Box 368, 145 West Wisconsin Avenue, Neenah, Wisconsin 54907-0368. Annual.

FEDERAL MOTOR CARRIER SAFETY REGULATIONS POCKETBOOK. United States Federal Highway Administration. J.J. Keller and Associates, Incorporated, P.O. Box 368, 145 West Wisconsin Avenue, Neenah, Wisconsin 54907-0368. 1990.

TEXTBOOKS AND GENERAL WORKS

THE CARRIAGE OF DANGEROUS GOODS BY SEA: THE ROLE OF THE INTERNATIONAL MARITIME ORGANIZATION IN INTERNATIONAL LEGISLATION. Cleopatra E. Henry. Saint Martin's Press, Incorporated, 175 Fifth Avenue, New York, New York 10010. 1985.

DESEGREGATION OF PUBLIC TRANSPORTATION, FACILITIES, AND PROGRAMS. Garland Publishing, Incorporated, 136 Madison Avenue, New York, New York 10016. 1991.

FREIGHT CLAIMS IN PLAIN ENGLISH. Second Edition. Shippers National Freight Claim Council, Incorporated, 120 Main Street, Box Z, Huntington, New York 11743. 1982.

INSTITUTIONAL DISABILITY: THE SAGA OF TRANSPORTATION POLICY FOR HANDICAPPED PEOPLE. Robert A. Katzmann. Brookings Institution, 1775 Massachusetts Avenue, Northwest, Washington, D.C. 20036-2188. 1986.

LAW AND ECONOMIC REGULATION IN TRANSPORTATION. Paul S. Dempsey and William E. Thomas. Greenwood Publishing Group, Incorporated, 88 Post Road West, P.O. Box 5007, Westport, Connecticut 06881. 1986.

RECOMMENDATIONS ON THE TRANSPORT OF DANGEROUS GOODS. Fifth Edition. United Nations Publishing Service, Room DC2-0853, New York, New York 10017. 1988.

TRANSPORT LAW OF THE EUROPEAN COMMUNITY. Rosa Greaves. Althone, Atlantic Highlands, New Jersey. 1991.

TRANSPORTATION INSURANCE IN PLAIN ENGLISH. Shippers National Freight Claim Council, Incorporated, 120 Main Street, Box Z, Huntington, New York 11743. 1985.

TRANSPORTATION LAW. Fourth Edition. John Guandolo. William C. Brown Company, 2460 Kerper Boulevard, Dubuque, Iowa 52001. 1983.

TRANSPORTATION LAW STUDY GUIDE. Association of Transportation Practitioners, 1725 K Street, Northwest, Suite 301, Washington, D.C. 20006. 1984.

TRANSPORTATION REGULATION. Ninth Edition. Marvin L. Fair and John Guandolo. William C. Brown Company, 2460 Kerper Boulevard, Dubuque, Iowa 52001. 1983.

ENCYCLOPEDIAS AND DICTIONARIES

DICTIONARY OF ROAD TRANSPORT TERMINOLOGY IN FOUR LANGUAGES: ENGLISH, FRENCH, GERMAN, AND SPANISH. International Road Transport Union, Elsevier Science Publishing Company, P.O.Box 882, Madison Square Station, New York, New York 10159. 1988.

TRANSPORTATION AND DISTRIBUTION DICTIONARY. J.J. Keller and Associates, Incorporated, P.O. Box 368, 145 West Wisconsin Avenue, Neenah, Wisconsin 54907-0368. 1987.

TRUCK AND BUS INDUSTRY GLOSSARY. Society of Automotive Engineers, 400 Commonwealth Drive, Warrendale, Pennsylvania 15096-0001. 1988.

URBAN PUBLIC TRANSPORTATION GLOSSARY. Benita H. Gray. Transportation Research Board, National Research Council, Washington, D.C. 1989.

ANNUALS AND SURVEYS

TRANSPORTATION LAW INSTITUTE, 1990: PAPERS AND PROCEEDINGS. Association of Transportation Practitioners, 1725 K Street, Northwest, Suite 301, Washington, D.C. 20006. 1990.

LAW REVIEWS AND PERIODICALS

TRANSPORTATION LAW JOURNAL. University of Denver, College of Law, Denver, Colorado 80220. Semiannual.

TRANSPORTATION PRACTITIONERS JOURNAL. Association of Transportation Practitioners, 1211 Connecticut Avenue, Northwest, Washington, D.C. 20036. Quarterly.

NEWSLETTERS AND NEWSPAPERS

HIGHWAY AND VEHICLE/SAFETY REPORT. Stamler Publishing Company, P.O. Box 3367, Brauford, Connecticut 06405. Biweekly.

INSIDE DOT/TRANSPORTATION WEEK. King Publishing Group, 627 National Press Building, Washington, D.C. 20005. Weekly.

MOTOR CARRIER SAFETY REPORT. J. J. Keller and Associates, Incorporated, 145 West Wisconsin Avenue, Neenah, Wisconsin 54956. Monthly.

TRANSAFETY REPORTER. Transafety Incorporated, 5811 Oak Leather Drive, Burke, Virginia 22015. Monthly.

TRANSPORT DE-REGULATION REPORT. Freight Traffic Institute, 960 Broadway, Hicksville, New York 11801. Monthly.

TRANSPORTATION COMMITTEE NEWSLETTER. American Bar Association, 750 North Lake Shore Drive, Chicago, Illinois 60611. Quarterly.

TRUCKING PERMIT AND TAX BULLETIN. J. J. Keller and Associates, 145 West Wisconsin Avenue, Neenah, Wisconsin 54956. Monthly.

YOUR LETTER OF THE LAW. Transportation Lawyers Association, P.O. Box 15122, Lenexa, Kansas 66215. Quarterly.

BIBLIOGRAPHIES

CITIZEN PARTICIPATION IN TRANSPORTATION DECISION MAKING: A BIBLIOGRAPHY. Frederick Frankena and Joann Koelln Frankena. Vance Bibliographies, P.O. Box 229, 112 North Charter Street, Monticello, Illinois 61856. 1987.

HIGHWAY TRANSPORTATION: MANAGEMENT OF TRAFFIC, ECONOMIC ASPECTS, LEGISLATION, TYPES OF HIGHWAYS. E. Willard Miller and Ruby M. Miller. Vance Bibliographies, P.O. Box 229, 112 North Charter Street, Monticello, Illinois 61856. 1987.

SOURCES OF INFORMATION IN TRANSPORTATION. Fourth Edition. Vance Bibliographies, P.O. Box 229, 112 North Charter Street, Monticello, Illinois 61856. 1990.

DIRECTORIES

DIRECTORY OF NATIONAL TRANSPORTATION POLICY CONTACTS. Second Edition. Robert A. Krause and Dinker I. Patel. Center for Transportation, State Government Research Institute, Lexington, Kentucky. 1987.

OFFICIAL DIRECTORY OF MOTOR CARRIER CONSULTANTS, 1989. Ben Silverstein and Linda S. Rothbart. American Trucking Associations, Information Center, 2200 Mill Road, Alexandria, Virginia 22314-4677. 1989.

ASSOCIATIONS AND PROFESSIONAL SOCIETIES

AMERICAN ASSOCIATION OF STATE HIGHWAY AND TRANSPORTATION OFFICIALS. 444 North Capital Street, Northwest, Suite 225, Washington, D.C. 20001. (202) 624-5800.

ASSOCIATION OF TRANSPORTATION PRACTITIONERS. 1725 K Street, Northwest, Suite 301, Washington, D.C. 20006. (202) 466-2080.

NATIONAL ASSOCIATION OF RAILROAD TRIAL COUNSEL. 88 Alma Roal Drive, Suite 218, Pacific Palisados, California 90272. (213) 459-7659.

TRANSPORTATION LAWYERS ASSOCIATIONS. 3310 Harrison, Topeka, Kansas 66611. (913) 266-7014.

ONLINE DATABASES

DRI TRANSPORTATION DATA BANK. Data Resources Incorporated, Data Products Division Headquarters, 1750 K Street, Northwest, Washington, D.C. 20006.

HIGHWAY RESEARCH INFORMATION SERVICE. National Academy of Sciences, National Research Council, 2101 Constitution Avenue, Northwest, Washington, D.C. 20418.

LEXIS FEDERAL TRANSPORTATION LIBRARY. Mead Data Central, P.O. Box 933, Dayton, Ohio 45401.

TRANSPORTATION INDUSTRY COMPETITIVE INTELLIGENCE TRACKING SERVICE. Strategic Intelligence Systems, Incorporated, 404 Park Avenue South, Suite 1301, New York, New York 10016.

TRANSPORTATION LIBRARY. National Academy of Sciences, National Research Council, 2101 Constitution Avenue, Northwest, Washington, D.C. 20418.

URBAN MASS TRANSPORTATION RESEARCH INFORMATION SERVICE. National Academy of Sciences, National Research Council, 2101 Constitution Avenue, Northwest, Washington, D.C. 20418.

WESTLAW TRANSPORTATION LIBRARY. West Publishing Company, 50 West Kellogg Boulevard, St. Paul, Minnesota 55164-0526.

TRANSPORTATION DEPARTMENT
See also: FEDERAL AVIATION ADMINISTRATION

STATUTES, CODES, STANDARDS, UNIFORM LAWS

CODE OF FEDERAL REGULATIONS, TITLE 14. Office of the Federal Register, National Archives and Records Administration, Superintendent of Documents, United States Government Printing Office, Washington, D.C. 20402. Annual. (Updated by use of monthly *List of Sections Affected* and daily *Federal Register.*)

FEDERAL LAWS AND MATERIAL RELATING TO THE FEDERAL HIGHWAY ADMINISTRATION. Transportation Department, Federal Highway Administration. Superintendent of Documents, United States Government Printing Office, Washington, D.C. 20402. 1983.

FEDERAL MOTOR CARRIER SAFETY REGULATIONS AND NOISE EMISSION REQUIREMENTS. Transportation Department, Office of Motor Carrier Safety. Superintendent of Documents, United States Government Printing Office, Washington, D.C. 20402. 1983.

NATIONAL TRAFFIC AND MOTOR VEHICLE SAFETY ACT OF 1966, LEGISLATIVE HISTORY. Transportation Department, National Highway Traffic Safety Administration. Superintendent of Documents, United States Government Printing Office, Washington, D.C. 20402. 1985.

NAVIGATION RULES: INTERNATIONAL AND INLAND. Transportation Department, Coast Guard. Gordon Press, P.O. Box 459, Bowling Green Station, New York, New York 10004. 1991.

RULES AND REGULATIONS FOR FOREIGN VESSELS OPERATING IN THE NAVIGABLE WATERS OF THE UNITED STATES. Transportation Department, Coast Guard. Superintendent of Documents, United States Government Printing Office, Washington, D.C. 20402. 1977- .

HANDBOOKS, MANUALS, FORMBOOKS

FEDERAL MOTOR CARRIER SAFETY REGULATIONS POCKETBOOK: AS PRESCRIBED BY THE U.S. DEPARTMENT OF TRANSPORTATION, FEDERAL HIGHWAY ADMINISTRATION. J.J. Keller and Associates, Incorporated, P.O. Box 368, 145 West Wisconsin Avenue, Neenah, Wisconsin 54907-0368. 1990.

GUIDE TO THE FEDERAL HAZARDOUS MATERIALS TRANSPORTATION REGULATORY PROGRAM. Transportation Department, Research and Special Programs Administration, Materials Transportation Bureau, and Office of the Secretary, Technology Sharing Program. Superintendent of Documents, United States Government Printing Office, Washington, D.C. 20402. 1983.

TEXTBOOKS AND GENERAL WORKS

DEPARTMENT OF TRANSPORTATION. Wallace Charles Stefany and Arthur Meier Schlesinger. Chelsea House Publishers, 1974 Sproul Road, Suite 400, Broomall, Pennsylvania 19008. 1988.

MOVING AMERICA: A LOOK AHEAD TO THE 21ST CENTURY: PROCEEDINGS OF THE CONFERENCE CONDUCTED BY THE TRANSPORTATION RESEARCH BOARD AND SPONSORED BY THE U.S. DEPARTMENT OF TRANSPORTATION, JULY 24, 1989, NATIONAL ACADEMY OF SCIENCES, WASHINGTON, D.C. United States Department of Transportation, Washington, D.C. 1989.

RESEARCH CENTERS, INSTITUTES, CLEARINGHOUSES

UNITED STATES DEPARTMENT OF TRANSPORTATION/FEDERAL HIGHWAY ADMINISTRATION, OFFICE OF CHIEF COUNSEL, LEGISLATIVE REFERENCE LIBRARY. 400 Seventh Street, Southwest, Room 4205, Washington, D.C. 20590. (202) 366-0761.

UNITED STATES DEPARTMENT OF TRANSPORTATION LAW LIBRARY. 400 Seventh Street, Southwest, Room 2215, Washington, D.C. 20590. (202) 366-2565.

ONLINE DATABASES

LEXIS FEDERAL TRANSPORTATION LIBRARY. Mead Data Central, P.O. Box 933, Dayton, Ohio 45401.

WESTLAW TRANSPORTATION LIBRARY. West Publishing Company, P.O. Box 64526, 50 West Kellogg Boulevard, St. Paul, Minnesota 55164-0526.

TRAVEL AND TRAVEL AGENCY
See also: TRANSPORTATION

LOOSELEAF SERVICES AND REPORTERS

TRAVEL LAW: THE COMPLETE LITIGATION GUIDE WITH RESPECT TO EVERY ASPECT OF THE TRAVEL INDUSTRY. Thomas A. Dickerson. Law Journal-Seminars Press, Incorporated, 111 Eighth Avenue, New York, New York 10011. 1981- .

HANDBOOKS, MANUALS, FORMBOOKS

LEGAL ASPECTS OF TRAVEL AGENCY OPERATION. Second Edition. Jeffrey R. Miller. Delmar Publishers, Incorporated, P.O. Box 15015, 2 Computer Drive, West Albany, New York 12212. 1987.

LEGAL FORMS FOR TRAVEL AGENTS. Jeffrey R. Miller. Merton House Publishing Company, 937 West Liberty Drive, Wheaton, Illinois 60187. 1985.

WORLD ALMANAC'S LEGAL GUIDE FOR AMERICAN TRAVELERS, EUROPE. Nack Novik. Pharos Books, Incorporated, 201 East Fiftieth, New York, New York 10022. 1986.

TEXTBOOKS AND GENERAL WORKS

CLAIMING TRAVEL EXPENSES. Holmes F. Crouch. Robert Erdmann Publishing, 28441 Highridge Road, Suite 101, Rolling Hills Estates, California 90274. 1991.

HOTEL, RESTAURANT, AND TRAVEL LAW. Third Edition. Norman G. Cournoyer and Anthony G. Marshall. Delmar Publishers, Incorporated, P.O. Box 15015, Two Computer Drive West, Albany, New York 12212. 1988.

INSTITUTIONAL DISABILITY: THE SAGA OF TRANS-PORTATION POLICY FOR THE DISABLED. Robert A. Katzmann. Brookings Institution, 1775 Massachusetts Avenue, Northwest, Washington, D.C. 20036-2188. 1986.

LEGAL ASPECTS OF TRAVEL AGENCY OPERATION. Second Edition. Jeffrey R. Miller. Delmar Publishers, Incorporated, P.O. Box 15015, Two Computer Drive West, Albany, New York 12212. 1987.

TRAVEL, TOURISM, AND HOSPITALITY LAW. Alexander Anolik. National Publishers of the Black Hills, Incorporated, 47 Nepperham Avenue, Elmsford, New York 10523. 1988.

NEWSLETTERS AND NEWSPAPERS

FROM THE STATE CAPITALS: TOURIST BUSINESS PROMOTION. Wakeman Walworth, Incorporated, 300 North Washington Street, Suite 204, Alexandria, Virginia 22314. Monthly.

DIRECTORIES

AMERICAN SOCIETY OF TRAVEL AGENTS, INCORPORATED, MEMBERSHIP ROSTER. American Society of Travel Agents, Incorporated, 1101 King Street, Alexandria, Virginia 22314. Annual.

RESEARCH CENTERS, INSTITUTES, CLEARINGHOUSES

UNITED STATES TRAVEL DATA CENTER. 2 Lafayette Center, 1133 Twenty-first Street, Northwest, Washington, D.C. 20036. (202) 293-1040.

ONLINE DATABASES

CITIZENS EMERGENCY TRAVEL ADVISORY SERVICE. United States Department of State, Citizens Emergency Service, 2201 C Street, Northwest, Washington, D.C. 20520.

VISA ADVISORS. 1808 Swann Street, Northwest, Suite 200, Washington, D.C. 20009.

TREASON
See also: CRIMINAL LAW

TEXTBOOKS AND GENERAL WORKS

THE AMERICAN LAW OF TREASON: REVOLUTIONARY AND EARLY NATIONAL ORIGINS. Bradley Chapin. University of Washington Press, P.O. Box 50096, Seattle, Washington 98145-5096. 1964.

AMERICAN SWASTIKA. Charles Hingham. Doubleday and Company, Incorporated, 666 Fifth Avenue, New York, New York 10103. 1985.

BEHIND EVERY BUSH. Richard H. Ichord and Boyd Upchurch. Seville Publishing, 16917 Enadia Way, Van Nuys, California 91406. 1982.

CAPTAIN OF INNOCENCE: FRANCE AND THE DREYFUS AFFAIR. Norman H. Finkelstein. Putnam Publishing Group, 200 Madison Avenue, New York, New York 10016. 1991.

THE DREYFUS AFFAIR: ART, TRUTH, AND JUSTICE. Norman L. Kleeblatt. University of California Press, 2120 Berkeley Way, Berkeley, California 94720. 1987.

THE GREAT RED MENACE: UNITED STATES PROSECUTION OF AMERICAN COMMUNISTS, 1947-1952. Peter L. Steinberg. Greenwood Publishing Group, Incorporated, 88 Post Road West, P.O. Box 5007, Westport, Connecticut 06881. 1984.

IN THE NAME OF THE VOLK: POLITICAL JUSTICE IN HITLER'S GERMANY. H. W. Koch. St. Martin's Press, 175 Fifth Avenue, New York, New York 10010. 1989.

THE LAW OF TREASON IN THE UNITED STATES: COLLECTED ESSAYS. James W. Hurst. Greenwood Publishing Group, Incorporated, 88 Post Road West, P.O. Box 5007, Westport, Connecticut 06881. 1971.

REPORT ON THE MURDER OF THE GENERAL SECRETARY. Karel Kaplan. Ohio State University Press, 1070 Carmack Road, Columbus, Ohio 43120-1002. 1990.

THE SPYCATCHER AFFAIR. Chapman Pincher. St. Martin's Press, 175 Fifth Avenue, New York, New York 10010. 1988.

VOLUNTARY AND STATUTORY COLLABORATION: RHETORIC OR REALITY. Diana Leat, Gerry Smolkaand and Judith Unell. Brookfield Publishing Company, Old Post Road, Brookfield, Vermont 05036. 1981.

TREASURY DEPARTMENT

STATUTES, CODES, STANDARDS, UNIFORM LAWS

CODE OF FEDERAL REGULATIONS, TITLE 31. Office of the Federal Register, National Archives and Records Administration. Superintendent of Documents, United States Government Printing Office, Washington, D.C. 20402. Annual. (Updated by use of monthly *List of Sections Affected* and daily *Federal Register*.)

TEXTBOOKS AND GENERAL WORKS

COMMENTARY ON THE AUDIT REQUIREMENTS OF THE LOCAL GOVERNMENT FISCAL ASSISTANCE AMENDMENTS OF 1983. Treasury Department, Office of Revenue Sharing. Superintendent of Documents, United States Government Printing Office, Washington, D.C. 20402. 1985.

THE DEPARTMENT OF THE TREASURY. Mark Walston. Chelsea House Publishers, 1974 Sproul Road, Suite 400, Broomall, Pennsylvania 19008. 1989.

FEDERAL - STATE - LOCAL FISCAL RELATIONS: REPORT TO THE PRESIDENT AND THE CONGRESS. Treasury Department, Office of State and Local Finance. Superintendent of Documents, United States Government Printing Office, Washington, D.C. 20402. 1985.

RECOMMENDATIONS FOR CHANGE IN THE FEDERAL DEPOSIT INSURANCE SYSTEM. Treasury Department, The Working Group of the Cabinet Council on Economic Affairs. Superintendent of Documents, United States Government Printing Office, Washington, D.C. 20402. 1985.

REPORT TO CONGRESS ON THE CAPITAL GAINS TAX REDUCTIONS OF 1978. Treasury Department, Office of the Secretary, Office of Tax Analysis. Superintendent of Documents, United States Government Printing Office, Washington, D.C. 20402. 1985.

SPECIAL AGENT: U.S. TREASURY DEPARTMENT. Sixth Edition. Eve P. Steinberg. Distributed by Prentice-Hall, Incorporated, 113 Sylvan Avenue, Englewood Cliffs, New Jersey 07632. 1989.

USE OF TAX SUBSIDIES FOR EMPLOYMENT: A REPORT TO CONGRESS BY THE DEPARTMENTS OF LABOR AND TREASURY. Treasury Department. Superintendent of Documents, United States Government Printing Office, Washington, D.C. 20402. 1986.

DIGESTS, INDEXES, ABSTRACTS, CITATORS

SHEPARD'S FEDERAL TAX CITATIONS. Shepard's/McGraw-Hill, P.O. Box 1235, Colorado Springs, Colorado 80901. Bimonthly.

SHEPARD'S UNITED STATES ADMINISTRATIVE CITATIONS. Shepard's/McGraw-Hill, P.O. Box 1235, Colorado Springs, Colorado 80901. Bimonthly.

RESEARCH CENTERS, INSTITUTES, CLEARINGHOUSES

UNITED STATES DEPARTMENT OF THE TREASURY LIBRARY. Main Treasury Building, Room 5310, Washington, D.C. 20220. (202) 566-2069.

TREATIES AND CONVENTIONS
See also: INTERNATIONAL LAW AND RELATIONS; STATE DEPARTMENT; TAXATION, INTERNATIONAL

COLLECTIONS

AIR AND AVIATION TREATIES OF THE WORLD. S. Houston Lay. Oceana Publications, Incorporated, 75 Main Street, Dobbs Ferry, New York 10522. 1984- .

BASIC DOCUMENTS OF INTERNATIONAL ECONOMIC LAW. Stephen Zamora and Ronald A. Brand. Commerce Clearing House, Incorporated, 4025 West Peterson Avenue, Chicago, Illinois 60646. 1990.

A COMPARISON OF STATE STATUTES AND INTERNATIONAL TREATIES IN TRUST AND ESTATE LAW: REFERENCE AND REFERRAL GUIDE FOR PRACTICING ATTORNEYS. M. Henner. Quorum Books, Imprint of Greenwood Publishing Group, Incorporated, 88 Post Road West, P.O. Box 5007, Westport, Connecticut 06881. 1985.

CONSOLIDATED TREATY SERIES, 1648-1918. Cliver Perry, Editor. Oceana Publications, Incorporated, 75 Main Street, Dobbs Ferry, New York 10522. 1977.

COPYRIGHT LAWS AND TREATIES OF THE WORLD. Bureau of National Affairs, 1231 Twenty-fifth Street, Northwest, Washington, D.C. 20037. 1956- .

DESIGN LAWS AND TREATIES OF THE WORLD. Bureau of National Affairs, 1231 Twenty-fifth Street, Northwest, Washington, D.C. 20037. 1960- .

EUROPEAN CONVENTIONS AND AGREEMENTS. Council of Europe, Directorate of Legal Affairs, Manhattan Publishing Company, 225 Lafayette Street, New York, New York 10012. 1983.

EUROPEAN TREATY SERIES. Council of Europe, Directorate of Legal Affairs, Manhattan Publishing Company, 225 Lafayette Street, New York, New York 10012. 1950- .

EXTRADITION LAWS AND TREATIES: UNITED STATES. Igor I. Kavass and Adolf Sprudzs. William S. Hein and Company, Incorporated, Hein Building, 1285 Main Street, Buffalo, New York 14209. 1980- .

INDUSTRIAL PROPERTY LAWS AND TREATIES. Unipub, A Xerox Publishing Company, 4611-F Assembly Drive, Lanham, Maryland 20706-4391. 1980- .

INSTRUMENTS OF ECONOMIC INTEGRATION IN LATIN AMERICA AND THE CARIBBEAN. F. V. Garcia-Amador, Editor. Oceana Publications, Incorporated, 75 Main Street, Dobbs Ferry, New York 10522. 1975.

INTERNATIONAL PROTECTION OF THE ENVIRONMENT: TREATIES AND RELATED DOCUMENTS. Bernard Ruster and Bruno Simma, Editors. Oceana Publications, Incorporated, 75 Main Street, Dobbs Ferry, New York 10522. 1990.

INTERNATIONAL TAX TREATIES OF ALL NATIONS. W. Diamond, Editor. Oceana Publications, Incorporated, 75 Main Street, Dobbs Ferry, New York 10522. 1975- .

INTERNATIONAL WITHHOLDING TAX TREATY GUIDE. Walter H. Diamond. Matthew Bender and Company, Incorporated, 11 Penn Plaza, New York, New York 10001. 1975- .

INVESTMENT TREATIES. Oceana Publications, Incorporated, 75 Main Street, Dobbs Ferry, New York 10522. 1983- .

THE LAWS OF ARMED CONFLICTS: A COLLECTION OF CONVENTIONS, RESOLUTIONS, AND OTHER DOCUMENTS. Third Edition. Dietrich Schindler and Jiri Toman. Martinus Nijhoff, Kluwer Academic Publishers, 101 Philip Drive, Assinippi Park, Norwell, Massachusetts 02061. 1988.

LEAGUE OF NATIONS TREATY SERIES AND GENERAL INDEXES TO THE TREATY SERIES, 1920-1946. Oceana Publications, Incorporated, 75 Main Street, Dobbs Ferry, New York 10522.

THE MAJOR INTERNATIONAL TREATIES, 1914-1973: A HISTORY AND GUIDE WITH TEXTS. J. Greenville, Editor. Stein and Day, Scarborough House, Briarcliff Manor, New York 10510. 1974.

MANUAL OF COLLECTIONS OF TREATIES AND COLLECTIONS RELATING TO TREATIES. Denys P. Myers, Editor. Burt Franklin, Publisher. Lenox Hill Publishing Corporation, 235 East Forty-fourth Street, New York, New York 10017. 1966.

ORGANIZATION OF AMERICAN STATES TREATY SERIES. OAS Department of Publications, 6840 Industrial Road, Springfield, Virginia 22151. 1957- .

PATENT COOPERATION TREATY AND REGULATIONS. Rules Service Company, 7658 Standish Place, Suite 106, Rockville, Maryland 20855. 1981- .

SWEET AND MAXWELL'S EUROPEAN COMMUNITY TREATIES, INCLUDING THE EUROPEAN COMMUNITIES ACT 1972. K. Simmonds, Editor. Sweet and Maxwell, Limited, Member of the Association of Book Publishers Group, South Quay Plaza, 183 Marsh Wall, London E14 9FT, England. 1977.

TAX TREATIES. Commerce Clearing House, Incorporated, 4025 West Peterson Avenue, Chicago, Illinois 60646. 1952- .

TAX TREATIES. Prentice-Hall, Incorporated, 113 Sylvan Avenue, Englewood Cliffs, New Jersey 07632. 1978- .

TRANSNATIONAL TERRORISM, CONVENTIONS AND COMMENTARY: A COMPILATION OF TREATIES, AGREEMENTS, AND DECLARATIONS OF ESPECIAL INTEREST TO THE UNITED STATES. Richard B. Lillich, Editor. The Michie Company, P.O. Box 7587, Charlottesville, Virginia 22906-7587. 1982.

TREATIES AND ALLIANCES OF THE WORLD. Fifth Edition. N. J. Rengger. Gale Research, Incorporated, 835 Penobscot Building, Detroit, Michigan 48226. 1990.

TREATIES AND OTHER INTERNATIONAL ACTS SERIES. United States Department of State. Superintendent of Documents, United States Government Printing Office, Washington, D.C. 20402. 1946- .

TREATIES AND OTHER INTERNATIONAL AGREEMENTS OF THE UNITED STATES OF AMERICA, 1776-1949. C. Bevins, Editor. Superintendent of Documents, United States Government Printing Office, Washington, D.C. 20402.

UNITED NATIONS TREATY SERIES: TREATIES AND INTERNATIONAL AGREEMENTS REGISTERED OR FILED AND RECORDED WITH THE SECRETARIAT OF THE UNITED NATIONS. United Nations, Sales Section, Room DC2-0853, Publishing Division, New York, New York 10017. 1946- .

UNITED STATES INCOME TAX TREATIES. Harry A. Shannon and Klaus Vogel. Kluwer Law Book Publishers, Incorporated, 36 West Forty-fourth Street, New York, New York 10036. 1989- .

UNITED STATES TREATIES AND OTHER INTERNATIONAL AGREEMENTS. United States Department of State. Superintendent of Documents, United States Government Printing Office, Washington, D.C. 20402. 1950- .

UNPERFECTED TREATIES OF THE UNITED STATES OF AMERICA, 1776-1976. Christian L. Wiktor, Editor. Oceana Publications, Incorporated, 75 Main Street, Dobbs Ferry, New York 10522. 1991.

LOOSELEAF SERVICES AND REPORTERS

ANNOTATED TOPICAL GUIDE TO U.S. INCOME TAX TREATIES. J. Ross Macdonald. Prentice-Hall, Incorporated, 113 Sylvan Avenue, Englewood Cliffs, New Jersey 07632. 1988- .

TEXTBOOKS AND GENERAL WORKS

THE ANTARCTIC TREATY SYSTEM: POLITICS, LAW, AND DIPLOMACY. Jeffrey D. Myhre. Westview Press, 5500 Central Avenue, Boulder, Colorado 80301. 1986.

BASIC DOCUMENTS IN INTERNATIONAL LAW. Third Edition. Clarendon Press, Oxford University Press, 200 Madison Avenue, New York, New York 10016. 1983.

A CALENDAR OF SOVIET TREATIES, 1974-1980. George Ginsburgs. Martinus Nijhoff, Kluwer Academic Publishers, 101 Philip Drive, Assinippi Park, Norwell, Massachusetts 02061. 1987.

THE CONSTITUTION AND THE TERMINATION OF TREATIES. David G. Adler. Garland Publishing, Incorporated, 136 Madison Avenue, New York, New York 10016. 1986.

CURRENT INTERNATIONAL TREATIES. T. B. Millar and Robin Ward, Editors. New York University Press, Distributed by Columbia University Press, 562 West One-Hundred Thirteenth Street, New York, New York 10025. 1984.

DEVELOPMENTS IN THE LAW OF TREATIES, 1945-1986. Shabtai Rosenne. Cambridge University Press, 40 West Twentieth Street, New York, New York 10011. 1989.

HUMAN RIGHTS TREATIES AND THE SENATE: A HISTORY OF OPPOSITION. Natalie Hevener Kaufman. University of North Carolina Press, P.O. Box 2288, 116 South Boundary Street, Chapel Hill, North Carolina 27515-2288. 1990.

INTERNATIONAL LAW GOVERNING COMMUNICATIONS AND INFORMATION: A COLLECTION OF DOCUMENTS. Edward W. Ploman, Editor. Greenwood Publishing Group, Incorporated, 88 Post Road West, P.O. Box 5007, Westport, Connecticut 06881. 1982.

INTERNATIONAL LAW: THE ESSENTIAL TREATIES AND OTHER RELEVANT DOCUMENTS. Ingo von Muench, Editor. Walter de Gruyter, Incorporated, 200 Saw Mill Road, Hawthorne, New York 10532. 1985.

INTERNATIONAL WILDLIFE LAW: AN ANALYSIS OF INTERNATIONAL TREATIES CONCERNED WITH THE CONSERVATION OF WILDLIFE. Simon Lyster. Butterworth Legal Publishers, 90 Stiles Road, Salem, New Hampshire 03079. 1985.

INTRODUCTION TO THE LAW OF TREATIES. Paul Reuter. Pinter Publishers, 562 West One Hundred Thirteenth Street, New York, New York 10025. 1989.

THE MAJOR INTERNATIONAL TREATIES, 1914-1945: A HISTORY AND GUIDE WITH TEXTS. J. A. S. Grenville. Methuen, New York, New York. 1987.

THE MAKING OF INTERNATIONAL AGREEMENTS: CONGRESS CONFRONTS THE EXECUTIVE. Lock K. Johnson. New York University Press, Distributed by Columbia University Press, 562 West One-Hundred Thirteenth Street, New York, New York 10025. 1985.

THE MODERN LAW OF TREATIES. T. O. Elias. Oceana Publications, Incorporated, 75 Main Street, Dobbs Ferry, New York 10522. 1974.

NORMATIVE POLITICS AND THE COMMUNITY OF NATIONS. Haskell Fain. Temple University Press, 1601 North Broad Street, University Services Building, Philadelphia, Pennsylvania 19122. 1987.

RESERVATIONS AND INTERPRETATIVE DECLARATIONS TO MULTILATERAL TREATIES. Frank Horn. Elsevier Science Publishing Company, P.O.Box 882, Madison Square Station, New York, New York 10159. 1988.

TREATY CONFLICT AND POLITICAL CONTRADICTION: THE DIALECTIC OF DUPLICITY. Guyora Binder. Praeger Publishers, One Madison Avenue, New York, New York 10010. 1988.

TREATY INTERPRETATION: THEORY AND REALITY. Edward Slavko Yambrusic. University Press of America, 4720 Boston Way, Lanham, Maryland 20706. 1987.

THE VIENNA CONVENTION ON THE LAW OF TREATIES. Second Edition. Ian Sinclair. St. Martin's Press, 175 Fifth Avenue, New York, New York 10010. 1988.

ENCYCLOPEDIAS AND DICTIONARIES

ENCYCLOPEDIAS OF THE UNITED NATIONS AND INTERNATIONAL AGREEMENTS. Edmund J. Osmanczyk, Editor. Taylor and Francis, Incorporated, 1990 Frost Road, Suite 101, Bristol, Pennsylvania 19007. 1985.

GLOSSARY OF INTERNATIONAL TREATIES. Yvette Renoux. North Holland Imprint of Elsevier, Elsevier Science Publishing Company, Incorporated, Division of Biomedical Division, P.O. Box 882, Madison Square Station, New York, New York 10159. 1970.

DIGESTS, INDEXES, ABSTRACTS, CITATORS

CATALOG OF TREATIES, 1814-1918. Oceana Publications, Incorporated, 75 Main Street, Dobbs Ferry, New York 10522. 1965.

CHART SHOWING SIGNATURES AND RATIFICATIONS OF EUROPEAN CONVENTIONS AND AGREEMENTS. Council of Europe, Directorate of Legal Affairs, Manhattan Publishing Company, 225 Lafayette Street, New York, New York 10012. 1984.

CUMULATIVE LIST AND INDEX TO TREATIES AND INTERNATIONAL AGREEMENTS REGISTERED OR FILED AND RECORDED WITH THE SECRETARIAT OF THE UNITED NATIONS, DECEMBER 1969-DECEMBER 1974. Joseph T. Vambery, Editor. Oceana Publications, Incorporated, 75 Main Street, Dobbs Ferry, New York 10522. 1977.

INDEX TO MULTI-LATERAL TREATIES: A CHRONOLOGICAL LIST OF MULTI-PARTY INTERNATIONAL AGREEMENTS FROM THE SIXTEENTH CENTURY THROUGH 1963, WITH CITATIONS TO THEIR TEXT. Vaclav Mostecky, Editor. Oceana Publications, Incorporated, 75 Main Street, Dobbs Ferry, New York 10522. 1965 (Supplement 1968).

MULTI-LATERAL TREATIES IN RESPECT OF WHICH THE SECRETARY-GENERAL PERFORMS DEPOSITORY FUNCTIONS: LIST OF SIGNATURES, RATIFICATIONS, ACCESSIONS, ETC. United Nations, Office of Legal Affairs, Sales Section, Publishing Division, Room DC2-0853, New York, New York 10017. Annual.

SHEPARD'S UNITED STATES CITATIONS: STATUTES AND COURT RULES: A COMPILATION OF CITATIONS TO UNITED STATES CONSTITUTION, UNITED STATES CODE, UNITED STATES STATUTES AT LARGE, UNITED STATES TREATIES AND OTHER INTERNATIONAL AGREEMENTS. Shepard's/McGraw-Hill, P.O. Box 1235, Colorado Springs, Colorado 80901. Monthly.

STATEMENT OF TREATIES AND INTERNATIONAL AGREEMENTS REGISTERED OR FILED AND RECORDED WITH THE SECRETARIAT OF THE UNITED NATIONS. United Nations, Office of Legal Affairs, Sales Section, Publishing Division, Room DC2-0853, New York, New York 10017. Monthly.

STATUS OF INTER-AMERICAN TREATIES AND CONVENTIONS. Organization of American States, Seventeenth Street and Constitution Avenue, Northwest, Washington, D.C. 20006. 1980.

TREATIES IN FORCE: A LIST OF TREATIES AND OTHER INTERNATIONAL AGREEMENTS OF THE UNITED STATES. United States Department of State, Superintendent of Documents, United States Government Printing Office, Washington, D.C. 20402. Annual.

TREATY PROFILES. Peter H. Rohn. ABC-Clio Information Services, Riviera Campus, P.O. Box 1911, Santa Barbara, California 93116-1911. 1976.

UNITED STATES TREATIES AND OTHER INTERNATIONAL AGREEMENTS CUMULATIVE INDEX, 1776-1949. Compiled by Igor I. Kavass and Mark A. Michael. William S. Hein and Company, Incorporated, Hein Building, 1285 Main Street, Buffalo, New York 14209. 1975.

UNITED STATES TREATIES AND OTHER INTERNATIONAL AGREEMENTS CUMULATIVE INDEX, 1950-1970. Compiled by Igor I. Kavass and Adolf Sprudzs. William S. Hein and Company, Incorporated, Hein Building, 1285 Main Street, Buffalo, New York 14209. 1973.

UNITED STATES TREATIES AND OTHER INTERNATIONAL AGREEMENTS CUMULATIVE INDEX, 1971-1975. Compiled by Igor I. Kavass and Adolf Sprudzs. William S. Hein and Company, Incorporated, Hein Building, 1285 Main Street, Buffalo, New York 14209. 1977. (Supplement 1985).

WORLD TREATY INDEX. Second Edition. Peter H. Rohn. ABC-Clio Information Services, Riviera Campus, P.O. Box 1911, Santa Barbara, California 93116-1911. 1984.

LAW REVIEWS AND PERIODICALS

AMERICAN JOURNAL OF INTERNATIONAL LAW. American Society of International Law, 2223 Massachusetts Avenue, Northwest, Washington, D.C. 20008. Quarterly.

DEPARTMENT OF STATE BULLETIN. United States Department of State. Superintendent of Documents, United States Government Printing Office, Washington, D.C. 20402. Monthly.

INTERNATIONAL LEGAL MATERIALS. American Society of International Law, 2223 Massachusetts Avenue, Northwest, Washington, D.C. 20008. Six issues per year.

DIRECTORIES

U.S. TAX TREATY REFERENCE LIBRARY INDEX: U.S. TAX TREATIES IN FORCE AND THEIR LEGISLATIVE HISTORIES, ONLINE AND MICROFICHE DATABASE CITATIONS. Tax Analysts, 6830 North Fairfax Drive, Arlington, Virginia 22213. 1990.

RESEARCH CENTERS, INSTITUTES, CLEARINGHOUSES

TREATY RESEARCH CENTER. University of Washington, Political Science Department, DO-30, Seattle, Washington 98195. (206) 543-8030.

TREES
See: FORESTS AND FORESTRY

TRIAL BY JURY, RIGHT TO
See: DUE PROCESS OF LAW

TRIAL PRACTICE
See also: APPELLATE PROCEDURE; CIVIL PROCEDURE; CRIMINAL PROCEDURE; CROSS-EXAMINATION; EVIDENCE; WITNESSES

LOOSELEAF SERVICES AND REPORTERS

ART OF ADVOCACY: CROSS EXAMINATION OF LAY WITNESSES. John E. Durst, Jr. and Fred Queller. Matthew Bender and Company, Incorporated, 11 Penn Plaza, New York, New York 10001. 1988- .

FEDERAL CIVIL TRIALBOOK. Cari P. Matthews. West Publishing Company, 50 West Kellogg Boulevard, St. Paul, Minnesota 55164-0526. 1991.

GOLDSTEIN TRIAL TECHNIQUE. Third Edition. Fred Lane. Callaghan and Company, 155 Pfingsten Road, Deerfield, Illinois 60015. 1984- .

LANE'S GOLDSTEIN LITIGATION FORMS. Fred Lane, Irving Goldstein, and Patricia A. Groble. Callaghan and Company, 155 Pfingsten Road, Deerfield, Illinois 60015. 1991.

MODERN VISUAL EVIDENCE. Gregory P. Joseph. Law Journal Seminars Press, Incorporated, 111 Eighth Avenue, New York, New York, 10011. 1984- .

THE PREPARATION AND TRIAL OF MEDICAL MALPRACTICE CASES. Richard E. Shandell and Patricia Smith. Law Journal Seminars-Press, Incorporated, 111 Eighth Avenue, Suite 900, New York, New York 10011. 1990- .

PRODUCTS LIABILITY LITIGATION:TRIAL STRATEGY AND PROCEDURE. Bob Gibbins and A. Russell Smith. Callaghan and Company, 155 Pfingsten Road, Deerfield, Illinois 60015. 1988- .

THE TRIAL LAWYER'S GUIDE. Revised Edition. John J. Kennelly, Editor. Callaghan and Company, 155 Pfingsten Road, Deerfield, Illinois 60015. 1981- .

HANDBOOKS, MANUALS, FORMBOOKS

THE ADVOCATE'S DESKBOOK: THE ESSENTIALS OF TRYING A CASE. Irving Younger. Prentice-Hall, Incorporated, 113 Sylvan Avenue, Englewood Cliffs, New Jersey 07632. 1988.

CIVIL TRIAL MANUAL II. American Law Institute-American Bar Association, Committee on Continuing Professional Education, 4025 Chestnut Street, Philadelphia, Pennsylvania 19104. 1980. (Supplement 1984 and 1987).

FEDERAL TRIAL HANDBOOK. Second Edition. Robert S. Hunter. Lawyers Co-Operative Publishing Company, Aqueduct Building, Rochester, New York 14694. 1984. (Annual Supplement).

TRIAL PRACTICE

FEDERAL TRIAL PROCEDURE HANDBOOK. James M. Fischer. John Wiley and Sons, Incorporated, 605 Third Avenue, New York, New York 10158. 1985.

GOING TO TRIAL: A STEP-BY-STEP GUIDE TO TRIAL PRACTICE AND PROCEDURE. Karl Beckmeyer. American Bar Association, Litigation Committee, Sole Practitioners and Small Firms Committee, Section of General Practice, 750 North Lake Shore Drive, Chicago, Illinois 60611. 1989.

THE LAWSUIT HANDBOOK. Richard Coombs. LawPrep Press, Incorporated, 17900 North Sky Park Circle, Suite 100, Irvine, California 92714. 1990.

THE LITIGATION MANUAL: A PRIMER FOR TRIAL LAWYERS. Second Edition. John G. Koeltl. American Bar Association, Section of Litigation, 750 North Lake Shore Drive, Chicago, Illinois 60611. 1989.

MANUAL FOR COMPLEX LITIGATION. Second Edition. Commerce Clearing House, Incorporated, 4025 West Peterson Avenue, Chicago, Illinois 60646. 1985.

MANUAL FOR COMPLEX LITIGATION. Second Edition. Clark Boardman Company, Limited, 435 Hudson Street, New York, New York 10014. 1986.

MASTERS ADVOCATES' HANDBOOK. D. Lake Rumsey, Editor. National Institute for Trial Advocacy, Notre Dame Law School, Notre Dame, Indiana 46556. 1986.

MCELHANEY'S TRIAL NOTEBOOK. Second Edition. James W. McElhaney. American Bar Association, Section of Litigation, 750 North Lake Shore Drive, Chicago, Illinois 60611. 1987.

PERSONAL INJURY TRIAL HANDBOOK. John A. Tarantino and David J. Oliveira. John Wiley and Sons, Incorporated, 605 Third Avenue, New York, New York 10158. 1989.

TRIAL HANDBOOK. Kent Sinclair. Practising Law Institute, 810 Seventh Avenue, New York, New York 10019. 1985.

TRIAL MANUAL FOR THE DEFENSE OF CRIMINAL CASES. Fourth Edition. American Law Institute-American Bar Association, Committee on Continuing Professional Education, 4025 Chestnut Street, Philadelphia, Pennsylvania 19104. 1984.

THE TRIAL MASTERS: A HANDBOOK OF STRATEGIES AND TECHNIQUES THAT WIN CASES. Bertram C. Warshaw, Editor. Prentice-Hall, Incorporated, 113 Sylvan Avenue, Englewood Cliffs, New Jersey 07632. 1984.

TRIAL PRACTICE CHECKLISTS. Douglas Danner and John W. Toothman. Lawyers Cooperative Publishing Company, Aqueduct Building, Rochester, New York 14694. 1989.

WINNING TRIAL ADVOCACY: HOW TO AVOID MISTAKES MADE BY MASTER TRIAL LAWYERS. Julius B. Levine. Prentice-Hall, Incorporated, 113 Sylvan Avenue, Englewood Cliffs, New Jersey 07632. 1989.

TEXTBOOKS AND GENERAL WORKS

ADVOCACY AND EVIDENCE: COURTROOM WARRIORS AND THEIR WEAPONS: ALI-ABA COURSE OF STUDY MATERIALS. American Bar Association, 750 North Lake Shore Drive, Chicago, Illinois 60611. 1983.

ADVOCACY, THE ART OF PLEADING A CAUSE. Second Edition. Richard A. Givens. Shepard's/McGraw-Hill, P.O. Box 1235, Colorado Springs, Colorado 80901. 1983.

ANATOMY OF A PERSONAL INJURY LAWSUIT. Third Edition. James S. Rogers. ATLA Press, 1050 Thiry-first Street, Northwest, Washington, D.C. 20007. 1991.

ART OF ADVOCACY: DIRECT EXAMINATION. Scott Baldwin. Matthew Bender and Company, Incorporated, 11 Penn Plaza, New York, New York 10001. 1982. (Annual Supplement).

ART OF ADVOCACY: OPENING STATEMENT. Leonard Decof. Matthew Bender and Company, Incorporated, 11 Penn Plaza, New York, New York 10001. 1982. (Annual Supplement).

ART OF ADVOCACY: SUMMATION. Lawrence J. Smith. Matthew Bender and Company, Incorporated, 11 Penn Plaza, New York, New York 10001. 1982. (Annual Supplement).

BASIC PERSONAL INJURY TRIAL PRACTICE. Neil T. Shayne. Practising Law Institute, 810 Seventh Avenue, New York, New York 10019. 1988.

BEST OF TRIAL. Association of Trial Lawyers of America. ATLA Press, 1050 Thirty-first Street, Northwest, Washington, D.C. 20007. 1990.

CANCER: CAUSES AND METHODS OF TREATMENT FOR TRIAL LAWYERS. John R. McLaren. Harrison Company, 3110 Crossing Park, Norcross, Georgia 30071. 1985.

CIVIL PRACTICE AND EFFECTIVE LITIGATION TECHNIQUES IN FEDERAL AND STATE COURTS: COURSE OF STUDY MATERIALS. American Law Institute-American Bar Association, Committee on Continuing Professional Education, 4025 Chestnut Street, Philadelphia, Pennsylvania 19104. 1985.

CLOSING ARGUMENT: THE ART AND THE LAW. Jacob A. Stein. Callaghan and Company, 155 Pfingsten Road, Deerfield, Illinois 60015. 1969. (Supplement 1985).

COMMUNICATION AND LITIGATION: CASE STUDIES OF FAMOUS TRIALS. Janice Schuetz and Kathryn Holmes Snedaker. Southern Illinois University Press, P.O. Box 3697, Carbondale, Illinois 62902-3697. 1988.

COMMUNICATION IN LEGAL ADVOCACY. Richard D. Rieke and Randall K. Stutman. University of South Carolina Press, Columbia, South Carolina 29208. 1990.

COMMUNICATION IN THE LEGAL PROCESS. Ronald J. Matlon. Holt, Rinehart, and Winston, Incorporated, 6277 Sea Harbor Drive, Orlando, Florida 32821. 1988.

CONFLICT, COURTS, AND TRIALS. Third Edition. Linda Riekes, Dolores B. Malcolm, and Michael A. Wolff. West Publishing Company, 50 West Kellogg Boulevard, St. Paul, Minnesota 55164-0526. 1991.

CONTRACT LAWSUITS: TRIAL STRATEGIES AND TECHNIQUES. Second Edition. Edward J. Imwinkelried. Michie Company, P.O. Box 7587, Charlottesville, Virginia 22906. 1989.

COORDINATION AND MANANAGEMENT OF MAJOR LITIGATION. Haley J. Froholz. Practising Law Institute, 810 Seventh Avenue, New York, New York 10019. 1982.

COURTROOM COMMUNICATION STRATEGIES. Lawrence J. Smith and Loretta A. Malandro. Michie Company, P.O. Box 7587, Charlottesville, Virginia 22906-7587. 1985. (1988 Supplement)

COURTROOM PSYCHOLOGY FOR TRIAL LAWYERS. Thomas Sannito and Peter J. McGovern. John Wiley and Sons, Incorporated, 605 Third Avenue, New York, New York 10158. 1985.

CREATIVE TRIAL TECHNIQUES: MASTERS IN THE COURTROOM. Thomas J. Murray. Professional Education Systems, 200 Spring Street, Eau Claire, Wisconsin 54702. 1983.

DOMBROFF ON UNFAIR TACTICS. Second Edition. Mark A. Dombroff. John Wiley and Sons, Incorporated, 605 Third Avenue, New York, New York 10158. 1988.

DYNAMICS OF TRIAL PRACTICE: PROBLEMS AND MATERIALS. Ronald L. Carlson and Edward J. Imwinkelried. West Publishing Company, 50 West Kellogg Boulevard, St. Paul, Minnesota 55164-0526. 1989.

EFFECTIVE OPENING STATEMENTS: THE ATTORNEY'S MASTER KEY TO VICTORY. Fredric G. Levin. Executive Reports Corporation, Subsidiary of Prentice-Hall, Incorporated, 113 Sylvan Avenue, Englewood Cliffs, New Jersey 07632. 1983.

ESSAYS ON ADVOCACY. Theodore I. Koskoff and Arnett J. Holloway. Association of Trial Lawyers of America, 1050 Thirty-first Street, Northwest, Washington, D.C. 20007. 1988.

EVIDENCE: HOW AND WHEN TO USE THE RULES TO WIN CASES. Edward T. Wright. Prentice-Hall, Incorporated, 113 Sylvan Avenue, Englewood Cliffs, New Jersey 07632. 1990.

FAMOUS AMERICAN JURY SPEECHES: ADDRESSES BEFORE JURIES AND FACT-FINDING TRIBUNALS. Frederick C. Hicks. Fred B. Rothman and Company, 10368 West Centennial Road, Littleton, Colorado 80127. 1990. (Reprint).

FEDERAL LITIGATION GUIDE. Matthew Bender and Company, Incorporated, 11 Penn Plaza, New York, New York 10001. 1985.

THE FIRST TRIAL: WHERE DO I SIT? WHAT DO I SAY? IN A NUTSHELL. Steven H. Goldberg. West Publishing Company, P.O. Box 64526, 50 West Kellogg Boulevard, St. Paul, Minnesota 55164-0526. 1982.

FUNDAMENTALS OF TRIAL TECHNIQUES. Second Edition. Thomas A. Mauet. Little, Brown and Company, 34 Beacon Street, Boston, Massachusetts 02108. 1988.

GUIDE TO MULTISTATE LITIGATION. Victor Schwartz, Patrick Lee, and Kathryn Kelly. Shepard's/McGraw-Hill, P.O. Box 1235, Colorado Springs, Colorado 80901. 1985.

HOW TO USE COURTROOM DRAMA TO WIN CASES. Edward T. Wright. Prentice-Hall, Incorporated, 113 Sylvan Avenue, Englewood Cliffs, New Jersey 07632. 1987.

INTRODUCTION TO ADVOCACY: BRIEF WRITING AND ORAL ARGUMENT IN MOOT COURT COMPETITION. Fourth Edition. Harvard Law School, Board of Student Advisors. Foundation Press, Incorporated, 615 Merrick Avenue, Westbury, New York 11590. 1985.

JULIEN ON SUMMATION. Alfred S. Julien. John Wiley and Sons, Incorporated, 605 Third Avenue, New York, New York 10158. 1986. (1991 Supplement).

KEY TRIAL CONTROL TACTICS: A GUIDE TO WINNING THE ULTIMATE VERDICT. Mark A. Dombroff. Executive Reports Corporation, Subsidiary of Prentice-Hall, Incorporated, 113 Sylvan Avenue, Englewood Cliffs, New Jersey 07632. 1984.

LITIGATION. James W. Jeans. Kluwer Law Book Publishers, Incorporated, 36 West Forty-fourth Street, New York, New York 10036. 1986.

LITIGATION AND TRIAL PRACTICE FOR THE LEGAL ASSISTANT. Third Edition. Roderick D. Blanchard. West Publishing Company, 50 West Kellogg Boulevard, St. Paul, Minnesota 55164-0526. 1990.

THE LITIGATION MANUAL: A PRIMER FOR TRIAL LAWYERS. American Bar Association, Section on Litigation, 750 North Lake Shore Drive, Chicago, Illinois 60611. 1989.

LITIGATION ORGANIZATION AND MANAGEMENT: EFFECTIVE TACTICS AND TECHNIQUES. Mark A. Dombroff. Law and Business, Harcourt Brace Jovanovich, Incorporated, 6277 Sea Harbor Drive, Orlando, Florida 32821. 1984.

MAKING TRIAL OBJECTIONS. James F. McCarthy, Sr., Editor. John Wiley and Sons, Incorporated, 605 Third Avenue, New York, New York 10158. 1986. (Periodic Supplements).

MANAGING COMPLEX LITIGATION: A PRACTICAL GUIDE TO SPECIAL MASTERS. American Bar Association, 750 North Lake Shore Drive, Chicago, Illinois 60611. 1983.

MASTERS OF TRIAL PRACTICE: TECHNIQUES OF 22 NATIONALLY RECOGNIZED ADVOCATES. Janine Warsaw. John Wiley and Sons, Incorporated, 605 Third Avenue, New York, New York 10158. 1988.

MATERIALS IN TRIAL ADVOCACY: PROBLEMS AND CASES. Second Edition. Thomas A. Mauet and Warren D. Wolfson. Little, Brown and Company, 34 Beacon Street, Boston, Massachusetts 02108. 1987.

MODERN TRIALS. Second Edition. Melvin M. Belli, Sr. West Publishing Company, P.O. Box 64526, 50 West Kellogg Boulevard, St. Paul, Minnesota 55164-0526. 1982. (Supplement 1984).

MOTION PRACTICE. David F. Herr, Roger S. Haydock, and Jeffrey W. Stempel. Little, Brown and Company, 34 Beacon Street, Boston, Massachusetts 02108. 1985.

NEW TECHNIQUES FOR WINNING JURY TRIALS. James Rasicot. AB Publishing, 6705 Woodedge Road, Mound, Minnesota 55364-8104. 1990.

NEWBERG ON CLASS ACTION. Herbert B. Newberg. Second Edition. Shepard's/McGraw-Hill, P.O. Box 1235, Colorado Springs, Colorado 80901. 1985.

THE PERSUASION EDGE: WINNING PSYCHOLOGICAL STRATEGIES AND TACTICS FOR LAWYERS. Richard J. Crawford. John Wiley and Sons, Incorporated, 605 Third Avenue, New York, New York 10158. 1991.

RESOURCE MATERIALS: CIVIL PRACTICE AND LITIGATION IN FEDERAL AND STATE COURTS. Fourth Edition. American Law Institute-American Bar Association, Committee on Continuing Professional Education, 4025 Chestnut Street, Philadelphia, Pennsylvania 19104. 1987.

THE ROLE OF COMMUNICATION IN THE PRACTICE OF LAW. Dirk Cameron Gibson. University Press of America, 4720 Boston Way, Lanham, Maryland 20706. 1992.

SOCIAL SCIENCE RESEARCH METHODS FOR LITIGATION. Donald E. Vinson and Phillip K. Anthony. The Michie Company, P.O. Box 7587, Charlottesville, Virginia 22906-7587. 1985.

SPONSORSHIP STRATEGY: EVIDENTIARY TACTICS FOR WINNING JURY TRIALS. Robert H. Klonoff and Paul L. Colby. Michie Company, P.O. Box 7587, Charlottesville, Virginia 22906. 1990.

STATISTICS IN LITIGATION: PRACTICAL APPLICATIONS FOR LAWYERS. Richard A. Wehmhoeffer. Shepard's/McGraw-Hill, P.O. Box 1235, Colorado Springs, Colorado 80901. 1985.

STRATEGIC USE OF SCIENTIFIC EVIDENCE. John A. Tarantino. Kluwer Law Book Publishers, Incorporated, 36 West Forty-fourth Street, New York, New York 10036. 1988.

SUCCESSFUL TECHNIQUES FOR CRIMINAL TRIALS. Second Edition. F. Lee Bailey and Henry B. Rothblatt. Lawyers Co-Operative Publishing Company, Aqueduct Building, Rochester, New York 14694. 1985.

SUCCESSFUL TRIAL TECHNIQUES OF EXPERT PRACTITIONERS. Robert V. Wells. Shepard's/McGraw-Hill, P.O. Box 1235, Colorado Springs, Colorado 80901. 1988.

TANGIBLE EVIDENCE: HOW TO USE EXHIBITS AT TRIAL. Deanne C. Siemer. Law and Business, Harcourt Brace Jovanovich, Incorporated, 6277 Sea Harbor Drive, Orlando, Florida 32821. 1984.

TRIAL ADVOCACY. James W. Jeans. West's Handbook Series. West Publishing Company, P.O. Box 64526, 50 West Kellogg Boulevard, St. Paul, Minnesota 55164-0526. 1975.

TRIAL ADVOCACY: A SYSTEMATIC APPROACH. American Law Institute-American Bar Association, Committee on Continuing Professional Education, 4025 Chestnut Street, Philadelphia, Pennsylvania 19104. 1984.

TRIAL ADVOCACY IN A NUTSHELL. Second Edition. Paul Bergman. West Publishing Company, P.O. Box 64526, 50 West Kellogg Boulevard, St. Paul, Minnesota 55164-0526. 1989.

TRIAL ADVOCACY MATERIALS. Kent Sinclair, Jr. Practising Law Institute, 810 Seventh Avenue, New York, New York 10019. 1985.

TRIAL ADVOCACY: PLANNING, ANALYSIS, AND STRATEGY. Marilyn J. Berger, John B. Mitchell, and Ronald H. Clark. Little, Brown and Company, 34 Beacon Street, Boston, Massachusetts 02108. 1989.

TRIAL BY JURY. Steven Brill. Simon and Schuster, Incorporated, 1230 Avenue of the Americas, New York, New York 10020. 1989.

TRIAL COMMUNICATIONS SKILLS. Roberto Aron, Julius Fast and Richard Klein. Shepard's/McGraw-Hill, P.O. Box 1235, Colorado Springs, Colorado 80901. 1986.

TRIAL DIPLOMACY: WITH TEXT, CASES AND ILLUSTRATIONS. Second Edition. Alan E. Morrill. Court Practice Institute, 30 West Washington, Room 530, Chicago, Illinois 60602. 1972. (1978 Printing).

TRIAL ETHICS. Richard H. Underwood and William H. Fortune. Little, Brown and Company, 34 Beacon Street, Boston, Massachusetts 02108. 1988.

THE TRIAL LAWYER'S BOOK: PREPARING AND WINNING CASES. Jonathan M. Purver. Lawyers Cooperative Publishing Company, Aqueduct Building, Rochester, New York 14694. 1990.

THE TRIAL LAWYERS: THE NATION'S TOP LITIGATORS TELL HOW THEY WIN. Emily Couric. St. Martin's Press, 175 Fifth Avenue, New York, New York 10010. 1988.

TRIAL PRACTICE: PROBLEMS AND CASE FILES. Edward R. Stein and Lawrence A. Dubin. Anderson Publishing Company, 2035 Reading Road, Cincinnati, Ohio 45202. 1990.

TRIAL PRACTICE SKILLS IN A NUTSHELL. Kenney P. Hegland. West Publishing Company, P.O. Box 64526, 50 West Kellogg Boulevard, St. Paul, Minnesota 55164-0526. 1978.

TRIAL PSYCHOLOGY: COMMUNICATION AND PERSUASION IN THE COURTROOM. Margaret C. Roberts. Butterworth Legal Publishers, 90 Stiles Road, Salem, New Hampshire 03079. 1987.

TRIAL TECHNIQUES: OPENING STATEMENTS AND CLOSING ARGUMENTS. Grace W. Holmes and Mary I. Hiniker. Institute of Continuing Legal Education, 1020 Greene Street, Ann Arbor, Michigan 48109-1444. 1987.

TRIAL: THEORIES, TACTICS, TECHNIQUES. Roger Haydock and John Sonsteng. West Publishing Company, 50 West Kellogg Boulevard, St. Paul, Minnesota 55164-0526. 1991.

TRIAL OBJECTIONS. Mark A. Dombroff. Ford Publishing Company, P.O. Box 626, Corona Del Mar, California 92625. 1985.

TRIAL PRACTICE FOR THE GENERAL PRACTITIONER. Leonard Packel, Editor. American Law Institute-American Bar Association, Committee on Continuing Professional Education, 4025 Chestnut Street, Philadelphia, Pennsylvania 19104. 1980.

THE TRIALBOOK: A TOTAL SYSTEM FOR THE PREPARATION AND PRESENTATION OF A CASE. John O. Sonsteng, Roger S. Haydock and James J. Boyd. West Publishing Company, P.O. Box 64526, 50 West Kellogg Boulevard, St. Paul, Minnesota 55164-0526. 1984.

TRYING CASES TO WIN. Herbert J. Stern. PSI Legal Publishers, Eau Claire, Wisconsin. 1991.

VIDEO TACTICS IN SETTLEMENT AND TRIAL. Alan S. Loewinsohn. John Wiley and Sons, Incorporated, 605 Third Avenue, New York, New York 10158. 1989.

VIDEO TECHNIQUES IN TRIAL AND PRETRIAL. Fred I. Heller, Chairman. Practising Law Institute, 810 Seventh Avenue, New York, New York 10019. 1983.

A WINNING CASE: HOW TO USE PERSUASIVE COMMUNICATION TECHNIQUES FOR SUCCESSFUL TRIAL WORK. Noelle C. Nelson. Prentice-Hall, Incorporated, 113 Sylvan Avenue, Englewood Cliffs, New Jersey 07632. 1991.

WOMEN TRIAL LAWYERS: HOW THEY SUCCEED IN PRACTICE AND IN THE COURTROOM. Janine N. Warsaw. Prentice-Hall, Incorporated, 113 Sylvan Avenue, Englewood Cliffs, New Jersey 07632. 1987.

ENCYCLOPEDIAS AND DICTIONARIES

AMERICAN JURISPRUDENCE TRIALS: AN ENCYCLOPEDIC GUIDE TO THE MODERN PRACTICES, TECHNIQUES AND TACTICS USED IN PREPARING AND TRYING CASES, WITH MODEL PROGRAMS FOR THE HANDLING OF ALL TYPES OF LITIGATION. Lawyers Co-Operative Publishing Company, Aqueduct Building, Rochester, New York 14694. 1964. (Annual Supplements).

CYCLOPEDIA OF TRIAL PRACTICE: PROOF OF TRAUMATIC INJURIES. Third Edition. Sydney C. Schweitzer. Lawyers Co-Operative Publishing Company, Aqueduct Building, Rochester, New York 14694. 1986. (Annual Supplements).

LAW REVIEWS AND PERIODICALS

AMERICAN JOURNAL OF TRIAL ADVOCACY. Cumberland School of Law of Samford University, 800 Lake Shore Drive, Birmingham, Alabama 35229. Quarterly.

THE BRIEF. American Bar Association, 750 North Lake Shore Drive, Chicago, Illinois 60611. Quarterly.

LITIGATION. Section of Litigation, American Bar Association, 750 North Lake Shore Drive, Chicago, Illinois 60611. Quarterly.

MEDICAL TRIAL TECHNIQUE QUARTERLY. Callaghan and Company, 155 Pfingsten Road, Deerfield, Illinois 60015. Quarterly.

REVIEW OF LITIGATION. University of Texas, School of Law, 727 East Twenty-sixth Street, Austin, Texas 78705. Semiannually.

TRIAL. Association of Trial Lawyers of America, 1050 Thirty-first Street, Northwest, Washington, D.C. 20007. Monthly.

TRIAL ADVOCATE QUARTERLY. Nova University Center for the Study of Law, 3100 Southwest Ninth Avenue, Fort Lauderdale, Florida 33315. Quarterly.

TRIAL DIPLOMACY JOURNAL. Court Practice Journal, Incorporated, P.O. Box 802, Danville, Illinois 61834. Quarterly.

TRIAL LAWYERS GUIDE. Callaghan and Company, 155 Pfingsten Road, Deerfield, Illinois 60015. Quarterly.

TRIAL LAWYERS QUARTERLY. New York State Trial Lawyers' Association, 132 Nassau Street, New York, New York 10038. Quarterly.

NEWSLETTERS AND NEWSPAPERS

ADVOCATE'S ADVOCATE. Advocacy Institute, 1730 Rhode Island Avenue, Northwest, Suite 600, Washington, D.C. 20036. Monthly.

ATLA ADVOCATE. Association of Trial Lawyers of America, 1050 Thirty-first Street, Northwest, Washington, D.C. 20007. Monthly.

ATLA LAW REPORTER. Association of Trial Lawyers of America, 1050 Thirty-first Street, Northwest, Washington, D.C. 20007. Monthly.

THE DOCKET. National Institute for Trial Advocacy, Notre Dame Law School, Notre Dame, Indiana 46556. Quarterly.

LITIGATION NEWS. Section on Litigation, American Bar Association, 750 North Lake Shore Drive, Chicago, Illinois 60611. Bimonthly.

IADC NEWS. International Association of Defense Counsel, 20 North Wacker Drive, Suite 3100, Chicago, Illinois 60606. Quarterly.

INSIDE LITIGATION. Prentice-Hall, Incorporated, 113 Sylvan Avenue, Englewood Cliffs, New Jersey 07632. Monthly.

LITIGATION COMMITTEE NEWSLETTER. American Bar Association, 750 North Lake Shore Drive, Chicago, Illinois 60611. Quarterly.

NOT GUILTY, THE NEWSLETTER FOR CRIMINAL DEFENSE ATTORNEYS. Kuehaus-Miller Publications, P.O. Box 88, Wossersburg, Missouri 64093. Monthly.

DIRECTORIES

NATIONAL BOARD OF TRIAL ADVOCACY: DIRECTORY OF BOARD MEMBERS AND CERTIFIED DIPLOMATS. National Board of Trial Advocacy, Association of Trial Lawyers of America, 1050 Thirty-first Street, Northwest, Washington, D.C. 20007. Annual.

ASSOCIATIONS AND PROFESSIONAL SOCIETIES

AMERICAN BAR ASSOCIATION, SECTION ON LITIGATION. 750 North Lake Shore Drive, Chicago, Illinois 60611. (312) 988-5000.

AMERICAN BOARD OF TRIAL ADVOCATES. 16633 Ventura Boulevard, Suite 730, Encino, California 91436. (818) 501-3250.

AMERICAN COLLEGE OF TRIAL LAWYERS. 8001 Irvine Center Drive, Suite 960, Irvine, California 92718. (714) 727-3194.

ASSOCIATION OF AMERICAN LAW SCHOOLS, SECTION ON LITIGATION, One Dupont Circle, Northwest, Washington, D.C. 20036. (202) 296-8851.

ASSOCIATION OF TRIAL LAWYERS OF AMERICA. 1050 Thirty-first Street, Northwest, Washington, D.C. 20007. (202) 965-3500.

DRI-DEFENSE RESEARCH AND TRIAL LAWYERS ASSOCIATION. 750 North Lake Shore Drive, Suite 500, Chicago, Illinois 60611. (312) 944-0575.

INTERNATIONAL ACADEMY OF TRIAL LAWYERS. 4 North Second Street, Suite 175, San Jose, California 95113. (408) 275-6767.

INTERNATIONAL ASSOCIATION OF DEFENSE COUNSEL. 20 North Wacker Drive, Suite 3100, Chicago, Illinois 60606. (312) 368-1494.

NATIONAL BOARD OF TRIAL ADVOCACY. Sulfolk University Law School, Beacon Hill, Boston, Massachusetts 02114. (617) 573-8700.

TRIAL LAWYERS FOR PUBLIC JUSTICE. 1625 Massachusetts Avenue, Suite 100, Washington, D.C. 20036. (202) 797-8600.

RESEARCH CENTERS, INSTITUTES, CLEARINGHOUSES

ADVOCACY INSTITUTE. 1730 Rhode Island Avenue, Northwest, Suite 600, Washington, D.C. 20036. (202) 659-8475.

NATIONAL INSTITUTE FOR TRIAL ADVOCACY. Notre Dame Law School, Notre Dame, Indiana 46556. (219) 239-7770.

NATIONAL JURY PROJECT. 1540 San Pablo Avenue, Ninth Floor, Oakland, California 94612. (415) 832-2583.

STATISTICS SOURCES

TRIALS - CIVIL AND CRIMINAL. Annual Report of the Director, Administrative Office of the United States Courts, United States Supreme Court Building, One First Street, Northeast, Washington, D.C. 20543.

AUDIOVISUALS

ADVOCACY AND THE ART OF STORYTELLING. National Institute for Trial Advocacy, Notre Dame Law School, Notre Dame, Indiana 46556. 1990. Videotape.

ART OF ADVOCACY: EXPERT WITNESSES. National Institute for Trial Advocacy, Notre Dame Law School, Notre Dame, Indiana 46556. 1988.

ART OF ADVOCACY: OPENING STATEMENTS AND CLOSING ARGUMENTS. National Institute for Trial Advocacy, Notre Dame Law School, Notre Dame, Indiana 46556. 1987.

ART OF ADVOCACY: SELECTING AND PERSUADING THE JURY. National Institute for Trial Advocacy, Notre Dame Law School, Notre Dame, Indiana 46556. 1988. Videotape.

ART OF CROSS-EXAMINATION. Henry B. Rothblatt. National Practice Institute, 330 Second Avenue South, Minneapolis, Minnesota 55401. Audiotape.

ATTORNEY'S GUIDE TO USING MEDICAL EVIDENCE. Harry Rein. National Practice Institute, 330 Second Avenue South, Minneapolis, Minnesota 55401. Audiotape.

BECOMING A 13TH JUROR: SUCCESSFUL TRIAL TECHNIQUES. Charles J. Ogletree. National Practice Institute, 330 Second Avenue South, Minneapolis, Minnesota 55401. Videotape.

BUSINESS LITIGATION. National Institute for Trial Advocacy, Notre Dame Law School, Notre Dame, Indiana 46556. 1987. Videotape.

CLOSING ARGUMENTS. National Institute for Trial Advocacy, Legal Education Center, 1507 Energy Park Drive, St. Paul, Minnesota 55108. 1983. Audio Series and Visual Series.

CLOSING ARGUMENTS: A LECTURE BY CHARLES BECTON. Consortium for Professional Education, American Bar Association, 750 North Lake Shore Drive, Chicago, Illinois 60611. 1980. Videotape.

DEMONSTRATIVE EVIDENCE. Mark A. Dombroff. National Practice Institute, 330 Second Avenue South, Minneapolis, Minnesota 55401. Videotape.

DIRECT AND CROSS-EXAMINATION OF A PLAINTIFF IN A CIVIL ASSAULT CASE. Consortium for Professional Education, American Bar Association, 750 North Lake Shore Drive, Chicago, Illinois 60611. 1979. Videotape.

DIRECT AND CROSS-EXAMINATION OF THE VICTIM IN A PURSE-SNATCHING CASE. Consortium for Professional Education, American Bar Association, 750 North Lake Shore Drive, Chicago, Illinois 60611. 1979. Videotape.

EFFECTIVE ARGUMENT TO THE COURT. American Bar Association, 750 North Lake Shore Drive, Chicago, Illinois 60611. 1989. Videotape.

EFFECTIVE COMMUNICATION IN THE COURTROOM. National Institute for Trial Advocacy, Legal Education Center, 1507 Energy Park Drive, St. Paul, Minnesota 55108. 1982. Videocassette Series.

EFFECTIVE COURTROOM PRACTICE: HOW TO HANDLE COMMON PROBLEMS. Practising Law Institute, 810 Seventh Avenue, New York, New York 10019. 1980. Videotapes.

EVIDENCE FOR THE TRIAL LAWYER. Faust F. Rossi. National Practice Institute, 330 Second Avenue South, Minneapolis, Minnesota 55401. Videotape.

EXHIBIT SERIES: 1. EVIDENTIARY OBJECTIONS; 2. DEMONSTRATIVE EVIDENCE; 3. LITURGY OF FOUNDATION LAYING. American Bar Association, Consortium for Professional Education, 750 North Lake Shore Drive, Chicago, Illinois 60611. 1979-80. Videotape.

JAMES JEANS TRIAL ADVOCACY SERIES. Consortium for Professional Education, American Bar Association, 750 North Lake Shore Drive, Chicago, Illinois 60611. 1980. Videotape.

JURY COMPREHENSION IN COMPLEX CASES. American Bar Association, 750 North Lake Shore Drive, Chicago, Illinois 60611. 1990. Videotape.

JURY SELECTION. National Institute for Trial Advocacy, Legal Education Center, 1507 Energy Park Drive, St. Paul, Minnesota 55108. Audio Series and Visual Series.

LASER DISC TECHNOLOGY IN THE COURTROOM. National Institute for Trial Advocacy, Notre Dame Law School, Notre Dame, Indiana 46556. 1990. Videotape.

LITIGATING "RULE OF REASON" CASES. American Bar Association, 750 North Lake Shore Drive, Chicago, Illinois 60611. 1987. Videotape.

LITIGATION MANAGEMENT AND ORGANIZATION: THE WINNING EDGE. Mark A. Dombroff. National Practice Institute, 330 Second Avenue South, Minneapolis, Minnesota 55401. Videotape.

MASTERING THE ART OF CROSS EXAMINATION. Irving Younger. National Institute for Trial Advocacy, Notre Dame Law School, Notre Dame, Indiana 46556. 1987. Videotape.

NEW PERSPECTIVES IN ADVOCACY: TRIAL AND APPELLATE. Myron Bright. National Practice Institute, 330 Second Avenue South, Minneapolis, Minnesota 55401. Videotape.

OPENING STATEMENTS. National Institute for Trial Advocacy, Legal Education Center, 1507 Energy Park Drive, St. Paul, Minnesota 55108. 1983. Audio Series and Visual Series.

OPENING STATEMENTS: CRIMINAL AND COMPLEX CIVIL. Consortium for Professional Education, American Bar Association, 750 North Lake Shore Drive, Chicago, Illinois 60611. 1980. Videotape.

PERSUASIVE EXPERT TESTIMONY. National Institute for Trial Advocacy, Notre Dame Law School, Notre Dame, Indiana 46556. 1988. Videotape.

PRACTICAL TRIAL EVIDENCE. Practising Law Institute, 810 Seventh Avenue, New York, New York 10019. 1977. Videotapes.

PRINCIPLES OF EXAMINATION: LECTURE BY JOHN A. BURGESS. Consortium for Professional Education, American Bar Association, 750 North Lake Shore Drive, Chicago, Illinois 60611. 1978 Videotape.

TRAINING THE ADVOCATE: 1. JURY SELECTION; 2. OPENING STATEMENTS; 3. LAYING THE FOUNDATION FOR EXHIBITS AND WITNESSES; 4. DIRECT EXAMINATION; 5. CROSS-EXAMINATION; 6. EXPERT WITNESS--LIABILITY; 7. EXPERT WITNESS--DAMAGES; 8. THE INTRODUCTION AND USE OF DEMON- STRATIVE EVIDENCE; 9. CLOSING ARGUMENTS; 10. JURY DELIBERATION. Consortium for Professional Education, American Bar Association, 750 North Lake Shore Drive, Chicago, Illinois 60611. 1983. Videotapes.

TRAINING THE ADVOCATE: THE PRETRIAL STAGE. National Institute for Trial Advocacy, Legal Education Center, 1507 Energy Park Drive, St. Paul, Minnesota 55108. 1985.

TRIAL EVIDENCE -- MAKING AND MEETING OBJECTIONS. National Institute for Trial Advocacy, Notre Dame Law School, Notre Dame, Indiana 46556. 1991. Videotape.

TRIAL NOTEBOOK. Consortium for Professional Education, American Bar Association, 750 North Lake Shore Drive, Chicago, Illinois 60611. 1979. Videotape.

TRIAL TACTICS. Mark A. Dombroff. National Practice Institute, 330 Second Avenue South, Minneapolis, Minnesota 55401. Videotape.

TRIAL TECHNIQUES WITH IRVING YOUNGER. National Practice Institute, 510 First Avenue North, Suite 205, Minneapolis, Minnesota 55403. 1978. Audio-cassettes.

UNFAIR TRIAL TACTICS: RECOGNIZING AND AVOIDING THEM IN LITIGATION. Mark A. Dombroff. National Practice Institute, 330 Second Avenue South, Minneapolis, Minnesota 55401. Videotape.

USE OF COMPUTERS IN COMPLEX LITIGATION. Consortium for Professional Education, American Bar Association, 750 North Lake Shore Drive, Chicago, Illinois 60611. 1980. Videotape.

USING FINANCIAL EXPERTS IN BUSINESS LITIGATION. National Institute for Trial Advocacy, Notre Dame Law School, Notre Dame, Indiana 46556. 1988. Videotape.

USING VIDEO IN LITIGATION. Practising Law Institute, 810 Seventh Avenue, New York, New York 10019. 1983. Videotape. VEHICLE COLLISION LITIGATION: TECHNIQUES AND EVALUATION. American Bar Association, 750 North Lake Shore Drive, Chicago, Illinois 60611. 1989. Videotape.

WINNING AT TRIAL. American Bar Association, 750 North Lake Shore Drive, Chicago, Illinois 60611. 1989. Videotape.

WINNING TRIAL TECHNIQUES. Richard "Racehorse" Haynes. National Practice Institute, 330 Second Avenue South, Minneapolis, Minnesota 55401. Videotape.

COMPUTER-ASSISTED LEGAL INSTRUCTION

BREW V. HARRIS I, II AND III. Interactive Video Library, Harvard Law School, Educational Technology Department, 18 Everett Street, Cambridge, Massachusetts 02138. Interactive videodisc.

BUFFALO CREEK: A GAME OF DISCOVERY. Owen M. Fiss, Thomas Glocer and Ronald F. Wright. Center for Computer-Assisted Instruction, 229 19th Avenue South, University of Minnesota, Minneapolis, Minnesota 55455. Machine-readable computer file.

COMPUGRAPH V. CHANG. Interactive Video Library, Harvard Law School, Educational Technology Department, 18 Everett Street, Cambridge, Massachusetts 02138. Interactive videodisc.

CONEY ISLAND: A GAME OF DISCOVERY. Owen M. Fiss, Thomas Glocer and Ronald F. Wright. Center for Computer-Assisted Instruction, 229 19th Avenue South, University of Minnesota, Minneapolis, Minnesota 55455. Machine-readable computer file.

CHARACTER EVIDENCE UNDER FEDERAL RULES. Roger C. Park. Center for Computer-Assisted Instruction, 229 19th Avenue South, University of Minnesota, Minneapolis, Minnesota 55455. Machine-readable computer file.

COMPUTER GAME OBJECTION! TransMedia Productions,Incorporated, c/o Center for Computer-Assisted Instruction, 229 19th Avenue South, University of Minnesota, Minneapolis, Minnesota 55455. Machine-readable computer file.

DECISIONS BEFORE TRIAL. Robert E. Keeton and Kenneth K. Kirwin. Center for Computer-Assisted Instruction, 229 19th Avenue South, University of Minnesota, Minneapolis, Minnesota 55455. Machine-readable computer file.

DEFENSE FUNCTION-CODE OF PROFESSIONAL RESPONSIBILITY VERSION. Kenneth K. Kirwin and Roger C. Park. Center for Computer-Assisted Instruction, 229 19th Avenue South, University of Minnesota, Minneapolis, Minnesota 55455. Machine-readable computer file.

DEFENSE FUNCTION-RULES OF PROFESSIONAL CONDUCT VERSION. Kenneth K. Kirwin and Roger C. Park. Center for Computer-Assisted Instruction, 229 19th Avenue South, University of Minnesota, Minneapolis, Minnesota 55455. Machine-readable computer file.

EASERLY V. LETWIN. Center for Computer-Assisted Instruction, 229 19th Avenue South, University of Minnesota, Minneapolis, Minnesota 55455. Interactive videodisc.

EVIDENCE OBJECTIONS. Roger W. Kirst. Center for Computer-Assisted Instruction, 229 19th Avenue South, University of Minnesota, Minneapolis, Minnesota 55455. Interactive videodisc.

EVIDENTIARY FOUNDATIONS ILLUSTRATED. CLE Group, 274 Willow Road, Menlo Park, California 94025. Interactive videodisc.

FRANCIS V. SPINDLER. Interactive Video Library, Harvard Law School, Educational Technology Department, 18 Everett Street, Cambridge, Massachusetts 02138. Interactive videodisc.

HEARSAY RULE AND ITS EXCEPTIONS. Roger C. Park. Center for Computer-Assisted Instruction, 229 19th Avenue South, University of Minnesota, Minneapolis, Minnesota 55455. Machine-readable computer file.

IMPEACHMENT AND REHABILITATION OF WITNESSES. Roger C. Park. Center for Computer-Assisted Instruction, 229 19th Avenue South, University of Minnesota, Minneapolis, Minnesota 55455. Machine-readable computer file.

MOTION SKILLS ILLUSTRATED. CLE Group, 274 Willow Road, Menlo Park, California 94025. Interactive videodisc.

OLCOTT V. OLCOTT. Center for Computer-Assisted Instruction, 229 19th Avenue South, University of Minnesota, Minneapolis, Minnesota 55455. Interactive videodisc.

ORTIZ V. FLEISHMAN I, II AND III. Center for Computer-Assisted Instruction, 229 19th Avenue South, University of Minnesota, Minneapolis, Minnesota 55455. Interactive videodisc.

SPRAGUE CASE: CHILD INJURY IN TORT LAW. Robert E. Keeton. Center for Computer-Assisted Instruction, 229 19th Avenue South, University of Minnesota, Minneapolis, Minnesota 55455. Machine-readable computer file.

STATE V. RODGERS. Center for Computer-Assisted Instruction, 229 19th Avenue South, University of Minnesota, Minneapolis, Minnesota 55455. Interactive videodisc.

STATE V. WILLIAMS I & II. Center for Computer-Assisted Instruction, 229 19th Avenue South, University of Minnesota, Minneapolis, Minnesota 55455. Interactive videodisc.

TRIAL EVIDENCE AND CROSS-EXAMINATION SKILLS. CLE Group, 274 Willow Road, Menlo Park, California 94025. Interactive videodisc.

TRIAL EVIDENCE AND DIRECT EXAMINATION SKILLS. CLE Group, 274 Willow Road, Menlo Park, California 94025. Interactive videodisc.

TRIAL SKILLS ILLUSTRATED I AND II. CLE Group, 274 Willow Road, Menlo Park, California 94025. Interactive videodisc.

YOU BE THE JUDGE. CLE Group, 274 Willow Road, Menlo Park, California 94025. Interactive videodisc.

TRIALS, NOTEWORTHY

TEXTBOOKS AND GENERAL WORKS

ACTUAL MALICE: TWENTY-FIVE YEARS AFTER TIMES V. SULLIVAN. W. Wat Hopkins. Praeger Publishers, One Madison Avenue, New York, New York 10010. 1989.

BEHIND BAKKE: AFFIRMATIVE ACTION AND THE SUPREME COURT. Bernard Schwartz. New York University Press, 70 Washington Square South, New York, New York 10012. 1988.

THE BELLI FILES: REFLECTIONS ON THE WAYWARD LAW. Melvin M. Belli. Prentice-Hall, Incorporated, 113 Sylvan Avenue, Englewood Cliffs, New Jersey 07632. 1983.

CHADHA: THE STORY OF AN EPIC CONSTITUTIONAL STRUGGLE. Barbara Hinkson Craig. Oxford University Press, 200 Madison Avenue, New York, New York 10016. 1988.

COMMUNICATION AND LITIGATION: CASE STUDIES OF FAMOUS TRIALS. Janice Schuetz and Kathryn Holmes Snedaker. Southern Illinois University Press, P.O. Box 3697, Carbondale, Illinois 62902-3697. 1988.

THE COURT-MARTIAL OF CLAYTON LONETREE. Lake Headley and William Hoffman. Holt, Rinehart, and Winston, Incorporated, 6277 Sea Harbor Drive, Orlando, Florida 32821. 1989.

A CRIME OF SELF-DEFENSE: BERNARD GOETZ AND THE LAW ON TRIAL. George P. Fletcher. University of Chicago Press, 5801 Ellis Avenue, Chicago, Illinois 60637. 1990.

FAMOUS JUDGES AND FAMOUS TRIALS. Charles Kingston. Fred B. Rothman and Company, 10368 West Centennial Road, Littleton, Colorado 80127. 1988. (Reprint).

FAMOUS TRIALS. John Mortimer, Editor. Penguin Books, Incorporated, 40 West Twenty-third Street, New York, New York 10010. 1986.

THE GOLDMARK CASE: AN AMERICAN LIBEL TRIAL. William L. Dwyer. University of Washington Press, P.O. Box 50096, Seattle, Washington 98145-5096. 1984.

GREAT TRIALS IN AMERICAN HISTORY: CIVIL WAR TO PRESENT. Lee Arbetman and Richard L. Roe. West Publishing Company, P.O. Box 64526, 50 West Kellogg Boulevard, St. Paul, Minnesota 55164-0526. 1984.

JERRY FALWELL V. LARRY FLYNT: THE FIRST AMENDMENT ON TRIAL. Rodney A. Smolla. St. Martin's Press, 175 Fifth Avenue, New York, New York 10010. 1988.

NO EASY ANSWERS: THE TRIAL AND CONVICTION OF BRUCE CURTIS. David Hayes. Viking-Penguin, Incorporated, 375 Hudson Street, New York, New York 10014. 1986.

THE PAPERS AND THE PAPERS: AN ACCOUNT OF THE LEGAL AND POLITICAL BATTLE OVER THE PENTAGON PAPERS. Sanford J. Ungar. Columbia University Press, 562 West One Hundred Thirteenth Street, New York, New York 10025. 1989. (Reprint).

A PICTORIAL HISTORY OF THE WORLD'S GREAT TRIALS: FROM SOCRATES TO JEAN HARRIS. Brandt Aymar and Edward Sagarin. Bonanza Books, Imprint of Outlet Book Company, 225 Park Avenue, New York, New York 10003. 1985.

POLITICAL TRIALS: GORDIAN KNOTS IN THE LAW. Ron Christenson. Transaction Books, Building 4051, Rutgers University, New Brunswick, New Jersey 08903. 1989.

POPULAR TRIALS: RHETORIC, MASS MEDIA, AND THE LAW. Robert Hariman. University of Alabama Press, P.O. Box 870380, Tuscaloosa, Alabama 35487. 1990.

ROE V. WADE: THE UNTOLD STORY OF THE LANDMARK SUPREME COURT DECISION THAT MADE ABORTION LEGAL. Marian Faux. Macmillan Publishing Company, Incorporated, 866 Third Avenue, New York, New York 10022. 1988.

A SCOTTSBORO CASE IN MISSISSIPPI: THE SUPREME COURT AND BROWN V. MISSISSIPPI. Richard C. Cortner. University Press of Mississippi, 3825 Ridgewood Road, Jackson, Mississippi 39211. 1986.

TEXACO AND THE $10 BILLION JURY. James Shannon. Prentice-Hall, Incorporated, 113 Sylvan Avenue, Englewood Cliffs, New Jersey 07632. 1988.

TOO OLD, TOO UGLY, AND NOT DEFERENTIAL TO MEN. Christine Craft. Prima Publishing and Communications, P.O. Box 1260, 4970 Topaz Avenue, Rocklin, California 95677. 1988.

THE TRIAL OF JOHN W. HINCKLEY, JR.: A CASE STUDY IN THE INSANITY DEFENSE. Peter W. Law, John Calvin Jeffries and Richard J. Bonnie. Foundation Press, Incorporated, 615 Merrick Avenue, Westbury, New York 11590. 1986.

THE U.S. WAR CRIMES TRIAL PROGRAM IN GERMANY, 1946-1955. Frank M. Buscher. Greenwood Publishing Group, Incorporated, 88 Post Road West, P.O. Box 5007, Westport, Connecticut 06881. 1989.

VIETNAM ON TRIAL: WESTMORELAND VS. CBS. Bob Brewin and Sydney Shaw. Atheneum Publishers, 597 Fifth Avenue, New York, New York 10017. 1986.

WE HAVE A DUTY: THE SUPREME COURT AND THE WATERGATE TAPES LITIGATION. Howard Ball. Greenwood Publishing Group, Incorporated, 88 Post Road West, P.O. Box 5007, Westport, Connecticut 06881. 1990.

WEBSTER VS. REPRODUCTIVE HEALTH SERVICES. Maria E. Protti. William S. Hein and Company, 1285 Main Street, Buffalo, New York 14209. 1990.

DIGESTS, INDEXES, ABSTRACTS, CITATORS

TRIALS IN COLLECTIONS: AN INDEX TO FAMOUS TRIALS THROUGHOUT THE WORLD. John M. Ross. Scarecrow Press, Incorporated, 52 Liberty Street, Box 4167, Metuchen, New Jersey 08840. 1983.

BIBLIOGRAPHIES

WESTMORELAND V. CBS: GUIDE TO THE MICROFICHE COLLECTION. Walter Schneir. Clearwater Publication Company, New York, New York. 1987.

TRUSTS AND TRUSTEES
See: WILLS, TRUSTS AND INHERITANCE

TRUSTS, INDUSTRIAL
See: ANTITRUST LAW

U

UNEMPLOYMENT
See: LABOR AND LABOR RELATIONS

UNFAIR COMPETITION
See: ANTITRUST LAW

UNFAIR LABOR PRACTICES
See: LABOR AND LABOR RELATIONS

UNIFORM AND MODEL ACTS

STATUTES, CODES, STANDARDS, UNIFORM LAWS

FEDERAL SECURITIES CODE ADOPTED BY THE AMERICAN LAW INSTITUTE. American Law Institute, 4025 Chestnut Street, Philadelphia, Pennsylvania 19104. 1980.

MODEL BUSINESS CORPORATION ACT (1969) AND REVISED MODEL BUSINESS CORPORATION ACT (1984). Committe on Corporate Laws, Section of Corporation, Banking and Business Law, American Bar Asssociation. Martindale-Hubbell Law Digest, Martindale-Hubbell, 121 Chanlon Road, New Providence, New Jersey 07974. Annual.

MODEL BUSINESS CORPORATION ACT ANNOTATED: REVISED MODEL BUSINESS CORPORATION ACT. Third Edition. Committee on Corporate Laws of the Section on Corporation, Banking and Business Law. American Bar Association. Prentice-Hall Law and Business, Incorporated, 855 Valley Road, Clifton, New Jersey 07013. 1984.

MODEL CLASS ACTIONS ACT. National Conference of Commissioners on Uniform State Laws. Uniform Laws Annotated. West Publishing Company, P.O. Box 64526, 50 West Kellogg Boulevard, St. Paul, Minnesota 55102-1611. 1976. (Annual Supplements).

MODEL CODE OF JUDICIAL CONDUCT. American Bar Association, 750 North Lake Shore Drive, Chicago, Illinois 60611.

MODEL EMINENT DOMAIN CODE. National Conference of Commissioners on Uniform State Laws. Uniform Laws Annotated. West Publishing Company, P.O. Box 64526, 50 West Kellogg Boulevard, St. Paul, Minnesota 55164-0526. 1976. (Annual Supplements).

MODEL HEALTH CARE CONSENT ACT. National Conference of Commissioners on Uniform State Laws. Uniform Laws Annotated. West Publishing Company, P.O. Box 64526, 50 West Kellogg Boulevard, St. Paul, Minnesota 55164-0526. 1976. (Annual Supplements).

MODEL INSANITY DEFENSE AND POST-TRIAL DISPOSITION ACT. National Conference of Commissioners on Uniform State Laws. Uniform Laws Annotated. West Publishing Company, P.O. Box 64526, 50 West Kellogg Boulevard, St. Paul, Minnesota 55164-0526. 1976. (Annual Supplements).

MODEL INTERPARTY AGREEMENT ACT. National Conference of Commissioners on Uniform State Laws. Martindale-Hubbell Law Digest, Martindale-Hubbell, 121 Chanlon Road, New Providence, New Jersey 07974. Annual.

MODEL JOINT OBLIGATIONS ACT. National Conference of Commissioners on Uniform State Laws. Martindale-Hubbell Law Digest, Martindale-Hubbell, 121 Chanlon Road, New Providence, New Jersey 07974. Annual.

MODEL JOINT OBLIGATIONS ACT. National Conference of Commissioners on Uniform State Laws. Uniform Laws Annotated. West Publishing Company, P.O. Box 64526, 50 West Kellogg Boulevard, St. Paul, Minnesota 55164-0526. 1976. (Annual Supplements).

MODEL JUVENILE COURT ACT. National Conference of Commissioners on Uniform State Laws. Uniform Laws Annotated. West Publishing Company, P.O. Box 64526, 50 West Kellogg Boulevard, St. Paul, Minnesota 55164-0526. 1976. (Annual Supplements).

MODEL LAND SALES PRACTICES ACT. National Conference of Commissioners on Uniform State Laws. Martindale-Hubbell Law Digest, Martindale-Hubbell, 121 Chanlon Road, New Providence, New Jersey 07974. Annual.

MODEL LAND SALES PRACTICES ACT. National Conference of Commissioners on Uniform State Laws. Uniform Laws Annotated. West Publishing Company, P.O. Box 64526, 50 West Kellogg Boulevard, St. Paul, Minnesota 55164-0526. 1976. (Annual Supplements).

MODEL METRIC PROCEDURE ACT. National Conference of Commissioners on Uniform State Laws. Uniform Laws Annotated. West Publishing Company, P.O. Box 64526, 50 West Kellogg Boulevard, St. Paul, Minnesota 55164-0526. 1976. (Annual Supplements).

MODEL MINOR STUDENT CAPACITY TO BORROW ACT. National Conference of Commissioners on Uniform State Laws. Uniform Laws Annotated. West Publishing Company, P.O. Box 64526, 50 West Kellogg Boulevard, St. Paul, Minnesota 55164-0526. 1976. (Annual Supplements).

MODEL PENAL CODE. National Conference of Commissioners on Uniform State Laws. Uniform Laws Annotated. West Publishing Company, P.O. Box 64526, 50 West Kellogg Boulevard, St. Paul, Minnesota 55164-0526. 1976. (Annual Supplements).

MODEL PERIODIC PAYMENT OF JUDGMENTS ACT (1990 AND 1980). National Conference of Commissioners on Uniform State Laws. Uniform Laws Annotated. West Publishing Company, P.O. Box 64526, 50 West Kellogg Boulevard, St. Paul, Minnesota 55164-0526. 1976. (Annual Supplements).

MODEL REAL ESTATE COOPERATIVE ACT. National Conference of Commissioners on Uniform State Laws. Uniform Laws Annotated. West Publishing Company, P.O. Box 64526, 50 West Kellogg Boulevard, St. Paul, Minnesota 55164-0526. 1976. (Annual Supplements).

MODEL REAL ESTATE TIME-SHARE ACT. National Conference of Commissioners on Uniform State Laws. Uniform Laws Annotated. West Publishing Company, P.O. Box 64526, 50 West Kellogg Boulevard, St. Paul, Minnesota 55164-0526. 1976. (Annual Supplements).

MODEL SENTENCING AND CORRECTIONS ACT. National Conference of Commissioners on Uniform State Laws. Uniform Laws Annotated. West Publishing Company, P.O. Box 64526, 50 West Kellogg Boulevard, St. Paul, Minnesota 55164-0526. 1976. (Annual Supplements).

MODEL STATE ADMINISTRATIVE PROCEDURE ACT (1961 AND 1981 ACT). National Conference of Commissioners on Uniform State Laws. Uniform Laws Annotated. West Publishing Company, P.O. Box 64526, 50 West Kellogg Boulevard, St. Paul, Minnesota 55164-0526. 1976. (Annual Supplements).

MODEL STATUTORY CONSTRUCTION ACT. National Conference of Commissioners on Uniform State Laws. Uniform Laws Annotated. West Publishing Company, P.O. Box 64526, 50 West Kellogg Boulevard, St. Paul, Minnesota 55164-0526. 1976. (Annual Supplements).

MODEL SURVIVAL AND DEATH ACT. National Conference of Commissioners on Uniform State Laws. Uniform Laws Annotated. West Publishing Company, P.O. Box 64526, 50 West Kellogg Boulevard, St. Paul, Minnesota 55164-0526. 1976. (Annual Supplements).

UNIFORM ABORTION ACT. National Conference of Commissioners on Uniform State Laws. Uniform Laws Annotated. West Publishing Company, P.O. Box 64526, 50 West Kellogg Boulevard, St. Paul, Minnesota 55164-0526. 1976. (Annual Supplements).

UNIFORM ABSENCE AS EVIDENCE OF DEATH AND ABSENTEE'S PROPERTY ACT. National Conference of Commissioners on Uniform State Laws. Uniform Laws Annotated. West Publishing Company, P.O. Box 64526, 50 West Kellogg Boulevard, St. Paul, Minnesota 55164-0526. 1976. (Annual Supplements).

UNIFORM ACKNOWLEDGEMENT ACT. National Conference of Commissioners on Uniform State Laws. Martindale-Hubbell Law Digest, Martindale-Hubbell, 121 Chanlon Road, New Providence, New Jersey 07974. Annual.

UNIFORM ACKNOWLEDGEMENT ACT. National Conference of Commissioners on Uniform State Laws. Uniform Laws Annotated. West Publishing Company, P.O. Box 64526, 50 West Kellogg Boulevard, St. Paul, Minnesota 55164-0526. 1976. (Annual Supplements).

UNIFORM ACT FOR SIMPLIFICATION OF FIDUCIARY SECURITY TRANSFERS. National Conference of Commissioners on Uniform State Laws. Martindale-Hubbell Law Directory, Volume Eight. Martindale-Hubbell, Incorporated, 121 Chanlon Road, New Providence, New Jersey 07974. Annual.

UNIFORM ACT FOR SIMPLIFICATION OF FIDUCIARY SECURITY TRANSFERS. National Conference of Commissioners on Uniform State Laws. Uniform Laws Annotated. West Publishing Company, P.O. Box 64526, 50 West Kellogg Boulevard, St. Paul, Minnesota 55164-0526. 1976. (Annual Supplements).

UNIFORM ACT ON PATERNITY. National Conference of Commissioners on Uniform State Laws. Uniform Laws Annotated. West Publishing Company, P.O. Box 64526, 50 West Kellogg Boulevard, St. Paul, Minnesota 55164-0526. 1976. (Annual Supplements).

UNIFORM ACT ON STATUS OF CONVICTED PERSONS. National Conference of Commissioners on Uniform State Laws. Uniform Laws Annotated. West Publishing Company, P.O. Box 64526, 50 West Kellogg Boulevard, St. Paul, Minnesota 55164-0526. 1976. (Annual Supplements).

UNIFORM ACT TO SECURE THE ATTENDANCE OF WITNESSES FROM WITHOUT A STATE IN CRIMINAL PROCEEDINGS. National Conference of Commissioners on Uniform State Laws. Martindale-Hubbell Law Digest, Martindale-Hubbell, 121 Chanlon Road, New Providence, New Jersey 07974. Annual.

UNIFORM ACT TO SECURE THE ATTENDANCE OF WITNESSES FROM WITHOUT A STATE IN CRIMINAL PROCEEDINGS. National Conference of Commissioners on Uniform State Laws. Uniform Laws Annotated. West Publishing Company, P.O. Box 64526, 50 West Kellogg Boulevard, St. Paul, Minnesota 55164-0526. 1976. (Annual Supplements).

UNIFORM ADOPTION ACT. National Conference of Commissioners on Uniform State Laws. Uniform Laws Annotated. West Publishing Company, P.O. Box 64526, 50 West Kellogg Boulevard, St. Paul, Minnesota 55164-0526. 1976. (Annual Supplements).

UNIFORM AIRCRAFT FINANCIAL RESPONSIBILITY ACT. National Conference of Commissioners on Uniform State Laws. Uniform Laws Annotated. West Publishing Company, P.O. Box 64526, 50 West Kellogg Boulevard, St. Paul, Minnesota 55164-0526. 1976. (Annual Supplements).

UNIFORM ALCOHOLISM AND INTOXICATION TREATMENT ACT. National Conference of Commissioners on Uniform State Laws. Uniform Laws Annotated. West Publishing Company, P.O. Box 64526, 50 West Kellogg Boulevard, St. Paul, Minnesota 55164-0526. 1976. (Annual Supplements).

UNIFORM ANATOMICAL GIFT ACT (1987 and 1968). National Conference of Commissioners on Uniform State Laws. Martindale-Hubbell Law Digest, Martindale-Hubbell, 121 Chanlon Road, New Providence, New Jersey 07974. Annual.

UNIFORM ANATOMICAL GIFT ACT (1987 AND 1968). National Conference of Commissioners on Uniform State Laws. Uniform Laws Annotated. West Publishing Company, P.O. Box 64526, 50 West Kellogg Boulevard, St. Paul, Minnesota 55164-0526. 1976. (Annual Supplements).

UNIFORM ANCILLARY ADMINISTRATION OF ESTATES ACT. National Conference of Commissioners on Uniform State Laws. Uniform Laws Annotated. West Publishing Company, P.O. Box 64526, 50 West Kellogg Boulevard, St. Paul, Minnesota 55164-0526. 1976. (Annual Supplements).

UNIFORM ARBITRATION ACT. National Conference of Commissioners on Uniform State Laws. Martindale-Hubbell Law Digest, Martindale-Hubbell, 121 Chanlon Road, New Providence, New Jersey 07974. Annual.

UNIFORM ARBITRATION ACT. National Conference of Commissioners on Uniform State Laws. Uniform Laws Annotated. West Publishing Company, P.O. Box 64526, 50 West Kellogg Boulevard, St. Paul, Minnesota 55164-0526. 1976. (Annual Supplements).

UNIFORM AUDIOVISUAL DEPOSITION ACT. National Conference of Commissioners on Uniform State Laws. Uniform Laws Annotated. West Publishing Company, P.O. Box 64526, 50 West Kellogg Boulevard, St. Paul, Minnesota 55164-0526. 1976. (Annual Supplements).

UNIFORM BRAIN DEATH ACT. National Conference of Commissioners on Uniform State Laws. Uniform Laws Annotated. West Publishing Company, P.O. Box 64526, 50 West Kellogg Boulevard, St. Paul, Minnesota 55164-0526. 1976. (Annual Supplements).

UNIFORM BUSINESS RECORDS AS EVIDENCE ACT. National Conference of Commissioners on Uniform State Laws. Martindale-Hubbell Law Digest, Martindale-Hubbell, 121 Chanlon Road, New Providence, New Jersey 07974. Annual.

UNIFORM CERTIFICATION OF QUESTIONS OF LAW ACT. National Conference of Commissioners on Uniform State Laws. Uniform Laws Annotated. West Publishing Company, P.O. Box 64526, 50 West Kellogg Boulevard, St. Paul, Minnesota 55164-0526. 1976. (Annual Supplements).

UNIFORM CHILD CUSTODY JURISDICTION ACT. National Conference of Commissioners on Uniform State Laws. Martindale-Hubbell Law Digest, Martindale-Hubbell, 121 Chanlon Road, New Providence, New Jersey 07974. Annual.

UNIFORM CHILD CUSTODY JURISDICTION ACT. National Conference of Commissioners on Uniform State Laws. Uniform Laws Annotated. West Publishing Company, P.O. Box 64526, 50 West Kellogg Boulevard, St. Paul, Minnesota 55164-0526. 1976. (Annual Supplements).

UNIFORM CIVIL LIABILITY FOR SUPPORT ACT. National Conference of Commissioners on Uniform State Laws. Uniform Laws Annotated. West Publishing Company, P.O. Box 64526, 50 West Kellogg Boulevard, St. Paul, Minnesota 55164-0526. 1976. (Annual Supplements).

UNIFORM CODE OF MILITARY JUSTICE. National Conference of Commissioners on Uniform State Laws. Uniform Laws Annotated. West Publishing Company, P.O. Box 64526, 50 West Kellogg Boulevard, St. Paul, Minnesota 55164-0526. 1976. (Annual Supplements).

UNIFORM COMMERCIAL CODE (ALL VERSIONS). National Conference of Commissioners on Uniform State Laws. Martindale-Hubbell Law Digest, Martindale-Hubbell, 121 Chanlon Road, New Providence, New Jersey 07974. Annual.

UNIFORM COMMERCIAL CODE (AND FORMS). National Conference of Commissioners on Uniform State Laws. Uniform Laws Annotated. West Publishing Company, P.O. Box 64526, 50 West Kellogg Boulevard, St. Paul, Minnesota 55164-0526. 1990. (Annual Supplements).

UNIFORM COMMON INTEREST OWNERSHIP ACT. National Conference of Commissioners on Uniform State Laws. Uniform Laws Annotated. West Publishing Company, P.O. Box 64526, 50 West Kellogg Boulevard, St. Paul, Minnesota 55164-0526. 1976. (Annual Supplements).

UNIFORM COMMON TRUST FUND ACT. National Conference of Commissioners on Uniform State Laws. Martindale-Hubbell Law Digest, Martindale-Hubbell, 121 Chanlon Road, New Providence, New Jersey 07974. Annual.

UNIFORM COMMON TRUST FUND ACT. National Conference of Commissioners on Uniform State Laws. Uniform Laws Annotated. West Publishing Company, P.O. Box 64526, 50 West Kellogg Boulevard, St. Paul, Minnesota 55164-0526. 1976. (Annual Supplements).

UNIFORM COMPARATIVE FAULT ACT. National Conference of Commissioners on Uniform State Laws. Uniform Laws Annotated. West Publishing Company, P.O. Box 64526, 50 West Kellogg Boulevard, St. Paul, Minnesota 55164-0526. 1976. (Annual Supplements).

UNIFORM CONDOMINIUM ACT. National Conference of Commissioners on Uniform State Laws. Uniform Laws Annotated. West Publishing Company, P.O. Box 64526, 50 West Kellogg Boulevard, St. Paul, Minnesota 55164-0526. 1976. (Annual Supplements).

UNIFORM CONFLICT OF LAWS- LIMITATIONS ACT. National Conference of Commissioners on Uniform State Laws. Uniform Laws Annotated. West Publishing Company, P.O. Box 64526, 50 West Kellogg Boulevard, St. Paul, Minnesota 55164-0526. 1976. (Annual Supplements).

UNIFORM CONSERVATION EASEMENT ACT. National Conference of Commissioners on Uniform State Laws. Uniform Laws Annotated. West Publishing Company, P.O. Box 64526, 50 West Kellogg Boulevard, St. Paul, Minnesota 55164-0526. 1976. (Annual Supplements).

UNIFORM CONSTRUCTION LIEN ACT. National Conference of Commissioners on Uniform State Laws. Uniform Laws Annotated. West Publishing Company, P.O. Box 64526, 50 West Kellogg Boulevard, St. Paul, Minnesota 55164-0526. 1976. (Annual Supplements).

UNIFORM CONSUMER CREDIT CODE (1974 AND 1968). National Conference of Commissioners on Uniform State Laws. Uniform Laws Annotated. West Publishing Company, P.O. Box 64526, 50 West Kellogg Boulevard, St. Paul, Minnesota 55164-0526. 1976. (Annual Supplements).

UNIFORM CONSUMER SALES PRACTICES ACT. National Conference of Commissioners on Uniform State Laws. Uniform Laws Annotated. West Publishing Company, P.O. Box 64526, 50 West Kellogg Boulevard, St. Paul, Minnesota 55164-0526. 1976. (Annual Supplements).

UNIFORM CONTRIBUTION AMONG TORTFEASORS ACT. National Conference of Commissioners on Uniform State Laws. Uniform Laws Annotated. West Publishing Company, P.O. Box 64526, 50 West Kellogg Boulevard, St. Paul, Minnesota 55164-0526. 1976. (Annual Supplements).

UNIFORM CONTROLLED SUBSTANCES ACT (1990 AND 1970). National Conference of Commissioners on Uniform State Laws. Uniform Laws Annotated. West Publishing Company, P.O. Box 64526, 50 West Kellogg Boulevard, St. Paul, Minnesota 55164-0526. 1976. (Annual Supplements).

UNIFORM CRIME VICTIMS REPARATIONS ACT. National Conference of Commissioners on Uniform State Laws. Uniform Laws Annotated. West Publishing Company, P.O. Box 64526, 50 West Kellogg Boulevard, St. Paul, Minnesota 55164-0526. 1976. (Annual Supplements).

UNIFORM CRIMINAL EXTRADITION ACT. National Conference of Commissioners on Uniform State Laws. Uniform Laws Annotated. West Publishing Company, P.O. Box 64526, 50 West Kellogg Boulevard, St. Paul, Minnesota 55164-0526. 1976. (Annual Supplements).

UNIFORM CRIMINAL STATISTICS ACT. National Conference of Commissioners on Uniform State Laws. Uniform Laws Annotated. West Publishing Company, P.O. Box 64526, 50 West Kellogg Boulevard, St. Paul, Minnesota 55164-0526. 1976. (Annual Supplements).

UNIFORM CUSTODIAL TRUST FUND ACT. National Conference of Commissioners on Uniform State Laws. Uniform Laws Annotated. West Publishing Company, P.O. Box 64526, 50 West Kellogg Boulevard, St. Paul, Minnesota 55164-0526. 1976. (Annual Supplements).

UNIFORM DEATH ACT. National Conference of Commissioners on Uniform State Laws. Uniform Laws Annotated. West Publishing Company, P.O. Box 64526, 50 West Kellogg Boulevard, St. Paul, Minnesota 55164-0526. 1976. (Annual Supplements).

UNIFORM DECEPTIVE TRADE PRACTICES ACT (REVISED). National Conference of Commissioners on Uniform State Laws. Martindale-Hubbell Law Digest, Martindale-Hubbell, 121 Chanlon Road, New Providence, New Jersey 07974. Annual.

UNIFORM DECEPTIVE TRADE PRACTICES ACT (1966 AND 1964). National Conference of Commissioners on Uniform State Laws. Uniform Laws Annotated. West Publishing Company, P.O. Box 64526, 50 West Kellogg Boulevard, St. Paul, Minnesota 55164-0526. 1976. (Annual Supplements).

UNIFORM DECLARATORY JUDGMENTS ACT. National Conference of Commissioners on Uniform State Laws. Martindale-Hubbell Law Digest, Martindale-Hubbell, 121 Chanlon Road, New Providence, New Jersey 07974. Annual.

UNIFORM DECLARATORY JUDGMENTS ACT. National Conference of Commissioners on Uniform State Laws. Uniform Laws Annotated. West Publishing Company, P.O. Box 64526, 50 West Kellogg Boulevard, St. Paul, Minnesota 55164-0526. 1976. (Annual Supplements).

UNIFORM DESERTION AND NON-SUPPORT ACT. National Conference of Commissioners on Uniform State Laws. Martindale-Hubbell Law Digest, Martindale-Hubbell, 121 Chanlon Road, New Providence, New Jersey 07974. Annual.

UNIFORM DETERMINATION OF DEATH ACT. National Conference of Commissioners on Uniform State Laws. Martindale-Hubbell Law Digest, Martindale-Hubbell, 121 Chanlon Road, New Providence, New Jersey 07974. Annual.

UNIFORM DETERMINATION OF DEATH ACT. National Conference of Commissioners on Uniform State Laws. Uniform Laws Annotated. West Publishing Company, P.O. Box 64526, 50 West Kellogg Boulevard, St. Paul, Minnesota 55164-0526. 1976. (Annual Supplements).

UNIFORM DISCLAIMER OF PROPERTY INTERESTS ACT. National Conference of Commissioners on Uniform State Laws. Uniform Laws Annotated. West Publishing Company, P.O. Box 64526, 50 West Kellogg Boulevard, St. Paul, Minnesota 55164-0526. 1976. (Annual Supplements).

UNIFORM DISCLAIMER OF TRANSFERS BY WILL, INTESTACY, OR APPOINTMENT ACT. National Conference of Commissioners on Uniform State Laws. Uniform Laws Annotated. West Publishing Company, P.O. Box 64526, 50 West Kellogg Boulevard, St. Paul, Minnesota 55164-0526. 1976. (Annual Supplements).

UNIFORM DISCLAIMER OF TRANSFERS UNDER NON-TESTAMENTARY INSTRUMENTS ACT. National Conference of Commissioners on Uniform State Laws. Uniform Laws Annotated. West Publishing Company, P.O. Box 64526, 50 West Kellogg Boulevard, St. Paul, Minnesota 55164-0526. 1976. (Annual Supplements).

UNIFORM DISPOSITION OF COMMUNITY PROPERTY RIGHTS AT DEATH ACT. National Conference of Commissioners on Uniform State Laws. Uniform Laws Annotated. West Publishing Company, P.O. Box 64526, 50 West Kellogg Boulevard, St. Paul, Minnesota 55164-0526. 1976. (Annual Supplements).

UNIFORM DISPOSITION OF UNCLAIMED PROPERTY ACT (1966 AND 1954). National Conference of Commissioners on Uniform State Laws. Martindale-Hubbell Law Digest, Martindale-Hubbell, 121 Chanlon Road, New Providence, New Jersey 07974. Annual.

UNIFORM DISPOSITION OF UNCLAIMED PROPERTY ACT (1966 AND 1954). National Conference of Commissioners on Uniform State Laws. Uniform Laws Annotated. West Publishing Company, P.O. Box 64526, 50 West Kellogg Boulevard, St. Paul, Minnesota 55164-0526. 1976. (Annual Supplements).

UNIFORM DIVISION OF INCOME FOR TAX PURPOSES ACT. National Conference of Commissioners on Uniform State Laws. Martindale-Hubbell Law Digest, Martindale-Hubbell, 121 Chanlon Road, New Providence, New Jersey 07974. Annual.

UNIFORM DIVISION OF INCOME FOR TAX PURPOSES ACT. National Conference of Commissioners on Uniform State Laws. Uniform Laws Annotated. West Publishing Company, P.O. Box 64526, 50 West Kellogg Boulevard, St. Paul, Minnesota 55164-0526. 1976. (Annual Supplements).

UNIFORM DIVORCE RECOGNITION ACT. National Conference of Commissioners on Uniform State Laws. Martindale-Hubbell Law Digest, Martindale-Hubbell, 121 Chanlon Road, New Providence, New Jersey 07974. Annual.

UNIFORM DIVORCE RECOGNITION ACT. National Conference of Commissioners on Uniform State Laws. Uniform Laws Annotated. West Publishing Company, P.O. Box 64526, 50 West Kellogg Boulevard, St. Paul, Minnesota 55164-0526. 1976. (Annual Supplements).

UNIFORM DORMANT MINERAL INTERESTS ACT. National Conference of Commissioners on Uniform State Laws. Uniform Laws Annotated. West Publishing Company, P.O. Box 64526, 50 West Kellogg Boulevard, St. Paul, Minnesota 55164-0526. 1976. (Annual Supplements).

UNIFORM DRUG DEPENDENCE TREATMENT AND REHABILITATION ACT. National Conference of Commissioners on Uniform State Laws. Uniform Laws Annotated. West Publishing Company, P.O. Box 64526, 50 West Kellogg Boulevard, St. Paul, Minnesota 55164-0526. 1976. (Annual Supplements).

UNIFORM DURABLE POWER OF ATTORNEY ACT. National Conference of Commissioners on Uniform State Laws. Martindale-Hubbell Law Digest, Martindale-Hubbell, 121 Chanlon Road, New Providence, New Jersey 07974. Annual.

UNIFORM DURABLE POWER OF ATTORNEY ACT. National Conference of Commissioners on Uniform State Laws. Uniform Laws Annotated. West Publishing Company, P.O. Box 64526, 50 West Kellogg Boulevard, St. Paul, Minnesota 55164-0526. 1976. (Annual Supplements).

UNIFORM DUTIES TO DISABLED PERSONS ACT. National Conference of Commissioners on Uniform State Laws. Uniform Laws Annotated. West Publishing Company, P.O. Box 64526, 50 West Kellogg Boulevard, St. Paul, Minnesota 55164-0526. 1976. (Annual Supplements).

UNIFORM ENFORCEMENT OF FOREIGN JUDGMENTS ACT (ORIGINAL AND REVISED). National Conference of Commissioners on Uniform State Laws. Martindale-Hubbell Law Digest, Martindale-Hubbell, 121 Chanlon Road, New Providence, New Jersey 07974. Annual.

UNIFORM ENFORCEMENT OF FOREIGN JUDGMENTS ACT (1948 AND 1964). National Conference of Commissioners on Uniform State Laws. Uniform Laws Annotated. West Publishing Company, P.O. Box 64526, 50 West Kellogg Boulevard, St. Paul, Minnesota 55164-0526. 1976. (Annual Supplements).

UNIFORM ESTATE TAX APPORTIONMENT ACT (1958 AND 1964). National Conference of Commissioners on Uniform State Laws. Uniform Laws Annotated. West Publishing Company, P.O. Box 64526, 50 West Kellogg Boulevard, St. Paul, Minnesota 55164-0526. 1976. (Annual Supplements).

UNIFORM EXEMPTIONS ACT. National Conference of Commissioners on Uniform State Laws. Uniform Laws Annotated. West Publishing Company, P.O. Box 64526, 50 West Kellogg Boulevard, St. Paul, Minnesota 55164-0526. 1976. (Annual Supplements).

UNIFORM EXTRADITION AND RENDITION ACT. National Conference of Commissioners on Uniform State Laws. Uniform Laws Annotated. West Publishing Company, P.O. Box 64526, 50 West Kellogg Boulevard, St. Paul, Minnesota 55164-0526. 1976. (Annual Supplements).

UNIFORM FACSIMILE SIGNATURES OF PUBLIC OFFICIALS ACT. National Conference of Commissioners on Uniform State Laws. Uniform Laws Annotated. West Publishing Company, P.O. Box 64526, 50 West Kellogg Boulevard, St. Paul, Minnesota 55164-0526. 1976. (Annual Supplements).

UNIFORM FEDERAL LIEN REGISTRATION ACT (1978 AND 1982). National Conference of Commissioners on Uniform State Laws. Martindale-Hubbell Law Digest, Martindale-Hubbell, 121 Chanlon Road, New Providence, New Jersey 07974. Annual.

UNIFORM FEDERAL LIEN REGISTRATION ACT. National Conference of Commissioners on Uniform State Laws. Uniform Laws Annotated. West Publishing Company, P.O. Box 64526, 50 West Kellogg Boulevard, St. Paul, Minnesota 55164-0526. 1976. (Annual Supplements).

UNIFORM FEDERAL TAX LIEN REGISTRATION ACT (REVISED). National Conference of Commissioners on Uniform State Laws. Martindale-Hubbell Law Digest, Martindale-Hubbell, 121 Chanlon Road, New Providence, New Jersey 07974. Annual.

UNIFORM FEDERAL TAX LIEN REGISTRATION ACT. National Conference of Commissioners on Uniform State Laws. Uniform Laws Annotated. West Publishing Company, P.O. Box 64526, 50 West Kellogg Boulevard, St. Paul, Minnesota 55164-0526. 1976. (Annual Supplements).

UNIFORM FIDUCIARIES ACT. National Conference of Commissioners on Uniform State Laws. Martindale-Hubbell Law Digest, Martindale-Hubbell, 121 Chanlon Road, New Providence, New Jersey 07974. Annual.

UNIFORM FIDUCIARIES ACT. National Conference of Commissioners on Uniform State Laws. Uniform Laws Annotated. West Publishing Company, P.O. Box 64526, 50 West Kellogg Boulevard, St. Paul, Minnesota 55164-0526. 1976. (Annual Supplements).

UNIFORM FOREIGN ACKNOWLEDGMENTS ACT. National Conference of Commissioners on Uniform State Laws. Martindale-Hubbell Law Digest, Martindale-Hubbell, 121 Chanlon Road, New Providence, New Jersey 07974. Annual.

UNIFORM FOREIGN DEPOSITIONS ACT. National Conference of Commissioners on Uniform State Laws. Martindale-Hubbell Law Digest, Martindale-Hubbell, 121 Chanlon Road, New Providence, New Jersey 07974. Annual.

UNIFORM FOREIGN EXECUTED WILLS ACT. National Conference of Commissioners on Uniform State Laws. Martindale-Hubbell Law Digest, Martindale-Hubbell, 121 Chanlon Road, New Providence, New Jersey 07974. Annual.

UNIFORM FOREIGN MONEY CLAIMS ACT. National Conference of Commissioners on Uniform State Laws. Uniform Laws Annotated. West Publishing Company, P.O. Box 64526, 50 West Kellogg Boulevard, St. Paul, Minnesota 55164-0526. 1976. (Annual Supplements).

UNIFORM FOREIGN MONEY JUDGMENTS RECOGNITION ACT. National Conference of Commissioners on Uniform State Laws. Uniform Laws Annotated. West Publishing Company, P.O. Box 64526, 50 West Kellogg Boulevard, St. Paul, Minnesota 55164-0526. 1976. (Annual Supplements).

UNIFORM FOREIGN PROBATED WILLS ACT. National Conference of Commissioners on Uniform State Laws. Martindale-Hubbell Law Directory, Volume Eight. Martindale-Hubbell, Incorporated, 121 Chanlon Road, New Providence, New Jersey 07974. Annual.

UNIFORM FRANCHISE AND BUSINESS OPPORTUNITIES ACT. National Conference of Commissioners on Uniform State Laws. Uniform Laws Annotated. West Publishing Company, P.O. Box 64526, 50 West Kellogg Boulevard, St. Paul, Minnesota 55164-0526. 1976. (Annual Supplements).

UNIFORM FRAUDULENT CONVEYANCES ACT. National Conference of Commissioners on Uniform State Laws. Martindale-Hubbell Law Digest, Martindale-Hubbell, 121 Chanlon Road, New Providence, New Jersey 07974. Annual.

UNIFORM FRAUDULENT CONVEYANCES ACT. National Conference of Commissioners on Uniform State Laws. Uniform Laws Annotated. West Publishing Company, P.O. Box 64526, 50 West Kellogg Boulevard, St. Paul, Minnesota 55164-0526. 1976. (Annual Supplements).

UNIFORM FRAUDULENT TRANSFER ACT. National Conference of Commissioners on Uniform State Laws. Martindale-Hubbell Law Digest, Martindale-Hubbell, 121 Chanlon Road, New Providence, New Jersey 07974. Annual.

UNIFORM FRAUDULENT TRANSFER ACT. National Conference of Commissioners on Uniform State Laws. Uniform Laws Annotated. West Publishing Company, P.O. Box 64526, 50 West Kellogg Boulevard, St. Paul, Minnesota 55164-0526. 1976. (Annual Supplements).

UNIFORM GIFTS TO MINORS ACT (REVISED WITH AMENDMENTS). National Conference of Commissioners on Uniform State Laws. Martindale-Hubbell Law Directory, Volume Eight. Martindale-Hubbell, Incorporated, 121 Chanlon Road, New Providence, New Jersey 07974. Annual.

UNIFORM GIFTS TO MINORS ACT (1956 AND 1966). National Conference of Commissioners on Uniform State Laws. Uniform Laws Annotated. West Publishing Company, P.O. Box 64526, 50 West Kellogg Boulevard, St. Paul, Minnesota 55164-0526. 1976. (Annual Supplements).

UNIFORM GUARDIANSHIP AND PROTECTIVE PROCEEDINGS ACT. National Conference of Commissioners on Uniform State Laws. Martindale-Hubbell Law Digest, Martindale-Hubbell, 121 Chanlon Road, New Providence, New Jersey 07974. Annual.

UNIFORM GUARDIANSHIP AND PROTECTIVE PROCEEDINGS ACT. National Conference of Commissioners on Uniform State Laws. Uniform Laws Annotated. West Publishing Company, P.O. Box 64526, 50 West Kellogg Boulevard, St. Paul, Minnesota 55164-0526. 1976. (Annual Supplements).

UNIFORM HEALTH-CARE INFORMATION ACT. Uniform Laws Annotated. West Publishing Company, P.O. Box 64526, 50 West Kellogg Boulevard, St. Paul, Minnesota 55164-0526. 1976. (Annual Supplements).

UNIFORM INFORMATION PRACTICES CODE. National Conference of Commissioners on Uniform State Laws. Uniform Laws Annotated. West Publishing Company, P.O. Box 64526, 50 West Kellogg Boulevard, St. Paul, Minnesota 55164-0526. 1976. (Annual Supplements).

UNIFORM INSURERS LIQUIDATION ACT. National Conference of Commissioners on Uniform State Laws. Uniform Laws Annotated. West Publishing Company, P.O. Box 64526, 50 West Kellogg Boulevard, St. Paul, Minnesota 55164-0526. 1976. (Annual Supplements).

UNIFORM INTERNATIONAL WILLS ACT. National Conference of Commissioners on Uniform State Laws. Martindale-Hubbell Law Digest, Martindale-Hubbell, 121 Chanlon Road, New Providence, New Jersey 07974. Annual.

UNIFORM INTERNATIONAL WILLS ACT. National Conference of Commissioners on Uniform State Laws. Uniform Laws Annotated. West Publishing Company, P.O. Box 64526, 50 West Kellogg Boulevard, St. Paul, Minnesota 55164-0526. 1976. (Annual Supplements).

UNIFORM INTERSTATE AND INTERNATIONAL PROCEDURE ACT. National Conference of Commissioners on Uniform State Laws. Uniform Laws Annotated. West Publishing Company, P.O. Box 64526, 50 West Kellogg Boulevard, St. Paul, Minnesota 55164-0526. 1976. (Annual Supplements).

UNIFORM INTERSTATE ARBITRATION OF DEATH TAXES ACT. National Conference of Commissioners on Uniform State Laws. Martindale-Hubbell Law Digest, Martindale-Hubbell, 121 Chanlon Road, New Providence, New Jersey 07974. Annual.

UNIFORM INTERSTATE ARBITRATION OF DEATH TAXES ACT. National Conference of Commissioners on Uniform State Laws. Uniform Laws Annotated. West Publishing Company, P.O. Box 64526, 50 West Kellogg Boulevard, St. Paul, Minnesota 55164-0526. 1976. (Annual Supplements).

UNIFORM INTERSTATE COMPROMISE OF DEATH TAXES ACT. National Conference of Commissioners on Uniform State Laws. Martindale-Hubbell Law Digest, Martindale-Hubbell, 121 Chanlon Road, New Providence, New Jersey 07974. Annual.

UNIFORM INTERSTATE COMPROMISE OF DEATH TAXES ACT. National Conference of Commissioners on Uniform State Laws. Uniform Laws Annotated. West Publishing Company, P.O. Box 64526, 50 West Kellogg Boulevard, St. Paul, Minnesota 55164-0526. 1976. (Annual Supplements).

UNIFORM JUDICIAL NOTICE OF FOREIGN LAW ACT. National Conference of Commissioners on Uniform State Laws. Martindale-Hubbell Law Digest, Martindale-Hubbell, 121 Chanlon Road, New Providence, New Jersey 07974. Annual.

UNIFORM JURY SELECTION AND SERVICE ACT. National Conference of Commissioners on Uniform State Laws. Uniform Laws Annotated. West Publishing Company, P.O. Box 64526, 50 West Kellogg Boulevard, St. Paul, Minnesota 55164-0526. 1976. (Annual Supplements).

UNIFORM LAND SECURITY INTEREST ACT. National Conference of Commissioners on Uniform Laws. Uniform Laws Annotated. West Publishing Company, P.O. Box 64526, 50 West Kellogg Boulevard, St. Paul, Minnesota 55164-0526. 1976. (Annual Supplements).

UNIFORM LAND TRANSACTIONS ACT. National Conference of Commissioners on Uniform State Laws. Uniform Laws Annotated. West Publishing Company, P.O. Box 64526, 50 West Kellogg Boulevard, St. Paul, Minnesota 55164-0526. 1976. (Annual Supplements).

UNIFORM LAW ON NOTARIAL ACTS. National Conference of Commissioners on Uniform State Laws. Martindale-Hubbell Law Digest, Martindale-Hubbell, 121 Chanlon Road, New Providence, New Jersey 07974. Annual.

UNIFORM LAW ON NOTARIAL ACTS. National Conference of Commissioners on Uniform State Laws. Uniform Laws Annotated. West Publishing Company, P.O. Box 64526, 50 West Kellogg Boulevard, St. Paul, Minnesota 55164-0526. 1976. (Annual Supplements).

UNIFORM LIMITED PARTNERSHIP ACT (1976 WITH AMENDMENTS). National Conference of Commissioners on Uniform State Laws. Martindale-Hubbell Law Digest, Martindale-Hubbell, 121 Chanlon Road, New Providence, New Jersey 07974. Annual.

UNIFORM LIMITED PARTNERSHIP ACT (1976 AND 1916). National Conference of Commissioners on Uniform State Laws. Uniform Laws Annotated. West Publishing Company, P.O. Box 64526, 50 West Kellogg Boulevard, St. Paul, Minnesota 55164-0526. 1976. (Annual Supplements).

UNIFORM MANAGEMENT OF INSTITUTIONAL FUNDS ACT. National Conference of Commissioners on Uniform State Laws. Martindale-Hubbell Law Digest, Martindale-Hubbell, 121 Chanlon Road, New Providence, New Jersey 07974. Annual.

UNIFORM MANAGEMENT OF INSTITUTIONAL FUNDS ACT. National Conference of Commissioners on Uniform State Laws. Uniform Laws Annotated. West Publishing Company, P.O. Box 64526, 50 West Kellogg Boulevard, St. Paul, Minnesota 55164-0526. 1976. (Annual Supplements).

UNIFORM MANDATORY DISPOSITION OF DETAINERS ACT. National Conference of Commissioners on Uniform State Laws. Uniform Laws Annotated. West Publishing Company, P.O. Box 64526, 50 West Kellogg Boulevard, St. Paul, Minnesota 55164-0526. 1976. (Annual Supplements).

UNIFORM MARITAL PROPERTY ACT. National Conference of Commissioners on Uniform State Laws. Uniform Laws Annotated. West Publishing Company, P.O. Box 64526, 50 West Kellogg Boulevard, St. Paul, Minnesota 55164-0526. 1976. (Annual Supplements).

UNIFORM MARKETABLE TITLE ACT. National Conference of Commissioners on Uniform State Laws. Uniform Laws Annotated. West Publishing Company, P.O. Box 64526, 50 West Kellogg Boulevard, St. Paul, Minnesota 55164-0526. 1976. (Annual Supplements).

UNIFORM MARRIAGE AND DIVORCE ACT. National Conference of Commissioners on Uniform State Laws. Uniform Laws Annotated. West Publishing Company, P.O. Box 64526, 50 West Kellogg Boulevard, St. Paul, Minnesota 55164-0526. 1976. (Annual Supplements).

UNIFORM MOTOR VEHICLE ACCIDENT REPARATIONS ACT. National Conference of Commissioners on Uniform State Laws. Uniform Laws Annotated. West Publishing Company, P.O. Box 64526, 50 West Kellogg Boulevard, St. Paul, Minnesota 55164-0526. 1976. (Annual Supplements).

UNIFORM MOTOR VEHICLE CERTIFICATE OF TITLE AND ANTITHEFT ACT. National Conference of Commissioners on Uniform State Laws. Uniform Laws Annotated. West Publishing Company, P.O. Box 64526, 50 West Kellogg Boulevard, St. Paul, Minnesota 55164-0526. 1976. (Annual Supplements).

UNIFORM MULTIPLE-PERSON ACCOUNTS ACT. National Conference of Commissioners on Uniform State Laws. Uniform Laws Annotated. West Publishing Company, P.O. Box 64526, 50 West Kellogg Boulevard, St. Paul, Minnesota 55164-0526. 1976. (Annual Supplements).

UNIFORM NARCOTIC DRUG ACT. National Conference of Commissioners on Uniform State Laws. Uniform Laws Annotated. West Publishing Company, P.O. Box 64526, 50 West Kellogg Boulevard, St. Paul, Minnesota 55164-0526. 1976. (Annual Supplements).

UNIFORM PARENTAGE ACT. National Conference of Commissioners on Uniform State Laws. Uniform Laws Annotated. West Publishing Company, P.O. Box 64526, 50 West Kellogg Boulevard, St. Paul, Minnesota 55164-0526. 1976. (Annual Supplements).

UNIFORM PARTNERSHIP ACT. National Conference of Commissioners on Uniform State Laws. Martindale-Hubbell Law Digest, Martindale-Hubbell, 121 Chanlon Road, New Providence, New Jersey 07974. Annual.

UNIFORM PARTNERSHIP ACT. National Conference of Commissioners on Uniform State Laws. Uniform Laws Annotated. West Publishing Company, P.O. Box 64526, 50 West Kellogg Boulevard, St. Paul, Minnesota 55164-0526. 1976. (Annual Supplements).

UNIFORM PATERNITY ACT. Uniform Laws Annotated. West Publishing Company, P.O. Box 64526, 50 West Kellogg Boulevard, St. Paul, Minnesota 55164-0526. 1976. (Annual Supplements).

UNIFORM PERPETUATION OF TESTIMONY ACT. National Conference of Commissioners on Uniform State Laws. Uniform Laws Annotated. West Publishing Company, P.O. Box 64526, 50 West Kellogg Boulevard, St. Paul, Minnesota 55164-0526. 1976. (Annual Supplements).

UNIFORM PHOTOGRAPHIC COPIES OF BUSINESS RECORDS AS EVIDENCE ACT. National Conference of Commissioners on Uniform State Laws. Martindale-Hubbell Law Digest, Martindale-Hubbell, 121 Chanlon Road, New Providence, New Jersey 07974. Annual.

UNIFORM PHOTOGRAPHIC COPIES OF BUSINESS RECORDS AS EVIDENCE ACT. National Conference of Commissioners on Uniform State Laws. Uniform Laws Annotated. West Publishing Company, P.O. Box 64526, 50 West Kellogg Boulevard, St. Paul, Minnesota 55164-0526. 1976. (Annual Supplements).

UNIFORM PLANNED COMMUNITY ACT. National Conference of Commissioners on Uniform State Laws. Uniform Laws Annotated. West Publishing Company, P.O. Box 64526, 50 West Kellogg Boulevard, St. Paul, Minnesota 55164-0526. 1976. (Annual Supplements).

UNIFORM POSTCONVICTION PROCEDURE ACT (1980 AND 1966). National Conference of Commissioners on Uniform State Laws. Uniform Laws Annotated. West Publishing Company, P.O. Box 64526, 50 West Kellogg Boulevard, St. Paul, Minnesota 55164-0526. 1976. (Annual Supplements).

UNIFORM PREMARITAL AGREEMENT ACT. National Conference of Commissioners on Uniform State Laws. Martindale-Hubbell Law Digest, Martindale-Hubbell, 121 Chanlon Road, New Providence, New Jersey 07974. Annual.

UNIFORM PREMARITAL AGREEMENT ACT. National Conference of Commissioners on Uniform State Laws. Uniform Laws Annotated. West Publishing Company, P.O. Box 64526, 50 West Kellogg Boulevard, St. Paul, Minnesota 55164-0526. 1976. (Annual Supplements).

UNIFORM PRETRIAL DETENTION ACT. National Conference of Commissioners on Uniform State Laws. Uniform Laws Annotated. West Publishing Company, P.O. Box 64526, 50 West Kellogg Boulevard, St. Paul, Minnesota 55164-0526. 1976. (Annual Supplements).

UNIFORM PRESERVATION OF PRIVATE BUSINESS RECORDS ACT. National Conference of Commissioners on Uniform State Laws. Uniform Laws Annotated. West Publishing Company, P.O. Box 64526, 50 West Kellogg Boulevard, St. Paul, Minnesota 55164-0526. 1976. (Annual Supplements).

UNIFORM PRINCIPAL AND INCOME ACT (ORIGINAL AND REVISED). National Conference of Commissioners on Uniform State Laws. Martindale-Hubbell Law Digest, Martindale-Hubbell, 121 Chanlon Road, New Providence, New Jersey 07974. Annual.

UNIFORM PRINCIPAL AND INCOME ACT (1962 AND 1931). National Conference of Commissioners on Uniform State Laws. Uniform Laws Annotated. West Publishing Company, P.O. Box 64526, 50 West Kellogg Boulevard, St. Paul, Minnesota 55164-0526. 1976. (Annual Supplements).

UNIFORM PROBATE CODE (WITH AMENDMENTS). National Conference of Commissioners on Uniform State Laws. Martindale-Hubbell Law Digest, Martindale-Hubbell, 121 Chanlon Road, New Providence, New Jersey 07974. Annual.

UNIFORM PROBATE CODE. National Conference of Commissioners on Uniform State Laws. Uniform Laws Annotated. West Publishing Company, P.O. Box 64526, 50 West Kellogg Boulevard, St. Paul, Minnesota 55164-0526. 1976. (Annual Supplements).

UNIFORM PROBATE OF FOREIGN WILLS ACT. National Conference of Commissioners on Uniform State Laws. Uniform Laws Annotated. West Publishing Company, P.O. Box 64526, 50 West Kellogg Boulevard, St. Paul, Minnesota 55164-0526. 1976. (Annual Supplements).

UNIFORM PUBLIC ASSEMBLY ACT. National Conference of Commissioners on Uniform State Laws. Uniform Laws Annotated. West Publishing Company, P.O. Box 64526, 50 West Kellogg Boulevard, St. Paul, Minnesota 55164-0526. 1976. (Annual Supplements).

UNIFORM PUTATIVE AND UNKNOWN FATHERS ACT. National Conference of Commissioners on Uniform State Laws. Uniform Laws Annotated. West Publishing Company, P.O. Box 64526, 50 West Kellogg Boulevard, St. Paul, Minnesota 55164-0526. 1976. (Annual Supplements).

UNIFORM RECIPROCAL ENFORCEMENT OF SUPPORT ACT (ORIGINAL AND REVISED 1968). National Conference of Commissioners on Uniform State Laws. Martindale-Hubbell Law Digest, Martindale-Hubbell, 121 Chanlon Road, New Providence, New Jersey 07974. Annual.

UNIFORM RECIPROCAL ENFORCEMENT OF SUPPORT ACT (1968 AND 1950). National Conference of Commissioners on Uniform State Laws. Uniform Laws Annotated. West Publishing Company, P.O. Box 64526, 50 West Kellogg Boulevard, St. Paul, Minnesota 55164-0526. 1976. (Annual Supplements).

UNIFORM RECIPROCAL TRANSFER TAX ACT. National Conference of Commissioners on Uniform State Laws. Martindale-Hubbell Law Digest, Martindale-Hubbell, 121 Chanlon Road, New Providence, New Jersey 07974. Annual.

UNIFORM RECIPROCAL TRANSFER TAX ACT. National Conference of Commissioners on Uniform State Laws. Uniform Laws Annotated. West Publishing Company, P.O. Box 64526, 50 West Kellogg Boulevard, St. Paul, Minnesota 55164-0526. 1976. (Annual Supplements).

UNIFORM RECOGNITION OF ACKNOWLEDGMENTS ACT. National Conference of Commissioners on Uniform State Laws. Martindale-Hubbell Law Digest, Martindale-Hubbell, 121 Chanlon Road, New Providence, New Jersey 07974. Annual.

UNIFORM RECOGNITION OF ACKNOWLEDGMENTS ACT. National Conference of Commissioners on Uniform State Laws. Uniform Laws Annotated. West Publishing Company, P.O. Box 64526, 50 West Kellogg Boulevard, St. Paul, Minnesota 55164-0526. 1976. (Annual Supplements).

UNIFORM RENDITION OF ACCUSED PERSONS ACT. National Conference of Commissioners on Uniform State Laws. Uniform Laws Annotated. West Publishing Company, P.O. Box 64526, 50 West Kellogg Boulevard, St. Paul, Minnesota 55164-0526. 1976. (Annual Supplements).

UNIFORM RENDITION OF PRISONERS AS WITNESSES IN CRIMINAL PROCEEDINGS ACT. National Conference of Commissioners on Uniform State Laws. Uniform Laws Annotated. West Publishing Company, P.O. Box 64526, 50 West Kellogg Boulevard, St. Paul, Minnesota 55164-0526. 1976. (Annual Supplements).

UNIFORM RESIDENTIAL LANDLORD AND TENANT ACT. National Conference of Commissioners on Uniform State Laws. Uniform Laws Annotated. West Publishing Company, P.O. Box 64526, 50 West Kellogg Boulevard, St. Paul, Minnesota 55164-0526. 1976. (Annual Supplements).

UNIFORM RIGHTS OF THE TERMINALLY ILL ACT (1989 AND 1985). Uniform Laws Annotated. West Publishing Company, P.O. Box 64526, 50 West Kellogg Boulevard, St. Paul, Minnesota 55164-0526. 1976. (Annual Supplements).

UNIFORM RULES OF CRIMINAL PROCEDURE (1987 AND 1974). National Conference of Commissioners on Uniform State Laws. Uniform Laws Annotated. West Publishing Company, P.O. Box 64526, 50 West Kellogg Boulevard, St. Paul, Minnesota 55164-0526. 1976. (Annual Supplements).

UNIFORM RULES OF EVIDENCE. National Conference of Commissioners on Uniform State Laws. Uniform Laws Annotated. West Publishing Company, P.O. Box 64526, 50 West Kellogg Boulevard, St. Paul, Minnesota 55164-0526. 1976. (Annual Supplements).

UNIFORM SECURITIES ACT. National Conference of Commissioners on Uniform State Laws. Martindale-Hubbell Law Digest, Martindale-Hubbell, 121 Chanlon Road, New Providence, New Jersey 07974. Annual.

UNIFORM SECURITIES ACT (1985 AND 1956). National Conference of Commissioners on Uniform State Laws. Uniform Laws Annotated. West Publishing Company, P.O. Box 64526, 50 West Kellogg Boulevard, St. Paul, Minnesota 55164-0526. 1976. (Annual Supplements).

UNIFORM SIMPLIFICATION OF FIDUCIARY SECURITY TRANSFERS ACT. National Conference of Commissioners on Uniform State Laws. Martindale-Hubbell Law Digest, Martindale-Hubbell, 121 Chanlon Road, New Providence, New Jersey 07974. Annual.

UNIFORM SIMPLIFICATION OF FIDUCIARY SECURITY TRANSFERS ACT. National Conference of Commissioners on Uniform State Laws. Uniform Laws Annotated. West Publishing Company, P.O. Box 64526, 50 West Kellogg Boulevard, St. Paul, Minnesota 55164-0526. 1976. (Annual Supplements).

UNIFORM SIMPLIFICATION OF LAND TRANSFERS ACT. National Conference of Commissioners on Uniform State Laws. Uniform Laws Annotated. Matindale-Hubbell Law Directory, Volume Eight. Martindale-Hubbell, Incorporated, 121 Chanlon Road, New Providence, New Jersey 07974. Annual.

UNIFORM SIMPLIFICATION OF LAND TRANSFERS ACT. National Conference of Commissioners on Uniform State Laws. Uniform Laws Annotated. West Publishing Company, P.O. Box 64526, 50 West Kellogg Boulevard, St. Paul, Minnesota 55164-0526. 1976. (Annual Supplements).

UNIFORM SIMULTANEOUS DEATH ACT. National Conference of Commissioners on Uniform State Laws. Martindale-Hubbell Law Digest, Martindale-Hubbell, 121 Chanlon Road, New Providence, New Jersey 07974. Annual.

UNIFORM SIMULTANEOUS DEATH ACT. National Conference of Commissioners on Uniform State Laws. Uniform Laws Annotated. West Publishing Company, P.O. Box 64526, 50 West Kellogg Boulevard, St. Paul, Minnesota 55164-0526. 1976. (Annual Supplements).

UNIFORM SINGLE PUBLICATION ACT. National Conference of Commissioners on Uniform State Laws. Uniform Laws Annotated. West Publishing Company, P.O. Box 64526, 50 West Kellogg Boulevard, St. Paul, Minnesota 55164-0526. 1976. (Annual Supplements).

UNIFORM STATE ANTITRUST ACT. National Conference of Commissioners on Uniform State Laws. Uniform Laws Annotated. West Publishing Company, P.O. Box 64526, 50 West Kellogg Boulevard, St. Paul, Minnesota 55164-0526. 1976. (Annual Supplements).

UNIFORM STATUS OF CHILDREN OF ASSISTED CONCEPTION ACT. National Conference of Commissioners on Uniform State Laws. Uniform Laws Annotated. West Publishing Company, P.O. Box 64526, 50 West Kellogg Boulevard, St. Paul, Minnesota 55164-0526. 1976. (Annual Supplements).

UNIFORM STATUTE OF LIMITATIONS ON FOREIGN CLAIMS ACT. National Conference of Commissioners on Uniform State Laws. Uniform Laws Annotated. West Publishing Company, P.O. Box 64526, 50 West Kellogg Boulevard, St. Paul, Minnesota 55164-0526. 1976. (Annual Supplements).

UNIFORM STATUTORY FORM POWER OF ATTORNEY ACT. National Conference of Commissioners on Uniform State Laws. Uniform Laws Annotated. West Publishing Company, P.O. Box 64526, 50 West Kellogg Boulevard, St. Paul, Minnesota 55164-0526. 1976. (Annual Supplements).

UNIFORM STATUTORY RULE AGAINST PERPETUITIES ACT. National Conference of Commissioners on Uniform State Laws. Martindale-Hubbell Law Digest, Martindale-Hubbell, 121 Chanlon Road, New Providence, New Jersey 07974. Annual.

UNIFORM STATUTORY RULE AGAINST PERPETUITIES ACT. National Conference of Commissioners on Uniform State Laws. Uniform Laws Annotated. West Publishing Company, P.O. Box 64526, 50 West Kellogg Boulevard, St. Paul, Minnesota 55164-0526. 1976. (Annual Supplements).

UNIFORM STATUTORY WILL ACT. National Conference of Commissioners on Uniform State Laws. Uniform Laws Annotated. West Publishing Company, P.O. Box 64526, 50 West Kellogg Boulevard, St. Paul, Minnesota 55164-0526. 1976. (Annual Supplements).

UNIFORM SUCCESSION WITHOUT ADMINISTRATION ACT. National Conference of Commissioners on Uniform State Laws. Uniform Laws Annotated. West Publishing Company, P.O. Box 64526, 50 West Kellogg Boulevard, St. Paul, Minnesota 55164-0526. 1976. (Annual Supplements).

UNIFORM SUPERVISION OF TRUSTEES FOR CHARITABLE PURPOSES ACT. National Conference of Commissioners on Uniform State Laws. Uniform Laws Annotated. West Publishing Company, P.O. Box 64526, 50 West Kellogg Boulevard, St. Paul, Minnesota 55164-0526. 1976. (Annual Supplements).

UNIFORM SURFACE USE AND MINERAL DEVELOPMENT ACCOMMODATION ACT. National Conference of Commissioners on Uniform State Laws. Uniform Laws Annotated. West Publishing Company, P.O. Box 64526, 50 West Kellogg Boulevard, St. Paul, Minnesota 55164-0526. 1976. (Annual Supplements).

UNIFORM TESTAMENTARY ADDITIONS TO TRUSTS ACT. National Conference of Commissioners on Uniform State Laws. Martindale-Hubbell Law Digest, Martindale-Hubbell, 121 Chanlon Road, New Providence, New Jersey 07974. Annual.

UNIFORM TESTAMENTARY ADDITIONS TO TRUSTS ACT. National Conference of Commissioners on Uniform State Laws. Uniform Laws Annotated. West Publishing Company, P.O. Box 64526, 50 West Kellogg Boulevard, St. Paul, Minnesota 55164-0526. 1976. (Annual Supplements).

UNIFORM TOD SECURITY REGISTRATION ACT. National Conference of Commissioners on Uniform State Laws. Uniform Laws Annotated. West Publishing Company, P.O. Box 64526, 50 West Kellogg Boulevard, St. Paul, Minnesota 55164-0526. 1976. (Annual Supplements).

UNIFORM TRADE SECRETS ACT. National Conference of Commissioners on Uniform State Laws. Martindale-Hubbell Law Digest, Martindale-Hubbell, 121 Chanlon Road, New Providence, New Jersey 07974. Annual.

UNIFORM TRADE SECRETS ACT. National Conference of Commissioners on Uniform State Laws. Uniform Laws Annotated. West Publishing Company, P.O. Box 64526, 50 West Kellogg Boulevard, St. Paul, Minnesota 55164-0526. 1976. (Annual Supplements).

UNIFORM TRANSBOUNDARY POLLUTION RECIPROCAL ACCESS ACT. National Conference of Commissioners on Uniform State Laws. Uniform Laws Annotated. West Publishing Company, P.O. Box 64526, 50 West Kellogg Boulevard, St. Paul, Minnesota 55164-0526. 1976. (Annual Supplements).

UNIFORM TRANSFERS TO MINORS ACT. National Conference of Commissioners on Uniform State Laws. Martindale-Hubbell Law Digest, Martindale-Hubbell, 121 Chanlon Road, New Providence, New Jersey 07974. Annual.

UNIFORM TRANSFERS TO MINORS ACT. National Conference of Commissioners on Uniform State Laws. Uniform Laws Annotated. West Publishing Company, P.O. Box 64526, 50 West Kellogg Boulevard, St. Paul, Minnesota 55164-0526. 1976. (Annual Supplements).

UNIFORM TRUSTEES' POWERS ACT. National Conference of Commissioners on Uniform State Laws. Uniform Laws Annotated. West Publishing Company, P.O. Box 64526, 50 West Kellogg Boulevard, St. Paul, Minnesota 55164-0526. 1976. (Annual Supplements).

UNIFORM TRUSTS ACT. National Conference of Commissioners on Uniform State Laws. Martindale-Hubbell Law Digest, Martindale-Hubbell, 121 Chanlon Road, New Providence, New Jersey 07974. Annual.

UNIFORM TRUSTS ACT. National Conference of Commissioners on Uniform State Laws. Uniform Laws Annotated. West Publishing Company, P.O. Box 64526, 50 West Kellogg Boulevard, St. Paul, Minnesota 55164-0526. 1976. (Annual Supplements).

UNIFORM UNCLAIMED PROPERTY ACT. National Conference of Commissioners on Uniform State Laws. Martindale-Hubbell Law Digest, Martindale-Hubbell, 121 Chanlon Road, New Providence, New Jersey 07974. Annual.

UNIFORM UNCLAIMED PROPERTY ACT (1986). National Conference of Commissioners on Uniform State Laws. Uniform Laws Annotated. West Publishing Company, P.O. Box 64526, 50 West Kellogg Boulevard, St. Paul, Minnesota 55164-0526. 1976. (Annual Supplements).

UNIFORM VENDOR AND PURCHASER RISK ACT. National Conference of Commissioners on Uniform State Laws. Martindale-Hubbell Law Digest, Martindale-Hubbell, 121 Chanlon Road, New Providence, New Jersey 07974. Annual.

UNIFORM VENDOR AND PURCHASER RISK ACT. National Conference of Commissioners on Uniform State Laws. Uniform Laws Annotated. West Publishing Company, P.O. Box 64526, 50 West Kellogg Boulevard, St. Paul, Minnesota 55164-0526. 1976. (Annual Supplements).

UNIFORM VETERANS GUARDIANSHIP ACT. National Conference of Commissioners on Uniform State Laws. Uniform Laws Annotated. West Publishing Company, P.O. Box 64526, 50 West Kellogg Boulevard, St. Paul, Minnesota 55164-0526. 1976. (Annual Supplements).

UNIFORM VOTING BY NEW RESIDENTS IN PRESIDENTIAL ELECTIONS ACT. National Conference of Commissioners on Uniform State Laws. Uniform Laws Annotated. West Publishing Company, P.O. Box 64526, 50 West Kellogg Boulevard, St. Paul, Minnesota 55164-0526. 1976. (Annual Supplements).

LOOSELEAF SERVICES AND REPORTERS

ADMINISTRATIVE INTERPRETATIONS OF THE UNIFORM COMMERCIAL CREDIT CODE. Frederick H. Miller. Butterworth Legal Publishers, 90 Stiles Road, Salem, New Hampshire 03079. 1989- .

COMMERCIAL TRANSACTIONS UNDER THE UNIFORM COMMERCIAL CODE. Donald B. King. Calvin A Kuenzel, and Bradford Stone. Matthew Bender and Company, 11 Penn Plaza, New York, New York 10001. 1987- . (Periodic supplements).

DAMAGES UNDER THE UNIFORM COMMERCIAL CODE. Roy R. Anderson. Callaghan and Company, 155 Pfingsten Road, Deerfield, Illinois 60015. 1988- . (Annual supplements).

UNIFORM COMMERCIAL CODE REPORTING SERVICE. Callaghan and Company, 155 Pfingsten Road, Deerfield, Illinois 60015. 1965- .

UNIFORM COMMERCIAL CODE TRANSACTION GUIDE. Peter A. Alces. Callaghan and Company, 155 Pfingsten Road, Deerfield, Illinois 60015. 1988- . (Annual supplements).

HANDBOOKS, MANUALS, FORMBOOKS

ANDERSON ON THE UNIFORM COMMERCIAL CODE: LEGAL FORMS. Second Edition. Ronald A. Anderson. Lawyers Co-Operative Publishing Company, Aqueduct Building, Rochester, New York 14694. 1974. (Annual Supplements).

ANDERSON ON THE UNIFORM COMMERCIAL CODE: PLEADING AND PRACTICE FORMS. Second Edition. Ronald A. Anderson. Lawyers Co-Operative Publishing Company, Aqueduct Building, Rochester, New York 14694. 1977. (Annual Supplements).

A GUIDE TO THE UNCITRAL MODEL LAW ON INTERNATIONAL COMMERCIAL ARBITRATION: LEGISLATIVE HISTORY AND COMMENTARY. Howard M. Holtzmann and Joseph E. Neuhaus. Kluwer Law and Taxation, 6 Bigelow Street, Cambridge, Massachusetts 02139. 1989.

MANUAL ON THE UNIFORM COMMERCIAL CODE. Second edition. Austin T. Stickells. West Publishing Company, P.O. Box 64526, 50 West Kellogg Boulevard, St. Paul, Minnesota 55164-0526. 1989.

UNIFORM COMMERCIAL CODE FORMS. Second edition. George I. Wallach and Richard W. Duesenberg. West Publishing Company, P.O. Box 64526, 50 West Kellogg Boulevard, St. Paul, Minnesota 55164-0526. 1987. (Annual Supplements).

UNIFORM COMMERCIAL CODE FORMS AND COMMENTARY. Second edition. Stephen W. Ramp and W. Harold Bigham. West Publishing Company, P.O. Box 64526, 50 West Kellogg Boulevard, St. Paul, Minnesota 55164-0526. 1987. (Annual Supplements).

TEXTBOOKS AND GENERAL WORKS

ANDERSON ON THE UNIFORM COMMERCIAL CODE. Third Edition. Ronald A. Anderson. Lawyers Co-Operative Publishing Company, Aqueduct Building, Rochester, New York 14694. 1981 (Annual Supplements).

COMMENTARY ON THE UNCITRAL MODEL LAW ON INTERNATIONAL COMMERCIAL ARBITRATION. Aron Broches. Kluwer Law Book Publishers, Incorporated, 36 West Forty-fourth Street, New York, New York 10036. 1990.

DISPOSITION OF REPOSSESSED COLLATERAL UNDER THE UNIFORM COMMERCIAL CODE. Christine A. Ferris and Bennett H. Goldstein. John Wiley and Sons, Incorporated, One Wiley Drive, Somerset, New Jersey 08873. 1990.

DOCUMENTARY HISTORY OF THE UNIFORM LAW FOR INTERNATIONAL SALES. John O. Honnold. Kluwer Law and Taxation, 6 Bigelow Street, Cambridge, Massachusetts 02139. 1989.

DOCUMENTS OF TITLE UNDER THE UNIFORM COMMERCIAL CODE. Second edition. Ray D. Henson. American Law Institute-American Bar Association Committee on Continuing Professional Education, 4025 Chestnut Street, Philadelphia, Pennsylvania 19104. 1990.

LAW OF SECURED TRANSACTIONS UNDER THE UNIFORM COMMERCIAL CODE. Second edition. Barkley Clark. Research Institute of America, Incorporated, 210 South Street, Boston, Massachusetts 02111. 1988.

UNIFORM COMMERCIAL CODE. Third edition. James J. White and Robert S. Summers. West Publishing Company, P.O. Box 64526, 50 West Kellogg Boulevard, St. Paul, Minnesota 55164-0526. 1989.

UNIFORM COMMERCIAL CODE. ARTICLE 2A, LEASES OF GOODS. Third edition. James J. White and Robert S. Summers. West Publishing Company, P.O. Box 64526, 50 West Kellogg Boulevard, St. Paul, Minnesota 55164-0526. 1991.

UNIFORM COMMERCIAL CODE IN A NUTSHELL. Third edition. Bradford Stone. West Publishing Company, P.O. Box 64526, 50 West Kellogg Boulevard, St. Paul, Minnesota 55164-0526. 1989.

UNIFORM COMMERCIAL CODE SERIES. William D. Hawkland. Callaghan and Company, 155 Pfingsten Road, Deerfield, Illinois 60015. 1990.

UNIFORM LAW FOR INTERNATIONAL SALES UNDER THE 1980 UNITED NATIONS CONVENTION. Second edition. John Honnold. Kluwer Law and Taxation, 6 Bigelow Street, Cambridge, Massachusetts 02139. 1991.

UNIFORM PROBATE CODE IN A NUTSHELL. Second edition. Lawrence H. Averill. West Publishing Company, P.O. Box 64526, 50 West Kellogg Boulevard, St. Paul, Minnesota 55164-0526 1987.

ENCYCLOPEDIAS AND DICTIONARIES

UNIFORM COMMERCIAL CODE: TERMS AND TRANSACTIONS IN COMMERCIAL LAW. John F. Dolan. Little Brown and Company, 34 Beacon Street, Boston, Massachusetts 02106. 1991.

DIGESTS, INDEXES, ABSTRACTS, CITATORS

ANNOTATIONS TO THE MODEL PROCUREMENT CODE FOR STATE AND LOCAL GOVERNMENTS. Louis F. Del Duca, Patrick J. Falvey, and Theodore A. Adler. Section of Urban, State, and Local Government Law, American Bar Association, 750 North Lake Shore Drive, Chicago, Illinois 60611. 1987.

MODEL BUSINESS CORPORATION ACT ANNOTATED: REVISED MODEL BUSINESS CORPORATION ACT. Third Edition. Committee on Corporate Laws of the Section on Corporation, Banking and Business Law. American Bar Association. Prentice-Hall Law and Business, Incorporated, 855 Valley Road, Clifton, New Jersey 07013. 1985.

NATIONAL CONFERENCE OF COMMISSIONERS ON UNIFORM STATE LAWS. Hardcopy Index to Microfiche of Archive Holdings. William S. Hein and Company, Incorporated, 1285 Main Street, Buffalo, New York 14209. 1982.

QUINN'S UNIFORM COMMERCIAL CODE COMMENTARY AND LAW DIGEST. Thomas M. Quinn. Research Institute of America, Incorporated, One Penn Plaza, New York, New York 10119. 1978. (Semi-annual Supplements).

SHEPARD'S UNIFORM COMMERCIAL CODE CITATIONS. Shepard's/McGraw-Hill, P.O. Box 1235, Colorado Springs, Colorado 80901. 1982. (Quarterly Supplements).

SHEPARD'S UNIFORM COMMERCIAL CODE CASE CITATIONS. Shepard's/McGraw-Hill, P.O. Box 1235, Colorado Springs, Colorado 80901. 1982. (Quarterly Supplements).

UNIFORM COMMERCIAL CODE: CASE DIGEST. Pike and Fischer, Incorporated, Editor. Callaghan and Company, 155 Pfingsten Road, Deerfield, Illinois 60015. 1976- .

UNIFORM LAWS ANNOTATED. National Conference of Commissioners on Uniform State Laws. West Publishing Company, P.O. Box 64526, 50 West Kellogg Boulevard, St. Paul, Minnesota 55164-0526. 1976. (Annual Supplements).

ANNUALS AND SURVEYS

NATIONAL CONFERENCE OF COMMISSIONERS ON UNIFORM STATE LAWS. Annual Meetings Proceedings. William S. Hein and Company, Incorporated, 1285 Main Street, Buffalo, New York 14209. Microfiche.

LAW REVIEWS AND PERIODICALS

UNIFORM COMMERCIAL CODE LAW JOURNAL. Research Institute of America, Incorporated, One Penn Plaza, New York, New York 10119. Quarterly.

NEWSLETTERS AND NEWSPAPERS

COMMERCIAL LAW ADVISER. Business Laws, Incorporated, 11630 Chillicothe Road, Chesterland, Ohio 44026. Monthly.

COMMERCIAL LAW REPORT. Matthew Bender and Company, Incorporated, 11 Penn Plaza, New York, New York 10001. Monthly.

UNIFORM COMMERCIAL CODE LAW LETTER. Research Institute of America, Incorporated, One Penn Plaza, New York, New York 10119. Monthly.

ASSOCIATIONS AND PROFESSIONAL SOCIETIES

AMERICAN BAR ASSOCIATION, COMMITTEE ON CORPORATE LAW OF THE SECTION ON CORPORATION, BUSINESS AND BANKING LAW. 750 North Lake Shore Drive, Chicago, Illinois 60611. (312) 988-5000.

NATIONAL CONFERENCE OF COMMISSIONERS ON UNIFORM STATE LAWS. 676 North St. Clair, Suite 1700, Chicago, Illinois 60611. (312) 915-0195.

OTHER SOURCES

A CENTURY OF SERVICE: A CENTENNIAL HISTORY OF THE NATIONAL CONFERENCE OF COMMISSIONERS ON UNIFORM STATE LAWS. Walter P. Armstrong. West Publishing Company, P.O. Box 64526, 50 West Kellogg Boulevard, St. Paul, Minnesota 55164-0526. 1991.

NATIONAL CONFERENCE OF COMMISSIONERS ON UNIFORM STATE LAWS. Archive Holdings. William S. Hein and Company, Incorporated, 1285 Main Street, Buffalo, New York 14209. 1982. Microfiche.

UNIONS
See: LABOR AND LABOR RELATIONS

UNITED NATIONS

TREATIES, JUDICIAL OPINIONS, RECORDS, DOCUMENTS

ACTS AND DOCUMENTS CONCERNING THE ORGANIZATION OF THE COURT. International Court of Justice, United Nations, Sales Section, Publishing Division, Room DC2-0853, New York, New York 10017. (Irregular).

BASIC DOCUMENTS ON UNITED NATIONS AND RELATED PEACE-KEEPING FORCES. Robert C. Siekmann. Kluwer Academic Publishers, 101 Philip Drive, Assinippi Park, Norwell, Massachusetts 02061.

HUMAN RIGHTS: A COMPILATION OF INTERNATIONAL INSTRUMENTS. United Nations, Sales Section, Publishing Division, Room DC2-0853, New York, New York 10017. 1988.

IIUMAN RIGHTS COMMITTEE: SELECTED DECISIONS UNDER THE OPTIONAL PROTOCOL. United Nations, Sales Section, Publishing Division, Room DC2-0853, New York, New York 10017. 1985.

INTERNATIONAL PROVISIONS PROTECTING THE HUMAN RIGHTS OF NON-CITIZENS. United Nations, Sales Section, Publishing Division, Room DC2-0853, New York, New York 10017. 1980.

THE LAW OF THE SEA: UNITED NATIONS CONVENTION ON THE LAW OF THE SEA WITH INDEX AND THE FINAL ACT OF THE THIRD UNITED NATIONS CONFERENCE ON THE LAW OF THE SEA. United Nations, Sales Section, Publishing Division, Room DC2-0853, New York, New York 10017. 1983.

PLEADINGS, ORAL ARGUMENTS AND DOCUMENTS. International Court of Justice. United Nations, Sales Section, Publishing Division, Room DC2-0853, New York, New York 10017. (Irregular).

REPERTORY OF PRACTICE OF UNITED NATIONS ORGANS. United Nations, Sales Section, Publishing Division, Room DC2-0853, New York, New York 10017. (Irregular).

REPORTS OF INTERNATIONAL ARBITRAL AWARDS. United Nations, Sales Section, Publishing Division, Room DC2-0853, New York, New York 10017. (Irregular).

REPORTS OF JUDGEMENTS, ADVISORY OPINIONS AND ORDERS. International Court of Justice, United Nations, Sales Section, Publishing Division, Room DC2-0853, New York, New York 10017. (Slip opinions and annual volumes).

THIRD UNITED NATIONS CONFERENCE ON THE LAW OF THE SEA: OFFICIAL RECORDS. United Nations, Sales Section, Publishing Division, Room DC2-0853, New York, New York 10017. 1975- .

UNITED NATIONS GENERAL ASSEMBLY RESOLUTIONS; A SELECTION OF THE MOST IMPORTANT RESOLUTIONS DURING THE PERIOD 1949 THROUGH 1974, SESSIONS I - XXVII. Knud Krakau. Fred B. Rothman and Company, 10368 West Centennial Road, Littleton, Colorado 80127. 1975.

UNITED NATIONS OFFICIAL RECORDS SERIES: GENERAL ASSEMBLY (AND MAIN COMMITTEES); SECURITY COUNCIL; ECONOMIC AND SOCIAL COUNCIL; DISARMAMENT COMMISSION. United Nations, Sales Section, Publishing Division, Room DC2-0853, New York, New York 10017. (Standing Orders to Classes of Records).

UNITED NATIONS TREATY SERIES. United Nations, Sales Section, Publishing Division, Room DC2-0853, New York, New York 10017. (Standing Orders).

HANDBOOKS, MANUAL, FORMBOOKS

BASIC DOCUMENTS ON UNITED NATIONS AND RELATED PEACE-KEEPING FORCES. Second Edition. Robert C.R. Siekmann. Martinus Nijhoff, Kluwer Academic Publishers, 101 Philip Drive, Assinippi Park, Norwell, Massachusetts 02061. 1989.

COMPLETE REFERENCE GUIDE TO UNITED NATIONS SALES PUBLICATIONS, 1946-1978. M. E. Birchfield and J. Coolman, Editors. UNIFO Publishers, Limited, P.O. Box 3858, Sarasota, Florida 34230-3858. 1982.

EVERYONE'S UNITED NATIONS. Tenth Edition. United Nations, Sales Section, Publishing Division, Room DC2-0853, New York, New York 10017. 1986.

GUIDE TO UNITED NATIONS CRIMINAL POLICY. Manuel Lopez-Rey. Gower Publishing Company, Old Post Road, Brookfield, Vermont 05036. 1985.

PETITIONING THE UNITED NATIONS: A STUDY IN HUMAN RIGHTS. Ton J. Zuijdwijk. Saint Martin's Press, Incorporated, 175 Fifth Avenue, New York, New York 10010. 1982.

POLITICS AND PROCESS IN THE SPECIALIZED AGENCIES OF THE UNITED NATIONS. Houshang Ameri. Gower Publishing Company, Old Post Road, Brookfield, Vermont 05036. 1982.

UNITED NATIONS CORRESPONDENCE MANUAL. United Nations, Sales Section, Publishing Division, Room DC2-0853, New York, New York 10017. 1984.

UNITED NATIONS EDITORIAL MANUAL: A COMPENDIUM OF RULES AND DIRECTIVES ON UNITED NATIONS EDITORIAL STYLE, PUBLICATION POLICIES, PROCEDURES AND PRACTICES. United Nations, Sales Section, Publishing Division, Room DC2-0853, New York, New York 10017. 1983.

THE UNITED NATIONS: HOW IT WORKS AND WHAT IT DOES. Evan Luard. Saint Martin's Press, Incorporated, 175 Fifth Avenue, New York, New York 10010. 1985.

TEXTBOOKS AND GENERAL WORKS

BASIC FACTS ABOUT THE UNITED NATIONS. United Nations, Sales Section, Publishing Division, Room DC2-0853, New York, New York 10017. 1990.

BENDING WITH THE WINDS. Kurt Waldheim, Seymour Maxwell Finger, and Arnold A. Saltzman. Praeger Publishers, One Madison Avenue, New York, New York 10010. 1990.

THE BLUE HELMETS: A REVIEW OF UNITED NATIONS PEACE-KEEPING. Second Edition. United Nations Publishing Service, Room DC2-0853, New York, New York 10017. 1990.

A CHILDREN'S CHORUS: CELEBRATING THE 30TH ANNIVERSARY OF THE DECLARATION OF THE RIGHTS OF THE CHILD. E.P. Dutton, 375 Hudson Street, New York, New York 10014. 1989.

A CHRONOLOGY AND FACT BOOK OF THE UNITED NATIONS, 1941-1985. Seventh Edition. Oceana Publications, Incorporated, 75 Main Street, Dobbs Ferry, New York 10522. 1986.

COUNTENANCE OF TRUTH: THE UNITED NATIONS AND THE WALDHEIM CASE. Shirley Hazzard. Viking Penguin, Incorporated, 375 Hudson Street, New York, New York 10014. 1990.

DISARMAMENT WITHOUT ORDER: THE POLITICS OF DISARMAMENT AT THE UNITED NATIONS. Avi Beker. Greenwood Publishing Group, Incorporated, 88 Post Road West, P.O. Box 5007, Westport, Connecticut 06881. 1985.

DUMBARTON OAKS: THE ORIGINS OF THE UNITED NATIONS AND THE SEARCH FOR POSTWAR SECURITY. Robert C. Hilderbrand. University of North Carolina Press, P.O. Box 2288, 116 South Boundary Street, Chapel Hill, North Carolina 27515-2288. 1990.

THE EVOLUTION OF THE UNITED NATIONS SYSTEM. Amos Yoder. Crane Russak, New York, New York. 1989.

EXPANDING JURISDICTION OF THE UNITED NATIONS. M. S. Rajan. Oceana Publications, Incorporated, 75 Main Street, Dobbs Ferry, New York 10522. 1982.

FIRES ALL AROUND THE HORIZON: THE UN'S UPHILL BATTLE TO PRESERVE THE PEACE. Max Harrelson. Praeger Publishers, One Madison Avenue, New York, New York 10010. 1989.

FROM THE LEAGUE TO U.N. Gilbert Murray. Greenwood Publishing Group, Incorporated, 88 Post Road West, P.O. Box 5007, Westport, Connecticut 06881. 1988. (Reprint).

THE GENERAL ASSEMBLY IN WORLD POLITICS. M. J. Peterson. Allen and Unwin, Incorporated, P.O. Box 442, Concord, Massachusetts 01742. 1986.

GLOBAL ISSUES IN THE UNITED NATIONS' FRAMEWORK. Paul Taylor and A.J.R. Groom. St. Martin's Press, 175 Fifth Avenue, New York, New York 10010. 1989.

GUIDE TO PRACTICAL APPLICATIONS OF THE UN CONVENTION ON CONTRACTS FOR THE INTERNATIONAL SALE OF GOODS. Albert H. Kritzer. Kluwer Law Book Publishers, Incorporated, 36 West Forty-fourth Street, New York, New York 10036. 1988.

HOW WARS END: THE UNITED NATIONS AND THE TERMINATION OF ARMED CONFLICT, 1946-1964. Sydney D. Bailey. New York University Press, Distributed by Oxford University Press, 200 Madison Avenue, New York, New York 10016. 1982.

HUMAN RIGHTS COMMITTEE: ITS ROLE IN THE DEVELOPMENT OF THE INTERNATIONAL COVENANT ON CIVIL AND POLITICAL RIGHTS. Dominic McGoldrick. Oxford University Press, 200 Madison Avenue, New York, New York 10016. 1990.

THE HUMAN RIGHTS ORGANS OF THE UNITED NATIONS: A CRITICAL APPRAISAL. Philip Alston. Oxford University Press, 200 Madison Avenue, New York, New York 10016. 1992.

HUMANITARIAN GOOD OFFICES IN INTERNATIONAL LAW: THE GOOD OFFICES OF THE UNITED NATIONS. Houshang Ameri. Gower Publishing Company, Old Post Road, Brookfield, Vermont 05036. 1982.

INTERNATIONAL CO-OPERATION: FROM THE VIENNA CONGRESS TO THE UNITED NATIONS. S.R. Gibbons. Longman Publishing Group, 95 Church Street, White Plains, New York 10601. 1991.

INTERNATIONAL INSTITUTIONS AT WORK. Paul Taylor and A.J.R. Groom. St. Martin's Press, 175 Fifth Avenue, New York, New York 10010. 1988.

KEEPING FAITH WITH THE UNITED NATIONS. B.G. Ramcharan. Martinus Nijhoff, Kluwer Academic Publishers, 101 Philip Drive, Assinippi Park, Norwell, Massachusetts 02061. 1987.

THE KIRKPATRICK MISSION: DIPLOMACY WITHOUT APOLOGY: AMERICA AT THE UNITED NATIONS, 1981-1985. Allan Gerson. Free Press, 866 Third Avenue, New York, New York 10022. 1991.

NATION AGAINST NATION: WHAT HAPPENED TO THE U.N. DREAM AND WHAT THE U.S. CAN DO ABOUT IT. Thomas M. Franck. Oxford University Press, Incorporated, 200 Madison Avenue, New York, New York 10016. 1985.

THE NON-ALIGNED, THE UNITED NATIONS, AND THE SUPERPOWERS. Richard L. Jackson. Praeger Publishers, One Madison Avenue, New York, New York 10010-3603. 1987.

POLITICS AND POVERTY: A CRITIQUE OF THE FOOD AND AGRICULTURE ORGANIZATION OF THE UNITED NATIONS. John C. Abbott. Routledge, Chapman & Hall, 29 West Thirty-fifth Street, New York, New York 10001. 1991.

POLITICS IN THE UNITED NATIONS SYSTEM. Lawrence S. Finkelstein. Duke University Press, Box 6697 College Station, Durham, North Carolina 27708. 1988.

THE PROCEDURE OF THE UN SECURITY COUNCIL. Second Edition. Sydney D. Bailey. Oxford University Press, 200 Madison Avenue, New York, New York 10016. 1988.

RALPH BUNCHE, THE MAN AND HIS TIMES. Benjamin Rivlin. Holmes and Meier Publishers, IUB Building, 30 Irving Place, New York, New York 10003. 1990.

THE REFORM OF THE UNITED NATIONS. Joachim W. Muller. Oceana Publications, 75 Main Street, Dobbs Ferry, New York 10522. 1992.

RESOLUTIONS OF THE UNITED NATIONS SECURITY COUNCIL. Renata Sonnenfeld. Martinus Nijhoff, Kluwer Academic Publishers, 101 Philip Drive, Assinippi Park, Norwell, Massachusetts 02061. 1988.

RETURN TO THE UN: UN DIPLOMACY IN REGIONAL CONFLICTS. G.R. Berridge. St. Martin's Press, 175 Fifth Avenue, New York, New York 10010. 1991.

THE RIGHT TO SELF DETERMINATION: HISTORICAL AND CURRENT DEVELOPMENT ON THE BASIS OF UNITED NATIONS INSTRUMENTS. United Nations, Sales Section, Publishing Division, Room DC2-0853, New York, New York 10017. 1983.

THE RISE OF ISRAEL: UNITED NATIONS DISCUSSIONS ON PALESTINE, 1947. Michael J. Cohen. Garland Publishing, Incorporated, 136 Madison Avenue, New York, New York 10016. 1987.

SHEATHING THE SWORD: THE UN SECRETARY-GENERAL AND THE PREVENTION OF INTERNATIONAL CONFLICT. Thomas E. Boudreau. Greenwood Publishing Group, Incorporated, 88 Post Road West, P.O. Box 5007, Westport, Connecticut 06881. 1991.

THE STRUCTURE OF THE UNITED NATIONS GENERAL ASSEMBLY: AN ORGANIZATIONAL APPROACH TO ITS WORK, 1974-1980S. Blanche Finley. Kraus International Publications, Route 100, Millwood, New York 10546. 1988.

THE STRUGGLE FOR STATEHOOD: FOCUS ON THE UNITED NATIONS. Aaron S. Klieman. Garland Publishing, Incorporated, 136 Madison Avenue, New York, New York 10016. 1991.

THE THIRD GENERATION WORLD ORGANIZATION. Maurice Bertrand. Martinus Nijhoff, Kluwer Academic Publishers, 101 Philip Drive, Assinippi Park, Norwell, Massachusetts 02061. 1989.

THE UNITED NATIONS. Harold and Geraldine Woods. Franklin Watts Company, Incorporated, 387 Park Avenue South, New York, New York 10016. 1985.

UNITED NATIONS ACTION IN THE FIELD OF HUMAN RIGHTS. United Nations, Sales Section, Publishing Division, Room DC2-0853, New York, New York 10017. 1989.

THE UNITED NATIONS AND A JUST WORLD ORDER. Richard A. Falk, Samuel S. Kim, and Saul H. Mendlovitz. Westview Press, Incorporated, 5500 Central Avenue, Boulder, Colorado 80301. 1991.

THE UNITED NATIONS AND HUMAN RIGHTS. Rowman-Allenheld, 420 Boston Way, Lanham, Maryland 20706. 1984.

THE UNITED NATIONS AND INTERNATIONAL BUSINESS. Sidney S. Dell. Duke University Press, Box 6697 College Station, Durham, North Carolina 27708. 1990.

THE UNITED NATIONS AND THE CONTROL OF INTERNATIONAL VIOLENCE: A LEGAL AND POLITICAL ANALYSIS. John F. Murphy. Manchester University Press, 175 Fifth Avenue, New York, New York 10010. 1983.

THE UNITED NATIONS AND THE MAINTENANCE OF INTERNATIONAL PEACE AND SECURITY. N. D. White. Manchester University Press. Distributed in the USA and Canada by St. Martin's Press, 175 Fifth Avenue, New York, New York 10010. 1990.

THE U. N. COMMISSION ON HUMAN RIGHTS. Howard Tolley, Jr. Westview Press, Incorporated, 5500 Central Avenue, Boulder, Colorado 80301. 1987.

UNITED NATIONS, DIVIDED WORLD: THE UN'S ROLES IN INTERNATIONAL RELATIONS. Adam Roberts and Benedict Kingsbury. Oxford University Press, 200 Madison Avenue, New York, New York 10016. 1988.

UNITED NATIONS GENERAL ASSEMBLY RESOLUTIONS IN OUR CHANGING WORLD. Blaine Sloan. Transnational Publishers, P.O. Box 7282, Ardsley-on-Hudson, New York 10503. 1991.

THE UNITED NATIONS IN THE WORLD POLITICAL ECONOMY: ESSAYS IN HONOUR OF LEON GORDENKER. David P. Forsythe. St. Martin's Press, 175 Fifth Avenue, New York, New York 10010. 1989.

THE UNITED NATIONS LAW MAKING: CULTURAL AND IDEOLOGICAL RELATIVISM AND INTERNATIONAL LAW MAKING FOR AN ERA OF TRANSITION. Edward McWhinney. Holmes and Meier Publishers, Incorporated, 30 Irving Place, IUB Building, New York, New York 10003. 1984.

THE UNITED NATIONS: REALITY AND IDEAL. Peter R. Bachr and Leon Gordenker. Praeger Publishers, One Madison Avenue, New York, New York 10010-3603. 1985.

THE UNITED NATIONS REBORN: CONFLICT CONTROL IN THE POST-COLD WAR WORLD. George L. Sherry. Council on Foreign Relations, 58 East Sixty-eighth Street, New York, New York 10021. 1990.

THE U.S., THE U.N. AND THE MANAGEMENT OF GLOBAL CHANGE. Toby T. Gati, Editor. New York University Press, Distributed by Columbia University Press, 562 West One-Hundred Thirteenth Street, New York, New York 10025. 1983.

ENCYCLOPEDIAS AND DICTIONARIES

THE ENCYCLOPEDIA OF THE UNITED NATIONS AND INTERNATIONAL RELATIONS. Second Edition. Edmund Jan Osmanczyk. Taylor and Francis, Incorporated, 1990 Frost Road, Suite 101, Bristol, Pennsylvania 19007. 1990.

UNITED NATIONS ORGANIZATION MULTILINGUAL GLOSSARY: ENGLISH, FRANCAIS, DEUTSCH-ITALIANO, ENGLISH-ARABIC. Angelo Miatello and Roberto Severino. Peter Lang Publishing, Incorporated, 62 West Forty-fifth Street, New York, New York 10036. 1988.

WORLDMARK ENCYCLOPEDIA OF THE NATIONS. Seventh Edition. John Wiley and Sons, Incorporated, 605 Third Avenue, New York, New York 10158. 1988.

DIGESTS, INDEXES, ABSTRACTS, CITATORS

INDEX TO PROCEEDINGS OF THE ECONOMIC AND SOCIAL COUNCIL. United Nations, Sales Section, Publishing Division, Room DC2-0853, New York, New York 10017. Annual.

INDEX TO PROCEEDINGS OF THE GENERAL ASSEMBLY. United Nations, Sales Section, Publishing Division, Room DC2-0853, New York, New York 10017. Annual.

INDEX TO PROCEEDINGS OF THE SECURITY COUNCIL. United Nations, Sales Section, Publishing Division, Room DC2-0853, New York, New York 10017. Annual.

INDEX TO PROCEEDINGS OF THE TRUSTEESHIP COUNCIL. United Nations, Sales Section, Publishing Division, Room DC2-0853, New York, New York 10017. Annual.

UNDOC: CURRENT INDEX (UNITED NATIONS DOCUMENTS INDEX). United Nations, Sales Section, Publishing Division, Room DC2-0853, New York, New York 10017. Ten Issues Per Year, Annual Cumulation.

UNITED NATIONS TREATY SERIES CUMULATIVE SUBJECT INDEXES. United Nations, Sales Section, Publishing Division, Room DC2-0853, New York, New York 10017. (Irregular).

ANNUALS AND SURVEYS

MULTILATERAL TREATIES DEPOSITED WITH THE SECRETARY-GENERAL. United Nations, Sales Section, Publishing Division, Room DC2-0853, New York, New York 10017. Annual.

UNITED NATIONS COMMISSION ON INTERNATIONAL TRADE LAW YEARBOOK. United Nations, Sales Section, Publishing Division, Room DC2-0853, New York, New York 10017. Annual.

UNITED NATIONS DISARMAMENT YEARBOOK. United Nations, Sales Section, Publishing Division, Room DC2-0853, New York, New York 10017. Annual.

UNITED NATIONS JURIDICIAL YEARBOOK. United Nations, Sales Section, Publishing Division, Room DC2-0853, New York, New York 10017. Irregular.

YEARBOOK OF THE INTERNATIONAL COURT OF JUSTICE. United Nations, Sales Section, Publishing Division, Room DC2-0853, New York, New York 10017. Annual.

YEARBOOK OF THE INTERNATIONAL LAW COMMISSION. United Nations, Sales Section, Publishing Division, Room DC2-0853, New York, New York 10017. Annual.

YEARBOOK OF THE UNITED NATIONS. United Nations, Sales Section, Publishing Division, Room DC2-0853, New York, New York 10017. Annual.

YEARBOOK ON HUMAN RIGHTS. United Nations, Sales Section, Publishing Division, Room DC2-0853, New York, New York 10017. Annual.

LAW REVIEWS AND PERIODICALS

CTC REPORTER. Centre on Transnational Corporations, United Nations, Sales Section, Publishing Division, Room DC2-0853, New York, New York 10017. Semiannual.

DISARMAMENT: A PERIODIC REVIEW BY THE UNITED NATIONS. United Nations, Sales Section, Publishing Division, Room DC2-0853, New York, New York 10017. Quarterly.

OBJECTIVE: JUSTICE. United Nations, Sales Section, Publishing Division, Room DC2-0853, New York, New York 10017. Semiannual.

UN CHRONICLE. United Nations, Sales Section, Publishing Division, Room DC2-0853, New York, New York 10017. Monthly.

NEWSLETTERS AND NEWSPAPERS

UNITED NATIONS LAW REPORTS. Walker and Company, 720 Fifth Avenue, New York, New York 10019. Monthly.

BIBLIOGRAPHIES

ACCIS GUIDE TO UNITED NATIONS INFORMATION SOURCES ON INTERNATIONAL TRADE AND DEVELOPMENT FINANCE. United Nations. Advisory Committee for the Coordination of Information Systems. United Nations Publishing Service, Room DC2-0853, New York, New York 10017. 1990.

BIBLIOGRAPHY OF THE INTERNATIONAL COURT OF JUSTICE. United Nations, Sales Section, Publishing Division, Room DC2-0853, New York, New York 10017. Annual.

CATALOGUE OF UNITED NATIONS PUBLICATIONS. United Nations, Sales Section, Publishing Division, Room DC2-0853, New York, New York 10017. Monthly and Annual.

CURRENT BIBLIOGRAPHIC INFORMATION. United Nations, Sales Section, Publishing Division, Room DC2-0853, New York, New York 10017. Monthly.

DIRECTORY OF UNITED NATIONS DOCUMENTARY AND ARCHIVAL SOURCES. Peter I. Hajnal. Kraus International Publications, Route 100, Millwood, New York 10546. 1991.

DIRECTORY OF UNITED NATIONS SYSTEM DATABASES ON NON-GOVERNMENTAL ORGANIZATIONS. United Nations. Advisory Committee for the Co-ordination of Information Systems. United Nations Publishing Service, Room DC2-0853, New York, New York 10017. 1988.

MONTHLY BIBLIOGRAPHY, PARTS I AND II. United Nations, Sales Section, Publishing Division, Room DC2-0853, New York, New York 10017. Monthly.

OFFICIAL RECORDS CATALOGUE. United Nations, Sales Section, Publishing Division, Room DC2-0853, New York, New York 10017. Irregular.

PEACE BY PIECES: UNITED NATIONS AGENCIES AND THEIR ROLES, A READER AND SELECTIVE BIBLIOGRAPHY. Robert N. Wells, Jr. Scarecrow Press, Incorporated, 52 Liberty Street, Box 4167, Metuchen, New Jersey 08840. 1991.

RESOLUTIONS AND STATEMENTS OF THE UNITED NATIONS SECURITY COUNCIL (1946-1989): A THEMATIC GUIDE. Karel C. Wellens. Martinus Nijhoff, Kluwer Academic Publishers, 101 Philip Drive, Assinippi Park, Norwell, Massachusetts 02061. 1990.

STRENGTHENING THE UNITED NATIONS: A BIBLIOGRAPHY ON U.N. REFORM AND WORLD FEDERALISM. Joseph Preston Baratta. Greenwood Publishing Group, Incorporated, 88 Post Road West, P.O. Box 5007, Westport, Connecticut 06881. 1987.

UNDOC: CURRENT INDEX (UNITED NATIONS DOCUMENTS INDEX). United Nations, Sales Section, Publishing Division, Room DC2-0853, New York, New York 10017. Ten Issues Per Year, Annual Cumulation.

UNITED NATIONS DOCUMENT SERIES SYMBOLS, 1978-1984. United Nations, Sales Section, Publishing Division, Room DC2-0853, New York, New York 10017. 1986.

DIRECTORIES

DIRECTORY OF UNITED NATIONS DATABASES AND INFORMATION SYSTEMS, 1990. Advisory Committee for the Co-ordination of Information Systems, United Nations, Sales Section, Publishing Division, Room DC2-0853, New York, New York 10017. 1990.

ASSOCIATIONS AND PROFESSIONAL SOCIETIES

AMERICAN FOREIGN LAW ASSOCIATION. Richard E. Lutringer, Whitman and Ransom, 200 Park Avenue, New York, New York 10166. (212) 351-3277.

BUSINESS COUNCIL FOR THE UNITED NATIONS. 60 East Forty-second Street, New York 10165. (212) 661-1772.

CAMPAIGN FOR UNITED NATIONS REFORM. 418 Seventh Street, Southeast, Washington, D.C. 20003. (202) 546-3956.

COMMUNICATIONS COORDINATION COMMITTEE FOR THE UNITED NATIONS. 301 East Forty-fifth Street, Suite 20B, New York, New York 10017. (212) 983-3353.

FRIENDS WORLD COMMITTEE FOR CONSULTATION. Sections of the Americas, 1506 Race Street, Philadelphia, Pennsylvania 19102. (215) 241-7250.

ORGANIZATION FOR INTERNATIONAL COOPERATION. 4 Winnipeg Court, Morganville, New Jersey 07751. (908) 536-5771.

PEOPLES' ASSEMBLY FOR THE UNITED NATIONS. The Delegate, 301 East Forty-fifth Street, Suite 20B, New York, New York 10017. (212) 983-3353.

UNESCO ASSOCIATION/U.S.A. 5815 Lawton Avenue, Oakland, California 94618. (510) 654-4638.

UNITED NATIONS ASSOCIATION OF THE UNITED STATES OF AMERICA. 485 Fifth Avenue, Second Floor, New York, New York 10017. (212) 697-3232.

RESEARCH CENTERS AND INSTITUTES

CENTER FOR UNITED NATIONS REFORM EDUCATION. 418 Seventh Street, Southwest, Washington, D.C. 20003. (202) 546-3956.

RALPH BUNCHE INSTITUTE ON THE UNITED NATIONS. City University of New York, 33 West Forty Second Street, New York, New York 10036. (212) 382-2114.

UNITED NATIONS INSTITUTE FOR TRAINING AND RESEARCH, 801 United Nations Plaza, New York, New York 10017. (212) 963-8621.

ONLINE DATABASES

ELECTRONIC INDEX TO UNITED NATIONS DOCUMENTS AND PUBLICATIONS. Readex, 58 Pine Street, New Canaan, Connecticut 06840.

UNITED NATIONS BIBLIOGRAPHIC INFORMATION SYSTEM (UNBIS). United Nations Headquarters, Dag Hammarskjold Library, United Nations Plaza, New York, New York 10017.

UNITED NATIONS COMMODITY TRADE STATISTICS. United Nations Statistical Office, Room DC2-1620, New York, New York 10017.

UNITED NATIONS REPORT. Newsnet Incorporated, 945 Haverford Road, Bryn Mawr, Pennsylvania 19010.

STATISTICS SOURCES

DIRECTORY OF INTERNATIONAL STATISTICS. United Nations, Sales Section, Publishing Division, Room DC2-0853, New York, New York 10017. 1982- .

MONTHLY BULLETIN OF STATISTICS. United Nations, Sales Section, Publishing Division, Room DC2-0853, New York, New York 10017. Monthly.

UNITED NATIONS IN BRIEF. United Nations, Sales Section, Publishing Division, Room DC2-0853, New York, New York 10017. Annual.

UNITED NATIONS STATISTICAL YEARBOOK. United Nations, Sales Section, Publishing Division, Room DC2-0853, New York, New York 10017. Annual.

OTHER SOURCES

UNIPUB. 4611-F Assembly Drive, Lanham, Maryland 20706-4391. (Private commercial publisher of United Nations publications.)

UNITED STATES GOVERNMENT
See: ATTORNEY-GENERAL (UNITED STATES); CIRCUIT COURTS OF APPEAL (UNITED STATES); DISTRICT COURTS (UNITED STATES); FEDERAL COURTS; PRESIDENT (UNITED STATES); SUPREME COURT (UNITED STATES)

UNIVERSITIES
See: EDUCATION; SCHOOL INTEGRATION; SCHOOL VIOLENCE AND DISCIPLINE

UNJUST ENRICHMENT
See: RESTITUTION

UNMARRIED COUPLES
See: COHABITATION

URBAN RENEWAL
See: HISTORIC PRESERVATION; LOCAL GOVERNMENT; ZONING AND PLANNING

USURY
See: BANKS AND BANKING

V

VEHICLES
See: MOTOR VEHICLES

VENUE
See: CIVIL PROCEDURE; TRIAL PRACTICE

VERDICTS
See: JURY

VETERANS
See also: DEFENSE DEPARTMENT; MILITARY LAW AND SERVICE

STATUTES, CODES, STANDARDS, UNIFORM LAWS

UNIFORM VETERANS' GUARDIANSHIP ACT. Uniform Laws Annotated. West Publishing Company, P.O. Box 64526, 50 West Kellogg Boulevard, St. Paul, Minnesota 55164-0526. 1976. (Annual Supplements).

HANDBOOKS, MANUALS, FORMBOOKS

A GUIDE TO VETERANS AFFAIRS LAW AND PRACTICE. Louis D. Coffelt and Janet G. Crews. Dewey Publications, Incorporated, P.O. Box 3423, Arlington, Virginia 22203. 1990.

MILITARY DISCHARGE UPGRADING, AND INTRODUCTION TO VETERANS ADMINISTRATION LAW: A PRACTICE MANUAL. David F. Addlestone, National Veterans Law Center, Washington College of Law. Veterans Education Project, P.O. Box 42130, Washington, D.C. 20015. 1982- .

TEXTBOOKS AND GENERAL WORKS

DEFENDING THE VIETNAM COMBAT VETERAN: RECOGNITION AND REPRESENTATION OF THE MILITARY HISTORY AND BACKGROUND OF THE COMBAT VETERAN LEGAL CLIENT. Barry Levin and David O. Ferrier. Vietnam Veterans Legal Assistance Project, Los Angeles, California. 1989.

FIGHTING BACK: LESBIAN AND GAY DRAFT, MILITARY AND VETERANS ISSUES. Midwest Committee for Military Counseling, National Lawyers Guild, 55 Sixth Avenue, New York, New York 10013. 1984.

FORGING LEGISLATION: THE POLITICS OF VETERANS REFORM. Paul C. Light. W. W. Norton and Company, Incorporated, 500 Fifth Avenue, New York, New York 10110. 1992.

HISTORY OF HOUSE COMMITTEES CONSIDERING VETERANS' LEGISLATION. Superintendent of Documents, United States Government Printing Office, Washington, D.C. 20402. 1990.

MILITARY RETIREMENT: THE ADMINISTRATION'S PLAN AND RELATED PROPOSALS. American Enterprise Institute for Public Policy Research, 1150 17th Street, Northwest, Washington, D.C. 20036 1980.

THE RIGHTS OF VETERANS: THE BASIC ACLU GUIDE TO A VETERAN'S RIGHTS. David F. Addlestone, Susan Hewman and Fredric Gross. Avon Books, 105 Madison Avenue, New York, New York 10016. 1978.

VIETNAM WAR ALMANAC. Harry G. Summers. Facts on File, Incorporated, 460 Park Avenue, South, New York, New York 10016. 1987.

WAR AND PEACE--LEGAL ISSUES FACING VETERANS OF DESERT STORM. Richard H. Sadowski. Massachusetts Continuing Legal Education, 20 West Street, Boston, Massachusetts 02111. 1991.

LAW REVIEWS AND PERIODICALS

DAV MAGAZINE. Disabled American Veterans, P.O. Box 14301, Cincinnati, Ohio 45250.

VVA VETERAN. 2001 S Street, Northwest, Suite 700, Washington, D.C. 20009. Monthly.

NEWSLETTERS AND NEWSPAPERS

V. A. DISABILITY REPORTER. Seak, Incorporated, P.O. Box 590, Falmouth, Massachusetts 02541. Monthly.

THE VETERAN. Vietnam Veterans Against the War, P.O. Box 408594, Chicago, Illinois 60640. Bimonthly.

THE VETERANS ADVOCATE. National Veterans Legal Services Project, 2001 S Street, Northwest, Suite 610, Washington, D.C. 20009. Quarterly.

VETERANS' LAW REPORTER. Veterans Education Project, Incorporated, P.O. Box 42130, Washington, D.C. 20015.

VETERANS RIGHTS NEWSLETTER. Veterans Education Project, P.O. Box 42130, Washington, D.C. 20015. Monthly.

BIBLIOGRAPHIES

AGENT ORANGE AND VIETNAM: AN ANNOTATED BIBLIOGRAPHY. Caroline D. Harnly. Scarecrow Press, Incorporated, 52 Liberty Street, Box 4167, Metuchen, New Jersey 08840. 1988.

DIRECTORIES

DIRECTORY OF FEDERAL AID FOR VETERANS. Ready Reference Press, P.O. Box 5249, Santa Monica, California 90405. 1982.

DIRECTORY OF VETERANS ADMINISTRATION FACILITIES, NUMBER AND TYPE. Veterans Administration, Office of Reports and Statistics, Reporting Policy and Review Service, Washington, D.C. 20420. Annual.

DIRECTORY OF VETERANS ORGANIZATIONS. Office of the Administrator, Veterans Service Organization Coordination, Veterans Administration, 810 Vermont Avenue, Northwest, Room 1018, Washington, D.C. 20420. 1984.

FEDERAL BENEFITS FOR VETERANS AND THEIR DEPENDANTS. Veterans Administration, Superintendent of Documents, United States Government Printing Office, Washington, D.C. 20402. Annual.

HOW TO LOCATE ANYONE WHO IS OR HAS BEEN IN THE MILITARY: ARMED FORCES LOCATOR DIRECTORY. Richard S. Johnson. Military Information Enterprises, Houston, Texas. 1988.

ASSOCIATIONS AND PROFESSIONAL SOCIETIES

COMBINED NATIONAL VETERANS ASSOCIATION OF AMERICA. 5413-C Backlick Road, Springfield, Virginia 22151. (703) 354-2140.

DISABLED AMERICAN VETERANS. P.O. Box 14301, Cincinnati, Ohio, 45250. (606) 441-7300.

NATIONAL ASSOCIATION OF STATE APPROVING AGENCIES. National Association of Veterans Program Administrators. c/o Metropolitan State College, 1006 Eleventh Street, Campus Box 16, Denver, Colorado 80204. (303) 556-2993.

NATIONAL ASSOCIATION OF STATE DIRECTORS OF VETERANS AFFAIRS. 941 North Capitol Street, Northeast, Room 1211F, Washington, D.C. 20421. (202) 737-5050.

NATIONAL ASSOCIATION OF VETERANS PROGRAM ADMINISTRATORS. c/o Metropolitan State College, 1006 Eleventh Street, Campus Box 16, Denver, Colorado 80204. (303) 556-2993.

NATIONAL VETERANS LEGAL SERVICES PROJECT. 2001 S Street, Northwest, Suite 610, Washington, D.C. 20009. (202) 265-8305.

REGULAR VETERANS ASSOCIATION OF THE UNITED STATES. RVA Building 219, 2470 Cardinal Loop, Del Valle, Texas 78617. (512) 389-2288.

VETERANS EDUCATION PROJECT. P.O. Box 42130, Washington, D.C. 20015. (202) 547-8387.

VIETNAM VETERANS AGAINST THE WAR. P.O. Box 408594, Chicago, Illinois 60640. (312) 761-8248.

VIETNAM VETERANS OF AMERICA. 2001 S Street, Northeast, Suite 700, Washington, D.C. 20009. (202) 332-2700.

RESEARCH CENTERS, INSTITUTES, CLEARINGHOUSES

WILLIAM JOINER CENTER FOR THE STUDY OF WAR AND SOCIAL CONSEQUENCES. University of Massachusetts at Boston, Wheatley Hall, Fourth Floor, Harbor Campus, Boston, Massachusetts 02125. (617) 287-5850.

ONLINE DATABASES

COMBINED HEALTH INFORMATION DATABASE. United States National Institutes of Health, P.O. Box NDIC, Bethesda, Maryland 20892.

MILITARY FORUM. 1041 Cavnation Drive, Rockville, Maryland 20850.

VA PATIENT EDUCATION DATABASE. United States Department of Veterans Affairs, VA Patient Health Education Clearinghouse, 810 Vermont Avenue, Northwest, Washington, D.C. 20420.

STATISTICS SOURCES

ANNUAL REPORT OF ADMINISTRATOR OF VETERANS AFFAIRS. United States Veterans Administration, 810 Vermont Avenue, Northwest, Washington, D.C. 20420.

VETERANS ADMINISTRATION FACT SHEETS. United States Veterans Administration, 810 Vermont Avenue, Northwest, Washington, D.C. 20420. Irregular.

VETERINARIANS

STATUTES, CODES, STANDARDS, UNIFORM LAWS

PREAMBLE COMPILATION: ANIMAL DRUGS, FEEDS, AND RELATED PRODUCTS, MARCH 1936-MARCH 1978. United States Food and Drug Administration. Superintendent of Documents, United States Government Printing Office, Washington, D.C. 20402. 1981.

TEXTBOOKS AND GENERAL WORKS

LEGAL BRIEFS FROM THE JOURNAL OF THE AMERICAN VETERINARY MEDICAL ASSOCIATION. Harold W. Hannah. American Veterinary Medical Association, 930 North Meacham Road, Shaumburg, Illinois 60196. 1986.

VETERINARY ETHICS. Jerrold Tannenbaum. Williams and Wilkins, 428 East Preston, Baltimore, Maryland 21202. 1989.

VETERINARY MEDICINE AND THE LAW. Orland A. Soave and Lester M. Crawford. Williams and Wilkins, 428 East Preston, Baltimore, Maryland 21202. 1981.

BIBLIOGRAPHIES

VETERINARY LAW AND MALPRACTICE: A BIBLIOGRAPHY. Tim J. Watts. Vance Bibliographies, P.O. Box 229, 112 North Charter Street, Monticello, Illinois 61856. 1989.

VICARIOUS LIABILITY
See: AGENCY

VICTIMS OF CRIME
See: CRIME VICTIMS

VIDEOGAMES
See: ENTERTAINMENT LAW

VIDEOTAPE
See: TELEVISION AND RADIO

VOTING
See: ELECTION LAW

W

WAGES
See: LABOR AND LABOR RELATIONS

WAR AND WAR CRIMES
See: INTERNATIONAL LAW AND RELATIONS; MILITARY LAW AND SERVICE

WARD
See: GUARDIAN AND WARD

WATER LAW
See also: ADMIRALTY; ENVIRONMENTAL LAW; ENVIRONMENTAL PROTECTION AGENCY; LAW OF THE SEA

STATUTES, CODES, STANDARDS, UNIFORM LAWS

COMPILATION OF SELECTED WATER RESOURCES AND WATER POLLUTION CONTROL LAWS: FEDERAL WATER POLLUTION CONTROL ACT. Committee on Public Works and Transportation. Superintendent of Documents, United States Government Printing Office, Washington, D.C. 20402. 1989.

FEDERAL RECLAMATION AND RELATED LAWS ANNOTATED: RECLAMATION REFORM ACT COMPILATION, 1982-1988. Paul B. Smyth. United States Department of Interior, Office of the Solicitor, Bureau of Reclamation, Washington, D.C. 1988.

A LEGISLATIVE HISTORY OF THE WATER QUALITY ACT OF 1987 (PUBLIC LAW 100-4). Library of Congress, Environment and Natural Resources Policy Division. Superintendent of Documents, United States Government Printing Office, Washington, D.C. 20402. 1988.

HANDBOOKS, MANUALS, FORMBOOKS

CLEAN WATER DESKBOOK. Environmental Law Reporter. Environmental Law Institute, 1616 P Street, Northwest, Suite 200, Washington, D.C. 20036. 1988.

CLEAN WATER HANDBOOK BY PATTON, BOGGS AND BLOW. J. Gordon Arbuckle and Russell V. Randle, editors. Government Institutes, Incorporated, 966 Hungerford Drive, Rockville, Maryland 20850. 1990.

RESERVED WATER RIGHTS SETTLEMENT MANUAL. Peter W. Sly. Island Press, 1718 Connecticut Avenue, Northwest, Suite 300, Washington, D.C. 20009. 1988.

TEXTBOOKS AND GENERAL WORKS

AMERICAN INDIAN WATER RIGHTS AND THE LIMITS OF LAW. Lloyd Burton. University Press of Kansas, 329 Carruth, Lawrence, Kansas 66045. 1991.

THE BOUNDARY WATERS CANOE AREA: WILDERNESS VALUES AND MOTORIZED RECREATION. James N. Gladden. Iowa State University Press, 2121 South State Avenue, Ames, Iowa 50010. 1990.

CANADA'S ARCTIC WATERS IN INTERNATIONAL LAW. Donat Pharand. Cambridge University Press, 40 West Twentieth Street, New York, New York 10011. 1988.

CLEAN WATER ACT: AS AMENDED BY THE WATER QUALITY ACT OF 1987. Michael A. Brown. Practising Law Institute, 810 Seventh Avenue, New York, New York 10019. 1987.

COMMAND OF THE WATERS: IRON TRIANGLES, FEDERAL WATER DEVELOPMENT, AND INDIAN WATER. Daniel McCool. University of California Press, 2120 Berkeley Way, Berkeley, California 94720. 1987.

THE CONSTITUTION, PROPERTY RIGHTS, AND THE FUTURE OF WATER LAW. Joseph L. Sax. University of Colorado School of Law, Natural Resources Law Center, Boulder, Colorado 80309. 1990.

CONTROLLING WATER USE: THE UNFINISHED BUSINESS OF WATER QUALITY PROTECTION. David H. Getches, Lawrence J. MacDonnell, and Teresa A. Rice. University of Colorado School of Law, Natural Resources Law Center, Boulder, Colorado 80309. 1991.

DISPUTED WATERS: NATIVE AMERICANS AND THE GREAT LAKES FISHERY. Robert Doherty. University Press of Kentucky, 663 South Limestone Street, Lexington, Kentucky 40506-0336. 1990.

ENGINEERING ASPECTS OF WATER LAW. Leonard Rice and Michael D. White. John Wiley and Sons, Incorporated, 605 Third Avenue, New York, New York 10158. 1987.

FORGING NEW RIGHTS IN WESTERN WATERS. Robert G. Dunbar. University of Nebraska Press, 901 North Seventeenth Street, Lincoln, Nebraska 68588-0520. 1983.

FUNDING WASTEWATER TREATMENT FACILITIES: THE COMPLETE GUIDE TO THE NEW STATE REVOLVING FUND PROGRAM. Beth L. Starr. Bureau of National Affairs, Incorporated, 1231 Twenty-fifth Street, Northwest, Washington, D.C. 20037. 1988.

GROUNDWATER: STRATEGIES FOR STATE ACTION. Timothy R. Henderson, Jeffrey Trauberman and Tara Gallagher. Environmental Law Institute, 1616 P Street, Northwest, Suite 200, Washington, D.C. 20036. 1984.

INTERNATIONAL MARITIME BOUNDARIES. Jonathan I. Charney and Lewis M. Alexander. Martinus Nijhoff, Kluwer Academic Publishers, 101 Philip Drive, Assinippi Park, Norwell, Massachusetts 02061. 1991.

LEASING INDIAN WATER: CHOICES IN THE COLORADO RIVER BASIN. Gary Weatherford, Mary Wallace, and Lee Herold Storey. Conservation Foundation, 1250 Twenty-fourth Street, Northwest, Washington, D.C. 20037. 1988.

LEGAL CONTROL OF WATER RESOURCES: CASES AND MATERIALS. Second Edition. Joseph L. Sax, Robert H. Abrams, and Barton H. Thompson, Jr. West Publishing Company, 50 West Kellogg Boulevard, St. Paul, Minnesota 55164-0526. 1991.

THE LEGAL DETERMINATION OF INTERNATIONAL MARITIME BOUNDARIES: THE PROGRESSIVE DEVELOPMENT OF CONTINENTAL SHELF, EFZ, AND EEZ LAW. Gerard J. Tanja. Kluwer Law Book Publishers, Incorporated, 36 West Forty-fourth Street, New York, New York 10036. 1990.

MANAGING TROUBLED WATERS: THE ROLE OF MARINE ENVIRONMENTAL MONITORING. National Research Council (U.S.) Committee on a Systems Assessment of Marine Environmental Monitoring. National Academy Press, 2101 Constitution Avenue, Northwest, P.O. Box 285, Washington, D.C. 20055. 1990.

MARKETS FOR FEDERAL WATER: SUBSIDIES, PROPERTY RIGHTS, AND THE BUREAU OF RECLAMATION. Richard W. Wahl. Resources for the Future. Distributed by Johns Hopkins University Press, 701 West Fortieth Street, Baltimore, Maryland 21211. 1989.

MEDITERRANEAN CONTINENTAL SHELF: DELIMITATIONS AND REGIMES, INTERNATIONAL AND LEGAL SOURCES. Umberto Leanza, Luigi Sico, and Maria Clelia Ciciriello. Oceana Publications, 75 Main Street, Dobbs Ferry, New York 10522. 1988.

NATURE INCORPORATED: INDUSTRIALIZATION AND THE WATERS OF NEW ENGLAND. Theodore Steinberg. Cambridge University Press, 40 West Twentieth Street, New York, New York 10011. 1991.

RIGHTS TO OCEANIC RESOURCES: DECIDING AND DRAWING MARITIME BOUNDARIES. Dorinda G. Dallmeyer and Louis DeVorsey, Jr. Martinus Nijhoff, Kluwer Academic Publishers, 101 Philip Drive, Assinippi Park, Norwell, Massachusetts 02061. 1989.

STRAIGHT BASELINES IN INTERNATIONAL MARITIME BOUNDARY DELIMITATION. W. Michael Reisman and Gayl S. Westerman. St. Martin's Press, 175 Fifth Avenue, New York, New York 10010. 1992.

STRAITS USED FOR INTERNATIONAL NAVIGATION: A SPANISH PERSPECTIVE. Jose A. de Yturriaga. Martinus Nijhoff, Kluwer Academic Publishers, 101 Philip Drive, Assinippi Park, Norwell, Massachusetts 02061. 1991.

TRADING WATER: AN ECONOMIC AND LEGAL FRAMEWORK FOR WATER MARKETING. Rodney T. Smith. Council of State Policy and Planning Association, Washington, D.C. 1988.

VIRGINIA TIDAL AND COASTAL LAW. Lynda Lee Butler and Margit Livingston. Michie Company, P.O. Box 7587, Charlottesville, Virginia 22906. 1988.

WATER AND THE AMERICAN WEST: ESSAYS IN HONOR OF RAPHAEL J. MOSES. David H. Getches. University of Colorado School of Law, Natural Resources Law Center, Boulder, Colorado 80309. 1988.

WATER AND THE FUTURE OF THE SOUTHWEST. Zachary A. Smith. University of New Mexico Press, 1720 Lomas Boulevard, Northeast, Albuquerque, New Mexico 87131. 1989.

WATER BOUNDARIES. George M. Cole. Landmark Enterprises, 10324 Newtown Way, Rancho Cordora, California 95670. 1984.

WATER CRISIS: ENDING THE POLICY DROUGHT. Terry L. Anderson. Johns Hopkins University Press, 701 West Fortieth Street, Suite 275, Baltimore, Maryland 21211-2190. 1983.

WATER LAW. Second Edition. William Goldfarb. John Wiley and Sons, Incorporated, 605 Third Avenue, New York, New York 10158. 1988.

WATER LAW IN A NUTSHELL. Third Edition. David H. Getches. West Publishing Company, P.O. Box 64526, 50 West Kellogg Boulevard, St. Paul, Minnesota 55164-0526. 1990.

WATER LAW IN HISTORICAL PERSPECTIVE. Ludwick A. Teclaff. W. S. Hein and Company, Incorporated, 1285 Main Street, Buffalo, New York 14209. 1985.

WATER RESOURCES, GEOGRAPHY AND LAW. Olen P. Matthews. Association of American Geographers, 1710 Sixteenth Street, Northwest, Washington, D.C. 20009-3198. 1984.

WATER RESOURCES MANAGEMENT: A CASEBOOK IN LAW AND PUBLIC POLICY. Charles J. Meyers. Foundation Press, 615 Merrick Avenue, Westbury, New York 11590. 1988.

WATER RESOURCES PLANNING. Andrew A. Dzurik. Rowman and Littlefield Publishers, Incorporated, 8705 Bollman Place, Savage, Maryland 20763. 1988.

WATER RIGHTS OF THE FIFTY STATES AND TERRITORIES. Kenneth R. Wright. American Water Works Association, 6666 West Quincy Avenue, Denver, Colorado 80235. 1990.

WATER RIGHTS: SCARCE RESOURCE ALLOCATION, BUREAUCRACY, AND THE ENVIRONMENT. Terry L. Anderson, Editor. Pacific Institute for Public Policy Research. Ballinger Publishing Company, Subsidiary of HarperCollins Publishers, 10 East Fifty-third Street, New York, New York 10022. 1983.

Encyclopedia of Legal Information Sources • 2nd Ed.   WILDLIFE

WATERS AND WATER RIGHTS: A TREATISE ON THE LAW OF WATERS AND ALLIED PROBLEMS: EASTERN, WESTERN, FEDERAL. Second Edition. Robert Emmet Clark, Editor. Allen Smith Company, Incorporated, 1435 North Meridian Street, Indianapolis, Indiana 46202. 1984. (Supplement 1985).

WESTERN TIMES AND WATER WARS: STATE, CULTURE, AND REBELLION IN CALIFORNIA. John Walton. University of California Press, 2120 Berkeley Way, Berkeley, California 94720. 1991.

DIGESTS, INDEXES, ABSTRACTS, CITATORS

SHEPARD'S FEDERAL ENERGY LAW CITATIONS. Shepard's/McGraw-Hill, P.O. Box 1235, Colorado Springs, Colorado 80901. 1982- .

LAW REVIEWS AND PERIODICALS

LAND AND WATER LAW REVIEW. University of Wyoming, College of Law, P.O. Box 3035, University Station, Laramie, Wyoming 82071. Semiannual.

LAW OF WATER RIGHTS AND RESOURCES. A. Dan Tarlock. Clark Boardman Company, Limited, 435 Hudson Street, New York, New York 10014. 1988- .

NEWSLETTERS AND NEWSPAPERS

FROM THE STATE CAPITALS: WATER SUPPLY. Wakeman, Walworth, Incorporated, 300 North Washington Street, Suite 204, Alexandria, Virginia 22314. Monthly.

WATER LAW NEWSLETTER. Rocky Mountain Mineral Law Foundation, 7039 East Eighteenth Avenue, Denver, Colorado 80220. Quarterly.

WATER NEWSLETTER. Water Information Center, Incorporated. 6800 Jericho Turnpike, Syosset, New York 11791. Semimonthly.

WATER RESOURCES REPORT. RPC Publications, Incorporated, 3200 Red River, Suite 302, Austin, Texas 78705. Semimonthly.

BIBLIOGRAPHIES

WATER LAW BIBLIOGRAPHY. SUPPLEMENT 4, 1978-1985: SOURCE BOOK ON U.S. WATER AND IRRIGATION STUDIES: LEGAL, ECONOMIC, AND POLITICAL. John E. Christensen, Deann E. Hupe, and Myron J. Jacobstein. Jefferson Lawbook Company, 1511 K Street, Northwest, Suite 635, Washington, D.C. 20005. 1987.

WATER RIGHTS IN THE UNITED STATES: A BIBLIOGRAPHY ARTICLES. Joseph J. Galin. Vance Bibliographies, P.O. Box 229, 112 North Charter Street, Monticello, Illinois 61856. 1986.

ASSOCIATIONS AND PROFESSIONAL SOCIETIES

INTERNATIONAL ASSOCIATION FOR WATER LAW. Via Montevideo 5, I-00198 Rome, Italy. (6) 8441247.

INTERSTATE CONFERENCE ON WATER PROBLEMS. 955 L'Enfant Plaza Square, Southwest, Washington, D.C. 20002. (202) 466-7287.

RESEARCH CENTERS, INSTITUTES, CLEARINGHOUSES

NORTHERN LIGHTS INSTITUTE. 210 North Higgins, Suite 328, Missoula, Montana 59802. (406) 721-7415.

ONLINE DATABASES

WATER RESOURCES ABSTRACTS. United States Department of the Interior, Geological Survey, Water Resources Scientific Information Center, 425 National Center, Reston, Virginia 22902.

WATERNET. American Water Works Association, Technical Library, 6666 West Quincy Avenue, Denver, Colorado 80235.

WEAPONS
See: CRIMINAL LAW; FIREARMS

WELFARE
See: INDIGENCE

WHITE COLLAR CRIME
See: BUSINESS CRIME

WIFE ABUSE
See: FAMILY VIOLENCE

WILDLIFE
See also: FISH AND FISHING; INTERIOR DEPARTMENT

STATUTES, CODES, STANDARDS, UNIFORM LAWS

ENDANGERED SPECIES ACT OF 1973, AS AMENDED THROUGH THE 100TH CONGRESS, DECEMBER 15, 1988. Superintendent of Documents, United States Government Printing Office, Washington, D.C. 20402. 1988.

HANDBOOKS, MANUALS, FORMBOOKS

CONTROLLED WILDLIFE: A THREE VOLUME GUIDE TO U.S. WILDLIFE LAWS AND PERMIT PROCEDURES. Carol Estes and Keith W. Sessions, Editors. Association of Systematics Collections, Museum of Natural History, University of Kansas, 602 Dyche Hall, Lawrence, Kansas 66045-2454. 1984.

THE ENDANGERED SPECIES ACT: A GUIDE TO ITS PROTECTION AND IMPLEMENTATION. Daniel J. Rohlf. Stanford Environmental Law Society, Stanford Law School, Stanford, California 94305. 1989.

TEXTBOOKS AND GENERAL WORKS

AMERICAN WILDLIFE LAW. Thomas A. Lund. University of California Press, 2120 Berkeley Way, Berkeley, California 94720. 1980.

BALANCING ON THE BRINK OF EXTINCTION: THE ENDANGERED SPECIES ACT AND LESSONS FOR THE FUTURE. Kathryn A. Kohm. Island Press, 1718 Connecticut Avenue, Northwest, Suite 300, Washington, D.C. 20009. 1991.

THE EVOLUTION OF NATIONAL WILDLIFE LAW. Revised Edition. Michael J. Beau. Praeger Publishers, One Madison Avenue, New York, New York 10010-3603. 1983.

FAIR GAME: THE LAW OF COUNTRY SPORTS AND THE PROTECTION OF WILDLIFE. Charlie Parkes and John Thornley. Pelham Books Limited, 27 Wright's Lane, London W8 5TZ, England. 1987.

INTERNATIONAL TRADE IN ENDANGERED SPECIES: A GUIDE TO CITES. David S. Favre. Martinus Nijhoff, Kluwer Academic Publishers, 101 Philip Drive, Assinippi Park, Norwell, Massachusetts 02061. 1989.

INTERNATIONAL WILDLIFE LAW: AN ANALYSIS OF INTERNATIONAL TREATIES CONCERNED WITH THE CONSERVATION OF WILDLIFE. Simon Lyster. Grotius Publications Limited, Llandysul, Dyfed SA44 4BQ, United Kingdom. 1985.

INTERNATIONAL WILDLIFE TRADE: WHOSE BUSINESS IS IT? Sarah Fitzgerald. World Wildlife Fund, 1250 Twenty-fourth Street, Northwest, Washington, D.C. 20037. 1989.

PROHIBITIVE POLICY: IMPLEMENTING THE FEDERAL ENDANGERED SPECIES ACT. Steven Lewis Yaffee. MIT Press, 55 Hayward Street, Cambridge, Massachusetts 02142. 1982.

RECONCILING CONFLICTS UNDER THE ENDANGERED SPECIES ACT: THE HABITAT CONSERVATION PLANNING EXPERIENCE. Michael J. Bean, Sarah G. Fitzgerald, and Michael A. O'Connell. World Wildlife Fund, 1250 Twenty-fourth Street, Northwest, Washington, D.C. 20037. 1991.

SAVING AMERICA'S WILDLIFE. Thomas R. Dunlap. Princeton University Press, 41 William Street, Princeton, New Jersey 08540. 1988.

WILDLIFE: CASES, LAW AND POLICY. David S. Favre. Associated Faculty Press, 19 West Thirty-sixth Street, New York, New York 10018. 1983.

BIBLIOGRAPHIES

GAME PROTECTION: MONOGRAPHS. Mary A. Vance. Vance Bibliographies, P.O. Box 229, 112 North Charter Street, Monticello, Illinois 61856. 1984.

DIRECTORIES

CONSERVATION DIRECTORY. National Wildlife Federation. 1412 Sixteenth Street, Northwest, Washington, D.C. 20036. Annual.

LAW REVIEWS AND PERIODICALS

CONSERVATION. National Wildlife Federation, 1412 Sixteenth Street, Northwest, Washington, D.C. 20036. Bi-weekly.

NEWSLETTERS AND NEWSPAPERS

FROM THE STATE CAPITALS--FISH AND GAME REGULATION. Wakeman, Walworth, Incorporated, P.O. Box 1939, New Haven, Connecticut 06509. Monthly.

ASSOCIATIONS AND PROFESSIONAL SOCIETIES

DEFENDERS OF WILDLIFE. 1244 Nineteenth Street, Northwest, Washington, D.C. 20036. (202) 659-9510.

INTERNATIONAL ASSOCIATION OF FISH AND WILDLIFE AGENCIES. 444 North Capitol Street, Northwest, Suite 534, Washington, D.C. 20001. (202) 624-7890.

INTERNATIONAL WILDLIFE COALITION. 634 North Falmouth Highway, P.O. Box 388, North Falmouth, Massachusetts 02556. (508) 564-9980.

NATIONAL AUDUBON SOCIETY. 950 Third Avenue, New York, New York 10022. (212) 832-3200.

NATIONAL WILDLIFE FEDERATION. 1400 Sixteenth Street, Northwest, Washington, D.C. 20036. (202) 797-6800.

WILDLIFE CONSERVATION FUND OF AMERICA, Legal Defense, Public Information and Research Section of the Wildlife Legislative Fund of America, 50 West Broad Street, Columbus, Ohio 43215. (614) 221-2684.

WILDLIFE PRESERVATION TRUST INTERNATIONAL. Thirty-fourth Street and Girard Avenue, Philadelphia, Pennsylvania 19104. (215) 222-3636.

THE WILDLIFE SOCIETY. 5410 Grosvenor Lane, Bethesda, Maryland 20814. (301) 897-9770.

WORLD WILDLIFE FUND. 1250 Twenty-fourth Street, Northwest, Washington, D.C. 20037. (202) 293-4800.

RESEARCH CENTERS, INSTITUTES, CLEARINGHOUSES

INSTITUTE FOR WILDLIFE RESEARCH. c/o National Wildlife Federation, 1400 Sixteenth Street, Northwest, Washington, D.C. 20036. (703) 790-4267.

NATIONAL INSTITUTE FOR URBAN WILDLIFE. 10921 Trotting Ridge Way, Columbia, Maryland 21044. (301) 596-3311.

WILDLIFE INFORMATION CENTER. 629 Green Street, Allentown, Pennsylvania 18102. (215) 434-1637.

WILDLIFE MANAGEMENT INSTITUTE. 1101 Fourteenth Street, Northwest, Suite 725, Washington, D.C. 20005. (202) 371-1808.

ONLINE DATABASES

ENVIRONMENTAL FORUM. Dana M. Armitage. 3 Paradise Street, Willimantic, Connecticut 06226.

FISHARD WILDLIFE REFERENCE SERVICE DATABASE. United States Fish and Wildlife Service, The Maxima Corporation, 5430 Grosvenor Lane, Suite 110, Bethesda, Maryland 20814.

WILDLIFE DATA BASE. Julie Moore and Associates, 9956 North Highway 85, Los Cruces, New Mexico 88005.

WILLS, TRUSTS AND INHERITANCE
See also: ESTATE, INHERITANCE AND TRANSFER TAXES

STATUTES, CODES, STANDARDS, UNIFORM LAWS

A COMPENDIUM OF STATE STATUTES AND INTERNATIONAL TREATIES IN TRUST AND ESTATE LAW: REFERENCE AND REFERRAL GUIDE FOR PRACTICING ATTORNEYS. Quorum Books, Imprint of Greenwood Publishing Group, Incorporated, 88 Post Road West, P.O. Box 5007, Westport, Connecticut 06881. 1985.

FEDERAL ESTATE AND GIFT TAXES: CODE AND REGULATIONS AS OF APRIL 1, 1988. Commerce Clearing House, Incorporated, 4025 West Peterson Avenue, Chicago, Illinois 60646. 1988.

MODEL SURVIVAL AND DEATH ACT. Uniform Laws Annotated, West Publishing Company, P.O. Box 64526, 50 West Kellogg Boulevard, St. Paul, Minnesota 55164-0526. 1976 (Annual Supplements).

SELECTED STATUTES ON TRUSTS AND ESTATES. John H. Langbein and Lawrence W. Waggoner. Foundation Press, 615 Merrick Avenue, Westbury, New York 11590. 1989.

UNIFORM COMMON TRUST FUND ACT. Uniform Laws Annotated, West Publishing Company, P.O. Box 64526, 50 West Kellogg Boulevard, St. Paul, Minnesota 55164-0526. 1976 (Annual Supplements).

UNIFORM COMMON TRUST FUND ACT. Martindale-Hubbell Law Directory, Volume Eight. Martindale-Hubbell, Incorporated, 121 Chanlon Road, New Providence, New Jersey 07974. Annual.

UNIFORM DISCLAIMER OF TRANSFERS BY WILL, INTESTACY, OR APPOINTMENT ACT. Uniform Laws Annotated, West Publishing Company, P.O. Box 64526, 50 West Kellogg Boulevard, St. Paul, Minnesota 55164-0526. 1976 (Annual Supplements).

UNIFORM DISPOSITION OF COMMUNITY PROPERTY RIGHTS AT DEATH ACT. Uniform Laws Annotated, West Publishing Company, P.O. Box 64526, 50 West Kellogg Boulevard, St. Paul, Minnesota 55164-0526. 1976 (Annual Supplements).

UNIFORM MANAGEMENT OF INSTITUTIONAL FUNDS ACT. Uniform Laws Annotated, West Publishing Company, P.O. Box 64526, 50 West Kellogg Boulevard, St. Paul, Minnesota 55164-0526. 1976 (Annual Supplements).

UNIFORM MANAGEMENT OF INSTITUTIONAL FUNDS ACT. Martindale-Hubbell Law Directory, Volume Eight. Martindale-Hubbell, Incorporated, 121 Chanlon Road, New Providence, New Jersey 07974. Annual.

UNIFORM PROBATE CODE. Uniform Laws Annotated, West Publishing Company, P.O. Box 64526, 50 West Kellogg Boulevard, St. Paul, Minnesota 55164-0526. 1976 (Annual Supplements).

UNIFORM PROBATE CODE. Martindale-Hubbell Law Directory, Volume Eight. Martindale-Hubbell, Incorporated, 121 Chanlon Road, New Providence, New Jersey 07974. Annual.

UNIFORM STATUTORY WILL ACT. Uniform Laws Annotated, West Publishing Company, P.O. Box 64526, 50 West Kellogg Boulevard, St. Paul, Minnesota 55164-0526. 1976 (Annual Supplements).

UNIFORM SUCCESSION WITHOUT ADMINISTRATION ACT. Uniform Laws Annotated, West Publishing Company, P.O. Box 64526, 50 West Kellogg Boulevard, St. Paul, Minnesota 55164-0526. 1976 (Annual Supplements).

UNIFORM SUPERVISION OF TRUSTEES FOR CHARITABLE PURPOSES ACT. Uniform Laws Annotated, West Publishing Company, P.O. Box 64526, 50 West Kellogg Boulevard, St. Paul, Minnesota 55164-0526. 1976 (Annual Supplements).

UNIFORM TESTAMENTARY ADDITIONS TO TRUSTS ACT. Uniform Laws Annotated, West Publishing Company, P.O. Box 64526, 50 West Kellogg Boulevard, St. Paul, Minnesota 55164-0526. 1976 (Annual Supplements).

UNIFORM TESTAMENTARY ADDITIONS TO TRUSTS ACT. Martindale-Hubbell Law Directory, Volume Eight. Martindale-Hubbell, Incorporated, 121 Chanlon Road, New Providence, New Jersey 07974. Annual.

UNIFORM TRUSTEES' POWERS ACT. Uniform Laws Annotated, West Publishing Company, P.O. Box 64526, 50 West Kellogg Boulevard, St. Paul, Minnesota 55164-0526. 1976 (Annual Supplements).

UNIFORM TRUSTS ACT. Uniform Laws Annotated, West Publishing Company, P.O. Box 64526, 50 West Kellogg Boulevard, St. Paul, Minnesota 55164-0526. 1976 (Annual Supplements).

UNIFORM TRUSTS ACT. Martindale-Hubbell Law Directory, Volume Eight. Martindale-Hubbell, Incorporated, 121 Chanlon Road, New Providence, New Jersey 07974. Annual.

RESTATEMENTS

RESTATEMENT OF THE LAW, SECOND, TRUSTS. Three Volumes. American Law Institute, 4025 Chestnut Street, Philadelphia, Pennsylvania 19104. 1957. (Volume 4, 1987 and Volume 5, 1987).

RESTATEMENT OF THE LAW, THIRD, TRUSTS--PRUDENT INVESTOR RULE. American Law Institute-American Bar Association, 4025 Chestnut Street, Philadelphia, Pennsylvania 19104. 1991.

WILLS, TRUSTS AND INHERITANCE

LOOSELEAF SERVICES AND REPORTERS

ANDERSON'S WILL FORMS AND CLAUSES. Robert A. Booth, Editor. Anderson Publishing Company, 2035 Reading Road, Cinncinati, Ohio 45202. 1984- .

CHANGING THE SITUS OF A TRUST. Robert A. Hendrickson and Neal R. Silverman. Law Journal-Seminars Press, Incorporated, 111 Eighth Avenue, New York, New York 10011. 1982- .

CURRENT LEGAL SYSTEMS: AUTOMATED WILL DRAFTING. Edward S. Schlesinger. Michie-Bobbs, The Michie Company, P.O. Box 7587, Charlottesville, Virginia 22906-7587. 1980- .

DRAFTING WILLS AND TRUST AGREEMENTS: A SYSTEMS APPROACH. Second Edition. Robert P. Wilkins. Shepard's/McGraw-Hill, P.O. Box 1235, Colorado Springs, Colorado 80901. 1989- .

ESTATE PLANNING. Gerald S. Sussman. Law Journal-Seminars Press, Incorporated, 111 Eighth Avenue, New York, New York 10011. 1981- .

ESTATE PLANNING. Fifth Edition. A. James Casner. Little, Brown and Company, 34 Beacon Street, Boston, Massachusetts 02108. 1983- .

ESTATE PLANNING LAW AND TAXATION. David Westfall. Research Institute of America, Incorporated, One Penn Plaza, New York, New York 10119. 1981- .

FIDUCIARY TAX GUIDE. Regis W. Campfield and Ted D. Englebrecht. Commerce Clearing House, Incorporated, 4025 West Peterson Avenue, Chicago, Illinois 60646. 1990.

GUIDE TO UNCLAIMED PROPERTY AND ESCHEAT LAWS. A. L. Andreoli and D. R. Shuman. Commonwealth Publishing Company, 101 North Westlake Boulevard, Suite 203, Westlake Village, California 91362. 1981- .

MODERN TRUST FORMS AND CHECKLISTS WITH COMMENTARY. Robert E. Parella and Joel E. Miller. Research Institute of America, Incorporated, One Penn Plaza, New York, New York 10119. 1980- .

MURPHY'S WILL CLAUSES: ANNOTATIONS AND FORMS WITH TAX EFFECTS. Joseph H. Murphy. The Michie Company, P.O. Box 7587, Charlottesville, Virginia 22906-7587. 1960- .

NEW YORK WILLS AND TRUSTS. Third Edition. John G. McQuaid, Frank W. Streng, and William P. LaPiana. Shepard's/McGraw-Hill, P.O. Box 1235, Colorado Springs, Colorado 80901. 1990.

TRUST ADMINISTRATION AND TAXATION. Second Edition. Walter L. Nossaman and Joseph L. Wyatt. Michie-Bobbs, The Michie Company, P.O. Box 7587, Charlottesville, Virginia 22906-7587. 1980- .

HANDBOOKS, MANUALS, FORMBOOKS

ADVANCED WILL DRAFTING 1985: A COURSE HANDBOOK. Practising Law Institute, 810 Seventh Avenue, New York, New York 10019. 1985.

AFFAIRS IN ORDER: A COMPLETE RESOURCE GUIDE TO DEATH AND DYING. Patricia Anderson. Macmillan Publishing Company, Incorporated, 866 Third Avenue, New York, New York 10022. 1991.

ALL-STATES WILLS AND ESTATE PLANNING GUIDE: BASIC PRINCIPLES AND A SUMMARY OF STATE AND TERRITORIAL WILL AND INTESTACY STATUTES. American Bar Association, Section of General Practice, 750 North Lake Shore Drive, Chicago, Illinois 60611. 1990.

ANDERSON'S WILL FORMS AND CLAUSES. Robert A. Booth, Editor. Anderson Publishing Company, 2035 Reading Road, Cincinnati, Ohio 45202. 1990. (Supplemented).

THE COMPLETE BOOK OF WILLS AND ESTATES. Alexander A. Bove, Jr. Henry Holt and Company, 115 West Eighteenth Street, New York, New York 10011. 1989.

THE COMPLETE WILL KIT. Jens C. Appel, III and F. Bruce Gentry. John Wiley and Sons, Incorporated, 605 Third Avenue, New York, New York 10158. 1990.

THE ESSENTIAL GUIDE TO WILLS, ESTATES, TRUSTS, AND DEATH TAXES. Alex J. Soled. Scott, Foresman and Company, Lifelong Learning Division, 1900 East Lake Avenue, Glenview, Illinois 60025. 1988.

AN ESTATE PLANNER'S HANDBOOK. Fourth Edition. James F. Farr and Jackson W. Wright, Junior. Little, Brown and Company, 34 Beacon Street, Boston, Massachusetts 02108. 1979. (Supplement 1985).

ESTATE PLANNING: COMPLETE GUIDE AND WORKBOOK. Alice F. Brod. Panel Publishers, Incorporated, 36 West Forty-fourth Street, New York, New York 10036. 1984.

ESTATE PLANNING HANDBOOK. Second Edition. William P.G. Allen and Thomas F.W. Allen. Carswell, Toronto, Ontario, Canada. 1991.

THE EXECUTOR'S MANUAL: EVERYTHING YOU NEED TO KNOW TO SETTLE AN ESTATE. Charles K. Plotnick and Stephan R. Leimberg. Doubleday and Company, Incorporated, 666 Fifth Avenue, New York, New York 10103. 1986.

THE FAMILY TRUST: A FINANCIAL CONSULTANT'S GUIDE TO TRUST FUNDS AND ESTATE PLANNING. Charles M. Aulino. Commerce Clearing House, Incorporated, 4025 West Peterson Avenue, Chicago, Illinois 60646. 1990.

FIDUCIARY ACCOUNTING GUIDE. Robert Whitman and Lawrence J. Kramer. American Law Institute-American Bar Association, 4025 Chestnut Street, Philadelphia, Pennsylvania 19104. 1990.

HANDBOOK ON WILLS AND ESTATES. Pravinchandra J. Patel. Legal Research Bureau, P.O. Box 374, Kew Gardens, New York 11415. 1983.

HOW TO SETTLE AN ESTATE OR PREPARE YOUR WILL. Toni P. Lester. Putnam Publishing Group, 200 Madison Avenue, New York, New York 10016. 1988.

HOW TO USE TRUSTS TO AVOID PROBATE AND TAXES: A GUIDE TO LIVING, MARITAL, SUPPORT, CHARITABLE, AND INSURANCE TRUSTS. Theresa Meehan Rudy, Kay Ostberg, and Jean Dimeo. HALT, Incorporated, 1319 F Street, Northwest, Suite 300, Washington, D.C. 20004. 1992.

HOW TO WRITE YOUR OWN WILL. John Cotton Howell. Liberty Publishing, 440 South Federal Highway, Suite 202, Deerfield Beach, Florida 33441. 1985.

THE JACOBY AND MEYERS GUIDE TO WILLS AND ESTATES. Gail J. Koff. Henry Holt and Company, 115 West Eighteenth Street, New York, New York 10011. 1991.

THE LAW OF TRUSTS AND TRUSTEES: A TREATISE COVERING THE LAW RELATING TO TRUSTS AND ALLIED SUBJECTS AFFECTING TRUST CREATION AND ADMINISTRATION, WITH FORMS. George G. Bogert, George T. Bogert and William K. Stevens. West Publishing Company, P.O. Box 64526, 50 West Kellogg Boulevard, St. Paul, Minnesota 55164-0526. 1977.

LAWYER'S COMPLETE GUIDE TO THE PERFECT WILL. Gilbert M. Cantor. Clarendon Press, Cato Press, 3 Bryn Mawr Avenue, Suite 205, P.O. Box 205, Bryn Mawr, Pennsylvania 19010. 1984.

NOLO'S SIMPLE WILL BOOK. Second Edition. Denis Clifford. Nolo Press, 950 Parker Street, Berkeley, California 94710. 1989.

PLANNING AN ESTATE: A GUIDEBOOK OF PRINCIPLES AND TECHNIQUES. Third Edition. Harold Weinstock. Shepard's/McGraw-Hill, P.O. Box 1235, Colorado Springs, Colorado 80901. 1988.

PLANNING AND ADMINISTRATION OF A LARGE ESTATE 1985: A COURSE HANDBOOK. Reginald S. Koehler III, Chairman. Practising Law Institute, 810 Seventh Avenue, New York, New York 10019. 1985.

A STUDENT'S GUIDE TO WILL DRAFTING. Leonard Levin. Matthew Bender and Company, Incorporated, 11 Penn Plaza, New York, New York 10001. 1987.

THY WILL BE DONE: A GUIDE TO WILLS, TAXATION, AND ESTATE PLANNING FOR OLDER PERSONS. Eugene J. Daly. Prometheus Books, 700 East Amherst Street, Buffalo, New York 14215. 1990.

USE OF TRUSTS IN ESTATE PLANNING 1985: A COURSE HANDBOOK. Practising Law Institute, 810 Seventh Avenue, New York, New York 10019. 1985.

YOUR WILL AND ESTATE PLANNING. Fred Tillman and Susan G. Parker. Houghton Mifflin Company, 1 Beacon Street, Boston, Massachusetts 02108. 1990.

TEXTBOOKS AND GENERAL WORKS

CASES AND MATERIALS ON DECEDENTS' ESTATES AND TRUSTS. Seventh Edition. John Ritchie, Neill H. Alford, Jr., and Richard W. Effland. Foundation Press, 615 Merrick Avenue, Westbury, New York 11590. 1988.

CASES AND TEXT ON THE LAW OF TRUSTS. Sixth Edition. George Gleason Bogert. Foundation Press, 615 Merrick Avenue, Westbury, New York 11590. 1991.

CHANGING THE SITUS OF A TRUST. Robert A. Hendrickson and Neal R. Silverman. Law Journal-Seminars Press, Incorporated, 111 Eighth Avenue, New York, New York 10011. 1982. (Supplemented).

CONTEMPORARY ESTATE PLANNING: TEXT AND PROBLEMS. John R. Price. Little, Brown and Company, 34 Beacon Street, Boston, Massachusetts 02108. 1982.

THE CURIOSITIES AND LAWS OF WILLS. John Proffatt. William S. Hein and Company, 1285 Main Street, Buffalo, New York 14209. 1989. (Reprint).

DEATH, DEEDS, AND DESCENDANTS: INHERITANCE IN MODERN AMERICA. Remi Clignet. Walter de Gruyter, Incorporated, 200 Saw Mill Road, Hawthorne, New York 10532. 1992.

DECEDANTS' ESTATES, WILLS, AND TRUSTS IN THE U.S.A. Frank G. Opton. Kluwer Law Book Publishers, Incorporated, 36 West Forty-fourth Street, New York, New York 10036. 1987.

ESTATE PLANNING. Third Edition. Jerome A. Manning. Practising Law Institute, 810 Seventh Avenue, New York, New York 10019. 1988. (Supplement 1989).

ESTATE PLANNING. Fifth Edition. A. James Casner. Little, Brown and Company, 34 Beacon Street, Boston, Massachusetts 02108. 1983. (Supplement 1985).

ESTATE PLANNING: A GUIDE FOR ADVISORS AND THEIR CLIENTS. D. Larry Crumbley and Edward E. Milam. Dow Jones-Irwin, 1818 Ridge Road, Homewood, Illinois 60430. 1986.

ESTATES AND TRUSTS: CASES, PROBLEMS, AND MATERIALS. John T. Gaubatz, Ira Mark Bloom, and Lewis D. Solomon. Matthew Bender and Company, Incorporated, 11 Penn Plaza, New York, New York 10001. 1989.

ESTATES, GIFTS, AND TRUSTS: PRIVATE FOUNDATIONS AND PUBLIC CHARITIES--SPECIAL RULES. Christopher L. Hartwell and Lauren Watson. Tax Management, 1231 Twenty-fifth Street, Northwest, Washington, D.C. 20037. 1990.

FEDERAL INCOME TAXATION OF ESTATES AND BENEFICIARIES. M. Carr Ferguson and James J. Freeland. Little, Brown and Company, 34 Beacon Street, Boston, Massachusetts 02108. 1970. (Supplement 1984).

FEDERAL INCOME TAXATION OF ESTATES AND TRUSTS. Norman H. Lane and Howard M. Zaritsky. Research Institute of America, Incorporated, One Penn Plaza, New York, New York 10119. 1988.

FEDERAL INCOME TAXES OF DECEDENTS AND ESTATES. Commerce Clearing House, Incorporated, 4025 West Peterson Avenue, Chicago, Illinois 60646. 1988.

FEDERAL TAXATION OF ESTATES, GIFTS, AND TRUSTS. Barry M. Nudelman, Max E. Blumenthal, and Stephen L. Owen. American Law Institute-American Bar Association, 4025 Chestnut Street, Philadelphia, Pennsylvania 19104. 1988.

FEDERAL TAXATION OF ESTATES, TRUSTS, AND GIFTS. Lewis D. Solomon, Ira Mark Bloom, and John T. Gaubatz. Matthew Bender and Company, Incorporated, 11 Penn Plaza, New York, New York 10001. 1989.

FEDERAL TAXATION OF TRUSTS, GRANTORS, AND BENEFICIARIES: INCOME, ESTATE, GIFT, GENERATION-SKIPPING TRANSFER. Second Edition. John L. Peschel and Edward D. Spurgeon. Research Institute of America, Incorporated, One Penn Plaza, New York, New York 10119. 1989.

FIDUCIARY OBLIGATION, AGENCY, AND PARTNERSHIP: DUTIES IN ONGOING BUSINESS RELATIONSHIPS. Deborah A. DeMott. West Publishing Company, 50 West Kellogg Boulevard, St. Paul, Minnesota 55164-0526. 1991.

FIDUCIARY STANDARDS IN PENSION AND TRUST FUND MANAGEMENT. Betty Linn Krikorian. Butterworth Legal Publishers, 90 Stiles Road, Salem, New Hampshire 03079. 1989.

FUTURE INTERESTS AND ESTATE PLANNING. William Schwartz and Robert A. Booth. Anderson Publishing Company, 2035 Reading Road, Cincinnati, Ohio 45202. 1965. (Supplement 1985).

FUTURE INTERESTS IN A NUTSHELL. Lawrence W. Waggoner. West Publishing Company, P.O. Box 64526, 50 West Kellogg Boulevard, St. Paul, Minnesota 55164-0526. 1980.

HANDBOOK OF THE LAW OF FUTURE INTERESTS. Second Edition. Lewis M. Simes. West Publishing Company, P.O. Box 64526, 50 West Kellogg Boulevard, St. Paul, Minnesota 55164-0526. 1966. (Hornbook).

HANDBOOK ON THE LAW OF TRUSTS. Fifth Edition. George G. Bogert and George T. Bogert. West Publishing Company, P.O. Box 64526, 50 West Kellogg Boulevard, St. Paul, Minnesota 55164-0526. 1973. (Hornbook).

HANDBOOK ON THE LAW OF WILLS AND OTHER PRINCIPLES OF SUCCESSION INCLUDING INTESTACY AND ADMINISTRATION OF DECEDENT'S ESTATES. Second Edition. Thomas E. Atkinson. West Publishing Company, P.O. Box 64526, 50 West Kellogg Boulevard, St. Paul, Minnesota 55164-0526. 1953. (Hornbook).

INCOME SHIFTING AFTER TAX REFORM. William A. Raabe, Karen J. Boucher, and Rick J. Taylor. Prentice-Hall, Incorporated, 113 Sylvan Avenue, Englewood Cliffs, New Jersey 07632. 1988.

INCOME TAXATION OF ESTATES AND TRUSTS. Thirteenth Edition. Arthur M. Michaelson and Jonathan G. Blattmachr. Practising Law Institute, 810 Seventh Avenue, New York, New York 10019. 1990.

INCOME TAXATION OF ESTATES AND TRUSTS. Hyman Gorenberg. American Institute of Certified Public Accountants, 1211 Avenue of the America, New York, New York 10036-8775. 1987.

INHERITANCE IN AMERICA: FROM COLONIAL TIMES TO THE PRESENT. Carole Shammas, Marylynn Salmon, and Michel Dahlin. Rutgers University Press, 109 Church Street, New Brunswick, New Jersey 08901. 1987.

INTERNATIONAL TAX TREATMENT OF COMMON LAW TRUSTS. International Fiscal Association. Kluwer Law Book Publishers, Incorporated, 36 West Forty-fourth Street, New York, New York 10036. 1988.

AN INTRODUCTION TO THE LAW OF TRUSTS. Simon Gardner. Oxford University Press, 200 Madison Avenue, New York, New York 10016. 1990.

IRREVOCABLE TRUSTS. George M. Turner. Shepard's/McGraw Hill, P.O. Box 1235, Colorado Springs, Colorado 80901. 1985.

KEYS TO PREPARING A WILL. James John Jurinski. Barron's Educational Series, Incorporated, 250 Wireless Boulevard, Hauppauge, New York 11788. 1991.

THE LAW OF TRUSTS. D.J. Hayton. Sweet and Maxwell Limited, South Quay Plaza, 183 Marsh Wall, London E14 9FT, England. 1989.

THE LAW OF TRUSTS. Fourth Edition. Austin Wakeman Scott and William Franklin Fratcher. Little, Brown and Company, 34 Beacon Street, Boston, Massachusetts 02108. 1987- .

LIFE INSURANCE IN ESTATE PLANNING. James C. Munch, Junior. Little, Brown and Company, 34 Beacon Street, Boston, Massachusetts 02108. 1981. (Supplements).

LIFETIME AND TESTAMENTARY ESTATE PLANNING. Tenth Edition. Harrison Tweed and William Parsons. American Law Institute-American Bar Association, 4025 Chestnut Street, Philadelphia, Pennsylvania 19104. 1988.

MULTISTATE AND MULTINATIONAL ESTATE PLANNING. Jeffrey A. Schoenblum. Little, Brown and Company, 34 Beacon Street, Boston, Massachusetts 02108. 1982. (Supplement 1985).

PLANNING AND DRAFTING FOR THE GENERATION-SKIPPING TRANSFER TAX. Jerold I. Horn. American Law Institute-American Bar Association, 4025 Chestnut Street, Philadelphia, Pennsylvania 19104. 1990.

THE PLANNING AND DRAFTING OF WILLS AND TRUSTS. Third Edition. Thomas L. Shaffer and Carol Ann Mooney. Foundation Press, 615 Merrick Avenue, Westbury, New York 11590. 1991.

PREFACE TO ESTATES IN LAND AND FUTURE INTERESTS. Thomas F. Bergin and Paul G. Haskell. Second Edition. Foundation Press, 615 Merrick Avenue, Westbury, New York 11590. 1989.

PREFACE TO THE LAW OF TRUSTS. Paul G. Haskell. Foundation Press, 615 Merrick Avenue, Westbury, New York 11590. 1975.

PREFACE TO WILLS, TRUSTS, AND ADMINISTRATION. Paul G. Haskell. Foundation Press, 615 Merrick Avenue, Westbury, New York 11590. 1987.

PROTECTING THE TRUSTEE AND EXECUTIVE IN THE 80'S. Section of Real Property, Probate, and Trust Law, American Bar Association, 750 North Lake Shore Drive, Chicago, Illinois 60611. 1985.

PROVIDING FIDUCIARY ACCOUNTING AND TAX SERVICES. Suzanne Clark-James. Matthew Bender and Company, Incorporated, 11 Penn Plaza, New York, New York 10001. 1990.

THE PSYCHIATRY OF WRITING A WILL. Nathan Roth. Charles C. Thomas, Publishers, 2600 South First Street, Springfield, Illinois 62794. 1989.

REVOCABLE TRUSTS. George M. Turner. Shepard's/McGraw Hill, P.O. Box 1235, Colorado Springs, Colorado 80901. 1983. (Annual Supplements).

THE ROMAN LAW OF TRUSTS. David Johnston. Oxford University Press, 200 Madison Avenue, New York, New York 10016. 1988.

SCOTT ON TRUST. Fourth Edition. Austin W. Scott. Little, Brown and Company, 34 Beacon Street, Boston, Massachusetts 02108.

TRUSTS. Sixth Edition. George T. Bogert. West Publishing Company, 50 West Kellogg Boulevard, St. Paul, Minnesota 55164. 1987.

UNIFORM PROBATE CODE IN A NUTSHELL. Second Edition. Lawrence H. Averill, Jr. West Publishing Company, P.O. Box 64526, 50 West Kellogg Boulevard, St. Paul Minnesota 55164-0526. 1987.

THE WAYS OF WILLS: TRUST AND ESTATE PLANNING FOR GOVERNMENT EMPLOYEES. G. Jerry Shaw, Thomas J. O'Rourke, and Virginia Hurt Johnson. MPC Publications, 715 Eighth Street, Southeast, Washington, D.C. 20003. 1991.

WHERE THERE'S A WILL--: WHO INHERITED WHAT AND WHY. Stephen M. Silverman. HarperCollins Publishers, 10 East Fifty-third Street, New York, New York 10022. 1991.

WILL DRAFTING. Dana Shilling. Prentice-Hall, Incorporated, 113 Sylvan Avenue, Englewood Cliffs, New Jersey 07632. 1987.

WILL POWER: DRAFTING EFFECTIVE WILLS. Linda R. Getzen and Edward F. Koren. Callaghan and Company, 155 Pfingsten Road, Deerfield, Illinois 60015. 1987.

WILLS AND TRUSTS. Ray E. Poplett. West Publishing Company, 50 West Kellogg Boulevard, St. Paul, Minnesota 55164-0526. 1988.

WILLS AND TRUSTS IN A NUTSHELL. Robert L. Mennell. West Publishing Company, P.O. Box 64526, 50 West Kellogg Boulevard, St. Paul Minnesota 55164-0526. 1979.

WILLS OF THE RICH AND FAMOUS: A FASCINATING LOOK AT THE RICH, OFTEN SURPRISING LEGACIES OF YESTERDAY'S CELEBRITIES. Herbert E. Nass. Warner Books, Incorporated, 666 Fifth Avenue, New York, New York 10103. 1991.

WILLS, TRUSTS, AND ESTATE ADMINISTRATION FOR THE PARALEGAL. Third Edition. Dennis R. Hower. West Publishing Company, 50 West Kellogg Boulevard, St. Paul, Minnesota 55164-0526. 1991.

WILLS, TRUSTS, AND ESTATE PLANNING: LAW AND TAXATION, CASES AND MATERIALS. Joseph M. Dodge. West Publishing Company, 50 West Kellogg Boulevard, St. Paul, Minnesota 55164-0526. 1988.

WILLS, TRUSTS AND ESTATES. Fourth Edition. Jesse Dukeminier and Stanley M. Johanson. Little, Brown and Company, 34 Beacon Street, Boston, Massachusetts 02108. 1990.

WILLS, TRUSTS, AND ESTATES: INCLUDING TAXATION AND FUTURE INTERESTS. William M. McGovern, Jr., Sheldon F. Kurtz, and Jan Ellen Rein. West Publishing Company, 50 West Kellogg Boulevard, St. Paul, Minnesota 55164-0526. 1988.

WILLS, TRUSTS, AND GIFTS. David T. Riedel. Butterworth Legal Publishers, 90 Stiles Road, Salem, New Hampshire 03079. 1991.

ENCYCLOPEDIAS AND DICTIONARIES

GLOSSARY OF FIDUCIARY TERMS. Fifth Edition. American Bankers Association, 1120 Connecticut Avenue, Northwest, Washington, D.C. 20036. 1990.

ANNUALS AND SURVEYS

ANNUAL ESTATE PLANNING INSTITUTE. Practising Law Institute, 810 Seventh Avenue, New York, New York 10019. Annual.

LAW REVIEWS AND PERIODICALS

ESTATE PLANNING. Research Institute of America, Incorporated, One Penn Plaza, New York, New York 10119. Bimonthly.

ESTATES, GIFTS AND TRUSTS JOURNAL. Tax Management, Incorporated, Bureau of National Affairs, 1231 Twenty-fifth Street, Northwest, Washington, D.C. 20007. Bimonthly.

PROBATE LAW JOURNAL. Boston University School of Law, 765 Commonwealth Avenue, Boston, Massachusetts 02215. Semiannually.

PROBATE LAWYER. American College of Probate Counsel, 10964 West Pico Boulevard, Los Angeles, California 90064. Bimonthly.

PROBATE NOTES. American College of Probate Counsel, 10964 West Pico Boulevard, Los Angeles, California 90064. Quarterly.

REAL PROPERTY, PROBATE AND TRUST JOURNAL. Section of Real Property, Probate and Trust Law. American Bar Association, 750 North Lake Shore Drive, Chicago, Illinois 60611. Quarterly.

TRUST AND ESTATE LAW BULLETIN. Dominion Publications, Incorporated, 4920 Millridge Parkway, Box 1847, Midlothian, Virginia 23113. Monthly.

TRUSTS AND ESTATES. Communications Channels, Incorporated, 6255 Barfield Road, Atlanta, Georgia 30328. Monthly.

NEWSLETTERS AND NEWSPAPERS

THE CHASE REVIEW. Chase Manhattan Bank, 1211 Avenue of the Americas, Thirty-fourth Floor, New York, New York 10036. Quarterly.

ELDER LAW REPORT. Little, Brown and Company, 34 Beacon Street, Boston, Massachusetts 02108. Monthly.

PROBATE AND PROPERTY. Section of Real Property, Probate and Trust Law, American Bar Association, 750 North Lake Shore Drive, Chicago, Illinois 60611. Bimonthly.

DIRECTORIES

DIRECTORY OF TRUST INSTITUTIONS. Trusts and Estates, Communication Channels, Incorporated, 6255 Barfield Road, Atlanta, Georgia 30328. Annual.

PROBATE COUNSEL. Royal Publishing Company, P.O. Box 2241, Palm Beach, Florida 33480. Annual.

SHEPARD'S ESTATE, PROBATE, TRUST, AND WILLS CITATIONS. Shepard's/McGraw-Hill, P.O. Box 1235, Colorado Springs, Colorado 80901. 1989.

ASSOCIATIONS AND PROFESSIONAL SOCIETIES

AMERICAN COLLEGE OF PROBATE COUNSEL. 2716 Ocean Park Boulevard, Suite 1080, Santa Monica, California 90405. (213) 450-2033.

NATIONAL ASSOCIATION OF ESTATE PLANNING COUNCILS. 98 Dennis Drive, Lexington, Kentucky 40503. (606) 276-4659.

SECTION OF REAL PROPERTY, PROBATE AND TRUST LAW, AMERICAN BAR ASSOCIATION. 750 North Lake Shore Drive, Chicago, Illinois 60611. (312) 988-5000.

AUDIOVISUALS

ADVANCED WILL DRAFTING. Practising Law Institute, 810 Seventh Avenue, New York, New York 10019. 1983. Audiocassette.

CHANGES INVOLVING THE ESTATE AND GIFT TAX AND RELATED AREAS: THE TAX REFORM ACT OF 1984. Section of Real Property, Probate and Trust Law, American Bar Association, 750 North Lake Shore Drive, Chicago, Illinois 60611. 1984. Audiocassette.

ESTATE AND FINANCIAL PLANNING FOR THE AGING OR INCAPACITATED CLIENT. Practising Law Institute, 810 Seventh Avenue, New York, New York 10019. 1985. Videotape.

THE ESTATE FREEZING RAGE. Section of Real Property, Probate and Trust Law, American Bar Association, 750 North Lake Shore Drive, Chicago, Illinois 60611. 1980. Audiocassette.

ESTATE PLANNING FOR SPOUSES IN AN UNCERTAIN MARITAL CLIMATE. Section of Real Property, Probate and Trust Law. American Bar Association, 750 North Lake Shore Drive, Chicago, Illinois 60611. 1984. Audiocassette.

ESTATE PLANNING: REVOCABLE TRUST. National Practice Institute, Consortium for Professional Education, American Bar Association, 750 North Lake Shore Drive, Chicago, Illinois 60611. 1983. Videocassettes.

HOW TO COMPUTERIZE YOUR ESTATE PLANNING AND PROBATE PRACTICE. American Bar Association, 750 North Lake Shore Drive, Chicago, Illinois 60611. 1990. Videotape.

OVERVIEW OF THE ESTATE AND GIFT TAX CHANGES ENACTED BY THE 1981 ERTA. Section of Real Property, Probate, and Trust Law, American Bar Association, 750 North Lake Shore Drive, Chicago, Illinois 60611. 1983. Audiocassette.

PERSONAL AND ESTATE PLANNING FOR THE ELDERLY. American Bar Association, 750 North Lake Shore Drive, Chicago, Illinois 60611. 1989. Videotape.

PLANNING FOR GENERATION SKIPPING TRANSFERS. Section of Real Property, Probate and Trust Law, American Bar Association, 750 North Lake Shore Drive, Chicago, Illinois 60611. Audiocassette.

POST-MORTEM ESTATE PLANNING. Practising Law Institute, 810 Seventh Avenue, New York, New York 10019. 1983. Audiocassette.

A PRACTITIONER'S GUIDE TO PREVENTING PROBATE LITIGATION: 1. ANTICIPATING THE DEFENSE OF WILLS CONTESTS; 2. A PRACTITIONER'S GUIDE TO DETERMINING BENEFICIARIES. Consortium for Professional Education, American Bar Association, 750 North Lake Shore Drive, Chicago, Illinois 60611. 1983. Videotape.

SELECTED COMMENTS ON THE USE OF INSURANCE IN ESTATE PLANNING AFTER ERTA. Section of Real Property, Probate, and Trust Law, American Bar Association, 750 North Lake Shore Drive, Chicago, Illinois 60611. 1983. Audiocassette.

THE USE OF TRUSTS IN ESTATE PLANNING. Practising Law Institute, 810 Seventh Avenue, New York, New York 10019. 1983. Audiocassette.

WILLS, TRUSTS, AND ESTATES: CLIENT COUNSELING VIDEOTAPE. American Bar Association, 750 North Lake Shore Drive, Chicago, Illinois 60611. 1985. Videotape.

COMPUTER-ASSISTED LEGAL INSTRUCTION

CALIFORNIA INTESTATE SUCCESSION. Charles I. Nelson. Center for Computer-Assisted Instruction, 229 19th Avenue South, University of Minnesota, Minneapolis, Minnesota 55455. Machine-readable computer file.

ESTATE PLANNING IN THE 90'S. National Practice Institute, 330 Second Avenue South, Minneapolis, Minnesota 55401. Audiotape.

ESTATE PLANNING SEMINAR SYSTEM. Benefit Analysis, Incorporated, c/o Center for Computer-Assisted Instruction, 229 19th Avenue South, University of Minnesota, Minneapolis, Minnesota 55455. Machine-readable computer file.

EXECUTION AND REVOCATION OF WILLS UNDER THE UPC. Charles I. Nelson. Center for Computer-Assisted Instruction, 229 19th Avenue South, University of Minnesota, Minneapolis, Minnesota 55455. Machine-readable computer file.

INTESTATE SUCCESSION UNDER THE UPC. Charles I. Nelson. Center for Computer-Assisted Instruction, 229 19th Avenue South, University of Minnesota, Minneapolis, Minnesota 55455. Machine-readable computer file.

PROBATE AND ESTATE PLANNING. National Practice Institute, 330 Second Avenue South, Minneapolis, Minnesota 55401. Audiotape.

WIRETAPPING
See: EAVESDROPPING

WITNESSES
See also: CONFIDENTIAL COMMUNICATIONS; CROSS-EXAMINATION

STATUTES, CODES, STANDARDS, UNIFORM LAWS

UNIFORM ACT TO SECURE THE ATTENDANCE OF WITNESSES FROM WITHOUT A STATE IN CRIMINAL PROCEEDINGS. Uniform Laws Annotated. West Publishing Company, P.O. Box 64526, 50 West Kellogg Boulevard, St. Paul, Minnesota 55164-0526. 1976. (Annual Supplements).

UNIFORM AUDIOVISUAL DEPOSITION ACT. Uniform Laws Annotated. West Publishing Company, P.O. Box 64526, 50 West Kellogg Boulevard, St. Paul, Minnesota 55164-0526. 1976. (Annual Supplements).

UNIFORM RENDITION OF PRISONERS AS WITNESSES IN CRIMINAL PROCEEDINGS ACT. Uniform Laws Annotated. West Publishing Company, P.O. Box 64526, 50 West Kellogg Boulevard, St. Paul, Minnesota 55164-0526. 1976. (Annual Supplements).

LOOSELEAF SERVICES AND REPORTERS

EXAMINATION OF WITNESSES. Richard A. Gonzales. Callaghan and Company, 155 Pfingsten Road, Deerfield, Illinois 60015. 1989- .

HANDBOOKS, MANUALS, FORMBOOKS

ABA GUIDELINES FOR FAIR TREATMENT OF VICTIMS AND WITNESSES IN THE CRIMINAL JUSTICE SYSTEM. Victims Committee, Criminal Justice Section, American Bar Association, 750 North Lake Shore Drive, Chicago, Illinois 60611. 1983.

DEPOSITION STRATEGY, LAW AND FORMS. Alexander Sann and S. Bellman, Editors. Matthew Bender and Company, Incorporated, 11 Penn Plaza, New York, New York 10001. 1981. (Supplemented Semi-Annually).

DEPOSITIONS, EXPERT WITNESSES, AND DEMONSTRATIVE EVIDENCE IN PERSONAL INJURY CASES. David G. Miller, Chairman. Practising Law Institute, 810 Seventh Avenue, New York, New York 10019. 1985.

EXPERT WITNESS CHECKLISTS. Douglas Danner. Lawyers Co-Operative Publishing Company, Aqueduct Building, Rochester, New York 14694. 1983. (Supplements).

EYEWITNESS IDENTIFICATION: A SYSTEM HANDBOOK. Gary L. Wells. Carswell, Toronto, Ontario, Canada. 1988.

PATTERN DEPOSITION CHECKLISTS. Second Edition. Lawyers Co-Operative Publishing Company, Aqueduct Building, Rochester, New York 14694. 1984. (Supplements).

REPRESENTATION OF WITNESSES BEFORE FEDERAL GRAND JURIES. Third Edition. Clark Boardman Company, Limited, 435 Hudson Street, New York, New York 10014. 1984.

SUCCEEDING AS AN EXPERT WITNESS: INCREASING YOUR IMPACT AND INCOME. Harold A. Feder. Van Nostrand Reinhold Company, Incorporated, 115 Fifth Avenue, New York, New York 10003. 1991.

THE TRUTH, THE WHOLE TRUTH, AND NOTHING BUT--: A POLICE OFFICER'S GUIDE TO TESTIFYING IN COURT. D.W. Reynolds. Charles C. Thomas, Publishers, 2600 South First Street, Springfield, Illinois 62794. 1990.

TEXTBOOKS AND GENERAL WORKS

CHILD WITNESS LAW AND PRACTICE. John E.B. Myers and Nancy W. Perry. John Wiley and Sons, Incorporated, 605 Third Avenue, New York, New York 10158. 1987.

THE CHILD WITNESS: LEGAL ISSUES AND DILEMMAS. Nancy Walker Perry and Lawrence S. Wrightsman. Sage Publications, 2455 Teller Road, Newbury Park, California 91320. 1991.

CHILDREN AS WITNESSES. Helen Dent and Rhona Flin. John Wiley and Sons, Incorporated, 605 Third Avenue, New York, New York 10158. 1992.

CHILDREN'S EYEWITNESS MEMORY. Stephen J. Ceci, Michael P. Toglia, and David F. Ross. Springer-Verlag New York, Incorporated, 175 Fifth Avenue, New York, New York 10010. 1987.

DIRECT AND CROSS-EXAMINATION OF ORTHOPEDIC SURGEONS. Thomas J. Murray, Jr. and Jeffrey D. Robertson. John Wiley and Sons, Incorporated, 605 Third Avenue, New York, New York 10158. 1991.

DOMBROFF ON DIRECT AND CROSS-EXAMINATION. Mark A. Dombroff. John Wiley and Sons, Incorporated, 605 Third Avenue, New York, New York 10158. 1985.

THE EXPERT WITNESS. Peter Dorram. American Planning Association, East Sixtieth Street, Chicago, Illinois 60637. 1982.

EXPERT WITNESSES: DIRECT AND CROSS-EXAMINATION. William G. Mulligan. John Wiley and Sons, Incorporated, 605 Third Avenue, New York, New York 10158. 1987.

EYE-WITNESS IDENTIFICATION. Second Edition. Nathan R. Sobel. Clark Boardman Company, 435 Hudson Street, New York, New York 10014. 1981. (Supplement 1984).

EYEWITNESS TESTIMONY: CIVIL AND CRIMINAL. Elizabeth F. Loftus and James M. Doyle. Kluwer Law Book Publishers, Incorporated, 36 West Forty-fourth Street, New York, New York 10036. 1987.

IMPEACHMENT OF WITNESSES: THE CROSS-EXAMINER'S ART. Roberto Aron, Kevin Thomas Duffy, and Jonathan L. Rosner. Shepard's/McGraw-Hill, P.O. Box 1235, Colorado Springs, Colorado 80901. 1990.

ON THE WITNESS STAND: CONTROVERSIES IN THE COURTROOM. Lawrence S. Wrightsman, Cynthia E. Willis, and Saul M. Kassin. Sage Publications, 2455 Teller Road, Newbury Park, California 91320. 1987.

PERSPECTIVES ON CHILDREN'S TESTIMONY. S.J. Ceci, D.F. Ross, and M.P. Toglia. Springer-Verlag New York, Incorporated, 175 Fifth Avenue, New York, New York 10010. 1989.

THE POLICE WITNESS: EFFECTIVENESS IN THE COURTROOM. Michael W. Whitaker. Charles C. Thomas Publishing, 2600 South First Street, Springfield, Illinois 62794-9265. 1985.

PSYCHOLOGICAL METHODS IN CRIMINAL INVESTIGATION AND EVIDENCE. David C. Raskin. Springer Publishing Company, 536 Broadway, New York, New York 10012. 1989.

PSYCHOLOGICAL TESTIMONY: A CASE FOR THE EXPERTS '91. Robert F. McGrath. Massachusetts Continuing Legal Education, 20 West Street, Boston, Massachusetts 02111. 1990.

SERVING CRIME VICTIMS AND WITNESSES. Peter Finn and Beverly N.W. Lee. United States Department of Justice, National Institute of Justice, Office of Communication and Research Utilization, Tenth Street and Pennsylvania Avenue, Northwest, Washington, D.C. 20530. 1987.

TESTIMONIAL PRIVILEGES. Scott N. Stone and Ronald S. Liebman, Editors. Shepard's/McGraw Hill, P.O. Box 1235, Colorado Springs, Colorado 80901. 1983. (Supplement 1984)

TESTIMONY: A PHILOSOPHICAL STUDY. C.A.J. Coady. Oxford University Press, 200 Madison Avenue, New York, New York 10016. 1992.

TRANCE ON TRIAL. Alan W. Scheflin and Jerrold Lee Shapiro. Guilford Publications, Incorporated, 72 Spring Street, New York, New York 10012. 1989.

TRIAL PSYCHOLOGY: COMMUNICATION AND PERSUASION IN THE COURTROOM. Margaret C. Roberts. Butterworth Legal Publishers, 90 Stiles Road, Salem, New Hampshire 03079. 1987.

WITNESS FOR THE DEFENSE: THE ACCUSED, THE EYEWITNESS, AND THE EXPERT WHO PUTS MEMORY ON TRIAL. Elizabeth Loftus and Katherine Ketcham. St. Martin's Press, 175 Fifth Avenue, New York, New York 10010. 1991.

WITNESS IMMUNITY. Lawrence Taylor. Charles C. Thomas Publishing, 2600 South First Street, Springfield, Illinois 62794-9265. 1983.

WITNESS INTIMIDATION: THE LAW'S RESPONSE. Michael H. Graham. Quorum Books, Imprint of Greenwood Publishing Group, Incorporated, 88 Post Road West, P.O. Box 5007, Westport, Connecticut 06881 1985

WITNESSES IN ARBITRATION: SELECTION, PREPARATION, AND PRESENTATION. Edward Levin and Donald Grody. Bureau of National Affairs, Incorporated, 1231 Twenty-fifth Street, Northwest, Washington, D.C. 20037. 1987.

NEWSLETTERS AND NEWSPAPERS

THE EXPERT AND THE LAW. National Forensic Center, 17 Temple Terrace, Lawrenceville, New Jersey 08648. Bimonthly.

THE EXPERT WITNESS JOURNAL. Seak, Incorporated, P O. Box 590, Falmouth, Massachusetts 02541. Monthly.

THE EXPERT WITNESS REPORTER. Harrow Communications, 6660 Dobbin Road, Columbia, Maryland 21045. Monthly.

BIBLIOGRAPHIES

THE CHILD WITNESS. Earleen H. Cook. Vance Bibliographies, P.O. Box 229, 112 North Charter Street, Monticello, Illinois 61856. 1987.

THE ECONOMIST/BUSINESS PROFESSIONAL AS EXPERT WITNESS: A BIBLIOGRAPHY. Frederick Frankena. Vance Bibliographies, P.O. Box 229, 112 North Charter Street, Monticello, Illinois 61856. 1985.

THE EXPERT MEDICAL WITNESS: A BIBLIOGRAPHY. Frederick Frankena. Vance Bibliographies, P.O. Box 229, 112 North Charter Street, Monticello, Illinois 61856. 1985.

THE EXPERT WITNESS: A GENERAL, MOSTLY LEGAL BIBLIOGRAPHY. Frederick Frankena. Vance Bibliographies, P.O. Box 229, 112 North Charter Street, Monticello, Illinois 61856. 1985.

HYPNOSIS AND THE COURTS. Earleen H. Cook. Vance Bibliographies, P.O. Box 229, 112 North Charter Street, Monticello, Illinois 61856. 1987.

THE MENTAL HEALTH PROFESSIONAL AS EXPERT WITNESS: A BIBLIOGRAPHY. Frederick Frankena. Vance Bibliographies, P.O. Box 229, 112 North Charter Street, Monticello, Illinois 61856. 1985.

THE SCIENTIST/TECHNICIAN AS EXPERT WITNESS: A BIBLIOGRAPHY. Frederick Frankena. Vance Bibliographies, P.O. Box 229, 112 North Charter Street, Monticello, Illinois 61856. 1985.

THE SOCIAL SCIENCE PRACTICIONER AS EXPERT WITNESS: A BIBLIOGRAPHY. Frederick Frankena. Vance Bibliographies, P.O. Box 229, 112 North Charter Street, Monticello, Illinois 61856. 1985.

DIRECTORIES

THE BEST LAWYERS IN AMERICA: DIRECTORY OF EXPERT WITNESSES. Steven W. Naifeh and Gregory White Smith. Woodward/White, New York, New York. 1990.

REGISTER OF EXPERT WITNESSES IN THE CONSTRUCTION INDUSTRY. Subcommittee on Register of Expert Witnesses, Section of Litigation, American Bar Association, 750 North Lake Shore Drive, Chicago, Illinois 60611. 1984.

ASSOCIATIONS AND PROFESSIONAL SOCIETIES

EXPERT WITNESS PROGRAM. Association of American Physicians and Surgeons, 9203 Lake Braddock Drive, Burke, Virginia 22015.

NATIONAL FORENSIC CENTER. 17 Temple Terrace, Lawrenceville, New Jersey 08648. (609) 883-0550.

RESEARCH CENTERS, INSTITUTES, CLEARINGHOUSES

CENTER FOR RESPONSIVE PSYCHOLOGY. Brooklyn College of the City University of New York, Brooklyn, New York 11210. (718) 780-5960.

ONLINE DATABASES

THE EXPERT AND THE LAW. National Forensic Center, 17 Temple Terrace, Lawrencevile, New Jersey 08648.

AUDIOVISUALS

ART OF ADVOCACY: EXPERT WITNESSES. National Institute for Trial Advocacy, Notre Dame Law School, Notre Dame, Indiana 46556. 1988. Videotape.

ATTORNEY'S GUIDE TO USING MEDICAL EVIDENCE. Harry Rein. National Practice Institute, 330 Second Avenue South, Minneapolis, Minnesota 55401. Audiotape.

EXPERT WITNESSES. Irving Younger. Professional Education Systems, Incorporated, 3410 Sky Park Boulevard, Eau Claire, Wisconsin 54702. 1985. Videocassettes.

PERSUASIVE EXPERT TESTIMONY. National Institute for Trial Advocacy, Notre Dame Law School, Notre Dame, Indiana 46556. 1988. Videotape.

PROBLEM WITNESS TACTICS: A LECTURE WITH DEMONSTRATION. Consortium for Professional Education, American Bar Association, 750 North Lake Shore Drive, Chicago, Illinois 60611. 1979. Videotape.

USING FINANCIAL EXPERTS IN BUSINESS LITIGATION. National Institute for Trial Advocacy, Notre Dame Law School, Notre Dame, Indiana 46556. 1988. Videotape.

WOMEN
See also: ABORTION; DISCRIMINATION, EMPLOYMENT; DISCRIMINATION, SEX; DIVORCE AND SEPARATION; EQUAL EMPLOYMENT OPPORTUNITY; FAMILY LAW; FAMILY VIOLENCE

LOOSELEAF SERVICES AND REPORTERS

SEX-BASED EMPLOYMENT DISCRIMINATION. Susan M. Omilian and Jean P. Kamp. Callaghan and Company, 155 Pfingsten Road, Deerfield, Illinois 60015. 1990.

HANDBOOKS, MANUALS, FORMBOOKS

COMPENDIUM OF INTERNATIONAL CONVENTIONS CONCERNING THE STATUS OF WOMEN. Centre for Social Development and Humanitarian Affairs. United Nations Publishing Service, Room DC2-0853, New York, New York 10017. 1988.

HOW TO PROTECT YOUR SPOUSAL RIGHTS. Tom Biracree. Contemporary Books, Incorporated, 180 North Michigan Avenue, Chicago, Illinois 60601. 1991.

THE LEGAL RIGHTS OF WOMEN: ADAPTED FOR USE IN EVERY STATE BY MEANS OF A BRIEF SYNOPSIS OF THE LAW RELATING TO PROPERTY RIGHTS, DOWER, DIVORCE, THE RIGHTS OF A WIDOW IN THE ESTATE OF HER HUSBAND. Lemuel H. Foster. Fred B. Rothman and Company, 10368 West Centennial Road, Littleton, Colorado 80127. 1986, c. 1913.

PREGNANCY AND EMPLOYMENT: THE COMPLETE HANDBOOK ON DISCRIMINATION, MATERNITY LEAVE, AND HEALTH AND SAFETY. Bureau of National Affairs, Incorporated, 1231 Twenty-fifth Street, Northwest, Washington, D.C. 20037. 1987.

SEXUAL HARASSMENT IN THE WORKPLACE: A GUIDE TO THE LAW. Third Edition. Ralph H. Baxter, Jr. and Lynne C. Hermle. Executive Enterprises Publications Company, 22 West Twenty-first Street, New York, New York 10010-6904. 1989.

THE STATE-BY-STATE GUIDE TO WOMEN'S LEGAL RIGHTS. National Organization of Women/Legal Defense and Education Fund, and Doctor Renee Cherow-O'Leary. Shepard's/McGraw-Hill, P.O. Box 1235, Colorado Springs, Colorado 80901. 1987.

WOMAN'S COUNSEL: A LEGAL GUIDE FOR WOMEN. Gayle L. Niles and Douglas H. Snider. Arden Press, P.O. Box 418, Denver, Colorado 80201. 1984.

WOMAN'S LEGAL GUIDE TO SEPARATION AND DIVORCE IN ALL FIFTY STATES. Norma Harwood. Charles Scribner's Sons, 115 Fifth Avenue, New York, New York 10003. 1985.

THE WOMEN'S GUIDE TO LEGAL RIGHTS. Jane Shay Lynch and Sara Lyn Smith. Contemporary Books, Incorporated, 180 North Michigan Avenue, Chicago, Illinois 60601. 1979.

WOMEN'S RIGHTS IN INTERNATIONAL DOCUMENTS: A SOURCEBOOK WITH COMMENTARY. Winston E. Langley. McFarland and Company, Incorporated, Box 611, Jefferson, North Carolina 28640. 1991.

A WORKING WOMAN'S GUIDE TO HER JOB RIGHTS. United States Department of Labor, Women's Bureau. Superintendent of Documents, United States Government Printing Office, Washington, D.C. 20402. 1988.

TEXTBOOKS AND GENERAL WORKS

ABORTION RIGHTS AS RELIGIOUS FREEDOM. Peter S. Wenz. Temple University Press, 1601 North Broad Street, University Services Building, Philadelphia, Pennsylvania 19122. 1992.

ACADEMIC WOMEN: WORKING TOWARDS EQUALITY. Angela Simeone. Bergin and Garvey, Incorporated, Rural Route 1, Box 105, Blue Hill, Maine 04614-9721. 1986.

AT THE BOUNDARIES OF LAW: FEMINISM AND LEGAL THEORY. Martha Albertson Fineman and Nancy Sweet Thomadsen. Routledge, Chapman & Hall, 29 West Thirty-fifth Street, New York, New York 10001. 1991.

BATTERED WOMEN WHO KILL: PSYCHOLOGICAL SELF-DEFENSE AS LEGAL JUSTIFICATION. Charles Patrick Ewing. Lexington Books, 125 Spring Street, Lexington, Massachusetts 02173. 1987.

BEYOND OPPRESSION: FEMINIST THEORY AND POLITICAL STRATEGY. M.E. Hawkesworth. Continuum Publishing Corporation, 370 Lexington Avenue, New York, New York 10017. 1990.

BIRTH POWER: THE CASE FOR SURROGACY. Carmel Shalev. Yale University Press, 302 Temple Street, New Haven, Connecticut 06520. 1989.

CENTURY OF STRUGGLE: THE WOMEN'S RIGHTS MOVEMENT IN THE UNITED STATES. Revised edition. Eleanor Flexner. The Belknap Press of Harvard University Press, 79 Garden Street, Cambridge, Massachusetts 02138. 1975.

THE CONSTITUTIONAL RIGHTS OF WOMEN: CASES IN LAW AND SOCIAL CHANGE. Second Edition. Leslie Friedman Goldstein. University of Wisconsin Press, 114 North Murray, Madison, Wisconsin 53706. 1988.

THE CRIMINALIZATION OF A WOMAN'S BODY. Clarice Feinman. Haworth Press, Incorporated, 10 Alice Street, Binghamton, New York 13904. 1991.

DISCRIMINATION AGAINST WOMEN: A GLOBAL SURVEY OF THE ECONOMIC, EDUCATIONAL, SOCIAL, AND POLITICAL STATUS OF WOMEN. Eschel M. Rhoodie. McFarland and Company, Incorporated, Box 611, Jefferson, North Carolina 28640. 1989.

DOMESTIC RELATIONS AND LAW. Nancy F. Cott. Meckler Corporation, 11 Ferry Lane West, Westport, Connecticut 06880. 1991.

A FEARFUL FREEDOM: WOMEN'S FLIGHT FROM EQUALITY. Wendy Kaminer. Addison-Wesley Publishing Company, Incorporated, Route 128, Reading, Massachusetts 01867. 1990.

THE FEMALE BODY AND THE LAW. Zillah R. Eisenstein. University of California Press, 2120 Berkeley Way, Berkeley, California 94720. 1988.

FEMALE REVOLT: WOMEN'S MOVEMENTS IN WORLD AND HISTORICAL PERSPECTIVE. Janet Saltzman Chafetz and Anthony Gary Dworkin. Rowman and Allanheld Publishers, 420 Boston Way, Lanham, Maryland 20706. 1986.

FEMINISM AND THE POWER OF LAW. Carol Smart. Routledge, Chapman & Hall, 29 West Thirty-fifth Street, New York, New York 10001. 1989.

FEMINISM, MARRIAGE, AND THE LAW IN VICTORIAN ENGLAND, 1850-1895. Mary Lyndon Shanley. Princeton University Press, 41 William Street, Princeton, New Jersey 08540. 1989.

FEMINISM UNMODIFIED: DISCOURSES ON LIFE AND LAW. Catharine A. MacKinnon. Harvard University Press, 79 Garden Street, Cambridge, Massachusetts 02138. 1987.

FEMINIST LEGAL THEORY: READINGS IN LAW AND GENDER. Katharine T. Bartlett and Rosanne Kennedy. Westview Press, Incorporated, 5500 Central Avenue, Boulder, Colorado 80301. 1991.

FOR ADULT USERS ONLY: THE DILEMMA OF VIOLENT PORNOGRAPHY. Susan Gubar and Joan Hoff. Indiana University Press, Tenth and Morton Streets, Bloomington, Indiana 47405. 1989.

FROM LADIES TO WOMEN: THE ORGANIZED STRUGGLE FOR WOMAN'S RIGHTS IN THE RECONSTRUCTION ERA. Israel Kugler. Greenwood Publishing Group, Incorporated, 88 Post Road West, P.O. Box 5007, Westport, Connecticut 06881. 1987.

GENDER DISCRIMINATION LAW OF THE EUROPEAN COMMUNITY. Sacha Prechal and Noreen Burrows. Gower Publishing Company, Old Post Road, Brookfield, Vermont 05036. 1990.

THE ILLUSION OF EQUALITY: THE RHETORIC AND REALITY OF DIVORCE REFORM. Martha Albertson Fineman. University of Chicago Press, 5801 Ellis Avenue, Chicago, Illinois 60637. 1991.

IN PURSUIT OF EQUALITY: WOMEN, PUBLIC POLICY, AND THE FEDERAL COURTS. Susan Gluck Mezey. St. Martin's Press, 175 Fifth Avenue, New York, New York 10010. 1992.

INTIMATE INTRUSIONS: WOMEN'S EXPERIENCES OF MALE VIOLENCE. Elizabeth Anne Stanko. Routledge and Kegan Paul, 29 West Thirty-fifth Street, New York, New York 10001. 1984.

THE INVISIBLE BAR: THE WOMAN LAWYER IN AMERICA: 1638 TO THE PRESENT. Karen Berger Morello. Random House Publicity, 201 East Fiftieth Street, New York, New York 10022. 1986.

JUSTICE AND GENDER: SEX DISCRIMINATION AND THE LAW. Deborah L. Rhode. Harvard University Press, 79 Garden Street, Cambridge, Massachusetts 02138. 1989.

JUSTIFIABLE HOMICIDE: BATTERED WOMEN, SELF-DEFENSE, AND THE LAW. Cynthia K. Gillespie. Ohio State University Press, 1070 Carmack Road, Columbus, Ohio 43120-1002. 1989.

LAW, GENDER, AND INJUSTICE: A LEGAL HISTORY OF U.S. WOMEN. Joan Hoff. New York University Press, 70 Washington Square South, New York, New York 10012. 1991.

THE LAW OF SEX DISCRIMINATION. J. Ralph Lindgren and Nadine Taub. West Publishing Company, 50 West Kellogg Boulevard, St. Paul, Minnesota 55164-0526. 1988.

THE LEGAL RELEVANCE OF GENDER: SOME ASPECTS OF SEX-BASED DISCRIMINATION. Sheila McLean and Noreen Burrows. Humanities Press International, Incorporated, 171 First Avenue, Atlantic Highlands, New Jersey 07716-1289. 1988.

A LESSER LIFE: THE MYTH OF WOMEN'S LIBERATION IN AMERICA. Sylvia Ann Hewlett. Warner Books, Incorporated, 866 Fifth Avenue, New York, New York 10103. 1987.

LITIGATION, COURTS, AND WOMEN WORKERS. Karen J. Maschke. Praeger Publishers, One Madison Avenue, New York, New York 10010. 1989.

MORAL VISION AND PROFESSIONAL DECISIONS: THE CHANGING VALUES OF WOMEN AND MEN LAWYERS. Rand Jack and Dana Crowley Jack. Cambridge University Press, 40 West Twentieth Street, New York, New York 10011. 1989.

MOTHER AND FETUS: CHANGING NOTIONS OF MATERNAL RESPONSIBILITY. Robert H. Blank. Greenwood Publishing Group, Incorporated, 88 Post Road West, P.O. Box 5007, Westport, Connecticut 06881. 1992.

MOTHERS ON TRIAL: WOMEN AND CHILD CUSTODY. Phyllis Chesler. HARV imprint of Harcourt, Brace, Jovanovich, Incorporated, 6277 Sea Harbor Drive, Orlando, Florida 32821. 1991.

ON ACCOUNT OF SEX: THE POLITICS OF WOMEN'S ISSUES, 1945-1968. Cynthia Ellen Harrison. University of California Press, 2120 Berkeley Way, Berkeley, California 94720. 1988.

ORIGINS OF PROTECTIVE LABOR LEGISLATION FOR WOMEN, 1905-1925. Susan Lehrer. State University of New York Press, State University Plaza, Albany, New York 12246. 1987.

PORNOGRAPHY AND CIVIL RIGHTS: A NEW DAY FOR WOMEN'S EQUALITY. Andrea Dworkin and Catharine A. MacKinnon. Organizing Against Pornography, 734 East Lake Street, Minneapolis, Minnesota 55407. 1988.

PREGNANCY AND CHILDCARE ISSUES IN THE WORKPLACE. Gerard P. Panaro. Executive Enterprises Publications Company, 22 West Twenty-first Street, New York, New York 10010-6904. 1987.

PREVENTING PRENATAL HARM: SHOULD THE STATE INVERVENE? Deborah Mathieu. Kluwer Academic Publishers, 101 Philip Drive, Assinippi Park, Norwell, Massachusetts 02061. 1991.

PROCEEDINGS OF THE NATIONAL CONFERENCE ON GENDER BIAS IN THE COURTS. Dixie K. Knoebel and Marilyn McCoy Roberts. National Association of Women Judges. National Center for State Courts, 300 Newport Avenue, Williamsburg, Virginia 23187. 1990.

REAL RAPE. Susan Estrich. Harvard University Press, 79 Garden Street, Cambridge, Massachusetts 02138. 1987.

REDRESS FOR SUCCESS: USING THE LAW TO ENFORCE YOUR RIGHTS AS A WOMAN. Dana Shilling. Viking Press, 375 Hudson Street, New York, New York 10014-3657. 1985.

REGULATING WOMANHOOD: HISTORICAL ESSAYS ON MARRIAGE, MOTHERHOOD, AND SEXUALITY. Carol Smart. Routledge, Chapman & Hall, 29 West Thirty-fifth Street, New York, New York 10001. 1992.

REPRESENTING--BATTERED WOMEN WHO KILL. Sara Lee Johann and Frank Osanka. Charles C. Thomas, Publishers, 2600 South First Street, Springfield, Illinois 62794. 1989.

REVOLT AGAINST CHIVALRY. Jacquelyn Dowd Hall. Columbia University Press, 562 West 113th Street, New York, New York 10025. 1979.

RIGHTS AND WRONGS: WOMEN'S STRUGGLE FOR LEGAL EQUALITY. Second edition. Susan Cary Nicholas, Alice M. Price, and Rachel Rubin. Feminist Press, 311 East 94th Street, New York, New York 10128. 1986.

RIGHTS OF PASSAGE: THE PAST AND FUTURE OF ERA. Joan Hoff-Wilson, Editor. Indiana University Press, Tenth and Morton Streets, Bloomington, Indiana 47405. 1986.

SEX DISCRIMINATION IN A NUTSHELL. Second Edition. Claire Sherman Thomas. West Publishing Company, 50 West Kellogg Boulevard, St. Paul, Minnesota 55164-0526. 1991.

SEX SEGREGATION IN THE WORKPLACE: TRENDS, EXPLANATION, AND REMEDIES. Barbara F. Reskin, Editor. National Academy Press, 2101 Constitution Avenue, N.W., Washington, D.C. 20418. 1984.

SEXISM, RACISM, AND OPPRESSION. Arthur Brittan and Mary Maynard. Basil Blackwell, 3 Cambridge Center, Cambridge, Massachusetts 02142. 1984.

SEXIST JUSTICE. Karen DeCrow. Random House Publicity, 201 East Fiftieth Street, New York, New York 10022. 1974.

SEXUAL DISTINCTIONS IN THE LAW: EARLY MAXIMUM HOUR DECISIONS OF THE UNITED STATES SUPREME COURT, 1905-1917. Candice Dalrymple. Garland Publishing, Incorporated, 136 Madison Avenue, New York, New York 10016. 1987.

SEXUAL HARASSMENT IN EMPLOYMENT. Susan M. Omilian. Callaghan and Company, 155 Pfingsten Road, Deerfield, Illinois 60015. 1987.

SEXUAL HARASSMENT IN EMPLOYMENT LAW. Barbara Lindemann Schlei and David D. Kadue. Bureau of National Affairs, Incorporated, 1231 Twenty-fifth Street, Northwest, Washington, D.C. 20037. 1992.

A SHORT HISTORY OF WOMEN. John Langdon-Davies. Norwood Editions, P.O. Box 38, Norwood, Pennsylvania 19074. 1928.

THE SOCIAL AND LEGAL STATUS OF WOMEN: A GLOBAL PERSPECTIVE. Winnie Hazou. Praeger Publishers, One Madison Avenue, New York, New York 10010. 1990.

THE STATUS OF WOMEN IN ISLAMIC LAW AND IN MODERN ISLAMIC LEGISLATION. Jamal J. Nasir. Graham and Trotman Limited, Sterling House, 66 Wilton Road, London SW1V 1DE, England. 1990.

STAYING SOLVENT: A COMPREHENSIVE GUIDE TO EQUAL CREDIT FOR WOMEN. Emily Card. Holt, Rinehart, and Winston, Incorporated, 6277 Sea Harbor Drive, Orlando, Florida 32821. 1985.

TOO OLD, TOO UGLY, AND NOT DEFERENTIAL TO MEN. Christine Craft. Prima Publishing and Communications, P.O. Box 1260, 4970 Topaz Avenue, Rocklin, California 95677. 1988.

UNEQUAL PROTECTION: WOMEN, CHILDREN, AND THE ELDERLY IN COURT. Lois G. Forer. W.W. Norton and Company, Incorporated, 500 Fifth Avenue, New York, New York 10110. 1991.

WHAT EVERY WOMAN NEEDS TO KNOW ABOUT THE LAW. Martha Pomroy. Doubleday and Company, Incorporated, 666 Fifth Avenue, New York, New York 10103. 1980.

WHY ERA FAILED: POLITICS, WOMEN'S RIGHTS AND THE AMENDING PROCESS OF THE CONSTITUTION. Mary Francis Berry. Indiana University Press, Tenth and Morton Streets, Bloomington, Indianan 47405. 1986.

WHY WE LOST ERA. Jane J. Mansbridge. University of Chicago Press, 5801 Ellis Avenue, Third Floor, South Chicago, Illinois 60637. 1986.

WOMAN AND THE LAW. E. Cary and K. W. Peratis. National Textbook Company, 4255 West Touhy Avenue, Lincolnwood, Illinois 60646-1975. 1983.

WOMAN AND THE LAW. T. N. Srivastava. Asia Book Corporation of America, 45-77 One hundred and fifty-seventh Street, Flushing, New York 11355. 1985.

WOMAN UNDER THE ENGLISH LAW, FROM THE LANDING OF THE SAXONS TO THE PRESENT TIME. Arthur Rackham Cleveland. Fred B. Rothman and Company, 10368 West Centennial Road, Littleton, Colorado 80127. 1987. (Reprint).

WOMANLAW: A GUIDE TO LEGAL MATTERS VITAL TO WOMEN. Anita M. Mephill and Charles F. Hemphill, Jr. Prentice-Hall, Incorporated, 113 Sylvan Avenue, Englewood Cliffs, New Jersey 07632. 1981.

WOMAN'S ISSUE: THE POLITICS OF FAMILY LAW REFORM IN ENGLAND. Dorothy M. Stetson. Greenwood Publishing Group, Incorporated, 88 Post Road West, P.O. Box 5007, Westport, Connecticut 06881. 1982.

WOMAN'S LEGACY: ESSAYS ON RACE, SEX, AND CLASS IN AMERICAN HISTORY. Bettina Aptheker. University of Massachusetts Press, P.O. Box 429, Amherst, Massachusetts 01004. 1982.

WOMEN AGAINST CENSORSHIP. Varda Burstyn, Editor. Merrimack Publishing Circle, Division of Salem House, Limited, 462 Boston Street, Topsfield, Massachusetts 09183. 1985.

WOMEN AND CRIME. Frances M. Heidensohn. Columbia University Press, 562 West 113th Street, New York, New York 10025. 1986.

WOMEN AND EQUAL PAY: THE EFFECTS OF LEGISLATION ON FEMALE EMPLOYMENT AND WAGES IN BRITAIN. A. Zabalza and Z. Tzannatos. Cambridge University Press, 40 West Twentieth Street, New York, New York 10011. 1985.

WOMEN AND LAW IN CLASSICAL GREECE. Raphael Sealey. University of North Carolina Press, P.O. Box 2288, 116 South Boundary Street, Chapel Hill, North Carolina 27515-2288. 1990.

WOMEN AND POWER. Lee Ellen Ford, Editor. Ford Associates, 824 East Seventh Street, Auburn, Indiana 46706. 1984.

WOMEN AND POWER. Rosalind Miles. Merrimack Publishing Circle, Division of Salem House, Limited, 462 Boston Street, Topsfield, Massachusetts 01983. 1986.

WOMEN AND PUBLIC POLICIES. Revised edition. Joyce Gelb and Marian Lief Palley. Princeton University Press, 41 William Street, Princeton, New Jersey 08540. 1986.

WOMEN AND THE LAW. Susan Atkins and Brenda Hoggett. Basil Blackwell, 3 Cambridge Center, Cambridge, Massachusetts 02142. 1985.

WOMEN AND THE LAW. Carol H. Lefcourt. Clark Boardman Company, Limited, 435 Hudson Street, New York, New York 10014. 1984- .

WOMEN AS CANDIDATES IN AMERICAN POLITICS. Susan J. Carroll. Indiana University Press, Tenth and Morton Streets, Bloomington, Indiana 47405. 1985.

WOMEN IN AMERICAN LAW: FROM COLONIAL TIMES TO THE NEW DEAL. Marlene S. Wortman, Editor. Holmes and Meier Publishers, Incorporated, 30 Irving Place, IBM Building, New York, New York 10003. 1985.

WOMEN IN AMERICAN LAW: THE STRUGGLE TOWARD EQUALITY, FROM THE NEW DEAL TO THE PRESENT. Judith Baer, Editor. Holmes and Meier Publishers, Incorporated, 30 Irving Place, IBM Building, New York, New York 10003. 1991.

WOMEN IN LAW. Cynthia F. Epstein. Doubleday and Company, Incorporated, 666 Fifth Avenue, New York, New York 10103. 1983.

WOMEN IN LAW: EXPLORATIONS IN LAW, FAMILY, AND SEXUALITY. Julea Brophy and Carol Smart, Editors. Methuen Incorporated, 29 West Thirty-fifth Street, New York, New York 10001. 1985.

WOMEN IN THE CRIMINAL JUSTICE SYSTEM. Second edition. Clarice Feinman. Praeger Publishers, One Madison Avenue, New York, New York 10010-3603. 1985.

WOMEN IN THE JUDICIARY: A SYMPOSIUM FOR WOMEN JUDGES. Marilyn M. Roberts and David Rhein. National Center for State Courts, 300 Newport Avenue, Williamsburg, Virginia 23187-8798.

WOMEN IN THE WORKPLACE. Phyllis A. Wallace, Editor. Auburn House Publishing Company, Greenwood Publishing Group, Incorporated, 88 Post Road West, P.O. Box 5007, Westport, Connecticut 06881. 1982.

WOMEN IN THE WORLD, 1975-1985: THE WOMEN'S DECADE. Second revised edition. Lynne B. Iglitzin and Ruth Ross. ABC-Clio Information Services, Riviera Campus, P.O. Box 1911, Santa Barbara, California 93116-1911. 1986.

WOMEN LAWYERS: PERSPECTIVES ON SUCCESS. Emily Couric. Harcourt, Brace, and Jovanovich, 6277 Sea Harbor Drive, Orlando, Florida 32821. 1984.

WOMEN ON TRIAL: A STUDY OF FEMALE SUSPECTS AND DEFENDANTS IN THE SYSTEM OF CRIMINAL JUSTICE. Susan S. Edwards. Manchester University Press, 175 Fifth Avenue, New York, New York 10010. 1988.

WOMEN PHYSICIANS: CAREERS, STATUS AND POWER. Judith Lorber. Routledge, Chapman & Hall, 29 West Thirty-fifth Street, New York, New York 10001. 1985.

WOMEN, POLITICS, AND THE CONSTITUTION. Naomi B. Lynn. Harrington Park Press, New York, New York. 1990.

WOMEN, SEX AND THE LAW. Rosemarie Tong. Rowman and Allenheld, 420 Boston Way, Lanham, Maryland 20706. 1984.

WOMEN, THE COURTS, AND EQUALITY. Laura L. Crites and Winifred L. Hepperle. Sage Publications, 2455 Teller Road, Newbury Park, California 91320. 1987.

WOMEN, THE LAW, AND THE CONSTITUTION: MAJOR HISTORICAL INTERPRETATIONS. Kermit L. Hall. Garland Publishing, Incorporated, 136 Madison Avenue, New York, New York 10016. 1987.

WOMEN, THE LAW, AND THE ECONOMY. E. Diane Pask and Kathleen E. Mahoney. Butterworth and Company, Limited, 75 Clegg Road, Markham, Ontario, Canada L3R 9Y6. 1985.

WOMEN'S LAW: AN INTRODUCTION TO FEMINIST JURISPRUDENCE. Tove Stang Dahl. Oxford University Press, 200 Madison Avenue, New York, New York 10016. 1987.

WOMEN'S LEGAL RIGHTS: INTERNATIONAL COVENANTS AN ALTERNATIVE TO ERA? Malvina Halberstam and Elizabeth F. Defeis. Transnational Publishers, P.O. Box 7282, Ardsley-on-Hudson, New York 10503. 1987.

WOMEN'S RIGHTS. Nancy McGlen and Karen O'Connor. Praeger Publishers, One Madison Avenue, New York, New York 10010-3603. 1983.

WOMEN'S RIGHTS AGENDA FOR THE STATES. Linda Tarr-Whelan, Editor. National Center for Policy Alternatives, 2000 Florida Avenue, Northwest, Washington, D.C. 20009. 1984.

WOMEN'S RIGHTS AT WORK: CAMPAIGNS AND POLICY IN BRITAIN AND THE UNITED STATES. Elizabeth M. Meehan. St. Martin's Press, Incorporated, 175 Fifth Avenue, New York, New York 10010. 1985.

WOMEN'S RIGHTS IN THE U.S.A.: POLICY DEBATES AND GENDER ROLES. Dorothy McBride Stetson. Brooks/Cole Publishing Company, 511 Forest Lodge Road, Pacific Grove, California 93950-5098. 1991.

WOMEN'S WELFARE--WOMEN'S RIGHTS. Jane Lewis, Editor. Longwood Publishing Group, Incorporated, 27 South Main Street, Wolfeboro, New Hampshire 03894-2069. 1982.

WORKING WOMEN AND THE LAW: EQUALITY AND DISCRIMINATION IN THEORY AND PRACTICE. Anne E. Morris and Susan M. Nott. Routledge, Chapman & Hall, 29 West Thirty-fifth Street, New York, New York 10001. 1990.

YOU'RE ENTITLED!: A DIVORCE LAWYER TALKS TO WOMEN. Sidney M. De Angelis. Contemporary Books, Incorporated, 180 North Michigan Avenue, Chicago, Illinois 60601. 1989.

ENCYCLOPEDIAS AND DICTIONARIES

ENCYCLOPEDIA OF FEMINISM. Lisa Tuttle. Facts on File, Incorporated, 460 Park Avenue, South, New York, New York 10016. 1986.

LAW REVIEWS AND PERIODICALS

BERKELEY'S WOMEN'S LAW JOURNAL. Boalt Hall School of Law, University of California, Berkeley, Berkeley, California 94720. Annual.

FEMINIST STUDIES. Feminist Studies, Incorporated, C/O Women Studies, University of Maryland, College Park, Maryland 20742. Quarterly.

HARVARD WOMEN'S LAW JOURNAL. Harvard Law School, Hastings Hall, Cambridge, Massachusetts 02138. 1978- . Annual.

HYPATIA: A JOURNAL OF FEMINIST PHILOSOPHY. Department of Philosophical Studies, Southern Illinois University at Edwardsville, Edwardsville, Illinois 62026-1001. Biannual.

WISCONSIN WOMEN'S LAW JOURNAL. University of Wisconsin Law School, 975 Bascon Mall, Madison, Wisconsin 53706. 1985- . Annual.

WOMEN'S LAW JOURNAL. Women's Law Journal, Incorporated, P.O. Box 130, 308 Westwood Plaza, Los Angeles, California 90024. Quarterly.

WOMEN'S RIGHTS LAW REPORTER. 15 Washington Street, Newark, New Jersey 07102. 1971- . Quarterly.

NEWSLETTERS AND NEWSPAPERS

ACTION ALERT. American Association of University Women, 1111 Sixteenth Street, Northwest, Washington, D.C. 20036. Monthly.

THE EQUAL RIGHTS ADVOCATE. Equal Rights Advocates, 1370 Mission Street, San Francisco, California 94103. Quarterly.

FROM THE STATE CAPITALS: WOMEN AND THE LAW. Wakeman Walworth, Incorporated, 300 North Washington Street, Suite 204, Alexandria, Virginia 22314. Monthly.

LEGISLATIVE UPDATE. National Council of Jewish Women, 1101 Fifteenth Street, Northwest, Suite 1012, Washington, D.C. 20005. Bimonthly.

LOYOLA QUARTERLY OF PUBLIC ISSUES AND THE LAW. Loyola University School of Law, 1 East Pearson Street, Chicago, Illinois 60611. 1987- . Quarterly.

WASHINGTON NEWSLETTER. National Council of Jewish Women, 1101 Fifteenth Street, Northwest, Suite 1012, Washington, D.C. 20005. Quarterly.

WBA NEWSLETTER. Women's Bar Association of the District of Columbia, 1819 H Street, Northwest, Suite 1250, Washington, D.C. 20006. Bimonthly.

THE WOMEN'S ADVOCATE. National Center on Women and Family Law, 799 Broadway, New York, New York 10003. Bimonthly.

WOMEN'S RIGHTS SECTION NEWSLETTER. New Jersey State Bar Association, One Constitution Square, New Brunswick, New Jersey 08901. Quarterly.

BIBLIOGRAPHIES

COMPARABLE WORTH. Joan Nordquist. Reference and Research Services, 511 Lincoln Street, Santa Cruz, California 95060. 1986.

COMPARABLE WORTH: AN ANNOTATED BIBLIOGRAPHY. June L. DeWeese and Jo Ann Humphreys. Compubibs, Division of Vantage Information Consultants, Brooklyn, New York. 1985.

THE EQUAL RIGHTS AMENDMENT: AN ANNOTATED BIBLIOGRAPHY OF THE ISSUES, 1976-1985. Renee Feinberg, Compiler. Greenwood Publishing Group, Incorporated, 88 Post Road West, P.O. Box 5007, Westport, Connecticut 06881. 1986.

FEMINIST LEGAL LITERATURE: A SELECTIVE ANNOTATED BIBLIOGRAPHY. F.C. DeCoste, K.M. Munro, and Lillian MacPherson. Garland Publishing, Incorporated, 136 Madison Avenue, New York, New York 10016. 1991.

LEGAL STATUS AND RIGHTS OF WOMEN: A SELECTED BIBLIOGRAPHY. Edward Stanek. Vance Bibliographies, P.O. Box 229, 112 North Charter Street, Monticello, Illinois 61856. 1987.

WOMEN'S ANNOTATED LEGAL BIBLIOGRAPHY. Yeshiva University, Benjamin N. Cardozo School of Law. Clark Boardman Company, Limited, 435 Hudson Street, New York, New York 10014. 1984.

WOMEN'S LEGAL RIGHTS IN THE UNITED STATES: A SELECTIVE BIBLIOGRAPHY. Joan Ariel. American Library Association, 50 East Huron Street, Chicago, Illinois 60611. 1985.

DIRECTORIES

DIRECTORY OF LOCAL WOMEN ELECTED OFFICIALS. Olivia Pickett. National League of Cities, 1301 Pennsylvania Avenue, Washington, D.C. 20004. Annual.

DIRECTORY OF SELECTED WOMEN'S RESEARCH AND POLICY CENTERS. Joan Button. Women's Research and Education Institute, Congressional Caucus for Women's Issues, 1700 Eighteenth Street, Northwest, Suite 400, Washington, D.C. 20009. Biennial.

FEMINIST PERIODICALS: A CURRENT LISTING OF CONTENTS. Susan E. Searing and Linda Shult, Editors. Women's Studies Librarian, University of Wisconsin System, Memorial Library, Room 112A, 728 State Street, Madison, Wisconsin 53706. Quarterly.

NATIONAL DIRECTORY OF WOMEN ELECTED OFFICIALS. National Women's Political Caucus, 1275 K Street, Northwest, Suite 750, Washington, D.C. 20005. Biennial.

RESOURCES FOR FEMINIST RESEARCH--INTERNATIONAL GUIDE TO WOMEN'S PERIODICALS AND RESOURCES ISSUES. Resources for Feminist Research/Documentation Sur la Recherche Feministe, Centre for Women's Studies in Education, Ontario Institute for Studies in Education, 252 Bloor Street West, Toronto, Ontario M55 IV6, Canada. 1982.

WOMAN'S YELLOW BOOK. Second edition. Federation of Organizations for Professional Women, 20001 South Street, Northwest, Suite 500, Washington, D.C. 20009. 1984.

WOMEN'S ORGANIZATIONS: A NATIONAL DIRECTORY. Martha Merrill Doss, Editor. Garrett Park Press, Box 190E, Garrett Park, Maryland 20896. 1986.

BIOGRAPHICAL SOURCES

BREAKTHROUGH: WOMEN IN LAW. Betsy Covington Smith. Walker and Company, 720 Fifth Avenue, New York, New York 10019. 1984.

FEMINISM ON TRIAL: THE GINNY FOAT CASE AND ITS MEANING FOR THE FUTURE OF THE WOMEN'S MOVEMENT. Ellen Hawkes. William Morrow and Company, Incorporated, 105 Madison Avenue, New York, New York 10016. 1986.

FROM EQUAL SUFFRAGE TO EQUAL RIGHTS: ALICE PAUL AND THE WOMAN'S PARTY, 1910-1928. Christine A. Lundardini. New York University Press, 70 Washington Square South, New York, New York 10012. 1988.

STATISTICS SOURCES

WOMEN LAWYERS: SUPPLEMENTARY DATA TO THE 1971 LAWYER STATISTICAL REPORT. American Bar Foundation. Books on Demand, Division of UMI, 300 North Zeeb Road, Ann Arbor, Michigan 48106-1346. 1973.

ASSOCIATIONS AND PROFESSIONAL SOCIETIES

AMERICAN ASSOCIATION OF UNIVERSITY WOMEN. 1111 Sixteenth Street, Northwest, Washington, D.C. 20036. (202) 785-7700.

ASSOCIATION OF AMERICAN LAW SCHOOLS, SECTION ON WOMEN IN LEGAL EDUCATION. Suite 370, One Dupont Circle, Northwest, Washington, D.C. 20036. (202) 296-8851.

CAPITOL HILL WOMEN'S POLITICAL CAUCUS. P.O. Box 599, Longworth House Office Building, Washington, D.C. 20515. (202) 225-2265.

COMPARABLE WORTH PROJECT. Institute of Industrial Relations, University of California, Berkeley, 12521 Channing Way, Berkeley, California 94720. (415) 642-0323.

CONGRESSIONAL CAUCUS FOR WOMEN'S ISSUES. 2471 Rayburn House Office Building, Washington, D.C. 20515. (202) 225-6740.

EQUAL RIGHTS ADVOCATES. 1370 Mission Street, San Francisco, California 94103. (415) 621-0505.

FEDERATION OF WOMEN LAWYERS, JUDICIAL SCREENING PANEL. 2000 P Street, Northwest, Suite 610, Washington, D.C. 20036. (202) 822-6644.

INTERNATIONAL FEDERATION OF WOMEN LAWYERS. 186 Fifth Avenue, New York, New York 10010. (212) 206-1666.

LEGAL EDUCATION. Suite 370, One Dupont Circle, Northwest, Washington, D. C. 20036. (202) 296-8851.

NATIONAL ASSOCIATION OF BLACK WOMEN ATTORNEYS. 3711 Macomb Street, Northwest, Second Floor, Washington, D.C. 20016. (202) 966-9693.

NATIONAL ASSOCIATION OF WOMEN JUDGES. c/o National Center for State Courts, 300 Newport Avenue, Williamsburg, Virginia 23187. (804) 253-2000.

NATIONAL ASSOCIATION OF WOMEN LAWYERS. American Bar Association, 750 North Lake Shore Drive, Chicago, Illinois 60611. (312) 988-5000.

NATIONAL CENTER ON WOMEN AND FAMILY LAW. 799 Broadway, Room 402, New York, New York 10003. (212) 674-8200.

NATIONAL COMMITTEE ON PAY EQUITY. 1201 Sixteenth Street, Northwest, Room 422, Washington, D.C. 20036. (202) 822-7304.

NATIONAL COUNCIL OF JEWISH WOMEN. 1101 Fifteenth Street, Northwest, Suite 1012, Washington, D.C. 20005. (202) 296-2588.

NATIONAL ORGANIZATION FOR WOMEN. 1000 Sixteenth Street, Northwest, Suite 700, Washington, D.C. 20036. (202) 331-0066.

NATIONAL TASK FORCE ON PROSTITUTION. 333 Valencia Street, Suite 101, San Francisco, California 94103. (415) 558-0450.

NATIONAL WOMAN'S PARTY. Sewall-Belmont House, 144 Constitution Avenue, Northeast, Washington, D.C. 20002. (202) 546-1210.

NATIONAL WOMEN AND THE LAW ASSOCIATION. 1810 Sixth Street, Berkeley, California 94710. (415) 704-0151.

NATIONAL WOMEN'S LAW CENTER. 1616 P Street, Northwest, Washington, D.C. 20036. (202) 328-5160.

NATIONAL WOMEN'S POLITICAL CAUCUS. 1275 K Street, Northwest, Suite 750, Washington, D.C. 20005. (202) 898-1100.

NATIONAL WOMEN'S STUDIES ASSOCIATION. c/o Caryn McTighe Musil, University of Maryland, College Park, Maryland 20742. (301) 405-5573.

NINE-TO-FIVE: NATIONAL ASSOCIATION OF WORKING WOMEN. 614 Superior Avenue, Northwest, Suite 852, Cleveland, Ohio 44113. (216) 566-9308.

NOW LEGAL DEFENSE AND EDUCATION FUND. 99 Hudson Street, Twelfth Floor, New York, New York 10013. (212) 925-6635.

RELIGIOUS NETWORK FOR EQUALITY FOR WOMEN. 475 Riverside Drive, Room 812-A, New York, New York 10115. (212) 870-2995.

SOCIETY FOR THE STUDY OF WOMEN IN LEGAL HISTORY. c/o Nancy S. Erickson, 619 Carroll Street, Brooklyn, New York 11215. (718) 783-8162.

WOMEN'S LAW FUND. c/o Nancy Krammer, 57 East Washington Street, Chagnin Falls, Ohio 44022. (216) 247-6167.

WOMEN'S LAW PROJECT. 125 South Ninth Street, Suite 401, Philadelphia, Pennsylvania 19107. (215) 928-9801.

WOMEN'S LEGAL DEFENSE FUND. 2000 P Street, Northwest, Suite 400, Washington, D.C. 20036. (202) 887-0364.

WOMEN'S RIGHTS PROJECT. c/o American Civil Liberties Union, 132 West Forty-third Street, New York, New York 10036. (212) 944-9800.

RESEARCH CENTERS, INSTITUTES, CLEARINGHOUSES

BUSINESS AND PROFESSIONAL WOMEN'S FOUNDATION. 2012 Massachusetts Avenue, Northwest, Washington, D.C. 20036. (202) 293-1200.

CENTER FOR THE STUDY OF CIVIL RIGHTS. University of Virginia, 1512 Jefferson Park Avenue, Charlottesville, Virginia 22903. (804) 924-3109.

CENTER FOR WOMEN POLICY STUDIES. 2000 P Street, Northwest, Suite 508, Washington, D.C. 20036. (202) 872-1770.

INSTITUTE FOR SCIENTIFIC ANALYSIS. 2235 Lombard Street, San Francisco, California 94123. (415) 921-4987.

NATIONAL CENTER FOR POLICY ALTERNATIVES. 2000 Florida Avenue, Northwest, Washington, D.C. 20009. (202) 387-6030.

NATIONAL CENTER ON WOMEN AND FAMILY LAW. 799 Broadway, Room 402, New York, New York 10003. (212) 674-8200.

NATIONAL WOMEN'S LAW CENTER. 1616 P Street, Northwest, Washington, D.C. 20036. (202) 328-5160.

NORTH CAROLINA CENTER FOR LAWS AFFECTING WOMEN, INCORPORATED. 1111 Brookstown Avenue, Winston-Salem, North Carolina 27101. (919) 722-0098.

WOMEN'S BUREAU. U.S. Department of Labor, 200 Constitution Avenue, Northwest, Washington, D.C. 20210. (202) 523-6611.

WOMEN'S RESEARCH AND EDUCATION INSTITUTE. 1700 Eighteenth Street, Northwest, Suite 400, Washington, D.C. 20009. (202) 328-7070.

WOMEN'S STUDIES PROGRAM AND POLICY CENTER. George Washington University, 2013 G Street, Northwest, Stuart Hall 202, Washington, D.C. 20052. (202) 994-6942.

WORKERS' COMPENSATION
See also: EMPLOYEES' COMPENSATION APPEALS BOARD

LOOSELEAF SERVICES AND REPORTERS

HANDLING OCCUPATIONAL DISEASE CASES. Frederick M. Baron. Callaghan and Company, 155 Pfingsten Road, Deerfield, Illinois 60015. 1989.

THE LAW OF WORKMEN'S COMPENSATION. Arthur Larson. Matthew Bender and Company, Incorporated, 11 Penn Plaza, New York, New York 10001. 1968- .

WORKERS' COMPENSATION LAW REPORTER. Commerce Clearing House, Incorporated, 4025 West Peterson Avenue, Chicago, Illinois 60646. 1957- .

HANDBOOKS, MANUALS, FORMBOOKS

NATIONAL COUNCIL WORKMEN'S COMPENSATION UNIT STATISTICAL PLAN MANUAL. National Council on Compensation Insurance, One Penn Plaza, New York, New York 10119. 1983.

PRENTICE-HALL'S WORKERS' COMPENSATION HANDBOOK. Jay E. Grenig. Prentice-Hall, Incorporated, 113 Sylvan Avenue, Englewood Cliffs, New Jersey 07632. 1987.

REFERENCE GUIDE TO WORKMEN'S COMPENSATION--A QUICK RETRIEVAL HANDBOOK. Elmer H. Blair. Thomas Law Book Company, Old Post Road, Brookfield, Vermont 05036. 1968- .

WORKER'S COMPENSATION HANDBOOK, SEVENTH EDITION. Stanford D. Herlick. Parker and Son Publications, Incorporated, Box 60001, Los Angeles, California 90060. 1985.

TEXTBOOKS AND GENERAL WORKS

AVOIDING THE CRACKS: A GUIDE TO THE WORKERS' COMPENSATION SYSTEM. Anne Tramposh. Praeger Publishers, One Madison Avenue, New York, New York 10010. 1991.

BENEFITS, COSTS, AND CYCLES IN WORKERS COMPENSATION. Philip S. Borba and David Appel. National Council on Compensation Insurance. Kluwer Academic Publishers, 101 Philip Drive, Assinippi Park, Norwell, Massachusetts 02061. 1990.

DESIGNING BENEFIT STRUCTURE FOR TEMPORARY DISABILITY: A GUIDE FOR POLICYMAKERS. Richard B. Victor and Charles A. Fleischman. Workers Compensation Research Institute, Cambridge, Massachusetts. 1989.

GUIDELINES FOR HANDLING PSYCHIATRIC ISSUES IN WORKERS' COMPENSATION CASES. Herbert Lasky. Lex-Com Enterprises, Rancho Palos Verdes, California. 1988.

AN INTERNATIONAL COMPARISON OF WORKERS' COMPENSATION. C. Arthur Williams, Jr. Kluwer Academic Publishers, 101 Philip Drive, Assinippi Park, Norwell, Massachusetts 02061. 1991.

THE LAW OF MARITIME PERSONAL INJURIES. Fourth Edition. Martin J. Norris. Lawyers Cooperative Publishing Company, Aqueduct Building, Rochester, New York 14694. 1990.

LOSS CONTROL FOR THE SMALL TO MEDIUM SIZE BUSINESS: REDUCING WORKERS' COMPENSATION COSTS. Robert E. Brisbin. Van Nostrand Reinhold Company, Incorporated, 115 Fifth Avenue, New York, New York 10003. 1990.

MEDICAL COST CONTAINMENT IN WORKERS' COMPENSATION: A NATIONAL INVENTORY. Leslie I. Boden, Joan M. DeFinis, and Charles A. Fleischman. Workers Compensation Research Institute, Cambridge, Massachusetts. 1990.

MEDICAL COSTS IN WORKERS' COMPENSATION: TRENDS AND INTERSTATE COMPARISONS. Leslie I. Boden and Charles A. Fleischman. Workers Compensation Research Institute, Cambridge, Massachusetts. 1989.

MODERN JOB SAFETY AND HEALTH. Wayne T. Brooks and Rich Arthurs. Prentice-Hall, Incorporated, 113 Sylvan Avenue, Englewood Cliffs, New Jersey 07632. 1987.

NEW PERSPECTIVES IN WORKERS' COMPENSATION. John F. Burton, Jr. New York State School of Industrial and Labor Relations. Cornell University Press, 124 Roberts Place, Ithaca, New York 14850. 1988.

OCCUPATIONAL HEARING LOSS. Robert Thayer Sataloff and Joseph Sataloff. Marcel Dekker, 720 Madison Avenue, New York, New York 10016. 1987.

PRIMER ON WORKERS' COMPENSATION. Second Edition. Jeffrey V. Nackley. Bureau of National Affairs, Incorporated, 1231 Twenty-fifth Street, Northwest, Washington, D.C. 20037. 1989.

REDUCING LITIGATION: USING PERMANENT PARTIAL DISABILITY GUIDELINES AND STATE EVALUATORS IN OREGON. Leslie I. Boden, Daniel E. Kern, and John A. Gardner. Workers Compensation Research Institute, Cambridge, Massachusetts. 1991.

RETURN TO WORK INCENTIVES: LESSONS FOR POLICYMAKERS FROM ECONOMIC STUDIES. John A. Gardner. Workers Compensation Research Institute, Cambridge, Massachusetts. 1989.

STRESS IN THE WORKPLACE: COSTS, LIABILITY, AND PREVENTION. Bureau of National Affairs, Incorporated, 1231 Twenty-fifth Street, Northwest, Washington, D.C. 20037. 1987.

WORKERS' COMPENSATION AND EMPLOYEE PROTECTION LAWS IN A NUTSHELL. Second Edition. Jack B. Hood, Benjamin A. Hardy, Jr., and Harold S. Lewis, Jr. West Publishing Company, P.O. Box 64526, 50 West Kellogg Boulevard, St. Paul, Minnesota 55164-0526-0526. 1990.

WORKERS' COMPENSATION BENEFITS: ADEQUACY, EQUITY, AND EFFICIENCY. John D. Worrall and David Appel, Editors. ILR Press, New York State School of Industrial Relations, Cornell University, Box 1000, Ithaca, New York 14851-0952. 1985.

WORKERS' COMPENSATION CLAIMS AND BENEFITS. David W. O'Brien and Bernadette M. O'Brien. Parker and Son Publications, Incorporated, P.O. Box 60001, Los Angeles, California 90060. 1990.

WORKERS' COMPENSATION IN CANADA. Second Edition. Terence G. Ison. Butterworths, 75 Clegg Road, Markham, Ontario, Canada L3R 9Y6. 1989.

WORKERS' COMPENSATION INSURANCE PRICING: CURRENT PROGRAMS AND PROPOSED REFORMS. Philip S. Borba and David Appel. Kluwer Academic Publishers, 101 Philip Drive, Assinippi Park, Norwell, Massachusetts 02061. 1988.

WORKERS' COMPENSATION LAW. Jon L. Gelman. West Publishing Company, 50 West Kellogg Boulevard, St. Paul, Minnesota 55164-0526. 1988.

WORKERS' COMPENSATION LAW AND PRACTICE. Karen A. Lerner. West Publishing Company, 50 West Kellogg Boulevard, St. Paul, Minnesota 55164-0526. 1989.

WORKERS' COMPENSATION: STRATEGIES FOR LOWERING COSTS AND REDUCING WORKERS' SUFFERING. Edward M. Welch. Michigan State University, School of Labor and Industrial Relations. LRP Publications, 747 Dresher Road, Horsham, Pennsylvania 19044. 1989.

WORKERS COMPENSATION: STRENGTHENING THE SOCIAL COMPACT. Orin Kramer and Richard Briffault. Insurance Information Institute Press. University Press of America, 4720 Boston Way, Lanham, Maryland 20706. 1991.

WORKMEN'S COMPENSATION FOR OCCUPATION INJURIES AND DEATH: AN ABRIDGMENT OF THE LAW OF WORKMEN'S COMPENSATION. Arthur Larson. Matthew Bender and Company, Incorporated, 11 Penn Plaza, New York, New York 10001. 1972.

WORKMEN'S COMPENSATION IN TWENTIETH CENTURY BRITAIN: LAW, HISTORY, AND SOCIAL POLICY. P.W.J. Bartrip. Avebury, Brookfield, Vermont. 1987.

ENCYCLOPEDIAS AND DICTIONARIES

THE BLR ENCYCLOPEDIA OF WORKERS' COMPENSATION. Business and Legal Reports, Incorporated, 64 Wall Street, Madison, Connecticut 06443. 1991.

LAW REVIEWS AND PERIODICALS

WORKMEN'S COMPENSATION LAW REVIEW. William S. Hein and Company, Incorporated, Hein Building, 1285 Main Street, Buffalo, New York, New York 14209. Annual.

NEWSLETTERS AND NEWSPAPERS

BNA'S WORKERS COMPENSATION REPORT. Bureau of National Affairs, Incorporated, 1231 Twenty-fifth Street, Northwest, Washington, D.C. 20037. Biweekly.

FROM THE STATE CAPITALS: WORKER'S COMPENSATION. Wakeman, Walworth, Incorporated, 300 North Washington Street, Suite 2011, Alexandria, Virginia 22314. Monthly.

JOHN BURTON'S WORKER'S COMPENSATION MONITOR. LRP Publications, 747 Dresher Road, Horsham, Pennsylvania 19044. Bimonthly.

WORKERS COMPENSATION BIWEEKLY. Quinlan Publishing Company, Incorporated, 23 Drydock Avenue, Boston, Massachusetts 02114. Biweekly.

WORKERS' COMPENSATION LAW BULLETIN. Quinlan Publishing Company, 23 Drydock Avenue, Boston, Massachusetts 02114. Monthly.

WORKERS' COMPENSATION MONTHLY. Seak, Incorporated, P.O. Box 590, Falmouth, Massachusetts 02541. Monthly.

DIRECTORIES

BUSINESS INSURANCE-EMPLOYEE BENEFITS CONSULTANTS SERVICES ISSUE. Crain Communications, Incorporated, 740 Rush Street, Chicago, Illinois 60611. Annual.

GROUP INSURANCE STANDARD DIRECTORY. ERISA Benefits Funds, Incorporated, 1341 G Street, Northwest, Suite 610, Washington, D.C. 20005. Annual.

WORKERS COMPENSATION, STATE ADMINISTRATIVE DIRECTORY. Alliance of American Insurers, 1501 Woodfield Road, Suite 400 W, Schaumburg, Illinois 60173. 1982- .

ASSOCIATIONS AND PROFESSIONAL SOCIETIES

INSURANCE SERVICES OFFICE. 160 Water Street, New York, New York 10038. (212) 487-5000.

INTERNATIONAL ASSOCIATION OF INDUSTRIAL ACCIDENT BOARDS AND COMMISSIONS. 1575 Aviation Center Parkway, Suite 519, Daytona Beach, Florida 32114. (904) 255-2915.

WORKERS' COMPENSATION (continued)

NATIONAL COUNCIL ON COMPENSATION INSURANCE. One Penn Plaza, New York, New York, 10119. (212) 560-1000.

RESEARCH CENTERS, INSTITUTES, CLEARINGHOUSES

BASIC RESEARCH, INCORPORATED. 16260 Ventura Boulevard, Suite LL30, Encino, California 91436. (205) 534-6844.

NATIONAL FOUNDATION FOR UNEMPLOYMENT COMPENSATION AND WORKERS COMPENSATION. 600 Maryland Avenue, Southwest, Suite 603, Washington, D.C. 20024. (202) 484-3346.

STATISTICS SOURCES

INSURANCE FACTS. Insurance Information Institute. 110 William Street, New York, New York 10038. Annual.

NATIONAL COUNCIL WORKMEN'S COMPENSATION UNIT STATISTICAL PLAN MANUAL. National Council on Compensation Insurance, One Penn Plaza, New York, New York 10001. 1983.

SOCIAL SECURITY BULLETIN--ANNUAL STATISTICAL SUPPLEMENT. U.S. Department of Health and Human Services. Social Security Administration. 6401 Security Boulevard, Baltimore, Maryland 21235. Annual.

WORLD TRADE
See: EXPORT AND IMPORT

WRITS
See: CIVIL PROCEDURE

WRONGFUL DEATH

HANDBOOKS, MANUALS, FORMBOOKS

MANUAL FOR LAWYERS AND LEGAL ASSISTANTS: WRONGFUL DEATH. L. Ray Bishop and Donald E. Shelton. University of Michigan, Law School Institute of Continuing Legal Education, 1020 Greene Street, Ann Arbor, Michigan 48109-1444. 1977.

RECOVERY FOR WRONGFUL DEATH AND INJURY: ECONOMIC HANDBOOK. Third Edition. Stuart M. Speiser. Lawyers Cooperative Publishing Company, Aqueduct Building, Rochester, New York 14694. 1988.

TEXTBOOKS AND GENERAL WORKS

HOW TO PROVE DAMAGES IN WRONGFUL PERSONAL INJURY AND DEATH SUITS. Second Edition. I. Duke Avnet. Prentice-Hall, Incorporated, 113 Sylvan Avenue, Englewood Cliffs, New Jersey 07632. 1978.

THE LAW OF MARITIME PERSONAL INJURIES. Fourth Edition. Martin J. Norris. Lawyers Cooperative Publishing Company, Aqueduct Building, Rochester, New York 14694. 1990.

RECOVERY FOR WRONGFUL DEATH: ECONOMIC HANDBOOK. Second Edition. Stuart M. Speiser. Lawyers Co-Operative Publishing Company, Aqueduct Building, Rochester, New York 14694. 1988. (Supplements).

WRONGFUL DEATH LITIGATION. Association of Trial Lawyers of America Education Fund, 1050 Thirty-first Street, Northwest, Washington, D.C. 20007. 1983.

STATISTICS SOURCES

NATIONAL WRONGFUL DEATH SURVEY. Kroll, Pomerantz, and Cameron, 500 Fifth Avenue, New York, New York 10110. 1983.

X Y Z

ZONING AND PLANNING
See also: HISTORIC PRESERVATION

LOOSELEAF SERVICES AND REPORTERS

CALIFORNIA LAND USE PROCEDURE. J.R. Ramos. Shepard's/McGraw-Hill, P.O. Box 1235, Colorado Springs, Colorado 80901. 1991- .

ENVIRONMENTAL AND NATURAL RESOURCES PERMITS: FEDERAL APPROVAL STANDARDS AND PROCEDURES. Robert L. Schmid. Butterworth Legal Publishers, 90 Stiles Road, Salem, New Hampshire 03079. 1991- .

ENVIRONMENTAL REGULATION OF LAND USE. Linda A. Malone. Clark Boardman Company, Limited, 435 Hudson Street, New York, New York 10014. 1990- .

HOUSING AND DEVELOPMENT REPORTER. Bureau of National Affairs, 1231 Twenty-fifth Street, Northwest, Washington, D.C. 20037. 1973- .

THE LAW OF ZONING AND PLANNING. Arden H. Rathkopf. Fourth Edition. Clark Boardman Company, Limited, 435 Hudson Street, New York, New York 10014. 1983- .

A PRACTICAL GUIDE TO WINNING LAND USE APPROVALS AND PERMITS. Nyal D. Deems and N. Stevenson Jennette, III. Matthew Bender and Company, Incorporated, 11 Penn Plaza, New York, New York 10001. 1989- .

ZONING AND LAND USE CONTROLS. Patrick J. Rohan. Matthew Bender and Company, Incorporated, 11 Penn Plaza, New York, New York 10001. 1978- .

HANDBOOKS, MANUALS, FORMBOOKS

CITIZEN'S GUIDE TO ZONING. Herbert H. Smith. Planners Press, 1313 East Sixtieth Street, Chicago, Illinois 60637. 1983.

THE SMALL TOWN PLANNING HANDBOOK. Thomas L. Daniels, John W. Keller, and Mark B. Lapping. Planners Press, 1313 East Sixtieth Street, Chicago, Illinois 60637. 1988.

ZONING AND PLANNING DESKBOOK. Douglas W. Kmiec. Clark Boardman Company, Limited, 435 Hudson Street, New York, New York 10014. 1986.

ZONING AND PLANNING LAW HANDBOOK. Noah J. Gordon, Editor. Clark Boardman Company, Limited, 435 Hudson Street, New York, New York 10014. 1988.

THE ZONING BOARD MANUAL. Planners Press, 1313 East Sixtieth Street, Chicago, Illinois 60637. 1984.

TEXTBOOKS AND GENERAL WORKS

AMERICAN LAND PLANNING LAW: 1974-1983. Norman Williams. Callaghan and Company, 155 Pfingsten Road, Deerfield, Illinois 60015. 1983 (1985 Supplement).

AMERICAN LAW OF ZONING. Second Edition. Robert M. Anderson. Lawyers Co-Operative Publishing Company, Aqueduct Building, Rochester, New York 14694. 1986. (Supplements).

CASES AND MATERIALS ON LAND USE. Fourth Edition. Robert R. Wright and Morton Gitelman. West Publishing Company, 50 West Kellogg Boulevard, St. Paul, Minnesota 55164. 1991.

CITIZEN'S GUIDE TO ZONING. Herbert H. Smith. Planners Press, 1313 East Sixtieth Street, Chicago, Illinois 60637. 1983.

ENFORCING ZONING AND LAND-USE CONTROLS. Eric Damian Kelly. American Planning Association, 1313 East Sixtieth Street, Chicago, Illinois 60637. 1988.

HANDLING ZONING AND LAND USE LITIGATION: A PRACTICAL GUIDE. Craig A. Peterson and Clair McCarthy. Michie/Bobbs-Merrill, The Michie Company, P.O. Box 7587, Charlottesville, Virginia 22906-7587. 1982. (1987 Supplement).

LAND OWNERSHIP AND USE, THIRD EDITION. Curtis J. Berger. Little, Brown, and Company, 34 Beacon Street, Boston, Massachusetts 02108. 1983.

LAND USE AND THE CONSTITUTION: PRINCIPLES FOR PLANNING PRACTICE. Brian W. Blaesser. Planners Press, 1313 East Sixtieth Street, Chicago, Illinois 60637. 1989.

LAND USE CONTROL: GEOGRAPHY, LAW, AND PUBLIC POLICY. Rutherford H. Platt. Prentice-Hall, Incorporated, 113 Sylvan Avenue, Englewood Cliffs, New Jersey 07632. 1991.

LAND USE LAW. Second Edition. Daniel R. Mandelker. Michie Company, P.O. Box 7587, Charlottesville, Virginia 22906-7587. 1988. (Supplement 1991).

LAND-USE PLANNING: A CASEBOOK ON THE USE, MISUSE, AND RE-USE OF URBAN LAND. Fourth Edition. Charles M. Haar and Michael Allan Wolf. Little, Brown and Company, 34 Beacon Street, Boston, Massachusetts 02108. 1989.

LAND USE PLANNING AND ZONING. Peter J. Loughlin. Equity Publishing Company, Main Street, Orford, New Hampshire 03777. 1990.

LAND USE REGULATION AND LITIGATION: ALI-ABA COURSE OF STUDY MATERIALS. American Law Institute, 4025 Chestnut Street, Philadelphia, Pennsylvania 19104. 1984.

LAND USE REGULATION: THE IMPACTS OF ALTERNATIVE LAND USE RIGHTS. Martin A. Garrett, Jr. Praeger Publishers, One Madison Avenue, New York, New York 10010. 1987.

LAND USE REGULATIONS: PLANNING, ZONING, SUBDIVISION REGULATION, AND ENVIRONMENTAL CONTROL. Peter W. Salsich. Shepard's/McGraw-Hill, P.O. Box 1235, Colorado Springs, Colorado 80901. 1991.

LANDMARK JUSTICE: THE INFLUENCE OF WILLIAM J. BRENNAN ON AMERICA'S COMMUNITIES. Charles M. Haar and Jerold S. Kayden. Preservation Press, National Trust for Historic Preservation, 1785 Massachusetts Avenue, Northwest, Washington, D.C. 20036. 1989.

THE LAW OF ZONING AND PLANNING, FOURTH EDITION. Arden H. Rathkopf and Daren A. Rathkopf. Clark Boardman Company, Limited, 435 Hudson Street, New York, New York 10014. 1985.

MANAGING LAND-USE CONFLICTS: CASE STUDIES IN SPECIAL AREA MANAGEMENT. David J. Brower and Daniel S. Carol. Duke University Press, Box 6697 College Station, Durham, North Carolina 27708. 1987.

PLANNING AND CONTROL OF LAND DEVELOPMENT: CASES AND MATERIALS. Third Edition. Daniel R. Mandelker and Roger A. Cunningham. Michie Company, P.O. Box 7587, Charlottesville, Virginia 22906. 1990.

PRIVATE SUPPLY OF PUBLIC SERVICES: EVALUATION OF REAL ESTATE EXACTIONS, LINKAGE, AND ALTERNATIVE LAND POLICIES. Rachelle Alterman. New York University Press, 70 Washington Square South, New York, New York 10012. 1988.

PROCEEDINGS OF THE INSTITUTE ON PLANNING, ZONING, AND EMINENT DOMAIN. Southwestern Legal Foundation, Municipal Legal Studies Center, Dallas, Texas, November 16-18, 1983. Matthew Bender and Company, Incorporated, 11 Penn Plaza, New York, New York 10001. 1984.

REAL ESTATE LAW. Second Edition. George J. Siedel, III. West Publishing Company, 50 West Kellogg Boulevard, St. Paul, Minnesota 55164. 1989.

REGULATING LAND USE: THE LAW OF ZONING. Irving J. Sloan. Oceana Publications, 75 Main Street, Dobbs Ferry, New York 10522. 1988.

REGULATORY TAKING: THE LIMITS OF LAND USE CONTROLS. G. Richard Hill. American Bar Association, Section of Urban, State, and Local Government, 750 North Lake Shore Drive, Chicago, Illinois 60611. 1990.

RESPONDING TO THE TAKINGS CHALLENGE. Richard J. Roddewig and Christopher J. Duerksen. American Planning Association, National Trust for Historic Preservation, 1776 Massachusetts Avenue, Northwest, Suite 704, Washington, D.C. 20036. 1989.

URBAN PLANNING AND LAND DEVELOPMENT CONTROL LAW. Second Edition. Donald G. Hagman and Julian Conrad Juergensmeyer. West Publishing Company, P.O. Box 64526, 50 West Kellogg Boulevard, St. Paul, Minnesota 55164-0526. 1986.

ZONING AND THE AMERICAN DREAM: PROMISES STILL TO KEEP. Charles M. Haar and Jerold S. Kayden. Planners Press, 1313 East Sixtieth Street, Chicago, Illinois 60637. 1989.

THE ZONING GAME REVISITED. Richard F. Babcock and Charles L. Siemon. Oelgeschlager, Gunn and Hain, Incorporated, 245 Mirriam Street, Weston, Massachusetts 02193. 1985.

ZONING LAW AND PRACTICE, FOURTH EDITION. E. C. Yokley. Michie/Bobbs-Merrill, The Michie Company, P.O. Box 7587, Charlottesville, Virginia 22906-7587. 1978. (Annual Supplement).

ENCYCLOPEDIAS AND DICTIONARIES

ENCYCLOPEDIA OF COMMUNITY PLANNING AND ENVIRONMENTAL PROTECTION. Marilyn S. Schultz and Vivian L. Kasen. Books on Demand, 300 North Zeeb Road, Ann Arbor, Michigan 48106-1346. 1983.

DIGESTS, INDEXES, ABSTRACTS, CITATORS

LAND USE DIGEST. Urban Land Institute, 625 Indiana Avenue, Washington, D.C. 20004. Monthly. 1968- .

LAND USE LAW AND ZONING DIGEST. American Planning Association, 1776 Massachusetts Avenue, Northwest, Washington, D.C. 20036. Monthly. 1948- .

ANNUALS AND SURVEYS

SECOND ANNUAL INSTITUTE: SECTION 1983 AND LAND USE. Richard G. Carlisle, Robert H. Freilich, and Clifford M. Greene. Prentice-Hall Law and Business, 855 Valley Road, Clifton, New Jersey 07013. 1989.

ZONING LAW ANTHOLOGY. International Library, 3865 Wilson Boulevard, Arlington, Virginia 22203. Annual.

LAW REVIEWS AND PERIODICALS

AMERICAN PLANNING ASSOCIATION JOURNAL. American Planning Association, 1313 Sixteenth Street, Chicago, Illinois 60637. Quarterly.

LAND USE AND ENVIRONMENTAL LAW REVIEW. Clark Boardman Company, Limited, 435 Hudson Street, New York, New York 10014. Annual.

PLANNING. American Planning Association. 1776 Massachusetts Avenue, Northwest, Washington, D.C. 20036. Monthly.

NEWSLETTERS AND NEWSPAPERS

FROM THE STATE CAPITALS: URBAN DEVELOPMENT. Wakeman Walworth, Incorporated, 300 North Washington Street, Suite 204, Alexandria, Virginia 22314. Monthly.

LAND USE LAW AND ZONING DIGEST. American Planning Association, 1313 East Sixteenth Street, Chicago, Illinois 60637. Monthly.

ZONING AND PLANNING LAW REPORT. Clark Boardman Company, Limited, 375 Hudson Street, New York, New York 10014. Monthly.

ZONING BULLETIN. Quinlan Publishing Company, 23 Drydock Avenue, Boston, Massachusetts 02110. Monthly.

ZONING NEWS. American Planning Association, 1313 East Sixteenth Street, Chicago, Illinois 60637. Monthly.

BIBLIOGRAPHIES

LEGAL ASPECTS OF ZONING PRACTICES: A CHECKLIST, 1980-1984. Dale E. Casper. Vance Bibliographies, P.O. Box 229, 112 North Charter Street, Monticello, Illinois 61856. 1985.

LEGAL PROBLEMS RELATING TO SCARCITY OF AGRICULTURAL AND URBAN HOUSING LAND: A SELECTIVE BIBLIOGRAPHY, 1970-1987. James Milles. Vance Bibliographies, P.O. Box 229, 112 North Charter Street, Monticello, Illinois 61856. 1988.

MEDIATION AND NEGOTIATION FOR PLANNING, LAND USE MANAGEMENT, AND ENVIRONMENTAL PROTECTION: AN ANNOTATED BIBLIOGRAPHY OF MATERIALS FOR THE PERIOD 1980-1989. Richard G. RuBino and Harvey M. Jacobs. Council of Planning Librarians, 1313 East Sixtieth Street, Chicago, Illinois 60637. 1990.

DIRECTORIES

DIRECTORY OF LOCAL AGENCIES; HOUSING, COMMUNITY DEVELOPMENT, REDEVELOPMENT. National Association of Housing and Redevelopment Officials (NAHRO), 1320 Eighteenth Street, Northwest, Washington, D.C. 20036. 1980.

ASSOCIATIONS AND PROFESSIONAL SOCIETIES

AMERICAN BAR ASSOCIATION, SPECIAL COMMITTEE ON HOUSING AND URBAN DEVELOPMENT LAW. 750 North Lake Shore Drive, Chicago, Illinois 60611. (312) 988-5000.

AMERICAN PLANNING ASSOCIATION. 1776 Massachusetts Avenue, Northwest, Suite 704, Washington, D.C. 20036. (202) 872-0611.

COUNCIL OF PLANNING LIBRARIANS. 1313 East Sixtieth Street, Chicago, Illinois 60637. (312) 947-2163.

NATIONAL ASSOCIATION OF COUNTY PLANNERS. 440 First Street, Northwest, Washington, D.C. 20001. (202) 393-6226.

NATIONAL ASSOCIATION OF HOUSING AND REDEVELOPMENT OFFICIALS. 1320 Eighteenth Street, Northwest, Washington, D.C. 20036. (202) 429-2960.

NATIONAL INDUSTRIAL ZONING COMMITTEE. P.O. Box 21398, Columbus, Ohio 43221. (614) 488-2643.

NATIONAL PLANNING ASSOCIATION. 1616 P Street, Northwest, Suite 400, Washington, D.C. 20036. (202) 265-7685.

PLANNING AND THE BLACK COMMUNITY. United States Corps of Engineers, P.O. Box C-3755, Seattle, Washington 98124. (206) 764-3614.

RESEARCH CENTERS, INSTITUTES, CLEARINGHOUSES

CENTER FOR URBAN POLICY RESEARCH. Rutgers University, Building 4051, Kilmer Area, New Brunswick, New Jersey 08903. (201) 932-3133.

INSTITUTE OF STATE AND REGIONAL AFFAIRS. University of Pennsylvania, Middletown, Pennsylvania 17057. (717) 948-6178.

INSTITUTE OF URBAN AND REGIONAL DEVELOPMENT. University of California, Berkeley, 316 Wunster Hall, Berkeley, California 94720. (415) 642-4874.

ULI-URBAN LAND INSTITUTE. 1090 Vermont Avenue, Northwest, Washington, D.C. 20005. (202) 289-8500.

ONLINE DATABASES

LAND USE PLANNING REPORT. Business Publishers, Incorporated, 951 Pershing Drive, Silver Spring, Maryland 20910.

COMPUTER-ASSISTED LEGAL INSTRUCTION

HAWKINS I & II. Center for Computer-Assisted Instruction, 229 19th Avenue South, University of Minnesota, Minneapolis, Minnesota 55455. Interactive videodisc.

OTHER SOURCES

APA PLANNING ADVISORY SERVICE REPORTS. American Planning Association, 1776 Massachusetts Avenue, Northwest, Suite 704, Washington, D.C. 20036. 10 issues per year.

RIDGEWATER COLLEGE LIBRARY
HUTCHINSON CAMPUS